C000128412

1 MONTH OF
FREE
READING

at

www.ForgottenBooks.com

By purchasing this book you are eligible for one month membership to ForgottenBooks.com, giving you unlimited access to our entire collection of over 1,000,000 titles via our web site and mobile apps.

To claim your free month visit:

www.forgottenbooks.com/free1249186

* Offer is valid for 45 days from date of purchase. Terms and conditions apply.

ISBN 978-0-428-61458-4
PIBN 11249186

This book is a reproduction of an important historical work. Forgotten Books uses
state-of-the-art technology to digitally reconstruct the work, preserving the original format
whilst repairing imperfections present in the aged copy. In rare cases, an imperfection in
the original, such as a blemish or missing page, may be replicated in our edition. We do,
however, repair the vast majority of imperfections successfully; any imperfections that
remain are intentionally left to preserve the state of such historical works.

Forgotten Books is a registered trademark of FB &c Ltd.
Copyright © 2018 FB &c Ltd.
FB &c Ltd, Dalton House, 60 Windsor Avenue, London, SW19 2RR.
Company number 08720141. Registered in England and Wales.

For support please visit www.forgottenbooks.com

Monthly Catalogue

United States

Public Documents

Nos. 343–354

July, 1923–June, 1924

ISSUED BY THE
SUPERINTENDENT OF DOCUMENTS

WASHINGTON
1923-24

Monthly Catalogue
United States
Public Documents

No. 343

July, 1923

ISSUED BY THE
SUPERINTENDENT OF DOCUMENTS

WASHINGTON
1923

Abbreviations

Appendix _____app.	Page, pages _____p.
Congress_____Cong.	Part, parts _____pt., pts.
Department _____Dept.	Plate, plates _____pl.
Document _____doc.	Portrait, portraits _____por.
Facsimile, facsimiles _____facsim.	Quarto_____4°
Folio_____f°	Report _____rp.
House_____H.	Saint_____St.
House bill _____H. k.	Section, sections _____sec.
House concurrent resolution__H. Con. Res.	Senate, Senate bill _____S.
House document_____H. doc.	Senate concurrent resolution___S. Con. Res.
House executive document_____H. ex. doc.	Senate document _____S. doc.
House joint resolution _____H. J. Res.	Senate executive document_____S. ex. doc.
House report _____H. rp.	Senate joint resolution _____S. J. Res.
House resolution (simple)_____H. Res.	Senate report _____S. rp.
Illustration, illustrations_____il.	Senate resolution (simple)_____S. Res.
Inch, inches _____in.	Session_____sess.
Latitude _____lat.	Sixteenmo _____16°
Longitude _____long.	Table, tables _____tab.
Mile, miles _____m.	Thirtytwo-mo _____32°
Miscellaneous_____mis., misc.	Treasury_____Treas.
Nautical _____naut.	Twelvemo _____12°
No date_____n. d.	Twentyfour-mo_____24°
No place_____n. p.	Versus_____vs., v.
Number, numbers _____no., nos.	Volume, volumes _____v., vol.
Octavo_____8°	Year _____yr.

Common abbreviations for names of States and months are also used.
* Document for sale by Superintendent of Documents.
† Distribution by office issuing document, free if unaccompanied by a price.
‡ Printed for official use.
NOTE.—Nearly all of the Departments of the Government make a limited free distribution of their publications. When an entry shows a * price, it is possible that upon application to the issuing office a copy may be obtained without charge.

Explanation

Words and figures inclosed in brackets [ ] are given for information, but do not appear on the title-pages of the publications catalogued. When size is not given octavo is to be understood. Size of maps is measured from outer edge of border, excluding margin. The dates, including day, month, and year, given with Senate and House documents and reports are the dates on which they were ordered to be printed. Usually the printing promptly follows the ordering, but various causes sometimes make delays.

2

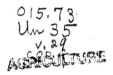

015.73
Um 35
v. 29
AGRICULTURE

SALES OF GOVERNMENT PUBLICATIONS

The Superintendent of Documents, Washington, D. C., is authorized to sell at cost of paper and printing, plus 10 per cent, any United States public document in his charge the distribution of which is not otherwise provided for.

Publications can not be supplied free to individuals nor forwarded in advance of payment.

Publications entered in this catalogue that are for sale by the Superintendent of Documents are indicated by a star (*) preceding the price. A dagger (†) indicates that application should be made to the Department, Bureau, or Division issuing the document. A double dagger (‡) indicates that the document is printed for official use. Whenever additional information concerning the method of procuring a document seems necessary, it will be found under the name of the Bureau by which it was published.

In ordering a publication from the Superintendent of Documents, give (if known) the name of the publishing Department, Bureau, or Division, and the title of the publication. If the publication is numbered, give the number also. Every such particular assists in quick identification. Do not order by the Library of Congress card number.

The accumulation of publications in this Office amounts to several millions, of which over two million are assorted, forming the sales stock. Many rare books are included, but under the law all must be sold regardless of their age or scarcity. Many of the books have been in stock some time, and are apt to be shop-worn. In filling orders the best copy available is sent. A general price-list of public documents is not available, but lists on special subjects will be furnished on application.

MONTHLY CATALOGUE DISTRIBUTION

The Monthly catalogue is sent to each Senator, Representative, Delegate, Resident Commissioner, and officer in Congress; to designated depositories and State and Territorial libraries if it is selected by them; to substantially all Government authors; and to as many school, college, and public libraries as the limited edition will supply.

Subscription price to individuals, 50c. a year, including index; foreign subscription, 75c. a year. Back numbers can not be supplied. Notify the Superintendent of Documents of any change of address.

LIBRARY OF CONGRESS CARDS

Numbers to be used in ordering the printed catalogue cards of the Library of Congress are given at the end of entries for the more important documents. Orders for these cards, remittances in payment for them, and requests for information about them should be addressed to the Librarian of Congress, *not* to the Superintendent of Documents.

INDEX

An Index to the Monthly catalogue is issued at the end of the fiscal year. This contains index entries for all the numbers issued from July to June, and can be bound with the numbers as an index to the volume. Persons desiring to bind the catalogue at the end of the year should be careful to retain the numbers received monthly, as duplicate copies can not be supplied.

HOW TO REMIT

Remittances for the documents marked with a star (*) should be made to the Superintendent of Documents, Washington, D. C., by coupons, postal money order, express order, or New York draft. Currency may be sent at sender's risk.

Postage stamps, foreign money, defaced or smooth coins, positively will not be accepted.

For the convenience of the general public, coupons that are good until used in exchange for Government publications sold by the Superintendent of Documents may be purchased from his Office in sets of 20 for $1.00. Address order to Superintendent of Documents, Government Printing Office.

No charge is made for postage on documents forwarded to points in United States, Alaska, Guam, Hawaii, Philippine Islands, Porto Rico, Samoa, or to Canada, Cuba, or Mexico. To other countries the regular rate of postage is charged, and remittances must cover such postage. In computing foreign postage, add one-third of the price of the publication.

MONTHLY CATALOGUE

No. 343   JULY   1923

AGRICULTURE DEPARTMENT

NOTE.—Those publications of the Department of Agriculture which are for sale will be supplied by the Superintendent of Documents, Washington, D. C. The Department issues a monthly list of publications, which is mailed to all applicants, enabling them to select such reports and bulletins as interest them.

Azotobacter. Protein synthesis by Azotobacter [with list of literature cited]; by O. W. Hunter. 1923. cover-title, p. 263-274. [From Journal of agricultural research, v. 24, no. 3, Apr. 21, 1923.] ‡

Cattle. [Bureau of Animal Industry] order 278, amendment 1 and 3 to regulations governing recognition of breeds and purebred animals, amending regulation 2, sec. 4, paragraph 1, recognizing breeds and books of record across the seas, effective Jan. 10 and May 25, 1923; Jan. 13-June 12, 1923. 1923. Each 1 p. †

Gummosis of citrus [with list of literature cited]; by Howard S. Fawcett. 1923. cover-title, 191-236+[7] p. 8 p. of pl. [From Journal of agricultural research, v. 24, no. 3, Apr. 21. 1923.] ‡

Journal of agricultural research, v. 24, no. 1-4; Apr. 7-28, 1923. 1923. cover-titles, 1-364+[28] p.+[9] leaves, il. 5 pl. 36 p. of pl. [Weekly. Text on p. 2 of covers.] * Paper, 10c. single copy, $4.00 a yr.; foreign subscription, $5.25.

Agr 13—1837

CONTENTS.—No. 1. Temperature relations of 11 species of Rhizopus [with list of literature cited; by] J. L. Weimer and L. L. Harter.—Nutrition of plants considered as electrical phenomenon; by James F. Breazeale.—Influence of soil temperature and soil moisture upon Fusarium disease in cabbage seedlings [with list of literature cited]; by William B. Tisdale.—Action of soap upon lead arsenates [with list of literature cited]; by R. M. Pinckney.—No. 2. Physiological requirements of Rocky Mountain trees [with list of literature cited]; by Carlos G. Bates.—Study of internal browning of yellow Newtown apple [with list of literature cited]; by A. J. Winkler.—On use of calcium carbonate in nitrogen fixation experiments [with list of literature cited]; by P. L. Gainey.—No. 3. Gummosis of citrus [with list of literature cited]; by Howard S. Fawcett.—Occurrence and significance of phloem necrosis in Irish potato [with list of literature cited]; by Ernst F. Artschwager.—Cultivated and wild hosts of sugar-cane or grass mosaic [with list of literature cited]; by E. W. Brandes and Peter J. Klaphaak.—Protein synthesis by Azotobacter [with list of literature cited]; by O. W. Hunter.—No. 4. Studies on temperature of individual insects, with special reference to honey bee [with list of literature cited]; by Gregor B. Pirsch.—Study of effect of changing absolute reaction of soils upon their Azotobacter content; by P. L. Gainey.—Oxidation of sulphur by microorganisms in black alkali soils [with list of literature cited]; by Selman A. Waksman, Clara H. Wark, Jacob Joffe, and Robert L. Starkey.—Peach rosette, infectious mosaic; by J. A. McClintock.—Toxicity and antagonism of various alkali salts in soil [with list of literature cited]; by F. S. Harris, M. D. Thomas, and D. W. Pittman.—Identification of certain species of Fusarium isolated from potato tubers in Montana [with list of literature cited]; by H. E. Morris and Grace B. Nutting.

NOTE.—This publication is published by authority of the Secretary of Agriculture, with the cooperation of the Association of Land-Grant Colleges. It is distributed free only to libraries of agricultural colleges and experiment stations, to large universities, technical schools, and to such institutions as make suitable exchanges with the Agriculture Department. Others desiring the Journal may obtain it from the Superintendent of Documents, Washington, D. C., at the prices stated above.

Market agencies. Amendment 1 to Circular 156 [Packers and stockyards act, 1921] general rules and regulations of Secretary of Agriculture with respect to stockyard owners, market agencies, and dealers; [June 14, 1923]. [1923.] 3 p. 16° ([Circular 156, amendment 1.]) †

Official record, Department of Agriculture, v. 2, no. 27-30; July 4-25, 1923. [1923.] Each 8 p. 4° [Weekly.] * Paper, 50c. a yr.; foreign subscription, $1.10.

Agr 22—146

Pasture-lands. Effect of burning on vegetation in Kansas pastures; by R. L. Hensel. 1923. cover-title, 631-644+[1] p. il. 2 p. of pl. [From Journal of agricultural research, v. 23, no. 8, Feb. 24, 1923.] ‡

Potatoes. Further studies on pathogenicity of Corticium vagum on potato as affected by soil temperature; by B. L. Richards. 1923. cover-title, p. 761–770+[1] leaf, il. 1 pl. [From Journal of agricultural research, v. 23, no. 9, Mar. 3, 1923.] ‡

Quarantine. Modification of gipsy moth and brown-tail moth quarantine, Amendment 4 to regulations supplemental to Notice of quarantine 45, effective July 1, 1923. [1923.] 4 p. (Federal Horticultural Board.) †

Report. Year in agriculture, annual report to the President [1922]; by Henry C. Wallace, Secretary of Agriculture. 1923. [1]+1–82 p. il. (Yearbook separate 883.) [From Yearbook, 1922.] * Paper, 10c.

NOTE.—This is the same, with the addition of illustrations, as the Report of the Secretary of Agriculture, 1922, for which see Monthly catalogue for Dec. 1922, p. 315.

Soils. Oxidation of sulphur by microörganisms in black alkali soils [with list of literature cited]; by Selman A. Waksman, Clara H. Wark, Jacob Joffe, and Robert L. Starkey. 1923. cover-title, p. 297–305. [From Journal of agricultural research, v. 24, no. 4, Apr. 28, 1923.] ‡

—— Study of effect of changing absolute reaction of soils upon their Azotobacter content; by P. L. Gainey. 1923. cover-title, p. 289–296. [From Journal of agricultural research, v. 24, no. 4, Apr. 28, 1923.] ‡

Weather, crops, and markets, weekly, July 7–28, 1923; v. 4, no. 1–4. [1923.] p. 1–112, il. 4° * Paper, $1.00 a yr.; foreign subscription, $2.00. Agr 22—147

AGRICULTURAL ECONOMICS BUREAU

Agricultural products. Imports and exports of agricultural products; compiled by Nat C. Murray, Lewis B. Flohr, O. A. Juve, and Caroline G. Gries, from reports of Bureau of Foreign and Domestic Commerce. 1923. [1]+949–982 p. (Yearbook separate 880.) [From Yearbook, 1922.] * Paper, 5c.

Agriculture. Distribution of types of farming in United States; [by W. J. Spillman]. [May, 1923.] ii+30 p. il. (Agriculture Dept. Farmers' bulletin 1289.) * Paper, 5c.   Agr 23—749

—— Miscellaneous agricultural statistics, 1922; compiled by Nat C. Murray, Lewis B. Flohr, and Preston C. Day. 1923. [1]+983–1044 p. (Yearbook separate 887.) [Prepared in cooperation with Weather Bureau. From Yearbook, 1922.] * Paper, 10c.

Crops. Statistics of crops other than grain crops, 1922; compiled by Nat C. Murray, Lewis B. Flohr, O. A. Juve, Emma S. Thompson, Lila Thompson, Caroline G. Gries, Birdella Miller, M. E. Murphy, James J. Window, and Perry Elliott. 1923. [1]+666–794 p. (Yearbook separate 884.) [From Yearbook, 1922.] * Paper, 5c.

Farm operations; compiled by O. A. Juve. 1923. [1]+1045–78 p. (Yearbook separate 890.) [From Yearbook, 1922.] * Paper, 5c.

Grain. Statistics of grain crops, 1922; compiled by Nat C. Murray, Lewis B. Flohr, O. A. Juve, Emma S. Thompson, Lila Thompson, Caroline G. Gries, John W. Strowbridge, and James J. Window. 1923. [1]+569–665 p. (Yearbook separate 881.) [From Yearbook, 1922.] * Paper, 10c.

Live stock, 1922; compiled by Nat C. Murray, Lewis B. Flohr, O. A. Juve, Emma S. Thompson, Florence C. Fitch, Lila Thompson, and James J. Window. 1923. [1]+795–913 p. (Yearbook separate 888.) [From Yearbook, 1922.] * Paper, 15c.

Rural planning, social aspects; [by Wayne C. Nason]. [May, 1923.] ii+30 p. il. (Agriculture Dept. Farmers' bulletin 1325.) * Paper, 5c.   Agr 23—802

Service announcements. Service and regulatory announcements, no. 75: Official wool standards of United States for grades of wool. July 16, 1923. 7 p. * Paper, 5c.   Agr 15—199

ANIMAL INDUSTRY BUREAU

Breeding. Essentials of animal breeding; [by George M. Rommel]. [Nov. 1920, revised May, 1923.] [1923.] 39 p. il. (Agriculture Dept. Farmers' bulletin 1167.) [Includes lists of Agriculture Department publications relating to breeding and raising livestock.] * Paper, 5c.

Cattle. Value of purebreds, why purebreds excel; [poster]. [1923.] 18×15 in. †

Dourine of horses; [by John R. Mohler and H. W. Schoening]. [Aug. 1920, revised June, 1923.] [1923.] ii+10 p. il. (Agriculture Dept. Farmers' bulletin 1146.) * Paper, 5c.

Foot-and-mouth disease; [by John R. Mohler]. [Apr. 22, 1915, revised Mar. 1923.] [1923.] 20 p. il. (Agriculture Dept. Farmers' bulletin 666.) [Includes lists of Agriculture Department publications relating to diseases of cattle.] * Paper, 5c.

Goose raising; [by Alfred R. Lee]. [Jan. 1921, revised Apr. 1922, reprint 1923.] 23 p. il. (Agriculture Dept. Farmers' bulletin 767.) [Imprint date incorrectly given on p. 23 as 1922. Includes list of Agriculture Department publications relating to poultry raising and egg production.]. * Paper, 5c.

Greasewood as poisonous plant; [by] C. Dwight Marsh, A. B. Clawson, and James F. Couch. July, 1923. 4 p. il. (Agriculture Dept. Department circular 279.) * Paper, 5c. Agr 23—800

Hog production and marketing; by E. Z. Russell, S. S. Buckley, O. E. Baker, C. E. Gibbons, R. H. Wilcox, H. W. Hawthorne, S. W. Mendum, O. C. Stine, G. K. Holmes, A. V. Swarthout, W. B. Bell, G. S. Jamieson, C. W. Warburton, [and] C. F. Langworthy. 1923. ii+181-280 p. il. (Yearbook separate 882.) [Prepared in cooperation with Agricultural Economics Bureau, Biological Survey Bureau, Chemistry Bureau, Plant Industry Bureau, and States Relations Service. From Yearbook, 1922.] * Paper, 15c.

Posters. More money for better hides, how to get it; [all lettered poster]. [1923.] 22×14 in. †

Poultry. Back-yard poultry keeping, [by Rob R. Slocum; revised by Alfred R. Lee]. [May, 1923.] ii+23 p. il. (Agriculture Dept. Farmers' bulletin 1331.) [Revision of Farmers' bulletin 889. Includes lists of Agriculture Department publications relating to poultry raising and egg production.] * Paper, 5c. Agr 23—803

BIOLOGICAL SURVEY BUREAU

Apterygota, Anoplura, and Heteroptera of Priblof Islands, Alaska; by W. L. McAtee.. June 20, 1923. p. [1], 139, 142, 145. [From North American fauna 46.] †

Birds. Report on bird censuses in United States, 1916-20; by May Thacher Cooke. July 20, 1923. cover-title, 36 p. il. (Agriculture Dept. Department bulletin 1165.) [Includes lists of Agriculture Department publications relating to distribution, migration, and attraction of wild birds.] * Paper, 5c. Agr 15—321

Chilopoda of Pribilof Islands, Alaska; by Ralph V. Chamberlin. June 20, 1923. [1]+240-244 p. [From North American fauna 46.] †

Coleoptera of Pribilof Islands, Alaska; by H. F. Wickham. June 20, 1923. [1]+150-157 p. [From North American fauna 46.] †

Diptera. Diptera [of Pribilof Islands, Alaska (Calliphoridae)]; by W. R. Walton. June 20, 1923. p. 228. [From North American fauna 46.] †

—— Diptera of Pribilof Islands, Alaska (except Tipulidae, Rhyphidae, and Calliphoridae); by J. R. Malloch. June 20, 1923. [1]+170-227 p. 4 p. of pl. [From North American fauna 46.] †

—— Diptera of Pribilof Islands, Alaska (Tipulidae and Rhyphidae); by Charles P. Alexander. June 20, 1923. [1]+159-169 p. 2 p. of pl. [From North American fauna 46.] †

Hymenoptera of Pribilof Islands, Alaska; by Henry L. Viereck. June 20, 1923. [1]+229-236 p. [From North American fauna 46.] †

Insects. Introduction to insects, arachnids, and chilopods of Pribilof Islands, Alaska; by W. L. McAtee. June 20, 1923. [1]+129-138 p. [From North American fauna 46.] †

Lepidoptera of Pribilof Islands, Alaska; by Wm. T. M. Forbes. June 20, 1923. [1]+147-149 p. [From North American fauna 46.] †

Mallophaga [of Pribilof Islands, Alaska]; by G. F. Ferris. June 20, 1923. p. 141. [From North American fauna 46.] †

Orthoptera [of Pribilof Islands, Alaska]; by Morgan Hebard. June 20, 1923. p. 140. [From North American fauna 46.] †

Poster. Open seasons for game, 1923–24, compiled by George A. Lawyer and Frank L. Earnshaw;. [all lettered poster]. July 17, 1923. 32×15 in. (Poster 42.) †

Pribilof Islands. Biological survey of Pribilof Islands, Alaska: 1, Birds and mammals [with bibliography, articles] by Edward A. Preble and W. L. McAtee; 2, Insects, arachnids, and chilopods, by various entomologists, with Introduction, by W. L. McAtee. June 20, 1923. iv+255 p. 5 pl. 10 p. of pl. and maps. (North American fauna 46.) * Paper, 40c.   Agr 23—807

Trichoptera, Mecoptera, and Arachnida of Pribilof Islands, Alaska; by Nathan Banks. June 20, 1923. p. [1], 146, 158, 237–239, 1 pl. [From North American fauna 46.] †

CHEMISTRY BUREAU

Apple by-products as stock foods [with list of literature cited]; by G. P. Walton and G. L. Bidwell. July 26, 1923. cover-title, 40 p. il. (Agriculture Dept. Department bulletin 1166.) * Paper, 5c.   Agr 23—797

Sweet-potato syrup. Production of sirup from sweet potatoes; by H. C. Gore, H. C. Reese, and J. O. Reed. July 3, 1923. 34 p. il. (Agriculture Dept. Department bulletin 1158.) * Paper, 10c.   Agr 23—796

ENTOMOLOGY BUREAU

Bees. Transferring bees to modern hives; [by] E. L. Sechrist. [July, 1918, reprint] 1923. 16 p. il. (Agriculture Dept. Farmers' bulletin 961.) [Includes lists of Agriculture Department publications relating to bees.] * Paper, 5c.   Agr 18—570

Wheat strawworm and its control; [by W. J. Phillips and F. W. Poos]. [May, 1923.] ii+10 p. il. (Agriculture Dept. Farmers' bulletin 1323.) * Paper, 5c.   Agr 23—750

FEDERAL HORTICULTURAL BOARD

Service announcements. Service and regulatory announcements, Jan.-Mar. 1923; [no.] 74. June, 1923. p. 1–56, il. * Paper, 10c.   Agr 14—383

FOREST SERVICE

Arbor day. Arbor day. June, 1923. 15 p. il. (Agriculture Dept. Department circular 265.) [Supersedes Department circular 8.] * Paper, 5c.   Agr 23—798

Forest fire prevention handbook for school children of California; prepared by Forest Service and State forester in cooperation with superintendent of public instruction of California. July 2, 1923. cover-title, 24 p. il. (Agriculture Dept. Miscellaneous circular 7.) [Text and illustration on p. 2 and 3 of cover.] * Paper, 10c.   Agr 23—805

Forest statistics; by Branch of Engineering, Louis S. Murphy, W. R. Mattoon, Harry Irion, Alice M. Meynes, C. R. Tillotson. 1023. ii+931–948 p. (Yearbook separate 889.) [From Yearbook, 1922. Tables 495–499 on lumber production have been omitted from this separate but may be found in the Yearbook for 1922.] * Paper, 5c.

Timber, mine or crop? by W. B. Greeley, Earle H. Clapp, Herbert A. Smith, Raphael Zon, W. N. Sparhawk, Ward Shepard, and J. Kittredge, jr. 1923. ii+83–180 p. il. (Yearbook separate 886.) [From Yearbook, 1922.] * Paper, 15c.

Trees. Physiological requirements of Rocky Mountain trees [with list of literature cited]; by Carlos G. Bates. 1923. cover-title, 97–164+[6] p.+[1] leaf, il. 7 p. of pl. [From Journal of agricultural research, v. 24, no. 2, Apr. 14, 1923.] ‡

Wood. Demonstration courses in kiln drying, boxing and crating, gluing of wood, wood properties and uses; prepared by Forest Products Laboratory. June, 1923. 20 p. il. (Agriculture Dept. Miscellaneous circular 8.) * Paper, 5c.   Agr 23—806

Maps

Wenatchee National Forest, Wash., information for mountain travelers. [1923.] 1 sheet (with map on verso), il. large 4°, folded into narrow 8° size and so printed as to number [1]+15+[1] p. †

PLANT INDUSTRY BUREAU

Flag smut of wheat; [by] W. H. Tisdale, G. H. Dungan, and C. E. Leighty. June, 1923. 7 p. 2 p. of pl. (Agriculture Dept. Department circular 273.) [Prepared in cooperation with Illinois Agricultural Experiment Station and Illinois Department of Agriculture.] * Paper, 5c. Agr 23—799

Horse beans; [by Roland McKee]. [May, 1918, revised Mar. 1923.] [1923.] 13 p. il. (Agriculture Dept. Farmers' bulletin 969.) * Paper, 5c.

Mosaic disease. Cultivated and wild hosts of sugar-cane or grass mosaic [with list of literature cited]; by E. W. Brandes and Peter J. Klaphaak. 1923. cover-title, 247–262+[3] p.+[1] leaf, 4 p. of pl. [From Journal of agricultural research, v. 24, no. 3, Apr. 21, 1923.] ‡

Newlands experiment farm. Work of Newlands reclamation project experiment farm in 1920 and 1921; [by] F. B. Headley and E. W. Knight. Mar. 1923. 26 p. il. (Agriculture Dept. Department circular 267.) * Paper, 5c. Agr 14—1380

Oats, barley, rye, rice, grain sorghums, seed flax, and buckwheat; by C. R. Ball, T. R. Stanton, H. V. Harlan, C. E. Leighty, C. E. Chambliss, A. C. Dillman, O. C. Stine, O. E. Baker, O. A. Juve, and W. J. Spillman. 1923· il+ 469–568 p. il. (Yearbook separate 891.) [Prepared in cooperation with Agricultural Economics Bureau. From Yearbook, 1922.] * Paper, 15c.

Potatoes. Occurrence and significance of phloem necrosis in Irish potato [with list of literature cited]; by Ernst F. Artschwager. 1923. cover-title, 237–246+[4] p. il. 5 p. of pl. [From Journal of agricultural research, v. 24, no. 3, Apr. 21, 1923.] ‡

Sorghum. Growing and utilizing sorghums for forage; [by H. N. Vinall and R. E. Getty]. [Nov. 1920, revised May, 1923.] [1923.] 32 p. il. (Agriculture Dept. Farmers' bulletin 1158.) * Paper, 5c. Agr 21—19

Tobacco. History and status of tobacco culture; by W. W. Garner, E. G. Moss, H. S. Yohe, F. B. Wilkinson, and O. C. Stine. 1923. [2]+395–468 p. il. (Yearbook separate 885.) [Prepared in cooperation with Agricultural Economics Bureau. From Yearbook, 1922.] * Paper, 10c.

Tomatoes as truck crop; [by W. R. Beattie]. [June, 1923.] ii+34 p. il. (Agriculture Dept. Farmers' bulletin 1338.) * Paper, 5c. Agr 23—804

PUBLICATIONS DIVISION

Agriculture Department. Monthly list of publications [of Agriculture Department], June, 1923. [1923.] 4 p. † Agr 9—1414

SOILS BUREAU

Duval County, Fla. Soil survey of Duval County, Fla.; by Arthur E. Taylor and T. J. Dunnewald. 1923. iii+21–48 p. il. map. [From Field operations, 1921.] * Paper, 25c.

STATES RELATIONS SERVICE

Canning and preserving. Home canning of fruits and vegetables; [prepared by Office of Home Economics]. [Oct. 1921, revised June, 1923.] [1923.] 48 p. il. (Agriculture Dept. Farmers' bulletin 1211.) *Paper, 5c.

Experiment station record. Experiment station record, v. 48, no. 8; June, 1923. 1923. cover-title, viii+701–800 p. [Text and illustration on p. 2 and 4 of cover.] *Paper, 10c. single copy, 75c. per vol. (2 vols. a yr.); foreign subscription, $1.25 per vol. Agr 9—832

NOTE.—Mainly made up of abstracts of reports and publications on agricultural science which have recently appeared in all countries, especially the United States. Extra numbers, called abstract numbers, are issued, 3 to each volume. These are made up almost exclusively of abstracts, that is, they contain no editorial notes and only a limited number of current notes.

—— Same, v. 48, no. 9; abstract number. June 26, 1923. cover-title, ix+ 801–900 p. [Text and illustration on p. 2 and 4 of cover.]

Farm kitchen as workshop; [by Anna Barrows]. [Revised Sept. 1921.] [Reprint 1923.] 24 p. il. (Agriculture Dept. Farmers' bulletin 607.) [Imprint date incorrectly given on p. 24 as 1921. Includes list of Agriculture Department publications of interest in connection with this bulletin.] * Paper, 5c.

Lamb and mutton and their use in diet; [prepared in Office of Home Economics]. [June, 1923.] ii+14 p. il. (Agriculture Dept. Farmers' bulletin 1324.) [Supersedes Farmers' bulletin 526.] * Paper, 5c.   Agr 23—801

VIRGIN ISLANDS AGRICULTURAL EXPERIMENT STATION

Insects. Truck-crop insect pests in Virgin Islands and methods of combating them; by Charles E. Wilson. June 21, 1923. ii+35 p. il. (Bulletin 4.) *Paper, 5c.   Agr 23—808

WEATHER BUREAU

Climatological data for United States by sections, v. 10, no. 3; Mar. 1923. [1923.] cover-title, [211] p. il. map, 2 p. of maps, 4° [Text on p. 2 of cover.] *Paper, 35c. complete monthly number, $4.00 a yr.   Agr 14—566
> NOTE.—Made up of separate Climatological data issued from 42 section centers of the United States. Printed at the several section centers and assembled and bound at the Washington Office. Issued principally for service use and exchange. The separate Climatological data are sold by the Superintendent of Documents, Washington, D. C., at the rate of 5c. single copy, 50c. a yr. for each section.

Lightning. Occurrence of lightning storms in relation to forest fires in California, by S. B. Show and E. I. Kotok; Discussion of thunderstorms and forest fires in California, by E. A. Beals. 1923. [1]+175-182 p. il. 4° [From Monthly weather review, Apr. 1923.] †

Meteorology. Monthly meteorological summary, Washington, D. C., June, 1923. [1923.] [2] p. f° †

Monthly weather review, v. 51, no. 4; Apr. 1923. [June] 1923. cover-title, p. 175-237, il. 2 maps, 8 p. of maps, 4° [Text on p. 2-4 of cover.] *Paper, 15c. single copy, $1.50 a yr.; foreign subscription, $2.25.   Agr 9—990
> NOTE.—The Monthly weather review contains (1) meteorological contributions, and bibliography including seismology, (2) an interpretative summary and charts of the weather of the month in the United States, and on adjacent oceans, and (3) climatological and seismological tables dealing with the weather and earthquakes of the month. The contributions are principally as follows: (a) results of observational or research work in meteorology carried on in the United States or other parts of the world, (b) abstracts or reviews of important meteorological papers and books, and (c) notes.
> SPECIAL ARTICLES.—Occurrence of lightning storms in relation to forest fires in California; by S. B. Show and E. I. Kotok.—Discussion of thunderstorms and forest fires in California; by E. A. Beals.—Forest fire weather in southern Appalachians; by E. F. McCarthy.—Solar radiation intensities and terrestrial weather; by Charles F. Marvin.—Weather forecasting from ships at sea; [by] Alfred J. Henry.—Concerning accuracy of free-air pressure maps; by C. Le Roy Meisinger.—[H. J.] Cox on thermal belts and fruit growing in North Carolina; [abstract] by Alfred J. Henry.—Rainfall of Jamaica; [by A. J. H.].—Double-walled waterspouts; [by H. L.].

Ocean. Weather of the oceans, Apr. 1923, with special reference to north Atlantic and north Pacific oceans (including charts), notes, abstracts, and reviews; issued by Marine Division. 1923. 7 p. 2 p. of maps, 4° [From Monthly weather review, Apr. 1923.] †

Sunshine-recorder. Instructions for care and management of electrical sunshine recorders, by C. F. Marvin; revised by B. C. Kadel. 1923. cover-title, 8 p. il. 1 pl. 2 p. of pl. (Circular G, Instrument Division, 5th edition.) *Paper, 5c.   Agr 23—809

Weather Bureau, by Henry E. Williams; revised by E. B. Calvert. 1923. iv+55 p. il. narrow 16° †   Agr 23—810

Weather map. Daily weather map [of United States, containing forecasts for all States east of Mississippi River except Illinois, Wisconsin, Indiana, upper Michigan, and lower Michigan], July 2-31, 1923. 1st edition. [1923.] Each 16.4×22.7 in. [Not issued Sundays or holidays.] *Editions issued at Washington, D. C., 25c. a month, $2.50 a yr.; editions issued at about 65 stations throughout the United States, 20c. a month, $2.00 a yr.

—— Same [containing forecasts for United States], July 1-31, 1923. 2d edition. [1923.] Each 16.4×22.7 in. [The Sunday edition does not contain as much information as the edition for week days.] *30c. a month, $3.00 a yr.

CIVIL SERVICE COMMISSION

Note.—The Commission furnishes its publications gratuitously to those who apply for them.

Porto Rico. Informes a los aspirantes a empleos en el servicio civil clasificado en Puerto Rico. Apr. 1923. 22 p. (Modelo 1372.) †

COAL COMMISSION

Coal mines and mining. Profit and loss, balance sheet, and surplus statements for semibituminous, bituminous, or subbituminous coal or lignite mines; [pepared in] Cost of Production and Investment Division. [1923.] 7 p. oblong large 8° (Form C–35.) [Blank form issued to operators of coal mines for purpose of securing information for use of Coal Commission.] †

Earnings of anthracite miners; by Anne Bezanson. [1923.] [2]+49 leaves, 4° [Mimeographed.] ‡

[*Report* of Coal Commission on anthracite industry to the President and Congress, July 5, 1923.] [1923.] 45+[1] leaves, f° [Mimeographed. This report has been reprinted by the National Coal Association, Southern Building, Washington, D. C.] ‡

COMMERCE DEPARTMENT

Note.—The Department of Commerce prints most of its publications in very limited editions, the distribution of which is confined to Government officers, libraries, etc. When a selling price is noted in this list, application for such publication should be submitted to the Superintendent of Documents, Washington, D. C., with remittance. For copies of charts, coast pilots, and tide tables, however, apply directly to the issuing office, the Coast and Geodetic Survey, Washington, D. C.

Trade association activities, prepared by L. E. Warford and Richard A. May, under direction of Julius Klein, director, Bureau of Foreign and Domestic Commerce; [with Trade association bibliography, by H. H. B. Meyer]. 1923. xii+368 p. il. 1 pl. (Elimination of waste series.) [This investigation was undertaken by the Census Bureau, Foreign and Domestic Commerce Bureau, and Standards Bureau.] *Cloth, 50c.   23—26722

CENSUS BUREAU

Note.—Persons desiring 14th census publications should address the Director of the Census, Department of Commerce, Washington, D. C. They are also sold by the Superintendent of Documents, Washington, D. C., at the price indicated.

Birth statistics for birth registration area of United States, [calendar year] 1921, 7th annual report. 1923. 269 p. il. 4° [Prepared under direction of William H. Davis, chief statistician for vital statistics, assisted by John B. Mitchell, expert chief of division.] *Paper, 35c.   17—26651

Centers of population, agriculture, and manufactures. 1923. 1 p. il. 4° †
    23—26655

Chemicals. 14th census of United States [1920]: Manufactures, 1919, chemicals and allied products. 1923. v+603–789 p. 4° [Prepared under supervision of Eugene F. Hartley, chief statistician for manufactures. From 14th census of United States, v. 10.] †

Cotton consumed, cotton on hand, active cotton spindles, and imports and exports of cotton, June, 1922 and 1923, with statistics of cotton consumed, imported, and exported for 11 months ending June 30. July 14, 1923. oblong 32° [Preliminary report. This publication is issued in postal card form.] †

Cottonseed received, crushed, and on hand, and cottonseed products manufactured, shipped out, on hand, and exported covering 11-month period ending June 30, 1923 and 1922. July 19, 1923. oblong 32° [Preliminary report. This publication is issued in postal card form.] †

Farm implements and machinery. Census of manufactures, 1921: Manufacture and sale of farm equipment. 1923. 22 p. * Paper, 5c.   23—26604

Manufactures. 14th census of United States, 1920: v. 10, Manufactures, 1919, reports for selected industries. 1923. 1059 p. il. 4° [Prepared under supervision of Eugene F. Hartley, chief statistician for manufactures, assisted by John F. Daly, William A. Ruff, William W. Sawyer, chiefs of division, Frank L. Sanford and Story B. Ladd, expert special agents, and Lucy Craycroft, statistical expert.] * Cloth, $2.50.

Motor-cycles. Census of manufactures, 1921: Motorcycles, bicycles, and parts. 1923. 9 p. * Paper, 5c.   23—26667

Official register of United States. Official register, 1923, key to abbreviations. [1923.] 14 p. 4° ‡

Textiles. 14th census of United States [1920]: Manufactures, 1919, textiles and their products. 1923. v+147–306 p. il. 4° [Prepared under supervision of Eugene F. Hartley, chief statistician for manufactures. From 14th census of United States, 1920, v. 10.] †

Turpentine. Census of manufactures, 1921: Turpentine and rosin; compiled in cooperation with Department of Agriculture, Bureau of Chemistry. 1923. 10 p. * Paper, 5c.   23—26668

Typewriters. Census of manufactures, 1921: Typewriters and supplies. 1923. 8 p. * Paper, 5c.   23—26669

Vital statistics. Physicians' pocket reference to international list of causes of death. 6th edition. 1923. 32 p. il. narrow 24° [Prepared under supervision of William H. Davis, chief statistician for vital statistics.] †
                                                            23—26670

Woman home-maker in city, study of statistics relating to married women in Rochester, N. Y., at census of 1920; by Bertha M. Nienburg. 1923. 49 p. * Paper, 10c.   23—26671

COAST AND GEODETIC SURVEY

NOTE.—The monthly Notice to mariners, formerly issued by the Coast and Geodetic Survey, has been consolidated with and made a part of the Notice to mariners issued by the Lighthouses Bureau, thus making it a joint publication. The charts, coast pilots, and tide tables of the Coast and Geodetic Survey are sold at the office of the Survey in Washington, and also by one or more sales agents in each of the important American seaports.

Coast and Geodetic Survey bulletin, June 30, 1923; no. 97. [1923.] 9 p. [Monthly.] ‡   15—26512

Coast pilots. Supplement to United States coast pilot, Atlantic Coast, section B, Cape Cod to Sandy Hook. Sept. 30, 1922, [reprint with slight change] 1923. 12 leaves. (Serial 219.) †

Charts

Columbia River, Oreg.-Wash., Grims Island to St. Helens, surveys by U. S. Engineers to Mar. 1923; chart 6153. Scale 1:40,000. Washington, Coast and Geodetic Survey, July, 1923. 38.9×32.9 in. † 75c.

Delaware River, Wilmington to Philadelphia, control by C. & G. Survey, surveys by U. S. Engineers to 1922 and other sources; chart 295. Scale 1:40,000. Washington, Coast and Geodetic Survey, July, 1923. 31.8×43.1 in. † 75c.

Gulf Coast, Habana [Cuba] to Tampa Bay [Fla., from] surveys to 1920 and other sources; chart 1113. [Scale 1:471,000.] Washington, Coast and Geodetic Survey, July, 1923. 43.1×29.1 in. [For offshore navigation only.] † 75c.

Jamaica Bay and Rockaway Inlet, N. Y., [from] surveys 1909–14, surveys by U. S. Engineers to 1923 and other sources; chart 542. Scale 1:20,000. Washington, Coast and Geodetic Survey, July, 1923. 31.1×39.6 in. † 75c.

Philippine Islands, southeastern part, surveys to 1922; chart 4708. [Scale 1:800,000.] Manila, P. I., Coast and Geodetic Survey, May, 1923. 31.2×32.7 in. † 75c.

FISHERIES BUREAU

Cold storage holdings of fish, June 15, 1923. [1923.] 1 p. oblong 8° (Statistical bulletin 577.) [Statistics furnished by Agricultural Economics Bureau.] †

Fisheries service bulletin, July 2, 1923; no. 98. [1923.] 7 p. [Monthly.] ‡
                         F 15—76

Fishery products. Statement of quantities and values of certain fishery products landed at Boston and Gloucester, Mass., and Portland, Me., by American fishing vessels, June, 1923. [1923.] 1 p. oblong f° (Statistical bulletin 578.) †

—— Statement of quantities and values of certain fishery products landed at Seattle, Wash., by American fishing vessels, May, 1923. [1923.] 1 p. oblong 8° (Statistical bulletin 576.) †

Report of commissioner of fisheries, fiscal year 1922, with appendixes [title-page, contents, etc.]. 1923. iv+2 p. ([Bureau of Fisheries doc. 913.]) †
                         F 10—2

Sciaenidae. Contributions to life histories of Sciænidæ of eastern United States coast [with bibliography]; by William W. Welsh and C. M. Breder, jr. 1923. [1]+141–201 p. il. large 8° ([Bureau of Fisheries] doc. 945.) [From Bulletin, v. 39.] *Paper, 15c.   F 23—199

FOREIGN AND DOMESTIC COMMERCE BUREAU

Agricultural Implements Division. Bringing American implement manufacturer and foreign customer together, [work of] Agricultural Implements Division. 1923. 8 p. narrow 12° †   23—26672

Automotive markets in China, British Malaya, and Chosen; by William I. Irvine. 1923. vi+105 p. 6 p. of pl. (Special agents series 221.) *Paper, 15c.   23—26673

Commerce. Monthly summary of foreign commerce of United States, May, 1923. 1923. 2 pts. p. 1–69 and ii+71–91 p. 4° *Paper, 10c. single copy (including pts. 1 and 2), $1.00 a yr.; foreign subscription, $1.60. 14—21465

—— Same. 1923. [2 pts. in 1], 91 p. 4° (H. doc. 437, 67th Cong. 3d sess.)

Commerce reports. Commerce reports, weekly survey of foreign trade, reports from American consular officers and representatives of Department of Commerce in foreign countries, no. 27–31; July 2–30, 1923. 1923. cover-titles, p. 1–328, 4° [Text and illustration on p. 2–4 of covers.] *Paper, 10c. single copy, $3.00 a yr.; foreign subscription, $5.00.

—— Supplement to Commerce reports. [Included in price of Commerce reports for subscribers.]

Trade and economic review for 1922, no. 10: Danzig; [by] Charles H. Albrecht. [1923.] 12 p. i
Same, no. 11: Algeria; [by] David C. Elkington. [1923.] 24 p.
Same, no. 12: Indo-China; [by] Leland L. Smith. [1923.] 8 p.
Same, no. 13: Venezuela; [by] S. J. Fletcher. [1923.] 20 p.
Same, no. 14: Finland; [by] Leslie A. Davis. [1923.] 11 p.
Same, no. 15: Uruguay; [by] Sherwood H. Avery. [1923.] 4 p.

—— Supplement to Commerce reports: Austrian trade in rubber products; by Carol H. Foster. July 30, 1923. ii+14 p. (Trade information bulletin 131; Rubber Division.) †   23—26674

—— Same: Bankruptcy and insolvency laws of Argentina; by W. Henry Robertson. July 23, 1923. ii+20 p. (Trade information bulletin 126; Division of Commercial Laws.) †   23—26675

—— Same: Brazilian market for paper and paper products; prepared from data furnished by W. L. Schurz, M. A. Cremer, Thomas H. Bevan, and C. R. Cameron. July 21, 1923. ii+14 p. (Trade information bulletin 127; Paper Division.) †   23—26676

—— Same: British banking, foreign policies of "Big Five" banks; by Leland Rex Robinson. July 2, 1923. ii+11 p. (Trade information bulletin 117; Finance and Investment Division.) †   23—26636

—— Same: Cost of protesting drafts in northern Africa and Egypt; compiled by A. J. Wolfe from information furnished by American consular officers. July 27, 1923. ii+10 p. (Trade information bulletin 128; Division of Commercial Laws.) †   23—26677

Commerce reports—Continued. Same: International trade in 1922; by J. J. Kral. July 16, 1923. [1]+22 p. (Trade information bulletin 123; Division of Research.) †   23—26678

—— Same: Italian Government finances; by H. C. MacLean. July 30, 1923. iii+15 p. (Trade information bulletin 130; Western European Division.) †
23—26679

—— Same: Legal aspects of construction enterprises in Asiatic countries; compiled by A. J. Wolfe from information furnished by American consular officers and Department of Commerce representatives. July 9, 1923. [1]+ 9 p. (Trade information bulletin 121; Division of Commercial Laws.) †
23—26640

—— Same: Legal aspects of construction enterprises in France; by Chester Lloyd Jones. July 16, 1923. ii+8 p. (Trade information bulletin 124; Division of Commercial Laws.) †   23—26680

—— Same: Legal aspects of construction enterprises in Latin America, with survey of laws on incorporation and registration of companies, taxation, and employers' liability for injury to workmen; prepared by A. J. Wolfe from information furnished by American Government representatives, in Latin America. July 2, 1923. ii+48 p. (Trade information bulletin 118; Division of Commercial Laws.) · †   23—26637

—— Same: Methods of handling lumber imports in Africa; by Perry J. Stevenson and American consular officers. July 2, 1923. iv+50 p. (Trade information bulletin 119; Lumber Division.) †   23—26638

—— Same: Methods of handling lumber imports in Australia, New Zealand, and Pacific islands, with report on lumber industry of New Zealand; compiled from information furnished by American trade commissioner at Melbourne and American consular officers. July 23, 1923. iv+23 p. (Trade information bulletin 125; Lumber Division.) †   23—26681

—— Same: Protesting drafts in Australia and New Zealand; compiled by A. J. Wolfe from information furnished by American consular officers in Australia and New Zealand. July 2, 1923. ii+7 p. (Trade information bulletin 120; Division of Commercial Laws.) †   23—26639

—— Same: Shipment of samples and advertising matter to British Empire; prepared by Division of Foreign Tariffs. July 9, 1923. ii+16 p. (Trade information bulletin 122.) †   23—26641

—— Same: Trade of United States in 1922 according to international statistical classification; prepared in Division of Statistics. July 31, 1923. [1]+ 9 p. (Trade information bulletin 129.) †   23—26682

—— Survey of current business, July, 1923, no. 23; compiled by Bureau of Census, Bureau of Foreign and Domestic Commerce, [and] Bureau of Standards. 1923. cover-title, 60 p. il. 4° (Monthly supplement to Commerce reports.) [Contains statistics for May, 1923, the date given above, July, 1923, being the date of issue. Text on p. 2–4 of cover.] * Paper, 10c. single copy, $1.00 a yr.; foreign subscription, $1.50.   21—26819

NOTE.—Realizing that current statistics are highly perishable and that to be of use they must reach the business man at the earliest possible moment, the Department has arranged to distribute advance leaflets twice each month to those subscribers who request them. One set of these leaflets is issued about the 20th of the month, giving such information as has been received up to that time, and another set of sheets is mailed at the end of the month giving those figures received since the 20th. The information contained in these leaflets is also published in Commerce reports issued weekly by the Foreign and Domestic Commerce Bureau. The advance sheets will be mailed free of charge to all subscribers to the Survey who request them. Such requests should be addressed to the Bureau of the Census, Department of Commerce, Washington, D. C. Subscriptions, however, should be sent to the Superintendent of Documents, Washington, D. C., at the prices stated above.

Publications. List of publications for sale by superintendent of documents and by district and cooperative offices of Bureau of Foreign and Domestic Commerce; corrected to June 1, 1923. 1923. 16 p. narrow 12° †   23—26657

Stave trade in foreign countries; [prepared in] Lumber Division. 1923. v+99 p. il. (Miscellaneous series 118.) [Includes lists of Foreign and Domestic Commerce Bureau publications relating to lumber industry.] *Paper, 15c.   23—26683

LIGHTHOUSES BUREAU

1st District. Atlantic Coast of United States, buoy list, Maine and New Hampshire, 1st lighthouse district; 1923, corrected to June 5. 1923. [1]+79 p. *Paper, 20c. 11—29015

17th District. Pacific Coast of United States, buoy list, Oregon and Washington, 17th lighthouse district; 1923, corrected to June 25. 1923. [1]+65 p. * Paper, 20c. 14—30348

18th District. Pacific Coast of United States, buoy list, California, 18th lighthouse district; 1923, corrected to June 15. 1923. [1]+35 p. * Paper, 20c. (price incorrectly given on p. 35 as 5c.). 16—25814

Lighthouse service bulletin, v. 2, no. 67; July 2, 1923. [1923.] p. 285–288. [Monthly.] † 12—35121

Notice to mariners, weekly, no. 27–30, 1923; July 6–27 [1923]. 1923. various paging. [Issued jointly with Coast and Geodetic Survey.] † 7—20609

NAVIGATION BUREAU

Ships. American documented seagoing merchant vessels of 500 gross tons and over, July 2, 1923. 1923. ii+64 p. 4° (Serial 68.) [Monthly.] *Paper, 10c. single copy, 75c. a yr.; foreign subscription, $1.25. 19—26597

RADIO SERVICE

Radio Service bulletin, July 2, 1923; no. 75. [1923.] 22 p. [Monthly.] *Paper, 5c. single copy, 25c. a yr.; foreign subscription, 40c. 15—26255

PUBLICATIONS DIVISION

Commerce Department. Supplement to annual List of publications [of Department of Commerce available for distribution], June 30, 1923. [1923.] 4 p. [Monthly.] †

STANDARDS BUREAU

NOTE.—The Scientific papers will be supplied on subscription as issued at $1.25 per volume, paper bound. These volumes will afterwards be issued bound in cloth at $2.00 per volume; foreign subscription, paper $2.50 (sent in single numbers), cloth $2.35 (bound volumes). Single numbers vary in price. Address the Superintendent of Documents, Washington, D. C.
The Technologic papers will be issued first as separates and later in volume form in the same manner as the Scientific papers. Subscriptions will be accepted by the Superintendent of Documents at $1.25 per volume; foreign subscription, $2.50. Single numbers vary in price.

Aeronautic instruments; by Franklin L. Hunt. May 16, 1923. [1]+447–511 p. il. large 8° (Technologic papers 237.) [From Technologic papers, v. 17.] *Paper, 20c. 23—26684

Bricks. Paving bricks. 2d revision, May 15, 1923. 1923. 10 p. (Simplified practice recommendation no. 1.) [Title on cover is: Elimination of waste, simplified practice, paving bricks.] *Paper, 5c. 23—26685

Limestone. Recommended specification for limestone and quicklime for use in manufacture of sulphite pulp. July 6, 1923. 7 p. large 8° (Circular 144.) *Paper, 5c. 23—26686

Metals. Standard samples, general information. 8th edition. June 26, 1923. [1]+14 p. (Circular 25.) [Supersedes 7th edition issued June 29, 1922.] *Paper, 5c. 23—26687

Quicklime. Recommended specification for quicklime for use in causticizing. June 25, 1923. 5 p. large 8° (Circular 143.) *Paper, 5c. 23—26605

STEAMBOAT-INSPECTION SERVICE

Steamboat Inspection Service bulletin, July 2, 1923; no. 93. [1923.] 3 p. [Monthly.] ‡ 15—26679

CONGRESS

POSTAL SERVICE JOINT COMMISSION

Postal service. Postal service, hearings. 1923. v. 2, ii+705-1213 p. † ·

—— [Report.] 1923. pts. 19–26, [xxxi]+1461-1562+[xv] p. [Part 18 is confidential and is not entered in this catalogue.] ‡ 21—27447

pt. 19. Special report on post office at Kansas City, Mo., by committee of postal service officials.

pt. 20. Special report on post office at Omaha, Nebr., by committee of postal service officials.

pt. 21. Special report on post office at Los Angeles, Calif., by committee of postal service officials.

pt. 22. Special report on post office at San Francisco, Calif., by committee of postal service officials.

pt. 23. Special report on post office at Seattle, Wash., by committee of postal service officials.

pt. 24. Special report on post office at St. Louis, Mo., by committee of postal service officials.

pt. 25. Special report on post office at Minneapolis, Minn., by committee of postal service officials.

pt. 26. Special report on post office at Milwaukee, Wis., by committee of postal service officials.

SENATE

GOLD AND SILVER INQUIRY COMMISSION

Silver purchases under Pittman act, hearings before subcommittee pursuant to S. Res. 469, creating Commission of Gold and Silver Inquiry, June 27 [–July 18], 1923. 1923. [xi]+111-250+ii p. (Serial 1, pts. 2–5.) †

REFORESTATION SELECT COMMITTEE

Reforestation, hearings pursuant to S. Res. 398, to investigate problems relating to reforestation, May 8–12, 1923. 1923. pt. 4, ii+423-637 p. †

COURT OF CLAIMS

Acme Die-Casting Corporation v. United States; evidence for plaintiff. [1923.] Congressional, no. 17330, p. 63–70. ‡

Chicago, Rock Island & Pacific Railway Co. v. United States; evidence for claimant. [1923.] no. 34706, p. 55–62. ‡

Consolidated Supply Company. Geo. M. Davis, doing business as Consolidated Supply Co., *v.* United States; evidence for plaintiff. [1923.] no. B-88, p. 15–21. ‡

Davis Sewing Machine Company v. United States; evidence for plaintiff. [1923.] no. B-17, p. 7-32. ‡

El Paso and Southwestern Company et al. *v.* United States; defendant's evidence. [1923.] no. 294–A, p. 37–38. ‡

Erie Specialty Company v. United States; evidence. [1923.] no. 34663, p. 289-292. ‡

Fairbanks, Morse & Company v. United States; evidence for plaintiff. [1923.] Congressional, no. 17332, p. 55–62. ‡

General Manufacturing Company v. United States; evidence for plaintiff. [1923.] no. B-424, p. 15–34. ‡

Gulf, Colorado & Santa Fe Railway Co. v. United States; defendant's evidence. [1923.] no. 2-B, p. 17–22. ‡ .

Kesler. Clarence I. Kesler *v.* United States; evidence. [1923.] no. B-369, p. 5–7. ‡

Louisville & Nashville Railroad Co. v. United States; defendant's evidence. [1923.] no. 206–B, p. 7–9. ‡

Missouri, Kansas and Texas Railway. Charles E. Schaff, receiver of Missouri, Kansas & Texas Railway Co. *v.* United States; defendants' evidence. [1923.] no. B-122, p. 7–14. ‡

Norfolk Southern Railroad Co. v. United States; evidence for defendant [claimant]. [1923.] no. B–190, p. 11–25. ‡

Peabody, Henry W., & Co. Henry W. Peabody & Co. *v.* United States; evidence for plaintiff. [1923.] no. B–425, p. 5–20. ‡

St. Louis, Brownsville and Mexico Railway. St. Louis, Brownsville & Mexico Railway Co. *v.* United States; defendant's evidence. [1923.] no. B–180, p. 15–17. ‡

—— St. Louis, Brownsville and Mexico Railway Company *v.* United States; defendant's evidence. [1923.] no. 159–B, p. 17–23. ‡

Smith. Terrence P. Smith *v.* United States; evidence [for claimant]. [1923.] no. B–370, p. 5–6. ‡

Southern Pacific Company v. United States; evidence for defendant. [1923.] no. B–368, p. 15–20. ‡

Thermal Syndicate (Ltd.) v. United States; evidence for plaintiff. [1923.] Congressional, no. 17333, p. 45–75. ‡

Western Pacific Railroad Company v. United States; evidence for defendant. [1923.] no. 30–A, p. 81–86. ‡

Wrigley, William, jr., Company. Wm. Wrigley, jr., Co. *v.* United States; Acme Die-Casting Corp. *v.* [same]; Sirio Match Co. *v.* [same]; Fairbanks, Morse & Co. *v.* [same]; Thermal Syndicate, Ltd., *v.* [same]; Drapery Hardware Co. *v.* [same]; Charles B. Chrystal *v.* [same]; P. L. Andrews Corp. *v.* [same]; R. S. Howard Co. *v.* [same]; evidence for defendant. [1923.] Congressional, no. 17329–337, 22 p. ‡

COURT OF CUSTOMS APPEALS

Press cloth. Nos. 2281 and 2283, United States *v.* M. J. Hogan; [same] *v.* Guy B. Barham, transcript of record on appeal from Board of General Appraisers. [1923.] cover-title, ii+26 p. ‡

Rules of Court of Customs Appeals, corrected to July 1, 1923, and provisions of chapter 8 of judicial code, act approved Mar. 3, 1911, relating to court. 1923. iii+13 p. * Paper, 10c. 23—26688

DISTRICT OF COLUMBIA

Public Utilities Commission. 10th annual report of Public Utilities Commission of District of Columbia, [calendar year] 1922. 1923. v+261 p. † Public Utilities Commission. 14—30633

FEDERAL RESERVE BOARD

Federal reserve bulletin. Federal reserve bulletin, July, 1923; [v. 9, no. 7]. 1st edition. 1923. ii+215–252 p. il. 4° [Monthly.] †Paper, $1.50 a yr. 15—26318

NOTE.—The Federal reserve bulletin is printed in 2 editions (a 1st edition and a final edition). The 1st edition is brief and contains the regular official announcements, the national review of business conditions, and other general matter, and is distributed without charge to the member banks of the Federal reserve system. The 2d or final edition contains detailed analyses of business conditions, special articles, review of foreign banking, and complete statistics showing condition of Federal reserve banks. Those desiring copies of either edition may obtain them from the Federal Reserve Board, Washington, D. C., at the prices stated above and below.

—— Same, July, 1923; [v. 9, no. 7]. Final edition. 1923. iv+767–870+iv p. il. 4° [Monthly.] † Paper, 40c. single copy, $4.00 a yr.

Federal reserve member banks. Federal reserve inter-district collection system, changes in list of banks upon which items will be received by Federal reserve banks for collection and credit, July 1, 1923. 1923. 12 p. 4° † 16—26370

Regulations [A-L], series of 1923. [Edition of] July, 1923. 1923. ii+41 p. 4° [These Regulations supersede all previous issues of Regulations A-L.] † 17—26561

58153—No. 343—23——3

GENERAL ACCOUNTING OFFICE

Decisions of comptroller general, v. 2, June, 1923; J. R. McCarl, comptroller general, Lurtin R. Ginn, assistant comptroller general. 1923. [1]+787–828 p. [Monthly.] †   21—26777

GOVERNMENT PRINTING OFFICE

Public printing. Abstract of contracts for material, etc., for public printing and binding, for 6 months and 1 year beginning July 1, 1923. 1923. 20 p. 4° ‡

DOCUMENTS OFFICE

Animal industry, farm animals, poultry, and dairying, list of publications for sale by superintendent of documents. June, 1923. [2]+19+[2] p. (Price list 38, 16th edition.) †   23—26689

Indians, including Government publications pertaining to mounds and antiquities, for sale by superintendent of documents. June, 1923. [2]+16+[2] p. (Price list 24, 7th edition.) †   23—26642

Monthly catalogue, United States public documents, no. 342; June, 1923. 1923. p. 757–814. * Paper, 5c. single copy, 50c. a yr.; foreign subscription, 75c. 4—18088

Weather, astronomy, and meteorology, list of publications for sale by superintendent of documents. June, 1923. [2]+9 p. (Price list 48, 13th edition.) †   23—26643

INTERIOR DEPARTMENT

EDUCATION BUREAU

Business education. Organization and conduct of business, report of conference held by Bureau of Education in conjunction with National Commercial Teachers' Federation, Chicago, Ill., Dec. 26, 1922; by Glen Levin Swiggett. June, 1923. 18 p. (Commercial education leaflet 5.) *Paper, 5c.   E 23—314

—— Statistics relating to business education in colleges and universities, 1921–22; by Glen Levin Swiggett. June, 1923. 8 p. (Commercial education leaflet 6.) * Paper, 5c.   E 23—315

Colleges and universities. Higher education, 1920–22; by George F. Zook. 1923. [1]+33 p. (Bulletin 34, 1923.) [Advance sheets from Biennial survey of education in United States, 1920–22.] * Paper, 5c.   E 21—496

Country schools. Educational progress and parents; [by] Orville G. Brim. May, 1923. 8 p. (Rural school leaflet 15.) *Paper, 5c.   E 23—317

Junior high schools. Junior high schools of Berkeley, Calif.; prepared by James T. Preston, chairman, W. B. Clark, H. H. Glessner, and D. L. Hennessey, in cooperation with H. B. Wilson, superintendent of schools. 1923. iii+48 p. il. (Bulletin 4, 1923.) * Paper, 10c.   E 23—311

—— Specimen junior high school programs of study [with list of references on junior high-school courses of study]; compiled by W. S. Deffenbaugh. 1923. [1]+28 p. (Bulletin 21, 1923.) *Paper, 5c.   E 23—269

Music. Recent advances in instruction in music; [articles] by Will Earhart and Charles N. Boyd. 1923. [1]+21 p. (Bulletin 20, 1923.) [Advance sheets from Biennial survey of education in United States, 1920–22.] *Paper, 5c.   E 23—312

CONTENTS.—Pt. 1, In public schools; by Will Earhart.—Pt. 2, General; by Charles N. Boyd.

Rural education; by Katherine M. Cook. 1923. ii+35 p. (Bulletin 36, 1923.) [Advance sheets from Biennial survey of education in United States, 1920–22.] *Paper, 5c.   E 23—313

St. Louis Manual Training School. History of manual training school of Washington University (St. Louis Manual Training School); by Charles Penney Coates. 1923. iii+86 p. il. 12 p. of pl. (Bulletin 3, 1923.) *Paper, 20c. E 23—268

School funds. School support and school indebtedness in cities; prepared by Statistical Division. June, 1923. 5 p. (Statistical circular 3.) * Paper, 5c.   E 23--318

Secondary education. Moral values in secondary education, report of Commission on Reorganization of Secondary Education appointed by National Education Association; prepared by Henry Neumann. [Reprint] 1923. 38 p. (Bulletin 51, 1917.) * Paper, 5c.   E 18—520

Sleep [with list of references]; by Harriet Wedgwood. [1923.] cover-title, 22 p. il. (Health education 12.) [Text on p. 2 and 3 of cover.] *Paper, 5c.
                                                                                                                E 23—316

Vocational education; by William T. Bawden. 1923. [1]+26 p. il. (Bulletin 28, 1923.) [Advance sheets from Biennial survey of education in United States, 1920–22.] * Paper, 5c.   E 19—228

Young Women's Christian Association. Educational work of Young Women's Christian Association; by Education and Research Division, National Board of Y. W. C. A. 1923. ii+24 p. (Bulletin 26, 1923.) [Advance sheets from Biennial survey of education in United States, 1920–22.] *Paper, 5c.
                                                                                                                E 23—273

GENERAL LAND OFFICE

NOTE.—The General Land Office publishes a large general map of the United States, which is sold at $2.00; and also separate maps of the States and Territories in which public lands are to be found, which are sold at 25c. per sheet. The map of California is in 2 sheets. Address the Superintendent of Documents, Washington, D. C.

Homestead. Soldiers' and sailors' homestead rights. June 12, 1923. 16 p. (Circular 302.) [This circular is a reprint of regulations of May 26, 1922, as revised Nov. 23, 1922, Circular 865, and Jan. 31, 1923, Circular 871.] †

GEOLOGICAL SURVEY

NOTE.—The publications of the United States Geological Survey consist of annual reports, Monographs, Professional papers, Bulletins, Water-supply papers, chapters and volumes of Mineral resources of the United States, folios of the Topographic atlas of the United States and topographic maps that bear descriptive text, and folios of the Geologic atlas of the United States and the World atlas of commercial geology. A wholesale rate has been established for topographic and geologic folios, so that a discount of 40 per cent from the retail price is now allowed on all orders the net cost of which amounts to $5.00 or more. This rate applies on an order for either maps or folios alone or for maps and folios together, but does not apply to the folios sold at 5c each on account of damage by fire. For maps and topographic and geologic folios address the Director of the Geological Survey, Washington, D. C. Other publications, with the exception of Monographs, are free at the Survey as long as the supply lasts and are also sold by the Superintendent of Documents at the price indicated. Orders for such publications as are for sale (excepting maps and folios) should be sent to the Superintendent of Documents, Washington, D. C.

Asphalt and related bitumens in 1922; by K. W. Cottrell. July 19, 1923. [1]+ 7–13 p. [From Mineral resources, 1922, pt. 2.] †

Atlantic Coastal Plain. Surface water supply of United States, 1919–20: pt. 1, North Atlantic slope drainage basins; Nathan C. Grover, chief hydraulic engineer, C. H. Pierce, C. C. Covert, O. W. Hartwell, and G. C. Stevens, district engineers. 1923. 330 p. 2 p. of pl. (Water-supply paper 501.) [Prepared in cooperation with Maine, New Hampshire, Vermont, Massachusetts, Connecticut, New York, and Pennsylvania.] * Paper, 30c.   GS 10—290
—— Same. (H. doc. 439, 67th Cong. 3d sess.)

Bismuth, selenium, and tellurium in 1922; by Victor C. Heikes. July 16, 1923. ii+15–25 p. [From Mineral resources, 1922, pt. 1.] †

Creede, Colo. Geology and ore deposits of Creede district, Colo. [with bibliography]; by William H. Emmons and Esper S. Larsen. 1923. ix+198 p. il. 2 pl. 8 p. of pl. 2 maps in pocket, 1 tab. (Bulletin 718.) * Paper, 40c.
                                                                                                                GS 23—203
—— Same. (H. doc. 1005, 66th Cong. 3d sess.)

Great Basin. Surface water supply of United States, 1919–20: pt. 10, Great Basin; Nathan C. Grover, chief hydraulic engineer, A. B. Purton, H. D. McGlashan, F. F. Henshaw, C. G. Paulsen, and Robert Follansbee, district engineers. 1923. vi+348 p. 2 p. of pl. (Water-supply paper 510.) [Prepared in cooperation with Utah, Nevada, California, Oregon, Wyoming, and Idaho.] * Paper, 30c.   GS 10—348
—— Same. (H. doc. 617, 67th Cong. 4th sess.)

Hot Springs, Ark. Hot Springs folio, Ark. [with bibliography]; by A. H. Purdue and H. D. Miser. [Library edition.] Washington, Geological Survey, 1923. cover-title, 12 p. il. 2 pl. 3 maps, large 4° (Geologic atlas of United States 215.) [Text and illustrations on p. 2-4 of cover.] † Paper, 25c.   GS 23—206

Ilsemannite at Ouray, Utah; by Frank L. Hess. June 28, 1923. ii+1-16 p. il. 2 p. of pl. (Bulletin 750 A.) †

Lead. Lead and zinc pigments and salts in 1922; by C. E. Siebenthal and A. Stoll. July 25, 1923. ii+77-85 p. il. [From Mineral resources, 1922, pt. 1.] †

—— Lead in 1922, general report; by C. E. Siebenthal and A. Stoll. July 17, 1923. ii+27-36 p. il. [From Mineral resources, 1922, pt. 1.] † :

Limestone. Lime belt of Massachusetts and parts of eastern New York and western Connecticut; by T. Nelson Dale. 1923. vi+71 p. il. 4 p. of pl. 4 maps in pocket. (Bulletin 744.) * Paper, 30c.   GS 23—207

—— Same. (H. doc. 466, 67th Cong. 3d sess.)

Mineral resources. Mineral resources of United States, 1920: pt. 1, Metals [with bibliographies]. 1922. 155a+611 p. il. 2 pl. * Cloth, 90c.   4—18124

—— Same. (H. doc. 403, 67th Cong. 2d sess.)

Pacific Coast. Surface water supply of United States, 1919–20: pt. 12, North Pacific slope drainage basins, A, Pacific basins in Washington and upper Columbia River basin; Nathan C. Grover, chief hydraulic engineer, G. L. Parker and W. A. Lamb, district engineers. 1923. v+262 p. 2 p. of pl. (Water-supply paper 512.) [Prepared in cooperation with Washington, Montana, and Idaho.] * Paper, 25c.   GS 10—167

—— Same. (H. doc. 619, 67th Cong. 4th sess.)

Petroleum. Progress report on subsurface study of Pershing oil and gas field, Osage County, Okla.; by W. W. Rubey. July 18, 1923. iv+23-70 p. il. 3 maps. (Bulletin 751 B.) †

Zinc in 1922; by C. E. Siebenthal and A. Stoll. July 18, 1923. ii+37-52 p. il. [From Mineral resources, 1922, pt. 1.] †

MINES BUREAU

Coke. Comparative tests of by-product coke and other fuels for house-heating boilers; by Henry Kreisinger, John Blizard, H. W. Jarrett, and J. J. McKitterick. [1st edition.] [May] 1923. ii+21 p. il. 1 pl. (Technical paper 315.) [Includes list of Mines Bureau publications on coal, as boiler fuel.] * Paper, 5c.   23—26690

PATENT OFFICE

NOTE.—The Patent Office publishes specifications and drawings of patents in single copies. These are not enumerated in this catalogue, but may be obtained for 10c. each at the Patent Office.
A variety of indexes, giving a complete view of the work of the Patent Office from 1790 to date, are published at prices ranging from 25c. to $10.00 per volume and may be obtained from the Superintendent of Documents, Washington, D. C. The Rules of practice and pamphlet Patent laws are furnished free of charge upon application to the Patent Office. The Patent Office issues coupon orders in packages of 20 at $2.00 per package or in books containing 100 coupons at $10.00 per book. These coupons are good until used, but are only to be used for orders sent to the Patent Office. For schedule of office fees, address Chief Clerk, Patent Office, Washington, D. C.

Decisions. [Decisions in patent and trade-mark cases, etc.]. July 3, 1923. p. 1-6, large 8° [From Official gazette, v. 312, no. 1.] † Paper, 5c. single copy, $2.00 a yr.

—— Same. July 10, 1923. p. 185-190, large 8° [From Official gazette, v. 312, no. 2.]

—— Same. July 17, 1923. p. 397-406, il. large 8° [From Official gazette, v. 312, no. 3.]

Decisions—Continued. Same. July 24, 1923. p. 615–624, large 8° [From Official gazette, v. 312, no. 4.]

—— Same. July 31, 1923. p. 823–832, large 8° [From Official gazette, v. 312, no. 5.]

Inventors. Alphabetical list of patentees to whom patents were issued, July 24, 1923 [with list of inventions and with Classification of patents issued July 24, 1923]. [1923.] p. xv–xxxvi, large 8°. [Weekly index to Official gazette. From Official gazette, v. 312, no. 4.] † Paper, $1.00 a yr.

—— Same. [July 31, 1923, with list of inventions, etc., and with Classification of patents issued July 31, 1923.] [1923.] xxxiv p. large 8° [Preceded by Alphabetical list of registrants of trade-marks, etc., which usually follows the Alphabetical list of patentees. Weekly index to Official gazette. From Official gazette, v. 312, no. 5.]

Official gazette. Official gazette, July 3–31, 1923; v. 312, no. 1–5. 1923. cover-titles, 1007+[clxxxiv] p. il. large 8° [Weekly.] * Paper, 10c. single copy, $5.00 a yr.; foreign subscription, $11.00.　　　　4—18256

NOTE.—Contains the patents, trade-marks, designs, and labels issued each week; also decisions of the commissioner of patents and of the United States courts in patent cases.

—— Same [title-page, contents, errata, etc., to] v. 311; June, 1923. 1923. [2] leaves, large 8° *Paper, 5c. single copy, included in price of Official gazette for subscribers.

Patents. Classification of patents issued July 3–31, 1923. [1923.] Each 2 p. large 8° [Weekly. From Official gazette, v. 312, no. 1–5.] †

Trade-marks. Trade-marks [etc., from] Official gazette, July 3, 1923. [1923.] 7–46+i–xi p. il. large 8° [From Official gazette, v. 312, no. 1.] † Paper, 5c. single copy, $2.50 a yr.

—— Same, July 10, 1923. [1923.] 191–246+i–xxi p. il. large 8° [From Official gazette, v. 312, no. 2.]

—— Same, July 17, 1923. [1923.] 407–452+i–xvii p. il. large 8° [From Official gazette, v. 312, no. 3.]

—— Same, July 24, 1923. [1923.] 625–667+i–xiv p. il. large 8° [From Official gazette, v. 312, no. 4.]

—— Same, July 31, 1923. [1923.] 833–870+i–xiv p. il. large 8° [From Official gazette, v. 312, no. 5.]

—— United States statutes concerning registration of trade-marks with rules of Patent Office relating thereto. Revised May 15, 1923 [8th revised edition]. 1923. iii+41 p. il. †　　　　23—26691

PENSION BUREAU

Civil service pensions. Handbook containing abstracts of decisions and opinions and rules of procedure relating to retirement act of May 22, 1920, and amendments; by John S. Beach and Marshall V. Andrews. 1923. x+82 p. [Title on cover is: Retirement act handbook.] *Paper, 10c.　　　　23—26692

RECLAMATION BUREAU

NOTE.—Formerly Reclamation Service.

Irrigation projects of Reclamation Service, national reclamation of arid lands; [revised to Mar. 15, 1923]. [1923.] 40 p. il. †　　　　23—26693

Reclamation record, v. 14, no. 7; July, 1923. [1923.] p. 233–264, il. large 8° [Monthly.]　　　　9—35252

NOTE.—The Reclamation record is published in the interest of the settlers on the reclamation projects, its aim being to raise the general average of success on these projects. It contains much valuable matter of interest to farmers, and will be sent without direct charge to any water user on the reclamation projects. The Record is sold to those who are not water users for 75 cents a year, payable in advance. Subscriptions may be forwarded to the Chief Clerk, U. S. Reclamation Bureau, Washington, D. C., and remittances (postal money order or New York draft) should be made payable to the Special Fiscal Agent, U. S. Reclamation Bureau. Postage stamps will not be accepted.

INTERSTATE COMMERCE COMMISSION

NOTE.—The bound volumes of the decisions, usually known as Interstate Commerce Commission reports, are sold by the Superintendent of Documents, Washington, D. C., at various prices, depending upon the size of the volume. Separate opinions are sold on subscription, price $1.00 per volume; foreign subscription, $1.50; single copies, usually 5c. each.

Batts. No. 13444' Chevrolet Motor Company of California, Incorporated, *v.* director general, as agent, Atchison, Topeka & Santa Fe Railway Company, et al.; decided June 26, 1923; report of commission. [1923.] p. 49–51. ([Opinion] 8597.) [From Interstate Commerce Commission reports, v. 81.] *Paper, 5c.

Bauxite and Northern Railway. Finance docket no. 304, guaranty settlement with Bauxite & Northern Ry.; [decided June 6, 1923; report of commission]. 1923. [1]+612–614 p. ([Finance decision] 727.) [From Interstate Commerce Commission reports, v. 79.] *Paper, 5c.

—— Finance docket no. 1294, deficit settlement with Bauxite & Northern Ry.; decided June 4, 1923; report of commission. [1923.] p. 579–580. ([Finance decision] 720.) [From Interstate Commerce Commission reports, v. 79.] *Paper, 5c.

Bedding, for cattle. No. 13107, National Live Stock Exchange *v.* Atchison, Topeka & Santa Fe Railway Company et al.; decided June 9, 1923; report of commission. [1923.] p. 747–750. ([Opinion] 8582.) [From Interstate Commerce Commission reports, v. 80.] *Paper, 5c.

Bills of lading. No. 4844, export bill of lading, in matter of bills of lading; decided June 6, 1923; report [and order] of commission on further hearing. [1923.] 305–308+ii p. ([Opinion] 8522.) [Report from Interstate Commerce Commission reports, v. 80.] *Paper, 5c.

Bricks. Investigation and suspension docket no. 1783, brick and clay products from El Paso, Tex., and related points to Arizona; [decided June 26, 1923; report and order of commission]. 1923. [1]+20–21+[1] p. ([Opinion] 8590.) [Report from Interstate Commerce Commission reports, v. 81.] *Paper, 5c.

Carbon. No. 13284, French Battery & Carbon Company *v.* Chicago & North Western Railway Company et al.; [decided May 31, 1923; report and order of commission]. 1923. [1]+344–346+[1] p. ([Opinion] 8532.) [Report from Interstate Commerce Commission reports, v. 80.] *Paper, 5c.

Carrollton and Worthville Railroad. Finance docket no. 123, deficit settlement with Carrollton & Worthville R. R.; decided June 1, 1923; report of commission. [1923.] p. 565–566. ([Finance decision] 714.) [From Interstate Commerce Commission reports, v. 79.] *Paper, 5c.

—— Finance docket no. 340, guaranty settlement with Carrollton & Worthville R. R.; [decided June 1, 1923; report of commission]. 1923. [1]+570–572 p. ([Finance decision] 717.) [From Interstate Commerce Commission reports, v. 79.] * Paper, 5c.

Castor-oil. No. 13316, Spencer Kellogg & Sons, Incorporated, *v.* West Shore Railroad Company et al.; decided May 31, 1923; report [and order] of commission. [1923.] 751–752+ii p. ([Opinion] 8583.) [Report from Interstate Commerce Commission reports, v. 80.] *Paper, 5c.

Cattle. No. 10583, North Packing & Provision Company et al. *v.* Chicago, Milwaukee & St. Paul Railway Company, director general, et al.; decided June 7, 1923; report of commission on reargument. [1923.] p. 737–742. ([Opinion] 8579.) [From Interstate Commerce Commission reports, v. 80.] *Paper, 5c.

—— No. 12975, Arizona Packing Company *v.* Arizona Eastern Railroad Company et al.; [no. 12975 (sub-no. 1), same *v.* same]; decided June 27, 1923; report [and order] of commission. [1923.] 115–127+iii p. ([Opinion] 8611.) [Report from Interstate Commerce Commission reports, v. 81.] *Paper, 5c.

Cement. No. 12710, Atlas Portland Cement Company *v.* Chicago, Burlington & Quincy Railroad Company et al.; decided June 6, 1923; [report and order of commission]. [1923.] 1–19+vii p. ([Opinion] 8589.) [Report from Interstate Commerce Commission reports, v. 81.] * Paper, 5c.

Central of Georgia Railway. Finance docket no. 2940, bonds of Central of Georgia Railway; decided June 4, 1923; report of commission. [1923.] p. 609–611. ([Finance decision] 726.) [From Interstate Commerce Commission reports, v. 79.] *Paper, 5c.

—— Finance docket no. 2949, Central of Georgia equipment trust. series O; approved June 1, 1923; supplemental order. 1923. p. 569. ([Finance decision] 716.) [From Interstate Commerce Commission reports, v. 79.] * Paper, 5c.

Chicago and Eastern Illinois Railway. Finance docket no. 2627, bonds of Chicago & Eastern Illinois Ry.; approved June 9, 1923; supplemental order. 1923. p. 627. ([Finance decision] 735.) [From Interstate Commerce Commission reports, v. 79.] * Paper, 5c.

Chicago, Burlington and Quincy Railroad. Finance docket no. 374, guaranty settlement with Chicago, Burlington & Quincy R. R.; decided June 6, 1923; report of commission. [1923.] p. 617–619. ([Finance decision] 730.) [From Interstate Commerce Commission reports, v. 79.] * Paper, 5c.

Chicago, Indianapolis and Louisville Railway. Before Interstate Commerce Commission, valuation dockets 168, 150, 210, 225, 19, 237, Chicago, Indianapolis and Louisville Railway Company et al.; memorandum on argument on original cost to date. 1923. cover-title, iii+223 p. il. 4 p. of pl. ‡

Chicago, Palatine and Wauconda Railroad. Finance docket no. 728, guaranty settlement with Chicago, Palatine & Wauconda R. R.; [decided June 8, 1923; report of commission]. 1923. [1]+600–602 p. ([Finance decision] 723.) [From Interstate Commerce Commission reports, v. 79.] * Paper, 5c.

Clay. No. 13620, Niles Fire Brick Company *v.* director general, as agent: [decided May 31, 1923; report of commission]. 1923. [1]+380–382 p. ([Opinion] 8539.) [From Interstate Commerce Commission reports, v. 80.] * Paper, 5c.

Coal. No. 12711, Perry County Coal Corporation et al. *v.* East St. Louis & Suburban Railway Company et al.; decided June 12, 1923; report [and order] of commission. [1923.] 711–716+[1] p. ([Opinion] 8575.) [Report from Interstate Commerce Commission reports, v. 80.] * Paper, 5c.

—— No. 12846, Dayton Malleable Iron Company *v.* Kanawha & Michigan Railway Company et al.; [decided June 9, 1923; report and order of commission]. 1923. [1]+22–24+[1] p. ([Opinion] 8591.) [Report from Interstate Commerce Commission reports, v. 81.] * Paper, 5c.

—— No. 13355, Northwestern Traffic & Service Bureau, Incorporated, et al. *v.* Central Wisconsin Railway Company et al.; decided June 9, 1923; report [and order] of commission. [1923.] 659–662+[1] p. ([Opinion] 8568.) [Report from Interstate Commerce Commission reports, v. 80.] *Paper, 5c.

—— No. 13603, Dewey Brothers Company *v.* Norfolk & Western Railway Company et al.; decided May 31, 1923; report [and orders] of commission. [1923.] 499–506+ii p. ([Opinion] 8547.) [Report from Interstate Commerce Commission reports, v. 80.] * Paper, 5c.

—— No. 13613, Elem Coal Company *v.* Lehigh Valley Railroad Company et al.; decided June 9, 1923; report [and order] of commission. [1923.] 647–650+[1] p. ([Opinion] 8564.) [Report from Interstate Commerce Commission reports, v. 80.] * Paper, 5c.

—— Ohio-Michigan coal cases, no. 12698, Southern Ohio Coal Exchange *v.* Chesapeake & Ohio Railway Company et al.; decided June 8, 1923; [report and orders of commission]. [1923.] 663–697+viii p. ([Opinion] 8569.) [Report from Interstate Commerce Commission reports, v. 80.] * Paper, 5c.

Coal-cars. Assigned cars for bituminous coal mines, no. 12530, in re distribution among coal mines of privately owned cars and cars for railroad fuel; [decided June 13, 1923; report and order of commission]. 1923. [1]+520–589+xxxvi p. ([Opinion] 8552.) [Report from Interstate Commerce Commission reports, v. 80.] *Paper, 10c.

Coconut-oil. No. 13279, Spencer Kellogg & Sons, Incorporated, *v.* director general, as agent; decided May 31, 1923; report of commission. [1923.] p. 507–509. ([Opinion] 8548.) [From Interstate Commerce Commission reports, v. 80.] *Paper, 5c.

Coke. No. 13106, Crookston Gas Company et al. *v.* Great Northern Railway Company; [no. 13106 (sub-no. 1), same *v.* director general, as agent; decided June 28, 1923; report and order of commission]. 1923. [1]+128–130+[1] p. ([Opinion] 8612.) [Report from Interstate Commerce Commission reports, v. 81.] *Paper, 5c.

—— No. 13124, Anaconda Copper Mining Company *v.* director general of railroads, as agent, Denver & Rio Grande Western Railroad Company, et al.; decided May 31, 1923; report [and order] of commission. [1923.] 481–482+ [1] p. ([Opinion] 8541.) [Report from Interstate Commerce Commission reports, v. 80.] *Paper, 5c.

—— No. 13763, Edward E. Marshall *v.* Pennsylvania Railroad Company et al.; decided May 31, 1923; report of commission. [1923.] p. 653–654. ([Opinion] 8566.) [From Interstate Commerce Commission reports, v. 80.] *Paper, 5c.

Colorado-Kansas Railway. Finance docket no. 404, guaranty settlement with Colorado-Kansas Ry.; decided June 2, 1923; report of commission. [1923.] p. 567–569. ([Finance decision] 715.) [From Interstate Commerce Commission reports, v. 79.] *Paper, 5c.

Copra. No. 13586, Spencer Kellogg & Sons, Incorporated, *v.* director general, as agent, Atchison, Topeka & Santa Fe Railway Company, et al.; decided May 31, 1923; report of commission. [1923.] p. 485–486. ([Opinion] 8543.) [From Interstate Commerce Commission reports, v. 80.] *Paper, 5c.

Corn-starch. No. 13996, A. E. Staley Manufacturing Company *v.* Canadian Pacific Railway Company, director general, as agent, et al.; [decided May 31, 1923; report of commission]. 1923. [1]+512–514 p. ([Opinion] 8550.) [From Interstate Commerce Commission reports, v. 80.] *Paper, 5c.

Cotton. No. 12229, H. Kempner *v.* director general, as agent, Galveston, Harrisburg & San Antonio Railway Company, et al.; decided May 31, 1923; report of commission. [1923.] p. 347–349. ([Opinion] 8533.) [From Interstate Commerce Commission reports, v. 80.] *Paper, 5c.

—— No. 12721, Anderson, Clayton & Company *v.* director general, as agent; [no. 12485, Southern Products Company *v.* director general, as agent, Alabama & Vicksburg Railway Company, et al.]; decided June 4, 1923; report of commission. [1923.] p. 323–326. ([Opinion] 8526.) [From Interstate Commerce Commission reports, v. 80.] *Paper, 5c.

Decisions of commission, Oct.–Dec. 1922, index-digest to [Interstate Commerce Commission reports], v. 74, with table of commodities and table of localities; [prepared in] Section of Indices. 1923, cover-title, p. 783–938. ‡   8–30656

Delaware and Hudson Company. In equity, no. E 26–388, in district court for southern district of New York, Delaware and Hudson Company *v.* United States and Interstate Commerce Commission; motion to dismiss. 1923. cover-title, 3 p. large 8° ‡

Demurrage. No. 12150, Cambria Steel Company et al. *v.* director general, as agent, Pennsylvania Railroad Company et al.; report [and order] of commission. [1923.] 633–639+[1] p., ([Opinion] 8561.) [Report from Interstate Commerce Commission reports, v. 80.] *Paper, 5c.

—— No. 12446, France *v.* director general, as agent; [decided July 2, 1923; report of commission]. 1923. [1]+174–180 p. ([Opinion] 8621.) [From Interstate Commerce Commission reports, v. 81.] *Paper, 5c.

—— No. 13118, Valley & Siletz Railroad Company *v.* Southern Pacific Company; [decided June 11, 1923; report and order of commission]. 1923. [1]+724–731+[1] p. ([Opinion] 8577.) [Report from Interstate Commerce Commission reports, v. 80.] *Paper, 5c.

—— No. 13723, United Paperboard Company *v.* Morristown & Erie Railroad Company et al.; [decided May 31, 1923; report and order of commission]. 1923. [1]+640–642+[1] p. ([Opinion] 8562.) [Report from Interstate Commerce Commission reports, v. 80.] *Paper, 5c.

Duluth and Northeastern Railroad. Finance docket no. 133, deficit settlement with Duluth & Northeastern R. R.; decided May 25, 1923; report of commission. [1923.] p. 563–564. ([Finance decision] 713.) [From Interstate Commerce Commission reports, v. 79.] *Paper, 5c.

Fertilizers. Investigation and suspension docket no. 1793, fertilizer and fertilizer material between points in western trunk line territory; [decided June 12, 1923; report and order of commission]. 1923. [1]+604–606+[1] p. ([Opinion] 8556.) [Report from Interstate Commerce Commission reports, v. 80.] *Paper, 5c.

Filters. No. 12985, Norman H. Schlieper *v.* Southern Pacific Company et al.; [decided May 31, 1923; report and order of commission]. 1923. [1]+630–632+ii p. ([Opinion] 8560.) [Report from Interstate Commerce Commission reports, v. 80.] *Paper, 5c.

Fort Wayne Union Railway. Finance docket no. 2987, Fort Wayne Union Railway stock; decided June 9, 1923; report of commission. [1923.] p. 623–624. ([Finance decision] 733.) [From Interstate Commerce Commission reports, v. 79.] *Paper, 5c.

Freight rates. Investigation and suspension docket no. 1788, class rates from points in Kansas to eastern Colorado; decided June 15, 1923; report [and order] of commission. [1923.] 709–710+[1] p. ([Opinion] 8574.) [Report from Interstate Commerce Commission reports, v. 80.] *Paper, 5c.

—— No. 11497, Owensboro Chamber of Commerce et al. *v.* Louisville, Henderson & St. Louis Railway Company et al.; portions of 4th section application no. 1065; decided June 29, 1923; report [and order] of commission. [1923.] 145–154+iii p. ([Opinion] 8615.) [Report from Interstate Commerce Commission reports, v. 81.] *Paper, 5c.

—— No. 12026, Board of Railroad Commissioners of South Dakota *v.* Ahnapee & Western Railway Company et al.; [decided June 7, 1923; report of commission on further argument]. 1923. [1]+332–334 p. ([Opinion] 8528.) [From Interstate Commerce Commission reports, v. 80.] *Paper, 5c.

—— No. 13139, Graham & Gila Counties Traffic Association *v.* Arizona Eastern Railroad Company et al.; [decided June 27, 1923; report and order of commission]. 1923. [1]+134–144+ii p. ([Opinion] 8614.) [Report from Interstate Commerce Commission reports, v. 81.] *Paper, 5c.

—— No. 13293 [reduced rates, 1922], in matter of rates, fares, and charges of carriers by railroad subject to interstate commerce act; [decided June 27, 1923; supplemental report of commission]. 1923. [1]+170–173 p. ([Opinion] 8620.) [From Interstate Commerce Commission reports, v. 81.] *Paper, 5c.

Fruit. No. 12680, American Fruit & Vegetable Shippers Association et al. *v.* American Railway Express Company et al.; decided June 26, 1923; report [and order] of commission. [1923.] 87–92+ii p. ([Opinion] 8606.) [Report from Interstate Commerce Commission reports, v. 81.] *Paper, 5c.

Gasoline. No. 13099, Producers Refining Company *v.* Missouri, Kansas & Texas Railway Company of Texas et al.; decided June 8, 1923; report [and order] of commission. [1923.] 339–340+[1] p. ([Opinion] 8530.) [Report from Interstate Commerce Commission reports, v. 80.] *Paper, 5c.

Grain. Investigation and suspension docket no. 1746' transit rules on grain products at Missouri Pacific Railroad stations in connection with back-haul traffic; decided June 19, 1923; report [and order] of commission. [1923.] 25–29+[1] p. ([Opinion] 8592.) [Report from Interstate Commerce Commission reports, v. 81.] *Paper, 5c.

—— No. 12669, Texas Grain Dealers Association et al. *v.* Abilene & Southern Railway Company et al.; [decided June 25, 1923; report and order of commission]. 1923. [1]+96–107+v p. ([Opinion] 8608.) [Report from Interstate Commerce Commission reports, v. 81.] *Paper, 5c.

—— No. 12929, interstate rates on grain, grain products, and hay, in carloads, between points in western and mountain-Pacific groups; [decided June 4, 1923; report of commission on further hearing]. 1923. [1]+362–370 p. ([Opinion] 8535.) [From Interstate Commerce Commission reports, v. 80.] *Paper, 5c.

—— No. 13215, Arkansas Jobbers & Manufacturers Association *v.* Chicago, Rock Island & Pacific Railway Company et al.; [decided June 11, 1923; report and order of commission]. 1923. [1]+620–626+ii p. ([Opinion] 8558.) [Report from Interstate Commerce Commission reports, v. 80.] *Paper, 5c.

58153—No. 343—23——4

Grain—Continued. No. 13406, Corporation Commission of Oklahoma *v.* Arkansas Railroad et al.; decided June 11, 1923; report [and orders] of commission. [1923.] 607–619+iii p.. ([Opinion] 8557.) [Report from Interstate Commerce Commission reports, v. 80.] * Paper, 5c.

Granite. No. 12556, J. F. Bloom & Company *v.* director general, as agent, Montpelier & Wells River Railroad, et al.; decided June 1, 1923; report of commission. [1923.] p. 283–284. ([Opinion] 8515.) [From Interstate Commerce Commission reports, v. 80.] *Paper, 5c.

Hair. No. 13441, Southern Cotton Oil Company *v.* director general, as agent; decided May 31, 1923; report [and order] of commission. [1923.] 627–629+[1] p. ([Opinion] 8559.) [Report from Interstate Commerce Commission reports, v. 80.] *Paper, 5c.

Horses. No. 13366, A. L. Derby *v.* Kansas City Southern Railway Company et al.; portions of 4th section applications nos. 621 and 629; [decided May 31, 1923; report and orders of commission]. 1923. [1]+374–376+ii p. ([Opinion] 8537.) [Report from Interstate Commerce Commission reports, v. 80.] *Paper, 5c.

Indiana Harbor Belt Railroad. Finance docket no. 2972, Indiana Harbor Belt equipment trust of 1923; decided June 13, 1923; report of commission. [1923.] p. 655–658. ([Finance decision] 747.) [From Interstate Commerce Commission reports, v. 79.] *Paper, 5c.

Inspectors. Instructions to inspectors, July, 1923 [with reference to investigation of railroad accidents, safety appliances, and hours of service]. 1923. [1]+32 p. 16° (Bureau of Safety circular 6.) [Supersedes circulars 3 and 4.] ‡

Iron. Investigation and suspension docket no. 1772, increased rates on iron and steel articles from St. Louis, Peoria, Chicago, St. Paul, and points taking same rates, to Kansas, Nebraska, and Colorado; [decided June 15, 1923; report and order of commission]. 1923. [1]+732–736+[1] p. ([Opinion] 8578.) [Report from Interstate Commerce Commission reports, v. 80.] *Paper, 5c.

Kansas City Northwestern Railroad. Finance docket no. 153, deficit settlement with Kansas City Northwestern R. R., Jay M. Lee, receiver; [decided Apr. 10, 1923; report of commission]. 1923. [1]+602–604 p. ([Finance decision] 724.) [From Interstate Commerce Commission reports, v. 79.] *Paper, 5c.

Kansas City Southern Railway. Finance docket no. 2495, construction of line by Kansas City Southern Railway; approved June 9, 1923; supplemental order [of commission]. 1923. p. 614. ([Finance decision] 728.) [From Interstate Commerce Commission reports, v. 79.] *Paper, 5c.

Kansas, Oklahoma and Gulf Railway. Finance docket no. 2914, Kansas, Oklahoma & Gulf equipment trust, series A; approved June 11, 1923; supplemental order [of commission]. 1923. p. 622. ([Finance decision] 732.) [From Interstate Commerce Commission reports, v. 79.] *Paper, 5c.

Lard substitutes. No. 14396, Interstate Cotton Oil Refining Company *v.* St. Louis Southwestern Railway Company et al.; decided June 26, 1923; report of commission. [1923.] p. 67–70. ([Opinion] 8602.) [From Interstate Commerce Commission reports, v. 81.] *Paper, 5c.

Leather. No. 13460, Max Gorewitz *v.* Pennsylvania Railroad Company et al.; decided May 31, 1923; report [and order] of commission. [1923.] 483–484+[1] p. ([Opinion] 8542.) [Report from Interstate Commerce Commission reports, v. 80.] *Paper, 5c.

Lighterage. No. 13030, Charles F. Gledhill Company *v.* director general, as agent, and Pennsylvania Railroad Company; decided June 9, 1923; report [and order] of commission. [1923.] 701–702+[1] p. ([Opinion] 8571.) [Report from Interstate Commerce Commission reports, v. 80.] *Paper, 5c.

Logs. Investigation and suspension docket no. 1743, increased rates on saw logs and bolts from stations on Copper Range Railroad; [decided June 12, 1923; report and order of commission]. 1923. [1]+590–594+[1] p. ([Opinion] 8553.) [Report from Interstate Commerce Commission reports, v. 80.] *Paper, 5c.

Logs—Continued. No. 13927, Lyons Lumber Company, Limited, *v.* director general, as agent, and New Orleans, Texas & Mexico Railway Company; decided May 31, 1923; report [and order] of commission. [1923.] 761–762+[1] p. ([Opinion] 8587.) [Report from Interstate Commerce Commission reports, v. 80.] *Paper, 5c.

Lumber. Investigation and suspension docket no. 1535, lumber from California to Minnesota and Wisconsin; [4th section application no. 349 and no. 12323]; decided June 8, 1923; report [and orders] of commission on further hearing. [1923.] 595–600+ii p. ([Opinion] 8554.) [Report from Interstate Commerce Commission reports, v. 80.] *Paper, 5c.

—— No. 13562, Indiana Quartered Oak Company *v.* Atlantic City Railroad Company et al.; decided June 26, 1923; report [and order] of commission. [1923.] 59–63+[1] p. ([Opinion] 8600.) [Report from Interstate Commerce Commission reports, v. 81.] *Paper, 5c.

—— No. 13728, J. R. Thames *v.* Alabama & Northwestern Railroad Company et al.; [no. 13649, same *v.* same]; decided June 9, 1923; report [and order] of commission. [1923.] 55–58+[1] p. ([Opinion] 8599.) [Report from Interstate Commerce Commission reports, v. 81.] *Paper, 5c.

—— No. 13765, Saginaw & Manistee Lumber Company et al. *v.* Atchison, Topeka & Santa Fe Railway et al.; decided May 31, 1923; report [and order] of commission. [1923.] 487–490+ii p. ([Opinion] 8544.) [Report from Interstate Commerce Commission reports, v. 80.] *Paper, 5c.

—— No. 13810, American Lumber & Manufacturing Company *v.* Georgia Railroad et al.; decided May 31, 1923; report [and order] of commission. [1923.] 759–760+[1] p. ([Opinion] 8586.) [Report from Interstate Commerce Commission reports, v. 80.] * Paper, 5c.

Macaroni. No. 12494, Skinner Manufacturing Company *v.* director general, as agent, Chicago, Burlington & Quincy Railroad Company, et al.; [decided June 28, 1923; report and order of commission]. 1923. [1]+108–112+ii p. ([Opinion] 8609.) [Report from Interstate Commerce Commission reports, v. 81.] *Paper, 5c.

Marble. No. 13152, Northwestern Marble & Tile Company *v.* director general, as agent, New York, New Haven & Hartford Railroad Company, et al.; portion of 4th section application no. 1481; decided June 30, 1923; report [and orders] of commission. [1923.] 167–168+ii p. ([Opinion] 8618.) [Report from Interstate. Commerce Commission reports, v. 81.] *Paper, 5c.

Massena Terminal Railroad. Finance docket no. 175, deficit settlement with Massena Terminal R. R.; decided June 9, 1923; report of commission. [1923.] p. 615–616. ([Finance decision] 729.) [From Interstate Commerce Commission reports, v. 79.] *Paper, 5c.

—— . Finance docket no. 616, guaranty settlement with Massena Terminal R. R.; decided June 9, 1923; report of commission. [1923.] p. 625–626. ([Finance decision] 734.) [From Interstate Commerce Commission reports, v. 79.] *Paper, 5c.

Meat. No. 12068, Wilson & Company, Incorporated, of Oklahoma, et al., *v.* director general, as agent, Chicago, Burlington & Quincy Railroad Company, et al.; decided June 27, 1923; report [and order] of commission. [1923.] 79–86+v p. ([Opinion] 8605.) [Report from Interstate Commerce Commission reports, v. 81.] *Paper, 5c.

Misrouting. No. 13114, E. W. Arthur *v.* director general, as agent; decided May 31, 1923; report [and order] of commission. [1923.] 707–708+[1] p. ([Opinion] 8573.) [Report from Interstate Commerce Commission reports, v. 80.] * Paper, 5c.

—— No. 13490, Lycoming Motors Corporation *v.* East Jordan & Southern Railroad Company et al.; [no. 13490 (sub-no. 1), same *v.* same]; decided May 31, 1923; report [and order] of commission. [1923.] 757–758+[1] p. ([Opinion] 8585.) [Report from Interstate Commerce Commission reports, v. 80.] *Paper, 5c.

Molasses. No. 13094, Grain Belt Mills Company *v.* Atchison, Topeka & Santa Fe Railway Company et al.; decided May 31, 1923; report [and order] of commission. [1923.] 745–746+[1] p. ([Opinion] 8581.) [Report from Interstate Commerce Commission reports, v. 80.] *Paper, 5c.

Morgantown and Kingwood Railroad. Finance docket no. 2463, deticit status of Morgantown & Kingwood R. R.; [decided June 11, 1923; report of commission]. 1923. [1]+628–630 p. ([Finance decision] 736.) [From Interstate Commerce Commission reports, v. 79.] *Paper, 5c.

New York Central Railroad. Finance docket no. 2973, New York Central lines equipment trust of 1923, in matter of application of New York Central Railroad Company, Michigan Central Railroad Company, and Cleveland, Cincinnati, Chicago & St. Louis Railway Company for authority to assume obligation and liability in respect of certain equipment-trust certificates; decided June 13, 1923; report of commission. [1923.] p. 659–663. ([Finance decision] 748.) [From Interstate Commerce Commission reports, v. 79.] * Paper, 5c.

New York, Chicago and St. Louis Railroad. Finance docket no. 2919, operation of lines and issue of capital stock by New York, Chicago & St. Louis Railroad Company; decided June 18, 1923; [report of commission]. [1923.] p. 581–596. ([Finance decision] 721.) [From Interstate Commerce Commission reports, v. 79.] *Paper, 5c.

New York, New Haven and Hartford Railroad. Finance docket no. 2226, loan to New York, New Haven & Hartford R. R.; decided June 1, 1923; supplemental report of commission. [1923.] p. 597–599. ([Finance decision] 722.) [From Interstate Commerce Commission reports, v. 79.] *Paper, 5c.

—— Finance docket no. 2938, bonds of New York, New Haven & Hartford R. R.; [decided June 11, 1923; report of commission]. 1923. [1]+640–642 p. ([Finance decision] 741.) [From Interstate Commerce Commission reports, v. 79.] * Paper, 5c.

Nickel. No. 12885, United States Nickel Company *v.* director general, as agent, and Raritan River Railroad Company; [decided June 29, 1923; report and order of commission]. 1923. [1]+162–166+[1] p. ([Opinion] 8617.) [Report from Interstate Commerce Commission reports, v. 81.] *Paper, 5c.

Oil-well supplies. No. 12228, Bradford Rig & Reel Company *v.* director general, as agent, Atchison, Topeka & Santa Fe Railway Company, et al.; decided May 31, 1923; report [and order] of commission. [1923.] 335–338+[1] p. ([Opinion] 8529.) [Report from Interstate Commerce Commission reports, v. 80.] * Paper, 5c.

—— No. 12365, Oklahoma Iron Works et al. *v.* director general, as agent, Akron, Canton & Youngstown Railway Company, et al.; decided June 4, 1923; report [and order] of commission. [1923.] 327–331+ii p. ([Opinion] 8527.) [Report from Interstate Commerce Commission reports, v. 80.] *Paper, 5c. ·

Ores. No. 13414, Arlington Silver Mining Company *v.* director general, as agent, and Great Northern Railway Company; decided May 31, 1923; report [and order] of commission. [1923.] 753–756+[1] p. ([Opinion] 8584.) [Report from Interstate Commerce Commission reports, v. 80.] *Paper, 5c.

Peanut-oil. No. 13335, Spencer Kellogg & Sons, Incorporated, *v.* director general, as agent, New York Central Railroad Company, et al.; decided May 31, 1923; report of commission. [1923.] p. 377–379. ([Opinion] 8538.) [From Interstate Commerce Commission reports, v. 80.] *Paper, 5c.

Petroleum. · Investigation and suspension docket no. 1795, petroleum and petroleum products, in carloads, from C. F. A. territory to El Paso, Tex., group; decided June 28, 1923; report [and order] of commission. [1923.] p. 71, [1]. ([Opinion] 8603.) [Report from Interstate Commerce Commission reports, v. 81.] *Paper, 5c.

—— No. 12813, Standard Oil Company (New Jersey) et al. *v.* director general, as agent; decided May 31, 1923; report of commission. [1923.] p. 643–646. ([Opinion] 8563.) [From Interstate Commerce Commission reports, v. 80.] *Paper, 5c.

—— No. 14122, Lubrite Refining Company *v.* Dayton-Goose Creek Railway Company et al.; decided May 31, 1923; report [and order] of commission. [1923.] 515–519+[1] p. ([Opinion] 8551.) [Report from Interstate Commerce Commission reports, v. 80.] *Paper, 5c.

Plumbers' supplies. Investigation and suspension docket no. 1690, cancellation of commodity rates on plumbers' supplies from Chattanooga, Tenn., and group points to south Atlantic ports and Florida junction points; decided May 29, 1923; report [and order] of commission. [1923.] 251–254+[1] p. ([Opinion] 8508.) [Report from Interstate Commerce Commission reports, v. 80.] *Paper, 5c.

—— No. 13792, Standard Sanitary Manufacturing Company *v.* Arcade & Attica Railroad Corporation et al.; [decided May 31, 1923; report and order of commission]. 1923. [1]+318–322+iii p. ([Opinion] 8525.) [Report from Interstate Commerce Commission reports, v. 80.] *Paper, 5c.

Potatoes. Investigation and suspension docket no. 1740, potatoes, in carloads, from D. & R. G. W. R. R, stations in Colorado to E. P. & S. W. stations in New Mexico; decided May 16, 1923; report [and order] of commission. [1923.] 191–193+[1] p. ([Opinion] 8492.) [Report from Interstate Commerce Commission reports, v. 80.] *Paper, 5c.

Pottery. Investigation and suspension docket no. 1791, earthenware or stoneware from Red Wing, Minn., to points in north Pacific Coast and intermediate territories, transcontinental; [decided June 27, 1923; report and order of commission]. 1923. [1]+64–66+[1] p. ([Opinion] 8601.) [Report from Interstate Commerce Commission reports, v. 81.] *Paper, 5c.

Quincy, Omaha and Kansas City Railroad. Finance docket no. 760, guaranty settlement with Quincy, Omaha & Kansas City R. R.; decided June 2, 1923; report of commission. [1923.]. p. 573–575. ([Finance decision] 718.) [From Interstate Commerce Commission reports, v. 79.] *Paper, 5c.

Railroad accidents. Summary of accident investigation reports, no. 15, Jan.–Mar. 1923; [prepared in] Bureau of Safety. 1923. iii+50 p. [Quarterly.] * Paper, 5c. single copy, 15c. a yr.; foreign subscription, 25c.   A20—942

Railroads. Freight and passenger train service unit costs (selected expense accounts) of class 1 steam roads in United States, including proportion of mixed-train and special-train service (compiled from 164 reports representing 177 steam roads, switching and terminal companies not included), May, 1923 and 1922, and 5 months [ended with May] 1923 and 1922; [prepared in] Bureau of Statistics. May, 1923. 1 p. oblong large 8° [Subject to revision.] †

—— Operating revenues and operating expenses of class 1 steam roads in United States (for 193 steam roads, including 15 switching and terminal companies), May, 1923 and 1922 [and] 5 months ending with May. 1923 and 1922; [prepared in] Bureau of Statistics. May, 1923. 1 p. oblong large 8° [Subject to revision.] †

—— Operating revenues and operating expenses of large steam roads. selected items for roads with annual operat'ng revenues above $25,000,000, May, 1922 and 1923 [and] 5 months ended with May, 1922 and 1923; [prepared in] Bureau of Statistics. May, 1923. [2] p. oblong large 8° [Subject to revision.] †

—— Operating statistics of large steam roads, selected items for May, 1923, compared with May, 1922, for roads with annual operating revenues above $25,000,000; [prepared in] Bureau of Statistics. May, 1923. [2] p. oblong large 8° [Subject to revision.] †

—— Revenue traffic statistics of class 1 steam roads in United States, including mixed-train service (compiled from 165 reports representing 178 steam roads, switching and terminal companies not included), Apr. 1923 and 1922 [and] 4 months ended with Apr. 1923 and 1922; [prepared in] Bureau of Statistics. Apr. 1923. 1 p. oblong large 8° [Subject to revision.] †

Rails. No. 13054, Hyman-Michaels Company et al. *v.* director general, as agent; decided May 31, 1923; report [and order] of commission. [1923.] 703–706+[1] p. ([Opinion] 8572.) [Report from Interstate Commerce Commission reports, v. 80.] * Paper, 5c.

—— No. 13670, Walter A. Zelnicker Supply Company *v.* Chesapeake & Ohio Railway Company et al.; decided May 31, 1923; report [and order] of commission. [1923.] 651–652+ii p. ([Opinion] 8565.). [Report from Interstate Commerce Commission reports, v. 80.] * Paper, 5c.

—— . Report on formation of transverse fissures in steel rails and their prevalence on certain railroads; [by James E. Howard]. 1923. [1]+169 p. il. * Paper, 30c.   A 23—1670

Reconsignment. No. 13459, Central Wisconsin Supply Company *v.* Chicago, Milwaukee & St. Paul Railway Company et·al.; decided May 31, 1923; report [and order] of commission. [1923.] 763–765+[1] p. ([Opinion] 8588.) [Report from Interstate Commerce Commiss:on reports, v. 80.] * Paper, 5c.

Refrigeration. Investigation and suspension docket no. 1762, protective service on perishable freight; decided June 27, 1923; report [and order] of commission. [1923.] 155–161+[1] p. ([Opinion] 8616.) [Report from Interstate Commerce Comm:ssion reports, v. 81.] * Paper, 5c.

—— No. 13119, S. G. Palmer Company *v.* director general, as agent, New York Central Railroad Company, et al.; decided May 31, 1923; report [and order] of commission. [1923.] p. 371–373+[1] p. ([Opinion] 8536.) [Report from Interstate Commerce Commission reports, v. 80.] * Paper, 5c.

Seaboard Air Line Railway. Finance docket no. 2869, Seaboard Air Line equipment trust, series v; [decided May 29, 1923; report of commission]. 1923. [1]+558–562 p. ([Finance decision] 712.) [Corrected print from Interstate Commerce Commiss:on reports, v. 79.]

—— Same. Corrected reprint. 1923. [1]+558–562 p. ([Finance dec:sion] 712.) [From Interstate Commerce Commission reports, v. 79.] * Paper, 5c.

Shales. No. 12816, Hocking Valley Brick Company *v.* director general, as agent, and Hocking valley Railway Company; decided June 9, 1923; report of commission. [1923.] p. 743–744. ([Opinion] 8580.) [From Interstate .Commerce Commission reports, v. 80.] * Paper, 5c.

Sodium cyanid. No. 13194, Compani de Real del Monte y Pachuca *v.* director general, as agent; [decided June 23, 1923; report and order of commission]. 1923. [1]+52–54+[1] p. ([Opinion] 8598.) [Report from Interstate Commerce Commission reports, v. 81.] * Paper, 5c.

Steamboats. Schedule of sailings (as furnished by steamship companies named herein) of steam vessels which are registered under laws of United States and which are intended to load general cargo at ports in United States for foreign destinations, July 15–Aug. 31, 1923, no. 11; issued by Section of Tariffs, Bureau of Traffic. 1923. ii+25 p. 4° [Monthly. No. 11 cancels no. 10.] †   22—26610

Steel. No. 13311, Wm. Cramp & Sons Ship & Engine Building Company *v.* director general, as·agent; decided May 31, 1923; report of commission. [1923.] p. 341–343. ([Opinion] 8531.) [From Interstate Commerce Commission reports, v. 80.] *Paper, 5c.

Swine. No. 11947, Armour & Company *v.* Central of Georgia Railway Company, director general, as agent, et al.; [no. 11947 (sub-no. 1), same *v.* Missouri Pacific Railroad Company, director general, as agent, et al.]; decided June 15, 1923; report [and order] of commission. [1923.] 33–38+ii p. ([Opinion] 8574 [8594].) [Report from Interstate Commerce Commission reports, v. 81.] *Paper, 5c.

—— No. 12598, Wilson & Company, Incorporated, of Oklahoma, *v.* director general, as agent, Nashville, Chattanooga & St. Louis Railway, et al.; decided June 15, 1923; report [and order] of commission. [1923.] 39–43+ [1] p. ([Opinion] 8595.) [Report from Interstate Commerce Commission reports, v. 81.] *Paper, 5c.

Switching charges. Investigation and suspension docket no. 1757, nonabsorption of switching charges on fish at Chicago, Ill., via express or passenger service; decided June 27, 1923; report [and order] of commission. [1923.] 113–114+[1] p. ([Opinion] 8610.) [Report from Interstate Commerce Commission reports, v. 81,] *Paper, 5c.

—— Investigation and suspension docket no. 1771, ice, in carloads, from points in Illinois, Iowa, Michigan, Minnesota, and Wisconsin to points within Chicago district; [decided June 27, 1923; report and order of commission]. 1923. [1]+30–32+[1] p. ([Opinion] 8593.) [Report from Interstate Commerce Commission reports, v. 81.] *Paper, 5c.

—— Investigation and suspension docket no. 1774, switching charges on grain in Rosedale, Kans., section of Kansas City, Mo.–Kans., switching district; decided June 12, 1923; report [and order] of commission. [1923.] 601–603+ [1] p. ([Opinion] 8555.) [Report from Interstate Commerce Commission reports, v. 80.] *Paper, 5c.

Switching charges—Continued. No. 11760, Frank P. Miller Paper Company et al. *v.* Pennsylvania Railroad Company et al.; [decided June 7, 1923; report of commission on further hearing]. 1923. [1]+314–317 p. ([Opinion] 8524.) [From Interstate Commerce Commission reports, v. 80.] * Paper, 5c.

—— No. 12917, Central Iron & Steel Company *v.* director general, as agent; [decided June 11, 1923; report of commission]. 1923. [1]+698–700 p. ([Opinion] 8570.) [From Interstate Commerce Commission reports, v. 80.] *Paper, 5c.

—— No. 13377, David Lupton's Sons Company *v.* Pennsylvania Railroad Company; decided June 26, 1923; report [and order] of commission. [1923.] 93–95+[1] p. ([Opinion] 8607.) [Report from Interstate Commerce Commission reports, v. 81.] *Paper, 5c.

—— No. 14226, Board of Trade of Detroit *v.* Wabash Railway Company et al.; decided June 9, 1923; report [and order] of commission. [1923.] 717–723+[1] p. ([Opinion] 8576.) [Report from Interstate Commerce Commission reports, v. 80.] *Paper, 5c.

Tin. No. 13103, Mitsui & Company, Limited, *v.* director general, as agent; decided June 27, 1923; report [and order] of commission. [1923.] 169–170+[1] p. ([Opinion] 8619.) [Report from Interstate Commerce Commission reports, v. 81.] * Paper, 5c.

Tires. No. 12705, Overland Tire & Rubber Company et al. *v.* Missouri Pacific Railroad Company et al.; decided May 31, 1923; report [and order] of commission. [1923.] 509–511+[1] p. ([Opinion] 8549.) [Report from Interstate Commerce Commission reports, v. 80.] *Paper, 5c.

Toledo, Angola and Western Railway. Finance docket no. 840, guaranty settlement with Toledo, Angola & Western Ry.; [decided June 8, 1923; report of commission]. 1923. [1]+620–622 p. ([Finance decision] 731.) [From Interstate Commerce Commission reports, v. 79.] *Paper, 5c.

Toys. No. 12739, Daisy Manufacturing Company *v.* Alabama & Vicksburg Railway Company et al.; [decided June 9, 1923; report and order of commission]. 1923. [1]+44–48+ii p. ([Opinion] 8596.) [Report from Interstate Commerce Commission reports, v. 81.] *Paper, 5c.

Unlading and lading. No. 13854, Gerard Ragone & Son *v.* director general, as agent, New York Central Railroad Company, et al.; decided May 31, 1923; report [and order] of commission. [1923.] 491–492+[1] p. ([Opinion] 8545.) [Report from Interstate Commerce Commission reports, v. 80.] *Paper, 5c.

Virginian Railway. Finance docket no. 2812, construction of extension by Virginian Ry.; decided June 25, 1923; report of commission. [1923.] p. 631–633. ([Finance decision] 737.) [From Interstate Commerce Commission reports, v. 79.] *Paper, 5c.

—— Finance docket no. 2975, Virginian Railway equipment trust, series D; decided June 4, 1923; report of commission. [1923.] p. 605–608. ([Finance decision] 725.) [From Interstate Commerce Commission reports, v. 79.] *Paper, 5c.

Wabash, Chester and Western Railroad. Finance docket no. 870, guaranty settlement with Wabash, Chester & Western R. R.; [decided June 1, 1923; report of commission]. 1923. [1]+576–578 p. ([Finance decision] 719.) [From Interstate Commerce Commission reports, v. 79.] *Paper, 5c.

Wharfage charges. No. 13487, Sugarland Industries *v.* Galveston Wharf Company; decided May 31, 1923; report [and order] of commission. [1923.] 655–658+[1] p. ([Opinion] 8567.) [Report from Interstate Commerce Commission reports, v. 80.] *Paper, 5c.

Wheat. No. 13033, Atchison Board of Trade et al. *v.* Atchison, Topeka & Santa Fe Railway Company et al.; [decided June 6, 1923; report and order of commission]. 1923. [1]+350–361+ii p. ([Opinion] 8534.) [Report from Interstate Commerce Commission reports, v. 80.] *Paper, 5c.

Wood-pulp. No. 13877, Tidewater Paper Mills Company *v.* Bush Terminal Railroad Company et al.; decided May 31, 1923; report [and order] of commission. [1923.] 493–498+[1] p. ([Opinion] 8546.) [Report from Interstate Commerce Commission reports, v. 80.] *Paper, 5c.

Wool. Investigation and suspension docket no. 1754, imported wool from New York and Boston to La Porte, Ind.; decided June 11, 1923; report [and order] of commission. [1923.] 309–313+[1] p. ([Opinion] 8523.) [Report from Interstate Commerce Commission reports, v. 80.] *Paper, 5c.

—— No. 13318, Boston Wool Trade Association *v.* director general, as agent; decided June 28, 1923; report of commission. [1923.] p. 131–133. ([Opinion] 8613.) [From Interstate Commerce Commission reports, v. 81.] *Paper, 5c.

LOCOMOTIVE INSPECTION BUREAU

Railroad accidents. Report covering investigation of accident to Pennsylvania Railroad locomotive 8255, which occurred at Wilmerding, Pa., May 5, 1923; by A. G. Pack, chief inspector. June 13, 1923. [1]+5 p. il. *Paper, 5c.

JUSTICE DEPARTMENT

Bentley, A., & Sons Company. At law no. 2178, in district court for southern district of Ohio, eastern division, United States *v.* A. Bentley & Sons Co.; brief and argument of plaintiff in resistance to defendants' motion. 1923. cover-title, 66 p. ‡

Gottesman, Joseph M. In Court of Claims, Joseph M. Gottesman *v.* United States, no. C–709; demurrer [and] brief. [1923.] p. 9–13, large 8° ‡

Illinois Central Railroad. No. 116–B, in Court of Claims, Illinois Central Railroad Company *v.* United States; defendant's request for findings of fact, and brief, [with] appendix, deposition of M. J. Ryan. 1923. cover-title, p. 27–49, il. large 8° ‡

International Harvester Company. In equity, no. 624, in district court of district of Minnesota, 3d division, United States *v.* International Harvester Company et al.; supplemental petition. 1923. cover-title, i+81 p. ‡

Johnston, James J. No. —, in Supreme Court, Oct. term, 1923, United States *v.* James J. Johnston; petition for writ of certiorari to circuit court of appeals for 2d circuit and brief in support thereof. 1923. cover-title, 7 p. ‡

Marks, Ernest E., & Co. No. 2235, Court of Customs Appeals, Ernest E. Marks & Co. et al. *v.* United States; brief for United States, 1923. cover-title, 15 p. ‡

Merritt & Chapman Derrick and Wrecking Company. No. C–713, in Court of Claims, Merritt & Chapman Derrick & Wrecking Company *v.* United States; counterclaim of United States. 1923. cover-title, p. 1–7, large 8° ‡

Newport Company. No. 2250, Court of Customs Appeals, Newport Co. *v.* United States; brief for United States. 1923. cover-title, 12 p. ‡

Ohio Savings Bank and Trust Company. United States district court, district of New Jersey, Ohio Savings Bank & Trust Company *v.* Willys Corporation; on bill, etc., proof of debt due United States, amount of claim, $1,548,224.38. 1923. cover-title, 27 p. ‡

Pearson, Mrs. Margaret E. In Court of Claims, Margaret E. Pearson and J. R. Pearson *v.* United States, no. C–738; demurrer [and brief]. [1923.] p. 21–26, large 8° ‡

Pressed Steel Car Company. No. 239–A, in Court of Claims, Pressed Steel Car Company *v.* United States; counterclaim. 1923. cover-title, p. 1–7, large 8° ‡

—— Same; defendant's motion for leave to file counterclaim. [1923.] p. 1–2, large 8° ‡

Scalione, Charles C. In Patent Office, before board of examiners in chief, interference no. 46407, [Charles C.] Scalione *v.* Mittasch and Kircher; brief for Scalione on appeal. 1923. cover-title, i+34 p. ‡

Scott, T. A., Company. No. C–713, in Court of Claims, T. A. Scott Company *v.* United States; counterclaim of United States against T. A. Scott Company and/or T. A. Scott Company, Inc. 1923. cover-title, p. 1–6, large 8° ‡

Southern Pacific Company. In Court of Claims, Southern Pacific Company *v.* United States, no. B–93; defendant's brief. [1923.] p. 35–38, large 8° ‡

Submarine Signal Company. In Court of Claims, Submarine Signal Company *v.* United States, no. C–318; demurrer [and brief]. [1923.] p. 23–37, large 8° ‡

Weitz', Charles, Sons. Law no. 296, in district court for southern district of Iowa, central division, United States *v.* Chas. Weitz' Sons et al.; brief and argument of plaintiff in resistance to defendants' motion to re-form plaintiff's petition. 1923. cover-title, 68 p. ‡

LABOR DEPARTMENT

CHILDREN'S BUREAU

Infants. Infant care. [Revised edition.] [Reprint with slight changes] 1923. 118 p. il. (Care of children series 2; Bureau publication 8 revised.) *Paper, 10c.   L 23—210·

—— Infant mortality, results of field study in Baltimore, Md., based on births in one year; by Anna Rochester. 1923. 400 p. il. map. (Bureau publication 119.) *Paper, 40c.   L 23—205·

Juvenile-court standards, report of committee appointed by Children's Bureau, Aug. 1921, to formulate juvenile-court standards, adopted by conference held under auspices of Children's Bureau and National Probation Association, Washington, D. C., May 18, 1923. 1923. vi+10 p. (Bureau publication 121.) *Paper, 5c.   L 23—206

Maternity and infant care in mountain county in Georgia; by Glenn Steele. 1923. v+58 p. 5 pl. (Bureau publication 120.) *Paper, 15c.   L 23—197

Playgrounds. Backyard playgrounds. 1923. 6 p. il. narrow 8° (Folder 2.) [From Bulletin of Recreation Department, Oakland, Calif.] †

EMPLOYMENT SERVICE

Industrial employment information bulletin, v. 3, no. 6; June, 1923. [1923.] 20 p. 4° [Monthly.] †   L 21—17

IMMIGRATION BUREAU

Immigration laws. Information relative to immigration laws and their enforcement in connection with admission of aliens. 1923. [1]+6 p. †

LABOR STATISTICS BUREAU

Accidents. Statistics of industrial accidents in United States; by Lucian W. Chaney. June, 1923. iii+60 p. (Bulletin 339; Industrial accidents and hygiene series.) *Paper, 10c.   L 23—207

—— Same. (H. doc. 639, 67th Cong. 4th sess.)

Hosiery. Wages and hours of labor in hosiery and underwear industry, 1922. May, 1923. iii+38 p. (Bulletin 328; Wages and hours of labor series.) *Paper, 5c.   L 23—208·

—— Same. (H. doc. 628, 67th Cong. 4th sess.)

Industrial betterment. Humanity in government; by James J. Davis. June, 1923. iii+39 p. (Bulletin 346; Miscellaneous series.) [Relates to the work of the Labor Department and the Federal Board for vocational Education. Previously issued as a general publication of the Labor Department, for which see Monthly catalogue for Apr. 1923, p. 675.] *Paper, 5c.   L 23—209·

—— Same. (H. doc. 25, 68th Cong. 1st sess.)

Monthly labor review, v. 17, no. 1; July, 1923. 1923. vi+1–295 p. il. *Paper, 15c. single copy, $1.50 a yr.; foreign subscription, $2.25.   15—26485·

SPECIAL ARTICLES.—Reclassification of United States 1920 occupation census, by industry; by Carl Hookstadt.—History of arbitration in American newspaper publishing industry; by David Weiss.—Agricultural wage earners in France; by Victoria B. Turner.—Building permits in principal cities of United States in 1922; by H. B. Byer.—Disease as compensable injury; by Lindley D. Clark.—Conciliation work of Department of Labor, May, 1923; by Hugh L. Kerwin.—Statistics of immigration,

Monthly labor review—Continued.

    Apr, 1923; by W. W. Husband.—Directory of labor officials in United States and foreign countries.

    NOTE.—The Review is the medium through which the Bureau publishes the results of original investigations too brief for bulletin purposes, notices of labor legislation by the States or by Congress, and Federal court decisions affecting labor, which from their importance should be given attention before they could ordinarily appear in the bulletins devoted to these subjects. One free subscription will be given to all labor departments and bureaus, workmen's compensation commissions, and other offices connected with the administration of labor laws and organizations exchanging publications with the Labor Statistics Bureau. Others desiring copies may obtain them from the Superintendent of Documents, Washington, D. C., at the prices stated above.

Prices. Prices and cost of living. [1923.] p. 51–79, il. [From Monthly labor review, July, 1923.] †

—— Wholesale prices of commodities for June, 1923. 1923. [1]+9 p. [Monthly.] †   L 22—229

WOMEN'S BUREAU

Kentucky. Women in Kentucky industries, study of hours, wages, and working conditions; [by Mary V. Robinson and Mrs. Mildred J. Gordon]. 1923. vi+114 p. (Bulletin 28 [29].) [The series number is incorrectly printed on this publication as 28. That number is assigned to Women's contributions in field of invention, for which see Monthly catalogue for Apr. 1923, p. 676.] *Paper, 15c.   L 23—199

LIBRARY OF CONGRESS

COPYRIGHT OFFICE

Copyright. [Catalogue of copyright entries, new series, pt. 1, group 1, Books, v. 20] no. 35–42; July, 1923. July 5–30, 1923. p. 273–400. [Issued several times a week.]   6—35347

    NOTE.—Each number is issued in 4 parts: pt. 1, group 1, relates to books; pt. 1, group 2, to pamphlets, leaflets, contributions to newspapers or periodicals, etc., lectures, sermons, addresses for oral delivery, dramatic compositions, maps, motion pictures; pt. 2, to periodicals; pt. 3, to musical compositions; pt. 4, to works of art, reproductions of a work of art, drawings or plastic works of scientific or technical character, photographs, prints, and pictorial illustrations.

    Subscriptions for the Catalogue of copyright entries should be made to the Superintendent of Documents, Washington, D. C., instead of to the Register of Copyrights. Prices are as follows: Paper, $3.00 a yr. (4 pts.), foreign subscription, $5.00; pt. 1 (groups 1 and 2), 5c. single copy (group 1, price of group 2 varies), $1.00 a yr., foreign subscription, $2.25; pt. 3, $1.00 a yr., foreign subscription, $1.50; pts. 2 and 4, each 10c. single copy, 50c. a yr., foreign subscription, 70c.

DOCUMENTS DIVISION

Government publications. Monthly check-list of State publications received during May, 1923; v. 14, no. 5. 1923. ii+205–244 p. *Paper, 10c. single copy, $1.00 a yr.; foreign subscription, $1.25.   10—8924

NATIONAL ADVISORY COMMITTEE FOR AERONAUTICS

Aerodynamic plane table; by A. F. Zahm. 1923. cover-title, 11 p. il. 4° (Report 166.) [Text and illustration on p. 2 and 3 of cover.] *Paper, 5c.
                                                   23—26694

Engine performance and determination of absolute ceiling [with list of references]; by Walter S. Diehl. 1923. cover-title, 12 p. il. 4° (Report 171.) [Prepared by Aeronautics Bureau. Text and illustration on p. 2 and 3 of cover.] *Paper, 5c.   23—26695

Wings. Distribution of lift over wing tips and ailerons [with bibliography]; by David L. Bacon. 1923. cover-title, 24 p. il. 4° (Report 161.) [Text and illustration on p. 2 and 3 of cover.] *Paper, 10c.   23—26696

—— Effect of airfoil thickness and plan form on lateral control; by H. I. Hoot. 1923. cover-title, 11 p. il. 4° (Report 169.) [Text and illustration on p. 2 and 3 of cover.] *Paper, 5c.   23—26697

NAVY DEPARTMENT

Court-martial order 5, 1923; May 31, 1923. [1923.] 11 p. 12° [Monthly.] ‡

Orders. General order 108 and 110 [6th series] ; June 6 and July 5, 1923.
* [1923.] 2 p. 4° [General order 109 to be printed separately.] ‡

AERONAUTICS BUREAU

Engines. Catalogue of assemblies and details of Curtiss D–12 engine without
hand starter. 1923. [1]+12 p. 4°, ‡

ENGINEERING BUREAU

Bulletin. Bulletin of engineering information 6; Mar. 1, 1923. 1923. [1]+52
p. il. ‡   22—26665

—— Same 7; May 1, 1923. 1923. [1]+37 p. il. ‡(price incorrectly given
in publication as *Paper, 5c.)

Marine engineering. Changes in Manual of engineering instructions, no. 14;
Apr. 16, 1923. [1923.] [1]+73 p. il. [Changes 14 is chapter 28 of the new
edition of the Manual of engineering instructions. This chapter has also
been issued in pamphlet form with title Instructions for operation, care,
and repair of storage batteries, for which see Monthly catalogue for June,
1923, p. 796.] *Paper, 10c.

MARINE CORPS

Orders. Marine Corps orders 3, 1923; June 21, 1923. 1923. 1 p. 4° ‡

Supplies. Changes [34] in System of accountability, Marine Corps, 1916; Aug.
5, 1922. [Reprint with slight change 1923.] 2 p. 4° [Accompanied by reprints of certain pages to be inserted in their proper places in the 1918 reprint
of the original publication. A list of these reprinted pages is given on the
first page.] ‡

—— Changes [35] in System of accountability, Marine Corps, 1916; June 27,
1922. [Reprint] 1923. 1 p. 4° [Accompanied by p. 81 to be inserted in
proper place in the 1918 reprint of the original publication.] ‡

—— Changes [39] in System of accountability, Marine Corps, 1916; June 1,
1923. [1923.] 1 p. 4° [Accompanied by p. 179 to be inserted in proper place
in the 1918 reprint of the original publication.] ‡

MEDICINE AND SURGERY BUREAU

Naval medical bulletin. United States naval medical bulletin, published for
information of Medical Department of service, July, 1923; v. 19, no. 1. 1923.
vi+1–114 p. 1 pl. 16 p. of pl. [Monthly. This is Dental number.] *Paper, 15c.
single copy, $1.50 a yr.; foreign subscription, $2.50.   8—35095

SPECIAL ARTICLES.—Navy Dental School; by the faculty.—Foreign bodies of dental
origin in air and food passages; by Louis H. Clerf.—Surgical treatment of chronic
suppurative pericementitis [with list of references]; by W. L. Darnall.—Manipulation
of amalgam; by H. E. Harvey.—Relation of modern dentistry to group diagnosis as
conducted at Naval Hospital, San Diego, Calif.; by L. C. Montgomery.—Tropical duty
as predisposing to gingivitis; by P. S. Tichey.—Manipulation of modeling compound
and sectional modeling compound impression technic; by J. J. Haas.—Wiring method
of treatment for fractures of mandible; by E. H. Tennent.—Use of modified Baker
anchorage in naval dental service; by W. L. Darnall.—Cementation; by H. E.
Harvey.—Clean cotton pellets; by H. E. Harvey.—Field service instruction for dental
officers of Navy; by J. V. McAlpin.—Case report [of iritis]; by L. C. Frost.—Notes
on preventive medicine for medical officers. Navy [including some sociological and
psychiatrical aspects of venereal disease problem; by Paul E. Bowers].

Navy as special field for medical work; [by E. R. Stitt]. May 1, 1923. 63 p. il.
4° †   23—26698

Navy Dental School; by the faculty. 1923. [1]+13 p. 8 p. of pl. [From United
States naval medical bulletin, v. 19, no. 1.] †

NAVIGATION BUREAU

English language. English for enlisted men, assignment 1; by William Oliver Stevens. 1923. ii+6 p. (Navy education-study courses.) ‡

—— Same, assignment 2; by William Oliver Stevens. 1923. [1]+8 p. (Navy education-study courses.) ‡

—— Same, assignment 3; by William Oliver Stevens. 1923. [1]+2 p. (Navy education-study courses.) ‡

—— Same, assignment 4; by William Oliver Stevens. 1923. [1]+2 p. (Navy education-study courses.) ‡

—— Same, assignment 5; by William Oliver Stevens. 1923. [1]+3 p. (Navy education-study courses.) ‡

—— Same, assignment 6; by William Oliver Stevens. 1923. [1]+4 p. (Navy education-study courses.) ‡

—— Same, assignment 7; by William Oliver Stevens. 1923. [1]+6 p. (Navy education-study courses.) ‡

—— Same, assignment 8; by William Oliver Stevens. 1923. [1]+4 p. (Navy education-study courses.) ‡

—— Same, assignment 9; by William Oliver Stevens. 1923. [1]+6 p. (Navy education-study courses.) ‡

—— Same, assignment 10; by William Oliver Stevens. 1923. [1]+6 p. (Navy education-study courses.) ‡

—— Same, assignment 11; by William Oliver Stevens. 1923. [1]+3 p. (Navy education-study courses.) ‡

—— Same, assignment 12; by William Oliver Stevens. 1923. [1]+6 p. (Navy education-study courses.) ‡

—— Same, assignment 13; by William Oliver Stevens. 1923. [1]+7 p. (Navy education-study courses.) ‡

—— Same, assignment 14; by William Oliver Stevens. 1923. [1]+4 p. (Navy education-study courses.) ‡

—— Same, assignment 15; by William Oliver Stevens. 1923. [1]+5 p. (Navy education-study courses.) ‡

—— Same, assignment 16; by William Oliver Stevens. 1923. [1]+2 p. (Navy education-study courses.) ‡

—— Same, assignment 17; by William Oliver Stevens. 1923. [1]+3 p. (Navy education-study courses.) ‡

—— Same, assignment 18; by William Oliver Stevens. 1923. [1]+4 p. (Navy education-study courses.) ‡

—— Same, assignment 19; by William Oliver Stevens. 1923. [1]+4 p. (Navy education-study courses.) ‡

—— Same, assignment 20; by William Oliver Stevens. 1923. [1]+1 p. (Navy education-study courses.) ‡

HYDROGRAPHIC OFFICE

·Note.—The charts, sailing directions, etc., of the Hydrographic Office are sold by the office in Washington and also by agents at the principal American and foreign seaports and American lake ports. Copies of the General catalogue of mariners' charts and books and of the Hydrographic bulletins, reprints, and Notice to mariners are supplied free on application at the Hydrographic Office in Washington and at the branch offices in Boston, New York, Philadelphia, Baltimore, Norfolk, Savannah, New Orleans, Galveston, San Francisco, Portland (Oreg.), Seattle, Chicago, Cleveland, Buffalo, Sault. Ste. Marie, and Duluth.

Hydrographic bulletin, weekly, no. 1765–68; July 3–25, 1923. [1923.] Each 1 p. large 4° [For Ice supplements to accompany nos. 1765–68, see below under center head *Charts* the subhead *Pilot charts*.] † ·

Notice to aviators 7, 1923; July 1 [1923]. 1923. 1 p. [Monthly.] †

20—26958·

Notice to mariners 27–30, 1923; July 7–28 [1923]. [1923.] [xxxvii]+703–806 leaves, 5 maps. [Weekly.] †

Tide calendars. Tide calendar [for Baltimore (Fells Point) and Cape Henry], July, 1923. [1923.] 1 p. 4° [Monthly.] †

—— Same, Aug. 1923. [1923.] 1 p. 4° [Monthly.] †

—— Tide calendar [for Norfolk (Navy Yard) and Newport News, Va.], Aug. 1923. [1923.] 1 p. 4° [Monthly.] †

.Charts

Honshu. Harbors and bays on north coast of Honshu, Japan, from Japanese surveys in 1914; chart 5315. Washington, Hydrographic Office, July, 1923. 25.7×41 in. † 50c.
Aomori Ko.
Mimmaya Wan.
Moura Ko.
Oma Wan.

Pilot charts. Ice supplement to north Atlantic pilot chart; issue 65. Scale 1° long.=0.3 in. Washington, Hydrographic Office [1923]. 8.9×11.8 in. [To accompany Hydrographic bulletin 1765, July 3, 1923.] †

—— Same; issue 66. Scale 1° long.=0.3 in. Washington, Hydrographic Office [1923]. 8.9×11.8 in. [To accompany Hydrographic bulletin 1766, July 11, 1923.] †

—— Same; issue 67. Scale 1° long.=0.3 in. Washington, Hydrographic Office [1923]. 8.9×11.8 in. [To accompany Hydrographic bulletin 1767, July 18, 1923.] †

—— Same; issue 68. Scale 1° long.=0.3 in. Washington, Hydrographic Office [1923]. 8.9×11.8 in. [To accompany Hydrographic bulletin 1768, July 25, 1923.] †

—— Pilot chart of Central American waters, Aug. 1923; chart 3500. Scale 1° long.=0.7 in. Washington, Hydrographic Office, July 12, 1923. 23.4×35.1 in. [Monthly. Certain portions of the data are furnished by the Weather Bureau.] † 10c.
NOTE.—Contains on reverse: Cyclonic storms.—Weather forecasting from ships at sea; by Alfred J. Henry.

—— Pilot chart of Indian Ocean, Sept. 1923; chart 2603. Scale 1° long.=0.2 in. Washington, Hydrographic Office, July 12, 1923. 22.6×31 in. [Monthly. Certain portions of the data are furnished by the Weather Bureau.] † 10c.
NOTE.—Contains on reverse: Cyclonic storms.—Weather forecasting from ships at sea; by Alfred J. Henry.

—— Pilot chart of north Atlantic Ocean, Aug. 1923; chart 1400. Scale 1° long.=0.27 in. Washington, Hydrographic Office, July 12, 1923. 23.2×31.8 in. [Monthly. Certain portions of the data are furnished by the Weather Bureau.] † 10c.   14—16339
NOTE.—Contains on reverse: Cyclonic storms.—Weather forecasting from ships at sea; by Alfred J. Henry.

—— Pilot chart of north Pacific Ocean, Aug. 1923; chart 1401. Scale 1° long.=0.2 in. Washington, Hydrographic Office, June 14, 1923. 23.7×35.3 in. [Monthly. Certain portions of the data are furnished by the Weather Bureau.] † 10c.
NOTE.—Contains on reverse: Cyclonic storms.

—— Same, Sept. 1923; chart 1401. Scale 1° long.=0.2 in. Washington, Hydrographic Office, July 12, 1923. 23.7×35.3 in. [Monthly. Certain portions of the data are furnished by the Weather Bureau.] † 10c.
NOTE.—Contains on reverse: Cyclonic storms.—Weather forecasting from ships at sea; by Alfred J. Henry.

—— Pilot chart of south Atlantic Ocean, Sept.–Nov. 1923; chart 2600. Scale 1° long.=0.3 in. Washington, Hydrographic Office, July 12, 1923. 23×31.9 in. [Quarterly. Certain portions of the data are furnished by the Weather Bureau.] † 10c.
NOTE.—Contains on reverse: Cyclonic storms.—Weather forecasting from ships at sea; by Alfred J. Henry.

—— Pilot chart of south Pacific Ocean, Sept.–Nov. 1923; chart 2601. Scale 1° long.=0.2 in. Washington, Hydrographic Office, July 12, 1923. 21.2× 35.5 in. [Quarterly. Certain portions of the data are furnished by the Weather Bureau.] † 10c.
NOTE.—Contains on reverse: Cyclonic storms.—Weather forecasting from ships at sea; by Alfred J. Henry.

NAUTICAL ALMANAC OFFICE

American nautical almanac, [calendar] year 1925. 1923. x+162 p. 1 pl. 2 maps. * Paper, 15c.

NOTE.—In the volumes of the American ephemeris and nautical almanac and the American nautical almanac, beginning with those for 1925, the hours of the day are counted from midnight to midnight instead of from noon to noon as was done in the volumes before 1925, and the time is designated civil time instead of mean time. By this change each day begins 12 hours earlier than formerly.

SUPPLIES AND ACCOUNTS BUREAU

Accounting numbers· for ships and stations. 1924 edition. July 1, 1923. v+39 p. 4° (Accounting bulletin 1, pt. 2.) ‡

Naval supplies. Index to specifications issued by Navy Department for naval stores and material. July 2, 1923. v+46 p. 12° [Quarterly.] †

—— Sale of Navy surplus, aeronautical equipment, Aug. 10, 1923, Central Sales Office, Navy Yard, Washington, D. C. 1923. cover-title, 17 p. (Catalogue 221B.) ·†

—— ,Sale of Navy surplus, metals, brass, bronze, copper, iron, lead, steel, tin, and zinc, Aug. 16, 1923, Central Sales Office, Navy Yard, Washington, D. C. 1923. cover-title, 104 p. (Catalogue 220B.) †

PAN AMERICAN UNION

NOTE.—The Pan American Union sells its own monthly bulletins, handbooks, etc., at prices usually ranging from 5c. to $2.50. The price of the English edition of the bulletin is 25c. a single copy or $2.50 a year, the Spanish edition $2.00 a year, the Portuguese edition $1.50 a year; there is an additional charge of 50c. a year on each edition for countries outside the Pan American Union. Address the Director General of the Pan American Union, Washington, D. C.

Asuncion, Paraguay's interesting capital; [by William A. Reid]. 1923. [1]+ 26 p. il. †   23—26699

Bulletin (English edition). Bulletin of Pan American Union, July, 1923; [v. 57, no. 1]. [1923.] iv+1–108 p. il. [Monthly.]   8—30967

—— Same. (H. doc. 6, pt. 1, 68th Cong. 1st sess.)

—— *(Portuguese edition).* Boletim da União Pan-Americana, Julho, 1923, edição portugueza; [v. 25, no. 1]. [Sun Job Print, Baltimore, Md., 1923.] [iv]+1–76 p. il. [Monthly.]   11—27014

—— *(Spanish edition).* Boletín de la Unión Panamericana, v. 52 [sección española]; Enero–Junio, 1921 [índice]. [1923.] [1]+xxv p.   12—12555

—— Same, Julio, 1923, sección española; [v. 57, no. 1]. [1923.] iv+1–108 p. il. [Monthly. This number is entitled La mortalidad infantil y métodos para combatirla.]

Ecuador. Commerce of Ecuador, latest reports from Ecuadorean official sources. 1923. [1]+4 p. †   23—6433

—— Ecuador, general descriptive data. 1923. [2]+30 p. il. †   16—26930

Latin America. What United States buys from Latin America, quantities and value. 1923. [1]+18 p. †   23—26700

Milk. Leche pura, importante problema en la alimentación; [por Ernest A. Sweet]. 1923. [1]+14 p. il. [From Boletín, July, 1923.] †

Rio de Janeiro, fair capital of Brazil; [by E. Albes]. 1923. [2]+22 p. il. †
                                                              23—26701

PANAMA CANAL

NOTE.—Although The Panama Canal makes its reports to, and is under the supervision of, the Secretary of War, it is not a part of the War Department.

Panama Canal. A great people's great canal, its achievements, its perils, where Government operation works, struggle against forces of nature, finest organization in world to-day, honor to our Presidents and Congress, what old-timers fear, greatest danger that threatens canal, appeal to Americans to prize what they have and be on guard; by Jay J. Morrow. Panama Canal Press, Mt. Hope, C. Z., [May 29] 1923. 16 p. il. [From Outlook, Feb. 28, 1923.] † 23—26702

Panama Canal record, v. 16, no. 47–50; July 4–25, 1923. Balboa Heights, C. Z. [1923]. p. 617–672. [Weekly.]   7—35328
- NOTE.—The Panama Canal record is furnished free to United States Government departments and bureaus. Members of Congress, representatives of foreign Governments, steamship lines, and public libraries. Others desiring this publication may obtain it at the subscription price of $1.50 per year in the Canal Zone, the United States, and the Republic of Panama; $2.00 per year elsewhere. Remittances for subscriptions may be forwarded to The Panama Canal, Washington, D. C., or to The Panama Canal Record, Balboa Heights, Canal Zone, Isthmus of Panama.

PURCHASING DEPARTMENT

Supplies. Circular [proposals for supplies] 1546; July 24, 1923. [1923.]   14+ [1] p. f°   †

—— Proposals [for supplies 1543, to accompany Circular proposals for supplies 1543]. [1923.]   1 p. 24°   ‡

POST OFFICE DEPARTMENT

Envelopes. Improper placement of name and address of senders on backs of envelopes; [issued by] 3d assistant Postmaster General. July 13, 1923.   1 p. oblong 32°   †

Money-orders. Numbers of C. O. D. parcels must be placed on money orders issued in payment of charges on C. O. D. parcels; [issued by] 3d assistant Postmaster General. July 7, 1923.   1 p. small 4°   †

Plants. Plants and plant products addressed to places in Georgia; [issued by] 3d assistant Postmaster General. July 26, 1923.   1 p. 4°   †

—— Terminal inspection of plants and plant products in Hawaii; [issued by] 3d assistant Postmaster General. July 7, 1923.   1 p. oblong 48°   †

Postal bulletin, v. 44, no. 13207–231; July 2–31, 1923.   1923.   various paging, f° [Daily except Sundays and holidays.]   * Paper, 5c. single copy, $2.00 a yr.
6—5810

Postal guide. United States official postal guide [4th series, v. 3, no. 1]; July, 1923.   [1923.]   975 p.   [Monthly.]   *Cloth, 75c.; with monthly supplements, $1.00, foreign subscription, $1.50; supplements published monthly (11 pamphlets) 25c., foreign subscription, 50c.   4—18254

Syracuse, N. Y. Scheme of primary distribution for use in Syracuse, N. Y., post office; corrected to July 15, 1923.   1923.   [1]+36 p. 12°   ‡

Telegraph. Rates of pay for communications by telegraph [during fiscal year 1924]. [1923.]   6 p. 4°   ‡

EQUIPMENT AND SUPPLIES DIVISION

Motor-vehicle supplies. List of motor-vehicle items furnished for use in motor-vehicle service, Government-operated star service, and motor-cycle service. July 15, 1923.   [1]+15 leaves.   ‡

RAILWAY MAIL SERVICE

Mail-trains. Schedule of mail trains, no. 365, May 23, 1923, 2d division, Railway Mail Service, comprising New York, New Jersey, Pennsylvania, Delaware, eastern shore of Maryland, Accomac and Northampton counties, Va., Porto Rico, and Virgin Islands. 1923.   296 p. narrow 8°   ‡

—— Schedule of mail trains, no. 444, July 3, 1923, 7th division, Railway Mail Service, comprising Kansas and Missouri. 1923.   164 p. narrow 8°   ‡

TOPOGRAPHY DIVISION

NOTE.—Since February, 1908, the Topography Division has been preparing rural-delivery maps of counties in which rural delivery is completely established. They are published in two forms, one giving simply the rural free delivery routes, starting from a single given post office, sold at 10 cents each; the other, the rural free delivery routes in an entire county, sold at 35 cents each. A uniform scale of 1 inch to 1 mile is used. Editions are not issued, but sun-print copies are produced in response to special calls addressed to the Disbursing Clerk, Post Office Department, Washington, D. C. These maps should not be confused with the post route maps, for which see Monthly catalogue for February, 1923, page 528.

PRESIDENT OF UNITED STATES

Addresses. Address of President of United States on agriculture, to be delivered at Hutchinson, Kans., June 23, 1923. 1923. [1]+11 p. †

23—26644

—— Address of President of United States on International Court of Justice, at St. Louis, June 21, 1923. 1923. [2]+12 p. †   23—26648

—— Address of President of United States on law enforcement, at Denver [Colo.], June 25, 1923. 1923. [2]+8 p. †   23—26645

—— Address of President of United States on Oregon trail, at Meacham, Oreg., July 3, 1923. 1923. [2]+5 p. †   23—26649

—— Address of President of United States on social justice, women, and labor, at Helena, Mont., June 29, 1923. 1923. [2]+10 p. †   23—26646

—— Address of President of United States on taxation and expenditure, at Salt Lake City, Utah, June 26, 1923. 1923. [2]+10 p. †   23—26647

—— Address of President of United States on transportation problem, to be delivered at Kansas City, Mo., June 22, 1923. 1923· [2]+14 p. † 23—26650

Ballard, Mrs. Lottie M. Executive order [authorizing appointment of Mrs. Lottie M. Ballard to position of printer's assistant in Engraving and Printing Bureau]. June 20, 1923. 1 p. f° (No. 3877.) ‡

Fortune, Mrs. Nellye C. Executive order [authorizing appointment of Mrs. Nellye C. Fortune as clerk in Supplies and Accounts Bureau, Navy Department]. June 20, 1923. 1 p. f° (No. 3876.) ‡

Guiton, Katie A. Executive order [authorizing appointment of Katie A. Guiton to clerical position in classified civil service]. June 20, 1923. 1 p. f° (No. 3875.) ‡

Interdepartmental Social Hygiene Board. Executive order [directing that chairman of Interdepartmental Social Hygiene Board on July 1, 1923, transfer all files, records, and filing cabinets to Public Health Service, and ordering that upon said transfer Interdepartmental Social Hygiene Board shall cease to exist]. June 20, 1923. 1 p. f° (No. 3874.) ‡

National forests. Carson National Forest, N. Mex., 4th proclamation. [June 16, 1923.] 2 p. map, f° ([No. 1667.]) †

—— Executive order, Routt National Forest, Colo. [modifying boundaries of Routt National Forest by excluding certain lands in Colorado, excluded lands to be subject only to homestead and desert land entry by ex-service men of War with Germany for period of 91 days, after which any remaining land may be open to general public under any public land law applicable thereto]. June 19, 1923. 1 p. f° (No. 3872.) ‡

—— Santa Fe National Forest, N. Mex., 3d proclamation. June 16, 1923. 1 p. map, f° (No. 1668.) †

Officers, Army. Executive order [directing that in absence of special instructions Secretary of War act for the President in approving or disapproving action of Final Classification Board and Honest and Faithful Board in placing an officer in class B, composed of those who should not be retained in service, and authorizing Secretary of War to place any case which he deems advisable before the President for disposition]. June 19, 1923. 1 p. f° (No. 3870.) ‡

Peelor, Philip R. Executive order [authorizing appointment of Philip R. Peelor to clerical position in postal service at New York, N. Y.]. June 20, 1923. 1 p. f° (No. 3873.) ‡

Strong, George E. Executive order [authorizing appointment of George E. Strong to position of chief clerk and administrative assistant in Justice Department]. June 19, 1923. 1 p. f° (No. 3872-A.) ‡

Virgin Islands. Executive order [transferring administration of national prohibition act in virgin Islands from Secretary of Treasury to Secretary of Navy]. June 19, 1923. 1 p. f° (No. 3871.) ‡

RAILROAD ADMINISTRATION

Beet-sugar. Before Interstate Commerce Commission, no. 14260 and sub nos. 1 and 2, Charles L. Bird et al. *v.* director general; exceptions on behalf of director general to report proposed by examiner. 1923. cover-title, 3 p. ‡

Box board. Before Interstate Commerce Commission no. 13249, Seneca Fibre Products Company *v.* director general; petition on behalf of director general for reargument, rehearing, or reconsideration. 1923. cover-title, i+16 p. ‡

Cabbage. Before Interstate Commerce Commission, no. 13806, Meyer-Vasquez Produce Company *v.* director general; exceptions on part of director general to report proposed by examiner. 1923. cover-title, 6 p. ‡

Cement. Before Interstate Commerce Commission, no. 14676, Riverside Portland Cement Company *v.* director general; brief for defendant. 1923. cover-title, 9 p. ‡

Copper. Before Interstate Commerce Commission, no. 14747, Afterthought Copper Company *v.* director general et al.; brief on behalf of director general. 1923. cover-title, 10 p. ‡

Demurrage. Before Interstate Commerce Commission, no. 14220, Getz Brothers & Company *v.* director general, as agent; answer to exceptions filed on behalf of complainant. 1923. cover-title, 8 p. ‡

Fluxing stone. Before Interstate Commerce Commission, no. 14485, Alan Wood Iron & Steel Company *v.* director general; brief on behalf of director general. 1923. cover-title, 8 p. ‡

Freight rates. Before Interstate Commerce Commission, no. 12820, West Virginia Pulp & Paper Co., Inc., *v.* director general, as agent; defendant's exceptions to attorney examiner's proposed report. 1923. cover-title, 1 p. ‡

—— No. 12497 and 12497 sub. no. 1, before Interstate Commerce Commission, United States *v.* director general, as agent, et al.; [same] *v.* Wharton & Northern Railroad Company and 92 other railroad companies, and receivers of certain thereof; suggestions on behalf of United States in opposition to application of Wharton & Northern Railroad for further hearing. 1923. cover-title, 5 p. ‡

Ice. Before Interstate Commerce Commission, no. 14448, Massachusetts Ice Dealers Association *v.* director general; exceptions on behalf of director general to report proposed by examiner. 1923. cover-title, 8 p. ‡

Linseed-meal. Before Interstate Commerce Commission, no. 12290, Midland Linseed Products Company *v.* director general et al.; brief on rehearing on behalf of director general. 1923. cover-title, 5 p. ‡

Matches. Before Interstate Commerce Commission, I. C. C. docket nos. 14599 and 14600, Diamond Match Company *v.* James C. Davis, director general of railroads, as agent, New York Central Railroad Company, and Philadelphia and Reading Railway Company; [same] *v.* director general, as agent, New York Central Railroad Company, et al.; defendants' brief. 1923. cover-title, i+29 p. ‡

Meat. Before Interstate Commerce Commission, no. 11012, Swift and Company *v.* director general et al.; no. 12174 [same *v.* same]; no. 12223, Armour and Company *v.* [same]; petition for further hearing. 1923. cover-title, 19 p. ‡

Molasses. Before Interstate Commerce Commission, no. 14611, Mason By-Products Company *v.* director general, as agent; brief filed on behalf of defendant. 1923. cover-title, 7 p. ‡

Sugar. Before Interstate Commerce Commission, no. 13635, Seavey & Flarsheim Brokerage Company *v.* director general; exceptions on behalf of director general to report proposed by examiner. 1923. cover-title, 6 p. ‡

Sugar-beet syrup. Before Interstate Commerce Commission, no. 14426, Wyoming Sugar Company *v.* director general; brief filed on behalf of director general. 1923. cover-title, 7 p. ‡

SHIPPING BOARD

Pusey & Jones Company. In equity, no. —, in district court for district of New
Jersey, United States *v.* Pusey and Jones Company et al.; bill of complaint.
1923. cover-title, 98 p. ‡

Shooters Island Shipyard Company. United States circuit court of appeals for
2d circuit, Shooters Island Shipyard Company *v.* Standard Shipbuilding Corporation et al., in equity, district court docket, no. 1044; United States *v.*
[same], in equity, district court docket, no. 1099 (foreclosure); [same] *v.*
[same], in equity, district court docket, no. 1101 (tax lien); petition for appeal to Supreme Court. 1923. cover-title, 15 p. ‡

SHIPPING BOARD EMERGENCY FLEET CORPORATION

Ships. Schedule of sailings of Shipping Board vessels in general cargo, passenger, and mail services, 1st of August to middle of September, 1923; issued
by Traffic Department. 1923. cover-title, ii+14 p. [Monthly. Text on p.
2–4 of cover.] †   23—26331

SMITHSONIAN INSTITUTION

NOTE.—In a recent price-list the Smithsonian Institution publishes this notice: "Applicants for the publications in this list are requested to state the grounds of their requests, as the Institution is able to supply papers only as an aid to the researches or
studies in which they are especially interested. These papers are distributed *gratis*,
except as otherwise indicated, and should be ordered by the *publication numbers* arranged in sequence. The serial publications of the Smithsonian Institution are as follows: 1, Smithsonian contributions to knowledge; 2, Smithsonian miscellaneous collections; 3, Smithsonian annual reports. No *sets* of these are for sale or distribution, as
most of the volumes are out of print. The papers issued in the series of Contributions to
knowledge and Miscellaneous collections are distributed without charge to public
libraries, educational establishments, learned societies, and specialists in this country
and abroad; and are supplied to other institutions and individuals at the prices indicated. Remittances should be made payable to the ' Smithsonian Institution.' The
Smithsonian report volumes and the papers reprinted in separate form therefrom are
distributed *gratuitously* by the Institution to libraries and individuals throughout the
world. Very few of the Report volumes are now available at the Institution, but many
of those of which the Smithsonian edition is exhausted can be purchased from the
Superintendent of Documents, Government Printing Office, Washington, D. C. The
Institution maintains mailing-lists of public libraries and other educational establishments, but no *general mailing-list of individuals.* A library making application to be
listed for Smithsonian publications should state the number of volumes which it contains and the date of its establishment, and have the endorsement of a Member of
Congress."
    The annual reports are the only Smithsonian publications that are regularly issued
as public documents. All the others are paid for from the private funds of the Institution, but as they are usually regarded as public documents and have free transmission
by mail they are listed in the Monthly catalogue.

Alimentary education of children, by Marcel Labbé; [translation]. 1923.
[1]+549–564 p. (Publication 2701.) [From Report, 1921.] †

Alkali problem in irrigation; by Carl S. Scofield. 1923. [1]+213–223 p. 3 p.
of pl. (Publication 2681.) [From Report, 1921.] †

Ant acacias and acacia ants of Mexico and Central America; by W. E. Safford.
1923. [1]+381–394 p. il. 15 p. of pl. (Publication 2692.) [From Report,
1921.] †

Astronomy. Daily influences of astronomy; by W. W. Campbell. 1923.
[1]+139–152 p. (Publication 2676.) [From Report, 1921.] †

Atomic weights and isotopes; by F. W. Aston. 1923. [1]+181–196 p. il.
(Publication 2679.) [From Report, 1921.] †

Birds. Descriptions of new East Indian birds of families Turdidae, Sylviidae,
Pycnonotidae. and Muscicapidae: by Harry C. Oberholser. Washington,
Smithsonian Institution, July 16, 1923. [2]+9 p. (Publication 2721; Smith-
sonian miscellaneous collections, v. 76, no. 6.) † Paper, 10c. • 23—26666

—— Some preliminary remarks on velocity of migratory flight among birds,
with special reference to Palæarctic region; by R. Meinertzhagen. 1923.
[1]+365–372 p. (Publication 2690.) [From Report, 1921.] †

Botanical reconnaissance in southeastern Asia; by A. S. Hitchcock. 1923. [1]+373–380 p. 11 p. of pl. (Publication 2691.) [From Report, 1921.] †

Cetaceans. Description of apparently new toothed cetacean from South Carolina; by Remington Kellogg. Washington, Smithsonian Institution, July 25, 1923. [2]+7 p. 2 p. of pl. (Publication 2723; Smithsonian miscellaneous collections, v. 76, no. 7.) † Paper, 10c.   23—26703

Costa Rica. Some observations on natural history of Costa Rica; by Robert Ridgway. 1923. [1]+303–324 p. 5 p. of pl. (Publication 2686.) [From Report, 1921.] †

Earth. Age of the earth; [articles] by Lord Rayleigh [W. J. Sollas, J. W. Gregory, and Harold Jeffreys]. 1923. [1]+249–260 p. (Publication 2684.) [From Report, 1921.] †

—— Yielding of the earth's crust; by William Bowie. 1923. [1]+235–247 p. il. (Publication 2683.) [From Report, 1921.] †

Entomology, Medical. Fifty-year sketch-history of medical entomology; by L. O. Howard. 1923. [1]+565–586 p. 10 p. of por. (Publication 2702.) [From Report, 1921.] †

Evolution. Historic development of evolutionary idea, by Branislav Petronievics; [translation]. 1923. [1]+325–334 p. (Publication 2687.) [From Report, 1921.] †

Fall webworm; by R. E. Snodgrass. 1923. [1]+395–414 p. il. 2 p. of pl. (Publication 2693.) [From Report, 1921.] †

Geology Department. Department of Geology of National Museum; by George P. Merrill. 1923. [1]+261–302 p. il. 2 pl. 18 p. of pl. and map. (Publication 2685.) [From Report, 1921.] †

Geophysical-chemistry. Outline of geophysical-chemical problems; by Robert B. Sosman. 1923. [1]+225–234 p. (Publication 2682.) [From Report, 1921.] †

Gorgas, William C. William Crawford Gorgas; by Robert E. Noble. 1923. [1]+615–624 p. 1 por. (Publication 2705.) [From Report, 1921.] †

Heredity of acquired characters, by L. Cuénot; [translation]. 1923. [1]+335–345 p. (Publication 2688.) [From Report, 1921.] †

Indians. Ancestor worship of Hopi Indians; by J. Walter Fewkes. 1923. [1]+485–506 p. il. 7 p. of pl. (Publication 2697.) [From Report, 1921.] †

—— Indian in literature, by Herman F. C. ten Kate; [translation]. 1923. [1]+507–528 p. (Publication 2698.) [From Report, 1921.] †

Insects. Collecting insects on Mount Rainier; by A. L. Melander. 1923. [1]+415–422 p. 9 p. of pl. (Publication 2694.) [From Report, 1921.] †

Lead; by Carl W. Mitman. 1923. [1]+595–614 p. il. 2 pl. 4 p. of pl. (Publication 2704.) [From Report, 1921.] †

Leopard-men in Naga Hills; by J. H. Hutton. 1923. [1]+529–540 p. (Publication 2699.) [From Report, 1921.] †

Man. Science of man, its needs and its prospects; by Karl Pearson. 1923. [1]+423–441 p. (Publication 2695.) [From Report, 1921.] †

Opossums. Breeding habits, development, and birth of opossum; by Carl Hartman. 1923. [1]+347–363 p. 10 p. of pl. (Publication 2689.) [From Report, 1921.] †

Palestine. New era in Palestine exploration; by Elihu Grant. 1923. [1]+541–547 p. 7 p. of pl. (Publication 2700.) [From Report, 1921.] †

Paper. Laid and wove [paper]; by Dard Hunter. 1923. [1]+587–593 p. il. 6 p. of pl. (Publication 2703.) [From Report, 1921.] †

Pigmentation in old Americans, with notes on graying and loss of hair; by Aleš Hrdlička. 1923. [1]+443–484 p. (Publication 2696.) [From Report, 1921.] †

Relativity. Modifying our ideas of nature, Einstein theory of relativity; by Henry Norris Russell. 1923. [1]+197–211 p. (Publication 2680.) [From Report, 1921.] †

Report. Annual report of board of regents of Smithsonian Institution, year ending June 30, 1921 [with report of secretary, etc., and appendix containing scientific papers]. 1922. xi+638 p. il. 1 por. 12 pl. 100 p. of por. pl. and map. (Publication 2675.) * Cloth, $1.50. 4—18264

    NOTE.—The 30 scientific papers contained in the appendix of this volume have been published also in separate pamphlets, each of which is entered in this catalogue.

—— Same. (H. doc. 230, 67th Cong. 2d sess.)

Stars. Cosmogony and stellar evolution; by J. H. Jeans. 1923. [1]+153–164 p. il. (Publication 2677.) [From Report, 1921.] †

—— Diameters of the stars, by A. Danjon; [translation]. 1923. [1]+165–179 p. il. 1 pl. (Publication 2678.) [From Report, 1921.] †

Work. Report on cooperative educational and research work carried on by Smithsonian Institution and its branches. Washington, Smithsonian Institution, July 28, 1923. [2]+30 p. (Publication 2719; Smithsonian miscellaneous collections, v. 76, no. 4.) † 23—26704

ETHNOLOGY BUREAU

Indian languages. Handbook of American Indian languages, [edited] by Franz Boas; with illustrative sketches, by Edward Sapir, Leo J. Frachtenberg, and Waldemar Bogoras. 1922. pt. 2, v+903 p. il. (Bulletin 40 [pt. 2].) *Cloth, $1.50. 11—8930

    CONTENTS.—Takelma language of southwestern Oregon; by Edward Sapir.—Coos; by Leo J. Frachtenberg.—Siuslawan (Lower Umpqua); by Leo J. Frachtenberg.—Chukchee; by Waldemar Bogoras.

—— Same. (H. doc. 1529, 60th Cong. 2d sess.)

Jibaro Indians. Blood revenge, war, and victory feasts among Jibaro Indians of eastern Ecuador; by Rafael Karsten. 1923. vii+94 p. il. 10 p. of pl. (Bulletin 79.) * Cloth, 60c. 23—26705

—— Same. (H. doc. 4, 68th Cong. 1st sess.)

NATIONAL MUSEUM

    NOTE.—The publications of the National Museum comprise an annual report and three scientific series, viz., Proceedings, Bulletins, and Contributions from national herbarium. The editions are distributed to established lists of libraries, scientific institutions, and specialists, any surplus copies being supplied on application. The volumes of Proceedings are made up of technical papers based on the Museum collections in biology, geology, and anthropology, and of each of these papers a small edition, in pamphlet form, is issued in advance of the volume, for prompt distribution to specialists. No sets of any of these series can now be furnished.

Polyzoa. North American later Tertiary and Quaternary bryozoa [with bibliographies]; by Ferdinand Canu and Ray S. Bassler. 1923. vii+302 p. il. 47 p. of pl. large 4° (Bulletin 125.) * Paper, 75c. 23—26706

Trees and shrubs of Mexico: Oxalidaceae-Turneraceae; by Paul C. Standley. 1923. xxviii+517–848 p. (Contributions from national herbarium, v. 23, pt. 3.) * Paper, 30c. Agr 20—1880

Water-craft. Catalogue of watercraft collection in National Museum; compiled by Carl W. Mitman. 1923. v+298 p. il. 1 pl. (Bulletin 127.) * Paper, 40c. 23—26707

STATE DEPARTMENT

[*Circulars*] 898–900; June 6–23, 1923. [1923.] Each 2 p. or 1 p. [General instruction circulars to consular officers.] ‡

Conference on Central American Affairs, Washington, Dec. 4, 1922–Feb. 7, 1923 [proceedings]. 1923. 403 p. [English and Spanish.] * Paper, 40c. 23—26660

Declaration of Independence and Constitution of United States [with amendments 1–19]. 1923. iii+55 p. 12° * Paper, 10c. 23—26708

Diplomatic list, July, 1923. [1923.] cover-title, ii+34 p. 24° [Monthly.] ‡ 10—16292

Haiti, American High Commissioner to. Report of American High Commissioner at Port au Prince, Haiti, submitted to Secretary of State, Jan. 1, 1923. 1923. [1]+25 p. map. † 23—26709

SUPREME COURT

Cases adjudged in Supreme Court at Oct. term, 1921, May 2–June 5, 1922; Ernest Knaebel, reporter. 1923. xxxiv+640 p. (United States reports, v. 259.) [Also issued in 4 preliminary prints.] * Cloth, $2.15.

Official reports of Supreme Court, v. 260 U. S., no. 4; Ernest Knaebel, reporter. Preliminary print. 1923. cover-title, [1]+438–760 p. 12° [Cases adjudged in Supreme Court at Oct. term, 1922. Text on p. 2–4 of cover. From United States reports, v. 260.] * Paper, 25c. single copy, $1.00 per vol. (4 nos. to a vol.; subscription price, $3.00 for 12 nos.) ; foreign subscription, 5c. added for each pamphlet.

TARIFF COMMISSION

Laws relating to Tariff Commission. [Reprint] 1923. 14 p. * Paper, 5c.
23—26710

Tariff. Tariff information surveys. Revised edition. 1923. [First edition was issued by Ways and Means Committee. Other parts of Tariff information surveys appeared in previous Monthly catalogues.] 20—27464
    K–6. On articles in paragraphs 293–303 of tariff act of 1913 and related articles in other paragraphs, Carpets and rugs of wool. vi + 151 p. il. * Paper, 15c.
—— Same, index. [1923.] [The index to the Tariff information surveys is being issued in separate parts.]
    Chemicals, oils, and paints, schedule A and free list, act of Oct. 3, 1913. [Reprint 1923.] 5 p. * Paper, 5c.
    Wood and manufactures of, schedule D and free list, act of Oct. 3, 1913. 1 p. * Paper, 5c.

TREASURY DEPARTMENT

Appeals pending before United States courts in customs cases, no. 71; July, 1923. 1923. [1]+10 p. [Quarterly.] * Paper, 5c. single copy, 15c. a yr.; foreign subscription, 20c. 10—4497

Coins. Values of foreign coins, July 1, 1923. [1923.] 1 p. 4° (Department circular 1; Director of Mint.) [Quarterly.] †

Finance. Daily statement of Treasury compiled from latest proved reports from Treasury offices and depositaries, July 2–31, 1923. [1923.] Each 4 p. or 3 p. f° [Daily except Sundays and holidays.] † 15—3303

Public debt. Statement of public debt of United States, Apr. 30, 1923. May 4, 1923. [2] p. narrow f° [Monthly.] † 10—21268

Treasury decisions under customs, internal-revenue, and other laws, including decisions of Board of General Appraisers and Court of Customs Appeals, v. 44, no. 1–4; July 5–26, 1923. 1923. various paging. [Weekly. Department decisions numbered 39709–745, general appraisers' decisions 8667–72, abstracts 46124–186, internal revenue decisions 3495–3500, Tariff Commission Notice 27, and later Tariff Commission Notices 4, 7, and 15.] * Paper, 5c. single copy, $1.00 a yr.; foreign subscription, $2.00. 10—30490

APPRAISERS

Reappraisements of merchandise by general appraisers [on June 27–July 16, 1923]; July 6–20, 1923. [1923.] various paging. (Reappraisement circulars 3470–71.) [Weekly; none issued July 13, 1923.] * Paper, 5c. single copy, 50c. a yr.; foreign subscription, $1.05. 13—2916

BOOKKEEPING AND WARRANTS DIVISION

Appropriations. Digest of appropriations, fiscal year 1924, and on account of deficiencies for prior years, made by 2d session of 67th Congress from July 2, 1922, and by 3d and 4th sessions of 67th Congress. 1923. vii+579 p. 4° (Treas. Dept. doc. 2923.) * Half-leather, $1.75. 6—35371
—— Recapitulation of digest of appropriations, fiscal year 1924. 1923. [1]+ 497–523 p. 4° [From Digest of appropriations, 1924.] ‡

BUDGET BUREAU

Report. 2d annual report of director of Bureau of Budget to President of United States [fiscal year 1923], containing report of operations of Bureau of Budget, reports of chief coordinator and chairmen of coordinating boards and agencies established by Executive order for coordination of routine business of Government, also special reports of economies effected by Departments and establishments. 1923. iv+243 p. il. [Title-page reads July 1, 1923, but reports cover year ended June 30, 1923.]   * Paper, 20c.   22—26686

COAST GUARD

Circular letter 250 amendment B, 292–294 [new series]; June 13–27, 1923. 1923. Each 1 p. or 2 p. ‡

Orders. General order 31 and 32; June 18 and 22, 1923. [1923.] 2 p. and 1 p. ‡

Radio communication. Amendment to Radio instructions, Coast Guard, 1916. [1923.] 2 p. ‡

COMPTROLLER OF CURRENCY

National banks. Monthly statement of capital stock of national banks, national bank notes, and Federal reserve bank notes outstanding, bonds on deposit, etc. [July 2, 1923]. July 2, 1923. 1 p. f° †   10—21266

GOVERNMENT ACTUARY

Bonds of United States. Market prices and investment values of outstanding bonds and notes [of United States, June, 1923]. July 1, 1923. 7 p. 4° (Form A.) [Monthly.] †

INTERNAL REVENUE BUREAU

Blank forms. Catalogue of blank forms, books, laws, and regulations, prepared for use of officers of Internal Revenue Bureau. July, 1923.. iii+21 p. ([Form] 155, revised 1923.) †

Internal revenue. Index to Mimeographs 1717–3073, Jan. 8, 1918–Mar. 14, 1923, and Collectors' circulars 1–352, July 7, 1920–Mar. 15, 1923. 1923. 112 p. ‡

Internal revenue bulletin, v. 2, no. 13–17; July 2–30, 1923. 1923. various paging. [Weekly.] * Paper, 5c. single copy (for subscription price see note below).   22—26051

    NOTE.—On May 7, 1923, the publication of weekly bulletins was resumed and the issuance of monthly bulletins (and special bulletins as occasion required) discontinued. Since May 1, therefore, the 1923 Internal revenue bulletin service consists of weekly bulletins of new rulings and decisions of the Bureau of Internal Revenue and internal revenue Treasury decisions of general importance, quarterly digests of such new rulings (cumulative from Jan. 1, 1922), and semiannual cumulative bulletins containing in full the new rulings and decisions published during the preceding 6 months. The complete bulletin service may be obtained, on a subscription basis, from the Superintendent of Documents, Government Printing Office, Washington, D. C., for $2.00 a yr.; foreign subscription, $2.75.

Oleomargarin. Regulations 9 relating to taxes on oleomargarine, adulterated butter, and process or renovated butter under act of Aug. 2, 1886, as amended by act of May 9, 1902. Revised June, 1923. 1923. vi+101 p. * Paper, 10c.   23—26711

LOANS AND CURRENCY DIVISION

Bonds of United States. Caveat list of United States registered bonds and notes, July 1, 1923. [1923.]. 54 p. f° [Monthly.] †

Money. Circulation statement, July 1, 1923. [1923.] 1 p. oblong 8° [Monthly.] †   10—21267

PUBLIC HEALTH SERVICE

Arsenic. Penetration of arsenic into cerebrospinal fluid, with particular reference to treatment of protozoal infections of central nervous system [with list of references]; by Carl Voegtlin, M. I. Smith, Helen Dyer, and J. W. Thompson. 1923. 20 p. il. (Reprint 835.) [From Public health reports, May 11, 1923.] * Paper, 5c.   23—26712

Health officers. Whole-time county health officers, 1923 [directory]. 1923. 6 p. (Reprint 837.) [From Public health reports, May 18, 1923.] * Paper, 5c.
23—26713

Mosquitos. Guide to mosquito identification for field workers engaged in malaria control in United States; by W. H. W. Komp. 1923. 22 p. il. (Reprint 836.) [From Public health reports, May 18, 1923.] * Paper, 5c.
23—26714

Public health reports, v. 38, no. 27–30; July 6–27, 1923. 1923. [xvi]+1519–1746 p. fl. 2 p. of pl. [Weekly.] *Paper, 5c. single copy, $1.50 a yr.; foreign subscription, $2.75.   6—25167

SPECIAL ARTICLES.—No. 27. Possible explanation of absence of bubonic plague in cold countries; by H. McG. Robertson.—Ventilation of ships after fumigation with poisonous gases; [abstract of report by Stephen Olop].—National Health Council as aid to organized health agencies.—Births, deaths, and marriages in Scotland, rates for first quarter of 1923 and for 1913–22 by quarters.—No. 28. Analysis of 6 annual seasons of fall hay fever in New Orleans, La.; by Wm. Scheppegrell.—Spleen and blood examinations for malaria, study of relative merits of spleen and blood parasite indices for determining malaria prevalence as found in Dunklin County, Mo. [with list of references] ; by M. V. Veldee.—East Harlem Health Center demonstration, successful coordination of health activities of 22 organizations in large city [New York].—No. 29. Intensive localized distribution of spore of B. botulinus and probable relation of preserved vegetables to type demonstrated; by J. C. Geiger and Harriet Benson.—Physiological effects of high temperatures and humidities with and without air movement, effects on body temperature and pulse rate of subjects at rest; by R. R. Sayers and D. Harrington.—Births, deaths, and infant mortality, 1921–22, provisional figures for 1922, and rates for 1921–22 in birth registration area of United States.—No. 30. Studies on oxidation-reduction: 4, Electrode potentials of indigo sulphonates, each in equilibrium with its reduction product [with list of references] ; by M. X. Sullivan, Barnett Cohen, and W. Mansfield Clark.

NOTE.—This publication is distributed gratuitously to State and municipal health officers, etc., by the Surgeon General of the Public Health Service, Treasury Department. Others desiring these reports may obtain them from the Superintendent of Documents, Washington, D. C., at the prices stated above.

Tuberculosis, its predisposing causes; by F. C. Smith. 1923. 8 p. (Reprint 829.) [Revision of Supplement 3 to Public health reports, Feb. 7, 1913. From Public health reports, Apr. 13, 1923.] *Paper, 5c.   23—26651

HYGIENIC LABORATORY

Streptococcus. 1, Study of alpha type of streptococcus from variety of sources [with list of literature cited], by Alice C. Evans; 2, Influence of complement upon tropins in antistreptococcic serums [with list of literature cited], by Alice C. Evans; 3, Testing of antistreptococcic serum by mouse protection method, by Ella M. A. Enlows; 4, Factors influencing standardization of antipneumococcic serums, by Ella M. A. Enlows. May, 1923. v+68 p. il. (Bulletin 134.) * Paper, 10c.   23—26715–718

—— Same. (H. doc. 5, 68th Cong. 1st sess.)

VENEREAL DISEASES DIVISION

Venereal disease information. venereal disease information, issued by Public Health Service for use in its cooperative work with State health departments, v. 4, no. 5; May 20, 1923. 1923. [2]+151–205+iv p. il. [Monthly. This information was formerly mimeographed, this number, v. 4, no. 5, being the first one printed.] * Paper, 5c. single copy, 50c. a yr. (subscription begins with the June number).   23—26719

SPECIAL ARTICLES.—General paresis; [by Paul E. Bowers].—Trend of venereal disease incidence.

—— Same, v. 4, no. 6; June 20, 1923. 1923. ii+207–238+iii p. [Monthly.]

SPECIAL ARTICLES.—Suggestions for history taking in syphilis; by Joseph Earle Moore and Albert Keidel.—State venereal disease regulations again sustained.

TREASURER OF UNITED STATES

Paper money. Monthly statement, paper currency of each denomination outstanding May 31, 1923. June 1 [1923]. 1 p. oblong 24° †

VETERANS' BUREAU

Life insurance. Premium rates and information regarding United States Government life insurance. [Revised] Apr. 1923. [1923.] 16 p. 16° (Form 752.) ‡   23—26720

Military and Naval Insurance Division. War risk insurance act, with amendments prior to Apr. 1, 1923, act to authorize establishment of Bureau of War Risk Insurance in Treasury Department, act to establish veterans' Bureau and to improve facilities and service of such bureau, and further to amend and modify war risk insurance act. Apr. 1923. [1]+47 p. [This publication contains only provisions relating to Division of Military and Naval Insurance.] *Paper, 5c.   23—26721

WAR DEPARTMENT

Army regulations. †

NOTE.—The Army regulations are issued in pamphlet form for insertion in loose-leaf binders. The names of such of the more important administrative subjects as may seem appropriate, arranged in proper sequence, are numbered in a single series and each name so numbered constitutes the title and number of a pamphlet containing certain administrative regulations pertaining thereto. Where more than one pamphlet is required for the administrative regulations pertaining to any such title, additional pamphlets will be issued in a separate sub-series.

40–210. Medical Department: Prevention of communicable diseases of man, general; Apr. 21, 1923. [1923.] 5 p.
40–215. Same: Prevention of communicable diseases of man, immunization; Apr. 21, 1923. [1923.] 10 p.
40–220. Same: Prevention of communicable diseases of man, diseases of respiratory system and other diseases transmitted by discharges from respiratory tract; Apr. 21, 1923. [1923.] 8 p.
40–225. Same: Prevention of communicable diseases of man, intestinal diseases; Apr. 21, 1923. [1923.] 4 p.
40–230. Same: Prevention of communicable diseases of man, insect-borne diseases; Apr. 21, 1923. [1923.] 5 p.
40–235. Same: Prevention of communicable diseases of man, venereal diseases; Apr. 21, 1923. [1923.] 5 p.
40–240. Same: Prevention of communicable diseases of man, miscellaneous diseases; Apr. 21, 1923. [1923.] 4 p.
40–245. Same: Prevention of communicable diseases of man, management of cases in hospitals and dispensaries; Apr. 21, 1923. [1923.] 5 p.
40–275. Same: Sanitary reports; Apr. 21, 1923. [1923.] 5 p.
90–50. Coast Artillery Corps: Fort command. Changes 1; June 9, 1923. 1923. 1 p.
105–20. Signal Corps: Administrative telephone and target-range signal communication systems; May 8, 1923. [1923.] 4 p. [Supersedes AR 105–20, Oct. 29, 1921.]
130–10. National Guard: Call and draft into Federal service; Apr. 25, 1923. [1923.] 38 p.
345–50. Military records: Strength returns, general; Apr. 26, 1923. [1923.] 5 p. [Supersedes AR 345–50. Mar. 31, 1922.]
345–100. Same: Diary; Apr. 26, 1923. [1923.] 2 p. [Supersedes AR 345–100, Mar. 10, 1922.]
600–375. Personnel: Prisoners, general provisions; May 19, 1923. [1923.] 12 p. [Supersedes AR 600–375. July 3, 1922.]
615–40. Enlisted men: Clothing, allowances, accounts, and disposition, Changes 3; May 9, 1923. [1923.] 2 p. [Supersedes AR 615–40, Changes 1 and 2. July 17, 1922, and Apr. 25, 1923.]
615–250. Same: Physical inspections, Changes 1; June 12, 1923. 1923. 1 p.
760–400. Basic allowances: Small arms targets and target material; Apr. 14, 1923. [1923.] 5 p.

Industrial mobilization. Notes on industrial mobilization [for procurement of supplies in time of war]. 1923. ii+5 p. narrow 8° †

Training regulations.

NOTE.—The Training regulations are issued in pamphlet form for insertion in loose-leaf binders.

50–15. Soldier: Instruction dismounted without arms, prepared under direction of chief of infantry; Apr. 14, 1923. [1923.] 12 p. il. *Paper, 5c.
50–20. Same: Instruction dismounted with rifle and automatic rifle, prepared under direction of chief of infantry; Apr. 14, 1923. [1923.] 26 p. il. *Paper, 5c.
150–15. Marksmanship: Individual score book for rifle [prepared under direction of chief of infantry; May 2, 1922]. [Reprint with omissions] 1923. 23+[4] p. il. 40 p. of pl. oblong 32° [Special edition for C. M. T. camps.] ‡
420–40. Infantry: Drill and combat signals, prepared under direction of chief of infantry; May 22, 1923. [1923.] 8 p. *Paper, 5c.
420–105. Same: Combat principles, rifle squad, prepared under direction of chief of infantry; Apr. 25, 1923. [1923.] 46 p. il. *Paper, 10c.
420–120. Same: Combat principles, rifle company, prepared under direction of chief of infantry; May 22, 1923. [1923.] 20 p. *Paper, 5c.
420–140. Same: Combat principles, howitzer company squads, prepared under direction of chief of infantry; May 22, 1923. [1923.] 20 p. *Paper, 5c.
430–155. Field artillery: Reconnaissance and occupation of position, prepared under direction of chief of field artillery; Apr. 30, 1923. [1923.] 54 p. il. *Paper, 10c.

ADJUTANT GENERAL'S DEPARTMENT

Army list and directory, July 1, 1923. 1923. vi+305 p. large 8° [Bimonthly.]
.* Paper, 25c. single copy; $1.25 a yr.; foreign subscription, $1.85.   9—35106

Military communications. Basic signal communication, instructors guide and [for] all arms; prepared under direction of chief signal officer, 1923. 1923. viii+140+[1] p. il. 1 pl. (United States Army training manual 21.) * Cloth, 30c.

—— Basic signal communication, students manual for all arms; prepared under direction of chief signal officer, 1923. 1923. v+68 p. il. 1 pl. (United States Army training manual 20.) * Cloth, 20c.

Officers, Army. Officers of Army stationed in or near District of Columbia, July, 1923. 1923. iv+38 p. [Quarterly.] * Paper, 5c. single copy, 20c a yr.; foreign subscription, 30c.   9—35107

Telephone switchboard operator, students manual for all arms; prepared under direction of chief signal officer, 1923. 1923. v+113+[1] p. il. 2 pl. (United States Army training manual 22.) * Cloth, 25c.

U. S. Army recruiting news, bulletin of recruiting information issued by direction of Adjutant General of Army, July 15, 1923. [Recruiting Publicity Bureau, Governors Island, N. Y., July 15, 1923.] 16 p. il. 4° [None issued July 1, 1923.] † Recruiting Publicity Bureau, Governors Island, N. Y. War 22—1

AIR SERVICE

Aeronautical bulletin, no. 31–41, State series; June 15, 1923. [1923.] Each 2 p. il. 12° (Airways Section.) * Paper, 5c. each.

ENGINEERING DIVISION

Stresses. Comparative mathematical analysis of stresses occurring in camshaft drive gears of liberty 12 and Packard 2025 engines. Power Plant Section report; by C. W. Iseler. 1923. ii+15 p. il. 4° (Air Service. Air Service information circular, aviation, v. 5, no. 423, Apr. 1, 1923.) ‡

ENGINEER DEPARTMENT

Chesapeake and Delaware Canal. Maintenance and improvement of existing river and harbor works, Chesapeake and Delaware Canal, advertisement [for excavating inland waterway from Delaware River to Chesapeake Bay, Del. and Md. (Chesapeake & Delaware Canal)]. [1923.] 16 p. 4° †

MISSISSIPPI RIVER COMMISSION

Dredges. Proposals for steel hull for sand dredge, advertisement. [1923.] 13 p. 4° †

NORTHERN AND NORTHWESTERN LAKES SURVEY

Note.—Charts of the Great Lakes and connecting waters and St. Lawrence River to the international boundary at St. Regis, of Lake Champlain, and of the New York State canals are prepared and sold by the U. S. Lake Survey Office, Old Custom-house, Detroit, Mich. Charts may also be purchased at the following U. S. engineer offices: 710 Army Building, New York, N. Y.; 467 Broadway, Albany, N. Y.; 540 Federal Building, Buffalo, N. Y.; and Canal Office, Sault Ste. Marie, Mich. A catalogue (with index map), showing localities, scales, prices, and conditions of sale, may be had upon application at any of these offices.
A descriptive bulletin, which supplements the charts and gives detailed information as to harbors, shore lines and shoals, magnetic determinations, and particulars of changing conditions affecting navigation, is issued free to chart purchasers, upon request. The bulletin is revised annually and issued at the opening of navigation (in April), and supplements thereto are published monthly during the navigation season.
Complete sets of the charts and publications may be seen at the U. S. engineer offices in Duluth, Minn., Milwaukee, Wis., Chicago, Ill., Grand Rapids, Mich., Cleveland, Ohio, and Oswego, N. Y., but they are obtainable only at the sales offices above mentioned.

Great Lakes. Supplement 3, July 21, 1923, corrections and additions to Bulletin 32; to supplement information given upon charts of Great Lakes. U. S. Lake Survey Office, Detroit, Mich. [July 16, 1923]. p. 1–3+leaves 4–11+[2] p. 4° †

GENERAL STAFF CORPS

Shooting. Changes 6 [for] Rifle marksmanship [June, 1920]; Mar. 21, 1923. 1923. 1 p. [Rifle marksmanship issued by Adjutant General's Department.] †

Special regulations. Changes 1 [for] Special regulations 58 [Instructions for preparation of Army pay rolls, 1916]; Mar. 13, 1923. . 1923. 1 p. 12°. [Special regulations issued by War Department.] †

—— Changes 4 [for] Special regulations 48 [Regulations for Enlisted Reserve Corps, 1921]; Apr. 18, 1923. 1923. 1 p. [Special regulations issued by War Department.] †

—— Changes 10 [for] Special regulations 77 [Salvage of materials and supplies for Army, 1918]; Mar. 23, 1923. 1923. 1 p. 12° [Special regulations issued by War Department.] †

QUARTERMASTER GENERAL OF ARMY

Circulars. Changes 45 [1923, to] Circulars; July 5, 1923. [1923.] 1 p. 4° [Mimeographed.] ‡

Specifications. Index to Army Quartermaster Corps specifications; revised to Nov. 15, 1922. 1923. 54 p. 12° ‡

SIGNAL OFFICE

Radio communication. Introduction to line radio communication [with list of references], Jan. 1923. 1923. v+51 p. il. (Radio communication pamphlet 41; War Dept. doc. 1114.) [Prepared in cooperation with Standards Bureau.] * Paper, 10c.   War 23—16

O

85

THE LIBRARY

Monthly Catalogue

United States UNIVERSITY OF

Public Documents

No. 344
August, 1923

ISSUED BY THE
SUPERINTENDENT OF DOCUMENTS

UNIVERSITY OF ILLINOIS LIBRARY

OCT 6 1923

WASHINGTON
1923

Abbreviations

Appendix	app.	Page, pages	p.
Congress	Cong.	Part, parts	pt., pts.
Department	Dept.	Plate, plates	pl.
Document	doc.	Portrait, portraits	por.
Facsimile, facsimiles	facsim.	Quarto	4°
Folio	f°	Report	rp.
House	H.	Saint	St.
House bill	H. R.	Section, sections	sec.
House concurrent resolution	H. Con. Res.	Senate, Senate bill	S.
House document	H. doc.	Senate concurrent resolution	S. Con. Res.
House executive document	H. ex. doc.	Senate document	S. doc.
House joint resolution	H. J. Res.	Senate executive document	S. ex. doc.
House report	H. rp.	Senate joint resolution	S. J. Res.
House resolution (simple)	H. Res.	Senate report	S. rp.
Illustration, illustrations	il.	Senate resolution (simple)	S. Res.
Inch, inches	in.	Session	sess.
Latitude	lat.	Sixteenmo	16°
Longitude	long.	Table, tables	tab.
Mile, miles	m.	Thirtytwo-mo	32°
Miscellaneous	mis., misc.	Treasury	Treas.
Nautical	naut.	Twelvemo	12°
No date	n. d.	Twentyfour-mo	24°
No place	n. p.	Versus	vs., v.
Number, numbers	no., nos.	Volume, volumes	v., vol.
Octavo	8°	Year	yr.

Common abbreviations for names of States and months are also used.
* Document for sale by Superintendent of Documents.
† Distribution by office issuing document, free if unaccompanied by a price.
‡ Printed for official use.
NOTE.—Nearly all of the Departments of the Government make a limited free distribution of their publications. When an entry shows a * price, it is possible that upon application to the issuing office a copy may be obtained without charge.

Explanation

Words and figures inclosed in brackets [ ] are given for information, but do not appear on the title-pages of the publications catalogued. When size is not given octavo is to be understood. Size of maps is measured from outer edge of border, excluding margin. The dates, including day, month, and year, given with Senate and House documents and reports are the dates on which they were ordered to be printed. Usually the printing promptly follows the ordering, but various causes sometimes make delays.

SALES OF GOVERNMENT PUBLICATIONS

The Superintendent of Documents, Washington, D. C., is authorized to sell at cost of paper and printing, plus 10 per cent, any United States public document in his charge the distribution of which is not otherwise provided for.

Publications can not be supplied free to individuals nor forwarded in advance of payment.

Publications entered in this catalogue that are for sale by the Superintendent of Documents are indicated by a star (*) preceding the price. A dagger (†) indicates that application should be made to the Department, Bureau, or Division issuing the document. A double dagger (‡) indicates that the document is printed for official use. Whenever additional information concerning the method of procuring a document seems necessary, it will be found under the name of the Bureau by which it was published.

In ordering a publication from the Superintendent of Documents, give (if known) the name of the publishing Department, Bureau, or Division, and the title of the publication. If the publication is numbered, give the number also. Every such particular assists in quick identification. Do not order by the Library of Congress card number.

The accumulation of publications in this Office amounts to several millions, of which over two million are assorted, forming the sales stock. Many rare books are included, but under the law all must be sold regardless of their age or scarcity. Many of the books have been in stock some time, and are apt to be shop-worn. In filling orders the best copy available is sent. A general price-list of public documents is not available, but lists on special subjects will be furnished on application.

MONTHLY CATALOGUE DISTRIBUTION

The Monthly catalogue is sent to each Senator, Representative, Delegate, Resident Commissioner, and officer in Congress; to designated depositories and State and Territorial libraries if it is selected by them; to substantially all Government authors; and to as many school, college, and public libraries as the limited edition will supply.

Subscription price to individuals, 50c. a year, including index; foreign subscription, 75c. a year. Back numbers can not be supplied. Notify the Superintendent of Documents of any change of address.

LIBRARY OF CONGRESS CARDS

Numbers to be used in ordering the printed catalogue cards of the Library of Congress are given at the end of entries for the more important documents. Orders for these cards, remittances in payment for them, and requests for information about them should be addressed to the Librarian of Congress, *not* to the Superintendent of Documents.

An Index to the Monthly catalogue is issued at the end of the fiscal year. This contains index entries for all the numbers issued from July to June, and can be bound with the numbers as an index to the volume. Persons desiring to bind the catalogue at the end of the year should be careful to retain the numbers received monthly, as duplicate copies can not be supplied.

HOW TO REMIT

Remittances for the documents marked with a star (*) should be made to the Superintendent of Documents, Washington, D. C., by coupons, postal money order, express order, or New York draft. Currency may be sent at sender's risk.

Postage stamps, foreign money, defaced or smooth coins, positively will not be accepted.

For the convenience of the general public, coupons that are good until used in exchange for Government publications sold by the Superintendent of Documents may be purchased from his Office in sets of 20 for $1.00. Address order to Superintendent of Documents, Government Printing Office.

No charge is made for postage on documents forwarded to points in United States, Alaska, Guam, Hawaii, Philippine Islands, Porto Rico, Samoa, or to Canada, Cuba, or Mexico. To other countries the regular rate of postage is charged, and remittances must cover such postage. In computing foreign postage, add one-third of the price of the publication.

MONTHLY CATALOGUE

AGRICULTURE DEPARTMENT

NOTE.—Those publications of the Department of Agriculture which are for sale will be supplied by the Superintendent of Documents, Washington, D. C. The Department issues a monthly list of publications, which is mailed to all applicants, enabling them to select such reports and bulletins as interest them.

Alkali lands. Toxicity and antagonism of various alkali salts in soil [with list of literature cited]; by F. S. Harris, M. D. Thomas, and D. W. Pittman. 1923. cover-title, p. 317–338, il. [From Journal of agricultural research, v. 24, no. 4, Apr. 28, 1923.] ‡

Bees. Studies on temperature of individual insects, with special reference to honey bee [with list of literature cited]; by Gregor B. Pirsch. 1923. cover-title, p. 275–288, il. 1 pl. [From Journal of agricultural research, v. 24, no. 4, Apr. 28, 1923.] ‡

Butter. Determination of fatty acids in butter fat, 2 [with list of literature cited]; by E. B. Holland. Mary E. Garvey, H. B. Pierce, Anne C. Messer, J. G. Archibald, and C. O. Dunbar. 1923. cover-title, p. 365–398. [From Journal of agricultural research, v. 24, no. 5, May 5, 1923.] ‡

Cattle. [Bureau of Animal Industry] order 278 [amendment 2] and 283; Apr. 26 and July 23, 1923. 1923. Each 1 p. [Consist of orders concerning quarantine of cattle, etc.] †

Drain-tiles. Effect of organic decomposition products from high vegetable content soils upon concrete drain tile [with list of literature cited]; by G. R. B. Elliott. 1923. cover-title, 471–500+[6] p.+[1] leaf, 7 p. of pl. [From Journal of agricultural research, v. 24, no. 6, May 12, 1923.] ‡

Fusarium. Identification of certain species of Fusarium isolated from potato tubers in Montana [with list of literature cited]; by H. E. Morris and Grace B. Nutting. 1923. cover-title, 339–364+[2] p.+[1] leaf, 3 p. of pl. [From Journal of agricultural research, v. 24, no. 4, Apr. 28, 1923.] ‡

Georgia velvet-bean. Nutritive value of Georgia velvet bean (Stizilobium [Stizolobium] deeringianum) [with list of literature cited]; by J. W. Read and Barnett Sure. 1923. cover-title, p. 433–440, il. [From Journal of agricultural research, v. 24, no. 5, May 5, 1923.] ‡

Journal of agricultural research, v. 24, no. 5–8; May 5–26, 1923. 1923. cover-titles, 365–740+[40] p.+[8] leaves, il. 5 pl. 50 p. of pl. [Weekly. Text on p. 2 of covers.] * Paper, 10c. single copy, $4.00 a yr.; foreign subscription, $5.25. Agr 13—1837

CONTENTS.—No. 5. Determination of fatty acids in butter fat, 2 [with list of literature cited]; by E. B. Holland, Mary E. Garvey, H. B. Pierce, Anne C. Messer, J. G. Archibald, and C. O. Dunbar.—Striped sod webworm, Crambus mutabilis Clemens [with list of literature cited]; by George G. Ainslie.—Silver-striped webworm, Crambus praefectellus Zincken [with list of literature cited]; by George G. Ainslie.—Movement of soil moisture from small capillaries to large capillaries of soil upon freezing; by George John Bouyoucos.—Nutritive value of Georgia velvet bean (Stizilobium [Stizolobium] deeringianum) [with list of literature cited]; by J. W. Read and Barnett Sure.—No. 6. Species of Rhizopus responsible for decay of sweet potatoes in storage house and at different temperatures in infection chambers [with list of literature cited]; by J. I. Lauritzen and L. L. Harter.—Inheritance of growth habit and resistance to stem rust in cross between 2 varieties of common wheat [with list of literature cited]; by Olaf S. Aamodt.—Effect of organic decomposition products from high vegetable content soils upon concrete drain tile [with list of literature cited]; by G. R. B. Elliott.—Injury to foliage by arsenical spray mixtures [with list of literature cited]; by D. B. Swingle, H. E. Morris, and Edmund Burke.—No. 7. Statistical study of comparative morphology of biologic forms of Puccinia graminis [with list of literature cited]; by

56 AUGUST, 1923

Journal of agricultural research—Continued.

M. N. Levine.—Relation of certain soil factors to infection of oats by loose smut; by Lucille K. Bartholomew and Edith Seymour Jones.—Influence of temperature, moisture, and oxygen on spore germination of Ustilago avenae [with list of literature cited]; by Edith Seymour Jones.—Influence of temperature on spore germination of Ustilago zeae [with list of literature cited]; by Edith Seymour Jones.—Spores in upper air; by Elvin C. Stakman, Arthur W. Henry, Gordon C. Curran, and Warren N. Christopher.—Studies on life history of stripe rust, Puccinia glumarum (Schm.) Erikss. & Henn. [with list of literature cited]; by Charles W. Hungerford.—Influence of some nitrogenous fertilizers on development of chlorosis in rice [with list of literature cited]; by L. G. Willis and J. O. Carrero.—No. 8. Some graminicolous species of Helminthosporium, 1 [with list of literature cited]; by Charles Drechsler.

NOTE.—This publication is published by authority of the Secretary of Agriculture, with the cooperation of the Association of Land-Grant Colleges. It is distributed free only to libraries of agricultural colleges and experiment stations, to large universities, technical schools, and to such institutions as make suitable exchanges with the Agriculture Department. Others desiring the Journal may obtain it from the Superintendent of Documents, Washington, D. C., at the prices stated above.

Official record, Department of Agriculture, v. 2, no. 31–35; Aug. 1–29, 1923. [1923.] Each 8 p. il. 4° [Weekly; nos. 32 and 33 are issued in one number, dated Aug. 15.] * Paper, 50c. a yr.; foreign subscription, $1.10. Agr 22—146

Peach rosette, infectious mosaic; by J. A. McClintock. 1923. cover-title, 307–316+[9] p. 10 p. of pl. [From Journal of agricultural research, v. 24, no. 4, Apr. 28, 1923.] ‡

Quarantine. Modification of quarantine on account of European corn borer and other dangerous insects and plant diseases, Amendment 1 to regulations supplemental to Notice of quarantine 41 (revised), effective Sept. 1, 1923. 1923. 1 p. (Federal Horticultural Board.) †

—— Seed or paddy rice quarantine, Notice of quarantine 55, with regulations, effective Sept. 1, 1923. [1923.] 3 p. (Federal Horticultural Board.) †

Soil moisture. Movement of soil moisture from small capillaries to large capillaries of soil upon freezing; by George John Bouyoucos. 1923. cover-title, p. 427–432, 1 pl. [From Journal of agricultural research, v. 24, no. 5, May 5, 1923.] ‡

Tea. Importation and inspection of tea [act of Mar. 2, 1897, as amended May 16, 1908, and May 31, 1920, with regulations effective May 1, 1923]. Aug. 1923. 12 p. (Miscellaneous circular 9.) * Paper, 5c. Agr 23—1117

Weather, crops, and markets, weekly, Aug. 4–25, 1923; v. 4, no. 5–8. [1923.] p. 113–216, il. 4° [Nos. 6 and 7 are issued in one number.] * Paper, $1.00 a yr.; foreign subscription, $2.00. Agr 22—147

AGRICULTURAL ECONOMICS BUREAU

Accounting records and business methods for live-stock shipping associations; by Frank Robotka. Aug. 8, 1923. cover-title, 52 p. il. 2 pl. (Agriculture Dept. Department bulletin 1150.) [Prepared in cooperation with Iowa State College of Agriculture and Mechanic Arts. Also published as Bulletin 209 of Iowa Agricultural Experiment Station.] * Paper, 10c. Agr 23—1113

Agricultural cooperation, selected and annotated reading list, with special reference to purchasing, marketing, and credit; compiled by Chastina Gardner. 1923. [1]+55 p. (Agriculture Dept. Miscellaneous circular 11.) [Includes only works printed in English, exclusive of periodical references except reprints and proceedings of associations.] * Paper, 10c. Agr 23—1030

Service announcements. Service and regulatory announcements, no 76: Regulations of Secretary of Agriculture under warehouse act of Aug. 11, 1916, as amended, revised regulations for cotton warehouses, approved May 29, 1923. July, 1923. iv+35 p. * Paper, 5c. Agr 15—199

—— Same, no. 77: Rules and regulations of Secretary of Agriculture governing inspection of hay under act approved Feb. 26, 1923 (public no. 446, 67th Congress). 1923. ii+6 p. * Paper, 5c.

ANIMAL INDUSTRY BUREAU

Blackleg, its nature, cause, and prevention; [by John R. Mohler]. [June, 1923.] ii+13 p. il. (Agriculture Dept. Farmers' bulletin 1355.) * Paper, 5c. Agr 23—1028

Cheese. Manufacture of Camembert cheese; by Kenneth J. Matheson and S. A. Hall. Aug. 30, 1923. 28 p. il. (Agriculture Dept. Department bulletin 1171.) * Paper, 5c. Agr 23—1114

Cockle-bur. Livestock poisoning by cocklebur; [by] C. Dwight Marsh, G. C. Roe, and A. B. Clawson. Aug. 1923. 4 p. il. (Agriculture Dept. Department circular 283.)　* Paper, 5c.　　　　　　　　　　　　Agr 23—1116
Dairy industry; by C. W. Larson, L. M. Davis, O. A. Juve, O. C. Stine, A. E. Wight, A. J. Pistor, and C. F. Langworthy. 1923. [2]+98 p. il. (Yearbook separate 879.) [Prepared in cooperation with Agricultural Economics Bureau and States Relations Service. From Yearbook, 1922.] * Paper, 15c.
　　NOTE.—In printing this separate from the Yearbook, some illustrations have been omitted. The page numbers and numbers of the illustrations have accordingly been changed. The text of the article remains the same.
Parasites and parasitic diseases of sheep; [by Maurice C. Hall]. [Apr. 1923.] 54 p. il. (Agriculture Dept. Farmers' bulletin 1330.) [Revision of Farmers' bulletin 1150.] * Paper, 10c.　　　　　　　　　　　Agr 23—1022
Posters. Purebred sires exclusively used on this farm, we are cooperating for better livestock with State college of agriculture and United States Department of Agriculture; [all lettered poster]. [1923.]　10.5×13.8 in. †
———— Standardbred poultry pays best, hear what hens say about it; [poster]. [1923.]　15.3×10.1 in. †
Service announcements. Service and regulatory announcements, June, 1923; [no.] 194. July, 1923. p. 53–59. [Monthly.] *Paper, 5c. single copy, 25c. a yr.; foreign subscription, 40c.　　　　　　　　　　　　Agr 7—1658
　　NOTE.—The free distribution of this publication will be limited to persons in the service of the Animal Industry Bureau, to proprietors of establishments at which the Federal meat inspection is conducted, to public officials whose duties render it necessary for them to have such information, and to journals especially concerned. Others desiring copies may obtain them from the Superintendent of Documents, Washington, D. C., at the prices stated above.
———— Same, July, 1923; [no.] 195. Aug. 1923. p. 61–68. [Monthly.]
Swine. Diseases, ailments, and abnormal conditions of swine; [by T. P. White]. [June, 1923.] ii+26 p. il. (Agriculture Dept. Farmers' bulletin 1244.) * Paper, 5c.　　　　　　　　　　　　　　　　　Agr 23—1024

BIOLOGICAL SURVEY BUREAU

Service announcements. Service and regulatory announcements, [no.] 55: Migratory bird treaty, act, and regulations [including amendments of regulations approved June 11, 1923]. Aug. 3, 1923. 13 p. * Paper, 5c. Agr 16—608

CHEMISTRY BUREAU

Leather, hides, and skins. Home tanning of leather and small fur skins; [by R. W. Frey, I. D. Clarke, and F. P. veitch]. [1923.] ii+29 p. il. (Agriculture Dept. Farmers' bulletin 1334.) [Includes lists of Agriculture Department publications relating to fur animals.] * Paper, 5c.　　　Agr 23—1021
Service announcements. Service and regulatory announcements, supplement 158. Aug. 10, 1923. p. 183–210. [Contains Notices of judgment under food and drugs act 11351–400.] * Paper, 5c.　　　　　　　　Agr 14—194
　　NOTE.—The free distribution of this publication will be limited to firms, establishments, and journals especially concerned. Others desiring copies may obtain them from the Superintendent of Documents, Washington, D. C., at the price stated above.

EDITORIAL AND DISTRIBUTION WORK OFFICES

Agriculture Department. Monthly list of publications [of Agriculture Department], July, 1923. [1923.] 4 p. †　　　　　　　　　　　Agr 9—1414
Farmers' bulletins [available for distribution] Aug. 1, 1923. [1923.] [4] p. †

ENTOMOLOGY BUREAU

Australian tomato weevil introduced in the South, preliminary account; [by] F. H. Chittenden. July 31, 1923. 8 p. il. (Agriculture Dept. Department circular 282.) * Paper, 5c.　　　　　　　　　　　　　Agr 23—815
Carpet beetles and their control; [by E. A. Back]. [July, 1923.] ii+14 p. il. (Agriculture Dept. Farmers' bulletin 1346.) * Paper, 5c.　　　Agr 23—1020
Silver-striped webworm, Crambus praefectellus Zincken [with list of literature cited]; by George G. Ainslie. 1923. cover-title, p. 415–426, il. 1 pl. [From Journal of agricultural research, v. 24, no. 5, May 5, 1923.] ‡

Strawberry rootworm as enemy of greenhouse rose; [by C. A. Weigel and C. F. Doucette]. [July,.1923.] ii+14 p. il. (Agriculture Dept. Farmers' bulletin 1344.) [Prepared in cooperation with Pennsylvania Department of Agriculture.] * Paper, 5c. Agr 23—1023

FOREST SERvICE

Maps

Cascade National Forest. Triangle trips in cool cascades, Cascade National Forest, information for mountain travelers. [1923.] 1 sheet (with map on verso), il. large 4°, folded into narrow 8° size and so printed as to number [1]+14 p. †

Umatilla National Forest. South half, Umatilla National Forest, Oreg. and Wash. [resources and recreation features, roads, trails, etc.]. [1923.] 1 sheet (with map on verso), il. f°, folded into narrow 8° size and so printed as to number [1]+14+[1] p. †

Umpqua National Forest, Oreg., information for mountain travelers. [1923.] 1 sheet (with map on verso), il. large 4°, folded into narrow 8° size and so printed as to number [1]+16+[1] p. †

HOME ECONOMICS BUREAU

NOTE.—Created under act making appropriations for Department of Agriculture, fiscal year 1924, approved Feb. 26, 1923. Formerly the work in home economics was carried on as a separate office in the States Relations Service. See also, below, States Relations Service.

Pectin. Homemade apple and citrus pectin extracts and their use in jelly making; [by] Minna C. Denton, Ruth Johnstin, and Fanny Walker Yeatman. [Mar.] 1923, revised Aug. 1923. [1923.] 11 p. (Agriculture Dept. Department circular 254.) [Date of original issue incorrectly given on this publication as July 1, 1923. This bulletin was originally issued by States Relations Service.] * Paper, 5c. Agr 23—1115

PLANT INDUSTRY BUREAU

Citrus fruit. Culture of citrus fruits in Gulf States; [by E. D. Vosbury and T. Ralph Robinson]. [July, 1923.] ii+42 p. il. (Agriculture Dept. Farmers' bulletin 1343.) [Supersedes Farmers' bulletin 1122. Includes lists of Agriculture Department publications on citrus fruits.] * Paper, 5c. Agr 23—1025

Helminthosporium. Some graminicolous species of Helminthosporium, 1 [with list of literature cited]; by Charles Drechsler. 1923. cover-title, 641–740+[32] p. 33 p. of pl. [From Journal of agricultural research, v. 24, no. 8, May 26, 1923.] ‡ (Publication not available in this form but sold as v. 24, no. 8, Journal of agricultural research, for which see p. 55.)

Rhizopus. Species of Rhizopus responsible for decay of sweet potatoes in storage house and at different temperatures in infection chambers [with list of literature cited]; by J. I. Lauritzen and L. L. Harter. 1923. cover-title, p. 441–456, il. [From Journal of agricultural research, v. 24, no. 6, May 12, 1923.] ‡

Rice experiments at Biggs Rice Field Station in California; by Jenkin W. Jones. June, 1923. cover-title, 60 p. il. (Agriculture Dept. Department bulletin 1155.) [Prepared in cooperation with Sacramento Valley Grain Association.] * Paper, 10c. Agr 23—748

Satsuma orange. Coloring Satsuma oranges in Alabama; by R. C. Wright. Aug. 22, 1923. 23 p. il. (Agriculture Dept. Department bulletin 1159.) * Paper, 5c. Agr 23—1027

Wheat. Inheritance of growth habit and resistance to stem rust in cross between 2 varieties of common wheat [with list of literature cited]; by Olaf S. Aamodt. 1923. cover-title, 457–470+[1] p. il. 2 p. of pl. [Prepared in cooperation with University of Minnesota Department of Agriculture. From Journal of agricultural research, v. 24, no. 6, May 12, 1923.] ‡

PUBLIC ROADS BUREAU

Pittsburg, Calif. Report of highway research at Pittsburg, Calif., 1921–22. California State Printing Office, Sacramento, 1923. 146 p. il. 4° [Prepared in cooperation with Columbia Steel Company and California Highway Commission.] † 23—26790

SOILS BUREAU

Emmet County, Iowa. Soil survey of Emmet County, Iowa; by D. S. Gray and F. W. Reich. 1923. iii+409–443 p. il. map. [Prepared in cooperation with Iowa Agricultural Experiment Station. From Field operations, 1920.] * Paper, 15c.

STATES RELATIONS SERVICE

Agricultural experiment stations. Work and expenditures of agricultural experiment stations, [fiscal year] 1921; prepared by Office of Experiment Stations. 1923. v+138 p. [Includes list of publications of experiment stations during fiscal year 1921.] * Paper, 15c. Agr 17—362

Milk and its uses in the home; [prepared by Office of Home Economics]. [July, 1923.] ii+20 p. il. (Agriculture Dept. Farmers' bulletin 1359.) [Revision of Farmers' bulletin 1207. Prepared in cooperation with Animal Industry Bureau.] * Paper, 5c. Agr 23—1029

HAWAII AGRICULTURAL EXPERIMENT STATION

Limes. Acid lime fruit in Hawaii; by W. T. Pope. July 9, 1923. ii+20 p. 6 p. of pl. (Bulletin 49.) * Paper, 10c. Agr 23—813

WEATHER BUREAU

Meteorology. Monthly meteorological summary, Washington, D. C., July, 1923. [1923.] [2] p. f° †

Monthly weather review, v. 51, no. 5; May, 1923. [Aug.] 1923. cover-title, p. 239–290, il. 2 pl. 8 p. of maps, 4° [Text on p. 2–4 of cover.] *Paper, 15c. single copy, $1.50 a yr.; foreign subscription, $2.25. Agr 9—990

NOTE.—The Monthly weather review contains (1) meteorological contributions, and bibliography including seismology, (2) an interpretative summary and charts of the weather of the month in the United States, and on adjacent oceans, and (3) climatological and seismological tables dealing with the weather and earthquakes of the month. The contributions are principally as follows: (a) results of observational or research work in meteorology carried on in the United States or other parts of the world, (b) abstracts or reviews of important meteorological papers and books, and (c) notes.

SPECIAL ARTICLES.—New form of thermoelectric recording pyrheliometer; by Herbert H. Kimball and Hermann E. Hobbs.—Sunspots and terrestrial temperature in United States; by Alfred J. Henry.—Some characteristics of Texas rainfall; by I. R. Tannehill.—Panama climate; by R. Z. Kirkpatrick.—Concerning halos of abnormal radii, [by] Louis Besson; [translated by C. LeRoy Meisinger].—Comments on halos of unusual radii; by W. J. Humphreys.—Winds and weather of central Greenland, meteorological results of Swiss Greenland expedition [1912–13]; by Charles F. Brooks.—Snowstorm of May 8–9, 1923, in Michigan; by B. B. Whittier.—Snowstorm of May 9, 1923, in Saginaw Valley, Mich.; by F. H. Coleman.—Tornado in Davidson County, Tenn., May 12, 1923; by R. M. Williamson.—Tornado at Little Rock, Ark., May 14, 1923; by H. S. Cole.—Torrential rains in extreme southeastern Texas; [by] Ernest Carson.—Water balance in Panama Canal, dry season of 1923; by R. Z. Kirkpatrick.—Mortality from heat and sunstroke.

Sunshine tables, edition of 1905 (reprinted), giving times of sunrise and sunset in mean solar time and total duration of sunshine for every day in year, latitudes 20° to 50° north; by C. F. Marvin. 1923. 3 pts. ([Publication] 805.) ‡

pt. 1. Latitudes 20° to 30° north. 25 p.
pt. 2. Latitudes 30° to 40° north. 25 p.
pt. 3. Latitude 40° to 50° north. 25 p.

Thermal belts. [H. J.] Cox on thermal belts and fruit growing in North Carolina; [abstract] by A. J. Henry. 1923. [1]+199–207 p. il. map, 4° [From Monthly weather review, Apr. 1923.] †

Weather map. Daily weather map [of United States, containing forecasts for all States east of Mississippi River except Illinois, Wisconsin, Indiana, upper Michigan, and lower Michigan], Aug. 1–31, 1923. 1st edition. [1923.] Each 16.4×22.7 in. [Not issued Sundays or holidays; none issued Aug. 8–10.] * Editions issued at Washington, D. C., 25c. a month, $2.50 a yr.; editions issued at about 65 stations throughout the United States, 20c. a month, $2.00 a yr.

—— Same [containing forecasts for United States], Aug. 1–31, 1923. 2d edition. [1923.] Each 16.4×22.7 in. [The Sunday edition does not contain as much information as the edition for week days.] * 30c. a month, $3.00 a yr.

CIVIL SERVICE COMMISSION

NOTE.—The Commission furnishes its publications gratuitously to those who apply for them.

Mechanics. Instructions to applicants for examination for mechanical trades and similar positions in Departmental and Indian services. June, 1923. 4 p. (Form 1250.) †

Navy-yards and naval stations. Regulations governing employment of civil personnel under naval service and administrative regulations in connection therewith promulgated by Secretary of Navy, authorized by Executive order, Dec. 7, 1912 [effective Sept. 15, 1923]. 1923. vii+30 p. (Form 2009.) †

Postmasters. Instructions to applicants for 4th-class postmaster examination. June, 1923. 8 p. (Form 1759.) †

Publications. List of publications. Apr. 1923. 5 p. (Form 2407.) †

23—26757

COMMERCE DEPARTMENT

CENSUS BUREAU

NOTE.—Persons desiring 14th census publications should address the Director of the Census, Department of Commerce, Washington. D. C. They are also sold by the Superintendent of Documents, Washington, D. C., at the price indicated.

Agriculture. 14th census of United States, 1920: v. 5, Agriculture, general report and analytical tables. 1922. 935 p. il. 4° [Prepared under supervision of William Lane Austin, chief statistician for agriculture, assisted by Leon E. Truesdell, special agent, and Arthur J. Hirsch, Thomas A. Devor, Bowen Crandall, and Sherman S. Slick, chiefs of division. The maps and diagrams were prepared under supervision of Charles S. Sloane, geographer.] *Cloth, $2.00.

Butter. Census of manufactures, 1921: Butter, cheese, and condensed milk. 1923. 21 p. *Paper, 5c.   23—26736

Buttons. Census of manufactures, 1921: Buttons. 1923. 11 p. *Paper, 5c.   23—26772

Cotton. Cotton consumed, cotton on hand, active cotton spindles, and imports and exports of cotton, July, 1922 and 1923, with statistics of cotton consumed, imported, and exported for 12 months ending July 31. Aug. 18, 1923. Oblong 32° [Preliminary report. This publication is issued in postal card form.] †

—— Report of cotton ginned, crops of 1922, 1921, and 1920. Mar. 20, 1923. oblong 32° [Preliminary report. This publication is issued in postal card form.]

Cottonseed received, crushed, and on hand, and cottonseed products manufactured, shipped out, on hand, and exported covering 12-month period ending July 31, 1923 and 1922. Aug. 20, 1923. oblong 32° [Preliminary report. This publication is issued in postal card form.] †

Engines. Census of manufactures, 1921: Engines and water wheels, locomotives, and aircraft. 1923. 22 p. *Paper, 5c.   23—26773

Essential oils. Census of manufactures, 1921: Essential oils. 1923. 8 p. *Paper, 5c.   23—26737

Explosives. Census of manufactures, 1921: Explosives. 1923. 10 p. *Paper, 5c.   23—26738

Forest products, 1921: Pulp-wood consumption and wood-pulp production. 1923. 15 p. [Compiled in cooperation with Forest Service.] * Paper, 5c.

23—26774

Ice. Census of manufactures, 1921: Manufactured ice. 1923. 14 p. * Paper, 5c.

23—26740

Machinery. Census of manufactures, 1921: Machinery, textile machinery, machine tools. 1923. 27 p. * Paper, 5c. 23—26739

Needles. Census of manufactures, 1921: Needles, pins, and hooks and eyes. 1923. 9 p. * Paper, 5c. 23—26741

Paper. Census of manufactures, 1921: Paper and wood pulp. 1923. 17 p. * Paper, 5c. 23—26742

Salt. Census of manufactures, 1921: Salt. 1923. 7 p. * Paper, 5c. 23—26775

Tobacco. Leaf tobacco held by manufacturers and dealers, July [1], 1923 and 1922, Apr. 1 and Jan. 1, 1923. July 31, 1923. oblong 32° [This publication is issued in postal card form.] †

COAST AND GEODETIC SURVEY

NOTE.—The monthly Notice to mariners, formerly issued by the Coast and Geodetic Survey, has been consolidated with and made a part of the Notice to mariners issued by the Lighthouses Bureau, thus making it a joint publication. The charts, coast pilots, and tide tables of the Coast and Geodetic Survey are sold at the office of the Survey in Washington, and also by one or more sales agents in each of the important American seaports.

Coast and Geodetic Survey bulletin, July 31, 1923; no. 98. [1923.] 8 p. [Monthly.] ‡ 15—26512

Terrestrial magnetism. Results of magnetic observations made by Coast and Geodetic Survey, [calendar year] 1922; by Daniel L. Hazard. 1923. [1]+41 p. (Special publication 94; serial 235.) * Paper, 5c. 5—35368

Charts

[*Florida*] St. Marys entrance to southward to latitude 30° n., surveys to 1917, corrections from U. S. Engineers to 1922; chart 158. Scale 1:80,000. Washington, Coast and Geodetic Survey, July, 1923. 41.9×33.5 in. † 75c.

Hudson River. Hudson and East rivers, from west 67th street to Blackwells Island, N. Y., surveys to 1899, surveys by U. S. Engineers to 1923 and other sources; chart 369⁴. Scale 1:10,000. Washington, Coast and Geodetic Survey, July, 1923. 45.5×30.8 in. † 75c.

Nawiliwili Bay, Kauai, Hawaii, surveys by U. S. Engineers to 1921; chart 4111. Scale 1:5,000. Washington, Coast and Geodetic Survey, June, 1923. 15.8×24.8 in. † 25c.

Newport Harbor, R. I., and entrance to Narragansett Bay, surveys 1861–1917, surveys by U. S. Engineers to 1922 and other sources; chart 353². Scale 1:20,000. Washington, Coast and Geodetic Survey, July, 1923. 37.2×24.7 in. † 50c.

Portsmouth Harbor, Me. and N. H., original surveys 1898 and 1917, additions from U. S. Engineers, 1916, additions from U. S. Navy to 1922 and other sources; chart 0329. Scale 1:10,000. Washington, Coast and Geodetic Survey, Aug. 1923. 29.8×33 in. † 50c.

Providence River and head of Narragansett Bay, surveys 1865–1913, surveys by U. S. Engineers to 1922 and other sources [with insets]; chart 278. Scale 1:20,000. Washington, Coast and Geodetic Survey, July, 1923. 38.2×31.4 in. † 75c.

Greenwich Cove, Head of.
Seekonk River, continuation to Pawtucket.

San Francisco Bay, Calif., surveys to 1921, surveys by U. S. Engineers to 1922 and other sources; chart 5530. Scale 1:80,000. Washington, Coast and Geodetic Survey, July, 1923. 41.5×34.1 in. † 75c.

Suisun Bay, Calif., surveys 1886–1915, surveys by U. S. Engineers to 1923; chart 5534. Scale 1:40,000. Washington, Coast and Geodetic Survey, Aug. 1923. 28.6×41.1 in. † 75c.

Tahoe, Lake. Lake Tahoe, Calif.-Nev., surveys to 1922 and other sources; chart 5001. Scale 1:40,000. Washington, Coast and Geodetic Survey, July, 1923. 42.8×28.1 in. † 75c.

Tybee Roads, Savannah River, and Wassaw Sound, Ga., surveys 1852–1920, surveys by U. S. Engineers to 1923; with inset, Continuation of Savannah River; chart 440. Scale 1:40,000. Washington, Coast and Geodetic Survey, July, 1923. 31×40.2 in. † 75c.

Willapa Bay, Wash., surveys to 1922, surveys by U. S. Engineers to 1922; with inset, Continuation of Willapa River; chart 6185. Scale 1:40,000. Washington, Coast and Geodetic Survey, July, 1923. 42.5×30.5 in. † 75c.

FISHERIES BUREAU

Bulletin of Bureau of Fisheries, 1921–22 [title-page, contents, errata, and index]. 1923. v. 38, iv+333–341 p. large 8° †

Fish-nets. Properties and values of certain fish-net preservatives [with bibliography] ; by Harden F. Taylor and Arthur W. Wells. 1923. [1]+69 p. il. 1 pl. 2 pl. of pl. 1 tab. (Bureau of Fisheries doc. 947.) [App. 1, report of commissioner of fisheries, 1923.] *Paper, 15c.   F 23—201

Fisheries service bulletin, Aug. 1, 1923; no. 99. [1923.] 6 p. [Monthly.] ‡
                                                                              F 15—76

Fishery products. Statement of quantities and values of certain fishery products landed at Seattle, Wash., by American fishing vessels, June, 1923. [1923.] 1 p. oblong 8° (Statistical bulletin 579.) †

Northwestern lakes of United States, biological and chemical studies with reference to possibilities in production of fish [with bibliography] ; by George Kemmerer, J. F. Bovard, and W. R. Boorman. 1923. [1]+51–140 p. il. 5 pl. 2 maps, large 8° ([Bureau of Fisheries] doc. 944.) [From Bulletin, v. 39.] *Paper, 25c.   F 23—200

Tagged fish. Reward for tagged fish, service circular. [1923.] 2 p. il. †

FOREIGN AND DOMESTIC COMMERCE BUREAU

Commerce. Monthly summary of foreign commerce of United States, June, 1923. 1923. 2 pts. p. 1–68 and ii+69–106 p. 4° *Paper, 10c. single copy (including pts. 1 and 2), $1.00 a yr. ; foreign subscription, $1.60.   14—21465

—— Same. 1923. [2 pts. in 1], 106 p. 4° (H. doc. 438, 67th Cong. 3d sess.)

Commerce reports. Commerce reports, weekly survey of foreign trade, reports from American consular officers and representatives of Department of Commerce in foreign countries, no. 32–35; Aug. 6–27, 1923. 1923. cover-titles, p. 329–576, il. 4° [Text and illustration on p. 2–4 of covers.] *Paper, 10c. single copy, $3.00 a yr. ; foreign subscription, $5.00.

—— Same, nos. 14–26 [series 1923], v. 2; 26th year; Apr.–June, 1923 [title-page and index]. 1923. [i]+xxxiii p. 4° [Quarterly.] *Paper, 5c. single copy, 20c. a yr. ; foreign subscription, 30c.

—— Supplement to Commerce reports. [Included in price of Commerce reports for subscribers.]

Trade and economic review for 1922, no. 16: Sweden, [by] Walter A. Leonard; [Goteborg, by Walter H. Sholes]. [1923.] 18 p.

—— Supplement to Commerce reports: British steel industry, brief study of important steel-plant areas, their characteristics and competitive advantages [with list of references] ; by H. B. Allin-Smith. Aug. 6, 1923. ii+22 p. (Trade information bulletin 133; Iron and Steel Division.)   23—26727

—— Same: Changes in monetary use of silver since 1914; by Leland Rex Robinson. Aug. 27, 1923. ii+66 p. (Trade information bulletin 140; Finance and Investment Division.) †   23—26776

—— Same: Consignment laws of Chile and Bolivia; [articles] by George A. Makinson and Dayle C. McDonough. Aug. 6, 1923. ii+10 p. (Trade information bulletin 134; Division of Commercial Laws.) †   23—26747

—— Same: French Government finance; by Charles E. Lyon. Aug. 13, 1923. ii+17 p. (Trade information bulletin 137; Western European Division.) †
                                                                              23—26750

Commerce reports—Continued. Same: Polish petroleum industry in 1922; compiled from reports by L. J. Keena, H. B. Smith, and Elbert H. Baldwin. Aug. 13, 1923. ii+9 p. (Trade information bulletin 135; Petroleum Division.) †
23—26748

—— Same: Promoting American machinery sales abroad; by W. H. Rastall. Aug. 20, 1923. ii+18 p. (Trade information bulletin 138; Industrial Machinery Division.) †
23—26751

—— Same: Protesting drafts in South, West, and East Africa, with brief discussion of South African laws and customs relating to insolvencies, merchandise, and insurance; compiled by A. J. Wolfe from information furnished by American consular officers. Aug. 13, 1923. ii+22 p. (Trade information bulletin 136; Division of Commercial Laws.) †
23—26749

—— Same: Use of statistics of machinery exports; by W. H. Rastall. Aug. 20, 1923. ii+4 p. (Trade information bulletin 139; Industrial Machinery Division.) †
23—26752

—— Same: Welsh coal trade in 1922; by John R. Bradley. Aug. 6, 1923. ii+26 p. (Trade information bulletin 132; Coal Division.) †
23—26726

Commercial and industrial organizations of United States. Revised edition, Mar. 1, 1923. 1923. iv+225 p. (Miscellaneous series 99.) * Paper, 20c.
23—26724

Foodstuffs Division, cooperating with American producers, manufacturers, and exporters of foodstuffs. 1923. [1]+8 p. narrow 12° †
23—26743

Lumber. Directory of exporters of American lumber and wood products; [compiled by] Lumber Division. 1923. iv+85 p. (Miscellaneous series 120.) * Paper, 10c.
23—26746

Petroleum in foreign trade and services of Petroleum Division. 1923. ii+8 p. narrow 12° [Includes list of Trade information bulletins on petroleum.] †
23—26744

LIGHTHOUSES BUREAU

Lighthouse service bulletin, v. 2, no. 68; Aug. 1, 1923. [1923.] p. 289–292. [Monthly.] †
12—35121

Notice to mariners, weekly, no. 31–35, 1923; Aug. 3–31 [1923]. 1923. various paging. [Issued jointly with Coast and Geodetic Survey.] †
7—20609

NAVIGATION BUREAU

Ships. American documented seagoing merchant vessels of 500 gross tons and over, Aug. 1, 1923. 1923. ii+67 p. 4° (Serial 69.) [Monthly.] * Paper, 10c. single copy, 75c a yr.; foreign subscription, $1.25.
19—26597

RADIO SERVICE·

Radio Service bulletin, Aug. 1, 1923; no. 76. [1923.] 15 p. [Monthly. This number is the 1st supplement to Commercial and Government radio stations, edition June 30, 1923, which has not yet been issued.] * Paper, 5c. single copy, 25c. a yr.; foreign subscription, 40c.
15—26255

PUBLICATIONS DIVISION

Commerce Department. Supplement to annual List of publications [of Department of Commerce available for distribution], July 31, 1923. [1923.] 4 p. [Monthly.] †

STANDARDS BUREAU ·

NOTE.—The Scientific papers will be supplied on subscription as issued at $1.25 per volume, paper bound. These volumes will afterwards be issued bound in cloth at $2.00 per volume; foreign subscription, paper $2.50 (sent in single numbers), cloth $2.35 (bound volumes). Single numbers vary in price. Address the Superintendent of Documents, Washington, D. C.

The Technologic papers will be issued first as separates and later in volume form in the same manner as the Scientific papers. Subscriptions will be accepted by the Superintendent of Documents at $1.25 per volume; foreign subscription, $2.50. Single numbers vary in price.

Electric resistance. Correction sheet for [Alternating-current resistance and inductance of single-layer coils; by C. N. Hickman]. [1923.] 1 p. (Scientific papers 472 [correction].) †

Invar and related nickel steels [with bibliography]. 2d edition. June 22, 1923. [1]+93 p. il. 2 p. of pl. large 8° (Circular 58.) * Paper, 30c.
23—26728

Molybdenum. Series in arc spectrum of molybdenum; by C. C. Kiess. July 10, 1923. [1]+113–129 p. il. 2 p. of pl. large 8° (Scientific papers 474.) [From Scientific papers, v. 19.] * Paper, 10c.   23—26777

Scientific papers of Bureau of Standards, v. 18 [title-page, contents, and index]. 1923. iv+763–766 p. large 8° * Paper, 5c.

Walls. Some compressive tests of hollow-tile walls; by Herbert L. Whittemore [and] Bernard D. Hathcock. July 21, 1923. [1]+513–527 p. il. 1 pl. large 8° (Technologic papers 238.) [From Technologic papers, v. 17.] * Paper, 5c.   23—26778

STEAMBOAT-INSPECTION SERVICE

Steamboat Inspection Service bulletin, Aug. 1, 1923; no. 94. [1923.] 2 p. [Monthly.] ‡   15—26679

CONGRESS

Congressional record, proceedings and debates of 4th session, 67th Congress [Mar. 3–4, 1923], and index [to pts. 1–6, including History of bills and resolutions], v. 64, pt. 6. 1923. [1]+5247–5716+237 p. 4° * Cloth, pts. 1, 3, and 4, each $1.50; pt. 2, $2.00; pts. 5 and 6, each $1.75.   12—36438

NOTE.—In this permanent bound edition, the paging differs from that of the daily numbers, the text being revised, rearranged, and printed without break. The bound volumes of the Record are sold by the Superintendent of Documents. Prices will be furnished on application for the proceedings and debates of the 67th Congress, 1st–3d sessions, and prior Congresses. Send remittances for the bound volumes to the Superintendent of Documents, Washington, D. C. Stamps and foreign money will not be accepted.

FEDERAL PRISONERS, JOINT COMMITTEE TO DETERMINE WHAT EMPLOYMENT MAY BE FURNISHED

Employment for Federal prisoners, hearing, H. Con. Res. 53, June 13, 1923. 1923. ii+14 p. †

HOUSE OF REPRESENTATIVES

Contested-election case of Don H. Clark *v.* R. Lee Moore from 1st Congressional district of Georgia. 1923. [1]+407 p. †

POSTAL SERVICE JOINT COMMISSION

Postal service. [Report.] 1923. pt. 27, iii+1563–1673+v p. 14 pl. 2 tab. †
21—27447

pt. 27. Final report: Motor vehicle service, New York, N. Y., Philadelphia, Pa., Boston, Mass., Detroit, Mich.: Inspection Service; Departmental organization and accounting; by W. B. Richards & Co.

SENATE

FOREIGN RELATIONS COMMITTEE

Treaties, conventions, international acts, protocols, and agreements between United States and other Powers, 1910–23, compiled under resolution of Senate of Aug. 19, 1921, v. 3, continuing Treaties, conventions, international acts, protocols, and agreements between United States and other Powers, 1776–1909. 1923. xxxii+2493–3918 p. il. (S. doc. 348, 67th Cong. 4th sess.) [This volume supersedes the v. 3 issued in 1913 as Senate document 1063, 62d Congress, 3d session, and covering the period from Jan. 1, 1910 to Mar. 4, 1913. volumes 1 and 2, covering the years 1776–1909, were issued as Senate document 357 of the 61st Congress, 2d session.] * Cloth, $1.50.

Silver purchases under Pittman act, hearings before subcommittee pursuant to S. Res. 469, creating Commission of Gold and Silver Inquiry, July 18, 1923. 1923. ii+251–266 p. (Serial 1, pt. 6.) †

INTERSTATE COMMERCE COMMITTEE

Railway transportation in United States; by Albert B. Cummins. 1923. [1]+29 p. (Senate committee print, 67th Congress.) †   23—26779

COURT OF CLAIMS

Brown. George R. Brown *v.* United States; evidence [for defendants]. [1923.] no. 34095, p. 87–89. ‡

Burton Coal Company v. United States; evidence for plaintiff [and] defendant. [1923.] no. B–80, p. 33–120. ‡

Chicago & Alton Railroad Co. v. United States; [evidence for claimant]. [1923.] no. B–114, p. 11–42. ‡

Chicago, Rock Island & Pacific Railway Company v. United States; [evidence for claimant]. [1923.] no. B–144, p. 17–55. ‡

Chrystal. Charles B. Chrystal *v.* United States; evidence for plaintiff. [1923.] Congressional no. 17335, p. 45–74. ‡

Clark. Harold Lyman Clark *v.* United States; evidence [for claimant]. [1923.] no. B–63, p. 5–8. ‡

Drapery Hardware Mfg. Company v. United States; evidence for plaintiff. [1923.] Cong. no. 17334, p. 59–96. ‡

Erie Iron and Metal Company v. United States; evidence for plaintiff. [1923.] no. B–95, p. 13–40. ‡

Garrison. Joshua Garrison, jr., *v.* United States; evidence [for plaintiff]. [1923.] [no.] A–116, p. 5–23. ‡

Lafayette Warehouse Company. Harris P. Rallston, William T [D]. Maginnis, liquidators of Lafayette Warehouse Co., *v.* United States; testimony for claimant. [1923.] no. 178–A, p. 7–15. ‡

McClintic-Marshall Co. v. United States; evidence for defendant. [1923.] no. 250–A, p. 147–167. ‡

Marshall. Thurman W. Marshall *v.* United States; evidence [for claimant]. [1923.] no. B–70, p. 5–7. ‡

Mason. Charles P. Mason *v.* United States; evidence [for claimant]. [1923.] no. B–55, p. 7–12. ‡

Matteson. George C. Matteson *v.* United States; evidence [for claimant]. [1923.] no. 334–A, p. 5–7. ‡

Nashville Protestant Hospital. William S. Booton, receiver of Nashville Protestant Hospital, *v.* United States; evidence for defendant (continued). [1923.] no. 71–A, p. 121–140. ‡

Reed's, Jacob, Sons, Incorporated. Jacob Reed's Sons (Inc.) *v.* United States; evidence for defendant. [1923.] no. B–42, p. 153–169. ‡

Salsman. Eugene Hazelip, admr. of James Salsman, *v.* United States; evidence [for claimant]. [1923.] no. B–53, p. 5–20. ‡

Wrigley, William, jr., Company. William Wrigley, jr., Co. *v.* United States; evidence for plaintiff. [1923.] Congressional, no. 17336, p. 63–158. ‡

COURT OF CUSTOMS APPEALS

Caviar. No. 2285, United States *v.* Neuman & Schwiers Co., transcript of record on appeal from Board of General Appraisers. [1923.] cover-title, i+14 p. ‡

DISTRICT OF COLUMBIA

Court of Appeals. Transcript of record, Oct. term, 1923, no. 4020, no. —, special calendar, Hubert Work, Secretary of Interior, *vs.* United States, ex rel. Logan Rives, appeal from Supreme Court of District of Columbia. 1923. cover-title, i+14 p. ‡

Laws. Acts of Congress affecting District of Columbia passed at 3d and 4th sessions of 67th Congress, Nov. 20, 1922–Mar. 4, 1923 [with index]. [1923.] 24+174 p. [Some of the pages are blank. Binder's title reads v. 27.] ‡

FEDERAL RESERVE BOARD

Agricultural credit facilities under Federal reserve act. Aug. 22, 1923. [1]+6 p. [From Federal reserve bulletin, Aug. 1923, final edition.] †

Federal reserve bulletin. Federal reserve bulletin, Aug. 1923; [v. 9, no. 8]. 1st edition. 1923. ii+253–307 p. il. map, 4° [Monthly.] † Paper, $1.50 a yr.   15—26318

> NOTE.—The Federal reserve bulletin is printed in 2 editions (a 1st edition and a final edition). The 1st edition is brief and contains the regular official announce-ments, the national review of business conditions, and other general matters, and is distributed without charge to the member banks of the Federal reserve system. The 2d or final edition contains detailed analyses of business conditions, special articles, review of foreign banking, and complete statistics showing condition of Federal re-serve banks. Those desiring copies of either edition may obtain them from the Federal Reserve Board, Washington, D. C., at the prices stated above and below.

—— Same, Aug. 1923; [v. 9, no. 8]. Final edition. 1923. iv+871–980+ii p. il. 4° [Monthly.] † Paper, 40c. single copy, $4.00 a yr.

Federal reserve member banks. Federal reserve inter-district collection system, changes in list of banks upon which items will be received by Federal reserve banks for collection and credit, Aug. 1, 1923. 1923. [1]+13 p. 4° †
                                                       16—26870

FEDERAL TRADE COMMISSION

> NOTE.—The bound volumes of the Federal Trade Commission decisions are sold by the Superintendent of Documents, Washington, D. C. Separate opinions are sold on sub-scription, price $1.00 per volume; foreign subscription, $1.50; single copies, 5c. each.

Aluminum Co. of America v. Federal Trade Commission; circuit court of ap-peals, 3d circuit, June 1, 1922, rehearing denied Nov. 22, 1922, no. 2721 [opinion of court]. [1923.] 13 p. ([Court decision] 1.) [From Federal Trade Commission decisions, v. 5.] * Paper, 5c.

Amalgamated Tire Stores Corporation. Federal Trade Commission *v.* Amalga-mated Tire Stores Corporation, complaint [report, findings, and order]; docket 888, Jan. 9, 1923. [1923.] p. 349–353. ([Decision] 326.) [From Federal Trade Commission decisions, v. 5.] * Paper, 5c.

Baltimore Grain Company. Federal Trade Commission *v.* Baltimore Grain Co. et al., district court, district of Maryland, Nov. 20, 1922, no. 301 [opinion of court]. [1923.] 6 p. ([Court decision] 6.) [From Federal Trade Com-mission decisions, v. 5.] * Paper, 5c. '

Chicago Portrait Company. Federal Trade Commission *v.* Chicago Portrait Company, complaint [report] findings, and order; docket 840, Jan. 26, 1923. 1923. [1]+396–409+[1] p. ([Decision] 338.) [From Federal Trade Com-mission decisions, v. 5. Includes list of Cases in which orders for discon-tinuance or dismissal have been entered, Jan. 30, 1923.] * Paper, 5c.

Claire Furnace Company. Federal Trade Commission et al. *v.* Claire Furnace Co. et al.; Court of Appeals of District of Columbia, Jan. 2, 1923, no. 3798 [opinion of court]. [1923.] 16 p. ([Court decision] 7.) [From Federal Trade Commission decisions, v. 5.] * Paper, 5c.

Curtis Publishing Company. Federal Trade Commission *v.* Curtis Publishing Co.; [circuit court of appeals, 3d circuit] Jan. 8, 1923, no. 86 [opinion of court]. [1923.] 9 p. ([Court decision] 8.) [From Federal Trade Com-mission decisions, v. 5.] * Paper, 5c.

Guarantee Veterinary Co. et al. *v.* Federal Trade Commission; circuit court of appeals, 2d circuit, Nov. 6, 1922, no. 8 [opinion of court]. [1923.] 11 p. ([Court decision] 5.) [From Federal Trade Commission decisions, v. 5.] * Paper, 5c.

Guaranty Fund Oil Company. Federal Trade Commission *v.* Guaranty Fund Oil Company, E. M. Thomasson, N. V. S. Mallory, and John C. Menke, individually and as trustees and officers of Guaranty Fund Oil Company, complaint [report, findings, and order]; docket 864, Jan. 16, 1923. [1923.] p. 361–371. ([Decision] 328.) [From Federal Trade Commission decisions v. 5.] * Paper, 5c.

King's Palace. Federal Trade Commission *v.* Philip King, Harry King, and Joseph King, partners, doing business under the name and style of King's Palace, complaint [report, findings, and order]; docket 799, Jan. 4, 1923. [1923.] p. 345–348. ([Decision] 325.) [From Federal Trade Commission decisions, v. 5.] * Paper, 5c.

Lorillard, P., Company. Federal Trade Commission *v.* P. Lorillard Co.; same *v.* American Tobacco Co., Inc.; district court, S. D. New York, Oct. 3, 1922 [opinion of court]. [1923.] 9 p. ([Court decision] 4.) [From Federal Trade Commission decisions, v. 5.] * Paper, 5c.

Mishawaka Woolen Manufacturing Co. v. Federal Trade Commission; circuit court of appeals, 7th circuit, Sept. 13, 1922, no. 2773 [opinion of court]. 1923. 1 p. ([Court decision] 3.) [From Federal Trade Commission decisions, v. 5.] * Paper, 5c.

Missoula, Mont. Federal Trade Commission *v.* Chamber of Commerce of Missoula, Mont., and Northwest Theatres Company, complaint [report, findings, and order]; docket 841, Feb. 7, 1923. [1923.] p. 451–464. ([Decision] 339.) [From Federal Trade Commission decisions, v. 5.] * Paper, 5c.

Music Publishers' Association of United States. Federal Trade Commission *v.* Music Publishers' Association of United States et al., complaint [report, findings, and order]; docket 400, Feb. 8, 1923. [1923.] p. 465–472. ([Decision] 340.) [From Federal Trade Commission decisions, v. 5.] * Paper, 5c.

North American Fibre Products Company. Federal Trade Commission *v.* American Turpentine Company, trading under name and style of North American Fibre Products Company, complaints [report] findings, and order; docket 938, Feb. 1, 1923. 1923. [1]+410–416 p. ([Decision] 334.) [From Federal Trade Commission decisions, v. 5.] * Paper, 5c.

Northern Hemlock and Hardwood Manufacturers Association. Report of Federal Trade Commission on Northern Hemlock and Hardwood Manufacturers Association, May 7, 1923. 1923. xii+52 p. * Paper, 10c.   23—26780

Orrell, L. C., & Co. Federal Trade Commission *v.* L. C. Orrell & Company, complaint [report, findings, and order]; docket 885, Jan. 23, 1923. [1923.] p. 391–395. ([Decision] 332.) [From Federal Trade Commission decisions, v. 5.] * Paper, 5c.

Premier Electric Company. Federal Trade Commission *v.* Premier Electric Company, complaint [report, findings, and order]; docket 921, Jan. 18, 1923. [1923.] p. 385–390. ([Decision] 331.) [From Federal Trade Commission decisions, v. 5.] * Paper, 5c.

Rex Hosiery Company. Federal Trade Commission *v.* Harry Freedman, trading under name and style of Rex Hosiery Company, complaints [report] findings, and order; docket 676, Jan. 17, 1923. 1923. [1]+372–375 p. ([Decision] 329.) [From Federal Trade Commission decisions, v. 5.] * Paper, 5c.

Russell, R. C. Federal Trade Commission *v.* R. C. Russell [et al.] and First National Oil Company, complaint [report] findings, and order; docket 866, Jan. 10, 1923. 1923. [1]+354–360 p. ([Decision] 327.) [From Federal Trade Commission decisions, v. 5.] * Paper, 5c.

Smith, Clifford, Company. Federal Trade Commission *v.* Clifford Smith, doing business under trade name and style of Clifford Smith Company, complaint [report, findings, and order]; docket 919, Feb. 5, 1923. [1923.] p. 435–438. ([Decision] 337.) [From Federal Trade Commission decisions, v. 5.] * Paper, 5c.

Standard Electric Manufacturing Company. Federal Trade Commission *v.*
Standard Electric Manufacturing Company, complaint [report] findings,
and order; docket 747, Jan. 17, 1923. 1923. [1]+376-384 p. ([Decision]
330.) [From Federal Trade Commission decisions, v. 5.] * Paper, 5c.

Standard Oil Co. of New Jersey et al. *v.* Federal Trade Commission; circuit
court of appeals, 3d circuit, July 14, 1922, nos. 2599, 2609, 2632 [opinion of
court]. [1923.] 15 p. ([Court decision] 2.) [From Federal Trade Commission decisions, v. 5.] * Paper, 5c.

Stinemetz, B. H., & Son Company. Federal Trade Commission *v.* B. H. Stinemetz & Son Company, complaint [report] findings, and order; docket 858,
Feb. 5, 1923. 1923. [1]+424-434+[1] p. ([From Fed-
eral Trade Commission decisions, v. 5. Includes list of Cases in which
orders for discontinuance or dismissal have been entered, Feb. 5, 1923.]
* Paper, 5c.

United States Hoffman Machinery Corporation. Federal Trade Commission
v. United States Hoffman Machinery Corporation et al., complaint [report,
findings, and order]; docket 923, Feb. 6, 1923. [1923.] p. 439-450. ([De-
cision] 338.) [From Federal Trade Commission decisions, v. 5.] * Paper, 5c.

Western Meat Company. Federal Trade Commission *v.* Western Meat Company, complaint [report, findings, and order]; docket 456, Feb. 2, 1923.
[1923.] 417-423+[1] p. ([Decision] 335.) [From Federal Trade Commission decisions, v. 5. Includes list of Cases in which orders for discontinuance or dismissal have been entered, Feb. 3, 1923.] * Paper, 5c.

Yellow Bell Taxi Company. Federal Trade Commission *v.* Fred A. Maltby
and Clarence W. Maltby, as individuals and as partners [doing business
under name and style of Yellow Bell Taxi Company and Yellow Ford Taxi
Company] complaint [report, findings, and order]; docket 944, Feb. 8, 1923.
[1923.] p. 473-481. ([Decision] 341.) [From Federal Trade Commission
decisions, v. 5.] *Paper, 5c. •

GENERAL ACCOUNTING OFFICE

Decisions of comptroller general, v. 3, July, 1923; J. R. McCarl, comptroller
general, Lurtin R. Ginn, assistant comptroller general. 1923. [1]+1-67 p.
[Monthly.] †   21—26777

GEOGRAPHIC BOARD

Decisions. Decisions of Geographic Board, July, 1920-June, 1923.   1923.
ii+31 p. †   10—26561
—— Decisions of Geographic Board, June 13, 1923. [1923.] 2 p. †

GOVERNMENT PRINTING OFFICE

Foreign words. Suggestions regarding division of foreign words in French,
Italian, Portuguese, German, and Spanish languages. 1923. [7] p. ‡ "

Supplies. Specifications and proposal for furnishing and installing complete
1 return-apron flat-work ironer or mangle, advertisement. 1923. [1]+4 p.
4° †

DOCUMENTS OFFICE

Foreign relations of United States, list of publications for sale by superintendent of documents. July, 1923. [2]+35+[2] p. (Price list 65, 6th
edition.), †   23—26781

Maps, list of publications for sale by superintendent of documents. July, 1923.
[2]+10 p. (Price list 53, 13th edition.) †   23—26754

Monthly catalogue, United States public documents, no. 343; July, 1923. 1923.
p. 1-50.. *Paper, 5c. single copy, 50c. a yr.; foreign subscription, 75c. '
                                                             14—18068

Public domain, Government publications concerning public lands, conservation,
railroad land grants, etc., for sale by superintendent of documents. Aug. 1923.
[2]+6 p. (Price list 20, 13th edition.) †   : 23—26782

INTERIOR DEPARTMENT

Note.—The decisions of the Department of the Interior in pension cases are issued in slips and in signatures, and the decisions in land cases are issued in signatures, both being published later in bound volumes. Subscribers may deposit $1.00 with the Superintendent of Documents and receive the contents of a volume of the decisions of either kind in separate parts as they are issued; foreign subscription, $1.25. Prices for bound volumes furnished upon application to the Superintendent of Documents, Washington, D. C.

Freedmen s Hospital. Proposal and specifications for erection and completion of pathological laboratory at Freedmen's Hospital, Washington, D. C. 1923. [1]+35 p. 4° †

Lawyers. Laws and regulations [Sept. 27, 1917] governing recognition of agents, attorneys, and other persons to represent claimants before Department of Interior and bureaus thereof. [1923.] 5 p. 4° †

Pensions. [Decisions of Department of Interior in appealed pension and bounty land claims, v. 21, slips] 80–83. [1923.] Each 2 p. or 8 p. [For price, see note above under center head.]   12—29422

—— Same [v. 21, slips] 57–61 retirement. [1923.] various paging.

Printing. Regulations relating to printing and binding [for Interior Department]. [Reprint 1923.] 3 p. †

EDUCATION BUREAU

Americanization. Americanization in United States; by John J. Mahoney. 1923. iv+42 p. il. (Bulletin 31, 1923.) [Includes lists of State publications used in Americanization work.] * Paper, 5c.   E 23—321

—— Americanization program [with bibliography]; by E. J. Irwin. 1923. iii+60 p. (Bulletin 30, 1923.) * Paper, 10c.   E 23—320

Bulletins. List of bulletins of Bureau of Education, 1906–22, with index by author, title, and subject; by Edith A. Wright. 1923. [1]+52 p. (Bulletin 35, 1923.) * Paper, 10c.   E 23—323

Business education. College entrance credits in commercial subjects; by Glen Levin Swiggett. Apr. 1923. 22 p. (Commercial education leaflet 4.) * Paper, 5c.   E 23—326

Citizenship and government, reading course; by George F. Zook. 1923. [1]+6 p. 12° (Reading course 24.) †

Consolidation of schools. Consolidated schools of Weld County, Colo.; by C. G. Sargent. 1923. cover-title, [1]+11 p. il. (Rural school leaflet 13.) * Paper, 5c.   E 23—329

—— Consolidation of schools in Randolph County, Ind.; [by O. H. Greist]. 1923. [1]+12 p. il. ([Rural school leaflet 12.]) * Paper, 5c.   E 23—328

Educational hygiene; by Willard S. Small. 1923. iii+36 p. (Bulletin 33, 1923.) * Paper, 5c.   E 23—322

Europe. Progressive tendencies in European education; by C. W. Washburne. 1923. iii+31 p. (Bulletin 37, 1923.) * Paper, 5c.   E 23—324

Hampton Normal and Agricultural Institute, its evolution and contribution to education as Federal land-grant college, prepared under direction of Walton C. John; with introduction by William Howard Taft. 1923 v+118 p. il. 3 pl. 10 p. of pl. (Bulletin 27, 1923.) * Paper, 25c.   E 23—319

High schools. Teaching load in 136 city high schools. June, 1923. 6 p. (City school leaflet 9.) [Survey made by committee from faculty of Polytechnic High School, San Francisco, Calif.] * Paper, 5c.   E 23—325

Home economics. List of references on home economics; prepared in Library Division. June, 1923. 21 p. (Library leaflet 21.) * Paper, 5c. E 23—327

Teachers, Training of. Iowa plan of observation and practice teaching in training of rural teachers; by Anna D. Cordts. June, 1923. 4 p. (Rural school leaflet 16.) * Paper, 5c.   E 23—330

—— Iowa plan of training superintendents and teachers for consolidated schools; by Macy Campbell. June, 1923. 5 p. (Rural school leaflet 17.) * Paper, 5c.   E 23—331

GEOLOGICAL SURVEY

NOTE.—The publications of the United States Geological Survey consist of annual reports, Monographs, Professional papers, Bulletins, Water-supply papers, chapters and volumes of Mineral resources of the United States, folios of the Topographic atlas of the United States and topographic maps that bear descriptive text, and folios of the Geologic atlas of the United States and the World atlas of commercial geology. A wholesale rate has been established for topographic and geologic folios, so that a discount of 40 per cent from the retail price is now allowed on all orders the net cost of which amounts to $5.00 or more. This rate applies on an order for either maps or folios alone or for maps and folios together, but does not apply to the folios sold at 5c. each on account of damage by fire. For maps and topographic and geologic folios address the Director of the Geological Survey, Washington, D. C. Other publications, with the exception of Monographs, are free at the Survey as long as the supply lasts and are also sold by the Superintendent of Documents at the price indicated. Orders for such publications as are for sale (excepting maps and folios) should be sent to the Superintendent of Documents, Washington, D. C. For topographic sheets see next page.

Alaska. Mineral resources of Alaska, report on progress of investigations in 1921; [articles] by A. H. Brooks and others. 1923. vi+169+xiv p. il. 3 maps. (Bulletin 739.) [Includes lists of recent Geological Survey publications on Alaska.] * Paper, 25c.   GS 5—752

    CONTENTS.—Preface; by Alfred H. Brooks.—Alaskan mining industry in 1921; by Alfred H. Brooks.—Administrative report; by Alfred H. Brooks.—Mineral deposits of Wrangell district; by A. F. Buddington.—Cold Bay district; by Stephen R. Capps.—Iniskin Bay district; by Fred H. Moffit.—Petroleum seepage near Anchorage; by Alfred H. Brooks.—Supposed petroleum seepage in Nenana coal field; by George C. Martin.—Occurrence of metalliferous deposits in Yukon and Kuskokwim regions [with bibliography]; by J. B. Mertie, Jr.—Index.

—— Same. (H. doc. 461, 67th Cong. 3d sess.)

Antimony in 1922; by Frank C. Schrader. Aug. 7, 1923. ii+97–105 p. [From Mineral resources, 1922, pt. 1.] †

Asbestos in 1922; by Edward Sampson. Aug. 29, 1923. ii+31–37 p. il. [From Mineral resources, 1922, pt. 2.] †

Bauxite and aluminum in 1922; by James M. Hill. Aug. 6, 1923. ii+87–96 p. [From Mineral resources, 1922, pt. 1.] †

Boundaries. Boundaries, areas, geographic centers, and altitudes of United States and the several States, with brief record of important changes in their territory [and with lists of references]; by Edward M. Douglas. 1923. vi+234 p. il. 1 pl. 2 p. of pl. 4 maps, 2 are in pocket. (Bulletin 689.) [Revision of Bulletin 226.] * Paper, 50c.   GS 23—250

—— Same. (H. doc. 1728, 65th Cong. 3d sess.)

Chromite in 1922; by Edward Sampson. Aug. 27, 1923. ii+107–112 p. il. [From Mineral resources, 1922, pt. 1.] †

Fluorspar and cryolite in 1922; by Hubert W. Davis. Aug. 10, 1923. ii+15–22 p. [From Mineral resources, 1922, pt. 2.] †

Graphite in 1922; by Arthur H. Redfield. Sept. 11, 1923. [1]+63–68 p. [From Mineral resources, 1922, pt. 2.] †

Hawaii. Surface water supply of Hawaii, July 1, 1918–June 30, 1919; Nathan C. Grover, chief hydraulic engineer, C. T. Bailey and James E. Stewart, acting district engineers. 1923. iv+123 p. (Water-supply paper 515.) [Prepared in cooperation with Hawaii.] *Paper, 15c.   GS 17—466

—— Same. (H. doc. 31, 68th Cóng. 1st sess.)

Mineral resources. Mineral resources of United States, 1920: pt. 1, Metals [title-page, contents, and index]. 1922. 1a–4a+597–611 p. †   4—18124

—— Mineral resources of United States in 1922, preliminary summary, introduction by G. F. Loughlin, statistics assembled by Martha B. Clark from data furnished by specialists of Division of Mineral Resources. Aug. 15, 1923. iv+1a–124a p. [From Mineral resources, 1922, pt. 1.] †

Nitrates in 1922; by George Rogers Mansfield. Aug. 24, 1923. [1]+39–40 p. [From Mineral resources, 1922, pt. 2.] †

Publications. New publications, list 184; July 1, 1923. [1923.] 3 p. [Monthly.] †

—— Same, list 185; Aug. 1, 1923. [1923.] 3 p. [Monthly.] †

Rock formations in Colorado Plateau of southeastern Utah and northern Arizona; by C. R. Longwell, H. D. Miser, R. C. Moore, Kirk Bryan, and Sidney Paige. July 27, 1923. ii+1–23 p. il. 2 pl. 8 p. of pl. 4° (Professional paper 132 A.) †

Salt, bromine, and calcium chloride in 1922; by K. W. Cottrell. Aug. 9, 1923. [1]+23-29 p. [From Mineral resources, 1922, pt. 2.] †
Surveying. Triangulation and primary traverse, 1916–18; C. H. Birdseye, chief topographic engineer. 1923. vi+914 p. 1 pl. map. (Bulletin 709.) *Paper, 75c. 4—1312

Topographic sheets

NOTE.—The Geological Survey is making a topographic map of the United States. The sheets of which it is composed are projected without reference to political divisions, and are designated by some prominent town or natural feature found on them. Three scales are ordinarily used, 1 : 62,500, 1 : 125,000, and 1 : 250,000. These correspond, approximately, to 1 mile, 2 miles, and 4 miles to 1 linear inch, covering, respectively, average areas of 230, 920, and 3,700 square miles. For some areas of particular importance special large-scale maps are published. The usual size, exclusive of the margin, is about 17.5 inches in height by 11.5 to 16 inches in width, the latter varying with the latitude. A description of the topographic map is printed on the reverse of each sheet.

More than two-fifths of the area of the country, excluding Alaska, has been mapped, every State being represented. Connecticut, Delaware, the District of Columbia, Maryland, Massachusetts, New Jersey, Ohio, Rhode Island, and West Virginia are completely mapped. Sheets of the regular size are sold by the Survey at 10c. each; but in lots of 50 or more copies, whether of the same sheet or of different sheets, the price is 6c. each. The discount is allowed on all orders the net cost of which amounts to $5.00 or more and applies on an order for either maps or folios alone or for maps and folios together, but does not apply to the folios sold at 5c. each on account of damage by fire.

California. California, Academy quadrangle, lat. 36° 52′ 30′′–37°, long. 119° 30′–119° 37′ 30′′. Scale 1 : 31,680, contour interval 5 ft. and 25 ft. [Washington, Geological Survey] edition of 1923. 17.3×13.9 in. † 10c.

—— California, Fresno quadrangle, lat. 36° 37′ 30′′–36° 45′, long. 119° 45′–119° 52′ 30′′. Scale 1 : 31,680, contour interval 5 ft. [Washington, Geological Survey] edition of 1923. 17.3×13.9 in. † 10c.

—— California, Little Panoche quadrangle, lat. 36° 45′–36° 52′ 30′′, long. 120° 37′ 30′′–120° 45′. Scale 1 : 31,680, contour interval 5 ft. [Washington, Geological Survey] edition of 1923. 17.3×13.9 in. † 10c.

—— California, Sanger quadrangle, lat. 36° 37′ 30′′–36° 45′, long. 119° 30′–119° 37′ 30′′. Scale 1 : 31,680, contour interval 5 ft. [Washington, Geological Survey] edition of 1923. 17.3×13.9 in. † 10c.

Illinois-Wisconsin, Grays Lake quadrangle, lat. 42° 15′–42° 30′, long. 88°–88° 15′. Scale 1 : 62,500, contour interval 10 ft. [Washington, Geological Survey] edition of 1923. 17.5×13.1 in. † 10c.

Kentucky, Bowling Green quadrangle, lat. 36° 45′–37°, long. 86° 15′–86° 30′. Scale 1 : 62,500, contour interval 20 ft. [Washington, Geological Survey] edition of 1923. 17.5×14.1 in. † 10c.

Oregon, Reedsport quadrangle, lat. 43° 30′–43° 45′, long. 124°–124° 15′. Scale 1 : 62,500, contour interval 50 ft. [Washington, Geological Survey] edition of 1923. 17.5×13.1 in. † 10c.

Pennsylvania. Pennsylvania, Lock Haven quadrangle, lat. 41°–41° 15′, long. 77° 15′–77° 30′. Scale 1 : 62,500, contour interval 20 ft. [Washington, Geological Survey] edition of 1923. 17.5×13.3 in. † 10c.

—— Pennsylvania, Williamsport quadrangle, lat. 41°–41° 15′, long. 77°–77° 15′. Scale 1 : 62,500, contour interval 20 ft. [Washington, Geological Survey] edition of 1923. 17.5×13.3 in. † 10c.

West Virginia. Virginia-West Virginia, Edinburg quadrangle, lat. 38° 45′–39°, long. 78° 30′–78° 45′. Scale 1 : 62,500, contour interval 50 ft. [Washington, Geological Survey] edition of 1923. 17.5×13.8 in. [Map covers only a portion of the sheet, the actual measurement being 6.8×9.8 in. Shows only the portion of Edinburg quadrangle that lies in West Virginia.] † 10c.

Wisconsin-Illinois, South Wayne quadrangle, lat. 42° 30′–42° 45′, long. 89° 45′–90°. Scale 1 : 62,500, contour interval 20 ft. [Washington, Geological Survey] edition of 1923. 17.5×13 in. † 10c.

MINES BUREAU

Barricades. Erection of barricades during mine fires or after explosions; by J. W. Paul, B. O. Pickard, and M. W. von Bernewitz. [1st edition.] [Aug.] 1923. iv+28 p. il. (Miner's circular 25.) *Paper, 5c. 23—26755

Water-gas tar emulsions; by W. W. Odell. [1st edition.] [May] 1923. iv+51
p. il. (Technical paper 304.) [This paper represents work done under a
cooperative agreement with the State Geological Survey Division of Illinois
and the Engineering Experiment Station of the University of Illinois.
Includes lists of Mines Bureau publications on industrial gases.]   *Paper,
10c.   23—26756

NATIONAL PARK SERVICE

Grand Canyon National Park. Summer trips, Grand Canyon National Park,
1923, supplement to Rules and regulations [Grand Canyon National Park,
Ariz.]. [Rand, McNally & Company, Chicago, 1923.] 24 p. il. [Includes
suggested list of books on Grand Canyon and the Southwest.] †

PATENT OFFICE

NOTE.—The Patent Office publishes Specifications and drawings of patents in single
copies. These are not enumerated in this catalogue, but may be obtained for 10c. each at
the Patent Office.
    A variety of indexes, giving a complete view of the work of the Patent Office from 1790
to date, are published at prices ranging from 25c. to $10.00 per volume and may be
obtained from the Superintendent of Documents, Washington, D. C. The Rules of
practice and pamphlet Patent laws are furnished free of charge upon application to the
Patent Office. The Patent Office issues coupon orders in packages of 20 at $2.00 per
package, or in books containing 100 coupons at $10.00 per book. These coupons are
good until used, but are only to be used for orders sent to the Patent Office. For schedule
of office fees, address Chief Clerk, Patent Office, Washington, D. C.

Classification bulletin [50], Jan. 1–June 30, 1923. containing classification of
- subjects of invention revised by Classification Division. 1923. 50 leaves,
large 8° *Paper, 15c.   8—16238

Decisions. [Decisions in patent and trade-mark cases, etc.] Aug. 7, 1923. p.
1–10, large 8° [From Official gazette, v.-313, no. 1.] †Paper, 5c. single copy,
$2.00 a yr.   23—7315

——— Same. Aug. 14, 1923. p. 229–238, il. large 8° [From Official gazette,
v. 313, no. 2.]

——— Same. Aug. 21, 1923. p. 451–460; large 8° [From Official gazette,
v. 313, no. 3.]

——— Same. Aug. 28, 1923. p. 661–670, il. large 8° [From Official gazette,
v. 313, no. 4.]

Inventions. Changes in classification [of inventions], order 2829, 2832–33;
July 3–Aug. 6. 1923. [1923.] 1 p. large 8° [From Official gazette, v. 312,
no. 4, and v. 313, no. 1 and no. 2.] ‡

Official gazette. Official gazette, Aug. 7–28, 1923; v. 313, no. 1–4. 1923. cover-
titles, 871+[cliv] p. il. large 8° [Weekly.] *Paper, 10c. single copy, $5.00
a yr.; foreign subscription, $11.00.   4—18256
    NOTE.—Contains the patents, trade-marks, designs, and labels issued each week; also
decisions of the commissioner of patents and of the United States courts in patent
cases.

——— Same [title-page, contents, errata, etc., to] v. 310; May, 1923. 1923.
[2] leaves, large 8° *Paper, 5c. single copy, included in price of Official
gazette for subscribers.

——— Same, weekly index, with title, Alphabetical list of registrants of trade-
marks [etc., Aug. 7, 1923.] xliv p. large 8° [From Official gazette,
v. 313, no. 1.] †Paper, $1.00 a yr.

——— Same [Aug. 14, 1923]. [1923.] xxxviii p. large 8°. [From Official
gazette, v. 313, no. 2.]

——— Same [Aug. 21, 1923]. [1923.] xxxiv p. large 8° [From Official gazette,
v. 313, no. 3.]

——— Same [Aug. 28, 1923]. [1923.] xxxviii p. large 8° [From Official
gazette, v. 313, no. 4.]

Patents. Classification of patents issued Aug. 7–28, 1923. [1923.] Each 2 p.
large 8° [Weekly. From Official gazette, v. 313, no. 1–4.] †

Trade-marks. Trade-marks [etc., from] Official gazette, Aug. 7, 1923. [1923.]
11–73+i–xxi p. il. large 8° [From Official gazette, v. 313, no. 1.] †Paper,
5c. single copy, $2.50 a yr.

——— Same, Aug. 14, 1923. Aug. 15, 1923. 239–295+i–xv p. il. large 8° [From
Official gazette, v. 313, no. 2.]

Trade-marks—Continued. Same, Aug. 21, 1923. [1923.] 461-513+i-xiv p. il. large 8°. [From Official gazette, v. 313, no. 3.]

—— Same, Aug. 28, 1923. [1923.] 671-718+i-xv p. il. large 8°. [From Official gazette, v. 313, no. 4.]

RECLAMATION BUREAU

NOTE.—Formerly Reclamation Service.

Specifications 419-421. 1923. Each 17 p. or 12 p. 4 pl. 4° [Consist of advertisements, proposals, specifications, and drawings for reclamation projects.] †

INTERSTATE COMMERCE COMMISSION

NOTE.—The bound volumes of the decisions, usually known as Interstate Commerce Commission reports, are sold by the Superintendent of Documents, Washington, D. C., at various prices, depending upon the size of the volume. Separate opinions are sold on subscription, price $1.00 per volume; foreign subscription, $1.50; single copies, usually 5c. each.

Abilene and Southern Railway. Finance docket no. 100, deficit status of Abilene & Southern Ry.; decided June 6, 1923; report of commission on hearing and further consideration. [1923.] p. 547-557. ([Finance decision] 711.) [From Interstate Commerce Commission reports, v. 79.] * Paper, 5c.

Akron, Canton and Youngstown Railway. Finance docket no. 2961, notes of Akron, Canton & Youngstown Ry.; decided June 29, 1923; report of commission. [1923.] p. 777-781. ([Finance decision] 788.) [From Interstate Commerce Commission reports, v. 79.] * Paper, 5c.

Alcolu Railroad. Finance docket no. 1597, deficit settlement with Alcolu R. R.; decided July 16, 1923; report of commission. [1923.] p. 1-2. ([Finance decision] 800.) [From Interstate Commerce Commission reports, v. 82.] * Paper, 5c.

Angelina and Neches River Railroad. Finance docket no. 106, deficit settlement with Angelina & Neches River R. R.; decided June 25, 1923; report of commission. [1923.] p. 719-720. ([Finance decision] 767.) [From Interstate Commerce Commission reports, v. 79.] * Paper, 5c.

—— Finance docket no. 270, guaranty settlement with Angelina & Neches River R. R.; [decided June 25, 1923; report of commission]. 1923. [1]+716-718 p. ([Finance decision] 766.) [From Interstate Commerce Commission reports, v. 79.] * Paper, 5c.

Asphalt. No. 13353, American Asphalt Roof Corporation et al v. Atchison, Topeka & Santa Fe Railway Company et al.; [portions of 4th section applications nos. 2174 and 2193; decided July 13, 1923; report and orders of commission]. 1923. [1]+522-528+ii p. ([Opinion] 8696.) [Report from Interstate Commerce Commission reports, v. 81.] * Paper, 5c.

Augusta Union Station Company. Before Interstate Commerce Commission, valuation docket no. 155, Augusta Union Station Company; brief in support of tentative valuation. 1923. cover-title, i+25 p. ‡

Automobiles. No. 14152, Apperson Brothers Automobile Company v. Lake Erie & Western Railroad Company et al.; [decided July 13, 1923; report and order of commission]. 1923. [1]+392-394+[1] p. ([Opinion] 8672.) [Report from Interstate Commerce Commission reports, v. 81.] * Paper, 5c.

Baltimore and Ohio Railroad. Finance docket no. 295, guaranty settlement with Baltimore & Ohio R. R.; [and finance docket no. 401]; decided June 13, 1923; report of commission. [1923.] p. 645-648. ([Finance decision] 743.) [From Interstate Commerce Commission reports, v. 79.] * Paper, 5c.

Barite. Investigation and suspension docket no. 1775, barytes from Central Freight Association to points in Canada; decided July 12, 1923; report [and order] of commission. [1923.] 399-400+[1] p. ([Opinion] 8675.) [Report from Interstate Commerce Commission reports, v. 81.] * Paper, 5c.

Beverages. No. 12326, Wichita Board of Commerce et al. v. director general, as agent, Atchison, Topeka & Santa Fe Railway Company, et al.; decided July 13, 1923; report of commission. [1923.] p. 423-430. ([Opinion] 8679.) [From Interstate Commerce Commission reports, v. 81.] * Paper, 5c.

Black Hills and Fort Pierre Railroad. Finance docket no. 317, guaranty status of Black Hills & Fort Pierre R. R.; [and finance docket no. 422]; decided June 13, 1923; report of commission. [1923.] p. 635–636. ([Finance decision] 739.) [From Interstate Commerce Commission reports, v. 79.] * Paper, 5c.

Bonlee and Western Railway. Finance docket no. 115, deficit settlement with Bonlee & Western Ry.; decided June 11, 1923; report of commission. [1923.] p. 643–644. ([Finance decision] 742.) [From Interstate Commerce Commission reports, v. 79.] * Paper, 5c.

Boston and Maine Railroad. Finance docket no. 2974,. Boston & Maine equipment trust no. 3; decided June 15, 1923; report of commission. [1923.] p. 669–672. ([Finance decision] 750.) [From Interstate Commerce Commission reports, v. 79.] * Paper, 5c.

Boyne City, Gaylord and Alpena Railroad. Finance docket no. 1300, deficit settlement with Boyne City, Gaylord & Alpena R. R.; decided July 2, 1923; report of commission on further consideration. [1923.] p. 749–750. ([Finance decision] 779.) [From Interstate Commerce Commission reports, v. 79.] * Paper, 5c.

Brass. No. 13666, Chase Companies, Incorporated, *v.* director general, as agent; decided June 28, 1923; report [and order] of commission. [1923.] 207–208+ [1] p. ([Opinion] 8631.) [Report from Interstate Commerce Commission reports, v. 81.] * Paper, 5c.

Bricks. No. 9702, Memphis-Southwestern investigation, commodity rates; decided July 24, 1923; supplemental report [and supplemental order] of commission. [1923.] 555–556+ii p. ([Opinion] 8703.) [Report from Interstate Commerce Commission reports, v. 81.] * Paper, 5c.

—— No. 13252, St. Clair Brick Company *v.* director general, as agent, Grand Trunk Western Railway Company, et al.; decided July 20, 1923; report [and order] of commission. [1923.] 567–568+[1] p. ([Opinion] 8708.) [Report from Interstate Commerce Commission reports, v. 81.] * Paper, 5c.

Camphor-oil. No. 13031, Antoine Chiris Company *v.* director general, as agent, Southern Pacific Company, et al.; decided July 13, 1923; report of commission. [1923.] p. 503–504. ([Opinion] 8692.) [From Interstate Commerce Commission reports, v. 81.] * Paper, 5c.

Cartage. No. 13452, Frank P. Dow Company, Incorporated, *v.* director general, as agent; decided July 11, 1923; report [and order] of commission. [1923.] p. 351, [1]. ([Opinion] 8661.) [Report from Interstate Commerce Commission reports, v. 81.] * Paper, 5c.

Cattle. No. 11699, National Live Stock Exchange *v.* Atchison, Topeka & Santa Fe Railway Company et al.; decided July 2, 1923; report [and order] of commission on reargument. [1923.] 305–308+iii p. ([Opinion] 8653.) [Report from Interstate Commerce Commission reports, v. 81.] * Paper, 5c.

—— No. 13002, Kansas City Live Stock Exchange *v.* Abilene & Southern Railway Company et al.; [decided July 13, 1923; report and order of commission]. 1923. [1]+482–486+ii p. ([Opinion] 8685.) [Report from Interstate Commerce Commission reports, v. 81.] * Paper, 5c.

Cayuga Southern Telephone Company. Finance docket no. 2962, purchase of properties by Cayuga Southern Telephone Co., in matter of joint application of Cayuga Southern Telephone Company, Farm & village Telephone Company, and New York Telephone Company for certificate of advantage and public interest; decided June 16, 1923; report of commission. [1923.] p. 691–693. ([Finance.decision] 758.) [From Interstate Commerce Commission reports, v. 79.] * Paper, 5c.

Central of Georgia Railway. Finance docket no. 3059, assumption of obligation by Central of Georgia Ry., in matter of application of Central of Georgia Railway Company for authority to assume obligation and liability in respect of bonds of Ocean Steamship Company of Savannah; [decided June 26, 1923; report of commission]. 1923. [1]+730–732 p. ([Finance decision] 772.) [From Interstate Commerce Commission reports, v. 79.] * Paper, 5c.

Chesapeake and Ohio Railway. Finance docket no. 3036, assumption of obligation and liability by Chesapeake & Ohio Railway; [decided June 18, 1923; report of commission]. 1923. [1]+694–696 p. ([Finance decision] 759.) [From Interstate Commerce Commission reports, v. 79.] * Paper, 5c.

Chicago and North Western Railway. Finance docket no. 1657, bonds of Chicago & North Western Ry.; decided July 16, 1923; supplemental report of commission. [1923.] p. 15–17. ([Finance decision] 805.) [From Interstate Commerce Commission reports, v. 82.] * Paper, 5c.

Chicago and Wabash Valley Railway. Before Interstate Commerce Commission, valuation docket no. 147, Chicago and Wabash valley Railway Company; brief in support of tentative valuation. 1923. cover-title, i+14 p. ‡

Chicago, Attica and Southern Railroad. Finance docket no. 2782, Chicago, Attica & Southern securities; decided Apr. 16, 1923; report of commission. [1923.] p. 209–213. ([Finance decision] 603.) [From Interstate Commerce Commission reports, v. 79.] * Paper, 5c.

Chicago Great Western Railroad. Finance docket no, 3046, Chicago Great Western notes; decided June 20, 1923; report of commission. [1923.] p. 713–715. ([Finance decision] 765.) [From Interstate Commerce Commission reports, v. 79.] * Paper, 5c.

Chicago, Indianapolis and Louisville Railway. Finance docket no. 2911, Chicago, Indianapolis & Louisville Railway bonds; [decided July 16, 1923; report of commission]. 1923. [1]+12–14 p. ([Finance decision] 804.) [From Interstate Commerce Commission reports, v. 82.] * Paper, 5c.

Chicago, Milwaukee and St. Paul Railway. Finance docket no. 2637, abandonment of part of branch line by Chicago, Milwaukee & St. Paul Ry.; decided July 9, 1923; report of commission. [1923.] p. 793–794. ([Finance decision] 791.) [From Interstate Commerce Commission reports, v. 79.] * Paper, 5c.

—— Finance docket no. 2810, abandonment of part of branch line by C., M. & St. P. Ry.; [decided June 18, 1923; report of commission]. 1923. [1]+684–686 p. ([Finance decision] 756.) [From Interstate Commerce Commission reports, v. 79.] * Paper, 5c.

—— Finance docket no. 2896, Chicago, Milwaukee & St. Paul bonds; decided Apr. 28, 1923; report of commission. [1923.] p. 243–246. ([Finance decision] 613.) [From Interstate Commerce Commission reports, v. 79.] * Paper, 5c.

Chicago, Rock Island and Pacific Railway. Finance docket no. 2985, Rock Island notes and bonds; [decided June 20, 1923; report of commission]. 1923. [1]+710–712 p. ([Finance decision] 764.) [From Interstate Commerce Commission reports, v. 79.] *Paper, 5c.

Chicago, Terre Haute and Southeastern Railway. Finance docket no. 389, guaranty settlement with Chicago, Terre Haute & Southeastern Ry.; decided June 18, 1923; report of commission. [1923.] p. 681–683. ([Finance decision] 755.) [From Interstate Commerce Commission reports, v. 79.] *Paper, 5c.

Clay. No. 12605, Refinite Company v. director general, as agent, and Chicago, Burlington & Quincy Railroad Company; decided July 11, 1923; supplemental report of commission. [1923.] p. 355–356. ([Opinion] 8663.) [From Interstate Commerce Commission reports, v. 81.] *Paper, 5c.

Cleveland Union Terminals Company. Finance docket no. 2971, Cleveland Union Terminals bonds, in matter of joint application of Cleveland Union Terminals Company for authority to issue bonds and of New York Central Railroad Company, Cleveland, Cincinnati, Chicago & St. Louis Railway Company and New York, Chicago & St. Louis Railroad Company for authority to assume obligation and liability, as guarantors, in respect of said bonds; [decided June 13, 1923; report of commission]. 1923. [1]+664–668 p. ([Finance decision] 749.) [From Interstate Commerce Commission reports, v. 79.] *Paper, 5c.

—— Same; decided July 5, 1923; supplemental report of commission. [1923.] p. 761–762. ([Finance decision] 784.) [From Interstate Commerce Commission reports, v. 79.] *Paper, 5c.

Coal. No. 12864, John A. Merritt & Company v. Central of Georgia Railway Company et al.; decided July 20, 1923; report [and order] of commission. [1923.] 559–561+[1] p. ([Opinion] 8705.) [Report from Interstate Commerce Commission reports, v. 81.] * Paper, 5c.

Coal—Continued. No. 13097, Standard Portland Cement Company *v.* director general, as agent; decided July 11, 1923; report of commission. [1923.] p. 357-360. ([Opin'on] 8664.) [From Interstate Commerce Commission reports, v. 81.] * Paper, 5c.

—— No. 13112, Clay County Coal Operators Association et al. *v.* Cumberland & Manchester Railroad Company et al.; [decided July 13, 1923, report and order of commission]. 1923. [1]+414-422+iii p. ([Opinion] 8678.) [Report from Interstate Commerce Commission reports, v. 81.] *Paper, 5c.

—— No. 13258, Webb Fuel Company *v.* director general, as agent; decided July 20, 1923; report [and order] of commission. [1923.] 631-633+[1] p. ([Opinion] 8725.) [Report from Interstate Commerce Commission reports, v. 81.] * Paper, 5c.

—— No. 13397, Melcroft Coal Company *v.* Indian Creek Valley Railway et al.; decided June 30, 1923; report [and order] of commission. [1923.] 251-260+ [1] p. ([Opinion] 8642.) [Report from Interstate Commerce Commission reports, v. 81.] *Paper, 5c.

—— No. 13471, Hamill Coal & Coke Company et al. *v.* Western Maryland Railway Company et al.; [decided June 25, 1923; report and order of commission]. 1923. [1]+72-78+iii p. ([Opinion] 8604.) [Report from Interstate Commerce Commission reports, v. 81.] *Paper, 5c.

—— No. 14064, St. Louis & O'Fallon Railway Company *v.* East St. Louis & Suburban Railway Company et al.; [no. 11415, same *v.* same; decided July 13, 1923; report and order of commission]. 1923. [1]+538-548+ii p. ([Opinion] 8700.) [Report from Interstate Commerce Commission reports,. v. 81.] * Paper, 5c.

Coke. Investigation and suspension docket no. 1814, coke, in carloads, from points in Pennsylvania and West Virginia to Moline and Rock Island, Ill., Davenport, Iowa, and Omaha, Nebr.; decided July 12, 1923; report [and order] of commission. [1923.] 309-311+[1] p. ([Opinion] 8654.) [Report from Interstate Commerce Commission reports, v. 81.] * Paper, 5c.

—— No. 13909, National Tube Company *v.* director general, as agent, and New York Central Railroad Company; decided July 11, 1923; report of commission. [1923.] p. 369-370. ([Opinion] 8668.) [From Interstate Commerce Commission reports, v. 81.] * Paper, 5c.

Colorado and Southeastern Railroad. Finance docket no. 1309, deficit settlement with Colorado & Southeastern R. R.; decided June 19, 1923; report of commission. [1923.] p. 697-698. ([Finance decision] 760.) [From Interstate Commerce Commission reports, v. 79.] * Paper, 5c.

Columbus and Greenville Railroad. Finance docket no. 799, guaranty settlement with Columbus & Greenville R. R., A. T. Stovall, receiver; decided May 19, 1923; report of commission. [1923.] p. 439-441. ([Finance decision] 677.) [From Interstate Commerce Commission reports, v. 79.] * Paper, 5c.

Copal. No. 13207, A. Klipstein & Company *v.* director general, as agent, Southern Pacific Company et al.; decided July 20, 1923; report [and order] of commission. [1923.] 565-566+[1] p. ([Opinion] 8707.) [Report from Interstate Commerce Commission reports, v. 81.] * Paper, 5c.

Cotton. 4th section application no. 12155, Cotton via Elberton & Eastern Railroad; decided June 27, 1923; report [and order] of commission. [1923.] 261-266+[1] p. ([Opinion] 8643.) [Report from Interstate Commerce Commission reports, v. 81.] * Paper, 5c.

Cotton-seed. No. 14149, Memphis Freight Bureau, for Crescent Cotton Oil Company, *v.* Columbus & Greenville Railroad Company et al.; decided June 27, 1923; report [and order] of commission. [1923.] 221-222+[1] p. ([Opinion] 8637.) [Report from Interstate Commerce Commission reports, v. 81.] * Paper, 5c.

Cotton-seed oil. No. 13438, Procter & Gamble Company *v.* director general, as agent, Atlanta & West Point Railroad Company, et al.; decided July 11, 1923; report of commission. [1923.] p. 361-364. ([Opinion] 8665.) [From Interstate Commerce Commission reports, v. 81.] * Paper, 5c.

Coudersport and Port Allegany Railroad. Finance docket no. 411, guaranty settlement with Coudersport & Port Allegany R. R.; decided July 14, 1923; report of commission. [1923.] p. 817-819. ([Finance decision] 798.) [From Interstate Commerce Commission reports, v. 79.] * Paper, 5c.

Davenport, Rock Island and Northwestern Railway. Finance docket no. 419, guaranty status of Davenport, Rock Island & Northwestern Railway; decided June 13, 1923; report of commission. [1923.] p. 651–652. ([Finance decision] 745.) [From Interstate Commerce Commission reports, v. 79.] * Paper, 5c.

Decisions. Decisions of commission, Dec. 1922–Mar. 1923, index-digest to [Interstate Commerce Commission reports], v. 77, with table of commodities and table of localities; [prepared in] Section of Indices. 1923. cover-title, p. 787–923. ‡   8—30656

—— Decisions of Interstate Commerce Commission, Oct.–Dec. 1922. 1923, xxx+938 p. (Interstate Commerce Commission reports, v. 74.) *Cloth, $2.00.

Demurrage. No. 13390, Fred G. Clark Company *v.* New York Central Railroad Company et al.; [decided July 13, 1923; report and order of commission]. 1923. [1]+500–502+[1] p. ([Opinion] 8691.) [Report from Interstate Commerce Commission reports, v. 81.] *Paper, 5c.

—— No. 13547, Allied Machinery Company of America *v.* director general, as agent, and Pennsylvania Railroad Company; [decided June 27, 1923; report and order of commission]. 1923. [1]+204–206+[1] p. ([Opinion] 8630.) [Report from Interstate Commerce Commission reports, v. 81.] *Paper, 5c.

Detroit and Mackinac Railway. Finance docket no. 2739, construction of extension by Detroit & Mackinac Ry.; decided July 2, 1923; report of commission. [1923.] p. 753–756. ([Finance decision] 782.) [From Interstate Commerce Commission reports, v. 79.] *Paper, 5c.

Erie Railroad. Finance docket no. 2875, Erie Railroad equipment trust, series II; decided Apr. 26, 1923; report of commission. [1923.] p. 239–242. ([Finance decision] 612.) [From Interstate Commerce Commission reports, v. 79.] *Paper, 5c.

Express. No. 12784, Southeastern Express Company *v.* American Railway Express Company; [no. 12786, Southern Fisheries Association *v.* American Railway Express Company et al.]; decided July 9, 1923; supplemental report [and order] of commission. [1923.] 247–250+ii p. ([Opinion] 8641.) [Report from Interstate Commerce Commission reports, v. 81.] *Paper, 5c.

Fire-brick. No. 12564, International Coal Products Corporation *v.* director general, as agent, Pennsylvania Railroad Company, et al.; [no. 12920, same *v.* director general, as agent]; decided July 13, 1923; report [and order] of commission. [1923.] 435–439+ii p. ([Opinion] 8682.) [Report from Interstate Commerce Commission reports, v. 81.] *Paper, 5c.

Florida East Coast Railway. Finance docket no. 3085, Florida East Coast equipment trust, series C; [decided July 11, 1923; report of commission]. 1923. [1]+798–801 p. ([Finance decision] 793.) [From Interstate Commerce Commission reports, v. 79.] * Paper, 5c.

Fluor-spar. No. 13579, Thomas R. Heyward, jr., trading as Thomas R. Heyward Company, *v.* director general, as agent; decided July 13, 1923; report of commission. [1923.] p. 529–532. ([Opinion] 8697.) [From Interstate Commerce Commission reports, v. 81.] *Paper, 5c.

Fordyce and Princeton Railroad. Finance docket no. 2548, deficit settlement with Fordyce & Princeton R. R.; decided June 16, 1923; report of commission. [1923.] p. 679–680. ([Finance decision] 754.) [From Interstate Commerce Commission reports, v. 79.] *Paper, 5c.

Fort Myers Southern Railroad. Finance docket no. 2751, construction of line by Fort Myers Southern R. R.; decided June 19, 1923; report of commission. 1923. [1]+702–706 p. ([Finance decision] 762.) [From Interstate Commerce Commission reports, v. 79.] *Paper, 5c.

Freight rates. Investigation and suspension docket no. 1812, catsup, cider, kraut, pickles, and vinegar, in carloads, between Michigan and Indiana points, and Chicago, Ill., and related points; [decided July 9, 1923; report and order of commission]. 1923. [1]+212–214+[1] p. ([Opinion] 8633.) [Report from Interstate Commerce Commission reports, v. 81.] * Paper, 5c.

—— Investigation and suspension dockets nos. 1511, 1597, 1655, and 1696, reduced rates from New York piers (1–4); [decided July 2, 1923; report and order of commission]. 1923. [1]+312–332+[1] p. ([Opinion] 8655.) [Report from Interstate Commerce Commission reports, v. 81.] * Paper, 5c.

Freight rates—Continued. No. 12090, Oklahoma Traffic Association *v.* Chicago, Rock Island & Pacific Railway Company et al.; [no. 12847 (sub-no. 1), Panhandle-Plains Chamber of Commerce *v.* Abilene & Southern Railway Company et al.]; decided July 20, 1923; report [and order] of commission. [1923.] 577–582+[1] p. ([Opinion] 8710.) [Report from Interstate Commerce Commission reports, v. 81.] * Paper, 5c.

Fuel-oil. No. 13607, Central Refining Company, Incorporated, *v.* director general, as agent; decided July 20, 1923; report of commission. [1923.] p. 597–598. ([Opinion] 8715.) [From Interstate Commerce Commission reports, v. 81.] * Paper, 5c.

Furniture polish. No. 9086, Channel Chemical Company *v.* Atchison, Topeka & Santa Fe Railway Company et al.; decided July 9, 1923; report [and order] of commission on further hearing. [1923.] 407–413+[1] p. ([Opinion] 8677.) [Report from Interstate Commerce Commission reports, v. 81.] * Paper, 5c.

Garbage. No. 11829, Nebraska rates, fares, and charges, in matter of intrastate rates, fares, and charges of Union Pacific Railroad Company and other carriers in Nebraska; [decided July 9, 1923; report and order of commission on further hearing]. 1923. [1]+290–292+[1] p. ([Opinion] 8649.) [Report from Interstate Commerce Commission reports, v. 81.] * Paper, 5c.

Gas oil. No. 13504, Standard Oil Company (Kentucky) *v.* Midland Valley Railroad Company et al.; decided June 27, 1923; report of commission. [1923.] p. 193–196. ([Opinion] 8627.) [From Interstate Commerce Commission reports, v. 81.] * Paper, 5c.

—— No. 13550, Sioux City Gas & Electric Company et al. *v.* Atchison, Topeka & Santa Fe Railway Company et al.; decided July 13, 1923; report of commission. [1923.] p. 397–398. ([Opinion] 8674.) [From Interstate Commerce Commission reports, v. 81.] * Paper, 5c.

Georgia, Florida and Alabama Railway. Finance docket no. 3070, Georgia, Florida & Alabama stock; decided July 11, 1923; report of commission. [1923.] p. 795–797. ([Finance decision] 792.) [From Interstate Commerce Commission reports, v. 79.] * Paper, 5c.

Glass. No. 14098, Kokomo Opalescent Glass Company *v.* Pittsburgh, Cincinnati, Chicago & St. Louis Railroad Company et al.; [decided July 11, 1923; report and order of commission]. 1923. [1]+352–354+[1] p. ([Opinion] 8662.) [Report from Interstate Commerce Commission reports, v. 81.] * Paper, 5c.

Grain. Investigation and suspension docket no. 1759, grain, grain products, and feed from Chicago, Joliet, and Lockport, Ill., to Texas points; decided July 5, 1923; report [and order] of commission. [1923.] 209–211+[1] p. ([Opinion] 8632.) [Report from Interstate Commerce Commission reports, v. 81.] * Paper, 5c.

—— Investigation and suspension docket no. 1778, grain and grain products between stations in Iowa and Minnesota, and Milwaukee, Wis., and Chicago and Peoria, Ill., group points; decided July 10, 1923; report [and order] of commission. [1923.] 267–271+[1] p. ([Opinion] 8644.) [Report from Interstate Commerce Commission reports, v. 81.] *Paper, 5c.

—— Investigation and suspension docket no. 1780, grain and grain products from St. Paul, Minneapolis, and Minnesota Transfer, Minn., to Kansas, Oklahoma, and Colorado points; [decided July 10, 1923; report and order of commission]. 1923. [1]+338–341+[1] p. ([Opinion] 8657.) [Report from Interstate Commerce Commission reports, v. 81.] *Paper, 5c.

—— Investigation and suspension docket no. 1792, grain and grain products from Minnesota and South Dakota points to Mississippi and Ohio River crossings and points in Mississippi Valley; [decided July 23, 1923; report and order of commission]. 1923. [1]+440–447+[1] p. ([Opinion] 8683.) [Report from Interstate Commerce Commission reports, v. 81.] *Paper, 5c.

Great Northern Railway. Finance docket no. 2853, bonds of Great Northern Ry.; decided June 22, 1923; report of commission. [1923.] p. 727–729. ([Finance decision] 771.) [From Interstate Commerce Commission reports, v. 79.] *Paper, 5c.

Great Western Railway. Finance docket no. 2469, deficit settlement with Great Western Ry.; [decided July 14, 1923; report of commission]. 1923. [1]+820–822 p. ([Finance decision] 799.) [From Interstate Commerce Commission reports, v. 79.] * Paper, 5c.

Ice-cream. No. 11948, Glacifer Company *v.* American Railway Express Company; decided June 6, 1923; report of commission on further hearing. [1923.] p. 223–226. ([Opinion] 8638.) [From Interstate Commerce Commission reports, v. 81.] *Paper, 5c.

Interstate Railroad. Finance docket no. 2838' securities of Interstate Railroad; [decided Apr. 25, 1923; report of commission]. 1923. [1]+228–232 p. ([Finance decision] 609.) [From Interstate Commerce Commission reports, v. 79.] *Paper, 5c.

Iron. No. 12415, Dave Levite *v.* director general, as agent, Texas & Pacific Railway Company, et al.; decided July 2, 1923; report of commission on further consideration. [1923.] p. 219–220. ([Opinion] 8636.) [From Interstate Commerce Commission reports, v. 81.] *Paper, 5c.

—— No. 12866, Standard Rail & Steel Company *v.* Terminal Railroad Association of St. Louis and director general, as agent; decided July 13,' 1923; report [and order] of commission. [1923.] 395–396+[1] p. ([Opinion] 8673.) [Report from Interstate Commerce Commission reports, v. 81.] *Paper, 5c.

—— No. 13860, Monroe Hardware Company et al. *v.* Alabama & Vicksburg Railway Company et al.; decided June 27, 1923; report of commission. [1923.] p. 187–188. ([Opinion] 8624.) [From Interstate Commerce Commission reports, v. 81.] *Paper, 5c.

Kansas City Southern Railway. Finance docket no. 2867, assumption of obligation by Kansas City Southern and Texarkana & Fort Smith railways; decided June 28, 1923; report of commission. [1923.] p. 733–736. ([Finance decision] 773.) [From Interstate Commerce Commission reports, v. 79.] *Paper, 5c.

Lawndale Railway and Industrial Company. Finance docket no. 576, guaranty settlement with Lawndale Railway & Industrial Co.; decided June 11, 1923; report of commission. [1923.] p. 649–651. ([Finance decision] 744.) [From Interstate Commerce Commission reports,' v. 79.] *Paper, 5c.

Lemons. No. 13598, Dickinson Grocery Company *v.* director general, as agent, Atchison, Topeka & Santa Fe Railway Company et al.; decided July 13, 1923; report [and order] of commission. [1923.] 533–534+[1] p. ([Opinion] 8698.) [Report from Interstate Commerce Commission reports, v. 81.] * Paper, 5c.

Lexington Terminal Railroad. Before Interstate Commerce Commission, valuation docket no. 176, Lexington Terminal Railroad Company; brief in support of tentative valuation. 1923. cover-title, ii+25 p. ‡

Locomotives. No. 13780, Walter A. Zelnicker Supply Company *v.* Denver & Rio Grande Western Railroad Company et al.; decided July 11, 1923; report [and order] of commission. [1923.] 367–368+[1] p. ([Opinion] 8667.) [Report from Interstate Commerce Commission reports, v. 81.] * Paper, 5c.

Logging-cars. No. 13527, Hartburg Lumber Company *v.* Beaumont, Sour Lake & Western Railway Company et al.; portion of 4th section application no. 462, logging cars or trucks from Kernan, La., to Mauriceville, Tex.; decided July 13, 1923; report [and orders] of commission. [1923.] 497–499+ii p. ([Opinion] 8690.) [Report from Interstate Commerce Commission reports, v. 81.] * Paper, 5c.

Longview, Portland and Northern Railway. Finance docket no. 2828, construction of line by Longview, Portland & Northern; decided July 11, 1923; report of commission. [1923.] p. 805–808. ([Finance decision] 795.) [From Interstate Commerce Commission reports, v. 79.] * Paper, 5c.

Louisiana and Arkansas Railway. Finance docket no. 2990, Louisiana & Arkansas Railway equipment notes; decided June 13, 1923; report of commission. [1923.] p. 637–639. ([Finance decision] 740.) [From Interstate Commerce Commission reports, v. 79.] * Paper, 5c.

Lumber. No. 12107, Ferd. Brenner Lumber Company, Incorporated, *v.* director general, as agent, Atchison, Topeka & Santa Fe Railway Company, et al.; decided June 7, 1923; report of commission on reargument. [1923.] p. 241–246. ([Opinion] 8640.) [From Interstate Commerce Commission reports, v. 81.] * Paper, 5c.

Lumber—Continued. No. 12459, White Pine Association of the Tonawandas et al. *v.* director general, as agent, New York Central Railroad Company, et al.; decided July 13, 1923; report [and order] of commission. [1923.] 401–406+[1] p. ([Opinion] 8676.) [Report from Interstate Commerce Commission reports, v. 81.] * Paper, 5c.

—— No. 12962, S. A. Foster Lumber Company *v.* Valley & Siletz Railroad Company et al.; decided July 13, 1923; report [and order] of commission. [1923.] 505–509+ii p. ([Opinion] 8693.) [Report from Interstate Commerce Commission reports, v. 81.] * Paper, 5c.

Marianna and Blountstown Railroad. Finance docket no. 2536, deficit status of Marianna & Blountstown R. R.; decided July 9, 1923; report of commission. [1923.] p. 751–752. ([Finance decision] 780.) [From Interstate Commerce Commission reports, v. 79.] * Paper, 5c.

Memphis, Dallas and Gulf Railroad. Finance docket no. 2254, application of [Martin Walsh], receiver of Memphis, Dallas & Gulf R. R.,' for loan; decided May 19, 1923; report of commission. [1923.] p. 675–676. ([Finance decision] 752.) [From Interstate Commerce Commission reports, v. 79.] * Paper, 5c.

Misrouting. No. 14088, Walter A. Zelnicker Supply Company *v.* Sugar Land Railway Company, director general, as agent, et al.; decided June 27, 1923; report [and order] of commission. [1923.] 189–190+[1] p. ([Opinion] 8625.) [Report from Interstate Commerce Commission reports, v. 81.] * Paper, 5c.

Nacogdoches and Southeastern Railroad. Finance docket no. 673,' guaranty settlement with Nacogdoches & Southeastern R. R.; decided June 20, 1923; report of commission. [1923.] p. 699–701. ([Finance decision] 761.) [From Interstate Commerce Commission reports, v. 79.] * Paper, 5c.

New York Central Railroad. Finance docket no. 3055, stock of New York Central Railroad; decided June 28, 1923; report of commission. [1923.] p. 739–740. ([Finance decision] 775.) [From Interstate Commerce Commission reports, v. 79.] * Paper, 5c.

New York, Chicago and St. Louis Railroad. Finance docket no. 2968, New York, Chicago & St. Louis equipment trust of 1923; [decided July 14, 1923; report of commission]. 1923. [1]+812–816 p. ([Finance decision] 797.) [From Interstate Commerce Commission reports, v. 79.] * Paper, 5c.

New York, Ontario and Western Railway. Before Interstate Commerce Commission, valuation docket no. 192, New York, Ontario and Western Railway Company, Rome and Clinton Railroad Company, Utica, Clinton and Binghamton Railroad Company, Wharton valley Railway Company, Ontario, Carbondale and Scranton Railway Company, Pecksport Connecting Railway Company, Ellenville and Kingston Railroad Company, and Port Jervis, Monticello and Summitville Railroad Company; brief in support of tentative valuation. 1923. cover-title, ii+101 p. il. ‡

Norfolk and Portsmouth Belt Line Railroad. Finance docket ho. 2988, note of Norfolk & Portsmouth Belt Line; decided June 13, 1923; report of commission. [1923.] p. 633–634. ([Finance decision] 738.) [From Interstate Commerce Commission reports, v. 79.] * Paper, 5c.

Norfolk Southern Railroad. Finance docket no. 2440, Norfolk Southern equipment notes; [approved July 9, 1923; supplemental order]. 1923. p. [1], 752. ([Finance decision] 781.) [From Interstate Commerce Commission reports, v. 79.] * Paper, 5c.

Northern Pacific Railway. Finance docket no. 2884, construction of branch line by Northern Pacific Ry.; decided June 14, 1923; report of commission. [1923.] p. 687–690. ([Finance decision] 757.) [From Interstate Commerce Commission reports, v. 79.] * Paper, 5c.

Northwestern Pacific Railroad. Finance docket no. 3033, Northwestern Pacific Railroad bonds; decided July 9, 1923; report of commission. [1923.] p. 763–766. ([Finance decision] 785.) [From Interstate Commerce Commission reports, v. 79.] * Paper, 5c.

Oil-well machinery. No. 13323, Parkersburg Rig & Reel Company *v.* Baltimore & Ohio Southwestern Railroad Company et al.; decided June 27, 1923; report of commission. [1923.] p. 197–199. ([Opinion] 8628.) [From Interstate Commerce Commission reports, v. 81.] * Paper, 5c.

Orangeburg Railway. Finance docket no. 201, deficit settlement with Orangeburg Ry., C. E. Denniston, receiver; decided July 18, 1923; report of commission. [1923.] p. 3–4. ([Finance decision] 801.) [From Interstate Commerce Commission reports, v. 82.] * Paper, 5c.

Oregon Short Line Railroad. Finance docket no. 2903, construction of line by Oregon Short Line R. R.; decided June 20, 1923; report of commission. [1923.] p. 707–709. ([Finance decision] 763.) [From Interstate Commerce Commission reports, v. 79.] * Paper, 5c.

—— Finance docket no. 2928, construction of extension by Oregon Short Line R. R.; [decided July 2, 1923; report of commission]. 1923. [1]+744–746 p. ([Finance decision] 777.) [From Interstate Commerce Commission reports, v. 79.] * Paper, 5c.

Osage Railway. Finance docket no. 2925, construction of extension by Osage Ry.; decided July 2, 1923; report of commission. [1923.] p. 757–760. ([Finance decision] 783.) [From Interstate Commerce Commission reports, v. 79.] ʹ* Paper, 5c.

Ouachita and Northwestern Railroad. Finance docket no. 182, deficit settlement with Ouachita & Northwestern R. R.; decided June 25, 1923; report of commission. [1923.] p. 721–722. ([Finance decision] 768.) [From Interstate Commerce Commission reports, v. 79.] * Paper, 5c.

Packing-house products. No. 9355, John Morrell & Company *v.* Chicago, Burlington & Quincy Railroad Company, director general, as agent, et al.; [decided June 30, 1923; report of commission on further hearing]. 1923. [1]+200–203 p. ([Opinion] 8629.) [From Interstate Commerce Commission reports, v. 81.] * Paper, 5c.

Paper. No. 13469, United Paperboard Company, Incorporated, *v.* Greenwich & Johnsonville Railway Company et al.; [no. 13470, same *v.* same]; decided July 20, 1923; report [and order] of commission. [1923.] 591–593+ii p. ([Opinion] 8713.) [Report from Interstate Commerce Commission reports, v. 81.] * Paper, 5c.

——No. 13651, Grimes & Friedman *v.* Atchison, Topeka & Santa Fe Railway Company et al.; [no. 13787. same *v.* same; decided July 13, 1923; report and order of commission]. 1923. [1]+552–554+[1] p. ([Opinion] 8702.) [Report from Interstate Commerce Commission reports, v. 81.] * Paper, 5c.

—— No. 13907, Tulsa Paper Company *v.* Chicago, Milwaukee & St. Paul Railway Company et al.; decided July 11, 1923; report [and order] of commission. [1923.] 293–294+[1] p. ([Opinion] 8650.) [Report from Interstate Commerce Commission reports, v. 81.] * Paper, 5c.

Peanuts. No. 13484, Fletcher & Wilson Coffee Company *v.* director general, as agent; [decided July 11, 1923; report of commission]. 1923. [1]+348–350 p. ([Opinion] 8660.) [From Interstate Commerce Commission reports, v. 81.] * Paper, 5c.

Petroleum. No. 10708, J. F. Campion *v.* director general, as agent, Atchison, Topeka & Santa Fe Railway Company, et al.; decided July 20, 1923; report [and order] of commission. [1923.] 557–558+[1] p. [Report from Interstate Commerce Commission reports, v. 81.] * Paper, 5c.

—— No. 12170, National Refining Company *v.* director general, as agent, Missouri, Kansas & Texas Railway Company, et al.; [decided July 11, 1923; report and order of commission]. 1923. [1]+342–344+[1] p. ([Opinion] 8658.) [Report from Interstate Commerce Commission reports, v. 81.] * Paper, 5c.

—— No. 12490, National Petroleum Association et al. *v.* director general, as agent, Pennsylvania Railroad Company, et al.; [no. 12552, same *v.* same]; decided July 20, 1923; supplemental report of commission. [1923.] p. 487–488. ([Opinion] 8686.) [From Interstate Commerce Commission reports, v. 81.] * Paper, 5c.

—— No. 12584, Indiahoma Refining Company *v.* director general, as agent Chicago & Alton Railroad Company, et al.; decided July 7, 1923; report [and order] of commission. [1923.] 287–289+[1] p. ([Opinion] 8648.) [Report from Interstate Commerce Commission reports, v. 81.] * Paper, 5c.

Philadelphia and Camden Ferry Company. Finance docket no. 738, guaranty status of Philadelphia & Camden Ferry Co.; decided June 25. 1923; report of commission. [1923.] p. 723–724. ([Finance decision] 769.) [From Interstate Commerce Commission reports, v. 79.] * Paper, 5c.

Plaster. No. 10912, Acme Cement Plaster Company *v.* director general, as agent, Pere Marquette Railway Company, et al.; [decided June 6, 1923; report of commission on further hearing]. 1923. [1]+298–304 p. ([Opinion] 8652.) [From Interstate Commerce Commission reports, v. 81.] * Paper, 5c.

Railroad accidents. Summary of accident investigation reports, no. 16, Apr.–June, 1923; [prepared in] Bureau of Safety. 1923. iii+28 p. [Quarterly.] * Paper, 5c. single copy, 15c. a yr.; foreign subscription, 25c.   A 20—942

Railroad, employees. Wage statistics, class 1 steam roads in United States, including 15 switching and terminal companies, May, 1923; [prepared in] Bureau of Statistics. May, 1923. [4] p. oblong large 8° †

Railroad switches. No. 14131, Pittsburgh & West Virginia Railway Company et al. *v.* Lake Erie, Alliance & Wheeling Railroad, New York Central Railroad Company, lessee; decided July 9, 1923; report [and order] of commission. [1923.] 333–337+[1] p. ([Opinion] 8656.) [Report from Interstate Commerce Commission reports, v. 81.] * Paper, 5c.

Railroads. Freight and passenger service operating statistics of class 1 steam roads in United States, compiled from 164 reports of freight statistics representing 177 roads and from 161 reports of passenger statistics representing 174 roads (switching and terminal companies not included), June, 1923 and 1922 [and 6 months ended with June, 1923 and 1922; [prepared in] Bureau of Statistics. June, 1923. [2] p. oblong large 8° [Subject to revision.] †

—— Freight and passenger train service unit costs (selected expense accounts) of class 1 steam roads in United States, including proportion of mixed-train and special-train service (compiled from 164 reports representing 177 steam roads, switching and terminal companies not included), June, 1923 and 1922, and 6 months [ended with June] 1923 and 1922; [prepared in] Bureau of Statistics. June, 1923. 1 p. oblong large 8° [Subject to revision.] †

—— No. 15100, depreciation charges of steam railroad companies [report of preliminary investigation of depreciation charges in connection with steam roads and tentative conclusions and recommendations of Depreciation Section, Accounts Bureau, for regulation of such charges] Aug. 23, 1923. [1923.] 31 p. * Paper, 5c.

—— Operating revenues and operating expenses of class 1 steam roads in United States (for 195 steam roads, including 15 switching and terminal companies), June, 1923 and 1922 [and] 6 months ending with June, 1923 and 1922; [prepared in] Bureau of Statistics. June, 1923. 1 p. oblong large 8° [Subject to revision.] †

—— Operating revenues and operating expenses of large steam roads, selected items for roads with annual operating revenues above $25,000,000, June, 1922 and 1923 [and] 6 months ended with June, 1922 and 1923; [prepared in] Bureau of Statistics. June, 1923. [2] p. oblong large 8° [Subject to revision.] †

—— Operating statistics of large steam roads, selected items for June, 1923, compared with June, 1922, for roads with annual operating revenues above $25,000,000; [prepared in] Bureau of Statistics. June, 1923. [2] p. oblong large 8° [Subject to revision.] †

—— Revenue traffic statistics of class 1 steam roads in United States, including mixed-train service (compiled from 165 reports representing 178 steam roads, switching and terminal companies not included), May, 1923 and 1922 [and] 5 months ended with May, 1923 and 1922; [prepared in] Bureau of Statistics. May, 1923. 1 p. oblong large 8° [Subject to revision.] †

Rails. No. 12226, Mid-Continent Equipment & Machinery Company *v.* Mobile & Ohio Railroad Company et al.; [portions of 4th section application no. 2138; decided July 13, 1923; report and orders of commission]. 1923. [1]+510–512+ii p. ([Opinion] 8694.) [Report from Interstate Commerce Commission reports, v. 81.] * Paper, 5c.

Raquette ·Lake Railway. Finance docket no. 765, guaranty settlement with Raquette Lake Ry.; decided June 29, 1923; report of commission. ' [1923.] p. 747-748.' ([Finance decision] 778.) [From Interstate Commerce Commission reports, v. 79.] * Paper, 5c.

Reading Company. Finance docket no. 3057, Reading equipment trust, series I; decided July 17, 1923; report of commission. [1923.] p. 5–8. ([Finance decision] 802.) [From Interstate Commerce Commission reports, v. 82.] * Paper, 5c.

Reconsignment. No. 13388, Ginocchio-Jones Fruit Company *v.* director general, as agent; decided July 13, 1923; report [and order] of commission. [1923.] 495–496+[1] p. ([Opinion] 8689.) [Report from Interstate Commerce Commission reports, v. 81.] * Paper, 5c.

Rice. No. 11220, Orange Rice Mill Company *v.* director general, as agent; Louisiana Western Railroad Company, et al.; decided June 7, 1923; report [and order] of commission on further hearing. [1923.] 285–286+ii p. ([Opinion] 8647.) [Report from Interstate Commerce Commission reports, v. 81.] * Paper, 5c.

Routing. Investigation and suspension docket no. 1766, intermediate routing via North Dakota junctions on transcontinental traffic; [decided July 7, 1923; report and order of commission. 1923. [1]+272–278+[1] p. ([Opinion] 8645.) [Report from Interstate Commerce Commission reports, v. 81.] * Paper, 5c.

Sacramento Northern Railway. Finance docket no. 1881, proposed control of Sacramento Northern by W. P. R. R.; [decided July 2, 1923; report of commission on ·rehearing]. 1923. [1]+782–790 p. ([Finance decision] 789.) [From Interstate Commerce Commission reports, v. 79.] * Paper, 5c.

Sand. Investigation and suspension docket no. 1810, sand and gravel from Covington and Kern, Ind., to Alvin and Rantoul, Ill.; decided July 12, 1923; report [and order] of commission. [1923.] 245–247+[1] p. ([Opinion] 8651.) .[Report from Interstate Commerce Commission reports, v. 81.] * Paper, 5c.

—— No. 12480, Davison & Namack Foundry Company *v.* Pennsylvania Railroad Company, director general, as agent, et al.; decided July 11, 1923; report of commission. [1923.] p. 345–347. ([Opinion] 8659.) [From Interstate· Commerce Commission reports, v. 81.] * Paper, 5c.

San Luis .Central Railroad. Finance docket no. 3044, San Luis Central Railroad bonds; decided June 28, 1923; report of commission. [1923.] p. 737–738. ([Finance decision] 774.) [From Interstate Commerce Commission reports, v. 79.] * Paper, 5c.

Sashes. Investigation and suspension docket no. 1559, sash and doors from Pacific Coast to New·York, N. Y.; decided June 6, 1923; report [and order] of commission. [1923.] 279–284+[1] p. ([Opinion] 8646.) [Report from Interstate Commerce Commission reports, v. 81.] * Paper, 5c.

Savannah and Statesboro Railway. Finance docket no. 1353, deficit settlement with Savannah & Statesboro Ry.; decided June 28, 1923; report of commission. [1923.] p. 725–726. ([Finance decision] 770.) [From Interstate Commerce Commission reports, v. 79.] * Paper, 5c.

Seaboard Air Line Railway. Finance docket no. 3056, issue and pledge of bonds by Seaboard Air Line Railway; decided June 29, 1923; report of commission. [1923.] p. 771–776. ([Finance decision] 787.) [From Interstate Commerce Commission reports, v. 79.] * Paper, 5c.

Silicate of soda. No. 13749, Philadelphia Quartz Company *v.* Pennsylvania Railroad Company et al.; decided July 13, 1923; report [and order] of commission. [1923.] 535–537+[1] p. ([Opinion] 8699.) [Report from Interstate Commerce Commission reports, v. 81.] * Paper, 5c.

Sodium. No. 13944, Hercules Powder Company *v.* Atchison, Topeka & Santa Fe Railway Company et al.; decided July 13, 1923; report [and order] of commission. [1923.] 431–432+[1] p. ([Opinion] 8680.) [Report from Interstate Commerce Commission reports, v. 81.] * Paper, 5c.

Springfield Terminal Railway. Finance docket no. 1436, Springfield Terminal Railway· stock; [decided· July 17, 1923; 2d supplemental report of commission]. 1923. [1]+18–19 p. ([Finance decision] 806.) [From Interstate Commerce Commission reports, v. 82.] * Paper, 5c.

Steamboats. Schedule of sailings (as furnished by steamship companies named herein) of steam vessels which are registered under laws of United States and which are intended to load general cargo at ports in United States for foreign destinations, Aug. 15–Sept. 30, 1923, no. 12; issued by Section of Tariffs, Bureau of Traffic. 1923. iii+19 p. 4° [Monthly. No. 12 cancels no. 11.] † 22—26610

Strawberries. No. 12378, Haley-Neeley Company *v.* director general, as agent, and American Railway Express Company; decided July 2, 1923; report [and order] of commission on further consideration. [1923]. p. 215, [1]. ([Opinion] 8634.) [Report from Interstate Commerce Commission reports, v. 81.] * Paper, 5c.

Sugar cases of 1922, no. 13098, Arbuckle Brothers et al. *v.* Ann Arbor Railroad Company et al.; [decided July 17, 1923; report and orders of commission]. 1923. [1]+448–481+ii p. ([Opinion] 8684.) [Report from Interstate Commerce Commission reports, v. 81.] * Paper, 5c.

Sulphur. No. 12773, Union Sulphur Company *v.* Ahnapee & Western Railway Company et al.; [decided July 13, 1923; report and order of commission]. 1923. [1]+382–391+[1] p. ([Opinion] 8671.) [Report from Interstate Commerce Commission reports, v. 81.] * Paper, 5c.

Swine. No. 14491, minimum carload weights on hogs in Missouri and other States; [no. 12945, in matter of minimum carload weight on shipments of hogs within Iowa]; decided July 9, 1923; [report and order of commission]. [1923.] 373–381+vi p. ([Opinion] 8670.) [Report from Interstate Commerce Commission reports, v. 81.] * Paper, 5c.

Switching. No. 11674, Hillsboro Coal Company *v.* Cleveland, Cincinnati, Chicago & St. Louis Railway Company et al.; [decided June 6, 1923; report of commission on reargument]. 1923. [1]+216–218 p. ([Opinion] 8635.) [From Interstate Commerce Commission reports, v. 81.] * Paper, 5c.

Switching charges. Investigation and suspension docket no. 1625, absorption of charges between Croxton and Jersey City, N. J.; decided July 2, 1923; report of commission on further hearing. [1923.] p. 181–184. ([Opinion] 8622.) [From Interstate Commerce Commission reports, v. 81.] *Paper, 5c.

—— No. 12505, Grasselli Chemical Company *v.* director general, as agent, and Central Railroad Company of New Jersey; [decided July 20, 1923; report and order of commission]. 1923. [1]+562–564+[1] p. ([Opinion] 8706.) [Report from Interstate Commerce Commission reports, v. 81.] *Paper, 5c.

—— No. 13317, Mitsui & Company, Limited, *v.* director general, as agent, and Oregon-Washington Railroad & Navigation Company; decided July 13, 1923; report [and order] of commission. [1923.] 489–491+[1] p. ([Opinion] 8687.) [Report from Interstate Commerce Commission reports, v. 81.] *Paper, 5c.

—— No. 13451, Sutherland Flour Mills Company *v.* director general, as agent; decided July 11, 1923; report [and order] of commission. [1923.] 365–366+ [1] p. ([Opinion] 8666.) [Report from Interstate Commerce Commission reports, v. 81.] *Paper, 5c.

—— No. 14355, Texas Chemical Company *v.* Galveston, Harrisburg & San Antonio Railway Company et al.; decided July 11, 1923; report [and order] of commission. [1923.] 371–372+[1] p. ([Opinion] 8669.) [Report from Interstate Commerce Commission reports, v. 81.] *Paper, 5c.

Tampa Southern Railroad. Finance docket no. 826, guaranty status of Tampa Southern Railroad; decided June 14, 1923; report of commission. [1923.] p. 653–654. ([Finance decision] 746.) [From Interstate Commerce Commission reports, v. 79.] *Paper, 5c.

Tennessee Central Railway. Finance docket no. 2223, Tennessee Central Railway loan; decided June 8, 1923; supplemental report of commission. [1923.] p. 673–674. ([Finance decision] 751.) [From Interstate Commerce Commission reports, v. 79.] *Paper, 5c.

Tobacco. No. 13873, G. J. Helmerichs Leaf Tobacco Company *v.* Cincinnati, Lebanon & Northern Railway Company et al.; [decided June 27, 1923; report and order of commission]. 1923. [1]+184–186+[1] p. ([Opinion] 8623.) [Report from Interstate Commerce Commission reports, v. 81.] *Paper, 5c.

Tonopah and Tidewater Railroad. Finance docket no. 2368, deficit settlement with Tonopah & Tidewater R. R.; decided June 9, 1923; report of commission. [1923.] p. 677–678. ([Finance decision] 753.) [From Interstate Commerce Commission reports, v. 79.] *Paper, 5c.

Train-control devices. Report of chief of Section of Signals and Train Control of Bureau of Safety upon tests of automatic train control system of Sprague Safety Control and Signal Corporation in electric zone, New York Central Lines. 1923. [1]+17 p. [This is an abstract of a joint report of inspectors of the Bureau of Safety and the American Railway Association.] *Paper, 5c.
A 23—1986

Unadilla Valley Railway. Finance docket no. 2994, Unadilla valley Railway notes; decided July 16, 1923; report of commission. [1923.] p. 9–11. ([Finance decision] 803.) [From Interstate Commerce Commission reports, v. 82.] *Paper, 5c.

Union Railway. Finance docket no. 858, guaranty settlement with Union Railway; decided June 29, 1923; report of commission. [1923.] p. 741–743. ([Finance decision] 776.) [From Interstate Commerce Commission reports, v. 79.] *Paper, 5c.

Union Terminal Company. Finance docket no. 3083, notes of Union Terminal Company [of Dallas, Tex.; decided July 11, 1923; report of commission]. 1923. [1]+802–804 p. ([Finance decision] 794.) [From Interstate Commerce Commission reports, v. 79.] *Paper, 5c.

Upper Merion and Plymouth Railroad. No. 14129, Upper Merion & Plymouth Railroad Company v. Pennsylvania Railroad Company et al.; decided June 27, 1923; report of commission. [1923.] p. 191–193. ([Opinion] 8626.) [From Interstate Commerce Commission reports, v. 81.] * Paper, 5c.

Veneers. No. 12887, National Veneer & Panel Manufacturers' Association et al. v. Aberdeen & Rockfish Railroad Company et al.; decided July 9, 1923; [report and orders of commission]. [1923.] 227–240+ix p. ([Opinion] 8639.) [Report from Interstate Commerce Commission reports, v. 81.] *Paper, 5c.

Wagons. No. 13998, State Highway Department of Texas v. Chicago, Burlington & Quincy Railroad Company et al.; decided July 13, 1923; report [and order] of commission. [1923.] 433–434+[1] p. ([Opinion] 8681.) [Report from Interstate Commerce Commission reports, v. 81.] *Paper, 5c.

Waycross and Southern Railroad. Finance docket no. 882, guaranty settlement with Waycross & Southern R. R.; decided July 14, 1923; report of commission. [1923.] p. 809–811. ([Finance decision] 796.) [From Interstate Commerce Commission reports, v. 79.] *Paper, 5c.

Western Maryland Railway. Finance docket no. 3054, Western Maryland equipment trust, series C; decided July 5, 1923; report of commission. [1923.] p. 767–770. ([Finance decision] 786.) [From Interstate Commerce Commission reports, v. 79.] *Paper, 5c.

Wheat. No. 13493, Acme Mills v. director general, as agent, Atlantic Coast Line Railroad Company, et al.; [decided July 13, 1923; report of commission]. 1923. [1]+492–494 p. ([Opinion] 8688.) [From Interstate Commerce Commission reports, v. 81.] *Paper, 5c.

Wisconsin Northwestern Railway. Finance docket no. 1866, deficit settlement with Wisconsin Northwestern Ry.; decided Mar. 29, 1923; report of commission. [1923.] p. 791–792. ([Finance decision] 790.) [From Interstate Commerce Commission reports, v. 79.] *Paper, 5c.

Wood-pulp. No. 11840, Inland Empire Paper Company v. Spokane International Railway Company and director general, as agent; decided July 20, 1923; report of commission. [1923.] p. 603–608. ([Opinion] 8718.) [From Interstate Commerce Commission reports, v. 81.] *Paper, 5c.

—— No. 13338, International Paper Company v. director general, as agent, New York Central Railroad Company, et al.; [no. 13369, same v. same]; decided July 13, 1923; report of commission. [1923.] p. 549–551. ([Opinion] 8701.) [From Interstate Commerce Commission reports, v. 81.] *Paper, 5c.

JUSTICE DEPARTMENT

Arndstein, Jules W. No. 404, in Supreme Court, Oct. term, 1922, Thomas D. McCarthy, United States marshal for southern district of New York, *v.* Jules W. Arndstein, on appeal from district court for southern district of New York; brief in support of petition for rehearing. 1923. cover-title, 16 p. ‡

Brown, Wm. A., & Co. No. 2232, Court of Customs Appeals, William A. Brown & Co. et al. *v.* United States; brief for United States. 1923. cover-title, 4 p. ‡

—— No. 2255, Court of Customs Appeals, Wm. A. Brown & Co. *v.* United States; brief for United States. 1923. cover-title, 6 p. ‡

Bush, George S., & Co., Incorporated. No. 2271, Court of Customs Appeals, George S. Bush & Co. (Inc.) *v.* United States; brief for United States. 1923. cover-title, 23 p. ‡

Byron, Joseph C. Docket no. 7191, in district court for northern district of West Virginia, Elkins, June term, 1923. United States *v.* Joseph C. Byron [et al.]; indictment, violation of sec. 37 of criminal code of United States. 1923. cover-title, 72 p. ‡

Central Railroad of New Jersey. In circuit court of appeals for 3d circuit, Oct. term, 1922, Charles V. Duffy, collector [of internal revenue for 5th district of New Jersey], *vs.* Central Railroad of New Jersey, no. 2925; [transcript of record]. [1923.] p. 38–44, large 8° ‡

—— No. —, in Supreme Court, Oct. term, 1923, Charles V. Duffy, collector of internal revenue for 5th district of New Jersey, *v.* Central Railroad Company of New Jersey; petition for writ of certiorari to circuit court of appeals for 3d circuit, and brief in support. 1923. cover-title, 14 p. ‡

Chevrolet Motor Company. No. C–717, in Court of Claims, Chevrolet Motor Company *v.* United States; demurrer and brief in support thereof. 1923. cover-title, p. 5–27, large 8° ‡

Consorzio Veneziano di Armanento e Navigazione. No. 34736, in Court of Claims, Consorzio Veneziano di Armanento e Navigazione *v.* United States; 1, defendant's objections to plaintiff's request for findings of fact, 2, defendant's request for findings of fact, statement, and brief. 1923. cover-title, 1+350–554 p. large 8° ‡

Darling & Co. No. 2244, Court of Customs Appeals, Darling & Company *v.* United States; brief for United States. 1923. cover-title, 37 p. ‡

Douglas Packing Company. [No. 3835, circuit court of appeals, 6th circuit, 95 barrels, more or less, apple cider vinegar (Douglas Packing Company, claimant), *vs.* United States, in error to district court, northern district of Ohio, eastern division] proceedings in circuit court of appeals for 6th circuit; [transcript of record]. [1923.] p. 42–53. [This is printed without title. The signature mark reads: 57627—23.] ‡

Driggs Ordnance Company, Incorporated. No. B–41 (2), in Court of Claims, Louis L. Driggs and John H. Sayres, as receivers of Driggs Ordnance Company, Incorporated, *v.* United States; demurrer to amended petition, memorandum thereon. 1923. cover-title, p. 1–8, large 8° ‡

Eidlitz, Marc, & Son, Incorporated. No. 2254, Court of Customs Appeals, Marc Eidlitz & Son (Inc.), as agent, *v.* United States; brief for United States. 1923. cover-title, 15 p. ‡

Fehl, Earl H. No. 704–C, in Court of Claims, Earl H. Fehl *v.* United States; demurrer and brief. 1923. cover-title, p. 5–8, large 8° ‡

Fish, O. B. No. 2266, Court of Customs Appeals, O. B. Fish *v.* United States; brief for United States. 1923. cover-title, 11 p. ‡

Habirshaw Electric Cable Company. In equity, in district court, southern district of New York, United States *v.* Habirshaw Electric Cable Company et al.; bill of complaint. 1923. cover-title, 169 p. large 8° ‡

Hale Company. No. 2195, Court of Customs Appeals, Hale Company et al. *v.* United States; petition for rehearing. 1923. cover-title, 9 p. ‡

Hendee Manufacturing Company. In Court of Claims, Hendee Manufacturing Company *v.* United States, no. B–99; defendant's brief. 1923. p. 1, large 8° ‡

Hudson Bay Knitting Company, Limited. In Court of Claims, Hudson Bay Knitting Co., Ltd., *v.* United States, no. C–59; demurrer [and] brief. [1923.] p. 5–10, large 8° ‡

Johnston, James J. United States circuit court of appeals for 2d circuit, James J. Johnston *against* United States; [transcript of record]. [1923.] p. 157–166. ‡

Keve & Young. No. 2231, Court of Customs Appeals, Keve & Young *v.* United States; brief for United States. 1923. cover-title, 35 p. ‡

Lilley Building and Loan Company. No. 1033, in Supreme Court, Oct. term, 1922, Lilley Building and Loan Company, corporation organized and existing under laws of Ohio, *v.* Newton M. Miller, as collector of internal revenue for 11th district of Ohio; memorandum in opposition to petition for writ of certiorari to circuit court of appeals for 6th circuit. 1923. cover-title, 4 p. ‡

Lutz Company, Incorporated. In Court of Claims, Lutz Company (Inc.) *v.* United States, no. C–691; answer and counterclaim. [1923.] p. 27–29, large 8° ‡

Mesta Machine Company. In Court of Claims, Mesta Machine Company *v.* United States, no. C–36; [answer and counterclaim]. [1923.] p. 39–64, large 8° ‡

Meyer & Lange. No. 2252, Court of Customs Appeals, Meyer & Lange *v.* United States; brief for United States. 1923. cover-title, 18 p. ‡

Mitsui & Co. No. 2256, Court of Customs Appeals, Mitsui & Co. *v.* United States; brief for United States. 1923. cover-title, 7 p. ‡

Pere Marquette Railway. In Court of Claims, Pere Marquette Railway Company *v.* United States, no. 255–A; defendant's objections to plaintiff's request for findings of fact, defendant's request for findings of fact, and brief. [1923.] p. 31–37, large 8° ‡

Pierce-Arrow Motor Car Company. In Court of Claims, Pierce-Arrow Motor Car Company *v.* United States, no. B–422; defendant's brief. 1923. p. 444, large 8° ‡

—— In Court of Claims, Pierce-Arrow Motor Car Company *v.* United States, no. C–123; defendant's brief. 1923. p. 25, large 8° ‡

Richmond Screw Anchor Company, Incorporated. No. 117–A, in Court of Claims, Richmond Screw Anchor Company, Inc., *v.* United States; defendant's motion for new trial and memorandum thereon. 1923. cover-title, i+1–9 p. large 8° ‡

Shaw, Alex. D., & Co. No. 338–A, in Court of Claims, Alex. D. Shaw & Company *v.* United States; defendant's objections to claimant's request for findings of fact, defendant's request for findings of fact, statement of case, brief. 1923. cover-title, i+43–64 p. ‡

Supplies. List of supplies, blank forms, and dockets for use of Federal judges, attorneys, marshals, and clerks, United States courts. Edition of May, 1923. 1923. ii+19 p. 4° ‡

Supreme Court. Records and briefs in United States cases decided by Supreme Court during Oct. term, 1922 [title-page and index]. 1923. [1]+9 p. ‡

—— United States Supreme Court, Oct. term, 1922, Government briefs in cases argued by solicitor general, 6 v., index. [1923.] 10 p. ‡

—— United States Supreme Court, Oct. term, 1922, Government briefs in cases argued by solicitor general (United States briefs only in this volume), index. [1923.] 3 p. ‡

Teets, Joseph W. No. 46, in Supreme Court, Oct. term, 1923, Title Guaranty & Trust Company and Minnie W. Teets, as executors of Joseph W. Teets, *v.* William H. Edwards, collector of internal revenue for 2d district of New York, in error to district court for southern district of New York; motion to dismiss or affirm. 1923. cover-title, 6 p. ‡

Trachtenberg, Aaron. No. 3970, in Court of Appeals of District of Columbia, Apr. term, 1923, no. —, special calendar, Aaron Trachtenberg *v.* United States; brief for appellee. 1923. cover-title, 13 p. ‡

Union Stock Yards Company of Omaha, Limited. [United States circuit court of appeals, 8th circuit, United States *vs.* Union Stock Yards Company of Omaha, Limited, no. 6057; transcript of record.] [1923.] p. 16–20. [This is printed without title. The signature mark reads: 55548—23.] ‡

—— [United States circuit court of appeals, 8th circuit, United States *vs.* Union Stock Yards Company of Omaha, Limited, no. 6058; transcript of record.] [1923.] p. 16–20. [This is printed without title. The signature mark reads: 55549—23.] ‡

—— [United States circuit court of appeals, 8th circuit, United States *vs.* Union Stock Yards Company of Omaha, Limited, no. 6059; transcript of record.] [1923.] p. 14–18. [This is printed without title. The signature mark reads: 55550—23.] ‡

Union Twist Drill Company. In Court of Claims, Union Twist Drill Company *v.* United States, no. 316–A; defendant's brief. 1923. 1 p. large 8° ‡.

Waldman, Szejwa. United States circuit court of appeals for 2d circuit, United States, ex rel. Szejwa Waldman and her 3 minor children, Zenia, Bessie, and Sophia, *against* Robert E. Tod, commissioner of immigration at port of New York, no. 202, Oct. term, 1922, appeal from district court for southern district of New York; [transcript of record]. [1923.] p. 23–32. ‡

LABOR DEPARTMENT

EMPLOYMENT SERVICE

Industrial employment information bulletin, v. 3, no. 7; July, 1923. [1923.] 22 p. 4° [Monthly.] †
L21—17

LABOR STATISTICS BUREAU

Directory of labor officials in United States and foreign countries. 1923. [1]+262–286 p. [From Monthly labor review, July, 1923.] †

Employment in selected industries, July, 1923. 1923. [1]+6 p. [From Monthly labor review, Sept. 1923.] †

Labor and laboring classes. Labor legislation of 1922. May, 1923. iii+102 p. (Bulletin 330; Labor laws of United States series.) [This bulletin contains a cumulative index to the laws in Bulletins 148, 166, 186, 213, 244, 257, 277, 292, 308, and 330.] *Paper, 10c.

—— Same. (H. doc. 630, 67th Cong. 4th sess.)

Monthly labor review. Monthly labor review, index, [title-page] and contents, v. 13; July–Dec. 1921. 1923. xxx+xiv p. * Paper, 5c.
15—26485

—— Same, v. 17, no. 2; Aug. 1923. 1923. v+297–570 p. il. 3 maps. * Paper, 15c. single copy, $1.50 a yr.; foreign subscription, $2.25.

SPECIAL ARTICLES.—Some effects of operation of California minimum wage law; by Louis Bloch.—Example of arbitration in San Francisco newspaper publishing industry; by David Weiss.—Individual and collective bargaining under Mexican State labor laws; by Martha Dobbin.—Conciliation work of Department of Labor. June, 1923; by Hugh L. Kerwin.—Statistics of immigration. May, 1923; by W. W. Husband.—Immigration during year ending June 30, 1923.—Immigrant aid, State activities, by Mary T. Waggaman.

NOTE.—The Review is the medium through which the Bureau publishes the results of original investigations too brief for bulletin purposes. notices of labor legislation by the States or by Congress, and Federal court decisions affecting labor, which from their importance should be given attention before they could ordinarily appear in the bulletins devoted to these subjects. One free subscription will be given to all labor departments and bureaus, workmen's compensation commissions, and other offices connected with the administration of labor laws and organizations exchanging publications with the Labor Statistics Bureau. Others desiring copies may obtain them from the Superintendent of Documents, Washington, D. C., at the prices stated above.

Prices. Prices and cost of living. [1923.] p. 341–400, il. [From Monthly labor review, Aug. 1923.]. †

—— Retail prices, 1913–Dec. 1922. June, 1923. v+224 p. il. (Bulletin 334; Retail prices and cost of living series.) * Paper, 25c.

—— Same. (H. doc. 634, 67th Cong. 4th sess.)

—— Wholesale prices of commodities for July, 1923. 1923. [1]+9 p. [Monthly.] †
L 22—229

LIBRARY OF CONGRESS

CATALOGUE DIVISION

Subject headings, monthly list [of additions and changes for 2d edition of L. C. subject headings], no. 9; July, 1923. [1923.] 8 leaves. 20—26009

NOTE.—This number includes those headings adopted since the publication, in June, 1922, of the 2d supplement to the 2d edition of Subject headings used in dictionary catalogues of Library of Congress, and covers the months, July, 1922–June, 1923. No. 8 contained the lists for June–Aug. 1921, which were incorporated in the above mentioned 2d supplement to the 2d edition. No. 9, here catalogued, is sent only to those having the 2d edition of the L. C. subject headings and can be obtained from the Card Division, Library of Congress.

COPYRIGHT OFFICE

Copyright. [Catalogue of copyright entries, new series, pt. 1, group 1, Books, v. 20] no. 43–51; Aug. 1923. Aug. 1–30, 1923. p. 401–544. [Issued several times a week.] 6—35347

NOTE.—Each number is issued in 4 parts: pt. 1, group 1, relates to books; pt. 1, group 2, to pamphlets, leaflets, contributions to newspapers or periodicals, etc., lectures, sermons, addresses for oral delivery, dramatic compositions, maps, motion pictures; pt. 2, to periodicals; pt. 3, to musical compositions; pt. 4, to works of art, reproductions of a work of art, drawings or plastic works of scientific or technical character, photographs, prints, and pictorial illustrations.
Subscriptions for the Catalogue of copyright entries should be made to the Superintendent of Documents, Washington, D. C., instead of to the Register of Copyrights. Prices are as follows: Paper, $3.00 a yr. (4 pts.), foreign subscription, $5.00; pt. 1 (groups 1 and 2), 5c. single copy (group 1, price of group 2 varies), $1.00 a yr., foreign subscription, $2.25; pt. 3, $1.00 a yr., foreign subscription, $1.50; pts. 2 and 4, each 10c. single copy, 50c. a yr., foreign subscription, 70c.

—— Same, pt. 1, group 2, Pamphlets, leaflets, contributions to newspapers or periodicals, etc., lectures, sermons, addresses for oral delivery, dramatic compositions; maps, motion pictures, v. 19, volume index [and title-pages, calendar] year 1922. 1923. iii+2089–2521 p.+[3]leaves+[2] p.

—— Same, pt. 1, group 2, Pamphlets, leaflets, contributions to newspapers or periodicals, etc., lectures, sermons, addresses for oral delivery, dramatic compositions, maps, motion pictures, v. 20, no. 4. 1923. iii+327–463 p. [Monthly.]

—— Same, pt. 3, Musical compositions, v. 18, no. 4. 1923. v+217–359 p. [Monthly.]

MIXED CLAIMS COMMISSION, UNITED STATES AND GERMANY

Bennett Trading Company, Incorporated. Nos. 8, 94, and 208, before Mixed Claims Commission, United States and Germany, United States *v.* Germany; United States on behalf of Bennett Trading Company, Incorporated, veterans' Bureau [et al.] *v.* [same]; United States, and United States on behalf of National Fire and Marine Insurance Company *v.* [same]; brief and additional brief on behalf of United States. 1923. cover-title, ii+163 p. 4° ‡

Carlton Machine Tool Company. No. 75, before Mixed Claims Commission, United States and Germany, United States on behalf of Carlton Machine Tool Company *v.* Germany; brief on behalf of United States. 1923. cover-title, 16 p. 4° ‡

NATIONAL ADVISORY COMMITTEE FOR AERONAUTICS

Dynamic stability as affected by longitudinal moment of inertia; by Edwin B. Wilson. 1923. cover-title, 8 p. 4° (Report 172.) [Text and illustration on p. 2 and 3 of cover.] * Paper, 5c. 23—26758

NATIONAL HOME FOR DISABLED VOLUNTEER SOLDIERS

Proceedings of board of managers of National Home for Disabled Volunteer Soldiers, June 19, 1923. June, 1923. [v. 4] p. 268–277. [Quarterly.] ‡

NAVY DEPARTMENT

Court-martial order 6, 1923; June 30, 1923. [1923.] 8 p. 12° [Monthly.] ‡
Orders. General order 109 and 111 [6th series]; June 13 and Aug. 3, 1923.
    [1923.] 19 p. and 1 p. 4° ‡
Wages. Schedule of wages for civil employees under naval establishment, with-
    in continental limits of United States and Pearl Harbor, Hawaii; revised
    to July 16, 1923. 1923. [1]+24 p. ‡

ENGINEERING BUREAU

[*Fuel*, reprint of chapter 38 of Manual of engineering instructions; corrected
    pages.] [1923.] p. 31–32A. [This is printed without title. The signature
    mark reads: 2121—23.] †

MARINE CORPS

Orders. Marine Corps orders 4 and 5, 1923; July 16 and 17, 1923. [1923.]
    2 p. and 1 p. 4° ‡

NAVAL INTELLIGENCE OFFICE

NAVAL RECORDS AND LIBRARY OFFICE

American Naval Planning Section, London; [prepared in] Historical Section.
    1923. v+537 p. il. 7 por. 2 pl. 9 maps, 8 are in pocket. (Publication 7.)
    * Cloth, 80c.   23—26760
    NOTE.—This monograph is virtually a reproduction of the formal records of the
    American Planning Section in London during the Great War, presented in numbered
    memoranda 1–71 (including 42a and 51a). Memoranda 21 and 67 have been omitted
    as being inappropriate for publication at this time.

NAVIGATION BUREAU

Education. Announcement of courses and manual of standard practice pre-
    pared for instruction of enlisted personnel. [Revised] July, 1923. 1923.
    ix+26 p. il. (Navy education-study courses.) [Educational work outlined
    in this pamphlet supplements that now being given in the Navy.] ‡
Naval training. Hints to instructors of recruits; compiled from notes pre-
    pared at [Naval] Training Station, Newport, R. I. 1923. iii+12 p. small
    4° ‡
Navy directory, officers of Navy and Marine Corps, including officers of Naval
    Reserve Force (active), Marine Corps Reserve (active), and foreign officers
    serving with Navy, July 1, 1923. 1923. ii+243 p. [Bimonthly.] * Paper,
    25c. single copy, $1.25 a yr.; foreign subscription, $1.75.
Panama Canal. General conditions on Canal Zone. [1923.] 7 p. † 23—26783

HYDROGRAPHIC OFFICE

    NOTE.—The charts, sailing directions, etc., of the Hydrographic Office are sold by the
office in Washington and also by agents at the principal American and foreign seaports
and American lake ports. Copies of the General catalogue of mariners' charts and books
and of the Hydrographic bulletins, reprints, and Notice to mariners are supplied free on
application at the Hydrographic Office in Washington and at the branch offices in Boston,
New York, Philadelphia, Baltimore, Norfolk, Savannah, New Orleans, Galveston, San
Francisco, Portland (Oreg.), Seattle, Chicago, Cleveland, Buffalo, Sault Ste. Marie,
and Duluth.

Hydrographic bulletin, weekly, no. 1769–73; Aug. 1–29, 1923. [1923.] Each 1
    p. large 4° and f° [For Ice supplements to accompany nos. 1769–73, see be-
    low under center head *Charts* the subhead *Pilot charts.*] †
Notice to aviators 8, 1923; Aug. 1 [1923]. 1923. 1 p. [Monthly.] †
                                                  20—26958
Notice to mariners. Index to Notices to mariners, nos. 1–26, 1923. 1923.
    [1]+34 p. †
—— Notice to mariners 31–34, 1923; Aug. 4–25 [1923]. [1923.] [xxxvi]+
    807–914 leaves. [Weekly.] †

Tide calendars. Tide calendar [for Baltimore (Fells Point) and Cape Henry], Sept. 1923. [1923.] 1 p. 4° [Monthly.] †

—— Tide calendar [for Norfolk (Navy Yard) and Newport News, Va.], Sept. 1923. [1923.] 1 p. 4° [Monthly.] †

Charts

Pilot charts. Ice supplement to north Atlantic pilot chart; issue 69. Scale 1° long.=0.3 in. Washington, Hydrographic Office [1923]. 8.9×11.8 in. [To accompany Hydrographic bulletin 1769, Aug. 1, 1923.] †

—— Same; issue 70. Scale 1° long.=0.3 in. Washington, Hydrographic Office [1923]. 8.9×11.8 in. [To accompany Hydrographic bulletin 1770, Aug. 8, 1923.] †

—— Same; issue 71. Scale 1° long.=0.3 in. Washington, Hydrographic Office [1923]. 8.9×11.8 in. [To accompany Hydrographic bulletin 1771, Aug. 15, 1923.] †

—— Same; issue 72. Scale 1° long.=0.3 in. Washington, Hydrographic Office. [1923]. 8.9×11.8 in. [To accompany Hydrographic bulletin 1772, Aug. 22, 1923.] †

—— Same; issue 73. Scale 1° long.=0.3 in. Washington, Hydrographic Office [1923]. 8.9×11.8 in. [To accompany Hydrographic bulletin 1773, Aug. 29, 1923.] †

—— Pilot chart of Central American waters, Sept. 1923; chart 3500. Scale 1° long.=0.7 in. Washington, Hydrographic Office, Aug. 13, 1923. 23.4×35.1 in. [Monthly. Certain portions of the data are furnished by the Weather Bureau.] † 10c.

NOTE.—Contains on reverse: Cyclonic storms.

—— Pilot chart of Indian Ocean, Oct. 1923; chart 2603. Scale 1° long.=0.2 in. Washington, Hydrographic Office, Aug. 13, 1923. 22.6×31 in. [Monthly. Certain portions of the data are furnished by the Weather Bureau.] † 10c.

NOTE.—Contains on reverse: Cyclonic storms.

—— Pilot chart of north Atlantic Ocean, Sept. 1923; chart 1400. Scale 1° long.=0.27 in. Washington, Hydrographic Office, Aug. 13, 1923. 23.2×31.8 in. [Monthly. Certain portions of the data are furnished by the Weather Bureau.] † 10c.　　　　14—16339

NOTE.—Contains on reverse: Cyclonic storms.

NAVAL ACADEMY

Electric engineering. Laboratory manual, manual for practical work and drills to be used in conjunction with course in electrical engineering at Naval Academy, 1st class; [prepared in] Department of Electrical Engineering and Physics. 1923. 56 p. il. 4° [Issued in loose-leaf form. Pages 10–56 have blank spaces for the recording of experiments with instructions for the performance of the same.] ‡

—— Laboratory manual, manual for practical work and drills to be used in conjunction with course in electrical engineering at Naval Academy, 2d class electricity, annex laboratory, B group, 1923–24; [prepared in] Department of Electrical Engineering and Physics. 1923. 47 p. il. 4° [Issued in loose-leaf form. Pages 7–47 have blank spaces for the recording of experiments with instructions for the performance of the same.] ‡

Regulations of Naval Academy, 1923; [pt. 1, Organization and general regulations; pt. 2, Interior discipline and government]. 1923. iv+87 p. il. ‡
　　　　9—35730

ORDNANCE BUREAU

Craven, Francis S. In Patent Office, interference no. 46578, Craven v. Foley; brief for Craven. 1923. cover-title, 23 p. ‡

—— Same; record and testimony of Craven. 1923. cover-title; 43 p. ‡

Harrison, John K. M. Interference no. 45648, in Patent Office, John K. M. Harrison v. Ralph C. Browne; record for Ralph C. Browne. 1923. v. 1, cover-title, ii+580 p. ‡

SUPPLIES AND ACCOUNTS BUREAU

Naval supplies. Sale of Navy surplus, instruments of precision, bids will be opened Sept. 7, 1923, Central Sales Office, Navy Yard, Washington, D. C. 1923. cover-title, 31 p. (Catalogue 222B.) †

Supply Corps, Navy. Memoranda for information of officers of Supply Corps, commanding officers of ships, and commandants 251; July 1, 1923. [1923.] p. 7413–7516, 12° [Monthly.] ‡

——. Same 252; Aug. 1, 1923. [1923.] p. 7517–96, il. 12° [Monthly.] ‡

PAN AMERICAN UNION

NOTE.—The Pan American Union sells its own monthly bulletins, handbooks, etc., at prices usually ranging from 5c. to $2.50. The price of the English edition of the bulletin is 25c. a single copy or $2.50 a year, the Spanish edition $2.00 a year, the Portuguese edition $1.50 a year; there is an additional charge of 50c. a year on each edition for countries outside the Pan American Union. Address the Director General of the Pan American Union, Washington, D. C.

Bulletin (English edition). Bulletin of Pan American Union, Aug. 1923; [v. 57, no. 2]. [1923.] iv+109–216 p. il. [Monthly. This number is entitled 5th International Conference of American States (5th Pan American Conference), Santiago, Chile, Mar. 25–May 3, 1923.] 8—30967

—— Same. (H. doc. 6, pt. 2, 68th Cong. 1st sess.)

—— *(Portuguese edition).* Boletim da União Pan-Americana, Agosto, 1923, edição portugueza; [v. 25, no. 2]. [Sun Job Print, Baltimore, Md., 1923.] [iv]+77–152 p. il. [Monthly. This number is entitled A mortalidade infantil e os meios de a reduzir.] 11—27014

—— *(Spanish edition).* Boletín de la Unión Panamericana, Agosto, 1923, edición española; [v. 57, no. 2]. [1923.] iv+109–216 p. il. [Monthly.] 12—12555

Dominican Republic. Commerce of Dominican Republic, latest reports from Dominican official sources. 1923. [1]+10+[1] p. † 13—7275

International Telephone and Telegraph Corporation (Corporación Internacional de Teléfonos y Telégrafos). 1923. [2]+14 p. il. [From Boletín, Aug. 1923.] †

Music. Indigenous music in Colombia; [by Emilio Murillo]. 1923. 4 p. [From Bulletin, July, 1923.] †

Nurses and nursing. La profesión de enfermera; [por Lucy E. Minnegerode]. 1923. [2]+14 p. il. [From Boletín, July, 1923.] †

PANAMA CANAL

NOTE.—Although The Panama Canal makes its reports to, and is under the supervision of, the Secretary of War, it is not a part of the War Department.

Panama Canal record. Panama Canal record, v. 16, no. 51 and 52; Aug. 1 and 8, 1923. Balboa Heights, C. Z. [1923]. p. 673–692. [Weekly.] 7—35328

NOTE.—The Panama Canal record is furnished free to United States Government departments and bureaus, Members of Congress, representatives of foreign Governments, steamship lines, and public libraries. Others desiring this publication may obtain it at the subscription price of $1.50 per year in the Canal Zone, the United States, and the Republic of Panama; $2.00 per year elsewhere. Remittances for subscriptions may be forwarded to The Panama Canal, Washington, D. C., or to The Panama Canal Record, Balboa Heights, Canal Zone, Isthmus of Panama.

—— Same, v. 17, no. 1–3; Aug. 15–29, 1923. Balboa Heights, C. Z. [1923]. p. 1–64. [Weekly.]

GOVERNOR

Maintenance and operation of The Panama Canal; by Jay J. Morrow. Panama Canal Press, Mount Hope, C. Z., 1923. 44 p. il. [Lecture delivered before New York section, American Society of Civil Engineers, New York City, Jan. 10, 1923, and repeated before Society of Civil Engineers, Washington, D. C., Jan. 17, 1923.] † 23—26784

HEALTH DEPARTMENT

Ancon Hospital, operated by Health Department of The Panama Canal, at Ancon, C. Z. Panama Canal Press, Mt. Hope, C. Z., 1923. cover-title, 8 p. il. large 8° †

PURCHASING DEPARTMENT

Supplies. Circular [proposals for supplies] 1549 and 1555; July 31 and Aug. 30, 1923. [1923.] 25+[1] p. and 32 p. f° † .

—— Proposals [for supplies 1549 and 1555, to accompany Circular proposals for supplies 1549 and 1555]. [1923.] Each 1 p. 24° ‡

POST OFFICE DEPARTMENT

Mail matter. Ascertainment of cost of handling and transporting the several classes of mail matter and conducting special services: Instruction letter D–a (series D), [June 15, 1923] revised Aug. 1, 1923, Time and expenditures, 1st-class post offices. [1923.] 10 p. ‡

—— Same: Instruction letter D–d (series D), [Dec. 1, 1922] revised Aug. 1, 1923, Time and expenditures, 2d-class post offices. [1923.] 8 p. ‡

—— Same: Instruction letter R [Aug. 1, 1923], Report of revenues represented by stamps affixed to Railway Mail Service drop mails and railroad station letter-box collections for 30 days at specially designated post offices, Sept. 21–Oct. 20, 1923. [1923.] 4 p. ‡

—— Same: Instruction letter R–dt [Aug. 24, 1923], Railway postal clerks' time report. [1923.] 3 p. ‡

—— Same: Instruction letter R–ps, Publications in publisher's sacks distributed by railway postal clerks in designated R. P. O.'s, terminals, and transfer offices. [1923.] 2 p. ‡

—— Same: Instruction letter R–t [Aug. 1, 1923], Railway Mail Service tests. [1923.] 5 p. ‡

—— Same: Instruction letter R–v-t [Aug. 1, 1923], Volume tests of sack mails distributed in railway post offices. [1923.] 5 p. ‡

Parcel post. Senders of refused parcels to be promptly notified if such parcels be presented for delivery second time they are subject to additional postage at local rate; [issued by] 3d assistant Postmaster General. Aug. 7, 1923. 1 p. †

—— Same, with correction. Aug. 14, 1923. 1 p. 12° †

Postage-stamps. New air mail stamps, series 1923; [issued by] 3d assistant Postmaster General. Aug. 15, 1923. 1 p. 12° †

—— New Harding memorial stamp, series 1923; [issued by] 3d assistant Postmaster General. Aug. 23, 1923. 1 p. 4° †

—— Where to buy stamps, and why; [issued by] 3d assistant Postmaster General. July 30, 1923. 1 p. †

Postal bulletin, v. 44, no. 13232–255; Aug. 1–31, 1923. 1923. various paging, f° [Daily except Sundays and holidays; none issued Aug. 8–10, 1923.]
 * Paper, 5c. single copy, $2.00 a yr. 6—5810

Postal guide. Abridged United States official postal guide [2d series, v. 3]; July, 1923. 1923. 675 p. [For official use only.] ‡

—— State list of post offices [3d series, v. 3]; July, 1923. 1923. cover-title, p. 225-663. [Text on p. 2 of cover. From United States official postal guide, July, 1923. The State list is for official use only.] ‡ 22—26854

—— United States official postal guide, 4th series, v. 3, no. 2; Aug. 1923, monthly supplement. 1923. cover-title, ii+61 p. il. [Includes Modification 22 of International money order list, pamphlet 14, and Inserts 821–832 to Postal laws and regulations of United States. Text on p. 2–4 of cover.]
 * Official postal guide, with supplements, $1.00; foreign subscription, $1.50; July issue, 75c.; supplements published monthly (11 pamphlets) 25c., foreign subscription, 50c.

FOREIGN MAILS DIVISION

Steamboats. ↘ Schedule of steamers appointed to convey mails to foreign countries during July, 1923. June 20, 1923. 1 p. f° [Monthly.] *Paper, 5c. single copy, 25c. a yr.; foreign subscription, 50c.

—— Same during Aug. 1923. July 21, 1923. 1 p. f° [Monthly.]

—— Same during Sept. 1923. Aug. 20, 1923. 1 p. f° [Monthly.]

MONEY ORDERS DIVISION

Money-orders. General instructions to postmaster at newly established domestic money order office. [1923, reprint with changes.] 4 p. 4° †

RAILWAY MAIL SERVICE

Mail-trains. Schedule of mail trains, no. 87, Aug. 1, 1923, 12th division, Railway Mail Service, comprising Louisiana and Mississippi. 1923. 80 p. narrow 8° ‡

—— Schedule of mail trains, no. 441, July 24, 1923, 3d division, Railway Mail Service, comprising District of Columbia, Maryland, North Carolina, Virginia, and West Virginia (except peninsula of Maryland and Virginia). 1923. 141+[1] p. narrow 8° ‡

TOPOGRAPHY DIVISION

NOTE.—Since February, 1908, the Topography Division has been preparing rural-delivery maps of counties in which rural delivery is completely established. They are published in two forms, one giving simply the rural free delivery routes, starting from a single given post office, sold at 10 cents each; the other, the rural free delivery routes in an entire county, sold at 35 cents each. A uniform scale of 1 inch to 1 mile is used. Editions are not issued, but sun-print copies are produced in response to special calls addressed to the Disbursing Clerk, Post Office Department, Washington, D. C. These maps should not be confused with the post route maps, for which see Monthly catalogue for February, 1923, page 528.

Rural mail delivery. Price list of rural delivery county maps, Apr. 1, 1923 [corrected to Aug. 1, 1923]. [1923.] 1 p. narrow f° [Manuscript corrections.] †

PRESIDENT OF UNITED STATES

Arizona. Executive order, Arizona [withdrawing certain described public lands in Arizona from settlement, etc., pending resurvey, such withdrawal to remain in effect until resurvey is accepted and approved plats thereof are officially filed in local land office.] July 27, 1923. 1 p. f° (No. 3882.) ‡

Arkansas. Executive order [transferring Arkansas from 45th (St. Louis) customs collection district to 43d (Tennessee) customs collection district, headquarters Memphis, Tenn., effective Oct. 1, 1923]. July 27, 1923. 1 p. f° (No. 3879.) ‡

Banks, William. Executive order [providing that trust period on allotment made to William Banks, deceased Sac and Fox allottee, located in Richardson County, Nebr., which expires Aug. 5, 1923, be extended for period of one year]. July 27, 1923. 1 p. f° (No. 3878.) ‡

Braddock, Ada. Executive order [authorizing Ada Braddock of General Land Office to sign land patents during absence of clerk designated for that service]. Aug. 4, 1923. 1 p. f° (No. 3887.) ‡

California. Executive order, California [temporarily withdrawing certain described lands in California for purpose of classification and pending enactment of appropriate legislation for their proper disposition]. Aug. 13, 1923. 1 p. f° (No. 3890.) ‡

—— Executive order, California [temporarily withdrawing certain described lands in California for use by Forest Service in connection with contemplated road construction in Cleveland National Forest, Calif.]. Aug. 13, 1923. 1 p. f° (No. 3891.) ‡

Colorado. Executive order, Colorado [withdrawing certain described public lands in Colorado from settlement, etc., pending resurvey, such withdrawal to remain in effect until resurvey is accepted and approved plats thereof are officially filed in local land office]. July 27, 1923. 1 p. f° (No. 3883.) ‡

Customs Service. Executive order [creating Cambridge, Md., as customs port of entry in 13th customs collection district (Maryland), with headquarters at Baltimore, Md., effective Oct. 1, 1923]. Aug. 13, 1923. 1 p. f° (No. 3888.) ‡

Harding, Warren G. Death of Warren Gamaliel Harding, President of United States, proclamation [appointing Aug. 10, 1923, as day of mourning and prayer]. Aug. 4, 1923. 1 p. f° (No. 1669.) †

Jefferson Barracks. Executive order [restoring to War Department for military purposes in connection with its occupancy and use of Jefferson Barracks military reservation certain described tract of land previously assigned by Executive order of Jan. 9, 1922, to veterans' Bureau]. July 27, 1923. 1 p. f° (No. 3884.) ‡

Michigan. Executive order, Michigan [temporarily withdrawing an island situated in Bud Lake, Mich., from all disposition until Mar. 5, 1925, for purpose of classification and in aid of proposed legislation]. July 27, 1923. 1 p. f° (No. 3880.) ‡

Military reservations. Executive order [authorizing that certain described military reservations in Washington and California, having become useless for military purposes, be placed under control of Secretary of Interior for disposition as provided by law]. [Aug. 13, 1923.] 2 p. f° ([No. 3893.]) ‡

—— Executive order [setting aside certain lands on island of Oahu, Hawaii, for military purposes]. [July 27, 1923.] 8 p. f° ([No. 3885.]) ‡

National forests. Executive order, administrative site, near Manzano National Forest, N. Mex. [temporarily withdrawing certain described lands from settlement, etc., and reserving same for use by Forest Service as ranger station in connection with administration of Manzano National Forest]. Aug. 13, 1923. 1 p. f° (No. 3889.) ‡

—— Executive order, Tongass National Forest, Alaska [directing that certain described lands heretofore occupied for fish cannery purposes, be excluded from Tongass National Forest and restored to entry under applicable public land laws]. July 27, 1923. 1 p. f° (No. 3881.) ‡

Pugh, Mrs. Viola B. Executive order [authorizing Mrs. Viola B. Pugh of General Land Office to sign land patents]. Aug. 4, 1923. 1 p. f° (No. 3886.) ‡

Utah. Executive order, Utah [withdrawing certain described public lands in Utah from settlement, etc., pending resurvey, such withdrawal to remain in effect until resurvey is accepted and approved plats thereof are officially filed in local land office]. Aug. 13, 1923. 1 p. f° (No. 3892.) ‡

RAILROAD ADMINISTRATION

Asbestos. Before Interstate Commerce Commission, no. 14233, Cutler-Hammer Manufacturing Company *v.* director general et al.; brief for director general. 1923. cover-title, 9 p. ‡

Cast-iron. Before Interstate Commerce Commission, no. 14841, Keystone Steel and Wire Company *v.* director general et al.; brief for director general. 1923. cover-title, 7 p. ‡

Central New England Railway. Final settlement between director general of railroads and Central New England Railway Company,—,1923. 1923. 3 p. 4° †

Clay. Before Interstate Commerce Commission, no. 14077, Louisville Pottery Company *v.* director general; exceptions on part of director general to report proposed by examiner. 1923. cover-title, 15 p. ‡

Coal. Before Interstate Commerce Commission, no. 12821, Utah Fuel Company *v.* director general; petition for further hearing on behalf of director general. 1923. cover-title, 24 p. ‡

Coal-tar. Before Interstate Commerce Commission, docket no. 14216, 14294–295, Barrett Company *v.* director general; exceptions on behalf of director general to report proposed by examiner. 1923. cover-title, 10 p. ‡

Coke. Before Interstate Commerce Commission, no. 14609, Delta Beet Sugar Corporation *v.* director general et al.; brief for director general. 1923. cover-title, 8 p. ‡

Corn. Before Interstate Commerce Commission, no. 14543, H. C. Farrell *v.* director general et al.; brief filed on behalf of director general. 1923. cover-title, 12 p. ‡

Creosote. Before Interstate Commerce Commission, no. 14514, Shreveport Creosoting Company *v.* director general; brief for director general. 1923. cover-title, 16 p. ‡

Detroit, Toledo and Ironton Railroad. Final settlement between director general of railroads and Detroit, Toledo and Ironton Railroad Company,—, 1923. 1923. 3 p. 4° †

Freight rates. Before Interstate Commerce Commission, no. 12195, Crown Willamette Paper Company *v.* director general et al.; exceptions on behalf of director general to examiner's proposed report. 1923. cover-title, 2 p. ‡

—— Before Interstate Commerce Commission, no. 14180, Doniphan Brick Works *v.* director general et al.; exceptions on behalf of director general to report proposed by examiner. 1923. cover-title, 3 p. ‡

—— Before Interstate Commerce Commission, no. 14210, Lindeteves-Stokvis *v.* director general et al.; brief on part of director general. 1923. cover-title, 16 p. ‡

—— Before Interstate Commerce Commission, no. 14694, Traffic Bureau of Nashville et al. *v.* director general et al.; brief for director general. 1923. cover-title, 6 p. ‡

Industrial railroads. Before Interstate Commerce Commission, no. 11275, Carneg'e Steel Company *v.* director general et al.; petition on part of director general for rehearing or reargument. 1923. cover-title, 10 p. ‡

Limestone. Before Interstate Commerce Commission, no. 14568, Amalgamated Sugar Company *v.* director general et al.; brief for director general. 1923. cover-title, 9 p. ‡

Locomotives. Before Interstate Commerce Commission, no. 14643, Colorado Fuel and Iron Company *v.* director general et al.; brief for director general. 1923. cover-title, 10 p. ‡

Lumber. Before Interstate Commerce Commission, no. 14242, Consolidated Lumber Company *v.* director general; answer to complainants' exceptions. [1923.] cover-title, 4 p. ‡

Paper. Before Interstate Commerce Commission, no. 14309, Kalamazoo Vegetable Parchment Company *v.* director general et al.; exceptions on behalf of director general. 1923. cover-title, 4 p. ‡

Reconsignment. Before Interstate Commerce Commission, no. 14176, Flanley Grain Company *v.* director general et al.; no. 14175, Turner Grain Company *v.* [same]; no. 13263, Washburn-Crosby Company *v.* [same]; exceptions on behalf of director general to report of examiners. 1923. cover-title, 6 p. ‡

St. Louis Southwestern Railway. Final settlement between director general of railroads and St. Louis Southwestern Railway Company and other corporations, —, 1923. 1923. 4 p. 4° †

Sand. Before Interstate Commerce Commission, no. 14755, United Engineering & Foundry Company *v.* director general; brief on part of director general. 1923. cover-title, 10 p. ‡

Tan-bark. Before Interstate Commerce Commission, no. 14937, American Hide & Leather Company *v.* director general; brief for director general. 1923. cover-title, 12 p. ‡

Wood. Before Interstate Commerce Commission, no. 14741, Phillips Excelsior Company *v.* director general et al.; brief for director general. 1923. cover-title, 5 p. ‡

Wool. Before Interstate Commerce Commission, no. 13318, Boston Wool Trade Association *v.* director general; petition for further consideration on part of director general. 1923. cover-title, 11 p. ‡

Zinc. Before Interstate Commerce Commission, no. 13227, New Jersey Zinc Company *v.* director general et al.; brief on part of director general on further hearing. 1923. cover-title, 9 p. ‡

RAILROAD LABOR BOARD

Decisions of Railroad Labor Board with addenda and interpretations, 1922, with appendix showing resolutions and announcements of Railroad Labor Board. 1923. v. 3, v+1252 p. * Paper, $1.00.   21—26844

SHIPPING BOARD

Cigarette papers. Docket no. 13, American Tobacco Company *v.* Compagnie Generale Transatlantique (French line) ; decided July 17, 1923; report of board. [1923.] p. 53–57. [From Shipping Board reports, v. 1.] †

Misrouting. Docket no. 12, Boston Wool Trade Association *v.* General Steamship Corporation, Oceanic Steamship Company, and Union Steamship Company; decided July 17, 1923; report [and order] of board. [1923.] 49–52+ [1] p. [Report from Shipping Board reports, v. 1.] †

SMITHSONIAN INSTITUTION

NOTE.—In a recent price-list the Smithsonian Institution publishes this notice: "Applicants for the publications in this list are requested to state the grounds of their requests, as the Institution is able to supply papers only as an aid to the researches or studies in which they are especially interested. These papers are distributed *gratis*, except as otherwise indicated, and should be ordered by the *publication numbers* arranged in sequence. The serial publications of the Smithsonian Institution are as follows: 1. Smithsonian contributions to knowledge; 2. Smithsonian miscellaneous collections; 3. Smithsonian annual reports. No *sets* of these are for sale or distribution, as most of the volumes are out of print. The papers issued in the series of Contributions to knowledge and Miscellaneous collections are distributed without charge to public libraries, educational establishments, learned societies, and specialists in this country and abroad; and are supplied to other institutions and individuals at the prices indicated. Remittances should be made payable to the 'Smithsonian Institution.' The Smithsonian report volumes and the papers reprinted in separate form therefrom are distributed *gratuitously* by the Institution to libraries and individuals throughout the world. Very few of the Report volumes are now available at the Institution, but many of those of which the Smithsonian edition is exhausted can be purchased from the Superintendent of Documents, Government Printing Office, Washington, D. C. The Institution maintains mailing-lists of public libraries and other educational establishments, but no *general mailing-list of individuals.* A library making application to be listed for Smithsonian publications should state the number of volumes which it contains and the date of its establishment, and have the endorsement of a Member of Congress.'

The annual reports are the only Smithsonian publications that are regularly issued as public documents. All the others are paid for from the private funds of the Institution, but as they are usually regarded as public documents and have free transmission by mail they are listed in the Monthly catalogue.

Cetaceans. Telescoping of cetacean skull; by Gerrit S. Miller, jr. Washington, Smithsonian Institution, Aug. 31, 1923. [2]+ 70 p. 8 pl. (Publication 2720; Smithsonian miscellaneous collections, v. 76, no. 5.) † Paper, 40c. 23—26785

Crinoids. On fossil crinoid family Catillocrinidae; by Frank Springer. Washington, Smithsonian Institution, Aug. 3, 1923. [2]+41 p. 5 pl. (Publication 2718; Smithsonian miscellaneous collections, v. 76, no. 3.) †Paper, 25c.
                                                                             23—26732

Electric lighting. History of electric light [with bibliography]; by Henry Schroeder. Washington, Smithsonian Institution, Aug. 15, 1923. xiii+94+ [1] p. il. (Publication 2717; Smithsonian miscellaneous collections, v. 76, no. 2.) †   23—26734

Publications of Smithsonian Institution, Apr. 15, 1922–Sept. 1, 1923. [1923.] 2 p. ([Publication] 2746.) [This list does not include publications issued by the National Museum or the Bureau of American Ethnology.] †

STATE DEPARTMENT

[*Circular*] 902; June 30, 1923. [1923.] 3 p. [General instruction circular to consular officers.] ‡

Consular courts. Manual of probate procedure in American consular courts in China; [by] John K. Davis and Walter E. Smith. 1923. vii+32 p. *Paper, 5c.   23—26763

Consuls. Foreign consular officers in United States; corrected to July 2, 1923. 1923. .[1]+42 p. *Paper, 10c.   23—26762

Diplomatic and consular service of United States; corrected to July 2, 1923. 1923. 68 p. ‡   10—16369

Diplomatic list, Aug. 1923. [1923.] cover-title, ii+34 p. 24° [Monthly.] ‡
                                                                                        10—16292

International American Conference. Report of delegates of United States to 5th International Conference of American States held at Santiago, Chile, Mar. 25–May 3, 1923. .1923. v+37 p. *Paper, 5c.   23—26761

NOTE.—Appendix 1 refers to personnel of United States delegation, which appears on p. 33 of this publication. Other appendices referred to herein will be published as soon as certified copies of the records of the conference have been received from the Chilean Government.

Narcotics. Traffic in habit-forming narcotic drugs, statement of attitude of Government of United States with documents relating thereto. 1923. viii+24 p. large 8° *Paper, 5c.   23—26786

PASSPORT CONTROL DIVISION .

Passports. Notice concerning use of passports [June 20, 1923]. [1923.] 8 p. †

SUPREME COURT

Official reports of Supreme Court, v. 261 U. S., no. 1; Ernest Knaebel, reporter. Preliminary print. 1923. cover-title, ix+1–164 p. ii. 12° [Cases adjudged in Supreme Court at Oct. term, 1922 (opinions of Feb. 19, 1923, in part). This number contains a list of cases reported in v. 260. Text on p. 2 and 4 of cover. From United States reports, v. 261.] * Paper, 25c. single copy, $1.00 per vol. (4 nos. to a vol.; subscription price, $3.00 for 12 nos.) ; foreign subscription, 5c. added for each pamphlet.

TREASURY DEPARTMENT

Finance. Daily statement of Treasury compiled from latest proved reports from Treasury offices and depositaries, Aug. 1–31, 1923. [1923.] Each 4 p. or 3 p. f° [Daily except Sundays and holidays.] †   15—3303

Public debt. Statement of public debt of United States. May 31, 1923. 1923. [2] p. narrow f° [Monthly. Date of issue incorrectly given as May 4, 1923.] †   10—21268

Telephone. Amendment to Telephone instructions [Coast Guard, 1919] no. 1 [new series] ; June 30, 1923. 1923. 1 p. [Accompanied by reprints of certain pages to be inserted in their proper places in the original instructions. A list of these reprinted pages is given on the first page. Telephone instructions issued by Coast Guard.] ‡

Treasury decisions. Index to Treasury decisions under customs and other laws, v. 43, Jan.–June, 1923. 1923. [1]+26 p. * Paper, 5c. single copy, included in price of Treasury decisions for subscribers.

—— Treasury decisions under customs, internal revenue, and other laws, including decisions of Board of General Appraisers and Court of Customs Appeals, v. 44, no. 5–9; Aug. 2–30, 1923. 1923. various paging. [Weekly. Department decisions numbered 39746–777, general appraisers' decisions 8673–79, abstracts 46187–217, internal revenue decisions 3501–9 (except 3507, which has been printed as supplement to Treasury decisions, for which see, below, under Internal Revenue Bureau), Tariff Commission Notices 28–31, and later Tariff Commission Notice 7.] * Paper, 5c. single copy, $1.00 a yr.; foreign subscription, $2.00.   10—30490

APPRAISERS

Reappraisements of merchandise by general appraisers [on July 17–Aug. 24, 1923]; Aug. 17–31, 1923. [1923.] 24 p. and 11 p. (Reappraisement circulars 3472–73.) [Weekly; none issued July 27, Aug. 3, 10, and 24, 1923.] * Paper, 5c. single copy, 50c. a yr.; foreign subscription, $1.05.   13—2916

BUDGET BUREAU

INTERDEPARTMENTAL BOARD OF CONTRACTS AND ADJUSTMENTS

Report. Annual report of chairman of Interdepartmental Board of Contracts and Adjustments to director of Bureau of Budget, July 1, 1923. 1923. iii+ 25 p. †   23—26787

COAST GUARD

Circular letter 295 [new series]; July 19, 1923. 1923. 1 p. ‡

Orders. General order 33; July 21, 1923. 1923. 1 p. [Accompanied by reprints of certain pages to be inserted in their proper places in the original regulations. A list of these reprinted pages is found on the first page.] ‡

Register of commissioned officers on active list of Coast Guard, July 1, 1923. 1923. [1]+10 p. * Paper, 5c.   15—26534

Uniforms. Regulations governing uniforms for commissioned and warrant officers of Coast Guard, 1923. 1923. iii+28 p. 10 p. of pl. [Issued in looseleaf form for insertion in binder.] * Paper, 10c.

COMPTROLLER OF CURRENCY

National banks. Monthly statement of capital stock of national banks, national bank notes, and Federal reserve bank notes outstanding, bonds on deposit, etc. [Aug. 1, 1923]. Aug. 1, 1923. 1 p. f° †   10—21266

FEDERAL FARM LOAN BUREAU

Agricultural credit. Farm loan primer, here you will find in brief form answers to questions most frequently asked about Federal farm loan act and amendments thereto. [Edition of] July, 1923. 1923. ii+10 p. (Circular 5 revised.) †   23—26765

Rulings and regulations of Federal Farm Loan Board to July 1, 1923, in matters pertaining to Federal farm loan act. Aug. 1923. ii+14 p. (Circular 10 revised.) †   23—26733

GOVERNMENT ACTUARY

Bonds of United States. Market prices and investment values of outstanding bonds and notes [of United States, July, 1923]. Aug. 1, 1923. 7 p. 4° (Form A.) [Monthly.] †

INTERNAL REVENUE BUREAU

Cider. Prohibition, manufacture of cider and vinegar, article 5, Regulations 60 amended. [1923.] 4 p. ([Treasury decision] 3498.) [From Treasury decisions, v. 44, no. 4.] †

Income tax, ownership certificates, articles 365, 367, 369–370, 1074, 1076–79 of Regulations 62 amended. [1923.] 3 p. ([Treasury decision] 3497.) [From Treasury decisions, v. 44, no. 3.] †

Internal revenue bulletin, v. 2, no. 18–21; Aug. 6–27, 1923. 1923. various paging. [Weekly.] *Paper, 5c. single copy (for subscription price see note below).   22—26051

NOTE.—On May 7, 1923, the publication of weekly bulletins was resumed and the issuance of monthly bulletins (and special bulletins as occasion required) discontinued. Since May 1, therefore, the 1923 Internal revenue bulletin service consists of weekly bulletins of new rulings and decisions of the Bureau of Internal Revenue and internal revenue Treasury decisions of general importance, quarterly digests of such new rulings (cumulative from Jan. 1, 1922), and semiannual cumulative bulletins containing in full the new rulings and decisions published during the preceding 6 months. The complete bulletin service may be obtained on a subscription basis, from the Superintendent of Documents, Government Printing Office, Washington, D. C., for $2.00 a yr.; foreign subscription, $2.75.

Oleomargarin. Regulations 9 relating to taxes on oleomargarine, adulterated butter, and process or renovated butter under act of Aug. 2, 1886, as amended by act of May 9, 1902. Revised June, 1923. 1923. vi+101 p. ([Treasury decision] 3507.) [Supplement to Treasury decisions, v. 44, no. 8.] *Paper, 10c.

FEDERAL PROHIBITION COMMISSIONER

Liquors. Instructions relative to reports on Form 1421 [report of alcohol and other liquor used for nonbeverage purposes, and sold on physicians' prescriptions by holders of permit on Form 1405, under national prohibition act]. [1923 reprint.] 4 p. (Pro-mimeograph, pro. no. 315.) †

LOANS AND CURRENCY DIVISION

Bonds of United States. Caveat list of United States registered bonds and notes, Aug. 1, 1923. [1923.] 54 p. f° [Monthly.] †

Money. Circulation statement, Aug. 1, 1923. [1923.] 1 p. oblong 8°
[Monthly.] †   10—21267

PUBLIC HEALTH SERVICE

Goiter. Prevention of simple goiter; by O. P. Kimball. 1923. 11 p. il. (Reprint 832.) [From Public health reports, Apr. 27, 1923.] *Paper, 5c.
                                                                23—26788

Hygiene, Public. State laws and regulations pertaining to public health, 1920; compiled by Jason Waterman and William Fowler. 1923. xv+457 p. (Supplement 43 to Public health reports.) *Paper, 25c.   20—26967

Malaria. Distribution of malaria in United States as indicated by mortality reports; by Kenneth F. Maxcy. 1923. 16 p. il. (Reprint 839.) [From Public health reports, May 25, 1923.] *Paper, 5c.   23—26789

Public health reports, v. 38, no. 31–35; Aug. 3–31, 1923. 1923. [xx]+1747–2051 p. il. [Weekly.] *Paper, 5c. single copy, $1.50 a yr.; foreign subscription, $2.75.   6—25167

SPECIAL ARTICLES.—No 31. Standardization of insulin: 1, Toxicity of insulin for white rats as influenced by temperature of room in which animals are kept; by Carl Voegtlin and Edith R. Dunn.—Dengue fever [with bibliography]; by C. Armstrong.—No. 32. Curative action of sulpharsphenamine in experimental syphilis [with list of references]; by Carl Voegtlin, C. Armstrong, and Helen A. Dyer.—Notifiable diseases, prevalence during 1922 in cities of over 100,000.—No. 33. Plague-infected rats without visible lesions, discovery of bubonic plague only in rats without lesions or with obscure or apparently trivial lesions, after subsidence of 2 recent epizootics [with list of references]; by C. L. Williams and T. W. Kemmerer.—On mechanism of action of arsenic upon protoplasm [with list of references]; by Carl Voegtlin, Helen A. Dyer, and C. S. Leonard.—No. 34. Nomenclature of melitensis-abortus group of bacterial organisms [with list of references]; by Alice C. Evans.—Serological classification of Brucella melitensis from human, bovine, caprine, porcine, and equine sources [with list of references]; by Alice C. Evans.—Devil's grip in Virginia; by C. Armstrong.—No. 35. On composition of precipitate from partially alkalinized alum solutions [with bibliography]; by Lewis B. Miller.—Collection and preservation of blood samples for determination of carbon monoxide; by R. R. Sayers, H. R. O'Brien, G. W. Jones, and W. P. Yant.—Automobile cost in rural health work, report on operation of automobiles in cooperative rural health work in Virginia; by H. McG. Robertson.—Sanitation of tourist camps.—Demand among sanitarians and practicing physicians for supplemental academic training.

NOTE.—This publication is distributed gratuitously to State and municipal health officers, etc., by the Surgeon General of the Public Health Service, Treasury Department. Others desiring these reports may obtain them from the Superintendent of Documents, Washington, D. C., at the prices stated above.

Publications. Public Health Service publications, list of publications issued Oct. 1922–Apr. 1923. 1923. 4 p. (Reprint 838.) [From Public health reports, May 18, 1923.] *Paper, 5c.   23—26767

VENEREAL DISEASES DIVISION

Venereal disease information, issued by Public Health Service for use in its cooperative work with State health departments, v. 4, no. 7; July 20, 1923. 1923. ii+239–283+iii p. [Monthly.] *Paper, 5c. single copy, 50c. a yr.
SPECIAL ARTICLE.—Report of Committee of Inquiry on Venereal Disease, England.

TREASURER OF UNITED STATES

Paper money. Monthly statement, paper currency of each denomination outstanding June 30, 1923. July 2 [1923]. 1 p. oblong 24° †

VETERANS' BUREAU

Life insurance. [Specimen policy — - -year endowment policy.] A. Hoen & Co., Baltimore [1923]. [4] p. il. f° (Form 751.) [Although this policy uses Bureau of War Risk Insurance in the text, it is signed by the director appointed for the veterans' Bureau in 1923.] †

WAR DEPARTMENT

Army regulations. †

NOTE.—The Army regulations are issued in pamphlet form for insertion in loose-leaf binders. The names of such of the more important administrative subjects as may seem appropriate, arranged in proper sequence, are numbered in a single series and each name so numbered constitutes the title and number of a pamphlet contain-ing certain administrative regulations pertaining thereto. Where more than one pamphlet is required for the administrative regulations pertaining to any such title, additional pamphlets will be issued in a separate sub-series.

30–1625. Quartermaster Corps: Electric plants and systems; Apr. 19, 1923. [1923.] 7 p.
30–1630. Same: Electricity for purposes other than lighting; June 6, 1923. [1923.] 2 p.
30–1635. Same: Charges for electricity and gas; June 6, 1923. [1923.] 3 p.
30–1840. Same: National cemeteries; June 6, 1923. [1923.] 2 p.
30–2110. Same: Salvage and laundry activities, general provisions; June 6, 1923. [1923.] 4 p.
30–2120. Same: Field printing; June 14, 1923. [1923.] 3 p.
30–2145. Same: Unserviceable property, including waste material, Changes 1; June 25, 1923. 1923. 1 p.
30–2200. Same: Classification of subsistence stores; June 6, 1923. 1923. 1 p.
30–2220. Same: Reclamation on subsistence stores; June 6, 1923. [1923.] 2 p.
30–2230. Same: Beef cattle; June 6, 1923. [1923.] 4 p.
30–2310. Same: Sales commissary units; June 6, 1923. 1923. 1 p.
30–2720. Same: Typewriters and similar office labor-saving devices; June 6, 1923. [1923.] 6 p.
35–1420. Finance Department: Burial expenses of military personnel and civilian employees; June 6, 1923. [1923.] 2 p.
40–105. Medical Department: Standards of physical examination for entrance into Regular Army, National Guard, and Organized Reserves; May 29, 1923. [1923.] 37 p. [Supersedes AR 40–105, June 20, 1921.]
40–1075. Same: Index to regulations regarding records of sick and wounded; July 2, 1923. [1923.] 8 p.
100–50. Corps of Engineers: Military railways; June 6, 1923. [1923.] 3 p.
340–15. Correspondence: How conducted, Changes 3; July 27, 1923. [1923.] 3 p. [Supersedes AR 340–15, Changes 1 and 2, June 15, 1922, and Mar. 3, 1923.]
345–55. Military records: Basic strength returns and record of events; Apr. 26, 1923. [1923.] 26 p. [Supersedes AR 345–55, 345–60, 345–65, and 345–70, Mar. 31, 1922.]
345–80. Same: Consolidated strength returns; Apr. 26, 1923. [1923.] 11 p. [Supersedes AR 345–80, Mar. 31, 1922.]
345–800. Same: Reports of changes, reports of casualties, and memoranda of trans-mittal, Changes 2; Apr. 17, 1923. [1923.] 2 p. [Supersedes AR 345–800, Changes 1, Mar. 7, 1923.]
500–50. Employment of troops: Enforcement of laws; June 6, 1923. [1923.] 12 p.
600–85. Personnel: Purpose of, and supply of, service ribbons, bronze stars, minia-tures, and lapel buttons, Changes 1; July 30, 1923. [1923.] 2 p.
605–115. Commissioned officers: Leaves of absence and delays, Changes 2; June 13, 1923. [1923.] 2 p. [Supersedes AR 605–115, Changes 1, May 22, 1922.]
605–120. Same: Personal reports, registration; June 20, 1923. [1923.] 7 p. [Super-sedes AR 605–120, June 26, 1922.]
605–175. Same: Foreign service; Apr. 20, 1923. [1923.] 2 p. [Supersedes AR 605–175, Sept. 1, 1922.]

Training regulations.

NOTE.—The Training regulations are issued in pamphlet form for insertion in loose-leaf binders.

240–20. Machine gun: Combat practice, prepared under direction of chief of in-fantry; June 6, 1923. [1923.] 23 p. il. *Paper, 5c.
420–60. Infantry: Drill, infantry battalion, prepared under direction of chief of in-fantry; June 2, 1923. [1923.] 7 p. il. *Paper, 5c.
420–85. Same: Extended order, rifle squad, section, and platoon, prepared under di-rection of chief of infantry; May 24, 1923. [1923.] 22 p. il. *Paper, 5c.
420–110. Same: Combat principles, rifle section, prepared under direction of chief of infantry; Apr. 25, 1923. [1923.] 34 p. il. *Paper, 5c.
420–115. Same: Combat principles, rifle platoon, prepared under direction of chief of infantry; Apr. 30, 1923. [1923.] 63 p. il. *Paper, 10c.
420–125. Same: Combat principles, machine-gun section, prepared under direction of chief of infantry; June 2, 1923. [1923.] 18 p. *Paper, 5c.
420–130. Same: Combat principles, machine-gun platoon, prepared under direction of chief of infantry; June 2, 1923. [1923.] 26 p. il. *Paper, 5c.
420–150. Same: Combat principles, howitzer company platoon, prepared under direc-tion of chief of infantry; May 29, 1923. [1923.] 15 p. il. *Paper, 5c.
430–75. Field artillery: Field artillery driver, prepared under direction of chief of field artillery; May 23, 1923. [1923.] 23 p. il. *Paper, 5c.

ADJUTANT GENERAL'S DEPARTMENT

Storage battery repair for military specialists; prepared under direction of quartermaster general, 1922. 1923. iv+119 p. il. (United States Army training manual 52.) ‡

Tire repair for military specialists; prepared under direction of quartermaster general, Army, 1922. 1923. vi+142 p. il. (United States Army training manual 51.) ‡

Typewriting for military specialists; prepared under direction of chief of finance, 1922. 1923. iv+111 p. 4 pl. 8 p. of pl. (United States Army training manual 71.) ‡

U. S. Army recruiting news, bulletin of recruiting information issued by direction of Adjutant General of Army, Aug. 1 and 15, 1923. [Recruiting Publicity Bureau, Governors Island, N. Y., Aug. 1 and 15, 1923.] Each 16 p. il. 4° †Recruiting Publicity Bureau, Governors Island, N. Y.   War 22—1

AIR SERVICE

ENGINEERING DIVISION

Aeroplanes. Handbook of instructions for airplane designers. [3d edition, June. 1922] revision June, 1923. [Dayton, Ohio, no publisher, June 21, 1923.] 4° [This June, 1923 revision consists of 1 p. of corrections and additional pages to be inserted in their proper places in the 3d edition. A list of the additional pages is found on the first page.] ‡

ENGINEER DEPARTMENT

Dredging. Standard form specifications for dredging; revised to July, 1923. [1923.] 18 leaves, 4° †

Milwaukee, Wis. Maintenance and improvement of existing river and harbor works, harbor at Milwaukee, Wis., advertisement [for constructing breakwater]. [1923.] 19 p. 4° †

Orders. Changes 9 [for] Orders and regulations [Corps of Engineers, Army, in force Dec. 31, 1916]; May 1, 1923. [1923.] iii p. 12° [Accompanied by reprints of certain pages to be inserted in their proper places in the original orders and regulations. A list of changes or new paragraphs because of which these pages have been reprinted is found on p. iii of Changes 9 here catalogued.] ‡

Pawcatuck River. Maintenance and improvement of existing river and harbor works, Pawcatuck River, R. I. and Conn., advertisement [for dredging]. [1923.] 14 p. 4° †

NORTHERN AND NORTHWESTERN LAKES SURVEY

NOTE.—Charts of the Great Lakes and connecting waters and St. Lawrence River to the international boundary at St. Regis, of Lake Champlain, and of the New York State canals are prepared and sold by the U. S. Lake Survey Office, Old Custom-house, Detroit, Mich. Charts may also be purchased at the following U. S. engineer offices: 710 Army Building, New York, N. Y.; 467 Broadway, Albany, N. Y.; 540 Federal Building, Buffalo, N. Y.; and Canal Office, Sault Ste. Marie, Mich. A catalogue (with index map), showing localities, scales, prices, and conditions of sale, may be had upon application at any of these offices.
    A descriptive bulletin, which supplements the charts and gives detailed information as to harbors, shore lines and shoals, magnetic determinations, and particulars of changing conditions affecting navigation, is issued free to chart purchasers, upon request. The bulletin is revised annually and issued at the opening of navigation (in April), and supplements thereto are published monthly during the navigation season.
    Complete sets of the charts and publications may be seen at the U. S. engineer offices in Duluth, Minn.. Milwaukee, Wis.. Chicago, Ill.. Grand Rapids. Mich.. Cleveland, Ohio, and Oswego, N. Y., but they are obtainable only at the sales offices above mentioned.

Great Lakes. Supplement 4, Aug. 21, 1923, corrections and additions to Bulletin 32; to supplement information given upon charts of Great Lakes. U. S. Lake Survey Office. Detroit, Mich. [Aug. 15, 1923]. p. 1–3+leaves 4–10+[2] p. 4° †

GENERAL STAFF CORPS

Army. Changes 135 [for] Army regulations [1913] ; July 6, 1923. [1923.] 3 leaves. [Regulations issued by War Department.] †

Courts-martial. Changes 3 [for] Manual for courts-martial, 1921; June 28, 1923. [1923.] 2 leaves. [Manual issued by Judge Advocate General's Department, Army.] †

Medical Department, Army. Changes 20 [for] Manual for Medical Department [1916] ; Feb. 21, 1923. 1923. 1 p. [Manual issued by Medical Department, Army.] †

Military law. Changes 3 [for] Military laws of United States, 1921; June 11, 1923. [1923.] 26 leaves. [Military laws issued by Judge Advocate General's Department.] * Paper, 5c.

Quartermaster Corps. Changes 23 [for] Manual for Quartermaster Corps [1916] ; June 7, 1923. 1923. 1 p. [Manual issued by Quartermaster General of Army.] †

Shooting. Changes 5 [for] Pistol marksmanship [Nov. 1920] ; June 22, 1923. 1923. 1 p. [Pistol marksmanship issued by Adjutant General's Department.] †

Special regulations. Changes 2 [for] Special regulations 32 [Allowances of ammunition for field artillery instruction and target practice, revised 1921] ; June 16, 1923. 1923. 1 p. [Special regulations issued by War Department.] †

—— Changes 2 [for] Special regulations 122 [Rifle and pistol competitions for Reserve Officers' Training Corps and other schools and colleges, 1921] ; May 25, 1923. 1923. 1 p. [Special regulations issued by War Department.] †

—— ˙ Changes 3 [for] Special regulations 43 [Regulations for Officers' Reserve Corps, 1921, with corrections to May 5, 1922] ; June 1, 1923. 1923. 1 p. [Special regulations issued by War Department.] †

—— Changes 9 [for] Special regulations 59 [Post exchange regulations, 1917] ; May 26, 1923. [1923.] 2 p. 12° [Special regulations issued by War Department.] † ¯

—— Changes 10 [for] Special regulations 44a [Training camps for Reserve Officers' Training Corps, revised 1920] ; July 30, 1923. 1923. 1 p. [Special regulations issued by War Department.] †

War Department. Changes 34 [for] Compilation of [General] orders [Circulars, and Bulletins of War Department, 1881–1915] ; May 4, 1923. 1923. 1 p. 12° [Compilation issued by Adjutant General's Department.] †

MEDICAL DEPARTMENT

Surgeon General's Office. Medical Department of United States Army in World War : v. 1, Surgeon General's Office [with lists of references] ; prepared by Charles Lynch, Frank W. Weed, [and] Loy McAfee. 1923. 1389 p. il. 2 pl. 2 p. of pl. large 8° * Cloth, $3.00.   S G 23—80

ORDNANCE DEPARTMENT

Orders. General orders 5 [1923] ; July 12, 1923. [1923.] 3 leaves, 12° ‡

QUARTERMASTER GENERAL OF ARMY

Circulars. Changes 44½, 46–48, 51–56 [1923, to] Circulars; July 3–Aug. 24, 1923. [1923.] Each 2 leaves or 1 p. 4° [Mimeographed. Changes 53 is a corrected copy.] ‡

○

UNIVERSITY OF ILLINOIS LIBRARY

OCT 6 1923

Monthly Catalogue

United States

Public Documents

No. 345
September, 1923

ISSUED BY THE
SUPERINTENDENT OF DOCUMENTS

WASHINGTON
1923

Abbreviations

Appendix	app.	Page, pages	p.
Congress	Cong.	Part, parts	pt., pts.
Department	Dept.	Plate, plates	pl.
Document	doc.	Portrait, portraits	por.
Facsimile, facsimiles	facsim.	Quarto	4°
Folio	f°	Report	rp.
House	H.	Saint	St.
House bill	H. R.	Section, sections	sec.
House concurrent resolution	H. Con. Res.	Senate, Senate bill	S.
House document	H. doc.	Senate concurrent resolution	S. Con. Res.
House executive document	H. ex. doc.	Senate document	S. doc.
House joint resolution	H. J. Res.	Senate executive document	S. ex. doc.
House report	H. rp.	Senate joint resolution	S. J. Res.
House resolution (simple)	H. Res.	Senate report	S. rp.
Illustration, illustrations	il.	Senate resolution (simple)	S. Res.
Inch, inches	in.	Session	sess.
Latitude	lat.	Sixteenmo	16°
Longitude	long.	Table, tables	tab.
Mile, miles	m.	Thirtytwo-mo	32°
Miscellaneous	mis., misc.	Treasury	Treas.
Nautical	naut.	Twelvemo	12°
No date	n. d.	Twentyfour-mo	24°
No place	n. p.	Versus	vs., v.
Number, numbers	no., nos.	Volume, volumes	v., vol.
Octavo	8°	Year	yr.

Common abbreviations for names of States and months are also used.
* Document for sale by Superintendent of Documents.
† Distribution by office issuing document, free if unaccompanied by a price.
‡ Printed for official use.
NOTE.—Nearly all of the Departments of the Government make a limited free distribution of their publications. When an entry shows a * price, it is possible that upon application to the issuing office a copy may be obtained without charge.

Explanation

Words and figures inclosed in brackets [ ] are given for information, but do not appear on the title-pages of the publications catalogued. When size is not given octavo is to be understood. Size of maps is measured from outer edge of border, excluding margin. The dates, including day, month, and year, given with Senate and House documents and reports are the dates on which they were ordered to be printed. Usually the printing promptly follows the ordering, but various causes sometimes make delays.

SALES OF GOVERNMENT PUBLICATIONS

The Superintendent of Documents, Washington, D. C., is authorized to sell at cost of paper and printing, plus 10 per cent, any United States public document in his charge the distribution of which is not otherwise provided for.

Publications can not be supplied free to individuals nor forwarded in advance of payment.

Publications entered in this catalogue that are for sale by the Superintendent of Documents are indicated by a star (*) preceding the price. A dagger (†) indicates that application should be made to the Department, Bureau, or Division issuing the document. A double dagger (‡) indicates that the document is printed for official use. Whenever additional information concerning the method of procuring a document seems necessary, it will be found under the name of the Bureau by which it was published.

In ordering a publication from the Superintendent of Documents, give (if known) the name of the publishing Department, Bureau, or Division, and the title of the publication. If the publication is numbered, give the number also. Every such particular assists in quick identification. Do not order by the Library of Congress card number.

The accumulation of publications in this Office amounts to several millions, of which over two million are assorted, forming the sales stock. Many rare books are included, but under the law all must be sold regardless of their age or scarcity. Many of the books have been in stock some time, and are apt to be shop-worn. In filling orders the best copy available is sent. A general price-list of public documents is not available, but lists on special subjects will be furnished on application.

MONTHLY CATALOGUE DISTRIBUTION

The Monthly catalogue is sent to each Senator, Representative, Delegate, Resident Commissioner, and officer in Congress; to designated depositories and State and Territorial libraries if it is selected by them; to substantially all Government authors; and to as many school, college, and public libraries as the limited edition will supply.

Subscription price to individuals, 50c. a year, including index; foreign subscription, 75c. a year. Back numbers can not be supplied. Notify the Superintendent of Documents of any change of address.

LIBRARY OF CONGRESS CARDS

Numbers to be used in ordering the printed catalogue cards of the Library of Congress are given at the end of entries for the more important documents. Orders for these cards, remittances in payment for them, and requests for information about them should be addressed to the Librarian of Congress, *not* to the Superintendent of Documents.

INDEX

An Index to the Monthly catalogue is issued at the end of the fiscal year. This contains index entries for all the numbers issued from July to June, and can be bound with the numbers as an index to the volume. Persons desiring to bind the catalogue at the end of the year should be careful to retain the numbers received monthly, as duplicate copies can not be supplied.

HOW TO REMIT

Remittances for the documents marked with a star (*) should be made to the Superintendent of Documents, Washington, D. C., by coupons, postal money order, express order, or New York draft. Currency may be sent at sender's risk.

Postage stamps, foreign money, defaced or smooth coins, positively will not be accepted.

For the convenience of the general public, coupons that are good until used in exchange for Government publications sold by the Superintendent of Documents may be purchased from his Office in sets of 20 for $1.00. Address order to Superintendent of Documents, Government Printing Office.

No charge is made for postage on documents forwarded to points in United States, Alaska, Guam, Hawaii, Philippine Islands, Porto Rico, Samoa, or to Canada, Cuba, or Mexico. To other countries the regular rate of postage is charged, and remittances must cover such postage. In computing foreign postage, add one-third of the price of the publication.

MONTHLY CATALOGUE

AGRICULTURE DEPARTMENT

NOTE.—Those publications of the Department of Agriculture which are for sale will be supplied by the Superintendent of Documents, Washington, D. C. The Department issues a monthly list of publications, which is mailed to all applicants, enabling them to select such reports and bulletins as interest them.

Azotobacter. Influence of absolute reaction of soil upon its Azotobacter flora and nitrogen fixing ability [with list of literature cited]; by P. L. Gainey. 1923. cover-title, p. 907–938. il. [From Journal of agricultural research, v. 24, no. 11, June 16, 1923.] ‡

Cattle. [Bureau of Animal Industry]‘ order 273, amendment 2, regulations governing interstate movement of livestock, modifying regulation 7, effective July 23, 1923; [July 16, 1923]. [1923.] 2 p. †

Intermediate credit for farmer, pamphlet containing questions and answers on intermediate credit as provided for in agricultural credits act of 1923 and essential facts showing need for it. 1923. [1]+5 p. narrow 8° †

Journal of agricultural research, v. 24, no. 9–12; June 2–23, 1923. 1923. cover-titles, 741–1048+[28] p.+[14] leaves, il. 8 pl. 38 p. of pl. [Weekly. Text on p. 2 of covers.] *Paper, 10c. single copy, $4.00 a yr.; foreign subscription, $5.25.   Agr 13—1837

CONTENTS.—No. 9. Control of snow molding in coniferous nursery stock; by C. F. Korstian.—Influence of moisture on bean wilt; by Lewis T. Leonard.—Pseudo-antagonism of sodium and calcium in dilute solutions [with list of literature cited]; by H. S. Reed and A. R. C. Haas.—Influence of hydrogen-ion concentration on growth and fixation of nitrogen by cultures of Azotobacter [with list of literature cited]; by P. L. Gainey and H. W. Batchelor.—Sunflower investigations; by Ray E. Neidig and Robert S. Snyder.—Effect of different concentrations of manganese sulphate on growth of plants in acid and neutral soils and necessity of manganese as plant nutrient [with list of literature cited]; by J. S. McHargue.—Sweet clover investigations; by Ray E. Neidig and Robert S. Snyder.—Growth and composition of orange trees in sand and soil cultures [with list of literature cited]; by H. S. Reed and A. R. C. Haas.—No. 10. Further studies of inheritance of rogue type in garden peas (Pisum sativum L.) [with list of literature cited]; by Wilber Brotherton, jr.—Method of treating maize seed to destroy adherent spores of downy mildew [with list of literature cited]; by William H. Weston, jr.—Influence of substrate and its hydrogen-ion concentration on pectinase production [with list of literature cited]; by L. L. Harter and J. L. Weimer.—Microscopic estimation of colloids in soil separates; by William H. Fry.—No. 11. Morphology and host relations of Pucciniastrum americanum [with list of literature cited]; by B. O. Dodge.—Watery-rot of tomato fruits, physiological form of Oospora lactis, effect on host, penetration of cell walls by enzymic action [with list of literature cited]; by Fred J. Pritchard and W. S. Porte.—Influence of absolute reaction of soil upon its Azotobacter flora and nitrogen fixing ability [with list of literature cited]; by P. L. Gainey.—Study of factors affecting nitrogen content of wheat and changes that occur during development of wheat [with list of literature cited]; by George A. Olson.—Relative susceptibility of citrus fruits and hybrids to Cladosporium citri Massee [with list of literature cited]; by G. L. Peltier and W. J. Frederich.—Improved method for determination of nicotine in tobacco and tobacco extracts; by O. M. Shedd.—Nutritive value of mixtures of proteins from corn and various concentrates [with list of literature cited]; by D. Breese Jones, A. J. Finks, and Carl O. Johns.—No. 12. Mode of inheritance of resistance to Puccinia graminis with relation to seed color in crosses between varieties of durum wheat [with list of literature cited]; by J. B. Harrington and O. S. Aamodt.—Study of rust resistance in cross between marquis and kota wheats [with list of literature cited]; by H. K. Hayes and O. S. Aamodt.—Biologic forms of Puccinia graminis on varieties of Avena spp. [with list of literature cited]; by E. C. Stakman, M. N. Levine, and D. L. Bailey.—Disease resistance to onion smudge [with list of literature cited]; by J. C. Walker.—Effect of respiration upon protein percentage of wheat, oats, and barley [with list of literature cited]; by F. W. McGinnis and G. S. Taylor.

NOTE.—This publication is published by authority of the Secretary of Agriculture, with the cooperation of the Association of Land-Grant Colleges. It is distributed free only to libraries of agricultural colleges and experiment stations, to large universities, technical schools, and to such institutions as make suitable exchanges with the Agriculture Department. Others desiring the Journal may obtain it from the Superintendent of Documents, Washington, D. C., at the prices stated above.

Journal of agricultural research—Continued. Same, v. 25, no. 1–4; July 7–28, 1923. 1923. cover-titles, 1–208+[25] p.+[6] leaves, il. 3 pl. 30 p. of pl. [Weekly. Text on p. 2 of covers.]

CONTENTS.—No. 1. Work and parasitism of Mediterranean fruit fly in Hawaii during 1919 and 1920; by H. F. Willard.—Acid production by Rhizopus tritici in decaying sweet potatoes; by H. A. Edson.—Temperature effects in plant metabolism [with list of literature cited]; by W. E. Tottingham.—Platygaster vernalis Myers, important parasite of Hessian fly; by Charles E. Hill.—No. 2. Transmission, variation, and control of certain degeneration diseases of Irish potatoes [with list of literature cited]; by E. S. Schultz and Donald Folsom.—No. 3. Some relations of crowngall organism to its host tissue [with list of literature cited]; by A. J. Riker.—Oxygen-supplying power of soil as indicated by color changes in alkaline pyrogallol solution; by Lee M. Hutchins and Burton E. Livingston.—Bacterial spot of lima bean [with list of literature cited]; by W. B. Tisdale and Maude Miller Williamson.—Hydrogen-ion changes induced by species of Rhizopus and by Botrytis cinerea [with list of literature cited]; by J. L. Weimer and L. L. Harter.—No. 4. Growth-promoting value of proteins of palm kernel, and vitamin content of palm-kernel meal; by A. J. Finks and D. Breese Jones.—Efficiencies of phosphatic fertilizers as affected by liming and by length of time phosphates remained in Porto Rican soils [with list of literature cited]; by P. L. Gile and J. O. Carrero.—Growth of fruiting parts in cotton plants; by R. D. Martin, W. W. Ballard, and D. M. Simpson.

Manganese. Effect of different concentrations of manganese sulphate on growth of plants in acid and neutral soils and necessity of manganese as plant nutrient [with list of literature cited]; by J. S. McHargue. 1923. cover-title, 781–794+[1] p.+[1] leaf, 2 p. of pl. [From Journal of agricultural research, v. 24, no. 9, June 2, 1923.] ‡

Official record, Department of Agriculture, v. 2, no. 36–39; Sept. 5–26, 1923. [1923.] Each 8 p. 4° [Weekly.] *Paper, 50c. a yr.; foreign subscription, $1.10.   Agr 22—146

Orange-trees. Growth and composition of orange trees in sand and soil cultures [with list of literature cited]; by H. S. Reed and A. R. C. Haas. 1923. cover-title, 801–814+[4] p.+[1] leaf, 5 p. of pl. [From Journal of agricultural research, v. 24, no. 9, June 2, 1923.] ‡

Quarantine. Fruit and vegetable quarantine, Notice of quarantine 56, with regulations, effective Nov. 1, 1923. [1923.] 8 p. (Federal Horticultural Board.) †

——— Modification of gypsy moth and brown-tail moth quarantine, Amendment 5 to regulations supplemental to Notice of quarantine 45, effective Aug. 21, 1923. [1923.] 2 p. (Federal Horticultural Board.) †

——— Quarantine on account of gypsy moth and brown-tail moth, Notice of quarantine 45 [with regulations], effective July 1, 1920. [Reprint 1923.] 6 p. (Federal Horticultural Board.) †

Sodium. Pseudo-antagonism of sodium and calcium in dilute solutions [with list of literature cited]; by H. S. Reed and A. R. C. Haas. 1923. cover-title, p. 753–758, 1 pl. [From Journal of agricultural research, v. 24, no. 9, June 2, 1923.] ‡

Sweet clover investigations; by Ray E. Neidig and Robert S. Snyder. 1923. cover-title, p. 795–799. [From Journal of agricultural research, v. 24, no. 9, June 2, 1923.] ‡

Warehousing farm products under warehouse act, pamphlet containing questions and answers about storage of agricultural products in warehouses under Federal supervision as provided for in warehouse act. 1923. [1]+12 p. narrow 8° †

Weather, crops, and markets, weekly, Sept. 1–29, 1923; v. 4, no. 9–13. [1923.] p. 217–344, il. 4° * Paper, $1.00 a yr.; foreign subscription, $2.00.
                                                                  Agr 22—147

AGRICULTURAL ECONOMICS BUREAU

Cold-storage holdings, year ending Jan. 1923, with comparable data for earlier years. Aug. [Sept.] 1923. cover-title, 32 p. (Agriculture Dept. Statistical bulletin 1.) [Text on p. 2 of cover.] * Paper, 5c.   Agr 23—1186

Farm management. Producing family and farm supplies on cotton farm; [by C. L. Goodrich]. [Jan. 1919, revised Aug. 1923.] [1923.] 16 p. il. (Agriculture Dept. Farmers' bulletin 1015.) [Includes list of Agriculture Department publications relating to farm home.] * Paper, 5c.

Potatoes. Marketing main-crop potatoes; [by Wells A. Sherman, George B. Fiske, and O. D. Miller]. [Aug. 1923.] ii+37 p. il. (Agriculture Dept. Farmers' bulletin 1317.) [Includes lists of Agriculture Department and State publications relating to potatoes and potato marketing.] * Paper, 5c.
                                                                  Agr 23—1183

Service announcements. Service and regulatory announcements, no. 78: Rules and regulations of Secretary of Agriculture governing inspection and certification of fruits, vegetables, and other products under act approved Feb. 26, 1923 (public no. 446, 67th Congress). Sept. 1923. ii+6 p. * Paper, 5c.
Agr 15—199

—— Same, no. 79: Rules and regulations of Secretary of Agriculture governing inspection and certification of butter, cheese, and eggs under act approved Feb. 26, 1923 (public no. 446, 67th Congress). Sept. 1923. ii+6 p. * Paper, 5c.

ANIMAL INDUSTRY BUREAU

Breeding. Principles of livestock breeding [with bibliography]; by Sewall Wright. Dec. 8, 1920, revised July, 1923. 1923. cover-title, 68 p. il. (Agriculture Dept. Department bulletin 905.) * Paper, 15c.
Agr 23—1220

Calves. Feeding and management of dairy calves and young dairy stock; [by W. K. Brainerd and H. P. Davis]. [June, 1923.] ii+18 p. il. (Agriculture Dept. Farmers' bulletin 1336.) [Revision of Farmers' bulletin 777.] * Paper, 5c.
Agr 23—1230

Milk. Inspection of milk supplies; [by] Ernest Kelly and C. S. Leete. July, 1923. 37 p. il. (Agriculture Dept. Department circular 276.) * Paper, 10c.
Agr 23—1181

Mule production; [by J. O. Williams]. [Aug. 1923.] ii+28 p. il. (Agriculture Dept. Farmers' bulletin 1341.) * Paper, 5c.
Agr 23—1233

Poultry. Diseases of poultry; [by Bernard A. Gallagher]. [July, 1923.] ii+41 p. il. (Agriculture Dept. Farmers' bulletin 1337.) [Supersedes Farmers' bulletin 957.] * Paper, 5c.
Agr 23—1231

—— Standard varieties of chickens: 1, American class, [by Rob R. Slocum; revised by Alfred R. Lee]. [July, 1923.] ii+18 p. il. (Agriculture Dept. Farmers' bulletin 1347.) [Revision of Farmers' bulletin 806.] * Paper, 5c.
Agr 23—1234

Service announcements. Service and regulatory announcements, Aug. 1923; [no.] 196. Sept. 1923. p. 69–75. [Monthly.] * Paper, 5c. single copy, 25c. a yr.; foreign subscription, 40c.
Agr 7—1658

NOTE.—The free distribution of this publication will be limited to persons in the service of the Animal Industry Bureau, to proprietors of establishments at which the Federal meat inspection is conducted, to public officials whose duties render it necessary for them to have such information, and to journals especially concerned. Others desiring copies may obtain them from the Superintendent of Documents, Washington, D. C., at the prices stated above.

BIOLOGICAL SURVEY BUREAU

Birds. Common birds of southeastern United States in relation to agriculture; [by F. E. L. Beal, W. L. McAtee, and E. R. Kalmbach]. [Oct. 26, 1916, revised June, 1923.] [1923.] 45 p. il. (Agriculture Dept. Farmers' bulletin 755.) [Includes lists of Agriculture Department publications relating to food habits of wild birds.] * Paper, 5c.

—— Some common birds useful to farmer; [by F. E. L. Beal]. [Feb. 13, 1915, revised May, 1923.] [1923.] ii+30 p. il. (Agriculture Dept. Farmers' bulletin 630.) [Includes lists of Agriculture Department publications relating to food habits of wild birds.] * Paper, 5c.

Game laws for season 1923–24, summary of provisions of Federal, State, and provincial statutes; [by Geo. A. Lawyer and Frank L. Earnshaw]. [Sept. 1923.] [2]+70 p. il. (Agriculture Dept. Farmers' bulletin 1375.) * Paper, 5c.
Agr 6—384

Service announcements. Service and regulatory announcements, [no.] 56: Regulations for protection of land fur-bearing animals in Alaska. Sept. 1, 1923. 4 p. il. * Paper, 5c.
Agr 16—608

—— Same, [no.] 57: Hunting migratory game birds on Cold Springs Reservation, Oreg. Sept. 1923. 1 p. * Paper, 5c.

CHEMISTRY BUREAU

Leather. Wearing qualities of shoe leathers; by F. P. Veitch, R. W. Frey, and I. D. Clarke. Sept. 5, 1923. 25 p. il. 2 p. of pl. (Agriculture Dept. Department bulletin 1168.) * Paper, 10c.
Agr 23—1178

EDITORIAL AND DISTRIBUTION WORK OFFICES

Agriculture Department. Monthly list of publications [of Agriculture Department], Aug. 1923. [1923.] 4 p. †   Agr 9—1414

ENTOMOLOGY BUREAU

Clothes moths and their control; [by E. A. Back]. [July, 1923.] ii+29 p. il. (Agriculture Dept. Farmers' bulletin 1353.) * Paper, 5c.   Agr 23—1237

Fowl tick and how premises may be freed from it; [by F. C. Bishopp]. [Dec. 1919, revised July, 1923.] [1923.] 16 p. il. (Agriculture Dept. Farmers' bulletin 1070.) * Paper, 5c.

Fumigation of citrus trees for control of insect pests; [by R. S. Woglum]. [July, 1923.] ii+59 p. il. (Agriculture Dept. Farmers' bulletin 1321.) [Supersedes Farmers' bulletin 923.] * Paper, 10c.   Agr 23—1184

Gipsy-moths. Controlling gipsy moth and brown-tail moth; [by A. F. Burgess]. [July, 1923.] ii+28 p. il. (Agriculture Dept. Farmers' bulletin 1335.) [Revision of Farmers' bulletin 845.] * Paper, 5c.   Agr 23—1229

Lead-cable borer or short-circuit beetle in California [with list of literature cited]; by H. E. Burke, R. D. Hartman, and T. E. Snyder. [Reprint] July, 1923. cover-title, 56 p. il. 10 p. of pl. (Agriculture Dept. Bulletin 1107.) * Paper, 15c.   Agr 23—243

Paradichlorobenzene. Further studies with paradichlorobenzene for peach borer control, with special reference to its use on young peach trees; by Oliver I. Snapp and Charles H. Alden. Sept. 13, 1923. 19 p. il. 1 pl. 2 p. of pl. (Agriculture Dept. Department bulletin 1169.) * Paper, 5c.   Agr 23—1224

Striped sod webworm, Crambus mutabilis Clemens [with list of literature cited]; by George G. Ainslie. 1923. cover-title, 399–414+[1] p.+[1] leaf, il. 2 p. of pl. [From Journal of agricultural research, v. 24, no. 5, May 5, 1923.] ‡

Tobacco flea-beetle in southern cigar-wrapper district; [by F. S. Chamberlin and J. N. Tenhet]. [July, 1923.] ii+10 p. il. (Agriculture Dept. Farmers' bulletin 1352.) * Paper, 5c.   Agr 23—1236

Tobacco hornworm insecticide, recommendations for use of powdered arsenate of lead in dark-tobacco district; [by A. C. Morgan]. [June, 1923.] ii+8 p. il. (Agriculture Dept. Farmers' bulletin 1356.) [Revision of Farmers' bulletin 867.] * Paper, 5c.   Agr 23—1026

FEDERAL HORTICULTURAL BOARD

Service announcements. Service and regulatory announcements, Apr.–June. 1923; [no.] 75. Sept. 1923. p. 57–98, map. * Paper, 10c.   Agr 14—383

FOREST SERVICE

Forests and forestry in United States; by Herbert A. Smith. [1923.] 16 p. il. [This publication, with slight changes, was previously issued by the State Department as a supplementary exhibit of the Forest Service at the Brazil Centennial Exposition, Rio de Janeiro, Brazil, 1922–23, for which see Monthly catalogue, Nov. 1922, p. 303.] * Paper, 5c.

National forest areas, June 30, 1923; compiled by Branch of Engineering. [1923.] 8 p. 4° †   Agr 16—330

Snow mold. Control of snow molding in coniferous nursery stock; by C. F. Korstian. 1923. cover-title, 741–748+[2] p. 3 p. of pl. [From Journal of agricultural research, v. 24, no. 9, June 2, 1923.] ‡

HOME ECONOMICS BUREAU

NOTE.—Created under act making appropriations for Department of Agriculture, fiscal year 1924, approved Feb. 26, 1923. Formerly the work in home economics was carried on as a separate office in the States Relations Service. See also, below, States Relations Service.

Kitchens. Well-planned kitchen; [by] Ruth Van Deman. Sept. 1921, revised Aug. 1923. [1923.] 4 p. (Agriculture Dept. Department circular 189.) [This circular was originally issued by States Relations Service. Includes list of Agriculture Department publications of interest in connection with this circular.] * Paper, 5c.   Agr 23—1238

Stains. Removal of stains from clothing and other textiles; [by Harold L. Lang and Anna H. Whittelsey]. [Sept. 1917, reprint with slight changes Sept. 1923.] ii+30 p. il. (Agriculture Dept. Farmers' bulletin 861.) [This bulletin was originally issued by States Relations Service.]   * Paper, 5c.

PLANT INDUSTRY BUREAU

Buckthorn. Rôle of genus Rhamnus in dissemination of crown rust [with list of literature cited]; by S. M. Dietz. Sept. 1923. 19 p. il. (Agriculture Dept. Department bulletin 1162.) [Prepared in cooperation with Iowa Agricultural Experiment Station.]   * Paper, 5c.   Agr 23—1221

Cabbage: by L. C. Corbett. Apr. 14, 1911, [reprint] 1923. 24 p. il. (Agriculture Dept. Farmers' bulletin 433.) [Mar. 1915, on title-page, is date of previous reprint.]   * Paper, 5c.

Cereal experiments at Chico, Calif.; by Victor H. Florell. Aug. 1923. cover-title, 34 p. il. (Agriculture Dept. Department bulletin 1172.)   * Paper, 10c.
          Agr 23—1180

Chayote, its culture and uses; [by] L. G. Hoover. Sept. 28, 1923. 11 p. il. 4 p. of pl. (Agriculture Dept. Department circular 286.)   * Paper, 5c.
          Agr 23—1239

Corn smut. Influence of temperature on spore germination of Ustilago zeae [with list of literature cited]; by Edith Seymour Jones. 1923. cover-title, p. 593–597, il. [Prepared in cooperation with Wisconsin Agricultural Experiment Station. From Journal of agricultural research, v. 24, no. 7, May 19, 1923.] ‡

Cotton diseases and their control; [by W. W. Gilbert]. [Mar. 1921, revised June, 1923.] [1923.] 32 p. il. (Agriculture Dept. Farmers' bulletin 1187.)   * Paper, 5c.   Agr 21—543

Douglas spruce. Study of decay in Douglas fir in Pacific Northwest [with list of literature cited]; by J. S. Boyce. July 21, 1923. 20 p. 8 p. of pl. (Agriculture Dept. Department bulletin 1163.) [Prepared in cooperation with Forest Service.]   * Paper, 10c.   Agr 23—1222

Grain-sorghum experiments at Woodward Field Station in Oklahoma; by John B. Sieglinger. Sept. 1923. cover-title, 66 p. il. 1 pl. 6 p. of pl. (Agriculture Dept. Department bulletin 1175.)   * Paper, 15c.   Agr 23—1226

Grazing. Effects of different systems and intensities of grazing upon native vegetation at Northern Great Plains Field Station; by J. T. Sarvis. July, 1923. cover-title, 46 p. il. 1 pl. 8 p. of pl. (Agriculture Dept. Department bulletin 1170.) [Prepared in cooperation with North Dakota Agricultural College.]   * Paper, 15c.   Agr 23—1179

Hungarian vetch; by Roland McKee and H. A. Schoth. Aug. 1923. 12 p. il. (Agriculture Dept. Department bulletin 1174.)   * Paper, 5c.   Agr 23—1225

Huntley experiment farm. Work of Huntley reclamation project experiment farm in 1921; [by] Dan Hansen. Aug. 1923. 27 p. il. (Agriculture Dept. Department circular 275.)   * Paper, 5c.   Agr 14—1379

Potatoes. Potato brown-rot; [by] F. C. Meier and G. K. K. Link. Aug. 1923. 6 p. il. (Agriculture Dept. Department circular 281.) [Pages 3 and 4 are numbered on one side of the leaf only, the unnumbered sides bearing the illustrations.]   * Paper, 5c.   Agr 23—1228

——— Transmission, variation, and control of certain degeneration diseases of Irish potatoes [with list of literature cited]; by E. S. Schultz and Donald Folsom. 1923. cover-title, 43–118+[14] p. 15 p. of pl. [Prepared in cooperation with Maine Agricultural Experiment Station. From Journal of agricultural research, v. 25, no. 2, July 14, 1923.] ‡

Pruning citrus trees in the Southwest; [by A. D. Shamel, C. S. Pomeroy, and R. E. Caryl]. [June, 1923.] ii+32 p. il. (Agriculture Dept. Farmers' bulletin 1333.)   * Paper, 5c.   Agr 23—1240

Puccinia graminis. Statistical study of comparative morphology of biologic forms of Puccinia graminis [with list of literature cited]; by M. N. Levine. 1923. cover-title, 539–568+[1] p. il. 2 p. of pl. [Prepared in cooperation with University of Minnesota Agricultural Experiment Station. From Journal of agricultural research, v. 24, no. 7, May 19, 1923.] ‡

Spores in upper air; by Elvin C. Stakman, Arthur W. Henry, Gordon C. Curran, and Warren N. Christopher. 1923. cover-title, 599–606+[1] p. 2 p. of pl. [From Journal of agricultural research, v. 24, no. 7, May 19, 1923.] ‡

Stripe rust. Studies on life history of stripe rust, Puccinia glumarum (Schm.) Erikss. & Henn. [with list of literature cited]; by Charles W. Hungerford. 1923. cover-title, 607–620+[3] p.+[1] leaf, il. 4 p. of pl. [Prepared in cooperation with Oregon Agricultural Experiment Station and Idaho Agricultural Experiment Station. From Journal of agricultural research, v. 24, no. 7, May 19, 1923.] ‡

Wheat. Kota wheat; [by] J. Allen Clark and L. R. Waldron. Aug. 1923. 16 p. il. (Agriculture Dept. Department circular 280.) * Paper, 5c.
　　　　　　　　　　　　　　　　　　　　　　　　　　Agr 23—1182

—— Polish and poulard wheats; [by John H. Martin]. [July, 1923.] ii+10 p. il. (Agriculture Dept. Farmers' bulletin 1340.) * Paper, 5c.
　　　　　　　　　　　　　　　　　　　　　　　　　　Agr 23—1232

Wilt-disease. Influence of moisture on bean wilt; by Lewis T. Leonard. 1923. cover-title, 749–752+[2] p.+[1] leaf, 3 p. of pl. [From Journal of agricultural research, v. 24, no. 9, June 2, 1923.] ‡

Yams. Cultivation of true yams in Gulf region; by Robert A. Young. Aug. 1923. 16 p. 10 p. of pl. (Agriculture Dept. Department bulletin 1167.) * Paper, 10c.
　　　　　　　　　　　　　　　　　　　　　　　　　　Agr 23—1223

PUBLIC ROADS BUREAU

Irrigation. Corrugation method of irrigation; [by James C. Marr]. [Aug. 1923.] 24 p. il. (Agriculture Dept. Farmers' bulletin 1348.) * Paper, 5c.
　　　　　　　　　　　　　　　　　　　　　　　　　　Agr 23—1235

—— Irrigation district operation and finance; by Wells A. Hutchins. Sept. 22, 1923. cover-title, 56 p. il. (Agriculture Dept. Department bulletin 1177.) * Paper, 10c.
　　　　　　　　　　　　　　　　　　　　　　　　　　Agr 23—1227

Tile-trenching machinery; [by D. L. Yarnell]. [May, 1920, revised Mar. 1923.] [1923.] ii+22 p. il. (Agriculture Dept. Farmers' bulletin 1131.) * Paper, 5c.

SOILS BUREAU

Bernardsville, N. J. Soil survey of Bernardsville area, N. J.; by Austin L. Patrick, E. B. Deeter, C. C. Engle, and L. L. Lee. 1923. iv+409–468 p. il. 2 pl. 2 maps. [Prepared in cooperation with Department of Conservation and Development of New Jersey. From Field operations, 1919.] * Paper, 25c.

Erath County, Tex. Soil survey of Erath County, Tex.; by T. M. Bushnell, H. W. Hawker, and D. B. Pratapas. 1923. iii+371–408 p. il. map. [Prepared in cooperation with Texas Agricultural Experiment Station. From Field operations, 1920.] * Paper, 25c.

Josephine County, Oreg. Soil survey of Josephine County, Oreg.; by A. E. Kocher and E. F. Torgerson. 1923. iii+349–408 p. il. 3 p. of pl. map. [Prepared in cooperation with Oregon Agricultural Experiment Station. From Field operations, 1919.] * Paper, 25c.

St. Joseph County, Mich. Soil survey of St. Joseph County, Mich.; by L. C. Wheeting and S. G. Bergquist. 1923. iii+49–72 p. il. 4 p. of pl. map. [Prepared in cooperation with Michigan Agricultural Experiment Station. From Field operations, 1921.] * Paper, 15c.

Smith County, Miss. Soil survey of Smith County, Miss.; by W. E. Tharp and William DeYoung. 1923. iii+445–492 p. il. map. [Prepared in cooperation with Mississippi Geological Survey. From Field operations, 1920.] * Paper, 15c.

Wayne County, N. Y. Soil survey of Wayne County, N. Y.; by Cornelius Van Duyne, N. M. Kirk, William Seltzer, John P. Gum, and H. W. Erde. 1923. iv+273–348 p. il. map. [Prepared in cooperation with New York State College of Agriculture. From Field operations, 1919.] * Paper, 25c.

STATES RELATIONS SERVICE

NOTE.—See also, above, Home Economics Bureau.

Experiment station record. Experiment station record, v. 49, no. 1; July, 1923. 1923. cover-title, viii+1–100 p. [Text and illustration on p. 2 and 4 of cover.] * Paper, 10c. single copy, 75c. per vol. (2 vols. a yr.) ; foreign subscription, $1.25 per vol. (subscription price incorrectly given in publication).

Agr 9—832

NOTE.—Mainly made up of abstracts of reports and publications on agricultural science which have recently appeared in all countries, especially the United States. Extra numbers, called abstract numbers, are issued, 3 to each volume. These are made up almost exclusively of abstracts, that is, they contain no editorial notes and only a limited number of current notes.

—— Same, v. 49, no. 2; Aug. 1923. 1923. cover-title, ix+101–200 p. [Text and illustration on p. 2 and 4 of cover.]

Home economics. Status and results of home demonstration work, Northern and Western States, 1921; [by] Florence E. Ward. July, 1923. 26 p. il. (Agriculture Dept. Department circular 285.) * Paper, 5c.   Agr 21—215

PORTO RICO AGRICULTURAL EXPERIMENT STATION

Chlorosis. Influence of some nitrogenous fertilizers on development of chlorosis in rice [with list of literature cited] ; by L. G. Willis and J. O. Carrero. 1923. cover-title, p. 621–640. [From Journal of agricultural research, v. 24, no. 7, May 19, 1923.] ‡

WEATHER BUREAU

Climatological data. Climatological data for United States by sections, v. 10, no. 4; Apr. 1923. [1923.] cover-title, [191] p. il. 2 maps, 2 p. of maps, 4° [Text on p. 2 of cover.] * Paper, 35c. complete monthly number, $4.00 a yr.

Agr 14—566

NOTE.—Made up of separate Climatological data issued from 42 section centers of the United States. Printed at the several section centers and assembled and bound at the Washington Office. Issued principally for service use and exchange. The separate Climatological data are sold by the Superintendent of Documents, Washington, D. C., at the rate of 5c. single copy, 50c. a yr. for each section.

—— Same, v. 10, no. 5; May, 1923. [1923.] cover-title, [192] p. il. 2 maps, 2 p. of maps, 4° [Text on p. 2 of cover.]

Greenland. Winds and weather of central Greenland, meteorological results of Swiss Greenland expedition [1912–13] ; by C. F. Brooks. 1923. [1]+256–260 p. il. 4° [From Monthly weather review, May, 1923.] †

Meteorology. Monthly meteorological summary, Washington, D. C., Aug. 1923. [1923.] [2] p. f° †

Monthly weather review. Monthly weather review, v. 51, no. 6; June, 1923. [Sept.] 1923. cover-title, p. 291–344, il. 2 pl. 10 p. of maps, 4° [Text on p. 2–4 of cover.] * Paper, 15c. single copy, $1.50 a yr; foreign subscription, $2.25.

Agr 9—990

NOTE.—The Monthly weather review contains (1) meteorological contributions, and bibliography including seismology, (2) an interpretative summary and charts of the weather of the month in the United States, and on adjacent oceans, and (3) climatological and seismological tables dealing with the weather and earthquakes of the month. The contributions are principally as follows: (a) results of observational or research work in meteorology carried on in the United States or other parts of the world, (b) abstracts or reviews of important meteorological papers and books, and (c) notes.

SPECIAL ARTICLES.—Rainfall interpolation ; by Robert E. Horton.—Concerning relation between duration, intensity, and periodicity of rainfall, by Peter Philipovitch Gorbatchev ; [with discussion by H. R. Leach and R. E. Horton].—City planning and prevailing winds ; [by] Clarence J. Root.—Stimulus and conservation of energy as bases of medical climatology ; by Franz Baur.—Fata morgana on the Nagyhortobágy [Hungary] ; by Antony Réthly.—Small tornadoes near Cheyenne, Wyo. ; by Geo. W. Pitman.—Tornado at Roswell, N. Mex. ; by Cleve Hallenbeck.—Five typhoons in far East in June, 1923 ; by José Coronas.—Low water in Mississippi River during June, 1923, in Davenport, Iowa, district ; by A. M. Hamrick.

—— Same, v. 51, no. 7; July, 1923. [Sept. 29] 1923. cover-title, p. 345–381, il. 8 p. of maps, 4° [Text on p. 2–4 of cover.]

SPECIAL ARTICLES.—Influence of Gulf water-surface temperatures on Texas weather ; by I. R. Tannehill.—Accuracy of areal rainfall estimates ; by Robert E. Horton.—Rainfall duration and intensity in India ; by Robert E. Horton.—Are we having less snowfall? by Clarence J. Root.—National elimination balloon race from Indianapolis, Ind., July 4, 1923 ; by L. T. Samuels.—Auroral spectrum and upper strata of atmosphere, by L. Vegard ; abstracted [by C. L. M.].—Characteristics of atmosphere up to 200 kilometers as indicated by observations of meteors, by G. M. B. Dobson ; [abstracted by C. F. B.].

Ocean. Weather of the oceans, May, 1923, with special reference to north Atlantic and north Pacific oceans (including charts), notes, abstracts, and reviews; issued by Marine Division. 1923. 4 p. 2 p. of maps, 4° [From Monthly weather review, May, 1923.] †

Pyrheliometer. New form of thermoelectric recording pyrheliometer; by Herbert H. Kimball & Hermann E. Hobbs. 1923. [1]+239–242 p. il. 1 pl. 4° [From Monthly weather review, May, 1923.] †

Rain. Concerning relation between duration, intensity, and periodicity of rainfall, by Peter Philipovitch Gorbatchev; with discussion by H. R. Leach and R. E. Horton. 1923. [1]+305–309 p. il. 4° [From Monthly weather review, June, 1923.] †

—— Rainfall interpolation; by Robert E. Horton. 1923. [1]+291–304 p. il. 4° [From Monthly weather review, June, 1923.] †

—— Some characteristics of Texas rainfall; by I. R. Tannehill. 1923. [1]+ 250–253 p. il. 4° [From Monthly weather review, May, 1923.] †

Sunspots and terrestrial temperature in United States; by A. J. Henry. 1923. [1]+243–249 p. il. 4° [From Monthly weather review, May, 1923.] †

Weather map. Daily weather map [of United States, containing forecasts for all States east of Mississippi River except Illinois, Wisconsin, Indiana, upper Michigan, and lower Michigan], Sept. 1–29, 1923. 1st edition. [1923.] Each 16.4×22.7 in. [Not issued Sundays or holidays.] * Editions issued at Washington, D. C., 25c. a month, $2.50 a yr.; editions issued at about 65 stations throughout the United States, 20c. a month, $2.00 a yr.

—— Same [containing forecasts for United States], Sept. 1–30, 1923. 2d edition. [1923.] Each 16.4×22.7 in. [The Sunday edition does not contain as much information as the edition for week days.] * 30c. a month, $3.00 a yr.

CIVIL SERVICE COMMISSION

NOTE.—The Commission furnishes its publications gratuitously to those who apply for them.

Civil service. General information in regard to civil service, including list of positions not subject to competitive civil service examination. May, 1923. ii+27 p. (Form 2346.) †   23—26800

COMMERCE DEPARTMENT

CENSUS BUREAU

NOTE.—Persons desiring 14th census publications should address the Director of the Census, Department of Commerce, Washington, D. C. They are also sold by the Superintendent of Documents, Washington, D. C., at the price indicated.

Cotton. Cotton consumed, cotton on hand, active cotton spindles, and imports and exports of cotton, Aug. 1922 and 1923, with statistics of cotton consumed, imported, and exported for 12 months ending July 31. Sept. 14, 1923. oblong 32° [Preliminary report. This publication is issued in postal card form.] †

—— Report on cotton ginning, number of bales of cotton ginned from growth of 1923 prior to Sept. 1, 1923, and comparative statistics to corresponding date in 1922 and 1921. Sept. 8, 1923. oblong 32° [Preliminary report. This publication is issued in postal card form.] †

Cottonseed received, crushed, and on hand, and cottonseed products manufactured, shipped out, on hand, and exported covering 1-month period ending Aug. 31, 1923 and 1922. Sept. 19, 1923. oblong 32° [Preliminary report. This publication is issued in postal card form.] †

Fertilizers. Census of manufactures, 1921: Fertilizers. 1923. 18 p. * Paper, 5c.   23—26801

Fuel. 14th census of United States [1920]: Manufactures, 1919, fuel consumed. 1923. [1]+130–141 p. 4° [Prepared under supervision of Eugene F. Hartley, chief statistician for manufactures. From 14th census of United States, 1920, v. 8.] †

Greensboro, N. C. Special census of population of Greensboro, N. C., Apr. 16, 1923. 1923. 6 p. [Prepared under supervision of Samuel D. Rhoads.] * Paper, 5c. 23—26802

Hours of labor. 14th census of United States [1920]: Manufactures, 1919, prevailing hours of labor. 1923. [1]+69–82 p. 4° [Prepared under supervision of Eugene F. Hartley, chief statistician for manufactures. From 14th census of United States, 1920, v. 8.] †

Lumber. Census of manufactures, 1921: Lumber industry, including lumber and timber products, planing mills, and wooden packing boxes. 1923. 59 p. il. [Compiled in cooperation with Forest Service.] * Paper, 10c. 23—26803

    NOTE.—Includes Forest resources, annual drain, and reforestation; prepared by Forest Service.

Manufactures. 14th census of United States [1920]: Manufactures, 1919, comparative summary for cities having 10,000 inhabitants or more, by States, 1919, 1914, and 1909. 1923. [1]+224–238 p. 4° [Prepared under supervision of Eugene F. Hartley, chief statistician for manufactures. From 14th census of United States, 1920, v. 8.] †

—— 14th census of United States [1920]: Manufactures, 1919, detailed statement for all industries, by States, 1919. 1923. [1]+298–509 p. 4° [Prepared under supervision of Eugene F. Hartley, chief statistician for manufactures. From 14th census of United States, 1920, v. 8.] †

—— 14th census of United States [1920]: Manufactures, 1919, detailed statement for United States, by geographic divisions and States, 1919. 1923. [1]+296–297 p. 4° [Prepared under supervision of Eugene F. Hartley, chief statistician for manufactures. From 14th census of United States, 1920, v. 8.] †

—— 14th census of United States [1920]: Manufactures, 1919, persons engaged in manufacturing industries. 1923. [1]+20–68 p. 4° [Prepared under supervision of Eugene F. Hartley, chief statistician for manufactures. From 14th census of United States, 1920, v. 8.] †

—— 14th census of United States [1920]: Manufactures, 1919, size of establishments. 1923. [1]+83–106 p. 4° [Prepared under supervision of Eugene F. Hartley, chief statistician for manufactures. From 14th census of United States, 1920, v. 8.] †

—— 14th census of United States [1920]: Manufactures, 1919, summary for counties by States, 1919. 1923. [1]+239–277 p. 4° [Prepared under supervision of Eugene F. Hartley, chief statistician for manufactures. From 14th census of United States, 1920, v. 8.] †

—— 14th census of United States, 1920: v. 8, Manufactures, 1919, general report and analytical tables. 1923. 543 p. il. 4° [Prepared under supervision of Eugene F. Hartley, chief statistician for manufactures, assisted by John F. Daly, William A. Ruff, William W. Sawyer, chiefs of divisions, Frank L. Sanford and Story B. Ladd, expert special agents, and Lucy Craycroft, statistical expert.] * Cloth, $1.50.

Occupations. 14th census of United States [1920]: Population, 1920, occupations, age of occupied persons. 1923. [1]+374–472 p. 4°. [Prepared under supervision of William C. Hunt, chief statistician for population. Chapter 4 from 14th census of United States, 1920, v. 4.] †

—— 14th census of United States [1920]: Population, 1920, occupations, enumeration and classification of occupations. 1923. [1]+8–30 p. 4° [Prepared under supervision of William C. Hunt, chief statistician for population. Chapter 1 from 14th census of United States, 1920, v. 4.] †

—— 14th census of United States [1920]: Population, 1920, occupations, number and sex of occupied persons. 1923. [1]+32–335 p. 4° [Prepared under supervision of William C. Hunt, chief statistician for population. Chapter 2 from 14th census of United States, 1920, v. 4.] †

Power. 14th census of United States [1920]: Manufactures, 1919, power used in manufacturing. 1923. [1]+121–129 p. 4° [Prepared under supervision of Eugene F. Hartley, chief statistician for manufactures. From 14th census of United States, 1920, v. 8.] †

Sugar. Census of manufactures, 1921: Sugar industries. 1923. 18 p. * Paper, 5c. 23—26804

Tobacco. Stocks of leaf tobacco, and American production, import, export, and consumption of tobacco and tobacco products, 1922. 1923. 45 p. il. (Bulletin 151.) [Compiled under supervision of William L. Austin, chief statistician for tobacco, assisted by Harvey J. Zimmerman, expert special agent.]
* Paper, 5c.   18—26607

COAST AND GEODETIC SURVEY

NOTE.—The monthly Notice to mariners, formerly issued by the Coast and Geodetic Survey, has been consolidated with and made a part of the Notice to mariners issued by the Lighthouses Bureau, thus making it a joint publication. The charts, coast pilots, and tide tables of the Coast and Geodetic Survey are sold at the office of the Survey in Washington, and also by one or more sales agents in each of the important American seaports.

Arkansas. Magnetic declination in Arkansas in 1923 [with bibliographies]; by W. N. McFarland. 1923. [1]+29 p. 1 pl. map. (Serial 237.) * Paper, 10c.
                                                                                23—26805
Coast and Geodetic Survey bulletin, Aug. 31, 1923; no. 99. [1923.] 7 p. [Monthly.] ‡   15—26512
Coast pilots. Supplement to United States coast pilot, Atlantic Coast, section E, Gulf of Mexico from Key West to Rio Grande. Mar. 30, 1923 [reprint with changes]. [1]+16 leaves. (Serial 231.) †
Current tables, Pacific Coast, North America, [calendar] year 1924. 1923. 56 p.+[5] folded leaves, il. (Serial 236.) † Paper, 10c.   22—26900

Charts

Alaska. Southeast Alaska, San Christoval Channel to Cape Lynch, surveys to 1922; chart 8157. Scale 1: 40,000. Washington, Coast and Geodetic Survey, Aug. 1923. 32.6×39.9 in. † 75c.
Buzzards Bay. Head of Buzzards Bay, Mass., original surveys 1895–1917, surveys by U. S. Engineers to 1922 and other sources; chart 251. Scale 1:20,000. Washington, Coast and Geodetic Survey, Sept. 1923. 33.6×41.3 in. † 75c.
Cagayan Islands, P. I., [from] surveys to 1923; with inset, Cagayan Anchorage, surveyed in 1921; chart 4356. Scale 1:60,000. Manila, P. I., Coast and Geodetic Survey, July, 1923. 38.5×33.5 in. † 75c.
Georgia Strait and Strait of Juan de Fuca, Wash., surveys 1852–1916 and other sources; chart 6300. Scale 1:200,000. Washington, Coast and Geodetic Survey, Aug. 1923. 28.3×41.8 in. † 75c.
Maine–New Hampshire, Cape Elizabeth to Portsmouth, surveys 1850–1917, surveys by U. S. Engineers to 1913 and other sources; chart 1205. Scale 1:80,000. Washington, Coast and Geodetic Survey, Sept. 1923. 30.4×37.1 in. † 75c.
New Bedford Harbor and approaches, Mass., surveys 1895–1915, surveys by U. S. Engineers to 1921 and other sources; chart 252. Scale 1:20,000. Washington, Coast and Geodetic Survey, Sept. 1923. 35.3×33.9 in. † 75c.
Pacific Coast. Northwest coast of America, Cape Flattery to Dixon Entrance, from United States and British sources; chart 7002. [Scale 1:198,000.] Washington, Coast and Geodetic Survey, Aug. 1923. 29×39.6 in. [For offshore navigation only.] † 75c.
—— Pacific Coast, San Diego to Point St. George, Calif.; chart 5002. [Scale 1:1,499,000.] Washington, Coast and Geodetic Survey, Sept. 1923. 32×41 in. [For offshore navigation only.] † 75c.
Port Royal Sound and inland passages, S. C., surveys 1853–1921; chart 571. Scale 1:40,000. Washington, Coast and Geodetic Survey, Aug. 1923. 41.7× 33.3 in. † 75c.

FISHERIES BUREAU

Cold storage holdings. Cold storage holdings of fish, July 15, 1923. [1923.] 1 p. oblong 8° (Statistical bulletin 580.) [Statistics furnished by Agricultural Economics Bureau.] †
—— Same, Aug. 15, 1923. [1923.] 1 p. oblong 8° (Statistical bulletin 583.) [Statistics furnished by Agricultural Economics Bureau.] †
Fisheries service bulletin, Sept. 1, 1923; no. 100. [1923.] 4 p. [Monthly.] ‡
                                                                                F15—76

Fishery products. Statement of quantities and values of certain fishery products landed at Boston and Gloucester, Mass., and Portland, Me., by American fishing vessels, July, 1923. [1923.] 1 p. oblong f° (Statistical bulletin 581.) †

—— Same, Aug. 1923. [1923.] 1 p. oblong f° (Statistical bulletin 584.) †

—— Statement of quantities and values of certain fishery products landed at Seattle, Wash., by American fishing vessels, July, 1923. [1923.] 1 p. oblong 12° (Statistical bulletin 582.) †

—— Same, Aug. 1923. [1923.] 1 p. oblong 8° (Statistical bulletin 585.) †

FOREIGN AND DOMESTIC COMMERCE BUREAU

Commerce. Monthly summary of foreign commerce of United States, July, 1923. 1923. 2 pts. p. 1–69 and ii+71–91 p. 4° *Paper, 10c. single copy (including pts. 1 and 2), $1.00 a yr.; foreign subscription, $1.60.   14—21465

—— Same. 1923. [2 pts. in 1], 91 p. 4° (H. doc. 7, 68th Cong. 1st sess.)

Commerce reports. Commerce reports, weekly survey of foreign trade, reports from American consular officers and representatives of Department of Commerce in foreign countries, no. 36–39; Sept. 3–24, 1923. 1923. cover-titles, p. 577–848, il. 4° [Text and illustration on p. 2–4 of covers.] *Paper, 10c. single copy, $3.00 a yr.; foreign subscription, $5.00.

—— Supplement to Commerce reports. [Included in price of Commerce reports for subscribers.]

—— Trade and economic review for 1922, no. 17: Portugal; [by] W. Stanley Hollis, H. Tobey Mooers, and Hernan C. Vogenitz. [1923.] 8 p.

—— Supplement to Commerce reports: Balance of international payments of United States in 1922, [by John H. Williams and Rufus S. Tucker]; with Foreword, by Herbert Hoover. Sept. 14, 1923. ii+25 p. (Trade information bulletin 144; Finance and Investment Division.) †   23—26806

—— Same: Belgian finance and industry; [articles] by S. H. Cross and Ellwood A. Welden. Sept. 20, 1923. ii+17 p. (Trade information bulletin 146; Western European Division.) †   23—26807

—— Same: German coal-tar chemical industry, production, export, and import statistics; by Frederick E. Breithut. Sept. 3, 1923. ii+12 p. (Trade information bulletin 141; Chemical Division.) †   23—26867

—— Same: Protesting drafts in China; compiled by A. J. Wolfe from information furnished by American consular officers. Sept. 3, 1923. ii+28 p. (Trade information bulletin 142; Division of Commercial Laws.) †   23—26792

—— Same: Protesting drafts in southeastern Asia; prepared by A. J. Wolfe from information furnished by American consular officers. Sept. 10, 1923. ii+20 p. (Trade information bulletin 143; Division of Commercial Laws.) †   23—26808

—— Same: Shipment of samples and advertising matter to Europe; by R. P. Wakefield. Sept. 20, 1923. iv + 30 p. (Trade information bulletin 145; [Foreign Tariffs Division].) †   23—26809

—— Survey of current business, Aug. 1923, no. 24; compiled by Bureau of Census, Bureau of Foreign and Domestic Commerce, [and] Bureau of Standards. 1923. cover-title, 211 p. il. 4° (Monthly supplement to Commerce reports.) [Contains statistics for June, 1923, the date given above, Aug. 1923, being the date of issue. Text on p. 2–4 of cover.] *Paper, 10c. single copy, $1.00 a yr.; foreign subscription, $1.50.   21—26819

NOTE.—Realizing that current statistics are highly perishable and that to be of use they must reach the business man at the earliest possible moment, the Department has arranged to distribute advance leaflets twice each month to those subscribers who request them. One set of these leaflets is issued about the 20th of the month, giving such information as has been received up to that time, and another set of sheets is mailed at the end of the month giving those figures received since the 20th. The information contained in these leaflets is also published in Commerce reports issued weekly by the Foreign and Domestic Commerce Bureau. The advance sheets will be mailed free of charge to all subscribers to the Survey who request them. Such request should be addressed to the Bureau of the Census, Department of Commerce. Washington, D. C. Subscriptions, however, should be sent to the Superintendent of Documents, Washington, D. C., at the prices stated above.

—— Same, Sept. 1923, no. 25; compiled by Bureau of Census, Bureau of Foreign and Domestic Commerce, [and] Bureau of Standards. 1923. cover-title, 63 p. il. 4° (Monthly supplement to Commerce reports.) [Contains statistics for July, 1923, the date given above, Sept. 1923, being the date of issue. Text on p. 2–4 of cover.]

Industrial machinery. Export helps; [prepared in] Industrial Machinery Division. 2d edition. 1923. ii+8 p. narrow 12° †

LIGHTHOUSES BUREAU

Lighthouse service bulletin, v. 2, no. 69; Sept. 1, 1923. [1923.] p. 293–297.
˜ [Monthly.] †   ˮ   12—35121
Notice to mariners, weekly, no. 36–39, 1923; Sept. 7–28 [1923]. 1923. various paging. [Issued jointly with Coast and Geodetic Survey.] † 7—20609

NAVIGATION BUREAU

Ships. American documented seagoing merchant vessels of 500 gross tons and over, Sept. 1, 1923. 1923. ii+69 p. 4° (Serial 70.) [Monthly.] *Paper, 10c. single copy, 75c. a yr.; foreign subscription, $1.25.   19—26597

RADIO SERVICE

Radio Service bulletin, Sept. 1, 1923; no. 77. [1923.] 15 p. [Monthly.]
*Paper, 5c. single copy, 25c. a yr.; foreign subscription, 40c.   15—26255

PUBLICATIONS DIVISION

Commerce Department. Supplement to annual List of publications [of Department of Commerce available for distribution], Aug. 31, 1923. [1923.] 4 p.
[Monthly.] †

STANDARDS BUREAU

NOTE.—The Scientific papers will be supplied on subscription as issued at $1.25 per volume, paper bound. These volumes will afterwards be issued bound in cloth at $2.00 per volume; foreign subscription, paper $2.50 (sent in single numbers), cloth $2.35 (bound volumes). Single numbers vary in price. Address the Superintendent of Documents, Washington, D. C.
The Technologic papers will be issued first as separates and later in volume form in the same manner as Scientific papers.. Subscriptions will be accepted by the. Superintendent of Documents at $1.25 per volume; foreign subscription, $2.50. Single numbers vary in price.

Homes. How to own your home, handbook for prospective home owners; by John M. Gries and James S. Taylor. 1923. viii+28 p. (Building and Housing Division.) [Includes lists of Commerce Department publications in relation to housing.] *Paper, 5c.   23—26810
Visibility of radiant energy [with bibliography]; by K. S. Gibson [and] E. P. T. Tyndall. Aug. 11, 1923. [1]+131–191 p. il. large 8° (Scientific papers 475.) [From Scientific papers, v. 19.] *Paper, 15c.   23—26811

STEAMBOAT-INSPECTION SERVICE

Pilot rules for rivers whose waters flow into Gulf of Mexico and their tributaries and Red River of the North. Edition, July 10, 1922. [Reprint with omissions 1923.] 22 p. il. †   11—35466
Steamboat Inspection Service bulletin, Sept. 1, 1923; no. 95. 1923. 1 p.
[Monthly.] ‡   15—26679

COURT OF CLAIMS

American Seating Company v. United States; [evidence for claimant]. [1923.] no. C–14, p. 25–43. ‡
Cases. Supplemental calendar, Oct. 1923 [cases ready for trial or hearing]. 1923. 49 p. [Part of the pages are blank.] ‡
Cherokee Nation v. United States; evidence for claimant. [1923.] no. 34449, p. 77–87. ‡
Chicago, Rock Island and Pacific Railway. Chicago, Rock Island and Pacific Railway Company *v.* United States; evidence for defendant. [1923.] no. B–144, p. 17–20. †
—— Chicago, Rock Island and Pacific Railway Company *v.* United States; stipulation [and evidence for claimant]. [1923.] no. B–33, p. 25–72. ‡

Depositions. Instructions for taking depositions to be used in Court of Claims. [1923.] 9 p. †

Federal Sugar Refining Company v. United States; evidence for plaintiff. [1923.] no. B–147, p. 11–70. ‡

Fidelity & Deposit Company of Maryland v. United States: testimony for claimant. [1923.] no. 33976, p. 9–17. ‡

Galveston, Harrisburg and San Antonio Railway. Galveston, Harrisburg & San Antonio Railway Co. *v.* United States; evidence for plaintiff. [1923.] no. B–186, p. 31–38. ‡

——— Galveston, Harrisburg & San Antonio Railway Co. *v.* United States; evidence for plaintiff. [1923.] no. C–263, p. 9–14. ‡

Guggenheim. S. D. Guggenheim et al. *v.* United States; evidence for plaintiffs. [1923.] no. B–101, p. 19–102. ‡

Houston and Texas Central Railroad Co. v. United States; evidence for plaintiff. [1923.] no. C–264, p. 9–10. ‡ ˒

Howard, R. S., & Co. R. S. Howard and Company *v.* United States; stipulation [and evidence for claimant]. [1923.] Congressional, no. 17329, p. 31–116. ‡

Iselin. Georgine Iselin *v.* United States; evidence for plaintiff. [1923.] no. B–96, p. 45–60. ‡

Kenilworth Co. v. United States; evidence for claimant. [1923.] no. 762-C, p. 25–36. ‡

Lafayette Warehouse Company. Harris P. Rallston, William F. McGinnis [William D. Maginnis], liquidators of Lafayette Warehouse Company *v.* United States; evidence for defendant. [1923.] no. 178–A, p. 17–29. ‡

La Vallette. Albert T. La Vallette *v.* United States; evidence for claimant. [1923.] no. 58–A, p. 9–65. ‡

Lawless. John Lawless, jr., *v.* United States; evidence for defendant. [1923.] no. 50–B, p. 37–44. ‡

Livingston. Thomas M. Livingston *v.* United States; evidence for plaintiff. [1923.] no. 298–A, p. 15–245. ‡

Marsh Manufacturing Co. v. United States; evidence for plaintiff. [1923.] no. 91–A, p. 17–65. ‡

Morgan's Louisiana & Texas Railroad & Steamship Company v. United States; evidence for plaintiff. [1923.] no. C–266, p. 9–12. ‡

National Contracting Company v. United States; evidence for defendant; [1923.] no. B–57, p. 87–131. ‡

New York State. State of New York *v.* United States; evidence for claimant. [1923.] no. 34022, p. 139–336. ‡

Northern Pacific Railway Company v. United States; defendant's evidence. [1923.] no. B–60, p. 9–30. ‡

Semple. John B. Semple *v.* United States; evidence for defendant. 1923. no. 34442, cover-title, p. 145–542. ‡

——— Same; evidence for plaintiff. [1923.] no. 34442, p. 15–144. ‡

Southern Pacific Company v. United States; evidence for plaintiff. [1923.] no. B–367, p. 11–18. ‡

Standard Transportation Co. v. United States; evidence for defendant [and] plaintiff's testimony in rebuttal. [1923.] no. 34216, p. 541–552. ‡

Streater. Wallace Streater *v.* United States; evidence for defendant. [1923.] no. 8–B, p. 45–47. ‡

Sughrue. Daniel H. Sughrue *v.* United States; evidence for defendant. 1923. no. 208–B, p. 21. ‡ ˑ

Texas & New Orleans Railroad Company v. United States; evidence for plaintiff. [1923.] no. C–265, p. 9–11. ‡

Towar Cotton Mills, Inc., v. United States; evidence for plaintiff. [1923.] no. C–209, p. 35–49. ‡

Turner, C. A. P., Company. C. A. P. Turner Company *v.* United States; evidence for plaintiff under rules. [1923.] no. 259–A, p. 9–254. ‡

Union Pacific Railroad Company v. United States; evidence for plaintiff. [1923.] no. 89–A, p. 37–41. ‡

Waite. Harry F. Waite *v.* United States; evidence for plaintiff. [1923.] no. B–129, p. 11–65. ‡

COURT OF CUSTOMS APPEALS

Calendar, Court of Customs Appeals, Oct. term, 1923. [1923.] xv+[94] p.
[Part of the pages are blank.] †

Cherries. No. 2309, United States *v.* M. J. & H. J. Meyer Co., transcript of
record on appeal from Board of General Appraisers. [1923.] cover-title,
i+7 p. ‡

Diamonds. No. 2314, United States *v.* J. R. Wood & Sons, transcript of record
on appeal from Board of General Appraisers. 1923. cover-title, i+8 p. ‡

Paper. No. 2312, United States *v.* Southern Paper Co., Ltd., transcript of
record on appeal from Board of General Appraisers. [1923.] cover-title,
i+8 p. ‡

DISTRICT OF COLUMBIA

Court of Appeals. Calendar, Oct. term, 1923. 1923. i+76 leaves. [Some of
these leaves are printed as pages.] ‡

—— Transcript of record, Oct. term, 1923, no. 4021, United States *vs.* Chichester
Chemical Company, proprietor and vendor of what is known as Chi-ches-ters
diamond brand new style pills; and no. 4022, [same] *vs.* [same], appeal from
Supreme Court of District of Columbia. [1923.] cover-title, ii+33 p. ‡

Supreme Court. Trial calendar, Oct. term, 1923. [1923.] [1]+71 p. ‡

FEDERAL BOARD FOR VOCATIONAL EDUCATION

Agriculture. Effectiveness of vocational education in agriculture, study of
value of vocational instruction in agriculture in secondary schools as indicated by occupational distribution of former students; [by Charles Everett
Myers]. May, 1923. v+63 p. il. (Bulletin 82; Agriculture [Agricultural]
series 13.) * Paper, 10c.   E 23—366

—— Principles underlying distribution of aid to vocational education in agriculture, bases of apportioning aid to local communities and limiting provisions
under which aid is granted [with bibliography; by Frank W. Lathrop].
June, 1923. vii+83 p. (Bulletin 84; Agricultural series 15.) * Paper, 10c.
                                                                 E 23—367

—— Supervised practice in agriculture, aims and values of such practice and
responsibilities of pupils, teachers, State administrators, and local boards of
education. June, 1923. v+55 p. (Bulletin 83; Agricultural series 14.)
* Paper, 10c.   E 23—365

Continuation schools. Program for training part-time-school teachers, organization and content of training program to prepare teachers for effective
service in part-time schools [with lists of references; by I. S. Noall]. June,
1923. vi+50 p. (Bulletin 85; Trade and industrial series 24.) * Paper, 5c.
                                                                 E 23—368

FEDERAL RESERVE BOARD

Cotton. Financing production and distribution of cotton; [by W. J. Carson].
1923. iii+72 p. il. [From Federal reserve bulletins, Feb.–June, 1923, final
edition.] †   23—26812

Federal reserve bulletin. Federal reserve bulletin, Sept. 1923; [v. 9, no. 9].
1st edition. 1923. ii+309–342 p. il. 4° [Monthly.] † Paper, $1.50 a yr.
                                                                 15—26318

NOTE.—The Federal reserve bulletin is printed in 2 editions (a 1st edition and a
final edition). The 1st edition is brief and contains the regular official announcements, the national review of business conditions, and other general matter, and is
distributed without charge to the member banks of the Federal reserve system. The
2d or final edition contains detailed analyses of business conditions, special articles,
review of foreign banking, and complete statistics showing condition of Federal reserve banks. Those desiring copies of either edition may obtain them from the Federal
Reserve Board, Washington, D. C., at the prices stated above and below.

—— Same, Sept. 1923; [v. 9, no. 9]. Final edition. 1923. iv+981–1084 p.
il. 4° [Monthly.] † Paper, 40c. single copy, $4.00 a yr.

Federal reserve member banks. Abstract of condition reports of State bank and trust company members, and of all member banks of Federal reserve system, June 30, 1923. Aug. 24, 1923. 12 p. f° (Report 21.) †
—— Federal reserve inter-district collection system, changes in list of banks upon which items will be received by Federal reserve banks for collection and credit, Sept. 1, 1923. 1923. [1]+16 p. 4° †   16—26870

FEDERAL TRADE COMMISSION

NOTE.—The bound volumes of the Federal Trade Commission decisions are sold by the Superintendent of Documents, Washington, D. C. Separate opinions are sold on subscription, price $1.00 per volume; foreign subscription, $1.50; single copies, 5c. each.

Claire Furnace Company. No. 250, in Supreme Court, Oct. term, 1923, Federal Trade Commission et al. *v.* Claire Furnace Company et al., on appeal from Court of Appeals of District of Columbia; motion by appellants to advance. 1923. cover-title, 2 p. ‡

International Paint and Oil Company. Federal Trade Commission *v.* International Paint & Oil Company et al., complaint [report] findings, and order; docket 734, Feb. 26, 1923. 1923. [1]+16–19 p. ([Decision] 344.) [From Federal Trade Commission decisions, v. 6.] * Paper, 5c.

Loeb Company. Federal Trade Commission *v.* Meyer J. Loeb and Harry J. Loeb, partners, trading under name and style of Loeb Company, and Joseph Hutner, trading under the name and style of P. Hutner & Co., complaint [report, findings, and order]; docket 834, Feb. 15, 1923. [1923.] p. 11–15. ([Decision] 343.) [From Federal Trade Commission decisions, v. 6.] * Paper, 5c.

McQuade, John, & Co., Incorporated. Federal Trade Commission *v.* John McQuade & Company, Inc., complaint [report, findings, and order]; docket 929, Feb. 14, 1923. [1923.] p. 1–10. ([Decision] 342.) [From Federal Trade Commission decisions, v. 6.] * Paper, 5c.

Maynard Coal Company. No. 3984, in Court of Appeals of District of Columbia, Federal Trade Commission et al. *v.* Maynard Coal Company; brief and argument for appellants. 1923. cover-title, ii+41 p. ‡

GENERAL ACCOUNTING OFFICE

Account numbers. General ledger account numbers. [1923.] [4] p. 4° (Post Office Department Division.) ‡

GOVERNMENT PRINTING OFFICE

Printing. Courses for training of apprentices in Government Printing Office. Revised edition, Sept. 1923. 1923. [2]+27 p. 16° * Paper, 5c.   23—26813

DOCUMENTS OFFICE

Health, diseases, drugs, and sanitation, list of publications for sale by superintendent of documents. July, 1923. [2]+50 p. (Price list 51, 13th edition.) †   23—26794

Monthly catalogue, United States public documents, no. 344; Aug. 1923. 1923. p. 51–103. * Paper, 5c. single copy, 50c. a yr.; foreign subscription, 75c.
                                                                        4—18088

INTERIOR DEPARTMENT

NOTE.—The decisions of the Department of the Interior in pension cases are issued in slips and in signatures, and the decisions in land cases are issued in signatures, both being published later in bound volumes. Subscribers may deposit $1.00 with the Superintendent of Documents and receive the contents of a volume of the decisions of either kind in separate parts as they are issued; foreign subscription, $1.25. Prices for bound volumes furnished upon application to the Superintendent of Documents, Washington, D. C.

Pensions. [Decisions of Department of Interior in appealed pension and bounty land claims, v. 21, slip] 84. [1923.] 2 p. [For price, see note above under center head.]   12—29422

Public lands. Decisions [of Department of Interior in cases] relating to public lands, v. 49, [signatures] 14-39. [1923.] p. 209-624. [For. price, see note above under center head.]   7—23651

EDUCATION BUREAU

Agriculture and country life [reading course]; prepared in cooperation with T. N. Carver and C. E. Ladd. [Reprint with additions] 1923. [1]+5 p. 12° (Home reading course 22.) †

Alaska. Work of Bureau of Education for natives of Alaska; by William Hamilton. 1923. [1]+4 p. (Bulletin 45, 1923.) [Advance sheets from Biennial survey of education in United States, 1920-22.] * Paper, 5c.
          E 13—1875

American education week. Suggestions for observance of American education week, Nov. 18-24, 1923 [with bibliographies]. 1923. [1]+20 p. * Paper, 5c.
          E 23—354

American history course; [prepared in] Home Education [Division]. [1923.] 4 p. 12° (Reading course 10 revised.) †

Boys. Reading course for boys; [prepared in] Home Education [Division]. [1923.] 4 p. 12° (Reading course 4 revised.) †

Fiction. Thirty books of great fiction; [prepared in] Home Education [Division]. [1923.] 4 p. 12° (Reading course 6 revised.) †

Foreign trade [reading course]; prepared by Glen Levin Swiggett. [Reprint with additions 1923.] [1]+5 p. 12° (Home reading course 17.) †

Girls. Reading course for girls; [prepared in] Home Education [Division]. [1923.] 4 p. 12° (Reading course 5 revised.) †

Heroes. Thirty American heroes; [prepared in] Home Education [Division]. [1923.] 4 p. 12° (Reading course 9 revised.) †

—— Thirty world heroes; [prepared in] Home Education [Division]. [1923.] 4 p. 12° (Reading course 7 revised.) †

Hygiene. Growing healthy children, study made for Child Health Organization of America, now part of American Child Health Association, by Mrs. Ina J. N. Perkins; revised by Julia Tappan. 1923. 35 p. il. ((School health studies 4.)) [Title on cover is: Growing healthy children, study of health supervision in Trenton, N. J., schools.] * Paper, 5c.   E 23—364

Kansas. Report of survey of State institutions of higher learning in Kansas; by commission composed of George F. Zook, Lotus D. Coffman [and] A. R. Mann. 1923. viii+160 p. (Bulletin 40, 1923.) * Paper, 20c.   E 23—353

Kindergarten. Kindergarten and health; [articles] by Arnold Gesell and Julia Wade Abbot. 1923. 38 p. il. (Health education 14.) * Paper, 5c.
          E 23—359

CONTENTS.—Pt. 1, Kindergarten as health agency; by Arnold Gesell.—Pt. 2, Health education in kindergarten; by Julia Wade Abbot.

—— Prefirst-grade training; by William Thomas Root. 1923. [1] +8 p. il. (Kindergarten circular 13.) * Paper, 5c.   E 23—360

NOTE.—This article previously appeared in School life, v. 8, no. 10, June, 1923, with title: Ample justification for the kindergarten.

—— Principles of kindergarten-primary education in consolidated rural school; by Katherine M. Cook. June, 1923. 9 p. (Rural school leaflet 18.) * Paper, 5c.   E 23—362

—— References on preschool and kindergarten-primary education; compiled by Nina C. Vandewalker and Harriet E. Howard. July, 1923. 11 p. (Kindergarten circular 14.) * Paper, 5c.   E 23—361

Literature. World's great literary bibles; [prepared in] Home Education [Division]. [1923.] 4 p. 12° (Reading course 1 revised.) †

National Conference on Consolidation of Rural Schools and Transportation of Pupils. Consolidation and transportation problems, report of 2d National Conference on Consolidation of Rural Schools and Transportation of Pupils, Cleveland, Ohio, Feb. 26, 1923; by J. F. Abel. 1923. ii+22 p. (Bulletin 39, 1923.) * Paper, 5c.   E 23—356.

Pageants. Gifts of nations, pageant for rural schools; by Maud C. Newbury. Sept. 1923. 12 p. (Rural school leaflet 20.) * Paper, 5c.   E 23—363

Parents. Reading course for parents (revised) ; [prepared in] Home Education [Division]. [1923.] 4 p. 12° (Reading course 3 revised) †

Platoon schools. Bibliography of work-study-play or platoon plan ; by Alice Barrows. July, 1923. 7 p. (City school leaflet 10.) * Paper, 5c.
                                                                    E 23—357

—— Training of teachers for platoon schools ; by W. J. Bankes. Aug. 1923. 5 p. (City school leaflet 11.) * Paper, 5c.   E 23—358

Roads. Main streets of the Nation, series of projects on highway transport for elementary schools [with bibliographies] ; by Florence C. Fox. 1923. viii+ 42 p. il. map. (Bulletin 38, 1923.) * Paper, 10c.   E 23—355

School life. School life, v. 8, Sept. 1922–June, 1923 [title-page and index]. 1923. [1] +7 p. 4° [Included in price of School life for subscribers.]
                                                                    E 18—902

—— Same, v. 9, no. 1 ; Sept. 1923. [1923.] p. 1–24, il. 4° [Monthly except July and August.] * Paper, 5c. single copy, 30c. yr. (10 months) ; foreign subscription, 55c.

Secondary education. List of references on secondary education in United States ; prepared in Library Division. June, 1923. 10 p. (Library leaflet 22.) * Paper, 5c.   E 13—1216

GENERAL LAND OFFICE

NOTE.—The General Land Office publishes a large general map of the United States, which is sold at $2.00 ; and also separate maps of the States and Territories in which public lands are to be found, which are sold at 25c. per sheet. The map of California is in 2 sheets. Address the Superintendent of Documents, Washington, D. C.

Roster of field officers, Sept. 1, 1923. [1923.] 4 p. †

GEOLOGICAL SURVEY

NOTE.—The publications of the United States Geological Survey consist of annual reports, Monographs, Professional papers, Bulletins, Water-supply papers, chapters and volumes of Mineral resources of the United States, folios of the Topographic atlas of the United States and topographic maps that bear descriptive text, and folios of the Geologic atlas of the United States and the World atlas of commercial geology. A wholesale rate has been established for topographic and geologic folios, so that a discount of 40 per cent from the retail price is now allowed on all orders the net cost of which amounts to $5.00 or more. This rate applies on an order for either maps or folios alone or for maps and folios together, but does not apply to the folios sold at 5c. each on account of damage by fire. For maps and topographic and geologic folios address the Director of the Geological Survey, Washington, D. C. Other publications, with the exception of Monographs, are free at the Survey as long as the supply lasts and are also sold by the Superintendent of Documents at the price indicated. Orders for such publications as are for sale (excepting maps and folios) should be sent to the Superintendent of Documents, Washington, D. C. For topographic sheets see next page.

Arsenic in 1922 ; by V. C. Heikes and G. F. Loughlin. Sept. 17, 1923. iv+53–76 p. il. [From Mineral resources, 1922, pt. 1.] †

Carlyle, Ill. Carlyle-Centralia folio, Ill. ; by E. W. Shaw. [Library edition.] Washington, Geological Survey, 1923. cover-title, 10 p. il. 4 maps, large 4° (Geologic atlas of United States 216.) [Prepared in cooperation with Geological Survey of Illinois. Text and illustrations on p. 2–4 of cover.] † Paper, 25c.   GS 23—262

Coal. Twentymile Park district of Yampa coal field, Routt County, Colo. ; by Marius R. Campbell. 1923. iv+82 p. il. 2 pl. 10 p. of pl. map in pocket. (Bulletin 748.) * Paper, 20c.   GS 23—261

—— Same. (H. doc. 28, 68th Cong. 1st sess.)

Fuller's earth in 1922 ; by Jefferson Middleton. Sept. 15, 1923. [1]+69–71 p. [From Mineral resources, 1922, pt. 2.] †

Magnesium and its compounds in 1922 ; by J. M. Hill and G. F. Loughlin. Sept. 20, 1923. ii+41–57 p. [From Mineral resources, 1922, pt. 2.] †

Missouri River. Surface water supply of United States, 1919–20 : pt. 6, Missouri River basin ; Nathan C. Grover, chief hydraulic engineer, W. A. Lamb, Robert Follansbee, W. G. Hoyt, and R. C. Rice, district engineers. 1923. 411 p. 2 p. of pl. (Water-supply paper 506.) [Prepared in cooperation with Montana, Wyoming, Iowa, Colorado, and Kansas.] * Paper, 35c. GS 10—383

—— Same. (H. doc. 444, 67th Cong. 3d sess.)

Publications. New publications, list 186 ; Sept. 1, 1923. [1923.] 3 p. [Monthly.] †

Quicksilver in 1922, by F. L. Ransome; with supplementary bibliography; by Isabel P. Evans. Sept. 18, 1923. [1]+113–124 p. [From Mineral resources, 1922, pt. 1.] †

Strontium in 1922; by George W. Stose. Sept. 12, 1923. [1]+59–61 p. [From Mineral resources, 1922, pt. 2.] †

Surveying. Triangulation and primary traverse, 1916–18; C. H. Birdseye, chief topographic engineer. 1923. vi+914 p. 1 pl. map. (Bulletin 709; H. doc. 830, 66th Cong. 3d sess.) * Paper, 75c.   4—1312

Topographic sheets

NOTE.—The Geological Survey is making a topographic map of the United States. The sheets of which it is composed are projected without reference to political divisions, and are designated by some prominent town or natural feature found on them. Three scales are ordinarily used, 1 : 62,500, 1 : 125,000, and 1 : 250,000. These correspond, approximately, to 1 mile, 2 miles, and 4 miles to 1 linear inch, covering, respectively, average areas of 230, 920, and 3,700 square miles. For some areas of particular importance special large-scale maps are published. The usual size, exclusive of the margin, is about 17.5 inches in height by 11.5 to 16 inches in width, the latter varying with the latitude. A description of the topographic map is printed on the reverse of each sheet.

More than two-fifths of the area of the country, excluding Alaska, has been mapped, every State being represented. Connecticut, Delaware, the District of Columbia, Maryland, Massachusetts, New Jersey, Ohio, Rhode Island, and West Virginia are completely mapped. Sheets of the regular size are sold by the Survey at 10c. each; but in lots of 50 or more copies, whether of the same sheet or of different sheets, the price is 6c. each. The discount is allowed on all orders the net cost of which amounts to $5.00 or more and applies on an order for either maps or folios alone or for maps and folios together, but does not apply to the folios sold at 5c. each on account of damage by fire.

California. California, Tierra Loma School quadrangle, lat. 36° 37′ 30″–36° 45′, long. 120° 37′ 30″–120° 45′. Scale 1 : 31,680, contour interval 5 ft. and 25 ft. Preliminary edition. [Washington, Geological Survey] edition of 1923. 17.3×13.9 in. † 10c.

—— California, Wisdom Well quadrangle, lat. 36° 45′–36° 52′ 30″, long. 120° 30′–120° 37′ 30″. Scale 1 : 31,680, contour interval 5 ft. [Washington, Geological Survey] edition of 1923. 17.3×13.9 in. † 10c.

Hawaii, Pahala quadrangle, lat. 19°–19° 15′, long. 155° 15′–155° 30′. Scale 1 : 62,500, contour interval 50 ft. [Washington, Geological Survey] edition of 1923. 17.5×16.6 in. † 10c.

Illinois. Illinois, Dongola quadrangle, lat. 37° 15′–37° 30′, long. 89°–89° 15′. Scale 1 : 62,500, contour interval 20 ft. [Washington, Geological Survey] edition of 1923. 17.5×14 in. † 10c.

—— Illinois, Monmouth quadrangle, lat. 40° 45′–41°, long. 90° 30′–90° 45′. Scale 1 : 62,500, contour interval 20 ft. [Washington, Geological Survey] edition of 1923. 17.5×13.4 in. † 10c.

Kentucky. Kentucky, Brownsville quadrangle, lat. 37°–37° 15′, long. 86° 15′–86° 30′. Scale 1 : 62,500, contour interval 20 ft. [Washington, Geological Survey] edition of 1923. 17.5×14.1 in. † 10c.

—— Kentucky, Mammoth Cave quadrangle, lat. 37°–37° 15′, long. 86°–86° 15′. Scale 1 : 62,500, contour interval 20 ft. [Washington, Geological Survey] edition of 1923. 17.5×14 in. † 10c.

Oregon, Mount Angel quadrangle, lat. 45°–45° 15′, long. 122° 45′–123°. Scale 1 : 62,500, contour interval 25 ft. [Washington, Geological Survey] edition of 1923. 17.5×12.4 in. † 10c.

Texas. Texas, Lopena Island quadrangle, lat. 26° 45′–27°, long. 97° 15′–97° 30′. Scale 1 : 62,500, contour interval on land 5 ft., off shore 20 ft. [Washington, Geological Survey] edition of 1923. 17.5×15.2 in. † 10c.

—— Texas, Saltillo Ranch quadrangle, lat. 26° 45′–27°, long. 97° 30′–97° 45′. Scale 1 : 62,500, contour interval 5 ft. [Washington, Geological Survey] edition of 1923. 17.5×15.2 in. † 10c.

—— Texas, Sierra Madera quadrangle, lat. 30° 30′–30° 45′, long. 102° 45′–103°. Scale 1 : 62,500, contour interval 25 ft. [Washington, Geological Survey] edition of 1923. 17.5×15.2 in. † 10c.

Virginia-West Virginia, Middletown quadrangle, lat. 39°–39° 15′, long. 78° 15′–78° 30′. Scale 1 : 62,500, contour interval 50 ft. [Washington, Geological Survey] edition of 1923. 17.5×13.6 in. [Map covers only a portion of the sheet, the actual measurement being 10.8×5.8 in. Shows only the portion of Middletown quadrangle that lies in West Virginia.] † 10c.

West Virginia-virginia, Ronceverte quadrangle, lat. 37° 30'–37° 45', long. 80° 15'–80° 30'. Scale 1 : 62,500, contour interval 50 ft. [Washington, Geological Survey] edition of 1923. 17.5×14 in. † 10c.

Wisconsin, Blanchardville quadrangle, lat. 42° 45'–43°, long. 89° 45'–90°. Scale 1 : 62,500, contour interval 20 ft. [Washington, Geological Survey] edition of 1923. 17.5×12.9 in. † 10c.

INDIAN AFFAIRS OFFICE

Inheritance. Regulations relating to determination of heirs and approval of wills except members of Five Civilized Tribes and Osage Indians; approved June 19, 1923. 1923. [1]+12 p. †

Leases. Regulations governing execution of leases of Indian allotted and tribal lands for farming, grazing, and business purposes; approved July 20, 1923. 1923. iii+15 p. †

MINES BUREAU

Coal mines and mining. Operating regulations to govern coal-mining methods and safety and welfare of miners on leased lands on public domain, under act of Feb. 25, 1920, public 146 [66th Congress]. [1st edition.] [May, 1921, reprint with changes] 1923. 48 p. [Changes appear only in index.] * Paper, 5c.

Leaching nonsulphide copper ores with sulphur dioxide; by Charles E. van Barneveld and Edmund S. Leaver. [1st edition.] [May] 1923. v+91 p. il. 3 pl. 2 p. of pl. (Technical paper 312.) [Includes lists of Mines Bureau publications on treatment of copper ores.] * Paper, 20c. 23—26797

Mine timbers. Timbering of metal mines; by E. A. Holbrook, Richard V. Ageton, and Harry E. Tufft. [1st edition.] [June] 1923. vii+72 p. il. 1 pl. 16 p. of pl. (Bulletin 215.) * Paper, 5c. 23—26797

Powdered-coal plants. Tests of powdered-coal plant, report of investigations at power plant of St. Joseph Lead Co., Rivermines, Mo.; by Henry Kreisinger, John Blizard, C. E. Augustine, and B. J. Cross. [1st edition.] [July] 1923. iv+22 p. il. 1 pl. (Technical paper 316.) [Includes lists of Mines Bureau publications on combustion of coal in boiler furnaces.] * Paper, 5c. 23—26814

Publications. Index of Bureau of Mines publications. [1st edition.] [July] 1923. ii+40 p. [This index covers all publications in list of July, 1923.] * Paper, 5c.

—— Publications of Bureau of Mines. [Edition of] July, 1923. [1923.] 35 p. † 12—35113

Zinc. Electrothermic metallurgy of zinc [with bibliography]; by B. M. O'Harra. [1st edition.] [May] 1923. vi+106 p. il. 2 p. of pl. (Bulletin 208.) [This bulletin represents work done under a cooperative agreement with Missouri School of Mines and Metallurgy.] * Paper, 15c. 23—26795

PATENT OFFICE

NOTE.—The Patent Office publishes Specifications and drawings of patents in single copies. These are not enumerated in this catalogue, but may be obtained for 10c. each at the Patent Office.

A variety of indexes, giving a complete view of the work of the Patent Office from 1790 to date, are published at prices ranging from 25c. to $10.00 per volume and may be obtained from the Superintendent of Documents, Washington, D. C. The Rules of practice and pamphlet Patent laws are furnished free of charge upon application to the Patent Office. The Patent Office issues coupon orders in packages of 20 at $2.00 per package, or in books containing 100 coupons at $10.00 per book. These coupons are good until used, but are only to be used for orders sent to the Patent Office. For schedule of office fees, address Chief Clerk, Patent Office, Washington, D. C.

Decisions. [Decisions in patent and trade-mark cases, etc.] Sept. 4, 1923. p. 1–10, il. large 8° [From Official gazette, v. 314, no. 1.] † Paper, 5c. single copy, $2.00 a yr.

—— Same. Sept. 11, 1923. p. 175–180, large 8° [From Official gazette, v. 314, no. 2.]

—— Same. Sept. 18, 1923. p. 377–384, il. large 8° [From Official gazette, v. 314, no. 3.]

—— Same. Sept. 25, 1923. p. 565–574, large 8° [From Official gazette, v. 314, no. 4.]

Decisions—Continued. Decisions of commissioner of patents and of United States courts in patent and trade-mark and copyright cases; compiled from Official gazette of Patent Office, [calendar] year 1922. 1923. xvi+301 p. il.
* Cloth, 75c.
23—7315
—— Same. (H. doc. 454, 67th Cong. 3d sess.)

Official gazette. Official gazette, Sept. 4–25, 1923; v. 314, no. 1–4. 1923. cover-titles. 750+[cxl] p. il. large 8° [Weekly.] * Paper, 10c. single copy, \$5.00 a yr.; foreign subscription, \$11.00.
4—18256
NOTE.—Contains the patents, trade-marks, designs, and labels issued each week; also decisions of the commissioner of patents and of the United States courts in patent cases.
—— Same [title-page, contents, errata, etc., to] v. 312; July, 1923. 1923. [2] leaves, large 8° * Paper, 5c. single copy, included in price of Official gazette for subscribers.
—— Same [title-page, contents, errata, etc., to] v. 313; Aug. 1923. 1923. [2] leaves, large 8°
—— Same, weekly index, with title. Alphabetical list of registrants of trade-marks [etc., Sept. 4, 1923]. [1923.] xxviii p. large 8° [From Official gazette, v. 314, no. 1.] † Paper, \$1.00 a yr.
—— Same [Sept. 11, 1923]. [1923.] xliv p. large 8° [From Official gazette, v. 314, no. 2.]
—— Same [Sept. 18, 1923]. [1923.] xxxiv p. large 8° [From Official gazette, v. 314, no. 3.]
—— Same [Sept. 25, 1923]. [1923.] xxxiv p. large 8° [From Official gazette, v. 314, no. 4.]

Patents. Classification of patents issued Sept. 4–25, 1923. [1923.] Each 2 p. large 8° [Weekly. From Official gazette, v. 314, no. 1–4.] †
—— General information concerning patents; by Karl Fenning [and] Wm. I. Wyman. [1923.] 23 p. il. 8°

Trade-marks. Trade-marks [etc., from] Official gazette, Sept. 4, 1923. [1923.] 11–42+i–viii p. il. large 8° [From Official gazette, v. 314, no. 1.] † Paper, 5c. single copy, \$2.50 a yr.
—— Same, Sept. 11. 1923. [1923.] 181–240+i–xxiii p. il. large 8° [From Official gazette, v. 314, no. 2.]
—— Same, Sept. 18, 1923. [1923.] 385–434+i–xiv p. il. large 8° [From Official gazette, v. 314, no. 3.]
—— Same, Sept. 25. 1923. [1923.] 575–630+i–xv p. il. large 8° [From Official gazette, v. 314, no. 4.]

RECLAMATION BUREAU

NOTE.—Formerly Reclamation Service.

Boise project, Idaho, [and] Riverton project, Wyo., gates, hoists, and miscellaneous metal work. [1923.] iii+15 p. 31 pl. 4° (Specifications 422.) [Consists of advertisement, proposal, specifications, and drawings for reclamation project.] † Paper, \$3.00.

Reclamation record. Reclamation record, v. 14, no. 8; Aug. 1923. [1923.] cover-title, p. 265–276, il. 4° [Monthly. Text and illustration on p. 2–4 of cover.]
9—35252
NOTE.—The Reclamation record is published in the interest of the settlers on the reclamation projects, its aim being to raise the general average of success on these projects. It contains much valuable matter of interest to farmers, and will be sent without direct charge to water users on the irrigation projects of the Reclamation Bureau. The Record is sold to those who are not water users for 75 cents a year, payable in advance. Subscriptions may be forwarded to the Chief Clerk, U. S. Reclamation Bureau, Washington, D. C., and remittances (postal money order or New York draft) should be made payable to the Special Fiscal Agent, U. S. Reclamation Bureau. Postage stamps will not be accepted.
—— Same, v. 14, no. 9; Sept. 1923. [1923.] cover-title, p. 277–292, il. 4° [Monthly. Text on p. 2–4 of cover.]

ST. ELIZABETHS HOSPITAL

Hospital attendants. Training school for attendants, session of 1923–24, announcement and calendar. 1923. [1]+11 p. small 4° †
Nurses. Training school for nurses, session of 1923–24, announcement and calendar. 1923. [1]+18 p. small 4° †

INTERSTATE COMMERCE COMMISSION

NOTE.—The bound volumes of the decisions, usually known as Interstate Commerce Commission reports, are sold by the Superintendent of Documents, Washington, D. C., at various prices, depending upon the size of the volume. Separate opinions are sold on subscription, price $1.00 per volume; foreign subscription, $1.50; single copies, usually 5c. each.

Adirondack and St. Lawrence Railroad. Finance docket no. 251, guaranty settlement with Adirondack & St. Lawrence R. R.; decided July 21, 1923; report of commission. [1923.] p. 47–49. ([Finance decision] 816.) [From Interstate Commerce Comm ssion reports, v. 82.] * Paper, 5c.

Andalusia, Florida and Gulf Railway. Finance docket no. 269, guaranty settlement with Andalusia, Florida & Gulf Ry.; decided Aug. 21, 1923; report of commission. [1923.] p. 175–176. ([Finance decision] 856.) [From Interstate Commerce Commission reports, v. 82.] * Paper, 5c.

Apache Railway. F'nance docket no. 2877, mortgage note of Apache Ry.; decided Aug. 22, 1923; report of commission. [1923.] p. 179–181. ([Finance decision] 858.) [From Interstate Commerce Commission reports, v. 82.] * Paper, 5c.

Arcade and Attica Railroad. Finance docket no. 3128, bonds of Arcade & Attica Railroad; decided Aug. 29, 1923; report of commiss:on. [1923.] p. 193–194. ([Finance decision] 862.) [From Interstate Commerce Commission reports, v. 82.] * Paper, 5c.

Atlanta, Birmingham and Atlantic Railroad. Valuation docket no. 1, Atlanta, Birmingham & Atlantic Railroad Company, Georgia Terminal Company, and Alabama Terminal Railroad Company; decided July 20, 1923; [report of commission]. [1923.] p. 645–743. (B–6.) [From Interstate Commerce Commission reports, v. 75.] * Paper, 10c.

Baltimore and Ohio Chicago Terminal Railroad. F'nance docket no. 296, guaranty settlement with Baltimore & Ohio Chicago Terminal R. R:; [decided Aug. 2, 1923; report of commission. 1923. [1]+58–60 p. ([Finance decision] 820.) [From Interstate Commerce Commission reports, v. 82.] * Paper, 5c.

Benzol. Investigation and suspension docket no. 1799, benzol and blended gasoline from Birmingham. Ala., group to southern points: decided Aug. 16, 1923; report [and order] of commission. [1923.] 735–737+[1] p. ([Opinion] 8748.) [Report from Interstate Commerce Commission reports, v. 81.] * Paper, 5c.

Bird gravel. No. 14520, Vincent Sanford *v.* Pennsylvania Railroad Company; [decided Aug. 7, 1923; report and order of commission]. 1923. [1]+7?0–732+[1] p. ([Opinion] 8746.) [Report from Interstate Commerce Commission reports, v. 81.] * Paper, 5c.

Boston and Maine Railroad. Finance docket no. 320, guaranty settlement with Boston & Maine R. R.; decided Aug. 15, 1923; report of commission. [1923.] p. 189–192. ([F:nance decision] 861.) [From Interstate Commerce Commission reports, v. 82.] * Paper, 5c.

Caddo and Choctaw Railroad. Finance docket no. 2932, abandonment of Caddo & Choctaw Railroad: [decided July 30, 1923; report of commission]. 1923. [1]+90–92 p. ([Finance decision] 834.) [From Interstate Commerce Commission reports, v. 82.] * Paper, 5c.

California Western Railroad and Navigation Company. Before Interstate Commerce Commission, valuation docket no. 323, California Western Railroad & Navigation Company; brief in support of tentative valuation. 1923. cover-title. i+25 p. *

Carolina Railroad. Finance docket no. 336, guaranty settlement with Carolina R. R.; decided Aug. 29, 1923; report of commission. [1923.] p. 173–174. ([Finance decision] 855.) [From Interstate Commerce Commission reports, v. 82.] * Paper, 5c.

Cattle. No. 13180, E. A. Tovrea & Company et al. *v.* director general, as agent; decided July 20, 1923; report of commission. [1923.] p. 583–587. ([Opinion] 8711.) [From Interstate Commerce Commission reports, v. 81.] * Paper, 5c.

Cement. Supplemental order [promulgated] at general session of Interstate Commerce Commission on 22d of August, 1923 [concerning western cement rates]. [1923.] iv p. * Paper, 5c.

Central of Georgia Railway. Finance docket no. 1120, bonds of Central of Georgia Ry.; approved Aug. 3, 1923; 3d supplemental order. 1923. p. 65. ([Finance decision] 823.) [From Interstate Commerce Commission reports, v. 82.] * **Paper, 5c.**

Central Pacific Railway. Finance docket no. 2873, construction of Natron cutoff by Central Pacific Ry.; decided Aug. 15, 1923; report of commission. [1923.] p. 185–188. ([Finance decision] 860.) [From Interstate Commerce Commission reports, v. 82.] * Paper, 5c.

Chicago and North Western Railway. Finance docket no. 3072, Chicago & North Western equipment trust of 1922; decided July 20, 1923; report of commission. [1923.] p. 23–26. ([Finance decision 808.]) [From Interstate Commerce Commission reports, v. 82.] * Paper, 5c.

—— Same; decided July 30, 1923; supplemental report of commission. [1923.] p. 93–94. ([Finance decision] 835.) [From Interstate Commerce Commission reports, v. 82.] * Paper, 5c.

Chicago, Indianapolis and Louisville Railway. Before Interstate Commerce Commission, valuation dockets nos. 19, 93, 150, 168, 210, 225, 237, Chicago, Indianapolis and Louisville Railway Company et al.; reply of Bureau of valuation to memorandum on original cost to date, filed July 23, 1923, by counsel for National Conference on Valuation of American Railroads et al. 1923. cover-title, i+22 p. ‡

Chicago, Kalamazoo and Saginaw Railway. Finance docket no. 379, guaranty settlement with Chicago, Kalamazoo & Saginaw Ry.; decided Aug. 6, 1923; report of commission. [1923.] p. 97-99. ([Finance decision] 837.) [From Interstate Commerce Commission reports, v. 82.] * Paper, 5c.

Chicago Short Line Railway. Finance docket no. 1308, deficit status of Chicago Short Line Ry.; decided Aug. 4, 1923; report of commission. [1923.] p. 61–62. ([Finance decision] 821.) [From Interstate Commerce Commission reports, v. 82.] * Paper, 5c.

Citizens Telephone Company. Finance docket no. 3102, purchase of properties of Citizens Telephone Company by Michigan State Telephone Company; [decided July 27, 1923; report of commission]. 1923. [1]+80–82 p. ([Finance decision] 829.) [From Interstate Commerce Commission reports, v. 82.] * Paper, 5c.

Coal. No. 13755, New Mexico Central Railway Company *v.* Atchison, Topeka, & Santa Fe Railway Company; [decided Aug. 7, 1923; report and order of commission]. 1923. [1]+718–724+[1] p. ([Opinion] 8744.) [Report from Interstate Commerce Commission reports, v. 81.] * Paper, 5c.

—— No. 13946, Indiana Power Company *v.* Pittsburgh, Cincinnati, Chicago & St. Louis Railroad Company, director general, as agent, et al.; decided July 20, 1923; report [and order] of commission. [1923.] 601–602+[1] p. ([Opinion] 8717.) [Report from Interstate Commerce Commission reports, v. 81.] * Paper, 5c.

Coffee. No. 14179, J. Henry Koenig Company *v.* Baltimore & Ohio Railroad Company; decided July 20, 1923; report [and order] of commission. [1923.] 683–684+[1] p. ([Opinion] 8738.) [Report from Interstate Commerce Commission reports, v. 81.] * Paper, 5c.

Copper Range Railroad. Before Interstate Commerce Commission, valuation docket 244, Copper Range Railroad Company; brief in support of tentative valuation. 1923. cover-title, i+21 p. ‡

Copra. No. 13659, Gorgas-Piere [Pierie] Manufacturing Company *v.* director general, as agent; decided July 26, 1923; report of commission. [1923.] p. 657–658. ([Opinion] 8730.) [From Interstate Commerce Commission reports, v. 81.] * Paper, 5c.

Cotton-seed. No. 11848, Apache Cotton Oil & Manufacturing Company *v.* director general, as agent, Arkansas Western Railway Company, et al.; decided July 20, 1923; report [and order] of commission. [1923.] 569–576+iii p. ([Opinion] 8709.) [Report from Interstate Commerce Commission reports, v. 81.] * Paper, 5c.

Cripple Creek and Colorado Springs Railroad. Finance docket no. 1311, deficit settlement with Cripple Creek & Colorado Springs R. R.; decided Aug. 4, 1923; report of commission. [1923.] p. 129–132. ([Finance decision] 842.) [From Interstate Commerce Commission reports, v. 82.] * Paper, 5c.

Cullet. No. 14037, Wright & Wimmer *v.* Baltimore & Ohio Railroad Company et al.; decided July 20, 1923; report [and order] of commission. [1923.] 685–687+[1] p. ([Opinion] 8739.) [Report from Interstate Commerce Commission reports, v. 81.] * Paper, 5c.

Dayton and Union Railroad. Finance docket no. 420, guaranty settlement with Dayton & Union R. R.; [decided Aug. 2, 1923; report of commission]. 1923. [1]+66–68 p. ([Finance decision] 824.) [From Interstate Commerce Commission reports, v. 82.] * Paper, 5c.

Dayton-Goose Creek Railway. Finance docket no. 2419, control of Dayton-Goose Creek Ry. by N. O., T. & M. Ry.; decided July 16, 1923; report of commission on further hearing. [1923.] p. 27–29. ([Finance decision] 809.) [From Interstate Commerce Commission reports, v. 82.] * Paper, 5c.

Decisions. Decisions of Interstate Commerce Commission, July–Oct. 1922. 1923. xxxiii+958 p. il. (Interstate Commerce Commission reports. v. 73.) [Contains also decision of June 26, 1922.] * Cloth, $2.00.   8—30656

—— Decisions of Interstate Commerce Commission (finance reports), June–Oct. 1922. 1923. xxix+934 p. (Interstate Commerce Commission reports, v. 72.) * Cloth, $2.00.

NOTE.—The Interstate Commerce Commission assigns a volume in the series of reports at various times which contains only finance dockets. This is true regarding v. 72 and 76 here catalogued.

—— Same, Nov. 1922–Mar. 1923. 1923. xxvii+891 p. (Interstate Commerce Commission reports, v. 76.) [Contains also decision of July 29, 1922.] * Cloth, $2.00.

Eggs. Investigation and suspension docket no. 1811, cancellation of mileage commodity rates on eggs, any quantity, on Mobile & Ohio Railroad; decided Aug. 30, 1923; report [and order] of commission. [1923.] 1–3+[1] p. ([Opinion] 8756.) [Report from Interstate Commerce Commission reports, v. 83.] * Paper, 5c.

Elgin, Joliet and Eastern Railway. Finance docket no. 3086, Joliet equipment-trust bonds; decided July 24, 1923; report of commission. [1923.] p. 55–57. ([Finance decision] 819.) [From Interstate Commerce Commission reports, v. 82.] * Paper, 5c.

Express. In equity, no. 245, in district court for northern district of Georgia, American Railway Express Company *v.* United States and Interstate Commerce Commission; answer of Interstate Commerce Commission. 1923. cover-title, 6 p. ‡

—— Same; brief for Interstate Commerce Commission. 1923. cover-title, i+27 p. ‡

Free time allowances. No. 13294, Pacific Grain Company *v.* director general, as agent, and Oregon-Washington Railroad & Navigation Company; decided July 20, 1923; report [and order] of commission. [1923.] 679–682+[1] p. ([Opinion] 8737.) [Report from Interstate Commerce Commission reports, v. 81.] * Paper, 5c.

Freight rates. Investigation and suspension docket no. 1824, class rates, Delaware, Maryland, and Virginia, to Buffalo, N. Y., also Baltimore, Md., to Delaware and Maryland; [decided Aug. 30, 1923; report and order of commission]. 1923. [1]+758–761+[1] p. ([Opinion] 8754.) [Report from Interstate Commerce Commission reports, v. 81.] * Paper, 5c.

—— No. 12004, Wichita Northwestern Railway Company et al. *v.* Chicago, Rock Island & Pacific Railway Company et al.; decided July 19, 1923; report [and order] of commission on further hearing. [1923.] 513–521+ii p. ([Opinion] 8695.) [Report from Interstate Commerce Commission reports, v. 81.] * Paper, 5c.

—— No. 12782, Rio Grande valley Chamber of Commerce et al. *v.* St. Louis, Brownsville & Mexico Railway Company et al.; portions of 4th section applications nos. 581 et seq.; decided Aug. 1, 1923; report [and order] of commission. [1923.] 703–717+[1] p. ([Opinion] 8743.) [Report from Interstate Commerce Commission reports, v. 81.] * Paper, 5c.

—— No. 14095, Carnation Milk Products Company *v.* Ahnapee & Western Railway Company et al.; decided Aug. 7, 1923; report [and order] of commission. [1923.] 699–702+[1] p. ([Opinion] 8742.) [Report from Interstate Commerce Commission reports, v. 81.] * Paper, 5c.

Grain. Investigation and suspension docket no. 1786, routing on grain and grain products from Chicago, Joliet, Lockport, and Peoria, Ill., to Texas points; decided Aug. 15, 1923; report [and order] of commission. [1923.] 725–729+[1] p. ([Opinion] 8745.) [Report from Interstate Commerce Commission reports, v. 81.] * Paper, 5c.

—— No. 12364, Southern Arizona Traffic Association et al. *v.* director general, as agent, Arizona Eastern Railroad Company, et al.; [no. 12391, same *v.* same]; decided July 20, 1923; report [and order] of commission on further hearing. [1923.] 609–613+[1] p. ([Opinion] 8719.) [Report from Interstate Commerce Commission reports. v. 81.] * Paper. 5c.

Graysonia, Nashville and Ashdown Railroad. Finance docket no. 2688, securities of Graysonia, Nashville & Ashdown R. R.; approved Aug. 2, 1923; supplemental order. [1923.] p. 89–90. ([Finance decision] 833.) [From Interstate Commerce Commission reports, v. 82.] * Paper, 5c.

Greenbrier and Eastern Railroad. Finance docket no. 2748, stock of Greenbrier & Eastern Railroad; decided Aug. 21, 1923; report of commission. [1923.] p. 177–178. ([Finance decision] 857.) [From Interstate Commerce Commission reports, v. 82.] * Paper, 5c.

Hamilton Belt Railway. Finance docket no. 513, guaranty settlement with Hamilton Belt Ry.; decided Aug. 2, 1923; report of commission. [1923.] p. 83–84. ([Finance decision] 830.) [From Interstate Commerce Commission reports, v. 82.] * Paper, 5c.

Illinois Central Railroad. Finance docket no. 2777, construction, etc., of cut-off for Illinois Central R. R., in matter of application of Southern Illinois & Kentucky Railroad Company and Chicago, St. Louis & New Orleans Railroad Company for authority to construct lines of railroad, and of Illinois Central Railroad Company for authority to acquire control. by purchase of stock, of Southern Illinois & Kentucky Railroad Company, and to purchase, lease, and/or acquire running rights over, and operate. said lines of railroad; [decided Aug. 3, 1923; report of commission]. 1923. [1]+100–119 p. ([Finance decision] 838.) [From Interstate Commerce Commission reports. v. 82.] * Paper, 5c.

Lake Erie, Franklin and Clarion Railroad. Finance docket no. 3092, notes of Lake Erie, Franklin & Clarion Railroad; decided July 24, 1923; report of commission. [1923.] p. 53–54. ([Finance decision] 818.) [From Interstate Commerce Commission reports, v. 82.] * Paper, 5c.

—— Finance docket no. 3115, notes of Lake Erie, Franklin & Clarion R. R.; decided July 27, 1923; report of commission. [1923.] p. 87–88. ([Finance decision] 832.) [From Interstate Commerce Commission reports. v. 82.] * Paper, 5c.

Leather. No. 14382. Union Tanning Company *v.* Southern Railway Company; decided Aug. 7, 1923; report [and order] of commission. [1923.] 741–742+[1] p. ([Opinion] 8750.) [Report from Interstate Commerce Commission reports, v. 81.] * Paper, 5c.

Lehigh Valley Railroad. Finance docket no. 3037, bonds of Lehigh Valley Railroad; decided July 26, 1923; report of commission. [1923.] p. 85–86. ([Finance decision] 831.) [From Interstate Commerce Commission reports. v. 82.] * Paper, 5c.

Little Kanawha Railroad. Finance docket no. 585, guaranty settlement with Little Kanawha R. R.; decided Aug. 2, 1923; report of commission. [1923.] p. 69–71. ([Finance decision] 825.) [From Interstate Commerce Commission reports, v. 82.] * Paper, 5c.

Logging-cars. No. 13008. Norton Lumber Company et al. *v.* Chicago, Milwaukee & St. Paul Railway Company; decided Sept. 10, 1923; report [and order] of commission. [1923.] 749–757+[1] p. ([Opinion] 8753.) [Report from Interstate Commerce Commission reports, v. 81.] * Paper, 5c.

Louisiana and Pacific Railway. Finance docket no. 1325, deficit settlement with Louisiana & Pacific Ry.; decided July 18, 1923; report of commission. [1923.] p. 43–44. ([Finance decision] 814.) [From Interstate Commerce Commission reports, v. 82.] * Paper, 5c.

Louisville, Henderson and St. Louis Railway. Finance docket no. 600, guaranty settlement with Louisville, Henderson & St. Louis Ry.; [decided Aug. 2, 1923; report of commission]. 1923. [1]+120–122 p. ([Finance decision] 839.) [From Interstate Commerce Commission reports, v. 82.] * Paper, 5c.

Lumber. Investigation and suspension docket no. 1802, cancellation rule for constructing combination rates on lumber between southern points and Ohio and Mississippi River crossings; decided Aug. 25, 1923; report [and order] of commission. [1923.] 745–748+[1] p. ([Opinion] 8752.) [Report from Interstate Commerce Commission reports, v. 81.] * Paper, 5c.

—— No. 38, in Supreme Court, Oct. term, 1923, Wyoming Railway Company *v.* United States and Interstate Commerce Commission, appeal from district court for district of Wyoming; brief for Interstate Commerce Commission. 1923. cover-title, ii+36 p. ‡

—— No. 13468, William Schuette Company *v.* director general, as agent, Seaboard Air Line Railway Company. et al.; decided July 20, 1923; report [and order] of commission. [1923.] 619–620+ii p. ([Opinion] 8721.) [Report from Interstate Commerce Commission reports, v. 81.] * Paper, 5c.

McKeesport, Connecting Railroad. Finance docket no. 2483, deficit status of McKeesport Connecting R. R.; decided Aug. 24, 1923; report of commission. [1923.] p. 195–196. ([Finance decision] 863.) [From Interstate Commerce Commission reports, v. 82.] * Paper, 5c.

Magnesite. No. 13424, Tulare Mining Company *v.* director general, as agent, and Southern Pacific Company; decided July 13, 1923; report [and order] of commission. [1923.] 675–676+[1] p. ([Opinion] 8735.) [Report from Interstate Commerce Commission reports, v. 81.] * Paper, 5c.

Manganese. No. 13925, R. B. Miller *v.* Norfolk & Western Railway Company et al.; [decided July 20, 1923; report and order of commission]. 1923. [1]+588–590+[1] p. ([Opinion] 8712.) [Report from Interstate Commerce Commission reports, v. 81.] * Paper, 5c.

Memphis Union Station Company. Before Interstate Commerce Commission, valuation docket no. 206, in matter of valuation of property of Memphis Union Station Company; brief in support of tentative valuation. 1923. cover-title, 10 p. ‡

Mine props. No. 13109, Star Timber Company *v.* Chicago & North Western Railway Company; decided July 20, 1923; report [and order] of commission. [1923.] 673–674+[1] p. ([Opinion] 8734.) [Report from Interstate Commerce Commission reports, v. 81.] * Paper, 5c.

Minneapolis Western Railway. Finance docket no. 637, guaranty settlement with Minneapolis Western Ry.; decided Aug. 6, 1923; report of commission. [1923] p. 95–97. ([Finance decision] 836.) [From Interstate Commerce Commission reports, v. 82.] * Paper, 5c.

Molasses. No. 13213, Tuscaloosa Cotton Seed Oil Company *v.* Southern Railway Company et al.; [no. 13213 (sub-no. 1), Gulfport Grocery Company *v.* Louisville & Nashville Railroad Company]; decided July 20, 1923; report [and order] of commission. [1923.] 629–630+[1] p. ([Opinion] 8724.) [Report from Interstate Commerce Commission reports, v. 81.] * Paper, 5c.

Montana, Wyoming and Southern Railroad. Finance docket no. 659, guaranty settlement with Montana, Wyoming & Southern R. R.; [decided July 24, 1923; report of commission]. 1923. [1]+50–52 p. ([Finance decision] 817.) [From Interstate Commerce Commission reports, v. 82.] * Paper, 5c.

Morgantown and Kingwood Railroad. Finance docket no. 663, guaranty settlement with Morgantown & Kingwood R. R.; [decided Aug. 2, 1923; report of commission]. 1923. [1]+72–74 p. ([Finance decision] 826.) [From Interstate Commerce Commission reports, v. 82.] * Paper, 5c.

Morristown and Erie Railroad. Finance docket no. 3150, Morristown & Erie Railroad bonds; [decided Aug. 30, 1923; report of commission]. 1923. [1]+182–184 p. ([Finance decision] 859.) [From Interstate Commerce Commission reports, v. 82.] * Paper, 5c.

Muncie Belt Railway. Finance docket no. 672, guaranty settlement with Muncie Belt Ry.; decided Aug. 21, 1923; report of commission. [1923.] p. 197–199. ([Finance decision] 864.) [From Interstate Commerce Commission reports, v. 82.] * Paper, 5c.

Munising, Marquette and Southeastern Railway. Before Interstate Commerce Commission, valuation docket no. 251, Munising, Marquette & Southeastern Railway; brief in support of tentative valuation. 1923. cover-title, 1+20 p. ‡

New York, New Haven and Hartford Railroad. Finance docket no 2960, abandonment of branch line by New York, New Haven & Hartford R. R.; decided July 18, 1923; report of commission. [1923.] p. 45–46. ([Finance decision] 815.) [From Interstate Commerce Commission reports, v. 82.] * Paper, 5c.

New York, Ontario and Western Railway. Finance docket no. 3105, assumption of obligation by N. Y., O. & W. Ry.; [decided July 21, 1923; report of commission]. 1923. [1]+20–22 p. ([Finance decision] 807.) [From Interstate Commerce Commission reports, v. 82.] * Paper, 5c.

Ocilla Southern Railroad. Finance docket no. 200, deficit settlement with Ocilla Southern R. R., W. T. Hargett and H. H. Hill, receivers; [decided Aug. 7, 1923; report of commission]. 1923. [1]+170–172 p. ([Finance decision] 854.) [From Interstate Commerce Commission reports, v. 82.] * Paper, 5c.

Onions. No. 14135, Memphis Freight Bureau, for D. Canale & Company, v. Chicago Great Western Railroad Company et al.; [decided July 20, 1923; report and order of commission]. 1923. [1]+626–628+ii p. ([Opinion] 8723.) [Report from Interstate Commerce Commission reports, v. 81.] * Paper, 5c.

Oregon Short Line Railroad. Finance docket no. 2903 (sub-no. 1), construction of line by Oregon Short Line R. R.; decided Aug. 2, 1923; report of commission. [1923.] p. 133–134. ([Finance decision] 843.) [From Interstate Commerce Commission reports, v. 82.] * Paper, 5c.

—— Finance docket no. 2979, construction of line by Oregon Short Line R. R.; [decided July 21, 1923; report of commission]. 1923. [1]+40–42 p. ([Finance decision] 813.) [From Interstate Commerce Commission reports, v. 82.] * Paper, 5c.

Osage County and Santa Fe Railway. Finance docket no. 3061, control of Osage County & Santa Fe Railway by Santa Fe; [decided Aug. 2, 1923; report of commission]. 1923. [1]+126–128 p. ([Finance decision] 841.) [From Interstate Commerce Commission reports, v. 82.] * Paper, 5c.

Ouachita Valley Railway. Finance docket no. 2597, deficit settlement with Ouachita Valley Ry.; decided Aug. 30, 1923; report of commission. [1923.] p. 165–166. ([Finance decision] 852.) [From Interstate Commerce Commission reports, v. 82.] * Paper, 5c.

Pacific and Idaho Northern Railway. Before Interstate Commerce Commission, valuation docket no. 100, Pacific & Idaho Northern Railway Company; brief in support of tentative valuation. 1923. cover-title, i+68 p. ‡

Paducah and Illinois Railroad. Finance docket no. 2783, assumption of obligation by Illinois Central R. R., in matter of application of Illinois Central Railroad Company for authority to assume obligation and liability in respect of 1st-mortgage bonds of Paducah & Illinois Railroad Company; decided Aug. 3, 1923; report of commission. [1923.] p. 139–143. ([Finance decision] 845.) [From Interstate Commerce Commission reports, v. 82.] * Paper, 5c.

Peanuts. No. 14151, Kelly Company v. Atlanta, Birmingham & Atlantic Railway Company et al.; decided July 26, 1923; report [and order] of commission. [1923.] 621–625+ii p. ([Opinion] 8722.) [Report from Interstate Commerce Commission reports, v. 81.] * Paper, 5c.

Petroleum. No. 14191, Ohio Refining Company v. Louisville & Nashville Railroad Company; [decided July 20, 1923; report and order of commission]. 1923. [1]+688–690+[1] p. ([Opinion] 8740.) [Report from Interstate Commerce Commission reports, v. 81.] * Paper, 5c.

Pipe. No. 14589, National Supply Company of Pennsylvania v. Baltimore & Ohio Railroad Company et al.; decided Aug. 7, 1923; report [and order] of commission. [1923.] 743–744+ii p. ([Opinion] 8751.) [Report from Interstate Commerce Commission reports, v. 81.] * Paper, 5c.

—— Portions of 4th section applications nos. 631 and 701, wrought-iron pipe and iron pipe fittings from and to points in the Southwest; decided July 18, 1923; report [and 2d supplemental 4th section order no. 7909] of commission on further hearing. [1923.] 691–698+[1] p. ([Opinion] 8741.) [Report from Interstate Commerce Commission reports, v. 81.] * Paper, 5c.

Poultry. No. 11640, Swift & Company v. director general, as agent; decided July 31, 1923; report of commission on further hearing. [1923.] p. 677–678. ([Opinion] 8736.) [From Interstate Commerce Commission reports, v. 81.] * Paper, 5c.

Railroad accidents. Accident bulletin 87, collisions, derailments, and other accidents resulting in injury to persons, equipment, or roadbed, arising from operation of steam roads used in interstate commerce, calendar year 1922; [prepared in] Bureau of Statistics. 1923. 107 p. il. 4° *Paper, 5c. single copy, 15c. a yr.; foreign subscription, 25c.   5—41547

NOTE.—For the first time, accidents statistics for the last quarter of the year and for the calendar year are published in separate bulletins. This is done for the purpose of making available the figures of the final quarter more promptly than could be done if they were held until the detailed analysis for the year is completed. Accident bulletin 86, covering the statistics for the quarter ending Dec. 1922, appeared in the Monthly catalogue, June, 1923. p. 788.

Railroad employees. No. 6404, in circuit court of appeals for 8th circuit, United States *v.* Colorado, Wyoming & Eastern Railway Company, in error to district court for district of Wyoming; brief and argument for plaintiff in error. 1923. cover-title, i+67 p. ‡

—— Wage statistics, class 1 steam roads in United States, including 15 switching and terminal companies, June, 1923; [prepared in] Bureau of Statistics. June, 1923. [4] p. oblong large 8° †

Railroads. 35th annual report on statistics of railways in United States, year ended Dec. 31, 1921, with abstracts of periodical reports, year ended Dec. 31, 1922; prepared by Bureau of Statistics. 1923. cxviii p. il. 4° [Cover and half title-page read: Text of 35th annual report.] *Paper, 15c.   5—11209

—— Freight and passenger service operating statistics of class 1 steam roads in United States, compiled from 161 reports of freight statistics representing 176 roads and from 158 reports of passenger statistics representing 173 roads (switching and terminal companies not included), July, 1923 and 1922 [and 7 months ending with July, 1923 and 1922; prepared in] Bureau of Statistics. July, 1923. [2] p. oblong large 8° [Subject to revision.] †

—— Operating revenues and operating expenses of class 1 steam roads in United States (for 194 steam roads, including 15 switching and terminal companies), July, 1923 and 1922 [and] 7 months ending with July, 1923 and 1922; [prepared in] Bureau of Statistics. July, 1923. 1 p. oblong large 8° [Subject to revision.] †

—— Operating revenues and operating expenses of large steam roads, selected items for roads with annual operating revenues above $25,000,000, July, 1922 and 1923 [and] 7 months ended with July, 1922 and 1923; [prepared in] Bureau of Statistics. July, 1923. [2] p. oblong large 8° [Subject to revision.] †

—— Operating statistics of large steam roads, selected items for July, 1923, compared with July, 1922, for roads with annual operating revenues above $25,000,000; [prepared in] Bureau of Statistics. July, 1923. [2] p. oblong large 8° [Subject to revision.] †

—— Preliminary abstract of statistics of common carriers, year ended Dec. 31, 1922; [prepared by] Bureau of Statistics. 1923. 30 p. 4° * Paper, 10c.

—— Revenue traffic statistics of class 1 steam roads in United States, including mixed-train service (compiled from 165 reports representing 178 steam roads, switching and terminal companies not included), June, 1923 and 1922 [and] 6 months ended with June, 1923 and 1922; [prepared in] Bureau of Statistics. June, 1923. 1 p. oblong large 8° [Subject to revision.] †

San Pedro, Los Angeles and Salt Lake Railroad. valuation docket no 26, San Pedro, Los Angeles & Salt Lake Railroad Company; decided June 7, 1923; report of commission. [1923.] p. 463–644. (B–5.) [From Interstate Commerce Commission reports, v. 75.] * Paper, 15c.

Sand. No. 13644, Muncie Sand Company *v.* director general, as agent; [decided July 20, 1923; report of commission]. 1923. [1]+594–596 p. ([Opinion] 8714.) [From Interstate Commerce Commission reports, v. 81.] * Paper, 5c.

Silica brick. No. 13955, Pittsburgh Crucible Steel Company *v.* director general, as agent, and Pennsylvania Railroad Company, western lines; decided July 26, 1923; report of commission. [1923.] p. 659–662. ([Opinion] 8731.) [From Interstate Commerce Commission reports, v. 81.] * Paper, 5c.

Silos. No. 13707, Western Silo Company *v.* Illinois Central Railroad Company et al.; [decided July 20, 1923; report and order of commission]. 1923. [1]+614–618+[1] p. ([Opinion] 8720.) [Report from Interstate Commerce Commission reports, v. 81.] * Paper, 5c.

South Manchester Railroad. Finance docket no. 795, guaranty settlement with South Manchester R. R.; decided Aug. 29, 1923; report of commission. [1923.] p. 167–169. ([Finance decision] 853.) [From Interstate Commerce Commission reports, v. 82.] * Paper, 5c.

Staten Island Rapid Transit Railway. Finance docket no. 816, guaranty settlement with Staten Island Rapid Transit Ry.; decided Aug. 2, 1923; report of commission. [1923.] p. 75–77. ([Finance decision] 827.) [From Interstate Commerce Commission reports, v. 82.] * Paper, 5c.

Steamboats. Schedule of sailings (as furnished by steamship companies named herein) of steam vessels which are registered under laws of United States and which are intended to load general cargo at ports in United States for foreign destinations. Sept. 15–Oct. 31, 1923, no. 13; issued by Section of Tariffs, Bureau of Traffic. 1923. iii+25 p. 4° [Monthly. No. 13 cancels no. 12.] †
                                                                22—26610

Strawberries. No. 12893, transportation of strawberries by express, in carload lots, in passenger trains, from Florida to northern markets; [no. 12981, Railroad Commissioners of Florida *v.* American Railway Express Company; decided July 31, 1923; report of commission. 1923. [1]+634–644 p. ([Opinion] 8726.) [From Interstate Commerce Commission reports, v. 81.] * Paper, 5c.

Sugar. No. 14670, Warfield-Pratt-Howell Company *v.* Texas & Pacific Railway Company et al.; decided Aug. 7, 1923; report [and order] of commission. [1923.] 733–734+[1] p. ([Opinion] 8747.) [Report from Interstate Commerce Commission reports, v. 81.] * Paper, 5c.

Tiles. No. 13928, Aluminum Company of American *v.* director general, as agent; decided July 20, 1923; report [and order] of commission. 1923. 599–600+[1] p. ([Opinion] 8716.) [Report from Interstate Commerce Commission reports, v. 81.] * Paper, 5c.

Tin. No. 14032, N. & G. Taylor Company, Incorporated, *v.* director general, as agent, Lehigh Valley Railroad Company, et al.; decided July 30, 1923; report of commission. [1923.] p. 663–665. ([Opinion] 8732.) [From Interstate Commerce Commission reports, v. 81.] * Paper, 5c.

Tin-plate. No. 13795, Metal & Thermit Corporation *v.* director general, as agent; [decided July 26, 1923; report of commission]. 1923. [1]+654–656 p. ([Opinion] 8729.) [From Interstate Commerce Commission reports, v. 81.] * Paper, 5c.

Trap Hill Telephone Company. Finance docket no. 3002, purchase of certain properties of Trap Hill Tel. Co. by Chesapeake & Potomac Tel. Co. of W. Va.; [decided July 14, 1923; report of commission]. [1923.] p. 37–39. ([Finance decision] 812.) [From Interstate Commerce Commission reports, v. 82.] * Paper, 5c.

Unlading and lading. No. 13943, Frank P. Dow Company, Incorporated, *v.* Great Northern Railway Company and Chicago, Milwaukee & St. Paul Railway Company; [no. 13943 (sub-no. 1), same *v.* director general, as agent]; decided July 20, 1923; report of commission. [1923.] p. 649–653. ([Opinion] 8728.) [From Interstate Commerce Commission reports, v. 81.] * Paper, 5c.

Vinegar. Investigation and suspension docket no. 1779, vinegar rates from Pacific Coast to middle West territory; [decided July 25, 1923, report and order of commission]. 1923. [1]+666–672+[1] p. ([Opinion] 8733.) [Report from Interstate Commerce Commission reports, v. 81.] * Paper, 5c.

Wabash Railway. Finance docket no. 2958, lease of line [owned by Missouri-Kansas-Texas Railroad Company] by Wabash Ry.; decided July 17, 1923; report of commission. [1923.] p. 33–36. ([Finance decision] 811.) [From Interstate Commerce Commission reports, v. 82.] * Paper, 5c.

—— Finance docket no. 3136, Wabash equipment trust, series C; decided Aug. 6, 1923; report of commission. [1923.] p. 135–138. ([Finance decision] 844.) [From Interstate Commerce Commission reports, v. 82.] * Paper, 5c.

Waco, Beaumont, Trinity and Sabine Railway. Finance docket no. 2950, acquisition of line by Waco, Beaumont, Trinity & Sabine Ry.; [decided July 16, 1923; report of commission]. 1923. [1]+30–32 p. ([Finance decision] 810.) [From Interstate Commerce Commission reports, v. 82.] * Paper, 5c.

Waco, Beaumont, Trinity and Sabine Railway—Continued. Finance docket no. 2978, securities of Waco, Beaumont, Trinity & Sabine Ry.; [decided Aug. 28, 1923; report of commission]. 1923. [1]+200–204 p. ([Finance decision] 865.) [From Interstate Commerce Commission reports, v. 82.] * Paper, 5c.

White Sulphur and Huntersville Railroad. Finance docket no. 889, guaranty settlement with White Sulphur & Huntersville R. R.; decided Aug. 7, 1923; report of commission. [1923.] p. 123–125. ([Finance decision] 840.) [From Interstate Commerce Commission reports, v. 82.] * Paper, 5c.

Wildwood and Delaware Bay Short Line Railroad. Before Interstate Commerce Commission, valuation docket no. 220, Wildwood and Delaware Bay Short Line Railroad Company; brief in support of tentative valuation. 1923. cover-title, i+46 p. ‡

Williamsport and North Branch Railroad. Finance docket no. 897, guaranty settlement with Williamsport & North Branch R. R., Edward Bailly, receiver; [decided July 25, 1923; report of commission]. 1923. [1]+78–80 p. ([Finance decision] 828.) [From Interstate Commerce Commission reports, v. 82.] * Paper, 5c.

Wyoming and Missouri River Railway. Finance docket no. 3103, stock of Wyoming & Missouri River Ry.; decided Aug. 2, 1923; report of commission. [1923.] p. 63–64. ([Finance decision] 822.) [From Interstate Commerce Commission reports, v. 82.] * Paper, 5c.

Zinc. No. 13508, B. Lissberger & Company et al. *v.* Pennsylvania Railroad Company et al.; decided July 10, 1923; report of commission on further consideration. [1923.] p. 645–648. ([Opinion] 8727.) [From Interstate Commerce Commission reports, v. 81.] * Paper, 5c.

JUSTICE DEPARTMENT

American Chain Company. No. —, in Supreme Court, Oct. term, 1923, American Chain Company *v.* Interstate Iron & Steel Company; petition for writ of certiorari to circuit court of appeals for 7th circuit. 1923. cover-title, 4 p. ‡

Arndstein, Jules W. No. 404, in Supreme Court, Oct. term, 1922, Thomas D. McCarthy, United States marshal for southern district of New York, *v.* Jules W. Arndstein, on appeal from district court for southern district of New York; petition for rehearing. 1923. cover-title, 5 p. ‡

Bertrose Company. No. 2265, Court of Customs Appeals, Bertrose Co. *v.* United States; brief for United States. 1923. cover-title, 13 p. ‡

Bondurant Construction Company, Incorporated. In Court of Claims, Bondurant Construction Company, Inc., *v.* United States, no. 34710; defendant's counterclaim. [1923.] p. 31–35, large 8° ‡

Brewer, William S. No. 492, in Supreme Court, Oct. term, 1923, William S. Brewer. *v.* United States, petition for writ of certiorari to circuit court of appeals for 2d circuit; brief of United States in opposition. 1923. cover-title, 4 p. ‡

Brown, Wm. A., & Co. No. 2232, Court of Customs Appeals, Wm. A. Brown & Co. *v.* United States; brief for United States on motion to dismiss. 1923. cover-title, 2 p. ‡

Burke, George W., jr. In Patent Office, interference no. 47272, George W. Burke, jr., *v.* William J. Ruff, fire-extinguishing apparatus; record for George W. Burke, jr. 1923. cover-title, 43 p. ‡

Bush, George S., & Co., Incorporated. No. 2308, Court of Customs Appeals, George S. Bush & Co. [Incorporated] *v.* United States; brief for United States on motion to dismiss. 1923. cover-title, 2 p. ‡

Chicago Cold Storage Warehouse Company. No. 69, in Supreme Court, Oct. term, 1923, Chicago Cold Storage Warehouse Company *v.* United States, appeal from Court of Claims; brief for United States. 1923. cover-title, 21 p. ‡

Driggs, Louis L. No. B-41 (1), in Court of Claims, Louis L. Driggs et al. *v.* United States; demurrer to amended petition as amplified by bill of particulars [and memorandum in support of demurrer]. 1923. cover-title, p. 1–5, large 8° ‡

Ensign, Ralph H. In Court of Claims, Joseph R. Ensign, executor of Ralph H. Ensign, *v.* United States, no. C–736; demurrer [and brief]. [1923.] p. 8–18, large 8° ‡

Fidelity Trust Company. United States circuit court of appeals for 3d circuit, Mar. term, 1923, Fidelity Trust Co. *v.* Ephraim Lederer, collector [of internal revenue for 1st district of Pennsylvania], no. 2960 (list 15); [transcript of record]. [1923.] p. 50–53. ‡

Finck, Jones & Libby, Incorporated. No. 2261, Court of Customs Appeals, Finck, Jones & Libby, Incorporated, *v.* United States; brief for United States. 1923. cover-title, 9 p. ‡

Fish, O. B. No. 2266, Court of Customs Appeals, O. B. Fish *v.* United States; brief for United States on motion to dismiss. 1923. cover-title, 2 p. ‡

Garland, Samuel. In Court of Claims, no. 30252, heirs of Samuel Garland. *v.* Choctaw Nation; defendant's objections to findings of fact requested by plaintiffs, request for findings of fact, and brief. 1923. cover-title, i+347–453 p. large 8° ‡

Geare, Reginald W. No. 3943, no. —, special calendar, in Court of Appeals of District of Columbia, Jan. term, 1923, United States *v.* Reginald W. Geare [et al.]; brief for appellant. 1923. cover-title, iii+48 p. ‡

Heitler, Michael. Nos. 387–389, in Supreme Court, Oct. term, 1923, Michael Heitler *v.* United States; Nathaniel Perlman *v.* [same]; Mandel Greenberg *v.* [same], petitions for writs of certiorari to circuit court of appeals for 7th circuit; brief for United States in opposition. 1923. cover-title, 2 p. ‡

Hogan, M. J. Nos. 2281, 2283, Court of Customs Appeals, United States *v.* M. J. Hogan; [same] *v.* Guy B. Barham; brief for United States. 1923. cover-title, 11 p. ‡

Hooton, H. H. No. 33856, in Court of Claims, H. R. Hooton, administrator of H. H. Hooton, *v.* United States; defendants' [request for findings of fact and] brief. 1923. cover-title, p. 1–35, large 8° ‡

Irwin & Leighton. At law, no. 3977, in district court for district of New Jersey, United States *v.* Irwin & Leighton, partnership [composed of] Alexander D. Irwin, jr., and Archibald O. Leighton; brief and argument of plaintiff on defendants' motion and answer. 1923. cover-title, 67 p. ‡

Jeddo-Highland Coal Company. No. C–790, in Court of Claims, Jeddo-Highland Coal Company *v.* United States; demurrer and brief in support thereof. 1923. cover-title, p. 6–12, large 8° ‡

Keve & Young. No. 2231, Court of Customs Appeals, Keve & Young *v.* United States; brief for United States on motion to dismiss. 1923. cover-title, 9 p. ‡

Lehigh Valley Coal Company. No. C–715, in Court of Claims, Lehigh valley Coal Company *v.* United States; demurrer and brief in support thereof. 1923. cover-title, p. 5–10, large 8° ‡

Lindsley Brothers Company. No. 2287, Court of Customs Appeals, Lindsley Brothers Co. *v.* United States; brief for United States on motion to dismiss. 1923. cover-title, 2 p. ‡

Lunham & Moore. No. 2227, Court of Customs Appeals, Lunham & Moore *v.* United States; brief for United States on motion to dismiss. 1923· cover-title, 12 p. ‡

Neuman & Schwiers Company. No. 2285, Court of Customs Appeals, United States *v.* Neuman & Schwiers Co.; brief for United States. 1923. cover-title, 32 p. ‡

Opinions. [Official opinions of Attorneys General] v. 33, [signatures] 21–22, 27–28, 30–32. [1923.] p. 321–352, 417–438, 465–512, il. [Previous prints of signatures 27 and 28 included a decision which is omitted from these reprints thus changing the pagination from 417–446 to 417–438.] † 12—40693

Pacific Orient Company. No. 2279, Court of Customs Appeals, Pacific Orient Co. *v.* United States; brief for United States on motion to dismiss. 1923. cover-title, 2 p. ‡

Parfums d'Orsay, Incorporated. No. 2236, Court of Customs Appeals, Parfums d'Orsay (Inc.) *v.* United States; brief for United States. 1923. cover-title, 1 p. ‡

—— Same; brief for United States on motion to dismiss. 1923. cover-title, 2 p. ‡

Phoenix Horseshoe Company, Incorporated. In Court of Claims, Phoenix Horseshoe Company (Inc.) *v.* United States, no. B–9; defendant's objections to plaintiff's request for findings of fact, defendant's request for findings of fact, and brief. [1923.] p. 52–56, large 8° ‡

Pitchlynn, Peter P. No. 30532, in Court of Claims, Sophia C. Pitchlynn et al., heirs at law of Peter P. Pitchlynn, *v.* Choctaw Nation; defendant's objections to findings of fact requested by plaintiffs, request for findings of fact, and brief. 1923. cover-title, p. 1–6. ‡

Pothier, Roland R. No. —, in Supreme Court, Oct. term, 1923, William R. Rodman, United States marshal [for district of Rhode Island], *v.* Roland R. Pothier; petition for writ of certiorari to circuit court of appeals for 1st circuit. 1923. cover-title, 12 p. ‡

—— United States circuit court of appeals for 1st circuit, Oct. term, 1922, Roland R. Pothier *v.* William R. Rodman, United States marshal [for district of Rhode Island], no. 1629; [transcript of record]. [1923.] p. 199–211. ‡

Rice & Fielding, Incorporated. No. 2286, Court of Customs Appeals, United States *v.* Rice & Fielding, Inc.; brief for United States. 1923. cover-title, 8 p. ‡

Sanguinetti, Stefano. No. 130, in Supreme Court, Oct. term, 1923, Stefano Sanguinetti *v.* United States, appeal from Court of Claims; brief for United States. 1923. cover-title, [1]+27 p. ‡

Scaramelli, Henry, Incorporated. No. 2300, Court of Customs Appeals, Henry Scaramelli (Inc.) *v.* United States; brief for United States on motion to dismiss. 1923. cover-title, 10 p. ‡

Schaefer, Charles, jr. No. 13–A, in Court of Claims, Charles Schaefer, jr., *v.* United States; defendant's objections to plaintiff's request for findings of fact, defendant's request for findings of fact, and brief. 1923. cover-title, p. 225–253, large 8° ‡

State Investment Company. No. 195, in Supreme Court, Oct. term, 1923, United States *v.* State Investment Company and Edward B. Wheeler, appeal from circuit court of appeals for 8th circuit; brief for United States. 1923. cover-title, i+27 p. ‡

Sumner Iron Works. No. 363, in Supreme Court, Oct. term, 1923, Sumner Iron Works *v.* Todd Drydock and Construction Corporation, on petition for writ of certiorari to circuit court of appeals for 9th circuit; brief in opposition. 1923. cover-title, 3 p. ‡

Sutton Chemical Company. In equity, no. —, in district court for southern district of West Virginia, United States *v.* Sutton Chemical Company, incorporated under laws of West Virginia; bill of complaint. 1923. cover-title, 55 p. ‡

Turner, Davies, & Co. No. 2264, Court of Customs Appeals, Davies Turner & Co. and C. G. Valentine & Co. *v.* United States; brief for United States. 1923. cover-title, 14 p. ‡

Walter, Leroy W. No. 20, in Supreme Court, Oct. term, 1923, United States *v.* Leroy W. Walter, in error to district court for southern district of Florida; brief for United States. 1923. cover-title, 20 p. ‡

Young, Allen M. No. 3953, in Court of Appeals of District of Columbia, Apr. term, 1923, no. —, special calendar, Allen Merrill Young *v.* United States; brief for appellee. 1923. cover-title, 10 p. ‡

LABOR DEPARTMENT

EMPLOYMENT SERVICE

Industrial employment information bulletin, v. 3, no. 8; Aug. 1923. [1923.] 19 p. 4° [Monthly.] †   L 21—17

LABOR STATISTICS BUREAU

Accidents. Errata [to Statistics of industrial accidents in United States; by Lucian W. Chaney]. [1923.] 1 p. oblong 48° (Bulletin 339 [errata; Industrial accidents and hygiene series].) †

Child labor. Trend of child labor in United States, 1920–23; [prepared in Children's Bureau]. [1923.] 5 p. [From Monthly labor review, Sept. 1923.] †

Chinese migrations, with special reference to labor conditions [with bibliographies and with list of reference books published in Chinese]; by Ta Chen. July, 1923. vi+237+vii p. il. 3 pl. 2 maps. (Bulletin 340; Miscellaneous series.) * Paper, 35c. L 23—236

Cotton goods. Wages and hours of labor in cotton-goods manufacturing, 1922. Aug. 1923. iii+27 p. (Bulletin 345; Wages and hours of labor series.) * Paper, 5c. L 18—12

—— Same. (H. doc. 24, 68th Cong. 1st sess.)

Employment in selected industries, Aug. 1923. 1923. 8 p. [From Monthly labor review, Oct. 1923.] †

Monthly labor review, v. 17, no. 3; Sept. 1923. 1923. v+571–776 p. il. * Paper, 15c. single copy, $1.50 a yr.; foreign subscription, $2.25. 15—26485

SPECIAL ARTICLES.—Purchasing power of the dollar, 1913–23, as computed by Bureau of Labor Statistics.—How Germany settles industrial disputes; by Emil Frankel.—Individual and collective bargaining under Mexican State labor laws [concluded]; by Martha Dobbin.—Conciliation work of Department of Labor, July, 1923; by Hugh L. Kerwin.—Statistics of immigration, fiscal year ended June 30, 1923; by W. W. Husband.

NOTE.—The Review is the medium through which the Bureau publishes the results of original investigations too brief for bulletin purposes, notices of labor legislation by the States or by Congress, and Federal court decisions affecting labor, which from their importance should be given attention before they could ordinarily appear in the bulletins devoted to these subjects. One free subscription will be given to all labor departments and bureaus, workmen's compensation commissions, and other offices connected with the administration of labor laws and organizations exchanging publications with the Labor Statistics Bureau. Others desiring copies may obtain them from the Superintendent of Documents, Washington, D. C., at the prices stated above.

Prices. Prices and cost of living. [1923.] p. 591–622, il. [From Monthly labor review, Sept. 1923.] †

—— Wholesale prices, 1890–1922. June, 1923. v+234 p. il. (Bulletin 335; Wholesale prices series.) * Paper, 25c. L 13—97

—— Same. (H. doc. 635, 67th Cong. 4th sess.)

Workmen's compensation. Workmen's compensation legislation of United States and Canada, 1920–22; by Lindley D. Clark. June, 1923. iv+260 p. (Bulletin 332; Workmen's insurance and compensation series.) * Paper, 25c. L 23—235

—— Same. (H. doc. 632, 67th Cong. 4th sess.)

NATURALIZATION BUREAU

Rulers. [List of foreign sovereignties and their rulers.] 16th edition. July 18, 1923. [2] p. 4° †

LIBRARY OF CONGRESS

COPYRIGHT OFFICE

Copyright. [Catalogue of copyright entries, new series, pt. 1, group 1, Books, v. 20] no. 52–61; Aug.–Sept. 1923. Aug. 31–Sept. 29, 1923. p. 545–704. [Issued several times a week.] 6—35347

NOTE.—Each number is issued in 4 parts: pt. 1, group 1, relates to books; pt. 1, group 2, to pamphlets, leaflets, contributions to newspapers or periodicals, etc., lectures, sermons, addresses for oral delivery, dramatic compositions, maps, motion pictures; pt. 2 to periodicals; pt. 3, to musical compositions; pt. 4, to works of art, reproductions of a work of art, drawings or plastic works of scientific or technical character, photographs, prints, and pictorial illustrations.

Subscriptions for the Catalogue of copyright entries should be made to the Superintendent of Documents, Washington, D. C., instead of to the Register of Copyrights. Prices are as follows: Paper, $3.00 a yr. (4 pts.), foreign subscription, $5.00; pt. 1 (groups 1 and 2), 5c. single copy (group 1, price of group 2 varies), $1.00 a yr., foreign subscription, $2.25; pt. 3, $1.00 a yr., foreign subscription, $1.50; pts. 2 and 4, each 10c. single copy, 50c. a yr., foreign subscription, 70c.

—— Same, pt. 1, group 2, Pamphlets, leaflets, contributions to newspapers or periodicals, etc., lectures, sermons, addresses for oral delivery, dramatic compositions, maps, motion pictures, v. 20, no. 5. 1923. iii+465–601 p. [Monthly.]

—— Same, pt. 3, Musical compositions, v. 17, no. 13 [with index and title-pages to new series, pt. 3, v. 17, calendar year 1922]. 1923. v+1539–2277 p.+[3] leaves+[2] p. [Monthly.]

DOCUMENTS DIVISION

Government publications. Monthly check-list of State publications received during June, 1923; v. 14, no. 6. 1923. ii+247–295 p. * Paper, 10c. single copy, $1.00 a yr.; foreign subscription, $1.25. 10—8924

NAVY DEPARTMENT

Court-martial order 7, 1923; July 31, 1923. [1923.] 12 p. 12° [Monthly.] ‡

Orders. General order 112–116 [6th series]; Aug. 13–22, 1923. [1923.] 2 p. 4° ‡

AERONAUTICS BUREAU

ZR–1, U. S. dirigible balloon. United States Navy ZR–1, general characteristics. [1923.] 1 p 4° †

ENGINEERING BUREAU

Bearings (machinery). Instructions for operation, care, and repair of bearings and shafting; reprint of chapter 9 of Manual of engineering instructions. 1923. [1]+23 p. il. [The edition of the Manual of engineering instructions of which this chapter forms a part has not yet been issued.] * Paper, 5c.
23—26815

Bulletin of engineering information 9; Sept. 1, 1923. 1923. [1]+27 p. ‡
22—26665

Marine engineering. Changes in Manual of engineering instructions, no. 15; Apr. 16, 1923. 1923. 1 p. [This is a corrected preliminary page for chapter 28 of the new edition of the Manual of engineering instructions. When chapter 28 was issued, see Monthly catalogue for July, 1923, p. 35, the accompanying preliminary page was designated as Changes 14, which was incorrect. The preliminary page here catalogued should be substituted for the one first issued.] †

MARINE CORPS

Orders. Marine Corps orders 3 and 4, 1922; Mar. 6 and June 20, 1922. [Reprint] 1923. 1 p. 4° ‡

Rain-coats. Marine Corps specifications: Coat, rubber, adopted Apr. 14, 1923. [1923.] 3 p. 12° ‡

Supplies. Changes [40] in System of accountability, Marine Corps, 1916; July 17, 1923. [1923.] 1 p. 4° .[Accompanied by reprints of certain pages to be inserted in their proper places in the 1918 reprint of the original publication. A list of these reprinted pages is given on the first page.] ‡

MEDICINE AND SURGERY BUREAU

Compression fractures of lower end of radius; by James H. Stevens. 1923. [1]+14 p. 18 p. of pl. [From United States naval medical bulletin, v. 19, no. 2.] †

Hospital Corps quarterly. Supplement to United States naval medical bulletin published for information of Hospital Corps of Navy, Apr. 1923, no. 25, old series, v. 7, no. 2, new series; edited by W. W. Behlow. 1923. v+141 p. il. 3 pl. 16 p. of pl. [Title on cover is: Hospital Corps quarterly.] * Paper, 25c.

SPECIAL ARTICLES.—Isolated duty on Cape Hatteras, N. C.; by M. B. Folb.—Iron, 2d great agent of civilization [with list of references]; by P. V. Tuttle.—Cruise in the Orient; by R. Martin.—Virgin Islands of United States; by B. E. Irwin.—Management of poison case, nature of poison being unknown; by C. Schaffer.—Blood test used at field hospital, San Pedro de Macoris, Dominican Republic; by J. O. Roberts.—Standard filing system; by P. V. Tuttle.—Article on water; by T. C. Hart.—Construction of dispensary building; by M. A. Banker.—Phthirius pubis; by F. O. Huntsinger.—Some aspects of naval pharmacy; by K. M. Smith.—Care of Government property; by A. B. Montgomery.—United States Naval Hospital, San Diego, Calif.; by W. T. Gildberg.—Personnel office, Naval Hospital, New York, N. Y.; by C. P. Dean.—Preparation of bills of fare at certain hospitals; by R. J. Youngkin.—Ionization; by A. S. Bagley.—The salute; by R. F. S. Puck.—Use of poison bottles; by P. V. Tuttle.—Service rifle as splint; by L. H. French.—Routine clerical procedure in connection with allotments, stub requisitions, open-purchase requisitions, and job orders; by N. F. Smith.—Testing of calibrations on glassware [with list of references]; by L. E. Bote.—Training of hospital corpsmen as dental technicians; by G. H. Reed.—Property accountability and stock accounting; by E. A. Rozea.

Juxtapyloric ulcer; by G. F. Cottle. 1923. [1]+18 p. [From United States naval medical bulletin, v. 19, no. 2.] †

Naval medical bulletin. United States naval medical bulletin, published for information of Medical Department of service, Aug. 1923, v. 19, no. 2; edited by W. M. Kerr. 1923. vi+115-256 p. 1 pl. 26 p. of pl. [Monthly.] * Paper, 15c. single copy, $1.50 a yr.; foreign subscription, $2.50.   8—35095

SPECIAL ARTICLES.—Compression fractures of lower end of radius; by James H. Stevens.—Juxtapyloric ulcer; by G. F. Cottle.—Samoan medicines and practices; by D. Hunt.—Deformities of nose; by F. E. Locy.—Notes on Dakin's solution; by J. Holden.—Surgical cases of especial interest; by A. H. Robnett.—Medical cases of especial interest; by J. Buckley.—Lipoma of ischlorectal fossa; by L. Humphreys.— Method of boiling drinking water for use in camp; by C. I. Wood.—Foreign body in nares; by C. B. Camerer.—Unusual nasal polyp; by P. M. Albright.—Report on sanitary conditions of 2d brigade, United States marines, Santo Domingo, for 1922; by J. J. Snyder.—Notes on preventive medicine for medical officers, Navy.

—— Same, Sept. 1923, v. 19, no. 3; edited by W. M. Kerr. 1923. vi+257-392 p. 2 p. of pl. [Monthly.]

SPECIAL ARTICLES.—Fear and worry; by H. Butts.—Psychoanalytic literature [with bibliography]; by J. C. Thompson.—Chronic colitis; by J. B. Pollard.—Cholecystitis of chemical origin in man following inhalations of poison gas; by H. M. Stenhouse.— Cancer of stomach [with list of references]; by L. H. Williams.—Present status of treatment of gonorrhea [with list of references]; by E. A. Daus.—Diagnosis and treatment of bronchial asthma; by J. E. Miller.—Diagnosis and treatment of fractures of leg; by C. L. Andrus.—Urology and its place in group medicine; by W. H. Connor.—Rôle of roentgenologist in modern hospital; [by] J. B. Farrior.—Case report of actinomycosis of liver and lungs; by G. F. Cottle and R. C. Satterlee.—Incidence of neurosyphilis in treated cases on island of St. Croix, Virgin Islands; by F. L. McDaniel.—Myiasis of ear; by L. L. Davis.—Notes on preventive medicine for medical officers, Navy.

Nose. Deformities of nose; by F. E. Locy. 1923. [1]+3 p. 2 p. of pl. [From United States naval medical bulletin, v. 19, no. 2.] † .

¡ NAVAL WAR COLLEGE

International law documents, Conference on Limitation of Armament, with notes and index, 1921; [compiled by George Grafton Wilson]. 1923. vii+392 p. * Cloth, 75c.   23—26816

NAVIGATION BUREAU

HYDROGRAPHIC OFFICE

NOTE.—The charts, sailing directions, etc., of the Hydrographic Office are sold by the office in Washington and also by agents at the principal American and foreign seaports and American lake ports. Copies of the General catalogue of mariners' charts and books and of the Hydrographic bulletins, reprints, and Notice to mariners are supplied free on application at the Hydrographic Office in Washington and at the branch offices in Boston, New York, Philadelphia, Baltimore, Norfolk, Savannah, New Orleans, Galveston, San Francisco, Portland (Oreg.), Seattle, Chicago, Cleveland, Buffalo, Sault Ste. Marie, and Duluth. .

Bengal, Bay of. Bay of Bengal pilot, comprising Bay of Bengal and coasts of India and Siam, including Nicobar and Andaman islands. 2d edition. 1923. vii+500 p.+[2] leaves, il. map. ([Publication] 160.) [The 2 leaves given in the collation consist of request coupons which are detachable.] † Cloth, 90c.

East Indies pilot: v. 2, Islands eastward of Celebes and Timor including New Guinea and Louisiade Archipelago. 2d edition. 1923. viii+708 p.+[2] leaves, il. 2 maps. ([Publication] 164.) [The 2 leaves given in the collation consist of request coupons which are detachable. Subtitle of 1st edition of v. 2 read: Southern part including New Guinea.] † Cloth, 90c.

Great Britain. British Islands pilot: v. 3, Coasts of Ireland. 2d edition. 1923. vi+585 p.+[2] leaves, il. map. ([Publication] 146.) [The 2 leaves given in the collation consist of request coupons which are detachable.] † Cloth, 90c.

Hydrographic bulletin, weekly, no. 1774-77; Sept. 5-26, 1923. [1923.] Each 1 p. large 4° and f° [For Ice supplements to accompany nos. 1774-77, see below under center head *Charts* the subhead *Pilot charts.*] †

Notice to aviators 9, 1923; Sept. 1[1923]. [1923.] 6 p. [Monthly.] †   20—26958

Notice to mariners 35-39, 1923; Sept. 1-29[1923]. [1923.] [xlvi]+915-1067 leaves. [Weekly.] †

Tide calendar [for Norfolk (Navy Yard) and Newport News, Va.]. Oct. 1923. [1923.] 1 p. 4° [Monthly.] †

Charts

Azores, north Atlantic Ocean, from British surveys in 1843 and 1844, with additions from other sources to 1922; [and] with inset, Princesse Alice Bank; chart 5384. Scale 1° long.=4.5 in. Washington, Hydrographic Office, Sept. 1923. 26.7×39.2 in. † 50c.

Haiti. Ports and anchorages in Republic of Haiti, island of Haiti, northwest coast, W. I., from British and other surveys; chart 950. Washington, Hydrographic Office, published Mar. 1885, 18th edition, Sept. 1923. 14.5×18.7 in. † 10c.

A'l'ecu, Port.
Chouchou & Salt River bays.
Juan Rabel Anchorage.
Moustique Bay.
St. Nicholas Mole, from British survey in 1830.
Tierra Baja Road.

Pilot charts. Ice supplement to north Atlantic pilot chart; issue 74. Scale 1° long.=0.3 in. Washington, Hydrographic Office [1923]. 8.9×11.8 in. [To accompany Hydrographic bulletin 1774, Sept. 5, 1923.] †

—— Same; issue 75. Scale 1° long.=0.3 in. Washington, Hydrographic Office [1923]. 8.9×11.8 in. [To accompany Hydrographic bulletin 1775, Sept. 12, 1923.] †

—— Same; issue 76. Scale 1° long.=0.3 in. Washington, Hydrographic Office [1923]. 8.9×11.8 in. [To accompany Hydrographic bulletin 1776, Sept. 19, 1923.] †

—— Same; issue 77. Scale 1° long.=0.3 in. Washington, Hydrographic Office [1923]. 8.9×11.8 in. [To accompany Hydrographic bulletin 1777, Sept. 26, 1923.] †

—— Pilot chart of Central American waters, Oct. 1923; chart 3500. Scale 1° long.=0.7 in. Washington, Hydrographic Office, Sept. 13, 1923. 23.4×35.1 in. [Monthly. Certain portions of the data are furnished by the Weather Bureau.] † 10c.

NOTE.—Contains on reverse: Cyclonic storms.

—— Pilot chart of Indian Ocean, Nov. 1923; chart 2603. Scale 1° long. =0.2 in. Washington, Hydrographic Office, Sept. 13, 1923. 22.6×31 in. [Monthly. Certain portions of the data are furnished by the Weather Bureau.] † 10c.

NOTE.—Contains on reverse: Cyclonic storms.

—— Pilot chart of north Atlantic Ocean, Oct. 1923; chart 1400. Scale 1° long. =0.27 in. Washington, Hydrographic Office, Sept. 13, 1923. 23.2×31.8 in. [Monthly. Certain portions of the data are furnished by the Weather Bureau.] † 10c.   14—16339

NOTE.—Contains on reverse: Cyclonic storms.

—— Pilot chart of north Pacific Ocean, Nov. 1923; chart 1401. Scale 1° long. =0.2 in. Washington, Hydrographic Office, Sept. 13, 1923. 23.7×35.3 in. [Monthly. Certain portions of the data are furnished by the Weather Bureau.] † 10c.

NOTE.—Contains on reverse: Cyclonic storms.

ORDNANCE BUREAU

Breech mechanisms, 16-inch breech mechanisms, mark 1 and mark 1 mod. 1, general description. May, 1923. [1]+i+14 p. il. 1 pl. 4° (Ordnance pamphlet 507.) ‡

Gearing. Specifications, hydraulic variable speed gears for use of Navy, inspection and manufacture. [Mar. 1912, 1st revision] June, 1923. 1923. [1]+i+5 p. 18 p. of pl. 4° (Ordnance pamphlet 66.) ‡

Ordnance. Index [to] Ordnance pamphlets with notes relative to their use and distribution. [Nov. 1905, 12th revision] June, 1923. 1923. [1]+ii+54 p. 4° (Ordnance pamphlet 0.) ‡

—— Ordnance allowances and instructions for supply of ordnance material to vessels. [Revised Jan. 1, 1922, reprinted] Mar. 1923. [1]+11 p. 4° (Ordnance pamphlet 19.) ‡

SUPPLIES AND ACCOUNTS BUREAU

Naval vessels. Sale of naval vessels for scrapping purposes, bids will be opened Nov. 1, 1923, and should be mailed to Room 1008, Navy Department, Washington, D. C. 1923. cover-title, 15 p. (Catalogue 225B.) †

—— Sale of naval vessels for scrapping purposes on ways at navy yards, bids will be opened Oct. 25, 1923, and should be mailed to Room 1008, Navy Department, Washington, D. C. 1923. cover-title, 10 p. (Catalogue 224B.) †

Radio stations. Sale of Navy radio stations [at] Alpena, Mich., Cleveland, Ohio, Detroit, Mich., Duluth, Minn., Manistique, Mich., Milwaukee, Wis., Mackinac Island, Mich., bids will be opened Oct. 2, 1923, Central Sales Office, Navy Yard, Washington, D. C. 1923. cover-title, 28 p. (Catalogue 227B.) †

Supply Corps, Navy. Memorandum for information of officers of Supply Corps, commanding officers of ships, and commandants 253; Sept. 1, 1923. [1923.] p. 7597–7652, 12° [Monthly.] ‡

PAN AMERICAN UNION

Note.—The Pan American Union sells its own monthly bulletins, handbooks, etc., at prices usually ranging from 5c. to $2.50. The price of the English edition of the bulletin is 25c. a single copy or $2.50 a year, the Spanish edition $1.50 a year, the Portuguese edition $1.50 a year; there is an additional charge of 50c. a year on each edition for countries outside the Pan American Union. Address the Director General of the Pan American Union, Washington, D. C.

Bulletin (English edition). Bulletin of Pan American Union, Sept. 1923; [v. 57, no. 3]. [1923.] iv+217–322 p. il. [Monthly.]   8—30967

—— Same. (H. doc. 6, pt. 3, 68th Cong. 1st sess.)

—— *(Portuguese edition).* Boletim da União Pan-Americana, Setembro, 1923, edição portugueza; [v. 25, no. 3]. [Sun Job Print, Baltimore, Md., 1923.] [iv]+153–230 p. il. [Monthly.]   11—27014

—— *(Spanish edition).* Boletín de la Unión Panamericana, v. 53 [edición española]; Julio–Diciembre, 1921 [índice]. [1923.] [1]+xvi p.   12—12555

—— Same, Septiembre, 1923, edición española; [v. 57, no. 3]. [1923.] iv+217–332 p. il. [Monthly. This number is entitled La quinta Conferencia Internacional Americana, Santiago de Chile, Marzo 25 a Mayo 3 de 1923.]

Coal resources of the Americas; [by Benjamin LeRoy Miller]. 1923. 24 p. il. map. †   23—26817

Peru, general descriptive data. 1923. [2]+30 p. il. †   11—35842

PANAMA CANAL

Note.—Although The Panama Canal makes its reports to, and is under the supervision of, the Secretary of War, it is not a part of the War Department.

Panama Canal record, v. 17, no. 4–7; Sept. 5–26, 1923. Balboa Heights, C. Z. [1923]. p. 65–120. [Weekly.]   7—35328

Note.—The Panama Canal record is furnished free to United States Government departments and bureaus, Members of Congress, representatives of foreign Governments, steamship lines, and public libraries. Others desiring this publication may obtain it at the subscription price of 50c. per year in the Canal Zone, the United States, and the Republic of Panama; $1.00 per year elsewhere. Remittances for subscriptions may be forwarded to The Panama Canal, Washington, D. C., or to The Panama Canal Record, Balboa Heights, Canal Zone, Isthmus of Panama.

PURCHASING DEPARTMENT

Supplies. Circular [proposals for supplies] 1558 and 1561; Sept. 21 and 27, 1923. [1923.] 30+[1] and 32+[1] p. f° †

—— Proposals [for supplies 1561, to accompany Circular proposals for supplies 1561]. [1923.] 1 p. small 4° ‡

POST OFFICE DEPARTMENT

Letter-writing. Preparation of correspondence for signature of 4th assistant Postmaster General. 1923. 21 p. ‡

Mail matter. Amendment to Postal laws and regulations [of United States] : Matter found in ordinary mail intended for registration or special delivery. Sept. 15, 1923. 1 p. narrow large 8° †

—— Ascertainment of cost of handling and transporting the several classes of mail matter and conducting special services: Instruction letter R–dx [Sept. 13, 1923], Time reports by items and tests of mixed items in specially designated terminal R. P. O.'s. [1923.] 5 p. ‡

Mail thefts. To stop mail thefts in apartment houses [regulations issued by Postmaster General, with accompanying instructions by 1st assistant Postmaster General]. [1923.] 1 p. narrow f° †

Money-orders. California conference-convention, June, 1923 [question discussed at convention concerning money-order for C. O. D. parcel, with answer]. [1923.] 1 p. oblong 32° †

Parcel post convention between United States and ——. 1923. [1]+10 p. [Specimen parcel post convention.] †

Post route maps. Proposal and specifications for photolithographing and printing post route maps for Post Office Department for term of 1, 2, or 4 years from Jan. 1, 1924. 1923. [1]+10 p. f° †

Postal bulletin, v. 44, no. 13256–279 ; Sept. 1–29, 1923. [1923.] various paging, f° [Daily except Sundays and holidays.] * Paper, 5c. single copy, $2.00 a yr.
6—5810

Postal guide. United States official postal guide, 4th series, v. 3, no. 3 ; Sept. 1923, monthly supplement. 1923. cover-title, ii+46 p. il. [Includes Modification 23 of International money order list, pamphlet 14. Text and illustration on p. 2 and 4 of cover.] * Official postal guide, with supplements, $1.00, foreign subscription, $1.50 ; July issue, 75c. ; supplements published monthly (11 pamphlets) 25c., foreign subscription, 50c.   4—18254

Registered mail. Amendment to Postal laws and regulations [of United States] : Registered matter remailed after delivery. Sept. 15, 1923. 1 p. narrow f° †

FOREIGN MAILS DIVISION

Steamboats. Schedule of steamers appointed to convey mails to foreign countries during Oct. 1923. Sept. 20, 1923. 1 p. f° [Monthly.] * Paper, 5c. single copy, 25c. a yr. ; foreign subscription, 50c.

MONEY ORDERS DIVISION

Money-orders. Register of money-order post offices in United States including Hawaii, Guam, Porto Rico, Tutuila (Samoa), and United States Virgin Islands, also Antigua, Bahamas, Barbados, Bermuda, British Guiana, British Honduras, Canada, Canal Zone, Cuba, Dominica, Grenada, Jamaica, Martinique, Montserrat, Nevis, Newfoundland, Philippine Islands, St. Kitts, St. Lucia, St. Vincent, Trinidad, Tobago, and British Virgin Islands [in operation July 2, 1923]. Aug. 1923. x+272 p. il. ‡   9—16602

RAILWAY MAIL SERVICE

Mail-trains. Schedule of mail trains, no. 366, Aug. 8, 1923, 2d division, Railway Mail Service, comprising New York, New Jersey, Pennsylvania, Delaware, eastern shore of Maryland, Accomac and Northampton counties, Va., Porto Rico, and Virgin Islands. 1923. 302+[1] p. narrow 8° ‡

—— Schedule of mail trains, no. 445, Aug. 22, 1923, 7th division, Railway Mail Service, comprising Kansas and Missouri. 1923. 168 p. narrow 8° ‡

TOPOGRAPHY DIVISION

NOTE.—Since February, 1908, the Topography Division has been preparing rural-delivery maps of counties in which rural delivery is completely established. They are published in two forms, one giving simply the rural free delivery routes, starting ,from a single given post office, sold at 10 cents each; the other, the rural free delivery routes in an entire county, sold at 35 cents each. A uniform scale of 1 inch to 1 mile is used. Editions are not issued, but sun-print copies are produced in response to special calls addressed to the Disbursing Clerk, Post Office Department, Washington, D. C. These maps should not be confused with the post route maps, for which see Monthly catalogue for February, 1923, page 528.

PRESIDENT OF UNITED STATES

Addresses. Address by President Warren G. Harding delivered at Pocatello, Idaho, June 28, 1923. 1923. [1]+8 p. †   23—26818

—— Address by President Warren G. Harding on Alaska, delivered at Seattle, Wash., July 27, 1923. 1923. [1]+14 p. †   23—26819

—— Address by President Warren G. Harding on Canadian-American relations, delivered at Vancouver, B. C., July 26, 1923. 1923. [1]+4 p. †
23—26820

—— Address by President Warren G. Harding on coal problem, delivered at Cheyenne, Wyo., June 25, 1923. 1923. [1]+6 p. †   23—26821

—— Address by President Warren G. Harding on development, reclamation, and water utilization, delivered at Spokane, Wash., July 2; 1923. 1923. [1]+ 7 p. †   23—26822

—— Address by President Warren G. Harding on immigration and Americanization, delivered at Portland, Oreg., July 4, 1923. 1923. [1]+5 p. †
23—26823

—— Address by President Warren G. Harding on merchant marine, delivered at Washington Stadium, Tacoma, Wash., July 5, 1923. 1923. [1]+4 p. †
23—26824

—— Address by President Warren G. Harding on national business conditions, delivered at Butte, Mont., June 29, 1923. 1923. [1]+7 p. †   23—26825

—— Address of President Warren G. Harding on cooperation in production and distribution, delivered at Idaho Falls, Idaho, June 28, 1923. 1923. [1]+5 p. †   23—26826

—— Address prepared by President Warren G. Harding on ideals of Christian fraternity, for delivery before Grand Commandery, Knights Templars of California, at Hollywood, Calif., Aug. 2, 1923. 1923. [1]+3 p. † 23—26827

NOTE.—This address was prepared by the President, but owing to his illness was read for him by George B. Christian, jr., secretary to the President, about 3 hours before the President's death. It was his last word to the American people.

—— Address prepared by President Warren G. Harding on our foreign relations, intended to be delivered at San Francisco, Calif., July 31, 1923. 1923. [1]+14 p. †   23—26828

NOTE.—This address was prepared by President Harding during his trip to Alaska, and but for his illness would have been delivered. When he found that his strength would not sustain the effort of delivery he directed that the address be released for publication.

Coal Commission. Executive order [designating date of termination of Coal Commission as Sept. 22, 1923, directing that records, files, and property of commission be transferred to Interior Department, designating Secretary of Interior as custodian of said records, etc., and authorizing director of Geological Survey to perform all duties incident to closing work of Coal Commission]. Sept. 13, 1923. 1 p. f° (No. 3901.) ‡

Consuls. Executive order [amending Regulations for consular service, 1896, concerning compensation of consular officers]. [Sept. 13, 1923.] 3 p. f° ([No. 3902.]) ‡

—— Executive order [amending Regulations for consular service, 1896, concerning privileges and powers under treaties and conventions, supervisory powers of consuls-general and diplomatic representatives, relations to naval officers of United States, and correspondence with Department of State]. [Sept. 6, 1923.] 4 p. f° ([No. 3899.]) ‡

—— Executive order [amending Regulations for consular service, 1896, under heading Miscellaneous instructions]. [Sept. 11, 1923.] 6 p. f° ([No. 3900.]) ‡

Federal Fuel Distributor. Executive order [directing that records, files, and property of Federal Fuel Distributor be transferred to Commerce Department, designating Secretary of Commerce as custodian of said records, etc., and further directing that Secretary of Commerce, acting Secretary of Commerce, or assistant Secretary of Commerce, each or either of them, shall approve for settlement any outstanding accounts due after expiration of Federal Fuel Distributor's organization on Sept. 21, 1923]. Sept. 15, 1923. 1 p. f° (No. 3905.) ‡

Fire prevention day. National fire prevention day, 1923, proclamation [designating Oct. 9, 1923, as National fire prevention day]. Sept. 17, 1923. 1 p. f° (No. 1674.) †

Idaho. Executive order, Idaho [temporarily withdrawing certain described lands in Idaho from settlement, etc., for classification and pending enactment of legislation for their proper disposition]. Sept. 6, 1923. 1 p. f° (No. 3898.) ‡

Katmai National Monument. Executive order [modifying proclamation of Sept. 24, 1918, establishing Katmai National Monument, Alaska, so as to eliminate certain described lands therefrom, to end that coal mining permit may be granted John J. Fostad]. Sept. 5, 1923. 1 p. f° (No. 3897.) ‡

National forests. Coconino National Forest, Ariz., 4th proclamation. Aug. 14, 1923. 1 p. map, f° (No. 1671.) †

—— Executive order, Dell administrative site, near Beaverhead National Forest, Mont. [temporarily withdrawing certain described lands from settlement, etc., and reserving same for use by Forest Service as ranger station in connection with administration of Beaverhead National Forest]. Aug. 31, 1923. 1 p. f° (No. 3896.) ‡

—— Prescott National Forest, Ariz., 7th proclamation. Aug. 14, 1923. 1 p. map, f° (No. 1673.) †

—— Tonto National Forest, Ariz., 5th proclamation. Aug. 14, 1923. 1 p. map, f° (No. 1672.) †

Panama Canal. Executive order amending Executive order of Feb. 6, 1917, relating to exclusion and deportation of undesirable persons from Canal Zone. [Sept. 13, 1923.] 2 p. f° ([No. 3903.]) ‡

Railroad Administration. Re-appointing James C. Davis director general of railroads and agent of the President, proclamation. Aug. 13, 1923. 1 p. f° (No. 1670.) †

Utah. Executive order [temporarily withdrawing certain described lands in Utah from settlement, etc., until Mar. 5, 1926, after which, if legislation be not enacted, they will become subject to disposal under any law applicable thereto]. Aug. 23, 1923. 1 p. f° (No. 3895.) ‡

Wyoming. Executive order, Wyoming [withdrawing certain described public lands in Wyoming from settlement, etc., pending resurvey, such withdrawal to remain in effect until resurvey is accepted and approved plat thereof is officially filed in local land office]. Aug. 21, 1923. 1 p. f° (No. 3894.) ‡

RAILROAD ADMINISTRATION

Coal. Before Interstate Commerce Commission, no. 14714, Whitaker-Glessner Manufacturing Company v. director general et al.; brief for director general. 1923. cover-title, i+30 p. ‡

Coal-cars. Before Interstate Commerce Commission, no. 11446, Northern West Virginia Coal Operators' Association v. Pennsylvania Railroad Company, director general, et al.; brief for director general. 1923. cover-title, i+15 p. 1 pl. ‡

Gainesville Midland Railway. Final settlement between director general of railroads and Gordon C. Carson and W. B. Veazey, receivers of Gainesville Midland Railway, —, 1923. 1923. 3 p. 4° †

Grain. Before Interstate Commerce Commission, no. 14849, S. W. Thaxter & Co. v. director general; brief for defendant. 1923. cover-title, 1 p. ‡

Graphite. Before Interstate Commerce Commission, no. 13836, 13945, United States Graphite Company v. director general; exceptions by director general to examiner's report. 1923. cover-title, 8 p. ‡

Huntingdon and Broad Top Mountain Railroad and Coal Company. Final set.
  tlement between director general of railroads and Huntingdon & Broad Top
  Mountain Railroad & Coal Company, Sept. —, 1923. 1923. 3 p. 4° †
Ice. Before Interstate Commerce Commission, no. 14388, Moline Ice Company
  v. director general; exceptions on behalf of director general to report pro-
  posed by examiner. 1923. cover-title, 4 p. ‡
Iron. Before Interstate Commerce Commission, no. 14386, Republic Iron &
  Steel Company *v.* director general et al.; exceptions on behalf of director
  general to examiner's proposed report. 1923. cover-title, 10 p. ‡
Logs. Before Interstate Commerce Commission, no. 14656, Murray & Nickell
  Manufacturing Company *v.* director general, as agent; exceptions on part of
  director general to report proposed by examiner. 1923. cover-title, 8 p. ‡
Sand. Before Interstate Commerce Commission, no. 14445, George A. Fuller
  Company et al. *v.* director general et al.; reply of director general to com-
  plainants' exceptions to proposed report of examiner. 1923. cover-title,
  3 p. ‡
Shales. Before Interstate Commerce Commission, no. 12816, Hocking valley
  Brick Company *v.* director general et al.; petition of director general for re-
  consideration. 1923. cover-title, 14 p. ‡
Shingles. Before Interstate Commerce Commission, no. 11982, A. & C. Mill
  Company et al. *v.* director general et al.; exceptions on part of director gen-
  eral to report proposed by examiner. 1923. cover-title, 2 p. ‡
Spotting charges. Before Interstate Commerce Commission, no. 11074, Jones &
  Laughlin Ore Company et al. *v.* director general et al.; brief for director
  general. 1923. cover-title, i+42 p. ‡
Storage. Before Interstate Commerce Commission, no. 14431, Hendee Manufacturing Company *v.* director general; defendant's exceptions to proposed
  report. 1923. cover-title, 9 p. ‡
Switching charges. Before Interstate Commerce Commission, no. 14769, Joseph
  Bancroft & Sons Company *v.* director general; brief for defendant. 1923.
  cover-title, 8 p. ‡
Tin. Before Interstate Commerce Commission, no. 14032, N. & G. Taylor Company (Inc.) *v.* director general, as agent; petition for further hearing and
  further consideration on part of director general. 1923. cover-title, 9 p. ‡
Tin-plate. Before Interstate Commerce Commission, no. 13795, Metal & Thermit Corporation *v.* director general, as agent; petition on part of director
  general for further consideration and further hearing. 1923. cover-title,
  5 p. ‡

SHIPPING BOARD

SHIPPING BOARD EMERGENCY FLEET CORPORATION

Ships. Schedule of sailings of Shipping Board vessels in general cargo, passenger, and mail services, 1st of September to middle of October, 1923; issued
  by Traffic Department. 1923. cover-title, ii+14 p. il. [Monthly. Text on
  p. 2–4 of cover.] †   23—26331

SMITHSONIAN INSTITUTION

NATIONAL MUSEUM

Note.—The publications of the National Museum comprise an annual report and
three scientific series, viz., Proceedings, Bulletins, and Contributions from national
herbarium. The editions are distributed to established lists of libraries, scientific institutions, and specialists, any surplus copies being supplied on application. The volumes
of Proceedings are made up of technical papers based on the Museum collections in
biology, geology, and anthropology, and of each of these papers a small edition, in
pamphlet form, is issued in advance of the volume, for prompt distribution to specialists.
No sets of any of these series can now be furnished.

Foraminifera of Atlantic Ocean: pt. 4, Lagenidae; by Joseph Augustine Cushman. 1923. x+228 p. 2 pl. 40 p. of pl. (Bulletin 104 [pt. 4].) * Paper,
  35c.   18—26668

STATE DEPARTMENT

[*Circulars*] 903–905; July 26–Aug. 14, 1923. [1923.] Each 2 p. or 5 p. [General instruction circulars to consular officers.] ‡

Diplomatic list, Sept. 1923. [1923.] cover-title, ii+34 p. 24° [Monthly.] ‡
10—16292

Pacific Islands Treaty. Agreement between United States, British Empire, France, and Japan, supplementary to treaty of Dec. 13, 1921, between same 4 Powers relating to their insular possessions and insular dominions in region of Pacific Ocean; signed Washington, Feb. 6, 1922, proclaimed Aug. 21, 1923. 1923. [1]+5 p. (Treaty series 670.) [French and English.] †
23—26829

—— Treaty between United States, British Empire, France, and Japan, relating to their insular possessions and insular dominions in region of Pacific Ocean; signed Washington, Dec. 13, 1921, proclaimed Aug. 21, 1923. 1923. [1]+8 p. (Treaty series 669.) [French and English.] †
23—26830

SUPREME COURT

Cases. Docket [of cases pending in] Supreme Court, Oct. term, 1923. [1923.] [1]+xxxi+218+[3] p. 4° [Half of the pages are blank. Issued in loose-leaf form.] ‡

Official reports. Official reports of Supreme Court, v. 261 U. S., no. 2; Ernest Knaebel, reporter. Preliminary print. 1923. cover-title, x+[2]+165–306 p. 12° [Cases adjudged in Supreme Court at Oct. term, 1922 (opinions of Feb. 19 in part–Mar. 5, 1923). This number contains lists of cases reported in v. 260 and in v. 261, pt. 1. Text on p. 2 and 4 of cover. From United States reports, v. 261.] * Paper, 25 c. single copy, $1.00 per vol. (4 nos. to a vol.; subscription price, $3.00 for 12 nos.); foreign subscription, 5c. added for each pamphlet.

—— Same, v. 261 U. S., no. 3; Ernest Knaebel, reporter. Preliminary print. 1923. cover-title, xi+[2]+307–445 p. 12° [Cases adjudged in Supreme Court at Oct. term, 1922 (opinions of Mar. 12–Apr. 9, 1923, in part). This number contains lists of cases reported in v. 260 and in v. 261, pts. 1 and 2. Text on p. 2 and 4 of cover. From United States reports, v. 261.]

—— Same, v. 261 U. S., no. 4; Ernest Knaebel, reporter. Preliminary print. 1923. cover-title, xii+[1]+446–630 p. 12° [Cases adjudged in Supreme Court at Oct. term, 1922 (opinions of Apr. 9, 1923, in part). This number contains lists of cases reported in v. 260 and in v. 261, pts. 1–3. Text on p. 2 and 4 of cover. From United States reports, v. 261.]

TREASURY DEPARTMENT

Bonds of officers. Companies holding certificates of authority from Secretary of Treasury, under acts of Aug. 13, 1894, and Mar. 23, 1910, as acceptable sureties on Federal bonds, also acceptable reinsuring companies under Department circular of July 5, 1922; revised as to process agents to Sept. 1, 1923. Sept. 1, 1923. 1 p. oblong large 8° [Semiannual.] †

Certificates of indebtedness. United States of America, 4¼ per cent Treasury certificates of indebtedness, series TM 2–1924, dated and bearing interest from Sept. 15, 1923, due Mar. 15, 1924. Sept. 10, 1923. 1 p. 4° (Department circular 328; Loans and Currency [Division].) †

Checks. Regulations and instructions governing issue of duplicate disbursing officers' checks. Aug. 15, 1923. 3 p. 4° (Department circular 327; Division of Bookkeeping and Warrants.) [This circular supersedes Treasury Department Form 1343, dated Apr. 14, 1916, and all previous regulations.] †

Claims. Laws and regulations governing recognition of attorneys, agents, and other persons representing claimants and others before Treasury Department and offices thereof. Aug. 15, 1923. 13 p. 4° (Department circular 230; Chief Clerk.) [This circular supersedes Department circular 230, dated Feb. 15, 1921, and its several supplements.] †

Finance. Daily statement of Treasury compiled from latest proved reports from Treasury offices and depositaries, Sept. 1–29, 1923. [1923.] Each 4 p. or 3 p. f° [Daily except Sundays and holidays.] †   15—3303

Gold (money). Instructions relative to deposits of gold coin and gold certificates for credit in gold fund account with Federal Reserve Board and payments therefrom under act of June 21, 1917. 2d edition. Aug. 15, 1923. 2 p. 4° (Department circular 86 amended and supplemented; Treasurer's Office.) †

Liberty bonds. [Notice to accompany leaflets giving information regarding outstanding issues of liberty bonds, Treasury bonds, Treasury notes, Treasury certificates of indebtedness, and current offering of Treasury savings certificates.] Aug. 15, 1923. 1 p. oblong 48° (Public Debt [Commissioner].) †

—— United States Government liberty bonds. July 15, 1923. [2] p. 4° †

Treasury bonds. United States Government Treasury bonds, Treasury notes, Treasury certificates of indebtedness, and Treasury savings certificates. July 15, 1923. [2] p. 4° †

Treasury decisions. Treasury decisions under customs and other laws, v. 43; Jan.–June, 1923. 1923. iii+748 p. * Cloth, $1.75.   10—11513

NOTE.—This volume contains Department decisions numbered 39387–453, 39455–716, including general appraisers' decisions 8595–8666, and abstracts 45512–46157. Department decision 39454 was withdrawn.

—— Treasury decisions under customs, internal-revenue, and other laws, including decisions of Board of General Appraisers and Court of Customs Appeals, v. 44, no. 10–13; Sept. 6–27, 1923. 1923. various paging. [Weekly. Department decisions numbered 39778–795, general appraisers' decisions 8680–83, abstracts 46218–234, internal revenue decisions 3510–19, and later Tariff Commission Notice 29.] * Paper, 5c. single copy, $1.00 a yr.; foreign subscription, $2.00.   10—30490

War-savings certificates. Regulations with respect to war-savings certificates. Aug. 1, 1923. 21 p. 4° (Department circular 108 revised; Public Debt [Commissioner].) †

APPRAISERS

Reappraisements. Index to Reappraisement circulars, showing reappraisements and re-reappraisements of merchandise made by general appraisers, Jan. 2–June 30, 1923. 1923. [1]+18 p. * Paper, 5c.

—— Reappraisements of merchandise by general appraisers [on Aug. 28– Sept. 24, 1923]; Sept. 14–28, 1923. [1923.] various paging. (Reappraisement circulars 3474–76.) [Weekly; none issued Sept. 7, 1923.] * Paper, 5c. single copy, 50c. a yr.; foreign subscription, $1.05.   13—2916

ARCHITECT, SUPERVISING

Public buildings. Specification, general conditions [for construction of public works under supervision of supervising chief engineer of building]. [1923.] 5 p. f° †

—— [Specification, general conditions for construction of public works under $2,000.] [1923.] 2 p. f° †

COAST GUARD

Circular letter 203 amendment A, 293 amendment A, 296 [new series]; July 16–Aug. 7, 1923. 1923. Each 1 p. ‡

Orders. General order 34; Aug. 7, 1923. [1923.] 8 p. ‡

COMPTROLLER OF CURRENCY

National banks. Abstract of reports of condition of national banks, June 30, 1923; no. 140. [1923.] 13 p. f° †

—— Monthly statement of capital stock of national banks, national bank notes, and Federal reserve bank notes outstanding, bonds on deposit, etc. [Sept. 1, 1923]. Sept. 1, 1923. 1 p. f° †   10—21266

GENERAL SUPPLY COMMITTEE

Government supplies. Contract for supplies listed in General schedule of supplies [fiscal year 1924]. [1923.] [2] leaves, 4° [Blank form.] †

—— General schedule of supplies, fiscal year 1924: 1st supplement of awards to class 7, Lumber, millwork, packing boxes, building materials, and tar for road building. [1923.] 7 p. 4° ‡   16—26857

—— Specifications and proposals for supplies [fiscal year 1924]: class 11, Forage, flour, and seed, Nov. 1, 1923–Feb. 29, 1924. [1923.] 8 p. 4° †

—— Supplemental specifications and proposals for supplies [fiscal year 1924]: class 7, Lumber, millwork, packing boxes, and building materials, Oct. 1–Dec. 31, 1923. [1923.] 12 p. 4° †

—— Same: class 10, Groceries and provisions, Nov. 1, 1923–June 30, 1924. [1923.] 16 p. 4° †

GOVERNMENT ACTUARY

Bonds of United States. Market prices and investment values of outstanding bonds and notes [of United States, Aug. 1923]. Sept. 1, 1923. 7 p. 4° (Form A.) [Monthly.] †

INTERNAL REVENUE BUREAU

Alcohol, Denatured. Appendix [to] Regulations 61, Formulae for completely and specially· denatured alcohol, Sept. 21, 1923. Revised [edition]. 1923. 15 p. [Title of no. 61 is: Regulations 61 relative to production, tax payment, etc., of industrial alcohol and to manufacture, sale, and use of denatured alcohol under title 3 of national prohibition act of Oct. 28, 1919.] †

Income Tax Unit. Training courses offered to members of Income Tax Unit, season 1923–24. 1923. iv+14 p. ‡

Internal revenue bulletin, v. 2, no. 22–25; Sept. 3–24, 1923. 1923. various paging. [Weekly.] * Paper, 5c. single copy (for subscription price see note below).   22—26051

NOTE.—On May 7, 1923, the publication of weekly bulletins was resumed and the issuance of monthly bulletins (and special bulletins as occasion required) discontinued. Since May 1, therefore, the 1923 Internal revenue bulletin service consists of weekly bulletins of new rulings and decisions of the Bureau of Internal Revenue and internal revenue Treasury decisions of general importance, quarterly digests of such new rulings (cumulative from Jan. 1. 1922), and semiannual cumulative bulletins containing in full the new rulings and decisions published during the preceding 6 months. The complete bulletin service may be obtained, on a subscription basis, from the Superintendent of Documents, Government Printing Office, Washington, D. C., for $2.00 a yr.; foreign subscription, $2.75.

LOANS AND CURRENCY DIVISION

Bonds of United States. Caveat list of United States registered bonds and notes, Sept. 1, 1923. [1923.] 55 p. f° [Monthly.] †

Money. Circulation statement of United States money, Sept. 1, 1923. [1923.] 1 p. oblong 8° [Monthly.] †   10—21267

PUBLIC HEALTH SERVICE

Arsphenamine. Effect of arsenic-fastness of Trypanosoma equiperdum on ratios between parasiticidal values of arsphenamine and neoarsphenamine; by G. C. Lake and T. F. Probey. 1923. 6 p. (Reprint 843.) [From Public health reports, June 15, 1923.] * Paper, 5c.   23—26831

Hygiene, Public. Report of committee on municipal·health department practice of American Public Health Association in cooperation with Public Health Service. July, 1923. x+468 p. il. 1 pl. (Public health bulletin 136.) * Paper, 50c.

Insulin. Standardization of insulin: 1, Toxicity of insulin for white rats as influenced by temperature of room in which animals are kept; by Carl Voegtlin and Edith R. Dunn. 1923. 4 p. (Reprint 855.) [From Public health reports, Aug. 3, 1923.] * Paper, 5c.   23—26832

Nutrition. Indices of nutrition, application of certain standards of nutrition to 506 native white children without physical defects and with good or excellent nutrition as judged from clinical evidence; by Taliaferro Clark, Edgar Sydenstricker, and Selwyn D. Collins. 1923. 35 p. (Reprint 842.) [From Public health reports, June 8, 1923.] * Paper, 5c.   23—26833

Oxidation. Studies on oxidation-reduction: 3, Electrode potentials of mixtures of 1-naphthol-2-sulphonic acid indophenol and reduction product [with list of references]; by W. Mansfield Clark and Barnett Cohen. 1923. 28 p. il. (Reprint 834.) [From Public health reports, May 4, 1923.] * Paper, 5c.
23—26652

Public health reports, v. 38, no. 36–39; Sept. 7–28, 1923. 1923. [xvi]+2053–2300 p. il. [Weekly.] * Paper, 5c. single copy, $1.50 a yr.; foreign subscription. $2.75.   6—25167

SPECIAL ARTICLES.—No. 36. Elimination of carbon monoxide from blood by treatment with air, with oxygen, and with mixture of carbon dioxide and oxygen; by R. R. Sayers and W. P. Yant.—Studies on permeability of living and dead cells: 3, Penetration of certain alkalies and ammonium salts into living and dead cells [with list of references]; by Matilda Moldenhauer Brooks.—No. 37. Application of partial correlation to health problem; by Frank M. Phillips, assisted by Faye Hollis Roberts.—Sugar-free medium for fermentation studies; by Ella M. A. Enlows.— No. 38. Vaccination technique and certification, experiment in making vaccination an insurance against delay as well as protection against disease; by S. B. Grubbs.— Effective publicity in rural health work [in Preston County, W. Va.].—Ship-borne plague during 1922.—No. 39. Effect of acidification on toxicity of B. botulinus toxin; by J. C. Geiger and W. E. Gouwens.—Malaria entering port of London, 1922.— Meeting of American Public Health Association, 52d annual meeting to be held in Boston, Oct. 8–11, 1923.—State and insular health authorities, 1923, directory, with data as to appropriations and publications.
NOTE—This publication is distributed gratuitously to State and municipal health officers, etc., by the Surgeon General of the Public Health Service, Treasury Department. Others desiring these reports may obtain them from the Superintendent of Documents, Washington, D. C., at the prices stated above.

School children. Physical care of rural school children; by Taliaferro Clark. 1923. 12 p. (Reprint 840.) [Supersedes Reprint 366. From Public health reports, June 1, 1923.] * Paper, 5c.   23—26834

Sewage treatment in United States, report on study of 15 representative sewage treatment plants [with lists of references]; by H. H. Wagenhals, E. J. Theriault, and H. B. Hommon. July,- 1923. iv+260 p. il. 23· pl. (Public health bulletin 132.) [Includes lists of Public Health Service publications on sewage disposal.] * Paper, 50c.   23—26799

Tuberculosis. Index to State tuberculosis laws; compiled by James A. Tobey. 1923. 12 p. (Reprint 841.) [From Public health reports, June 1, 1923.] * Paper, 5c.   23—26798

Venereal diseases. Incidence of venereal diseases among American seamen in the Orient; by M. R. King. 1923. 4 p. il. (Reprint 847.) [From Public health reports, June 29, 1923.] * Paper, 5c.   23—26835

Ventilation of ships after fumigation with poisonous gases; [abstract of report by Stephen Olop]. 1923. 4 p. (Reprint 849.) [From Public health reports, July 6, 1923.] * Paper, 5c.   23—26836

Water pollution. Principles underlying movement of Bacillus coli in groundwater, with resulting pollution of wells; by C. W. Stiles and Harry R. Crohurst. 1923. 6 p. (Reprint 844.) [From Public health reports, June 15, 1923.] * Paper, 5c.   23—26837

VENEREAL DISEASES DIVISION

Venereal disease information, issued by Public Health Service for use in its cooperative work with State health departments. v. 4, no. 8; Aug. 20, 1923. 1923. ii+285–329+iv p. [Monthly.] * Paper, 5c. single copy, 50c. a yr.
23—26719

SPECIAL ARTICLES.—Treatment of syphilis on Mediterranean station; by G. B. Scott.—Treatment of syphilis afloat; by J. H. Fergussen.—The Trevethin report [resolution adopted by Society for Prevention of Venereal Disease accepting report of Committee of Inquiry on Venereal Disease].

SAVINGS SYSTEM

Treasury savings securities. Opportunity knocks at your door [and shows way to security and independence through investment in Treasury savings certificates]. [1923.] [4] p. il. narrow S° ([T. S. S. 24–23.]) †

TREASURER OF UNITED STATES

Money. Issue, exchange, and redemption of money. Aug. 25, 1923. 3 p. 4°
(Treasury Dept. Department circular 55 amended and supplemented.) †

Paper money. Monthly statement, paper currency of each denomination outstanding July 31, 1923. Aug. 1 [1923]. 1 p. oblong 24° †

VETERANS' BUREAU

Life insurance. [Specimen policy, ordinary life policy.] [1923.] [4] p. il. f°
([Form] 741.) [Although this policy uses Bureau of War Risk Insurance in the text, it is signed by the director appointed for the veterans' Bureau in 1923.] †

—— [Specimen policy, 20-payment life policy.] [1923.] [4] p. il. f° ([Form] 747.) [Although this policy uses Bureau of War Risk Insurance in the text, it is signed by the director appointed for the veterans' Bureau in 1923.] †

—— [Specimen policy, 30-year endowment policy.] [1923.] [4] p. il. f° ([Form] 750.) [Although this policy uses Bureau of War Risk Insurance in the text, it is signed by the director appointed for the veterans' Bureau in 1923.] †

WAR DEPARTMENT

Army regulations. †

NOTE.—The Army regulations are issued in pamphlet form for insertion in loose-leaf binders. The names of such of the more important administrative subjects as may seem appropriate, arranged in proper sequence, are numbered in a single series and each name so numbered constitutes the title and number of a pamphlet containing certain administrative regulations pertaining thereto. Where more than one pamphlet is required for the administrative regulations pertaining to any such title, additional pamphlets will be issued in a separate sub-series.

30–440. Quartermaster Corps: Classification of and specifications for public animals, Changes 1; Aug. 3, 1923. 1923. 1 p.
30–1195. Same: Transportation of individuals on transports, Changes 1; Feb. 1, 1923. 1923. 1 p.
35–840. Finance Department: Procurement authorities, general, Changes 1; July 24, 1923. 1923. 1 p.
45–400. Ordnance Department: Allowances of small-arms ammunition; Mar. 21, 1923. [1923.] 11 p.
105–40. Signal Corps: Operation and maintenance of United States military telegraph lines, Changes 2; July 3, 1923. [1923.] 2 p. [Supersedes AR 105–40, Changes 1, Apr. 20, 1922.]
105–200. Same: Pigeon service, Changes 1; Mar. 2, 1923. 1923. 1 p.
260–10. Flags, colors, standards, and guidons: Description and use; Feb. 8, 1923. [1923.] 22 p.
600–35. Personnel: Specifications for uniform, Changes 8; Aug. 23, 1923. [1923.] 7 p. [Supersedes AR 600–35, Changes 1–7, Jan. 6, 1922–Apr. 10, 1923.]
600–40. Same: Wearing of uniform, Changes 9; Aug. 23, 1923. [1923.] 9 p. [Supersedes 600–40, Changes 1–8, Jan. 31, 1922–Apr. 16, 1923.]
600–375. Same: Prisoners, general provisions, Changes 1; July 26, 1923. 1923. 1 p.
605–135. Commissioned officers: Specifications and requirements for private mounts, Changes 1; Aug. 3, 1923. 1923. 1 p.
850–5. Marking of clothing, equipment, animals, vehicles, and property; June 6, 1923. [1923.] 19 p. il.

Conference on Moral and Religious Work in Army. Report of Conference on Moral and Religious Work in Army [held at Washington, D. C., June 6–7] 1923. 1923. v+24 p. * Paper, 5c.   23—26838

Training regulations.

NOTE.—The Training regulations are issued in pamphlet form for insertion in loose-leaf binders.

150–5. Marksmanship: Rifle, individual, prepared under direction of chief of infantry; June 6, 1923. [1923.] 45 p. il. * Paper, 10c.
150–10. Same: Rifle, general, prepared under direction of chief of infantry; June 6, 1923. [1923.] 44 p. il. * Paper, 5c.
190–10. Topography and surveying: Conventional signs, prepared under direction of chief of engineers; Oct. 30, 1922. [1923.] 31 p. il. map. * Paper, 10c.
420–90. Infantry: Extended order, machine-gun squad, section, and platoon, prepared under direction of chief of infantry; June 6, 1923. [1923.] 18 p. il. * Paper, 5c.
420–135. Same: Combat principles, machine-gun company, prepared under direction of chief of infantry; June 20, 1923. [1923.] 51 p. * Paper, 10c.
420–155. Same: Combat principles, howitzer company, prepared under direction of chief of infantry; June 20, 1923. [1923.] 26 p. * Paper, 5c.
430–80. Field artillery: Maneuvers limbered, prepared under direction of chief of field artillery; May 29, 1923. [1923.] 43 p. il. * Paper, 10c.
435–98. Coast Artillery Corps: Separate battalion, antiaircraft artillery (75-mm., 3-inch, or 4.7-inch guns), peace strength, prepared under direction of chief of coast artillery; June 7, 1923. [1923.] 11 p. il. * Paper, 5c.

ADJUTANT GENERAL'S DEPARTMENT

Army list and directory, Sept. 1, 1923. 1923. vi+274 p. large 8° [Bi-monthly.] * Paper, 25c. single copy, $1.25 a yr.; foreign subscription, $1.85.
9—35106

U. S. Army recruiting news, bulletin of recruiting information issued by direction of Adjutant General of Army, Sept. 1 and 15, 1923. [Recruiting Publicity Bureau, Governors Island, N. Y., Sept. 1 and 15, 1923.] Each 16 p. il. 4° † Recruiting Publicity Bureau, Governors Island, N. Y.
War 22—1

AIR SERVICE

Aeronautical bulletins. Aeronautical bulletin, no. 1–10, Route information series; Aug. 15–Sept. 15, 1923. [1923.] various paging, 12° (Airways Section.) * Paper, 5c. each.
23—26231

—— Aeronautical bulletin, no. 42–66, State series; July 15–Sept. 15, 1923. [1923.] various paging, il. 12° (Airways Section.) [No. 50 is Index to Aeronautical bulletins 1–50.] * Paper, 5c. each.

ENGINEERING DIVISION

Aeroplanes. Handbook of instructions for airplane designers. [3d edition, June, 1922] revision Aug. 1923. [Dayton, Ohio, no publisher, Aug. 3, 1923.] 4° [This Aug. 1923 revision consists of 1 p. and an additional page to be inserted in its proper place in the 3d edition.] ‡

ENGINEER DEPARTMENT

Bridgeport, Conn. Maintenance and improvement of existing river and harbor works for Bridgeport Harbor, Conn., advertisement [for dredging]. [1923.] 14 p. 4° †

New Rochelle, N. Y. Maintenance and improvement of existing river and harbor works, New Rochelle Harbor, N. Y., dredging, advertisement. [1923.] 14 p. 4° †

New York Harbor. Act to prevent obstructive and injurious deposits within harbor and adjacent waters of New York City, by dumping or otherwise, and to punish and prevent such offenses [approved June 29, 1888, as amended]. [1923.] 5 p. 4° †

Port Chester, N. Y. Maintenance and improvement of existing river and harbor works, Port Chester Harbor, N. Y., dredging and rock removal, advertisement. [1923.] 14 p. 4° †

NORTHERN AND NORTHWESTERN LAKES SURVEY

NOTE.—Charts of the Great Lakes and connecting waters and St. Lawrence River to the international boundary at St. Regis of Lake Champlain, and of the New York State canals are prepared and sold by the U. S. Lake Survey Office, Old Custom-house, Detroit, Mich. Charts may also be purchased at the following U. S. engineer offices: 710 Army Building, New York, N. Y.; 467 Broadway, Albany, N. Y.; 540 Federal Building, Buffalo. N. Y.; and Canal Office, Sault Ste. Marie, Mich. A catalogue (with index map), showing localities, scales, prices, and conditions of sale, may be had upon application at any of these offices.
A descriptive bulletin, which supplements the charts and gives detailed information as to harbors, shore lines and shoals, magnetic determinations, and particulars of changing conditions affecting navigation, is issued free to chart purchasers, upon request. The bulletin is revised annually and issued at the opening of navigation (in April), and supplements thereto are published monthly during the navigation season.
Complete sets of the charts and publications may be seen at the U. S. engineer offices in Duluth, Minn., Milwaukee, Wis., Chicago, Ill., Grand Rapids, Mich., Cleveland, Ohio, and Oswego, N. Y., but they are obtainable only at the sales offices above mentioned.

Great Lakes. Supplement 5, Sept. 20, 1923, corrections and additions to Bulletin 32; to supplement information given upon charts of Great Lakes. U. S. Lake Survey Office, Detroit, Mich. [Sept. 14, 1923]. p. 1–3+leaves 4–11+ [2] p. 4° †

FINANCE DEPARTMENT

Finance circular 6 [1923] ; June 30, 1923.   [1923.]   8 p. 12°   ‡

ORDNANCE DEPARTMENT

Ordnance provision system. Ordnance provision system : Group B, Automatic pistol, cal. .45, M 1911 ; Apr. 12, 1923. [1923.] 13 p. il. (Standard nomenclature list B–6.) [Supersedes Standard nomenclature list B–6, Jan. 15. 1923.] ‡

—— Same : Group B, Colt revolver, cal. .45, M 1917, Smith & Wesson revolver, cal. .45, M 1917 ; June 5, 1923. [1923.] 17 p. il. (Standard nomenclature list B–7.) [Supersedes Standard nomenclature list B–7, Nov. 15, 1922.] ‡

—— Same : Group F, Clinometer, Mk. 2, for 3″ Stokes trench mortar, Mk. 1 ; May 21, 1923. [1923.] 4 p. il. (Standard nomenclature list F–37.) [Supersedes Standard nomenclature list F–37, Nov. 15, 1922.] ‡

QUARTERMASTER GENERAL OF ARMY

Circulars. Changes 57 [1923, to] Circulars ; Sept. 10, 1923. [1923.] 1 p. 4° [Mimeographed.] ‡

O

35

Monthly Catalogue

United States

Public Documents

UNIVERSITY OF ILLINOIS L
DEC 12 1923

No. 346

October, 1923

ISSUED BY THE
SUPERINTENDENT OF DOCUMENTS

WASHINGTON
1923

Abbreviations

Common abbreviations for names of States and months are also used.
* Document for sale by Superintendent of Documents.
† Distribution by office issuing document, free if unaccompanied by a price.
‡ Printed for official use.
NOTE.—Nearly all of the Departments of the Government make a limited free distribution of their publications. When an entry shows a * price, it is possible that upon application to the issuing office a copy may be obtained without charge.

Explanation

Words and figures inclosed in brackets [ ] are given for information, but do not appear on the title-pages of the publications catalogued. When size is not given octavo is to be understood. Size of maps is measured from outer edge of border, excluding margin. The dates, including day, month, and year, given with Senate and House documents and reports are the dates on which they were ordered to be printed. Usually the printing promptly follows the ordering, but various causes sometimes make delays.

SALES OF GOVERNMENT PUBLICATIONS

The Superintendent of Documents, Washington, D. C., is authorized to sell at cost of paper and printing, plus 10 per cent, any United States public document in his charge the distribution of which is not otherwise provided for.

Publications can not be supplied free to individuals nor forwarded in advance of payment.

Publications entered in this catalogue that are for sale by the Superintendent of Documents are indicated by a star (*) preceding the price. A dagger (†) indicates that application should be made to the Department, Bureau, or Division issuing the document. A double dagger (‡) indicates that the document is printed for official use. Whenever additional information concerning the method of procuring a document seems necessary, it will be found under the name of the Bureau by which it was published.

In ordering a publication from the Superintendent of Documents, give (if known) the name of the publishing Department, Bureau, or Division, and the title of the publication. If the publication is numbered, give the number also. Every such particular assists in quick identification. Do not order by the Library of Congress card number.

The accumulation of publications in this Office amounts to several millions, of which over two million are assorted, forming the sales stock. Many rare books are included, but under the law all must be sold regardless of their age or scarcity. Many of the books have been in stock some time, and are apt to be shop-worn. In filling orders the best copy available is sent. A general price-list of public documents is not available, but lists on special subjects will be furnished on application.

MONTHLY CATALOGUE DISTRIBUTION

The Monthly catalogue is sent to each Senator, Representative, Delegate, Resident Commissioner, and officer in Congress; to designated depositories and State and Territorial libraries if it is selected by them; to substantially all Government authors; and to as many school, college, and public libraries as the limited edition will supply.

Subscription price to individuals, 50c. a year, including index; foreign subscription, 75c. a year. Back numbers can not be supplied. Notify the Superintendent of Documents of any change of address.

LIBRARY OF CONGRESS CARDS

Numbers to be used in ordering the printed catalogue cards of the Library of Congress are given at the end of entries for the more important documents. Orders for these cards, remittances in payment for them, and requests for information about them should be addressed to the Librarian of Congress, not to the Superintendent of Documents.

INDEX

An Index to the Monthly catalogue is issued at the end of the fiscal year. This contains index entries for all the numbers issued from July to June, and can be bound with the numbers as an index to the volume. Persons desiring to bind the catalogue at the end of the year should be careful to retain the numbers received monthly, as duplicate copies can not be supplied.

HOW TO REMIT

Remittances'for the documents marked with a star (*) should be made to the Superintendent of Documents, Washington, D. C., by coupons, postal money order, express order, or New York draft. Currency may be sent at sender's risk.

Postage stamps, foreign money, defaced or smooth coins, positively will not be accepted.

For the convenience of the general public, coupons that are good until used in exchange for Government publications sold by the Superintendent of Documents may be purchased from his Office in sets of 20 for $1.00. Address order to Superintendent of Documents, Government Printing Office, Washington, D. C.

No charge is made for postage on documents forwarded to points in United States, Alaska, Guam, Hawaii, Philippine Islands, Porto Rico, Samoa, or to Canada, Cuba, or Mexico. To other countries the regular rate of postage is charged, and remittances must cover such postage. In computing foreign postage, add one-third of the price of the publication.

MONTHLY CATALOGUE

AGRICULTURE DEPARTMENT

NOTE.—Those publications of the Department of Agriculture which are for sale will be supplied by the Superintendent of Documents, Washington, D. C. The Department issues a monthly list of publications, which is mailed to all applicants, enabling them to select such reports and bulletins as interest them.

Bacterial spot of lima bean [with list of literature cited]; by W. B. Tisdale and Maude Miller Williamson. 1923. cover-title, 141–154+[2] p. 3 p. of pl. [From Journal of agricultural research, v. 25, no. 3, July 21, 1923.] ‡

Crown-gall. Some relations of crowngall organism to its host tissue [with list of literature cited]; by A. J. Riker. 1923. cover-title, 119–132+[4] p.+[1] leaf, 5 p. of pl. [From Journal of agricultural research, v. 25, no. 3, July 21, 1923.] ‡

Grain futures act [of Sept. 21] 1922, general rules and regulations of Secretary of Agriculture with respect to contract markets. June 22, 1923. [1]+65 p. narrow 16° (Miscellaneous circular 10.) * Paper, 10c.   Agr 23—1308

Journal of agricultural research, v. 25, no. 5–8; Aug. 4–25, 1923. 1923. cover-titles, 209–362+[32] p.+[10] leaves, il. 5 pl. 40 p. of pl. [Weekly. Text on p. 2 of covers.] * Paper, 10c. single copy, $4.00 a yr.; foreign subscription, $5.25.   Agr 13—1837

CONTENTS.—No. 5, Systemic infections of Rubus with orange-rust [with list of literature cited]; by B. O. Dodge.—Resistance in rye to leaf rust, Puccinia dispersa Erikss [with list of literature cited]; by E. B. Mains and C. E. Leighty.—Undescribed orange pest from Honduras; by A. C. Baker.—No. 6. Correlation of foliage degeneration diseases of Irish potato with variations of tuber and sprout [with list of literature cited]; by Alfred H. Gilbert.—Comparative study of Phytophthora faberi on coconut and cacao in Philippine Islands [with list of literature cited]; by Otto August Reinking.—No. 7. Quantitative variation of gossypol and its relation to oil content of cottonseed [with list of literature cited]; by Erich W. Schwartze and Carl L. Alsberg.—Inheritance of dwarfing in maize [with list of literature cited]; by J. H. Kempton.—Determination of sulphur compounds in dry lime-sulphur [with list of literature cited]; by Carleton Parker Jones.—No. 8. Twinning and monembryonic development of Platygaster hiemalis, parasite of Hessian fly [with list of literature cited]; by R. W. Leiby and C. C. Hill.—Pathogenicity of Ophiobolus cariceti in its relationship to weakened plants [with list of literature cited]; by H. R. Rosen and J. A. Elliott.—Pharynx and alimentary canal of hookworm larva, Necator americanus; by N. A. Cobb.

NOTE.—This publication is published by authority of the Secretary of Agriculture, with the cooperation of the Association of Land-Grant Colleges. It is distributed free only to libraries of agricultural colleges and experiment stations, to large universities, technical schools, and to such institutions as make suitable exchanges with the Agriculture Department. Others desiring the Journal may obtain it from the Superintendent of Documents, Washington, D. C., at the prices stated above.

Nicotin. Improved method for determination of nicotine in tobacco and tobacco extracts; by O. M. Shedd. 1923. cover-title, p. 961–970. [From Journal of agricultural research, v. 24, no. 11, June 16, 1923.] ‡

Official record, Department of Agriculture, v. 2, no. 40–44; Oct. 3–31, 1923. [1923.] Each 8 p. 4° [Weekly.] * Paper, 50c. a yr.; foreign subscription, $1.10.   Agr 22—146

Weather, crops, and markets, weekly, Oct. 6–27, 1923; v. 4, no. 14–17. [1923.] p. 345–456, il. 4° * Paper, $1.00 a yr.; foreign subscription, $2.00.   Agr 22—147

Wheat. Effect of respiration upon protein percentage of wheat, oats, and barley [with list of literature cited]; by F. W. McGinnis and G. S. Taylor. 1923. cover-title, p. 1041–48. [From Journal of agricultural research, v. 24, no. 12, June 23, 1923.] ‡

—— Study of factors affecting nitrogen content of wheat and of changes that occur during development of wheat [with list of literature cited]; by George A. Olson. 1923. cover-title, p. 939–953, il. [From Journal of agricultural research, v. 24, no. 11, June 23, 1923.] ‡

Yearbook, 1922. 1923. v + 1137 p. il. (H. doc. 606, 67th Cong. 4th sess.) [For contents see entry of this publication without Congressional document number in Monthly catalogue for May, 1923, p. 698.] * Cloth, $1.25.   Agr 7—1035

AGRICULTURAL ECONOMICS BUREAU

Accounting. Farm household accounts; [by] W. C. Funk. [June, 1918, reprint Aug. 1923.] 12 p. il. (Agriculture Dept. Farmers' bulletin 964.) [Imprint date incorrectly given on title-page as 1921. Previous reprint issued by Farm Management and Farm Economics Office.] * Paper, 5c.

Hides and skins. Country hides and skins, skinning, curing, and marketing; [by R. W. Frey, F. P. veitch, R. W. Hickman, and C. v. Whalen]. [Aug. 1919, revised July, 1923.] [1923.] 56 p. il. (Agriculture Dept. Farmers' bulletin 1055.) [Prepared in cooperation with Chemistry Bureau and Animal Industry Bureau. Previously issued by Markets and Crop Estimates Bureau.] * Paper, 5c.

Service announcements. Service and regulatory announcements, no. 80: Regulations of Secretary of Agriculture under cotton standards act, effective Aug. 1, 1923. 1923. iv + 21 p. * Paper, 5c.   Agr 15—199

ANIMAL INDUSTRY BUREAU

Cotton-seed. Feeding cottonseed products to livestock; [by E. W. Sheets and E. H. Thompson]. [Nov. 1920, revised Sept. 1923.] [1923.] 20 p. il. (Agriculture Dept. Farmers' bulletin 1179.) [Includes lists of Agriculture Department publications relating to feeding of livestock.] * Paper, 5c.

Cows. Feeding of dairy cows; [by Helmer Rabild, H. P. Davis, and W. K. Brainerd]. [July, 1916, revised Mar. 1923.] [1923.] 28 p. il. (Agriculture Dept. Farmers' bulletin 743.) * Paper, 5c.

Dairy-barn construction; [by K. E. Parks]. [Oct. 1923.] ii+22 p. il. (Agriculture Dept. Farmers' bulletin 1342.) * Paper, 5c.   Agr 23—1301

Hog lice and hog mange, methods of control and eradication; [by Marion Imes]. [May, 1920, revised Sept. 1923.] [1923.] 28 p. il. (Agriculture Dept. Farmers' bulletin 1085.) * Paper, 5c.

Milk. Cooling milk & cream on farm; [by J. A. Gamble]. [May, 1918, revised Sept. 1923.] [1923.] 16 p. il. (Agriculture Dept. Farmers' bulletin 976.) * Paper, 5c.

Service announcements. Service and regulatory announcements. Sept. 1923; [no.] 197. Oct. 1923. p. 77–84. [Monthly.] * Paper, 5c. single copy, 25c. a yr.; foreign subscription, 40c.   Agr 7—1658

NOTE.—The free distribution of this publication will be limited to persons in the service of the Animal Industry Bureau, to proprietors of establishments at which the Federal meat inspection is conducted, to public officials whose duties render it necessary for them to have such information, and to journals especially concerned. Others desiring copies may obtain them from the Superintendent of Documents, Washington, D. C., at the prices stated above.

BIOLOGICAL SURVEY BUREAU

Game-birds. Local names of migratory game birds; [by] W. L. McAtee. Oct. 1923. cover-title, 95 p. il. (Agriculture Dept. Miscellaneous circular 13.) * Paper, 20c.   Agr 23—1309

Game laws. Substitute for p. 24 [of] Game laws for season 1923-24 [summary of provisions of Federal, State, and provincial statutes; by Geo. A. Lawyer and Frank L. Earnshaw]. [1923.] p. 24. (Agriculture Dept. Farmers' bulletin 1375 [corrected page].) †

CHEMISTRY BUREAU

Calcium arsenate. Method for preparing commercial grade of calcium arsenate; by J. K. Haywood and C. M. Smith. Oct. 5, 1918, revised Sept. 1923. [1923.] 10 p. (Agriculture Dept. Department bulletin 750.) [Prepared in cooperation with Insecticide and Fungicide Board.] * Paper, 5c.

Proteins. Nutritive value of mixtures of proteins from corn and various concentrates [with list of literature cited]; by D. Breese Jones, A. J. Finks, and Carl O. Johns. 1923. cover-title, p. 971–978, il. [From Journal of agricultural research, v. 24, no. 11, June 16, 1923.] ‡

Service announcements. Service and regulatory announcements, Jan. 1914, [no.] 1; [reprint of p. 1–5]. Feb. 19, 1914 [reprint with omissions 1923]. p. 1–5. [The original print of no. 1 included p. 1–19.] * Paper, 5c.

Agr 14—194

—— Same, supplement 159. Oct. 4, 1923. p. 211–244. [Contains Notices of judgment under food and drugs act 11401–450.] * Paper, 5c.

NOTE.—The free distribution of this publication will be limited to firms, establishments, and journals especially concerned. Others desiring copies may obtain them from the Superintendent of Documents, Washington, D. C., at the prices stated above and below.

—— Same, supplement 160. Sept. 21, 1923. p. 245–271. [Contains Notices of judgment under food and drugs act 11451–500.] * Paper, 5c.

—— Same, supplement 161. Oct. 25, 1923. p. 273–300. [Contains Notices of judgment under food and drugs act 11501–550.] * Paper, 5c.

EDITORIAL AND DISTRIBUTION WORK OFFICES

Agriculture Department. Monthly list of publications [of Agriculture Department], Sept. 1923. [1923.] 4 p. †

Agr 9—1414

Department bulletins. Department bulletins 951–975, [title-page] with contents and index; prepared in Office of Editorial Work. 1923. 10+16 p. * Paper, 5c.

—— Same 1001–25, [title-page] with contents and index; prepared in Office of Editorial Work. 1923. viii+15 p. * Paper, 5c.

—— Same 1051–75, [title-page] with contents and index; prepared in Office of Editorial Work. 1923. 8+17 p. * Paper, 5c.

Farmers' bulletins [available for distribution] Oct. 1923. [1923.] [4] p. †

ENTOMOLOGY BUREAU

Grasshoppers and their control on sugar beets and truck crops; [by F. B. Milliken]. [Nov. 11, 1915, revised July, 1923.] [1923.] 20 p. il. (Agriculture Dept. Farmers' bulletin 691.) * Paper, 5c.

Mosquitos. Yellow-fever mosquito; [by L. O. Howard]. [Oct. 1923.] ii+14 p. il. (Agriculture Dept. Farmers' bulletin 1354.) [Revision of Farmers' bulletin 547.] * Paper, 5c.

Potatoes. Increasing potato crop by spraying; [by F. H. Chittenden and W. A. Orton]. [Oct. 1923.] ii+22 p. il. (Agriculture Dept. Farmers' bulletin 1349.) [Prepared in cooperation with Plant Industry Bureau. Revision of Farmers' bulletin 868; publication reads incorrectly, revision of Farmers' bulletin 863.] * Paper, 5c.

Agr 23—1302

Rat mite attacking man; [by] F. C. Bishopp. Oct. 1923. 4 p. (Agriculture Dept. Department circular 294.) * Paper, 5c.

Agr 23—1297

EXPERIMENT STATIONS OFFICE

NOTE.—The Experiment Stations Office was created Oct. 1, 1888, and was merged into the States Relations Service July 1, 1915. The States Relations Service ceased to exist as such July 1, 1923, and the Experiment Stations Office has again become a publishing office.

Experiment station record. Experiment station record, v. 49, no. 3; abstract number. Oct. 6, 1923. cover-title, x+201–300 p. [Text and illustration on p. 2 and 4 of cover.] * Paper, 10c. single copy, 75c. per vol. (2 vols. a yr.); foreign subscription, $1.25 per vol.

Agr 9—832

NOTE.—Mainly made up of abstracts of reports and publications on agricultural science which have recently appeared in all countries, especially the United States. Extra numbers, called abstract numbers, are issued, 3 to each volume. These are made up almost exclusively of abstracts, that is, they contain no editorial notes and only a limited number of current notes.

—— Same, v. 49, no. 4; Sept. 1923. 1923. cover-title, ix+301–400 p. [Text and illustration on p. 2 and 4 of cover.]

ALASKA AGRICULTURAL EXPERIMENT STATIONS

Alaska. Information for prospective settlers in Alaska; by C. C. Georgeson. May 11, 1916, revised Oct. 15, 1923. 1923. ii+18 p. 6 p. of pl. map. (Circular 1.) * Paper, 10c.

Agr 23—1305

FOREST SERVICE

Cattle. Constitution and by-laws of — Stóck Association, · adopted at —,
—, 19–. [1923.] [1]+10 p. 12° [Suggested constitution and by-laws for
livestock association working in cooperation with the Forest Service in the
administration and use of national forest grazing lands.] . †

Lumber. Standard grading specifications for yard lumber, as recommended by
Department of Agriculture; [by] Edward P. Ivory, David G. White, and
Arthur T. Upson. Oct. 1923. 75 p. il. 2 pl. 20 p.' of pl. 1 tab. (Agriculture
Dept. Department circular 296.) * Paper, 20c.   Agr 23—1299

National forests. National forests of southern Appalachians. [Aug. 1923.]
22+[2] p. il. oblong 8° folded into narrow 8° size. * Paper, 15c. Agr 23—1310

—— Washington National Forest, mountain vacation land. [1923.] 15 p. il.
4° folded ·into narrow 8° size. ([Agriculture Dept. Department circular 132
revised.]) * Paper, 10c.   Agr 23—1307

Timber. Basic grading rules and working stresses for structural timbers as
recommended by Department of Agriculture; [by] J. A. Newlin and R. P. A.
Johnson. Oct. 1923. 23 p. il. (Agriculture Dept. Department circular 295.)
* Paper, ·5c.   Agr 23—1298

Maps

Chelan National Forest, information for mountain travelers, recreation map.
[1923.] 1 sheet (with map on verso), il. large 4°, folded into narrow 8° size
and so printed as to number [1]+16+[1] p. †

PLANT INDUSTRY BUREAU

Cabbage diseases [by L. L. Harter and L. R. Jones; revised by J. C. Walker].
[Sept. 1923.] ii+29 p. il. (Agriculture Dept. Farmers' bulletin 1351.)
[Revision of Farmers' bulletin 925.] * Paper, 5c.   Agr 23—1303

Citrus melanose. Commercial control of citrus melanose; [by] John R. Winston
and John J. Bowman. [Reprint] Oct. 1923. 8 p. (Agriculture Dept. Department circular 259.) * Paper, 5c.   Agr 23—405

Citrus stem-end rot. Commercial control of citrus stem-end rot; [by] John R.
Winston, Harry R. Fulton, and John J. Bowman. Oct. 1923. 10 p. il. (Agriculture Dept. Department circular 293.) * Paper, 5c.   Agr 23—1296

Cladosporium citri. Relative susceptibility of citrus fruits and hybrids to
Cladosporium citri Massee [with list of literature cited]; by G: L. Peltier and
W. L. Frederich. 1923. cover-title, p. 955–959.· [Prepared in cooperation
with Alabama Agricultural Experiment Station. From Journal of agricultural research, v. 24, no. 11, June 16, 1923.] ‡

Corn. Method of treating maize seed to destroy adherent spores of· downy
mildew [with list of literature cited]; by William H. Weston, jr. 1923.
cover-title, p. 853–860. [From Journal of agricultural research, v. 24, no. 10,
June 9, 1923.] ‡

Cotton. Segregation and correlation of characters in upland-Egyptian cotton
hybrid [with list of literature cited]; by Thomas H. Kearney. Aug. 10,·
1923. cover-title, 58 p. il. 3 pl. 18 p. of pl. (Agriculture Dept. Department
bulletin 1164.) * Paper, 25c.   Agr 23—1306

Eelworm disease, menace to alfalfa in America; [by] G. H. Godfrey. Oct. 1923.
8 p. il. (Agriculture Dept. Department circular 297.) * Paper, 5c.
     Agr 23—1300

Hydrogen-ion changes induced by species of Rhizopus and by Botrytis cinerea
[with list of ·literature cited]; by J. L. Weimer and L. L. Harter. 1923.
cover-title, p. 155–164. [From Journal of agricultural research, v. 25, no. 3,
July 21, 1923.] ‡

Loose smut. Relation of certain soil factors to infection of oats by loose smut;
by Lucille· K. Bartholomew and Edith Seymour Jones. 1923. cover-title,
p. 569–575, il. [Prepared in cooperation with Wisconsin Agricultural Experiment Station. From Journal of agricultural research, v. 24, no. 7, May 19,
1923.] ‡

Onion smudge. Disease resistance to onion smudge [with list of literature
cited]; by J. C. Walker. 1923. cover-title, 1019–40+[3] p. il. 2 pl. 2 p. of
pl. [Prepared in cooperation with University of Wisconsin. From Journal
of agricultural research, v. 24, no. 12, June 23, 1923.] ‡

Peaches. Growing peaches, sites and cultural methods; [by H. P. Gould]. [Mar. 1918, revised July, 1923.] [1923.] 44 p. il. (Agriculture Dept. Farmers' bulletin 917.)　* Paper, 5c.

Peas. Further studies on inheritance of rogue type in garden peas (Pisum sativum L.) [with list of literature cited]; by Wilber Brotherton, jr. 1923. cover-title, 815–852+[7] p.+[1] leaf, il. 8 p. of pl. [Prepared in cooperation with University of Michigan. From Journal of agricultural research, v. 24, no. 10, June 9, 1923.] ‡

Puccinia graminis. Biologic forms of Puccinia graminis on varieties of Avena spp. [with list of literature cited]; by E. C. Stakman, M. N. Levine, and D. L. Bailey. 1923. cover-title, 1013–18+[3] p.+[1] leaf, 4 p. of pl. [Prepared in cooperation with University of Minnesota Agricultural Experiment Station. From Journal of agricultural research, v. 24, no. 12, June 23, 1923.] ‡

Pucciniastrum americanum. Morphology and host relations of Pucciniastrum americum [americanum, with list of literature cited]; by B. O. Dodge. 1923. cover-title, 885–894+[4] p.+[1] leaf, 5 p. of pl. [From Journal of agricultural research, v. 24, no. 11, June 16, 1923.] ‡

Sacaton Cooperative Testing Station. Crop tests at Cooperative Testing Station, Sacaton, Ariz.; [by] C. J. King. Sept. 1923. 40 p. il. (Agriculture Dept. Department circular 277.)　* Paper, 10c.　　　　Agr 23—1295

Soils. Oxygen-supplying power of soil as indicated by color changes in alkaline pyrogallol solution; by Lee M. Hutchins and Burton E. Livingston. 1923. cover-title, p. 133–140. [From Journal of agricultural research, v. 25, no. 3, July 21, 1923.] ‡

Ustilago avenae. Influence of temperature, moisture, and oxygen on spore germination of Ustilago avenae [with list of literature cited]; by Edith Seymour Jones. 1923. cover-title, p. 577–591, il. [Prepared in cooperation with Wisconsin Agricultural Experiment Station. From Journal of agricultural research, v. 24, no. 7, May 19, 1923.] ‡

Watery rot of tomato fruits [physiological form of Oospora lactis, effect on host, penetration of cell walls by enzymic action, with list of literature cited]; by Fred J. Pritchard and W. S. Porté. 1923. cover-title, 895–906+[3] p. 4 p. of pl. [From Journal of agricultural research, v. 24, no. 11, June 16, 1923.] ‡

Wheat. Experiments in wheat production on dry lands of western United States; by David E. Stephens, Max A. McCall, and Aaron F. Bracken. Sept. 1923. cover-title, 60 p. il. (Agriculture Dept. Department bulletin 1173.) [Prepared in cooperation with Oregon, Washington, and Utah Agricultural Experiment Stations.]　* Paper, 10c.　　　　Agr 23—1294

—— Mode of inheritance of resistance to Puccinia graminis with relation to seed color in crosses between varieties of durum wheat [with list of literature cited], by J. B. Harrington and O. S. Aamodt; Study of rust resistance in cross between marquis and kota wheats [with list of literature cited], by H. K. Hayes and O. S. Aamodt. 1923. cover-title, 979–1012+[4] p.+[3] leaves, 1 pl. 6 p. of pl. [Prepared in cooperation with Minnesota Agricultural Experiment Station. From Journal of agricultural research, v. 24, no. 12, June 23, 1923.] ‡

PUBLIC ROADS BUREAU

Roads. District no. —, specifications, proposal, contract, and bond for forest road construction. 1923. iv+41 p. 4° †

SOILS BUREAU

Colloids. Microscopic estimation of colloids in soil separates; by William H. Fry. 1923. cover-title, p. 879–883. [From Journal of agricultural research, v. 24, no. 10, June 9, 1923.] ‡

Rockdale County, Ga. Soil survey of Rockdale County, Ga.; by A. H. Meyer [W. Edward Hearn, and David D. Long]. 1923. iii+537–553 p. il. map. [Prepared in cooperation with Georgia State College of Agriculture. From Field operations, 1920.]　* Paper, 15c.

69825—No. 346—23——2

WEATHER BUREAU

Climatological data. Climatological data for United States by sections, v. 10, no. 6 ;
June, 1923. [1923.] cover-title, [192] p. il. 2 maps, 2 p. of maps, 4° [Text on p. 2
of cover.] * Paper, 35c. complete monthly number, $4.00 a yr.   Agr 14—566
    NOTE.—Made up of separate Climatological data issued from 42 section centers of
the United States.   Printed at the several section centers and assembled and bound at
the Washington Office. Issued principally for service use and exchange.   The separate
Climatological data are sold by the Superintendent of Documents, Washington, D. C.,
at the rate of 5c. single copy, 50c. a yr. for each section.
—— Same, v. 10, no. 7; July, 1923. [1923.] cover-title, [188] p. il. 2 maps,
2 p. of maps, 4° [Text on p. 2 of cover.]
Meteorology. Monthly meteorological summary, Washington, D. C., Sept. 1923.
[1923.] [2] p. f° †
Monthly weather review, v. 51, no. 8; Aug. 1923. [Oct. 23] 1923. cover-title,
p. 383–435, il. 10 p. of maps, 4° [Text on p. 2–4 of cover.] * Paper, 15c.
single copy, $1.50 a yr.; foreign subscription, $2.25.   Agr 9—990
    NOTE.—The Monthly weather review contains (1) meteorological contributions, and
bibliography including seismology, (2) an interpretative summary and charts of the
weather of the month in the United States, and on adjacent oceans, and (3) climatological and seismological tables dealing with the weather and earthquakes of the month.
The contributions are principally as follows; (a) results of observational or research
work in meteorology carried on in the United States or other parts of the world,
(b) abstracts or reviews of important meteorological papers and books, and (c) notes.
    SPECIAL ARTICLES.—Concerning normals, secular trends, and climatic changes; by
Charles F. Marvin.—Improved method of computing meteorological normals; by H. W.
Clough.—Hourly precipitation at Syracuse, N. Y.; by Morgan R. Sanford.—Efficiency
of smoke screens as protection from frost; by H. H. Kimball and B. G. MacIntire.—
Cloud dissipated by kite; [by] J. A. Riley.—Forecasting rain on west Texas coast;
[by] Joseph P. McAuliffe.—Waterspouts near Corpus Christi, Tex.; by Joseph P.
McAuliffe.—First cool wave of 1923 in the Dakotas and Lake region; by Alfred J.
Henry.—Fires caused by lightning in Iowa, 1919–22; by Roy N. Covert.—Daily
weather bulletins transmitted by radio from United States to France; by E. B. Cal-
vert.—Ground surface temperatures as dependent on insolation and as controlling
diurnal temperature unrest and gustiness, by M. Robitzch: abstracted [by C. F. B.].—
One depression and one typhoon in Philippines during July, 1923; by José Coronas.—
Tropical storm west of Hawaii; by Thomas A. Blair.
Ocean. Weather of the oceans, June, 1923, with special reference to north
Atlantic and north Pacific oceans (including charts), notes, abstracts, and
reviews; issued by Marine Division. 1923. 6 p. 4 p. of maps, 4° [From
Monthly weather review, June, 1923.] †
—— Same, July, 1923, with special reference to north Atlantic and north
Pacific oceans (including charts), notes, abstracts, and reviews; issued by
Marine Division. 1923. 4 p. 2 p. of maps, 4° [From Monthly weather re-
view, July, 1923.] †
Rain. Accuracy of areal rainfall estimates: Rainfall duration and intensity
in India: by Robert E. Horton. 1923. [1]+348–355 p. il. 4° [From Monthly
weather review, July, 1923.] †
Texas. Influence of Gulf water-surface temperatures on Texas weather: by
I. R. Tannehill. 1923. [1]+345–347 p. 4° [From Monthly weather review,
July, 1923.] †
Weather map. Daily weather map [of United States, containing forecasts for
all States east of Mississippi River, except Illinois, Wisconsin, Indiana, upper Michigan, and lower Michigan], Oct. 1–31, 1923. 1st edition. [1923.]
Each 16.4×22.7 in. [Not issued Sundays or holidays.] * Editions issued at
Washington, D. C., 25c. a month, $2.50 a yr.; editions issued at about 65
stations throughout the United States, 20c. a month, $2.00 a yr.
—— Same [containing forecasts for United States], Oct. 1–31, 1923. 2d edition. [1923.] Each 16.4×22.7 in. [The Sunday edition does not contain as
much information as the edition for week days.] * 30c. a month, $3.00 a yr.

CIVIL SERVICE COMMISSION

    NOTE.—The Commission furnishes its publications gratuitously to those who apply
for them.
Posters. Wanted for civil service, Government always needs men and women
for employment in civil service, in force so large vacancies are constantly
occurring; [all lettered poster]. Sept. 1923. 16×12.5 in. (Form 2227.)
[Cancels previous issues.] †
Veteran preference [in appointment to civil offices under United States Gov-
ernment]. Aug. 1923. 8 p. (Form 1481.) †

COMMERCE DEPARTMENT

CENSUS BUREAU

Note.—Persons desiring 14th census publications should address the Director of the Census, Department of Commerce, Washington, D. C. They are also sold by the Superintendent of Documents, Washington, D. C., at the price indicated.

Automobiles. Census of manufactures, 1921: Motor vehicles, including bodies and parts. 1923. 23 p. * Paper, 5c.

Chocolate. Census of manufactures, 1921: Chocolate and cocoa products and confectionery and ice cream. 1923. 15 p. * Paper, 5c.   23—26887

Cotton. Cotton consumed, cotton on hand, active cotton spindles, and imports and exports of cotton, Sept. 1922 and 1923, with statistics of cotton consumed, imported, and exported for 2 months ending Sept. 30. Oct. 13, 1923. oblong 32° [Preliminary report. This publication is issued in postal card form.] †

—— Report on cotton ginning, number of bales of cotton ginned from growth of 1923 prior to Sept. 25, 1923, and comparative statistics to corresponding date in 1922 and 1921. Oct. 2, 1923. oblong 32° [Preliminary report. This publication is issued in postal card form.] †

—— Same prior to Oct. 18, 1923, and comparative statistics to corresponding date in 1922 and 1921. Oct. 25, 1923. oblong 32° [Preliminary report. This publication is issued in postal card form.] †

Cottonseed received, crushed, and on hand, and cottonseed products manufactured, shipped out, on hand, and exported covering 2-month periods ending Sept. 30, 1923 and 1922. Oct. 18, 1923. oblong 24° [Preliminary report. This publication is issued in postal card form.] †

Dyes and dyeing. Census of manufactures, 1921: Natural dyestuffs and extracts. 1923. 11 p. * Paper, 5c.   23—26888

Electric machinery. Census of manufactures, 1921: Electrical machinery, apparatus, and supplies. 1923. 19 p. * Paper, 5c.   23—26869

Farm implements and machinery. Manufacture and sale of farm equipment, 1922. 1923. ii+10 p. * Paper, 5c.   23—26892

Fats. Animal and vegetable fats and oils, production, consumption, imports, exports, and stocks by quarters, calendar years 1919–22. 1923. 24 p. [Prepared under supervision of William L. Austin, chief statistician, assisted by Harvey J. Zimmerman, expert special agent.] * Paper, 5c.   22—26370

Flour-mills. Census of manufactures, 1921: Flour-mill products and bread and other bakery products. 1923. 30 p. * Paper, 5c.   23—26870

Occupations. 14th census of United States [1920]: Population, 1920, occupations, color or race, nativity, and parentage of occupied persons. 1923. [1]+338–372 p. 4° [Prepared under supervision of William C. Hunt, chief statistician for population. Chapter 3 from 14th census of United States, 1920, v. 4.] †

—— 14th census of United States [1920]: Population, 1920, occupations, males and females in selected occupations. 1923. [1]+872–1257 p. 4° [Prepared under supervision of William C. Hunt, chief statistician for population. Chapter 7 from 14th census of United States, 1920, v. 4.] †

—— 14th census of United States [1920]: Population, 1920, occupations, marital condition of occupied women. 1923. [1]+690–870 p. 4° [Prepared under supervision of William C. Hunt, chief statistician for population. Chapter 6 from 14th census of United States, 1920, v. 4.] †

—— 14th census of United States [1920]: Population, 1920, occupations, occupation statistics for Alaska, Hawaii, and Porto Rico. 1923. [1]+1260–1309 p. 4° [Prepared under supervision of William C. Hunt, chief statistician for population. Chapter 8 from 14th census of United States, 1920, v. 4.] †

Paint. Census of manufactures, 1921: Paint and varnish, bone black, carbon black, and lampblack. 1923. 24 p. * Paper, 5c.   23—26889

Petroleum. Census of manufactures, 1921: Petroleum refining. 1923. 15 p. * Paper, 5c.   23—26890

Railroad-cars. Census of manufactures, 1921: Steam and electric railroad cars and railroad repair shops. 1923. 26 p. * Paper, 5c.   23—26580

Ship-building. Census of manufactures, 1921: Shipbuilding, including boat building. 1923. 26 p. * Paper, 5c.
23—26585

Slaughtering. Census of manufactures, 1921: Slaughtering and meat packing. 1923. 24 p. * Paper, 5c.
23—26891

Smelting. Census of manufactures, 1921: Smelting and refining (nonferrous metals). 1923. 12 p. * Paper, 5c.
23—26588

Soap. Census of manufactures, 1921: Soap industry. 1923. 11 p. * Paper, 5c.
23—26591

Vital statistics. United States abridged life tables, 1919–20. 1923. 84 p. il. 4° [Prepared under direction of William H. Davis, chief statistician for vital statistics, by Elbertie Foudray, expert special agent.] * Paper, 20c.
23—26873

Wood distillation. Census of manufactures, 1921: Wood distillation. 1923. 11 p. * Paper, 5c.
23—26872

COAST AND GEODETIC SURVEY

NOTE.—The monthly Notice to mariners, formerly issued by the Coast and Geodetic Survey, has been consolidated with and made a part of the Notice to mariners issued by the Lighthouses Bureau, thus making it a joint publication. The charts, coast pilots, and tide tables of the Coast and Geodetic Survey are sold at the office of the Survey in Washington, and also by one or more sales agents in each of the important American seaports.

Coast and Geodetic Survey bulletin, Sept. 30, 1923; no. 100. [1923.] 8 p. [Monthly.] ‡
15—26512

Coast pilots. United States coast pilot, Atlantic Coast: section C, Sandy Hook to Cape Henry, including Delaware and Chesapeake bays; [prepared by L. A. Potter]. [Reprint] 1923. 284 p. map. (Serial 32.) † Cloth, 75c.
23—26325

Deep-sea soundings, Atlantic and Pacific oceans and Caribbean Sea, 1919 and 1922; [by J. T. Watkins]. 1923. iv+30 p. il. 2 pl. 6 p. of pl. (Special publication 97; serial 241.) * Paper, 15c.
23—26934

Magnetic observatories. Results of observations made at Coast and Geodetic Survey magnetic observatory at Vieques, P. R., 1919–20; by Daniel L. Hazard. 1923. [1]+100 p. 10 pl. (Serial 239.) * Paper, 20c.
10—35894

Publications. Catalogue of U. S. Coast and Geodetic Survey charts, coast pilots, tide tables, current tables (Philippine Islands charts catalogued separately). [Edition of] Aug. 1, 1923. 1923. 47 p. il. 4° (Serial 243.) †
7—6923

Charts

Buzzards Bay, Mass., original surveys 1888–1917, surveys by U. S. Engineers to 1922 and other sources; chart 249. Scale 1:40,000. Washington, Coast and Geodetic Survey, Sept. 1923. 43.5×33.4 in. † 75c.

Coos Bay, Oreg., surveys 1861–90, surveys by Port of Coos Bay in 1915, surveys by U. S. Engineers to June, 1922; chart 5984. Scale 1:20,000. Washington, Coast and Geodetic Survey, Oct. 1923. 29.4×38.2 in. † 75c.

Icy Strait and Cross Sound, Port Frederick to Cape Spencer, Alaska, surveys to 1923 and other sources; with inset, Inian Cove; chart 8304. Scale 1:80,000 Washington, Coast and Geodetic Survey, Sept. 1923. 27.6×39 in. † 75c.

New York Harbor. Approaches to New York, Fire Island light to Sea Girt light, N. Y.–N. J., surveys 1835–1915, surveys by U. S. Engineers to 1923; chart 1215. Scale 1:80,000. Washington, Coast and Geodetic Survey, Oct. 1923. 33×41.4 in. † 75c.

Philadelphia water front, Schuylkill River, Pa., surveys to 1915, surveys by Department of Public Works to 1913, surveys by U. S. Engineers to 1922, surveys by Navy Department to 1922; chart 381. Scale 1:96,000. Washington, Coast and Geodetic Survey, Oct. 1923. 45.1×26 in. † 75c.

Sabine Pass and Lake, La. and Tex., surveys 1874–85, surveys by U. S. Engineers to 1923; chart 517. Scale 1:40,000. Washington, Coast and Geodetic Survey, Oct. 1923. 41×25.7 in. † 75c.

FISHERIES BUREAU

Bulletin of Bureau of Fisheries, 1921–22. 1923. v. 38, iv+341 p. il. 16 pl. 42 p. of pl. large 8° * Cloth, $1.50. 9—35239
CONTENTS.—Ecological study of aquatic midges and some related insects with special reference to feeding habits [with bibliography]; by Adelbert L. Leathers.—Experiments in culture of fresh-water mussels [with list of literature cited]; by Arthur Day Howard.—Further notes on natural history and artificial propagation of diamond-back terrapin; by R. L. Barney.—Notes on habits and development of eggs and larvæ of silversides Menidia menidia and Menidia beryllina; by Samuel F. Hildebrand.—Deductions concerning air bladder and specific gravity of fishes [with list of literature cited]; by Harden F. Taylor.—Biology and economic value of sea mussel, Mytilus edulis [with bibliography]; by Irving A. Field.—New bacterial disease of fresh-water fishes; by H. S. Davis.—Spiny lobster, Panulirus argus, of southern Florida, its natural history and utilization; by D. R. Crawford and W. J. J. De Smidt.—Some embryonic and larval stages of winter flounder; by C. M. Breder, jr.—Salmon of Yukon River; by Charles H. Gilbert.—General index.
Cold storage holdings of fish, Sept. 15, 1923. [1923.] 1 p. oblong 12° (Statistical bulletin 586.) [Statistics furnished by Agricultural Economics Bureau.] †
Fisheries service bulletin, Oct. 1, 1923; no 101. [1923.] 6 p. [Monthly.] ‡
F 15—76

Fishery products. Statement of quantities and values of certain fishery products landed at Boston and Gloucester, Mass., and Portland, Me., by American fishing vessels, Sept. 1923. [1923.] 1 p. oblong f° (Statistical bulletin 587.) †
—— Statement of quantities and values of certain fishery products landed at Seattle, Wash., by American fishing vessels, Sept. 1923. [1923.] 1 p. oblong 12° (Statistical bulletin 588.) †
Report of commissioner of fisheries, fiscal year 1922, with appendixes; Henry O'Malley, commissioner. 1923. iv+[762] p. il. 14 pl. 24 p. of pl. 2 maps. [Manuscript corrections.] ‡ F 10—2
CONTENTS.—Report of commissioner of fisheries.—Fresh-water Crustacea as food for young fishes [with bibliography]; by William Converse Kendall.—Principles involved in preservation of fish by salt; by Harden F. Taylor.—Shellfish resources of northwest coast of United States; by Charles H. Edmondson.—Use of fishes for control of mosquitoes in northern fresh waters of United States [with list of literature cited]; by J. Percy Moore.—Mortality in pike-perch eggs in hatcheries [with bibliography]; by Franz Schrader and Sally Hughes Schrader.—Sources, preparation, and properties of some algal gelatines; by Irving A. Field.—Trade in fresh and frozen fishery products and related marketing considerations in Seattle, Wash.; by L. T. Hopkinson and W. P. Studdert.—Fisheries and market for fishery products in Mexico, Central America, South America, West Indies, and Bermudas [reports from American consular officers, with bibliography]; compiled by Lewis Radcliffe.—Fishery industries of United States, report of Division of Fishery Industries for 1921 [with list of earlier publications relating to fisheries of Maryland and Virginia]; by Lewis Radcliffe.—Alaska fishery and fur-seal industries in 1921; by Ward T. Bower.—Kentucky River and its mussel resources; by Ernest Danglade.—Goldfish, their care in small aquaria [with bibliography]; by E. C. Fearnow.—Progress in biological inquiries, 1922, report of Division of Scientific Inquiry, fiscal year 1922; by R. E. Coker, with collaboration of investigators.—Fisheries prosecuted by California fishermen in Mexican waters [with bibliography relating to fisheries of Lower California and west coast of Mexico]; by R. A. Coleman.—Life history and ecology of orange-spotted sunfish, Lepomis humilis [with bibliography]; by R. L. Barney and B. J. Anson.—Trade in fresh and frozen fishery products and related marketing considerations in Boston, Mass.; by L. T. Hopkinson.—Propagation and distribution of food fishes, 1922, report of Division of Fish Culture, fiscal year 1922; by Glen C. Leach.

FOREIGN AND DOMESTIC COMMERCE BUREAU

Commerce. Monthly summary of foreign commerce of United States, Aug. 1923. 1923. 2 pts. p. 1–69 and ii+71–91 p. 4° * Paper, 10c. single copy (including pts. 1 and 2), $1.00 a yr.; foreign subscription, $1.60. 14—21465
—— Same. 1923. [2 pts. in 1], 91 p. 4° · (H. doc. 8, 68th Cong. 1st sess.)
Commerce reports. Commerce reports, weekly survey of foreign trade, reports from American consular officers and representatives of Department of Commerce in foreign countries, no. 40–44; Oct. 1–29, 1923. 1923. cover-titles, p. 1–328, il, 4° [Text and illustrations on p. 2–4 of covers.] * Paper, 10c. single copy, $3.00 a yr.; foreign subscription, $5.00.
—— Supplement to Commerce reports. [Included in price of Commerce reports for subscribers.]
Trade and economic review for 1922, no. 18: Australia; [by] Romeyn Wormuth, P. H. Moseley, and Walter F. Costello. [1923.] 24 p.
Same, no. 19: Canada; [by] John G. Foster. [1923.] 20 p.
Same, no. 20: Hongkong; [by] William H. Gale. [1923.] 12 p.
Same, no. 21: Virgin Islands of United States; compiled by Division of Statistics. [1923.] 15 p.
Same, no. 22: Norway; [by] Alban G. Snyder. [1923.] 14 p.
Same, no. 23: Ecuador, by Frederic W. Goding; with supplementary data prepared in Latin American Division. [1923.] 8 p.

Commerce reports—Continued. Supplement to Commerce reports: American trade with Germany, 1914, 1921, and 1922; [articles] by C. E. Herring and Edward G. Eichelberger. Oct. 8, 1923. ii+19 p. (Trade information bulletin 150; Western European Division.) †
23—26895

—— Same: Belgian Kongo; by Ellwood A. Welden. Oct. 15, 1923. ii+17 p. (Trade information bulletin 154; Western European Division.) † 23—26899

—— Same: British Honduras, brief review of its resources, trade, and industry; by L. W. James, based on reports of W. W. Early, on British colonial reports, and other material. Oct. 29, 1923. ii+13 p. (Trade information bulletin 158; Latin American Division.) †
23—26935

—— Same: Economic development in Argentina since 1921; by M. A. Phoebus. Oct. 29, 1923. ii+14 p. (Trade information bulletin 156; Latin American Division.) †
23—26936

—— Same: Electrical equipment in Italy; by H. C. MacLean. Oct. 15, 1923. ii+18 p. (Trade information bulletin 151; Electrical Equipment Division.) †
23—26896

—— Same: Foreign trade of United States, fiscal year 1922-23; [by H. C. Campbell]. Oct. 29, 1923. [1]+51 p. (Trade information bulletin 157; [Research Division].) †
A 22—1744

—— Same: German agricultural implement industry and trade; by Ernest M. Zwickel. Oct. 15, 1923. ii+25 p. (Trade information bulletin 153; Agricultural Implements Division.) †
23—26898

—— Same: Japan after earthquake [of Sept. 1, 1923]; by F. R. Eldridge, jr. Oct. 1, 1923. ii+9 p. (Trade information bulletin 147; Far Eastern Division.) †
23—26874

—— Same: Markets for American pharmaceutical, medicinal, and biological preparations. Oct. 8, 1923. ii+10 p. (Trade information bulletin 149; Chemical Division.) †
23—26894

—— Same: Notes on forest resources of Central Europe. Oct. 15, 1923. ii+16 p. (Trade information bulletin 152; Lumber Division.) †
23—26897

—— Same: States of Brazil; prepared by George R. Coxe, based on reports from [various consular officers] in Brazil, and other sources. Oct. 8, 1923. ii+28 p. (Trade information bulletin 148; Latin American Division.) †
23—26875

—— Same: Trade-mark protection in Europe; by Bernard A. Kosicki. Oct. 22, 1923. ii+29 p. (Trade information bulletin 155; Division of Foreign Tariffs.) †
23—26900

—— Survey of current business, Oct. 1923, no. 26; compiled by Bureau of Census, Bureau of Foreign and Domestic Commerce, [and] Bureau of Standards. 1923. cover-title, 67 p. ii. 4° (Monthly supplement to Commerce reports.) [Contains statistics for Aug. 1923, the date given above, Oct. 1923, being the date of issue. Text on p. 2–4 of cover.] * Paper, 10c. single copy. $1.00 a yr.; foreign subscription, $1.50.
21—26819

NOTE.—Realizing that current statistics are highly perishable and that to be of use they must reach the business man at the earliest possible moment, the Department has arranged to distribute advance leaflets twice each month to those subscribers who request them. One set of these leaflets is issued about the 20th of the month, giving such information as has been received up to that time, and another set of sheets is mailed at the end of the month giving those figures received since the 20th. The information contained in these leaflets is also published in Commerce reports issued weekly by the Foreign and Domestic Commerce Bureau. The advance sheets will be mailed free of charge to all subscribers to the Survey who request them. Such requests should be addressed to the Bureau of the Census, Department of Commerce, Washington, D. C. Subscriptions, however, should be sent to the Superintendent of Documents, Washington, D. C., at the prices stated above.

Inland water transportation in United States [with list of references; prepared in] Transportation Division. 1923. v+95 p. 3 maps. (Miscellaneous series 119.) * Paper, 15c.
23—26893

International communications and International telegraph convention (St. Petersburg, 1875, Lisbon, 1908); by P. E. D. Nagle. 1923. iv+68 p. il. map. (Miscellaneous series 121.) * Paper, 10c.
23—26937

LIGHTHOUSES BUREAU

14th District. Light list, Ohio, Tennessee, Kanawha, and Monongahela rivers, 14th lighthouse district; 1923, corrected to Sept. 15. 1923. 112 p. narrow 16° [About half of the pages are blank.] * Paper, 20c.
11—35302

Light-ships. Specifications for machinery installation and completion of single-screw, steel, Diesel-engine-propelled 2d-class light vessel, no. 111, 1923. 1923. [1]+75 p. †

Lighthouse service bulletin. Lighthouse service bulletin, v. 2, no. 70; Oct. 1, 1923. [1923.] p. 299–302. [Monthly.] †   12—35121

—— Same, v. 2, no. 71; Nov. 1, 1923. [1923.] p. 303–311. [Monthly.] †

Massachusetts, Nantucket Sound, east entrance, Great Round Shoal light vessel, light to be changed; [all lettered poster]. Oct. 27, 1923. 16×10.5 in. ([Poster] notice to mariners 89.) †

Notice to mariners, weekly, no. 40–43, 1923; Oct. 5–26 [1923]. 1923. various paging. [Issued jointly with Coast and Geodetic Survey.] †   7—20609

NAVIGATION BUREAU

Ships. American documented seagoing merchant vessels of 500 gross tons and over, Oct. 1, 1923. 1923. ii+69 p. 4° (Serial 71.) [Monthly.] * Paper, 10c. single copy, 75c. a yr.; foreign subscription, $1.25.   19—26597

—— Seagoing vessels of United States, with official numbers and signal letters, 1923; pt. 6 of 55th annual list of merchant vessels of United States, year ended June 30, 1923. 1923. 162 p. il. 14 pl. 4° * Paper, 35c.   7—27311

RADIO SERVICE

Radio Service bulletin, Oct. 1, 1923; no. 78. [1923.] 14 p. [Monthly.] * Paper, 5c. single copy, 25c. a yr.; foreign subscription, 40c.   15—26255

Radio stations. Amateur radio stations of United States. Edition, June 30, 1923. 1923. iv+314 p. * Paper, 25c.   20—26897

—— Commercial and Government radio stations of United States. Edition, June 30, 1923. 1923. iv+122 p. [The 1st supplement to this publication was issued as Radio Service bulletin, Aug. 1, 1923, no. 76, which was entered in the Monthly catalogue for Aug. 1923, p. 63.] * Paper, 15c.   14—30838

PUBLICATIONS DIVISION

Commerce Department. Supplement to annual List of publications [of Department of Commerce available for distribution], Sept. 29, 1923. [1923.] 4 p. [Monthly.] †   •

STANDARDS BUREAU

NOTE.—The Scientific papers will be supplied on subscription as issued at $1.25 per volume, paper bound. These volumes will afterwards be issued bound in cloth at $2.00 per volume; foreign subscription, paper $2.50 (sent in single numbers), cloth $2.35 (bound volumes). Single numbers vary in price. Address the Superintendent of Documents, Washington, D. C.

The Technologic papers will be issued first as separates and later in volume form in the same manner as the Scientific papers. Subscriptions will be accepted by the Superintendent of Documents at $1.25 per volume; foreign subscription, $2.50. Single numbers vary in price.

Caustic magnesia. Tests of caustic magnesia made from magnesite from several sources; by P. H. Bates, Roy N. Young, [and] Paul Rapp. Sept. 14, 1923. [1]+529–558 p. il. large 8° (Technologic papers 239.) [From Technologic papers, v. 17.] * Paper, 10c.   23—26904

Detector for water vapor in closed pipes; by E. R. Weaver [and] P. G. Ledig. Oct. 1, 1923. [1]+637–644 p. il. 1 pl. (Technologic papers 242.) [From Technologic papers, v. 17.] * Paper, 5c.   23—26527

Enamel. United States Government specification for water-resisting red enamel, Federal Specifications Board, Standard specification 66, officially adopted by Federal Specifications Board, Sept. 1, 1923, for use of Departments and independent establishments of Government in purchase of water-resisting red enamel. Sept. 25, 1923. 6 p. (Circular 146.) * Paper, 5c.   23—26902

Paint. United States Government specification for gloss interior lithopone paint, white and light tints. Federal Specifications Board, Standard specification 67, officially adopted by Federal Specifications Board, Sept. 1, 1923, for use of Departments and independent establishments of Government in purchase of gloss interior lithopone paint, white and light tints. Sept. 19, 1923. 8 p. (Circular 147.) * Paper, 5c.   23—26903

Radio communication. Sources of elementary radio information. 2d [edition]. Sept. 12, 1923. [1]+16 p. il. large 8° (Circular 122.) * Paper, 5c.

23—26901

—— Study of radio signal fading; by J. H. Dellinger, L. E. Whittemore, [and] S. Kruse. Sept. 25, 1923. [1]+193–230 p. il. (Scientific papers 476.) [From Scientific papers, v. 19.] * Paper, 10c.

23—26525

Scientific papers. Scientific papers, v. 16, 1920. 1921. iv+762 p. il. 17 pl. 10 p. of pl. [Scientific papers 369–404 are included in this volume. Each paper is also published separately in advance.] * Cloth, $2.00.

CONTENTS.—Vapor pressure of ammonia; by Carl S. Cragoe, Cyril H. Meyers, and Cyril S. Taylor.—New form of vibration galvanometer; by P. G. Agnew.—New cadmium-vapor arc lamp; by Frederick Bates.—Wave lengths longer than 5500 A in arc spectra of 7 elements; by C. C. Kiess and W. F. Meggers.—Characteristics of striæ in optical glass; by T. T. Smith, A. H. Bennett, and G. E. Merritt.—Integration method of deriving alternating-current resistance and inductance of conductors; by Harvey L. Curtis.—Double-polarization method for estimation of sucrose and evaluation of Clerget divisor; by Richard F. Jackson and Clara L. Gillis.—Critical ranges of some commercial nickel steels; by Howard Scott.—Intercrystalline brittleness of lead; by Henry S. Rawdon.—New spectropyrheliometer and measurements of component radiations from the sun and from quartz-mercury vapor lamp; by W. W. Coblentz and H. Kahler.—Reflecting power of monel metal, stellite, and zinc; by W. W. Coblentz.—Spectrophotoelectric sensitivity of thalofide; by W. W. Coblentz.—Electron tube transmitter of completely modulated waves; by Lewis M. Hull.—Testing of magnetic compasses; by R. L. Sanford.—Measurements of hysteresis values from high magnetizing forces; by W. L. Cheney.—Variation of residual induction and coercive force with magnetizing force; by R. L. Sanford and W. L. Cheney.—New microphotometer for photographic densities; by W. F. Meggers and Paul D. Foote.—Atomic theory and low-voltage arcs in cæsium vapor; by Paul D. Foote and W. F. Meggers.—Permeability of rubber to gases; by Junius David Edwards and S. F. Pickering.—Adjustment of parabolic and linear curves to observations taken at equal intervals of independent variable; by Harry M. Roeser.—Relative spectral transmission of atmosphere; by Enoch Karrer and E. P. T. Tyndall.—Two common failures of Clark standard cell; by E. C. McKelvy and M. P. Shoemaker.—Measurement of diffuse reflection factors, and new absolute reflectometer [with bibliography]; by A. H. Taylor.—Photographic method of detecting changes in complicated group of objects; by M. H. Stillman.—Measurements on thermal dilatation of glass at high temperatures; by C. G. Peters and C. H. Cragoe.—Air forces on circular cylinders, axes normal to wind, with special reference to dynamical similarity; by Hugh L. Dryden.—Relation of high-temperature treatment of high-speed steel to secondary hardening and red hardness; by Howard Scott.—Thermal and physical changes accompanying heating of hardened carbon steels; by Howard Scott and H. Gretchen Movius.—Study of relation between Brinell hardness and grain size of annealed carbon steels; by Henry S. Rawdon and Emilio Jimeno-Gil.—Positive and negative photoelectrical properties of molybdenite and several other substances; by W. W. Coblentz.—Metallographic etching reagents: 1, For copper; by Henry S. Rawdon and Marjorie G. Lorentz.—Ionization and resonance potentials of some nonmetallic elements; by F. L. Mohler and Paul D. Foote.—Infra-red transmission and refraction data on standard lens and prism material [with bibliography]; by W. W. Coblentz.—Use of ammonium persulphate for revealing macrostructure of iron and steel; by Henry S. Rawdon.—Resonance potentials and low-voltage arcs for metals of 2d group of periodic table; by F. L. Mohler, Paul D. Foote, and W. F. Meggers.—Magnetic reluctivity relationship as related to certain structures of eutectoid-carbon steel; by C. Nusbaum, W. L. Cheney, and H. Scott.—Index.

—— Same, v. 17, 1922. 1922. iv+753 p. il. 12 pl. 40 p. of pl. [Corrections made with rubber stamp on p. 363. Scientific papers 405–438 are included in this volume. Each paper is also published separately in advance.] * Cloth, $2.00.

CONTENTS.—Simple portable instrument for absolute measurement of reflection and transmission factors; by A. H. Taylor.—Present status of constants and verification of laws of thermal radiation of uniformly heated inclosure [with bibliography]; by W. W. Coblentz.—Recent modifications in construction of platinum resistance thermometers; by T. S. Sligh, jr.—Effect of rate of cooling on magnetic and other properties of annealed eutectoid carbon steel; by C. Nusbaum and W. L. Cheney.—New method for measurement of photographic filter factors; by Raymond Davis.—Thermal expansion of copper and some of its important industrial alloys; by Peter Hidnert.—Wave-length measurements in arc spectra photographed in yellow, red, and infra-red; by F. M. Walters, jr.—Spectrophotoelectrical sensitivity of proustite; by W. W. Coblentz.—Portable vacuum thermopile; by W. W. Coblentz.—Interference measurements in spectra of argon, krypton, and xenon; by W. F. Meggers.—Use of Ulbricht sphere in measuring reflection and transmission factors; by Enoch Karrer.—Preparation of galactose; by E. P. Clark.—Spectral distribution of energy required to evoke gray sensation [with bibliography]; by Irwin G. Priest.—Spectroradiometric investigation of transmission of various substances, 2; by W. W. Coblentz.—Production of liquid air on laboratory scale; by J. W. Cook.—Specific volume of liquid ammonia; by C. S. Cragoe and D. R. Harper, 3d.—Wave lengths longer than 5,500 A in arc spectra of yttrium, lanthanum, and cerium [by C. C. Kiess]; and Preparation of pure rare earth elements [by B. S. Hopkins and H. C. Kremers].—Studies in color sensitive photographic plates and methods of sensitizing by bathing; by Francis M. Walters, jr, and Raymond Davis.—Operation of modulator tube in radio telephone sets; by E. S. Purington.—Mathematical theory of induced voltage in high-tension magneto; by Francis B. Silsbee.—Characteristic soft X-rays from arcs in gases and vapors; by F. L. Mohler and Paul D. Foote.—Thermal expansion of nickel, monel metal, stellite, stainless steel, and aluminum; by Wilmer H. Souder and Peter Hidnert.—Some effects of distributed capacity between inductance coils and ground; by Gregory Breit.—Radio direction

Scientific papers—Continued.
finder and its application to navigation; by Frederick A. Kolster and Francis W. Dunmore.—Note on preparation of mannose; by E. P. Clark.—High-frequency resistance of inductance coils; by Gregory Breit.—Field radiated from 2 horizontal coils; by Gregory Breit.—Improved method for preparing raffinose; by E. P. Clark.—Thermal expansion of a few steels; by Wilmer Souder and Peter Hidnert.—Electromotive force of cells at low temperature; by G. W. Vinal and F. W. Altrup.—Metallographic etching reagents: 2, For copper alloys. nickel, and alpha alloys of nickel; by Henry S. Rawdon and Marjorie G. Lorentz.—Interference methods for standardizing and testing precision gage blocks; by C. G. Peters and H. S. Boyd.—Solubility of dextrose in water; by Richard F. Jackson and Clara Gillis Silsbee.—Tests of stellar radiometers and measurements of energy distribution in spectra of 16 stars; by W. W. Coblentz.—Index.

Soap. United States Government specification for grit cake soap, Federal Specifications Board, Standard specification 33, officially adopted by Federal Specifications Board, June 20, 1922, for use of Departments and independent establishments of Government in purchase of materials covered by it. July 27, 1922 [reprint with changes 1923]. 5 p. large 8°. (Circular 130.) * Paper, 5c.   23—26938

STEAMBOAT-INSPECTION SERVICE

Pilot rules for inland waters of Atlantic and Pacific coasts and of coast of Gulf of Mexico. Edition, June 1, 1923. 1923. 32 p. il. †   10—35955
Steamboat Inspection Service bulletin, Oct. 1, 1923; no. 96. [1923.] 2 p. [Monthly.] ‡   15—26679
Steamboats. 33d supplement to General rules and regulations [edition of 1923], circular letter. Oct. 19, 1923. 2 p. †

CONGRESS

HOUSE OF REPRESENTATIVES

Committees. Standing and select committees of House of Representatives, 67th Congress, 4th session, corrected to Oct. 26, 1923; compiled by Wm. Tyler Page. [1923.] 24 p. ‡

Members. Alphabetical list of Members and Delegates of House of Representatives, with committee assignments, 68th Congress, 1st session, corrected to Oct. 16, 1923; compiled by Wm. Tyler Page. [1923.] 21 p. [Unofficial.] ‡

—— Unofficial list of Members of House of Representatives and their places of residence [with List of Senators by States], 68th Congress, corrected to Oct. 16, 1923; compiled by Wm. Tyler Page. 1923. 16 p. ‡

War risk insurance, soldiers' compensation and insurance laws, and soldiers and sailors civil rights act (65th Congress): public no. 193, 63d Congress; public no. 209, 64th Congress; public no. 387, 64th Congress; public no. 20, 65th Congress; public no. 90, 65th Congress; public res. 22, 65th Congress; public res. 27, 65th Congress; public res. 52, 65th Congress; public no. 103, 65th Congress; public no. 151, 65th Congress; public no. 175, 65th Congress; public no. 178, 65th Congress; public no. 195, 65th Congress; public no. 272, 65th Congress; public no. 312, 65th Congress; public no. 104, 66th Congress; public no. 26, 66th Congress; public no. 47, 67th Congress; public no. 370, 67th Congress; public no. 460, 67th Congress; public no. 542, 67th Congress. 1923. 85 p. * Paper, 10c.

SENATE

PUBLIC LANDS AND SURVEYS COMMITTEE

Naval petroleum reserves. Leases upon naval oil reserves, hearing on S. Res. 282 and S. Res. 294, Oct. 22, 1923. 1923. [pt. 1], ii+1–174 p. †

COURT OF CLAIMS

Andrus. John E. Andrus *v.* United States; evidence for defendant. [1923.] no. 242–A, p. 161–248. ‡

Atlantic Gulf Oil Corporation v. United States; evidence for claimant. [1923.] no. B–150, p. 21–682. ‡

69825—No. 346—23——3

Austern. Lester Austern *v.* United States; evidence for plaintiff. [1923.] no. 12–A, p. 11–69. ‡

Baltimore & Ohio Railroad Company v. United States; evidence for claimant [defendant]. [1923.] no. B–73, p. 11–46. ‡

Brodie. John L. Brodie *v.* United States; testimony for plaintiff. [1923.] no. 34726, p. 7–77. ‡

Central Vermont Railway. Central vermont Railway Company *v.* United States; defendant's evidence. [1923.] no. B–209, p. 41–42. ‡

—— Same; evidence for plaintiff. [1923.] no. B–209, p. 19–40. ‡

Chicago, Milwaukee & St. Paul Railway Co. v. United States; evidence for plaintiff. [1923.] no. B–200, p. 11–51. ‡

Cohen, Endel & Co. Chas. W. Endel, Jacob Endel, and Irving Endel, doing business under firm name and style of Cohen, Endel & Co., *v.* United States; evidence for plaintiff. [1923.] no. 266–A, p. 73–166. ‡

Electric Cable Company. John S. Worley and John B. Johnston, receivers of Electric Cable Company, *v.* United States; evidence for plaintiff. [1923.] no. B–374, p. 47–126. ‡

El Paso & Southwestern Co. et al. *v.* United States; evidence for plaintiff. [1923.] no. B–417, p. 11–18. ‡

Glenwood Park Corporation. Glenwood Park Corporation [*v.* United States]; Glenwood Annex Corporation [*v.* same]; Terminal Heights Corporation [*v.* same]; evidence for defendant. [1923.] no. 270–A, 268–[A], 269–A, p. 133–204. ‡

—— Same; evidence for plaintiffs. [1923.] no. 270–A, 268–A, 269–A, p. 13–132. ‡

Hygienic Fibre Company v. United States; evidence for claimant. [1923.] no. 287–A, p. 15–96. ‡

Iselin, William, & Co. William E. Iselin [et al.], copartners doing business under firm name of William Iselin & Company, *v.* United States; evidence for defendant. [1923.] no. B–13, p. 83–272. ‡

Livingston. Thomas M. Livingston *v.* United States; evidence for defendant. [1923.] no. 298–A, p. 247–411. ‡

Louisville & Nashville Railroad Company v. United States; evidence for claimant. [1923.] no. 33824, p. 43–49. ‡

Luckenbach Steamship Company, Incorporated. Luckenbach Steamship Company (Inc.) *v.* United States; evidence for defendants. [1923.] no. 33962, p. 1001–1115. ‡

—— Same; evidence for plaintiff in rebuttal. [1923.] no. 33962, p. 1117–39. ‡

Marconi Wireless Telegraph Company of America v. United States; evidence for plaintiff. [1923.] no. 33642, p. 9–316. ‡

Montgomery. Regina C. Montgomery, heir, and Richard J. Montgomery, assignee of Ellen Montgomery, heir of John J. Montgomery, *v.* United States; evidence for defendant. [1923.] no. 33852, p. 607–858, 3 pl. ‡

Mottram. George William Mottram *v.* United States; evidence for defendant. [1923.] no. 52–B, p. 207–280. [Publication reads incorrectly: In Court of Claims.] ‡

National Contract Company v. United States; evidence for defendants. [1923.] no. B–259, p. 59–87. ‡

New York Central Railroad Company v. United States; defendant's evidence. [1923.] no. B–151, p. 65–74. ‡

Nugent Construction Corporation v. United States; evidence for plaintiff. [1923.] no. B–100, p. 157–205. ‡

Ocean Steamship Company of Savannah v. United States; evidence for claimant. [1923.] no. 343–A, p. 199–224. ‡

Oregon Short Line Railroad Company v. United States; evidence for plaintiff. [1923.] no. B–76, p. 7–32. ‡

Packard Motor Car Company v. United States; evidence for plaintiff. [1923.] no. B–85, p. 413–476. ‡

Pere Marquette Railway Co. v. United States; evidence for plaintiff [and] defendant. [1923.] no. 336–A, p. 27–104. ‡

Poole Engineering & Machine Company v. United States; evidence for claimant. [1923.] no. 331–A, p. 23–207. ‡

Rome Brass & Copper Co. v. United States; evidence for defendant. [1923.] no. 228–A, p. 133–161. ‡

Sirio Match Co. v. United States; evidence for plaintiff. [1923.] Congressional, no. 17331, p. 49–66. ‡

Southern Pacific Company. Southern Pacific Company *v.* United States; evidence for defendant. [1923.] no. B–69, p. 87–97. ‡

—— Southern Pacific Co. *v.* United States; evidence for plaintiff. [1923.] no. B–367, p. 19–25. ‡

—— Southern Pacific Company *v.* United States; evidence for plaintiff. [1923.] no. B–368, p. 21–34. ‡

—— Southern Pacific Company *v.* United States; evidence for plaintiff. [1923.] no. B–371, p. 15–18. ‡

—— Southern Pacific Company *v.* United States; evidence for plaintiff. [1923.] no. B–420, p. 11–22. ‡

—— Southern Pacific Co. *v.* United States; evidence for plaintiff. [1923.] no. C–41, p. 9–12. ‡

—— Southern Pacific Company *v.* United States; evidence for plaintiff. [1923.] no. C–348, p. 7–24. ‡

—— Southern Pacific Company *v.* United States; evidence for plaintiff. [1923.] no. 33946, p. 195–221. ‡

—— Southern Pacific Company *v.* United States; evidence for plaintiff. [1923.] no. 34717, p. 89–98. ‡

—— Southern Pacific Company *v.* United States; evidence for plaintiff. [1923.] no. 34757, p. 37–45. ‡

Spreckles. John D. Spreckles *v.* United States; evidence for plaintiff. [1923.] no. 111–A, p. 13–309. ‡

Texas and Pacific Railway. J. L. Lancaster and Charles L. Wallace, receivers of Texas & Pacific Railway, *v.* United States; evidence for defendants. [1923.] no. C–48, p. 7–10. ‡.

Union Insulating Construction Company v. United States; evidence for plaintiff [and] defendant. [1923.] no. B–92, p. 67–117. ‡ .·.

Wilmerding. William E. Wilmerding *v.* United States; evidence for defendant. [1923.] no. 55–A, p. 23–30. ‡

DISTRICT OF COLUMBIA

Court of Appeals. Return to writ of certiorari, Oct. term, 1923, no. 3943, no. 3, special calendar, United States *v.* Reginald W. Geare et al., appeal from Supreme Court of District of Columbia; motion to quash indictment. [1923.] 4 p. ‡

FEDERAL BOARD FOR VOCATIONAL EDUCATION

Health of the family, program for study of personal, home, and community health problems [with lists of references, by Florence Brown Sherbon; edited by Anna R. Van Meter]. June, 1923. viii+303 p. (Bulletin 86; Home economics series 8.) * Paper, 25c. E 23—383

Policies. [Insert containing additional sections 21 and 22 to pt. 1 of Statement of policies, revised edition, May, 1922.] [1923.] p. [1], 16A–B. ([Bulletin 1, insert.]) †

FEDERAL FUEL DISTRIBUTOR

Report. Final report of Federal Fuel Distributor to President of United States, Sept. 21, 1923. 1923. v+51 p. il. 4 pl. ;* Paper, 10c. 23—26905

FEDERAL RESERVE BOARD

Federal reserve bulletin. Federal reserve bulletin, Oct. 1923; [v. 9, no. 10]. 1st edition. 1923. ii+343–370 p. il. map, 4° [Monthly.] † Paper, $1.50 a yr.

15—26318

NOTE.—The Federal reserve bulletin is printed in 2 editions (a 1st edition and a final edition). The 1st edition is brief and contains the regular official announcements, the national review of business conditions, and other general matter, and is distributed without charge to the member banks of the Federal reserve system. The 2d or final edition contains detailed analyses of business conditions, special articles, review of foreign banking, and complete statistics showing condition of Federal reserve banks. Those desiring copies of either edition may obtain them from the Federal Reserve Board, Washington, D. C., at the prices stated above and below.

—— Same, Oct. 1923; [v. 9, no. 10]. Final edition. 1923. iv+1085–1174+[2] p. il. 4° [Monthly.] † Paper, 40c. single copy, $4.00 a yr.

Federal reserve member banks. Federal reserve inter-district collection system, changes in list of banks upon which items will be received by Federal reserve banks for collection and credit, Oct. 1, 1923. 1923. [1]+18 p. 4° †

16—26870

FEDERAL TRADE COMMISSION

NOTE.—The bound volumes of the Federal Trade Commission decisions are sold by the Superintendent of Documents, Washington, D. C. Separate opinions are sold on subscription, price $1.00 per volume; foreign subscription, $1.50; single copies, 5c. each.

Aluminum Company of America. No. 2721, in circuit court of appeals for 3d circuit, Oct. term, 1921, Aluminum Company of America *v.* Federal Trade Commission, on petition for review from Federal Trade Commission; application by Federal Trade Commission for modification of order. 1923. cover-title, 55 p. large 8° ‡

Boyden, George E., & Son. Federal Trade Commission *v.* Everett F. Boyden, trading under name and style of George E. Boyden & Son, complaint [report] findings, and order; docket 689, Mar. 9, 1923. 1923. [1]+20–23 p. ([Decision] 345.) [From Federal Trade Commission decisions, v. 6.] *Paper, 5c.

Decisions. Table of cases in v. 5 [of Federal Trade Commission decisions]. [1923.] 11 p. ‡

Juvenile Shoe Company, Incorporated. No. 470, in Supreme Court, Oct. term, 1923, Juvenile Shoe Company, Incorporated, *v.* Federal Trade Commission, petition for writ of certiorari to circuit court of appeals for 9th circuit; brief in opposition. 1923. cover-title, ii+8 p. ‡

Raymond Brothers-Clark Company. No. 102, in Supreme Court, Oct. term, 1923, Federal Trade Commission *v.* Raymond Bros.-Clark Company, on writ of certiorari to circuit court of appeals for 8th circuit; brief for petitioner. 1923. cover-title, ii+33 p. ‡

Southgate, T. S., & Co. Federal Trade Commission *v.* T. S. Southgate, trading under name and style of T. S. Southgate & Co., and Lexington Grocery Co. and Taylor Bros. & Co., Inc., trading under name and style of Southern Salt Co., complaints [report] findings, and order; docket 935, Mar. 9, 1923. 1923. [1]+28–34 p. ([Decision] 347.) [From Federal Trade Commission decisions, v. 6.] * Paper, 5c.

United States Refining Company. Federal Trade Commission *v.* Simon Adelson, trading under name and style of United States Refining Company, complaint [report] findings, and order; docket 716, Mar. 9, 1923. 1923. [1]+24–27 p. ([Decision] 346.) [From Federal Trade Commission decisions, v. 6.] * Paper, 5c.

GENERAL ACCOUNTING OFFICE

Decisions of comptroller general, v. 3, Aug. 1923; J. R. McCarl, comptroller general, Lurtin R. Ginn, assistant comptroller general. 1923. [1]+67–115 p. [Monthly.] †

21—26777

GOVERNMENT PRINTING OFFICE

Supplies. Specifications and proposal for furnishing and installing complete 2 pile sheet feeders, advertisement. Oct. 8, 1923. 6 p. 4° †

DOCUMENTS OFFICE

Army. Supplement to Price list 19 [13th edition]. Army and Militia [aviation and pensions, list of publications for sale by superintendent of documents]. Revised edition 1923. 2 p. ([Price list 19, 13th edition, supplement.]) †

Congressional documents. Index to reports and documents of 67th Congress, 3d and 4th sessions, Nov. 20, 1922–Mar. 4, 1923, with numerical lists and schedule of volumes. 1923. no. 33; vi+135 p. * Cloth, 50c. 6—20448

—— Same. (H. doc. 640, 67th Cong. 3d & 4th sess.)

Depository libraries. Report on designated depository libraries, showing conditions, Apr. 16, 1923, under selective plan first authorized by public act 171, 67th Congress, with List of designated depository libraries revised to July 1, 1923; by Mary A. Hartwell. 1923. 29 p. 2 maps in pocket. † 23—26505

Education, list of publications for sale by superintendent of documents. Aug. 1923. [2]+38 p. (Price list 31, 10th edition.) † 23—26906

Forestry, tree planting, wood tests, and lumber industries, list of publications for sale by superintendent of documents. Sept. 1923. [2]+14 p. (Price list 43, 16th edition.) † 23—26908

Insular possessions (Philippines, Porto Rico, Hawaii, Guam, Samoa, Virgin Islands), and Cuba and Panama Canal, list of publications for sale by superintendent of documents. Sept. 1923. [2]+22 p. (Price list 32, 10th edition.) † 23—26907

Monthly catalogue, United States public documents, no. 345; Sept. 1923. 1923. p. 105-155. * Paper, 5c. single copy, 50c. a yr.; foreign subscription, 75c. 4—18088

Political science, documents and debates relating to initiative, referendum, lynching, elections, prohibition, woman suffrage, political parties, District of Columbia, list of publications for sale by superintendent of documents. Aug. 1923. [2]+30 p. (Price list 54, 9th edition.) † 23—26909

INTERIOR DEPARTMENT

NOTE.—The decisions of the Department of the Interior in pension cases are issued in slips and in signatures, and the decisions in land cases are issued in signatures, both being published later in bound volumes. Subscribers may deposit $1.00 with the Superintendent of Documents and receive the contents of a volume of the decisions of either kind in separate parts as they are issued; foreign subscription, $1.25. Prices for bound volumes furnished upon application to the Superintendent of Documents, Washington, D. C.

Letter-writing. Preparation of correspondence for signature of the Secretary. 1923. iv+10 p. ‡

Pensions. [Decisions of Department of Interior in appealed pension and bounty land claims, v. 21, slip] 62 retirement. [1923.] 3 p. [For price, see note above under center head.] 12—29422

Rives, Logan. In Court of Appeals of District of Columbia, Oct. term, 1923, no. 4020, no. 28, special calendar, Hubert Work, Secretary of Interior, *v.* U. S. *ex rel.* Logan Rives, appeal from Supreme Court of District of Columbia; brief for appellant. 1923. cover-title, i+23 p. ‡

Santa Fe Pacific Railroad. No. 3966, Court of Appeals of District of Columbia, Oct. term, 1923, Santa Fe Pacific Railroad Company *v.* Hubert Work, Secretary of Interior, appeal from Supreme Court of District of Columbia; brief for appellee. 1923. cover-title, 13 p. ‡

EDUCATION BUREAU

American literature; [prepared in] Home Education [Division]. [1923.] 4 p. 12° (Reading course 8 revised.) †

Art. Art as vocation [with list of references]; by William T. Bawden. Oct. 1923. 18 p. (Industrial education circular 20.) [This circular is a report of a conference called by commissioner of education and held in cooperation with annual convention of American Federation of Arts at St. Louis, Mo., May 22, 1923.] * Paper, 5c. E 23—376

—— Need of art training in college and its application in after life; by George C. Nimmons. Oct. 1923. 7 p. (Higher education circular 27.) * Paper, 5c. E 23—380

Children. Classroom weight record [blank form]. [1923.] 1 p. narrow f° * Paper, 5c.

Children—Continued. Weight-height-age tables for boys and girls [revised tables, 1923; prepared by Bird T. Baldwin and Thomas D. Wood]. [1923.] 1 p. il. large 4° (Health education poster 4.) [Courtesy of American Child Health Association.] * Paper, 5c.

Colleges and universities. Statistics of State universities and State colleges, year ended June 30, 1922; prepared in Division of Statistics. 1923. [1]+16 p. (Bulletin 49, 1923.) * Paper, 5c.   E 9—429

Commercial education, school opportunities and business needs; by Glen Levin Swiggett. Sept. 1923. 10 p. (Commercial education leaflet 7.) [This leaflet is a summarized report of a conference held under joint auspices of Bureau of Education and State Teachers Association of South Carolina, Columbia, S. C., Apr. 12, 1923.] * Paper, 5c.   E 23—381

Consolidation of schools. Suggestions for consolidating rural schools of Beaufort County, N. C., digest of report [made orally to board of education and superintendent of schools of Beaufort County]; by Katherine M. Cook and E. E. Windes. 1923. iii+23 p. il. (Bulletin 48, 1923.) * Paper, 5c.
                                                        E 23—379

Dramatics for health teaching [with bibliographies]; by Harriet Wedgwood. 1923. 16 p. il. (Health education 13.) [Includes lists of Education Department publications on health education.] * Paper, 5c.   E 23—382

Home economics. Training teachers of home economics, report on basic principles underlying courses in training of teachers of home economics, made by committee on home economics education of American Home Economics Association. 1923. 1 p. 4° [From School life, v. 9, no. 1, Sept. 1923.] †

Manual training. Standards of 8th-grade attainment in shop work [with lists of references]; by William T. Bawden. Oct. 1923. 15 p. (Industrial education circular 18.) [This circular is a report of a conference of shop teachers and supervisors in public schools, called by commissioner of education, in cooperation with annual convention of Western Arts Association, and held in St. Louis, Mo., Apr. 30, 1923.] * Paper, 5c.   E 23—378

Publications available Sept. 1923. [1923.] 24 p. †   E 15—1070

School life, v. 9, no. 2; Oct. 1923. [1923.] p. 25–48, 4° [Monthly except July and August. This is Parent-teacher association number.] * Paper, 5c. single copy, 30c. a yr. (10 months); foreign subscription, 55c.   E 18—902

Teachers. Means of improvement for teachers in service [with list of references]; by William T. Bawden. Oct. 1923. 18 p. (Industrial education circular 19.) [This circular is a report of a conference of shop teachers and supervisors in public schools, called by commissioner of education, in cooperation with annual convention of Eastern Arts Association, and held in Providence, R. I., May 2, 1923.] * Paper, 5c.   E 23—377

GENERAL LAND OFFICE
Maps

NOTE.—The General Land Office publishes a large general map of the United States, which is sold at $2.00; and also separate maps of the States and Territories in which public lands are to be found, which are sold at 25c. per sheet. The map of California is in 2 sheets. Address the Superintendent of Documents, Washington, D. C.

Wyoming. State of Wyoming, from official records of General Land Office, with supplemental data from other map making agencies; compiled and drawn by I. P. Berthrong, revised, traced, and lettered by J. J. Black. Scale 12 m.= 1 in. Columbia Planograph Co., Washington, D. C., 1923. 29×32.9 in. * 25c.

GEOLOGICAL SURVEY

NOTE.—The publications of the United States Geological Survey consist of Annual reports, Monographs, Professional papers, Bulletins, Water-supply papers, chapters and volumes of Mineral resources of the United States, folios of the Topographic atlas of the United States and topographic maps that bear descriptive text, and folios of the Geologic atlas of the United States and the World atlas of commercial geology. The Monographs, folios, and maps are sold. Other publications are generally free as long as the Survey's supply lasts. Copies are also sold by the Superintendent of Documents, Washington, D. C., at the prices indicated. For maps and folios address the Director of the Geological Survey, Washington, D. C. A discount of 40 per cent is allowed on any order for maps or folios that amounts to $5.00 or more at the retail price. This discount applies to an order for either maps or folios alone or for maps and folios together but is not allowed on a few folios that are sold at 5c. each on account of damage by fire. Orders for other publications that are for sale should be sent to the Superintendent of Documents, Washington, D. C.

Clay in 1922; by Jefferson Middleton. Oct. 10, 1923. [1]+73–80 p. [From Mineral resources, 1922, pt. 2.] †

Gypsum in 1922; by K. W. Cottrell. Oct. 18, 1923. [1]+133–139 p. [From Mineral resources, 1922, pt. 2.] †

Mineral resources. Mineral resources of United States, 1920: pt. 2, Nonmetals [with bibliography on potash]. 1923. iv+529 p. il. 2 maps, 1 tab. in pocket. * Cloth, $1.00.

—— Same. (H. doc. 403, pt. 2, 67th Cong. 2d sess.)

Mississippi River. Surface water supply of United States, 1921: pt. 7, Lower Mississippi River basin; Nathan C. Grover, chief hydraulic engineer, Robert Follansbee and E. L. Williams, district engineers. 1923. iii+39 p. 2 p. of pl. (Water-supply paper 527.) [Prepared in cooperation with Colorado, Missouri, and Kansas.] * Paper, 5c.   GS10—345

—— Same. (H. doc. 43, 68th Cong. 1st sess.)

Phosphate rock in 1922 [with bibliography]; by George Rogers Mansfield. Oct. 16, 1923. ii+109–132 p. [From Mineral resources, 1922, pt. 2.] †

Platinum and allied metals in 1922; by James M. Hill. Oct. 8, 1923. ii+125–135 p. [From Mineral resources, 1922, pt. 1.] †

Potash in 1922 [with bibliography]; by George Rogers Mansfield. Oct. 12, 1923. ii+87–107 p. [From Mineral resources, 1922, pt. 2.] †

Publications. New publications, list 187; Oct. 1, 1923. [1923.] 3 p. [Monthly.] †

Silver, copper, lead, and zinc in Central States in 1922, mines report; [articles] by J. P. Dunlop and F. Begeman. Oct. 10, 1923. ii+137–168 p. [From Mineral resources, 1922, pt. 1.] †

Slate in 1922; by G. F. Loughlin and A. T. Coons. Nov. 6, 1923. [1]+165–175 p. [From Mineral resources, 1922, pt. 2.] †

Talc and soapstone in 1922; by Edward Sampson. Oct. 11, 1923. ii+81–86 p. il. [From Mineral resources, 1922, pt. 2.] †

Tin in 1922; by Bertrand Leroy Johnson. Oct. 11, 1923. [1]+169–172 p. [From Mineral resources, 1922, pt. 1.] †

Water. Outline of ground-water hydrology, with definitions; by Oscar E. Meinzer. 1923. iv+71 p. il. (Water-supply paper 494.) * Paper, 15c.
                                                               GS 23—282

—— Same. (H. doc. 209, 67th Cong. 2d sess.)

Maps

Oregon. State of Oregon. Scale 1:500,000. [Washington] Geological Survey, 1923. 40.2×53 in. † 25c.

INDIAN COMMISSIONERS BOARD

Indians. Some memoranda concerning American Indians; compiled by Malcolm McDowell. 1923. [1]+20 p. * Paper, 5c.   23—26911

MINES BUREAU

Coke-oven accidents in United States, calendar year 1922; by William W. Adams. [1st edition.] [Sept.] 1923. iii+37 p. (Technical paper 349.) [Includes list of Mines Bureau publications on coke-oven accidents statistics.] * Paper, 5c.   15—26409

Petroleum. Bibliography of petroleum and allied substances, 1921; by E. H. Burroughs. [1st edition.] [June] 1923. xii+230 p. (Bulletin 220.) [Includes lists of Mines Bureau publications on petroleum and natural gas.] * Paper, 20c.   18—26432

—— Manual for oil and gas operations, including Operating regulations to govern production of oil and gas under acts of Feb. 25, 1920, June 4, 1920, and Mar. 4, 1923, and under special agreement by United States; by T. E. Swigart and C. E. Beecher. [1st edition.] [Aug.] 1923. 2 pts. xi+145 p. il. 9 pl. 12 p. of pl. and (in pocket) iii+19 p.+[1] folded leaf. (Bulletin 232.) [Includes lists of Mines Bureau publications on oil field technology. Part 2, Operating regulations to govern production of oil and gas, is in pocket; these regulations were also issued separately, see Monthly catalogue for Apr. 1923, p. 659.] * Paper, 40c.   23—26912

CONTENTS.—Pt. 1. Prevention of losses in oil and gas production [with list of recent articles on diamond drilling; by T. E. Swigart and C. E. Beecher].—Pt. 2. Operating regulations to govern production of oil and gas under acts of Feb. 25, 1920, June 4, 1920, and Mar. 4, 1923, and under special agreement by United States.

Smoke abatement'; by Osborn Monnett. ' [1st edition.] [Aug.] 1923. iv+31 p. il. 12 p. of pl. (Technical paper 273.) [Includes lists of Mines Bureau publications relating to coal smoke.] * Paper, 15c. 23—26913

PATENT OFFICE

NOTE.—The Patent Office publishes Specifications and drawings of patents in single copies. These are not enumerated in this catalogue, but may be obtained for 10c. each at the Patent Office.
A variety of indexes, giving a complete view of the work of the Patent Office from 1790 to date, are published at prices ranging from 25c. to $10.00 per volume and may be obtained from the Superintendent of Documents, Washington, D. C. The Rules of practice and pamphlet Patent laws are furnished free of charge upon application to the Patent Office. The Patent Office issues coupon orders in packages of 20 at $2.00 per package, or in books containing 100 coupons at $10.00 per book. These coupons are good until used, but are only to be used for orders sent to the Patent Office. For schedule of office fees, address Chief Clerk, Patent Office, Washington, D. C.

Carr, Edward G. In Court of Appeals of District of Columbia, Oct. term, 1923, patent appeal no. 1632; *in re* Edward G. Carr, method and apparatus for compacting concrete; brief for commissioner of patents. 1923. cover-title, 12 p. ‡

Decisions. [Decisions in patent and trade-mark cases, etc.] Oct. 2, 1923. p. 1–10, large 8° [From Official gazette, v. 315, no. 1.] † Paper, 5c. single copy, $2.00 a yr. 23—7315

—— Same. Oct. 9, 1923. p. 193–200, large 8° [From Official gazette, v. 315, no. 2.]

—— Same. Oct. 16, 1923. p. 395–404, large 8° [From Official gazette, v. 315, no. 3.]

—— Same. Oct. 23, 1923. p. 609–618, il. large 8° [From Official gazette, v. 315, no. 4.]

—— Same. Oct. 30, 1923. p. 809–816, large 8° [From Official gazette, v. 315, no. 5.]

Deutz & Ortenberg, Incorporated. In Court of Appeals of District of Columbia, Oct. term, 1923, patent appeal no. 1637, *in re* Deutz & Ortenberg (Inc.), trade-mark for blouses, waists, gowns, and dresses; brief for commissioner of patents. 1923. cover-title, 5 p. ‡

Drew, Irving, Company. In Court of Appeals of District of Columbia, Oct. term, 1923, patent appeal no. 1620, *in re* Irving Drew Company, trade-mark for boots, shoes, and slippers; brief for commissioner of patents. 1923. cover-title, 6 p. ‡

Inventions. Changes in classification [of inventions], order 2836 and 2837; Sept. 7 and 8, 1923. [1923.] 2 leaves, large 8° [From Official gazette, v. 315, no. 1.] ‡

Official gazette. Official gazette, Oct, 2–30, 1923; v. 315. no. 1–5. 1923. cover-titles, 1038+[clxxxiv] p. il. large 8° [Weekly.] * Paper, 10c. single copy, $5.00 a yr.; foreign subscription, $11.00. 4—18256
NOTE.—Contains the patents, trade-marks, designs, and labels issued each week; also decisions of the commissioner of patents and of the United States courts in patent cases.

—— Same [title-page, contents, errata, etc., to] v. 314; Sept. 1923. 1923. [2] leaves. large 8° * Paper, 5c. single copy, included in price of Official gazette for subscribers.

—— Same, weekly index with title, Alphabetical list of registrants of trade-marks [etc., Oct. 2, 1923]. [1923.] xl p. large 8° [From Official gazette, v. 315, no. 1.] † Paper, $1.00 a yr.

—— Same [Oct. 9, 1923]. [1923.] xxx p. large 8° [From Official gazette, v. 315, no. 2.]

—— Same [Oct. 16, 1923]. [1923.] xxxvi p. large 8° [From Official gazette, v. 315, no. 3.]

—— Same [Oct. 23, 1923]. [1923.] xxxvi p. large 8° [From Official gazette, v. 315, no. 4.]

—— Same [Oct. 30, 1923]. [1923.] xiii p. large 8° [From Official gazette, v. 315, no. 5.]

Patents. Classification of patents issued Oct. 2–30, 1923. [1923.] Each 2 p. large 8° [Weekly. From Official gazette, v. 315, no. 1–5.] †

Shaffer, Ernest J. In Court of Appeals of District of Columbia, Oct. term, 1923, patent appeal no. 1649, *in re* Ernest J. Shaffer, improvements in slip sockets; brief for commissioner of patents. 1923. cover-title, 7 p. ‡

Trade-marks. Trade-marks [etc., from] Official gazette, Oct. 2, 1923. [1923.] 11–66+i–xxii p. il. large 8° [From Official gazette, v. 315, no. 1.] † Paper, 5c. single copy, $2.50 a yr.

—— Same, Oct. 9, 1923. [1923.] 201–227+i–viii p. il. large 8° [From Official gazette, v. 315, no. 2.]

—— Same, Oct. 16, 1923. [1923.] 405–456+i–xv p. il. large 8° [From Official gazette, v. 315, no. 3.]

—— Same, Oct. 23, 1923. [1923.] 619–659+i–xvi p. il. large 8° [From Official gazette, v. 315, no. 4.]

—— Same, Oct. 30, 1923. [1923.] 817–878+i–xviii p. il. large 8° [From Official gazette, v. 315, no. 5.]

RECLAMATION BUREAU

Engineering. List of engineering articles [relating to work of Reclamation Bureau] no. 5. 1923. [1]+141–175 p. [From High-pressure reservoir outlets, report on Bureau of Reclamation installations.] †   16—8962

Minidoka irrigation project. Minidoka project, Idaho, Reclamation Addition, American Falls, constructing sewer system. [1923.] 19 p. 3 pl. map, 4° (Specifications 424.) [Consists of advertisement, proposal, specifications, and drawings for reclamation project.] † Paper, 30c.

—— Minidoka project, Idaho, Reclamation Addition, American Falls, constructing water system. [1923.] 22 p. map, 4° (Specifications 426.) [Consists of advertisement, proposal, specifications, and drawing for reclamation project.] † Paper, 25c.

—— Minidoka project, Idaho, Reclamation Addition, American Falls, sewer pipe. [1923.] 13 p. 4° (Specifications 423.) [Consists of advertisement, proposal, and specifications for reclamation project.] † Paper, 20c.

—— Minidoka project, Idaho, Reclamation Addition, American Falls, water pipe. [1923.] 32 p. 4° (Specifications 425.) [Consists of advertisement, proposal, and specifications for reclamation project.] † Paper, 20c.

Reclamation record, v. 14, no. 10; Oct. 1923. [1923.] cover-title, p. 293–308, il. 4° [Monthly. Text on p. 2–4 of cover.]   9—35252

> NOTE.—The Reclamation record is published in the interest of the settlers on the reclamation projects, its aim being to raise the general average of success on these projects. It contains much valuable matter of interest to farmers, and will be sent without direct charge to water users on the irrigation projects of the Reclamation Bureau. The Record is sold to those who are not water users for 75 cents a year, payable in advance. Subscriptions may be forwarded to the Chief Clerk, U. S. Reclamation Bureau, Washington, D. C., and remittances (postal money order or New York draft) should be made payable to the Special Fiscal Agent, U. S. Reclamation Bureau. Postage stamps will not be accepted.

Reservoirs. High-pressure reservoir outlets, report on Bureau of Reclamation installations; by J. M. Gaylord and J. L. Savage. 1923. [pt. 1], x+179 p. il. 10 pl. 22 p. of pl. 8° [Includes Partial list of articles in technical and other periodicals on Bureau of Reclamation and list of books on irrigation published separately under title, List of engineering articles, no. 5.] † Cloth, $5.00, Chief Engineer, Bureau of Reclamation, Denver, Colo.

—— Same: Detail drawings. 1923. pt. 2, iii p. 88 pl. 4° † Cloth, $10.00, Chief Engineer, Bureau of Reclamation, Denver, Colo.

INTERSTATE COMMERCE COMMISSION

> NOTE.—The bound volumes of the decisions, usually known as Interstate Commerce Commission reports, are sold by the Superintendent of Documents, Washington, D. C., at various prices, depending upon the size of the volume. Separate opinions are sold on subscription, price $1.00 per volume; foreign subscription, $1.50; single copies, usually 5c. each.

Apples. No. 13246, Wenatchee Valley Fruit Exchange *v.* Northern Pacific Railway Company et al.; decided Aug. 30, 1923; report [and order] of commission. [1923.] 71–79+[1] p. ([Opinion] 8774.) [Report from Interstate Commerce Commission reports, v. 83.] * Paper, 5c.

Cement. Investigation and suspension docket no. 1821, minimum weights on coal-tar paving cement and asbestos or magnesia cement and asbestos millboard in straight and mixed carloads from defined territory to southwestern points; [decided Sept. 7, 1923; report and order of commission]. 1923. [1]+762–763+[1] p. ([Opinion] 8755.) [Report from Interstate Commerce Commission reports, v. 81.] * Paper, 5c.

——. No. 12710, Atlas Portland Cement Company *v.* Chicago, Burlington & Quincy Railroad Company et al.; [decided Oct. 2, 1923; supplemental report and 3d supplemental order of commission]. 1923. [1]+80–81+[1] p. · ([Opinion] 8775.) [Report from Interstate Commerce Commission reports, v. 83.] * Paper, 5c.

Cherry Tree and Dixonville Railroad. Finance docket no. 361, guaranty status of Cherry Tree & Dixonville R. R.; decided Sept. 14, 1923; report of commission. [1923.] p. 257–258. ([Finance decision] 885.) [From Interstate Commerce Commission reports, v. 82.] * Paper, 5c.

Chesapeake and Ohio Railway. Finance docket no. 2541, Chesapeake & Ohio Railway capital stock; approved Sept. 14, 1923; supplemental order. 1923. p. 273. ([Finance decision] 890.) [From Interstate Commerce Commission reports, v. 82.] * Paper, 5c.   ·

Chicago and North Western Railway. Finance docket no. 1657, bonds of Chicago & North Western Ry.; approved Sept. 24, 1923; amended supplemental order. 1923. p. 289. ([Finance decision] 897.) [From Interstate Commerce Commission reports, v. 82.] * Paper, 5c.

Chicago, Milwaukee and St. Paul Railway. Finance docket no. 2901, abandonment of line by Chicago, Milwaukee & St. Paul Ry.; [decided Sept. 11, 1923; report of commission]. 1923. [1]+274–276 p. ([Finance decision] 891.) [From Interstate Commerce Commission reports, v. 82.] * Paper, 5c.

Chicago, Peoria and St. Louis Railroad. Finance docket no. 2258, loan to [Bluford Wilson and William Cotter],· receivers of Chicago, Peoria & St. Louis R. R.; approved July 30, 1923; order. 1923. p. 213. ([Finance decision] 869.) [From Interstate Commerce Commission reports, v. 82.] * Paper, 5c.

Cimarron and Northwestern Railway. Finance docket no. 2980, abandonment of part of line by Cimarron & Northwestern Ry.; decided Aug. 29, 1923; report of commission. [1923.] p. 217–218. ([Finance decision] 871.) [From Interstate Commerce Commission reports, v. 82.] * Paper, 5c.   ·

Clay. No. 12461, Peninsular Portland Cement Company *v.* director general, as agent, and Cincinnati Northern Railroad Company; [decided Sept. 7, 1923; report of commission]. 1923. [1]+10–13 p. ([Opinion] 8758.) [From Interstate Commerce Commission reports, v. 83.] * Paper, 5c.

Coal. No. 12994, Wm. Cramp & Sons Ship & Engine Building Company *v.* director general, as agent; decided Sept. 12, 1923; report of commission. [1923.] p. 55–59. ([Opinion] 8770.) [From Interstate Commerce Commission reports, v. 83.] * Paper, 5c.

Colorado and Southern Railway. Finance docket no. 1572, abandonment of branch line by Colorado & Southern Ry.; [decided Sept. 24, 1923; report of commission on further hearing]. 1923. [1]+310–312 p. ([Finance decision] 904.) [From Interstate Commerce Commission reports, v. 82.] * Paper, 5c.

Copper River and Northwestern Railway. Finance docket no. 410, guaranty status of Copper River & Northwestern Ry.; decided Sept. 11, 1923; report of commission. [1923.] p. 219–220. ([Finance decision] 872.) [From Interstate Commerce Commission reports, v. 82.] * Paper, 5c.

Cotton. Investigation and suspension docket no. 1817, restrictions in transit privileges on cotton, cotton linters, or regins at certain southern points; [decided Sept. 14, 1923; report and order of commission].· 1923. [1]+60–63+[1] p. ([Opinion] 8771.) [Manuscript correction on p. 63. Report from Interstate Commerce Commission reports, v. 83.] * Paper, 5c.

—— Investigation and suspension docket no. 1846, concentration of cotton at New Orleans, La.; [decided Sept. 7, 1923; report and order of commission]. 1923. [1]+18–21+[1] p. ([Opinion] 8760.) [Report from Interstate Commerce Commission reports, v. 83.] * Paper, 5c.

Creosote-oil. Investigation and suspension docket no. 1841. creosote oil from Birmingham, Ala., group points to Ohio and Mississippi River crossings; decided Sept. 8, 1923; report [and order] of commission. [1923.]   41–45+[1] p. ([Opinion] 8767.) [Report from Interstate Commerce Commission reports, v. 83.]   * Paper, 5c.

Dayton-Goose Creek Railway. In equity, no. 330, in Supreme Court, Oct. term, 1923, Dayton-Goose Creek Railway Company *v.* United States, Interstate Commerce Commission, et al.; brief for Interstate Commerce Commission. 1923. cover-title, ii+45 p. ‡

Decisions of Interstate Commerce Commission, Dec. 1922–Mar. 1923. 1923. xxvii+923 p. (Interstate Commerce Commission reports, v. 77.)   * Cloth, $2.00.   8—30656

Detroit Terminal Railroad. Finance docket no. 440, guaranty settlement with Detroit Terminal R. R.; [decided Sept. 11, 1923; report of commission]. 1923. [1]+304–306 p.   ([Finance decision] 902.) [From Interstate Commerce Commission reports, v. 82.]   * Paper, 5c.

Erie and Michigan Railway and Navigation Company. Finance docket no. 1315, deficit settlement with Erie & Michigan Ry. & Nav. Co.; decided Sept. 21, 1923; report of commission. [1923.] p. 287–289.   ([Finance decision] 896.) [From Interstate Commerce Commission reports, v. 82.]   * Paper, 5c.

Erie and Pittsburgh Railroad. Finance docket no. 3212, stock of Erie & Pittsburgh Railroad, in matter of joint application of Erie & Pittsburgh Railroad Company for authority to issue special stock and Pennsylvania Railroad Company, as guarantor, to assume obligation and liability in respect thereof; decided Sept. 26, 1923; report of commission. [1923.] p. 337–339. ([Finance decision] 914.)   [From Interstate Commerce Commission reports, v. 82.]   * Paper, 5c.

Fernwood, Columbia and Gulf Railroad. Finance docket no. 956, loan to Fernwood, Columbia & Gulf R. R.; decided Sept. 24, 1923; supplemental report of commission. [1923.] p. 307–309.   ([Finance decision] 903.) [From Interstate Commerce Commission reports, v. 82.]   * Paper, 5c.

Flour. Investigation and suspension docket no. 1809, transit of phosphated flour at Nashville, Tenn., and points on Tennessee Central R. R.; [decided Aug. 29, 1923; report and order of commission]. 1923. [1]+738–740+ii p. ([Opinion] 8749.)   [Report from Interstate Commerce Commission reports, v. 81.]   * Paper, 5c.

Freight-cars. No. 4080, in circuit court of appeals for 9th circuit, United States *v.* Northern Pacific Railway Company, error to district court for western district of Washington, northern division; brief and argument for plaintiff in error. 1923.   cover-title, i+101 p. ‡

Freight rates. Investigation and suspension docket no. 1782, proportional class rates between upper Mississippi River crossings and points in Iowa, Minnesota, Missouri, and South Dakota; decided Oct. 3, 1923; report [and order] of commission. [1923.]   93–97+[1] p. ([Opinion] 8777.)   [Report from Interstate Commerce Commission reports, v. 83.]   * Paper, 5c.

—— No. 13738, Idaho, ex rel. Public Utilities Commission of Idaho, *v.* Oregon Short Line Railroad Company et al.; [decided July 13, 1923; report and order of commission]. 1923.   [1]+4–9+[1] p. · ([Opinion] 8757.)   [Report from Interstate Commerce Commission reports, v. 83.]   * Paper, 5c.

Furniture. Investigation and suspension docket no. 1834, minimum weights on furniture between points in western trunk-line territory; [investigation and suspension docket no. 1859; decided Sept. 6, 1923; report and order of commission.] 1923.   [1]+64–67+[1] p.   ([Opinion] 8772.) [Report from Interstate Commerce Commission reports, v. 83.]   * Paper, 5c.

Grain. Investigation and suspension docket no. 1847, grain from Chicago, Burlington & Quincy Railroad points in Illinois to Cairo, Ill., and St. Louis, Mo.; [decided Oct. 10, 1923; report and order of commission]. 1923.   [1]+118–124+[1] p.   ([Opinion] 8780.) [Report from Interstate Commerce Commission reports, v. 83.]   * Paper, 5c.

—— No. 14393, Public Utilities Commission of Kansas *v.* Atchison, Topeka & Santa Fe Railway Company et al.; decided Oct. 11, 1923; report [and order] of commission. [1923].   105–117+[1] p.   ([Opinion] 8779.)   [Report from Interstate Commerce Commission reports, v. 83.]   * Paper, 5c.

Gulf, Mobile and Northern Railroad. Finance docket no. 966, loan to Gulf, Mobile & Northern Railroad [and finance docket no. 2219]; decided July 17, 1923; supplemental report of commission. [1923.] p. 207-208. ([Finance decision] 867.) [From Interstate Commerce Commission reports, v. 82.] * Paper, 5c.

Gulf, Texas and Western Railway. Finance docket no. 512, guaranty settlement with Gulf, Texas & Western Ry., W. Frank Knox, receiver; decided Sept. 11, 1923; report of commission. [1923.] p. 221-223. ([Finance decision] 873.) [From Interstate Commerce Commission reports, v. 82.] * Paper, 5c.

Hay. Investigation and suspension docket no. 1815, proportional rates on hay from T., St. L. & W. R. R. stations to Cairo, Ill., and Evansville, Ind., when destined to southeastern and Carolina territories; [decided Sept. 8, 1923; report and order of commission]. 1923. [1]+38-40+[1] p. ([Opinion] 8766.) [Report from Interstate Commerce Commission reports, v. 83.] * Paper, 5c.

Iron. Investigation and suspension docket no. 1837, iron and steel, Pittsburgh-Buffalo territories and related points to virginia cities; [decided Sept. 29, 1923; report and order of commission]. 1923. [1]+82-92+[1] p. ([Opinion] 8776.) [Report from Interstate Commerce Commission reports, v. 83.] * Paper, 5c.

Jonesboro, Lake City and Eastern Railway. Finance docket no. 1323, deficit status of Jonesboro, Lake City & Eastern R. R.; decided Sept. 25, 1923; report of commission. [1923.] p. 319-320. ([Finance decision] 907.) [From Interstate Commerce Commission reports, v. 82.] * Paper, 5c.

Kansas City Southern Railway. Finance docket no. 2867, assumption of obligation by Kansas City Southern and Texarkana & Fort Smith Railways; decided Sept. 25, 1923; supplemental report of commission. [1923.] p. 325-327. ([Finance decision] 910.) [From Interstate Commerce Commission reports, v. 82.] * Paper, 5c.

Kansas, Oklahoma and Gulf Railway. Finance docket no. 49, bonds, stock, and notes of Kansas, Oklahoma & Gulf Ry.; [decided Sept. 26, 1923; 2d supplemental report of commission]. 1923. [1]+316-318 p. ([Finance decision] 906.) [From Interstate Commerce Commission reports, v. 82.] * Paper, 5c.

Kinston Carolina Railroad. Finance docket no. 564, guaranty settlement with Kinston Carolina R. R.; [decided Sept. 11, 1923; report of commission]. 1923. [1]+224-226 p. ([Finance decision] 874.) [From Interstate Commerce Commission reports, v. 82.] * Paper, 5c.

Lime. No. 12940, Glencoe Lime & Cement Company et al. *v.* Akron, Canton & Youngstown Railway Company et al.; [decided Sept. 7, 1923; report and order of commission]. 1923. [1]+46-50+iii p. ([Opinion] 8768.) [Report from Interstate Commerce Commission reports, v. 83.] * Paper, 5c.

Long Island Railroad. Finance docket no. 3192, Long Island equipment trust, series E; decided Sept. 13, 1923; report of commission. [1923.] p. 259-262. ([Finance decision] 886.) [From Interstate Commerce Commission reports, v. 82.] * Paper, 5c.

Lorain and West Virginia Railway. Finance docket no. 589, guaranty settlement with Lorain & West virginia Ry.; [decided Sept. 21, 1923; report of commission]. 1923. [1]+282-284 p. ([Finance decision] 894.) [From Interstate Commerce Commission reports, v. 82.] * Paper, 5c.

Loranger, Louisiana and Northeastern Railroad. Finance docket no. 168, deficit settlement with Loranger, Louisiana & Northeastern R. R.; decided July 30, 1923; report of commission. [1923.] p. 255-256. ([Finance decision] 884.) [From Interstate Commerce Commission reports, v. 82.] * Paper, 5c.

—— Finance docket no. 591, guaranty settlement with Loranger, Louisiana & Northeastern R. R., A. Loranger, receiver; decided Sept. 11, 1923; report of commission. [1923.] p. 227-228. ([Finance decision] 875.) [From Interstate Commerce Commission reports, v. 82.] * Paper, 5c.

Louisville and Nashville Railroad. Finance docket no. 3199, bonds of Louisville & Nashville R. R.; decided Sept. 11, 1923; report of commission. [1923.] p. 249-251. ([Finance decision] 882.) [From Interstate Commerce Commission reports, v. 82.] * Paper, 5c.

Louisville and Nashville Railroad—Continued. Finance docket no. 3200, Louisville & Nashville equipment trust, series F; decided Sept. 14, 1923; report of commission. [1923.] p. 263-266. ([Finance decision] 887.) [From Interstate Commerce Commission reports, v. 82.] * Paper, 5c.

Lumber. Investigation and suspension docket no. 1827, agricultural implement, sleigh, and vehicle wood from Arkansas to Kansas; decided Sept. 7, 1923; report [and order] of commission. [1923.] 25-28+[1] p. ([Opinion] 8763.) [Report from Interstate Commerce Commission reports, v. 83.] * Paper, 5c.

—— No. 40, in Supreme Court, Oct. term, 1923, United States, Interstate Commerce Commission, et al., *v.* Illinois Central Railroad Company et al.; brief for Interstate Commerce Commission. 1923. cover-title, ii+34 p. map. ‡

Midland and Northwestern Railway. Finance docket no. 179, deficit status of Midland & Northwestern Ry., Homer W. Rowe, receiver; decided Sept. 22, 1923; report of commission. [1923.] p. 285-286. ([Finance decision] 895.) [From Interstate Commerce Commission reports, v. 82.] * Paper, 5c.

Minnesota Transfer Railway. Finance docket no. 3179, bonds of Minnesota Transfer Railway; [decided Sept. 11, 1923; report of commission]. 1923. [1]+238-240 p. ([Finance decision] 879.) [From Interstate Commerce Commission reports, v. 82.] * Paper, 5c.

Mississippi Central Railroad. Finance docket no. 3176, notes of Mississippi Central R. R.; [decided Sept. 21, 1923; report of commission]. 1923. [1]+290-292 p. ([Finance decision] 898.) [From Interstate Commerce Commission reports, v. 82.] * Paper, 5c.

Muncie and Western Railroad. Finance docket no. 188, deficit settlement with Muncie & Western R. R.; decided Aug. 15, 1923; report of commission. [1923.] p. 205-206. ([Finance decision] 866.) [From Interstate Commerce Commission reports, v. 82.] * Paper, 5c.

Naphtha. No. 13914, Tidal-Western Oil Corporation et al. *v.* Wichita Falls & Northwestern Railway et al.; decided Sept. 13, 1923; report [and order] of commission. [1923.] 51-54+[1] p. ([Opinion] 8769.) [Report from Interstate Commerce Commission reports, v. 83.] * Paper, 5c.

New York Central Railroad. Finance docket no. 3181, construction of line by New York Central R. R.; decided Sept. 18, 1923; report of commission. [1923.] p. 267-269. ([Finance decision] 888.) [From Interstate Commerce Commission reports, v. 82.] * Paper, 5c.

New York Connecting Railroad. Finance docket no. 693, guaranty settlement with New York Connecting R. R.; [decided Sept. 26, 1923; report of commission]. 1923. [1]+322-324 p. ([Finance decision] 909.) [From Interstate Commerce Commission reports, v. 82.] * Paper, 5c.

New York Telephone Company. Finance docket no. 3201, purchase of properties by New York Telephone Co. and [victor B. Malby and Mabel Malby, doing business as] Allegany Telephone Co.; decided Sept. 22, 1923; report of commission. [1923.] p. 313-315. ([Finance decision] 905.) [From Interstate Commerce Commission reports, v. 82.] .* Paper, 5c.

Northern Maryland and Tidewater Railroad. Finance docket no. 3132, operation of Northern Maryland & Tidewater R. R., in matter of application of William A. Morgart, individually and in behalf of Castleman valley Railroad Company, for certificate of public convenience and necessity authorizing operation of line of railroad; decided Sept. 21, 1923; report of commission. [1923.] p. 301-304. ([Finance decision] 901.) [From Interstate Commerce Commission reports, v. 82.] * Paper, 5c.

Oswego and Syracuse Railroad. Finance docket no. 3204, bonds of Oswego & Syracuse Railroad, in matter of joint application of Oswego & Syracuse Railroad Company for authority to issue certain bonds and Delaware, Lackawanna & Western Railroad Company to guarantee them; decided Sept. 20, 1923; report of commission. [1923.] p. 297-300. ([Finance decision] 900.) [From Interstate Commerce Commission reports, v. 82.] * Paper, 5c.

Pacific Southwestern Railroad Company. Finance docket no. 3071, acquisition and operation of line by Southern Pacific Co., in matter of application of Southern Pacific Company for certificate of public convenience and necessity authorizing it to acquire, by purchase, all of franchises, properties, and appurtenances of Pacific Southwestern Railroad Company, including line of railroad to be constructed in Santa Barbara County, Calif., and to operate said railroad; decided Sept. 11, 1923; report of commission. [1923.] p. 245-248. ([Finance decision] 881.) [From Interstate Commerce Commission reports, v. 82.] * Paper, 5c.

Paper. Investigation and suspension docket no. 1856, waste paper, in carloads, from Long Island Railroad stations to Austin, Pa.; decided Sept. 8, 1923; report [and order] of commission. [1923.] 35–37+[1]p. ([Opinion] 8765.) [Report from Interstate Commerce Commission reports, v. 83.] * Paper, 5c.

Peanuts. No. 12664, A. A. Jackson & Company et al. *v.* Atlantic Coast Line Railroad Company, director general, as agent, et al.; [decided Sept. 7, 1923; report and order of commission]. 1923. [1]+14–17+ii p. ([Opinion] 8759.) [Report from Interstate Commerce Commission reports, v. 83.] * Paper, 5c.

Pearl River Valley Railroad. Finance docket no. 3217, notes of Pearl River Valley Railroad; decided Sept. 18, 1923; report of commission. [1923.] p. 279–281. ([Finance decision] 893.) [From Interstate Commerce Commission reports, v. 82.] * Paper, 5c.

Petroleum. Investigation and suspension docket no. 1819, petroleum and its products between lower Mississippi River crossings and various Mississippi valley points; [decided Sept. 28, 1923; report and order ·of commission]. 1923. [1]+98–104+[1] p. ([Opinion] 8778.) [Report from Interstate Commerce Commission reports, v. 83.] * Paper, 5c.

—— Investigation and suspension docket no. 1845, crude, fuel, and gas oils from Kansas, Missouri, and Oklahoma to Nebraska and South Dakota; decided Sept. 7, 1923; report [and order] of commission. [1923.] 29–34+[1] p. ([Opinion] 8764.) [Report from Interstate Commerce Commission reports, v. 83.] * Paper, 5c.

Poteau and Cavanal Mountain Railroad. Finance docket no. 2863, acquisition of line by Poteau & Cavanal Mountain R. R.; [decided Sept. 11, 1923; report of commission]. 1923. [1]+270–272 p. ([Finance decision] 889.) [From Interstate Commerce Commission reports, v. 82.] * Paper, 5c.

Radiators. Investigation and suspension docket no. 1835, radiators from Dunkirk, N. Y., to interstate destinations; decided Sept. 7, 1923; report [and order] of commission. [1923.] 21–22+[1] p. ([Opinion] 8761.) [Report from Interstate Commerce Commission reports, v. 83.] * Paper, 5c.

Railroad accidents. Report of director of Bureau of Safety in re investigation of accident which occurred on Grand Trunk Western Railway near Durand, Mich., June 5, 1923. [1923.] 8 p. il. * Paper, 5c.　　　　　　A 23—2233

Railroad employees. Wage statistics, class 1 steam roads in United States, including 15 switching and terminal companies, July, 1923; [prepared in] Bureau of Statistics. July, 1923. [4] p. oblong large 8° †

—— Same, Aug. 1923; [prepared in] Bureau of Statistics. Aug. 1923. [4] p. oblong large 8° †

Railroads. 35th annual report on statistics of railways in United States, year ended Dec. 31, 1921, with abstracts of periodical reports, year ended Dec. 31, 1922 [and with addition of statistical tables]; prepared by Bureau of Statistics. ˋ1923· cxviii+476 p. il. 4° * Cloth, $1.50.　　　　5—11209

—— Freight and passenger service operating statistics of class 1 steam roads in United States, compiled from 161 reports of freight statistics representing 176 roads and from 158 reports of passenger statistics representing 173 roads (switching and terminal companies not included), Aug. 1923 and 1922 [and 8 months ended with Aug. 1923 and 1922; prepared in] Bureau of Statistics. Aug. 1923. [2] p. oblong large 8° [Subject to revision.] †

—— Freight and passenger train service unit costs (selected expense accounts) of class 1 steam roads in United States, including proportion of mixed-train and special-train service (compiled from 161 reports representing 176 steam roads, switching and terminal companies not included), July, 1923 and 1922, and 7 months [ended with July] 1923 and 1922; [prepared in] Bureau of Statistics. July, 1923. 1 p. oblong large 8° [Subject to revision.] †

—— Same, Aug. 1923 and 1922, and 8 months [ended with Aug.] 1923 and 1922; [prepared in] Bureau of Statistics. Aug. 1923. 1 p. oblong large 8° [Subject to revision.] †

—— Operating revenues and operating expenses of class 1 steam roads in United States (for 194 steam roads, including 15 switching and terminal companies), Aug. 1923 and 1922 [and] 8 months ending with Aug. 1923 and 1922; [prepared in] Bureau of Statistics. Aug. 1923. 1 p. oblong large 8° [Subject to revision.] †

Railroads—Continued. Operating revenues and operating expenses of large steam roads, selected items for roads with annual operating revenues above $25,000,000, Aug. 1922 and 1923 [and] 8 months ended with Aug. 1922 and 1923; [prepared in] Bureau of Statistics. Aug. 1923. [2] p. oblong large 8° [Subject to revision.] †

—— Operating statistics of large steam roads, selected items for Aug. 1923, compared with Aug. 1922, for roads with annual operating revenues above $25,000,000; [prepared in] Bureau of Statistics. Aug. 1923. [2] p. oblong large 8° [Subject to revision.] †

San Diego and Arizona Railway. Finance docket no. 3198, notes of San Diego & Arizona Railway; decided Sept. 20, 1923; report of commission. [1923.] p. 293–296. ([Finance decision] 899.) [From Interstate Commerce Commission reports, v. 82.] * Paper, 5c.

Seaboard Air Line Railway. Finance docket no. 3202, Seaboard Air Line Railway bonds; [decided Sept. 12, 1923; report of commission]. 1923. [1]+ 252–254 p. ([Finance decision] 883.) [From Interstate Commerce Commission reports, v. 82.] * Paper, 5c.

Steamboats. Schedule of sailings (as furnished by steamship companies named herein) of steam vessels which are registered under laws of United States and which are intended to load general cargo at ports in United States for foreign destinations, Oct. 15–Nov. 30, 1923, no. 14; issued by Section of Tariffs, Bureau of Traffic. 1923. iii+33 p. 4° [Monthly. No. 14 cancels no. 13.] †　　　　　　　　　　　　　　　　　　　　　　22—26610

Stone. No. 12810, Columbia Quarry Company *v.* director general, as agent; decided Oct. 5, 1923; report [and order] of commission. [1923.] 173–175+ [1] p. ([Opinion] 8788.) [Report from Interstate Commerce Commission reports, v. 83.] * Paper, 5c.

Superior and Southeastern Railway. Finance docket no. 2619, operation of line by Superior & Southeastern Ry.; [decided Aug. 24, 1923; report of commission]. 1923. [1]+214–216 p. ([Finance decision] 870.) [From Interstate Commerce Commission reports, v. 82.] * Paper, 5c.

Sussex Railroad. Finance docket no. 1566, control of Sussex R. R. by D., L. & W. R. R.; [decided Aug. 30, 1923; report of commission]. 1923. [1]+232– 235 p. ([Finance decision] 877.) [From Interstate Commerce Commission reports, v. 82.] * Paper, 5c.

Switching. Investigation and suspension docket no. 1825, cancellation of South Georgia Railway switching arrangements at Perry, Fla.; decided Sept. 7, 1923; report [and order] of commission. [1923.] 23–25+[1] p. ([Opinion] 8762.) [Report from Interstate Commerce Commission reports, v. 83.] * Paper, 5c.

Switching charges. Investigation and suspension docket no. 1844, switching charges on ferry cars at Boston, Mass.; [decided Sept. 7, 1923; report and order of commission]. 1923. [1]+68–70+[1] p. ([Opinion] 8773.) [Report from Interstate Commerce Commission reports, v. 83.] * Paper, 5c.

Tennessee, Alabama and Georgia Railroad. Finance docket no. 3035, securities of Tennessee, Alabama & Georgia Railway; decided Aug. 30, 1923; report of commission. [1923.] p. 235–238. ([Finance decision] 878.) [From Interstate Commerce Commission reports, v. 82.] * Paper, 5c.

—— Finance docket no. 3193, notes of Tennessee, Alabama & Georgia Railway; decided Sept. 26, 1923; report of commission. [1923.] p. 331–332. ([Finance decision] 912.) [From Interstate Commerce Commission reports, v. 82.] * Paper, 5c.

Tennessee Central Railroad. Finance docket no. 2223, Tennessee Central Railway loan; decided July 26, 1923; supplemental report of commission. [1923.] p. 209–212. ([Finance decision] 868.) [From Interstate Commerce Commission reports, v. 82.] * Paper, 5c.

Uintah Railway. Finance docket no. 2580, deficit settlement with Uintah Ry.; decided Sept. 13, 1923; report of commission. [1923.] p. 277–278. ([Finance decision] 892.) [From Interstate Commerce Commission reports, v. 82.] * Paper, 5c.

Union Pacific Railroad. Finance docket no. 3220, bonds of Union Pacific Railroad; decided Sept. 26, 1923; report of commission. [1923.] p. 333–336. ([Finance decision] 913.) [From Interstate Commerce Commission reports, v. 82.] * Paper, 5c.

United New Jersey Railroad and Canal Company. Finance docket no. 3211, bonds of United New Jersey Railroad & Canal Co., in matter of joint application of United New Jersey Railroad & Canal Company for authority to issue bonds, and Pennsylvania Railroad Company, as lessee, to assume obligation and liability in respect thereof; [decided Sept. 26, 1923; report of commission]. 1923. [1]+328-330 p. ([Finance decision] 911.) [From Interstate Commerce Commission reports, v. 82.] * Paper, 5c.

Wabash Railway. Finance docket no. 2840, Wabash Railway Company terminal bonds; decided Sept. 11, 1923; report of commission. [1923.] p. 241-244. ([Finance decision] 880.) [From Interstate Commerce Commission reports, v. 82.] * Paper, 5c.

Woodworth and Louisiana Central Railway. Finance docket no. 909, guaranty settlement with Woodworth & Louisiana Central Ry.; decided Aug. 29, 1923; report of commission. [1923.] p. 229-231. ([Finance decision] 876.) [From Interstate Commerce Commission reports, v. 82.] * Paper, 5c.

LOCOMOTIvE INSPECTION BUREAU

Railroad accidents. Report covering investigation of accident to Chicago, Rock Island and Pacific Railway locomotive 2132, which occurred near Harrah, Okla., July 3, 1923; by A. G. Pack, chief inspector. Aug. 15, 1923. [1]+3 p. il. * Paper, 5c.   A 23—2211

JUSTICE DEPARTMENT

Addy, Matthew, Company. Nos. 84 and 85, in Supreme Court, Oct. term, 1923, Matthew Addy Company *v.* United States; Benjamin Ford *v.* [same], on writs of certiorari to circuit court of appeals for 6th circuit; brief for United States. 1923. cover-title, iii+56 p. ‡

Alaska. No. 514, in Supreme Court, Oct. term, 1923, Alaska *v.* Annette Island Packing Company and Albert B. Fall, Secretary of Interior, for and on behalf of people of Annette Islands Reserve, Alaska, petition for writ of certiorari to circuit court of appeals for 9th circuit; brief for respondents in opposition. 1923. cover-title, 9 p. ‡

Atchison, Topeka and Santa Fe Railway. In Court of Claims, Atchison, Topeka & Santa Fe Railroad Co. *v.* United States, no. 22-A; defendant's objections to plaintiff's requested findings of fact, defendant's request for findings of fact, and brief thereon. [1923.] p. 1-5, large 8° ‡

—— In Court of Claims, Atchison, Topeka & Santa Fe Railway Company *v.* United States, no. 37-A; defendant's supplemental brief. [1923.] p. 57-62, large 8° ‡

Atlantic Refining Company. No. C-978, in Court of Claims, Atlantic Refining Co. *v.* United States; counterclaim of United States. 1923. cover-title, p. 1-5, large 8° ‡

Baer, Harry I. In Court of Appeals of District of Columbia, Oct. term, 1923, no. 3991, no. 17, special calendar, Harry I. Baer *v.* United States; brief for appellee. 1923. cover-title, 7 p. ‡

Bailey, Luther J. In Court of Claims, Luther J. Bailey and James E. Fulgham *v.* United States, no. C-778; demurrer [and] brief. 1923. p. 1, large 8° ‡

Banco Mexicano de Commercio e Industria. No. 361, in Supreme Court, Oct. term, 1923, Banco Mexicano de Commercio e Industria and Elias S. A. de Lima, Francisco de P. Cardona, and Edwin J. Parkinson, as liquidators of Banco Mexicano de Commercio e Industria, *v.* Deutsche Bank, Thomas W. Miller, Alien Property Custodian, and Frank White, Treasurer of United States, appeal from Court of Appeals of District of Columbia; motion to advance. 1923. cover-title, 3 p. ‡

Beaumont, Sour Lake and Western Railway. In Court of Claims, Beaumont, Sour Lake & Western Railway Company *v.* United States, no. 301-A; defendant's request for findings of fact and brief. 1923. p. 17, large 8° ‡

Bentley, A., & Sons Company. No. 2178, in district court for northern district of Ohio, western division, United States *v.* A. Bentley & Sons Company; supplemental memorandum in behalf of United States. 1923. cover-title, 18 p. ‡

Berg, Thorvald. In Court of Claims, Thorvald Berg and David C. Reid *v.* United States, no. C–914; demurrer [and brief]. [1923.] p. 27–31, large 8° ‡

Bilokumsky, Michael. No. 92, in Supreme Court, Oct. term, 1923, United States ex rel, Michael Bilokumsky *v.* Robert E. Tod, commissioner of immigration at port of New York, et al., appeal from district court for southern district of New York; brief for United States. 1923. cover-title, 12 p. ‡

Blum, Mrs. Rosa. No. 705, in Supreme Court, Oct. term, 1921, Justus S. Wardell, as collector of internal revenue for 1st district of California, *v.* James B. Blum and Anglo-California Trust Company, as executors of Rosa Blum; motion for leave to withdraw motion heretofore made to revoke order denying petition for writ of certiorari. 1923. cover-title, 2 p. ‡

Boston Insurance Company. No. B–166, in Court of Claims, Boston Insurance Company *v.* United States; defendant's objections to claimant's request for findings of fact, findings requested in lieu thereof, and brief. 1923. cover-title, i+77–108 p. large 8° ‡

Brabandt, L., & Co. In Court of Claims, L. Brabandt, Paul Hye, and Ch. de Baets, doing business under firm name and style of L. Brabandt & Company, Brussels, Belgium, *v.* United States, no. C–1006; demurrer [and] brief. [1923.] p. 1–6, large 8° ‡

Brady, Thomas N. No. 121, in Supreme Court, Oct. term, 1923, Thomas N. Brady *v.* Hubert Work, Secretary of Interior, and William Spry, commissioner of General Land Office, appeal from Court of Appeals of District of Columbia; brief for appellees. 1923. cover-title, 12 p. ‡

Brede, John H. No. 45, in Supreme Court, Oct. term, 1923, John H. Brede *v.* James H. Powers, as United States marshal for eastern district of New York, appeal from district court for eastern district of New York; brief for appellee. 1923. cover-title, ii+26 p. ‡

Brown, DeWitt G. Nos. 97 and 98, in Supreme Court, Oct. term, 1923; DeWitt Garrison Brown and Roosa C. Brown *v.* United States; United States *v.* DeWitt Garrison Brown and Roosa C. Brown, in error to district court for district of Idaho; brief for United States. 1923. cover-title, ii+24 p. ‡

Burgess, Arthur B. No. 3955, in Court of Appeals of District of Columbia, Apr. term, 1923, no. —, special calendar, Arthur B. Burgess *v.* United States; brief for appellee. 1923. cover-title, 9 p. ‡

Burke, George W., jr. Interference no. 44272, in Patent Office, before examiner of interferences, George W. Burke, jr., *v.* William J. Ruff; brief for George W. Burke, jr. 1923. cover-title, i+18 p. ‡

Cady, William. No. 4011, in Court of Appeals of District of Columbia, Oct. term, 1923, William Cady and Roland Clifton *v.* United States; brief for appellee. 1923. cover-title, 8 p. ‡

California Midway Oil Company. No. 62, in Supreme Court, Oct. term, 1923, United States *v.* California Midway Oil Company et al., appeal from circuit court of appeals for 9th circuit; brief for United States. 1923. cover-title, i+21 p. ‡

Central New England Railway. No. B–45, in Court of Claims, Central New England Ry. Co. *v.* United States: defendant's objections to plaintiff's request for findings of fact, defendant's request for findings of fact, and briefs. 1923. cover-title, p. 57–74, large 8° ‡

Chemical Foundation, Incorporated. In equity, no. 502, 'n district court for district of Delaware, United States *v.* Chemical Foundation, Incorporated; reply brief on behalf of United States. 1923. cover-title, iii+108 p. large 8° ‡

Choy Jee Tong & Co. No. 2284, Court of Customs Appeals, Choy Jee Tong & Company *v.* United States; brief for United States. 1923. cover-title, 7 p. ‡

Clallam County, Wash. No. 255, in Supreme Court, Oct. term, 1923, Clallam County, Wash., William A. Nelson, sheriff of Clallam County, E. C. Stewart, treasurer of Clallam County, et al. *v.* United States and United States Spruce Production Corporation, on certificate from circuit court of appeals for 9th circuit; brief for United States. 1923. cover-title, ii+29 p. ‡

Clifton, James. In Court of Appeals of District of Columbia, Apr. term, 1923, no. 3946, no. 4, special calendar, James Clifton *v.* United States; brief for appellee. 1923. cover-title, 15 p. ‡

Craig, Charles L. No. 82, in Supreme Court, Oct. term, 1923, Charles L. Craig *v.* William C. Hecht, United States marshal for southern district of New York, on writ of certiorari to circuit court of appeals for 2d circuit; brief for respondent. 1923. cover-title, iii+64 p. ‡

Douglas Packing Company. No. —, in Supreme Court Oct. term, 1923. United States *v.* 95 barrels, more or less, alleged apple cider vinegar, Douglas Packing Company, claimant; petition for writ of certiorari to circuit court of appeals for 6th circuit, and brief in support thereof. 1923. cover-title, i+23 p. ‡

Ducas, Benjamin P. In Court of Claims, Farmers' Loan and Trust Company [et al.], as executors of Benjamin P. Ducas *v.* United States, no. C–735; demurrer [and brief]. [1923.] p. 11–21, large 8° ‡

Duckett, A. W., & Co., Incorporated. No. 409, in Supreme Court, Oct. term, 1923, A. W. Duckett & Co. (Inc.) *v.* United States, appeal from Court of Claims; motion by United States to advance. 1923. cover-title, 3 p. ‡

Erie Specialty Company. In Court of Claims, Erie Specialty Company *v.* United States, no. 34663; defendant's objections to claimant's requests for findings of fact, defendant's request for findings of fact, and brief. [1923.] p. 333–334, large 8° ‡

Federal Reserve Bank of Richmond. No. 553, in Supreme Court, Oct. term, 1923, Federal Reserve Bank of Richmond *v.* D. J. Malloy and J. H. Malloy, trading as Malloy Brothers, in error to circuit court of appeals for 4th circuit; motion by plaintiff in error to advance. 1923. cover-title, 4 p. ‡

Fidelity Trust Company. No. —, in Supreme Court, Oct. term, 1923, Ephraim Lederer, collector of internal revenue of 1st district of Pennsylvania, *v.* Fidelity Trust Company; petition for writ of certiorari to circuit court of appeals for 3d circuit, and brief in support thereof. 1923. cover-title, 10 p. ‡

Fulgham, Jesse W. In Court of Claims, Jesse W. Fulgham *v.* United States, no. C–777; demurrer [and] brief. [1923.] p. 1–14, large 8° ‡

Greylock Mills. In Court of Appeals of District of Columbia, Oct. term, 1923, no. 4015, United States, ex relatione Greylock Mills, *v.* David H. Blair, commissioner of internal revenue; brief for appellee. 1923. cover-title, 12 p. ‡

Gulf Refining Company. In Court of Claims, Gulf Refining Company *v.* United States, no. C–943; demurrer. [1923.] p. 95–103, large 8° ‡

Harris Brothers Company. In Court of Claims, Harris Brothers Company *v.* United States, no. C–714; defendant's counterclaim. [1923.] p. 11–13, large 8° ‡

Hatchet, John. No. 3992, no. 18, special calendar, in Court of Appeals of District of Columbia, Apr. term, 1923, John Hatchet, otherwise known as John Brown, *v.* United States; brief for appellee. 1923. cover-title, 18 p. ‡

Hines, Edward, Yellow Pine Trustees. No. 91, in Supreme Court, Oct. term, 1923, Edward Hines Yellow Pine Trustees, Edward Hines, C. F. Wiehe, and L. L. Barth, trustees, *v.* United States and Interstate Commerce Commission, appeal from district court for northern district of Illinois; brief for United States. 1923. cover-title, 6 p. ‡

Hoyt, Shepston & Sciaroni. No. 2276, Court of Customs Appeals, Hoyt, Shepston & Sciaroni *v.* United States; brief for United States. 1923. cover-title, 12 p. ‡

Hurst, Adolph, & Co. No. 2274, Court of Customs Appeals, Adolph Hurst & Co. *v.* United States; brief for United States. 1923. cover-title, 12 p. ‡

International Harvester Company. In equity, no. 624, in district court, district of Minnesota, 3d division, United States *v.* International Harvester Company et al.; supplemental petition. 1923. cover-title, i+81 p. ‡

Jackson, R. No. 3979, no. —, special calendar, in Court of Appeals of District of Columbia, Oct. term, 1923, R. Jackson, alias Red Jackson, *v.* Edgar C. Snyder, United States marshal in and for District of Columbia, appeal from Supreme Court of District of Columbia; brief on behalf of appellee. 1923. cover-title, 9 p. ‡

Judges. List of United States judges, attorneys, and marshals; compiled by appointment clerk [Charles B. Sornborger]. Oct. 13, 1923. ii+24 p. †

11—35284

Kenilworth Company. In Court of Claims, Kenilworth Company *v.* United States, no. 305–A; defendant's objections to plaintiff's request for findings of fact, defendant's request for findings of fact, and brief. [1923.] p. 1–5, large 8°. ‡

Keve & Young. No. 2231, Court of Customs Appeals, Keve & Young *v.* United States; supplemental brief for United States on motion to dismiss. 1923. cover-title, 4 p. ‡

Laney, William. In Court of Appeals of District of Columbia, Oct. term, 1923, no. 4000, special calendar no. —, William Laney *v.* United States; brief for appellee. 1923. cover-title, i+34 p. ‡

Linder, Charles O. No. 581, in Supreme Court, Oct. term, 1923, Charles O. Linder *v.* United States, petition for writ of certiorari to circuit court of appeals for 9th circuit; brief for United States in opposition. 1923. cover-title, 2 p. ‡

May Company. No. 2277, Court of Customs Appeals, May Company *v.* United States; brief for United States. 1923. cover-title, 11 p. ‡

Mays, Jack. No. 496, in Supreme Court, Oct. term, 1923, Jack Mays *v.* United States, petition for writ of certiorari to circuit court of appeals for 4th circuit; brief for United States in opposition. 1923. cover-title, 4 p. ‡

Merchants and Miners Bank of Bisbee, Ariz. In Court of Claims, Merchants and Miners Bank of Bisbee, Ariz. *v.* United States, no. C–737; demurrer [and brief]. [1923.] p. 10–20, large 8° ‡

Meyer, M. J. & H. J., Company. No. 2309, Court of Customs Appeals, United States *v.* M. J. & H. J. Meyer Co.; brief for United States. 1923. cover-title, 12 p. ‡

Missouri, Kansas and Texas Railway. In Court of Claims, [Charles E.] Schaff, receiver of Missouri, Kansas & Texas Railway Company, *v.* United States, no. B–122; defendant's objections to plaintiff's request for findings of fact, defendant's request for findings of fact, and brief. [1923.] p. 21–27, large 8° ‡

Missouri Pacific Railroad. In Court of Claims, Missouri Pacific Railroad Co. *v.* United States, no. 697–C; brief on demurrer. [1923.] p. 17–25, large 8° ‡

National Council of Traveling Salesmen's Associations. No. 469, in Supreme Court, Oct. term, 1923, United States, Interstate Commerce Commission, National Council of Traveling Salesmen's Associations, et al., *v.* New York Central Railroad Company et al., appeal from district court for district of Massachusetts; motion to advance. 1923. cover-title, 3 p. ‡

New England Steamship Company. In Court of Claims, New England Steamship Co. *v.* United States, no. B–46; [defendant's] objections to plaintiff's request for findings of fact, defendant's request for findings of fact, and brief. [1923.] p. 23–29, large 8° ‡

New York Coffee and Sugar Exchange, Incorporated. In equity no. 331, in Supreme Court, Oct. term, 1923, United States *v.* New York Coffee and Sugar Exchange (Inc.), New York Coffee and Sugar Clearing Association (Inc.), et al., appeal from district court for southern district of New York; brief for United States. 1923. cover-title, ii+162 p. ‡

Nippon Yusen Kaisha. No. 2275, Court of Customs Appeals, Nippon Yusen Kaisha *v.* United States; brief for United States. 1923. cover-title, 7 p. ‡

Opinions. [Official opinions of Attorneys General] v. 33, [signatures] 33–35, 37. [1923.] p. 513–560, 577–583. †   12—40693

Perrygo, Edgar R. No. 3954, no. 12, special calendar, in Court of Appeals of District of Columbia, Oct. term, 1923, Edgar Randolph Perrygo *v.* United States; brief for appellee. 1923. cover-title, ii+30 p. ‡

Pope, August. No. 437, in Supreme Court, Oct. term, 1923, August Pope, Henry Pope, and Leo Pope *v.* United States, petition for writ of certiorari to circuit court of appeals for 3d circuit; brief for United States in opposition. 1923. cover-title, 4 p. ‡

Prohibition. Report submitted to President Coolidge by Attorney General H. M. Daugherty concerning prohibition litigation throughout United States, Jan. 16, 1920–June 16, 1923. Sept. 11, 1923. 12 p. * Paper, 5c.   23—26883

Rae, Algional H. In Supreme Court, Oct. term, 1923, no. 567, Algional H. Rae, claimant of 1,250 cases of intoxicating liquors. *v.* United States; no. 568, Charles Eugene Albury, claimant of schooner Henry L. Marshall, *v.* [same]; no. 569, [same] *v.* [same], petitions for writs of certiorari to circuit court of appeals for 2d circuit; brief for United States in opposition. 1923. cover-title, i+21 p. ‡

Read, William J. No. 3971, in Court of Appeals of District of Columbia, Apr. term, 1923, no. 18, special calendar, William J. Read [alias C. B. Morse, alias C. D. Morse, alias A. C. Morse] *v.* United States; brief for appellee. 1923. cover-title, 9 p. ‡

Robinson, Ray E. No. 378, in Supreme Court, Oct. term, 1923, Ray E. Robinson [et al.] *v.* United States, petition for writ of certiorari to circuit court of appeals for 2d circuit; brief on behalf of United States in opposition. 1923. cover-title, 5 p. ‡

Rumely, Edward A. No. —, in Supreme Court, Oct. term, 1923, Edward A. Rumely, S. Walter Kaufmann, and Norvin R. Lindheim *v.* United States, petition for writ of certiorari to circuit court of appeals for 2d circuit; brief for United States in opposition. 1923. cover-title, 6 p. ‡

Sage, Mrs. Margaret O. No. 276, in Supreme Court, Oct. term, 1923, William H. Edwards, formerly collector of internal revenue [for 2d district of New York] *v.* Joseph Jermain Slocum et al., executors [of Margaret Olivia Sage], on writ of certiorari to circuit court of appeals for 2d circuit; motion by petitioner to advance. 1923. cover-title, 2 p. ‡

St. Louis, Mo. No. 252, in Supreme Court, Oct. term, 1923, First National Bank of St. Louis, petitioner for certiorari, *v.* Missouri, at information of Jesse W. Barrett, attorney general, respondent for certiorari, on writ of error and petition for writ of certiorari to Supreme Court of Missouri; motion of United States for leave to appear as amicus curiae. 1923. cover-title, 3 p. ‡

Schencks, Maude P. No. 3936, in Court of Appeals of District of Columbia, Oct. term, 1923, no. 1 special calendar, Maude P. Schencks *v.* United States; brief on behalf of appellee. 1923. cover-title, ii+31 p. ‡

Simpson, J. B. No. 506, in Supreme Court, Oct. term, 1923, J. B. Simpson *v.* United States, petition for writ of certiorari to circuit court of appeals for 9th circuit; brief for United States in opposition. 1923. cover-title, 6 p. ‡

Slaymaker, William W. No. 87, in Supreme Court, Oct. term, 1923, United States *v.* William W. Slaymaker, appeal from Court of Claims; brief and argument for United States. 1923. cover-title, 13 p. ‡

Standard Oil Company. No. 549, in Supreme Court, Oct. term, 1923, Standard Oil Company of New Jersey *v.* United States, petition for writ of certiorari to circuit court of appeals for 3d circuit; brief for United States in opposition. 1923. cover-title, 11 p. ‡

Starrett, William A. Criminal, no. 40384, in Supreme Court of District of Columbia, holding criminal term, Oct. term, 1922, United States *v.* Wiliam A. Starrett et al.; brief on sufficiency of indictment. 1923. cover-title, iv+122 p. ‡

Stewart, James, & Co., Incorporated. Law no. 6365, in district court for eastern district of Arkansas, western division, United States *v.* James Stewart & Co. (Inc.); brief of plaintiff in support of application and motion to be relieved from order and to modify order. 1923. cover-title, 69 p. large 8° ‡

Stone & Downer Company. No. 2245, Court of Customs Appeals, Stone & Downer Co. et al. *v.* United States; brief for United States. 1923. cover-title, 71 p. ‡

Swift Lumber Company. No. 40, in Supreme Court, Oct. term, 1923, United States, Interstate Commerce Commission, and Swift Lumber Company *v.* Illinois Central Railroad Company and Fernwood, Columbia & Gulf Railroad Company, appeal from district court for southern district of Mississippi; brief for United States. 1923. cover-title, ii+24 p. ‡

Teets, Joseph W. No. 46, in Supreme Court, Oct. term, 1923, Title Guaranty & Trust Company and Winnie [Minnie] W. Teets, as executors of Joseph W. Teets, *v.* William H. Edwards, collector of internal revenue for southern [2d] district of New York, in error to district court for southern district of New York; brief for defendant in error. 1923. cover-title, 12 p. ‡

Thompson-Starrett Company. No. 2262, Court of Customs Appeals, Thompson-Starrett Co. *v.* United States; brief for United States. 1923. cover-title, 13 p. ‡

—— No. 2263, Court of Customs Appeals, United States *v.* Thompson-Starrett Co.; brief for United States on motion to dismiss. 1923. cover-title, 4 p. ‡

Tilden Produce Company. No. 139, in Supreme Court, Oct. term, 1923, Margaret C. Lynch, executrix of E. J. Lynch, collector of internal revenue [for district of Minnesota], *v.* Tilden Produce Company, on writ of certiorari to circuit court of appeals for 8th circuit; brief for United States. 1923. cover-title, i+33 p. ‡

Trueba, Frank. No. 543, in Supreme Court, Oct. term, 1923, Frank Trueba *v.* United States, petition for writ of certiorari to circuit court of appeals for 9th circuit; brief for United States in opposition. 1923. cover-title, 5 p. ‡

Union Pacific Railroad. In Court of Claims, Union Pacific Railway Company *v.* United States, no. 209-A; defendant's objections to plaintiff's request for findings of fact, defendant's request for findings of fact, and brief. [1923.] p. 43–51, large 8° ‡

—— No. C–789, in Court of Claims, Union Pacific Railroad Company *v.* United States; demurrer [and brief]. 1923. cover-title, p. 1–3, large 8° ‡

United Products Corporation of America. In Court of Claims, United Products Corporation of America *v.* United States, no. C–964; demurrer [and] memorandum brief. [1923.] p. 1–12, large 8° ‡

Weaver, Walter W. No. 3997, special calendar no. —, in Court of Appeals of District of Columbia, Oct. term, 1923, Walter W. Weaver *v.* United States; brief for appellee. 1923. cover-title, i+26 p. ‡

Weill, Andre, & Co., Incorporated. No. 2289, Court of Customs Appeals, Andre Weill & Co., Inc., *v.* United States; brief for United States. 1923. cover-title, 18 p. ‡

West Coast Rubber Corporation, Incorporated. No. 574, in Supreme Court, Oct. term, 1923, A. J. Oliver, as trustee in bankruptcy of West Coast Rubber Corporation, Inc., and Oscar Courtin [et al.] *v.* United States and city and county of San Francisco, petition for writ of certiorari to circuit court of appeals for 9th circuit; brief on behalf of United States in opposition. 1923. cover-title, 5 p. ‡

Woodbridge, William E. No. 51, in Supreme Court, Oct. term, 1923, Samuel Homer Woodbridge and Edward Woodbridge Barnes, executors of William E. Woodbridge, *v.* United States, appeal from Court of Claims; brief on behalf of appellee. 1923. cover-title, i+43 p. ‡

Wyman, Joe. No. 140, in Supreme Court, Oct. term, 1923, Joe Wyman *v.* United States, in error to district court for eastern district of New York; motion to advance. 1923. cover-title, 2 p. ‡

Wyoming Railway. No. 38, in Supreme Court, Oct. term, 1923, Wyoming Railway Company *v.* United States and Interstate Commerce Commission, appeal from district court for district of Wyoming; brief for United States. 1923. cover-title, ii+18 p. ‡

Yale & Towne Manufacturing Company. In Court of Claims, Yale & Towne Manufacturing Company *v.* United States, no. 67-A; defendant's brief. [1923.] p. 1–6, large 8° ‡

LABOR DEPARTMENT

CHILDREN'S BUREAU

Food. Breast feeding. [1923.] [4] p. il. 4° ([Dodger no. 4 revised.]) †

Juvenile courts. List of references on juvenile courts and probation in United States, and selected list of foreign references; [by Irma C. Lonegren and Eliza Tonks]. 1923. v+41 p. (Bureau publication 124.) * Paper, 10c.

L 23—241

Malnutrition. What is malnutrition? Hundreds of thousands of American children are undernourished [with list of references]; by Lydia Roberts. [Reprint 1923.] 20 p. il. ([Children's year follow-up series 1]; Bureau publication 59.) * Paper, 5c.

19—26683

Market-gardening. Child labor on Maryland truck farms; by Alice Channing.
   1923. v+52 p. 3 pl. 2 p. of pl. (Bureau publication 123.)   * Paper, 10c.
                                                              L 23—240
Publications. Publications. [Edition of] Sept. 15, 1923. 1923. 12 p. narrow
   12° †

Work. Ten years' work for children [by Children's Bureau]; by Grace Abbott.
   1923. [1]+10 p. [Reprinted, by permission, from North American review
   for Aug. 1923.]   * Paper, 5c.   L 23—237

EMPLOYMENT SERVICE

Industrial employment information bulletin, v. 3, no. 9; Sept. 1923. [1923.]
   20 p. 4° [Monthly.] †   L 21—17

LABOR STATISTICS BUREAU

Child labor. U. S. Children's Bureau leaflet, Trend of child labor in United
   States, 1920–23, errata. [1923.] 1 p. oblong 48° [Also issued in postal card
   form. The article which this corrects was prepared by the Children's Bureau
   and appeared in the Monthly labor review, Sept. 1923, and also as a separate
   therefrom.] †

Employment in selected industries, Sept. 1923. 1923. [1]+8 p. [From Monthly
   labor review, Nov. 1923.] †

Headlights. Rules governing approval of head lighting devices for motor vehi-
   cles, Illuminating Engineering Society, New York, N. Y., sponsor; tentative
   American standard, approved Nov. 1922, by American Engineering Standards
   Committee. Sept. 1923. vii+7 p. il. (Bulletin 350; Safety code series.)
   * Paper, 5c.   L 23—239
—— Same. (H. doc. 57, 68th Cong. 1st sess.)

International Seamen's Union of America. International Seamen's Union of
   America, study of its history and problems; [by] Arthur Emil Albrecht. June,
   1923. vi+120+vi p. (Bulletin 342; Miscellaneous series.)   * Paper, 15c.
                                                              L 23—238
—— Same. (H. doc. 21' 68th Cong. 1st sess.)

Monthly labor review, v. 17, no. 4; Oct. 1923. 1923. v+777–989 p. il. * Paper,
   15c. single copy, $1.50 a yr.; foreign subscription, $2.25.   15—26485
   SPECIAL ARTICLES.—Expansion of family-wage system in France and Belgium; by
   Mary T. Waggaman.—Accident occurrence in iron and steel industry, 1922; by Lucian W. Chaney.—Review of compensation legislation for 1923; by Lindley D. Clark.—
   Conciliation work of Department of Labor, Aug. 1923; by Hugh L. Kerwin.—Statistics of immigration, fiscal year 1923, and July, 1923; by W. W. Husband.
   NOTE.—The Review is the medium through which the Bureau publishes the results
   of original investigations too brief for bulletin purposes, notices of labor legislation by
   the States or by Congress, and Federal court decisions affecting labor, which from
   their importance should be given attention before they could ordinarily appear in the
   bulletins devoted to these subjects. One free subscription will be given to all labor
   departments and bureaus, workmen's compensation commissions, and other offices connected with the administration of labor laws and organizations exchanging publications with the Labor Statistics Bureau. Others desiring copies may obtain them
   from the Superintendent of Documents, Washington, D. C., at the prices stated above.

Prices. Prices and cost of living. 1923. [1]+802–832 p. il. [From Monthly
   labor review, Oct. 1923.] †
—— Wholesale prices of commodities for Aug. 1923. 1923. [1]+9 p.
   [Monthly.] †   L 22—229
—— Same for Sept. 1923. 1923. [1]+9 p. [Monthly.] †

NATURALIZATION BUREAU

Federal citizenship textbook: Government of United States [chart]. 2d revised
   edition. [Apr. 27, 1923.] 1 p. large 4° †

PUBLICATIONS AND SUPPLIES DIVISION

Labor Department. Publications of Department of Labor. [Edition of] Nov. 1,
   1923. 1923. ii+30 p. †   16—26563

LIBRARY OF CONGRESS

COPYRIGHT OFFICE

Copyright. [Catalogue of copyright entries, new series, pt. 1, group 1, Books, v. 20] no. 62–72; Oct. 1923. Oct. 3–31, 1923. p. 705–880. [Issued several times a week.]   6—35347

NOTE.—Each number is issued in 4 parts: pt. 1, group 1, relates to books; pt. 1, group 2, to pamphlets, leaflets, contributions to newspapers or periodicals, etc., lectures, sermons, addresses for oral delivery, dramatic compositions, maps, motion pictures; pt. 2, to periodicals; pt. 3, to musical compositions; pt. 4, to works of art, reproductions of a work of art, drawings or plastic works of scientific or technical character, photographs, prints and pictorial illustrations.
Subscriptions for the Catalogue of copyright entries should be made to the Superintendent of Documents, Washington, D. C., instead of to the Register of Copyrights. Prices are as follows: Paper, $3.00 a yr. (4 pts.), foreign subscription, $5.00; pt. 1 (groups 1 and 2), 5c. single copy (group 1, price of group 2 varies), $1.00 a yr., foreign subscription, $2.25; pt. 3, $1.00 a yr., foreign subscription, $1.50; pts. 2 and 4, each 10c. single copy, 50c. a yr., foreign subscription, 70c.

—— Same, pt. 2, Periodicals, v. 18, no. 1. 1923. iii+1–95 p. [Quarterly.]

—— Same, pt. 3, Musical compositions, v. 18, no. 5. 1923. v+361–492 p. [Monthly.]

—— Same, pt. 4, Works of art, reproductions of a work of art, drawings or plastic works of scientific or technical character, photographs, prints, and pictorial illustrations, v. 18, no. 1. 1923. iii+1–85 p. [Quarterly.]

—— Same, pt. 4, Works of art, reproductions of a work of art, drawings or plastic works of scientific or technical character, photographs, prints, and pictorial illustrations, v. 18, no. 2. 1923. iii+87–191 p. [Quarterly.]

DOCUMENTS DIVISION

Government publications. Monthly check-list of State publications received during July–Aug, 1923; v. 14, nos. 7–8. 1923. p. 297–352. * Paper, 10c. single copy, $1.00 a yr.; foreign subscription, $1.25.   10—8924

Law. Popular names of Federal statutes, tentative list based on records of American Law Section, Legislative Reference Service, Library of Congress. July 1, 1923. [1]+20 p. large 8° * Paper, 10c.   22—26004

NATIONAL HOME FOR DISABLED VOLUNTEER SOLDIERS

Proceedings of board of managers of National Home for Disabled Volunteer Soliders, Sept. 14, 1923. Sept. 1923. [v. 4] p. 278–286. [Quarterly.] ‡

NAVY DEPARTMENT

Court-martial order 8, 1923; Aug. 31, 1923. [1923.] 8 p. 12° [Monthly.] ‡
Orders. General order 117 [6th series]; Sept. 13, 1923. [1923.] 1 p. 4° ‡

AERONAUTICS BUREAU

Naval aviation, eyes of the fleet. 1923 [reprint with slight changes]. [1]+13 p. il. †

CONSTRUCTION AND REPAIR BUREAU

Displacement (ships). Instructions for displacement and stability calculations under Bureau of Construction and Repair. [1st revision.] 1923. iii+257 p. il. 9 pl. 13 tab. * Cloth, 75c.   23—26553

Paint. Sailors' manual of paints and painting. Edition of 1923. 1923. v+21 p. ‡   23—26530

ENGINEERING BUREAU

Bulletin of engineering information 8; July 1, 1923. 1923. [1]+49 p. il. 11 pl. 1 tab. ‡   22—26665

Reciprocating steam engines. Instructions for operation, care, and repair of main propelling machinery: sec. 3, Reciprocating steam engines; reprint of sec. 3, chapter 7, of Manual of engineering instructions. 1923. [1]+300–354 p. il. [The edition of the Manual of engineering instructions of which this chapter forms a part has not yet been issued.] * Paper, 10c.   23—26537

Turbines. Instructions for operation, care, and repair of main propelling machinery: sec. 1, Turbines; reprint of sec. 1, chapter 7, of Manual of engineering instructions. 1923. [1]+1–56 p. il. 1 pl. [The edition of the Manual of engineering instructions of which this chapter forms a part has not yet been issued.] * Paper, 10c.   23—26939

JUDGE ADVOCATE GENERAL

Prisons. Manual for government of United States naval prisons. 1923. iii+42 p. 16° [Supersedes Manual promulgated Feb. 4, 1918.] ‡

MEDICINE AND SURGERY BUREAU

Arthritis. Roentgenological study of infectious arthritis [with bibliography]; by F. W. Muller. 1923. [1]+9 p. 6 p. of pl. [From United States naval medical bulletin, v. 19, no. 4.] †

Asthma. Diagnosis and treatment of bronchial asthma; by J. E. Miller. 1923. [1]+10 p. [From United States naval medical bulletin, v. 19, no. 3.] †

Cancer of stomach [with list of references]; by L. H. Williams. 1923. [1]+5 p. [From United States naval medical bulletin, v. 19, no. 3.] †

Cholecystitis of chemical origin in man following inhalations of poison gas; ·by H. M. Stenhouse. 1923. [1]+6 p. [From United States naval medical bulletin, v. 19, no. 3.] †

Colitis. Chronic colitis; by J. B. Pollard. 1923. [1]+6 p. [From United States naval medical bulletin, v. 19, no. 3.] †

Conjunctivitis. Samoan conjunctivitis, study of causative organism; by· D. Hunt. 1923. [1]+4 p. [From United States naval medical bulletin, v. 19, no. 4.] †

Dysentery. Amœbic and bacillary dysentery, review of recent literature; by J. G. Smith. 1923. [1]+8 p. [From United States naval medical bulletin, v. 19, no. 4.] †

Fear and worry; by H. Butts. 1923. [1]+25 p. [From United States naval medical bulletin, v. 19, no. 3.] †

Gonorrhea. Present status of treatment of gonorrhea [with list of references]; by E. A. Daus. 1923. [1]+11 p. [From United States naval medical bulletin, v. 19, no. 3.] †

Instructions to medical· officers issued by Bureau of Medicine and Surgery. [1923.] 162 p. [From United States naval medical bulletin, v. 19, no. 4.] †

Leg. Diagnosis and treatment of fractures of leg; by C. L. Andrus. 1923. [1]+9 ·p. [From United States naval medical bulletin, v. 19, no. 3.] †

Malaria. Malaria parasite in Haiti [with list of references]; by R. B. Storch. 1923. 4 p. [From United States naval medical bulletin, v. 19, no. 4.] †

—— Personal experiences with malaria among natives of Republic of Haiti; by R. B. Storch. 1923. [1]+8 p. [From United States naval medical bulletin, v. 19, no. 4.] †

—— Report of antimalarial campaign conducted by medical officers of 1st brigade, United States marines, in Haiti; by A. H. Allen. 1923. [1]+6 p. il. [From United States naval medical bulletin, v. 19, no. 4.] †

Medical compend for commanders of naval vessels to which no member of Medical Department of Navy is attached, and others, to accompany medicine box. 1923. v+97 p. il. ‡   23—26940

Naval medical bulletin. United States naval medical bulletin, published for information of Medical Department of service, Oct. 1923, v. 19, no. 4; edited by W. M. Kerr. 1923. vi+393–650 p. il. 6 p. of pl. [Monthly.] * Paper, 15c, single copy, $1.50 a yr.; foreign subscription, $2.50.   8—35095

SPECIAL ARTICLES.—Roentgenological study of infectious arthritis [with bibliography]; by F. W. Muller.—Report of antimalarial campaign conducted by medical officers of 1st brigade, United States marines, in Haiti; by A. H. Allen.—Malaria parasite in Haiti [with list of references]; by R. B. Storch.—Samoan conjunctivitis,

Naval medical bulletin—Continued.
study of causative organism; by D. Hunt.—Blackwater fever; by G. E. Robertson and W. Moore.—Personal experiences with malaria among natives of Republic of Haiti; by R. B. Storch.—Amœbic and bacillary dysentary, review of recent literature; by J. G. Smith.—Instructions to medical officers issued by Bureau of Medicine and Surgery.—Notes on preventive medicine for medical officers, Navy [including Report of work carried on during 1922 by bureau of laboratories, Department of Health, New York City, under direction of William H. Park].

Psychoanalytic literature [with bibliography]; by J. C. Thompson. 1923. [1]+5 p. [From United States naval medical bulletin, v. 19, no. 3.] †

Urology and its place in group medicine; by W. H. Connor. 1923. [1]+5 p. [From United States naval medical bulletin, v. 19, no. 3.] †

NAVAL OPERATIONS OFFICE

Marine engineering. Rules for engineering performances, 1923–24, Navy. 1923. v+195 p.+[3] folded leaves, 1 pl. small 4° [Includes lists of publications prepared by Naval Operations Office on gunnery exercises and engineering performances.] ‡

NAVIGATION BUREAU

Bearings (machinery). Bearings and lubrication, assignment 1; prepared by Bureau of Engineering. 1923. [1]+8 p. il. (Navy education-study courses.) ‡

—— Same, assignment 2; prepared by Bureau of Engineering. 1923. [1]+8 p. il. (Navy education-study courses.) ‡

—— Same, assignment 3; prepared by Bureau of Engineering. 1923. [1]+7 p. (Navy education-study courses.) ‡

—— Same, assignment 4; prepared by Bureau of Engineering. 1923. [1]+7 p. (Navy education-study courses.) ‡

—— Same, assignment 5; prepared by Bureau of Engineering. 1923. [1]+5 p. il. (Navy education-study courses.) ‡

—— Same, assignment 6; prepared by Bureau of Engineering. 1923. [1]+7 p. (Navy education-study courses.) ‡

Naval Academy, Annapolis. Examination papers for admission to Naval Academy, Annapolis, Md.; series 30–46, 48–54, Feb. 1914–Apr. 1923. 1923. [1]+49 p. † Naval Academy.   8—35154

Navy directory, officers of Navy and Marine Corps, including officers of Naval Reserve Force (active), Marine Corps Reserve (active), and foreign officers serving with Navy, Sept. 1, 1923. 1923. iii+241 p. [Bimonthly.] * Paper, 25c. single copy, $1.25 a yr.; foreign subscription, $1.75.

Storage batteries. Storage batteries, care and repair, assignment 1; prepared by Bureau of Engineering. 1923. iii+9 p. (Navy education-study courses.) ‡

—— Same, assignment 2; prepared by Bureau of Engineering. 1923. [1]+8 p. (Navy education-study courses.) ‡

—— Same, assignment 3; prepared by Bureau of Engineering. 1923. [1]+9 p. (Navy education-study courses.) ‡

—— Same, assignment 4; prepared by Bureau of Engineering. 1923. [1]+10 p. (Navy education-study courses.) ‡

—— Same, assignment 5; prepared by Bureau of Engineering. 1923. [1]+8 p. (Navy education-study courses.) ‡

—— Same, assignment 6; prepared by Bureau of Engineering. 1923. [1]+8 p. (Navy education-study courses.) ‡

—— Same, assignment 7; prepared by Bureau of Engineering. 1923. [1]+12 p. (Navy education-study courses.) ‡

—— Same, assignment 8; prepared by Bureau of Engineering. 1923. [1]+10 p. (Navy education-study courses.) ‡

—— Same, assignment 9; prepared by Bureau of Engineering. 1923. [1]+8 p. (Navy education-study courses.) ‡

NOTE.—The charts, sailing directions, etc., of the Hydrographic Office are sold by the office in Washington and also by agents at the principal American and foreign seaports and American lake ports. Copies of the General catalogue of mariners' charts and books and of the Hydrographic bulletins, reprints, and Notice to mariners are supplied free on application at the Hydrographic Office in Washington and at the branch offices in Boston, New York, Philadelphia, Baltimore, Norfolk, Savannah, New Orleans, Galveston. San Francisco, Portland (Oreg.), Seattle, Chicago, Cleveland, Buffalo, Sault Ste. Marie, and Duluth.

Africa pilot: v. 1, West coast from Cape Palmas to Cape of Good Hope. 2d edition. 1923. v+661 p.+[2] leaves, il. map. ([Publication] 105.) [The 2 leaves given in the collation consist of request coupons which are detachable.] †Cloth, 90c.

Altitude, azimuth. and line of position, comprising tables for working sight of heavenly body for line of position by cosine-haversine formula, Marcq St. Hilaire method, and also Aquino's altitude and azimuth tables for line of position, Marcq St. Hilaire method. 4th reprint [with changes] 1923. cover-title, p. 3–320, il. 1 pl. large 8° ([Publication] 200.) [Page of text pasted on inside of cover.] † Cloth, 60c. 23—26549

Hydrographic bulletin, weekly, no. 1778–82; Oct. 3–31, 1923. [1923.] Each 1 p. large 4° and f° [For Ice supplements to accompany nos. 1778–82, see below under center head *Charts* the subhead *Pilot charts.*] †

Lights. List of lights, with fog signals and visible time signals, including uniform time system, radio time signals, radio weather bulletins, and radio compass stations of the world; v. 3, West coast of Europe and Africa, including Mediterranean Sea, Black Sea, and Sea of Azov; corrected to July 7, 1923. 1923. 560 p. map. ([Publication] 32.) † Paper, 60c. 7—24403

Notice to aviators 10, 1923; Oct. 1 [1923]. [1923.] 5 p. [Monthly.] † 20—26958

Notice to mariners 40–43. 1923; Oct. 6–27 [1923]. [1923.] [xxxviii]+1068–1178 leaves, 9 maps. [Weekly.] †

Tide calendars. Tide calendar [for Baltimore (Fort McHenry) and Cape Henry], Nov. 1923. [1923.] 1 p. 4° [Monthly.] †

—— Tide calendar [for Norfolk (Navy Yard) and Newport News, Va.], Nov. 1923. [1923.] 1 p. 4° [Monthly.] †

Charts

Nicaragua. East coast of Nicaragua, Central America, False Cape to Brangmans Bluff, including Morrison Dennis and Miskito cays, from U. S. naval surveys between 1910 and 1923, and British surveys between 1830 and 1843; chart 5382. Scale naut. m.=0.5 in. Washington, Hydrographic Office, Oct. 1923. 40.7×29 in. †50c.

Pilot charts. Ice supplement to north Atlantic pilot chart; issue 78. Scale 1° long.=0.3 in. Washington, Hydrographic Office [1923]. 8.9×11.8 in. [To accompany Hydrographic bulletin 1778, Oct 3, 1923.] †

—— Same; issue 79. Scale 1° long.=0.3 in. Washington, Hydrographic Office [1923]. 8.9×11.8 in. [To accompany Hydrographic bulletin 1779, Oct. 10, 1923.] †

—— Same; issue 80. Scale 1° long.=0.3 in. Washington, Hydrographic Office [1923]. 8.9×11.8 in. [To accompany Hydrographic bulletin 1780, Oct. 17, 1923.] †

—— Same; issue 81. Scale 1° long.=0.3 in. Washington, Hydrographic Office [1923]. 8.9×11.8 in. [To accompany Hydrographic bulletin 1781, Oct. 24, 1923.] †

—— Same; issue 82. Scale 1° long.=0.3 in. Washington, Hydrographic Office [1923]. 8.9×11.8 in. [To accompany Hydrographic bulletin 1782, Oct. 31, 1923.] †

—— Pilot chart of Central American waters, Nov. 1923; chart 3500. Scale 1° long.=0.7 in. Washington, Hydrographic Office, Oct. 12, 1923. 23.4×35.1 in. [Monthly. Certain portions of the data are furnished by the Weather Bureau.] † 10c.

NOTE.—Contains on reverse: Navigator's time-distance-speed diagram.—Daily weather bulletins transmitted by radio from United States to France.

Pilot charts—Continued. Pilot chart of Indian Ocean, Dec. 1923; chart 2603. Scale 1° long.=0.2 in. Washington, Hydrographic Office, Oct. 12, 1923. 22.6×31 in. [Monthly. Certain portions of the data are furnished by the Weather Bureau.] † 10c.

    Note.—Contains on reverse: Navigator's time-distance-speed diagram.—Daily weather bulletins transmitted by radio from United States to France.

—— Pilot chart of north Atlantic Ocean, Nov. 1923; chart 1400. Scale 1° long.=0.27 in. Washington, Hydrographic Office, Oct. 12, 1923. 23.2×31.8 in. [Monthly. Certain portions of the data are furnished by the Weather Bureau.] † 10c.

                                                                              14—16339

    Note.—Contains on reverse: Navigator's time-distance-speed diagram.—Daily weather bulletins transmitted by radio from United States to France.

—— Pilot chart of north Pacific Ocean, Oct. 1923; chart 1401. Scale 1° long.=0.2 in. Washington, Hydrographic Office, Aug. 13, 1923. 23.7×35.3 in. [Monthly. Certain portions of the data are furnished by the Weather Bureau.] † 10c.

    Note.—Contains on reverse: Cyclonic storms.

—— Same, Dec. 1923; chart 1401. Scale 1° long.=0.2 in. Washington. Hydrographic Office, Oct. 12, 1923. 23.7×35.3 in. [Monthly. Certain portions of the data are furnished by the Weather Bureau.] † 10c.

    Note.—Contains on reverse: Navigator's time-distance-speed diagram.—Daily weather bulletins transmitted by radio from United States to France.

—— Pilot chart of south Atlantic Ocean, Dec. 1923–Feb. 1924; chart 2600. Scale 1° long.=0.3 in. Washington, Hydrographic Office, Oct. 12, 1923. 23×31.9 in. [Quarterly. Certain portions of the data are furnished by the Weather Bureau.] † 10c.

    Note.—Contains on reverse: Navigator's time-distance-speed diagram.—Daily weather bulletins transmitted by radio from United States to France.

—— Pilot chart of south Pacific Ocean, Dec. 1923–Feb. 1924; chart 2601. Scale 1° long.=0.2 in. Washington, Hydrographic Office, Oct. 12, 1923. 21.2×35.5 in. [Quarterly. Certain portions of the data are furnished by the Weather Bureau.] † 10c.

    Note.—Contains on reverse: Navigator's time-distance-speed diagram.—Daily weather bulletins transmitted by radio from United States to France.

Telegraph chart of the world, showing submarine cables, principal land lines, and radio stations; [with insets]; chart 2180a–c. Scale 1° long.=0.2 in. Washington, Hydrographic Office. Sept. 1923. 3 sheets, each 37.9×25.8 in. † 40c. per sheet.

British Isles, North Sea and Baltic.
Newfoundland to Chesapeake Bay.
West Indies and Central America.

ORDNANCE BUREAU

Harrison, John K. M. Interference no. 45648, in Patent Office, John K. M. Harrison *v.* Ralph C. Browne; index of exhibits and copies of documentary exhibits. 1923. v. 2, cover-title, iii+581–674 p. il. ‡

SUPPLIES AND ACCOUNTS BUREAU

Naval supplies. Index to specifications issued by Navy Department for naval stores and material. Oct. 1. 1923. vi+45 p. 12° [Quarterly.]. †

Naval vessels. Sale of naval vessels for scrapping purposes, bids will be opened Nov. 30, 1923, and should be mailed to Room 1008, Navy Department, Washington, D. C. 1923. cover-title, 12 p. (Catalogue 228B.) [Text on p. 2 of cover.] †

—— Sale of naval vessels for scrapping purposes on ways at shipbuilding plants, bids will be opened Nov. 8, 1923, and should be mailed to Room 1008, Navy Department, Washington, D. C. 1923. cover-title, 8 p. (Catalogue 226B.) [Text on p. 2 of cover.] †

Pay, Navy. Instructions for carrying into effect joint service pay bill (act of June 10, 1922) sec. A–H; revised to Sept. 21, 1923. 1923. [66] p. ‡

Supply Corps, Navy. Memorandum for information of officers of Supply Corps, commanding officers of ships, and commandants 254; Oct. 1, 1923. [1923.] p. 7653–7732, 12° [Monthly.] ‡

YARDS AND DOCKS BUREAU

Public works of Navy under cognizance of Bureau of Yards and Docks and Corps of Civil Engineers, U. S. Navy, Oct. 1923. 1923. iii+58 p. il. 10 pl. 8 p. of pl. (Bulletin 33.) [Quarterly; none issued July, 1923.] ‡

PAN AMERICAN UNION

NOTE.—The Pan American Union sells its own monthly bulletins, handbooks, etc., at prices usually ranging from 5c. to $2.50. The price of the English edition of the bulletin is 25c. a single copy or $2.50 a year, the Spanish edition $2.00 a year, the Portuguese edition $1.50 a year; there is an additional charge of 50c. a year on each edition for countries outside the Pan American Union. Address the Director General of the Pan American Union, Washington, D. C.

Bulletin (*English edition*). Bulletin of Pan American Union, Oct. 1923; [v. 57, no. 4]. [1923.] iv+323–428 p. il. [Monthly. This number is entitled The Red Cross of the Americas.]   8—30967

—— Same. (H. doc. 6, pt. 4, 68th Cong. 1st sess.)

—— (*Portuguese edition*). Boletim da União Pan-Americana, Outubro, 1923, edição portugueza; [v. 25, no. 4]. [Sun Job Print, Baltimore, Md.. 1923.] [iv]+231–314 p. il. [Monthly. This number is entitled A quinta Conferencia Internacional Americana, Santiago, Chile, Março 25–Maio 3, 1923.]   11—27014

—— (*Spanish edition*). Boletín de la Unión Panamericana, Octubre, 1923, edición española; [v. 57, no. 4]. [1923.] iv+333–440 p. il. [Monthly.]   12—12555

Chocolate age, Dominican cacao; [by William E. Pulliam]. 1923. [2]+6 p. il. [From Bulletin, Sept. 1923.] †

International American Conference. Quinta Conferencia Internacional Americana, Santiago de Chile, 25 de Marzo-3 de Mayo, 1923, tratado, convenciones, y resoluciones. 1923. v+63 p. †   23—26572

International Telephone and Telegraph Corporation (Corporación Internacional de Teléfonos y Telégrafos). 1923. [2]+14 p. il. [From Boletín, Oct. 1923. The print of this publication for which entry was made in the Monthly catalogue for Aug. 1923, p. 92, stated incorrectly that it was reprinted from the Boletín for Aug. instead of Oct. 1923.] †

Monroe doctrine. Observaciones acerca de la doctrina ·de Monroe, discurso del Charles E. Hughes, Secretario de Estado de los Estados Unidos, pronunciado ante la Asociación del Foro Americano, en la ciudad de Minneapolis el 30 de Agosto de 1923. 1923. 23 p. [For English edition issued by the State Department, see p. 205.] †   23—26559

Nicaragua. Commerce of Nicaragua, latest reports from Nicaraguan official sources. 1923. [1]+10 p. †   20—21429

Paraguay, general descriptive data. 1923. [2]+30 p. il. †   11—35841

PANAMA CANAL

NOTE.—Although The Panama Canal makes its reports to, and is under the supervision of, the Secretary of War, it is not a part of the War Department.

Panama Canal record, v. 17, no. 8–12; Oct. 3–31, 1923. Balboa Heights, C. Z. [1923]. p. 121–196. [Weekly.]   7—35328

NOTE.—The yearly subscription rate of the Panama Canal record is 50c. domestic, and $1.00 foreign, (single issues 2c.), except in the case of Government departments and bureaus, Members of Congress, representatives of foreign governments, steamship lines, chambers of commerce, boards of trade, and university and public libraries, to whom the Record is distributed free. The word "domestic" refers to the United States, Canada, Canal Zone, Cuba, Guam, Hawaii, Manua, Mexico, the Philippines, Porto Rico, Republic of Panama, Tutuila, and the Virgin Islands. Subscriptions will commence with the first issue of the Record in the month in which the subscriptions are received, unless otherwise requested. Remittances should be made payable to Disbursing Clerk, The Panama Canal, but should be forwarded to the Chief of Office, The Panama Canal, Washington, D. C. The name and address to which the Record is to be sent should be plainly written. Postage stamps, foreign money, and defaced or smooth coins will not be accepted.

EXECUTIVE DEPARTMENT

EXECUTIVE OFFICE

Executive orders. Supplement 2 [to] Executive orders relating to Panama Canal [Mar. 8, 1904–Dec. 31, 1921, annotated 1921]. [Balboa Heights, C. Z., Oct. 9, 1923.] [1]+336–338 p. [Executive orders relating to Panama Canal published by The Panama Canal. This supplement includes Executive orders dated May 16–Sept. 13, 1923.] †

HEALTH DEPARTMENT

Medical Association of Isthmian Canal Zone. Proceedings of Medical Association of Isthmian Canal Zone, Jan.–Dec. 1920. Panama Canal Press, Mount Hope, C. Z., 1923. v. 13, pts. 1 and 2, 139 p. il. 5 pl. map. [Discontinued with this issue.] ‡

CONTENTS.—Hookworm disease; [by] Frederick A. Miller.—Types of general paralysis of insane, with presentation of cases; [by] Louis Wender.—Bacteriology of influenza epidemic on Canal Zone, Mar.–Apr. 1920; [by] Lewis B. Bates and J. H. St. John.—Anopheles breeding among water lettuce, new habitat [with list of references; by] James Zetek.—Panama Canal species of genus Anopheles [with list of references; by] James Zetek.—Some remaining problems of malaria control on Isthmus; [by] Dalferes P. Curry.—Sinusitis, otitis media, and mastoiditis, incidence at autopsy in Panama Canal Zone; [by] Herbert C. Clark.—Gauze sponge in abdominal cavity for 14 years, with simulation of ectopic gestation; [by] Fred C. Watson and P. H. Desnoes.—1920 epidemic influenza at Ancon Hospital; [by] Roland C. Connor.—Lethargic encephalitis, case report and brief review of literature; [by] Cornelius D. Briscoe.—Case of yaws; [by] John R. Ernst.—Influenza quarantine; [by] John C. Hubbard.—Clonorchus sinensis in Panama; [by] George M. Gehringer.—Vaginal hysterectomy and vaginal suspension; [by] C C. Brin.—Treatment of hookworm disease, chenopodium vs. thymol; [by] Fred. C. Caldwell.—Preliminary report upon administration of 10,000 doses of arsphenamine; [by] Troy W. Earhart and Nathan B. Kupfer.—Fracture of symphysis pubis, case report; [by] Hiram S. Liggett.—Diaphragmatic hernia with case report [and with reference; by] Troy W. Earhart.—Unilateral renal hemorrhage, case report; [by] Holland G. Hambleton.—Intra-abdominal pregnancy, 3 cases, and ablatio placentae, 1 case; [by] Howard K. Tuttle.—Mediastinal disease, review of cases encountered in 6,000 autopsies; [by] Nathan B. Kupfer.

PURCHASING DEPARTMENT

Supplies. Circular [proposals for supplies] 1564; Oct. 6, 1923. [1923.] 21+[1] p. f° †

—— Proposals [for supplies 1564, to accompany Circular proposals for supplies 1564]. [1923.] 1 p. 24° ‡

POST OFFICE DEPARTMENT

Envelopes. Proposal and specifications for envelopes for departments of Government, for one year, beginning July 1, 1923. 1923. 19 p. f° †

—— Requisitions for special-request envelopes; [issued by] 3d assistant Postmaster General. Sept. 28, 1923. 1 p. †

European corn-borers. Extension of quarantine on account of European corn borer; [issued by] 3d assistant Postmaster General. Oct. 6, 1923. 1 p. 4° †

Mail contracts. Advertisement inviting proposals for carrying mails on steamboat or other power-boat routes in North Carolina, South Carolina, Georgia, Florida, Alabama, Mississippi, Tennessee, Kentucky, and Porto Rico, July 1, 1924–June 30, 1928. Oct. 30, 1923. 30 p. †

Mail matter. Questions brought up at South Dakota postal conference convention. [1923.] 1 p. narrow 8° †

Parcel post. Amendment to Postal laws and regulations [of United States]: Collect-on-delivery service with Philippine Islands discontinued Dec. 1, 1923. Oct. 25, 1923. 1 p. †

—— Same, without preliminary paragraph and with title, Collect-on-delivery service with Philippine Islands discontinued Dec. 1, 1923; [issued by] 3d assistant Postmaster General. Oct. 25, 1923. 1 p. †

Pneumatic tubes. Before Interstate Commerce Commission, no. 14969, New York Pneumatic Service Company *v.* United States; brief for Postmaster General. 1923. cover-title, 18 p. ‡

Postal bulletin, v. 44, no. 13280–306; Oct. 1–31, 1923. [1923.] various paging, f° [Daily except Sundays and holidays.] * Paper, 5c. single copy, $2.00 a yr.　　　　　　　　　　　　　　　　　　　　　　　　　　　6—5810

Postal cards. Improper defacement of reply portions of undeliverable double postal cards; [issued by] 3d assistant Postmaster General. Oct. 6, 1923. 1 p. oblong 48° †

Postal guide. United States official postal guide, 4th series, v. 3, no. 4; Oct. 1923, monthly supplement. 1923. cover-title. 52 p. il. [Includes Modifications 24–26 of International money order list, pamphlet 14, and Inserts 833–835 to Postal laws and regulations of United States. Text and illustration on p. 2–4 of cover.] * Official postal guide, with supplements, $1.00, foreign subscription, $1.50; July issue, 75c.; supplements published monthly (11 pamphlets) 25c., foreign subscription, 50c.　　　　　　　4—18254

RAILWAY MAIL SERVICE

Mail-trains. Schedule of mail trains, no. 88, Oct. 1, 1923, 12th division, Railway Mail Service, comprising Louisiana and Mississippi. 1923. 81+[1] p. narrow 8° ‡

—— Schedule of mail trains, no. 446, Oct. 9, 1923, 7th division, Railway Mail Service, comprising Kansas and Missouri. 1923. 170+[1] p. narrow 8° ‡

TOPOGRAPHY DIVISION

NOTE.—Since February, 1908, the Topography Division has been preparing rural-delivery maps of counties in which rural delivery is completely established. They are published in two forms, one giving simply the rural free delivery routes, starting from a single given post office, sold at 10 cents each; the other, the rural free delivery routes in an entire county, sold at 35 cents each. A uniform scale of 1 inch to 1 mile is used. Editions are not issued, but sun-print copies are produced in response to special calls addressed to the Disbursing Clerk, Post Office Department, Washington, D. C. These maps should not be confused with the post route maps, for which see Monthly catalogue for February, 1923, page 528.

PRESIDENT OF UNITED STATES

Alien property. Executive order authorizing Alien Property Custodian to sell certain property at private sale [being real estate in New York City belonging to Anton Birkle of Germany]. Sept. 22, 1923. 1 p. f° (No. 3907.) ‡

—— Executive order authorizing Alien Property Custodian to sell certain property at private sale [being real estate in New York City belonging to Ernst Haertel of Leipzig, Germany]. Sept. 19, 1923. 1 p. f° (No. 3906.) ‡

Birds. Third executive order, Deer Flat bird reservation, Idaho [revoking Executive order of Feb. 25, 1909, setting apart certain lands in Idaho as preserves and breeding grounds for native birds, in so far as it affects certain described lands in Idaho]. Sept. 13, 1923. 1 p. map, f° (No. 3904.) ‡

Civil service. Executive order [amending civil service rules relating to reinstatement and adding new section to said rules so as to permit former classified employee, retired upon annuity by reason of total disability but who is eligible by reason of recovery and termination of annuity, to be reinstated to appropriate position in any part of classified service]. Sept. 28, 1923. 1 p. f° (No. 3908A.) ‡

—— Executive order [amending civil service rules relating to reinstatement so as to permit reinstatement in any part of classified service, thus utilizing training and experience acquired in any part of classified service in any other part when such action is necessary]. Oct. 5, 1923. 1 p. f° (No. 3912.) ‡

Education week. National education week, 1923, proclamation [designating week beginning on Nov. 18, 1923, as National education week]. [Sept. 26, 1923.] [2] p. f° ([No. 1676.]) †

Idaho. Executive order, Idaho [amending proclamation dated June 4, 1912, concerning St. Joe National Forest, so as to permit Idaho to select certain described lands in order to consummate exchange authorized by said proclamation]. Oct. 5, 1923. 1 p. f° (No. 3913.) ‡

Iron ores. Executive order [authorizing Secretary of Commerce to pay all expenses in connection with liquidation of account from sale or other disposition of Swedish iron ore purchased from Great Britain from money accruing from disposition of said ore, directing Secretary of Commerce to deposit such moneys in Treasury for payment of necessary expenses, and further directing that remaining balance be transferred and covered into general fund of Treasury]. Oct. 3, 1923. 1 p. f°. (No. 3910.) ‡

National forests. Allegheny National Forest, Pa., proclamation. Sept. 24, 1923. 1 p. map, f° (No. 1675.) †

—— Executive order, administrative site, near Custer National Forest, Mont. [temporarily withdrawing certain described lands from settlement, etc., and reserving same for use by Forest Service as driveway and watering place for stock grazed on Custer National Forest]. Oct. 4. 1923. 1 p. f° (No. 3911.) ‡

—— Executive order, Fishlake-Fillmore National Forest, Utah [merging into one national forest, to be known as Fishlake National Forest, all lands heretofore within Fillmore National Forest and Fishlake National Forest]. Sept. 24, 1923. 1 p. f° (No. 3908.) ‡

—— Executive order, Harney National Forest, S. Dak. [excluding certain described tract of land in South Dakota used by city of Custer as cemetery, from Harney National Forest, and restoring same to entry under applicable public land laws]. Oct. 15, 1923. 1 p. f° (No. 3916.) ‡

—— Executive order, La Sal National Forest, Utah and Colo. [excluding certain described tract of unsurveyed land in Utah, occupied in part by Piute Indians, from La Sal National Forest, and restoring said lands to public domain subject to rights of said Indians and other valid existing claims]. Oct. 12, 1923. 1 p. f° (No. 3915.) ‡

—— Sitgreaves National Forest, Ariz., 3d proclamation. [Oct. 13, 1923.] 2 p. map, f° ([No. 1677.]) †

Panama Canal. Executive order, order of transfer [of certain buildings at Cristobal, Canal Zone, from The Panama Canal to War Department]. Oct. 16, 1923. 1 p. f° (No. 3917.) ‡

Wyoming. Executive order, Wyoming [withdrawing certain described public lands in Wyoming from settlement, etc., pending resurvey, such withdrawal to remain in effect until resurvey is accepted and approved plat thereof is officially filed in local land office]. Sept. 29, 1923. 1 p. f° (No. 3909.) ‡

—— Executive order, Wyoming [withdrawing certain other described public lands in Wyoming from settlement, etc., pending resurvey, such withdrawal to remain in effect until resurvey is accepted and approved plats thereof are officially filed in local land office]. Oct. 5, 1923. 1 p. f° (No. 3914.) ‡

RAILROAD ADMINISTRATION

Beet final molasses. Before Interstate Commerce Commission, no. 14575, Utah-Idaho Sugar Company *v.* director general; exceptions to examiner's proposed report filed on behalf of defendant. 1923. cover-title, 7 p. ‡

Brooklyn Eastern District Terminal. Final settlement between director general of railroads and Brooklyn Eastern District Terminal, Oct. —, 1923. 1922 [1923]. 3 p. 4° [Imprint date incorrectly given on title-page as 1922.] †

Cast-iron. Before Interstate Commerce Commission, no. 14654, sub-no. 1, Keystone Steel & Wire Company *v.* director general et al.; exceptions on behalf of director general to report proposed by examiner. 1923. cover-title, 2 p. ‡

Cattle. Before Interstate Commerce Commission, no. 13180, E. A. Tovrea & Company et al. *v.* director general; petition by director general for rehearing, reargument, or reconsideration. 1923. cover-title, 19 p. ‡

Central Vermont Railway. Final settlement between director general of railroads and Central Vermont Railway Company and Central Vermont Transportation Company, —, 1923. 3 p. 4° †

Cleveland, Cincinnati, Chicago and St. Louis Railway. Final settlement between director general of railroads and Cleveland, Cincinnati, Chicago & St. Louis Railway Company and Muncie Belt Railway Company, —, 1923. 1923. 3 p. 4° †

Coal. Before Interstate Commerce Commission, no. 14030, Michigan Tanning and Extract Company *v.* director general; reply to complainant's exceptions to examiner's proposed report. 1923. cover-title, 3 p. ‡

Coke. Before Interstate Commerce Commission, no. 14609, Delta Beet Sugar Corporation *v.* director general; exceptions on behalf of director general to report proposed by examiner. 1923. cover-title, 9 p. ‡

Copper. Before Interstate Commerce Commission, no. 11755, Raritan Copper Works *v.* director general et al.; exceptions on part of director general to report proposed by examiner. 1923. cover-title, 3 p. ‡

Demurrage. Before Interstate Commerce Commission, no. .11881, Krauss Brothers Lumber Company *v.* director general; brief for director general. 1923. cover-title, 5 p. ‡

Fluxing stone. Before Interstate Commerce Commission, no. 14485, Alan Wood Iron and Steel Company *v.* director general; exceptions on part of director general to report proposed by examiner. 1923. cover-title, 3 p. ‡

Freight rates. Before Interstate Commerce Commission, no. 14044, Metropolitan Utilities District of Omaha [Nebr.] *v.* director general et al; defendants' answer to complainant's exceptions to report proposed by examiner. 1923. cover-title, 11 p. ‡

Ice. Before Interstate Commerce Commission, no. 14339, City Ice and Fuel Company *v.* director general; exceptions on part of director general to report proposed by examiner. 1923. cover-title, 5 p. ‡

Kentucky and Indiana Terminal Railroad. Final settlement between director general of railroads and Kentucky & Indiana Terminal Railroad Company, Oct. —, 1923. 1923. 3 p. 4° †

Michigan Central Railroad. Final settlement between director general of railroads and Michigan Central Railroad Company and Chicago, Kalamazoo & Saginaw Railway Company, Sept. 11, 1923. 1923. 4 p. 4° †

New York, New Haven and Hartford Railroad. Final settlement between director general of railroads and New York, New Haven and Hartford Railroad Company, Oct. —, 1923. 1923. 3 p. 4° †

Petroleum. Before Interstate Commerce Commission, no. 10804, Barnett Oil and Gas Company *v.* director general et al.; brief for defendants. 1923. cover-title, 8 p. ‡

—— Before Interstate Commerce Commission, no. 12813, Standard Oil Company (New Jersey) et al. *v.* director general et al.; reply to complainant's petition for rehearing. 1923. cover-title, 6 p. ‡

Silica brick. Before Interstate Commerce Commission, no. 13955, Pittsburgh Crucible Steel Co. *v.* director general; petition for reargument. 1923. cover-title, 7 p. ‡

Switching charges. Before Interstate Commerce Commission, no. 14123, Diamond Coal and Coke Company *v.* director general; exceptions on part of director general to report proposed by examiner. 1923. cover-title, 8 p. ‡

Syrups. Before Interstate Commerce Commission, no. 14610, Steuart, Son & Company *v.* director general; exceptions on part of director general to report proposed by examiner. 1923. cover-title, 3 p. ‡

Wheat. Before Interstate Commerce Commission, no. 13493, Acme Mills *v.* director general et al.; petition for reargument or reconsideration. 1923. cover-title, 11 p. ‡

SHIPPING BOARD

Eastern Shore Shipbuilding Corporation. No. 314, in Supreme Court, Oct. term, 1923, United States *v.* Roger B. Wood, trustee in bankruptcy of Eastern Shore Shipbuilding Corporation, on appeal from circuit court of appeals for 2d circuit; memorandum for United States in opposition to motion to affirm under rule 6, subdivision 5. 1923. cover-title, i+13 p. ‡

South Atlantic Dry Dock Company. [In circuit court of appeals, 5th circuit, Shipping Board Emergency Fleet Corporation *vs.* South Atlantic Dry Dock Company, no. 4171, error to district court for southern district of Florida; placita, evidence for plaintiff and defendant, etc.] [1923.] iii+322 p. 1 tab. ‡

SHIPPING BOARD EMERGENCY FLEET CORPORATION

Ships. Schedule of sailings of Shipping Board vessels in general cargo, passenger, and mail services, 1st of October to middle of November, 1923; issued by Traffic Department. 1923. cover-title, ii+14 p. il. [Monthly. Text on p. 2–4 of cover.] †   23—26331

SMITHSONIAN INSTITUTION

AMERICAN HISTORICAL ASSOCIATION

Reports. Annual report of American Historical Association, 1919. 1923. v. 1, 486 p. * Cloth, 75c.   4—18261

CONTENTS.—Proceedings of 34th annual meeting of American Historical Association, Cleveland, Ohio, Dec. 29–31, 1919.—Proceedings of 15th annual meeting of Pacific Coast Branch of American Historical Association, San Francisco, Calif., Nov. 28–29, 1919; [reported by William A. Morris].—Joint conference of historical societies and National Association of State War History Organizations [Cleveland, Ohio, Dec. 29, 1919].—American historical activities during World War; edited by Newton D. Mereness.—Roman policy in Armenia and Transcaucasia and its significance; by David Magie.—Epeiros-Albania boundary dispute in ancient times; by Herbert Wing.—Peter of Abano, medieval scientist; by Lynn Thorndike.—Abstract of commissions and instructions to colonial governors in America, 1740; by Arthur H. Basye.—Lincoln and progress of nationality in the North; by N. W. Stephenson.—Strategy of concentration of Confederate forces in Mississippi Valley in spring of 1862; by Alfred P. James.—Possibilities of intensive research in agricultural history; by R. W. Kelsey.—Some features of tobacco history; by George K. Holmes.—Notes on agricultural history of maize; by G. N. Collins.—Earliest American book on kitchen gardening; by Marjorie Fleming Warner.—Early agricultural periodical; by Mary G. Lacy.—Index; compiled by H. S. Parsons.

—— Same. (H. doc. 1039, 66th Cong. 3d sess.)

—— Same, 1920, supplement. 1923. xxiii+267 p. * Cloth, 60c.

CONTENTS.—Writings on American history, 1920, bibliography of books and articles on United States and Canadian history published during 1920, with some memoranda on other portions of America; compiled by Grace Gardner Griffin.

—— Same. (H. doc. 400, 67th Cong. 2d sess.)

STATE DEPARTMENT

[*Circular*] 906–911; Aug. 17–Oct. 4, 1923. [1923.] Each 2 p. or 1 p. [General instruction circulars to consular officers.] ‡

Diplomatic list, Oct. 1923. [1923.] cover-title, ii+34 p. 24° [Monthly.] ‡
                                                             10—16292

Monroe doctrine. Observations on Monroe doctrine, address by Charles E. Hughes, Secretary of State, delivered before American Bar Association, Minneapolis, Minn., Aug. 30, 1923. 1923. [1]+20 p. [For Spanish edition issued by the Pan American Union, see p. 200.] † ,   23—26941

War-ships. Treaty between United States, British Empire, France, Italy, and Japan, limitation of naval armament; signed Washington, Feb. 6, 1922, proclaimed Aug. 21, 1923. 1923. [1]+36 p. (Treaty series 671.) [French and English.] †   23—26877

SUPREME COURT

[*Journal*, Oct. 1–]22, 1923; [slips]1–19. [1923.] leaves 1–60. ‡

National Council of Traveling Salesmen's Associations. Transcript of record, Oct. term, 1923, no. 469, United States, Interstate Commerce Commission, National Council of Traveling Salesmen's Associations, et al., vs. New York Central Railroad Company et al., appeal from district court for district of Massachusetts. [1923.] cover-title, iii+165 p. 6 tab. ‡

Official reports. Official reports of Supreme Court, v. 262 U. S., no. 1; Ernest Knaebel, reporter. Preliminary print. · 1923. cover-title, v+1–146 p. 12° [Cases adjudged in Supreme Court at Oct. term, 1922 (opinions of Apr. 16, 23, and 30, 1923). This number contains lists of cases reported in v. 261. Text on p. 2 and 4 of cover. From United States reports, v. 262.] *Paper, 25c. single copy, $1.00 per vol. (4 nos. to a vol.; subscription price, $3.00 for 12 nos.); foreign subscription, 5c. added for each pamphlet.

Official reports—Continued. Same v. 262 U. S., no. 2; Ernest Knaebel, reporter. Preliminary prnt. 1923. cover-title, [1]+147–312 p. 12° [Cases adjudged in Supreme Court at Oct. term, 1922 (opinions of May 7 and 21, 1923, in part). This number contains a list of cases reported in v. 262, pt. 1. Text on p. 2–4 of cover. From United States reports, v. 262.]

Swift Lumber Company. Transcript of record, Oct. term, 1923, no. 40, United States, Interstate Commerce Commission, and Swift Lumber Company *vs.* Illinois Central Railroad Company and Fernwood, Columbia & Gulf Railroad Company, appeal from district court for southern district of Mississippi. [1923.] cover-title, iv+186 p. ‡

TARIFF COMMISSION

Dyes and dyeing. Census of dyes and other synthetic organic chemicals, 1922. 1923. vii+185 p. (Tariff information series 31.) *Paper, 20c. 23—26914

TREASURY DEPARTMENT

Appeals pending before United States courts in customs cases, no. 72; Oct. 1923. 1923. [1]+12 p. [Quarterly.] * Paper, 5c. single copy, 15c. a yr.; foreign subscription, 20c. 10—4497

Bonds of United States. Regulations with respect to United States bonds and notes. July 31, 1923. vi+156 p. 4° (Department circular 300; [Public Debt Commissioner].) †

—— Same, extract, with title, Extract [1] from Regulations of Treasury Department with respect to United States bonds and notes (Treasury Department circular 300, dated July 31, 1923). [1923.] 3 p. 4° †

Coins. values of foreign coins, Oct. 1, 1923. [1923.] 1 p.+4° (Department circular 1; Director of Mint.) [Quarterly.] †.

Finance. Daily statement of Treasury compiled from latest proved reports from Treasury offices and depositaries, Oct. 1–31, 1923. [1923.] Each 4 p. or 3 p. f° [Daily except Sundays and holidays.] † 15—3303

Mail regulations, revision of joint departmental regulations governing treatment of merchandise imported through mails. [1923.] 11 p. ([Treasury decision] 39805.) [From Treasury decisions, v. 44, no. 15.] †

Public debt. Statement of public debt of United States, June 30, 1923. 1923. [2] p. narrow f° [Monthly. Date of issue incorrectly given as May 4, 1923.] † 10—21268

—— Same. July 31, 1923. [1923.] [2] p. narrow f° [Monthly.] †

Treasury decisions under customs, internal-revenue, and other laws, including decisions of Board of General Appraisers and Court of Customs Appeals, v. 44, no. 14–17; Oct. 4–25, 1923. 1923. various paging. [Weekly. Department decisions numbered 39796–833, general appraisers' decisions 8684–94, abstracts 46235–378, internal revenue decisions 3520–25, and later Tariff Commission Notices 1–3, 5–6, 12–15.] * Paper, 5c. single copy, $1.00 a yr.; foreign subscription, $2.00. 10—30490

APPRAISERS

Reappraisements of merchandise by general appraisers [on Sept. 25–Oct. 20, 1923]; Oct. 5–26, 1923. [1923.] various paging. (Reappraisement circulars 3477–80.) [Weekly.] *Paper, 5c. single copy, 50c. a yr.; foreign subscription, $1.05. 13—2916

ARCHITECT, SUPERVISING

Public buildings. Specification, general conditions [for construction of public works under supervision of custodian of building]. [Reprint with changes 1923.] 4 p. f° †

COMPTROLLER OF CURRENCY

National banks. Monthly statement of capital stock of national banks, national bank notes, and Federal reserve bank notes outstanding, bonds on deposit, etc. [Oct. 1, 1923]. Oct. 1, 1923. 1 p. f° †   10—21266

GOVERNMENT ACTUARY

Bonds of United States. Market prices and investment values of outstanding bonds and notes [of United States, Sept. 1923]. Oct. 1, 1923. 7 p. 4° (Form A.) [Monthly.] †

INTER-AMERICAN HIGH COMMISSION

Trade-marks. Convention for protection of commercial, industrial, and agricultural trade marks and commercial names, signed in Santiago, Chile, Apr. 28, 1923. 1923. iv+68 p. [English, Spanish, Portuguese, and French.] †
23—26910

INTERNAL REVENUE BUREAU

Income. Statistics of income from returns of net income for [calendar year] 1921, including statistics from Federal estate tax returns [Jan. 16–Dec. 31, 1922]. 1923. iv+185 p. 1 pl. *Paper, 20c.   .18—26569

Income Tax Unit. Laws, regulations, and rules of ethics governing members of Income Tax Unit, July, 1923. 1923. [1]+30 p. 24° ‡   23—26878

Internal revenue bulletin. Internal revenue bulletin, v. 2, no. 26–30; Oct. 1-29, 1923. 1923. various paging. [Weekly.] *Paper, 5c. single copy (for subscription price see note below).   22—26051

NOTE.—On May 7, 1923, the publication of weekly bulletins was resumed and the issuance of monthly bulletins (and special bulletins as occasion required) discontinued. Since May 1, therefore, the 1923 Internal revenue bulletin service consists of weekly bulletins of new rulings and decisions of the Bureau of Internal Revenue and internal revenue Treasury decisions of general importance, quarterly digests of such new rulings (cumulative from Jan. 1, 1922), and semiannual cumulative bulletins containing in full the new rulings and decisions published during the preceding 6 months. The complete bulletin service may be obtained, on a subscription basis, from the Superintendent of Documents, Government Printing Office, Washington, D. C., for $2.00 a yr.; foreign subscription, $2.75.

—— Internal revenue bulletin, digest no. 7; Jan. 1922–June, 1923. 1923. xi+ 313 p. *Paper, 20c. (for subscription price see note above).   22—26463

NOTE.—In spite of information published in recent Internal revenue bulletins to the effect that the digests were to be quarterly, this number covers the semiannual period which follows the last digest numbered 6.

LOANS AND CURRENCY DIVISION

Bonds of United States. Caveat list of United States registered bonds and notes, Oct. 1, 1923. [1923.] 55 p. f° [Monthly.] †

Money. Circulation statement of United States money, Oct. 1, 1923. [1923.] 1 p. oblong 8° [Monthly.] †   10—21267

PUBLIC HEALTH SERVICE

Alum. On composition of precipitate from partially alkalinized alum solutions [with bibliography]; by Lewis B. Miller. 1923. 12 p. il. (Reprint 862.) [From Public health reports, Aug. 31, 1923.] *Paper, 5c.   23—26942

Arsenic. Mechanism of action of arsenic upon protoplasm [with list of references]; by Carl Voegtlin, Helen A. Dyer, and C. S. Leonard. 1923. 32 p. il. (Reprint 860.) [From Public health reports, Aug. 17, 1923.] *Paper, 5c.
23—26943

Automobile cost in rural health work, report on operation of automobiles in cooperative rural health in Virginia; by H. McG. Robertson. 1923. 8 p. (Reprint 864.) [From Public health reports, Aug. 31, 1923.] *Paper, 5c.
23—26944

Bacillus botulinus. Intensive localized distribution of spore of B. botulinus and probable relation of preserved vegetables to type demonstrated; by J. C. Geiger and Harriet Benson. 1923. 7 p. (Reprint 853.) [From Public health reports, July 20, 1923.] *Paper, 5c.   23—26919

Carbon monoxid. Collection and preservation of blood samples for determination of carbon monoxide; by R. R. Sayers, H. R. O'Brien, G. W. Jones, and W. P. Yant. 1923. 8 p. il. (Reprint 863.) [Prepared in cooperation with Mines Bureau. From Public health reports, Aug. 31, 1923.] *Paper, 5c. 23—26945

—— Elimination of carbon monoxide from blood by treatment with air, with oxygen, and with mixture of carbon dioxide and oxygen; by R. R. Sayers and W. P. Yant. 1923. 24 p. il. (Reprint 865.) [Prepared in cooperation with Mines Bureau. From Public health reports, Sept. 7, 1923.] *Paper, 5c. 23—26946

Cells. Studies on permeability of living and dead cells: 1, New quantitative observations on penetration of acids into living and dead cells [with list of references]; by Matilda Moldenhauer Brooks. 1923. 24 p. il. (Reprint 845.) [From Public health reports, June 29, 1923.] *Paper, 5c. 23—26916

—— Same: 3, Penetration of certain alkalies and ammonium salts into living and dead cells [with list of references]; by Matilda Moldenhauer Brooks. 1923. 14 p. il. (Reprint 866.) [From Public health reports, Sept. 7, 1923.] *Paper, 5c.

Contagious diseases. Notifiable diseases, prevalence in cities of over 100,000, 1922. 1923. 28 p. (Reprint 858.) [From Public health reports, Aug. 10, 1923.] *Paper, 5c. 23—26947

Dengue fever [with bibliography]; by C. Armstrong. 1923. 36 p. il. (Reprint 856.) [From Public health reports, Aug. 3, 1923.] *Paper, 5c. 23—26948

Hay fever. Analysis of 6 annual seasons of fall hay fever in New Orleans, La.; by Wm. Scheppegrell. 1923. 12 p. (Reprint 851.) [From Public health reports, July 13, 1923.] *Paper, 5c. 23—26949

Infants. Heat and infant mortality [with bibliography]; by J. W. Schereschewsky. Edition of May, 1923. 1923. [1]+27 p. il. (Reprint 155.) [Original article from Public health reports, Dec. 5, 1913.] *Paper, 5c. 23—26915

Malaria. Spleen and blood examinations for malaria, study of relative merits of spleen and blood parasite indices for determining malaria prevalence as found in Dunklin County, Mo. [with list of references]; by M. V. Veldee. 1923. 8 p. (Reprint 852.) [From Public health reports, July 13, 1923.] *Paper, 5c. 23—26918

Melitensis-abortus bacteria. Nomenclature of melitensis-abortus group of bacterial organisms [with list of references]; Serological classification of Brucella melitensis from human, bovine, carpine, porcine, and equine sources [with list of references]: by Alice C. Evans. 1923. 24 p. il. (Reprint 861.) [From Public health reports, Aug. 24, 1923.] *Paper, 5c. 23—26950

Oxidation. Studies on oxidation-reduction: 4, Electrode potentials of indigo sulphonates, each in equilibrium with its reduction product [with list of references]; by M. X. Sullivan, Barnett Cohen, and W. Mansfield Clark. 1923. 52 p. il. (Reprint 848.) [From Public health reports, July 27, 1923.] *Paper, 10c. 23—26951

Public health reports. Public health reports, v. 38, pt. 1, nos. 1–26, Jan.–June, 1923 [title-page and index]. 1923. xxxii p. *Paper, 5c. single copy, included in price of Public health reports for subscribers.

—— Same, v. 38, no. 40–43; Oct. 5–26, 1923. 1923. [xvi]+2311–2512 p. il. 2 pl. [Weekly.] *Paper, 5c. single copy, $1.50 a yr.; foreign subscription, $2.75. 6—25167

SPECIAL ARTICLES.—No. 40. Pyro-tannic acid method for quantitative determination of carbon monoxide in blood and air; by R. R. Sayers, W. P. Yant, and G. W. Jones.—Health conditions among chemical workers, with respect to earnings; by Frank M. Phillips and Gertrude A. Sager.—Trend of cancer mortality rate in group of insured persons.—Educational campaign against cancer, American Society for Control of Cancer announces series of local campaigns for 1923–24.—No. 41. Pellagra prevention by diet among institutional inmates [with list of references]; by Joseph Goldberger, C. H. Waring, and W. F. Tanner.—Campaign against hookworm in province of Cebu, Philippine Islands.—Report of law division of New York City Department of Health for 1922.—No. 42. Thyroid enlargement among school children of Grand Rapids, Mich.—City health officers, 1923, directory of those in cities of 10,000 or more population.—No. 43. Results of 3-year trachoma campaign begun in Knott County, Ky., in 1913, as shown by survey made in same locality 10 years later; by John McMullen.—Spleen rate of school boys in Mississippi Delta [with bibliography]; by K. F. Maxcy and C. P. Coogle.—Milk to be served in individual containers in Chicago [Ill.].

Public health reports—Continued.

NOTE.—This publication is distributed gratuitously to State and municipal health officers, etc., by the Surgeon General of the Public Health Service, Treasury Department. Others desiring these reports may obtain them from the Superintendent of Documents, Washington, D. C., at the prices stated above.

Rats. Plague-infected rats without visible lesions, discovery of bubonic plague only in rats without lesions or with obscure or apparently trivial lesions, after subsidence of 2 recent epizootics [with list of references] ; by C. L. Williams and T. W. Kemmerer. 1923. 11 p. (Reprint 859.) [From Public health reports, Aug. 17, 1923.] * Paper, 5c.   23—26922

Sulpharsphenamine. Curative action of sulpharsphenamine in experimental syphilis [with list of references] ; by Carl Voegtlin, C. Armstrong, and Helen A. Dyer. 1923. 4 p. (Reprint 857.) [From Public health reports, Aug. 10, 1923.] * Paper, 5c.   23—26921

Temperature. Physiological effects of high temperatures and humidities with and without air movement, effects on body temperature and pulse rate of subjects at rest; by R. R. Sayers and D. Harrington. 1923. 23 p. il. (Reprint 854.) [From Public health reports, July 20, 1923.] * Paper, 5c.
                                                                            23—26920

Virus. Regulations for sale of viruses, serums, toxins, and analogous products in District of Columbia and interstate traffic [in said articles, prepared by board consisting of surgeon general of Army, surgeon general of Navy, and surgeon general of Public Health Service] ; approved Aug. 1, 1923. 1923. [1]+13 p. (Miscellaneous publication 10.) [Supersedes Regulations issued Feb. 12, 1919, and amendments thereto.] * Paper, 5c.   23—26952

VENEREAL DISEASES DIVISION

Sex instruction. Need for sex education for parents and their children. [1923.] [2] p. il. large 8° (v. D. 74.) [Includes lists of books on sex education and venereal disease control for general use recommended by Public Health Service and Education Bureau.] †

Venereal disease information, issued by Public Health Service for use in its cooperative work with State health departments, v. 4, no. 9; Sept. 20, 1923. 1923. ii+331–382 p. [Monthly.] *Paper, 5c. single copy, 50c. a yr.; foreign subscription, 75c.   23—26719

SPECIAL ARTICLES.—Syphilitic headache ; by Paul E. Bowers.—Treatment of syphilis in woman of child-bearing age; [by] Margaret Rorke.

TREASURER OF UNITED STATES

Paper money. Monthly statement, paper currency of each denomination outstanding Aug. 31, 1923. Sept. 1 [1923]. 1 p. oblong 24° †

—— Same Sept. 29, 1923. Oct. 1 [1923]. 1 p. oblong 24° †

VETERANS' BUREAU

Life insurance. Every world war veteran should own United States Government life insurance policy. [1923.] 8 p. il. 24° (Form 705, revised July, 1923.) [Accompanied by a detachable return post card calling for information concerning insurance. This is a combination of Form 705 and 705a, previously issued.] †

Regulations, Veterans' Bureau, 1923; [prepared in Legal Division]. 1923. iv+189 p. ‡   23—26881

NOTE.—This codification of regulations includes all Treasury decisions, Bureau of War Risk Insurance regulations, and such other of Bureau of War Risk Insurance issues as are in the nature of regulations, and all Veterans' Bureau regulations and other orders in the nature of regulations as were in effect at the date of the adoption of the code, June 1, 1923. From time to time cumulative indices will be issued. It is also contemplated that a check system to verify the substitution of pages containing amendments will be instituted, so that the field officers will always be in a position to verify that the regulations as appearing in the field books are the latest issued on any given subject.

WAR DEPARTMENT

Army regulations. †

NOTE.—The Army regulations are issued in pamphlet form for insertion in loose-leaf binders. The names of such of the more important administrative subjects as may seem appropriate, arranged in proper sequence, are numbered in a single series and each name so numbered constitutes the title and number of a pamphlet containing certain administrative regulations pertaining thereto. Where more than one pamphlet is required for the administrative regulations pertaining to any such title, additional pamphlets will be issued in a separate sub-series.

20–35.   Inspector General's Department: Inspection of property for condemnation; Aug. 7, 1923. [1923.] 5 p.
30–905.   Quartermaster Corps: Rail transportation and water transportation on commercial vessels, general; June 1, 1923. [1923.] 3 p.
30–910.   Same: Transportation requests; June 1, 1923. [1923.] 14 p.
30–920.   Same: Transportation of individuals; June 1, 1923. [1923.] 15 p.
30–925.   Same: Sleeping car and similar accommodations; June 1, 1923. [1923.] 6 p.
30–930.   Same: Transportation of troops, general; June 1, 1923. 1923. 6 p.
30–935.   Same: Transportation of troops, railway equipment; June 1, 1923. [1923.] 3 p.
30–940.   Same: Transportation of troops, preparation and listing of property for shipment; June 1, 1923. [1923.] 3 p.
30–945.   Same: Transportation of troops, entraining, duties en route, and detraining; June 1, 1923. [1923.] 14 p.
30–950.   Same: Bills of lading; June 1, 1923. [1923.] 15 p.
30–955.   Same: Transportation of supplies; June 1, 1923. [1923.] 19 p.
30–960.   Same: Transportation of baggage; June 1, 1923. [1923.] 15 p.
30–965.   Same: Transportation of animals; June 1, 1923. [1923.] 27 p.
30–970.   Same: Embargoes; June 1, 1923. [1923.] 3 p.
30–975.   Same: Demurrage; June 1, 1923. [1923.] 7 p. [Corrected print.]
30–1195.   Same: Transportation of individuals on transports, Changes 2; Oct. 1, 1923. 1923. 1 p. [Supersedes AR 30–1195, Changes 1, Feb. 1, 1923.]
30–2110.   Same: Salvage and laundry activities, general provisions; June 6, 1923. [1923.] 4 p.
30–2135.   Same: Laundries; July 1, 1923. [1923.] 11 p.
35–2380.   Finance Department: Additional compensation for enlisted men, except Philippine Scouts, for special qualification in use of arms, Changes 1; Sept. 5, 1923. 1923. 1 p.
35–4520.   Same: Monetary allowances in lieu of rations and quarters for enlisted men, Changes 1; Sept. 1, 1923. 1923. 1 p.
35–6640.   Same: Lost, destroyed, damaged, or unserviceable property; June 13, 1923. [1923.] 13 p.
40–100.   Medical Department: Standards of miscellaneous physical examinations, Changes 1; Sept. 5, 1923. [1923.] 3 p.
45–5.   Ordnance Department: General provisions; June 6, 1923. [1923.] 2 p.
350–1400.   Military education: Army Music School, Changes 1; Sept. 13, 1923. [1923.] 2 p.
615–395.   Enlisted men: Retirement, Changes 3; Aug. 14, 1923. 1923. 1 p. [Supersedes AR 615–395, Changes 1 and 2, June 6 and Aug. 3, 1922.]

Training regulations.

NOTE.—The Training regulations are issued in pamphlet form for insertion in loose-leaf binders.

190–45.   Topography and surveying: Meridian determination, prepared under direction of chief of engineers; July 13, 1923. [1923.] 47 p. il. * Paper, 10c.
420–50.   Infantry: Drill, rifle squad, platoon, and company, prepared under direction of chief of infantry; May 24, 1923. [1923.] 54 p. il. * Paper, 10c.
445–220.   Bridging: Stringer bridges and use of pile and trestle supports, prepared under direction of chief of engineers; July 13, 1923. [1923.] 24 p. il. * Paper, 5c.
445–235.   Bridges: Portable footbridges, prepared under direction of chief of engineers; July 13, 1923. [1923.] 14 p. il. * Paper, 5c.

ADJUTANT GENERAL'S DEPARTMENT

Officers, Army. Officers of Army stationed in or near District of Columbia, Oct. 1923. 1923. iv+39 p. [Quarterly.] * Paper, 5c. single copy, 20c. a yr.; foreign subscription, 30c.   9—35107

U. S. Army recruiting news, bulletin of recruiting information issued by direction of Adjutant General of Army Oct. 1 and 15, 1923. [Recruiting Publicity Bureau, Governors Island, N. Y., Oct. 1 and 15, 1923.] Each 16 p. il. 4° †
Recruiting Publicity Bureau, Governors Island, N. Y.   War 22—1

AIR SERVICE

Aeronautical bulletins. Aeronautical bulletin, no. 11–14, 16–28, 38, Route information series; Sept. 15, 1923. [1923.] various paging, 12°. (Airways Section.) * Paper, 5c. each.   23—26231

—— Aeronautical bulletin,. no. 67–70, State series; Sept. 15, 1923. [1923.] Each 2 p. il. 12° (Airways Section.) * Paper, 5c. each.

ENGINEER DEPARTMENT

Bronx River. Maintenance and improvement of existing river and harbor works, Bronx River, N. Y., dredging and rock removal. [1923.] 15 p. 4° †

Chattahoochee River, Ga. and Ala., proposals for steel-hull stern-wheel towboat, advertisement. [1923.] 35 p. 4°. †

Chicago, Ill. Anchorage ground in harbor at Chicago, Ill., and rules and regulations relating thereto, July 19, 1923. 1923. [1]+6 p. il. †

Officers. Statement showing rank, duties, and addresses of officers of Corps of Engineers, Army, Oct. 1, 1923. 1923. [1]+26 p. 4° [Quarterly; none issued for July. 1923.] ‡ War 14—114

St. Marys River. Maintenance and improvement of existing river and harbor works, St. Marys River, Mich., advertisement [for dredging]. [1923.] 13 p. †

Tacoma, Wash. Maintenance and improvement of existing river and harbor works, Tacoma Harbor (City Waterway), Wash., advertisement [for dredging]. [1923.] 13 p. 4° †

NORTHERN AND NORTHWESTERN LAKES SURVEY

NOTE.—Charts of the Great Lakes and connecting waters and St. Lawrence River to the international boundary at St. Regis, of Lake Champlain, and of the New York State canals are prepared and sold by the U. S. Lake Survey Office, Old Custom-house, Detroit, Mich. Charts may also be purchased at the following U. S. engineer offices: 710 Army Building, New York, N. Y.; 467 Broadway, Albany, N. Y.; 540 Federal Building, Buffalo, N. Y.; and Canal Office, Sault Ste. Marie, Mich. A catalogue (with index map), showing localities, scales, prices, and conditions of sale, may be had upon application at any of these offices.

A descriptive bulletin, which supplements the charts and gives detailed information as to harbors, shore lines and shoals, magnetic determinations, and particulars of changing conditions affecting navigation, is issued free to chart purchasers, upon request. The bulletin is revised annually and issued at the opening of navigation (in April), and supplements thereto are published monthly during the navigation season.

Complete sets of the charts and publications may be seen at the U. S. engineer offices in Duluth, Minn., Milwaukee, Wis., Chicago, Ill., Grand Rapids, Mich., Cleveland, Ohio, and Oswego, N. Y., but they are obtainable only at the sales offices above mentioned.

Great Lakes. Supplement 6, Oct. 20, 1923, corrections and additions to Bulleton 32; to supplement information given upon charts of Great Lakes. U. S. Lake Survey Office, Detroit, Mich. [Oct. 15, 1923.] p. 1–3+leaves 4–10+[2] p. 4° †

Charts

Ashland and Washburn harbors, Wis. Scale 1:15,000. 3d edition. [U. S. Lake Survey Office, Detroit, Mich.] June 11, 1923. 30.1×26 in. †15c.

Beaver Island Group, including north shore of Lake Michigan from Waugoshance Point to Seul Choix Point. Scale 1:80,000. 3d edition. [U. S. Lake Survey Office, Detroit, Mich.] May 10, 1923. 32.4×39.5 in. †25c.

Champlain, Lake. Lake Champlain, from Cumberland Head to Ligonier Point; chart 2. Scale 1:40,000. 4th edition. [U. S. Lake Survey Office, Detroit, Mich.] June 2, 1923. 37.1×27.6 in. †20c.

Cleveland Harbor, Ohio, including lower Cuyahoga River and Ohio Canal. Scale 1:15,000. 4th edition. [U. S. Lake Survey Office, Detroit, Mich.] July 20, 1923. 30×30 in. †20c.

Grand Haven, Mich. Harbor at Grand Haven, Mich., including Spring Lake and lower Grand River. Scale 1:15,000. 3d edition. [U. S. Lake Survey Office, Detroit, Mich.] Sept. 8, 1923. 26.5×30.6 in. †15c.

Green Bay. Head of Green Bay, including Fox River below Depere, Wis. Scale 1:25,000. 4th edition. [U. S. Lake Survey Office, Detroit, Mich.] Sept. 20, 1923. 33.1×24 in. †15c.

Huron, Lake. South end of Lake Huron from Harbor Beach, Mich., and Port Albert, Ont., to head of St. Clair River; coast chart 1. Scale 1:120,000. 4th edition. [U. S. Lake Survey Office, Detroit, Mich.] Oct. 20, 1923. 34.6×27.7 in. †25c.

Mackinac, Straits of. Straits of Mackinac from Presque Isle, Lake Huron, to Charlevoix, Lake Michigan. Scale 1:120,000. 3d edition. [U. S. Lake Survey Office, Detroit, Mich.] May 17, 1923. 28.9×49.1 in. †25c.

Maumee Bay and Maumee River, including Toledo, Ohio. Scale 1:30,000. 2d edition. [U. S. Lake Survey Office, Detroit, Mich.] Aug. 16, 1923. 26.3×34.1 in. †20c.

Michigan, Lake. General chart of Lake Michigan. Scale 1:500,000. 9th edition. [U. S. Lake Survey Office, Detroit, Mich.] July 31, 1923. 44.2×26 in. †25c.

Niagara River. Upper Niagara River from Lake Erie to the Falls. Scale 1:30,000. 4th edition. [U. S. Lake Survey Office, Detroit, Mich.] June 29, 1923. 45×28.4 in. †25c.

St. Clair, Lake. Lake St. Clair. Scale 1:50,000. 9th edition. [U. S. Lake Survey Office, Detroit, Mich.] Oct. 11, 1923. 38×33.3 in. †25c.

St. Lawrence River. St. Lawrence River; chart 4. Scale 1:30,000. 6th edition. [U. S. Lake Survey Office, Detroit, Mich.] June 19, 1923. 24.7×29.7 in. †20c.

—— St. Lawrence River; chart 5. Scale 1:30,000. 8th edition. [U. S. Lake Survey Office, Detroit, Mich.] Aug. 24, 1923. 27×40 in. †20c.

—— St. Lawrence River; with inset, Harbors at Ogdensburg, N. Y., and Prescott, Ontario; chart 3. Scale 1:30,000. 6th edition. [U. S. Lake Survey Office, Detroit, Mich.] Aug. 14, 1923. 26×35.8 in. †25c.

RIVERS AND HARBORS BOARD

Mobile, Ala. Ports of Mobile, Ala., and Pensacola, Fla. 1922. ix+220 p. il. 8 pl. 14 p. of pl. 6 maps, 2 mosaic maps. 5 tab. (Port series 3.) [Prepared in cooperation with Research Bureau, Shipping Board.] *Paper, 75c.

FINANCE DEPARTMENT

Finance circular. Finance circular 5, 7–8 [1923]; May 31–Aug. 31, 1923. [1923.] various paging, 12° ‡

—— Index, Finance circulars, 1922. [1923.] 28 p. 12° ‡

GENERAL STAFF CORPS

Army. Changes 136 [for] Army regulations [1913]; Aug. 29, 1923. [1923.] 2 leaves. [Regulations issued by War Department.] †

Special regulations. Changes 5 [for] Special regulations 33 [Allowances of ammunition for coast artillery target practice, revised 1920]; June 16, 1923. 1923. 1 p. [Special regulations issued by War Department.] †

—— Changes 9 [for] Special regulations 44, pt. 1 [Reserve Officers' Training Corps, revised 1921]; Aug. 7, 1923. 1923. 1 p. [Special regulations issued by War Department.] †

JUDGE ADVOCATE GENERAL'S DEPARTMENT

Opinions. Digest of opinions of judge advocate general of Army, Jan.–Dec. 1922, with decisions of board of review in Office of Judge Advocate General, from its organization, Feb. 4, 1921, to Dec. 31, 1922, opinions of Attorney General, decisions of comptroller general, [and] recent publications and decisions of courts. 1923. iv+156 p. ‡ 18—26585

NOTE.—The Notes on administration of military justice, which have been published with the Digest of opinions of judge advocate general since about 1913, are discontinued as a separate section, beginning Jan. 1, 1922, and such notes are now found in sec. 1 under Digest of opinions of judge advocate general. The section entitled Regulations of Bureau of War Risk Insurance, which has been incorporated in the Digest since 1918, has been discontinued beginning Jan. 1, 1922. The data contained in that section are omitted.

ORDNANCE DEPARTMENT

Ordnance provision system: Group B, Bayonets, bolos, sabers, and their scabbards; July 20, 1923. [1923.] 11 p. (Standard nomenclature list B–8.) [Supersedes Standard nomenclature list B–8, Oct. 25, 1922.] ‡

Monthly Catalogue
United States
Public Documents

No. 347
November, 1923

ISSUED BY THE
SUPERINTENDENT OF DOCUMENTS

WASHINGTON
1924

Abbreviations

Appendix	app.	Page, pages	p.
Congress	Cong.	Part, parts	pt., pts.
Department	Dept.	Plate, plates	pl.
Document	doc.	Portrait, portraits	por.
Facsimile, facsimiles	facsim.	Quarto	4°
Folio	f°	Report	rp.
House	H.	Saint	St.
House bill	H. R.	Section, sections	sec.
House concurrent resolution	H. Con. Res.	Senate, Senate bill	S.
House document	H. doc.	Senate concurrent resolution	S. Con. Res.
House executive document	H. ex. doc.	Senate document	S. doc.
House joint resolution	H. J. Res.	Senate executive document	S. ex. doc.
House report	H. rp.	Senate joint resolution	S. J. Res.
House resolution (simple)	H. Res.	Senate report	S. rp.
Illustration, illustrations	il.	Senate resolution (simple)	S. Res.
Inch, inches	in.	Session	sess.
Latitude	lat.	Sixteenmo	16°
Longitude	long.	Table, tables	tab.
Mile, miles	m.	Thirtytwo-mo	32°
Miscellaneous	mis., misc.	Treasury	Treas.
Nautical	naut.	Twelvemo	12°
No date	n. d.	Twentyfour-mo	24°
No place	n. p.	Versus	vs., v.
Number, numbers	no., nos.	Volume, volumes	v., vol.
Octavo	8°	Year	yr.

Common abbreviations for names of States and months are also used.
*Document for sale by Superintendent of Documents.
†Distribution by office issuing document, free if unaccompanied by a price.
‡Printed for official use.
NOTE.—Nearly all of the Departments of the Government make a limited free distribution of their publications. When an entry shows a * price, it is possible that upon application to the issuing office a copy may be obtained without charge.

Explanation

Words and figures inclosed in brackets [ ] are given for information, but do not appear on the title-pages of the publications catalogued. When size is not given octavo is to be understood. Size of maps is measured from outer edge of border, excluding margin. The dates, including day, month, and year, given with Senate and House documents and reports are the dates on which they were ordered to be printed. Usually the printing promptly follows the ordering, but various causes sometimes make delays.

SALES OF GOVERNMENT PUBLICATIONS

The Superintendent of Documents, Washington, D. C., is authorized to sell at cost of paper and printing, plus 10 per cent, any United States public document in his charge the distribution of which is not otherwise provided for.

Publications can not be supplied free to individuals nor forwarded in advance of payment.

Publications entered in this catalogue that are for sale by the Superintendent of Documents are indicated by a star (*) preceding the price. A dagger (†) indicates that application should be made to the Department, Bureau, or Division issuing the document. A double dagger (‡) indicates that the document is printed for official use. Whenever additional information concerning the method of procuring a document seems necessary, it will be found under the name of the Bureau by which it was published.

In ordering a publication from the Superintendent of Documents, give (if known) the name of the publishing Department, Bureau, or Division, and the title of the publication. If the publication is numbered, give the number also. Every such particular assists in quick identification. Do not order by the Library of Congress card number.

The accumulation of publications in this Office amounts to several millions, of which over two million are assorted, forming the sales stock. Many rare books are included, but under the law all must be sold regardless of their age or scarcity. Many of the books have been in stock some time, and are apt to be shop-worn. In filling orders the best copy available is sent. A general price-list of public documents is not available, but lists on special subjects will be furnished on application.

MONTHLY CATALOGUE DISTRIBUTION

The Monthly catalogue is sent to each Senator, Representative, Delegate, Resident Commissioner, and officer in Congress; to designated depositories and State and Territorial libraries if it is selected by them; to substantially all Government authors; and to as many school, college, and public libraries as the limited edition will supply.

Subscription price to individuals, 50c. a year, including index; foreign subscription, 75c. a year. Back numbers can not be supplied. Notify the Superintendent of Documents of any change of address.

LIBRARY OF CONGRESS CARDS

Numbers to be used in ordering the printed catalogue cards of the Library of Congress are given at the end of entries for the more important documents. Orders for these cards, remittances in payment for them, and requests for information about them should be addressed to the Librarian of Congress, *not* to the Superintendent of Documents.

INDEX

An Index to the Monthly catalogue is issued at the end of the fiscal year. This contains index entries for all the numbers issued from July to June, and can be bound with the numbers as an index to the volume. Persons desiring to bind the catalogue at the end of the year should be careful to retain the numbers received monthly, as duplicate copies can not be supplied.

Remittances for the documents marked with a star (*) should be made to the **Superintendent of Documents, Washington, D. C.**, by coupons, postal money order, express order, or New York draft.; Currency may be sent at sender's risk.

Postage stamps, foreign money, defaced or smooth coins, positively will not be accepted.

For the convenience of the general public, coupons that are good until used in exchange for Government publications sold by the Superintendent of Documents may be purchased from his Office in sets of 20 for $1.00. Address order to Superintendent of Documents, Government Printing Office.

No charge is made for postage on documents forwarded to points in United States, Alaska, Guam, Hawaii, Philippine Islands, Porto Rico, Samoa, or to Canada, Cuba, or Mexico. To other countries the regular rate of postage is charged, and remittances must cover such postage. In computing foreign postage, add one-third of the price of the publication.

AGRICULTURE DEPARTMENT

NOTE.—Those publications of the Department of Agriculture which are for sale will be supplied by the Superintendent of Documents, Washington, D. C. The Department issues a monthly list of publications, which is mailed to all applicants, enabling them to select such reports and bulletins as interest them.

Journal of agricultural research, v. 25, no. 9–12; Sept. 1–22, 1923. 1923. cover-titles, 363–500+[10] p.+[8] leaves, il. 3 pl. 18 p. of pl. [Weekly; Text on p. 2 of covers.], *Paper, 10c. single copy, $4.00 a yr.; foreign subscription, $5.25.   Agr 13—1837

CONTENTS.—No. 9. Specialized varieties of Puccinia glumarum, and hosts for variety tritici [with list of literature cited]; by Charles W. Hungerford and C. E. Owens.—No. 10. Origin and control of apple-blotch cankers [with list of literature cited]; by Max W. Gardner.—Determination of surface area of cattle and swine [with list of literature cited]; by Albert G. Hogan and Charles I. Skouby.—No. 11. Soil temperature as factor affecting pathogenicity of Corticium vagum on pea and bean [with list of literature cited]; by B. L. Richards.—Growing experimental chickens in confinement; by C. A. Herrick, J. E. Ackert, and Bertha L. Danheim.—Acidity of corn and its relation to vegetative vigor [with list of literature cited]; by Annie May Hurd.—No. 12. Bacterial leafspot of clovers [with list of literature cited]; by L. R. Jones, Maude Miller Williamson, F. A. Wolf, and Lucia McCulloch.—New type of orange-rust on blackberry; by B. O. Dodge.—Effect of orange-rusts of Rubus on development and distribution of stomata; by B. O. Dodge.

NOTE.—This publication is published by authority of the Secretary of Agriculture, with the cooperation of the Association of Land-Grant Colleges. It is distributed free only to libraries of agricultural colleges and experiment stations, to large universities, technical schools, and to such institutions as make suitable exchanges with the Agriculture Department. Others desiring the Journal may obtain it from the Superintendent of Documents, Washington, D. C., at the prices stated above.

Official record, Department of Agriculture, v. 2, no. 45–48; Nov. 7–28, 1923. [1923.] Each 8 p. 4° [Weekly.] *Paper, 50c. a yr.; foreign subscription, $1.10.   Agr 22—146

Quarantine. Extension of European corn borer quarantine, Amendment 5 to regulations supplemental to Notice of quarantine 43 (2d revision), as amended, effective Oct. 1, 1923. [1923.] 2 p. (Federal Horticultural Board.) †

——— Modification of pink bollworm quarantine, Amendment 1 to 2d revision of regulations supplemental to Notice of quarantine 52, effective Oct. 15, 1923. [1923.] 2 p. (Federal Horticultural Board.) †

Sunflower investigations; by Ray E. Neidig and Robert S. Snyder. 1923. cover-title, p. 769–780. [From Journal of agricultural research, v. 24, no. 9, June 2, 1923.] ‡

Temperature effects in plant metabolism [with list of literature cited]; by W. E. Tottingham. 1923. cover-title, 13–30+[3] p.+[1] leaf, il. 4 p. of pl. [From Journal of agricultural research, v. 25, no. 1, July 7, 1923.] ‡

Weather, crops, and markets, weekly, Nov. 3–24, 1923; v. 4, no. 18–21. [1923.] p. 457–568, il. 4° *Paper, $1.00 a yr.; foreign subscription, $2.00.
                                                              Agr 22—147

AGRICULTURAL ECONOMICS BUREAU

Rice. United States grades for milled rice recommended by Department of Agriculture, effective Aug. 1, 1923; [by] H. J. Besley, E. G. Boerner, and W. D. Smith. Oct. 1923. 17 p. (Agriculture Dept. Department circular 291.) [Supersedes Markets document 15 and Department circular 133.] *Paper, 5c.   Agr 23—1482

——— United States grades for rough rice recommended by Department of Agriculture, effective Aug. 1, 1923; [by] H. J. Besley, E. G. Boerner, and W. D. Smith. Oct. 1923. 10 p. (Agriculture Dept. Department circular 290.) *Paper, 5c.   Agr 23—1481

Warehouses. United States warehouse act, as amended July 25 [24], 1919, and Feb. 23, 1923. 1923 [reprint]. [1] + 7 p. †

ANIMAL INDUSTRY BUREAU

Barns. Beef-cattle barns; [by E. W. Sheets and M. A. R. Kelley]. [Sept. 1923.]
ii + 17 p. il. (Agriculture [Dept. Farmers' bulletin 1350.) *Paper, 5c.
                                                           Agr 23—1485
Cattle. Judging beef cattle; [by E. H. Thompson]. [Nov. 1919, revised Oct.
1923.] [1923.] ii + 18 p. il. (Agriculture Dept. Farmers' bulletin 1068.)
[Includes lists of Agriculture Department publications relating to beef cattle
industry.] *Paper, 5c.
Directory of Bureau of Animal Industry; corrected to Oct. 1, 1923. 1923. ii +
107 p. *Paper, 15c.   ..   Agr 10—511
Eggs. Natural and artificial incubation of hens' eggs; [by Alfred R. Lee]. [Oct.
1923.] ii + 18 p. il. (Agriculture, Dept. Farmers' bulletin 1363.) [Revi-
sion of Farmers' bulletin 585. Includes lists of Agriculture Department
publications relating to poultry.] *Paper, 5c. ·   Agr 23—1486
Milk. Effect of feeding green alfalfa and green corn on flavor and odor of
milk; by C. J. Babcock. Nov. 16, 1923. 12 p. il. (Agriculture Dept. Department bulletin 1190.) *Paper, 5c.   Agr 23—1478
——— Effect of feeding turnips on flavor and odor of milk; by C. J. Babcock.
Nov. 15' 1923. 8 p. il. (Agriculture Dept. Department bulletin 1208.)
. *Paper, 5c.   Agr 23—1479
Service announcements. Service and regulatory announcements, Oct. 1923;
. [no.] 198. Nov. 1923. p. 85–92. [Monthly.] *Paper, 5c. single copy, 25c. a
. yr.; foreign subscription, 40c...   Agr 7—1658
' Note.—The free distribution of this publication will be limited to persons in the service of the Animal
Industry Bureau, to proprietors of establishments at which the Federal meat inspection is conducted,
to public officials whose duties render it necessary for them to have such information, and to journals
especially concerned. Others desiring copies may obtain them from the Superintendent of Documents,
Washington, D. C., at the prices stated above.
Tuberculosis in animals. Tuberculosis in live stock, detection, control & eradication; [by John A. Kiernan and Alexander E. Wight]. [Nov. 1919, slightly
revised Nov. 1923.] [1923.] 32 p. il. (Agriculture Dept. Farmers' bulletin
1069.) *Paper, 5c.
——— Tuberculosis of hogs; [by John R. Mohler and Henry J. Washburn].
[Feb. 1917, revised Sept. 1923.] [1923.] [2] + 18 p. il. (Agriculture' Dept.
Farmers' bulletin 781.) [Date of original issue incorrectly given on this publication as May, 1917.' Includes lists of Agriculture Department publications
relating to hogs.] *Paper, 5c.

BIOLOGICAL SURVEY BUREAU

Bird houses and how to build them; [by Ned Dearborn]. [Sept. 11, 1914, revised
Nov. 1923.] [1923.] 23 p. il. (Agriculture Dept. Farmers' bulletin 609.)
[Includes lists of Agriculture Department publications relating to protection
and attraction of wild birds.] *Paper, 5c.
Directory of officials and organizations concerned with protection of birds and
game, 1923; [by] George A. Lawyer and Frank L. Earnshaw. Nov. 28, 1923.
16 p. (Agriculture Dept. Department circular 298.) *Paper, 5c. Agr14—1377
Fur-bearing animals. Laws relating to fur animals, for season 1923–24; [by
George A. Lawyer and Frank L. Earnshaw]. [Nov. 1923.] ii+34 p. il.
(Agriculture Dept. Farmers' bulletin 1387.) [Includes lists of Agriculture
Department publications relating to fur animals.] *Paper, 5c. Agr 16—245

CHEMISTRY BUREAU

Palm-kernels. Growth-promoting value of proteins of palm kernel, and vitamin
content of palm-kernel meal; by A. J. Finks and D. Breese Jones. 1923. cover-
title, p. 165–169, il. [From Journal of agricultural research, v. 25, no. 4,
July 28, 1923.] ‡
Service announcements. Service and regulatory announcements, supplement 162.
Nov. 1923. p. 301–324. [Contains Notices of judgment under food and drugs
act 11551–600.] *Paper, 5c.   Agr 14—194
Note.—The free distribution of this publication will be limited to firms, establishments, and journals
especially concerned. Others desiring copies may obtain them from the Superintendent of Documents,
Washington, D. C., at the prices stated above and below.
——— Same, supplement 163. Nov. 28, 1923. p. 325–349. [Contains Notices
of judgment under food and drugs act 11601–650.] *Paper, 5c.

EDITORIAL AND DISTRIBUTION WORK OFFICES

Department bulletins. Department bulletins 1026–50, [title-page] with contents and index; prepared in Office of Editorial Work. 1923. 9+21 p. *Paper, 5c.
—— Same 1076–1100, [title-page] with contents and index; prepared in Office of Editorial Work. 1923. 9+14 p. *Paper, 5c.
—— Same 1101–25, [title-page] with contents and index; prepared in Office of Editorial Work. 1923. 8+16 p. *Paper, 5c.
Farmers' bulletins. Farmers' bulletins [available for distribution] Dec. 1923. [1923.] [4] p. †
—— List of available Farmers' bulletins, Dec. 1, 1923 [classified by subjects; prepared in] Office of Publications. [1923.] [4] p. †

ENTOMOLOGY BUREAU

Bees. Occurrence of diseases of adult bees, 2 [with list of literature cited; by] E. F. Phillips. Nov. 1923. 34 p. (Agriculture Dept. Department circular 287.) *Paper, 5c.   Agr 22—367
Grasshopper control in Pacific States; [by T. D. Urbahns]. [Oct. 1920, revised Sept. 1923.] [1923.] 16 p. il. (Agriculture Dept. Farmers' bulletin 1140.) *Paper, 5c.
Mediterranean fruit-flies. Work and parasitism of Mediterranean fruit fly in Hawaii during 1919 and 1920; by H. F. Willard. 1923. cover-title, p. 1–7. [From Journal of agricultural research, v. 25, no. 1, July 7, 1923.] ‡
Platygaster vernalis Myers, important parasite of Hessian fly; by Charles C. Hill. 1923. cover-title, 31–42+[3] p.+[1] leaf, il. 4 p. of pl. [From Journal of agricultural research, v. 25, no. 1, July 7, 1923.] ‡
Puss caterpillar and effects of its sting on man; [by] F. C. Bishopp. Sept. 1923. 14 p. il. (Agriculture Dept. Department circular 288.) *Paper, 5c.
                                                                      Agr 23—1480

EXPERIMENT STATIONS OFFICE

NOTE.—The Experiment Stations Office was created Oct. 1, 1888, and was merged into the States Relations Service July 1, 1915. The States Relations Service ceased to exist as such July 1, 1923, and the Experiment Stations Office has again become a publishing office.
Experiment station record, v. 49, no. 5; Oct. 1923. 1923. cover-title, ix+401–500 p. [Text and illustration on p. 2 and 4 of cover.] *Paper, 10c. single copy, 75c. per vol. (2 vols. a yr.); foreign subscription, $1.25 per vol. (subscription price incorrectly given in publication).   Agr 9—832
NOTE.—Mainly made up of abstracts of reports and publications on agricultural science which have recently appeared in all countries, especially the United States. Extra numbers called abstract numbers, are issued, 3 to each volume. These are made up almost exclusively of abstracts, that is, they contain no editorial notes and only a limited number of current notes.

ALASKA AGRICULTURAL EXPERIMENT STATIONS

Strawberries. Production of improved hardy strawberries for Alaska; by C. C. Georgeson. Oct. 1923. ii+13 p. 10 p. of pl. (Bulletin 4.) *Paper, 10c.
                                                                      Agr 23—1416

HAWAII AGRICULTURAL EXPERIMENT STATION

Sweet potato in Hawaii; by H. L. Chung. Oct. 1923. ii+20 p. 4 p. of pl. (Bulletin 50.) *Paper, 10c.   Agr 23—1417

PORTO RICO AGRICULTURAL EXPERIMENT STATION

Phosphates. Efficiencies of phosphatic fertilizers as affected by liming and by length of time phosphates remained in Porto Rican soils [with list of literature cited]; by P. L. Gile and J. O. Carrero. 1923. cover-title, p. 171–194, il. [From Journal of agricultural research, v. 25, no. 4, July 28, 1923.] ‡

FEDERAL HORTICULTURAL BOARD

Service announcements. Service and regulatory announcements, July–Sept. 1923; [no.] 76. Nov. 1923. p. 99–131. *Paper, 5c.   Agr 14—383

.ı) ıı.   FOREST SERVICE

Basket willow culture; by George N. Lamb.   Dec. 10, 1914, revised July, 1923.
. [1923.]ˊ. 32 p. il.   (Agriculture Dept. .Farmers' bulletin 622.)   *Paper, 5c.
Forest Service directory, Oct. 1923; no. 7. .[1923.] .43 p. .16° [Semiannual.] ‡
Agr 21—224
Wood preservation. , Preservative treatment of farm timbers; by George M.
Hunt. Sept. 21, 1916, revised Sept. 1923. [1923.]   32 p. il.   (Agriculture
, Dep_t. Farmers' bulletin 744.) .*Paper, 5c.

Maps

Fremont National Forest, Oreg., its purpose and its resources, information map.
[1923.]   1 sheet (with map on verso), il. large 4°, folded into narrow 8° size
and so printed as to number [1]+15+[1] p. †
National forests.. Vacation in national forests [including lists of national forests
, by districts].. [1923.]   1 sheet (with map on verso), oblong large 8°, folded
into 24° size and so printed as to number [3]+7 p. †
Olympic National .Forest. Map of Olympic National Forest [resources and
recreation features, roads, trails, etc.]. [1923.]   1 sheet (with map on verso),
'il. oblong f°, folded into narrow 8° size and so printed as to number 20+[2]
p. †
Oregon. Road and recreation map, Oregon. [1923.] 1 sheet (with map on
verso); il. f°, folded into narrow 8° size and so printed as to number [1]+16 + [1]
p. †
Santiam National Forest, Oreg. [resources and recreation features, trails, etc.].
' [1923.] 1 sheet (with map on verso), il. large 4°, folded into narrow 8° size
and so printed as to number [1]+13+[1] p. †
Whitman National Forest, Oreg. [resources and recreation features, roads,'
trails, .etc.]. ' [1923.] 1 sheet (with map on verso), il. large 4°, folded into
narrow 8° size and so printed as to number [1]+12+[1] p. †

PLANT INDUSTRY BUREAU

Bordeaux-oil emulsion [with list of literature cited]; by John R. Winston, John
J. Bowman, and W. W. Yothers. Nov. 21, 1923.   24 p. il.   (Agriculture
Dept. Department bulletin 1178.)   [Prepared in cooperation with Entomol-
ogy Bureau.] *Paper, 5c.ˊ   Agr 23—1476
Chrysanthemums for the home; [by B. Y. Morrison]. [Nov. 1923.] .ii+17
p. il. (Agriculture Dept. Farmers' bulletin 1311.) *Paper, 5c. Agr 23-1483
Cotton. Growth of fruiting parts in cotton plant; by R. D. Martin, W. W. Ballard,
and D. M. Simpson. 1923. cover-title, 195–208+[1] p.+[1] leaf, 2 p. of pl.
[From Journal of agricultural research, v. 25, no. 4, July 28, 1923.] ‡
Cucumbers; [by L. C. Corbett]. [1906, revised Oct. 1923.] [1923.] 31 p. il.
(Agriculture Dept. Farmers' .bulletin 254.) , *Paper, 5c.
Dahlias for the home; [by B. Y. Morrison]. [Nov. 1923.] ii+17 p. il. (Agri-
culture Dept. Farmers' bulletin 1370.) *Paper, 5c.   Agr 23-1499
Fig growing in South Atlantic and Gulf States, [by H. P. Gould; with contribu-
tions by others]. [Mar. 1919, revised Oct. 1923.] [1923.]. 48 p. il. (Agriculture Dept. Farmers' bulletin 1031.) [Includes lists of Agriculture Department publications on subjects related to fruit growing.] *Paper, 10c.
Flax-stem anatomy in relation to retting; by Robert L. Davis. Oct. 1923. 27 p.
il. (Agriculture Dept. Department bulletin 1185.) *Paper, 5c.   Agr 23-1479
Pectinase. Influence of substrate and its hydrogen-ion concentration on pectinase production [with list of literature cited]; by L. L. Harter and J. L. Weimer.
1923. cover-title, p. 861–878. [From Journal of agricultural research, v. 24,
no. 10, June 9, 1923.] ‡
Root-knot, its cause and control; [by G. H. Godfrey]. [Oct. 1923.] ii+27 p. il.
(Agriculture Dept. Farmers' bulletin 1345.) [Revision of Farmers' bulletin
648.] *Paper, 5c.   ,   .   Agr 23-1484
Seeds. Inventory of seeds and plants imported by Office of Foreign Seed and
Plant Introduction, Apr. 1–June 30, 1921, no. 67; nos. 52855–53895. Oct. 1923.
iv+100 p. il. 6 p. of pl. * Paper, 15c.   .Agr 7-1331

Seeds—Continued. Same,' July 1–Sept. 30, 1921; no. 68; nos. 53896–54425. Oct. 1923. iii+65 p. 4 p. of pl. *Paper, 10c.
—— Same, Oct. 1–Dec. 31, 1921, no. 69; nos. 54426–676. Oct. 1923. iii+41 p. il. 6 p. of pl. *Paper, 10c.

Stripe rust. Specialized varieties of Puccinia glumarum and hosts for variety tritici [with list of literature cited]; by Charles W. Hungerford and C. E. Owens. 1923. cover-title, 363–402+[5] p. 6 p. of pl. [Prepared in coöperation with Oregon and Idaho Agricultural Experiment Stations. From Journal of agricultural research, v. 25, no. 9, Sept. 1, 1923.] ‡

Sweet potatoes. Acid production by Rhizopus tritici in decaying sweet potatoes; by H. A. Edson. 1923. cover-title, p. 9–12. [From Journal of agricultural research, v. 25, no. 1, July 7, 1923.] ‡

WEATHER BUREAU

Climate. Concerning normals, secular trends, and climatic changes; by Charles F. Marvin. 1923. [1]+383–390 p. il. 4° [From Monthly weather review, Aug. 1923.] †

Climatological data for United States by sections, v. 10, no. 8; Aug. 1923. [1923.] cover-title, [188] p. il. 2 maps, 2 p. of maps, 4° [Text on p. 2 of cover.] *Paper, 35c. complete monthly number, $4.00 a yr.   Agr 14–566

NOTE.—Made up of separate Climatological data issued from 42 section centers of the United States. Printed at the several section centers and assembled and bound at the Washington Office. Issued principally for service use and exchange. The separate Climatological data are sold by the Superintendent of Documents, Washington, D. C., at the rate of 5c. single copy, 50c. a yr. for each section.

Electric wiring. Instructions for wiring meteorological instruments; by Roy N. Covert. 1923. iii+44 p. il. 3 pl. 2 p. of pl. (App. 2, Circular D, Instrument Division.) *Paper, 15c.

Frost. Efficiency of smoke screens as protection from frost; by H. H. Kimball and B. G. MacIntire. 1923. [1]+396–399 p. il. 4° [From Monthly weather review, Aug. 1923.] †

Meteorology. Improved method of computing meteorological normals; by H. W. Clough. 1923. [1]+391–395 p. il. 4° [From Monthly weather review, Aug. 1923.] †

—— Monthly meteorological summary, Washington, D. C., Oct. 1923. [1923.] [2] p. large 8° †

Mexico. Temperature of Mexico, by Jesus Hernández; [translated by W. W. Reed]. July 16, 1923. iii+24 p. il. 4 maps, 48 p. of maps, 4° (Monthly weather review supplement 23.) *Paper, 25c. (incorrectly given in publication as 10c.).

Ocean. Weather of the oceans, Aug. 1923, with special reference to north Atlantic and north Pacific oceans (including charts), notes, abstracts, and reviews; issued by Marine Division. 1923. 7 p. 4 p. of maps, 4° [From Monthly weather review, Aug. 1923.] †

Weather map. Daily weather map [of United States, containing forecasts for all States east of Mississippi River except Illinois, Wisconsin, Indiana, upper Michigan, and lower Michigan], Nov. 1–30, 1923. 1st edition. [1923.] Each 16.4×22.7 in. [Not issued Sundays or holidays.] *Editions issued at Washington, D. C., 25c. a month, $2.50 a yr.; editions issued at about 65 stations throughout the United States, 20c. a month, $2.00 a yr.

—— Same [containing forecasts for United States], Nov. 1–30, 1923. 2d edition. [1923.] Each 16.4×22.7 in. [The Sunday edition does not contain as much information as the edition for week days.] *30c. a month, $3.00 a yr.

CIVIL SERVICE COMMISSION

NOTE.—The commission furnishes its publications gratuitously to those who apply for them.

Civil service act and rules, retirement and classification acts, statutes, Executive orders, and regulations, with notes and legal decisions; amended to Sept. 1, 1923. 1923. iii+154 p. †   23–26953

Deaf and dumb. Circular in regard to admission of deaf-mutes to civil-service examinations. Oct. 1923. 4 p. (Form 1786.) †

Post offices. [Instructions relative to manner of making nominations for original appointments in post offices.] July, 1921 [reprint 1923]. 4 p. (Form 1576.) †

Postal service. Instructions to applicants for post-office service, 11th civil-service district, headquarters, Seattle, Wash. Sept. 1923. 16+[1] p. (Form 1898.) †

Pos'ers. Wanted for civil service, Government always needs men and women for employment in civil service, in force so large, vacancies are constantly occurring; [all lettered poster]. Nov. 1923. 16×12.5 in. (Form 2227.) [Cancels previous issues.] †

Reentry in classified service. Oct. 1923. 8 p. (Form 126.) †

Removals. Information concerning removals, reductions, suspensions, and furloughs. Oct. 1923. 8 p. (Form 505.) †

COMMERCE DEPARTMENT

CENSUS BUREAU

NOTE.—Persons desiring 14th census publications should address the Director of the Census, Department of Commerce, Washington, D. C. They are also sold by the Superintendent of Documents, Washington, D. C., at the price indicated.

Abstract of 14th census of United States, 1920. 1923. 1303 p. il. *Cloth, $1.50. 23–26954

NOTE.—This volume contains all of the essential statistics collected at the census of 1920 for population, occupations, agriculture, irrigation, drainage, manufactures, and mines and quarries.

Canning and preserving. Census of manufactures, 1921: Canning and preserving. 1923. 30 p. *Paper, 5c. 23–26988

Coke. Census of manufactures, 1921: Coke. 1923. 11 p. *Paper, 5c. 23–26973

Cotton. Cotton consumed, cotton on hand, active cotton spindles, and imports and exports of cotton, Oct. 1922 and 1923, with statistics of cotton consumed, imported, and exported for 3 months ending Oct. 31. Nov. 14, 1923. oblong 32° [Preliminary report. This publication is issued in postal card form.] †

—— Report on cotton ginning, number of bales of cotton ginned from growth of 1923 prior to Nov. 1, 1923 and comparative statistics to corresponding date in 1922 and 1921. Nov. 8, 1923. oblong 32° [Preliminary report. This publication is issued in postal card form.] †

—— Same prior to Nov. 14, 1923; and comparative statistics to corresponding date in 1922 and 1921. Nov. 21, 1923. oblong 32° [Preliminary report. This publication is issued in postal card form.] †

Cottonseed received, crushed, and on hand, and cottonseed products manufactured, shipped out, on hand, and exported covering 3-month period ending Oct. 31, 1923 and 1922. Nov. 19, 1923. oblong 32° [Preliminary report. This publication is issued in postal card form.] †

Knit goods. Census of manufactures, 1921: Knit goods. 1923. 16 p. *Paper, 5c. 23–26974

Mortality statistics, [calendar year] 1921. 1923. 112 p. 4° (Bulletin 152.) [Prepared under direction of William H. Davis, chief statistician for vital statistics, assisted by John B. Mitchell, expert chief of division.] *Paper, 25c. 23–26989

Pipe. Census of manufactures, 1921: Cast-iron pipe. 1923. 7 p. *Paper, 5c. 23–26990

Population. Estimates of population of United States by States and cities, 1910–23, and area, July 1, 1922. 1923. 140 p. [Prepared under supervision of Charles S. Sloane, geographer of the census.] *Paper, 15c. 23–26975

—— 14th census of United States, 1920: Center of population and median lines, and centers of area, agriculture, manufactures, and cotton. 1923. 41 p. il. 4° [Prepared under supervision of Charles S. Sloane, geographer of the census.] *Paper, 10c. 23–26991

—— 14th census of United States, 1920: v. 2, Population, 1920, general report and analytical tables. 1922. 1410 p. il. 4° [Prepared under supervision of William C. Hunt, chief statistician for population, assisted by Olive M. Riddleberger and LeVerne Beales, special agents for population, and Walter Laidlaw.] *Cloth, $2.50.

Tobacco. Leaf tobacco held by manufacturers and dealers, Oct. 1, 1923 and 1922, and July 1 and Apr. 1, 1923. Oct. 30, 1923. oblong 32° [This publication is issued in postal card form.] †

COAST AND GEODETIC SURVEY

NOTE.—The monthly Notice to mariners, formerly issued by the Coast and Geodetic Survey, has been consolidated with and made a part of the Notice to mariners issued by the Lighthouses Bureau, thus making it a joint publication. The charts, coast pilots, and tide tables of the Coast and Geodetic Survey are sold at the office of the Survey in Washington, and also by one or more sales agents in each of the important American seaports.

Coast and Geodetic Survey bulletin, Oct. 31, 1923; no. 101. [1923.] 8 p. [Monthly.] †‡
15–26512

Compass. Instructions for compensation of magnetic compass [with list of references]; by N. H. Heck, with cooperation of W. E. Parker. 1923. iv+49 p. il. 3 pl. 8 p. of pl. (Special publication 96; serial 238.) *Paper, 15c.
23–26992

Charts

Great Harbor, Culebra Island, W. I., surveys to 1923 and other sources; chart 913. Scale 1:6,500. Washington, Coast and Geodetic Survey, Nov. 1923. 31.4×38.1 in. †75c.

Hampton Roads, Va., surveys to 1920, surveys by U. S. Engineers to 1921, surveys by U. S. Navy to 1923; [with inset, Continuation to Norfolk, Va.]; chart 400. Scale 1:20,000. Washington, Coast and Geodetic Survey, Oct. 1923. 34×40.9 in. †75c.

Houston ship channel, Tex., surveys by U. S. Engineers to 1920, surveys by Geological Survey and other sources; chart 532. Scale 1:25,000. Washington, Coast and Geodetic Survey, Oct. 1923. 29.2×34.7 in. [Map is divided into 2 sections.] †75c.

Hudson River, Days Point to Fort Washington Point, N. Y.-N. J., original surveys 1885–86, surveys by U. S. Engineers to 1923 and other sources; chart 369³. Scale 1:10,000. Washington, Coast and Geodetic Survey, Nov. 1923. 40.8×28.1 in. †75c.

Massachusetts, Ipswich Bay to Gloucester Harbor, original surveys 1853–1919, surveys by Mass. Harbor and Land Commission to 1916, surveys by U. S. Engineers to 1914 and other sources; chart 243. Scale 1:20,000. Washington, Coast and Geodetic Survey, Oct. 1923. 33.8×38.7 in. †75c.

Mendocino, Cape. Cape Mendocino and vicinity, Calif., surveys to 1921; chart 5795. Scale 1:40,000. Washington, Coast and Geodetic Survey, Nov. 1923. 37.9×24.9 in. †50c.

New York Harbor, upper bay and Narrows, anchorage chart, surveys 1885–1919, surveys by U. S. Engineers to 1923 and other sources; chart 541. Scale 1:10,000. Washington, Coast and Geodetic Survey, Oct. 1923. 43.6×34.3 in. †75c.

Oregon-Washington, Columbia River to Destruction Island, surveys to 1922, surveys by U. S. Engineers to 1923 and other sources; chart 6002. [Scale 1:200,000.] Washington, Coast and Geodetic Survey, Nov. 1923. 39.1×31.7 in. †75c.

Port Orchard, Wash., southern part, surveys 1875–1915, surveys by U. S. Engineers to 1904, surveys by U. S. Navy to 1923; chart 6444. Scale 1:20,000. Washington, Coast and Geodetic Survey, Oct. 1923. 33.5×38.3 in. †75c.

Porto Rico, east coast, San Juan Passage to Port Humacao, and western part of Vieques Island, original surveys 1900–23; chart 917. Scale 1:40,000. Washington, Coast and Geodetic Survey, Oct. 1923. 41.5×33.8 in. †75c.

San Miguel Bay. San Miguel and Lamit bays, east coast of Luzon, P. I., original surveys 1906–21, Bicol River from survey by Bureau of Navigation in 1911; with inset, Bicol River from mouth of Naga; chart 4223. [Scale 1:100,000.] Manila, P. I., Coast and Geodetic Survey, Aug. 1923. 40.9×29.3 in. †75c.

Sinclair Inlet, Puget Sound, Wash., Navy Yard from survey by U. S. Navy in 1923; chart 6440. Scale 1:10,000. Washington, Coast and Geodetic Survey, Nov. 1923. 22.9×31.8 in. †25c.

Surigao Strait and vicinity, northeast coast of Mindanao, P. I., surveys 1907–11 and other sources; chart 4603. Scale naut. m.=0.4 in. Washington, Coast and Geodetic Survey, Feb. 1913, reissued at Manila, P. I., June, 1923. 43.7×34.9 in. †75c.

Tillamook Bay, Oreg., surveys 1866–1902, surveys from U. S. Engineers to July, 1923; chart 6112. Scale 1:20,000. Washington, Coast and Geodetic Survey, Nov. 1923. 32.3×26 in. †50c.

Umpqua River, Oreg., entrance bar to Reedsport, surveys to 1920, surveys by U. S. Engineers to June, 1923; chart 6004. Scale 1:20,000. Washington, Coast and Geodetic Survey, Nov. 1923. 23.9×27.8 in. †25c.

Zamboanga Peninsula, Mindanao, west coast, P. I., surveys to 1922; chart 4605. [Scale 1:200,000.] Manila, P. I., Coast and Geodetic Survey, Aug. †1923. 41.1×33.8 in. †75c.

FISHERIES BUREAU

Aquatic plants in pond culture; by John W. Titcomb. 2d edition. 1923. [1]+ 24 p. il. 1 pl. (Bureau of Fisheries doc. 948.) [App. 2, report of commissioner of fisheries, 1923. The 1st edition of this paper, Bureau of Fisheries document 643, was published separately in 1909, and also as part of the Fisheries Bureau report for 1907.] *Paper, 10c.   F 23–276

Cold storage holdings, of fish, Oct. 15, 1923. [1923.] 1 p. oblong 8° (Statistical bulletin 589.) [Statistics furnished by Agricultural Economics Bureau.]   †

Creosote. Toxicities of coal tar creosote, creosote distillates, and individual constituents for marine wood borer, Limnoria lignorum; by L. F. Shackell. 1923. ii+221–230 p. il. large 8° ([Bureau of Fisheries] doc. 952.) [From Bulletin, v. 39.] *Paper, 5c.   F 23–279

Fisheries service bulletin, Nov. 1, 1923; no. 102. [1923.] 7 p. [Monthly]. †
                                                                        F 15–76

Fishery products. Statement of quantities and values of certain fishery products landed at Boston and Gloucester, Mass., and Portland, Me., by American fishing vessels, Oct. 1923. [1923.] 1 p. oblong f° (Statistical bulletin 590.) †

—— Statement of quantities and values of certain fishery products landed at Seattle, Wash., by American fishing vessels, Oct. 1923. [1923.] 1 p. oblong 12° (Statistical bulletin 591.) †

Mussels. Significance of larval mantle of fresh-water mussels during parasitism, with notes on new mantle condition exhibited by Lampsilis luteola [and with list of literature cited]; by Chester N. Blystad. 1923. [1]+203–219 p. il. large 8° ([Bureau of Fisheries] doc. 950.) [From Bulletin, v. 39.] *Paper, 10c.   F23–278

Whitefish. Artificial propagation of whitefish, grayling, and lake trout; by Glen C. Leach. 1923. [1]+32 p. il. 6 pl. 10 p. of pl. (Bureau of Fisheries doc. 949.) [App. 3, report of commissioner of fisheries, 1923.] *Paper, 15c.
                                                                        F23–277

FOREIGN AND DOMESTIC COMMERCE BUREAU

Commerce. Commerce yearbook, 1922 (including early part of 1923). 1923. viii+692 p. il. 5 maps. [Prepared in cooperation with Census Bureau.] *Cloth, 60 c.   23—26993

—— Monthly summary of foreign commerce of United States, Sept. 1923. 1923. 2 pts. p. 1–69 and ii+71–91 p. 4° *Paper, 10 c. single copy (including pts. 1 and 2), $1.00 a yr.; foreign subscription, $1.60.   14—21465

—— Same. 1923. [2 pts. in 1], 91 p. 4° (H. doc. 9, 68th Cong. 1st sess.)

Commerce reports. Commerce reports, weekly survey of foreign trade, reports from American consular officers and representatives of Department of Commerce in foreign countries, no. 45–48; Nov. 5–26, 1923. 1923. cover-titles, p. 329–592, il. 4° [Text and illustrations on p. 2–4 of covers.] *Paper, 10c. single copy, $3.00 a yr.; foreign subscription, $5.00.

—— Supplement to Commerce reports. [Included in price of Commerce reports for subscribers.]

Trade and economic review for 1922, no. 24: Chile; prepared in Latin American Division from report by George A. Makinson. [1923.] 22 p.
Same, no. 25: Bolivia; [by] Dayle C. McDonough. [1923.] 16 p.
Same, no. 26: Guatemala; [by] Robert C. Frost. [1923.] 15 p.
Same, no. 27: Costa Rica; prepared by Latin American Division from reports by Henry S. Waterman, John J. Meily, and from various supplemental material. [1923.] 22 p.
Same, no. 28: Union of South Africa; [by] Charles J. Pisar. [1923.] 36 p.
Same, no. 29: Salvador; by Lynn W. Franklin. [1923.] 6 p.
Same, no. 30: Netherlands East Indies; by Charles L. Hoover. [1923.] 26 p.
Same, no. 31: Madagascar; [by] James G. Carter. [1923.] 4 p.
Same, no. 32: Dominican Republic; by Charles Bridgham Hosmer. [1923.] 11 p.

Commerce reports—Continued. Supplement to Commerce reports: Belgian wool industry; by S. H. Cross. Nov. 1923. ii+15 p. (Trade information bulletin 160; Textile Division.) †		23—26958

——— Same: Economic conditions in Cuba; by Paul L. Edwards. Oct. 29, 1923. ii+18 p. (Trade information bulletin 159; Latin American Division.) †		23—26957

——— Same: London market for American textiles; by Hugh D. Butler. Nov. 5, 1923. ii+16 p. (Trade information bulletin 161; Textile Division.) †		23—26959

——— Same: Principal features of Chilean finances; by Charles A. McQueen. Nov. 26, 1923. ii+24 p. (Trade information bulletin 162; Finance and Investment Division.) †		23—26994

Mexican west coast and Lower California, commercial and industrial survey [with list of reference material]; by P. L. Bell and H. Bentley Mackenzie, with assistance of Francis J. Dyer, Bartley F. Yost, and W. E. Chapman. 1923. xvi+340 p. 10 p. of pl. map. (Special agents series 220.) *Cloth, 85c.		23—26960

Oils. World trade in vegetable oils and animal fats; by J. E. Wrenn. 1923. vi+214 p. il. (Miscellaneous series 123.) *Paper, 25c.		23—26956

Organization. Helping exporter, service story step by step [organization and service of Foreign and Domestic Commerce Bureau]. 1923. [1]+50 p. il. †		23—26955

LIGHTHOUSES BUREAU

7th District. Atlantic Coast of United States, buoy list, Florida Reefs and Gulf Coast to Cedar Keys, 7th lighthouse district; 1923, corrected to Oct. 1. 1923. [1]+72 p. *Paper, 20c.		11—28290

8th District. Gulf Coast of United States, buoy list, Cedar Keys to Rio Grande, 8th lighthouse district; 1923, corrected to Oct. 15. 1923. 75 p. *Paper, 20c.		11—29933

19th District. Pacific islands of United States, buoy list, Hawaiian, [Midway, Guam, and American] Samoan islands, 19th lighthouse district; 1923, corrected to Nov. 1, 1923. [1]+14 p. [Of the American Samoan Islands only Tutuila is included in this publication.] *Paper, 20c.		11—34531

Notice to mariners, weekly, no. 44—48, 1923; Nov. 2–30 [1923]. 1923. various paging. [Issued jointly with Coast and Geodetic Survey.] †		7—20609

NAVIGATION BUREAU

Ships. American documented seagoing merchant vessels of 500 gross tons and over, Nov. 1, 1923. 1923. ii+69 p. 4° (Serial 72.) [Monthly.] *Paper, 10c. single copy, 75c. a yr.; foreign subscription, $1.25.		19—26597

RADIO SERVICE

Radio Service bulletin, Nov. 1, 1923; no. 79. [1923.] 18 p. [Monthly.] *Paper, 5c. single copy, 25c. a yr.; foreign subscription, 40c.		15—26255

PUBLICATIONS DIVISION

Commerce Department. Supplement to annual List of publications [of Department of Commerce available for distribution], Oct. 31, 1923. [1923.] 4 p. [Monthly.] †

STANDARDS BUREAU

NOTE.—The Scientific papers will be supplied on subscription as issued at $1.25 per volume, paper bound. These volumes will afterwards be issued bound in cloth at $2.00 per volume; foreign subscription, paper $2.50 (sent in single numbers), cloth $2.35 (bound volumes). Single numbers vary in price. Address the Superintendent of Documents, Washington, D. C.
    The Technologic papers will be issued first as separates and later in volume form in the same manner as the Scientific papers. Subscriptions will be accepted by the Superintendent of Documents at $1.25 per volume; foreign subscription, $2.50. Single numbers vary in price.

Asphalt. Asphalt. 1923. 6 p. (Simplified practice recommendation no. 4.) [Title on cover is: Elimination of waste, simplified practice, asphalt. Recommendation becomes effective Jan. 1, 1924.] *Paper, 5c.

Belting. United States Government specification for leather belting, Federal Specifications Board,* Standard specification 37, officially adopted by Federal Specifications Board, July 3, 1922, for use of Departments and independent establishments of Government in purchase of leather belting. Oct. 10, 1923. 9 p. il. large 8° (Circular 148.) *Paper, 5c. 23—26961

Electricity. Standards for electric service [with bibliography]. 2d edition. Sept. 26, 1923. [1]+344 p. (Circular 56.) *Paper, 60c. 23—26976

Fences. Woven-wire fencing. Sept. 1, 1923. 7 p. (Simplified practice recommendation no. 9.) [Title on cover is: Elimination of waste, simplified practice, woven-wire fencing.] *Paper, 5c.

Radio communication. Spectroradiométric analysis of radio signals; by Chester Snow. Oct. 22, 1923. [1]+231–261 p. il. (Scientific papers 477.) [From Scientific papers, v. 19.] *Paper, 10c. 23—26997

Steel. Comparison of deoxidation effects of titanium and silicon on properties of rail steel; by George K. Burgess [and] G. Willard Quick. Oct. 1, 1923. [1]+581–635 p. il. (Technologic papers 241.) [From Technologic papers, v. 17.] *Paper, 10c. 23—26977

Tires.[1] Dynamometer tests of automobile tires; by W. L. Holt [and] P. L. Wormeley. Sept. 24, 1923. [1]+559–579 p. il. 1 pl. 2 p. of pl. (Technologic papers 240.) [From Technologic papers, v. 17.] *Paper, 10c. 23—26998

STEAMBOAT INSPECTION SERVICE

Licenses. Provisional licenses [canceled and not surrendered], circular letter, Aug. 28, 1923. [1923.] 11 p. ‡

Steamboat Inspection Service bulletin, Nov. 1, 1923; no. 97. [1923.] 2 p. [Monthly.] ‡ 15—26679

CONGRESS

Statutes at large, Apr. 1921–Mar. 1923, concurrent resolutions, and recent treaties, conventions, and Executive proclamations; edited under direction of Secretary of State. 1923. v. 42, 2 pts. [ccclxix]+2684 p. il. 10 maps, 8 p. of maps, large 8° [Pt. 1 contains the public acts and resolutions; pt. 2, the private acts and resolutions, concurrent resolutions, treaties, and proclamations. The contents are the same as those of the Pamphlet or Session laws, for the four sessions of the 67th Congress, but with a different arrangement.] *Cloth, pt. 1, $3.25; pt. 2, $2.00. 7—35353

FEDERAL PRISONERS, JOINT COMMITTEE TO DETERMINE WHAT EMPLOYMENT MAY BE FURNISHED

Employment for Federal prisoners, memorandum of Heber H. Votaw, superintendent of prisons, H. Con. Res. 53, Nov. 3, 1923. 1923. pt. 2, ii+15–19 p. [Part 1, which is the hearing of June 13, 1923, appeared in Monthly catalogue for Aug. 1923, p. 64.] †

HOUSE OF REPRESENTATIVES

Life insurance. Laws of 65th, 66th, and 67th Congresses relating to insurance: public law 20, 90, 151, 175, 195, 272, 312 [65th Congress]; public res. 22, 27, 52 [65th Congress]; proclamations nos. 1366, 1386, and public law 193, 63d Congress; public law 209, 64th Congress; public law 387, 64th Congress; public res. 44, 66th Congress; public law 11, 66th Congress; public law 99, 66th Congress; public law 26, 66th Congress; public law 104, 66th Congress; [extract from] public law 105, 66th Congress; public law 47, 67th Congress; [extract from] public law 109, 67th Congress; public law 194, 67th Congress; public law 216, 67th Congress; public law 273, 67th Congress; public law 361, 67th Congress; public law 370, 67th Congress; public law 460, 67th Congress; [and] public law 542, 67th Congress. 1923. 86 p. [These laws include war risk insurance and soldiers' compensation and insurance laws.] * Paper, 10c.

AGRICULTURE COMMITTEE

Nitrate, statement relative to production of nitrates; by Gray Silver, Washington representative American Farm Bureau Federation. 1923. cover-title, x+ 75 p. il. 4 pl. 6 maps. (Series HH, 2d supplement.) †

SENATE

Prohibition amendment to Constitution of United States. [Reprint] 1923. 4 p. (State Dept.) ‡

GOLD AND SILVER INQUIRY COMMISSION

Gold and silver statistics, Commission of Gold and Silver Inquiry, Senate, pursuant to S. Res. 469, creating Commission of Gold and Silver Inquiry, Aug. 28, 1923; prepared by H. N. Lawrie, assistant to commission. 1923. vii + 182 p. il. (Serial 3.) †

Silver Producers' Convention, report of hearings before Commission of Gold and Silver Inquiry, Senate, and proceedings of Pan-American Silver Producers' Convention at Reno, Nev., Sept. 4 and 5, 1923, pursuant to S. Res. 469, creating Commission of Gold and Silver Inquiry. 1923. ii+64 p. (Serial 4.) †

PUBLIC LANDS AND SURVEYS COMMITTEE

Naval petroleum reserves. Leases upon naval oil reserves, hearings on S. Res. 282, S. Res. 294, and S. Res. 434, Oct. 23 [-Nov. 2], 1923. 1923. pts. 2, 3, [v]+175-821 p. †

VETERANS' BUREAU INVESTIGATION SELECT COMMITTEE

Veterans' Bureau. Investigation of Veterans' Bureau, hearings pursuant to S. Res. 466, authorizing appointment of committee to investigate leases and contracts executed by Veterans' Bureau, and for other purposes, Oct. 22 [-Nov. 1], 1923. 1923. pts. 1, 2, [iv]+1-559 p. 15 pl. 3 tab. †

COURT OF CLAIMS

Ætna Casualty and Surety Company v. United States; agreed statement of facts. [1923.] no. C-8, p. 9-18. ‡

Allgrunn. Carl G. Allgrunn *v.* United States; evidence for plaintiff. [1923.] p. 31-407. ‡

Cadwalader. John Cadwalader *v.* United States; evidence for plaintiff [and] defendant. [1923.] no. B-20, p. 17-75. ‡

Chicago Great Western Railway Company v. United States; evidence for defendant. [1923.] no. B-72, p. 45-48. ‡

Cygnet Manufacturing Co. v. United States; evidence for plaintiff. [1923.] 115-A, p. 13-75. ‡

Denver & Rio Grande Railway Company v. United States; defendant's evidence. [1923.] no. 153-B, p. 25-32. ‡

Dewey Brothers Co. v. United States; evidence for plaintiff. [1923.] no. B-47, p. 15-81. ‡

El Paso and Southwestern Company. El Paso and Southwestern Company et al. *v.* United States; evidence for plaintiff. [1923.] no. 38-A, p. 49-87. ‡

—— El Paso and Southwestern Co. et al. *v.* United States; evidence for plaintiff. [1923.] no. 278-A, p. 43-63. ‡

—— El Paso & Southwestern Co. et al. *v.* United States; evidence for plaintiff. [1923.] no. 279-A, p. 25-51. ‡

—— El Paso and Southwestern Company et al. *v.* United States; evidence for plaintiff. [1923.] no. 294-A, p. 39-70. ‡

—— El Paso and Southwestern Co. et al. *v.* United States; evidence for plaintiff. [1923.] no. 310-A, p. 47-54. ‡

—— El Paso & Southwestern Company et al. *v.* United States; evidence for plaintiff. [1923.] no. B-66, p. 37-54. ‡

—— El Paso and Southwestern Company et al. *v.* United States; evidence for plaintiff. [1923.] no. B-77, p. 19-26. ‡

—— El Paso and Southwestern Co. et al. *v.* United States; evidence for plaintiff. [1923.] no. 34753, p. 47-61. ‡

El Paso and Southwestern System. El Paso and Southwestern Company et al., doing business as El Paso Southwestern System, *v.* United States; evidence for defendant. [1923.] no. B-66, p. 21-24. ‡

Illinois Central Railroad Company v. United States; findings of fact [conclusion of law, and opinion of court], decided Nov. 5, 1923. [1923.] no. B-116, 8 p. ‡

Iselin, William, & Co. William E. Iselin et al., copartners, doing business under firm name of William Iselin & Company, *v.* United States; evidence for defendant. [1923.] ' no. B–13, 'p. 273–296. ‡

Locomobile Company. Elmer H. Havens, trustee in bankruptcy of Locomobile Company, *v.* United States; evidence for plaintiff. [1923.]   no. B–355, . p. 65–84. ‡

Maguire & Co. (*Inc.*), *v.* United States; evidence for plaintiff [and] defendant. [1923.] no. 75–B, p. 11–90. ‡

Marr. Walter L. Marr *v.* United States; findings of fact [conclusion of law, and memorandum], decided Nov. 21, 1923. [1923.] no. C–12, 5 p. ‡

Meagher, S. A., Company. S. A. Meagher Company *v.* United States; evidence for plaintiff. [1923.] no. B–431, p. 23–190. ‡

Miller, James S., Company. Fred E. Hummel, trustee in bankruptcy of James S. Miller Company, *v.* United States; findings of fact [conclusion of law, and opinion of court], decided Oct. 29, 1923. [1923.] no. B–61, 7 p. ‡

Nugent Construction Company v. United States; evidence for defendant. [1923.] no. B–100, p. 207–209. ‡

Ordnance Engineering Corporation. Ordnance Engineering Corporation *v.* United States; evidence for claimant. [1923.] no. B–5, p. 79–142. ‡

—— Ordnance Engineering Corporation *v.* United States; evidence for defendants. [1923.] no. 34680, p. 967–1346. ‡

Osage Nation of Indians *v.* United States; evidence for plaintiff. [1923.] no. B–38, p. 89–117. ‡

Products Manufacturing Company v. United States; evidence for plaintiff. [1923.] no. B–392, p. 15–35. ‡

Snare. Frederick, Corporation. Frederick Snare Corporation *v.* United States; testimony for plaintiff. [1923.] no. B–199, p. 21–52. ‡

Southern Pacific Company. Southern Pacific Company *v.* United States; evidence for defendant. [1923.] no. B–37, p. 23–27. ‡

—— Southern Pacific Company *v.* United States; evidence for plaintiff. [1923.] no. B–418, p. 7–22. ‡

—— Southern Pacific Co. *v.* United States; evidence for plaintiff. [1923.] no. C–356, p. 7–26. ‡

Swartz. Nell R. Swartz *v.* United States; evidence. [1923.] no. B–271, p. 5–17. ‡

Turner, C. A. P., Company. C. A. P. Turner Company *v.* United States; defendant's evidence. [1923.] no. 259–A, p. 255–771, il. ‡

Twin City Forge & Foundry Company v. United States; evidence for plaintiff. [1923.] no. A–212, p. 131–561. ‡

COURT OF CUSTOMS APPEALS

Camel's hair. No. 2286, United States *v.* Rice & Fielding, Inc., transcript of record on appeal from Board of General Appraisers. [1923.] cover-title, i+28 p. ‡

Cases adjudged in Court of Customs Appeals, Feb. 1921–July, 1923, Alex. H. Clark, reporter; [with Rules of Court of Customs Appeals, corrected to July 1, 1923]. 1923. xx+713 p. (Court of Customs Appeals reports, v. 11.) *Cloth, $1.00.

Linen. No. 2306, United States *v.* Glendinning, McLeish & Co., Inc., transcript of record on appeal from Board of General Appraisers. 1923. cover-title, i+7 p. ‡

DISTRICT OF COLUMBIA

Weights, Measures, and Markets Department. Public no. 358; 66th Congress [H. R. 8067, act to establish standard weights and measures for District of Columbia, to define duties of superintendent of weights, measures, and markets of District of Columbia, and for other purposes] as amended by public no. 72, 67th Congress. [1923.] 10 p. ‡

FEDERAL BOARD FOR VOCATIONAL EDUCATION

Farm management. Analysis of management of a farm business, managerial-training content of type jobs of farm as business unit; [by C. H. Schopmeyer]. Oct. 1923. v +28 p. (Bulletin 88; Agricultural series 16.) [Includes lists of Agriculture Department publications relating to farm management.] *Paper, 5c.   E 23–406

FEDERAL RESERVE BOARD

Federal reserve bulletin. Federal reserve bulletin, Nov. 1923; [v. 9, no. 11]. 1st edition. 1923. ii +371–405 p. il. map, 4° [Monthly.] † Paper, $1.50 a yr.
                                                                            15–26318.

> NOTE.—The Federal reserve bulletin is printed in 2 editions (a 1st edition and a final edition). The 1st edition is brief and contains the regular official announcements, the national review of business conditions, and other general matter, and is distributed without charge to the member banks of the Federal reserve system. The 2d or final edition contains detailed analyses of business conditions, special articles, review of foreign banking, and complete statistics showing condition of Federal reserve banks. Those desiring copies of either edition may obtain them from the Federal Reserve Board, Washington, D. C., at the prices stated above and below.

—— Same, Nov. 1923; [v. 9, no. 11]. Final edition. 1923. iv +1175–1249 + ii p. il. map, 4° [Monthly.] † Paper, 40c. single copy, $4.00 a yr.

Federal reserve member banks. Abstract of condition reports of State bank and trust company members, and of all member banks of Federal reserve system, Sept. 14, 1923. Nov. 9, 1923. 12 p. f° (Report 22.) †

—— Federal reserve inter-district collection system, changes in list of banks upon which items will be received by Federal reserve banks for collection and credit, Nov. 1, 1923. 1923. [1]+18 p. 4° †   16–26870

FEDERAL TRADE COMMISSION

> NOTE.—The bound volumes of the Federal Trade Commission decisions are sold by the Superintendent of Documents, Washington, D. C. Separate opinions are sold on subscription, price $1.00 per volume; foreign subscription, $1.50; single copies, 5c. each.

American Film Company. Federal Trade Commission *v.* American Film Company, complaint [report, findings, and order]; docket 903, Apr. 11, 1923. [1923.] p. 89–96. ([Decision] 356.) [From Federal Trade Commission decisions, v. 6.] *Paper, 5c.

Aristo Hosiery Company. Federal Trade Commission *v.* Aristo Hosiery Company, complaint [report] findings, and order; docket 685, Apr. 11, 1923. 1923. [1]+84–88 p. ([Decision] 355.) [From Federal Trade Commission decisions, v. 6.] *Paper, 5c.

Austin-Western Road Machinery Company. Federal Trade Commission *v.* Austin-Western Road Machinery Company, complaint [report, modified findings, and order]; docket 434, Mar. 29, 1923. [1923.] p. 69–73. ([Decision] 352.) [From Federal Trade Commission decisions, v. 6.] *Paper, 5c.

Big Diamond Oil and Refining Company. Federal Trade Commission *v.* Big Diamond Oil & Refining Co. et al., complaint [report, findings, and order]; docket 795, Mar. 16, 1923. [1923.] p. 51–59. ([Decision] 350.) [From Federal Trade Commission decisions, v. 6.] *Paper, 5c.

Brown Durrell Company. Federal Trade Commission *v.* Brown Durrell Company, complaint [report, findings, and order]; docket 678, Apr. 11, 1923. [1923.] 79–83 +[1] p. ([Decision] 354.) [From Federal Trade Commission decisions, v. 6. Includes list of Cases in which orders for discontinuance or dismissal have been entered, Apr. 11, 1923.] *Paper, 5c.

Claire Furnace Company. No. 250, in Supreme Court, Oct. term, 1923, Federal Trade Commission et al. *v.* Claire Furnace Company et al., on appeal from Court of Appeals of District of Columbia; brief for appellants. 1923. cover-title, v +105 p. ‡

Hyman & Zaslav. Federal Trade Commission *v.* Eli Hyman and Louis M. Zaslav, partners, doing business under name and style of Hyman and Zaslav, complaint [report, findings, and order]; docket 948, Apr. 11, 1923. [1923.] p. 97–100. ([Decision] 357.) [From Federal Trade Commission decisions, v. 6.] *Paper, 5c.

Lone Star Oil Company. Federal Trade Commission *v.* Lone Star Oil Company et al., complaint [report] findings, and order; docket 796, Mar. 23, 1923. 1923. [1]+60–68+[1] p. ([Decision] 351.) [From Federal Trade Commission decisions, v. 6. Includes list of Cases in which orders for discontinuance or dismissal have been entered, Mar. 24, 1923.] *Paper, 5c.

Pilling & Madeley. Federal Trade Commission *v.* Pilling and Madeley, complaint [report] findings, and order; docket 698, Apr. 5, 1923. 1923. [1]+74–78+[1] p. ([Decision] 353.) [From Federal Trade Commission decisions, v. 6. Includes list of Cases in which orders for discontinuance or dismissal have been entered, Apr. 10, 1923.] *Paper, 5c.

Sizz Chemical Company. Federal Trade Commission *v.* Sizz Chemical Co. et al., complaint [report, findings, and order]; docket 942, Mar. 9, 1923. [1923.] 35–42+[1] p. ([Decision] 348.) [From Federal Trade Commission decisions, v. 6. Includes list of Cases in which orders for discontinuance or dismissal have been entered, Mar. 12, 1923.] *Paper, 5c.

United Fibre Works. Federal Trade Commission *v.* John T. Bailey, trading under name and style of United Fibre Works, complaint [report, findings, and order]; docket 955, Apr. 11, 1923. [1923.] p. 101–106. ([Decision] 358.) [From Federal Trade Commission decisions, v. 6.] *Paper, 5c.

GENERAL ACCOUNTING OFFICE

Decisions. Decisions of comptroller general, v. 3, Sept. 1923, and index, July–Sept. 1923; J. R. McCarl, comptroller general, Lurtin R. Ginn, assistant comptroller general. 1923. [1]+115–179+xvii p. [Monthly.] † 21–26777

——— Same, v. 3, Oct. 1923; J. R. McCarl, comptroller general, Lurtin R. Ginn, assistant comptroller general. 1923. [1]+179–281 p. [Monthly.] †

GOVERNMENT PRINTING OFFICE

DOCUMENTS OFFICE

Census publications, statistics for population, agriculture, manufactures, and mining, with abstracts and compendiums, list of publications for sale by superintendent of documents. Oct. 1923. [2]+30 p. (Price list 70, 3d edition.) † 23–26962

Children. Children's Bureau [publications] and other publications relating to children for sale by superintendent of documents. Oct. 1923. [2]+10 p. (Price list 71, 3d edition.) † 23–26963

Dwellings. Publications of interest to home seekers and housekeepers [for sale by superintendent of documents]. [1923.] 1 p. 4° [Manuscript correction.] †

Monthly catalogue, United States public documents, no. 346; Oct. 1923. 1923. p. 157–212. *Paper, 5c. single copy, 50c. a yr.; foreign subscription, 75c.
4–18088

Radio communication. Important radio publications [for sale by superintendent of documents]. [1923.] 1 p. 4° [This list contains 39 titles. Rubber stamp corrections have been made.] † 23–26999

INTERIOR DEPARTMENT

NOTE.—The decisions of the Department of the Interior in pension cases are issued in slips and in signatures, and the decisions in land cases are issued in signatures, both being published later in bound volumes. Subscribers may deposit $1.00 with the Superintendent of Documents and receive the contents of a volume of the decisions of either kind in separate parts as they are issued; foreign subscription, $1.25. Prices for bound volumes furnished upon application to the Superintendent of Documents, Washington, D. C.

Pensions. [Decisions of Department of Interior in appealed pension and bounty land claims, v. 21, slip] 85–87 pension. [1923.] Each 2 p. or 3 p. [For price, see note above under center head.] 12–29422

Public lands. Decisions [of Department of Interior in cases] relating to public lands, v. 49, [signatures] 40–42. [1923.] p. 625–672. [For price, see note above under center head.] 7–23651

St. Elizabeths Hospital. Proposal and specifications for erection and completion of 7 bungalows at St. Elizabeths Hospital, Washington, D. C. 1923. 13 p. 4° †

EDUCATION BUREAU

Consolidation of schools and transportation of pupils in Lafayette Parish, La.; [by J. W. Faulk]. 1923. [1]+10 p. il. ([Rural school leaflet 19.]) *Paper, 5c. E23–405

Education. Biennial survey of education, 1918–20: Statistics. 1923. iii+597 p. il. (Bulletin 29, 1923.) *Cloth, $1.00. E21–504

CONTENTS.—Statistical survey of education, 1919–20; [by Florence DuBois].—Statistics of State school systems, 1919–20; [by Florence DuBois and H. R. Bonner].—City school systems, 1919–20.—Statistics of universities, colleges, and professional schools, 1919–20.—Teachers' colleges and normal schools, 1919–20.—Statistics of public high schools. 1919–20.—Private high schools and academies, 1919–20.—Private commercial and business schools, 1919–20.—Nurse training schools, 1919–20.—Statistics of kindergartens, 1919–20.—Index.

Latin America. Outline of education systems and school conditions in Latin America; by George W. A. Luckey. 1923. iii+111 p. il. (Bulletin 44, 1923.) *Paper, 15c. E23–404

School life, v. 9, no. 3; Nov. 1923. [1923.] p. 49–72, il. 4° [Monthly except July and August.] *Paper, 5c. single copy, 30c. a yr. (10 months); foreign subscription, 55c. E18–902

GENERAL LAND OFFICE

NOTE.—The General Land Office publishes a large general map of the United States, which is sold at $2.00; and also separate maps of the States and Territories in which public lands are to be found, which are sold at 25c. per sheet. The map of California is in 2 sheets. Address the Superintendent of Documents, Washington, D. C.

Public lands. Vacant public lands on July 1, 1923. [1923.] 22 p. (Circular 901.) †

GEOLOGICAL SURVEY

NOTE.—The publications of the United States Geological Survey consist of Annual reports, Monographs, Professional papers, Bulletins, Water-supply papers, chapters and volumes of Mineral resources of the United States, folios of the Topographic atlas of the United States and topographic maps that bear descriptive text, and folios of the Geologic atlas of the United States and the World atlas of commercial geology. The Monographs, folios, and maps are sold. Other publications are generally free: as long as the Survey's supply lasts. Copies are also sold by the Superintendent of Documents, Washington, D. C., at the prices indicated. For maps and folios address the Director of the Geological Survey, Washington, D. C. A discount of 40 per cent is allowed on any order for maps or folios that amounts to $5.00 or more at the retail price. This discount applies to an order for either maps or folios alone or for maps and folios together but is not allowed on a few folios that are sold at 5c. each on account of damage by fire. Orders for other publications that are for sale should be sent to the Superintendent of Documents, Washington, D. C. For topographic maps see p. 232.

Abrasive materials in 1922; by L. M. Beach and A. T. Coons. Dec. 3, 1923. [1]+221–225 p. [From Mineral resources, 1922, pt. 2.] †

Alaskan mining industry in 1922; by Alfred H. Brooks and Stephen R. Capps. 1923. ii+1–56+xiv p. (Bulletin 755 A.) [Includes lists of recent Geological Survey publications on Alaska.] †

CONTENTS.—Preface; by Alfred H. Brooks.—Alaskan mining industry in 1922; by Alfred H. Brooks and S. R. Capps.—Administrative report; by Alfred H. Brooks and George C. Martin.

Animals, Fossil. New fauna from Colorado group of southern Montana; by John B. Reeside, jr. Nov. 5, 1923. ii+25–33 p. 11 p. of pl. 4° (Professional paper 132 B.) †

Barytes and barium products in 1922; by George W. Stose. Nov. 3, 1923. [1]+141–152 p. [From Mineral resources, 1922, pt. 2.] †

Coal in 1919, 1920, and 1921; by F. G. Tryon and Sydney A. Hale. Oct. 24, 1923. v+445–662 p. il. map, 1 tab. in pocket. [From Mineral resources, 1921, pt. 2.] †

Geology. Contributions to economic geology, 1922: pt. 1, Metals and nonmetals except fuels; F. L. Ransome, G. R. Mansfield, and E. F. Burchard, geologists in charge. 1923. x+336 p. il. 4 pl. 8 p. of pl. 3 maps. (Bulletin 735.) *Paper, 55c. GS 5–748

CONTENTS.—Introduction.—Candelaria silver district, Nev.; by Adolph Knopf.—Colemanite in Clark County, Nev.; by L. F. Noble.—Bonanza ores of Comstock lode, Virginia City, Nev.; by Edson S. Bastin.—Silver enrichment in San Juan Mountains, Colo.; by Edson S. Bastin.—Primary native-silver ores near Wickenburg, Ariz., and their bearing on genesis of silver ores of Cobalt, Ontario; by E. S. Bastin.—General features of brown hematite ores of western North Carolina; by W. S. Bayley.—General features of magnetite ores of western North Carolina and eastern Tennessee; by W. S. Bayley.—Peridotite dikes in Scott County, Ark.; by Hugh D. Miser and Clarence S. Ross.—Diamond-bearing peridotite in Pike County, Ark. [with bibliography]; by Hugh D. Miser and Clarence S. Ross.—Los Burros district, Monterey County, Calif.; by James M. Hill.—Index.

—— Same. (H. doc. 457, 67th Cong. 3d sess.)

Geology—Continued.

Same: pt. 2, Mineral fuels; K. C. Heald, geologist in charge. 1923. vi+254 p. il. 13 pl. 4 are in pocket, 11 maps, 4 are in pocket, 1 tab. (Bulletin 736.) *Paper, 60c.

CONTENTS.—Introduction.—Structure of Madill-Denison area, Okla. and Tex., with notes on oil and gas development; by O. B. Hopkins, Sidney Powers, and H. M. Robinson.—Oil and gas prospects in and near Crow Indian Reservation, Mont.; by W. T. Thom, jr.—Geology of Wiles area, Ranger district, Tex.; by Carroll E. Dobbin.—Osage oil field, Weston County, Wyo.; by A. J. Collier.— Geology of Ranger oil field, Tex.; by Frank Reeves.—Possibility of finding oil in laccolithic domes south of Little Rocky Mountains, Mont.; by A. J. Collier and S. H. Cathcart.—Brooks, Steen, and Grand Saline salt domes, Smith and Van Zandt counties, Tex.: by Sidney Powers and Oliver B. Hopkins.—Stratigraphy of El Dorado oil field, Ark., as determined by drill cuttings; by James Gilluly and K. C. Heald.—Index.

—— Same. (H. doc. 458, 67th Cong. 3d sess.)

—— Shorter contributions to general geology, 1922; David White, chief geologist. 1923. iv+212 p. il. 5 pl. 44 p. of pl. map, I tab. 4° (Professional paper 131.)·*Paper, 60c.   GS15–90

CONTENTS.—Additions to flora of Wilcox group; by Edward Wilber Berry.—Section of Paleozoic formations of Grand Canyon at Bass trail; by L. F. Noble.—Shapes of beach pebbles; by Chester K. Wentworth.—Geologic reconnaissance in Gulf Coastal Plain of Texas near Rio Grande; by A. C. Trowbridge.—New species of Mollusca from Eocene deposits of southwestern Texas; by Julia Gardner.—Preliminary report on fossil vertebrates of San Pedro Valley, Ariz., with descriptions of new species of Rodentia and Lagomorpha; by James W. Gidley.—Revision of flora of Green River formation, with descriptions of new species; by F. H. Knowlton.—Fossil plants from Tertiary lake beds of south-central Colorado; by F. H. Knowlton.—Fauna of so-called Dakota formation of northern central Colorado and its equivalent in southeastern Wyoming; by John B. Reeside, jr.—Index.

—— Same. (H. doc. 62, 68th Cong. 1st sess.)

Gold. Gold, silver, copper, and lead in South Dakota and Wyoming in 1922, mines report; by C. W. Henderson. Nov. 20, 1923. ii+193–198 p. [From Mineral resources, 1922, pt. 1.] †

—— Gold, silver, copper, lead, and zinc in New Mexico and Texas in 1922, mines report; by Charles W. Henderson. Nov. 28, 1923. ii+199–215 p. [From Mineral resources, 1922, pt. 1.] †

Green River Valley. Notes on geology of Green River Valley between Green River, Wyo., and Green River, Utah; by John B. Reeside, jr. Nov. 30, 1923. ii+35–50 p. il. 4° (Professional paper 132 C.) †

Lime in 1922; by G. F. Loughlin and A. T. Coons. Dec. 1, 1923. [1]+195–206 p. [From Mineral resources, 1922, pt. 2.] †

Mica in 1922 [with bibliography]; by B. H. Stoddard. Nov. 14, 1923. [1]+153–164 p. [From Mineral resources, 1922, pt. 2.] †

Oligocene period. . Correlation of Vicksburg group, by C. Wythe Cooke; and Foraminifera of Vicksburg group, by Joseph A. Cushman. 1923. ii+71 p. 8 p. of pl. 1 tab. 4° (Professional paper 133.) *Paper, 20c.   GS23–331

.—┐ Same. (H. doc. 75, 68th Cong. 1st sess.)

Publications. New publications, list 188; Nov. 1, 1923. [1923.] 4 p. [Monthly.] †

Secondary metals in 1922, by J. P. Dunlop; [with Secondary nonferrous metals, by W. M. Corse]. Nov. 7, 1923. ii+173–191 p. [From Mineral resources, 1922, pt. 1.] †

Silica in 1922; by Frank J. Katz. Nov. 27, 1923. [1]+183–186 p. [From Mineral resources, 1922, pt. 2.] †

Sulphur and pyrites in 1922; by H. A. C. Jenison and H. M. Meyer. Nov. 16, 1923. [1]+177–181 p. [From Mineral resources, 1922, pt. 2.] †

Topographic maps

NOTE.—The Geological Survey is making a topographic map of the United States. The individual maps of which it is composed are projected without reference to political divisions, and each map is designated by the name of some prominent town or natural feature in the area mapped. Three scales are ordinarily used, 1:62,500, 1:125,000, and 1:250,000. These correspond, approximately, to 1 mile, 2 miles, and 4 miles to 1 linear inch, covering, respectively, average areas of 230, 920, and 3,700 square miles. For some areas of particular importance special large-scale maps are published. The usual size, exclusive of the margin, is 17.5 inches in height by 11.5 to 16 inches in width, the width varying with the latitude. The sheets measure 20 by 16½ inches. A description of the topographic map is printed on the reverse of each sheet.

More than two-fifths of the area of the country, excluding Alaska, has been mapped, every State being represented. Connecticut, Delaware, the District of Columbia, Maryland, Massachusetts, New Jersey, Ohio, Rhode Island, and West Virginia are completely mapped. Maps of the regular size are sold by the Survey at 10c. each, but a discount of 40 per cent is allowed on any order which amounts to $5.00 or more at the retail price. The discount is allowed on an order for either maps or folios alone or for maps and folios together, but does not apply to a few folios that are sold at 5c. each on account of damage by fire.

California. California, Bullard quadrangle, lat. 36° 45′–36° 52′ 30″, long. 119° 45′–119° 52′ 30″. Scale 1:31,680, contour interval 5 ft. [Washington, Geological Survey] edition of 1923. 17.2×13.9 in. †10c.

California—Continued.   California, Englebrecht Ranch quadrangle, lat. 36°
 30'–36°·37' 30'', long. 120° 15'–120° 22' 30''. Scale 1:31,680, contour interval
 5 ft. [Washington, Geological Survey] edition of 1923. 17.2×13.9 in. †10c.

Illinois.   Illinois, Buda quadrangle, lat. 41° 15'–41° 30', long. 89° 30'–89° 45'.
 Scale 1:62,500, contour interval 20 ft. [Washington, Geological Survey]
 edition of 1923. 17.5 ×13.2 in. †10c.

—— Illinois-Missouri, Jonesboro quadrangle, lat. 37° 15'–37° 30', long. 89°
 15'–89° 30'. Scale 1:62,500, contour interval 20 ft., [Washington, Geological
 Survey] edition of 1923. 17.5×14 in. †10c.

Michigan, Marshall quadrangle, lat. 42° 15'–42° 30', long. 84° 45'–85°. Scale
 1:62,500, contour interval 10 ft. [Washington, Geological Survey] edition of
 1923. 17.5×13 in. †10c.

Mississippi, Tupelo quadrangle, lat. 34° 15'–34° 30', long. 88° 30'–88° 45'.
 Scale 1:62,500, contour interval 20 ft. [Washington, Geological Survey]
 edition of 1923. 17.5×14.5 in. †10c.

New York State.   New York, Cattaraugus quadrangle, lat. 42° 15'–42° 30', long.
 78° 45'–79°. Scale 1:62,500, contour interval 20 ft. [Washington, Geological
 Survey] edition of 1923. 17.5×13 in. †10c.

—— New York, Santa Clara quadrangle, lat. 44° 30'–44° 45', long. 74° 15'–
 74° 30'. Scale 1:62,500, contour interval 20 ft. [Washington, Geological
 Survey] edition of 1923. 17.5×12.5 in. †10c.

Pennsylvania; Trout Run quadrangle, lat. 41° 15'–41° 30', long.· 77°–77° 15'.
 Scale 1:62,500, contour interval 20 ft. [Washington, Geological Survey]
 edition of 1923. 17.5×13.2 in. †10c.

Texas, Ketchum Mountain quadrangle, lat. 31° 15'–31° 30', long. 101°–101° 15'.
 Scale 1:62,500, contour interval 25 ft. [Washington, Geological Survey]
 edition of 1923. 17.5×15 in. †10c.

West Virginia.   Virginia-West Virginia, Callaghan quadrangle, lat. 37° 45'–38°,
 long. 80°–80° 15'. Scale 1:62,500, contour interval 50 ft. [Washington, Geological Survey] edition of 1923. 17.5×13.9 in. [Map covers only a portion of
 the sheet,the actual measurement being 16.9 ×13.9 in. Shows only the portion of Callaghan quadrangle that lies in West Virginia.] ‡10c.

—— Virginia-West Virginia, Pearisburg quadrangle, lat. 37° 15'–37° 30', long.
 80° 30'–80° 45'. Scale 1:62,500, contour interval 50 ft. [Washington,
 Geological Survey] edition of 1923. 17.5×14 in. [Map covers only a portion
 of the sheet, the actual measurement being 8.4×14 in. Shows only the portion
 of Pearisburg quadrangle that lies in West Virginia.] †10c.

—— West Virginia, Alderson quadrangle, lat. 37° 30'–37° 45', long. 80° 30'–
 80° 45'. Scale 1:62,500, contour interval 50 ft. [Washington, Geological
 Survey] edition of 1923. 17.5×14 in. †10c.

—— West Virginia, Hanging Rock quadrangle, lat. 39° 15'–39° 30', long.
 78° 30'–78° 45'. Scale 1:62,500, contour interval 50 ft. [Washington,
 Geological Survey] edition of 1923. 17.5×13.6 in. †10c.

—— West Virginia, White Sulphur Springs quadrangle, lat. 37° 45'–38°, long.
 80° 15'–80° 30'. Scale 1:62,500, contour interval 50 ft. [Washington, Geological Survey] edition of 1923. 17.5×13.9 in. †10c.

—— West Virginia-Virginia, Orkney Springs quadrangle. lat. 38° 45'–39°, long.
 78° 45'–79°. Scale 1:62,500, contour interval 50 ft. [Washington, Geological
 Survey] edition of 1923. 17.5×13.7 in. [Map covers only a portion of the
 sheet, the actual measurement being 16.7×13.7 in. Shows only the portion
 of Orkney Springs quadrangle that lies in West Virginia.] †10c.

MINES BUREAU

Breathing-apparatus.   Self-contained mine rescue oxygen breathing apparatus,
 handbook for miners; by D. J. Parker, G. S. McCaa, and E. H. Denny. [1st
 edition.] [Sept.] 1923. xiv +139 p. il. 3 pl. small 4° *Paper, 20c. 23–26979

Change houses in Lake Superior region; by Cleve E. Kindall. [1st edition.]
 [Sept.] 1923. iv +31 p. il. 2 pl. 10 p. of pl. (Technical paper 289.) [Includes
 lists of Mines Bureau publications on wash and change houses.] *Paper, 15c.
 23—26964

Flotation. Certain interfacial tension equilibria important in flotation; by Will
H. Coghill and Carl O. Anderson. [1st edition.] [Sept.] 1923. vi+55 p. il. 1
pl. (Technical paper 262.) [This report was prepared under a cooperative
agreement with the University of Washington. Includes lists of MinesBureau
publications on flotation.] *Paper, 10c.   23—26980

Petroleum. Methods of decreasing evaporation losses of petroleum; by J. H.
Wiggins. [1st edition.] [Aug.] 1923. vi+57 p. il. 1 pl. 10 p. of pl. (Technical paper 319.) [Includes lists of Mines Bureau publications on oil-field
technology.] * Paper, 15c.   23—26981

PATENT OFFICE

NOTE.—The Patent Office publishes Specifications and drawings of patents in single copies. These are
not enumerated in this catalogue, but may be obtained for 10c. each at the Patent Office.
   A variety of indexes, giving a complete view of the work of the Patent Office from 1790 to date, are published at prices ranging from 25c. to $10.00 per volume and may be obtained from the Superintendent of
Documents, Washington, D. C.   The Rules of practice and pamphlet Patent laws are furnished free of
charge upon application to the Patent Office. The Patent Office issues coupon orders in packages of 20 at
$2.00 per package, or in books containing 100 coupons at $10.00 per book. These coupons are good until
used, but are only to be used for orders sent to the Patent Office. For schedule of office fees, address Chief
Clerk, Patent Office, Washington, D. C.

Carr, Edward G. In Court of Appeals of District of Columbia, Oct. term, 1923,
patent appeal no. 1650, *in re* Edward G. Carr, construction car; brief for
commissioner of patents. 1923. cover-title, 9 p. ‡

Decisions. [Decisions in patent· and trade-mark cases, etc.] Nov. 6, 1923.
p. 1–8, large 8° [From Official gazette, v. 316, no. 1.] †Paper, 5c. single
copy, $2.00 a yr.   23—7315

—— Same. Nov. 13, 1923. p. 231–238, large 8° [From Official gazette, v.
316, no. 2.]

—— Same. Nov. 20, 1923. p. 453–462, large 8° [From Official gazette, v.
316, no. 3.]

—— Same. Nov. 27, 1923. p. 701–710, large 8° [From Official gazette, v.
316, no. 4.]

Official gazette. Official gazette, Nov. 6–27, 1923; v. 316, no. 1–4. 1923. cover-
titles, 924+[clxvi] p. il. large 8° [Weekly.] *Paper, 10c. single copy, $5.00
a yr.; foreign subscription, $11.00.   4—18256

   NOTE.—Contains the patents, trade-marks, designs, and labels issued each week; also decisions of
the commissioner of patents and of the United States courts in patent cases.

—— Same, weekly index, with title, Alphabetical list of registrants of trade-
marks [etc., Nov. 6, 1923]. [1923.] xlii p. large 8° [From Official gazette,
v. 316, no. 1.] †Paper, $1.00 a yr.

—— Same [Nov. 13, 1923]. [1923.] xlii p. large 8° [From Official gazette,
v. 316, no. 2.]

—— Same [Nov. 20, 1923]. [1923.] xlii p. large 8° [From Official gazette,
v. 316, no. 3.]

—— Same [Nov. 27, 1923]. [1923.] xl p. large 8° [From Official gazette,
v. 316, no. 4.]

Patents. Classification of patents issued Nov. 6–27, 1923. [1923.] Each 2 p.
large 8° [Weekly. From Official gazette, v. 316, no. 1–4.] †

Pupin, Michael I. In Court of Appeals of District of Columbia, Oct. term,
1923, *in re* Michael I. Pupin, electromagnetic production of direct current
without fluctuations; brief for commissioner of patents. 1923. cover-title,
11 p. †

Trade-marks. Trade-marks [etc., from] Official gazette, Nov. 6, 1923. [1923.]
9–58+i–xviii p. il. large 8° [From Official gazette, v. 316, no. 1.] †Paper,
5c. single copy, $2.50 a yr.

—— Same, Nov. 13, 1923. [1923.] 239–300+i–xix p. il. large 8° [From
Official gazette, v. 316, no. 2.]

—— Same, Nov. 20, 1923. [1923.] 463–520+i–xvii p. il. large 8° [From
Official gazette, v. 316, no. 3.]

—— Same, Nov. 27, 1923. [1923.] 711–763+i–xviii p. il. large 8° [From
Official gazette, v. 316, no. 4.]

Van Horning, Harry L. In Court of Appeals of District of Columbia, Oct. term,
1923, patent appeal no. 1617, *in re* Harry Le Van Horning, improvement in
internal-combustion engine; brief for commissioner of patents. 1923. cover-
title, 7 p. ‡

PENSION BUREAU

Pensions. Laws of United States governing granting of Army and Navy pensions, with regulations and instructions relating thereto, in effect Nov. 1, 1923. 1923. xix+236 p. *Paper, 25c. 23–26978

RECLAMATION BUREAU

Yakima project, Wash., high-pressure emergency gates for Tieton Dam. [1923.] 14 p. 12 pl. 4° (Specifications 427.) [Consists of advertisement, proposal, specifications, and drawings for reclamation project.] †Paper, 55c.

INTERSTATE COMMERCE COMMISSION

Note.—The bound volumes of the decisions, usually known as Interstate Commerce Commission reports, are sold by the Superintendent of Documents, Washington, D. C., at various prices, depending upon the size of the volume. Separate opinions are sold on subscription, price $1.00 per volume; foreign subscription, $1.50; single copies, usually 5c. each.

Acid condensing rings. No. 14117, B. Mifflin-Hood Brick Company *v.* director general, as agent; decided Oct. 27, 1923; report [and order] of commission. [1923.] 553–554+[1] p. ([Opinion] 8903.) [Report from Interstate Commerce Commission reports, v. 83.] *Paper, 5c.

Alton and Southern Railroad. Finance docket no. 266, guaranty settlement with Alton & Southern Railroad; [decided Oct. 20, 1923; report of commission]. 1923. [1]+502–504 p. ([Finance decision] 972.) [From Interstate Commerce Commission reports, v. 82.] *Paper, 5c.

Alum. No. 14328, Crown Willamette Paper Company *v.* director general, as agent; [decided Oct. 10, 1923; report of commission]. 1923. [1]+320–322 p. ([Opinion] 8828.) [From Interstate Commerce Commission reports, v. 83.] *Paper, 5c.

American Niagara Railroad. Finance docket no. 3148, construction of line by American Niagara R. R.; [decided Oct. 10, 1923; report of commission]. 1923. [1]+420–424 p. ([Finance decision] 944.) [From Interstate Commerce Commission reports, v. 82.] *Paper, 5c.

Ammonium nitrate. No. 13962, E. I. du Pont de Nemours & Company *v.* director general, as agent; [decided Oct. 11, 1923; report and order of commission]. 1923. [1]+374–376+[1] p. ([Opinion] 8849.) [Report from Interstate Commerce Commission reports, v. 83.] *Paper, 5c.

Ammonium sulphate. No. 14275, Seaboard By-Product Coke Company *v.* Delaware, Lackawanna & Western Railroad Company; [no. 14348, same *v.* Erie Railroad Company]; decided Oct. 27, 1923; report [and order] of commission. [1923.] 527–529+[1] p. ([Opinion] 8895.) [Report from Interstate Commerce Commission reports, v. 83.] *Paper, 5c.

Antimony regulus. No. 13543, Arthur E. Winter and Frank B. Ross *v.* Great Northern Railway Company et al.; decided Oct. 10, 1923; report [and order] of commission. [1923.] 331–332+[1] p. ([Opinion] 8832.) [Report from Interstate Commerce Commission reports, v. 83.] *Paper, 5c.

Apples. No. 14231, Klein-Simpson Fruit Company *v.* Atchison, Topeka & Santa Fe Railway Company; decided Oct. 10, 1923; report [and order] of commission. [1923.] 285–286+[1] p. ([Opinion] 8816.) [Report from Interstate Commerce Commission reports, v. 83.] *Paper, 5c.

Aransas Harbor Terminal Railway. Finance docket no. 2148, deficit status of Aransas Harbor Terminal Ry.; decided Oct. 3, 1923; report of commission. [1923.] p. 357–358. ([Finance decision] 921.) [From Interstate Commerce Commission reports, v. 82.] *Paper, 5c.

Arcade and Attica Railroad. Finance docket no. 3128, bonds of Arcade & Attica R. R.; [approved Oct. 13, 1923; supplemental order]. 1923. p. [1], 434. ([Finance decision] 948.) [From Interstate Commerce Commission reports, v. 82.] *Paper, 5c.

Asphalt. Investigation and suspension docket no. 1855, asphalt from New Orleans and related points to points in Arkansas; [decided Oct. 31, 1923; report and order of commission]. 1923. [1]+424–426+[1] p. ([Opinion] 8864.) [Report from Interstate Commerce Commission reports, v. 83.] *Paper, 5c.

Augusta and Summerville Railroad. Before Interstate Commerce Commission, valuation docket no. 247, Augusta and Summerville Railroad Company; brief in support of tentative valuation. 1923. cover-title, i+39 p. ‡

Augusta Belt Railway. Before Interstate Commerce Commission, valuation docket no. 234, Augusta Belt Railway Company; brief in support of tentative valuation. 1923. cover-title, i+28 p. ‡

Automatic Telephone Company of New Bedford. Finance docket no. 3208, purchase by New England Telephone & Telegraph Company of properties of Automatic Telephone Co. of New Bedford; decided Oct. 16, 1923; report of commission. [1923.] p. 499–501. ([Finance decision] 971.) [From Interstate Commerce Commission reports, v. 82.] *Paper, 5c.

Automobiles. No. 13858, Barnes Automobile Company *v.* Detroit, Toledo & Ironton Railroad Company et al.; [decided Oct. 11, 1923; report and order of commission]. 1923. [1]+350–352+[1] p. ([Opinion] 8841.) [Report from Interstate Commerce Commission reports, v. 83.] *Paper, 5c.

Barley. No. 13906, Globe Grain & Milling Company *v.* director general, as agent; decided Oct. 27, 1923; report of commission. [1923.] p. 483–484. ([Opinion] 8879.) [From Interstate Commerce Commission reports, v. 83.] *Paper, 5c.

—— No. 14298, Morgan & Miller *v.* director general, as agent; decided Oct. 10, 1913 [1923]; report [and order] of commission. [1923.] 287–288+[1] p. ([Opinion] 8817.) [Report from Interstate Commerce Commission reports, v. 83.] *Paper, 5c.

Beaver Valley Railroad. Finance docket no. 1281, deficit settlement with Beaver Valley R. R.; decided Aug. 21, 1923; report of commission. [1923.] p. 409–410. ([Finance decision] 942.) [From Interstate Commerce Commission reports, v. 82.] *Paper, 5c.

Berry boxes. No. 13538, Sebastopol Berry Growers Association *v.* American Railway Express Company; decided Oct. 13, 1923; report [and order] of commission. [1923.] 345–346+[1] p. ([Opinion] 8839.) [Report from Interstate Commerce Commission reports, v. 83.] *Paper, 5c.

Boxes. No. 13940, Iten Biscuit Company *v.* Atchison, Topeka & Santa Fe Railway Company et al.; decided Oct. 10, 1923; report of commission. [1923.] p. 317–319. ([Opinion] 8827.) [From Interstate Commerce Commission reports, v. 83.] *Paper, 5c.

Bricks. No. 14463, Indiana State Highway Commission *v.* Chicago, Rock Island & Pacific Railway Company et al.; decided Oct. 27, 1923; report [and order] of commission. [1923.] 577–578+[1] p. ([Opinion] 8912.) [Report from Interstate Commerce Commission reports, v. 83.] *Paper, 5c.

Building stones. No. 11488, I. G. Lawrence *v.* director general, as agent; decided Oct. 15, 1923; report [and order] of commission. [1923.] 369–370+[1] p. ([Opinion] 8847.) [Report from Interstate Commerce Commission reports, v. 83.] *Paper, 5c.

Canned food. Investigation and suspension docket no. 1912, canned goods from Princeton, Ind., to Evansville, Ind., and other C. F. A. points; decided Nov. 6, 1923; report [and order] of commission. [1923.] 547–548+[1] p. ([Opinion] 8900.) [Report from Interstate Commerce Commission reports, v. 83.] *Paper, 5c.

Cape Girardeau Northern Railway. Finance docket no. 335, guaranty settlement with Cape Girardeau Northern Ry., J. W. Fristoe, receiver; decided Oct. 9, 1923; report of commission. [1923.] p. 405–406. ([Finance decision] 940.) [From Interstate Commerce Commission reports, v. 82.] *Paper, 5c.

Cast-iron. No. 12455, Homer Furnace Company *v.* director general, as agent, New York Central Railroad Company, et al.; [decided Oct. 27, 1923; report and order of commission]. 1923. [1]+468–472+ii p. ([Opinion] 8875.) [Report from Interstate Commerce Commission reports, v. 83.] *Paper, 5c.

Cattle. No. 12941, Western Meat Company et al. *v.* director general, as agent, Southern Pacific Company, et al.; [decided Oct. 10, 1923; report of commission]. 1923. [1]+218–222 p. ([Opinion] 8798.) [From Interstate Commerce Commission reports, v. 83.] *Paper, 5c.

—— No. 13461, Sioux City Live Stock Exchange *v.* Chicago, St. Paul, Minneapolis & Omaha Railway Company et al.; decided Oct. 10, 1923; report [and order] of commission. [1923.] 243–247+ii p. ([Opinion] 8806.) [Report from Interstate Commerce Commission reports, v. 83.] *Paper, 5c.

Cement. Investigation and suspension docket no. 1805, cement from Bonner Springs, Kans., to Kansas City, Mo.; [decided Oct. 9, 1923; report and order of commission]. 1923. [1]+176-179+[1] p. ([Opinion] 8789.) [Report from Interstate Commerce Commission reports, v. 83.] *Paper, 5c.

Central New England Railway. Finance docket no. 346, guaranty settlement with Central New England Ry. [decided Oct. 19, 1923; report of commission]. 1923. [1]+456-458 p. ([Finance decision] 957.) [From Interstate Commerce Commission reports, v. 82.] *Paper, 5c.

Charlotte, Monroe and Columbia Railroad. Finance docket no. 357, guaranty settlement with Charlotte, Monroe & Columbia R. R.; decided Oct. 18, 1923; report of commission. [1923.] p. 459-461. ([Finance decision] 958.) [From Interstate Commerce Commission reports, v. 82.] *Paper, 5c.

Chesterfield and Lancaster Railroad. Finance docket no. 367, guaranty settlement with Chesterfield & Lancaster R. R.; [decided Oct. 18, 1923; report o commission]. 1923. [1]+462-464 p. ([Finance decision] 959.) [From Interstate Commerce Commission reports, v. 82.]. *Paper, 5c.

Chicago and Illinois Midland Railway. Finance docket no. 1304, deficit status of Chicago & Illinois Midland Ry.; decided Oct. 10, 1923; report of commission. [1923.] p. 407-408. ([Finance decision] 941.) [From Interstate Commerce Commission reports, v. 82.] *Paper, 5c.

Chicago and North Western Railway. Finance docket no. 3243, bonds of Chicago & North Western Ry.; decided Oct. 15, 1923; report of commission. [1923.] p. 453-455. ([Finance decision] 956.) [From Interstate Commerce Commission reports, v. 82.] *Paper, 5c.

Chip board. No. 13938, Weldon, Williams & Lick v. Atchison, Topeka & Santa Fe Railway Company et al.; decided Oct. 11, 1923; report of commission. [1923.] p. 371-374. ([Opinion] 8848.) [From Interstate Commerce Commission reports, v. 83.] *Paper, 5c.

Cimarron and Northwestern Railway. Finance docket no. 1918, deficit settlement with Cimarron & Northwestern Ry.; decided Oct. 13, 1923; report of commission. [1923.] p. 441-442. ([Finance decision] 951.) [From Interstate Commerce Commission reports, v. 82.] *Paper, 5c.

Cincinnati Northern Railroad. Finance docket no. 397, guaranty settlement with Cincinnati Northern R. R.; decided Oct. 16, 1923; report of commission. [1923.] p. 465-467. ([Finance decision] 960.) [From Interstate Commerce Commission reports, v. 82.] *Paper, 5c.

Cinders. No. 13634, Omaha Chamber of Commerce v. director general, as agent; [decided Oct. 10, 1923; report of commission]. 1923. [1]+310-312 p. ([Opinion] 8824.) [From Interstate Commerce Commission reports, v. 83.] *Paper, 5c.

Clay. No. 13370, Clay Products Company, Incorporated, v. director general, as agent; decided Oct. 5, 1923; report of commission. [1923.] p. 193-195. ([Opinion] 8792.) [From Interstate Commerce Commission reports, v. 83.] *Paper, 5c.

Cleveland, Cincinnati, Chicago and St. Louis Railway. Finance docket no. 400, guaranty settlement with Cleveland, Cincinnati, Chicago & St. Louis Railway; [decided Oct. 18, 1923; report of commission]. 1923. [1]+468-470 p. ([Finance decision] 961.) [From Interstate Commerce Commission reports, v. 82.] *Paper, 5c.

Coal. No. 12134, Manufacturers Association of Connecticut, Incorporated, v. director general, as agent; decided Oct. 27, 1923; report of commission. [1923.] p. 563-565. ([Opinion] 8907.) [From Interstate Commerce Commission reports, v. 83.] *Paper, 5c.

—— No. 12774, Republic Iron & Steel Company v. Baltimore & Ohio Railroad Company et al.; decided Oct. 18, 1923; report [and order] of commission. [1923.] 429-431+[1] p. ([Opinion] 8866.) [Report from Interstate Commerce Commission reports, v. 83.] *Paper, 5c.

—— No. 12862, Commerce Club of St. Joseph, Mo., v. Alton & Southern Railroad Company et al.; decided Oct. 5, 1923; report [and order] of commission. [1923.] 185-192+ii p. ([Opinion] 8791.) [Report from Interstate Commerce Commission reports, v. 83.] *Paper, 5c.

—— No. 13271, M. L. Butcher v. director general, as agent, Atchison, Topeka & Santa Fe Railway Company, et al.; decided Oct. 11, 1923; report [and order] of commission. [1923.] 359-360+[1] p. ([Opinion] 8844.) [Report from Interstate Commerce Commission reports, v. 83.] *Paper, 5c.

Coal—Continued.   No. 13308, L'Anguille River Railway Company et al. *v.* Illinois
Central Railroad Company et al.; decided Oct. 27, 1923; report[and order] of
commission. [1923.]   521–524+[1] p. ([Opinion] 8893.)· [Report from Interstate Commerce Commission reports, v. 83.]   *Paper, 5c.

—— No. 13453, Pittsburgh Coal Producers' Association *v.* Pittsburgh, Cincinnati, Chicago & St. Louis Railroad Company; decided Oct. 10, 1923;
report of commission. [1923.]   p. 145–159.   ([Opinion] 8784.)i   [From·Inter-
state Commerce Commission reports, v. 83.]   *Paper, 5c.

—— No. 13501, Southern Appalachian Coal Operators Association *v.* Louisville & Nashville Railroad Company;· [decided Oct. 5, 1923; report and order
of commission]. 1923.   [1]+136–144+[1] p.. ([Opinion] 8783.) [Report
from Interstate Commerce Commission reports, v. 83.]   *Paper, 5c.

—— No. 13594, Megeath Coal Company *v.* director general, as agent; [no. 13594
(sub-no. 1), same *v.* same]; decided Oct. 5, 1923; report of commission.
[1923.]   p. 165–166.   ([Opinion] 8786.)· [From Interstate Commerce Commission reports, v. 83.]   *Paper, 5c.

—— No. 13826, West Kentucky Coal Bureau *v.* Louisville & Nashville Railroad Company et·al.; [decided Oct. 15, 1923; report and order of commis-
sion]. 1923. ·[1]+180–184+iii p. ([Opinion] 8790.) [Report from Interstate Commerce Commission reports, v. 83.]. *Paper, 5c.

—— No. 14005, Seaboard By-Product Coke Company *v.* director general, as
agent; decided Oct. 10, 1923; report of commission. [1923.]   p. 315–316.
([Opinion] 8826.) [From Interstate Commerce Commission reports, v. 83.]
*Paper, 5c.

—— No. 14075, Commercial Coal Company et al. *v.* Louisville & Nashville
Railroad Company et al.; [decided Oct. 23, 1923; report and order of com-
mission]. 1923.   [1]+464–467+ii p.. ([Opinion] 8874.) [Report from Interstate Commerce Commission reports, v. 83.]   *Paper, 5c.

Coal-tar oil.   No. 13137, Semet-Solvay Company *v.* director general, as agent;
[decided Oct. 27, 1923; report of commission]. 1923.   [1]+492–495 p.
([Opinion] 8883.) [From Interstate Commerce Commission reports, v. 83.]
*Paper, 5c.

Coffee.   Investigation and suspension docket no. ·1828; roasted coffee, in less
than carloads, Atlantic Seaboard to Galveston, Tex., and related points;
decided Oct. 10, 1923; report [and order] of commission. ·[1923.]   131–135+
[1] p. ([Opinion] 8782.) [Report from Interstate Commerce Commission
reports, v. 83.]   *Paper, 5c.

Coke.   No. 13238, Citizens Gas Company *v.* Cleveland, Cincinnati, Chicago &
St. Louis Railway Company et al.; decided Oct. 10, 1923; report [and order]
of commission. [1923.]   323–324+[1] p. ([Opinion] 8829.) [Report from
Interstate Commerce Commission reports, v. 83.]   *Paper, 5c.

—— No. 13690, New Jersey Zinc Company et al. *v.* Boston & Albany Railroad
Company (New·York Central Railroad Company, lessee), et al.; [decided
Oct. 11, 1923; report and order of commission]. 1923.   [1]+356–358+ii p.
([Opinion] 8843.) [Report from Interstate Commerce Commission reports,
v. 83.]   *Paper, 5c.

—— No. 13838, Tuffli Bros. ·Pig Iron & Coke Company *v.* Pittsburgh, Cincinnati, Chicago & St. Louis Railroad Company et al.; decided Oct. 10, 1923;
report [and order] of commission. [1923.]   341–342+[1] p. ([Opinion] 8837.)
[Report from Interstate Commerce Commission reports, v. 83.] ·*Paper, 5c.

Condensed milk.   No. 13141, Larimer County Cooperative Milk Condensery
Company *v.* director general, as agent; decided Oct. 10, 1923; report of
commission. [1923.]   p. 225–227. ([Opinion] 8800.) [From Interstate Commerce Commission reports, v. 83.]   *Paper, 5c.

Cotton.   No. 13251, M. H. Wolfe & Company *v.* director general, as agent,
International & Great Northern Railway Company, et al.; decided Oct. 10,
1923; report of commission. [1923.]   p. 301–304. ([Opinion] 8821.) [From
Interstate Commerce Commission reports, v. 83.]   *Paper, 5c.

—— No. 14319, Floyd & Company *v.* Alabama & Mississippi Railroad Company et al; decided Oct. 23, 1923; report [and order] of commission. [1923.]
485–487+[1] p. ([Opinion] 8880.) [Report from Interstate Commerce Commission reports, v. 83.] ·*Paper, 5c.

Cotton goods.   No. 13609, Hamilton Carhartt Cotton Mills *v.* Alabama & Vicksburg Railway Company et al.; [decided Oct. 10, 1923; report and order of
commission]. 1923.   [1]+212–214+[1] p. ([Opinion] 8796.) [Report from
Interstate Commerce Commission reports, v. 83.]   *Paper, 5c.

Crates. No. 14422, Texas Chamber of Commerce et al. *v.* director general, as agent, Atchison, Topeka & Santa Fe Railway Company, et al.; [decided Oct. 20, 1923; report and order of commission]. 1923. [1]+538–542+[1] p. ([Opinion] 8898.) [Report from Interstate Commerce Commission reports, v. 83.] *Paper, 5c.

Culverts. No. 13420, Colorado Culvert & Flume Company *v.* Atchison, Topeka & Santa Fe Railway Company et al.; decided Oct. 11, 1923; report [and order] of commission. [1923.] 267–270+ii p. ([Opinion] 8812.) [Report from Interstate Commerce Commission reports, v. 83.] *Paper, 5c.

Demurrage. No. 13574, Watters-Tonge Lumber Company *v.* director general, as agent, South Georgia Railway Company, et al.; [decided Oct. 27, 1923; report and order of commission]. 1923. [1]+512–513+[1] p. ([Opinion] 8889.) [Report from Interstate Commerce Commission reports, v. 83.] *Paper, 5c.

—— No. 13706, Kaw Boiler Works Company *v.* director general, as agent; decided Oct. 10, 1923; report [and order] of commission. [1923.] 339–340+ [1] p. ([Opinion] 8836.) [Report from Interstate Commerce Commission reports, v. 83.] *Paper, 5c.

Detroit and Huron Railway. Finance docket no. 435, guaranty settlement with Detroit & Huron Ry.; [decided Sept. 29, 1923; report of commission]. 1923. [1]+362–364 p. ([Finance decision] 923.) [From Interstate Commerce Commission reports, v. 82.] *Paper, 5c.

Detroit, Grand Haven and Milwaukee Railway. Finance docket no. 439, guaranty settlement with Detroit, Grand Haven & Milwaukee Ry.; [and finance dockets nos. 495 and 497]; decided Sept. 29, 1923; report of commission. [1923.] p. 375–378. ([Finance decision] 927.) [From Interstate Commerce Commission reports, v. 82.] *Paper, 5c.

Detroit, Toledo and Ironton Railroad. Finance docket no. 2648, Detroit, Toledo & Ironton investment certificates, decided Oct. 9, 1923; report of commission. [1923.] p. 411–419. ([Finance decision] 943.) [From Interstate Commerce Commission reports, v. 82.] *Paper, 5c.

East and West Coast Railway. Finance docket no. 449, guaranty settlement with East & West Coast Ry.; decided Oct. 18, 1923; report of commission. [1923.] p. 471–473. ([Finance decision] 962.) [From Interstate Commerce Commission reports, v. 82.] *Paper, 5c.

Eggs. No. 13079, H. J. Keith Company et al. *v.* director general, as agent; decided Oct. 5, 1923; report of commission. [1923.] p. 167–172. ([Opinion] 8787.) [From Interstate Commerce Commission reports, v. 83.] *Paper, 5c.

Excavating machinery. No. 13727, Fidelity Lumber Company *v.* Louisiana & Pacific Railway Company and director general, as agent; decided Oct. 27, 1923; report [and order] of commission. [1923.] 499–500+[1] p. ([Opinion] 8885.) [Report from Interstate Commerce Commission reports, v. 83.] *Paper, 5c.

Flint River and Northeastern Railroad. Finance docket no. 1320, deficit settlement with Flint River & Northeastern R. R.; decided Sept. 28, 1923; report of commission. [1923.] p. 387–388. ([Finance decision] 931.) [From Interstate Commerce Commission reports, v. 82.] *Paper, 5c.

Flour. No. 13462, Aunt Jemima Mills Company *v.* director general, as agent, Chicago, Burlington & Quincy Railroad Company, et al.; decided Oct. 20, 1923; report of commission. [1923.] p. 549–551. ([Opinion] 8901.) [From Interstate Commerce Commission reports, v. 83.] *Paper, 5c.

Food for cattle. No. 13457, American Stockmen's Supplies Association *v.* Chicago, Rock Island & Pacific Railway Company et al.; [decided Oct. 10, 1923; report and order of commission]. 1923. [1]+334–336+[1] p. ([Opinion] 8834.) [Report from Interstate Commerce Commission reports, v. 83.] *Paper, 5c.

Franklin and Pittsylvania Railroad. Finance docket no. 141, deficit settlement with Franklin & Pittsylvania R. R.; decided Oct. 9, 1923; report of commission. [1923.] p. 403–404. ([Finance decision] 939.) [From Interstate Commerce Commission reports, v. 82.] *Paper, 5c.

—— Finance docket no. 476, guaranty settlement with Franklin & Pittsylvania R. R.; [decided Oct. 9, 1923; report of commission]. 1923. [1]+400–402 p. ([Finance decision] 938.) [From Interstate Commerce Commission reports, v. 82.] *Paper, 5c.

Freight-cars. Decisions under safety appliance acts, circuit court of appeals, 6th circuit, no. 2959, Baltimore & Ohio Southwestern Railroad Company *v.* United States, error to district court for southern district of Ohio, western division [opinion of court]; decided May 18, 1917. [Reprint with changes 1923.] 6 p. [This print carries designation 242 Fed. 420.] †.

Freight rates. 4th section application no. 12378, commodity rates from Jacksonville to Miami, Fla.; decided Oct. 3, 1923; report [and order] of commission. [1923.] 207–211+[1] p. ([Opinion] 8795.) [Report from Interstate Commerce Commission reports, v. 83.] *Paper, 5c.

—— No. 14576, White Star Line *v.* New York Central Railroad Company et al.; decided Oct. 30, 1923; report [and order] of commission. [1923.] 473–478+[1] p. ([Opinion] 8876.) [Report from Interstate Commerce Commission reports, v. 83.] *Paper, 5c.

Fruit. No. 14164, California Packing Corporation *v.* director general, as agent; decided Oct. 27, 1923; report [and order] of commission. 1923. [1]+490–491 +[1] p. ([Opinion] 8882.) [Report from Interstate Commerce Commission reports, v. 83.] *Paper, 5c.

Fruit-jars. No. 13702, Boren-Stewart Company *v.* Baltimore & Ohio Railroad Company et al.; decided Oct. 10, 1923; report [and order] of commission. [1923.] 215–217+[1] p. ([Opinion] 8797.) [Report from Interstate Commerce Commission reports, v. 83.] *Paper, 5c.

Fuel-oil. No. 12896, East Bay Water Company *v.* director general, as agent; [no. 12966, East Bay Water Company et al. *v.* same; decided Oct. 10, 1923; report and order of commission]. 1923. [1]+238–242+[1] p. ([Opinion] 8805.) [Report from Interstate Commerce Commission reports, v. 83.] *Paper, 5c.

—— No. 12897, Eastern Texas Electric Company *v.* director general, as agent, Texas & New Orleans Railroad Company, et al.; [decided Oct. 27, 1923; report and order of commission]. 1923. [1]+518–520+[1] p. ([Opinion] 8892.) [Report from Interstate Commerce Commission reports, v. 83.] *Paper, 5c.

—— No. 13360, Moline Oil Company *v.* director general, as agent; [no. 13360 (sub-no. 1), Mobile Oil Co. *v.* Atchison, Topeka & Santa Fe Railway Company et al.]; decided Oct. 10, 1923; report of commission. [1923.] p. 227–228. ([Opinion] 8801.) [From Interstate Commerce Commission reports, v. 83.] *Paper, 5c.

Furniture. Investigation and suspension docket no. 1861, furniture, Western Trunk Line territory on and east of Missouri River to Denver, Colo., and related points; decided Oct. 24, 1923; report [and order] of commission. [1923.] 293–297+[1] p. ([Opinion] 8819.) [Report from Interstate Commerce Commission reports, v. 83.] *Paper, 5c.

Galveston and Western Railway. Finance docket no. 3158, acquisition and operation of [Galveston & Western Railway Company) by Gulf, Colorado & Santa Fe Ry.; decided Oct. 18, 1923; report of commission. [1923.] p. 527–530. ([Finance decision] 980.) [From Interstate Commerce Commission reports, v. 82.] *Paper, 5c.

Gas masks. No. 12292, Carnie-Goudie Manufacturing Company *v.* director general, as agent; decided Oct. 27, 1923; report [and order] of commission. [1923.] 573–574+[1] p. ([Opinion] 8910.) [Report from Interstate Commerce Commission reports, v. 83.] *Paper, 5c.

Gas oil. No. 13617, Empire Refineries, Incorporated, et al., *v.* director general, as agent, Atchison, Topeka & Santa Fe Railway Company, et al.; decided Oct. 10, 1923; report of commission. [1923.] p. 223–224. ([Opinion] 8799.) [From Interstate Commerce Commission reports, v. 83.] *Paper, 5c.

Grain. Investigation and suspension docket no. 1870, grain and grain products, Illinois to Clarksville and Nashville, Tenn.; portion of 4th section application no. 1952; decided Nov. 6, 1923; report [and order] of commission. [1923.] 543–546+ii p. ([Opinion] 8899.) [Report from Interstate Commerce Commission reports, v. 83.] *Paper, 5c.

Grand Rapids and Indiana Railway. Finance docket no. 1465, lease of Grand Rapids & Indiana Ry., [by] Pennsylvania Railroad Company; approved Oct. 2, 1923; amendatory order. 1923. p. 391. ([Finance decision] 933.) [From Interstate Commerce Commission reports, v. 82.] *Paper, 5c.

Grand Trunk Railway of Canada. Finance docket no. 287, guaranty settlement with Grand Trunk Ry. Co. of Canada, lessee of Lewiston & Auburn Railroad, Michigan Air Line Railway, Cincinnati, Saginaw & Mackinaw Railroad (including Bay City Terminal Railway), Chicago, Detroit & Canada Grand Junction Railroad, and Atlantic & St. Lawrence Railroad, including Norway

Grand Trunk Railway of Canada—Continued.
  Branch Railroad, under sec. 209 of transportation act; 1920; [and finance dockets nos. 305, 375, 398, 583, 622, and 712; decided Sept. 29, 1923; report of commission]. 1923. [1]+340–346 p. ([Finance decision] 915.) [From Interstate Commerce Commission reports, v. 82.] *Paper, 5c.

Grand Trunk Western Railway. Finance docket no. 498, guaranty settlement with Grand Trunk Western Ry.; [and finance docket no. 371; decided Sept. 29, 1923; report of commission]. 1923. [1]+348–350 p. ([Finance decision] 917.) [From Interstate Commerce Commission reports, v. 82.] *Paper, 5c.

Gravel. No. 12186, General Motors Corporation *v.* director general, as agent; decided Oct. 27, 1923; report of commission. [1923.] p. 479–480. ([Opinion] 8877.) [From Interstate Commerce Commission reports, v. 83.] *Paper, 5c.

—— No. 13637, Alfred T. Wagner *v.* director general, as agent, Pere Marquette Railway Company, et al.; decided Oct. 27, 1923; report of commission. [1923.] p. 501–502. ([Opinion] 8886.) [From Interstate Commerce Commission reports, v. 83.] *Paper, 5c.

Great Northern Railway. Finance docket no. 3224, Great Northern equipment trust, series B; decided Oct. 8, 1923; report of commission. [1923.] p. 369–372. ([Finance decision] 925.) [From Interstate Commerce Commission reports, v. 82.] *Paper, 5c.

Handles. No. 13417, Geo. W. Pittman Company et al. *v.* director general, as agent; [decided Oct. 16, 1923; report of commission]. 1923. [1]+380–382 p. ([Opinion] 8851.) [From Interstate Commerce Commission reports, v. 83.] *Paper, 5c.

Hartford and Connecticut Western Railroad. Finance docket no. 3213, bonds of Hartford & Connecticut Western R. R.; [and finance docket no. 3213 (sub-no. 1)]; decided Oct. 20, 1923; report of commission. [1923.] p. 531–534. ([Finance decision] 981.) [From Interstate Commerce Commission reports, v. 82.] *Paper, 5c.

Horses. No. 13851, Fies & Sons *v.* Missouri Pacific Railroad Company et al.; decided Oct. 11, 1923; report [and order] of commission. [1923.] 421–423+ [1] p. ([Opinion] 8863.) [Report from Interstate Commerce Commission reports, v. 83.] *Paper, 5c.

Hours of labor. Decisions under hours of service act, circuit court of appeals, 8th circuit, no. 6404, Sept. term, 1923, United States *v.* Colorado, Wyoming and Eastern Railway Company, error to district court for district of Wyoming [opinion of court]; decided Oct. 22, 1923. [1923.] 8 p. *Paper, 5c.

Ice. No. 13809, Hazard Jellico Coal Company *v.* director general, as agent; decided Oct. 5, 1923; report of commission. [1923.] p. 383–384. ([Opinion] 8852.) [From Interstate Commerce Commission reports, v. 83.] *Paper, 5c.

Indiana Harbor Belt Railroad. Finance docket no. 534, guaranty settlement with Indiana Harbor Belt R. R.; decided Oct. 16, 1923; report of commission. [1923.] p. 447–449. ([Finance decision] 954.) [From Interstate Commerce Commission reports, v. 82.] *Paper, 5c.

Interstate commerce act, including text or related sections of [other acts]; revised to Aug. 1, 1923. 1923. 304 p. *Paper, 20c.

  The included sections are:
   Accident reports act.
   Ash pan act.
   Bills of lading act.
   Block signal-resolution.
   Boiler inspection act, as amended.
   Clayton antitrust act.
   Compulsory testimony act.
   District court jurisdiction act.
   Elkins act, as amended.
   Emergency coal act.
   Expediting act, as amended.
   Federal control act, as amended.
   Federal possession and control act.
   Government-aided railroad and telegraph act.
   Hours of service act, as amended.
   Immunity of witnesses act.
   Lake Erie and Ohio River Ship Canal act.
   Medals of honor act, [with] regulations as amended.
   Merchant marine act, 1920.
   Miscellaneous provisions.
   Parcel-post acts.
   Railway mail service pay acts.
   Reimbursement of United States for motive power and equipment.
   Safety appliance acts, as amended.
   Standard time act, as amended.
   Transportation act, 1920, as amended.
   Transportation of explosives act, as amended.

Interstate Railroad. Finance docket no. 2890, stock of Interstate Railroad;
, decided Sept. 29, 1923; report of commission. [1923.] p. 359-361. ([Finance
decision] 922.) [From Interstate Commerce Commission reports, v. 82.]
*Paper, 5c.

Kanawha and Michigan Railway. Finance docket no. 545, guaranty settlement
with Kanawha & Michigan Ry.; [decided Oct. 18, 1923; report of commission].
1923. [1]+474-476 p. ([Finance decision] 963.) [From Interstate Com-
, merce Commission reports, v. 82.] *Paper, 5c.

Kanawha and West Virginia Railroad. Finance docket no. 546, guafanty settlement with Kanawha & West Virginia R. R.; decided Oct. 16, 1923; report of
commission. [1923.] p. 477-479. ([Finance decision] 964.) [From Interstate Commerce Commission reports, v. 82.] *Paper, 5c.

Kansas City and Grandview Railway. Finance docket no. 3125, construction
of line by Kansas City & Grandview Ry.; [decided Oct. 6, 1923; report of
commission]. 1923. [1]+392-394 p. ([Finance decision] 934.) [From Interstate Commerce Commission reports, v. 82.] *Paper, 5c.

—— Finance docket no. 3126, stock of Kansas City & Grandview Ry.; decided
Oct. 18, 1923; report of commission. [1923.] p. 525-526. ([Finance decision]
979.) [From Interstate Commerce Commission reports, v. 82.] *Paper, 5c.

Kansas City Southern Railway. Finance docket no. 2867, assumption of obligation by Kansas City Southern and Texarkana & Fort Smith railways; approved
Oct. 4, 1923; 2d supplemental order. 1923. p. 399. ([Finance decision]
937.) [From Interstate Commerce Commission reports, v. 82.] *Paper, 5c.

—— Finance docket no. 3230, Kansas City Southern equipment trust, series E;
decided Oct. 10, 1923; report of commission. [1923.] p. 427-430. ([Finance
decision] 946.) [From Interstate Commerce Commission reports, v. 82.]
*Paper, 5c.

Kishacoquillas Valley Railroad. Finance docket no. 565, guaranty settlement
with Kishacoquillas Valley R. R.; decided Oct. 24, 1923; report of commission.
[1923.] p. 565-566. ([Finance decision] 993.) [From Interstate Commerce
Commission reports, v. 82.] *Paper, 5c.

Lambs. No. 14212, Armour & Company v. Pennsylvania Railroad Company;
decided Oct. 17, 1923; report [and order] of commission. [1923.] 289-292+
[1] p. ([Opinion] 8818.) [Report from Interstate Commerce Commission
reports, v. 83.] *Paper, 5c.

Leavenworth Terminal Railway and Bridge Company. Finance docket no. 579,
guaranty status of Leavenworth Terminal Railway & Bridge Co.; [decided
Apr. 21, 1923; report of commission]. 1923. [1]+824-825 p. ([Finance
decision] 799-B.) [From Interstate Commerce Commission reports, v. 79.]
*Paper, 5c.

Lewiston, Nezperce and Eastern Railroad. Finance docket no. 2232, deficit
status of Lewiston, Nezperce & Eastern R. R.; decided Oct. 13, 1923; report
of commission. [1923.] p. 443-444. ([Finance decision] 952.) [From Interstate Commerce Commission reports, v. 82.] *Paper, 5c.

Limestone. No. 13319, Sunderland Brothers Company v. director general, as
agent, Chicago, Burlington & Quincy Railroad Company, et al.; decided Oct.
10, 1923; report [and order] of commission. [1923.] 337-338+[1] p. ([Opin-
ion] 8835.) [Report from Interstate Commerce Commission reports, v. 83.]
*Paper, 5c.

—— No. 14327, Olympic Portland Cement Company, Limited, v. director
general, as agent; [decided Oct. 10, 1923; report and order of commission].
1923. [1]+402-406+[1] p. ([Opinion] 8857.) [Report from Interstate Commerce Commission reports, v. 83.] *Paper, 5c.

Locomotives. No. 13780, Walter A. Zelnicker Supply Company v. Denver &
Rio Grande Western Railroad Company et al.; decided July 11, 1923; report
[and order] of commission. Corrected reprint. [1923.] 367-368+[1] p.
([Opinion] 8667.) [Report from Interstate Commerce Commission reports,
v. 81.] *Paper, 5c.

Lumber. Investigation and suspension docket no. 1852, transit on lumber and
forest products, in carloads, in Washington, Idaho, and Montana; decided
Oct. 25, 1923; report [and order] of commission. [1923.] 451-459+[1] p.
([Opinion] 8872.) [Report from Interstate Commerce Commission reports,
v. 83.] *Paper, 5c.

Lumber.—Continued.   No. 11025, Pritchard-Wheeler Lumber Company et al. *v.* director general, Missouri Pacific Railroad Company, et al.; [no. 11025 (subno. 1), Desha Lumber Company et al. *v.* same; decided Oct. 16, 1923; report and order of commission]. 1923. [1]+260-263+ii p. ([Opinion] 8810.) [Report from Interstate Commerce Commission reports, v. 83.] *Paper, 5c.

—— No. 13566, Central Pennsylvania Lumber Company *v.* director general, as agent, Susquehanna & New York Railroad Company, et al.; decided Oct. 10, 1923; report [and order] of commission. [1923.] 333-334+[1] p. ([Opinion] 8833.) [Report from Interstate Commerce Commission reports, v. 83.] *Paper, 5c.

Manganese.   No. 13113, Donner Steel Company, Incorporated, *v.* director general, as agent; decided Oct. 10, 1923; report [and order] of commission. [1923.] 203-206+[1] p. ([Opinion] 8794.) [Report from Interstate Commerce Commission reports, v. 83.] *Paper, 5c.

Marble.   No. 13322, Sunderland Brothers Company *v,* director general, as agent, Chicago, Burlington & Quincy Railroad Company, et al.; decided Oct. 10, 1923; report [and order] of commission. [1923.] 229-232+[1] p. ([Opinion] 8802.) [Report from Interstate Commerce Commission reports, v. 83.] *Paper, 5c.

Michigan Central Railroad.   Finance docket no. 623, guaranty settlement with Michigan Central Railroad; decided Oct. 18, 1923; report of commission. [1923.] p. 507-509. ([Finance decision] 974.) [From Interstate Commerce Commission reports, v. 82.] *Paper, 5c.

Midland Railway.   Finance docket no. 178, deficit settlement with Midland Ry., George M. Brinson, receiver; decided Oct. 23, 1923; report of commission. [1923.] p. 543-544. ([Finance decision] 985.) [From Interstate Commerce Commission reports, v. 82.] *Paper, 5c.

—— Finance docket no. 626, guaranty settlement with Midland Railway [George M. Brinson, receiver; decided Oct. 23, 1923; report of commission]. 1923. [1]+550-552 p. ([Finance decision] 987.) [From Interstate Commerce Commission reports, v. 82.] *Paper, 5c.

Misrouting.   No. 11997, Dixie Portland Cement Company *v.* director general, as agent; decided Oct. 15, 1923; report [and order] of commission. [1923.] 417-420+[1] p. ([Opinion] 8862.) [Report from Interstate Commerce Commission reports, v. 83.] *Paper, 5c.

Molasses.   No. 14021, American Sugar Refining Company *v.* director general, as agent; [decided Nov. 1, 1923; report and order of commission]. 1923. [1]+560-562+[1] p. ([Opinion] 8906.) [Report from Interstate Commerce Commission reports, v. 83.] *Paper, 5c.

Money.   No. 13920, John F. Koine *v.* Michigan Central Railroad Company; decided Oct. 11, 1923; report [and order] of commission. [1923.] 407-408+[1] p. ([Opinion] 8858.) [Report from Interstate Commerce Commission reports, v. 83.] *Paper, 5c.

Muscatine, Burlington and Southern Railroad.   Finance docket no. 1339, deficit status of Muscatine, Burlington & Southern R. R., Theo. W. Krein, receiver; decided Oct. 11, 1923; report of commission. [1923.] p. 425-426. ([Finance decision] 945.) [From Interstate Commerce Commission reports, v. 82.] *Paper, 5c.

Natchez, Columbia and Mobile Railroad.   Finance docket no. 190, deficit status of Natchez, Columbia & Mobile R. R.; decided Oct. 20, 1923; report of commission. [1923.] p. 505-506. ([Finance decision] 973.) [From Interstate Commerce Commission reports, v. 82.] *Paper, 5c.

—— Finance docket no. 678, guaranty settlement with Natchez, Columbia & Mobile R. R.; [decided Oct. 20, 1923; report of commission]. 1923. [1]+510-512 p. ([Finance decision] 975.) [From Interstate Commerce Commission reports, v. 82.] *Paper, 5c.

New Orleans, Texas and Mexico Railway.   Finance docket no. 688, guaranty settlement with New Orleans, Texas & Mexico Railway and affiliated companies, in matter of settlement with New Orleans, Texas & Mexico Railway Company, Beaumont, Sour Lake & Western Railway Company, New Iberia & Northern Railroad Company, Orange & Northwestern Railroad Company, and St. Louis, Brownsville & Mexico Railway Company under sec. 209 of transportation act, 1920; [and finance dockets nos. 306, 684, 719, and 807]; decided Oct. 20, 1923; report of commission. [1923.] p. 513-518. ([Finance decision] 976.) [From Interstate Commerce Commission reports, v. 82.] *Paper, 5c.

New York Central Railroad. Finance docket no. 2973, New York Central lines
equipment trust of 1923, in matter of application of New York Central Railroad Company, Michigan Central Railroad Company, and Cleveland, Cincinnati, Chicago & St. Louis Railway Company for authority to assume obligation and liability in respect of certain equipment-trust certificates; approved
Oct. 3, 1923; supplemental order. 1923. p. 351. ([Finance decision]
918.) [From Interstate Commerce Commission reports, v. 82.] *Paper, 5c.

New York, Chicago and St. Louis Railroad. Finance docket no. 2967, New York,
Chicago & St. Louis R. R. bonds; decided Oct. 3, 1923; report of commission.
[1923.] p. 365–368. ([Finance decision] 924.) [From Interstate Commerce
Commission reports, v. 82.] *Paper, 5c.

New York, New Haven and Hartford Railroad. Finance docket no. 695, guaranty
settlement with New York, New Haven & Hartford R. R. and affiliated Cos.;
[and finance dockets nos. 518, 682, and 683]; decided Oct. 22, 1923; report
of commission. [1923.] p. 545–550. ([Finance decision] 986.) [From
Interstate Commerce Commission reports, v. 82.] *Paper, 5c.

Oakdale and Gulf Railway. Finance docket no. 2996, abandonment of operation
of line by Oakdale & Gulf Railway; [decided Oct. 13, 1923; report of commis-
sion]. 1923. [1]+450–452 p. ([Finance decision] 955.) [From Interstate
Commerce Commission reports, v. 82.] *Paper, 5c.

Ores. No. 13315, Arlington Silver Mining Company v. Great Northern Railway
Company et al.; decided Oct. 10, 1923; report-[and order] of commission.
[1923.] 255–259+[1] p. ([Opinion] 8809.) [Report from Interstate Commerce Commission reports, v. 83.] *Paper, 5c.

Overshoes. No. 13837, Haywood Brothers Shoe Company v. Chicago, Milwaukee & St. Paul Railway Company; decided Oct. 27, 1923; report [and
order] of commission. [1923.] 525–526+[1] p. ([Opinion] 8894.) [Report
from Interstate Commerce Commission reports, v. 83.] *Paper, 5c.

Paducah and Illinois Railroad. Finance docket no. 727, guaranty status of
Paducah & Illinois R. R.; decided Oct. 2, 1923; report of commission. [1923.]
p. 379–380. ([Finance decision] 928.) [From Interstate Commerce Commission reports, v. 82.] *Paper, 5c.

Paper. No. 13818, Hale-Halsell Company v. Chicago, Rock Island & Pacific
Railway Company et al.; decided Oct. 10, 1923; report of commission. [1923.]
p. 313–314. ([Opinion] 8825.) [From Interstate Commerce Commission
reports, v. 83.] *Paper, 5c.

——— No. 13947, L. Scharff & Company v. Southern Railway Company et al.;
decided Oct. 11, 1923; report [and order] of commission. [1923.] 409–410+
[1] p. ([Opinion] 8859.) [Report from Interstate Commerce Commission
reports, v. 83.] *Paper, 5c.

——— No. 14305, Pioneer Paper Company v. director general, as agent; decided
Oct. 11, 1923; report [and order] of commission. [1923.] 377–379+[1] p.
([Opinion] 8850.) [Report from Interstate Commerce Commission reports,
v. 83.] *Paper, 5c.

Pennsylvania-Detroit Railroad. Finance docket no. 3164, lease of Pennsylvania-
Detroit R. R., [by] Pennsylvania Railroad Company; [decided Sept. 29, 1923;
report of commission]. 1923. [1]+396–398 p. ([Finance decision] 936.)
[From Interstate Commerce Commission reports, v. 82.] *Paper, 5c.

Petroleum. No. 14074, Elk Refining Company v. Baltimore & Ohio Railroad
Company et al.; [decided Oct. 11, 1923; report and order of commission].
1923. [1]+414–416+[1] p. ([Opinion] 8861.) [Report from Interstate
Commerce Commission reports, v. 83.] *Paper, 5c.

Phonographs. No. 13577, Sonora, Incorporated, v. Delaware, Lackawanna &
Western Railroad Company et al.; decided Oct. 11, 1923; report [and order]
of commission. [1923.] 399–401+[1] p. ([Opinion] 8856.) [Report from
Interstate Commerce Commission reports, v. 83.] *Paper, 5c.

Pipe. No. 13590, Mexican Gulf Oil Company v. director general, as agent,
Pittsburgh & Lake Erie Railroad Company, et. al.; [no. 13590 (sub-no. 1), same
v. Wheeling & Lake Erie Railway Company et al.]; decided Oct. 11, 1923;
report [and order] of commission. [1923.] 411–413+[1] p. ([Opinion] 8860.)
[Report from Interstate Commerce Commission reports, v. 83.] *Paper, 5c.

Pittsburg and Shawmut Railroad. Finance docket no. 744, guaranty settlement
with Pittsburg & Shawmut R. R.; decided Oct. 13, 1923; report of commission.
[1923.] p. 435–437. ([Finance decision] 949.) [From Interstate Commerce
Commission reports, v. 82.] *Paper, 5c.

Pittsburgh and West Virginia Railway. In equity, no. 3986, in Court of Appeals of District of Columbia, Apr. term, 1923, Pittsburgh & West Virginia Railway Company and West Side Belt Railroad Company *v.* Interstate Commerce Commission and Harry M. Daugherty, Attorney General; brief for Interstate Commerce Commission. 1923. cover-title, iii+78 p. ‡

Pittsburgh, Cincinnati, Chicago and St. Louis Railroad. Finance docket no. 1466, lease of Pan Handle by Pennsylvania R. R.; approved Oct. 2, 1923; amendatory order. . 1923, p. 395. ([Finance decision] 935.) [From Interstate Commerce Commission reports, v. 82.] *Paper, 5c.

Pontiac, Oxford and Northern Railroad. Finance docket no. 749, guaranty settlement with Pontiac, Oxford & Northern R. R.; decided Sept. 29, 1923; report of commission. p. 381-383. [1923.] ([Finance decision] 929.) [From Interstate Commerce Commission reports, v. 82.] *Paper, 5c.

Railroad accidents. Report of director of Bureau of Safety in re investigation of accident which occurred on New York, New Haven & Hartford Railroad at Readville, Mass., on Sept. 11, 1923. [1923.] 15 p. il. *Paper, 5c.
                                                                              A23-2346

Railroad employees. Decisions under hours of service act, circuit court of appeals, 8th circuit, no. 4880, May term, 1917, Minneapolis & St. Louis Railroad Co. *v.* United States, in error to district court for southern district of Iowa [opinion of court]; decided Aug. 9, 1917. [Reprint 1923.] 9 p. [This print carries designation 245 Fed. 60.] †

—— Wage statistics, class 1 steam roads in United States, including 15 switching and terminal companies, Sept. 1923; [prepared in] Bureau of Statistics. Sept. 1923. [4] p. oblong large 8° †

Railroad tickets. In equity, no. 469, in Supreme Court, Oct. term, 1923, United States, Interstate Commerce Commission, et al., *v.* New York Central Railroad Company et al.; brief for Interstate Commerce Commission. 1923. cover-title, ii+33 p. ‡

Railroads. Before Interstate Commerce Commission, valuation docket nos. 192, 149, 164, 180, New York, Ontario and Western Railway Company, Mobile and Ohio Railroad Company, Charleston and Western Carolina Railway, Norfolk and Portsmouth Belt Line Railway, et al.; memorandum on argument relative to presidents' conference committee general studies. 1923. cover-title, i+90 p. il. ‡

—— Freight and passenger service operating statistics of class 1 steam roads in United States, compiled from 161 reports of freight statistics representing 176 roads and from 158 reports of passenger statistics representing 173 roads (switching and terminal companies not included), Sept. 1923 and 1922 [and 9 months ended with Sept. 1923 and 1922; prepared in] Bureau of Statistics. Sept. 1923. [2] p. oblong 8° [Subject to revision.] †

—— Freight and passenger train service unit costs (selected expense accounts) of class 1 steam roads in United States, including proportion of mixed-train and special-train service (compiled from 161 reports representing 176 steam roads, switching and terminal companies not included), Sept. 1923 amd 1922, and 9 months [ended with Sept.] 1923 and 1922; [prepared in] Bureau of Statistics. Sept. 1923. 1 p. oblong large 8° [Subject to revision.] †

—— Operating revenues and operating expenses of class 1 steam roads in United States (for 194 steam roads, including 15 switching and terminal companies), Sept. 1923 and 1922 [and] 9 months ending with Sept. 1923 and 1922; [prepared in] Bureau of Statistics. Sept. 1923. 1 p. oblong large 8° [Subject to revision.] †

—— Operating statistics of large steam roads, selected items for Sept. 1923, compared with Sept. 1922, for roads with annual operating revenues above $25,000,000; [prepared in] Bureau of Statistics. Sept. 1923. [2] p. oblong large 8° [Subject to revision.] †

Rails. No. 13871, Mid-Continent Equipment & Machinery Company *v.* Missouri Southern Railroad Company et al.; decided Oct. 10, 1923; report [and order] of commission. [1923.] 393-398+ii p. ([Opinion] 8855.) [Report from Interstate Commerce Commission reports, v. 83.] *Paper, 5c.

Raleigh and Charleston Railroad. Finance docket no. 762, guaranty settlement with Raleigh & Charleston R. R.; [decided Oct. 18, 1923; report of commission]. 1923. [1]+480-482 p. ([Finance decision] 965.) [From Interstate Commerce Commission reports, v. 82.] *Paper, 5c.

Reconsignment. No. 13242, D. Kellerman *v.* director general, as agent; decided Oct. 10, 1923; report [and order] of commission. [1923.] 347–349+[1] p. ([Opinion] 8840.) [Report from Interstate Commerce Commission, v. 83.] *Paper, 5c.

—— No. 13835, Carolina Portland Cement Company *v.* director general, as agent; [no. 13835 (sub-no. 1), same *v.* Chicago, Milwaukee & St. Paul Railway Company et al; decided Oct. 11, 1923; report and order of commission]. 1923. [1]+388–392+ii p. ([Opinion] 8854.) [Report from Interstate Commerce Commission reports, v. 83.] *Paper, 5c.

Refrigeration. Investigation and suspension docket no. 1842, rules, regulations, and charges for protective service on perishable freight; decided Oct. 16, 1923; report [and order] of commission. [1923.] 275–281+ii p. ([Opinion] 8814.) [Report from Interstate Commerce Commission reports, v. 83.] *Paper, 5c.

Refrigerator-cars. No. 13901, Portland Flouring Mills Company *v.* Northern Pacific Railway Company et al.; [decided Oct. 11, 1923; report of commission]. 1923. [1]+366–368 p. ([Opinion] 8846.) [From Interstate Commerce Commission reports, v. 83.] *Paper, 5c.

Rice. No. 12341, Rosenberg Bros. & Company et al. *v.* director general, as agent; decided Nov. 5, 1923; report of commission on further hearing. [1923.] p. 557–559. ([Opinion] 8905.) [From Interstate Commerce Commission reports, v. 83.] *Paper, 5c.

—— No. 13051, R. L. Abbott et al. *v.* director general, as agent, Chicago, Rock Island & Pacific Railway Company, et al.; [decided Oct. 27, 1923; report of commission]. 1923. [1]+508–511 p. ([Opinion] 8888.) [From Interstate Commerce Commission reports, v. 83.] *Paper, 5c.

—— No. 13720, Standard Rice Company, Incorporated, *v.* Galveston, Harrisburg & San Antonio Railway Company et al.; decided Oct. 13, 1923; report [and order] of commission. [1923.] 305–306+[1] p. ([Opinion] 8822.) [Report from Interstate Commerce Commission reports, v. 83.] *Paper, 5c.

Rome and Northern Railroad. Finance docket no. 1198, deficit settlement with Rome & Northern R. R., D. B. Carson, receiver; [decided June 18, 1923; report of commission]. 1923. [1]+822–823 p. ([Finance decision] 799–A.) [From Interstate Commerce Commission reports, v. 79.] *Paper, 5c.

Routing. No. 14347, Boston Wool Trade Association *v.* Atchison, Topeka & Santa Fe Railway Company et al.; decided Oct. 22, 1923; report [and order] of commission. [1923.] 445–450+[1] p. ([Opinion] 8871.) [Report from Interstate Commerce Commission reports, v. 83.] *Paper, 5c.

Rutland Railroad. Finance docket no. 775, guaranty settlement with Rutland R. R.; decided Oct. 20, 1923; report of commission. [1923.] p. 519–521. ([Finance decision] 977.) [From Interstate Commerce Commission reports, v. 82.] *Paper, 5c.

Salem, Winona and Southern Railroad. Finance docket no. 1351, deficit status of Salem, Winona & Southern R. R.; decided Oct. 23, 1923; report of commission. [1923.] p. 541–542. ([Finance decision] 984.) [From Interstate Commerce Commission reports, v. 82.] *Paper, 5c.

Saltpeter, Chile. No. 13278, Trojan Powder Company *v.* Philadelphia & Reading Railway Company et al.; decided Oct. 27, 1923; report [and order] of commission. [1923.] 481–482+[1] p. ([Opinion] 8878.) [Report from Interstate Commerce Commission reports, v. 83.] *Paper, 5c.

Sand. Investigation and suspension docket no. 1848, sand and gravel from stations on Charleston & Western Carolina Railway to Southeast; [decided Oct. 27, 1923; report and order of commission]. 1923. [1]+436–442+[1] p. ([Opinion] 8869.) [Report from Interstate Commerce Commission reports, v. 83.] *Paper, 5c.

—— No. 12727, Fairbanks, Morse & Company *v.* director general, as agent; [decided Oct. 27, 1923; report of commission]. 1923. [1]+496–498 p. ([Opinion] 8884.) [From Interstate Commerce Commission reports, v. 83.] *Paper, 5c.

—— No. 13261, United Iron Works, Incorporated, *v.* director general, as agent, et al.; [decided Oct. 10, 1923; report and order of commission]. 1923. [1]+282–284+[1] p. ([Opinion] 8815.) [Report from Interstate Commerce Commission reports, v. 83.] *Paper, 5c.

Sand—Continued. No. 13814, Barnes Foundry Company *v.* director general, as agent; decided Oct. 10, 1923; report [and order] of commission. [1923.] 233–234+ [1] p. ([Opinion] 8803.) [Report from Interstate Commerce Commission reports, v. 83.] *Paper, 5c.

Shells (conchology). No. 13433, Lester & Toner, Incorporated, *v.* Long Island Railroad Company et al.; decided Oct. 10, 1923; report [and order] of commission. [1923.] 251–254+ii p. ([Opinion] 8808.) [Report from Interstate Commerce Commission reports, v. 83.] *Paper, 5c.

Sisal hemp. No. 13212, Erie Corporation *v.* International & Great Northern Railway Company et al.; decided Oct. 10, 1923; report [and order] of commission. [1923.] 325–327+[1] p. ([Opinion] 8830.) [Report from Interstate Commerce Commission reports, v. 83.] *Paper, 5c.

Smoky Mountain Railway. Finance docket no. 221, deficit settlement with Smoky Mountain Railway; decided Oct. 3, 1923; report of commission. [1923.] p. 355–356. ([Finance decision] 920.) [From Interstate Commerce Commission reports, v. 82.] *Paper, 5c.

Soda (caustic). No. 13544, Hooker Electro Chemical Company et al. *v.* Atlantic City Railroad Company et al.; [decided Oct. 5, 1923; report and order of commission]. 1923. [1]+196–202+ii p. ([Opinion] 8793.) [Report from Interstate Commerce Commission reports, v. 83.] *Paper, 5c.

Speedometers. No. 13628, Olney-Hart, Incorporated, *v.* Chicago, Milwaukee & St. Paul Railway Company et al.; [decided Oct. 27, 1923; report of commission]. 1923. [1]+514–515 p. ([Opinion] 8890.) [From Interstate Commerce Commission reports, v. 83.] *Paper, 5c.

Staves. No. 14207, Sandusky Cooperage & Lumber Company *v.* Nashville, Chattanooga & St. Louis Railway et al.; portions of 4th section applications nos. 458, 1548, and 2494; decided Oct. 10, 1923; report [and order] of commission. [1923.] 271–274+ii p. ([Opinion] 8813.) [Report from Interstate Commerce Commission reports, v. 83.] *Paper, 5c.

Steam-turbines. No.11417, Northwest Steel Company et al. *v.* director general, as agent, et al.; [decided Oct. 10, 1923; report and order of commission]. 1923. [1]+298–300+[1] p. ([Opinion] 8820.) [Report from Interstate Commerce Commission reports. v. 83.] *Paper, 5c.

Steamboats. Schedule of sailings (as furnished by steamship companies named herein) of steam vessels which are registered under laws of United States and which are intended to load general cargo at ports in United States for foreign destinations, Nov. 15–Dec. 31, 1923, no. 15; issued by Section of Tariffs, Bureau of Traffic. 1923. iii+29 p. 4° [Monthly. No. 15 cancels no. 14.] †
22—26610

Steel. No. 13967, Alan Wood Iron & Steel Company et al. *v.* Pennsylvania Railroad Company et al.; decided Oct. 26, 1923; report [and order] of commission. [1923.] 503–507+[1] p. ([Opinion] 8887.) [Report from Interstate Commerce Commission reports, v. 83.] *Paper, 5c.

Stoves. No. 13283, General Gas Light Company *v.* Alabama Great Southern Railroad Company et al.; decided Oct. 11, 1923; report [and order] of commission. [1923.] 361–365+iii p. ([Opinion] 8845.) [Report from Interstate Commerce Commission reports, v. 83.] *Paper, 5c.

Straw. No. 13405, Lafayette Box Board & Paper Company *v.* director general, as agent; decided Oct. 10, 1923; report of commission. [1923.] p. 307–310. ([Opinion] 8823.) [From Interstate Commerce Commission reports, v. 83.] *Paper, 5c.

Strawberries. No. 11995, Charles C. Oyler & Son et al. *v.* American Railway Express Company; [decided Oct. 2, 1923; report and order of commission]. 1923. [1]+160–164+[1] p. ([Opinion] 8785.) [Report from Interstate Commerce Commission reports, v. 83.] *Paper, 5c.

Sugar. No. 11902, Beaumont Chamber of Commerce et al. *v.* director general, as agent, Beaumont, Sour Lake & Western Railway Company, et al.; decided Oct. 2, 1923; report of commission. [1923.] p. 125–130. ([Opinion] 8781.) [From Interstate Commerce Commission reports, v. 83.] *Paper, 5c.

—— No. 13805, Hale-Halsell Company *v.* Alabama & Vicksburg Railway Company et al.; decided Oct. 27, 1923; report [and orders] of commission. [1923.] 535–537+iii p. ([Opinion] 8897.) [Report from Interstate Commerce Commission reports, v. 83.] *Paper, 5c.

Sugar-beet syrup. No. 13808, Holly Sugar Corporation *v.* director general, as agent; [decided Oct. 27, 1923; report and order of commission]. 1923.. [1]+488–490+[1] p. ([Opinion] 8881.) [Report from Interstate Commerce: Commission reports, v. 83.] *Paper, 5c.

Sulphuric acid. No. 13381, Wilson & Toomer Fertilizer Company *v.* director general, as agent; [decided Oct. 10, 1923; report and order of commission]. 1923. [1]+264–266+[1] p. ([Opinion] 8811.) [Report from Interstate Commerce Commission reports, v. 83.] *Paper, 5c.

Surry, Sussex and Southampton Railway. Finance docket no. 228, deficit status. of Surry, Sussex & Southampton Ry.; decided Aug. 11, 1923; report of commission. [1923.] p. 491–492. ([Finance decision] 968.) [From Interstate. Commerce Commission reports, v. 82.] *Paper, 5c.

Switching charges. No. 318, in Supreme Court, Oct. term, 1923, Peoria & Pekin Union Railway Company *v.* United States, Interstate Commerce Commission, et al.; brief for Interstate Commerce Commission. 1923. covertitle, ii+35 p. ‡

—— . No. 13734, Cyrus C. Shafer Lumber Company *v.* director general, as agent, and Illinois Central Railroad Company; decided Oct. 11, 1923; report [and order] of commission. [1923.] 427–428+[1] p. ([Opinion] 8865.) [Report from Interstate Commerce Commission reports, v. 83.] *Paper, 5c.

—— No. 13811, Weber Flour Mills Corporation et al. *v.* Union Pacific Railroad Company; decided Oct. 11, 1923; report of commission. [1923.] p. 385–388. ([Opinion] 8853.) [From Interstate Commerce Commission reports, v. 83.] *Paper, 5c.

Tampa and Gulf Coast Railroad. Finance docket no. 824, guaranty settlement. with Tampa & Gulf Coast R. R.; decided Oct. 18, 1923; report of. commission. [1923.] p. 483–485. ([Finance decision] 966.) [From Interstate Commerce. Commission reports, v. 82.] *Paper, 5c.

Tampa Northern Railroad. Finance docket no. 825, guaranty settlement with Tampa Northern R. R.; decided Oct. 18, 1923; report of commission. [1923.] p. 493–495. ([Finance decision] 969.) [From Interstate Commerce Commission reports, v. 82.] *Paper, 5c.

Tavares and Gulf Railroad. Finance docket no. 229, deficit settlement with Tavares & Gulf R. R.; decided Oct. 6, 1923; report of commission. [1923.] p. 373–374. ([Finance decision] 926.) [From Interstate Commerce Commission reports, v. 82.] *Paper, 5c.

Toledo and Ohio Central Railway. Finance docket no. 839, guaranty settlement with Toledo & Ohio Central Ry.; [decided Oct. 18, 1923; report of commission]. 1923. [1]+496–498 p. ([Finance decision] 970.) [From Interstate Commerce Commission reports, v. 82.] *Paper, 5c.

Toledo and Western Railroad. Finance docket no. 1455, deficit status of Toledo. & Western R. R. [J. Frank Johnson, Harry A. Dunn, and Joseph A. Yoger, receivers]; decided Sept. 29, 1923; report of commission. [1923.] p. 389–390. ([Finance decision] 932.) [From Interstate Commerce Commission reports, v. 82.] *Paper, 5c.

Toledo, Saginaw and Muskegon Railway. Finance docket no. 842, guaranty settlement with Toledo, Saginaw & Muskegon Ry.; [decided Sept. 29, 1923; report of commission]. 1923. [1]+352–354 p. ([Finance decision] 919.) [From Interstate Commerce Commission reports, v. 82.] *Paper, 5c.

Union Freight Railroad. Finance docket no. 3178, note of Union Freight Railroad; decided Oct. 23, 1923; report of commission. [1923.] p. 597–598. ([Finance decision] 1005.) [From Interstate Commerce Commission reports, v. 82.] *Paper, 5c.

Union Pacific Railroad. Finance docket no. 855, guaranty settlement with Union Pacific Railroad and affiliated companies, in matter of settlement with Union Pacific Railroad Company, Los Angeles & Salt Lake Railroad Company, Oregon Short Line Railroad Company, and Oregon-Washington Railroad & Navigation Company (including Des Chutes Railroad Company) under sec. 209 of transportation act, 1920; [and finance dockets nos. 434, 592, 721, and 723; decided Oct. 16, 1923; report of commission]. 1923. [1]+486–490 p. ([Finance decision] 967.) [From Interstate Commerce Commission reports, v. 82.] *Paper, 5c.

Unlading and lading. Investigation and suspension docket no. 1851, loading and unloading live stock at Chicago, Ill.; [decided Oct. 17, 1923; report and order of commission]. 1923. [1]+248–250+ [1] p. ([Opinion] 8807.) [Report from Interstate Commerce Commission reports, v. 83.] *Paper, 5c.

Vicksburg, Shreveport and Pacific Railway. Finance docket no. 3218, Vicksburg, Shreveport & Pacific Railway bonds; decided Oct. 18, 1923; report of commission. [1923.] p. 535–538. ([Finance decision] 982.) [From Interstate Commerce Commission reports, v. 82.] *Paper, 5c.

Virginia Blue Ridge Railroad.. Finance docket no. 867, guaranty settlement with Virginia Blue Ridge Ry.; [decided Oct. 4, 1923; report of commission]. 1923. [1]+438–440 p. ([Finance decision] 950.) [From Interstate Commerce Commission reports, v. 82.] *Paper, 5c.

Washington Run Railroad. Finance docket no. 1364, deficit settlement with Washington Run R. R.; decided Oct. 15, 1923; report of commission. [1923.] p. 445–446. ([Finance decision] 953.) [From Interstate Commerce Commission reports, v. 82.] *Paper, 5c.

Watermelons. No. 13458, Ben D. Anguish et al. *v.* Alabama & Vicksburg Railway Company et al.; decided Oct. 11, 1923; report [and order] of commission. [1923.] 353–355+iii p. ([Opinion] 8842.) [Report from Interstate Commerce Commission reports, v. 83.] *Paper, 5c.

Waupaca-Green Bay Railway. Finance docket no. 881, guaranty settlement with Waupaca-Green Bay Ry.; [decided Oct. 20, 1923; report of commission]. 1923. [1]+522–524 p. ([Finance decision) 978.) [From Interstate Commerce Commission reports, v. 82.] *Paper, 5c.

Weights and measures. No. 13383, National Retail Coal Merchants' Association *v.* Baltimore & Ohio Railroad Company et al.; [decided Oct. 10, 1923; report and order of commission]. 1923. [1]+328–330+[1] p. ([Opinion] 8831.) [Report from Interstate Commerce Commission reports, v. 83.] *Paper, 5c.

West Virginia Northern Railroad. Finance docket no. 242, deficit status of West Virginia Northern R. R.; decided Oct. 11, 1923; report of commission. [1923.] p. 431–434. ([Finance decision] 947.) [From Interstate Commerce Commission reports, v. 82.] *Paper, 5c.

Western Maryland Railway. Finance docket no. 3234, securities of Western Maryland Railway; decided Oct. 19, 1923; report of commission. [1923.] p. 539–540. ([Finance decision] 983). [From Interstate Commerce Commission reports, v. 82.] *Paper, 5c.

Wheat. No. 13411, Saginaw Milling Company et al. *v.* director general, as agent, Pere Marquette Railway Company, et al.; decided Oct. 11, 1923; report [and order] of commission. [1923.] 343–344+[1] p. ([Opinion] 8838.) [Report from Interstate Commerce Commission reports, v. 83.] *Paper, 5c.

Wheeling Terminal Railway. Finance docket no. 2515, lease of properties of subsidiary companies by Pennsylvania R. R.. in matter of application of Pennsylvania Railroad Company for authority to acquire control, by lease, of railroad and property of Wheeling Terminal Railway Company; [and finance dockets nos. 2516–19]; approved Oct. 2, 1923; amendatory order. 1923. p. 347. ([Finance decision] 916.) [From Interstate Commerce Commission reports, v. 82.] *Paper, 5c.

Wood-pulp. No. 14529, International Paper Company *v.* Maine Central Railroad Company et al.; decided Oct. 10, 1923; report of commission. [1923.] p. 235–237. ([Opinion] 8804.) [From Interstate Commerce Commission reports, v. 83.] *Paper, 5c.

York Harbor and Beach Railroad. Finance docket no. 914, guaranty settlement with York Harbor & Beach R. R.; [decided Oct. 2, 1923; report of commission]. 1923. [1]+384–386 p. ([Finance decision] 930.) [From Interstate Commerce Commission reports, v. 82.] *Paper, 5c.

JUSTICE DEPARTMENT

Archer, John. In Court of Claims, John Archer *v.* United States, no. C–1147; demurrer [and] brief. [1923.] p. 1–4, large 8° ‡

Baltimore and Ohio Railroad. In Court of Claims, Baltimore & Ohio R. R. Co. *v.* United States, no. 56–A; defendant's objections to plaintiff's request for findings of fact, defendant's request for findings of fact, and brief thereon. [1923.] p. 1–7, large 8° ‡

Baltimore and Ohio Railroad—Continued. No. 12497 and 12497 sub-no. 1, before Interstate Commerce Commission, United States *v.* director general, as agent, Baltimore & Ohio Railroad Company, et al.; [same] *v.* Wharton & Northern Railroad Company et al.; supplemental petition. 1923. cover-title, 4 p. ‡

Barrow, David W. No. 3996, in Court of Appeals of District of Columbia, Oct. term, 1923, no. —, special calendar, David W. Barrow *v.* United States; brief for appellee. 1923. cover-title, i+27 p. ‡

Bascobal, steam tug. No. —, in circuit court of appeals for 5th circuit, United States, claimant of steam tug Bascobal, *v.* Berwind-White Coal Mining Company, owner of cargo on barge Richmond, appeal from district court for southern district of Texas; brief for United States. 1923. cover-title, i+20 p. ‡

Bay, Emily W. In Court of Claims, Emily W. Bay *v.* United States, no. C–1155; demurrer [and] brief. [1923.] p. 1–6, large 8° ‡

Behn, Meyer & Co., Limited. No. 4014, Court of Appeals of District of Columbia, Oct. term, 1923, Behn, Meyer & Company, Limited, *v.* Thomas W. Miller, as Alien Property Custodian, and Frank White, as Treasurer of United States; brief on behalf of Thomas W. Miller, as Alien Property Custodian, and Frank White, as Treasurer of United States. 1923. cover-title, i+56 p. ‡

Bond, H. B. In Court of Claims, H. B. Bond *v.* United States, no. B–155; demurrer [and] brief. [1923.] p. 5–8, large 8° ‡

Cape Cruz Company. In Court of Claims, Cape Cruz Company *v.* United States, no. C–701; demurrer [and brief]. [1923.] p. 1–9, large 8° ‡

Carr, James M. In Court of Claims, James M. Carr *v.* United States, no. C–1142; demurrer [and brief]. [1923.] p.1–6, large 8° ‡

Carroll, George. No. 117, in Supreme Court, Oct. term, 1923, George Carroll and John Kiro *v.* United States, in error to district court for western district of Michigan; brief for United States. 1923. cover-title, ii+21 p. ‡

Chemical Foundation, Incorporated. In equity, no. 502, in district court for district of Delaware, United States *v.* Chemical Foundation, Incorporated; reply brief on behalf of United States. 1923. cover-title, viii +399 p. 4° ‡

Chichester Chemical Company. In Court of Appeals of District of Columbia, Oct. term, 1923, no. 4021, United States *v.* Chichester Chemical Company, proprietor and vendor of what is known as Chi-ches-ters diamond brand new style pills; no. 4022, [same] *v.* [same]; brief for appellant. 1923. cover-title, 17 p. ‡

Clallam County, Wash. [No. 255, in Supreme Court, Oct. term, 1923, Clallam County, Wash., William A. Nelson, sheriff of Clallam County, E. C. Stewart, treasurer of Clallam County, et al. *v.* United States and United States Spruce Production Corporation, on certificate from circuit court of appeals for 9th circuit; brief for United States] addendum. [1923.] 3 p. [This is printed without title. The signature mark reads: 69681–23.] ‡

Clemmings, Grover E. No. 223, in Supreme Court, Oct. term, 1923, Grover E. Clemmings *v.* United States, in error to district court for district of Minnesota; motion by United States to transfer to circuit court of appeals for 8th circuit. 1923. cover-title, 3 p. ‡

Consolidated Supply Company. In Court of Claims, George M. Davis, doing business as Consolidated Supply Company, *v.* United States, no. B–88; objections to plaintiff's request for findings of fact [and brief]. [1923.] p. 27–38, large 8° ‡

Dayton-Goose Creek Railway. Recapture of excess earnings case, no. 330, in Supreme Court, Oct. term, 1923, Dayton-Goose Creek Railway Company *v.* United States, appeal from district court for eastern district of Texas; brief for United States. 1923. cover-title, iv+162 p. ‡

DeWitt, Theodore. No. 620, in Supreme Court, Oct. term, 1923, Theodore DeWitt *v.* United States, on petition for writ of certiorari to circuit court of appeals for 6th circuit; brief for United States in opposition. 1923. cover-title, 5 p. ‡

Douglas Packing Company. No. 559, in Supreme Court, Oct. term, 1923, United States *v.* 95 barrels, more or less, alleged apple cider vinegar, Douglas Packing Company, claimant, on writ of certiorari to circuit court of appeals for 6th circuit; motion by United States to advance. 1923. cover-title, 3 p. ‡

Durnford, Nelida A. No. 173, in Supreme Court, Oct. term, 1923, United States ex rel. Nelida A. Durnford *v.* Hubert Work, Secretary of Interior, in error to Court of Appeals of District of Columbia; brief for defendant in error. 1923. cover-title, 7 p. ‡

Fehl, Earl H. In Court of Claims, Earl H. Fehl *v.* United States, no. C–704; demurrer [and] brief. [1923.] p. 13–18, large 8° ‡

Frye, James A. No. 3968, in Court of Appeals of District of Columbia, Oct. term, 1923, no.—, special calendar, James Alphonzo Frye *v.* United States; brief for appellee. 1923. cover-title, 9 p. ‡

Goltra, Edward F. No. 23, original, in Supreme Court, Oct. term, 1923, in matter of petition of United States, as owner of 19 barges and 4 towboats [leased to Edward F. Goltra]; brief for United States. 1923. cover-title, ii +47 p. ‹

Graham, Samuel J. No. 311, in Supreme Court, Oct. term, 1923, Joshua W. Miles collector [of internal revenue for district of Maryland], *v.* Samuel J. Graham, in error to district court for district of Maryland; motion by plaintiff in error to advance. 1923. cover-title, 3 p. ‡

Heintz, Joseph G. Nos. 599–602, in Supreme Court, Oct. term, 1923, Joseph G. Heintz et al. *v.* United States, on petition for writ of certiorari to circuit court of appeals for 7th circuit; brief for United States in opposition. 1923. cover-title, 5 p. ‡

Hewitt, Erskine. In Court of Claims, Erskine Hewitt *v.* United States, no. C–769; demurrer [and] brief. [1923.] p. 17–30, large 8° ‡

Industrial Association of San Francisco. In equity, no. 1044, in southern division of district court for northern district of California, 3d division, United States *v.* Industrial Association of San Francisco et al.; bill of complaint. [1923.] cover-title, 13 p. ‡

—— Same; opinion by Judge Dooling. [1923.] cover-title, 6 p. ‡

Johnston, James J. No. —, in Supreme Court, Oct. term, 1923, United States *v.* James J. Johnston; petition for writ of certiorari to circuit court of appeals for 2d circuit and brief in support thereof. 1923. cover-title, 4 p. ‡

Keve & Young. Nos. 2231, 2232, 2236, Court of Customs Appeals, Keve & Young *v.* United States; William A. Brown & Co. et al. *v.* [same]; Parfums d'Orsay (Inc.) *v.* [same]; supplemental brief for United States. 1923. cover-title, 8 p. ‡

Kirby, Thomas E. In Court of Claims, Thomas E. Kirby *v.* United States, [no.] C–1144; demurrer [and] brief. [1923.] p. 1–6, large 8° ‡

Leather, William. No. 172, in Supreme Court, Oct. term, 1923, William Leather and Leon K. Leigh *v.* Mark J. White [assistant surgeon general, Public Health Service] et al., appeal from circuit court of appeals for 7th circuit; motion of appellee, Mark J. White, to dismiss appeal, and brief in support. 1923. cover-title, 13 p. ‡

Lehigh Valley Railroad. In equity, no. 11–129, in district court, southern district of New York, United States *v.* Lehigh Valley Railroad Company et al.; final decree. 1923. cover-title, 35 p. ‡

Lexington Utilities Company. In Court of Claims, Lexington Utilities Company *v.* United States, no. C–1162; demurrer [and] brief. [1923.] p. 1–5, large 8° ‡

Liggins, George R. No. 4023, in Court of Appeals of District of Columbia, Oct. term, 1923, no. 29, special calendar, George Raymond Liggins *v.* United States; brief for appellee. 1923. cover-title, 6 p. ‡

Marr, Walter L. No. C–12, in Court of Claims, Walter L. Marr *v.* United States defendant's request for findings of fact, statement of case, brief. 1923. cover-title, i+45–73 p. large 8° ‡

Mensevich, Nicolai. No. 148, in Supreme Court, Oct. term, 1923, United States ex rel. Nicolai Mensevich *v.* Robert E. Tod, commissioner of immigration at port of New York, appeal from district court for southern district of New York; motion by appellee to dismiss or affirm. 1923. cover-title, 8 p. ‡

Midland Land and Improvement Company. In Court of Claims, Midland Land & Improvement Company *v.* United States, no. 33713; defendant's answer to plaintiff's motion for new trial. [1923.] p. 395–398, large 8° ‡

National Association of Window Glass Manufacturers. No. 353, in Supreme
Court, Oct. term, 1923, National Association of Window Glass Manufacturers,
National Window Glass Workers, et al., *v.* United States, appeal from district
court for northern district of Ohio; brief for United States. 1923. cover-
title, i+54 p. ‡

New York Coffee and Sugar Exchange, Incorporated. No. 331, in Supreme Court,
Oct. term, 1923, United States *v.* New York Coffee and Sugar Exchange (Inc.),
New York Coffee and Sugar Clearing Association (Inc.), et al., appeal from
district court for southern district of New York; reply brief for United States.
1923. cover-title, 12 p. ‡

New York, New Haven and Hartford Railroad. No. 44–B, in Court of Claims,
New York, New Haven & Hartford Railroad Company *v.* United States;
defendant's objections to plaintiff's request for findings of fact, defendant's
request for findings of fact, and brief. 1923. cover-title, p. 51–66, large
8° ‡

Oklahoma. No. 15, original, in Supreme Court, Oct. term, 1923, Oklahoma *v.*
Texas, United States, intervener; response of United States to motion of
Charles West for leave to intervene. 1923. cover-title, 2 p. ‡

Opinions. [Official opinions of Attorneys General] v. 33, [signature] 36. [1923.]
p. 561–576. ‡   12—40693

Peoria and Pekin Union Railway. No. 318, in Supreme Court, Oct. term, 1923,
Peoria & Pekin Union Railway Company *v.* United States, Interstate Commerce Commission, and Minneapolis & St. Louis Railroad Company, appeal
from district court for southern district of Illinois; brief for United States.
1923. cover-title, i+33 p. ‡

Pittsburgh and West Virginia Railway. In equity, no. 945, in district court for
western district of Pennsylvania, Pittsburgh and West Virginia Railway Company and James C. Davis, director general of railroads, *v.* United States and
Avella Coal Company et al.; brief for United States on motion to dismiss bill.
1923. cover-title, 17 p. ‡

—— No. 3986, in Court of Appeals of District of Columbia, Pittsburgh &
West Virginia Railway Company and West Side Belt Railroad Company *v.*
Interstate Commerce Commission and Harry M. Daugherty, Attorney General,
appeal from Supreme Court of District of Columbia; brief on behalf of Attorney General. 1923. cover-title, 15 p. ‡

Prince Line, Limited. Nos. 644 and 645, in Supreme Court, Oct. term, 1923,
United States *v.* Prince Line (Ltd.); [same] *v.* American-Hawaiian Steamship
Company, writs of error to district court for eastern district of New York;
motion by United States to vacate orders dismissing these cases and to enlarge
time for docketing writs of error. 1923. cover-title, 7 p. ‡

Remus, George. No. 638, in Supreme Court, Oct. term, 1923, George Remus et al.
v. United States, on petition for writ of certiorari to circuit court of appeals for
6th circuit; brief for United States in opposition. 1923. cover-title, 8 p. ‡

—— No. 639, in Supreme Court, Oct. term, 1923, George Remus et al. *v.*
United States, on petition for writ of certiorari to circuit court of appeals for
6th circuit; brief for United States in opposition. 1923. cover-title. 6 p. ‡

Rhodia Chemical Company. No. 2288, Court of Customs Appeals, Rhodia
Chemical Company *v.* United States; brief for United States on motion to
dismiss appeal. 1923. cover-title, 4 p. ‡

Ringk, A. H., & Co. No. 2318, Court of Customs Appeals, A. H. Ringk & Co. *v.*
United States; brief for United States. 1923. cover-title, 9 p. ‡

Rodman, Hugh. In Patent Office, interference no. 46630, Rodman *v.* Woodruff;
Woodruff evidence. 1923. cover-title, 46 p. ‡

Royer, Elmo R. In Court of Claims, Elmo R. Royer *v.* United States, no. 34193;
defendant's brief. [1923.] p. 77–81, large 8° ‡

Ruston, William H. In Court of Claims, William H. Ruston *v.* Department of
Internal Revenue, no. C–521; demurrer [and brief]. [1923.] p. 1–3, large
8° ‡

St. Louis, Brownsville and Mexico Railway. In Court of Claims, St. Louis,
Brownsville & Mexico Railway Company *v.* United States, no. 180–B; defendant's objections to plaintiff's request for findings of fact, defendant's request
for findings of fact, and brief. [1923.] p. 1–9, large 8° ‡

Sanday, Saml., & Co. In Court of Claims, Saml. Sanday [et al.] doing business under firm name and style of Saml. Sanday & Company, with office and principal place of business in London, England, *v.* United States, no. C–712; demurrer [and brief]. [1923.] p. 1–4, large 8° ‡

Schrader's, A., Son, Incorporated. In district court for eastern district of New York, United States *v.* A. Schrader's Son, Incorporated [et al.]; final decree. 1923. cover-title, 4 p. ‡

Shaw, Alex. D., & Co. No. 2298, Court of Customs Appeals, Alex. D. Shaw & Co. *v.* United States; brief for United States. 1923. cover-title, 16 p. ‡

Southern Pacific Company. In Court of Claims, no. 33946, Southern Pacific Company *v.* United States; defendant's brief on resubmission. [1923.] p. 241–255, large 8° ‡

Stoehr, Max W. United States circuit court of appeals for 2d circuit, Max W. Stoehr *v.* Thomas W. Miller, Alien Property Custodian; brief on behalf of Thomas W. Miller, as Alien Property Custodian. 1923. cover-title, i + 85 p. large 8° ‡

Swan, Charles T. In Court of Appeals of District of Columbia, Oct. term, 1923, no. 3980, no. 15, special calendar, Charles T. Swan *v.* United States; brief for appellee. 1923. cover-title, iii + 38 p. ‡

Terminal Railroad Association of St. Louis. No. 425, in Supreme Court, Oct. term, 1923, Terminal Railroad Association of St. Louis et al. *v.* United States et al., appeal from district court for eastern district of Missouri, eastern division; motion to advance. 1923. cover-title, 4 p. ‡

Texas-Pacific Coal and Oil Company. In Court of Claims, Texas-Pacific Coal & Oil Company, Texas-Pacific Mercantile and Manufacturing Company, and Thurber Brick Company *v.* United States, no. C–678; demurrer [and brief]. [1923.] p. 151–159, large 8° ‡

Tisi, Catoni. No. 132, in Supreme Court, Oct. term, 1923, United States ex rel. Catoni Tisi, alias Lista Cortina, *v.* Robert E. Tod, commissioner of immigration at port of New York, appeal from district court for southern district of New York; brief for respondent. 1923. cover-title, 10 p. ‡

Union Pacific Railway. In Court of Claims, Union Pacific Railway Co. *v.* United States, no. 89–A; defendant's objections to plaintiff's request for findings of fact, defendant's request for findings of fact, and brief. [1923.] p. 53–64, large 8° ‡

Vue de l'Eau Company. No. 109, in Supreme Court, Oct. term, 1923, Guaranty Title & Trust Corporation, receiver of Vue de l'Eau Company, intervener, *v.* United States, appeal from Court of Claims; brief for United States. 1923, cover-title, 3 p. ‡

Western Pacific Railway. In Court of Claims, Western Pacific Railway Company *v.* United States, no. 30–A; defendant's objections to plaintiff's request for findings of fact, defendant's request for findings of fact, and brief. [1923.] p. 101–107, large 8° ‡

Worcester Pressed Steel Company. In Court of Claims, Worcester Pressed Steel Company *v.* United States, no. C–750; demurrer [and brief]. [1923.] p. 8–29, large 8° ‡

LABOR DEPARTMENT

CHILDREN'S BUREAU

Children. Books and pamphlets on child care. [1923.] [4] p. 4° ([Dodger no. 1 revised.]) †

Gary, Ind. Children of preschool age in Gary, Ind.: pt. 1, General conditions affecting child welfare, by Elizabeth Hughes; pt. 2, Diet of the children, by Lydia Roberts. 1922. ix + 175 p. il. 3 pl. 4 p. of pl. map. (Bureau publication 122.) *Paper, 20c.   L23—269

Unemployment and child welfare, study made in middle-western [Racine, Wis.] and eastern city [Springfield, Mass.], during industrial depression of 1921 and 1922; by Emma Octavia Lundberg. 1923. ix + 173 p. il. (Bureau publication 125.) *Paper, 20c.   L23—270

EMPLOYMENT SERVICE

Industrial employment information bulletin, v. 3, no. 10; Oct. 1923   [1923.] 20 p. 4° [Monthly.] †   L21—17

, LABOR STATISTICS BUREAU

Chinese migrations, with special reference to labor conditions [with bibliographies and with list of reference books published in Chinese]; by Ta Chen. July, 1923. vi+237+vii p. il. 3 pl. 2 maps. (Bulletin 340; Miscellaneous series; H. doc. 19, 68th Cong. 1st sess.) *Paper, 35c. L23—236

Employment in selected industries, Oct. 1923. 1923. 10 p. [From Monthly labor review, Dec. 1923.] †

Foundry work. Wages and hours of labor in foundries and machine shops, 1923. [1923.] p. 835–837. [From Monthly labor review, Oct. 1923.] †

Labor and laboring classes. Decisions of courts and opinions affecting labor, 1922; [compiled by] Lindley D. Clark and Daniel F. Callahan. Sept. 1923. xiv+421 p. (Bulletin 344; Labor laws of United States series.) *Paper, 50c.

—— Same. (H. doc. 23, 68th Con. 1st sess.) ·

Labor bureaus. Laws providing for bureaus of labor statistics, etc. Aug. 1923. iv+170 p. (Bulletin 343; Labor laws of United States series.) *Paper, 20c.
L23—281

—— Same. (H. doc. 22, 68th Cong. 1st sess.)

Monthly labor review, v. 17, no. 5; Nov. 1923. 1923. v+991–1223 p. il. *Paper. 15c. single copy, $1.50 a yr.; foreign subscription, $2.25. 15—26485

SPECIAL ARTICLES.—Estimated annual number and cost of industrial accidents in United States; by Carl Hookstadt.—Present economic situation of German student body; by E. Boehler.—Analysis of Mexican State laws on wages and hours of labor, and employment of women and children; by John Ritchie, 3d.—Conciliation work of Department of Labor, Sept. 1923; by Hugh L. Kerwin.—Statistics of immigration, July–Aug. 1923; by W. W. Husband.

NOTE.—The Review is the medium through which the Bureau publishes the results of original investigations too brief for bulletin purposes, notices of labor legislation by the States or by Congress, and Federal court decisions affecting labor, which from their importance should be given attention before they could ordinarily appear in the bulletins devoted to these subjects. One free subscription will be given to all labor departments and bureaus, workmen's compensation commissions. and other offices connected with the administration of labor laws and organizations exchanging publications with the Labor Statistics Bureau. Others desiring copies may obtain them from the Superintendent of Documents, Washington, D. C., at the prices stated above.

Prices. Prices and cost of living. 1923. [1]+1022–76 p. il. [From Monthly labor review, Nov. 1923.] †

—— Wholesale prices of commodities for Oct. 1923. 1923. [1]+9 p. [Monthly.] †
L22—229

LIBRARY OF CONGRESS
COPYRIGHT OFFICE

Copyright. [Catalogue of copyright entries, new series, pt. 1, group 1, Books, v. 20] no. 73–80; Nov. 1923. Nov. 3–28, 1923. p. 881–1008. [Issued several times a week.] · 6—35347

NOTE.—Each number is issued in 4 parts: pt. 1, group 1, relates to books; pt. 1, group 2, to pamphlets, leaflets, contributions to newspapers or periodicals, etc., lectures, sermons, addresses for oral delivery, dramatic compositions, maps, motion pictures; pt. 2, to periodicals; pt. 3, to musical compositions; pt. 4, to works of art, reproductions of a work of art, drawings or plastic works of scientific or technical character, photographs, prints, and pictorial illustrations.

Subscriptions for the Catalogue of copyright entries should be made to the Superintendent of Documents, Washington, D. C., instead of to the Register of Copyrights. Prices are as follows: Paper, $3.00 a yr. (4 pts.), foreign subscription, $5.00: pt. 1 (groups 1 and 2), 5c. single copy (group 1, price of group 2 varies), $1.00 a yr., foreign subscription, $2.25: pt. 3, $1.00 a yr., foreign subscription, $1.50; pts. 2 and 4, each 10c. single copy, 50c. a yr., foreign subscription, 70c.

—— Same, pt. 1, group 2, Pamphlets, leaflets, contributions to newspapers or periodicals, etc., lectures, sermons, addresses for oral delivery, dramatic compositions, maps, motion pictures, v. 20, no. 6. 1923. iii+603–824 p. [Monthly.]

—— Same, pt. 1, group 2, Pamphlets, leaflets, contributions to newspapers or periodicals, etc., lectures, sermons, addresses for oral delivery, dramatic compositions, maps, motion pictures, v. 20, no. 7. 1923. iii+825–1023 p. [Monthly.]

—— Same, pt. 2, Periodicals, v. 18, no. 2. 1923. iii+97–186 p. [Quarterly.]

—— Same, pt. 3, Musical compositions, v. 18, no. 6. 1923. v+493–592 p. [Monthly.]

DOCUMENTS DIVISION

Government publications. Monthly check-list of State publications received during Sept. 1923; v. 14, no. 9. 1923. p. 353–400. *Paper, 10c. single copy, $1.00 a yr.; foreign subscription, $1.25. 10—8924

—— Same [title-page and index to] v. 13, 1922. 1923. [1]+481–535 p. *Paper, 10c.

MIXED CLAIMS COMMISSION, UNITED STATES AND GERMANY

Allegiance. Before Mixed Claims Commission, United States and Germany; brief on behalf of United States on question of diverse nationality. 1923. cover-title, 15 p. 4° ‡

Provident Mutual Life Insurance Company. Nos. 19, 248–256, before Mixed Claims Commission, United States and Germany, United States on behalf of Provident Mutual Life Insurance Company *v.* Germany; United States on behalf of New York Life Insurance Company *v.* [same]; United States on behalf of Mutual Life Insurance Company *v.* [same]; United States on behalf of Penn Mutual Life Insurance Company *v.* [same]; United States on behalf of Aetna Life Insurance Company *v.* [same]; United States on behalf of State Mutual Life Assurance Company *v.* [same]; United States on behalf of Northwestern Mutual Life Insurance Company *v.* [same]; United States on behalf of Equitable Life Assurance Society *v.* [same]; United States on behalf of Manhattan Life Insurance Company, Prudential Insurance Company, Metropolitan Life Insurance Company, *v.* [same]; United States on behalf of Travelers Insurance Company *v.* [same]; brief of United States. 1923. cover-title, viii+234 p. 4° ‡

NATIONAL ADVISORY COMMITTEE FOR AERONAUTICS

Flight. Reliable formulae for estimating airplane performance and effects of changes in weight, wing area, or power; by Walter S. Diehl. 1923. cover-title, 22 p. il. 4° (Report 173.) [Prepared by Aeronautics Bureau, Navy Department. Text and illustration on p. 2 and 3 of cover.] *Paper, 5c. 23—26965

—— Small angular oscillations of airplanes in steady flight; by F. H. Norton. 1923. cover-title, 8 p. il. 4° (Report 174.) [Text and illustration on p. 2 and 3 of cover.] *Paper, 5c. 23—27000

Propellers. Analysis of W. F. Durand's and E. P. Lesley's propeller tests [with list of references]; by Max M. Munk. 1923. cover-title, 14 p. il. 4° (Report 175.) [Text and illustration on p. 2 and 3 of cover.] *Paper, 5c. 23—26966

Report. Aeronautics, 8th annual report of National Advisory Committee for Aeronautics, [fiscal year] 1922, including Technical reports 133–158. 1923. ix+708 p. il. 4 pl. 1 tab. 4° [Each report is also published separately in advance.] *Paper, $1.50. 16—26395

CONTENTS.—8th annual report.—Report 133. Tail plane; by Max M. Munk.—Report 134. Performance of Maybach 300-horsepower airplane engine; by S. W. Sparrow.—Report 135. Performance of B. M. W. 185-horsepower airplane engine; by S. W. Sparrow.—Report 136. Damping coefficients due to tail surfaces in aircraft, by Lynn Chu; condensed and modified by Edward P. Warner.—Report 137. Point drag and total drag of Navy struts no. 1 modified; by A. F. Zahm, R. H. Smith, and G. C. Hill.—Report 138. Drag of C class airship hull with varying length of cylindric midships; by A. F. Zahm, R. H. Smith, and G. C. Hill.—Report 139. Influence of model surface and air flow texture on resistance of aerodynamic bodies; by A. F. Zahm.—Report 140. Lift and drag effects of wing-tip rake; by A. F. Zahm, R. M. Bear, and G. C. Hill.—Report 141. Experimental research on air propellers, 5; by W. F. Durand and E. P. Lesley.—Report 142. General theory of thin wing sections [with list of references]; by Max M. Munk.—Report 143. Analysis of stresses in German airplanes [with bibliography]; by Wilhelm Hoff.—Report 144. Decay of simple eddy; by H. Bateman.—Report 145. Internal stresses in laminated construction; by A. L. Heim, A. C. Knauss, and Louis Seutter.—Report 146. Six-component wind balance; by A. F. Zahm.—Report 147. Standard atmosphere; by Willis Ray Gregg.—Report 148. Pressure distribution over horizontal tail surfaces of airplane, 3; by F. H. Norton and W. G. Brown.—Report 149. Pressure distribution over rudder and fin of airplane in flight; by F. H. Norton and W. G. Brown.—Report 150. Pressure distribution over thick airfoils, model tests [with bibliography]; by F. H. Norton and D. L. Bacon.—Report 151. General biplane theory [with list of references]; by Max M. Munk.—Report 152. Aerodynamic properties of thick airfoils, 2, (continuation of Report 75); by F. H. Norton and D. L. Bacon.—Report 153. Controllability and maneuverability of airplanes; by F. H. Norton and W. G. Brown.—Report 154. Study of taking off and landing an airplane; by T. Carroll.—Report 155. Study of airplane maneuvers with special reference to angular velocities [with bibliography]; by H. J. E. Reid.—Report 156. Altitude effect on air speed indicators, 2 [with bibliography], (continuation of Report 110); by H. N. Eaton and W. A. MacNair.—Report 157. Nomenclature for aeronautics; [revision of Report 91].—Report 158. Mathematical equations for heat conduction in fins of air-cooled engines; by D. R. Harper, 3d, and W. B. Brown.

NAVY DEPARTMENT

ENGINEERING BUREAU

Marine engineering. Changes in Manual of engineering instructions, no. 20; Sept. 20, 1923. [1923.] 1 p. [Accompanied by reprints of certain pages to be inserted in their proper places in the new edition of the Manual of engineering instructions. A list of these reprinted pages is found on the first page of Changes 20 here catalogued.] †

MARINE CORPS

Orders. Marine Corps orders 6, 1923; Oct. 1, 1923. [1923.] 40 p. 4° ‡

Supplies. Changes [36] in System of accountability, Marine Corps, 1916; Sept. 25, 1922. [Reprint] 1923. 1 p. 4° ‡

—— Changes [41] in System of accountability, Marine Corps, 1916; Oct. 9, 1923. [1923.] 1 p. 4° [Accompanied by reprints of certain pages to be inserted in their proper places in the 1918 reprint of the original publication. A list of these reprinted pages is given on the first page.] ‡

MEDICINE AND SURGERY BUREAU

Heart diseases. Analysis of 360 cases of valvular heart disease discharged from naval service; by W. A. Bloedorn and L. J. Roberts. 1923. 12 p. il. [From United States naval medical bulletin, v. 19, no. 5.] †

Hospital Corps handbook, Navy, 1923 [with lists of references]; compiled by W. J. C. Agnew, W. W. Behlow, and N. L. Saunders]. 1923. v+717 p. il. [This is a revision of Handy book for Hospital Corps, Navy.] *Cloth, $1.00.
23—27460

Instructions issued by Bureau of Medicine and Surgery (for office files). 1923. 8 p. [From United States naval medical bulletin, v. 19, no. 5.] †

Malaria. Complement fixation test and other findings in malaria [with list of references]; by J. H. Chambers. 1923. 8 p. [From United States naval medical bulletin, v. 19, no. 5.] †

Manual. Changes in Manual for Medical Department [Navy, 1922], no. 1; July, 1923. [1923.] iii p. [Accompanied by reprints of certain pages to be inserted in their proper places in the original manual. A list of these reprinted pages is found on p. ii and iii of Changes 1 here catalogued.] ‡

Naval medical bulletin. United States naval medical bulletin, published for information of Medical Department of service, Nov. 1923, v. 19, no. 5; edited by W. M. Kerr. 1923. vi+651–734 p. il. 5 p. of pl. [Monthly.] *Paper, 15c. single copy, $1.50 a yr.; foreign subscription, $2.50.
8—35095

SPECIAL ARTICLES.—Analysis of 360 cases of valvular heart disease discharged from naval service; by W. A. Bloedorn and L. J. Roberts.—Complement fixation test and other findings in malaria [with list of references]; by J. H. Chambers.—Illumination of dental offices ashore and afloat; by H. E. Harvey.—Open operation for extraction of teeth; by S. H. Reed.—Deep X-ray therapy; by G. U. Pillmore.—Case of subphrenic abscess; by G. F. Cottle.—Instructions issued by Bureau of Medicine and Surgery.—Notes on preventive medicine for medical officers, Navy [including Convalescents' serum and measles virus in immunization of children against measles, with list of references; by T. W. Kemmerer].

X-rays. Deep X-ray therapy; by G. U. Pillmore. 1923. 8 p. [From United States naval medical bulletin, v. 19, no. 5.] †

NAVIGATION BUREAU

Chemistry, assignments 1–33, course based on Foundations of chemistry, by Blanchard and Wade; syllabus prepared by Elliot Snow. 1923. [1]+29 p. (Navy education-study courses.) ‡

Navy. American naval history, assignments 1–17, course based on Story of our navy (1918 edition); course and text by William Oliver Stevens. 1923. [1]+ 30 p. 12° (Navy education-study courses.) ‡

Navy directory, officers of Navy and Marine Corps, including officers of Naval Reserve Force (active), Marine Corps Reserve (active), and foreign officers serving with Navy, Nov. 1, 1923. 1923. iii+243 p. [Bimonthly.] *Paper, 25c. single copy, $1.25 a yr.; foreign subscription, $1.75.

Officers of Navy and Marine Corps in District of Columbia, Nov. 1, 1923. 1923. [1]+23 p. *Paper, 5c.
9—24810

HYDROGRAPHIC OFFICE

NOTE.—The charts, sailing directions, etc., of the Hydrographic Office are sold by the office in Washington and also by agents at the principal American and foreign seaports and American lake ports. Copies of the General catalogue of mariners' charts and books and of the Hydrographic bulletins, reprints, and Notice to mariners are supplied free on application at the Hydrographic Office in Washington and at the branch offices in Boston, New York, Philadelphia, Baltimore, Norfolk, Savannah, New Orleans, Galveston, San Francisco, Portland (Oreg.), Seattle, Chicago, Cleveland, Buffalo, Sault Ste. Marie, and Duluth.

Hydrographic bulletin, weekly, no. 1783–86; Nov. 7–28, 1923. [1923.] Each 1 p. f° and large 4° [For Ice supplements to accompany nos. 1783–86, see below under center head *Charts* the subhead *Pilot charts.*] †

Notice to aviators 11, 1923; Nov. 1 [1923]. [1923.] 5 p. [Monthly.] †
20–26958

Notice to mariners 44–47, 1923; Nov. 3–24 [1923]. [1923.] [xxxvi]+1179–1283 leaves. [Weekly.] †

Sumner line of position furnished ready to lay down upon chart by means of tables of simultaneous hour angle and azimuth of celestial bodies, latitude 60° N. to 60° S., declination 27° N. to 27° S. 1923. xviii+869 p. il. 4° ([Publication] 203.) †Cloth, $2.25. 23–26986

Tide calendars. Tide calendar [for Baltimore (Fort McHenry) and Cape Henry], Dec. 1923. [1923.] 1 p. 4° [Monthly.] †

—— Tide calendar [for Norfolk (Navy Yard) and Newport News, Va.], Dec. 1923. [1923.] 1 p. 4° [Monthly.] †

Charts

Castilletes Anchorage, Guajira Peninsula, Venezuela, from surveys by Caribbean Petroleum Co., in 1922; chart 5438. Scale naut. m. = 4.9 in. Washington, Hydrographic Office, Oct. 1923. 20.2×27.3 in. †20c.

Chishima Retto (Kuril Islands), Japan, Ketoi To to Shasukotan To, from Japanese surveys in 1916 and 1917 [with insets]; chart 5324. Scale naut. m. = 0.3 in. Washington, Hydrographic Office, Oct. 1923. 26.7×38.2 in. †50c.
Ushishiru To.
Yamato Wan, Matsuwa To.

Earth. Outline chart of the world [showing in Pacific groups of islands belonging to various countries, and mandate areas]; chart 1262a. Scale 10° long.=1.2 in. Washington, Hydrographic Office, Oct. 1923. 27.1×47.9 in. †50c.

Pilot charts. Ice supplement to north Atlantic pilot .chart; issue 83. Scale 1° long.=0.3 in. Washington, Hydrographic Office [1923]. 8.9×11.8 in. [To accompany Hydrographic bulletin 1783, Nov. 7, 1923.] †

—— Same; issue 84. Scale 1° long.=0.3 in. Washington, Hydrographic Office [1923]. ` 8.9×11.8 in. [To accompany Hydrographic bulletin 1784, Nov. 14, 1923.] †

—— Same; issue 85. Scale 1° long.=0.3 in. Washington, Hydrographic Office [1923]. 8.9×11.8 in. [To accompany Hydrographic bulletin 1785, Nov. 21, 1923.] †

—— Same; issue 86. Scale 1° long.=0.3 in. Washington, Hydrographic Office [1923]. 8.9×11.8 in. [To accompany Hydrographic bulletin 1786, Nov. 28, 1923.] †

—— Pilot chart of Central American waters, Dec. 1923; chart 3500. Scale 1° long.=0.7 in. Washington, Hydrographic Office, Nov. 15, 1923. 23.4× 35.1 in. [Monthly. Certain portions of the data are furnished by the Weather Bureau.] †10c.
NOTE.—Contains on reverse: New and shorter method for finding position [note concerning Hydrographic Office publication 203, Sumner line of position].

—— Pilot chart of Indian Ocean, Jan. 1924; chart 2603. Scale 1° long.=0.2 in. Washington, Hydrographic Office, Nov. 15, 1923. 22.6×31 in. [Monthly. Certain portions of the data are furnished by the Weather Bureau.] †10c.
NOTE.—Contains on reverse: New and shorter method for finding position [note concerning Hydrographic Office publication 203, Sumner line of position].

—— Pilot chart of north Atlantic Ocean, Dec. 1923; chart 1400. Scale 1° long.=0.27 in. Washington, Hydrographic Office, Nov. 15, 1923. 23.2× 31.8 in. [Monthly. Certain portions of the data are furnished by the Weather Bureau.] †10c. 14–16339
NOTE.—Contains on reverse: New and shorter method for finding position [note concerning Hydrographic Office publication 203, Sumner line of position].

—— Pilot chart of north Pacific Ocean, Jan. 1924; chart 1401. Scale 1° long.= 0.2 in. Washington, Hydrographic Office, Nov. 15, 1923. 23.7×35.3 in. [Monthly. Certain portions of the data are furnished by the Weather Bureau.] †10c.
NOTE.—Contains on reverse: New and shorter method for finding position [note concerning Hydrographic Office publication 203, Sumner line of position].

NAUTICAL ALMANAC OFFICE

Eclipses. Total eclipse of the sun, Jan. 24, 1925. 1923. 31 p. 1 pl. 2 maps (1 is in pocket). [Supplement to American ephemeris and nautical almanac, 1925.] *Paper, 30c. 23–27421

Register. Annual register of Naval Academy, Annapolis, Md., 79th academic year, 1923–24. 1923. iv+196 p. *Paper, 20c.   7–32067

RECRUITING BUREAU

Posters. [Poster] 228. n. p. [July 5, 1923]. 14×17 in. [Title is: Bluejackets meet king of Greece.] †

NOTE.—Entries for Posters 219–227 have not appeared in the Monthly catalogue.

—— Same 229. n. p. [July 9, 1923]. 14×17 in. [Title is: Foreign cruises for new scout cruisers.] †

—— Same 230. n. p. [May 26, 1923]. 14×17 in. [Title is: Among ruins of Pompeii.] †

—— Same 231. n. p. [July 6, 1923]. 14×17 in. [Title is: At the home of Hallide Hanoum.] †

—— Same 232. n. p. [July 27, 1923]. 14×17 in. [Title is: Cruising in the desert.] †

—— Same 233. n. p. [Aug. 7, 1923]. 14×17 in. [Title is: Chinese flivvers.] †

—— Same 234. n. p. [Aug. 13, 1923]. 14×17 in. [Title is: Chinese gargoyle.] †

—— Same 235. n. p. [Aug. 7, 1923]. 14×17 in. [Title is: Meeting king of Denmark.] †

—— Same 236. n. p. [Aug. 16, 1923]. 14×17 in. [Title is: Fine whale boat crew.] †

—— Same 237. n. p. [Aug. 17, 1923]. 14×17 in. [Title is: Fit to carry the flag.] †

—— Same 238. n. p. [Aug. 24, 1923]. 14×17 in. [Title is: Around Cape of Good Hope.] †

—— Same 239. n. p. [Sept. 20, 1923]. 14×17 in. [Title is: Battle fleet champions.] †

—— Same 240. n. p. [Sept. 12, 1923]. 14×17 in. [Title is: Sight-seeing in Morocco.] †

—— Same 241. n. p. [Sept. 20, 1923]. 14×17 in. [Title is: At Naval Training Station, Newport, R. I.] †

—— Same 242. n. p. [Oct. 10, 1923]. 14×17 in. [Title is: Roosevelt and Navy.] †

—— Same 243. n. p. [Oct. 11, 1923]. 14×17 in. [Title is: Navy aviation leads the world.] †

—— Same 244. n. p. [Oct. 25, 1923]. 14×17 in. [Title is: Learning a trade in Navy.] †

—— Same 245. n. p. [Nov. 6, 1923]. 14×17 in. [Title is: Training Navy radiomen.] †

—— Same 246. n. p. [Nov. 6, 1923]. 14×17 in. [Title is: Football at sea.] †

SUPPLIES AND ACCOUNTS BUREAU

Supply Corps, Navy. Memorandum for information of officers of Supply Corps, commanding officers of ships, and commandants 255; Nov. 1, 1923. [1923.] p. 7733–7825, 12°. [Monthly.] ‡

PAN AMERICAN UNION

NOTE.—The Pan American Union sells its own monthly bulletins, handbooks, etc., at prices usually ranging from 5c. to $2.50. The price of the English edition of the bulletin is 25c. a single copy or $2.50 a year, the Spanish edition $2.00 a year, the Portuguese edition $1.50 a year; there is an additional charge of 50c. a year on each edition for countries outside the Pan American Union. Address the Director General of the Pan American Union, Washington, D. C.

Bulletin (English edition). Bulletin of Pan American Union, Nov. 1923; [v. 57, no. 5]. [1923.] iv+429–536 p. il. [Monthly.]   8–30967

—— Same. (H. doc. 6, pt. 5, 68th Cong. 1st sess.)

—— *(Portuguese edition).* Boletim da União Pan-Americana, Novembro, 1923, edição portugueza; [v. 25, no. 5]. [Sun Job Print, Baltimore, Md., 1923.] [iv]+315–390 p. il. [Monthly.]   11–27014

Bulletin—Continued. (*Spanish edition*). Boletín de la Unión Panamericana, v. 54 [sección española]; Enero-Junio, 1922 [índice]. [1923.] [1]+xvi p.
12–12555

—— Same, Noviembre, 1923, edición española; [v. 57, no. 5]. [1923.] iv+441–552 p. il. [Monthly. This number is entitled La Cruz Roja en las Américas.]

Chile, general descriptive data. 1923. [2]+30 p. il. †   11–35833

Colombia, general descriptive data. 1923. [2]+30 p. il. †   11–35834

Junior Red Cross. La Cruz Roja Juvenil; [por W. S. Gard]. 1923. [2]+10 p. il. [From Boletín, Nov. 1923.] †

Pan American Student League. Pan American Student League. 1923. [1]+2 p. [From Bulletin, Nov. 1923.] †

Panama. Commerce of Panama, latest reports from Panaman official sources. 1923. [1]+4+[1] p. †   13–6845

PANAMA CANAL

NOTE.—Although The Panama Canal makes its reports to, and is under the supervision of, the Secretary of War, it is not a part of the War Department.

Panama Canal record, v. 17, no. 13–16; Nov. 7–28, 1923. Balboa Heights, C. Z. [1923]. p. 197–248. [Weekly.]   7–35328

NOTE.—The yearly subscription rate of the Panama Canal record is 50c. domestic, and $1.00 foreign, (single issues 2c.), except in the case of Government departments and bureaus, Members of Congress, representatives of foreign governments, steamship lines, chambers of commerce, boards of trade, and university and public libraries, to whom the Record is distributed free. The word "domestic" refers to the United States. Canada, Canal Zone, Cuba, Guam. Hawaii, Manua, Mexico, the Philippines, Porto Rico, Republic of Panama, Tutuila, and the Virgin Islands. Subscriptions will commence with the first issue of the Record in the month in which the subscriptions are received, unless otherwise requested. Remittances should be made payable to Disbursing Clerk, The Panama Canal, but should be forwarded to the Chief of Office, The Panama Canal, Washington, D. C. The name and address to which the Record is to be sent should be plainly written. Postage stamps, foreign money, and defaced or smooth coins will not be accepted.

Vehicles. Vehicle and traffic laws and regulations in force in Canal Zone, Aug. 15, 1921, amended Oct. 15, 1923. Panama Canal Press, Mount Hope, C. Z., [Nov. 13] 1923. 42 p. small 4° †

POST OFFICE DEPARTMENT

Insured mail. Receipts to be taken for all insured mail delivered, effective Dec. 1, 1923; [issued by] 3d assistant Postmaster General. Nov. 21, 1923. 1 p. narrow large 8° †

Mail contracts. Advertisement inviting proposals for carrying mails on star routes in Alabama, July 1, 1924–June 30, 1928. Oct. 26, 1923. [1]+70 p. [Interleaved.] †

—— Advertisement inviting proposals for carrying mails on star routes in Florida, July 1, 1924–June 30, 1928. Oct. 26, 1923. [1]+45 p. [Interleaved.] †

—— Advertisement inviting proposals for carrying mails on star routes in Georgia, July 1, 1924–June 30, 1928. Oct. 26, 1923. [1]+49 p. [Interleaved.] †

—— Advertisement inviting proposals for carrying mails on star routes in Kentucky, July 1, 1924–June 30, 1928. Oct. 26, 1923. [1]+182 p. [Interleaved.] †

—— Advertisement inviting proposals for carrying mails on star routes in Mississippi, July 1, 1924–June 30, 1928. Oct. 26, 1923. [1]+59 p. [Interleaved.] †

—— Advertisement inviting proposals for carrying mails on star routes in North Carolina, July 1, 1924–June 30, 1928. Oct. 26, 1923. [1]+97 p. [Interleaved.] †

—— Advertisement inviting proposals for carrying mails on star routes in South Carolina, July 1, 1924–June 30, 1928. Oct. 26, 1923. [1]+39 p. [Interleaved.] †

—— Advertisement inviting proposals for carrying mails on star routes in Tennessee, July 1, 1924–June 30, 1928. Oct. 26, 1923. [1]+62 p. [Interleaved.] †

Mail matter. Inserts [837] to Postal laws and regulations [of United States]; Sept. 29, 1923. [1923.] 4 p. [This is Joint regulations adopted by Secretary of Treasury and Postmaster General governing treatment of mail matter received from foreign countries involving customs revenue. From United States official postal guide, Nov. 1923.] ‡

Money-orders. Further change in conversion rates for international money orders; [issued by] 3d assistant Postmaster General. Nov. 9, 1923. 1 p. ' †

Parcel post. Abstract from United States official postal guide for [July] 1923: International (foreign) parcel post. 1923. [1]+172-224 p. ‡

Postage due on all mail must be collected; [issued by] 3d assistant Postmaster General. Nov. 19, 1923. 1 p. oblong 32° †

Postage-stamps. Use of precanceled stamps on holiday mail; [issued by] 3d assistant Postmaster General. Oct. 30, 1923. 1 p. narrow 8° †

Postal bulletin, v. 44, no. 13307–331; Nov. 1–30, 1923. [1923.] various paging, f° [Daily except Sundays and holidays.] *Paper, 5c. single copy, $2.00 a yr.
                                                                          6–5810

Postal guide. United States official postal guide, 4th series, v. 3, no. 5; Nov. 1923, monthly supplement. 1923. cover-title, 67+[1] p. 1 pl. [Includes Modifications 27 and 28 of International money order list, pamphlet 14, and Inserts 836–839 to Postal laws and regulations of United States. Text on p. 2–4 of cover.] *Official postal guide, with supplements, $1.00, foreign subscription, $1.50; July issue, 75c.; supplements published monthly (11 pamphlets) 25c., foreign subscription, 50c.   4–18254

RAILWAY MAIL SERVICE

Iowa. Alphabetical scheme of Iowa, for use of publishers in distribution of 2d-class mail, 1924. 1923. 21 p. ‡

Mail-trains. Schedule of mail trains. no. 367, Oct. 25, 1923, 2d division, Railway Mail Service, comprising New York, New Jersey, Pennsylvania, Delaware, eastern shore of Maryland, Accomac and Northampton counties, Va., Porto Rico, and Virgin Islands. 1923. 313+[1] p. narrow 8° ‡

—— Schedule of mail trains, no. 442, Oct. 16, 1923, 3d division, Railway Mail Service, comprising District of Columbia, Maryland, North Carolina, Virginia, and West Virginia (except peninsula of Maryland and Virginia). 1923. 144 p. narrow 8° ‡

TOPOGRAPHY DIVISION

NOTE.—Since February, 1908, the Topography Division has been preparing rural-delivery maps of counties in which rural delivery is completely established. They are published in two forms, one giving simply the rural free delivery routes, starting from a single given post office, sold at 10 cents each; the other, the rural free delivery routes in an entire county, sold at 35 cents each. A uniform scale of 1 inch to 1 mile is used. Editions are not issued, but sun-print copies are produced in response to special calls addressed to the Disbursing Clerk, Post Office Department, Washington, D. C. These maps should not be confused with the post route maps, for which see Monthly catalogue for February, 1923, page 528.

PRESIDENT OF UNITED STATES

Alaska. Executive order, Alaska [temporarily withdrawing certain described lands in Alaska, from settlement, etc., to be reserved for use by Agriculture Department as agricultural experiment station]. Nov. 9, 1923. 1 p. f° (No. 3924.) ‡

Alien property. Executive order, amending order of Oct. 23, 1923, authorizing Alien Property Custodian to sell certain property at private sale [being 2098.21 shares of Stoehr & Sons, Inc., representing 6,090 shares of Botany Worsted Mills stock, and authorizing sale of said shares of Stoehr & Sons, Inc., for $1,218,000]. [Nov. 7, 1923.] 2 p. f° ([No. 3923.]) ‡

—— Executive order, authorizing Alien Property Custodian to sell certain property at private sale [being 14,910 shares of stock of Botany Worsted Mills, corporation of New Jersey, and 6,090 shares of said company's stock represented by 2098.21 shares of Stoehr & Sons, Inc., a holding company, of par value of $100 each, at price of $200 per share for each share of said Botany Worsted Mills stock]. Oct. 23, 1923. 1 p. f° (No. 3917A.) ‡

Army supply bases. Executive order, transferring portion of Army supply base, at Charleston, S. C., from control of War Department to control of Shipping Board [and reserving to War Department certain described rights, privileges, and easements in said property]. [Nov. 3, 1923.] [2] p. f° ([No. 3920.]) ‡

Bailey, Mrs. Blanche N. Executive order [authorizing appointment of Mrs. Blanche N. Bailey to clerical position in Agriculture Department]. Nov. 17, 1923. 1 p. f° (No. 3926.) ‡

California. Executive order, California [withdrawing certain described public lands in California from settlement, etc., pending resurvey, such withdrawal to remain in effect until resurvey is accepted and approved plat thereof is officially filed in local land office]. Oct. 29, 1923. 1 p. f° (No. 3918.) ‡

Customs Service. Executive order [abolishing port of entry at St. Andrews in customs collection district no. 18 (Florida), and creating port of entry at Panama City in same district, with headquarters at Tampa, Fla., effective Nov. 15, 1923]. Nov. 1, 1923. 1 p. f° (No. 3919.) [An incorrect print of this order was also issued.] ‡

—— Executive order [abolishing ports of St. Albans, Swanton, and Highgate, in customs collection district no. 2 (Vermont), and establishing port of entry at St. Albans, headquarters port of same district, which shall comprise townships of St. Albans, Swanton, Highgate, and Franklin, effective Dec. 1, 1923]. Nov. 13, 1923. 1 p. f° (No. 3925.) ‡

National forests. Executive order, Uinta National Forest, Utah [modifying boundaries of Uinta National Forest as defined by proclamation of June 23, 1915, so as to include certain described lands embraced within boundaries of Mt. Nebo division of Manti National Forest, Utah, as defined by proclamation of Oct. 23, 1917]. Nov. 6, 1923. 1 p. f° (No. 3922.) ‡

Smith, Mrs. Lyne P. Executive order [authorizing appointment of Mrs. Lyne Pepper Smith to clerical position in War Department]. Nov. 3, 1923. 1 p. f° (No. 3921.) ‡

Thanksgiving, 1923, proclamation. Nov. 5, 1923. 1 p. f° (No. 1680.) †

Virgin Islands. Further extending [period from Nov. 1, 1923, to May 1, 1924, for] establishment of adequate shipping service in, and deferring extension of coastwise laws of United States to Virgin Islands, proclamation. [Oct. 25, 1923.] 2 p. f° ([No. 1678.]) †

RAILROAD ADMINISTRATION

Automobiles. Before Interstate Commerce Commission, no. 13923 (sub. no. 1), Chevrolet Motor Company of Texas *v.* director general et al.; brief for director general. 1923. cover-title, 4 p. ‡

Beet final molasses. Before Interstate Commerce Commission, no. 14426, Wyoming Sugar Company *v.* director general; exceptions filed on behalf of defendant to examiner's proposed report. 1923. cover-title, 7 p. ‡

Celery. Before Interstate Commerce Commission, no. 14733, A. G. Zulfer & Co. *v.* director general; defendant's brief. 1923. cover-title, 7 p. ‡

Coke. Before Interstate Commerce Commission, no. 14675, Delta Beet Sugar Corporation *v.* director general; exceptions on behalf of defendant to examiner's proposed report. 1923. cover-title, 7 p. ‡

Copper. Before Interstate Commerce Commission, no. 14747, Afterthought Copper Company *v.* director general et al.; exceptions filed on behalf of director general to examiner's proposed report. 1923. cover-title, 3 p. ‡

Flour. Before Interstate Commerce Commission, no. 14503, Larabee Flour Mills Corporation *v.* director general et al.; brief on behalf of director general. 1923. cover-title, 18 p. ‡

Freight rates. Before Interstate Commerce Commission, no. 14210, Lindeteves-Stokvis *v.* director general; exceptions on part of director general to report proposed by examiner. 1923. cover-title, 11 p. ‡

Industrial railroads. Before Interstate Commerce Commission, no. 12596, Pressed Steel Car Company *v.* director general; brief for director general. [1923.] cover-title, ii+53 p. ‡

Iron. In district court in and for southern division of northern district of California, no. 16692, Arthur Erb et al., substituted plaintiffs for A. O. Anderson & Company [et al.] *v.* James C. Davis, director general of railroads, as agent; brief of defendant. 1923. cover-title, i+35 p. ‡

Kansas City Southern Railway. Final settlement between director general of railroads and Kansas City Southern Railway Company and other corporations, Nov. —, 1923. 1923. 3 p. 4° †

Limestone. Before Interstate Commerce Commission, no. 14568, Amalgamated Sugar Company *v.* director general; exceptions on behalf of director general to report proposed by examiner. 1923. cover-title, 6 p. ‡

Muriate of potash. Before Interstate Commerce Commission, no. 12942, Diamond Match Company *v.* director general; brief on part of director general on rehearing. 1923. cover-title, 9 p. ‡

New Orleans and Northeastern Railroad. Final settlement between director general of railroads and New Orleans & Northeastern Railroad Company, Nov. —, 1923. 1923. 3 p. 4° †

New Orleans Terminal Company. Final settlement between director general of railroads and New Orleans Terminal Company, Nov. —, 1923. 1923. 3 p. 4° †

Petroleum coke. Before Interstate Commerce Commission, no. 14333, Aluminum Company of America et al. *v.* director general; no. 14861, Tallassee Power Company *v.* director general et al.; exceptions on part of director general to examiner's proposed report. 1923. cover-title, 8 p. ‡

Pipe. No. 6412, in circuit court of appeals, 8th circuit, James C. Davis, director general of railroads, as agent of the President, *v.* Prairie Pipe Line Company; brief for plaintiff in error. 1923. cover-title, i+31 p. ‡

Pittsburg and Shawmut Railroad. Final settlement between director general of railroads and Pittsburg & Shawmut Railroad Company, Nov. —, 1923. 1923. 3 p. 4° †

Rabbit skin. Before Interstate Commerce Commission, no. 13012, American Trading Company *v.* director general; brief on part of director general on rehearing. 1923. cover-title, 12 p. ‡

St. John's River Terminal Company. Final settlement between director general of railroads and St. John's River Terminal Company, Nov. —, 1923. 1923. 3 p. 4° †

Starch. Before Interstate Commerce Commission, no. 14223, A. Klipstein & Company *v.* director general et al.; exceptions on behalf of director general to report proposed by examiner. 1923. cover-title, 9 p. ‡

Sugar-beets. Before Interstate Commerce Commission, no. 14562, Amalgamated Sugar Company *v.* director general et al.; exceptions filed on behalf of director general to report proposed by examiner. 1923. cover-title, 5 p. ‡

Switching charges. Before Interstate Commerce Commission, no. 14769, Joseph Bancroft & Sons Company *v.* director general et al.; exceptions on behalf of director general to examiner's proposed report. 1923. cover-title, 5 p. ‡

—— Before Interstate Commerce Commission, no. 15139, United States *v.* Springfield Street Railway Company; amendment to complaint. 1923. cover-title, 3 p. ‡

Tanks (military science). Before Interstate Commerce Commission, [investigation and suspension docket no.] 1895, classification rating on Army tractor tanks; brief for protestant. 1923. cover-title, 11 p. ‡

Wood flour. Before Interstate Commerce Commission, no. 14467, Hercules Powder Company *v.* director general; brief on part of director general. 1923. cover-title, 12 p. ‡

SHIPPING BOARD

South Atlantic Dry Dock Company. No. 4171, circuit court of appeals, 5th circuit, Shipping Board Emergency Fleet Corporation *v.* South Atlantic Dry Dock Company, error to district court for southern district of Florida; brief of plaintiff in error. 1923. cover-title, iv+98 p. ‡

SHIPPING BOARD EMERGENCY FLEET CORPORATION

Ships. Schedule of sailings of Shipping Board vessels in general cargo, passenger, and mail services, 1st of November to middle of December, 1923; issued by Traffic Department. 1923. cover-title, ii+14 p. il. [Monthly. Text on p. 2–4 of cover.] † 23–26331

Travel. Going abroad [information compiled for convenience and guidance of travellers to foreign countries, with list of ships in passenger services of, and managing operators for, Shipping Board]. United States Shipping Board Emergency Fleet Corporation, Washington, D. C. [1923]. 14+[2] p. 16° †

SMITHSONIAN INSTITUTION

AMERICAN HISTORICAL ASSOCIATION

Agriculture. Agricultural History Society papers. 1923. v. 2, iii+375–454 p. [From Report, 1919, v. 1.] †

CONTENTS.—Possibilities of intensive research in agricultural history; by R. W. Kelsey.—Some features of tobacco history; by George K. Holmes.—Notes on agricultural history of maize; by G. N. Collins.—Earliest American book on kitchen gardening; by Marjorie Fleming Warner.—Early agricultural periodical; by Mary G. Lacy.

—— Early agricultural periodical; by Mary G. Lacy. 1923. [1]+443–454 p. [From Report, 1919, v. 1.] †

—— Possibilities of intensive research in agricultural history; by R. W. Kelsey. 1923. [1]+375–383 p. [From Report, 1919, v. 1.] †

American colonies. Abstract of commissions and instructions to colonial governors in America, 1740; by Arthur H. Basye. 1923. [1]+327–349 p. [From Report, 1919, v. 1.] †

Armenia. Roman policy in Armenia and Transcaucasia and its significance; by David Magie. 1923. [1]+295–304 p. [From Report, 1919, v. 1.] †

Civil War, 1861–65. Strategy of concentration of Confederate forces in Mississippi Valley in spring of 1862; by Alfred P. James. 1923. [1]+365–374 p. [From Report, 1919, v. 1.] †

Corn. Notes on agricultural history of maize; by G. N. Collins. 1923. [1]+409–429 p. [From Report, 1919, v. 1.] †

Epeiros-Albania boundary dispute in ancient times; by Herbert Wing. 1923. [1]+305–313 p. [From Report, 1919, v. 1.] †

European War, 1914–18. American historical activities during World War; edited by Newton D. Mereness. 1923. [1]+137–293 p. [From Report, 1919, v. 1.] †

Gardening. Earliest American book on kitchen gardening; by Marjorie Fleming Warner. 1923. [1]+431–442 p. [From Report, 1919, v. 1.] †

Historical societies. Proceedings of joint conference of historical societies and National Association of State War History Organizations, Cleveland, Ohio, Dec. 29, 1919. 1923. [1]+121–136 p. [From Report, 1919, v. 1.] †

Introductory pages [letter of submittal, contents, organization and activities, etc.]. 1923. p. 1–32. [From Report, 1919, v. 1.] †

Lincoln and progress of nationality in the North; by N. W. Stephenson. 1923. [1]+351–363 p. [From Report, 1919, v. 1.] †

National Board for Historical Service; by Waldo G. Leland. 1923. [1]+161–189 p. [From Report, 1919, v. 1.] †

Pacific Coast Branch. Report of proceedings of 15th annual meeting of Pacific Coast Branch of American Historical Association, San Francisco, Calif., Nov. 28–29, 1919; reported by [William A. Morris]. 1923. [1]+105–120 p. [Title-page reads incorrectly, reported by J. J. Van Nostrand, jr. From Report, 1919, v. 1.] †

Proceedings of 34th annual meeting of American Historical Association, Cleveland, Ohio, Dec. 29–31, 1919; reported by John Spencer Bassett. 1923. [1]+33–103 p. [From Report, 1919, v. 1.] †

Tobacco. Some features of tobacco history; by George K. Holmes. 1923. [1]+385–407 p. [From Report, 1919, v. 1.] †

STATE DEPARTMENT

[Circulars] 912 and 913; Oct. 23 and 30, 1923. [1923.] 2 p. and 1 p. [General instruction circulars to consular officers.] ‡

Diplomatic and consular service of United States; corrected to Oct. 3, 1923. 1923. 67 p. ‡   10–16369

Diplomatic list, Nov. 1923. [1923.] cover-title, i+34 p. 24° [Monthly.] ‡
                                                                                                        10–16292

Tariff. Agreement effected by exchange of notes between United States and Brazil according mutual unconditional most-favored-nation treatment in customs matters; signed [Washington] Oct. 18, 1923. 1923. 4 p. (Treaty series 672.) [Note from ambassador of Brazil to Secretary of State in Portuguese and English.] †   23–26984

Weights and measures. Convention between United States and other Powers, amending convention relating to weights and measures, signed at Paris, May 20, 1875, and regulations annexed thereto; signed Sevres, Oct. 6, 1921, proclaimed Oct. 27, 1923. 1923. [1]+10 p. (Treaty series 673.) [French and English.] †

23–26985

SUPREME COURT

Cases. Cases adjudged in Supreme Court at Oct. term, 1922, Oct. 2, 1922–Jan. 29, 1923; Ernest Knaebel, reporter. 1923. lxx+827 p. (United States reports v. 260.) [Also issued in 4 preliminary prints.] *Cloth, $2.50.

—— Docket [of cases pending in Supreme Court], Oct. term, 1923. [1923.] p. 217–236, 4° [Issued in loose leaf form.] ‡

Ferris, Charles J. Transcript of record, Oct. term, 1923, no. 217, United States *vs.* Charles J. Ferris, appeal from Court of Claims. [1923.] cover-title, [1]+5 p. ‡

Gay, Alphonse. Transcript of record, Oct. term, 1923, no. 205, United States *vs.* Alphonse Gay, appeal from Court of Claims. [1923.] cover-title, i+11 p. ‡

Gray, E. W. Transcript of record, Oct. term, 1923, no. 177, United States *vs.* E. W. Gray et al., appeal from circuit court of appeals for 8th circuit. [1923.] cover-title, i+42 p. ‡

Intercity Radio Company, Incorporated. Transcript of record, Oct. term, 1923, no. 244, Herbert Hoover, Secretary of Commerce, *vs.* Intercity Radio Company, Inc., in error to Court of Appeals of District of Columbia. [1923.] cover-title, i+26 p. ‡

[Journal] Nov. 12–28, 1923; [slips]. 20–33. [1923.] leaves 61–92. [A corrected print of the Journal for Nov. 23 was also issued.] ‡

Lasley, Rosa. Transcript of record; Oct. term, 1923, no. 166, Albert B. Fall, Secretary of Interior, *vs.* United States ex rel. W. G. Lynn, guardian of Rosa Lasley, incompetent Osage Indian allottee, appeal from Court of Appeals of District of Columbia. [1923.] cover-title, [1]+17 p. ‡

Official reports. Official reports of Supreme Court, v. 262 U. S., no. 3; Ernest Knaebel, reporter. Preliminary print. 1923. cover-title, [1]+312–506 p. 12° [Cases adjudged in Supreme Court at Oct. term, 1922 (opinions of May 21 in part, and June 4, 1923). This number contains lists of cases reported in v. 262, pts. 1 and 2. Text on p. 2–4 of cover. From United States reports, v. 262.] *Paper, 25c. single copy, $1.00 per vol. (4 nos. to a vol.; subscription price, $3.00 for 12 nos.); foreign subscription, 5c. added for each pamphlet.

—— Same, v. 262 U. S., no. 4; Ernest Knaebel, reporter. Preliminary print. 1923. cover-title, [1]+506–762 p. 12° [Cases adjudged in Supreme Court at Oct. term, 1922 (opinions of June 11, 1923). This number contains lists of cases reported in v. 262, pts. 1–3. Text on p. 2–4 of cover. From United States reports, v. 262.]

Pennsylvania-Ohio Power and Light Company. Transcript of record, Oct. term, 1923, no. 228, United States, Interstate Commerce Commission, and Pennsylvania-Ohio Power & Light Company *vs.* Hubbard, Ohio, appeal from district court for northern district of Ohio. [1923.] cover-title, ii+58 p. ‡

Ransom, J. P. Transcript of record, Oct. term, 1923, no. 178, United States *vs.* J. P. Ransom, in error to circuit court of appeals for 8th circuit. [1923.] cover-title, ii+55 p. ‡

Reed, James. Transcript of record, Oct. term, 1923, no. 227, United States *vs.* James Reed, appeal from Court of Claims. [1923.] cover-title, i+9 p. ‡

Sage, Mrs. Margaret O. Transcript of record, Oct. term, 1923, no. 276, William H. Edwards, formerly collector of internal revenue for 2d district of New York, *vs.* Joseph Jermain Slocum et al. [executors of Margaret Olivia Sage], on writ of certiorari to circuit court of appeals for 2d circuit. [1923.] cover-title, i+38 p. ‡

Steubenville, East Liverpool and Beaver Valley Traction Company. Transcript of record, Oct. term, 1923, no. 229, United States, Steubenville, East Liverpool and Beaver Valley Traction Company, and Interstate Commerce Commission *vs.* Wellsville, Ohio, appeal from district court for northern district of Ohio. [1923.] cover-title, ii+78 p. ‡

Valante, John. Transcript of record, Oct. term, 1923, no. 218, United States *vs.* John Valante, appeal from district court for southern district of New York. [1923.] cover-title, i+12 p. ‡

TREASURY DEPARTMENT

Bonds of United States. Extract from Regulations of Treasury Department with respect to United States bonds and notes (Treasury Department circular 300, dated July 31, 1923): Extract 2, Exchanges of coupon bonds and notes. [1923.] 4 p. 4° †

——— Same: Extract 4, Registered bonds owned by minors or persons under legal disability. . [1923.] 3 p. 4° †

———: Same: Extract 5, Transfers and exchanges of registered bonds. [1923.] 4 p. 4° †

——— Same: Extract 6, Assignments of registered bonds under power of attorney. [1923.] 2 p. 4° †

——— Same: Extract 14, Payment of interest on United States bonds. . [1923.] 2 p. 4° †

Finance. Daily statement of Treasury compiled from latest proved reports from Treasury offices and depositaries, Nov. 1–30, 1923. [1923.] Each 4 p. or 3 p. f° [Daily except Sundays and holidays.] † 15–3303

Public debt. Statement of public debt of United States, Aug. 31, 1923. [1923.] [2] p. narrow f° [Monthly.] † 10–21268

Taxation. Letter from Secretary of Treasury to acting chairman of Committee on Ways and Means [concerning possibilities of tax revision and giving recommendations for simplification of the law]. Nov. 10, 1923. 6 p. 4° ‡

Treasury decisions under customs, internal-revenue, and other laws, including decisions of Board of General Appraisers and Court of Customs Appeals, v. 44, no. 18–22; Nov. 1–29, 1923. 1923. various paging. [Weekly. Department decisions numbered 39834–897, general appraisers' decisions 8695–8707, abstracts 46379–494, internal revenue decisions 3526–32, Tariff Commission Notices 32 and 33, and later Tariff Commission Notice 12.] *Paper, 5c. single copy, $1.00 a yr.; foreign subscription, $2.00. 10–30490

Treasury savings certificates. Redemption and exchange of Treasury savings certificates, series of 1919. Nov. 15, 1923. 4 p. 4° (Department circular 331; Public Debt [Commissioner].) †

———: United States of America, new offering of Treasury savings certificates, issue of Dec. 1, 1923. Nov. 15, 1923. 10 p. 4° (Department circular 329; Public Debt [Commissioner].) †

Virus. United States Public Health Service decision no. 3 under sec. 63 of Regulations for sale of viruses, serums, toxins, and analogous products [in District of Columbia and interstate traffic, approved Aug. 1, 1923, regarding dating of special products in accordance with tests made therein]. [1923.] 2 p. ([Public Health Service.]) †

APPRAISERS

Reappraisements of merchandise by general appraisers [on Oct. 23–Nov. 23, 1923]; Nov. 2–30, 1923. [1923.] various paging. (Reappraisement circulars 3481–85.) [Weekly.] *Paper, 5c. single copy, 50c. a yr.; foreign subscription, $1.05. 13–2916

COAST GUARD

Orders. General order 35; Oct. 11, 1923. 1923. 1 p. ‡

COMPTROLLER OF CURRENCY

National banks. Abstract of reports of condition of national banks, Sept. 14, 1923; no. 141. [1923.] 13 p. f° †

——— Monthly statement of capital stock of national banks, national bank notes, and Federal reserve bank notes outstanding, bonds on deposit, etc. [Nov. 1, 1923]. Nov. 1, 1923. 1 p. f° † 10–21266

FEDERAL FARM LOAN BUREAU

Federal intermediate credit banks. Text of law providing for Federal intermediate credit banks; Rules and regulations of Federal Farm Loan Board to Aug. 15, 1923 [in matters pertaining to Federal intermediate credit banks]. Washington, National Capital Press, 1923. 15 p. (Circular 15.) † 23–27422

GENERAL SUPPLY COMMITTEE

Government supplies. Supplemental specifications and proposals for supplies [fiscal year 1924]; classes 1, 6, 8, 9, 17 [Jan. 1–June 30, 1924]. [1923.] 20 p. 4° †

GOVERNMENT ACTUARY

Bonds of United States. Market prices and investment values of outstanding bonds and notes [of United States, Oct. 1923]. Nov. 1, 1923. 7 p. 4° (Form A.) [Monthly.] †

INTERNAL REVENUE BUREAU

Income tax. Treasury decisions amending or relating to Regulations 62 promulgated under income tax and war profits and excess profits tax provisions of revenue act of 1921; compiled Nov. 15, 1923. 1923. v+50 p. [Contains Treasury decisions issued Jan. 19, 1922–Nov. 15, 1923.] *Paper, 5c.

Internal revenue bulletin. Internal revenue bulletin, v. 2, no. 31–34; Nov. 5–26, 1923. 1923. various paging. [Weekly.] *Paper, 5c. single copy (for subscription price see note below). 22–26051

NOTE.—On May 7, 1923, the publication of weekly bulletins was resumed and the issuance of monthly bulletins (and special bulletins as occasion required) discontinued. Since May 1, therefore, the 1923 Internal revenue bulletin service consists of weekly bulletins of new rulings and decisions of the Bureau of Internal Revenue and internal revenue Treasury decisions of general importance, quarterly digests of such new rulings (cumulative from Jan. 1, 1922), and semiannual cumulative bulletins containing in full the new rulings and decisions published during the preceding 6 months. The complete bulletin service may be obtained, on a subscription basis, from the Superintendent of Documents, Government Printing Office, Washington, D. C., for $2.00 a yr.; foreign subscription, $2.75.

—— Internal revenue bulletin; cumulative bulletin II–1, Jan.–June, 1923. 1923. vii+364 p. [Semiannual.] *Paper, 30c. (for subscription price see note above). 22–27420

LOANS AND CURRENCY DIVISION

Bonds of United States. Caveat list of United States registered bonds and notes, Nov. 1, 1923. [1923.] 55 p. f° [Monthly.] †

Money. Circulation statement of United States money, Nov. 1, 1923. [1923.] 1 p. oblong 8° [Monthly.] † 10–21267

PUBLIC HEALTH SERVICE

Arsphenamine. Regulations for control of manufacture, importation, and sale of arsphenamine and its derivatives, neoarsphenamine, sodium arsphenamine, silver arsphenamine, neosilverarsphenamine, phospharsphenamine, and sulpharsphenamine, referred to collectively as arsphenamines, supplementary to Regulations for sale of viruses, serums, toxins, and analogous products, approved Aug. 1, 1923. 1923. ii+3 p. (Miscellaneous publication 22 revised.) *Paper, 5c. 23–26983

Botulism. Effect of acidification on toxicity of B. botulinus toxin; by J. C. Geiger and W. E. Gouwens. 1923. 6 p. (Reprint 870.) [Prepared in cooperation with University of Chicago. From Public health reports, Sept. 28, 1923.] * Paper, 5c. 23–26970

Carbon monoxid. Pyro-tannic acid method for quantitative determination of carbon monoxide in blood and air; by R. R. Sayers, W. P. Yant, and G. W. Jones. 1923. 12 p. il. 1 pl. (Reprint 872.) [Prepared in cooperation with Mines Bureau. From Public health reports, Oct. 5, 1923.] * Paper, 5c. 23–27423

Fermentation. Sugar-free medium for fermentation studies; by Ella M. A. Enlows. 1923. 6 p. (Reprint 868.) [From Public health reports, Sept. 14, 1923.] * Paper, 5c. 23–26968

Hygiene. Prevention of disease and care of sick, how to keep well and what to do in case of sudden illness, by W. G. Stimpson; including First aid to injured, by M. H. Foster. 4th edition. 1923. 318 p.il. 80 p. of pl. (Miscellaneous publication 17.) * Paper, 75c. 23–26971

Malaria. Transactions of 4th annual conference of malaria field workers[Antimalaria Conference], held at Chattanooga, Tenn., Nov. 14–16, 1922. Sept. 1923. vi+183 p. il. 2 pl. 2 p. of pl. (Public health bulletin 137.) [Includes lists of Public Health Service publications on malaria.] * Paper, 20c. 19–27671

Malnutrition. Campaign against malnutrition; prepared by advisory committee on foods and nutrition of National Child Health Council in cooperation with Public Health Service. 1923 [reprint with slight changes]. iii + 39 p. (Public health bulletin 134.) * Paper, 5c. 23–27424

Public health reports, v. 38, no. 44–48; Nov. 2–30, 1923. 1923. [xx] + 2513–2876 p. [Weekly.] * Paper, 5c. single copy, $1.50 a yr.; foreign subscription, $2.75. 6–25167

> SPECIAL ARTICLES.—No. 44. Prevalence of poliomyelitis in 1923.—Notifiable diseases, prevalence during 1922 in States.—No. 45. Home nursing of pneumonia cases.— Cancer mortality by certain divisions in group of insured persons, 1911–22.—General health conditions as reported by health section of League of Nations.—Public Health Service publications, list of publications issued Apr.–Oct. 1923.—No. 46. Case of black tongue, with post-mortem findings: by Jos. Goldberger, W. F. Tanner, and E. B. Saye.—Fundamentals of rural health work: by W. F. Draper.—Antimalaria campaign conducted in Haiti by naval medical officers; [by A. H. Allen].—Analysis of 163 mild cases of smallpox in Doncaster, England.—No. 47. Fleas found on wild animals in Bitterroot Valley, Mont.; by L. H. Dunn and R. R. Parker.—Epidemiological study of whooping cough in Amsterdam [Netherlands].—No. 48. Collection of morbidity data and other sanitary information by Public Health Service: by Brock C. Hampton.—Powers, duties, and policies of Sanitary Water Board of Commonwealth of Pennsylvania: by W. L. Stevenson.—National Board bulletin, new publication issued by National Board of Medical Examiners.
>
> NOTE.—This publication is distributed gratuitously to State and municipal health officers, etc., by the Surgeon General of the Public Health Service, Treasury Department. Others desiring these reports may obtain them from the Superintendent of Documents, Washington, D. C., at the prices stated above.

Sickness. Application of partial correlation to health problem; by Frank M. Phillips, assisted by Faye Hollis Roberts. 1923. 15 p. il. (Reprint 867.) [From Public health reports, Sept. 14, 1923.] * Paper, 5c. 23–27425

Trachoma, its nature and prevention; by John McMullen. Revised edition, Sept. 1915. [Reprint with slight change] 1923. [1] + 4 p. 2 p. of pl. (Supplement 8 to Public health reports.) * Paper, 5c. 23–27426

Vaccination technique and certification, experiment in making vaccination an insurance against delay as well as protection against disease; by S. B. Grubbs. 1923. 8 p. (Reprint 869.) [From Public health reports, Sept. 21, 1923.] * Paper, 5c. 23–26969

Vital statistics. Model State law for morbidity reports as amended by 13th annual Conference of State and Territorial Health Authorities with Public Health Service, Washington, May 13, 1915. [Reprint] 1923. ii + 6 p. (Reprint 285.) [From Public health reports, July 2, 1915.] * Paper, 5c. 23–27427

VENEREAL DISEASES DIVISION

Venereal disease information, issued by Public Health Service for use in its cooperative work with State health departments, v. 4, no. 10; Oct. 20, 1923. 1923. ii + 383–434 + iv p. [Monthly.] * Paper, 5c. single copy, 50c. a yr.; foreign subscription, 75c.

> SPECIAL ARTICLES.—Review of venereal disease activities, fiscal year 1923.—Venereal diseases in Germany, by Dr. Berger; [translation].

SAVINGS SYSTEM

Saving and thrift. How other people get ahead. 1923 [reprint with changes]. 16 p. 12° ([T. S. S. 23–23.]) †

VETERANS' BUREAU

Regulations, Veterans' Bureau [1923], supplement 1; Sept. 30, 1923. [1] + 19 p. ‡

WAR DEPARTMENT

Army regulations. †

> NOTE.—The Army regulations are issued in pamphlet form for insertion in loose-leaf binders. The names of such of the more important administrative subjects as may seem appropriate, arranged in proper sequence, are numbered in a single series and each name so numbered constitutes the title and number of a pamphlet containing certain administrative regulations pertaining thereto. Where more than one pamphlet is required for the administrative regulations pertaining to any such title, additional pamphlets will be issued in a separate sub-series.

30–1285. Quartermaster Corps: Transportation of animals on transports; Oct. 5, 1923. [1923.] 10 p. [Supersedes AR 30–1285, Mar. 4, 1922.]

35–2360. Finance Department: Pay of enlisted men, longevity pay; Oct. 2, 1923. [1923.] 2 p.

40–205. Medical Department: Military hygiene and sanitation, Changes 1; Oct. 19, 1923. 1923. 1 p

100–20. Corps of Engineers: Seacoast fortifications, Changes 2; Oct. 20, 1923. [1923.] 2 p. [Supersede AR 100–20, Changes 1, Oct. 27, 1922.]

105–5. Signal Corps: General provisions, Changes 1; Oct. 20, 1923. 1923. 1 p.

Army regulations—Continued.

600–35. Personnel: Specifications for uniform, Changes 9; Oct. 16, 1923. [1923.] 10 p. [Supersedes AR 600–35, Changes 1–8, Jan. 6, 1922–Aug. 23, 1923.]
600–40. Same: Wearing of uniform, Changes 10; Oct. 16, 1923. [1923.] 9 p. [Supersedes AR 600–40, Changes 1–9. Jan. 31, 1922–Aug. 23, 1923.]
600–375. Same: Prisoners, general provisions, Changes 2: Sept. 6, 1923. 1923. 1 p. [Supersedes AR 600–375, Changes 1, July 26, 1923.]
605–115. Commissioned officers: Leaves of absence and delays, Changes 3: Oct. 5, 1923. [1923.] 3 p. [Supersedes AR 605–115, Changes 1 and 2, May 22, 1922, and June 13, 1923.]
605–120. Same: Personal reports, registration, Changes 1; Oct. 5, 1923. 1923. 1 p.
615–40. Enlisted men: Clothing, allowances, accounts, and disposition, Changes 4; Oct. 16, 1923. [1923.] 3 p. [Supersedes AR 615–40, Changes 1–3, July 17, 1922–May 9, 1923.]
615–160. Same: Flying cadets, Changes 2; July 31, 1923. [1923.] 2 p. [Supersedes AR 615–160, Changes 1, June 15, 1922.]

Training regulations.

NOTE.—The Training regulations are issued in pamphlet form for insertion in loose-leaf binders.

190–14. Topography and surveying: Drafting, basic, prepared under direction of chief of engineers; June 21, 1923. [1923.] 33 p.il. *Paper, 10c.
435–90. Coast Artillery Corps: Gun battery, antiaircraft artillery, prepared under direction of chief of coast artillery; June 25, 1923. [1923.] 24 p. il. 1 pl. *Paper, 5c.
435–95. Same: Service battery, antiaircraft regiment, prepared under direction of chief of coast artillery; July 30, 1923. [1923.] 6 p. il. 2 pl. *Paper, 5c.
435–105. Same: Battalion and battalion headquarters, machine-gun battalion, antiaircraft regiment, prepared under direction of chief of coast artillery; July 30, 1923. [1923.] 8 p. il. *Paper, 5c.
435–120. Same: Antiaircraft regiment, artillery, prepared under direction of chief of coast artillery; July 31, 1923. [1923.] 7 p. il. *Paper, 5c.

ADJUTANT GENERAL'S DEPARTMENT

Army list and directory, Nov. 1, 1923. 1923. vi+314 p. large 8° [Bimonthly.] *Paper, 25c. single copy, $1.25 a yr.; foreign subscription, $1.85. 9–35106

Telephone switchboard operator, instructors guide for all arms; prepared under direction of chief signal officer, 1923. 1923. xxii+266 p. il. 1 pl. (United States Army training manual 23.) *Cloth, 45c.

U. S. Army recruiting news, bulletin of recruiting information issued by direction of Adjutant General of Army, Nov. 1 and 15, 1923. [Recruiting Publicity Bureau, Governors Island, N. Y., Nov. 1 and 15, 1923.] Each 16 p. il. 4° †Recruiting Publicity Bureau, Governors Island, N. Y. War 22—21

AIR SERVICE

Aeronautical bulletin, no. 39, Route information series; Nov. 1, 1923. [1923.] 3 p. 12° (Airways Section.) *Paper, 5c. 23–26231

ENGINEER DEPARTMENT

East River. Maintenance and improvement of existing river and harbor works, East River, N. Y., dredging and rock removal, advertisement. [1923.] 14 p. 4° †

Savannah, Ga. Maintenance and improvement of existing river and harbor works, Savannah Harbor, Ga., advertisement [for dredging]. [1923.] 14 p. 4° †

MISSISSIPPI RIVER COMMISSION

Tugboats. Proposals for stern-wheel steel towboat, advertisement. [1923.] 34 p. 4° †

NORTHERN AND NORTHWESTERN LAKES SURVEY

NOTE.—Charts of the Great Lakes and connecting waters and St. Lawrence River to the international boundary at St. Regis, of Lake Champlain, and of the New York State canals are prepared and sold by the U. S. Lake Survey Office, Old Custom-house, Detroit, Mich. Charts may also be purchased at the following U. S. engineer offices: 710 Army Building, New York, N. Y.; 467 Broadway, Albany, N. Y.; 540 Federal Building, Buffalo, N. Y.; and Canal Office, Sault Ste. Marie, Mich. A catalogue (with index map), showing localities, scales, prices, and conditions of sale, may be had upon application at any of these offices.

A descriptive bulletin, which supplements the charts and gives detailed information as to harbors, shore lines and shoals, magnetic determinations, and particulars of changing conditions affecting navigation, is issued free to chart purchasers, upon request. The bulletin is revised annually and issued at the opening of navigation (in April), and supplements thereto are published monthly during the navigation season.

Complete sets of the charts and publications may be seen at the U. S. engineer offices in Duluth, Minn., Milwaukee, Wis., Chicago, Ill., Grand Rapids, Mich., Cleveland, Ohio, and Oswego, N. Y., but they are obtainable only at the sales offices above mentioned.

Great Lakes. Supplement 7, Nov. 19, 1923, corrections and additions to Bulletin 32; to supplement information given upon charts of Great Lakes. U. S. Lake Survey Office, Detroit, Mich. [Nov. 13, 1923]. p. 1–3 +leaves 4–12+ [2] p. 4° †

Charts

Marquette, Mich. Chart of Marquette and Presque Isle harbors, Mich. Scale 1:15,000. 5th edition. [U. S. Lake Survey Office, Detroit, Mich.] Nov. 6, 1923. 35.6×22.2 in. †15c.

Superior, Lake. Lake Superior, from Grand Portal to Big Bay Point, Mich., including Manitou Island and Stannard Rock; coast chart 3. Scale 1:120,000. 2d edition. [U. S. Lakes Survey Office, Detroit, Mich.] Nov. 21, 1923. 43.1× 32 in. †25c.

RIVERS AND HARBORS BOARD

Philadelphia, Pa. Port of Philadelphia, Pa., including Camden, N. J., Chester, Pa., Wilmington, Del. 1922. viii+374 p. il. 2 pl. 6 p. of pl. 3 maps, 1 mosaic map, 8 tab. (Port series 4.) [Prepared in cooperation with Research Bureau, Shipping Board.] *Paper, 75c. 23–26982

GENERAL STAFF CORPS

Army. Changes 137 [for] Army regulations [1913]; Oct. 19, 1923. [1923.] 3 leaves. [Regulations issued by War Department.] †

Medical Department, Army. Changes 21 [for] Manual for Medical Department [1916]; Sept. 26, 1923. [1923.] 4 leaves. [Manual issued by Medical Department, Army.] †

Special regulations. Rescissions [of] Special regulations 28, 40, 40a, 44b, 55, 57a; Oct. 4, 1923. 1923. 1 p. [Special regulations issued by War Department.] †

War Department. Changes 35 [for] Compilation of [General] orders [Circulars, and Bulletins of War Department, 1881–1915]; Oct. 1, 1923. 1923. 1 p. 12° ₁Compilation issued by Adjutant General's Department.] †

JUDGE ADVOCATE GENERAL'S DEPARTMENT

Opinions. Index of Opinions of judge advocate general of Army, Jan. 1–Dec. 31, 1919. 1923. [1]+66 p. ‡

MEDICAL DEPARTMENT

Medical Corps, Army. Circular of information [relative to] appointment as 1st lieutenant in Medical Corps of Regular Army. Revised Oct. 13, 1923. [1923.] 10 p. narrow 12° †

Military hospitals. Medical Department of United States Army in World War: v. 5, Military hospitals in United States [with lists of references]; by Frank W. Weed. 1923. 857 p. il. large 8° *Cloth, $2.25. SG 22-2

NATIONAL BOARD FOR PROMOTION OF RIFLE PRACTICE

National Rifle Association of America. Program of N. R. A., annual gallery rifle and pistol competitions, 1923–24. [1923.] 47+[4] p. il. small 4° †

SIGNAL OFFICE

Circular 1, 4–8, 10–11 [1923]; Jan. 12–July 13, 1923. [1923.] Each 7 p. or 1 p. 12° [Circular 6 is mimeographed.] ‡

Orders 8–27 [1923]; Mar. 12–Sept. 22, 1923. 1923. Each 1 p. 12° ‡

WAR FINANCE CORPORATION

Wheat. Report to the President on wheat situation, Nov. 5, 1923; by Eugene Meyer, jr., and Frank W. Mondell. 1923. [1]+14 p. † 23—27428

Monthly Catalogue

United States

Public Documents

No. 348
December, 1923

THE LIBRARY OF THE

ISSUED BY THE NOV 2 1923
SUPERINTENDENT OF DOCUMENTS
UNIVERSITY OF ILLINOIS

Abbreviations

Appendix _____app.	Page, pages _____p.
Congress_____Cong.	Part, parts _____pt., pts.
Department _____Dept.	Plate, plates _____pl.
Document _____doc.	Portrait, portraits_____por.
Facsimile, facsimiles _____facsim.	Quarto _____4°
Folio_____f°	Report _____rp.
House_____H.	Saint_____St.
House bill_____H. R.	Section, sections _____sec.
House concurrent resolution__H. Con. Res.	Senate, Senate bill _____S.
House document_____H. doc.	Senate concurrent resolution___S. Con. Res.
House executive document_____H. ex. doc.	Senate document _____S. doc.
House joint resolution _____H. J. Res.	Senate executive document_____S. ex. doc.
House report _____H. rp.	Senate joint resolution _____S. J. Res.
House resolution (simple)_____H. Res.	Senate report _____S. rp.
Illustration, illustrations_____il.	Senate resolution (simple)_____S. Res.
Inch, inches _____in.	Session_____sess.
Latitude _____lat.	Sixteenmo _____16°
Longitude _____long.	Table, tables _____tab.
Mile, miles _____m.	Thirtytwo-mo _____32°
Miscellaneous_____mis., misc.	Treasury_____Treas.
Nautical _____naut.	Twelvemo _____12°
No date_____n. d.	Twentyfour-mo_____24°
No place_____n. p.	Versus_____vs., v.
Number, numbers _____no., nos.	Volume, volumes _____v., vol.
Octavo_____8°	Year _____yr.

Common abbreviations for names of States and months are also used.
* Document for sale by Superintendent of Documents.
† Distribution by office issuing document, free if unaccompanied by a price.
‡ Printed for official use.
  NOTE.—Nearly all of the Departments of the Government make a limited free distribution of their publications. When an entry shows a * price, it is possible that upon application to the issuing office a copy may be obtained without charge.

Explanation

Words and figures inclosed in brackets [ ] are given for information, but do not appear on the title-pages of the publications catalogued. When size is not given octavo is to be understood. Size of maps is measured from outer edge of border, excluding margin. The dates, including day, month, and year, given with Senate and House documents and reports are the dates on which they were ordered to be printed. Usually the printing promptly follows the ordering, but various causes sometimes make delays.

SALES OF GOVERNMENT PUBLICATIONS

The Superintendent of Documents, Washington, D. C., is authorized to sell at cost, plus 10 per cent, without limit as to the number of copies to any one applicant who agrees not to resell or distribute the same for profit, any United States Government publication not confidential in character.

Publications can not be supplied free to individuals nor forwarded in advance of payment.

Publications entered in this catalogue that are for sale by the Superintendent of Documents are indicated by a star (*) preceding the price. A dagger (†) indicates that application should be made to the Department, Bureau, or Division issuing the document. A double dagger (‡) indicates that the document is printed for official use. Whenever additional information concerning the method of procuring a document seems necessary, it will be found under the name of the Bureau by which it was published.

In ordering a publication from the Superintendent of Documents, give (if known) the name of the publishing Department, Bureau, or Division, and the title of the publication. If the publication is numbered, give the number also. Every such particular assists in quick identification. Do not order by the Library of Congress card number.

The accumulation of publications in this Office amounts to several millions, of which over two million are assorted, forming the sales stock. Many rare books are included, but under the law all must be sold regardless of their age or scarcity. Many of the books have been in stock some time, and are apt to be shop-worn. In filling orders the best copy available is sent. A general price-list of public documents is not available, but lists on special subjects will be furnished on application.

MONTHLY CATALOGUE DISTRIBUTION

The Monthly catalogue is sent to each Senator, Representative, Delegate, Resident Commissioner, and officer in Congress; to designated depositories and State and Territorial libraries if it is selected by them; to substantially all Government authors; and to as many school, college, and public libraries as the limited edition will supply.

Subscription price to individuals, 50c. a year, including index; foreign subscription, 75c. a year. Back numbers can not be supplied. Notify the Superintendent of Documents of any change of address.

LIBRARY OF CONGRESS CARDS

Numbers to be used in ordering the printed catalogue cards of the Library of Congress are given at the end of entries for the more important documents. Orders for these cards, remittances in payment for them, and requests for information about them should be addressed to the Librarian of Congress, *not* to the Superintendent of Documents.

INDEX

An Index to the Monthly catalogue is issued at the end of the fiscal year. This contains index entries for all the numbers issued from July to June, and can be bound with the numbers as an index to the volume. Persons desiring to bind the catalogue at the end of the year should be careful to retain the numbers received monthly, as duplicate copies can not be supplied.

HOW TO REMIT

Remittances for the documents marked with a star (*) should be made to the Superintendent of Documents, Washington, D. C., by coupons, postal money order, express order, or New York draft. Currency may be sent at sender's risk.

Postage stamps, foreign money, defaced or smooth coins, positively will not be accepted.

For the convenience of the general public, coupons that are good until used in exchange for Government publications sold by the Superintendent of Documents may be purchased from his Office in sets of 20 for $1.00. Address order to Superintendent of Documents, Government Printing Office, Washington, D. C.

No charge is made for postage on documents forwarded to points in United States, Alaska, Guam, Hawaii, Philippine Islands, Porto Rico, Samoa, or to Canada, Cuba, or Mexico. To other countries the regular rate of postage is charged, and remittances must cover such postage. In computing foreign postage, add one-third of the price of the publication.

MONTHLY CATALOGUE

AGRICULTURE DEPARTMENT

NOTE.—Those publications of the Department of Agriculture which are for sale will be supplied by the Superintendent of Documents, Washington, D. C. The Department issues a monthly list of publications, which is mailed to all applicants, enabling them to select such reports and bulletins as interest them.

Apple-blotch canker. Origin and control of apple-blotch cankers [with list of literature cited] ; by Max W. Gardner. 1923. cover-title, 403–418+[2] p. + [1] leaf, 3 p. of pl. [From Journal of agricultural research, v. 25, no. 10, Sept. 8, 1923.] ‡

Cattle. [Bureau of Animal Industry] order 285, rule 1, revision 22, to prevent spread of splenetic, southern, or Texas fever in cattle, effective Dec. 31, 1923; [Dec. 5, 1923]. [1923.] 5 p. †

——. Determination of surface area of cattle and swine [with list of literature cited] ; by Albert G. Hogan and Charles I. Skouby. 1923. cover-title, p. 419–430+[1] leaf, 1 pl. [From Journal of agricultural research, v. 25, no. 10, Sept. 8, 1923.] ‡

Journal of agricultural research, v. 26, no. 1–4; Oct. 6–27, 1923. 1923. cover-titles, 1–194+[14] p. +[1] leaf, il. 4 pl. 14 p. of pl. [Weekly. Text on p. 2 of covers.] * Paper, 10c. single copy, $4.00 a yr. ; foreign subscription, $5.25.

                                              Agr 13—1837

CONTENTS.—No. 1. Action of sodium nitrite in soil [with list of literature cited] ; by R. H. Robinson.—Effect of autoclaving upon toxicity of cottonseed meal ; by C. T. Dowell and Paul Menaul.—Auxotaxic curve as means of classifying soils and studying their colloidal properties; by A. E. Vinson and C. N. Catlin.—Some observations on temperature of leaves of crop plants [with list of literature cited] ; by Edwin C. Miller and A. R. Saunders.—No. 2. New tumor of apricot [with list of literature cited] ; by Amram Khazanoff.—Notes on biology of cadelle, Tenebroides mauritanicus Linné; by Richard T. Cotton.—Chemical examination of chufa, tubers of Cyperus esculentus Linné [with list of literature cited] ; by Frederick B. Power and Victor K. Chestnut.—Constituents of chufa oil, fatty oil from tubers of Cyperus esculentus Linné [with list of literature cited] ; by Walter F. Baughman and George S. Jamieson.—No. 3. Soil reaction in relation to calcium adsorption [with list of literature cited] ; by C. O. Swanson.—Time for testing mother beets; by Dean A. Pack.— No. 4. Bacterial stripe disease of proso millet [with list of literature cited] ; by Charlotte Elliott.—Factors which determine otocephaly in guinea pigs [with list of literature cited] ; by Sewall Wright and Orson N. Eaton.—Method of automatic control of low temperatures employed by Department of Agriculture; by John T. Bowen.— Excretions from leaves as factor in arsenical injury to plants; by C. M. Smith.
    NOTE.—This publication is published by authority of the Secretary of Agriculture, with the cooperation of the Association of Land-Grant Colleges. It is distributed free only to libraries of agricultural colleges and experiment stations, to large universities, technical schools, and to such institutions as make suitable exchanges with the Agriculture Department. Others desiring the Journal may obtain it from the Superintendent of Documents, Washington, D. C., at the prices stated above.

Official record, Department of Agriculture, v. 2, no. 49–52; Dec. 5–26, 1923. [1923.] Each 8 p. 4° [Weekly.] * Paper, 50c. a yr. ; foreign subscription, $1.10.   Agr 22—146

Ophiobolus cariceti. Pathogenicity of Ophiobolus cariceti in its relationship to weakened plants [with list of literature cited] ; by H. R. Rosen and J. A. Elliott. 1923. cover-title, 351–358+[4] p. +[1] leaf, 5 p. of pl. [From Journal of agricultural research, v. 25, no. 8, Aug. 25, 1923.] ‡

Potatoes. Correlation of foliage degeneration diseases of Irish potato with variations of tuber and sprout [with list of literature cited] ; by Alfred H. Gilbert. 1923. cover-title, 255–266+[5] p.+[1] leaf, 6 p. of pl. [From Journal of agricultural research, v. 25, no. 6, Aug. 11, 1923.] ‡

Poultry. Growing experimental chickens in confinement; by C. A. Herrick, J. E. Ackert, and Bertha L. Danheim. 1923. cover-title. 451–456+[1] p. 2 p. of pl. [From Journal of agricultural research, v. 25, no. 11, Sept. 15, 1923.] ‡

Quarantine. Modification of fruit and vegetable quarantine, Amendment 1 to regulations supplemental to Notice of quarantine 56, effective Nov. 1, 1923. [1923.] 1 p. (Federal Horticultural Board.) †

—— Modification of satin moth quarantine, Amendment 1 to regulations supplemental to Notice of quarantine 53, effective Nov. 15, 1923. 1923. 1 p. (Federal Horticultural Board.) †

—— Quarantine on account of Japanese beetle [revised rules and regulations supplemental to Notice of quarantine 48 (2d revision), effective Nov. 27, 1923]. [1923.] 5 p. (Federal Horticultural Board.) †

Report of Secretary of Agriculture, 1923. 1923. iv+100 p. †   Agr 9—987

Sulphur. Determination of sulphur compounds in dry lime-sulphur [with list of literature cited]; by Carleton Parker Jones. 1923. cover-title, p. 323–336, il. [From Journal of agricultural research, v. 25, no. 7, Aug. 18, 1923.] ‡

Weather, crops, and markets. Weather, crops, and markets, v. 3, Jan.–June, 1923 [title-page, corrections, and index]. [1923.] ii+7 p. 4° * Paper, 5c.
                                                                    Agr 22—147

—— Same, weekly, Dec. 1–29, 1923; v. 4, no. 22–26. [1923–24.] p. 569–712, il. 4° * Paper, $1.00 a yr.; foreign subscription, $2.00.

Wheat situation, report to the President; by Henry C. Wallace, Secretary of Agriculture. 1923. iv+126 p. il. †   Agr 24—36

ACCOUNTS AND DISBURSEMENTS DIVISION

Report of chief of Division of Accounts and Disbursements [fiscal year 1923]. [1923.] 7 p. †   8—30669

AGRICULTURAL ECONOMICS BUREAU

Crop systems for Arkansas; [by] A. D. McNair. Aug. 1918 [revised Oct. 1923]. [1923.] 24 p. il. (Agriculture Dept. Farmers' bulletin 1000.) [Formerly issued by Farm Management Office.] * Paper, 5c.

Report of chief of Bureau of Agricultural Economics [fiscal year 1923]. [1923.] 67 p. †   Agr 24—37

Service announcements. Service and regulatory announcements, no. 81: Regulations of Secretary of Agriculture under warehouse act of Aug. 11, 1916, as amended, regulations for peanut warehouses, approved Sept. 29, 1923. 1923. iv+33 p. *Paper, 5c.   Agr 15—199

ANIMAL INDUSTRY BUREAU

Cattle. Brahman (Zebu) cattle; [by Virgil V. Parr]. [Oct. 1923.] ii+21 p. il. (Agriculture Dept. Farmers' bulletin 1361.) *Paper, 5c.   Agr 24—33

Horses. Breaking and training colts; [by V. G. Stambaugh; revised by J. O. Williams and Earl B. Krantz]. [Oct. 1923.] ii+21 p. il. (Agriculture Dept. Farmers' bulletin 1368.) [Revision of Farmers' bulletin 667. Includes list of Agriculture Department publications relating to horses.] *Paper, 5c.
                                                                    Agr 24—34

Milk. Production of clean milk; [by Ernest Kelly]. [Aug. 1914, revised Nov. 1923.] [1923.] 24 p. il. (Agriculture Dept. Farmers' bulletin 602.) [Includes lists of Agriculture Department publications relating to production and care of milk.] *Paper, 5c.

Report of chief of Bureau of Animal Industry [fiscal year 1923]. [1923.] 56 p. †   Agr 12—377

Silage. Making and feeding of silage: [articles by T. E. Woodward and J. B. McNulty, George M. Rommel, E. W. Sheets, and F. R. Marshall]. [July, 1918, revised Nov.1923.] [1923.] 32 p. il. (Agriculture Dept. Farmers' bulletin 578.) [Includes list of Agriculture Department publications relating to silage.] *Paper, 5c.

CONTENTS.—Silage, its preparation and feeding value; [by] T. E. Woodward and J. B. McNulty.—Silage for dairy cattle; [by] T. E. Woodward and J. B. McNulty.—Silage for horses; [by] George M. Rommel.—Silage for beef cattle; [by] E. W. Sheets.—Silage for sheep; [by] F. R. Marshall.

BIOLOGICAL SURVEY BUREAU

Report of chief of Bureau of Biological Survey [fiscal year 1923]. [1923.]
44 p. †   Agr 12—378

Service announcements. Service and regulatory announcements, [no.] 58: Use
of headlights on Big Lake Reservation, Ark., prohibited. Dec. 14, 1923.
1 p. *Paper, 5c.   Agr 16—608

CHEMISTRY BUREAU

Gossypol. Quantitative variation of gossypol and its relation to oil content
of cottonseed [with list of literature cited] ; by Erich W. Schwartze and Carl
L. Alsberg. 1923. cover-title, p. 285–295, il. [From Journal of agricultural
research, v. 25, no. 7, Aug. 18, 1923.] ‡

Mesquite beans. Chemical and structural study of mesquite, carob, and honey
locust beans [with list of literature cited] ; by G. P. Walton. Dec. 22, 1923.
20 p. 2 p. of pl. (Agriculture Dept. Department bulletin 1194.)
                                                               Agr 24—29

Report of chemist [fiscal year 1923]. [1923.] 28 p. †   Agr 12—382

Straw-gas. Experimental production of straw gas; by Harry E. Roethe. Nov.
30, 1923. 11 p. il. (Agriculture Dept. Department bulletin 1203.) * Paper, 5c.
                                                               Agr 24—30

EDITORIAL AND DISTRIBUTION WORK OFFICES

NOTE.—See also Publications Division, p. 279.

Agriculture Department. Monthly list of publications [of Agriculture Depart-
ment], Oct. 1923. [1923.] 4 p. †

ENTOMOLOGY BUREAU

Aleurodicus manni. Undescribed orange pest [Aleurodicus manni] from Honduras; by A. C. Baker. 1923. cover-title, 253–254+[1] p.+[1] leaf, 2 p. of pl.
[From Journal of agricultural research, v. 25, no. 5, Aug. 4, 1923.] ‡

Imported pine sawfly; by William Middleton. Dec. 12, 1923. 22 p. il. (Agriculture Dept. Department bulletin 1182.) * Paper, 5c.   Agr 24—26

Report of entomologist [fiscal year 1923]. [1923.] 37 p. †   8—9985

EXPERIMENT STATIONS OFFICE

NOTE.—The Experiment Stations Office was created Oct. 1, 1888, and was merged
into the States Relations Service July 1, 1915. The States Relations Service ceased to
exist as such July 1, 1923, and the Experiment Stations Office has again become a publishing office. See also for reports of the States Relations Service and its subordinate
offices covering the period previous to July 1, 1923, p. 280.

Experiment station record. Experiment station record, v. 48; index number.
Nov. 28, 1923. cover-title, xvi+901–992 p. [Text and illustration on p. 2 and
4 of cover.] * Paper, 10c. single copy, 75c. per vol. (2 vols. a yr.) ; foreign
subscription, $1.25 per vol.   Agr 9—832

NOTE.—Mainly made up of abstracts of reports and publications on agricultural
science which have recently appeared in all countries, especially the United States.
Extra numbers, called abstract numbers, are issued, 3 to each volume. These are made
up almost exclusively of abstracts, that is, they contain no editorial notes and only a
limited number of current notes.

—— Same, v. 49, no. 6; abstract number. Dec. 15, 1923. cover-title, ix+501–
600 p. [Text and illustration on p. 2 and 4 of cover.] * Paper, 10c. single
copy, 75c. per vol. (2 vols. a yr.) ; foreign subscription, $1.25 per vol. (sub-
scription price incorrectly given in publication).

FEDERAL HORTICULTURAL BOARD

Report of Federal Horticultural Board [fiscal year 1923]. [1923.] 36 p. †
                                                               Agr 15—530

FIXED NITROGEN RESEARCH LABORATORY

Report of director of Fixed Nitrogen Research Laboratory [fiscal year 1923].
[1923.] 12 p. †   23—18745

FOREST SERVICE

Report of forester [fiscal year 1923]. [1923.] 56 p. †   Agr 12—394
Sierra Nevada. Some results of cutting in Sierra forests of California [with list of references] ; by Duncan Dunning. Nov. 24. 1923. 27 p. il. 8 p. of pl. (Agriculture Dept. Department bulletin 1176.) * Paper, 10c.   Agr 24—25

Maps

Deschutes National Forest. Recreation map, Deschutes National Forest [resources and recreation features]. [1923.] 1 sheet (with map on verso), il. f°, folded into narrow 8° size and so printed as to number [1]+18+[1] p. †
Rainier National Forest, Wash. [resources and recreation features, roads, etc.]. [1923.] 1 sheet (with map on verso), il. large 4°, folded into narrow 8° size and so printed as to number [1]+16+[1] p. †
Snoqualmie National Forest, Wash. [resources and recreation features, roads, trails, etc.]. [1923.] 1 sheet (with map on verso), il. f°, folded into narrow 8° size and so printed as to number [1]+13+[1] p. †

GRAIN FUTURES ADMINISTRATION

Report of administration of grain futures act [fiscal year 1923]. [1923.] 4 p. †   Agr 24—38

HOME ECONOMICS BUREAU

NOTE.—Created under act making appropriations for Department of Agriculture, fiscal year 1924, approved Feb. 26, 1923. Formerly the work in home economics was carried on as a separate office in the States Relations Service. See also, below, States Relations Service.

Canning and preserving. Home canning of fruits and vegetables. [Oct. 1921, revised June. 1923, corrected Dec. 1923.] [1923.] 48 p. il. (Agriculture Dept. Farmers' bulletin 1211.) [Formerly issued by States Relations Service.] * Paper, 5c.
Food. Care of food in the home. [Nov. 1923.] ii+13 p. (Agriculture Dept. Farmers' bulletin 1374.) [Revision of Farmers' bulletin 375, which was originally issued Nov. 30, 1909.] * Paper, 5c.   Agr 24—35
—— 100-calorie portions of a few familiar foods in terms of ordinary household measurements and of quantities commonly purchased ; [poster]. [1923.] 19×24 in. * 10c.

INSECTICIDE AND FUNGICIDE BOARD

Report of Insecticide and Fungicide Board [fiscal year 1923]. [1923.] 6 p. †   Agr 12—2227
Service announcements. Service and regulatory announcements, no. 45. Oct. 1923. p. 1057–87. [Contains Notices of insecticide act judgments 851–875.] * Paper, 5c.   Agr 14—384

NOTE.—The free distribution of this publication will be limited to firms, establishments, and journals especially concerned. Others desiring copies may obtain them from the Superintendent of Documents at the prices stated above and below.

—— Same, no. 46. Dec. 1923. p. 1089–1109. [Contains Notices of insecticide act judgments 876–900.] * Paper, 5c.

LIBRARY

Report of librarian [fiscal year 1923]. [1923.] 16 p. †   8—26939

PACKERS AND STOCKYARDS ADMINISTRATION

Report of Packers and Stockyards Administration [fiscal year 1923]. [1923.] 31 p. †   Agr 23—399

PLANT INDUSTRY BUREAU   •

Alfalfa, ns ruc ons adapted to New England States and New York. [1923.] 5 p. ti t ti

Corn. Inheritance of dwarfing in maize [with list of literature cited] ; by J. H. Kempton. 1923. cover-title, 297–322+[4] p. il. 5 p. of pl. [From Journal of agricultural research, v. 25, no. 7, Aug. 18, 1923.] ‡

Cotton. Utilization of Pima cotton [with list of literature cited] ; by Horace H. Willis. Nov. 1923. 27 p. il. 1 pl. 12 p. of pl. (Agriculture Dept. Bulletin 1184.) [Prepared in cooperation with Agricultural Economics Bureau.] * Paper, 15c. Agr 24—27

Cow-pea. Cowpeas. [1923.] 4 p. †

Hookworms. Pharynx and alimentary canal of hookworm larva, Necator americanus ; by N. A. Cobb. 1923. cover-title, p. 359–362. 1 pl. [From Journal of agricultural research, v. 25, no. 8, Aug. 25, 1923.] ‡

Orange-rust. New type of orange-rust on blackberry ; by B. O. Dodge. [1923.] p. 491–494. [From Journal of agricultural research, v. 25, no. 12, Sept. 22, 1923.] ‡

Phytophthora faberi. Comparative study of Phytophthora faberi on coconut and cacao in Philippine Islands [with list of literature cited] ; by Otto A. Reinking. 1923. cover-title, 267–284+[11] leaf, il. 12 p. of pl. [From Journal of agricultural research, v. 25, no. 6, Aug. 11, 1923.] ‡

Red clover culture [by A. J. Pieters ; with notes on insect enemies of red clover, by W. R. Walton]. [1923.] ii+33 p. il. (Agriculture Dept. Farmers' bulletin 1339.) [Revision of Farmers' bulletin 455.] * Paper, 5c. Agr 24—32

Report of chief of Bureau of Plant Industry [fiscal year 1923]. [1923.] 34 p. † 8—12625

Rye. Resistance in rye to leaf rust, Puccinia dispersa Erikss [with list of literature cited] ; by E. B. Mains and C. E. Leighty. 1923. cover-title, 243–252 +[1] p.+[1] leaf, 2 p. of pl. [Prepared in cooperation with Purdue University Agricultural Experiment Station. From Journal of agricultural research, v. 25, no. 5, Aug. 4, 1923.] ‡

Seeds. Inventory of seeds and plants imported by Office of Foreign Seed and Plant Introduction. Jan. 1–Mar. 31, 1922, no. 70 ; nos. 54677–968. Nov. 1923. iii+37 p. 4 p. of pl. * Paper, 5c. Agr 7—1331

—— Same, Apr. 1–June 30, 1922, no. 71 ; nos. 54969–55568. Dec. 1923. iii+ 62 p. 6 p. of pl. * Paper, 10c.

Soy-bean. Soy beans. [1923.] 4 p. †

Sugar-cane. Hot-water treatment of sugar cane for insect pests, a precaution ; [by] P. A. Yoder and J. W. Ingram. Dec. 1923. 4 p. (Agriculture Dept. Department circular 303.) [Prepared in cooperation with Entomology Bureau.] * Paper, 5c. Agr 24—31

Velvet-bean. velvet beans. [1923.] 3 p. †

Wheat. Improvement of Kubanka durum wheat by pure-line selection ; by Ralph W. Smith, L. R. Waldron, and J. Allen Clark. Nov. 1923. 15 p. il. (Agriculture Dept. Department bulletin 1192.) [Prepared in cooperation with North Dakota Agricultural Experiment Station.] * Paper, 5c. Agr 24—28

PUBLIC ROADS BUREAU

Drainage of irrigated farms ; [by R. A. Hart]. [June, 1917, revised June, 1923.] [1923.] 32 p. il. (Agriculture Dept. Farmers' bulletin 805.) * Paper, 5c.

Irrigation of orchards ; [by Samuel Fortier]. [Revised Oct. 1923.] [1923.] 40 p. il. (Agriculture Dept. Farmers' bulletin 882.) [June, 1910, on page 2, is the original date of issue of Farmers' bulletin 404, which Farmers' bulletin 882 revised.] * Paper, 5c.

Report of chief of Bureau of Public Roads [fiscal year 1923]. [1923.] 32 p. † 7—14969

PUBLICATIONS DIVISION

NOTE.—See also Editorial and Distribution Work Offices, p. 277.

Reports of chief of Division of Publications. Office of Motion Pictures, and Office of Exhibits [fiscal year 1923]. [1923.] 22 p. †

SOILS BUREAU

Chatsworth, N. J. Soil survey of Chatsworth area, N. J.; by L. L. Lee, C. C. Engle, William Seltzer, Austin L. Patrick, and E. B. Deeter. 1923. iv+469–515 p. il. 3 maps. [Prepared in cooperation with Department of Conservation and Development of New Jersey. From Field operations, 1919.] *.Paper, 25c.

Marengo County, Ala. Soil survey of Marengo County, Ala.; by S. W. Phillips, R. E. Devereux, R. A. Winston, R. W. McClure, and E. W. Knobel. 1923. iii+555–597 p. il. map. [Prepared in cooperation with Alabama Department of Agriculture and Industries. From Field operations, 1920.] * Paper, 25c.

Ontonagon County, Mich. Reconnaissance soil survey of Ontonagon County, Mich.; by J. O. Veatch, James Tyson, and W. D. Lee. 1923. iii+73–100 p. il. map. [Prepared in cooperation with Michigan Agricultural Experiment Station. From Field operations, 1921.] * Paper, 15c.

Report of chief of Bureau of Soils [fiscal year 1923]. [1923.] 7 p. †

8—30670

SOLICITOR OF DEPARTMENT OF AGRICULTURE

Report of solicitor [of Department of Agriculture, fiscal year 1923]. [1923.] 24 p. †

8—9984

STATES RELATIONS SERVICE

NOTE.—The States Relations Service ceased to exist as such July 1, 1923. See also notes under Experiment Stations Office, p. 277, and Home Economics Office, p. 278.

Report of director of States Relations Service [fiscal year 1923]. [1923.] 62 p. †

Agr 16—1352

PORTO RICO AGRICULTURAL EXPERIMENT STATION

Report of Porto Rico Agricultural Experiment Station, 1922. Dec. 14, 1923. [2]+18 p. il. 4 p. of pl. * Paper, 10c.

Agr 6—1362

VIRGIN ISLANDS AGRICULTURAL EXPERIMENT STATION

Report of Virgin Islands Agricultural Experiment Station, 1922. Dec. 15, 1923. cover-title. 18 p. il. * Paper, 5c.

Agr 20—1776

WEATHER BUREAU

Atmospheric pressure. Law of pressure ratios and its application to charting of isobars in lower levels of troposphere; by C. LeRoy Meisinger. 1923. [1]+437–448 p. il. 4° [From Monthly weather review, Sept. 1923.] †

Climatological data for United States by sections, v. 10, no. 9; Sept. 1923. [1923.] cover-title, [192] p. il. map. 2 p. of maps, 4° [Text on p. 2 of cover.] * Paper, 35c. complete monthly number, $4.00 a yr.

Agr 14—566

NOTE.—Made up of separate Climatological data issued from 42 section centers of the United States. Printed at the several section centers and assembled and bound at the Washington Office. Issued principally for service use and exchange. The separate Climatological data are sold by the Superintendent of Documents, Washington, D. C., at the rate of 5c. single copy, 50c. a yr. for each section.

Meteorology. Monthly meteorological summary, Washington, D. C., Nov. 1923. [1923.] [2] p. f° †

Monthly weather review, v. 51, no. 9; Sept. 1923. [Dec. 5] 1923. cover-title, p. 437–495, il. 11 p. of maps, 4° [Text on p. 2–4 of cover.] *Paper, 15c. single copy, $1.50 a yr.; foreign subscription, $2.25.

Agr 9—990

NOTE.—The Monthly weather review contains (1) meteorological contributions, and bibliography including seismology, (2) an interpretative summary and charts of the weather of the month in the United States, and on adjacent oceans, and (3) climatological and seismological tables dealing with the weather and earthquakes of the month. The contributions are principally as follows; (a) results of observational or research work in meteorology carried on in the United States or other parts of the world, (b) abstracts or reviews of important meteorological papers and books, and (c) notes. SPECIAL ARTICLES.—Law of pressure ratios and its application to charting of isobars in lower levels of troposphere; [by] C. LeRoy Meisinger.—Winds of Oklahoma and east Texas; by John A. Riley.—Anticyclone of Sept. 12–18, 1923; by Alfred J. Henry.—Frequencies of monthly and seasonal rainfalls of various depths at San Jose, Calif.; by Esek S. Nichols.—Typhoon at Guam, M. I., Mar. 19–27, 1923; by J. H. West and J. D. Swartwout.—Weather and Berkeley [Calif.] fire; by George W. Alexander.—Record-breaking rainfall in southern Michigan; [by] R. M. Dole.—Tornado at Council Bluffs, Iowa, Sept. 28, 1923; by M. V. Robins.—International Meteorological Conference at Utrecht [Sept. 7–14, 1923].—Eight typhoons in far East during Aug. 1923; by José Coronas.

New England highway bulletin, Dec. 18 and 26, 1923: no. 1 and 2 [season of 1923–24]. [Boston, Mass., 1923.] Each 1 p. il. large 8° [Weekly.] *Paper, 50c. per season.

Ocean. Weather of the oceans, Sept. 1923, with special reference to north Atlantic and north Pacific oceans (including charts), notes, abstracts, and reviews; issued by Marine Division. 1923. 8 p. il. 5 p. of maps, 4° [From Monthly weather review, Sept. 1923.] †

Report of chief of Weather Bureau [fiscal year 1923]. [1923.] 28 p. †
                                                                  Agr 9—1419

Snow and ice bulletin, no. 1–3, winter 1923–24; Dec. 10–24, 1923. Dec. 11–26, 1923. Each [2] p. il. large 4° [Weekly during winter.] †   12—1660

Weather map. Daily weather map [of United States, containing forecasts for all States east of Mississippi River, except Illinois, Wisconsin, Indiana, upper Michigan, and lower Michigan], Dec. 1–31, 1923. 1st edition. [1923.] Each 16.4×22.7 in. [Not issued Sundays or holidays.] * Editions issued at Washington, D. C., 25c. a month, $2.50 a yr.; editions issued at about 65 stations throughout the United States, 20c. a month, $2.00 a yr.

—— Same [containing forecasts for United States], Dec. 1–31. 1923. 2d edition. [1923.] Each 16.4×22.7 in. [The Sunday edition does not contain as much information as the edition for week days.] *30c. a month, $3.00 a yr.

Winds of Oklahoma and east Texas; by John A. Riley. 1923. [1]+448–455 p. il. 4° [From Monthly weather review, Sept. 1923.] †

ALIEN PROPERTY CUSTODIAN

Enemy property. Accrued interest under trading with the enemy act, letter transmitting, in response to resolution, information as to accrued interest under trading with the enemy act. Dec. 18, 1923. 2 p. (S. doc. 10, 68th Cong. 1st sess.) * Paper, 5c.

CIVIL SERVICE COMMISSION

NOTE.—The Commission furnishes its publications gratuitously to those who apply for them.

Postal service. Instructions to applicants for post-office service, 10th civil-service district, headquarters, New Orleans, La. Oct. 1923. 17+[1] p. (Form 1898.) †

Reports. 40th annual report of Civil Service Commission, fiscal year 1923. 1923. c p. il. †   4—18119

—— Same [with report of chief examiner, and with appendix], fiscal year 1923. 1923. c+206 p. il. †
    NOTE.—Contains civil service acts, rules, and regulations.

—— Same. (H. doc. 84, 68th Cong. 1st sess.).

—— Annual reports of chief examiner and director of research of Civil Service Commission, fiscal year 1923. 1923. lxiv p. il. †

COMMERCE DEPARTMENT

NOTE.—The Department of Commerce prints most of its publications in very limited editions, the distribution of which is confined to Government officers, libraries, etc. When a selling price is noted in this list, application for such publication should be submitted to the Superintendent of Documents, Washington, D. C., with remittance. For copies of charts, coast pilots, and tide tables, however, apply directly to the issuing office, the Coast and Geodetic Survey, Washington, D. C.

Commerce. Amendments to Schedule B, statistical classification of domestic commodities exported [from United States and regulations governing statistical returns of exports of domestic commodities, effective Jan. 1, 1924]. [1923.] 2 p. (Foreign and Domestic Commerce Bureau.) [No revised edition of Schedule B for 1924 will be printed.] †

Report. 11th annual report of Secretary of Commerce [with condensed reports of bureaus, fiscal year] 1923. 1923. viii+235 p. * Paper, 20c.   14—30030

APPOINTMENT DIVISION

Report. Annual report of chief of Appointment Division, fiscal year 1923.
1923. ii+14 p. †   14—7029

CENSUS BUREAU

Cement. Census of manufactures, 1921: Cement, lime, and sand-lime brick.
1923. 20 p. * Paper, 5c.   23—27472
Clay industries. Census of manufactures, 1921: Clay-products industries, brick,
tile, and terra-cotta and fire-clay products, pottery. 1923. 24 p. * Paper, 5c.
                                                                      23—27473
Cotton. Cotton consumed, cotton on hand, active cotton spindles, and imports
and exports of cotton, Nov. 1922 and 1923, with statistics of cotton consumed,
imported, and exported for 4 months ending Nov. 30. Dec. 14, 1923. oblong
32° [Preliminary report. This publication is issued in postal card form.] †
—— Report on cotton ginning, number of bales of cotton ginned from growth
of 1923 prior to Dec. 1, 1923, and comparative statistics to corresponding
date in 1922 and 1921. Dec. 8, 1923. oblong 32° [Preliminary report. This
publication is issued in postal card form.] †
—— Same prior to Dec. 13, 1923, and comparative statistics to corresponding
date in 1922 and 1921. Dec. 20, 1923. oblong 32° [Preliminary report. This
publication is issued in postal card form.] †
Cottonseed received, crushed, and on hand, and cottonseed products manufactured, shipped out, on hand, and exported covering 4-month period ending
Nov. 30, 1923 and 1922. Dec. 19, 1923. oblong 32° [Preliminary report.
This publication is issued in postal card form.] †
Mortality rates, 1910–20, with population of Federal censuses of 1910 and
1920 and intercensal estimates of population. 1923. 681 p. il. 4° [Prepared
under direction of William H. Davis, chief statistician for vital statistics,
and under supervision of Richard C. Lappin, expert special agent.] * Cloth,
$1.75.   23—27474
Report. Annual report of director of census, fiscal year 1923. 1923. iv+
46 p. †   8—20800

COAST AND GEODETIC SURVEY

NOTE.—The monthly Notice to mariners, formerly issued by the Coast and Geodetic
Survey, has been consolidated with and made a part of the Notice to mariners issued by
the Lighthouses Bureau, thus making it a joint publication. The charts, coast pilots, and
tide tables of the Coast and Geodetic Survey are sold at the office of the Survey in Washington, and also by one or more sales agents in each of the important American seaports.

Coast and Geodetic Survey bulletin, Nov. 30, 1923; no. 102. [1923.] 8 p.
 [Monthly.] ‡   15—26512
Georgia. Precise leveling in Georgia; by Henry G. Avers. 1923. ii+107 p. il.
1 pl. map. (Special publication 95; serial 240.) * Paper, 15c.   23—27449
Magnetic observatories. Results of observations made at Coast and Geodetic
Survey magnetic observatory at Sitka, Alaska, in 1919 and 1920; by Daniel L.
Hazard. 1923. [1]+102 p. 20 pl. (Serial 242.) * Paper, 25c.   11—35478
Maps and charts. Rules and practice relating to construction of nautical
charts; [by George L. Flower]. [Reprint] 1923. 34 p. (Special publication
66; serial 141.) * Russet cloth lined, 5c.   23—27475
Regulations. Supplement to Regulations for government of Coast and Geodetic
Survey, Nov. 24, 1923. 1923. [1]+32 leaves, 12° (Serial 252.) [This sup-
plement of Nov. 24, 1923, contains all the additions and corrections to the
Regulations since Feb. 1, 1921.] ‡
Report. Annual report of director, Coast and Geodetic Survey, fiscal year 1923.
1923. 4 pts. in 1. v+149 p. 4 pl. 35 maps. * Paper, 30c.
—— Same. (H. doc. 68, 68th Cong. 1st sess.)
Tide tables, Atlantic Coast, North America, [calendar] year 1925; from Tide
tables, United States and foreign ports [calendar year 1925]. 1923. 1–104+
339–364+416–425+432–438+445–448 p. il. (Serial 245.) † Paper, 15c.
                                                                      7—35329

Charts

Bering Sea, eastern part, Alaska, west coast, from United States, British, and foreign authorities; chart 9302. [Scale 1:1, 600,000.] Washington, Coast and Geodetic Survey, Nov. 1923. 38.1×29.7 in. †75c.

Boston Harbor, Mass., surveys 1892–1915, surveys by Boston authorities to 1921, surveys by U. S. Engineers to 1922, surveys by Navy to 1921; chart 246. Scale 1: 20,000. Washington, Coast and Geodetic Survey, Nov. 1923. 34.2× 43.5 in. †75c.

California, San Diego to Point Fermin, surveys 1851–1914 and other sources; chart 5102. [Scale 1: 222,000.] Washington, Coast and Geodetic Survey, Dec. 1923. 31.3×41.1 in. [Not intended for inside navigation.] †75c.

Delaware River, Philadelphia to Trenton, surveys by U. S. Engineers to 1923 and other sources; with inset, Trenton; chart 296. Scale 1: 40,000. Washington, Coast and Geodetic Survey, Nov. 1923. 28×32.7 in. †50c.

Nehalem River, Oreg., surveys 1875–89, surveys by U. S. Engineers to July, 1923; chart 6122. Scale 1: 20,000. Washington, Coast and Geodetic Survey, Nov. 1923. 19.1×15.8 in. †25c.

Philadelphia water front, Delaware River. Pa., surveys 1878–1915, surveys by Dept. of Public Works to 1923, surveys by U. S. Engineers to 1923; chart 380. Scale 1: 9,600. Washington, Coast and Geodetic Survey, Nov. 1923. 49.7× 26.1 in. †75c.

Siuslaw Inlet, Oreg., from reconnaissance by Coast and Geodetic Survey in 1883 and 1887, and surveys by Corps of Engrs. to June, 1923; chart 6023. Scale 1: 20,000. Washington, Coast and Geodetic Survey, Dec. 1923. 17.6×17.3 in. †25c.

Target Bay and vicinity, Culebra Island, W. I,. surveys 1900–04 and other sources; chart 915. Scale 1: 10,000. Washington, Coast and Geodetic Survey, Dec. 1923. 25.3×37 in. †50c.

Yaquina River and approaches. Oreg.. surveys 1868–1914, surveys by U. S. Engineers to 1923; chart 6058. Scale 1: 20,000. Washington, Coast and Geodetic Survey, Dec. 1923. 26.4×30.5 in. †50c.

FISHERIES BUREAU

Alaska fishery and fur-seal industries in 1922; by Ward T. Bower. 1923. [1]+ 118 p. il. 7 pl. 2 maps. (Bureau of Fisheries doc. 951.) [App. 4, report of commissioner of fisheries, 1923.] *Paper, 20c. F 13—212

NOTE.—Includes Fur-seal census, Pribilof Islands, 1922; by Edward C. Johnston.

Cold storage holdings of fish, Nov. 15, 1923. [1923.] 1 p. oblong 8° (Statistical bulletin 592.) [Statistics furnished by Agricultural Economics Bureau.] †

Fisheries service bulletin, Dec. 1, 1923; no. 103. [1923.] 13 p. [Monthly.] ‡ F 15—76

Fishery industries of United States. report of Division of Fishery Industries for 1922 [with list of earlier publications relating to fisheries of New York, New Jersey, Pennsylvania, and Delaware]; by Harden F. Taylor, with collaboration of division staff. 1923. [1]+111 p. il. 2 p. of pl. (Bureau of Fisheries doc 954.) [App. 5, report of commissioner of fisheries, 1923.] *Paper, 15c. F 19—41

Fishery products. Statement of quantities and values of certain fishery products landed at Boston and Gloucester, Mass., and Portland, Me., by American fishing vessels, Nov. 1923. [1923.] 1 p. oblong f° (Statistical bulletin 593.) †

—— Statement of quantities and values of certain fishery products landed at Seattle, Wash., by American fishing vessels, Nov. 1923. [1923.] 1 p. oblong 12° (Statistical bulletin 594.) †

Report. Annual report of commissioner of fisheries, fiscal year 1923. 1923. ii+47 p. (Bureau of Fisheries doc. 946.) † F 10—2

Water beetles in relation to pondfish culture, with life histories of those found in fishponds at Fairport, Iowa [and with bibliography]; by Charles Branch Wilson. 1923. [1]+231-345 p. il. 5 pl. large 8° ([Bureau of Fisheries] doc. 953.) [Manuscript correction on p. 262. From Bulletin, v. 39.] * Paper, 30c.

F 24—1

FOREIGN AND DOMESTIC COMMERCE BUREAU

Commerce. Foreign commerce and navigation of United States, calendar year 1922. 1923. lxxiv+672 p. 4° * Cloth, $1.50.   14—21466

—— Same. (H. doc. 609, 67th Cong. 4th sess.)

—— Monthly summary of foreign commerce of United States, Oct. 1923. 1923. 2 pts. p. 1-69 and ii+71-91 p. 4° * Paper, 10c. single copy (including pts. 1 and 2), $1.00 a yr.; foreign subscription, $1.60.   14—21465

—— Same. 1923. [2 pts. in 1], 91 p. 4° (H. doc. 10, 68th Cong. 1st sess.)

Commerce reports. Commerce reports, weekly survey of foreign trade, reports from American consular officers and representatives of Department of Commerce in foreign countries, no. 49-53; Dec. 3-31, 1923. 1923. cover-titles, p. 593-920, il. 4° [Text and illustrations on p. 2-4 of covers.] * Paper, 10c. single copy, $3.00 a yr.; foreign subscription, $5.00.

—— Same, nos. 27-39 [series 1923], v. 3, 26th year; July-Sept. 1923 [title-page and index]. 1923. [2]+xxix p. 4° [Quarterly.] * Paper, 5c. single copy, 20c. a yr.; foreign subscription, 30c.

—— Supplement to Commerce reports. [Included in price of Commerce reports for subscribers.]

Trade and economic review for 1922, no. 33: Switzerland; by James R. Wilkinson. [1923.] 10 p.
Same, no. 34: India; by Harold Shantz. [1923.] 51 p.
Same, no. 35: Turkey; by G. Bie Ravndal. [1923.] 28 p.
Same, no. 36: Aden; by Raymond Davis. [1923.] 14 p.
Same, no. 37: Chosen; [by] Foster M. Beck. [1923.] 8 p.
Same, no. 38: China: Canton, by R. P. Tenney; Hankow, by P. S. Heintzelman; Tientsin, by F. P. Dormady. [1923.] 37 p.
Same, no. 39: Poland; [by] L. J. Keena, assisted by L. H. Gourley, Donald R. Heath, and R. Y. Jarvis. [1923.] 42 p.
Same, no. 40: Greece; by John G. Ehrhardt. [1923.] 24 p.

—— Supplement to Commerce reports: Foreign markets for paints and paint materials with complete statistics of United States exports for 1922 and first 6 months of 1923; by William M. Taylor. Dec. 3, 1923. ii+26 p. (Trade information bulletin 164; Chemical Division.) †   23—27452

—— Same: Industrial machinery trade of Italy; largely derived from report by A. A. Osborne. Dec. 10, 1923. ii+20 p. (Trade information bulletin 169; Industrial Machinery Division.) †   23—27476

—— Same: Market for prepared medicines in Brazil; by M. A. Cremer. Dec. 3, 1923. ii+14 p. (Trade information bulletin 165; Chemical Division.) †   23—27453

—— Same: Markets for paper and paper products in Chile and Peru; prepared from data furnished by W. E. Embry, C. F. Deichman, Homer Brett, Stewart E. McMillin, Samuel R. Thompson, [and] W. N. Pearce. Dec. 10, 1923. ii+21 p. (Trade information bulletin 168; Paper Division.) †   23—27456

—— Same: Nitrogen survey, pt. 1, Cost of Chilean nitrate; by H. Foster Bain and H. S. Mulliken. Jan. 7, 1924, [published] 1923. ii+69 p. il. (Trade information bulletin 170.) [Prepared as part of investigation of essential raw materials authorized by 67th Congress.] †   23—27477

—— Same: Ramie or China grass; by J. Frank Gillen, in collaboration with J. Orlo Hayes. Dec. 3, 1923. ii+9 p. (Trade information bulletin 166; Far Eastern Division.) †   23—27454

—— Same: Turkish cotton-goods market; by Julian E. Gillespie. Dec. 24, 1923. ii+18 p. (Trade information bulletin 171; Textile Division.) †   23—27478

—— Same: Use of statistics of rubber-goods exports; prepared in Rubber Division. Dec. 31, 1923. ii+10 p. (Trade information bulletin 172; Rubber Division.) †   23—27470

Commerce reports—Continued. Survey of current business, Nov. 1923, no. 27; compiled by Bureau of Census, Bureau of Foreign and Domestic Commerce, [and] Bureau of Standards. 1923. cover-title, 217 p. il. 4° (Monthly supplement to Commerce reports.) [Contains statistics for Sept. 1923, the date given above, Nov. 1923, being the date of issue. Text on p. 2–4 of cover.]
* Paper, 10c. single copy, $1.00 a yr.; foreign subscription, $1.50.   21—26819

> NOTE.—Realizing that current statistics are highly perishable and that to be of use they must reach the business man at the earliest possible moment, the Department has arranged to distribute advance leaflets twice each month to those subscribers who request them. One set of these leaflets is issued about the 20th of the month, giving such information as has been received up to that time, and another set of sheets is mailed at the end of the month giving those figures received since the 20th. The information contained in these leaflets is also published in Commerce reports issued weekly by the Foreign and Domestic Commerce Bureau. The advance sheets will be mailed free of charge to all subscribers to the Survey who request them. Such requests should be addressed to the Bureau of the Census, Department of Commerce, Washington, D. C. Subscriptions, however, should be sent to the Superintendent of Documents, Washington, D. C., at the prices stated above.

Report. Annual report of director of Bureau of Foreign and Domestic Commerce, fiscal year 1923. 1923. ix+170 p. il. map. †   14—30033

Russia. Foreign capital investments in Russian industries and commerce; by Leonard J. Lewery. 1923. iv+28 p. (Miscellaneous series 124.) *Paper, 5c.   23—27480

Statistical abstract. Statistical abstract of United States, 1922. 1923. no. 45; xx+755 p. * Paper, 75c.   4—18089

—— Same. (H. doc. 613, 67th Cong. 4th sess.)

LIGHTHOUSES BUREAU

Bahama Islands, Little Bahama Banks, Matanilla Shoal, light and whistling buoy to be established; [all lettered poster]. Dec. 7, 1923. 16×10.5 in. ([Poster] notice to mariners 90.) †

9th District. West Indies of United States, buoy list, Porto Rico and adjacent islands, 9th lighthouse district; 1923, corrected to Nov. 1. 1923. 21 p. [Includes Guantanamo Bay on south coast of Cuba, and Virgin Islands.] *Paper, 20c.   14—30034

15th District. Light list, lower Mississippi River and tributaries, 15th lighthouse district; 1923, corrected to Nov. 15. 1923. 84 p. narrow 16° [About half of the pages are blank.] *Paper, 20c.   12—29023

Lighthouse service bulletin, v. 2, no. 72; Dec. 1, 1923. [1923.] p. 313–319. [Monthly.] †   12—35121

Notice to mariners, weekly, no. 49–52, 1923; Dec. 7–28 [1923]. 1923. various paging. [Issued jointly with Coast and Geodetic Survey.] †   7—20609

Report. Annual report of commissioner of lighthouses, fiscal year 1923. 1923. ii+82 p. †   12—4661

NAVIGATION BUREAU

Report. Annual report of commissioner of navigation, fiscal year 1923. 1923. v+166 p. *Paper, 15c.   4—18255

—— Same. (H. doc. 69, 68th Cong. 1st sess.)

Ships. American documented seagoing merchant vessels of 500 gross tons and over, Dec. 1, 1923. 1923. ii+68 p. 4° (Serial 73.) [Monthly.] *Paper, 10c. single copy, 75c. a yr.; foreign subscription, $1.25.   19—26597

—— 55th annual list of merchant vessels of United States, with official numbers and signal letters, and lists of vessels belonging to Government with distinguishing signals, year ended June 30, 1923. 1923. [pts. 1–5] vi+572 p. 4° *Cloth, $1.25.   6—35358

—— Same. 1923. [6 pts.] vi+572+162 p. il. 14 pl. 4° ‡ (prices as given on publication are prices of pts. 1–5 and pt. 6 published separately).

—— Same. (H. doc. 30, 68th Cong. 1st sess.)

RADIO SERVICE

Radio Service bulletin, Dec. 1, 1923; no. 80. [1923.] 16 p. [Monthly.]
* Paper, 5c. single copy, 25c. a yr.; foreign subscription, 40c.   15—26255

PUBLICATIONS DIVISION

Commerce Department. Supplement to annual List of publications [of Department of Commerce available for distribution], Nov. 30, 1923. [1923.] 4 p. [Monthly.] †

Report. Annual report of chief, Division of Publications, fiscal year 1923. 1923. ii+25 p. †   14—11645

STANDARDS BUREAU

NOTE.—The Scientific papers will be supplied on subscription as issued at $1.25 per volume, paper bound. These volumes will afterwards be issued bound in cloth at $2.00 per volume; foreign subscription, paper $2.50 (sent in single numbers), cloth $2.35 (bound volumes). Single numbers vary in price. Address the Superintendent of Documents, Washington, D. C.

The Technologic papers will be issued first as separates and later in volume form in the same manner as the Scientific papers. Subscriptions will be accepted by the Superintendent of Documents at $1.25 per volume; foreign subscription, $2.50. Single numbers vary in price.

Paper. Measure of color characteristics of white papers; by R. E. Lofton. Nov. 17, 1923. [1]+667–676 p. il. (Technologic papers 244.) [From Technologic papers, v. 17.] * Paper, 5c.   23—27481

Report. Annual report of director of Bureau of Standards, fiscal year 1923. 1923. xvi+330 p. il. (Miscellaneous publications 53.) †   6—23979

Tanks. Stresses in a few welded and riveted tanks tested under hydrostatic pressure; by A. H. Stang [and] T. W. Greene. Oct. 13, 1923. [1]+645–666 p. il. 1 pl. 2 p. of pl. large 8° (Technologic papers 243.) [From Technologic papers, v. 17.] * Paper, 10c.   23—27450

Tires. United States Government specification for pneumatic tires, solid tires, and inner tubes, Federal Specifications Board. Standard specification 3, officially adopted by Federal Specifications Board, Feb. 3, 1922, for use of Departments and independent establishments of Government in purchase of pneumatic tires, solid tires, and inner tubes. Reprinted [with changes] Nov. 20, 1923. 16 p. large 8° (Circular 115.) [No change from original issuance except correction of typographical errors and slight change in title of circular.] * Paper, 5c.   23—27482

Whiting. Recommended specification for ceramic whiting. Dec. 8, 1923. 7 p. large 8° (Circular 152.) * Paper, 5c.   23—27483

STEAMBOAT INSPECTION SERVICE

Report. Annual report of supervising inspector general, Steamboat Inspection Service, fiscal year 1923. 1923. ii+23 p. †   8—9657

Steamboat Inspection Service bulletin, Dec. 1, 1923; no. 98. [1923.] 2 p. [Monthly.] ‡   15—26679

CONGRESS

Congressional record. Congressional record, 68th Congress, 1st session, v. 65, no. 1–14; Dec. 3–20, 1923. [1923.] 1–496+[16] p. 4°   12—36438

NOTE.—The Congressional record, containing the proceedings and debates of Congress, is issued daily when Congress is in session, and indexes thereto are published fortnightly.

The Record is sold by the Superintendent of Documents on the following terms: Single copy, 3 cents, if not more than 24 pages, and 1 cent more for each additional 8 pages; per month, $1.50, foreign subscription, $2.50. Subscriptions are payable in advance. Prices for the bound volumes of the Record, 67th Congress, 1st–4th sessions, and prior Congresses, will be furnished on application. Send remittances to the Superintendent of Documents, Washington, D. C. Stamps and foreign money will not be accepted.

—— Same, index, with title, Congressional record index, 68th Congress, 1st session, v. 65, nos. 1–14; Dec. 3–20, 1923. [1923.] no. 1; 125+90 p. 4° [Includes History of bills and resolutions.]

Directory. 68th Congress, 1st session, beginning Dec. 3, 1923, official Congressional directory; compiled by Elmer C. Hess. 1st edition, Dec. 1923. [1923.] xvi+551 p. il. 1 pl. * Cloth, 60c.   6—35330

Members. Duplicate names [of members in Senate and House of Representatives, with lists of Senators, Representatives, etc.], 68th Congress, 1st session; corrected to Dec. 3, 1923. 1923. [4] p. f° ‡

PUBLIC LAWS

NOTE.—Public acts in slip form in the first prints may be obtained from the Superintendent of Documents, Washington, D. C., at a subscription price of $1.00 for the 68th Congress, 1st session, foreign subscription $1.25; single copies are usually 5c. each.

Public [joint] resolution 1, 68th Congress.

Congress. H. J. Res. 70, joint resolution authorizing payment of salaries of officers and employees of Congress for Dec. 1923, on 20th day of that month. Approved Dec. 18, 1923. 1 p. (Public resolution 1.)

FEDERAL PRISONERS, JOINT COMMITTEE TO DETERMINE WHAT EMPLOYMENT MAY BE FURNISHED

Employment. Employment of Federal prisoners, report, Dec. 3, 1923. 1923. ii+39 p. [Includes hearings of June 13 and Nov. 3, 1923.] * Paper, 5c.
23—27469

—— Same; submitted by Mr. Overman. 1923. ii+39 p. (S. rp. 1, 68th Cong. 1st sess.) [Title differs slightly.] * Paper, 5c.

HOUSE OF REPRESENTATIVES

Accounts. Annual report of clerk of House of Representatives, Wm. Tyler Page, giving names of statutory and contingent-fund employees of House and their respective compensations, including clerks to Members, expenditures from contingent fund and from certain specific appropriations, amounts drawn from Treasury, stationery accounts, and unexpended balances for year ended June 30, 1923. 1923. iii+501 p. (H. doc. 2, 68th Cong. 1st sess.) * Paper, 5c.
11—12005

Calendars of House of Representatives, 68th Congress, 1st session, Dec. 3–20, 1923; no. 1–10. 1923. Each 12 p. or 16 p. large 8° [Daily when House of Representatives is in session.] ‡

Contested elections. Contested-election case of Martin C. Ansorge *v.* Royal H. Weller from 21st Congressional district of New York. 1923. [1]+655 p. ‡

—— Contested-election case of Walter M. Chandler *v.* Sol Bloom, from 19th Congressional district of New York. 1923. [1]+1097 p. ‡

Reports to be made to Congress, letter from clerk of House of Representatives transmitting list of reports to be made to Congress by public officers during 68th Congress. Dec. 5, 1923. 32 p. (H. doc. 96, 68th Cong. 1st sess.) * Paper, 5c.

IMMIGRATION AND NATURALIZATION COMMITTEE

Immigration. Selection of immigrants at the source, brief submitted by John C. Box. 1923. [1]+10 p. †
23—27410

JUDICIARY COMMITTEE

Calendar. Legislative calendar, 68th Congress, Dec. —, 1923; no. 1. 1923. 43 p. 4° ‡

PENSIONS COMMITTEE

Pensions. U. S. S. Maine pension bill, report to accompany H. R. 74 [to extend benefits of certain pension laws to officers, sailors, and marines on board U. S. S. Maine when that vessel was wrecked in harbor of Habana, Feb. 15, 1898, and to their widows and dependent relatives]; submitted by Mr. Knutson. Dec. 20, 1923. 2 p. (H. rp. 3, 68th Cong. 1st sess.) * Paper, 5c.

PRINTING COMMITTEE

Government Printing Office. Wages of Government Printing Office employees, report to accompany H. R. 506 [to authorize Public Printer to fix rates of wages for employees of Government Printing Office]; submitted by Mr. Kiess. Dec. 17, 1923. 5 p. (H. rp. 1, 68th Cong. 1st sess.) * Paper, 5c.

Calendar. Legislative calendar, 68th Congress, Dec. 22, 1923; no. 1. 1923. 26 p. 4° ‡

Revenue act of 1924, containing proposed amendments to existing law suggested by Secretary of Treasury. Dec. 17, 1923, reprinted Dec. 28, 1923, with certain typographical changes. 344 p. large 8° (Committee print no. 1.) [1st print, Dec. 17, 1923, is Confidential committee print no. 1.] * Paper, 25c. 23—27484

PRINTING JOINT COMMITTEE

Paper. Proposal for furnishing paper for public printing and binding for term of 6 months or 1 year beginning Mar. 1, 1924, including specifications and standards of paper as fixed upon by Joint Committee on Printing, Dec. 14, 1923. Dec. 14, 1923. 48 p. 4° †

SENATE

Accounts. Report of secretary of Senate submitting full and complete statement of receipts and expenditures, July 1, 1922–June 30, 1923. 1923. iii+372 p. (S. doc. 1, 68th Cong. 1st sess.) * Paper, 5c. 9—16161

Calendar of business, Senate, 68th Congress, 1st session, Dec. 11–20, 1923; no. 2–8. [1923.] Each 7 p. large 8° [Daily when Senate is in session; none issued Dec. 3–10, 1923. No calendar was printed bearing the number 1.] ‡

Monroe doctrine. One hundred years of Monroe doctrine, by Henry Cabot Lodge; presented by Mr. Moses. 1923. [1]+14 p. (S. doc. 8, 68th Cong. 1st sess.) [From Scribner's magazine, Oct. 1923.] * Paper, 5c. 23—27485

Permanent Court of International Justice. League of Nations, its court, and its law [and] American cooperation for world peace, by David Jayne Hill; presented by Mr. Moses. 1923. [1]+24 p. (S. doc. 9, 68th Cong. 1st sess.) [From Saturday evening post, Aug. 11 and Nov. 3, 1923.] * Paper, 5c. 23—27486

Property. Property report of secretary of Senate, letter from secretary of Senate submitting account of all property, including stationery, in his possession on 3d of December, 1923. Dec. 10, 1923. 5 p. (S. doc. 4, 68th Cong. 1st sess.) * Paper, 5c.

—— Property report of sergeant at arms of Senate, letter transmitting full and complete account of all property in his possession and in Senate Office Building belonging to Senate, Dec. 3, 1923. 1923. ii+62 p. (S. doc. 13, 68th Cong. 1st sess.) * Paper, 5c.

—— Sale of condemned property, letter from sergeant at arms of Senate [Dec. 3, 1923] submitting report of sale of property condemned in accordance with statutes and deposit of proceeds with financial clerk of Senate, Dec. 20, 1923. 1 p. (S. doc. 12, 68th Cong. 1st sess.) *Paper, 5c.

Rules. Senate manual containing standing rules and orders of Senate, Constitution of United States, Declaration of Independence, Articles of Confederation, Ordinance of 1787, Jefferson's manual, etc. [Revised edition.] 1923. 1–20B+21–726 p. (S. doc. 349, 67th Cong. 4th sess.) *Paper, $1.00. 1—9223

Automobiles. Tax on motor-vehicle fuel sold in District of Columbia, report to accompany S. 120; submitted by Mr. Ball. Dec. 19, 1923. 3 p. (S. rp. 3, 68th Cong. 1st sess.) *Paper, 5c.

Calendar. Legislative calendar, 68th Congress, Dec. 28, 1923; no. 1. 1923. 11 p. 4° ‡

Calendar, 68th Congress, 1st session, Dec. 18, 1923; no. 1. 1923. 7 p. 4° ‡

JUDICIARY COMMITTEE

Calendar. Legislative calendar, 68th Congress, Dec. 17, 1923; no. 1. 1923. 15 p. 4° ‡

PRINTING COMMITTEE

District of Columbia. Laws relating to District of Columbia in force Mar. 4, 1923, report to accompany S. Res. 65 [to have recompiled laws relating to District of Columbia in force Mar. 4, 1923]; submitted by Mr. Moses. Dec. 15, 1923. 1 p. (S. rp. 2, 68th Cong. 1st sess.) *Paper, 5c.

PUBLIC LANDS AND SURVEYS COMMITTEE

Calendar. Legislative calendar, 68th Congress, Dec. 11 and 19, 1923; no. 1 and 2. [1923.] 8 p. and 16 p. 4° ‡

REFORESTATION SELECT COMMITTEE

Reforestation, hearings, 67th Congress, 4th session, pursuant to S. Res. 398, to investigate problems relating to reforestation, Sept. 6 [-27], 1923. 1923. pts. 5, 6, [iv]+639-1252 p. il. †

VETERANS' BUREAU INVESTIGATION SELECT COMMITTEE

Veterans' Bureau. Investigation of Veterans' Bureau, hearings, 67th Congress, 4th session, pursuant to S. Res. 466, authorizing appointment of committee to investigate leases and contracts executed by Veterans' Bureau, and for other purposes, Nov. 5 [-15], 1923. 1923. pts. 3, 4, [iv]+561-1145 p. †

COURT OF CLAIMS

American Rolling Mills Company v. United States; evidence for plaintiff. [1923.] no. C-460, p. 27-71. ‡

American Tobacco Company v. United States; evidence for defendant. [1923.] no. 34477, p. 89-130. ‡

Atlantic Works v. United States, findings in case of Atlantic Works against United States. Dec. 10, 1923. 6 p. (S. doc. 5, 68th Cong. 1st sess.) * Paper, 5c.

Axe, B., & Co. B. Axe and Company *v.* United States; evidence for plaintiff. [1923.] no. C-319, p. 7-24. ‡

Baltimore and Ohio Railroad Company v. United States; testimony for plaintiff. [1923.] [no.] B-87, p. 23-45. ‡

Campbell. Bruce R. Campbell *v.* United States; evidence. [1923.] no. C-791, p. 5-12. ‡

Carleton. Wayne L. Carleton *v.* United States; evidence. [1923.] no. C-702, p. 5-12. ‡

Carlisle Commission Company. Charles D. Carlisle, trading as Carlisle Commission Co., *v.* United States; evidence for plaintiff. [1923.] no. B-204, p. 11-39. ‡

Cases. December calendar [of cases ready for trial or hearing], term 1923 [-24]. 1923. 47 p. [Part of the pages are blank.] ‡

—— Docket of cases pending in Court of Claims, general jurisdiction, [year ending] Dec. 1923. 1923. [1]+90 p. 4° †

Cherokee Nation v. United States; evidence for defendant. [1923.] no. 34449, p. 89-90. ‡

Chicago, Milwaukee & St. Paul Railway Co. v. United States; evidence. [1923.] no. C-63, p. 9-11. ‡

Chicago, Rock Island and Pacific Railway. Dickinson, receiver, Chicago, Rock Island & Pacific Railway Co. *v.* United States; evidence for defendant. [1923.] no. 33612, p. 43-46. ‡

Crook, H. E., Company. H. E. Crook Company *v.* United States; stipulation. [1923.] no. B-194, p. 55-58. ‡

—— H. E. Crook Company *v.* United States; stipulation. [1923.] no. B-195, p. 81-84. ‡

Denver & Rio Grande Western Railroad Co. v. United States; evidence for plaintiff. [1923.] [no.] B–153, p. 15–53. ‡

Erie Railroad Company v. United States; defendant's evidence. [1923.] no. B–169, p. 71–74. ‡

Hygienic Fiber Company v. United States; evidence for defendant. [1923.] no. 287–A, p. 97–119. ‡

Illinois Central Railroad Co. v. United States; defendant's evidence. [1923.] no. B–74, p. 13–20. ‡

Judgments of Court of Claims, letter transmitting statement of all judgments rendered by Court of Claims for year ended Dec. 2, 1923, amounts, parties, and synopsis of nature of claims. Dec. 10, 1923. 10 p. (S. doc. 6, 68th Cong, 1st sess.) * Paper, 5c.   9—6546

Kenny. Thomas Kenny *v.* United States; evidence. [1923.] no. B–388, p. 7–28. ‡

Lecorchick. George Lecorchick *v.* United States; evidence. [1923.] no. C–372, p. 5–9. ‡

Louisville & Nashville Railroad Co. v. United States; defendant's evidence. [1923.] no. B–179, p. 1–2. ‡

Midland Land and Improvement Company v. United States; findings of fact [conclusion of law, and opinion of court], decided Apr. 2, 1923. [1923.] no. 33713, 12 p. ‡

Missouri, Kansas and Texas Railway of Texas. Receiver of Missouri, Kansas and Texas Railway Company of Texas *v.* United States; report of General Accounting Office. [1923.] no. C–16, p. 11–13. ‡

Moore. Louise [Louis] W. Moore and Lilly C. Stone *v.* United States; evidence for plaintiff. [1923.] no. B–246, p. 11–25. ‡

Morgan. Joseph F. Morgan *v.* United States; evidence in behalf of defendant. [1923.] no. B–211, p. 65–71. ‡

Norfolk Southern Railroad Company v. United States; evidence for defendant. [1923.] no. B–190, p. 45–46. ‡

Pressed Steel Car Company v. United States; evidence for defendant. [1923.] no. 239–A, p. 333–585. ‡

St. Louis, Iron Mountain and Southern Railway. Benjamin F. Bush, receiver of St. Louis, Iron Mountain & Southern Railway Company *v.* United States; defendant's evidence. [1923.] no. 340–A, p. 5–7. ‡

Schneider. E. William Schneider *v.* United States; evidence for claimant. [1923.] no. B–135, p. 5–14. ‡

Skinner and Eddy Corporation v. United States, on plaintiff's motion to dismiss; [opinion of court] decided Nov. 28, 1923. [1923.] no. 199–A, 5 p. ‡

Southern Pacific Company v. United States; evidence for defendant. [1923.] no. 34757, p. 47–55. ‡

Stilz. Harry B. Stilz *v.* United States; amended findings of fact [conclusion of law, and opinion of court], decided Dec. 17, 1923. [1923.] no. B–25, 12 p. il. ‡

Wabash Railway Company v. United States; evidence for claimant [and] defendants. [1923.] no. C–74, p. 11–17. ‡

Western Cartridge Co. v. United States; evidence for plaintiff. [1923.] no. 320–A, p. 23–90. ‡

Western Pacific Railroad. Western Pacific Railroad Company *v.* United States; defendant's evidence. [1923.] no. 187–B, p. 15–32. ‡

—— Same; plaintiff's evidence. [1923.] no. B–187, p. 15–54. ‡

Wright. David A. Wright *v.* United States; evidence for plaintiff. [1923.] no. 261–A, p. 7–194. ‡

—— David A. Wright *v.* United States; evidence for plaintiff. [1923.] no. 300–A, p. 23–69. ‡

COURT OF CUSTOMS APPEALS

Amber. No. 2325, United States *v.* National Importing Co., Inc., et al., transcript of record on appeal from Board of General Appraisers. [1923.] cover-title, 1+19 p. ‡

Embroidery. No. 2322, United States *v.* J. D. Smith & Co., transcript of record on appeal from Board of General Appraisers. 1923. cover-title, i+12 p. ‡

DISTRICT OF COLUMBIA

NOTE.—For annual report on sinking fund and funded debt see Treasurer of United States (p. 328).

Charities Board. Report of Board of Charities of District of Columbia [on charitable and reformatory institutions, fiscal year] 1923. 1923. [1]+29 p. † Charities Board.   9—4374

—— Same [with reports of the several institutions, fiscal year] 1923. 1923. [1]+135 p. † Charities Board.

Commissioners. Annual report of commissioners of District of Columbia, year ended June 30, 1923. 1923. v. 2, iv+97 p. [This is the report of the Engineer Department of the District.] † Commissioners.

—— Same. (H. doc. 61, 68th Cong. 1st sess.)

—— Annual report of commissioners of District of Columbia, year ended June 30, 1923. 1923. v. 3, iii+110 p. [This is the report of the Health Department of the District.] † Commissioners.

—— (H. doc. 61, 68th Cong. 1st sess.)

—— Annual report of commissioners of District of Columbia, year ended June 30, 1923. 1923. v. 4, iv+108 p. [This is the report of the Board of Education of the District.] † Commissioners.

—— Same. (H. doc. 61, 68th Cong. 1st sess.)

—— Annual report of commissioners of District of Columbia, year ended June 30, 1923. 1923. v. 5, iii+91 p. [This is the report of the Insurance Department of the District, calendar year 1922.] † Commissioners.

—— Same. (H. doc. 61, 68th Cong. 1st sess.)

—— Report of commissioners of District of Columbia, year ended June 30, 1923. 1923. [1]+56 p. † Commissioners.   8—16038

Court of Appeals. Calendar, Jan. term, 1924. 1923. 61 leaves. [Some of these leaves are printed as pages.] ‡

—— Transcript of record, — term, 192–, no. 4061, no. —, special calendar, United States *vs.* John B. Keleher, appeal from Supreme Court of District of Columbia. 1923. cover-title, i+8 p. ‡

—— Transcript of record, — term, 192–, no. 4062, no. —, special calendar, United States *vs.* Claude L. Burrows, appeal from Supreme Court of District of Columbia. [1923.] cover-title, i+10 p. ‡

Education Board. Report of Board of Education of District of Columbia [with report of superintendent of schools, fiscal year] 1922–23. 1923. iv+108 p. † Education Board.   6—20322

Engineer Department. Report of operations of Engineer Department of District of Columbia, year ended June 30, 1923. 1923. iv+97 p. † Engineer Department.   CA 8—1121

Finances of District of Columbia, fiscal year 1923, embracing annual reports of auditor, assessor, and collector of taxes. 1923. [1]+29 p. † Auditor.

Fire Department. Report of chief engineer of Fire Department of District of Columbia, fiscal year 1923. 1923. [1]+12 p. † Fire Department.   6—35350

Playgrounds Department. 12th annual report of Department of Playgrounds of District of Columbia, year ended June 30, 1923. 1923. [1]+18 p. † Playgrounds Department.   12—40033

Police Department. Report of major and superintendent of Metropolitan police, District of Columbia, [fiscal year] 1923. 1923. [1]+45 p. † Police Department.   8—30781

Public Library. 26th annual report of board of trustees and 25th annual report of librarian of Public Library of District of Columbia, fiscal year 1923. 1923. ii+30 p. † Public Library.   7—35450

EFFICIENCY BUREAU

Report. Report of Bureau of Efficiency, Nov. 1, 1922–Oct. 31, 1923. 1923.
v+6 p. †   17—26040
—— Same. (H. doc. 89, 68th Cong. 1st sess.)

EMPLOYEES' COMPENSATION COMMISSION

Report. 7th annual report of United States Employees' Compensation Commission, July 1, 1922–June 30, 1923. 1923. iii+131 p. †   18—26057
—— Same. (H. doc. 86, 68th Cong. 1st sess.)

FEDERAL BOARD FOR VOCATIONAL EDUCATION

Apprentice education, survey of part-time education and other forms of extension training in their relation to apprenticeship in United States; [by Jennie McMullin Turner]. June, 1923. xiii+521 p. il. 1 tab. (Bulletin 87; Trade and industrial series 25.) * Paper, 55c.   E 24—2

Report. 7th annual report of Federal Board for Vocational Education, [fiscal year] 1923. 1923. ix+186 p. il. 3 pl. * Paper, 15c.   18—26041

CONTENTS.—Sec. 1, General survey of work of board, administrative activities in 1923.—Sec. 2, Vocational Education Division.—Sec. 3, Civilian vocational rehabilitation.—Sec. 4, Statistical report.

—— Same. (H. doc. 88, 68th Cong. 1st sess.)

FEDERAL POWER COMMISSION

Report. 3d annual report of Federal Power Commission, fiscal year 1923. 1923. iii+282 p. * Paper, 20c.   21—27492
—— Same. (H. doc. 73, 68th Cong. 1st sess.)

FEDERAL RESERVE BOARD

Federal reserve bulletin. Federal reserve bulletin, Dec. 1923; [v. 9, no. 12]. 1st edition. 1923. ii+407–440 p. il. 4° [Monthly.] † Paper, $1.50 a yr.
                                                           15—26318
NOTE.—The Federal reserve bulletin is printed in 2 editions (a 1st edition and a final edition). The 1st edition is brief and contains the regular official announcements, the national review of business conditions, and other general matter, and is distributed without charge to the member banks of the Federal reserve system. The 2d or final edition contains detailed analyses of business conditions, special articles, review of foreign banking, and complete statistics showing condition of Federal reserve banks. Those desiring copies of either edition may obtain them from the Federal Reserve Board, Washington, D. C., at the prices stated above and below.

—— Same, Dec. 1923; [v. 9, no. 12]. Final edition. 1923. iv+1251–1376 p. il. map, 4° [Monthly. Includes Index to v. 9.] † Paper, 40c. single copy, $4.00 a yr.

Federal reserve member banks. Federal reserve inter-district collection system, changes in list of banks upon which items will be received by Federal reserve banks for collection and credit, Dec. 1, 1923. 1923. [1]+19 p. 4° †
                                                           16—26870

FEDERAL TRADE COMMISSION

NOTE.—The bound volumes of the Federal Trade Commission decisions are sold by the Superintendent of Documents, Washington, D. C. Separate opinions are sold on subscription, price $1.00 per volume; foreign subscription, $1.50; single copies, 5c. each.

Aluminum Company of America. No. 84, in circuit court of appeals for 3d circuit, Oct. term, 1923, Aluminum Company of America v. Federal Trade Commission, on application by Federal Trade Commission for modification of order; transcript of testimony. 1923. cover-title, i+188 p. large 8° ‡

Decisions. Index to v. 5 [of Federal Trade Commission decisions]. [1923.]
10 p. * Paper, 5c.

Lederer, Henry, & Bros., Incorporated. Federal Trade Commission *v.* Henry
Lederer & Bros., Inc., complaint [report] findings, and order; docket 946, Apr.
30, 1923. 1923. [1]+126–130 p. ([Decision] 361.) [From Federal Trade
Commission decisions, v. 6.] * Paper, 5c.

Report. Annual report of Federal Trade Commission, fiscal year 1923. 1923.
iv+218 p. * Paper, 15c.   15—26727

—— Same. (H. doc. 85, 68th Cong. 1st sess.)

Signet Films, Incorporated. Federal Trade Commission *v.* Signet Films, Inc.,
complaint [report, findings, and order]; docket 936, Apr. 30, 1923. [1923.]
p. 119–125. ([Decision] 360.) [From Federal Trade Commission decisions,
v. 6.] * Paper, 5c.

Williams Soap Company. Federal Trade Commission *v.* Williams Soap Company, complaint [report, findings, and order]; docket 896, Apr. 12, 1923.
[1923.] 107–118+[1] p. ([Decision] 359.) [From Federal Trade Commission decisions, v. 6. Includes list of Cases in which orders for discontinuance or dismissal have been entered, Apr. 18–28, 1923.] * Paper, 5c.

GENERAL ACCOUNTING OFFICE

Decisions of comptroller general, v. 2, July 1, 1922–June 30, 1923; J. R. McCarl,
comptroller general, Lurtin R. Ginn, assistant comptroller general. 1923.
xvii+876 p. * Cloth, $1.75.   22—24145

Report. Annual report of General Accounting Office, [fiscal year] 1923. Dec.
5, 1923. 42 p. (H. doc. 101, 68th Cong. 1st sess.) * Paper, 5c.   22—27353

GOVERNMENT PRINTING OFFICE

Supplies. Specifications and proposal for furnishing and installing complete 1
rotary web perfecting job printing press, advertisement. Dec. 3, 1923.
8 p. 4° †

—— Specifications and proposal for furnishing and installing complete postal
card presses, advertisement. [1923.] [1]+7 p. 4° †

DOCUMENTS OFFICE

American history and biography, list of publications for sale by superintendent
of documents. Oct. 1923. [2]+30 p. (Price list 50, 10th edition.) †
                                                                          23—27461

Birds and wild animals, list of publications for sale by superintendent of documents. Nov. 1923. [2]+8+[1] p. (Price list 39, 14th edition.) †
                                                                          23—27487

Geography and explorations, natural wonders, scenery, and national parks, list
of publications for sale by superintendent of documents. Nov. 1923. [2]+
14 p. (Price list 35, 8th edition.) †   23—27462

Irrigation, drainage, and water power, list of publications for sale by superintendent of documents. Nov. 1923. [2]+22 p. (Price list 42, 14th edition.) †   23—27488

Monthly catalogue, United States public documents, no. 347; Nov. 1923. 1924.
p. 213–269. * Paper, 5c. single copy, 50c. a yr.; foreign subscription, 75c.
                                                                           4—18088

Tariff and taxation, list of publications for sale by superintendent of documents. Nov. 1923. [2]+40+[2] p. (Price list 37, 10th edition.) †
                                                                          23—27489

INTERIOR DEPARTMENT

NOTE.—The decisions of the Department of the Interior in pension cases are issued in
slips and in signatures, and the decisions in land cases are issued in signatures, both
being published later in bound volumes. Subscribers may deposit $1.00 with the Super-
intendent of Documents and receive the contents of a volume of the decisions of either
kind in separate parts as they are issued; foreign subscriptions, $1.25. Prices for bound
volumes furnished upon application to the Superintendent of Documents, Washington,
D. C.

Santa Fe Pacific Railroad. In Court of Appeals of District of Columbia, Oct. term, 1923, Santa Fe Pacific Railroad Company *v.* Hubert Work, Secretary of Interior, no. 3966; reply brief for appellee. [1923.] 4 p. ‡

ALASKA.

Report of governor of Alaska, [fiscal year] 1923. 1923. v+104 p. map. † Interior Dept. 14—30044

COLUMBIA INSTITUTION FOR THE DEAF

Report. 66th annual report of Columbia Institution for the Deaf, fiscal year 1923. 1923. v+7 p. † 6—35346

EDUCATION BUREAU

All-year schools. Bibliography of all-year schools and vacation schools in United States; by Florence Savannah Webb. Nov. 1923. 15 p. (Library leaflet 23.) * Paper, 5c. E 24—4
Blind. Schools and classes for blind, 1921–22; prepared in Division of Statistics. 1923. [1]+12 p. (Bulletin 51, 1923.) [Advance sheets from Biennial survey of education in United States, 1920–22.] * Paper, 5c. E 20—357
Consolidation of schools and transportation of pupils; by J. F. Abel. 1923. iv+135 p. il. 1 pl. 12 p. of pl. (Bulletin 41, 1923.) * Paper, 25c. E 23—420
Hygiene. Health education publications. 1923. [4] p. il. narrow 12° [Same, rearranged, and with additional matter, as edition of same date entered in Monthly catalogue for Feb. 1923, p. 511.] † E 22—568
—— Pathways to health, reading course for parents; by Harriet Wedgwood. 1923. [1]+6 p. il. 12° (Home education reading course 25.) * Paper, 5c.
Junior high schools in cities having population of 2,500 and over; compiled by Bertha Y. Hebb. Sept. 1923. 6 p. (City school leaflet 12.) * Paper, 5c. E 23—431
Kindergarten. How to arouse public interest in kindergartens. Nov. 1919, revised Nov. 1923. 1923. [1]+2 p. narrow 8° (Kindergarten extension series 1.) †
—— Organizing kindergartens in city school systems. Revised Nov. 1923. [1923.] 4 p. (Kindergarten education circular 2.) [Includes list of Education Bureau Bulletins on kindergarten organization.] * Paper, 5c.
—— Why your child should go to kindergarten; by Julia Wade Abbot. [1923.] 6 p. narrow 16° † E 24—8
Parents. Reading course for parents [(revised); prepared in] Home Education [Division]. [1923, reprint with slight changes.] 4 p. 12° (Reading course 3 revised.) †
Pictures. Appreciation of pictures [with bibliographies]; compiled by Bertha Y. Hebb. Oct. 1923. 15 p. (City school leaflet 13.) *Paper, 5c. E 24—1
Report. Report of commissioner of education, year ended June 30, 1923. 1923. iii+34 p. il. *Paper, 5c. 4—18120
—— Same. (H. doc. 64, 68th Cong. 1st sess.)
School funds. Biennial survey of public school finance in United States, 1920–22; by Fletcher Harper Swift. 1923. [1]+34 p. (Bulletin 47, 1923.) [Advance sheets from Biennial survey of education in United States, 1920–22.] *Paper, 5c. E 23—439
School life, v. 9, no. 4; Dec. 1923. [1923.] p. 73–96, 4° [Monthly except July and August.] *Paper, 5c. single copy, 30c. a yr. (10 months); foreign subscription, 55c. E 18—902
Sleep, one thing you surely must do is to sleep enough; [poster]. [1923.] 30×17 in. (Health education poster 5.) *Paper, 5c.
Taxpaying as lesson in citizenship; by Macy Campbell. Oct. 1923. 8 p. (Rural school leaflet 21.) * Paper, 5c. E 23—424

FREEDMAN'S HOSPITAL

Report of Freedman's Hospital, fiscal year 1923. 1923. iv+8 p. † Interior Dept. 8—6339

GENERAL LAND OFFICE

NOTE.—The General Land Office publishes a large general map of the United States, which is sold at $2.00; and also separate maps of the States and Territories in which public lands are to be found, which are sold at 25c. per sheet. The map of California is in 2 sheets. Address the Superintendent of Documents, Washington, D. C.

Alaska. Instructions relating to acquisition of title to public lands in Alaska; revision approved. Sept. 8, 1923. 1923. iii+108 p. (Circular 491.) †
23—27409

Harding, Fla. Town lots in townsite of Harding, Fla., near Miami Beach, Fla., to be sold at public auction by Government. 1923. 4 p. il. 4° †

Report of commissioner of General Land Office [with Statistics relating to disposition of public domain], fiscal year 1923. 1923. vi+76 p. † 6—35355

GEOLOGICAL SURVEY

NOTE.—The publications of the United States Geological Survey consist of Annual reports, Monographs, Professional papers, Bulletins, Water-supply papers, chapters and volumes of Mineral resources of the United States, folios of the Topographic atlas of the United States and topographic maps that bear descriptive text, and folios of the Geologic atlas of the United States and the World atlas of commercial geology. The Monographs, folios, and maps are sold. Other publications are generally free as long as the Survey's supply lasts. Copies are also sold by the Superintendent of Documents, Washington, D. C., at the prices indicated. For maps and folios address the Director of the Geological Survey, Washington, D. C. A discount of 40 per cent is allowed on any order for maps or folios that amounts to $5.00 or more at the retail price. This discount applies to an order for either maps or folios alone or for maps and folios together but is not allowed on a few folios that are sold at 5c. each on account of damage by fire. Orders for other publications should be sent to the Superintendent of Documents, Washington, D. C. For topographic maps see next page.

Alaska. Metalliferous deposits of Chitina Valley, Alaska; by Fred H. Moffit. 1923. [1]+57–72 p. (Bulletin 755 B.) †

Atlantic Coastal Plain. Surface water supply of United States, 1919–20: pt. 2, South Atlantic slope and eastern Gulf of Mexico basins; Nathan C. Grover, chief hydraulic engineer, Guy C. Stevens, C. G. Paulsen, and Warren E. Hall, district engineers. 1923. iv+80 p. 2 p. of pl. (Water-supply paper 502.) * Paper, 10c. GS 9—363

—— Same. (H. doc. 440, 67th Cong. 3d sess.)

Cement in 1922; by E. F. Burchard and B. W. Bagley. Dec. 31, 1923. ii+227–249 p. il. [From Mineral resources, 1922, pt. 2.] †

Gold, silver, copper, lead and zinc in Idaho and Washington in 1922, mines report; by C. N. Gerry. Dec. 18, 1923. ii+217–256 p. [From Mineral resources, 1922, pt. 1.] †

Gulf Coastal Plain. Surface water supply of United States, 1921: pt. 8, Western Gulf of Mexico basins; Nathan C. Grover, chief hydraulic engineer, C. E. Ellsworth, district engineer. 1923. iv+96 p. 2 p. of pl. (Water-supply paper 528.) [Prepared in cooperation with Texas.] * Paper, 10c. GS 10—346

—— Same. (H. doc. 44, 68th Cong. 1st sess.)

Hudson Bay. Surface water supply of United States, 1919–20: pt. 5, Hudson Bay and upper Mississippi River basins; Nathan C. Grover, chief hydraulic engineer, W. A. Lamb and W. G. Hoyt, district engineers. 1923. v+287 p. 2 p. of pl. (Water-supply paper 505.) [Prepared in cooperation with Minnesota, Wisconsin, Iowa, and Illinois.] * Paper, 30c. GS 10—344

—— Same. (H. doc. 443, 67th Cong. 3d sess.)

Mineral waters in 1922; by W. D. Collins. Dec. 20, 1923. [1]+207–220 p. [From Mineral resources, 1922, pt. 2.] †

Pedestal rocks in arid Southwest; by Kirk Bryan. Dec. 15, 1923. ii+1–11 p. 5 p. of pl. (Bulletin 760 A.) †

Publications. List of publications of Geological Survey, not including topographic maps. [Edition of] Nov. 1923. 1923. 201 p. †

—— New publications, list 189; Dec. 1, 1923. [1923.] 3 p. [Monthly.] †

Report. 44th annual report of director of Geological Survey, fiscal year 1923. 1923. ii+89 p. map. † 4—18125

Rocky Mountains. Variation in annual run-off in Rocky Mountain region; by Robert Follansbee. Dec. 21, 1923. ii+1–14 p. il. 2 pl. (Water-supply paper 520 A.) †

78186—No. 348—24——4.

Rosebud County, Mont. Geology of Tullock Creek coal field, Rosebud and Big Horn counties, Mont.; by G. Sherburne Rogers and Wallace Lee. 1923. vi+ 181 p. il. 5 pl. 6 p. of pl. 5 maps in pocket. (Bulletin 749.) * Paper, 50c.
                                                            GS 23—352
—— Same. (H. doc. 47, 68th Cong. 1st sess.)

St. Lawrence River. Surface water supply of United States, 1921: pt. 4, St. Lawrence River basin; Nathan C. Grover, chief hydraulic engineer, S. B. Soulé, A. H. Horton, C. C. Covert, and C. H. Pierce, district engineers. 1923. iv+112 p. 2 p. of pl. (Water-supply paper 524.) [Prepared in cooperation with Wisconsin, New York, and Vermont.] * Paper, 10c.   GS 10—294
—— Same. (H. doc. 40, 68th Cong. 1st sess.)

Sand and gravel in 1922; by L. M. Beach. Dec. 18, 1923. [1]+187–194 p. [From Mineral resources, 1922, pt. 2.] †

Maps

United States. United States. [Scale 1:16,000,000.] [Washington] Geological Survey, edition of Mar. 1911, reprinted 1923. 7.5×11.6 in. † 1c.

Topographic maps

NOTE.—The Geological Survey is making a topographic map of the United States. The individual maps of which it is composed are projected without reference to political divisions, and each map is designated by the name of some prominent town or natural feature in the area mapped. Three scales are ordinarily used, 1:62,500, 1:125,000, and 1:250,000. These correspond, approximately, to 1 mile, 2 miles, and 4 miles to 1 linear inch, covering, respectively, average areas to 230, 920, and 3,700 square miles. For some areas of particular importance special large-scale maps are published. The usual size, exclusive of the margin, is 17.5 inches in height by 11.5 to 16 inches in width, the width varying with the latitude. The sheets measure 20 by 16½ inches. A description of the topographic map is printed on the reverse of each sheet.

More than two-fifths of the area of the country, excluding Alaska, has been mapped, every State being represented. Connecticut, Delaware, the District of Columbia, Maryland, Massachusetts, New Jersey, Ohio, Rhode Island, and West Virginia are completely mapped. Maps of the regular size are sold by the Survey at 10c. each, but a discount of 40 per cent is allowed on an order which amounts to $5.00 or more at the retail price. The discount is allowed on an order for either maps or folios alone or for maps and folios together, but does not apply to a few folios that are sold at 5c. each on account of damage by fire.

California. California, Clovis quadrangle, lat. 36° 45'–36° 52' 30'', long. 119° 37' 30''–119° 45. Scale 1:31,680, contour interval 5 ft. [Washington, Geological Survey] edition of 1923. 17.3×13.9 in. † 10c.

—— California, Laguna Seca Ranch quadrangle, lat. 36° 45'–36° 52' 30'', long. 120° 45'–120° 52' 30''. Scale 1:31,680, contour interval 5 ft. and 25 ft. [Washington, Geological Survey] edition of 1923. 17.3×13.9 in. [Map covers only a portion of the sheet, the actual measurement being 14.3× 7.8 in.] † 10c.

—— California, Levis quadrangle, lat. 36° 30'–36° 37' 30'', long. 120° 22' 30''– 120° 30'. Scale 1:31,680, contour interval 5 ft. and 25 ft. [Washington, Geological Survey] edition of 1923. 17.3×13.9 in. † 10c.

—— California, Malaga quadrangle, lat. 36° 37' 30''–36° 45', long. 119° 37' 30''–119° 45'. Scale 1:31,680, contour interval 5 ft. [Washington, Geological Survey] edition of 1923. 17.3×13.9 in. † 10c.

—— California, Monocline Ridge quadrangle, lat. 36° 30'–36° 37' 30'', long. 120° 30'–120° 37' 30''. Scale 1:31,680, contour interval 5 ft. and 25 ft. [Washington Geological Survey] edition of 1923. 17.3×13.9 in. [Map covers only a portion of the sheet, the actual measurement being 15.7×13.9 in.] † 10c.

—— California, Orangedale School quadrangle, lat. 36° 45'–36° 52' 30'', long. 119° 22' 30''–119° 30'. Scale 1:31,680, contour interval 5 ft. [Washington, Geological Survey] edition of 1923. 17.3×13.9 in. [Map covers only a portion of the sheet, the actual measurement being 14×13.9 in.] † 10c.

—— California, Sultana quadrangle, lat. 36° 30'–36° 37' 30'', long. 119° 15'– 119° 22' 30''. Scale 1:31,680, contour interval 5 ft. and 25 ft. [Washington, Geological Survey] edition of 1923. 17.3×13.9 in. † 10c.

New York, Rochester quadrangle, lat. 43°–43° 20', long. 77° 30'–77° 45'. Scale 1:62,500, contour interval 20 ft. [Washington, Geological Survey] edition of 1920 reprinted 1923. 23.4×12.9 in. † 10c.

Pennsylvania, Shippensburg quadrangle, lat. 40°–40° 15′, long. 77° 30′–77° 45′. Scale 1 : 62,500, contour interval 20 ft. [Washington, Geological Survey] edition of 1923. 17.5×13.5 in. † 10c.

Texas, Chisos Mountains quadrangle, lat. 29°–29° 30′, long. 102° 40′–103° 30′. Scale 1 : 125,000, contour interval 100 ft. [Washington, Geological Survey] edition of 1905 reprinted 1923. 18.6×25.6 in. † 10c.

Washington, Corfu quadrangle, lat. 46° 45′–47°, long. 119° 15′–119° 30′. Scale 1 : 62,500, contour interval 25 ft. [Washington, Geological Survey] edition of 1923. 17.5×12.1 in. † 10c.

West Virginia. West Virginia, Clintonville quadrangle, lat. 37° 45′–38°, long. 80° 30′–80° 45′ Scale 1 : 62,500, contour interval 50 ft. [Washington, Geological Survey] edition of 1923. 17.5×13.9 in. † 10c.

—— West Virginia, Richwood quadrangle, lat. 38°–38° 15′, long. 80° 30′–80° 45′. Scale 1 : 62,500, contour interval 50 ft. [Washington, Geological Survey] edition of 1923. 17.5×13.9 in. † 10c.

HAWAII

Report of governor of Hawaii, [fiscal year] 1923. 1923. iv+124 p. map. † Interior Dept.   GS 12—562

HOWARD UNIVERSITY

Report of president of Howard University, fiscal year 1923. 1923. iii+12 p. † 8—15409

INDIAN AFFAIRS OFFICE

Report of commissioner of Indian affairs, fiscal year 1923. 1923. vi+46 p. map. †   8—33623

INDIAN COMMISSIONERS BOARD

Report. 54th annual report of Board of Indian Commissioners, fiscal year 1923. 1923. iii+51 p. †   11—11229

MINES BUREAU

Coal. Analyses of Ohio coals [with bibliography; articles by M. R. Campbell, J. W. Paul, and others]. [1st edition.] [Dec.] 1923. v+40 p. il. (Technical paper 344.) * Paper, 5c.   23—27490

    CONTENTS.—Coal fields of Ohio; by M. R. Campbell.—Mining and transportation; by J. W. Paul.—Analyses of mine and car samples; by A. C. Fieldner, H. M. Cooper, and F. D. Osgood.—Analyses of delivered coal; by N. H. Snyder.

—— Efficiencies in use of bituminous coking coal as water-gas generator fuel, Illinois coal mining investigations cooperative agreement; by W. W. Odell. [1st edition.] [Oct.] 1923. iv+39 p. il. 1 pl. (Technical paper 274.) [This paper represents work done under a cooperative agreement with the State Geological Survey Division of Illinois and the Engineering Experiment Station of the University of Illinois. Includes lists of Mines Bureau publications on producer gas and water gas.] * Paper, 10c.   23—27458

—— Investigation of powdered coal as fuel for power-plant boilers, tests at Oneida street power station, Milwaukee, Wis.; by Henry Kreisinger, John Blizard, C. E. Augustine, and B. J. Cross. [1st edition.] [Nov.] 1923. v+92 p. il. (Bulletin 223.) [Includes list of Mines Bureau publications on powdered coal.] * Paper, 15c.   23—27491

Gasoline. Recovery of gasoline from uncondensed still vapors; by D. B. Dow. [1st edition.] [Aug.] 1923. v+53 p. il. 6 pl. 4 p. of pl. (Technical paper 310.) [Includes lists of Mines Bureau publications on production and use of gasoline.] * Paper, 15c.

Lignite. Production and briquetting of carbonized lignite; by E. J. Babcock and W. W. Odell. [1st edition.] [Oct.] 1923. vi+82 p. il. 4 pl. 4 p. of pl. (Bulletin 221.) [This bulletin represents work done under a cooperative agreement with the School of Mines of the University of North Dakota. Includes lists of Mines Bureau publications on lignite briquetting.] * Paper, 20c.   23—27492

Metals. Analytical methods for certain metals, including cerium, thorium. molybdenum, tungsten, radium, uranium, vanadium, titanium, and zirconium [with bibliographies; articles] by R. B. Moore, S. C. Lind, J. W. Marden, J. P. Bonardi, C. W. Davis, and J. E. Conley. [1st edition.] [Aug.] 1923. xviii+325 p. il. 2 pl. (Bulletin 212.)   * Paper, 40c.   23—27457

Report. 13th annual report by director of Bureau of Mines, fiscal year 1923. [1st edition.] [Nov.] 1923. ii+21 p. 1 pl. . * Paper, 5c.   GS 12—481

Water. Uses of water in oil-shale industry with particular reference to engineering [and sanitary] requirements [with bibliography], by J. J. Jakosky; [and] with chapter on Sanitation of oil-shale camps, by A. L. Murray. [1st edition.] [Sept.] 1923. vi+57 p. il. (Technical paper 324.)   * Paper, 10c.
                                                                        23—27493

NATIONAL PARK SERVICE

Report of director of National Park Service, fiscal year 1923 and travel season 1923. 1923. vii+198 p. il. 12 p. of pl. * Paper, 20c.   18—26060

PATENT OFFICE

NOTE.—The Patent Office publishes Specifications and drawings of patents in single copies. These are not enumerated in this catalogue, but may be obtained for 10c. each at the Patent Office.
    A variety of indexes, giving a complete view of the work of the Patent Office from 1790 to date, are published at prices ranging from 25c. to $10.00 per volume and may be obtained from the Superintendent of Documents, Washington, D. C. The Rules of practice and pamphlet Patent laws are furnished free of charge upon application to the Patent Office. The Patent Office issues coupon orders in packages of 20 at $2.00 per package, or in books containing 100 coupons at $10.00 per book. These coupons are good until used, but are only to be used for orders sent to the Patent Office. For schedule of office fees, address Chief Clerk, Patent Office, Washington, D. C.

Decisions. [Decisions in patent and trade-mark cases, etc.] Dec. 4, 1923. p. 1–12, large 8° [From Official gazette, 1. 317, no. 1.] † Paper, 5c. single copy, $2.00 a yr.   23—7315

—— Same. Dec. 11, 1923. p. 229–242, large 8° [From Official gazette, v. 317, no. 2.]

—— Same. Dec. 18, 1923. p. 489–516, large 8° [From Official gazette, v. 317, no. 3.]

—— Same. Dec. 25, 1923. p. 751–809, il. large 8° [From Official gazette. v. 317, no. 4.]

Official gazette. Official gazette, Dec. 4–25, 1923; v. 317, no. 1–4. 1923. covertitles, 1008+[clvi] p. il. large 8° [Weekly.] * Paper, 10c. single copy, $5.00 a yr.; foreign subscription, $11.00.   4—18256

NOTE.—Contains the patents, trade-marks, designs, and labels issued each week; also decisions of the commissioner of patents and of the United States courts in patent cases.

—— Same [title-page, contents, errata, etc., to] v. 315; Oct. 1923. 1923. [2] leaves, large 8° * Paper, 5c. single copy, included in price of Official gazette for subscribers.

—— Same [title-page, contents, etc., to] v. 316; Nov. 1923. 1923. [2] leaves, large 8°

—— Same, weekly index, with title, Alphabetical list of registrants of trademarks [etc., Dec. 4, 1923]. xxxvi p. large 8° [From Official gazette, v. 317, no. 1.] † Paper, $1.00 a yr.

—— Same [Dec. 11, 1923]. [1923.] xliv p. large 8° [From Official gazette, v. 317, no. 2.]

—— Same [Dec. 18, 1923]. [1923.] xl p. large 8° [From Official gazette, v. 317, no. 3.]

—— Same [Dec. 25, 1923]. [1923.] xxxvi p. large 8° [From Official gazette, v. 317, no. 4.]

Patents. Classification of patents issued Dec. 4–25, 1923. [1923.] Each 2 p. large 8° [Weekly. From Official gazette, v. 317, no. 1–4.] †

Report of commissioner of patents to Secretary of Interior, fiscal year 1923. 1923. [1]+7 p. †   12—3671

Trade-marks. Trade-marks [etc., from] Official gazette, Dec. 4, 1923. [1923.] 13–67+i–xii p. il. large 8° [From Official gazette, v. 317, no. 1.] † Paper, 5c. single copy, $2.50 a yr.

Trade-marks—Continued. Same, Dec. 11, 1923. [1923.] 243–296+i–xviii p. il. large 8° [From Official gazette, v. 317, no. 2.]

—— Same, Dec. 18, 1923. [1923.] 517–570+i–xxxviii p. il. large 8° [From Official gazette, v. 317, no. 3.]

—— Same, Dec. 25, 1923. [1923.] 811–868+i–xv p. il. large 8° [From Official gazette, v. 317, no. 4.]

Wasserfallen, Charles F. In Court of Appeals of District of Columbia, Oct. term, 1923, patent appeal no. 1626, *in re* Charles F. Wasserfallen, spare tire carrier; brief for commissioner of patents. 1923. cover-title, 7 p. ‡

PENSION BUREAU

Pensions. Synopsis of pension laws of United States, also regulations and instructions relating thereto, with tables of rates and information in regard to soldiers' homes in effect Nov. 1, 1923. 1923. [1]+49 p. * Paper, 10c.
23—27494

Report of commissioner of pensions, fiscal year 1923. 1923. iii+33 p. †
8—9363

RECLAMATION BUREAU

Irrigation projects. Proposed work on reclamation projects, fiscal year 1925, with estimates of appropriation as included in budget. 1923. iv+42 p. †
17—26092

Reclamation record, v. 14, nos. 11 and 12; Nov.–Dec. 1923. [1923.] cover-title, p. 309–332, il. 4° [Monthly. Text on p. 2–4 of cover.]
9—35252

NOTE.—The Reclamation record is published in the interest of the settlers on the reclamation projects, its aim being to raise the general average of success on these projects. It contains much valuable matter of interest to farmers, and will be sent without direct charge to water users on the irrigation projects of the Reclamation Bureau. The Record is sold to those who are not water users for 75 cents a year, payable in advance. Subscriptions may be forwarded to the Chief Clerk, U. S. Reclamation Bureau, Washington, D. C., and remittances (postal money order or New York draft) should be made payable to the Special Fiscal Agent, U. S. Reclamation Bureau. Postage stamps will not be accepted.

Report. 22d annual report of Bureau of Reclamation, [fiscal year] 1922–23. 1923. ii+178 p. * Paper, 15c.   GS 6—71

—— Same. (H. doc. 67, 68th Cong. 1st sess.)

—— Extracts from 22d annual report of Bureau of Reclamation, [fiscal year 1922–23]. [1923.] 47 p. †

ST. ELIZABETHS HOSPITAL

Report of St. Elizabeths Hospital, fiscal year 1923. 1923. vii+18 p. †
6—35354

INTERSTATE COMMERCE COMMISSION

NOTE.—The bound volumes of the decisions, usually known as Interstate Commerce Commission reports, are sold by the Superintendent of Documents, Washington, D. C., at various prices, depending upon the size of the volume. Separate opinions are sold on subscription, price $1.00 per volume; foreign subscription, $1.50; single copies, usually 5c. each.

Acids. Investigation and suspension docket no. 1854, acid between points in Chicago switching district; [decided Oct. 25, 1923; report and order of commission]. 1923. [1]+432–434+[1] p. ([Opinion] 8867.) [Report from Interstate Commerce Commission reports, v. 83.] * Paper, 5c.

Alabama Great Southern Railroad. Finance docket no. 3318, bonds of Alabama Great Southern R. R.; decided Nov. 22, 1923; report of commission. [1923.] p. 721–722. ([Finance decision] 1045.) [From Interstate Commerce Commission reports, v. 82.] * Paper, 5c.

Ann Arbor Railroad. Finance docket no. 3286, notes of Ann Arbor R. R.; decided Nov. 22, 1923; report of commission. [1923.] p. 719–720. ([Finance decision] 1044.) [From Interstate Commerce Commission reports, v. 82.] * Paper, 5c.

Arcade and Attica Railroad. Finance docket no. 3146, securities of Arcade & Attica R. R.; decided Nov. 10, 1923; report of commission. [1923.] p. 663–664. ([Finance decision] 1029.) [From Interstate Commerce Commission reports, v. 82.] * Paper, 5c.

Arkansas Short Line. Finance docket no. 2883, construction and operation of line by Arkansas Short Line; decided Nov. 7, 1923; report of commission. [1923.] p. 651–657. ([Finance decision] 1026.) [From Interstate Commerce Commission reports, v. 82.] * Paper, 5c.

Back-haul charges. Investigation and suspension docket no. 1904, back-haul charges on grain, grain products and feed transited at Huntington, W. Va.; decided Nov. 9, 1923; report [and order] of commission. [1923.] 693–694+ [1] p. ([Opinion] 8924.) [Report from Interstate Commerce Commission reports, v. 83.] * Paper, 5c.

Bangor and Aroostook Railroad. Finance docket no. 926, loan to Bangor & Aroostook R. R.; decided Nov. 2, 1923; supplemental report of commission. [1923.] p. 617–618. ([Finance decision] 1011.) [From Interstate Commerce Commission reports, v. 82.] * Paper, 5c.

Bay Terminal Railroad. Finance docket no. 1511, deficit settlement with Bay Terminal R. R.; decided Nov. 6, 1923; report of commission. [1923.] p. 629–630. ([Finance decision] 1017.) [From Interstate Commerce Commission reports, v. 82.] * Paper, 5c.

Birmingham and Northwestern Railway. Before Interstate Commerce Commission, valuation docket no. 290, in matter of tentative valuation of Birmingham .& Northwestern Railway Company; in re hearing on carrier's protest. 1923. cover-title, i+36 p. ‡

Box-cars. No. 4002, in circuit court of appeals for 6th circuit, United States *v.* Louisville & Jeffersonville Bridge & Railroad Company, in error to district court for western district of Kentucky; brief and.argument for plaintiff in error. 1923. cover-title, i+24 p. ‡

California State Board of Harbor Commissioners Belt Railroad. No. 4130, in circuit court of appeals for 9th circuit, John H. McCallum, Fred S. Moody, and Harry H. Cosgriff, constituting Board of State Harbor Commissioners of California, operating State Belt Railroad, *v.* United States, in error to district court for northern district of California, southern division; brief and argument for defendant in error. 1923. cover-title, i+36 p. ‡

Campbell's Creek Railroad. Finance docket no. 3310, stock of Campbell's Creek Railroad; [decided Nov. 28, 1923; report of commission]. 1923. [1]+ 734–735 p. ([Finance decision] 1049.) [From Interstate Commerce Commission reports, v. 82.] * Paper, 5c.

Cartage. No. 13120, National League of Commission Merchants of United States *v.* Pennsylvania Railroad Company et al.; decided Oct. 26, 1923; report [and order] of commission. [1923.] 723–730+ii p. ([Opinion] 8934.) [Report from Interstate Commerce Commission reports, v. 83.] * Paper, 5c.

Cheese. Investigation and suspension docket no. 1874, cheese from Wisconsin points to Ohio River crossings; [no. 15114, Armour & Company *v.* Ahnapee & Western Railway Company et al.; decided Nov. 28, 1923; report and order of commission]. 1923. [1]+18–24+[1] p. ([Opinion] 8944.) [Report from Interstate Commerce Commission reports, v. 85.] *Paper, 5c.

Chicago and Alton Railroad. Finance docket no. 3317, Chicago & Alton equipment trust, series A [William W. Wheelock and William G. Bierd, receivers; decided Nov. 22, 1923; report of commission. 1923. [1]+708–713 p. ([Finance decision] 1042.) [From Interstate Commerce Commission reports, v. 82.] *Paper, 5c.

Chicago, Indianapolis and Louisville Railway. In matter of petition of National Conference on Valuation of American Railroads, valuation dockets nos. 168, 19, 93, 150, 210, 225, and 237, Chicago, Indianapolis & Louisville Railway Company et al.; decided Nov. 13, 1923; report of commission. [1923.] p. 9–23. (B–8.) [From Interstate Commerce Commission reports, v. 84.] *Paper, 5c.

Chicago, Terra Haute and Southeastern Railway. Finance docket no. 1383, acquisition of C., T. H. & S. E. Ry. by C., M. & St. P. Ry.; [decided Nov. 22, 1923; 3d supplemental report of commission]. 1923. [1]+728–731 p. ([Finance decision] 1047.) [From Interstate Commerce Commission reports, v. 82.] *Paper, 5c.

Cincinnati, Indianapolis and Western Railroad. Finance docket no. 3117, bonds of Cincinnati, Indianapolis & Western R. R.; [decided Nov. 10, 1923; report of commission]. 1923. [1]+658–660 p. ([Finance decision] 1027.) [From Interstate Commerce Commission reports, v. 82.] *Paper, 5c.

Clay. No. 13997, Western Terra Cotta Company of Kansas City, Kans., *v.* Missouri, Kansas & Texas Railway Company et al.; decided Oct. 27, 1923; report [and order] of commission. [1923.] 555–556+[1] p. ([Opinion] 8904.) [Report from Interstate Commerce Commission reports, v. 83.] *Paper, 5c.

Coal. Investigation and suspension docket no. 1898, coal from Tennessee Railroad stations to interstate destinations; decided Dec. 5, 1923; report [and order] of commission. [1923.] 25–29+[1] p. ([Opinion] 8945.) [Report from Interstate Commerce Commission reports, v. 85.] *Paper, 5c.

—— No. 13158, Nelson Fuel Company et al. *v.* Chesapeake & Ohio Railway Company et al.; decided Nov. 2, 1923; report [and order] of commission. [1923.] 737–741+iii p. ([Opinion] 8937.) [Report from Interstate Commerce Commission reports, v. 83.] *Paper, 5c.

—— No. 13472, United Paperboard Company, Incorporated, *v.* Greenwich & Johnsonville Railway Company et al.; [decided Oct. 9, 1923; report and order of commission]. 1923. [1]+712–714+[1] p. ([Opinion] 8931.) [Date of order incorrectly given as Nov. 9, 1923, instead of Oct. 9, 1923. Report from Interstate Commerce Commission reports, v. 83.] *Paper, 5c.

—— No. 13841, Indiana State Chamber of Commerce *v.* Baltimore & Ohio Railroad Company et al.; decided Oct. 31, 1923; report [and order] of commission. [1923.] 591–602+ii p. ([Opinion] 8918.) [Report from Interstate Commerce Commission reports, v. 83.] *Paper, 5c.

Corn. No. 13931, R. A. Heacock Company *v.* Chicago, Burlington & Quincy Railroad Company et al.; decided Oct. 27, 1923; report [and order] of commission. [1923.] 691–692+[1] p. ([Opinion] 8923.) [Report from Interstate Commerce Commission reports, v. 83.] *Paper, 5c.

Cotton. Investigation and suspension docket no. 1858, cotton and cotton linters from Louisiana and Arkansas points to Louisiana and Texas gulf ports; decided Nov. 23, 1923; report [and order] of commission. [1923.] 5–14+[1] p. ([Opinion] 8942.) [Report from Interstate Commerce Commission reports, v. 85.] * Paper, 5c.

Cotton-seed oil. No. 12422, Lookout Oil & Refining Company *v.* Alabama & Vicksburg Railway Company, director general, as agent, et al.; decided Oct. 25, 1923; report [and order] of commission. [1923.] 715–718+[1] p. ([Opinion] 8932.) [Report from Interstate Commerce Commission reports, v. 83.] * Paper, 5c.

Eagles Mere Railway. Finance docket no. 2843, securities of Eagles Mere Ry.; [decided Nov. 17, 1923; report of commission]. 1923. [1]+648–650 p. ([Finance decision] 1025.) [From Interstate Commerce Commission reports, v. 82.] * Paper, 5c.

Electric railroads. Regulations to govern destruction of records of electric railway companies as prescribed by Interstate Commerce Commission in accordance with sec. 20 of act to regulate commerce, effective May 1, 1913. 1st issue. [Reprint with slight changes] 1923. 16 p. * Paper, 5c.

Evansville and Indianapolis Railroad. Finance docket no. 462, guaranty settlement with Evansville & Indianapolis R. R., Wm. P. Kappes, receiver; [decided Nov. 26, 1923; report of commission]. 1923. [1]+690–692 p. ([Finance decision] 1036.) [From Interstate Commerce Commission reports, v. 82.] * Paper, 5c.

Express. No. 13930, express rates, 1922; [no. 14349, Ypsilanti Reed Furniture Company et al. *v.* American Railway Express Company; decided Nov. 10, 1923; report and orders of commission]. 1923. [1]+606–681+iii p. map. ([Opinion] 8920.) [Report from Interstate Commerce Commission reports, v. 83.] * Paper, 5c.

Federal Valley Railroad. Finance docket no. 3305, Federal Valley Railroad notes; [decided Nov. 22, 1923; report of commission]. 1923. [1]+732–733 p. ([Finance decision] 1048.) [From Interstate Commerce Commission reports, v. 82.] * Paper, 5c.

Florida Central and Gulf Railway. Finance docket no. 466, guaranty settlement with Florida Central & Gulf Ry.; decided Oct. 24. 1923; report of commission. [1923.] p. 557–559. ([Finance decision] 990.) [From Interstate Commerce Commission reports, v. 82.] ·* Paper, 5c.

Freight·rates. Investigation and suspension docket no. 1877, minimum class rates from Atlantic seaboard to Arkansas and Louisiana; decided Nov. 23, 1923; report [and order] of commission. [1923.] p. 711, [1]. ([Opinion] 8930.) [Report from Interstate Commerce Commission reports, v. 83.] * Paper, 5c.

—— Investigation and suspension docket no. 1896, proportional commodity rates between upper Mississippi River crossings and points west thereof; [decided Dec. 6, 1923; report and order of commission]. 1923. [1]+40–42+ [1] p. ([Opinion] 8949.) [Report from Interstate Commerce Commission reports, v. 85.] * Paper, 5c.

—— No. 11893, War Department, inland waterways, Mississippi-Warrior service v. Abilene & Southern Railway et al.; [decided Nov. 12, 1923; report of commission on further hearing]. 1923. [1]+742–752 p. ([Opinion] 8938.) [From Interstate Commerce Commission reports, v. 83.] * Paper, 5c.

Gas oil. No. 13552, Empire Refineries, Incorporated, et al. v. Atchison, Topeka & Santa Fe Railway Company et al.; [no. 13553, same v. same; decided Nov. 9, 1923; report of commission]. 1923. [1]+706–708 p. ([Opinion] 8928.) [From Interstate Commerce Commission reports, v. 83.] ·*·Paper, 5c.

Gasoline. No. 13926, Standard Oil Company (Kentucky) v. director general, as agent, et al.; decided Oct. 23, 1923; report of commission. [1923.] p. 705–706. ([Opinion] 8927.) [From Interstate Commerce Commission reports, v. 83.] * Paper, 5c.

Glenmora and Western Railway. Finance docket no. 490. guaranty settlement with Glenmora & Western Ry.; [decided Oct. 30, 1923; report of commismission]. 1923. [1]+560–562 p. ([Finance decision] 991.) [From Interstate Commerce Commission reports, v. 82.] * Paper, 5c.

Goldsboro Union Station Company. Finance docket no. 3048, bonds of Goldsboro Union Station; [decided Nov. 17, 1923; report of commission]. 1923. [1]+676–678 p. ([Finance decision] 1034.) [From Interstate Commerce Commission reports, v. 82.] * Paper, 5c.

Grain. Investigation and suspension docket no. 1866, grain and grain products from Iowa, Minnesota, and South Dakota to Texas; decided Nov. 14, 1923; report [and order] of commission. [1923.] 695–701+[1] p. ([Opinion] 8925.) [Report from Interstate Commerce Commission reports, v. 83.] * Paper, 5c.

—— Investigation and suspension docket no. 1890, transit privileges on transcontinental grain at stations on St. L.-S. F. Ry.; decided Dec. 5, 1923; report [and order] of commission. [1923.] 43–46+[1] p. ([Opinion] 8950.) [Report from Interstate Commerce Commission reports, v. 85.] * Paper, 5c.

—— No. 14109, Board of Trade of Cairo, Ill., v. Alabama Great Southern Railroad Company et al.; decided Nov. 23, 1923; report [and order] of commission. [1923.] 761–768+[1] p. ([Opinion] 8940.) [Report from Interstate Commerce Commission reports, v. 83.] * Paper, 5c.

Greenwich and Johnsonville Railway. Finance docket no. 3293, bonds of Greenwich & Johnsonville Railway; decided Nov. 6, 1923; report of commission. [1923.] p. 637–639. ([Finance decision] 1020.) [From Interstate Commerce Commission reports, v. 82.] * Paper, 5c.

Gypsum. Investigation and suspension docket no. 1868, gypsum, plaster, et cetera, Montana to north Pacific Coast destinations; decided Nov. 20, 1923; report [and order] of commission. [1923.] 753–760+[1] p. ([Opinion] 8939.) [Report from Interstate Commerce Commission reports, v. 83.] * Paper, 5c.

Ice-cream cones. No. 13988. American Cone & Pretzel Company v. Chicago. Burlington & Quincy Railroad Company et al.; decided Oct. 27, 1923; report [and order] of commission. [1923.] 575–576+[1] p. ([Opinion] 8911.) [Report from Interstate Commerce Commission reports, v. 83.] * Paper, 5c.

Illinois Central Railroad. Finance docket no. 3278, stock of Illinois Central Railroad; decided Oct. 23. 1923: report of commission. [1923.] p. 609–611. ([Finance decision] 1009.) [From Interstate Commerce Commission reports, v. 82.] * Paper, 5c.

Iron County Telephone Company. Finance docket no. 3274, purchase of properties of Iron County Telephone Co. by Mountain States Telephone & Telegraph Co.; [decided Nov. 6, 1923; report of commission]. 1923. [1]+640–642 p.. ([Finance decision] 1021.) [From Interstate Commerce Commission reports, v. 82.] * Paper, 5c.

Ironton Railroad. Finance docket no. 3168, control of Ironton R. R. by Lehigh valley R. R. and Reading Co.; decided Nov. 8, 1923; report of commission. [1923.] p. 665–667. ([Finance decision] 1030.) [From Interstate Commerce Commission reports, v. 82.] * Paper, 5c.

Kane and Elk Railroad. Finance docket no. 547, guaranty settlement with Kane & Elk R. R.; decided Oct. 31, 1923; report of commission. [1923.] p. 563–565. ([Finance decision] 992.) [From Interstate Commerce Commission reports, v. 82.] * Paper, 5c.

Kansas and Missouri Railway and Terminal Company. Finance docket no. 3129, construction of line by Kansas & Missouri Railway & Terminal Co.; [decided Oct. 31, 1923; report of commission]. 1923. [1]+612–616 p. ([Finance decision] 1010.) [From Interstate Commerce Commission reports, v. 82.] * Paper, 5c.

Kansas City Terminal Railway. Finance docket no. 3159, Kansas City Terminal Railway secured notes; decided Oct. 26, 1923; report of commission. [1923.] p. 593–596. ([Finance decision] 1004.) [From Interstate Commerce Commission reports, v. 82.] * Paper, 5c.

Kapok. No. 13817, Bernstein Manufacturing Company *v.* director general, as agent; decided Oct. 27, 1923; report [and order] of commission. [1923.] 551–552+[1] p. ([Opinion] 8902.) [Report from Interstate Commerce Commission reports, v. 83.] * Paper, 5c.

Limestone. No. 12884, Brier Hill Steel Company et al. *v.* Baltimore & Ohio Railroad Company et al.; decided Nov. 9, 1923; report [and order] of commission. [1923.] 709–710+[1] p. ([Opinion] 8929.) [Report from Interstate Commerce Commission reports, v. 83.] * Paper, 5c.

Long Island Railroad. Finance docket no. 588, guaranty settlement with Long Island R. R.; decided Oct. 31, 1923; report of commission. [1923.] p. 567–569. ([Finance decision] 994.) [From Interstate Commerce Commission reports, v. 82.] * Paper, 5c.

Macon, Dublin and Savannah Railroad. Finance docket no. 603, guaranty settlement with Macon, Dublin & Savannah R. R.; [decided Oct. 24, 1923; report of commission]. 1923. [1]+570–572 p. ([Finance decision] 995.) [From Interstate Commerce Commission reports, v. 82.] * Paper, 5c.

Mineral Point and Northern Railway. Finance docket no. 181, deficit settlement with Mineral Point & Northern Ry.; [decided Nov. 21, 1923; report of commission]. 1923. [1]+702–703 p. ([Finance decision] 1040.) [From Interstate Commerce Commission reports, v. 82.] * Paper, 5c.

Misrouting. No. 13853, Whalen Pulp & Paper Mills, Limited, *v.* director general, as agent, and Grand Trunk Pacific Railway Company; [decided Oct. 26, 1923; report and order of commission]. 1923. [1]+516–517+[1] p. ([Opinion] 8891.) [Report from Interstate·Commerce Commission reports, v. 83.] * Paper, 5c.

Mississippian Railway. Finance docket no. 3188, construction of line by Mississippian Railway; [decided Nov. 22, 1923; report of commission]. 1923. [1]+698–701 p. ([Finance decision] 1039.) [From Interstate.Commerce Commission reports, v. 82.] * Paper, 5c.

Missouri and Kansas Railway. Finance docket no. 645, guaranty settlement with Missouri & Kansas Ry.; decided Nov. 7, 1923; report of commission. [1923.] p. 647–648. ([Finance decision] 1024.) [From Interstate Commerce Commission reports, v. 82.] * Paper, 5c.

Missouri Pacific Railroad. Finance docket no. 3306, Missouri Pacific equipment trust, series B; [decided Nov. 20, 1923; report of commission]. 1923. [1]+672–675 p. ([Finance decision] 1033.) [From Interstate Commerce Commission reports, v. 82.] * Paper, 5c.

Monson Railroad. Finance docket no. 656, guaranty settlement with Monson R. R.; decided Nov. 5, 1923; report of commission. [1923.] p. 631–633. ([Finance decision] 1018.) [From Interstate Commerce Commission reports. v. 82.] * Paper, 5c.

Morenci Southern Railway. Finance docket no. 661, guaranty settlement with Morenci Southern Railway; [decided Nov. 21, 1923; report of commission]. 1923. [1]+692–694 p. ([Finance decision] 1037.) [From Interstate Commerce Commission reports, v. 82.] * Paper, 5c.

Morristown and Erie Railroad. Finance docket no. 1337, deficit status of Morristown & Erie R. R.; decided Oct. 24, 1923; report of commission. [1923.] p. 581–582. ([Finance decision] 999.) [From Interstate Commerce Commission reports, v. 82.] * Paper, 5c.

Naphtha. No. 14221, Caddo Central Oil & Refining Corporation *v.* director general, as agent, Pennsylvania Railroad Company, et al.; [decided Nov. 9, 1923; report and order of commission. 1923. [1]+734–736+[1] p. ([Opinion] 8936.) [Report from Interstate Commerce Commission reports, v. 83.] * Paper, 5c.

Natchez and Louisiana Railway and Transfer Company. Finance docket no. 676, guaranty status of Natchez & Louisiana Railway & Transfer Co.; decided Oct. 30, 1923; report of commission. [1923.] p. 573–574. ([Finance decision] 996.) [From Interstate Commerce Commission reports, v. 82.] * Paper, 5c.

New Holland, Higginsport and Mount Vernon Railroad. Finance docket no. 3069, securities of New Holland, Higginsport & Mount vernon R. R.; decided Nov. 9, 1923; report of commission. [1923.] p. 661–662. ([Finance decision] 1028.) [From Interstate Commerce Commission reports, v. 82.] * Paper, 5c.

New York Central Railroad. Finance docket no. 692, guaranty settlement with New York Central R. R.; [and finance docket no. 570; decided Oct. 26, 1923; report of commission]. 1923. [1]+586–588 p. ([Finance decision] 1002.) [From Interstate Commerce Commission reports, v. 82.] * Paper, 5c.

Norfolk Southern Railroad. Finance docket no. 3281, notes of Norfolk Southern R. R.; decided Nov. 3, 1923; report of commission. [1923.] p. 627–629. ([Finance decision] 1016.) [From Interstate Commerce Commission reports, v. 82.] * Paper, 5c.

—— Finance docket no. 3282, Norfolk Southern equipment trust, series D; [decided Nov. 3, 1923; report of commission]. 1923. [1]+622–624 p. ([Finance decision] 1014.) [From Interstate Commerce Commission reports, v. 82.] * Paper, 5c.

North Louisiana and Gulf Railroad. Finance docket no. 705, guaranty settlement with North Louisiana & Gulf R. R.; decided Oct. 31, 1923; report of commission. [1923.] p. 619–620. ([Finance decision] 1012.) [From Interstate Commerce Commission reports, v. 82.] * Paper, 5c.

Passenger rates. No. 14628, Wichita Falls & Southern passenger fares and charges, in matter of intrastate passenger fares and charges of Wichita Falls & Southern Railroad Company in Texas; decided Nov. 5, 1923; report [and order] of commission. [1923.] 603–605+[1] p. ([Opinion] 8919.) [Report from Interstate Commerce Commission reports, v. 83.] * Paper, 5c.

Penn Yan and Lake Shore Railway. Finance docket no. 207, deficit settlement with Penn Yan & Lake Shore Ry., William J. Tylee, receiver; decided Nov. 5, 1923; report of commission. [1923.] p. 625–626. ([Finance decision] 1015.) [From Interstate Commerce Commission reports, v. 82.] * Paper, 5c.

—— Finance docket no. 733, guaranty settlement with Penn Yan & Lake Shore Ry., William J. Tylee, receiver; [decided Nov. 5, 1923; report of commission]. 1923. [1]+634–636 p. ([Finance decision] 1019.) [From Interstate Commerce Commission reports, v. 82.] * Paper, 5c.

Pennsylvania-Ohio Power and Light Company. Nos. 228 and 229, in Supreme Court, Oct. term, 1923, United States, Interstate Commerce Commission, and Pennsylvania[-Ohio] Power & Light Company *v.* Hubbard, Ohio; United States, Steubenville, East Liverpool and Beaver valley Traction Company, and Interstate Commerce Commission *v.* Wellsville, Ohio; brief for Interstate Commerce Commission. 1923. cover-title, i+55 p. ‡

Pere Marquette Railway. Finance docket no. 2740, Pere Marquette 5 per cent bonds of 1923; approved Oct. 27, 1923; supplemental order. 1923. p. 585. ([Finance decision] 1001.) [From Interstate Commerce Commission reports, v. 82.] * Paper, 5c.

Petroleum. No. 11225, Lawton Refining Company *v.* director general, as agent, and Chicago, Rock Island & Pacific Railway Company; decided Oct. 22, 1923; report of commission on further argument. [1923.] p. 443–444. ([Opinion] 8870.) [From Interstate Commerce Commission reports, v. 83.] * Paper, 5c.

—— No. 13564, Western Petroleum Refiners Association *v.* St. Louis-San Francisco Railway Company et al.; [decided Nov. 7, 1923; report and order of commission]. 1923. [1]+702–704+[1] p. ([Opinion] 8926.) [Report from Interstate Commerce Commission reports, v. 83.] * Paper, 5c.

—— No. 13801, National Petroleum Association et al. *v.* Atchison, Topeka & Santa Fe Railway Company et al.; [decided Oct. 27, 1923; report and order of commission]. 1923. [1]+ 530–534+ ii p. ([Opinion] 8896.) [Report from Interstate Commerce Commission reports, v. 83.] * Paper, 5c.

Pittsburgh and Lake Erie Railroad. Finance docket no. 743, guaranty settlement with Pittsburgh & Lake Erie R. R.; decided Oct. 29, 1923; report of commission. [1923.] p. 575–577. ([Finance decision] 997.) [From Interstate Commerce Commission reports, v. 82.] * Paper, 5c.

Pittsburgh and West Virginia Railway. Finance docket no. 2531, capital stock of Pittsburgh & West Virginia Ry.; [decided Nov. 21, 1923; report of commission]. 1923. [1]+704–707 p. ([Finance decision] 1041.) [From Interstate Commerce Commission reports, v. 82.] * Paper, 5c.

Pittsburgh, Fort Wayne and Chicago Railway. Finance docket no. 3297, stock of P., F. W. & C. Ry., in matter of application of Pittsburgh, Fort Wayne & Chicago Railway Company for authority to issue stock and of Pennsylvania Railroad Company to assume obligation and liability, as lessee, in respect thereof; [decided Nov. 12, 1923; report of commission]. 1923. [1]+714–718 p. ([Finance decision] 1043.) [From Interstate Commerce Commission reports, v. 82.] * Paper, 5c.

Plaster. No. 5626, Grand Rapids Plaster Company *v.* Lake Shore & Michigan Southern Railway Company et al.; 4th section applications nos. 1883, 10596, and 12025; [decided Oct. 27, 1923; report and order of commission on 2d supplemental hearing]. 1923. [1]+682–685+[1] p. ([Opinion] 8921.) [Report from Interstate Commerce Commission reports, v. 83.] * Paper, 5c.

Railroad accidents. Accident bulletin 88, collisions, derailments, and other accidents resulting in injury to persons, equipment, or roadbed. arising from operation of steam roads used in interstate commerce, Jan.–Mar. 1923; [prepared in] Bureau of Statistics. 1923. iii+28 p. il. 4° [Quarterly.] * Paper, 5c. single copy quarterly issue, 25c. a yr.; foreign subscription, 40c.

5—41547

Railroad tickets. No. 14524, F. Hohlfelder *v.* Denver & Rio Grande Western Railroad Company et al.; decided Oct. 27, 1923; report [and order] of commission. [1923.] 587–588+[1] p. ([Opinion] 8916.) [Report from Interstate Commerce Commission reports, v. 83.] * Paper, 5c.

Railroads. Before Interstate Commerce Commission, in re hearings before valuation examiners under sec. 19a of interstate commerce act; brief in reply to brief of W. G. Brantley for presidents' conference committee, dated Nov. 1923. 1923. cover-title, ii+68 p. ‡

—— Freight and passenger service operating statistics of class 1 steam roads in United States, compiled from 161 reports of freight statistics representing 176 roads and from 158 reports of passenger statistics representing 173 roads (switching and terminal companies not included), Oct. 1923 and 1922 [and 10 months ended with Oct. 1923 and 1922; prepared in] Bureau of Statistics. Oct. 1923. [2] p. oblong large 8° [Subject to revision.] †

—— Freight and passenger train service unit costs (selected expense accounts) of class 1 steam roads in United States, including proportion of mixed-train and special-train service (compiled from 161 reports representing 176 steam roads, switching and terminal companies not included), Oct. 1923 and 1922, and 10 months [ended with Oct.] 1923 and 1922; [prepared in] Bureau of Statistics. Oct. 1923. 1 p. oblong large 8° [Subject to revision.] †

—— Operating revenues and operating expenses of class 1 steam roads in United States (for 194 steam roads, including 15 switching and terminal companies), Oct. 1923 and 1922 [and] 10 months ending with Oct. 1923 and 1922; [prepared in] Bureau of Statistics. Oct. 1923. 1 p. oblong large 8° [Subject to revision.] †

Railroads—Continued. Operating revenues and operating expenses of large steam roads, selected items for roads with annual operating revenues above $25,000,000, Sept. 1922 and 1923 [and] 9 months ended with Sept. 1922 and 1923; [prepared in] Bureau of Statistics. Sept. 1923. [2] p. oblong large 8° [Subject to revision.] †

—— Same, Oct. 1922 and 1923 [and] 10 months ended with Oct. 1922 and 1923; [prepared in] Bureau of Statistics. Oct. 1923. [2] p. oblong large 8° [Subject to revision.] †

—— Operating statistics of large steam roads, selected items for Oct. 1923, compared with Oct. 1922, for roads with annual operating revenues above $25,000,000; [prepared in] Bureau of Statistics. Oct. 1923. [2] p. oblong large 8° [Subject to revision.] †

—— Revenue traffic statistics of class 1 steam roads in United States, including mixed-train service (compiled from 162 reports representing 177 steam roads, switching and terminal companies not included), July, 1923 and 1922 [and] 7 months ended with July, 1923 and 1922: [prepared in] Bureau of Statistics. July, 1923. 1 p. oblong large 8° [Subject to revision.] †

—— Same. Aug. 1923 and 1922 [and] 8 months ended with Aug. 1923 and 1922; [prepared in] Bureau of Statistics. Aug. 1923. 1 p. oblong large 8° [Subject to revision.] †

—— Same, Sept. 1923 and 1922 [and] 9 months ended with Sept. 1923 and 1922; [prepared in] Bureau of Statistics. Sept. 1923. 1 p. oblong large 8° [Subject to revision.] †

Randolph and Cumberland Railway. Finance docket no. 212, deficit settlement with Randolph & Cumberland Ry., J. S. Crews, receiver; decided Oct. 29, 1923; report of commission. [1923.] p. 553–554. ([Finance decision] 988.) [From Interstate Commerce Commission reports, v. 82.] * Paper, 5c.

—— Finance docket no. 763, guaranty settlement with Randolph & Cumberland Ry., J. S. Crews, receiver; [decided Oct. 29, 1923; report of commission]. 1923. [1]+578–580 p. ([Finance decision] 998.) [From Interstate Commerce Commission reports, v. 82.] * Paper, 5c.

Reconsignment. No. 14499, Memphis Freight Bureau. for Brown Coal Company, *v.* Louisville & Nashville Railroad Company et al.; decided Oct. 27, 1923; report [and order] of commission. [1923.] 589–590+[1] p. ([Opinion] 8917.) [Report from Interstate Commerce Commission reports. v. 83.] * Paper, 5c.

Refrigeration. Investigation and suspension docket no. 1867, absorption of icing and re-icing charges on less-than-carload shipments of dairy products; [decided Nov. 9, 1923; report and order of commission]. 1923. [1]+686–690+[1] p. ([Opinion] 8922.) [Report from Interstate Commerce Commission reports, v. 83.] * Paper, 5c.

Report. 37th annual report of Interstate Commerce Commission, Dec. 1, 1923. 1923. [pt. 1], iv+256 p. il. [Report covers the period from Nov. 1, 1922, to Oct. 31, 1923.] * Cloth, 50c.　　　　　　　　　　　　　　9—14672

—— Same [with Statement of appropriations and expenditures and of persons employed by commission, fiscal year 1923]. 1923. 2 pts. in 1, iv+322 p. il. ‡　　　　　　　　　　　　　　　　　　9—14679

—— Same. (H. doc. 70, 68th Cong. 1st sess.)

Roscoe, Snyder and Pacific Company. Finance docket no. 1348. deficit settlement with Roscoe, Snyder & Pacific Ry.; decided Oct. 27, 1923; report of commission. [1923.] p. 583–584. ([Finance decision] 1000.) [From Interstate Commerce Commission reports, v. 82.] * Paper, 5c.

Safety Bureau. Report of director of Bureau of Safety, fiscal year 1923, and extracts from 37th annual report of Interstate Commerce Commission pertaining to safety appliances, hours of service, investigation of accidents, and investigation of safety devices. 1923. [1]+44 p. * Paper, 5c.　17—26073

St. Louis Southwestern Railway. No. 398, in Supreme Court, Oct. term, 1923, United States at relation of St. Louis Southwestern Railway Company *v.* Interstate Commerce Commission; brief for Interstate Commerce Commission. 1923. cover-title, ii+29 p. ‡

St. Louis, Troy and Eastern Railroad. Finance docket no. 3232, St. Louis. Troy & Eastern equipment trust, series A; decided Oct. 24, 1923; report of commission. [1923.] p. 599–602. ([Finance decision] 1006.) [From Interstate Commerce Commission reports, v. 82.] * Paper, 5c.

Salvage. Treatment of salvage, piecework, and prices in accounting, finance docket no. 2797; [and finance docket no. 839; decided Aug. 15, 1923; report of commission]. 1923. [1]+678–689 p. ([Finance decision] 1035.) [From Interstate Commerce Commission reports, v. 82.]   * Paper, 5c.

Sand. Investigation and suspension docket no. 1864, sand and gravel from Canada to points in New York and Pennsylvania; [decided Nov. 6, 1923; report and order of commission]. 1923. [1]+460–463+[1] p. ([Opinion] 8873.) [Report from Interstate Commerce Commission reports, v. 83.]   * Paper, 5c.

—— No. 12480, Davison & Namack Foundry Company *v.* Pennsylvania Railroad Company, director general, as agent, et al.; decided July 11, 1923; report of commission. Corrected reprint. [1923.] p. 345–347. ([Opinion] 8659.) [From Interstate Commerce Commission reports, v. 81.]   * Paper, 5c.

Seaboard Air Line Railway. Finance docket no. 3144, bonds of Seaboard Air Line Ry.; decided Oct. 27, 1923; report of commission. [1923.] p. 589–592. ([Finance decision] 1003.) [From Interstate Commerce Commission reports, v. 82.]   * Paper, 5c.

Silica. Investigation and suspension docket no. 1897, minimum weight on silica from southern Illinois to eastern destinations; [decided Dec. 6, 1923; report and order of commission]. 1923. [1]+30–32+[1] p. ([Opinion] 8946.) [Report from Interstate Commerce Commission reports, v. 85.]   * Paper, 5c.

South Georgia Railway. Finance docket no. 2615, South Georgia Railway capital stock; [and finance docket no. 2761]; decided Nov. 21, 1923; supplemental report of commission. [1923.] p. 723–727. ([Finance decision] 1046.) [From Interstate Commerce Commission reports, v. 82.]   * Paper, 5c.

Southern Railway. Finance docket no. 3277, bonds of Southern Ry.; [decided Oct. 25, 1923; report of commission]. 1923. [1]+606–608 p. ([Finance decision] 1008.) [From Interstate Commerce Commission reports, v. 82.]   * Paper, 5c.

Speedometers. No. 11669, Stewart-Warner Speedometer Corporation et al. *v.* director general, as agent, Chicago & North Western Railway Company, et al.; decided Oct. 22, 1923; report of commission on further hearing. [1923.] p. 435–436. ([Opinion] 8868.) [From Interstate Commerce Commission reports, v. 83.]   * Paper, 5c.

Spotting (freight). No. 13531. What Cheer Beef Company *v.* New York, New Haven & Hartford Railroad Company; decided Oct. 27, 1923; report [and order] of commission. [1923.] 569–572+[1] p. ([Opinion] 8909.) [Report from Interstate Commerce Commission reports, v. 83.]   * Paper, 5c.

Steamboats. Schedule of sailings (as furnished by steamship companies named herein) of steam vessels which are registered under laws of United States and which are intended to load general cargo at ports in United States for foreign destinations, Dec. 15, 1923–Jan. 31, 1924, no. 16; issued by Section of Tariffs, Bureau of Traffic. 1923. iii+27 p. 4° [Monthly. No. 16 cancels no. 15.] †   22—26610

Sugar. No. 14027, Utah-Idaho Sugar Company *v.* director general, as agent, Los Angeles & Salt Lake Railroad Company, et al.; [decided Oct. 27, 1923; report of commission]. 1923. [1]+566–568 p. ([Opinion] 8908.) [From Interstate Commerce Commission reports, v. 83.]   * Paper, 5c.

Sulphur. No. 14062, General Chemical Company *v.* Baltimore & Ohio Railroad Company et al.; [decided Oct. 27, 1923; report and order of commission]. 1923. [1]+582–584+[1] p. ([Opinion] 8914.) [Report from Interstate Commerce Commission reports, v. 83.]   * Paper, 5c.

Sunflower seed. No. 14410, Amendt Milling Company *v.* Michigan Central Railroad Company et al.; decided Oct. 27, 1923; report [and order] of commission. [1923.] 585–586+[1] p. ([Opinion] 8915.) [Report from Interstate Commerce Commission reports, v. 83.]   * Paper, 5c.

Switching charges. Investigation and suspension docket no. 1863, switching at stations in North Dakota; decided Nov. 13, 1923; report [and order] of commission. [1923.] 731–734+[1] p. ([Opinion] 8935.) [Report from Interstate Commerce Commission reports, v. 83.]   * Paper, 5c.

Telegraph. Ex parte no. 42, in matter of making of inventories under provisions of sec. 19a of interstate commerce act of property used by telegraph companies and by other carriers for common carrier purposes; decided Nov. 6, 1923; [report of commission]. [1923.] p. 1–8. (B–7.) [From Interstate Commerce Commission reports, v. 84.] * Paper, 5c.

—— No. 12159, Consolidated Press Association *v.* Western Union Telegraph Company; decided Nov. 12, 1923; report of commission on reargument. [1923.] p. 15–17. ([Opinion] 8943.) [From Interstate Commerce Commission reports, p. 85.] * Paper, 5c.

Thornton and Alexandria Railway. Finance docket no. 2438, deficit settlement with Thornton & Alexandria Ry.; decided Nov. 8, 1923; report of commission. [1923.] p. 645–646. ([Finance decision] 1023.) [From Interstate Commerce Commission reports, v. 82.] * Paper, 5c.

Tobacco. No. 13912, G. J. Helmerichs Tobacco Company *v.* East St. Louis Connecting Railway Company et al.; [no. 13913, same *v.* same; no. 13916. same *v.* Chicago & Alton Railroad Company et al.]; decided Oct. 27, 1923; report [and order] of commission. [1923.] 579–581+[1] p. ([Opinion] 8913.) [Report from Interstate Commerce Commission reports, v. 83.] * Paper, 5c.

Trans-Mississippi Terminal Railroad. Finance docket no. 3267, notes of Trans-Mississippi Terminal Railroad, in matter of application of Trans-Mississippi Terminal Railroad Company, Texas & Pacific Railway Company, Missouri Pacific Railroad Company, and J. L. Lancaster and Charles L. Wallace, as receivers of Texas & Pacific Railway Company, for authority to extend maturity of and to guarantee certain notes of Trans-Mississippi Terminal Railroad Company; decided Oct. 26, 1923; report of commission. [1923.] p. 603–606. ([Finance decision] 1007.) [From Interstate Commerce Commission reports, v. 82.] * Paper, 5c.

—— Same; approved Nov. 1, 1923; amendatory order. 1923. p. 621. ([Finance decision] 1013.) [From Interstate Commerce Commission reports, v. 82.] * Paper, 5c.

Tripoli. Investigation and suspension docket no. 1862, tripoli from Kansas and Missouri to western trunk line territory; decided Nov. 30, 1923; report [and order] of commission. [1923.] 35–39+[1] p. ([Opinion] 8948.) [Report from Interstate Commerce Commission reports, v. 85.] * Paper, 5c.

Unloading and lading. No. 13171, Mutual Products Trading Company *v.* Oregon-Washington Railroad & Navigation Company; decided Nov. 22, 1923; report of commission. [1923.] p. 1–4. ([Opinion] 8941.) [From Interstate Commerce Commission reports, v. 85.] * Paper, 5c.

Varnish. Investigation and suspension docket no. 1876, varnish, Chicago, Memphis, and St. Louis to Texas; decided Dec. 1, 1923; report [and order] of commission. [1923.] 33–34+[1] p. ([Opinion] 8947.) [Report from Interstate Commerce Commission reports, v. 85.] * Paper, 5c.

Williams Valley Railroad. Finance docket no. 3303, Williams Valley Railroad bonds; [and finance docket no. 3303 (sub-no. 1); decided Nov. 20, 1923; report of commission]. 1923. [1]+668–670 p. ([Finance decision] 1031.) [From Interstate Commerce Commission reports, v. 82.] * Paper, 5c.

Williamson and Pond Creek Railroad. Before Interstate Commerce Commission, valuation docket no. 233, Williamson and Pond Creek Railroad; reply to Memorandum of argument of counsel for carrier dated Nov. 17, 1923. 1923. cover-title, i+33 p. ‡

Wood flour. No. 13978, E. I. du Pont de Nemours & Company *v.* director general, as agent; decided Nov. 10, 1923; report of commission. [1923.] p. 719–722. ([Opinion] 8933.) [From Interstate Commerce Commission reports, v. 83.] * Paper, 5c.

LOCOMOTIVE INSPECTION BUREAU

Report. 12th annual report of chief inspector, Bureau of Locomotive Inspection, fiscal year 1923. 1923. [1]+115 p. il. * Paper, 25c. 12—29929

JUSTICE DEPARTMENT

Abilene and Southern Railway. No. 456, in Supreme Court, Oct. term, 1923, United States et al. *v.* Abilene & Southern Railway Company et al., appeal from district court for district of Kansas, 2d division; motion to advance. 1923. cover-title, 3 p. ‡

Arnstein, Jules. No. 4025, in Court of Appeals of District of Columbia, Oct. term, 1923, Jules Arnstein et al. *v.* United States; brief on behalf of appellee. 1923. cover-title, 18 p. ‡

Atchison, Topeka and Santa Fe Railway. In Court of Claims, Atchison, Topeka & Santa Fe Railway Company *v.* United States, no. 319–A; defendant's objections to plaintiff's request for findings of fact [defendant's request for findings of fact, and brief]. [1923.] p. 55–59, large 8° ‡

Bankruptcy. United States district court, district of Indiana, rules in bankruptcy. 1923. 3 p. †

Bartlett, Frank W. In Court of Claims, Frank W. Bartlett *v.* United States, no. 193–B; defendant's brief. [1923.] p. 43–49, large 8° ‡

Berryman, Robert. No. 629, in Supreme Court, Oct. term, 1923, Robert Berryman *v.* United States, on petition for writ of certiorari to circuit court of appeals for 6th circuit; brief for United States in opposition. 1923. cover-title, 4 p. ‡

Burton Coal Company. No. B–80, in Court of Claims, Burton Coal Company *v.* United States; defendant's objections to claimant's request for findings of fact, findings of fact requested by defendant, statement of case, and brief. 1923. cover-title, p. 265–296. ‡

Cement Manufacturers Protective Association. In equity, no. E 22–25, in district court for southern district of New York, United States *v.* Cement Manufacturers Protective Association et al.; final decree. 1923. cover-title, 8 p. ‡

Chicago Great Western Railroad. In Court of Claims, Chicago Great Western Railroad Company *v.* United States, no. B–72; defendant's objections to plaintiff's request for findings of fact, defendant's request for findings of fact, and brief. [1923.] p. 1–10, large 8° ‡

Chicago, Rock Island and Pacific Railway. In Court of Claims, Chicago, Rock Island & Pacific Railway Company *v.* United States, no. 34706; defendant's objections to plaintiff's supplemental request for finding of fact, defendant's supplemental request for findings of fact, and brief on resubmission. [1923.] p. 69–82, large 8° ‡

Clausen, Catharina. No. 6448, circuit court of appeals for 8th circuit, Thomas W. Miller, as Alien Property Custodian, and Frank White, as Treasurer of United States, *v.* Catharina Clausen; brief on behalf of Thomas W. Miller, as Alien Property Custodian, and Frank White, as Treasurer of United States. 1923. cover-title, ii+33 p. ‡

Dayton-Goose Creek Railway. Recapture clause case [of Dayton-Goose Creek Railway Company *v.* United States]; oral argument by James M. Beck, Solicitor General, in Supreme Court, Nov. 19, 1923. 1923. cover-title, 29 p. ‡

Dominion Canners, Limited. Nos. 2218 and 2316, Court of Customs Appeals, Dominion Canners (Ltd.) *v.* United States; Lewis Hubbard & Co. et al *v.* [same]; brief for United States. 1923. cover-title, 18 p. ‡

Everard's, James, Breweries. No. 200, in Supreme Court, Oct. term, 1923, James Everard's Breweries *v.* Ralph A. Day, prohibition director of State of New York, et al., appeal from district court for southern district of New York; brief for appellees. 1923. cover-title, ii+28 p. ‡

Farmers' Cotton Oil and Fertilizer Company. In Court of Claims, Farmers' Cotton Oil and Fertilizer Company *v.* United States, no. C–1179; demurrer [and brief]. [1923.] p. 99–145, large 8° ‡

Feibleman, L., & Co., Incorporated. No. 2319, Court of Customs Appeals, L. Feibleman & Co. (Inc.) *v.* United States; brief for United States. 1923. cover-title, 12 p. ‡

Fensterer & Voss, Incorporated. No. 2317, Court of Customs Appeals, Fensterer & Voss, Inc., v. United States; brief for United States. 1923. cover-title, 5 p. ‡

Gottlieb, Gittel. No. 221. in Supreme Court, Oct. term, 1923, commissioner of immigration of port of New York v. Gittel Gottlieb and Israel Gottlieb, on writ of certiorari to circuit court of appeals for 2d circuit; brief for petitioner. 1923. cover-title, i+38 p. ‡

Hopkins, Lewis C., Company. No. 2282, Court of Customs Appeals, Lewis C. Hopkins Co. v. United States; brief for United States. 1923. cover-title 19 p. ‡

Keleher, John B. Nos. 4061 and 4062, in Court of Appeals of District of Columbia, Oct. term. 1923, nos. — and —, special calendar, United States v. John B. Keleher; and [same] v. Claude L. Burrows; brief for appellant. 1923. cover-title, 16 p. ‡

Kwock Seu Lum. No. 650, in Supreme Court, Oct. term, 1923, Kwock Seu Lum v. Edward White, commissioner of immigration [port of San Francisco] petition for writ of certiorari to circuit court of appeals for 9th circuit: brief for respondent in opposition. 1923. cover-title, 4 p. ‡

Lasley, Rosa. No. 166, in Supreme Court, Oct. term, 1923, Hubert Work, Secretary of Interior, v. United States ex rel. W. G. Lynn, guardian of Rosa Lasley, on writ of error to Court of Appeals of District of Columbia; brief for plaintiff in error. 1923. cover-title, i+23 p. ‡

La Vallette, Albert T. No. 58–A, in Court of Claims, Albert T. La Vallette v. United States; defendants' objections to plaintiff's proposed findings of fact, defendants' request for findings of fact, and brief. 1923. cover-title, p. 84–94. ‡

Lawless, John, jr. In Court of Claims, John Lawless, jr., v. United States, no. 50–B; defendant's brief. [1923.] p. 45–53, large 8° ‡

Leather, William. No. 172, in Supreme Court, Oct. term, 1923, William Leather and Leon K. Leigh v. Mark J. White [assistant surgeon general, Public Health Service] et al., appeal from circuit court of appeals for 7th circuit; brief for Mark J. White. 1923. cover-title, 23 p. ‡

—— Same. 1923 [reprint with slight changes and addition of index]. cover-title, i+23 p. ‡

McIntosh County, Okla. No. 177, in Supreme Court, Oct. term, 1923, United States v. McIntosh County, Okla., et al., appeal from circuit court of appeals for 8th circuit; brief for United States. 1923. cover-title, 16 p. ‡

—— No. 178, in Supreme Court, Oct. term, 1923, United States v. J. P. Ransom as county treasurer of McIntosh County, Okla., error to circuit court of appeals for 8th circuit; brief for United States. 1923. cover-title, 17 p. ‡

Magg, Joseph. No. 4407, in Court of Appeals of District of Columbia, Oct. term, 1923, Joseph Magg v. Thomas W. Miller, as Alien Property Custodian, and Frank White, Treasurer of United States; brief for appellees. 1923. cover-title, i+31 p. [A corrected copy of page 31, entitled Money values, and with signature mark 77022—23, was also issued.] ‡

Mensevich, Nicolai. No. 148, in Supreme Court, Oct. term, 1923, United States ex rel. Nicolai Mensevich v. Robert E. Tod, commissioner of immigration at port of New York, appeal from district court for southern district of New York; brief for appellee. [1923.] cover-title, 19 p. ÷

Metal Products Company. No. 34685, in Court of Claims, Metal Products Company v. United States; motion to amend defendant's motion for new trial filed June 22, error of fact, error of law, newly discovered evidence, and fraud, wrong, and injustice done United States, statement and argument. 1923. cover-title, ii+1–140 p. large 8° ‡

—— Same, exhibit 21. [1923.] p. 141–142, large 8° [This is printed without title or signature mark.] ‡

—— Same. exhibit 22. 1923. 1 p. large 8° ‡

Meyer, M. J. & H. J., Company. No. 2309, Court of Customs Appeals, United States v. M. J. & H. J. Meyer Co.; reply brief for United States. 1923. cover-title, 6 p. ‡

Missouri, Kansas and Texas Railway of Texas. In Court of Claims, [Charles E.] Schaff, receiver of Missouri, Kansas & Texas Railway Company of Texas, *v.* United States, no. 106–A; defendant's objections to plaintiff's request for findings of fact, defendant's request for findings of fact, and brief. [1923.] p. 31–42, large 8°. ‡

Mottram, George W. No. B–52, in Court of Claims, George William Mottram *v.* United States; defendant's objections to plaintiff's request for findings of fact, findings requested in lieu thereof, and brief. 1923. cover-title, ii+311–380 p. large 8° ‡

National Council of Traveling Salesmen's Associations. No. 469, interchangeable script coupon ticket case, in Supreme Court, Oct. term, 1923, United States, Interstate Commerce Commission, National Council of Traveling Salesmen's Associations, et al. *v.* New York Central Railroad Company et al., appeal from district court for district of Massachusetts; brief for United States. 1923. cover-title, vi+111 p. ‡

National Shorthand Reporting Company. In Court of Claims, Robert F. Rose and Walter H. Lee, partners, trading as National Shorthand Reporting Company, *v.* United States, no. B–109; defendant's objections to claimants' request for findings of fact, defendant's request for finding of fact, and brief. [1923.] p. 27–29, large 8° ‡

Neal-Blun Company. No. 327–A, in Court of Claims, Neal-Blun [Company] *v.* United States; defendant's objections to claimant's request for findings of fact, findings of fact requested by defendant, statement of case, and brief. 1923. cover-title, p. 1–19. ‡

Nixon, S. M. No. 436, in Supreme Court, Oct. term, 1923, S. M. Nixon and Earl L. Nixon *v.* United States, petition for writ of certiorari to circuit court of appeals for 9th circuit; brief for United States in opposition. 1923. cover-title, 5 p. ‡

Noce, Daniel. In Court of Claims, Daniel Noce *v.* United States, no. 152–B; defendant's motion for new trial [and brief in support thereof]. [1923.] p. 27–55, large 8° ‡

Northern Pacific Railroad. No. 60–B, in Court of Claims, Northern Pacific R. R. Co. *v.* United States; defendant's objections to plaintiff's request for findings of fact, defendant's request for findings of fact, and brief. 1923. cover-title, p. 91–106, large 8° ‡

Opinions. Advance sheets, Official opinions of Attorneys General, v. 34, [signature] 1. 1923. [1]+1–16 p. ‡

Pacific Mail Steamship Company. In Court of Claims, Pacific Mail Steamship Company *v.* United States, no. C–1132; demurrer. [1923.] p. 1–8, large 8° ‡

Porter Brothers. No. 6823, in district court for eastern district of Michigan, southern division, United States *v.* Porter Bros. et al.; brief and argument of plaintiff in resistance to defendants' motion for bill of particulars. 1923. cover-title, 34 p. ‡

Pothier, Roland R. No. 546, in Supreme Court, Oct. term, 1923, William R. Rodman, United States marshal [for district of Rhode Island], *v.* Roland R. Pothier, on writ of certiorari to circuit court of appeals for 1st circuit; motion by petitioner to advance. 1923. cover-title, 3 p. ‡

Prince Line, Limited. Nos. 644 and 645, in Supreme Court, Oct. term, 1923, United States *v.* Prince Line (Ltd.) ; [same] *v.* American-Hawaiian Steamship Company, writs of error to district court for eastern district of New York; memorandum in reply to that of defendants in error in opposition to motion by United States to vacate orders dismissing these cases, etc. 1923. cover-title, 3 p. ‡

Report. Annual report of Attorney General, fiscal year 1923 [with exhibits]. 1923. v+426 p. 1 tab. * Cloth, 65c. 17—9090

—— Same. (H. doc. 91, 68th Cong. 1st sess.)

River Rouge Improvement Company. No. 204, in Supreme Court, Oct. term, 1923, United States *v.* River Rouge Improvement Company et al., in error to circuit court of appeals for 6th circuit; brief for United States. 1923. cover-title, ii+53 p. ‡

Robilio, Joe. No. 631, in Supreme Court, Oct. term, 1923, Joe Robilio et al. *v.* United States, on petition for writ of certiorari to circuit court of appeals for 6th circuit; brief for United States in opposition. 1923. cover-title, 2 p. ‡

Rodman, Hugh. In Patent Office, before examiner of interferences at final hearing, interference no. 46630, Hugh Rodman *v.* John C. Woodruff, method of making activated carbon; brief for Woodruff. 1923. cover-title. 26 p. ‡

Sage, Mrs. Margaret O. No. 276, in Supreme Court, Oct. term, 1923, William H. Edwards, formerly collector of internal revenue for 2d district of New York, *v.* Joseph Germain [Jermain] Slocum et al., [executors of Margaret Olivia Sage], on writ of certiorari to circuit court of appeals for 2d circuit; brief for petitioner. 1923. cover-title, 18 p. ‡

St. Louis Car Company. No. B-146, in Court of Claims, St. Louis Car Company *v.* United States; defendant's objections to plaintiff's request for findings of fact, defendant's request for findings of fact, and brief. 1923. cover-title, p. 1-14. ‡

Semple, John B. No. 34442, in Court of Claims, John B. Semple *v.* United States; defendant's brief and request for finding of facts. 1923. cover-title, ii+543-634 p. large 8° ‡

Sisson, Robert W. No. 4009, in Court of Appeals of District of Columbia, Oct. term, 1923, no. —, special calendar, Robert W. Sisson, Maurice Sullivan, and Earl D. Dean *v.* United States; brief for appellee. 1923. cover-title, 13 p. ‡

Skinner & Eddy Corporation. In Court of Claims, Skinner & Eddy Corporation *v.* United States, no. A-199; answer and counterclaim. [1923.] p. 591-592, large 8° ‡

Sperry Oil and Gas Company. No. 164, in Supreme Court. Oct. term, 1923, Sperry Oil & Gas Company and Oklahoma Producing & Refining Corporation of America *v.* Pearl Chisholm and Webster Chisholm, appeal from and certiorari to circuit court of appeals for 8th circuit; brief for United States. 1923. cover-title, 18 p. ‡

Standard Oil Company. In Court of Claims, Standard Oil Company (New Jersey) *v.* United States, no. B-22; defendant's brief. 1923. p. 1-3, large 8° ‡

State Savings Bank of Ortley, S. Dak. In Court of Claims, State Savings Bank of Ortley, S. Dak., *v.* United States, no. 35-B; defendant's brief [and] facts. [1923.] p. 1-22, large 8° ‡

Streater, Wallace. In Court of Claims, Wallace Streater *v.* United States, no. 8-B; defendant's brief. [1923.] p. 49-59, large 8° ‡

Sughrue, Daniel H. In Court of Claims, Daniel H. Sughrue *v.* United States, no. 208-B; defendant's brief. [1923.] p. 23-28, large 8° ‡

Swartz, Nell R. In Court of Claims, Nell R. Swartz *v.* United States, no. 271-B; defendant's brief. [1923.] p. 29-34, large 8° ‡

Tile Manufacturers Credit Association. In district court, no. 201, in district court, southern district of Ohio, United States *v.* Tile Manufacturers Credit Association et al.; final decree. 1923. cover-title, 9 p. ‡

Trusts. Federal antitrust law with amendments, list of cases instituted by United States, and citations of cases decided thereunder or relating thereto, Dec. 15, 1923. 1923. ix+182 p. * Paper, 10c.   23—27495

Tuckerman, Jake. No. 630, in Supreme Court, Oct. term, 1923, Jake Tuckerman *v.* United States, on petition for writ of certiorari to circuit court of appeals for 6th circuit; brief for United States in opposition. 1923. cover-title, 2 p. ‡

United Gas and Electric Engineering Corporation. In Court of Claims, United Gas & Electric Engineering Corporation *v.* United States, no. B-173; defendant's objections to claimant's request for findings of fact, defendant's request for findings of fact, and brief. [1923.] p. 1-22, large 8° ‡

Waialua Agricultural Company, Limited. In Court of Claims, Waialua Agricultural Company, Ltd., *v.* United States, no. C-965; demurrer [and] brief. [1923.] p. 11-26, large 8° ‡

Wilkes, Loftis. No. 632, in Supreme Court, Oct. term, 1923, Loftis Wilkes et al. *v.* United States, on petition for writ of certiorari to circuit court of appeals for 6th circuit; brief for United States in opposition. 1923. cover-title, 6 p. ‡

Witcombe, McGeachin & Co. No. 2280, Court of Customs Appeals. Witcombe, McGeachin & Co., et al. *v.* United States; brief for United States. 1923. cover-title, 13 p. ‡

Wood, J. R., & Sons. No. 2314, Court of Customs Appeals, United States *v.* J. R. Wood & Sons; brief for United States. 1923. cover-title, 12 p. ‡

LABOR DEPARTMENT

Moran Towing and Transportation Company. Claim of Moran Towing & Transportation Co., New York, N. Y. Dec. 13, 1923. 2 p. (H. doc. 106, 68th Cong. 1st sess.) * Paper, 5c.

Report. 11th annual report of Secretary of Labor, fiscal year 1923. 1923. v+149 p. il. 1 tab. * Paper, 15c.   14—30221

CHILDREN'S BUREAU

Automobiles. Minors in automobile and metal-manufacturing industries in Michigan [with bibliography; by Helen M. Dart and Ella Arvilla Merritt]. 1923. vii+131 p. 1 pl. 18 p. of pl. (Bureau publication 126.) * Paper, 25c.
                                                                          L 24—3

Child labor in North Dakota. 1923. v+67 p. 4 pl. 2 p. of pl. (Bureau publication 129.) * Paper, 15c.   L 24—1

Child welfare in insular possessions of United States: pt. 1, Porto Rico; by Helen v. Bary. 1923. v+75 p. il. 5 pl. 2 p. of pl. (Bureau publication 127.) * Paper, 15c. ·   L 23—282

Play and recreation, outlines for study [with lists of references, by George E. Johnson] ; separate 3 [from] Child care and child welfare. 2d edition. 1923. iii+5–10+373–418 p. (Bureau publication 92.) [Prepared in cooperation with Federal Board for Vocational Education. Original article from Federal Board for Vocational Education, Bulletin 65, Home economics series 5. Title-page rearranged from that of previous edition.] * Paper, 5c.   L 24—2

Report. 11th annual report of chief, Children's Bureau, fiscal year 1923. 1923. iii+38 p. †   14—8115

EMPLOYMENT SERVICE

Industrial employment information bulletin, v. 3, no. 11; Nov. 1923. [1923.] 22 p. 4° [Monthly.] †   L 21—17

IMMIGRATION BUREAU

Report. Annual report of commissioner general of immigration, fiscal year 1923. 1923. vi+161 p. * Paper, 15c.   8—14486

LABOR STATISTICS BUREAU

Automobiles. Wages and hours of labor in automobile industry, 1922. Oct. 1923. iii+70 p. (Bulletin 348; Wages and hours of labor series.) * Paper, 10c.   L 24—4

—— Same. (H. doc. 55, 68th Cong. 1st sess.)

Buildings. Building permits in principal cities of United States in 1922. Oct. 1923. iii+120+vi p. (Bulletin 347; Miscellaneous series.) * Paper, 15c.
                                                                          L 22—165

—— Same. (H. doc. 54, 68th Cong. 1st sess.)

Cost of living. Changes in cost of living in United States. [1923.] p. 1077–90. [From Monthly labor review, Nov. 1923.] †

Ladders. Safety code for construction, care, and use of ladders, American Society of Safety Engineers, sponsor; tentative American standard, approved July 25, 1923, by American Engineering Standards Committee. Oct. 1923. iii+16 p. (Bulletin 351; Safety code series.) * Paper, 5c.   L 24—5

—— Same. (H. doc. 58, 68th Cong. 1st sess.)

Monthly labor review, v. 17, no. 6; Dec. 1923. 1923.´ v+1225–1449+vi p. il.
* Paper, 15c. single copy, $1.50 a yr.; foreign subscription, $2.25.   15—26485

SPECIAL ARTICLES.—Bread making in modern bakery; by Robert S. Billups.—Protection of workers under Mexican State labor laws; by Ethel C. Yohe.—48-hour week in industry; by J. C. Bowen.—Conciliation work of Department of Labor, Oct. 1923; by Hugh L. Kerwin.—Statistics of immigration, Sept. 1923; by W. W. Husband.

NOTE.—The Review is the medium through which the Bureau publishes the results of original investigations too brief for bulletin purposes, notices of labor legislation by the States or by Congress, and Federal court decisions affecting labor, which from their importance should be given attention before they could ordinarily appear in the bulletins devoted to these subjects. One free subscription will be given to all labor departments and bureaus, workmen's compensation commissions, and other offices connected with the administration of labor laws and organizations exchanging publications with the Labor Statistics Bureau. Others desiring copies may obtain them from the Superintendent of Documents, Washington, D. C., at the prices stated above.

Prices. Prices and cost of living. 1923. [1]+1276–1303 p. il. [From Monthly labor review, Dec. 1923.] †

—— Wholesale prices of commodities for Nov. 1923. 1923. [1]+9 p.
[Monthly.] †   L 22—229

Ribbon. Trade agreement in silk-ribbon industry of New York City; by Margaret Gadsby. Oct. 1923. iii+95 p. il. 1 pl. (Bulletin 341; Conciliation and arbitration series.) * Paper, 15c.   L 24—6

—— Same. (H. doc. 20, 68th Cong. 1st sess.)

NATURALIZATION BUREAU

Posters. United States Government and public schools are helping our foreign-born friends who are applicants for American citizenship to learn our language and principles of our Government in preparation for good citizenship; [all lettered poster]. [Reprint with slight changes 1923.] 20.9×14 in. †

—— Same, Italian. †

Report. Annual report of commissioner of naturalization, fiscal year 1923. 1923. [1]+31 p. †   14—6278

WOMEN'S BUREAU

Report. 5th annual report of director of Women's Bureau, fiscal year 1923. 1923. [1]+20 p. †   L 20—1

South Carolina. Women in South Carolina industries, study of hours, wages, and working conditions; [by Mary V. Robinson]. 1923. v+128 p. (Bulletin 32.) * Paper, 15c.   L 24—7

LIBRARY OF CONGRESS

Orientalia added 1922–23; [by Walter T. Swingle]. [1923.] [1]+171–195 p. [From Report of librarian of Congress, 1923.] †

Report. Report of librarian of Congress, fiscal year 1923. 1923. vi+217 p. 2 pl. 4 p. of pl. * Cloth, 60c.   6—6273

—— Same. (H. doc. 79, 68th Cong. 1st sess.)

COPYRIGHT OFFICE

Copyright. [Catalogue of copyright entries, new series, pt. 1, group 1, Books, v. 20] no. 81–89; Dec. 1923. Dec. 4–31, 1923. p. 1009–1120. [Issued several times a week.]   6—35347

NOTE.—Each number is issued in 4 parts: pt. 1. group 1, relates to books; pt. 1, group 2, to pamphlets, leaflets, contributions to newspapers or periodicals, etc., lectures, sermons, addresses for oral delivery, dramatic compositions, maps, motion pictures; pt. 2, to periodicals; pt. 3, to musical compositions; pt. 4, to works of art, reproductions of a work of art, drawings or plastic works of scientific or technical character, photographs, prints, and pictorial illustrations.

Subscriptions for the Catalogue of copyright entries should be made to the Superintendent of Documents, Washington, D. C., instead of to the Register of Copyrights. Prices are as follows: Paper, $3.00 a yr. (4 pts.), foreign subscription, $5.00; pt. 1 (groups 1 and 2), 5c. single copy (group 1, price of group 2 varies), $1.00 a yr., foreign subscription, $2.25; pt. 3, $1.00 a yr., foreign subscription, $1.50; pts. 2 and 4, each 10c. single copy, 50c. a yr., foreign subscription, 70c.

—— Same, pt. 3, Musical compositions, v. 18, no. 7. 1923. v+593–746 p. [Monthly.]

Copyright—Continued. Copyright law of United States, act of Mar. 4, 1909, in force July 1, 1909, as amended by acts of Aug. 24, 1912, Mar. 2, 1913, and Mar. 28, 1914; with Rules for practice and procedure under sec. 25, by Supreme Court, [and] with act of Dec. 18, 1919. [Edition of] Nov. 1923. 1923. 1–34B+35–68A+69–80 p. (Bulletin 14.) * Paper, 10c.　　　12—35200

DOCUMENTS DIVISION

Government publications. Monthly check-list of State publications received during Oct. 1923; v. 14, no. 10. 1923. p. 401–443. * Paper, 10c. single copy, $1.00 a yr.; foreign subscription, $1.25.　　　10—8924

MIXED CLAIMS COMMISSION, UNITED STATES AND GERMANY

Functions. Dealing with functions of commission and announcing fundamental rules of decision, Nov. 1, 1923. 1923. ii+5–15 p. . (Administrative decision 2.) ‡

Germany. Dealing with liabilities of Germany on all claims (save those expressly excepted) asserted by United States in behalf of its nationals, Nov. 1, 1923. 1923. ii+1–3 p. (Administrative decision 1.) ‡　　　23—27496

Gilmer, Mrs. May D. H. No. 4, before Mixed Claims Commission [United States and Germany], United States on behalf of May Davies Hopkins Gilmer, administratrix [of Albert Lloyd Hopkins], *v.* Germany; brief on behalf of United States. 1923 [reprint]. cover-title, ii+160 p. 4° [The case number has been used on this reprint, there have been other additions to the cover-title, and because of resetting the type, the page numbers have had to be changed in the list of contents.] ‡

Lusitania, steamship. Opinion in the Lusitania cases, Nov. 1, 1923. 1923. ii+17–32 p. ‡

Selliger, Max. Before Mixed Claims Commission, United States and Germany, no. 10, United States on behalf of Max Selliger *v.* Germany; no. 11, United States on behalf of Kentucky Distilleries & Warehouse Company *v.* [same]; no. 12, United States on behalf of William Bergenthal Company *v.* [same]; brief on behalf of United States. 1923. cover-title, 17 p. 4° [Manuscript corrections on p. 2 and 17.] ‡

War risk insurance. Opinion in war-risk insurance premium claims, Nov. 1, 1923. 1923. ii+33–59 p. ‡

NATIONAL ADVISORY COMMITTEE FOR AERONAUTICS

Electrodes. Effect of electrode temperature on sparking voltage of short spark gaps; by F. B. Silsbee. 1923. cover-title, 10 p. il. 4° (Report 179.) [Prepared by Standards Bureau. Text and illustration on p. 2 and 3 of cover.] * Paper, 5c.　　.　　　23—27497

Report. Aeronautics, 9th annual report of National Advisory Committee for Aeronautics, [fiscal year] 1923, administrative report without technical reports. 1923. viii+56 p. 4° * Paper, 10c.　　　16—26395

—— Same. (S. doc. 2, 68th Cong. 1st sess.)

NAVY DEPARTMENT

Claims. Appropriation to pay claims which have been adjusted, communication from Secretary of Navy submitting estimate of appropriation to pay claims which he has adjusted under provisions of act of Dec. 28, 1922, and which require appropriation for their payment. Dec. 20, 1923. 4 p. (H. doc. 119, 68th Cong. 1st sess.) * Paper, 5c.

—— Claims adjusted by Secretary of Navy which require appropriation. Dec. 15, 1923. 5 p. (H. doc. 115, 68th Cong. 1st sess.) * Paper, 5c.

Court-martial orders. Court-martial order 9, 1923; Sept. 30, 1923. [1923.] 12 p. 12° [Monthly.] ‡

—— Same 10, 1923; Oct. 31, 1923. [1923.] 16 p. 12° [Monthly.] ‡

Orders. General order 118 and 119 [6th series] ; Nov. 1 and 19, 1923. [1923.]
2 p. 4° ‡

Report. Annual report of Secretary of Navy, fiscal year 1923. 1923. iii+
117 p. [Includes operations to Nov. 15, 1923.] †   8—8477

Wages. Schedule of wages for civil employees under naval establishment,
within continental limits of United States and Pearl Harbor, Hawaii, calendar year 1924. 1923. [1]+26 p. ‡   23—27408

AERONAUTICS BUREAU

Report. Annual report of chief of Bureau of Aeronautics, fiscal year 1923.
1923. [1]+45 p. †   27—27369

CONSTRUCTION AND REPAIR BUREAU

Report. Annual report to chief of Bureau of Construction and Repair, fiscal
year 1923. 1923. [1]+6 p. †   .

ENGINEERING BUREAU

Report. Annual report of chief of Bureau of Engineering, fiscal year 1923.
1923. [1]+31 p. †   8—32063

JUDGE ADVOCATE GENERAL

Report. Annual report of judge advocate general of Navy, fiscal year 1923.
1923. [1]+31 p. 1 pl. †   8—12050

MARINE CORPS

Orders. Marine Corps orders 7, 1923; Dec. 11, 1923. [1923.] 1 p. oblong 48°
[Mimeographed.] ‡

Report. Annual report of major general commandant of Marine Corps, fiscal
year 1923. 1923. [1]+23 p. †   8—8002

MEDICINE AND SURGERY BUREAU

Naval medical bulletin. United States naval medical bulletin, published for
information of Medical Department of service, Dec. 1923, v. 19, no. 6;
edited by W. M. Kerr. 1923. vi+735-873+xi p. il. [Monthly.] * Paper,
15c. single copy, $1.50 a yr.; foreign subscription, $2.50.   8—35095

SPECIAL ARTICLES.—Some of functions of naval medical personnel serving in the
field, with special reference to field sanitary measures; by W. L. Mann.—Notes on
preventive medicine for medical officers, Navy [including Evaluation of methods in
public health education].—Index to United States naval medical bulletin, v. 19.

Report. Annual report of surgeon general, Navy, chief of Bureau of Medicine
and Surgery, fiscal year 1923. 1923. iii+182 p. il. †   8—9360

NAVAL INTELLIGENCE OFFICE

Holidays. List of national holidays of maritime countries. 1923. [1]+v+6 p.
[The first page given in the collation is a blank form for corrections which
is detachable.] ‡   23—26995

NAVAL OPERATIONS OFFICE

Report. Annual report of chief of naval operations, fiscal year 1923. 1923.
[1]+45 p. †

NAVIGATION BUREAU

Boat book of Navy, 1920. 1921 [reprint with omission of illustration and with
additional matter, 1922]. 258 p.+4 leaves, il. 5 pl. 24° [This publication
includes Change 1.] * Cloth, 50c.   23—27498

Medical Corps, Navy. Circular for information of persons desiring to enter
Medical Corps of Navy. Revised Oct. 1923. 1923. 7 p. 4° †   17—26234

Philippine Islands. Information regarding living conditions at naval stations
in Philippine Islands, Sept. 1923. [1923.] 7 p. †   23—26996

Pipe-fitting. Piping, fittings, and packing, clothing and lagging, assignment 1; prepared by Bureau of Engineering. 1923. [1]+1–14 p. il. (Navy education-study courses.) ‡

—— Same, assignment 2; prepared by Bureau of Engineering. 1923. [1]+ 14–22+2 p. (Navy education-study courses.) ‡

Report. Annual report of chief of Bureau of Navigation, fiscal year 1923. 1923. [1]+26 p. †   8—9359

HYDROGRAPHIC OFFICE

NOTE.—The charts, sailing directions, etc., of the Hydrographic Office are sold by the office in Washington and also by agents at the principal American and foreign seaports and American lake ports. Copies of the General catalogue of mariners' charts and books and of the Hydrographic bulletins, reprints, and Notice to mariners are supplied free on application at the Hydrographic Office in Washington and at the branch offices in Boston, New York, Philadelphia, Baltimore, Norfolk, Savannah, New Orleans, Galveston, San Francisco, Portland (Oreg.), Seattle, Chicago, Cleveland, Buffalo, Sault Ste. Marie, and Duluth.

Distances. Table of distances between ports via shortest navigable routes as determined by Hydrographic Office. 1923. 288 p. 1 tab. ([Publication] 117.) † Paper, 45c.   23—27499

Hydrographic bulletin, weekly, no. 1787–90; Dec. 5–26, 1923. [1923.] Each 1 p. f° and large 4° [For Ice supplements to accompany nos. 1787–90, see below under center head *Charts* the subhead *Pilot charts.*] †

Lights. List of lights, with fog signals and visible time signals, including uniform time system, radio time signals, radio weather bulletins, and radio compass stations of the world: v. 4, British Islands, English Channel, and North Sea; corrected to Nov. 3, 1923. 1923. ii+507 p. map. ([Publication] 33.) † Paper, 60c.

Notice to aviators 12, 1923; Dec. 1 [1923]. [1923.] 12 p. [Monthly.] †
                                                               20—26958

Notice to mariners 48–52, 1923; Dec. 1–29 [1923]. [1923.] [xlix]+1284–1415 leaves. [Weekly.] †

Report. Annual report of Hydrographic Office, fiscal year 1923. 1923. ii+34 p. il. †   8—12043

Tide calendars. Tide calendar [for Baltimore (Fort McHenry) and Cape Henry], Jan. 1924. [1923.] 1 p. 4° [Monthly.] †

—— Tide calendar [for Norfolk (Navy Yard) and Newport News, Va.], Jan. 1924. [1923.] 1 p. 4° [Monthly.] †

Charts

Bahama Islands. Islands and anchorages in the Bahamas, W. I., mainly from British surveys in 1832; chart 2805. Washington, Hydrographic Office, Nov. 1923. 26.5×19.7 in. † 20c.
Acklin Island, Anchorage on sw. side of.
Crooked Island Anchorage.
Crooked Island anchorages.
Mariguana Island.
Nelson, Port, Rum Cay, from survey by U. S. F. C. S. Albatross in 1886.
San Salvador or Watling Island (landfall of Columbus, 1492).

Pilot charts. Ice supplement to north Atlantic pilot chart; issue 87. Scale 1° long.=0.3 in. Washington, Hydrographic Office [1923]. 8.9×11.8 in. [To accompany Hydrographic bulletin 1787, Dec. 5, 1923.] †

—— Same; issue 88. Scale 1° long.=0.3 in. Washington, Hydrographic Office [1923]. 8.9×11.8 in. [To accompany Hydrographic bulletin 1789, Dec. 12, 1923.] †

—— Same; issue 89. Scale 1° long.=0.3 in. Washington, Hydrographic Office [1923]. 8.9×11.8 in. [To accompany Hydrographic bulletin 1789, Dec. 19, 1923.] †

—— Same; issue 90. Scale 1° long.=0.3 in. Washington, Hydrographic Office [1923]. 8.9×11.8 in. [To accompany Hydrographic bulletin 1790, Dec. 26, 1923.] †

—— Pilot chart of Central American waters, Jan. 1924; chart 3500. Scale 1° long.=0.7 in. Washington, Hydrographic Office, Dec. 13, 1923. 23.4×35.1 in. [Monthly. Certain portions of the data are furnished by the Weather Bureau.] † 10c.

NOTE.—Contains on reverse: New and shorter method for finding position [note concerning Hydrographic Office publication 203, Sumner line of position].

Pilot charts—Continued. Pilot chart of Indian Ocean, Feb. 1924; chart 2603.
Scale 1° long.=0.2 in. Washington, Hydrographic Office, Dec. 13, 1923.
22.6×31 in. [Monthly. Certain portions of the data are furnished by the
Weather Bureau.] † 10c.

NOTE.—Contains on reverse: New and shorter method for finding position [note
concerning Hydrographic Office publication 203, Sumner line of position].

—— Pilot chart of north Atlantic Ocean, Jan. 1924; chart 1400. Scale 1°
long.=0.27 in. Washington, Hydrographic Office, Dec. 13, 1923. 23.2×
31.8 in. [Monthly. Certain portions of the data are furnished by the
Weather Bureau.] † 10c.   14—16339

NOTE.—Contains on reverse: New and shorter method for finding position [note
concerning Hydrographic Office publication 203, Sumner line of position].

—— Pilot chart of north Pacific Ocean, Feb. 1924; chart 1401. Scale 1°
long.=0.2 in. Washington, Hydrographic Office, Dec. 13, 1923. 23.7×35.3 in.
[Monthly. Certain portions of the data are furnished by the Weather
Bureau.] † 10c.

NOTE.—Contains on reverse: New and shorter method for finding position [note
concerning Hydrographic Office publication 203, Sumner line of position].

NAVAL OBSERVATORY

Report. Annual report of Naval Observatory, fiscal year 1923. 1923. [1]+
25 p. †   8—7054

ORDNANCE BUREAU

Report. Annual report of chief of Bureau of Ordnance, fiscal year 1923. 1923.
[1]+14 p. †   9—4633

SUPPLIES AND ACCOUNTS BUREAU

Report. Annual report of paymaster general of Navy, fiscal year 1923. 1923.
xii p. †   11—20038

—— Same [with tabulated statements]. 1923. 3 v. xv+361+960+386 p. †

Supply Corps, Navy. Memorandum for information of officers of Supply Corps,
commanding officers of ships, and commandants 256; Dec. 1, 1923. [1923.]
p. 7826–7901, 12° [Monthly.] ‡

YARDS AND DOCKS BUREAU

Report. Annual report of chief of Bureau of Yards and Docks, fiscal year
1923. 1923. [1]+14 p. †   8—1786

PAN AMERICAN UNION

NOTE.—The Pan American Union sells its own monthly bulletins, handbooks, etc., at
prices usually ranging from 5c. to $2.50. The price of the English edition of the bulle-
tin is 25c. a single copy or $2.50 a year, the Spanish edition $2.00 a year, the Portuguese
edition $1.50 a year; there is an additional charge of 50c. a year on each edition for
countries outside the Pan American Union. Address the Director General of the Pan
American Union, Washington, D. C.

Banana. Story of the banana; [by Philip K. Reynolds]. 1923. [2]+30 p.
il. †   23—27500

Buenos Aires, metropolis of Southern Hemisphere. 1923. [2]+22 p. il. †
                                                                    23—27411

Bulletin (English edition). Bulletin of Pan American Union, Dec. 1923; [v.
57, no. 6]. [1923.] iv+537–644 p. il. [Monthly.]   8—30967

—— Same. (H. doc. 6, pt. 6, 68th Cong. 1st sess.)

—— *(Portuguese edition).* Boletim da União Pan-Americana, Dezembro,
1923, edição portugueza; [v. 25, no. 6]. [Sun Job Print, Baltimore, Md.,
1923.] [iv]+391–474 p. il. [Monthly. This number is entitled A Cruz
Vermelha nas Americas.]   11—27014

—— *(Spanish edition).* Boletín de la Unión Panamericana, Diciembre, 1923,
sección española; [v. 57, no. 6]. [1923.] iv+553–660 p. il. [Monthly.]
                                                                    12—12555

Haiti. Recent progress, social and economic, in Haiti. 1923. [2]+22 p. il. [From Bulletin, Nov. 1923.] †
Mexico, general descriptive data. 1923. [2]+46 p. il. †   10—35021
Peru. Commerce of Peru, latest reports from Peruvian official sources. 1923. 12 p. †   22—26690

PANAMA CANAL

NOTE.—Although The Panama Canal makes its reports to, and is under the supervision of, the Secretary of War, it is not a part of the War Department.

Panama Canal record, v. 17, no. 17–20; Dec. 5–26, 1923: Balboa Heights, C. Z. [1923]. p. 249–302. [Weekly.]   7—35328

NOTE.—The yearly subscription rate of the Panama Canal record is 50c. domestic, and $1.00 foreign, (single issues 2c.), except in the case of Government departments and bureaus, Members of Congress, representatives of foreign governments, steamship lines, chambers of commerce, boards of trade, and university and public libraries, to whom the Record is distributed free. The word "domestic" refers to the United States, Canada, Canal Zone, Cuba, Guam, Hawaii, Manua, Mexico, the Philippines, Porto Rico, Republic of Panama, Tutuila, and the Virgin Islands. Subscriptions will commence with the first issue of the Record in the month in which the subscriptions are received, unless otherwise requested. Remittances should be made payable to Disbursing Clerk, The Panama Canal, but should be forwarded to the Chief of Office, The Panama Canal, Washington, D. C. The name and address to which the Record is to be sent should be plainly written. Postage stamps, foreign money, and defaced or smooth coins will not be accepted.

Steamship lines through Panama Canal and to its terminal ports, and passenger connections from Panama Canal. Panama Canal Press, Mount Hope, C. Z., Oct. 1923. cover-title, 19 p. †

GOVERNOR

Report. Annual report of governor of The Panama Canal, fiscal year 1923. 1923. v+102 p. †   15—26761

—— Same. (H. doc. 72, 68th Cong. 1st sess.)

PURCHASING DEPARTMENT

Supplies. Circular [proposals for supplies] 1580 and 1581; Dec. 10 and 21, 1923. [1923.] 18+[1] and 28 p. f° †

POST OFFICE DEPARTMENT

Claims. Claims adjusted under act of Dec. 28, 1922, 4 communications from Postmaster General submitting estimates of appropriations to pay claims which he has adjusted and which require appropriation for their payment. Dec. 13, 1923. 25 p. (H. doc. 107, 68th Cong. 1st sess.) * Paper, 5c.

—— Estimate of appropriation to pay claims adjusted under act of Dec. 28, 1922, communication from Postmaster General submitting estimate of appropriation to pay claims which he has adjusted and which requires appropriation for its payment. Dec. 13, 1923. 6 p. (H. doc. 113, 68th Cong. 1st sess.) * Paper, 5c.

Postal bulletin, v. 44, no. 13332–356; Dec. 1–31, 1923. 1923. Each 1 p. or 2 leaves, f° [Daily except Sundays and holidays.] * Paper, 5c. single copy, $2.00 a yr.   6—5810

Postal cards. Double post cards to be folded with address on reply portion inside; [issued by] 3d assistant Postmaster General. Dec. 14, 1923. 1 p. small 4° †

Postal guide. United States official postal guide, 4th series, v. 3, no. 6; Dec. 1923, monthly supplement. 1923. cover-title, ii+45 p. il. [Includes Modification 29 of International money order list, pamphlet 14, and Inserts 840–845 to Postal laws and regulations of United States. Text on p. 2–4 of cover.] * Official postal guide, with supplements, $1.00, foreign subscription, $1.50; July issue, 75c.; supplements published monthly (11 pamphlets) 25c., foreign subscription, 50c.   4—18254

Postal savings. Amendment to Postal laws and regulations [of United States: Interest to be paid on postal savings certificates]. Dec. 27, 1923. 1 p. oblong 32° †

Report. Annual report of Postmaster General, fiscal year 1923. 1923. viii+149 p. †

         8—10371

—— Same. (H. doc. 82, 68th Cong. 1st sess.)

Universal Postal Union. Report of committee to rearrange universal postal convention of Madrid and recommend any changes deemed necessary in anticipation of Stockholm congress to meet June 4, 1924. 1923. [1]+91 p. ‡

         23—27412

War-savings certificates. Registered 1919 war-savings certificates; [issued by] 3d assistant Postmaster General. Dec. 17, 1923. 1 p. oblong 32° †

FOREIGN MAILS DIVISION

Steamboats. Schedule of steamers appointed to convey mails to foreign countries during Nov. 1923. Oct. 19, 1923. 1 p. f° [Monthly.] * Paper, 5c. single copy, 25c. a yr.; foreign subscription, 50c.

—— Same during Dec. 1923. Nov. 19, 1923. 1 p. f° [Monthly.]

—— Same during Jan. 1924. Dec. 20, 1923. 1 p. f° [Monthly.]

POSTAL SAVINGS SYSTEM

Postal savings. Interest payments on postal savings deposits. Dec. 28, 1923. 1 p. oblong 24° †

Report. Annual report of operations, Postal Savings System, [fiscal year] 1923. Dec. 10, 1923. 49 p. (H. doc. 102, 68th Cong. 1st sess.) * Paper, 5c.

Statement of operations of Postal Savings System by Postmaster General, as chairman, board of trustees Postal Savings System, fiscal year 1923. 1923. 50 p. †

         13—35115

RAILWAY MAIL SERVICE

Mail-trains. Schedule of mail trains, no. 89, Dec. 1, 1923, 12th division, Railway Mail Service, comprising Louisiana and Mississippi. 1923. 80+[1] p. narrow 8° ‡

—— Schedule of mail trains, no. 447, Nov. 24, 1923, 7th division, Railway Mail Service, comprising Kansas and Missouri. 1923. 172 p. narrow 8° ‡

TOPOGRAPHY DIVISION

NOTE.—Since February, 1908, the Topography Division has been preparing rural-delivery maps of counties in which rural delivery is completely established. They are published in two forms, one giving simply the rural free delivery routes, starting from a single given post office, sold at 10 cents each; the other, the rural free delivery routes in an entire county, sold at 35 cents each. A uniform scale of 1 inch to 1 mile is used. Editions are not issued, but sun-print copies are produced in response to special calls addressed to the Disbursing Clerk, Post Office Department, Washington, D. C. These maps should not be confused with the post route maps, for which see Monthly catalogue for February, 1923, page 528.

PRESIDENT OF UNITED STATES

Alien property. Executive order authorizing Alien Property Custodian to sell certain property at private sale [being 510 shares of common stock of National Liberty Insurance Company, corporation of New York State]. Nov. 22, 1923. 1 p. f° (No. 3929.) ‡

—— Executive order authorizing Alien Property Custodian to sell certain property at private sale [being 9,920 shares of common stock of Roessler & Hasslacher Chemical Company, corporation of New York State, and 2,200 shares of common stock of Niagara Electro Chemical Company. said stock belonging to Deutsche Gold und Silber Scheidenanstalt Vormals Roessler, subsidiary corporation of said Roessler & Hasslacher Chemical Company, also 4,900 shares of common stock of Perth Amboy Chemical Works, said stock belonging to Holzverkolungs-Industrie Aktiengesellschaft, subsidiary corporation of said Roessler & Hasslacher Chemical Company]. Nov. 22, 1923. 1 p. f° (No. 3928.) ‡

Alien property—Continued. Executive order authorizing Alien Property Custodian to sell certain property at private sale [being real estate in New York City, belonging to Anna Nink, Jean Nink, Katharina Nink, and Oswald Nink, of Germany]. Nov. 22, 1923. 1 p. f° (No. 3930.) ‡

—— Executive order authorizing Alien Property Custodian to sell certain property at private sale [being real estate in New York City, belonging to Jenny Faber of Austria]. Nov. 22, 1923. 1 p. f° (No. 3931.) ‡

—— Executive order authorizing Alien Property Custodian to sell certain property at private sale [being real estate in New York City, belonging to Waldemar Conrad Von Zedtwitz of Germany]. Nov. 22, 1923. 1 p, f° (No. 3932.) ‡

Customs Service. Executive order [abolishing port of Chopaka in 30th customs collection district (Washington), and creating Nighthawk as customs port of entry in said district, effective Dec. 1, 1923]. Nov. 22, 1923. 1 p. f° (No. 3927.) ‡

Government officials and employees. Executive order [amending Executive order of Dec. 12, 1923, authorizing that beginning at 9 a. m., on Dec. 24, 1923, 4 hours, exclusive of time for luncheon, shall constitute a day's work, so as to direct that on Dec. 24, 1923, beginning with time fixed by heads of Executive establishments for entering on duty, and exclusive of time for luncheon. 4 hours shall constitute a day's work for all clerks and other employees of Federal Government and government of District of Columbia, in District of Columbia]. Dec. 17, 1923. 1 p. f° (No. 3935.) ‡

—— Executive order [authorizing that beginning at 9 a. m., on Dec. 24, 1923, 4 hours, exclusive of time for luncheon, shall constitute a day's work for all clerks and other employees. including per diem employees, of Federal Government and government of District of Columbia, in District of Columbia]. Dec. 12, 1923. 1 p. f° (No. 3934.) ‡

McMillin, Frank E. Executive order [authorizing reinstatement of Frank E. McMillin to position of post-office inspector]. Dec. 19, 1923. 1 p. f° (No. 3937.) ‡

Message. Annual message of President of United States to joint session of Senate and House of Representatives, Dec. 6, 1923 [1st session, 68th Congress]. 1923. [2]+16 p. * Paper, 5c. 23—27466

—— Same. 1923. [2]+14 p. (H. doc. 1, 68th Cong. 1st sess.)

Plate printers. Executive order [authorizing that plate printers in Engraving and Printing Bureau, separated by reduction of force during first 10 months of 1923, may be transferred to other parts of classified civil service subject to appropriate examinations and to 3-year and other statutory requirements]. Dec. 19, 1923. 1 p. f° (No. 3936.) ‡

Wyoming. Executive order, Wyoming [revoking Executive order of Jan. 6, 1912, withdrawing certain described lands in Wyoming near Washakie National Forest (which embraces former Bonneville National Forest) for use by Forest Service as Geyser Springs ranger station, and authorizing that said lands be subject only to homestead and desert land entry by ex-service men of War with Germany for period of 91 days, after which remaining land may be open to general public under any public land law applicable thereto]. Nov. 23, 1923. 1 p. f° (No. 3933.) ‡

RAILROAD ADMINISTRATION

Atlanta and West Point Railroad. Final settlement between director general of railroads and Atlanta and West Point Railroad Company, —, 192–, 1923. 3 p. 4° †

Augusta and Summerville Railroad. Final settlement between director general of railroads and Augusta & Summerville Railroad Company, —, 192–. 1923. 3 p. 4° †

Cement. Before Interstate Commerce Commission. no. 14721, Utah *v.* director general et al.; no. 14721, sub. no. 1, Union Portland Cement Company *v.* [same]; brief on behalf of director general. 1923. cover-title, 13 p. ‡

Central Railroad of New Jersey. Final settlement between director general of railroads and Central Railroad Company of New Jersey, Dec. —, 1923. 1923. 3 p. 4° †

Chesapeake and Ohio Railway. Final settlement between director general of railroads and Chesapeake and Ohio Railway. Company and other corporations, Dec. —, 1923. 1923. 3 p. 4° †

Clay. Before Interstate Commerce Commission, no. 12461, Peninsular Portland Cement Co. *v.* director general et al.; petition for reargument before full commission. 1923. cover-title, 2 p. ‡

Demurrage. Before Interstate Commerce Commission, no. 14209, Mitsui and Company (Ltd.) *v.* director general et al.; no. 12725, United States Steel Products Company *v.* [same]; exceptions on behalf of director general to examiner's proposed report. 1923. cover-title, 30 p. ‡

Detroit, Bay City and Western Railroad. Final settlement between director general of railroads and Detroit Trust Company, receiver of Detroit, Bay City & Western Railroad Company, Dec. 10, 1923. 1923. 3 p. 4° †

Freight rates. Before Interstate Commerce Commission, no. 14765, McCloud River Lumber Company *v.* director general; exceptions to examiner's proposed report filed on behalf of director general. 1923. cover-title, 6 p. ‡

Georgia Railroad. Final settlement between director general of railroads and Louisville and Nashville Railroad Company and Atlantic Coast Line Railroad Company as joint lessees of Georgia Railroad, —, 192-. 1923. 3 p. 4° †

Leather, Imitation. Before Interstate Commerce Commission, no. 14889, Chevrolet Motor Company of California *v.* director general; brief on part of director general. 1923. cover-title, 9 p. ‡

Litchfield and Madison Railway. Final settlement between director general of railroads and Litchfield & Madison Railway Company, —, 192-. 1923. 3 p. 4° †

Minnesota Transfer Railway. Final settlement between director general of railroads and Minnesota Transfer Railway Company, Dec. —, 1923. 1923. 3 p. 4° †

Molasses. Before Interstate Commerce Commission, no. 14444, Wash-Co. Alfalfa Milling Company and L. W. Rice, trustee in bankruptcy for Wash-Co. Alfalfa Milling Company. *v.* director general; exceptions on behalf of director general to examiner's proposed report. 1923. cover-title, 12 p. ‡

New York and Long Branch Railroad. Final settlement between director general of railroads and New York and Long Branch Railroad Company, Dec.—, 1923. 1923. 3 p. 4° †

Sand. Before Interstate Commerce Commission, no. 13936, Richardson Sand Company *v.* director general et al.; exceptions on part of director general to report proposed by examiner. 1923. cover-title, 7 p. ‡

Steel. Before Interstate Commerce Commission, no. 14561, R. E. Givens *v.* director general; exceptions to examiner's proposed report filed on behalf of defendant. 1923. cover-title, 7 p. ‡

Stone. Before district court for eastern district of Oklahoma, cause no. 3775, law, Oklahoma Portland Cement Company *v.* James C. Davis, director general, agent of St. Louis-San Francisco Railroad Company; brief for defendant. 1923. cover-title, ii+44 p. ‡

Switching charges. Before Interstate Commerce Commission, no. 14805, Otto Krueger *v.* Northern Pacific Railway Company and director general, as agent; exceptions filed on behalf of director general to examiner's proposed report. 1923. cover-title, 7 p. ‡

Western Railway of Alabama. Final settlement between director general of railroads and Western Railway of Alabama, —, 192-. 1923. 3 p. 4° †

SHIPPING BOARD

Commerce. Report on volume of water-borne foreign commerce of United States by foreign ports of origin and destination, fiscal year 1922; [prepared in] Bureau of Research. 1923. pt. 2, xii leaves+111 p. oblong 8° [Part 2 shows commodity movement arranged by foreign ports; for pt. 1, showing movement by United States ports, see Monthly catalogue for May, 1923, p. 748.] * Paper, 20c. 23—26420

Report. 7th annual report of Shipping Board, fiscal year 1923. 1923. ix+204 p. 1 pl. † 18—26039

—— Same. (H. doc. 78, 68th Cong. 1st sess.)

SHIPPING BOARD EMERGENCY FLEET CORPORATION

Ships. Schedule of sailings of Shipping Board vessels in general cargo, passenger, and mail services, 1st of December [1923] to middle of January, 1924; issued by Traffic Department. 1923. cover-title, ii+14 p. il. [Monthly. Text on p. 2-4 of cover.] † 23—26331

SMITHSONIAN INSTITUTION

NOTE.—In a recent price-list the Smithsonian Institution publishes this notice: "Applicants for the publications in this list are requested to state the grounds of their requests, as the Institution is able to supply papers only as an aid to the researches or studies in which they are especially interested. These papers are distributed *gratis,* except as otherwise indicated, and should be ordered by the *publication numbers* arranged in sequence. The serial publications of the Smithsonian Institution are as follows: 1, Smithsonian contributions to knowledge; 2, Smithsonian miscellaneous collections; 3, Smithsonian annual reports. No *sets* of these are for sale or distribution, as most of the volumes are out of print. The papers issued in the series of Contributions to knowledge and Miscellaneous collections are distributed without charge to public libraries, educational establishments, learned societies, and specialists in this country and abroad: and are supplied to other institutions and individuals at the prices indicated. Remittances should be made payable to the 'Smithsonian Institution.' The Smithsonian report volumes and the papers reprinted in separate form therefrom are distributed *gratuitously* by the Institution to libraries and individuals throughout the world. Very few of the Report volumes are now available at the Institution, but many of those of which the Smithsonian edition is exhausted can be purchased from the Superintendent of Documents, Government Printing Office, Washington, D. C. The Institution maintains mailing-lists of public libraries and other educational establishments, but no *general mailing-list of individuals.* A library making application to be listed for Smithsonian publications should state the number of volumes which it contains and the date of its establishment, and have the endorsement of a Member of Congress."
The annual reports are the only Smithsonian publications that are regularly issued as public documents. All the others are paid for from the private funds of the Institution, but as they are usually regarded as public documents and have free transmission by mail they are listed in the Monthly catalogue.

International catalogue of scientific literature. Report of United States Regional Bureau of International Catalogue of Scientific Literature, fiscal year 1923. 1923. iii+111-113 p. [From Report, 1923.] † 15—29821

Mathematics. Smithsonian mathematical formulae and Tables of elliptic functions: Mathematical formulae [with bibliography], prepared by Edwin P. Adams; Tables of elliptic functions, prepared under direction of Sir George Greenhill by R. L. Hippisley. Washington, Smithsonian Institution. 1922 [published 1923]. viii+314 p. il. (Publication 2672; Smithsonian miscellaneous collections, v. 73 [74], no. 1.) [A printed figure 74 on gummed paper was sent out for use in correcting the title-page which read incorrectly. volume 73.] † Cloth, $3.00. 23—27471

Physics. Smithsonian physical tables; [by Thomas Gray]. 2d reprint [with changes and additions] of 7th revised edition, prepared by Frederick E. Fowle. Washington, Smithsonian Institution. 1923. xlvi+458+[1] p. il. (Publication 2539; Smithsonian miscellaneous collections, v. 71, no. 1.) † Cloth, $3.00. 23—27413

Reports. Annual report of board of regents of Smithsonian Institution, year ending June 30, 1923: [pt. 2] Report of National Museum. 1923. ix+205 p. 1 pl. ([Publication 2754.]) * Cloth, 50c. 4—18266

—— Same. (H. doc. 80, 68th Cong. 1st sess.)

—— Report of executive committee and proceedings of board of regents of Smithsonian Institution, year ending June 30, 1923. 1923. [1]+13 p. (Publication 2750.) † 10—18350

—— Report of secretary of Smithsonian Institution [with reports of subordinate bureaus, including library, and editor's report on publications issued] year ending June 30, 1923. 1923. iv+125 p. (Publication 2749.) † CA 18—3

ETHNOLOGY BUREAU

Publications. List of publications of Bureau of American Ethnology, with index to authors and titles. 1923. [1]+45 p. † 23—27414

NATIONAL GALLERY OF ART

Report on National Gallery of Art, including Freer Gallery of Art, year ending June 30, 1923. 1923. [2]+45–62 p. [From Smithsonian Institution report, 1923.] †

NATIONAL ZOOLOGICAL PARK

Report of superintendent of National Zoological Park, fiscal year 1923. 1923. [1]+87–104 p. [From Smithsonian Institution report, 1923.] † S 15—720a

STATE DEPARTMENT

[*Circulars*] 914–917; Oct. 31–Dec. 7, 1923. [1923.] various paging. [Nos. 914 and 917 are General instruction circulars to consular officers, and nos. 915 and 916 are Special instruction circulars to consular officers.] ‡

Claim of Government of Netherlands against United States, letter recommending appropriation to pay Arend Kamp and Francis Gort, subjects of Netherlands, for personal injuries sustained while U. S. S. Canibas was loading at Rotterdam. Dec. 20, 1923. 4 p. (S. doc. 11, 68th Cong. 1st sess.) * Paper, 5c.

Diplomatic list, Dec. 1923. [1923.] cover-title, ii+34 p. 24° [Monthly.] ‡
                                                                    10—16292

SUPREME COURT

Cases adjudged in Supreme Court at Oct. term, 1922, Jan. 30–Apr. 9, 1923; Ernest Knaebel, reporter. 1923. xlvii+676 p. il. (United States reports, v. 261.) [Also issued in 4 preliminary prints.] * Cloth, $2.50.

[*Journal*] Dec. 3–10, 1923; [slips] 34–39. [1923.] leaves 93–108. ‡

TREASURY DEPARTMENT

Bonds of United States. Cumulative sinking fund, report on cumulative sinking fund [fiscal year 1923]. Dec. 6, 1923. 9 p. (H. doc. 99, 68th Cong. 1st sess.) * Paper, 5c.

—— Extract from Regulations of Treasury Department with respect to United States bonds and notes (Treasury Department circular 300, dated July 31, 1923) : Extract 8, Assignments of registered bonds by corporations, unincorporated bodies, and partnerships.. [1923.] 4 p. 4° †

Certificates of indebtedness. United States of America, Treasury certificates of indebtedness, dated and bearing interest from Dec. 15, 1923, series TJ–1924, 4 per cent, due June 16, 1924, series TD–1924, 4¼ per cent, due Dec. 15, 1924. 1923. 1 p. 4° (Department circular 332; Loans and Currency [Division].) †

Finance. Daily statement of Treasury compiled from latest proved reports from Treasury offices and depositaries, Dec. 1–31, 1923. [1923–24.] Each 4 p. or 3 p. f° [Daily except Sundays and holidays.] †   15—3303

Government bonds. Obligations of foreign Governments, report on purchase of obligations of foreign Governments and purchase of United States bonds from repayments by foreign Governments. Dec. 6, 1923. 3 p. (H. doc. 98, 68th Cong. 1st sess.) * Paper, 5c.   23—27467

Loans. Expenses of loans, report on expenses of loans through fiscal year 1923. Dec. 6, 1923. 7 p. (H. doc. 97, 68th Cong. 1st sess.) * Paper, 5c.

Public debt. Statement of public debt of United States, Sept. 30, 1923. [1923.] [2] p. narrow f° [Monthly.] †   10—21268

Receipts and expenditures, and Refunding short-dated debt; extracts from Report of Secretary of Treasury on state of finances, fiscal year 1923. 1923. [1]+15 p. il. †

Report. Annual report of Secretary of Treasury on state of finances, fiscal year 1923. 1923. xi+580 p. il. (Treas. Dept. doc. 2925.) †   8—9648

Taxation; extract from Report of Secretary of Treasury on state of finances, fiscal year 1923. 1923. [1]+26 p. †

Treasury decisions under customs, internal revenue, and other laws, including decisions of Board of General Appraisers and Court of Customs Appeals, v. 44, no. 23–26; Dec. 6–27. 1923. 1923. various paging. [Weekly. Department decisions numbered 39898–929, general appraisers' decisions 8708–20, abstracts 46495–624, internal revenue decisions 3533–41, and later Tariff Commission Notices 18, 21–22, 24–25.]   * Paper, 5c. single copy, $1.00 a yr.; foreign subscription, $2.00.   10—30490

World War Foreign Debt Commission and obligations of foreign Governments; extract from Report of Secretary of Treasury on state of finances, fiscal year 1923. 1923. 29 p. †

APPRAISERS

Reappraisements of merchandise by general appraisers [on Nov. 26–Dec. 21, 1923]; Dec. 7–28, 1923. [1923–24.] various paging. (Reappraisement circulars 3486–89.) [Weekly.] * Paper, 5c. single copy, 50c. a yr.; foreign subscription, $1.05.   13—2916

BUDGET BUREAU

Appropriations. Message of President of United States transmitting budget for service of fiscal year 1925. 1923. ix+96+1024 p. 1 pl. 1 tab. 4° * Paper, $1.25.   21—27488

—— Same. (H. doc. 76, 68th Cong. 1st sess.)

—— Message of President of United States transmitting budget for service of fiscal year 1925, and Budget statements [fiscal year 1925]. 1923. ix+96 p. 1 pl. 1 tab. 4° [Message of transmittal and Budget statements only.] * Paper, 15c. (price incorrectly given in publication as $1.25).   22—27384

COAST GUARD

Cadets. Appointment of cadets and cadet engineers, regulations effective Dec. 1, 1923. 1923. 30 p. †   23—26218

Report. Annual report of Coast Guard, fiscal year 1923. 1923. v+50 p. (Treas. Dept. doc. 2931.) †   15—26648

COMPTROLLER OF CURRENCY

National banks. Monthly statement of capital stock of national banks, national bank notes, and Federal reserve bank notes outstanding, bonds on deposit, etc. [Dec. 1, 1923]. Dec. 1, 1923. 1 p. f° †   10—21266

Report. Text of annual report of comptroller of currency, Dec. 3, 1923. 1923. v+155 p. (Treas. Dept. doc. 2935.) [Report covers year ended Oct. 31, 1923.] †   10—11566

ENGRAVING AND PRINTING BUREAU

Report. Annual report of director of Bureau of Engraving and Printing, fiscal year 1923. 1923. ii+31 p. (Treas. Dept. doc. 2927.) †   CA 5—1360

FEDERAL FARM LOAN BUREAU

Agricultural credit. Amendments to Federal farm loan act, with comments and notes by Farm Loan Board. Nov. 1923. ii+15 p. (Circular 11.) * Paper, 5c.   23—27415

GENERAL SUPPLY COMMITTEE

Government supplies. Specifications and proposals for supplies [fiscal year 1925]: class 4, Drugs and medicines, and chemicals. [1923.] 32 p. 4° †

—— Same: class 12, Photographic supplies, meteorological instruments, towers, etc., and meat-inspection supplies. [1923.] 28 p. 4° †

—— Supplements to general schedule of supplies, fiscal year 1924. [1923.] 22 p. 4° [Includes 1st supplements to class 1, 6, and 17, 2d supplement to class 9, 4th supplement to class 8, Jan. 1–June 30, 1924.] †

GOVERNMENT ACTUARY

Bonds of United States. Market prices and investment values of outstanding bonds and notes [of United States, Nov. 1923]. Dec. 1, 1923. 7 p. 4° (Form A.) [Monthly.] †

INTER-AMERICAN HIGH COMMISSION

Program of activities of Inter American High Commission, Oct. 22, 1923. 1923. v+63 p. 1 tab. [English and Spanish.] ‡　　　　　　23—27416

Reports. Inter American High Commission, United States Section, reports of secretary submitted Jan. 10 and Oct. 22, 1923. 1923. v+78 p. [English and Spanish.] †　　　　　　　　　　　　　　23—27417

INTERNAL REVENUE BUREAU

Internal revenue bulletin, v. 2, no. 35–39; Dec. 3–31, 1923. 1923. various paging. [Weekly.] * Paper, 5c. single copy (for subscription price see note below).
　　　　　　　　　　　　　　　　　　　　　　　22—26051

Note.—On May 7, 1923, the publication of weekly bulletins was resumed and the issuance of monthly bulletins (and special bulletins as occasion required) discontinued. Since May 1, therefore, the 1923 Internal revenue bulletin service consists of weekly bulletins of new rulings and decisions of the Bureau of Internal Revenue and internal revenue Treasury decisions of general importance, quarterly digests of such new rulings (cumulative from Jan. 1, 1922), and semiannual cumulative bulletins containing in full the new rulings and decisions published during the preceding 6 months. The complete bulletin service may be obtained, on a subscription basis, from the Superintendent of Documents, Government Printing Office, Washington, D. C., for $2.00 a yr.; foreign subscription, $2.75.

Report. Annual report of commissioner of internal revenue, fiscal year 1923 [with statistical tables]. 1923. vii+215 p. (Treas. Dept. doc. 2929.) * Cloth, 60c.　　　　　　　　　　　　　　　　　　　9—35242

—— Same. (H. doc. 71, 68th Cong. 1st sess.)

LOANS AND CURRENCY DIVISION

Bonds of United States. Caveat list of United States registered bonds and notes, Dec. 1, 1923. [1923.] 56 p. f° [Monthly.] †

Money. Circulation statement of United States money, Dec. 1, 1923. [1923.] 1 p. oblong 8° [Monthly.] †　　　　　　　　　　　10—21267

MINT BUREAU

Money. The world's monetary stocks and production of gold and silver [1921 and 1922]. 1923. [1]+221–236 p. [From Report, 1923.] †

Report. Annual report of director of mint, fiscal year 1923, including Report on production of precious metals, calendar year 1922. 1923. 248 p. 1 pl. (Treas. Dept. doc. 2928.) * Cloth, 50c.　　　　　　　9—34686

PUBLIC HEALTH SERVICE

General information. United States Public Health Service, information for persons desiring to enter regular corps of service; [by R. C. Williams]. Edition of 1923. 1923. [1]+12 p. 6 p. of pl. (Reprint 719.) [Original article from Public health reports, Dec. 23, 1921.] * Paper, 5c.　23—27418

Hookworm disease. Campaign against hookworm in province of Cebu, Philippine Islands. 1923. 4 p. (Reprint 875.) [From Public health reports, Oct. 12, 1923.] * Paper, 5c.　　　　　　　　　　23—27419

Official list of commissioned and other officers of Public Health Service, also list of marine hospitals, quarantine, immigration, relief stations, and quarantine vessels, July 1, 1923. 1923. v+86 p. (Miscellaneous publication 11.) * Paper, 10c.　　　　　　　　　　　　　　　　6—40500

Public health reports, v. 38, no. 49–52; Dec. 7–28, 1923. 1923. [xvi]+2877–3154 p. il. 1 pl. 2 p. of pl. [Weekly.] * Paper, 5c. single copy, $1.50 a yr.; foreign subscription, $2.75. 6—25167

SPECIAL ARTICLES.—No. 49. Epidemiological study of folliculosis of conjunctiva [with list of references] ; by Milton V. Veldee.—Tuberculosis mortality in Colorado [1908–20].—Vital statistics for England and Wales, 1922.—Automobile fatalities in United States, 1917–22.—No. 50. Cooperative rural health work of Public Health Service, fiscal year 1923 ; by L. L. Lumsden.—Studies on permeability of living and dead cells ; 4, Penetration of trivalent and pentavalent arsenic into living and dead cells [with list of references] ; by Matilda Moldenhauer Brooks.—Death rates in registration area, 1922.—No. 51. Preliminary note on observations made on physical condition of persons engaged in measuring radium preparations [with bibliography] ; by R. C. Williams.—Program for oral hygiene in public schools of Minneapolis, Minn.; by F. E. Harrington.—Mortality from cancer, United States registration area, 1922.—Mortality from tuberculosis, United States registration area, 1922.—No. 52. Biological products, establishments licensed for propagation and sale of viruses, serums, toxins, and analogous products.—Current court decisions pertaining to public health.

NOTE.—This publication is distributed gratuitously to State and municipal health officers, etc., by the Surgeon General of the Public Health Service, Treasury Department. Others desiring these reports may obtain them from the Superintendent of Documents, Washington, D. C., at the prices stated above.

Publications. Public Health Service publications, list of publications issued Apr.–Oct. 1923. 1923. 4 p. (Reprint 880.) [From Public health reports, Nov. 9, 1923.] * Paper, 5c. 23—27420

Report. Annual report of surgeon general of Public Health Service, fiscal year 1923. 1923. vi+316 p. il. (Treas. Dept. doc. 2933.) * Cloth, 75c. 6—5954

—— Same. (H. doc. 83, 68th Cong. 1st sess.)

VENEREAL DISEASES DIVISION

Adolescence and sex education, exhibit for high school teachers; prepared by Public Health Service : [posters] 1–34 [in 5 parts]. [1923.] Each 12 × 9 in. †

pt. 1. Problems of adolescence; [posters] 2–6.
pt. 2. Fruits of ignorance; [posters] 7–12.
pt. 3. Scope of sex education; [posters] 13–20.
pt. 4. Sex education in courses of study; [posters] 21–29.
pt. 5. Teacher and his training [with lists of selected readings; posters] 30–34.

Venereal disease information. venereal disease information, issued by Public Health Service for use in its cooperative work with State health departments, v. 4, no. 11 ; Nov. 20, 1923. 1923. ii+435–494+iv p. il. [Monthly.] * Paper, 5c. single copy, 50c. a yr.; foreign subscription. 75c.

SPECIAL ARTICLES.—Incidence of venereal disease at different ages, study of 23,170 separate case reports of syphilis and gonorrhea in New York State, exclusive of New York City ; by Jos. S. Lawrence and Russell B. Tewksbury.—Present status of treatment of gonorrhea [with list of references] ; by E. A. Daus.—Venereal diseases in Germany [continued] ; by Dr. Berger.

—— Same, v. 4, no. 12 ; Dec. 20, 1923. 1923. ii+495–550+iii p. [Monthly.]

SPECIAL ARTICLES.—Psychoses with cerebral syphilis ; by Paul E. Bowers.—Enforcement of regulations relating to interstate travel of venereally infected persons.—Venereal diseases in United States, number of cases of venereal diseases reported to State boards of health for 3 months, July 1–Sept. 30. 1923.—Standards of infectivity pertaining to venereal diseases [adopted by State director of public health of Illinois].

Venereal diseases. Outdoing the ostrich, pamphlet for good citizens. [Reprint] 1923. 10 p. narrow 12° ([V. D. 62.]) †

REGISTER OF TREASURY

Report. Annual report of register of Treasury, fiscal year 1923. 1923. iv+54 p. il. 5 pl. (Treas. Dept. doc. 2930.) * Paper, 10c. 10—11514

TAX SIMPLIFICATION BOARD

Report of Tax Simplification Board, letter transmitting report as to recommendations made to bureau, condition of work, and recommendations as to legislation regarding simplification of administration of internal revenue laws [Dec. 3, 1923]. Dec. 10, 1923. 20 p. (H. doc. 103, 68th Cong. 1st sess.) * Paper, 5c. 22—27395

TREASURER OF UNITED STATES

District of Columbia. 46th annual report of treasurer of United States on sinking fund and funded debt of District of Columbia, fiscal year 1923. 1923. [2]+14 p. (Treas. Dept. doc. 2934.) †   8—10350

Report. Annual report of treasurer of United States, fiscal year 1923. 1923. vi+47 p. (Treas. Dept. doc. 2932.) †   8—9968

VETERANS' BUREAU

Report. Annual report of director, Veterans' Bureau, fiscal year 1923. 1923. xxiv+1082 p. il. 8 pl. map, 3 tab. * Paper, $1.00.   22—27396

—— Same. (H. doc. 87, 68th Cong. 1st sess.)

WAR DEPARTMENT

Army regulations. †

NOTE.—The Army regulations are issued in pamphlet form for insertion in loose-leaf binders. The names of such of the more important administrative subjects as may seem appropriate, arranged in proper sequence, are numbered in a single series, and each name so numbered constitutes the title and number of a pamphlet containing certain administrative regulations pertaining thereto. Where more than one pamphlet is required for the administrative regulations pertaining to any such title, additional pamphlets will be issued in a separate sub-series.

1–10. Army regulations: List of current pamphlets and changes, distribution; Oct. 1, 1923. [1923.] 9 p. [Supersedes AR 1–10, Mar. 31, 1923.]
10–15. General Staff: Organization and general duties, Changes 4; Oct. 26, 1923. [1923.] 2 p. [Supersedes AR 10–15, Changes 1–3, June 7–Nov. 15, 1922.]
30–1195. Quartermaster Corps: Transportation of individuals on transports, Changes 3; Nov. 9, 1923. 1923. 1 p. [Supersedes AR 30–1195, Changes 1 and 2, Feb. 1 and Oct. 9, 1923.]
35–820. Finance Department: Payments of expenses and refunds in connection with sales of public property; Dec. 1, 1923. [1923.] 3 p. [Supersedes AR 35–820, Mar. 24, 1922.]
35–2320. Same: Payments to enlisted men, general provisions; Oct. 2, 1923. [1923.] 6 p.
35–2340. Same: Pay of enlisted men, rates of pay; Oct. 2, 1923. [1923.] 3 p.
35–2400. Same: Pay of enlisted men, specialist rating; Oct. 2, 1923. [1923.] 2 p.
35–2420. Same: Pay of enlisted men, enlistment allowance; Oct. 2, 1923. [1923.] 5 p.
35–3070. Same: Payments to cadets, Military Academy; Sept. 21, 1923. [1923.] 2 p.
35–6120. Same: Payment of transportation accounts; July 20, 1923. [1923.] 4 p. [Supersedes AR 35–6120, Mar. 31, 1922.]
40–215. Medical Department: Prevention of communicable diseases of man, immunization, Changes 1; Nov. 28. 1923. 1923. 1 p.
40–235. Same: Prevention of communicable diseases of man, venereal diseases, Changes 1; Oct. 22, 1923. 1923. 1 p.
45–30. Ordnance Department: Ordnance field service in time of peace; Sept. 10, 1923. [1923.] 6 p.
90–150. Coast Artillery Corps: Army mine planters, general, Changes 2; Oct. 2. 1923. [1923.] 3 p. [Supersedes AR 90–150, Changes 1, Sept. 1, 1922.]
90–155. Same: Assignment, control, and use of Army mine planters; Oct. 2, 1923. [1923.] 2 p. [Supersedes AR 90–155, Jan. 21, 1922.]
100–15. Corps of Engineers: Maps and mapping, Changes 1; Nov. 5, 1923. 1923. 1 p.
310–200. Military publications: War Department publications, including binders therefor, and blank forms (A. G. O.), allowance and distribution of; Nov. 12, 1923. [1923.] 7 p. [Supersedes AR 310–200, June 2, 1922.]

Organization. Department of War. [1923.] 10 p. [Information concerning organization of Department reprinted from the 1st edition, Dec. 1923, of 68th Congress, 1st session, official Congressional directory.] ii‡

Report of Secretary of War, [fiscal year] 1923. 1923. i +187 p. il. 5 tab. †
     8—15847

Training regulations.

NOTE.—The Training regulations are issued in pamphlet form for insertion in loose-leaf binders.

150–40. Marksmanship: 37-mm. gun and 3-inch trench mortar, prepared under direction of chief of infantry; June 22, 1923. [1923.] 39 p. il. * Paper, 5c.
190–15. Topography and surveying: Military sketching, prepared under direction of chief of engineers; June 21, 1923. [1923.] 39 p. il. * Paper, 10c.
190–25. Same: Topographic drafting, prepared under direction of chief of engineers; June 21, 1923. [1923.] 23 p. il. * Paper, 5c.
190–30. Same: Use of map in firing, prepared under direction of chief of engineers; June 21, 1923. [1923.] 32 p. il. 1 pl. * Paper, 10c.
435–85. Coast Artillery Corps: Machine-gun battery, antiaircraft artillery, prepared under direction of chief of coast artillery; July 24, 1923. [1923.] 23 p. il. *Paper, 5c.
435–110. Same: Battalion (gun) antiaircraft artillery, prepared under direction of chief of coast artillery; July 31, 1923. [1923.] 7 p. il. * Paper, 5c.

ADJUTANT GENERAL'S DEPARTMENT

Message center specialist, instructors guide for all arms; prepared under direction of chief signal officer, 1923. 1923. ix+318 p. il. (United States Army training manual 25.) ‡

U. S. Army recruiting news, bulletin of recruiting information issued by direction of Adjutant General of Army, Dec. 1 and 15, 1923. [Recruiting Publicity Bureau, Governors Island. N. Y., Dec. 1 and 15, 1923.] Each 16 p. il. 4°
† Recruiting Publicity Bureau, Governors Island, N. Y.   War 22—1

AIR SERvICE

Aeronautical bulletins. Aeronautical bulletin, no. 15, 29–33, 35–37, 40–52, Route information series; Sept. 15–Nov. 1, 1923. [1923.] various paging, 12° (Airways Section.) *Paper, 5c. each,   23—26231

—— Aeronautical bulletin, no. 71–86, State series; Nov. 1, 1923. [1923.] Each 2 p. il. 12° (Airways Section.) *Paper, 5c. each.

ENGINEER DEPARTMENT

Floating plant. Statement of floating plant owned by United States and employed in Engineer Department at Large, calendar year 1922. 1923. iii+ 345 p. [Extract from annual report of chief of engineers, 1923.] *Cloth, 55c.

Flushing Bay. Harbor at Flushing Bay, N. Y., advertisement [for dredging]. [1923.] 14 p. 4° †

Report. Report of chief of engineers, [fiscal year] 1923. 1923. [1]+2107+ xxxviii p. map. *Cloth, $2.00.   9—6836

—— Same [with Commercial statistics of water-borne commerce and Statement of floating plant, calendar year 1922]. 1923. 3 pts. [xi]+2107+1425 +345+xxxviii p. map. *Cloth, pt. 1, $2.00; pt. 2, $1.50; pt. 3, 55c.   9—6836

pt. 1. Annual report of chief of engineers. [i] + 2107 + xxxviii p. map.
pt. 2. Commercial statistics [of water-borne commerce], calendar year 1922; compiled by Statistical Division, Board of Engineers for Rivers and Harbors. vii + 1425 p.
pt. 3. Statement of floating plant owned by United States and employed in Engineer Department at Large, calendar year 1922. iii + 345 p.

—— Same. (H. doc. 60 [3 pts.], 68th Cong. 1st sess.)

NORTHERN AND NORTHWESTERN LAKES SURVEY

NOTE.—Charts of the Great Lakes and connecting waters and St. Lawrence River to the international boundary at St. Regis, of Lake Champlain, and of the New York State canals are prepared and sold by the U. S. Lake Survey Office, Old Custom-house, Detroit, Mich. Charts may also be purchased at the following U. S. engineer offices : 710 Army Building, New York, N. Y. ; 467 Broadway, Albany, N. Y .; 540 Federal Building, Buffalo, N. Y.; and Canal Office, Sault Ste. Marie, Mich. A catalogue (with index map), showing localities, scales, prices, and conditions of sale, may be had upon application at any of these offices.
A descriptive bulletin, which supplements the charts and gives detailed information as to harbors, shore lines and shoals, magnetic determinations, and particulars of changing conditions affecting navigation, is issued free to chart purchasers, upon request. The bulletin is revised annually and issued at the opening of navigation (in April), and supplements thereto are published monthly during the navigation season.
Complete sets of the charts and publications may be seen at the U. S. engineer offices in Duluth, Minn., Milwaukee, Wis., Chicago, Ill., Grand Rapids. Mich., Cleveland, Ohio, and Oswego, N. Y., but they are obtainable only at the sales offices above mentioned.

Charts

Les Cheneaux Islands and northeasterly approaches to Straits of Mackinac. from Beaver Tail Reef to St. Martin Bay, including Mackinac and Round islands and northerly shore of Bois Blanc Island. Scale 1 : 40.000. 4th edition. [U. S. Lake Survey Office, Detroit, Mich.] Dec. 7. 1923. 28.3 × 41.4 in. † 25c.

RIVERS AND HARBORS BOARD

Commercial statistics [of water-borne commerce], calendar year 1922; compiled by Statistical Division, Board of Engineers for Rivers and Harbors. 1923. vii+1425 p. [Extract from annual report of chief of engineers, 1923.] * Cloth, $1.50.   22—18731

Shore control and port administration, investigation of status of national, State, and municipal authority over port affairs: pt. 1, Control of the port [study of legal phases of public administration of port traffic and water-front property], by Edmund Brown, jr.; pt. 2, Organization and duties of administrative bodies at ports of United States. 1923. xii+232 p. * Paper, 30c.   23—27464

FINANCE DEPARTMENT

Finance circulars. Changes 2 and 3 [to] Finance circulars; June 12 and Nov. 22, 1923. [1923.] Each 2 leaves, 12° [Changes 3 is an advance copy.] ‡
—— Finance circular 9 and 10 [1923]; Sept. 30 and Oct. 31, 1923. [1923.] 4 p. and 8 p. 12° ‡

GENERAL SERVICE SCHOOLS

Report. Annual report of Major General H. E. Ely, commandant, General Service Schools, Fort Leavenworth, Kans., [Sept. 12, 1922–June 30] 1923. General Service Schools Press, Fort Leavenworth, Kans., [Nov. 10] 1923. 77 p. 2 pl. †

GENERAL STAFF CORPS

Special regulations. Changes 1 and 2 [for] Special regulations 53 [Examination and classification of gunners of field artillery, 1921] ; July 2 and Oct. 10, 1923. 1923. 1 p. and 8 leaves. [Special regulations issued by War Department.] †

INLAND AND COASTWISE WATERWAYS SERVICE

Report. Annual report of chief of Inland and Coastwise Waterways Service, fiscal year 1923. 1923. [1]+75 p. †

INSULAR AFFAIRS BUREAU

Filipinos in United States. Philippine Government students; [prepared by W. W. Marquardt, Philippine educational agent, and revised by Georgia S. Williams, secretary]. 1923. ii+12 p. ‡
Report of chief of Bureau of Insular Affairs, [fiscal year] 1923. 1923. [1]+ 15 p. †

MEDICAL DEPARTMENT

Report of surgeon general, Army, [fiscal year] 1923 [with statistical tables for calendar year 1922]. 1923. x+393 p. il. †   6—35357

MILITIA BUREAU

Report. Annual report of chief of Militia Bureau, [fiscal year] 1923. 1923 iv+65 p. 4 tab. †   War 10—1

ORDNANCE DEPARTMENT

Ordnance. American coast artillery matériel, June, 1922 [with bibliography]. 1923. vii+513 p. il. 1 pl. (Ordnance Dept. doc. 2042.) * Cloth, $1.00.
                                                                    War 24—1

PHILIPPINE ISLANDS

Governor general. Annual report of governor general of Philippine Islands, message from President of United States transmitting annual report of governor general of Philippine Islands, with reports of heads of departments of Philippine Government, fiscal year ended Dec. 31, 1922. 1923. iv+66 p. (H. doc. 118, 68th Cong. 1st sess.) [Message of transmittal and annual report of governor general only.] * Paper, 10c.   23—6553

PORTO RICO

Governor. 23d annual report of governor of Porto Rico, message from President of United States transmitting 23d annual report of governor of Porto Rico, with reports of heads of the several departments of Porto Rican Government, also that of auditor, fiscal year 1923. 1923. iii+40 p. (H. doc. 117, 68th Cong. 1st sess.) [Message of transmittal and annual report of governor only.] * Paper, 5c. 6—35095

SIGNAL OFFICE

Orders 28–29, 31 [1923] ; Oct. 17–Nov. 10, 1923. 1923. Each 1 p. 12° ‡

WAR FINANCE CORPORATION

Report. 6th annual report of War Finance Corporation, year ended Nov. 30, 1923. 1923. [2]+20 p. † 19—26060

—— Same. (H. doc. 116, 68th Cong. 1st sess.)

O

Monthly Catalogue
United States
Public Documents

No. 349

January, 1924

UNIVERSITY CF ILLINOIS LIBRARY

APR 1 1924

ISSUED BY THE
SUPERINTENDENT OF DOCUMENTS

WASHINGTON
1924

Abbreviations

Appendix	app.	Page, pages	p.
Congress	Cong.	Part, parts	pt., pts.
Department	Dept.	Plate, plates	pl.
Document	doc.	Portrait, portraits	por.
Facsimile, facsimiles	facsim.	Quarto	4°
Folio	f°	Report	rp.
House	H.	Saint	St.
House bill	H. R.	Section, sections	sec.
House concurrent resolution	H. Con. Res.	Senate, Senate bill	S.
House document	H. doc.	Senate concurrent resolution	S. Con. Res.
House executive document	H. ex. doc.	Senate document	S. doc.
House joint resolution	H. J. Res.	Senate executive document	S. ex. doc.
House report	H. rp.	Senate joint resolution	S. J. Res.
House resolution (simple)	H. Res.	Senate report	S. rp.
Illustration, illustrations	il.	Senate resolution (simple)	S. Res.
Inch, inches	in.	Session	sess.
Latitude	lat.	Sixteenmo	16°
Longitude	long.	Table, tables	tab.
Mile, miles	m.	Thirtytwo-mo	32°
Miscellaneous	mis., misc.	Treasury	Treas.
Nautical	naut.	Twelvemo	12°
No date	n. d.	Twentyfour-mo	24°
No place	n. p.	Versus	vs., v.
Number, numbers	no., nos.	Volume, volumes	v., vol.
Octavo	8°	Year	yr.

Common abbreviations for names of States and months are also used.
*Document for sale by Superintendent of Documents.
†Distribution by office issuing document, free if unaccompanied by a price.
‡Printed for official use.
NOTE.—Nearly all of the Departments of the Government make a limited free distribution of their publications. When an entry shows a * price, it is possible that upon application to the issuing office a copy may be obtained without charge.

Explanation

Words and figures inclosed in brackets [ ] are given for information, but do not appear on the title-pages of the publications catalogued. When size is not given octavo is to be understood. Size of maps is measured from outer edge of border, excluding margin. The dates, including day, month, and year, given with Senate and House documents and reports are the dates on which they were ordered to be printed. Usually the printing promptly follows the ordering, but various causes sometimes make delays.

SALES OF GOVERNMENT PUBLICATIONS

The Superintendent of Documents, Washington, D. C., is authorized to sell at cost, plus 10 per cent, without limit as to the number of copies to any one applicant who agrees not to resell or distribute the same for profit, any United States Government publication not confidential in character.

Publications can not be supplied free to individuals nor forwarded in advance of payment.

Publications entered in this catalogue that are for sale by the Superintendent of Documents are indicated by a star (*) preceding the price. A dagger (†) indicates that application should be made to the Department, Bureau, or Division issuing the document. A double dagger (‡) indicates that the document is printed for official use. Whenever additional information concerning the method of procuring a document seems necessary, it will be found under the name of the Bureau by which it was published.

In ordering a publication from the Superintendent of Documents, give (if known) the name of the publishing Department, Bureau, or Division, and the title of the publication. If the publication is numbered, give the number also. Every such particular assists in quick identification. Do not order by the Library of Congress card number.

The accumulation of publications in this Office amounts to several millions, of which over two million are assorted, forming the sales stock. Many rare books are included, but under the law all must be sold regardless of their age or scarcity. Many of the books have been in stock some time, and are apt to be shop-worn. In filling orders the best copy available is sent. A general price-list of public documents is not available, but lists on special subjects will be furnished on application.

MONTHLY CATALOGUE DISTRIBUTION

The Monthly catalogue is sent to each Senator, Representative, Delegate, Resident Commissioner, and officer in Congress; to designated depositories and State and Territorial libraries if it is selected by them; to substantially all Government authors; and to as many school, college, and public libraries as the limited edition will supply.

Subscription price to individuals, 50c. a year, including index; foreign subscription, 75c. a year. Back numbers can not be supplied. Notify the Superintendent of Documents of any change of address.

LIBRARY OF CONGRESS CARDS

Numbers to be used in ordering the printed catalogue cards of the Library of Congress are given at the end of entries for the more important documents. Orders for these cards, remittances in payment for them, and requests for information about them should be addressed to the Librarian of Congress, *not* to the Superintendent of Documents.

INDEX

An Index to the Monthly catalogue is issued at the end of the fiscal year. This contains index entries for all the numbers issued from July to June, and can be

bound with the numbers as an index to the volume.   Persons desiring to bind the catalogue at the end of the year should be careful to retain the numbers received monthly, as duplicate copies can not be supplied.

HOW TO REMIT

Remittances for the documents marked with a star (*) should be made to the **Superintendent of Documents, Washington, D. C.**, by coupons, postal money order, express order, or New York draft.   Currency may be sent at sender's risk.

Postage stamps, foreign money, defaced or smooth coins, positively will not be accepted.

For the convenience of the general public, coupons that are good until used in exchange for Government publications sold by the Superintendent of Documents may be purchased from his Office in sets of 20 for $1.00.   Address order to Superintendent of Documents, Government Printing Office, Washington, D. C.

No charge is made for postage on documents forwarded to points in United States, Alaska, Guam, Hawaii, Philippine Islands, Porto Rico, Samoa, or to Canada, Cuba, or Mexico.   To other countries the regular rate of postage is charged, and remittances must cover such postage.   In computing foreign postage, add one-third of the price of the publication.

Monthly Catalogue

AGRICULTURE DEPARTMENT

NOTE.—Those publications of the Department of Agriculture which are for sale will be supplied by the Superintendent of Documents, Washington, D. C. The Department issues a monthly list of publications, which is mailed to all applicants, enabling them to select such reports and bulletins as interest them.

Accounts. Fiscal regulations of Department of Agriculture [effective Oct. 1, 1922, amendments and reprints]. 1923. iii p. 12° [Accompanied by re-·· prints of 20 variously numbered pages to be inserted in their proper places in the original publication.] ‡

Bacterial leafspot of clovers [with list of literature cited] ; by L. R. Jones, Maude M. Williamson, F. A. Wolf, and Lucia McCulloch. 1923. cover-title, 471–490+[5] p.+[1] leaf, il. 6 p. of pl. [Contribution from Wisconsin and North Carolina Agricultural Experiment Stations and Plant Industry Bureau. From Journal of agricultural research, v. 25, no. 12, Sept. 22, 1923.] ‡

Cattle. [Bureau of Animal Industry] order 273 revised, regulations governing interstate movement of live stock, effective July 1, 1921 [with amendments]. [1923.] 35 p. [Supersedes previous regulations and includes amendment 1, effective Mar. 1, 1922, and amendment 2, effective July 23, 1923.] †

Corticium vagum. Soil temperature as factor affecting pathogenicity of Corticium vagum on pea and bean [with list of literature cited] ; by B. L. Richards. 1923. cover-title, 431–450+[1] p. il. 2 p. of pl. [From Journal of agricultural research, v. 25, no. 11, Sept. 15, 1923.] ‡

Cotton-seed meal. Effect of autoclaving upon toxicity of cottonseed meal; by C. T. Dowell and Paul Menaul. [1923.] p. 9–10. [From Journal of agricultural research, v. 26, no. 1, Oct. 6, 1923.] ‡

Crop report regulations, regulations governing publication of reports and information utilized in compilation of reports, prepared by Bureau of Agricultural Economics, concerning acreages, conditions, yields, farm reserves, or quality of products of soil grown within United States, effective Jan. 1, 1924. Dec. 1923. 4 p. (Miscellaneous circular 20.) [Publication has rubber-stamp correction and note to the effect that the report on intentions to plant Mar. 18, will not include cotton.] ‡

Crops and markets. Crops and markets, weekly, Jan. 5–26, 1924; v. 1, no. 1–4. [1924.] p. 1–64, il. 4° * Paper, $1.00 a yr.; foreign subscription, $2.00 (including monthly supplement). Agr 24—113

NOTE.—This publication continues the weekly formerly entitled Weather, crops, and markets. With this issue the weekly weather review is discontinued and will not appear in this publication hereafter, but the information will be distributed in another form to those ·particularly interested who will make application to the Weather Bureau, Washington, D. C. The weekly issues of Crops and markets will be sent on special request to crop reporters only when necessary to their work.

—— Same, monthly supplement, Jan. 1924; v. 1, supplement 1. [1924.] 40 p. il. 4° [Included in price of weekly Crops and markets.]

NOTE.—The monthly supplement, containing crop reports and monthly statistical summaries, will be issued about the 3d week each month. It will be distributed free only to crop reporters and other cooperators, as provided by the law and regulations.

Journal of agricultural research, v. 26, no. 5–8; Nov. 3–24, 1923. 1923–24. cover-titles, 195–382+[16] p.+[9] leaves, il. 5 pl. 24 p. of pl. [Weekly. Text on p. 2 of covers.] * Paper, 10c. single copy, $4.00 a yr.; foreign subscription, $5.25. Agr 13—1837

CONTENTS.—No. 5. Influence of soil temperature and moisture on infection of wheat seedlings by Helminthosporium sativum [with list of literature cited]; by H. H. McKinney.—Five molds and their penetration into wood [with list of literature cited]; by Eloise Gerry.—Common earthenware jars source of error in pot experiments; by J. S. McHargue.—Physiological effect of gossypol [with list of literature cited]; by Paul Menaul.—Iron content of blood and spleen in infectious equine anemia; by Lewis H. Wright.—No. 6. Further observations on osmotic pressure of juices of potato plant; by B. F. Lutman.—Method for quantitative estimation of tannin in plant tissue; by Paul Menaul.—Chemical analysis of Jatropha stimulosa; by Paul Menaul.—Varietal resistance in winter wheat to rosette disease; by R. W. Webb, C. E. Leighty, G. H. Dungan, and J. B. Kendrick.—Two diseases of udo (Aralia cordata Thunb.) [with list of literature cited]; by J. L. Weimer.—No. 7. Biological notes on termites of Canal Zone and adjoining parts of Republic of Panama [with list of literature cited]; by Harry Frederic Dietz and Thomas Elliott Snyder.—Absorption of carbon by roots of plants; by J. F. Breazeale.—Oak sapling borer. Goes tesselatus Haldeman; by Fred E. Brooks.—Bud selection as related to quantity production in Washington navel orange; by A. D. Shamel, C. S. Pomeroy, and R. E. Caryl.—No. 8. Compounds developed in rancid fats, with observations on mechanism of their formation [with list of literature cited]: by Wilmer C. Powick.—Some physiological variations in strains of Rhizopus nigricans [with list of literature cited]; by L. L. Harter and J. L. Weimer.—Preparation and properties of colloidal arsenate of lead; by F. J. Brinley.—Active chlorin as germicide for milk and milk products; by Harrison Hale and William L. Bleecker.

NOTE.—This publication is published by authority of the Secretary of Agriculture. with the cooperation of the Association of Land-Grant Colleges. It is distributed free only to libraries of agricultural colleges and experiment stations, to large universities, technical schools, and to such institutions as make suitable exchanges with the Agriculture Department. Others desiring the Journal may obtain it from the Superintendent of Documents, Washington, D. C., at the prices stated above.

Leaves. Some observations on temperature of leaves of crop plants [with list of literature cited]; by Edwin C. Miller and A. R. Saunders. 1923. cover-title, p. 15–43, il. [From Journal of agricultural research, v. 26, no. 1, Oct. 6, 1923.] ‡

Official record, Department of Agriculture, v. 3, no. 1–5; Jan. 2–30, 1924. [1924.] Each 8 p. 4° [Weekly.] * Paper, 50c. a yr.; foreign subscription, $1.10.
Agr 22—146

Quarantine. Modification of quarantine on account of European corn borer and other dangerous insects and plant diseases. Amendment 2 to regulations supplemental to Notice of quarantine 41 (revised), effective Nov. 30, 1923. [1923.] 2 p. (Federal Horticultural Board.) †

Sodium nitrite. Action of sodium nitrite in soil [with list of literature cited]; by R. H. Robinson. [1923.] p. 1–7. [From Journal of agricultural research, v. 26, no. 1, Oct. 6, 1923.] ‡

Soils. Auxotaxic curve as means of classifying soils and studying their colloidal properties; by A. E. Vinson and C. N. Catlin. [1923.] p. 11–13, il. [From Journal of agricultural research, v. 26, no. 1, Oct. 6, 1923.] ‡

AGRICULTURAL ECONOMICS BUREAU

Bookkeeping. Farm bookkeeping [with Selected list of references on farm business analysis, by Edward H. Thomson; revised by James S. Ball]. [Oct. 1912, revised June. 1920, corrected Dec. 1923.] [1923.] 43 p. il. (Agriculture Dept. Farmers' bulletin 511.) * Paper, 5c.

Cotton. Commercial classification of American cotton with reference to standards for grade, color. and staple; [by] Arthur W. Palmer. Jan. 1924. 35 p. il. 4 p. of pl. (Agriculture Dept. Department circular 278.) * Paper, 10c.
Agr 24—107

Family living in farm homes. economic study of 402 farm families in Livingston County, N. Y.; by E. L. Kirkpatrick, Helen W. Atwater, and Ilena M. Bailey. Jan. 1924. cover-title, 36 p. (Agriculture Dept. Department bulletin 1214.) [Prepared in cooperation with Home Economics Bureau and New York State College of Agriculture.] * Paper, 5c. Agr 24—104

Farms. Buying a farm in undeveloped region; [by] B. Henderson]. [Jan. 1924.] ii+30 p. il. (Agriculture Dept. Farmers' bulletin 1385.) * Paper, 5c. Agr 24—112

ANIMAL INDUSTRY BUREAU

Beef production in cotton belt; [by Arthur T. Semple]. [Nov. 1923.] ii+19 p. il. (Agriculture Dept. Farmers' bulletin 1379.) [Includes list of Farmers' bulletins relating to beef production.] *Paper, 5c. Agr 24—110

Horses. Breeding Morgan horses at U. S. Morgan horse farm; [by H. H. Reese]. [Nov. 1921, revised Sept. 1923.] [1923.] 22+[1] p. il. 1 tab. (Agriculture Dept. Department circular 199.) *Paper, 10c. Agr 24—106

—— Special report on diseases of horse; [articles] by Drs. Pearson, Michener, Law, Harbaugh, Trumbower, Liautard, Holcombe. Huidekoper, Mohler, Eichhorn, Hall, and Adams. Revised edition, 1923. 1923. 629 p. il. 24 pl. 18 p. of pl. *Cloth, $1.00. Agr 24—114

CONTENTS.—Examination of sick horse; by Leonard Pearson.—Fundamental principles of disease, by Rush Shippen Huidekoper; revised by Leonard Pearson.—Methods of administering medicines, by Ch. B. Michener; revised by Leonard Pearson.—Diseases of digestive organs, by Ch. B. Michener, revised by John R. Mohler; [with Gastrointestinal parasites, by Maurice C. Hall].—Diseases of respiratory organs, by W. H. Harbaugh; revised by Leonard Pearson.—Diseases of urinary organs; by James Law.—Diseases of generative organs; by James Law.—Diseases of nervous system, by M. R. Trumbower; revised by John R. Mohler.—Diseases of heart, blood vessels, and lymphatics, by M. R. Trumbower; revised by Leonard Pearson.—Diseases of eye; by James Law.—Lameness, its causes and treatment, by A. Liautard; revised by John R. Mohler.—Diseases of fetlock, ankle, and foot; by A. A. Holcombe.—Diseases of skin; by James Law.—Wounds and their treatment, by Ch. B. Michener; revised by John R. Mohler.—Infectious diseases, by Rush Shippen Huidekoper, revised by A. Eichhorn; [with articles on Sporotrichosis (mycotic lymphangitis), by John R. Mohler, Dourine, by John R. Mohler, Infectious anemia or swamp fever, by John R. Mohler, Surra, by Ch. Wardell Stiles, Osteoporosis or bighead, by John R. Mohler].—Horseshoeing; by John W. Adams.—Index.

Larkspur, or poison weed; [by C. Dwight Marsh, A. B. Clawson, and Hadleigh Marsh]. [Revised July, 1918, corrected Dec. 1923.] [1923.] 16 p. il. (Agriculture Dept. Farmers' bulletin 988.) *Paper, 5c.

Poultry. Diseases of poultry; [by Bernard A. Gallagher]. [July, 1923, revised Nov. 1923.] [1923.] ii+41 p. il. (Agriculture Dept. Farmers' bulletin 1337.) *Paper, 5c. Agr 23—1231

Service announcements. Service and regulatory announcements, Nov. 1923; [no.] 199. Jan. 1924. p. 93–102. [Monthly.] *Paper, 5c. single copy, 25c. a yr.; foreign subscription, 40c. Agr 7—1658

NOTE.—The free distribution of this publication will be limited to persons in the service of the Animal Industry Bureau, to proprietors of establishments at which the Federal meat inspection is conducted, to public officials whose duties render it necessary for them to have such information, and to journals especially concerned. Others desiring copies may obtain them from the Superintendent of Documents, Washington, D. C., at the prices stated above.

—— Same, Dec. 1923; [no.] 200. Jan. 1924. p. 103–109. [Monthly.]

Sheep. Flushing and other means of increasing lamb yields; by F. R. Marshall and C. G. Potts. Oct. 12, 1921, revised Jan. 8, 1924. [1924.] 15 p. (Agriculture Dept. Bulletin 996.) *Paper, 5c.

CHEMISTRY BUREAU

Arsenicals. Excretions from leaves as factor in arsenical injury to plants; by C. M. Smith. [1924.] p. 191–194. [From Journal of agricultural research, v. 26, no. 4, Oct. 27, 1923.] ‡

Chufa. Chemical examination of chufa, tubers of Cyperus esculentus Linné [with list of literature cited], by Frederick B. Power and Victor K. Chesnut; Constituents of chufa oil, fatty oil from tubers of Cyperus esculentus Linné [with list of literature cited], by Walter F. Baughman and George S. Jamieson. 1923. cover-title. p. 69–82. [From Journal of agricultural research, v. 26, no. 2, Oct. 13, 1923.] ‡

Service announcements. Service and regulatory announcements, supplement 164. Jan. 5, 1924. p. 351–386. [Contains Notices of judgment under food and drugs act 11651–700.] *Paper, 5c. Agr 14—194

NOTE.—The free distribution of this publication will be limited to firms, establishments, and journals especially concerned. Others desiring copies may obtain them from the Superintendent of Documents, Washington, D. C., at the prices stated above and below.

—— Same, supplement 165. Dec. 1923. p. 387–423. [Contains Notices of judgment under food and drugs act 11701–750.] *Paper, 5c.

COOPERATIVE EXTENSION WORK OFFICE

Extension program in range livestock, dairying, and human nutrition for Western States [recommended by Western States Extension Conference, held at Fort Collins, Colo., Nov. 5–9, 1923; by] W. A. Lloyd. Jan. 1924. 14 p. il. (Agriculture Dept. Department circular 308.) * Paper, 5c.

Agr 24—108

Records. System of field and office records for county extension workers; [by] M. C. Wilson. Oct. 1920, revised Jan. 1924. [1924.] 13 p. il. (Agriculture Dept. Department circular 107.) * Paper, 5c.

EDITORIAL AND DISTRIBUTION WORK OFFICES

Agriculture Department. Publications issued in Nov. 1923; [prepared in Office of Publications]. [1923.] oblong 48° [Monthly. This publication is issued in postal card form, and takes the place of the 4-page leaflet of monthly publications formerly issued.] †

—— Same Dec. 1923; [prepared in Office of Publications]. [1924.] oblong 48° [Monthly. This publication is issued in postal card form.] †

Farmers' bulletins. Subject list of Farmers' bulletins [available] Jan. 15, 1924. [1924.] [4] p. [The blank space at top of p. 1 is for correspondence.] †

—— Same, with title, Farmers' bulletins. Jan. 15, 1924; [prepared in] Office of Publications. [1924.] [4] p. [No blank space at top of p. 1.] †

ENTOMOLOGY BUREAU

Cadelles. Notes on biology of cadelle. Tenebroides mauritanicus Linné; by Richard T. Cotton. [1923.] p. 61–68. [From Journal of agricultural research, v. 26, no. 2, Oct. 13, 1923.] ‡

Chicken-ticks. Results of experiments with miscellaneous substances against chicken mite; by W. M. Davidson. Jan. 23, 1924. 11 p. (Agriculture Dept. Department bulletin 1228.) [Prepared in cooperation with Insecticide and Fungicide Board.] * Paper, 5c.

Agr 24—105

Dusting. Dusting and spraying peach trees after harvest for control of plum curculio; by Oliver I. Snapp and C. H. Alden. Jan. 25, 1924. 19 p. il. 2 p. of pl. (Agriculture Dept. Department bulletin 1205.) * Paper, 5c.

Agr 24—103

—— Dusting cotton from airplanes; by B. R. Coad, E. Johnson, and G. L. McNeil. Jan. 1924. 40 p. il. (Agriculture Dept. Department bulletin 1204.) [Prepared in cooperation with Public Roads Bureau and Air Service.] * Paper, 10c.

Agr 24—102

Platygaster hiemalis. Twinning and monembryonic development of Platygaster hiemalis, parasite of Hessian fly [with list of literature cited]; by R. W. Leiby and C. C. Hill. 1923. cover-title, 337–350+[4] p. 5 p. of pl. [From Journal of agricultural research, v. 25, no. 8, Aug. 25, 1923.] ‡

Screw-worms and other maggots affecting animals; [by F. C. Bishopp, J. D. Mitchell, and D. C. Parman]. [Sept. 1917, revised July, 1923.] [1923.] ii+16 p. il. (Agriculture Dept. Farmers' bulletin 857.) [Date of original issue incorrectly given on this publication as Dec. 1919.] * Paper, 5c.

EXPERIMENT STATIONS OFFICE

NOTE.—The Experiment Stations Office was created Oct. 1, 1888, and was merged into the States Relations Service July 1, 1915. The States Relations Service ceased to exist as such July 1, 1923, and the Experiment Stations Office has again become a publishing office. See also for report of subordinate office of States Relations Service covering the period previous to July 1, 1923, p. 342.

Experiment station record. Experiment station record, v. 49, no. 7; Nov. 1923. 1923. cover-title, viii+601–700 p. [Text and illustration on p. 2 and 4 of cover.] * Paper, 10c. single copy, 75c. per vol. (2 vols. a yr.); foreign subscription, $1.25 per vol.

Agr 9—832

NOTE.—Mainly made up of abstracts of reports and publications on agricultural science which have recently appeared in all countries, especially the United States. Extra numbers, called abstract numbers, are issued, 3 to each volume. These are made up almost exclusively of abstracts, that is, they contain no editorial notes and only a limited number of current notes.

—— Same, v. 49, no. 8; Dec. 1923. 1924. cover-title, ix+701–800 p. il. [Text and illustration on p. 2 and 4 of cover.]

FOREST SERVICE

Wood. Mechanical properties of woods grown in United States; by J. A. Newlin and Thomas R. C. Wilson. Sept. 15, 1917, [reprint] 1923. cover-title, 47 p. 1 pl. 2 p. of pl. (Agriculture Dept. Bulletin 556.) [Includes lists of publications and papers dealing with mechanical properties of timber.] * Paper, 10c. Agr 17–976

PLANT INDUSTRY BUREAU

Apple scald and its control; [by Charles Brooks, J. S. Cooley, and D. F. Fisher]. [Oct. 1923.] [2]+17 p. il. (Agriculture Dept. Farmers' bulletin 1380.) * Paper, 5c. Agr 24–111

Corn. Acidity of corn and its relation to vegetative vigor [with list of literature cited]; by Annie May Hurd. [1923.] p. 457–469, il. [From Journal of agricultural research, v. 25, no. 11, Sept. 15, 1923.] ‡

Dodder; [by Albert A. Hansen]. [Jan. 1921, revised Aug. 1923.] [1923.] 22+[1] p. il. (Agriculture Dept. Farmers' bulletin 1161.) * Paper, 5c.

Fertilizers. Field experiments with atmospheric-nitrogen fertilizers; by F. E. Allison, J. M. Braham, and J. E. McMurtrey, jr. Jan. 22, 1924. cover-title, 44 p. il. 14 p. of pl. (Agriculture Dept. Department bulletin 1180.) [Prepared in cooperation with Fixed Nitrogen Research Laboratory.] * Paper, 10c. Agr 24–99

Fruits in West Virginia, Kentucky, and Tennessee [with list of literature cited]; by George M. Darrow. Dec. 1923. cover-title, 82 p. il. (Agriculture Dept. Department bulletin 1189.) * Paper, 15c. · Agr 24–101

Grafting. Bridge grafting; [by Guy E. Yerkes, H. P. Gould collaborating]. [Nov. 1923.] ii+20 p. il. (Agriculture Dept. Farmers' bulletin 1369.) [Revision of Farmers' bulletin 710.] * Paper, 5c. Agr 24–109

Oats. Spring oat production; [by C. W. Warburton]. [Nov. 1917, revised June, 1923.] [1923.] 24 p. il. (Agriculture Dept. Farmers' bulletin 892.) [Includes list of Agriculture Department publications treating of various phases of oat production.] * Paper, 5c.

Orange-rust. Effect of orange-rusts of Rubus on development and distribution of stomata; by B. O. Dodge. 1923. cover-title, p. 495–500+[1] leaf, il. 1 pl. [From Journal of agricultural research, v. 25, no. 12, Sept. 22, 1923.] ‡

—— Systemic infections of Rubus with orange-rusts [with list of literature cited]; by B. O. Dodge. 1923. cover-title, 209–242+[6] p.+[1] leaf, il. 7 p. of pl. [From Journal of agricultural research, v. 25, no. 5, Aug. 4, 1923.] ‡

Peas. Field peas. [1923.] 4 p. †

Sweet clover: Harvesting and thrashing seed crop; [by H. S. Coe]. [July, 1917, reprint 1923.] 24 p. il. (Agriculture Dept. Farmers' bulletin 836.) * Paper, 5c. Agr 17–717

PUBLIC ROADS BUREAU

Irrigation of alfalfa; [by Samuel Fortier]. [Revised Aug. 1923.] [1923.] ii+36 p. il. (Agriculture Dept. Farmers' bulletin 865.) [Nov. 1909, on page ii, is the original date of issue of Farmers' bulletin 373, which Farmers' bulletin 865 revised.] * Paper, 5c.

SOILS BUREAU

Brawley, Calif. Soil survey of Brawley area, Calif.; by A. E. Kocher, E. J. Carpenter, Walter C. Dean, Alfred Smith, S. W. Cosby, and M. E. Wank. 1923. iv+641–716 p. il. 1 pl. 4 p. of pl. 2 maps. [Prepared in cooperation with University of California Agricultural Experiment Station. From Field operations, 1920.] * Paper, 25c.

Dickinson County, Iowa. Soil survey of Dickinson County, Iowa; by J. Ambrose Elwell and J. L. Boatman. 1923. iii+599–639 p. il. map. [Prepared in cooperation with Iowa Agricultural Experiment Station. From Field operations, 1920.] * Paper, 15c.

Dubuque County, Iowa. Soil survey of Dubuque County, Iowa; by J. O. Veatch and C. L. Orrben. 1923. iii+345–369 p. il. map. [Prepared in cooperation with Iowa Agricultural Experiment Station. From Field operations, 1920.] * Paper, 25c.

Kelp. Potash from kelp: Early development and growth of giant kelp, Macrocystis pyrifera [with list of literature cited], by R. P. Brandt; with introduction, by J. W. Turrentine. Dec. 1923. cover-title, 40 p. il. (Agriculture Dept. Department bulletin 1191.) *Paper, 5c.   Agr 24—100

Onslow County, N. C. Soil survey of Onslow County, N. C.; by R. C. Jurney, R. E. Devereux, E. H. Stevens, S. F. Davidson, and W. D. Lee. 1923. iii+101–127 p. il. map. [Prepared in cooperation with North Carolina Department of Agriculture and State Agricultural Experiment Station. From Field operations, 1921.] *Paper, 25c.

Perry County, Ark. Soil survey of Perry County, Ark.; by E. B. Deeter, T. M. Bushnell, and Louis A. Wolfanger. 1923. iii+493–536 p. il. map. [From Field operations, 1920.] *Paper, 25c.

Phosphoric acid. Investigations of manufacture of phosphoric acid by volatilization process; by William H. Waggaman, Henry W. Easterwood, and Thomas B. Turley. Dec. 1923. cover-title, 55 p. il. 2 pl. 10 p. of pl. (Agriculture Dept. Department bulletin 1179.) *Paper, 15c.   Agr 24—98

St. Louis County, Mo. Soil survey of St. Louis, Mo.; by H. H. Krusekopf and D. B. Pratapas. 1923. iii+517–562 p. il. 4 p. of pl. map. [Prepared in cooperation with University of Missouri Agricultural Experiment Station. From Field operations, 1919.] *Paper, 25c.

STATES RELATIONS SERVICE

Note.—The States Relations Service ceased to exist as such July 1, 1923. See also note under Experiment Stations Office, p. 340.

ALASKA AGRICULTURAL EXPERIMENT STATIONS

Report of Alaska Agricultural Experiment Stations, [calendar year] 1922. Dec. 1923. cover-title, 25 p. il. 2 pl. *Paper, 5c.   Agr 6—1413

WEATHER BUREAU

Climatological data for United States by sections, v. 10, no. 10; Oct. 1923. [1924.] cover-title, [190] p. il. 2 maps, 2 p of maps, 4° [Text on p. 2 of cover.] *Paper, 35c. complete monthly number, $4.00 a yr. /   Agr 14—566

Note.—Made up of separate Climatological data issued from 42 section centers of the United States. Printed at the several section centers and assembled and bound at the Washington Office. Issued principally for service use and exchange. The separate Climatological data are sold by the Superintendent of Documents, Washington, D. C., at the rate of 5c. single copy, 50c. a yr. for each section.

Meteorology. Monthly meteorological summary, Washington, D. C., Dec. 1923. [1924.] [2] p. f°   †

Monthly weather review, v. 51, no. 10; Oct. 1923. [Dec. 31] 1923. cover-title, p. 497–560, il. 2 maps, 32 p. of maps, 4° [Text on p. 2–4 of cover.] *Paper. 15c. single copy, $1.50 a yr.; foreign subscription, $2.25.   Agr 9—990

Note.—The Monthly weather review contains (1) meteorological contributions, and bibliography including seismology, (2) an interpretative summary and charts of the weather of the month in the United States, and on adjacent oceans, and (3) climatological and seismological tables dealing with the weather and earthquakes of the month. The contributions are principally as follows: (a) results of observational or research work in meteorology carried on in the United States or other parts of the world, (b) abstracts or reviews of important meteorological papers and books, and (c) notes.

Special articles.—[Jesus] Hernandez on temperature of Mexico; [abstract] by Alfred J. Henry.—Climate of San Jose, Calif.; [by] Esek S. Nichols.—Group distribution and periodicity of annual rainfall amounts; by Robert E. Horton.—East winds on north Pacific Coast; by Edward Lansing Wells.—Note on trade winds in Hawaii; by Thomas Arthur Blair.—Meeting of Commission for Radiation Researches [Utrecht, Holland, Sept. 1923, abstract of proceedings; by H. H. K.].—Warm fall weather in Alaska and Russia, 1923; [by A. J. Henry].—Six or seven typhoons in far East during Sept. 1923; by José Coronas.

New England highway weather bulletin, Jan. 2–29, 1924; no. 3–7 [season of 1923–24]. [Boston, Mass., 1924.] Each 1 p. il. large 8° [Weekly.] *Paper, 50c. per season.

Ocean. Weather of the oceans, Oct. 1923, with special reference to north Atlantic and north Pacific oceans (including charts), notes, abstracts, and reviews; issued by Marine Division. 1924. 10 p. 8 p. of maps, 4° [From Monthly weather review, Oct. 1923.] †

Rain. Group distribution and periodicity of annual rainfall amounts; by R. E. Horton. 1924. [1]+515–521 p. il. 4° [From Monthly weather review, Oct. 1923.] †

Rivers. Daily river stages at river gage stations on principal rivers of United States, v. 20, [calendar] year 1922; by H. C. Frankenfield. 1923. iii +268 p. 4° ([Publication] 819.) * Paper, 40c.   Agr 6—372

Snow and ice bulletin, no. 4–8, winter 1923–24; Dec. 31, 1923–Jan. 28, 1924. Jan. 2–29, 1924. Each [2] p. il. large 4° [Weekly during winter.] †
    12—1660

Weather map. Daily weather map [of United States, containing forecasts for all States east of Mississippi River except Illinois, Wisconsin, Indiana, upper Michigan, and lower Michigan], Jan. 2–31, 1924. 1st edition. [1924.] Each 16.4×22.7 in. [Not issued Sundays or holidays.] * Editions issued at Washington, D. C., 25c. a month, $2.50 a yr.; editions issued at about 65 stations throughout the United States, 20c. a month, $2.00 a yr.

—— Same [containing forecasts for United States], Jan. 1–31, 1924. 2d edition. [1924.] Each 16.4×22.7 in. [The Sunday edition does not contain as much information as the edition for week days.] * 30c. a month, $3.00 a yr.

ALIEN PROPERTY CUSTODIAN

Report. Annual report of Alien Property Custodian, communication submitting annual report of proceedings had under trading with the enemy act, year ended Dec. 31, 1923. Jan. 14, 1924. 8 p. (H. doc. 155, 68th Cong. 1st sess.) * Paper, 5c.   18—26123

CIVIL SERVICE COMMISSION

NOTE.—The Commission furnishes its publications gratuitously to those who apply for them.

Postmasters. Information regarding postmaster positions filled through nomination by the President for confirmation by Senate [corrected pages for edition of May, 1922]. Jan. 1924. p. 5–6. (Form 2223, corrections p. 5 and 6.) †

Retirement act of May 22, 1920, with amendments and notes. Jan. 1924. 23 p. (Form 2368.) †   24—26069

Steamboat Inspection Service. Information concerning examinations for entrance to Steamboat Inspection Service. Dec. 1923 [published 1924]. (Form 1405.) †

COMMERCE DEPARTMENT

NOTE.—The Department of Commerce prints most of its publications in very limited editions, the distribution of which is confined to Government officers, libraries, etc. When a selling price is noted in this list, application for such publication should be submitted to the Superintendent of Documents, Washington, D. C., with remittance. For copies of charts, coast pilots, and tide tables, however, apply directly to the issuing office, the Coast and Geodetic Survey, Washington, D. C.

Claims. Adjusted claim requiring appropriation, communication from assistant Secretary of Commerce submitting claim [of C. E. Moran] for damages to privately owned property, which he has adjusted and which requires appropriation for its payment. Jan. 3, 1924. 2 p. (H. doc. 127, 68th Cong. 1st sess.) * Paper, 5c.

—— Adjusted claim requiring appropriation, communication submitting claim [of R. C. Stark] for damages to privately owned property, which claim has been adjusted by director of Coast and Geodetic Survey and which requires appropriation for its payment. Jan. 3, 1924. 2 p. (H. doc. 128, 68th Cong. 1st sess.) * Paper, 5c.

—— Adjusted claims requiring appropriation, communication submitting claims for damages to privately owned property, which claims have been adjusted by commissioner of lighthouses and which require appropriation for their payment. Jan. 3, 1924. 2 p. (H. doc. 129, 68th Cong. 1st sess.) * Paper, 5c.

Commerce. Schedule A, statistical classification of imports into United States, with rates of duty, and regulations governing preparation of monthly and quarterly statements of imports; approved and effective Sept. 22, 1922. 3d edition, Jan. 1, 1924. 1924. 112 p. (Foreign and Domestic Commerce Bureau.) * Paper, 15c.   24—26070

CENSUS BUREAU

Cotton. Cotton consumed, cotton on hand, active cotton spindles, and imports and exports of cotton, Dec. 1922 and 1923, with statistics of cotton consumed, imported, and exported for 5 months ending Dec. 31. Jan. 15, 1924. oblong 32° [Preliminary report. This publication is issued in postal card form.] †

—— Report on cotton ginning, number of bales of cotton ginned from growth of 1923 prior to Jan. 1, 1924, and comparative statistics to corresponding date in 1923 and 1922. Jan. 9, 1924. oblong 32° [Preliminary report. This publication is issued in postal card form.] †

—— Same prior to Jan. 16, 1924, and comparative statistics to corresponding date in 1923 and 1922. Jan. 23, 1924. oblong 32° [Preliminary report. This publication is issued in postal card form.] †

Cottonseed received, crushed, and on hand, and cottonseed products manufactured, shipped out, on hand, and exported covering 5-month period ending Dec. 31, 1923 and 1922. Jan. 19, 1924. oblong 32° [Preliminary report. This publication is issued in postal card form.] † .

Drugs. Census of manufactures, 1921: Drug industries, druggists' preparations, patent medicines and compounds, and perfumery and cosmetics, drug grinding. 1924. 26 p. * Paper, 5c.   24—26102

Iron. Census of manufactures, 1921: Iron and steel, blast furnaces, steel works and rolling mills, wire, tin plate and terneplate. 1923. 63 p. * Paper, 10c.
24—26103

Musical instruments. Census of manufactures, 1921: Musical instruments and phonographs. 1924. 28 p. * Paper, 5c.   24—26104

Printing. Census of manufactures, 1921: Printing and publishing and allied industries, printing and publishing, bookbinding and blank-book making, engraving and plate printing. lithographing. 1924. 53 p. * Paper, 5c.
24—26105

Turpentine. Forest products. 1922: Turpentine and rosin; compiled in cooperation with Department of Agriculture, Forest Service. 1924. 6 p. * Paper, 5c.
24—26106

Wool. Census of manufactures, 1921: Wool manufactures and allied industries, woolen goods, worsted goods, carpets and rugs, felt goods, wool-felt hats, wool shoddy, wool pulling, wool scouring. 1923. 39 p. * Paper, 5c.   23—27392

COAST AND GEODETIC SURVEY

NOTE.—The monthly Notice to mariners, formerly issued by the Coast and Geodetic Survey, has been consolidated with and made a part of the Notice to mariners issued by the Lighthouses Bureau, thus making it a joint publication. The charts, coast pilots, and tide tables of the Coast and Geodetic Survey are sold at the office of the Survey in Washington, and also by one or more sales agents in each of the important American seaports.

Coast and Geodetic Survey bulletin. Dec. 31, 1923; no. 103. [1924.] 8 p. [Monthly.] ‡   15—26512

Coast pilots. Supplement to United States coast pilot. Atlantic Coast, section B, Cape Cod to Sandy Hook. Dec. 14, 1923. [1]+16 leaves. (Serial 251.) †

—— Supplement to United States coast pilot, Pacific Coast: California, Oregon, and Washington. Jan. 2. 1924. 23 leaves. (Serial 253.) †

Tide tables, Pacific Coast, North America, eastern Asia, and island groups, [calendar] year 1925; from Tide tables, United States and foreign ports [calendar year 1925]. 1923. 1–8+121–222+231–234+339–340+370–394+ 416–433+439–448 p. il. (Serial 247.) † Paper, 15c.   7—35369

Charts

Admiralty Inlet and Puget Sound to Seattle, Wash., surveys to 1917, surveys by U. S. Engineers to 1923 and other sources; chart 6450. Scale 1:80,000. Washington, Coast and Geodetic Survey, Dec. 1923. 42.1×33 in. † 75c.

Baker Island. Baker, Noyes, and Lulu islands and adjacent waters, southeast Alaska, surveys to 1922; chart 8158. Scale 1:40,000. Washington, Coast and Geodetic Survey, Dec. 1923. 43×32.5 in. † 75c.

Grays Harbor, Wash., surveys in 1911 with additions from older surveys, surveys by U. S. Engineers and port of Grays Harbor to July, 1923; with inset, Continuation of Chehalis River; chart 6195. Scale 1 : 40,000. Washington, Coast and Geodetic Survey, Jan. 1924. 24.5×38.6 in. † 50c.

Los Angeles Harbor. Los Angeles and Long Beach harbors [San Pedro Bay], Calif., surveys to 1921, surveys by U. S. Engineers to 1923 and other sources; chart 5146. Scale 1 : 10,000. Washington, Coast and Geodetic Survey, Jan. 1924. 39.6×33.8 in. † 75c.

New Bedford Harbor and approaches, Mass., surveys 1895–1915, surveys by U. S. Engineers to 1923 and other sources; chart 252. Scale 1 : 20,000. Washington, Coast and Geodetic Survey, Jan. 1924. 35.3×33.8 in. † 75c.

Raritan Bay and southern part of Arthur Kill, N. Y., and N. J., surveys to 1915, surveys by U. S. Engineers to 1923 and other sources; chart 286. Scale 1 : 15,000. Washington, Coast and Geodetic Survey, Jan. 1924. 44×30.1 in. † 75c.

Tlevak Strait. Northern part of Tlevak Strait and Ulloa Channel, southeast Alaska, surveys to 1920; chart 8151. Scale 1 : 40,000. Washington, Coast and Geodetic Survey, Jan. 1924. 30.1×40.5 in. † 75c.

FISHERIES BUREAU

Biology. Progress in biological inquiries, 1923, report of Division of Scientific Inquiry, fiscal year 1923; by Willis H. Rich, with collaboration of investigators. 1924. [1]+27 p. (Bureau of Fisheries doc. 956.) [App. 7, report of commissioner of fisheries, 1923.] * Paper, 5c.   F 21—2

Cold storage holdings of fish, Dec. 15, 1923. [1924.] 1 p. oblong 12° (Statistical bulletin 595.) [Statistics furnished by Agricultural Economics Bureau.] †

Fisheries service bulletin, Jan. 2, 1924; no. 104. [1924.] 6 p. [Monthly.] ‡
F15—76

Fishery products. Statement of quantities and values of certain fishery products landed at Boston and Gloucester, Mass., and Portland, Me., by American fishing vessels, Dec. 1923. [1924.] 1 p. oblong f° (Statistical bulletin 596.) †

—— Statement of quantities and values of certain fishery products landed at Seattle, Wash., by American fishing vessels, Dec. 1923. [1924.] 1 p. oblong 12° (Statistical bulletin 597.) †

Myxosporidia. New myxosporidian parasite, cause of wormy halibut [with bibliography]; by H. S. Davis. 1924. [1]+5 p. il. (Bureau of Fisheries doc. 957.) [App. 8, report of commissioner of fisheries, 1923.] * Paper, 5c.
F 24—3

Trout. Artificial propagation of brook trout and rainbow trout, with notes on 3 other species; revised and enlarged by Glen C. Leach. . 1923. [1]+74 p. il. 5 pl. 8 p. of pl. (Bureau of Fisheries doc. 955.) [App. 6, report of commissioner of fisheries, 1923. This document represents a revision and enlargement of chapters from Manual of fish-culture, revised edition, published in 1900.] * Paper, 20c.   F 24—4

FOREIGN AND DOMESTIC COMMERCE BUREAU

Automobiles. American automotive products in India; by C. C. Batchelder. 1923. vi+61 p. (Special agents series 223.) * Paper, 10c.

China wood oil; by William M. Taylor. 1923. iv+21 p. il. map. (Miscellaneous series 125.) * Paper, 5c.   23—27376

Commerce. Monthly summary of foreign commerce of United States, Nov. 1923. 1924. 2 pts. p. 1–69 and ii+71–91 p. 4° * Paper, 10c. single copy (including pts. 1 and 2), $1.00 a yr.; foreign subscription, $1.60.

—— Same. 1924. [2 pts. in 1], 91 p. 4° (H. doc. 11, 68th Cong. 1st sess.)

Commerce reports. Commerce reports,weekly survey of foreign trade, reports from American consular officers and representatives of Department of Commerce in foreign countries, no. 1–4; Jan. 7–28, 1924. 1924. cover-titles, p. 1–264, 4° [Text and illustrations on p. 2–4 of covers.] * Paper, 10c. single copy, $3.00 a yr.; foreign subscription, $5.00.

Commerce reports—Continued. Supplement to Commerce reports. [Included in price of Commerce reports for subscribers.]

Trade and economic review for 1922, no. 41: Hungary; [by] Edwin C. Kemp and Digby A. Willson. [1923.] 14 p.
Same, no. 42: Mexico; compiled in Latin American Division, based on reports from Claude I. Dawson, E. E. Evans, H. B. MacKenzie, and from other sources. [1923.] 32 p. [Supplemented by data for first months of 1923.]
Same, no. 43: Peru; by C. E. Guyant. [1923.] 14 p.
Same, no. 44: Italy; [by] John Ball Osborne. [1924.] 14 p.
Same, no. 45: Japan; [by] Emmett A. Chapman. [1924.] 20 p. [Includes trade statistics for first 6 months of 1923.]
Same, no. 46: Brazil; by A. Gaulin, in collaboration with Jack Dewey Hickerson. [1924.] 22 p.
Same, no. 47: France; [by] A. M. Thackara. [1924.] 14 p.
Same, no. 48: Latvia; by John P. Hurley. [1924.] 28 p.
Same, no. 49: Yugoslavia; by Kenneth S. Patton. [1924.] 14 p.

—— Supplement to Commerce reports: British possessions in East Africa; by Thomas R. Wilson. Jan. 7, 1924. ii+25 p. (Trade information bulletin 173; Western European Division.) †   23—27393

—— Same: Comparative progress of rival British ports; by H. B. Allin-Smith. Jan. 14, 1924. ii+10 p. (Trade information bulletin 174; Transportation Division.) †   24—26124

—— Same: Crude rubber survey, no. 1, Marketing of plantation rubber; by J. J. Blandin. Jan. 24, 1924. iv+24 p. (Trade information bulletin 180; Rubber Division.) [Prepared as part of survey of essential raw materials authorized by 67th Congress.] †   24—26037

—— Same: European market for sporting and athletic goods; by C. J. North, prepared from reports by American consular officers and representatives of Department of Commerce. Jan. 21, 1924. ii+30 p. (Trade information bulletin 179; [Specialties Division].) †   24—26036

—— Same: Magnesite, commercial sources and trade; [articles] by Charles G. Yale, R. O. Hall, [and] E. Baldwin, with supplemental data from other reliable sources. Feb. 4, 1924. ii+19 p. ⟨Trade information bulletin 184; Mineral Section, Iron and Steel Division.⟩ †   24—26041
CONTENTS.—United States; by Charles G. Yale.—Austria; by E. Baldwin.—Greece; by R. O. Hall.—India.—Canada.—Australia.—Union of South Africa.—Margarita Island.

—— Same: Market for rubber-soled footwear in China; prepared from reports of consular representatives of Department of State stationed in China. Jan. 21, 1924. ii+11 p. (Trade information bulletin 181; Rubber Division.) †   24—26038

—— Same: Petroleum industry and trade of Peru and Equador [Ecuador]; by William W. Dobkin. Jan. 21, 1924. ii+26 p. (Trade information bulletin 178; Petroleum Division.) †   24—26035

—— Same: Protesting drafts in western and northern Europe; compiled by A. J. Wolfe from information furnished by consular officers of Department of State and officers of Department of Commerce stationed abroad. Jan. 28, 1924. ii+18 p. (Trade information bulletin 182; Division of Commercial Laws.) †   24—26039

—— Same: Survey of world trade in agricultural products, no. 1, Distribution of agricultural exports from United States; by H. M. Strong. Jan. 28, 1924. iv+42 p. il. (Trade information bulletin 177; Foodstuffs Division.) [Prepared as part of study of world trade in agricultural products authorized by 67th Congress.] †.   24—26034

—— Same: Survey of world trade in agricultural products, no. 2, Methods of merchandising American wheat in export trade, pt. 1, Buying wheat for export; by Theo. D. Hammatt. Feb. 4, 1924. ii+74 p. il. (Trade information bulletin 183; Foodstuffs Division.) [Prepared as part of study of world trade in agricultural products authorized by 67th Congress.] †   24—26040

—— Same: Swiss dyestuffs industry, production, export, and import statistics [with bibliography]; by Frederick E. Breithut. Jan. 14, 1924. ii+16 p. (Trade information bulletin 175; Chemical Division.) [Imprint date incorrectly given at bottom of title-page as 1923.] †   24—26032

—— Same: Tanning materials survey, pt. 1, Problem of our commercial independence in tanning materials. Jan. 2, 1924. ii+18 p. (Trade information bulletin 167; Hide and Leather Division.) [Prepared as part of the study of essential raw materials authorized by the 67th Congress.] †   24—26107

Commerce reports—Continued. Same: Tire trade practices in Australia; by J. W. Sanger. Jan. 14, 1924. ii+6 p. (Trade information bulletin 176; Rubber Division.) † 24—26033

—— Survey of current business, Dec. 1923, no. 28; compiled by Bureau of Census, Bureau of Foreign and Domestic Commerce, [and] Bureau of Standards. 1924. cover-title, 62 p. il. 4° (Monthly supplement to Commerce reports.) [Contains statistics for Oct. 1923, the date given above, Dec. 1923, being the date of issue. Text on p. 2–4 of cover.] * Paper, 10c. single copy, $1.00 a yr.; foreign subscription, $1.50. 21—26819

NOTE.—Realizing that current statistics are highly perishable and that to be of use they must reach the business man at the earliest possible moment, the Department has arranged to distribute advance leaflets twice each month to those subscribers who request them. One set of these leaflets is issued about the 20th of the month, giving such information as has been received up to that time, and another set of sheets is mailed at the end of the month giving those figures received since the 20th. The information contained in these leaflets is also published in Commerce reports issued weekly by the Foreign and Domestic Commerce Bureau. The advance sheets will be mailed free of charge to all subscribers to the Survey who request them. Such requests should be addressed to the Bureau of the Census, Department of Commerce, Washington, D. C. Subscriptions, however, should be sent to the Superintendent of Documents, Washington, D. C., at the prices stated above.

—— Same, Jan. 1924, no. 29; compiled by Bureau of Census, Bureau of Foreign and Domestic Commerce, [and] Bureau of Standards. 1924. cover-title, 56 p. il. 4° (Monthly supplement to Commerce reports.) [Contains statistics for Nov. 1923, the date given above, Jan. 1924, being the date of issue. Text on p. 2–4 of cover.]

Electrical apparatus and appliances. Glossary of electrical terms and instructions to exporters for guidance in properly listing and classifying electrical apparatus and supplies in shippers' export declarations; compiled by Electrical Equipment Division, Bureau of Foreign and Domestic Commerce, in conference with Electrical Manufacturers' Council. Revised Jan. 1, 1924. 1923. viii+15 p. (Miscellaneous series 117.) * Paper, 5c. 23—27400

Market methods and trade usages in London; compiled in American consulate general, London. 1923. vi+82 p. (Special consular reports 86.) * Paper, 10c. 23—27377

Specialties Division. Services of Specialties Division. 1923. ii+8+[1] p. narrow 12° †

Tunis, its resources, industries, and commerce with reference to United States trade [with list of principal economic and statistical sources]; by James Raider Mood. 1923. vi+57 p. il. (Miscellaneous series 122.) * Paper, 10c. 23—27401

LIGHTHOUSES BUREAU

Lighthouse service bulletin, v. 3, no. 1; Jan. 1, 1924. [1924.] p. 1–7. [Monthly.] † 12—35121

Louisiana Gulf Coast, Sabine Pass East Jetty light to be moved, fog signal to be established; [all lettered poster]. Jan 19, 1924. 16×10.5 in. ([Poster] notice to mariners 91.) †

Notice to mariners, weekly, no. 1–4, 1924; Jan.·4–25 [1924]. 1924. various paging. [Issued jointly with Coast and Geodetic Survey.] † 7—20609

NAVIGATION BUREAU

Navigation laws of United States, 1923. 1923. x+557 p. * Cloth, $1.00. 24—26108

Ships. American documented seagoing merchant vessels of 500 gross tons and over, Jan. 1, 1924. 1924. ii+67 p. 4° (Serial 74.) [Monthly.] * Paper, 10c. single copy, 75c. a yr.; foreign subscription, $1.25. 19—26597

RADIO SERVICE

Radio Service bulletin, Jan. 2, 1924; no. 81. [1924.] 14 p. [Monthly.] * Paper, 5c. single copy, 25c. a yr.; foreign subscription, 40c. 15—26255

PUBLICATIONS DIVISION

Commerce Department. Supplement to annual List of publications [of Department of Commerce available for distribution], Dec. 31, 1923. [1924.] 4 p. [Monthly.] †

STANDARDS BUREAU

NOTE.—The Scientific papers will be supplied on subscription as issued at $1.25 per volume, paper bound. These volumes will afterwards be issued bound in cloth at $2.00 per volume; foreign subscription, paper $2.50 (sent in single numbers), cloth $2.35 (bound volumes). Single numbers vary in price. Address the Superintendent of Documents, Washington, D. C.
The Technologic papers will be issued first as separates and later in volume form in the same manner as the Scientific papers. Subscriptions will be accepted by the Superintendent of Documents at $1.25 per volume; foreign subscription, $2.50. Single numbers vary in price.

Cast-iron. Embrittlement of malleable cast iron resulting from heat treatment; by Leslie H. Marshall. Nov. 26, 1923. [1]+677–693 p. il. (Technologic papers 245.) [From Technologic papers, v. 17.] * Paper, 5c.   24—26046

Enamel. Wet-process enamels for cast iron; by R. R. Danielson [and] H. P. Reinecker. Dec. 19, 1923. [1]+695–735 p. (Technologic papers 246.) [From Technologic papers, v. 17.] * Paper, 10c.   24—26047

Iron. Interferometer measurements of longer waves in iron arc spectrum; by W. F. Meggers [and] C. C. Kiess. Jan. 5, 1924. [1]+273–280 p. il. (Scientific papers 479.) [From Scientific papers, v. 19.] * Paper, 5c.   24—26045

Lumber. Elimination of waste: Lumber, [circular] to all organized consumers, technical experts, distributors, and manufacturers interested in lumber [asking indorsement of recommendations and pledge of their support for fiscal year 1925]. [1923.] 15 p. 4° †   24—26109

—— Same. [Reprint with slight changes 1924.] 15 p. 4° †

Publications. 1924 (January) supplement to Circular 24 [6th edition], Publications of Bureau of Standards. [1923, published 1924.] 49 p. ([Circular 24, 6th edition, Jan. 1924, supplement.]) [Office correction has been made on p. 3.] †

Quicklime. Recommended specification for quicklime and hydrated lime for manufacture of silica brick. Dec. 27, 1923. 7 p. (Circular 153.) * Paper, 5c.   23—27395

—— Recommended specification for quicklime and hydrated lime for use in manufacture of sand-lime brick. Dec. 28, 1923. 6 p. (Circular 150.) * Paper, 5c.   24—26044

Scouring powder. United States Government specification for scouring compounds for floors (a) and (b), and soap scouring compound (c), Federal Specifications Board, Standard specification 34, officially adopted by Federal Specifications Board, July 3, 1922, for use of Departments and independent establishments of Government in purchase of scouring compounds for floors (a) and (b), and soap scouring compound (c). Reprinted [with changes] Dec. 21, 1923. 5 p. (Circular 131.) * Paper, 5c.   24—26043

Soap. United States Government specification for ordinary laundry soap, Federal Specifications Board, Standard specification 32, officially adopted by Federal Specifications Board, July 3, 1922, for use of Departments and independent establishments of Government in purchase of ordinary laundry soap. Reprinted [with changes] Dec. 21, 1923. 5 p. large S° (Circular 129.) * Paper, 5c.   23—27394

STEAMBOAT INSPECTION SERVICE

Steamboat Inspection Service bulletin, Jan. 2, 1924; no. 99. [1924.] 2 p. [Monthly.] ‡   15—26679

Steamboats. 33d supplement to General rules and regulations [edition of 1923], circular letter. Oct. 19, 1923 [reprint 1924]. 2 p. †

CONGRESS

Congressional record. Congressional record, 68th Congress, 1st session, v. 65, no. 15–37; Jan. 3–31, 1924. [1924.] 497–1806+[47] p. 4°   12—36438

NOTE.—The Congressional record, containing the proceedings and debates of Congress, is issued daily when Congress is in session, and indexes thereto are published fortnightly.
The Record is sold by the Superintendent of Documents on the following terms: Single copy, 3 cents, if not more than 24 pages, and 1 cent more for each additional 8 pages; per month, $1.50, foreign subscription, $2.50. Subscriptions are payable in advance. Prices for the bound volumes of the Record, from 67th Congress, 1st–4th sessions, and prior Congresses, will be furnished on application. Send remittances to the Superintendent of Documents, Washington, D. C. Stamps and foreign money will not be accepted.

Congressional record—Continued. Same, index, with title, Congressional record index, 68th Congress, 1st session, v. 65, nos. 15–27; Jan. 3–19, 1924. [1924.] no. 2; 59+34 p. 4° · [Includes History of bills and resolutions.]

Directory. 68th Congress, 1st session, beginning Dec. 3, 1923, official Congressional directory; compiled by Elmer C. Hess. 2d edition, Jan. 1924. [1924.] xvi+583 p. il. 1 pl. * Cloth, 60c. ·   6—35330

PRIVATE LAWS

NOTE.—The Publications Division, State Department, receives a small supply of the private acts which it distributes free upon application.

Private [act] 1, 68th Congress.

Harding, Mrs. Florence K. S. 2, act granting franking privilege to Florence Kling Harding. Approved Jan. 25, 1924. 1 p. (Private 1.)

ADJUSTMENT OF SALARIES OF OFFICERS AND EMPLOYEES OF CONGRESS, JOINT SELECT COMMITTEE ON

Salaries. Adjustment of salaries of officers and employees of Congress, report pursuant to sec. 10 of act (H. R. 14435), 67th Congress, directing select committee to submit to Congress on 1st day of next regular session what adjustments, if any, should be made in compensation of officers and employees of Senate and House, including joint committees, joint commissions, Office of Architect of Capitol, Legislative Drafting Service, and Capitol police. 1923. iii+13 p. (S. doc. 3, 68th Cong. 1st sess.) * Paper, 5c.
,   23—27468

—— Same, with title, Adjustment of salaries, officers and employees of Congress, letter transmitting report of Joint Committee for Readjustment of Salaries of Officers and Employees of Congress as required by sec. 10 of act approved Mar. 4, 1923. Jan. 3, 1924. 14 p. (H. doc. 131, 68th Cong. 1st sess.) * Paper, 5c.

CONFERENCE COMMITTEES

Cattle. Return of certain domestic animals into United States duty free, conference report to accompany H. J. Res. 82; submitted by Mr. Hawley. Jan. 22, 1924. 2 p. (H. rp. 76, 68th Cong. 1st sess.) * Paper, 5c.

HOUSE OF REPRESENTATIVES

Appropriations. Legislative establishment, deficiency and supplemental estimates of appropriations for legislative establishment for fiscal year 1923, and fiscal year 1924. Jan. 7, 1924. 3 p. (H. doc. 136, 68th Cong. 1st sess.) * Paper, 5c.

Calendars of House of Representatives, 68th Congress, 1st session, Jan. 3–31, 1924; no. 11–33. 1924. various paging, large 8° [Daily when House of Representatives is in session.] ‡

Contested elections. Don H. Clark v. R. Lee Moore, letter from clerk of House of Representatives transmitting contested-election case of Don H. Clark v. R. Lee Moore for seat in House of Representatives for 1st district, Georgia. Dec. 20, 1923. 1 p. (H. doc. 122, 68th Cong. 1st sess.) [Letter of transmittal only.] * Paper, 5c.

—— John J. Gorman v. James R. Buckley, letter from clerk of House of Representatives transmitting contested-election case of John J. Gorman v. James R. Buckley from 6th district of Illinois. Jan. 3, 1924. 1 p. (H. doc. 132, 68th Cong. 1st sess.) [Letter of transmittal only.] * Paper, 5c.

—— Martin C. Ansorge v. Royal H. Weller, letter from clerk of House of Representatives transmitting contested-election case of Martin C. Ansorge v. Royal H. Weller for 21st district, State of New York. Dec. 20, 1923. 1 p. (H. doc. 121, 68th Cong. 1st sess.) [Letter of transmittal only.] * Paper, 5c.

—— Walter M. Chandler v. Sol Bloom, letter from clerk of House of Representatives transmitting contested-election case of Walter M. Chandler v. Sol Bloom for seat in House of Representatives for 19th district, State of New York. Dec. 20, 1923. 1 p. (H. doc. 123, 68th Cong. 1st sess.) [Letter of transmittal only.] * Paper, 5c.

England, C. H. To pay C. H. England $266.66, report to accompany H. Res. 30; submitted by Mr. MacGregor. Dec. 20, 1923. 1 p. (H. rp. 6, 68th Cong. 1st sess.) * Paper, 5c.

Hahn, George W. To pay George W. Hahn $186.66 and Mary Clark $120, report to accompany H. Res. 32; submitted by Mr. MacGregor. Dec. 20, 1923. 1 p. (H. rp. 11, 68th Cong. 1st sess.) * Paper, 5c.

Holland, Eugene J. To pay Eugene J. Holland $186.66 and Jeremiah [Jermiah] P. Holland $120, report to accompany H. Res. 38; submitted by Mr. Mac-Gregor. Dec. 20, 1923. 1 p. (H. rp. 15, 68th Cong. 1st sess.) * Paper, 5c.

House of Representatives. Attendant for ladies' reception room, report to accompany H. Res. 46 [authorizing doorkeeper to appoint attendant for ladies' reception room of House of Representatives]; submitted by Mr. MacGregor. Dec. 20, 1923. 1 p. (H. rp. 9, 68th Cong. 1st sess.) * Paper, 5c.

Landon, Harry F. To pay Harry Fay Landon $186.66 and Leota W. Landon $120, report to accompany H. Res. 39; submitted by Mr. MacGregor. Dec. 20, 1923. 1 p. (H. rp. 16, 68th Cong. 1st sess.) * Paper, 5c.

McCullough, E. M. To pay E. M. McCullough $206.66 and Theda Miller $100, report to accompany H. Res. 84; submitted by Mr. MacGregor. Dec. 20, 1923. 1 p. (H. rp. 17, 68th Cong. 1st sess.) * Paper, 5c.

Morris, Joseph W. To pay Joe W. Morris $186.66 and Marguerite Free $120, report to accompany H. Res. 87; submitted by Mr. MacGregor. Dec. 20, 1923. 1 p. (H. rp. 18, 68th Cong. 1st sess.) * Paper, 5c.

Mountjoy, Nellie. To pay Nelly [Nellie] Mountjoy $206.66 and W. Y. Humphreys $100, report to accompany H. Res. 33; submitted by Mr. MacGregor. Dec. 20, 1923. 1 p. (H. rp. 12, 68th Cong. 1st sess.) * Paper, 5c.

Murphy, Kenneth. To pay Kenneth Murphy $228.33 and Dorsey T. Murphy $78.33, report to accompany H. Res. 37; submitted by Mr. MacGregor. Dec. 20, 1923. 1 p. (H. rp. 14, 68th Cong. 1st sess.) * Paper, 5c.

Reilly, Edward J. To pay to Edward J. Reilly $186.66 and to Dennis F. Shea $120, report to accompany H. Res. 98; submitted by Mr. MacGregor. Dec. 20, 1923. 1 p. (H. rp. 10, 68th Cong. 1st sess.) * Paper, 5c.

Reynolds, Blanche G. To pay Blanche G. Reynolds $186.66, report to accompany H. Res. 36; submitted by Mr. MacGregor. Dec. 20, 1923. 1 p. (H. rp. 13, 68th Cong. 1st sess.) * Paper, 5c.

Ways and Means Committee, House. Authorizing Committee on Ways and Means to sit during sessions and recesses of Congress and to employ such assistance as is necessary, report to accompany H. Res. 44; submitted by Mr. MacGregor. Dec. 20, 1923. 1 p. (H. rp. 7, 68th Cong. 1st sess.) * Paper, 5c.

—— Providing clerk for minority members of Ways and Means Committee, report to accompany H. Res. 88; submitted by Mr. MacGregor. Dec. 20, 1923. 1 p. (H. rp. 8, 68th Cong. 1st sess.) * Paper, 5c.

Agricultural credit. Diversification loan bill, hearings on H. R. 4159, to provide loan of $50,000,000 to encourage diversification in wheat areas, Jan. 11–15, 1924. 1924. iii+130 p. (Serial B.) * Paper, 15c.

Agricultural experiment stations. Purnell agricultural experiment stations bill, hearings on H. R. 157, to endow agricultural experiment stations, Jan. 22, 1924. 1924. iii+29 p. (Serial F.) * Paper, 5c.

Cattle. Tick-infested cattle, report to accompany H. R. 5791 [to repeal that part of act making appropriations for Department of Agriculture, fiscal year 1912, relating to admission of tick-infested cattle from Mexico into Texas]; submitted by Mr. Haugen. Jan. 29, 1924. 2 p. (H. rp. 126, 68th Cong. 1st sess.) * Paper, 5c.

Containers. Haugen slack-filled package bill, hearings on H. R. 762, amending pure food and drugs act, Jan. 23, 1924. 1924. iii+60 p. (Serial G.) * Paper, 10c.

Containers—Continued. Slack filled package bill, report to accompany H. R. 762 [to amend act for preventing manufacture, sale, or transportation of adulterated or misbranded or poisonous or deleterious foods, drugs, medicines, and liquors, and for regulating traffic therein, as amended, so as to prohibit use of certain types of packages]; submitted by Mr. Haugen. Jan. 29, 1924. 6 p. (H. rp. 125, 68th Cong. 1st sess.) * Paper, 5c.   24—26049

Game. Protection of wild game on refuges, report to accompany H. R. 5946 [to amend sec. 84 of penal code of United States, relating to trespasses on bird reservations, so as to make provisions applicable to wild animal refuges and to protect United States property on any such lands]; submitted by Mr. Haugen. Jan. 29, 1924. 2 p. (H. rp. 127, 68th Cong. 1st sess.) * Paper, 5c.

Marketing of farm produce. Norris-Sinclair marketing bill, hearings on H. R. 2659, for purchase and sale of farm products, Jan. 8–18, 1924. 1924. iii+ 135 p. (Serial A.) * Paper, 15c.

Seeds. Langley free-seed bill, hearings on H. R. 602, authorizing distribution of free seeds, Jan. 16 and 17, 1924. 1924. iii+36 p. (Serial C.) * Paper 5c.

Warehouses. Swank warehouse bill, hearings on H. R. 4149, for building of warehouses by United States, Jan. 17, 1924; [statement of F. B. Swank]. 1924. iii+28 p. (Serial D.) * Paper, 5c.

Willow Creek ranger station, Mont., report to accompany H. R. 5941 [to complete construction of Willow Creek ranger station, Mont.]; submitted by Mr. Haugen. Jan. 29, 1924. 1 p. (H. rp. 124, 68th Cong. 1st sess.) * Paper, 5c.

APPROPRIATIONS COMMITTEE

Interior Department. Interior Department appropriation bill, [fiscal year] 1925, hearing before subcommittee in charge of Interior Department appropriation bill, 1925. 1924. [2]+1073 p. il. * Paper, 85c.

—— Interior Department appropriation bill, [fiscal year] 1925, report to accompany H. R. 5078; submitted by Mr. Cramton. Jan. 9, 1924. 32 p. (H. rp. 22, 68th Cong. 1st sess.) * Paper, 5c.

Post Office Department. Post Office appropriation bill, [fiscal year] 1925, hearings before subcomittee in charge of Post Office appropriation bill for 1925. 1924. ii+272 p. * Paper, 25c.

Treasury Department. Treasury and Post Office Departments appropriation bill, fiscal year 1925, report to accompany H. R. 6349; submitted by Mr. Madden. Jan. 29, 1924. 35 p. (H. rp. 116, 68th Cong. 1st sess.) * Paper, 5c.

—— Treasury Department appropriation bill, [fiscal year] 1925, hearing before subcommittee in charge of Treasury Department appropriation bill for 1925. 1924. ii+905 p. * Paper, 80c.

BANKING AND CURRENCY COMMITTEE

Federal Reserve System, Joint Committee of Inquiry on Membership in. Extension of time for final report of Joint Committee of Inquiry on Membership in Federal Reserve System, report to accompany H. J. Res. 151; submitted by Mr. McFadden. Jan. 23, 1924. 1 p. (H. rp. 86, 68th Cong. 1st sess.) * Paper, 5c.

CIVIL SERVICE REFORM COMMITTEE

Personnel Classification Board. Requesting information from Personnel Classification Board, report to accompany H. Res. 78; submitted by Mr. Lehlbach. Dec. 20, 1923. 1 p. (H. rp. 4, 68th Cong. 1st sess.) * Paper, 5c.

CLAIMS COMMITTEE

Con Rein, schooner. East La Have Transportation Co. (Ltd.), owner of schooner Con Rein, report to accompany H. R. 2498 [for relief of East La Have Transportation Company, Limited, owner, A. Picard and Company, owner of cargo, and George H. Corkum, Leopold S. Conrad, Wilson Zinck, Freeman Beck, Sidney Knickle, and Norman E. LeGay, crew of schooner Con Rein, sunk by United States submarine K–4]; submitted by Mr. Thomas of Oklahoma. Jan. 28, 1924. 2 p. (H. rp. 113, 68th Cong. 1st sess.) * Paper, 5c.

Fellows, Rush O.   Rush O. Fellows, report to accompany H. R. 3183 [for relief of Rush O. Fellows] ; submitted by Mr. Sears of Nebraska. Jan. 21, 1924. 5 p. (H. rp. 73, 68th Cong. 1st sess.)   * Paper, 5c.

Higgins, Fannie M.   Fannie M. Higgins, report to accompany H. R. 1860 [for relief of Fannie M. Higgins] ; submitted by Mr. Box. Jan. 28, 1924. 18 p. (H. rp. 111, 68th Cong. 1st sess.)   * Paper, 5c.

Long Island Railroad Co., report to accompany H. R. 1823 [for relief of Long Island Railroad Company] ; submitted by Mr. Underhill. Jan. 28, 1924. 2 p. (H. rp. 110, 68th Cong. 1st sess.)   * Paper, 5c.

MacAdam, D. H.   D. H. MacAdam, report to accompany H. R. 1438 [for relief of D. H. MacAdam] ; submitted by Mr. Edmonds. Jan. 29, 1924. 4 p. (H. rp. 119, 68th Cong. 1st sess.)   * Paper, 5c.

Reynolds, Hubert.   Hubert Reynolds, report to accompany H. R. 5541 [for relief of Hubert Reynolds] ; submitted by Mr. Edmonds. Jan. 29, 1924. 21 p. (H. rp. 120, 68th Cong. 1st sess.)   * Paper, 5c.

Seibel, Clifford W.   Clifford W. Seibel and Frank A. Vestal, report to accompany H. R. 5448 [for relief of Clifford W. Seibel and Frank A. Vestal] ; submitted by Mr. Thomas of Oklahoma. Jan. 21, 1924. 6 p. (H. rp. 75, 68th Cong. 1st sess.)   * Paper, 5c.

Thornton, Elizabeth.   Elizabeth Thornton, foster mother of Edward Short, report to accompany H. R. 3386 [authorizing Secretary of Treasury to pay war-risk insurance to Elizabeth Thornton, foster mother of Edward Short] ; submitted by Mr. Bulwinkle. Jan. 22, 1924. 8 p. (H. rp. 77, 68th Cong. 1st sess.)   * Paper, 5c.

Underwood Typewriter Co. and Frank P. Trott, report to accompany H. R. 4647 [for relief of Underwood Typewriter Company and Frank P. Trott] ; submitted by Mr. McReynolds. Jan. 21, 1924. 3 p. (H. rp. 74, 68th Cong. 1st sess.)   * Paper, 5c.

DISTRICT OF COLUMBIA COMMITTEE

Automobiles.   Tax on motor-vehicle fuels sold within District of Columbia, minority report to accompany H. R. 655 ; submitted by Mr. Blanton. Jan. 26, 1924. 13 p. (H. rp. 80, pt. 2, 68th Cong. 1st sess.) [Corrected print.]   * Paper, 5c.

——   Tax on motor-vehicle fuels sold within District of Columbia, report to accompany H. R. 655 ; submitted by Mr. Zihlman. Jan. 23, 1924. 4 p. (H. rp. 80 [pt. 1], 68th Cong. 1st sess.)   * Paper, 5c.

Police Department.   Salaries of officers and members of Metropolitan Police Force and Fire Department of District of Columbia, report to accompany H. R. 5855 ; submitted by Mr. Zihlman. Jan. 26, 1924. 6 p. (H. rp. 108, 68th Cong. 1st sess.)   * Paper, 5c.

Venereal diseases.   Prevention of venereal diseases in District of Columbia, report to accompany H. R. 491 ; submitted by Mr. Gilbert. Jan. 17, 1924. 2 p. (H. rp. 52, 68th Cong. 1st sess.)   * Paper, 5c.

ELECTIONS COMMITTEE, NO. 3

Miller, Edward E.   Eligibility of Edward E. Miller, Representative elect from Illinois, arguments and hearings on House resolution 2. 1924. ii+41 p.   * Paper, 5c.

——   Eligibility of Representative Edward E. Miller, adverse report to accompany H. Res. 2 [appointing committee to investigate eligibility of Edward E. Miller, Member of House of Representatives] ; submitted by Mr. Elliott. Jan. 18, 1924. 1 p. (H. rp. 56, 68th Cong. 1st sess.)   * Paper, 5c.

FOREIGN AFFAIRS COMMITTEE

Foreign service of United States, hearings on H. R. 17 and H. R. 6357 (H. R. 6357 reported favorably), for reorganization and improvement of foreign service of United States, Jan. 14–18, 1924. 1924. x+226 p. [Includes hearings before 67th Congress,.4th session, on H. R..12543, and Activities and needs for reorganization and improvement of Nation's foreign service, by W. F. Lineberger.]   * Paper, 20c.   .

INDIAN AFFAIRS COMMITTEE

Bell, Richard. Cancellation of allotments made to Richard Bell, deceased, report to accompany H. R. 3900 [to cancel 2 allotments made to Richard Bell, deceased, embracing land within Round Valley Indian Reservation in California]; submitted by Mr. Howard of Nebraska. Jan. 25, 1924. 2 p. (H. rp. 101, 68th Cong. 1st sess.) * Paper, 5c.

Blackfeet Reservation. Disposal of homestead allotments of deceased allottees , in Blackfeet Indian Reservation, Mont., report to accompany H. R. 2879; submitted by Mr. Leavitt. Jan. 11, 1924. 2 p. (H. rp. 33, 68th Cong. 1st sess.) * Paper, 5c.

Cherokee Indians. Claims of Cherokee Indians against United States, report to accompany H. R. 4457 [conferring jurisdiction upon Court of Claims to hear. examine, adjudicate, and enter judgment in any claims which Cherokee Indians may have against United States]; submitted by Mr. Hastings. Jan. 19, 1924. 2 p. (H. rp. 68, 68th Cong. 1st sess.) * Paper, 5c.

—— Final disposition of affairs of eastern band of Cherokee Indians of North Carolina, report to accompany H. R. 3852; submitted by Mr. Dallinger. Jan. 19, 1924. 4 p. (H. rp. 67, 68th Cong. 1st sess.) * Paper, 5c.

Chilocco Indian School. Construction of highway from Kansas State line to Chilocco Indian School, report to accompany H. R. 5714; submitted by Mr. Garber. Jan. 19, 1924. 1 p. (H. rp. 65, 68th Cong. 1st sess.) * Paper, 5c.

Chippewa Indians. Enrollment and allotment of members of Lac du Flambeau band of Lake Superior Chippewas, Wisconsin, report to accompany H. R. 3684; submitted by Mr. Roach. Jan. 18, 1924. 3 p. (H. rp. 61, 68th Cong. 1st sess.) * Paper, 5c.

—— Payment of claims of·Chippewa Indians of Minnesota for back annuities, report to accompany H. R. 2876; submitted by Mr. Snyder. Jan. 18, 1924. 1 p. (H. rp. 62, 68th Cong. 1st sess.) * Paper, 5c.

—— Per capita payment of $100 to each enrolled member of Chippewa tribe of Minnesota, report to accompany H. R. 185 [for per capita payment of $100 to each enrolled member of Chippewa tribe of Minnesota from funds standing to their credit in Treasury]; submitted by Mr. Snyder. Jan. 12, 1924. 2 p. (H. rp. 42, 68th Cong. 1st sess.) * Paper, 5c.

Colville Reservation. Sale of lands allotted to Indians under Moses agreement, report to accompany H. R. 2878; submitted by Mr. Hill of Washington. Jan. 17, 1924. 2 p. (H. rp. 54, 68th Cong. 1st sess.) * Paper, 5c.

Comanche Indians. Compensation to 3 Comanche Indians of Kiowa Reservation, report to accompany H. R. 2881 [to compensate Nehio or Len Parker, Arrushe, and Neho, Comanche Indians of Kiowa Reservation]; submitted by Mr. Howard of Oklahoma. Jan. 19, 1924. 2 p. (H. rp. 66, 68th Cong. 1st sess.) * Paper, 5c.

Crane, Mary. Cancellation of allotment of land made to Mary Crane, deceased Indian, report to accompany H. R. 3800 [to cancel allotment of land made to Mary Crane or Ho-tah-kah-win-kaw, deceased Indian, embracing land within Winnebago Indian Reservation·in Nebraska]; submitted by Mr. Howard of Nebraska. Jan. 25, 1924. 2 p. (H. rp. 100, 68th Cong. 1st sess.) * Paper, 5c.

Indians. Relief of certain nations or tribes of Indians in Montana, Idaho, and Washington, report to accompany H. R. 3444; submitted by Mr. Leavitt. Jan. 19, 1924. 4 p. (H. rp. 64, 68th Cong. 1st sess.) * Paper, 5c.

—— Sale of lands and plants no longer needed for Indian administrative or allotment purposes, report to accompany H. R. 4803; submitted by Mr. Snyder. Jan. 18, 1924. 2 p. (H. rp. 63, 68th Cong. 1st sess.) * Paper, 5c.

Jack, Isaac. Isaac Jack, Seneca Indian, report to accompany H. R. 1629 [authorizing removal of restrictions from 40 acres of allotment of Isaac Jack, Seneca Indian]; submitted by Mr. Howard of Oklahoma. Jan. 10, 1924. 1 p. (H. rp. 24, 68th Cong. 1st sess.) * Paper, 5c.

Lac Court Oreille Reservation. Allotments of land to Indians on Lac Courte Oreille Indian Reservation in Wisconsin, report to accompany H. R. 2883; submitted by Mr. Snyder. Jan. 10, 1924. 2 p. (H. rp. 28, 68th Cong. 1st sess.) * Paper, 5c.

Quinaielt Reservation. Setting aside tribal lands within Quinaielt Indian Reservation in Washington for lighthouse purposes, report to accompany H. R. 5416; submitted by Mr. Snyder. Jan. 25, 1924. 2 p. (H. rp. 106; 68th Cong. 1st sess.) * Paper, 5c.

Red Lake Reservation. Payment to members of Red Lake band of Chippewa Indians, report to accompany H. R. 25 [authorizing per capita payment of $50 each to members of Red Lake band of Chippewa Indians from proceeds of sale of timber and lumber on Red Lake Reservation]; submitted by Mr. Knutson. Jan. 23, 1924. 2 p. (H. rp. 81, 68th Cong. 1st sess.) * Paper, 5c.

Sia Indians. Reservation of lands in New Mexico for Zia Pueblo Indians, report to accompany H. R. 2877; submitted by Mr. Morrow. Jan. 23, 1924. 1 p. (H. rp. 79, 68th Cong. 1st sess.) * Paper, 5c.

INTERSTATE AND FOREIGN COMMERCE COMMITTEE

Arkansas River. Bridge across Arkansas River between Little Rock and Argenta, Ark., report to accompany S. 602 [to extend time for construction of bridge across Arkansas River between Little Rock and Argenta, Ark., by Pulaski County]; submitted by Mr. Parks of Arkansas. Jan. 23, 1924. 1 p. (H. rp. 83, 68th Cong. 1st sess.) * Paper, 5c.

Chattahoochee River. Bridge across Chattahoochee River, near Eufaula, Ala., report to accompany H. R. 3198 [to authorize Alabama and Georgia, through their respective Highway Departments, to construct bridge across Chattahoochee River at or near Eufaula, Ala., connecting Barbour County, Ala., and Quitman County, Ga.]; submitted by Mr. Huddleston. Jan. 12, 1924. 2 p. (H. rp. 37, 68th Cong. 1st sess.) * Paper, 5c.

—— Bridge across Chattahoochie [Chattahoochee] River near Fort Gaines, Ga., report to accompany H. R. 477 [to authorize Georgia through its Highway Department to construct bridge across Chattahoochee River at or near Fort Gaines, Ga., connecting Clay County, Ga., and Henry County, Ala.]; submitted by Mr. Huddleston. Jan. 12, 1924. 2 p. (H. rp. 36, 68th Cong. 1st sess.) * Paper, 5c.

Columbia River. Bridge across Columbia River between Oregon and Washington, report to accompany H. R. 726 [to extend time for completion of construction of bridge across Columbia River between Oregon and Washington at or within 2 miles westerly from Cascade Locks, Oreg., by Interstate Construction Corporation]; submitted by Mr. Burtness. Jan. 12, 1924. 2 p. (H. rp. 46, 68th Cong. 1st sess.) * Paper, 5c.

—— Bridge across Columbia River, report to accompany H. R. 4120 [granting consent of Congress to Greater Wenatchee Irrigation District to construct bridge across Columbia River, Wash.]; submitted by Mr. Burtness. Jan. 24, 1924. 1 p. (H. rp. 95, 68th Cong. 1st sess.) * Paper, 5c.

Current River. Bridge across Current River near Finleys Ferry, Ark., report to accompany H. R. 4984 [to authorize Clay County bridge district, Ark., to construct bridge over Current River near Finley's Ferry, Ark.]; submitted by Mr. Parks of Arkansas. Jan. 24, 1924. 2 p. (H. rp. 92, 68th Cong. 1st sess.) * Paper, 5c.

Fox River. Bridge across Fox River in Kendall County, Ill., report to accompany H. R. 4498 [to authorize Illinois to construct bridge across Fox River in county of Kendall, Ill., between Yorkville and Bristol]; submitted by Mr. Denison. Jan. 23, 1924. 2 p. (H. rp. 87, 68th Cong. 1st sess.) * Paper, 5c.

Hudson River. Bridge across Hudson River at Poughkeepsie, N. Y., report to accompany S. 733 [granting consent of Congress to construction of bridge over Hudson River at Poughkeepsie, N. Y., by commissioner of highways of New York State]; submitted by Mr. Corning. Jan. 23, 1924. 1 p. (H. rp. 85, 68th Cong. 1st sess.) * Paper, 5c.

—— Extending time for completion of bridge across Hudson River, N. Y., report to accompany H. R. 4796 [to extend time of Hudson River Connecting Railroad Corporation for completion of its bridge across Hudson River, N. Y., at point between Castleton and Schodack Landing]; submitted by Mr. Parker. Jan. 10, 1924. 1 p. (H. rp. 25, 68th Cong. 1st sess.) * Paper, 5c.

Kingston Lake. Bridge across Kingston Lake at Conway, S. C., report to accompany H. R. 3680 [authorizing building of bridge across Kingston Lake at Conway, S. C., by Horry County]; submitted by Mr. Huddleston. Jan. 12, 1924. 2 p. (H. rp. 39, 68th Cong. 1st sess.) * Paper, 5c.

Little Calumet River. Bridge across Little Calumet River at Riverdale, Ill., report to accompany H. R. 3845 [to authorize construction of bridge across Little Calumet River at Riverdale, Ill., by Acme Steel Goods Company]; submitted by Mr. Graham of Illinois. Jan. 23, 1924. 2 p. (H. rp. 82, 68th Cong. 1st sess.) * Paper, 5c.

Lumber River. Bridge across Lumber River between Marion and Horry counties, S. C., report to accompany S. 1634 [to authorize building of bridge across Columbia River, S. C., between Marion and Horry counties near Nichols, S. C., by Highway Department of South Carolina]; submitted by Mr. Huddleston. Jan. 24, 1924. (H. rp. 94, 68th Cong. 1st sess.) * Paper, 5c.

Mississippi River. Bridge across Mississippi River between Hennepin and Ramsey counties, Minn., report to accompany S. 801 [granting consent of Congress to construction by Valley Transfer Railway Company of bridge across Mississippi River between Hennepin and Ramsey counties, Minn.]; submitted by Mr. Newton of Minnesota. Jan. 15, 1924. 1 p. (H. rp. 51, 68th Cong. 1st sess.) * Paper, 5c.

—— Bridge across Mississippi River between St. Paul and Minneapolis, Minn., report to accompany H. R. 5273 [granting consent of Congress to Chicago, Milwaukee and St. Paul Railway Company to construct bridge over Mississippi River between St. Paul and Minneapolis, Minn.]; submitted by Mr. Newton of Minnesota. Jan. 29, 1924. 2 p. (H. rp. 123, 68th Cong. 1st sess.) * Paper, 5c.

—— Bridge across Mississippi River connecting county of Whiteside, Ill., and county of Clinton, Iowa, report to accompany H. R. 4817 [granting consent of Congress to Illinois and Iowa, or either of them, to construct bridge across Mississippi River connecting county of Whiteside, Ill., and county of Clinton, Iowa]; submitted by Mr. Shallenberger. Jan. 25, 1924. 2 p. (H. rp. 99, 68th Cong., 1st sess.) * Paper, 5c.

—— Bridge across Mississippi River, Minneapolis, Minn., report to accompany H. R. 4366 [granting consent of Congress to Great Northern Railway Company to maintain and operate or reconstruct, maintain and operate bridge across Mississippi River within Minneapolis, Minn.]; submitted by Mr. Newton of Minnesota. Jan. 22, 1924. 2 p. (H. rp. 78, 68th Cong. 1st sess.) * Paper, 5c.

Missouri River. Bridge across Missouri River between Brule and Lyman counties, S. Dak., report to accompany S. 1367 [granting consent of Congress to South Dakota for construction of bridge across Missouri River between Brule County and Lyman County, S. Dak.]; submitted by Mr. Burtness. Jan. 10, 1924. 1 p. (H. rp. 26, 68th Cong. 1st sess.) * Paper, 5c.

—— Bridge across Missouri River, S. Dak., report to accompany S. 1368 [granting consent of Congress to South Dakota for construction of bridge across Missouri River between Walworth County and Corson County, S. Dak.]; submitted by Mr. Burtness. Jan. 10, 1924. 1 p. (H. rp. 27, 68th Cong. 1st sess.) * Paper, 5c.

Newtown Creek. Bridge between boroughs of Brooklyn and Queens, N. Y., report to accompany H. R. 3265 [to authorize construction of bridge by New York City across Newtown Creek between boroughs of Brooklyn and Queens, in city and State of New York]; submitted by Mr. Parker. Jan. 12, 1924. 2 p. (H. rp. 48, 68th Cong. 1st sess.) * Paper, 5c.

Ohio River. Extending time for construction of bridge across Ohio River, between Benwood, W. Va., and Bellaire, Ohio, report to accompany H. R. 5624 [authorizing construction of bridge across Ohio River to connect Benwood, W. Va. ,and Bellaire, Ohio, by Interstate Bridge Company]; submitted by Mr. Cooper of Ohio. Jan. 24, 1924. 2 p. (H. rp. 93, 68th Cong. 1st sess.) * Paper, 5c.

Pamunkey River. Bridge across Pamunkey River, Va., report to accompany S. 643 [to extend time for construction of bridge across Pamunkey River, Va., by Pamunkey Ferry Company, near Sweet Hall, Va.]; submitted by Mr. Wyant. Jan. 23, 1924. 1 p. (H. rp. 84, 68th Cong. 1st sess.) * Paper, 5c.

Pearl River. Bridge across Pearl River between St. Tammany Parish, La., and Hancock County, Miss., report to accompany H. R. 4808 [granting consent of Congress to construction of bridge across Pearl River between St. Tammany Parish, La., and Hancock County, Miss., by Highway Commission of Louisiana in cooperation with Mississippi or Hancock County]; submitted by Mr. Huddleston. Jan. 24, 1924. 2 p. (H. rp. 91 68th Cong. 1st sess.) * Paper, 5c.

Pearl River—Continued. Bridge across Pearl River, Miss., report to accompany H. R. 657 [granting consent of Congress to boards of supervisors of Rankin and Madison counties, Miss., to construct bridge across Pearl River, Miss., at Meeks Ferry]; submitted by Mr. Rayburn. Jan. 12, 1924. 2 p. (H. rp. 34, 68th Cong. 1st sess.)   *Paper, 5c.

Peedee River. Bridge across Pee Dee River, S. C., report to accompany H. R. 3679 [to authorize building of bridge across Pee Dee River, S. C., at Yawhannah Ferry by Horry and Georgetown counties, S. C.]; submitted by Mr. Huddleston. Jan. 12, 1924. 2 p. (H. rp. 38, 68th Cong. 1st sess.)   * Paper, 5c.

Pere Marquette Lake. Bridge across arm of Pere Marquette Lake, Mich., report to accompany H. R. 4182 [authorizing Ludington, Mason County, Mich., to construct bridge across arm of Pere Marquette Lake]; submitted by Mr. Mapes. Jan. 25, 1924. 2 p. (H. rp. 103, 68th Cong. 1st sess.). * Paper, 5c.

Ratigan, Luke. Luke Ratigan, report to accompany H. R. 1475 [for relief of Luke Ratigan]; submitted by Mr. Lea of California. Jan. 21, 1924. 2 p. (H. rp. 72, 68th Cong. 1st sess.)   * Paper, 5c.

Rio Grande. Bridge across Rio Grande, report to accompany H. R. 5196 [granting consent of Congress to construction of bridge across Rio Grande, by El Paso Electric Railway Company and El Paso and Juarez Traction Company, at El Paso, Tex.]; submitted by Mr. Rayburn. Jan. 12, 1924. 2 p. (H. rp. 35, 68th Cong. 1st sess.)   * Paper, 5c.

Rock River. Bridge across Rock River in county of Winnebago, Ill., report to accompany H. R. 4499 [granting consent of Congress to Illinois to construct bridge across Rock River in county of Winnebago, Ill., in section 24, township 46 north, range 1 east, of 3d principal meridian]; submitted by Mr. Denison. Jan. 23, 1924. 2 p. (H. rp. 88, 68th Cong. 1st sess.)   * Paper, 5c.

St. Croix River. Bridge across St. Croix River, report to accompany H. R. 5337 [granting consent of Congress to Maine to construct, jointly with Canada, bridge over St. Croix River between Vanceboro, Me., and St. Croix, New Brunswick]; submitted by Mr. Merritt. Jan. 30, 1924. 2 p. (H. rp. 128, 68th Cong. 1st sess.)   * Paper, 5c.

St. Francis River. Bridge across St. Francis River, Ark., report to accompany S. 604 [to authorize construction of bridge across St. Francis River near St. Francis, Ark., by St. Louis Southwestern Railway Company]; submitted by Mr. Parks of Arkansas. Jan. 12, 1924. 1 p. (H. rp. 43, 68th Cong. 1st sess.) * Paper, 5c.

St. John River. Bridge across St. John River, report to accompany H. R. 5348 [granting consent of Congress for construction of bridge across St. John River between Fort Kent, Me., and Clairs, New Brunswick, by Maine and Canada jointly]; submitted by Mr. Merritt. Jan. 30, 1924. 2 p. (H. rp. 129, 68th Cong. 1st sess.) * Paper, 5c.

St. Louis, Mo. Completion of approaches to bridge across Mississippi River between St. Louis, Mo., and East St. Louis, Ill., report to accompany H. R. 486 [to extend time for completion of municipal bridge approaches, and extensions or additions thereto, by St. Louis, within Illinois and Missouri]; submitted by Mr. Winslow. Jan. 24, 1924. 2 p. (H. rp. 97, 68th Cong. 1st sess.)   * Paper, 5c.

—— St. Louis municipal bridge, hearings on H. R. 486, to extend time for completion of municipal bridge approaches, and extensions or additions thereto, by St. Louis, within Illinois and Missouri, Jan. 18 and 19, 1924. 1924. iii+68 p. * Paper, 5c.

St. Louis River. Bridge across St. Louis River in Carlton County, Minn., report to accompany H. R. 4187 [to legalize bridge across St. Louis River in Carlton County, Minn., constructed by Minnesota]; submitted by Mr. Newton of Minnesota. Jan. 29, 1924. 1 p. (H. rp. 122, 68th Cong. 1st sess.) * Paper, 5c.

Tittmann, Otto H. O. H. Tittmann, report to accompany H. R. 1917 [for relief of O. H. Tittmann]; submitted by Mr. Hawes. Jan. 28, 1924. 2 p. (H. rp. 112, 68th Cong. 1st sess.)   * Paper, 5c.

Tug Fork. Bridge across Tug Fork of Big Sandy River near Williamson,
W. Va., report to accompany S. 1374 [to authorize Norfolk and Western Rail-
way Company to construct bridge across Tug Fork of Big Sandy River at
or near point about mile and a half west of Williamson, Mingo County, W.
Va., and near mouth of Turkey Creek, Pike County, Ky.]; submitted by
Mr. Huddleston. Jan. 12, 1924. 1 p. (H. rp. 41, 68th Cong. 1st sess.)
* Paper, 5c.

Waccamaw River. Bridge across Waccamaw River, S. C., report to accompany
H. R. 3681 [to authorize building of bridge across Waccamaw River, S. C., by
Horry County, at or near Star Bluff, or at or near Bellamys Landing]; submitted by Mr. Huddleston. Jan. 12, 1924. 2 p. (H. rp. 40, 68th Cong. 1st
sess.) * Paper, 5c.

—— Bridge across Waccamaw River, S. C., report to accompany S. 384 [to
authorize building of bridge across Waccamaw River, S. C., near North
Carolina State line by North and South Carolina Waccamaw Bridge Com-
pany]; submitted by Mr. Wyant. Jan. 25, 1924. 1 p. (H. rp. 104, 68th
Cong. 1st sess.) * Paper, 5c.

—— Spillway across Waccamaw River, N. C., report to accompany H. R.
2818 [to grant consent of Congress to K. C. Council, F. B. Gault, and Oscar
High to construct dam and spillway across Waccamaw River, N. C.]; submitted by Mr. Huddleston. Jan. 18, 1924. 2 p. (H. rp. 60, 68th Cong. 1st
sess.) * Paper, 5c.

West Pearl River. Bridge across West Pearl River, La., report to accompany
H. R. 4807 [granting consent of Congress to Highway Commission of Louisiana
to construct bridge across West Pearl River, La., near Pearl River station];
submitted by Mr. Rayburn. Jan. 25, 1924. 2 p. (H. rp. 105, 68th Cong. 1st
sess.) * Paper, 5c.

Willamette River. Bridge across Willamette River near Sellwood Ferry, Portland, Oreg., report to accompany H. R. 584 [to authorize county of Multnomah, Oreg., to construct bridge across Willamette River in Portland, Oreg.,
in vicinity of present site of Sellwood Ferry]; submitted by Mr. Burtness.
Jan. 12, 1924. 2 p. (H. rp. 44, 68th Cong. 1st sess.) * Paper, 5c.

—— Bridge across Willamette River, Portland, Oreg., near Ross Island, report to accompany H. R. 585 [to authorize county of Multnomah, Oreg., to
construct bridge across Willamette River in Portland, Oreg., to replace present Burnside Street Bridge in Portland, and also to authorize county of
Multnomah to construct bridge across Willamette River in Portland, in vicinity of Ross Island]; submitted by Mr. Burtness. Jan. 12, 1924. 2 p. (H.
rp. 45, 68th Cong. 1st sess.) * Paper, 5c.

Yellowstone River. Bridge across Yellowstone River at Glendive, Mont., report to accompany S. 1170 [to authorize Highway Commission of Montana to
construct bridge across Yellowstone River at or near Glendive, Mont.]; submitted by Mr. Burtness. Jan. 12, 1924. 1 p. (H. rp. 47, 68th Cong. 1st
sess.) * Paper, 5c.

JUDICIARY COMMITTEE

Arbitration. To validate certain agreements for arbitration, report to accompany H. R. 646 [to make valid and enforceable written provisions or agreements for arbitration of disputes arising out of contracts, maritime transactions, or commerce among States or Territories or with foreign nations];
submitted by Mr. Graham of Pennsylvania. Jan. 24, 1924. 2 p. (H. rp. 96,
68th Cong. 1st sess.) * Paper, 5c.

Calendar. Legislative calendar, 68th Congress, Jan. 3–21, 1924; no. 2–4. 1924.
Each 45 p. or 48 p. 4° ‡

Convict labor. Employment for Federal prisoners, report to accompany S. 704
[to equip Penitentiary, Leavenworth, Kans., for manufacture of supplies for
use of Government, for compensation of prisoners for their labor, and for
other purposes]; submitted by Mr. Hersey. Jan. 7, 1924. 2 p. (H. rp. 21,
68th Cong. 1st sess.) * Paper, 5c.

District Courts. Create 2 judicial districts within Indiana, report to accompany
H. R. 62; submitted by Mr. Hickey. Jan. 3, 1924. 4 p. (H. rp. 20, 68th
Cong. 1st sess.) [Corrected print.] * Paper, 5c.

—— To transfer Chicot County from eastern to western division of eastern
judicial district of Arkansas, report to accompany H. R. 4439; submitted by
Mr. Tillman. Jan. 17, 1924. 1 p. (H. rp. 55, 68th Cong. 1st sess.) * Paper,
5c.

Internal revenue claims. Amend paragraph 20 of sec. 24 of judicial code, report to accompany H. R. 2716 [to amend paragraph 20 of sec. 24 of judicial code as amended by act of Nov. 23, 1921, to reduce and equalize taxation, to provide revenue, and for other purposes]; submitted by Mr. Graham of Pennsylvania. Jan. 29, 1924. 1 p. (H. rp. 121, 68th Cong. 1st sess.) * Paper, 5c.

Judges. Additional judges for 8th circuit, hearing on H. R. 661, Jan. 23, 1924. 1924. ii+12 p. (Serial 2.) * Paper, 5c.

—— Additional judges for 8th circuit, report to accompany H. R. 661 [authorizing the President to appoint 2 additional circuit judges for 8th circuit]; submitted by Mr. Graham of Pennsylvania. Jan. 25, 1924. 12 p. (H. rp. 102, 68th Cong. 1st sess.) * Paper, 5c.

—— To amend act for appointment of additional circuit court judge, etc., report to accompany H. R. 4507 [to amend act for appointment of additional circuit court judge for 4th judicial circuit, for appointment of additional district judges for certain districts, providing for annual conference of certain judges, and for other purposes]; submitted by Mr. Graham of Pennsylvania. Jan. 18, 1924. 1 p. (H. rp. 58, 68th Cong. 1st sess.) * Paper, 5c.

Lynch law. Antilynching bill, report to accompany H. R. 1 [to assure to persons within jurisdiction of every State equal protection of laws, and to punish crime of lynching]; submitted by Mr. Dyer. Jan. 19, 1924. 22 p. (H. rp. 71, 68th Cong. 1st sess.) [Includes views of minority signed by Mr. Thomas and others.] * Paper, 5c.   23—27384

Pay, Army. Pay claims of Army officers, report to accompany H. R. 703 [to confer jurisdiction on Court of Claims to certify findings of fact heretofore made for claimants in claims of officers of Army for longevity pay]; submitted by Mr. Graham of Pennsylvania. Jan. 18, 1924. 3 p. (H. rp. 57, 68th Cong. 1st sess.) * Paper, 5c.

Reformatories. Establishment of industrial reformatory and Federal industrial farm for women, hearing on H. R. 2869, H. R. 685, and H. R. 4125, Jan. 9, 1924. 1924. ii+19 p. (Serial 1.) * Paper, 5c.

—— Establishment of industrial reformatory, report to accompany H. R. 2869; submitted by Mr. Foster. Jan. 19, 1924. 4 p. (H. rp. 70, 68th Cong. 1st sess.) * Paper, 5c.

—— Federal industrial institution for women, report to accompany S. 790 [for establishment of Federal industrial institution for women]; submitted by Mr. Foster. Jan. 19, 1924. 2 p. (H. rp. 69, 68th Cong. 1st sess.) * Paper, 5c.

LAWS, COMMITTEE ON REVISION OF

Code of laws of United States, report to accompany H. R. 12 [to consolidate, codify, revise, and reenact general and permanent laws of United States in force Dec. 2, 1923]; submitted by Mr. Little. Dec. 20, 1923. 37 p. (H. rp. 2, 68th Cong. 1st sess.) * Paper, 5c.   23—27402

LIBRARY COMMITTEE

District of Columbia. Bronze tablet on Francis Scott Key Bridge, report to accompany S. 627 [to authorize National Society United States Daughters of 1812 to place bronze tablet on Francis Scott Key Bridge]; submitted by Mr. Luce. Jan. 17, 1924. 1 p. (H. rp. 53, 68th Cong. 1st sess.) * Paper, 5c.

Navy and Marine Memorial to Americans Lost at Sea, report to accompany H. J. Res. 129 [authorizing erection on public grounds in Washington, D. C., of memorial to Navy and Marine services, to be known as Navy and Marine Memorial Dedicated to Americans Lost at Sea]; submitted by Mr. Luce. Jan. 26, 1924. 1 p. (H. rp. 109, 68th Cong. 1st sess.) * Paper, 5c.

Women. Monument to commemorate services and sacrifices of women in World War, report to accompany H. J. Res. 107 [in relation to erection of American Red Cross memorial building as monument to commemorate services and sacrifices of women of United States, its insular possessions, and District of Columbia in World War]; submitted by Mr. Luce. Jan. 26, 1924. 2 p. (H. rp. 107, 68th Cong. 1st sess.) * Paper, 5c.

MERCHANT MARINE AND FISHERIES COMMITTEE

Shipping Board. Conversion of ships into motor types, hearings on H. J. Res. 41 [permitting use of certain funds by Shipping Board for conversion of present-owned ships of United States into motor ships], Jan. 10 and 11, 1924. 1924. ii+143 p. 1 tab. * Paper, 20c.

MILITARY AFFAIRS COMMITTEE

Boy Scouts of America. Sale or transfer of Army and Navy equipment to Boy Scouts of America, hearings, 67th Congress, 2d session, on H. R. 11492, June 15 [and] 19, 1922; statements of John W. Weeks [and] James G. Strong. 1924. ii+8 p. * Paper, 5c.

Siam. Two Siamese subjects for instruction at Military Academy, report to accompany H. J. Res. 144 [authorizing Secretary of War to receive, for instruction at Military Academy, West Point, 2 Siamese subjects, to be designated hereafter by Government of Siam]; submitted by Mr. Kahn. Jan. 18, 1924. 2 p. (H. rp. 59, 68th Cong. 1st sess.) * Paper, 5c.

War Department. To restrict expenditures of War Department and military establishment, report to accompany H. R. 517; submitted by Mr. McKenzie. Jan. 11, 1924. 3 p. (H. rp. 29, 68th Cong. 1st sess.) * Paper, 5c.

War trophies. Distribution of war devices and trophies, report to accompany H. R. 3675 [for equitable distribution of captured war devices and trophies to States and Territories and to District of Columbia]; submitted by Mr. Kahn. Jan. 9, 1924. 21 p. (H. rp. 23, 68th Cong. 1st sess.) * Paper, 5c.

24—26110

NAVAL AFFAIRS COMMITTEE

Navy. Providing for sundry matters affecting naval service, and for other purposes, report to accompany H. R. 2688; submitted by Mr. Butler. Jan. 11, 1924. 35 p. (H. rp. 31, 68th Cong. 1st sess.) * Paper, 5c.

Public works. To authorize Secretary of Navy to proceed with construction of certain public works, report to accompany H. R. 5721; submitted by Mr. Britten. Jan. 23, 1924. 4 p. (H. rp. 90, 68th Cong. 1st sess.) * Paper, 5c.

PENSIONS COMMITTEE

Pensions. Pensions and increase of pensions for certain soldiers and sailors of Regular Army and Navy, etc., report to accompany H. R. 6426 [substituted for H. R. 792 and other bills]; submitted by Mr. Knutson. Jan. 30, 1924. 287 p. (H. rp. 130, 68th Cong. 1st sess.) * Paper, 25c.

POST OFFICE AND POST ROADS COMMITTEE

Harding, Mrs. Florence K. Florence Kling Harding, report to accompany H. R. 4617 [granting franking privilege to Florence Kling Harding]; submitted by Mr. Griest. Jan. 15, 1924. 1 p. (H. rp. 50, 68th Cong. 1st sess.) * Paper, 5c.

Mail matter. Extend insurance and collect-on-delivery service to 3d-class mail, report to accompany H. R. 4442; submitted by Mr. Kelly. Jan. 29, 1924. 2 p. (H. rp. 118, 68th Cong. 1st sess.) * Paper, 5c.

PUBLIC BUILDINGS AND GROUNDS COMMITTEE

Kenosha, Wis. Post-office site, Kenosha, Wis., report to accompany H. Res. 51 [authorizing Secretary of Treasury to negotiate with authorities of Kenosha, Wis., to ascertain terms and conditions upon which can be secured site for Federal building located in accordance with plan for civic center adopted by Kenosha]; submitted by Mr. Langley. Jan. 11, 1924. 2 p. (H. rp. 32, 68th Cong. 1st sess.) * Paper, 5c.

Veterans' Bureau. Additional hospital facilities for patients of veterans' Bureau, report to accompany H. R. 5209; submitted by Mr. Langley. Jan. 28, 1924. 3 p. (H. rp. 117, 68th Cong. 1st sess.) * Paper, 5c.

PUBLIC LANDS COMMITTEE

Calendar. Legislative calendar, 68th Congress, Jan. 22, 1924; no. 2. 1923 [1924]. 30 p. 4° [Imprint date incorrectly given as 1923.] ‡

RIVERS AND HARBORS COMMITTEE

Illinois River. Illinois and Mississippi rivers and diversion of water from Lake Michigan, hearings, Sept. 14, 1922. 1924. [1]+35 p. * Paper, 5c.
Mill Cut and Clubfoot Creek, N. C., report to accompany H. R. 4577 [for examination and survey of Mill Cut and Clubfoot Creek, N. C.]; submitted by Mr. Lyon. Jan. 24, 1924. 1 p. (H. rp. 98, 68th Cong. 1st sess.) * Paper, 5c.

RULES COMMITTEE

Rules. Revision of rules, hearings. 1924. pts. 1, 2, [3]+1–136 p. * Paper, pt. 1, 5c.; * pt. 2, 10c.

TERRITORIES COMMITTEE

Hawaii. Hawaiian bill of rights, hearings on H. R. 4121, to extend provisions of certain [Federal aid] laws to Hawaii, Dec. 22 [and] 29, 1923. 1924. [1]+42 p. * Paper, 5c.
—— Hawaiian bill of rights, report to accompany H. R. 4121 [to extend provisions of certain Federal aid laws to Hawaii]; submitted by Mr. Curry. Jan. 3. 1924. 4 p. (H. rp. 19, 68th Cong. 1st sess.) * Paper, 5c.

WAR CLAIMS COMMITTEE

Flagg, William H. William H. Flagg and others, report to accompany H. R. 4012 [to reimburse William H. Flagg and others]; submitted by Mr. Bulwinkle. Jan. 28, 1924. 7 p. (H. rp. 114, 68th Cong. 1st sess.) * Paper, 5c.

WAYS AND MEANS COMMITTEE

Finland. Settlement of debt of Finland to United States, report to accompany H. R. 5557 [to authorize settlement of indebtedness of Republic of Finland to United States]; submitted by Mr. Crisp. Jan. 23, 1924. 7 p. (H. rp. 89, 68th Cong. 1st sess.) * Paper, 5c.
Revenue act of 1924. Jan. 22, 1924. 262 p. large 8° (Committee print no. 2.) [Certain indicated portions of the bill, containing suggestions of Secretary of Treasury shown in stricken-through type and italics, have not been considered by the committee.] * Paper, 25c.   24—26111
Securities. Tax-exempt securities, report to accompany H. J. Res. 136 [proposing amendment to Constitution of United States relative to taxation of income from securities issued by or under authority of United States or any State]; submitted by Mr. Green of Iowa. Jan. 11, 1924. 10 p. (H. rp. 30, 68th Cong. 1st sess.) * Paper, 5c.   23—27389

SENATE

Appropriations. Supplemental estimate of appropriation for legislative establishment. Jan. 12, 1924. 2 p. (H. doc. 152, 68th Cong. 1st sess.) * Paper, 5c.
Calendar of business, Senate, 68th Congress, 1st session, Jan. 3–legislative day Jan. 28, calendar day Jan. 31, 1924; no. 9–25. [1924.] various paging, large 8° [Daily when Senate is in session.] ‡
Communism. Attempt by communists to seize American labor movement, prepared by United Mine Workers of America and published in newspapers of United States; presented by Mr. Lodge. 1924. ii+43 p. (S. doc. 14. 68th Cong. 1st sess.) * Paper, 5c.   23—27404
Library. Catalogue of library of Senate; compiled by Edward C. Goodwin. 1924. 1210 p. large 8° ‡   24—1209
Ruhr Valley. Conditions in Ruhr and Rhineland, report on present conditions in Ruhr and Rhineland made to council, New York commandery, Military Order of Foreign Wars of United States, by William Seaman Bainbridge, commander; presented by Mr. Pepper. 1924. [1]+16 p. (S. doc. 26, 68th Cong. 1st sess.) * Paper, 5c.   24—26050

APPROPRIATIONS COMMITTEE

Naval petroleum reserves. Appropriation to cancel leases, report to accompany H. J. Res. 160 [to provide appropriation for prosecution of suits to cancel leases on oil lands in former naval reserves]; submitted by Mr. Warren. Jan. 28, calendar day Jan. 30, 1924. 2 p. (S. rp. 110, 68th Cong. 1st sess.). * Paper, 5c.

BANKING AND CURRENCY COMMITTEE

Federal Farm Loan Board, hearings on nominations of members of board. 1924. ii+20 p. [Confidential.] * Paper, 5c.

CLAIMS COMMITTEE

Baltimore, Md. City of Baltimore, State of Maryland, report to accompany S. 1761 [to reimburse Baltimore, Md., for moneys expended to aid United States in construction of works of defense during Civil War]; submitted by Mr. Stanfield. Jan. 14, 1924. 18 p. (S. rp. 42, 68th Cong. 1st sess.) * Paper, 5c.

Bradley, William R. William R. Bradley, report to accompany S. 383 [for relief of William R. Bradley]; submitted by Mr. Capper. Jan. 24, 1924. 3 p. (S. rp. 98, 68th Cong. 1st sess.) * Paper, 5c.

Brock, C. LeRoy. Dr. C. LeRoy Brock, report to accompany S. 1664 [for relief of C. LeRoy Brock]; submitted by Mr. Harreld. Jan. 14, 1924. 5 p. (S. rp. 34, 68th Cong. 1st sess.) * Paper, 5c.

Canniff, Mrs. Kate. Kate Canniff, report to accompany S. 334 [for relief of Kate Canniff]; submitted by Mr. Capper. Jan. 21, 1924. 2 p. (S. rp. 80, 68th Cong. 1st sess.) * Paper, 5c.

Cleveland State Bank, Cleveland, Miss., report to accompany S. 75 [for relief of Cleveland State Bank, Cleveland, Miss.]; submitted by Mr. Bayard. Jan. 7, 1924. 4 p. (S. rp. 14, 68th Cong. 1st sess.) * Paper, 5c.

Cobb, Murray A. Capt. Murray A. Cobb, report to accompany S. 1815 [for relief of Murray A. Cobb]; submitted by Mr. Capper. Jan. 22, 1924. 7 p. (S. rp. 89, 68th Cong. 1st sess.) * Paper, 5c.

De Kimpke Construction Co., report to accompany S. 970 [for relief of De Kimpke Construction Company; West Hoboken, N. J.]; submitted by Mr. Bayard. Jan. 22, 1924. 3 p. (S. rp. 88, 68th Cong. 1st sess.) * Paper, 5c.

Eddy, Charles G. Elizabeth B. Eddy, report to accompany S. 85 [to carry into effect finding of Court of Claims in claim of Elizabeth B. Eddy, widow of Charles G. Eddy]; submitted by Mr. Spencer. Jan. 22, 1924. 4 p. (S. rp. 86, 68th Cong. 1st sess.) * Paper, 5c.

Fallon, Henry N. Lieut. Henry N. Fallon. report to accompany S. 946 [for relief of family of Henry N. Fallon]; submitted by Mr. Trammell. Jan. 14, 1924. 6 p. (S. rp. 55, 68th Cong. 1st sess.) * Paper, 5c.

Faxon, Horton & Gallagher, Long Bros. Grocery Co., A. Rieger, Rothenberg & Schloss, Ryley, Wilson & Co., and Van Noy News Co., report to accompany S. 1435 [for relief of Faxon, Horton and Gallagher, Long Brothers Grocery Company, A. Rieger, Rothenberg and Schloss, Ryley, Wilson and Company, and Van Noy News Company]; submitted by Mr. Spencer. Jan. 14, 1924. 3 p. (S. rp. 50, 68th Cong. 1st sess.) * Paper, 5c.

Fore River Shipbuilding Co., report to accompany S. 1769 [to carry out findings of Court of Claims in case of Fore River Shipbuilding Company]; submitted by Mr. Spencer. Jan. 14, 1924. 10 p. (S. rp. 49, 68th Cong. 1st sess.) * Paper, 5c.

French spoliations, report to accompany S. 56 [for allowance of certain claims for indemnity for spoliations by French prior to July 31, 1801, as reported by Court of Claims]: submitted by Mr. Spencer. Jan. 14, 1924. 6 p. (S. rp. 45, 68th Cong. 1st sess.) * Paper, 5c.

Frost, Arthur. Arthur Frost, report to accompany S. 105 [for relief of Arthur Frost]: submitted by Mr. Harreld for Mr. Stanfield. Jan. 21, 1924. 8 p. (S. rp. 78, 68th Cong. 1st sess.) * Paper, 5c.

Glanville, J. B. J. B. Glanville and others, report to accompany S. 1253 [to reimburse J. B. Glanville and others for losses and damages sustained by them through negligent dipping of tick-infested cattle by Bureau of Animal Industry, Department of Agriculture]; submitted by Mr. Capper. Jan. 14, 1924. 16 p. (S. rp. 41, 68th Cong. 1st sess.) * Paper, 5c.

Grissinger, Elwood. Elwood Grissinger, report to accompany S. 1861 [authorizing Court of Claims to hear, determine, and render final judgment in claim of Elwood Grissinger]; submitted by Mr. Spencer. Jan. 14, 1924. 6 p. (S. rp. 51, 68th Cong. 1st sess.) * Paper, 5c.

Hartmann, Edward T. Capt. Edward T. Hartmann, report to accompany S. 1506 [for relief of Edward T. Hartmann and others]; submitted by Mr. Spencer. Jan. 14, 1924. 9 p. (S. rp. 48, 68th Cong. 1st sess.) * Paper, 5c.

Hunter, Reuben R. Reuben R. Hunter, report to accompany S. 353 [for relief of Reuben R. Hunter]; submitted by Mr. Spencer. Jan. 22, 1924. 3 p. (S. rp. 87, 68th Cong. 1st sess.) * Paper, 5c.

Hurst, Charles. Charles Hurst, report to accompany S. 661 [for relief of Charles Hurst]; submitted by Mr. Spencer. Jan. 14, 1924. 10 p. (S. rp. 46, 68th Cong. 1st sess.) * Paper, 5c.

Ingels, Mrs. Agnes. Relief of heirs of Agnes Ingels, report to accompany S. 1765; submitted by Mr. Capper. Jan. 15, 1924. 7 p. (S. rp. 60, 68th Cong. 1st sess.) * Paper, 5c.

Inheritance and transfer tax. To extend time for refunding of taxes erroneously collected from certain estates, report to accompany S. 894; submitted by Mr. Spencer. Jan. 14, 1924. 2 p. (S. rp. 47, 68th Cong. 1st sess.) * Paper, 5c.

Keegan, Peter C. Peter C. Keegan and others, report to accompany S. 210 [for relief of Peter C. Keegan and others]; submitted by Mr. Capper. Jan. 8, 1924. 3 p. (S. rp. 18, 68th Cong. 1st sess.) * Paper, 5c.

Kernan, Harold. Harold Kernan, report to accompany S. 1213 [for relief of Harold Kernan]; submitted by Mr. Capper. Jan. 28, calendar day Jan. 30, 1924. 2 p. (S. rp. 109, 68th Cong. 1st sess.) * Paper, 5c.

Kiener, Christian. Emma Kiener, report to accompany S. 1605 [for relief of Emma Kiener, widow of Christian Kiener]; submitted by Mr. Gooding. Jan. 14, 1924. 3 p. (S. rp. 44, 68th Cong. 1st sess.) * Paper, 5c.

Kin-Dave, steamship. Owners of steamship Kin-Dave, report to accompany S. 1894 [for relief of owners of steamship Kin-Dave]; submitted by Mr. Capper. Jan. 21, 1924. 3 p. (S. rp. 83, 68th Cong. 1st sess.) * Paper, 5c.

Leavitt, Louis. Claim of Louis Leavitt, report to accompany S. 88 [for relief of Louis Leavitt]; submitted by Mr. Capper. Jan. 14, 1924. 22 p. (S. rp. 35, 68th Cong. 1st sess.) * Paper, 5c.

Lee, William H. William H. Lee, report to accompany S. 796 [for relief of William H. Lee]; submitted by Mr. Capper. Jan. 14, 1924. 3 p. (S. rp. 38, 68th Cong. 1st sess.) * Paper, 5c.

McCarty, Edward N. Edward N. McCarty, report to accompany S. 225 [to extend benefits of employees' compensation act to Edward N. McCarty]; submitted by Mr. Capper. Jan. 28, calendar day Jan. 30, 1924. 7 p. (S. rp. 108, 68th Cong. 1st sess.) * Paper, 5c.

McColgan, Mrs. Annie. Annie McColgan, report to accompany S. 1353 [for relief of Annie McColgan]; submitted by Mr. Capper. Jan. 24, 1924. 5 p. (S. rp. 99, 68th Cong. 1st sess.) * Paper, 5c.

Massachusetts. Claim of Massachusetts, report to accompany S. 55 [making appropriation to pay Massachusetts for expenses incurred and paid at request of the President in protecting harbors and fortifying coast during Civil War, in accordance with findings of Court of Claims and Senate report numbered 764, 66th Congress, 3d session]; submitted by Mr. Spencer. Jan. 22, 1924. 12 p. (S. rp. 85, 68th Cong. 1st sess.) * Paper, 5c.

Mullen, William D., Company. William D. Mullen Co., report to accompany S. 129 [for relief of William D. Mullen Company]; submitted by Mr. Bruce. Jan. 7, 1924. 2 p. (S. rp. 16, 68th Cong. 1st sess.) * Paper, 5c.

New Jersey Shipbuilding and Dredging Company. New Jersey Shipbuilding and Dredging Company, hearing on S. 1572, for relief of New Jersey Shipbuilding and Dredging Company, Bayonne, N. J., Jan. 10, 1924. 1924. ii+13 p. * Paper, 5c.

New Jersey Shipbuilding and Dredging Company—Continued. New Jersey Shipbuilding & Dredging Co., report to accompany S. 1572 [for relief of New Jersey Shipbuilding and Dredging Company, Bayonne, N. J.]; submitted by Mr. Capper. Jan. 15, 1924. 4 p. (S. rp. 59, 68th Cong. 1st sess.) * Paper, 5c.

New York City. City of New York, report to accompany S. 1035 [for relief of city of New York]; submitted by Mr. Harreld. Jan. 14, 1924. 25 p. (S. rp. 33, 68th Cong. 1st sess.) * Paper, 5c.

Nolan, Thomas. Margaret Nolan, report to accompany S. 1219 [for relief of Margaret Nolan, mother of Thomas Nolan]; submitted by Mr. Stanfield. Jan. 14, 1924. 4 p. (S. rp. 40, 68th Cong. 1st sess.) * Paper, 5c.

Old National Bank of Martinsburg, Martinsburg, W. Va., report to accompany S. 214 [for relief of Old National Bank of Martinsburg, Martinsburg, W. Va.]; submitted by Mr. Mayfield. Jan. 8, 1924. 5 p. (S. rp. 19, 68th Cong. 1st sess.) * Paper, 5c.

Patterson, Robert F. Marion B. Patterson, report to accompany S. 244 [for relief of Marion B. Patterson, widow of Robert F. Patterson]; submitted by Mr. Bayard. Jan. 14, 1924. 12 p. (S. rp. 53, 68th Cong. 1st sess.) * Paper, 5c.

Plomteaux, Fred V. Fred V. Plomteaux, report to accompany S. 361 [for relief of Fred V. Plomteaux]; submitted by Mr. Capper. Jan. 24, 1924. 3 p. (S. rp. 97, 68th Cong. 1st sess.) * Paper, 5c.

Plummer, Mrs. Rosa E. Rosa E. Plummer, report to accompany S. 1249 [for relief of Rosa E. Plummer]; submitted by Mr. Capper. Jan. 21, 1924. 2 p. (S. rp. 82, 68th Cong. 1st sess.) * Paper, 5c.

Rice, Elizabeth H. Elizabeth H. Rice, report to accompany S. 49 [for relief of Elizabeth H. Rice]; submitted by Mr. Stephens. Jan. 15, 1924. 2 p. (S. rp. 58, 68th Cong. 1st sess.) * Paper, 5c.

Sonnenstrahl, Ely N. Estate of Ely N. Sonnenstrahl, report to accompany S. 1330 [for relief of estate of Ely N. Sonnenstrahl]; submitted by Mr. Capper. Jan. 15, 1924. 4 p. (S. rp. 65, 68th Cong. 1st sess.) * Paper, 5c.

Spates, Benjamin F. Benjamin F. Spates, report to accompany S. 1732 [for relief of Benjamin F. Spates]; submitted by Mr. Trammell. Jan. 14, 1924. 3 p. (S. rp. 57, 68th Cong. 1st sess.) * Paper, 5c.

Spiller, C. C. Estate of C. C. Spiller, report to accompany S. 967 [for relief of estate of C. C. Spiller]; submitted by Mr. Capper. Jan. 14, 1924. 9 p. (S. rp. 39, 68th Cong. 1st sess.) * Paper, 5c.

Stewart, John. Estate of John Stewart, report to accompany S. 1867 [for relief of estate of John Stewart]; submitted by Mr. Harreld. Jan. 21, 1924. 8 p. (S. rp. 77, 68th Cong. 1st sess.) * Paper, 5c.

Stoudemire, Eugene K. Eugene K. Stoudemire, report to accompany S. 1323 [for relief of Eugene K. Stoudemire]; submitted by Mr. Trammell. Jan. 14, 1924. 4 p. (S. rp. 56, 68th Cong. 1st sess.) * Paper, 5c.

Stout, Harry B. H. B. Stout, report to accompany S. 831 [for relief of H. B. Stout]; submitted by Mr. Capper. Jan. 15, 1924. (S. rp. 64, 68th Cong. 1st sess.) * Paper, 5c.

Swenson, Franklin A. Franklin A. Swenson, report to accompany S. 925 [for relief of Franklin A. Swenson]; submitted by Mr. Gooding. Jan. 14, 1924. 5 p. (S. rp. 43, 68th Cong. 1st sess.) * Paper, 5c.

Tobin, George T., & Son. George T. Tobin & Son, report to accompany S. 130 [for relief of George T. Tobin and Son]; submitted by Mr. Bayard. Jan. 14, 1924. 2 p. (S. rp. 52, 68th Cong. 1st sess.) * Paper, 5c.

United Dredging Co., report to accompany S. 593 [for relief of United Dredging Company]; submitted by Mr. Capper. Jan. 14, 1924. 4 p. (S. rp. 36, 68th Cong. 1st sess.) * Paper, 5c.

Vumbaca, Frank. Frank Vumbaca, report to accompany S. 243 [for relief of Frank Vumbaca]; submitted by Mr. Capper. Jan. 21, 1924. 2 p. (S. rp. 79, 68th Cong. 1st sess.) * Paper, 5c.

Walker, John H. John H. Walker, report to accompany S. 356 [for relief of John H. Walker]; submitted by Mr. Capper. Jan. 21, 1924. 2 p. (S. rp. 81, 68th Cong. 1st sess.) * Paper, 5c.

White, Mrs. Jessie M. Jessie M. White, report to accompany S. 827 [for relief of Jessie M. White]; submitted by Mr. Trammell. Jan. 14, 1924. 6 p. (S. rp. 54, 68th Cong. 1st sess.) * Paper, 5c.

Williams, Mrs. Ethel. Ethel Williams, report to accompany S. 646 [for relief of Ethel Williams]; submitted by Mr. Capper. Jan. 14, 1924. 8 p. (S. rp. 37, 68th Cong. 1st sess.) * Paper, 5c.

COMMERCE COMMITTEE

Arkansas River. Bridge across Arkansas River, report to accompany S. 602 [to extend time for construction of bridge across Arkansas River between Little Rock and Argenta, Ark., by Pulaski County]; submitted by Mr. Ladd. Jan. 8, 1924. 2 p. (S. rp. 20, 68th Cong. 1st sess.) * Paper, 5c.

Chattahoochee River. Bridge across Chattahoochee River, report to accompany S. 160 [authorizing Georgia to construct bridge across Chattahoochee River between Georgia and Alabama at or near Fort Gaines, Ga.]; submitted by Mr. Ladd. Jan. 15, 1924. 1 p. (S. rp. 62, 68th Cong. 1st sess.) * Paper, 5c.

Civil Aeronautics Bureau. Bureau of Civil Aeronautics in Department of Commerce, report to accompany S. 76 [to create Bureau of Civil Aeronautics in Department of Commerce, to encourage and regulate operation of civil aircraft in commerce, and for other purposes]; submitted by Mr. Jones of Washington. Jan. 7, 1924. 32 p. (S. rp. 15, 68th Cong. 1st sess.) * Paper, 5c.
23—27390

Columbia River. Bridge across Columbia River between Oregon and Washington, report to accompany S. 484 [to extend time for completion of construction of bridge across Columbia River between Oregon and Washington at or within 2 miles westerly from Cascade Locks, Oreg., by Interstate Construction Corporation]; submitted by Mr. Ladd. Jan. 15, 1924. 1 p. (S. rp. 63, 68th Cong. 1st sess.) * Paper, 5c.

—— Bridge across Columbia River, Wash., report to accompany S. 1225 [granting consent of Congress to Elbert M. Chandler to construct bridge across Columbia River at or near vantage Ferry, Wash.]; submitted by Mr. Ladd. Jan. 8, 1924. 1 p. (S. rp. 24, 68th Cong. 1st sess.) * Paper, 5c.

Fox River. Bridge across Fox River, Ill., report to accompany S. 1539 [extending time for construction of bridge across Fox River by Aurora, Ill., and granting consent of Congress to removal of existing dam and to its replacement with new structure]; submitted by Mr. Ladd. Jan. 3, 1924. 1 p. (S. rp. 11, 68th Cong. 1st sess.) * Paper, 5c.

—— To permit Aurora, Ill., to operate bridges across Fox River, report to accompany S. 1540 [granting consent of Congress to Aurora, Kane County, Ill., to construct bridges across Fox River]; submitted by Mr. Ladd. Jan. 3, 1924. 1 p. (S. rp. 12, 68th Cong. 1st sess.) * Paper, 5c.

Hudson River. Bridge over Hudson River, report to accompany S. 733 [granting consent of Congress to construction of bridge over Hudson River at Poughkeepsie, N. Y., by commissioner of highways of New York State]; submitted by Mr. Ladd. Jan. 8, 1924. 2 p. (S. rp. 22, 68th Cong. 1st sess.) * Paper, 5c.

Kingston Lake. Bridge across Kingston Lake, Conway, S. C., report to accompany H. R. 3680 [authorizing building of bridge across Kingston Lake at Conway, S. C., by Horry County]; submitted by Mr. Ladd. Jan. 24, 1924. 2 p. (S. rp. 94, 68th Cong. 1st sess.) * Paper, 5c.

Lumber River. Bridge across Lumber River, report to accompany S. 1634 [to authorize building of bridge across Lumber River, S. C., between Marion and Horry counties near Nichols, S. C., by Highway Department of South Carolina]; submitted by Mr. Ladd. Jan. 17, 1924. 1 p. (S. rp. 76, 68th Cong. 1st sess.) * Paper, 5c.

Mississippi River. Bridge across Mississippi River, Minn., report to accompany S. 801 [granting consent of Congress to construction by Valley Transfer Railway Company of bridge across Mississippi River between Hennepin and Ramsey counties, Minn.]; submitted by Mr. Ladd. Jan. 3, 1924. 1 p. (S. rp. 6, 68th Cong. 1st sess.) * Paper, 5c.

—— Bridge across Mississippi River, report to accompany S. 802 [granting consent of Congress to maintenance and operation or reconstruction, maintenance and operation of existing bridge owned and operated by Great Northern Railway Company across Mississippi River, within Minneapolis, Minn.]; submitted by Mr. Ladd. Jan. 23, 1924. 2 p. (S. rp. 92, 68th Cong. 1st sess.) * Paper, 5c.

Mississippi River—Continued.   Bridge across Mississippi River, report to accompany S. 1980 [granting consent of Congress to construction by Chicago, Milwaukee and St. Paul Railway Company of bridge across Mississippi River between Minneapolis and St. Paul, Minn.]; submitted by Mr. Ladd.   Jan. 28, calendar day Jan. 29, 1924. 1 p. (S. rp. 107, 68th Cong. 1st sess.) * Paper, 5c.

Missouri River.   Bridge across Missouri River, S. Dak., report to accompany S. 1367 [granting consent of Congress to South Dakota for construction of bridge across Missouri River between Brule County and Lyman County, S. Dak.]; submitted by Mr. Ladd.   Jan. 3, 1924. 1 p. (S. rp. 8, 68th Cong. 1st sess.) * Paper, 5c.

—— Bridge across Missouri River, S. Dak., report to accompany S. 1368 [granting consent of Congress to South Dakota for construction of bridge across Missouri River between Walworth County and Corson County, S. Dak.]; submitted by Mr. Ladd.   Jan. 3, 1924. 1 p. (S. rp. 9, 68th Cong. 1st sess.) * Paper, 5c.

Newtown Creek.   Bridge between boroughs of Brooklyn and Queens, N. Y., report to accompany H. R. 3265 [to authorize construction of bridge by New York City across Newtown Creek between boroughs of Brooklyn and Queens, in city and State of New York]; submitted by Mr. Ladd.   Jan. 24, 1924. 1 p. (S. rp. 96, 68th Cong. 1st sess.) * Paper, 5c.

Pamunkey River.   Bridge across Pamunkey River, report to accompany S. 643 [to extend time for construction of bridge across Pamunkey River, Va., by Pamunkey Ferry Company near Sweet Hall, Va.]; submitted by Mr. Ladd. Jan. 15, 1924. 1 p. (S. rp. 61, 68th Cong. 1st sess.) * Paper, 5c.

Pearl River.   Bridge across Pearl River, Miss., report to accompany H. R. 657 [granting consent of Congress to boards of supervisors of Rankin and Madison counties, Miss., to construct bridge across Pearl River, Miss., at Meeks Ferry]; submitted by Mr. Ladd.   Jan. 24, 1924. 1 p. (S. rp. 95, 68th Cong. 1st sess.) * Paper, 5c.

Peedee River.   Bridge across Peedee River, S. C., report to accompany H. R. 3679 [to authorize building of bridge across Pee Dee River, S. C., at Yawhannah Ferry by Horry and Georgetown counties, S. C.]; submitted by Mr. Ladd.   Jan. 24, 1924. 1 p. (S. rp. 93, 68th Cong. 1st sess.) * Paper, 5c.

Red River.   Bridge across Red River, report to accompany S. 1837 [granting consent of Congress to Fulton Ferry and Bridge Company to construct bridge across Red River at or near Fulton, Ark.]; submitted by Mr. Ladd.   Jan. 23, 1924. 1 p. (S. rp. 91, 68th Cong. 1st sess.) * Paper, 5c.

Rio Grande.   Bridge across Rio Grande River, report to accompany H. R. 5196 [granting consent of Congress to construction of bridge across Rio Grande. by El Paso Electric Railway Company and El Paso and Juarez Traction Company, at El Paso, Tex.]; submitted by Mr. Sheppard.   Jan. 23, 1924. 2 p. (S. rp. 90, 68th Cong. 1st sess.) * Paper, 5c.

St. Francis River.   Bridge across St. Francis River near St. Francis, Ark., report to accompany S. 604 [to authorize construction of bridge across St. Francis River near St. Francis, Ark., by St. Louis Southwestern Railway Company]; submitted by Mr. Ladd.   Jan. 3, 1924. 1 p. (S. rp. 5, 68th Cong. 1st sess.) * Paper, 5c.

St. Louis, Mo.   Completion of municipal bridge approaches within Illinois and Missouri, report to accompany S. 987 [to extend time for completion of municipal bridge approaches and extensions or additions thereto, by St. Louis, within Illinois and Missouri]; submitted by Mr. Ladd.   Jan. 8, 1924. 1 p. (S. rp. 23, 68th Cong. 1st sess.) * Paper, 5c.

Steamboat Inspection Service.   To abolish inspection districts of Apalachicola, Fla., and Burlington, Vt., Steamboat Inspection Service, report to accompany S. 1724 [to amend sec. 4414, Revised statutes, as amended, to abolish inspection districts of Apalachicola, Fla., and Burlington, Vt., Steamboat Inspection Service]; submitted by Mr. Jones of Washington.   Jan. 28, 1924. 1 p. (S. rp. 102, 68th Cong. 1st sess.) * Paper, 5c.

—— To amend sec. 4404, Revised statutes, report to accompany S. 1718 [to amend sec. 4404, Revised statutes, as amended, placing supervising inspectors of Steamboat Inspection Service under classified civil service]; submitted by Mr. Jones of Washington.   Jan. 28, 1924. 1 p. (S. rp. 101, 68th Cong. 1st sess.) * Paper, 5c.

Tug Fork. Bridge across Tug Fork of Big Sandy River, Ky., report to accompany S. 1374 [to authorize Norfolk and Western Railway Company to construct bridge across Tug Fork of Big Sandy River at or near point about mile and a half west of Williamson, Mingo County, W. Va., and near mouth of Turkey Creek, Pike County, Ky]; submitted by Mr. Ladd. Jan. 3, 1924. 1 p. (S. rp. 10, 68th Cong. 1st sess.) * Paper, 5c.

Waccamaw River. Bridge across Waccamaw River, S. C., report to accompany S. 384 [to authorize building of bridge across Waccamaw River, S. C., near North Carolina State line by North and South Carolina Waccamaw Bridge Company]; submitted by Mr. Dial. Jan. 3, 1924. 1 p. (S. rp. 13, 68th Cong. 1st sess.) * Paper, 5c.

Water pollution. Pollution of navigable waters, hearing before subcommittee on S. 42, S. 936, and S. 1388, bills relative to pollution of navigable waters, Jan. 9, 1924. 1924. iii+114 p. * Paper, 10c.

—— Preventing oil pollution of navigable coastal waters of United States, report to accompany S. 1942 [to protect navigation from obstruction and injury by preventing discharge of oil into coastal navigable waters of United States]; submitted by Mr. Willis. Jan. 15, 1924. 4 p. (S. rp. 66, 68th Cong. 1st sess.) * Paper, 5c.

White River. Bridge across White River, Ark., report to accompany S. 625 [to extend time for construction of bridge across White River at or near Batesville, Ark., by Independence County]; submitted by Mr. Ladd. Jan. 8, 1924. 2 p. (S. rp. 21, 68th Cong. 1st sess.) * Paper, 5c.

—— Bridge across White River near Des Arc, Ark., report to accompany S. 603 [to extend time for constructing bridge to be built by Gordon N. Peay, jr., across White River at or near Des Arc, Ark.]; submitted by Mr. Ladd. Jan. 3, 1924. 1 p. (S. rp. 4, 68th Cong. 1st sess.) * Paper, 5c.

Yellowstone River. Bridge across Yellowstone River, report to accompany S. 1170 [to authorize Highway Commission of Montana to construct bridge across Yellowstone River at or near Glendive, Mont.]; submitted by Mr. Ladd. Jan. 3, 1924. 1 p. (S. rp. 7, 68th Cong. 1st sess.) * Paper, 5c.

DISTRICT OF COLUMBIA COMMITTEE

Capital punishment in District of Columbia, report to accompany S. 387 [to prescribe method of capital punishment in District of Columbia to be electricution]; submitted by Mr. Jones of Washington. Jan. 16, 1924. 2 p. (S. rp. 67, 68th Cong. 1st sess.) * Paper, 5c.

Parks. Anacostia Park for nursery site, report to accompany S. 932 [authorizing transfer to jurisdiction of commissioners of District of Columbia of portion of Anacostia Park for nursery purposes]; submitted by Mr. Jones of Washington. Jan. 16, 1924. 2 p. (S. rp. 68, 68th Cong. 1st sess.) * Paper, 5c.

—— Glover parkway, report to accompany S. 1971 [to authorize commissioners of District of Columbia to accept land in District of Columbia dedicated by Charles C. Glover for park purposes]; submitted by Mr. Ball. Jan. 28, calendar day Jan. 29, 1924. 1 p. (S. rp. 105, 68th Cong. 1st sess.) * Paper, 5c.

Public works. Payment of claims, report to accompany S. 1342 [to amend act relative to payment of claims for material and labor furnished for District of Columbia buildings]; submitted by Mr. Capper. Jan. 9, 1924. 2 p. (S. rp. 27, 68th Cong. 1st sess.) * Paper, 5c.

Recorder of deeds. Fireproof addition to courthouse of District of Columbia, report to accompany S. 1972 [for erection of fireproof addition to courthouse of District of Columbia in Judiciary square for use of office of recorder of deeds]; submitted by Mr. Ball. Jan. 28, calendar day Jan. 29, 1924. 2 p. (S. rp. 106, 68th Cong. 1st sess.) * Paper, 5c.

Streets. Changing name of street, report to accompany S. 113 [changing name of Keokuk street, county of Washington, District of Columbia, to Military road]; submitted by Mr. Weller. Jan. 17, 1924. 1 p. (S. rp. 71, 68th Cong. 1st sess.) * Paper, 5c.

—— Closing of portion of Massachusetts avenue nw., report to accompany S. 1784 [for closing of portion of Massachusetts avenue northwest, District of Columbia]; submitted by Mr. Weller. Jan. 17, 1924. 1 p. (S. rp. 75, 68th Cong. 1st sess.) * Paper, 5c.

Streets—Continued. Opening of minor street, report to accompany S. 1341 [to authorize opening of minor street from Georgia avenue to 9th street northwest through squares 2875 and 2877]; submitted by Mr. Weller. Jan. 17, 1924. 2 p. (S. rp. 73, 68th Cong. 1st sess.) * Paper, 5c.

——— Widening of 4th street, report to accompany S. 1343 [to authorize widening of 4th street, south of Cedar street northwest, District of Columbia]; submitted by Mr. Weller. Jan. 17, 1924. 2 p. (S. rp. 74, 68th Cong. 1st sess.) * Paper, 5c.

——— Widening of Georgia avenue, report to accompany S. 1339 [to authorize widening of Georgia avenue between Fairmont street and Gresham place northwest]; submitted by Mr. Weller. Jan. 17, 1924. 2 p. (S. rp. 72, 68th Cong. 1st sess.) * Paper, 5c.

Taxation. Assistant assessors for District of Columbia, etc., report to accompany S. 1786 [to amend sec. 5, 6, and 7 of act making appropriations for expenses of government of District of Columbia, fiscal year 1903, relating to taxation and licenses]; submitted by Mr. Jones of Washington. Jan. 28, calendar day Jan. 29, 1924. 2 p. (S. rp. 104, 68th Cong. 1st sess.) * Paper, 5c.

Traffic regulations. Traffic conditions in District of Columbia, hearings before subcommittee, 67th Congress, 4th session, pursuant to S. Res. 419, for investigation of traffic conditions in Washington, D. C., and of accidents resulting therefrom, and better measures for protecting the public against injury and · damage arising from negligence, Nov. 5–Dec. 20, 1923. 1923. iii+372 p. il. 2 p. of pl. * Paper, 25c.

——— Traffic conditions in District of Columbia, report pursuant to S. Res. 419, 67th Cong. [for investigation of traffic conditions in Washington, D. C., and of accidents resulting therefrom, and better measures for protecting the public against injury and damage arising from negligence]; submitted by Mr. Ball. Jan. 22, 1924. 23 p. (S. rp. 84, 68th Cong. 1st sess.) [Corrected print.] * Paper, 5c.

FINANCE COMMITTEE

Calendar. Legislative calendar, 68th Congress, Jan. 5–29, 1924; no. 2–4. 1924. Each 19 p. or 23 p. 4° ‡

Cattle. Extending time for return of certain domestic animals into United States without payment of duties, report to accompany H. J. Res. 82; submitted by Mr. Smoot. Jan. 16, 1924. 2 p. (S. rp. 70, 68th Cong. 1st sess.) * Paper, 5c.

FOREIGN RELATIONS COMMITTEE

Calendar, 68th Congress, 1st session, Jan. 7, 1924; no. 2. 1924. 8 p. 4° ‡

Russia. Recognition of Russia, hearings before subcommittee pursuant to S. Res. 50, declaring that Senate favors recognition of present Soviet Government in Russia, Jan. 21–23, 1924. 1924. pt. 1, ii+1–158 p. * Paper, 15c.

GOLD AND SILVER INQUIRY COMMISSION

Money. Foreign currency and exchange investigation, foreign exchange quotations and curves, Commission of Gold and Silver Inquiry, Senate, pursuant to S. Res. 469, creating Commission of Gold and Silver Inquiry; prepared by H. N. Lawrie, assistant to commission. 1923. ii+125 p. 18 pl. (Serial 2.) * Paper, 60c.

Silver purchases under Pittman act, Commission of Gold and Silver Inquiry, Senate, 67th Congress, 4th session, pursuant to S. Res. 469, creating Commission of Gold and Silver Inquiry, Sept. 4, 1923, reply of comptroller general to argument of Senator Key Pittman for rehearing by comptroller general on revocation of allocations. 1924. ii+267–268 p. (Serial 1, pt. 7.) * Paper, 5c.

JUDICIARY COMMITTEE

Arbitration of interstate commercial disputes, joint hearings before subcommittees of Committees on Judiciary, on S. 1005 and H. R. 646, bills to make valid and enforceable written provisions or agreements for arbitration of disputes arising out of contracts, maritime transactions, or commerce among States or Territories or with foreign nations, Jan. 9, 1924. 1924. iii+41 p. * Paper, 5c.

Calendar. Legislative calendar, 68th Congress, Jan. 7–28, 1924; no. 2–5. 1924. various paging, 4° ‡

Marriage and divorce, amendment to Constitution, hearing before subcommittee on S. J. Res. 5, proposing amendment to Constitution of United States relative to marriage and divorce laws, Jan. 11, 1924. 1924. iii+28 p. * Paper, 5c.

Reformatories. For establishment of Federal industrial farm for women, report to accompany S. 790 [for establishment of Federal industrial institution for women]; submitted by Mr. Brandegee. Jan. 9, 1924. 3 p. (S. rp. 26, 68th Cong. 1st sess.) * Paper, 5c.

MILITARY AFFAIRS COMMITTEE

War trophies. To provide for equitable distribution of war devices, report to accompany S. 1376 [for equitable distribution of captured war devices and trophies to States and Territories and to District of Columbia]; submitted by Mr. Wadsworth. Jan. 7, 1924. 2 p. (S. rp. 17, 68th Cong. 1st sess.) * Paper, 5c.

Woodruff, William S. William Schuyler Woodruff, report to accompany S. 1199 [authorizing appointment of William Schuyler Woodruff as infantry officer, Army]; submitted by Mr. Reed of Pennsylvania. Jan. 9, 1924. 2 p. (S. rp. 25, 68th Cong. 1st sess.) * Paper, 5c.

NAVAL AFFAIRS COMMITTEE

Calendar. Legislative calendar, 68th Congress, 1st session, Jan. 8, 1924; no. 1. 1924. 6 p. large 8° ‡

POST OFFICES AND POST ROADS COMMITTEE

Poisons. To amend sec. 217 of penal laws, report to accompany S. 1750 [to amend sec. 217, as amended, of act to codify, revise, and amend penal laws of United States, so as to permit poisons prepared as disinfectants, germicides, or insecticides to be accepted for mailing]; submitted by Mr. Sterling. Jan. 16, 1924. 1 p. (S. rp. 69, 68th Cong. 1st sess.) * Paper, 5c.

PUBLIC LANDS AND SURVEYS COMMITTEE

Arizona University. To authorize Secretary of Interior to issue patent in fee-simple to board of regents of University of Arizona, Tucson, Ariz., for described tract of land, report to accompany S. 511; submitted by Mr. Cameron. Jan. 14, 1924. 2 p. (S. rp. 30, 68th Cong. 1st sess.) * Paper, 5c.

Calendar. Legislative calendar, 68th Congress, Jan. 17 and 23, 1924; no. 3 and 4. [1924.] 24 p. and 27 p. 4° ‡

Homestead. To amend sec. 2 of act for stock-raising homesteads, report to accompany S. 381; submitted by Mr. Jones of New Mexico. Jan. 14, 1924. 2 p. (S. rp. 32, 68th Cong. 1st sess.) * Paper, 5c.

Indian reservations. To amend sec. 13, chapter 431, of act approved June 25, 1910 (36 Stat. L. 855), report to accompany S. 665 [to amend sec. 13, chapter 431, of act approved June 25, 1910 (36 Statutes at large, p. 855), so as to authorize Secretary of Interior to issue trust and final patents on lands in Indian reservations withdrawn or classified as power or reservoir sites, with reservation of right of United States or its permittees to enter upon and use any part of such land for reservoir or power site purposes]; submitted by Mr. Smoot. Jan. 14, 1924. 1 p. (S. rp. 29, 68th Cong. 1st sess.) * Paper, 5c.

National forests. Limiting creation or extension of forest reserves in New Mexico and Arizona, report to accompany S. 377; submitted by Mr. Jones of New Mexico. Jan. 14, 1924. 2 p. (S. rp. 31, 68th Cong. 1st sess.) * Paper, 5c.

Naval petroleum reserves. Leases upon naval oil reserves, hearings, 67th Congress, 4th session, pursuant to S. Res. 282, S. Res. 294, and S. Res. 434, Nov. 30, 1923 [–Jan. 29, 1924]. 1923–24. pts. 4–6, [vi]+823–1909 p. il. * Paper, pt. 4, 30c.; * pt. 5, 35c.; * pt. 6, 20c.

REFORESTATION SELECT COMMITTEE

Reforestation, report pursuant to S. Res. 398 of 67th Congress [to investigate problems relating to reforestation]; submitted by Mr. McNary. Jan. 10, 1924. 29 p. (S. rp. 28, 68th Cong. 1st sess.) [Includes additional views of Mr. Moses and Mr. Couzens] * Paper, 5c.   23—27391

TERRITORIES AND INSULAR POSSESSIONS COMMITTEE

Hawaii. Federal farm loan act, report to accompany H. R. 4121 [to extend provisions of certain Federal aid laws to Hawaii]; submitted by Mr. Johnson of California. Jan. 28, 1924. 1 p. (S. rp.'100, 68th Cong. 1st sess.) * Paper, 5c.

VETERANS' BUREAU INVESTIGATION SELECT COMMITTEE

Veterans' Bureau. Investigation of veterans' Bureau, hearings, 67th Congress, 4th session, pursuant to S. Res. 466, authorizing appointment of committee to investigate leases and contracts executed by veterans' Bureau, and for other purposes, Oct. 22 [–Dec. 5], 1923. 1923. 2 v. [iv]+1791 p. 15 pl. 3 tab. [These hearings were also published in separate numbered parts.] * Paper, v. 1, 80c.; * v. 2, 75c.

——— Investigation of Veterans' Bureau, preliminary report, pursuant to S. Res. 466, 67th Cong. 4th sess.; submitted by Mr. Reed of Pennsylvania. Jan. 28, calendar day Jan. 29, 1924. 3 p. (S. rp. 103 [pt. 1], 68th Cong. 1st sess.) * Paper, 5c.   24—26052

COURT OF CLAIMS

Austin. Charles M. Austin *v.* United States; evidence [for claimant]. [1924.] no. C–792, p. 5–14. ‡

Chicago, Wilmington & Franklin Coal Co. v. United States; evidence for defendant. [1923.] no. B–11, p. 141–151. ‡

Darling. Jesse M. Darling *v.* United States; evidence for claimant. [1924.] no. B–131, p. 1–10. ‡

Federal Sugar Refining Company v. United States; evidence for defendant. [1924.] · no. B–147, p. 71–96. ‡

Hart. William H. H. Hart, findings in case of William H. H. Hart against United States. Jan. 3, 1924. 14 p. (S. doc. 16, 68th Cong. 1st sess.) * Paper, 5c.

Manhattan Sponging Works v. United States; evidence for plaintiff. [1924.] no. C–89, p. 11–40. ‡

Marion & Rye Valley Railway Company v. United States; stipulation. [1924.] no. C–699, p.· 45–60. ‡

Markley. John M. Markley *v.* United States; evidence [for claimant]. [1923.] no. C–936, p. 5–12. ‡

Marshall. Thurman W. Marshall *v.* United States; evidence [for claimant]. [1923.] no. B–70, p. 9–16. ‡

Mason. Charles P. Mason *v.* United States; evidence [for claimant]. [1924.] no. B–55, p. 13–31. ‡

Meyer. Robert R. Meyer *v.* United States; evidence for plaintiff. [1923.] no. 34233, p. 5–100. ‡

Missouri Pacific Railroad Company vs. United States; evidence for claimant. [1924.] no. 341–A, p. 9–15. ‡

Nashville, Chattanooga & St. Louis Railway Co. v. United States; defendant's evidence. [1924.] no. ·B–172, p. 1–4. ‡

National Fruit Products Company v. United States; evidence for plaintiff. [1924.] no. B–78, p. 17–36. ‡

Ordnance Engineering Corporation v. United States; evidence on defendant's counterclaim. [1924.] no. B–5, p. 143–215. ‡

Osage Nation of Indians *v.* United States; evidence for· plaintiff. [1924.] no. B–38, p. 119–132. ‡

Preil. Alvin O. Preil *v.* United States; evidence. [1923.] no. C–1027, p. 5–12. ‡

Reed's, Jacob, Sons, Incorporated. Jacob Reed's Sons *v.* United States; rebuttal evidence for plaintiff. [1923.] no. B–42, p. 171–184. ‡

Rettig. August Rettig *v.* United States; evidence [for claimant]. [1924.] no. C–698. p. 7–18. ‡

Robinson. Edgar S. Robinson *v.* United States; evidence for claimant. [1924.] no. B–133, p. 1–12. ‡

Rogers. Wilbur Rogers *v.* United States; evidence for claimant [and] defendant. [1924.] no. B–16, p. 25–148. ‡

St. Louis, Iron Mountain and Southern Railway. Benjamin F. Bush, receiver of St. Louis, Iron Mountain & Southern Railway Company, *v.* United States; evidence for claimant [and] defendant. [1924.] no. C–44. p. 11–20. ‡

Schaefer. Charles Schaefer, jr., *v.* United States; evidence for plaintiff. [1923.] no. 13–A, p. 261–264. ‡

Southern Products Company v. United States; evidence for plaintiff. [1923.] no. A–87, p. 7–37. ‡

Texas and Pacific Railway. J. L. Lancaster and Charles L. Wallace, receivers of Texas & Pacific Railway, *v.* United States; evidence for claimants [and] defendants. [1924.] no. C–112, p. 11–24. ‡

Thompson. John W. Thompson *v.* United States; evidence for defendant. [1923.] no. 34097, p. 891–988. ‡

COURT OF CUSTOMS APPEALS

Fish as food. No. 2331, United States *v.* R. U. Delapenha & Co. et al., transcript of record on appeal from Board of General Appraisers. [1923.] cover-title, i+26 p. ‡

Fringe. No. 2330, United States *v.* Wm. R. Noe & Sons et al., transcript of record on appeal from Board of General Appraisers. 1923. cover-title, i+18 p. ‡

Lasts. No. 2340, United States *v.* W. A. Mitchell, transcript of record on appeal from Board of General Appraisers. [1924.] cover-title, i+5 p. ‡

Wool. No. 2328, United States *v.* James C. Malone, Inc., transcript of record on appeal from Board of General Appraisers. [1923.] cover-title, i+23 p. ‡

FEDERAL BOARD FOR VOCATIONAL EDUCATION

Agriculture. Agricultural evening schools, methods of organizing and conducting evening schools and suggestions for content of courses; [by J. A. Linke]. Nov. 1923. v+41 p. 1 pl. (Bulletin 89; Agricultural series 17.) * Paper, 10c.   E 24—55

—— Agricultural teacher training. principles of organization for training of teachers of agriculture; [by Theodore H. Eaton]. Dec. 1923, [published] 1924. v+45 p. (Bulletin 90; Agricultural series 18.) * Paper, 10c. E 24—56

FEDERAL RESERVE BOARD

Federal reserve bulletin, Jan. 1924; [v. 10, no. 1]. 1924. iv+1–74+ii p. il. 4° [Monthly.] † Paper, 20c. single copy, $2.00 a yr.   15—26318

NOTE.—Beginning with the current issue of the Federal reserve bulletin, the 1st and final editions will be consolidated and all member banks and subscribers will receive current copies of the consolidated edition.

The bulletin contains, in addition to the regular official announcements, the national review of business conditions, detailed analyses of business conditions, research studies, reviews of foreign banking, and complete statistics showing the condition of Federal reserve banks and member banks. It will be sent to all member banks without charge. Others desiring copies may obtain them from the Federal Reserve Board, Washington, D. C., at the prices stated above.

FEDERAL TRADE COMMISSION

NOTE.—The bound volumes of the Federal Trade Commission decisions are sold by the Superintendent of Documents, Washington, D. C. Separate opinions are sold on subscription, price $1.00 per volume; foreign subscription, $1.50; single copies, 5c. each.

Aluminum Company of America. No. 2721, in circuit court of appeals for 3d circuit, Oct. term, 1921, Aluminum Company of America *v.* Federal Trade Commission; application by Federal Trade Commission for modification of order, Federal Trade Commission's brief. 1924. cover-title, 35 p. large 8° ‡

Hemler, G. F. Federal Trade Commission *v.* G. F. Hemler, complaint [report, findings, and order]; docket 1001, May 15, 1923. [1923.] p. 159–162. ([Decision] 366.) [From Federal Trade Commission decisions, v. 6.] * Paper, 5c.

Kahn & Frank. Federal Trade Commission *v.* Joseph Kahn, Jacob Frank, and Jerome Frank, partners, styling themselves as Kahn & Frank, complaint [report, modified] findings and order; docket 682, May 12, 1923. 1923. [1]+ 144–148+[1] p. ([Decision] 363.) [From Federal Trade Commission decisions, v. 6. Includes list of Cases in which orders for discontinuance or dismissal have been entered, May 14–15, 1923.] .* Paper, 5c.

Minneapolis, Minn. Federal Trade Commission *v.* Chamber of Commerce of Minneapolis et al., complaint [report, findings, and order]; docket 694, Dec. 28, 1923. [1924.] 39 p. * Paper, 5c.

Old Dominion Oil Company. Federal Trade Commission *v.* Old Dominion Oil Co. et al., complaint [report, findings, and order]; docket 861, May 4, 1923. [1923.] 131–143+[1] p. ([Decision] 362.) [From Federal Trade Commission decisions, v. 6. Includes list of Cases in which orders for discontinuance or dismissal have been entered, May 7, 1923.] * Paper, 5c.

Royal Duke Oil Company. Federal Trade Commission *v.* Royal Duke Oil Co., complaint [report, findings, and order]; docket 364, May 15, 1923. [1923.] p. 149–154. ([Decision] 364.) [From Federal Trade Commission decisions, v. 6.] * Paper, 5c.

United Woolen Mills of Washington. Federal Trade Commission *v.* Jack Bernstein, doing business as United Woolen Mills of Washington, complaint [report, findings, and order]; docket 926, May 15, 1923. [1923.] p. 155–158. ([Decision] 365.) [From Federal Trade Commission decisions, v. 6.] * Paper, 5c.

GENERAL ACCOUNTING OFFICE

Claims requiring appropriations for their payment, schedules of claims allowed by the various divisions of General Accounting Office, which require appropriations for their payment. Jan. 3, 1924. 187 p. (H. doc. 130, 68th Cong. 1st sess.) * Paper, 15c.   '24—26112

Decisions of comptroller general, v. 3, Nov. 1923; J. R. McCarl, comptroller general, Lurtin R. Ginn, assistant comptroller general. 1923. [1]+281–347 p. [Monthly.] †   21—26777

Navy Department. Salaries and expenses of Board of Survey, Appraisal, and Sale, with headquarters at Navy Yard, Washington, D. C., letter transmitting report of use by Navy Department of public moneys, proceeds of sales of Government property, to pay certain expenses, including salaries of civilian employees, of board created without authority of law therefor. Jan. 21, 1924. 2 p. (H. doc. 157, 68th Cong. 1st sess.) * Paper, 5c.

Reclamation of land. Augmenting reclamation fund by crediting thereto repayments by water users, etc. Jan. 3, 1924. 5 p. (H. doc. 125, 68th Cong. 1st sess.) * Paper, 5c.

Surety bonds in favor of United States, letter submitting draft of proposed legislation for standardization of procedure with reference to surety bonds running in favor of United States. Jan. 16, 1924. 5 p. (S. doc. 21, 68th Cong. 1st sess.) * Paper, 5c.

GEOGRAPHIC BOARD

Decisions of Geographic Board, Oct. 3–Dec. 5, 1923. [1924.] 3 p. † '10—26561

GOVERNMENT PRINTING OFFICE

Report. Annual report of Public Printer, fiscal year 1923. 1924. ii+76 p. [The cover of this edition has illustrations on p. 2 and 3 which are not given with the document edition.] †
                                                                        11—29491
—— Same. (S. doc. 15, 68th Cong. 1st sess.)

Supplies. Specifications and proposal for furnishing and installing complete 1 wax-ruling machine, advertisement. [1924.] [1]+4 p. 4° †

DOCUMENTS OFFICE

Immigration, naturalization, citizenship, Chinese, Japanese, negroes, and aliens, list of publications for sale by superintendent of documents. Nov. 1923. [2] +10 p. (Price list 67, 7th edition.) †   24—26055

Labor, child labor, cost of living, reconstruction, employers' liability. insurance, wages, women wage earners, strikes, list of publications for sale by superintendent of documents. Dec. 1923. [2]+27+[2] p. (Price list 33, 9th edition.) †   24—26053

Monthly catalogue. Index to Monthly catalogue. United States public documents, nos. 331–342; July, 1922–June, 1923. 1923. [1]+clxxix+[1] p. [Accompanied by an errata sheet, 1 p. oblong 24°, multigraphed.] * Paper, 20c. single copy, included in price of Monthly catalogue for subscribers.
      NOTE.—A volume title-page for nos. 331–342 is included.

—— Monthly catalogue, United States public documents. no. 348; Dec. 1923. 1924. p. 271–331. * Paper, 5c. single copy, 50c. a yr.; foreign subscription, 75c.   4—18088

Periodicals. Government periodicals, subscriptions are taken for these periodicals by superintendent of documents. Jan. 1924. [2]+6 p. (Price list 36, 15th edition.) †   24—26054

INTERIOR DEPARTMENT

      NOTE.—The decisions of the Department of the Interior in pension cases are issued in slips and in signatures, and the decisions in land cases are issued in signatures, both being published later in bound volumes. Subscribers may deposit $1.00 with the Superintendent of Documents and receive the contents of a volume of the decisions of either kind in separate parts as they are issued; foreign subscription, $1.25. Prices for bound volumes furnished upon application to the Superintendent of Documents, Washington, D. C.

Claims. Adjusted claims requiring appropriation, communication submitting claims which have been adjusted and which require appropriation for their payment. Jan. 8, 1924. 2 p. (H. doc. 151, 68th Cong. 1st sess.) * Paper, 5c.

Indian problem, resolution of committee of 100 appointed by Secretary of Interior and Review of Indian problem, by Joseph E. Otis, member of the committee; presented by Mr. Snyder. 1924. [1]+49 p. (H. doc. 149, 68th Cong. 1st sess.) * Paper, 5c.   23—27380

Pensions. [Decisions of Department of Interior in appealed pension and bounty land claims, v. 21, slips] 88–93 pension. [1923.] Each 2 p. or 3 p. [For price, see note above under center head.]   12—29422

—— Same. [v. 21, slip] 63 retirement. [1923.] 2 p.

ARCHITECT OF CAPITOL

Appropriations. Deficiency and supplemental estimates of appropriations for legislative establishment. Jan. 22, 1924. 2 p. (H. doc. 162, 68th Cong. 1st sess.) * Paper, 5c.

Library of Congress. Legislative establishment, supplemental estimate of appropriation for legislative establishment for fiscal year 1925 [for construction of new bookstacks in northeast court, Congressional Library Building]. Jan. 7, 1924. 2 p. (H. doc. 138, 68th Cong. 1st sess.) * Paper, 5c.

EDUCATION BUREAU

Art. Suggestions on art education for elementary schools, report of illustrated paper read before American Federation of Arts. St. Louis, Mo., May 24, 1923 [with bibliography]; by Jane Betsy Welling. Oct. 1923. 18 p. il. (Industrial education circular 21.) * Paper, 5c.   E 24—53

Citizenship. Community score card; prepared by Federal Council of Citizenship Training. 1924. iii+31 p. [Constructive suggestions to secure more effective citizenship training.] * Paper, 5c.   E 24—51

Cooperative Education Association of Virginia; by George W. Guy. 1924 iv+ 23 p. il. (Bulletin 53, 1923.) * Paper, 5c.   E 24—50

Education. Record of current educational publications, comprising publications received to Oct. 15, 1923 [subsequent to May 1, 1923]; compiled by Library Division. 1923. [1]+44 p. (Bulletin 54, 1923.) * Paper, 5c.   E 12—227

Educational research [with bibliographies]; by Bird T. Baldwin, assisted by Madorah Smith. 1923. iii+76 p. (Bulletin 42, 1923.) [Advance sheets from Biennial survey of education, 1920–22.] * Paper, 10c.   E 24—49

English language. Games and other devices for improving pupils' English; compiled by W. W. Charters and Harry G. Paul. 1923. ix+88 p. (Bulletin 43, 1923) * Paper, 10c.   E 24—11

Hygiene. Suggestions for program for health teaching in high school [with bibliography]; by Dorothy Hutchinson. 1923. iv+40 p. il. (Health education 15.) * Paper, 5c.   E 24—12

Master builders of to-day. [Reprint with changes] 1923. 6 p. 12° (Reading course 19.) [Publication reads: Home education reading course 19.] †

Parents. Twenty good books for parents. [Reprint with additions] 1922 [published 1923]. 6 p. 12° (Reading course 21.) †

Physical education and training. Suggestions for physical education program for small secondary schools arranged with special consideration of problems in physical education which face local school officials where there is no director of physical education [with bibliography]; by Walter F. Cobb and Dorothy Hutchinson. 1923. vi+79 p. il. (Physical education series 3.) * Paper, 10c.   E 24—54

Research bureaus. Organization of research bureaus in city school systems; by Elise H. Martens. Jan. 1924. 15 p. (City school leaflet 14) * Paper, 5c.   E 24—52

Salaries of elementary, junior high, and high school teachers in certain cities; [compiled] by Bertha Y. Hebb. Jan. 1924. 16 p. (City school leaflet 15.) * Paper, 5c.   E 24—24

School life. v. 9, no. 5; Jan. 1924 [1924.] p. 97–120, il. 4° [Monthly except July and August. This is Health education number.] * Paper, 5c. single copy. 30c. a year. (10 months); foreign subscription, 55c.   E 18—902

Teaching [short reading course for use of teachers and others who would keep abreast of times in the profession]; by George D. Strayer. [Reprint with changes] 1924. 6 p. 12° (Reading course 20.) †

GENERAL LAND OFFICE

Maps

NOTE.—The General Land office publishes a large general map of the United States, which is sold at $2.00; and also separate maps of the States and Territories in which public lands are to be found, which are sold at 25c. per sheet. The map of California is in 2 sheets. Address the Superintendent of Documents, Washington, D. C.

United States. Part of United States west of Mississippi River showing activities of bureaus of Department of Interior; compiled by M. Hendges. Scale 50 m.=0.7 in. [Washington] Geological Survey, 1923. 17.8×26.5 in. * 15c.

GEOLOGICAL SURVEY

NOTE.—The publications of the United States Geological Survey consist of Annual reports, Monographs, Professional papers, Bulletins, Water-supply papers, chapters and volumes of Mineral resources of the United States, folios of the Topographic atlas of the United States and topographic maps that bear descriptive text, and folios of the Geologic atlas of the United States and the World atlas of commercial geology. The Monographs, folios, and maps are sold. Other publications are generally free as long as the Survey's supply lasts. Copies are also sold by the Superintendent of Documents. Washington, D. C., at the prices indicated. For maps and folios address the Director of the Geological Survey, Washington, D. C. A discount of 40 per cent is allowed on any order for maps or folios that amounts to $5.00 or more at the retail price. This discount applies to an order for either maps or folios alone or for maps and folios together but is not allowed on a few folios that are sold at 5c. each on account of damage by fire. Orders for other publications that are for sale should be sent to the Superintendent of Documents, Washington, D. C. For topographic maps see next page.

Arsenic deposits in United States, in response to resolution. [report] containing information on arsenic deposits in United States available for manufacture of white arsenic; [by V. C. Heikes and G. F. Loughlin]. Jan. 24, 1924. 7 p. (S. doc. 27, 68th Cong. 1st sess.) * Paper, 5c.   24—26051

Gold, silver, copper, lead, and zinc in Nevada in 1922, mines report; by V. C. Heikes. Jan. 14, 1924. ii+305–339 p. [From Mineral resources, 1922, pt. 1.] †

Iron ore, pig iron, and steel in 1922; by Ernest F. Burchard and Hubert W. Davis. Jan. 25, 1924. ii+341–376 p. il. [From Mineral resources, 1922, pt. 1.] †

Pacific Coast. Surface water supply of United States, 1919–20: pt. 11, Pacific slope basins in California; Nathan C. Grover, chief hydraulic engineer, H. D. McGlashan and F. F. Henshaw, district engineers. 1923. vii+456 p. 2 p. of pl. (Water-supply paper 511.) [Prepared in cooperation with California and Oregon.] * Paper, 40c.   GS 10—439

——— Same. (H. doc. 618, 67th Cong. 4th sess.)

Publications. New publications, list 190; Jan. 1, 1924. [1924.] 3 p. [Monthly.] †

Maps

Montana. State of Montana. Scale 1 : 500,000. [Washington] Geological Survey, 1923. 2 sheets, each 43.3×38.1 in. † 25c.

Topographic maps

NOTE.—The Geological Survey is making a topographic map of the United States. The individual maps of which it is composed are projected without reference to political divisions, and each map is designated by the name of some prominent town or natural feature in the area mapped. Three scales are ordinarily used, 1 : 62,500, 1 : 125,000, and 1 : 250,000. These correspond, approximately, to 1 mile, 2 miles, and 4 miles to 1 linear inch, covering, respectively, average areas of 230, 920, and 3,700 square miles. For some areas of particular importance special large-scale maps are published. The usual size, exclusive of the margin, is 17.5 inches in height by 11.5 to 16 inches in width, the width varying with the latitude. The sheets measure 20 by 16½ inches. A description of the topographic map is printed on the reverse of each sheet.
More than two-fifths of the area of the country, excluding Alaska, has been mapped, every State being represented. Connecticut, Delaware, the District of Columbia, Maryland, Massachusetts, New Jersey, Ohio, Rhode Island, and West Virginia are completely mapped. Maps of the regular size are sold by the Survey at 10c. each, but a discount of 40 per cent is allowed on any order which amounts to $5.00 or more at the retail price. The discount is allowed on an order for either maps or folios alone or for maps and folios together, but does not apply to a few folios that are sold at 5c. each on account of damage by fire.

California, Herndon quadrangle, lat. 36° 45′–36° 52′ 30′′, long. 119° 52′ 30′′–120°. Scale 1 : 31,680, contour interval 5 ft. [Washington, Geological Survey] edition of 1923. 17.2×13.9 in. † 10c.

Pennsylvania, Howard quadrangle, lat. 41°–41° 15′, long. 77° 30′–77° 45′. Scale 1 : 62,500, contour interval 20 ft. [Washington, Geological Survey] edition of 1923. 17.5×13.3 in. † 10c.

*West Virginia–*Virginia. Capon Bridge quadrangle, lat 39° 15′–39° 30′, long. 78° 15′–78° 30′. Scale 1 : 62,500, contour interval 50 ft. [Washington, Geological Survey] edition of 1923. 17.5×13.6 in. [Map shows only the portion of Capon Bridge quadrangle that lies in West Virginia.] † 10c.

INDIAN AFFAIRS OFFICE

Indian trust funds. Regulations for applications for tribal funds under act of Mar. 2, 1907, as amended by Indian appropriation act approved May 18, 1916. [Reprint 1924.] 3 p. †

MINES BUREAU

Carbon monoxide hazards from house heaters burning natural gas; by G. W. Jones, L. B. Berger, and W. F. Holbrook. [1st edition.] [Dec.] 1923. iv+31 p. il. 1 pl. (Technical paper 337.) [Includes lists of Mines Bureau publications on utilization of natural gas.] * Paper, 10c.   24—26057

Coal. Analyses of samples of delivered coal collected, July 1, 1915–Jan. 1, 1922, with chapter on Tidewater pool classifications; by Ned H. Snyder. [1st edition.] [Nov.] 1923. iii+174 p. (Bulletin 230.) [Includes list of Mines Bureau publications giving analyses of coal.] * Paper, 20c.   24—26056

Gas masks. Procedure for establishing list of permissible gas masks. fees, character of tests, and conditions under which gas masks will be tested. Aug. 25, 1923. iii+15 p. (Schedule 14A.) [Supersedes Schedule 14 and supplement thereto.] * Paper, 5c.   24—26113

Metallurgical plants. Accidents at metallurgical works in United States, calendar year 1922; by William W. Adams. [1st edition.] [Oct.] 1923. iii+ 31 p. (Technical paper 350.) [Date of publication on verso of title-page incorrectly given as Oct. 1922. Includes lists of Mines Bureau publications on accident statistics.] * Paper, 5c.   15—26600

PATENT OFFICE

NOTE.—The Patent Office publishes Specifications and drawings of patents in single copies. These are not enumerated in this catalogue, but may be obtained for 10c. each at the Patent Office.

A variety of indexes giving a complete view of the work of the Patent Office from 1790 to date, are published at prices ranging from 25c. to $10.00 per volume and may be obtained from the Superintendent of Documents, Washington, D. C. The Rules of practice and pamphlet Patent laws are furnished free of charge upon application to the Patent Office. The Patent Office issues coupon orders in packages of 20 at $2.00 per package, or in books containing 100 coupons at $10.00 per book. These coupons are good until used, but are only to be used for orders sent to the Patent Office. For schedule of office fees, address Chief Clerk, Patent Office, Washington, D. C.

Decisions. [Decisions in patent and trade-mark cases, etc.] Jan. 1, 1924. p. 1–8, large 8° [From Official gazette, v. 318, no. 1.] † Paper, 5c. single copy, $2.00 a yr.   23—7315

—— Same. Jan. 8, 1924. p. 235–242, large 8° [From Official gazette, v. 318, no. 2.]

—— Same. Jan. 15, 1924. p. 473–478, large 8° [From Official gazette, v. 318, no. 3.]

—— Same. Jan. 22, 1924. p. 685–690, large 8° [From Official gazette, v. 318, no. 4.]

—— Same. Jan. 29, 1924. p. 843–849, large 8° [From Official gazette, v. 318, no. 5.]

Heany, John A. In Court of Appeals of District of Columbia, Jan. term, 1924, patent appeal no. 1587, *in re* John Allen Heany, improvement in automatic control mechanism for electric starter [for automobile]; brief for commissioner of patents. 1924. cover-title, i+45 p. ‡

Myers, Wilson R. In Court of Appeals of District of Columbia, Jan. term, 1924, patent appeal no. 1660, *in re* Wilson R. Myers, improvement in process of positioning materials; brief for commissioner of patents. 1924. cover-title, 10 p. ‡

Official gazette. Official gazette, Jan. 1–29, 1924; v. 318, no. 1–5. 1924. cover-titles, 1017+[clxxi] p. il. large 8° [Weekly.] * Paper, 10c. single copy, $5.00 a yr.; foreign subscription, $11.00.   4—18256

NOTE.—Contains the patents, trade-marks, designs, and labels issued each week; also decisions of the commissioner of patents and of the United States courts in patent cases.

—— Same, weekly index, with title, Alphabetical list of registrants of trade-marks [etc., Jan. 1, 1924]. [1924.] xxxviii p. large 8° [From Official gazette, v. 318, no. 1.] † Paper, $1.00 a yr.

—— Same [Jan. 8, 1924]. [1924.] xliv p. large 8° [From Official gazette, v. 318, no. 2.]

—— Same [Jan. 15, 1924]. [1924.] xxxvi p. large 8° [From Official gazette, v. 318, no. 3.]

—— Same [Jan. 22, 1924]. [1924.] xxiii p. large 8° [From Official gazette, v. 318, no. 4.]

—— Same [Jan. 29, 1924]. [1924.] xxx p. large 8° [From Official gazette, v. 318, no. 5.]

Patents. Classification of patents issued Jan. 1–29, 1924. [1924.] Each 2 p. or 1 p. large 8° [Weekly. From Official gazette, v. 318, no. 1–5.] †

—— Manual of classification of patents. 1923. 231 p. oblong 16° * Cloth, $1.00.

NOTE.—This publication is bound in a loose-leaf binder. Definitions of revised classes, published in 1912, and Classification bulletins, numbered consecutively beginning with no. 28 and published semiannually, are referred to in the body of the book in connection with each class defined. Substitute pages will be published from time to time as changes are made. An index is being prepared for publication. The Superintendent of Documents, Washington, D. C., will sell the Manual at $1.00 per copy, including the index, on publication, and copies of such pages as may be reprinted during the calendar years 1924 and 1925.

Trade-marks. Trade-marks [etc., from] Official gazette, Jan. 1, 1924. [1924.] 9–70+i–xv p. il. large 8° [From Official gazette, v. 318, no. 1.] † Paper, 5c. single copy, $2.50 a yr.

—— Same, Jan. 8, 1924. [1924.] 243–302+i–xix p. il. large 8° [From Official gazette, v. 318, no. 2.]

—— Same, Jan. 15, 1924. [1924.] 479–534+i–xiv p. il. large 8° [From Official gazette, v. 318, no. 3.]

—— Same, Jan. 22, 1924. [1924.] 691–727+i–viii p. il. large 8° [From Official gazette, v. 318, no. 4.]

—— Same, Jan. 29, 1924. [1924.] 851–892+i–xii p. il. large 8° [From Official gazette, v. 318, no. 5.]

RECLAMATION BUREAU

Inspection work, engineering materials and machinery. [1924.] 7 p. 4° (Specifications 428.) [Consists of advertisement, proposal, and specifications for inspection of engineering materials and machinery for Reclamation Bureau.] † Paper, 20c.

Reclamation record. Index [to] Reclamation record, v. 14, 1923. [1924.] viii p. large 8°

—— Reclamation record, v. 15, no. 1; Jan. 1924. [1924.] cover-title, p. 1–16, il. 4° [Monthly. Text on p. 2–4 of cover.]   9—35252

NOTE.—The Reclamation record is published in the interest of the settlers on the reclamation projects, its aim being to raise the general average of success on these projects. It contains much valuable matter of interest to farmers, and will be sent without direct charge to water users on the irrigation projects of the Reclamation Bureau. The Record is sold to those who are not water users for 75 cents a year, payable in advance. Subscriptions may be forwarded to the Chief Clerk, U. S. Reclamation Bureau, Washington, D. C., and remittances (postal money order or New York draft) should be made payable to the Special Fiscal Agent, U. S. Reclamation Bureau. Postage stamps will not be accepted.

INTERSTATE COMMERCE COMMISSION

NOTE.—The bound volumes of the decisions, usually known as Interstate Commerce Commission reports, are sold by the Superintendent of Documents, Washington. D. C., at various prices, depending upon the size of the volume. Separate opinions are sold on subscription, price $1.00 per volume; foreign subscription, $1.50; single copies, usually 5c. each.

Alabama and Vicksburg Railway. Finance docket no. 257, guaranty settlement with Alabama & Vicksburg Ry.; [and finance docket no. 593]; decided Dec. 8, 1923; report of commission. [1923.] p. 3–6. ([Finance decision] 1078.) [From Interstate Commerce Commission reports, v. 86.] * Paper, 5c.

Alabama Central Railroad. Finance docket no. 258, guaranty settlement with Alabama Central R. R.; decided Dec. 14, 1923; report of commission. [1924.] p. 49–51. ([Finance decision] 1092.) [From Interstate Commerce Commission reports, v. 86.] * Paper, 5c.

Alabama, Florida and Gulf Railroad. Finance docket no. 2250, loan to Alabama, Florida & Gulf R. R.; [decided Nov. 24, 1923]; report of commission]. 1923. [1]+736–739 p. ([Finance decision] 1050.) [From Interstate Commerce Commission reports. v. 82.] * Paper, 5c.

Anthracene. No. 11895, E. I. du Pont de Nemours & Company *v.* director general, as agent; [no. 12072, Barrett Company *v.* director general, as agent, Pennsylvania Railroad Company, et al.; no. 12234, same *v.* director general, as agent, Baltimore & Ohio Railroad Company, et al.]; decided Dec. 11, 1923; report of commission on further consideration. [1924.] p. 475–477. ([Opinion] 9021.) [From Interstate Commerce Commission reports, v. 85.] * Paper, 5c.

Apples. No. 13844, Bell & Company *v.* Chicago, Milwaukee & St. Paul Railway Company et al.; [decided Dec. 27, 1923; report and order of commission]. 1924. [1]+520–522+[1] p. ([Opinion] 9026.) [Report from Interstate Commerce Commission reports, v. 85.] * Paper, 5c.

Arkansas Central Railroad. Finance docket no. 279, guaranty settlement with Arkansas Central R. R.; [decided Dec. 21, 1923; report of commission]. 1924. [1]+68–70 p. ([Finance decision] 1098.) [From Interstate Commerce Commission reports, v. 86.] * Paper, 5c.

Asphalt. No. 13754, El Paso Bitulithic Company *v.* El Paso & Southwestern Railroad Company et al.; decided Dec. 7, 1923; report of commission. [1923.] p. 425–428. ([Opinion] 9006.) [From Interstate Commerce Commission reports, v. 85.] * Paper, 5c.

Atlanta and St. Andrews Bay Railway. Finance docket no. 284, guaranty settlement with Atlanta & St. Andrews Bay Ry.; decided Dec. 20, 1923; report of commission. [1924.] p. 71–73. ([Finance decision] 1099.) [From Interstate Commerce Commission reports, v. 86.] * Paper, 5c.

Baggage. No. 12959, Coit-Alber Chautauqua Company et al. *v.* Albany & Susquehanna Railroad Company et al.; decided Dec. 20, 1923; report [and order] of commission. [1924.] 357–365+[1] p. ([Opinion] 8989.) [Report from Interstate Commerce Commission reports, v. 85.] * Paper, 5c.

Baltimore and Ohio Railroad. Finance docket no. 3353, Baltimore & Ohio Railroad equipment trust, series A; decided Dec. 13, 1923; report of commission. [1924.] p. 45–48. ([Finance decision] 1091.) [From Interstate Commerce Commission reports, v. 86.] * Paper, 5c.

Bangor and Aroostook Railroad. Finance docket no. 3345, Bangor & Aroostook equipment trust, series I; decided Dec. 5, 1923; report of commission. [1924.] p. 837–838. ([Finance decision] 1076.) [From Interstate Commerce Commission reports, v. 82.] * Paper, 5c.

Barracks bags. No. 14009, American Mills Company *v.* Canton Railroad Company et al.; [decided Dec. 8, 1923; report and order of commission]. 1924. [1]+214–216+[1] p. ([Opinion] 8975.) [Report from Interstate Commerce Commission reports, v. 85.] * Paper, 5c.

Barrels. Investigation and suspension docket no. 1911, cancellation of interstate classification rating on empty wooden barrels; [decided Dec. 18, 1923; report and order of commission]. 1923. [1]+154–156+[1] p. ([Opinion] 8966.) [Report from Interstate Commerce Commission reports, v. 85.] * Paper, 5c.

Belt Railway of Chicago. Finance docket no. 3273, stock of Belt Railway of Chicago; decided Nov. 30, 1923; report of commission. [1923.] p. 771–773. ([Finance decision] 1054.) [From Interstate Commerce Commission reports, v. 82.] * Paper, 5c.

Binder's board. Investigation and suspension docket no. 1926, strawboard and other paper articles, in carloads, from transcontinental defined territory to south Pacific Coast points; [decided Dec. 31, 1923; report and order of commission]. 1924. [1]+470–474+[1] p. ([Opinion] 9020.) [Report from Interstate Commerce Commission reports, v. 85.] * Paper, 5c.

Boston and Maine Railroad. Finance docket no. 3355, bonds of Boston & Maine Railroad; [decided Dec. 19, 1923; report of commission]. 1924. [1]+86–88 p. ([Finance decision] 1105.) [From Interstate Commerce Commission reports, v. 86.] * Paper, 5c.

Boxes. No. 14712, Ludwig Friedlander *v.* director general, as agent. Pennsylvania Railroad Company, et al.; decided Dec. 21, 1923; report [and order] of commission. [1924.] 465–466+[1] p. ([Opinion] 9018.) [Report from Interstate Commerce Commission reports, v. 85.] * Paper, 5c.

Brakes. No. 4174, in circuit court of appeals for 9th circuit. Great Northern Railway Company *v.* United States, error to district court for eastern district of Washington, northern division; brief and argument for defendant in error. 1924. cover-title, i+24 p. ‡

Bricks. Investigation and suspension docket no. 1915, cancellation of rates on brick and draintile from St. Louis. Mo., to C., St. P., M. & O. Nebraska stations; decided Dec. 20, 1923; report [and order] of commission. [1924.] 353–356+[1] p. ([Opinion] 8988.) [Report from Interstate Commerce Commission reports, v. 85.] * Paper, 5c.

Brownstone and Middletown Railroad. Finance docket no. 117, deficit settlement with Brownstone & Middletown R. R.; decided Nov. 30, 1923; report of commission. [1923.] p. 777–778. ([Finance decision] 1056.) [From Interstate Commerce Commission reports, v. 82.] * Paper, 5c.

Buffalo, Rochester and Pittsburgh Railway. Finance docket no. 3327, bonds of Buffalo, Rochester & Pittsburgh Ry.; decided Dec. 5, 1923; report of commission. 1924. [1]+830–832 p. ([Finance decision] 1073.) [Last page incorrectly numbered 232 instead of 832, From Interstate Commerce Commission reports, v. 82.] * Paper, 5c.

Central of Georgia Railway. Finance docket no. 3307, stock of Central of Georgia Railway; decided Dec. 5, 1923; report of commission. [1924.] p. 833–834. ([Finance decision] 1074.) [From Interstate Commerce Commission reports, v. 82.] * Paper, 5c.

Chicago and Alton Railroad. Finance docket no. 3317, Chicago & Alton equipment trust, series A [William W. Wheelock and William G. Bierd, receivers] ; approved Dec. 6, 1923; supplemental order. [1924.] p. 835–836. ([Finance decision] 1075.) [From Interstate Commerce Commission reports, v. 82.] * Paper, 5c.

Chicago and North Western Railway. Finance docket no. 3329, bonds of Chicago & North Western Ry.; decided Nov. 30, 1923; report of commission. [1923.] p. 769–770. ([Finance decision] 1053.) [From Interstate Commerce Commission reports, v. 82.] * Paper, 5c.

—— Finance docket no. 3342, Chicago & North Western equipment trust of 1923; decided Dec. 17, 1923; report of commission. [1924.] p. 61–64. ([Finance decision] 1096.) [From Interstate Commerce Commission reports, v. 86.] * Paper, 5c.

Chicago, Milwaukee and St. Paul Railway. Finance docket no. 3291, operation of line by Chicago, Milwaukee & St. Paul Ry.; decided Dec. 8, 1923; report of commission. [1924.] p. 33–34. ([Finance decision] 1086.) [From Interstate Commerce Commission reports, v. 86.] * Paper, 5c.

Chicago, Rock Island and Pacific Railway. Finance docket no. 2794, acquisition of line and bond issue by Chicago, Rock Island & Pacific Ry.; [decided Dec. 18, 1923; report of commission]. 1924. [1]+96–100 p. ([Finance decision] 1110.) [From Interstate Commerce Commission reports, v. 86.] * Paper, 5c.

Clay. No. 14077, Louisville Fire Brick Works *v.* director general, as agent, et al.; [no. 14677, Louisville Pottery Company *v.* director general, as agent] ; decided Dec. 21, 1923; report [and order] of commission. [1924.] 457–460+[1] p. ([Opinion] 9015.) [Report from Interstate Commerce Commission reports, v. 85.] * Paper, 5c.

Coal. Investigation and suspension docket no. 1886, bituminous coal from mines in Illinois to certain stations in Missouri; decided Dec. 6, 1923; report [and order] of commission. [1923.] 105–107+[1] p. ([Opinion] 8957.) [Report from Interstate Commerce Commission reports, v. 85.] * Paper, 5c.

—— No. 5504, Cotton Manufacturers' Association of South Carolina *v.* Carolina, Clinchfield & Ohio Railway [of South Carolina] et al.; decided Dec. 10, 1923; report of commission on rehearing. [1923.] p. 131–136. ([Opinion] 8961.) [From Interstate Commerce Commission reports, v. 85.] * Paper, 5c.

—— No. 12112, Sloss-Sheffield Steel & Iron Company *v.* director general, as agent; decided Dec. 7, 1923; report of commission. [1924.] p. 367–369. ([Opinion] 8991.) [From Interstate Commerce Commission reports, v. 85.] * Paper, 5c.

—— No. 13289, Mark McFadden *v.* director general, as agent; decided Dec. 7, 1923; report of commission. [1924.] p. 365–366. ([Opinion] 8990.) [From Interstate Commerce Commission reports, v. 85.] * Paper, 5c.

—— No. 14316, Municipal Electric and Water Departments, Anderson [Ind.] *v.* Cincinnati, Indianapolis & Western Railroad Company et al.; [decided Dec. 8, 1923; report of commission]. 1924. [1]+446–448 p. ([Opinion] 9012.) [From Interstate Commerce Commission reports, v. 85.] * Paper, 5c.

—— No. 14887, Midland Coal Company *v.* Fort Smith & Western Railroad Company, Arthur .L. Mills, receiver, director general, as agent, et al.; [decided Dec. 8, 1923; report of commission]. 1923. [1]+146–148 p. ([Opinion] 8964.) [From Interstate Commerce Commission reports, v. 85.] * Paper, 5c.

Colorado, Columbus and Mexican Railroad. Finance docket no. 2625, securities of Colorado, Columbus & Mexican R. R.; [decided Dec. 18, 1923; report of commission]. 1924. [1]+94[-95] p. ([Finance decision] 1109.) [From Interstate Commerce Commission reports, v. 86.] * Paper, 5c.

—— Finance docket no. 2626, public convenience application of Colorado, Columbus & Mexican R. R.; [decided Dec. 10, 1923; report of commission]. 1924. [1]+18–26 p. ([Finance decision] 1084.) [From Interstate Commerce Commission reports, v. 86.] * Paper, 5c.

Commerce. Rules of practice before commission in proceedings under act to regulate commerce, as amended, otherwise known as interstate commerce act, with approved forms; revised, amended, and adopted Dec. 10, 1923. 1923. [1]+45 p. * Paper, 5c. 24—26141

Contractors' outfits. No. 13342, Gila Water Company et al. *v.* Arizona Eastern Railroad Company et al.; [decided Dec. 7, 1923; report and order of commission]. 1924. [1]+408–411+[1] p. ([Opinion] 9000.) [Report from Interstate Commerce Commission reports, v. 85.] * Paper, 5c.

Cotton goods. No. 13740, Elk Brand Shirt & Overall Company, Incorporated, et al. *v.* Durham & Southern Railway Company et al.; portions of 4th section applications nos. 1952, 2045, and 3912; [decided Dec. 7, 1923; report and order of commission]. 1924. [1]+320–326+iii p. ([Opinion] 8982.) [Report from Interstate Commerce Commission reports, v. 85.] * Paper, 5c.

Cotton-seed meal. No. 12366, John W. Eshelman & Sons et al. *v.* director general, as agent, Mobile & Ohio Railroad Company et al.; [decided Dec. 31, 1923; report of commission]. 1924. [1]+578–582 p. ([Opinion] 9035.) [From Interstate Commerce Commission reports, v. 85.] * Paper, 5c.

Coudersport and Port Allegany Railroad. Finance docket no. 1310, deficit settlement with Coudersport & Port Allegany R. R.; decided Dec. 21, 1923; report of commission. [1924.] p. 89–90. ([Finance decision] 1106.) [From Interstate Commerce Commission reports, v. 86.] * Paper, 5c.

Cream. No. 13432, Beatrice Creamery Company *v.* Louisville & Nashville Railroad Company; decided Dec. 7, 1923; report [and order] of commission. [1924.] 377–382+ii p. ([Opinion] 8994.) [Report from Interstate Commerce Commission reports, v. 85.] * Paper, 5c.

Creosote-oil. No. 13709, E. T. Chapin Company et al. *v.* Chicago, Milwaukee & St. Paul Railway Company et al.; decided Dec. 7, 1923; report [and order] of commission. [1924.] 263–266+[1] p. ([Opinion] 8979.) [Report from Interstate Commerce Commission reports, v. 85.] * Paper, 5c.

Cumberland and Pennsylvania Railroad. Finance docket no. 413, guaranty settlement with Cumberland & Pennsylvania R. R.; decided Dec. 12, 1923; report of commission. [1924.] p. 9–11. ([Finance decision] 1081.) [From Interstate Commerce Commission reports, v. 86.] * Paper, 5c.

Decisions. Decisions of Interstate Commerce Commission. Mar.–Apr. 1923. 1923. xxviii+940 p. 1 pl. map. (Interstate Commerce Commission reports, v. 78.) [Contains also decisions of Jan. 16, Feb. 6, and May 7, 1923.] * Cloth, $2.00. 8—30656

—— Same, May–June, 1923. 1923. xxvii+925 p. 1 tab. (Interstate Commerce Commission reports, v. 80.) [Contains also decisions of Apr. 27, 1923.] * Cloth, $2.00.

Demurrage. No. 11606, John E. Murray *v.* director general, as agent; [decided Sept. 18, 1923; report and order of commission on further hearing]. 1924. [1]+422–424+[1] p. ([Opinion] 9005.) [Report from Interstate Commerce Commission reports, v. 85.] * Paper, 5c.

—— No. 13281, Smokeless Fuel Company et al. *v.* Norfolk & Western Railway Company; decided Dec. 21, 1923; report [and order] of commission. [1924.] 395–402+[1] p. ([Opinion] 8998.) [Report from Interstate Commerce Commission reports, v. 85.] * Paper, 5c.

—— No. 13464, Republic Coal Company *v.* Chicago, St. Paul, Minneapolis & Omaha Railway Company; decided Dec. 3, 1923; report of commission. [1924.] p. 331–336. ([Opinion] 8984.) [From Interstate Commerce Commission reports, v. 85.] * Paper, 5c.

Denver and Rio Grande Western Railroad. Finance docket no. 3169, Denver & Rio Grande Western reorganization; decided Dec. 12, 1923; report of commission. [1923.] p. 745–768. ([Finance decision] 1052.) [Imprint date incorrectly given on p. 768 as 1922. From Interstate Commerce Commission reports, v. 82.] * Paper, 5c.

—— Finance docket no. 3290, acquisition of line by Denver & Rio Grande Western R. R. [T. H. Beacom, receiver]; decided Dec. 19, 1923; report of commission. [1924.] p. 105–107. ([Finance decision] 1112.) [From Interstate Commerce Commission reports, v. 86.] * Paper, 5c.

· *Detroit and Mackinac Railway.* Finance docket no. 2739, construction of extension by Detroit & Mackinac Ry.; [decided Dec. 20, 1923; report of commission on further hearing]. 1924. [1]+80–82 p. ([Finance decision] 1102.) [From Interstate Commerce Commission reports, v. 86.] . * Paper, 5c.

Dodge City. and Cimarron Valley Railway. Finance docket no. 2182, public convenience certificate to D. C. & C. V. Ry.; approved Dec. 12, 1923; order. 1924. p. 39. ([Finance decision] 1088.) [From Interstate Commerce Commission reports, v. 86.] * Paper, 5c.

Duluth, South Shore and Atlantic Railway. Before Interstate Commerce Commission, valuation dockets nos. 256, 228. Duluth, South Shore and Atlantic Railway Company, Mineral Range Railroad Company and Hancock and Calumet Railroad Company; brief in support of tentative valuation. 1923. cover-title, i+75 p. il. ‡

Elberton and Eastern Railroad. Finance docket no. 452, guaranty settlement with Elberton & Eastern R. R.; [decided Dec. 17, 1923; report of commission]. 1924. [1]+52–54 p. ([Finance decision] 1093.) [From Interstate Commerce Commission reports, v. 86.] * Paper, 5c.

Erie Railroad. Finance docket no. 3269, Erie Railroad equipment trust, series. KK; decided Dec. 17, 1923; report of commission. [1924.] p. 101–104. ([Finance decision] 1111.) [From Interstate Commerce Commission reports, v. 86.] * Paper, 5c.

Floor-sweeping compound. No. 13779, Fitch Dustdown Company v. Ann Arbor Railroad Company et al.; [decided Dec. 7, 1923; report and order of commission]. 1924. [1]+416–417+[1] p. ([Opinion] 9002.) [Report from Interstate Commerce Commission reports. v. 85.] * Paper, 5c.

Forest products. No. 12899, Pacific Coast Shippers Association, Incorporated,. et al. v. director general, as agent, Arizona Eastern Railroad Company et al.; [decided Dec. 7, 1923; report and order of commission]. 1924. [1]+386–388+[1] p. ([Opinion] 8996.) [Report from Interstate Commerce Commission reports. v. 85.] * Paper, 5c.

Freight-cars. No. 4080, in circuit court of appeals for 9th circuit, United States: v. Northern Pacific Railway Company; petition for rehearing. 1923. cover-title, 20 p. ‡

Freight rates. New England divisions, no. 11756. Bangor & Aroostook Railroad Company et al. v. Aberdeen & Rockfish Railroad Company et al.; [decided Jan. 5, 1924; report of commission construing amended order]. 1924. [1]+482–495 p. ([Opinion] 9023.) [From Interstate Commerce Commission reports, v. 85.] * Paper, 5c.

—— No. 12709, Chamber of Commerce of Grand Island. Nebr., et al. v. Aberdeen & Rockfish Railroad Company et al.; [decided Dec. 18, 1923; report and order of commission]. 1924. [1]+502–519+vi p. ([Opinion] 9025.) [Report from Interstate Commerce Commission reports, v. 85.] * Paper, 5c.

—— No. 13313, Michigan Traffic League v. Ann Arbor Railroad Company et al.; decided Dec. 3, 1923; report [and order] of commission. [1923.] 47–85+ 11 p. ([Opinion] 8951.) [Report from Interstate Commerce Commission reports, v. 85.] * Paper, 5c.

—— No. 14323, cities of Marshall and Jefferson, Tex., et al. v. Texas & Pacific Railway Company et al.; [portions of 4th section applications nos. 629, 635, 677, and 696 of F. A. Leland, agent]; decided Dec. 8, 1923; report [and orders] of commission. [1923.] 115–125+vi p. ([Opinion] 8959.) [Report from Interstate Commerce Commission reports, v. 85.] * Paper, 5c.

Furniture polish. No. 12624. O-So-Ezy Products Company et al. v. director general, as agent, Abilene & Southern Railway Company, et al.; decided Dec. 7, 1923; report [and order] of commission. [1924.] 187–194+xi p. ([Opinion]. 8969.) [Report from Interstate Commerce Commission reports, v. 85.] * Paper, 5c.

Gas oil. No. 12506, Greater Des Moines Committee. Incorporated, et al. v. director general. as agent. Arkansas Central Railroad Company, et al.; [decided Jan. 9, 1924; report and order of commission]. 1924. [1]+478–481 +ii p. ([Opinion] 9022.) [Report from Interstate Commerce Commission reports, v. 85.] * Paper, 5c.

—— No. 14003, Citizens Gas & Electric Company of Council Bluffs v. Atchison, Topeka & Santa Fe Railway Company et al.; decided Dec. 8, 1923; report of commission. [1924.] p. 435–438. ([Opinion] 9009.) [From Interstate Commerce Commission reports, v. 85.] * Paper, 5c.

Gasoline. No. 13926, Standard Oil Company (Kentucky) *v.* director general, as agent, et al.; decided Oct. 23, 1923; report of commission. Corrected reprint. [1923.] p. 705–706. ([Opinion] 8927.) [From Interstate Commerce Commission reports, v. 83.] * Paper, 5c.

Herington Co-operative Telephone Exchange. Finance docket no. 3296, purchase of properties of Herington Co-operative Telephone Exchange by United Telephone Co.; decided Dec. 1, 1923; report of commission. [1924.] p. 809–811. ([Finance decision] 1068.) [From Interstate Commerce Commission reports, v. 82.] * Paper, 5c.

Horses. No. 13621, Fies & Sons *v.* director general, as agent; decided Dec. 7, 1923; report [and order] of commission. [1924.] 195–196+[1] p. ([Opinion] 8970.) [Report from Interstate Commerce Commission reports, v. 85.] * Paper, 5c.

Inter-California Railway. Finance docket no. 2798, construction of branch line by Inter-California Ry.; approved Dec. 19, 1923; order. 1924. p. 85. ([Finance decision] 1104.) [From Interstate Commerce Commission reports, v. 86.] * Paper, 5c.

Iron. No. 12396, Chicago Bridge & Iron Works *v.* director general, as agent, Erie Railroad Company, et al.; decided Dec. 7, 1923; report of commission on further hearing. [1923.] p. 99–100. ([Opinion] 8955.) [From Interstate Commerce Commission reports, v. 85.] * Paper, 5c.

——. No. 12425, Fort Wayne Rolling Mill Corporation *v.* director general, as agent, Chicago, Milwaukee & St. Paul Railway Company, et al.; decided Dec. 11, 1923; report [and order] of commission on further hearing. [1924.] 523–526+[1] p. ([Opinion] 9027.) [Report from Interstate Commerce Commission reports, v. 85.] * Paper, 5c.

Kansas, Oklahoma and Gulf Railway. Finance docket no. 154, deficit settlement with Kansas, Oklahoma & Gulf Ry.; decided Dec. 18, 1923; report of commission. [1924.] p. 65–67. ([Finance decision] 1097.) [From Interstate Commerce Commission reports, v. 86.] * Paper, 5c.

Kentwood and Eastern Railway. Finance docket no. 560, guaranty settlement with Kentwood & Eastern Ry.; decided Dec. 1, 1923; report of commission. [1924.] p. 779–781. ([Finance decision] 1057.) [Corrected print. Changes have been made on p. 780. From Interstate Commerce Commission reports, v. 82.] * Paper, 5c.

Kitchen cabinets. No. 13695. Wasmuth-Endicott Company *v.* Wabash Railway Company et al.; [decided Dec. 7, 1923; report and order of commission]. 1924. [1]+370–372+[1] p. ([Opinion] 8992.) [Report from Interstate Commerce Commission reports, v. 85.] * Paper, 5c.

Lard substitutes. No. 13969, Southern Cotton Oil Company *v.* director general, as agent; decided Dec. 8, 1923; report [and order] of commission. [1924.] 433–434+[1] p. ([Opinion] 9008.) [Report from Interstate Commerce Commission reports, v. 85.] * Paper, 5c.

Leavenworth and Topeka Railroad. Finance docket no. 578, guaranty settlement with Leavenworth & Topeka R. R.; [decided Dec. 13, 1923; report of commission]. 1924. [1]+40–42 p. ([Finance decision] 1089.) [From Interstate Commerce Commission reports, v. 86.] * Paper, 5c.

Lighterage. No. 13339, Coastwise Lumber & Supply Company, Incorporated, *v.* Baltimore & Ohio Railroad Company; decided Dec. 7, 1923; report of commission. [1924.] p. 441–445. ([Opinion] 9011.) [From Interstate Commerce Commission reports, v. 85.] * Paper, 5c.

Lime. No. 13014, Lehigh Lime Company *v.* Akron, Canton & Youngstown Railway Company et al.; decided Dec. 21, 1923; report [and orders] of commission. [1924.] 341–352+iv p. ([Opinion] 8987.) [Report from Interstate Commerce Commission reports, v. 85.] * Paper, 5c.

Logs. No. 13679, Public Service Commission of Indiana *v.* Ann Arbor Railroad Company et al.; decided Dec. 28, 1923; report [and order] of commission. [1924.] 533–536+ii p. ([Opinion] 9029.) [Report from Interstate Commerce Commission reports, v. 85.] * Paper, 5c.

Lumber. Investigation and suspension docket no. 1888, cancellation of rule for constructing combination rates on forest products, north Pacific Coast to eastern destinations; decided Dec. 5, 1923; report [and order] of commission. [1923.] 101–104+[1] p. ([Opinion] 8956.) [Report from Interstate Commerce Commission reports, v. 85.] * Paper, 5c.

—— No. 13193, Ingram Day Lumber Company *v.* Gulf & Ship Island Railroad Company et al.; decided Dec. 7, 1923; report [and order]· of. commission. [1924.] 373–376+[1] p. ([Opinion] 8993.) [Report from Interstate Commerce Commission reports, v. 85.] * Paper, 5c.

—— No. 13449, North Carolina Pine Association et al. *v.* Atlantic Coast Line Railroad Company et al.; 4th section applications no. 600 et seq.; [decided Dec. 8, 1923; report and orders of commission]. 1924. [1]+270–319+xvi p. ([Opinion] 8981.) [Report from Interstate Commerce Commission reports, v. 85.] * Paper, 5c.

—— No. 13689, R. L. Muse Lumber Company *v.* director general, as agent; decided Dec. 7, 1923; report [and order] of commission. [1923.] 267–269+ [1] p. ([Opinion] 8980.) [Report from Interstate Commerce Commission reports, v. 85.] * Paper, 5c.

—— No. 13829, Settle Lumber Company *v.* Alabama & Vicksburg Railway Company et al.; decided Dec. 7, 1923; report [and order] of commission. [1924.] 197–199+ii p. ([Opinion] 8971.) [Report from Interstate Commerce Commission reports, v. 85.] * Paper, 5c.

—— No. 13999, Traffic Bureau of Nashville, Tenn., *v.* director general, as agent; decided Dec. 8, 1923; report [and order] of commission. [1924.] 261–262+[1] p. ([Opinion] 8978.) [Report from Interstate Commerce Commission reports, v. 85.] * Paper, 5c.

Mail matter. No. 14969, transmission of mail by pneumatic tubes in city of New York; decided Dec. 10, 1923; report [and order] of commission. [1923.] 207–213+[1] p. ([Opinion] 8974.) [Report from Interstate Commerce Commission reports, v. 85.] * Paper, 5c.

Manistique and Lake Superior Railroad. Finance docket no. 608, guaranty settlement with Manistique & Lake Superior R. R.; [decided Dec. 17, 1923; report of commission]. 1924. [1]+74–76 p. ([Finance decision] 1100.) [From Interstate Commerce Commission reports, v. 86.] * Paper,. 5c.

Meat. No. 11667, Jacob E. Decker & Sons *v.* director general, as agent, Chicago Great Western Railroad Company, et al.; decided Dec. 11, 1923; report [and order] of commission on further hearing. [1924.] 389–394+ii p. ([Opinion] 8997.) [Report from Interstate Commerce Commission reports, v. 85.] * Paper, 5c.

—— No. 14288, Oscar Mayer & Company *v.* Chicago & North Western Railway Company et al.; decided Dec. 29, 1923; report [and order] of commission. [1924.] 549–556+ii p. ([Opinion] 9033.) [Report from Interstate Commerce Commission reports, v. 85.] * Paper, 5c.

Mill waste. No. 13408, Atwood-Crawford Company, Incorporated, *v.* Maine Central Railroad Company et al.; decided Dec. 20, 1923; report [and order] of commission. [1924.] 651–653+[1] p. ([Opinion] 9054.) [Report from Interstate Commerce Commission reports,. v. 85.] * Paper, 5c.

Minneapolis and. St. Louis Railroad. Finance docket no. 2614, securities of Minneapolis & St. Louis Railroad; [and finance docket no. 2726]; decided Dec. 8, 1923; report of commission. [1924.] p. 1–2. ([Finance decision] 1077.) [From Interstate Commerce Commission reports, v. 86.] * Paper, 5c.

Minnesota Northwestern Electric Railway. Finance. docket no. 640,. guaranty settlement with Minnesota Northwestern Electric Ry.; [decided Dec. 13, 1923; report of commission]. 1924. [1]+12–14 p. ([Finance decision] 1082.) [From Interstate Commerce Commission reports, v. 86.] *Paper, 5c.

Misrouting. No. 14395, West End Chemical Company *v.* Los Angeles & Salt Lake Railroad Company et al.; decided Dec. 8, 1923; report [and order] of commission. [1924.] 339–340+[1] p. ([Opinion] 8986.) [Report from Interstate Commerce Commission reports, v. 85.] * Paper, 5c.

—— No. 14646, Brownell Improvement Company et al. *v.* Baltimore & Ohio Chicago Terminal Railroad Company et al.; decided Dec. 21, 1923; report [and order] of commission. [1924.] 461–462+[1] p. ([Opinion] 9016.) [Report from Interstate Commerce Commission reports, v. 85.] * Paper, 5c.

Misrouting—Continued. No. 14998, Ridenour-Baker Mercantile Company *v.* director general, as agent; decided Dec. 8, 1923; report of commission. [1924.] p. 463-464. ([Opinion] 9017.) [From Interstate Commerce Commission reports, v. 85.] * Paper, 5c.

Mississippian Railway. Finance docket no. 3298, securities of Mississippian Ry.; decided Dec. 6, 1923; report of commission. [1924.] p. 827-829. ([Finance decision] 1072.) [From Interstate Commerce Commission reports, v. 82.] * Paper, 5c.

Monongahela Railway. Finance docket no. 655, guaranty settlement with Monongahela Ry.; decided Dec. 20, 1923; report of commission. [1924.] p. 77-79. ([Finance decision] 1101.) [From Interstate Commerce Commission reports, v. 86.] * Paper, 5c.

Montour Railroad. Finance docket no. 1335, deficit settlement with Montour R. R.; decided Dec. 20, 1923; report of commission. [1924.] p. 91-92. ([Finance decision] 1107.) [From Interstate Commerce Commission reports, v. 86.] * Paper, 5c.

Morenci Southern Railway. Finance docket no. 1338, deficit settlement with Morenci Southern Ry.; decided Dec. 8, 1923; report of commission. [1924.] p. 7-8. ([Finance decision] 1080.) [From Interstate Commerce Commission reports, v. 86.] * Paper, 5c.

Natchez, Columbia and Mobile Railroad. Before Interstate Commerce Commission, valuation docket no. 319, Natchez, Columbia & Mobile Railroad Company; reply to brief filed by Illinois Central Railroad Company in support of its protest to tentative valuation. 1924. cover-title, i+28 p. ‡

New Hope Telephone Company. Finance docket no. 3295, purchase of properties of New Hope Tel. Co. by United Tel. Co.; [decided Nov. 30, 1923; report of commission]. 1923. [1]+774-776 p. ([Finance decision] 1055.) [From Interstate Commerce Commission reports, v. 82.] * Paper, 5c.

New York Central Railroad. No. 489, in Supreme Court, Oct. term, 1923, Baltimore & Ohio Railroad Company et al. *v.* United States, Interstate Commerce Commission, New York Central Railroad Company, et al.; brief for Interstate Commerce Commission. 1924. cover-title, ii+30 p. ‡

Paper. No. 14403, Express Publishing Company *v.* Galveston, Harrisburg and San Antonio Railway Company et al.; decided Dec. 15, 1923; report [and order] of commission. [1923.] 203-206+[1] p. ([Opinion] 8973.) [Report from Interstate Commerce Commission reports, v. 85.] * Paper, 5c.

Passenger rates. No. 11541, Arizona Corporation Commission et al. *v.* Arizona Eastern Railroad Company et al.; [decided Nov. 13, 1923; report and order of commission on further hearing]. 1923. [1]+76-94+ii p. ([Opinion] 8953.) [Report from Interstate Commerce Commission reports, v. 85.] * Paper, 5c.

Petroleum. Investigation and suspension docket no. 1903, petroleum oils from Philadelphia to Swedeland, Pa., and intermediate points; decided Jan. 2, 1924; report [and order] of commission. [1924.] 583-585+[1] p. ([Opinion] 9036.) [Report from Interstate Commerce Commission reports, v. 85.] * Paper, 5c.

—— No. 13990, Kanotex Refining Company *v.* Midland Valley Railroad Company; [decided Dec. 8, 1923; report and order of commission]. 1924. [1]+200-202+[1] p. ([Opinion] 8972.) [Report from Interstate Commerce Commission reports, v. 85.] * Paper, 5c.

Pipe. No. 14008, Simms Oil Company *v.* Houston & Texas Central Railroad Company et al.; decided Dec. 27, 1923; report [and order] of commission. [1924.] 537-541+ii p. ([Opinion] 9030.) [Report from Interstate Commerce Commission reports, v. 85.] * Paper, 5c.

Pittsburgh, Chartiers and Youghiogheny Railway. Finance docket no. 746, guaranty settlement with Pittsburgh, Chartiers & Youghiogheny Ry.; decided Dec. 17, 1923; report of commission. [1924.] p. 83-85. ([Finance decision] 1103.) [From Interstate Commerce Commission reports, v. 86.] * Paper, 5c.

Posts. No. 12308, Nebraska Bridge Supply & Lumber Company *v.* director general, as agent; decided Dec. 8, 1923; report [and order] of commission. [1924.] 327-330+[1] p. ([Opinion] 8983.) [Report from Interstate Commerce Commission reports, v. 85.] * Paper, 5c.

Railroad employees. Wage statistics, class 1 steam roads in United States, including 15 switching and terminal companies, Oct. 1923; [prepared in] Bureau of Statistics. Oct. 1923. [4] p. oblong large 8° †

—— Same, Nov. 1923; [prepared in] Bureau of Statistics. Nov. 1923. [4] p. il. oblong large 8° †

Railroad ties. No. 14790, Germain Company v. Louisville & Nashville Railroad Company; decided Dec. 8, 1923; report [and order] of commission. [1924.] 449–451+[1] p. ([Opinion] 9013.) [Report from Interstate Commerce Commission reports, v. 85.] * Paper, 5c.

Railroads. Freight and passenger service operating statistics of class 1 steam roads in United States, compiled from 161 reports of freight statistics representing 176 roads and from 158 reports of passenger statistics representing 173 roads (switching and terminal companies not included), Nov. 1923 and 1922 [and 11 months ended with Nov. 1923 and 1922; prepared in] Bureau of Statistics. Nov. 1923. [2] p. oblong large 8° [Subject to revision. Office correction has been made on p. 2.] †

—— Freight and passenger train service unit costs (selected expense accounts) of class 1 steam roads in United States, including proportion of mixed-train and special-train service (compiled from 161 reports representing 176 steam roads, switching and terminal companies not included), Nov. 1923 and 1922, and 11 months [ended with Nov.] 1923 and 1922; [prepared in] Bureau of Statistics. Nov. 1923. 1 p. oblong large 8° [Subject to revision.] †

—— In matter of regulations to govern destruction of records of steam roads, issue of 1914, [order promulgated] at general session of Interstate Commerce Commission on 4th of November, 1919 [amending item 5 of paragraph 20, concerning corporate elections]. [Reprint] 1924. 1 p. . * Paper, 5c.

—— Operating revenues and operating expenses of class 1 steam roads in United States (for 194 steam roads, including 15 switching and terminal companies), Nov. 1923 and 1922 [and] 11 months ending with Nov. 1923 and 1922; [prepared in] Bureau of Statistics. Nov. 1923. 1 p. oblong large 8° [Subject to revision.] †

—— Operating revenues and operating expenses of large steam roads, selected items for roads with annual operating revenues above $25,000,000, Nov. 1923 and 1922 [and] 11 months ended with Nov. 1923 and 1922; [prepared in] Bureau of Statistics. Nov. 1923. [2] p. oblong large 8° [Subject to revision.] †

—— Operating statistics of large steam roads, selected items for Nov. 1923, compared with Nov. 1922, for roads with annual operating revenues above $25,000,000; [prepared in] Bureau of Statistics. Nov. 1923. [2] p. oblong large 8° [Subject to revision.] †

—— Revenue traffic statistics of class 1 steam roads in United States, including mixed-train service (compiled from 162 reports representing 177 steam roads, switching and terminal companies not included), Oct. 1923 and 1922 [and] 10 months ended with Oct. 1923 and 1922; [prepared in] Bureau of Statistics. Oct. 1923. 1 p. oblong large 8° [Subject to revision.] †

Railway Mail Service. No. 9200, railway mail pay, in matter of application of New England lines for increased rates of railway mail pay; decided Dec. 13, 1923; report [and order] of commission. [1924.] 157–183+ii p. ([Opinion] 8967.) [Report from Interstate Commerce Commission reports, v. 85.] * Paper, 5c.

Refrigeration. Investigation and suspension docket no. 1878, refrigeration charges from Florida, Maryland, Pennsylvania, and West Virginia to interstate destinations; decided Dec. 17, 1923; report [and order] of commission. [1924.] 247–260+[1] p. ([Opinion] 8977.) [Report from Interstate Commerce Commission reports, v. 85.] * Paper, 5c.

—— No. 14081, St. Louis Fruit & vegetable Dealers Traffic Association v. Wabash Railway Company et al.; [decided Dec. 27, 1923; report and order of commission]. 1924. [1]+496–501+[1] p. ([Opinion] 9024.) [Report from Interstate Commerce Commission reports, v. 85.] * Paper, 5c.

Rice. No. 11898, Beaumont Chamber of Commerce v. director general, as agent, Beaumont, Sour Lake & Western Railway Company, et al.; decided Dec. 7, 1923; report [and order] of commission. [1923.] 139–145+ii p. ([Opinion] 8963.) [Report from Interstate Commerce Commission reports, v. 85.] * Paper, 5c.

Rome and Northern Railroad. Finance docket no. 773, guaranty settlement with Rome & Northern R. R., D. B. Carson, receiver; decided Dec. 10, 1923; report of commission. [1924.] p. 15–17. ([Finance decision] 1083.) [From Interstate Commerce Commission reports, v. 86.] * Paper, 5c.

Routing. Investigation and suspension docket no. 1910, elimination of routing transcontinental traffic via Illinois junctions destined to southeastern points; [decided Nov. 26, 1923; report and order of commission]. 1923. [1]+108–114+[1] p. ([Opinion] 8958.) [Report from Interstate Commerce Commission reports, v. 85.] * Paper, 5c.

St. Joseph and Grand Island Railway. Finance docket no. 803, guaranty settlement with St. Joseph & Grand Island Ry.; decided Dec. 17, 1923; report of commission. [1924.] p. 55–57. ([Finance decision] 1094.) [From Interstate Commerce Commission reports, v. 86.] * Paper, 5c.

St. Paul Union Depot Company. Finance docket no. 2530, bonds of St. Paul Union Depot Company; [decided Nov. 22, 1923; report of commission]. 1923. [1]+740–744 p. ([Finance decision] 1051.) [From Interstate Commerce Commission reports, v. 82.] * Paper, 5c.

Saltpeter, Chile. Investigation and suspension docket no. 1913, nitrate of soda in carloads, from Gulf ports to Central Freight Association territory destinations; [decided Dec. 27, 1923; report and order of commission]. 1924. [1]+586–590+[1] p. ([Opinion] 9037.) [Report from Interstate Commerce Commission reports, v. 85.] * Paper, 5c.

Sand. No. 13365, Roquemore Gravel Company *v.* Atlanta & West Point Railroad Company et al.; [decided Dec. 7, 1923; report and order of commission]. 1924. [1]+184–186+[1] p. ([Opinion] 8968.) [Report from Interstate Commerce Commission reports, v. 85.] * Paper, 5c.

—— No. 13821, A. E. Staley Manufacturing Company *v.* director general, as agent; [decided Dec. 7, 1923; report and order of commission]. 1924. [1]+418–419+[1] p. ([Opinion] 9003.) [Report from Interstate Commerce Commission reports, v. 85.] * Paper, 5c.

—— No. 14055, Charles Boldt Glass Company *v.* Chicago, Burlington & Quincy Railroad Company et al.; [decided Dec. 10, 1923; report and order of commission]. 1924. [1]+412–415+[1] p. ([Opinion] 9001.) [Report from Interstate Commerce Commission reports, v. 85.] * Paper, 5c.

—— No. 14252, in matter of intrastate rates on sand, gravel, crushed stone, and vitrified paving blocks within Ohio; [decided Dec. 3, 1923; report and order of commission]. 1923. [1]+66–75+[1] p. ([Opinion] 8952.) [Report from Interstate Commerce Commission reports, v. 85.] * Paper, 5c.

San Pedro, Los Angeles & Salt Lake Railroad Co., dissenting opinion of Commissioner Eastman in case of San Pedro, Los Angeles & Salt Lake Railroad Co., tentative valuation; presented by Mr. McNary. 1924. [1]+62 p. (S. doc. 17, 68th Cong. 1st sess.) [Includes views of Commissioner Potter and Chairman Meyer.] * Paper, 5c.

Seaboard Air Line Railway. Finance docket no. 789, guaranty settlement with Seaboard Air Line Ry.; [and finance docket no. 298]; decided Dec. 4, 1923; report of commission. [1924.] p. 793–796. ([Finance decision] 1062.) [From Interstate Commerce Commission reports, v. 82.] * Paper, 5c.

Sisal hemp. Investigation and suspension docket no. 1922, cancellation application on through rate via Pennsylvania Railroad on sisal from Gulf ports, stored at Indianapolis, Ind., destined to Chicago, Ill., and Michigan City, Ind.; decided Dec. 24, 1923; report [and order] of commission. [1924.] 467–469+[1] p. ([Opinion] 9019.) [Report from Interstate Commerce Commission reports, v. 85.] * Paper, 5c.

Southern Pacific Company. Finance docket no. 3331, Southern Pacific equipment trust, series F; decided Dec. 8, 1923; report of commission. [1924.] p. 35–38. ([Finance decision] 1087.) [From Interstate Commerce Commission reports, v. 86.] * Paper, 5c.

Southern Railway. Finance docket no. 3323, bonds of Southern Ry.; [decided Dec. 1, 1923; report of commission]. 1924. [1]+788–790 p. ([Finance decision] 1060.) [From Interstate Commerce Commission reports, v. 82.] * Paper, 5c.

—— Same; [approved Dec. 8, 1923; supplemental order]. 1924. p. [1], 6. ([Finance decision] 1079.) [From Interstate Commerce Commission reports, v. 86.] * Paper, 5c.

Staley System of Electrified Railway. Finance docket no. 2587, public convenience application of Staley System of Electrified Ry.; [decided Dec. 5, 1923; report of commission]. 1924. [1]+820-824 p. ([Finance decision] 1070.) [From Interstate Commerce Commission reports, v. 82.] * Paper, 5c.

Steamboats. Schedule of sailings (as furnished by steamship companies. named herein) of steam vessels which are registered under laws of United States and which are intended to load general cargo at ports in United States for foreign destinations, Jan. 15-Feb. 29, 1924, no. 17; issued by Section of Tariffs, Bureau of Traffic. 1924. iii+32 p. 4° [Monthly. No. 17 cancels no. 16.] †

22—26610

Stewartstown Railroad. Finance docket no. 2661, Stewartstown Railroad stock; decided Dec. 17, 1923; report of commission. [1924.] p. 93-94. ([Finance decision] 1108.) [From Interstate Commerce Commission reports, v. 86.] * Paper, 5c.

Sugar. No. 13868, John W. Focke et al. *v.* Galveston, Harrisburg & San Antonio Railway Company et al.; decided Dec. 8, 1923; report [and order] of commission. [1923.] 137-138+[1] p. ([Opinion] 8962.) [Report from Interstate Commerce Commission reports, v. 85.] * Paper, 5c.

Sulphuric acid. Investigation and suspension docket no. 1883, acid from Moundsville, W. Va., and Pittsburgh district to points in Pennsylvania, West Virginia, and Ohio; [investigation and suspension docket no. 1917]; decided Dec. 12, 1923; report [and order] of commission. [1924.] 149-153+[1] p. ([Opinion] 8965.) [Report from Interstate Commerce Commission reports, v. 85.] * Paper, 5c.

Switching charges. No. 14040, Shearman Concrete Pipe Company *v.* director general, as agent; decided Dec. 8, 1923; report [and order] of commission. [1924.] 337-338+[1] p. ([Opinion] 8985.) [Report from Interstate Commerce Commission reports, v. 85.] * Paper, 5c.

Tanks. No. 11842, General Iron Works *v.* director general, as agent, Cleveland, Cincinnati, Chicago & St. Louis Railway Company, et al.; [decided Dec. 10, 1923; report of commission on further hearing]. 1924. [1]+452-456 p. ([Opinion] 9014.) [From Interstate Commerce Commission reports, v. 85.] * Paper, 5c.

Tanks (military science). Investigation and suspension docket no. 1895. classification ratings on army tractor tanks; decided Dec. 18, 1923; report [and order] of commission. [1924.] 383-385+[1] p. ([Opinion] 8995.) [Report from Interstate Commerce Commission reports, v. 85.] * Paper, 5c.

Tiles. No. 14405, Southwest Cotton Company *v.* Southern Pacific Company et al.; [decided Dec. 8, 1923; report and order of commission]. 1924. [1]+420-421+[1] p. ([Opinion] 9004.) [Report from Interstate Commerce Commission reports, v. 85.] * Paper, 5c.

Tobacco. No. 14257, Imperial Tobacco Company (of Great Britain and Ireland), Limited, *v.* director general, as agent; [no. 14257 (sub-nos. 1 and 2), same *v.* same]; decided Dec. 8, 1923; report [and order] of commission. [1924.] 439-440+[1] p. ([Opinion] 9010.) [Report from Interstate Commerce Commission reports, v. 85.] * Paper, 5c.

Toilet paper. No. 13834, Albany Perforated Wrapping Paper Company *v.* Ahnapee & Western Railway Company et al.; decided Dec. 7, 1923; report [and order] of commission. [1924.] 429-432+[1] p. ([Opinion] 9007.) [Report from Interstate Commerce Commission reports, v. 85.] * Paper, 5c.

Train-control devices. No. 13413, in matter of automatic train-control devices; no. 13413 (sub-no. 1), in matter of automatic train-control device of Regan Safety Devices Company, Incorporated, on Chicago, Rock Island & Pacific Railway; decided Dec. 17, 1923; report of commission. [1924.] p. 403-408. ([Opinion] 8999.) [From Interstate Commerce Commission reports, v. 85.] * Paper, 5c.

Washington and Lincolnton Railroad. Finance docket no. 874, guaranty settlement with Washington & Lincolnton R. R.; [decided Dec. 17, 1923; report of commission]. 1924. [1]+58-60 p. ([Finance decision] 1095.) [From Interstate Commerce Commission reports, v. 86.] * Paper, 5c.

Washington Railway and Electric Company. No. 13135, in matter of jurisdiction over depreciation charges of Washington Railway & Electric Company; [decided Dec. 8, 1923; report and order of commission]. 1923. [1]+126-130 +[1] p. ([Opinion] 8960.) [Report from Interstate Commerce Commission reports, v. 85.] * Paper, 5c.

Wheat. No. 14387, Sperry Flour Company *v.* director general, as agent; decided Dec. 27, 1923; report [and order] of commission; [1924.] 675–676+ [1] p. ([Opinion] 9060.) [Report from Interstate Commerce Commission reports, v. 85.] *Paper, 5c.

Wildwood and Delaware Bay Short Line Railroad. Finance docket no. 2785, Wildwood & Delaware Bay Short Line bonds; decided Dec. 7, 1923; report of commission. [1924.] p. 825–826. ([Finance decision] 1071.) [From Interstate Commerce Commission reports, v. 82.] *Paper, 5c.

Williamson and Pond Creek Railroad. Before Interstate Commerce Commission, valuation docket no. 233, Williamson and Pond Creek Railroad; reply to brief filed by counsel for carrier, Dec. —, 1923, entitled Some suggestions touching procedural and evidential problems of constitutional hearing under sec. 19a of act to regulate commerce. 1923. cover-title, 14 p. ‡

Wood-pulp. Investigation and suspension docket no. 1921, wood pulp from International Falls, Minn., group to C. F. A. territory; decided Dec. 5, 1923; report [and order] of commission. [1923.] 95–98+[1] p. ([Opinion] 8954.) [Report from Interstate Commerce Commission reports, v. 85.] * Paper, 5c.

Woodworth and Louisiana Central Railway. Finance docket no. 247, deficit settlement with Woodworth & Louisiana Central Ry.; decided Dec. 14, 1923; report of commission. [1924.] p. 43–44. ([Finance decision] 1090.) [From Interstate Commerce Commission reports, v. 86.] * Paper, 5c.

LOCOMOTIVE INSPECTION BUREAU

Railroad accidents. Report covering investigation of accident to Chicago, Rock Island & Pacific Railway locomotive 254, which occurred at Biddle, Ark., Sept. 24, 1923; by A. G. Pack, chief inspector. Nov. 17, 1923. [1]+9 p. il. * Paper, 5c.

JUSTICE DEPARTMENT

American Linseed Oil Company. In equity, no. 1490, in district court for northern district of Illinois, United States *v.* American Linseed Oil Company et al.; final decree. 1923. cover-title, 3 p. ‡

Atchison, Topeka and Santa Fe Railway. In Court of Claims, Atchison, Topeka & Santa Fe Railway Company *v.* United States, no. A–158; defendant's request for findings of fact and brief on new trial. [1924.] p. 55–58, large 8° ‡

—— In Court of Claims, Atchison, Topeka and Santa Fe Railway Company *v.* United States, no. B–90; defendant's brief in opposition to claimant's motion for new trial. [1924.] p. 47–50, large 8° ‡

Baltimore and Ohio Railroad. No. 489, in Supreme Court, Oct. term, 1923, Baltimore & Ohio Railroad Company [et al.] *v.* United States, New York Central Railroad Company [et al.] and Interstate Commerce Commission, appeal from district court for northern district of Illinois; brief for United States. 1924. cover-title, ii+21 p. ·‡

Banco Mexicano de Commercio e Industria. No. 361, in Supreme Court, Oct. term, 1923, Banco Mexicano de Commercio e Industria and Elias S. A. de Lima, Francisco de O [P]. Cardona, and Edwin J. Parkinson, as liquidators of Banco Mexicano de Commercio e Industria, *v.* Deutsche Bank, Thomas W. Miller, Alien Property Custodian, and Frank White, Treasurer of United States, appeal from Court of Appeals of District of Columbia; brief for Thomas W. Miller, Alien Property Custodian, and Frank White, Treasurer of United States. 1923. cover-title, i+17 p. ‡

Berg, Thorvald. In Court of Claims, Thorvald Berg and David C. Reid *v.* United States, no. C–914; brief on demurrer. [1924.] p. 33–37, large 8° ‡

Burke, Edward & John, Limited. No. 245, in Supreme Court, Oct. term, 1923, Edward and John Burke (Limited) *v.* David H. Blair, commissioner of internal revenue, et al., appeal from district court for southern district of New York; brief for appellees. 1924. cover-title, i+24 p. ‡

—— Same; motion for appellees to advance. 1924. cover-title, 2 p. ‡

Chamberlain Machine Works. In Court of Claims, Chamberlain Machine Works *v.* United States, no. C–1176; demurrer [and] brief. [1924.] p. 41–60, large 8° ‡

Claims. Judgments rendered against Government by district court of New Mexico. Jan. 7, 1924. 4 p. (H. doc. 144, 68th Cong. 1st sess.) * Paper, 5c.

—— Judgments rendered against Government by District Courts, list of judgments rendered against Government by District Courts as submitted by Attorney General, which require appropriation for their payment. Jan. 7, 1924. 13 p. (H. doc. 146, 68th Cong. 1st sess.) * Paper, 5c.

—— Judgments rendered against Government by District Courts requiring appropriation for their payment. Jan. 7, 1924. 4 p. (H. doc. 143, 68th Cong. 1st sess.) * Paper, 5c.

—— Judgments rendered against Government in admiralty, records of judgments rendered against Government by district court for eastern district of New York sitting in admiralty, requiring appropriation. Jan. 7, 1924. 4 p. (H. doc. 145, 68th Cong. 1st sess.) * Paper, 5c.

Clark, Chapman S. In Court of Claims, Chapman S. Clark *v.* United States, no. C–1153; demurrer [and] brief. [1924.] p. 1–11, large 8° ‡

Crook, H. E., Company, Incorporated. In Court of Claims, H. E. Crook Company, Inc., *v.* United States, no. B–194; defendant's objections to plaintiff's request for findings of fact, defendant's request for additional findings of fact, and brief. [1924.] p. 68–74, large 8° ‡

—— In Court of Claims, H. E. Crook Company [Inc.] *v.* United States, no. B–195; defendant's objections to plaintiff's request for findings of fact, defendant's request for additional findings of fact, and brief. [1924.] p. 94–101, large 8° ‡

Delaney, Thomas A. No. 354, in Supreme Court, Oct. term, 1923, Thomas A. Delaney *v.* United States, on writ of certiorari to circuit court of appeals for 7th circuit; brief for United States. 1923. cover-title, 20 p. ‡

Dunbar, Oliver E. In Court of Claims, no. C–1201, Oliver E. Dunbar *v.* United States; answer and counterclaim. [1924.] p. 62–73, large 8° ‡

Electric Boat Company. No. 159, in Supreme Court, Oct. term, 1923, Electric Boat Company *v.* United States, appeal from Court of Claims; brief for appellee. 1924. cover-title, iii+157 p. il. ‡

Field, Walter S. In circuit court of appeals for 2d circuit, Walter S. Field *v.* Thomas W. Miller, as Alien Property Custodian, Frank White, as Treasurer of United States, Hugo Stinnes, Edward Wagenknecht, and Albert Jensen; brief on behalf of Thomas W. Miller, as Alien Property Custodian, and Frank White, as Treasurer of United States. 1924. cover-title, i+24 p. large 8° ‡

Fisher, Michael H. In Court of Claims. Frank Schatz, administrator of Michael H. Fisher, *v.* United States, no. C–1157; demurrer [and] brief. [1924.] p. 1–5, large 8° ‡

Fougera, E., & Co. No. 2295, Court of Customs Appeals. E. Fougera & Company *v.* United States; brief for United States. 1924. cover-title, 15 p. ‡

Gay, Alphonse. No. 205, in Supreme Court, Oct. term, 1923, United States *v.* Alphonse Gay, appeal from Court of Claims; brief for United States. 1924. cover-title, ii+63 p. ‡

Goltra, Edward F. No. 23, original, in Supreme Court, Oct. term, 1923, in matter of petition of United States as owner of 19 barges and 4 towboats [leased to Edward F. Goltra]; motion of United States to set aside order denying writ of prohibition and for rehearing. 1923. cover-title, 3 p. ‡

Holloway, W. Carl. In Court of Claims, W. Carl Holloway *v.* United States, no. C–1085; demurrer [and] brief. [1923.] p. 1–6, large 8° ‡

Illinois Central Railroad. In Court of Claims, Illinois Central Railroad Co. *v.* United States. no. B–207; defendant's request for findings of fact and brief. [1923.] p. 3–4, large 8° ‡

Independent Bridge Company. In Court of Claims. Independent Bridge Company *v.* United States. no. 353–B; defendant's objections to claimant's request for findings of fact and brief. [1924.] p. 96–102, large 8° ‡

Industrial Association of San Francisco. In equity. no. 1044, in southern division of district court for northern district of California. 3d division. United States *v.* Industrial Association of San Francisco et al.; final decree. 1924. cover-title, 4 p. ‡

Jebsen, Rhederei M., Company. In Court of Claims, Rhederei M. Jebsen Company *v.* United States. no. C–786; demurrer [and] brief. [1924.] p. 1–12, large 8° ‡

Kirby, Harry. In Court of Claims, Harry Kirby *v.* United States, no C–1146; demurrer [and] brief. [1924.] p. 1–6, large 8° ‡

Ladenburg, Thalmann & Co. United States circuit court of appeals for 2d circuit, Benjamin Guinness [et al.], copartners, doing business under firm name and style of Ladenburg, Thalmann & Company, *v.* Thomas W, Miller, as Alien Property Custodian, Frank White, as Treasurer of United States, and Carl Joerger [et al.], copartners, doing business under firm name and style of Delbruck, Schickler & Company; brief on behalf of Thomas W. Miller, as Alien Property Custodian, and Frank White, as Treasurer of United States. 1924. cover-title, ii+44 p. large 8° ‡

Littauer Brothers. In Court of Claims, Lucius N. and Eugene Littauer, copartners trading under firm name and style of Littauer Brothers, *v.* United States, no. C–761; demurrer [and] brief. [1924.] p. 27–37, large 8° ‡

Louisville and Nashville Railroad. No. B–179, in Court of Claims, Louisville & Nashville Railroad Company *v.* United States; defendant's objections to plaintiff's request for findings of fact, defendant's request for findings of fact, and brief. 1924. cover-title, p. 1–10, large 8° ‡

Louisville Bedding Company. In Court of Claims, Louisville Bedding Company *v.* United States, no B–178; defendant's objections to plaintiff's request for findings of fact, findings requested in lieu thereof, and brief. [1924.] p. 42–54, large 8° ‡

Mahler, Herbert. No. 184, in Supreme Court, Oct. term, 1923, Herbert Mahler et al. *v.* Howard Eby, inspector in charge immigration service, Department of Labor, at Chicago, Ill., appeal from district court for northern district of Illinois; brief for respondent. 1924. cover-title, ii+24 p. ‡

Malone, James C., Incorporated. No. 2328, Court of Customs Appeals, United States *v.* James C. Malone, Inc.; brief for United States. 1924. cover-title, 4 p. ‡

Manufacturers' Land and Improvement Company. No. 181, in Supreme Court, Oct. term, 1923, Manufacturers' Land & Improvement Company *v.* Shipping Board Emergency Fleet Corporation and Public Service Railway Company, in error to circuit court of appeals for 3d circuit; brief for defendants in error. 1923. cover-title, 14 p. ‡

Maple Flooring Manufacturers Association. In district court, western district of Michigan, United States *v.* Maple Flooring Manufacturers Association et al., [equity no. 1979]; final decree. 1924. cover-title, 4 p. ‡

—— In equity, in district court for western district of Michigan, southern division, United States *v.* Maple Flooring Manufacturers Association et al.; opinion. 1923. cover-title, 8 p. ‡

Marr, Walter L. No. 686, in Supreme Court, Oct. term, 1923, Walter L. Marr *v.* United States, appeal from Court of Claims; motion to advance. 1923. cover-title, 3 p. ‡

Metal Products Company. In Court of Claims, Metal Products Company *v.* United States, no. 34685; motion to file affidavits in support of motion for new trial. [1924.] p. 1–24, large 8° ‡

Michael, J. Edmund. In Court of Claims, J. Edmund Michael *v.* United States. no. C–10820; demurrer [and] brief. [1923.] p. 1–4, large 8° ‡

Midland Land and Improvement Company. In Court of Claims, Midland Land & Improvement Company *v.* United States, no. 33713; defendant's amended answer to plaintiff's motion for new trial. [1923.] p. 399–431, large 8° ‡

Minnesota. No. 24, original, in Supreme Court, Oct. term, 1923, United States *v.* Minnesota; reply to defendant's claims of offset. 1924. cover-title, 8 p. ‡

Missouri Pacific Railroad. In Court of Claims, Missouri Pacific R. R. Co. *v.* United States, no. A–341; defendant's request for findings of fact and brief. [1924.] p. 1–2, large 8° ‡

—— Same. [1924.] p. 9–10, large 8° ‡

—— In Court of Claims, Missouri Pacific Railroad Company *v.* United States, no. C–697; defendant's reply brief. [1924.] p. 101–109, large 8° ‡

Myers, Warren. No. 158, in Supreme Court, Oct. term, 1923, Warren Myers and Bill Summers *v.* United States. in error to district court for western district of Missouri; brief for United States. 1923. cover-title, ii+26 p. ‡

National Contracting Company. In Court of Claims, National Contracting Company *v.* United States, no. B–57; defendant's objections to plaintiff's request for findings of fact, and defendant's request for findings of fact, and brief. [1924.] p. 1–14, large 8° ‡.

New Jersey. No. 27, original, in Supreme Court, Oct. term. 1923, New Jersey *v.* Harry M. Daugherty, personally and as Attorney General, John W. Weeks, personally and as Secretary of War, Hubert Work, personally and as Secretary of Interior, Henry C. Wallace, personally and as Secretary of Agriculture, and John W. Weeks, Hubert Work, and Henry C. Wallace, as members of and constituting Federal Power Commission; motion by defendants to dismiss bill of complaint, and brief in support thereof. 1924. cover-title, ii+22 p. ‡

New York Central Railroad. No. 169, certificate, in Supreme Court, Oct. term, 1923, New York Central Railroad Company *v.* United States, on certificate from circuit court of appeals for 3d circuit; brief for United States. 1924. cover-title, ii+34 p. ‡

Norfolk Southern Railroad. No. B–190, in Court of Claims, Norfolk Southern Railway Co. *v.* United States; defendant's objections to plaintiff's request for findings of fact, defendant's request for findings of fact, and brief. 1923. cover-title, p. 47–65, large 8° ‡

North German Lloyd Steamship Company. In Court of Claims, North German Lloyd *v.* United States, no. C–313; demurrer [and] brief. [1924.] p. 1–18, large 8° ‡

Pacific Mail Steamship Company. In Court of Claims, Pacific Mail Steamship Company *v.* United States, no. C–1132; amended demurrer [and Government's reply to claimant's brief]. [1924.] p. 125–132, large 8° ‡

Packard Motor Car Company. In Court of Claims, Packard Motor Car Company *v.* United States, no. 85–B; defendant's objections to plaintiff's request for findings of fact, with brief. 1924. p. 1, large 8° ‡

Perkins Campbell Company. No. 183, in Supreme Court, Oct. term, 1923, Perkins Campbell Company *v.* United States, appeal from Court of Claims; brief for United States. 1924. cover-title, 17 p. ‡

Piel Brothers. No. 95, in Supreme Court, Oct. term, 1923, Piel Bros. *v.* Ralph A. Day, Federal prohibition director for State of New York, et al., appeal from circuit court of appeals for 2d circuit; brief for appellees. 1924. cover-title, 5 p. ‡

Rice & Fielding, Incorporated. No. 2286, Court of Customs Appeals, United States *v.* Rice & Fielding, Inc.; brief for United States in opposition to application for rehearing. 1924. cover-title, 7 p. ‡

St. Louis, Iron Mountain and Southern Railway. In Court of Claims, Benjamin F. Bush, receiver of St. Louis, Iron Mountain & Southern Railway Company, *v.* United States, no. 340–A; defendant's request for findings of fact, and brief. [1924.] p. 13–14, large 8° ‡

Salinger, B. I., jr. Nos. 341, 342, and 705, in Supreme Court, Oct. term, 1923. B. I. Salinger, jr., *v.* Victor Loisel, United States marshal for eastern district of Louisiana; [same] *v.* [same], appeals from district court for eastern district of Louisiana; [same] *v.* United States and Victor Loisel, as United States marshal, eastern district of Louisiana, on writ of certiorari to circuit court of appeals for 5th circuit; brief for appellee and respondents. 1923. cover-title, i+32 p. ‡.

Seaboard Air Line Railway. In Court of Claims, Seaboard Air Line Railway Company *v.* United States, no. 24915; defendant's objections to plaintiff's request for findings of fact, defendant's request for findings of fact, and brief. [1924.] p. 87–136, large 8° ‡

Snare, Frederick, Corporation. In Court of Claims, Frederick Snare Corporation *v.* United States, [no.] B–199; objections to plaintiff's request for findings of fact, findings requested in lieu thereof, and brief. [1924.] p. 73–90, large 8° ‡

Southern Railway. No. B–118, in Court of Claims, Southern Railway Company *v.* United States; defendant's objections to plaintiff's request for findings of fact, defendant's request for findings of fact, and brief. 1924. cover-title, p. 57–71, large 8° ‡

Starrett, William A. Criminal no. 40384, in Supreme Court of District of Columbia holding criminal term, Oct. term, 1922, United States *v.* William A. Starrett [et al.]; reply brief for United States. 1923. cover-title, iv+155 p. ‡

State Savings Bank of Ortley, S. Dak. In Court of Claims, State Savings Bank of Ortley, S. Dak., *v.* United States, no. 35-B; Treasury brief. [1923.] p. 1-16. large 8° ‡

Stewart, James, & Co., Incorporated. In Court of Claims, James Stewart & Co. (Inc.) *v.* United States, no. B-21; defendant's brief. [1923.] p. 1-7, large 8° ‡

Stone & Downer Company. No. 2245, Court of Customs Appeals, Stone & Downer Co. et al. *v.* United States; application for rehearing on behalf of United States and brief in support thereof. 1924. cover-title, 31 p. ‡

Title Insurance and Trust Company. No. 358, in Supreme Court, Oct. term, 1923, United States *v.* Title Insurance and Trust Company et al., appeal from circuit court of appeals for 9th circuit; brief for United States. 1924. cover-title, iv+99 p. ‡

Union Twist Drill Company. No. 316-A, in Court of Claims, Union Twist Drill Company *v.* United States; defendant's motion for new trial, and brief in support thereof. 1924. cover-title, i+1-33 p. large 8° ‡

Vandiver, Annie C. In Court of Claims, Annie C. Vandiver, Dorothy C. Vandiver, and Robert M. Vandiver *v.* United States, no. C-1081; demurrer [and] brief. [1924.] p. 1-6, large 8° ‡

Wabash Railway. In Court of Claims, Wabash Railway Company *v.* United States, no. C-74; defendant's objections to plaintiff's request for findings of fact, defendant's request for findings of fact, and brief. [1924.] p. 29-32, large 8° ‡

Westmoreland Brewing Company, Incorporated. No. 713, in Supreme Court, Oct. term, 1923, Westmoreland Brewing Company (Inc.) [et al.] *v.* United States, on petition for writ of certiorari to circuit court of appeals for 3d circuit; brief for United States in opposition. 1924. cover-title, 11 p. ‡

Wilkes, Loftis. No. 694, in Supreme Court, Oct. term, 1923, Loftis Wilkes *v.* United States, on petition for writ of certiorari to circuit court of appeals for 6th circuit; brief for United States in opposition. 1923. cover-title, 3 p. ‡

Williams, J. E. No. 751, in Supreme Court, Oct. term, 1923, J. E. Williams et al. *v.* United States, petition for writ of certiorari to circuit court of appeals for 5th circuit; brief for United States in opposition. 1924. cover-title, 5 p. ‡

LABOR DEPARTMENT

Government Hotels. United States Housing Corporation, supplemental estimate of appropriation for Housing Corporation, fiscal years 1923 and 1924, for ground rent for Government Hotels for Government workers, Nov. 15, 1922–June 30, 1924. Jan. 7, 1924. 4 p. (H. doc. 137, 68th Cong. 1st sess.) * Paper, 5c.

Immigration. Letter from Secretary of Labor to chairman of Committee on Immigration and Naturalization, House of Representatives, transmitting suggestions in connection with impending immigration legislation. 1924. [1]+ 20 p. † L 24—8

CHILDREN'S BUREAU

Infants. Care of the baby. [1923.] [1]+5 p. il. 4° ([Dodger no. 9 revised.]) †

EMPLOYMENT SERVICE

Directory of public employment offices, Jan. 1924. 1924. 16 p. narrow 12° † L 24—9

Employment conditions. Special survey of 44 States based on information received from Federal-State directors of Employment Service and commissioners of labor showing present employment conditions of country and general, industrial, and agricultural employment prospects for 1924. 1924. [1]+ 15 p. † L 24—10

Farm Labor Bureau. Report of Farm Labor Bureau of Employment Service·
[Jan. 1–Nov. 30, 1923]. [1924.] 4 p. †

Industrial employment information bulletin, v. 3. no. 12; Dec. 1923. [1924.]
19 p. 4° [Monthly.] †   L 21—17

News-letter. News-letter 6, Aug. and Sept. 1923; [prepared in] Junior Division..
1923. [1]+14 p. [Nos. 1–5 were issued in mimeographed form only and
have not been entered in this catalogue.] †

—— Same 7, Oct. and Nov. 1923; [prepared in] Junior Division. 1923. [1]+
17 p. †

IMMIGRATION BUREAU

Blank forms. Catalogue of books and blanks used by immigration service,.
Jan. 1924. 1924. [1]+1–2 p.+leaves 3–12. ‡

LABOR STATISTICS BUREAU

Association of Governmental Labor Officials of United States and Canada.
Proceedings of 10th annual convention of Association of Governmental.
Labor Officials of United States and Canada, held at Richmond, Va., May
1–4, 1923. Dec. 1923. x+212+vi p. (Bulletin 352; Miscellaneous series.)
*Paper, 25c.   15—27231·

—— Same. (H. doc. 59, 68th Cong. 1st sess.)

Employment. Employment in selected industries, Nov. 1923. 1923. [1]+ 8 p..
[From Monthly labor review, Jan. 1924.] †

—— Same, Dec. 1923. 1924. [1]+8 p. [From Monthly labor review, Feb.
1924.] †

Monthly labor review. Monthly labor review, index, [title-page] and contents, v. 14; Jan.–June, 1922. 1924. lvi+xvi p. *Paper, 10c.

—— Same, v. 18, no. 1; Jan. 1924. 1924. iv+1–215 p. il. 1 tab. *Paper, 15c.
single copy, $1.50 a yr.; foreign subscription, $2.25.   15—26485·

    SPECIAL ARTICLES.—Century of immigration.—Family-wage system in Germany and .
certain other European countries; by Mary T. Waggaman.—Record of industrial·
accidents in United States, 1922; by Carl Hookstadt.—Conciliation work of De-·
partment of Labor, Nov. 1923; by Hugh L. Kerwin.—Statistics of immigration, Oct.
1923; by W. W. Husband.—Immigrant aid: National, nongovernmental activities; ·
by Mary T. Waggaman.
    NOTE.—The Review is the medium through which the Bureau publishes the results
of original investigations too brief for bulletin purposes, notices of labor legislation by
the States or by Congress, and Federal court decisions affecting labor, which from their·
importance should be given attention before they could ordinarily appear in the bulletins devoted to these subjects. One free subscription will be given to all labor departments and bureaus, workmen's compensation commissions, and other offices connected with the administration of labor laws and organizations exchanging publications with the Labor Statistics Bureau. Others desiring copies may obtain them from
the Superintendent of Documents, Washington, D. C., at the prices stated above.

Prices. Prices and cost of living. 1924. [1]+36–64 p. il. [From Monthly
labor review, Jan. 1924.] †

—— Wholesale prices of commodities for· Dec. 1923. 1924. [1]+9 p.
[Monthly.] †   L 22—229·

NATURALIZATION BUREAU

Citizenship. Federal citizenship textbook. course of instruction for use in
public schools by candidate for citizenship; by Raymond F. Crist. [Reprint
with additions] 1923. pt. 3, 104 p. 2 por. 3 pl. †   22—26786··

    CONTENTS.—The American's creed.; [by] William Tyler Page.—Pledge to the flag.—
Declaration of Independence, simplified form and original text, arranged in 6 lessons.—Constitution of United States, with short history of America from 1492 to
1789, 24 lessons in simple language; [by Edgar M. Ross].

WOMEN'S BUREAU

Women's Industrial Conference. Proceedings of Women's Industrial Conference called by Women's Bureau, Washington, D. C., Jan. 11–13, 1923.
1923. xvii+190 p. (Bulletin 33.) *Paper, 20c.   L 24—12··

LIBRARY OF CONGRESS

COPYRIGHT OFFICE

Copyright. [Catalogue of copyright entries, new series, pt. 1, group 1, Books, v. 20] no. 90–102; Jan. 1924. Jan. 2–30, 1924. p. 1121–1248. [Issued several times a week.]
       6—35347

  Note.—Each number is issued in 4 parts: pt. 1, group 1, relates to books; pt. 1, group 2, to pamphlets, leaflets, contributions to newspapers or periodicals, etc., lectures, sermons, addresses for oral delivery, dramatic compositions, maps, motion pictures; pt. 2, to periodicals; pt. 3, to musical compositions; pt. 4, to works of art, reproductions of a work of art, drawings or plastic works of scientific or technical character, photographs, prints, and pictorial illustrations.
  Subscriptions for the Catalogue of copyright entries should be made to the Superintendent of Documents, Washington, D. C., instead of to the Register of Copyrights. Prices are as follows: Paper, $3.00 a yr. (4 pts.), foreign subscription, $5.00; pt. 1 (groups 1 and 2), 5c. single copy (group 1, price of group 2 varies), $1.00 a yr., foreign subscription, $2.25; pt. 3, $1.00 a yr., foreign subscription, $1.50; pts. 2 and 4, each 10c. single copy, 50c. a yr., foreign subscription, 70c.

—— Same, pt. 1, group 2, Pamphlets, leaflets, contributions to newspapers or periodicals, etc., lectures, sermons, addresses for oral delivery, dramatic compositions, maps, motion pictures, v. 20, no. 8. 1923. vi+1025–1227 p. [Monthly.]

—— Same, pt. 2, Periodicals, v. 18, no. 3. 1924. iii+187–266 p. [Quarterly.]

—— Same, pt. 4, Works of art, reproductions of a work of art, drawings or plastic works of scientific or technical character, photographs, prints, and pictorial illustrations, v. 18, no. 3. 1923. iii+193–273 p. [Quarterly.]

DOCUMENTS DIVISION

Government publications. Monthly check-list of State publications received during Nov. 1923; v. 14, no. 11. 1924. p. 445–490. * Paper, 10c. single copy. $1.00 a yr.; foreign subscription, $1.25.
       10–8924

MIXED CLAIMS COMMISSION, UNITED STATES AND GERMANY

Bache, Semon, & Co. Docket no. 72, list no. 3119, before Mixed Claims Commission, United States and Germany, United States on behalf of Semon Bache and Company *v.* Germany; brief on behalf of United States. 1924. cover-title, 8 p. 4° ‡

Germany. Dealing with liability of Germany for damages in nature of interest in all claims falling within Administrative decision 1, and measure of damages in all claims for property taken, Dec. 11, 1923. 1924. iii+61–70 p. (Administrative decision 3.) [Includes list of decisions and opinions of Mixed Claims Commission, United States and Germany, published to Dec. 31, 1923.] ‡

Gilmer, Mrs. May D. H. Before Mixed Claims Commission, United States and Germany, docket no. 4, United States on behalf of May Davies Hopkins Gilmer, administratrix [of Albert Lloyd Hopkins], *v.* Germany; supplemental brief on behalf of United States in connection with claims arising out of sinking of steamship Lusitania on May 7, 1915. 1924. cover-title, 12 p. 4° ‡

NATIONAL ADVISORY COMMITTEE FOR AERONAUTICS

Bombs. Constant pressure bomb; by F. W. Stevens. 1923. cover-title, 8 p. il. 4° (Report 176.) [Prepared by Standards Bureau. Text and illustration on p. 2 and 3 of cover.] * Paper, 5c.
       23–27379

Propellers. Relative efficiency of direct and geared drive propellers; by Walter S. Diehl. 1923. cover-title, 9 p. il. 4° (Report 178.) [Prepared by Aeronautics Bureau, Navy Department. Text and illustration on p. 2 and 3 of cover.] * Paper, 5c.
       23–27405

NATIONAL HOME FOR DISABLED VOLUNTEER SOLDIERS

Proceedings of board of managers of National Home for Disabled Volunteer Soldiers, Dec. 2, 1923. Dec. 1923. [v. 4] p. 287–299. [Quarterly.] ‡

NAVY DEPARTMENT

Appropriations. Supplemental estimate of appropriation for Navy Department for gunnery and engineering exercises. Jan. 25, 1924. 6 p. (H. doc. 172, 68th Cong. 1st sess.) * Paper, 5c.

Court-martial order 11, 1923; Nov. 30, 1923. [1924.] 10 p. 12° [Monthly.] ‡

AERONAUTICS BUREAU

Manual. Bureau of Aeronautics manual, 1923. 1923. vi+122 p. [Issued in loose-leaf form for insertion in binder.] ‡   24—26114

ENGINEERING BUREAU

Bulletin of engineering information 10; Nov. 1, 1923. 1923. [1]+37 p. il. ‡
                                                    22—26665

MEDICINE AND SURGERY BUREAU

Appendectomy. Notes on 350 appendectomies; by L. W. Johnson. 1924. 12 p. [From United States naval medical bulletin, v. 20, no. 1.] †

Cancer in St. Croix, Virgin Islands; by C. B. Van Gaasbeek. 1924. 7 p. [From United States naval medical bulletin, v. 20, no. 1.] †

Climatic bubo, by C. S. Butler; [with comments by Raymond Spear and J. R. Phelps]. 1924. 8 p. [From United States naval medical bulletin, v. 20. no. 1.] †

Instructions issued by Bureau of Medicine and Surgery (for office files). 1924. 24 p. il. 2 p. of pl. [From United States naval medical bulletin, v. 20, no. 1.] †

Naval medical bulletin. United States naval medical bulletin, published for information of Medical Department of service, Jan. 1924, v. 20, no. 1; edited by W. M. Kerr. 1923 [published 1924]. vi+1–148 p. il. 2 pl. 6 p. of pl. [Monthly.] * Paper, 15c. single copy, $1.50 a yr.; foreign subscription, $2.50.
                                                    8—35095

SPECIAL ARTICLES.—Climatic bubo, by C. S. Butler; [with comment by Raymond Spear and J. R. Phelps].—Notes on 350 appendectomies; by L. W. Johnson.—Clinical trial of Ellis test for tuberculosis; by David Ferguson.—Cancer in St. Croix, Virgin Islands; by C. B. Van Gaasbeek.—Sugar in urine [with bibliography]; by C. W. O. Bunker and R. L. Thrasher.—Endothelioma [with list of references]; by L. H. Williams.—Glanders in man; by L. H. Williams and R. C. Satterlee.—Acute appendicitis within hernia sac; by C. B. Van Gaasbeek.—Chancre of palmar surface of hand; by J. E. Root, jr.—Report of case of recurrent diffuse scleroderma; by C. W. Lane.—Case of acute yellow atrophy of liver [with list of references]; by G. L. McClintock.—Instructions issued by Bureau of Medicine and Surgery.—Notes on preventive medicine for medical officers, Navy [including Pneumonia, bronchitis, and tonsillitis season, housing, ventilation, and contact, by J. R. Phelps; Some of factors which lead to increase and decline of communicable diseases among men and animals, by W. H. Park].

Pneumonia, bronchitis and tonsillitis season, housing, ventilation, and contact, by J. R. Phelps; [Some of factors which lead to increase and decline of communicable diseases among men and animals, by W. H. Park]. 1924. 32 p. [From United States naval medical bulletin, v. 20, no. 1.] †

Sanitation. Some of functions of naval medical personnel serving in the field, with special reference to field sanitary measures; by W. L. Mann. 1923. [1]+79 p. il. [From United States naval medical bulletin, v. 19, no. 6.] †

Surgeons. Circular for information of persons desiring to enroll in Naval Reserve Force as medical officers. Nov. 1923. [1]+4 p. 4° †

Tuberculosis. Clinical trial of Ellis test for tuberculosis; by David Ferguson. 1924. 16 p. [From United States naval medical bulletin, v. 20, no. 1.] †

NAVIGATION BUREAU

Drill. Ship and gun drills, Navy, 1922. 1922 [published 1923]. xiii+213 p. il. 16° * Cloth, 50c. (incorrectly given in publication as 25c).   24—26115

Navy directory, officers of Navy and Marine Corps, including officers of Naval Reserve Force (active), Marine Corps Reserve (active), and foreign officers serving with Navy, Jan. 1, 1924. 1924. iii+246 p. [Bimonthly.] * Paper, 25c. single copy, $1.25 a yr.; foreign subscription, $1.75.

Personnel management. Personnel management, assignment 1. 1923. [1]+9 p. (Navy education-study courses.) ‡
—— Same, assignment 2. 1923. [1]+16 p. (Navy education-study courses.) ‡
—— Same, assignment 3. 1923. [1]+16 p. (Navy education-study courses.) ‡
—— Same, assignment 4. 1923. [1]+16 p. (Navy education-study courses.) ‡
—— Same, assignment 5. 1923. [1]+18 p. (Navy education-study courses.) ‡
—— Same, assignment 6. 1923. [1]+15 p. (Navy education-study courses.) ‡
—— Same, assignment 7. 1923. [1]+15 p. (Navy education-study courses.) ‡
—— Same, assignment 8. 1923. [1]+15 p. (Navy education-study courses.) ‡
—— Same, assignment 9. 1923. [1]+21 p. (Navy education-study courses.) ‡
—— Same, assignment 10. 1923. [1]+10 p. (Navy education-study courses.) ‡
—— Same, assignment 11. 1923. [1]+21 p. (Navy education-study courses.) ‡

Refrigeration and refrigerating machinery. Refrigeration and refrigerating machines, assignment 1; by J. L. King. 1923. [1]+11 p. (Navy education-study courses.) ‡
—— Same, assignment 2; by J. L. King. 1923. [1]+8 p. 2 pl. (Navy education-study courses.) ‡
—— Same, assignment 3; by J. L. King. 1923. [1]+5 p. 1 pl. (Navy education-study courses.) ‡
—— Same, assignment 4; by J. L. King. 1923. [1]+5 p. 5 pl. (Navy education-study courses.) ‡
—— Same, assignment 5; by J. L. King. 1923. [1]+4 p. 2 pl. (Navy education-study courses.) ‡
—— Same, assignment 6; by J. L. King. 1923. [1]+7 p. 3 pl. (Navy education-study courses.) ‡
—— Same, assignment 7; by J. L. King. 1923. [1]+6 p. 1 pl. (Navy education-study courses.) ‡

HYDROGRAPHIC OFFICE

NOTE.—The charts, sailing directions, etc., of the Hydrographic Office are sold by the office in Washington and also by agents at the principal American and foreign seaports and American lake ports. Copies of the General catalogue of mariners' charts and books and of the Hydrographic bulletins, reprints, and Notice to mariners are supplied free on application at the Hydrographic Office in Washington and at the branch offices in Boston, New York, Philadelphia, Baltimore, Norfolk, Savannah, New Orleans, Galveston, San Francisco, Portland (Oreg.), Seattle, Chicago, Cleveland, Buffalo, Sault Ste. Marie, and Duluth.

Hydrographic bulletin, weekly, no. 1791–95; Jan. 2–30, 1924. [1924.] Each 1 p. large 4° and f° [For Ice supplements to accompany nos. 1791–95, see below under center head *Charts* the subhead *Pilot charts.*] †

Notice to aviators 1, 1924; Jan. 1 [1924]. [1924.] 7 p. [Monthly.] †

Notice to mariners 1–4, 1924; Jan. 5–26 [1924]. [1924.] [xxxvi]+1–118 leaves, 6 maps. [Weekly.] †

Tide calendars. Tide calendar [for Baltimore (Fort McHenry) and Cape Henry], Feb. 1924. [1924.] 1 p. 4° [Monthly.] †
—— Tide calendar [for Norfolk (Navy Yard) and Newport News, Va.], Feb. 1924. [1924.] 1 p. 4° [Monthly.] †

Charts

Hwangpoo River. Hwangpoo River (Woosung River), China, east coast, Kaokiao Creek to Yangtzepoo Creek, from surveys by Hwangpoo Conservancy Board between 1914 and 1920, with additions from municipal plans; chart 5391. Scale naut. m.=7 in. Washington, Hydrographic Office, Dec. 1923. 39.4×27.3 in. † 50c.

Hwangpoo River—Continued. Hwangpoo River (Woosung River), China, east coast, Woosung to Kaokiao Creek, from surveys by Hwangpoo Conservancy Board between 1914 and 1920, soundings in Yangtze River from Chinese Maritime Customs surveys in 1920; chart 5390. Scale naut. m.=7 in. Washington, Hydrographic Office, Nov. 1923. 39.4×26.7 in. † 50c.

New Guinea, west coast, Patipi Bay (Solat Len) to Cape van den Bosch (Tanjung Katumin), from Netherlands Government survey in 1911 and 1912 [with insets]; chart 2981. Scale naut. m.=0.4 in. Washington. Hydrographic Office, Jan. 1924. 38.7×25.9 in. † 40c.

Panjang, Channels near, from Netherlands Government survey in 1911 and 1912. Sanggala and Wap bays, from Neth. Govt. survey in 1911 and 1912.

Pilot charts. Ice supplement to north Atlantic pilot chart; issue 91. Scale 1° long.=0.3 in. Washington, Hydrographic Office [1924]. 8.9×11.8 in. [To accompany Hydrographic bulletin 1791, Jan. 2, 1924.] †

—— Same; issue 92. Scale 1° long.=0.3 in. Washington, Hydrographic Office [1924]. 8.9×11.8 in. [To accompany Hydrographic bulletin 1792, Jan. 9, 1924.] †

—— Same; issue 93. Scale 1° long.=0.3 in. Washington, Hydrographic Office [1924]. 8.9×11.8 in. [To accompany Hydrographic bulletin 1793, Jan. 16, 1924.] †

—— Same; issue 94. Scale 1° long.=0.3 in. Washington, Hydrographic Office [1924]. 8.9×11.8 in. [To accompany Hydrographic bulletin 1794, Jan. 23, 1924.] †

—— Same; issue 95. Scale 1° long.=0.3 in. Washington, Hydrographic Office [1924]. 8.9×11.8 in. [To accompany Hydrographic bulletin 1795, Jan. 30, 1924.] †

—— Pilot chart of Central American waters. Feb. 1924; chart 3500. Scale 1° long.=0.7 in. Washington, Hydrographic Office, Jan. 12, 1924. 23.4×35.1 in. [Monthly. Certain portions of the data are furnished by the Weather Bureau.] † 10c.

NOTE.—Contains on reverse: Index charts of Hydrographic Office publications.

—— Pilot chart of Indian Ocean, Mar. 1924; chart 2603. Scale 1° long.=0.2 in. Washington, Hydrographic Office, Jan. 12, 1924. 22.6×31 in. [Monthly. Certain portions of the data are furnished by the Weather Bureau.] † 10c.

NOTE.—Contains on reverse: Index charts of Hydrographic Office publications.

—— Pilot chart of north Atlantic Ocean, Feb. 1924; chart 1400. Scale 1° long.=0.27 in. Washington, Hydrographic Office, Jan. 12, 1924. 23.2×31 8 in. [Monthly. Certain portions of the data are furnished by the Weather Bureau.] † 10c.
                                                                14—16339

NOTE.—Contains on reverse: Index charts of Hydrographic Office publications.

—— Pilot chart of south Atlantic Ocean, Mar.–May, 1924; chart 2600. Scale 1° long.=0.3 in. Washington, Hydrographic Office, Jan. 12, 1924. 23×31.9 in. [Quarterly. Certain portions of the data are furnished by the Weather Bureau.] † 10c.

NOTE.—Contains on reverse: Index charts of Hydrographic Office publications.

—— Pilot chart of south Pacific Ocean, Mar.–May, 1924; chart 2601. Scale 1° long.=0.2 in. Washington, Hydrographic Office, Jan. 12, 1924. 21.2×35.5 in. [Quarterly. Certain portions of the data are furnished by the Weather Bureau.] † 10c.

NOTE.—Contains on reverse: Index charts of Hydrographic Office publications.

ORDNANCE BUREAU

Craven, Francis S. In Patent Office, interference no. 46578, Craven *r.* Foley: brief for Craven on appeal to board of examiners in chief. 1924. cover-title, 15 p. ‡

SUPPLIES AND ACCOUNTS BUREAU

Income tax. For information of all persons in naval service relative to income tax. [1924.] 4 p. 4° ‡

PAN AMERICAN UNION

NOTE.—The Pan American Union sells its own monthly bulletins, handbooks, etc., at prices usually ranging from 5c. to $2.50. The price of the English edition of the bulletin is 25c. a single copy or $2.50 a year, the Spanish edition $2.00 a year, the Portuguese edition $1.50 a year; there is an additional charge of 50c. a year on each edition for countries outside the Pan American Union. Address the Director General of the Pan American Union, Washington, D. C.

Bulletin (*English edition*). Bulletin of Pan American Union, Jan. 1924; [v. 58, no. 1]. [1924.] iv+1–108 p. il. [Monthly.] 8—30967

—— Same. (H. doc. 6, pt. 7, 68th Cong. 1st sess.)

—— (*Portuguese edition*). Boletim da União Pan-Americana, Janeiro, 1924, edição portugueza; [v. 26, no. 1]. [Sun Job Print, Baltimore, Md., 1923.] [iv]+1–76 p. il. [Monthly.] 11—27014

—— (*Spanish edition*). Boletín de la Unión Panamericana, Enero, 1924, sección española; [v. 58, no. 1]. [1923.] iv+1–108 p. il. [Monthly.] 12—12555

Commerce. Latin American foreign trade in 1922, general survey. 1924. ii+8+[1] p. [From Bulletin, Jan. 1924.] †

Cuba, general descriptive data. 1924. ii+30 p. il. † 11—35835

Guatemala, general descriptive data. 1924. [2]+30 p. il. † 16—26951

Honduras. Commerce of Honduras, latest reports from Honduran official sources. 1924. [1]+ 6 p. † 22—26934

Puebla, third city in Mexican Union; [by Carlos M. Ibarra]. 1924. [2]+14 p. il. [From Bulletin, Jan. 1924.] †

PANAMA CANAL

NOTE.—Although The Panama Canal makes its reports to, and is under the supervision of, the Secretary of War, it is not a part of the War Department.

Appropriations. Estimates for The Panama Canal, 1925. 1924. cover-title, [1]+420–434+870–877 p. 4° [Extracts from Appropriations Committee, House, subcommittee print of War Department appropriation bill, 1925, and from Budget Bureau Budget, 1925.] ‡

Panama Canal record, v. 17, no. 21–25; Jan. 2–30, 1924. Balboa Heights, C. Z. [1924.] p. 303–370, il. [Weekly.] 7—35328

NOTE.—The yearly subscription rate of the Panama Canal record is 50c. domestic, and $1.00 foreign, (single issues 2c.), except in the case of Government departments and bureaus, Members of Congress, representatives of foreign governments, steamship lines, chambers of commerce, boards of trade, and university and public libraries, to whom the Record is distributed free. The word "domestic" refers to the United States, Canada, Canal Zone, Cuba, Guam, Hawaii, Manua, Mexico, the Philippines, Porto Rico, Republic of Panama, Tutuila, and the Virgin Islands. Subscriptions will commence with the first issue of the Record in the month in which the subscriptions are received unless otherwise requested. Remittances should be made payable to Disbursing Clerk, The Panama Canal, but should be forwarded to the Chief of Office, The Panama Canal, Washington, D. C. The name and address to which the Record is to be sent should be plainly written. Postage stamps, foreign money, and defaced or smooth coins will not be accepted.

EXECUTIVE DEPARTMENT

EXECUTIVE OFFICE

Telephone directory. The Panama Canal, telephone directory, Nov. 1, 1923. Panama Canal Press, Mount Hope, C. Z., 1923. 180 p. † Paper, 40c., Panama Canal, Balboa Heights, Canal Zone.

SUPPLY DEPARTMENT

Rules. Book of rules, Supply Department storehouses. Revised 1923. Panama Canal Press, Mount Hope, C. Z., 1923. 185 p. ‡

POST OFFICE DEPARTMENT

Advertising. Folded advertising cards; [issued by] 3d assistant Postmaster General. Jan. 22, 1924. 1 p. oblong 32° †

Claims. Claims adjusted by Postmaster General requiring appropriation, communication submitting claims for damages to privately owned property which have been adjusted and which require appropriation for their payment. Jan. 7, 1924. 6 p. (H. doc. 142, 68th Cong. 1st sess.) * Paper, 5c.

—— Claims settled by Postmaster General requiring appropriation for their payment. Jan. 29, 1924. 6 p. (H. doc. 180, 68th Cong. 1st sess.) * Paper, 5c.

Mail matter. Correction of objectionable practices in addressing and preparing 2d-class matter for mailing; [issued by] 3d assistant Postmaster General. 1924. 1 p. narrow f° †

Postal bulletin, v. '45, no. 13357–382; Jan. 2–31, 1924. 1924. Each 1 p. or 2 leaves, f° [Daily except Sundays and holidays.] * Paper, 5c. single copy, $2.00 a yr.   6—5810

Postal guide. United States official postal guide, 4th series, v. 3, no. 7; Jan. 1924, monthly supplement. 1924. cover-title, 47 p. il. [Includes Modifications 30–32 of International money order list, pamphlet 14, and Inserts 846 and 847 to Postal laws and regulations of United States. Text on p. 2–4 of cover.] * Official postal guide, with supplements, $1.00, foreign subscription, $1.50; July issue, 75c.; supplements published monthly (11 pamphlets) 25c.; foreign subscription, 50c.   4—18254

Seals (fasteners). Use of paper seals for holding together edges of pamphlets, folders, etc.; [issued by] 3d assistant Postmaster General. Jan. 28, 1924. 1 p. 12° †

POSTAL SAVINGS SYSTEM

Postal savings. United States Postal Savings System. Aug. 1923. [4] p. il. narrow 16° (P. S. 4.) †

RAILWAY MAIL SERVICE

Mail-trains. Schedule of mail trains, no. 443, Dec. 18, 1923, 3d division, Railway Mail Service, comprising District of Columbia, Maryland, North Carolina, Virginia, and West Virginia (except peninsula of Maryland and Virginia). 1924. 160+[1] p. narrow 8° ‡

TOPOGRAPHY DIVISION

NOTE.—Since February, 1908, the Topography Division has been preparing rural-delivery maps of counties in which rural delivery is completely established. They are published in two forms, one giving simply the rural free delivery routes starting from a single given post office, sold at 10 cents each; the other, the rural free delivery routes in an entire county, sold at 35 cents each. A uniform scale of 1 inch to 1 mile is used. Editions are not issued, but sun-print copies are produced in response to special calls addressed to the Disbursing Clerk, Post Office Department, Washington, D. C. These maps should not be confused with the post route maps, for which see Monthly catalogue for February, 1923, page 528.

PRESIDENT OF UNITED STATES

Agricultural distress in United States, message transmitting special recommendations for legislation by Congress for relief of distress in agricultural districts in United States. Jan. 23, 1924. 3 p. (H. doc. 167, 68th Cong. 1st sess.) * Paper, 5c.   23—27383

Copyright, Canada, proclamation [extending to citizens of Canada all benefits of act of Mar. 4, 1909, including copyright controlling parts of instruments serving to reproduce mechanically musical works, same to be effective Jan. 1, 1924]. Dec. 27, 1923. 1 p. f° (No. 1682.) †

Crabbe, C. C. Executive order [waiving provisions of Executive order of Jan. 17, 1873, prohibiting Federal employees from holding office under any State, Territorial or municipal government, so as to permit C. C. Crabbe. attorney general of Ohio, to hold position of special assistant to Attorney General of United States]. Jan. 11, 1924. 1 p. f° (No. 3941.) ‡

Crow Reservation. Extension of time for payments for Crow Indian lands, Mont., proclamation. [Dec. 18, 1923.] 2 p. f° ([No. 1681.]) †

Government officials and employees. Executive order [of President Grant relative to employees of Federal Government assuming duties of State, Territorial, or municipal office at same time that they are charged with duties of civil office held under Federal authority]. Jan. 17, 1873 [reprint 1923]. 1 p. f° (No. 9.) ‡

Harding, Warren G. Warren Gamaliel Harding, eulogy delivered by Calvin Coolidge, broadcasted by radio in behalf of Harding Memorial Association, Dec. 10, 1923; presented by Mr. Willis. Dec. 15, 1923. 6 p. (S. doc. 7, 68th Cong. 1st sess.) * Paper, 5c.   23—27406

Mexico. Exportation of arms or munitions of war to Mexico unlawful, proclamation. Jan. 7, 1924. 1 p. f° (No. 1683.) †

Naval petroleum reserves. Oil leases made on naval reserves, estimate of appropriation, fiscal year 1924, to enable Chief Executive to take such action as may be required for purpose of insuring enforcement of either civil or criminal liability pertaining to oil leases made on naval reserves and protection of interests of United States in such reserves. Jan. 29, 1924. 2 p. (H. doc. 174, 68th Cong. 1st sess.) * Paper, 5c.

Panama Canal. Executive order, transit and harbor regulations for The Panama Canal and approaches thereto, including all waters under its jurisdiction [effective Jan. 1, 1924]. [Dec. 20, 1923.] 23 p. f° ([No. 3938.]) ‡

Townsend, Charles H. Executive order [waiving time limitation upon eligibility for reinstatement so as to permit reinstatement of Charles H. Townsend to Railway Mail Service]. Dec. 21, 1923. 1 p. f° (No. 3939.) ‡

Wilmeth, James L. Executive order [directing that James L. Wilmeth and James E. Chamberlain are eligible to reenter any part of classified service in appropriate positions for period of 5 years from Mar. 31, 1922]. Dec. 24, 1923. 1 p. f° (No. 3940.) ‡

RAILROAD ADMINISTRATION

Alfalfa. No. 114, in Supreme Court, Oct. term, 1923, James C. Davis, agent of the President and director general of railroads *v.* Portland Seed Company, upon writ of error to circuit court of appeals for 9th circuit; supplemental brief for director general of railroads, damages under 4th section of act to regulate commerce, was director general subject to 4th section? 1924. cover-title, ii+86 p. ‡

Aluminium sulphate. Before Interstate Commerce Commission, no. 14328, Crown Willamette Paper Company *v.* director general; petition for reconsideration and reargument on behalf of director general. 1923. cover-title, 9 p. ‡

Barley. Before Interstate Commerce Commission, no. 14298, Morgan & Miller *v.* director general; petition for reconsideration and reargument on behalf of director general. 1923. cover-title, 14 p. ‡

Corn syrup. Before Interstate Commerce Commission, no. 14812 and sub-no. 1. American Maize-Products Company *v.* director general, as agent; exceptions to examiner's proposed report filed on behalf of defendant. 1923. cover-title, 6 p. ‡

Flour. Before Interstate Commerce Commission, no. 13462, Aunt Jemima Mills Company et al. *v.* director general et al.; petition for rehearing or reargument. 1924. cover-title, 7 p. ‡

Freight rates. Before Interstate Commerce Commission, no. 15125, Crown Cork & Seal Company *v.* director general et al.; exceptions to examiner's proposed report filed on behalf of director general, 1924. cover-title, 3 p. ‡

—— No. 209, in Supreme Court, Oct. term, 1923, Great Northern Railway Company *v.* McCaull-Dinsmore Company, upon writ of certiorari to Supreme Court of Minnesota; brief for director general of railroads as amicus curiae. 1924. cover-title, ii+67 p. ‡

Matches. Before Interstate Commerce Commission, I. C. C. dockets nos. 14599 and 14600, Diamond Match Company *v.* James C. Davis, director general of railroads, as agent, New York Central Railroad Company, and Philadelphia and Reading Railroad Company; [same] *v.* director general, as agent, New York Central Railroad, et al.; exceptions of defendants to report proposed by examiner. 1923. cover-title, 32 p. ‡

Paper. Before Interstate Commerce Commission, no. 15316, Texas Farm and Ranch Publishing Company et al. *v.* director general; brief for director general. 1924. cover-title, 7 p. ‡

Peoria Railway Terminal Company. Final settlement between director general of railroads and W. G. Bierd and H. I. Battles, receivers of Peoria Railway Terminal Company, Jan. 3, 1924. 1924. 3 p. 4° †

Rails. Before Interstate Commerce Commission, no. 14230, Duluth Iron and Metal Company *v.* director general; exceptions on behalf of director general to report proposed by examiner. 1924. cover-title, 11 p. ‡

Report. Disputes arising incident to Federal control that have been liquidated, communication submitting summary of progress made to Dec. 31, 1923, in liquidating all matters, including compensation, and all questions and disputes arising out of or incident to Federal control, as provided for in sec. 202 of transportation act of 1920. Jan. 7, 1924. 4 p. (H. doc. 148, 68th Cong. 1st sess.) * Paper, 5c.

Sand. Before Interstate Commerce Commission, no. 12727, Fairbanks, Morse & Co. *v.* director general; petition of defendant for reargument, reconsideration, or revision of report. 1924. cover-title, i+24 p. ‡

—— Before Interstate Commerce Commission, no. 15088, Owens Bottle Company *v.* director general et al.; exceptions to examiner's proposed report filed on behalf of director general. 1924. cover-title, 4 p. ‡

Sugar. No. 123, in Supreme Court, Oct. term, 1923, James C. Davis, agent of the President and director general of railroads, *v.* A. J. Parington, upon writ of error to circuit court of appeals for 9th circuit; supplemental brief for director general of railroads, damages under 4th section of act to regulate commerce, was director general subject to 4th section? 1924. cover-title, ii+86 p. ‡

Swine. Before Interstate Commerce Commission, no. 12386, North Packing & Provision Company et al. *v.* director general et al.; exceptions on part of director general to report proposed by examiners. 1924. cover-title, i+18 p. ‡

Switching charges. Before Interstate Commerce Commission, no. 11040, Boston Wool Trade Association *v.* director general; exceptions on part of director general to report proposed by examiner. 1924. cover-title, i+29 p. ‡

Weighing charges. Before Interstate Commerce Commission, no. 15150, Walsh Fire Clay Products Company et al. *v.* director general et al.; defendant's brief. 1924. cover-title, 11 p. ‡

Wool. Before Interstate Commerce Commission, no. 13318, Boston Wool Trade Association *v.* director general; brief on part of director general. 1924. cover-title, 10 p. ‡

SHIPPING BOARD

Brooks-Scanlon Corporation. Nos. 367 and 385, in Supreme Court, Oct. term, 1923, Brooks-Scanlon Corporation *v.* United States; United States *v.* Brooks-Scanlon Corporation, appeals from Court of Claims; brief for United States. 1924. cover-title, i+41 p. ‡

Skinner & Eddy Corporation. In Supreme Court, Oct. term, 1923, original, in matter of Skinner & Eddy Corporation; brief for United States in opposition to motion for leave to file petition for writ of mandamus, etc. 1924. cover-title, i+22 p. ‡

SHIPPING BOARD EMERGENCY FLEET CORPORATION

Ships. Schedule of sailings of Shipping Board vessels in general cargo, passenger, and mail services, 1st of January to middle of February, 1924; issued by Traffic Department. 1923. cover-title, vi+14 p. il. [Monthly. Text on p. 2–4 of cover.] †   23—26331

SMITHSONIAN INSTITUTION

Note.—In a recent price-list the Smithsonian Institution publishes this notice: " Applicants for the publications in this list are requested to state the grounds of their requests, as the Institution is able to supply papers only as an aid to the researches or studies in which they are especially interested. These papers are distributed *gratis*, except as otherwise indicated, and should be ordered by the *publication numbers* arranged in sequence. The serial publications of the Smithsonian Institution are as follows: 1, Smithsonian contributions to knowledge; 2, Smithsonian miscellaneous collections; 3, Smithsonian annual reports. No *sets* of these are for sale or distribution, as most of the volumes are out of print. The papers issued in the series of Contributions to knowledge and Miscellaneous collections are distributed without charge to public libraries, educational establishments, learned societies, and specialists in this country and abroad; and are supplied to other institutions and individuals at the prices indicated. Remittances should be made payable to the ' Smithsonian Institution.' The Smithsonian report volumes and the papers reprinted in separate form therefrom are distributed *gratuitously* by the Institution to libraries and individuals throughout the world. Very few of the Report volumes are now available at the Institution, but many of those of which the Smithsonian edition is exhausted can be purchased from the Superintendent of Documents, Government Printing Office, Washington, D. C. The Institution maintains mailing-lists of public libraries and other educational establishments, but no *general mailing-list of individuals*. A library making application to be listed for Smithsonian publications should state the number of volumes which it contains and the date of its establishment, and have the endorsement of a Member of Congress."

The annual reports are the only Smithsonian publications that are regularly issued as public documents. All the others are paid for from the private funds of the Institution, but as they are usually regarded as public documents and have free transmission by mail they are listed in the Monthly catalogue.

Pottery. Additional designs on prehistoric Mimbres pottery; by J. Walter Fewkes. Washington, Smithsonian Institution, Jan. 22. 1924. [2]+46 p. il. (Publication 2748; Smithsonian miscellaneous collections, v. 76, no. 8.) † Paper, 30c.   24—26062

ETHNOLOGY BUREAU

Chama Valley. Excavations in Chama valley, N. Mex.; by J. A. Jeancon. 1923. ix+80 p. il. 1 pl. 64 p. of pl. map. (Bulletin 81.)   * Cloth, 75c.   24—26060

—— Same. (H. doc. 46, 68th Cong. 1st sess.)

Mandan Indians. Mandan and Hidatsa music [with list of authorities cited]; by Frances Densmore. 1923. xx+192 p. il. 1 pl. 18 p. of por. and pl. (Bulletin 80.)   * Cloth, 60c.   23—27407

—— Same. (H. doc. 45, 68th Cong. 1st sess.)

INTERNATIONAL EXCHANGE SERVICE

Report on International Exchange Service, fiscal year 1923. 1923. [1]+78– 86 p. [From Smithsonian Institution report, 1923.] †   15—10108

NATIONAL MUSEUM

Note.—The publications of the National Museum comprise an annual report and three scientific series, viz., Proceedings, Bulletins, and Contributions from national herbarium. The editions are distributed to established lists of libraries, scientific institutions, and specialists, any surplus copies being supplied on application. The volumes of Proceedings are made up of technical papers based on the Museum collections in biology, geology, and anthropology, and of each of these papers a small edition, in pamphlet form, is issued in advance of the volume, for prompt distribution to specialists. No sets of any of these series can now be furnished.

Annelids. Heteronereis phase of new species of polychaetous annelid from Uruguay; by Aaron L. Treadwell. 1923. cover-title, 4 p. il. [From Proceedings, v. 64; no. 2499.] †

Birds, Fossil. Fossil birds from southeastern Arizona; by Alexander Wetmore. 1924. cover-title, 18 p. il. [From Proceedings, v. 64; no. 2495.] †

Dolichopus. Notes and descriptions of 2-winged flies of family Dolichopodidae from Alaska; by M. C. Van Duzee. 1923. cover-title, 16 p. 1 pl. [From Proceedings, v. 63; no. 2490.] †

Fishes. Descriptions of 18 new species of fishes from Wilkes exploring expedition preserved in National Museum; by Henry W. Fowler and Barton A. Bean. 1923. cover-title, 27 p. [From Proceedings, v. 63; no. 2488.] †

Ichneumon-flies. New genera and species of ichneumon-flies; by R. A. Cushman. 1924. cover-title, 16 p. il. [From Proceedings, v. 64; no. 2494.] †

Insects, Fossil. Fossil insects in National Museum; by T. D. A. Cockerell. 1924. cover-title, 15 p. il. 2 p. of pl. [From Proceedings, v. 64; no. 2503.] †

Meteorites. Sharps meteorite, Richmond County, Va.; by Thomas L. Watson. 1923. cover-title, 4 p. 2 p. of pl. [From Proceedings, v. 64; no. 2492.] †

Mollusks. Tertiary mollusks of genus Orthaulax from Republic of Haiti, Porto Rico, and Cuba; by Wendell P. Woodring. 1923. cover-title, 12 p. 2 p. of pl. [From Proceedings, v. 64; no. 2491.] †

Mussels. New pearly fresh-water mussels from Mexico and Uruguay; by William B. Marshall. 1923. cover-title, 4 p. 3 p. of pl. [From Proceedings, v. 63; no. 2485.] †

Polyclads. . Contributions to biology of Philippine Archipelago and adjacent regions; Polyclad turbellarians from Philippine Islands; by Tokio Kaburaki. 1923. [1]+635–649 p. il. 2 p. of pl. (Bulletin 100, v. 1, pt. 10.) * Paper, 5c.
                                                                        24—26061

Report on progress and condition of National Museum, year ending June 30, 1923. 1923. ix+205 p. 1 pl. ([Smithsonian Institution. . Annual report, pt. 2.]) * Cloth, 50c.
                                                                        6—6378

Spider-crabs. New species and subspecies of spider crabs; by Mary J. Rathbun. 1923. cover-title, 5 p. [From Proceedings, v. 64; no. 2504.] †

STATE DEPARTMENT

Arbitration. . Agreement between United States and Great Britain, arbitration, further extending duration of convention of Apr. 4, 1908; signed Washington, June 23, 1923, proclaimed Dec. 29, 1923. 1924. [1]+3 p. (Treaty series 674.) †
                                                                        24—26064

[*Circulars*] 1918 and 1920; Dec. 11, 1923 and Jan. 8, 1924. 1923 [–24]. 1 p. and 2 p. [General instruction circulars to consular officers.] ‡

Claims. Claim for death of Samuel Richardson, report respecting claim presented by British Government for death of Samuel Richardson, Nov. 1, 1921, at Consuelo, Dominican Republic. Jan. 14, 1924. 3 p. (S. doc. 20, 68th Cong. 1st sess.) * Paper, 5c.

—— Claim of Salvador Buitrago Diaz, report respecting claim against United States on account of damage done by United States marines to property of Salvador Buitrago Diaz, owner of newspaper La Tribuna, of Managua, Nicaragua. Jan. 10, 1924. 3 p. (S. doc. 18, 68th Cong. 1st sess.) * Paper, 5c.

—— Claims for death of several Nicaraguans, report respecting claims against United States on account of several Nicaraguans killed or injured in encounters with American marines. Jan. 21, 1924. 5 p. (S. doc. 24, 68th Cong. 1st sess.) * Paper, 5c.

Consuls. Regulations governing consular service of United States; annotated to Dec. 31, 1922. 1923. xi+[194] p. [Includes Articles 1–9, 11–21, 24, 25. and 28. Issued in loose-leaf form for insertion in binder.] ‡   24—26116

NOTE.—There has been no reprint of the consular regulations since the publication of the edition of 1896, although in some instances the text has undergone modification as the result of statutory enactments and Executive orders. It has become necessary for administrative purposes to reprint the consular regulations of 1896, as well as to provide a dependable digest of general instructions. This edition, therefore, is a reprint of the consular regulations of 1896, with the above-mentioned modifications in the text, and with accompanying notes, which latter are not to be considered as in anywise modifying the regulations themselves, but as explanatory and interpretative.

—— Reprint of Consular regulations [circular letter, Jan. 18, 1924, to American consular officers concerning issuance of Regulations governing consular service of United States, annotated to Dec. 31, 1922, with instructions as to the care of the same]. [1924.] 3 p. ‡

Diplomatic list, Jan. 1924. [1924.] cover-title, i+34 p. 24° [Monthly.] ‡
                                                                        10—16292

Europe. Index to political map of Europe and Asia Minor [issued by] Military Intelligence Division, General Staff, Army, Jan. 15, 1922 [1921], with indices of insert maps of Africa and Oceanica; prepared by Division of Political and Economic Information, Department of State. 1923. iii+79 p. large 8° [The map which this indexes was issued in 2 sheets, and was entered in the Monthly catalogue for Sept. 1921, p. 178.] * Paper, 15c.

Extradition. Treaty and additional article between United States and Venezuela, extradition; signed Caracas, Jan. 19 and 21, 1922, proclaimed Jan. 2, 1924. 1924. [1]+11 p. (Treaty series 675.) [English and Spanish.] †

International relations. Recent questions and negotiations, address by Charles E. Hughes, Secretary of State, before meeting of Council on Foreign Relations, held at Ritz-Carlton Hotel, New York City, Jan. 23, 1924. [1924.] [1]+19 p. †   24—26063

International Sanitary Conference of American Republics. 7th International Sanitary Conference, report concerning representation by United States in 7th International Sanitary Conference of American States to be held at Habana, Cuba, in Nov. 1924. Jan. 16, 1924. 3 p. (S. doc. 22, 68th Cong. 1st sess.) * Paper, 5c.   23—27385

International Statistical Institute at The Hague, report concerning legislation to enable United States to maintain membership in [International Statistical Bureau of] International Statistical Institute at The Hague. Jan. 14, 1924. 2 p. (S. doc. 19, 68th Cong. 1st sess.). * Paper, 5c.

INTERNATIONAL JOINT COMMISSION ON BOUNDARY WATERS BETWEEN UNITED STATES AND CANADA

St. Mary River. Hearing in matter of measurement and apportionment of waters of St. Mary and Milk rivers and their tributaries in United States and Canada under article 6 of treaty of Jan. 11, 1909, between United States and Great Britain, Chinook, Mont., Lethbridge, Alberta, Sept. 15 and 17, 1921. 1923. ii+91 p. †   23—26291

SUPREME COURT

Abilene and Southern Railway. Transcript of record, Oct. term, 1923, no. 456, United States and Interstate Commerce Commission *vs.* Abilene & Southern Railway Company et al., appeal from district court for district of Kansas. [1923.] cover-title, v+76 p. ‡

Cases. Cases adjudged in Supreme Court at Oct. term, 1922, Apr. 10–June 11, 1923; Ernest Knaebel, reporter. 1923. L+814 p. (United States reports, v. 262.) [Also issued in 4 preliminary prints.] * Cloth, $2.50.

—— Docket [of cases pending in Supreme Court], Oct. term, 1923. [1923.] p. 237–256, 4° [Issued in loose leaf form.] ‡

[*Journal*] Jan. 2–28, 1924; [slips] 40–59. [1924.] leaves 109–153. ‡

New River Company. Transcript of record, Oct. term, 1923, no. 627, United States and Interstate Commerce Commission *vs.* New River Company et al., appeal from district court for southern district of West Virginia. [1923.] cover-title, ii+67 p. ‡

Official reports of Supreme Court, v. 263 U. S., no. 1; Ernest Knaebel, reporter. Preliminary print. 1924. cover-title, p. 1–161, 12° [Cases adjudged in Supreme Court at Oct. term, 1923 (opinions of Oct. 15–Nov. 12, 1923, in part). Text on p. 2 and 4 of cover. From United States reports, v. 263.] * Paper, 25c. single copy, $1.00 per vol. (4 nos. to a vol.; subscription price, $3.00 for 12 nos.) ; foreign subscription, 5c. added for each pamphlet.

Title Insurance and Trust Company. Transcript of record, Oct. term, 1923, no. 358, United States *vs.* Title Insurance & Trust Company et al., appeal from circuit court of appeals for 9th circuit. [1923.] cover-title, i+30 p. map. ‡

TREASURY DEPARTMENT

Claims. Claims requiring appropriation for their payment. Jan. 14, 1924. 4 p. (H. doc. 154, 68th Cong. 1st sess.) * Paper, 5c.

—— Judgments rendered by Court of Claims, list of judgments rendered by Court of Claims, which have been submitted by Secretary of Treasury and which require appropriation for their payment. Jan. 7, 1924. 7 p. (H. doc. 147, 68th Cong. 1st sess.) * Paper, 5c.   9—6546

Coins. values of foreign coins, Jan. 1, 1924. [1924.] 1 p. 4° (Department circular 1; Director of Mint.) [Quarterly.] †

Finance. Daily statement of Treasury compiled from latest proved reports from Treasury offices and depositaries, Jan. 2–31, 1924. [1924.] Each 4 p. or 3 p. f° [Daily except Sundays and holidays.] †   15—3303

Public buildings. Erection of public buildings, in response to resolution, information relative to sites acquired and appropriations necessary for erection of public buildings. Jan. 28, calendar day Jan. 29, 1924. 8 p. (S. doc. 28, 68th Cong. 1st sess.) * Paper, 5c.

Public debt. Statement of public debt of United States, Oct. 31, 1923. [1923.] [2] p. narrow f° [Monthly.] †   10—21268

Public property. Rents from properties on Government-owned sites, report as to rents received from properties on sites of proposed public buildings purchased by Government in Washington. Jan. 23, 1924. 3 p. (S. doc. 25, 68th Cong. 1st sess.) * Paper, 5c.

Treasury decisions, under customs, internal revenue. and other laws, including decisions of Board of General Appraisers and Court of Customs Appeals. v. 45, no. 1–5; Jan. 3–31. 1924. 1924. various paging. [Weekly. Department decisions numbered 39930–981, general appraisers' decisions 8721–33. abstracts, 46625–785, internal revenue decisions 3542–44. and later Tariff Commission Notice 11.] * Paper. 5c. single copy, $1.00 a yr.; foreign subscription, $2.00.   10—30490

APPRAISERS

Reappraisements of merchandise by general appraisers [on Dec. 27, 1923–Jan. 19, 1924]; Jan. 4–25, 1924. [1924.] various paging. (Reappraisement circulars 3490–93.) [Weekly.] * Paper, 5c. single copy, 50c. a yr.; foreign subscription, $1.05.   13—2916

BOOKKEEPING AND WARRANTS DIVISION

Receipts and expenditures. Combined statement of receipts and disbursements, balances. etc.. of United States, fiscal year 1923. 1924. 278 p. 4° (Treas. Dept. doc. 2936.) ‡   10—11510

—— Same. (Treas. Dept. doc. 2936; H. doc. 95, 68th Cong. 1st sess.)

BUDGET BUREAU

Addresses of President of United States and director of Bureau of Budget at 6th regular meeting of business organization of Government at Memorial Continental Hall, Jan. 21, 1924. 1924. [1]+22 p. †   24—26117

Agriculture Department. Estimates of appropriations for Department of Agriculture. doc. Jan. 29, 1924. 3 p. (H. doc. 178, 68th Cong. 1st sess.) * Paper, 5c.

—— Supplemental estimates of appropriations for Department of Agriculture and draft of proposed legislation. Jan. 22, 1924. 4 p. (H. doc. 163. 68th Cong. 1st sess.) * Paper, 5c.

Alien Property Custodian. Supplemental estimate of appropriation for Alien Property Custodian. fiscal year 1924, for expenses of protection and return of works of art loaned by Austro-Hungarian Government to Panama-Pacific International Exposition. Jan. 25, 1924. 3 p. (H. doc. 169, 68th Cong. 1st sess.) * Paper, 5c.

American Battle Monuments Commission. Supplemental estimate of appropriation for American Battle Monuments Commission. Jan. 7, 1924. 4 p. (H. doc. 133, 68th Cong. 1st sess.) * Paper, 5c.

Commerce Department. Supplemental estimates of appropriations for Department of Commerce. Jan. 25. 1924. 2 p. (H. doc. 171, 68th Cong. 1st sess.) * Paper, 5c.

District of Columbia. Supplemental estimate of appropriation for District of Columbia. Jan. 29, 1924. 2 p. (H. doc. 181, 68th Cong. 1st sess.) * Paper, 5c.

—— Supplemental estimates of appropriations for District of Columbia. Jan. 25, 1924. 7 p. (H. doc. 170, 68th Cong. 1st sess.) * Paper, 5c.

Dove, J. Maury, Company. To pay claim of J. Maury Dove Co., supplemental estimate of appropriation, fiscal year 1924, submitted by War Department for payment of claim of J. Maury Dove Co. Jan. 7, 1924. 2 p. (H. doc. 140, 68th Cong. 1st sess.) * Paper, 5c.

Federal Board for Vocational Education. deficiency estimates of appropriations for Federal Board for Vocational Education, fiscal year 1924. Jan. 7, 1924. 3 p. (H. doc. 141, 68th Cong. 1st sess.)   * Paper, 5c.

Federal Power Commission, supplemental estimate of appropriation for Federal Power Commission, fiscal year 1924, for printing and binding. Jan. 7, 1924. 2 p. (H. doc. 135, 68th Cong. 1st sess.)   * Paper, 5c.

Harding, Warren G. Expenses incurred on account of sickness and death of President Harding, supplemental estimate of appropriation for fiscal year 1924, to defray expenses incurred on account of sickness and death of President Harding. Jan. 7, 1924. 2 p. (H. doc. 139, 68th Cong. 1st sess.) * Paper, 5c.

Interior Department. Estimates of appropriations for Department of Interior. Jan. 29, 1924. 6 p. (H. doc. 175, 68th Cong. 1st sess.)   * Paper, 5c.

Judge Advocate General's Department, Army. Appropriation for special service in Office of Judge Advocate General. Jan. 25, 1924. 2 p. (H. doc. 168, 68th Cong. 1st sess.)   * Paper, 5c.   -

Justice Department. Estimates of appropriations for Department of Justice and draft of proposed legislation. Jan. 22, 1924. 7 p. (H. doc. 160, 68th Cong. 1st sess.)   * Paper, 5c.

Labor Department. Estimates of appropriations for Department of Labor. Jan. 22, 1924. 6 p. (H. doc. 165, 68th Cong. 1st sess.)   * Paper, 5c.

Post Office Department. Estimates of appropriations for Post Office Department. Jan. 29, 1924. 9 p. (H. doc. 177, 68th Cong. 1st sess.)   * Paper, 5c.

Smithsonian Institution. Smithsonian Institution, supplemental estimate of appropriation for Smithsonian Institution, fiscal year 1924, for laying of water mains and erection of fire hydrants in Smithsonian grounds. Jan. 7, 1924. 2 p. (H. doc. 134, 68th Cong. 1st sess.)   * Paper, 5c.

—— Supplemental estimates of appropriation for Smithsonian Institution. Jan. 21, 1924. 2 p. (H. doc. 159, 68th Cong. 1st sess.)   * Paper, 5c.

Treasury Department. Deficiency and supplemental estimates of appropriations for Treasury Department. Jan. 22, 1924. 10 p. (H. doc. 164, 68th Cong. 1st sess.)   * Paper, 5c.

—— Proposed authorization to permit Treasury Department to use appropriation. " Collecting internal revenue, 1924," for rental of quarters in District of Columbia. Jan 29, 1924. 3 p. (H. doc. 176, 68th Cong. 1st sess.) *Paper, 5c.

War Department. Supplemental estimate of appropriation for War Department, fiscal year 1924, for water and sewers at military posts. Jan. 29, 1924. 2 p. (H. doc. 179, 68th Cong. 1st sess.) *Paper, 5c.

—— Supplemental estimates of appropriations for War Department, fiscal year 1924. Jan. 12, 1924. 3 p. (H. doc. 153, 68th Cong. 1st sess.) *Paper, 5c.

COAST GUARD

Uniforms. Amendments to uniform regulations, commissioned and warrant officers [of Coast Guard, 1923] no. 1; Jan. 3, 1924. 1924. 1 p. †

COMPTROLLER OF CURRENCY

National banks. Monthly statement of capital stock of national banks, national bank notes, and Federal reserve bank notes outstanding, bonds on deposit, etc. [Jan. 2, 1924]. Jan. 2, 1924. 1 p. f° †   10—21266

GENERAL SUPPLY COMMITTEE

Government supplies. Advertisement, instructions, and proposal [for Class 1–2, 4–6, 8, 10, 12–13, 16–18, fiscal year 1925]: Form A. [1924.] 4 p. 4° †

—— Specifications and proposals for supplies [fiscal year 1925]: class 1, Stationery, paper articles, and drafting supplies. [1924.] 58 p. 4° [Office correction has been made on p. 1.] †

—— Same: class 2, Hardware, metals, leather and leather goods. [1924.] 82 p. 4° †

Government supplies—Continued. Same: class 5, Laboratory apparatus, and hospital appliances and surgical instruments. [1924.] 35 p. 4° †

—— Same: class 6, Electrical, engineering, and plumbing supplies. [1924.] 31 p. 4° †

—— Same: class 8, Brushes, glass, lubricants, fuel oils, and paints and painters' supplies. [1923.] 21 p. 4° †

—— Same: class 10, Cleaner, polish, floor wax and polishing compound, scouring compound, soap and soap dispensers, and household supplies. [1924.] 18 p. 4° †

—— Same: class 13, Engraving, printing, and lithographic supplies (excluding supplies for Government Printing Office and Bureau of Engraving and Printing). [1923.] 3 p. 4° †

—— Same: class 16, Incandescent gas-lamp supplies. [1924.] 3 p. 4° †

—— Same: class 18, Computing, dictating, transcribing, duplicating, folding, sealing, and typewriting machines; labor-saving devices; typewriter exchange allowances, repair parts, and equipment. [1924.] 14 p. 4° †

GOVERNMENT ACTUARY

Bonds of United States. Market prices and investment values of outstanding bonds and notes [of United States, Dec. 1923]. Jan. 2, 1924· 7 p. 4° (Form A.) [Monthly.] †

INTERNAL REVENUE BUREAU

Internal revenue bulletin. Internal revenue bulletin, v. 3, no. 1–4; Jan. 7–28, 1924. 1924. various paging. [Weekly.] *Paper, 5c. single copy (for subscription price see note below). 22—26051

NOTE.—The Internal revenue bulletin service for 1924 will consist of weekly bulletins, quarterly digests, and semiannual cumulative bulletins. The weekly bulletins will contain the rulings to be made public and all internal revenue Treasury decisions. The quarterly digests, with the exception of the one to be published at the end of 1924, will contain digests of the rulings previously published in the weekly bulletins for 1924. The last digest for 1924 will also contain digests of the rulings published during 1922 and 1923. The semiannual cumulative bulletins will contain all new rulings published during the previous 6 months. The complete bulletin service may be obtained, on a subscription basis, from the Superintendent of Documents, Government Printing Office, Washington, D. C., for $2.00 a yr.; foreign subscription, $2.75.

—— Internal revenue bulletin, digest no. 8; Jan. 1922–Sept. 1923. 1923. xii+356 p. [Quarterly.] * Paper, 25c. (for subscription price see note above). 22—26463

Narcotics. Extracts from Report of commissioner of internal revenue, 1923, in regard to enforcement of internal revenue narcotic laws. [1923.] 16 p. †

LOANS AND CURRENCY DIVISION

Bonds of United States. Caveat list of United States registered bonds and notes, Jan. 1, 1924. [1924.] 56 p. f° [Monthly.] †

Money. Circulation statement of United States money, Jan. 1, 1924. [1924.] 1 p. oblong 8° [Monthly.] † 10—21267

PUBLIC HEALTH SERVICE

Black tongue. Case of black tongue, with post-mortem findings; by Jos. Goldberger, W. F. Tanner, and E. B. Saye. 1923. 7 p. (Reprint 881.) [From Public health reports, Nov. 16, 1923.] * Paper, 5c. 23—27396

Chemical industries. Health conditions among chemical workers, with respect to earnings; by Frank M. Phillips and Gertrude A. Sager. 1923. 4 p. (Reprint 873.) [From Public health reports, Oct. 5, 1923.] * Paper, 5c. 23—27465

Contagious diseases. Notifiable diseases, prevalence in States, 1922. 1924. 115 p. (Reprint 879.) [From Public health reports, Nov. 2, 1923.] * Paper, 10c. 24—26066

Health officers. City health officers, 1923, directory of those in cities of 10,000 or more population. 1923. 12 p. (Reprint 876.) [From Public health reports, Oct. 19, 1923.] * Paper, 5c. 24—26065

Hygiene, Public. Fundamentals of rural health work; by W. F. Draper. 1924.
8 p. (Reprint 882.) [From Public health reports, Nov. 16, 1923.] * Paper,
5c. 24—26067

Public health reports, v. 39, no. 1–4; Jan. 4–25, 1924. 1924. [xv]+1–177 p.
[Weekly.] * Paper, 5c. single copy, $1.50 a yr.; foreign subscription, $2.75.
6—25167

SPECIAL ARTICLES.—No. 1. Hydrogen sulphide literature [with bibliography on
hydrogen sulphide poisoning]; by C. W. Mitchell and S. J. Davenport.—Mortality
from typhoid fever in United States registration area, 1922.—Mortality from diabetes
in United States registration area, 1922.—Death rates of mothers from childbirth in
birth registration area, 1922.—No. 2. Methods of administering iodine for prophylaxis of endemic goiter [with list of references]; by Robert Olesen.—Rocky Mountain
spotted fever: Viability of virus in animal tissues; by R. R. Spencer and R. R. Parker.—No. 3. Study of treatment and prevention of pellagra, experiments showing
value of fresh meat and milk, therapeutic failure of gelatin and preventive failure of
butter and of cod-liver oil [with list of references]; by Joseph Goldberger and W. F.
Tanner.—Importance of our knowledge of thyroid physiology in control of thyroid
diseases [by David Marine]; abstract by Taliaferro Clark.—No. 4. Some notes on
relation of domestic animals to Anopheles; by M. A. Barber and T. B. Hayne.—
General health conditions as reported by Health Section of League of Nations.—Principal causes of death, 1922.—Mortality from typhoid fever, tuberculosis, and pneumonia in large cities, 1923.—Health news, new publication issued by New York State
Department of Health.
NOTE.—This publication is distributed gratuitously to State and municipal health
officers, etc., by the Surgeon General of the Public Health Service, Treasury Department. Others desiring these reports may obtain them from the Superintendent of
Documents, Washington, D. C., at the prices stated above.

Spleen rate of school boys in Mississippi Delta [with bibliography]; by K. F.
Maxcy and C. P. Coogle. 1923. 8 p. (Reprint 878.) [From Public health
reports, Oct. 26, 1923.] * Paper, 5c. 24—26118

Trachoma. Results of 3-year trachoma campaign begun in Knott County, Ky.,
in 1913, as shown by survey made in same locality 10 years later; by John
McMullen. 1923. 6 p. (Reprint 877.) [From Public health reports, Oct.
26, 1923.] * Paper, 5c. 24—26119

HYGIENIC LABORATORY

Parasites. Studies on various intestinal parasites (especially amoebae) of man
[with bibliography; articles] by William C. Boeck and Ch. Wardell Stiles.
Oct. 1923. xxvi+202 p. il. 1 pl. 4 p. of pl. (Bulletin 133.) [Title on p. xi is:
Report upon possible bearing of World War in spread of zooparasitic infections, especially amoebic dysentery, in United States.] * Paper, 25c.
23—27399

CONTENTS.—Summary.—Introduction; by C. W. Stiles.—Survey of 8,029 persons in
United States for intestinal parasites, with special reference to amoebic dysentry
among returned soldiers; by Wm. C. Boeck.—Technique of fecal examination for pro-
tozoan infections; by W. C. Boeck.—Descriptions of more common intestinal protozoa
of man; by Wm. C. Boeck.—Nomenclatorial status of certain protozoa parasitic in
man; by C. W. Stiles and W. C. Boeck.

—— Same. (H. doc. 450, 67th Cong. 3d sess.)

SAVINGS SYSTEM·

Treasury savings certificates. Exchange your 1919 war savings stamps for
Treasury savings certificates, renew your investment at higher interest rate.
[1923.] [2] p. oblong 48° (T. S. S. 21–23R.) †

—— How to save your savings [by investing in Treasury savings certificates].
1924. cover-title, 16 p. 12° ([T. S. S. 34–23.]) [Text on p. 2–4 of cover.] †

TREASURER OF UNITED STATES

Paper money. Monthly statement, paper currency of each denomination outstanding Oct. 31, 1923. Nov. 1 [1923]. 1 p. oblong 24° †
—— Same, Nov. 30, 1923. Dec. 1 [1923]. 1 p. oblong 24° †

VETERANS' BUREAU

Appropriations. Deficiency estimates of appropriations for Veterans' Bureau.
Jan. 22, 1924. 4 p. (H. doc. 161, 68th Cong. 1st sess.) * Paper, 5c.

WAR DEPARTMENT

Army regulations. †

NOTE.—The Army regulations are issued in pamphlet form for insertion in loose-leaf binders. The names of such of the more important administrative subjects as may seem appropriate, arranged in proper sequence, are numbered in a single series, and each name so numbered constitutes the title and number of a pamphlet containing certain administrative regulations pertaining thereto. Where more than one pamphlet is required for the administrative regulations pertaining to any such title, additional pamphlets will be issued in a separate sub-series.

30–1515. Quartermaster Corps: Water-supply systems; Sept. 21, 1923. [1924.] 4 p.
30–2145. Same: Unserviceable property, including waste material, changes 2; Dec. 8, 1923. 1924. 1 p. [Supersedes AR 30–2145, changes 1, June 25, 1923.]
35–1420. Finance Department: Burial expenses of military personnel and civilian employees; June 21, 1923. [1924.] 2 p.
40–275. Medical Department: Sanitary reports, Changes 1; Dec. 4, 1923. 1923. 1 p.
45–65. Ordnance Department: Definition and classification of property; Dec. 4, 1923. [1924.] 2 p.
605–10. Commissioned officers: Appointment in Medical Corps, Regular Army, Changes 1; Nov. 14, 1923. [1924.] 4 p.
605–15. Same: Appointment in Dental Corps, Regular Army; Nov. 14, 1923. [1924.] 8 p. [Supersedes AR 605–15, Feb. 24, 1921.]
605–20. Same: Appointment in Veterinary Corps, Regular Army, Changes 1; Nov. 14, 1923. [1924.] 4 p.
605–25. Same: Appointment in Medical Administrative Corps, Regular Army; Nov. 14, 1923. [1924.] 6 p. [Supersedes AR 605–25, Feb. 24, 1921.]
615–40. Enlisted men: Clothing, allowances, accounts, and disposition. Changes 5; Nov. 24, 1923. [1924.] 4 p. [Supersedes AR 615–40, Changes 1–4, July 17, 1922–Oct. 16, 1923.]

Muscle Shoals. Additional offer made by Tennessee Electric Power Co. [and its associates] to manufacture nitrogen and fertilizers at Muscle Shoals. Jan. 25, 1924. 4 p. (H. doc. 173, 68th Cong. 1st sess.) * Paper, 5c.   24—26048

—— Offer of Union Carbide Co. for Muscle Shoals, proposition submitted by Union Carbide Co. of New York to manufacture nitrates at Muscle Shoals. Jan. 23, 1924. 6 p. (H. doc. 166, 68th Cong. 1st sess.) * Paper, 5c.
      23—27382

—— Plan for development of Muscle Shoals presented jointly by Tennessee Electric Power Co., Memphis Power & Light Co., and Alabama Power Co. Jan. 21, 1924. 6 p. (H. doc. 158, 68th Cong. 1st sess.) * Paper, 5c.
      23—27381

Training regulations.

NOTE.—The Training regulations are issued in pamphlet form for insertion in loose-leaf binders.

150–35. Marksmanship: Machine gun, prepared under direction of chief of infantry; June 22, 1923. [1923.] 84 p. il. * Paper, 15c.
435–100. Coast Artillery Corps: Battalion headquarters and combat train, gun battalion, antiaircraft artillery, prepared under direction of chief of coast artillery; Aug. 2, 1923. [1923.] 7 p. il. 2 pl. * Paper, 5c.
445–205. Bridges: General bridging considerations, prepared under direction of chief of engineers; July 13, 1923. [1924.] 47 p. il. * Paper, 10c.

Work of War Department. 1924. iv+42 p. 1 pl. †   24—26068

ADJUTANT GENERAL'S DEPARTMENT

Army list and directory, Jan. 1, 1924. 1924. vi+276 p. large 8° [Bimonthly.] * Paper, 25c. single copy, $1.25 a yr.; foreign subscription, $1.85.   9—35106

Officers, Army. Officers of Army stationed in or near District of Columbia, Jan. 1924. 1924. iv+40 p. [Quarterly.] * Paper, 5c. single copy, 2c. a yr.; foreign subscription, 30c.   9—35107

Oxyacetylene welding for military purposes; prepared under direction of quartermaster general, 1923. 1923. vi+199 p. il. (United States Army training manual 53.) * Cloth, 40c.

U. S. Army recruiting news, bulletin of recruiting information issued by direction of Adjutant General of Army, Jan. 1 and 15, 1924. [Recruiting Publicity Bureau, Governors Island, N. Y., Jan. 1 and 15, 1924.] Each 16 p. il. 4° † Recruiting Publicity Bureau, Governors Island, N. Y.   War 22—1

AIR SERVICE

Aeronautical bulletins. Aeronautical bulletin, no. 34, 53–70, 72, 81, 83, 85, 99–100, 102–104, Route information series; Nov. 1, 1923–Jan. 15, 1924. [1923–24.] various paging, 12° (Airways Section.) * Paper, 5c. each.   23—26231

—— Aeronautical bulletin, no. 87–121, 135–137, 140, State series; Dec. 1, 1923–Jan. 15, 1924. [1923–24.] Each 2 p. or 7 p. il. 12° (Airways Section.) [No. 100 is Index to Aeronautical bulletins 1–100.] * Paper, 5c. each.

ENGINEER DEPARTMENT

Anacostia Park and reclamation and development of Anacostia River and flats from mouth of river to District line, D. C.; Repairs to Aqueduct Bridge, D. C.; Construction of bridge across Potomac River at Georgetown, D. C. (Francis Scott Key Bridge); Maintenance and repair of Washington Aqueduct, D. C., and Washington Aqueduct filtration plant; Increasing water supply, District of Columbia; M. C. Tyler in charge. 1923. [1]+1989–2019 p. map. [Extract WW from annual report of chief of engineers, 1923.] †

Baltimore, Md. Report upon improvement of rivers and harbors in Baltimore. Md., district; F. C. Harrington in charge. 1923. [1]+404–443 p. [Extract G from annual report of chief of engineers, 1923.] †

Boston, Mass. Report upon improvement of rivers and harbors in Boston, Mass., district; Wildurr Willing in charge. 1923. [1]+15–61 p. [Extract A from annual report of chief of engineers, 1923.] †

Buffalo, N. Y. Report upon improvement of rivers and harbors in Buffalo, N. Y., district; P. S. Reinecke in charge. 1923. [1]+1520–1609 p. [Extract JJ from annual report of chief of engineers, 1923.] †

Charleston, S. C. Report upon improvement of rivers and harbors in Charleston, S. C., district; Edgar Jadwin in charge. 1923. iii+577–604 p. [Extract K from annual report of chief of engineers, 1923.] †

Chattanooga, Tenn. Report upon improvement of rivers and harbors in Chattanooga, Tenn., district; H. C. Fiske in charge. 1923. [1]+1177–99 p. [Extract Y from annual report of chief of engineers, 1923.] †

Chicago, Ill. Report upon improvement of rivers and harbors in Chicago, Ill., district; Rufus W. Putnam in charge. 1923. [1]+1423–58 p. [Extract HH from annual report of chief of engineers, 1923.] †

Cincinnati, Ohio. Report upon improvement of rivers and harbors in Cincinnati, Ohio, district; A. K. B. Lyman in charge. 1923. [1]+1259–68 p. [Extract DD from annual report of chief of engineers, 1923.] †

Columbia River between mouth of Willamette River and Vancouver, Wash., reports on preliminary examination and survey of Columbia River between mouth of Willamette River and Vancouver, Wash., with view to determine whether United States should maintain channel if it is deepened to 25 feet by Port Commission of Vancouver, Wash. Jan. 3, 1924. 19 p. (H. doc. 126, 68th Cong. 1st sess.) * Paper, 5c.

Detroit, Mich. Report upon improvement of rivers and harbors in Detroit, Mich.. district; E. M. Markham in charge. 1923. [1]+1458–1520 p. [Extract II from annual report of chief of engineers, 1923.] †

District of Columbia. Report upon improvements of rivers and harbors in Washington, D. C., district; M. C. Tyler in charge. 1923. [1]+443–467 p. [Extract H from annual report of chief of engineers, 1923.] †

Duluth, Minn. Report upon improvement of rivers and harbors in Duluth, Minn., district; E. H. Marks in charge. 1923. [1]+1279–1327 p. [Extract FF from annual report of chief of engineers, 1923.] †

Duwamish waterway, Seattle Harbor, Wash., reports on preliminary examination and survey of Duwamish waterway, Seattle Harbor, Wash., with view of widening or deepening, or both widening and deepening, channel to accommodate present and future commerce. Dec. 13, 1923. 23 p. (H. doc. 108, 68th Cong. 1st sess.) * Paper, 5c.

Florence, Ala. Report upon improvement of rivers and harbors in Florence, Ala., district; G. R. Spalding in charge. 1923. [1]+1199–1212 p. [Extract Z from annual report of chief of engineers, 1923.] †

Flushing Bay and Creek. N. Y., reports on preliminary examination and survey of Flushing Bay and Creek, N. Y. Jan. 3, 1924. 20 p. (H. doc. 124, 68th Cong. 1st sess.) * Paper, 5c.

Galveston, Tex. Report upon improvement of rivers and harbors in Galveston, Tex., district; L. M. Adams in charge. 1923. [1]+918–1020 p. [Extract Q from annual report of chief of engineers, 1923.] †

Hawaii. Report upon river and harbor improvement in district of Hawaii; W. A. Johnson in charge. 1923. [1]+1827–40 p. [Extract RR from annual report of chief of engineers, 1923.] †

Huntington, W. Va. Report upon improvement of rivers and harbors in Huntington. W. Va., district; W. P. Stokey in charge. 1923. iii+1246–59 p. [Extract CC from annual report of chief of engineers, 1923.] †

Jacksonville, Fla. Report upon improvement of rivers and harbors in Jacksonville, Fla., district; Gilbert A. Youngberg in charge. 1923. [1]+651–727 p. [Extract M from annual report of chief of engineers. 1923.] †

Juneau, Alaska. Report upon improvement of rivers and harbors in Juneau, Alaska, district; J. G. Steese in charge. 1923. [1]+1822–27 p. [Extract QQ from annual report of chief of engineers, 1923.] †

Kansas City, Mo. Report upon improvement of rivers and harbors in Kansas City, Mo., district; C. C. Gee in charge. 1923. [1]+1132–58 p. [Extract W from annual report of chief of engineers, 1923.] †

Los Angeles, Calif. Report upon improvement of rivers and harbors in Los Angeles, Calif., district; Edward D. Ardery in charge. 1923. [1]+1609–19 p. [Extract KK from annual report of chief of engineers, 1923.] †

Louisville, Ky. Report upon improvement of rivers and harbors in Louisville, Ky., district; G. R. Lukesh in charge. 1923. [1]+1268–79 p. [Extract EE from annual report of chief of engineers, 1923.] †

Memphis, Tenn. Report upon improvement of rivers and harbors in Memphis, Tenn., district; George J. Richards in charge. 1923. [1]+1056–78 p. [Extract S from annual report of chief of engineers, 1923.] †

Milwaukee, Wis. Report upon improvement of rivers and harbors in Milwaukee, Wis., district; F. S. Skinner in charge. 1923. [1]+1327–1423 p. [Extract GG from annual report of chief of engineers, 1923.] †

Mississippi River at Nauvoo, Ill., reports on preliminary examination and survey of Mississippi River at Nauvoo, Ill. Dec. 13, 1923. 14 p. map. (H. doc. 112, 68th Cong. 1st sess.) * Paper, 5c.

Mobile, Ala. Report upon improvement of rivers and harbors in Mobile, Ala., district; Earl North in charge. 1923. [1]+783–830 p. [Extract O from annual report of chief of engineers, 1923.] †

Montgomery, Ala. Report upon improvement of rivers and harbors in Montgomery, Ala., district; J. J. Loving in charge. 1923. [1]+727–783 p. [Extract N from annual report of chief of engineers, 1923.] †

Muscle Shoals. Dam no. 2, Muscle Shoals, Ala., advertisement [for furnishing structural steel roof trusses, columns, etc., for power house of Wilson Dam, Tennessee River]. [1923.] 10 p. 4°. †

Nashville, Tenn. Report upon improvement of rivers and harbors in Nashville, Tenn., district; Harold C. Fiske in charge. 1923. [1]+1158–77 p. [Extract X from annual report of chief of engineers, 1923.] †

New Orleans, La. Report upon improvement of rivers and harbors in New Orleans, La., district; E. J. Dent in charge. 1923. [1]+830–918 p. [Extract P from annual report of chief of engineers, 1923.] †

New York City. Report upon improvement of rivers and harbors in 1st New York, N. Y., district; J. R. Slattery in charge. 1923. [1]+137–276 p. [Extract C from annual report of chief of engineers, 1923.] †

—— Report upon improvement of rivers and harbors in 2d New York, N. Y., district; H. C. Newcomer in charge. 1923. [1]+276–311 p. [Extract D from annual report of chief of engineers, 1923.] †

Norfolk, Va. Report upon improvement of rivers and harbors in Norfolk, Va., district; D. D. Pullen in charge. 1923. [1]+467–518 p. [Extract I from annual report of chief of engineers, 1923.] †

Ohio River. Report upon improvement of Ohio River by construction and operation of locks and dams. 1923. [1]+1212–31 p. [Extract AA from annual report of chief of engineers, 1923.] †

Philadelphia, Pa. Report upon improvement of rivers and harbors in Philadelphia, Pa., district; F. C. Boggs in charge. 1923. [1]+311–337 p. [Extract E from annual report of chief of engineers, 1923.] †

Pittsburgh, Pa. Report upon improvement of rivers and harbors in Pittsburgh, Pa., district; C. W. Kutz in charge. 1923. [1]+1231–45 p. [Extract BB from annual report of chief of engineers, 1923.] †

Port Orchard Bay, Wash., report on preliminary examination and survey of entrance to Port Orchard Bay, Wash. Dec. 13, 1923. 9 p. map. (H. doc. 109, 68th Cong. 1st sess.) * Paper, 5c.

Portland, Oreg. Report upon improvement of rivers and harbors in 1st Portland, Oreg., district; George Mayo in charge. 1923. [1]+1686–1743 p. [Extract NN from annual report of chief of engineers, 1923.] †

Portland, Oreg.—Continued. Report upon improvement of rivers and harbors in 2d Portland, Oreg., district; R. Park in charge. ·1923. [1]+1743–77 p. [Extract OO from annual report of chief of engineers, 1923.] †

Porto Rico. Report upon river and harbor improvement in district of Porto Rico; H. C. Newcomer in charge. 1923. [1]+1840–45 p. [Extract SS from annual report of chief of engineers, 1923.] †

Providence, R. I. Report upon improvement of rivers and harbors in Providence, R. I., district; V. L. Peterson in charge. 1923. [1]+61–137 p. [Extract B from annual report of chief of engineers, 1923.] †

Rock Island, Ill. Report upon improvement of rivers and harbors in Rock Island, Ill., district; B. C. Dunn in charge. 1923. [1]+1088–1111 p. [Extract U from annual report of chief of engineers, 1923.] †

St. Louis, Mo. Report upon improvement of rivers and harbors in St. Louis, Mo., district; Lunsford E. Oliver in charge. 1923. [1]+1078–88 p. [Extract T from annual report of chief of engineers, 1923.] †

St. Paul, Minn. Report upon improvement of rivers and harbors in St. Paul, Minn., district; C. F. Williams in charge. 1923. [1]+1111–32 p. [Extract V from annual report of chief of engineers, 1923.] †

Salem River, N. J., report on preliminary examination and survey of Salem River, N. J. Dec. 13, 1923. 14 p. 2 maps. (H. doc. 110, 68th Cong. 1st sess.) * Paper, 5c.

San Francisco, Calif. Report upon improvement of rivers and harbors in 1st San Francisco, Calif., district; Herbert Deakyne in charge. 1923. [1]+1619–66 p. [Extract LL from annual report of chief of engineers, 1923.] †

—— Report upon improvement of rivers and harbors in 2d San Francisco, Calif., district; U. S. Grant, 3d, in charge. 1923. iii+1667–86 p. [Extract MM from annual report of chief of engineers, 1923.] †

Savannah, Ga. Report upon improvement of rivers and harbors in Savannah, Ga., district; F. W. Altstaetter. in charge. 1923. iii+605–651 p. [Extract L from annual report of chief of engineers, 1923.] †

Seattle, Wash. Report upon improvement of rivers and harbors in Seattle, Wash., district; W. J. Barden in charge. 1923. [1]+1777–1822 p. [Extract PP from annual report of chief of engineers, 1923.] †

Vicksburg, Miss. Report upon improvement of rivers and harbors in Vicksburg, Miss., district; R. P. Howell in charge. 1923. [1]+1020–56 p. [Extract R from annual report of chief of engineers, 1923.] †

Wilmington, Del. Report upon improvement of rivers and harbors in Wilmington, Del., district; Earl I. Brown in charge. 1923. [1]+337–404 p. [Extract F from annual report of chief of engineers, 1923.] †

Wilmington, N. C. Report upon improvement of rivers and harbors in Wilmington, N. C., district; Oscar O. Kuentz in charge. 1923. [1]+518–576 p. [Extract J from annual report of chief of engineers, 1923.] †

. ALASKA ROAD COMMISSIONERS BOARD

Report. Report upon construction and maintenance of military and post roads, bridges, and trails, Alaska [fiscal year 1923]; Board of Road Commissioners for Alaska [in charge]. 1923. [pt. 1, 1]+2084–2104 p. [Extract ZZ from annual report of chief of engineers, 1923. For pt. 2, see following entry.] †

—— Same, pt. 2, with title, Report upon construction and maintenance of military and post roads, bridges, and trails, and of other roads, tramways. ferries, bridges, trails, and related works, Alaska, 19th annual report, [fiscal year] 1923; Board of Road Commissioners for Alaska [in charge]. Juneau, Alaska, Alaska Daily Empire Print, [Aug. 27] 1923. pt. 2, 131 p. 12 pl. 11 maps. [Part 1 was printed as a part of the annual report of chief of engineers, 1923, for which see above.] †

Roads. Alaska Road Commission, [extract] from speech of President Harding in Seattle, July 27, 1923· [concerning road building in Alaska]. [1923.] 1 p. †

CALIFORNIA DÉBRIS COMMISSION

Report of California Débris Commission [fiscal year 1923]. 1923. [1]+1845–59 p. [Extract TT from annual report of chief of engineers, 1923.] †

MISSISSIPPI RIVER COMMISSION

Report of Mississippi River Commission [fiscal year 1923]. 1923. iii+1860–1954 p. [Extract UU from report of chief of engineers, 1923.] † 6—13873

NEW YORK HARBOR SUPERVISOR

Report. Supervision of harbor of New York, N. Y. [fiscal year 1923]; P. N. Olmsted, supervisor. 1923. [1]+1976–89 p. [Extract VV from annual report of chief of engineers, 1923.] †

NORTHERN AND NORTHWESTERN LAKES SURVEY

NOTE.—Charts of the Great Lakes and connecting waters and St. Lawrence River to the international boundary at St. Regis, of Lake Champlain, and of the New York State canals are prepared and sold by the U. S. Lake Survey Office, Old Custom-house, Detroit, Mich. Charts may also be purchased at the following U. S. engineer offices: 710 Army Building, New York, N. Y.; 467 Broadway, Albany, N. Y.; 540 Federal Building, Buffalo, N. Y.; and Canal Office, Sault Ste. Marie, Mich. A catalogue (with index map), showing localities, scales, prices, and conditions of sale, may be had upon application at any of these offices.

A descriptive bulletin, which supplements the charts and gives detailed information as to harbors, shore lines and shoals, magnetic determinations, and particulars of changing conditions affecting navigation, is issued free to chart purchasers, upon request. The bulletin is revised annually and issued at the opening of navigation (in April), and supplements thereto are published monthly during the navigation season.

Complete sets of the charts and publications may be seen at the U. S. engineer offices in Duluth, Minn., Milwaukee, Wis., Chicago, Ill., Grand Rapids, Mich., Cleveland, Ohio, and Oswego, N. Y., but they are obtainable only at the sales offices above mentioned.

Reports. Survey of northern and northwestern lakes; Survey of St. Lawrence River; Preservation of Niagara Falls and supervision of power companies diverting water from Niagara River; Investigations regarding certain boundary waters; [E. M. Markham, J. G. Warren, and Spencer Cosby in charge]. 1923. [1]+2062–84 p. [Extract YY from annual report of chief of engineers, 1923.] †

Charts

Fairport Harbor, Ohio. Fairport Harbor, Ohio. Scale 1:8,000. 5th edition. [U. S. Lake Survey Office, Detroit, Mich.] Jan. 7, 1924. 24.5×16.2 in. † 10c.

PUBLIC BUILDINGS AND GROUNDS OFFICE

Report. Improvement and care of public buildings and grounds, care and maintenance of Washington Monument and of Lincoln Memorial, and erection of monuments, memorials, etc., Washington, D. C.; C. O. Sherrill in charge. 1923. iii+2020–62 p. [Extract XX from annual report of chief of engineers, 1923.] †

FINANCE DEPARTMENT

Finance circulars. Changes 1 [to] Finance circular 5, 1923; Nov. 28, 1923. [1924.] 5 leaves, 12° ‡

GENERAL STAFF CORPS

Special regulations. Recissions [of] Special regulations [65b, Physical standards for Reserve Officers' Training Corps, 1919]; Nov. 1, 1923. 1923. 1 p. [Special regulations issued by War Department.] ‡

MEDICAL DEPARTMENT

Vaccination. Prevention of typhoid fever and smallpox by vaccination, for information of applicants to attend citizens' military training camp, their parents, and others interested in physical welfare of Americans. [Reprint with changes 1924.] 6 p. narrow 8° †

ORDNANCE DEPARTMENT

Orders. General orders 6 [1923]; Dec. 31, 1923. [1923.] 1 p. 12° [Multigraphed.] ‡

Ordnance. Schedule of instruction for student officers in artillery design. 1923. iii+10 p. (Design manual, note 5, artillery; Ordnance Dept. doc. 2047.) * Paper, 5c.

WORLD WAR FOREIGN DEBT COMMISSION

Finland. Report of World War Foreign Debt Commission, letter from Secretary of Treasury submitting report of World War Foreign Debt Commission, May 2, 1923, with agreement referred to, therein providing for settlement of indebtedness of Republic of Finland to United States, and letter of approval of President Harding. Jan. 16, 1924. 9 p. (S. doc. 23, 68th Cong. 1st sess.) * Paper, 5c.   23—27386

Monthly Catalogue
United States
Public Documents

No. 350

February, 1924

ISSUED BY THE
SUPERINTENDENT OF DOCUMENTS

UNIVERSITY OF ILLINOIS LIBRARY

MAY 1 0 l...

WASHINGTON
1924

Abbreviations

Appendix....................................app.	Page, pages......................................p.
Congress....................................Cong.	Part, parts.............................pt., pts.
Department....................................Dept.	Plate, plates....................................pl∘
Document....................................doc.	Portrait, portraits...........................por.
Facsimile, facsimiles........................facsim.	Quarto.......................................4.
Folio......................................f∘	Report.......................................rp.
House..H.	Saint.......................................St.
House bill................................H. R.	Section, sections.............................sec.
House concurrent resolution..........H. Con. Res.	Senate, Senate bill..............................S.
House document................:.....H. doc.	Senate concurrent resolution..........S. Con. Res.
House executive document.............H. ex. doc.	Senate document.......................S. doc.
House joint resolution..................H. J. Res.	Senate executive document...........S. ex. doc.
House report.................................H. rp.	Senate joint resolution..................S. J. Res.
House resolution (simple)..................H. Res.	Senate report...............................S. rp.
Illustration, illustrations.....................il.	Senate resolution (simple)..................S. Res.
Inch, inches....................................in.	Session.......................................sess.
Latitude.......................................lat.	Sixteenmo.....................................16∘
Longitude....................................long.	Table, tables....................................tab.
Mile, miles....................................m.	Thirtytwo-mo..............................32∘
Miscellaneous...........................mis., misc.	Treasury.....................................Treas
Nautical......................................naut.	Twelvemo...................................12∘
No date....................................n. d.	Twentyfour-mo..............................24∘
No place....................................n. p.	Versus......................................vs., v.
Number, numbers......................no., nos.	Volume, volumes.......................v., vol.
Octavo.......................................8∘	Year..yr.

Common abbreviations for names of States and months are also used.
*Document for sale by Superintendent of Documents.
†Distribution by office issuing document, free if unaccompanied by a price.
‡Printed for official use.

NOTE.—Nearly all of the Departments of the Government make a limited free distribution of their publications. When an entry shows a * price, it is possible that upon application to the issuing office a copy may be obtained without charge.

Explanation

Words and figures inclosed in brackets [ ] are given for information, but do not appear on the title-pages of the publications catalogued. When size is not given octavo is to be understood. Size of maps is measured from outer edge of border, excluding margin. The dates, including day, month, and year, given with Senate and House documents and reports are the dates on which they were ordered to be printed. Usually the printing promptly follows the ordering, but various causes sometimes make delays.

SALES OF GOVERNMENT PUBLICATIONS

The Superintendent of Documents, Washington, D. C., is authorized to sell at cost, plus 10 per cent, without limit as to the number of copies to any one applicant who agrees not to resell or distribute the same for profit, any United States Government publication not confidential in character.

Publications can not be supplied free to individuals nor forwarded in advance of payment.

Publications entered in this catalogue that are for sale by the Superintendent of Documents are indicated by a star (*) preceding the price. A dagger (†) indicates that application should be made to the Department, Bureau, or Division issuing the document. A double dagger (‡) indicates that the document is printed for official use. Whenever additional information concerning the method of procuring a document seems necessary, it will be found under the name of the Bureau by which it was published.

In ordering a publication from the Superintendent of Documents, give (if known) the name of the publishing Department, Bureau, or Division, and the title of the publication. If the publication is numbered, give the number also. Every such particular assists in quick identification. Do not order by the Library of Congress card number.

The accumulation of publications in this Office amounts to several millions, of which over two million are assorted, forming the sales stock. Many rare books are included, but under the law all must be sold regardless of their age or scarcity. Many of the books have been in stock some time, and are apt to be shop-worn. In filling orders the best copy available is sent. A general price-list of public documents is not available, but lists on special subjects will be furnished on application.

MONTHLY CATALOGUE DISTRIBUTION

The Monthly catalogue is sent to each Senator, Representative, Delegate, Resident Commissioner, and officer in Congress; to designated depositories and State and Territorial libraries if it is selected by them; to substantially all Government authors; and to as many school, college, and public libraries as the limited edition will supply.

Subscription price to individuals, 50c. a year, including index; foreign subscription, 75c. a year. Back numbers can not be supplied. Notify the Superintendent of Documents of any change of address.

LIBRARY OF CONGRESS CARDS

Numbers to be used in ordering the printed catalogue cards of the Library of Congress are given at the end of entries for the more important documents. Orders for these cards, remittances in payment for them, and requests for information about them should be addressed to the Librarian of Congress, not to the Superintendent of Documents.

INDEX

An Index to the Monthly catalogue is issued at the end of the fiscal year. This contains index entries for all the numbers issued from July to June, and can be

bound with the numbers as an index to the volume.   Persons desiring to bind the catalogue at the end of the year should be careful to retain the numbers received monthly, as duplicate copies can not be supplied.

HOW TO REMIT

Remittances for the documents marked with a star (*) should be made to the Superintendent of Documents, Washington, D. C., by coupons, postal money order, express order, or New York draft.   Currency may be sent at sender's risk.

Postage stamps, foreign money, defaced or smooth coins, positively will not be accepted.

For the convenience of the general public, coupons that are good until used in exchange for Government publications sold by the Superintendent of Documents may be purchased from his Office in sets of 20 for $1.00.   Address order to Superintendent of Documents, Government Printing Office, Washington, D. C.

No charge is made for postage on documents forwarded to points in United States, Alaska, Guam, Hawaii, Philippine Islands, Porto Rico, Samoa, or to Canada, Cuba, or Mexico.   To other countries the regular rate of postage is charged, and remittances must cover such postage.   In computing foreign postage, add one-third of the price of the publication.

CORRECTION · FOR JANUARY, 1924, MONTHLY CATALOGUE

For " [Circulars] 1918 and 1920 " in 1st line of 2d entry under State Department on p. 402, read " [Circulars] 918 and 920."

MONTHLY CATALOGUE

AGRICULTURE DEPARTMENT

NOTE.—Those publications of the Department of Agriculture which are for sale will be supplied by the Superintendent of Documents, Washington, D. C. The Department issues a monthly list of publications, which is mailed to all applicants, enabling them to select such reports and bulletins as interest them.

Accounts. [Fiscal regulations of Department of Agriculture, effective Oct. 1, 1922, amendments and reprints.] [1924.] [14] p. 12° [These are reprints of variously numbered pages to be inserted in their proper places in the original publication.] ‡

Anemia. Iron content of blood and spleen in infectious equine anemia ; by Lewis H. Wright. [1924.] p. 239–242. [From Journal of agricultural research, v. 26, no. 5, Nov. 3, 1923.] ‡

Cattle. [Bureau of Animal Industry] order 237, regulations governing purchase and destruction of animals and materials, disinfection, and expenditures on account of arrest and eradication of foot-and-mouth disease and other contagious or infectious diseases of animals, effective Mar. 29, 1915 ; Mar. 19, 1915. [Reprint 1924.] 7 p. ‡

—— Same 287 and 287 amendment 1 ; [Feb. 23 and] 25, 1924. [1924.] 2 p. and 1 p. [Consist of orders concerning quarantine of cattle, etc.] †

Chlorin. Active chlorin as germicide for milk and milk products ; by Harrison Hale and William L. Bleecker. 1924, cover-title, 375–382+[2] p. il. 3 p. of pl. [From Journal of agricultural research, v. 26, no. 8, Nov. 24, 1923.] ‡

Claim adjusted by Secretary of Agriculture, communication submitting claim [of Nathan Marks Company, Incorporated] for damages to privately owned property which has been adjusted and which requires appropriation for its payment. Feb. 9, 1924. 2 p. (H. doc. 191, 68th Cong. 1st sess.) * Paper, 5c.

Cotton. Amendment 1 to Regulations pursuant to joint resolution of House of Representatives and Senate entitled For relief of States in cotton belt that have given aid to cotton farmers, approved Aug. 9, 1921, effective Dec. 28, 1923. 1924. 1 p. (Federal Horticultural Board.) [This amends regulations dated Mar. 22, 1922, with title, Compensation on account of noncotton zones, joint resolution of Congress and regulations, effective Apr. 1, 1922.] †

Crops and markets. Crops and markets, weekly. Feb. 2–23, 1924 ; v. 1, no. 5–8. [1924.] p. 65–128, il. 4° * Paper, $1.00 a yr. ; foreign subscription, $2.00 (including monthly supplement).   Agr 24—113

—— Same. monthly supplement, Feb. 1924 : v. 1, supplement 2. [1924.] p. 41–80. il. 4° [Included in price of weekly Crops and markets.]

Flower-pots. Common earthenware jars source of error in pot experiments ; by J. S. McHargue. 1924. cover-title, p. 231–232+[1] leaf, 1 pl. [From Journal of agricultural research, v. 26, no. 5, Nov. 3, 1923.] ‡

Gossypol. Physiological effect of gossypol [with list of literature cited] ; by Paul Menaul. [1924.] p. 233–237. [From Journal of agricultural research, v. 26, no. 5, Nov. 3, 1923.] ‡

Jatropha stimulosa. Chemical analysis of Jatropha stimulosa ; by Paul Menaul. [1924.] p. 259–260. [From Journal of agricultural research, v. 26, no. 6, Nov. 10, 1923.] ‡

Journal of agricultural research, v. 26, no. 9–12; Dec. 1–22, 1923. 1924. cover-titles, 383–616+[24]p.+[12] leaves, il. 9 pl. 32 p. of pl. [Weekly. Text on p. 2 of covers.] *Paper, 10c. single copy, $4.00 a yr.; foreign subscription, $5.25.

Agr 13—1837

CONTENTS.—No. 9. Quantitative determination of carotin by means of spectrophotometer and colorimeter [with list of literature cited; by] F. M. Schertz.—Our only common North American chigger, its distribution and nomenclature; by H. E. Ewing.—Habits of cotton rootrot fungus [with list of literature cited]; by C. J. King.—Three-banded grape leafhopper and other leafhoppers injuring grapes [with list of literature cited]; by G. A. Runner and C. I. Bliss.—Some morphological responses of host tissue of crowngall organism [with list of literature cited]; by A. J. Riker.—Minimum milk requirement for calf raising; by A. C. Ragsdale and C. W. Turner.—No. 10. Red stain in wood of boxelder; by Ernest E. Hubert.—Stem and rootrot of peas in United States caused by species of Fusarium [with list of literature cited]; by Fred Reuel Jones.—Hornworm septicemia [with list of literature cited]; by G. F. White.—Cutworm septicemia; by G. F. White.—Study of serology, cerebrospinal fluid, and pathological changes in spinal cord in dourine; by Harry W. Schoening and Robert J. Formad.—Budrot of peach caused by species of Fusarium; by John W. Roberts.—No. 11. Oiled wrappers, oils, and waxes in control of apple scald; by Charles Brooks, J. S. Cooley, and D. F. Fisher.—Influence of temperature and initial weight of seeds upon growth-rate of Phaseolus vulgaris seedlings; by Willem Rudolfs.—Some factors which influence feathering of cream in coffee; by L. H. Burgwald.—Biology of false wireworm Eleodes suturalis Say [with list of literature cited]; by J. S. Wade and R. A. St. George.—Eggplant leaf-miner, Phtherimaea glochinella Zeller [with list of literature cited]; by Thomas H. Jones.—No. 12. Cytological studies of infection of Baart, Kanred, and Mindum wheats by Puccinia graminis tritici forms 3 and 19 [with list of literature cited]; by Ruth F. Allen.—Intracellular bodies associated with rosette disease and mosaiclike leaf mottling of wheat; by Harold H. McKinney, Sophia H. Eckerson, and Robert W. Webb.—Notes on biolcgy of 4-spotted bean weevil, Bruchus quadrimaculatus Fab.; by A. O. Larson and Perez Simmons.

NOTE.—This publication is published by authority of the Secretary of Agriculture, with the cooperation of the Association of Land-Grant Colleges. It is distributed free only to libraries of agricultural colleges and experiment stations, to large universities, technical schools, and to such institutions as make suitable exchanges with the Agriculture Department. Others desiring the Journal may obtain it from the Superintendent of Documents, Washington, D. C., at the prices stated above.

Official record, Department of Agriculture. v. 3, no. 6–9; Feb. 6–27, 1924. [1924.] Each 8 p. 4° [Weekly.] *Paper, 50c. a yr.; foreign subscription, $1.10.

Agr 22—146

Quarantine. Citrus fruit quarantine, Notice of quarantine 28, with regulations, effective Aug. 1, 1917. [Reprint with slight changes 1924.] 5 p. (Federal Horticultural Board.) †

—— Modification of fruit and vegetable quarantine, Amendment 2 of regulations supplemental to Notice of quarantine 56, effective Jan. 18, 1924. [1924.] 2 p. (Federal Horticultural Board.) †

—— Modification of pink bollworm quarantine, Amendment 2 to 2d revision of regulations supplemental to Notice of quarantine 52, effective Jan. 17, 1924. [1924.] 2 p. (Federal Horticultural Board.) †

Soil reaction in relation to calcium adsorption [with list of literature cited]; by C. O. Swanson. 1924. cover-title, p. 83–123, il. [From Journal of agricultural research, v. 26, no. 3, Oct. 20, 1923.] ‡

Tannins. Method for quantitative estimation of tannin in plant tissue; by Paul Menaul. [1924.] p. 257–258. [From Journal of agricultural research, v. 26, no. 6, Nov. 10, 1923.] ‡

World's Poultry Congress. 3d World's Poultry Congress, report from Secretary of State with accompanying letter to him from Secretary of Agriculture favoring legislation by Congress sanctioning Governmental participation in holding 3d World's Poultry Congress in United States in 1927. Feb. 13, 1924. 4 p. (S. doc. 45, 68th Cong. 1st sess.) *Paper, 5c.

AGRICULTURAL ECONOMICS BUREAU

Hay. United States grades for timothy hay, clover hay, clover mixed hay, and grass mixed hay, revised, effective Feb. 1, 1924 (tabulated and abridged). Jan. 1924. [2] p. oblong 24° folded into narrow 24° size. †

Poultry. Marketing poultry; [by Rob R. Slocum]. [Feb. 1924.] ii+30 p. il. (Agriculture Dept. Farmers' bulletin 1377.) * Paper, 5c.

Agr 24—243

Wheat. Milling and baking experiments with American wheat varieties; by J. H. Shollenberger and J. Allen Clark. Feb. 7, 1924. cover-title. 94 p. il. 5 pl. (Agriculture Dept. Department bulletin 1183.) [Prepared in cooperation with Plant Industry Bureau. Includes lists of Agriculture Department publications treating on American wheat varieties.] * Paper, 15c.

Agr 24—204

ANIMAL INDUSTRY BUREAU

Cattle. Special report on diseases of cattle; [articles] by Drs.' Atkinson, Dickson, Eichhorn, Hickman, Law, Lowe, Marsh, Mohler, Murray, Pearson, Ransom, Trumbower, and Woodward. Revised edition, 1923. 1923. 563 p. il. 26 pl. 24 p. of pl. * Cloth, $1.00. Agr 24—255

CONTENTS.—Administration of medicines; by Leonard Pearson.—Diseases of digestive organs, by A. J. Murray; revised by R. W. Hickman.—Poisons and poisoning, by V. T. Atkinson; revised by C. Dwight Marsh.—Diseases of heart, blood vessels, and lymphatics, by W. H. Harbaugh; revised by Leonard Pearson.—Noncontagious diseases of organs of respiration; by William Herbert Lowe.—Diseases of nervous systems, by W. H. Harbaugh; revised by John R. Mohler.—Diseases of urinary organs; by James Law.—Diseases of generative organs, by James Law; revised by Adolph Eichhorn.—Diseases following parturition; by James Law.—Diseases of young calves; by James Law.—Bones, diseases and accidents, by V. T. Atkinson; revised by John R. Mohler.—Surgical operations, by William Dickson and William Herbert Lowe; revised by B. T. Woodward.—Tumors affecting cattle; by John R. Mohler.—Diseases of skin, by M. R. Trumbower; revised by John R. Mohler.—Diseases of foot, by M. R. Trumbower; revised by Leonard Pearson.—Diseases of eye and its appendages, by M. R. Trumbower; revised by Leonard Pearson.—Diseases of ear, by M. R. Trumbower; revised by Leonard Pearson.—Infectious diseases of cattle; revised by John. R. Mohler.—Animal parasites of cattle; by B. H. Ransom.—Mycotic stomatitis of cattle; by John R. Mohler.—Index.

Cattle scab and methods of control and eradication; [by Marion Imes]. [Dec. 1918, slightly revised Feb. 1924.] [1924.] 30 p. il. (Agriculture Dept. Farmers' bulletin 1017.) * Paper, 5c.

Fats. Compounds developed in rancid fats, with observations on mechanism of their formation [with list of literature cited]; by Wilmer C. Powick. 1924. cover-title, p. 323–362, il. [From Journal of agricultural research, v. 26, no. 8, Nov. 24, 1923.] ‡

Food for cattle. Handbook for better feeding of livestock; [compiled by E. W. Sheets and William Jackson]. [1924.] cover-title, 48 p. 16° (Agriculture Dept. Miscellaneous circular 12.) [Text on p. 2–4 of cover. Includes list of Farmers' bulletins relating to feeding of livestock.] * Paper, 5c. Agr 24—212

Foot-and-mouth disease; [by John R. Mohler]. [Apr. 22, 1915, revised Mar. 1923, reprinted with slight revision Dec. 1923.] 20 p. il. (Agriculture Dept. Farmers' bulletin 666.) [Includes lists of Agriculture Department publications relating to diseases of cattle.] * Paper, 5c.

Garbage. Feeding garbage to hogs; [by F. G. Ashbrook and A. Wilson]. [Aug. 1920, revised Dec. 1923.] [1923.] 27 p. il. (Agriculture Dept. Farmers' bulletin 1133.) [Includes lists of Agriculture Department publications relating to swine management.] * Paper, 5c.

Otocephaly. Factors which determine otocephaly in guinea pigs [with list of literature cited]; by Sewall Wright and Orson N. Eaton. 1924. cover-title, p. 161–182, il. 1 pl. [From Journal of agricultural research, v. 26, no. 4, Oct. 27, 1923.] ‡

Posters. Ten points in better feeding, make every pound of feed yield profit; [poster]. [1924.] 26.1×18.2 in. †

Poultry. Back-yard poultry keeping, [by Rob R. Slocum; revised by Alfred R. Lee]. [May, 1923, reprint with changes 1924.] ii+18 p. il. (Agriculture Dept. Farmers' bulletin 1331.) * Paper, 5c.

—— Natural and artificial brooding of chickens; [by Alfred R. Lee]. [Jan. 1924.] ii+17 p. il. (Agriculture Dept. Farmers' bulletin 1376.) [Revision of Farmers' bulletin 624. Includes list of Farmers' bulletins relating to poultry.] * Paper, 5c. Agr 24—210

Service announcements. Index to Service and regulatory announcements. 1923. [1924.] p. 111–115. * Paper, 5c. single copy, included in price of Service and regulatory announcements to subscribers.

—— Service and regulatory announcements, Jan. 1924; [no.] 201. Feb. 1924. p. 1–12. [Monthly.] * Paper, 5c. single copy, 25c, a yr.; foreign subscription, 40c. Agr 7—1658

Sheep. Farm sheep raising for beginners, [by F. R. Marshall and R. B. Millin; revised by D. A. Spencer]. [July, 1917, revised Dec. 1923.] [1923.] 24 p. il. (Agriculture Dept. Farmers' bulletin 840.) * Paper, 5c.

Swine. Castration of hogs; [by S. S. Buckley]. [Dec. 1923.] ii+8 p. il. (Agriculture Dept. Farmers' bulletin 1357.) [Supersedes Farmers' bulletin 780. Includes list of Agriculture Department publications relating to hogs.]
* Paper, 5c.   Agr 24—262
Temperature. Method of automatic control of low temperatures employed by Department of Agriculture; by John T. Bowen. [1924.] p. 183–190, il. [From Journal of agricultural research, v. 26, no. 4, Oct. 27, 1923.] ‡

BIOLOGICAL SURVEY BUREAU

Grebes. Food and economic relations of North American grebes; by Alexander Wetmore. Jan. 1924. 24 p. il. (Agriculture Dept. Department bulletin 1196.) * Paper, 5c.   Agr 24—205

CHEMISTRY BUREAU

Maple syrup. Production of maple sirup and sugar; [by A. Hugh Bryan, William F. Hubbard, and Sidney F. Sherwood]. [1923.] 35 p. il. (Agriculture Dept. Farmers' bulletin 1366.) [Prepared in cooperation with Forest Service and Plant Industry Bureau. Revision of Farmers' bulletin 516.] * Paper, 5c.
                                                              Agr 24—209
Service announcements. Service and regulatory announcements, Feb. 1914, [no.] 2; [reprint of p. 21–25]. Apr. 2, 1914 [reprint with omissions 1924]. 4 p. [The original print of no. 2 included p. 21–108.] * Paper, 5c.
                                                              Agr 14—194
—— Same, June, 1914; [no.] 6. July 17, 1914 [reprint 1924]. p. 415–421. * Paper, 5c.

—— Same, Oct. 1914, [no.] 10; [reprint of p. 741–743]. Nov. 25, 1914 [reprint with omissions 1924]. p. 741–743. [The original print of no. 10 included p. 741–750.] * Paper, 5c.

—— Same, no. 15. Nov. 4, 1915 [reprint 1923]. p. 21–24. * Paper, 5c.

—— Same, supplement 166. Feb. 1924. p. 425–454. [Contains Notices of judgment under food and drugs act 11751–800.] * Paper, 5c.

—— Same, supplement 167. Mar. 3, 1924. p. 455–479. [Contains Notices of judgment under food and drugs act 11801–850.] * Paper, 5c.

EDITORIAL AND DISTRIBUTION WORK OFFICES

Farmers' bulletins 1251–75, [title-page] with contents and index; prepared in Office of Editorial Work. 1924. 9+24 p. * Paper, 5c.

ENTOMOLOGY BUREAU

Insects injurious to ornamental greenhouse plants; [by C. A. Weigel and E. R. Sasscer]. [1924.] ii+81 p. il. (Agriculture Dept. Farmers' bulletin 1362.) * Paper, 15c.   Agr 24—244
Oak sapling borer, Goes tesselatus Haldeman; by Fred E. Brooks. [1924.] 313–318+[2] p. 3 p. of pl. [From Journal of agricultural research, v. 26, no. 7, Nov. 17, 1923.] ‡

EXPERIMENT STATIONS OFFICE

Experiment station record, v. 49, no. 9; abstract number. Feb. 1924. cover-title, x+801–900 p. [Text and illustration on p. 2 and 4 of cover.] * Paper, 10c. single copy, 75c. per vol. (2 vols. a yr.); foreign subscription, $1.25 per vol.   Agr 9—832
    NOTE.—Mainly made up of abstracts of reports and publications on agricultural science which have recently appeared in all countries. especially the United States. Extra numbers, called abstract numbers, are issued, 3 to each volume. These are made up almost exclusively of abstracts, that is, they contain no editorial notes and only a limited number of current notes.

ALASKA AGRICULTURAL EXPERIMENT STATIONS

Tuberculosis in animals. Eradication of tuberculosis in cattle at Kodiak Experiment Station; by C. C. Georgeson and W. T. White. Jan. 1924. cover-title, 11 p. il. (Bulletin 5.) [Text on p. 2 of cover.] * Paper, 5c.
                                                              Agr 24—202

FOREST SERVICE

Molds (*botany*). Five molds and their penetration into wood [with list of literature cited] ; by Eloise Gerry. 1924. cover-title, 219–230+[3] p. 4 p. of pl. [From Journal of agricultural research, v. 26, no. 5, Nov. 3, 1923.] ‡

Maps

Medicine Bow National Forest, Wyo. [resources and recreation features, roads, trails, etc.]. [1924.] 1 sheet (with map on verso), il. oblong f°, folded into narrow 8° size and so printed as to number [1]+10+[1] p. †

HOME ECONOMICS BUREAU

Digestibility of raw starches and carbohydrates; by C. F. Langworthy and Alice Thompson Merrill. Feb. 28, 1924. 16 p. (Agriculture Dept. Department bulletin 1213.) * Paper, 5c.   Agr 24—259

Food values and body needs, shown graphically; [by Emma A. Winslow]. [1924.] ii+36 p. il. (Agriculture Dept. Farmers' bulletin 1383.) * Paper, 10c.   Agr 24—211

Milk and its uses in the home. [July, 1923, revised Jan. 1924.] [1924.] ii+18 p. il. (Agriculture Dept. Farmers' bulletin 1359.) [Prepared in cooperation with Animal Industry Bureau.] * Paper, 5c.

PLANT INDUSTRY BUREAU

Alfalfa. Alfalfa, instructions adapted to Ohio, Indiana, Illinois, Iowa, Missouri, and Kentucky. [1924.] 4 p. †

—— Alfalfa, instructions adapted to Pennsylvania, West Virginia, northwestern Maryland, and northern New Jersey. [1924.] 4 p. †

—— Alfalfa, instructions adapted to southern New Jersey, Delaware, southern Maryland, Virginia, Arkansas, Tennessee, and south Atlantic and Gulf States. [1924.] 4 p. †

—— Peruvian alfalfa. [1924.] 4 p. †

Bacterial stripe disease of proso millet [with list of literature cited] ; by Charlotte Elliott. 1924. cover-title, 151–160+[3] p. 2 pl. 2 p. of pl. [From Journal of agricultural research, v. 26, no. 4, Oct. 27, 1923.] ‡

Bermuda grass. Eradication of Bermuda grass; [by Albert A. Hansen]. [Sept. 1918, revised Sept. 1923.] [1924.] 12 p. il. (Agriculture Dept. Farmers' bulletin 945.) *Paper, 5c.

Corn. Effects of selection on yield of cross between varieties of corn; by Frederick D. Richey. Feb. 1924. 20 p. il. (Agriculture Dept. Department bulletin 1209.) *Paper, 5c.   Agr 24—248

Helminthosporium sativum. Influence of soil temperature and moisture on infection of wheat seedlings by Helminthosporium sativum [with list of literature cited] ; by H. H. McKinney. 1924. cover-title, 195–218+[3] p. il. 2 pl. 2 p. of pl. [Prepared in cooperation with Wisconsin Agricultural Experiment Station. From Journal of agricultural research, v. 26, no. 5, Nov. 3, 1923.] ‡

Pear and how to grow it; [by G. B. Brackett]. [Feb. 14, 1912, revised Nov. 1923.] [1923.] 32 p. il. (Agriculture Dept. Farmers' bulletin 482.) *Paper, 5c.

Quarantine procedure to safeguard introduction of citrus plants, system of aseptic plant propagation; [by] Walter T. Swingle, T. Ralph Robinson, and Eugene May, jr. Jan. 1924. 15 p. il. (Agriculture Dept. Department circular 299.) *Paper, 5c.   Agr 24—207

Rye. Growing rye in western half of United States; [by John H. Martin and Ralph W. Smith]. [Sept. 1923.] 19 p. il. (Agriculture Dept. Farmers' bulletin 1358.) *Paper, 5c.   Agr 24—208

Strawberry culture, eastern United States; [by George M. Darrow]. [Apr. 1919, revised Nov. 1923.] [1923.] 52 p. il. (Agriculture Dept. Farmers' bulletin 1028.) *Paper, 5c.

Sugar; by E. W. Brandes, C. O. Townsend, P. A. Yoder, S. F. Sherwood, R. S. Washburn, G. B. L. Arner, O. E. Baker, F. C. Stevens, F. H. Chittenden, and C. F. Langworthy. 1924. [1]+98 p. il. (Yearbook separate 893.) [Prepared in cooperation with Agricultural Economics Bureau, Entomology Bureau, Home Economics Bureau, and Louisiana College of Agriculture. From Yearbook, 1923.] *Paper, 20c.

Sugar-beets. Time for testing mother beets; by Dean A. Pack. 1924. cover-title, p. 125–150. [From Journal of agricultural research, v. 26, no. 3, Oct. 20, 1923.] ‡

Trees for town & city streets; [by Furman Lloyd Mulford]. [Mar. 1922, revised Nov. 1923.] [1923.] 41 p. il. (Agriculture Dept. Farmers' bulletin 1208.) * Paper, 5c. (incorrectly given in publication as 10c.).

Udo. Two diseases of udo (Aralia cordata Thunb.) [with list of literature cited]; by J. L. Weimer. 1924. cover-title. 271–278+[3] p.+[1] leaf, 4 p. of pl. [From Journal of agricultural research, v. 26, no. 6, Nov. 10, 1923.] ‡

Vegetables. Diseases and insects of garden vegetables; [by W. W. Gilbert and C. H. Popenoe. [Jan. 1924.] ii+46 p. il. (Agriculture Dept. Farmers' bulletin 1371.) [Prepared in cooperation with Entomology Bureau.] *Paper, 10c.
Agr 24—257

Wheat. Electrochemical treatment of seed wheat [with list of literature cited; by] C. E. Leighty and J. W. Taylor. Feb. 1924. 7 p. il. (Agriculture Dept. Department circular 305.) *Paper, 5c.
Agr 24—245

White-pine blister rust in western Europe [with list of literature cited]; by W. Stuart Moir. Feb. 8, 1924. 32 p. il. 4 p. of pl. (Agriculture Dept. Department bulletin 1186.) [Imprint date incorrectly given on last page of publication as 1923.] *Paper, 10c.
Agr 24—246

PUBLIC ROADS BUREAU

Drainage district assessments, study of present practices in assessing benefits under State drainage laws; by George R. Boyd, in collaboration with R. A. Hart. Feb. 1924. cover-title, 70 p. (Agriculture Dept. Department bulletin 1207.) *Paper, 10c.
Agr 24—258

SOILS BUREAU

Ashley Creek Valley. Soil survey of Ashley valley, Utah; by A. T. Strahorn, Scott Ewing, and D. S. Jennings. 1924. iii+907–937 p. il. 1 pl. map. [Prepared in cooperation with Utah Agricultural Experiment Station. From Field operations, 1920.] * Paper. 15c.

Buncombe County, N. C. Soil survey of Buncombe County, N. C.; by S. O. Perkins, R. E. Devereux, S. F. Davidson, and W. A. Davis. 1923. iii+785–812 p. il. map. [Prepared in cooperation with North Carolina Department of Agriculture and State Agricultural Experiment Station. From Field operations, 1920.] * Paper, 25c.

Colloids. Estimation of colloidal material in soils by adsorption [with list of literature cited]; by P. L. Gile. H. E. Middleton, W. O. Robinson, W. H. Fry, and M. S. Anderson. Feb. 15, 1924. cover-title, 42 p. (Agriculture Dept. Bulletin 1193.) * Paper, 5c.
Agr 24—247

Geneva County, Ala. Soil survey of Geneva County, Ala.; by A. H. Meyer, C. O. Jaeckel, and L. R. Schoenmann. 1924. iii+287–314 p. il. map. [Prepared in cooperation with Alabama Department of Agriculture and Industries. From Field operations, 1920.] * Paper. 15c.

Hardin County, Iowa. Soil survey of Hardin County, Iowa; by T. H. Benton and W. W. Strike. 1923. iii+717–757 p. il. map. [Prepared in cooperation with Iowa Agricultural Experiment Station. From Field operations, 1920.] * Paper, 15c.

Lafayette County, Mo. Soil survey of Lafayette County, Mo.; by William De Young and H. v. Jordan. 1923. iii+813–837 p. il. map. [Prepared in cooperation with University of Missouri Agricultural Experiment Station. From Field operations, 1920.] * Paper, 25c.

Tyrrell County, N. C.   Soil survey of Tyrrell County, N. C.; by W. B. Cobb and W. A. Davis. 1924. iii+839–858 p. il. map. [Prepared in cooperation with North Carolina Department of Agriculture and Agricultural Experiment Station. From Field operations, 1920.]   * Paper, 15c.

Woodbury County, Iowa.   Soil survey of Woodbury County, Iowa; by J. O. Veatch, E. I. Angell. A. M. O'Neal, jr., H. W. Warner, C. L. Orrben, and D. S. Gray. 1923. iii+759–784 p. il. map. [Prepared in cooperation with Iowa Agricultural Experiment Station. From Field operations, 1920.]   * Paper, 25c.

WEATHER BUREAU

Climatological data for United States by sections, v. 10, no. 11; Nov. 1923. [1924.]   cover-title, [188] p. il. 2 maps, 2 p. of maps, 4°   [Text on p. 2 of cover.]   * Paper, 35c. complete monthly number, $4.00 a yr.   Agr 14—566

NOTE.—Made up of separate Climatological data issued from 42 section centers of the United States. Printed at the several section centers and assembled and bound at the Washington Office. Issued principally for service use and exchange. The separate Climatological data are sold by the Superintendent of Documents, Washington, D. C., at the rate of 5c. single copy, 50c. a yr. for each section.

Forest fires.   Symposium on fire-weather forecasting: 1, Intensive studies of local conditions as aid to forecasting fire-weather, [by] G. W. Alexander; 2, Relation of weather forecasts to prediction of dangerous forest-fire conditions, [by] R. H. Weidman; 3, Forest-fire weather in western Washington, [by] G. C. Joy; 4, Lightning and forest fires in California; [by] S. B. Show; 5, How weather forecasting can aid in forest-fire control, [by] H. R. Flint; 6, Meteorological factors and forest fires, [by] J. v. Hofmann; 7, Evaporation as simple index to weather conditions, [by] C. G. Bates. 1924. [1]+561–571 p. 4°   [From Monthly weather review, Nov. 1923.]   †

Frost.   Notes on 1922 freeze in southern California; by F. D. Young. 1924. [1]+581–585 p. il. 2 p. of pl. 4°   [From Monthly weather review, Nov. 1923.]   †

Meteorology.   Monthly meteorological summary, Washington, D. C., Jan. 1924. [1924.]   [2] p. large 8°   †

Monthly weather review, v. 51, no. 11; Nov. 1923. [Feb. 7] 1924. cover-title, p. 561–616, il. 13 p. of pl. and maps, 4°   [Text on p. 2–4 of cover.]   * Paper, 15c. single copy, $1.50 a yr,; foreign subscription, $2.25.   Agr 9—990

NOTE.—The Monthly weather review contains (1) meteorological contributions and bibliography including seismology, (2) an interpretative summary and charts of the weather of the month in the United States, and on adjacent oceans, and (3) climatological and seismological tables dealing with the weather and earthquakes of the month. The contributions are principally as follows: (a) results of observational or research work in meteorology carried on in the United States or other parts of the world, (b) abstracts or reviews of important meteorological papers and books, and (c) notes.

SPECIAL ARTICLES.—Intensive studies of local conditions as aid to forecasting fire weather; by George W. Alexander.—Relation of weather forecasts to prediction of dangerous forest fire conditions; by R. H. Weidman.—Forest fire weather in western Washington: [by] George C. Joy.—Lightning and forest fires in California; by S. B. Show.—How weather forecasting can aid in forest fire control; by Howard R. Flint.—Meteorological factors and forest fires; by J. V. Hofmann.—Evaporation as simple index to weather conditions; by Carlos G. Bates.—Transpiration by forest trees; by Robert E. Horton.—Notes on 1922 freeze in southern California; by Floyd D. Young.—Sonora storms; by Dean Blake.—Work of Weather Bureau for river interests along Ohio River; by W. C. Devereaux.

New England highway weather bulletin, Feb. 5–26, 1924; no. 8–11 [season of 1923–24.] [Boston, Mass., 1924.] Each 1 p. il. large 8° [Weekly.] * Paper, 50c. per season.

Snow and ice bulletin, no. 9–12, winter 1923–24; Feb. 4–25, 1924. Feb. 5–26, 1924. Each [2] p. il. large 4° [Weekly during winter.] †   12—1660

Trees.   Transpiration by forest trees; by R. E. Horton. 1924. [1]+571–581 p. il. 4°   [From Monthly weather review, Nov. 1923.]   †

Weather.   Weekly weather and crop bulletin, Feb. 5–26, 1924; no. 6–9, 1924. Feb. 6–27, 1924. Each 4 p. il. 4°   * Paper, 25c a yr.   Agr 24—260

NOTE.—The weekly weather and crop summaries, published in Weather, crops, and markets during the 2 years ending with 1923, and prior thereto in the National weather and crop bulletin, will in the future constitute a separate publication by the Weather Bureau entitled Weekly weather and crop bulletin, of which this is the first regular issue. Tabular data, similar to that contained in the table on p. 3, for the weeks ending Jan. 1. 8. 15, 22, and 29 respectively, will be published later in a single issue, designated nos. 1–5, 1924.

Weather map. Daily weather map [of United States, containing forecasts for all States east of Mississippi River except Illinois, Wisconsin, Indiana, upper Michigan, and lower Michigan], Feb. 1–29, 1924. 1st edition. [1924.] Each 16.4×22.7 in. [Not issued Sundays or holidays.] *Editions issued at Washington, D. C., 25c. a month, $2.50 a yr.; editions issued at about 65 stations throughout the United States, 20c. a month, $2.00 a yr.

—— Same [containing forecasts for United States], Feb. 1–29, 1924. 2d edition. [1924.] Each 16.4×22.7 in. [The Sunday edition does not contain as much information as the edition for week days.] *30c. a month, $3.00 a yr.

CIVIL SERVICE COMMISSION

NOTE.—The Commission furnishes its publications gratuitously to those who apply for them.

Civil service. Instructions to applicants, 11th civil service district, headquarters. Seattle. Wash. Oct. 1923, [published] 1924. ii+30+[1] p. (Form 1372.) †

—— Instructions to applicants, 12th civil service district, headquarters, San Francisco, Calif. Oct. 1923, [published] 1924. [2]+32+[1] p. (Form 1372.) †

—— Miscellaneous information. Jan. 1924. 8 p. (Form 1089.) †

Postal service. Instructions to applicants for post-office service, 2d civil-service district, headquarters, New York, N. Y. Nov. 1923 [published 1924]. 16+[1] p. (Form 1898.) †

—— Instructions to applicants for post-office service, 12th civil-service district, headquarters, San Francisco, Calif. Nov. 1923. 16+[1] p. (Form 1898.) †

COMMERCE DEPARTMENT

CENSUS BUREAU

NOTE.—Persons desiring 14th census publications should address the Director of the Census, Department of Commerce, Washington, D. C. They are also sold by the Superintendent of Documents, Washington, D. C., at the price indicated.

Alabama. 14th census of United States: State compendium, Alabama, statistics of population, occupations, agriculture, manufactures, and mines and quarries for State, counties, and cities. 1924. cover-title, 121 p. il. 4° [Text on p. 2–4 of cover.] *Paper, 20c.   24—26198

Arizona. 14th census of United States: State compendium, Arizona, statistics of population, occupations, agriculture, irrigation, manufactures, and mines and quarries for State, counties, and cities. 1924. cover-title, 89 p. il. 4° [Text on p. 2–4 of cover.] *Paper, 15c.   24—26199

Cotton. Cotton consumed, cotton on hand, active cotton spindles, and imports and exports of cotton, Jan. 1923 and 1924, with statistics of cotton consumed, imported, and exported for 6 months ending Jan. 31. Feb. 14, 1924. oblong 32° [Preliminary report. This publication is issued in postal card form.] †

Cotton goods. Census of manufactures, 1921: Cotton manufactures. 1924. 29 p. *Paper, 5c.   24—26155

Cottonseed received, crushed, and on hand, and cottonseed products manufactured, shipped out, on hand, and exported covering 6-month period ending Jan. 31, 1924 and 1923. Feb. 19, 1924. oblong 32° [Preliminary report. This publication is issued in postal card form.] †

Gas (illuminating). Census of manufactures, 1921: Manufactured gas. 1924. 35 p. *Paper, 5c.   24—26157

Leather. Census of manufactures. 1921: Leather industries 1924. 53 p. *Paper, 10c.   24—26156

Manufactures. Census of manufactures, 1923, instructions to special agents. 1924. iv+44 p. narrow 12° ‡   24—26225

Mortgages on homes, report on results of inquiry as to mortgage debt on homes other than farm homes at 14th census, 1920. 1923. 277 p. il. large 8° (Census monographs 2.) [Prepared under supervision of Charles S. Sloane, geographer of census, by Thomas J. Fitzgerald, special agent, edited and revised under supervision of Richard T. Ely.] *Cloth, $1.25. · 24—26159

Silk. Census of manufactures, 1921: Silk manufactures. 1924. 13 p. *Paper, 5c. 24—26158

Tobacco. Leaf tobacco held by manufacturers and dealers, Jan. 1, 1924 and 1923, and Oct. 1 and July 1, 1923. Jan. 31, 1924. oblong 32° [This publication is issued in postal card form.] †

COAST AND GEODETIC SURVEY

NOTE.—The monthly Notice to mariners, formerly issued by the Coast and Geodetic Survey, has been consolidated with and made a part of the Notice to mariners issued by the Lighthouses Bureau, thus making it a joint publication. The charts, coast pilots, and tide tables of the Coast and Geodetic Survey are sold at the office of the Survey in Washington, and also by one or more sales agents in each of the important American seaports.

Coast and Geodetic Survey bulletin, Jan. 31, 1924; no. 104. 1924. 8 p. [Monthly.] ‡ 15—26512

Coast pilots. Supplement to United States coast pilot, Atlantic Coast, section A, St. Croix River to Cape Cod. Jan. 11, 1924. [1]+16 leaves. (Serial 256.) †

Magnetic observatories. Results of observations made at Coast and Geodetic Survey magnetic observatory near Tucson, Ariz., in 1919 and 1920; by Daniel L. Hazard. 1924. [1]+98 p. 8 pl. (Serial 248.) *Paper, 20c. 13—35172

Charts

Chandeleur Sound. Chandeleur and Breton sounds, La., surveys to 1922; chart 1270. Scale 1:80,000. Washington, Coast and Geodetic Survey, Feb. 1924. 32.2×43.1 in. †75c.

Galveston entrance, Tex., surveys 1851–1900, surveys by U. S. Engineers to 1923; chart 520. Scale 1:40,000. Washington, Coast and Geodetic Survey, Jan. 1924. 15.9×21.6 in. †25c.

Porto Rico, east coast, San Juan Passage to Port Humacao, and western part of Vieques Island, original surveys 1900–23; chart 917. Scale 1:40,000. Washington, Coast and Geodetic Survey, Jan. 1924. 41.4×33.8 in. † 75c.

Prince of Wales Island. West coast of Prince of Wales Island, southeast Alaska, Ulloa Channel to San Christoval Channel, surveys 1912–21; chart 8155. Scale 1:40,000. Washington, Coast and Geodetic Survey, Jan. 1924. 30.2×36.3 in. † 75c.

San Diego Bay, Calif., San Diego Bay and entrance surveys to 1923, surveys by U. S. Engineers to 1922 and U. S. Navy to 1923, approaches, surveys to 1923; chart 5107. Scale 1:20,000. Washington, Coast and Geodetic Survey, Jan. 1924. 37.4×33.4 in. † 75c.

· *Virgin Passage* and Vieques Sound, W. I., surveys to 1923 and other sources; chart 904. [Scale 1:100,000.] Washington, Coast and Geodetic Survey, Feb. 1924. 30.8×43 in. † 75c. •

FISHERIES BUREAU

Fisheries service bulletin, Feb. 1, 1924; no. 105. [1924.] 9 p. [Monthly.] ‡ F15—76

Fishery products. Statement, by fishing grounds, of quantities and values of certain fishery products landed at Boston and Gloucester, Mass., and Portland, Me., by American fishing vessels, calendar year 1923. [1924.] 1 p. oblong f° (Statistical bulletin 600.) †

—— Statement, by fishing grounds [etc.], of quantities and values of certain fishery products landed at Seattle, Wash., by American fishing vessels, calendar year 1923. [1924.] 1 p. oblong f° (Statistical bulletin 598.) †

—— Statement, by months, of quantities and values of certain fishery products landed at Boston and Gloucester, Mass., and Portland, Me., by American fishing vessels, [calendar] year 1923. [1924.] 1 p. oblong f° (Statistical bulletin 599.) †

FOREIGN AND DOMESTIC COMMERCE BUREAU

Commerce. Monthly summary of foreign commerce of United States; Dec. 1923. 1924. 2 pts. p. 1–69 and ii+71–110 p. 4° *Paper, 10c. single copy (including pts. 1 and 2), $1.00 a yr.; foreign subscription, $1.60. 14—21465

—— Same. 1924. [2 pts. in 1], 110 p. 4° (H. doc. 12, 68th Cong. 1st sess.)

Commerce reports. Commerce reports, weekly survey of foreign trade, reports from American consular officers and representatives of Department of Commerce in foreign countries, no. 5–8; Feb. 4–25; 1924. 1924. cover-titles, p. 265–536, il. 4° [Text and illustrations on p. 2–4 of covers.] *Paper, 10c. single copy, $3.00 a yr.; foreign subscription, $5.00.

—— Same, nos. 40–53 [series 1923], v. 4, 26th year; Oct.–Dec. 1923 [title-page and index]. 1924. [2]+xxxiii p. 4° [Quarterly.] *Paper, 5c. single copy, 20c. a yr.; foreign subscription, 30c.

—— Supplement to Commerce reports. [Included in price of Commerce reports for subscribers.]

Trade and economic review for 1922, no. 50: China; by Edwin S. Cunningham. [1924.] 20 p.
Same, no. 51: Cuba; [by] Arthur C. Frost. [1924.] 16 p.
Same, no. 52: Panama; [by] George Orr. [1924.] 8 p.
Same, no. 53: Siam; [by] Charles H. Albrecht. [1924.] 18 p.

—— Supplement to Commerce reports: Austrian and Czechoslovak lumber and woodworking industries; [articles] by Carol H. Foster, Walter A. Foote, and C. M. Ravndal. Feb. 18, 1924. ii+16 p. (Trade information bulletin 196; Lumber Division.) † 24—26165

—— Same: Bolivian public debt, with survey of Bolivian financial history; by Charles A. McQueen. Feb. 18, 1924. ii+27 p. (Trade information bulletin 194; Finance and Investment Division.) † 24—26163

—— Same: Boot and shoe industry and trade of Australia; by Elmer G. Pauly. Feb. 18, 1924. ii+7 p. (Trade information bulletin 195; Shoe and Leather Manufactures Division.) † 24—26164

—— Same: Chicle and chewing gum, review of chicle production and sources of supply, and chewing gum industry and trade [with list of references]; by H. M. Hoar. Feb. 25. 1924. ii+10 p. (Trade information bulletin 197; Foodstuffs Division.) † 24—26166

—— Same: Cuban economic improvement [from reports dated Dec. 19, 1923]; by C. A. Livengood and Frank E. Coombs. Feb. 11, 1924. ii+8 p. (Trade information bulletin 191; Latin American Division.) † 24—26129

—— Same: Cuban market for paper and paper products; by Charles A. Livengood. Feb. 18, 1924. ii+15 p. (Trade information bulletin 192; Paper Division.) † 24—26161

—— Same: England's trade with Russia; by L. J. Lewery. Feb. 25, 1924. ii+11 p. (Trade information bulletin 199; Eastern European Division.) † 24—26200

—— Same: Geneva conference and ocean shipping; by Eugene Tyler Chamberlain. Mar. 3, 1924. ii+24 p. (Trade information bulletin 202; Transportation Division.) † 24—26201

Note.—Includes text of convention and statute on international régime of maritime ports agreed upon at Geneva conference.

—— Same: German electrical industry as revealed by exhibits at Leipzig Fall Fair, 1923; by Arthur J. Gray. Feb. 11, 1924. ii+16 p. (Trade information bulletin 187; Electrical Equipment Division.) † 24—26126

—— Same: Honduras; compiled by Hector Lazo from reports from Robert L. Keiser, Alexander K. Sloan, W. L. Beaulac, G. P. Shaw, and other sources. Feb. 18, 1924. ii+18 p. (Trade information bulletin 193; Latin American Division.) † 24—26162

—— Same: Ireland, its agricultural, industrial, and commercial resources; by Fred A. Christoph. Feb. 11, 1924. ii+44 p. (Trade information bulletin 188; Western European Division.) † 24—26127

—— Same: Protesting drafts in Spain, Portugal, and Italy; compiled by A. J. Wolfe from information furnished by consular officers of Department of State. Feb. 11, 1924. ii+23 p. (Trade information bulletin 189; Division of Commercial Laws.) † 24—26160

Commerce reports—Continued. Same: Road construction in Peru; by W. E. Dunn. Feb. 25, 1924. ii+16 p. (Trade information bulletin 198; Transportation Division.) †   24—26167

——— Same: Sisal, production, prices, and marketing; by Louis Crossette. Feb. 25, 1924. ii+7 p. (Trade information bulletin 200; Textile Division.) [Prepared as part of investigation of essential raw materials authorized by 67th Congress.] . †   24—26202

——— Same: Survey of world trade in agricultural products, no. 2; Methods of merchandising American wheat in export trade, pt. 2, Selling American wheat abroad; by Theo. D. Hammatt. Feb. 11, 1924; ii+78 p. il. (Trade information bulletin 185; Foodstuffs Division.) [Prepared as part of study of world trade in agricultural products authorized by 67th Congress.] †   24—26040

——— Same: Trade organizations in French metallurgy; by Chester Lloyd Jones. Feb. 4. 1924. ii+10 p. (Trade information bulletin 186; Iron and Steel Division.) †   24—26125

——— Same: Trading under laws of Union of South Africa, by Leslie Blackwell; with Supplementary notes, by A. J. Wolfe. Feb. 11, 1924. ii+32 p. (Trade information bulletin 190; Division of Commercial Laws.) †   24—26128

——— Survey of current business, Feb. 1924, no. 30; compiled by Bureau of Census, Bureau of Foreign and Domestic Commerce, [and] Bureau of Standards. 1924. cover-title, 224 p. il. 4° (Monthly supplement to Commerce reports.) [Contains statistics for Dec. 1923, the date given above, Feb. 1924, being the date of issue. Text on p. 2–4 of cover.] * Paper, 10c. single copy, $1.00 a yr.; foreign subscription, $1.50.   21—26819

NOTE.—Realizing that current statistics are highly perishable and that to be of use they must reach the business man at the earliest possible moment, the Department has arranged to distribute advance leaflets twice each month to those subscribers who request them. One set of these leaflets is issued about the 20th of the month, giving such information as has been received up to that time, and another set of sheets is mailed at the end of the month giving those figures received since the 20th. The information contained in these leaflets is also published in Commerce reports issued weekly by the Foreign and Domestic Commerce Bureau. The advance sheets will be mailed free of charge to all subscribers to the Survey who request them. Such requests should be addressed to the Bureau of the Census, Department of Commerce, Washington, D. C. Subscriptions, however, should be sent to the Superintendent of Documents, Washington, D. C., at the prices stated above.

Rumania, economic handbook [with bibliography]; prepared in Eastern European and Levantine Division. 1924. viii+167 p. il. 10 p. of pl. (Special agents series 222.) * Cloth, 65c.   24—26130

LIGHTHOUSES BUREAU

13th District. Light list, upper Mississippi River and tributaries, 13th lighthouse district; 1924, corrected to Jan. 15. 1924. 211 p. narrow 16° [About half of the pages are blank.] * Paper, 20c.   10—34309

Lighthouse service bulletin, v. 3, no. 2; Feb. 1, 1924. [1924.] p. 9–12. [Monthly.] †   12—35121

Notice to mariners, weekly, no. 5–9, 1924; Feb. 1–29 [1924]. 1924. various paging. [Issued jointly with Coast and Geodetic Survey.] †   7—20609

Willow, lighthouse tender. Specifications for side-wheel. steel, steam-propelled lighthouse tender Willow, 1924. 1924. [1]+76 p. †

NAVIGATION BUREAU

Ships. American documented seagoing merchant vessels of 500 gross tons and over, Feb. 1, 1924. 1924. ii+68 p. 4° (Serial 75.) [Monthly.] * Paper, 10c. single copy, 75c. a yr.; foreign subscription, $1.25.   19—26597

RADIO SERVICE

Radio Service bulletin, Feb. 1, 1924; no. 82. [1924.] 27 p. [Monthly.] * Paper, 5c. single copy, 25c. a yr.; foreign subscription, 40c.   15—26255

PUBLICATIONS DIVISION

Commerce Department. Supplement to annual List of publications [of Department of Commerce available for distribution], Jan. 31, 1924. [1924.] 4 p. [Monthly.] †

STANDARDS BUREAU

· NOTE.—The Scientific papers will be supplied on subscription·as issued at $1.25 per volume, paper bound. These volumes will afterwards be issued bound in cloth at $2.00 per volume; foreign subscription, paper $2.50 (sent in single numbers), cloth $2.35 (bound volumes).· Single numbers vary in price. Address the Superintendent of Documents, Washington, D. C.

The Technologic papers will be issued first as separates and later in volume form in the same manner as the Scientific papers. Subscriptions will be accepted by the Superintendent of Documents at $1.25 per volume; foreign subscription, $2.50. Single numbers vary in price.

Bottles. Milk and cream bottles and bottle caps. Oct. 1. 1923, [published] .1924.' ii+3 p. (Simplified practice recommendation no. 10.) [Title on ·cover is: Elimination of' waste, simplified practice, milk and cream bottles and bottle caps.] * Paper, 5c. ·

Bushel. Legal weights (in pounds) per bushel of various commodities. 4th edition. Jan. 22, 1924. [1]+18 p. (Circular 10.) * Paper, 5c.   24—26131

Duck (cloth). United States Government specification for numbered cotton duck, Federal Specifications Board, Standard specification 53, officially adopted by Federal Specifications Board, Feb. 1, 1923, for use of Departments and independent establishments of Government in purchase of numbered cotton duck. 2d edition.: Jan.'12, 1924. 4 p. (Circular 136.) [This specification was drawn up by the Cotton Duck Association and several of the large Government Departments.] * Paper, 5c.   24—26132

Electric resistance. Measurement of low resistance by means of wheatstone bridge; by Frank Wenner,[and] Alva Smith. Jan. 11, 1924. [1]+297-305 p. il. large 8° (Scientific papers 481.) [From Scientific papers, v. 19.] *Paper, 5c.   24—26135

Gases. Thermal-conductivity method for analysis of gases; by P. E. Palmer [and] E. R. Weaver. Jan. 7, 1924. [1]+35-100 p. il. large 8° (Technologic papers 249.) [From Technologic papers, v. 18.] *Paper, 20c.   24—26138

Hosiery. Standardized method of measuring size of hosiery. Feb. 1, 1924. [1]+5 p. il. (Circular 149.) [Prepared in cooperation with National Association of Hosiery and Underwear Manufacturers.] *Paper, 5c.   24—26169

Radio beacons. Directive type of radio beacon and its application to navigation; by F. H. Engel [and] F. W. Dunmore. Jan. 5, 1924. [1]+281-295 p. il. 1 pl. (Scientific papers 480.) [From Scientific papers, v. 19.] *Paper, 5c.   24—26134

Soap. United States Government specification for hand grit soap, Federal Specifications Board, Standard specification 35, officially adopted by Federal Specifications Board, July 3, 1922, for use of Departments and independent establishments of Government in purchase of hand grit soap. 2d [edition]. Feb. 1, 1924. 4 p. (Circular 132.) *Paper, 5c.   24—26203

Spectra. Redetermination of secondary standards of wave length from new international iron arc; by W. F. Meggers, C. C. Kiess, [and] Keivin Burns. Jan. 5, 1924. [1]+263-272 p. 1 pl. (Scientific papers 478.) [From Scientific papers, v. 19.] *Paper, 5c.   24—26133

Telemeters. New electrical telemeter; by Burton McCollum [and] O. S. Peters. Jan. 4, 1924. [1]+737-777 p. il. 6 p. of pl. (Technologic papers 247.) [From Technologic papers, v. 17.] *Paper, 15c.   24—26136

Wall plaster, its ingredients, preparation, and properties [report of Bureau of Standards Plastering Conference]. Jan. 9, 1924. [1]+66 p. (Circular 151.) *Paper, 15c.   24—26170

Waterproofing. Exposure tests on colorless waterproofing materials; by D. W. Kessler. Jan. 7, 1924. [1]+1-33 p. il. 1 pl. 2 p. of pl. (Technologic papers 248.) [From Technologic papers, v. 18.] *Paper, 15c.   24—26137

STEAMBOAT INSPECTION SERVICE

Steamboat Inspection Service bulletin, Feb. 1, 1924; no. 100. [1924.] 2 p. [Monthly.] ‡   15—26679

CONGRESS

Congressional record. Congressional record, 68th Congress, 1st session, v. 65, no. 38–61; Feb. 1–29, 1924. [1924.] 1807–3498+[59] p. 4° 12—36438

NOTE.—The Congressional record, containing the proceedings and debates of Congress, is issued daily when Congress is in session, and indexes thereto are published fortnightly.

The Record is sold by the Superintendent of Documents on the following terms: Single copy, 3 cents, if not more than 24 pages, and 1 cent more for each additional 8 pages; per month, $1.50, foreign subscription, $2.50. Subscriptions are payable in advance. Prices for the bound volumes of the Record, 67th Congress, 1st–4th sessions, and prior Congresses, will be furnished on application. Send remittances to the Superintendent of Documents, Washington, D. C. Stamps and foreign money will not be accepted.

—— Same, index, with title, Congressional record index, 68th Congress, 1st session, v. 65, nos. 28–39; Jan. 21–Feb. 2, 1924. [1924.] no. 3; 47+22 p. 4° [Includes History of bills and resolutions.]

—— Same, v. 65, nos. 40–50; Feb. 4–16, 1924. [1924.] no. 4; 37+16 p. 4° [Includes History of bills and resolutions.]

PUBLIC LAWS

NOTE.—Public acts in slip form in the first prints may be obtained from the Superintendent of Documents, Washington, D. C., at a subscription price of $1.00 for the 68th Congress, 1st session, foreign subscription $1.25; single copies are usually 5c. each.

Public [act] 1–32, 68th Congress.

Arkansas River. S. 602, act to extend time for construction of bridge across Arkansas River between Little Rock and Argenta, Ark. [Pulaski County]. Approved Feb. 16, 1924. 1 p. (Public 18.)

Chattahoochee River. S. 160, act authorizing Georgia to construct bridge across Chattahoochee River between Georgia and Alabama at or near Fort Gaines, Ga. Approved Feb. 1, 1924. 1 p. (Public 8.)

Chippewa Indians. H. R. 185, act for per capita payment of $100 to each enrolled member of Chippewa tribe of Minnesota from funds standing to their credit in Treasury. Approved Jan. 25, 1924. 1 p. (Public 1.)

Columbia River. S. 484, act to extend time for completion of construction of bridge across Columbia River between Oregon and Washington at or within 2 miles westerly from Cascade Locks, Oreg. [by Interstate Construction Corporation]. Approved Jan. 30, 1924. 1 p. (Public 2.)

Convict labor. S. 794, act to equip Penitentiary, Leavenworth, Kans., for manufacture of supplies for use of Government, for compensation of prisoners for their labor, and for other purposes. [Approved Feb. 11, 1924.] 2 p. (Public 12.)

District of Columbia. S. 627, act to authorize National Society United States Daughters of 1812 to place bronze tablet on Francis Scott Key Bridge. Approved Jan. 30, 1924. 1 p. (Public 6.)

Dog River. H. R. 3770, act for examination and survey of Dog River, Ala., from Louisville and Nashville Railroad bridge to mouth of said river including connection with Mobile Bay ship channel. Approved Feb. 2, 1924. 1 p. (Public 11.)

Fox River. H. R. 4498, act to authorize Illinois to construct bridge across Fox River in county of Kendall, Ill. [between Yorkville and Bristol]. Approved Feb. 16, 1924. 1 p. (Public 28.)

—— S. 1539, act extending time for construction of bridge across Fox River by Aurora, Ill., and granting consent of Congress to removal of existing dam and to its replacement with new structure. Approved Feb. 16, 1924. 1 p. (Public 24.)

—— S. 1540, act granting consent of Congress to Aurora, Kane County, Ill., to construct bridges across Fox River. Approved Feb. 16, 1924. 1 p. (Public 25.)

Hudson River. H. R. 4796, act to extend time of Hudson River Connecting Railroad Corporation for completion of its bridge across Hudson River, N. Y. [at point between Castleton and Schodack Landing]. Approved Feb. 14, 1924. 1 p. (Public 15.)

—— S. 733, act granting consent of Congress to construction of bridge over Hudson River at Poughkeepsie, N. Y. [by commissioner of highways of New York State]. Approved Feb. 16, 1924. 1 p. (Public 21.)

Kingston Lake. H. R. 3680, act authorizing building of bridge across Kingston Lake at Conway, S. C. [by Horry County]. Approved Feb. 2, 1924. 1 p. (Public 10.)

Lumber River. H. R. 1634, act to authorize building of bridge across Lumber River, S. C., between Marion and Horry counties [near Nichols, S. C., by Highway Department of South Carolina]. Approved Feb. 16, 1924. 1 p. (Public 26.)

Mississippi River. H. R. 4366, act granting consent of Congress to Great Northern Railway Company to maintain and operate or reconstruct, maintain, and operate bridge across Mississippi River [within Minneapolis, Minn.]. Approved Feb. 16, 1924. 1 p. (Public 27.)

—— H. R. 4817, act granting consent of Congress to Illinois and Iowa, or either of them, to construct bridge across Mississippi River connecting county of Whiteside, Ill., and county of Clinton, Iowa. Approved Feb. 20, 1924. 1 p. (Public 32.)

—— H. R. 5273, act granting consent of Congress to Chicago, Milwaukee and St. Paul Railway Company to construct bridge over Mississippi River between St. Paul and Minneapolis, Minn. Approved Feb. 16, 1924. 1 p. (Public 30.)

—— S. 801, act granting consent of Congress to construction by Valley Transfer Railway Company of bridge across Mississippi River between Hennepin and Ramsey counties, Minn. Approved Jan. 30, 1924. 1 p. (Public 3.)

Public [act] 1–32, 68th Congress—Continued.

Missouri River. S. 1367, act granting consent of Congress to South Dakota for construction of bridge across Missouri River between Brule County and Lyman County, S. Dak. Approved Jan. 30, 1924. 1 p. (Public 4.)

——. S. 1368, act granting consent of Congress to South Dakota for construction of bridge across Missouri River between Walworth County and Corson County, S. Dak. Approved Jan. 30, 1924. 1 p. (Public 5.)

Pamunkey River. S. 643, act to extend time for construction of bridge across Pamunkey River, Va. [by Pamunkey Ferry Company, near Sweet Hall, Va.]. Approved Feb. 16, 1924. 1 p. (Public 20.)

Pearl River. H. R. 657, act granting consent of Congress to boards of supervisors of Rankin and Madison counties, Miss., to construct bridge across Pearl River, Miss. [at Meeks Ferry]. Approved Feb. 13, 1924. 1 p. (Public 14.)

Peedee River. H. R. 3679, act to authorize building of bridge across Pee Dee River, S. C. [at Yawhannah Ferry by Horry and Georgetown counties, S. C.]. Approved Feb. 2, 1924. 1 p. (Public 9.)

Rio Grande. H. R. 5196, act granting consent of Congress to construction of bridge across Rio Grande [by El Paso Electric Railway Company and El Paso and Jaurez Traction Company, at El Paso, Tex.]. Approved Feb. 1, 1924. 1 p. (Public 7.)

Rock River. H. R. 4499, act granting consent of Congress to Illinois to construct bridge across Rock River in county of Winnebago, Ill., in section 24, township 46 north, range 1 east, of 3d principal meridian. Approved Feb. 16, 1924. 1 p. (Public 29.)

St. Francis River. S. 604, act to authorize construction of bridge across St. Francis River near St. Francis, Ark. [by St. Louis Southwestern Railway Company]. Approved Feb. 16, 1924. 1 p. (Public 19.)

St. Louis, Mo. H. R. 486, act to extend time for completion of municipal bridge approaches, and extensions or additions thereto, by St. Louis, within Illinois and Missouri. Approved Feb. 13, 1924. 1 p. (Public 13.)

Tug Fork. S. 1374, act to authorize Norfolk and Western Railway Company to construct bridge across Tug Fork of Big Sandy River at or near point about mile and a half west of Williamson, Mingo County, W. Va., and near mouth of Turkey Creek, Pike County, Ky. Approved Feb. 16, 1924. 1 p. (Public 23.)

Waccamaw River. S. 384, act to authorize building of bridge across Waccamaw River, S. C., near North Carolina State line [by North and South Carolina Waccamaw Bridge Company]. Approved Feb. 16, 1924. 1 p. (Public 17.)

War Finance Corporation. S. 2249, act to extend for 9 months power of War Finance Corporation to make advances under provisions of War Finance Corporation act, as amended [relative to relief for producers of and dealers in agricultural products], and for other purposes. Approved Feb. 20, 1924. 1 p. (Public 31.)

Willamette River. S. 152, act to authorize county of Multnomah, Oreg., to construct bridge across Willamette River in Portland, Oreg., to replace present Burnside Street Bridge in Portland, and also to authorize county of Multnomah to construct bridge across Willamette River in Portland, in vicinity of Ross Island. Approved Feb. 16, 1924. 1 p. (Public 16.)

Yellowstone River. S. 1170, act to authorize Highway Commission of Montana to construct bridge across Yellowstone River at or near Glendive, Mont. Approved Feb. 16, 1924. 1 p. (Public 22.)

Public [joint] resolution 2–5, 68th Congress.

Cattle. H. J. Res. 82, joint resolution extending time during which certain domestic animals which have crossed boundary line into foreign countries may be returned duty free. Approved Jan. 25, 1924. 1 p. (Public resolution 2.)

Federal Reserve System, Joint Committee of Inquiry on Membership in. H. J. Res. 151, joint resolution extending time for final report of joint congressional committee created by agricultural credits act of 1923. Approved Jan. 31, 1924. 1 p. (Public resolution 3.)

Naval petroleum reserves. S. J. Res. 54, joint resolution directing President to institute and prosecute suits to cancel certain leases of oil lands and incidental contracts. [Approved Feb. 8, 1924.] 2 p. (Public resolution 4.)

Navy and Marine Memorial Dedicated to Americans Lost at Sea. S. J. Res. 68, joint resolution authorizing erection on public grounds in Washington, D. C., of memorial to Navy and Marine services, to be known as Navy and Marine Memorial Dedicated to Americans Lost at Sea. Approved Feb. 16, 1924. 1 p. (Public resolution 5.)

HARDING, WARREN G., JOINT SELECT COMMITTEE ON ARRANGEMENTS OF MEMORIAL SERVICES FOR

Harding, Warren G. Memorial services for Warren G. Harding, report pursuant to S. Res. 21; submitted by Mr. Willis. Feb. 16, calendar day Feb. 20, 1924. 2 p. (S. rp. 163, 68th Cong. 1st sess.) *Paper, 5c.

HOUSE OF REPRESENTATIVES

Appropriations. Legislative establishment, supplemental estimates of appropriations for legislative establishment, fiscal year 1924 and fiscal year 1925. Feb. 2, 1924. 3 p. (H. doc. 185, 68th Cong. 1st sess.) *Paper, 5c.

Bankruptcy laws of United States: public law 171, July 1, 1898, 55th Congress; public law 62, Feb. 5, 1903, 57th Congress; public law 232, June 15, 1906, 59th Congress; public law 294, June 25, 1910, 61st Congress; public law 241 (extract), Jan. 28, 1915, 63d Congress; public law 258 (extract), Sept. 6, 1916, 64th Congress; public law 376, Mar. 2, 1917, 64th Congress; public law 121, Jan. 7, 1922, 67th Congress. 1924. [1]+40 p. *Paper, 5c.   24—26222

Boy Scouts of America. 13th annual report of Boy Scouts of America, letter from chief scout executive transmitting 13th annual report of Boy Scouts of America [year ending Dec. 31, 1922]. 1924. iii+153 p. (H. doc. 114, 68th Cong. 1st sess.) * Paper, 15c.   E 13—532

Calendars of House of Representatives, 68th Congress, 1st session, Feb. 1–29, 1924; no. 34–57. 1924. various paging, large 8° [Daily when House of Representatives is in session.] ‡

Commerce. Laws of 65th, 66th, and 67th Congresses relating to interstate and foreign commerce: 1, Railroads; 2, Wire control; 3, Proclamations; 4, Executive orders; 5, Termination of Federal control of railroads; 6, Relinquishment of Federal control, proclamation. 1924. 124 p. [Includes extract from public law 242, 64th Congress.] *Paper, 15c.

Revenue laws with amendments: public law no. 217, approved Oct. 22, 1914, 63d Congress; public law no. 271, approved Sept. 8, 1916, 64th Congress; public law no. 377, approved Mar. 3, 1917, 64th Congress; public law no. 50, approved Oct. 3, 1917, 65th Congress; public law no. 254, approved Feb. 24, 1919, 65th Congress; public law no. 98, approved Nov. 23, 1921, 67th Congress; public law no. 527, approved Mar. 4, 1923, 67th Congress; public law no. 531, approved Mar. 4, 1923, 67th Congress; public law no. 545, approved Mar. 4, 1923, 67th Congress. 1924. [1]+345 p. *Paper, 35c.

ACCOUNTS COMMITTEE

Johnson, James. To pay James Johnson for extra services, report to accompany H. Res. 55; submitted by Mr. MacGregor. Feb. 9, 1924. 1 p. (H. rp. 174, 68th Cong. 1st sess.) * Paper, 5c.

Mileage Committee, House. Appointing session clerk to Committee on Mileage, report to accompany H. Res. 111; submitted by Mr. MacGregor. Feb. 9, 1924. 1 p. (H. rp. 175, 68th Cong. 1st sess.) * Paper, 5c.

World War Veterans' Legislation Committee, House. To provide clerks for Committee on World War veterans' Legislation, report to accompany H. Res. 170; submitted by Mr. Underhill. Feb. 14, 1924. 1 p. (H. rp. 193, 68th Cong. 1st sess.) * Paper, 5c.

AGRICULTURE COMMITTEE

Agricultural attachés. Ketcham foreign crop marketing and report bill, hearings on H. R. 5568, to gather and disseminate information on agricultural production, competition, and demand in foreign countries, Jan. 28 and 30, 1924. 1924. ii+34 p. (Serial H.) * Paper, 5c.

Agricultural products. McNary-Haugen export bill, hearings on H. R. 5563, declaring emergency in respect to certain agricultural commodities and to promote equality between agricultural commodities and other commodities, Jan. 21[–Feb. 16]. 1924. 1924. [pts. 1–4], [xii]+1–288 p. (Serial E, pts. [1]–4.) * Paper, pts. 1 and 4, each 5c.; * pts. 2 and 3. each 15c.

Agriculture Department. Department bills, hearings on H. R. 5791, H. R. 5941, H. R. 5939, H. R. 5946, H. R. 5937, H. R. 762 [bills providing for sundry matters affecting Department of Agriculture] Jan. 29, 1924. 1924. iii+31 p. (Serial I.) * Paper, 5c.

Dairy Bureau. Bureau of Dairying. hearings on H. R. 7113, to establish Dairy Bureau in Department of Agriculture, Feb. 13, 1924. 1924. iii+16 p. (Serial L.) * Paper, 5c.

Forest Service administration. report to accompany H. R. 5939 [to facilitate and simplify work of Forest Service, Department of Agriculture, and to promote reforestation]; submitted by Mr. Haugen. Feb. 5, 1924. 4 p. (H. rp. 153, 68th Cong. 1st sess.) * Paper, 5c.

McGuire, Henry. Henry McGuire, report to accompany H. R. 1306 [for relief of Henry McGuire]; submitted by Mr. Haugen. Feb. 5, 1924. 2 p. (H. rp. 152, 68th Cong. 1st sess.) * Paper, 5c.

Seed distribution, report to accompany H. R. 5559 [to authorize appropriation to enable Secretary of Agriculture to purchase and distribute valuable seeds]; submitted by Mr. Haugen. Feb. 14, 1924. 2 p. (H. rp. 205, 68th Cong. 1st sess.) * Paper, 5c.

Smith, Albert W. A. W. Smith, report to accompany H. R. 6557 [to allow credit in accounts of A. W. Smith]; submitted by Mr. Haugen. Feb. 5, 1924. 2 p. (H. rp. 154, 68th Cong. 1st sess.) * Paper, 5c.

432 FEBRUARY, 1924

APPROPRIATIONS COMMITTEE

Agriculture Department. Agricultural appropriation bill, [fiscal year] 1925, hearings before subcommittee in charge of agricultural appropriation bill for 1925. 1924. ii+1168 p. * Paper, 85c.

—— Agricultural appropriation bill, [fiscal year] 1925, report to accompany H. R. 7220; submitted by Mr. Anderson. Feb. 22, 1924. 26 p. (H. rp. 223, 68th Cong. 1st sess.) * Paper, 5c.

Naval petroleum reserves. Navy Department appropriation bill, [fiscal year] 1925, supplemental hearing before subcommittee in charge of Navy Department appropriation bill for 1925, naval petroleum reserves. 1924. pt. 2, ii+57 p. * Paper, 5c.

Navy Department. Navy Department and naval service appropriation bill, fiscal year 1925, report to accompany H. R. 6820; submitted by Mr. French. Feb. 9, 1924. 24 p. (H. rp. 178, 68th Cong. 1st sess.) * Paper, 5c.

—— Navy Department appropriation bill, [fiscal year] 1925, hearing before subcommittee in charge of Navy Department appropriation bill for 1925. 1924. [pt. 1], ii+928 p. * Paper, 60c.

BANKING AND CURRENCY COMMITTEE

War Finance Corporation. Extend power of War Finance Corporation, report to accompany S. 2249 [to extend for 9 months power of War Finance Corporation to make advances under provisions of War Finance Corporation act, as amended relative to relief for producers of and dealers in agricultural products, and for other purposes]; submitted by Mr. McFadden. Feb. 12, 1924. 1 p. (H. rp. 185, 68th Cong. 1st sess.) * Paper, 5c.

CLAIMS COMMITTEE

American Surety Co. of New York, report to accompany H. R. 4374 [for relief of American Surety Company of New York]; submitted by Mr. Fredericks. Feb. 14, 1924. 5 p. (H. rp. 201, 68th Cong. 1st sess.) * Paper, 5c.

Bradley, William R. William R. Bradley, report to accompany H. R. 1316 [for relief of William R. Bradley]; submitted by Mr. Celler. Feb. 2, 1924. 3 p. (H. rp. 147, 68th Cong. 1st sess.) * Paper, 5c.

Buxton, Grace. Grace Buxton, report to accompany H. R. 5967 [for relief of Grace Buxton]; submitted by Mr. Edmonds. Feb. 14, 1924. 3 p. (H. rp. 204, 68th Cong. 1st sess.) * Paper, 5c.

Cleveland State Bank, Cleveland, Miss., report to accompany S. 75 [for relief of Cleveland State Bank, Cleveland, Miss.]; submitted by Mr. Thomas of Oklahoma. Feb. 2, 1924. 5 p. (H. rp. 148, 68th Cong. 1st sess.) * Paper, 5c.

Cole, C. M. Estate of C. M. Cole, report to accompany H. R. 4760 [for relief of estate of C. M. Cole]; submitted by Mr. Fredericks. Feb. 14, 1924. 14 p. (H. rp. 202, 68th Cong. 1st sess.) * Paper, 5c.

Fuller, Stansfield A. Stansfield A. and Elizabeth G. Fuller, report to accompany H. R. 914 [granting 6 months' gratuity pay to Stansfield A. and Elizabeth G. Fuller, parents of Stansfield A. Fuller]; submitted by Mr. Beck. Feb. 14, 1924. 2 p. (H. rp. 196, 68th Cong. 1st sess.) * Paper, 5c.

Greenport Basin & Construction Co., report to accompany H. R. 3348 [to pay claim as result of damage sustained to marine railway of Greenport Basin and Construction Company]; submitted by Mr. Edmonds. Feb. 14, 1924. 4 p. (H. rp. 198, 68th Cong. 1st sess.) * Paper, 5c.

Hutcheson, Bernice. Bernice Hutcheson, report to accompany H. R. 3143 [for relief of Bernice Hutcheson]; submitted by Mr. vincent of Michigan. Feb. 2, 1924. 9 p. (H. rp. 144, 68th Cong. 1st sess.) * Paper, 5c.

Jonas, Julius. Julius Jonas, report to accompany H. R. 5762 [for relief of Julius Jonas]; submitted by Mr. Fredericks. Feb. 14, 1924. 12 p. (H. rp. 203, 68th Cong. 1st sess.) * Paper, 5c.

Lebanon National Bank, Lebanon, Tenn., report to accompany H. R. 3748 [for relief of Lebanon National Bank]; submitted by Mr. Thomas of Oklahoma. Feb. 2, 1924. 7 p. (H. rp. 145, 68th Cong. 1st sess.) * Paper, 5c.

New Jersey Shipbuilding & Dredging Co., report to accompany S. 1572 [for relief of New Jersey Shipbuilding and Dredging Company, Bayonne, N. J.]; submitted by Mr. Underhill. Feb. 14, 1924. 7 p. (H. rp. 195, 68th Cong. 1st sess.) * Paper, 5c.

Nickles, George A. George A. Nickles, report to accompany H. R. 3761 [for relief of George A. Nickles]; submitted by Mr. Vincent of Michigan. Feb. 14. 1924. 8 p. (H. rp. 200, 68th Cong. 1st sess.) * Paper, 5c.

Old National Bank of Martinsburg, Martinsburg, W. Va., report to accompany S. 214 [for relief of Old National Bank of Martinsburg, Martinsburg, W. Va.]; submitted by Mr. Thomas of Oklahoma. Feb. 2, 1924. 6 p. (H. rp. 149, 68th Cong. 1st sess.) * Paper, 5c.

Stone Towing Line, report to accompany H. R. 1682 [for relief of Stone Towing Line]; submitted by Mr. Bulwinkle. Feb. 18, 1924. 7 p. (H. rp. 209, 68th Cong. 1st sess.) * Paper, 5c.

Thompson-Vache Boat Co., report to accompany H. R. 2123 [for relief of Thompson-Vache Boat Company, Bonnots Mill, Mo.]; submitted by Mr. Little. Feb. 14, 1924. 20 p. (H. rp. 197, 68th Cong. 1st sess.) * Paper, 5c.

Tower, Mrs. Cornelia M. A. Cornelia M. A. Tower, report to accompany H. R. 3504 [for relief of Cornelia M. A. Tower]; submitted by Mr. McReynolds. Feb. 14, 1924. 4 p. (H. rp. 199, 68th Cong. 1st sess.) * Paper, 5c.

Williams, Edward T. Edward T. Williams, report to accompany H. R. 5808 [for relief of Edward T. Williams]; submitted by Mr. Edmonds. Feb. 2, 1924. 11 p. (H. rp. 146, 68th Cong. 1st sess.) * Paper, 5c.

COINAGE, WEIGHTS, AND MEASURES COMMITTEE

Weights and measures. Standard of weights and measures for certain agricultural products, hearings on H. R. 3241, to establish standard of weights and measures for following wheat-mill, rye-mill, and corn-mill products, namely, flours, hominy, grits, and meals and all commercial feeding stuffs, Jan. 25 and 29, 1924. 1924. [1]+25 p. * Paper, 5c.

DISTRICT OF COLUMBIA COMMITTEE

Capital punishment in District of Columbia, report to accompany S. 387 [to prescribe method of capital punishment in District of Columbia to be electricution]; submitted by Mr. Gasque. Feb. 5, 1924. 2 p. (H. rp. 156, 68th Cong. 1st sess.) * Paper, 5c.

Grand Army of the Republic. Incorporation of Grand Army of the Republic, report to accompany H. R. 1869; submitted by Mr. Jost. Feb. 28, 1924. 2 p. (H. rp. 242, 68th Cong. 1st sess.) * Paper, 5c.

Insurance. To amend insurance laws of District of Columbia, report to accompany H. R. 3689; submitted by Mr. Jost. Feb. 26, 1924. 7 p. (H. rp. 231, 68th Cong. 1st sess.) * Paper, 5c.

Lincoln, Abraham. Lincoln's birthday a holiday in District of Columbia, minority report to accompany H. R. 20; submitted by Mr. Blanton. Feb. 5, 1924. 7 p. (H. rp. 140, pt. 2, 68th Cong. 1st sess.) * Paper, 5c.

—— Lincoln's birthday a holiday in District of Columbia, report to accompany H. R. 20; submitted by Mr. Keller. Feb. 1, 1924. 6 p. (H. rp. 140 [pt. 1], 68th Cong. 1st sess.) * Paper, 5c.

—— Lincoln's birthday, hearing on H. R. 20, to declare Lincoln's birthday legal holiday in District of Columbia, Jan. 23, 1924. 1924. ii+27 p. * Paper, 5c.

National Society of Daughters of American Revolution. Exemption from taxation of certain property of Daughters of American Revolution, report to accompany H. R. 837 [to exempt from taxation certain property of Daughters of American Revolution in Washington, D. C.]; submitted by Mr. Gibson. Feb. 11, 1924. 1 p. (H. rp. 183, 68th Cong. 1st sess.) * Paper, 5c.

Police Department. Salaries of officers and members of Police Force and Fire Department, District of Columbia, hearing before subcommittee on H. R. 4486, to fix salaries of officers and members of Metropolitan Police Force and Fire Department of District of Columbia, Jan. 14 [-21], 1924. 1924. [1]+62 p. * Paper, 5c.

Streets. Change of certain streets in District of Columbia, report to accompany H. R. 4531 [to vacate streets and alleys within area known as Walter Reed General Hospital, District of Columbia, and to authorize extension and widening of 14th street from Montague street to its southern terminus south of Dahlia street, Nicholson street from 13th street to 16th street, Colorado avenue from Montague street to 13th street, Concord avenue from 16th street to its western terminus west of 8th street west, 13th street from Nicholson street to Piney Branch road, and Piney Branch road from 13th street to Blair road]; submitted by Mr. Zihlman. Feb. 25, 1924. 5 p. (H. rp. 227, 68th Cong. 1st sess.) *Paper, 5c.

Workmen's compensation. District of Columbia insurance fund, hearing on H. R. 487, creating District of Columbia insurance fund for benefit of employees injured and dependents of employees killed in employments, providing for administration of such fund by Employees' Compensation Commission, and making appropriation therefor, Jan. 26, 1924. 1924. ii+58 p. *Paper, 5c.

EDUCATION COMMITTEE

Library Service Division. Library information service, hearing on H. R. 633, for library information service in Bureau of Education. 1924. [1]+26 p. *Paper, 5c.

—— Library information service in Bureau of Education, report to accompany H. R. 633; submitted by Mr. Dallinger. Feb. 7, 1924. 3 p. (H. rp. 161. 68th Cong. 1st sess.) *Paper, 5c. 24—26223

Rehabilitation of the disabled. Industrial vocational rehabilitation, report to accompany H. R. 5478 [to amend sec. 1, 3, and 6 of act for promotion of vocational rehabilitation of persons disabled in industry or otherwise and their return to civil employment]; submitted by Mr. Dallinger. Feb. 7, 1924. 7 p. (H. rp. 164, 68th Cong. 1st sess.) [Includes views of minority signed by Mr. Tucker and Mr. Black of New York.] *Paper, 5c. 24—26149

—— vocational rehabilitation of persons disabled in industry or otherwise and their return to civil employment, hearing on H. R. 5478, to amend sec. 1, 3, and 6 of act for promotion of vocational rehabilitation of persons disabled in industry or otherwise and their return to civil employment. 1924. [1]+47 p. *Paper, 5c.

ELECTION OF PRESIDENT, VICE PRESIDENT, AND REPRESENTATIVES COMMITTEE

President of United States. Proposed amendment to Constitution of United States fixing commencement of terms of President and Vice President and Members of Congress, and fixing time of assembling of Congress, hearings, H. J. Res. 93, Jan. 10 and 24 [1924]. 1924. ii+36 p. *Paper, 5c.

—— Proposing amendment to Constitution of United States, report to accompany H. J. Res. 93 [proposing amendment to Constitution of United States fixing commencement of terms of President and Vice President and Members of Congress, and fixing time of assembling of Congress]; submitted by Mr. White of Kansas. Feb. 19, 1924. 4 p. (H. rp. 211 [pt. 1], 68th Cong. 1st sess.) *Paper, 5c. 24—26177

ELECTIONS COMMITTEE, NO. 3

Contested elections. Arguments and hearings, contested-election case of Walter M. Chandler *v.* Sol Bloom from 19th Congressional district of New York. 1924. ii+452 p. * Paper, 40c.

—— Chandler *v.* Bloom, minority report on contested-election case of Walter M. Chandler *v.* Sol Bloom, 19th Congressional district of New York; submitted by Mr. Williams of Texas. Feb. 28, 1924. 12 p. (H. rp. 224, pt. 2, 68th Cong. 1st sess.) * Paper, 5c.

—— Chandler *v.* Bloom, report on contested election case of Walter M. Chandler *v.* Sol Bloom, 19th Congressional district of New York; submitted by Mr. Elliott. Feb. 23, 1924. 8 p. (H. rp. 224 [pt. 1] 68th Cong. 1st sess.) * Paper, 5c.

—— Contested-election case of Walter M. Chandler *v.* Sol. Bloom, report to accompany H. Res. 166 [relating to taking of testimony before Committee on Elections Numbered 3, in contested election case of Walter M. Chandler *v.* Sol Bloom]; submitted by Mr. Elliott. Jan. 30, 1924. 1 p. (H. rp. 131, 68th Cong. 1st sess.) * Paper, 5c.

Diplomatic and consular service. Reorganization and improvement of foreign service of United States, report to accompany H. R. 6357; submitted by Mr. Rogers of Massachusetts. Feb. 5, 1924. '18 p. (H. rp. 157, 68th Cong. 1st sess.) * Paper, 5c.   24—26151

Germany. Relief for women and children of Germany, hearings on H. J. Res. 180, for relief of distressed and starving women and children of Germany, Jan. 29–Feb. 13, 1924. 1924. ii+156 p. il. * Paper, 15c.

Narcotics. Appropriation for participation of United States in 2 international conferences for control of narcotic drugs, report to accompany H. J. Res. 195; submitted by Mr. Porter. Feb. 28, 1924. 1 p. (H. rp. 244, 68th Cong. 1st sess.) * Paper, 5c.

Calendar. Legislative calendar, 68th Congress, Jan. 3 and Feb. 25, 1924; no. 1 and 2. 1923–24. 8 p. and 12 p. large 8° ‡

Citizenship of wives of Americans in foreign service, hearings on H. R. 6073, Feb. 12, 1924. 1924. ii+24 p. * Paper, 5c.

Immigration. Restriction of immigration, hearings on H. R. 5, H. R. 101, and H. R. 561, Dec. 26, 1923–Jan. 19, 1924. 1924. ii+914 p. il. (Serial 1–A.) * Paper, 60c.

—— Restriction of immigration, minority report to accompany H. R. 6540; submitted by Mr. Sabath. Feb. 15, 1924. 20 p. (H. rp. 176, pt. 2, 68th Cong. 1st sess.) * Paper, 5c.

—— Restriction of immigration, report to accompany H. R. 6540; submitted by Mr. Johnson of Washington. Feb. 9, 1924. 29 p. (H. rp. 176 [pt. 1], 68th Cong. 1st sess.) [Includes views of Mr. Bacon.] * Paper, 5c.   24—26150

Andes, Lake. Spillway and drainage ditch, Lake Andes, S. Dak., report to accompany H. R. 4161 [to acquire necessary rights of way across private lands, by purchase or condemnation proceedings, needed in constructing spillway and drainage ditch to lower and maintain level of Lake Andes, S. Dak.]; submitted by Mr. Johnson of South Dakota. Feb. 1, 1924. 2 p. (H. rp. 139, 68th Cong. 1st sess.) * Paper, 5c.

Chester Calf, Indian. Chester Calf and Crooked Nose Woman, report to accompany H. R. 6857 [for addition of names of Chester Calf and Crooked Nose Woman to final roll of Cheyenne and Arapaho Indians, Seger jurisdiction, Okla.]; submitted by Mr. Snyder. Feb. 21, 1924. 1 p. (H. rp. 220, 68th Cong. 1st sess.) * Paper, 5c.

Fort Apache Reservation. Appropriation for construction of road, Fort Apache Indian Reservation, Ariz. [and for agency building], report to accompany H. R. 4117; submitted by Mr. Hayden. Feb. 11, 1924. 3 p. (H. rp. 182, 68th Cong. 1st sess.) * Paper, 5c.

Indians. Administration of Indian affairs in Oklahoma, report to accompany H. J. Res. 181 [creating joint committee of 3 Members of Senate and 3 Members of House to investigate administration of Indian affairs in Oklahoma]; submitted by Mr. Snyder. Feb. 23, 1924. 3 p. (H. rp. 225, 68th Cong. 1st sess.) * Paper, 5c.

—— Certificates of citizenship to Indians, report to accompany H. R. 6355; submitted by Mr. Snyder. Feb. 22, 1924. 3 p. (H. rp. 222, 68th Cong. 1st sess.) * Paper, 5c.

—— Indian tribes of Washington, hearing on H. R. 2694 [authorizing Indian tribes and individual Indians residing in State of Washington and west of summit of Cascade Mountains to submit to Court of Claims certain claims growing out of treaties and otherwise], Feb. 2, 1924. 1924. [1]+72 p. * Paper, 10c.

Lapwai Indian Sanatorium. Girls' dormitory at Lapwai Indian Sanatorium, report to accompany H. R. 192; submitted by Mr. Leavitt. Jan. 31, 1924. 1 p. (H. rp. 133, 68th Cong. 1st sess.) * Paper, 5c.

Navajo Indians. Deposit of certain funds to credit of Navajo tribe of Indians, report to accompany H. R. 472; submitted by Mr. Hayden. Jan. 31, 1924. 2 p. (H. rp. 135, 68th Cong. 1st sess.) * Paper, 5c.

Osage Indians. Amending act for division of lands and funds of Osage Indians in Oklahoma, report to accompany H. R. 6483 [amending act for division of lands and funds of Osage Indians in Oklahoma, and acts amendatory thereof and supplemental thereto, relative to lands, money, or mineral interests inherited by persons not Osage Indians by blood]; submitted by Mr. Howard of Oklahoma. Feb. 28, 1924. 2 p. (H. rp. 243, 68th Cong. 1st sess.) * Paper, 5c.

—— Division of lands and funds of Osage Indians in Oklahoma, report to accompany H. R. 6483 [amending act for division of lands and funds of Osage : Indians in Oklahoma, and acts amendatory thereof and supplemental thereto, relative to lands, money, or mineral interests inherited by persons not Osage Indians by blood]; submitted by Mr. Howard of Oklahoma. Feb. 7, 1924. 1 p. (H. rp. 165, 68th Cong. 1st sess.) * Paper, 5c.

—— Modifying Osage fund restrictions, hearings on H. R. 5726, Jan. 25–Feb. 7, 1924. 1924. [1]+329 p. (Serial 1.) * Paper, 30c.

Paiute Indians. Reservation of lands in Utah for Paiute Indians, report to accompany H. R. 2884; submitted by Mr. Snyder. Feb. 7, 1924. 2 p. (H. rp. 163, 68th Cong. 1st sess.) * Paper, 5c.

Rapid City Indian School. Sale of certain lands of Rapid City Indian School [S. Dak.], report to accompany H. R. 2812; submitted by Mr. Johnson of South Dakota. Feb. 19, 1924. 2 p. (H. rp. 213, 68th Cong. 1st sess.) * Paper, 5c.

Seminole Indians. Claims which Seminole Indians may have against United States, report to accompany H. R. 5799 [conferring jurisdiction upon Court of Claims to hear, examine, adjudicate, and enter judgment in any claims which Seminole Indians may have against United States]; submitted by Mr. Hastings. Jan. 31, 1924. 1 p. (H. rp. 134, 68th Cong. 1st sess.) * Paper, 5c.

Seupelt, J. G. J. G. Seupelt, report to accompany H. R. 5525 [for relief of J. G. Seupelt]; submitted by Mr. Snyder. Feb. 21, 1924. 2 p. (H. rp. 219, 68th Cong. 1st sess.) *Paper, 5c.

Ute Indians. Reservation of land in Utah as school site for Ute Indians, report to accompany H. R. 2882; submitted by Mr. Snyder. Feb. 7, 1924. 2 p. (H. rp. 162, 68th Cong. 1st sess.) *Paper, 5c.

Yuma Reservation. Allotment of certain lands within Fort Yuma Indian Reservation, Calif., report to accompany H. R. 4804; submitted by Mr. Hayden. Jan. 31, 1924. 1 p. (H. rp. 136, 68th Cong. 1st sess.) *Paper, 5c.

INSULAR AFFAIRS COMMITTEE

Porto Rico. Extension of provisions of certain [Federal aid] laws to Porto Rico, hearing on H. R. 6294, Jan. 31, 1924. 1924. [1]+29 p. *Paper, 5c.

—— Purchase ground and erect and repair Government buildings in Porto Rico, hearing on H. R. 6143, Jan. 31, 1924. 1924. [1]+7 p. *Paper, 5c.

—— Site for customhouse in Porto Rico, report to accompany H. R. 6143 [to purchase grounds, erect, and repair buildings for customhouses, offices, and warehouses in Porto Rico]; submitted by Mr. Fairfield. Feb. 20, 1924. 2 p. (H. rp. 216, 68th Cong. 1st sess.) *Paper, 5c.

INTERSTATE AND FOREIGN COMMERCE COMMITTEE

Apalachicola River–St. Andrews Bay Canal. Bridge across canal connecting Apalachicola River and St. Andrews Bay, Fla., report to accompany S. 2014 [to authorize Park-Wood Lumber Company to construct 2 bridges across canal which connects Apalachicola River and St. Andrews Bay, Fla.]; submitted by Mr. Huddleston. Feb. 13, 1924. 1 p. (H. rp. 191, 68th Cong. 1st sess.) .*Paper, 5c.

Byram River. Dam across Byram River, report to accompany H. R. 6943 [granting consent of Congress to Port Chester, N. Y., and town of Greenwich, Conn., or either of them, to construct dam across Byram River]; submitted by Mr. Merritt. Feb. 28, 1924. 1 p. (H. rp. 240, 68th Cong. 1st sess.) *Paper, 5c.

Calumet River. Bridge across Calumet River at Chicago, Ill., report to accompany H. R. 6925 [granting consent of Congress to Chicago to construct bridge across Calumet River at or near 130th street in Chicago, county of Cook, Ill.]; submitted by Mr. Denison. Feb. 13, 1924. 2 p. (H. rp. 190, 68th Cong. 1st sess.) *Paper, 5c.

Cape Cod Canal. Purchase of Cape Cod Canal property, report to accompany H. R. 3933; submitted by Mr. Winslow. Feb. 11, 1924. 23 p. (H. rp. 181, 68th Cong. 1st sess.) [Includes views of Mr. Huddleston.] *Paper, 5c.

Coast Guard. Temporary increase of Coast Guard for law enforcement, report to accompany H. R. 6815; submitted by Mr. Winslow. Feb. 25, 1924. 3 p. (H. rp. 228, 68th Cong. 1st sess.) *Paper, 5c.

Coast Guard cutters. vessel for Coast Guard duty in Alaska, report to accompany H. R. 6817; submitted by Mr. Winslow. Feb. 20, 1924. 1 p. (H. rp. 215, 68th Cong. 1st sess.) *Paper, 5c.

Foreign Commerce Service. To establish in Bureau of Foreign and Domestic Commerce a Foreign Commerce Service, report to accompany H. R. 7034; submitted by Mr. Winslow. Feb. 20, 1924. 4 p. (H. rp. 214, 68th Cong. 1st sess.) [Corrected print.] *Paper, 5c. 24—26178

Fox River. Bridge across Fox River, ., report to accompany S. 1539 [extending time for construction of bridge across Fox River by Aurora, Ill., and granting consent of Congress to removal of existing dam and to its replacement with new structure]; submitted by Mr. Graham of Illinois. Feb. 2, 1924. 1 p. (H. rp. 141, 68th Cong. 1st sess.) *Paper, 5c.

—— To permit Aurora, Ill., to operate bridges across Fox River, report to accompany S. 1540 [granting consent of Congress to Aurora, Kane County, Ill., to construct bridges across Fox River]; submitted by Mr. Graham of Illinois. Feb. 2, 1924. 1 p. (H. rp. 142, 68th Cong. 1st sess.) * Paper, 5c.

Kankakee River. Bridge across Kankakee River between Illinois and Indiana, report to accompany H. R. 5737 [granting consent of Congress to county of Kankakee, Ill., and counties of Lake and Newton, Ind., to construct bridge across Kankakee River at or near State line between section 19, township 31 north, range 15 east of 3d principal meridian, in county of Kankakee, Ill., and section 1, township 31 north, range 10 west of 2d principal meridian, in counties of Lake and Newton, Ind.]; submitted by Mr. Denison. Feb. 8, 1924. 2 p. (H. rp. 171, 68th Cong. 1st sess.) * Paper, 5c.

Mississippi River. Bridge across Mississippi River between Minneapolis and St. Paul, Minn., report to accompany H. R. 6420 [to extend time for construction of bridge across Mississippi River in section 17, township 28 north, range 23 west of 4th principal meridian in Minnesota by Minneapolis and St. Paul, Minn., or either of them]; submitted by Mr. Newton of Minnesota. Feb. 8, 1924. 1 p. (H. rp. 172, 68th Cong. 1st sess.) * Paper, 5c.

Pearl River. Bridge across Pearl River, Miss., report to accompany H. R. 5633 [granting consent of Congress to board of supervisors of Hinds County, Miss., to construct bridge across Pearl River, Miss., at or near Jackson]; submitted by Mr. Rayburn. Feb. 8, 1924. 1 p. (H. rp. 169, 68th Cong. 1st sess.) * Paper, 5c.

Peedee River. Bridge across Peedee River between Anson and Richmond counties, N. C., report to accompany H. R. 6717 [granting consent of Congress to Highway Department of North Carolina to construct bridge across Peedee River, N. C., between Anson and Richmond counties, at or near Pee Dee]; submitted by Mr. Wyant. Feb. 9, 1924. 2 p. (H. rp. 177, 68th Cong. 1st sess.) * Paper, 5c.

St. Marys River. Bridge across St. Marys River near Wilds Landing, Fla., report to accompany H. R. 6725 [granting consent of Congress to Georgia and Florida, through their respective highway departments, to construct bridge across St. Marys River at or near Wilds Landing, Fla.]; submitted by Mr. Huddleston. Feb. 11, 1924. 2 p. (H. rp. 180, 68th Cong. 1st sess.) * Paper, 5c.

Securities. To prevent use of mails and other agencies of interstate commerce for transporting and for promoting or procuring sale of securities contrary to laws of States, report to accompany H. R. 4; submitted by Mr. Denison. Jan. 31, 1924. 23 p. (H. rp. 132, 68th Cong. 1st sess.) * Paper, 5c.

24—26121

Susquehanna River. Bridge across Susquehanna River near Clarks Ferry, Pa., report to accompany H. R. 6487 [granting consent of Congress to Clarks Ferry Bridge Company to construct bridge across Susquehanna River at or near railroad station of Clarks Ferry, Pa.]; submitted by M. Wyant. Feb. 15, 1924. 2 p. (H. rp. 208, 68th Cong. 1st sess.) * Paper, 5c.

Tennessee River. Bridge across Tennessee River at Knoxville, Tenn., report to accompany H. R. 5727 [to grant consent of Congress to Southern Railway Company to maintain bridge across Tennessee River at Knoxville, in county of Knox, Tenn.]; submitted by Mr. Barkley. Feb. 8, 1924. 1 p. (H. rp. 170, 68th Cong. 1st sess.) * Paper, 5c.

Tug Fork. Bridge across Tug Fork of Big Sandy River between West Virginia and Kentucky, report to accompany H. R. 5218 [granting consent of Congress to Pittsburgh Coal, Land and Railroad Company to construct bridge across Tug Fork of Big Sandy River at or near Nolan, in Mingo County, W. Va., to Kentucky side, in Pike County, Ky.]; submitted by Mr. Barkley. Feb. 1, 1924. 2 p. (H. rp. 137, 68th Cong. 1st sess.) * Paper, 5c.

—— Bridge across Tug Fork of Big Sandy River near Williamson, W. Va., report to accompany H. R. 5219 [to authorize Norfolk and Western Railway Company to construct bridge across Tug Fork of Big Sandy River at or near point about mile and a half west of Williamson, Mingo County, W. Va., and near mouth of Turkey Creek, Pike County, Ky.]; submitted by Mr. Barkley. Feb. 1, 1924. 2 p. (H. rp. 138, 68th Cong. 1st sess.) * Paper, 5c.

White River. Bridge across White River near Batesville, Ark., report to accompany S. 625 [to extend time for construction of bridge across White River at or near Batesville, Ark., by Independence County]; submitted by Mr. Parks of Arkansas. Feb. 13. 1924. 1 p. (H. rp. 189, 68th Cong. 1st sess.) * Paper, 5c.

INVALID PENSIONS COMMITTEE

Pensions and increase of pensions to certain soldiers and sailors of Civil War, etc., report to accompany H. R. 6941 [substituted for H. R. 768 and other bills]; submitted by Mr. Fuller. Feb. 13, 1924. 421 p. (H. rp. 188, 68th Cong. 1st sess.) * Paper, 35c.

JUDICIARY COMMITTEE

American Bar Association. Incorporation of American Bar Association, hearing on H. R. 513, Jan. 23, 1924. 1924. ii+8 p. (Serial 6.) * Paper, 5c.

Calendar. Legislative calendar, 68th Congress, Feb. 4 and 18, 1924; no. 5 and 6. 1924. 48 p. and 51 p. 4° ‡

Circuit Courts of Appeals. Court of appeals for 1st circuit to hold sittings at San Juan, P. R., report to accompany H. R. 704; submitted by Mr. Graham [of Pennsylvania]. Feb. 5, 1924. 4 p. (H. rp. 155, 68th Cong. 1st sess.) * Paper, 5c.

Commerce. To amend China trade act of 1922 and revenue act of 1921, hearing on H. J. Res. 149, Jan. 30 and 31, 1924. 1924. ii+34 p. (Serial 8.) * Paper, 5c.

Constitution of United States. Proposal and ratification of amendments to Constitution of United States, hearing on H. J. Res. 68, Jan. 24, 1924; statement of Finis J. Garrett. 1924. ii+16 p. (Serial 5.) * Paper, 5c.

District Courts. Southern judicial district of Texas, report to accompany H. R. 5549 [to detach Jim Hogg County from Corpus Christi division of southern judicial district of Texas, and attach same to Laredo division of southern judicial district of said State]; submitted by Mr. Sumners of Texas. Feb. 14, 1924. 1 p. (H. rp. 192, 68th Cong. 1st sess.) * Paper, 5c.

Judges. Additional judge for district of Maryland, hearing on H. R. 5083, Jan. 30, 1924. 1924. ii+28 p. (Serial 7.) * Paper, 5c.

—— Additional judges for southern district of New York, hearings on H. R. 3318, Feb. 13, 1924. 1924. ii+19 p. (Serial 9.) * Paper, 5c.

—— Two additional judges for southern district of New York, report to accompany H. R. 3318; submitted by Mr. Perlman. Feb. 26, 1924. 4 p. (H. rp. 234, 68th Cong. 1st sess.) * Paper, 5c.

Jury. Fees of jurors and witnesses, hearing on H. R. 2860, H. R. 2909, and H. R. 6578, Jan. 22 and 29, 1924. 1924. ii+18 p. (Serial 3.) * Paper, 5c.

Probation system. Establishment of probation system in United States courts, hearing on H. R. 5195, H. R. 137, and H. R. 138, Feb. 21, 1924. 1924. ii+ 29 p. (Serial 10.) * Paper, 5c.

LABOR COMMITTEE

Convict labor in United States, report to accompany H. Res. 176 [directing Secretary of Labor to make report on subject of convict labor in United States]; submitted by Mr. Zihlman. Feb. 19, 1924. 1 p. (H. rp. 210, 68th Cong. 1st sess.) * Paper, 5c.

LIBRARY COMMITTEE

District of Columbia. Statue of " Serenity," report to accompany S. J. Res. 57 [authorizing erection on public grounds in District of Columbia of statue by Jose Clara personifying " Serenity "]; submitted by Mr. Luce. Feb. 14, 1924. 1 p. (H. rp. 207, 68th Cong. 1st sess.) * Paper, 5c.

MERCHANT MARINE AND FISHERIES COMMITTEE

Alaska. Fisheries of Alaska, hearings on H. R. 2714, Jan. 31–Feb. 8, 1924. 1924. ii+346 p. * Paper, 35c.

Ships. Conversion of ships, report to accompany H. R. 6202 [to amend sec. 11 and 12 of merchant marine act, 1920, so as to permit use of certain funds of Shipping Board for conversion of ships into motor ships]; submitted by Mr. Greene of Massachusetts. Feb. 5, 1924. 4 p. (H. rp. 151, 68th Cong. 1st sess.) * Paper, 5c.

MILITARY AFFAIRS COMMITTEE

Jackson, Camp. Transfer of lands at Camp Jackson, S. C., report to accompany H. R. 490 [to transfer to trustees to be named by Chamber of Commerce of Columbia, S. C., lands at Camp Jackson, S. C.]; submitted by Mr. McSwain. Feb. 28, 1924. 3 p. (H. rp. 238, 68th Cong. 1st sess.) * Paper, 5c.

Lagrange, Ga. Sufferers from cyclone at La Grange and West Point, Ga., report to accompany H. J. Res. 115 [approving action of Secretary of War in directing issuance of quartermaster stores for relief of sufferers from cyclone at Lagrange and West Point, Ga., and vicinity, Mar. 1920]; submitted by Mr. Wright. Feb. 8, 1924. 2 p. (H. rp. 173, 68th Cong. 1st sess.) * Paper, 5c.

Medals to 2 Texas cavalry brigades, report to accompany H. R. 593 [authorizing issuance of service medals to officers and enlisted men of 2 brigades of Texas cavalry organized under authority from War Department under date of Dec. 8, 1917, and authorizing appropriation therefor, and further authorizing wearing by such officers and enlisted men on occasions of ceremony of uniform lawfully prescribed to be worn by them during their service]; submitted by Mr. Wurzbach. Feb. 20, 1924. 4 p. (H. rp. 217, 68th Cong. 1st sess.) * Paper, 5c.

Moriarty, Ambrose I. Ambrose I. Moriarty, report to accompany H. R. 5465 [for advancement on retired list of Regular Army of Ambrose I. Moriarty]; submitted by Mr. Hill of Maryland. Feb. 27, 1924. 4 p. (H. rp. 237, 68th Cong. 1st sess.) * Paper, 5c.

Muscle Shoals. Muscle Shoals, minority views to accompany H. R. 518 [to authorize and direct Secretary of War, for national defense in time of war and for production of fertilizers and other useful products in time of peace, to sell to Henry Ford, or corporation to be incorporated by him, nitrate plant numbered 1, at Sheffield, Ala., nitrate plant numbered 2, at Muscle Shoals, Ala., Waco Quarry, near Russellville, Ala., steam power plant to be located and constructed at or near lock and dam numbered 17 on Black Warrior River, Ala., with right of way and transmission line to nitrate plant numbered 2, Muscle Shoals, Ala., and to lease to Henry Ford, or corporation to be incorporated by him, dam numbered 2 and dam numbered 3 (as designated in House document 1262, 64th Congress, 1st session), including power stations when constructed as provided herein]; submitted by Mr. Hull of Iowa. Feb. 9, 1924. 27 p. (H. rp. 143, pt. 2, 68th Cong. 1st sess.) * Paper, 5c.

*Muscle Shoals—*Continued. Muscle Shoals, report to accompany H. R. 518 [to authorize and direct Secretary of War, for national defense in time of war and for production of fertilizers and other useful products in time of peace, to sell to Henry Ford, or corporation to be incorporated by him, nitrate plant numbered 1, at Sheffield, Ala., nitrate plant numbered 2, at Muscle Shoals, Ala., Waco Quarry, near Russellville, Ala., steam power plant to be located and constructed at or near lock and dam numbered 17 on Black Warrior River, Ala., with right of way and transmission line to nitrate plant numbered 2, Muscle Shoals, Ala., and to lease to Henry Ford, or corporation to be incorporated by him, dam numbered 2 and dam numbered 3 (as designated in House document 1262, 64th Congress, 1st session), including power stations when constructed as provided herein]; submitted by Mr. McKenzie. Feb. 2, 1924. 62 p. (H. rp. 143 [pt. 1], 68th Cong. 1st sess.) * Paper, 10c. 24—26122

—— Muscle Shoals propositions, hearings, Jan. 29, 1924; statement of Elon H. Hooker, representing United States Muscle Shoals Power & Nitrates Corporation. 1924. 16 p. * Paper, 5c.

National Home for Disabled Volunteer Soldiers. Appointment of [John J. Steadman as] member of board of managers of National Home for Disabled Volunteer Soldiers, report to accompany H. J. Res. 97; submitted by Mr. Sherwood. Feb. 7, 1924. 1 p. (H. rp. 168, 68th Cong. 1st sess.) * Paper, 5c.

Pay, Army. Readjust pay and allowances of commissioned and enlisted personnel of Army, Navy, Marine Corps, etc., report to accompany H. R. 4820 [to amend act to readjust pay and allowances of commissioned and enlisted personnel of Army, Navy, Marine Corps, Coast Guard, Coast and Geodetic Survey, and Public Health Service]; submitted by Mr. McKenzie. Feb. 27, 1924. 4 p. (H. rp. 236, 68th Cong. 1st sess.) * Paper, 5c.

William and Mary College. To loan College of William and Mary in Virginia 2 of cannon surrendered by British at Yorktown on Oct. 19, 1781, report to accompany H. R. 1831; submitted by Mr. Hill of Maryland. Feb. 14, 1924. 3 p. (H. rp. 194, 68th Cong. 1st sess.) * Paper, 5c.

MINES AND MINING COMMITTEE

Mineral lands. Suspension of annual assessment work on certain mining claims, hearing on H. J. Res. 142, to suspend requirements of annual assessment work on certain mining claims for period of 3 years, Feb. 5, 1924. 1924. [1]+25 p. * Paper, 5c.

NAVAL AFFAIRS COMMITTEE

Albany Institute and Historical and Art Society. Disposition of silver service which was presented to cruiser Albany, report to accompany H. R. 1018 [authorizing Secretary of Navy to deliver to custody of Albany Institute and Historical and Art Society of Albany, N. Y., silver service which was presented to cruiser Albany by citizens of Albany, N. Y.]; submitted by Mr. Logan. Feb. 2, 1924. 1 p. (H. rp. 150, 68th Cong. 1st sess.) * Paper, 5c.

Calendar. Legislative calendar, 68th Congress, 1923–24; no. 1, Feb. 12, 1924. 1924. 28 p. 4° ‡

PENSIONS COMMITTEE

McAndrew, Mrs. Nellie R. Nellie Roche McAndrew, report to accompany H. R. 2574 [granting pension to Nellie Roche McAndrew]; submitted by Mr. Knutson. Feb. 7, 1924. 5 p. (H. rp. 159, 68th Cong. 1st sess.) * Paper, 5c.

Pensions. Spanish War pension bill, report to accompany H. R. 5934 [to pension soldiers and sailors of War with Spain, Philippine insurrection, or China Relief Expedition]; submitted by Mr. Robsion of Kentucky. Feb. 26, 1924. 3 p. (H. rp. 233, 68th Cong. 1st sess.) * Paper, 5c.

POST OFFICE AND POST ROADS COMMITTEE

Mail delivery. Establishing length of rural postal routes, report to accompany H. R. 4448 [authorizing establishment of rural routes of from 36 to 75 miles in length]; submitted by Mr. Moore of Ohio. Feb. 12, 1924. 2 p. (H. rp. 186, 68th Cong. 1st sess.) * Paper, 5c.

Money-orders. Quarterly money-order account to be rendered by district postmasters, report to accompany H. R. 4441 [to provide for quarterly instead of monthly money-order accounts to be rendered by district postmasters at 3d and 4th class post offices]; submitted by Mr. Kendall. Feb. 12, 1924. 2 p. (H. rp. 187, 68th Cong. 1st sess.) * Paper, 5c.

Postal service. Mail messenger service, report to accompany H. R. 6482 [authorizing Postmaster General to contract for mail messenger service]; submitted by Mr. Sproul of Illinois. Feb. 19, 1924. 2 p. (H. rp. 212, 68th Cong. 1st sess.) * Paper, 5c.

Registered mail matter, report to accompany H. R. 6352 [to authorize Postmaster General to fix fees chargeable for registration of mail matter, and for other purposes]; submitted by Mr. Kelly. Feb. 26, 1924. 2 p. (H. rp. 232, 68th Cong. 1st sess.) * Paper, 5c.

Wilson, Mrs. Edith B. Granting franking privilege to Edith Bolling Wilson, report to accompany H. R. 6750; submitted by Mr. Griest. Feb. 12, 1924. 1 p. (H. rp. 184, 68th Cong. 1st sess.) * Paper, 5c.

PRINTING COMMITTEE

Government publications. To amend sec. 72 of chapter 23 of printing act of Jan. 12, 1895 [relative to disposal of Congressional allotment of public documents at close of term]; submitted by Mr. Kiess. Feb. 20, 1924. 1 p. (H. rp. 218, 68th Cong. 1st sess.) * Paper, 5c.

Rivers. Amending sec. 6 of river and harbor act of 1920, report to accompany H. R. 695 [to amend sec. 6 of act making appropriations for construction, repair, and preservation of certain public works on rivers and harbors, approved June 5, 1920, providing for printing of laws relating to improvement of rivers and harbors, so as to include laws of 67th Congress]; submitted by Mr. Kiess. Feb. 28, 1924. 1 p. (H. rp. 239, 68th Cong. 1st sess.) * Paper, 5c.

PUBLIC BUILDINGS AND GROUNDS COMMITTEE

Centerville, Iowa. Correction of title to certain lands adjacent to and including portion of Federal building site, Centerville, Iowa, report to accompany H. R. 6895; submitted by Mr. Langley. Feb. 28, 1924. 2 p. (H. rp. 246, 68th Cong. 1st sess.) * Paper, 5c.

Cincinnati, Ohio. Cleaning of exterior of post-office building, Cincinnati, Ohio, report to accompany H. R. 4200; submitted by Mr. Langley. Feb. 28, 1924. 1 p. (H. rp. 247, 68th Cong. 1st sess.) * Paper, 5c.

Donora, Pa. Post-office site, Donora, Pa., report to accompany H. R. 5352 [to accept title to site for post office at Donora, Pa., which excepts and reserves natural gas and oil underlying land]; submitted by Mr. Langley. Feb. 25, 1924. 1 p. (H. rp. 230, 68th Cong. 1st sess.) * Paper, 5c.

Hospitals. Public buildings and grounds, hearings on H. R. 2821, hospital, Santa Monica, Calif., H. R. 5209, additional hospital facilities, Battle Mountain Sanitarium, Custer [Hot Springs], S. Dak., hospital, Portland, Oreg., Jan. 18–25, 1924. 1924. ii+120 p. 2 pl. 2 tab. (No. 2.) * Paper, 20c.

Kenosha, Wis. Public buildings and grounds, hearings on H. Res. 51, post-office site, Kenosha, Wis., Jan. 11, 1924. 1924. ii+4 p. (No. 1.) * Paper, 5c.

Lincoln, Abraham. Public buildings and grounds, hearing on H. R. 5728, Oldroyd collection of Lincoln relics, Jan. 25, 1924. 1924. ii+4 p. (No. 4.) * Paper, 5c.

National Botanic Gardens. Public buildings and grounds, hearing on H. R. 46, additional land, Botanic Garden, S. 211, conservatory and other necessary buildings, Botanic Garden, Jan. 26[29], 1924. 1924. ii+18 p. (No. 5.) * Paper, 5c.

Osborne, Kans. Public buildings and grounds, hearings on H. R. 5483, public building, Osborne, Kans., Jan. 22, 1924. 1924. ii+4 p. (No. 3.) * Paper, 5c.

Philadelphia, Pa. Widen Haines street in front of national cemetery, Philadelphia, Pa., report to accompany H. R. 4981; submitted by Mr. Langley. Feb. 25, 1924. 2 p. (H. rp. 229, 68th Cong. 1st sess.) * Paper, 5c.

Washington, Mo. Conveyance of portion of Federal building site to Washington, Mo., report to accompany H. R. 6059; submitted by Mr. Langley. Feb. 28, 1924. 2 p. (H. rp. 245, 68th Cong. 1st sess.) * Paper, 5c.

Calendar. Legislative calendar, 68th Congress, Feb. 5, 1924; no. 3. 1924. 32 p. 4° ‡

Crook National Forest. Recreational area within Crook National Forest, Ariz., report to accompany H. R. 498; submitted by Mr. Morrow. Feb. 7, 1924. 2 p. (H. rp. 160, 68th Cong. 1st sess.) * Paper, 5c.

National forests. Limiting creation or extension of forest reserves in New Mexico and Arizona, report to accompany S. 377; submitted by Mr. Morrow. Feb. 7, 1924. 2 p. (H. rp. 166, 68th Cong. 1st sess.) * Paper, 5c.

Western State College of Colorado. Granting 160 acres of land to Western State College of Colorado, Gunnison, Colo., for use of Rocky Mountain Biological Station of said college, report to accompany H. R. 3104; submitted by Mr. Evans of Montana. Feb. 7, 1924. 4 p. (H. rp. 167, 68th Cong. 1st sess.) * Paper, 5c.

Water pollution. Pollution of navigable waters, hearings on subject of pollution of navigable waters. Jan. 23–30, 1924. 1924. v+300 p. * Paper, 30c.

Air Service. Appointment of special committee to inquire into Army Air Service, Naval Bureau of Aeronautics, and Mail Air Service, report to accompany H. Res. 192; submitted by Mr. Snell. Feb. 28, 1924. 1 p. (H. rp. 241, 68th Cong. 1st sess.) * Paper, 5c.

—— Investigation of Air Service, hearings, Feb. 16 and 20, 1924. 1924. ii+28 p. * Paper, 5c.

House of Representatives. Rules of 68th Congress, report to accompany H. Res. 146 [amending rules of House of Representatives]; submitted by Mr. Snell. Jan. 14, 1924. 3 p. (H. rp. 49, 68th Cong. 1st sess.) . * Paper, 5c.

Securities. Consideration of House joint resolution 136, report to accompany H. Res. 173 [for consideration of H. J. Res. 136, proposing amendment to Constitution relative to taxation of income from securities issued by or under authority of United States or any State]; submitted by Mr. Snell. Feb. 5, 1924. 1 p. (H. rp. 158, 68th Cong. 1st sess.) * Paper, 5c.

Shipping Board. Operations and policies of Shipping Board, etc., report to accompany H. Res. 186 [directing Speaker of House to appoint select committee to inquire into operations, policies, and affairs of Shipping Board and Shipping Board Emergency Fleet Corporation]; submitted by Mr. Snell. Feb. 22, 1924. 1 p. (H. rp. 221, 68th Cong. 1st sess.) * Paper, 5c.

Amusements. Tax on admissions; statement of Joseph R. Denniston, Jan. 15, 1924. 1924. [2]+9 p. * Paper, 5c.

Internal revenue. Comparison of revenue acts of 1918 and 1921, with index; by Clayton F. Moore. Revised edition. 1924. v+240 p. * Paper, 30c.
24—26204

—— Revenue act of 1924. Feb. 7, 1924. 242 p. large 8° (Committee print no. 3.) * Paper, 20c.
24—26111

—— Revenue bill of 1924, report to accompany H. R. 6715; submitted by Mr. Green of Iowa. Feb. 11, 1924. 87 p. 1 tab. (H. rp. 179, 68th Cong. 1st sess.) [Includes views signed by Mr. Hawley and others, views of Mr. Frear. and minority views signed by Mr. Garner and others.] * Paper, 10c. 24—26152

—— Revenue revision, 1924, hearings. 1924. [2]+528 p. * Paper, 45c.

Report. Postal service, report relative to methods and systems of handling, dispatching, transporting, and delivering mails; presented by Mr. Sterling. 1924. ii+41 p. (S. doc. 36, 68th Cong. 1st sess.) [Previous report on this subject published as Senate document 306, 67th Congress, 4th session.] * Paper, 5c.
24—26123

PUBLIC BUILDINGS COMMISSION

Appropriation for legislative establishment, Public Buildings Commission, supplemental estimate of appropriation for legislative establishment, Public Buildings Commission, fiscal year 1924. Feb. 7, 1924. 2 p. (H. doc. 188, 68th Cong. 1st sess.) * Paper, 5c.

REORGANIZATION JOINT COMMITTEE

Executive Departments. Reorganization of Executive Departments, hearings on S. J. Res. 282, 67th Congress, to amend joint resolution to create Joint Committee on Reorganization of Administrative Branch of Government, Jan. 7 [-31], 1924. 1924. pts. 1-3, [vi]+1-765 p. il. 1 tab. * Paper, pt. 1, 20c; * pts. 2 and 3, each 30c.

SENATE

American prosperity and peace, address of Medill McCormick, Chicago, Jan. 28, 1924; presented by Mr. McKinley. 1924. 8 p. (S. doc. 51, 68th Cong. 1st sess.) * Paper, 5c.   24—26182

Calendar of business, Senate, 68th Congress, 1st session, Feb. 1-29, 1924; no. 26–46. [1924.] various paging, large 8° [Daily when Senate is in session.] ‡

Democracy. Discontent with democracy, address by Nicholas Murray Butler before midwinter meeting of Republican State Editorial Association at Indianapolis, Ind., Feb. 8, 1924; presented by Mr. Lodge. 1924. [1]+10 p. (S. doc. 55, 68th Cong. 1st sess.) * Paper, 5c.   24—26205

District of Columbia. Public utilities companies, annual reports of. public utility companies of District of Columbia, year ending Dec. 31, 1923. 1924. iii+67 p. (S. doc. 30, 68th Cong. 1st sess.) * Paper, 10c.   14—30633

European War, 1914–18. Secret history of a great betrayal, by E. D. Morel, with preface by Raymond Beazley; presented by Mr. Owen. 1924. vi+34 p. (S. doc. 40, 68th Cong. 1st sess.) * Paper, 5c.   24—26179

Stationery for Senators, committees, and officers of Senate, supplemental estimate of appropriation for legislative establishment, fiscal year 1924. Feb. 23, 1924. 2 p. (H. doc. 205, 68th Cong. 1st sess.) * Paper, 5c.

AGRICULTURE AND FORESTRY COMMITTEE

Agricultural credit. Emergency commission to promote permanent system of self-supporting agriculture, hearings on S. 1597, for emergency commission to promote permanent system of self-supporting agriculture in regions adversely affected by stimulation of wheat production during the war, and aggravated by many years of small yields and high production costs of wheat, Jan. 11–24, 1924. 1924. ii+206 p. il. * Paper, 20c.

—— Federal livestock loans, report to accompany S. 2250 [to promote permanent system of self-supporting agriculture in regions adversely affected by stimulation of wheat production during the war, and aggravated by many years of small yields and high production costs of wheat]; submitted by Mr. Ladd. Feb. 1, 1924. 2 p. (S. rp. 124, 68th Cong. 1st sess.) * Paper, 5c.

Calendar. Legislative calendar, 68th Congress, Feb, 9-19, 1924; no. 1-3. 1924. Each 15 leaves or 15 p. 4° ‡

Loans. Relief of drought-stricken. farm areas of New Mexico, hearing on S. J. Res. 52, Jan. 21, 1924. 1924. ii+24 p. * Paper, 5c.

Marketing of farm produce. Purchase and sale of farm products, hearings on S. 1642, for purchase and sale of farm products, and S. 2012, declaring emergency in respect of certain agricultural commodities, to promote equality between agricultural commodities and other commodities, and for other purposes, Jan. 7-26, 1924. 1924. pt. 1, ii+1-376 p. * Paper, 30c.

APPROPRIATIONS COMMITTEE

Interior Department. Interior Department appropriation bill, [fiscal year] 1925, hearings before subcommittee on H. R. 5078. 1924. ii+154 p. * Paper, 15c,

—— Interior Department appropriation bill, [fiscal year] 1925, report to accompany H. R. 5078; submitted by Mr. Smoot. Feb. 7, calendar day Feb. 9, 1924. 4 p. (S. rp. 134, 68th Cong. 1st sess.) * Paper, 5c.

Treasury Department. Treasury and Post Office Departments appropriation bill, [fiscal year] 1925, hearings before subcommittee on H. R. 6349. 1924. ii+166 p. * Paper, 15c.

—— Treasury and Post Office Departments appropriation bill, fiscal year 1925, report to accompany H. R. 6349; submitted by Mr. Warren. Feb. 26, 1924. 4 p. (S. rp. 172, 68th Cong. 1st sess.) * Paper, 5c.

BANKING AND CURRENCY COMMITTEE

War Finance Corporation. To extend time (power) of War Finance Corporation, report to accompany S. 2249 [to extend for 9 months power of War Finance Corporation to make advances under provisions of War Finance Corporation act, as amended relative to relief for producers of and dealers in agricultural products, and for other purposes]; submitted by Mr. McLean. Feb. 7, calendar day Feb. 9, 1924. 2 p. (S. rp. 137, 68th Cong. 1st sess.) * Paper, 5c.

CIVIL SERVICE COMMITTEE

Civil service pensions. Retirement of Federal employees, extracts from joint hearings before Committees on Civil Service relative to amendments to act for retirement of employees in classified civil service, Jan. 15, 16, and 23, 1924; statements of Thomas F. Flaherty, Harry C. Weinstock, and Leo E. George. 1924. ii+10 p. *Paper, 5c.

—— Retirement of Federal employees, joint hearings before Committees on Civil Service relative to amendments to act for retirement of employees in classified civil service, Jan. 14–23, 1924. 1924. iv+227 p. 1 tab. [These hearings were held at a joint meeting of the Senate Civil Service Committee and the House Civil Service Committee.] * Paper, 25c.

CLAIMS COMMITTEE

Alaska Commercial Co., report to accompany S. 1021 [for relief of Alaska Commercial Company]; submitted by Mr. Capper. Feb. 1, 1924. 3 p. (S. rp. 122, 68th Cong. 1st sess.) *Paper, 5c.

Alaska Steamship Co., report to accompany S. 732 [for relief of Alaska Steamship Company]; submitted by Mr. Capper. Feb. 16, calendar day Feb. 21, 1924. 4 p. (S. rp. 169, 68th Cong. 1st sess.) *Paper, 5c.

Belding, Paul B. Paul B. Belding, report to accompany S. 611 [for relief of Paul B. Belding]; submitted by Mr. Mayfield. Feb. 1, 1924. 5 p. (S. rp. 119, 68th Cong. 1st sess.) *Paper, 5c.

Commercial Pacific Cable Co., report to accompany S. 709 [for relief of Commercial Pacific Cable Company]; submitted by Mr. Stephens. Feb. 29, 1924. 7 p. (S. rp. 187, 68th Cong. 1st sess.) *Paper, 5c.

Desmare, Alphonse. Estate of Alphonse Desmare, and others, report to accompany S. 2219 [for relief of legal representatives of estate of Alphonse Desmare, and others]; submitted by Mr. Capper. Feb. 29, 1924. 2 p. (S. rp. 184, 68th Cong. 1st sess.) *Paper, 5c.

Disbursing officers. To allow credit to certain disbursing officers, report to accompany S. 1763 [to validate certain payments made to George M. Apple and to authorize General Accounting Office to allow credit to certain disbursing officers for payments of salaries made on properly certified and approved vouchers]; submitted by Mr. Capper. Feb. 13, 1924. 5 p. (S. rp. 144, 68th Cong. 1st sess.) *Paper, 5c.

Eaton, John T. John T. Eaton, report to accompany S. 335 [for relief of John T. Eaton]; submitted by Mr. Capper. Feb. 29, 1924. 2 p. (S. rp. 181, 68th Cong. 1st sess.) *Paper, 5c.

Ewing, William J. William J. Ewing, report to accompany S. 964 [for relief of William J. Ewing]; submitted by Mr. Bayard. Feb. 29, 1924. 5 p. (S. rp. 191, 68th Cong. 1st sess.) *Paper, 5c.

Fletcher, Ed. F. J. Belcher, jr., trustee, report to accompany S. 1014 [for relief of F. J. Belcher, jr., trustee for Ed Fletcher]; submitted by Mr. Capper. Feb. 13, 1924. 9 p. (S. rp. 143, 68th Cong. 1st sess.) *Paper, 5c.

Glisson, Mrs. Janie B. Janie Beasley Glisson, report to accompany S. 648 [for relief of Janie Beasley Glisson]; submitted by Mr. Capper. Feb. 29, 1924. 6 p. (S. rp. 182, 68th Cong. 1st sess.) *Paper, 5c.

Hensley, William. . William Hensley, report to accompany S. 2562 [for relief of William Hensley]; submitted by Mr. Capper. Feb. 29, 1924. 11 p. (S. rp. 186, 68th Cong. 1st sess.) *Paper, 5c.

Jarvis, W. Ernest. W. Ernest Jarvis, report to accompany S. 131 [for relief of W. Ernest Jarvis]; submitted by Mr. Capper. Feb. 29, 1924. 2 p. (S. rp. 180, 68th Cong. 1st sess.) *Paper, 5c.

LaMee, Mrs. Emma. Emma La Mee, report to accompany S. 833 [for relief of Emma LaMee]; submitted by Mr. Capper. Feb. 1, 1924. 10 p. (S. rp. 121, 68th Cong. 1st sess.) *Paper, 5c.

Lapene & Ferré, report to accompany S. 2220 [for relief of Louise St. Gez, executrix of Auguste Ferré, surviving partner of Lapene and Ferré]; submitted by Mr. Capper. Feb. 29, 1924. 2 p. (S. rp. 185, 68th Cong. 1st sess.) *Paper, 5c.

Maron, Frank A. F. A. Maron, report to accompany S. 799 [for relief of F. A. Maron]; submitted by Mr. Brookhart. Feb. 1, 1924. 5 p. (S. rp. 118, 68th Cong. 1st sess.) *Paper, 5c.

Near East Relief, hearing on S. 87, for relief of Near East Relief (Inc.), Jan. 24, 1924. 1924. ii+10 p. * Paper, 5c.

Pacific Commissary Company, report to accompany S. 2357 [for relief of Pacific Commissary Company]; submitted by Mr. Stanfield. Feb. 29, 1924. 8 p. (S. rp. 192, 68th Cong. 1st sess.) * Paper, 5c.

Van Voorhis, David C. David C. Van voorhis, report to accompany S. 2168 [for relief of David C. Van voorhis]; submitted by Mr. Capper. Feb. 29, 1924. 3 p. (S. rp. 183, 68th Cong. 1st sess.) * Paper, 5c.

Walker, Mrs. Ellen B. Ellen B. Walker, report to accompany S. 365 [for relief of Ellen B. Walker]; submitted by Mr. Capper. Feb. 1, 1924. 3 p. (S. rp. 120, 68th Cong. 1st sess.) * Paper, 5c.

COMMERCE COMMITTEE

Apalachicola River–St. Andrews Bay Canal. Bridge across canal which connects Apalachicola River and St. Andrews Bay, Fla., report to accompany S. 2014 [to authorize Park-Wood Lumber Company to construct 2 bridges across canal which connects Apalachicola River and St. Andrews Bay, Fla.]; submitted by Mr. Ladd. Feb. 1, 1924. 1 p. (S. rp. 125, 68th Cong. 1st sess.) * Paper, 5c.

Chattahoochee River. Bridge across Chattahoochee River between Alabama and Georgia, report to accompany H. R. 3198 [to authorize Alabama and Georgia, through their respective highway departments, to construct bridge across Chattahoochee River at or near Eufaula, Ala., connecting Barbour County, Ala.. and Quitman County, Ga.]; submitted by Mr. Ladd. Feb. 7, calendar day Feb. 9, 1924. 2 p. (S. rp. 131, 68th Cong. 1st sess.) * Paper, 5c.

Columbia River. Bridge across Columbia River, report to accompany H. R. 4120 [granting consent of Congress to Greater Wenatchee Irrigation District to construct bridge across Columbia River, Wash.]; submitted by Mr. Ladd. Feb. 16, calendar day Feb. 18, 1924. 2 p. (S. rp. 151, 68th Cong. 1st sess.) * Paper, 5c.

Cumberland River. Bridge across Cumberland River in Montgomery County, Tenn., report to accompany S. 431 [to extend time for construction of bridge across Cumberland River in Montgomery County, Tenn., by said county. within 7 miles of Clarksville]; submitted by Mr. Ladd. Feb. 7, calendar day Feb. 9, 1924. 1 p. (S. rp. 130, 68th Cong. 1st sess.) * Paper, 5c.

Current River. Bridge over Current River, report to accompany H. R. 4984 [to authorize Clay County bridge district, Ark., to construct bridge over Current River near Finley's Ferry, Ark.]; submitted by Mr. Ladd. Feb. 16, calendar day Feb. 18, 1924. 1 p. (S. rp. 154, 68th Cong. 1st sess.) * Paper, 5c.

Kanawha River. Bridges across Great Kanawha River, report to accompany S. 1614 [to repeal act authorizing construction of bridges across Great Kanawha River]; submitted by Mr. Ladd. Feb. 7, calendar day Feb. 9, 1924. 2 p. (S. rp. 133, 68th Cong. 1st sess.) * Paper, 5c.

Little Calumet River. Bridge across [Little] Calumet River, report to accompany H. R. 3845 [to authorize construction of bridge across Little Calumet River at Riverdale, Ill., by Acme Steel Goods Company]; submitted by Mr. Ladd. Feb. 16, calendar day Feb. 18, 1924. 1 p. (S. rp. 150, 68th Cong. 1st sess.) * Paper, 5c.

Mill Cut. Survey of Mill Cut and Clubfoot Creek, N. C., report to accompany H. R. 4577 [for examination and survey of Mill Cut and Clubfoot Creek, N. C.]; submitted by Mr. Simmons. Feb. 29, 1924. 1 p. (S. rp. 189, 68th Cong. 1st sess.) * Paper, 5c.

Mississippi River. Bridge across Mississippi River connecting county of Whiteside, Ill., and county of Clinton, Iowa, report to accompany H. R. 4817 [granting consent of Congress to Illinois and Iowa, or either of them, to construct bridge across Mississippi River connecting county of Whiteside, Ill., and county of Clinton, Iowa]; submitted by Mr. Ladd. Feb. 7, calendar day Feb. 9, 1924. 2 p. (S. rp. 132, 68th Cong. 1st sess.) * Paper, 5c.

Missouri River. Bridge across Missouri River, report to accompany S. 2420 [granting consent of Congress to South Dakota for construction of bridge across Missouri River between Potter County and Dewey County, S. Dak.]; submitted by Mr. Ladd. Feb. 16, calendar day Feb. 20, 1924. 2 p. (S. rp. 164, 68th Cong. 1st sess.) * Paper, 5c.

—— Bridge across Missouri River, S. Dak., report to accompany S. 2332 [granting consent of Congress to South Dakota for construction of bridge across Missouri River between Hughes County and Stanley County, S. Dak.]; submitted by Mr. Ladd. Feb. 16, calendar day Feb. 18, 1924. 2 p. (S. rp. 158, 68th Cong. 1st sess.) * Paper, 5c.

Ohio River. Bridge across Ohio River, report to accompany H. R. 5624 [authorizing construction of bridge across Ohio River to connect Benwood, W. Va., and Bellaire, Ohio, by Interstate Bridge Company]; submitted by Mr. Ladd. Feb. 16, calendar day Feb. 18, 1924. 2 p. (S. rp. 157, 68th Cong. 1st sess.) * Paper, 5c.

Pearl River. Bridge across Pearl River, report to accompany H. R. 4808 [granting consent of Congress to construction of bridge across Pearl River between St. Tammany Parish, La., and Hancock County, Miss., by Highway Commission of Louisiana in cooperation with Mississippi or Hancock County]; submitted by Mr. Sheppard. Feb. 28, 1924. 2 p. (S. rp. 175, 68th Cong. 1st sess.) * Paper, 5c.

—— Bridge across Pearl River, report to accompany S. 2436 [granting consent of Congress to board of supervisors of Leake County, Miss., to construct bridge across Pearl River, Miss., at or near Grigsbys Ferry]; submitted by Mr. Ladd. Feb. 16, calendar day Feb. 20, 1924. 2 p. (S. rp. 165, 68th Cong. 1st sess.) * Paper, 5c.

—— Bridge across Pearl River, report to accompany S. 2437 [granting consent of Congress to board of supervisors of Leake County, Miss., to construct bridge across Pearl River, Miss., at or near Battle Bluff Crossing]; submitted by Mr. Ladd. Feb. 16, calendar day Feb. 20, 1924. 2 p. (S. rp. 166, 68th Cong. 1st sess.) * Paper, 5c.

Peedee River. Bridge across Peedee River, N. C., report to accompany S. 2189 [to authorize building of bridge across Peedee River, N. C., between Anson and Richmond counties, near Pee Dee, by Highway Commission of North Carolina]; submitted by Mr. Sheppard. Feb. 7, calendar day Feb. 9, 1924. 2 p. (S. rp. 136, 68th Cong. 1st sess.) * Paper, 5c.

Pere Marquette Lake. Bridge across Pere Marquette River [Lake], report to accompany H. R. 4182 [authorizing Ludington, Mason County, Mich., to construct bridge across arm of Pere Marquette Lake]; submitted by Mr. Ladd. Feb. 16, calendar day Feb. 18, 1924. 2 p. (S. rp. 152, 68th Cong. 1st sess.) * Paper, 5c.

Pribilof Islands, hearing before subcommittee on S. 2122, to create Pribilof Islands fund and to provide for disposition of surplus revenue from Pribilof Islands, Alaska, Feb. 25, 1924. 1924. ii+16 p. * Paper, 5c.

St. Croix River. Bridge over St. Croix River, report to accompany H. R. 5337 [granting consent of Congress to Maine to construct, jointly with Canada, bridge over St. Croix River between Vanceboro, Me., and St. Croix, New Brunswick]; submitted by Mr. Ladd. Feb. 16, calendar day Feb. 18, 1924. 2 p. (S. rp. 155, 68th Cong. 1st sess.) * Paper, 5c.

St. John River. Bridge across St. John River, report to accompany H. R. 5348 [granting consent of Congress for construction of bridge across St. John River between Fort Kent, Me., and Clairs, New Brunswick, by Maine and Canada jointly]; submitted by Mr. Ladd. Feb. 16, calendar day Feb. 18, 1924. 2 p. (S. rp. 156, 68th Cong. 1st sess.) * Paper, 5c.

St. Louis River. Bridge across St. Louis River, report to accompany H. R. 4187 [to legalize bridge across St. Louis River in Carlton County, Minn., constructed by Minnesota]; submitted by Mr. Ladd. Feb. 16, calendar day Feb. 18, 1924. 1 p. (S. rp. 153, 68th Cong. 1st sess.) * Paper, 5c.

Susquehanna River. Bridge across Susquehanna River, report to accompany S. 2446 [granting consent of Congress to Clarks Ferry Bridge Company to construct bridge across Susquehanna River at or near railroad station of Clarks Ferry, Pa.]; submitted by Mr. Ladd. Feb. 16, calendar day Feb. 20, 1924. 2 p. (S. rp. 167, 68th Cong. 1st sess.) * Paper, 5c.

Tennessee River. Bridge across Tennessee River, report to accompany S. 2108 [to grant consent of Congress to Southern Railway Company to maintain bridge across Tennessee River at Knoxville, in county of Knox, Tenn.]; submitted by Mr. Ladd. Feb. 16, calendar day Feb. 18, 1924. 1 p. (S. rp. 148, 68th Cong. 1st sess.) * Paper, 5c.

Waccamaw River. Bridge across Waccamaw River, S. C., report to accompany H. R. 3681 [to authorize building of bridge across Waccamaw River, S. C., by Horry County, at or near Star Bluff, or at or near Bellamys Landing]; submitted by Mr. Ladd. Feb. 1, 1924. 1 p. (S. rp. 126, 68th Cong. 1st sess.) * Paper, 5c.

—— Bridge [dam] across Waccamaw River, report to accompany H. R. 2818 [to grant consent of Congress to K. C. Council, F. B. Gault, and Oscar High to construct dam and spillway across Waccamaw River, N. C.]; submitted by Mr. Ladd. Feb. 16, calendar day Feb. 18, 1924. 1 p. (S. rp. 149, 68th Cong. 1st sess.) * Paper, 5c.

West Pearl River. Bridge across West Pearl River, report to accompany H. R. 4807 [granting consent of Congress to Highway Commission of Louisiana to construct bridge across West Pearl River, La., near Pearl River station]; submitted by Mr. Sheppard. Feb. 28, 1924. 2 p. (S. rp. 176, 68th Cong. 1st sess.) * Paper, 5c.

Willamette River. Bridge across Willamette River, report to accompany H. R. 584 [to authorize county of Multnomah, Oreg., to construct bridge across Willamette River in Portland, Oreg., in vicinity of present site of Sellwood Ferry]; submitted by Mr. McNary for Mr. Ladd. Feb. 16, 1924. 2 p. (S. rp. 147, 68th Cong. 1st sess.) * Paper, 5c.

DISTRICT OF COLUMBIA COMMITTEE

Accounts. Adjustment of accounts between United States and District of Columbia, report to accompany S. 703; submitted by Mr. Ball. Feb. 28, 1924. 8 p. (S. rp. 177, 68th Cong. 1st sess.) * Paper, 5c.

Lincoln, Abraham. To declare Lincoln's birthday legal holiday [in District of Columbia], report to accompany S. 1641; submitted by Mr. Ball. Feb. 22, calendar day Feb. 23, 1924. 2 p. (S. rp. 171, 68th Cong. 1st sess.) * Paper, 5c.

Parks. Authorizing extension of park system of District of Columbia, report to accompany S. 1787; submitted by Mr. Ball. Feb. 28, 1924. 4 p. (S. rp. 178, 68th Cong. 1st sess.) * Paper, 5c.

Potomac River. Hydroelectric energy at Great Falls, report to accompany S. 746 [for development of hydroelectric energy at Great Falls]; submitted by Mr. Ball. Feb. 29, 1924. 3 p. (S. rp. 188, 68th Cong. 1st sess.) * Paper, 5c.

Streets. To change name of part of street, report to accompany S. 1932 [to change name of 37th street between Chevy Chase circle and Reno road to Chevy Chase drive]; submitted by Mr. Ball. Feb. 13, calendar day Feb. 14, 1924. 2 p. (S. rp. 145, 68th Cong. 1st sess.) * Paper, 5c.

Streets—Continued. vacate and extend streets near Walter Reed General Hospital, report to accompany S. 114 [to vacate streets and alleys within area known as Walter Reed General Hospital, District of Columbia, and to authorize extension and widening of 14th street from Montague street to its southern terminus south of Dahlia street, Nicholson street from 13th street to 16th street, Colorado avenue from Montague street to 13th street, Concord avenue from 16th street to its western terminus west of 8th street west, 13th street from Nicholson street to Piney Branch road, and Piney Branch road from 13th street to Blair road] ; submitted by Mr. Ball. Feb. 1, 1924. 3 p. (S. rp. 114, 68th Cong. 1st sess.) * Paper, 5c.

FINANCE COMMITTEE

Calendar. Legislative calendar, 68th Congress, Feb. 12–27, 1924; no. 5–9. 1924. Each 24 p. or 28 p. 4° ‡

Naiden, Earl L. Authorizing granting of war risk insurance to Earl L. Naiden, report to accompany S. 1370; submitted by Mr. Reed of Pennsylvania. Feb. 16, calendar day Feb. 21, 1924. 2 p. (S. rp. 168, 68th Cong. 1st sess.) * Paper, 5c.

FOREIGN RELATIONS COMMITTEE

Calendar, 68th Congress, 1st session, Feb. 11 and 20, 1924; no. 3 and 4. 1924. 10 p. and 15 p. 4° ‡ .

Crignier, Madame. Relief of Madame Crignier, of France, report to accompany S. 2392 [authorizing appropriation to indemnify damages to property of Madame Crignier, caused by search for body of John Paul Jones] ; submitted by Mr. Pepper. Feb. 16, 1924. 13 p. (S. rp. 146, 68th Cong. 1st sess.) * Paper, 5c.

Inter-American Electrical Communications Committee. Representation of United States at Inter-American Committee on Electrical Communications in Mexico City, report to accompany S. J. Res. 79; submitted by Mr. Lodge. Feb. 16, calendar day Feb. 19, 1924. 3 p. (S. rp. 161, 68th Cong. 1st sess.) * Paper, 5c.

International Sanitary Conference of American Republics. Authorizing appointment of delegates to 7th Pan American Sanitary Conference to be held at Habana, Cuba, report to accompany S. J. Res. 77; submitted by Mr. Lodge. Feb. 16, calendar day Feb. 19, 1924. 2 p. (S. rp. 160, 68th Cong. 1st sess.) * Paper, 5c.

International Statistical Bureau. Maintenance of membership in International Statistical Bureau at The Hague, report to accompany S. J. Res. 76 [authorizing maintenance by United States of membership in International Statistical Bureau at The Hague] ; submitted by Mr. Lodge. Feb. 16, calendar day Feb. 19, 1924. 2 p. (S. rp. 159, 68th Cong. 1st sess.) * Paper, 5c.

GOLD AND SILVER INQUIRY COMMISSION

Report. Progress report, Commission of Gold and Silver Inquiry, Senate, pursuant to Senate resolution 460, 67th Congress, 4th session, creating Commission of Gold and Silver Inquiry, Feb. 1, 1924. 1924. iii+45 p. (Serial 5.) * Paper, 5c. 24—26154

—— Same; presented by Mr. Oddie. (S. doc. 38, 68th Cong. 1st sess.) [Title differs slightly.]

IMMIGRATION COMMITTEE

Calendar. Legislative calendar, 68th Congress, Feb. 12, 1924; no. 1 and 2. 1924. 4 p. and 6 p. 4° ‡

INDIAN AFFAIRS COMMITTEE

Cherokee Indians. Claims of Cherokee Indians against United States, report to accompany S. 2115 [conferring jurisdiction upon Court of Claims to hear, examine, adjudicate, and enter judgment in any claims which Cherokee Indians may have against United States] ; submitted by Mr. Wheeler. Feb. 1, 1924. 2 p. (S. rp. 116, 68th Cong. 1st sess.) * Paper, 5c.

Indians. ,Relief of certain nations or tribes of Indians in Montana, Idaho, and Washington, report to accompany H. R. 3444; submitted by Mr. Harreld. Feb. 13, 1924. 4 p. , (S. rp. 141, 68th Cong. 1st sess.) * Paper, 5c.

—— Relief of certain tribes and nations of Indians in Montana, report to accompany S. 321 [for relief of certain nations or tribes of Indians in Montana, Idaho, and Washington]; submitted by Mr. Wheeler. Feb. 1, 1924. 4 p. (S. rp. 115, 68th Cong. 1st sess.) * Paper, 5c.

Osage Indians. To amend act for division of lands and funds of Osage Indians in Oklahoma, and acts amendatory thereof and supplemental thereto [relative to lands, money, or mineral interests inherited by persons not Osage Indians by blood], report to accompany,S. 2315; submitted by Mr. Harreld. Feb. 13, 1924. 1 p. (S. rp. 142, 68th Cong. 1st sess.) * Paper, 5c.

San Carlos Federal irrigation project, Ariz., report to accompany S. 966 [for continuance of construction work on San Carlos Federal irrigation project, Ariz.]; submitted by Mr. Cameron. Feb. 7, calendar day Feb. 8, 1924. 6 p. (S. rp. 129, 68th Cong. 1st sess.) [Corrected print.] * Paper, 5c.

Seupelt, J. G. J. G. Seupelt, report to accompany S. 1703 [for relief of J. G. Seupelt]; submitted by Mr. Harreld. Feb. 13, 1924. 2 p. (S. rp. 140, 68th Cong. 1st sess.) * Paper, 5c.

IRRIGATION AND RECLAMATION COMMITTEE

Reclamation of land. Payments of reclamation charges, report to accompany S. 1631 [to authorize deferring of payments of reclamation charges]; submitted by Mr. McNary. Jan. 28, calendar day Jan. 31, 1924. 2 p. (S. rp. 111. 68th Cong. 1st sess.) * Paper, 5c.

JUDICIARY COMMITTEE

Calendar. Legislative calendar, 68th Congress, Feb. 4 and 18, 1924; no. 6 and 7. 1924. Each 27 p. 4°. ‡

Courts of United States. Procedure in Federal courts, hearing before subcommittee on S. 2060, to amend judicial code, and S. 2061, to give Supreme Court authority to make and publish rules in common law actions, Feb. 2, 1924. 1924. iii+82 p. * Paper, 10c.

President of United States. Fixing commencement of terms of President, Vice President, and Members of Congress, report to accompany S. J. Res. 22 [proposing amendment to Constitution of United States fixing commencement of terms of President and Vice President and Members of Congress, and fixing time of assembling of Congress]; submitted by Mr. Norris. Feb. 22. calendar day Feb. 23, 1924. 5 p. (S. rp. 170, 68th Cong. 1st sess.) * Paper, 5c. 24—26184

Probation system in United States courts, hearing before subcommittee on S. 1042 and S. 1729, for establishment of probation system in United States courts, except in District of Columbia, Feb. 21, 1924. 1924. iii+36 p. * Paper, 5c .

LIBRARY COMMITTEE

National Botanic Garden. United States Botanic Garden, Washington, D. C., plants for Congressional distribution, 1924. [1924.] 5 p. †

MILITARY AFFAIRS COMMITTEE

Army. Amendments to national defense act, report to accompany S. 2169 [to amend in certain particulars national defense act, as amended]; submitted by Mr. Brookhart. Feb. 13, 1924. 3 p. (S. rp. 139, 68th Cong. 1st sess.) [Corrected print.] * Paper, 5c. 24—26183

Harrison, Ramon B. Ramon B. Harrison, report to accompany S. J. Res. 46 [for relief of Ramon B. Harrison]; submitted by Mr. Reed of Pennsylvania. Feb. 13, 1924. 4 p. (S. rp. 138, 68th Cong. 1st sess.) * Paper, 5c.

McAtee, John H. John H. McAtee, report to accompany S. 107 [for relief of John H. McAtee]; submitted by Mr. Sheppard. Feb. 1, 1924. 4 p. (S. rp. 117, 68th Cong. 1st sess.) * Paper, 5c.

Moriarty, Ambrose I. Second Lieut. Ambrose I. Moriarty, report to accompany S. 2090 [for advancement on retired list of Regular Army of Ambrose I. Moriarty]; submitted by Mr. Bruce. Feb. 7, calendar day Feb. 9, 1924. 4 p. (S. rp. 135, 68th Cong. 1st sess.) * Paper, 5c.

Panama Canal. Compensation for retired warrant officers and enlisted men employed by Panama Canal, report to accompany S. 2401; submitted by Mr. Bursum. Feb. 28, 1924. 3 p. (S. rp. 179, 68th Cong. 1st sess.) * Paper, 5c.

Siam. Admission of 2 Siamese subjects to West Point, report to accompany S. J. Res. 63 [authorizing Secretary of War to receive, for instruction at . Military Academy, West Point, 2 Siamese subjects, to be designated hereafter by Government of Siam]; submitted by Mr. Wadsworth. Jan. 28, calendar day Jan. 31, 1924. 1 p. (S. rp. 112, 68th Cong. 1st sess.) * Paper, 5c.

Southern Pacific Railroad. Right of way over Government levee at Yuma, .Ariz., report to accompany S. 514 [to grant right of way over Government levee at Yuma, Ariz., to Southern Pacific Railroad Company]; submitted by Mr. Cameron. Feb. 29, 1924. 2 p. (S. rp. 190, 68th Cong. 1st sess.) * Paper, 5c.

World War emergency officers retired list. Retirement of disabled emergency officers, report to accompany S. 33 [making eligible for retirement under certain conditions officers and former officers of Army, other than officers of Regular Army, who incurred physical disability in line of duty while in service of United .States during World War]; submitted by Mr. Bursum. Feb. 1, 1924. 15 p. (S. rp. 123, 68th Cong. 1st sess.) * Paper, 5c.

NAVAL AFFAIRS COMMITTEE

Calendar. Legislative calendar, 68th Congress, 1st session, Feb. 5 and 19, 1924; no. 2 and 3. 1924. .8 p. and 11 p. large 8° ‡

MacDonald, Gordon G. Gordon G. MacDonald, report to accompany S. 1013 [for relief of Gordon G. MacDonald]; submitted by Mr. Hale. Feb. 26, 1924. 2 p. (S. rp. 174, 68th Cong. 1st sess.) * Paper, 5c.

Willey, Charles H. Charles H. Willey, report to accompany S. 264 [for relief of Charles H. Willey]; submitted by Mr. Hale. Feb. 26, 1924. 2 p. (S. rp. 173, 68th Cong. 1st sess.) * Paper, 5c.

PENSIONS COMMITTEE

Pensions. Amending act of Sept. 22, 1922, so as to make pension laws applicable to certain class of persons, report to accompany S. 2154 [to amend act to provide for applicability of pension laws to certain classes of persons in military and naval services not entitled to benefits of article 3 of war risk insurance act, as amended]; submitted by Mr. Bursum. Feb. 7, 1924. 3 p. (S. rp. 127, 68th Cong. 1st sess.) * Paper, 5c.

—— Pensions and increase of pensions to soldiers and sailors of Civil War, etc., report to accompany S. 5 [granting pensions and increase of pensions to soldiers and sailors of Civil and Mexican wars and to widows, former widows, minor children, and helpless children of said soldiers and sailors, and to widows of War of 1812, and to Indian war veterans and widows]; submitted by Mr. Bursum. Feb. 7, 1924. 15 p. (S. rp. 128, 68th Cong. 1st sess.) * Paper, 5c.

POST OFFICES AND POST ROADS COMMITTEE

Marketing of farm produce. Authorizing Postmaster General to conduct experiment in rural mail service, report to accompany S. 2111 [authorizing Postmaster General to conduct experiment in rural mail service to encourage transportation of food products directly from producers to consumers or vendors]; submitted by Mr. George. Jan. 28, calendar day Jan. 31, 1924. 2 p. (S. rp. 113, 68th Cong. 1st sess.) * Paper, 5c.

PRINTING COMMITTEE

Calendar of bills, resolutions, petitions, manuscripts, communications, etc., referred to Committee on Printing for its consideration and action thereon, Feb. 11, 1924; no. 1, 68th Congress, 1st session. 1924. 7 p. 4° ‡

Medicine Bow National Forest. To authorize addition of certain lands to Medicine Bow National Forest in Wyoming, and for other purposes, report to accompany S. 699; submitted by Mr. Kendrick. Feb. 16, calendar day Feb. 19, 1924. 3 p. (S. rp. 162, 68th Cong. 1st sess.) * Paper, 5c.

Naval petroleum reserves. Leases upon naval oil reserves, hearings pursuant to S. Res. 147, Feb. 12–15, 1924. 1924. pt. 8, ii+2071–2336 p. * Paper, 25c.

—— Leases upon naval oil reserves, hearings pursuant to S. Res. 282, S. Res. 294, and S. Res. 434, 67th Congress, 4th session, Feb. 1–11, 1924. 1924. pt. 7, ii+1911–2070 p. * Paper, 15c.

Veterans' Bureau. Investigation of Veterans' Bureau, 2d preliminary report, pursuant to S. Res. 466, 67th Cong. 4th sess.; submitted by Mr. Reed of Pennsylvania. Feb. 7, calendar day Feb. 9, 1924. 75 p. il. (S. rp. 103, pt. 2, 68th Cong. 1st sess.) * Paper, 10c.

USELESS EXECUTIVE PAPERS, JOINT SELECT COMMITTEE ON DISPOSITION OF

Interior Department. Disposition of useless executive papers in Department of Interior, report; submitted by Mr. Moores of Indiana. Feb. 25, 1924. 12 p. (H. rp. 226, 68th Cong. 1st sess.) * Paper, 5c.

Post Office Department. Disposition of useless executive papers in Post-Office Department, report; submitted by Mr. Moores of Indiana. Feb. 14, 1924. 6 p. (H. rp. 206, 68th Cong. 1st sess.) * Paper, 5c.

COURT OF CLAIMS

American Electro Products Company, Limited, and Shawinigan Water and Power Company *v.* United States; evidence for plaintiffs. [1924.] no. B–188, p. 81–158, il. ‡

Baltimore & Ohio Railroad v. United States; evidence for defendant. [1924.] no. 6–A, p. 307–494. ‡

Barrett Company v. United States; evidence for defendant. [1924.] no. 107–A, p. 297–339. ‡

Carley Life Float Company v. United States; evidence for defendant. [1924.] no. 34647, p. 150–402. ‡

Culver. Clarence O. Culver *v.* United States; evidence [for claimant]. [1924.] no. C–375, p. 7–21. ‡

Cygnet Manufacturing Company. Cyguet [Cygnet] Manufacturing Co. *v.* United States; evidence for defendant. [1924.] no. 115–A, p. 77–96. ‡

Garlock. George A. Garlock *v.* United States; evidence for claimant. [1924.] no. B–132, p. 1–10. ‡

Howard Brothers. Henry Howard, trading as Howard Brothers, *v.* United States; evidence for claimant. [1924.] no. C–532, p. 29–96. ‡

Ingalls. Charles B. Ingalls *v.* United States; evidence for claimant. [1924.] no. B–130, p. 5–63. ‡

Kenilworth Company v. United States; findings of fact [conclusion of law, and opinion of court], decided Jan. 21, 1924. [1924.] no. C–762, 25 p. ‡

Montgomery. Regina Cleary Montgomery et al. *v.* United States; rebuttal evidence for plaintiffs. [1924.] no. 33852, p. 859–922. ‡

Mosler Metal Products Corporation v. United States; evidence for plaintiff. [1924.] no. C–940, p. 47–56. ‡

Ohio Public Service Company v. United States; evidence for plaintiff. [1924.] no. C–90, p. 7–18. ‡

Osage Nation of Indians *v.* United States; evidence for defendant. [1924.] no. B–38, p. 119–124. ‡

Philadelphia, Pa. City of Philadelphia *v.* United States, findings of court in case of Philadelphia against United States. Jan. 28, calendar day Jan. 30, 1924. 9 p. (S. doc. 29, 68th Cong. 1st sess.) * Paper, 5c.

Philadelphia, Baltimore & Washington Railroad Company v. United States; evidence for defendant. [1924.] no. 113–A, p. 165–262. ‡

Schaefer. Charles Schaefer, jr., *v.* United States; findings of fact [conclusion of law, and opinion of court], decided Jan. 21, 1924. [1924.] no. 13–A, 4 p. ‡

Schaufler. Albert B. Schaufler *v.* United States; evidence for claimant. [1924.] no. B–134, p. 1–16. ‡

Seaboard Air Line Railway v. United States; findings of fact [conclusion of law, and opinion of court], decided Feb. 11, 1924. [1924.] no. 24915, 20 p. ‡

Sherman. Clayton L. Sherman *v.* United States; evidence for claimant. [1924.] no. B–136, p. 1–13. ‡

Smith. Terrence P. Smith *v.* United States; evidence [for claimant]. [1924.] no. B–370, p. 7–9. ‡

Sun Shipbuilding Company v. United States; evidence for defendant. [1924.] no. B–317, p. 111–148. ‡

Turk. Charles R. Turk *v.* United States; evidence for claimant. [1924.] no. B–137, p. 1–9. ‡

Wyckoff Pipe & Creosoting Co. [Inc.] v. United States; evidence for plaintiff [and] defendant. [1924.] no. C–19, p. 49–126. ‡

DISTRICT OF COLUMBIA

Court of Appeals. Transcript of record, Jan. term, 1924, no. 4094, no. 25 special calendar, United States *vs.* Arthur A. O'Brien and David J. Maloney, appeal from Supreme Court of District of Columbia. [1924.] cover-title, i+13 p. ‡

—— Transcript of record, Jan. term, 1924, no. 4096, Hubert Work, Secretary of Interior, *vs.* W. H. Mason, appeal from Supreme Court of District of Columbia. [1924.] cover-title, i+11 p. ‡

—— Transcript of record, Jan. term, 1924, no. 4116, no. —, special calendar, Hubert Work, Secretary of Interior, *vs.* United States ex rel. Chestatee Pyrites & Chemical Corporation, appeal from Supreme Court of District of Columbia. [1924.] cover-title, i+14 p. ‡

EMPLOYEES' COMPENSATION COMMISSION

Employers' liability and workmen's compensation. Opinion of Attorney General of May 16, 1923, and decision of comptroller general of Feb. 11, 1924, affecting administration of employees' compensation act. 1924. [1]+10 p. †   24—26206

FEDERAL BOARD FOR VOCATIONAL EDUCATION

Building. Apprentice education in construction industry, discussions and papers presented at 17th annual convention of National Society for Vocational Education, at Buffalo, N. Y., Dec. 6, 1923. 1924. v+45 p. (Bulletin 92; Trade and industrial series 26.) * Paper, 10c.   E 24—81

Market-gardening. Job lesson units for selected truck and fruit crops adapted to southern conditions, suggestions to teachers for organizing instruction on basis of job analyses of crop production; [by F. A. Merrill]. Jan. 1924. vii+61 p. (Bulletin 91; Agricultural series 19.) [Prepared in cooperation with Agriculture Department.] * Paper, 10c.   E 24—78

FEDERAL RESERVE BOARD

Federal reserve bulletin, Feb. 1924; [v. 10, no. 2]. 1924. iv+75–145+ii p. il. map, 4° [Monthly.] † Paper, 20c. single copy, $2.00 a yr. 15—26318

Nᴏᴛᴇ.—The bulletin contains, in addition to the regular official announcements, the national review of business conditions, detailed analyses of business conditions, research studies, reviews of foreign banking, and complete statistics showing the condition of Federal reserve banks and member banks. It will be sent to all member banks without charge. Others desiring copies may obtain them from the Federal Reserve Board, Washington, D. C., at the prices stated above.

Federal reserve member banks. Federal reserve inter-district collection system, banks upon which items will be received by Federal reserve banks for collection and credit, Jan. 1, 1924. 1924. iii+129 p. 4° † 24—26207

—— Federal reserve inter-district collection system, changes in list of banks upon which items will be received by Federal reserve banks for collection and credit, Feb. 1, 1924. 1924. [1]+9 p. 4° † 16—26870

FEDERAL TRADE COMMISSION

Nᴏᴛᴇ.—The bound volumes of the Federal Trade Commission decisions are sold by the Superintendent of Documents, Washington, D. C. Separate opinions are sold on subscription, price $1.00 per volume; foreign subscription, $1.50; single copies, 5c. each.

Grain. Report of Federal Trade Commission on methods and operations of grain exporters: v. 2, Speculation, competition, and prices, June 18, 1923. 1923. xli+264 p. 12 pl. map. * Paper, 40c. 22—26926

Juvenile Shoe Co., Inc., v. Federal Trade Commission; circuit court of appeals, 9th circuit, May 14, 1923, no. 3927 [opinion of court]. [1924.] 4 p. ([Court decision] 5.) [From Federal Trade Commission decisions, v. 6.] * Paper, 5c.

Melhuish & Co. Federal Trade Commission *v.* Melhuish & Company et al., complaint [report, findings, and order]; docket 872, May 17, 1923. [1923.] 163–179+[1] p. ([Decision] 367.) [From Federal Trade Commission decisions, v. 6. Includes list of Cases in which orders for discontinuance or dismissal have been entered, May 18, 1923.] * Paper, 5c.

National Biscuit Company. No. 8205, in circuit court of appeals for 2d circuit, National Biscuit Company *v.* Federal Trade Commission; answer in nature of cross bill. 1924. cover-title, 4 p. large 8° ‡

Silver, L. B., Company. L. B. Silver Co. *v.* Federal Trade Commission; circuit court of appeals, 6th circuit, Feb. 16, 1923, no. 3648 [opinion of court]. [1923.] 16 p. ([Court decision]1.) [From Federal Trade Commission decisions, v. 6.] * Paper, 5c.

Sinclair Refining Company. Federal Trade Commission *v.* Sinclair Refining Co.; same *v.* Standard Oil Co. (New Jersey); same *v.* Gulf Refining Co.; same *v.* Maloney Oil & Mfg. Co.; [Supreme Court] Apr. 9, 1923, nos. 213, 637–639 [opinion of court]. [1924.] 7 p. ([Court decision]4.) [From Federal Trade Commission decisions, v. 6.] * Paper, 5c.

GENERAL ACCOUNTING OFFICE

Decisions. Decisions of comptroller general, v. 3, Dec. 1923, and index, Oct.–Dec. 1923; J. R. McCarl, comptroller general, Lurtin R. Ginn, assistant comptroller general. 1924. [1]+347–401+xv p. [Monthly.] † 21-26777

—— Same, v. 3, Jan. 1924; J. R. McCarl, comptroller general, Lurtin R. Ginn, assistant comptroller general. 1924. [1]+401–465 p. [Monthly.] †

GOVERNMENT PRINTING OFFICE

DOCUMENTS OFFICE

Congress. Proceedings of Congress, Annals of Congress, Register of debates, Congressional globe, Congressional record [for sale by superintendent of documents]. Jan. 1924. [2]+14 p. (Price list 49, 11th edition.) † 24-26172

Engineering and surveying [publications relating to] coasts, rivers, harbors, engines, tides, compass, terrestrial magnetism, for sale by superintendent of documents. Jan. 1924. [2]+19+[2] p. (Price list 18, 13th edition.) †
24–26171

Farm management, farm accounts, credits, marketing, homes, and statistics, list of publications for sale by superintendent of documents. Jan. 1924. [2] +22 p. (Price list 68, 9th edition.) †
24–26208

Monthly catalogue, United States public documents, no. 349; Jan. 1924. 1924. p. 333–412. * Paper, 5c. single copy, 50c. a yr.; foreign subscription, 75c.
4–18088

Soils and fertilizers, publications for sale by superintendent of documents. Jan. 1924. [2]+14 p. (Price list 46, 17th edition.) †
, 24–26209

Transportation, railroad and shipping problems, postal service, telegraphs, telephones, Government ownership and control, list of publications for sale by superintendent of documents. Dec. 1923. [2]+18 p. (Price list 25, 11th edition.) †
24–26139

INTERIOR DEPARTMENT

NOTE.—The decisions of the Department of the Interior in pension cases are issued in slips and in signatures, and the decisions in land cases are issued in signatures, both being published later in bound volumes. Subscribers may deposit $1.00 with the Superintendent of Documents and receive the contents of a volume of the decisions of either kind in separate parts as they are issued; foreign subscription, $1.25. Prices for bound volumes furnished upon application to the Superintendent of Documents, Washington, D. C.

Pensions. [Decisions of Department of Interior in appealed pension and bounty land claims, v. 21, slips] 94 and 96 pension. [1924.] 2 p. and 3 p. [For price, see note above under center head.]
12–29422

Public lands. Decisions of Department of Interior in cases relating to public lands, May 1, 1922–July 31, 1923; edited by Daniel M. Greene. 1923. v. 49, xxxi+698 p. [Also issued in separate signatures. These decisions are made up in the Office of the Solicitor for the Department of Interior, but are promulgated by the Secretary of the Interior.] * Cloth, $1.75. .7–23651

—— Decisions of Department of Interior in cases relating to public lands, v. 49, [signatures] i and ii. 1923. xxxi p. [Title-page, table of cases, etc., for v. 49. For price, see note above under center head.]

—— Same, v. 49, [signatures]43 and 44. [1924.] p. 673–698. [Index to v. 49.]

ARCHITECT OF CAPITOL

Report. Annual report of architect of capitol, year ending June 30, 1923. 1924. iii+16 p. (S. doc: 46, 68th Cong. 1st sess.) * Paper, 5c.

EDUCATION BUREAU

Children's literature. Poetical literature for boys and girls [in first 6 grades, reading course]; by Florence C. Fox. 1924. [1]+10 p. il. 12° (Home education reading course 27.) †

—— Sixty selected stories for boys and girls [grades 1–6, reading course]; by Florence C. Fox. 1924. [1]+11 p. il. 12° (Home education reading course 26.) †

Feeble-minded. Schools and classes for feeble-minded and subnormal children, 1922; prepared by Division of Statistics. 1924. [1]+22 p. (Bulletin 59, 1923.) [Advance sheets from Biennial survey of education in United States, 1920–22.] * Paper, 5c.
E 20–406

Hygiene. Health education publications. [1924.] [4] p. il. narrow 8° †
E 22–568

—— Health promotion in continuation school; by Harriet Wedgwood. 1924. [1]+25 p. il. 1 pl. (School health studies 5.) [Includes list of health education publications issued by Education Bureau.] * Paper, 5c. E 24–80

Kindergarten. How kindergarten prepares children for primary work; by Mary G. Waite. Jan. 1924. 6 p. (Kindergarten circular 15.) [From School life, v. 9, no. 4, Dec. 1923.] * Paper, 5c.
E 24–79

School life, v. 9, no. 6; Feb. 1924. [1924.] p. 121–144, il. 4° [Monthly except July and August. This is Rural education number.] * Paper, 5c. single copy, 30c. a yr. (10 months) ; foreign subscription, 55c. E 18–902

GEOLOGICAL SURVEY

NOTE.—The publications of the United States Geological Survey consist of Annual reports, Monographs, Professional papers, Bulletins, Water-supply papers, chapters and volumes of Mineral resources of the United States, folios of the Topographic atlas of the United States and topographic maps that bear descriptive text, and folios of the Geologic atlas of the United States and the World atlas of commercial geology. The Monographs, folios, and maps are sold. Other publications are generally free as long as the Survey's supply lasts. Copies are also sold by the Superintendent of Documents, Washington, D. C., at the prices indicated. For maps and folios address the Director of the Geological Survey, Washington, D. C. A discount of 40 per cent is allowed on any order for maps or folios that amounts to $5.00 or more at the retail price. This discount applies to an order for either maps or folios alone or for maps and folios together but is not allowed on a few folios that are sold at 5c. each on account of damage by fire. Orders for other publications that are for sale should be sent to the Superintendent of Documents, Washington, D, C. For topographic maps see next page.

Gila River Valley. Lower Gila region, Ariz., geographic, geologic, and hydrologic reconnaissance, with guide to desert watering places [and with bibliography] ; by Clyde P. Ross. 1923. xiv+237 p. il. 4 pl. 14 p. of pl. 5 maps, 3 are in pocket. (Water-supply paper 498.) GS 24–1
NOTE.—Includes Preface ; by O. E. Meinzer.—Types of surface water supplies ; by Kirk Bryan.—History of irrigation along Gila River west of Gila River Reservation ; by C. R. Olberg.—Irrigation with ground water in Colorado River Indian Reservation, by A. L. Harris ; [abstracted by Clyde P. Ross].

—— Same. (H. doc. 213, 67th Cong. 2d sess.)

Manganese and manganiferous ores in 1922 ; by H. A. C. Jenison and H. M. Meyer. Feb. 25, 1924. ii+585–594 p. il. [From Mineral resources, 1922, pt. 1.] †

Publications. New publications, list 191 ; Feb. 1, 1924. [1924.] 3 p. [Monthly.] †

Ray, Ariz. Ray folio, Ariz. ; by F. L. Ransome. [Library edition.] Washington, Geological Survey, 1923. cover-title, 24 p. il. 1 pl. 4 maps, large 4° (Geologic atlas of United States 217.) [Text and illustrations on p. 2–4 of cover.] †Paper, 25c. GS24—53

Rivers. Summary of hydrometric data in Washington, 1878–1919 [with bibliography] ; by Glenn L. Parker and Lasley Lee. 1923. viii+363 p. 8 p. of pl. map in pocket. (Water-supply paper 492.) [Prepared in cooperation with Washington State Board of Geological Survey.] *Paper, 40c. GS24—31

—— Same. (H. doc. 207, 67th Cong. 2d sess.)

Salton Sea region. Salton Sea region, Calif., geographic, geologic, and hydrologic reconnaissance with guide to desert watering places [and with bibliography of southeastern California] ; by John S. Brown. 1923. xv+292 p. il. 1 pl. 14 p. of pl. 4 maps, 3 are in pocket. (Water-supply paper 497.) [Prepared in cooperation with Department of Engineering of California.] *Paper, 50c. GS24—24

—— Same. (H. doc. 212, 67th Cong. 2d sess.)

Silver. Origin of certain rich silver ores near Chloride and Kingman, Ariz. ; by Edson S. Bastin. Feb. 23, 1924. ii+17–39 p. il. (Bulletin 750 B.) * Paper, 5c.

Water (underground). Occurrence of ground water in United States, with discussion of principles ; by Oscar Edward Meinzer. 1923. xi+321 p. il. 4 pl. 22 p. of pl. 5 maps. (Water-supply paper 489.) [Includes lists of Geological Survey and State publications which give information relating to water in the various rock systems of the United States.] *Paper, 60c. GS24—30
—— Same. (H. doc. 846, 66th Cong. 3d sess.)

Maps

Alaska. Map of Alaska in relief ; with inset, Aleutian Islands. Scale 1 : 2,500,000. [Washington] Geological Survey, edition 1923. 33.1×49 in. [Relief shading by Jno. H. Renshawe.] †50c.

Topographic maps

NOTE.—The Geological Survey is making a topographic map of the United States. The individual maps of which it is composed are projected without reference to political divisions, and each map is designated by the name of some prominent town or natural feature in the area mapped. Three scales are ordinarily used. 1 : 62,500, 1 : 125,000, and 1 : 250,000. These correspond, approximately, to 1 mile, 2 miles, and 4 miles to 1 linear inch, covering, respectively, average areas of 230, 920, and 3,700 square miles. For some areas of particular importance special large-scale maps are published. The usual size, exclusive of the margin, is 17.5 inches in height by 11.5 to 16 inches in width. the width varying with the latitude. The sheets measure 20 by 16½ inches. A description of the topographic map is printed on the reverse of each sheet.

More than two-fifths of the area of the country, excluding Alaska, has been mapped,: every State being represented. Connecticut, Delaware, the District of Columbia, Maryland, Massachusetts, New Jersey, Ohio, Rhode Island, and West Virginia are completely mapped. Maps of the regular size are sold by the Survey at 10c. each, but a discount of, 40 per cent is allowed on any order which amounts to $5.00 or more at the retail price. The discount is allowed on an order for either maps or folios alone or for maps and folios together, but does not apply to a few folios that are sold at 5c. each on account of damage by fire.

Pennsylvania. Pennsylvania, Howard quadrangle, lat. 41°–41°15′, long. 77°30′–77°45′. Scale 1 : 62,500, contour interval 20 ft. [Washington, Geological Survey] edition of 1923. 17.5×13.3 in. [Contour map with relief shading.] †10c.

—— Pennsylvania, Lock Haven quadrangle, lat. 41°–41°15′, long. 77°15′–77°30′. Scale 1 : 62,500, contour interval 20 ft. [Washington, Geological Survey] edition of 1923. 17.5×13.3 in. [Contour map with relief shading.] †10c.

—— Pennsylvania, Tyrone quadrangle, lat. 40°30′–40°45′, long. 78°–78°15′. Scale 1 : 62,500, contour interval 20 ft. [Washington, Geological Survey] edition of 1923. 17.5×13.4 in. †10c.

—— Same, contour map with relief shading. †10c.

West Virginia. West Virginia, Clintonville quadrangle, lat. 37° 45′–38°, long. 80° 30′–80° 45′. Scale 1 : 62,500, contour interval 50 ft. [Washington, Geological Survey] edition of 1923. 17.5×13.9 in. [Contour map with relief shading.] † 10c.

—— West Virginia-Virginia, Ronceverte quadrangle, lat. 37° 30′–37° 45′, long. 80° 15′–80° 30′. Scale 1 : 62,500, contour interval 50 ft. [Washington, Geological Survey] edition of 1923. 17.5×15.5 in. [Contour map with relief shading.] † 10c.

INDIAN AFFAIRS OFFICE

Leases. Regulations governing execution of leases of Indian allotted and tribal lands for farming, grazing, and business purposes; approved July 20, 1923. [Reprint] 1924. iii+ 15 p. †

MINES BUREAU

Mine accidents. Metal-mine accidents in United States, calendar year 1922; by William W. Adams. [1st edition.] [Nov, 1923. published] 1924. v+72 p. (Technical paper 354.) [Includes lists of Mines Bureau publications on mine and quarry accident statistics.] * Paper, 10c. 13—35245

Platinum. Methods for recovery of platinum, iridium, palladium, gold, and silver from jewelers' waste; by C. W. Davis. [1st edition.] [Jan.] 1924. iii+14 p. (Technical paper 342.) * Paper, 5c. 24—26140

PATENT OFFICE

NOTE.—The Patent Office publishes Specifications and drawings of patents in single copies. These are not enumerated in this catalogue, and may be obtained for 10c. each at the Patent Office.

A variety of indexes, giving a complete view of the work of the Patent Office from 1790 to date. are published at prices ranging from 25c. to $10.00 per volume and may be obtained from the Superintendent of Documents. Washington, D. C. The Rules of practice and pamphlet Patent laws are furnished free of charge upon application to the Patent Office. The Patent Office issues coupon orders in packages of 20 at $2.00 per package, or in books containing 100 coupons at $10.00 per book. These coupons are good until used, but are only to be used for orders sent to the Patent Office. For schedule of office fees, address Chief Clerk, Patent Office, Washington, D. C.

Cowles, Alfred H. Patent appeal no. 1645, in Court of Appeals of District of Columbia, Jan. term, 1924, in re Alfred H. Cowles [improvement in process for treating substances adapted to form alkali-aluminum-silicates and calcium-silico-aluminates] ; brief for commissioner of patents. 1924. cover-title, 31 p. ‡

Decisions. [Decisions in patent and trade-mark cases, etc.] Feb. 5, 1924. p. 1–8, large 8° [From Official gazette, v. 319, no. 1.] † Paper, 5c. single copy, $2.00 a yr.   23—7315

—— Same. Feb. 12, 1924. p. 223–236, large 8° [Includes also the Report of commissioner of patents to Congress, year ended Dec. 31, 1923. From Official gazette, v. 319, no. 2.]

—— Same. Feb. 19, 1924. p. 471–478, large 8° [From Official gazette, v. 319, no. 3.]

—— Same. Feb. 26, 1924. p. 705–712, il. large 8° [From Official gazette, v. 319, no. 4.]

Official gazette. Official gazette, Feb. 5–26, 1924; v. 319, no. 1–4. 1924. cover-titles, 931+[clxviii] p. il. large 8° [Weekly. The Report of the commissioner of patents to Congress, year ended Dec. 31, 1923, is included in v. 319, no. 2, p. 225–235.] * Paper, 10c. single copy, $5.00 a yr.; foreign subscription, $11.00.   4—18256

    Note.—Contains the patents, trade-marks, designs, and labels issued each week; also decisions of the commissioner of patents and of the United States courts in patent cases.

—— Same [title-page, contents, errata, etc., to] v. 318; Jan. 1924. 1924. [2] leaves, large 8° * Paper, 5c. single copy, included in price of Official gazette for subscribers.

—— Same, weekly index, with title, Alphabetical list of registrants of trade-marks [etc., Feb. 5, 1924]. [1924.] xlii p. large 8° [From Official gazette, v. 319, no. 1.] † Paper, $1.00 a yr.

—— Same [Feb. 12, 1924]. [1924.] xliv p. large 8° [From Official gazette, v. 319, no. 2.]

—— Same [Feb. 19, 1924]. [1924.] xlii p. large 8° [From Official gazette, v. 319, no. 3.]

—— Same [Feb. 26, 1924]. [1924.] xl p. large 8° [From Official gazette, v. 319, no. 4.]

Patent attorneys. Rules and regulations in regard to attorneys practicing before Patent Office, May 3, 1922, extracts from Rules of practice. [Reprint with additions 1924.] 4 p. †

Patents. Classification of patents issued Feb. 5–26, 1924. [1924.] Each 2 p. large 8° [Weekly. From Official gazette, v. 319, no. 1–4.] †

—— Index of patents issued from Patent Office, [calendar year] 1923. 1924. 1598 p. large 8° [This index is the same as p. ii, 3–1598 of the Annual report to Congress, 1923, for which see below.] * Paper, $1.00.   24—26174

Report. Report of commissioner of patents to Congress, year ended Dec. 31, 1923. 1924. [1]+16 p. †

—— Same, with letter of transmittal. Jan. 28, 1924. 17 p. (H. doc. 104, 68th Cong. 1st sess.) †

—— Same, with indexes to patentees, inventions, etc., and with title, Annual report of commissioner of patents [to Congress, calendar] year 1923. 1924. xiii+3–1598 p. large 8° * Paper, $1.00.

—— Same. (H. doc. 104, 68th Cong. 1st sess.) [For the 1st print of House document 104, issued without indexes to patentees, inventions, etc., see above.]

Smithey, Marvin. No. 2164, circuit court of appeals, 4th circuit, Marvin Smithey v. Thomas E. Robertson, commissioner of patents; brief for appellee. 1924. cover-title, i+13 p. large 8° ‡

Trade-marks. Trade-marks [etc., from] Official gazette, Feb. 5, 1924. [1924.] 9–71+i–xxi p. il. large 8° [From Official gazette, v. 319, no. 1.] † Paper, 5c. single copy, $2.50 a yr.

—— Same, Feb. 12, 1924. [1924.] 237–297+i–xix p. il. large 8° [From Official gazette, v. 319, no. 2.]

—— Same, Feb. 19, 1924. [1924.] 479–540+i–xix p. il. large 8° [From Official gazette, v. 319, no. 3.]

—— Same, Feb. 26, 1924. [1924.] 713–767+i–xvii p. il. large 8° [From Official gazette, v. 319, no. 4.]

PENSION BUREAU

ACTUARIES BOARD

Report. Civil service retirement and disability fund, letter from Secretary of Interior transmitting communication from commissioner of pensions submitting 3d annual report of Board of Actuaries upon operation of act for retirement of employees in classified civil service [Jan. 11, 1924]. 1924. iv+24 p. (S. doc. 32, 68th Cong. 1st sess.) * Paper, 5c.   22—26097

RECLAMATION BUREAU

Klamath project, Oreg.-Calif., earthwork, north canal, Langell Valley division. [1924.] 17 p. 3 pl. map. 4° (Specifications 429.) [Consists of advertisement, proposal, specifications, and drawings for reclamation project.] † Paper, 30c.

Reclamation record, v. 15, no. 2; Feb. 1924. [1924.] cover-title, p. 17–32, il. 4° [Monthly. Text on p. 2–4 of cover.]   9—35252

> NOTE.—The Reclamation record is published in the interest of the settlers on the reclamation projects, its aim being to raise the general average of success on these projects. It contains much valuable matter of interest to farmers, and will be sent without direct charge to water users on the irrigation projects of the Reclamation Bureau. The Record is sold to those who are not water users for 75 cents a year, payable in advance. Subscriptions may be forwarded to the Chief Clerk, U. S. Reclamation Bureau, Washington, D. C., and remittances (postal money order or New York draft) should be made payable to the Special Fiscal Agent, U. S. Reclamation Bureau. Postage stamps will not be accepted.

INTERSTATE COMMERCE COMMISSION

> NOTE.—The bound volumes of the decisions, usually known as Interstate Commerce Commission reports, are sold by the Superintendent of Documents, Washington D. C., at various prices, depending upon the size of the volume. Separate opinions are sold on subscription, price $1.00 per volume; foreign subscription, $1.50; single copies, usually 5c. each.

Alcohol. No. 13865, Anheuser-Busch, Incorporated, *v.* Chicago & Alton Railroad Company et al.; decided Jan. 17, 1924; report [and order] of commission. [1924.] 307–309+[1] p. ([Opinion]9180.) [Report from Interstate Commerce Commission reports, v. 87.] * Paper, 5c.

Alfalfa. No. 14111, Swift & Company *v.* director general, as agent, Spokane, Portland & Seattle Railway Company, et al.; [decided Dec. 31, 1923; report of commission]. 1924. [1]+154–156 p. ([Opinion]9141.) [From Interstate Commerce Commission reports, v. 87.] * Paper, 5c.

Alsike clover. No. 13872, Chas. H. Lilly Company *v.* Oregon Short Line Railroad Company and Oregon-Washington Railroad & Navigation Company; [decided Dec. 27, 1923; report and order of commission]. 1924. [1]+644–646+[1] p. ([Opinion]9051.) [Report from Interstate Commerce Commission reports, v. 85.] * Paper, 5c.

American Niagara Railroad Corporation. Finance docket no. 3351, stock of American Niagara R. R. Corporation; decided Dec. 29, 1923; report of commission. [1924.] p. 177–178. ([Finance decision]1127.) [From Interstate Commerce Commission reports, v. 86.] * Paper, 5c.

Arkansas and Louisiana Midland Railway. Finance docket no. 108, deficit settlement with Arkansas & Louisiana Midland Ry. [H. B. Hearn and H. R. Speed, receivers; decided Jan. 11, 1924; report of commission]. 1924. [1]+232–234 p. ([Finance decision]1148.) [From Interstate Commerce Commission reports, v. 86.] * Paper, 5c.

—— Finance docket no. 277, guaranty settlement with Arkansas & Louisiana Midland Ry. [H. B. Hearn and H. R. Speed, receivers; decided Dec. 27, 1923; report of commission]. 1924. [1]+148–150 p. ([Finance decision]1121.) [From Interstate Commerce Commission reports, v. 86.] * Paper, 5c.

Barite. No. 14145, Rollin Chemical Corporation *v.* director general, as agent; decided Jan. 17, 1924; report [and order] of commission. [1924.] 263–264+[1] p. ([Opinion] 9169.) [Report from Interstate Commerce Commission reports, v. 87.] * Paper, 5c.

Barley. No. 12800, A. B. Haslacher and F. G. E. Lange, doing business as California Grain Company, *v.* director general, as agent, and Sacramento Northern Railroad; [decided Dec. 28, 1923; report and order of commission]. 1924. [1]+680-682+[1] p. ([Opinion]9062.) [Report from Interstate Commerce Commission reports, v. 85.] * Paper, 5c.

—— No. 13768, Garrette & Agnew *v.* Southern Pacific Company et al.; decided Jan. 17, 1924; report [and order] of commission. [1924.] 199-200+ [1] p. ([Opinion]9149.) [Report from Interstate Commerce Commission reports, v. 87.] * Paper, 5c.

Beans. No. 13554, J. C. Sewell & Company *v.* director general, as agent; decided Dec. 27, 1923; report [and order] of commission. [1924.] 641-642+ [1] p. ([Opinion]9049.) [Report from Interstate Commerce Commission reports, v. 85.] * Paper 5c.

—— No. 13640, Rosser &.Fitch *v.* Seaboard Air Line Railway Company et al.; decided Dec. 27, 1923; report [and order] of commission. .[1924.] 93-94+ [1] p. ([Opinion]9120.) [Report from Interstate Commerce Commission reports, v. 87.] * Paper, 5c.

Beaver, Meade and Englewood Railroad. Finance docket no. 3183, construction of extension by Beaver, Meade & Englewood R. R.;. [decided Jan. 29, 1924; report of commission]. 1924. [1]+286-290 p. ([Finance decision]1168.) [From Interstate Commerce Commission reports, v. 86.] * Paper, 5c.

Bedding, for cattle. No. 13107, National Live Stock Exchange *v.* Atchison, Topeka & Santa Fe Railway Company et al.; decided Jan. 14, 1924; report of commission on further argument. [1924.] p. 157-158. ([Opinion]9142.) [From Interstate Commerce Commission reports, v. 87.] * Paper, 5c.

Beet final molasses. No. 14575, Utah-Idaho Sugar Company *v.* director general, as agent; decided Jan. 17, 1924; report of commission. [1924.] p. 361-362. ([Opinion]9198.) [From Interstate Commerce Commission reports, v. 87.] * Paper, 5c.

Beverages. No. 12115, Helena Traffic Bureau et al. *v.* Missouri Pacific Railroad Company, director general, as agent, et al.; [decided Jan. 17, 1924; report of commission], 1924. [1]+216-221 p. .([Opinion]9155.) [From Interstate Commerce Commission reports, v. 87.] * Paper, 5c.

Blytheville, Burdette and Mississippi River Railway. Finance docket no. 3275, abandonment of line by Blytheville, Burdette &.Mississippi River Ry.; [decided Dec.. 27, 1923; report of commission]. .1924. [1]+150-152 p. ([Finance decision]1122.) [From Interstate Commerce Commission reports, v. 86.] * Paper, 5c.

Boots and shoes. No. 14557, W. H. McElwain Company, trading as McElwain, Morse & Rogers, *v.* director general, as agent; decided Jan. 17, 1924; report [and order] of commission. [1924.] 359-360+[1] p. ([Opinion]9197.) [Report from Interstate Commerce Commission reports, v. 87.] * Paper, 5c.

Bricks. No. 14421, Galena Signal Oil Company (of Texas) *v.* director general, as agent; decided Dec. 28, 1923; report of commission. [1924.] p. 105-106. ([Opinion]9125.) [From Interstate Commerce Commission reports, v. 87.] * Paper, 5c.

—— No. 14555, T. L. Herbert & Sons et al. *v.* Norfolk & Western Railway Company et al.; decided Dec. 31, 1923; report [and order] of commission. [1924.] 139-141+[1] p. ([Opinion]9137.) [Report from Interstate Commerce Commission reports, v. 87.] * Paper, 5c.

Buffalo Creek Railroad. Finance. docket no. 3406, bonds of Buffalo Creek R. R.; [decided Jan. 12, 1924; report of commission]. .1924. [1]+208-210 p. ([Finance decision]1140.) [From Interstate Commerce Commission reports, v. 86.] * Paper, 5c.

Car-door boards. No. 14370, Colorado & Utah Coal Company et al. *v.* Denver & Salt Lake Railroad Company et al.; decided Dec. 28, 1923; report [and order] of commission. [1924.] 545-548+ii p. ([Opinion]9032.) [Report from Interstate Commerce Commission reports, v. 85.] * Paper, 5c.

Cast-iron. No. 14604, Elevator Supplies Company, Incorporated, *v.* director general, as agent, Southern Railway Company, et al.; [decided Dec. 31, 1923; report and order of commission]. 1924. [1]+102-104+[1] p. ([Opinion] 9124.) [Report from Interstate Commerce Commission reports, v. 87.] * Paper, 5c.

Castings. No. 14206, American Foundry & Machine Company *v.* Oregon Short Line Railroad Company, director general, as agent, et al.; decided Dec. 28, 1923; report [and order] of commission. [1924.] p. 3, [1]. ([Opinion] 9091.) [Report from Interstate Commerce Commission reports, v. 87.] * Paper, 5c.

Cement. No. 13891, Atlas Portland Cement Company *v.* Central Railroad Company of New Jersey et al.; portions of 4th section application. no. 1774; decided Dec. 27, 1923; report [and orders] of commission. [1924.] 611–616+ ii p. ([Opinion]9043.) [Report from Interstate Commerce Commission reports, v. 85.] * Paper, 5c.

Central Railway of Arkansas. Finance docket no. 2175, deficit settlement with Central Ry. Co. of Arkansas; decided Dec. 28, 1923; report of commission. [1924.] p. 271–272. ([Finance decision]1161.) [From Interstate Commerce Commission reports, v. 86.] * Paper, 5c.

Chicago and Eastern Illinois Railroad. Finance docket no. 2627, bonds of Chicago & Eastern Illinois Ry.; approved Jan. 19, 1924; 2d supplemental order. 1924. p. 263. ([Finance decision] 1158.) [From Interstate Commerce Commission reports, v. 86.] * Paper, 5c.

—— Finance docket no. 3361, bonds of Chicago & Eastern Illinois Railway; decided Jan. 16, 1924; report of commission. [1924.] p. 247–250. ([Finance decision] 1153.) [From Interstate Commerce Commission reports, v. 86.] * Paper, 5c.

Chicago and North Western Railway. Finance docket no. 3400, bonds of Chicago & North Western Ry.; decided Jan. 7, 1924; report of commission. [1924.] p. 201–203. ([Finance decision] 1138.) [From Interstate Commerce Commission reports, v. 86.] * Paper, 5c.

Chicago, Milwaukee and St. Paul Railway. Finance docket no. 3359, Chicago, Milwaukee & St. Paul bonds; decided Dec. 27, 1923; report of commission. [1924.] p. 181–183. ([Finance decision] 1129.) [From Interstate Commerce Commission reports, v. 86.] * Paper, 5c.

Cleveland, Cincinnati, Chicago and St. Louis Railway. Finance docket no. 3336, bonds of C., C., C. & St. L. Ry.; decided Dec. 29, 1923; report of commission. [1924.] p. 169–171. ([Finance decision] 1125.) [From Interstate Commerce Commission reports, v. 86.] * Paper, 5c.

Clothing. No. 14504, Camp Grant Laundering & Cleaning Company *v.* director general, as agent, and Chicago, Burlington & Quincy Railroad Company; decided Jan. 17, 1924; report [and order] of commission. [1924.] 265–267+[1] p. ([Opinion] 9170.) [Report from Interstate Commerce Commission reports, v. 87.] * Paper, 5c.

Coal. No. 13055, M'Grew Coal Company *v.* director general, as agent, and Missouri Pacific Railroad Company; decided Dec. 28, 1923; report [and order] of commission. [1924.] 735–736+[1] p. ([Opinion] 9080.) [Report from Interstate Commerce Commission reports, v. 85.] * Paper, 5c.

—— No. 13570, divisions between carriers of rates on bituminous coal to destinations in Michigan, Ohio, Indiana, Illinois, and Wisconsin under report of commission in ex parte. no. 74; decided Jan. 5, 1924; report [and order] of commission. [1924.] 617–625+[1] p. ([Opinion] 9044.) [Report from Interstate Commerce Commission reports, v. 85.] * Paper, 5c.

—— No. 13825, Hartland Railroad Company *v.* Baltimore & Ohio Railroad Company et al.; [decided Dec. 31, 1923; report and order of commission]. 1924. [1]+36–40+[1] p. ([Opinion] 9102.) [Report from Interstate Commerce Commission reports, v. 87.] * Paper, 5c.

—— No. 13968, National Tube Company *v.* director general, as agent, and Baltimore & Ohio Railroad Company; decided Dec. 28, 1923; report [and order] of commission. [1924.] 689–692+[1] p. ([Opinion] 9066.) [Report from Interstate Commerce Commission reports, v. 85.] * Paper, 5c.

—— No. 13982, Parker Brothers Company, Limited, *v.* director general, as agent; decided Dec. 27, 1923; report of commission. [1924.] p. 721–722. ([Opinion] 9076.) [From Interstate Commerce Commission reports, v. 85.] * Paper, 5c.

—— No. 14070, Central Wisconsin Supply Company *v.* Chicago, Milwaukee & St. Paul Railway Company et al.; decided Dec. 31, 1923; report [and order] of commission. [1924.] 63–64+[1] p. ([Opinion] 9111.) [Report from Interstate Commerce Commission reports, v. 87.] * Paper, 5c.

Coal—Continued. No. 14222, Corona Coal Company *v.* Southern Railway Company et al.; [no. 14213, same *v.* same; decided Dec. 31, 1923; report and order of commission]. 1924. [1]+126–129+[1] p. ([Opinion] 9132.) [Report from Interstate Commerce Commission reports, v. 87.] * Paper, 5c.

—— No. 14246, Corona Coal Company *v.* St. Louis–San Francisco Railway Company et al.; decided Dec. 27, 1923; report [and order] of commission. [1924.] 723–724+[1] p. ([Opinion] 9077.) [Report from Interstate Commerce Commission reports, v. 85.] * Paper, 5c.

—— No. 14272, Cambria Steel Company *v.* director general, as agent; [no. 14272 (sub-nos. 1 and 2), same *v.* same; decided Jan. 17, 1924; report of commission]. 1924. [1]+336–338 p. ([Opinion] 9190.) [From Interstate Commerce Commission reports, v. 87.] * Paper, 5c.

—— No. 14805, Otto Krueger *v.* Northern Pacific Railway Company and director general, as agent; decided Jan. 23, 1924; report [and order] of commission. [1924.] 399–400+[1] p. ([Opinion] 9206.) [Report from Interstate Commerce Commission reports, v. 87.] * Paper, 5c.

Colemanite. No. 14394, West End Chemical Company *v.* Los Angeles & Salt Lake Railroad Company et al.; decided Jan. 17, 1924; report [and order] of commission. [1924.] 327–330+[1] p. ([Opinion] 9178.) [Report from Interstate Commerce Commission reports, v. 87.] * Paper, 5c.

Colorado and Southern Railway. Finance docket no. 2657, securities of Colorado & Southern and subsidiaries and control by Colorado & Southern; decided Jan. 8, 1924; report of commission. [1924.] p. 213–220. ([Finance decision] 1142.) [From Interstate Commerce Commission reports, v. 86.] * Paper, 5c.

Columbus and Greenville Railway. Finance docket no. 3279, equipment notes of Columbus & Greenville Ry.; [decided Dec. 29, 1923; report of commission]. 1924. [1]+184–186 p. ([Finance decision] 1130.) [From Interstate Commerce Commission reports, v. 86.] * Paper, 5c.

—— Finance docket no. 3280, Columbus & Greenville Ry. stock; decided Dec. 29, 1923; report of commission. [1924.] p. 153–156. ([Finance decision] 1123.) [From Interstate Commerce Commission reports, v. 86.] * Paper, 5c.

Corn. No. 13918, Pacific Grain Company *v.* director general, as agent, Northern Pacific Railway Company, et al.; decided Jan. 17, 1924; report [and order] of commission. [1924.] 333–335+[1] p. ([Opinion] 9189.) [Report from Interstate Commerce Commission reports, v. 87.] * Paper, 5c.

—— No. 13964, T. B. Hord Grain Company *v.* director general, as agent; [decided Jan. 17, 1924; report of commission]. 1924. [1]+310–312 p. ([Opinion] 9181.) [From Interstate Commerce Commission reports, v. 87.] * Paper, 5c.

—— No. 14031, Edward A. Glenn *v.* director general, as agent; decided Dec. 28, 1923; report [and order] of commission. [1924.] 743–744+[1] p. ([Opinion] 9083.) [Report from Interstate Commerce Commission reports, v. 85.] * Paper, 5c.

Cotton. No. 13418, Houston Cotton Exchange & Board of Trade et al. *v.* Arcade & Attica Railroad Corporation et al.; [decided Jan. 23, 1924; report of commission]. 1924. [1]+392–398 p. ([Opinion] 9205.) [From Interstate Commerce Commission reports, v. 87.] * Paper, 5c.

—— No. 13631, Royall & Borden Manufacturing Company *v.* Atlantic Coast Line Railroad Company et al.; [no. 13632, same *v.* same; no. 13633, same *v.* same]; decided Dec. 27, 1923; report [and order] of commission. [1924.] 715–718+[1] p. ([Opinion] 9074.) [Report from Interstate Commerce Commission reports, v. 85.] * Paper, 5c.

Cotton goods. No. 13182, Wichita Board of Commerce *v.* Atchison, Topeka & Santa Fe Railway Company et al.; decided Jan. 21, 1924; report [and order] of commission. [1924.] 249–256+ii p. ([Opinion] 9165.) [Report from Interstate Commerce Commission reports, v. 87.] * Paper, 5c.

Cotton-seed. No. 14365, Prairie Cotton Oil Company *v.* Chicago, Rock Island & Gulf Railway Company et al.; [decided Dec. 31, 1923; report and order of commission]. 1924. [1]+88–89+[1] p. ([Opinion] 9118.) [Report from Interstate Commerce Commission reports, v. 87.] * Paper, 5c.

Cotton-seed—Continued. No. 14565, Nara Visa Lumber Company *v.* director general, as agent, Chicago, Rock Island & Pacific Railway Company, et al.; decided Dec. 31, 1923; report [and order] of commission. [1924.] 111–112+[1] p. ([Opinion] 9128.) [Report from Interstate Commerce Commission reports, v. 87.] * Paper, 5c.

Cotton-seed meal. Investigation and suspension docket no. 1923, cottonseed products from Texas to Louisville, Ky., and points in West Virginia; [portions of 4th section application no. 676]; decided Jan. 24, 1924; report [and orders] of commission. [1924.] 351–356+ii p. ([Opinion] 9195.) [Report from Interstate Commerce Commission reports, v. 87.] * Paper, 5c.

Cotton-seed oil. No. 14703, Palmine Company, Incorporated, *v.* Illinois Central Railroad Company et al.; decided Jan. 17, 1924; report [and order] of commission. [1924.] 279–284+[1] p. ([Opinion] 9174.) [Report from Interstate Commerce Commission reports, v. 87.] * Paper, 5c.

Damages. No. 14217, Brown Coal Company *v.* director general, as agent; [decided Dec. 31, 1923; report and order of commission]. 1924. [1]+130–131+[1] p. ([Opinion] 9133.) [Report from Interstate Commerce Commission reports, v. 87.] * Paper, 5c.

Decisions. Decisions of commission, May–June, 1923, index-digest to [Interstate Commerce Commission reports], v. 80, with table of commodities and table of localities; [prepared in] Section of Indices. 1924. cover-title, p. 779–925. ‡

—— Decisions of Interstate Commerce Commission (valuation reports), July, 1918–July, 1923. 1924. x+846 p. il. 5 maps. (Interstate Commerce Commission reports, v. 75.) * Cloth, $2.00.   8—30656

NOTE.—The Interstate Commerce Commission has decided to assign a volume in the series of reports at various times which will contain only valuation dockets. This is true regarding v. 75, which is the first volume of valuation dockets to be issued. The individual decisions contained in this volume have been printed separately.

Demurrage. No. 12033, Louisa Schaefer et al. *v.* Lehigh Valley Railroad Company; decided Dec. 20, 1923; report [and order] of commission on further hearing. [1924.] p. [605, 1]. ([Opinion] 9040.) [Volume number incorrectly given on publication as 87. Report from Interstate Commerce Commission reports, v. 85.] * Paper, 5c.

—— No. 13589, Gadsden Lumber Company *v.* Apalachicola Northern Railroad Company, director general, as agent, et al.; [decided Dec. 27, 1923; report and order of commission]. 1924. [1]+626–628+[1] p. ([Opinion] 9045.) [Report from Interstate Commerce Commission reports, v. 85.] * Paper, 5c.

—— No. 14208, Grenada Oil Mills *v.* director general of railroads, as agent, Illinois Central Railroad Company, et al.; decided Jan. 17, 1924; report [and order] of commission. [1924.] 325–326+[1] p. ([Opinion] 9186.) [Report from Interstate Commerce Commission reports, v. 87.] * Paper, 5c.

—— No. 14220, Getz Brothers & Company *v.* director general, as agent; decided Dec. 27, 1923; report [and order] of commission. [1924.] 673–674+[1] p. ([Opinion] 9059.) [Report from Interstate Commerce Commission reports, v. 85.] * Paper, 5c.

—— No. 14322, Gammill Lumber Company *v.* Alabama & Vicksburg Railway Company et al.; decided Dec. 31, 1923; report [and order] of commission. [1924.] 41–42+[1] p. ([Opinion] 9103.) [Report from Interstate Commerce Commission reports, v. 87.] * Paper, 5c.

—— No. 14626, Republic Coal Company *v.* Chicago, Milwaukee & St. Paul Railway Company; decided Jan. 23, 1924; report [and order] of commission. [1924.] 415–416+[1] p. ([Opinion] 9212.) [Report from Interstate Commerce Commission reports, v. 87.] * Paper, 5c.

—— No. 14716, P. Koenig Coal Company *v.* Grand Trunk Western Railway Company et al.; decided Dec. 29, 1923; report [and order] of commission. [1924.] 33–35+[1] p. ([Opinion] 9101.) [Report from Interstate Commerce Commission reports, v. 87.] * Paper, 5c.

Derricks. No. 14697, Indiana State Highway Commission *v.* Cleveland, Cincinnati, Chicago & St. Louis Railway Company et al.; decided Dec. 28, 1923; report [and order] of commission. [1924.] 95–97+[1] p. ([Opinion] 9121.) [Report from Interstate Commerce Commission reports, v. 87.] * Paper, 5c.

Dyewoods. No. 13402, American Dyewood Company *v.* Atlantic Coast Line Railroad Company et al.; decided Jan. 17, 1924; report [and order] of commission. [1924.] 297–302+[1] p. ([Opinion] 9178.) [Report from Interstate Commerce Commission reports, v. 87.] * Paper, 5c.

El Paso and Southwestern System. Finance docket no. 3135, control and securities of El Paso & Southwestern subsidiaries; [decided Dec. 26, 1923; report of commission]. 1924. [1]+122–134 p. ([Finance decision] 1118.) [From Interstate Commerce Commission reports, v. 86.] * Paper, 5c.

Evansville, Indianapolis and Terre Haute Railway. Finance docket no. 3330, acquisition and operation of line by Evansville, Indianapolis & Terre Haute Ry.; decided Jan. 24, 1924; report of commission. [1924.] p. 291–293. ([Finance decision] 1169.) [From Interstate Commerce Commission reports, v. 86.] * Paper, 5c.

Express. In equity, no 666, in Supreme Court, Oct. term, 1923, United States, Interstate Commerce Commission, et al. *v.* American Railway Express Company et al.; brief for Interstate Commerce Commission. 1924. cover-title, i+29 p. ‡

Fence-posts. No. 14329, Nebraska Bridge Supply & Lumber Company *v.* director general, as agent; [decided Jan. 17, 1924; report of commission]. 1924. [1]+234–238 p. ([Opinion] 9160.) [From Interstate Commerce Commission reports, v. 87.] * Paper, 5c.

Fire-brick. No. 13712, Barnsdall Refining Company et al. *v.* Atchison, Topeka & Santa Fe Railway Company et al.; decided Dec. 27, 1923; report of commission. [1924.] p. 685–686. ([Opinion] 9064.) [From Interstate Commerce Commission reports, v. 85.] * Paper, 5c.

Fluxing stone. No. 14232, Cambria Steel Company *v.* director general, as agent; [decided Jan. 17, 1924; report of commission]. 1924. [1]+342–344 p. ([Opinion] 9192.) [From Interstate Commerce Commission reports, v. 87.] * Paper, 5c.

Food for cattle. No. 12996, John W. Eshelman & Sons et al. *v.* Arkansas Central Railroad Company et al.; decided Jan. 21, 1924; report of commission. [1924.] p. 285–290. ([Opinion] 9175.) [From Interstate Commerce Commission reports, v. 87.] * Paper, 5c.

—— No. 13616, Josey-Miller Company *v.* Brimstone Railroad & Canal Company et al.; [no. 13616 (sub-no. 3), Orange Rice Mill Company *v.* Beaumont, Sour Lake & Western Railway Company et al.]; decided Jan. 17, 1924; report [and order] of commission. [1924.] 207–210+ii p. ([Opinion] 9152.) [Report from Interstate Commerce Commission reports, v. 87.] * Paper, 5c.

Fredericksburg and Northern Railway. Finance docket no. 3412, Fredericksburg & Northern Ry. notes; decided Jan. 18, 1924; report of commission. [1924.] p. 267–270. ([Finance decision] 1160.) [From Interstate Commerce Commission reports, v. 86.] * Paper, 5c.

Freight-cars. No. 14633, W. J. Stahlberg, doing business as Winter's Metallic Paint Company, *v.* Chicago, Milwaukee & St. Paul Railway Company; decided Dec. 31, 1923; report [and order] of commission. [1924.] 113–114+ [1] p. ([Opinion] 9129.) [Report from Interstate Commerce Commission reports, v. 87.] * Paper, 5c.

Freight rates. No. 456, in Supreme Court, Oct. term, 1923, United States and Interstate Commerce Commission *v.* Abilene & Southern Railway Company et al., appeal from district court for district of Kansas; brief for Interstate Commerce Commission. 1924. cover-title, iii+62 p. map. ‡

—— No. 13267, San Luis Valley Federation of Commerce et al. *v.* director general, as agent, Denver & Rio Grande Western Railroad Company, et al.; decided Jan. 17, 1924; report [and order] of commission. [1924.] 291–293+ [1] p. ([Opinion] 9176.) [Report from Interstate Commerce Commission reports, v. 87.] * Paper, 5c.

—— No. 13614, Hanging Rock Iron Company *v.* Norfolk & Western Railway Company et al.; decided Jan. 23, 1924; report [and order] of commission. [1924.] 373–382+iii p. ([Opinion] 9203.) [Report from Interstate Commerce Commission reports, v. 87.] * Paper, 5c.

—— No. 14079, Theo. W. Krein, receiver, Muscatine, Burlington & Southern Railroad Company, *v.* Chicago, Burlington & Quincy Railroad Company et al.; [decided Dec. 31, 1923; report and order of commission]. 1924. [1]+118– 125+[1] p. ([Opinion] 9131.) [Report from Interstate Commerce Commission reports, v. 87.] * Paper, 5c.

Freight rates—Continued. Short and long distance hauls, interstate commerce law, letter transmitting, in response to resolution, 67th Congress, 4th session, report on administration of sec. 4 of interstate commerce act. Feb. 13, calendar day Feb. 14, 1924. 42 p. (S. doc. 50, 68th Cong. 1st sess.)   * Paper, 5c.   24—26181

Fuel-oil. No. 13889, Midwest Refining Company *v.* director general, as agent; decided Dec. 27, 1923; report [and order] of commission. [1924.] 719–720+[1] p. ([Opinion] 9075.) [Report from Interstate Commerce Commission reports, v. 85.] * Paper, 5c.

Gas oil. No. 13888, Omaha Blaugas Company et al. *v.* Atchison, Topeka & Santa Fe Railway Company et al.; decided Dec. 28, 1923; report of commission. [1924.] p. 737–739. ([Opinion] 9081.) [From Interstate Commerce Commission reports, v. 85.] * Paper, 5c.

Gasoline. No. 14187, Standard Oil Company *v.* director general, as agent, and Missouri Pacific Railroad Company; [decided Dec. 31, 1923; report and order of commission]. 1924. [1]+214–215+[1] p. ([Opinion] 9154.) [Report from Interstate Commerce Commission reports, v. 87.] * Paper, 5c.

Georgia Northern Railway. Finance docket no. 3308, Georgia Northern Railway bonds; decided Jan. 11, 1924; report of commission. [1924.] p. 221–222. ([Finance decision] 1143.) [From Interstate Commerce Commission reports, v. 86.] * Paper, 5c.   .

Gilsonite. No. 12716, Utah Gilsonite Company *v.* Atchison, Topeka & Santa Fe Railway Company et al.; decided Dec. 28, 1923; report [and order] of commission. [1924.] 557–577+ii p. ([Opinion] 9034.) [Report from Interstate Commerce Commission reports, v. 85.] * Paper, 5c.

Grain. Investigation and suspension docket no. 1931, grain from Oklahoma points to Memphis, Tenn., and to Texas and Louisiana ports for export; [decided Dec. 28, 1923.] report and order of commission]. 1924. [1]+602–604+[1] p. ([Opinion] 9039.) [Report from Interstate Commerce Commission reports, v. 85.] * Paper, 5c.   ·

—— No. 13000, Board of Railroad Commissioners of South Dakota *v.* Chicago & North Western Railway Company et al.; decided Dec. 14, 1923; [report and order of commission]. [1924.] 217–246+iv p. ([Opinion] 8976.) [Report from Interstate Commerce Commission reports, v. 85.] * Paper, 5c.

—— No. 13595, Albert H. Buehrle Company *v.* Baltimore & Ohio Railroad Company et al.; decided Jan. 17, 1924; report [and order] of commission. [1924.] 303–306+ii p. ([Opinion] 9179.) [Report from Interstate Commerce Commission reports, v. 87.] * Paper, 5c.

—— No. 13658, C. B. Westrope et al. *v.* director general, as agent; decided Jan. 17, 1924; report [and order] of commission. [1924.] 225–228+[1] p. ([Opinion] 9157.) [Report from Interstate Commerce Commission reports, v. 87.] * Paper, 5c.

Hay. No. 14093, Burge-Doyle Live Stock Company et al. *v.* Arizona Eastern Railroad Company et al.; decided Jan. 17, 1924; report [and order] of commission. [1924.] 319–321+[1] p. ([Opinion] 9184.) [Report from Interstate Commerce Commission reports, v. 87.] * Paper, 5c.

Hoop-poles. No. 13639, Creamery Package Manufacturing Company *v.* director general, as agent, Pere Marquette Railway Company, et al.; [no. 13684, same *v.* same]; decided Jan. 17, 1924; report [and order] of commission. [1924.] 201–202+[1] p. ([Opinion] 9150.) [Report from Interstate Commerce Commission reports, v. 87.] * Paper, 5c.

Ice. No. 12062, Wilson & Company, Incorporated, *v.* director general, as agent; decided Dec. 11, 1923; report of commission. [1924.] p. 81–85. ([Opinion] 9116.) [From Interstate Commerce Commission reports, v. 87.] * Paper, 5c.

—— No. 14339, City Ice & Fuel Company *v.* director general, as agent; decided Dec. 29, 1923; report of commission. [1924.] p. 55–57. ([Opinion] 9108.) [From Interstate Commerce Commission reports, v. 87.] * Paper, 5c.

Iron. No. 13608, Southern Wire & Iron Company et al. *v.* Akron, Canton & Youngstown Railway Company et al.; decided Dec. 31, 1923; report of commission. [1924.] p. 115–117. ([Opinion] 9130.) [From Interstate Commerce Commission reports, v. 87.] * Paper, 5c. ñ

—— No. 14290, Briggs & Turivas *v.* Michigan Central Railroad Company et al.; decided Dec. 31, 1923; report [and order] of commission. [1924.] 109–110+[1] p. ([Opinion] 9127.) [Report from Interstate Commerce Commission reports, v. 87.] * Paper, 5c.   · ·

Jackson and Eastern·Railway. Finance docket no. 9, public convenience certificate to Jackson & Eastern Railway; approved Jan. 18, 1924; supplemental order. 1924. p. 259. ([Finance decision] 1156.) [From Interstate Commerce Commission reports, v. 86.] * Paper, 5c.

Kansas and Oklahoma Southern Railway. Finance docket no. 1621, public convenience certificate to Kansas & Oklahoma Southern Ry.; approved Jan. 5, 1924; order. 1924. p. 195. ([Finance decision] 1135.) [From Interstate Commerce Commission reports, v. 86.] * Paper, 5c.

—— Finance docket no. 2422, Kansas & Oklahoma Southern bonds and notes; approved Jan. 7, 1924; 2d supplemental order. 1924. p. 187. ([Finance decision] 1131.) [From Interstate Commerce Commission reports, v. 86.] * Paper, 5c.

Kentucky and Indiana Terminal Railroad. Finance docket no. 3283, Kentucky & Indiana Terminal Railroad bonds; [and finance docket no. 3283 (sub–nos. 1-3)]; decided Dec. 27, 1923; corrected report of commission. [1924.] p. 113–115. ([Finance decision] 1115.) [From Interstate Commerce Commission reports. v. 86.] * Paper, 5c.

Keokuk and Des Moines Railway. Finance docket no. 3377, lease of Keokuk & Des Moines Ry. by Chicago, Rock Island & Pacific Ry.; decided Dec. 22, 1923; report of commission. [1924.] p. 119–121. ([Finance decision] 1117.) [From Interstate Commerce Commission reports, v. 86.] * Paper, 5c.

Lake Tahoe Railway and Transportation Company. Finance docket no. 3398, notes of Lake Tahoe Railway & Transportation Company; decided Jan. 5, 1924; report of commission. [1924.] p. 193–195. ([Finance decision] 1134.) [From Interstate Commerce Commission reports, v. 86.] * Paper, 5c.

Lamps. No. 14343, Larkin Company, Incorporated, *v.* Chicago & Erie Railroad Company et al.; decided Dec. 27, 1923; report [and order] of commission. [1924.] 649–650+[1] p. ([Opinion] 9053.) [Report from Interstate Commerce Commission reports, v. 85.] **Paper, 5c.**

Lessees Buffalo Creek Railroad. Finance docket no. 328, guaranty settlement with Lessees Buffalo Creek R. R.; [decided Dec. 24, 1923; report of commission]. 1924. [1]+108–110 p. ([Finance decision] 1113.) [From Interstate Commerce Commission reports, v. 86.] * Paper, 5c.

Lime. No. 13304, Utah Lime & Stone Company *v.* Atchison, Topeka & Santa Fe Railway Company et al.; decided Jan. 16, 1924; report [and order] of commission. [1924.] 181–188+ii p. ([Opinion] 9145.) [Report from Interstate Commerce Commission reports, v. 87.] * Paper, 5c.

—— No. 13305, Utah Lime & Stone Company *v.* Atchison, Topeka & Santa Fe Railway Company et al.; [decided Jan. 16, 1924; report and order of commission]. 1924. [1]+170–180+ii p. ([Opinion] 9144.) [Report from Interstate Commerce Commission reports, v. 87.] * Paper, 5c.

—— No. 14001, Hoosier Lime Company *v.* director general, as agent; decided Jan. 17, 1924; report [and order] of commission. [1924.] 261–262+[1] p. ([Opinion] 9168.) [Report from Interstate Commerce Commission reports, v. 87.] * Paper, 5c.

Logs. No. 12373, Kneeland-Bigelow Company et al. *v.* director general, as agent, and Michigan Central Railroad Company; [no. 13111, same *v.* Michigan Central Railroad Company; no. 13903, Bay City Transportation Association et al. *v.* director general, as agent, and Michigan Central Railroad Company]; decided Jan. 8, 1924; report [and order] of commission. [1924.] 659–664+[1] p. ([Opinion] 9057.) [Report from Interstate Commerce Commission reports, v. 85.] * Paper, 5c.

—— No. 14059, West Coast Shingle Company *v.* Northern Pacific Railway Company; decided Jan. 17, 1924; report [and order] of commission. [1924.] 317–318+[1] p. ([Opinion] 9183.) [Report from Interstate Commerce Commission reports, v. 87.] * Paper, 5c.

—— No. 14679, Diamond Match Company *v.* director general, as agent; decided Dec. 31, 1923; report [and order] of commission. [1924.] 107–108+[1] p. ([Opinion] 9126.) [Report from Interstate Commerce Commission reports, v. 87.] * Paper, 5c.

Los Angeles and Salt Lake Railroad. In equity, no. H–44–T, in district court for southern district of California, southern division, Los Angeles & Salt Lake Railroad Company *v.* United States and Interstate Commerce Commission; answer of Interstate Commerce Commission. 1924. cover-title, 15 p. ‡

Lumber. No. 14024, Allegheny Lumber Company *v.* Pittsburg, Shawmut & Northern Railroad Company et al.; decided Dec. 27, 1923; report [and order] of commission. [1924.] p. 643, [1]. ([Opinion] 9050.) [Report from Interstate Commerce Commission reports, v. 85.] * Paper, 5c.

—— No. 14170, American Box Company *v.* director general, as agent, Hampton & Branchville Railroad Company, et al.; [decided Dec. 28, 1923; report and order of commission]. 1924. [1]+750-752+[1] p. ([Opinion] 9086.) [Report from Interstate Commerce Commission reports, v. 85.] * Paper, 5c.

—— No. 14242, Consolidated Lumber Company *v.* director general, as agent, et al.; decided Dec. 28, 1923; report [and order] of commission. [1924.] 1-2+[1] p. ([Opinion] 9090.) [Report from Interstate Commerce Commission reports, v. 87.] * Paper, 5c.

—— No. 14279, Arizona Corporation Commission *v.* Atchison, Topeka & Santa Fe Railway Company et al.; decided Jan. 17, 1924; report [and order] of commission. [1924.] 271-274+ii p. ([Opinion] 9172.) [Report from Interstate Commerce Commission reports, v. 87.] * Paper, 5c.

—— No. 14293, Edward Hines Lumber Company *v.* director general, as agent; decided Dec. 28, 1923; report [and order] of commission. [1924.] 17-18+ [1] p. ([Opinion] 9095.) [Report from Interstate Commerce Commission reports, v. 87.] * Paper, 5c.

Marion Railway Corporation. Finance docket no. 613, guaranty settlement with Marion Ry.; decided Jan. 29, 1924; report of commission. [1924.] p. 277-279. ([Finance decision] 1164.) [From Interstate Commerce Commission reports, v. 86.] * Paper, 5c.

Meat. No. 13426, Guggenheim Brothers *v.* director general, as agent, et al.; decided Dec. 27, 1923; report of commission. [1924.] p. 725-727. ([Opinion] 9078.) [From Interstate Commerce Commission reports, v. 85.] * Paper, 5c.

Mine props. No. 14094, Lafayette Lumber Company *v.* director general, as agent, Erie Railroad Company, et al.; decided Dec. 27, 1923; report [and order] of commission. [1924.] 647-648+[1] p. ([Opinion] 9052.) [Report from Interstate Commerce Commission reports, v. 85.] * Paper, 5c.

Misrouting. No. 13729, Dells Paper & Pulp Company *v.* director general, as agent, Houston & Brazos Valley Railway Company, et al.; decided Dec. 27, 1923; report [and order] of commission. [1924.] 609-610+[1] p. ([Opinion] 9042.) [Report from Interstate Commerce Commission reports, v. 85.] * Paper, 5c.

—— No. 14100, H. G. Prince & Company *v.* director general, as agent; decided Jan. 17, 1924; report [and order] of commission. [1924.] 229-230+[1] p. ([Opinion] 9158.) [Report from Interstate Commerce Commission reports, v. 87.] * Paper, 5c.

—— No. 14112, E. E. Howe et al. *v.* Chicago & North Western Railway Company et al.; [decided Dec. 28, 1923; report and order of commission]. 1924. [1]+760-762+[1] p. ([Opinion] 9089.) [Report from Interstate Commerce Commission reports, v. 85.] * Paper, 5c.

—— No. 14851, L. G. Everist, Incorporated, et al. *v.* Chicago, Milwaukee & St. Paul Railway Company; decided Dec. 29, 1923; report of commission. [1924.] p. 31-32. ([Opinion] 9100.) [From Interstate Commerce Commission reports, v. 87.] * Paper, 5c.

Mobile and Ohio Railroad. Finance docket no. 3391, Mobile & Ohio equipment trust, series M; [decided Dec. 31, 1923; report of commission]. 1924. [1]+204-207 p. ([Finance decision] 1139.) [From Interstate Commerce Commission reports, v. 86.] * Paper, 5c.

Molasses. No. 13732, H. L. Halliday Milling Company *v.* director general, as agent, and Mobile & Ohio Railroad Company; decided Dec. 27, 1923; report [and order] of commission. [1924.] 687-688+[1] p. ([Opinion] 9065.) [Report from Interstate Commerce Commission reports, v. 85.] * Paper, 5c.

—— No. 13870, Arcady Farms Milling Company *v.* Nashville, Chattanooga & St. Louis Railway et al.; decided Dec. 31, 1923; report [and order] of commission. [1924.] 67-69+[1] p. ([Opinion] 9113.) [Report from Interstate Commerce Commission reports, v. 87.] * Paper, 5c.

Monongahela Railway. Finance docket no. 3379, Monongahela Railway bonds; [decided Jan. 18, 1924; report of commission]. 1924. [1]+260-262 p. ([Finance decision] 1157.) [From Interstate Commerce Commission reports, v. 86.] * Paper, 5c.

Nails. No. 14336, Charles G. Bard *v.* director general, Toledo, St. Louis & Western Railroad Company, et al.; decided Dec. 31, 1923; report [and order] of commission. [1924.] 65–66+[1] p. ([Opinion], 9112.) [Report from Interstate Commerce Commission reports, v. 87.] * Paper, 5c.

New Jersey and New York Railroad. Finance docket no. 685, guaranty status of New Jersey & New York R. R.; decided Jan. 10, 1924; report of commission. [1924.] p. 211–212. ([Finance decision] 1141.) [From Interstate Commerce Commission reports, v. 86.] * Paper, 5c.

New York Central Railroad. Finance docket no. 3381, New York Central Railroad stock; [decided Dec. 31, 1923; report of commission]. 1924. [1]+196–198 p. ([Finance decision] 1136.) [From Interstate Commerce Commission reports, v. 86.] * Paper, 5c.

New York, New Haven and Hartford Railroad. Finance docket no. 3384, bonds of N. Y., N. H. & H. Railroad; decided Dec. 27, 1923; report of commission. [1924.] p. 179–180. ([Finance decision] 1128.) [From Interstate Commerce Commission reports, v. 86.] * Paper, 5c.

Northwest (U. S.). Movements of products of northwest Pacific States, letter transmitting report concerning adequacy of transportation facilities in 1922 for movement of products of northwest Pacific States. Feb. 7, 1924. 28 p. (S. doc. 35, 68th Cong. 1st sess.) * Paper, 5c.   24—26153

Northwestern Bell Telephone Company. Finance docket no. 3335, acquisition of properties by Northwestern Bell Telephone Co. and Adel Mutual Telephone Co.; decided Jan. 15, 1924; report of commission. [1924.] p. 251–253. ([Finance decision] 1154.) [From Interstate Commerce Commission reports, v. 86.] * **Paper, 5c.**

Norwood and St. Lawrence Railroad. Finance docket no. 3356, notes of Norwood & St. Lawrence R. R.; [decided Jan. 3, 1924; report of commission]. 1924. [1]+188–190 p. ([Finance decision] 1132.) [From Interstate Commerce Commission reports, v. 86.] * Paper, 5c.

Oahu Railway and Land Company. Finance docket no. 3195, stock dividend of Oahu Railway & Land Company; decided Dec. 24, 1923; report of commission. [1924.] p. 137–147. ([Finance decision] 1120.) [From Interstate Commerce Commission reports, v. 86.] * Paper, 5c.

Oats. No. 13597, Pacific Grain Company *v.* director general, as agent, Northern Pacific Railway Company, et al.; [decided Dec. 31, 1923; report of commission]. 1924. [1]+58–60 p. ([Opinion] 9109.) [From Interstate Commerce Commission reports, v. 87.] * Paper, 5c.

—— No. 14864, Callahan & Sons *v.* director general, as agent; decided Jan. 21, 1924; report [and order] of commission. [1924.] 331–332+[1] p. ([Opinion] 9188.) [Report from Interstate Commerce Commission reports, v. 87.] * Paper, 5c.

Ocher. No. 14442, Meridian Fertilizer Factory *v.* director general, as agent, Nashville, Chattanooga & St. Louis Railway, et al.; portion of 4th section application no. 458; decided Jan. 17, 1924; report [and orders] of commission. [1924.] 275–278+ii p. ([Opinion] 9173.) [Report from Interstate Commerce Commission reports, v. 87.] * Paper, 5c.

Oil-well machinery. No. 14238, Layne & Bowler Company *v.* director general, as agent; [decided Dec. 31, 1923; report and order of commission]. 1924. [1]+86–87+[1] p. ([Opinion] 9117.) [Report from Interstate Commerce Commission reports, v. 87.] * Paper, 5c.

Oklahoma City-Ada-Atoka Railway. Finance docket no. 3309, acquisition of line by Oklahoma City-Ada-Atoka Railway; [decided Jan. 16, 1924; report of commission]. 1924. [1]+240–242 p. ([Finance decision] 1151.) [From Interstate Commerce Commission reports, v. 86.] * Paper, 5c.

Oklahoma City Shawnee Interurban Railway. Finance docket no. 3325, acquisition of line by Oklahoma City Shawnee Interurban Railway; decided Jan. 16, 1924; report of commission. [1924.] p. 273–274. ([Finance decision] 1162.) [From Interstate Commerce Commission reports, v. 86.] * Paper, 5c.

Oregon-Washington Railroad and Navigation Company. Finance docket no. 3339, construction of extension by Oregon-Washington Railroad & Navigation Co.; [decided Jan. 16, 1924; report of commission]. 1924. [1]+264–266 p. ([Finance decision] 1159.) [From Interstate Commerce Commission reports, v. 86.] * Paper, 5c.

Osage orange. No. 12820, West Virginia Pulp & Paper Company, Incorporated, *v.* director general, as agent; decided Jan. 17, 1924; report [and order] of commission. [1924.] 203–206+[1] p. ([Opinion]. 9151.) [Report from Interstate Commerce Commission reports, v. 87.] * Paper, 5c.

Paper. No. 14309, Kalamazoo Vegetable Parchment Company *v.* director general, as agent, Chicago, Kalamazoo & Saginaw Railway Company, et al.; decided Dec. 28, 1923; report of commission. [1924.] p. 19–20. ([Opinion] 9096.) [From Interstate Commerce Commission reports, v. 87.] * Paper, 5c.

Paraffin. No. 13890, Midwest Refining Company *v.* director general, as agent; [decided Jan. 17, 1924; report and order of commission]. 1924. [1]+256–257+[1] p. ([Opinion] 9166.) [Report from Interstate Commerce Commission reports, v. 87.] * Paper, 5c.

Patterns (wooden). No. 13993, American Manganese Steel Company *v.* Atchison, Topeka & Santa Fe Railway Company et al.; [decided Dec. 31, 1923; report and order of commission]. 1924. [1]+78–80+ii p. ([Opinion] 9115.) [Report from Interstate Commerce Commission reports, v. 87.] * Paper, 5c.

Peanuts. No. 13981, Albers Bros. Milling Company *v.* director general, as agent; decided Dec. 28, 1923; report of commission. [1924.] p. 747–749. ([Opinion] 9085.) [From Interstate Commerce Commission reports, v. 85.] * Paper, 5c.

Pere Marquette Railway. Finance docket no. 3319, bonds of Pere Marquette Railway; decided Jan. 9, 1924; report of commission. [1924.] p. 223–225. ([Finance decision] 1144.) [From Interstate Commerce Commission reports, v. 86.] * Paper, 5c.

Petroleum. Investigation and suspension docket no. 1831, petroleum, Kansas and Oklahoma to El Paso, Tex., and group; [decided Jan. 7, 1924; report and order of commission]. 1924. [1]+70–77+[1] p. ([Opinion] 9114.) [Report from Interstate Commerce Commission reports, v. 87.] * Paper, 5c.

—— No. 12566, Magnolia Petroleum Company *v.* director general, as agent, Oklahoma, New Mexico & Pacific Railway Company, et al.; [no. 12566 (sub-no. 1), same *v.* same; decided Dec. 27, 1923; report of commission]. 1924. [1]+712–715 p. ([Opinion] 9073.) [From Interstate Commerce Commission reports, v. 85.] * Paper, 5c.

—— No. 13206, Minneapolis Gas Light Company et al. *v.* director general, as agent; decided Jan. 15, 1924; report of commission. [1924.] p. 149–153. ([Opinion] 9140.) [From Interstate Commerce Commission reports, v. 87.] * Paper, 5c.

—— No. 13428, Utah Oil Refining Company *v.* director general, as agent; [decided Dec. 27, 1923; report and order of commission]. 1924. [1]+654–656+[1] p. ([Opinion] 9055.) [Report from Interstate Commerce Commission reports, v. 85.] * Paper, 5c.

—— No. 13498, North American Oil & Refining Corporation *v.* director general, as agent, Kansas City, Mexico & Orient Railroad Company, et al.; [no. 13498 (sub-no. 1), same *v.* Kansas City, Mexico & Orient Railroad Company et al.; no. 13498 (sub-no. 2), same *v.* same]; decided Dec. 28, 1923; report of commission. [1924.] p. 697–701. ([Opinion] 9069.) [From Interstate Commerce Commission reports, v. 85.] * Paper, 5c.

—— No. 13862, W. P. Fuller & Company *v.* director general, as agent; [decided Jan. 17, 1924; report of commission]. 1924. [1]+294–296 p. ([Opinion] 9177.) [From Interstate Commerce Commission reports, v. 87.] * Paper, 5c.

—— No. 14247, Wadhams Oil Company et al. *v.* Chicago & North Western Railway Company et al.; [no. 14247 (sub-no. 1), O'Neil Oil & Paint Company *v.* same]; decided Dec. 28, 1923; report of commission. [1924.] p. 705–709. ([Opinion] 9071.) [From Interstate Commerce Commission reports, v. 85.] * Paper, 5c.

Philadelphia and Beach Haven Railroad. Finance docket no. 737, guaranty settlement with Philadelphia & Beach Haven Railroad; decided Jan. 23, 1924; report of commission. [1924.] p. 281–282. ([Finance decision] 1166.) [From Interstate Commerce Commission reports, v. 86.] * Paper, 5c.

Phosphates. No. 14141, Tennessee Chemical Company *v.* Louisville & Nashville Railroad Company et al.; [no. 13591, Read Phosphate Company *v.* director general, as agent; decided Dec. 29, 1923; report of commission]. 1924. [1]+46-50 p. ([Opinion] 9105.) [From Interstate Commerce Commission reports, v. 87.] * Paper, 5c.

Pipe. No. 12845, Harry A. Pitts *v.* Texas & Pacific Railway Company et al.; decided Dec. 27, 1923; report [and order] of commission. [1924.] 635-636 +[1] p. ([Opinion] 9047.) [Report from Interstate Commerce Commission reports, v. 85.] * Paper, 5c.

—— No. 13389, Lynchburg Foundry Company *v.* Norfolk & Western Railway Company et al.; [decided Dec. 27, 1923; report and order of commission]. 1924. [1]+90-92+[1] p. ([Opinion] 9119.) [Report from Interstate Commerce Commission reports, v. 87.] * Paper, 5c.

—— No. 13756, Southern Carbon Company *v.* Arkansas & Louisiana Missouri Railway Company et al.; [decided Dec. 27, 1923; report and order of commission]. 1924. [1]+542-544+ii p. ([Opinion] 9031.) [Report from Interstate Commerce Commission reports, v. 85.] * Paper, 5c.

—— No. 13784, Crawford & Sebastian *v.* Chicago, Rock Island & Pacific Railway Company et al.; decided Dec. 28, 1923; report [and order] of commission. [1924.] 753-756+[1] p. ([Opinion] 9087.) [Report from Interstate Commerce Commission reports, v. 85.] * Paper, 5c.

—— No. 13828, General Fire Extinguisher Company *v.* director general, as agent; decided Jan. 17, 1924; report [and order] of commission. [1924.] 241-242+[1] p. ([Opinion] 9162.). [Report from Interstate Commerce Commission reports, v. 87.] * Paper, 5c.

—— No. 14596, Shearman Concrete Pipe Company *v.* Southern Railway Company et al.; [decided Jan. 17, 1924; report of commission]. 1924. [1]+344-346 p. ([Opinion] 9193.) [From Interstate Commerce Commission reports, v. 87.] * Paper, 5c.

Pittsburg, Shawmut and Northern Railroad. Finance docket no. 748, guaranty settlement with Pittsburg, Shawmut & Northern R. R. [John D. Dickson, receiver]; decided Jan. 12, 1924; report of commission. [1924.] p. 227-229. ([Finance decision] 1146.) [From Interstate Commerce Commission reports, v. 86.] * Paper, 5c.

Plaster. No. 13337, Nephi Plaster & Manufacturing Company *v.* Denver & Rio Grande Western Railroad Company et al.; decided Jan. 16, 1924; report [and order] of commission. [1924.] 159-169+ii p. ([Opinion] 9143.) [Report from Interstate Commerce Commission reports, v. 87.] * Paper, 5c.

Plates, Steel. No. 12428, Willamette Iron & Steel Works et al. *v.* director general, as agent, Baltimore & Ohio Railroad Company, et al.; decided Dec. 20, 1923; report of commission. [1924.] p. 629-634. ([Opinion] 9046.) [From Interstate Commerce Commission reports, v. 85.] * Paper, 5c.

—— No. 14299, Worth Steel Company *v.* director general, as agent; decided Dec. 31, 1923; report [and order] of commission. [1924.] 29-30+[1] p. ([Opinion] 9099.) [Report from Interstate Commerce Commission reports, v. 87.] * Paper, 5c.

Poles. No. 13646, Walter A. Zelnicker Supply Company *v.* director general, as agent, Southern Railway Company, et al.; decided Jan. 17, 1924; report [and order] of commission. [1924.] 239-240+[1] p. ([Opinion] 9161.) [Report from Interstate Commerce Commission reports, v. 87.] * Paper, 5c.

Poultry. No. 13379, Southern Poultry & Egg Shippers' Association et al. *v.* Alabama & Mississippi Railroad Company et al; decided Dec. 28, 1923; report [and order] of commission. [1924.] 11-16+[1] p. ([Opinion] 9094.) [Report from Interstate Commerce Commission reports, v. 87.] * Paper, 5c.

Press cloth. No. 12946, Charles Harley Company *v.* director general, as agent; decided Dec. 31, 1923; report [and order] of commission. [1924.] 61-62+[1] p. ([Opinion] 9110.) [Report from Interstate Commerce Commission reports, v. 87.] * Paper, 5c.

Railroad accidents. Accident bulletin 89, collisions, derailments, and other accidents resulting in injury to persons, equipment, or roadbed, arising from operation of steam roads used in interstate commerce, Apr.–June, 1923; [prepared in] Bureau of Statistics. 1924. iv+14 p. 4° [Quarterly.] * Paper, 5c. single copy quarterly issue, 25c. a yr.; foreign subscription, 40c. (10c. per copy on publication incorrect). 5—41547

Railroad accidents—Continued. Report of director of Bureau of Safety in re investigation of accident which occurred on New York Central Railroad near Forsyth, N. Y., on Dec. 9, 1923. [1924.] 16 p. il. * Paper, 5c.

—— Summary of accident investigation reports, no. 17, July–Sept. 1923; [prepared in] Bureau of Safety. 1924. iii+38 p. [Quarterly.] * Paper, 5c. single copy, 15c. a yr.; foreign subscription, 25c. A20—942

Railroad employees. Statistical analysis of carriers' monthly hours of service reports covering all railroads which reported, year ending June 30, 1923, instances in which employees were on duty for periods other than those provided by Federal hours of service act, with comparative summary covering fiscal years 1919–23. Nov. 1923. 36 p. oblong large 8° * Paper, 10c. A24—242

Railroads. Freight and passenger service operating statistics of class 1 steam roads in United States, compiled from 161 reports of freight statistics representing 176 roads and from 158 reports of passenger statistics representing 173 roads (switching and terminal companies not included), Dec. 1923 and 1922 [and 12 months ended with Dec. 1923 and 1922; prepared in] Bureau of Statistics. Dec. 1923 [published 1924]. [2] p. oblong large 8° [Subject to revision.] †

—— Operating revenues and operating expenses of class 1 steam roads in United States (for 194 steam roads, including 15 switching and terminal companies), Dec. 1923 and 1922 [and] 12 months ending with Dec. 1923 and 1922; [prepared in] Bureau of Statistics. Dec. 1923 [published 1924].. 1 p. oblong large 8° [Subject to revision.] †

—— Operating revenues and operating expenses of large steam roads, selected items for roads with annual operating revenues above $25,000,000, Dec. 1923 and 1922 [and] 12 months ended with Dec. 1923 and 1922; [prepared in] Bureau of Statistics. Dec. 1923 [published 1924]. [2] p. oblong large 8° [Subject to revision.] †

—— Operating statistics of large steam roads, selected items for Dec. 1923, compared with Dec. 1922, for roads with annual operating revenues above $25,000,000; [prepared in] Bureau of Statistics. Dec. 1923 [published 1924]. [2] p. oblong large 8° [Subject to revision.] †

—— Revenue traffic statistics of class 1 steam roads in United States, including mixed-train service (compiled from 162 reports representing 177 steam roads, switching and terminal companies not included), Nov. 1923 and 1922 [and] 11 months ended with Nov. 1923 and 1922; [prepared in] Bureau of Statistics. Nov. 1923. 1 p. oblong large 8° [Subject to revision.] †

Rails. No. 13625, Mid-Continent Equipment & Machinery Company *v.* Mobile & Ohio Railroad Company et al.; decided Dec. 27, 1923; report [and order] of commission. [1924.] 683–684+[1] p. ([Opinion] 9063.) [Report from Interstate Commerce Commission reports, v. 85.] * Paper, 5c.

Reading Company. Finance docket no. 3320, operation of lines and bond issue by Reading Company; [and finance docket no. 3321]; decided Dec. 26, 1923; report of commission. [1924.] p. 157–168. ([Finance decision] 1124.) [From Interstate Commerce Commission reports, v. 86.] * Paper, 5c.

Registers (heating systems). No. 14066, Monitor Stove Company *v.* Chesapeake & Ohio Railway Company et al.; decided Dec. 28, 1923; report [and order] of commission. [1924.] 757–759+[1] p. ([Opinion] 9088.) [Report from Interstate Commerce Commission reports, v. 85.] * Paper, 5c.

Rice. No. 14354, Interstate Rice Milling Company *v.* Louisiana Western Railroad Company et al.; [no. 14468, Industrial Rice Milling Company *v.* Beaumont, Sour Lake & Western Railway Company et al.; decided Dec. 27, 1923; report and order of commission]. 1924. [1]+606–608+ii p. ([Opinion] 9041.) [Report from Interstate Commerce Commission reports, v. 85.] * Paper, 5c.

Rosin. No. 14108, Sales Department Gillican-Chipley Company, Incorporated, *v.* director general, as agent, and Gulf & Northern Railroad Company; [no. 14108 (sub-no. 1), same *v.* director general, as agent, and Angelina & Neches River Railroad Company; decided Dec. 28, 1923; report and order of commission]. 1924. [1]+702–704+[1] p. ([Opinion] 9070.) [Report from Interstate Commerce Commission reports, v. 85.] * Paper, 5c.

Routing. Investigation and suspension docket no. 1920, restriction in routing on grain and grain products from Kansas City, Mo., to Texas; [decided Jan. 12, 1924; report and order of commission]. 1924. [1]+144–148+[1] p. ([Opinion] 9139.) [Report from Interstate Commerce Commission reports, v. 87.] * Paper, 5c.

—— Investigation and suspension docket no. 1928, routing of lumber from Alabama, Tennessee & Northern Railroad to C. F. A. and western trunk line territories; decided Dec. 27, 1923; report [and order] of commission. [1924.] 527–532+[1] p. ([Opinion] 9028.) [Report from Interstate Commerce Commission reports, v. 85.] * Paper, 5c.

Saltpeter, Chile. No. 14979, E. I. du Pont de Nemours & Company *v.* Galveston, Harrisburg & San Antonio Railway Company et al.; decided Jan. 14, 1924; report [and order] of commission. [1924.] 189–192+[1] p. ([Opinion] 9146.) [Report from Interstate Commerce Commission reports, v. 87.] * Paper, 5c.

Sand. No. 14057, General Chemical Company *v.* director general, as agent; decided Dec. 27, 1923; report of commission. [1924.] p. 693–694. ([Opinion] 9067.) [From Interstate Commerce Commission reports, v. 85.] * Paper, 5c.

—— No. 14512, American Radiator Company *v.* director general, as agent; decided Jan. 17, 1924; report [and order] of commission. [1924.] 231–233+ [1] p. ([Opinion] 9159.) [Report from Interstate Commerce Commission reports, v. 87.] * Paper, 5c.

Seaboard Air Line Railway. Finance docket no. 3337, Seaboard Air Line Railway bonds; [decided Dec. 29, 1923; report of commission]. 1924. [1]+ 172–176 p. ([Finance decision] 1126.) [From Interstate Commerce Commission reports, v. 86.] * Paper, 5c.

Sheep. No. 13686, Chas. S. Hardy *v.* director general, as agent; decided Jan. 17, 1924; report [and order] of commission. [1924.] 247–248+[1] p. ([Opinion] 9164.) [Report from Interstate Commerce Commission reports, v. 87.] * Paper, 5c.

Sodium sulphate. No. 13601, Pacific Mills, Limited, *v.* director general, as agent, Southern Pacific Company, et al.; decided Dec. 27, 1923; report of commission. [1924.] p. 677–679. ([Opinion] 9061.) [From Interstate Commerce Commission reports, v. 85.] * Paper, 5c.

Southern Pacific Company. Finance docket no. 3276, operation of line by Southern Pacific; decided Dec. 24, 1923; report of commission. [1924.] p. 111–112. ([Finance decision] 1114.) [From Interstate Commerce Commission reports, v. 86.] * Paper, 5c.

Southern Railway. Finance docket no. 3393, bonds of Southern Railway; decided Jan. 5, 1924; report of commission. [1924.] p. 199–201. ([Finance decision] 1137.) [From Interstate Commerce Commission reports, v. 86.] * Paper, 5c.

Springfield Electric Railway. Finance docket no. 1356, deficit settlement with Springfield Electric Ry. [E. S. French, receiver]; decided Dec. 28, 1923; report of commission. [1924.] p. 135–136. ([Finance decision] 1119.) [From Interstate Commerce Commission reports, v. 86.] * Paper, 5c.

Steamboats. Schedule of sailings (as furnished by steamship companies named herein) of steam vessels which are registered under laws of United States and which are intended to load general cargo at ports in United States for foreign destinations, Feb. 15–Mar. 31, 1924, no. 18; issued by Section of Tariffs, Bureau of Traffic. 1924. iii+37 p. 4° [Monthly. No. 18 cancels no. 17.] † 22—26610

Stokers (mechanical). No. 13883, Anheuser-Busch, Incorporated, *v.* Baltimore & Ohio Chicago Terminal Railway Company et al.; [decided Dec. 31, 1923; report of commission]. 1924. [1]+132–134 p. ([Opinion] 9134.) [From Interstate Commerce Commission reports, v. 87.] * Paper, 5c.

Stoneware. No. 13277, American Clay Products Company *v.* Pennsylvania Railroad Company et al.; [decided Jan. 17, 1924; report and order of commission]. 1924. [1]+268–270+ii p. ([Opinion] 9171.) [Report from Interstate Commerce Commission reports, v. 87.] * Paper, 5c.

Strawberries. No. 13995, Wm. F. Helm and Edward Helm *v.* Kansas City Southern Railway Company; decided Dec. 31, 1923; report [and order] of commission. [1924.] 135–136+[1] p. ([Opinion] 9135.) [Report from Interstate Commerce Commission reports, v. 87.] * Paper, 5c.

Sugar. No. 13652, William D. Cleveland & Sons et al. *v.* Beaumont, Sour Lake & Western Railway Company et al.; decided Jan. 17, 1924; report of commission. [1924.] p. 193–194. ([Opinion] 9147.) [From Interstate Commerce Commission reports, v. 87.] * Paper, 5c.

Switching charges. Investigation and suspension docket no. 1908 [and 1949], terminal allowance to St. Louis Coke & Iron Company at Cochem, Ill.; decided Dec. 31, 1923; report [and order] of commission. [1924.] 591–601+ ii p. ([Opinion] 9038.) [Report from Interstate Commerce Commission reports, v. 85.] * Paper, 5c.

—— No. 12968, Judson Manufacturing Company *v.* director general, as agent, and Southern Pacific Company; decided Dec. 20, 1923; report of commission. [1924.] p. 637–640. ([Opinion] 9048.) [From Interstate Commerce Commission reports, v. 85.] * Paper, 5c.

—— No. 13507, Colorado Fuel & Iron Company *v.* director general, as agent; [no. 13542, same *v.* same]; decided Jan. 17, 1924; report of commission. [1924.] p. 211–213. ([Opinion] 9153.) [From Interstate Commerce Commission reports, v. 87.] * Paper, 5c.

—— No. 13886, Globe Iron Company *v.* director general, as agent; decided Jan. 22, 1924; report of commission. [1924.] p. 313–316. ([Opinion] 9182.) [From Interstate Commerce Commission reports, v. 87.] * Paper, 5c.

—— No. 14259, Flushing Farmers Elevator Company *v.* director general, as agent, Great Northern Railway Company, et al.; decided Dec. 28, 1923; report [and order] of commission. [1924.] 9–10+[1] p. ([Opinion] 9093.) [Report from Interstate Commerce Commission reports, v. 87.] * Paper, 5c.

—— No. 14330, Standard Forgings Company *v.* Indiana Harbor Belt Railroad Company; decided Dec. 31, 1923; report of commission. [1924.] p. 53–55. ([Opinion] 9107.) [From Interstate Commerce Commission reports, v. 87.] * Paper, 5c.

Tan-bark. No. 14603, Michigan Tanning & Extract Company *v.* Chicago, Milwaukee & St. Paul Railway Company et al.; [decided Jan. 17, 1924; report and order of commission]. 1924. [1]+322–324+[1] p. ([Opinion] 9185.) [Report from Interstate Commerce Commission reports, v. 87.] * Paper, 5c.

Tank-cars. No. 13895, Mathieson Alkali Works, Incorporated, et al. *v.* Baltimore & Ohio Railroad Company et al.; [no. 13895 (sub-no. 1), same *v.* Buffalo, Rochester & Pittsburgh Railway Company et al.; no. 13895 (sub-no. 2), same *v.* Erie Railroad Company et al.; decided Dec. 28, 1923; report of commission]. 1924. [1]+728–734 p. ([Opinion] 9079.) [From Interstate Commerce Commission reports, v. 85.] * Paper, 5c.

Tanks. No. 12437, Parkersburg Rig & Reel Company *v.* director general, as agent, Atchison, Topeka & Santa Fe Railway Company, et al.; decided Dec. 27, 1923; report of commission. [1924.] p. 665–672. ([Opinion] 9058.) [From Interstate Commerce Commission reports, v. 85.] * Paper, 5c.

—— No. 14522, Walford Forwarding Corporation *v.* Pennsylvania Railroad Company; decided Dec. 31, 1923; report [and order] of commission. [1924.] 43–45+[1] p. ([Opinion] 9104.) [Report from Interstate Commerce Commission reports, v. 87.] * Paper, 5c.

Terminal charges. No. 14434, Western Stock Yards Company et al. *v.* New York Central Railroad Company; [decided Dec. 29, 1923; report and order of commission]. 1924. [1]+4–8+[1] p. ([Opinion] 9092.) [Report from Interstate Commerce Commission reports, v. 87.] * Paper, 5c.

Texas Short Line Railway. Finance docket no. 1361, deficit status of Texas Short Line Ry.; decided Jan. 11, 1924; report of commission. [1924.] p. 235–236. ([Finance decision] 1149.) [From Interstate Commerce Commission reports, v. 86.] * Paper, 5c.

Tiles. No. 14133, Chicago Fire Brick Company *v.* director general, as agent, Chicago & North Western Railway Company, et al.; decided Jan. 17, 1924; report [and order] of commission. [1924.] 365–367+[1] p. ([Opinion] 9200.) [Report from Interstate Commerce Commission reports, v. 87.] * Paper, 5c.

Train-control devices. No. 13413, in matter of automatic train control devices, order [promulgated] at general session of Interstate Commerce Commission on 14th of January, 1924. [1924.] 8 p. * Paper, 5c.

Train service. No. 14967. Railroad Commission of Wisconsin et al. *v.* Chicago & North Western Railway Company; [no. 14967 (sub–no. 1), same *v.* Minneapolis, St. Paul· & Sault Ste. Marie Railway Company]; decided Jan. 14, 1924; report [and order] of commission. [1924.] 195–198+[1] p. ([Opinion] 9148.) [Report from Interstate Commerce Commission reports, v. 87.] * Paper, 5c.

Treenail wood. No. 13874, J. S. Hoskins Lumber Company *v.* director general, as agent, Pennsylvania Railroad Company, et al.; [decided Dec. 28, 1923; report and order of commission]. 1924. [1]+740–742+[1] p. ([Opinion] 9082.) [Report from Interstate Commerce Commission reports, v. 85.] * Paper, 5c.

Unlading and lading. No. 14105, I. Hershman & Company *v.* director general, as agent. New York Central Railroad Company, et al.; [no. 14105 (sub–no. 1), Kelly & Company *v.* director general, as agent, und Baltimore & Ohio Railroad Company]; decided Dec. 28, 1923; report [and order] of commission. [1924.] 695–696+[1] p. ([Opinion] 9068.) [Report from Interstate Commerce Commission reports, v. 85.] * Paper, 5c.

Utica, Clinton and Binghamton Railroad. Finance docket no. 3294, lease of lines [of Utica. Clinton & Binghamton Railroad Company and Rome & Clinton Railroad Company] by New York, Ontario & Western Ry.; [decided Dec. 24, 1923; report of commission]. 1924. [1]+116–118 p. ([Finance decision] 1116.) [From Interstate Commerce Commission reports, v. 86.] * Paper, 5c.

Vanadium. No. 14437, Vanadium Corporation of America *v.* Baltimore & Ohio Railroad Company et al.; [decided Dec. 31, 1923; report and order of commission]. 1924. [1]+98–100+[1]. p. ([Opinion] 9122.) [Report from Interstate Commerce Commission reports, v. 87.] *Paper, 5c.

Virginian Railway. Finance docket no. 869, guaranty settlement with Virginian Ry.; decided Jan. 23, 1924; report of commission. [1924.] p. 283–285. ([Opinion] 1167.) [From Interstate Commerce Commission reports, v. 86.] *Paper, 5c.

Virginian Terminal Railway. Finance docket no. 3390, bonds of Virginian Terminal Railway; [and finance docket no. 3390 (sub–no. 1); decided Jan. 18, 1924; report of commission]. 1924. [1]+254–258 p. ([Finance decision] 1155.) [From Interstate Commerce Commission reports, v. 86.] *Paper, 5c.

Waukegan, Rockford and Elgin Traction Company. Finance docket no. 1282, deficit settlement with Waukegan, Rockford & Elgin Traction Co.; [and finance docket no. 205]; decided Jan. 12, 1924; report of commission. [1924.] p. 243–246. ([Finance decision] 1152.) [From Interstate Commerce Commission reports, v. 86.] *Paper, 5c.

—— Finance docket no. 1282, deficit settlement with Waukegan, Rockford & Elgin Traction Co., Ralph L. Peck, receiver; decided June 26, 1923; report of commission. [1924.] p. 839–841. ([Finance decision] 1076 A.) [From Interstate Commerce Commission reports, v. 82.] *Paper, 5c.

Waycross and Southern Railroad. Finance docket no. 240, deficit settlement with Waycross & Southern R. R.; decided Jan. 24, 1924; report of commission. [1924.] p. 275–276. ([Finance decision] 1163.) [From Interstate Commerce Commission reports, v. 86.] *Paper, 5c.

Wellington and Powellsville Railroad. Finance docket no. 2415, deficit settlement with Wellington & Powellsville R. R. [J. A. Pretlow, receiver]; decided Jan. 14, 1924; report of commission. [1924.] p. 225–226. ([Finance decision] 1145.) [From Interstate Commerce Commission reports, v. 86.] *Paper, 5c.

Wheat. No. 13596, Pacific Grain Company *v.* director general, as agent, Oregon-Washington Railroad & Navigation Company. et al.; [decided Dec. 27, 1923; report of commission]. 1924. [1]+710–712 p. ([Opinion] 9072.) [From Interstate Commerce Commission reports, v. 85.] *Paper, 5c.

—— No. 13678, Colorado Milling & Elevator Company *v.* director general, as agent; [decided Jan. 17, 1924; report and order of commission]. 1924. [1]+222–224+[1] p. ([Opinion] 9156.) [Report from Interstate Commerce Commission reports, v. 87.] *Paper, 5c.

Wheat—Continued. No. 13769, Globe Grain & Milling Company *v.* director general, as agent; decided Jan. 17, 1924; report [and order] of commission. [1924.] 243–246+[1] p. ([Opinion] 9163.) [Report from Interstate Commerce Commission reports, v. 87.] * Paper, 5c.

Wichita Northwestern Railway. Finance docket no. 244, deficit settlement with Wichita Northwestern Ry. [O. P. Byers and J. E. Conklin, receivers]; decided Dec. 10, 1923; report of commission. [1924.] p. 229–231. ([Finance decision] 1147.) [From Interstate Commerce Commission reports, v. 86.] *Paper, 5c.

Williamsport and North Branch Railroad. Finance docket no. 1367, deficit settlement with Williamsport & North Branch R. R. [Edward Bailey, receiver]; decided Jan. 3, 1924; report of commission. [1924.] p. 191–192. ([Finance decision] 1133.) [From Interstate Commerce Commission reports, v. 86.] *Paper, 5c.

Wood-pulp. No. 12195, Crown Willamette Paper Company *v.* director general, as agent, Spokane, Portland & Seattle Railway Company, et al; decided Dec. 27, 1923; report of commission. [1924.] p. 657–658. ([Opinion] 9056.) [From Interstate Commerce Commission reports, v. 87.] *Paper, 5c.

—— No. 12983, Crown Willamette Paper Company *v.* director general, as agent, Western Transportation Company, et al.; decided Dec. 31, 1923; report of commission. [1924.] p. 51–52. ([Opinion] 9106.) [From Interstate Commerce Commission reports, v. 87.] *Paper, 5c.

—— No. 13867, International Paper Company *v.* director general, as agent, Erie Railroad Company, et al.; [decided Dec. 28, 1923; report and order of commission]. 1924. [1]+142–143+[1] p. ([Opinion] 9138.) [Report from Interstate Commerce Commission reports, v. 87.] * Paper, 5c.

—— No. 14281, Monadnock Paper Mills *v.* Boston & Maine Railroad et al.; decided Dec. 31, 1923; report of commission. [1924.] p. 137–138. ([Opinion] 9136.) [From Interstate Commerce Commission reports, v. 87.] * Paper, 5c.

Wyandotte Terminal Railroad. Finance docket no. 1200, deficit settlement with Wyandotte Terminal R. R.; decided Jan. 26, 1924; report of commission. [1924.] p. 279–280. ([Finance decision] 1165.) [From Interstate Commerce Commission reports, v. 86.] * Paper, 5c.

Zinc. No. 14035, Alaska Junk Company *v.* director general, as agent, Northern Pacific Railway Company, et al.; decided Dec. 27, 1923; report [and order] of commission. [1924.] 745–746+[1] p. ([Opinion] 9084.) [Report from Interstate Commerce Commission reports, v. 85.] * Paper, 5c.

JUSTICE DEPARTMENT

Abilene and Southern Railway. No. 456, in Supreme Court, Oct. term, 1923, United States and Interstate Commerce Commission *v.* Abilene & Southern Railway Company et al., appeal from district court for district of Kansas; brief for United States. 1924. cover-title, ii+41 p. ‡

Alworth-Stephens Company. No. —, in Supreme Court, Oct. term, 1924, Margaret C. Lynch, executrix of E. J. Lynch [collector of internal revenue for district of Minnesota], *v.* Alworth-Stephens Company, petition for writ of certiorari to circuit court of appeals for 8th circuit and brief in support thereof; petition for writ of certiorari and brief in support thereof. 1924. cover-title, 14 p. ‡

—— [United States circuit court of appeals, 8th circuit, no. 6219, Sept. term, 1923, Margaret C. Lynch, executrix of E. J. Lynch, collector of internal revenue for district of Minnesota, *vs.* Alworth-Stephens Company, in error to district court of Minnesota, proceedings in circuit court of appeals, 8th circuit; transcript of record.] [1924.] p. 262–273. [This is printed without title. The signature mark reads: 82299—24.] ‡

American Railway Express Company. No. 666–668, in Supreme Court, Oct. term, 1923, United States et al. *v.* American Railway Express Company; Southeastern Express Company *v.* American Railway Express Company et al.; Southern Traffic League et al. *v.* [same], appeals from district court for northern district of Georgia; motion to advance. 1924. cover-title, 3 p. ‡

American Tobacco Company. In Court of Claims, American Tobacco Company *v.* United States, no. 34477; defendant's exhibits. [1924.] p. 131–133, large 8° ‡

Atlas Line Steamship Company. In Court of Claims, Atlas Line Steamship Company *v.* United States, no. C–316; demurrer [and brief]. [1924.] p. 19–43, large 8° ‡

—— In Court of Claims, Atlas Line Steamship Company *v.* United States, no. C–317; demurrer [and] brief. [1924.] p. 29–61, large 8° ‡

Avery, Will. No. 749, in Supreme Court, Oct. term, 1923, Will Avery *v.* United States, on petition for writ of certiorari to circuit court of appeals for 5th circuit; brief for United States in opposition. 1924. cover-title, 3 p. ‡

Blount, Henry F. No. B–86, in Court of Claims, Lucia E. Blount, executrix in her own right and as administratrix c. t. a. of Henry F. Blount, *v.* United States; defendant's request for findings of fact and brief. 1924. cover-title, i+25–49 p. large 8° ‡

Blumenthal, Sidney, & Co., Incorporated. No. 2296, Court of Customs Appeals. Sidney Blumenthal & Co., Inc., *v.* United States, brief for United States. 1924. cover-title, 9 p. ‡

Burnes National Bank. No. 762, in Supreme Court, Oct. term, 1923, Missouri, at relation of Burnes National Bank of St. Joseph, Mo., *v.* A. B. Duncan, judge of probate court of Buchanan County, Mo., in error to Supreme Court of Missouri; motion for leave to appear as amicus curiæ and to participate in oral argument. 1924. cover-title, 5 p. ‡

Cadwalader, John. In Court of Claims, John Cadwalader *v.* United States, no. B–20; defendant's objections to claimant's request for findings of fact, defendant's request for findings of fact, and brief. [1924.] p. 98–107, large 8° ‡

Campbell, Bruce R. In Court of Claims, Bruce R. Campbell *v.* United States, No. C–791; defendant's brief. [1924.] p. 29–46, large 8° ‡

Central New England Railway. In Court of Claims, Central New England Railway Company *v.* United States, no. B–45; defendant's brief on demand. [1924.] p. 93–99, large 8° ‡

Chase National Bank. No. 787, in Supreme Court, Oct. term, 1923, Shipping Board Emergency Fleet Corporation *v.* Chase National Bank of city of New York et al.; supplemental memorandum in support of petition for writ of certiorari, opinion of District Judge Bean, district court for district of Oregon, in Astoria Marine Iron Works *v.* Shipping Board Emergency Fleet Corporation. 1924. cover-title, 7 p. ‡

Cherokee Indians. No. 34449, in Court of Claims, Cherokee Nation *v.* United States; defendant's statement of case, objections to findings of fact requested by plaintiff, request for findings of fact, and brief. 1924. cover-title, i+127–190 p. large 8° ‡

Chicago, Rock Island and Pacific Railway. [No.] B–33, in Court of Claims, Chicago, Rock Island & Pacific Railway Co. *v.* United States; defendant's objections to plaintiff's request for findings of fact, defendant's request for findings of fact, and brief. 1924. cover-title, p. 89–108, large 8° ‡

Cohen, Louis. No. 801, in Supreme Court, Oct. term, 1923, Louis Cohen *v.* United States, on petition for writ of certiorari to circuit court of appeals for 6th circuit; brief for United States in opposition. 1924. cover-title, 4 p. ‡

Delapenha, R. U., & Co. No. 2331, Court of Customs Appeals, United States *v.* R. U. Delapenha & Co. et al.; brief for United States. 1924. cover-title, 13 p. ‡

Eagle-Picher Lead Company. In Court of Claims, Eagle-Picher Lead Company, for use and benefit of Pennsylvania Railroad Company and Philadelphia and Reading Railway Company, *v.* United States, no. 189–B; stipulation of facts. [1924.] p. 9–15, large 8° ‡

Erickson, C. J. No. 125, in Supreme Court, Oct. term, 1923, C. J. Erickson and United States Fidelity and Guaranty Company *v.* United States and United States Spruce Production Corporation, in error to district court for western district of Washington; brief for defendants in error. 1924. cover-title, ii+35 p. ‡

Farmers and Ginners Cotton Oil Company. In Court of Claims, Farmers and Ginners Cotton Oil Company *v.* United States, no. D–21; demurrer [and] brief. [1924.] p. 13–19, large 8° ‡

Flannery, James J. In Court of Claims, Harriet Rogers Flannery and J. Rogers Flannery, executors of James J. Flannery, *v.* United States, no. C–1080; defendant's request for findings of fact and brief. [1924.] p. 40–43, large 8° ‡

Glenwood Annex Corporation. In Court of Claims, Glenwood Annex Corporation *v.* United States, no. 268–A; defendant's objections to plaintiff's request for findings of fact, defendant's request for findings of fact, and brief. [1924.] p. 225–248, large 8° ‡

Glenwood Park Corporation. In Court of Claims, Glenwood Park, a corporation, *v.* United States, no. 270–A; defendant's objections to plaintiff's request for findings of fact, defendant's request for findings of fact, and brief. [1924.] p. 221–244, large 8° ‡

Goto, I. No. 463, in Supreme Court, Oct. term, 1923, I. Goto et al. *v.* John C. Lane, high sheriff of Hawaii, appeal from district court for district of Hawaii; brief for United States as amicus curiae. 1924. cover-title, ii+80 p. ‡

Great Britain. In Court of Claims, George V, king of United Kingdom of Great Britain and Ireland and British Dominions beyond the Seas, Emperor of India, *v.* United States, no. C–1001; stipulation of facts. [1924.] p. 7–10, large 8° ‡

Hamburg-American Line Terminal and Navigation Company. In Court of Claims, Hamburg-American Line Terminal & Navigation Company *v.* United States, no. C–314; demurrer [and] brief. [1924.] p. 23–46, large 8° ‡

—— In Court of Claims, Hamburg-American Line Terminal & Navigation Co. *v.* United States, [no.] C–315; demurrer [and] brief. [1924.] p. 23–46, large 8° ‡

Howard, R. S., Company. In Court of Claims, R. S. Howard Company *v.* United States, Cong. 17329; defendant's brief. [1924.] p. 133–150, large 8° ‡

International and Great Northern Railway. In Court of Claims, James A. Baker, receiver of International and Great Northern Railway Co., *vs.* United States, no. 34463; demurrer [and] brief. [1924.] p. 11–18, large 8° ‡

Judges. List of United States judges, attorneys, and marshals; compiled by appointment clerk [Charles B. Sornborger]. Jan. 30, 1924. ii+24 p. †

11—35284

Law, DeWitt T. No. 4158, circuit court of appeals for 9th circuit, United States *v.* DeWitt T. Law, writ of error to district court for district of Montana; brief on behalf of United States. 1924. cover-title, ii+79 p. ‡

Levensaler, C. No. 4080, in Court of Appeals of District of Columbia, C. Levensaler et al. *v.* Shipping Board Emergency Fleet Corporation; brief for appellee. 1924. cover-title, 2 p. ‡

Livingston, Thomas M. No. 298–A, in Court of Claims, Thomas M. Livingston *v.* United States; defendant's objections to claimant's request for findings of fact, findings requested in lieu thereof, and brief. 1924. cover-title, i+444–474 p. large 8° ‡

Long, F. R., & Co. In Court of Claims, F. R. Long and Company *v.* United States, [no.] C–1330; demurrer [and] brief. [1924.] p. 14–17, large 8° ‡

Los Angeles and Salt Lake Railroad. In equity, no. H–44–T, in district court, southern district of California, southern division, Los Angeles & Salt Lake Railroad Company *v.* United States; answer of United States. 1924. cover-title, 9 p. ‡

Louisville and Nashville Railroad. In Court of Claims, Lou'sville and Nashville Railroad Company *v.* United States. no. 299–A; defendant's objections to plaintiff's request for findings of fact, defendant's request for findings of fact, and brief. [1924.] p. 43–62, large 8° ‡

Luckenbach Steamship Company, Incorporated. No. 33962, in Court of Claims, Luckenbach Steamship Company, Inc., *v.* United States; objections to plaintiff's request for findings of fact, defendant's proposed substituted findings of fact, and request therefor, statement, reply to plaintiff's brief, with brief for United States. 1924. cover-title, iv+1321–1471 p. 1 tab. large 8° ‡

McKay, Gordon. In Court of Claims, George E. Gilbert and Arthur H. Brooks, trustees under deed of Gordon McKay, dated Nov. 30, 1887, *v.* United States, no. B–34; defendant's objections to plaintiff's request for findings of fact, defendant's request for findings of fact, and brief. [1924.] p. 115–122, large 8° ‡

Maple Flooring Manufacturers Association. In district court for northern district of Illinois, eastern division, United States *v.* Maple Flooring Manufacturers Association et al.; indictment. 1924. cover-title, 9 p. ‡

Mitchell, W. A. No. 2340, Court of Customs Appeals, United States *v.* W. A. Mitchell; brief for United States. 1924. cover-title, 11 p. ‡

Napoleon, Rena. No. 4142, circuit court of appeals for 5th circuit, United States *v.* Rena Napoleon and Rosa Napoleon, writ of error to district court for southern district of Florida; brief on behalf of United States. 1924. cover-title, ii+87 p. ‡

National Contract Company. In Court of Claims, National Contract Company *vs.* United States, no. B–259; defendant's objections to plaintiff's request for findings of fact, defendant's request for findings of fact, and argument. [1924.] p. 115–136, large 8° ‡

National Importing Company, Incorporated. No. 2325, Court of Customs Appeals, United States *v.* National Importing Co., Inc., et al.; brief for United States. 1924. cover-title, 14 p. ‡

New England Steamship Company. In Court of Claims, New England Steamship Company *v.* United States, no. B–46; defendant's brief on remand. [1924.] p. 41–47, large 8° ‡

New York and Baltimore Transportation Line. In Court of Claims, New York & Baltimore Transportation Line *v.* United States, no. C–927; demurrer [and] brief. [1924.] p. 15–36, large 8° ‡

New York, New Haven and Hartford Railroad. In Court of Claims, New York, New Haven & Hartford Railroad Company *v.* United States, no. B–44; defendant's brief of remand. [1924.] p. 85–92, large 8° ‡.

North American Mercantile Company. No. 2320, Court of Customs Appeals, North American Mercantile Co. *v.* United States; brief for United States. 1924. cover-title, 15 p. ‡

North German Lloyd Steamship Company. In Court of Claims, North German Lloyd *v.* United States, no. C–311; demurrer. [1924.] p. 11–36, large 8° ‡

—— In Court of Claims, North German Lloyd *v.* United States, [no.] C–312; demurrer [and] brief. [1924.] p. 13–30, large 8° ‡

Owens, Henry D. No. 235, in Supreme Court, Oct. term, 1923, Henry D. Owens *v.* United States, appeal from Court of Claims; brief for United States. 1924. cover-title, 12 p. ‡

Paleais, Adolph. No. 743, in Supreme Court, Oct. term, 1923, Adolph Paleais *v.* Jesse D. Moore, United States marshal for eastern district of New York, on petition for writ of certiorari to circuit court of appeals for 2d circuit; brief for United States in opposition. 1924. cover-title, 8 p. ‡

Panhandle and Santa Fe Railway. In Court of Claims, Panhandle & Santa Fe Railway Company *v.* United States, no. B–442; defendant's request for findings of fact and brief. [1924.] p. 17–19, large 8° ‡

Payne, Tommy. No. 240, in Supreme Court, Oct. term, 1923, United States *v.* Tommy Payne, appeal from circuit court of appeals for 9th circuit; brief for United States. 1924. cover-title, i+22 p. ‡

Pennsylvania-Ohio Power and Light Company. No. 228, in Supreme Court, Oct. term, 1923, United States, Interstate Commerce Commission, and Pennsylvania-Ohio Power & Light Company *v.* Hubbard, Ohio, appeal from district court for northern district of Ohio; brief for United States. 1924. cover-title, iii+28 p. ‡

Robinson, George. No. 732, in Supreme Court, Oct. term, 1923, George Robinson *v.* United States, on petition for writ of certiorari to circuit court of appeals for 9th circuit; brief for United States in opposition. 1924. cover-title, 8 p. ‡

St. Louis, Mo. No. 252, in Supreme Court, Oct. term, 1923, First National Bank in St. Louis *v.* Missouri, on information of Jesse W. Barrett, attorney general, in error to Supreme Court of Missouri; suggestion of United States on petition for rehearing. 1924. cover-title, 4 p. ‡

St. Louis, Brownsville and Mexico Railway. In Court of Claims, no. A-236, St. Louis, Brownsville & Mexico Railway Company *v.* United States; defendant's objections to plaintiff's request for findings of fact, defendant's request for findings of fact, and brief. [1924.] p. 41–54, large 8° ‡

St. Louis, San Francisco and Texas Railway. In Court of Claims, St. Louis, San Francisco & Texas Railway Company *v.* United States, no. C-58; defendant's request for findings of fact and brief. [1924.] p. 13–14, large 8° ‡

Standard Steel Car Company. In Court of Claims. Standard Steel Car Company *v.* United States, no. 307–A; motion of defendant for leave to file counterclaim. [1924.] p. 1279–1304, large 8° ‡

Sternfeld, J., Incorporated. No. 2304, Court of Customs Appeals, J. Sternfeld, Inc., *v.* United States; brief for United States. 1924. cover-title, 9 p. ‡

Steubenville, East Liverpool and Beaver Valley Traction Company. No. 229, in Supreme Court, Oct. term, 1923, United States, Steubenville, East Liverpool and Beaver Valley Traction Company, and Interstate Commerce Commission *v.* Wellsville, Ohio, appeal from district court for northern district of Ohio; brief for United States. 1924. cover-title, iii+29 p. ‡

Supplee-Biddle Hardware Company. No. 447, in Supreme Court, Oct. term, 1923, United States *v.* Supplee-Biddle Hardware Company, appeal from Court of Claims; motion to advance. 1924 cover-title, 2 p. ‡

Terminal Heights Corporation. In Court of Claims, Terminal Heights, a corporation, *v.* United States, no. 269–A; defendant's objections to plaintiff's request for findings of fact, defendant's request for findings of fact, and brief. [1924.] p. 221–243, large 8° ‡

Turner, C. A. P., Company. No. 259–A, in Court of Claims, C. A. P. Turner Company *v.* United States; defendant's objections to plaintiff's request for findings of fact, defendant's request for findings of fact, and defendant's brief. 1924. cover-title, iv+943–1067 p. 1 pl. large 8° ‡

Union Insulating and Construction Company. In Court of Claims, Union Insulating and Construction Company *v.* United States, no. B–92; defendant's objections to plaintiff's request for findings of fact, defendant's request for findings of fact, and defendant's brief. [1924.] p. 157–169, large 8° ‡

Unit Construction Company. In Court of Claims, Unit Construction Company *v.* United States, no. B–448; defendant's brief. 1924. p. 1, large 8° ‡

Valante, John. No. 218, in Supreme Court, Oct. term, 1923, United States *v.* John Valante, appeal from district court for southern district of New York; brief for United States. 1924· cover-title, ii+32 p. ‡

Van Doorn, W. No. 2302, Court of Customs Appeals, W. Van Doorn *v.* United States; brief for United States. 1924. cover-title, 3 p. ‡

Violette, Fred P. No. 143, in Supreme Court, Oct. term, 1923, Fred P. Violette *v.* James A. Walsh, collector of internal revenue for district of Montana, appeal from circuit court of appeals for 9th circuit; memorandum on behalf of appellee. 1924. cover-title, 8 p. ‡

Wheeler, Thomas R. No. 758, in Supreme Court, Oct. term, 1923, Thomas R. Wheeler *v.* United States, on petition for writ of certiorari to circuit court of appeals for 5th circuit; brief for United States in opposition. 1924. cover-title, 5 p. ‡

LABOR DEPARTMENT

CHILDREN'S BUREAU

Child labor in United States, 10 questions answered. 2d edition. [1924.] 31 p. il. (Bureau publication 114.) [Includes list of Children's Bureau publications on subject of child labor.] * Paper, 5c.   L 24—51

Dependent children. What child dependency means in District of Columbia and how it can be prevented; by Emma O. Lundberg and Mary E. Milburn. 1924. iii+16 p. [From Child dependency in District of Columbia.] †   L 24—52

Market-gardening. Child labor and work of mothers on Norfolk truck farms. 1924. iv+27 p. 1 pl. (Bureau publication 130.) * Paper, 5c.   L 24—46

Mothers. Laws relating to mothers' pensions in United States passed 1920–23 [with list of references by States; compiled by Lulu L. Eckman]. 1924. viii+99 p. * Paper, 10c.   L 24—49

Publications. Publications. [Edition of] Feb. 15, 1924. 1924. 12 p. narrow 12° †

State commissions for study and revision of child-welfare laws; by Emma O. Lundberg. 1924. v+156 p. map. (Bureau publication 131.) [Revision of Children's year follow-up series 6, Bureau publication 71.] * Paper, 15c.
                                                                   L 24—47

NOTE.—Lists included are: Reports and articles relating to work of commissions.—Child-welfare standards and recommendations for uniform legislation.—Compilations and summaries of laws on special subjects.—Compilations and summaries of State laws relating to children in need of special care.—Bibliographies and lists of references on child welfare.

EMPLOYMENT SERVICE

Industrial employment information bulletin, v. 4, no. 1; Jan. 1924. [1924.] 18 p. 4° [Monthly] †   L 21–17

IMMIGRATION BUREAU

Immigration laws and rules of Feb. 1, 1924. 1924. [1]+168 p. map. * Paper, 15c.   12–35065

LABOR STATISTICS BUREAU

Employment in selected industries, Jan. 1924. 1924. [1]+9 p. [From Monthly labor review, Mar. 1924.] †

Lumbering. Industrial relations in West Coast lumber industry [with bibliography]; by Cloice R. Howd. Dec. 1923, [published] 1924. vi+120+vi p. il. (Bulletin 349; Miscellaneous series.) * Paper, 15c.   L 24—48

——— Same. (H. doc. 56, 68th Cong. 1st sess.)

Monthly labor review, v. 18, no. 2; Feb. 1924. 1924. v+217–473 p. il. * Paper, 15c. single copy, $1.50 a yr.; foreign subscription, $2.25.   15–26485

SPECIAL ARTICLES.—Comparison of workmen's compensation laws of Mexican States; by Ethel C. Yohe.—Eugenics as viewed by sociologist; by Warren S. Thompson.—Status of maritime workers injured in course of employment; by Lindley D. Clark.—Conciliation work of Department of Labor, Dec. 1923; by Hugh L. Kerwin.—Statistics of immigration, Nov. 1923; by W. W. Husband.

NOTE.—The Review is the medium through which the Bureau publishes the results of original investigations too brief for bulletin purposes, notices of labor legislation by the States or by Congress, and Federal court decisions affecting labor, which from their importance should be given attention before they could ordinarily appear in the bulletins devoted to these subjects. One free subscription will be given to all labor departments and bureaus, workmen's compensation commissions, and other offices connected with the administration of labor laws and organizations exchanging publications with the Labor Statistics Bureau. Others desiring copies may obtain them from the Superintendent of Documents, Washington, D. C., at the prices stated above.

Prices and cost of living. [1924.] p. 245–310, il. [From Monthly labor review, Feb. 1924.] †

NATURALIZATION BUREAU

Penmanship. Federal citizenship textbook, course of instruction for use in public schools by candidate for citizenship: Penmanship sheets; [by Raymond F. Crist]. [Reprint with slight changes] 1923. [2]+15 p. [Issued in loose-leaf form.] †   22–26786

WOMEN'S BUREAU

ι *Women in industry.* Married women in industry; by Mary N. Winslow. 1924. iii+8 p. (Bulletin 38.) * Paper, 5c.   L 24–50

——— Supplement to Bulletin 16 [State laws affecting working women]: Changes since 1921 in State laws affecting women's hours and wages. [1924.] 10 p. ([Bulletin 16 supplement.]) [This supplement makes available information pertaining to these laws as of July 1, 1923.] ; * Paper, 5c.

LIBRARY OF CONGRESS

COPYRIGHT OFFICE

Copyright. [Catalogue of copyright entries, new series, pt. 1, group 1, Books, v. 20] no. 103–114; Feb. 1924. Feb. 1–29, 1924. p. 1249–1344. [Issued several times a week.]
6—35347

Nᴏᴛᴇ.—Each number is issued in 4 parts: pt. 1, group 1, relates to books; pt. 1, group 2, to pamphlets, leaflets, contributions to newspapers or periodicals, etc., lectures, sermons, addresses for oral delivery, dramatic compositions, maps, motion pictures; pt. 2, to periodicals; pt. 3, to musical compositions; pt. 4, to works of art, reproductions of a work of art, drawings or plastic works of scientific or technical character, photographs, prints, and pictorial illustrations.

Subscriptions for the Catalogue of copyright entries should be made to the Superintendent of Documents, Washington, D. C., instead of to the Register of Copyrights. Prices are as follows: Paper, $3.00 a yr. (4 pts.), foreign subscription, $5.00; pt. 1 (groups 1 and 2), 5c. single copy (group 1, price of group 2 varies), $1.00 a yr., foreign subscription, $2.25; pt. 3, $1.00 a yr., foreign subscription, $1.50; pts. 2 and 4, each 10c. single copy, 50c. a yr., foreign subscription, 70c.

—— Same, pt. 3, Musical compositions, v. 18, no. 8. 1924. viii+747–858 p. [Monthly.]

DOCUMENTS DIVISION

Government publications. Monthly check-list of State publications received during Dec. 1923; v. 14, no. 12. 1924. p. 491–536. * Paper, 10c. single copy, $1.00 a yr.; foreign subscription, $1.25.
10—8924

Nᴏᴛᴇ.—Includes Tentative list of directories of State officials, Jan. 1, 1924.

MIXED CLAIMS COMMISSION, UNITED STATES AND GERMANY

American Congo Company. Docket nos. 173, 540 and 544 [504], before Mixed Claims Commission, United States and Germany, United States on behalf of American Congo Company, H. Herrmann Manufacturing Company, A. Klipstein and Company, *v.* Germany; brief of United States on question of right of American corporation to recover full compensation for losses sustained by it regardless of nationality of owners of majority of capital stock of corporation. 1924. cover-title, 21 p. 4° [Docket no. 504 incorrectly given on cover and p. 1 as 544. An office correction has also been made on p. 19.] ‡

Baylies, Gladys M. No. 93, before Mixed Claims Commission, United States and Germany, United States on behalf of Gladys Mary Baylies *v.* Germany; brief on behalf of United States. 1924. cover-title, 4 p. 4° ‡

Hilson, Edward A. List no. 6770, docket no. 26, before Mixed Claims Commission, United States and Germany, United States on behalf of Edward A. Hilson *v.* Germany; brief on behalf of United States on question of protection of alien seamen employed in American merchant marine. 1924. cover-title, 10 p. 4° ‡

Pickard, Frederick J. No. 207, before Mixed Claims Commission, United States and Germany, United States on behalf of Frederick J. Pickard *v.* Germany; brief on behalf of United States. 1924. cover-title, 6 p. 4° ‡

Reports. 1st report [Apr. 10–June 16, 1923] of Marshall Morgan, assistant to agent of United States before Mixed Claims Commission, United States and Germany, established under agreement of Aug. 10, 1922, between United States and Germany. 1924. viii+55 p. * Paper, 10c.
24—26147

Shipping Board. Nos. 29, 127, and 546–556, before Mixed Claims Commission, United States and Germany, United States on its own behalf, acting through Shipping Board and/or Shipping Board Emergency Fleet Corporation, and on behalf of certain of its nationals suffering losses at sea, *v.* Germany; memorandum brief in relation to liability of Germany under Treaty of Berlin for shipping losses suffered by United States and/or its nationals. 1924. cover-title, ii+83 p. 4° ‡

NAVY DEPARTMENT

Japan. Relief of earthquake sufferers in Japan, draft of proposed legislation, to be included in one of deficiency bills: "Paymaster general of Navy is hereby authorized and directed to expend from naval supply account fund issues made by order of Secretary of Navy, pursuant to directions of the President, for relief of sufferers in Japan following earthquake which occurred Sept. 1, 1923." Feb. 14, 1924. 2 p. (H. doc. 195, 68th Cong. 1st sess.) * Paper, 5c.

Washington Navy-Yard. Local telephone system, Navy Yard, Washington, D. C.; [corrected to Jan. 1] 1924. 1924. [1]+6 p. ‡

ENGINEERING BUREAU

Electric propulsion installations. Instructions for operation, care, and repair of main propelling machinery; sec. 2, Electric propulsion installations; reprint of sec. 2, chapter 7, of Manual of engineering instructions. 1924. [1]+14 p. [The edition of the Manual of engineering instructions of which this chapter forms a part has not yet been issued.] * Paper, 5c.   24—26142

Marine engineering. Changes in Manual of engineering instructions, no. 19; Nov. 15, 1923. [1924.] i+14 p. [Changes 19 is section 2, chapter 7 of the new edition of the Manual of engineering instructions. This section has also been issued in pamphlet form with the title Instructions for operation, care, and repair of main propelling machinery: sec. 2, Electric propulsion installations, for which see above.] * Paper, 5c.

MARINE CORPS

Orders. Marine Corps orders 1, 1924; Jan. 3, 1924. 1924. 1 p. 4° ‡

MEDICINE AND SURGERY BUREAU

Diseases. Nomenclature of diseases and injuries, general instructions for use. 1923. cover-title, p. 231–264°. [Revision of chapter 15 from Manual of Medical Department, 1922.] ‡

Mental diseases. Detection of psychopath and classification of naval recruits in accordance with their intelligence; by A. W. Stearns. 1924. [1]+21 p. [From United States naval medical bulletin, v. 20, no. 2.] †

Naval medical bulletin. United States naval medical bulletin, published for information of Medical Department of service, Feb. 1924; v. 20, no. 2; edited by W. M. Kerr. 1924. vi+149–284 p. il. [Monthly.] * Paper, 15c. single copy, $1.50 a yr.; foreign subscription, $2.50.   8—35095

SPECIAL ARTICLES.—Detection of psychopath and classification of naval recruits in accordance with their intelligence; by A. W. Stearns.—Insulin treatment of diabetes mellitus; by W. D. Owens.—Novocaine anesthesia; by G. F. Cottle.—Observations concerning yaws in Haiti; by P. W. Wilson.—Relation of clinical laboratory to modern hospital [with list of references]; by H. S. Sumerlin.—Gas mask for head and chest injury cases; by F. F. Lane.—Improved technique in spinal puncture; by T. W. Raison.—Cystoscopy and report of 3 unusual cases; by L. B. Marshall.—Notes on preventive medicine for medical officers, Navy [including Eradication of vermin on board ship, with list of references; Supplementary report, review of literature relating to prophylaxis of measles, with bibliography, by T. W. Kemmerer].

Vermin. Eradication of vermin on board ship [with list of references]. 1924. [1]+22 p. [From United States naval medical bulletin, v. 20, no. 2.] †

NAVIGATION BUREAU

HYDROGRAPHIC OFFICE

NOTE.—The charts, sailing directions, etc., of the Hydrographic Office are sold by the office in Washington and also by agents at the principal American and foreign seaports and American lake ports. Copies of the General catalogue of mariners' charts and books and of the Hydrographic bulletins, reprints, and Notice to mariners are supplied free on application at the Hydrographic Office in Washington and at the branch offices in Boston, New York, Philadelphia, Baltimore, Norfolk, Savannah, New Orleans, Galveston, San Francisco, Portland (Oreg.), Seattle, Chicago, Cleveland, Buffalo, Sault Ste. Marie, and Duluth,

Asiatic pilot: v. 6. Malakka Strait and west coast of Sumatra with adjacent islands. 2d edition. 1923, [published] 1924. vii+649 p.+[2] leaves, il. map. ([Publication] 162.) [The 2 leaves given in the collation consist of request coupons which are detachable.] †Cloth, 90c.   19—2755

Hydrographic bulletin, weekly, no. 1796–99; Feb. 6–27, 1924. [1924.] Each 1 p.
.large 4° and f° [For Ice supplements to accompany nos. 1796–99, see below
under center head *Charts* the subhead *Pilot charts.*] † .

Lights. List of lights, with fog signals and visible time signals, including uni-
. form time system, radio time signals, radio weather bulletins, and radio compass stations of the world: v. 2, South and east coasts of Africa and Asia,
East Indies, Australia, New Zealand, and South Sea Isles; corrected to Dec.
29, 1923. 1924. ii+564 p. map. ([Publication] 31.) †Paper, 60c. 7—24402

Notice to aviators 2, 1924; Feb. 1 [1924]. [1924.] 2 p. [Monthly.] †
20—26958

Notice to mariners. Index to Notice to mariners, nos. 27–52, 1923. 1924.
[1]+34 p. †

—— .Notice to mariners 5–8, 1924; Feb. 2–23 [1924]. [1924.]. [xxxvi]+119–,
.224 leaves. [Weekly.] †

Tide calendars. Tide calendar [for Baltimore (Fort McHenry) and Cape
Henry], Mar. 1924. [1924.] 1 p. 4° [Monthly.] †

—— Tide calendar [for Norfolk (Navy Yard) and Newport News, Va.], Mar.
.1924. [1924.] 1 p. 4° [Monthly.] †

Charts

Africa. West coast of Africa, Cape Lopez to Loanda, from latest information;
chart 2203. Scale 1° long.= 4.5 in. Washington, Hydrographic Office, published Nov. 1905, 4th edition, Jan. 1924. 40.8×28.1 in. †50c.

Australia, east coast, Cape Byron to Port Jackson, from British surveys between 1862 and 1871; chart 3428. Scale 1° lat.= 7.9 in. Washington, Hydrographic Office, Jan. 1924. 43×25.7 in. †50c.

Bering Sea and Strait, Siberia and Alaska, compiled from latest information;
chart 68. Scale 1° long.=0.6 in. Washington, Hydrographic Office, pub-
.~lished Mar. 1917, 11th edition, Feb. 1924. 34.5×32.3 in. †50c.

Dover Strait and southern approaches, English Channel, from latest British
and French surveys; chart 4810. Scale naut. m.=0.4 in. Washington, Hydrographic Office, published Mar. 1917, 9th edition, Feb. 1924. 41.8×25.8 in.
.c † 40c. .

Elbe River, Germany, North Sea, outer light vessel to Brunsbuttelkoog, from
latest German surveys [with insets]; chart 4908. Scale naut. m.=1.4 in.
. Washington, Hydrographic Office, published Mar. 1915, 9th edition, Jan.
. 1924. 25×47.3 in. †50c.
. Brunsbuttelkoog, Kaiser Wilhelm Canal entrance.
.̩ Cuxhaven Road.

France, north coast, Cape Levi to Fecamp, from latest French surveys; chart
.4324. Scale naut. m.=0.5 in. Washington, Hydrographic Office, published
.: Nov. 1915, 15th edition, Feb. 1924. 27.3×41.2 in. †40c.

Great Britain, south coast, Dungeness to the Thames, including Dover Strait,
from latest British and French surveys; chart 4445. Scale naut. m.=0.7 in.
. Washington, Hydrographic Office, published Jan. 1915, 18th edition, Feb.
. 1924. 33.4×25.9 in. †40c.

Hwangpoo River (Woosung River), China, east coast, Yangtzepoo Creek to
Lunghwa Creek, from surveys by Hwangpoo Conservancy Board between
1914 and 1921, with additions from municipal plans; chart 5392. Scale
naut. m.=7 in. Washington, Hydrographic Office, Jan. 1924. 39.4×26.7 in.
† 50c.

Nanaimo Harbor, Vancouver Island, British Columbia, Canada, from British
. survey in 1899; chart 1774. Scale 1000 yds.=6 in. Washington, Hydrographic Office, published Mar. 1902, 14th edition, Feb. 1924. 27.6×33.1 in.
.† 40c.

New Zealand, Pacific Ocean, from British surveys between 1848 and 1855, with
additions from local and topographic surveys between 1870 and 1885; chart
3335. Scale naut. m.=0.2 in. Washington, Hydrographic Office, Jan. 1924.
38.6×25.5 in. † 40c.

Pei Ho (Hai Ho) or Peking River, Gulf of Pechili, China, sheet 1 from en-
. trance to Koku, from surveys by Hai Ho Conservancy Commission between
1905 and 1907; chart 1870. Scale naut. m.=2.3 in. Washington, Hydrographic Office, published June. 1907, 7th edition, Feb. 1924. 26.3×43.8 in.
† 50c.

Pilot charts. Ice supplement to north Atlantic pilot chart; issue 96. Scale 1° long.=0.3 in. Washington, Hydrographic Office [1924]. 8.9×11.8 in. [To accompany Hydrographic bulletin 1796, Feb. 6, 1924.] †

—— Same; issue 97. Scale 1° long.=0.3 in. Washington, Hydrographic Office [1924]. 8.9×11.8 in. [To accompany Hydrographic bulletin 1797, Feb. 13, 1924.] †

—— Same; issue 98. Scale 1° long.=0.3 in. Washington, Hydrographic Office [1924]. 8.9×11.8 in. [To accompany Hydrographic bulletin 1798. Feb. 20, 1924.] †

—— Same; issue 99. Scale 1° long.=0.3 in. Washington, Hydrographic Office [1924]. 8.9×11.8 in. [To accompany Hydrographic bulletin 1799, Feb. 27, 1924.] †

—— Pilot chart of Central American waters, Mar. 1924; chart 3500. Scale 1° long.=0.7 in. Washington, Hydrographic Office, Feb. 12, 1924. 23.4×35.1 in. [Monthly. Certain portions of the data are furnished by the Weather Bureau.] † 10c.
NOTE.—Contains on reverse: Reports on currents experienced: [Reproduction of] current report for record in Hydrographic Office.—Table of fishing banks in north Atlantic Ocean.—Table of fishing banks in north Pacific Ocean.—Ocean currents.

—— Pilot chart of Indian Ocean, Apr. 1924; chart 2603. Scale 1° long.=0.2 in. Washington, Hydrographic Office, Feb. 12, 1924. 22.6×31 in. [Monthly. Certain portions of the data are furnished by the Weather Bureau.] † 10c.
NOTE.—Contains on reverse: Reports on currents experienced: [Reproduction of] current report for record in Hydrographic Office.—Table of fishing banks in north Atlantic Ocean.—Table of fishing banks in north Pacific Ocean.—Ocean currents.

—— Pilot chart of north Atlantic Ocean, Mar. 1924; chart 1400. Scale 1° long.=0.27 in. Washington, Hydrographic Office, Feb. 12, 1924. 23.2×31.8 in. [Monthly. Certain portions of the data are furnished by the Weather Bureau.] † 10c.   14—16339
NOTE.—Contains on reverse: Reports on currents experienced: [Reproduction of] current report for record in Hydrographic Office.—Table of fishing banks in north Atlantic Ocean.—Table of fishing banks in north Pacific Ocean.—Ocean currents.

—— Same, supplement, with title, Ice drift in north Atlantic; by Edward H. Smith. Washington, Hydrographic Office, Feb. 21, 1924. 1 p. il. oblong f° (Supplement to Pilot chart of north Atlantic Ocean for Mar. 1924.) † Included in price of Pilot chart for north Atlantic Ocean.

—— Pilot chart of north Pacific Ocean. Mar. 1924; chart 1401. Scale 1° long.=0.2 in. Washington, Hydrographic Office, Jan. 12, 1924. 23.7×35.3 in. [Monthly. Certain portions of the data are furnished by the Weather Bureau.] † 10c.
NOTE.—Contains on reverse: Index charts of Hydrographic Office publications.

—— Same, Apr. 1924; chart 1401. Scale 1° long.=0.2 in. Washington, Hydrographic Office, Feb. 12, 1924. 23.7×35.3 in. [Monthly. Certain portions of the data are furnished by the Weather Bureau.] † 10c.
NOTE.—Contains on reverse: Reports on currents experienced: [Reproduction of] current report for record in Hydrographic Office.—Table of fishing banks in north Atlantic Ocean.—Table of fishing banks in north Pacific Ocean.—Ocean currents.

Port Antonio, Jamaica, W. I., from British survey in 1921; chart 1286. Scale 2000 yds.=9.6 in. Washington, Hydrographic Office, published Sept. 1891, 18th edition, Feb. 1924. 22×25.6 in. † 30c.

Radio stations. Chart showing location of Army and Navy radio stations and Navy radio compass stations, and naval district boundaries with their terminal points [with insets]; chart 5172. Scale 5° long.=3.9 in. Washington, Hydrographic Office, published June, 1919, 9th edition, Jan. 1924. 28.1×44.8 in. † 20c.
Alaska; with inset, Aleutian Islands.
Guam.
Haiti, Island of.
Hawaiian Islands.
[Massachusetts, Southeastern, and entrance to Long Island Sound.]-
[New York City, Vicinity of.]
[Norfolk, Vicinity of.]
Panama Canal.
Philippine Islands; with inset, Manila Bay.
Porto Rico and Virgin Islands.
[Puget Sound Navy-Yard, Vicinity of.]
[San Francisco, Vicinity of.]
Tutuila.

Syria. Coast of Syria, Mediterranean, Markhab to Ras en-Nakura, from British survey in 1860; with inset, Juneh Bay, from Ottoman Government plan, 1912; chart 3973. Scale naut. m.=0.3 in. Washington, Hydrographic Office, published Nov. 1914, 4th edition, Feb. 1924. 39.5×25.4 in. † 40c.

RECRUITING BUREAU

Posters. [Poster] 247. n. p. [Nov. 7, 1923]. 14×17 in. [Title is: Tribute to Roosevelt.] †

—— Same 248. n. p. [Nov. 23, 1923]. 14×17 in. [Title is: Divine service in Navy.] †

—— Same 249. n. p. [Dec. 5, 1923]. 14×17 in. [Title is: On parade at Hampton Roads.] †

—— Same 250. n. p. [Dec. 10, 1923]. 14×17 in. [Title is: One of the Nation's shields.] †

—— Same 251. n. p. [Nov. 12, 1923]. 14×17 in. [Title is: Sight-seeing in south seas.] †

—— Same 252. n. p. [Dec. 15, 1923]. 14×17 in. [Title is: Our Navy in Hawaii.] †

—— Same 253. n. p. [Dec. 29, 1923]. 14×17 in. [Title is: New sights in far lands.] †

—— Same 254. n. p. [Jan. 9, 1924]. 14×17 in. [Title is: Training for championship.] †

—— Same 255. n. p. [Jan. 9, 1924]. 14×17 in. [Title is: U. S. S. Detroit at Venice.] †

—— Same 256. n. p. [Jan. 28, 1924]. 14×17 in. [Title is: Atop the Great Pyramid at Gizeh.] †

SUPPLIES AND ACCOUNTS BUREAU

Naval supplies. Index to specifications issued by Navy Department for naval stores and material. Jan. 2, 1924. vi+46 p. 12° [Quarterly.] †

Naval vessels. Sale of targets, Indiana, Alabama, San Marcos, by public auction at [Central Sales Office], Navy Yard, Washington, D. C., Mar. 19, 1924. 1924. cover-title, 4 p. 4 p. of pl. (Catalogue 551A.) †

Supply Corps, Navy. Memorandum for information of officers of Supply Corps, commanding officers [of ships], and commandants 257; Jan. 2, 1924. [1924.] p. 7902–99, 12° [Monthly.] ‡

—— Same 258; Feb. 1, 1924. [1924.] p. 8000–77, 12° [Monthly.] ‡

PAN AMERICAN UNION

NOTE.—The Pan American Union sells its own monthly bulletins, handbooks, etc., at prices usually ranging from 5c. to $2.50. The price of the English edition of the bulletin is 25c. a single copy or $2.50 a year, the Spanish edition $2.00 a year, the Portuguese edition $1.50 a year; there is an additional charge of 50c. a year on each edition for countries outside the Pan American Union. Address the Director General of the Pan American Union, Washington, D. C.

Bulletin (English edition). Bulletin of Pan American Union, Feb. 1924; [v. 58, no. 2] [1924.] iv+109–215 p. il. [Monthly.]   8—30967

—— Same. (H doc. 6, pt. 8, 68th Cong. 1st, sess.)

—— Same, index [to] v. 57, July-Dec. 1923. [1924.] [1]+xxxiii p.

—— Same. (H. doc. 6, 68th Cong. 1st sess.)

Bulletin (Portuguese edition). Boletim da União Pan-Americana, Fevereiro, 1924, edição portugueza; [v. 26, no. 2]. [Sun Job Print, Baltimore, Md., 1924.] [iv]+77–151 p. il. [Monthly.]   11—27014

Bulletin (Spanish edition). Boletín de la Unión Panamericana, v. 55. [sección española]; Julio-Diciembre, 1922 [índice]. [1924.] [1]+xiv p.   12—12555

—— Same, Febrero, 1924, sección española; [v. 58, no. 2]. [1924.] iv+109–219 p. il. [Monthly. This number is entitled Casas obreras en las Américas.]

Pan American Pedagogical Congress, to be held in Santiago, Chile, Sept. 1925.
1924. [2]+6 p. il. [From Bulletin, Feb. 1924.] †
Panama, general descriptive data. 1924. [2]+30 p. il. †   11—35840

PANAMA CANAL

Note.—Although The Panama Canal makes its reports to, and is under the supervision of, the Secretary of War, it is not a part of the War Department.

Panama Canal record, v. 17, no. 26–29; Feb. 6–27, 1924. Balboa Heights, C. Z.
[1924.] p. 371–424. [Weekly.]   7—35328

Note.—The yearly subscription rate of the Panama Canal record is 50c. domestic, and $1.00 foreign, (single issues 2c.), except in the case of Government departments and bureaus, Members of Congress, representatives of foreign Governments, steamship lines, chambers of commerce, boards of trade, and university and public libraries, to whom the Record is distributed free. The word "domestic" refers to the United States, Canada, Canal Zone, Cuba, Guam, Hawaii, Manua, Mexico, the Philippines, Porto Rico, Republic of Panama, Tutuila, and the Virgin Islands. Subscriptions will commence with the first issue of the Record in the month in which the subscriptions are received, unless otherwise requested. Remittances should be made payable to Disbursing Clerk, The Panama Canal, but should be forwarded to the Chief of Office, The Panama Canal, Washington, D. C. The name and address to which the Record is to be sent should be plainly written. Postage stamps, foreign money, and defaced or smooth coins will not be accepted.

EXECUTIVE DEPARTMENT

EXECUTIVE OFFICE

Navigation. Transit and harbor regulations of Panama Canal and approaches thereto, including all waters under its jurisdiction. Panama Canal Press, Mount Hope, C. Z., 1923 [published 1924]. 68 p. †

PANAMA RAILROAD COMPANY

Accounts. Classification of accounts no. 3, operations carried on through Panama Railroad Company on Isthmus of Panama; revised to July 1, 1923. The Panama Canal, Mount Hope, C. Z., 1924. 39 p. ‡.

PURCHASING DEPARTMENT

Supplies. Circular [proposals for supplies] 1588, 1591–92; Feb. 6–23, 1924. [1924.] various paging, f° †

—— Proposals [for supplies 1588 and 1592 to accompany Circular proposals for supplies 1588 and 1592]. [1924.] Each 1 p. 24° and 32° ‡

POST OFFICE DEPARTMENT

Advertising. Treatment to be accorded undeliverable advertising matter not bearing return postage pledge with which are inclosed reply postal cards or post cards having uncanceled 1-cent stamps attached; [issued by] 3d assistant Postmaster General. Feb. 25, 1924. 1 p. 16° †

Confessions, test of admissibility, searches and seizures [decision rendered by circuit court of appeals, 7th circuit, in docket nos. 3065–68, Chicago, Ill., Jan. 2, 1923, Murphy *v.* United States and 3 other cases]. 1923. [1] +14 p. ‡   24—26233

Mail contracts. Advertisement inviting proposals for service of carrying mails in regulation screen wagons and for furnishing equipments for delivery, collection, and transportation of mail at cities and towns named in North Carolina, South Carolina, Georgia, Florida, Alabama, Mississippi, Tennessee, and Kentucky, July 1, 1924–June 30, 1928. Feb. 12, 1924. [1]+92 p. †

Newspapers. What are newspapers? [definition of newspaper as defined by Postmaster General]. Feb. 11, 1924. 1 p. 12°. †

Plants. Additional plant-inspection place in Utah; [issued by] 3d assistant Postmaster General. Feb. 28, 1924. 1 p. 16° †

Post offices, by classes, in each State and Territory, Jan. 1, 1924. 1924. 1 p. †

Postal bulletin, v. 45, no. 13383–406; Feb. 1–29, 1924. 1924. various paging, f°. [Daily except Sundays and holidays.] * Paper, 5c. single copy, $2.00 a yr.

6—5810,

Postal guide. United States official postal guide, 4th series, v. 3, no. 8; Feb. 1924, monthly supplement. 1924. cover-title, ii+44 p. il. [Includes Inserts 848–851 to Postal laws and regulations of United States. Text on p. 2–4 of cover.] * Official postal guide, with supplements, $1.00, foreign subscription, $1.50; July issue, 75c.; supplements published monthly (11 pamphlets) 25c., foreign subscription, 50c.

4—18254

Postal savings. Interest payments on postal savings deposits; [issued by] 3d assistant Postmaster General. Feb. 18, 1924. 1 p. 16° †

Railway mail pay. Before Interstate Commerce Commission, docket no. 9200, in re railway mail pay, application of short line railroads in intermountain and Pacific Coast States in matter of railway mail pay; brief for Postmaster General. 1924. cover-title, vi+156 p. ‡

POSTAL SAVINGS SYSTEM

Postal savings. Informace stranou Spojených Státu Poštovni Spořitelni Soustavy. Jan. 1924. 2 p. (Form PS 20.) [Same, in Bohemian, as publication entitled Information about Postal Savings System.] †

RAILWAY MAIL SERVICE

Mail-trains. Schedule of mail trains, no. 90, Feb. 1, 1924, 12th division, Railway Mail Service, comprising Louisiana and Mississippi. 1924. 80 p. narrow 8° ‡

—— Schedule of mail trains, no. 368, Dec. 26, 1923, 2d division, Railway Mail Service, comprising New York, New Jersey, Pennsylvania, Delaware, eastern shore of Maryland, Accomac and Northampton counties, Va., Porto Rico, and Virgin Islands. 1924. 330+[1] p. narrow 8° ‡

—— Schedule of mail trains, no. 448, Jan. 19, 1924, 7th division, Railway Mail Service, comprising Kansas and Missouri. 1924. 172 p. narrow 8° ‡

SOLICITOR FOR POST OFFICE DEPARTMENT

Fraud order [against Madame E. A. Fisher, E. A. Fisher, E. A. Fisher, C. A., and Edward Fisher, at Somerville, Tenn.]. Feb. 16, 1924. 1 p. 16° †

TOPOGRAPHY DIVISION

NOTE.—Post route maps corrected to Jan. 1 will be distributed in February to the postal service. For a list of the maps composing the set, with prices, see below. Orders for the maps should be addressed to the Disbursing Clerk, Post Office Department, Washington, D. C., and money orders should be made payable to him.

Since February, 1908, the Topography Division has been preparing rural-delivery maps of counties in which rural-delivery is completely established. They are published in two forms, one giving simply the rural free delivery routes starting from a single given post office, sold at 10 cents each; the other, the rural free delivery routes in an entire county, sold at 35 cents each. A uniform scale of 1 inch to 1 mile is used. Editions are not issued, but sun-print copies are produced in response to special calls addressed to the Disbursing Clerk, Post Office Department, Washington, D. C. These maps should not be confused with the post route maps described in the preceding paragraph.

Post route maps. Post route maps of—

Alabama. Scale 8 m.=1 in. 60c.

Alaska. Scale 40 m.=1 in. 60c.

Arizona. Scale 12 m.= 1 in. 60c.

Arkansas. Scale 9 m.=1 in. 60c.

California, Nevada. Scale 12 m.=1 in. 2 sheets, $1.20.

Canal Zone, Isthmus of Panama. Scale 1.6 m.=1 in. 60c.

Colorado. Scale 10 m.=1 in. 60c.

Florida. Scale 10 m.=1 in. 60c.

Georgia. Scale 8 m.=1 in. 60c.

Hawaii, Samoan Islands, Guam. Scale 9 m.=1 in. 60c.

Idaho. Scale 12 m.=1 in. 60c.

Post route maps. Post route maps of—Continued.

Illinois. Scale 8 m.=1 in. 60c.
Indiana. Scale 7 m.=1 in. 60c.
Iowa. Scale 7 m.= 1 in. 60c.
Kansas. Scale 10 m.=1 in. 60c.
Kentucky. Scale 7 m.=1 in. 60c.
Louisiana. Scale, 9 m.=1 in. 60c.
Maine. Scale 6.5 m.=1 in. 60c.
Maryland, Delaware, District of Columbia. Scale 5 m.=1 in. 60c.
Massachusetts, Rhode Island, Connecticut. Scale 5 m.=1 in. 60c.
Michigan. Scale 9 m.=1 in. 60c.
Minnesota. Scale 10 m.=1 in. 60c.
Mississippi. Scale 8 m.=1 in. 60c.
Missouri. Scale 9 m.=1 in. 60c.
Montana. Scale 12 m.=1 in. 60c.
Nebraska. Scale 10 m.=1 in. 60c.
New Hampshire, vermont. Scale 5 m.=1 in. 60c.
New Jersey. Scale 4 m.=1 in. 60c.
New Mexico. Scale 12 m.=1 in. 60c.
New York. Scale 6.5 m.=1 in. 2 sheets, $1.20.
North Carolina. Scale 8 m.=1 in. 60c.
North Dakota. Scale 10 m.=1 in. 60c.
Ohio. Scale 7 m.=1 in. 60c·
Oklahoma. Scale 10 m.=1 in. 60c.
Oregon. Scale 10 m.=1 in. 60c.
Pennsylvania. Scale 5 m.=1 in. 2 sheets, $1.20.
Philippine Islands. Scale 14 m.=1 in. 2 sheets, $1.20.
Porto Rico, virgin Islands. Scale 5 m.=1 in. 60c.
South Carolina. Scale 8 m.=1 in. 60c.
South Dakota. Scale 10 m.=1 in, 60c.
Tennessee. Scale 7 m.=1 in. 60c.
Texas. Scale 12 m.=1 in. 2 sheets, $1.20.
Utah. Scale 10 m.=1 in. 60c.
Virginia. Scale 7 m.=1 in. 60c.
Washington. Scale 9 m.=1 in. 60c.
West Virginia. Scale 6 m.=1 in. 60c.
Wisconsin. Scale 9 m.=1 in. 60c.
Wyoming. Scale 12 m.=1 in. 60c.
—— Price list of post route maps. [1924.] 1 p. 4° †

Rural mail delivery. Price list of rural delivery county maps, Jan. 1, 1924. [1924.] 1 p. narrow f° [Manuscript corrections.]. †

PRESIDENT OF UNITED STATES

Addresses. Address of President of United States before National Republican Club at Waldorf-Astoria [New York City], Feb. 12, 1924. 1924. [2]+12 p.
  * Paper, 5c. 24—26143
—— Same. (S. doc. 42, 68th Cong. 1st sess.)

Alaska. Executive order, Alaska [revoking Executive order of Jan. 13, 1922, which authorized temporary withdrawal of certain lands in Alaska for use in connection with administration of Mount McKinley National Park, in so far as it affects certain described lands, and authorizing that said lands, with certain described adjoining land, be withdrawn from settlement, etc., and reserved for use in connection with construction and operation of railroad lines]. Jan. 21, 1924. 1 p. f° (No. 3946.) ‡

Alien property. Executive order authorizing Alien Property Custodian to sell certain property at private sale [being 1,132 shares of 8% preferred stock of Stern Brothers, corporation of New York State, formerly belonging to A. Schaaffhausenscher Bankverein A. G., Cologne, Germany]. Feb. 19, 1924. 1 p. f° (No. 3961.) ‡

Blackbeard Island Reservation. 3d Executive order [vacating Executive order of May 25, 1915, which abolished Blackbeard Island Reservation, Ga., as bird refuge, and restoring said reservation as created by Executive order of July 17, 1914, as preserve and breeding ground for native birds, under jurisdiction of Agriculture Department, subject to use of island for quarantine purposes by Treasury Department]. Feb. 15, 1924. 1 p. f° (No. 3957.) ‡

California. Executive order, California [withdrawing certain described public lands in California from settlement, etc., pending resurvey, such withdrawal to remain in effect until resurvey is accepted and approved plat thereof is officially filed in local land office]. Jan. 21, 1924. 1 p. f° (No. 3945.) ‡

Colorado. Executive order, Colorado [withdrawing certain described public lands in Colorado from settlement, etc., pending resurvey, such withdrawal to remain in effect until resurvey is accepted and approved plats thereof are officially filed in local land office]. Feb. 6, 1924. 1 p. f° (No. 3954.) ‡

Diplomatic and consular service. Executive order [of President Roosevelt relative to charges and criticisms against officers of diplomatic and consular services]. Apr. 25, 1902 [reprint 1924]. 1 p. f° (No. 171.) ‡

Entriken, Harvey. Executive order [authorizing appointment of Harvey Entriken to position of private secretary in office of Board of General Appraisers of New York]. Jan. 15, 1924. 1 p. f° (No. 3941 A.) ‡

Forest protection week and Arbor day, 1924, proclamation [urging that Apr. 21-27, 1924, be designated and set apart as Forest protection week, and that Arbor day be observed within the same week wherever practicable and not in conflict with State law or accepted customs]. Feb. 15, 1924. 1 p. f° (No. 1686.) †

Forest service. Executive order [amending civil service rules relating to Agriculture Department so as to except from examination foremen engaged upon road or trail construction and telephone operators employed temporarily by Forest Service during season of danger from fires or when special work requires additions to regular forest force]. Feb. 15, 1924. 1 p. f° (No. 3956.) ‡

Henderson, Mrs. Olive C. Executive order [authorizing appointment of Mrs. Olive Crook Henderson to clerical position in classified civil service]. Feb. 20, 1924. 1 p. f° (No. 3963.) ‡

Kraemer, Edward K. Executive order [authorizing reinstatement of Edward K. Kraemer to position of rural carrier at Elmer, N. J.]. Feb. 5, 1924. 1 p. f° (No. 3953.) ‡

Marcks, Louis. Executive order [authorizing reinstatement of Louis Marcks as clerk or carrier in post office service]. Feb. 16, 1924. 1 p. f° (No. 3959.) ‡

Military reservations. Executive order [authorizing that remaining part of Fort Keogh military reservation, Mont., having become useless for military purposes, be placed under control of Secretary of Interior for disposition as provided by law]. Feb. 2, 1924. 1 p. f° (No. 3952.) ‡

Murphy, Mrs. Margaret. Executive order [authorizing appointment of Mrs. Margaret Murphy as money counter or to similar position]. Jan. 29, 1924. 1 p. f° (No. 3950.) ‡

National forests. Executive order, Mount Baker National Forest, Wash. [directing that Washington National Forest, Wash., shall hereafter be known as Mount Baker National Forest]. Jan. 21, 1924. 1 p. f° (No. 3943.) ‡

—— Executive order, Mount Hood National Forest, Oreg. [directing that Oregon National Forest, Oreg., shall hereafter be known as Mount Hood National Forest]. Jan. 21, 1924. 1 p. f° (No. 3944.) ‡

—— Executive order, Roberts administrative site, near Blackfeet National Forest, Mont. [temporarily withdrawing certain described lands from settlement, etc., and reserving same for use by Forest Service as lookout station in connection with administration of Blackfeet National Forest]. Jan. 25, 1924. 1 p. f° (No. 3948.) ‡

National forests—Continued. Executive order, Santa Barbara National Forest, Calif. [modifying boundaries of Santa Barbara National Forest by excluding therefrom certain described lands in California, excluded lands to be subject only to homestead and desert land entry by ex-service men of War with Germany for period of 91 days, after which any remaining land may be open to general public under any public land law applicable thereto]. Feb. 9, 1924. 1 p. f° (No. 3955.) ‡

—— National forests in State of Washington, proclamation [modifying Executive order of Dec. 31, 1920, affecting boundaries of Chelan National Forest so as to exclude certain designated areas and so as to allow State of Washington to make selections of lands as indemnity in satisfaction of its common school grant]. [Jan. 16, 1924.] 4 p. f° ([No. 1684.]) †

Oregon. Executive order, Oregon [withdrawing certain described public lands in Oregon from settlement, etc., pending resurvey, such withdrawal to remain in effect until resurvey is accepted and approved plats thereof are officially filed in local land office]. Feb. 15, 1924. 1 p. f° (No. 3958.) ‡

Passports. Executive order [of President McKinley amending certain designated paragraphs of Instructions to diplomatic officers of United States, 1897, and of Regulations prescribed for use of consular service, 1896, concerning passports]. Jan. 31, 1901 [reprint 1924]. 1 p. f° (No. 135.) ‡

Pay, Army. Executive order [authorizing that enlisted men of Army who have established special qualifications in use of arms which they may be required to use, shall receive additional compensation]. Feb. 19, 1924. 1 p. f° (No. 3962.) ‡

Shaughnessy, Mrs. Myrtle. Executive order [authorizing appointment of Mrs. Myrtle Shaughnessy to clerical position in classified civil service]. Jan. 24, 1924. 1 p. f° (No. 3947.) ‡

Steamboat Inspection Service. Executive order [authorizing reinstatement of assistant inspectors of hulls and assistant inspectors of boilers, Steamboat Inspection Service, whose services were dispensed with July 31, 1921, in response to call for economy in Federal service, to appropriate positions in classified service]. Jan. 30, 1924. 1 p. f° (No. 3951.) ‡

Stringfellow, James R. Executive order [waiving age limit for operatives in Secret Service so as to permit James R. Stringfellow to enter examination]. Jan. 19, 1924. 1 p. f° (No. 3942.) ‡

Washington State. Executive order, Washington [modifying Executive order of Aug. 13, 1923, which transferred to Secretary of Interior certain lands in abandoned military reservations in Washington and California, in so far as it concerns certain described lands in Washington, and authorizing that said lands be placed under control of Treasury Department for Coast Guard purposes]. Jan. 28, 1924. 1 p. f° (No. 3949.) ‡

Wilson, Woodrow. Announcing death of Woodrow Wilson, proclamation. Feb. 3, 1924. 1 p. f° (No. 1685.) †

Wyoming. Executive order, Wyoming [withdrawing certain described public lands in Wyoming from settlement, etc., pending resurvey, such withdrawal to remain in effect until resurvey is accepted and approved plats thereof are officially filed in local land office]. Feb. 18, 1924. 1 p. f° (No. 3960.) ‡

RAILROAD ADMINISTRATION

Clay. Before Interstate Commerce Commission, no. 12461, Peninsular Portland Cement Company *v.* director general et al.; supplemental petition for reargument before full commission. 1924. cover-title, 5 p. ‡

Coal. Before Interstate Commerce Commission, no. 14714, Whitaker-Glessner Company et al. *v.* director general et al.; exception on behalf of director general to examiner's report. 1924. cover-title, 12 p. ‡

Coal-cars. Before Interstate Commerce Commission, no. 11446, Northern West Virginia Coal Operators' Association *v.* Pennsylvania Railroad Company, director general, et al.; exceptions of director general to proposed report. 1924. cover-title, i+24 p. ‡

Coke. Before Interstate Commerce Commission, no. 14189 and sub. nos. 1 and 2, Acheson Graphite Company *v.* director general; director general's exceptions to report proposed by examiner. 1924. cover-title, 5 p. ‡

Cotton goods. Before Interstate Commerce Commission, no. 14722, H. D. Lee Mercantile Company *v.* director general; exceptions filed on behalf of director general to examiner's proposed report. 1924. cover-title, 5 p. ‡

Dried beef. Before Interstate Commerce Commission, no. 11130, Indian Packing Corporation *v.* director general et al.; exceptions on behalf of director general to portion of proposed report relating to reparation. 1924. cover-title, 4 p. ‡

Fullers' earth. Before Interstate Commerce Commission, no. 14581, White Oil Corporation *v.* director general et al.; brief for director general. 1924. cover-title, 16 p. ‡

Grain. Before Interstate Commerce Commission, no. 14849, S. W. Thaxter & Company *v.* director general; defendant's exceptions to proposed report. 1924. cover-title, 10 p. ‡

Lighterage. Before Interstate Commerce Commission, no. 15067, American Pulpwood Corporation *v.* director general et al.; exceptions filed on behalf of director general to examiner's proposed report. 1924. cover-title, 4 p. ‡

Paper. Before Interstate Commerce Commission, no. 14443, Minnesota & Ontario Paper Company *v.* director general; no. 14376, Seaman Paper Company *v.* [same]; brief on part of director general. 1924. cover-title, 16 p. ‡

Wire-rods. Before Interstate Commerce Commission, no. 15149, New England Drawn Steel Co. *v.* director general et al.; brief for director general. 1924. cover-title, 2 p. ‡

SHIPPING BOARD

American Metals Company. No. 8170, in district court, eastern district of Pennsylvania, Harry A. Robinson and Henry B. Robinson, trading as American Metals Company, *v.* Shipping Board Emergency Fleet Corporation; defendant's brief. 1924. cover-title, 34 p. · ‡

South Atlantic Dry Dock Company. No. 4171, in circuit court of appeals, 5th circu't, Shipping Board Emergency Fleet Corporation *vs.* South Atlantic Dry Dock Company, error to district court for southern district of Florida; answer and reply brief of plaintiff in error. 1924. cover-title, 42 p. ‡

SHIPPING BOARD EMERGENCY FLEET CORPORATION

Ships. Schedule of sailings of Shipping Board vessels in general cargo, passenger & mail services, 1st of February to middle of March, 1924; issued by Traffic Department. [1924.] cover-title, iv+14+[1] p. il. [Monthly. Text on p. 2 and 3 of cover.] †   23—26331

SMITHSONIAN INSTITUTION

NOTE.—In a recent price-list the Smithsonian Institution publishes this notice: "Applicants for the publications in this list are requested to state the grounds of their requests, as the Institution is able to supply papers only as an aid to the researches or studies in which they are especially interested. These papers are distributed *gratis,* except as otherwise indicated, and should be ordered by the *publication numbers* arranged in sequence. The serial publications of the Smithsonian-Institution are as follows. 1, Smithsonian contributions to knowledge; 2, Smithsonian miscellaneous collections; 3, Smithsonian annual reports. No *sets* of these are for sale or distribution, as most of the volumes are out of print. The papers issued in the series of Contributions to knowledge and Miscellaneous collections are distributed without charge to public libraries, educational establishments, learned societies, and specialists in this country and abroad; and are supplied to other institutions and individuals at the prices indicated. Remittances should be made payable to the 'Smithsonian Institution.' The Smithsonian report volumes and the papers reprinted in separate form therefrom are distributed *gratuitously* by the Institution to libraries and individuals throughout the world. Very few of the Report volumes are now available at the Institution, but many of those of which the Smithsonian edition is exhausted can be purchased from the Superintendent of Documents, Government Printing Office. Washington, D. C. The Institution maintains mailing-lists of public libraries and other educational establishments, but no *general mailing-list of individuals.* A library making application to be listed for Smithsonian publications should state the number of volumes which it contains and the date of its establishment, and have the endorsement of a Member of Congress."

The annual reports are the only Smithsonian publications that are regularly issued as public documents. All the others are paid for from the private funds of the Institution, but as they are usually regarded as public documents and have free transmission by mail they are listed in the Monthly catalogue.

Eclipses. Brightness of lunar eclipses, 1860–1922 [with lists of references] ; by Willard J. Fisher. Washington, Smithsonian Institution, Feb. 18, 1924. [2]+61 p. il. (Publication 2751; Smithsonian miscellaneous collections, v. 76, no. 9.) † Paper, 40c.   24—26175

Zoology. Opinions [78–81] rendered by International Commission on Zoological Nomenclature. Washington, Smithsonian Institution, Feb. 9, 1924. [2]+32 p. (Publication 2747; Smithsonian miscellaneous collections, v. 73, no. 2.) † Paper, 20c.   10—35963

AMERICAN HISTORICAL ASSOCIATION

Peter of Abano, medieval scientist; by Lynn Thorndike. 1923. [1]+315–326 p. [From Report, 1919, v. 1.] †

NATIONAL MUSEUM

NOTE.—The publications of the National Museum comprise an annual report and three scientific series, viz., Proceedings, Bulletins, and Contributions from national herbarium. The editions are distributed to established lists of libraries, scientific institutions, and specialists, any surplus copies being supplied on application. The volumes of Proceedings are made up of technical papers based on the Museum collections in biology, geology, and anthropology, and of each of these papers a small edition, in pamphlet form, is issued in advance of the volume, for prompt distribution to specialists. No sets of any of these series can now be furnished.

Phorocera. North American species of parasitic 2-winged flies belonging to genus Phorocera and allied genera; by J. M. Aldrich and Ray T. Webber. 1924. cover-title, 90 p. il. [From Proceedings, v. 63; no. 2486.] †

Proceedings. Proceedings of National Museum. 1923. v. 62, xvi+[750] p. il. 11 pl. 50 p. of pl. [Articles 2447–68 are included in this volume. Each article is also published separately in advance.] * Paper, $1.50.   11—20830

CONTENTS.—Mosquitoes of United States; by Harrison G. Dyar.—Fishes from Formosa and Philippine Islands; by Henry W. Fowler and Barton A. Bean.—Seven new species of fish of order Malacopterygii, by W. W. Welsh; [edited by C. M. Breder, jr.].—Revision of North American 2-winged flies of family Therevidæ [with list of references to literature] ; by Frank R. Cole.—New fossil turtle, Kinosternon arizonense, from Arizona ; by Charles W. Gilmore.—Rehabilitation of hitherto overlooked species of musk turtle of Southern States; by Leonhard Stejneger.—Two new Lithothamnieae, calcareous algae, from Lower Miocene of Trinidad, British West Indies ; by Marshall A. Howe.— Leaf and twig mining buprestid beetles of Mexico and Central America ; by Warren S. Fisher.—Mineralogic notes on pucherite, pyrite, trichalcite, and wavellite ; by Earl V. Shannon.—Species of round worm (Gongylonema) from domestic swine in United States; by Edward A. Chapin.—Neotropical muscoid genus Mesembrinella Giglio-Tos and other testaceous muscoid flies [with list of literature] ; by J. M. Aldrich.—On siderite and associated minerals from Columbia River basalt at Spokane, Wash.; by Earl V. Shannon.—Dermanyssid mites of North America ; by H. E. Ewing.—Tertiary fossil plants from Republic of Haiti ; by Edward W. Berry.—Notes on mineralogy of 3 gouge clays from precious metal veins ; by Earl V. Shannon.—Description of 2 squalodonts recently discovered in Calvert Cliffs, Md., and notes on shark-toothed cetaceans ; by Remington Kellogg.—Scale insects of subfamilies Monophlebinae and Margarodinae treated by Maskell ; by Harold Morrison and Emily Morrison.—Meteoric metabolite from Dungannon, Va.; by George P. Merrill.—Miocene plants from southern Mexico; by Edward W. Berry.—New genera of 2-winged flies of subfamily Leptogastrinae of family Asilidae; by J. M. Aldrich.—Dragonflies (Odonata) of Burma and Lower Siam; 3. Subfamily Aeschninae [with bibliography] ; by Frank Fortescue Laidlaw.—Steiroxys hendersoni, new katydid from Utah ; by A. N. Caudell.

—— Same, [title-page, contents, and list of illustrations to] v. 62. 1923. xv p. † (price given on this publication is that of bound volume catalogued above).

Spiders. Descriptions of new American and Chinese spiders, with notes on other Chinese species; by Ralph v. Chamberlin. [1924.] 38 p. 7 p. of pl. [From Proceedings, v. 63; no. 2481.] †

Whales. Description of new genus and species of whalebone whale from Calvert Cliffs, Md.; by Remington Kellogg. 1924. cover-title, 14 p. 6 p. of pl. [From Proceedings, v. 63; no. 2483.] †

STATE DEPARTMENT

[*Circulars*] 919 and 921; Nov. 24, 1923 and Jan. 19, 1924. [1924.] 7 p. and 2 p. [General instruction circulars to consular officers.] ‡

Claims. British steamship Baron Berwick, report with reference to claim by British Government on account of losses sustained by British steamship Baron Berwick as result of collision between that vessel and U. S. S. Iroquois (now Freedom) and further collision with U. S. destroyer Truxton. Feb. 28, 1924. 4 p. (S. doc. 56, 68th. Cong. 1st sess.) * Paper, 5c.

—— Claim of Government of Norway, report in relation to claim presented by Government of Norway against Government of United States on account of losses sustained by owners of Norwegian steamship Hassel in collision between it and American steamship Ausable, operated by War Department. Feb. 22, calendar day Feb. 25, 1924. 4 p. (S. doc. 52, 68th Cong. 1st sess.) * Paper, 5c.

—— Claim of Madame Crignier, report with reference to claim presented by Government of France on account of losses sustained by Madam Crignier, French citizen, in search for body of John Paul Jones. Feb. 7, calendar day Feb. 11, 1924. 3 p. (S. doc. 41, 68th Cong. 1st sess.) * Paper, 5c.

—— Claims arising out of occupation of Vera Cruz, report requesting submission to present Congress [of] claims arising out of occupation of Vera Cruz, Mexico, by American forces in 1914, and requesting legislation for appropriation to pay same. Feb. 7, 1924. 10 p. (S. doc. 33, 68th Cong. 1st sess.) * Paper, 5c.

—— Swedish fishing boat Lilly, report relative to claim presented by Swedish Government on account of sinking of Swedish fishing boat Lilly by U. S. Army transport Antigone. Feb. 7, calendar day Feb. 11, 1924. 3 p. (S. doc. 39, 68th Cong. 1st sess.) * Paper, 5c.

Diplomatic and consular service of United States; corrected to Jan. 1, 1924. 1924. 67 p. ‡   10—16369

Diplomatic list, Feb. 1924. [1924.] cover-title, i+34 p. 24° [Monthly.] ‡
10—16292

Harding, Warren G. Memorial address in honor of the late President Warren ●G. Harding delivered by Charles E. Hughes, Secretary of State, at official memorial exercises in honor of the late President Harding, held in Hall of House of Representatives, Feb. 27, 1924. 1924. cover-title, [2]+18 p. †
24—26210

Inter-American Electrical Communications Committee, report concerning meeting of Inter-American Electrical Communications Committee at city of Mexico, Mar. 27, 1924, and requesting legislation authorizing appropriation for purposes of participation by Government. Feb. 7, 1924. 3 p. (S. doc. 34, 68th Cong. 1st sess.) [Corrected print.] * Paper, 5c.

Russia. Reports on Russian affairs, in response to resolution, report touching [reports on] Russian affairs by William Boyce Thompson, Colonel Raymond Robins, General Graves, Governor J. P. Goodrich, Major Slaughter, and Major Faymonville. Feb. 1, 1924. 2 p. (S. doc. 31, 68th Cong. 1st sess.) * Paper, 5c.

San Martin, José de. Equestrian statue of General San Martin, letter recommending authorization of erection in Washington of equestrian statue of General San Martin, gift by people of Argentina. Feb. 13, 1924. 2 p. (S. doc. 43, 68th Cong. 1st sess.) * Paper, 5c.

PASSPORT CONTROL DIVISION

Passports. Notice concerning use of passports [Feb. 1, 1924]. [1924.] 8 p. †

SUPREME COURT

Coamo, steamship. Certificate, Oct. term, 1923, no. 301, United States *vs.* steamship Coamo, her engines, etc., New York & Porto Rico Steamship Company, on certificate from circuit court of appeals for 2d circuit. [1924.] cover-title, i+2 p. ‡

Douglas Packing Company. Transcript of record, Oct. term, 1923, no. 559, United States *vs.* 95 barrels, more or less, alleged apple cider vinegar, Douglas Packing Company, claimant, on writ of certiorari to circuit court of appeals for 6th circuit. [1924.] cover-title, ii+41 p. ‡

Foumakis, Peter. Transcript of record, Oct. term, 1923, no. 735, Flo La-Chapelle, as administratrix of Peter Foumakis, *vs.* Union Pacific Coal Company, in error to Supreme Court of Wyoming. [1924.] cover-title, ii+38 p. ‡

[*Journal*] Jan. 28–Feb. 29, 1924; [slips] 59–69. [1924.] leaves 149–178. [Corrected prints of the Journal for Jan. 28 and Feb. 26 were also issued.] ‡

Louisiana. Transcript of record, Oct. term, 1923, no. 289, Hubert Work, Secretary of Interior, *vs.* Louisiana, appeal from ·Court of Appeals of District of Columbia. [1924.] cover-title, i+47 p. ‡

Lowe, Matthew. · Transcript of record, Oct. term, 1923, no. 615, Matthew Lowe *vs.* Benjamin E. Dyson, United States marshal in and for southern district of Florida, in error to district court for southern district of Florida. [1924.] cover-title, i+18 p. ‡

McCarthy, William P. Transcript of record, Oct. term, 1923, no. 616, William P. McCarthy *vs.* Benjamin E. Dyson, United States marshal in and for southern district of Florida, in error to district court for southern district of Florida. [1924.] cover-title, iii+17 p. ‡

Stearn, Louis. Transcript of record, Oct. term, 1923, no. 262, Harry H. Weiss, collector of internal revenue [for 18th district of Ohio] *vs.* Louis Stearn, on writ of certiorari to circuit court of appeals for 6th circuit. [1924.] cover-title, ii+37 p. ‡

White, John G. Transcript of record, Oct. term, 1923, no. 263, Harry H. Weiss, collector of internal revenue [for 18th district of Ohio] *vs.* John G. White, on writ of certiorari to circuit court of appeals for 6th circuit. [1924.] cover-title, i+32 p. ‡

TARIFF COMMISSION

Report. 7th annual report of Tariff Commission, [fiscal year] 1923. 1924. v+117 p. 1 pl. * Paper, 10c.   18—26040

—— Same. (H. doc. 105, 68th Cong. 1st sess.)

TREASURY DEPARTMENT

Appeals pending before United States courts in customs cases,· no. 73; Jan. 1924. 1924. [1]+14 p. [Quarterly.] * Paper, 5c. single copy, 15c. a yr.; foreign subscription, 20c.   10—4497

Claims. Claim of Powell Grocery Co., Asheville, N. C., communication· submitting claim of Powell Grocery Co., Asheville, N. C., against United States for damages caused by negligence of employee of ·Public Health Service, which requires appropriation for its payment. Feb. 26, 1924. 2 p. (H. doc. 206, 68th Cong. 1st sess.) * Paper, 5c.

—— Laws and regulations governing recognition of attorneys, agents, and other persons representing claimants and others before Treasury Department and offices thereof. Jan. 4, 1924. 1 p. 4° (1st supplement to Department circular 230 dated Aug. 15, 1923; Chief Clerk.) †

—— Same. Feb. 15, 1924. 1 p. 4° (2d supplement to Department circular 230 dated Aug. 15, 1923; Chief Clerk.) †

Finance. Daily statement of Treasury compiled from latest proved reports from Treasury offices and depositaries, Feb. 1–29, 1924. [1924.] Each 4 p. or 3 p. f° [Daily except Sundays and holidays.] †   15—3303

Personnel Classification Board. Treasury Department Personnel Classification Board. Jan. 29, 1924. 1 p. 4° (Department circular 324 amended; Chief Clerk.) †

Public debt. Statement of public debt of United States, Nov. 30, 1923. [1924.] [2] p. narrow f° [Monthly.] †   10—21268

Sabine, Tex. Boundaries of quarantine anchorage at Sabine Pass, Sabine, Tex. Feb. 5, 1924. 1 p. 4° (Department circular 336; Publ c Health Service.) †

S8421—No. 350—24——6

Treasury decisions. Index to Treasury decisions under customs, internal-revenue, and other laws; v. 44, Customs, July–Dec. 1923; and v. 25, Internal
revenue, Jan.–Dec. 1923. 1924. [1]+36 p. * Paper, 5c. single copy, included
in price of Treasury decisions for subscribers.

—— Treasury decisions under customs, internal revenue, and other laws,
including decisions of Board of General Appraisers and Court of Customs
Appeals, v. 45, no. 6–9; Feb. 7–28, 1924. 1924. various paging. [Weekly.
Department decisions numbered 39982–40036, general appraisers' decisions
8734–47, abstracts 46786–886, internal revenue decis'ons 3545–58, Tariff Commission Notice 34, and later Tariff Commission Notice 12.] * Paper, 5c.
single copy, $1.00 a yr.; foreign subscription, $2.00.   10—30490

APPRAISERS

Reappraisements. Index to reappraisement circulars, showing reappraisements
and decisions on appeals for review by general appraisers, July 1–Dec. 31,
1923. 1924. [1]+17 p. * Paper, 5c.

—— Reappraisements of merchandise by general appraisers [on Jan. 21–
Feb. 21, 1924]; Feb. 1–29, 1924. [1924.] various paging. (Reappraisement
circulars 3494–98.) [Weekly.] * Paper, 5c. single copy, 50c. a yr.; foreign
subscription, $1.05.   13—2916

BUDGET BUREAU

Chilocco Indian School, Chilocco, Okla., supplemental estimate of appropriation
for Department of Interior, fiscal year 1924, for making replacement of
losses occasioned by fire at Chilocco Indian School, Chilocco, Okla. Feb.
21, 1924. 2 p. (H. doc. 203, 68th Cong. 1st sess.) * Paper, 5c.

Coast Guard. United States Coast Guard, supplemental estimates of appropriations for Treasury Department, fiscal year 1924, for increasing equipment and personnel of Coast Guard. Feb. 1, 1924. 5 p. (H. doc. 182, 68th
Cong. 1st sess.) * Paper, 5c.

Commerce Department. Printing and binding, Department of Commerce, supplemental estimate of appropriation for Department of Commerce, fiscal
year 1924, for printing and binding. Feb. 19, 1924. 2 p. (H. doc. 201, 68th
Cong. 1st sess.) * Paper, 5c.

District of Columbia. District of Columbia, supplemental estimate for District
of Columbia, fiscal year 1924 [for treatment of patients under contract made
by Board of Charities with Children's Hospital]. Feb. 7, 1924. 2 p. (H. doc.
187, 68th Cong. 1st sess.) * Paper, 5c.

—— Special legal services for Public Utilities Commission, supplemental estimate of appropriation for District of Columbia for employment of special
legal services for Public Utilities Commission, fiscal year 1924. Feb. 16,
1924. 3 p. (H. doc. 198, 68th Cong. 1st sess.) * Paper, 5c.

Gila River Reservation. Indian service, supplemental estimate of appropriation for Department of Interior, fiscal year 1924, pertaining to Indian service.
Feb. 16, 1924. 3 p. (H. doc. 197, 68th Cong. 1st sess.) * Paper, 5c.

Military reservations. Acquiring land at certain military reservations, supplemental estimates of appropriations for War Department, fiscal year 1924,
for completion of acquisition of land at certain military reservations. Feb.
21, 1924. 3 p. (H. doc. 204, 68th Cong. 1st sess.) * Paper, 5c.

National Home for Disabled Volunteer Soldiers at Battle Mountain Sanitarium,
Hot Springs, S. Dak., supplemental estimate of appropriation for War Department, fiscal year 1924, for National Home for Disabled Soldiers at Battle
Mountain Sanitarium, Hot Springs, S. Dak. Feb. 2, 1924. 2 p. (H. doc.
184, 68th Cong. 1st sess.) * Paper, 5c.

National Park Service, supplemental estimate of appropriation for Department
of Interior pertaining to National Park Service, fiscal year 1924. Feb. 7,
1924. 2 p. (H. doc. 186, 68th Cong. 1st sess.) * Paper, 5c.

Penitentiary, Leavenworth. Appropriation for Department of Justice, supplemental estimate of appropriation for Department of Justice, fiscal year 1924,
to be available during fiscal year 1925 [for factory at Penitentiary, Leaven-
worth]. Feb. 14, 1924. 2 p. (H. doc. 194, 68th Cong. 1st sess.) * Paper, 5c.

Penitentiary, McNeil Island. United States Penitentiary, McNeil Island, Wash., supplemental estimate of appropriation for Department of Justice, fiscal year 1924, for McNeil Island Penitentiary, Wash. Feb. 19, 1924. 2 p. (H. doc. 202, 68th Cong. 1st sess.)   * Paper, 5c.

Standards Bureau. Department of Commerce, supplemental estimate of appropriation for Department of Commerce [for investigation of performance of automotive power plants, etc., Bureau of Standards], fiscal year 1924. Feb. 8, 1924. 2 p. (H. doc. 190, 68th Cong. 1st sess.)   * Paper, 5c.

State, War, and Navy Department Building Office. Central heating plant for State, War, and Navy Department buildings, draft of proposed legislation making available until June 30, 1925, $75,000 of appropriations for fiscal year 1924 for salaries, Office of Superintendent State, War, and Navy Department Buildings, for purpose of erecting central heating plant to connect with 12 buildings now heated by 8 separate plants. Feb. 19, 1924. 3 p. (H. doc. 200, 68th Cong. 1st sess.)   * Paper, 5c.

COAST GUARD

Circular letter 1–4, 6–7; Dec. 12, 1923. 1924. various paging. ‡
Orders. General order 2; Dec. 12, 1923. 1924. 1 p. ‡

COMPTROLLER OF CURRENCY

National banks. Abstract of reports of condition of national banks, Dec. 31, 1923; no. 142. [1924.] 13 p. f° †

—— Individual statements of condition of national banks at close of business, Sept. 14, 1923. 1924. 261 p. [Table 89, report of comptroller of currency, 1923.] †

    NOTE.—This table has been published heretofore in the Annual report of the comptroller of the currency. For convenience, and because of less demand for the information contained in it than in the full report, it is printed in this form. For Annual report, see below.

—— Monthly statement of capital stock of national banks, national bank notes, and Federal reserve bank notes outstanding, bonds on deposit, etc. [Feb. 1, 1924.] Feb. 1, 1924. 1 p. f° †   10—21266

—— National-bank act as amended and other laws relating to national banks. Dec. 1. 1923. vi+148 p. * Cloth, 50c.   24—26144

Report. Annual report of comptroller of currency, Dec. 3, 1923 [with appendix]. 1924. ix+523 p. (Treas. Dept. doc. 2935.) [Report covers year ended Oct. 31, 1923. Table 89 of the appendix is omitted from this report and is published as a separate table, for which see, above, under *National banks.*] * Cloth. 75c.   9—34683

—— Same. (Treas. Dept. doc. 2935; H. doc. 90, 68th Cong. 1st sess.)

FEDERAL FARM LOAN BUREAU

Report. Annual report of Federal Farm Loan Board, letter from Secretary of Treasury transmitting 7th annual report of Federal Farm Loan Board, year ending Dec. 31, 1923. Feb. 12, 1924. 43 p. (H. doc. 196, 68th Cong. 1st sess.) * Paper, 5c.   18—26147

GENERAL SUPPLY COMMITTEE

Government supplies. General schedule of supplies, fiscal year 1924: class 11, Forage, flour, and seed, Mar. 1–June 30, 1924. [1924.] 4 p. 4° ‡   16—26857

—— Specifications and proposals for supplies [fiscal year 1925]: class 1, Paper. [1924.] 9 p. 4° †

—— Same: class 3, Dry goods, clothing, boots and shoes, cloth bags, flags, wearing apparel, window shades, and cordage. [1924.] 32 p. 4° †

—— Same: class 7, Lumber, millwork, excelsior, sawdust, packing boxes, building materials, road oils, and tar for road building. [1924.] 26 p. 4° †

GOVERNMENT ACTUARY

Bonds of United States. Market prices and investment values of outstanding bonds and notes [of United States, Jan. 1924]. Feb. 1, 1924. 7 p. 4° (Form A.) [Monthly.] †

INTERNAL REVENUE BUREAU

Alcohol Trades Advisory Committee. Statement and recommendations prepared for Bureau of Internal Revenue by its Alcohol Trades Advisory Committee appointed by commissioner of internal revenue in respect to administration of national prohibition act; presented by Mr. Bayard. 1924. [1]+ 9 p. 1 pl. (S. doc. 44, 68th Cong. 1st sess.) * Paper, 5c.   24—26180

Decisions. Treasury decisions under internal-revenue laws of United States, v. 25; Jan.–Dec. 1923. 1924. iii+376 p. il. * Cloth, $1.00.   10—11509

NOTE.—This volume contains internal revenue decisions 3421–74, 3476–77, 3479–3541 and all regulations and rulings during calendar year 1923. Internal revenue decisions .3475 and 3478 were withdrawn.

Income tax. Federal income tax on estates and trusts, issued under direction of Training Section, Staff Division, Income Tax Unit; by L. J. Outlaw. Dec. 1923. iii+49 p. * Paper, 5c.   24—26211

—— Treasury decisions amending or relating to Regulations 45 (1920 edition) promulgated under income tax and war-profits and excess-profits tax provisions of revenue act of 1918; compiled Dec. 31, 1923. 1924. v+55 p. [Contains Treasury decisions issued Jan. 28, 1921–Dec. 31, 1923.] * Paper, 10c.   24—26212

Internal revenue bulletin, v. 3, no. 5–8; Feb. 4–25, 1924. 1924. various paging. [Weekly.] * Paper. 5c. single copy (for subscription price see note below).   22—26051

NOTE.—The Internal revenue bulletin service for 1924 will consist of weekly bulletins, quarterly digests, and semiannual cumulative bulletins. The weekly bulletins will contain the rulings to be made public and all internal revenue Treasury decisions. The quarterly digests, with the exception of the one to be published at the end of 1924, will contain digests of the rulings previously published in the weekly bulletins for 1924. The last digest for 1924 will also contain digests of the rulings published during 1922 and 1923. The semiannual cumulative bulletins will contain all new rulings published during the previous 6 months. The complete bulletin service may be obtained, on a subscription basis, from the Superintendent of Documents, Government Printing Office, Washington, D. C., for $2.00 a yr.; foreign subscription, $2.75.

LOANS AND CURRENCY DIVISION

Bonds of United States. Caveat list of United States registered bonds and notes, Feb. 1, 1924. [1924.] 56 p. f° [Monthly.] †

Money. Circulation statement of United States money, Feb. 1, 1924. [1924.] 1 p. oblong 8° [Monthly.] †   10—21267

PUBLIC HEALTH SERVICE

Biological products, establishments licensed for propagation and sale of viruses, serums, toxins, and analogous products, Dec. 1923. 1924. 11 p. (Reprint 891.) [From Public health reports, Dec. 28, 1923.] * Paper, 5c.   24—26213

Cells. Studies on permeability of living and dead cells: 2, Observations on penetration of alkali bicarbonates into living and dead cells [with list of references]; by Matilda Moldenhauer Brooks. 1923. 8 p. il. (Reprint 846.) [From Public health reports, June 29, 1923.] * Paper, 5c.   24—26214

—— Same: 4, Penetration of trivalent and pentavalent arsenic into living and dead cells [with list of references]; by Matilda Moldenhauer Brooks. 1924. 16 p. il. (Reprint 888.) [From Public health reports, Dec. 14, 1923.] * Paper, 5c.   24—26215

Diseases. Collection of morbidity data and other sanitary information by Public Health Service; by Brock C. Hampton. 1924. 16 p. (Reprint 884.) [From Public health reports, Nov. 30, 1923.] * Paper, 5c.   24—26216

Fleas found on wild animals in Bitterroot valley, Mont.; by L. H. Dunn and R. R. Parker. 1924. 15 p. (Reprint 883.) [From Public health reports, Nov. 23, 1923.] * Paper, 5c.   24—26217

Health boards. State and insular health authorities, 1923, directory, with data as to appropriations and publications. 1923. 23 p. (Reprint 871.) [From Public health reports, Sept. 28, 1923.] .* Paper, 5c.   24—26218

National Health Council as aid to organized health agenc'es. 1923. 8 p. (Reprint 850.) [From Public health reports, July 6, 1923.] * Paper, 5c.
24—26219

Pellagra prevention by diet among institutional inmates [with list of references]; by Joseph Goldberger, C. H. Waring, and W. F. Tanner. 1923. 10 p. (Reprint 874.) [From Public health reports, Oct. 12, 1923.] * Paper, 5c.
· 24—26220

Public health reports, v. 39, no. 5–9; Feb. 1–29, 1924. 1924. [19]+179–446 p. il. 1 pl. [Weekly.] * Paper, 5c. single copy, $1.50 a yr.; foreign subscription, $2.75.   6—25167

SPECIAL ARTICLES.—No. 5. Viscosity and toxicity of arsphenamine solutions [with bibliography]; by Carl Voegtlin, James M. Johnson and Helen Dyer.—Some observations on dispersal of adult Anopheles; by M. A. Barber and T. B. Hayne.—No. 6. Some observations on winter activities of Anopheles in southern United States; by M. A. Barber, W. H. W. Komp, and T. B. Hayne.—Annual reports of marine hospitals [no. 21. Stapleton, N. Y., and no. 9. Fort Stanton, N. Mex.] fiscal year 1923.—No. 7. Is prophylactic use of.diphtheria antitoxin justified? [with list of references]; by James A. Doull and Roy P. Sandidge.—Preparation of crystalline picrate having antineuritic properties of vitamine B; by Atherton Seidell.—Irish vital statistics and population changes.—No. 8. Mercurial poisoning, report on poisoning from small quantities of mercurial vapor; by J. A. Turner.—Training of midwives, [by Janet M. Campbell]; abstract by Tallaferro Clark.—Typhoid fever in large cities of United States, 1923.—No. 9. Studies on oxidation-reduction: 5, Electrode potentials of simple indophenols, each in equilibrium with its reduction product [with list of references]; by Barnett Cohen, H. D. Gibbs, and W. Mansfield Clark.—Health Section of League of Nations, work being done by Service of Epidemiological Intelligence and Public Health Statistics.—Trichinosis and typhoid carriers in New York State.

NOTE.—This publication is distributed gratuitously to State and municipal health officers, etc., by the Surgeon General of the Public Health Service. Treasury Department. Others desiring these reports may obtain them from the Superintendent of Documents, Washington, D. C., at the prices stated above.

Sanitary Water Board of Commonwealth of Pennsylvania. Powers, duties, and policies of Sanitary Water Board of Commonwealth of Pennsylvania; by W. L. Stevenson. 1924. 11 p. (Reprint 885.) [From Public health reports, Nov. 30, 1923.] * Paper, 5c.   24—26221

VENEREAL DISEASES DIVISION

Venereal disease information. venereal disease information. issued by Public Health Service for use in its cooperative work with State health departments, v. 5, no. 1; Jan. 20, 1924. 1924. ii+1–55+iv p. [Monthly.] * Paper, 5c. single copy, 50c. a yr; foreign subscription, 75c.   23—26719

SPECIAL ARTICLES.—Venereal disease control in Pennsylvania, plan utilizing State police, genito-urinary division; by Edgar S. Everhart.—On personal prophylaxis in combating venereal diseases [with bibliography]; by P. Manteufel.

—— Same, v. 5, no. 2; Feb. 20, 1924. 1924. [1]+61–108 p. il. [Monthly.]

SPECIAL ARTICLES.—Venereal disease prophylaxis in foreign countries [with bibliography]; reviewed by B. Bickel.—Venereal diseases in Switzerland, results of inquiry undertaken by Swiss Association for Combating Venereal Diseases; by Hubert Jaeger.

SPECIAL AGENCY SERVICE, CUSTOMS

Manual for use of United States customs representatives. 1924. cover-title. 15 p. small 4° ‡

TREASURER OF UNITED STATES

Paper money. Monthly statement, paper currency of each denomination outstanding Dec. 31, 1923. Jan. 2 [1924]. 1 p. oblong 24° †

VETERANS' BUREAU

Claims adjusted by director of veterans' Bureau, communication from director of veterans' Bureau, submitting claims for damages to or loss of privately owned property which have been adjusted by him and which require appropriation for their payment. Feb. 2, 1924. 6 p. (H. doc. 183, 68th Cong. 1st sess.) * Paper, 5c.

Opinions. Digests of legal opinions relating to Veterans' Bureau, including opinions of general counsel of veterans' Bureau, comptroller general, and Attorney General, Sept. 1923; no. 1. 1924. v+23 p. [Monthly.] * Paper, 5c.

24—26146

Regulations, Veterans' Bureau [1923], supplement 2; Dec. 31, 1923. 1924. iii+9 p. ‡

WAR DEPARTMENT

Army regulations. †

NOTE.—The Army regulations are issued in pamphlet form for insertion in loose-leaf binders. The names of such of the more important administrative subjects as may seem appropriate, arranged in proper sequence, are numbered in a single series, and each name so numbered constitutes the title and number of a pamphlet containing certain administrative regulations pertaining thereto. Where more than one pamphlet is required for the administrative regulations pertaining to any such title, additional pamphlets will be issued in a separate sub-series.

30–3000. Quartermaster Corps: Price list of clothing and equipage, Changes 1; Dec. 20, 1923. 1924. 1 p.
40–215. Medical Department: Prevention of communicable diseases of man, immunization, Changes 2; Dec. 18, 1923. [1924.] 2 p. [Supersedes AR 40–215, Changes 1, Nov. 28, 1923.]
40–270. Same: Medical inspector (heretofore known as sanitary inspector), Changes 1; Dec. 22, 1923. 1924. 1 p.
350–1400. Military education : Army Music School, Changes 2; Dec. 21, 1923. [1924.] 2 p. [Supersedes AR 350–1400, Changes 1. Sept. 13, 1923. Date of Changes 1 incorrectly given on p. 1 as Sept. 13, 1913.]

Claims adjusted and settled by chief of engineers, Army, communication submitting claims for damages by collisions which have been adjusted and settled by chief of engineers, Army. Feb. 7, 1924. 2 p. (H. doc. 189, 68th Cong. 1st sess.) * Paper, 5c.

Training regulations.

NOTE.—The Training regulations are issued in pamphlet form for insertion in loose-leaf binders.

420–160. Infantry : Combat principles, infantry battalion, prepared under direction of chief of infantry; Dec. 10, 1923. [1924.] 20 p. * Paper, 5c.
435–85. [Coast Artillery Corps : Machine-gun battery, antiaircraft artillery, prepared under direction of chief of coast artillery, fig. 1; July 24, 1923.] [1923.] 1 pl. oblong 8° [This plate is folded to 8° size and is to be inserted opposite p. 2 of Training regulations 435–85, for which see Monthly catalogue for Dec. 1923, p. 328.] †

ADJUTANT GENERAL'S DEPARTMENT

Army. Official Army register, Jan. 1, 1924. 1924. vi+814 p. (War Dept. doc. 1118.) [Title on p. 1 reads: Register of Army for 1924.] * Paper, 65c.

4—18250

—— Same. (War Dept. doc. 1118; H. doc. 29, 68th Cong. 1st sess.)

Automobile mechanics, students' manual for military specialists; prepared under direction of quartermaster general, 1923. 1923. xii+308 p. il. (United States Army training manual 55.) * Cloth, 55c.

Message center specialist, students manual for all arms; prepared under direction of chief signal officer, 1923. 1924. vi+162 p. il. (United States Army training manual 24.) * Cloth, 40c.

Motor cycle repairer for military specialists, 1923. 1924. vi+154 p. il. (United States Army training manual 58.) * Cloth, 40c.

Pay tables [1924]. [1924.] [1]+808–814 p. [From Official army register, 1924.] ‡

Pigeoneer, students manual for all arms; prepared under direction of chief signal officer, 1923. 1924. viii+131 p. il. (United States Army training manual 32.) * Cloth, 35c.

U. S. Army recruiting news, bulletin of recruiting information issued by direction of Adjutant General of Army, Feb. 1 and 15, 1924. [Recruiting Publicity Bureau, Governors Island, N. Y., Feb. 1 and 15, 1924.] Each 16 p. il. 4° † Recruiting Publicity Bureau, Governors Island, N. Y. 22—27502

AIR SERVICE

Aeronautical bulletins. Aeronautical bulletin, no. 71, 73–80, 82, 84, 86–92, 94–96, 98, 101, 105–108, 118, Route information series; Jan. 2–Feb. 15, 1924. [1924.] various paging, il. 12° (Airways Section.) [No. 118 is index of sections of proposed airways of United States.] * Paper, 5c. each. 23—26231

—— Aeronautical bulletin, no. 122–123, 125–126, 128–130, 132–134, 138–139. 141, 149, State series; Jan. 2–Feb. 1, 1924. [1924.] Each 2 p. or 1 p. il. 12° (Airways Section.) * Paper, 5c. each.

Index [to] Air Service orders and circulars, Jan. 1, 1919–Dec. 31, 1923. 1924. 14 p. 4° (Air Service information circular, aviation, v. 5, no. 459, Mar. 15, 1924.) ‡

ENGINEERING DIVISION

Alloys. Investigation of Z-D process for treatment of light alloys to inhibit corrosion, to minimize porosity, and to effect desired physical properties, Material Section report; by A. C. Zimmerman and Samuel Daniels. 1924. ii+22 p. il. 4° (Air Service. Air Service information circular, aviation, v. 5, no. 448, Mar. 1, 1924.) ‡

ENGINEER DEPARTMENT

Anacostia River and flats, report of board on reclamation and development of Anacostia River and flats; presented by Mr. Ball. 1924. [1]+20 p. (S. doc. 37, 68th Cong. 1st sess.) * Paper, 5c.

Connecticut River. Maintenance and improvement of existing river and harbor works for Connecticut River below Hartford, Conn., advertisement [for maintenance dredging]. [1924.] 14 p. 4° †

Gravesend Bay. Waterway connecting Gravesend Bay with Jamaica Bay, N. Y., reports on preliminary examination and survey of waterway connecting Gravesend Bay with Jamaica Bay, N. Y., including consideration of any proposition for cooperation on part of local or State interests, or both. Dec. 13, 1923. 15 p. 2 maps. (H. doc. 111, 68th Cong. 1st sess.) * Paper, 15c.

Navigable waters. Information circular, applications for permits for work in navigable waters of United States, 1923. 1924. [1]+10 p. il. 4° †

GENERAL STAFF CORPS

Army. Changes 138 [for] Army regulations [1913]; Dec. 31, 1923. [1924.] 2 leaves. [Regulations issued by War Department.] †

War Department. Changes 36 [for] Compilation of [General] orders [Circulars, and Bulletins of War Department, 1881–1915]; Dec. 31, 1923. [1924.] 4 leaves, 12° [Compilation issued by Adjutant General's Department.] †

INSULAR AFFAIRS BUREAU

Filipinos in United States. Directory of Filipino students in United States, Jan. 1, 1924. 1924. [1]+52 p. 16° †   20—26267

MEDICAL DEPARTMENT

Index-catalogue of library of Surgeon General's Office, Army, authors and subjects; 3d series, v. 4, Coffee-Dzubenko. 1923. iii+10+857 p. large 8° * Cloth, $2.00.   1—2344

ORDNANCE DEPARTMENT

Gun mounts. Supplement to Instructions for mounting, using, and caring for disappearing carriages, L. F., models of 1907 and 1907 M1, for 14-inch guns, models of 1907 and 1907 M1 and model of 1910; approved by Secretary of War, Dec. 5, 1923. 1924. [1]+15 p. ([Form] 1712A.) ‡

Orders. General orders 1 [1924]; Feb. 4, 1924. [1924.] [2] leaves, 12° [Mimeographed.] ‡

Ordnance provision system. Ordnance provision system: Group A, Browning automatic rifle, cal. .30, M1918; May 22, 1923. [1923.] 23 p. il. 1 pl. (Standard nomenclature list A–4.) [Supersedes Standard nomenclature list A–4, Jan. 6, 1923.] ‡

—— Same: Group A, Browning machine gun, cal. .30, M1917; Sept. 14, 1923. [1924.] 86 p. il. (Standard nomenclature list A–5.) [Supersedes Standard nomenclature list A–5, Jan. 15, 1923.] ‡

QUARTERMASTER GENERAL OF ARMY

Tombstones. Instructions and regulation governing erection of monuments, markers, etc., in national cemeteries. July 1, 1918, revised Dec. 6, 1923. [1924.] 4 p. 12° †

O

Monthly Catalogue
United States
Public Documents

No. 351
March, 1924

ISSUED BY THE
SUPERINTENDENT OF DOCUMENTS-

WASHINGTON
1924

Abbreviations

Appendix	app.	Page, pages	p.
Congress	Cong.	Part, parts	pt., pts.
Department	Dept.	Plate, plates	pl.
Document	doc.	Portrait, portraits	por.
Facsimile, facsimiles	facsim.	Quarto	4°
Folio	f°	Report	rp.
House	H.	Saint	St.
House bill	H. R.	Section, sections	sec.
House concurrent resolution	H. Con. Res.	Senate, Senate bill	S.
House document	H. doc.	Senate concurrent resolution	S. Con. Res.
House executive document	H. ex. doc.	Senate document	S. doc.
House joint resolution	H. J. Res.	Senate executive document	S. ex. doc.
House report	H. rp.	Senate joint resolution	S. J. Res.
House resolution (simple)	H. Res.	Senate report	S. rp.
Illustration, illustrations	il.	Senate resolution (simple)	S. Res.
Inch, inches	in.	Session	sess.
Latitude	lat.	Sixteenmo	16°
Longitude	long.	Table, tables	tab
Mile, miles	m.	Thirtytwo-mo	32°
Miscellaneous	mis., misc.	Treasury	Treas.
Nautical	naut.	Twelvemo	12°
No date	n. d.	Twentyfour-mo	24°
No place	n. p.	Versus	vs., v.
Number, numbers	no., nos.	Volume, volumes	v., vol.
Octavo	8°	Year	yr.

Common abbreviations for names of States and months are also used.
*Document for sale by Superintendent of Documents.
†Distribution by office issuing document, free if unaccompanied by a price.
‡Printed for official use.
NOTE.—Nearly all of the Departments of the Government make a limited free distribution of their publications. When an entry shows a * price, it is possible that upon application to the issuing office a copy may be obtained without charge.

Explanation

Words and figures inclosed in brackets [ ] are given for information, but do not appear on the title-pages of the publications catalogued. When size is not given octavo is to be understood. Size of maps is measured from outer edge of border, excluding margin. The dates, including day, month, and year, given with Senate and House documents and reports are the dates on which they were ordered to be printed. Usually the printing promptly follows the ordering, but various causes sometimes make delays.

SALES OF GOVERNMENT PUBLICATIONS

The Superintendent of Documents, Washington, D. C., is authorized to sell at cost, plus 10 per cent, without limit as to the number of copies to any one applicant who agrees not to resell or distribute the same for profit, any United States Government publication not confidential in character.

Publications can not be supplied free to individuals nor forwarded in advance of payment.

Publications entered in this catalogue that are for sale by the Superintendent of Documents are indicated by a star (*) preceding the price. A dagger (†) indicates that application should be made to the Department, Bureau, or Division issuing the document. A double dagger (‡) indicates that the document is printed for official use. Whenever additional information concerning the method of procuring a document seems necessary, it will be found under the name of the Bureau by which it was published.

In ordering a publication from the Superintendent of Documents, give (if known) the name of the publishing Department, Bureau, or Division, and the title of the publication. If the publication is numbered, give the number also. Every such particular assists in quick identification. Do not order by the Library of Congress card number.

The accumulation of publications in this Office amounts to several millions, of which over two million are assorted, forming the sales stock. Many rare books are included, but under the law all must be sold regardless of their age or scarcity. Many of the books have been in stock some time, and are apt to be shop-worn. In filling orders the best copy available is sent. A general price-list of public documents is not available, but lists on special subjects will be furnished on application.

MONTHLY CATALOGUE DISTRIBUTION

The Monthly catalogue is sent to each Senator, Representative, Delegate, Resident Commissioner, and officer in Congress; to designated depositories and State and Territorial libraries if it is selected by them; to substantially all Government authors; and to as many school, college, and public libraries as the limited edition will supply.

Subscription price to individuals, 50c. a year, including index; foreign subscription, 75c. a year. Back numbers can not be supplied. Notify the Superintendent of Documents of any change of address.

LIBRARY OF CONGRESS CARDS

Numbers to be used in ordering the printed catalogue cards of the Library of Congress are given at the end of entries for the more important documents. Orders for these cards, remittances in payment for them, and requests for information about them should be addressed to the Librarian of Congress, not to the Superintendent of Documents.

INDEX

An Index to the Monthly catalogue is issued at the end of the fiscal year. This contains index entries for all the numbers issued from July to June, and can be bound with the numbers as an index to the volume. Persons desiring to bind the catalogue at the end of the year should be careful to retain the numbers received monthly, as duplicate copies can not be supplied.

HOW TO REMIT

Remittances for the documents marked with a star (*) should be made to the **Superintendent of Documents, Washington, D. C.**, by coupons, postal money order, express order, or New York draft. Currency may be sent at sender's risk.

Postage stamps, foreign money, defaced or smooth coins, positively will not be accepted.

For the convenience of the general public, coupons that are good until used in exchange for Government publications sold by the Superintendent of Documents may be purchased from his Office in sets of 20 for $1.00. Address order to Superintendent of Documents, Government Printing Office, Washington, D. C.

No charge is made for postage on documents forwarded to points in United States, Alaska, Guam, Hawaii, Philippine Islands, Porto Rico, Samoa, or to Canada, Cuba, or Mexico. To other countries the regular rate of postage is charged, and remittances must cover such postage. In computing foreign postage, add one-third of the price of the publication.

MONTHLY CATALOGUE

AGRICULTURE DEPARTMENT

Note.—Those publications of the Department of Agriculture which are for sale will be supplied by the Superintendent of Documents, Washington, D. C. The Department issues a monthly list of publications, which is mailed to all applicants, enabling them to select such reports and bulletins as interest them.

Agriculture. Statistics of cooperative extension work, 1923–24 [under Smith-Lever act approved May 8, 1914; by] Eugene Merritt. Mar. 1, 1924. 22 p. (Department circular 306.)   * Paper, 5c.   Agr 19—232

Beans. Influence of temperature and initial weight of seeds upon growth-rate of Phaseolus vulgaris seedlings; by Willem Rudolfs. [1924.] p. 537–539, il. [From Journal of agricultural research, v. 26, no. 11, Dec. 15, 1923.] ‡

Calves. Minimum milk requirement for calf raising; by A. C. Ragsdale and C. W. Turner. [1924.] p. 437–446, il. [From Journal of agricultural research, v. 26, no. 9, Dec. 1, 1923.] ‡

Crops and markets. Crops and markets, weekly, Mar. 1–29, 1924; v. 1, no. 9–13. [1924.] p. 129–208, il. 4°   * Paper, $1.00 a yr.; foreign subscription, $2.00 (including monthly supplement).   Agr 24—113

—— Same, monthly supplement, Mar. 1924; v. 1, supplement 3. [1924.] p. 81–112, il. 4° [Included in price of weekly Crops and markets.]

Crown-gall. Some morphological responses of host tissue to crowngall organism [with list of literature cited]; by A. J. Riker. 1924. cover-title, 425–436+[5] p. 6 p. of pl. [From Journal of agricultural research, v. 26, no. 9, Dec. 1, 1923.] ‡

Gipsy-moths. Supplemental estimate of appropriation for Department of Agriculture [for preventing spread of gipsy-moths]. Mar. 19, 1924. 4 p. (S. doc. 74, 68th Cong. 1st sess.)   * Paper, 5c.

Journal of agricultural research, v. 27, no. 1–4; Jan. 5–26, 1924. 1924. cover-titles, 1–230+[11] p.+[6] leaves, il. 7 pl. 14 p. of pl. [Weekly. Text on p. 2 of covers.]   * Paper, 10c. single copy, $4.00 a yr.; foreign subscription, $5.25.   Agr 13—1837

CONTENTS.—No. 1. Physiological studies on apples in storage [with list of literature cited]; by J. R. Magness and H. C. Diehl.—Study of effects of pumpkin seeds on growth of rats; by Benjamin Masurovsky.—Argus tortoise beetle [with list of literature cited]; by F. H. Chittenden.—Seed-color inheritance in certain grain-sorghum crosses [with list of literature cited]; by John B. Sieglinger.—European corn borer, Pyrausta nubilalis Hbn., versus corn earworm, Heliothis obsoleta Fab.; by Geo. W. Barber.—No. 2. Anchorage and extent of corn root systems; by James R. Holbert and Benjamin Koehler.—Adjusting yields to their regression on moving average, as means of correcting for soil heterogeneity; by Frederick D. Richey.—Soybean mosaic, seed transmission and effect on yield [with list of literature cited]; by James B. Kendrick and Max W. Gardner.—Insecticidal effect of cold storage on bean weevils [with list of literature cited]; by A. O. Larson and Perez Simmons.—Effect of rust infection upon water requirement of wheat [with list of literature cited]; by Freeman Weiss.—No. 3. Photoperiodism in relation to hydrogen-ion concentration of cell sap and carbohydrate content of plant [with list of literature cited]; by W. W. Garner, C. W. Bacon, and F. A. Allard.—On anatomy of sweet potato root, with notes on internal breakdown [and with list of literature cited]; by Ernst Artschwager.—Influence of low temperatures and of disinfectants on eggs of Ascaris lumbricoides [with list of literature cited]; by Eloise B. Cram.—No. 4. Black-bundle disease of corn [with list of literature cited]; by Charles S. Reddy and James R. Holbert.—Changes in hydrogen-ion concentration produced by growing seedlings in acid solutions [with list of literature cited]; by Jehiel Davidson and Edgar T. Wherry.—Nutritive properties of wild rice (Zizania aquatica); by Cornelia Kennedy.—Bacterial blight of gladioli; by Lucia McCulloch.

NOTE.—This publication is published by authority of the Secretary of Agriculture, with the cooperation of the Association of Land-Grant Colleges. It is distributed free only to libraries of agricultural colleges and experiment stations, to large universities, technical schools, and to such institutions as make suitable exchanges with the Agriculture Department. Others desiring the Journal may obtain it from the Superintendent of Documents, Washington, D. C., at the prices stated above.

Naval stores act [approved Mar. 3, 1923], and regulations for its enforcement
[effective Mar. 1, 1024]. Mar. 1924. 8 p. (Miscellaneous circular 22.)
* Paper, 5c.   Agr 24—266
Official record, Department of Agriculture, v. 3, no. 10–13; Mar. 5–26, 1924.
[1924.] Each 8 p. 4° [Weekly.] * Paper, 50c. a yr.; foreign subscription,
$1.10.   Agr 22—146
Pumpkin seeds. Study of effects of pumpkin seeds on growth of rats; by
Benjamin Masurovsky. [1924.] p. 39–42, il. [From Journal of agricul-
tural research, v. 27, no. 1, Jan. 5, 1924.] ‡

AGRICULTURAL ECONOMICS BUREAU

Agricultural outlook for 1924· Mar. 1924. [1]+22 p. (Agriculture Dept.
Miscellaneous circular 23.) * Paper, 5c.   Agr 24—277
Eggs. Marketing eggs; [by Rob R. Slocum]. [Mar. 1924.] ii+29 p. il.
(Agriculture Dept. Farmers' bulletin 1378.) * Paper, 5c.   Agr 24—280
Farm management. Method of testing farm-management and cost-of-produc-
tion data for validity of conclusions; [by] H. R. Tolley and S. W. Mendum.
Mar. 31, 1924. 13 p. il. (Agriculture Dept. Department circular 307.)
* Paper, 5c.   Agr 24—274
Labor requirements of Arkansas crops; by A. D. McNair. Mar. 15, 1924.
cover-title, 64 p. il. (Agriculture Dept. Department bulletin 1181.) [Pre-
pared in cooperation with Arkansas College of Agriculture.] * Paper, 15c.
                                                                     Agr 24—2(7
Meat. Commercial cuts of meat; [by] W. C. Davis. Mar. 1924. 9 p. 4 p. of pl.
(Agriculture Dept. Department circular 300.) * Paper, 5c.   Agr 24—285
Rural planning. social aspects of recreation places; [by Wayne C. Nason].
[Mar. 1924.] ii+30 p. il. (Agriculture Dept. Farmers' bulletin 1388.)
* Paper, 5c.   Agr 24—281
Service announcements. Service and regulatory announcements, no. 82: United
States cotton standards act and universal standards. Mar. 1924. 28 p.
* Paper, 5c.   Agr 15—199
Sweet potatoes. Marketing southern-grown sweet potatoes; by George O.
Gatlin. Mar. 13, 1924. cover-title, 48 p. il. (Agriculture Dept. Department
bulletin 1206.) [Includes list of Agriculture Department publications relat-
ing to sweet potato.] * Paper, 10c.   Agr 24—269

ANIMAL INDUSTRY BUREAU

Cattle. State sanitary requirements governing admission of livestock. Feb.
1924. ii+91 p. narrow 16° (Miscellaneous circular 14.) [Supersedes issue
of Mar. 30, 1922.] * Paper, 10c.   Agr 24—276
Dairy-houses. Farm dairy houses; [by Ernest Kelly and K. E. Parks]. [Oct.
1921, revised Mar. 1924.] [1924.] 15 p. il. (Agriculture Dept. Farmers'
bulletin 1214.) * Paper, 5c.
Dourine. Study of serology, cerebrospinal fluid, and pathological changes in
spinal cord in dourine; by Harry W. Schoening and Robert J. Formad.
[1924.] p. 497–505, il. [From Journal of agricultural research, v. 26, no.
10, Dec. 8, 1923.] ‡
Guinea fowl, [by Andrew S. Weiant; revised by Alfred R. Lee]. [Mar. 1924.]
ii+13 p. il. · (Agriculture Dept.   Farmers' bulletin 1391.) [Revision of
Farmers' bulletin 858,] * Paper, 5c.   Agr 24—280
Homing pigeons, their care and training; [by Alfred R. Lee]. [1923.] ii+16
p. il. (Agriculture Dept. Farmers' bulletin 1373.) * Paper, 5c. Agr 24—279
Posters. For the children's sake, better sires, better stock; [poster]. [Reprint
1924.] 18×12 in. †
—— value of purebreds, why purebreds excel; [poster]. [Reprint 1924.]
18×15 in. .†
Poultry. Feeding hens for egg production; [by Alfred R. Lee]. [Revised edition.] [Mar. 1924.] ii+14 p. il. (Agriculture Dept. Farmers' bulletin
1067.) * Paper, 5c. ·
—— Standard varieties of chickens: 3. Asiatic, English, and French classes;
[by] Rob R. Slocum. [Aug. 1919, revised Mar. 1920, reprint] 1924. 32 p.
il. (Agriculture Dept. Farmers' bulletin 1052.) [Includes lists of Agriculture Department publications relating to poultry.] * Paper, 5c.
                                                                     Agr 23—1234

BIOLOGICAL SURVEY BUREAU

Posters. Vandals of night, while America sleeps, rats destroy entire labor of 200,000 men and pestilence lurks in their wake; [poster]. [1924.] 13×15.6 in. †

CHEMISTRY BUREAU

Service announcements. Service and regulatory announcements, supplement 168. Mar. 1924. p. 481–508. [Contains Notices of judgment under food and drugs act 11851–900.] * Paper, 5c. Agr 14—194
Sorgo-sirup manufacture; [by A. Hugh Bryan and Sidney F. Sherwood]. [Feb. 1924.] ii+29 p. il. (Agriculture Dept. Farmers' bulletin 1389.) [Prepared in cooperation with Plant Industry Bureau. Revision of Farmers' bulletin 477.] * Paper, 5c. Agr 24—264

COOPERATIVE EXTENSION WORK OFFICE

Agricultural engineering. Extension work in agricultural engineering, 1922; [by] George R. Boyd. Mar. 1924. 16 p. il. (Agriculture Dept. Department circular 270.) [Prepared in cooperation with Public Roads Bureau.] * Paper, 5c. Agr 24—272
Farm management extension, early development, and status in 1922; [by] H. M. Dixon. Mar. 12, 1924. 27 p. il. (Agriculture Dept. Department circular 302.) [Prepared in cooperation with Agricultural Economics Bureau.] * Paper, 5c. Agr 24—273

EDITORIAL AND DISTRIBUTION WORK OFFICES

Agriculture Department. Publications issued in Jan. 1924; [prepared in Office of Publications]. [1924.] oblong 48° [Monthly. This publication is issued in postal card form.] †
—— Same Feb. 1924; [prepared in Office of Publications]. [1924.] oblong 48° [Monthly. This publication is issued in postal card form.] . †
Department bulletins 1126–50, [title-page] with contents and index; prepared in Office of Editorial Work. 1924. 8+15 p. * Paper, 5c.

ENTOMOLOGY BUREAU

Bees. Growth and feeding of honeybee larvae; [articles] by James A. Nelson, Arnold P. Sturtevant, and Bruce Lineburg. Mar. 14, 1924. cover-title, 38 p. il. (Agriculture Dept. Department bulletin 1222.) * Paper, 10c. Agr 24—270

CONTENTS.—Pt. 1, Rate of growth of honeybee larva [with list of literature cited; by] James A. Nelson and Arnold P. Sturtevant.—Pt. 2, Feeding of honeybee larvæ; [by] Bruce Lineburg.
Chiggers. Our only common North American chigger, its distribution and nomenclature; by H. E. Ewing. [1924.] p. 401–403. [From Journal of agricultural research, v. 26, no. 9, Dec. 1, 1923.] ‡
Codling-moths. Control of codling moth in Pacific Northwest; [by E. J. Newcomer, M. A. Yothers, and W. D. Whitcomb]. [Mar. 1924.] ii+27 p. il. 1 pl. (Agriculture Dept. Farmers' bulletin 1326.) * Paper, 10c. Agr 24—278
Lead arsenate. Preparation and properties of colloidal arsenate of lead; by F. J. Brinley. [1924.] p. 373–374. [From Journal of agricultural research, v. 26, no. 8, Nov. 24, 1923.] ‡
Plants tested for or reported to possess insecticidal properties [with list of literature cited]; by N. E. McIndoo and A. F. Sievers. Mar. 19, 1924. cover-title, 62 p. (Agriculture Dept. Department bulletin 1201.) [Prepared in cooperation with Plant Industry Bureau.] * Paper, 10c. Agr 24—268
Termites. Biological notes on termites of Canal Zone and adjoining parts of Republic of Panama [with list of literature cited]; by Harry Frederic Dietz and Thomas Elliott Snyder. 1924. cover-title, 279–302+[6] p.+[2] leaves, 8 p. of pl. [From Journal of agricultural research, v. 26, no. 7, Nov. 17, 1923.] ‡
Three-banded grape leafhopper and other leafhoppers injuring grapes [with list of literature cited]; by G. A. Runner and C. I. Bliss. 1924. cover-title, 419–424+[1] p.+[1] leaf, 2 p. of pl. [From Journal of agricultural research, v. 26, no. 9, Dec. 1, 1923.] ‡

EXPERIMENT STATIONS OFFICE

Experiment station record, v. 50, no. 1; Jan. 1924. 1924. cover-title, ix+
1–100 p. [Text and illustration on p. 2 and 4 of cover.] * Paper, 10c. single
copy, 75c. per vol. (2 vols. a yr.) ; foreign subscription, $1.25 per vol.
                                                          Agr 9—832
NOTE.—Mainly made up of abstracts of reports and publications on agricultural
science which have recently appeared in all countries, especially the United States.
Extra numbers, called abstract numbers, are issued, 3 to each volume. These are made
up almost exclusively of abstracts, that is, they contain no editorial notes and only a
limited number of current notes.

FOREST SERVICE

Forest protection, national necessity, summary for use by speakers during
forest protection week [with list of references; by Geo. E. Griffith]. [1924.]
[4] p. il. narrow 8° †

Windbreak as farm asset; [by Carlos G. Bates]. [Jan.. 1924.] 16 p. il.
(Agriculture Dept. Farmers' bulletin 1405.) [Revision of Farmers' bulletin
788.] * Paper, 5c.   Agr 24—283

PLANT INDUSTRY BUREAU

Alfalfa. [Grimm] alfalfa. [1924.] 4 p. †.

Brown rot. Control of brown-rot of prunes and cherries in Pacific Northwest;
[by D. F. Fisher and Charles Brooks]. [Mar. 1924.] ii+13 p. il. (Agriculture Dept. Farmers' bulletin 1410.) * Paper, 5c.   Agr 24—284

Carbon. Absorption of carbon by roots of plants; by J. F. Breazeale. [1924.]
p. 303–311. [From Journal of agricultural research, v. 26, no. 7, Nov. 17,
1923.] ‡

Carotin. Quantitative determination of carotin by means of spectrophotometer and colorimeter [with list of literature cited]; by F. M. Schertz. 1924.
cover-title, p. 383–400, il. [From Journal of agricultural research, v. 26, no.
9, Dec. 1, 1923.] ‡

Cherries. Growing cherries east of Rocky Mountains; [by] H. P. Gould. [Dec. ↲
1916, revised Nov. 1923.] [1923.] 36 p. il. (Agriculture Dept. Farmers'
bulletin 776.) * Paper, 5c.

Corn. Better seed corn; [by] C. P. Hartley]. [Sept. 1920, reprint 1924.] 15 p.
il. (Agriculture Dept. Farmers' bulletin 1175.) * Paper, 5c. Agr 20—1744

Fruit. Growing fruit for home use in Great Plains area; by H. P. Gould and
Oliver J. Grace. June 30, 1916 [reprint 1923]. 40 p. il. (Agriculture Dept.
Farmers' bulletin 727.) * Paper, 5c.   Agr 16—890

Grain sorghums, how to grow them; [by Benton E. Rothgeb]. [Oct. 1920,
reprint 1924.] 28 p. il. (Agriculture Dept. Farmers' bulletin 1137.) [In-
cludes lists of Agriculture Department publications of interest in connection
with this bulletin.] * Paper, 5c.   Agr 20—1796

Oranges. Bud selection as related to quantity production in Washington navel
orange; by A. D. Shamel, C. S. Pomeroy, and R. E. Caryl. [1924.] p. 319–
322+[2] leaves, 2 p. of pl. [From Journal of agricultural research, v. 26,
no. 7, Nov. 17, 1923.] ‡

Potatoes. Control of potato-tuber diseases; [by] Michael Shapovalov and
George K. K. Link]. [Jan. 1924.] ii+38 p. il. (Agriculture Dept. Farmers' bulletin 1367.) [Revision of Farmers' bulletin 544.] * Paper, 10c.
                                                          Agr 24—263

Rhizopus nigricans. Some physiological variations in strains of Rhizopus
nigricans [with list of literature cited]; by L. L. Harter and J. L. Weimer.
[1924.] p. 363–371. [From Journal of agricultural research, v. 26, no. 8,
Nov. 24, 1923.] ‡

Scottsbluff experiment farm. Work of Scottsbluff experiment farm in 1920
and 1921; [by] James A. Holden. Mar. 1924. 38 p. il. (Agriculture Dept.
Department circular 289.) * Paper, 5c.   Agr 14—1460

Spraying strawberries for control of fruit rots; [by] E. M. Stoddard, D. H.
Rose. and N. E. Stevens. Mar. 1924. 4 p. (Agriculture Dept. Department
circular 309.) * Paper, 5c.   Agr 24—275

Tylenchus dipsaci. Stem nematode Tylenchus dipsaci on wild hosts in the Northwest [with list of literature cited]; by G. H. Godfrey and M. B. McKay. Mar. 1, 1924. 10 p. il. 3 p. of pl. (Agriculture Dept. Department bulletin 1229.) [Prepared in cooperation with Oregon Agricultural Experiment Station.] * Paper, 5c. Agr 24—265

Wheat. Varietal resistance in winter wheat to rosette disease; by R. W. Webb, C. E. Leighty, G. H. Dungan, and J. B. Kendrick. [1924.] p. 261-270. [Prepared in cooperation with Illinois and Indiana agricultural experiment stations. From Journal of agricultural research, v. 26, no. 6, Nov. 10. 1923.] ‡

PUBLIC ROADS BUREAU

Public roads, journal of highway research, v. 5, no. 1; Mar. 1924. 1924. cover-title, 35 p. il. 4° [Monthly; none issued Jan. 1922–Feb. 1924. Text on p. 2–4 of cover.] * Paper, 10c. single copy, $1.00 a yr.; foreign subscription, $1.50.
Agr 18—322

SOILS BUREAU

Carroll County, Ga. Soil survey of Carroll County, Ga.; by H. G. Lewis, A. T. Sweet, Mark Baldwin, J. M. Snyder, R. L. Gillett, R. T. Avon Burke, and A. H. Meyer. 1924. iii+129–154 p. il. map. [Prepared in cooperation with Georgia State College of Agriculture. From Field operations, 1921.] * Paper, 25c.

Potash. Recovery of potash as by-product in blast-furnace industry [with bibliography]; by Albert R. Merz and William H. Ross. Mar. 1924. 22 p. (Agriculture Dept. Department bulletin 1226.) * Paper, 5c. Agr 24—271

WEATHER BUREAU

Climatological data for United States by sections, v. 10, no. 12; Dec. 1923. [1924.] cover-title, [198] p. il. 2 maps, 2 p. of maps, 4° [Text on p. 2 of cover. Manuscript corrections have been made in the Virginia section.] * Paper, 35c. complete monthly number, $4.00 a yr. Agr 14—566

NOTE.—Made up of separate Climatological data issued from 42 section centers of the United States. Printed at the several section centers and assembled and bound at the Washington Office. Issued principally for service use and exchange. The separate Climatological data are sold by the Superintendent of Documents, Washington, D. C., at the rate of 5c. single copy, 50c. a yr. for each section.

Meteorology. Monthly meteorological summary, Washington, D. C., Feb. 1924. [1924.] [2] p. f° †

Monthly weather review, v. 51, no. 12; Dec. 1923. [Mar. 10] 1924. cover-title, p. 617–683, il. 6 p. of pl. 2 maps, 14 p. of maps, 4° [Text on p. 2–4 of cover.] * Paper, 15c. single copy, $1.50 a yr.; foreign subscription, $2.25.
Agr 9—990

NOTE.—The Monthly weather review contains (1) meteorological contributions, and bibliography including seismology, (2) an interpretative summary and charts of the weather of the month in the United States, and on adjacent oceans, and (3) climatological and seismological tables dealing with the weather and earthquakes of the month. The contributions are principally as follows: (a) results of observational or research work in meteorology carried on in the United States or other parts of the world, (b) abstracts or reviews of important meteorological papers and books, and (c) notes.

SPECIAL ARTICLES.—Damaging temperatures and orchard heating in Rogue River Valley, Oreg.; by Floyd D. Young and Claude C. Cate.—Mountain snowfall and flood crests in the Colorado; by J. M. Sherier.—Flood of Oct. 22–25, 1923, in Canal Zone; by R. Z. Kirkpatrick.—Is there an antitrade wind in equatorial regions? by S. Sarasola; [translated by W. W. Reed].—Development of meteorology, as illustrative of rôle of mathematics in progress of science; by Edgar W. Woolard.—Using weather records; by J. Cecil Alter.—Weather of 1923; by Alfred J. Henry.—Tropical disturbances during hurricane season of 1923; by W. P. Day.—Earthquakes felt in United States during 1923; by Edgar W. Woolard.

New England highway weather bulletin, Mar. 4–25, 1924; no. 12–15 [season of 1923–24]. [Boston, Mass., 1924.] Each 1 p. il. large 8° [Weekly.] * Paper, 50c. per season.

Ocean. Weather of the oceans, Nov. 1923, with special reference to north Atlantic and north Pacific oceans (including charts), notes, abstracts, and reviews; issued by Marine Division. 1924. 8 p. 4 p. of maps, 4° [From Monthly weather review, Nov. 1923.] †

Snow and ice bulletin, no. 13–16, winter 1923–24; Mar. 3–24, 1924. Mar. 4–25. 1924. Each [2] p. il. large 4° [Weekly during winter.] † 12—1660

93602—No. 351—24——2

Weather. Weekly weather and crop bulletin, Mar. 4–25, 1924; no. 10–13, 1924. Mar. 5–26, 1924. Each 4 p. il. 4°. * Paper, 25c. a yr.   Agr 24—260

Weather map. Daily weather map [of United States, containing forecasts for all States east of Mississippi River except Illinois, Wisconsin, Indiana. upper Michigan. and lower Michigan], Mar. 1–31, 1924. 1st edition. [1924.] Each 16.4 × 22.7 in. [Not issued Sundays or holidays.] * Editions issued at Washington, D. C., 25c. a month, $2.50 a yr.; editions issued at about 65 stations throughout the United States. 20c. a month, $2.00 a yr.

—— Same [containing forecasts for United States], Mar. 1–31, 1924. 2d edition. [1924.] Each 16.4 × 22.7 in. [The Sunday edition does not contain as much information as the edition for week days.] * 30c. a month, $3.00 a yr.

ALIEN PROPERTY CUSTODIAN

Report. Annual report of Alien Property Custodian for year 1923, communication submitting annual report of proceedings had under trading with the enemy act, year ended Dec. 31, 1923 [with reports of divisions, etc.]. 1924. xii+261 p. (S. doc. 49, 68th Cong. 1st sess.) * Paper, 30c.   18—26123

CIVIL SERVICE COMMISSION

NOTE.—The Commission furnishes its publications gratuitously to those who apply for them.

Customs Service. Regulations governing promotions and transfers in Customs Service in districts other than that of New York. Jan. 1924. 3 p. (Form 1556.) †

Letter-carriers. Instructions to applicants for rural carrier examinations. Feb. 1924. 12 p. (Form 1977.) †

Postmasters. Instructions to applicants for 4th-class postmaster examination. Feb. 1924. 8 p. (Form 1759.) †

COMMERCE DEPARTMENT

NOTE.—The Department of Commerce prints most of its publications in very limited editions, the distribution of which is confined to Government officers, libraries, etc. When a selling price is noted in this list, application for such publication should be submitted to the Superintendent of Documents, Washington, D. C., with remittance. For copies of charts, coast pilots, and tide tables, however, apply directly to the issuing office, the Coast and Geodetic Survey, Washington, D. C.

Walrus. Protection of walruses and sea lions in Alaska [laws and regulations]. Mar. 1, 1924. 3 p. 4° (Department circular 286, 2d edition; Bureau of Fisheries, Alaska Fisheries Service.) [Supersedes 1st edition.] †

CENSUS BUREAU

NOTE.—Persons desiring 14th census publications should address the Director of the Census, Department of Commerce, Washington, D. C. They are also sold by the Superintendent of Documents, Washington, D. C., at the price indicated.

California. 14th census of United States: State compendium. California, statistics of population, occupations, agriculture, irrigation. drainage, manufactures, and mines and quarries for State, counties, and cities. 1924. cover-title, 196 p. il. 4° [Text on p. 2–4 of cover.] * Paper, 30c.   24—26247

Chemicals. Census of manufactures, 1921; Chemicals and acids, chemicals, sulphuric, nitric, and mixed acids. 1924. 48 p. * Paper, 5c.   24—26241

Children in gainful occupations at 14th census of United States. 1924. 276 p. 4° [Prepared under supervision of William C. Hunt, chief statistician for population, by Alba M. Edwards, expert special agent.] * Paper, 50c.
                                                                    24—26192

Clay and refractory products, 1922. 1924. 23 p. * Paper, 5c.   24—26244

Clothing. Census of manufactures, 1921: Wearing apparel. 1924. 46 p. * Paper, 5c.   24—26243

Connecticut. 14th census of United States: State compendium, Connecticut, statistics of population, occupations, agriculture, manufactures, and mines and quarries for State, counties, and cities. 1924. cover-title, 108 p. il. 4° [Text on p. 2–4 of cover.] *Paper, 20c. 24—26296

Cordage. Census of manufactures, 1921: Cordage, twine, jute goods, linen goods, fur-felt hats, dyeing and finishing textiles, oilcloth and linoleum, flax and hemp dressed, haircloth, mats and matting. 1924. 36 p. *Paper, 5c. 24—26242

Cotton. Cotton consumed, cotton on hand, active cotton spindles, and imports and exports of cotton, Feb. 1923 and 1924, with statistics of cotton consumed, imported, and exported for 7 months ending Feb. 29. Mar. 14, 1924. oblong 32° [Preliminary report. This publication is issued in postal card form.] †

—— Report of cotton ginned, crops of 1923, 1922, and 1921. Mar. 20, 1924. oblong 32° [Preliminary report. This publication is issued in postal card form.] †

Cottonseed received, crushed, and on hand, and cottonseed products manufactured, shipped out, on hand, and exported covering 7-month period ending Feb. 29, 1924 and 1923. Mar. 19, 1924. oblong 32° [Preliminary report. This publication is issued in postal card form.] †

Financial statistics of cities of 30,000 population and over, 1922, assessed valuation of property subject to general property taxes, total revenues, governmental-cost payments, and net debt. [1924.] 15 p. [Preliminary statement.] † 24—26245

Population. 14th census of United States, 1920: v. 4, Population, 1920, occupations. 1923. 1309 p. 4° [Prepared under supervision of William C. Hunt, chief statistician for population, assisted by Alba M. Edwards, special agent.] *Cloth, $2.25.

Wood-pulp. Forest products, 1922: Pulp-wood consumption and wood-pulp production; compiled in cooperation with Department of Agriculture, Forest Service. 1924. 16 p. *Paper, 5c. 24—26246

COAST AND GEODETIC SURVEY

NOTE.—The monthly Notice to mariners, formerly issued by the Coast and Geodetic Survey, has been consolidated with and made a part of the Notice to mariners issued by the Lighthouses Bureau, thus making it a joint publication. The charts, coast pilots, and tide tables of the Coast and Geodetic Survey are sold at the office of the Survey in Washington, and also by one or more sales agents in each of the important American seaports.

Coast and Geodetic Survey bulletin, Feb. 29, 1924; no. 105. [1924.] 8 p. [Monthly.] ‡ 15—26512

Coast pilots. Supplement to United States coast pilot, Atlantic Coast, section D, Cape Henry to Key West. Mar. 1, 1924. [1]+11 leaves. (Serial 261.) †

—— Supplement to United States coast pilot, Philippine Islands: pt. 2, Palawan, Mindanao, and Sulu Archipelago, 1st edition. Jan. 1, 1924. 10 leaves. (Serial 263.) †

Current tables, Atlantic Coast, North America, [calendar] year 1925. 1924. 88 p.+[6] folded leaves, il. (Serial 249.) †Paper, 10c. 22—26822

Least squares. Some elementary examples of least squares; by Oscar S. Adams. 1924. [1]+17 p. (Serial 250.) *Paper, 5c. 24—26226

Charts

Brazos River entrance, Tex., surveys in 1897, surveys by U. S. engineers to 1924; chart 525. Scale 1:10,000. Washington, Coast and Geodetic Survey, Feb. 1924. 28.5×38.9 in. † 75c.

Columbia River, Oreg.-Wash., entrance to Harrington Point, surveys 1868–99, surveys by U. S. Engineers to Nov. 1923; chart 6151. Scale 1:40,000. Washington, Coast and Geodetic Survey, Mar. 1924. 24.5×41.1 in. † 75c.

Fajardo Harbor and approaches, P. R., surveys to 1923; chart 921. Scale 1:10,000. Washington, Coast and Geodetic Survey, Feb. 1924. 41.6×32.4 in. † 75c.

Kill Van Kull and northern part of Arthur Kill, N. Y.-N. J., surveys to 1915, surveys by U. S. Engineers to 1923 and other sources; chart 285. Scale 1:15,000. Washington, Coast and Geodetic Survey, Feb. 1924. 31.9×37 in. † 75c.

Manila Bay and coast of Luzon to Capones Islands, P. I., surveys to 1921 and other authorities; with inset, Mariveles Harbor, west coast of Luzon, surveyed 1918; chart 4255. [Scale 1 : 125,000.] Washington, Coast and Geodetic Survey, Jan. 1924. 26.6×36.4 in. † 75c.

North Edisto River, S. C., surveys 1851–1921 and other sources: chart 434. Scale 1 : 50,000. Washington. Coast and Geodetic Survey, Feb. 1924. 17.4× 13.9 in. † 25c.

Oregon, Cape Blanco to Yaquina Head, surveys to 1922, surveys by U. S. Engineers to 1923 and other sources; chart 5802. [Scale 1 : 191,000.] Washington, Coast and Geodetic Survey, Feb. 1924. 43.4×31.5 in. [Not intended for inside navigation.] † 75c.

FISHERIES BUREAU

Cold storage holdings. Cold storage holdings of fish, Jan. 15, 1924. [1924.] 1 p. oblong 8° (Statistical bulletin 601.) [Statistics furnished by Agricultural Economics Bureau.] †

—— Same, Feb. 15, 1924. [1924.] 1 p. oblong 8° (Statistical bulletin 604.) [Statistics furnished by Agricultural Economics Bureau.] †

Fisheries service bulletin, Mar. 1, 1924; no. 106. [1924.] 6 p. [Monthly.] ‡
F 15—76

Fishery products. Statement of quantities and values of certain fishery products landed at Boston and Gloucester, Mass., and Portland, Me., by American fishing vessels, Jan. 1924. [1924.] 1 p. oblong large 8° (Statistical bulletin 602.) †

—— Same, Feb. 1924. [1924.] 1 p. oblong large 8°. (Statistical bulletin 605.) †

—— Statement of quantities and values of certain fishery products landed at Seattle, Wash., by American fishing vessels. Jan. 1924. [1924.] 1 p. oblong 12° (Statistical bulletin 603.) †

Mississippi River. Limnological observations in the upper Mississippi, 1921 [with bibliography]; by P. S. Galtsoff. 1924. [1]+347–438 p. fl. 3 pl. map, large 8° ([Bureau of Fisheries] doc. 958.) [From Bulletin, v. 39.] *Paper, 25c.
F 24—7

Salmon. Pacific Coast salmon pack, 1923. [1924.] 1 p. oblong 8° †

FOREIGN AND DOMESTIC COMMERCE BUREAU

Agricultural implements and farm equipment in South Africa; by Perry J. Stevenson. 1924. vii+86 p. (Special agents series 225.) *Paper, 10c.
24—26297

Chilean public finance [with bibliography]; by Charles A. McQueen. 1924. vi+121 p. il. (Special agents series 224.) *Paper, 15c.   24—26254

Commerce. Monthly summary of foreign commerce of United States. Jan. 1924. 1924. 2 pts. p. 1–76 and ii+77–98 p. 4° *Paper, 10c. single copy (including pts. 1 and 2), $1.00 a yr.; foreign subscription, $1.60.   14—21465

—— Same. 1924. [2 pts. in 1], 98 p. 4° (H. doc. 13, 68th Cong. 1st sess.)

Commerce reports. Commerce reports, weekly survey of foreign trade, reports from American consular officers and representatives of Department of Commerce in foreign countries, no. 9–13; Mar. 3–31, 1924. 1924. cover-titles, p. 537–872, il. 4° [Text and illustrations on p. 2–4 of covers.] *Paper, 10c. single copy, $3.00 a yr.; foreign subscription, $5.00.

—— Supplement to Commerce reports: Bolivian fiscal system, revenue, expenditure. and taxation; by Charles A. McQueen. Mar. 3, 1924. ii+23 p. (Trade information bulletin 201; Finance and Investment Division.) †
24—26227

—— Same: British financial conditions in 1923: by Charles E. Lyon. Mar. 10, 1924. ii+21 p. (Trade information bulletin 206; Finance and Investment Division.) †   24—26230

—— Same: Currency, exchange, and banking in Bolivia; by Charles A. McQueen. Mar. 10, 1924. ii+22 p. (Trade information bulletin 207; Finance and Investment Division.) †   24—26249

Commerce reports—Continued. Same: German alkali and sulphuric acid industries, production, export, and import statistics; by William T. Daugherty. Mar. 3, 1924. ii+7 p. (Trade information bulletin 203; Chemical Division.) †
24—26228

—— Same: Ice-making and cold-storage plants in South America, reports of ' American consular officers. Mar. 10, 1924. ii+41 p. (Trade information bulletin 209; Industrial Machinery Division.) †
24—26251

—— Same: International trade in cement, pt. 1, North and South America, compiled by Reigart M. Santmyers from official statistics, reports of American consular officers, and other sources; with report on United States produc-tion and trade, by Ernest F. Burchard. Mar. 10, 1924. ii+36 p. (Trade information bulletin 205; Mineral Section, Iron and Steel Division.) †
24—26248

—— Same: International trade in cement, pt. 2, Europe; compiled by Reigart M. Santmyers from official statistics, reports of American consular officers of Department of State, and from other sources. Mar. 17, 1924. ii+38 p. (Trade information bulletin 213; Mineral Section, Iron and Steel Division.) †
24—26248

—— Same: Mexican market for paper and paper products; prepared from data furnished by Warren Ullrich, and from reports by Claude I. Dawson, O. J. McConnico, James B. Stewart, Walter F. Boyle, John Q. Wood, and Bartley F. Yost. Mar. 31, 1924. ii+13 p. (Trade information bulletin 214: Paper Division.) †
24—26253

—— Same: 1924 plans for machinery exports: by W. H. Rastall. Mar. 17, 1924. ii+28 p. (Trade information bulletin 212; Industrial Machinery Division.) †
24—26252

—— Same: Packing for foreign markets, some general considerations; by J. F. Keeley. Mar. 10, 1924. ii+29 p. (Trade information bulletin 208; Transportation Division.) †
24—26250

—— Same: Survey of world trade in agricultural products, no. 3, Interna-tional competition in production of wheat for export. Mar. 17, 1924. ii+25 p. (Trade information bulletin 210; Foodstuffs Division.) [Prepared as part of study of world trade in agricultural products authorized by 67th Congress.] †
24—26295

—— Same: Tanning materials survey, pt. 2, Wattle culture, its development within British Empire and economic importance of growing wattle in United States and adjacent territory; by H. M. Hoar. Mar. 17, 1924. ii+22 p. (Trade information bulletin 211; Hide and Leather Division.) [Prepared as part of the study of essential raw materials authorized by the 67th Congress.] †
24—26107

—— Same: value of machinery export statistics; by Wm. Althoff. Mar. 3, 1924. ii+6 p. (Trade information bulletin 204; Industrial Machinery Division.) †
24—26229

—— Survey of current business, Mar. 1924, no. 31; compiled by Bureau of Census, Bureau of Foreign and Domestic Commerce, [and] Bureau of Stand-ards. 1924. cover-title, 62 p. il. 4° (Monthly supplement to Commerce reports.) [Contains statistics for Jan. 1924, the date given above, Mar. 1924, being the date of issue. Text on p. 2–4 of cover.] * Paper, 10c. single copy, $1.00 a yr.; foreign subscription, $1.50.
21—26819

NOTE.—Realizing that current statistics are highly perishable and that to be of use they must reach the business man at the earliest possible moment, the Depart-ment has arranged to distribute advance leaflets twice each month to those sub-scribers who request them. One set of these leaflets is issued about the 20th of the month, giving such information as has been received up to that time, and another set of sheets is mailed at the end of the month giving those figures received since the 20th. The information contained in these leaflets is also published in Commerce reports issued weekly by the Foreign and Domestic Commerce Bureau. The advance sheets will be mailed free of charge to all subscribers to the Survey who re-quest them. Such requests should be addressed to the Bureau of the Census, Depart-ment of Commerce, Washington, D. C. Subscriptions, however, should be sent to the Superintendent of Documents, Washington, D. C., at the prices stated above.

LIGHTHOUSES BUREAU

1st–9th Districts. Light list, Atlantic and Gulf coasts of United States; 1924, corrected to Dec. 15, 1923. 1924. 465 p. [Porto Rico, the Virgin Islands, Cuba, and Navassa Island are included in this publication. Also includes lists of light lists and buoy lists. Map usually included in publication is printed on verso of front cover.] * Paper, 30c.
11—15353

16th–19th Districts. Light list, Pacific Coast, United States, Canada, Hawaiian, [Midway, Guam, and American] Samoan islands; 1924, corrected to Jan. 1. 1924. 228 p. [Of the American Samoan Islands only Tutuila is included in this publication. Also includes lists of light lists and buoy lists. Map usually included in publication is printed on verso of front cover.] * Paper. 30c.
14—30372

Lighthouse service bulletin, v. 3, no. 3; Mar. 1, 1924. [1924.] p. 13–16. [Monthly.] †
12—35121

Notice to mariners, weekly, no. 10–13, 1924; Mar. 7–28 [1924]. 1924. various paging. [Issued jointly with Coast and Geodetic Survey.] †   7—20609

NAVIGATION BUREAU

Ships. American documented seagoing merchant vessels of 500 gross tons and over, Mar. 1, 1924. 1924. ii+67 p. 4° (Serial 75 [76].) [Monthly.] * Paper, 10c. single copy, 75c. a yr.; foreign subscription, $1.25.   19—26597

RADIO SERVICE

Radio Service bulletin, Mar. 1, 1924; no. 83. [1924.] 32 p. [Monthly.] * Paper, 5c. single copy, 25c. a yr.; foreign subscription, 40c.   15—26255

PUBLICATIONS DIVISION

Commerce Department. Supplement to annual List of publications [of Department of Commerce available for distribution], Feb. 29, 1924. [1924.] 4 p. [Monthly.] †

STANDARDS BUREAU

NOTE.—The Scientific papers will be supplied on subscription as issued at $1.25 per volume, paper bound. These volumes will afterwards be issued bound in cloth at $2.00 per volume; foreign subscription, paper $2.50 (sent in single numbers), cloth $2.35 (bound volumes). Single numbers vary in price. Address the Superintendent of Documents, Washington, D. C.
The Technologic papers will be issued first as separates and later in volume form in the same manner as the Scientific papers. Subscriptions will be accepted by the Superintendent of Documents at $1.25 per volume; foreign subscription, $2.50. Single numbers vary in price.

Equalizer apparatus for transverse tests of bricks; by H. L. Whittemore. Feb. 5, 1924. [1]+107–113 p. il. 1 pl. 4 p. of pl. (Technologic papers 251.) [From Technologic papers, v. 18.] *Paper, 10c.   24—26259

Felt. United States Government specification for asphalt-saturated rag felt for roofing and waterproofing, Federal Specifications Board. Standard specification 86, officially adopted by Federal Specifications Board, Dec. 29, 1923, for use of Departments and independent establishments of Government in purchase of asphalt-saturated rag felt for roofing and waterproofing. Mar. 1, 1924. 5 p. (Circular 161.) *Paper, 5c.   24—26257

—— United States Government specification for coal-tar saturated rag felt for roofing and waterproofing, Federal Specifications Board, Standard specification 81, officially adopted by Federal Specifications Board, Dec. 29, 1923, for use of Departments and independent establishments of Government in purchase of coal-tar saturated rag felt for roofing and waterproofing. Mar. 1, 1924. 4 p. (Circular 156.) *Paper, 5c.   24—26256

Gas-fixtures. Tentative program for testing gas appliances. [1924.] 8 p. 4° †

Load requirements (building). Minimum live-load requirements for use in design of buildings, tentative report of Building Code Committee, 1924. 1924. iv+23 p. †   24—26240

Metals. Standard samples issued or in preparation. Mar. 3, 1924. 6 p. large 8° (Circular 25, supplement.) [Supersedes supplement issued Mar. 2, 1923.] †

Molasses. Summary of technical methods for utilization of molasses; collated from patent literature. Jan. 28, 1924. [1]+72 p. il. (Circular 145.) *Paper, 15c.   24—26255

Soap. United States Government specification for chip soap, Federal Specifications Board, Standard specification 31, officially adopted by Federal Specifications Board, July 3, 1922, for use of Departments and independent establishments of Government in purchase of chip soap. 2d edition. Feb. 1, 1924. 5 p. large 8° (Circular 128.) *Paper, 5c.   24—26168

Technologic papers of Bureau of Standards, v. 17 [nos. 221-247, title-page, contents, and index]. 1924. iv+779-781 p. large 8° *Paper, 5c.

Titanium. United States Government specification for titanium pigment, dry and paste, Federal Specifications Board, Standard specification 115, officially adopted by Federal Specifications Board, Feb. 20, 1924, for use of Departments, and independent establishments of Government in purchase of titanium pigment, dry and paste. Feb. 20, 1924. 11 p. (Circular 163.) *Paper, 5c. 24—26258

Zoning. Standard State zoning enabling act under which municipalities may adopt zoning regulations, by Advisory Committee on Zoning; [prepared in] Division of Building and Housing. 1924. iv+12 p. [A list of Commerce Department publications in relation to housing and municipal regulation is given on p. 4 of cover.] *Paper, 5c. 24—26239

STEAMBOAT INSPECTION SERVICE

Steamboat Inspection Service bulletin, Mar. 1, 1924; no. 101. 1924. 1 p. [Monthly.] ‡ 15—26679

CONGRESS

Congressional record. Congressional record, 68th Congress, 1st session, v. 65, no. 62-88; Mar. 1-31, 1924. [1924.] 3499-5518+[62] p. il. 4° 12—36438

NOTE.—The Congressional record, containing the proceedings and debates of Congress. is issued daily when Congress is in session, and indexes thereto are published fortnightly.

The Record is sold by the Superintendent of Documents on the following terms: Single copy, 3 cents. if not more than 24 pages, and 1 cent more for each additional 8 pages; per month, $1.50, foreign subscription, $2.50. Subscriptions are payable in advance. Prices for the bound volumes of the Record, 67th Congress, 1st–4th sessions, and prior Congresses, will be furnished on application. Send remittances to the Superintendent of Documents, Washington, D. C. Stamps and foreign money will not be accepted.

—— Same, index, with title, Congressional record index, 68th Congress, 1st session, v. 65, nos. 51-62; Feb. 18-Mar. 1, 1924. [1924.] no. 5; 38+17 p. 4° [Includes History of bills and resolutions.]

—— Same, v. 65, nos. 63-75; Mar. 3-15, 1924. [1924.] no. 6; 38+42 p. 4° [Includes History of bills and resolutions.]

—— Same, v. 65, nos. 76-87; Mar. 17-29, 1924. [1924.] no. 7; 49+19 p. 4° [Includes History of bills and resolutions.]

Directory. Congressional vest pocket directory, 68th Congress, 1st session; corrected to Feb. 9, 1924. 1924. 299 p. narrow 24° ‡

PRIVATE LAWS

NOTE.—The Publications Division, State Department, receives a small supply of the private acts which it distributes free upon application.

Private [act] 2, 68th Congress.

Wilson, Mrs. Edith B. S. 2583, act granting franking privilege to Edith Bolling Wilson. Approved Mar. 4, 1924. 1 p. (Private 2.)

PUBLIC LAWS.

NOTE.—Public acts in slip form in the first prints may be obtained from the Superintendent of Documents, Washington, D. C., at a subscription price of $1.00 for the 68th Congress, 1st session, foreign subscription $1.25; single copies are usually 5c. each.

Public [act] 33-61, 68th Congress.

Apalachicola River-St. Andrews Bay Canal. S. 2014. act to authorize Park Wood Lumber Company to construct 2 bridges across canal which connects Apalachicola River and St. Andrews Bay, Fla. Approved Mar. 14, 1924. 1 p. (Public 44.)

Calumet River. H. R. 6925, act granting consent of Congress to Chicago to construct bridge across Calumet River at or near 130th street in Chicago, county of Cook, Ill. Approved Mar. 21, 1924. 1 p. (Public 61.)

Chattahoochee River. H. R. 3198, act to authorize Alabama and Georgia, through their respective Highway Departments, to construct bridge across Chattahoochee River at or near Eufaula, Ala., connecting Barbour County, Ala.; and Quitman County, Ga. Approved Feb. 27, 1924. 1 p. (Public 33.)

Cherokee Indians. H. R. 4457, act conferring jurisdiction upon Court of Claims to hear, examine, adjudicate, and enter judgment in any claims which Cherokee Indians may have against United States. [Approved Mar. 19, 1924.] 2 p. (Public 57.)

Public [act] 33–61, 68th Congress—Continued.

Columbia River. H. R. 4120, act granting consent of Congress to Greater Wenatchee Irrigation District to construct bridge across Columbia River [Wash.]. Approved Mar. 18, 1924. 1 p. (Public 50.)

Current River. H. R. 4984, act to authorize Clay County bridge district, Ark., to construct bridge over Current River [near Finley's Ferry, Ark.]. Approved Mar. 18, 1924. 1 p. (Public 53.)

Finland. H. R. 5557, act to authorize settlement of indebtedness of Republic of Finland to United States. Approved Mar. 12, 1924. 1 p. (Public 41.)

Government publications. H. R. 7039, act to amend sec. 72 of chapter 23, printing act, approved Jan. 12, 1895, relative to allotment of public documents. Approved Mar. 18, 1924. 1 p. (Public 47.)

Half-dollar. S. 684, act to authorize coinage of 50-cent pieces in commemoration of commencement on June 18, 1923, of work of carving on Stone Mountain, Ga., monument to valor of soldiers of the South, which was the inspiration of their sons and daughters and grandsons and granddaughters in Spanish-American and World Wars, and in memory of Warren G. Harding, President of United States, in whose administration the work was begun. Approved Mar. 17, 1924. 1 p. (Public 46.)

Hawaii. H. R. 4121, act to extend provisions of certain [Federal aid] laws to Hawaii. [Approved Mar. 10, 1924.] 2 p. (Public 44.)

Income tax. H. R. 6901, act to amend sec. 252 of revenue act of 1921 in respect of credit and refunds. Approved Mar. 13, 1924. 1 p. (Public 43.)

Indians. H. R. 3444, act for relief of certain nations or tribes of Indians in Montana, Idaho, and Washington. [Approved Mar. 13, 1924.] 2 p. (Public 42.)

Kankakee River. H. R. 5737, act granting consent of Congress to county of Kankakee, Ill., and counties of Lake and Newton, Ind., to construct bridge across Kankakee River at or near State line between section 19, township 31 north, range 15 east of 3d principal meridian, in county of Kankakee, Ill., and section 1, township 31 north, range 10 west of 2d principal meridian, in counties of Lake and Newton, Ind. Approved Mar. 21, 1924. 1 p. (Public 59.)

Little Calumet River. H. R. 3845, act to authorize construction of bridge across Little Calumet River at Riverdale, Ill. [by Acme Steel Goods Company]. Approved Mar. 18, 1924. 1 p. (Public 49.)

Mill Cut. H. R. 4577, act for examination and survey of Mill Cut and Clubfoot Creek, N. C. Approved Mar. 14, 1924. 1 p. (Public 45.)

Mississippi River. H. R. 6420, act to extend time for construction of bridge across Mississippi River in section 17, township 28 north, range 23 west of 4th principal meridian in Minnesota [by Minneapolis and St. Paul, Minn., or either of them]. Approved Mar. 21, 1924. 1 p. (Public 60.)

Newtown Creek. H. R. 3265, act to authorize construction of bridge [by New York City across Newtown Creek] between boroughs of Brooklyn and Queens, in city and State of New York. Approved Mar. 11, 1924. 1 p. (Public 37.)

Ohio River. H. R. 5624, act authorizing construction of bridge across Ohio River to connect Benwood, W. Va., and Bellaire, Ohio [by Interstate Bridge Company]. Approved Mar. 18, 1924. 1 p. (Public 56.)

Pearl River. H. R. 4808, act granting consent of Congress to construction of bridge across Pearl River between St. Tammany Parish, La., and Hancock County, Miss. [by Highway Commission of Louisiana in cooperation with Mississippi or Hancock County]. Approved Mar. 11, 1924. 1 p. (Public 40.)

—— H. R. 5633, act granting consent of Congress to board of supervisors of Hinds County, Miss., to construct bridge across Pearl River, Miss. [at or near Jackson]. Approved Mar. 21, 1924. 1 p. (Public 58.)

Peedee River. S. 2189, act granting consent of Congress to Highway Department of North Carolina to construct bridge across Pedee [Peedee] River, N. C., between Anson and Richmond counties [at or near Pee Dee]. Approved Feb. 29, 1924. 1 p. (Public 34.)

Pere Marquette Lake. H. R. 4182, act authorizing Ludington, Mason County, Mich., to construct bridge across arm of Pere Marquette Lake. Approved Mar. 18, 1924. 1 p. (Public 51.)

St. Croix River. H. R. 5337, act granting consent of Congress [to Maine] to construct [jointly with Canada] bridge over St. Croix River between Vanceboro, Me., and St. Croix, New Brunswick. Approved Mar. 18, 1924. 1 p. (Public 54.)

St. John River. H. R. 5348, act granting consent of Congress for construction of bridge across St. John River between Fort Kent, Me., and Clairs, New Brunswick [by Maine and Canada jointly]. Approved Mar. 18, 1924. 1 p. (Public 55.)

St. Louis River. H. R. 4187, act to legalize bridge across St. Louis River in Carlton County, Minn. [constructed by Minnesota]. Approved Mar. 18, 1924. 1 p. (Public 52.)

Waccamaw River. H. R. 2818, act to grant consent of Congress [to K. C. Council, F. B. Gault, and Oscar High] to construct dam and spillway across Waccamaw River, N. C. Approved Mar. 18, 1924. 1 p. (Public 48.)

—— H. R. 3681, act to authorize building of bridge across Waccamaw River. S. C., [by Horry County, at or near Star Bluff, or at or near Bellamys Landing]. Approved Mar. 11, 1924. 1 p. (Public 38.)

West Pearl River. H. R. 4807, act granting consent of Congress to Highway Commission of Louisiana to construct bridge across West Pearl River, La. [near Pearl River station]. Approved Mar. 11, 1924. 1 p. (Public 39.)

Willamette River. H. R. 584, act to authorize county of Multnomah, Oreg., to construct bridge across Willamette River in Portland, Oreg., in vicinity of present site of Sellwood Ferry. Approved Mar. 11, 1924. 1 p. (Public 36.)

Public [joint] resolution 6–11, 68th Congress.

District of Columbia. S. J. Res. 57, joint resolution authorizing erection on public grounds in District of Columbia of statue of Jose Clara personifying " Serenity." Approved Mar. 12, 1924. 1 p. (Public resolution 10.)

—— S. J. Res. 91, joint resolution to authorize National Society United States Daughters of 1812 to place marble tablet on Francis Scott Key Bridge. Approved Mar. 17, 1924. 1 p. (Public resolution 11.)

Public [joint] resolution 6–11, 68th Congress—Continued.
National Home for Disabled Volunteer Soldiers. S. J. Res. 83, joint resolution for appointment of [John J. Steadman as] member of board of managers of National Home for Disabled Volunteer Soldiers. Approved Feb. 29, 1924. 1 p. (Public resolution 9.)
Naval petroleum reserves. H. J. Res. 160, joint resolution to provide appropriation for prosecution of suits to cancel leases [on oil lands in former naval reserves]. Approved Feb. 27, 1924. 1 p. (Public resolution 8.)
—— S. J. Res. 71, joint resolution directing Secretary of Interior to institute proceedings touching sections 16 and 36, township 30 south, range 23 east, Mount Diablo meridian [within exterior limits of naval reserve numbered 1 in California]. Approved Feb. 21, 1924. 1 p. (Public resolution 6.)
Senate. S. J. Res. 84, joint resolution making appropriation for contingent expenses of Senate, fiscal year 1924. Approved Feb. 27, 1924. 1 p. (Public resolution 7.)

CONFERENCE COMMITTEES

Appropriations. First deficiency appropriation bill, [fiscal year] 1924 [and prior fiscal years], conference report to accompany H. R. 7449; submitted by Mr. Madden, Mar. 27, 1924. 4 p. (H. rp. 390, 68th Cong. 1st sess.) * Paper, 5c.

Interior Department. Interior Department appropriation bill, [fiscal year] 1925, conference report to accompany H. R. 5078; submitted by Mr. Cramton. Mar. 6, 1924. 7 p. (H. rp. 268, 68th Cong. 1st sess.) * Paper, 5c.

—— Interior Department appropriation bill, [fiscal year] 1925, conference report to accompany H. R. 5078; submitted by Mr. Cramton. Mar. 24, 1924. 2+[1] p. (H. rp. 358, 68th Cong. 1st sess.) * Paper, 5c.

Treasury Department. Treasury and Post Office Departments appropriation bill, [fiscal year] 1925, conference report to accompany H. R. 6349; submitted by Mr. Madden. Mar. 28, 1924. 5 p. (H. rp. 391, 68th Cong. 1st sess.) * Paper, 5c.

HOUSE OF REPRESENTATIVES

Calendars of House of Representatives, 68th Congress, 1st session, Mar. 1–31, 1924; no. 58–83. 1924. various paging, large 8° [Daily when House of Representatives is in session.] ‡

Oil land leasing acts with amendments, 57th Congress–67th Congress, Indian and public lands: public law no. 86, approved Feb. 12, 1903, 57th Congress; public res. no. 8, approved Mar. 7, 1906, 59th Congress; public law no. 234 (extract from), approved June 16, 1906, 59th Congress; public law no. 321 (extract from), approved June 28, 1906, 59th Congress; public law no. 140, approved May 27, 1908, 60th Congress; public law no. 303, approved June 25, 1910, 61st Congress; public law no. 450, approved Mar. 2, 1911, 61st Congress; public law no. 314, approved Aug. 24, 1912, 62d Congress; public law no. 316, approved Aug. 24, 1912, 62d Congress; public law no. 393, approved Feb. 27, 1913, 62d Congress; public law no. 187, approved Aug. 25, 1914, 63d Congress; public law no. 218, approved Aug. 21, 1916, 64th Congress; public law no. 146, approved Feb. 25, 1920, 66th Congress; public law no. 127, approved Jan. 11, 1922, 67th Congress; public law no. 302, approved Sept. 15, 1922, 67th Congress; public law no. 500, approved Mar. 4, 1923, 67th Congress; public res. no. 4, approved Feb. 8, 1924, 68th Congress. 1924. [1]+41 p. * Paper, 5c.   24—26298

Rules. Constitution, Jefferson's manual, and Rules of House of Representatives, with digest of practice, 68th Congress, 1st session; [compiled] by Lehr Fess. 1923. viii+709 p. (H. doc. 100, 68th Cong. 1st sess.) * Paper, 75c.   6—17027

ACCOUNTS COMMITTEE

Enrolled Bills Committee, House. Assistant clerk to Committee on Enrolled Bills, report to accompany H. Res. 195; submitted by Mr. MacGregor. Mar. 1, 1924. 1 p. (H. rp. 251, 68th Cong. 1st sess.) * Paper, 5c.

Fulham, William H. William H. Fulham and Belle Dupré, report to accompany H. Res. 200 [to pay to William H. Fulham $203.33 and to Belle Dupré $103.33 as clerk hire to late H. Garland Dupré]; submitted by Mr. MacGregor. Mar. 1, 1924. 1 p. (H. rp. 250, 68th Cong. 1st sess.) * Paper, 5c.

House of Representatives. Authorizing select committee appointed under House resolution 217 to employ stenographic and other assistance, and for other purposes, report to accompany H. Res. 221; submitted by Mr. MacGregor. Mar. 18, 1924. 1 p. (H. rp. 323, 68th Cong. 1st sess.) *Paper, 5c.

—— Enrolling clerk to act during illness of present incumbent, report to accompany H. Res. 199; submitted by Mr. MacGregor. Mar. 1, 1924. 1 p. (H. rp. 252, 68th Cong. 1st sess.) *Paper, 5c.

Shipping Board. Authorizing select committee appointed under House resolution 186 [to investigate Shipping Board, etc.] to employ stenographic and other assistance, and for other purposes, report to accompany H. Res. 212; submitted by Mr. MacGregor. Mar. 18, 1924. 1 p. (H. rp. 322, 68th Cong. 1st sess.) *Paper, 5c.

AGRICULTURE COMMITTEE

Agricultural attachés. Promoting sale of farm products abroad, report to accompany H. R. 7111 [to promote American agriculture by making more extensively available by expanding service now rendered by Department of Agriculture in gathering and disseminating information regarding agricultural production, competition, and demand in foreign countries in promoting sale of farm products abroad, and in other ways]; submitted by Mr. Haugen. Mar. 1, 1924. 15 p. (H. rp. 248, 68th Cong. 1st sess.) *Paper, 5c. 24—26090

Agricultural products. McNary-Haugen bill, hearings on H. R. 5563, declaring emergency in respect to certain agricultural commodities and to promote equality between agricultural commodities and other commodities, Feb. 20 [–Mar. 12], 1924. 1924. [pts. 5–11, xxvii]+289–530 p. (Serial E. pts. 5–11.) *Paper, each pt. 5c.

Bread bill, hearings on H. R. 4533, to establish standard weights for loaves of bread, Feb. 18 and 19, 1924. 1924. iii+66 p. (Serial M.) *Paper, 5c.

Cotton. Cotton crop reports, report to accompany S. 2112 [authorizing Department of Agriculture to issue semimonthly cotton crop reports and providing for their publication simultaneously with ginning reports of Department of Commerce]; submitted by Mr. Haugen. Mar. 27, 1924. 2 p. (H. rp. 384, 68th Cong. 1st sess.) [Corrected print.] *Paper, 5c.

—— Swank cotton crop reports bill, hearings on H. R. 5842, authorizing Department of Agriculture to issue semimonthly cotton crop reports and providing for their publication simultaneously with ginning reports of Department of Commerce, Feb. 14–16, 1924. 1924. iii+83 p. (Serial K.) *Paper, 10c.

Dairy Bureau. To establish Dairy Bureau in Department of Agriculture, report to accompany H. R. 7113; submitted by Mr. Haugen. Mar. 29, 1924. 6 p. (H. rp. 399, 68th Cong. 1st sess.) *Paper, 5c.

Mississippi River Wild Life and Fish Refuge, hearings on H. R. 4088, to establish Upper Mississippi River Wild Life and Fish Refuge, Feb. 11–13, 1924. 1924. iii+104 p. (Serial J.) *Paper, 10c.

Wheat. Little export bill, hearings on H. R. 78, to authorize Secretary of Agriculture to purchase, store, and sell wheat, and to secure and maintain to producer reasonable price for wheat and to consumer reasonable price for bread, and to stabilize wheat prices, Mar. 5, 1924. 1924. ii+23 p. (Serial P.) *Paper, 5c.

—— Wheat prices in 1917, 1918, and 1919, hearings on H. R. 7062, to determine and refund difference between price received for wheat of 1917, 1918, and 1919 fixed by United States and its agents, and price which wheat of 1917, 1918, and 1919 would have brought unfixed thereby, Feb. 27, 1924; [statement of Sterling P. Bond]. 1924. iii+14 p. (Serial O.) *Paper, 5c.

World's Poultry Congress. Extending invitations to Governments to participate in World's Poultry Congress, report to accompany H. J. Res. 189; submitted by Mr. Haugen. Mar. 29, 1924. 3 p. (H. rp. 400, 68th Cong. 1st sess.) *Paper, 5c.

APPROPRIATIONS COMMITTEE

Appropriations. First deficiency appropriation bill, [fiscal year] 1924 [and prior fiscal years], hearing before subcommittee in charge of deficiency appropriations. 1924. ii+811 p. *Paper, 55c.

Appropriations—Continued. First deficiency appropriation bill, fiscal year 1924 [and prior fiscal years], report to accompany H. R. 7449; submitted by Mr. Madden. Mar. 1, 1924. 24 p. (H. rp. 249, 68th Cong. 1st sess.) * Paper, 5c.

—— Independent offices appropriation bill, [fiscal year] 1925, hearing before subcommittee in charge of independent offices appropriation bill for 1925. 1924. ii+736 p. * Paper, 75c.

—— Independent offices appropriation bill, [fiscal year] 1925, report to accompany H. R. 8233; submitted by Mr. Madden. Mar. 26, 1924. 29 p. (H. rp. 380, 68th Cong. 1st sess.) * Paper, 5c.

War Department. War Department appropriation bill, [fiscal year] 1925, hearings before subcommittee in charge of War Department appropriation bill for 1925. 1924. 2 pts. [iv]+1794+[xxii] p. * Paper, pt. 1 ,$1.00; * pt. 2, 50c.

pt. 1. Testimony on title 1 of bill comprising military activities of War Department.
pt. 2. Testimony on title 2 of bill comprising nonmilitary activities of War Department.

—— War Department appropriation bill, fiscal year 1925, report to accompany H. R. 7877; submitted by Mr. Anthony. Mar. 13, 1924. 52 p. (H. rp. 288, 68th Cong. 1st sess.) * Paper, 5c.

CENSUS COMMITTEE

Cotton. Collection and publication of cotton statistics, report to accompany S. 2113 [to amend act authorizing director of census to collect and publish statistics of cotton]; submitted by Mr. Rankin. Mar. 3, 1924. 1 p. (H. rp. 255, 68th Cong. 1st sess.) .* Paper, 5c.

CIVIL SERVICE COMMITTEE

Civil service pensions. Retirement of employees in classified civil service, report to accompany H. R. 8202 [to amend act for retirement of employees in classified civil service and acts in amendment thereof]; submitted by Mr. Lehlbach. Mar. 28, 1924. 4 p. (H. rp. 394, 68th Cong. 1st sess.) * Paper, 5c.   24—26299

Personnel Classification Board. The law and the Personnel Classification Board, hearings on H. R. 6896 [to amend classification act of 1923, by abolishing Personnel Classification Board and transferring powers and duties of said board to Civil Service Commission], Feb. 25–Mar. 1, 1924. 1924. ii+146 p. * Paper, 15c.

—— To abolish Personnel Classification Board, report to accompany H. R. 6896 [to amend classification act of 1923, by abolishing Personnel Classification Board and transferring powers and duties of said board to Civil Service Commission]; submitted by Mr. Lehlbach. Mar. 18, 1924. 4 p. (H. rp. 315, 68th Cong. 1st sess.) * Paper, 5c.   24—26300

CLAIMS COMMITTEE,

Alaska Commercial Co., report to accompany S. 1021 [for relief of Alaska Commercial Company]; submitted by Mr. Bulwinkle. Mar. 24, 1924. 3 p. (H. rp. 356, 68th Cong. 1st sess.) * Paper, 5c.

Bess, Gerard E. Gerard E. Bess, report to accompany H. R. 905 [for relief of Gerard E. Bess]; submitted by Mr. Underhill. Mar. 24, 1924. 5 p. (H. rp. 354, 68th Cong. 1st sess.) * Paper, 5c.

Lee, William H. William H. Lee, report to accompany S. 790 [for relief of William H. Lee]; submitted by Mr. Bulwinkle. Mar. 24, 1924. 3 p. (H. rp. 355, 68th Cong. 1st sess.) * Paper, 5c.

Maryland Casualty Company. Maryland Casualty Co. et al., report to accompany H. R. 6384 [for relief of Maryland Casualty Company, Fidelity and Deposit Company of Maryland, United States Fidelity and Guaranty Company, Baltimore, Md.]; submitted by Mr. Edmonds. Mar. 20, 1924. 18 p. (H. rp. 330, 68th Cong. 1st sess.) * Paper, 5c.

—— Maryland Casualty Co., United States Fidelity & Guaranty Co., Baltimore, Md., and National Surety Co., report to accompany H. R. 6383 [for relief of Maryland Casualty Company, United States Fidelity and Guaranty Company, Baltimore, Md., and National Surety Company]; submitted by Mr. Edmonds. Mar. 20, 1924. 7 p. (H. rp. 329, 68th Cong. 1st sess.) * Paper, 5c.

Nolan, Thomas. Margaret Nolan. guardian of Thomas Nolan. report to accompany S. 1219 [for relief of Margaret Nolan. mother of Thomas Nolan] ; submitted by Mr. Box. Mar. 13. 1924. 6 p. (H. rp. 298, 68th Cong. 1st sess.) * Paper, 5c.

Paul. Orville. Orville Paul. report to accompany H. R. 4432 [for relief of Orville Paul. son and ward of Jennie Kingston] ; submitted by Mr. Box. Mar. 20, 1924. 10 p. (H. rp. 335. 68th Cong. 1st sess.) * Paper, 5c.

Sharon. Mrs. Eva B. Eva B. Sharon. report to accompany H. R. 5136 [for relief of Eva B. Sharon] ; submitted by Mr. Sears of Nebraska. Mar. 20, 1924. 5 p. (H. rp. 328. 68th Cong. 1st sess.) * Paper, 5c.

Southern Pacific Company. To ascertain cost to Southern Pacific Co. in closing breaks in Colorado River. report to accompany H. R. 6012 ; submitted by Mr. Fredericks. Mar. 27. 1924. 19 p. (H. rp. 383. 68th Cong. 1st sess.) [Includes views of Mr. Box.] * Paper, 5c.

Williams. Mrs. Ethel. Ethel Williams. report to accompany S. 646 [for relief of Ethel Williams] ; submitted by Mr. McReynolds. Mar. 20. 1924. 8 p. (H. rp. 326, 68th Cong. 1st sess.) * Paper, 5c.

COINAGE. WEIGHTS. AND MEASURES COMMITTEE

Baskets. Standards for hampers, round stave baskets. and splint baskets for fruit, hearing on H. R. 4085. to fix standards for hampers. round stave baskets, and splint baskets for fruit and vegetables. and for other purposes, Mar. 21. 1924. 1924. [1]+14 p. * Paper, 5c.

Half-dollar. Coinage of 50-cent pieces in commemoration of carving on Stone Mountain. Ga.. report to accompany H. R. 5259 [to authorize coinage of 50-cent pieces in commemoration of commencement on June 18, 1923, of work of carving on Stone Mountain. Ga., monument to valor of soldiers of the South. which was the inspiration of their sons and daughters and grandsons and granddaughters in Spanish-American and World Wars. and in memory of Warren G. Harding. President of United States. in whose administration the work was begun] ; submitted by Mr. vestal. Mar. 8. 1924. 1 p. (H. rp. 277. 68th Cong. 1st sess.) * Paper. 5c.

Weights and measures. Standard of weights and measures for certain agricultural products, hearing on H. R. 3241. to establish standard of weights and measures for following wheat-mill, rye-mill, and corn-mill products. namely, flours, hominy. grits. and meals and all commercial feeding stuffs, Feb. 21, 1924. 1924. pt. 2. [1]+6 p. [Part 1 appeared in Monthly catalogue for Feb. 1924. p. 433.] * Paper, 5c.

—— To establish standard of weights and measures for flours. hominy. grits. and meals, and all commercial feeding stuffs, report to accompany H. R. 3241 [to establish standard of weights and measures for following wheat-mill. rye-mill. and corn-mill products. namely, flours. hominy. grits, and meals. and all commercial feeding stuffs] : submitted by Mr. vestal. Mar. 14. 1924. 2 p. (H. rp. 309, 68th Cong. 1st sess.) * Paper. 5c.

DISTRICT OF COLUMBIA COMMITTEE

Insurance. Bill to amend insurance laws of District of Columbia. minority report to accompany H. R. 3689 ; submitted by Mr. Blanton. Mar. 24. 1924. 35 p. (H. rp. 231. pt. 2, 68th Cong. 1st sess.) [Part 1 appeared in Monthly catalogue for Feb. 1924. p. 433.] * Paper, 5c.

Medical Society of District of Columbia. Amending charter of Medical Society of District of Columbia. report to accompany H. R. 4122 ; submitted by Mr. McLeod. Mar. 6. 1924. 3 p. (H. rp. 264. 68th Cong. 1st sess.) * Paper, 5c.

Optometry. Practice of optometry in District of Columbia. report to accompany H. R. 3236 [to regulate practice of optometry in District of Columbia] ; submitted by Mr. Fitzgerald. Mar. 31. 1924. 1 p. (H. rp. 410, 68th Cong. 1st sess.) * Paper, 5c.

Parks. Extension of park system of District of Columbia. report to accompany H. R. 4805 ; submitted by Mr. Gibson. Mar. 10. 1924. 4 p. (H. rp. 278, 68th Cong. 1st sess.) * Paper, 5c.

—— Extension of park system of District of Columbia. report to accompany S. 1787 ; submitted by Mr. Gibson. Mar. 21. 1924. 1 p. (H. rp. 337, 68th Cong. 1st sess.) * Paper, 5c.

Rent Commission. District of Columbia Rent Commission, hearings before subcommittee on H. R. 7962 (H. R. 23 amended)`, to create and establish commission, as independent establishment of Federal Government, to regulate rents in District of Columbia, Feb. 11 [-27]. 1924. 1924. pts. 1-3. [vi]+1-450 p. il. * Paper, each pt. 15c.

Streets. Changing name of Keokuk street to Military road, report to accompany S. 113; submitted by Mr. Blanton. Mar. 29, 1924. 1 p. (H. rp. 408, 68th Cong. 1st sess.) * Paper, 5c.

—— Changing name of 37th street between Chevy Chase circle and Reno road [to Chevy Chase drive], report to accompany H. R. 6296; submitted by Mr. Beers. Mar. 24, 1924. 2 p. (H. rp. 351, 68th Cong. 1st sess.) * Paper, 5c.

—— Vacate and extend streets near Walter Reed General Hospital, report to accompany S. 114 [to vacate streets and alleys within area known as Walter Reed General Hospital, District of Columbia, and to authorize extension and widening of 14th street from Montague street to its southern terminus south of Dahlia street, Nicholson street from 13th street to 16th street. Colorado avenue from Montague street to 13th street, Concord avenue from 16th street to its western terminus west of 8th street west, 13th street from Nicholson street to Piney Branch road, and Piney Branch road from 13th street to Butternut street]; submitted by Mr. Zihlman. Mar. 26, 1924. 1 p. (H. rp. 373, 68th Cong. 1st sess.) * Paper, 5c.

—— Widening of 4th street nw., report to accompany S. 1343 [to authorize widening of 4th street, south of Cedar street northwest, District of Columbia]; submitted by Mr. Kent. Mar. 21, 1924. 2 p. (H. rp. 338, 68th Cong. 1st sess.) * Paper, 5c.

—— Widening of Georgia avenue, report to accompany S. 1339 [to authorize widening of Georgia avenue between Fairmont street and Gresham place northwest]; submitted by Mr. Gibson. Mar. 13, 1924. 2 p. (H. rp. 301, 68th Cong. 1st sess.) * Paper, 5c.

Teachers. Teachers' salary and school reorganization bill for District of Columbia, minority report to accompany H. R. 6721 [to amend act to fix and regulate salaries of teachers, school officers, and other employees of Board of Education of District of Columbia, as amended, and for other purposes]; submitted by Mr. Blanton. Mar. 29, 1924. 12 p. (H. rp. 302, pt. 2. 68th Cong. 1st sess.) * Paper, 5c.

—— Teachers' salary and school reorganization bill for District of Columbia, report to accompany H. R. 6721 [to amend act to fix and regulate salaries of teachers, school officers, and other employees of Board of Education of District of Columbia, as amended, and for other purposes]; submitted by Mr. Lampert. Mar. 14, 1924. 9 p. (H. rp. 302 [pt. 1], 68th Cong. 1st sess.) * Paper, 5c.

ELECTION OF PRESIDENT, VICE PRESIDENT, AND REPRESENTATIVES COMMITTEE

President of United States. Proposing amendment to Constitution of United States, minority report to accompany H. J. Res. 93 [proposing amendment to Constitution of United States fixing commencement of terms of President and Vice President and Members of Congress, and fixing time of assembling of Congress]; submitted by Mr. Jeffers. Mar. 3, 1924. 4 p. (H. rp. 211, pt. 2, 68th Cong. 1st sess.) * Paper, 5c.

—— Providing for meeting of electors of President and Vice President, for issuance and transmission of certificates of their selection and result of their determination. hearing on H. R. 7108 and H. R. 8054, Feb. 21, 1924; testimony of Hatton W. Sumners [and] William Tyler Page. 1924. ii+3 p. * Paper, 5c.

ELECTIONS COMMITTEE, NO. 2

Cole, E. W. Case of E. W. Cole, hearings on claim of E. W. Cole to seat in House of Representatives as representative at large from Texas, Mar. 18, 1924; [statement of Carlos Bee]. 1924. ii+14 p. * Paper, 5c.

—— Claim of E. W. Cole for seat in House of Representatives as representative at large from Texas, report; submitted by Mr. Nelson of Wisconsin. Mar. 29, 1924. 4 p. (H. rp. 398, 68th Cong. 1st sess.) * Paper, 5c.

Contested elections. Clark *v.* Moore, report on contested-election case of Don H. Clark *v.* R. Lee Moore from 1st Congressional district of Georgia; submitted by Mr. Nelson of Wisconsin. Mar. 26, 1924. 4 p. (H. rp. 367, 68th Cong. 1st sess.) * Paper, 5c.

FLOOD CONTROL COMMITTEE

Floods. Preliminary examinations of sundry streams, report to accompany H. R. 8070 [authorizing preliminary examinations and surveys of sundry streams with view to control of their floods]; submitted by Mr. Schall. Mar. 20, 1924. 6 p. (H. rp. 334, 68th Cong. 1st sess.) [Corrected print. 1st print has 6 pages.] * Paper, 5c.

FOREIGN AFFAIRS COMMITTEE

Crignier, Madame. Relief of Madame Crignier, of France, report to accompany S. 2392 [authorizing appropriation to indemnify damages to property of Madame Crignier, caused by search for body of John Paul Jones]; submitted by Mr. Begg. Mar. 18, 1924. 10 p. (H. rp. 319, 68th Cong. 1st sess.) * Paper, 5c.

Germany. Relief of distressed and starving women and children of Germany, report to accompany H. J. Res. 180; submitted by Mr. Fish. Mar. 3, 1924. 3 p. (H. rp. 256, 68th Cong. 1st sess.) * Paper, 5c.

Great Britain. In re treaty between Great Britain and United States having for its purpose abolition of smuggling intoxicating liquors from Great Britain into America, hearings on H. Res. 174, requesting President of United States to transmit to House of Representatives copy of treaty between Great Britain and United States having for its purpose abolition of smuggling intoxicating liquors from Great Britain into America; statement of Henry St. George Tucker, Feb. 20 and Mar. 7, 1924. 1924. ii+32 p. [The hearing of Feb. 20, p. 1–7, was first issued as pt. 1.] * Paper, 5c.

Inter-American Electrical Communications Committee, report to accompany S. J. Res. 79 [for representation of United States at meeting of Inter-American Committee on Electrical Communications to be held in Mexico City in 1924]; submitted by Mr. Fairchild. Mar. 29, 1924. 3 p. (H. rp. 403, 68th Cong. 1st sess.) * Paper, 5c.

International Institute of Agriculture. Appropriations for payment of expenses of delegates to represent United States at general assembly of International Institute of Agriculture to be held at Rome in May, 1924, etc.. report to accompany S. J. Res. 96 [authorizing appropriations for payment of expenses of delegates to represent United States at general assembly of International Institute of Agriculture to be held at Rome in May, 1924, and for payment of quotas of Hawaii, the Philippines, Porto Rico, and Virgin Islands for support of Institute, calendar year 1924]; submitted by Mr. Cole of Iowa. Mar. 18 1924. 5 p. (H. rp. 320, 68th Cong. 1st sess.) * Paper, 5c.

International Sanitary Conference of American Republics. 7th Pan American Sanitary Conference, report to accompany S. J. Res. 77 [authorizing appropriation to provide for representation of United States at 7th Pan American Sanitary Conference to be held at Habana, Cuba]; submitted by Mr. Porter. Mar. 29, 1924. 2 p. (H. rp. 402, 68th Cong. 1st sess.) * Paper, 5c.

International Statistical Bureau.. International Statistical Institute at The Hague, report to accompany S. J. Res. 76 [authorizing appropriations for maintenance by United States of membership in International Statistical Bureau at The Hague]; submitted by Mr. Browne of Wisconsin. Mar. 28, 1924. 4 p. (H. rp. 396, 68th Cong. 1st sess.) * Paper, 5c.

Sharp, Mrs. May A. May Adelaide Sharp, report to accompany H. R. 6498 [for relief of May Adelaide Sharp]; submitted by Mr. Moores of Indiana. Mar. 29, 1924. 2 p. (H. rp. 404, 68th Cong. 1st sess.) * Paper, 5c.

IMMIGRATION AND NATURALIZATION COMMITTEE

Immigration. Restriction of immigration, hearings on H. R. 5, H. R. 101, H. R. 561, H. R. 6540, Jan. 14–Feb. 12, 1924. 1924. ii+915–1175+ii p. (Serial 2-A.) * Paper, 25c.

—— Restriction of immigration, minority report to accompany H. R. 7995; submitted by Mr. Sabath. Mar. 27, 1924. 34 p. (H. rp. 350, pt. 2, 68th Cong. 1st sess.) * Paper, 5c.

Immigration—Continued. Restriction of immigration, report to accompany H. R. 7995; submitted by Mr. Johnson of Washington. Mar. 24, 1924. 41 p. (H. rp. 350 [pt. 1], 68th Cong. 1st sess.) * Paper, 5c.

INDIAN AFFAIRS COMMITTEE

Chippewa Indians. Payment of claims against Chippewa Indians of Minnesota, report to accompany H. R. 4461; submitted by Mr. Hudson. Mar. 7, 1924. 2 p. (H. rp. 275, 68th Cong. 1st sess.) * Paper, 5c.

—— To compensate [Chippewa] Indians of Minnesota for lands disposed of by free homestead act, report to accompany H. R. 26; submitted by Mr. Hudson. Mar. 7, 1924. 3 p. (H. rp. 272, 68th Cong. 1st sess.) * Paper, 5c.

Choctaw Indians. Amend act authorizing payment of Choctaw and Chickasaw town-site fund, etc. [so as to provide for payment of shares of deceased Indians to their heirs], report to accompany H. R. 4462; submitted by Mr. Hastings. Mar. 13, 1924. 2 p. (H. rp. 293, 68th Cong. 1st sess.) * Paper, 5c.

—— To adjudicate claims of Choctaw and Chickasaw Indians, report to accompany H. R. 5325 [conferring jurisdiction upon Court of Claims to hear, examine, adjudicate, and enter judgment in any claims which Choctaw and Chickasaw Indians may have against United States]; submitted by Mr. Garber. Mar. 13, 1924. 2 p. (H. rp. 295, 68th Cong. 1st sess.) * Paper, 5c.

Creek Indians. Authorizing Court of Claims to adjudicate claims of Creek Indians, report to accompany H. R. 7913; submitted by Mr. Hastings. Mar. 20, 1924. 2 p. (H. rp. 333, 68th Cong. 1st sess.) * Paper, 5c.

Five Civilized Tribes. To amend act fulfilling treaty stipulations with various Indian tribes, report to accompany H. R. 7077 [to amend act to amend act making appropriations for current and contingent expenses of Bureau of Indian Affairs, for fulfilling treaty stipulations with various Indian tribes, and for other purposes, fiscal year 1914, relating to certain payments from funds of Five Civilized Tribes of Oklahoma for cost of street paving and construction of sidewalks and sewers]; submitted by Mr. Howard of Oklahoma. Mar. 6, 1924. 2 p. (H. rp. 271, 68th Cong. 1st sess.) * Paper, 5c.

Indian reservations. Leasing of unallotted lands of Indians for oil and gas, report to accompany H. R. 6298; submitted by Mr. Garber. Mar. 27, 1924. 2 p. (H. rp. 386, 68th Cong. 1st sess.) * Paper, 5c.

Indians. Administration of Indian affairs in Oklahoma, hearing on H. J. Res. 181, Feb. 21, 1924. 1924. [1]+32 p. *Paper, 5c.

—— Pay tuition of Indian children in public schools, report to accompany H. R. 4835; submitted by Mr. Leavitt. Mar. 6, 1924. 2 p. (H. rp. 270, 68th Cong. 1st sess.) *Paper, 5c.

Jocko Reservation. Additional names to final roll of Indians, Flathead [or Jocko] Reservation, Mont., report to accompany H. R. 2875; submitted by Mr. Snyder. Mar. 13, 1924. 2 p. (H. rp. 296, 68th Cong. 1st sess.) *Paper, 5c.

Kansa Indians. Extension of period of restriction against alienation on homestead allotments, Kansas or Kaw tribe of Indians in Oklahoma, report to accompany H. R. 2887; submitted by Mr. Garber. Mar. 6, 1924. 3 p. (H. rp. 269, 68th Cong. 1st sess.) *Paper, 5c.

Nisqualli Reservation. Relief of dispossessed allotted Indians of Nisqually Reservation, Wash., report to accompany H. R. 6490; submitted by Mr. Leavitt. Mar. 27, 1924. 2 p. (H. rp. 387, 68th Cong. 1st sess.) *Paper, 5c.

Osage Indians. Division of lands and funds of Osage Indians in Oklahoma, report to accompany H. R. 5726 [to amend act to amend sec. 3 of act for division of lands and funds of Osage Indians in Oklahoma]; submitted by Mr. Snyder. Mar. 5, 1924. 5 p. (H. rp. 260, 68th Cong. 1st sess.) *Paper, 5c.

—— Modifying Osage fund restrictions, hearings on H. R. 5726, Feb. 22-29, 1924. 1924. [1]+331-389 p. (Serial 2.) *Paper, 10c.

Peirce, Charles F. Charles F. Peirce, Frank T. Mann, and Mollie V. Gaither, report to accompany H. R. 6328 [for relief of Charles F. Peirce, Frank T. Mann, and Mollie V. Gaither]; submitted by Mr. Howard of Nebraska. Mar. 13, 1924. 2 p. (H. rp. 297, 68th Cong. 1st sess.) *Paper, 5c.

Potawatomi Indians. Pay certain funds to various Wisconsin Pottawatomi Indians, report to accompany H. R. 7239; submitted by Mr. Hudson. Mar. 20, 1924. 2 p. (H. rp. 331, 68th Cong. 1st sess.) *Paper, 5c.

Quapaw Agency. Removal of restrictions on alienation of lands of allottees of Quapaw Agency, Okla., report to accompany H. R. 7453 [to amend act for removal of restrictions on alienation of lands of allottees of Quapaw Agency, Okla., and sale of all tribal lands, school, agency, or other buildings on any of reservations within jurisdiction of such agency, so as to permit sale of homestead allotments]; submitted by Mr. Howard of Oklahoma. Mar. 20, 1924. 1 p. (H. rp. 332, 68th Cong. 1st sess.) *Paper, 5c.

——— To perfect title of purchasers of Indian lands, report to accompany H. R. 4818 [to perfect title of purchasers of Indian lands sold under provisions of act of Congress of Mar. 3, 1909, and regulations pursuant thereto as applied to Indians of Quapaw Agency]; submitted by Mr. Howard of Oklahoma. Mar. 13, 1924. 2 p. (H. rp. 294, 68th Cong. 1st sess.) *Paper, 5c.

Red Lake Reservation. Payment to Red Lake Indians for lands surrendered for school farm use, report to accompany H. R. 4460 [authorizing payment to Red Lake Indians, out of tribal trust funds, for garden plats surrendered for school-farm use]; submitted by Mr. Hudson. Mar. 7, 1924. 2 p. (H. rp. 274, 68th Cong. 1st sess.) *Paper, 5c.

Saginaw Indians. To amend act for relief of Chippewa Indians in Michigan, report to accompany H. R. 694 [to amend act for relief of Saginaw, Swan Creek, and Black River Band of Chippewa Indians in Michigan, so as to increase limit of attorneys' fees]: submitted by Mr. Hudson. Mar. 7. 1924. 2 p. (H. rp. 273, 68th Cong. 1st sess.) *Paper, 5c.

Seupelt, J. G. J. G. Seupelt. report to accompany S. 1703 [for relief of J. G. Seupelt]; submitted by Mr. Snyder. Mar. 20, 1924. 2 p. (H. rp. 327, 68th Cong. 1st sess.) *Paper, 5c.

INSULAR AFFAIRS COMMITTEE

Philippine independence, hearing on H. J. Res. 131, to enable people of Philippine Islands to form constitution and national government and to provide for recognition of their independence, H. R. 3924, for withdrawal of United States from Philippine Islands. H. J. Res. 127, to grant complete independence to Philippine Islands and to effect treaty of recognition therewith, H. R. 2817, for independence of Philippine Islands, Feb. 17 and 25, 1924. 1924. [1]+99 p. *Paper, 10c.

Porto Rico. Amend organic act of Porto Rico, hearing on H. R. 6583, Feb. 26, 1924. 1924. [1]+22 p. *Paper, 5c.

——— Amend organic act of Porto Rico, report to accompany H. R. 6583; submitted by Mr. Fairfield. Mar. 13. 1924. 6 p. (H. rp. 291, 68th Cong. 1st sess.) *Paper, 5c.

——— Civil government of Porto Rico, hearings on H. R. 4087, to amend and reenact sec. 20, 22, and 50 of act to provide civil government for Porto Rico [relating to salaries], and H. R. 6583 to amend organic act of Porto Rico, Feb. 13 and 14, 1924. 1924. [1]+100 p. *Paper, 10c.

INTERSTATE AND FOREIGN COMMERCE COMMITTEE

Anthrax. To prohibit importation and interstate shipment of certain articles contaminated with anthrax, report to accompany H. R. 6425; submitted by Mr. Winslow. Mar. 26. 1924. 2 p. (H. rp. 369, 68th Cong. 1st sess.) * Paper. 5c.

Calumet River. Bridge across Calumet River, report to accompany H. R. 2665 [granting consent of Congress to Chicago to construct bridge across Calumet River in vicinity of 134th street in Chicago, county of Cook. Ill.]; submitted by Mr. Graham of Illinois. Mar. 26, 1924. 2 p. (H. rp. 370, 68th Cong. 1st sess.) * Paper, 5c.

Coast Guard. United States Coast Guard law enforcement, hearing on H. R. 6815, to authorize temporary increase of Coast Guard for law enforcement. 1924. iii+23 p. * Paper, 5c.

Coast Guard cutters. United States Coast Guard legislation, hearing on H. R. 6817, for construction of vessel for Coast Guard [for duty in Alaskan waters], Feb. 20. 1924. 1924. iii+7 p. * Paper, 5c.

Foreign Commerce Service. To establish in Bureau of Foreign and Domestic Commerce of Department of Commerce a Foreign Commerce Service, hearings on H. R. 4517, Feb. 7–14, 1924. 1924. iii+171 p. * Paper, 15c.

Fox River. Bridge across Fox River in St. Charles Township, Kane County, Ill., report to accompany H. R. 7104 [granting consent of Congress to Aurora, Elgin, and Fox River Electric Company to construct bridge across Fox River in St. Charles Township, Kane County, Ill.]; submitted by Mr. Graham of Illinois. Mar. 26, 1924. 2 p. (H. rp. 372, 68th Cong. 1st sess.) * Paper, 5c.

Inland Waterways Corporation. Inland Waterways Corporation, hearings on H. R. 6647, to create Inland Waterways Corporation for purpose of carrying out mandate and purpose of Congress as expressed in sec. 201 and 500 of transportation act, Feb. 26–Mar. 7, 1924. 1924. iii+201 p. * Paper, 25c.

—— To create Inland Waterways Corporation for purpose of carrying out mandate and purpose of Congress as expressed in sec. 201 and 500 of transportation act, report to accompany H. R. 8209; submitted by Mr. Denison. Mar. 26, 1924. 14 p. (H. rp. 375, 68th Cong. 1st sess.) * Paper, 5c.

Mahoning River. Bridge across Mahoning River, Ohio, report to accompany H. R. 6623 [granting consent of Congress to Pittsburgh, Youngstown & Ashtabula Railway Company to construct bridge across Mahoning River, Ohio, at or near Haselton]; submitted by Mr. Cooper of Ohio. Mar. 13, 1924. 2 p. (H. rp. 292, 68th Cong. 1st sess.) * Paper, 5c.

Minnesota River. Bridge across Minnesota River, report to accompany H. R. 6724 [granting consent of Congress to counties of Sibley and Scott, Minn., to construct bridge across Minnesota River at or near Blakely]; submitted by Mr. Newton of Minnesota. Mar. 13, 1924. 2 p. (H. rp. 299, 68th Cong. 1st sess.) * Paper, 5c.

Mississippi River. Bridge across Mississippi River between Carroll County, Ill., and Jackson County, Iowa, report to accompany H. R. 7063 [granting consent of Congress to Illinois and Iowa, or either of them, to construct bridge across Mississippi River, connecting county of Carroll, Ill., and county of Jackson, Iowa]; submitted by Mr. Graham of Illinois. Mar. 26, 1924. 2 p. (H. rp. 371, 68th Cong. 1st sess.) * Paper, 5c.

—— Bridge across Mississippi River, report to accompany S. 2488 [to authorize Minneapolis, Minn., to construct bridge across Mississippi River in said city]; submitted by Mr. Newton of Minnesota. Mar. 27, 1924. 2 p. (H. rp. 382, 68th Cong. 1st sess.) * Paper, 5c.

—— Bridge across Mississippi River, report to accompany S. 2656 [granting consent of Congress to construction of bridge across Mississippi River near and above New Orleans, La., by said city through its Public Belt Railroad Commission]; submitted by Mr. Parks of Arkansas. Mar. 26, 1924. 2 p. (H. rp. 368, 68th Cong. 1st sess.) * Paper, 5c.

Missouri River. Bridge across Missouri River between Potter and Dewey counties, S. Dak., report to accompany H. R. 6955 [granting consent of Congress to South Dakota for construction of bridge across Missouri River between Potter County and Dewey County, S. Dak.]; submitted by Mr. Burtness. Mar. 13, 1924. 2 p. (H. rp. 300, 68th Cong. 1st sess.) * Paper, 5c.

—— Bridge across Missouri River, report to accompany S. 2332 [granting consent of Congress to South Dakota for construction of bridge across Missouri River between Hughes County and Stanley County, S. Dak.]; submitted by Mr. Burtness. Mar. 26, 1924. 2 p. (H. rp. 374, 68th Cong. 1st sess.) * Paper, 5c.

Panama Canal. Compensation to retired warrant officers and enlisted men employed by Panama Canal, report to accompany H. R. 6816; submitted by Mr. Rayburn. Mar. 22, 1924. 3 p. (H. rp. 348, 68th Cong. 1st sess.) * Paper, 5c.

—— Open-market purchases of supplies for use on Panama Canal and in Canal Zone, report to accompany H. R. 7015; submitted by Mr. Winslow. Mar. 25, 1924. 3 p. (H. rp. 363, 68th Cong. 1st sess.) * Paper, 5c.

—— Panama Canal Zone, proposed legislation, hearing on H. R. 7015, H. R. 7307, H. R. 6816, and H. R. 7762, open market purchases, liability of owners of motor vehicles, compensation of retired warrant officers and enlisted men, and measurement of vessels, Mar. 12 and 13, 1924. 1924. ii+33 p. * Paper, 5c.

93602—No. 351—24——4

Pearl River. Bridge across Pearl River, Miss., report to accompany H. R. 6902 [granting consent of Congress to board of supervisors of Leake County, Miss., to construct bridge across Pearl River, Miss., at or near Battle Bluff Crossing] ; submitted by Mr. Rayburn. Mar. 14, 1924. 2 p. (H. rp. 308, 68th Cong. 1st sess.) * Paper, 5c.

—— Bridge across Pearl River, Miss., report to accompany H. R. 6903 [granting consent of Congress to board of supervisors of Leake County, Miss., to construct bridge across Pearl River, Miss., at or near Grigsbys Ferry] ; submitted by Mr. Huddleston. Mar. 14, 1924. 2 p. (H. rp. 303, 68th Cong. 1st sess.) * Paper, 5c.

Porto Rico. Extension of welfare of maternity and infancy act to Porto Rico, report to accompany H. R. 6142 [to extend to Porto Rico benefits of act for promotion of welfare and hygiene of maternity and infancy, as amended] ; submitted by Mr. Burtness. Mar. 22, 1924. 2 p. (H. rp. 346, 68th Cong. 1st sess.) * Paper, 5c.

—— Public protection of maternity and infancy, Porto Rico, hearings on H. R. 6142, amending act for promotion of welfare of maternity and infancy [by extending provisions of act to Porto Rico], Feb. 19. 1924. 1924. iii+20 p. * Paper, 5c.

Savannah River. Bridge across Savannah River near Augusta, Ga., report to accompany H. R. 8180 [to revive and reenact act authorizing counties of Aiken, S. C., and Richmond, Ga., to construct bridge across Savannah River at or near Augusta, Ga.] ; submitted by Mr. Huddleston. Mar. 26, 1924. 2 p. (H. rp. 378, 68th Cong. 1st sess.) * Paper, 5c.

Susquehanna River. Bridge across Susquehanna River at Millersburg, Pa., report to accompany H. R. 6810 [granting consent of Congress to Millersburg and Liverpool Bridge Corporation to construct bridge across Susquehanna River, at Millersburg, Pa.] ; submitted by Mr. Wyant. Mar. 18, 1924. 2 p. (H. rp. 317, 68th Cong. 1st sess.) * Paper, 5c.

INVALID PENSIONS COMMITTEE

Militia. Pensions for Militia organizations of the several States, report to accompany H. R. 5936 [to extend provisions of pension act of May 11, 1912, to officers and enlisted men of all State Militia and other State organizations that rendered service to the Union cause during Civil War for period of 90 days or more, and providing pensions for their widows, minor children, and dependent parents] ; submitted by Mr. Fulbright. Mar. 12, 1924. 69 p. (H. rp. 287, 68th Cong. 1st sess.) * Paper, 5c.

Pensions. Granting pensions and increase of pensions to certain soldiers and sailors of Civil War, etc., report to accompany H. R. 7816 [substituted for H. R. 812 and other bills] ; submitted by Mr. Elliott. Mar. 11, 1924. 105 p. (H. rp. 283, 68th Cong. 1st sess.) * Paper, 10c.

—— Increase of Civil War pensions, minority report to accompany H. R. 7963 [to increase pensions of persons who served in Army, Navy, or Marine Corps during Civil War, and of widows and former widows of such persons, and Army nurses of said war] ; submitted by Mr. O'Brien. Mar. 26, 1924. 2 p. (H. rp. 314, pt. 2, 68th Cong. 1st sess.) * Paper, 5c.

—— Increase of Civil War pensions, report to accompany H. R. 7963 [to increase pensions of persons who served in Army, Navy, or Marine Corps during Civil War, and of widows and former widows of such persons, and Army nurses of said war] ; submitted by Mr. Fuller. Mar. 17, 1924. 3 p. (H. rp. 314 [pt. 1], 68th Cong. 1st sess.) * Paper, 5c.

IRRIGATION AND RECLAMATION COMMITTEE

Reclamation of land. Extension of charges on reclamation projects, hearings on S. 1631, to extend time for payment of charges due on reclamation projects, Mar. 8, 1924. 1924. ii+51 p. * Paper, 10c.

—— Relief of settlers on Government reclamation projects, report to accompany S. 1631 [to authorize deferring of payments of reclamation charges] ; submitted by Mr. Smith. Mar. 14, 1924. 3 p. (H. rp. 312, 68th Cong. 1st sess.) * Paper, 5c.

JUDICIARY COMMITTEE

Alaska. Amending law providing for special taxes on business and trades in Alaska, hearing on H. R. 6584, Mar. 15, 1924. 1924. ii+11 p. (Serial 17.) * Paper, 5c.

Bankruptcy. To amend bankruptcy law, hearings on H. R. 5426 and H. R. 5193, Feb. 20, 1924. 1924. ii+20 p. (Serial 11.) * Paper, 5c.

Calendar. Legislative calendar, 68th Congress, Mar. 3–24, 1924; no. 7–9. 1924. Each 56 p. or 66 p. 4° ‡

Child labor. Child-labor amendment to Constitution of United States, minority report to accompany H. J. Res. 184; submitted by Mr. Graham, of Pennsylvania. Mar. 29, 1924. 10 p. (H. rp. 395, pt. 2, 68th Cong., 1st sess.) * Paper, 5c.

—— Child-labor amendment to Constitution of United States, report to accompany H. J. Res. 184; submitted by Mr. Foster. Mar. 28, 1924. 21 p. (H. rp. 395 [pt. 1], 68th Cong. 1st sess.) * Paper, 5c.   24—26301

—— Proposed child-labor amendments to Constitution of United States, hearings, Feb. 7–Mar. 8, 1924. 1924. iv+307 p. (Serial 16.) * Paper, 30c.

Commerce. To amend China trade act of 1922, report to accompany H. R. 7190; submitted by Mr. Dyer. Mar. 18, 1924. 20 p. (H. rp. 321, 68th Cong. 1st sess.) * Paper, 5c.

Constitution of United States. Proposal and ratification of amendments to Constitution of United States, hearing on H. J. Res. 68, Mar. 5, 1924. 1924. [pt. 2], ii+15 p. (Serial 5, pt. 2) * Paper, 5c.

—— Proposal and ratification of amendments to Constitution of United States, hearing on H. J. Res. 68, Mar. 5, 1924; statement of Louis A. Coolidge. 1924. [pt. 3], ii+3 p. (Serial 5, pt. 3.) * Paper, 5c.

Courts of United States. To limit power of United States courts to express opinions as to credibility of witnesses or weight of testimony, report to accompany H. R. 3260 [to amend practice and procedure in Federal courts, so. that in jury trials presiding judge shall not express his opinion as to credibility of witnesses or weight of testimony involved in issue]; submitted by Mr. Graham of Pennsylvania. Mar. 25, 1924. 1 p. (H. rp. 365, 68th Cong. 1st sess.) * Paper, 5c.

District Courts. Providing for additional place for holding United States court in eastern district of Oklahoma at Ada, Okla., report to accompany H. R. 714; submitted by Mr. Yates. Mar. 26, 1924. 2 p. (H. rp. 377, 68th Cong. 1st sess.) * Paper, 5c.

—— Providing for holding of district and circuit courts at Poteau, Okla., report to accompany H. R. 644; submitted by Mr. Yates. Mar. 27, 1924. 2 p. (H. rp. 388, 68th Cong. 1st sess.) [Corrected print.] * Paper, 5c.

—— Providing terms of court to be held at Pauls Valley, Okla., report to accompany H. R. 162; submitted by Mr. Yates. Mar. 28, 1924. 2 p. (H. rp. 392, 68th Cong. 1st sess.) * Paper, 5c.

—— Term of court at Ada, Okla., hearing on H. R. 714, Jan. 22, 1924. 1924. ii+11 p. (Serial 18.) * Paper, 5c.

—— Term of court at Casper, Wyo., hearing on H. R. 4445, Mar. 5, 1924; statement of Charles E. Winter. 1924. [1]+6 p. (Serial 21.) * Paper. 5c.

—— Term of court at Casper, Wyo., report to accompany H. R. 4445; submitted by Mr. Graham of Pennsylvania. Mar. 27, 1924. 1 p. (H. rp. 385, 68th Cong. 1st sess.) * Paper, 5c.

Employers' liability and workmen's compensation. To amend employees' compensation act, report to accompany H. R. 7041 [to amend act to provide compensation for employees of United States suffering injuries while in performance of their duties]; submitted by Mr. Graham of Pennsylvania. Mar. 10, 1924. 3 p. (H. rp. 280. 68th Cong. 1st sess.) * Paper, 5c.

—— To amend United States employees' compensation act, hearing on H. R. 7041, Mar. 5, 1924. 1924. ii+17 p. (Serial 14.) * Paper, 5c.

House of Representatives. Alleged charge against 2 Members of Congress, report on communication of Attorney General in reply to H. Res. 211 [directing Attorney General to transmit names of 2 Members of Congress and nature of charges made against them]; submitted by Mr. Graham of Pennsylvania. Mar. 10, 1924. 3 p. (H. rp. 282, 68th Cong. 1st sess.) * Paper, 5c.

International Federation of Catholic Alumnæ. To incorporate International Federation of Catholic Alumnæ, hearing on H. R. 6061, Feb. 21, 1924. 1924. ii+16 p. (Serial 15.) * Paper, 5c.

Judges. To limit power of judges of United States courts, hearing on H. R. 2910, H. R. 3260, H. R. 4509, and H. R. 4821, Feb. 14, 1924. 1924. ii+20 p. (Serial 13.) * Paper, 5c.

Jury. To authorize grand juries to sit during succeeding term to continue business unfinished by such grand jury, report to accompany H. R. 7271: submitted by Mr. Graham of Pennsylvania. Mar. 25, 1924. 3 p. (H. rp. 366, 68th Cong. 1st sess.) * Paper, 5c.

—— To permit clerks or stenographers employed to assist United States attorneys to be in attendance before grand juries, report to accompany H. R. 7270 [to amend sec. 1025, Revised statutes, so as to permit clerks or stenographers employed to assist United States attorneys to be in attendance before grand juries]; submitted by Mr. Graham of Pennsylvania. Mar. 24, 1924. 4 p. (H. rp. 352, 68th Cong. 1st sess.) * Paper, 5c.

Justice Department. Directing Attorney General to furnish certain information to House of Representatives, report to accompany H. Res. 162 [requesting Attorney General to furnish to House of Representatives certain information regarding $500,000 appropriated by Congress to prosecute war frauds, and for other purposes]; submitted by Mr. Graham of Pennsylvania. Mar. 6, 1924. 1 p. (H. rp. 267, 68th Cong. 1st sess.) * Paper, 5c.

—— Requiring certain information from Attorney General, report to accompany H. Res. 155 [requesting information from Attorney General regarding special attorneys appointed during 1922 and 1923 for prosecution of war frauds, and for other purposes]; submitted by Mr. Graham of Pennsylvania. Mar. 6, 1924. 1 p. (H. rp. 266, 68th Cong. 1st sess.) * Paper, 5c.

Larceny. To amend act of Feb. 13 1913 (37 Stat. 670), report to accompany H. R. 4168 [to amend act to punish unlawful breaking of seals of railroad cars containing interstate or foreign shipments, unlawful entering of such cars, stealing of freight and express packages or baggage or articles in process of transportation in interstate shipment, and felonious asportation of such freight or express packages or baggage or articles therefrom into another district of United States, and felonious possession or reception of same]; submitted by Mr. Dyer. Mar. 27, 1924. 7 p. (H. rp. 389, 68th Cong. 1st sess.) * Paper, 5c.

—— Transportation of interstate shipments from wagons, automobiles, trucks, etc., hearing on H. R. 4168 [to amend act to punish unlawful breaking of seals of railroad cars containing interstate or foreign shipments, unlawful entering of such cars, stealing of freight and express packages or baggage or articles in process of transportation in interstate shipment, and felonious asportation of such freight or express packages or baggage or articles therefrom into another district of United States, and felonious possession or reception of same], Feb. 20, 1924. 1924. ii+27 p. (Serial 12.) * Paper, 5c.

Marshals. Granting pension to deputy marshals of district court for western district of Arkansas, hearings on H. R. 767 and H. R. 4456, Feb. 25 and Mar. 19, 1924. 1924. ii+20 p. (Serial 20.) * Paper, 5c.

National Society of Sons of American Revolution. To amend act to incorporate National Society of Sons of American Revolution, report to accompany H. R. 7399; submitted by Mr. Graham of Pennsylvania. Mar. 26, 1924. 1 p. (H. rp. 379, 68th Cong. 1st sess.) * Paper, 5c.

Prohibition. To provide punishment by fine and imprisonment for violations of national prohibition act, as amended, hearing on H. R. 728, Mar. 11, 1924. 1924. ii+25 p. (Serial 19.) * Paper, 5c.

Seal and seal fisheries. Unlawful seizure of vessels in Bering Sea, report to accompany S. 1192 [to confer jurisdiction upon district court, northern district of California, to adjudicate claims of American citizens who suffered damages or loss resulting from seizure, detention, sale, or interference by United States of vessels charged with unlawful sealing in Bering Sea during years 1886–96]; submitted by Mr. Graham of Pennsylvania. Mar. 1, 1924. 4 p. (H. rp. 253, 68th Cong. 1st sess.) * Paper, 5c.

Alaska. Protection of fisheries of Alaska, report to accompany H. R. 8143; submitted by Mr. White of Maine. Mar. 24, 1924. 3 p. (H. rp. 357, 68th Cong. 1st sess.) * Paper, 5c.

Ships. Admission of foreign-built ships to American registry, hearings on H. R. 3216 [to amend sec. 4132, Revised statutes, and to repeal act for admission of foreign-built ships to American registry for foreign trade], Feb. 28 and Mar. 4, 1924. 1924. ii+36 p. * Paper, 5c.

Steamboat Inspection Service. To abolish inspection districts of Apalachicola, Fla., and Burlington, Vt., Steamboat-Inspection Service, report to accompany S. 1724 [to amend sec. 4414, Revised statutes, as amended, to abolish inspection districts of Apalachicola, Fla., and Burlington, Vt., Steamboat Inspection Service]; submitted by Mr. Greene of Massachusetts. Mar. 22, 1924. 1 p. (H. rp. 347, 68th Cong. 1st sess.) * Paper, 5c.

Army. To amend in certain particulars national defense act, report to accompany S. 2169; submitted by Mr. Wainwright. Mar. 28. 1924. 9 p. (H. rp. 397, 68th Cong. 1st sess.) [Corrected print.] * Paper, 5c.

Capron, Albert J. Albert J. Capron, report to accompany H. R. 3030 [to allow and credit accounts of Albert J. Capron, formerly captain, Quartermaster Corps, Army, sum of $84.52, disallowed by comptroller general]; submitted by Mr. Hill of Alabama. Mar. 6, 1924. 2 p. (H. rp. 263, 68th Cong. 1st sess.) * Paper, 5c.

Howard, Mrs. Warren V. Widow of Warren V. Howard, report to accompany H. R. 3453 [for relief of widow of Warren V. Howard]; submitted by Mr. Wurzbach. Mar. 6, 1924. 2 p. (H. rp. 265, 68th Cong. 1st sess.) * Paper, 5c.

La Bare, J. W. J. W. La Bare, report to accompany H. R. 1359 [for relief of J. W. La Bare]; submitted by Mr. Wurzbach. Mar. 18, 1924. 2 p. (H. rp. 318, 68th Cong. 1st sess.) * Paper, 5c.

Leavenworth, Fort. Transfer to jurisdiction of Department of Justice portion of Fort Leavenworth reservation in Missouri, report to accompany H. R. 6207; submitted by Mr. McKenzie. Mar. 26, 1924. 2 p. (H. rp. 376, 68th Cong. 1st sess.) * Paper, 5c.

McAtee, John H. John H. McAtee, report to accompany H. R. 2319 [for relief of John H. McAtee]; submitted by Mr. McSwain. Mar. 25, 1924. 4 p. (H. rp. 362, 68th Cong. 1st sess.) * Paper, 5c.

Mothers. To authorize mothers of deceased World War veterans buried in Europe to visit the graves, hearings, Feb. 19, 1924. 1924. ii+26 p. * Paper, 5c.

Nelson, William H. William H. Nelson, report to accompany H. R. 6972 [for relief of William H. Nelson]; submitted by Mr. Reece. Mar. 5, 1924. 3 p. (H. rp. 261, 68th Cong. 1st sess.) * Paper, 5c.

New Orleans, La. To lease New Orleans quartermaster depot no. 2 to New Orleans Association of Commerce, report to accompany H. J. Res. 171 [to lease New Orleans quartermaster depot numbered 2 to New Orleans Association of Commerce]; submitted by Mr. Quin. Mar. 6. 1924. 2 p. (H. rp. 262, 68th Cong. 1st sess.) * Paper, 5c.

Pay, Army. To amend pay readjustment act, hearings on H. R. 4820 [to amend act to readjust pay and allowances of commissioned and enlisted personnel of Army. Navy, Marine Corps, Coast Guard, Coast and Geodetic Survey, and Public Health Service], Feb. 7 and 14, 1924. 1924. ii+28 p. * Paper, 5c.

Robert E. L. Michie, Camp. Reconveying camp site of Camp Robert E. L. Michie, report to accompany H. R. 7805 [reconveying to Elizabeth Moore camp site of Camp Robert E. L. Michie]; submitted by Mr. Wurzbach, Mar. 21, 1924. 1 p. (H. rp. 339, 68th Cong. 1st sess.) * Paper, 5c.

Rock Island Arsenal. Sale of surplus electric power at Rock Island Arsenal, Ill., report to accompany H. R. 5477; submitted by Mr. Hull of Iowa. Mar. 28, 1924. 6 p. (H. rp. 393, 68th Cong. 1st sess.) * Paper, 5c.

Snelling, Fort. Railway across Fort Snelling military reservation, Minn., report to accompany H. R. 5274 [to authorize Chicago, Milwaukee and St. Paul Railway Company to construct line of railroad across Fort Snelling military reservation, Minn.]; submitted by Mr. Hull of Iowa. Mar. 12, 1924. 2 p. (H. rp. 285, 68th Cong. 1st sess.) * Paper, 5c.

Southern Pacific Railroad. Right of way over Government levee at Yuma, Ariz., report to accompany H. R. 58 [to grant right of way over Government levee at Yuma, Ariz., to Southern Pacific Railroad Company]; submitted by Mr. Garrett of Texas. Mar. 10, 1924. 2 p. (H. rp. 281, 68th Cong. 1st sess.) * Paper, 5c.

United Confederate Veterans. Loan of tents, etc., to United Confederate Veterans, report to accompany H. J. Res. 163 [authorizing Secretary of War to loan tents, cots, chairs, and so forth, to executive committee of United Confederate Veterans for use at 34th annual reunion to be held at Memphis. Tenn., June, 1924]; submitted by Mr. Fisher. Mar. 25. 1924. 1 p. (H. rp. 359, 68th Cong. 1st sess.) * Paper, 5c.

MINES AND MINING COMMITTEE

Mining claims. To suspend annual assessment work on certain mining claims for 3 years, report to accompany H. J. Res. 142 [to suspend requirements of annual assessment work on mining claims, located and held on discovery of carnotite or other radium-bearing ore, for period of 3 years]; submitted by Mr. Brumm. Mar. 18, 1924. 1 p. (H. rp. 316, 68th Cong. 1st sess.) * Paper, 5c.

NAVAL AFFAIRS COMMITTEE

Calendar. Legislative calendar, 68th Congress, 1923–24; no. 2, Mar. 12, 1924. 1924. 32 p. 4° ‡

Navy-yards. Naval paper no. 250, 1923, extract from hearings on H. R. 10967, to relieve unemployment among civilian workers of Government, to remove financial incentives to war, to stabilize production in Federal industrial plants, to promote economical and efficient operation of these plants, and for other purposes; statement of N. P. Alifas, Feb. 14, 1923. 1924. 16 p. [The hearings in no. 250, from which this is an extract, were held. Nov. 28, 1922–Feb. 16, 1923, before the subcommittee on yards and docks.] * Paper, 5c.

PENSIONS COMMITTEE

Pensions and increase of pensions for certain soldiers and sailors of Regular Army and Navy, etc., report to accompany H. R. 7783 [substituted for H. R. 984 and other bills]; submitted by Mr. Knutson. Mar. 10, 1924. 136 p. (H. rp. 279, 68th Cong. 1st sess.) * Paper, 15c.

POST OFFICE AND POST ROADS COMMITTEE

Post-offices. Appointment of superintendent of delivery and assistant superintendents in certain offices of 1st class, report to accompany H. R. 579; submitted by Mr. Sproul of Illinois. Mar. 15, 1924. 1 p. (H. rp. 311, 68th Cong. 1st sess.) * Paper, 5c.

PRINTING COMMITTEE

Hughes, Charles E. Compiling and printing oration delivered by Charles Evans Hughes in memory of late President Harding, report to accompany S. Con. Res. 5; submitted by Mr. Kiess. Mar. 15, 1924. 1 p. (H. rp. 310. 68th Cong. 1st sess.) * Paper, 5c.

PUBLIC BUILDINGS AND GROUNDS COMMITTEE

National Botanic Garden. Conservatory and other buildings, and additional land, Botanic Garden, report to accompany S. 211 [for acquisition of property in District of Columbia for Botanic Garden and for building thereon of conservatory and other necessary buildings]; submitted by Mr. Langley. Mar. 12, 1924. 2 p. (H. rp. 286, 68th Cong. 1st sess.) * Paper, 5c.

Cordova Bay Harbor Improvement and Town Site Company. Change of condition of grant of Cordova Bay town site, report to accompany H. R. 2811 [to amend sec. 7 of act authorizing sale of lands at head of Cordova (or Orca) Bay, Alaska, relative to building of dock required under provisions of act]; submitted by Mr. Vaile. Mar. 22, 1924. 3 p. (H. rp. 349, 68th Cong. 1st sess.) * Paper, 5c.

Custer County, Mont. Granting Custer County, Mont., land for use as fairground, report to accompany H. R. 3756; submitted by Mr. Leavitt. Mar. 25, 1924. 2 p. (H. rp. 360, 68th Cong. 1st sess.) * Paper, 5c.

Flomaton, Ala. To quiet titles to land in Flomaton, Ala., report to accompany H. R. 4437; submitted by Mr. Abernethy. Mar. 21, 1924. 2 p. (H. rp. 340, 68th Cong. 1st sess.) * Paper, 5c.

Fort Berthold Reservation. Extension of time for payment of purchase money due on Government land, Fort Berthold Indian Reservation, N. Dak., report to accompany H. R. 4494; submitted by Mr. Winter. Mar. 5, 1924. 3 p. (H. rp. 259, 68th Cong. 1st sess.) * Paper, 5c.

Homestead. Adjustment for relief of homestead entrymen in Montana, to allow them patent to lands necessary to give them total acreage their original entries were believed to contain, report to accompany H. R. 3511 [to extend relief to claimants in township 16 north, ranges 32 and 33 east, Montana meridian, Montana]; submitted by Mr. Leavitt. Mar. 21, 1924. 2 p. (H. rp. 336, 68th Cong. 1st sess.) * Paper, 5c.

Keogh, Fort. Transfer of Fort Keogh military reservation, Mont., to Department of Agriculture, report to accompany H. R. 4840 [authorizing Secretary of Interior to transfer jurisdiction over portion of Fort Keogh military reservation, Mont., to Department of Agriculture for experiments in stock raising and growing of forage crops in connection therewith]; submitted by Mr. Leavitt. Mar. 11, 1924. 5 p. (H. rp. 284, 68th Cong. 1st sess.) *Paper, 5c.

Miles City, Mont. Conveyance of land to Miles City, Mont., for park purposes, report to accompany H. R. 4319; submitted by Mr. Leavitt. Mar. 25, 1924. 2 p. (H. rp. 361, 68th Cong. 1st sess.) *Paper, 5c.

National parks. Construction and improvement of roads, trails, and bridges in national parks, report to accompany H. R. 3682 [authorizing construction, reconstruction, and improvement of roads and trails, inclusive of necessary bridges, in national parks and monuments under jurisdiction of Department of Interior]; submitted by Mr. Sinnott. Mar. 5, 1924. 6 p. (H. rp. 258, 68th Cong. 1st sess.) *Paper, 5c.

—— Construction of roads, etc., in national parks and monuments, hearings on H. R. 3682, authorizing construction, reconstruction, and improvement of roads and trails, inclusive of necessary bridges, in national parks and monuments under jurisdiction of Department of Interior, Feb. 7–14, 1924. 1924. iii+136 p. il. *Paper, 15c.

Polk County, Fla. Authorizing Secretary of Interior to adjust certain disputes in Florida, report to accompany H. R. 5204 [to authorize Secretary of Interior to adjust disputes or claims by settlers, entrymen, selectors, grantees, and patentees of United States against United States and between each other, arising from incomplete or faulty surveys in township 28 south, ranges 26 and 27 east, Tallahassee meridian, Polk County, Fla.]; submitted by Mr. Vinson of Kentucky. Mar. 21, 1924. 2 p. (H. rp. 341, 68th Cong. 1st sess.) *Paper, 5c.

Rocky Mountain National Park. Transfer of certain lands from Rocky Mountain National Park to Colorado National Forest, report to accompany H. R. 2713; submitted by Mr. Vaile. Mar. 19, 1924. 3 p. (H. rp. 324, 68th Cong. 1st sess.) *Paper, 5c.

—— Transferring lands from Rocky Mountain National Park to Colorado National Forest, Colo., hearings on H. R. 2713, Mar. 18, 1924. 1924. iii+20 p. *Paper, 5c.

Shreveport, La. Granting lands to Shreveport, La., for reservoir purposes, report to accompany H. R. 5573; submitted by Mr. Vinson of Kentucky. Mar. 21, 1924. 2 p. (H. rp. 342, 68th Cong. 1st sess.) *Paper, 5c.

Silverton, Colo.   Purchase of public land for park purposes by Silverton, Colo., report to accompany H. R. 3927 [granting public lands to Silverton, Colo., for public park purposes]; submitted by Mr. Vaile. Mar. 25, 1924. 2 p. (H. rp. 364, 68th Cong. 1st sess.)   *Paper, 5c.

RULES COMMITTEE

Germany.   Consideration of House joint resolution 180, report to accompany H. Res. 232 [for consideration of joint resolution (H. J. Res. 180) for relief of distressed and starving women and children of Germany]; submitted by Mr. Bixler. Mar. 21, 1924. 1 p. (H. rp. 345, 68th Cong. 1st sess.) *Paper, 5c.

Government securities.   Appointment of special committee to investigate certain matters relating to Government bonds and other securities, report to accompany H. Res. 231 [for special committee to investigate preparation, distribution, sale, payment, retirement, surrender, cancellation, and destruction of Government bonds and other securities]; submitted by Mr. Bixler. Mar. 21. 1924. 1 p. (H. rp. 344, 68th Cong. 1st sess.) *Paper, 5c.

Immigration.   Consideration of H. R. 7995, report to accompany H. Res. 236 [for consideration of H. R. 7995, to limit immigration]; submitted by Mr. Snell. Mar. 27, 1924. 1 p. (H. rp. 331, 68th Cong. 1st sess.) *Paper, 5c.

Muscle Shoals.   Consideration of H. R. 518, report to accompany H. Res. 169 [for immediate consideration of H. R. 518, to authorize and direct Secretary of War, for national defense in time of war and for production of fertilizers and other useful products in time of peace, to sell to Henry Ford, or corporation to be incorporated by him. nitrate plant numbered 1, at Sheffield, Ala., nitrate plant numbered 2, at Muscle Shoals, Ala., Waco quarry, near Russellville, Ala., steam power plant to be located and constructed at or near lock and dam numbered 17 on Black Warrior River, Ala., with right of way and transmission line to nitrate plant numbered 2, Muscle Shoals, Ala., and to lease to Henry Ford, or corporation to be incorporated by him, dam numbered 2 and dam numbered 3 (as designated in House document 1262, 64th Congress, 1st session), including power stations when constructed as provided herein]; submitted by Mr. Snell. Mar. 1, 1924. 1 p. (H. rp. 254, 68th Cong. 1st sess.) *Paper, 5c.

WAR CLAIMS COMMITTEE

Barrett, John H.   John H. Barrett and Ada H. Barrett, report to accompany H. R. 912 [for relief of John H. Barrett and Ada H. Barrett]; submitted by Mr. Winter. Mar. 13, 1924. 4 p. (H. rp. 290, 68th Cong. 1st sess.) * Paper, 5c.

Carson, C. C.   C. C. Carson, report to accompany H. R. 2126 [for relief of C. C. Carson]; submitted by Mr. Simmons. Mar. 24, 1924. 3 p. (H. rp. 353, 68th Cong. 1st sess.) * Paper, 5c.

Grissinger, Elwood.   Elwood Grissinger, report to accompany S. 1861 [authorizing Court of Claims to hear and determine claim of Elwood Grissinger]; submitted by Mr. Williams of Michigan. Mar. 21, 1924. 7 p. (H. rp. 343, 68th Cong. 1st sess.) * Paper, 5c.

Jessop. J.   J. Jessop & sons. report to accompany H. R. 2335 [for relief of J. Jessop and sons]; submitted by Mr. Roach. Mar. 14, 1924. 3 p. (H. rp. 304, 68th Cong. 1st sess.) * Paper, 5c.

Mullen. William D., Company.   William D. Mullen Co., report to accompany S. 129 [for relief of William D. Mullen Company]; submitted by Mr. Roach. Mar. 8, 1924. 2 p. (H. rp. 276, 68th Cong. 1st sess.) * Paper, 5c.

Rhode Island.   Claim of Rhode Island for unpaid balance of expenditures during War with Spain, report to accompany H. R. 913; submitted by Mr. Winter. Mar. 13, 1924. 2 p. (H. rp. 289, 68th Cong. 1st sess.) * Paper, 5c.

Tobin. George T., & Son.   George T. Tobin & Son, report to accompany S. 130 [for relief of George T. Tobin and Son]; submitted by Mr. Roach. Mar. 14. 1924. 2 p. (H. rp. 305, 68th Cong. 1st sess.) * Paper, 5c.

WAYS AND MEANS COMMITTEE

Income tax.   Amend revenue act of 1921, report to accompany H. R. 6901 [to amend sec. 252 of revenue act of 1921 in respect of credits and refunds]; submitted by Mr. Green of Iowa. Mar. 4. 1924. 3 p. (H. rp. 257, 68th Cong. 1st sess.) * Paper, 5c.

Jewelry tax, extract from hearings; statement of Edward H. Hufnagel, Jan. 15, 1924. 1924. [1]+9 p. * Paper, 5c.

Soldiers. Soldiers' adjusted compensation, 1924, hearings. Mar. 3-5, 1924. 1924. iv+189 p. * Paper, 15c.

—— Soldiers' adjusted compensation, report to accompany H. R. 7959 [to provide adjusted compensation for veterans of World War]; submitted by Mr. Green of Iowa. Mar. 17, 1924. 8 p. (H. rp. 313, 68th Cong. 1st sess.) [Includes minority views signed by Mr. Treadway, Mr. Tilson, Mr. Watson, and Mr. Mills.] * Paper, 5c.

WORLD WAR VETERANS' LEGISLATION COMMITTEE.

World War emergency officers retired list. World War veterans' legislation (officers who incurred physical disability), hearings on H. R. 6484, making eligible for retirement under certain conditions officers, and former officers of World War, other than officers of Regular Army, who incurred physical disability in line of duty while in service of United States, during World War, Mar. 11, 1924. 1924. iii+74 p. * Paper, 5c.

World War veterans' legislation, hearings on proposed legislation as recommended by director of Veterans' Bureau and American Legion, Disabled American Veterans, and Veterans of Foreign Wars. 1924. iii+172 p. * Paper, 15c.

REORGANIZATION JOINT COMMITTEE

Public Works Department. Reorganization of Executive Departments [hearing] Jan. 28. 1924 [on proposed Department of Public Works]. [1924.] p. 573-618. * Paper, 5c.

SENATE

Appropriations. Appropriation to maintain automobile for the Vice President, supplemental estimate of appropriation for legislative branch of Government, fiscal year 1925, said estimate is for driving, maintenance, and operation of automobile for the Vice President, which automobile is now used by president pro tempore. Mar. 8, 1924. 2 p. (H. doc. 213, 68th Cong. 1st sess.) * Paper, 5c.

—— Contingent expenses, Senate, supplemental estimate of appropriation required for legislative establishment, fiscal year 1924. Mar. 14, calendar day Mar. 15, 1924. 2 p. (S. doc. 65, 68th Cong. 1st sess.) * Paper, 5c.

Calendar of business, Senate, 68th Congress, 1st session, Mar. 1-31, 1924; no. 41-71. [1924.] Each 20 p. or 24 p. large 8°. [Daily, when Senate is in session. The legislative day of Feb. 29 extended through the calendar day Mar. 1. Two calendars numbered 53 and 54 were issued for Mar. 10, 1924.] ‡

Chase, Clarence C. Senate resolution 195, regarding Clarence C. Chase, message transmitting copy of Senate resolution (S. Res. 195) relating to Clarence C. Chase, collector of customs at port of El Paso, Tex., together with certain testimony adduced before Senate Committee on Public Lands and Surveys. Mar. 25, 1924. 2 p. (H. doc. 230, 68th Cong. 1st sess.) [Text of resolution only.] * Paper, 5c.

Income tax. Proposed tax plans, comparison of Mellon, Garner, and Longworth tax plans with present law, married persons without dependents on basis of unearned income; submitted by Mr. Simmons. 1924. [1]+3 p. (S. doc. 62, 68th Cong. 1st sess.) * Paper, 5c.   24—26237

Judicial salaries, report of committee to consider salaries of Federal and State judges made to and adopted by American Bar Association, by Alexander B. Andrews, chairman of special committee; presented by Mr. Overman. 1924. [1]+6 p. (S. doc. 53, 68th Cong. 1st sess.) * Paper, 5c.   24—26302

Opium and narcotic laws: public no. 221, 60th Congress; public no. 46, 63d Congress; public no. 47. 63d Congress; public no. 223, 63d Congress; public no. 254 (extract revenue law), 65th Congress; public no. 227, 67th Congress; public resolution no. 96, 67th Congress. 1924. [27] p. * Paper, 5c.

AGRICULTURE AND FORESTRY COMMITTEE

Agricultural products. Agricultural export bill, report to accompany S. 2012 [declaring emergency in respect of certain agricultural commodities, to promote equality between agricultural commodities and other commodities, and for other purposes] ; submitted by Mr. McNary. Feb. 29, calendar day Mar. 1, 1924. 7 p. (S. rp. 193 [pt. 1], 68th Cong. 1st sess.) *Paper, 5c.

—— Agricultural export bill, views of minority to accompany S. 2012 [declaring emergency in respect of certain agricultural commodities, to promote equality between agricultural commodities and other commodities, and for other purposes] ; submitted by Mr. Norris. Mar. 3, calendar day Mar. 5, 1924. 6 p. (S. rp. 193, pt. 2, 68th Cong. 1st sess.) [The minority report recommends the enactment of S. 1642, for purchase and sale of farm products, instead of S. 2012.] *Paper, 5c.

Agriculture Department. Authorize arrests by employees of Department of Agriculture, report to accompany S. 2150 [to authorize arrests by officers and employees of Department of Agriculture in certain cases and to amend sec. 62 of act to codify, revise, and amend penal laws of United States, relative to assaults on employees of Department of Agriculture] ; submitted by Mr. Norris. Mar. 14, calendar day Mar. 15, 1924. 2 p. (S. rp. 260, 68th Cong. 1st sess.) *Paper, 5c.

—— To empower certain employees of Department of Agriculture to administer oaths, report to accompany S. 2148 [to empower certain officers, agents, or employees of Department of Agriculture to administer and take oaths, affirmations, and affidavits in certain cases] ; submitted by Mr. Norris. Mar. 14, calendar day Mar. 15, 1924. 2 p. (S. rp. 258, 68th Cong. 1st sess.) *Paper, 5c.

—— To increase subsistence and per diem allowances of certain officers and employees of Department of Agriculture, report to accompany S. 2151 ; submitted by Mr. Norris. Mar. 14, calendar day Mar. 15, 1924. 2 p. (S. rp. 261, 68th Cong. 1st sess.) *Paper, 5c.

Calendar. Legislative calendar, 68th Congress, Mar. 12 and 25, 1924 ; no. 4 and 5. 1924. Each 19 p. 4° †

Cattle. Admission of tick-infested cattle from Mexico into Texas, report to accompany S. 2164 [to repeal that part of act making appropriations for Department of Agriculture, fiscal year 1912, relating to admission of tick-infested cattle from Mexico into Texas] ; submitted by Mr. Norris. Mar. 14, calendar day Mar. 15, 1924. 2 p. (S. rp. 262, 68th Cong. 1st sess.) *Paper, 5c.

Forest experiment station in southern pine region, report to accompany S. 824 ; submitted by Mr. Harrison. Mar. 19, 1924. 4 p. (S. rp. 283, 68th Cong. 1st sess.) *Paper, 5c.

Forest Service, report to accompany S. 2149 [to facilitate and simplify work of Forest Service, Department of Agriculture, and to promote reforestation] ; submitted by Mr. Norris. Mar. 14, calendar day Mar. 15, 1924. 2 p. (S. rp. 259, 68th Cong. 1st sess.) *Paper, 5c.

Forests and forestry. Experimental and demonstration forest in Florida, report to accompany S. 1667 [to authorize purchase of lands in Florida for experimental and demonstration forest for production of naval stores] ; submitted by Mr. Harrison. Mar. 19, 1924. 3 p. (S. rp. 284, 68th Cong. 1st sess.) *Paper, 5c.

Game. To amend sec. 84 of penal code of United States, report to accompany S. 2146 [to amend sec. 84 of penal code of United States, relating to trespasses on bird reservations, so as to make provisions applicable to wild animal refuges and to protect United States property on any such lands] ; submitted by Mr. Norris. Mar. 14, calendar day Mar. 15, 1924. 1 p. (S. rp. 256, 68th Cong. 1st sess.) *Paper, 5c.

Marketing of farm produce. Purchase and sale of farm products, hearings on S. 1642, for purchase and sale of farm products, and S. 2012, declaring emergency in respect of certain agricultural commodities, to promote equality between agricultural commodities and other commodities, and for other purposes, Jan. 30–Feb. 15, 1924. 1924. pt. 2, ii+377–720 p. *Paper, 35c.

Pitt River Power Co., report to accompany S. 2711 [for relief of Pitt River Power Company] ; submitted by Mr. Norris. Mar. 14, calendar day Mar. 15, 1924. 2 p. (S. rp. 264, 68th Cong. 1st sess.) *Paper, 5c.

Smith, Albert W. To allow credit in accounts of A. W. Smith, report to accompany S. 2316; submitted by Mr. Norris. Mar. 14, calendar day Mar. 15, 1924. 2 p. (S. rp. 263, 68th Cong. 1st sess.). * Paper, 5c.

Sugar. To adjust certain sugar transactions, report to accompany S. J. Res. 49 [authorizing the President to require Sugar Equalization Board (Incorporated) to adjust transaction relating to 3,500 tons of sugar imported from Argentine Republic]; submitted by Mr. McNary. Mar. 12, calendar day Mar. 13, 1924. 3 p. (S. rp. 246, 68th Cong. 1st sess.) * Paper, 5c.

Willow Creek ranger station, Mont., report to accompany S. 2147 [to complete construction of Willow Creek ranger station, Mont.] ; submitted by Mr. Norris. Mar. 14, calendar day Mar. 15, 1924. 1 p. (S. rp. 257, 68th Cong. 1st sess.) * Paper, 5c.

World's Poultry Congress. 3d World's Poultry Congress in United States in 1927, report to accompany S. J. Res. 98 [authorizing the President to extend invitation for holding of 3d World's Poultry Congress in United States in 1927, and to extend invitations to foreign Governments to participate in this congress]; submitted by Mr. Norris. Mar. 22, 1924. 1 p. (S. rp. 297, 68th Cong. 1st sess.) * Paper, 5c.

APPROPRIATIONS COMMITTEE

Appropriations. First deficiency appropriation bill, [fiscal year] 1924 [and prior fiscal years], hearings before subcommittee, on H. R. 7449. 1924. [2]+65+i p. * Paper, 5c.

—— First deficiency appropriation bill, [fiscal year] 1924 [and prior fiscal years], report to accompany H. R. 7449; submitted by Mr. Warren. Mar. 20, 1924. 3 p. (S. rp. 285, 68th Cong. 1st sess.) * Paper, 5c.

Charles Fort, S. C. Monument on site of Charles Fort, S. C., report to accompany S. 1530 [for marking with enduring monument site of Charles Fort, S. C.]; submitted by Mr. Warren. Mar. 21, 1924. 1 p. (S. rp. 291, 68th Cong. 1st sess.) * Paper, 5c.

CIVIL SERVICE COMMITTEE

Civil service pensions. Retirement of Federal employees, extracts from joint hearings before Committees on Civil Service, relative to amendments to act for retirement of employees in classified civil service; statement of N. P. Alifas, Jan. 21 and 22, 1924. 1924. ii+21 p. * Paper, 5c.

CLAIMS COMMITTEE

Andrews, Albert. Albert Andrews, report to accompany S. 1307 [for relief of Albert Andrews for loss of personal effects while serving with military forces of United States] ; submitted by Mr. Johnson of Minnesota. Mar. 10, 1924. 6 p. (S. rp. 226, 68th Cong. 1st sess.) * Paper, 5c.

Anode, barge. Owners of barge Anode, report to accompany S. 78 [for relief of Raritan Copper Works, owners of barge Anode]; submitted by Mr. Bruce. Mar. 3, calendar day Mar. 4, 1924. 3 p. (S. rp. 203, 68th Cong. 1st sess.) * Paper, 5c.

Archer, Samuel S. Samuel S. Archer, report to accompany S. 1643 [for relief of Samuel S. Archer] ; submitted by Mr. Brookhart. Mar. 3, 1924. 4 p. (S. rp. 197, 68th Cong. 1st sess.) * Paper. 5c.

Army. Claims for damages to and loss of private property incident to training, practice, operation, or maintenance of Army, report to accompany S. 2527; submitted by Mr. Capper. Mar. 10, 1924. 3 p. (S. rp. 233, 68th Cong. 1st sess.) * Paper, 5c.

Ceylon Maru, steamship. Owners of steamship Ceylon Maru, report to accompany S. 84 [for relief of Nippon Yusen Kabushiki Kaisha, owners of steamship Ceylon Maru] ; submitted by Mr. Bruce. Mar. 3, calendar day Mar. 4, 1924. 13 p. (S. rp. 205, 68th Cong. 1st sess.) * Paper, 5c.

Comanche, steamship. Owners of steamship Comanche, report to accompany S. 82 [for relief of Clyde Steamship Company, owners of steamship Comanche] ; submitted by Mr. Bruce. Mar. 3, calendar day Mar. 4, 1924. 2 p. (S. rp. 204, 68th Cong. 1st sess.) * Paper, 5c.

Edgar, Clinton G. Clinton G. Edgar, report to accompany S. 1929 [to refund to Clinton G. Edgar income tax erroneously and illegally collected]; submitted by Mr. Mayfield. Mar. 11, 1924. 2 p. (S. rp. 240, 68th Cong. 1st sess.) * Paper, 5c.

Erie Railroad Co., report to accompany S. 935 [for relief of Erie Railroad Company]; submitted by Mr. Stanfield. Mar. 10, 1924. 7 p. (S. rp. 219, 68th Cong. 1st sess.) * Paper, 5c.

Fitzgerald, James B. James B. Fitzgerald, report to accompany S. 608 [for relief of James B. Fitzgerald]; submitted by Mr. Capper. Mar. 10, 1924. 3 p. (S. rp. 234, 68th Cong. 1st sess.) * Paper, 5c.

Freund, Clotilda. Clotilda Freund. report to accompany S. 969 [for relief of Clotilda Freund]; submitted by Mr. Brookhart. Mar. 10, 1924. 3 p. (S. rp. 229. 68th Cong. 1st sess.) * Paper, 5c.

Fries, Charles S. Charles S. Fries, report to accompany S. 196 [for relief of Charles S. Fries]; submitted by Mr. Capper. Mar. 10, 1924. 6 p. (S. rp. 231, 68th Cong. 1st sess.). * Paper, 5c.

Gattis, John H. John H. Gattis, report to accompany S. 2481 [for relief of John H. Gattis]; submitted by Mr. Harreld. Mar. 10, 1924. 3 p. (S. rp. 218, 68th Cong. 1st sess.) * Paper, 5c.

Glover, Daniel S. Daniel S. Glover, report to accompany S. 788 [to extend benefits of employers' liability act of Sept. 7, 1916, to Daniel S. Glover]; submitted by Mr. Bruce. Mar. 3. calendar day Mar. 4, 1924. 2 p. (S. rp. 206, 68th Cong. 1st sess.) * Paper, 5c.

Grygla, Frank. Frank Grygla, report to accompany S. 362 [for relief of Frank Grygla]; submitted by Mr. Capper. Mar. 14, 1924. 2 p. (S. rp. 249, 68th Cong. 1st sess.) * Paper, 5c.

Gulf, Florida & Alabama Railway Co., report to accompany S. 828 [for relief of receiver of Gulf, Florida and Alabama Railway Company]; submitted by Mr. Capper. Mar. 10, 1924. 8 p. (S. rp. 232, 68th Cong. 1st sess.) * Paper, 5c.

Hall, John D. Mrs. John D. Hall, report to accompany S. 2187 [authorizing comptroller general to consider and settle claim of Mrs. John D. Hall, widow of Colonel John D. Hall, Army, retired, for personal property destroyed in earthquake at San Francisco, Calif.]; submitted by Mr. Harreld. Mar. 10, 1924. 6 p. (S. rp. 217, 68th Cong. 1st sess.) * Paper, 5c.

Hastings Brothers. G. T. and W. B. Hastings, report to accompany S. 763 [for relief of G. T. and W. B. Hastings. partners. trading as Hastings Brothers]; submitted by Mr. Capper. Mar. 14, 1924. 2 p. (S. rp. 250, 68th Cong. 1st sess.) * Paper, 5c.

Lexington, steamship. Owners of steamship Lexington. report to accompany S. 81 [for relief of Colonial Navigation Company, owners of steamship Lexington]; submitted by Mr. Capper. Mar. 14, 1924. 3 p. (S. rp. 248, 68th Cong. 1st sess.) * Paper, 5c.

Long Island Railroad. Long Island Railroad Co., report to accompany H. R. 1823 [for relief of Long Island Railroad Company]; submitted by Mr. Capper. Mar. 28, 1924. 2 p. (S. rp. 318, 68th Cong. 1st sess.) * Paper, 5c.

—— Long Island Railroad Co., report to accompany S. 80 [for relief of Long Island Railroad Company]; submitted by Mr. Capper. Mar. 24, 1924. 3 p. (S. rp. 300, 68th Cong. 1st sess.) * Paper, 5c.

Mansfield, George C., Company. Permission for George C. Mansfield Company to prosecute claim before Court of Claims. hearing before subcommittee on S. 2145, for relief of George C. Mansfield Co. and George D. Mansfield. Mar. 3, 1924. 1924. ii+34 p. * Paper, 5c.

Martin, Annie H. Annie H. Martin. report to accompany S. 1316 [for relief of Annie H. Martin]; submitted by Mr. Spencer. Mar. 10, 1924. 2 p. (S. rp. 236, 68th Cong. 1st sess.). * Paper, 5c.

Mortesen, William. William Mortesen, report to accompany S. 148 [for relief of William Mortesen]; submitted by Mr. Brookhart. Mar. 3. calendar day Mar. 5, 1924. 3 p. (S. rp. 207, 68th Cong. 1st sess.). * Paper, 5c.

Near East Relief (Inc.), report to accompany S. 87 [for relief of Near East Relief (Incorporated)]; submitted by Mr. Stephens. Mar. 6, 1924. 18 p. (S. rp. 208, 68th Cong. 1st sess.) [Includes hearing of Jan. 24. 1924.] * Paper, 5c.   24—26238

Officers, Army. Relief of certain officers in Army, report to accompany S. 1568 [for relief of Horace P. Hobbs, Charles B. Stone, Henry M. Bankhead, and Louis F. Garrard, jr., officers in Army]; submitted by Mr. Spencer. Mar. 10, 1924. 2 p. (S. rp. 237, 68th Cong. 1st sess.) * Paper, 5c.

Platt, J. B. J. B. Platt, report to accompany S. 1180 [for relief of J. B. Platt]; submitted by Mr. Bayard. Feb. 29, calendar day Mar. 1, 1924. 2 p. (S. rp. 194, 68th Cong. 1st sess.) * Paper, 5c.

Pond, Ezra S. Ezra S. Pond, report to accompany S. 1941 [for relief of Ezra S. Pond]; submitted by Mr. Stanfield. Mar. 10, 1924. 4 p. (S. rp. 221, 68th. Cong. 1st sess.) * Paper, 5c.

Proud, Mrs. Florence. Florence Proud, report to accompany S. 1017 [for relief of Florence Proud]; submitted by Mr. Brookhart. Mar. 14, 1924. 5 p. (S. rp. 253, 68th Cong. 1st sess.) * Paper, 5c.

Rio Grande. Relief of sufferers in New Mexico from flood due to overflow of Rio Grande and its tributaries, report to accompany S. 349; submitted by Mr. Bayard. Mar. 6, calendar day Mar. 7, 1924. 5 p. (S. rp. 210, 68th Cong. 1st sess.) * Paper, 5c.

San Diego Consolidated Gas & Electric Co., report to accompany S. 1930 [for relief of San Diego Consolidated Gas and Electric Company]; submitted by Mr. Stanfield. Mar. 10, 1924. 3 p. (S. rp. 220, 68th Cong. 1st sess.) * Paper, 5c.

Strecker, Charles B. Charles B. Strecker, report to accompany S. 47 [to permit correction of general account of Charles B. Strecker, former assistant treasurer United States at Boston, Mass.]; submitted by Mr. Capper. Mar. 10, 1924. 5 p. (S. rp. 230, 68th Cong. 1st sess.) * Paper, 5c.

Weaver, Samuel S. Samuel S. Weaver, report to accompany S. 1573 [for relief of Samuel S. Weaver]; submitted by Mr. Johnson of Minnesota. Mar. 10, 1924. 4 p. (S. rp. 227, 68th Cong. 1st sess.) * Paper, 5c.

COMMERCE COMMITTEE.

Automobiles. Providing and adjusting penalties for violation of navigation laws [relative to transportation of automobiles on vessels]. report to accompany S. 2399; submitted by Mr. Jones of Washington for Mr. Edge. Mar. 14, 1924. 2 p. (S. rp. 252, 68th Cong. 1st sess.) * Paper, 5c.

Byram River. To construct dam across Byram River, report to accompany H. R. 6943 [granting consent of Congress to Port Chester, N. Y., and town of Greenwich, Conn., or either of them, to construct dam across Byram River]; submitted by Mr. Jones of Washington. Mar. 20, 1924. 2 p. (S. rp. 289, 68th Cong. 1st sess.) * Paper, 5c.

Calumet River. Bridge across Calumet River at Chicago, Ill., report to accompany H. R. 6925 [granting consent of Congress to Chicago to construct bridge across Calumet River at or near 130th street in Chicago, county of Cook, Ill.]; submitted by Mr. Ladd. Mar. 10, 1924. 2 p. (S. rp. 225, 68th Cong. 1st sess.) * Paper, 5c.

Coast Guard. Temporary increase of Coast Guard for law enforcement, report to accompany H. R. 6815; submitted by Mr. Jones of Washington. Mar. 21, 1924. 2 p. (S. rp. 293, 68th Cong. 1st sess.) * Paper, 5c.

Detroit River. Bridge across Detroit River, Mich., report to accompany S. 2825 [to extend time of American Transit Company for commencing and completing construction of bridge across Detroit River within or near Detroit, Mich.]; submitted by Mr. Ladd. Mar. 24, calendar day Mar. 26, 1924. 1 p. (S. rp. 305, 68th Cong. 1st sess.) * Paper, 5c.

Dixie Power Company. To amend permit issued to Dixie Power Co., report to accompany S. 2686 [to authorize Federal Power Commission to amend permit numbered 1, project numbered 1, issued to Dixie Power Company, by extending time of permit]; submitted by Mr. Fletcher. Mar. 21, 1924. 2 p. (S. rp. 290, 68th Cong. 1st sess.) * Paper, 5c.

Fox River. Bridge across Fox River, Ill., report to accompany S. 2597 [to authorize construction of bridge across Fox River in St. Charles Township, Kane County, Ill., by Aurora, Elgin, and Fox River Electric Company]; submitted by Mr. Ladd. Mar. 20, 1924. 1 p. (S. rp. 288, 68th Cong. 1st sess.) * Paper, 5c.

• *Kankakee River.* Bridge across Kankakee River between Illinois and Indiana, report to accompany H. R. 5737 [granting consent of Congress to county of Kankakee, Ill., and counties of Lake and Newton. Ind., to construct bridge across Kankakee River at or near State line between section 19, township 31 north, range 15 east of 3d principal meridian, in county of Kankakee, Ill., and section 1, township 31 north, range 10 west of 2d principal meridian, in counties of Lake and Newton, Ind.]; submitted by Mr. Ladd. Mar. 10, 1924, 2 p. (S. rp. 223, 68th Cong. 1st sess.)   * Paper, 5c.

Mahoning River. Bridge across Mahoning River, Ohio, report to accompany H. R. 6623 [granting consent of Congress to Pittsburgh, Youngstown & Ashtabula Railway Company to construct bridge across Mahoning River, Ohio, at or near Haselton]; submitted by Mr. Willis. Mar. 24, 1924: 2 p. (S. rp. 301, 68th Cong. 1st sess.)   * Paper, 5c.

Minnesota River. Bridge across Minnesota River, Minn., report to accompany H. R. 6724 [granting consent of Congress to counties of Sibley and Scott, Minn., to construct bridge across Minnesota River at or near Blakely]; submitted by Mr. Ladd. Mar. 24. calendar day Mar. 25, 1924. 1 p. (S. rp. 303, 68th Cong. 1st sess.)   * Paper, 5c.

—— Bridge across Minnesota River, Minn., report to accompany S. 2512 [granting consent of Congress to counties of Sibley and Scott, Minn., to construct bridge across Minnesota River at or near Blakely]; submitted by Mr. Ladd. Mar. 20, 1924. 1 p. (S. rp. 287, 68th Cong. 1st sess.)   * Paper, 5c.

Mississippi River. Bridge across Mississippi River between Minneapolis and St. Paul, Minn., report to accompany H. R. 6420 [to extend time for construction of bridge across Mississippi River in section 17, township 28 north, range 23 west of 4th principal meridian in Minnesota by Minneapolis and St. Paul, Minn., or either of them]; submitted by Mr. Ladd. Mar. 10, 1924. 2 p. (S. rp. 224, 68th Cong. 1st sess.)   * Paper, 5c.

—— Bridge across Mississippi River in Minneapolis. report to accompany S. 2488 [to authorize Minneapolis, Minn., to construct bridge across Mississippi River in said city]; submitted by Mr. Ladd. Mar. 12, 1924. 2 p. (S. rp. 242, 68th Cong. 1st sess.).   * Paper, 5c.

—— Bridge across Mississippi River near and above New Orleans, La., report to accompany S. 2656 [granting consent of Congress to construction of bridge across Mississippi River near and above New Orleans. La., by said city through its Public Belt Railroad Commission]; submitted by Mr. Ransdell. Mar. 22, 1024. 2 p. (S. rp. 296, 68th Cong. 1st sess.)   * Paper; 5c.

Pearl River. Bridge across Pearl River, Miss., report to accompany H. R. 5633 [granting consent of Congress to board of supervisors of Hinds County, Miss., to construct bridge across Pearl River, Miss., at or near Jackson]; submitted by Mr. Ladd. Mar. 10, 1924. 2 p. (S. rp. 222, 68th Cong. 1st sess.)   * Paper, 5c.

Pribilof Islands. To create Pribilof Islands fund, report to accompany S. 2122 [to create Pribilof Islands fund and to provide for disposition of surplus revenue from Pribilof Islands. Alaska]; submitted by Mr. Jones of Washington. Mar. 3, calendar day Mar. 4, 1924. 4 p. (S. rp. 200, 68th Cong. 1st sess.)   * Paper, 5c.

Savannah River. Bridge across Savannah River at or near Augusta, Ga., report to accompany S. 2538 [to revive and reenact act authorizing counties of Aiken, S. C., and Richmond, Ga., to construct bridge across Savannah River at or near Augusta, Ga.]; submitted by Mr. Ladd. Mar. 12, 1924. 2 p. (S. rp. 243, 68th Cong. 1st sess.)   * Paper, 5c.

Upper Mississippi River Wild Life and Fish Refuge, hearing on S. 1558, to establish Upper Mississippi River Wild Life and Fish Refuge, Feb. 15, 1924. ii+27 p.   * Paper, 5c.

Water pollution. Oil pollution of navigable waters, hearing before subcommittee on S. 2414, to prevent pollution by oil of navigable rivers of United States, Mar. 17, 1924. 1924. ii+16 p.   * Paper, 5c.

DISTRICT OF COLUMBIA COMMITTEE

Automobiles. Gasoline tax in District of Columbia, hearings before subcommittee on H. R. 655, for tax on motor-vehicle fuels sold within District of Columbia, and for other purposes, Feb. 23–Mar. 8, 1924. . 1924. ii+76 p.   * Paper, 10c.

Automobiles—Continued. Tax on motor-vehicle fuel sold in District of Columbia, report to accompany H. R. 655; submitted by Mr. Ball. Mar. 14, calendar day Mar. 15, 1924. 4 p. (S. rp. 267, 68th Cong. 1st sess.) . * Paper, 5c.

Flag. To create commission to procure design for flag for District of Columbia, report to accompany S. 2430; submitted by Mr. Ball. Mar. 12, calendar day Mar. 13, 1924. 1 p. (S. rp. 244, 68th Cong. 1st sess.) *:Paper, 5c. ··—··

Parks. Comprehensive development of park and playground system of National Capital, report to accompany S. 112; submitted by Mr. Ball. Mar. 12, calendar day Mar. 13, 1924. 7 p. (S. rp. 245, 68th Cong. 1st sess.) * Paper, 5c.

Teachers. Salaries of teachers, school officers, and other employees of Board of Education of District of Columbia, hearings before subcommittee on H. R. 6576 and H. R. 6721, to amend act to fix and regulate salaries of teachers, school officers, and other employees of Board of Education of District of Columbia, as amended, and for other purposes, Mar. 1 and 3, 1924. 1924. ii+81 p. * Paper, 10c.

FINANCE COMMITTEE

Boyce, William H., sr. For relief of William Henry Boyce, sr., report to accompany S. 2510; submitted by Mr. Simmons. Mar. 3, calendar day Mar. 4, 1924. 1 p. (S. rp. 201, 68th Cong. 1st sess.) *,Paper, 5c.

Calendar. Legislative calendar, 68th Congress, Mar. 6–31, 1924; no. 10–14. 1924. various paging, 4° ‡

Half-dollar. Coinage of 50-cent pieces in commemoration of work of carving in Stone Mountain, near Atlanta, Ga., monument to valor of soldiers of the South, etc., report to accompany S. 684 [to authorize coinage of 50-cent pieces in commemoration of commencement on June 18, 1923, of work of carving on Stone Mountain, Ga., monument to valor of soldiers of the South,] which was the inspiration of their sons and daughters and grandsons and granddaughters in Spanish-American and World Wars, and in memory of Warren G. Harding, President of United States, in whose administration the work was begun]; submitted by Mr. Simmons. Feb. 29, calendar day Mar. 1, 1924. 1 p. (S. rp. 196, 68th Cong. 1st sess.) * Paper, 5c.

FOREIGN RELATIONS COMMITTEE

Blattmann & Co., report to accompany S. 555 [for relief of Blattmann and Company]; submitted by Mr. Pepper. Mar. 14, calendar day Mar. 18, 1924. 2 p. (S. rp. 282, 68th Cong. 1st sess.) * Paper, 5c.

Calendar, 68th Congress, 1st session, Mar. 19, 1924; no. 5. 1924. 15 p. 4° ‡

International Institute of Agriculture. Appropriations providing for quotas of Hawaii, the Philippines, Porto Rico, and Virgin Islands in support of International Institute of Agriculture at Rome, and for expense of representation thereat, report to accompany S. J. Res. 96 [making appropriations for payment of expenses of delegates to represent United States at general assembly of International Institute of Agriculture to be held at Rome in May, 1924, and for payment of quotas of Hawaii, the Philippines, Porto Rico, and Virgin Islands for support of Institute, calendar year 1924]; submitted by Mr. Lodge. Mar. 14, 1924. 4 p. (S. rp. 247, 68th Cong. 1st sess.) * Paper, 5c.

Turner, George. For relief of George Turner, report to accompany S. 2839; submitted by Mr. Willis. Mar. 28, 1924. 2 p. (S. rp. 312, 68th Cong. 1st sess.) * Paper, 5c.

Vera Cruz, Mexico. Authorizing appropriation for payment of claims arising out of occupation of Vera Cruz, Mexico, by American forces in 1914, report to accompany S. 2506; submitted by Mr. Lodge. Mar. 14, calendar day Mar. 18, 1924. 10 p. (S. rp. 281, 68th Cong. 1st sess.) * Paper, 5c.

INDIAN AFFAIRS COMMITTEE

Andes, Lake. Authorizing commissioner of Indian affairs to acquire necessary rights of way across private lands, by purchase or condemnation proceedings, needed in constructing spillway and drainage ditch to lower and maintain level of Lake Andes, S. Dak., report to accompany H. R. 4161; submitted by Mr. Harreld. Mar. 14, calendar day Mar. 15, 1924. 2 p. (S. rp. 266, 68th Cong. 1st sess.) * Paper, 5c.

Chippewa Indians. For enrollment and allotment of members of Lac du Flambeau band of Lake Superior Chippewas in Wisconsin, and for other purposes, report to accompany H. R. 3684; submitted by Mr. Harreld. Mar. 14, calendar day Mar. 17, 1924. 3 p. (S. rp. 277, 68th Cong. 1st sess.) *Paper, 5c.

—— To provide for payment of claims of Chippewa Indians of Minnesota for back annuities, report to accompany H. R. 2876; submitted by Mr. Harreld. Mar. 14, calendar day Mar. 17, 1924. 2 p. (S. rp. 270, 68th Cong. 1st sess.) *Paper, 5c.

Clallam Indians. Appropriating money to purchase lands for Clallam tribe of Indians in State of Washington, report to accompany S. 1707; submitted by Mr. Harreld. Mar. 27, 1924. 3 p. (S. rp. 308, 68th Cong. 1st sess.) [The committee recommends amendment of the bill so as to authorize appropria- tion for per capita payments to Clallam Indians, but the title of the bill was not amended.] *Paper, 5c.

Colville Reservation. To authorize sale of lands allotted to Indians under Moses agreement of July 7, 1883, report to accompany H. R. 2878; submitted by Mr. Harreld. Mar. 14, calendar day Mar. 17, 1924. 2 p. (S. rp. 275, 68th Cong. 1st sess.) *Paper, 5c.

Dakota Indians. Authorizing Secretary of Interior to consider, ascertain, ad- just, and determine claims of members of Sioux Nation of Indians for dam- ages occasioned by destruction of their horses, report to accompany S. 1174; submitted by Mr. Harreld. Mar. 14, calendar day Mar. 15, 1924. 2 p. (S. rp. 265, 68th Cong. 1st sess.). *Paper, 5c.

Fort Apache Reservation. Authorizing appropriation for construction of road within Fort Apache Indian Reservation, Ariz. [and for agency building], report to accompany H. R. 4117; submitted by Mr. Harreld. Mar. 14, calen- dar day Mar. 17, 1924. 3 p. (S. rp. 278, 68th Cong. 1st sess.) *Paper, 5c.

Indians. To authorize sale of lands and plants not longer needed for Indian administrative or allotment purposes, report to accompany H. R. 4803; sub- mitted by Mr. Harreld. Mar. 14, calendar day Mar. 17, 1924. 2 p. (S. rp. 279, 68th Cong. 1st sess.) *Paper, 5c.

Lac Court Oreille Reservation. To validate allotments of land made to Indians on Lac Courte Oreille Indian Reservation in Wisconsin, report to accompany H. R. 2883; submitted by Mr. Harreld. Mar. 14, calendar day Mar. 17, 1924. 2 p. (S. rp. 276, 68th Cong. 1st sess.) *Paper, 5c.

Lapwai Indian Sanatorium. To provide for girls' dormitory at Fort Lapwai Sanatorium, Lapwai, Idaho, report to accompany H. R. 192; submitted by Mr. Harreld. Mar. 14, calendar day Mar. 17, 1924. 2 p. (S. rp. 271, 68th Cong. 1st sess.) †Paper, 5c.

McCanna, P. F. For relief of Nelly McCanna, residuary legatee and devisee under last will and testament of P. F. McCanna, report to accompany S. 368; submitted by Mr. Harreld. Mar. 27, 1924. 2 p. (S. rp. 307, 68th Cong. 1st sess.) *Paper, 5c.

Navajo Indians. To authorize deposit of certain funds in Treasury to credit of Navajo tribe of Indians and to make same available for appropriation for benefit of said Indians, report to accompany H. R. 472; submitted by Mr. Harreld. Mar. 14, calendar day Mar. 17, 1924. 2 p. (S. rp. 272, 68th Cong. 1st sess.) *Paper, 5c.

Navajo Reservation. Authorizing annual appropriations for maintenance of that portion of Gallup-Durango highway across Navajo Indian Reservation and providing reimbursement therefor, report to accompany S. 2159; sub- mitted by Mr. Harreld. Mar. 17 [14], calendar day Mar. 17, 1924. 2 p. (S. rp. 269, 68th Cong. 1st sess.) *Paper, 5c.

Nisqualli Reservation. For relief of dispossessed allotted Indians of Nisqually Reservation, Wash., report to accompany S. 1704; submitted by Mr. Harreld. Mar. 31, 1924. 2 p. (S. rp. 329, 68th Cong. 1st sess.) *Paper, 5c.

Osage Indians. Amending act for division of lands and funds of Osage In- dians in Oklahoma, report to accompany H. R. 6483 [amending act for divi- sion of lands and funds of Osage Indians in Oklahoma, and acts amenda- tory thereof and supplemental thereto, relative to lands, money, or mineral interests inherited by persons not Osage Indians by blood]; submitted by Mr. Harreld. Mar. 27, 1924. 2 p. (S. rp. 310, 68th Cong. 1st sess.) *Paper, 5c.

Rapid City Indian School. To authorize Secretary of Interior to sell certain lands not longer needed for Rapid City Indian School [S. Dak.], report to accompany H. R. 2812; submitted by Mr. Harreld. Mar. 14, calendar day Mar. 17, 1924. 2 p. (S. rp. 273, 68th Cong. 1st sess.) *Paper, 5c.

Seminole Indians. Claims which Seminole Indians may have against United States, report to accompany H. R. 5799 [conferring jurisdiction upon Court of Claims to hear, examine, adjudicate, and enter judgment in any claims which Seminole Indians may have against United States]; submitted by Mr. Harreld. Mar. 27, 1924. 2 p. (S. rp. 309, 68th Cong. 1st sess.) *Paper, 5c.

Sia Indians. Providing for reservation of certain lands in New Mexico for Indians of Zia Pueblo, report to accompany H. R. 2877; submitted by Mr. Harreld. Mar. 14, calendar day Mar. 17, 1924. 2 p. (S. rp. 274, 68th Cong. 1st sess.) *Paper, 5c.

Yuma Reservation. To authorize allotment of certain lands within Fort Yuma Indian Reservation, Calif., and for other purposes, report to accompany H. R. 4804; submitted by Mr. Harreld. Mar. 14, calendar day Mar. 17, 1924. 2 p. (S. rp. 280, 68th Cong. 1st sess.) *Paper, 5c.

INTERSTATE COMMERCE COMMITTEE

Agriculture. Declaring agriculture to be basic industry of the country [and directing Interstate Commerce Commission to lower rates on agricultural products], report to accompany S. J. Res. 107; submitted by Mr. Smith. Mar. 28, 1924. 1 p. (S. rp. 313, 68th Cong. 1st sess.) *Paper, 5c.

Freight rates. Long and short haul charges, hearings on S. 2327, to amend sec. 4 of interstate commerce act, Feb. 18 [–Mar. 6], 1924. 1924. 3 pts. [vii]+887 p. il. 2 pl. map. * Paper, pt. 1, 25c.; * pt. 2, 40c.; * pt. 3, 50c.

—— To amend paragraph (3), sec. 16, of interstate commerce act [so as to extend time of filing claims for overcharge], report to accompany S 2704; submitted by Mr. Smith. Mar. 20, 1924. 2 p. (S. rp. 286, 68th Cong. 1st sess.) * Paper, 5c.

—— To amend sec. 4 of interstate commerce act (long and short haul rule), report to accompany S. 2327; submitted by Mr. Gooding. Mar. 24, calendar day Mar. 25, 1924. 6 p. (S. rp. 302, 68th Cong. 1st sess.) [Corrected print.] * Paper, 5c.

Radio communication. Respecting use of the ether, report to accompany S. 2930 [reaffirming use of the ether for radio communication or otherwise to be inalienable possession of the people of United States and their Government, and for other purposes]; submitted by Mr. Smith. Mar. 27, 1924. 2 p. (S. rp. 311, 68th Cong. 1st sess.) * Paper, 5c.

Railroad-cars. Use of wooden cars on railroads, report to accompany S. 1499 [to promote safety of passengers and employees upon railroads by prohibiting use of wooden cars under certain circumstances]; submitted by Mr. Smith. Mar. 3, 1924. 1 p. (S. rp. 198, 68th Cong. 1st sess.) * Paper, 5c.

Railroads. Investigation of railroad propaganda, report to accompany S. Res. 124 [directing Interstate Commerce Commission to secure information relative to amount of money expended for purpose of creating public interest favorable to railroad sentiment]; submitted by Mr. Smith. Mar. 3, 1924. 2 p. (S. rp. 199, 68th Cong. 1st sess.) * Paper, 5c.

Wool. Truth in fabric and misbranding bills, hearings before subcommittee on S. 1024 and S. 1188, to prevent sale and transportation in interstate commerce of misbranded woolen fabrics and falsely described articles, Feb. 28–Mar. 12, 1924. 1924. iii+171 p. * Paper, 15c.

IRRIGATION AND RECLAMATION COMMITTEE

Reclamation of land. Development of irrigation projects, hearing on development of irrigation projects and deferring of payments of reclamation charges, Mar. 11, 1924. 1924. ii+20 p. * Paper, 5c.

JUDICIARY COMMITTEE

Calendar. Legislative calendar, 68th Congress, Mar. 3–29, 1924; no. 8–11. 1924. Each 30 p. or 31 p. 4° ‡

Constitution of United States. Amendment to Constitution of United States relative to adoption of amendments thereto, report to accompany S. J. Res. 4; submitted by Mr. Walsh of Montana. Mar. 3, calendar day Mar. 4, 1924. 1 p. (S. rp. 202, 68th Cong. 1st sess.) * Paper, 5c.

MILITARY AFFAIRS COMMITTEE

Army. Sundry matters affecting military establishment, report to accompany S. 1974; submitted by Mr. George. Feb. 29, calendar day Mar. 1, 1924. 2 p. (S. rp. 195, 68th Cong. 1st sess.) * Paper, 5c.

Cemeteries, National. Approaches to national cemeteries and national military parks, report to accompany S. 2745 [to authorize Secretary of War to convey to States in which located Government owned or controlled approach roads to national cemeteries and national military parks]; submitted by Mr. Wadsworth. Mar. 6, calendar day Mar. 7, 1924. 1 p. (S. rp. 211, 68th Cong. 1st sess.) * Paper, 5c.

Collins, Henry P. Henry P. Collins, alias Patrick Collins, report to accompany S. 245 [for relief of Henry P. Collins, alias Patrick Collins]; submitted by Mr. Bruce. Mar. 10, 1924. 1 p. (S. rp. 235, 68th Cong. 1st sess.) * Paper, 5c.

Kruschke, Herman O. For relief of Herman O. Kruschke, report to accompany S. 1790; submitted by Mr. Ralston. Mar. 11, 1924. 2 p. (S. rp. 238, 68th Cong. 1st sess.) * Paper, 5c.

McClary, Fort. Transfer of land to Kittery, Me., report to accompany S. 2634 [authorizing Secretary of War to convey to Maine land in Kittery, Me., formerly part of abandoned military reservation of Fort McClary]; submitted by Mr. Fletcher. Mar. 28, 1924. 1 p. (S. rp. 320, 68th Cong. 1st sess.) * Paper, 5c.

Moran, James. James Moran, report to accompany S. 589 [for relief of James Moran]; submitted by Mr. Cameron. Mar. 6, calendar day Mar. 7, 1924. 2 p. (S. rp. 209, 68th Cong. 1st sess.) * Paper, 5c.

New Orleans, La. Lease of storage warehouse at New Orleans, La., to New Orleans Association of Commerce, report to accompany S. J. Res. 72 [to lease to New Orleans Association of Commerce New Orleans quartermaster intermediate depot unit numbered 2]; submitted by Mr. Wadsworth. Mar. 6, calendar day Mar. 7, 1924. 2 p. (S. rp. 213, 68th Cong. 1st sess.) * Paper, 5c.

Officers, Army. validating payments to officers of Army and enlisted men of National Guard, report to accompany S. 2299 [to validate payment of commutation of quarters, heat, and light under act of Apr. 16, 1918, and of rental and subsistence allowances under act of June 10, 1922, and for other purposes]; submitted by Mr. Wadsworth. Mar. 14, 1924. 3 p. (S. rp. 255, 68th Cong. 1st sess.) * Paper, 5c.

Pay, Army. Recovery of allotments, report to accompany S. 2746 [regulating recovery of allotments and allowances heretofore paid to designated beneficiaries]; submitted by Mr. Wadsworth. Mar. 6, calendar day Mar. 7, 1924. 2 p. (S. rp. 212, 68th Cong. 1st sess.) * Paper, 5c.

Quinn, Leo P. Leo P. Quinn, report to accompany S. 2764 [authorizing President to order Leo P. Quinn before retiring board for rehearing of his case and upon findings of such board either confirm his discharge or place him on retired list with rank and pay held by him at time of his discharge]; submitted by Mr. Fletcher. Mar. 10, 1924. 3 p. (S. rp. 215, 68th Cong. 1st sess.) * Paper, 5c.

Retired list, Army. validating payments to retired enlisted men, report to accompany S. 2450 [to amend sec. 2 of legislative, executive, and judicial appropriation act, approved July 31, 1894, relative to holding of Government office by retired enlisted men of Army, Navy, Marine Corps, or Coast Guard]; submitted by Mr. Wadsworth. Mar. 14, 1924. 2 p. (S. rp. 254, 68th Cong. 1st sess.) * Paper, 5c.

Russian Railway Service Corps, report to accompany S. 1557 [to give military status and discharges to members of Russian Railway Service Corps organized by War Department under authority of President of United States for service during war with Germany]; submitted by Mr. Brookhart. Mar. 10, 1924. 2 p. (S. rp. 228, 68th Cong. 1st sess.) * Paper, 5c.

Snelling, Fort. Construction of railroad across Fort Snelling military reservation, report to accompany S. 1982 [granting consent of Congress to construction by Chicago, Milwaukee and St. Paul Railway Company of line of railroad across northeasterly portion of Fort Snelling military reservation, Minn.]; submitted by Mr. Ralston. Mar. 11, 1924. 2 p. (S. rp. 239, 68th Cong. 1st sess.) . * Paper, 5c.

Sussex County, Del. Conveying of lands to Delaware, report to accompany S. 2431 [conveying to Delaware land in county of Sussex, in that State]; submitted by Mr. Reed of Pennsylvania. Mar. 10, 1924. 2 p. (S. rp. 214, 68th Cong. 1st sess.) * Paper, 5c.

Sweeney, Michael. Michael Sweeney, report to accompany S. 1011 [for relief of Michael Sweeney]; submitted by Mr. Sheppard. Mar. 10, 1924. 2 p. (S. rp. 216, 68th Cong. 1st sess.) * Paper, 5c.

Thornton, Orin. Orion [Orin] Thornton, report to accompany S. 606 [for relief of Orin Thornton]; submitted by Mr. Walsh of Massachusetts. Mar. 14, 1924. 2 p. (S. rp. 251, 68th Cong. 1st sess.) * Paper, 5c.

Yarbrough, Mrs. Rosa L. Rosa L. Yarbrough, report to accompany S. 1427 [for relief of Rosa L. Yarbrough]; submitted by Mr. Walsh of Massachusetts. Mar. 28, 1924. 2 p. (S. rp. 319, 68th Cong. 1st sess.) * Paper, 5c.

MINES AND MINING COMMITTEE

Claims. To authorize payment of claims under provisions of so-called war minerals relief act, report to accompany S. 2797; submitted by Mr. Oddie. Mar. 18, 1924. 8 p. (S. rp. 292, 68th Cong. 1st sess.) * Paper, 5c.

NAVAL AFFAIRS COMMITTEE

Books. To authorize transfer of surplus books from Navy Department to Interior Department, report to accompany S. 350; submitted by Mr. Hale. Mar. 11, 1924. 2 p. (S. rp. 241, 68th Cong. 1st sess.) * Paper, 5c.

Calendar. Legislative calendar, 68th Congress, 1st session, Mar. 4, 1924; no. 4. 1924. 8 p. large 8° ‡

Naval omnibus bill, hearings before subcommittee on S. 1808, providing for sundry matters affecting naval establishment, Jan. 16–22, 1924. 1924. iii+ 144 p. * Paper, 15c.

Tozier, Emelus S. Emelus S. Tozier, report to accompany S. 1809 [for relief of Emelus S. Tozier]; submitted by Mr. Hale. Mar. 28, 1924. 2 p. (S. rp. 317, 68th Cong. 1st sess.) * Paper, 5c.

PUBLIC LANDS AND SURVEYS COMMITTEE

Calendar. Legislative calendar, 68th Congress, Mar. 10 and 31, 1924; no. 5 and 6. [1924.] Each 31 p. 4° ‡

Custer County, Mont. Granting to county of Custer, Mont., land in said county for use as fair ground, report to accompany S. 306; submitted by Mr. Walsh of Montana. Mar. 28, 1924. 1 p. (S. rp. 314, 68th Cong. 1st sess.) * Paper, 5c.

Dakota Indians. Authorizing Secretary of Interior to acquire land and erect monument on site of battle with Sioux Indians in which commands of Major Reno and Major Benteen were engaged, report to accompany S. 310; submitted by Mr. Walsh of Montana. Mar. 28, 1924. 1 p. (S. rp. 315, 68th Cong. 1st sess.) * Paper, 5c.

Duchesne, Fort. Granting to Utah Fort Duchesne reservation for its use as branch agricultural college, report to accompany S. 667; submitted by Mr. Smoot. Mar. 21, 1924. 2 p. (S. rp. 295, 68th Cong. 1st sess.) * Paper, 5c.

Keogh, Fort. To transfer jurisdiction over portion of Fort Keogh military reservation, Mont., from Department of Interior to Department of Agriculture for experiments in stock raising and growing of forage crops in connection therewith; report to accompany S. 2690; submitted by Mr. Walsh of Montana. Mar. 28, 1924. 2 p. (S. rp. 316, 68th Cong. 1st sess.) * Paper, 5c.

Naval petroleum reserves. Leases upon naval oil reserves, hearings pursuant to S. Res. 147, Feb. 25 [–Mar. 11], 1924. 1924. pts. 9, 10, [vii]+2337–2665 p. * Paper, pt. 9, 15c.; * pt. 10, 20c.

Pensacola, Fla. Authorizing Secretary of Interior to determine and confirm by patent in nature of deed of quitclaim title to lots in Pensacola, Fla., report to accompany S. 807; submitted by Mr. Ladd. Mar. 24, calendar day Mar. 26, 1924. 1 p. (S. rp. 306, 68th Cong. 1st sess.) * Paper, 5c.

Rainier, Mount. Change of name of Mount Rainier to Mount Tacoma, report to accompany S. J. Res. 64; submitted by Mr. Dill. Mar. 14, calendar day Mar. 15, 1924. 2 p. (S. rp. 268, 68th Cong. 1st sess.) * Paper, 5c.

Sinclair, Harry F. Leases upon naval oil reserves, Harry F. Sinclair, special report; submitted by Mr. Ladd. Mar. 24, 1924. 2 pts. in 1, 9 p. (S. rp. 299 [2 pts.], 68th Cong. 1st sess.) * Paper, 5c.

Taos County, N. Mex. Providing for acquirement by United States of privately owned lands within Taos County, N. Mex., known as Santa Barbara grant, by exchanging therefor timber, or lands and timber, within exterior boundaries of any national forest situated within New Mexico, report to accompany S. 1762; submitted by Mr. Bursum. Mar. 22, 1924. 3 p. (S. rp. 298, 68th Cong. 1st sess.) * Paper, 5c.

Utah National Park. To establish Utah National Park in Utah, report to accompany S. 668; submitted by Mr. Smoot. Mar. 21, 1924. 3 p. (S. rp. 294, 68th Cong. 1st sess.) * Paper, 5c.

REFORESTATION SELECT COMMITTEE

Reforestation, hearings, 67th Congress, 4th session, pursuant to S. Res. 398, to investigate problems relating to reforestation, Nov. 19 [-23], 1923. 1923-24. pts. 7, 8, [iv]+1253-1447 p. il. * Paper, each pt. 10c.

TERRITORIES AND INSULAR POSSESSIONS COMMITTEE

Porto Rico. Act to amend act to provide civil government for Porto Rico. etc., report to accompany S. 2573 [to amend and reenact sec. 20, 22, and 50 of act to provide civil government for Porto Rico, relating to salaries]; submitted by Mr. Willis. Mar. 24, calendar day Mar. 26, 1924. 2 p. (S. rp. 304, 68th Cong. 1st sess.) [Corrected print.] * Paper, 5c.

USELESS EXECUTIVE PAPERS, JOINT SELECT COMMITTEE ON DISPOSITION OF

Civil Service Commission. Disposition of useless executive papers in Civil Service Commission, report; submitted by Mr. Moores of Indiana. Mar. 14, 1924. 4 p. (H. rp. 307, 68th Cong. 1st sess.) * Paper, 5c.

Commerce Department. Disposition of useless executive papers in Department of Commerce, report; submitted by Mr. Moores of Indiana. Mar. 14, 1924. 10 p. (H. rp. 306, 68th Cong. 1st sess.) * Paper, 5c.

Executive Departments. Disposition of useless executive papers, report on disposition of useless papers during 67th Congress [3d and 4th sessions]; submitted by Mr. Moores of Indiana. Mar. 19, 1924. 1 p. (H. rp. 325, 68th Cong. 1st sess.) * Paper, 5c.

COURT OF CLAIMS

Calumet & Chicago Canal & Dock Co. v. United States; evidence for plaintiff. [1924.] no. B-111, p. 5-25. ‡

Cleveland, Cincinnati, Chicago and St. Louis Railway. Cleveland, Cincinnati, Chicago & St. Louis Railway *v.* United States; evidence for plaintiff [and] defendant. [1924.] no. B-145, p. 55-97. ‡

—— Cleveland, Cincinnati, Chicago and St. Louis Railway Co. *v.* United States; evidence for plaintiff. [1924.] no. B-419, p. 51-61. ‡

Crook, H. E., Company, Incorporated. H. E. Crook Company, Inc., *v.* United States; findings of fact [conclusion of law, and memorandum] decided Mar. 3, 1924. [1924.] no. B-195, 2 p. ‡

Dorris Motor Car Company v. United States; evidence for plaintiff. [1924.] no. B-389, p. 19-42. ‡

Galveston, Harrisburg & San Antonio Railway Company v. United States; defendant's evidence. [1924.] no. B-186, p. 31-46. ‡

Huron Navigation Corporation v. United States; evidence for plaintiff. [1924.] no. 34755, p. 19–148. ‡

Missouri-Kansas-Texas Railroad Company of Texas v. United States; report of General Accounting Office. [1924.] no. C–527, p. 9–12. ‡

National Fruit Products Company v. United States; evidence for defendant. [1924.] no. B–78, p. 37–47. ‡

New York Central Railroad. New York Central Railroad Company *v.* United States; defendant's evidence. [1924.] no. B–151, p. 115–124. ‡

—— Same; evidence for plaintiff. [1924.] no. B–151, p. 75–113. ‡

Provost Brothers & Co. George D. Provost and Cornelius W. Provost, copartners composing firm of Provost Bros. & Co., *v.* United States; evidence for plaintiffs. [1924.] no. B–112, p. 9–47. ‡

Ray Consolidated Copper Company v. United States; amended agreed statement of facts. [1924.] no. B–160, p. 23–32. ‡

Swift & Company v. United States; findings of fact [conclusion of law, and opinion of court], decided Mar. 17, 1924. [1924.] no. 4–A, 54 p. ‡

Wall Rope Works, Inc., v. United States; evidence for plaintiff [and] defendant. [1924.] no. B–448, p. 19–52. ‡

COURT OF CUSTOMS APPEALS

Bitters. No. 2364, United States *v.* L. Gandolfi & Co., transcript of record on appeal from Board of General Appraisers. [1924.] cover-title, i+6 p. ‡

Curling-stones. No. 2355, United States *v.* Kelley Hardware Co., transcript of record on appeal from Board of General Appraisers. [1924.] cover-title, i+12 p. ‡

Gelatin. No. 2367, United States *v.* E. Stegemann, jr., transcript of record on appeal from Board of General Appraisers. [1924.] cover-title, i+10 p. ‡

Meat. No. 2359, United States *v.* Sobrinos de Villamil, transcript of record on appeal from Board of General Appraisers. [1924.] cover-title, i+9 p. ‡

Toys. No. 2354, United States *v.* D. C. Andrews & Co., transcript of record on appeal from Board of General Appraisers. [1924.] cover-title, i+46 p. ‡

DISTRICT OF COLUMBIA

Court of Appeals. Calendar, Apr. term, 1924. [1924.] 63 leaves. [Some of these leaves are printed as pages.] ‡

—— Transcript of record, Jan. term, 1924, no. 4114, no. 27, special calendar, United States *vs.* Ward W. Griffith et al., appeal from Supreme Court of District of Columbia. [1924.] cover-title, i+29 p. ‡

—— Transcript of record, Apr. term, 1924, no. 4123, no. —, special calendar, Louis M. Croson *vs.* District of Columbia, in error to Police Court of District of Columbia. [1924.] cover-title, i+14 p. ‡

FEDERAL BOARD FOR VOCATIONAL EDUCATION

Home economics education, organization and administration [by Josephine T. Berry; revised by Anna E. Richardson]. Revised edition, Feb. 1924. 1924. v+54 p. (Bulletin 28; Home economics series 2.) * Paper, 10c. E 24—388

FEDERAL RESERVE BOARD

Banks and banking. Digest of rulings of Federal Reserve Board, 1914–23, with appendices containing text of Federal reserve act, regulations of Federal Reserve Board, and related matters; compiled in Office of its General Counsel. 1924. xiv+407 p. il. † Cloth, $2.00.   24—26260

Federal reserve bulletin, Mar. 1924; [v. 10, no. 3]. 1924. iv+147–242+ii p. il. map, 4° [Monthly.] † Paper, 20c. single copy, $2.00 a yr. 15—26318

NOTE.—The bulletin contains, in addition to the regular official announcements, the national review of business conditions, detailed analyses of business conditions, research studies, reviews of foreign banking, and complete statistics showing the condition of Federal reserve banks and member banks. It will be sent to all member banks without charge. Others desiring copies may obtain them from the Federal Reserve Board, Washington, D. C., at the prices stated above.

Federal reserve member banks. Abstract of condition reports of State bank and trust company members, and of all member banks of Federal reserve system, Dec. 31, 1923. Feb. 14, 1924. 12 p. f° (Report 23.) †

—— *Federal reserve inter-district collection system, changes in list of banks upon which items will be received by Federal reserve banks for collection and credit, Mar. 1, 1924. 12 p. 4° † : 16—26870

Prices in United States and abroad, 1919–23, Federal Reserve Board price indexes, international price comparisons, foreign exchange rates. 1924. v+63 p. il. 4° † 24—26261

FEDERAL TRADE COMMISSION

NOTE.—The bound volumes of the Federal Trade Commission decisions are sold by the superintendent of Documents, Washington, D. C. Separate opinions are sold on subscription, price $1.00 per volume; foreign subscription, $1.50; single copies, 5c. each.

Chicago Portrait Company. No. 3276. in circuit court of appeals for 7th circuit, Chicago Portrait Company *v.* Federal Trade Commission, original petition to review order of Federal Trade Commission; brief and argument for respondent. 1924. cover-title. 36 p. ‡

Douglas Fir Exploitation and Export Company, Incorporated. Before Federal Trade Commission, Federal Trade Commission *v.* Douglas Fir Exploitation & Export Company, Incorporated, and 107 others, docket 880; brief and argument of facts and law in support of complaint charging 108 respondents with conspiring to hinder and obstruct competition in manufacture, sale, and distribution of lumber in interstate and foreign commerce, all in violation of sec. 5 of act approved Sept. 26, 1914 (Federal Trade Commission act). 1924. cover-title, vii+360 p. +[7] folded leaves, il. 1 pl. ‡

Maynard Coal Co. v. Federal Trade Commission; Supreme Court of District of Columbia, Mar. 6, 1923. in equity 37659, opinion [of court]. [1924.] 4 p. ([Court decision] 2.) [From Federal Trade Commission decisions, v. 6.] * Paper, 5c.

Mennen Co. v. Federal Trade Commission; circuit court of appeals, 2d circuit, Mar. 13, 1923, no. 69 [opinion of court]. [1924.] 9 p. ([Court decision] 3.) [From Federal Trade Commission decisions, v. 6.] * Paper, 5c.

Pearsall, B. S., Butter Company. B. S. Pearsall Butter Co. *v.* Federal Trade Commission; circuit court of appeals, 7th circuit, July 19, 1923, no. 3190 [opinion of court]. [1924.] 4 p. ([Court decision] 7.) [From Federal Trade Commission decisions, v. 6.] * Paper, 5c.

Radio communication. Report of Federal Trade Commission on radio industry in response to House resolution 548, 67th Congress, 4th session, Dec. 1, 1923. 1924. vii+347 p. * Paper, 40c. 24—26262

Rules of practice before commission, adopted June 17, 1915, with amendments to Feb. 1, 1924. 1924. 11 p. * Paper, 5c. 24—26263

Southern Hardware Jobbers' Ass'n. et al. *v.* Federal Trade Commission; circuit court of appeals, 5th circuit, June 13, 1923, no. 3887 [opinion of court]. [1924.] 8 p. ([Court decision] 6.) [From Federal Trade Commission decisions, v. 6.] * Paper, 5c.

Thatcher Manufacturing Company. No. —. in circuit court of appeals for 3d circuit, Mar. term, 1924, Federal Trade Commission *v.* Thatcher Manufacturing Company; application for enforcement of order of Federal Trade Commission. 1924. cover-title, i+44 p. large 8° ‡

GEOGRAPHIC BOARD

Report. Index to 5th report [1890–1920], and supplement, 1920–23, of Geographic Board, arranged by countries, States, counties (excluding Europe, Hawaii, and Philippines). 1924. iii+111 p. [Prepared in cooperation with Geological Survey.] * Paper, 10c.

GOVERNMENT 'PRINTING OFFICE

Paper. Abstract of contracts approved by Joint Committee on Printing for
paper for public printing and binding for term of 6' months and 1 year, beginning Mar. 1, 1924; corrected Mar. 1, 1924. '[1924.] 40 p.' 4° †
—— Table showing substance number, relative weight, thickness, and burst-
ing 'strength of paper, 1924–25; [prepared in] Stores Division'. ' [1924.]
8· p. 4° ‡   24—26303

DOCUMENTS OFFICE

Agriculture Department., Farmers' bulletins, Department bulletins, circulars,
agriculture yearbooks, list of publications for sale by superintendent of
documents. Feb. 1924. [2]+59+[2] p. (Price list 16, 19th edition.) .†
                                                                 24—26264
Fishes, including publications relating to whales, shellfish, lobsters, sponges,
list of publications for sale by superintendent of documents. Jan. 1924.
[2]+18 p. (Price list 21, 10th edition.) †   24—26265
Monthly catalogue, United States public documents, no. 350; Feb. 1924. 1924.
p.' 413–500. * Paper, 5c. single copy, 50c. a yr.; foreign subscription, 75c.
                                                                  4—18088
Pacific States: California, Oregon, Washington, list of publications relating to
above States for sale by superintendent of documents. Feb. 1924. [2]+14 p.
(Price list 69, 4th edition.) †   24—26266
Radio communication. Important radio publications [for sale by superintendent of documents]. Revised Feb. 1924. [1924.] 1 p. 4° [Office correction.] †

INTERIOR DEPARTMENT

NOTE.—The decisions of the Department of the Interior in pension cases are issued in
slips and in signatures, and the decisions in land cases are issued in signatures, both
being published later in bound volumes. Subscribers may deposit $1.00 with the Super-
intendent of Documents and receive the contents of a volume of the decisions of either
kind in separate parts as they are issued; foreign subscription, $1.25. Prices for bound
volumes furnished upon application to the Superintendent of Documents, Washington,
D. C.

Chestatee Pyrites and Chemical Corporation. No. 4116, no. —, special calendar,
in Court of Appeals of District of Columbia, Jan. term, 1924, Hubert Work,
Secretary of Interior, *v.* United States ex rel. Chestatee Pyrites & Chemical
Corporation, appeal from Supreme Court of District of Columbia; brief and
argument for appellant. 1924. cover-title, i+26 p. ‡
Mason,, W. H. No. 4096, in Court of Appeals of District of Columbia, Jan.
term, 1924, Hubert Work, Secretary of Interior, *v.* W. H. Mason, appeal
from Supreme Court of District of Columbia; brief and argument for ap-
pellant. 1924. cover-title, i+26 p. ‡
Pensions. [Decisions of Department of Interior in appealed pension and
bounty land claims, v. 21, slips] 95, 98–100 pension. [1924.] various paging.
[For price, see note above under center head.]   12—29422
—— Same, [v. 21, slips] 65 and 66 retirement. [1924.] Each 3 p.

ARCHITECT OF CAPITOL

Capitol power plant and Capitol grounds, supplemental estimate of appropriation for legislative establishment providing $166,000 for Capitol power plant
and Capitol grounds. Mar. 3, 1924. 3 p. (H. doc. 212, 68th Cong. 1st sess.)
*Paper, 5c.
Senate Office Building. Maintenance, Senate Office Building, supplemental
estimate of appropriation required for legislative establishment, fiscal year
1924. Mar. 14, calendar day Mar. 15, 1924. 2 p. (S. doc. 66, 68th Cong.
1st sess.) *Paper, 5c.
—— Maintenance, Senate Office Building, 1925, supplemental estimate of
appropriation for legislative establishment for maintenance, Senate Office
Building, fiscal year 1925. Mar. 29, 1924. 2 p. (H. doc. 231, 68th Cong.
1st sess.) *Paper, 5c.

EDUCATION BUREAU

Alexandria, Va. Survey of schools of Alexandria, Va. 1924. iii+62 p. (Bulletin 56, 1923.) *Paper, 10c.   E 24—396

Country schools. Training courses in consolidation of schools and transportation of pupils; by J. F. Abel. Mar. 1924. 6 p. (Rural school leaflet 23.) *Paper, 5c.   E 24—391

Deaf. Schools for deaf, 1921–22; prepared in Division of Statistics. 1924. [1]+29 p. (Bulletin 52, 1923.) [Advance sheets from Biennial survey of education, 1920–22.] *Paper, 5c.   E 20—408

Educational cooperation. New order in educational cooperation; by Margaretta Wills Reeve. Feb. 1924. 7 p. (Home education circular 4.) [From School life, v. 9, no. 2, Oct. 1923.] *Paper, 5c.   E 24—390

Educational directory, 1924. 1924. iii+191 p. (Bulletin 1, 1924.) *Paper, 20c.   E 13—213

Educational tests; by Stephen S. Colvin. 1924. [1]+28 p. (Bulletin 57, 1923.) [Advance sheets from Biennial survey of education in United States, 1920–22.] *Paper, 5c.   E 24—393

Free textbooks for public-school pupils; by William R. Hood. 1924. [1]+14 p. (Bulletin 50, 1923.) *Paper, 5c.   E 24—395

High schools. Study of distinguished high-school pupils in Iowa [with bibliography on gifted children]; by Charles Deich and Elmer E. Jones. 1924. iii+58 p. (Bulletin 46, 1923.) *Paper, 10c.   E 24—394

Home economics. National conference of city supervisors of home economics called by Commissioner of Education John J. Tigert, Washington, D. C., Apr. 21–24, 1924, program. [1924.] [4] p.

Hygiene. Child health program for parent-teacher associations and women's clubs [with list of useful references]; by Lucy Wood Collier; revised by Harriet Wedgwood. 1924. iv+22 p. il. (Health education 5.) [Revised in cooperation with Child Health Organization of America (now American Child Health Association).] *Paper, 5c.   E 24—397

—— Continuing need for teachers of child health; by Dorothy Hutchinson and Harriet Wedgwood. 1924. [2]+18 p. il. (Health education 16.) [Includes lists of Education Bureau publications on health education.] *Paper, 5c.   E 24—389

Playgrounds. Municipal and school playgrounds and their management, introduction and summary; by J. F. Rogers. Jan. 1924. 22 p. (School health studies 6.) *Paper, 5c.   E 24—392

Publications available Feb. 1924. [1924.] 24 p. †   E 15—1070

Rhodes scholarships, regulations for United States, 1924. Feb. 1924. 4 p. 4° (Higher education circular 28.) *Paper, 5c.   E 19—579

School life, v. 9, no. 7; Mar. 1924. [1924.] p. 145–168, il. 4° [Monthly except July and August.] *Paper, 5c. single copy, 30c. a yr. (10 months); foreign subscription, 55c.   E 18—902

GEOLOGICAL SURVEY

NOTE.—The publications of the United States Geological Survey consist of Annual reports, Monographs, Professional papers, Bulletins, Water-supply papers, chapters and volumes of Mineral resources of the United States, folios of the Topographic atlas of the United States and topographic maps that bear descriptive text, and folios of the Geologic atlas of the United States and the World atlas, of, commercial geology. The Monographs, folios, and maps are sold. Other publications are generally free as long as the Survey's supply lasts. Copies are also sold by the Superintendent of Documents, Washington, D. C., at the prices indicated. For maps and folios address the Director of the Geological Survey, Washington, D. C. A discount of 40 per cent is allowed on any order for maps or folios that amounts to $5.00 or more at the retail price. This discount applies to an order for either maps or folios alone or for maps and folios together but is not allowed on a few folios that are sold at 5c. each on account of damage by fire. Orders for other publications that are for sale should be sent to the Superintendent of Documents, Washington, D. C. For topographic maps see next page.

Coal resources of Raton coal field, Colfax County, N. Mex.; by Willis T. Lee. 1924. vi+254 p. il. 18 pl. 2 p. of pl. 2 maps, 1 is in pocket. (Bulletin 752.) *Paper, 50c.   GS 24—39

Cobalt, molybdenum, nickel, tantalum, titanium, tungsten, radium, uranium, and vanadium in 1922; by Frank L. Hess. Mar. 14, 1924. [1]+557–583 p. [From Mineral resources, 1922, pt. 1.] †

Copper in 1922, general report; by H. A. C. Jenison. Feb. 29, 1924. iv+257–304 p. il. [From Mineral resources, 1922, pt. 1.] †

Feldspar in 1922; by Frank J. Katz. Mar. 6, 1924. ii+251–259 p. il. [From Mineral resources, 1922, pt. 2.] †

Geology. Geological literature on North America, 1785–1918; pt. 1, Bibliography; by John M. Nickles. 1923. ii+1167 p. (Bulletin 746.) * Paper, $1.25.
G S 24–38

—— Same. (H. doc. 26, 68th Cong. 1st sess.)

Gold. Gold, silver, copper, lead, and zinc in Arizona in 1922, mines report; by V. C. Heikes. Mar. 15, 1924. ii+489–518 p. [From Mineral resources, 1922, pt. 1.] †

—— Gold, silver, copper, lead, and zinc in California and Oregon in 1922, mines report; by James M. Hill. Mar. 10, 1924. ii+405–451 p. [From Mineral resources, 1922, pt. 1.] †

—— Gold, silver, copper, lead, and zinc in Colorado in 1922, mines report; by Charles W. Henderson. Mar. 20, 1924. ii+519–556 p. [From Mineral resources, 1922, pt. 1.] †

—— Gold, silver, copper, lead, and zinc in Montana in 1922, mines report; by C. N. Gerry. Mar. 12, 1924. ii+453–488 p. [From Mineral resources, 1922, pt. 1.] †

—— Gold, silver, copper, lead, and zinc in Utah in 1922, mines report; by V. C. Heikes. Mar. 8, 1924. ii+377–403 p. [From Mineral resources, 1922, pt. 1.] †

Mineral resources of United States, 1920: pt. 2, Nonmetals [title-page, contents, and index]. 1923. iv+499–529 p. †
4—18124

Publications. New publications, list 192; Mar. 1, 1924. [1924.] 2 p. [Monthly.] †

Maps

Arizona. State of Arizona. Scale 1 : 500,000. [Washington] Geological Survey, 1924. 51×42 in. †25c.

Topographic maps

NOTE.—The Geological Survey is making a topographic map of the United States. The individual maps of which it is composed are projected without reference to political divisions, and each map is designated by the name of some prominent town or natural feature in the area mapped. Three scales are ordinarily used, 1 : 62,500, 1 : 125,000, and 1 : 250,000. These correspond approximately to 1 mile, 2 miles, and 4 miles to 1 linear inch, covering, respectively, average areas of 230, 920, and 3,700 square miles. For some areas of particular importance special large-scale maps are published. The usual size, exclusive of the margin, is 17.5 inches in height by 11.5 to 16 inches in width, the width varying with the latitude. The sheets measure 20 by 16½ inches. A description of the topographic map is printed on the reverse of each sheet.
More than two-fifths of the area of the country, excluding Alaska, has been mapped, every State being represented. Connecticut, Delaware, the District of Columbia, Maryland, Massachusetts, New Jersey, Ohio, Rhode Island, and West Virginia are completely mapped. Maps of the regular size are sold by the Survey at 10c. each, but a discount of 40 per cent is allowed on any order which amounts to $5.00 or more at the retail price. The discount is allowed on an order for either maps or folios alone or for maps and folios together, but does not apply to a few folios that are sold at 5c. each on account of damage by fire.

California. California, Torrance quadrangle, lat. 33° 48'–33° 54', long. 118° 18'– 118° 26'. Scale 1 : 24,000, contour interval 5 ft. [Washington, Geological Survey] edition of 1924. 18.2×20.2 in. †10c.

—— California, Tumey Hills quadrangle, lat. 36° 32' 30''–36° 37' 30'', long. 120° 37' 30''–120° 45'. Scale 1 : 31,680, contour interval 5 and 25 ft. [Washington, Geological Survey] edition of 1924. 11.5×15.9 in. †10c.

Snake River. Plan and profile of Snake River, Lewiston, Idaho, to Huntington, Oreg. Scale 1 : 31,680, contour interval 25 ft., vertical scale 20 ft.=1 in. [Washington, Geological Survey] 1923. 17 sheets (A–Q) each 15×18 in. or 15×20.9 in. †10c. per sheet.

MINES BUREAU

Coal. Central district bituminous coals as water-gas generator fuel; by W. W. Odell and W. A. Dunkley. [1st edition.] [Jan.] 1924. v+92 p. il. (Bulletin 203.) [This bulletin represents work done under a cooperative agreement with the State Geological Survey Division of Illinois and the Engineering Experiment Station of the University of Illinois. Includes lists of Mines Bureau publications on gas producers and industrial gases.]
* Paper, 15c.
24—26267

Lubricating-oils. United States Government specification for lubricants and liquid fuels and methods for testing, Federal Specifications Board, Standard specification .2c, officially adopted by Federal Specifications Board. Feb. 3, 1922 [revised Mar. 18, 1924] for use of Departments and independent establishments of Government in purchase of materials covered by it. [1st edition.] [Feb.] 1924. vii+89 p. il. (Technical paper 323A.) [The latest date on which this specification shall become mandatory for all Departments and independent establishments of the Government is June 18, 1924.] * Paper, 15c.
                                                                              24—26269
Motion pictures. List of motion picture films and plan of, distribution, Feb. 1924: [prepared in] Pittsburgh Experiment. Station. , [1924.] [2]+12 p. narrow 12° †
                                                                              24—26304
Publications. New publications, list 98; Mar. 1924. [1924.] oblong 48° [This publication is issued in postal card form.] †.
Quarry accidents in United States, calendar year 1922; by William W, Adams. [1st edition.] [Dec. 1923, published] 1924. v+61 p. (Technical paper 353.) [Includes lists of Mines Bureau publications on statistics, of mine accidents.] * Paper, 10c.
                                                                              13—35364
Stone dusting or rock dusting to prevent coal-dust explosions, as practiced in Great Britain and France; by George S. Rice. [1st edition.], [Feb.] 1924. iv+57 p. (Bulletin 225.) [Includes lists of Mines Bureau publications on explosibility of coal dust and prevention of coal-dust explosions.] * Paper, 10c.
                                                                              24—26268

PATENT OFFICE

NOTE.—The Patent Office publishes Specifications and drawings of patents in single copies. These are not enumerated in this catalogue, but may be obtained for 10c. each at the Patent Office.
A variety of indexes, giving a complete view of the work of the Patent Office from 1790 to date, are published at prices ranging from 25c. to $10.00 per volume and may be obtained from the Superintendent of Documents, Washington, D. C. The Rules of practice and pamphlet Patent laws are furnished free of charge upon application to the Patent Office. The Patent Office issues coupon orders in packages of 20 at $2.00 per package, or in books containing 100 coupons at $10.00 per book. These coupons are good until used, but are only to be used for orders sent to the Patent Office. For schedule of office fees, address Chief Clerk, Patent Office, Washington, D. C.

Decisions. [Decisions in patent and trade-mark cases, etc.] Mar. 4, 1924. p. 1–8, large 8° [From Official gazette, v. 320, no. 1.] † Paper, 5c. single copy, $2.00 a yr.
                                                                              23—7315
—— Same. Mar. 11, 1924. p. 225–232, large 8°. [From Official gazette, v. 320, no. 2.]
—— Same. Mar. 18, 1924. p. 447–454, il. large 8°. [From Official gazette, v. 320, no. 3.]
—— Same. Mar. 25, 1924. p. 695–702, large 8° [From Official gazette, v. 320, no. 4.]
Malocsay, Frank. In Court of Appeals of District of Columbia, Jan. term, 1924, patent appeal no. 1619, *in re* Frank Malocsay, improvement in talking machine; brief for commissioner of patents. 1924. cover-title, 16 p. †
Official gazette. Official gazette, Mar. 4–25, 1924; v. 320, no. 1–4. 1924. cover-titles, 917+[clviii] p. il. large 8° [Weekly.] * Paper, 10c. single copy, $5.00 a yr. foreign subscription, $11.00.
                                                                              4—18256
NOTE.—Contains the patents, trade-marks, designs, and labels issued each week; also decisions of the commissioner of patents and of the United States courts in patent cases.

—— Same [title-page, contents, errata, etc., to] v. 319; Feb. 1924. 1924. [2] leaves, large 8° * Paper, 5c. single copy, included in price of Official gazette for subscribers.
—— Same, weekly index, with title, Alphabetical list of registrants of trade-marks [etc., Mar. 4, 1924]. [1924.] xl p. large 8° [From Official gazette, v. 320, no. 1.] † Paper, $1.00 a yr.
—— Same [Mar. 11, 1924]. [1924.] xxxviii p. large 8° [From Official gazette, v. 320, no. 2.]
—— Same [Mar. 18, 1924]. [1924.] xlii p. large 8° [From Official gazette. v. 320, no. 3.]
—— Same [Mar. 25, 1924]. [1924.] xxxviii p. large 8° [From Official gazette, v. 320, no. 4.]

Patents. Classification of patents issued Mar. 4–25, 1924. [1924.] Each 2 p. large 8° [Weekly. From Official gazette, v. 320, no. 1–4.] †

Trade-marks. Trade-marks [etc., from] Official gazette, Mar. 4, 1924. '[1924.] 9–60+i–xvii p. il. large 8° [From Official gazette, v. 320, no. 1.] † Paper, 5c. single copy, $2.50 a yr.

—— Same, Mar. 11, 1924. [1924.] 233–282+i–xvi p. il. large 8° [From Official gazette, v. 320, no. 2.]

—— Same, Mar. 18, 1924. [1924.] 455–508+i–xvii p. il. large 8° [From Official gazette, v. 320, no. 3.]

—— Same, Mar 25, 1924. [1924.] 703–752+i–xvi p. il. large 8° [From Official gazette, v. 320, no. 4.]

Tufford, John G. In Court of Appeals of District of Columbia, Jan. term, 1924, patent appeal no. 1655, *in re* John G. Tufford, heel lift; brief for commissioner of patents. 1924. cover-title, 16 p. il. ‡

RECLAMATION BUREAU

New reclamation era; v. 15, no. 3; Mar. 1924. [1924.] cover-title, p. 33–48, il. 4° [Monthly. Formerly Reclamation record. Text on p. 2–4 of cover.]
9—35252

NOTE.—The New reclamation era is a magazine for the farmers and the personnel of the service. Its aim is to assist the settlers in the proper use of water, to help them in overcoming their agricultural difficulties, to instruct them in diversifying and marketing their crops, to inspire the employees of the service and chronicle engineering problems and achievements, and to promote a wholehearted spirit of cooperation, so that reclamation shall attain the greatest heights of success. The Era is sent without direct charge to water users of the reclamation projects constructed and operated by the Government. Persons desiring to subscribe for the New reclamation era, other than water users, may secure it for the price of 75c. a year, payable in advance. Subscriptions should be sent to the Chief Clerk, Reclamation Bureau, Washington, D. C., and remittances in the form of postal money order or New York draft should be made payable to the Special Fiscal Agent, Reclamation Bureau. Postage stamps are not acceptable in payment of subscription.

Shoshone irrigation project, Frannie division, acceptance of conditions of suspension order no. 30, dated Feb. 7, 1924, agreement to pay past-due and future water charges, and application for temporary water service. [1924.] 1 p. 4° [Blank form.] †

INTERSTATE COMMERCE COMMISSION

NOTE.—The bound volumes of the decisions, usually known as Interstate Commerce Commission reports, are sold by the Superintendent of Documents, Washington, D. C., at various prices, depending upon the size of the volume. Separate opinions are sold on subscription, price $1.00 per volume; foreign subscription, $1.50; single copies, usually 5c. each.

Alaska Anthracite Railroad. Finance docket no. 1664, stock of Alaska Anthracite Railroad; decided Feb. 14, 1924; report of commission. [1924.] p. 399–400. ([Finance decision] 1202.) [From Interstate Commerce Commission reports, v. 86.] * Paper, 5c.

Amador Central Railroad. Finance docket no. 2195, deficit settlement with Amador Central R. R.; decided Feb. 14, 1924; report of commission. [1924.] p. 401–402. ·([Finance decision] 1203.) [From Interstate Commerce Commission reports, v. 86.] * Paper, 5c.

Ann Arbor Railroad. Finance docket no. 3415. Ann Arbor equipment trust; decided Jan. 19, 1924; report of commission. [1924.] p. 321–324. ([Finance decision] 1178.) [From Interstate Commerce Commission reports, v. 86.] * Paper, 5c.

Atchison, Topeka and Santa Fe Railway. Finance docket no. 3360, abandonment of branch line by Atchison, Topeka & Santa Fe and California, Arizona & Santa Fe railways; [decided Feb. 18, 1924; report of commission]. 1924. [1]+422–424 p. ([Finance decision] 1210.) [From Interstate Commerce Commission reports, v. 86.] * Paper, 5c.

—— Finance docket no. 3433, construction of extension by Atchison, Topeka & Santa Fe Ry.; [decided Feb. 26, 1924; report of commission]. 1924. [1]+462–464 p. ([Finance decision] 1223.) [From Interstate Commerce Commission reports, v. 86.] * Paper, 5c.

Automobiles. No. 14482, W. A. Patterson Company *v.* Pere Marquette Railway Company et al.; decided Jan. 17, 1924; report [and order] of commission. [1924.] 357–358+[1] p. ([Opinion] 9196.) [Report from Interstate Commerce Commission reports, v. 87.] * Paper, 5c.

—— No. 14707, C. S. Howard *v.* Pere Marquette Railway Company et al.; decided Feb. 18, 1924; report [and order] of commission. [1924.] 723–724 +[1] p. ([Opinion] 9266.) [Report from Interstate Commerce Commission reports, v. 87.] * Paper, 5c.

Bagging. No. 14255, Jackson Traffic Bureau, for R. H. Green *v.* Alabama & Vicksburg Railway Company et al.; portions of 4th section applications nos. 601, 703, 1548, and 1573; [decided Jan. 17, 1924; report and orders of commission]. 1924. [1]+258–260+ii p. ([Opinion] 9167.) [Report from Interstate Commerce Commission reports, v. 87.] * Paper, 5c.

Baltimore and Ohio Railroad. Finance docket no. 3368, abandonment of branch line by Baltimore & Ohio R. R.; decided Jan. 29, 1924; report of commission. [1924.] p. 327–328. ([Finance decision] 1180.) [From Interstate Commerce Commission reports, v. 86.] * Paper, 5c.

Bananas. No. 12426, Acme Fruit Company et al. *v.* Canadian Pacific Railway Company, director general, as agent, et al.; decided Jan. 28, 1924; report [and order] of commission. [1924.] 401–402+[1] p. ([Opinion] 9207.) [Report from Interstate Commerce Commission reports, v. 87.] * Paper, 5c.

Birmingham and Southeastern Railway. Finance docket no. 315, guaranty settlement with Birmingham & Southeastern Ry. [John T. Cochrane and Winton M. Blount, receivers]; decided Feb. 7, 1924; report of commission. [1924.] p. 341–343. ([Finance decision] 1185.) [From Interstate Commerce Commission reports, v. 86.] * Paper, 5c.

Box board. No. 13249, Seneca Fibre Products Company *v.* director general, as agent; decided Feb. 5, 1924; report of commission on reconsideration. [1924.] p. 521–522. ([Opinion] 9225.) [From Interstate Commerce Commission reports, v. 87.] * Paper, 5c.

Casks. No. 13192, Lucas E. Moore Stave Company *v.* director general, as agent, Atchison, Topeka & Santa Fe Railway Company, et al.; decided Feb. 4, 1924; report of commission. [1924.] p. 503–506. ([Opinion] 9221.) [From Interstate Commerce Commission reports, v. 87.] * Paper, 5c.

Cement. No. 14936, Iola Cement Mills Traffic Association et al. *v.* Arkansas Western Railway Company et al.; decided Jan. 22, 1924; [report and orders of commission]. [1924.] 451–471+v p. ([Opinion] 9219.) [Report from Interstate Commerce Commission reports, v. 87.] * Paper, 5c.

Central Indiana Railway. Finance docket no. 344, guaranty settlement with Central Indiana Ry. [Wm. P. Herod, receiver; decided Feb. 19, 1924; report of commission]. 1924· [1]+416–418 p. ([Finance decision] 1208.) [From Interstate Commerce Commission reports, v. 86.] * Paper, 5c.

Chicago, Burlington and Quincy Railroad. Finance docket no. 3394, bonds of Chicago, Burlington & Quincy R. R.; [decided Feb. 11, 1924; report of commission]. 1924. [1]+362–365 p. ([Finance decision] 1193.) [From Interstate Commerce Commission reports, v. 86.] * Paper, 5c.

Chicago Great Western Railroad. Finance docket no. 376, guaranty settlement with Chicago Great Western R. R.; [decided Jan. 31, 1924; report of commission]. 1924· [1]+338–340 p. ([Finance decision] 1184.) [From Interstate Commerce Commission reports, v. 86.] * Paper, 5c.

Chicago, Milwaukee and St. Paul Railway. Finance docket no. 3432, Chicago Milwaukee & St. Paul bonds; [decided Feb. 7, 1924; report of commission]. 1924· [1]+358–360 p. ([Finance decision] 1191.) [From Interstate Commerce Commission reports, v. 86.] * Paper, 5c.

Chicago River and Indiana Railroad. Finance docket no. 385, guaranty settlement with Chicago River & Indiana R. R.; [decided Feb. 29, 1924; report of commission]. 1924. [1]+468–470 p. ([Finance decision] 1226.) [From Interstate Commerce Commission reports, v. 86.] * Paper, 5c.

Chicago, West Pullman and Southern Railroad. Finance docket no. 393, guaranty settlement with Chicago, West Pullman & Southern R. R.; [decided Feb. 9, 1924; report of commission]. 1924. [1]+344–346 p. ([Finance decision] 1186.) [From Interstate Commerce Commission reports, v. 86.] * Paper, 5c.

Coal. No. 12560. Lackawanna Steel Company et al. *v.* director general, as agent, Pennsylvania Railroad Company, et al.; [no. 12560 (sub-no. 1), Seneca Iron & Steel Company et al. *v.* Pennsylvania Railroad Company et al.; no. 13287, Covert Gear Company. Incorporated. et al. *v.* same]; decided Jan. 26, 1924; report [and order] of commission. [1924.] 383–391+ii p. ([Opinion] 9204.) [Report from Interstate Commerce Commission reports. v. 87.] * Paper, 5c.

—— No. 13588, western coal rates; decided Mar. 3, 1924; supplemental report of commission. [1924.] p. 13–16. ([Opinion] 9274.) [From Interstate Commerce Commission reports, v. 88.] * Paper, 5c.

—— No. 13713, C. Reiss Coal Company *v.* Pere Marquette Railway Company, director general, as agent, et al.; [no. 14273. Flour City Fuel & Transfer Company *v.* director general, as agent; decided Feb. 2, 1924; report and orders of commission]. 1924. [1]+438–442+[1] p. ([Opinion] 9217.) [Report from Interstate Commerce Commission reports, v. 87.] * Paper, 5c.

—— No. 14000, Hoosier Lime Company *v.* director general, as agent; [decided Feb. 18, 1924; report of commission]. 1924. [1]+718–720 p. ([Opinion] 9264.) [From Interstate Commerce Commission reports, v. 87.] * Paper, 5c.

—— *v.* No. 14012, Sewell valley Railroad Company *v.* Chesapeake & Ohio Railway Company; decided Feb. 12. 1924; report [and order] of commission. [1924.] 21–26+[1] p. ([Opinion] 9097.) [Report from Interstate Commerce Commission reports, v. 87.] * Paper, 5c.

—— No. 14033, Amalgamated Sugar Company *v.* director general, as agent, and Oregon Short Line Railroad Company; decided Feb. 18, 1924; report of commission. [1924.] p. 705–706. ([Opinion] 9259.) [From Interstate Commerce reports, v. 87.] * Paper, 5c.

—— No. 14640, Midland Coal Company et al. *v.* Chicago, Rock Island & Pacific Railway Company, director general, as agent, et al.; decided Feb. 8, 1924; report [and order] of commission. [1924.] 533–534+[1] p.• ([Opinion] 9228.) [Report from Interstate Commerce Commission reports, v. 87.] * Paper, 5c.

—— No. 15011, Arnold, Hoffman & Company *v.* New York. New Haven & Hartford Railroad Company; decided Jan. 23, 1924; report of commission. [1924.] p. 417–418. ([Opinion] 9213.) [From Interstate Commerce Commission reports, v. 87.] * Paper, 5c.

Coal-tar oil. No. 13830, By-Products Coke Corporation *v.* director general, as agent; decided Feb. 18, 1924; report of commission. [1924.] p. 683–686. ([Opinion] 9253.) [From Interstate Commerce Commission reports, v. 87.] * Paper, 5c.

Coke. No. 13491, Fairbanks Company *v.* Boston & Albany Railroad Company et al.; decided Feb. 27, 1924; report of commission. [1924.] p. 725–728. ([Opinion] 9267.) [From Interstate Commerce Commission reports, v. 87.] * Paper, 5c.

Colorado and Southern Railway. Finance docket no. 1572. abandonment of branch line by Colorado & Southern Ry.; decided Feb. 11, 1924; report of commission on further argument. [1924.] p. 393–398. ([Finance decision] 1201.) [From Interstate Commerce Commission reports, v. 86.] * Paper, 5c.

Cotton goods. No. 15023, Graniteville Manufacturing Company *v.* director general, as agent; decided Feb. 8, 1924; report [and order] of commission. [1924.] 541–542+[1] p. ([Opinion] 9232.) [Report from Interstate Commerce Commission reports, v. 87.] * Paper, 5c.

Crates. No. 12569, Chevrolet Motor Company of Michigan *v.* director general, as agent, Atchison, Topeka & Santa Fe Railway Company, et al.; decided Feb. 5, 1924; report [and order] of commission. [1924.] 517–520+ii p. ([Opinion] 9224.) [Report from Interstate Commerce Commission reports. v. 87.] * Paper, 5c.

Decisions of Interstate Commerce Commission (finance reports), Mar.–July, 1923. 1924. xxviii+914 p. (Interstate Commerce Commission reports, v. 79.) * Cloth, $2.00.　　　　8–30656

NOTE.—The Interstate Commerce Commission assigns a volume in the series of reports at various times which contains only finance dockets. This is true regarding v. 79 here catalogued.

Delaware and Hudson Company. In equity, no. 633, in Supreme Court, Oct. term, 1923, Delaware and Hudson Company et al. *v.* United States and Interstate Commerce Commission; brief for Interstate Commerce Commission. 1924. cover-title, i+19 p. ‡

Delaware and Northern Railroad. Finance docket no. 132, deficit settlement with Delaware & Northern R. R. [Andrew M. Moreland and James J. Welch, receivers]; decided Jan. 31, 1924; report of commission. [1924.] p. 325–326. ([Finance decision] 1179.) [From Interstate Commerce Commission reports, v. 86.] * Paper, 5c.

—— Finance docket no. 425, guaranty settlement with Delaware & Northern R. R. [Andrew M. Moreland and James J. Welch, receivers]; decided Jan. 31, 1924; report of commission. [1924.] p. 329–331. ([Finance decision] 1181.) [From Interstate Commerce Commission reports, v. 86.] * Paper, 5c.

Demurrage. No. 13529, Atlantic Bithulithic Company *v.* Monongahela Power & Railway Company, director general, as agent, et al.; decided Feb. 18, 1924; report [and order] of commission. [1924.] 687–689+[1] p. ([Opinion] 9254.) [Report from Interstate Commerce Commission reports, v. 87.] * Paper, 5c.

—— No. 14237, Krauss Brothers Lumber Company *v.* Gulf, Mobile & Northern Railroad Company et al.; [decided Jan. 17, 1924; report of commission]. 1924. [1]+412–414 p. ([Opinion] 9211.) [From Interstate Commerce Commission reports, v. 87.] * Paper, 5c.

—— No. 14241, Krauss Brothers Lumber Company *v.* director general, as agent, Atlantic Coast Line Railroad Company, et al.; decided Feb. 18, 1924; report [and order] of commission. [1924.] 707–708+[1] p. ([Opinion] 9260.) [Report from Interstate Commerce Commission reports, v. 87.] * Paper, 5c.

—— No. 14409, Vickers Petroleum Company, Incorporated, *v.* Sand Springs Railway Company; [decided Feb. 18, 1924; report and order of commission]. 1924. [1]+676–677+[1] p. ([Opinion] 9250.) [Report from Interstate Commerce Commission reports, v. 87.] * Paper, 5c.

Denver and Rio Grande Western Railroad. Finance docket no. 3443, Denver & Rio Grande Western receiver's certificates, series no. 2 [T. H. Beacom, receiver]; decided Feb. 11, 1924; report of commission. [1924.] p. 389–392. ([Finance decision] 1200.) [From Interstate Commerce Commission reports, v. 86.] * Paper, 5c.

Detroit, Toledo and Ironton Railroad. Finance docket no. 3421, bonds of Detroit, Toledo & Ironton R. R.; decided Feb. 20, 1924; report of commission. [1924.] p. 437–438. ([Finance decision] 1215.) [From Interstate Commerce Commission reports, v. 86.] * Paper, 5c.

Fertilizers. No. 13514, Blackshear Manufacturing Company *v.* Atlantic Coast Line Railroad Company et al.; [decided Feb. 18, 1924; report and order of commission]. 1924. [1]+654–667+iv p. ([Opinion] 9247.) [Report from Interstate Commerce Commission reports, v. 87.] * Paper, 5c.

Fire-brick. No. 14019, Davis Fire Brick Company et al. *v.* Baltimore & Ohio Railroad Company et al.; [no. 14249, Chicago Retort & Fire Brick Company *v.* Chicago, Rock Island & Pacific Railway Company et al.]; decided Feb. 5, 1924; report [and orders] of commission. [1924.] 523–528+ii p. ([Opinion] 9226.) [Report from Interstate Commerce Commission reports, v. 87.] * Paper, 5c.

—— No. 14263, Jointless Fire Brick Company *v.* Chicago, Indianapolis & Louisville Railway Company et al.; [decided Feb. 18, 1924; report of commission].. 1924. [1]+702–704 p. ([Opinion] 9258.) [From Interstate Commerce Commission reports, v. 87.] * Paper, 5c.

Fish as food. Investigation and suspension docket no. 1975, nonapplication of class rates on fish between stations on Maine Central Railroad; [decided Feb. 15, 1924; report and order of commission]. 1924. [1]+640–642+[1] p. ([Opinion] 9242.) [Report from Interstate Commerce Commission reports, v. 87.] * Paper, 5c.

Fonda, Johnstown and Gloversville Railroad. Finance docket no. 2479, Fonda, Johnstown & Gloversville bonds; [decided Feb. 9, 1924; supplemental report of commission]. 1924. [1]+378–380 p. ([Finance decision] 1196.) [From Interstate Commerce Commission reports, v. 86.] * Paper, 5c.

Fort Smith, Subiaco and Rock Island Railroad. No. 13850, Fort Smith, Subiaco & Rock Island Railroad Company *v.* Arkansas Central Railroad Company et al.; decided Feb. 12, 1924; report of commission. [1924.] p. 617–621. ([Opinion] 9239.) [From Interstate Commerce Commission reports, v. 87.] * Paper, 5c.

Freeo Valley Railroad. Finance docket no. 2552, deficit settlement with Freeo valley R. R.; decided Feb. 11, 1924; report of commission. [1924.] p. 383–384. ([Finance decision] 1198.) [From Interstate Commerce Commission reports, v. 86.] * Paper, 5c.

Freight. Summary of freight commodity statistics of class 1 roads [having annual operating revenues above $1,000,000], quarter ended Dec. 31, 1923; [prepared in] Bureau of Statistics. [1924.] [4] p. oblong large 8° †

—— Same, year ended Dec. 31, 1923; [prepared in] Bureau of Statistics. [1924.] [4] p. oblong large 8° †

Freight-cars. No. 14784, adequacy of transportation facilities in northwest Pacific States; [report of commission to Senate, Feb. 4, 1924, and order of commission]. 1924. [1]+472–502+[1] p. ([Opinion] 9220.) [Report from Interstate Commerce Commission reports, v. 87.] * Paper, 5c.

Freight rates. No. 456, in Supreme Court, Oct. term, 1923, United States and Interstate Commerce Commission *v.* Abilene & Southern Railway Company et al., appeal from district court for district of Kansas; memorandum reply brief for Interstate Commerce Commission. 1924. cover-title, 14 p. ‡

—— No. 14011, United verde Extension Mining Company *v.* Atchison, Topeka & Santa Fe Railway Company et al.; decided Feb. 29, 1924; report [and order] of commission. [1924.] 5–13+iii p. ([Opinion] 9273.) [Report from Interstate Commerce Commission reports, v. 88.] * Paper, 5c.

—— No. 14941, administration of sec. 4 of interstate commerce act; [report of commission to Senate, Feb. 11, 1924, and order of commission]. 1924. [1]+564–612+[1] p. ([Opinion] 9236.) [Report from Interstate Commerce Commission reports, v. 87.] * Paper, 5c.

Fuel-oil. No. 12812, Gulf Refining Company *v.* director general, as agent, and Pennsylvania Railroad Company; [decided Feb. 18, 1924; report and order of commission]. 1924. [1]+690–694+[1] p. ([Opinion] 9255.) [Report from Interstate Commerce Commission reports, v. 87.] * Paper, 5c.

—— No. 14614, Kansas City Brick Company *v.* Kansas City Southern Railway Company et al.; [decided Feb. 14, 1924; report and order of commission]. 1924. [1]+646–648+[1] p. ([Opinion] 9244.) [Report from Interstate Commerce Commission reports, v. 87.] * Paper, 5c.

Gas-engines. No. 13064, H. M. Spence *v.* director general, as agent, Baltimore & Ohio Railroad Company et al.; decided Jan. 17, 1924; report [and order] of commission. [1924.] 339–341+[1] p. ([Opinion] 9191.) [Report from Interstate Commerce Commission reports, v. 87.] * Paper, 5c.

—— No. 14369, Moreland Motor Truck Company et al. *v.* Pennsylvania Railroad Company et al.; decided Feb. 18, 1924; report [and order] of commission. [1924.] 715–717+[1] p. ([Opinion] 9263.) [Report from Interstate Commerce Commission reports, v. 87.] * Paper, 5c.

Gas oil. No. 14384, Omaha Steel Works et al. *v.* Atchison, Topeka & Santa Fe Railway Company et al.; decided Jan. 23, 1924; report of commission. [1924.] p. 403–406. ([Opinion] 9208.) [From Interstate Commerce Commission reports, v. 87.] * Paper, 5c.

Grain. Investigation and suspension docket no. 1946, grain and grain products from Chicago and Peoria, Ill., and St. Louis, Mo., to Indiana; [investigation and suspension docket no. 2015]; decided Feb. 27, 1924; report [and order] of commission. [1924.] 731–739+[1] p. ([Opinion] 9269.) [Report from Interstate Commerce Commission reports, v. 87.] * Paper, 5c.

—— Investigation and suspension docket no. 1958, cancellation of transit privileges on grain and grain products at New Orleans, La.; [decided Feb. 15, 1924; report and order of commission]. 1924. [1]+652–653+[1] p. ([Opinion] 9246.) [Report from Interstate Commerce Commission reports, v. 87.] * Paper, 5c.

—— No. 12965, Merchants Exchange of St. Louis et al. *v.* Aberdeen & Rockfish Railroad Company et al.; decided Feb. 5, 1924; [report and order of commission]. [1924.] 547–563+[1] p. ([Opinion] 9235.) [Report from Interstate Commerce Commission reports, v. 87.] * Paper, 5c.

Grain—Continued. No. 14665, Bruning Mill & Elevator *v.* Chicago, Burlington & Quincy Railroad Company; decided Jan. 17, 1924; report of commission. [1924] p. 363–364. ([Opinion] 9199.) [From Interstate Commerce Commission reports, v. 87.] * Paper, 5c.

Grand Canyon Railway. Finance docket no. 3369, acquisition of control of line [Grand Canyon Railway Company] by Atchison, Topeka & Santa Fe Ry.; decided Feb. 1, 1924; report of commission. [1924.] p. 355–357. ([Finance decision] 1190.) [From Interstate Commerce Commission reports, v. 86.] * Paper, 5c.

Grape-fruit. No. 14727, Jacobs, Malcolm & Burtt *v.* Arizona Eastern Railroad Company et al.; decided Jan. 23, 1924; report of commission. [1924.] p. 419–421. ([Opinion] 9214.) [From Interstate Commerce Commission reports, v. 87.] * Paper, 5c.

Greenstone. No. 14496, Lockport Paper Company *v.* Western Maryland Railway Company et al.; decided Jan. 17, 1924; report of commission. [1924.] p. 347–350. ([Opinion] 9194.) [From Interstate Commerce Commission reports, v. 87.] * Paper, 5c.

Gulf and Ship Island Railroad. Before Interstate Commerce Commission, valuation docket no. 302, Gulf and Ship Island Railroad Company; brief in support of tentative valuation. 1924. cover-title, i+24 p. ‡

Hampton and Branchville Railroad and Lumber Company. Finance docket no. 2633, bonds of Hampton & Branchville Railroad & Lumber Co.; decided Feb. 7, 1924; report of commission. [1924.] p. 349–351. ([Finance decision] 1188.) [From Interstate Commerce Commission reports, v. 86.] * Paper, 5c.

Hay. No. 14308, M. J. Hyland, trading as Omaha Hay & Feed Company, et al. *v.* director general, as agent, Chicago, Burlington & Quincy Railroad Company, et al.; [decided Dec. 31, 1923; report and order of commission]. 1924. [1]+26–28+[1] p. ([Opinion] 9098.) [Report from Interstate Commerce Commission reports, v. 87.] * Paper, 5c.

—— No. 14853, Scott, Magner & Miller *v.* director general, as agent; decided Jan. 23, 1924; report [and order] of commission. [1924.] 409–411+[1] p. ([Opinion] 9210.) [Report from Interstate Commerce Commission reports, v. 87.] * Paper, 5c.

Hocking Valley Railway. Finance docket no. 3451, notes of Hocking valley Ry.; decided Feb. 18, 1924; report of commission. [1924.] p. 413–415. ([Finance decision] 1207.) [From Interstate Commerce Commission reports, v. 86.] * Paper, 5c.

Illinois Bell Telephone Company. Finance docket no. 3425, purchase of properties by Illinois Bell Telephone Co.; decided Feb. 19, 1924; report of commission. [1924.] p. 439–440. ([Finance decision] 1216.) [From Interstate Commerce Commission reports, v. 86.] * Paper, 5c.

Illinois Central Railroad. Finance docket no. 2777, construction of cut-off for Illinois Central Railroad; [and finance dockets nos. 2783 and 2817]; decided Feb. 5, 1924; report of commission on reargument. [1924.] p. 371–377. ([Finance decision] 1195.) [From Interstate Commerce Commission reports, v. 86.] * Paper, 5c.

—— Finance docket no. 3455, joint bonds of Illinois Central and Chicago, St. Louis & New Orleans; decided Feb. 27, 1924; report of commission. [1924.] p. 457–461. ([Finance decision] 1222.) [From Interstate Commerce Commission reports, v. 86.] * Paper, 5c.

Kahului Railroad. Finance docket no. 3370, stock dividend of Kahului Railroad; decided Jan. 22, 1924; report of commission. [1924.] p. 309–312. ([Finance decision] 1175.) [From Interstate Commerce Commission reports, v. 86.] * Paper, 5c.

Kansas, Oklahoma and Gulf Railway. Finance docket no. 557, guaranty settlement with Kansas, Oklahoma & Gulf Ry.; [and finance dockets nos. 649 and 650]; decided Jan. 21, 1924; report of commission. [1924.] p. 297–300. ([Finance decision] 1171.) [From Interstate Commerce Commission reports, v. 86.] *Paper, 5c.

Lehigh Valley Harbor Terminal Railway. Finance docket no. 3418, bonds of Lehigh valley Harbor Terminal Ry.; [decided Jan. 31, 1924; report of commission]. 1924. [1]+332–335 p. ([Finance decision] 1182.) [From Interstate Commerce Commission reports, v. 86.] *Paper, 5c.

Lighterage. No. 12876, Compagnie Auxiliare de Chemins de Fer au Bresil *v.* Delaware, Lackawanna & Western Railroad Company, director general, as agent, et al.; decided Jan. 14, 1924; report of commission on further argument. [1924.] p. 443-450. ([Opinion] 9218.) [From Interstate Commerce Commission reports, v. 87.] *Paper, 5c.

Lumber. No. 14411, William Schuette Company *v.* Chicago, Milwaukee & St. Paul Railway Company et al.; decided Feb. 18, 1924; report [and order] of commission. [1924.] 709-710+[1] p. ([Opinion] 9261.) [Report from Interstate Commerce Commission reports, v. 87.] *Paper, 5c.

—— No. 14526, Marshall Tie Company *v.* Southern Railway Company et al.; decided Feb. 18, 1924; report of commission. [1924.] p. 681-682. ([Opinion] 9252.) [From Interstate Commerce Commission reports, v. 87.] *Paper, 5c.

Manistee and Northeastern Railroad. Finance docket no. 3216, abandonment of branch line by receiver of Manistee & Northeastern R. R.; [decided Feb. 11, 1924; report of commission]. 1924. [1]+406-408 p. ([Finance decision] 1205.) [From Interstate Commerce Commission reports, v. 86.] *Paper, 5c.

Marshall, Elysian Fields and Southeastern Railway. Finance docket no. 2970, construction of extension by Marshall, Elysian Fields & Southeastern Ry.; decided Feb. 9, 1924; report of commission. [1924.] p. 385-388. ([Finance decision] 1199.) [From Interstate Commerce Commission reports, v. 86.] *Paper, 5c.

—— Finance docket no. 3222, operation of line by Marshall, Elysian Fields & Southeastern Ry.; [decided Feb. 2, 1924; report of commission]. 1924. [1]+352-354 p. ([Finance decision] 1189.) [From Interstate Commerce Commission reports, v. 86.] *Paper, 5c.

Mine timbers. No. 13915, E. L. Palmer *v.* Missouri Pacific Railroad Company et al.; [no. 13915 (sub-no. 1), Nokomis Coal Company *v.* same; decided Feb. 11, 1924; report and order of commission]. 1924. [1]+622-633+ii p. ([Opinion] 9240.) [Report from Interstate Commerce Commission reports, v. 87.] *Paper, 5c.

Misrouting. No. 14448, Massachusetts Ice Dealers Association *v.* director general, as agent; decided Jan. 17, 1924; report of commission. [1924.] p. 407-409. ([Opinion] 9209.) [From Interstate Commerce Commission reports, v. 87.] *Paper, 5c.

—— No. 14601, Ichabod T. Williams & Sons *v.* Virginia Blue Ridge Railway Company et al.; decided Feb. 18, 1924; report [and order] of commission. [1924.] 721-722+[1] p. ([Opinion] 9265.) [Report from Interstate Commerce Commission reports, v. 87.] *Paper, 5c.

—— No. 14774, Unit Stove & Furnace Company *v.* Chesapeake & Ohio Railroad Company et al.; decided Feb. 8, 1924; report [and order] of commission. [1924.] 543-544+[1] p. ([Opinion] 9233.) [Report from Interstate Commerce Commission reports, v. 87.] *Paper, 5c.

Morristown and Erie Railroad. Finance docket no. 664, guaranty settlement with Morristown & Erie R. R.; decided Jan. 22, 1924; report of commission. [1924.] p. 301-303. ([Finance decision] 1172.) [From Interstate Commerce Commission reports, v. 86.] *Paper, 5c.

Motor-trucks. No. 12954, State Highway Department of Texas *v.* director general, as agent, Chicago & North Western Railway Company et al.; [decided Feb. 18, 1924; report of commission]. 1924. [1]+678-681 p. ([Opinion] 9251.) [From Interstate Commerce Commission reports, v. 87.] *Paper, 5c.

Mount Hood Railroad. Finance docket no. 668, guaranty settlement with Mount Hood R. R.; decided Jan. 31, 1924; report of commission. [1924.] p. 335-337. ([Finance decision] 1183.) [From Interstate Commerce Commission reports, v. 86.] *Paper, 5c.

Naval stores. Investigation and suspension docket no. 1900, naval stores from southern producing points to various destinations; 4th section applications no. 2174, etc.; [decided Mar. 5, 1924; report and orders of commission]. 1924. [1]+740-758+ii p. ([Opinion] 9270.) [Report from Interstate Commerce Commission reports, v. 87.] *Paper, 5c.

Nevada County Narrow Gauge Railroad. Before Interstate Commerce Commission, valuation docket no. 313, Nevada County Narrow Gauge Railroad Company; brief in support of tentative valuation. 1924. cover-title, 18 p. ‡

New York, Chicago and St. Louis Railroad. Finance docket no. 3454, New York, Chicago & St. Louis equipment trust of 1924; report of commission. [1924.] p. 445–448. ([Finance decision] 1218.) [From Interstate Commerce Commission reports. v. 86.] * Paper, 5c.

—— Finance docket no. 3464, pledge of Toledo, St. Louis & Western bonds by New York, Chicago & St. Louis Railroad; decided Feb. 26, 1924; report of commission. [1924.] p. 465–467. ([Finance decision] 1224.) [From Interstate Commerce Commission reports, v. 86.] * Paper, 5c.

New York, New Haven and Hartford Railroad. Finance docket no. 2939, equipment notes of New York, New Haven & Hartford R. R.; decided Jan. 21, 1924; supplemental report of commission. [1924.] p. 307–308. ([Finance decision] 1174.) [From Interstate Commerce Commission reports. v. 86.] * Paper, 5c.

—— Finance docket no. 3374, abandonment of part of branch line by New York, New Haven & Hartford R. R.; decided Feb. 25, 1924; report of commission. [1924.] p. 471–472. ([Finance decision] 1227.) [From Interstate Commerce Commission reports. v. 86.] * Paper, 5c.

—— Finance docket no. 3375, abandonment of part of branch line by New York, New Haven & Hartford R. R; decided Feb. 29, 1924; report of commission. [1924.] p. 473–474. ([Finance decision] 1228.) [From Interstate Commerce Commission reports. v. 86.] * Paper, 5c.

Nezperce and Idaho Railroad. Finance docket no. 699, guaranty settlement with Nezperce & Idaho R. R.; decided Feb. 21, 1924; report of commission. [1924.] p. 429–431. ([Finance decision] 1212.) [From Interstate.Commerce Commission reports, v. 86.] * Paper, 5c.

Old Colony Railroad. Finance docket no. 3397, bonds of Old Colony Railroad; [decided Jan. 21, 1924; report of commission]. 1924. [1]+318–320 p. ([Finance decision] 1177.) [From Interstate Commerce Commission reports, v. 86.] * Paper, 5c.

Packing-house products. No. 13941, Jonesboro Freight Bureau *v.* Houston East & West Texas Railway Company et al.; decided Feb. 18, 1924; report [and order] of commission. [1924.] 699–701+[1] p. ([Opinion] 9257.) [Report from Interstate Commerce Commission reports. v. 87.] * Paper, 5c.

Paper. No. 13255, American Publishing Company *r.* director general, as agent, et al.; decided Feb. 18, 1924; report of commission. [1924.] p. 711–714. ([Opinion] 9262.) [From Interstate Commerce Commission reports, v. 87.] * Paper, 5c.

—— No. 14666, Jackson Traffic Bureau *v.* Alabama & vicksburg Railway Company et al.; decided Feb. 8, 1924; report [and order] of commission. [1924.] 535–536+[1] p. ([Opinion] 9229.) [Report from Interstate Commerce Commission reports, v. 87.] * Paper, 5c.

—— No. 14704. Jackson Paper Company *v.* Alabama & vicksburg Railway Company et al.; decided Feb. 5. 1924; report [and order] of commission. [1924.] 529–532+[1] p. ([Opinion] 9227.) [Report from Interstate Commerce Commission reports. v. 87.] * Paper, 5c.

—— No. 15015, Minnesota & Ontario Paper Company *v.* Missouri. Kansas & Texas Railway Company et al.; decided Feb. 8. 1924; report [and order] of commission. [1924.] 539–540+[1] p. ([Opinion] 9231.) [Report from Interstate Commerce Commission reports, v. 87.] * Paper, 5c.

Petroleum. No. 12536. Automobile Gasoline Company *r.* director general, as agent, et al.; [decided Feb. 7, 1924; report of commission]. 1924. [1]+514–516 p. ([Opinion] 9223.) [From Interstate Commerce Commission reports. v. 87.] * Paper, 5c.

Petroleum coke. No. 14333. Aluminum Company of America et al *v.* director general, as agent; [no. 14861, Tallassee Power Company *r.* director general, as agent. Cincinnati, New Orleans & Texas Pacific Railway Company, et al.]; decided Feb. 12, 1924; report of commission. [1924.] p. 615–617. ([Opinion] 9238.) [From Interstate Commerce Commission reports, v. 87.] * Paper, 5c.

Philadelphia, Baltimore and Washington Railroad. Finance docket no. 3456, bonds of Philadelphia, Baltimore & Washington R. R.; decided Feb. 21, 1924; report of commission. [1924.] p. 449–452. ([Finance decision] 1219.) [From Interstate Commerce Commission reports. v. 86.] * Paper, 5c.

Pittsburgh, Youngstown and Ashtabula Railway. Finance docket no. 2829, Pittsburgh, Youngstown & Ashtabula bonds; approved Feb. 29, 1924; supplemental order. 1924. p. 452. ([Finance decision] 1220.) [From Interstate Commerce Commission reports, v. 86.] * Paper, 5c.

—— Finance docket no. 3458, bonds of Pittsburgh, Youngstown & Ashtabula Railway; decided Feb. 21, 1924; report of commission. [1924.] p. 453–456. ([Finance decision] 1221.) [From Interstate Commerce Commission reports, v. 86.] * Paper, 5c.

Poles. No. 14698, Western Electric Company *v.* director general, as agent, et al.; decided Feb. 8, 1924; report of commission. [1924.] p. 545–546. ([Opinion] 9234.) [From Interstate Commerce Commission reports, v. 87.] * Paper, 5c.

Potassium sulphate. No. 14515, Salt Lake Potash Company *v.* Atlantic Coast Line Railroad, director general, as agent, et al.; decided Feb. 18, 1924; report of commission. [1924.] p. 695–698. ([Opinion] 9256.) [From Interstate Commerce Commission reports, v. 87.] * Paper, 5c.

Poteau and Cavanal Mountain Railroad. Finance docket no. 2983, stock of Poteau & Cavanal Mountain Railroad; decided Feb. 20, 1924; report of commission. [1924.] p. 419–421. ([Finance decision] 1209.) [From Interstate Commerce Commission reports, v. 86.] * Paper, 5c.

Prescott and Northwestern Railroad. Finance docket no. 3227, construction of extension by Prescott & Northwestern R. R.; decided Feb. 7, 1924; report of commission. [1924.] p. 365–370. ([Finance decision] 1194.) [From Interstate Commerce Commission reports, v. 86.] * Paper, 5c.

Railroad accidents. Report of director of Bureau of Safety in re investigation of accident which occurred on Philadelphia & Reading Railway near Annville, Pa., Nov. 21, 1923 [accompanied by report of engineer-physicist]. [1924.] 28 p. il. * Paper, 10c. A 24—655

Railroad employees. Wage statistics, class 1 steam roads in United States, including 15 switching and terminal companies, Dec. 1923; [prepared in] Bureau of Statistics. [1924.] [4] p. il. oblong large 8° †

Railroads. Freight and passenger service operating statistics of class 1 steam roads in United States, compiled from 161 reports of freight statistics representing 176 roads and from 158 reports of passenger statistics representing 173 roads (switching and terminal companies not included), Jan. 1924 and 1923; [prepared in] Bureau of Statistics. Jan. 1924. 1 p. oblong large 8° [Subject to revision.] †

—— Operating revenues and operating expenses of class 1 steam roads in United States (for 194 steam roads, including 15 switching and terminal companies), Jan. 1924 and 1923; [prepared in] Bureau of Statistics. Jan. 1924. 1 p. oblong large 8° [Subject to revision.] †

—— Operating revenues and operating expenses of large steam roads, selected items for roads with annual operating revenues above $25,000,000, Jan. 1924 and 1923; [prepared in] Bureau of Statistics. Jan. 1924. [2] p. oblong large 8° [Subject to revision.] †

—— Operating statistics of large steam roads, selected items for Jan. 1924, compared with Jan. 1923, for roads with annual operating revenues above $25,000,000; [prepared in] Bureau of Statistics. Jan. 1924. [2] p. oblong large 8° [Subject to revision.] †

—— Revenue traffic statistics of class 1 steam roads in United States, including mixed-train service (compiled from 162 reports representing 177 steam roads, switching and terminal companies not included), Dec. 1923 and 1922 [and] 12 months ended with Dec. 1923 and 1922; [prepared in] Bureau of Statistics. Dec. 1923 [published 1924]. 1 p. oblong large 8° [Subject to revision.] †

Refrigeration. Investigation and suspension docket no. 1934, icing of less-than-carload shipments of milk, cream, and other dairy products at points on New York, New Haven & Hartford Railroad; [decided Feb. 12, 1924; report and order of commission]. [1924.] [1]+634–639+[1] p. ([Opinion] 9241.) [Report from Interstate Commerce Commission reports, v. 87.] * Paper, 5c.

Rice bran. No. 14957, J. Zimmern's Company *v.* Beaumont, Sour Lake & Western Railway Company et al; decided Feb. 8, 1924; report [and order] of commission. [1924.] 537–538+[1] p. ([Opinion] 9230.) [Report from Interstate Commerce Commission reports, v. 87.] * Paper, 5c.

Rockingham Railroad. Finance docket no. 771, guaranty settlement with Rockingham R. R.; [decided Jan. 22, 1924; report of commission]. 1924. [1]+304–306 p. ([Finance decision] 1173.) [From Interstate Commerce Commission reports, v. 86.] * Paper, 5c.

Rocky Mountain and Santa Fe Railway. Finance docket no. 3299, acquisition of line by Rocky Mountain & Santa Fe Ry.; [and finance docket no. 3300]; decided Feb. 14, 1924; report of commission. [1924.] p. 409–412. ([Finance decision] 1206.) [From Interstate Commerce Commission reports, v. 86.] * Paper, 5c.

Rumford Falls and Rangeley Lakes Railroad. Finance docket no. 3440, bonds of Rumford Falls & Rangeley Lakes Railroad; decided Feb. 18, 1924; report of commission. [1924.] p. 425–428. ([Finance decision] 1211.) [From Interstate Commerce Commission reports, v. 86.] * Paper, 5c.

St. Louis Southwestern Railway. Finance docket no. 3450, St. Louis Southwestern equipment trust, series I; decided Feb. 19, 1924; report of commission. [1924.] p. 441–444. ([Finance decision] 1217.) [From Interstate Commerce Commission reports, v. 86.] * Paper, 5c.

Sand. No. 14754, American Sand & Gravel Company v. Chicago & North Western Railway Company et al.; decided Feb. 27, 1924; report [and order] of commission. [1924.] 1–4+ii p. ([Opinion] 9272.) [Report from Interstate Commerce Commission reports, v. 88.] * Paper, 5c.

Sewell Valley Railroad. Finance docket no. 3441, notes of Sewell Valley Railroad; decided Feb. 29. 1924; report of commission. [1924.] p. 481–482. ([Finance decision] 1231.) [From Interstate Commerce Commission reports, v. 86.] * Paper, 5c.

Sisal hemp. No. 14875, Eric Corporation v. Delaware, Lackawanna & Western Railroad Company et al.; decided Jan. 23, 1924; report [and order] of commission. [1924.] 371–372+ii p. ([Opinion] 9202.) [Report from Interstate Commerce Commission reports, v. 87.] * Paper, 5c.

Soda (baking). No. 12686, Paxton & Gallagher Company et al. v. director general, as agent, Chicago, Burlington & Quincy Railroad Company, et al.; [decided Feb. 18, 1924; report and order of commission]. 1924. [1]+668–673+[1] p. ([Opinion] 9248.) [Report from Interstate Commerce Commission reports, v. 87.] * Paper, 5c.

Southern Railway. Finance docket no. 3395, construction of line by Southern Ry.; [decided Feb. 18, 1924; report of commission]. 1924. [1]+432–434 p. ([Finance decision] 1213.) [From Interstate Commerce Commission reports, v. 86.] * Paper, 5c.

—— Finance docket no. 3410, construction of line by Southern Ry.; decided Feb. 18. 1924; report of commission. [1924.] p. 435–437. ([Finance decision] 1214.) [From Interstate Commerce Commission reports, v. 86.] * Paper, 5c.

Steamboats. Schedule of sailings (as furnished by steamship companies named herein) of steam vessels which are registered under laws of United States and which are intended to load general cargo at ports in United States for foreign destinations. Mar. 15–Apr. 30, 1924. no. 19; issued by Section of Tariffs, Bureau of Traffic. 1924. iii+28 p. 4° [Monthly. No. 19 cancels no. 18.] †　　　　　　　　　　　　　　　　　　22—26610

Stone. Investigation and suspension docket no. 1973. crushed stone from Thornton, Ill., to points in Chicago district: decided Feb. 28, 1924; report [and order] of commission. [1924.] 759–762+[1] p. ([Opinion] 9271.) [Report from Interstate Commerce Commission reports. v. 87.] * Paper, 5c.

Sugar. No. 14670, Warfield-Pratt-Howell Company v. Texas & Pacific Railway Company et al.; decided Feb. 27, 1924; report [and order] of commission on further hearing. [1924.] 729–730+[1] p. ([Opinion] 9268.) [Report from Interstate Commerce Commission reports, v. 87.] * Paper, 5c.

—— No. 14745, West Cache Sugar Company v. director general, as agent; [decided Jan. 23. 1924; report and order of commission]. 1924. [1]+368–370+[1] p. ([Opinion] 9201.) [Report from Interstate Commerce Commission reports, v. 87.] * Paper, 5c.

Sulphur. No. 13975. Texas Gulf Sulphur Company v. Central Railroad Company of New Jersey et al.; decided Jan. 14. 1924: report of commission. [1924.] p. 613–615. ([Opinion] 9237.) [From Interstate Commerce Commission reports, v. 87.] * Paper, 5c.

Superior and Southeastern Railway. Finance docket no. 2619, operation of line by Superior & Southeastern Ry.; decided Feb. 14, 1924; report of commission on further hearing. [1924.] p. 403–405. ([Finance decision] 1204.) [From Interstate Commerce Commission reports, v. 86.] * Paper, 5c.

Switching. No. 13761, Traffic & Transportation Bureau of Tacoma Commercial Club & Chamber of Commerce *v.* Northern Pacific Railway Company et al.; decided Feb. 4, 1924; report [and order] of commission. [1924.] 507–513+[1] p. ([Opinion] 9222.) [Report from Interstate Commerce Commission reports, v. 87.] * Paper, 5c.

Switching charges. No. 14485, Alan Wood Iron & Steel Company *v.* director general, as agent; decided Feb. 14, 1924; report of commission. [1924.] p. 643–645. ([Opinion] 9243.) [From Interstate Commerce Commission reports, v. 87.] * Paper, 5c.

—— No. 14769, Joseph Bancroft & Sons Company *v.* director general, as agent, Philadelphia & Reading Railway Company, et al.; decided Jan. 30, 1924; report of commission. [1924.] p. 421–424. ([Opinion] 9215.) [From Interstate Commerce Commission reports, v. 87.] * Paper, 5c.

Tin-plate. No. 14788, Newport Milling Company *v.* director general, as agent, and Chicago & North Western Railway Company; decided Mar. 5, 1924; report [and order] of commission. [1924.] 17–18+[1] p. ([Opinion] 9275.) [Report from Interstate Commerce Commission reports, v. 88.] * Paper, 5c.

Union Pacific Railroad. Finance docket no. 3350, construction of extension by Union Pacific R. R.; [decided Feb. 11, 1924; report of commission]. 1924. [1]+380–382 p. ([Finance decision] 1197.) [From Interstate Commerce Commission reports, v. 86.] * Paper, 5c.

Windows. No. 13095, Anderson Lumber Company *v.* Northern Pacific Railway Company et al.; decided Jan. 24, 1924; report [and order] of commission. [1924.] 425–437+iii p. ([Opinion] 9216.) [Report from Interstate Commerce Commission reports, v. 87.] * Paper, 5c.

Wood-pulp. No. 14280, Ryegate Paper Company *v.* Boston & Maine Railroad et al.; decided Feb. 18, 1924; report [and order] of commission. [1924.] 673–675+[1] p. ([Opinion] 9249.) [Report from Interstate Commerce Commission reports, v. 87.] * Paper, 5c.

JUSTICE DEPARTMENT

American Tobacco Company. In Supreme Court, Oct. term, 1923, no. 206, Federal Trade Commission *v.* American Tobacco Company; no. 207, [same] *v.* P. Lorrilard [Lorillard] Company, Inc., on writs of error to district court for southern district of New York; brief for plaintiff in error. 1924. cover-title, iv+56 p. ‡

B. & S. Drug Company. No. 79, in Supreme Court, Oct. term, 1923, Waldemar Gnerich and Jeremiah T. Regan, copartners, doing business under firm name and style of B. & S. Drug Company, *v.* S. F. Rutter, as prohibition director in and for district of California, appeal from circuit court of appeals for 9th circuit; brief for appellee. 1924. cover-title, ii+36 p. ‡

Bek, Mrs. Emilie. Equity, no. 41530, in Supreme Court of District of Columbia holding equity court, Emilie Bek *v.* Thomas W. Miller, as Alien Property Custodian, and Frank White, as Treasurer of United States; brief on behalf of Thomas W. Miller, as Alien Property Custodian, and Frank White, as Treasurer of United States. 1924. cover-title, 25 p. ‡

Bentley, A., & Sons Company. No. 2178 in district court for southern district of Ohio, eastern division, action at law, United States *v.* A. Bentley & Sons Co.; amended petition. 1924. cover-title, 101 p. ‡

Brilliant Coal Company. In Court of Claims, Brilliant Coal Company *vs.* United States, no. C-671; defendant's request for findings of fact and brief. [1924.] p. 56–62, large 8° ‡

Carroll, George. No. 117, in Supreme Court, Oct. term, 1923, George Carroll and John Kiro *v.* United States, in error to district court for western district of Michigan; substituted brief for United States on reargument. 1924. cover-title, iv+101 p. ‡

Cheney Brothers. No. 2323, Court of Customs Appeals, Cheney Brothers *v.* United States; brief for United States. 1924. cover-title. 18 p. ‡

Chicago, Ill. No. 529, in Supreme Court, Oct. term, 1923, sanitary district of Chicago *v.* United States, appeal from district court for northern district of Illinois; motion ·by appellee to advance case. 1924. cover-title, 5 p. ‡

Chicago and Alton Railroad. In Court of Claims, Wm. W. Wheelock & Wm. G. Bierd, receivers of Chicago & Alton Railroad Company, *v.* United States, no. B–114; defendant's request for findings of fact, and brief. [1924.] p. 43–44, large 8° ‡

Chung Fook. No. 299, in Supreme Court, Oct. term, 1923, Chung Fook *v.* Edward White, as commissioner of immigration, port of San Francisco, on writ of certiorari to circuit court of appeals for 9th circuit; brief on behalf of respondent. 1924. cover-title, 7 p. ‡

Claims. Judgments against Government by District Courts, list of judgments rendered against Government by District Courts. Mar. 14, calendar day Mar. 18, 1924. 4 p. (S. doc. 69, 68th Cong. 1st sess.) * Paper, 5c.

Cook, George W. No. 220, in Supreme Court, Oct. term, 1923, George W. Cook *v.* Galen L. Tait, collector of internal revenue for district of Maryland, in error to district court for district of Maryland; brief for defendant in error. 1924. cover-title, ii+26 p. ‡

Diana, Andrea. No. 2324, Court of Customs Appeals, Andrea Diana et al. *v.* United States; brief for United States. 1924. cover-title, 8 p. ‡

Douglas, John, jr. No. 832, in Supreme Court, John Douglas, jr., *v.* United States, on petition for writ of certiorari to circuit court of appeals for 3d circuit; brief for United States in opposition. 1924. cover-title, 10 p. ‡

Douglas Packing Company. No. 559, in Supreme Court, Oct. term, 1923, United States *v.* 95 barrels, more or less, alleged apple cider vinegar, Douglas Packing Company, claimant, on writ of certiorari to circuit court of appeals for 6th circuit; brief and argument on behalf of United States. 1924. cover-title, ii+57 p. ‡

Eagle-Picher Lead Company. In Court of Claims, Eagle-Picher Lead Co., for use and benefit of Pennsylvania R. R. Co. and Philadelphia and Reading R. R. Co., *v.* United States, no. B–189; defendant's objections to plaintiff's request for findings of fact, defendant's request for findings of fact, and brief. [1924.] p. 21–28, large 8° ‡

Fehl, Earl H. In Court of Claims, Earl H. Fehl *v.* United States, no. C–704; demurrer to 2d amended petition [and] brief. [1924.] p. 23–26, large 8° ‡

Ferris, Charles J. No. 217, in Supreme Court, Oct. term, 1923, United States *v.* Charles J. Ferris, appeal from Court of Claims; brief for United 'States. 1924. cover-title, 9 p. ‡

Forbes, Charles R. No. 12227, in district court for northern district of Illinois, eastern division, United States *v.* Charles R. Forbes and John W. Thompson; indictment, viol. sec. 37, criminal code, conspiracy to defraud United States in construction of U. S. veterans' hospitals. 1924. cover-title, 13 p. ‡

—— No. 12228, in district court for northern district of Illinois, eastern division, United States *v.* Charles R. Forbes and John W. Thompson; indictment, viol.·sec. 37, criminal code, conspiracy to commit bribery offenses. 1924. cover-title, 8 p. ‡

—— No. 12229, in district court for northern district of Illinois, eastern division, United States *v.* Charles R. Forbes; indictment, viol. sec. 117, criminal code. 1924. cover-title, 5 p. ‡

Ford Motor Company. No. 2329, Court of Customs Appeals, Ford Motor Company *v.* United States; brief for United States. 1924. cover-title, 7 p. ‡

Gavit, E. Palmer. No. —, in Supreme Court, Oct. term, 1923, Roscoe Irwin, former collector of internal revenue [for 14th district of New York], *v.* E. Palmer Gavit; petition for writ of certiorari to circuit court of appeals for 2d circuit, and brief in support thereof. 1924. cover-title, 11 p. ‡

—— United States circuit court of appeals for 2d circuit, Oct. term, 1923, Roscoe Irwin, collector of internal revenue for 14th district of New York, *v.* E. Palmer Gavit, no. 70, in error to district court for northern district of New York; [transcript of record]. [1924.] p. 57–62. ‡

General Electric Company. In equity, no. —, in district court for northern district of Ohio, eastern division, United States *v.* General Electric Company, Westinghouse Electric and Manufacturing Company, and Westinghouse Lamp Company; petition. 1924. cover-title, 29 p. ‡

Glendinning, McLeish & Co., Incorporated. No. 2306, Court of Customs Appeals, United States v. Glendinning, McLeish & Co., Inc.; brief for United States. 1924. cover-title, 6 p. ‡

Gottesman, Joseph M. In Court of Claims, Joseph M. Gottesman v. United States, no. C–709; demurrer to amended petition [and] brief. [1924.] p. 13–17, large 8° ‡

Greylock Mills. No. 808, in Supreme Court, Oct. term, 1923, United States ex relatione Greylock Mills v. David H. Blair, commissioner of internal revenue. petition for writ of certiorari to Court of Appeals of District of Columbia; brief for United States in opposition. 1924. cover-title, 12 p. ‡

Hammerschmidt, Thomas. No. 254, in Supreme Court, Oct. term, 1923, Thomas Hammerschmidt et al. v. United States, on writ of certiorari to circuit court of appeals for 6th circuit; brief on behalf of United States. 1924. cover-title, 10 p. ‡

House of Representatives. Charges against 2 Members of Congress, letter from Attorney General transmitting letter in response to resolution directing him to transmit to the House names of 2 Members of Congress mentioned in report of grand jury of district court for northern district of Illinois and nature of charges made against such Members of Congress [stating that request can not be complied with]. Mar. 8, 1924. 2 p. (H. doc. 216, 68th Cong. 1st sess.) * Paper, 5c.

Hygienic Fibre Company. No. 287–A, in Court of Claims, Hygienic Fiber [Fibre] Co. v. United States; defendant's objections to plaintiff's request for findings of fact, defendant's request for findings of fact, and brief. 1924. cover-title, i+171–225 p. large 8° ‡

Illinois Central Railroad. In Court of Claims, Illinois Central Railroad Co. v. United States, no. B–74; defendant's objections to plaintiff's request for findings of fact, defendant's request for findings of fact, and brief. [1924.] p. 61–69, large 8° ‡

International Sales Company. No. 2299, Court of Customs Appeals, International Sales Co. et al. v. United States; brief for United States. 1924. cover-title, 16 p. ‡

Iselin, Georgine. No. B–96, in Court of Claims, Georgine Iselin v. United States; defendant's request for findings of fact and brief. 1924. cover-title. i+95–132 p. large 8° ‡

Jenkins, John F. In Court of Claims, John F. Jenkins v. United States, no. A–112; defendant's objections to plaintiff's request for findings of fact, defendant's request for findings of fact, and brief. [1924.] p. 77–100, large 8° ‡

Kennedy, A. P. No. 222, in Supreme Court, Oct. term, 1923, A. P. Kennedy and John Kennedy v. United States, on certificate from circuit court of appeals for 8th circuit; brief for United States. 1924. cover-title, ii+26 p. ‡

Kny, Richard. No. 4079, in Court of Appeals of District of Columbia, Jan. term, 1924, Helene A. Kny, sole executrix of Richard Kny, v. Thomas W. Miller, as Alien Property Custodian, and Frank White, as Treasurer of United States; brief on behalf of Thomas W. Miller, as Alien Property Custodian. and Frank White, as Treasurer of United States. 1924. cover-title, i+28 p. ‡

Ladenburg, Thalmann & Co. In circuit court of appeals for 2d circuit, Benjamin Guiness [Guinness, et al.], copartners, doing business under firm name and style of Ladenburg, Thalmann & Company, v. Thomas W. Miller, as Alien Property Custodian, Frank White, as Treasurer of United States, and Carl Joerger [et al.], copartners, doing business under firm name and style of Delbruck, Schickler & Company; supplemental brief on behalf of Thomas W. Miller, as Alien Property Custodian, and Frank White, as Treasurer of United States. 1924. cover-title, 35 p. large 8° ‡

Lawrence, A. C., Leather Company. In Court of Claims, A. C. Lawrence Leather Company v. United States, no. D–4; demurrer [and] brief in support of demurrer. [1924.] p. 11–14, large 8° ‡

Maguire & Co., Incorporated. No. 75–B, in Court of Claims, Maguire & Company v. United States; objections to plaintiff's requests for findings of fact, defendant's request for findings of fact, statement. reply to plaintiff's brief, and brief. 1924. cover-title, ii+103–148 p. large 8° ‡

Nashville Protestant Hospital, Incorporated. No. 71–A, in Court of Claims. Nashville Protestant Hospital, Incorporated, v. United States: defendant's objections to plaintiff's request for findings of fact. defendant's request for findings of fact, defendant's brief. 1924. cover-title. i+157–186 p. large 8° ‡

New River Company. No. 627 and 628, in Supreme Court, Oct. term, 1923. United States et al. *v.* New River Company et al.; Slab Fork Coal Company et al. *v.* [same], appeals from district court for southern district of West Virginia; motion to advance. 1924. cover-title, 3 p. ‡

Newport Company. No. 2250, Court of Customs Appeals. Newport Co. *v.* United States; petition for rehearing on behalf of United States. 1924. cover-title, 3 p. ‡

Noe, Wm. R., & Sons. No. 2330, Court of Customs Appeals. United States *v.* Wm. R. Noe & Sons et al.; brief for United States. 1924. cover-title, 18 p. ‡

Oklahoma. No. 15, original, in Supreme Court, Oct. term, 1923, Oklahoma *v.* Texas, United States, intervener; response of United States to motion of Mrs. Lillis Morgan and others for return to them of patented flood plain lands and for payment to them of proceeds of oil wells thereon. 1924. cover-title, 4 p. ‡

Opinions. Official opinions of Attorneys General [July 11, 1921–Sept. 19, 1923], edited by George Kearney; indexes and tables by Emily A. Spilman. 1924. v. 33. xliv+643 p. il. [Includes opinions of Oct. 23, 1915 and Apr. 25, 1919.]
* Cloth, $1.50.   12—40693

—— Same. (H. doc. 199, 68th Cong. 1st sess.)

—— Same, v. 34, [signatures] 2–4. [1924.] p. 17–64. †

Pere Marquette Railway. No. 336–A, in Court of Claims, Pere Marquette Railway Company *v.* United States; defendant's objections to plaintiff's request for findings of fact, defendant's request for findings of fact, and brief. 1924. cover-title, ii+129–174 p. large 8° ‡

Piel Brothers. The beer cases, nos. 95, 200, 245, in Supreme Court, Oct. term, 1923, Piel Bros. *v.* Ralph A. Day, Federal prohibition director for State of New York, John Rafferty, collector of internal revenue for 1st district of New York, et al., appeal from circuit court of appeals for 2d circuit; James Everard's Breweries *v.* Ralph A. Day, prohibition director of New York, et al.; Edward and John Burke (Limited) *v.* David H. Blair, commissioner of internal revenue, et al., appeals from district court for southern district of New York; memorandum on behalf of appellees. 1924. cover-title, 15 p. ‡

—— Same; supplemental brief for appellees. 1924. cover-title, 19 p. ‡

Pothier, Roland R. No. 546, in Supreme Court, Oct. term, 1923, William R. Rodman, United States marshal [for district of Rhode Island], *v.* Roland R. Pothier, on writ of certiorari to circuit court of appeals for 1st circuit; brief in behalf of petitioner. 1924. cover-title, ii+35 p. ‡

Ray Consolidated Copper Company. No. B–160, in Court of Claims, Ray Consolidated Copper Company *v.* United States; Government's request for findings of fact and brief. 1924. cover-title, i+181–227 p. large 8° ‡

Reed, James. No. 227, in Supreme Court, Oct. term, 1923, United States *v.* James Reed, appeal from Court of Claims; brief for United States. 1924. cover-title, 14 p. ‡

Report. Appendix to Annual report of Attorney General, fiscal year 1922 [containing correspondence relating to action of Government with reference to interruption by force of interstate commerce, carriage of mails, etc., in 1922, printed pursuant to concurrent resolution of Mar. 3, 1923]. 1924. v+690 p. [This edition is bound in cloth with side-lettering on cover which reads: Lawless disorders and their suppression.] *Cloth. $1.00.

—— Same. (H. doc. 409, pt. 2, 67th Cong. 3d sess.)

River Rouge Improvement Company. No. 204, in Supreme Court, Oct. term, 1923, United States *v.* River Rouge Improvement Company et al., in error to circuit court of appeals for 6th circuit; reply brief for United States. 1924. cover-title, ii+25 p. ‡

Robertson, Frederick Y. No. 273, in Supreme Court, Oct. term, 1923, Thomas W. Miller, as Alien Property Custodian, and Frank White, as Treasurer of United States, *v.* Frederick Y. Robertson, appeal from circuit court of appeals for 2d circuit; brief on behalf of Alien Property Custodian and Treasurer of United States. 1924. cover-title, iv+136 p. [Cover-title reads incorrectly Frank W. White.] ‡

—— No. 493, in Supreme Court, Oct. term, 1923, Frederick Y. Robertson *v.* Thomas W. Miller, as Alien Property Custodian, and Frank White, as Treasurer of United States, appeal from circuit court of appeals for 2d circuit; brief on behalf of Alien Property Custodian and Treasurer of United States. 1924. cover-title, 14 p. ‡

Rogers, Wilbur. In Court of Claims, Wilbur Rogers *v.* United States, no. 16-B; defendant's brief. [1924.] p. 1-16, large 8° ‡

Ross, Waldo A. Interference no. 47229, in Patent Office, Waldo A. Ross *v.* George W. Burke, jr.; record for George W. Burke, jr. 1924. cover-title. i+82 p. ‡

Schutte, Fritz. No. 4099, in Court of Appeals of District of Columbia, Jan. term, 1924, Fritz Schutte *v.* Thomas W. Miller, as Alien Property Custodian, and Frank White, as Treasurer of United States; brief on behalf of Thomas W. Miller, as Alien Property Custodian, and Frank White, as Treasurer of United States. 1924. cover-title, i+40 p. ‡

Smith, J. D., & Co. No. 2322, Court of Customs Appeals, United States *v.* J. D. Smith & Co.; brief for United States. 1924. cover-title, 14 p. ‡

Smith, Hauser & McIsaac, Incorporated. In district court for district of Maryland, United States *v.* Smith, Hauser and McIsaac, Inc.; declaration. 1924. cover-title, 25 p. ‡

Super, Steve. No. 4110, in Court of Appeals of District of Columbia, Jan. term, 1924, Steve Super and Benjamin H. Wilder *v.* Hubert Work, Secretary of Interior, as member of Federal Power Commission, and Henry C. Wallace, Secretary of Agriculture, as member of Federal Power Commission, appeal from Supreme Court of District of Columbia; brief for appellees. 1924. cover-title, 16 p. ‡

Supplee-Biddle Hardware Company. No. 447, in Supreme Court, Oct. term, 1923, United States *v.* Supplee-Biddle Hardware Company, appeal from Court of Claims; brief for appellant. [1924.] cover-title, i+21 p. ‡

Swift & Co. Big Five meat packing companies, report in response to S. Res. 145 and S. Res. 167, containing information and data relating to suit of United States *v.* Swift & Co. et al., in Supreme Court of District of Columbia. Mar. 10, 1924. 39 p. (S. doc. 61, 68th Cong. 1st sess.) *Paper, 5c. 24—26236

Terminal Railroad Association of St. Louis. No. 425, in Supreme Court, Oct. term, 1923, Terminal Railroad Association of St. Louis et al. *v.* United States, Missouri, Kansas & Texas Railway Company et al., appeal from district court for eastern district of Missouri; brief for United States. 1924. cover-title, ii+20 p. ‡

Thompson, John W. No. 12230, in district court for northern district of Illinois, eastern division, United States *v.* John W. Thompson; indictment, viol. sec. 39, criminal code. 1924. cover-title, 6 p. ‡

Willoughby, John A. Patent appeal docket no. 1662, interference no. 44156, Court of Appeals of District of Columbia, Oct. term, 1923, Willoughby and Lowell *v.* James Harris Rogers, subject, submarine radio; brief for Willoughby and Lowell. 1924. cover-title, vi+242 p. il. ‡

Ziang Sun Wan. No. 451, in Supreme Court, Oct. term, 1923, Ziang Sung [Sun] Wan *v.* United States, on certiorari from Court of Appeals of District of Columbia; brief for United States. 1924. cover-title, iv+67 p. ‡

ATTORNEY GENERAL, ASSISTANT, FOR COURT OF CLAIMS AND DISTRICT COURTS

Report. Bureau for defense of suits against United States in Court of Claims and District Courts. [1924.] 13 p. [From Annual report of Attorney General, 1923.] †

LABOR DEPARTMENT

CHILDREN'S BUREAU

Child mentality and management, outlines for study [with lists of references, by Helen Thompson Woolley]; separate 2 [from] Child care and child welfare. [Reprint] 1924. 1-10+329-372 p. (Bureau publication 91.) [Prepared in cooperation with Federal Board for vocational Education. From Federal Board for vocational Education, Bulletin 65, Home economics series 5. Title-page rearranged from that of previous print.] * Paper, 5c.

Market-gardening. Work of children on truck and small-fruit farms in southern New Jersey. 1924. v+58 p. 1 pl. 2 p. of pl. (Bureau publication 132.) * Paper, 10c. L 24—60

EMPLOYMENT SERVICE

Employment agencies. Monthly report of activities of State and municipal employment services cooperating with U. S. Employment Service, Jan. 1924. 1924. 12 p. † L 24—62
—— Same, Feb. 1924. 1924. 16 p. †
Industrial employment information bulletin, v. 4, no. 2; Feb. 1924. [1924.] 18+[1] p. 4° [Monthly.] † L 21—17
News-letter 8, Jan. and Feb. 1924; [prepared in] Junior Division. 1924. [1]+20 p. †

LABOR STATISTICS BUREAU

Convict labor, 1923. 1924. [1]+33 p. * Paper, 5c. L 24—61
Employment in selected industries. Feb. 1924. 1924. [1]+13 p. [Monthly.] † L 23—234
Eugenics as viewed by sociologist; by Warren S. Thompson. [1924.] p. 227–239. [From Monthly labor review, Feb. 1924.] †
Monthly labor review, v. 18, no. 3; Mar. 1924. 1924. vi+475–697 p. il. * Paper. 15c. single copy, $1.50 a yr.; foreign subscription, $2.25. 15—26485
SPECIAL ARTICLES.—Recent northward migration of negro; by Joseph A. Hill.—Labor productivity in slaughtering; by Ethelbert Stewart.—Labor legislation of 1923; by Lindley D. Clark.—Conciliation work of Department of Labor, Jan. 1924; by Hugh L. Kerwin.—Statistics of immigration, Dec. 1923; by W. W. Husband.
NOTE.—The Review is the medium through which the Bureau publishes the results of original investigations too brief for bulletin purposes, notices of labor legislation by the States or by Congress, and Federal court decisions affecting labor, which from their importance should be given attention before they could ordinarily appear in the bulletins devoted to these subjects. One free subscription will be given to all labor departments and bureaus, workmen's compensation commissions, and other offices connected with the administration of labor laws and organizations exchanging publications with the Labor Statistics Bureau. Others desiring copies may obtain them from the Superintendent of Documents, Washington, D. C., at the prices stated above.
Negroes. Recent northward migration of negro; by Joseph A. Hill. [1924.] p. 475–488, il. [From Monthly labor review, Mar. 1924.] †
Prices. Prices and cost of living. 1924. [1]+500–528 p. il. [From Monthly labor review, Mar. 1924.] †
—— Wholesale prices of commodities for Jan. 1924. 1924. [1]+9 p. [Monthly.] † L 22—229
—— Same for Feb. 1924. [1924.] [1]+9 p. [Monthly.] †

NATURALIZATION BUREAU

Posters. O Governo dos Estados Unidos e as escolas publicas estão ajudando os nossos amigos nascidos no estranjeiro que são requerentes aos direitos de cidadão Americano a aprender a nossa lingua e os principios do nosso Governo afim de os preparar a serem bons cidadãos; [all lettered poster]. [1924.] 21×14 in. [Same, in Portuguese, as poster entitled United States Government and public schools are helping our foreign-born friends who are applicants for American citizenship to learn our language and principles of our Government in preparation for good citizenship, for which see Monthly catalogue for Mar. 1922, p. 544.] †

LIBRARY OF CONGRESS

COPYRIGHT OFFICE

Copyright. [Catalogue of copyright entries, new series. pt. 1, group 1, Books. v. 20] no. 115–122; Mar. 1924. Mar. 1–28, 1924. p. 1345–1408. [Issued several times a week; nos. 123–125 will be issued later.] 6—35347
NOTE.—Each number is issued in 4 parts: pt. 1, group 1, relates to books; pt. 1, group 2. to pamphlets, leaflets, contributions to newspapers or periodicals, etc., lectures, sermons, addresses for oral delivery, dramatic compositions, maps, motion pictures; pt. 2, to periodicals; pt. 3, to musical compositions; pt. 4, to works of art, reproductions of a work of art, drawings or plastic works of scientific or technical character. photographs, prints, and pictorial illustrations.
Subscriptions for the Catalogue of copyright entries should be made to the Superintendent of Documents, Washington, D. C., instead of to the Register of Copyrights. Prices are as follows: Paper, $3.00 a yr. (4 pts.), foreign subscription, $5.00; pt. 1 (groups 1 and 2), 5c. single copy (group 1, price of group 2 varies), $1.00 a yr., foreign subscription, $2.25; pt. 3, $1.00 a yr., foreign subscription, $1.50; pts. 2 and 4. each 10c. single copy, 50c. a yr., foreign subscription, 70c.

Copyright—Continued. Same, pt. 1, group 2, Pamphlets, leaflets, contributions to newspapers or periodicals, etc., lectures, sermons, addresses for oral delivery, dramatic compositions, maps, motion pictures, v. 20, no. 9. 1924. iii+1229–1443 p. [Monthly.]

MIXED CLAIMS COMMISSION, UNITED STATES AND GERMANY

Boyer, Henry. No. 276, before Mixed Claims Commission, United States and Germany, United States on behalf of Henry Boyer *v.* Germany; brief on behalf of United States. 1924. cover-title, 12 p. 4° ‡

NATIONAL ADVISORY COMMITTEE FOR AERONAUTICS

Aerofoils. Aerodynamic characteristics of airfoils, 3 [continuation of Reports 93 and 124]. 1924. cover-title, p. 143–186, il. 4° (Report 182.) [Text and illustration on p. 2 and 3 of cover.] * Paper, 15c.   21—26356

Propellers. Effect of slipstream obstructions on air propellers; by E. P. Lesley and B. M. Woods. 1924. cover-title, 24 p. il. 4° (Report 177.) [Text and illustration on p. 2 and 3 of cover.] * Paper, 10c.   24—26305

NAVY DEPARTMENT

Court-martial orders. Court-martial order 12, 1923; Dec. 31, 1923. [1924.] 13 p. 12° [Monthly.] ‡

—— Same 1, 1924; Jan. 31, 1924. [1924.] 8 p. 12° [Monthly.] ‡

Maritime law. Instructions for Navy governing maritime warfare, June, 1917. [Reprint] 1924. 79 p. ‡   24—26271

Orders. General order 120–126 [6th series]; Jan. 10–Mar. 12, 1924. [1924.] Each 2 p. 4° ‡

Virgin Islands of United States, draft of proposed legislation to extend provisions of national bank act to Virgin Islands of United States. Mar. 25, 1924. 3 p. (H. doc. 229, 68th Cong. 1st sess.) * Paper, 5c.

MARINE CORPS

Shooting. Instructions in pistol marksmanship, Marine Corps, 1924. 1924. ii+39 p. il. 12° [This is a reprint, with slight modifications, of a non-Government publication entitled Instructions in learning accurate pistol shooting, copyrighted and published by Gunnery Sergeant John M. Thomas, Marine Corps, 1922.] ‡

MEDICINE AND SURGERY BUREAU

Dental Corps, Navy. Circular for information of persons desiring to enter Dental Corps of Navy. Revised Jan. 1924. 1924. [1]+4 p. 4° †

Hospital Corps quarterly. Supplement to United States naval medical bulletin published for information of Hospital Corps of Navy, July and Oct. 1923, nos. 26 and 27, old series, v. 7, nos. 3 and 4, new series; edited by W. W. Behlow. 1924. v+121 p. il. 3 pl. 4 p. of pl. [Title on cover is: Hospital Corps quarterly. Two numbers issued as one publication.] * Paper, 20c. (price given on verso of title-page incorrect).

SPECIAL ARTICLES.—Hospital Corps handbook, Navy, 1923; by E. R. Stitt.—Another drop of blood; by Ivor Griffith.—Medicinal plant garden at Pharmacist's Mates' School; by E. G. Swann.—From recruit to hospital corpsman; by D. Gunter.—Some pointers on liquor magnesii citratis, U. S. P., and some facts relative to melting point of cocoa butter not found in pharmacopœia or dispensatories; by A. H. Benhard.—Regarding requisitions; by B. E. Irwin.—Medical department aboard U. S. S. Arkansas; [by] M. O. Warns.—Test for methyl in ethyl alcohol; by L. Rowe.—Pharmacist's mate on recruiting duty; by A. B. Brown.—Reactions and technique involved in chemical analysis of blood; by P. S. Gault.—Coal; by J. I. Wexlin.—United States naval radio station, Wailupe, Hawaii; by H. B. Felton.—Outline on embalming as aid for Navy hospital corpsmen; by R. J. Isreall.—Index, 1923.

Naval medical bulletin. United States naval medical bulletin. published for
information of Medical Department of service. Mar. 1924, v. 20, no. 3; edited
by W. M. Kerr. 1924. vi+285–422 p. 16 p. of pl. 1 tab. [Monthly.]
* Paper, 15c. single copy, $1.50 a yr.; foreign subscription, $2.50.   8—35095

SPECIAL ARTICLES.—Aviation accidents and methods of prevention; by J. F.
Neuberger.—Ophthalmology in its relation to aviation; [1. Some eye problems special
to the services with particular reference to flying, by David Munro; 2. Judgment of
distance, by Cecil Clements].—Notes on course for instructors of nursing [given at
Leland Stanford University summer course, June 19–July 15, 1923, with lists of
references; compiled by Elizabeth M. O'Brien].—Notes on preventive medicine for
medical officers, Navy [including Remarks on epidemiology of smallpox and preventive
value of vaccination with cowpox virus].

NAVIGATION BUREAU

Navy directory, officers of Navy and Marine Corps, including officers of Naval
Reserve Force (active), Marine Corps Reserve (active), and foreign officers
serving with Navy, Mar. 1, 1924. 1924. iii+244 p. [Bimonthly.] * Paper,
25c. single copy, $1.25 a yr.; foreign subscription, $1.75.

HYDROGRAPHIC OFFICE

NOTE.—The charts, sailing directions, etc., of the Hydrographic Office are sold by the
office in Washington and also by agents at the principal American and foreign seaports
and American lake ports. Copies of the General catalogue of mariners' charts and books
and of the Hydrographic bulletins. reprints, and Notice to mariners are supplied free on
application at the Hydrographic Office in Washington and at the branch offices in Boston,
New York, Philadelphia, Baltimore, Norfolk, Savannah, New Orleans, Galveston, San
Francisco, Portland (Oreg.), Seattle, Chicago, Cleveland, Buffalo, Sault Ste. Marie,
and Duluth.

Africa. Supplement to publication 156, Africa pilot, v. 2. including summary
of Notices to mariners and other information from date of publication (Apr.
16, 1916) to Dec. 31, 1923. 1924. ii+43 leaves. †
Australia. Supplement to publication 168, Australian pilot, v. 2, including
summary of Notices to mariners and other information from date of publication (Apr. 10, 1920) to Dec. 31, 1923. 1924. ii+15 leaves, il. map. †
—— Supplement to publication 170, Australian pilot, v. 4, including summary
of Notices to mariners and other information from date of publication (Mdy
14, 1920) to Dec. 31, 1923. 1924. ii+18 leaves, map. †
Baltic Sea. Supplement to publication 142, Baltic pilot, v. 1, including summary of Notices to mariners and other information from date of publication
(Jan. 29, 1920) to Dec. 31, 1923. 1924. ii+46 leaves, map. †
—— Supplement to publication 143, Baltic pilot, v. 2, including summary of
Notices to mariners and other information from date of publication (Jan. 2,
1920) to Dec. 31, 1923. 1924. ii+34 leaves, il. map. †
Bengal, Bay of. Supplement to publication 160, Bay of Bengal pilot, including
summary of Notices to mariners and other information from date of publication (May 7, 1923) to Dec. 31, 1923. 1924. ii+2 leaves. †
Black Sea. Supplement to publication 155, Black Sea pilot, including summary
of Notices to mariners and other information from date of publication (Mar.
12, 1920) to Dec. 31, 1923. 1924. ii+44 leaves, map. †
British Columbia. Supplement to publication 175, British Columbia pilot, v. 1,
including summary of Notices to mariners and other information from date
of publication (Mar. 1, 1920) to Dec. 31, 1923. 1924. ii+30 leaves, il. map. †
—— Supplement to publication 176, British Columbia pilot. v. 2. including
summary of Notices to mariners and other information from date of publication (Mar. 5, 1920) to Dec. 31, 1923. 1924. ii+15 leaves, il. map. †
Central America. Supplement to publication 130, Central America and Mexico
pilot (east coast), including summary of Notices to mariners and other information from date of publication (Feb. 5, 1920) to Dec. 31, 1923. 1924.
ii+34 leaves, 2 maps. †
East Indies. Supplement to publication 163, East Indies pilot, v. 1. including
summary of Notices to mariners and other information from date of publication (May 17, 1916) to Dec. 31, 1923. 1924. ii+35 leaves, il. †
Great Britain. Supplement to publication 144, British Islands pilot. v. 1. including summary of Notices to mariners and other information from date of
publication (Mar. 19, 1920) to Dec. 31, 1923. 1924. ii+35 leaves, map. †
—— Supplement to publication 150, British Isles pilot. v. 7. including summary of Notices to mariners and other information from date of publication
(Oct. 22, 1917) to Dec. 31, 1923. 1924. ii+49 leaves. †

Hydrographic bulletin, weekly, no. 1800–3; Mar. 5–26, 1924. [1924.] Each 1 p. large 4° and f° [For Ice supplements to accompany nos. 1800–3, see below under center head *Charts* the subhead *Pilot charts*.] †

India. Supplement to publication 159, West coast of India pilot, including summary of Notices to mariners and other information from date of publication (June 1, 1920) to Dec. 31, 1923. 1924. ii+17 leaves, 2 maps. †

Indian Ocean. Supplement to publication 161, South Indian Ocean pilot, including summary of Notices to mariners and other information from date of publication (Apr. 17, 1917) to Dec. 31, 1923. 1924. ii+23 leaves. † ·

Lights. List of lights, with fog signals and visible time signals, including uniform time system, radio time signals, radio weather bulletins, and radio compass stations of the world; v. 1, Coasts of North and South America (excepting United States), West Indies, and Hawaiian Islands; corrected to Jan. 12, 1924. 1924. 546 p. map. ([Publication] 30.) † Paper, 60c.   7—24401

——— Same: v. 5, Norway, Iceland, and Arctic Ocean; corrected to Dec. 29, 1923. 1924. 576 p. map. ([Publication] 34.) † Paper, 60c.   7—24404

Mediterranean Sea. Supplement to publication 151, Mediterranean pilot, v. 1, including summary of Notices to mariners and other information from date of publication (Mar. 5, 1920) to Dec. 31, 1923. 1924.. ii+21 leaves, il. map. †

——— Supplement to publication 152, Mediterranean pilot, v. 2, including summary of Notices to mariners and other information from date of publication (Jan. 1, 1917) to Dec. 31, 1923. 1924. ii+36 leaves, il. map. †

——— Supplement to publication 153, Mediterranean pilot, v. 3, including summary of Notices to mariners and other information from date of publication (June 4, 1917) to Dec. 31, 1923. 1924. ii+40 leaves, il. map. †

North Sea. Supplement to publication 135, North Sea pilot, including summary of Notices to mariners and other information from date of publication (May 28, 1922) to Dec. 31, 1923. . 1924. ii+17 leaves, 2 maps. †

Notice to aviators 3, 1924; Mar. 1 [1924]. [1924.] 4 p. [Monthly.] †
20—26958

Notice to mariners 9–13. 1924; Mar. 1–29 [1924]. [1924.] [xlv]+225–358 leaves. [Weekly.] †

Pacific Ocean. Supplement to publication 165, Pacific Islands pilot, v. 1, including summary of Notices to mariners and other information from date of publication (Aug. 20, 1920) to Dec. 31, 1923. 1924. ii+20 leaves, il. †

——— Supplement to publication 166, Pacific Islands pilot, v. 2, including summary of Notices to mariners and other information from date of publication (June 18, 1920) to Dec. 31, 1923. 1924. ii+33 leaves, il. 2 maps. †

Persian Gulf. Supplement to publication 158, Persian Gulf pilot, including summary of Notices to mariners and other information from date of publication (Mar. 19, 1920) to Dec. 31, 1923. 1924. ii+21 leaves, il. map. †

Scandinavia. Supplement to publication 141, Scandinavia pilot, v. 2, including summary of Notices to mariners and other information from date of publication (Jan. 29, 1920) to Dec. 31, 1923. 1924. ii+67 leaves, map. †

Tide calendar [for Norfolk (Navy Yard) and Newport News, Va.], Apr. 1924. [1924.] 1 p. 4° [Monthly.] †

West Indies. Supplement to publication 128, West Indies pilot, v. 1, including summary of Notices to mariners and other information from date of publication (Apr. 15, 1922) to Dec. 31, 1923. 1924. ii+18 leaves, map. †

Charts

Africa. South coast of Africa, Algoa Bay to Cape Town, from British surveys between 1853 and 1870; chart 1601. Scale 1° long.=4.6 in. Washington, Hydrographic Office, published May, 1897, 14th edition, Mar. [1924]. 32.9× 44 in. † 60c.

Australia. Australia, east coast, Lady Elliot Island to Cape Byron, mainly from British surveys between 1863 and 1870; chart 3429. Scale 1° long.= 6.8 in. Washington, Hydrographic Office, Mar. 1924. 38.6×25.7 in. † 40c.

——— Australia, south coast, Rivoli Bay to Cape Jervis, from British survey in 1870 and 1871; chart 3438. Scale 1° long.=12 in. Washington, Hydrographic Office, Feb. 1924. 39×26.1 in. † 40c.

Earth. Outline chart of the world [showing Pacific groups of islands belonging to various countries, and mandate areas] ; chart 1262a. Scale 10° long.=1.2 in. Washington, Hydrographic Office, published Oct. 1923, 2d edition, Feb. 1924. 27.2×47.9 in. † 50c.

Guanabara, Bay of. Bahia de Guanabara, including Rio∙de Janeiro Harbor, east coast of Brazil, from Brazilian Government chart published in 1922 [with insets] ; chart 5385. Scale naut. m.=1.5 in. Washington, Hydrographic Office, published Mar. 1923, 2d edition, Mar. 1924. 39.9×29.9 in. † 50c:

Channels between Ilha de Mocangue and Maruhy.
Commercial quays and approaches [Rio de Janeiro].

Haro Strait and adjacent channels, Wash., and British Columbia, compiled from latest United States and British surveys; chart 1769. Scale naut. m.=1 in. Washington, Hydrographic Office, published Feb. 1900, 24th edition, Feb. [1924]. 41.3×31.6 in. † 60c.

Medway River. ∙River Medway, England, east coast, Bishops Ness to Rochester, from latest British surveys; chart 4487. Scale naut. m.=6 in. Washington, Hydrographic Office, published Oct. 1915, 5th edition, Feb. 1924. 26.4×39.8 in. † 40c.

Miramichi Bay, New Brunswick, Gulf of St. Lawrence, original British survey in 1885; chart 1179. Scale naut. m.=1.5 in. Washington, Hydrographic Office, published Dec. 1889, 20th edition. Feb. [1924]. 23.8×34.9 in. † 40c.

New Guinea, southwest coast, Cape van den Bosch (Tanjong Katumin) to Lakahia Bay, from Netherlands Government survey in 1910 and 1911 [with insets] ; chart 2982. Scale naut. m.=0.4 in. Washington, Hydrographic Office, Feb. 1924. 26×41.8 in. † 50c.

Arguni Bay.
Etna Bay (Kiruru Bay), from Netherlands Government survey in 1905.

Newfoundland. Newfoundland, northern part, and adjacent coast of Labrador, from latest British and French surveys; chart 2440a. Scale 1° long.=4.6 in. Washington, Hydrographic Office, Feb. 1924. 28.9×38.1 in. † 40c.

——— Newfoundland, southern part, from latest British and French surveys; chart 2440b. Scale 1° long.=4.6 in. ┆ Washington, Hydrographic Office, Feb. 1924. 27.1×38.1 in. † 40c.

Nova Scotia, west coast, Tusket Islands to Brier Island, from British surveys between 1850 and 1862; chart 2134. Scale naut. m.=1 in. Washington, Hydrographic Office, published June, 1905, 12th edition, Mar. [1924]. 41.2× 32 in. † 60c.

Pacific Ocean. North Pacific Ocean, sheet 2; chart 527. Scale 1° long.=0.6 in. Washington, Hydrographic Office, published Jan. 1874, 120th edition, Mar. 1924. 47.6×21.9 in. † 70c.

Panama Canal. Panama Canal, Canal Zone, Central America, Gamboa Reach to Panama Bay, from Isthmian Canal Commission and other United States Government surveys [with insets] ; chart 5001. Scale naut. m.=1.9 in. Washington, Hydrographic Office, published Dec. 1914, 13th edition, Feb. 1924. 36.6×28.6 in. † 30c.

Balboa Harbor, Outline plan of.
Gaillard Cut, Enlarged plan of.

——— Panama Canal, Canal Zone, Central America, Limon Bay to Gamboa Reach, from Isthmian Canal Commission and other United States Government surveys; chart 5000. Scale naut.∙m.=1.8 in. Washington, Hydrographic Office, published Dec. 1914, 12th edition, Feb. 1924. 40.2×28.5 in. † 30c.

Para River, channel to Para, Brazil, from latest information ; chart 1375. Scale naut. m.=1.5 in. Washington, Hydrographic Office, published June, 1893, 15th edition, Mar. 1924. 38.3×25 in. † 40c.

Pilot charts. Ice supplement to north Atlantic pilot chart; issue 100. Scale 1° long.=0.3 in. Washington, Hydrographic Office [1924]. 8.9×11.8 in. [To accompany Hydrographic bulletin 1800, Mar. 5, 1924.] †

——— Same; issue 101. Scale 1° long.=0.3 in. Washington, Hydrographic Office [1924]. 8.9×11.8 in. [To accompany Hydrographic bulletin 1801, Mar. 12, 1924.] †

——— Same; issue 102. Scale 1° long.=0.3 in. Washington, Hydrographic Office [1924]. 8.9×11.8 in. [To accompany Hydrographic bulletin 1802, Mar. 19, 1924.] †

Pilot charts—Continued. Same; issue 103. Scale 1° long.=0.3 in. Washington, Hydrographic Office [1924]. 8.9×11.8 in. [To accompany Hydrographic bulletin 1803, Mar. 26, 1924.] †
—— Pilot chart of Central American waters, Apr. 1924; chart 3500. Scale 1° long.=0.7 in. Washington, Hydrographic Office, Mar. 12, 1924. 23.4×35.1 in. [Monthly. Certain portions of the data are furnished by the Weather Bureau.] † 10c.
NOTE.—Contains on reverse : Currents and navigational details in waters of Gulf of Mexico, Caribbean Sea, and west coast of Central America; by John C. Soley.
—— Pilot chart of Indian Ocean, May, 1924; chart 2603. Scale 1° long.=0.2 in. Washington, Hydrographic Office, Mar. 12, 1924. 22.6×31 in. [Monthly. Certain portions of the data are furnished by the Weather Bureau.] † 10c.
NOTE.—Contains on reverse : Great circle sailing chart of Indian Ocean, [with] Supplementary method for finding courses.
—— Pilot chart of north Atlantic Ocean, Apr. 1924; chart 1400. Scale 1° long.=0 27 in. Washington, Hydrographic Office, Mar. 12, 1924. 23.2×31.8 in. [Monthly. Certain portions of the data are furnished by the Weather Bureau.] † 10c.   14—16339
NOTE.—Contains on reverse : Great circle sailing chart of north Atlantic Ocean, [with] Supplementary method for finding courses.
—— Pilot chart of north Pacific Ocean, May, 1924; chart 1401. Scale 1° long.=0.2 in. Washington, Hydrographic Office, Mar. 12, 1924. 23.7×35.3 in. [Monthly. Certain portions of the data are furnished by the Weather Bureau.] † 10c.
NOTE.—Contains on reverse : Great circle sailing chart of north Pacific Ocean, [with] Supplementary method for finding courses.
Rio Grande do Sul, Brazil, from Brazilian survey in 1915, with additions to 1923 [with insets] ; chart 1191. Scale naut. m.=2.3 in. Washington, Hydrographic Office, published Nov. 1916, 3d edition, Mar. [1924]. 30.8×18.9 in. † 30c.
Castillo and Polonio anchorages, Uruguay, from latest information.
Paloma Roads and harbor, Uruguay, from latest information.
San Antonio, Argentina. Port San Antonio, Argentina, from Argentine Government surveys to 1911; chart 2357. Scale naut. m.=1.5 in. Washington, Hydrographic Office, published Dec. 1917, 2d edition, Mar. 1924. 29.7×20.1 in. † 20c.
Suez, Gulf of. Suez Bay, Red Sea, from British and Suez Canal Company's surveys to 1920; chart 5435. Scale naut. m.=2 in. Washington, Hydrographic Office, Feb. 1924. 33.8×26.9 in. † 40c.
Tarakan Road, Borneo, east coast, from Netherlands Government surveys to 1921, with additions from survey by Capt. von der Biesen, Dutch S. S. J. B. Aug. Kessler in 1913; chart 3095. Scale naut. m.=2 in. Washington, Hydrographic Office, published Oct. 1913, 4th edition, Mar. 1924. 12×17.2 in. † 10c.
Topolobampo Harbor, Gulf of California, original survey by U. S. S. Narragansett in 1875; chart 1335. Scale naut. m.=2 in. Washington, Hydrographic Office, published June, 1892, 16th edition, Mar. [1924]. 30.6×40.4 in. † 50c.
Yarmouth Harbor, Nova Scotia, from Canadian survey in 1922; with inset, Yarmouth inner harbor; chart 5441. Scale 2000 yds.=6.3 in. Washington, Hydrographic Office, Feb. 1924. 26.9×18.2 in. † 20c.

NAUTICAL ALMANAC OFFICE

American ephemeris and nautical almanac, [calendar] year 1926. 1924. xviii+ 804 p. il. 2 maps. * Cloth, $1.00.   7—35435
NOTE.—In the volumes of the American ephemeris and nautical almanac and the American nautical almanac, beginning with those for 1925, the hours of the day are counted from midnight to midnight instead of from noon to noon as was done in the volumes before 1925, and the time is designated civil time instead of mean time. By this change each day begins 12 hours earlier than formerly.

RECRUITING BUREAU

[*Poster*] 257. n. p. [Feb. 29, 1924]. 14×17 in. [Title is : Navy ashore.] †

SUPPLIES AND ACCOUNTS BUREAU

Manual. Changes in Manual of Supply Corps [Navy, 1922], no. 2; July 1 1923. [1923.] iii p. 4° [Accompanied by 100 variously numbered pages to be inserted in their proper places in the Manual.] ‡

572   MARCH, 1924

OIL CASES, SPECIAL COUNSEL FOR UNITED STATES IN

Mammoth Oil Company. In district court for district of Wyoming, United States *v.* Mammoth Oil Company, corporation of Delaware, Sinclair Crude Oil Purchasing Company, corporation of Delaware, and Sinclair Pipe Line Company, corporation of Maine; bill of complaint. 1924. cover-title, 53 p. ‡

Pan American Petroleum Company. No. —, in equity. in district court for southern district of California. northern division, United States *v.* Pan American Petroleum Company and Pan American Petroleum and Transport Company; bill of complaint. 1924. cover-title, 38 p. ‡

PAN AMERICAN UNION

NOTE.—The Pan American Union sells its own monthly bulletins, handbooks, etc., at prices usually ranging from 5c. to $2.50. The price of the English edition of the bulletin is 25c. a single copy or $2.50 a year, the Spanish edition $2.00 a year, the Portuguese edition $1.50 a year; there is an additional charge of 50c. a year on each edition for countries outside the Pan American Union. Address the Director General of the Pan American Union, Washington, D. C.

Bulletin (English edition). Bulletin of Pan American Union, Mar. 1924; [v. 58, no. 3]. [1924.] iv+217–324 p. il. [Monthly.]
8—30967

—— Same. (H. doc. 6, pt. 9, 68th Cong. 1st sess.)

—— *(Portuguese edition).* Boletim da União Pan-Americana, Março, 1924, edição portugueza; [v. 26, no. 3]. [Sun Job Print, Baltimore, Md., 1924.] [iv]+153–228 p. il. [Monthly. This number is entitled O problema da habitação obreira nas Americas.]
11—27014

—— *(Spanish edition).* Boletín de la Unión Panamericana, Marzo, 1924. sección española; [v. 58, no. 3]. [1924.] iv+221–327 p. il. [Monthly.]
12—12555

—— Same, index to v. 56, with title, Índice del Boletín de la Unión Panamericana. v. 56 [sección española]; Enero–Junio, 1923. [1924.] [1]+xiv p.

—— Same, index to v. 57, with title, Boletín de la Unión Panamericana, v. 57 [sección española]; Julio–Diciembre, 1923 [índice]. [1924.] [1]+xxiv p.

Chile. Commerce of Chile, latest reports from Chilean official sources. 1924. [1]+16 p. †
20—15504

Costa Rica, general descriptive data. 1924. [2]+30 p. il. †   17—14293

Guatemala. Commerce of Guatemala, latest reports from Guatemalan official sources. 1924. 8 p. †
13—6844

Mexico City, city of palaces; [by Wm. A. Reid]. 1924. [2]+30 p. il. †
24—26272

Pan American Child Congress. 4th Pan American Child Congress, to be held in Santiago, Chile. Oct. 12–19, 1924. 1924. [2]+6 p. il. [From Bulletin, Mar. 1924.] †

PANAMA CANAL

NOTE.—Although The Panama Canal makes its reports to, and is under the supervision of. the Secretary of War, it is not a part of the War Department..

Panama Canal record. Panama Canal record, Aug. 16, 1922–Aug. 8, 1923; v. 16' [title-page] with index. The Panama Canal, Balboa Heights, Canal Zone, 1923. 6 p.
7—35328

—— Same, v. 17, no. 30–33; Mar. 5–26, 1924. Balboa Heights, C. Z. [1924]. p. 425–482. [Weekly.]

NOTE.—The yearly subscription rate of the Panama Canal record is 50c. domestic, and $1.00 foreign, (single issues 2c.), except in the case of Government departments and bureaus, Members of Congress, representatives of foreign Governments, steamship lines, chambers of commerce, boards of trade, and university and public libraries; to whom the Record is distributed free. The word "domestic" refers to the United States, Canada, Canal Zone, Cuba, Guam, Hawaii, Manua, Mexico, the Philippines, Porto Rico, Republic of Panama, Tutuila, and the Virgin Islands. Subscriptions will commence with the first issue of the Record in the month in which the subscriptions are received, unless otherwise requested. Remittances should be made payable to Disbursing Clerk. The Panama Canal, but should be forwarded to the Chief of Office, The Panama Canal, Washington, D. C. The name and address to which the Record is to be sent should be plainly written. Postage stamps, foreign money, and defaced or smooth coins will not be accepted.

HEALTH DEPARTMENT

Report of Health Department of The Panama Canal, calendar year 1922. Panama Canal Press, Mount Hope, C. Z., 1923. 120 p. il. 7 pl. 12° †   9—22388

PURCHASING DEPARTMENT

Supplies. Circular [proposals for supplies] 1596 and 1598; Mar. 17 and 25, 1924. [1924.] 37+[1] p. and 28 p. f° †

SUPPLY DEPARTMENT

COMMISSARY DIVISION

Employees' manual, Apr. 1923. Panama Canal Press, Mount Hope, C. Z. [1923]. 44 p. small 4° ‡

POST OFFICE DEPARTMENT

Foot-and-mouth disease. Restrictions on shipment of carcasses, hides, skins, or hoofs of cattle, sheep, and other animals, and of hay, straw, or similar fodder from area in California quarantined on account of foot-and-mouth disease; [issued by] 3d assistant Postmaster General. Mar. 1, 1924. 1 p. oblong 32° †

Mail matter. Six weeks to be allowed for return from Hawaii of notices regarding mail held for postage; Individually addressed copies of publications inclosed in packages should include name of post office: [issued by] 3d assistant Postmaster General. Feb. 25, 1924. 1 p. 12° †

Postal bulletin, v. 45, no. 13407–432; Mar. 1–31, 1924. 1924. Each 1 p. or 2 leaves, f° [Daily except Sundays and holidays.] *Paper, 5c. single copy, $2.00 a yr.   6—5810

Postal guide. United States official postal guide, 4th series, v. 3, no. 9; Mar. 1924, monthly supplement. 1924. cover-title, 39 p. [Includes Insert 852 to Postal laws and regulations of United States. Text on p. 2–4 of cover.] *Official postal guide, with supplements, $1.00, foreign subscription, $1.50; July issue, 75c.; supplements published monthly (11 pamphlets) 25c., foreign subscription, 50c.   4—18254

Postal service. United States postal system, 1639–1924, biggest single business in the world, its job. [1924.] [4] p. il. 4° †

RAILWAY MAIL SERVICE

Illinois. Alphabetical scheme of Illinois for use of publishers in distribution of 2d-class mail, 1924. 1924. 29 p. ‡

Louisiana. Alphabetical scheme of Louisiana, for use of publishers in distribution of 2d-class mail, 1924. 1924. 19 p. ‡

Mail-trains. Schedule of mail trains, no. 369, Feb. 26, 1924, 2d division, Railway Mail Service, comprising New York, New Jersey, Pennsylvania, Delaware, eastern shore of Maryland, Accomac and Northampton counties, Va., Porto Rico, and Virgin Islands. 1924. 297+[1] p. narrow 8° ‡

—— Schedule of mail trains, no. 444, Feb. 19, 1924, 3d division, Railway Mail Service, comprising District of Columbia, Maryland, North Carolina, Virginia, and West Virginia (except peninsula of Maryland and virginia). 1924. 149+ [1] p. narrow 8° ‡

TOPOGRAPHY DIVISION

Note.—Since February, 1908, the Topography Division has been preparing rural-delivery maps of counties in which rural delivery is completely established. They are published in two forms, one giving simply rural free delivery routes, starting from a single given post office, and sold at 10 cents each; the other, the rural free delivery routes in an entire county, sold at 35 cents each. A uniform scale of 1 inch to 1 mile is used. Editions are not issued, but sun-print copies are produced in response to special calls addressed to the Disbursing Clerk, Post Office Department, Washington, D. C. These maps should not be confused with the post route maps, for which see Monthly catalogue for February, 1924, page 486.

PRESIDENT OF UNITED STATES

Amnesty and pardon, proclamation. [Mar. 5, 1924.] [2] p. f° ([No. 1687.]) †

Barnett, De Warren B. Executive order [authorizing appointment of De Warren B. Barnett and Charles F. Cortelyou in Special Agency Service of Customs of Treasury Department]. Feb. 28, 1924. 1 p. f° (No. 3966.) ‡

Big Lake Reservation. 3d Executive order [modifying boundaries of Big Lake Reservation, Ark., as defined by Executive order dated May 31, 1918]. Feb. 23, 1924. 1 p. map. f° (No. 3964.) ‡

Income tax. Income tax returns of certain individuals and corporations, communication transmitting, in response to resolution, reply declining, under advice of acting assistant Attorney General, request to direct Secretary of Treasury to turn over to Senate Committee on Public Lands and Surveys all income tax returns filed by certain individuals and corporations named in above resolution. Mar. 6. 1924. 5 p. (S. doc. 57, 68th Cong. 1st sess.) * Paper, 5c.

—— Twenty-five per cent reduction in taxes, message recommending enactment of resolution for reduction of 25 per cent in taxes to be paid before 15th of March for current year. Mar. 11, 1924. 1 p. (S. doc. 63, 68th Cong. 1st sess.) * Paper, 5c.

National forests. Executive order. Grand Mesa National Forest, Colo. [directing that Battlement National Forest, Colo., shall hereafter be known as Grand Mesa National Forest]. Mar. 11, 1924. 1 p. f° (No. 3970.) ‡

—— Executive order, Kaibab National Forest, Ariz. [transferring Mt. Trumbull division of Dixie National Forest, as defined by proclamation of May 10. 1916, to Kaibab National Forest]. Mar. 18, 1924. 1 p. f° (No. 3972.) ‡

Officers, Army. Detail of officers of United States, proposed bill to authorize temporary Executive disposition, in public interest, of services of officers subject to Executive control. Mar. 24, calendar day Mar. 26, 1924. 2 p. (S. doc. 79. 68th Cong. 1st sess.) * Paper, 5c.

Panama Canal. Executive order concerning costs and taxation thereof in District Court and Magistrate Courts of Panama Canal Zone, and notices in probate and guardianship proceedings [amending Executive order of Jan. 9. 1920, concerning costs and security for costs in District Court and Magistrate Courts in Panama Canal Zone]. [Mar. 5. 1924.] 2 p. f° ([No. 3960.]) ‡

—— Executive order relating to division of Canal Zone into 2 judicial districts, and amending Executive order promulgated Mar. 12, 1914 [relating to establishment of Canal Zone judiciary, so as to include certain described additional territory in Balboa Division of District Court of Canal Zone]. Feb. 26, 1924. 1 p. f° (No. 3965.) ‡

—— Executive order relating to pardons, paroles. remission of fines and forfeitures, and kindred subjects [and setting forth powers granted to governor of The Panama Canal concerning said subjects]. Mar. 5, 1924. 1 p. f° (No. 3968.) ‡

Utah. Executive order. Utah [withdrawing certain described public lands in Utah from settlement. etc.. pending resurvey, such withdrawal to remain in effect until resurvey is accepted and approved plat thereof is officially filed in local land office]. Mar. 12, 1924. 1 p. f° (No. 3971.) ‡

Wheat and wheat products, proclamation [authorizing certain increase in duty on wheat and certain wheat products and certain decrease in duty on bran, shorts, and by-product feeds obtained in milling wheat, in order to equalize differences in costs of production in United States and in Canada]. [Mar. 7. 1924.] [2] p. f° ([No. 1688.]) †

Wyoming. Executive order. Wyoming [withdrawing certain described public lands in Wyoming from settlement. etc., pending resurvey, such withdrawal to remain in effect until resurvey is accepted and approved plat thereof is officially filed in local land office]. Mar. 5. 1924. 1 p. f° (No. 3967.) ‡

RAILROAD ADMINISTRATION

Bills of lading. No. 15201, before Interstate Commerce Commission, Liggett & Myers Tobacco Company *v.* director general; brief on behalf of director general. 1924. cover-title, 11 p. ‡

Coal. Before Interstate Commerce Commission, no. 14641, Midland Coal Company *v.* director general; exceptions on behalf of director general to report proposed by examiner. 1924. cover-title, 3 p. ‡

Cotton-seed oil. Before Interstate Commerce Commission, no. 14815, Los Angeles Soap Company *v.* director general; exceptions to examiner's proposed report filed on behalf of director general. 1924. cover-title, 4 p. ‡

Creosote. Before Interstate Commerce Commission, no. 14514, Shreveport Creosoting Company *v.* Louisiana & Pacific Railway Company and James C. Davis, director general of railroads, as agent; exceptions on part of director general to report proposed by examiner. 1923[1924]. cover-title, 15 p. [Imprint date incorrectly given as 1923.]

Demurrage. Before Interstate Commerce Commission, no. 14991, General Motors Corporation *v.* director general et al.; brief on behalf of director general. 1924. cover-title, ii+31 p. ‡

—— No. 517, in Supreme Court, Oct. term, 1923, James C. Davis, director general of railroads, as agent, *v.* E. I. du Pont de Nemours & Company; brief for respondent. 1924. cover-title, ii+39 p. ‡

Freight rates. Before Interstate Commerce Commission, no. 14215, Omaha Refining Company et al. *v.* director general; exceptions on behalf of director general to proposed report of examiner. 1924. cover-title, 7 p. ‡

—— Before Interstate Commerce Commission, no. 14891, Geo. H. McFadden & Brother's Agency *v.* director general; no. 14891, sub no. 1, Edward M. Fowler *v.* [same]; director general's exceptions to report proposed by examiner. 1924. cover-title, 3 p. ‡

—— Before Interstate Commerce Commission, no. 15106, Pendleton & Gilkey et al. *v.* director general et al.; exceptions on behalf of director general to report proposed by examiner. 1924. cover-title, 5 p. ‡

—— Before Interstate Commerce Commission, no. 15131, Minneapolis Steel and Machinery Company *v.* director general; exceptions on behalf of director general to report of examiner. 1924. cover-title, 1 p. ‡

Fruit. Before Interstate Commerce Commission, no. 15240, Sid F. Mauk Produce Company *v.* director general; brief for director general. 1924. cover-title, 4 p. ‡

Gasoline. Before Interstate Commerce Commission, no. 12536, Automobile Gasoline Co. *v.* director general et al.; petition by director general for rehearing, reargument, or reconsideration. 1924. cover-title, 4 p. ‡

Gravel. Before Interstate Commerce Commission, no. 15454, county of Becker [Minn.] *v.* director general; brief for defendant. 1924. cover-title, 3 p. ‡

Peanuts. Before Interstate Commerce Commission, no. 14501, Universal Oil Company et al. *v.* director general; exceptions on part of director general to report proposed by examiner. 1924. cover-title, 7 p. ‡

Potassium chlorid. Before Interstate Commerce Commission, no. 12942, Diamond Match Company *v.* director general; exceptions on part of director general to report on further hearing proposed by examiner. 1924. cover-title, 4 p. ‡

Sugar. No. 123, in Supreme Court, James C. Davis, agent, Railroad Administration, *v.* A. J. Parrington; brief for plaintiff in error in opposition to motion of defendant in error for order to reconsider rule announced in Kansas City Southern *v.* Wolf, 43 S. C. R. 259, with reference to limitation of actions in view of subsequent legislation of Congress and to receive and consider accompanying argument on said reconsideration. 1924. cover-title, 10 p. ‡

Toledo, St. Louis and Western Railroad. Final settlement between director general of railroads and W. L. Ross, receiver of Toledo, St. Louis & Western Railroad Company, Mar. —, 1924. 1924. 3 p. 4° †

Turpentine. Before Interstate Commerce Commission, no. 15355, Dill-Crosett, Incorporated, *v.* director general; brief for director general. 1924. cover-title, 12 p. ‡

SHIPPING BOARD

SHIPPING BOARD EMERGENCY FLEET CORPORATION

Ships. Schedule of sailings of Shipping Board vessels in general cargo, passenger & mail services, Mar. 1–Apr. 15, 1924; issued by Traffic Department. [1924.] cover-title, iv+16 p. il. [Monthly. Text on p. 2–4 of cover.] †
23—26331

SMITHSONIAN INSTITUTION

NOTE.—In a recent price-list the Smithsonian Institution publishes this notice: "Applicants for the publications in this list are requested to state the grounds for their requests, as the Institution is able to supply papers only as an aid to the researches or studies in which they are *especially* interested. These papers are distributed *gratis*, except as otherwise indicated, and should be ordered by the *publication numbers* arranged in sequence. The serial publications of the Smithsonian Institution are as follows: 1, Smithsonian contributions to knowledge; 2, Smithsonian miscellaneous collections; 3, Smithsonian annual reports. No *sets* of these are for sale or distribution, as most of the volumes are out of print. The papers issued in the series of Contributions to knowledge and Miscellaneous collections are distributed without charge to public libraries, educational establishments, learned societies, and specialists in this country and abroad; and are supplied to other institutions and individuals at the prices indicated. Remittances should be made payable to the 'Smithsonian Institution.' The Smithsonian report volumes and the papers reprinted in separate form therefrom are distributed *gratuitously* by the Institution to libraries and individuals throughout the world. Very few of the Report volumes are now available at the Institution, but many of those of which the Smithsonian edition is exhausted can be purchased from the Superintendent of Documents, Government Printing Office, Washington, D. C. The Institution maintains mailing-lists of public libraries and other educational establishments, but no *general mailing-list of individuals*. A library making application to be listed for Smithsonian publications should state the number of volumes which it contains and the date of its establishment, and have the endorsement of a Member of Congress."
The annual reports are the only Smithsonian publications that are regularly issued as public documents. All the others are paid for from the private funds of the Institution, but as they are usually regarded as public documents and have free transmission by mail they are listed in the Monthly catalogue.

Publications. Classified list of Smithsonian publications available for distribution, Mar. 1, 1924; compiled by Helen Munroe. Washington, Smithsonian Institution, 1924. iv+[1]+30 p. (Publication 2755.) [This list does not include publications issued by the National Museum and the Bureau of American Ethnology.] †
24—26306

NATIONAL MUSEUM

NOTE.—The publications of the National Museum comprise an annual report and three scientific series, viz., Proceedings, Bulletins, and Contributions from national herbarium. The editions are distributed to established lists of libraries, scientific institutions, and specialists, any surplus copies being supplied on application. The volumes of Proceedings are made up of technical papers based on the Museum collections in biology, geology, and anthropology, and of each of these papers a small edition, in pamphlet form, is issued in advance of the volume, for prompt distribution to specialists. No sets of any of these series can now be furnished.

Amastridium, neglected genus of snakes; by E. R. Dunn. 1924. cover-title, 3 p. [From Proceedings, v. 65; no. 2524.] †

Birds. Notes on birds collected by W. L. Abbott on Karimata Islands, off West Borneo; by Harry C. Oberholser. 1924. cover-title, 4 p. [From Proceedings, v. 64; no. 2512.] †

Boeckella. Synopsis of species of Boeckella and Pseudoboeckella, with key to genera of fresh-water Centropagidae [and with list of literature]; by C. Dwight Marsh. 1924. cover-title, 28 p. il. [From Proceedings, v. 64; no. 2498.] †

Catostomids. Notes on certain catostomids of Bonneville system, including type of Pantosteus virescens Cope; by John Otterbein Snyder. 1924. cover-title, 6 p. [From Proceedings, v. 64; no. 2508.] †

Crabs. Studies on larvae of crabs of family Pinnotheridae [with bibliography]; by O. W. Hyman. 1924. cover-title, 9 p. 6 p. of pl. [From Proceedings, v. 64; no. 2497.] †

Crane-flies. New species of 2-winged flies from western North America belonging to family Tipulidae; by Charles P. Alexander. 1924. cover-title, 16 p. [From Proceedings, v. 64; no. 2500.] †

Dragon-flies. Notes and descriptions of naiads belonging to dragonfly genus Helocordulia; by Clarence Hamilton Kennedy. 1924. cover-title, 4 p. 1 pl. [From Proceedings, v. 64; no. 2502.] †

Lice. On taxonomy, biology, and distribution of biting lice of family Gyropidae; by H. E. Ewing. 1924. cover-title, 42 p. il. 1 pl. [From Proceedings, v. 63; no. 2489.] †

Meteorites. Recently found meteoric irons from Mesa verde Park, Colo., and Savannah, Tenn.; by George P. Merrill. 1923. cover-title, 4 p. 3 p. of pl. [From Proceedings, v. 63; no. 2487.] †

Mordenite and associated minerals from near Challis, Custer County, Idaho; by Clarence S. Ross and Earl V. Shannon. 1924. cover-title, 19 p. il. 3 p. of pl. [From Proceedings. v. 64; no. 2509.] †

Porpoises. Fossil porpoise from Calvert formation of Maryland; by Remington Kellogg. 1924. cover-title, 39 p. 18 p. of pl. [From Proceedings, v. 63; 2482.] †

Skull. Catalogue of human crania in National Museum collections: Eskimo, Alaska and related Indians, north eastern Asiatics; by Aleš Hrdlička. 1924. cover-title, 51 p. [From Proceedings, v. 63; no. 2480.] †

Starfish. Remarkable new sea star from Japan; by W. K. Fisher. 1924. cover-title, 6 p. il. 2 p. of pl. [From Proceedings, v. 64; no. 2493.] †

STATE DEPARTMENT

Arbitration. Agreement between United States and France, arbitration, further extending duration of convention of Feb. 10, 1908; signed Washington, July 19, 1923, proclaimed Mar. 4, 1924. 1924. [1]+4 p. (Treaty series 679.) [English and French.] †   24—26276

Colombia. Diplomatic correspondence with Colombia in connection with treaty of 1914, and certain oil concessions, in response to resolution, letter submitting diplomatic correspondence in connection with ratification of treaty concluded between United States and Colombia, Apr. 6, 1914, and in connection with securing of any oil concessions for American citizens. Mar. 14, 1924. 71 p. (S. doc. 64, 68th Cong. 1st sess.) *Paper, 5c.   24—26307

Diplomatic list, Mar. 1924. [1924.] cover-title, i+34 p. 24° [Monthly.] ‡   10—16292

Extradition. Treaty between United States and Latvia, extradition; signed Riga, Oct. 16, 1923, proclaimed Mar. 3, 1924. 1924. [1]+6 p. (Treaty series 677.) †   24—26333

International Institute of Agriculture. General assembly of International Institute of Agriculture, report concurring in requests made by Secretary of Agriculture for legislation to enable appropriation to be made for expenses of delegates to meeting of general assembly of International Institute of Agriculture at Rome in May next, and to secure admission to Institute of Hawaii, the Philippines, Porto Rico, and Virgin Islands. Mar. 6, calendar day Mar. 7, 1924. 4 p. (S. doc. 58, 68th Cong. 1st sess.) *Paper, 5c.

Mexico. Convention between United States and Mexico, general claims; signed Washington, Sept. 8, 1923, proclaimed Mar. 3, 1924. 1924. [1]+9 p. (Treaty series 678.) [English and Spanish.] †   24—26275

—— Special claims convention between United States and Mexico for settlement of claims of American citizens arising from revolutionary acts in Mexico, Nov. 20, 1910–May 31, 1920; signed Mexico City, Sept. 10, 1923, proclaimed Feb. 23, 1924. 1924. [1]+9 p. (Treaty series 676.) [English and Spanish.] †   24—26274

Parcel post agreement between United States and Netherlands East India; [signed Washington, Feb. 15, 1924, Batavia, Oct. 2, 1922, approved Feb. 20] 1924. 1924. [1]+6 p. †   24—26273

INTERNATIONAL JOINT COMMISSION ON BOUNDARY WATERS BETWEEN UNITED STATES AND CANADA

Work. International Joint Commission, organization, jurisdiction, and operation under treaty of Jan. 11, 1909, between United States and Great Britain. 1924. v+55 p. *Paper, 10c.   24—26270

PASSPORT CONTROL DIVISION

Passports. To clerks of courts who take passport applications, regulation 10; Mar. 1, 1924. [1924.] 1 p. 4° [Most of the Regulations of the Passport Control Division have been multigraphed and have not been entered in this catalogue.] ‡

SUPREME COURT

American Railway Express Company. Stipulated record, Oct. term, 1923, no. 666, United States and Interstate Commerce Commission *vs.* American Railway Express Company and Seaboard Air Line Railway Company; appeal from district court for northern district of Georgia. [1924.] cover-title, i+8 p. ‡

Cases. Docket [of cases pending in Supreme Court], Oct. term, 1923. [1924.] p. 257–284, 4° [Issued in loose-leaf form.] ‡

[*Journal*] Mar. 3–17, 1924; [slips] 70–80. [1924.] leaves 179–203. ‡

Official reports of Supreme Court, v. 263 U. S., no. 2; Ernest Knaebel, reporter. Preliminary print. 1924. cover-title, [1]+162–365 p. 12° [Cases adjudged in Supreme Court at Oct. term, 1923 (opinions of Nov. 12, in part,–Dec. 3. 1923). Text on p. 2 and 4 of cover. From United States reports, v. 263.] * Paper, 25c. single copy, $1.00 per vol. (4 nos. to a vol.; subscription price, $3.00 for 12 nos.); foreign subscription, 5c. added for each pamphlet.

Pothier, Roland R. Transcript of record, Oct. term, 1923, no. 546, William R. Rodman, United States marshal [for district of Rhode Island], *vs.* Roland R. Pothier, on writ of certiorari to circuit court of appeals for 1st circuit. [1924.] cover-title, ii+160 p. ‡

Stilz, Harry B. Transcript of record, Oct. term, 1923, no. 830. Harry B. Stilz *vs.* United States, appeal from Court of Claims. [1924.] cover-title, i+16 p. il. ‡

Supplee-Biddle Hardware Company. Transcript of record, Oct. term, 1923, no. 447, United States *vs.* Supplee-Biddle Hardware Company, appeal from Court of Claims. [1924.] cover-title, i+10 p. ‡

TREASURY DEPARTMENT

Appraisers. Schedule for hearings by Board of General Appraisers at ports other than port of New York, calendar year 1924. [1924.] 2 p. ([Treasury decision] 39952.) [From Treasury decisions, v. 45, no. 3.] †

Certificates of indebtedness. United States of America, 4 per cent Treasury certificates of indebtedness, series TM–1925, dated and bearing interest from Mar. 15' 1924, due Mar. 15, 1925. Mar. 10, 1924. 1 p. 4° (Department circular 337; Public Debt [Commissioner].) †

Claims. Judgments of Court of Claims, list of judgments rendered by Court of Claims submitted by Secretary of Treasury and requiring appropriation. Mar. 14, calendar day Mar. 18, 1924. 5 p. (S. doc. 70, 68th Cong. 1st sess.) * Paper, 5c.
9—6546

Excess profits tax. Corporate income and excess-profits tax for 1921, in response to resolution, information showing amounts of net income and excess profits tax, by industrial divisions and excess-profits tax brackets, reported to Treasury Department in corporate income and excess-profits tax returns for 1921. Mar. 15, calendar day Mar. 17, 1924. 82 p. (S. doc. 67, 68th Cong. 1st sess.) * Paper, 10c.
24—26308

Finance. Daily statement of Treasury compiled from latest proved reports from Treasury offices and depositaries, Mar. 1–31, 1924. [1924.] Each 4 p. or 3 p. f° [Daily except Sundays and holidays.] †
15—3303

Ports, revision of lists of ports at which bonded warehouses are established and of ports at which no bonded warehouse of class 3 is established, but where the customhouse premises are used for storage of bonded merchandise; [List of customs districts, headquarters, and ports of entry]. [1924.] 4 p. ([Treasury decision] 39478 [and 39974].) [From Treasury decisions, v. 43, no. 10, and v. 45, no. 5.] †

Public debt. Statement of public debt of United States, Dec. 31, 1923. [1924.] [2] p. narrow f° [Monthly.] † 10—21268

Soldiers. Cash bonus, letter from Secretary of Treasury in response to letter from chairman of Committee on Finance in regard to bill (S. 1969) to provide adjusted compensation for veterans of World War; presented by Mr. Copeland. 1924. [1]+2 p. (S. doc. 60, 68th Cong. 1st sess.) * Paper, 5c. 24—26148

Treasury decisions. Treasury decisions under customs and other laws, v. 44; July–Dec. 1923. 1924. iii+528 p. * Cloth, $1.50. 10—11513

NOTE.—This volume contains Department decisions numbered 39717–737, 39739–938, including general appraisers' decisions 8667–8722, and abstracts 46158–678. Department decision 39738 was withdrawn.

—— Treasury decisions under customs, internal revenue, and other laws, including decisions of Board of General Appraisers and Court of Customs Appeals. v. 45, no. 10–13; Mar. 6–27, 1924. 1924. various paging. [Weekly. Department decisions numbered 40037–86, general appraisers' decisions 8748–66, abstracts 46887–47005, internal revenue decisions 3559–67, and later Tariff Commission Notice 12.] * Paper, 5c. single copy, $1.00 a yr.; foreign subscription, $2.00. 10—30490

APPRAISERS

Reappraisements of merchandise by general appraisers [on Feb. 25–Mar. 22, 1924]; Mar. 7–28, 1924. [1924.] various paging. (Reappraisement circulars 3499–3502.) [Weekly.] * Paper, 5c. single copy, 50c. a yr.; foreign subscription, $1.05. 13—2916

BUDGET BUREAU

Boise, Idaho. Mint and assay offices, supplemental estimate of appropriation for Treasury Department, fiscal year 1924, pertaining to mints and assay offices [for contingent expenses of assay office at Boise, Idaho]. Mar. 14, 1924. 2 p. (H. doc. 221, 68th Cong. 1st sess.) * Paper, 5c.

District of Columbia. Maintenance of public convenience stations, supplemental estimate of appropriation for District of Columbia, fiscal year 1924, for maintenance of public convenience stations. Mar. 20, 1924. 2 p. (S. doc. 76, 68th Cong. 1st sess.) * Paper, 5c.

Federal Farm Loan Bureau. Miscellaneous expenses of Federal Farm Loan Board, supplemental estimate of appropriation for Treasury Department, fiscal year 1924, for miscellaneous expenses pertaining to activities of Federal Farm Loan Board. Mar. 8, 1924. 2 p. (H. doc. 215, 68th Cong. 1st sess.) * Paper, 5c.

Foot-and-mouth disease. Eradication of foot-and-mouth and other contagious [contagious] diseases of animals, supplemental estimate of appropriation for Department of Agriculture, fiscal year 1924, to remain available until June 30, 1925, for eradication of foot-and-mouth and other contagious diseases of animals, $1,000,000. Mar. 1, 1924. 2 p. (H. doc. 211, 68th Cong. 1st sess.) * Paper, 5c.

Guam Agricultural Experiment Station. Agricultural experiment station on island of Guam, Oregon and California Railroad lands, and Coos Bay wagon road lands, supplemental estimate of appropriation for Department of Agriculture, fiscal year 1924, to repair damage by typhoon to buildings, fences, etc., of agricultural experiment station on island of Guam, and for protection of so-called Oregon and California Railroad lands and Coos Bay wagon road lands. Mar. 8, 1924. 3 p. (H. doc. 214, 68th Cong. 1st sess.) * Paper, 5c.

Internal revenue. Refunding internal-revenue collections, supplemental estimate of appropriation for Treasury Department, fiscal year 1924. Mar. 19, 1924. 3 p. (S. doc. 75, 68th Cong. 1st sess.) * Paper, 5c.

Marine hospital, Key West, Fla., supplemental estimate of appropriation for Treasury Department, fiscal year 1924, for providing water supply at Key West, Fla., marine hospital. Mar. 14, calendar day Mar. 18, 1924. 2 p. (S. doc. 72, 68th Cong. 1st sess.) * Paper, 5c.

State Department. Deficiency and supplemental estimates for State Department, deficiency estimates of appropriations for Department of State, fiscal years 1922, 1923, and supplemental estimates, fiscal year 1924. Mar. 14, calendar day Mar. 18, 1924. 7 p. (S. doc. 71, 68th Cong. 1st sess.) * Paper, 5c.

COAST GUARD

Examinations. Standards of examinations for promotion of personnel of Coast Guard, Nov. 1923. 1924. ii+42 p. ‡

Regulations for Coast Guard, 1923. 1924. v+366 p. [Issued in loose-leaf form for insertion in binder.] ‡

COMPTROLLER OF CURRENCY

National banks. Monthly statement of capital stock of national banks, national bank notes, and Federal reserve bank notes outstanding, bonds on deposit, etc. [Mar. 1, 1924].. Mar. 1, 1924. 1 p. f° †   10—21266

ENGRAVING AND PRINTING BUREAU

Supplies. Engraving and printing supplies: Paper, etc. [specifications and proposal for fiscal year 1925]. Mar. 1, 1924. 3 p. f° †

FEDERAL FARM LOAN BUREAU

Agricultural credit. Federal farm loan act as amended to Jan. 1, 1924. Jan. 1924. ii+34 p. (Circular 20.) †   24—26279

GENERAL SUPPLY COMMITTEE

Government supplies. Specifications and proposals for supplies [fiscal year 1925]: class 9, Furniture and floor coverings. [1924.] 65 p. 4° †

—— Same: class 10, Groceries and provisions, July 1–Oct. 31, 1924. [1924.] 12 p. 4° †

—— Same: class 11, Forage. flour, and seed, July 1–Oct. 31, 1924. [1924.] 5 p. 4° †

—— Same: class 15. Incandescent electric lamps. [1924.] 7 p. 4° †

GOVERNMENT ACTUARY

Bonds of United States. Market prices and investment values of outstanding bonds and notes [of United States, Feb. 1924]. Mar. 1, 1924. 7 p. 4° (Form A.) [Monthly.] †

INTERNAL REVENUE BUREAU

Income tax forms, revenue act of 1921, copies of forms used for taxable year 1923 in administration of title 2 of revenue act of 1921. 1924. cover-title, 111 p. f° (Bulletin A [income tax] revised Jan. 1, 1924.) *Paper, 30c.
                    24—26280

Internal revenue bulletin, v. 3, no. 9–13; Mar. 3–31, 1924. 1924. various paging. [Weekly.] *Paper, 5c. single copy (for subscription price see note below).   22—26051

NOTE.—The Internal revenue bulletin service for 1924 will consist of weekly bulletins, quarterly digests, and semiannual cumulative bulletins. The weekly bulletins will contain the rulings to be made public and all internal revenue Treasury decisions. The quarterly digests, with the exception of the one to be published at the end of 1924, will contain digests of the rulings previously published in the weekly bulletins for 1924. The last digest for 1924 will also contain digests of the rulings published during 1922 and 1923. The semiannual cumulative bulletins will contain all new rulings published during the previous 6 months. The complete bulletin service may be obtained, on a subscription basis, from the Superintendent of Documents, Government Printing Office, Washington, D. C., for $2.00 a yr.; foreign subscription, $2.75.

Internal revenue tax information service, 1924 [rates of subscription and detachable form to forward with remittance]. [1924.] 1 p. 4° [This supersedes Income tax and Sales tax information services formerly issued as separate publications.] †

LOANS AND CURRENCY DIVISION

Bonds of United States. Caveat list of United States registered bonds and notes, Mar. 1, 1924. [1924.] 56 p. f° [Monthly.] †

Money. Circulation statement of United States money, Mar. 1, 1924. [1924.] 1 p. oblong 8° [Monthly.] †   10—21267

PUBLIC HEALTH SERVICE

Arsphenamine. Viscosity and toxicity of arsphenamine solutions [with bibliography]; by Carl Voegtlin, James M. Johnson, and Helen Dyer. 1924. [1]+ 17 p. il. (Reprint 898.) [From Public health reports, Feb 1, 1924.] *Paper, 5c.   24—26309

Folliculosis. Epidemiological study of folliculosis of conjunctiva [with list of references]; by Milton V. Veldee. 1924. 12 p. il. (Reprint 886.) [From Public health reports, Dec. 7, 1923.] *Paper, 5c.   24—26283

Hydrogen sulphide literature [with bibliography on hydrogen sulphide poisoning]; by C. W. Mitchell and S. J. Davenport. 1924. [1]+13 p. (Reprint 892.) [Prepared in cooperation with Mines Bureau. From Public health reports, Jan. 4, 1924.] *Paper, 5c.   24—26287

Hygiene, Public. Changes in small town [West Point, Va.] brought about by Health Department; by B. B. Bagby. [Reprint] 1924. 4 p. (Reprint 821.) [From Public health reports, Mar. 9, 1923.] *Paper, 5c.   24—26310

—— Cooperative rural health work of Public Health Service, fiscal year 1923; by L. L. Lumsden. 1924. 24 p. (Reprint 887.) [From Public health reports, Dec. 14, 1923.] * Paper, 5c.   24—26284

—— Transactions of 21st annual Conference of State and Territorial Health Officers with United States Public Health Service, Washington, D. C., May 16 and 17, 1923. Jan. 1924. vii+176 p. (Public health bulletin 139.) * Paper, 20c.   6—35322

Iodin. Methods of administering iodine for prophylaxis of endemic goiter [with list of references]; by Robert Olesen. 1924. [1]+11 p. (Reprint 893.) [From Public health reports, Jan. 11, 1924.] * Paper, 5c. 24—26288

Mosquitos. Some notes on relation of domestic animals to Anopheles; by M. A. Barber and T. B. Hayne. 1924. [1]+6 p. (Reprint 897.) [From Public health reports, Jan. 25, 1924.] * Paper, 5c.   24—26291

Negroes. National negro health week, Mar. 30–Apr. 5, 1924, 10th annual observance, under auspices of Annual Tuskegee Negro Conference and National Negro Business League, in cooperation with Public Health Service, State health departments, county health departments, city health departments, and various health, civic, and other organizations. 1924. iii+12 p. *Paper, 5c.

Oral hygiene. Program for oral hygiene in public schools of Minneapolis, Minn.; by F. Denton White. 1924. 6 p. 1 pl. (Reprint 890.) [From Public health reports, Dec. 21, 1923. This article was erroneously credited to F. E. Harrington when it was printed in the Public health reports.] * Paper, 5c.   24—26286

Pellagra. Study of treatment and prevention of pellagra, experiments showing value of fresh meat and of milk, therapeutic failure of gelatin, and preventive failure of butter and of cod-liver oil [with list of references]; by Joseph Goldberger and W. F. Tanner. 1924. [1]+21 p. (Reprint 895.) [From Public health reports, Jan. 18, 1924.] * Paper, 5c.   24—26311

Public health reports, v. 39, no. 10–13; Mar. 7–28, 1924. 1924. [xvi]+447– 653 p. il. [Weekly.] * Paper, 5c. single copy, $1.50 a yr.; foreign subscription, $2.75.   6—25167

SPECIAL ARTICLES.—No. 10. Factors in mental health of girls of foreign parentage, study of 210 girls of foreign parentage who received advice and assistance from social agency [Boston Society for Care of Girls], 1919–22; by Mary C. Jarrett.—World health conditions as reported by Health Section of League of Nations.—No. 11. Malta fever, cattle suggested as possible source of infection, following serological study of human serums [with list of references]; by Alice C. Evans.—New Baldwin-Wood weight-height-age tables as index of nutrition, application of Baldwin-Wood standard of nutrition to 506 native white children without physical defects and with good or excellent nutrition as judged from clinical evidence; by Taliaferro Clark, Edgar Sydenstricker, and Selwyn D. Collins.—Improved health conditions in New York City in past 50 years.—No. 12. Absenteeism among white and negro school

Public health reports—Continued.

children in Cleveland [Ohio], 1922–23; by G. E. Harmon and G. E. Whitman.—Workmen's compensation acts in United States, medical aspect, review [of Research report 61, of National Industrial Conference Board]; by E. C. Ernst.—Reports of Health Section of League of Nations.—No. 13. Epidemic of typhoid fever and other intestinal diseases in Everett, Wash., July, 1923; by C. E. Dorisy.—Effect of Chara robbinsii on mosquito larvæ [with list of references]; by M. A. Barber.—Work of Madison County (Ala.) Health Department.—Rural health work in New York State. Cattaraugus County demonstration establishes first county health unit in State.—Death rates in group of insured persons, comparison of principal causes of death, Jan. 1924, Jan., Dec., and year 1923, and last quarter of 1923.

NOTE.—This publication is distributed gratuitously to State and municipal health officers, etc., by the Surgeon General of the Public Health Service, Treasury Department. Others desiring these reports may obtain them from the Superintendent of Documents, Washington, D. C., at the prices stated above.

Radium. Preliminary note on observations made on physical condition of persons engaged in measuring radium preparations [with bibliography]; by R. C. Williams. 1924. 24 p. il. 2 p. of pl. (Reprint 889.) [From Public health reports, Dec. 21, 1923.] * Paper, 5c.
24—26285

Rocky Mountain spotted fever: viability of virus in animal tissues; by R. R. Spencer and R. R. Parker. 1924. 4 p. (Reprint 894.) [From Public health reports, Jan. 11, 1924.] * Paper, 5c.
24—26289

Thyroid gland. Importance of our knowledge of thyroid physiology in control of thyroid diseases, [by David Marine]; abstract by Taliaferro Clark. 1924. [1]+4 p. (Reprint 896.) [From Public health reports, Jan. 18, 1924.] * Paper, 5c.
24—26290

Tuberculosis survey of Porto Rico, Oct. 11, 1922–Apr. 18, 1923; by J. G. Townsend. Dec. 1923. [published] 1924. vi+98 p. il. 12 pl. 24 p. of pl. 2 maps, 4 tab. (Public health bulletin 138.) * Paper, 35c.
24—26281

Vaccination. Specific leprous reactions and abnormal vaccinia induced in lepers by smallpox vaccination; by Oswald E. Denney and Ralph Hopkins. [Reprint] 1924. 11 p. 2 p. of pl. (Reprint 805.) [From Public health reports, Dec. 22, 1922.] * Paper, 5c.
24—26282

HYGIENIC LABORATORY

Arsphenamine. '1' Study of acid-base equilibria of arsphenamine solutions [with list of references], by Elias Elvove and W. Mansfield Clark; 2 Biological standardization of arsphenamine and neoarsphenamine, by George B. Roth; 3, Osmotic pressure of arsphenamine and neoarsphenamine solutions, by James M. Johnson. Mar. 1924. v+41 p. il. (Bulletin 135.) * Paper. 10c.
24—26292–294

—— Same. (H. doc. 65. 68th Cong. 1st sess.)

VENEREAL DISEASES DIVISION

Venereal disease information, issued by Public Health Service for use in its cooperative work with State health departments, v. 5, no. 3; Mar. 20, 1924. 1924. ii+109–157+iv p. [Monthly.] * Paper, 5c. single copy, 50c. a yr.; foreign subscription, 75c.
23—26719

SPECIAL ARTICLES.—Diagnosis and treatment of syphilis, not including neurosyphilis; by John H. Stokes.—General paralysis in New York State, 1913–22; by Horatio M. Pollock.—Report of inquiry concerning present incidence of venereal diseases in Hamilton County, Ohio.—Venereal disease clinics statistics, July 1–Dec. 31, 1923 [as reported to State departments of health].

Venereal diseases. Enforcement of regulations relating to interstate travel of venereally infected persons. [1924.] [1]+6 p. [From Venereal disease information, v. 4, no. 12, Dec. 20, 1923.] †

TREASURER OF UNITED STATES

Paper money. Monthly statement, paper currency of each denomination out standing Jan. 31, 1924. Feb. 1 [1924]. 1 p. oblong 24° †

—— Same. Feb. 29, 1924. Mar. 1 [1924]. 1 p. oblong 24° †

WAR DEPARTMENT

Army regulations. †

NOTE.—The Army regulations are issued in pamphlet form for insertion in loose-leaf binders. The names of such of the more important administrative subjects as may seem appropriate, arranged in proper sequence, are numbered in a single series, and each name so numbered constitutes the title and number of a pamphlet containing certain administrative regulations pertaining thereto. Where more than one pamphlet is required for the administrative regulations pertaining to any such title, additional pamphlets will be issued in a separate sub-series.

1–10. Army regulations: List of current pamphlets and changes, distribution; Dec. 31, 1923. [1924.] 10 p. [Supersedes AR 1–10, Oct. 1, 1923.]
20–10. Inspector General's Department: Inspection of posts and camps; Dec. 13, 1923. [1924.] 4 p. [Supersedes AR 20–10, Apr. 23, 1923.]
30–430. Quartermaster Corps: Remount purchasing and breeding headquarters, Changes 2; Jan. 9, 1924. [1924.] 2 p. [Supersedes AR 30–430, Changes 1, Jan. 3, 1923.]
30–1155. Same: Transport chaplain; Jan. 28, 1924. 1924. 1 p. [Supersedes AR 30–1155, Mar. 16, 1922.]
30–2135. Same: Laundries, Changes 1; Jan. 29, 1924. 1924. 1 p.
340–10. Correspondence: Penalty envelopes and labels, use of mails, Changes 1; Jan. 3, 1924. 1924. 1 p.
500–50. Employment of troops: Enforcement of laws, Changes 1; Jan. 31, 1924. 1924. 1 p.
605–120. Commissioned officers: Personal reports, registration, Changes 2; Jan. 18, 1924. [1924.] 2 p. [Supersedes AR 605–120, Changes 1, Oct. 5, 1923.]
615–10. Enlisted men: Rating and disrating of specialists, except in Medical Department; Dec. 13, 1923. [1924.] 6 p.
615–250. Same: Physical inspections, Changes 2; Jan. 14, 1924. 1924. 1 p. [Supersedes AR 615–250, Changes 1, June 12, 1923.]

Training regulations.

NOTE.—The Training regulations are issued in pamphlet form for insertion in loose-leaf binders.

150–30. Marksmanship: Automatic rifle, prepared under direction of chief of infantry; Nov. 21, 1923. [1924.] 42 p. il. * Paper, 10c.
200–5. Scouting and patrolling: Scouting and patrolling, dismounted, prepared under direction of chief of infantry; Sept. 29, 1923. [1924.] 83 p. il. * Paper, 10c.
435–30. Coast Artillery Corps: Tactical employment of antiaircraft artillery (includes machine guns, guns, and searchlights), prepared under direction of chief of coast artillery; Jan. 7, 1924. [1924.] 23 p. il. * Paper, 5c.

ADJUTANT GENERAL'S DEPARTMENT

Army list and directory, Mar. 1, 1924. 1924. v+314 p. large 8° [Bimonthly.] * Paper, 25c. single copy, $1.25 a yr.; foreign subscription, $1.85. 9—35106

Ignition and carburetion for military specialists, 1923. 1924. vii+240 p. il. (United States Army training manual 56.) * Cloth, 50c.

Officers, Army. Officers of Army stationed in or near District of Columbia, Apr. 1924. 1924. iv+41 p. [Quarterly.] * Paper, 5c. single copy, 20c. a yr.; foreign subscription, 30c. 9—35107

U. S. Army recruiting news, bulletin of recruiting information issued by direction of Adjutant General of Army, Mar. 1 and 15, 1924. [Recruiting Publicity Bureau, Governors Island, N. Y., Mar. 1 and 15, 1924.] Each 16 p. il. 4° † Recruiting Publicity Bureau, Governors Island, N. Y. War 22—1

AIR SERVICE

Aeronautical bulletins. Aeronautical bulletin, no. 93, 97, 109–117, 119–124, Route information series; Jan. 15–Mar. 1, 1924. [1924.] various paging, 12° (Airways Section.) * Paper, 5c. each. 23—26231

—— Aeronautical bulletin, no. 124, 127, 131, 142–148, 150–157, 159–169, 171–184, State series; Jan. 15–Mar. 1, 1924. [1924.] various paging, il. 12° (Airways Section.) * Paper, 5c. each.

ENGINEERING DIVISION

Alcohol-gasoline mixtures, Material Section report; by A. C. Zimmerman. 1924. ii+3 p. il. 4° (Air Service. Air Service information circular, aviation, v. 5, no. 450, Mar. 1, 1924.) ‡

Engines. Comparison tests of storage preparations for aviation engine storage of less than 6 months, Power Plant Section report; by S. A. Christiansen. 1924. ii+9 p. il. 4° (Air Service. Air Service information circular, aviation, v. 5, no. 451, Mar. 1, 1924.) ‡

ENGINEER DEPARTMENT

Duluth, Minn. Duluth-Superior Harbor, statistical report of marine commerce of Duluth, Minn., and Superior, Wis., calendar year 1923, with supplementary report of commerce of Keweenaw Waterway, Mich. 1924. [1]+28 p. il. †

Frankfort Harbor, Mich., reports on preliminary examination and survey of Frankfort Harbor, Mich. Feb. 26, 1924. 25 p. map. (H. doc. 208, 68th Cong. 1st sess.) * Paper, 5c.

Glencove Creek, N. Y., reports on preliminary examination and survey of Glencove Creek, N. Y. Feb. 26, 1924. 14 p. map. (H. doc. 207, 68th Cong. 1st sess.) * Paper, 5c.

Hackensack River. Maintenance and improvement of existing river and harbor works, Hackensack River, N. J., advertisement [for dredging and rock removal]. [1924.] 14 p. 4° †

Providence River. Maintenance and improvement of existing river and harbor works for Providence River and Harbor, R. I,. advertisement [for dredging]. [1924.] 13 p. 4° †

Shoal Harbor. Maintenance and improvement of existing river and harbor works, Shoal Harbor and Compton Creek and Keyport Harbor, N. J., advertisement [for maintenance dredging]. [1924.] 15 p. 4° †

Tolovana River, Alaska, reports on preliminary examination and survey of Tolovana River, Alaska. Feb. 9, 1924. 12 p. map. (H. doc. 193, 68th Cong. 1st sess.) * Paper, 5c.

FINANCE DEPARTMENT

Finance circular. Changes 2 [to] Finance circular 5, 1923; Jan. 12, 1924. [1924.] 3 leaves, 12° ‡

—— Finance circular 1 [1924]; Jan. 14, 1924. [1924.] 5 p. 12° ‡

—— Index, Finance circulars, 1923. [1924.] 18 p. 12° ‡

MEDICAL DEPARTMENT

Veterinary Corps, Army. Circular of information in relation to appointment in veterinary Corps, Army, requisite qualifications, examination of applicants, etc. Revised Feb. 19, 1924. [1924.] 7 p. narrow 8° †

ORDNANCE DEPARTMENT

Gun mounts. Elements of mobile carriage design (supplement), Dec. 12, 1923: [Determination of forces brought upon principal parts of 75 mm. gun carriage. model of 1921, by discharge of gun]. 1924. iii+25 p. il. (Design manual, note no. 2, artillery; Ordnance Dept. doc. 2046.) ‡

    NOTE.—This set of calculations on the 75 mm. gun carriage, model of 1921, issued as note no. 2, is intended to supplement Elements of mobile carriage design (Ordnance Department document 2043) which is note no. 1 of this series.

Ordnance. Handbook of 75-mm. gun matériel, model of 1897 M1 (French), with instructions for its care. [Edition of] July 8, 1918. [Reprint] 1924. 142 p. il. 17 pl. 18 p. of pl. ([Form] no. 1817.) ‡

Ordnance field service bulletin. Ordnance field service bulletins, general instructions, introduction; Oct. 15, 1923. 1924. 1 p. ‡

    NOTE.—In order to provide a vehicle for conveying instructions and information from the chief of field service to the ordnance field service, four bulletins, entitled Ordnance field service bulletins, will be issued. These bulletins replace all former field service bulletins. The bulletins will be divided in the following headings: Bulletin 1, General instructions; Bulletin 2, Supply; Bulletin 3, Ammunition; Bulletin 4, Maintenance.

—— Ordnance field service bulletin 1, sec. 1; Oct. 15, 1923. [1924.] 10 p. il. ‡

—— Same 2, introduction [and sec. 1-] 12; Oct. 15, 1923. [1924.] various paging, il. ‡

—— Same 3, introduction [and sec. 1-] 6; Oct. 15, 1923. [1924.] various paging. ‡

—— Same 4, introduction [and sec. 1-] 10; Oct. 15, 1923. 1924. various paging. ‡

Monthly Catalogue
United States
Public Documents

No. 352
April, 1924

TIIE LIBRARY OF THE

JUN 3 1924

ISSUED BY THE
SUPERINTENDENT OF DOCUMENTS

UNIVERSITY OF

WASHINGTON
1924

Abbreviations

Appendix	app.	Page, pages	p
Congress	Cong.	Part, parts	pt., pts.
Department	Dept.	Plate, plates	pl.
Document	doc.	Portrait, portraits	por.
Facsimile, facsimiles	facsim.	Quarto	4°
Folio	f°	Report	rp.
House	H.	Saint	St.
House bill	H. R.	Section, sections	sec.
House concurrent resolution	H. Con. Res.	Senate, Senate bill	S.
House document	H. doc.	Senate concurrent resolution	S. Con. Res.
House executive document	H. ex. doc.	Senate document	S. doc.
House joint resolution	H. J. Res.	Senate executive document	S. ex. doc.
House report	H. rp.	Senate joint resolution	S. J. Res.
House resolution (simple)	H. Res.	Senate report	S. rp.
Illustration, illustrations	il.	Senate resolution (simple)	S. Res.
Inch, inches	in.	Session	sess.
Latitude	lat.	Sixteenmo	16°
Longitude	long.	Table, tables	tab
Mile, miles	m.	Thirtytwo-mo	32°
Miscellaneous	mis., misc.	Treasury	Treas.
Nautical	naut.	Twelvemo	12°
No date	n. d.	Twentyfour-mo	24°
No place	n. p.	Versus	vs., v.
Number, numbers	no., nos.	Volume, volumes	v., vol.
Octavo	8°	Year	yr.

Common abbreviations for names of States and months are also used.
*Document for sale by Superintendent of Documents.
†Distribution by office issuing document, free if unaccompanied by a price.
‡Printed for official use.

NOTE.—Nearly all of the Departments of the Government make a limited free distribution of their publications. When an entry shows a * price, it is possible that upon application to the issuing office a copy may be obtained without charge.

Explanation

Words and figures inclosed in brackets [ ] are given for information, but do not appear on the title-pages of the publications catalogued. When size is not given octavo is to be understood. Size of maps is measured from outer edge of border, excluding margin. The dates, including day, month, and year, given with Senate and House documents and reports are the dates on which they were ordered to be printed. Usually the printing promptly follows the ordering, but various causes sometimes make delays.

586

SALES OF GOVERNMENT PUBLICATIONS

The Superintendent of Documents, Washington, D. C., is authorized to sell at cost, plus 10 per cent, without limit as to the number of copies to any one applicant who agrees not to resell or distribute the same for profit, any United States Government publication not confidential in character.

Publications can not be supplied free to individuals nor forwarded in advance of payment.

Publications entered in this catalogue that are for sale by the Superintendent of Documents are indicated by a star (*) preceding the price. A dagger (†) indicates that application should be made to the Department, Bureau, or Division issuing the document. A double dagger (‡) indicates that the document is printed for official use. Whenever additional information concerning the method of procuring a document seems necessary, it will be found under the name of the Bureau by which it was published.

In ordering a publication from the Superintendent of Documents, give (if known) the name of the publishing Department, Bureau, or Division, and the title of the publication. If the publication is numbered, give the number also. Every such particular assists in quick identification. Do not order by the Library of Congress card number.

The accumulation of publications in this Office amounts to several millions, of which over two million are assorted, forming the sales stock. Many rare books are included, but under the law all must be sold regardless of their age or scarcity. Many of the books have been in stock some time, and are apt to be shop-worn. In filling orders the best copy available is sent. A general price-list of public documents is not available, but lists on special subjects will be furnished on application.

MONTHLY CATALOGUE DISTRIBUTION

The Monthly catalogue is sent to each Senator, Representative, Delegate, Resident Commissioner, and officer in Congress; to designated depositories and State and Territorial libraries if it is selected by them; to substantially all Government authors; and to as many school, college, and public libraries as the limited edition will supply.

Subscription price to individuals, 50c. a year, including index; foreign subscription, 75c. a year. Back numbers can not be supplied. Notify the Superintendent of Documents of any change of address.

LIBRARY OF CONGRESS CARDS

Numbers to be used in ordering the printed catalogue cards of the Library of Congress are given at the end of entries for the more important documents. Orders for these cards, remittances in payment for them, and requests for information about them should be addressed to the Librarian of Congress, *not* to the Superintendent of Documents.

INDEX

An Index to the Monthly catalogue is issued at the end of the fiscal year. This contains index entries for all the numbers issued from July to June, and can be

bound with the numbers as an index to the volume.   Persons desiring to bind the catalogue at the end of the year should be careful to retain the numbers received monthly, as duplicate copies can not be supplied.

HOW TO REMIT

Remittances for the documents marked with a star (*) should be made to the Superintendent of Documents, Washington, D. C., by coupons, postal money order, express order, or New York draft.   Currency may be sent at sender's risk.

Postage stamps, foreign money, defaced or smooth coins, positively will not be accepted.

For the convenience of the general public, coupons that are good until used in exchange for Government publications sold by the Superintendent of Documents may be purchased from his Office in sets of 20 for $1.00.   Address order to Superintendent of Documents, Government Printing Office, Washington, D. C.

No charge is made for postage on documents forwarded to points in United States, Alaska, Guam, Hawaii, Philippine Islands, Porto Rico, Samoa, or to Canada, Cuba, or Mexico.   To other countries the regular rate of postage is charged, and remittances must cover such postage.   In computing foreign postage, add one-third of the price of the publication.

AGRICULTURE DEPARTMENT

NOTE.—Those publications of the Department of Agriculture which are for sale will be supplied by the Superintendent of Documents, Washington, D. C. The Department issues a monthly list of publications, which is mailed to all applicants, enabling them to select such reports and bulletins as interest them.

Cattle. [Bureau of Animal Industry] order 278 [amendment 4 and 5], 287 [amendment 2–6]; Feb. 20–Apr. 22, 1924. 1924. Each 1 p. or 2 p. [Consist of orders concerning quarantine of cattle, etc.] †

Crops and markets. Crops and markets, weekly, Apr. 5–26, 1924; v. 1, no. 14–17. [1924.] p. 209–272, 4° *Paper, $1.00 a yr.; foreign subscription, $2.00 (including monthly supplement).   Agr 24—113

—— Same, monthly supplement, Apr. 1924; v. 1, supplement 4. [1924.] p. 113–144, il. 4° [Included in price of weekly Crops and markets.]

Official record, Department of Agriculture, v. 3, no. 14–18; Apr. 2–30, 1924. [1924.] Each 8 p. 4° [Weekly.] *Paper, 50c. a yr.; foreign subscription, $1.10.   Agr 22—146

Weather, crops, and markets, v. 4, July–Dec. 1923 [title-page, corrections, and index]. [1924.] ii+8 p. 4° *Paper, 5c.

Wild rice. Nutritive properties of wild rice (Zizania aquatica); by Cornelia Kennedy. [1924.] p. 219–224. il. [From Journal of agricultural research, v. 27, no. 4, Jan. 26, 1924.] ‡

AGRICULTURAL ECONOMICS BUREAU

Farm labor. Conditions affecting demand for harvest labor in wheat belt; by Don D. Lescohier. Apr. 1924. cover-title, 46 p. il. (Agriculture Dept. Department bulletin 1230.) *Paper, 10c.   Agr 24—329

Potatoes. Costs and farm practices in producing potatoes on 461 farms in Minnesota, Wisconsin, Michigan, New York, and Maine for crop year 1919; by W. C. Funk. Apr. 9, 1924. cover-title, 40 p. il. (Agriculture Dept. Department bulletin 1188.) *Paper, 10c.   Agr 24—322

Sorghum. Handbook of United States grades for grain sorghums (tabulated and abridged); recommended by Bureau of Agricultural Economics. Mar. 1924. cover-title, 8 p. 24° [Text on p. 2 of cover.] *Paper, 5c.   Agr 24—338

Tractors and horses in winter wheat belt, Oklahoma, Kansas, Nebraska; by H. R. Tolley and W. R. Humphries. Apr. 25, 1924. cover-title, 60 p. il. (Agriculture Dept. Department bulletin 1202.) [Prepared in cooperation with Public Roads Bureau and Animal Industry Bureau.] *Paper, 10c.
                                                                    Agr 24—326

Wheat. Cost of producing winter wheat in central Great Plains region of United States; by R. S. Washburn. Apr. 16, 1924. cover-title, 36 p. il. (Agriculture Dept. Department bulletin 1198.) *Paper, 10c.   Agr 24—324

ANIMAL INDUSTRY BUREAU

Cream. Some factors which influence feathering of cream in coffee; by L. H. Burgwald. [1924.] p. 541–546. [From Journal of agricultural research, v. 26, no. 11, Dec. 15, 1923.] ‡

Eggs. Natural and artificial incubation of hens' eggs; [by Alfred R. Lee]. [Reprint with changes Mar. 1924.] ii+14 p. il. (Agriculture Dept. Farmers' bulletin 1363.) *Paper, 5c

Hemorrhagic septicemia, stockyards fever, swine plague, fowl cholera, etc.; [by] Henry J. Washburn. [Oct. 1918, reprinted with slight revision Mar.] 1924. 8 p. il. (Agriculture Dept. Farmers' bulletin 1018.) * Paper, 5c.

Roundworms. Influence of low temperatures and of disinfectants on eggs of Ascaris lumbricoides [with list of literature cited]; by Eloise B. Cram. [1924.] p. 167–175. [Prepared in cooperation with Armour & Co., Chicago, Ill. From Journal of agricultural research, v. 27, no. 3, Jan. 19, 1924.] ‡

Service announcements. Service and regulatory announcements, Feb. 1924; [no.] 202. Mar. 1924. p. 13–24. [Monthly.] * Paper, 5c. single copy, 25c. a yr.; foreign subscription, 40c.   Agr 7—1658

—— Same, Mar. 1924; [no.] 203. Apr. 1924. p. 25–39. [Monthly.]

BIOLOGICAL SURVEY BUREAU

Birds. Some common game, aquatic, and rapacious birds in relation to man; [by W. L. McAtee and F. E. L. Beal]. [May 6, 1912, revised Mar. 1924.] [1924.] 28 p. il. (Agriculture Dept. Farmers' bulletin 497.) * Paper, 5c.

Mouse control in field and orchard; [by James Silver]. [Mar. 1924.] ii+14 p. il. (Agriculture Dept. Farmers' bulletin 1397.) [Supersedes Farmers' bulletin 670.] * Paper, 5c.   Agr 24—334

CHEMISTRY BUREAU

Food. Chart showing import food and drug control of United States [with Chart showing interstate food and drug control of United States]; by W. W. Skinner and W. L. Morrison. [1924.] [2] p. il. oblong 12° †

Hydrogen-ion concentration. Changes in hydrogen-ion concentration produced by growing seedlings in acid solutions [with list of literature cited]; by Jehiel Davidson and Edgar T. Wherry. [1924.] p. 207–217. [From Journal of agricultural research, v. 27, no. 4, Jan. 26, 1924.] ‡

Service announcements. Service and regulatory announcements, supplement 169. Apr. 1924. p. 509–531. [Contains Notices of judgment under food and drugs act 11901–950.] * Paper, 5c.   Agr 14—194

Work. Bureau of Chemistry of Department of Agriculture, organization, enforcement of food and drugs act, enforcement of tea act, research work. Dec. 1920, revised Feb. 1924. [1924.] 23 p. il. narrow 12° (Agriculture Dept. Department circular 137.) * Paper, 5c.   Agr 24—330

EDITORIAL AND DISTRIBUTION WORK OFFICES

Agriculture Department. Publications issued in Mar. 1924; [prepared in Office of Publications]. [1924.] oblong 48° [Monthly. This publication is issued in postal card form.] †

Farmers' bulletins. Classified list of Farmers' bulletins of Department of Agriculture, Apr. 25, 1924. [1924.] [4] p. (List no. 2.) †

—— [Farmers'] bulletins of Department of Agriculture of interest to persons who live in cities and towns, Apr. 15, 1924. 1924. 1 p. (List no. 3.) †

—— Numerical list of Farmers' bulletins of Department of Agriculture, Apr. 25, 1924. [1924.] [4] p. (List no. 1.) †

ENTOMOLOGY BUREAU

Ants. House ants, kinds and methods of control; [by] C. L. Marlatt. [July 8, 1916, revised reprint Apr. 1922, reprint] 1924. 15 p. il. (Agriculture Dept. Farmers' bulletin 740.) * Paper, 5c.

Argus tortoise beetle [with list of literature cited]; by F. H. Chittenden. [1924.] p. 43–52, il. 1 pl. [From Journal of agricultural research, v. 27, no. 1, Jan. 5, 1924.] ‡

Bagworm, injurious shade-tree insect; by L. O. Howard and F. H. Chittenden. Jan. 15, 1916 [reprint 1924]. 12 p. il. (Agriculture Dept. Farmers' bulletin 701.) [Apr. 1922, on p. 1, is date of previous reprint. Includes lists of Agriculture Department publications relating to insects affecting shade and ornamental trees.] * Paper, 5c.

Bean-weevils. Insecticidal effect of cold storage on bean weevils [with list of literature cited]; by A. O. Larson and Perez Simmons. [1924.] p. 99–105. [From Journal of agricultural research, v. 27, no. 2, Jan. 12, 1924.] ‡

—— Notes on biology of 4-spotted bean weevil, Bruchus quadrimaculatus Fab.; by A. O. Larson and Perez Simmons. [1924.] p. 609–616, il. [From Journal of agricultural research, v. 26, no. 12, Dec. 22, 1923.] ‡

Cranberry insect problems and suggestions for solving them; [by] H. B. Scammell. [Dec. 1917, reprint] 1924. 43 p. il. (Agriculture Dept. Farmers' bulletin 860.) *Paper, 5c.

Cutworm septicemia; by G. F. White. 1924. cover-title, 487–496+[1] p. il. 2 p. of pl. [From Journal of agricultural research, v. 26, no. 10, Dec. 8, 1923.] ‡

Eggplant leaf-miner, Phthorimaea-glochinella Zeller [with list of literature cited]; by Thomas H. Jones. [1924.] p. 567–570+[1] leaf, 1 pl. [From Journal of agricultural research, v. 26, no. 11, Dec. 15, 1923.] ‡

European corn borer, Pyrausta nubilalis Hbn., versus corn earworm, Heliothis obsoleta Fab.; by Geo. W. Barber. [1924.] p. 65–70, 1 pl. [From Journal of agricultural research, v. 27, no. 1, Jan. 5, 1924.] ‡

False wireworms. Biology of false wireworm Eleodes suturalis Say [with list of literature cited]; by J. S. Wade and R. A. St. George. 1924. cover-title, 547–566+[1] p.+[1] leaf, il. 2 p. of pl. [From Journal of agricultural research, v. 26, no. 11, Dec. 15, 1923.] ‡

Hornworm septicemia [with list of literature cited]; by G. F. White. 1924. cover-title, p. 477–486+[1] leaf, il. 1 pl. [From Journal of agricultural research, v. 26, no. 10, Dec. 8, 1923.] ‡

Pecans. Important pecan insects and their control; [by John B. Gill]. [Jan. 1924.] ii+49 p. il. (Agriculture Dept. Farmers' Bulletin 1364.) [Revision of Farmers' bulletin 843.] *Paper, 10c. Agr 24—331

Rice. How insects affect rice crop; [by J. L. Webb]. [Mar. 1920, revised Feb. 1924.] [1924.] ii+10 p. il. (Agriculture Dept. Farmers' bulletin 1086.) *Paper, 5c.

Rough-headed corn stalk-beetle in Southern States and its control; [by] W. J. Phillips and Henry Fox. Oct. 1917, revised reprint July, 1918, [reprint] 1924. 12 p. il. (Agriculture Dept. Farmers' bulletin 875.) [Includes lists of Agriculture Department publications relating to insects injurious to cereal and forage crops.] *Paper, 5c.

EXPERIMENT STATIONS OFFICE

Experiment station record, v. 50, no. 2; Feb. 1924. 1924. cover-title, x+101–200 p. [Text and illustration on p. 2 and 4 of cover.] *Paper, 10c. single copy, 75c. per vol. (2 vols. a yr.); foreign subscription, $1.25 per vol. (subscription price incorrectly given in publication). Agr 9—832

NOTE.—Mainly made up of abstracts of reports and publications on agricultural science which have recently appeared in all countries, especially the United States. Extra numbers, called abstract numbers, are issued, 3 to each volume. These are made up almost exclusively of abstracts, that is, they contain no editorial notes and only a limited number of current notes.

FEDERAL HORTICULTURAL BOARD

Service announcements. Service and regulatory announcements, Oct.–Dec. 1923; [no.] 77. Apr. 23, 1924. p. 133–174. *Paper, 5c. Agr 14—383

FOREST SERVICE

Douglas spruce. Natural regeneration of Douglas fir in Pacific Northwest [with bibliography]; by Julius V. Hofmann. Apr. 1924. cover-title, 63 p. il. 1 pl. 20 p. of pl. 2 maps. (Agriculture Dept. Department bulletin 1200.) *Paper, 25c. Agr 24—325

Forest fires in the intermountain region; prepared by Intermountain District of Forest Service. Apr. 1924. 16 p. il. (Agriculture Dept. Miscellaneous circular 19.) *Paper, 5c. Agr 24—387

Forests and forestry. Idle land and costly timber; [by W. B. Greeley]. [Apr. 1924.] ii+22 p. il. (Agriculture Dept. Farmers' bulletin 1417.) *Paper, 5c.   Agr 24—335

—— Importance of forestry and national forests, information for social and civic organizations in the Southwest; [prepared in] Forest Service, District 3, Albuquerque, N. Mex. Mar. 1924. 16 p. il. (Agriculture Dept. Miscellaneous circular 15.) [Includes list of Agriculture Department publications of interest in connection with this circular.] * Paper, 5c.   Agr 24—336

Oregon Caves, Siskiyou National Forest [with bibliography]. [1923.] 16 p. il. 4°, folded into narrow 8° size. †

Maps

Carson National Forest, N. Mex. [resources and recreation features, roads, trails, etc.]. [1924.] 1 sheet (with map on verso), il. oblong 8°, folded into narrow 8° size and so printed as to number [3] pages. †

Colville National Forest, Wash. [resources and recreation features, roads, trails, etc.]. [1924.] 1 sheet (with map on verso), il. narrow f°, folded into narrow 8° size and so printed as to number 11 + [1] p. †

Gila National Forest, N. Mex., information for tourists. [1924.] 1 sheet (with map on verso), il. 4°, folded into narrow 8° size, and so printed as to number [2] pages. †

National forests. National forests of Clearwater region, Nezperce-Selway-Clearwater, Oreg. [Idaho, resources and recreation features, roads, trails, etc.]. [1924.] 1 sheet (with map on verso), il. large 4°, folded into narrow 8° size and so printed as to number 14 + [1] p. [Publication reads incorrectly Oregon instead of Idaho.] †

—— National forests of Utah [including Arizona north of Colorado River, how to see them with automobile]. [1924.] 1 sheet (with map on verso), il. f°, folded into narrow 8° size and so printed as to number [1]+21+[1] p. †

Tonto National Forest, Ariz. [resources and recreation features]. [1924.] 1 sheet (with map on verso), il. oblong 8°, folded into narrow 8° size and so printed as to number [3] pages. †

HOME ECONOMICS BUREAU

Food. Food values and body needs shown graphically; [by Emma A. Winslow]. [Reprint Mar. 1924.] ii+36 p. il. (Agriculture Dept. Farmers' bulletin 1383.) * Paper, 10c.   Agr 24—211

—— How to select foods: 1, What body needs; [by] Caroline L. Hunt and Helen W. Atwater. [Mar. 1917; revised Sept. 1922, reprint] 1924. 15 p. il. (Agriculture Dept. Farmers' bulletin 808.) [Formerly issued by States Relations Service. Includes list of Agriculture Department publications of interest in connection with this bulletin.] * Paper, 5c.

PLANT INDUSTRY BUREAU

Apple bitter-rot and its control; [by] John W. Roberts and Leslie Pierce. Apr. 1918, [reprint with slight changes] 1924. (Agriculture Dept. Farmers' bulletin 938.) [Includes lists of Agriculture Department publications relating to production of apples.] * Paper, 5c.

Apple-scald. Oiled wrappers, oils, and waxes in control of apple scald; by Charles Brooks, J. S. Cooley, and D. F. Fisher. 1924. cover-title, p. 513–536. [From Journal of agricultural research, v. 26, no. 11, Dec. 15, 1923.] ‡

Apples. Physiological studies on apples in storage [with list of literature cited]; by J. R. Magness and H. C. Diehl. 1924. cover-title, p. 1–38, il. [From Journal of agricultural research, v. 27, no. 1, Jan. 5, 1924.] ‡

Black-bundle disease of corn [with list of literature cited]; by Charles S. Reddy and James R. Holbert. 1924. cover-title, 177–206+[5] p. il. 2 pl. 4 p. of pl. [Prepared in cooperation with Funk Brothers Seed Company, Bloomington, Ill., and Wisconsin and Illinois Agricultural Experiment Stations. From Journal of agricultural research, v. 27, no. 4, Jan. 26, 1924.] ‡

Chinese jujube [with list of literature cited], by C. C. Thomas; [and] with chapter on Composition of Chinese jujube, by C. G. Church. Apr. 1924. 31 p. il. 8 p. of pl. (Agriculture Dept. Department bulletin 1215.) [Prepared in cooperation with Chemistry Bureau.] *Paper, 10c. Agr 24—327

Clover failure; [by A. J. Pieters]. [1924.] ii+25 p. il. (Agriculture Dept. Farmers' bulletin 1365.) *Paper, 5c. Agr 24—332

Cotton root-rot. Habits of cotton rootrot fungus [with list of literature cited]; by C. J. King. 1924. cover-title, 405–418+[6] p.+[1] leaf, il. 7 p. of pl. [From Journal of agricultural research, v. 26, no. 9, Dec. 1, 1923.] ‡

Crops. Adjusting yields to their regression on moving average, as means of correcting for soil heterogeneity; by Frederick D. Richey. [1924.] p. 79–90. il. [From Journal of agricultural research, v. 27, no. 2, Jan. 12, 1924.] ‡

Forage for cotton belt; [by S. M. Tracy.] [Oct. 1912, revised May, 1920, reprint 1924.] 64 p. il. (Agriculture Dept. Farmers' bulletin 1125.) *Paper, 5c.

Fusarium. Stem and rootrot of peas in United States caused by species of Fusarium [with list of literature cited]; by Fred Reuel Jones. 1924. cover-title, 459–476 p. il. 1 pl. [From Journal of agricultural research, v. 26, no. 10, Dec. 8, 1923.] ‡

Gardening. City home garden; [by W. R. Beattie]. [Mar. 1919, revised Feb. 1922, reprint with changes 1924.] ii+33 p. il. (Agriculture Dept. Farmers' bulletin 1044.) *Paper, 5c.

Gladiolus. Bacterial blight of gladioli; by Lucia McCulloch. [1924.] 225–230+[1] p. 2 p. of pl. [From Journal of agricultural research, v. 27, no. 4, Jan. 26, 1924.] ‡

Intracellular bodies associated with rosette disease and mosaiclike leaf mottling of wheat; by Harold H. McKinney, Sophia H. Eckerson, and Robert W. Webb. 1924. cover-title, 605–608+[7] p.+[1] leaf, 8 p. of pl. [Prepared in cooperation with Wisconsin and Illinois Agricultural Experiment Stations. From Journal of agricultural research, v. 26, no. 12, Dec. 22, 1923.] ‡

Muscadine grape paste; [by Charles Dearing]. [Mar. 1919, reprint with additions Sept. 1921, reprint 1924.] 16 p. il. (Agriculture Dept. Farmers' bulletin 1033.) [Includes lists of Agriculture Department publications of interest in connection with this bulletin.] *Paper, 5c.

Onion culture; [by] W. R. Beattie. [Apr. 1909, revised Mar. 1924.] 1924. 35 p. il. (Agriculture Dept. Farmers' bulletin 354.) *Paper, 5c.

Peaches. Budrot of peach caused by species of Fusarium; by John W. Roberts. 1924. cover-title, p. 507–512, il. 1 pl. [From Journal of agricultural research, v. 26, no. 10, Dec. 8, 1923.] ‡

Photoperiodism in relation to hydrogen-ion concentration of cell sap and carbohydrate content of plant [with list of literature cited]; by W. W. Garner, C. W. Bacon, and H. A. Allard. 1924. cover-title, 119–156+[1] p.+[1] leaf, il. 2 p. of pl. [From Journal of agricultural research, v. 27, no. 3, Jan. 19, 1924.] ‡

Potatoes. Sterilities of wild and cultivated potatoes with reference to breeding from seed [with list of literature cited]; by A. B. Stout and C. F. Clark. Mar. 1924. 32 p. 8 p. of pl. (Agriculture Dept. Department bulletin 1195.) [Prepared in cooperation with New York Botanical Garden.] *Paper, 10c. Agr 24—323

Red clover culture. [by A. J. Pieters; with notes on insect enemies of red clover, by W. R. Walton]. [Reprint with omissions 1924.] ii+30 p. il. (Agriculture Dept. Farmers' bulletin 1339.) *Paper, 5c.

Service announcements. Service and regulatory announcement, Apr. 1924 [no.] 7: Adulteration and misbranding of seeds of orchard grass and hairy vetch. Apr. 30, 1924. 2 p. *Paper, 5c. Agr 14—1059

Sorghum. Seed-color inheritance in certain grain-sorghum crosses [with list of literature cited]; by John B. Sieglinger. [1924.] p. 53–64. [From Journal of agricultural research, v. 27, no. 1, Jan. 5, 1924.] ‡

Sweet potatoes. On anatomy of sweet potato root, with notes on internal breakdown [and with list of literature cited]; by Ernst Artschwager. [1924.] 157–166+[3] p.+[1] leaf. il. 2 pl. 2 p. of pl. [From Journal of agricultural research, v. 27, no. 3, Jan. 19, 1924.] ‡

Watermelons; [by] W. R. Beattie. [Apr. 1924.] ii+22 p. il. (Agriculture Dept. Farmers' bulletin 1394.) *Paper, 5c. Agr 24—333

Wheat. Cytological studies of infection of Baart, Kanred, and Mindum wheats by Puccinia graminis tritici forms 3 and 19 [with list of literature cited]; by Ruth F. Allen. 1924. cover-title, 571–604+[6]p.+[1] leaf, 7 p. of pl. [Prepared in cooperation with California Agricultural Experiment Station. From Journal of agricultural research, v. 26, no. 12, Dec. 22, 1923.] ‡

—— Effect of rust infection upon water requirement of wheat [with list of literature cited]; by Freeman Weiss. [1924.] p. 107–118. [Prepared in cooperation with Department of Agriculture of University of Minnesota. From Journal of agricultural research, v. 27, no. 2, Jan. 12, 1924.] ‡

PUBLIC ROADS BUREAU

Gas-engines. Practical hints on running gas engine; [by A. P. Yerkes]. [Jan. 1919, reprint 1923.] 16 p. il. (Agriculture Dept. Farmers' bulletin 1013.) [Previous reprint issued by Farm Management and Farm Economics Office.] * Paper, 5c.

Road under construction, map of detour, passable but drive with care [signs erected at dangerous points in Federal-aid highway system and forest highways]. [1924.] [4] p. narrow 8° †

Soil moisture. Capillary distribution of moisture in soil columns of small cross section; by W. W. McLaughlin. Apr. 23, 1924. 23 p. il. (Agriculture Dept. Department bulletin 1221.) * Paper, 5c. Agr 24—328

SOILS BUREAU

Field operations. Field operations of Bureau of Soils, [calendar year] 1917, 19th report, by Milton Whitney; with accompanying papers by assistants in charge of field parties. 1923. xiv+2644 p. il. 18 pl. 48 p. of pl. and map, 2 maps, and portfolio of 60 maps. Text and portfolio; * cloth $9.00. Agr 8—875

—— Same. (H. doc. 1356, 65th Cong. 2d sess.)

Howard County, Nebr. Soil survey of Howard County, Nebr.; by F. A. Hayes, L. S. Paine, D. L. Gross, and O. M. Krueger. 1924. iii+965–1004 p. il. map. [Prepared in cooperation with State Soil Survey of University of Nebraska. From Field operations, 1920.] * Paper, 25c.

Muhlenberg County, Ky. Soil survey of Muhlenberg County, Ky.; by J. A. Kerr, Grove B. Jones, S. W. Phillips, and P. E. Karraker. 1924. iii+939–964 p. il. map. [Prepared in cooperation with Kentucky Agricultural Experiment Station. From Field operations, 1920.] * Paper, 25c.

Tarrant County, Tex. Soil survey of Tarrant County, Tex.; by H. W. Hawker, Neal Gearreald, and M. W. Beck. 1924. iv+859–905 p. il. 4 p of pl. map. [Prepared in cooperation with Texas Agricultural Experiment Station. From Field operations, 1920.] * Paper, 25c.

WEATHER BUREAU

Atmospheric pressure. Monthly normal sea-level pressure for United States, Canada, Alaska, and West Indies; by P. C. Day. 1924. [1]+30–35 p. 4° [From Monthly weather review, Jan. 1924.] †

Balloon project and what we hope to accomplish; by C. L. Meisinger. 1924. [1]+27–29 p. 4° [From Monthly weather review, Jan. 1924.] †

Climatological data for United States by sections, v. 11, no. 1; Jan. 1924. [1924.] cover-title, [200] p. il. 2 maps, 2 p. of maps, 4° [Text on p. 2 of cover.] * Paper, 35c. complete monthly number, $4.00 a yr. Agr 14—566

NOTE.—Made up of separate Climatological data issued from 42 section centers of the United States. Printed at the several section centers and assembled and bound at the Washington Office. Issued principally for service use and exchange. The separate Climatological data are sold by the Superintendent of Documents, Washington, D. C., at the rate of 5c. single copy, 50c. a yr. for each section.

Frost protection. Damaging temperatures and orchard heating in Rogue River Valley, Oreg.; by F. D. Young and C. C. Cate. 1924. [1]+617–639 p. il. 6 p. of pl. 4° [From Monthly weather review, Dec. 1923.] †

Meteorology. Monthly meteorological summary, Washington, D. C., Mar. 1924. [1924.] [2] p. large 8° †

Monthly weather review, v. 52, no. 1; Jan. 1924. [Apr. 4] 1924. cover-title, p. 1–69, il. 11 p. of maps, 4° [Text on p. 2–4 of cover.] * Paper, 15c. single copy, $1.50 a yr.; foreign subscription, $2.25. Agr 9—990

NOTE.—The Monthly weather review contains (1) meteorological contributions, and bibliography including seismology, (2) an interpretative summary and charts of the weather of the month in the United States, and on adjacent oceans, and (3) climatological and seismological tables dealing with the weather and earthquakes of the month. The contributions are principally as follows: (a) results of observational or research work in meteorology carried on in the United States or other parts of the world, (b) abstracts or reviews of important meteorological papers and books, and (c) notes.

SPECIAL ARTICLES.—Relations between free-air temperatures and wind directions; by Willis Ray Gregg.—Preliminary study of precipitation in relation to winds and temperature; by V. E. Jakl.—Pilot-balloon observations at San Juan, P. R., by Oliver L. Fassig, abstract [by A. J. Henry; with discussion by W. R. Gregg and W. C. Haines].—Balloon project and what we hope to accomplish; by C. LeRoy Meisinger.—Method for locating decimal point in slide-rule computation; by Nelson W. Haas.—Monthly normals of sea-level pressure for United States, Canada, Alaska, and West Indies; by P. C. Day.—V. H. Ryd on travelling cyclones; by Edgar W. Woolard.—On mechanism of cyclones and anticyclones, by T. Kobayasi; abstracted [by C. L. M.].—Two-and-a-half year cycle in weather and solar phenomena, [by] H. W. Clough; author's abstract.

New England highway weather bulletin, Apr. 1, 1924; no. 16 [season of 1923–24]. [Boston, Mass., 1924.] 1 p. il. large 8° [Weekly.] * Paper, 50c. per season.

NOTE.—As snowfall of quantity sufficient to impede traffic is improbable henceforth, publication of this bulletin will be suspended until November.

Ocean. Weather of the oceans, Dec. 1923, with special reference to north Atlantic and north Pacific oceans (including charts), notes, abstracts, and reviews; issued by Marine Division. 1924. 8 p. 6 p. of maps, 4°. [From Monthly weather review, Dec. 1923.] †

—— Same, Jan. 1924, with special reference to north Atlantic and north Pacific oceans (including charts), notes, abstracts, and reviews; issued by Marine Division. 1924. 6 p. 4 p. of maps, 4° [From Monthly weather review, Jan. 1924.] †

Precipitation. Preliminary study of precipitation in relation to winds and temperature; by V. E. Jakl. 1924. [1]+18–22 p. il. 4° [From Monthly weather review, Jan. 1924.] †

Report. Report of chief of Weather Bureau, 1922–23 [administrative report, fiscal year 1923, with meteorological tables, calendar year 1922]. 1924. [4 pts.] iii+268 p. 7 maps, 4° * Cloth, 85c. Agr 9—1419

—— Same. (H. doc. 81, 68th Cong. 1st sess.)

Snow and ice bulletin, no. 17, winter 1923–24; Mar. 31, 1924. Apr. 1, 1924. [2] p. il. large 4° [Weekly during winter. No. 17 is the last issue for winter of 1923–24.] † 12—1660

NOTE.—A brief report on ice conditions over the Great Lakes will be issued for several weeks from the Weather Bureau office in Detroit, Mich. Copies of this may be secured by addressing that office.

Temperature. Relations between free-air temperatures and wind directions; by W. R. Gregg. 1924. [1]+1–18 p. il. 4°. [From Monthly weather review, Jan. 1924.] †

Weather. Weekly weather and crop bulletin, Apr. 1–29, 1924; no. 14–18, 1924. Apr. 2–30, 1924. Each 4 p. il. 4° * Paper, 25c. a yr. Agr 24—260

Weather map. Daily weather map [of United States, containing forecasts for all States east of Mississippi River except Illinois, Wisconsin, Indiana, upper Michigan, and lower Michigan], Apr. 1–30, 1924. 1st edition. [1924.] Each 16.4×22.7 in. [Not issued Sundays or holidays.] * Editions issued at Washington, D. C., 25c. a month, $2.50 a yr.; editions issued at about 65 stations throughout the United States, 20c. a month, $2.00 a yr.

—— Same [containing forecasts for United States], Apr. 1–30, 1924. 2d edition. [1924.] Each 16.4×22.7 in. [The Sunday edition does not contain as much information as the edition for week days.] * 30c. a month, $3.00 a yr.

CIVIL SERVICE COMMISSION

NOTE.—The Commission furnishes its publications gratuitously to those who apply for them.

Civil service. Information for boards of examiners and nominating officers concerning applications, examinations, and appointments. Jan. 1924. ii+66 p. (Form 131.) ‡ 24—26335

Postal service. Instructions to applicants for postal service. Apr. 1924. 16 p. (Form 1898.) †

COMMERCE DEPARTMENT

NOTE.—The Department of Commerce prints most of its publications in very limited editions, the distribution of which is confined to Government officers, libraries, etc. When a selling price is noted in this list, application for such publication should be submitted to the Superintendent of Documents, Washington, D. C., with remittance. For copies of charts, coast pilots, and tide tables, however, apply directly to the issuing office, the Coast and Geodetic Survey, Washington, D. C.

Aids to navigation. Rules and regulations governing private aids to navigation. Apr. 12, 1924. 2 p. 4° (Department circular 213, 4th edition; Bureau of Light-houses.) [Supersedes 3d edition issued Sept. 24. 1918. and Department circulars 144, Feb. 26, 1907; 164, Mar. 21, 1908; 199, Nov. 4, 1909; and 203, Feb. 3, 1910.] †

CENSUS BUREAU

NOTE.—Persons desiring 14th census publications should address the Director of the Census, Department of Commerce, Washington, D. C. They are also sold by the Super-intendent of Documents, Washington, D. C., at the price indicated.

Arkansas. 14th census of United States: State compendium. Arkansas, statistics of population, occupations, agriculture, irrigation, drainage. manufactures, and mines and quarries for State, counties. and cities. 1924. cover-title, 141 p. il. 4° [Text on p. 2–4 of cover.] * Paper, 25c. 24—26314

Colorado. 14th census of United States: State compendium, Colorado, statistics of population. occupations, agriculture, irrigation, drainage, manufactures, and mines and quarries for State, counties, and cities. 1924. cover-title, 145 p. il. 4° [Text on p. 2–4 of cover.] * Paper, 25c. 24—26337

Cotton consumed, cotton on hand, active cotton spindles, and imports and exports of cotton, Mar. 1923 and 1924, with statistics of cotton consumed. imported, and exported for 8 months ending Mar. 31. Apr. 14, 1924. oblong 32° [Preliminary report. This publication is issued in postal card form.] †

Cottonseed received, crushed, and on hand, and cottonseed products manufactured, shipped out, on hand, and exported covering 8-month period ending Mar. 31, 1924 and 1923. Apr. 21, 1924. oblong 32° [Preliminary report. This publication is issued in postal card form.] †

Manufactures. Census of manufactures, 1921: Summary for United States by industries, geographic divisions, and States. 1924. 141 p. * Paper. 15c.
24—26349

—— Census of manufactures, 1923: Classifications by industries. 1924. ii+78 p. 12° [Prepared under supervision of Eugene F. Hartley, chief statistician for manufactures.] ‡ 24—26396

COAST AND GEODETIC SURVEY

NOTE.—The monthly Notice to mariners, formerly issued by the Coast and Geodetic Survey, has been consolidated with and made a part of the Notice to mariners issued by the Lighthouses Bureau, thus making it a joint publication. The charts, coast pilots, and tide tables of the Coast and Geodetic Survey are sold at the office of the Survey in Washington, and also by one or more sales agents in each of the important American seaports.

Coast and Geodetic Survey bulletin, Mar. 31, 1924; no. 106. [1924.] 11 p. [Monthly.] ‡ 15—26512

Geodetic surveys, methods, instruments, and purposes. 1924. [1]+18 p. 24° (Serial 257.) † 24—26397

Isostatic investigations and data for gravity stations in United States established since 1915 [with bibliography]; by William Bowie. 1924. iv+91 p. il. 2 maps, 4° (Special publication 99; serial 246.) * Paper, 25c. 24—26336

Publications. Catalogue of U. S. Coast and Geodetic Survey charts, coast pilots. tide tables, current tables (Philippine Islands charts catalogued separately). [Edition of] Apr. 1, 1924. 1924. 47 p. il. 4° (Serial 259.) †
7—6923

Tide tables, United States and foreign ports, [calendar] year 1925. 1924. 451 p. il. (Serial 254.) † Paper, 75c. 11—35919

Charts

Atlantic Coast, Cape Sable to Cape Hatteras; chart 1000. Mercator projection. Washington. Coast and Geodetic Survey, Apr. 1924. 41.1×33.1 in. [For offshore navigation only.] † 75c.

Florida, East Cape to Mormon Key, surveys to 1890 and other sources; chart 1253. Scale 1: 80,000. Washington, Coast and Geodetic Survey, Mar. 1924. 42×33.4 in. † 75c.

Hudson River, Days.Point to Fort Washington Point, N. Y.-N. J., original surveys 1885–86, surveys by U. S. Engineers to 1923 and other sources; chart 369⁸. Scale 1: 10,000. Washington, Coast and Geodetic Survey, Apr. 1924. 40.7×28 in. † 75c.

Mare Island Strait, Calif., original surveys to 1923, surveys by U. S. Navy to 1924, surveys by U. S. Engrs. to 1923, and other sources; chart 5525. Scale 1: 10, 000. Washington, Coast and Geodetic Survey, Mar. 1924. 34.9×23 in. † 50c.

FISHERIES BUREAU

Canned fishery products and by-products of United States and Alaska, 1923. [1924.] 1 p. narrow f° (Statistical bulletin 608.) †

Cold storage holdings of fish, Mar. 15, 1924. [1924.] 1 p. oblong 8° (Statistical bulletin 609.) [Statistics furnished by Agricultural Economics Bureau.] †

Fisheries service bulletin, Apr. 1, 1924; no. 107. [1924.] 11 p. [Monthly.] †
F.15—76

Fishery products. Statement of quantities and values of certain fishery products landed at Seattle ,Wash., by American fishing vessels, Feb. 1924. [1924.] 1 p. oblong 12° (Statistical bulletin 606.) †

Ichthyophthirius disease of fishes and methods of control; by Herbert F. Prytherch. 1924. [1]+6 p. il. (Bureau of Fisheries doc. 959.) [App. 9, report of commissioner of fisheries, 1923.] * Paper, 5c.   F 24—8

Mississippi River. Fisheries of Mississippi River and tributaries, 1922. [1924.] 1 p. oblong f° (Statistical bulletin 607.) †

FOREIGN AND DOMESTIC COMMERCE BUREAU

Boots and shoes. Directory of United States exporters of boots and shoes and other leather manufactures; compiled in Shoe and Leather Manufactures Division. 1924. ii+30 p. (Miscellaneous series 127.) * Paper, 10c.
24—26338

Commerce. Monthly summary of foreign commerce of United States, Feb. 1924. 1924. 2 pts. p. 1–76 and ii+77–98 p. 4° * Paper, 10c. single copy. (including pts. 1 and 2), $1.00 a yr.; foreign subscription, $1.60.   14—21465

—— Same. 1924. [2 pts. in 1], 98 p. 4° (H. doc. 14, 68th Cong. 1st sess.)

Commerce reports. Commerce reports, weekly survey of foreign trade, reports from American consular officers and representatives of Department of Commerce in foreign countries, no. 14–17; Apr. 7–28, 1924. 1924. cover-titles, p. 1–264, il. 4° [Text and illustrations on p. 2–4 of covers.] * Paper, 10c. single copy, $3.00 a yr.; foreign subscription, $5.00.

—— Supplement to Commerce reports. [Included in price of Commerce reports for subscribers.]

Trade and economic review for 1922. no. 54: Esthonia; by Harold B. Quarton. [1924.] 37 p.

—— Supplement to Commerce reports: Balance of international payments of United States in 1923, by Rufus S. Tucker; with foreword by Herbert Hoover. Apr. 7, 1924. iv+19 p. (Trade information bulletin 215; Finance and Investment Division.) †   23—26806

—— Same: Budgets of western European countries; by R. C. Miller. Apr. 21, 1924. ii+31 p. (Trade information bulletin 222; Western European Division.) †   24—26398

—— Same: Chemical trade of Japan [with bibliography]; by Thomas W. Delahanty and Charles C. Concannon. Apr. 14, 1924. ii+44 p. (Trade information bulletin 217; Chemical Division.) †   24—26341

—— Same: Export trade in rubber footwear; by E. G. Holt. Apr. 14, 1924. ii+24 p. (Trade information bulletin 218; Rubber Division.) †   24—26342

—— Same: International trade in cement, pt. 3, Asia, Australia, and Africa; compiled by Reigart M. Santmyers from official statistics, reports of consular officers of State Department, and from other sources. Apr. 14, 1924. ii+25 p. (Trade information bulletin 220; Mineral Section, Iron and Steel Division.) †   24—26248

Commerce reports—Continued. Same: Rate procedure of steamship conferences; by E. S. Gregg. Apr. 21, 1924. ii+16 p. (Trade information bulletin 221; Transportation Division.) †
                                                                    24—26344
—— Same: Survey of world trade in agricultural products, no. 4, Transporta-
tion in relation to export trade in agricultural products; by Roland M.
Kramer. Apr. 14, 1924. ii+74 p. il. (Trade information bulletin 216;
Foodstuffs and Transportation Divisions.) [Prepared as part of the study
of world trade in agricultural products authorized by the 67th Congress.] †
                                                                    24—26340
—— Same: Trade-mark protection in Latin America; by Bernard A. Kosicki.
Apr. 14, 1924. ii+28 p. (Trade information bulletin 219; Division of For-
eign Tariffs.) †
                                                                    24—26343
—— Survey of current business, Apr. 1924, no. 32; compiled by Bureau of
Census, Bureau of Foreign and Domestic Commerce, [and] Bureau of Standards. 1924. cover-title, 67 p. il. 4° (Monthly supplement to Commerce reports.) [Contains statistics for Feb. 1924, the date given above, Apr. 1924,
being the date of issue. Text on p. 2–4 of cover.] *Paper, 10c. single copy,
$1.00 a yr.; foreign subscription, $1.50.
                                                                    21—26819

NOTE.—Realizing that current statistics are highly perishable and that to be of
use they must reach the business man at the earliest possible moment, the Department has arranged to distribute advance leaflets twice each month to those subscribers who request them. One set of these leaflets is issued about the 20th of
the month, giving such information as has been received up to that time, and
another set of sheets is mailed at the end of the month giving those figures received
since the 20th. The information contained in these leaflets is also published in
Commerce reports issued weekly by the Foreign and Domestic Commerce Bureau. The
advance sheets will be mailed free of charge to all subscribers to the Survey who request
them. Such requests should be addressed to the Bureau of the Census, Department
of Commerce, Washington, D. C. Subscriptions, however, should be sent to the
Superintendent of Documents, Washington, D. C., at the prices stated above.

LIGHTHOUSES BUREAU

10th–12th Districts. Light list, Great Lakes, United States and Canada; 1924,
corrected to Mar. 1. 1924. 239 p. *Paper, 30c.   12—29082
Lighthouse service bulletin, v. 3, no. 4; Apr. 1, 1924. [1924.] p. 17–19.
[Monthly.] †   12—35121
Notice to mariners, weekly, no. 14–17, 1924; Apr. 4–25 [1924]. 1924. various
paging, il. [Issued jointly with Coast and Geodetic Survey.] †   7—20609

NAVIGATION BUREAU

Ships. American documented seagoing merchant vessels of 500 gross tons and
over, Apr. 1, 1924. 1924. ii+67 p. 4° (Serial 77.) [Monthly.] *Paper,
10c. single copy, 75c. a yr.; foreign subscription, $1.25.   19—26597

RADIO SERVICE

Radio Service bulletin, Apr. 1, 1924; no. 84. [1924.] 20 p. [Monthly.] *Paper,
5c. single copy, 25c a yr.; foreign subscription, 40c.   15—26255

PUBLICATIONS DIVISION

Commerce Department. Supplement to annual List of publications [of Department of Commerce available for distribution], Mar. 31, 1924. [1924.] 4 p.
[Monthly.] †

STANDARDS BUREAU

NOTE.—The Scientific papers will be supplied on subscription as issued at $1.25 per
volume, paper bound. These volumes will afterwards be issued bound in cloth at $2.00
per volume; foreign subscription, paper $2.50 (sent in single numbers), cloth $2.35
(bound volumes). Single numbers vary in price. Address the Superintendent of Documents, Washington, D. C.
   The Technologic papers will be issued first as separates and later in volume form in the
same manner as the Scientific papers. Subscriptions will be accepted by the Superintendent of Documents at $1.25 per volume; foreign subscription, $2.50. Single numbers
vary in price.

Bricks. Face brick and common brick. June 21, 1923, [published] 1924. 5 p.
(Simplified practice recommendation no. 7.) [Title on cover is: Elimination of waste, simplified practice, face brick and common brick.] *Paper, 5c.

Camera for studying projectiles in flight; by H. L. Curtis, W. H. Wadleigh, [and] A. H. Sellman. Mar. 19, 1924. [1]+189–202 p. il. 1 pl. 4 p. of pl. (Technologic papers 255.) [From Technologic papers, v. 18.] * Paper, 10c.
24—26399

Coal-tar pitch. United States Government master specification for coal-tar pitch for waterproofing and damp proofing, Federal Specifications Board, Specification 83, officially adopted by Federal Specifications Board, Dec. 29, 1923, for use of Departments and independent establishments of Government in purchase of coal-tar pitch for waterproofing and damp proofing. Apr. 8, 1924. 11 p. il. (Circular 155.) * Paper, 5c.   24—26400

Crystals. Gravitational anisotropy in crystals; by Paul R. Heyl. Feb. 16, 1924. [1]+307–324 p. il. 1 pl. 2 p. of pl. large 8° (Scientific papers 482.) [From Scientific papers, v. 19.] * Paper, 10c.   24—26347

Hollow tile. Hollow building tile. Jan. 1, 1924. 6 p. (Simplified practice recommendation no. 12.) [Title on cover is: Elimination of waste, simplified practice, hollow building tile.] * Paper, 5c.

Hosiery boxes. Standardization of hosiery box dimensions; by Charles W. Schoffstall [and] E. M. Schenke. Mar. 1, 1924. [1]+157–169 p. il. 1 pl. 4 p. of pl. large 8° (Technologic papers 253.) [Prepared in cooperation with National Association of Hosiery and Underwear Manufacturers. From Technologic papers, v. 18.] * Paper, 10c.   24—26352

Iridium. Investigations on platinum metals: 4, Determination of iridium in platinum alloys by method of fusion with lead; by Raleigh Gilchrist. Feb. 28, 1924. [1]+325–345 p. large 8° (Scientific papers 483.) [From Scientific papers, v. 19.] * Paper, 5c.   24—26348

Iron. Preparation and properties of pure iron alloys: 4, Determination of critical ranges of pure iron-carbon alloys by thermoelectric method; by J. F. T. Berliner. Mar. 5, 1924. [1]+347–356 p. il. large 8° (Scientific papers 484.) [From Scientific papers, v. 19.] * Paper, 5c.   22—27473

Lathing. Metal lath. Dec. 12, 1922, [published] 1924. 6 p. (Simplified practice recommendation no. 3.) [Title on cover is: Elimination of waste, simplified practice, metal lath. Recommendation becomes effective July 1, 1924.] * Paper, 5c.

Paint. Emissive tests of paints for decreasing or increasing heat radiation from surfaces; by W. W. Coblentz [and] C. W. Hughes. Mar. 13, 1924. [1]+171–187 p. il. (Technologic papers 254.) [From Technologic papers, v. 18.] * Paper, 5c.   24—26401

Pottery. Application of interferometer to measurements of thermal dilatation of ceramic materials; by George E. Merritt. Mar. 7, 1924. [1]+357–373 p. il. large 8° (Scientific papers 485.) [From Scientific papers, v. 19.] * Paper, 5c.   24—26350

Radio instruments and measurements [with bibliography]. 2d edition. Mar. 10, 1924. 345 p. il. 2 pl. 8 p. of pl. large 8° (Circular 74.) * Paper, 60c.
24—26345

Roofing. United States Government master specification for surfacing materials for bituminous built-up roofing, Federal Specifications Board, Specification 82, officially adopted by Federal Specifications Board, Dec. 29, 1923, for use of Departments and independent establishments of Government in purchase of surfacing materials for bituminous built-up roofing. Mar. 25, 1924. 3 p. (Circular 158.) * Paper, 5c.   24—26346

Wrought-iron. Nick-bend test for wrought iron; by Henry S. Rawdon [and] Samuel Epstein. Feb. 29, 1924. [1]+115–155 p. il. large 8° (Technologic papers 252.) [From Technologic papers, v. 18.] * Paper, 10c.   24—26351

STEAMBOAT INSPECTION SERVICE

Laws governing Steamboat-Inspection Service, Revised statutes as modified by acts of Congress. Edition, July 21, 1920. [Reprint with changes] 1924. 91 p. †   11—35015

Steamboat Inspection Service bulletin, Apr. 1, 1924; no. 102. [1924.] 2 p. [Monthly.] ‡   15—26679

Steamboats. 34th supplement to General rules and regulations [edition of 1923], circular letter. Mar. 4, 1924. 15 p. †

—— 1st supplement to General rules and regulations, 1924 edition, circular letter. Mar. 27, 1924. 1 p. †

NOTE.—The 1924 edition of General rules and regulations is now in press. This supplement, therefore, amends the 1923 edition while that edition is effective.

CONGRESS

Congressional record. Congressional record, proceedings and debates of 1st session, 68th Congress, and index. v. 65, pt. 1; Dec. 3, 1923–Jan. 15, 1924. [Permanent edition.] 1924. p. 1–1018. 4° [The index does not appear with this part but will be issued in the last volume.] * Price will be quoted when set is completed.
12—36438

NOTE.—In this permanent bound edition the paging differs from that of the daily numbers, the text being revised, rearranged, and printed without break. The bound volumes of the Record are sold by the Superintendent of Documents. Prices will be furnished on application for the proceedings and debates of the 67th Congress, 1st–4th sessions, and prior Congresses. Send remittances for the bound volumes to the Superintendent of Documents, Washington. D. C. Stamps and foreign money will not be accepted.

—— Congressional record, 68th Congress, 1st session, v. 65, no. 89–116; Apr. 1–30, 1924. [1924.] 5519–7825+[73] p. il. 4°.

NOTE.—The Congressional record, containing the proceedings and debates of Congress, is issued daily when Congress is in session, and indexes thereto are published fortnightly.

The Record is sold by the Superintendent of Documents on the following terms: Single copy, 3 cents, if not more than 24 pages, and 1 cent more for each additional 8 pages; per month, $1.50, foreign subscription, $2.50. Subscriptions are payable in advance. Prices for the bound volumes of the Record, 67th Congress, 1st–4th sessions, and prior Congresses, will be furnished on application. Send remittances to the Superintendent of Documents, Washington, D. C. Stamps and foreign money will not be accepted.

—— Same, index, with title, Congressional record index, 68th Congress, 1st session, v. 65, nos. 88–100; Mar. 31–Apr. 12, 1924. [1924.] no. 8; 39+19 p. 4° [Includes History of bills and resolutions.]

—— Same, v. 65, nos. 101–113; Apr. 14–27, 1924. [1924.] no. 9; 37+17 p. 4° [Includes History of bills and resolutions.]

Eulogies. Thomas E. Watson, memorial addresses. 1924. iii+[1]+250 p. 1 por. ‡
24—26353

PRIVATE LAWS

NOTE.—The Publications Division, State Department, receives a small supply of the private acts which it distributes free upon application.

Private [act] 3–15, 68th Congress.

Alaska Commercial Company. S. 1021, act for relief of Alaska Commercial Company. Approved Apr. 12, 1924. 1 p. (Private 8.)

Bradley, William R. H. R. 1316, act for relief of William R. Bradley. Approved Apr. 3. 1924. 1 p. (Private 5.)

Cleveland State Bank. S. 75, act for relief of Cleveland State Bank, Cleveland, Miss. Approved Mar. 31, 1924. 1 p. (Private 3.)

Grissinger, Elwood. S. 1861, act authorizing Court of Claims to hear and determine claim of Elwood Grissinger. Approved Apr. 18, 1924. 1 p. (Private 15.)

Hurst, Fred. S. 661, act for relief of Fred Hurst. Approved Apr. 15, 1924. 1 p. (Private 13.)

Lee, William H. S. 796, act for relief of William H. Lee. Approved Apr. 12, 1924. 1 p. (Private 7.)

McAtee, John H. S. 107, act for relief of John H. McAtee. Approved Apr. 15, 1924. 1 p. (Private 11.)

Moriarty, Ambrose I. S. 2090, act for advancement on retired list of Regular Army of Ambrose I. Moriarty. Approved Apr. 14. 1924. 1 p. (Private 10.)

Nolan, Thomas. S. 1219. act for relief of Thomas Nolan [son of Margaret Nolan]. Approved Apr. 15. 1924. 1 p. (Private 14.)

Old National Bank of Martinsburg. S. 214. act for relief of Old National Bank of Martinsburg, Martinsburg, W. Va. Approved Apr. 1, 1924. 1 p. (Private 4.)

Seupelt, J. G. S. 1703, act for relief of J. G. Seupelt. Approved Apr. 14, 1924. 1 p. (Private 9.)

Strecker, Charles B. S. 47. act to permit correction of general account of Charles B. Strecker, former assistant treasurer, United States [at Boston, Mass.]. Approved Apr. 12, 1924. 1 p. (Private 6.)

Williams, Mrs. Ethel. S. 646, act for relief of Ethel Williams. Approved Apr. 15. 1924. 1 p. (Private 12.)

PUBLIC LAWS

NOTE.—Public acts in slip form in the first prints may be obtained from the Superintendent of Documents, Washington, D. C., at a subscription price of $1.00 for the 68th Congress, 1st session, foreign subscription $1.25; single copies are usually 5c. each.

Public [act] 62–104, 68th Congress.

Appropriations. H. R. 7449, act making appropriations to supply deficiencies in certain appropriations for fiscal year 1924 and prior fiscal years, to provide supplemental appropriations for fiscal year 1924, and for other purposes. [Approved Apr. 2, 1924.] 35 p. (Public 66.)

Byram River. H. R. 6943, act granting consent of Congress to Port Chester, N. Y., and town of Greenwich, Conn., or either of them, to construct dam across Byram River. Approved Apr. 12, 1924. 1 p. (Public 81.)

Cattle. S. 2164, act to repeal that part of act making appropriations for Department of Agriculture, fiscal year 1912, relating to admission of tick-infested cattle from Mexico into Texas. Approved Apr. 15, 1924. 1 p. (Public 89.)

Chippewa Indians. H. R. 2876, act to provide for payment of claims of Chippewa Indians of Minnesota for back annuities. Approved Apr. 14, 1924. 1 p. (Public 82.)

Coast Guard. H. R. 6815, act to authorize temporary increase of Coast Guard for law enforcement. [Approved Apr. 21, 1924.] 2 p. (Public 103.)

Cotton. S. 2113, act authorizing director of census to collect and publish statistics of cotton. [Approved Apr. 2, 1924.] 2 p. (Public 65.)

Custer County, Mont. S. 306, act granting to county of Custer, Mont., land in said county for use as fair ground. Approved Apr. 15, 1924. 1 p. (Public 86.)

Detroit River. S. 2825, act to extend time [of American Transit Company] for commencing and completing construction of bridge across Detroit River within or near Detroit, Mich. Approved Apr. 17, 1924. 1 p. (Public 99.)

District Courts. H. R. 4439, act to amend sec. 71 of judicial code, as amended [so as to transfer Chicot County from eastern division to western division of eastern judicial district of Arkansas. [Approved Apr. 12, 1924.] 2 p. (Public 71.)

—— S. 2625, act to detach Jim Hogg County from Corpus Christi division of southern judicial district of Texas, and attach same to Laredo division of southern judicial district of said State. Approved Apr. 3, 1924. 1 p. (Public 67.)

District of Columbia. H. R. 655, act for tax on motor-vehicle fuels sold within District of Columbia, and for other purposes. [Approved Apr. 23, 1924.] 4 p. (Public 104.)

—— S 1339, act to authorize widening of Georgia avenue between Fairmont street and Gresham place northwest. Approved Apr. 14, 1924. 1 p. (Public 83.)

Dixie Power Company. S. 2686, act to authorize Federal Power Commission to amend permit numbered 1, project numbered 1, issued to Dixie Power Company [by extending time of permit]. Approved Apr. 15, 1924. 1 p. (Public 84.)

Fort Apache Reservation. H. R. 4117, act authorizing appropriation for construction of road within Fort Apache Indian Reservation, Ariz. [and for agency\ building]. Approved Apr. 12, 1924. 1 p. (Public 76.)

Fox River. S 2597, act to authorize construction of bridge across Fox River in St. Charles Township, Kane County, Ill. [by Aurora, Elgin, and Fox River Electric Company]. Approved Apr. 18, 1924. 1 p. (Public 101.)

Game. S. 2146, act to amend sec. 84 of penal code of United States [relating to trespasses on bird reservations, so as to make provisions applicable to wild animal refuges and to protect United States property on any such lands]. Approved Apr. 15, 1924. 1 p. (Public 87.)

Indians. H. R. 4803, act to authorize sale of lands and plants not longer needed for Indian administrative or allotment purposes. Approved Apr. 12, 1924. 1 p. (Public 77.)

Keogh, Fort. S. 2690, act to transfer jurisdiction over portion of Fort Keogh military reservation, Mont., from Department of Interior to Department of Agriculture for experiments in stock raising and growing of forage crops in connection therewith. [Approved Apr. 15, 1924.] 2 p. (Public 90.)

Lac Court Oreille Reservation. H. R. 2883, act to validate allotments of land made to Indians on Lac Court Oreille Indian Reservation, Wis. Approved Apr. 12, 1924. 1 p. (Public 75.)

Mahoning River. H. R. 6623, act granting consent of Congress to Pittsburgh, Youngstown & Ashtabula Railway Company to construct bridge across Mahoning River, Ohio [at or near Haselton]. Approved Apr. 7, 1924. 1 p. (Public 69.)

Medals. H. R. 593, act authorizing issuance of service medals to officers and enlisted men of 2 brigades of Texas cavalry organized under authority from War Department under date of Dec. 8, 1917, and authorizing appropriation therefor, and further authorizing wearing by such officers and enlisted men on occasions of ceremony of uniform lawfully prescribed to be worn by them during their service. Approved Apr. 16, 1924. 1 p. (Public 91.)

Miles City, Mont. S. 303, act authorizing conveyance of land to Miles City, Mont., for park purposes. Approved Apr. 15, 1924. 1 p. (Public 85.)

Minnesota River. H. R. 6724, act granting consent of Congress to counties of Sibley and Scott, Minn., to construct bridge across Minnesota River [at or near Blakely]. Approved Apr. 12, 1924. 1 p. (Public 80.)

Mississippi River. S. 2488, act to authorize Minneapolis, Minn., to construct bridge across Mississippi River in said city. Approved Apr. 17, 1924. 1 p. (Public 96.)

—— S. 2656, act granting consent of Congress to construction of bridge across Mississippi River near and above New Orleans, La. [by said city through its Public Belt Railroad Commission]. Approved Apr. 17, 1924. 1 p. (Public 98.)

Missouri River. S. 2332, act granting consent of Congress to South Dakota for construction of bridge across Missouri River between Hughes County and Stanley County, S. Dak. Approved Apr. 17, 1924. 1 p. (Public 93.)

—— S. 2420, act granting consent of Congress to South Dakota for construction of bridge across Missouri River between Potter County and Dewey County, S. Dak. Approved Mar. 27, 1924. 1 p. (Public 62.)

Public [act] 62-104, 68th Congress—Continued.

National parks. H. R. 3682, act authorizing construction, reconstruction, and improvement of roads and trails, inclusive of necessary bridges, in national parks and monuments under jurisdiction of Department of Interior. Approved Apr. 9, 1924. 1 p. (Public 70.)

Navajo Indians. H. R. 472, act to authorize deposit of certain funds in Treasury to credit of Navajo tribe of Indians and to make same available for appropriation for benefit of said Indians. Approved Apr. 12, 1924. 1 p. (Public 72.)

Ohio River. S. 2914, act authorizing construction of bridge across Ohio River approximately midway between Owensboro, Ky., and Rockport, Ind. [by Edward T. Franks and Thomas H. Hazelrigg]. Approved Apr. 17, 1924. 1 p. (Public 100.)

Osage Indians. H. R. 6483, act amending act for division of lands and funds of Osage Indians in Oklahoma, and acts amendatory thereof and supplemental thereto [relative to lands, money, or mineral interests inherited by persons not Osage Indians by blood]. Approved Apr. 12, 1924. 1 p. (Public 79.)

Pearl River. S. 2436, act granting consent of Congress to board of supervisors of Leake County, Miss., to construct bridge across Pearl River, Miss. [at or near Grigsbys Ferry]. Approved Apr. 17, 1924. 1 p. (Public 94.)

——— , S. 2437, act granting consent of Congress to board of supervisors of Leake County, Miss., to construct bridge across Pearl River, Miss. [at or near Battle Bluff Crossing]. Approved Apr. 17, 1924. 1 p. (Public 95.)

Rapid City Indian School. H. R. 2812, act to authorize Secretary of Interior to sell certain lands not longer needed for Rapid City Indian School [S. Dak.]. Approved Apr. 12, 1924. 1 p. (Public 73.)

Savannah River. S. 2538, act to revive and reenact act authorizing counties of Aiken, S. C., and Richmond, Ga., to construct bridge across Savannah River at or near Augusta, Ga. Approved Apr. 17, 1924. 1 p. (Public 97.)

Kia Indians. H. R. 2877, act providing for reservation of certain lands in New Mexico for Indians of Zia Pueblo. Approved Apr. 12, 1924. 1 p. (Public 74.)

Snelling, Fort. S. 1982, act granting consent of Congress to construction by Chicago, Milwaukee and St. Paul Railway Company of line of railroad across northeasterly portion of Fort Snelling military reservation, Minn. Approved Mar. 28, 1924. 1 p. (Public 64.)

Southern Pacific Railroad. S. 514, act to grant right of way over Government levee at Yuma, Ariz. [to Southern Pacific Railroad Company]. Approved Apr. 17, 1924. 1 p. (Public 92.)

Steamboat Inspection Service. S. 1724, act to amend sec. 4414, Revised statutes, as amended, to abolish inspection districts of Apalachicola, Fla., and Burlington, Vt., Steamboat Inspection Service. Approved Apr. 19, 1924. 1 p. (Public 102.)

Susquehanna River. S. 2446, act granting consent of Congress to Clarks Ferry Bridge Company to construct bridge across Susquehanna River at or near railroad station of Clarks Ferry, Pa. Approved Mar. 27, 1924. 1 p. (Public 63.)

Treasury Department. H. R. 6349, act making appropriations for Treasury and Post Office Departments, fiscal year 1925. [Approved Apr. 4, 1924.] 29 p. (Public 68.)

Willow Creek ranger station. S. 2147, act to complete construction of Willow Creek ranger station, Mont. Approved Apr. 15, 1924. 1 p. (Public 88.)

Yuma Reservation. H. R. 4804, act to authorize allotment of certain lands within Fort Yuma Indian Reservation, Calif., and for other purposes. Approved Apr. 12, 1924. 1 p. (Public 78.)

Public [joint] resolution 12, 68th Congress.

New Orleans, La. S. J. Res. 72, joint resolution to lease to New Orleans Association of Commerce New Orleans quartermaster intermediate depot unit numbered 2. Approved Apr. 15, 1924. 1 p. (Public resolution 12.)

ADJUSTMENT OF SALARIES OF OFFICERS AND EMPLOYEES OF CONGRESS, JOINT SELECT COMMITTEE ON

Salaries. Adjustment of salaries of officers and employees of Congress, report to accompany H. R. 8262 [to fix compensation of officers and employees of legislative branch of Government]; submitted by Mr. Madden. Apr. 3, 1924. 3 p. (H. rp. 447, 68th Cong. 1st sess.) * Paper, 5c.

ARLINGTON MEMORIAL AMPHITHEATER COMMISSION

Report. Report of Arlington Memorial Amphitheater Commission, letter from chairman transmitting final report upon construction and completion of memorial amphitheater and chapel which has been erected in national cemetery at Arlington, Va., by authority of Congress. 1923. 75 p. 14 por. 7 pl. large 8° * Paper, 35c.

24—26402

——— Same (H. doc. 623, 67th Cong. 4th sess.)

CONFERENCE COMMITTEES

District of Columbia gasoline tax, conference report to accompany H. R. 655 [for tax on motor-vehicle fuels sold within District of Columbia, and for other purposes]; submitted by Mr. Zihlman. Apr. 8, 1924. 6 p. (H. rp. 476, 68th Cong. 1st sess.) * Paper, 5c.

Loans. Relief of drought-stricken areas of New Mexico. conference report to accompany S. J. Res. 52; submitted by Mr. Haugen. Apr. 18, 1924. 2 p. (H. rp. 532, 68th Cong. 1st sess.) * Paper, 5c.

Reclamation of land. Deferring of payments of reclamation charges, conference report to accompany S. 1631; submitted by Mr. Smith. Apr. 28, 1924. 3 p. (H. rp. 591, 68th Cong. 1st sess.) * Paper, 5c.

HOUSE OF REPRESENTATIVES

Calendars of House of Representatives, 68th Congress, 1st session, Apr. 1–30, 1924; no. 84–109. 1924. various paging, large 8° [Daily when House of Representatives is in session.] ‡

National defense acts with amendments, 1916–23: public law no. 85, approved June 3, 1916, 64th Congress; public res. no. 23, approved July 1, 1916, 64th Congress; public law no. 242 (extract from), approved Aug. 29, 1916. 64th Congress; public law no. 391 (extract from), approved Mar. 4, 1917, 64th Congress; public law no. 11 ([1st] extract from), approved May 12. 1917, 65th Congress; public law no. 11 ([2d] extract from), approved May 12, 1917, 65th Congress; public law no. 132, approved Apr. 17, 1918, 65th Congress; public law no. 158, approved May 25, 1918, 65th Congress; public law no. 185 (extract from), approved July 2, 1918, 65th Congress; public law no. 193 ([1st] extract from), approved July 9. 1918, 65th Congress; public law no. 193 ([2d] extract from), approved July 9, 1918, 65th Congress; public law no. 300, approved Feb. 28, 1919, 65th Congress; public law no. 242, approved June 4, 1920, 66th Congress; public law. no. 344, approved Sept. 22, 1922, 67th Congress; public law no. 358, approved Sept. 22. 1922, 67th Congress. 1924. [147] p. [The entire text of public laws 132 and 158 is given and not extracts as stated on title-page.] * Paper, 10c.

War Finance Corporation laws with amendments: public law no. 121, approved Apr. 5, 1918, 65th Congress; public law no. 243, approved Nov. 21, 1918, 65th Congress; public law no. 328, approved Mar. 3, 1919. 65th Congress; public law no. 62, approved Oct. 22, 1919, 66th Congress; public law. no. 195 (extract from), approved May 8' 1920, 66th Congress; public res. no. 55, Jan. 4, 1921, 66th Congress; public law no. 60, approved Aug. 24. 1921. 67th Congress; public law no. 503 (extract from), approved Mar. 4, 1923, 67th Congress; public law no. 31, approved Feb. 20, 1924, 68th Congress. 1924. [1]+33 p. * Paper, 5c.

ACCOUNTS COMMITTEE

Air Service. Authorizing select committee appointed under House resolution 192 [to make inquiry into operations of Army Air Service, Naval Bureau of Aeronautics, and Mail Air Service] to employ stenographic and other assistance, report to accompany H. Res. 243; submitted by Mr. MacGregor. Apr. 22, 1924. 1 p. (H. rp. 547, 68th Cong. 1st sess.) * Paper, 5c.

Government securities. Authorizing select committee appointed under House resolution 231 [for purpose of investigating preparation, distribution, sale, payment, retirement, surrender, cancellation, and destruction of Government bonds and other securities] to employ stenographic and other assistance, report to accompany H. Res. 239; submitted by Mr. MacGregor. Apr. 4, 1924. 1 p. (H. rp. 452, 68th Cong. 1st sess.) * Paper, 5c.

House of Representatives. Appropriating additional funds for select committee appointed under provisions of House resolution 217 [to investigate charges that 2 Members of Congress improperly accepted money in connection with securing paroles and pardons of persons convicted of crimes], report to accompany H. Res. 251; submitted by Mr. MacGregor. Apr. 22, 1924. 1 p. (H. rp. 544, 68th Cong. 1st sess.) * Paper, 5c.

—— Providing for employment of substitute telephone operator when required, report to accompany H. Res. 240; submitted by Mr. MacGregor. Apr. 4, 1924. 1 p. (H. rp. 453, 68th Cong. 1st sess.) * Paper, 5c.

Ives, Norman E. Norman E. Ives, report to accompany H. Res. 152 [to pay Norman E. Ives]; submitted by Mr. MacGregor. Apr. 22, 1924. 1 p. (H. rp. 545, 68th Cong. 1st sess.) * Paper, 5c.

Neilson, Walter C. Walter C. Neilson, report to accompany H. Res. 148 [to pay Walter C. Neilson]; submitted by Mr. MacGregor. Apr. 22, 1924. 1 p. (H. rp. 546, 68th Cong. 1st sess.) * Paper, 5c.

Agricultural products. McNary-Haugen bill, hearings on H. R. 5563, declaring emergency in respect to certain agricultural commodities and to promote equality between agricultural commodities and other commodities, Mar. 6 [–19], 1924. 1924. [pts. 12–14, xi]+531–728 p. (Serial E, pts. 12–14.) * Paper, pt. 12, 15c.; pts. 13 and 14, each 5c.

Agriculture. Aswell agricultural extension bill, hearings on H. R. 45, for apportionment of expenditures for extension and demonstration work in agriculture and home economics, Mar. 10 and 11, 1924. 1924. iii+66 p. (Serial Q.)   * Paper, 10c.

Alaska game act, hearings on H. R. 5949, to establish Alaska Game Commission, to protect game animals, land fur-bearing animals, and birds in Alaska, and for other purposes, Mar. 29, 1924. 1924. iii+16 p. (Serial V.)   * Paper, 5c.

Birds. Migratory bird refuge act, hearings on H. R. 745, for establishment of migratory-bird refuges to furnish in perpetuity homes for migratory birds, establishment of public shooting grounds to preserve American system of free shooting, provision of funds for establishing such areas, and furnishing of adequate protection for migratory birds, Mar. 29, 1924. 1924. iii+63 p. (Serial U.)   * Paper, 5c.

Forests and forestry. Protection of forest lands, etc., report to accompany H. R. 4830 [for protection of forest lands, for reforestation of denuded areas, for extension of national forests, and for other purposes, in order to promote continuous production of timber on lands chiefly suitable therefor]; submitted by Mr. Clarke of New York. Apr. 3, 1924. 8 p. (H. rp. 439, 68th Cong. 1st sess.)   * Paper, 5c.   24—26403

—— Reforestation, hearings on H. R. 4830, for protection of forest lands, for reforestation of denuded areas, for extension of national forests, and for other purposes, in order to promote continuous production of timber on lands chiefly suitable therefor, Mar. 25–27, 1924. 1924. iii+98 p.   * Paper, 10c.

International Livestock Exposition. Medals to exhibitors winning prizes at International Livestock Exposition of Chicago, Ill., report to accompany H. J. Res. 239; submitted by Mr. Haugen. Apr. 18, 1924. 2 p. (H. rp. 531, 68th Cong. 1st sess.)   * Paper, 5c.

Loans. New Mexico relief, hearings on S. J. Res. 52, for relief of drought-stricken farm areas of New Mexico, Mar. 28, 1924. 1924. iii+12 p. (Serial S.)   * Paper, 5c.

—— Relief of boll weevil, drought, and flood-stricken farm areas of Oklahoma, report to accompany H. J. Res. 202; submitted by Mr. Haugen. Apr. 3, 1924. 4 p. (H. rp. 438, 68th Cong. 1st sess.). * Paper, 5c.

—— Relief of drought-stricken farm areas of New Mexico, report to accompany S. J. Res. 52; submitted by Mr. Haugen. Mar. 29, 1924. 3 p. (H. rp. 401, 68th Cong. 1st sess.). * Paper, 5c.

Marketing of farm produce. Curtis-Aswell cooperative marketing bill, hearings on H. R. 8108, to place agricultural industry on sound commercial basis, to encourage agricultural cooperative associations, and for other purposes, the Yoakum plan, Apr. 1, 1924. 1924. iii+31 p. (Serial W.) * Paper, 5c.

—— Norris-Sinclair marketing bill, hearings on H. R. 2659, for purchase and sale of farm products, Feb. 15 [and Apr. 1], 1924. 1924. [pts. 2, 3, vi]+137–167 p. (Serial A, pts. 2, 3.) [Part 1 appeared in Monthly catalogue for Jan. 1924, p. 351.] * Paper; pts. 2 and 3, each 5c.

Packing industry. Packer act amendments, hearings on H. R. 4823, H. R. 4824, H. R. 5093, H. R. 5944, H. R. 6424, H. R. 7110, Feb. 28–Mar. 10, 1924. 1924. iii+181 p. (Serial N.)   * Paper, 20c.

—— Packer act amendments, report to accompany H. R. 6424 [to amend packers and stockyards act, 1921]; submitted by Mr. Haugen. Apr. 19, 1924. 3 p. (H. rp. 537, 68th Cong. 1st sess.)   * Paper, 5c.

—— Packer act amendments, report to accompany H. R. 8942 [to amend packers and stockyards act, 1921]; submitted by Mr. Haugen. Apr. 28, 1924. 3 p. (H. rp. 593, 68th Cong. 1st sess.)   * Paper, 5c.

APPROPRIATIONS COMMITTEE

Commerce Department. Department of Commerce appropriation bill, [fiscal year] 1925, hearing before subcommittee in charge of Department of Commerce appropriation bill for 1925. 1924. ii+496 p. *Paper, 50c.

District of Columbia. District of Columbia appropriation bill, [fiscal year] 1925, hearings before subcommittee in charge of District of Columbia appropriation bill for 1925. 1924. ii+606 p. *Paper, 60c.

—— District of Columbia appropriation bill, fiscal year 1925, report to accompany H. R. 8839; submitted by Mr. Davis of Minnesota. Apr. 22, 1924. 30 p. (H. rp. 548, 68th Cong. 1st sess.) *Paper, 5c.

Foot-and-mouth disease. Additional appropriation for Department of Agriculture [fiscal years 1924 and 1925, for expenditures in connection with eradication of foot-and-mouth disease and other diseases of animals], report to accompany H. J. Res. 247; submitted by Mr. Madden. Apr. 18, 1924. 2 p. (H. rp. 533, 68th Cong. 1st sess.) *Paper, 5c.

Justice Department. Appropriations, Department of Justice, [fiscal year] 1925, hearing before subcommittee in charge of Department of Justice appropriation bill. 1925. 1924. ii+378 p. *Paper, 40c.

Labor Department. Department of Labor appropriation bill, [fiscal year] 1925, hearing before subcommittee in charge of Department of Labor appropriation bill for 1925. 1924. ii+161 p. *Paper, 15c.

State Department. Department of State appropriation bill, [fiscal year] 1925, hearings before subcommittee in charge of Department of State appropriation bill for 1925. 1924. ii+277 p. *Paper, 30c.

—— Departments of State, Justice, Commerce, and Labor appropriation bill, [fiscal year] 1925, report to accompany H. R. 8350; submitted by Mr. Shreve. Apr. 1, 1924. 36 p. (H. rp. 419, 68th Cong. 1st sess.) [Corrected print. 1st print has 34 pages.] *Paper, 5c.

BANKING AND CURRENCY COMMITTEE

National banks. Consolidation of national banking associations, etc., hearings on H. R. 6855, to amend act for consolidation of national banking associations, to amend sec. 5136 as amended, 5137, 5138 as amended, 5142, 5150, 5155, 5190, 5200 as amended, 5202 as amended, 5208 as amended, 5211 as amended, Revised statutes, and to amend sec. 9, 13, 22, and 24 of Federal reserve act, Apr. 9–18, 1924. 1924. iii+253 p. *Paper, 5c.

——, Consolidation of national banking associations, report to accompany H. R. 8887 [to amend act for consolidation of national banking associations, to amend sec. 5136 as amended, 5137, 5138 as amended, 5142, 5150, 5155, 5190, 5200 as amended, 5202 as amended, 5208 as amended, 5211 as amended, Revised statutes, and to amend sec. 9, 13, 22, and 24 of Federal reserve act]; submitted by Mr. McFadden. Apr. 26, 1924. 5 p. (H. rp. 583, 68th Cong. 1st sess.) *Paper, 5c.

CENSUS COMMITTEE

Cotton. Census of cotton in manufacturing establishments and warehouses, report to accompany H. J. Res. 231 [directing census to be taken of bales of cotton now held at various places]; submitted by Mr. Rankin. Mar. 29, 1924. 2 p. (H. rp. 406, 68th Cong. 1st sess.) *Paper, 5c.

CIVIL SERVICE COMMITTEE

Prohibition agents. Extension of civil service regulations to prohibition agents, hearings on H. R. 6147, Feb. 28, 1924. 1924. ii+71 p. *Paper, 10c.

CLAIMS COMMITTEE

Aktieselskabet Marie di Giorgio, report to accompany H. R. 8235 [for relief of Aktieselskabet Marie di Giorgio, Norwegian corporation of Christiania, Norway]; submitted by Mr. Edmonds. Apr. 2, 1924. 1 p. (H. rp. 430, 68th Cong. 1st sess.) *Paper, 5c.

Bethlehem Steel Company. Award of National War Labor Board in favor of certain employees of Bethlehem Steel Co., report to accompany H. R. 5481 [for carrying out of award of National War Labor Board of July 31, 1918, in favor of certain employees of Bethlehem Steel Company, Bethlehem, Pa.]; submitted by Mr. Keller. Apr. 11, 1924. 29 p. (H. rp. 493, 68th Cong. 1st sess.) * Paper, 5c.

Bingham, John A. John A. Bingham, report to accompany H. R. 5803 [for relief of John A. Bingham]; submitted by Mr. Black of New York. Apr. 28, 1924. 2 p. (H. rp. 587, 68th Cong. 1st sess.) * Paper, 5c.

Black, Clara T. Clara T. Black, report to accompany H. R. 1326 [for relief of Clara T. Black]; submitted by Mr. Underhill. Apr. 14, 1924. 9 p. (H. rp. 508, 68th Cong. 1st sess.) * Paper, 5c.

Bruusgaard Kiosteruds Dampskibs Aktieselskab, report to accompany H. R. 8237 [for relief of Bruusgaard Kiosteruds Dampskibs Aktieselskab, Norwegian corporation of Drammen, Norway]; submitted by Mr. Edmonds. Apr. 2, 1924. 2 p. (H. rp. 431, 68th Cong. 1st sess.) * Paper, 5c.

Canada. Relief of Government of Canada, report to accompany H. R. 8236; submitted by Mr. Edmonds. Mar. 31, 1924. 6 p. (H. rp. 413, 68th Cong. 1st sess.) * Paper, 5c.

Flaten, Emil L. Emil L. Flaten, report to accompany H. R. 2806 [for relief of Emil L. Flaten]; submitted by Mr. Vincent of Michigan. Apr. 17, 1924. 14 p. (H. rp. 523, 68th Cong. 1st sess.) * Paper, 5c.

Frost, Arthur. Arthur Frost, report to accompany S. 105 [for relief of Arthur Frost]; submitted by Mr. Thomas of Oklahoma. Apr. 12, 1924. 9 p. (H. rp. 503, 68th Cong. 1st sess.) * Paper, 5c.

Hilton, Robert G. Robert G. Hilton, report to accompany H. R. 2656 [to permit correction of general account of Robert G. Hilton, former assistant treasurer of United States at Baltimore, Md.]; submitted by Mr. Edmonds. Mar. 31, 1924. 3 p. (H. rp. 414, 68th Cong. 1st sess.) * Paper, 5c.

Hopkins, Mrs. Evalyn. Mrs. John P. Hopkins, report to accompany H. R. 3411 [for relief of Mrs. John P. Hopkins]; submitted by Mr. McReynolds. Apr. 28, 1924. 13 p. (H. rp. 592, 68th Cong. 1st sess.) * Paper, 5c.

Hunt, Geston P. Geston P. Hunt, report to accompany H. R. 7052 [for relief of Geston P. Hunt]; submitted by Mr. Vincent of Michigan. Apr. 14, 1924. 8 p. (H. rp. 510, 68th Cong. 1st sess.) * Paper, 5c.

Hunter, Reuben R. Reuben R. Hunter, report to accompany S. 353 [for relief of Reuben R. Hunter]; submitted by Mr. Sears of Nebraska. Apr. 17, 1924. 5 p. (H. rp. 521, 68th Cong. 1st sess.) [Includes minority report signed by Mr. Box, Mr. Underhill, and Mr. McReynolds.] * Paper, 5c.

Hurst, Fred. Fred Hurst, report to accompany S. 661 [for relief of Fred Hurst]; submitted by Mr. Bulwinkle. Mar. 31, 1924. 10 p. (H. rp. 418, 68th Cong. 1st sess.) * Paper, 5c.

Ingels, Mrs. Agnes. Heirs of Agnes Ingels, report to accompany S. 1765 [for relief of heirs of Agnes Ingels]; submitted by Mr. Browne of New Jersey. Apr. 17, 1924. 22 p. (H. rp. 522, 68th Cong. 1st sess.) * Paper, 5c.

Jones, Fred E., Dredging Company. Fred E. Jones Dredging Co., report to accompany H. R. 1078 [for relief of Fred E. Jones Dredging Company]; submitted by Mr. Thomas of Oklahoma. Apr. 17, 1924. 5 p. (H. rp. 517, 68th Cong. 1st sess.) * Paper, 5c.

Keegan, Peter C. Peter Keegan and others, report to accompany S. 210 [for relief of Peter C. Keegan and others]; submitted by Mr. Thomas of Oklahoma. Mar. 31, 1924. 6 p. (H. rp. 417, 68th Cong. 1st sess.) * Paper, 5c.

Kirk, Robert J. Robert J. Kirk, report to accompany H. R. 3009 [for relief of Robert J. Kirk]; submitted by Mr. Underhill. Apr. 14, 1924. 3 p. (H. rp. 509, 68th Cong. 1st sess.) * Paper, 5c.

Laxton, Albert E. Albert E. Laxton, report to accompany H. R. 7420 [for relief of Albert E. Laxton]; submitted by Mr. Thomas of Oklahoma. Apr. 28, 1924. 6 p. (H. rp. 588, 68th Cong. 1st sess.) * Paper, 5c.

Leavitt, Louis. Claim of Louis Leavitt, report to accompany S. 88 [for relief of Louis Leavitt]; submitted by Mr. Fredericks. Apr. 12, 1924. 71 p. (H. rp. 502, 68th Cong. 1st sess.) [Includes views of Mr. Box.] * Paper, 5c.

Lexington, steamship. Owners of steamship Lexington, report to accompany S. 81 [for relief of Colonial Navigation Company, owners of steamship Lexington]; submitted by Mr. Underhill. Apr. 28, 1924. 3 p. (H. rp. 590, 68th Cong. 1st sess.) * Paper, 5c.

McGee, William J. William G [J]. McGee, report to accompany H. R. 2005 [for relief of William J. McGee]; submitted by Mr. Edmonds. Apr. 12, 1924. 12 p. (H. rp. 505, 68th Cong. 1st sess.) * Paper, 5c.

Norfleet, J. Frank. Relief of J. Frank Norfleet, hearing on H. R. 8096, Mar. 25, 1924. 1924. ii+28 p. * Paper, 5c.

Oliver, William J., Company. William J. Oliver Co. and William J. Oliver, hearings before subcommittee on H. R. 3132, for relief of William J. Oliver Co. and William J. Oliver, of Knoxville, Tenn., Mar. 11 and Feb. 22, 1924. 1924. [1]+82 p. * Paper, 10c.

Owens, Mrs. Lena G. Lena Garagnon Owens, report to accompany H. R. 2647 [for relief of Lena Garagnon Owens]; submitted by Mr. Underhill. Apr. 2, 1924. 24 p. (H. rp. 429, 68th Cong. 1st sess.) * Paper, 5c.

Porter, James B. James B. Porter, report to accompany H. R. 3477 [for relief of J. B. Porter]; submitted by Mr. vincent of Michigan. Apr. 21, 1924. 6 p. (H. rp. 543, 68th Cong. 1st sess.) * Paper, 5c.

Scheibe, Edward S. Edward S. Scheibe, report to accompany H. R. 4318 [for relief of Edward S. Scheibe]; submitted by Mr. McReynolds. Apr. 28, 1924. 12 p. (H. rp. 586, 68th Cong. 1st sess.) * Paper, 5c.

Schermerhorn, V. E. V. E. Schermerhorn and others, report to accompany H. R. 6049 [for relief of v. E. Schermerhorn, E. C. Caley, G. W. Campbell, and Philip Hudspeth]; submitted by Mr. Sears of Nebraska. Mar. 31, 1924. 2 p. (H. rp. 415, 68th Cong. 1st sess.) * Paper, 5c.

Scott, L. A. L. A. Scott, report to accompany H. R. 3537 [for relief of L. A. Scott]; submitted by Mr. McReynolds. Apr. 1, 1924. 4 p. (H. rp. 422, 68th Cong. 1st sess.) * Paper, 5c.

Stickney, Fred W. Fred W. Stickney and H. A. Reynolds, report to accompany H. R. 3505 [for relief of Fred W. Stickney and H. A. Reynolds]; submitted by Mr. Fredericks. Apr. 28, 1924. 1 p. (H. rp. 585, 68th Cong. 1st sess.) * Paper, 5c.

Strecker, Charles B. Charles B. Strecker, report to accompany S. 47 [to permit correction of general account of Charles B. Strecker, former assistant treasurer United States at Boston, Mass.]; submitted by Mr. Edmonds. Mar. 31. 1924. 5 p. (H. rp. 416, 68th Cong. 1st sess.) * Paper, 5c.

United Dredging Co., report to accompany S. 593 [for relief of United Dredging Company]; submitted by Mr. Box. Apr. 28, 1924. 4 p. (H. rp. 584, 68th Cong. 1st sess.) * Paper, 5c.

Walker, Mrs. Ellen B. Ellen B. Walker, report to accompany S. 365 [for relief of Ellen B. Walker]; submitted by Mr. McReynolds. Apr. 12, 1924. 4 p. (H. rp. 504, 68th Cong. 1st sess.) * Paper, 5c.

COINAGE, WEIGHTS, AND MEASURES COMMITTEE

Weights and measures. Standardization of weights and measures used in trade and commerce, hearings on H. R. 4465, to regulate and control manufacture. sale, and use of weights and measures and weighing and measuring devices for use or used in trade or commerce, Mar. 28 and Apr. 4, 1924. 1924. ii+46 p. * Paper, 5c.

DISTRICT OF COLUMBIA COMMITTEE

Coroners. To amend sec. 196 of code of law for District of Columbia [relating to appointment of deputy coroners], report to accompany H. R. 3220; submitted by Mr. Z'hlman. Apr. 5, 1924. 1 p. (H. rp. 464, 68th Cong. 1st sess.) * Paper, 5c.

Dentistry. Practice of dentistry in District of Columbia, report to accompany H. R. 8524 [to amend act for regulation of practice of dentistry in District of Columbia, and for protection of the people from empiricism in relation thereto, and acts amendatory thereof]; submitted by Mr. Keller. Apr. 21, 1924. 3 p. (H. rp. 541, 68th Cong. 1st sess.) * Paper, 5c.

Land. Authorizing sale of certain Government property in District of Columbia to Jeremiah O'Connor, report to accompany H. R. 5517 [authorizing sale of certain Government property in Distrct of Columbia]; submitted by Mr. Keller. Apr. 11, 1924. 1 p. (H. rp. 489, 68th Cong. 1st sess.) * Paper, 5c.

Parks. Comprehensive development of park and playground system of National Capital, report to accompany H. R. 8055; submitted by Mr. Gibson. Apr. 25, 1924. 7 p. (H. rp. 571, 68th Cong. 1st sess.) * Paper, 5c.

Railroads. Providing addit'onal terminal facilities in District of Columbia, report to accompany H. R. 597 [providing additional terminal facilities in square east of 710 and square 712 n District of Columbia for freight, traffic]; submitted by Mr. Zihlman. Apr. 3, 1924. 2 p. (H. rp. 436, 68th Cong. 1st sess.) *Paper, 5c.

Rent Commission. District of Columbia rent act, minority report to accompany, H. R. 7962 [to create and establish commission, as independent establishment of Federal Government, to regulate rents in District of Columbia]; submitted by Mr. Blanton. Apr. 12, 1924. 27 p. (H. rp. 467, pt. 3, 68th Cong. 1st sess.) * Paper, 5c.

—— District of Columbia rents act, m'nority report to accompany H. R. 7962 [to create and establish commission, as independent establishment of Federal Government, to regulate rents in District of Columbia]; subm tted by Mr. Underhill. Apr. 11, 1924. 2 p. (H. rp. 467, pt. 2, 68th Cong. 1st sess.) * Paper, 5c.

—— District of Columbia rent act, report to accompany H. R. 7962 [to create and establish commission, as independent establ shment of Federal Government, to regulate rents in District of Columbia]; submitted by Mr. Lampert. Apr. 7, 1924. 4 p. (H. rp. 467 [pt. 1], 68th Cong. 1st sess.) * Paper, 5c.

Streets. Changing name of Jewett street to Cathedral avenue, report to accompany H. R. 6628; submitted by Mr. Gasque. Apr. 7, 1924. 1 p. (H. rp. 468, 68th Cong. 1st sess.) * Paper, 5c.

Traffic regulations. D'strict of Columbia traffic regulations, report to accompany H. R. 8305 [to regulate use by vehicles of streets, alleys, and public places within District of Columb'a]; submitted by Mr. McLeod. Apr. 12, 1924. 2 p. (H. rp. 501, 68th Cong. 1st sess.) * Paper, 5c.

Workmen's compensation. District of Columb'a insurance fund, hearing on H. R. 487, creating District of Columbia insurance fund for benefit of employees injured and dependents of employees killed in employments, providing for administration of such fund by Employees' Compensation Commiss on, and making appropriation therefor, Feb. 11–18, 1924. 1924. pt. 2, ii+59–125 p. [Part 1 appeared in Monthly catalogue for Feb. 1924, p. 434.] * Paper, 10c.

—— Workmen's accident compensat on for District of Columbia, report to accompany H. R. 487 [creating District of Columbia insurance fund for benefit of employees injured and dependents of employees killed in employment, providing for admin stration of such fund by United States Employees' Compensation Commission, and authorizing, appropriation therefor]; submitted by Mr. Fitzgerald. Apr. 24, 1924. 10 p. (H. rp. 562, 68th Cong. 1st sess.) * Paper, 5c.

24—26404

—EDUCATION COMMITTEE

National Conservatory of Music, hearing on H. R. 7011, to create commission to ascertain feasibility of establishing National Conservatory of Music. 1924. ii+32 p. * Paper, 5c.

ELECTION OF PRESIDENT, VICE PRESIDENT, AND REPRESENTATIVES COMMITTEE

Campaign funds. Additional publicity of campaign contributions, made to political parties, and limiting amount of campaign expenditures by amending corrupt practices act, hearings on H. R. 6851, Feb. 21–Mar. 13, 1924; testimony of William Tyler Page [and] John L. Cable. 1924. ii+38 p. * Paper, 5c.

President of United States. Proposed amendment to Constitution of United States fixing commencement of terms of President and vice President and Members of Congress, and fixing time of assembling of Congress, hearings on S. J. Res. 22 and H. J. Res. 93, Mar. 27, 1924; testimony of George W. Norris. 1924. pt. 2, ii+37–52 p. [Part 1 appeared in Monthly catalogue for Feb. 1924, p. 434.] * Paper, 5c.

President of United States—Continued. Proposing amendment to Constitution of United States, report to accompany S. J. Res. 22 [proposing amendment to Constitution of United States fixing commencement of terms of President and vice President and Members of Congress, and fixing time of assembling of Congress]; submitted by Mr. White of Kansas. Apr. 15, 1924. 7 p. (H. rp. 513, 68th Cong. 1st sess.) * Paper, 5c. 24—26405

ELECTIONS COMMITTEE, NO. 1

Contested elections. Martin C. Ansorge *v.* Royal H. Weller, argument of counsel on contested-election case of Martin C. Ansorge *v.* Royal H. Weller from 21st Congressional district of New York. 1924. ii+245 p. [Pages 1–130 were also published separately.] * Paper, 25c.

FLOOD CONTROL COMMITTEE

Floods. Surveys for flood control, hearings on preliminary surveys and surveys with view to flood control on sundry streams, Mar. 5. 1924. 1924. ii+59 p. * Paper, 10c.

FOREIGN AFFAIRS COMMITTEE

China. Chinese indemnity, hearings on H. J. Res. 201, for remission of further payments of annual installments of Chinese indemnity, Mar. 31–Apr. 2, 1924. 1924. ii+98 p. * Paper, 10c.
—— Chinese indemnity, report to accompany H. J. Res. 248 [for remission of further payments of annual installments of Chinese indemnity]; submitted by Mr. Porter. Apr. 29, 1924. 6 p. (H. rp. 600, 68th Cong. 1st sess.) * Paper, 5c.
Cumming, Hugh S. Decorations bestowed upon Surg. Gen. Hugh S. Cumming by Republics of France and Poland, report to accompany H. J. Res. 222; submitted by Mr. Moore of Virginia. Mar. 29, 1924. 1 p. (H. rp. 405, 68th Cong. 1st sess.) * Paper, 5c.
Interparliamentary Union, report to accompany H. J. Res. 204 [requesting the President to invite Interparliamentary Union to meet in city of Washington in 1925 and authorizing appropriation to defray expenses of meeting]; submitted by Mr. Temple. Apr. 8, 1924. 2 p. (H. rp. 475, 68th Cong. 1st sess.) * Paper, 5c.
Tozier, Dorr F. Granting permission to Commander Dorr F. Tozier to accept gift from King of Great Britain, report to accompany S. 1698; submitted by Mr. Cole of Iowa. Apr. 8, 1924. 1 p. (H. rp. 473, 68th Cong. 1st sess.) * Paper, 5c.

IMMIGRATION AND NATURALIZATION COMMITTEE

Immigration Bureau. Overtime pay of immigrant inspectors, hearings on H. R. 7694, proposed amendment to H. R. 7995. Feb. 22, 1924; statement of W. J. Coyne. 1924. ii+1177–92 p. 1 pl. (Serial 3–A.) * Paper, 5c.

INDIAN AFFAIRS COMMITTEE

Chippewa Indians. To compensate Chippewa Indians of Minnesota for timber and interest, report to accompany H. R. 27 [to compensate Chippewa Indians of Minnesota for timber and interest in connection with settlement for Minnesota National Forest]; submitted by Mr. Hudson. Apr. 24, 1924. 2 p. (H. rp. 568, 68th Cong. 1st sess.) * Paper, 5c.
Cowlitz Indians. Authorizing Cowlitz tribe of Indians in State of Washington to submit claims to Court of Claims, report to accompany H. R. 71; submitted by Mr. Brumm. Apr. 4. 1924. 2 p. (H. rp. 454, 68th Cong. 1st sess.) * Paper, 5c.
Dakota Indians. Authorizing Secretary of Interior to determine claims of certain members of Sioux Nation in South Dakota. report to accompany H. R. 7400 [authorizing Secretary of Interior to consider, ascertain, adjust, and determine claims of certain members of Sioux Nation of Indians for damages occasioned by destruction of their horses]; submitted by Mr. Leavitt. Apr. 3. 1924. 2 p. (H. rp. 443, 68th Cong. 1st sess.) * Paper, 5c.

Delaware Indians. Refer claims of Delaware Indians to Court of Claims, report to accompany H. R. 3913 [to refer claims of Delaware Indians to Court of Claims, with right of appeal to Supreme Court of United States]; submitted by Mr. Leavitt. Apr. 19, 1924. 3 p. (H. rp. 536, 68th Cong. 1st sess.) * Paper, 5c.

Five Civilized Tribes in Oklahoma, hearings before subcommittee on H. R. 6900 [for protection of restricted lands and funds of Indians of Five Civilized Tribes], Mar. 22 and 28, 1924. 1924. [1]+80 p. * Paper, 10c.

Fort Hall Reservation. Authorizing use of Indian lands for reservoir purposes, report to accompany H. R. 6864 [authorizing acquiring of lands on Fort Hall Indian Reservation, Idaho, for reservoir purposes in connection with Minidoka irrigation project]; submitted by Mr. Garber. Apr. 3, 1924. 3 p. (H. rp. 446, 68th Cong. 1st sess.) * Paper, 5c.

—— Minidoka irrigation project, Idaho, hearing before subcommittee on H. R. 6864 [authorizing use of Indian lands on Fort Hall Indian Reservation, Idaho, for reservoir purposes in connection with Minidoka irrigation project], Mar. 6–13, 1924. 1924. [1]+67 p. * Paper, 5c.

Indian Affairs Office. Quarters, fuel, and light for employees of Indian field service, report to accompany H. R. 7887; submitted by Mr. Snyder. Apr. 19, 1924. 2 p. (H. rp. 534, 68th Cong. 1st sess.) * Paper, 5c.

Indians. Authority to certain Indians and Indian tribes to submit claims to Court of Claims, report to accompany H. R. 2694 [authorizing certain Indian tribes, or any of them, residing in State of Washington to submit to Court of Claims certain claims growing out of treaties or otherwise]; submitted by Mr. Brumm. Apr. 4, 1924. 3 p. (H. rp. 456, 68th Cong. 1st sess.) * Paper, 5c.

Kansa Reservation. To lease for mining purposes unallotted lands in Kaw [or Kansa] Reservation, report to accompany S. 2798; submitted by Mr. Snyder. Apr. 10, 1924. 2 p. (H. rp. 480, 68th Cong. 1st sess.) * Paper, 5c.

Kramer, Forrest J. Forrest J. Kramer, report to accompany H. R. 7249 [for relief of Forrest J. Kramer]; submitted by Mr. Howard of Oklahoma. Apr. 10, 1924. 2 p. (H. rp. 482, 68th Cong. 1st sess.) [Report reads, incorrectly, "to accompany H. R. 7294."] * Paper, 5c.

Kuca, H. E. H. E. Kuca and V. J. Koupal, report to accompany H. R. 2977 [for relief of H. E. Kuca and V. J. Koupal]; submitted by Mr. Johnson of South Dakota. Apr. 24, 1924. 3 p. (H. rp. 570, 68th Cong. 1st sess.) * Paper, 5c.

Paiute Indians. To amend act authorizing appropriation to meet proportionate expenses of providing drainage system for Piute Indian lands in Nevada within Newlands reclamation project of Reclamation Service, report to accompany S. 1203; submitted by Mr. Snyder. Apr. 17, 1924. 2 p. (H. rp. 526, 68th Cong. 1st sess.) * Paper, 5c.

Ponca Indians. Authorizing Ponca tribe of Indians in Oklahoma and Nebraska to submit claims to Court of Claims, report to accompany H. R. 4275; submitted by Mr. Leavitt. Apr. 4, 1924. 2 p. (H. rp. 457, 68th Cong. 1st sess.) * Paper, 5c.

Pyramid Lake Reservation For relief of settlers and town-site occupants of lands in Pyramid Lake Indian Reservation. Nev., report to accompany S. 1309; submitted by Mr. Snyder. Apr. 24, 1924. 2 p. (H. rp. 567, 68th Cong. 1st sess.) * Paper, 5c.

Reclamation of land. Extension of water charges in connection with Indian irrigation projects, report to accompany H. R. 8581; submitted by Mr. Leavitt. Apr. 24, 1924. 2 p. (H. rp. 569, 68th Cong. 1st sess.) * Paper. 5c.

Red Pipestone Quarries. Interest, title, ownership, and right of possession of Red Pipestone Quarries, Minn., report to accompany H. R. 8545 [conferring jurisdiction on Court of Claims to determine and report upon interest, title, ownership, and right of possession of Yankton band of Santee Sioux Indians to Red Pipestone Quarries, Minn.]; submitted by Mr. Johnson of South Dakota. Apr. 24, 1924. 2 p. (H. rp. 565, 68th Cong. 1st sess.) * Paper, 5c.

San Carlos irrigation project. Pima Indians and San Carlos irrigation project, hearings on S. 966, Apr. 10 and 18. 1924. 1924. ii+40 p. * Paper, 5c.

Stevens County, Wash. Claims of Stevens and Ferry counties. Wash., hearings before subcommittee on H. R. 1414, Feb. 9 and Apr. 1, 1924. 1924. ii+33 p. * Paper, 5c.

Stevens County, Wash.—Continued. Payment of certain taxes to Stevens and
Ferry counties, Wash., report to accompany H. R. 1414; submitted by
Mr. Roach. Apr. 24, 1924. 5 p. (H. rp. 566, 68th Cong. 1st sess.) * Paper, 5c.
Temoak Indians. Authorizing Secretary of Interior to purchase tract of land,
with sufficient water right attached, for use and occupancy of Temoak band
of homeless Indians located at Ruby valley, Nev., report to accompany S.
1308; submitted by Mr. Snyder. Apr. 17, 1924. 2 p. (H. rp. 527, 68th Cong.
1st sess.) * Paper, 5c.
Wichita Indians. Wichita band of Indians to submit claims to Court of
Claims, report to accompany H. R. 731 [authorizing Wichita and affiliated
bands of Indians in Oklahoma to submit claims to Court of Claims]; submitted by Mr. Hastings. Apr. 4, 1924. 3 p. (H. rp. 455, 68th Cong. 1st
sess.) * Paper, 5c.

INSULAR AFFAIRS COMMITTEE

Porto Rico. To amend and reenact secs. 20, 22, and 50 of act to provide civil
government for Porto Rico [relating to salaries], report to accompany S. 2573;
submitted by Mr. Fairfield. Apr. 23, 1924. 2 p. (H. rp, 551, 68th Cong.
1st sess.) * Paper, 5c.

INTERSTATE AND FOREIGN COMMERCE COMMITTEE

Calumet River. Bridge across Calumet River at Chicago, Ill., report to accompany H. R. 8304 [granting consent of Congress to Chicago to construct
bridge across Calumet River at or near 100th street in Chicago, county of
Cook, Ill.]; submitted by Mr. Graham of Illinois. Apr. 11, 1924. 2 p. (H.
rp. 497, 68th Cong. 1st sess.) * Paper, 5c.
Coast and Geodetic Survey seismological investigations, report to accompany
H. R. 8308 [authorizing Coast and Geodetic Survey to make seismological investigations, including such investigations as have been heretofore performed
by Weather Bureau]; submitted by Mr. Lea of California. Apr. 21, 1924.
2 p. (H. rp. 540, 68th Cong. 1st sess.) * Paper, 5c.
Cumberland River. Bridge across Cumberland River, report to accompany
S. 431 [to extend time for construction of bridge across Cumberland River
in Montgomery County, Tenn., by said county, within 7 miles of Clarksville];
submitted by Mr. Barkley. Apr. 2, 1924. 1 p. (H. rp. 433, 68th Cong. 1st
sess.) * Paper, 5c.
Detroit River. Bridge across Detroit River, report to accompany H. R. 8084
[to extend times of American Transit Company for commencing and completing construction of bridge across Detroit River within or near Detroit,
Mich.]; submitted by Mr. Mapes. Apr. 3, 1924. 1 p. (H. rp. 441, 68th
Cong. 1st sess.) * Paper, 5c.
Dixie Power Company. To amend permit issued to Dixie Power Co., report
to accompany S. 2686 [to authorize Federal Power Commission to amend
permit numbered 1, project numbered 1, issued to Dixie Power Company];
submitted by Mr. Parks of Arkansas. Apr. 3, 1924. 3 p. (H. rp. 437, 68th
Cong. 1st sess.) * Paper, 5c.
Freight rates. Railroad rate structure survey, hearings on H. J. Res. 141,
directing Interstate Commerce Commission to take action relative to ad-
justments in rate structure of common carriers subject to interstate com-
merce act, and fixing of rates and charges, Apr. 3–9, 1924. 1924. iii+65 p.
* Paper, 5c.
——— Same, supplement, Apr. 12 and 14, 1924. 1924. iii+47 p. * Paper, 5c.
Kanawha River. To repeal act authorizing construction of bridges across Great
Kanawha River, report to accompany S. 1614; submitted by Mr. Wyant.
Apr. 2, 1924. 2 p. (H. rp. 425, 68th Cong. 1st sess.) * Paper, 5c.
Lighthouse service personnel bill, hearings on H. R. 6866, for protection of aids
to navigation in lighthouse service and for other purposes, Mar. 27, 1924.
1924. iii+31 p. * Paper, 5c.
Locomotives. Additional Government railroad locomotive inspectors, hearings
on H. R. 5836, to amend act to promote safety of employees and travelers
upon railroads by compelling common carriers engaged in interstate commerce to equip their locomotives with safe and suitable boilers and appurtenances thereto, as amended; Mar. 28–Apr. 1, 1924. 1924. iii+66 p. * Paper,
5c.

Locomotives—Continued. To promote safety of employees and travelers on railroads, report to accompany H. R. 8578 [to amend act to promote safety of employees and travelers upon railroads by compelling common carriers engaged in interstate commerce to equip their locomotives with safe and suitable boilers and appurtenances thereto, as amended]; submitted by Mr. Cooper of Ohio. Apr. 11, 1924. 8 p. (H. rp. 490, 68th Cong. 1st sess.) * Paper, 5c.

Mississippi River. Bridge across Mississippi River at St. Paul, Minn., report to accompany H. R. 8229 [granting consent of Congress to St. Paul, Minn., to construct bridge across Mississippi River in said city]; submitted by Mr. Newton of Minnesota. Apr. 11, 1924. 2 p. (H. rp. 496, 68th Cong. 1st sess.) * Paper, 5c.

Ohio River. Bridge across Ohio River, report to accompany H. R. 8181 [granting consent of Congress to Edward T. Franks and Thomas H. Hazelrigg to construct bridge across Ohio River approximately midway between Owensboro, Ky., and Rockport, Ind.]; submitted by Mr. Barkley. Apr. 2, 1924. 2 p. (H. rp. 432, 68th Cong. 1st sess.) * Paper, 5c.

Panama Canal. Measurement of vessels using Panama Canal, report to accompany H. R. 7762; submitted by Mr. Hoch. Apr. 25, 1924. 6 p. (H. rp. 573, 68th Cong. 1st sess.) * Paper, 5c.

Susquehanna River. Bridge across Susquehanna River, report to accompany H. R. 7846 [to extend time for construction of bridge across North Branch of Susquehanna River from Wilkes-Barre to borough of Dorranceton, Pa., by county of Luzerne, Pa.]; submitted by Mr. Wyant. Apr. 1, 1924. 1 p. (H. rp. 420, 68th Cong. 1st sess.) * Paper, 5c.

INVALID PENSIONS COMMITTEE

Pensions and increase of pensions to soldiers and sailors of Civil War, etc., report to accompany S. 5 [granting pensions and increase of pensions to soldiers and sailors of Civil and Mexican wars and to widows, former widows, minor children, and helpless children of 'said soldiers and sailors, and to widows of War of 1812, and to Indian war veterans and widows, and to Spanish War soldiers, and certain maimed soldiers, and for other purposes]; submitted by Mr. Fuller. Apr. 5, 1924. 15 p. (H. rp. 463, 68th Cong. 1st sess.) * Paper, 5c.

IRRIGATION AND RECLAMATION COMMITTEE

Colorado River. Protection and development of lower Colorado River basin, hearings on H. R. 2903. 1924. pts. 1–3; [vi]+1–539 p. * Paper, pt. 1, 25c.; * pt. 2, 20c.; * pt. 3, 10c.

JUDICIARY COMMITTEE

Alaska. Amendment to law providing for special taxes on business and trades in Alaska, report to accompany H. R. 6584; submitted by Mr. Michener. Apr. 1, 1924. 2 p. (H. rp. 424, 68th Cong. 1st sess.) * Paper, 5c.

Calendar. Legislative calendar, 68th Congress, Apr. 7 and 21, 1924; no. 10 and 11. 1924. 69 p. and 71 p. 4°

Clerks of United States courts. Fees of clerks of United States courts, etc., hearing on H. R. 5420, H. R. 5421, H. R. 5422, H. R. 5423, H. R. 5424, H. R. 5425, and H. R. 5428, Apr. 10, 1924. 1924. ii+30 p. (Serial 30.) [Includes hearings before subcommittee of Senate Committee on Judiciary on corresponding Senate bills.] * Paper, 5c.

Disbursing officers. To continue life of act granting relief to certain disbursing officers of War and Navy Departments, report to accompany H. R. 8369; submitted by Mr. Graham of Pennsylvania. Apr. 3, 1924. 3 p. (H. rp. 448, 68th Cong. 1st sess.) * Paper, 5c.

District Courts. Judges of district court for district of Hawaii, report to accompany H. R. 6860 [to authorize each of the judges of district court for district of Hawaii to hold sessions of said court separately at same time]; submitted by Mr. Graham of Pennsylvania. Apr. 29, 1924. 3 p. (H. rp. 595, 68th Cong. 1st sess.) * Paper, 5c.

—— Judicial districts in Texas, report to accompany H. R. 8050 [to detach Reagan County, Tex., from El Paso division of western judicial district of Texas and attach said county to San Angelo division of northern judicial district of said State]; submitted by Mr. Sumners of Texas. Mar. 29, 1924. 1 p. (H. rp. 407, 68th Cong. 1st sess.) * Paper, 5c.

District Courts—Continued. Providing terms of court at Durant, Okla., report to accompany H. R. 6646; submitted by Mr. Yates. Apr. 10, 1924. 1 p. (H. rp. 487, 68th Cong. 1st sess.) * Paper, 5c.

—— Providing terms of court to be held at Sterling, Colo., report to accompany H. R. 169; submitted by Mr. Yates. Apr. 10, 1924. 3 p. (H. rp. 486, 68th Cong. 1st sess.) *Paper, 5c.

—— Term of court at Poteau, Okla., hearing on H. R. 644, Feb. 13, 1924; statement of Charles D. Carter. 1924. [1]+7 p. (Serial 22.) *Paper, 5c.

—— Terms of court at Albuquerque, Roswell, Las Vegas, Silver City, and Las Cruces, N. Mex., hearing on H. R. 7523, Apr. 18, 1924; statement of John Morrow. 1924. [1]+10 p. (Serial 31.) *Paper, 5c.

—— Terms of court at Bartlesville and Pawhuska, Okla., report to accompany H. R. 64; submitted by Mr. Yates. Apr. 10, 1924. 1 p. (H. rp. 485, 68th Cong. 1st sess.) *Paper, 5c.

—— Terms of court at Pawhuska, Bartlesville, and Pauls Valley, Okla., hearing on H. R. 64 and H. R. 162, Mar. 3, 1924. 1924. ii+11 p. (Serial 23.) *Paper, 5c.

—— Terms of court at Shelby, N. C., report to accompany H. R. 8657 [to amend sec. 98 of judicial code, providing for holding of district court at Shelby, N. C.]; submitted by Mr. Graham of Pennsylvania. Apr. 29, 1924. 1 p. (H. rp. 596, 68th Cong. 1st sess.) *Paper, 5c.

—— Time and place for holding terms of court in New Mexico, report to accompany H. R. 7523 [designating New Mexico as judicial district, fixing time and place for holding terms of court therein, and for other purposes]; submitted by Mr. Yates. Apr. 21, 1924. 1 p. (H. rp. 542, 68th Cong. 1st sess.) *Paper, 5c.

—— Time of holding court in Mississippi, report to accompany H. R. 466 [to amend sec. 90 of judicial code so as to change time of holding certain terms of district court of Mississippi]; submitted by Mr. Graham of Pennsylvania. Apr. 29, 1924. 2 p. (H. rp. 594, 68th Cong. 1st sess.) *Paper, 5c.

—— To fix time for terms of district courts in western district of Virginia, report to accompany S. 1609; submitted by Mr. Montague. Apr. 3, 1924. 1 p. (H. rp. 450, 68th Cong. 1st sess.) *Paper, 5c.

General Supply Committee. To enlarge functions of General Supply Committee, hearing on H. R. 7493, Apr. 3, 1924. 1924. ii+9 p. (Serial 27.) *Paper, 5c.

—— To enlarge functions of General Supply Committee, report to accompany H. R. 8711 [to authorize consolidation and coordination of Government purchases, to enlarge functions of General Supply Committee, and for other purposes]; submitted by Mr. Graham of Pennsylvania. Apr. 29, 1924. 2 p. (H. rp. 597, 68th Cong. 1st sess.) *Paper, 5c.

Internal revenue. To provide for recording of tax liens in Connecticut, Rhode Island, Vermont, and Louisiana, hearing on H. R. 4202, Mar. 24, 1924; statement of Clark Burdick. 1924. [1]+6 p. (Serial 25.) *Paper, 5c.

Leavenworth, Fort. Transfer to jurisdiction of Department of Justice portion of Fort Leavenworth reservation in Missouri, report to accompany H. R. 6207; submitted by Mr. Graham of Pennsylvania. Apr. 3, 1924. 2 p. (H. rp. 445, 68th Cong. 1st sess.) *Paper, 5c.

National McKinley Birthplace Memorial Association. To amend sec. 3 of act to incorporate National McKinley Birthplace Memorial Association, report to accompany S. 2821; submitted by Mr. Foster. Apr. 3, 1924. 1 p. (H. rp. 440, 68th Cong. 1st sess.) * Paper, 5c.

Probation system in United States courts, report to accompany H. R. 5195; submitted by Mr. Graham of Pennsylvania. Apr. 1, 1924. 11 p. (H. rp. 423, 68th Cong. 1st sess.) * Paper, 5c.   24—26406

Prohibition Bureau. To provide for Bureau of Prohibition in Treasury Department, hearing on H. R. 6645, Mar. 13–Apr. 2, 1924. 1924. iv+250 p. 1 pl. (Serial 28.) * Paper, 25c.

Star-spangled banner. Legislation to make Star-spangled banner the national anthem, hearing on H. R. 6429 and H. J. Res. 69, Mar. 20, 1924. 1924. ii+33 p. (Serial 24.) * Paper, 5c.

United States Blind Veterans of World War. To incorporate Blind Veterans of World War, hearing on H. R. 4526, Apr. 10, 1924. 1924. ii+4 p. (Serial 29.) * Paper, 5c.

United States Blind Veterans of World War—Continued. To incorporate United States Blind Veterans of World War, report to accompany H. R. 4526; submitted by Mr. Graham of Pennsylvania. Apr. 10, 1924. 1 p. (H. rp. 483, 68th Cong. 1st sess.) *Paper, 5c.

Witnesses. Relating to examination of witnesses in suits in equity in courts of United States, report to accompany H. R. 8546; submitted by Mr. Graham of Pennsylvania. Apr. 10, 1924. 2 p. (H. rp. 484, 68th Cong. 1st sess.) *Paper, 5c.

LABOR COMMITTEE

Strikes and lockouts. Regulating transportation of labor in interstate commerce. report to accompany H. R. 7698 [to regulate transportation and importation of labor from one State to any point in another State or District of Columbia, or any territorial possession of United States, or from District of Columbia or any territorial possession of United States into any State where labor lockout or strike is then in progress]; submitted by Mr. Zihlman. Apr. 12, 1924.. 2 p. (H. rp. 500, 68th Cong. 1st sess.) *Paper, 5c.

MERCHANT MARINE AND FISHERIES COMMITTEE

Radio communication. To regulate radio communication, hearings on H. R. 7357. Mar. 11–14. 1924. 1924. ii+254 p. *Paper, 25c.

MILITARY AFFAIRS COMMITTEE

Alexandria Light and Power Company. Sale of electric current from Government-owned transmission line, report to accompany H. R. 526 [authorizing Secretary of War to enter into arrangement, on behalf of United States, with Alexandria Light and Power Company, whereby civilians may obtain electric current from Government-owned transmission line extending from Alexandria to Fort Humphreys. Va.]; submitted by Mr. Speaks. Apr. 9, 1924. 2 p. (H. rp. 477, 68th Cong. 1st sess.) *Paper, 5c.

Army. To amend national defense act, as amended, hearings on H. R. 6354 and S. 2169, to amend in certain particulars national defense act, as amended, Feb. 12–Mar. 10, 1924. 1924. ii+135 p. *Paper, 15c.

Crockett, Fort. Authorizing use of Government buildings at Fort Crockett. Tex., report to accompany S. 2736 [authorizing use of Government buildings at Fort Crockett, Tex., for occupancy during State convention of Texas Shriners]; submitted by Mr. Garrett of Texas. Apr. 8, 1924. 1 p. (H. rp. 471, 68th Cong. 1st sess.) *Paper, 5c.

Dilks, John W. John W. Dilks, report to accompany H. R. 7296 [for relief of John W. Dilks]; submitted by Mr. McSwain. Apr. 3, 1924. 1 p. (H. rp. 451, 68th Cong. 1st sess.) [Corrected print.] *Paper, 5c.

—— Relief of John W. Dilks, hearings on H. R. 7296, Apr. 1, 1924; statement of Richard Yates. 1924 ii+6 p. *Paper, 5c.

Helium. Conservation of helium gas, hearings on H. R. 5722, authorizing conservation, production, and exploitation of helium gas, mineral resource pertaining to national defense, and to development of commercial aeronautics, Mar. 20, 1924. 1924. ii+35 p. *Paper, 5c.

Hughes, James A. James A. Hughes, report to accompany H. R. 6737 [for relief of James A. Hughes]; submitted by Mr. Boylan. Apr. 11, 1924. 3 p. (H. rp. 491, 68th Cong. 1st sess.) *Paper, 5c.

Long, Frederic K. Frederic K. Long, report to accompany H. R. 8259 [to authorize the President to reconsider case of Frederic K. Long and to reappoint him captain in Regular Army]; submitted by Mr. Wainright [Wainwright]. Apr. 15, 1924. 2 p. (H. rp. 514, 68th Cong. 1st sess.) *Paper, 5c.

Macon, Fort. Granting Fort Macon military reservation to North Carolina, report to accompany H. R. 7145; submitted by Mr. Hill of Alabama. Apr. 15, 1924. 2 p. (H. rp. 515, 68th Cong. 1st sess.) *Paper, 5c.

Meeks, Jesse L. Jesse L. Meeks, report to accompany H. R. 2607 [for relief of Jesse L. Meeks]; submitted by Mr. Gerau. Apr. 3, 1924. 2 p. (H. rp. 444, 68th Cong. 1st sess.) *Paper, 5c.

Moran, James. James Moran, report to accompany S. 589 [for relief of James Moran]; submitted by Mr. McSwain. Apr. 4, 1924. 2 p. (H. rp. 460, 68th Cong. 1st sess.) *Paper, 5c.

Pay, Navy. Pay of warrant and commissioned warrant officers, Navy, hearings, Mar. 18, 1924. 1924. ii+50 p. *Paper, 5c.

Petersburg, Va. Inspection of battle fields of siege of Petersburg, Va., report to accompany H. R. 3669; submitted by Mr. Sherwood. , Apr. 29, 1924. 1 p. (H. rp. 599, 68th Cong. 1st sess.) * Paper, 5c.

Rethers, Harry F. Permission to Col. Harry F. Rethers to accept statuette Le courage militaire, report to accompany H. R. 5661 [granting permission to Colonel Harry F. Rethers, Quartermaster Corps, Army, to accept gift of Sevres statuette entitled Le courage militaire tendered by, President of French Republic] ; submitted by Mr. Wainwright. Apr. 25, 1924. 2 p. (H. rp. 574. 68th Cong. 1st sess.) * Paper, 5c.

Retired list, Army. Equalize pay of retired officers of Army, etc., report to accompany H. R. 5097 [to equalize pay of retired officers of Army, Navy, Marine Corps, Coast Guard, Coast and Geodetic Survey, and Public Health Service] ; submitted by Mr. Hull of Iowa. Apr. 12, 1924. 4 p. (H. rp. 499. 68th Cong. 1st sess.) * Paper, 5c.

—— National defense act, report to accompany H. R. 5084 [to amend national defense act, as amended, relative to retirement of certain officers] ; submitted by Mr. Wurzbach. Apr. 11, 1924. 5 p. (H. rp. 495. 68th Cong. 1st sess.) * Paper, 5c.

—— To equalize pay of retired officers, hearings on H. R. 5097 [to equalize pay of retired officers of Army, Navy, Marine Corps, Coast Guard, Coast and Geodetic Survey, and Public Health Service], Mar. 25, 1924. 1924. ii+17 p. * Paper, 5c.

—— validating payments to retired enlisted men, to accompany S. 2450 [to amend sec. 2 of legislative, executive, and judicial appropriation act, approved July 31, 1894, relative to holding of Government office by retired enlisted men of Army, Navy, Marine Corps, or Coast Guard] ; submitted by Mr. Speaks. Apr. 12, 1924. 2 p. (H. rp. 498. 68th Cong. 1st sess.) * Paper, 5c.

Revere, Fort. Sale of portion of Fort Revere reservation at Hull, Mass. [to said city], report to accompany H. R. 6095; submitted by Mr. Frothingham. Apr. 24. 1924. 1 p. (H. rp. 563. 68th Cong. 1st sess.) * Paper, 5c.

Shevlin, Dennis. Dennis Shevlin, report to accompany H. R. 1332 [for relief of Dennis Shevlin] ; submitted by Mr. Boylan, Apr. 7, 1924. 3 p. (H. rp. 469, 68th Cong. 1st sess.) . * Paper, 5c.

Snelling, Fort. Railroad right of way at Fort Snelling, hearings before subcommittee 6 on, H. R. 5274, Feb. 13, 1924; statements of Oscar E. Keller [and] C. F. Loweth. 1924. ii+12 p. * Paper, 5c.

Tombstones. Durable markers in form of crosses for graves of American soldiers in Europe, hearings, Mar. 13 [and] 25, 1924. 1924. ii+36 p. * Paper, 5c.

Vicksburg, Miss. Construct water mains on National Cemetery road at Vicksburg, Miss., report to accompany H. R. 4816 [to permit Vicksburg, Miss., to construct water mains on and under National Cemetery road, Vicksburg, Miss.] ; submitted by Mr. Quin, Apr. 3, 1924. 2 p. (H. rp. 449, 68th Cong. 1st sess.) * Paper, 5c.

MINES AND MINING COMMITTEE

Claims. To authorize payment of claims under provisions of so-called war minerals relief act, report to accompany S. 2797; submitted by Mr. Robsion of Kentucky. Apr. 29, 1924. 9 p. (H. rp. 601, 68th Cong. 1st sess.) * Paper, 5c.

NAVAL AFFAIRS COMMITTEE

Calendar. Legislative calendar, 68th Congress, 1923–24; no. 3, Apr. 5, 1924. 1924. 32 p. 4° ‡

Navy Department. To authorize disposition of lands no longer needed and acquisition of other lands required for naval purposes, report to accompany H. R. 8732; submitted by Mr. Britten. Apr. 18, 1924. 9 p. (H. rp. 529. 68th Cong. 1st sess.) * Paper, 5c.

War-ships. To authorize alterations to certain naval vessels and to provide for construction of additional vessels, report to accompany H. R. 8687 ; submitted by Mr. Butler. Apr. 19, 1924. 10 p. (H. rp. 535, 68th Cong. 1st sess.) * Paper, 5c.

Girayosxian. Garabed T. K. Garabed free-energy generator, report to accompany H. J. Res. 190 [to amend sec. 3 of joint resolution for purpose of promoting efficiency, for utilization of resources and industries of United States, for lessening expenses of the war, and restoring loss caused by the war by providing for employment of discovery or invention called the "Garabed," claiming to make possible utilization of free energy] ; submitted by Mr. McLeod. Apr. 17, 1924. 4 p. (H. rp. 524, 68th Cong. 1st sess.) * Paper, 5c.

Patents. To amend patent and trade-mark laws. and for other purposes, report to accompany H. R. 21 ; submitted by Mr. Lanham. Apr. 8, 1924. 1 p. (H. rp. 470.168th Cong. 1st sess.) * Paper, 5c.

Pensions. Amending act of Sept. 22, 1922, so as to make pension laws applicable to certain class of persons, report to accompany S. 2154 [to amend act to provide for applicability of pension laws to certain classes of persons in military and naval services not entitled to benefits of article 3 of war risk insurance act, as amended] ; submitted by Mr. Robsion of Kentucky. Apr. 2, 1924. 4 p. (H. rp. 426, 68th Cong. 1st sess.) * Paper, 5c.

Air Mail, flying fields and hangars, report to accompany H. R. 3261 [to authorize and provide for payment of amounts expended in construction of hangars and maintenance of flying fields for use of Air Mail Service of Post Office Department] ; submitted by Mr. LaGuardia. Apr. 8, 1924. 3 p. (H. rp. 472, 68th Cong. 1st sess.) [Corrected print.] * Paper, 5c.

Alaska. Mail service in Alaska, report to accompany H. R. 6581 [authorizing Postmaster General to provide emergency mail service in Alaska] ; submitted by Mr. Moore of Ohio. Apr. 26, 1924. 4 p. (H. rp. 582, 68th Cong. 1st sess.) * Paper, 5c.

Marketing of farm produce. Rural mail service, report to accompany S. 2111 [authorizing Postmaster General to conduct experiment in rural mail service to encourage transportation of food products directly from producers to consumers or vendors] ; submitted by Mr. Moore of Ohio. Apr. 11, 1924. 4 p. (H. rp. 492, 68th Cong. 1st sess.) . * Paper, 5c.

Government Printing Office. Regulation of Government Printing Office wages, report to accompany H. R. 7996 ; submitted by Mr. Kiess. Mar. 31, 1924. 3 p. (H. rp. 412, 68th Cong. 1st sess.) * Paper, 5c.

Grand Army of the Republic. National encampment proceedings of Grand Army of the Republic, Spanish War veterans, and American Legion, report to accompany H. J. Res. 194 [to print as House document proceedings of national encampments of Grand Army of the Republic, United Spanish War veterans, and American Legion, for use of House and Senate] ; submitted by Mr. Kiess. Apr. 17, 1924. 1 p. (H. rp. 518, 68th Cong. 1st sess.) * Paper, 5c.

Philippine Islands. Printing report of governor general of Philippine Islands [fiscal year ended Dec. 31, 1922] as House document, report to accompany H. Res. 238 : submitted by Mr. Kiess. Apr. 17, 1924. 1 p. (H. rp. 520, 68th Cong. 1st sess.) * Paper, 5c.

Porto Rico. Printing annual report of governor of Porto Rico [fiscal year 1923], report to accompany H. Res. 237 ; submitted by Mr. Kiess. Apr. 17, 1924. 1 p. (H. rp. 519, 68th Cong. 1st sess.) * Paper, 5c.

Astoria, Oreg. Conveyance of land to Astoria, Oreg., report to accompany H. R. 7821 : submitted by Mr. Langley. Apr. 10, 1924. 2 p. (H. rp. 488, 68th Cong. 1st sess.) * Paper, 5c.

District of Columbia. Glover parkway, report to accompany S. 1971 [to author-
ize commissioners of District of Columbia to accept land in District of
Columbia dedicated by Charles C. Glover for park purposes]; submitted by
Mr. Langley. Apr. 15, 1924. 2 p. (H. rp. 511, 68th Cong. 1st sess.)
* Paper, 5c.

Duluth, Minn. Conveyance of land to Duluth, Minn., report to accompany
H. R. 8110; submitted by Mr. Langley. Apr. 12, 1924. 2 p. (H. rp, 506,
68th Cong. 1st sess.) * Paper, 5c.

National Home for Disabled Volunteer Soldiers. Hospital at National Home
for Disabled volunteer Soldiers, Santa Monica, Calif., report to accompany
H. R. 2821; submitted by Mr. Langley. Apr. 14, 1924. 2 p. (H. rp. 507,
68th Cong. 1st sess.) * Paper, 5c.

Public buildings. Officers in charge of public buildings and grounds, District of
Columbia, report to accompany S. 1918; submitted by Mr. Langley. Apr. 16,
1924. 1 p. (H. rp. 516, 68th Cong. 1st sess.) [S. 1918 changes name of
Office of Superintendent, State, War, and Navy Department Buildings to
Office of Public Buildings in District of Columbia, and of Office of Public
Buildings and Grounds to Office of Public Parks in District of Columbia.]
* Paper, 5c.

PUBLIC LANDS COMMITTEE

Adger, Idaho. Purchase of lands for railroad right of way purposes, report to
accompany H. R. 7500 [to authorize sale of lands at or near Adger, Ada
County, Idaho, for railroad purposes, to Oregon Short Line Railroad Com-
pany]; submitted by Mr. Smith, Apr. 2, 1924. 1 p. (H. rp. 428, 68th Cong.
1st sess.) * Paper, 5c.

Alaska. Sale of timber on public lands in Alaska, hearings on H. R. 7696, to
amend sec. 11 of act approved May 14, 1898 (30th Statutes at large, p. 409–
415) [relating to sale of timber on public lands in Alaska], Apr. 9, 1924.
1924. ii+28 p. * Paper, 5c.

Brown, William. William Brown, report to accompany H. R. 2313 [authorizing
issuance of patent to William Brown]; submitted by Mr. White of Kansas.
Apr. 4, 1924. 3 p. (H. rp. 461, 68th Cong. 1st sess.) * Paper, 5c.

Calendar. Legislative calendar, 68th Congress, 1st session, Mar. 8 and Apr. 15,
1924; no. 4 and 5. 1924. 40 p. and 47 p. 4° ‡

Columbia Reservation. Authorizing acquisition of unreserved public lands in
Columbia or Moses Reservation, Wash., report to accompany H. R. 7109 [to
authorize acquisition of unreserved public lands in Columbia or Moses Reservation, Wash., under acts of Mar. 28, 1912 (isolated tract) and Mar. 3,
1877 (desert land)]; submitted by Mr. Hill of Washington. Apr. 4, 1924.
2 p. (H. rp. 458, 68th Cong. 1st sess.) * Paper, 5c.

Custer State Park Game Sanctuary, report to accompany H. R. 7494 [to amend
act creating Custer State Park Game Sanctuary in South Dakota so as to
authorize enlargement]; submitted by Mr. Winter. Apr. 26, 1924. 3 p.
(H. rp. 580, 68th Cong. 1st sess.) * Paper, 5c.

Duchesne, Fort. Granting to Utah Fort Duchesne reservation for use as branch
agricultural college, report to accompany S. 667; submitted by Mr. Colton.
Apr. 23, 1924. 2 p. (H. rp. 553, 68th Cong. 1st sess.) * Paper, 5c.

Eldorado National Forest. Exchange of lands and adjustment of boundaries,
Eldorado National Forest, Calif., report to accompany H. R. 104 [for inclu-
sion of certain lands in Eldorado National Forest, Calif.]; submitted by
Mr. Raker. Apr. 23, 1924. 2 p. (H. rp. 558, 68th Cong. 1st sess.) * Paper, 5c.

—— Lake Tahoe, Eldorado National Forest, Calif., report to accompany H. R.
5555 [to include certain lands in county of Eldorado, Calif., on shore of Lake
Tahoe, in Eldorado National Forest, Calif.]; submitted by Mr. Raker. Apr.
22, 1924. 4 p. (H. rp. 550, 68th Cong. 1st sess.) * Paper, 5c.

Golden, Colo. Sale of lands to Golden, Colo., for water supply, report to accompany H. R. 7998; submitted by Mr. Vaile. Apr. 23, 1924. 2 p. (H.
rp. 556, 68th Cong. 1st sess.) *Paper, 5c.

Hawaii National Park. To repeal 1st proviso of sec. 4 of act to establish
national park in Hawaii [relating to limitation on appropriations which may
be made for improvement of said park], report to accompany H. R. 4985;
submitted by Mr. Jarrett. Apr. 3, 1924. 2 p. (H. rp. 442, 68th Cong. 1st
sess.) * Paper, 5c.

Homestead. Provide for stock-raising homesteads, report to accompany S. 381 [to amend sec. 2 of act to provide for stock-raising homesteads]; submitted by Mr. Morrow. Apr. 4, 1924. 2 p. (H. rp. 459, 68th Cong. 1st sess.) *Paper, 5c.

Lutsch, Johann J. Johann Jacob Lutsch, report to accompany H. R. 5169 [to grant patent to certain lands to Johann Jacob Lutsch]; submitted by Mr. Smith. Apr. 2, 1924. 1 p. (H. rp. 427, 68th Cong. 1st sess.) *Paper, 5c.

Medicine Bow National Forest. To authorize addition of certain lands to Medicine Bow National Forest, Wyo., and for other purposes, report to accompany S. 699; submitted by Mr. Winter. Apr. 24, 1924. 3 p. (H. rp. 564, 68th Cong. 1st sess.) *Paper, 5c.

Northern Pacific Railway. Northern Pacific land grant. 1924. pts. [1-]5.

[pt. 1.] Letter from President of United States with reference to Northern Pacific land grant, also letter from Secretary of Agriculture and Secretary of Interior, with brief and statutes, pertaining to said grant. ii+115 p. il. *Paper, 10c.

pts. 2-4. Hearings on H. J. Res. 183, directing Secretary of Interior to w bhold his approval of adjustment of Northern Pacific land grants, Mar. 1[-18], 1924. [vii]+1-326 p. *Paper, pt. 2, 5c.; *pt. 3, 10c.; *pt. 4. 15c.

[pt. 5.] Reply of Department of Agriculture, Forest Service, to pamphlet of Charles Donnelly, president of Northern Pacific Railway Company. iii+327-356 p. *Paper, 5c.

—— Northern Pacific land grants, report to accompany H. J. Res. 237 [directing Secretary of Interior to withhold his approval of adjustment of Northern Pacific land grants, and creating joint committee to investigate said land grants]; submitted by Mr. Sinnott. Apr. 15, 1924. 5 p. (H. rp. 512, 68th Cong. 1st sess.) *Paper, 5c.

Pensacola, Fla. Authorizing Secretary of Interior to determine and confirm by patent in nature of deed of quitclaim title to lots in Pensacola, Fla., report to accompany S. 807; submitted by Mr. Abernethy. Apr. 29, 1924. 2 p. (H. rp. 598, 68th Cong. 1st sess.) *Paper, 5c.

Plumas National Forest. Exchange of lands and adjustment of boundaries, Plumas National Forest, Calif., report to accompany H. R. 103 [for inclusion of certain lands in Plumas National Forest, Calif.]; submitted by Mr. Raker. Apr. 23, 1924. 4 p. (H. rp. 557, 68th Cong. 1st sess.) *Paper, 5c.

—— Plumas and Lassen national forests, Calif., report to accompany H. R. 656 [to add lands to Plumas and to Lassen national forests, Calif.]; submitted by Mr. Raker. Apr. 10, 1924. 4 p. (H. rp. 481, 68th Cong. 1st sess.) *Paper, 5c.

Point of Woods Range Lights. Authorizing exchange of lands with Robert P. Hudson, report to accompany H. R. 4481 [authorizing Secretary of Commerce to exchange land formerly used as site for Point of Woods Range Lights, Mich., for other lands in vicinity owned by Robert P. Hudson]; submitted by Mr. Williams of Michigan. Apr. 9, 1924. 2 p. (H. rp. 478, 68th Cong. 1st sess.) *Paper, 5c.

Santiam National Forest. Adding lands to Santiam National Forest, report to accompany H. R. 8366; submitted by Mr. Sinnott. Apr. 8, 1924. 3 p. (H. rp. 474, 68th Cong. 1st sess.) *Paper, 5c.

Shasta National Forest. Exchange of lands and adjustment of boundaries, Shasta National Forest, Calif., report to accompany H. R. 106 [for inclusion of certain lands in Shasta National Forest, Calif.]; submitted by Mr. Raker. Apr. 23, 1924. 2 p. (H. rp. 560, 68th Cong. 1st sess.) *Paper, 5c.

Shreveport, La. Granting lands to Shreveport, La., hearings on H. R. 5573, granting public lands to Shreveport, La., for reservoir purposes, Mar. 11, 1924. 1924. ii+32 p. *Paper, 5c.

Stanislaus National Forest. Exchange of lands and adjustment of boundaries, Stanislaus National Forest, Calif., report to accompany H. R. 105 [for inclusion of certain lands in Stanislaus National Forest, Calif.]; submitted by Mr. Raker. Apr. 23, 1924. 2 p. (H. rp. 559, 68th Cong. 1st sess.) *Paper, 5c.

Swanson, Charles. Issuance of patent to Charles Swanson, report to accompany H. R. 1442; submitted by Mr. Colton. Apr. 23, 1924. 3 p. (H. rp. 555, 68th Cong. 1st sess.) *Paper, 5c.

Tahoe National Forest. Exchange of lands and adjustment of boundaries, Tahoe National Forest, Calif. and Nev., report to accompany H. R. 107 [for inclusion of certain lands in Tahoe National Forest, Calif. and Nev.]; submitted by Mr. Raker. Apr. 23, 1924. 3 p. (H. rp. 561, 68th Cong. 1st sess.) *Paper, 5c.

Utah National Park. Establish Utah National Park, report to accompany S. 668 [to establish Utah National Park in Utah]; submitted by Mr. Colton. Apr. 23, 1924. 3 p. (H. rp. 554, 68th Cong. 1st sess.) *Paper, 5c.

Washington State. Authorizing exchange of lands with State of Washington, report to accompany H. R. 5318; submitted by Mr. Hill of Washington. Apr. 10, 1924. 3 p. (H. rp. 479, 68th Cong. 1st sess.) *Paper, 5c.

RIVERS AND HARBORS COMMITTEE

Frankfort Harbor, Mich., hearings on subject of improvement of Frankfort Harbor, Mich., Mar. 6, 1924. 1924. [1]+19 p. *Paper, 5c.

Illinois River. Illinois and Mississippi rivers and diversion of water from Lake Michigan, hearings, Mar. 17-20, 1924. 1924. pt. 1, iv+1-259 p. *Paper, 25c.

Rivers. River and harbor bill, report to accompany H. R. 8914; submitted by Mr. Dempsey. Apr. 26, 1924. 52 p. (H. rp. 581, 68th Cong. 1st sess.) *Paper, 5c.

Water pollution. Pollution of navigable waters, hearings on subject of pollution of navigable waters, Mar. 14, 1924. 1924. pt. 2, [1]+301-326 p. [Part 1 appeared in Monthly catalogue for Feb. 1924, p. 442.] *Paper, 5c.

RULES COMMITTEE

Child labor. For consideration of House joint resolution 184, report to accompany H. Res. 268 [for consideration of joint resolution proposing amendment to Constitution relating to child labor]; submitted by Mr. Snell. Apr. 23, 1924. 1 p. (H. rp. 552, 68th Cong. 1st sess.) *Paper, 5c.

District of Columbia. For consideration of H. R. 7962, report to accompany H. Res. 270 [for consideration of H. R. 7962, to establish and create Rent Commission for District of Columbia]; submitted by Mr. Snell. Apr. 26, 1924. 1 p. (H. rp. 575, 68th Cong. 1st sess.) *Paper, 5c.

Employers' liability and workmen's compensation. Consideration of H. R. 7041, report to accompany H. Res. 245 [for consideration of bill (H. R. 7041) to amend act to provide compensation for employees of United States suffering injuries while in performance of their duties]; submitted by Mr. Snell. Apr. 2, 1924. 1 p. (H. rp. 434, 68th Cong. 1st sess.) *Paper, 5c.

Loans. Consideration of Senate joint resolution 52, report to accompany H. Res. 246 [for consideration of S. J. Res. 52, for relief of drought-stricken farm areas of New Mexico]; submitted by Mr. Snell. Apr. 2, 1924. 1 p. (H. rp. 435, 68th Cong. 1st sess.) *Paper, 5c.

Personnel Classification Board. Consideration of H. R. 6896, report to accompany H. Res. 250 [for immediate consideration of H. R. 6896, to amend classification act of 1923, by abolishing Personnel Classification Board and transferring powers and duties of said board to Civil Service Commission]; submitted by Mr. Snell. Apr. 5, 1924. 1 p. (H. rp. 466, 68th Cong. 1st sess.) *Paper, 5c.

Reclamation of land. Consideration of S. 1631, report to accompany H. Res. 223 [for consideration of bill (S. 1631) to authorize deferring of payments of reclamation charges]; submitted by Mr. Snell. Apr. 5, 1924. 1 p. (H. rp. 465, 68th Cong. 1st sess.) *Paper, 5c.

TERRITORIES COMMITTEE

Alaska Railroad. Relief of special disbursing agents of Alaskan Engineering Commission, report to accompany H. J. Res. 226 [for relief of special disbursing agents of Alaskan Engineering Commission, authorizing payment of certain claims, and for other purposes, affecting management of Alaska Railroad]; submitted by Mr. Curry. Apr. 25, 1924. 23 p. (H. rp. 572, 68th Cong. 1st sess.) *Paper, 5c.

Cordova, Alaska. Public school bond issue, Cordova, Alaska, hearings on H. R. 6950, to authorize Cordova, Alaska, to issue bonds in any sum not exceeding $100,000 for purpose of constructing and equipping public school building in Cordova, Alaska, Mar. 29, 1924. 1924. ii+4 p. *Paper, 5c.

—— Public school bond issue, Cordova, Alaska, report to accompany H. R. 6950 [to authorize Cordova, Alaska, to issue bonds in any sum not exceeding $100,000 for purpose of constructing and equipping public school building in Cordova, Alaska]; submitted by Mr. Moore of Illinois. Apr. 11, 1924. 1 p. (H. rp. 494, 68th Cong. 1st sess.) *Paper, 5c.

Hawaii. Electric light and power within district of Hamakua, report to accompany H. R. 6070 [for manufacture, maintenance, distribution, and supply of electric current for light and power within district of Hamakua, on island of Hawaii, Hawaii, by M. S. Botelho]; submitted by Mr. Jarrett. Apr. 10, 1924. 2 p. (H. rp. 538, 68th Cong. 1st sess.) * Paper, 5c.

—— Title to certain lands in Hawaii, report to accompany H. R. 6303 [to issue patents to certain persons who purchased government lots in district of Waiakea, island of Hawaii, in accordance with act 33, session laws of 1915, Legislature of Hawaii]; submitted by Mr. Jarrett. Apr. 19, 1924. 2 p. (H. rp. 539, 68th Cong. 1st sess.) * Paper, 5c.

Ketchikan, Alaska. Public school bond issue, Ketchikan, Alaska, hearings on H. R. 6255, to amend act to authorize Ketchikan, Alaska, to issue bonds in any sum not to exceed $100,000 for purpose of constructing schoolhouse in said town and equipping same so as to permit increase in amount of bond issue], Mar. 29, 1924. 1924. ii+2 p. * Paper, 5c.

—— Schoolhouse at Ketchikan, Alaska, report to accompany H. R. 6255 [to amend act to authorize Ketchikan, Alaska, to issue bonds in any sum not to exceed $100,000 for purpose of constructing schoolhouse in said town and equipping same, so as to permit increase in amount of bond issue]; submitted by Mr. Driver. Apr. 1, 1924. 2 p. (H. rp. 421, 68th Cong. 1st sess.) * Paper, 5c.

Seward Peninsula. Improvement of system of overland communication on Seward Peninsula, Alaska, report to accompany H. J. Res. 60; submitted by Mr. Curry. Apr. 18, 1924. 14 p. (H. rp. 530, 68th Cong. 1st sess.) [H. J. Res. 60 provides for the adoption of the Nome-Shelton-Kugruk River-Keewalik project.] * Paper, 5c.

Sitka, Alaska. Public-school bond issue, report to accompany H. R. 5096 [to authorize Sitka, Alaska, to issue bonds in any sum not exceeding $25,000 for purpose of constructing public school building in Sitka, Alaska]; submitted by Mr. Cummings. Apr. 22, 1924. 1 p. (H. rp. 549, 68th Cong. 1st sess.) * Paper, 5c.

Technical education. Establishment of industrial schools for Alaskan native children, and for other purposes, report to accompany H. R. 4825; submitted by Mr. Elliott. Apr. 18, 1924. 4 p. (H. rp. 528, 68th Cong. 1st sess.) * Paper, 5c.

WAR CLAIMS COMMITTEE

Fallon, Henry N. Lieut. Henry N. Fallon, report to accompany S. 946 [for relief of Amy L. Fallon, mother of Henry N. Fallon]; submitted by Mr. Roach. Mar. 31, 1924. 6 p. (H. rp. 411, 68th Cong. 1st sess.) * Paper, 5c.

Geere, Frank. Capt. Frank Geere, report to accompany H. R. 8258 [for relief of Frank Geere]; submitted by Mr. Winter. Apr. 26, 1924. 4 p. (H. rp. 579, 68th Cong. 1st sess.) * Paper, 5c.

Kernan, Harold. Harold Kernan, report to accompany S. 1213 [for relief of Harold Kernan]; submitted by Mr. Winter. Apr. 26, 1924. 2 p. (H. rp. 576, 68th Cong. 1st sess.) * Paper, 5c.

McAllister, Edwin J. Lieut. E. J. McAllister, report to accompany H. R. 6241 [for relief of E. J. McAllister]; submitted by Mr. Roach. Apr. 26, 1924. 2 p. (H. rp. 578, 68th Cong. 1st sess.) * Paper, 5c.

Sonnenstrahl, Ely N. Estate of Ely N. Sonnenstrahl, report to accompany S. 1330 [for relief of estate of Ely N. Sonnenstrahl]; submitted by Mr. Roach. Apr. 26, 1924. 4 p. (H. rp. 577, 68th Cong. 1st sess.) * Paper, 5c.

WAYS AND MEANS COMMITTEE

Agricultural products. Tariff provisions of H. R. 5563, McNary-Haugen export bill, hearings on tariff provisions of H. R. 5563, declaring emergency in respect to certain agricultural commodities and to promote equality between agricultural commodities and other commodities, and report of Tariff Commission thereon, Apr. 2 and 11, 1924. 1924. ii+42 p. * Paper, 5c.

Freer, Charles L. Relief of estate of Charles L. Freer, report to accompany H. R. 8100; submitted by Mr. Green of Iowa. Apr. 4, 1924. 2 p. (H. rp. 462, 68th Cong. 1st sess.) * Paper, 5c.

Heroin. Prohibiting importation of crude opium for manufacture of heroin, report to accompany H. R. 7079; submitted by Mr. Hadley. Apr. 17, 1924. 3 p. (H. rp. 525, 68th Cong. 1st sess.) * Paper, 5c.

—— Prohibiting importation of opium for manufacture of heroin, hearings on H. R. 7079, Apr. 3, 1924. 1924. iii+55 p. * Paper, 5c.

WORLD WAR VETERANS' LEGISLATION COMMITTEE

Veterans' Bureau. To amend act to establish veterans' Bureau, etc., report to accompany H. R. 8869 [to amend act to establish veterans' Bureau and to improve facilities and service of such bureau, and further to amend and modify war risk insurance act, approved Aug. 9, 1921, and to amend and modify war risk insurance act, and to amend vocational rehabilitation act]; submitted by Mr. Johnson of South Dakota. Apr. 28, 1924. 7 p. (H. rp. 589, 68th Cong. 1st sess.) * Paper, 5c.

World War veterans' legislation, hearings on proposed legislation as recommended by director of Veterans' Bureau, American Legion, Disabled American veterans, and veterans of Foreign Wars, and H. R. 7320. 1924. pt. 2, iii+173–678 p. [Part 1 appeared in Monthly catalogue for Mar. 1924, p. 533.] * Paper, 50c.

NATIONAL FOREST RESERVATION COMMISSION

Report. National Forest Reservation Commission, report of National Forest Reservation Commission, year ending June 30, 1923. 1924. v+37 p. il. 8 p. of pl. (S. doc. 59, 68th Cong. 1st sess.) * Paper, 15c.   11—35944

REORGANIZATION JOINT COMMITTEE

Executive Departments. Reorganization of Executive Departments, hearings on S. J. Res. 282, 67th Congress, to amend joint resolution to create Joint Committee on Reorganization of Administrative Branch of Government, Jan. 7–31, 1924. 1924. iii+786 p. il. 1 pl. [These hearings were also published in separate numbered parts.] * Paper, 80c.

SENATE

Appropriations. Expenses of inquiries and investigations ordered by Senate, supplemental estimate of appropriation for legislative establishment, fiscal year 1925, for expenses of inquiries and investigations ordered by Senate. Apr. 15, 1924. 2 p. (H. doc. 239, 68th Cong. 1st sess.) * Paper, 5c.

Calendar of business, Senate, 68th Congress, 1st session, Apr. 1–30, 1924; no. 72–96. [1924.] various paging, large 8° [Daily when Senate is in session. The legislative day of Mar. 31 extended through the calendar day Apr. 1.] ‡

Income tax. Comparison of tax on specified incomes, table showing tax to be paid on specified incomes under the several revenue laws, present law, Mellon plan, House bill, [and] Simmons amendment; presented by Mr. Simmons. 1924. [1]+1 p. (S. doc. 86, 68th Cong. 1st sess.) * Paper, 5c.

AGRICULTURE AND FORESTRY COMMITTEE

Agricultural attachés. To promote sale of American agricultural products in foreign countries, report to accompany H. R. 7111 [to promote American agriculture by making more extensively available by expanding service now rendered by Department of Agriculture in gathering and disseminating information regarding agricultural production, competition, and demand in foreign countries in promoting sale of farm products abroad, and in other ways]; submitted by Mr. Norris. Apr. 21, 1924. 2 p. (S. rp. 448, 68th Cong. 1st sess.) [Corrected print.] * Paper, 5c.

Agricultural products. Agricultural export bill, report to accompany S. 3091 [declaring emergency in respect of certain agricultural commodities to promote equality between agricultural commodities and other commodities, and for other purposes]; submitted by Mr. McNary. Apr. 10, calendar day Apr. 16, 1924. 6 p. (S. rp. 410, 68th Cong. 1st sess.) * Paper, 5c.

Alaska Game Commission. Establishment of Alaska Game Commission, report to accompany S. 2559 [to establish Alaska Game Commission to protect game animals, land fur-bearing animals, and birds, in Alaska, and for other purposes]; submitted by Mr. Norbeck. Apr. 24, calendar day Apr. 29, 1924. 5 p. (S. rp. 480, 68th Cong. 1st sess.) * Paper, 5c.

Calendar. Legislative calendar, 68th Congress, Apr. 9–25, 1924; no. 6–8. 1924. Each 19 p. or 22 p. 4° ‡

Custer State Park Game Sanctuary, report to accompany S. 2699 [to amend act creating Custer State Park Game Sanctuary in South Dakota, so as to authorize enlargement]; submitted by Mr. Norbeck. Apr. 24, calendar day Apr. 29, 1924. 3 p. (S. rp. 479, 68th Cong. 1st sess.) * Paper, 5c.

Forest experimental station, hearing on S. 824, to establish and maintain forest experiment station in Florida, and S. 1667, to authorize purchase of lands in Florida for experimental and demonstration forest for production of naval stores, Mar. 18, 1924. 1924. ii+8 p. * Paper, 5c.

Forest lands, report to accompany S. 1182 [for protection of forest lands, for reforestation of denuded areas, for extension of national forests, and for other purposes, in order to promote continuous production of timber on lands chiefly suitable therefor]; submitted by Mr. McNary. Apr. 10, calendar day Apr. 15, 1924. 1 p. (S. rp. 405, 68th Cong. 1st sess.) * Paper, 5c.

Loans. Relief of drought-stricken farm areas of New Mexico, hearing on S. J. Res. 52. Feb. 1, 1924. 1924. pt. 2, ii+25–33 p. [Part 1 appeared in Monthly catalogue for Feb. 1924, p. 443.] * Paper, 5c.

Marketing of farm produce. Purchase and sale of farm products, report to accompany S. 1642; submitted by Mr. Norris. Apr. 24, 1924. 3 p. (S. rp. 463. 68th Cong. 1st sess.) * Paper, 5c.

APPROPRIATIONS COMMITTEE

Appropriations. Independent offices appropriation bill, [fiscal year] 1925, report to accompany H. R. 8233; submitted by Mr. Warren. Apr. 8, 1924. 2 p. (S. rp. 361, 68th Cong. 1st sess.) * Paper, 5c.

Navy Department. Navy Department and naval service appropriation bill, fiscal year 1925, report to accompany H. R. 6820; submitted by Mr. Hale. Apr. 7, calendar day Apr. 9, 1924. 26 p. (S. rp. 363, 68th Cong. 1st sess.) * Paper, 5c.

24—26407

—— Navy Department appropriation bill, [fiscal year] 1925, hearings before subcommittee on H. R. 6820. 1924. ii+287 p. * Paper, 30c.

State Department. Departments of State, Justice, Commerce, and Labor appropriation bill, [fiscal year] 1925, report to accompany H. R. 8350; submitted by Mr. Jones of Washington. Apr. 21. calendar day Apr. 23, 1924. 3 p. (S. rp. 457, 68th Cong. 1st sess.) * Paper, 5c.

War Department. War Department appropriation bill, [fiscal year] 1925, hearings before subcommittee on H. R. 7877. 1924. ii+283 p. * Paper, 30c.

—— War Department appropriation bill, [fiscal year] 1925, report to accompany H. R. 7877; submitted by Mr. Wadsworth. Apr. 10, calendar day Apr. 11, 1924. 5 p. (S. rp. 396, 68th Cong. 1st sess.) * Paper, 5c.

BANKING AND CURRENCY COMMITTEE

Banks and banking. To amend sec. 25 (a) of act approved Dec. 23, 1913, known as Federal reserve act [relative to reserves of corporations organized under provisions of sec. 25 (a) to engage in international or foreign banking], report to accompany S. 2905; submitted by Mr. Weller. Apr. 2, 1924. 2 p. (S. rp. 345, 68th Cong. 1st sess.) * Paper, 5c.

Virgin Islands. To extend provisions of national bank act to Virgin Islands of United States, report to accompany S. 2919; submitted by Mr. Weller. Apr. 2, 1924. 3 p. (S. rp. 346, 68th Cong. 1st sess.) * Paper, 5c.

CLAIMS COMMITTEE

A. A. Raven, steamship. American Transportation Co., report to accompany S. 2052 [to carry out decree of district court for eastern district of Pennsylvania in case of United States, owner of steam dredge Delaware, against steamship A. A. Raven, American Transportation Company, claimant, and to pay amount decreed to be due said company]; submitted by Mr. Bayard. Apr. 10, calendar day Apr. 11, 1924. 5 p. (S. rp. 381, 68th Cong. 1st sess.) * Paper, 5c.

Aktieselskabet Marie di Giorgio, report to accompany H. R. 8235 [for relief of Aktieselskabet Marie di Giorgio, Norwegian corporation of Christiania, Norway]; submitted by Mr. Capper. Apr. 10, calendar day Apr. 11, 1924. 2 p. (S. rp. 378, 68th Cong. 1st sess.) * Paper, 5c.

Brooklyn Eastern District Terminal, report to accompany S. 1038 [for relief of Brooklyn Eastern District Terminal]; submitted by Mr. Bruce. Apr. 21, 1924. 2 p. (S. rp. 444, 68th Cong. 1st sess,) * Paper, 5c.

Bruusgaard Kiosteruds Dampskibs Aktieselskab, report to accompany H. R. 8237 [for relief of Bruusgaard Kiosteruds Dampskibs Aktieselskab, Norwegian corporation of Drammen, Norway]; submitted by Mr. Capper. Apr. 10, calendar day Apr. 11, 1924. 2 p. (S. rp. 379, 68th Cong. 1st sess.) * Paper, 5c.

Carson, C. C. C. C. Carson, report to accompany H. R. 2126 [for relief of C. C. Carson]; submitted by Mr. Spencer. Apr. 10, calendar day Apr. 11, 1924. 3 p. (S. rp. 385, 68th Cong. 1st sess.) * Paper, 5c.

Charlesworth, William T. Owner of scow W. T. C. no. 35, report to accompany S. 1039 [for relief of William T. Charlesworth, owner of scow W. T. C. numbered 35]; submitted by Mr. Bruce. Apr. 21, 1924. 2 p. (S. rp. 445, 68th Cong. 1st sess.) * Paper, 5c.

Commercial Union Assurance Company, Limited. Commercial Union Assurance Co. (Ltd.) and others, report to accompany S. 1975 [for relief of Commercial Union Assurance Company (Limited), Federal Insurance Company, American and Foreign Marine Insurance Company, Queen Insurance Company. St. Paul Fire and Marine Insurance Company, and United States Lloyds, and St. Paul Fire and Marine Insurance Company]; submitted by Mr. Bayard. Apr. 10, calendar day Apr. 18, 1924. 15 p. (S. rp. 420, 68th Cong. 1st sess.) * Paper, 5c.

—— Commercial Union Assurance Co. (Ltd.) and others, report to accompany S. 1976 [for relief of Commercial Union Assurance Company (Limited), Federal Insurance Company, American and Foreign Marine Insurance Company, Queen Insurance Company of America, Fireman's Fund Insurance Company, St. Paul Fire and Marine Insurance Company, and United States Lloyds]; submitted by Mr. Bayard. Apr. 10, calendar day Apr. 18, 1924. 18 p. (S. rp. 421, 68th Cong. 1st sess.) * Paper, 5c.

Con Rein, schooner. East La Have Transportation Co. (Ltd.) owner of schooner Con Rein, report to accompany H. R. 2498 [for relief of East LaHave Transportation Company, Limited, owner, A. Picard and Company, owner of cargo, and George H. Corkum, Leopold S. Conrad, Wilson Zinck, Freeman Beck, Sidney Knickle, and Norman E. LeGay, crew of schooner Con Rein, sunk by United States submarine K–4]; submitted by Mr. Bayard. Apr. 10, calendar day Apr. 11, 1924. 3 p. (S. rp. 383, 68th Cong. 1st sess.) * Paper, 5c.

Davis Construction Co., report to accompany S. 2685 [for relief of Davis Construction Company]; submitted by Mr. Stanfield. Mar. 31, calendar day Apr. 1, 1924. 11 p. (S. rp. 337, 68th Cong. 1st sess.) * Paper, 5c.

Dillon, Robert. Legal representatives of Robert Dillon, report to accompany S. 1834 [for relief of legal representatives of Robert Dillon]; submitted by Mr. Bayard. Apr. 10, calendar day Apr. 11, 1924. 4 p. (S. rp. 380, 68th Cong. 1st sess.) * Paper, 5c.

Eastern Transportation Co., report to accompany S. 785 [for relief of Eastern Transportation Company]; submitted by Mr. Bruce. Apr. 21, 1924. 2 p. (S. rp. 443, 68th Cong. 1st sess.) * Paper, 5c.

Fellows, Rush O. Rush O. Fellows, report to accompany H. R. 3183 [for relief of Rush O. Fellows]; submitted by Mr. Capper. Apr. 10, calendar day Apr. 11, 1924. 5 p. (S. rp. 375, 68th Cong. 1st sess.) * Paper, 5c.

Flagg, William H. William H. Flagg and others, report to accompany H. R. 4012 [to reimburse William H. Flagg and others]; submitted by Mr. Capper. Apr. 24, calendar day Apr. 25, 1924. 7 p. (S. rp. 465, 68th Cong. 1st sess.) * Paper, 5c.

French spoliation claims. French spoliation claims, hearing on S. 56, for allowance of certain claims for indemnity for spoliations by French prior to July 31. 1801, as reported by Court of Claims, Mar. 20, 1924. 1924. ii+23 p. * Paper, 5c.

—— French spoliations, report to accompany S. 56 [for allowance of certain claims for indemnity for spoliations by French prior to July 31, 1801, as reported by Court of Claims]; submitted by Mr. Spencer. Apr. 10, calendar day Apr. 15, 1924. 9 p. (S. rp. 404, 68th Cong. 1st sess.) * Paper, 5c.

Grace, W. R., & Co. W. R. Grace & Co., report to accompany S. 1037 [for relief of W. R. Grace and Company]; submitted by Mr. Trammell. Mar. 31, 1924. 2 p. (S. rp. 333, 68th Cong. 1st sess.) * Paper, 5c.

Great Lakes Engineering Works, report to accompany S. 698 [for relief of Great Lakes Engineering Works]; submitted by Mr. Bruce. Apr. 10, calendar day Apr. 18, 1924. 2 p. (S. rp. 418, 68th Cong. 1st sess.) * Paper, 5c.

Hubbard, Harry R. Harry Ross Hubbard, report to accompany S. 336 [for relief of Harry Ross Hubbard]; submitted by Mr. Caraway. Apr. 10, calendar day Apr. 14, 1924. 6 p. (S. rp. 401, 68th Cong. 1st sess.) * Paper, 5c.

Hutcheson, Bernice. Bernice Hutcheson, report to accompany H. R. 3143 [for relief of Bernice Hutcheson]; submitted by Mr. Capper. Apr. 10, calendar day Apr. 17, 1924. 9 p. (S. rp. 413, 68th Cong. 1st sess.) * Paper, 5c.

Italian Government, report to accompany S. 2826 [for relief of Italian Government]; submitted by Mr. Bayard. Apr. 10, calendar day Apr. 11, 1924. 6 p. (S. rp. 382, 68th Cong. 1st sess.) * Paper, 5c.

Itasca, schooner. Owner of schooner Itasca, report to accompany S. 51 [for relief of owner of schooner Itasca and her master and crew]; submitted by Mr. Bruce. Apr. 21, 1924. 2 p. (S. rp. 442, 68th Cong. 1st sess.) * Paper, 5c.

King, J. R. J. R. King, report to accompany S. 2669 [for relief of J. R. King]; submitted by Mr. Spencer. Apr. 10, calendar day Apr. 11, 1924. 7 p. (S. rp. 386, 68th Cong. 1st sess.) * Paper, 5c.

Langin Field. Relief for victims of airplane accident at Langin Field, report to accompany S. 1740; submitted by Mr. Capper. Apr. 21, calendar day Apr. 23, 1924. 4 p. (S. rp. 456, 68th Cong. 1st sess.) * Paper, 5c.

Loveland, John W., jr. Capt. John W. Loveland, jr., report to accompany S. 1387 [for payment of amount of war risk insurance policy to beneficiary designated by John W. Loveland, jr.]; submitted by Mr. Spencer. Mar. 31, calendar day Apr. 1, 1924. 6 p. (S. rp. 335, 68th Cong. 1st sess.) *Paper, 5c.

Macnair, Archibald L. Archibald L. Macnair, report to accompany S. 825 [for relief of Archibald L. Macnair]; submitted by Mr. Mayfield. Apr. 10, calendar day Apr. 16, 1924. 6 p. (S. rp. 409, 68th Cong. 1st sess.) *Paper, 5c. ·

Merrill, Mrs. Ivy L. Ivy L. Merrill, report to accompany S. 2201 [for relief of Ivy L. Merrill]; submitted by Mr. Capper. Apr. 2, 1924. 9 p. (S. rp. 350, 68th Cong. 1st sess.) *Paper, 5c.

Morse, Perley, & Co. Perley Morse & Co., report to accompany S. 2124 [for relief of Perley Morse and Company]; submitted by Mr. Mayfield. Apr. 10, calendar day Apr. 18, 1924. 10 p. (S. rp. 417, 68th Cong. 1st sess.) *Paper, 5c.

New York Sanitary Utilization Company. Owners of New York Sanitary Utilization Co. scow no. 14, report to accompany S. 1040 [for relief of owners of New York Sanitary Utilization Company scow number 14]; submitted by Mr. Bruce. Apr. 21, 1924. 3 p. (S. rp. 446, 68th Cong. 1st sess.) *Paper, 5c.

Nickles, George A. George A. Nickles, report to accompany H. R. 3761 [for relief of George A. Nickles]; submitted by Mr. Capper. Apr. 10, calendar day Apr. 11, 1924. 8 p. (S. rp. 376, 68th Cong. 1st sess.) *Paper, 5c.

O'Neil, Mrs. Alice E. Alice E. O'Neil, report to accompany S. 1574 [for relief of Alice E. O'Neil]; submitted by Mr. Capper. Apr. 24, 1924. 2 p. (S. rp. 459, 68th Cong. 1st sess.) *Paper, 5c.

Owens, Mrs. Lena G. Lena Garagnon Owens, report to accompany H. R. 2647 [for relief of Lena Garagnon Owens]; submitted by Mr. Capper. Apr. 24, calendar day Apr. 25, 1924. 24 p. (S. rp. 464, 68th Cong. 1st sess.) *Paper, 5c.

Patten, Thomas G. Thomas G. Patten, report to accompany S. 2301 [for relief of Thomas G. Patten]; submitted by Mr. Stanfield. Mar. 31, calendar day Apr. 1, 1924. 8 p. (S. rp. 336, 68th Cong. 1st sess.) *Paper, 5c.

Reynolds, Hubert. Hubert Reynolds, report to accompany H. R. 5541 [for relief of Hubert Reynolds]; submitted by Mr. Capper. Apr. 10, calendar day Apr. 17, 1924. 21 p. (S. rp. 414, 68th Cong. 1st sess.) *Paper, 5c.

Rogers, Harry L., jr. First Lieut. Harry L. Rogers, jr., report to accompany S. 2138 [for relief of Harry L. Rogers, jr.]; submitted by Mr. Harreld. Apr. 10, calendar day Apr. 14, 1924. 7 p. (S. rp. 399, 68th Cong. 1st sess.) *Paper, 5c.

Schermerhorn, V. E. V. E. Schermerhorn and others, report to accompany H. R. 6049 [for relief of v. E. Schermerhorn, E. C. Caley, G. W. Campbell, and Philip Hudspeth]; submitted by Mr. Capper. Apr. 10, calendar day Apr. 11, 1924. 2 p. (S. rp. 377, 68th Cong. 1st sess.) *Paper, 5c.

Sharon, Mrs. Eva B. Eva B. Sharon, report to accompany H. R. 5136 [for relief of Eva B. Sharon] ; submitted by Mr. Capper. Apr. 24, calendar day Apr. 25, 1924. 5 p. (S. rp. 466, 68th Cong. 1st sess.) *Paper, 5c.

Shearer, David M. Capt. David McD. Shearer, report to accompany S. 1638 [authorizing Court of Claims to adjudicate claim of David McD. Shearer for compensation for adoption and use and acquisition by Government of his patented inventions] ; submitted by Mr. Capper. Apr. 21, calendar day Apr. 23, 1924. 7 p. (S. rp. 455, 68th Cong. 1st sess.) *Paper, 5c.

Shymer, Mrs. Anne C. Estate of Anne C. Shymer, report to accompany S. 2793 [for relief of estate of Anne C. Shymer] ; submitted by Mr. Harreld. Apr. 10, calendar day Apr. 14, 1924. 6 p. (S. rp. 400, 68th Cong. 1st sess.) *Paper, 5c.

Simpson, Harry. Harry Simpson, report to accompany S. 773 [to extend benefits of employees' compensation act to Harry Simpson] ; submitted by Mr. Bruce. Apr. 21, 1924. 2 p. (S. rp. 447, 68th Cong. 1st sess.) * Paper, 5c.

Smith, Arthur A. Arthur A. Smith, report to accompany S. 2261 [for relief of Arthur A. Smith] ; submitted by Mr. Bayard. Mar. 31, 1924. 4 p. (S. rp. 332, 68th Cong. 1st sess.) * Paper, 5c.

Southern Pacific Company. To ascertain cost to Southern Pacific Co. in closing breaks in Colorado River, report to accompany H. R. 6012; submitted by Mr. Spencer. Apr. 10, calendar day Apr. 18, 1924. 19 p. (S. rp. 419, 68th Cong. 1st sess.) * Paper, 5c.

Spaight, Daniel A. Daniel A. Spaight et al., report to accompany S. 588 [for relief of Daniel A. Spaight and others] ; submitted by Mr. Stephens. Apr. 4, 1924. 18 p. (S. rp. 352, 68th Cong. 1st sess.) * Paper, 5c.

Tainter, Austin G. Austin G. Tainter, report to accompany S. 2518 [for relief of Austin G. Tainter] ; submitted by Mr. Bruce. Apr. 24, calendar day Apr. 25, 1924. 8 p. (S. rp. 467, 68th Cong. 1st sess.) * Paper, 5c.

Thompson-Vache Boat Co., report to accompany H. R. 2123 [for relief of Thompson-vache Boat Company, Bonnots Mill, Mo.] ; submitted by Mr. Spencer. Apr. 10, calendar day Apr. 11, 1924. 20 p. (S. rp. 384, 68th Cong. 1st sess.) * Paper, 5c.

Toulouse, J. H. J. H. Toulouse, report to accompany S. 354 [for relief of J. H. Toulouse] ; submitted by Mr. Mayfield. Apr. 10, calendar day Apr. 16, 1924. 2 p. (S. rp. 408, 68th Cong. 1st sess.) * Paper, 5c.

Underwood Typewriter Co. and Frank P. Trott, report to accompany H. R. 4647 [for relief of Underwood Typewriter Company and Frank P. Trott] ; submitted by Mr. Stephens. Apr. 10, calendar day Apr. 18, 1924. 3 p. (S. rp. 416, 68th Cong. 1st sess.) * Paper, 5c.

Williams, Edward T. Edward T. Williams, report to accompany H. R. 5808 [for relief of Edward T. Williams] ; submitted by Mr. Capper. Apr. 10, calendar day Apr. 17, 1924. 11 p. (S. rp. 415, 68th Cong. 1st sess.) * Paper, 5c.

Wood, Albert. Albert Wood, report to accompany S. 147 [for relief of Albert Wood] ; submitted by Mr. Trammell. Apr. 24, 1924. 4 p. (S. rp. 458, 68th Cong. 1st sess.) * Paper, 5c.

Wooten, Mrs. Elizabeth. Elizabeth Wooten, report to accompany S. 830 [for relief of Elizabeth Wooten] ; submitted by Mr. Trammell. Apr. 10, calendar day Apr. 14, 1924. 12 p. (S. rp. 402, 68th Cong. 1st sess.) * Paper, 5c.

COMMERCE COMMITTEE

Alaska. Protection of fisheries of Alaska, report to accompany H. R. 8143; submitted by Mr. Jones of Washington. Apr. 21, calendar day Apr. 22, 1924. 6 p. (S. rp. 449, 68th Cong. 1st sess.) * Paper, 5c.

Calumet River. Bridge across Calumet River at Chicago, Ill., report to accompany H. R. 8304 [granting consent of Congress to Chicago to construct bridge across Calumet River at or near 100th street in Chicago, county of Cook, Ill.] ; submitted by Mr. Ladd. Apr. 21, calendar day Apr. 23, 1924. 1 p. (S. rp. 453, 68th Cong. 1st sess.) * Paper, 5c.

—— Bridge across Calumet River, report to accompany H. R. 2665 [granting consent of Congress to Chicago to construct bridge across Calumet River in vicinity of 134th street in Chicago, county of Cook, Ill.] ; submitted by Mr. Ladd. Apr. 10, 1924. 2 p. (S. rp. 369, 68th Cong. 1st sess.) * Paper, 5c.

Free zones. Foreign trade zones in ports of United States, report to accompany S. 2570 [to provide for establishment, operation and maintenance of foreign trade zones in ports of entry of United States, to expedite and encourage foreign commerce, and for other purposes]; submitted by Mr. Jones of Washington. Apr. 24. calendar day Apr. 28, 1924. 36 p. (S. rp. 477, 68th Cong. 1st sess.) * Paper, 5c. 24—26408

Mississippi River. Bridge across Mississippi River at St. Paul, Minn., report to accompany H. R. 8229 [granting consent of Congress to St. Paul, Minn., to construct bridge across Mississippi River in said city]; submitted by Mr. Ladd. Apr. 21, calendar day Apr. 23, 1924. 2 p. (S. rp. 452, 68th Cong. 1st sess.) * Paper, 5c.

——— Bridge across Mississippi River between Carroll County, Ill., and Jackson County, Iowa, report to accompany H. R. 7063 [granting consent of Congress to Illinois and Iowa, or either of them, to construct bridge across Mississippi River, connecting county of Carroll, Ill., and county of. Jackson, Iowa]; submitted by Mr. Ladd. Apr. 10, 1924. 2 p. (S. rp. 371, 68th Cong. 1st sess.) * Paper, 5c.

——— Bridge across Mississippi River, St. Paul, Minn., report to accompany S. 2977 [granting consent of Congress to St. Paul, Minn., to construct bridge across Mississippi River in said city]; submitted by Mr. Ladd. Apr. 10, calendar day Apr. 11, 1924. 2 p. (S. rp. 391, 68th Cong. 1st sess.) * Paper, 5c.

Ohio River. Bridge across Ohio River, Ky. and Ind., report to accompany S. 2914 [authorizing construction of bridge across Ohio River approximately midway between Owensboro, Ky., and Rockport, Ind., by Edward T. Franks and Thomas H. Hazelrigg]; submitted by Mr. Ladd. Apr. 2, 1924. 2 p. (S. rp. 351, 68th Cong. 1st sess.) * Paper, 5c.

Oostanaula River. Bridge across Oostanaula River, Ga., report to accompany S. 3025 [to authorize construction of bridge across Oostanaula River in Gordon County, Ga., by Highway Department of Georgia]; submitted by Mr. Ladd. Apr. 10, calendar day Apr. 18, 1924. 2 p. (S. rp. 424, 68th Cong. 1st sess.) * Paper, 5c.

Pointe aux Barques Resort Association. Conveying land to Pointe aux Barques Resort Association, Michigan, report to accompany S. 696 [authorizing and directing Secretary of. Commerce to convey land in section 21, township 19 north, range 13 east, Huron County, Mich., to Pointe aux Barques Resort Association]; submitted by Mr. Couzens. Mar. 31, 1924. 2 p. (S. rp. 328, 68th Cong. 1st sess.) * Paper, 5c.

St. Marys River. Bridge across St. Marys River, Fla., report to accompany S. 2929 [granting consent of Congress to Georgia and Florida, through their respective highway departments, to construct bridge across St. Marys River at or near Wilds Landing, Fla.]; submitted by Mr. Fletcher. Apr. 10, 1924. 2 p. (S. rp. 368, 68th Cong. 1st sess.) * Paper, 5c.

Ships. To amend sec. 11 and 12 of merchant marine act, 1920, [so as to permit use of certain funds of Shipping Board for conversion of ships into motor ships]. report to accompany H. R. 6202: submitted by Mr. Jones of Washington. Apr. 21. calendar day Apr. 22, 1924. 5 p. (S. rp. 450, 68th Cong. 1st sess.) * Paper, 5c.

Susquehanna River. Bridge across Susquehanna River at Millersburg, Pa., report to accompany H. R. 6810 [granting consent of Congress to Millersburg and Liverpool Bridge Corporation to construct bridge across Susquehanna River at Millersburg, Pa.]; submitted by Mr. Ladd. Apr. 10, 1924. 2 p. (S. rp. 370, 68th Cong. 1st sess.) * Paper, 5c.

——— Bridge across Susquehanna River, report to accompany H. R. 7846 [to extend time for construction of bridge across North Branch of Susquehanna River from Wilkes-Barre to borough of Dorranceton, Pa.]; submitted by Mr. Ladd. Apr. 10, 1924. 1 p. (S. rp. 372, 68th Cong. 1st sess.) * Paper, 5c.

Tug Fork. Bridge across Tug Fork of Big Sandy River between West Virginia and Kentucky, report to accompany H. R. 5218 [granting consent of Congress to Pittsburgh Coal, Land and Railroad Company to construct bridge across Tug Fork of Big Sandy River at or near Nolan, in Mingo County, W. Va., to Kentucky side, in Pike County, Ky.]; submitted by Mr. Ladd. Apr. 21. calendar day Apr. 23, 1924. 2 p. (S. rp. 451, 68th Cong. 1st sess.) * Paper, 5c.

White River. Bridge across White River, report to accompany S. 3116 [to authorize Choctaw, Oklahoma and Gulf Railway Company and Chicago, Rock Island and Pacific Railway Company-to construct bridge across White River near De valls Bluff, Ark.]; submitted by Mr. Sheppard. Apr. 21, calendar day Apr. 23, 1924. 2 p. (S. rp. 454, 68th Cong. 1st sess.) * Paper, 5c.

DISTRICT OF COLUMBIA COMMITTEE

Alleys. Public alley facilities in square 616 in District of Columbia, report to accompany S. 2265 [for rearrangement of public alley facilities in square 616 in District of Columbia]; submitted by Mr. Ball. Mar. 31, 1924. 2 p. (S. rp. 324, 68th Cong. 1st sess.) * Paper, 5c.

Architects. and architecture in District of Columbia, report to accompany S. 933 [for examination and registration of architects and to regulate practice of architecture in District of Columbia]; submitted by Mr. Ball. Apr. 10, calendar day Apr. 11, 1924. 2 p. (S. rp. 390, 68th Cong. 1st sess.) * Paper, 5c.

Coroners. To amend sec. 196 of code of law for District of Columbia [relating to appointment of deputy coroners], report to accompany S. 116; submitted by Mr. Ball. Mar. 31, 1924. 1 p. (S. rp. 323, 68th Cong. 1st sess.) * Paper, 5c.

Dentistry. Practice of dentistry in District of Columbia, report to accompany S. 1785 [to amend act for regulation of practice of dentistry in District of Columbia, and for protection of the people from empiricism in relation thereto, and acts amendatory thereof]; submitted by Mr. Ball. Apr. 10, calendar day Apr. 19, 1924. 3 p. (S. rp. 426, 68th Cong. 1st sess.) [Corrected print.] * Paper, 5c.

Medical Society of District of Columbia, report to accompany H. R. 4122 [to amend act to revive, with amendments, act to incorporate Medical Society of District of Columbia, as amended]; submitted by Mr. Ball. Apr. 10, calendar day Apr. 17, 1924. 3 p. (S. rp. 411, 68th Cong. 1st sess.) * Paper, 5c.

National Society of Daughters of American Revolution. Daughters of American Revolution in Washington, D. C., report to accompany H. R. 837 [to exempt from taxation certain property of Daughters of American Revolution in Washington, D. C.]; submitted by Mr. Ball. Apr. 10, calendar day Apr. 11, 1924. 1 p. (S. rp. 389, 68th Cong. 1st sess.) * Paper, 5c.

Optometry. To regulate practice of optometry in District of Columbia, report to accompany S. 1027; submitted by Mr. Ball. Apr. 10, calendar day Apr. 11, 1924. 1 p. (S. rp. 388, 68th Cong. 1st sess.) * Paper, 5c.

Streets. Extension of Rittenhouse street in District of Columbia, report to accompany S. 2593; submitted by Mr. Ball. Apr. 10, calendar day Apr. 17, 1924. 4 p. (S. rp. 412, 68th Cong. 1st sess.) * Paper, 5c.

—— Widening of Nichols avenue between Good Hope road and S street se., report to accompany S. 1782; submitted by Mr. Ball. Mar. 31, 1924. 2 p. (S. rp. 326, 68th Cong. 1st sess.) * Paper, 5c.

Teachers. Retirement of public-school teachers in District of Columbia, report to accompany S. 1230 [to amend sec. 11 of act for retirement of public-school teachers in District of Columbia, so that provisions of this act shall apply to certain teachers who resigned or were retired from school service prior to June 1, 1919]; submitted by Mr. Ball. Apr. 24, 1924. 2 p. (S. rp. 461, 68th Cong. 1st sess.) * Paper, 5c.

Washington Gaslight Company. Agreement between Secretary of War and Washington Gas Light Co., report to accompany S. 2848 [to validate agreement between Secretary of War, acting on behalf of United States, and Washington Gas Light Company]; submitted by Mr. Ball. Mar. 31, 1924. 3 p. (S. rp. 325, 68th Cong. 1st sess.) * Paper, 5c.

EDUCATION AND LABOR COMMITTEE

Education Department. To create Department of Education and to encourage education and to encourage States in promotion and support of education, hearings on S. 1337, to create Department of Education, to authorize appropriations for conduct of said Department, to authorize appropriation of money to encourage States in promotion and support of education, and for other purposes. 1924. iv+402 p. il. 2 pl. * Paper, 45c.

National Conservatory of Music, hearing before subcommittee on S. 1320, to establish National Conservatory of Music for education of pupils in music in all its branches, vocal and instrumental, Mar. 25, 1924. 1924. ii+44 p. *Paper, 5c.

Rehabilitation of the disabled. Industrial vocational rehabilitation, report to accompany S. 2590 [to amend sec. 1, 3, and 6 of act for promotion of vocational rehabilitation of persons disabled in industry or otherwise and their return to civil employment]; submitted by Mr. Sterling. Apr. 21, 1924. 5 p. (S. rp. 429, 68th Cong. 1st sess.) *Paper, 5c.

FINANCE COMMITTEE

Calendar. Legislative calendar, 68th Congress, Apr. 7–29, 1924; no. 15–18. 1924. various paging, 4° ‡

Internal revenue. Internal revenue bill of 1924, minority views to accompany H. R. 6715; submitted by Mr. Jones of New Mexico. Apr. 21, calendar day Apr. 22, 1924. 16 p. 1 tab. (S. rp. 398, pt. 2, 68th Cong. 1st sess.) *Paper, 5c.

—— Internal revenue bill of 1924, report to accompany H. R. 6715; submitted by Mr. Smoot. Apr. 10, calendar day Apr. 12, 1924. 48 p. (S. rp. 398 [pt. 1], 68th Cong. 1st sess.) *Paper, 5c.   24—26409

Soldiers. To provide adjusted compensation for veterans of World War, minority views to accompany H. R. 7959; submitted by Mr. Walsh of Massachusetts. Apr. 21, 1924. 4 p, (S. rp. 403, pt. 2, 68th Cong. 1st sess.) *Paper, 5c.

—— To provide adjusted compensation for veterans of World War, report to accompany H. R. 7959; submitted by Mr. Curtis. Apr. 10, calendar day Apr. 15, 1924. 11 p. (S. rp. 403 [pt. 1], 68th Cong. 1st sess.) *Paper, 5c.

Veterans' Bureau. United States Veterans' Bureau (war risk insurance act); report to accompany S. 2257 [to consolidate, codify, revise, and reenact laws affecting establishment of Veterans' Bureau and administration of war risk insurance act, as amended, and vocational rehabilitation act, as amended]; submitted by Mr. Reed of Pennsylvania. Apr. 10, calendar day Apr. 11, 1924. 9 p. (S. rp. 397, 68th Cong. 1st sess.) *Paper, 5c.

—— Veterans' Bureau codification act, hearings before subcommittee on S. 2257, to consolidate, codify, revise, and reenact laws affecting establishment of veterans' Bureau and administration of war risk insurance act, as amended, and vocational rehabilitation act, as amended, Feb. 21–Mar. 6, 1924, with letter and critique of bill from director of Veterans' Bureau. 1924. ii+175 p. *Paper, 15c.

FOREIGN RELATIONS COMMITTEE

Calendar, 68th Congress, 1st session, Apr. 9, 1924; no. 6. 1924. 16 p. 4° ‡

Cumming, Hugh S. Granting permission to Hugh S. Cumming, surgeon general of Public Health Service, to accept certain decorations bestowed upon him by Republics of France and Poland, report to accompany S. J. Res. 100; submitted by Mr. Swanson. Apr. 2, 1924. 1 p. (S. rp. 349, 68th Cong. 1st sess.) *Paper, 5c.

Diaz, Salvador B. To authorize payment of indemnity to Government of Nicaragua on account of damages alleged to have been done to property of Salvador Buitrago Diaz by United States marines, on Feb. 6, 1921, report to accompany S. 2455; submitted by Mr. Shipstead. Apr. 4, 1924. 3 p. (S. rp. 355, 68th Cong. 1st sess.) *Paper, 5c.

Interparliamentary Union, report to accompany S. J. Res. 104 [requesting the President to invite Interparliamentary Union to meet in Washington City in 1925, and authorizing appropriation to defray expenses of meeting]; submitted by Mr. Lodge. Apr. 10, calendar day Apr. 18, 1924. 2 p. (S. rp. 425, 68th Cong. 1st sess.) *Paper, 5c.

Murphy, Dominic I. Authorizing Dominic I. Murphy, consul general of United States, to accept silver fruit bowl presented to him by British Government, report to accompany S. 1699; submitted by Mr. Swanson. Apr. 2, 1924. 1 p. (S. rp. 348, 68th Cong. 1st sess.) *Paper, 5c.

Nicaragua. To authorize payment of indemnity to Government of Nicaragua on account of killing and wounding of Nicaraguans in encounters with United States marines, report to accompany S. 2457; submitted by Mr. Shipstead. Apr. 4, 1924. 5 p. (S. rp. 354, 68th Cong. 1st sess.) *Paper, 5c.

Rio Grande. Providing for study of equitable use of Rio Grande with Mexico, below Fort Quitman, Tex., report to accompany S. 2998; submitted by Mr. Lodge. Apr. 24, calendar day Apr. 26, 1924. 2 p. (S. rp. 474, 68th Cong. 1st sess.) * Paper, 5c.

Tozier, Dorr F. Granting permission to Commander Dorr F. Tozier to accept gift from King of Great Britain, report to accompany S. 1698; submitted by Mr. Swanson. Apr. 2, 1924. 1 p. (S. rp. 347, 68th Cong. 1st sess.) * Paper, 5c.

IMMIGRATION COMMITTEE

Immigration. Selective immigration legislation, extracts from hearings on S. 2365 and S. 2576: [Social and economic aspects of immigration, statement on behalf of Railway Business Association, Mar. 8, 1924, by Frank W. Noxon, secretary]. 1924. [1]+2 p. * Paper, 5c.

—— Selective immigration legislation, hearings on S. 2365 and S. 2576, to limit immigration of aliens into United States and to provide system of selection in connection therewith, Feb. 13–Apr. 8, 1924· 1924. iii+314 p. * Paper, 30c.

Japanese immigration legislation, hearings on S. 2576, to limit immigration of aliens into United States, Mar. 11–15, 1924. 1924. iii+170 p. * Paper, 15c.

INDIAN AFFAIRS COMMITTEE

Bell, Richard. Cancellation of allotments made to Richard Bell, deceased, report to accompany H. R. 3900 [to cancel 2 allotments made to Richard Bell, deceased, embracing land within Round Valley Indian Reservation, Calif.]; submitted by Mr. Harreld. Apr. 21, 1924. 2 p. (S. rp. 435, 68th Cong. 1st sess.) * Paper, 5c.

Blackfeet Reservation. Disposal of homestead allotments of deceased allottees within Blackfeet Indian Reservation, Mont., report to accompany H. R. 2879; submitted by Mr. Harreld. Apr. 24, 1924. 2 p. (S. rp. 460, 68th Cong. 1st sess.) * Paper, 5c.

Cherokee Indians. Providing for final disposition of affairs of eastern band of Cherokee Indians of North Carolina, report to accompany H. R. 3852; submitted by Mr. Harreld. Mar. 31, 1924. 4 p. (S. rp. 331, 68th Cong. 1st sess.) * Paper, 5c.

Choctaw Indians. . To adjudicate claims of Choctaw and Chickasaw Indians, report to accompany H. R. 5325 [conferring jurisdiction upon Court of Claims to hear, examine, adjudicate, and enter judgment in any claims which Choctaw and Chickasaw Indians may have against United States]; submitted by Mr. Harreld. Apr. 21, 1924. 4 p. (S. rp. 440, 68th Cong. 1st sess.) * Paper, 5c.

—— To amend act authorizing payment of Choctaw and Chickasaw townsite fund, and for other purposes [so as to provide for payment of shares of deceased Indians to their heirs], report to accompany H. R. 4462; submitted by Mr. Harreld. Apr. 21, 1924. 3 p. (S. rp. 436, 68th Cong. 1st sess.) * Paper, 5c.

Comanche Indians. To compensate 3 Comanche Indians of Kiowa Reservation, report to accompany H. R. 2881 [to compensate Nehio or Len Parker, Arrushe, and Neho, Comanche Indians of Kiowa Reservation]; submitted by Mr. Harreld. Apr. 21, 1924. 2 p. (S. rp. 432, 68th Cong. 1st sess.) * Paper, 5c.

Crane, Mary. Cancellation of allotment of land made to Mary Crane, deceased Indian, report to accompany H. R. 3800 [to cancel all allotment of land made to Mary Crane or Ho-tah-kah-win-kaw, deceased Indian, embracing land within Winnebago Indian Reservation, Nebr.]; submitted by Mr. Harreld. Apr. 21, 1924. 2 p. (S. rp. 434, 68th Cong. 1st sess.) * Paper, 5c.

Creek Indians. Authorizing Court of Claims to adjudicate claims of Creek Indians, report to accompany H. R. 7913; submitted by Mr. Harreld. Apr. 21, 1924. 2 p. (S. rp. 437, 68th Cong. 1st sess.) * Paper, 5c.

Fort Hall Reservation. Authorizing acquiring of Indian lands on Fort Hall Indian Reservation, Idaho, for reservoir purposes in connection with Minidoka irrigation project. report to accompany S. 2002; submitted by Mr. Harreld. Mar. 31, 1924. 3 p. (S. rp. 330, 68th Cong. 1st sess.) * Paper, 5c.

Fort Peck Reservation. Authorizing expenditure of Fort Peck 4 per cent fund now standing to credit of Fort Peck Indians of Montana in Treasury, report to accompany S. J. Res. 103; submitted by Mr. Harreld. Apr. 21, 1924. 2 p. (S. rp. 438, 68th Cong. 1st sess.) *Paper, 5c.

Indian reservations. To permit leasing of unallotted lands of Indians for oil and gas purposes for stated term and as long thereafter as oil or gas is found in paying quantities, report to accompany S. 2814; submitted by Mr. Harreld. Apr. 2, 1924. 2 p. (S. rp. 344, 68th Cong. 1st sess.) *Paper, 5c.

Indians. To authorize Secretary of Interior to issue certificates of citizenship to Indians, report to accompany H. R. 6355 [granting citizenship to Indians]; submitted by Mr. Harreld. Apr. 21, 1924. 3 p. (S. rp. 441, 68th Cong. 1st sess.) *Paper, 5c.

Jack, Isaac. Authorizing removal of restrictions from 40 acres of allotment of Isaac Jack, Seneca Indian, report to accompany H. R. 1629; submitted by Mr. Harreld. Apr. 7, 1924. 2 p. (S. rp. 358, 68th Cong. 1st sess.) *Paper, 5c.

Kansa Indians. To authorize extension of period of restriction against alienation on homestead allotments made to members of Kansas or Kaw tribe of Indians in Oklahoma, report to accompany H. R. 2887; submitted by Mr. Harreld. Apr. 21, 1924. 3 p. (S. rp. 433, 68th Cong. 1st sess.) *Paper, 5c.

Kansa Reservation. To authorize leasing for mining purposes of unallotted lands in Kaw [or Kansa] Reservation, Okla., report to accompany S. 2798; submitted by Mr. Harreld. Apr. 2, 1924. 1 p. (S. rp. 342, 68th Cong. 1st sess.) *Paper, 5c.

L'Anse Reservation. For relief of settlers and claimants to section 16, lands in L'Anse and Vieux Desert Indian Reservation, Mich., report to accompany S. 1237; submitted by Mr. Harreld. Apr. 2, 1924. 2 p. (S. rp. 340, 68th Cong. 1st sess.) *Paper, 5c.

Paiute Indians. To amend act authorizing appropriation to meet proportionate expenses of providing drainage system for Piute Indian lands in Nevada within Newlands reclamation project of Reclamation Service, report to accompany S. 1203; submitted by Mr. Harreld. Apr. 2, 1924. 2 p. (S. rp. 339, 68th Cong. 1st sess.) *Paper, 5c.

Pyramid Lake Reservation. For relief of settlers and town-site occupants of lands in Pyramid Lake Indian Reservation, Nev., report to accompany S. 1309; submitted by Mr. Harreld. Apr. 2, 1924. 2 p. (S. rp. 341, 68th Cong. 1st sess.) *Paper, 5c.

Rowell, James F. Providing for allotment of land from Kiowa, Comanche, and Apache Indian Reservation, Okla., to J. F. Rowell, enrolled member of Kiowa tribe, report to accompany S. 2526; submitted by Mr. Harreld. Apr. 21, 1924. 2 p. (S. rp. 439, 68th Cong. 1st sess.) *Paper, 5c.

Saginaw Indians. To amend act for relief of Chippewa Indians in Michigan, report to accompany H. R. 694 [to amend act for relief of Saginaw, Swan Creek, and Black River Band of Chippewa Indians in Michigan, so as to increase limit of attorneys' fees]; submitted by Mr. Harreld. Apr. 21, 1924. 2 p. (S. rp. 431, 68th Cong. 1st sess.) *Paper, 5c.

Temoak Indians. Authorizing Secretary of Interior to purchase tract of land with sufficient water right attached, for use and occupancy of Temoak band of homeless Indians located at Ruby Valley, Nev., report to accompany S. 1308; submitted by Mr. Harreld. Apr. 2, 1924. 2 p. (S. rp. 343, 68th Cong. 1st sess.) *Paper, 5c.

INTERNAL REVENUE BUREAU, SELECT COMMITTEE ON INVESTIGATION OF

Internal Revenue Bureau. Investigation of Bureau of Internal Revenue, hearings pursuant to S. Res. 168, authorizing appointment of special committee to investigate Bureau of Internal Revenue. Mar. 14[-Apr. 2], 1924. 1924. pts. 1, 2, [vii]+1–463 p. *Paper, each pt. 25c.

INTERSTATE COMMERCE COMMITTEE

Industrial arbitration. Arbitration between carriers and employees, boards of adjustment, hearings before subcommittee on S. 2646, for expeditious and prompt settlement, mediation, conciliation, and arbitration of disputes between carriers and their employees and subordinate officials, Mar. 18–Apr. 7, 1924. 1924. iii+364 p. *Paper, 35c.

Railroad-cars. Protection of railway baggage and express car employees, hearings before subcommittee on S. 863 and H. R. 4107, bills for protection of persons employed on railway baggage cars and railway express cars, Mar. 11, 1924. 1924. iii+168 p. [Hearings held on Mar. 20 and 21, 1924, are included.] * Paper, 15c.

—— Safety of passengers and employees on railroads, hearing before subcommittee on S. 1499, to promote safety of passengers and employees upon railroads by prohibiting use of wooden cars under certain circumstances, Mar. 21, 1924. 1924. ii+8 p. * Paper, 5c.

IRRIGATION AND RECLAMATION COMMITTEE

Reclamation of land. Development of irrigation projects, hearing on development of irrigation projects and deferring of payments of reclamation charges, Mar. 21, 1924. 1924. pt. 2, ii+21–55 p. [Part 1 appeared in Monthly catalogue for Mar. 1924, p. 541.] * Paper, 5c.

—— Funds for maintenance of reclamation projects, report to accompany S. 2836 [relating to deposit of funds available for maintenance of reclamation projects]; submitted by Mr. McNary. Apr. 21, 1924. 2 p. (S. rp. 430, 68th Cong. 1st sess.) * Paper, 5c.

JUDICIARY COMMITTEE

American Academy in Rome. Relating to American Academy in Rome, report to accompany S. 2834; submitted by Mr. Brandegee. Apr. 24, calendar day Apr. 26, 1924. 2 p. (S. rp. 473, 68th Cong. 1st sess.) * Paper, 5c.

Child labor amendment, report to accompany S. J. Res. 1 [proposing amendment to Constitution of United States giving Congress power to limit or prohibit child labor]; submitted by Mr. Shortridge. Apr. 10, calendar day Apr. 15, 1924. 16 p. (S. rp. 406, 68th Cong. 1st sess.) * Paper, 5c.   24—26410

Clerks of United States courts. Fees of clerks of United States courts, etc., hearing before subcommittee on S. 2173, S. 2174, S. 2175, S. 2176, S. 2177, S. 2178, and 2179, Mar. 25, 1924. 1924. ii+16 p. * Paper, 5c.

Courts of United States. Appellate jurisdiction of Federal courts, report to accompany S. 2060 [to amend judicial code, further to define jurisdiction of Circuit Courts of Appeal and of Supreme Court, and for other purposes]; submitted by Mr. Cummins. Apr. 7, calendar day Apr. 8, 1924. 4 p. (S. rp. 362, 68th Cong. 1st sess.) * Paper, 5c.

National banks. Escheat of unclaimed moneys in national banks, hearing before subcommittee on S. 111, to amend sec. 5219, Revised statutes, Mar. 25, 1924; [statement of Frank M. Eastman]. 1924. ii+7 p. * Paper, 5c.

JUSTICE DEPARTMENT, SELECT COMMITTEE ON INVESTIGATION OF

Daugherty, Harry M. Investigation of Attorney General, hearings pursuant to S. Res. 157, directing committee to investigate failure of Attorney General to prosecute or defend certain criminal and civil actions wherein the Government is interested, Mar. 12 [–Apr. 4], 1924. 1924. pts. 1–4, [xv]+1–1034 p. il. [Pt. 4 has title: Investigation of Hon. Harry M. Daugherty, formerly Attorney General of United States.] * Paper, pt. 1, 25c.; * pts. 2 and 4, each 30c.; * pt. 3, 20c.

Daugherty, Mal S. M. S. Daugherty, report [that M. S. Daugherty is in contempt of authority of committee and of Senate]; submitted by Mr. Brookhart. Apr. 24, calendar day Apr. 26, 1924. 5 p. (S. rp. 475, 68th Cong. 1st sess.) * Paper, 5c.

LIBRARY COMMITTEE

San Martin, José de. Equestrian statue of General San Martin, report to accompany S. J. Res. 106 [authorizing erection on public grounds in Washington, D. C., of equestrian statue of General San Martin which the people of Argentina have presented to United States]; submitted by Mr. Pepper. Apr. 10, 1924. 2 p. (S. rp. 367, 68th Cong. 1st sess.) * Paper, 5c.

Carlisle Barracks reservation, report to accompany S. 2949 [authorizing Secretary of War to sell portion of Carlisle Barracks reservation]; submitted by Mr. Wadsworth. Apr. 7, 1924. 2 p. (S. rp. 359, 68th Cong. 1st sess.) * Paper, 5c.

Corinth, Miss. Construction of water and sewer mains in Corinth, Miss., report to accompany S. 3026 [to permit Corinth, Miss., to construct water and sewer mains under and along Government approach roadway to Corinth National Cemetery]; submitted by Mr. Fletcher. Apr. 24, calendar day Apr. 26, 1924. 1 p. (S. rp. 472, 68th Cong. 1st sess.) * Paper, 5c.

Crockett, Fort. Authorizing use of Government buildings at Fort Crockett, Tex., report to accompany S. 2736 [authorizing use of Government buildings at Fort Crockett, Tex., for occupancy during State convention of Texas Shriners]; submitted by Mr. Sheppard. Mar. 31, 1924. 1 p. (S. rp. 321, 68th Cong. 1st sess.) * Paper, 5c.

Davison, Eustacio B. Eustacio B. Davison, report to accompany S. 513 [for relief of Eustacio B. Davison]; submitted by Mr. Sheppard. Apr. 7, 1924. 3 p. (S. rp. 357, 68th Cong. 1st sess.) * Paper, 5c.

Hamilton, Robert F. Robert F. Hamilton, report to accompany S. 106 [for relief of Robert F. Hamilton]; submitted by Mr. Sheppard. Apr. 10, calendar day Apr. 19, 1924. 2 p. (S. rp. 427, 68th Cong. 1st sess.) * Paper, 5c.

Hoboken Manufacturers' Railroad. Sale of Hoboken Shore Line, hearing on S. 2287, to permit Secretary of War to dispose of and Port of New York Authority to acquire Hoboken Shore Line, Mar. 21, 1924. 1924. iii+76 p. * Paper, 10c.

—— Sale of Hoboken Shore Line, report to accompany S. 2287 [to permit Secretary of War to dispose of and Port of New York Authority to acquire Hoboken Manufacturers' Railroad]; submitted by Mr. Wadsworth. Apr. 4, 1924. 5 p. (S. rp. 353, 68th Cong. 1st sess.) * Paper, 5c.

Leavenworth, Fort. Transfer to jurisdiction of Department of Justice of portion of Fort Leavenworth reservation in Missouri, report to accompany H. R. 6207; submitted by Mr. Cappér. Apr. 24, calendar day Apr. 25, 1924. 2 p. (S. rp. 470, 68th Cong. 1st sess.) * Paper, 5c.

Long, Frederic K. Frederic K. Long, report to accompany S. 2922 [to authorize the President to reconsider case of Frederic K. Long and to reappoint him captain in Regular Army]; submitted by Mr. Wadsworth. Apr. 10, calendar day Apr. 18, 1924. 2 p. (S. rp. 422, 68th Cong. 1st sess.) * Paper, 5c.

Medals to 2 Texas cavalry brigades, report to accompany H. R. 593 [authorizing issuance of service medals to officers and enlisted men of 2 brigades of Texas cavalry organized under authority from War Department under date of Dec. 8, 1917, and authorizing appropriation therefor, and further authorizing wearing by such officers and enlisted men on occasions of ceremony of uniform lawfully prescribed to be worn by them during their service]; submitted by Mr. Sheppard. Mar. 31, 1924. 4 p. (S. rp. 322, 68th Cong. 1st sess.) * Paper, 5c.

Miller, Edgar W. Edgar William Miller, report to accompany S. 3170 [for relief of Edgar William Miller]; submitted by Mr. Wadsworth. Apr. 24, calendar day Apr. 25, 1924. 3 p. (S. rp. 471, 68th Cong. 1st sess.) * Paper, 5c.

National defense. To provide for national defense, hearing on S. 2561, to provide further for national security and defense [by authorizing, in national emergency, drafting of unorganized militia, conscription of material resources and industrial organizations and services, and regulation of prices], Apr. 10, 1924. 1924. ii+33 p. * Paper, 5c.

New York Canal and Great Lakes Corporation. Modification of contracts with New York Canal and Great Lakes Corporation, hearing on S. J. Res. 102, authorizing Secretary of War to modify certain contracts entered into for sale of boats, barges, tugs, and other transportation facilities intended for operation upon New York State Barge Canal, Mar. 28, 1924. 1924. ii+36 p. * Paper, 5c.

New York Canal and Great Lakes Corporation—Continued. Modification of contracts with New York Canal & Great Lakes Corporation, report to accompany S. J. Res. 102 [authorizing Secretary of War to modify certain contracts entered into for sale of boats, barges, tugs, and other transportation facilities intended for operation upon New York State Barge Canal]; submitted by Mr. Wadsworth. Apr. 21, 1924. 9 p. (S. rp. 428, 68th Cong. 1st sess.). * Paper, 5c.

Philadelphia, Pa. Widen Haines street in front of national cemetery, Philadelphia, Pa., report to accompany H. R. 4981; submitted by Mr. Reed of Pennsylvania. Apr. 24, calendar day Apr. 26, 1924. 2 p. (S. rp. 476, 68th Cong. 1st sess.) *Paper, 5c.

Tucker, Albert O. Albert O. Tucker, report to accompany S. 2035 [for relief of Albert O. Tucker]; submitted by Mr. Cameron. Apr. 10, calendar day Apr. 18, 1924. 3 p. (S. rp. 423, 68th Cong. 1st sess.) *Paper, 5c.

Varnum, Mrs. Margaret I. Margaret I. varnum, report to accompany S. 246 [for relief of Margaret I. varnum]; submitted by Mr. Bursum. Apr. 10, calendar day Apr. 15, 1924. 3 p. (S. rp. 407, 68th Cong. 1st sess.) *Paper, 5c.

William and Mary College. To loan to College of William and Mary in Virginia 2 of cannon surrendered by British at Yorktown on Oct. 19, 1781, report to accompany H. R. 1831; submitted by Mr. Wadsworth. Apr. 7, 1924. 3 p. (S. rp. 360, 68th Cong. 1st sess.) *Paper, 5c.

NAVAL AFFAIRS COMMITTEE

Naval Air Station, Pensacola. Authorizing Secretary of Navy to accept lands in vicinity of Pensacola, Fla., to assure suitable water supply for Naval Air Station at Pensacola, report to accompany S. 2928; submitted by Mr. Trammell. Apr. 10, 1924.. 2 p. (S. rp. 373, 68th Cong. 1st sess.) *Paper, 5c.

—— United States Naval Air Station, Pensacola, Fla., report to accompany amendment intended to be proposed by Mr. Trammell to H. R. 6820 [making appropriations for Navy Department and naval service, fiscal year 1925]; submitted by Mr. Trammell. Apr. 10, 1924. 2 p. (S. rp. 374, 68th Cong. 1st sess.) [Proposed amendment is to authorize Secretary of Navy to accept lands in vicinity of Pensacola, Fla., to assure suitable water supply for Naval Air Station at Pensacola, Fla.] *Paper, 5c.

Naval Reserve and Marine Corps Reserve, hearings before subcommittee on S. 1807, for creation, organization, administration, and maintenance of Naval Reserve and Marine Corps Reserve, Mar. 12–19, 1924. 1924. ii+133 p. *Paper, 15c.

Officers, Navy. Equalization of promotion of officers of Navy, hearings before subcommittee on S. 1806, for equalization of promotion of officers of staff corps of Navy with officers of the line, Mar. 17–19, 1924. 1924. ii+122 p. *Paper, 15c.

POST OFFICES, AND POST ROADS COMMITTEE

Mail matter. Providing that unpaid letters of 1st-class shall be transmitted to destination and postage thereon paid upon delivery, report to accompany S. 2513; submitted by Mr. Sterling. Apr. 7, calendar day Apr. 9, 1924. 1 p. (S. rp. 365, 68th Cong. 1st sess.) *Paper, 5c.

—— To extend insurance and collect-on-delivery service to 3d-class mail, report to accompany H. R. 4442; submitted by Mr. Sterling. Apr. 7, calendar day Apr. 9, 1924. 1 p. (S. rp. 366, 68th Cong. 1st sess.) *Paper, 5c.

Postal salaries, joint hearings before subcommittee of Committees on Post Offices and Post Roads on S. 1898, H. R. 4123, and H. R. 7016, bills relative to salaries and compensation of employees in postal service, Mar. 3–10, 1924. 1924. pt. 1, ii+1–766+xxxi p. [These hearings were held at joint meetings of the subcommittees of the Senate Committee on Post Offices and Post Roads and the House Committee on Post Office and Post Roads.] * Paper, 75c.

Postmasters. Prescribing certain qualifications of postmasters of offices of 1st, 2d, and 3d class, report to accompany S. 819; submitted by Mr. Sterling. Apr. 7, calendar day Apr. 9, 1924. 2 p. (S. rp. 364, 68th Cong. 1st sess.) *Paper, 5c.

PUBLIC BUILDINGS AND GROUNDS COMMITTEE

Corpus Christi, Tex. Authorizing sale of veterans' Bureau hospital at Corpus Christi, Tex., report to accompany S. 2100; submitted by Mr. Shipstead. Mar. 31, calendar day Apr. 1, 1924. 2 p. (S. rp. 334, 68th Cong. 1st sess.) * Paper, 5c.

PUBLIC LANDS AND SURVEYS COMMITTEE

Adger, Idaho. Sale of lands for railroad purposes, report to accompany H. R. 7500 [to authorize sale of lands at or near Adger, Ada County, Idaho, for railroad purposes, to Oregon Short Line Railroad Company]; submitted by Mr. Smoot. Apr. 24, 1924. 2 p. (S. rp. 462, 68th Cong. 1st sess.) * Paper, 5c.

Assinniboine, Fort. Fort Assinniboine abandoned military reservation, Mont., report to accompany S. J. Res. 90 [providing extension of time for payment by entrymen of lands on Fort Assinniboine abandoned military reservation, Mont.]; submitted by Mr. Ladd. Apr. 10, calendar day Apr. 11, 1924. 1 p. (S. rp. 395, 68th Cong. 1st sess.) ..* Paper, 5c.

Calendar. Legislative calendar, 68th Congress, Apr. 25, 1924; no. 7. [1924.] 34 p. 4° ‡

Flomaton, Ala. To quiet titles to land in Flomaton, Ala., report to accompany H. R. 4437; submitted by Mr. Ladd. Apr. 24, calendar day Apr. 25, 1924. 2 p. (S. rp. 469, 68th Cong. 1st sess.) * Paper, 5c.

Fort Berthold Indian Reservation, N. Dak., report to accompany H. R. 4494 [authorizing extensions of time for payment of purchase money due under homestead entries and Government land purchases within Fort Berthold Indian Reservation, N. Dak.]; submitted by Mr. Ladd. Apr. 10, calendar day Apr. 11, 1924. 3 p. (S. rp. 394, 68th Cong. 1st sess.) * Paper, 5c.

Game. Withdrawal of lands for protection of game animals and birds [in South Dakota], report to accompany S. 2761; submitted by Mr. Norbeck. Apr. 24, calendar day Apr. 28, 1924. 2 p. (S. rp. 478, 68th Cong. 1st sess.) * Paper, 5c.

Homestead. validating certain applications for and entries of public lands, report to accompany S. 2975; submitted by Mr. Ladd. Apr. 10, calendar day Apr. 11, 1924. 9 p. (S. rp. 393, 68th Cong. 1st sess.) * Paper, 5c.

Kaup, William. William Kaup, report to accompany S. 953 [for relief of William Kaup]; submitted by Mr. Ladd. Apr. 10, calendar day Apr. 11, 1924. 2 p. (S. rp. 392, 68th Cong. 1st sess.) * Paper, 5c.

Militia Target Range Reservation, Utah, report to accompany S. 1733 [to authorize Secretary of War to secure for United States title to certain private lands contiguous to and within Militia Target Range Reservation, Utah]; submitted by Mr. Smoot. Apr. 10, calendar day Apr. 11, 1924. 2 p. (S. rp. 387, 68th Cong. 1st sess.) * Paper, 5c.

Naval petroleum reserves. Leases upon naval oil reserves, hearings pursuant to S. Res. 147, Mar. 12 [–Apr. 2], 1924. 1924. pts. 11, 12, [vii]+2667–3072 p. * Paper, pt. 11, 15c.; * pt. 12, 25c.

—— Same, index, pts. 1–8. 1924. ix p. * Paper, 5c.

New Mexico. To amend act to enable people of New Mexico to form constitution and State Government and be admitted into the Union on equal footing with original States [relative to payment of drainage assessments on lands granted under this act], report to accompany S. 1660; submitted by Mr. Bursum. Apr. 2, 1924. 1 p. (S. rp. 338, 68th Cong. 1st sess.) * Paper, 5c.

Northern Pacific Railway. Directing Secretary of Interior to withhold his approval of adjustment of Northern Pacific land grants, report to accompany S. J. Res. 82; submitted by Mr. Ladd. Mar. 31, 1924. 5 p. (S. rp. 327, 68th Cong. 1st sess.) * Paper, 5c.

Rocky Mountain National Park. Transfer of certain lands from Rocky Mountain National Park to Colorado National Forest, report to accompany H. R. 2713; submitted by Mr. Ladd. Apr. 24, calendar day Apr. 25, 1924. 2 p. (S. rp. 468, 68th Cong. 1st sess.) * Paper, 5c.

TERRITORIES AND INSULAR POSSESSIONS COMMITTEE

Philippine independence, hearings on S. 912, providing for withdrawal of United States from Philippine Islands. Feb. 11–Mar. 3, 1924. 1924. ii+119 p. [The hearing held on Mar. 6, 1924, is included.] * Paper, 10c.

Porto Rico. Civil government of Porto Rico, hearings on S. 2448, to amend organic act of Porto Rico, S. 2571, to extend provisions of certain [Federal aid] laws to Porto Rico, S. 2572, to purchase grounds, erect and repair buildings for customhouses, offices, and warehouses in Porto Rico, S. 2573, to amend and reenact sec. 20, 22, and 50 of act to provide civil government for Porto Rico [relating to salaries], Feb. 16–Mar. 7, 1924. 1924. ii+85 p.
* Paper, 10c.

——— To amend organic act of Porto Rico, report to accompany S. 2448; submitted by Mr. Willis. Apr. 7, 1924. 9 p. (S. rp. 356, 68th Cong. 1st sess.)
* Paper, 5c.

WHEELER, BURTON K., SELECT COMMITTEE ON INVESTIGATION OF CHARGES AGAINST

Wheeler, Burton K. Charges against Senator Burton K. Wheeler, of Montana, hearings pursuant to S. Res. 206, to investigate facts in relation to charges made in indictment returned against Senator Burton K. Wheeler in district court for Montana, Apr. 17, 1924. 1924. pt. 1, ii+1–41 p.
* Paper, 5c.

COURT OF CLAIMS

Beckstrom, Ross P., Company. Ross P. Beckstrom Company v. United States; evidence for plaintiff. [1924.] no. C–1019, p. 23–45. ‡

Cases decided in Court of Claims at term of 1922–23, with abstract of decisions of Supreme Court in appealed cases, Oct. 1922–June, 1923; reported by Harry N. Stull. 1924. v. 58, xxiv+754 p. il. * Cloth, $1.75.

Cheyenne Milling Company v. United States; evidence for defendant. [1924.] no. 34739, p. 67–98. ‡

Clark. Harold Lyman Clark v. United States; evidence [for claimant]. [1924.] no. B–63, p. 9–10. ‡

Cuyahoga Stamping & Machine Co. v. United States; findings of fact [conclusion of law and memorandum], decided Apr. 14, 1924. [1924.] Law no. 114–A, 2 p. ‡

DeGroot. John DeGroot v. United States; evidence [for claimant]. 1924. no. C–889, p. 5. ‡

Early & Daniel Company v. United States; evidence for defendant. [1924.] no. 238–A, p. 83–94. ‡

Garrison. Joshua Garrison, jr., v. United States; evidence for claimant. [1924.] no. 116–A, p. 25–27. ‡

Harris. Smith A. Harris v. United States; evidence [for claimant]. [1924.] no. C–938, p. 5–6. ‡

Houston and Texas Central Railroad Company v. United States; evidence for defendant. [1924.] no. C–264, p. 11–17. ‡

Morgan's Louisiana and Texas Railroad and Steamship Co. v. United States; evidence for defendant. [1924.] no. C–266, p. 13–18. ‡

Peabody, Henry W., & Co. Henry W. Peabody & Company v. United States; [evidence for defendant]. [1924.] no. B–425, p. 23–34. ‡

Pittsburgh & West Virginia Railroad Co. v. United States; evidence for plaintiff. [1924.] no. C–32, p. 21–44. ‡

Reading Company [successor to Philadelphia & Reading Railway] v. United States; evidence for claimant. [1924.] no. 34747, p. 219–225. ‡

Southern Pacific Company v. United States; evidence for defendant. [1924.] no. B–418, p. 23–33. ‡

Texas & New Orleans Railroad Company v. United States; evidence for defendant. [1924.] no. C–265, p. 13–15. ‡

Towar Cotton Mills, Inc., v. United States; evidence for defendant. [1924.] no. C–209, p. 51–65. ‡

Western Cartridge Company v. United States; evidence for defendant [and] rebuttal evidence for plaintiff. [1924.] no. 320–A, p. 91–108. ‡

White, J. G., Engineering Corporation. J. G. White Engineering Corporation v. United States; testimony for defendant. [1924.] no. 34754, p. 325–411. ‡

Wilson, C. R., Body Company. C. R. Wilson Body Company v. United States; findings of fact [conclusion of law, and opinion of court], decided Apr. 28, 1924. [1924.] no. 79–A, 7 p. ‡

COURT OF CUSTOMS APPEALS

Foreign exchange. No. 2373, United States *v.* Brown & Roese, transcript of record on appeal from Board of General Appraisers. 1924. cover-title, i+6 p. ‡

Jewelry. No. 2368, United States *v.* Barnard Hirsch Company, transcript of record on appeal from Board of General Appraisers. [1924.] cover-title, i+8 p. ‡

Knitting-machines. No. 2311, United States *v.* C. B. Richard & Co. et al., transcript of record on appeal from Board of General Appraisers.' [1924.] cover-title, i+71 p. ‡

Tomatoes. No. 2369, United States· *v.* Hamilton Michaelson & Co. et al., transcript of record on appeal from Board of General Appraisers. [1924.] cover-title, i+49 p. ‡

DISTRICT OF COLUMBIA

Court of Appeals. Jan. term, 1924, no. 4114, no. 27, special calendar, United States *v.* Ward W. Griffith et al., appeal from Supreme Court of District of Columbia; brief for appellant. 1924. cover-title, v+1–48a+49–99 p. ‡

—— Apr. term, 1924, no. 4123, no. —, special calendar, Louis M. Croson *v.* District of Columbia, in error to Police Court of District of Columbia; brief for plaintiff in error. 1924. cover-title, ii+22 p. ‡ .

FEDERAL POWER COMMISSION

Rules and regulations governing administration of Federal water power act, with copy of act and of amendment thereto. 2d revised issue. 1924. vi+ 69 p. [Contains all amendments to and including Apr. 1, 1924, but does not include commission's accounting rules and regulations approved Nov. 20, 1922, which are published separately.] * Paper, 10c. · 24—26354

FEDERAL RESERVE BOARD

Banks and banking. Provisions of State laws relating to bank reserves; prepared in Office of its General Counsel. 1924. [1]+154–181 p. 4°. [From Federal reserve bulletin, Mar. 1924.] †

Federal reserve bulletin, Apr. 1924; [v. 10, no. 4]. 1924. iv+243–323+iv p. il. 4° [Monthly.] † Paper, 20c. single copy, $2.00 a yr. 15—26318
   NOTE.—The bulletin contains, in addition to the regular official announcements, the national review of business conditions, detailed analyses of business conditions, research studies, reviews of foreign banking, and complete statistics showing the condition of Federal reserve banks and member banks. It·will be sent to all member banks without charge. Others desiring copies may obtain them from the Federal Reserve Board, Washington, D. C., at the prices stated above.

Federal reserve member banks. Federal reserve inter-district collection system, changes in list of banks upon which items will be received by Federal reserve banks for collection and credit, Apr. 1, 1924. 1924. 15 p. 4° † 16—26870

Report. 10th annual report of Federal Reserve Board, covering operations for [calendar] year 1923. 1924. iv+80 p. il. † 15—26170

FEDERAL TRADE COMMISSION

   NOTE.—The bound volumes of the Federal Trade Commission decisions are sold by the Superintendent of Documents, Washington, D. C. Separate opinions are sold on subscription, price $1.00 per volume; foreign subscription, $1.50; single copies, 5c. each.

Bene, John, & Sons, Incorporated. In circuit court of circuit, Oct. term, 1923, original petition to revise order of Federal Trade Commission, John Bene & Sons, Inc., *v.* Federal Trade Commission; brief and argument for respondent. 1924. cover-title, 25 p. large 8°. ‡

Loose-Wiles Biscuit Company. No. 8218, in circuit court of appeals for 2d circuit, Loose-Wiles Biscuit Company *v.* Federal Trade Commission; brief for respondent. 1924. cover-title, i+45 p. large 8° ‡

National Biscuit Company. No. 8205, in circuit court of appeals for 2d circuit, National Biscuit Company *v.* Federal Trade Commission; answer in nature of cross bill. 1924. cover-title, 3 p. large 8° [1st edition of 4 pages entered in the Monthly catalogue for Feb. 1924, p. 453, incorrectly printed.] ‡

—— Same; brief for respondent. 1924. cover-title, ii+69 p. large 8° ‡

Stoves. Report of Federal Trade Commission on house furnishings industries: v. 2, Household stoves, Oct. 1, 1923. 1924. ix+187 p. il. 1 pl. * Paper, 20c.
23—26305

Swift & Co. No. 3215, in circuit court of appeals for 7th circuit, Oct. term, 1922, Swift & Company *v.* Federal Trade Commission; brief and argument for respondent. 1924. cover-title, ii+60 p. ‡

Thatcher Manufacturing Company. Transcript of record, in circuit court of appeals for 3d circuit, no. —, Mar. term, 1924, Federal Trade Commission *v.* Thatcher Manufacturing Company, on application for enforcement of order of Federal Trade Commission. 1924. cover-title, ii+258 p. large 8° ‡

GENERAL ACCOUNTING OFFICE

Claims. Schedule of claims against United States, schedules of claims allowed by various divisions of General Accounting Office under appropriations balances of which have been exhausted or carried to surplus fund. Mar. 14, calendar day Mar. 18, 1924. 121 p. (S. doc. 68, 68th Cong. 1st sess.) * Paper, 10c.

Decisions. Appendix [and subject index to Decisions of comptroller general, v. 1, July 1, 1921–June 30, 1922]. [1924.] p. 775–820. †

—— Same [v. 2, July 1, 1922–June 30, 1923]. [1924.] p. 829–876. †

—— Decisions of comptroller general, v. 3, Feb. 1924; J. R. McCarl, comptroller general, Lurtin R. Ginn, assistant comptroller general. 1924. [1]+465-562 p. [Monthly.] †
21—26777

GEOGRAPHIC BOARD

Decisions of Geographic Board, Jan. 9–Mar. 5, 1924. [1924.] 2 p. †   10—26561

GOVERNMENT PRINTING OFFICE

Public printing. Proposals for material for public printing and binding for term of 1 year beginning July 1, 1924. Apr. 21, 1924. 21 p. 4° †

DOCUMENTS OFFICE

Agricultural chemistry, list of publications for sale by superintendent of documents, Feb. 1924. [2]+6 p. (Price list 40, 16th edition.) †   24—26355

Alaska, list of publications for sale by superintendent of documents. Mar. 1924. [2]+22 p. (Price list 60, 8th edition.) †   24—26358

Army and Militia, aviation and pensions, list of publications for sale by superintendent of documents. Feb. 1924. [2]+36+[1] p. (Price list 19, 14th edition.) †   24—26411

Indians, including Government publications pertaining to mounds and antiquities, for sale by superintendent of documents. Mar. 1924. [2]+16+[1] p. (Price list 24, 8th edition.) †   24—26412

Monthly catalogue, United States public documents, no. 351; Mar. 1924. 1924. p. 501–584. * Paper, 5c. single copy, 50c. a yr.; foreign subscription, 75c.
4—18088

Plants, [publications relating to] culture of fruits, vegetables, grain, grasses, and seeds, for sale by superintendent of documents. Feb. 1924. [2]+38 p. (Price list 44, 15th edition.) †   24—26356

Roads, list of publications for sale by superintendent of documents. Mar. 1924. [2]+4+[2] p. (Price list 45, 13th edition.) †   24—26357

INTERDEPARTMENTAL PATENTS BOARD

Report. Interdepartmental Patents Board, report of Interdepartmental Patents Board, with drafts of bills to authorize the President to withhold from publication any patent which in his opinion would be detrimental to national defense. 1924. iii+7 p. (S. doc. 83, 68th Cong. 1st sess.) *Paper, 5c.

24—26431

INTERIOR DEPARTMENT

NOTE.—The decisions of the Department of the Interior in pension cases are issued in slips and in signatures, and the decisions in land cases are issued in signatures, both being published later in bound volumes. Subscribers may deposit $1.00 with the Superintendent of Documents and receive the contents of a volume of the decisions of either kind in separate parts as they are issued; foreign subscription, $1.25. Prices for bound volumes furnished upon application to the Superintendent of Documents, Washington, D. C.

Pensions. [Decisions of Department of Interior in appealed pension and bounty land claims, v. 21, slips] 101 and 102 pension. [1924.] 4 p. and 3 p. [For price, see note above under center head.]

12—29422

Public lands. Decisions [of Department of Interior in cases] relating to public lands, v. 50, [signatures] 1–13. [1924.] p. 1–208. [For price, see note above under center head.]

7—23651

EDUCATION BUREAU

Consolidated schools of Bernalillo County, N. Mex.; by A. Montoya. 1924. [1]+8 p. il. 1 pl. (Rural school leaflet 22.) *Paper, 5c.

E 24—419

Kindergarten. Statistics of kindergartens, 1921–22; prepared by Statistical Division. 1924. [1]+7 p. (Bulletin 58, 1923.) [Advance sheets from Biennial survey of education in United States, 1920–22.] *Paper, 5c.

E 22—569

National Conference on Home Education. Program, 2d National Conference on Home Education called by Commissioner of Education Jno. J. Tigert, to be held in conjunction with annual meeting of National Congress of Mothers and Parent-Teacher Associations, May 7, 1924, University of Minnesota, Minneapolis, Minn. [1924.] [2] leaves+[4] p. †

School life, v. 9, no. 8; Apr. 1924. [1924.] p. 169–192, 4° [Monthly except July and August.] *Paper, 5c. single copy, 30c. a yr. (10 months); foreign subscription, 55c.

E 18—902

GENERAL LAND OFFICE

Maps

NOTE.—The General Land Office publishes a large general map of the United States, which is sold at $2.00; and also separate maps of the States and Territories in which public lands are to be found, which are sold at 25c. per sheet. The map of California is in 2 sheets. Address the Superintendent of Documents, Washington, D. C.

Washington State. State of Washington, compiled chiefly from official records of General Land Office with supplemental data from other map making agencies; compiled by George A. Daidy. Scale 12 m.=1 in. Columbia Planograph Co., Washington, D. C., 1924. 24.3×35 in. *25c.

GEOLOGICAL SURVEY

NOTE.—The publications of the United States Geological Survey consist of Annual reports, Monographs, Professional papers, Bulletins, Water-supply papers, chapters and volumes of Mineral resources of the United States, folios of the Topographic atlas of the United States and topographic maps that bear descriptive text, and folios of the Geologic atlas of the United States and the World atlas of commercial geology. The Monographs, folios, and maps are sold.. Other publications are generally free as long as the Survey's supply lasts. Copies are also sold by the Superintendent of Documents, Washington, D. C., at the prices indicated. For maps and folios address the Director of the Geological Survey, Washington, D. C. A discount of 40 per cent is allowed on any order for maps or folios that amounts to $5.00 or more at the retail price. This discount applies to an order for either maps or folios alone or for maps and folios together but is not allowed on a few folios that are sold at 5c. each on account of damage by fire. Orders for other publications that are for sale should be sent to the Superintendent of Documents, Washington, D. C. For topographic maps see next page.

Carbon black produced from natural gas in 1922; by G. B. Richardson. Apr 7, 1924. [1]+345–346 p. [From Mineral resources, 1922, pt. 2.] †

Eocene period. Early Eocene florule from central Texas; by Edward Wilber Berry. Apr. 10, 1924. ii+87–92 p. il. 1 pl. 4° (Professional paper 132 E.) * Paper, 5c.

Gasoline. Natural-gas gasoline in 1922; by G. B. Richardson. Apr. 24, 1924. [1]+347–351 p. [From Mineral resources, 1922, pt. 2.] †

Geology. Geologic literature on North America, 1785–1918: pt. 2, Index; by John M. Nickles. 1924. [1]+658 p. (Bulletin 747.) * Paper, 65c. GS 24—38

—— Same. (H. doc. 27, 68th Cong. 1st sess.)

Manhattan, Nev. Geology and ore deposits of Manhattan district, Nev. [with bibliography]; by Henry G. Ferguson. 1924. ix+163 p. il. 4 pl. 10 p. of pl. 4 maps, 1 is in pocket. (Bulletin 723.) * Paper, 50c. GS 24—67

—— Same. (H. doc. 310, 67th Cong. 2d sess.)

Matter. Evolution and disintegration of matter; by Frank Wigglesworth Clarke. Apr. 9, 1924. ii+51–86 p. 1 pl. 4° (Professional paper 132 D.) * Paper, 10c.

Mineral resources. Mineral resources of United States, 1921: pt. 1, Metals [with bibliographies]. 1924. iv+130A+617 p. il. 1 pl. * Cloth, $1.00.
4—18124

—— Same. (H. doc. 610, 67th Cong. 4th sess.)

—— Same: pt. 2, Nonmetals [with bibliographies]. 1924. v+682 p. il. map, 1 tab. in pocket. * Cloth, $1.00.

—— Same. (H. doc. 610, 67th Cong. 4th sess.)

Natural gas in 1922; by G. B. Richardson. Apr. 26, 1924. [1]+353–358 p. [From Mineral resources, 1922, pt. 2.] †

Publications. New publications, list 193; Apr. 1, 1924. [1924.] 3 p. [Monthly.] †

Stone in 1922; by G. F. Loughlin and A. T. Coons. Apr. 10, 1924. ii+261–344 p. il. [From Mineral resources, 1922, pt. 2.] †

Sulphur and pyrites in 1923; by H. M. Meyer. Apr. 21, 1924. [1]+1–6 p. [From Mineral resources, 1923, pt. 2.] †

Topographic maps

NOTE.—The Geological Survey is making a topographic map of the United States. The individual maps of which it is composed are projected without reference to political divisions, and each map is designated by the name of some prominent town or natural feature in the area mapped. Three scales are ordinarily used, 1 : 62,500, 1 : 125,000, and 1 : 250,000. These correspond, approximately, to 1 mile, 2 miles, and 4 miles to 1 linear inch, covering, respectively, average areas of 230, 920, and 3,700 square miles. For some areas of particular importance special large-scale maps are published. The usual size, exclusive of the margin, is 17.5 inches in height by 11.5 to 16 inches in width, the width varying with the latitude. The sheets measure 20 by 16½ inches. A description of the topographic map is printed on the reverse of each sheet.

More than two-fifths of the area of the country, excluding Alaska, has been mapped, every State being represented. Connecticut, Delaware, the District of Columbia, Maryland, Massachusetts, New Jersey, Ohio, Rhode Island, and West Virginia are completely mapped. Maps of the regular size are sold by the Survey at 10c. each, but a discount of 40 per cent is allowed on any order which amounts to $5.00 or more at the retail price. The discount is allowed on an order for either maps or folios alone or for maps and folios together, but does not apply to a few folios that are sold at 5c. each on account of damage by fire.

California. California, Citrus Cove quadrangle, lat. 36° 37′ 30″–36° 45′, long. 119° 15′–119° 22′ 30″. Scale 1 : 31,680, contour interval 5 ft. [Washington, Geological Survey] edition of 1924. 18.4×13.9 in. † 10c.

—— California, Mendota quadrangle, lat. 36° 45′–36° 52′ 30″, long. 120° 15′–120° 22′ 30″. Scale 1 : 31,680, contour interval 5 ft. [Washington, Geological Survey] edition of 1924. 17.3×13.9 in. † 10c.

—— California. Reedley quadrangle, lat. 36° 30′–36° 37′ 30″, long. 119° 22′ 30″–119° 30′. Scale 1 : 31,680, contour interval 5 ft. [Washington, Geological Survey] edition of 1924. 17.3×13.9 in. † 10c.

—— California, Stokes Mountain quadrangle, lat. 36° 30′–36° 37′ 30″, long. 119° 07′ 30″–119° 15′. Scale 1 : 31,680, controur interval 5 feet. [Washington, Geological Survey] edition of 1924. 17.2×15.4 in. † 10c.

California—Continued. California, Wahtoke quadrangle, lat. 36° 37′ 30′′-36° 45′, long. 119° 22′ 30′′-119° 30′. Scale 1:31,680, contour interval 5 and 25 ft. [Washington, Geological Survey] edition of 1923. 17.3×13.9 in. † 10c.

Hawaii. Hawaii, Honuapo quadrangle. lat. 19°-19° 15′, long. 155° 30′-155° 45′. Scale 1:62,500, contour interval 50 ft. [Washington, Geological Survey] edition of 1924. 17.5×16.6 in. † 10c.

—— Hawaii, Kalae quadrangle, lat. 18° 45′-19°, long. 155° 35′-155° 50′. Scale 1:62,500, contour interval 50 ft. [Washington, Geological Survey] edition of 1924. 17.5×16.6 in. † 10c.

Mississippi, Pelahatchee quadrangle, lat. 32° 15′-32° 30′, long. 89° 45′-90°. Scale 1:62,500, contour interval 20 ft. [Washington, Geological Survey] edition of 1924. 17.5×14.9 in. † 10c.

New York, Randolph quadrangle, lat. 42°-42° 15′, long. 78° 45′-79°. Scale 1:62,500, contour interval 20 ft. [Washington, Geological Survey] edition of 1923. 17.6×13.1 in. † 10c.

Pennsylvania, Milton quadrangle, lat. 41°-41° 15′, long. 76° 45′-77°. Scale 1:62,500, contour interval 20 ft. [Washington, Geological Survey] edition of 1924. 17.5×13.3 in. † 10c.

Vermont, Camels Hump quadrangle, lat. 44° 15′-44° 30′, long. 72° 45′-73°. Scale 1:62,500, contour interval 20 ft. [Washington, Geological Survey] edition of 1924. 17.5×12.6 in. † 10c.

INDIAN AFFAIRS OFFICE

Mineral lands. Regulations to govern prospecting for and mining of metalliferous minerals on unallotted lands of Indian reservations. [1924.] 19 p. †

Supplies. Advertisement [inviting proposals for hardware for Indian service, fiscal year 1925]. Mar. 25, 1924. p. 3–4, 4° †

—— Proposal for hardware, iron, nails, and plumber's and steam and gas fitter's tools, fittings, and supplies for Indian service [fiscal year 1925]. [1924.] 56+[1] p. 4° †

—— Proposal [for] medical supplies for Indian service [fiscal year 1925]. [1924.] 22+[1] p. 4° †

MINES BUREAU

Oil shale, historical, technical, and economic study, by Martin J. Gavin; [with selected bibliography, compiled by Elizabeth H. Burroughs]. [Revised edition.] [Jan.] 1924. x+201 p. il. 8 pl. 10 p. of pl. (Bulletin 210.) [This bulletin represents work done under a cooperative agreement with Colorado.] * Paper, 35c. 24—26413

Publications. New publications, special, 1924. [1924.] oblong 48° [This publication is issued in postal card form.] †

Silver in chloride volatilization; by C. M. Bouton, W. C. Riddell, and L. H. Duschak. [1st edition.] [Feb.] 1924. iv+56 p. il. (Technical paper 317.) [Includes lists of Mines Bureau publications on chloride volatilization.] * Paper, 10c. 24—26359

NATIONAL PARK SERVICE

Crater Lake National Park. Rules and regulations, Crater Lake National Park, Oreg., 1924, season July 1–Sept. 30 [with list of literature]. [1924.] vi+21 p. il. 2 p. of pl. map. † 21—26512

Glacier National Park. Rules and regulations, Glacier National Park, Mont., 1924, season June 15–Sept. 15 [with list of literature]. [1924.] vi+53 p. il. 2 p. of pl. map. † 21—26513

Mount Rainier National Park. Rules and regulations, Mount Rainier National Park, Wash., 1924, season June 15–Sept. 15 [with list of literature]. [1924.] 43 p. il. 2 p. of pl. map. † 21—26443

Rocky Mountain National Park. Rules and regulations, Rocky Mountain National Park, Colo., 1924, open all year, summer season June 15–Oct. 1 [with list of literature]. [1924.] vi+41 p. il. 2 p. of pl. map. † 21—26444

PATENT OFFICE

NOTE. — Patent Office publishes Specifications and drawings of patents in single copies. These are not enumerated in this catalogue, but may be obtained for 10c. each at the Patent Office.

A variety of indexes, giving a complete view of the work of the Patent Office from 1790 to date, are published at prices ranging from 25c. to $10.00 per volume and may be obtained from the Superintendent of Documents, Washington, D. C. The Rules of practice and pamphlet Patent laws are furnished free of charge upon application to the Patent Office. The Patent Office issues coupon orders in packages of 20 at $2.00 per package, or in books containing 100 coupons at $10.00 per book. These coupons are good until used, but are only to be used for orders sent to the Patent Office. For schedule of office fees, address Chief Clerk, Patent Office, Washington, D. C.

Decisions. [Decisions in patent and trade-mark cases, etc.] Apr. 1, 1924. p. 1–8, large 8° [From Official gazette, v. 321, no. 1.] † Paper, 5c. single copy, $2.00 a yr.

—— Same. Apr. 8, 1924. p. 221–228, il. large 8° [From Official gazette, v. 321, no. 2.]

—— Same. Apr. 15, 1924. p. 459–466, il. large 8° [From Official gazette, v. 321, no. 3.]

—— Same. Apr. 22, 1924. p. 703–708, large 8° [From Official gazette, v. 321, no. 4.]

—— Same. Apr. 29, 1924. p. 951–956, large 8° [From Official gazette, v. 321, no. 5.]

Dolly Varden Chocolate Company. In Court of Appeals of District of Columbia, Apr. term, 1924, patent appeal no. 1651, *in re* Dolly Varden Chocolate Company, trade mark for candy; brief for commissioner of patents. 1924. cover-title, 5 p. ‡

Foster, Bertram G. In Court of Appeals of District of Columbia, Apr. term, 1924, patent appeal no. 1682, *in re* Bertram G. Foster, improvement in hoists; brief for commissioner of patents. 1924. cover-title, 5 p. ‡

Hernandez-Mejia, Arturo. In Court of Appeals of District of Columbia, Apr. term, 1924, patent appeal no. 1663, *in re* Arturo Hernandez-Mejia, color photography; brief for commissioner of patents. 1924. cover-title, 9 p. ‡

Johns-Manville, Incorporated. In Court of Appeals of District of Columbia, Apr. term, 1924, patent appeal no. 1686, *in re* Johns-Manville, Incorporated, trade-mark for sectional pipe covering; brief for commissioner of patents. 1924. cover-title, 10 p. ‡

Landis Machine Company. In Court of Appeals of District of Columbia, Apr. term, 1924, patent appeal no. 1661, *in re* Landis Machine Company, trademark for certain machines; brief for commissioner of patents. 1924. cover-title, 7 p. ‡

Official gazette. Official gazette, Apr. 1–29, 1924; v. 321, no. 1–5. 1924. cover-titles, 1173+[ccii] p. il. large 8° [Weekly.] * Paper, 10c. single copy, $5.00 a yr.; foreign subscription, $11.00.   4—18256

NOTE.—Contains the patents, trade-marks, designs, and labels issued each week; also decisions of the commissioner of patents and of the United States courts in patent cases.

—— Same [title-page, contents, etc., to] v. 320; Mar. 1924. 1924. [2] leaves, large 8° * Paper, 5c. single copy, included in price of Official gazette for subscribers.

—— Same, weekly index, with title, Alphabetical list of registrants of trademarks [etc., Apr. 1, 1924]. [1924.] xxxviii p. large 8° [From Official gazette, v. 321, no. 1.] † Paper, $1.00 a yr.

—— Same [Apr. 8, 1924]. [1924.] xl p. large 8° [From Official gazette, v. 321, no. 2.]

—— Same [Apr. 15, 1924]. [1924.] xlii p. large 8° [From Official gazette, v. 321, no. 3.]

—— Same [Apr. 22, 1924]. [1924.] xliv p. large 8° [From Official gazette, v. 321, no. 4.]

—— Same [Apr. 29, 1924]. [1924.] xxxviii p. large 8° [From Official gazette, v. 321, no. 5.]

Patents. Classification of patents issued Apr. 1–29, 1924. [1924.] Each 2 p. large 8° [Weekly. From Official gazette, v. 321, no. 1–5.] †

—— Index to classification of patents, to accompany Manual of classification of patents; revised to Jan. 1, 1924. 1924. ii+58 p.+[1] folded leaf, oblong 24° [Included in price of Manual, for which see the Monthly catalogue for Jan. 1924, p. 375.]

Trade-marks. Trade-marks [etc., from] Official gazette, Apr. 1, 1924. [1924.] 9–54+i–xvi p. il. large 8° [From Official gazette, v. 321, no. 1.] † Paper, 5c. single copy, $2.50 a yr.

—— Same, Apr. 8, 1924. [1924.] 229–277+i–xv p. il. large 8° [From Official gazette, v. 321, no. 2.]

—— Same, Apr. 15, 1924. [1924.] 467–525+i–xvii p. il. large 8° [From Official gazette, v. 321, no. 3.]

—— Same, Apr. 22, 1924. [1924.] 709–763+i–xvii p. il. large 8° [From Official gazette, v. 321, no. 4.]

—— Same, Apr. 29, 1924. [1924.] 957–1008+i–xv p. il. large 8° [From Official gazette, v. 321, no. 5.]

RECLAMATION BUREAU

New reclamation era, v. 15, no. 4; Apr. 1924. [1924.] cover-title, p. 49–64, il. 4° [Monthly. Text on p. 2–4 of cover.]

NOTE.—The New reclamation era is a magazine for the farmers and the personnel of the service. Its aim is to assist the settlers in the proper use of water, to help them in overcoming their agricultural difficulties, to instruct them in diversifying and marketing their crops, to inspire the employees of the service and chronicle engineering problems and achievements, and to promote a wholehearted spirit of cooperation, so that reclamation shall attain the greatest heights of success. The Era is sent without direct charge to water users of the reclamation projects constructed and operated by the Government. Persons desiring to subscribe for the New reclamation era, other than water users, may secure it for the price of 75c. a year, payable in advance. Subscriptions should be sent to the Chief Clerk, Reclamation Bureau, Washington, D. C., and remittances in the form of postal money order or New York draft should be made payable to the Special Fiscal Agent, Reclamation Bureau. Postage stamps are not acceptable in payment of subscription.

INTERSTATE COMMERCE COMMISSION

NOTE.—The bound volumes of the decisions, usually known as Interstate Commerce Commission reports, are sold by the Superintendent of Documents, Washington, D. C., at various prices, depending upon the size of the volume. Separate opinions are sold on subscription, price $1.00 per volume; foreign subscription, $1.50; single copies, usually 5c. each.

Ann Arbor Railroad. Finance docket no. 3415, Ann Arbor equipment trust; [decided Feb. 29, 1924; supplemental report of commission]. 1924. [1]+478–480 p. ([Finance decision] 1230.) [From Interstate Commerce Commission reports, v. 86.] * Paper, 5c.

Boiler-preservative compounds. No. 14136, Garratt-Callahan Company *v.* Atlantic Coast Line Railroad Company et al.; [no. 14136 (sub-no. 1), Perolin Company of America *v.* same; no. 14039, Brooks Oil Company *v.* Baltimore & Ohio Railroad Company et al.]; decided Mar 7, 1924; report [and order] of commission. [1924.] 103–106+ii p. ([Opinion] 9291.) [Report from Interstate Commerce Commission reports, v. 88.] * Paper, 5c.

Boston Terminal Company. Before Interstate Commerce Commission, valuation docket no. 166, Boston Terminal Company; brief in support of tentative valuation. 1924. cover-title, i+49 p. ‡

Bowdon Railway. Finance docket no. 322, guaranty settlement with Bowdon Ry.; decided Mar. 19, 1924; report of commission. [1924.] p. 543–545. ([Finance decision] 1251.) [From Interstate Commerce Commission reports, v. 86.] * Paper, 5c.

Brimstone Railroad and Canal Company. No. 12969, divisions received by Brimstone Railroad & Canal Company; [decided Mar. 10, 1924; report and order of commission on further hearing]. 1924. [1]+62–76+[1] p. ([Opinion] 9286.) [Report from Interstate Commerce Commission reports, v. 88.] * Paper, 5c.

Cantaloupes. Investigation and suspension docket no. 1979, cantaloupes and melons from California to points in Arizona and New Mexico, and to El Paso, Tex.; [decided Mar. 24, 1924; report and order of commission]. 1924. [1]+340–342+[1] p. ([Opinion] 9356.) [Report from Interstate Commerce Commission reports, v. 88.] * Paper, 5c.

Carriers. No. 15780, depreciation charges of carriers by water [report of preliminary investigation of depreciation charges in connection with carriers by water and tentative conclusions and recommendations of Depreciation Section, Accounts Bureau, for regulation of such charges] Apr. 12, 1924. [1924.] 18 p. * Paper, 5c.

Cement. No. 12701, Atlas Portland Cement Company *v.* Chicago, Burlington & Quincy Railroad Company et al.; decided Mar. 3, 1924; report [and order] of commission. [1924.] 27–32+ii p. ([Opinion] 9279.) [Report from Interstate Commerce Commission reports, v. 88.] * Paper, 5c.

Central of Georgia Railway. Finance docket no. 3474, bonds of Central of Georgia Ry.; [decided Mar. 4, 1924; report of commission]. 1924. [1]+ 488–490 p. ([Finance decision] 1235.) [From Interstate Commerce Commission reports, v. 86.] * Paper, 5c.

—— Finance docket no. 3475, notes of Central of Georgia Ry.; decided Mar. 4, 1924; report of commission. [1924.] p. 485–487. ([Finance decision] 1233.) [From Interstate Commerce Commission reports, v. 86.] * Paper, 5c.

Chicago Great Western Railroad. Finance docket no. 3466, bonds of Chicago Great Western R. R.; decided Mar. 17, 1924; report of commission. [1924.] p. 541–543. ([Finance decision] 1250.) [From Interstate Commerce Commission reports, v. 86.] * Paper, 5c.

Chicago, New York and Boston Refrigerator Company. No. 288, in Supreme Court, Oct. term, 1923, United States ex rel. Chicago, New York & Boston Refrigerator Company *v.* Interstate Commerce Commission, from Court of Appeals of District of Columbia on writ of error; brief for Interstate Commerce Commission. 1924. cover-title, ii+45 p. ‡

Chicago, Rock Island and Pacific Railway. Finance docket no. 3485, Rock Island Railway bonds; decided Mar. 15, 1924; report of commission. [1924.] p. 509–511. ([Finance dec'sion] 1241.) [From Interstate Commerce Commission reports, v. 86.] * Paper, 5c.

Cincinnati, New Orleans and Texas Pacific Railway. Finance docket no. 3413, assumption of obligation by Cincinnati, New Orleans & Texas Pacific Railway [as lessee of Cincinnati Southern Railway]; decided Feb. 29, 1924; report of commission. [1924.] p. 475–477. ([Finance decision] 1229.) [From Interstate Commerce Commission reports. v. 86.] * Paper, 5c.

Coal. Before Interstate Commerce Commission, docket 15006, in matter of rates, charges, classifications, regulations, and practices governing transportation of anthracite coal; brief prepared by commission's attorney. 1924. cover-title, iii+128 p. ‡

—— No. 12737, Slogo Coal Corporation *v.* Missouri Pacific Railroad Company et al.; [no. 12737 (sub-no. 1), Perry County Coal Corporation *v.* Baltimore & Ohio Railroad Company et al.]; decided Mar. 7, 1924; report [and orders] of commission. [1924.] 111–114+iii p. ([Opinion] 9293.) [Report from Interstate Commerce Commission reports, v. 88.] * Paper, 5c.

—— No. 13845, Gottlieb-Bertsch Company et al. *v.* director general, as agent; decided Mar. 7, 1924; report [and order] of commission. [1924.] 177–178+[1] p. ([Opinion] 9306.) [Report from Interstate Commerce Commission reports, v. 88.] * Paper, 5c.

—— No. 13899, Dixie Portland Cement Company *v.* Nashville, Chattanooga & St. Louis Railway; decided Mar. 7, 1924; report [and order] of commission. [1924.] 147–151+[1] p. ([Opinion] 9301.) [Report from Interstate Commerce Commission reports, v. 88.] * Paper, 5c.

—— No. 14030, Michigan Tanning & Extract Company *v.* director general, as agent; [decided Mar. 7, 1924; report and order of commission]. 1924. [1]+298–300+[1] p. ([Opinion] 9344.) [Report from Interstate Commerce Commission reports, v. 88.] * Paper, 5c.

—— No. 14516, Wickwire Spencer Steel Corporation *v.* director general, as agent; [decided Mar. 8, 1924; report of commission]. 1924. [1]+54–56 p. ([Opinion] 9284.) [From Interstate Commerce Commission reports, v. 88.] * Paper, 5c.

—— No. 14672, Northwestern Clay Manufacturing Company *v.* Rock Island Southern Railway Company, director general, as agent, et al.; decided Mar. 7, 1924; report of commission. [1924.] p. 131–134. ([Opinion] 9298.) [From Interstate Commerce Commission reports, v. 88.] * Paper, 5c.

Coal-cars. No. 627, in Supreme Court. Oct. term, 1923, United States and Interstate Commerce Commission *v.* New River Company et al., appeal from district court for southern district of West Virginia; brief for Interstate Commerce Commission. 1924. cover-title, ii+38 p. ‡

Coffins. No. 14736, Wichita Board of Commerce et al. *v.* Atchison, Topeka & Santa Fe Railway Company et al.; decided Feb. 12, 1924; report of commission. [1924.] p. 649–652. ([Opinion] 9245.) [From Interstate Commerce Commission reports, v. 87.] *Paper, 5c.

Demurrage. No. 12725, United States Steel Products Company *v.* director general, as agent, Alabama & Vicksburg Railway Company, et al.; [no. 14209, Mitsui & Company, Limited, *v.* director general, as agent]; decided Mar. 10, 1924; report [and order] of commission. [1924.] 57–61+[1] p. ([Opinion] 9285.) [Report from Interstate Commerce Commission reports, v. 88.] *Paper, 5c.

—— No. 14188, Gerhard & Hey, Incorporated, *v.* director general, as agent, Delaware, Lackawanna & Western Railroad Company, et al.; decided Mar. 7, 1924; report [and order] of commission. [1924.] 293–294+[1] p. ([Opinion] 9342.) [Report from Interstate Commerce Commission reports, v. 88.] *Paper, 5c.

—— No.14456, James W. Person *v.* Illinois Central Railroad Company; decided Mar. 7, 1924; report of commission. [1924.] p. 21–23. ([Opinion] 9277.) [From Interstate Commerce Commission reports, v. 88.] *Paper, 5c.

—— No. 14738, Marfield Grain Company *v.* Ahnapee & Western Railway Company; [decided Mar. 7, 1924; report and order of commission]. 1924. [1]+126–128+[1] p. ([Opinion] 9296.) [Report from Interstate Commerce Commission reports, v. 88.] *Paper, 5c.

—— No. 14932, John A. McGarry & Company *v.* Wabash Railway Company; decided Mar. 26, 1924; report [and order] of commission. [1924.] 301–302+[1] p. ([Opinion] 9345.) [Report from Interstate Commerce Commission reports, v. 88.] *Paper, 5c.

Dock charges. Investigation and suspension docket no. 1960, dockage, handling, and storage charges at Duluth, Minn., and other Lake Superior ports; [decided Mar. 10, 1924; report and order of commission]. 1924. [1]+24–26+[1] p. ([Opinion] 9278.) [Report from Interstate Commerce Commission reports, v. 88.] *Paper, 5c.

Drain-tiles. No. 12801, Mason City Brick & Tile Company et al. *v.* director general, as agent; decided Mar. 8, 1924; report of commission. [1924.] p. 37–45. ([Opinion] 9281.) [From Interstate Commerce Commission reports, v. 88.] *Paper, 5c.

Explosives. Supplement 1 to Regulations for transportation of explosives and other dangerous articles by freight and express and as baggage, including specifications for shipping containers prescribed under act of Mar. 4, 1921, binding upon all common carriers engaged in interstate or foreign commerce, and upon all shippers making shipments via such carriers by land. 1924. iv+62 p. il. [Contains all outstanding amendments to Regulations revised, effective Jan. 1, 1923.] *Paper, 5c.

Fourth section order, general, no. 21; Mar. 4, 1924. [1924.] 8 p. [Relates to 4th section of act to regulate commerce as amended. This is Fourth section order 8900, superseding Fourth section order 383 as amended, general, no. 7, and Fourth section circular 5.] *Paper, 5c.

Freight rates. Proposed report, no. 13494, southern class rate investigation. [1924.] [1]+182 p. il. 1 pl. 4 maps. *Paper, 35c.

Grain. Investigation and suspension docket no. 2000, grain and grain products from Minnesota and Wisconsin to various destinations; decided Mar. 31, 1924; report [and order] of commission. [1924.] 365–367+ii p. ([Opinion] 9362.) [Report from Interstate Commerce Commission reports, v. 88.] *Paper, 5c.

—— No. 13406, Corporation Commission of Oklahoma *v.* Arkansas Railroad et al.; decided Mar. 8, 1924; supplemental report [and supplemental order] of commission. [1924.] p. 101, [1]. ([Opinion] 9123.) [Report from Interstate Commerce Commission reports, v. 87.] *Paper, 5c.

—— No. 13788, Portland Flouring Mills Company *v.* Spokane, Portland & Seattle Railway Company et al.; decided Mar. 7, 1924; report [and order] of commission. [1924.] 99–102+[1] p. ([Opinion] 9290.) [Report from Interstate Commerce Commission reports, v. 88.] *Paper, 5c.

Graphite. No. 13836, United States Graphite Company *v.* director general, as agent, and Southern Pacific Railroad Company of Mexico; [no. 13945, same *v.* same]; decided Mar. 7, 1924; report [and order] of commission. [1924.] 157–160+[1] p. ([Opinion] 9303.) [Report from Interstate Commerce Commission reports, v. 88.] *Paper, 5c.

Insecticides. No. 12751, Sweet Dreams Company *v.* Louisville & Nashville Railroad Company et al.; decided Mar. 8, 1924; report [and order] of commission. [1924.] 33–36+[1] p. ([Opinion] 9280.) [Report from Interstate Commerce Commission reports, v. 88.] *Paper, 5c.

Iron. No. 11733, Parkersburg Rig & Reel Company *v.* Baltimore & Ohio Railroad Company et al.; [no. 13980, same *v.* same]; decided Mar. 4, 1924; report [and order] of commission on further hearing. [1924.] 49–53+[1] p. ([Opinion] 9283.) [Report from Interstate Commerce Commission reports, v. 88.] *Paper, 5c.

Jackson and Eastern Railway. Finance docket no. 1539, bonds of Jackson & Eastern Railway; decided Mar. 10, 1924; supplemental report of commission. [1924.] p. 515–516. ([Finance decision] 1243.) [From Interstate Commerce Commission reports, v. 86.] *Paper, 5c.

Kansas City Telephone Company. Finance docket no. 3453, purchase of stock of Kansas City Telephone Co. by Southwestern Bell Telephone Co.; decided Mar. 15, 1924; report of commission. [1924.] p. 525–528. ([Finance decision] 1246.) [From Interstate Commerce Commission reports, v. 86.] *Paper, 5c.

Kentwood and Eastern Railway. Before Interstate Commerce Commission, valuation docket no. 130, Kentwood & Eastern Railway Company, *in re* protest of Illinois Central Railroad Company, lessor; brief in support of tentative valuation. 1924. cover-title, 10 p. ‡

Lighterage. No. 12104, Midland Linseed Products Company *v.* director general, as agent, Erie Railroad Company, et al.; decided Mar. 14, 1924; report [and order] of commission. [1924.] 247–249+[1] p. ([Opinion] 9327.) [Report from Interstate Commerce Commission reports, v. 88.] *Paper, 5c.

Linseed-oil. No. 15403, Midland Linseed Products Company *v.* New York, Susquehanna & Western Railroad Company et al.; decided Mar. 20, 1924; report of commission. [1924.] p. 329–330. ([Opinion] 9353.) [From Interstate Commerce Commission reports, v. 88.] *Paper, 5c.

Lufkin, Hemphill and Gulf Railway. Before Interstate Commerce Commission, valuation docket no. 97, Lufkin, Hemphill & Gulf Railway Company; brief in support of tentative valuation. 1924. cover-title, 11 p. ‡

Lumber. No. 13833, Hampton & Branchville Railroad & Lumber Company *v.* Atlantic Coast Line Railroad Company et al.; decided Mar. 7, 1924; report [and order] of commission. [1924.] 77–89+[1] p. ([Opinion] 9287.) [Report from Interstate Commerce Commission reports, v. 88.] *Paper, 5c.

—— No. 14834, National Lumber Company *v.* Norfolk & Western Railway Company; decided Mar. 26, 1924; report [and order] of commission. [1924.] 357–360+[1] p. ([Opinion] 9360.) [Report from Interstate Commerce Commission reports, v. 88.] *Paper, 5c.

Magnolia leaves. No. 13977, Walter Armacost & Company *v.* Merchants & Miners Transportation Company, director general, as agent, et al.; decided Mar. 7, 1924; report [and order] of commission. [1924.] 185–187+[1] p. ([Opinion] 9309.) [Report from Interstate Commerce Commission reports, v. 88.] *Paper, 5c.

Matches. No. 14569, American Splint Corporation *v.* Canadian Pacific Railway Company et al.; decided Mar. 7, 1924; report [and order] of commission. [1924.] 221–224+[1] p. ([Opinion] 9321.) [Report from Interstate Commerce Commission reports, v. 88.] *Paper, 5c.

Meat. No. 14146, Cleveland Provision Company *v.* Alabama Great Southern Railroad Company et al.; decided Mar. 7, 1924; report [and order] of commission. [1924.] 161–166+ii p. ([Opinion] 9304.) [Report from Interstate Commerce Commission reports, v. 88.] *Paper, 5c.

Missouri Pacific Railroad. Finance docket no. 651, guaranty settlement with Missouri Pacific R. R.; decided Mar. 17, 1924; report of commission. [1924.] p. 549–552. ([Finance decision] 1253.) [From Interstate Commerce Commission reports, v. 86.] *Paper, 5c.

Muncie and Western Railroad. Before Interstate Commerce · Commission, valuation docket no. 158, Muncie and Western Railroad Company; brief in support of tentative valuation. 1924. cover-title, 10 p. ‡

New Orleans Great Northern Railroad. Before Interstate Commerce Commission, valuation docket no. 305, New Orleans Great Northern Railroad Company; brief in support of tentative valuation. 1924. cover-title, i+36 p. ‡

New Park and Fawn Grove Railroad. Finance docket no. 689, guaranty settlement with New Park & Fawn Grove R. R.; decided Mar. 13, 1924; report of commission. [1924.] p. 507–509. ([Finance decision] 1240.) [From Interstate Commerce Commission reports, v. 86.] * Paper, 5c.

Norfolk and Western Railway. Finance docket no. 3497, Norfolk & Western equipment trust; 1924; decided Mar. 19, 1924; report of commission. [1924.] p. 553–556. ([Finance decision] 1254.) [From Interstate Commerce Commission reports, v. 86.] * Paper, 5c.

Norwood and St. Lawrence Railroad. Finance docket no. 3356, notes of Norwood & St. Lawrence R. R.; approved Mar. 3, 1924; amendatory order. [1924.] p. 487. ([Finance decision] 1234.) [From Interstate Commerce Commission reports, v. 86.] * Paper, 5c.

Oklahoma City Shawnee Interurban Railway. Finance docket no. 3326, securities of Oklahoma City Shawnee Interurban Railway; decided Mar. 10, 1924; report of commission. [1924.] p. 517–520. ([Finance decision] 1244.) [From Interstate Commerce Commission reports, v. 86.] * Paper, 5c.

Oregon-Washington Railroad and Navigation Company. Finance docket no. 3429, construction of branch by Oregon-Washington R. R. & Nav. Co.; decided Mar. 12, 1924; report of commission. [1924.] p. 521–524. ([Finance decision] 1245.). [From Interstate Commerce Commission reports, v. 86.] * Paper, 5c.

Paper. Fourth section application no. 12278, paper and paper articles from Wisconsin, Minnesota, Michigan, and Canada to New Orleans, La.; decided Mar. 11, 1924; report [and 4th section order] no. 8891] of commission. [1924.] 345–353+[1] p. ([Opinion] 9358.) [Report from Interstate Commerce Commission reports, v. 88.] * Paper, 5c.

Passenger rates. No. 11541, Arizona Corporation Commission et al. v. Arizona Eastern Railroad Company et al.; [decided Mar. 10, 1924; supplemental report and supplemental order of commission]. 1924. [1]+90–93+[1] p. ([Opinion] 9288.) [Report from Interstate Commerce Commission reports, v. 88.] * Paper, 5c.

Petroleum. No. 14620, Lincoln Oil Refining Company v. Cleveland, Cincinnati, Chicago & St. Louis Railway Company et al.; decided Mar. 7, 1924; report [and order] of commission. [1924.] 269–272+[1] p. ([Opinion] 9334.) [Report from Interstate Commerce Commission reports, v. 88.] * Paper, 5c.

Portland Terminal Company. Finance docket no. 3476, Portland Terminal notes; [decided Mar. 17, 1924; report of commission]. 1924. [1]+546–548 p. ([Finance decision] 1252.) [From Interstate Commerce Commission reports, v. 86.] * Paper, 5c.

Pullman car surcharges, data with reference to surcharges on Pullman cars by rail carriers; presented by Mr. Smith; 1924. 13 p. (S. doc. 81. 68th Cong. 1st sess.) * Paper, 5c.

Railroad accidents. Accident bulletin 90, collisions, derailments, and other accidents resulting in injury to persons, equipment, or roadbed, arising from operation of steam roads used in interstate commerce, July–Sept. 1923; [prepared in] Bureau of Statistics. 1924. iii+16 p. 4° [Quarterly.] * Paper, 5c. single copy quarterly issue, 25c. a yr.; foreign subscription, 40c.
5—41547

—— Report of director of Bureau of Safety in re investigation of accident which occurred on line of Union Traction Company of Indiana near Ingalls, Ind., on Feb. 2, 1924. [1924.]. 16 p. il. * Paper, 5c.   A 24—690

—— Report of director of Bureau of Safety in re investigation of accident which occurred on Nashville, Chattanooga and St. Louis Railway at Kennesaw, Ga., on Dec. 22, 1923 [accompanied by report of engineer-physicist]. [1924.] 28 p. il. * Paper, 10c.   A 24—689

—— Summary of accident investigation reports, no. 18, Oct.–Dec. 1923; [prepared in] Bureau of Safety. 1924. iii+51 p. [Quarterly.] * Paper, 5c. single copy, 15c. a yr.; foreign subscription, 25c.   A 20—942

Railroad employees. Wage statistics, class 1 steam roads in United States, including 15 switching and terminal companies, Feb. 1924; [prepared in] Bureau of Statistics. [1924.] [4] p. il. oblong large 8° †

Railroads. Freight and passenger service operating statistics of class 1 steam roads in United States, compiled from 160 reports of freight statistics representing 175 roads and from 158 reports of passenger statistics representing 173 roads (switching and terminal companies not included), Feb. 1924 and 1923 [and 2 months ended with Feb. 1924 and 1923; prepared in] Bureau of Statistics. Feb. 1924. [2] p. oblong large 8° [Subject to revision.] †

—— Operating revenues and operating expenses of class 1 steam roads in United States (for 193 steam roads, including 15 switching and terminal companies), Feb. 1924 and 1923 [and] 2 months ended with Feb. 1924 and 1923; [prepared in] Bureau of Statistics. Feb. 1924. 1 p. oblong large 8° [Subject to revision.] †

—— Operating revenues and operating expenses of large steam roads, selected items for roads with annual operating revenues above $25,000,000, Feb. 1924 and 1923 [and] 2 months ended with Feb. 1924 and 1923; [prepared in] Bureau of Statistics. Feb. 1924. [2] p. oblong large 8° [Subject to revision.] †

—— Operating statistics of large steam roads, selected items for Feb. 1924, compared with Feb. 1923, for roads with annual operating revenues above $25,000.000; [prepared in] Bureau of Statistics. Feb. 1924. [2] p. oblong large 8° [Subject to revision.] †

—— Order [promulgated] at session of Interstate Commerce Commission, division 4, held on 17th of March, 1924, in matter of recovery and payment of excess net railway operating income under provisions of sec. 15A of interstate commerce act, year ended Dec. 31, 1923. [1924.] 10 p. * Paper, 5c.

—— Revenue traffic statistics of class 1 steam roads in United States, including mixed-train service (compiled from 162 reports representing 177 steam roads, switching and terminal companies not included), Jan. 1924 and 1923; [prepared in] Bureau of Statistics. Jan. 1924. 1 p. oblong large 8° [Subject to revision.] †

Refrigeration. Investigation and suspension docket no. 1990, furnishing ice and salt for protection of perishable freight; decided Mar. 31, 1924; report [and order] of commission. [1924.] 361–364+[1] p. ([Opinion] 9361.) [Report from Interstate Commerce Commission reports, v. 88.] * Paper, 5c.

St. Johnsbury and Lake Champlain Railroad. Finance docket no. 802, guaranty settlement with St. Johnsbury & Lake Champlain R. R.; [decided Mar. 13, 1924; report of commission]. 1924. [1]+504–506 p. ([Finance decision] 1239.) [From Interstate Commerce Commission reports, v. 86.] * Paper, 5c.

St. Louis, Kennett and Southeastern Railroad. Finance docket no. 3480, bonds of St. Louis, Kennett & Southeastern R. R.; decided Mar. 10, 1924; report of commission. [1924.] p. 535–536. ([Finance decision] 1248.) [From Interstate Commerce Commission reports, v. 86.] * Paper, 5c.

Salmon. No. 14351, Traffic Bureau of Phoenix Chamber of Commerce et al. v. Atchison, Topeka & Santa Fe Railway Company et al.; [decided Mar. 7, 1924; report and order of commission]. 1924. [1]+178–182+ii p. ([Opinion] 9307.) [Report from Interstate Commerce Commission reports, v. 88.] * Paper, 5c.

Sorghum. No. 12653, Mangelsdorf Seed Company v. Atchison, Topeka & Santa Fe Railway Company et. al.; [decided Mar. 13, 1924; report and order of commission]. 1924. [1]+120–126+ii p. ([Opinion] 9295.) [Report from Interstate Commerce Commission reports, v. 88.] * Paper, 5c.

Steamboats. Schedule of sailings (as furnished by steamship companies named herein) of steam vessels which are registered under laws of United States and which are intended to load general cargo at ports in United States for foreign destinations, Apr. 15–May 31, 1924; no. 20; issued by Section of Tariffs, Bureau of Traffic. 1924. iii+49 p. 4° [Monthly. No. 20 cancels no. 19.] †

Steel. No. 14163, National Car Coupler Company v. Baltimore & Ohio Railroad Company et al.; decided Mar. 7, 1924; report [and order] of commission. [1924.] 325–328+[1] p. ([Opinion] 9352.) [Report from Interstate Commerce Commission reports, v. 88.] * Paper, 5c.

Sugar. No. 13369. Burlington Shippers' Association *v*. Atchison, Topeka & Santa Fe Railway Company et al.; [decided Mar. 8, 1924; report and order of commission]. 1924. [1]+46–48+[1] p. ([Opinion] 9282.) [Report from Interstate Commerce Commission reports, v. 88.] * Paper, 5c.

Sulphur. No. 12831, Butterworth-Judson Corporation *v*. director general, as agent, and Central Railroad Company of New Jersey; decided Jan. 14 ,1924; report of commission on further argument. [1924.] p. 19–20. ([Opinion] 9276.) [From Interstate Commerce Commission reports, v. 88.] * Paper, 5c.

Texas Southeastern Railroad. Finance docket no. 2299, deficit settlement with Texas South-Eastern R. R.; decided Mar. 6, 1924; report of commission. [1924.] p. 483–484. ([Finance decision] 1232.) [From Interstate Commerce Commission reports, v. 86.] * Paper, 5c.

Time. No. 10122, standard time zone investigation; decided Mar. 13, 1924; 10th supplemental report [and order] of commission. [1924.] 135–142+ [1] p. ([Opinion] 9299.) [Report from Interstate Commerce Commission reports, v. 88.] * Paper, 5c.

Valley Railroad. Finance docket no. 3484, bonds of Valley Railroad; decided Mar. 15, 1924; report of commission. [1924.] p. 537–540. ([Finance decision] 1240.) [From Interstate Commerce Commission reports, v. 86.] * Paper, 5c.

Wheat. No. 13776. Portland Flouring Mills Company *v*. Great Northern Railway Company et al.; [decided Mar. 7, 1924; report and order of commission]. 1924. [1]+94–98+[1] p. ([Opinion] 9289.) [Report from Interstate Commerce Commission reports, v. 88.] * Paper, 5c.

JUSTICE DEPARTMENT

American Railway Express Company. No. 666, in Supreme Court, Oct. term, 1923, United States and Interstate Commerce Commission *v*. American Railway Express Company and Seaboard Air Line Railway Company, appeal from district court for northern district of Georgia; brief for United States. 1924. cover-title, ii+46 p. ‡

Arnstein, Jules. No. 895, in Supreme Court, Oct. term, 1923, Jules Arnstein, alias Nicky Arnstein [et al.] *v*. United States, on petition for writ of certiorari to Court of Appeals of District of Columbia; brief in opposition to petition. 1924. cover-title, 8 p. ‡

Bickett Coal and Coke Company. In Court of Claims, Bickett Coal and Coke Company *v*. United States, no. D–1; demurrer to petition [and brief in support of demurrer]. [1924.] p. 29–40, large 8° ‡

Briesen, Fritz von. No. 4101, Court of Appeals of District of Columbia, Jan. term, 1924, Fritz von Briesen, Hans von Briesen, and Otto von Schrenk *v*. Thomas W. Miller, as Alien Property Custodian, Frank White, as Treasurer of United States, and certain fund; brief on behalf of Thomas W. Miller, as Alien Property Custodian, and Frank White, as Treasurer of United States. 1924. cover-title, iii+34 p. ‡

Brown, Wm. A., & Co. No. 946, in Supreme Court, Oct. term, 1923, William A. Brown & Company et al. *v*. United States, on petition for writ of certiorari to Court of Customs Appeals; brief for United States. 1924. cover-title, 8 p. ‡

Burnes National Bank. No. 762, in Supreme Court, Oct. term, 1923, Missouri, at relation of Burnes National Bank of St. Joseph, *v*. A. B. Duncan, judge of probate court of Buchanan County, Mo., in error to Supreme Court of Missouri; brief for United States as amicus curiae. 1924. cover-title, ii+35 p. ‡

California Cooperative Canneries. No. 4071, in Court of Appeals of District of Columbia, Jan. term, 1924, California Cooperative Canneries *v*. United States, Swift & Company, et al., appeal from Supreme Court of District of Columbia; brief on behalf of United States. 1924. cover-title, ii+47 p. ‡

California Wholesale Grocers' Association. In equity, no —, in district court in and for southern district of California, southern division, United States *v*. California Wholesale Grocers' Association et al.; bill of complaint. 1924. cover-title, 17 p. ‡

Central New England Railway. In Court of Claims, Central New England Railway Company *v.* United States. no. B–45; defendant's supplemental request for findings of fact and brief on remand. [1924.] p. 107–119, large 8° ‡

Chicago, Wilmington and Franklin Coal Company. In Court of Claims, Chicago, Wilmington and Franklin Coal Company *v.* United States, no. B–11; defendant's brief. [1924.] p. 189–192. large 8° ‡

Coast Coaling and Engineering Company. In Court of Claims, Coast Coaling & Engineering Co. *v.* United States; no. C–909; defendant's amended answer and counterclaim. [1924.] p. 17–20, large 8° ‡

Crosland, John G. No. 841, in Supreme Court, Oct. term, 1923, John G. Crosland *v.* United States, on petition for writ of certiorari to circuit court of appeals for 3d circuit; brief for United States in opposition. 1924. cover-title, 6 p. ‡

Cuyahoga Stamping and Machine Company. In Court of Claims, Cuyahoga Stamping & Machine Co. *v.* United States. no. 114–A; defendant's objections to plaintiff's request for findings of fact and brief. [1924.] p. 43–47, large 8° ‡

Davis Sewing Machine Company. In Court of Claims, Davis Sewing Machine Company *v.* United States, no. B–17; defendant's objections to plaintiff's request for findings of fact, defendant's request for findings of fact, and brief. [1924.] p. 49–74, large 8° ‡

Deutsch-Australische Dampfschiffs-Gesellschaft. In Court of Claims, May 11, 1923, Deutsch-Australische Dampfschiffs-Gesellschaft *v.* United States, no. C–576; demurrer [and] brief. [1924.] p. 9–30. large 8° ‡

Dong Yick Yuen. No. 961, in Supreme Court. Oct. term, 1923, Dong Yick Yuen *v.* John F. Dunton, Chinese inspector in charge, port of New York, on petition for writ of certiorari to circuit court of appeals for 2d circuit; brief for respondent in opposition. 1924. cover-title, 4 p. ‡

Durbrow & Hearne. No. 2338, Court of Customs Appeals, Durbrow & Hearne *v.* United States; brief for United States. 1924. cover-title. 16 p. ‡

Eaton, William A. Interference no. 49384. in Patent Office, before board of examiners in chief, William A. Eaton *v.* Ralph R. Beal *v.* Ernst F. W. Alexanderson; brief for William A. Eaton. 1924. cover-title, i+26 p. il. ‡

Falconer, Raleigh M. No. 882, in Supreme Court, Oct. term, 1923, Raleigh Monroe Falconer *v.* United States, on petition for writ of certiorari to circuit court of appeals for 9th circuit; brief for United States in opposition. 1924. cover-title, 4 p. ‡

Gandolfi, L., & Co. No. 2364, Court of Customs Appeals, United States *v.* L. Gandolfi & Co.; brief for United States. 1924. cover-title, 12 p. ‡

Government officials. Practice by ex-officials before Department of Justice, letter, in response to resolution, furnishing information relative to ex-Members of Congress and ex-Cabinet officers who, since Jan. 1. 1918, have appeared as attorneys or agents before Department of Justice advocating claims against Government. Apr. 7. 1924. 20 p. (S. doc. 82, 68th Cong. 1st sess.) *Paper, 5c.* 24—26414

Great Britain. In Court of Claims. George V, king of United Kingdom of Great Britain and Ireland and of Dominions beyond the Seas, Emperor of India, *v.* United States, no. C–1001; defendant's objections to plaintiff's request for findings of fact, defendant's request for findings of fact, and brief. [1924.] p. 17–25, large 8° ‡

Hester, Charlie. No. 243, in Supreme Court. Oct. term, 1923, Charlie Hester *v.* United States, in error to district court for western district of South Carolina; brief for defendant in error. 1924. cover-title, ii+23 p. ‡

Hewitt, Erskine. No. C–769, in Court of Claims, Erskine Hewitt *v.* United States; defendant's supplemental brief on demurrer. 1924. cover-title, i+89–130 p. large 8° ‡

International Arms and Fuze Company. In Court of Claims. International Arms & Fuze Company *v.* United States, no. C–220; defendant's demurrer to claimant's petition [and brief on demurrer]. [1924.] p. 41–47, large 8° ‡

Joyce, Thomas. No. 831, in Supreme Court, Oct. term, 1923. Thomas Joyce *v.* United States, on petition for writ of certiorari to circuit court of appeals for 9th circuit; brief for United States in opposition. 1924. cover-title, 5 p. ‡

Kelley Hardware Company. No. 2355, Court of Customs Appeals, United States *v.* Kelley Hardware Co.; brief for United States. 1924. cover-title, 14 p. ‡

Koeller-Struss Company. No. 2332, Court of Customs Appeals. Koeller-Struss Company *v.* United States; brief for United States. 1924. cover-title, 10 p. ‡

Lake Fairlie, steamship. In circuit court of appeals for 5th circuit, United States, owner of steamships Lake Fairlie [etc.] *vs.* Sugarland Industries [et al.], no. 4126, appeal from district court for southern district of Texas; [transcript of record]. [1924.] p. 240–247. ‡

—— No. —, in Supreme Court, Oct. term, 1923, United States, owner steamships Lake Fairlie, etc., *v.* Sugarland Industries; petition for writ of certiorari to circuit court of appeals for 5th circuit, and brief in support thereof. 1924. cover-title, 9 p. ‡

Levy, J. W., Corporation. Nos. 2333 and 2337, Court of Customs Appeals, J. W. Levy Corporation et al. *v.* United States; United States *v.* J. W. Levy Corporation et al.; brief for United States. 1924. cover-title, 15 p. ‡

Louisiana. No. 289, in Supreme Court, Oct. term, 1923, Hubert Work, Secretary of Interior, *v.* Louisiana, appeal from Court of Appeals of District of Columbia; brief for appellant. 1924. cover-title, ii+40 p. ‡

Marion and Rye Valley Railway. No. C–699, in Court of Claims, Marion & Rye valley Railway Company *v.* United States; defendant's objections to plaintiff's request for findings of fact, defendant's request for findings of fact, defendant's brief. 1924. cover-title, p. 97–167, large 8° ‡

Marks, Ernest E., & Co. No. 2235, Court of Customs Appeals, Ernest E. Marks & Co. et al. *v.* United States; brief for United States, appellee, in opposition to appellants' petition for rehearing. 1924. cover-title, 4 p. ‡

Marshall, Thurman W. In Court of Claims, Thurman W. Marshall *v.* United States, no. 70–B; defendant's brief. [1924.] p. 21–23, large 8° ‡

Meadows, Wye & Co. No. 2248, Court of Customs Appeals, Meadows, Wye & Company *v.* United States; brief for United States. 1924. cover-title, 8 p. ‡

Missouri, Kansas and Texas Railway of Texas. In Court of Claims, [Charles E.] Schaff, receiver of Missouri, Kansas & Texas Railway Company of Texas, *v.* United States, no. A–257; defendant's objections to plaintiff's request for findings of fact, defendant's request for findings of fact, and brief on remand. [1924.] p. 43–52, large 8° ‡

Mitchell, Irvine. In Court of Claims, Irvine Mitchell *v.* United States, no. B–356; defendant's brief. [1924.] p. 14–17, large 8° ‡

Moore, Alfred F. No. C–972, in Court of Claims, Girard Trust Company, George Stevenson, Walter R. verner, Robert Glendinning, trustees of estate of Alfred F. Moore, *v.* United States; defendant's request for findings of fact, statement of case, brief. 1924. cover-title, p. 35–58, large 8° ‡

Morgan, Joseph F. In Court of Claims, Joseph F. Morgan *v.* United States, no. B–211; defendant's objection to plaintiff's request for finding of fact, defendant's request for findings of fact, and brief. [1924.] p. 107–113, large 8° ‡

National Malleable and Steel Castings Company. In district court for northern district of Ohio, eastern division, United States *v.* National Malleable and Steel Castings Company et al.; indictment. 1924. cover-title, 10 p. ‡

National Paper and Type Company. No. 877, in Supreme Court, Oct. term, 1923, National Paper and Type Company *v.* Frank K. Bowers, collector of internal revenue [for 2d district of New York], in error to district court for southern district of New York; motion to advance. 1924. cover-title, 2 p. ‡

New Creek Company. No. 923, in Supreme Court, Oct. term, 1923, New Creek Company *v.* Ephraim Lederer, collector of internal revenue [for 1st district of Pennsylvania], petition for writ of certiorari to circuit court of appeals for 3d circuit; brief for United States in opposition. 1924. cover-title, 6 p. ‡

New England Steamship Company. In Court of Claims, New England Steamship Co. *v.* United States, no. B–46; defendant's supplemental request for findings of fact and brief on remand. [1924.] p. 53–65. large 8° ‡

New River Company. No. 627. in Supreme Court, Oct. term, 1923, United States and Interstate Commerce Commission *v.* New River Company [et al.], appeal from district court for southern district of West Virginia; brief for United States. 1924. cover-title, iii+23 p. ‡

New York, New Haven and Hartford Railroad. In Court of Claims, New York, New Haven and Hartford Railroad Company *v.* United States, no. B–44; defendant's supplemental request for findings of fact and brief on remand. [1924.] p. 99–112, large 8° ‡

Nixon, Lewis. In Court of Claims, Lewis Nixon *v.* United States, no. D–175; demurrer [and] brief. [1924.] p. 7–10, large 8° ‡

Norcross Audit and Statistical Bureau. No. 302. in district court for western division of western district of Missouri, United States *vs.* Hiram Norcross, operating as Norcross Audit & Statistical Bureau [et al.]; final decree. 1924. cover-title, 12 p. ‡

Nugent Construction Corporation. In Court of Claims, Nugent Construction Corporation *r.* United States, no. B–100; defendant's objections to plaintiff's request for findings of fact. defendant's request for findings of fact, defendant's brief. [1924.] p. 217–231, large 8° ‡

Peabody, Henry W., & Co. In Court of Claims. Henry W. Peabody & Co. *v.* United States, no. B–425; defendant's brief. [1924.] p. 30–38, large 8°. ‡

Prohibition. Memorandum in regard to enforcement of national prohibition act by State and municipal officers [of New York State]. [1924.] 3 p. †

Roger & Gallet. No. 2335. Court of Customs Appeals, Roger & Gallet *v.* United States; brief for United States. 1924. cover-title, 10 p. ‡

St. Louis, San Francisco and Texas Railway. In Court of Claims, St. Louis, San Francisco & Texas Railway Company *v.* United States, no. C–58; defendant's motion for new trial. and brief in support thereof. [1924.] p. 15–16, large 8° ‡

Schaefer, Charles. jr. In Court of Claims, Charles Schaefer, jr., *v.* United States, no. 13–A; defendant's motion for amendment of findings of fact and for new trial. [1924.] p. 254–281, large 8° ‡

Sigman. Leon. No. 916. in Supreme Court, Oct. term, 1923, Leon Sigman *v.* Mabel G. Reinecke, individually and as collector of internal revenue, on petition for writ of certiorari to circuit court of appeals for 7th circuit; memorandum in opposition to petition. 1924. cover-title, 2 p. ‡

Skinner & Eddy Corporation. Original, no. 28, in Supreme Court, Oct. term, 1923. in matter of Skinner & Eddy Corporation; brief of solicitor general in behalf of Court of Claims on return to rule to show cause. 1924. cover-title, i+21 p. ‡

Southern California Wholesale Grocers' Association. In equity, no. —, in district court in and for southern district of California, southern, division, United States *v.* Southern California Wholesale Grocers' Association, et al.; bill of complaint. 1924. cover-title, 15 p. ‡

Southern Pacific Company. In Supreme Court, Southern Pacific Company *v.* United States, no. B–367; defendant's objection to plaintiff's request for findings of fact. defendant's request for findings of fact, defendant's brief. [1924.] p. 43–46, large 8°. ‡

Southern Paper Company, Limited. No. 2312. Court of Customs Appeals. United States *v.* Southern Paper Co. Ltd.; brief for United States. 1924. cover-title, 11 p. ‡

Stearn, Louis. Nos. 262. 263. in Supreme Court, Oct. term, 1923. Harry H. Weiss, collector of internal revenue [for 18th district of Ohio], *v.* Louis Stearn; [same] *r.* John G. White. on writ of certiorari to circuit court of appeals for 6th circuit; brief for petitioner. 1924. cover-title, i+30 p. ‡

Utah-Idaho Wholesale Grocers' Association. In equity no. —. in district court in and for district of Utah, United States *v.* Utah-Idaho Wholesale Grocers' Association et al.; bill of complaint. 1924. cover-title, 18 p. ‡

Vandegrift, F. B., & Co. No. 2310. Court of Customs Appeals, F. B. vandegrift & Co. *v.* United States; brief for United States. 1924. cover-title, 14 p. ‡

Villamil, Sobrinos de. No. 2359. Court of Customs Appeals. United States *v.* Sobrinos de villamil; brief for United States. 1924. cover-title, 12 p. ‡

Wall Rope Works, Incorporated. In Court of Claims, Wall Rope Works (Inc.), *v.* United States, no. B–448; objections to plaintiff's request for findings of fact [defendant's request for findings of fact, and brief]. [1924.] p. 68–82, large 8° ‡

West Virginia Pulp and Paper Company. No. —, in Supreme Court, Oct. term, 1923, Frank K. Bowers, collector of internal revenue [for 2d district of New York], *v.* West Virginia Pulp and Paper Company; petition for writ of certiorari to circuit court of appeals for 2d circuit, and brief in support thereof. 1924. cover-title, 12 p. ‡

—— United States circuit court of appeals for 2d circuit, Oct. term, 1923, decided Feb. 4, 1924, Frank K. Bowers, collector of internal revenue for 2d circuit of New York, *v.* West Virginia Pulp & Paper Company, no. 211, in error to district court for southern district of New York; [transcript of record]. [1924.] 2 p. ‡

Whittemore, Herbert L. Interference no. 48089, in Patent Office, before examiner of interferences, Whittemore *v.* Rapp and vanorio; brief for Whittemore. 1924. cover-title, 7 p. ‡

—— Interference no. 48089, in Patent Office, Herbert L. Whittemore *v.* John W. Rapp and Joseph L. Vanorio; record for Herbert L. Whittemore. 1924. cover-title, i+14 p. ‡

Wigington, Joe. No. 907, in Supreme Court, Oct. term, 1923, Joe Wigington *v.* United States, on petition for writ of certiorari to circuit court of appeals for 4th circuit; brief for United States in opposition. 1924. cover-title, 5 p. ‡

Wilson, C. R., Body Company. In Court of Claims, C. R. Wilson Body Company *v.* United States, no. 79–A; objections to plaintiff's request for findings of fact, defendant's request for findings of fact, and brief thereon. [1924.] p. 185–218, large 8° ‡

Wisconsin. No. —, original, in Supreme Court, Oct. term, 1923, United States *v.* Wisconsin; motion for leave to file bill of complaint, and bill of complaint. 1924. cover-title, 19 p. ‡

Wong Doo. No. 736, in Supreme Court, Oct. term, 1923, Wong Doo *v.* United States, on writ of certiorari to circuit court of appeals for 6th circuit; brief for United States. 1924. cover-title, 14 p. ‡

LABOR DEPARTMENT

CHILDREN'S BUREAU.

Child labor, outlines for study [with lists of references, by Ellen N. Matthews. Nettie P. McGill, and Ella A. Merritt]; separate 4 [from] Child care and child welfare. 3d edition. 1924. vi+61 p. 1 tab. (Bureau publication 93.) [Prepared in cooperation with Federal Board for Vocational Education. Original article from Federal Board for Vocational Education, Bulletin 65. Home economics series 5.] *Paper, 10c.

Hygiene of maternity and childhood, outlines for study [with lists of references]; separate 1 [from] Child care and child welfare. [Reprint with slight changes] 1924. 327 p. il. (Bureau publication 90.) [Prepared in cooperation with Federal Board for Vocational Education. Original article from Federal Board for Vocational Education, Bulletin 65, Home economics series 5. Title-page rearranged from that of previous print.] *Paper, 30c.

EMPLOYMENT SERVICE

Employment agencies. Monthly report of activities of State and municipal employment services cooperating with U. S. Employment Service, Mar. 1924. 1924. iv+9+[1] p. †
L 24—62

Industrial employment information bulletin, v. 4, no. 3; Mar. 1924. [1924.] 20 p. 4° [Monthly.] †
L 21—17

LABOR STATISTICS BUREAU

Employment in selected industries, Mar. 1924. 1924. [1]+12 p. [Monthly.] †

International Association of Public Employment Services. Proceedings of 11th annual meeting of International Association of Public Employment Services, held at Toronto, Canada, Sept. 4–7, 1923. Mar. 1924. vi+56 p. (Bulletin 355; Employment and unemployment series.) * Paper, 10c.
L 16—28

International Association of Public Employment Services—Continued.　Same.
(H. doc. 94, 68th Cong. 1st sess.)
Monthly labor review, v. 18, no. 4; Apr. 1924.　1924.　v+699–931 p. il.　* Paper,
15c. single copy, $1.50 a yr.; foreign subscription, $2.25.　　　　15—26485

SPECIAL ARTICLES.—Convict labor, 1923.—Shifting of occupations among wage earners as determined by occupational history of industrial policyholders; by Louis I. Dublin and Robert J. Vane, jr.—German Metal Workers' Federation, by Fritz Kummer; [translated by Alfred Maylander].—Land law of Esthonia; by Andrew Pranspill.—Steadying worker's income: Establishment unemployment insurance plans; by Margaret Gadsby.—Labor law of Durango, Mexico; by Ethel C. Yohe.—Conciliation work of Department of Labor, Feb. 1924; by Hugh L. Kerwin.—Statistics of immigration, Jan. 1924; by W. W. Husband.

NOTE.—The Review is the medium through which the Bureau publishes the results of original investigations too brief for bulletin purposes, notices of labor legislation by the States or by Congress, and Federal court decisions affecting labor, which from their importance should be given attention before they could ordinarily appear in the bulletins devoted to these subjects. One free subscription will be given to all labor departments and bureaus, workmen's compensation commissions, and other offices connected with the administration of labor laws and organizations exchanging publications with the Labor Statistics Bureau. Others desiring copies may obtain them from the Superintendent of Documents, Washington, D. C., at the prices stated above.

Occupations. Shift ng of occupations among industrial insurance policyholders; [by Louis I. Dublin and Robert J. vane, jr.].　1924.　[1]+732–740 p.　[From Monthly labor review, Apr. 1924.] †

Prices. Prices and cost of living, [1924.] p. 765–793, il. [From Monthly labor review, Apr. 1924.] †

——, Wholesale prices of commodities for Mar. 1924.　1924.　[1]+9 p.
[Monthly.] †　　　　　　　　　　　　　　　　　　　　　　　　L 22—229

NATURALIZATION BUREAU

Citizenship. Suggested program for welcome to new citizens or citizenship graduation exercises. [1924.] 2 p. †

English language. Teaching our language to beg'nners, directions to teachers of candidates for citizenship who are learning to speak English in public schools [with l st of references for teachers]; by Lillian P. Clark; to accompany Federal textbook on citizenship training, pt. 1, Our language. 1924. [1]+51 p. †　　　　　　　　　　　　　　　　　　　　　　L 24—63

PUBLICATIONS AND SUPPLIES DIVISION

Labor Department. Publications of Department of Labor. [Edition of] Apr. 15, 1924. 1924. ii+30 p.　　　　　　　　　　　　　　　　16—26563

LIBRARY OF CONGRESS

Reading room. Information for readers in main reading room; [by Frederick W. Ashley]. 1924. 16 p. 1 pl. †　　　　　　　　　　　　14—30003

COPYRIGHT OFFICE

Canada: Copyright in Canada, act 11 and 12 Geo. V. ch. 24, act to amend and consolidate law relating to copyright; assented to June 4, 1921, and amended June 13, 1923; in effect Jan. 1, 1924. 1924. iii+55 p. (Bulletin 20.)　* Paper, 10c.　　　　　　　　　　　　　　　　　　　　　　　24—26415

Copyright. [Catalogue of copyright entries, new series, pt. 1; group 1, Books, v. 20] no. 123 and 124; Apr. 1924. Apr. 4 and 14, 1924. p. 1409–24. [Issued several times a week.]　　　　　　　　　　　　　　　　6—35347

NOTE.—Each number is issued in 4 parts: pt. 1, group 1, relates to books; pt 1, group 2, to pamphlets, leaflets, contributions to newspapers or periodicals, etc., lectures, sermons, addresses for oral delivery, dramatic compositions, maps, motion pictures; pt. 2, to periodicals; pt. 3, to musical compositions; pt. 4, to works of art, reproductions of a work of art, drawings or plastic works of scientific or technical character, photographs, prints, and pictorial illustrations. Subscriptions for the Catalogue of copyright entries should be made to the Superintendent of Documents, Washington, D. C., instead of to the Register of Copyrights. Prices are as follows: Paper, $3.00 a yr. (4 pts.), foreign subscription, $5.00; pt. 1 (groups 1 and 2), 5c. single copy (group 1, price of group 2 varies), $1.00 a yr., foreign subscription, $2.25; pt. 3, $1.00 a yr., foreign subscription, $1.50; pts. 2 and 4, each 10c. single copy, 50c. a yr., foreign subscription, 70c.

—— Same [pt. 1, group 1, Books, v. 21] no. 1–15; Mar.–Apr. 1924. Mar. 13–Apr. 29, 1924. p. 1–120. [Issued several times a week.]

Copyright—Continued. Same, pt. 1, group 2, Pamphlets, leaflets, contributions to newspapers or periodicals, etc., lectures, sermons, addresses for oral delivery, dramatic compositions, maps, motion pictures, v. 20, no. 10. 1924. ii+1445-1644 p. [Monthly.]

DOCUMENTS DIVISION

Government publications. Monthly check-list of State publications received during Jan. 1924; v. 15, no. 1. 1924. p. 1–51. * Paper, 10c. single copy, $1.00 a yr.; foreign subscription, $1.25.   10—8924
—— Same received during Feb. 1924; v. 15, no. 2. 1924. p. 53–95.

MIXED CLAIMS COMMISSION, UNITED STATES AND GERMANY

Eastern Steamship Lines, Incorporated. Opinion in war-risk insurance premium claim, Mar. 11, 1924, United States on behalf of Eastern Steamship Lines, Inc., v. Germany [docket no. 436]. 1924. iii+71-74 p. ‡
Provident Mutual Life Insurance Company. Nos. 19, 248–256, before Mixed Claims Commission, United States and Germany. United States on behalf of Provident Mutual Life Insurance Company. New York Life Insurance Company, Mutual Life Insurance Company, Penn Mutual Life Insurance Company, Aetna Life Insurance Company, State Mutual Life Assurance Company, Northwestern Mutual Life Insurance Company, Equitable Life Assurance Society, Manhattan Life Insurance Company, Prudential Insurance Company, Metropolitan Life Insurance Company, Travelers Insurance Company, v. Germany; amended reply brief on behalf of United States. 1924. cover-title, ii+122 p. 4° ‡
Shipping Board. Opinion construing phrase "naval and military works or materials" as applied to hull losses and also dealing with requisitioned Dutch ships, Mar. 25, 1924 [United States on its own behalf, acting through Shipping Board and/or Shipping Board Emergency Fleet Corporation, and on behalf of certain of its nationals suffering losses at sea, v. Germany, docket nos. 29, 127, 546–556]. 1924. iii+75-101 p. ‡

NATIONAL ACADEMY OF SCIENCES

Report. Report of National Academy of Sciences [fiscal] year 1923. 1924. vii+156 p. * Paper, 15c.   15—10608
—— Same.., (S. doc. 54, 68th Cong. 1st sess.)

NATIONAL ADVISORY COMMITTEE FOR AERONAUTICS

Aerodynamic forces on airship hulls [with list of references]; by Max M. Munk. 1924. cover-title, 20 p. il. 4° (Report 184.) [Text and illustration on p. 2 and 3 of cover.] *Paper, 10c.   24—26361
Aeronautics. Relation between aeronautic research and aircraft design; by Joseph S. Ames. 1924. cover-title, 15 p. il. 4° [Appendix to Administrative report, 1923.] *Paper, 10c.   24—26416
Beams. Influence of form of wooden beam on its stiffness and strength: 1, Deflection of beams with special reference to shear deformations; by J. A. Newlin and G. W. Trayer. 1924. cover-title. 19 p. il. 4° (Report 180.) [Prepared by Forest Products Laboratory. Text and illustration on p. 2 and 3 of cover.] *Paper, 10c.   24—26417
—— Same: 2, Form factors of beams subjected to transverse loading only; by J. A. Newlin and G. W. Trayer. 1924. cover-title, 19 p. il. 4° (Report 181.) [Prepared by Forest Products Laboratory. Text and illustration on p. 2 and 3 of cover.] *Paper, 10c.
Propellers. Analysis of free flight propeller tests and its application to design [with list of references]; by Max M. Munk. 1924. cover-title. 12 p. il. 4° (Report 183.) [Text and illustration on p. 2 and 3 of cover.] *Paper, 5c.
                                      24—26360

Propellers—Continued. Application of propeller test data to design and performance calculations [with list of references] ; by Walter S. Diehl. 1924. cover-title, 11 p. il. 4° (Report 186.) [Prepared by Aeronautics Bureau, Navy Department. Text and illustration on p. 2 and 3 of cover.] * Paper, 5c.
24—26363

Sphere resistance. Resistance of spheres in wind tunnels and in air [with bibliography] ; by D. L. Bacon and E. G. Reid. 1924. cover-title, 21 p. il. 4° (Report 185.) [Text and illustration on p. 2 and 3 of cover.] *Paper, 10c.
24—26362

NAVY DEPARTMENT

Court-martial order 2, 1924; Feb. 29, 1924. [1924.] 18 p. 12° [Monthly.] ‡

Government officials. Practice of ex-officials before Navy Department, in response to resolution, report relative to appearance of ex-Members of Senate or ex-Cabinet officers as attorneys or agents before Navy Department in advocacy of claims against United States. Apr. 10, calendar day Apr. 19, 1924. 3 p. (S. doc. 91, 68th Cong. 1st sess.) *Paper, 5c. 24—26418

CONSTRUCTION AND REPAIR BUREAU

Manual of Bureau of Construction and Repair [1922], index. [Reprint 1924.] 8 p. [Issued in loose-leaf form for insertion in binder.] ‡

ENGINEERING BUREAU

Eagle boats. Machinery installation, operation, and care of eagle boats [200-foot patrol boats]. 1924. iii+78 p. il. ‡

Lubricating-oils. Test of lubricating oils, laboratory test of lubricating oils at engineering experiment station, Annapolis. Md., instructions for conducting service tests of lubricating oils. 1924. [1]+17 p. 12° ‡ 24—26419

MARINE CORPS

Orders. Marine Corps orders 2, 1924; Feb. 14, 1924. [1924.] 2 p. 4° ‡

MEDICINE AND SURGERY BUREAU

Naval medical bulletin. United States naval medical bulletin. published for information of Medical Department of service. Apr. 1924, v. 20, no. 4; edited by W. M. Kerr. 1924. vi+423–529.p. il. 8 p. of pl. [Monthly.] * Paper, 15c. single copy, $1.50 a yr.; foreign subscription, $2.50. 8—35095

SPECIAL ARTICLES.—Value of electrocardiograph in prognosis; by W. A. Bloedorn and L. J. Roberts.—Use of ethylene for general anesthesia; by C. W. Moots.—Hydronephrosis; by R. Cuthbertson.—Unsuspected syphilis; by W. H. Connor.—Rise of local anesthesia; [by] Charles A. Ingraham.—Sarcoma, with report of 2 interesting cases; by R. M. Choisser.—Avulsion of scrotum, left testicle. and sheath of penis; by G. F. Cottle.—Case of hydatidiform mole; by C. C. Kress and H. C. Bishop, jr.—Notes on preventive medicine for medical officers. Navy [including Prevention and control of cerebrospinal fever in British army as reviewed in official history of the war, by R. J. Reece; abstract].

Nurses and nursing. Notes on course for instructors of nursing [given at Leland Stanford University summer course, June 19–July 15, 1923. with lists of references; compiled by Elizabeth M. O'Brien]. 1924. 32 p. [From United States naval medical bulletin. v. 20, no. 3.] †

Smallpox. Remarks on epidemiology of smallpox and preventive value of vaccination with cowpox virus. 1924. [1]+18 p. [From United States naval medical bulletin. v. 20, no. 3.] †

NAVAL COMMUNICATION SERVICE

Coastal radio and landline rate sheet of United States. Jan. 1, 1924. [1924.] 1 p. large 4° * 10c.

NAVAL WAR COLLEGE

International law, decisions and notes. 1922. 1924. v+212 p. * Cloth, 60c.
24—26364

NAVIGATION BUREAU

HYDROGRAPHIC OFFICE

NOTE.—The charts, sailing directions, etc., of the Hydrographic Office are sold by the office in Washington and also by agents at the principal American and foreign seaports and American lake ports. Copies of the General catalogue of mariners' charts and books and of the Hydrographic bulletins, reprints, and Notice to mariners are supplied free on application at the Hydrographic Office in Washington and at the branch offices in Boston, New York, Philadelphia, Baltimore, Norfolk, Savannah, New Orleans, Galveston, San Francisco, Portland (Oreg.), Seattle, Chicago, Cleveland, Buffalo, Sault Ste. Marie, and Duluth.

Biscay, Bay of. Supplement to publication 133, Bay of Biscay pilot, including summary of Notices to mariners and other information from date of publication (Nov. 5, 1917) to Dec. 31, 1923. 1924. ii+45 leaves, map. †

East Indies. Supplement to publication 164, East Indies pilot, v. 2, including summary of Notices to mariners and other information from date of publication (May 28, 1923) to Dec. 31, 1923. 1924. ii+3 leaves. †

Hydrographic bulletin, weekly, no. 1804–8; Apr. 2–30. 1924. [1924.] Each 1 p. f° and large 4° [For Ice supplements to accompany nos. 1804–8, see below under center head *Charts* the subhead *Pilot charts.*] †

Notice to aviators 4, 1924; Apr. 1 [1924]. [1924.] 2 p. [Monthly.] †
20—26958

Notice to mariners 14–17, 1924; Apr. 5–26 [1924]. [1924.] [xxxvi]+359–476 leaves, 6 maps. [Weekly.] †

Tide calendars. Tide calendar [for Baltimore (Fort McHenry) and Cape Henry], Apr. 1924. [1924.] 1 p. 4° [Monthly.] †

—— Same, May, 1924. [1924.] 1 p. 4° [Monthly.] †

—— Tide calendar [for Norfolk (Navy Yard) and Newport News. Va.], May. 1924. [1924.] 1 p. 4° [Monthly.] †

Charts

Africa. West coast of Africa, Cape Three Points to Niger River. from latest information; chart 2201. Scale 1° long.=4.6 in. Washington, Hydrographic Office, published Oct. 1905, 6th edition, Mar. 1924. 28.4×44.2 in. † 50c.

Annatto Bay, Jamaica, from British survey in 1879; with inset, Hope Bay Anchorage, from British survey in 1896; chart 1289. Scale naut. m.=6.1 in. Washington, Hydrographic Office, published Oct. 1891, 13th edition, Mar. 1924. 19.4×13.3 in. † 10c.

Bombay, India. Port of Bombay, west coast of India, from survey by Royal Indian Marine in 1920 and 1921, with additions from Bombay Port Trust in 1922; chart 2462. Scale naut. m.=6 in. Washington. Hydrographic Office, published May, 1908, 5th edition, Mar. 1924. 39.9×26.9 in. † 40c.

Brazil. Plans on north coast of Brazil, from Brazilian and other sources to 1920; chart 480. Washington, Hydrographic Office, published Dec. 1917, 2d edition, Apr. 1924. 12.9×22.1 in. † 20c.
Amarracao Bar.
Tutoya Bar.

Chile. Anchorages on coast of Chile; chart 1569. Washington, Hydrographic Office, published Dec. 1896, 8th edition, Mar. [1924]. 19.1×16 in. † 10c.
Montt, Port, Reloncavi Sound, from Chilean surveys to 1922.
San Pedro, Port, Corcovado Gulf, from Chilean plan published in 1916.
Sheep and Samuel (Small) coves, Huafo Island, from British surveys in 1835.

—— Channels between gulfs of Trinidad and Peñas, lower part, Chile; with inset, Port Rosario; chart 447. Scale 1° long.=9.4 in. Washington, Hydrographic Office. published Apr. 1885, 20th edition. Apr. 1924. 23.5×25.9 in. † 30c.

Fraser River [from its mouth to Harrison River] and Burrard Inlet, British Columbia, compiled from latest information; chart 1768. Scale naut. m.=0.8 in. Washington, Hydrographic Office, published Feb. 1900, 14th edition, Apr. [1924]. 26.7×45.5 in. † 60c.

Hawaiian Islands, Lisianski Island to Ocean Island; chart 4. Washington, Hydrographic Office, published Jan. 1868, 14th edition, Apr. 1924. 20.8×30.8 in. † 30c.

[Hawaiian Islands, Lisianski Island to Ocean Island.]
Lisianski Island. from Hawaiian Government survey, with additions from Russian survey in 1805.
Ocean Island (Cure Island), surveyed by U. S. S. Lackawanna in 1867, with additions by U. S. S. Tanager in 1923.
Pearl and Hermes Reef. surveyed by U. S. S. Lackawanna in 1867, with additions by U. S. S. Tanager in 1923.

Hongkong Harbor, China, south coast, from British survey in 1912 and 1913; chart 1254. Scale naut. m.=12 in. Washington, Hydrographic Office, published Feb. 1918, 4th edition, Mar. 1924. 26.3×39.4 in. † 50c.

Kusaie Island. Kusaie or Ualan Island, Carol'ne Islands, north Pacific Ocean, from Japanese surveys in 1920 [with insets] ; chart 5420. Scale naut. m.=1 in. Washington, Hydrographic Office, Mar. 1924. 19.6×26.8 in. † 20c.

Chabrol (Lele) Harbor.
Coquille (Okaato) Harbor.
Lottin (Utwa), Port.

Leghorn, Italy. Leghorn (Livorno) Roadstead, Italy, west coast, Mediterranean, from latest Italian surveys; with inset, Port of Leghorn (Livorno) ; chart 4027. Scale naut. m.=2.9 in. Washington, Hydrographic Office, published Mar. 1915, 7th edition, Apr. 1924. 25.8×38.7 in. † 40c.

Magdalen Islands, Gulf of St. Lawrence, Canada, original British survey in 1833; chart 1092. Scale 1° long.=9.8 in. Washington, Hydrographic Office, published July, 1888, 22d edition, Mar. [1924]. 23.9×19.5 :n. † 20c.

Magellan Strait. Harbors and anchorages in Magellan Strait, original British surveys in 1868 and 1880; chart 264. Washington. Hydrographic Office, published Apr. 1884, 16th edition, Mar. [1924]. 16.8×22.9. † 20c.

Angosto, Port, Long Reach.
Borja Bay, Crooked Reach.
Mussel Bay, English Reach.
Playa Parda Cove, Long Reach.
Pollard Cove, Sketch of.
Swallow Bay and Condesa Bay between Crooked and Long Reach.
Tilly Bay, Crooked Reach.
Upright, Port, Sketch of.

Mersina, Asia Minor. Mersina (Mersin) Roadstead, Mediterranean Sea, Asia Minor, from French survey in 1921, with additions from U. S. naval survey in 1896, Mezetli from British survey in 1812; chart 1549. Scale naut. m.=2.9 in. Washington, Hydrographic Office, published June, 1897, 3d edition, Apr. 1924. 19.7×32.2 in. † 30c.

North Island. North and South islands, New Zealand, Hokitika to Otago Harbor, including Cook Strait, from British surveys between 1849 and 1854, with additions from New Zealand Government surveys; chart 3336. Scale 1° long.=4.8 in. Washington, Hydrographic Office, Mar. 1924. 38.5×25.6 in. † 40c.

Nova Scotia, south coast, Port Medway to Lockeport Harbor, from British surveys in 1861 and 1862; chart 2131. Scale naut. m.=1 in. Washington. Hydrographic Office, published Oct. 1903, 15th edition, Mar. [1924]. 41.2× 32.1 in. † 60c.

Pilot charts. Ice supplement to north Atlantic pilot chart; issue 104. Scale 1° long.=0.3 in. Washington. Hydrographic Office [1924]. 8.9×11.8 in. [To accompany Hydrographic bulletin 1804, Apr. 2, 1924.] †

—— Same; issue 105. Scale 1° long.=0.3 in. Washington, Hydrographic Office [1924]. 8.9×11.8 in. [To accompany Hydrographic bulletin 1805, Apr. 9 1924.] †

—— Same; issue 106. Scale 1° long.=0.3 in. Washington, Hydrographic Office [1924]. 8.9×11.8 in. [To accompany Hydrographic bulletin 1806, Apr. 16, 1924.] †

—— Same; issue 107. Scale 1° long.=0.3 in. Washington, Hydrographic Office [1924]. 8.9×11.8 in. [To accompany Hydrographic bulletin 1807, Apr. 23, 1924.] †

—— Same; issue 108. Scale 1° long.=0.3 in. Washington, Hydrographic Office [1924]. 8.9×11.8 in. [To accompany Hydrographic bulletin 1808, Apr. 30, 1924.] †

Pilot charts—Continued. Pilot chart of Central American waters, May, 1924; chart 3500. Scale 1° long.=0.7 in. Washington, Hydrographic Office, Apr. 14, 1924. 23.4×35.1 in. [Monthly. Certain portions of the data are furnished by the Weather Bureau.] † 10c.

NOTE. — Contains on reverse: Description of activities of Hydrographic Office. — Assistance of shipmasters requested; [Reproduction of] current report, route report, and port facilities report for record in Hydrographic Office.

—— Pilot chart of Indian Ocean, June, 1924; chart 2603. Scale 1° long.= 0.2 in. Washington, Hydrographic Office, Apr. 14, 1924. 22.6×31 in. [Monthly. Certain portions of the data are furnished by the Weather Bureau.] † 10c.

NOTE. — Contains on reverse: Description of activities of Hydrographic Office. — Assistance of shipmasters requested; [Reproduction of] current report, marine data report, route report, and port facilities report for record in Hydrographic Office.

—— Pilot chart of north Atlantic Ocean, May, 1924; chart 1400. Scale 1° long.=0.27 in. Washington, Hydrographic Office. Apr. 14, 1924. 23.2×31.8 in. [Monthly. Certain portions of the data are furnished by the Weather Bureau.] † 10c.

14—16339

NOTE. — Contains on reverse: Description of activities of Hydrographic Office. — Assistance of shipmasters requested; [Reproduction of] current report, marine data report, route report, and port facilities report for record in Hydrographic Office.

—— Pilot chart of north Pacific Ocean, June, 1924; chart 1401. Scale 1° long.=0.2 in. Washington, Hydrographic Office. Apr. 14. 1924. 23.7×35.3 in. [Monthly. Certain portions of the data are furnished by the Weather Bureau.] † 10c.

NOTE. — Contains on reverse: Description of activities of Hydrographic Office. — Assistance of shipmasters requested; [Reproduction of] current report, marine data report, route report, and port facilities report for record in Hydrographic Office.

—— Pilot chart of south Atlantic Ocean, June–Aug. 1924; chart 2600. Scale 1° long.=0.3 in. Washington, Hydrographic Office, Apr. 14. 1924. 23×31.9 in. [Quarterly. Certain portions of the data are furnished by the Weather Bureau.] † 10c.

NOTE. — Contains on reverse: Description of activities of Hydrographic Office. — Assistance of shipmasters requested; [Reproduction of] current report, marine data report, route report, and port facilities report for record in Hydrographic Office.

—— Pilot chart of south Pacific Ocean, June–Aug. 1924; chart 2601. Scale 1° long.=0.2 in. Washington, Hydrographic Office. Apr. 14. 1924. 21.2×35.5 in. [Quarterly. Certain portions of the data are furnished by the Weather Bureau.] † 10c.

NOTE. — Contains on reverse: Description of activities of Hydrographic Office. — Assistance of shipmasters requested; [Reproduction of] current report, marine data report, route report, and port facilities report for record in Hydrographic Office.

St. Lawrence River, McKies Point to eastern entrance of Soulanges Canal, from Canadian surveys to 1910, with additions from other sources; chart 1351. Scale naut. m.=2 in. Washington, Hydrographic Office, published Feb. 1893, 19th edition, Mar. 1924. 26.9×37.5 in. † 40c.

Sakhalin Island. Anchorages on north part of Sakhalin Island, Siberia, Asia, from Japanese sketch surveys in 1920; chart 5431. Washington, Hydrographic Office, Mar. 1924. 20.6×32.6 in. † 30c.

Baikal Bay, West entrance to.
Chaivo Anchorage.
Kuegda Road.
Kyakrvo Anchorage.
Urkt Road.

Santa Anna Harbor, Island of Curaçao, W. I., from Netherlands Government chart of 1922, with additions from other sources; chart 1049. Scale 1.500 yds.=6.8 in. Washington, Hydrographic Office, published Sept. 1887, 24th edition, Apr. 1924. 27.9×25.2 in. † 30c.

Sermata Islands. Anchorages in Sermata and Tanimbar Is., Eastern Archipelago, from Netherlands Government surveys between 1859 and 1914; chart 3023. Washington, Hydrographic Office, published Nov. 1913, 3d edition, Mar. 1924. 25.3×19.5 in. † 20c.

Babar Strait, Sermata Islands.
Batu Merah Anch., Damma I., n. w. coast, Sermata Islands.
Egeron Strait, Tanimbar Islands, from Netherlands Government surveys between 1874 and 1914, with corrections to 1921.
Lawawang Road, Masela I., w. coast, Sermata Islands.
Nika Anchorage, Nila or Asap Bediri I., n. coast, Sermata Islands.
Ritabel Bay and approaches, Tanimbar Islands.

Sermata, Islands—Continued.

Rumah Kuda Bay and Nusa Mitan. Roma, s. q. coast. Sermata Islands.
Sabiani Anchorage. Vordate I., west coast, Tanimbar Islands.
Tepa Road. Babar I., Sermata Islands.
Wailutu (Uratan) Road. Sera I., north coast. Tanimbar Islands.
Watteweh Road, Dawelur I., Sermata Islands.
Staten Island, South America. original Brit'sh survey; chart 12. Scale naut. m.=0.6 in. Washington. Hydrographic Office, published June, 1883. 13th edition. Mar. [1924]. 17.4×22.8 in. † 20c.
Timor Island. Plans in Timor. Eastern Archipelago; chart 3021. Washington, Hydrographic Office, Mar. 1924. 18.1×26 in. † 20c.

Hainsisi Anchorage, Semau Island, from Netherlands Government survey in 1910.
Kupang Bay and Roti Strait. from Netherlands Government survey in 1910.
Kupang Road, from Netherlands Government survey in 1910.
Tomini, Gulf of. Gulf of Tomini. Celebes, east coast, Tilamuta Bay to Tanjung Tuladenggi, from latest Netherlands Government surveys; chart 3074. Scale naut. m.=0 5 in. Washington, Hydrographic Office, Mar. 1924. 26.1× 39.1 in. † 40c.
West Frisian Islands. Netherlands, North Sea, Terschelling Zeegat to Friesche Zeegat, from latest Netherlands and German surveys; chart 4858. Scale naut. m.=0.7 in. Washington. Hydrographic Office, published Aug. 1915, 8th edition, Mar. 1924. 25.9×44.3 in † 50c.

RECRUITING BUREAU

[*Poster*] 258. n. p. [Mar. 20, 1924]. 14×17 in. [Title is: Navy at play.] †

ORDNANCE BUREAU

Harrison, John K. M. Interference no. 45648, in Patent Office, John K. M. Harr:son *v.* Ralph C. Browne; brief for Browne on final hearing. 1924. cover-title. 112 p. ‡

SUPPLIES AND ACCOUNTS BUREAU

Naval supplies. Index to specifications issued by Navy Department for naval stores and material. Apr. 1. 1924. vi+47 p. 12° [Quarterly.] †
Pay, Navy. Instructions relative to payment of travel allowance and furnishing transportation to enlisted men on discharge. 1924. [1]+11 p. 4° ‡
Supply Corps, Navy. Memorandum for information of officers of Supply Corps. commanding officers [of ships], and commandants 259; Mar. 1, 1924. [1924.] p. 8078–8171, 12° [Monthly.] ‡

OIL CASES, SPECIAL COUNSEL FOR UNITED STATES IN

Pan American Petroleum Company. No. B100M, in equity, in district court for southern district of California, northern division, United States *v* Pan American Petroleum Company and Pan American Petroleum and Transport Company; amended bill of complaint. 1924. cover-title. 51 p. ‡

PAN AMERICAN UNION

Note.—The Pan American Union sells its own monthly bulletins, handbooks, etc., at prices usually ranging from 5c. to $2.50. The price of the English edition of the bulletin is 25c. a single copy or $2.50 a year, the Spanish edition $2.00 a year, the Portuguese edition $1.50 a year; there is an additional charge of 50c. a year on each edition for countries outside the Pan American Union. Address the Director General of the Pan American Union, Washington. D. C.
Bulletin (English edition). Bulletin of Pan American Union, Apr. 1924; [v. 58. no. 4]. [1924.] iv+325–430 p. il. [Monthly.]   8—30967
—— Same. (H. doc. 6. pt. 10. 68th Cong. 1st sess.)
—— (*Portuguese edition*). Boletim da União Pan-Americana, Avril, 1924, edição portuguesa; [v. 26, no. 4]. [1924.] [iv]+229–304 p. il. [Monthly.]   11—27014
—— (*Spanish edition*). Boletin de la Unión Panamericana, Abril, 1924, sección española; [v. 58. no. 4]. [1924.]. iv+329–436 .p. il. [Monthly. This number is entitled La vialidad en las Américas.]   12—12555

Calendars. Evolution of calendars and how to improve them; [by Moses B.
Cotsworth]. [Reprint with changes] 1924. ii+28+[1] p. il. [Original
article from Bulletin, June, 1922.] †

Cuba. Commerce of Cuba, latest reports from Cuban official sources. 1924.
12 p. †
                                                                        13—35123

Panama and Colón, gateway cities between greatest oceans; [by W. A. R.].
1924. [1]+27+[1] p. il. †
                                                                        24—26369

Santiago, Chile's interesting capital. 1924. [2]+30 p. il. †   24—26370

Venezuela, general descriptive data. 1924. [2]+30 p. il. †   10—35040

PANAMA CANAL

NOTE.—Although The Panama Canal makes its reports to, and is under the supervision of, the Secretary of War, it is not a part of the War Department.

Panama Canal record, v. 17. no. 34–38; Apr. 2–30, 1924. Balboa Heights, C. Z.
[1924]. p. 483–552, il. [Weekly.]
                                                                        7—35328

NOTE.—The yearly subscription rate of the Panama Canal record is 50c. domestic,
and $1.00 foreign (single issues 2c.), except in the case of Government departments
and bureaus, Members of Congress, representatives of foreign Governments, steamship
lines, chambers of commerce, boards of trade, and university and public libraries, to
whom the Record is distributed free. The word "domestic" refers to the United
States, Canada, Canal Zone, Cuba, Guam, Hawaii, Manua, Mexico, the Philippines,
Porto Rico, Republic of Panama, Tutuila, and the Virgin Islands. Subscriptions will
commence with the first issue of the Record in the month in which the subscriptions
are received, unless otherwise requested. Remittances should be made payable to Disbursing Clerk, The Panama Canal, but should be forwarded to the Chief of Office, The
Panama Canal, Washington, D. C. The name and address to which the Record is to
be sent should be plainly written. Postage stamps, foreign money, and defaced or
smooth coins will not be accepted.

PURCHASING DEPARTMENT

Supplies. Circular [proposals for supplies] 1602; Apr. 10, 1924. [1924.]
28+[1] p. f° †

POST OFFICE DEPARTMENT

Electric railway mail pay. Before Interstate Commerce Commission. docket no.
10227, in re electric railway mail pay, petition of American Electric Railway
Association in matter of electric railway mail pay; brief for Postmaster General. 1924. cover-title, iv+127 p. 1 tab. ‡

Envelopes. Proposal and specifications for envelopes for departments of Government, for one year, beginning July 1, 1924. 1924. 22 p. f° †

Mail matter. Conditions upon which mailings of certain matter will be accepted
under permit without stamps affixed as provided by sec. 459, Postal laws and
regulations; [issued by] 3d assistant Postmaster General. Apr. 19, 1924.
1 p. il, narrow f° [Supersedes all regulations governing acceptance of permit
matter heretofore issued.] †

Postal bulletin, v. 45. no. 13433–458; Apr. 1–30, 1924. 1924. Each 1 p. or 2
leaves. il. f° [Daily except Sundays and holidays.] * Paper, 5c. single copy,
$2.00 a yr.
                                                                        6—5810

Postal guide. United States official postal guide, 4th series, v. 3, no. 10; Apr.
1924. monthly supplement. 1924. cover-title, 48 p. [Includes Modifications
33 and 34 of International money order list, pamphlet 14. and Insert 853 to
Postal laws and regulations of United States. Text on p. 2–4 of cover.] * Official postal guide, with supplements, $1.00, foreign subscription, $1.50; July
issue, 75c.; supplements published monthly (11 pamphlets) 25c.; foreign
subscription, 50c.
                                                                        4—18254

Spokane, Wash. Partial scheme of distribution for Spokane, Wash., Aug. 1923.
1924. 36 p. 12° ‡

FOREIGN MAILS DIVISION

Steamboats. Schedule of steamers appointed to convey mails to foreign countries during Feb. 1924. Jan. 21, 1924. 1 p. f° [Monthly.] * Paper, 5c.
single copy, 25c. a yr.; foreign subscription, 50c.

—— Same during Mar. 1924. Feb. 21, 1924. 1 p. f° [Monthly.]

—— Same during Apr. 1924. Mar. 20, 1924. 1 p. f° [Monthly.]

—— Same during May, 1924. Apr. 21, 1924. 1 p. f° [Monthly.]

RAILWAY MAIL SERVICE

Arizona. Alphabetical scheme of Arizona, for use of publishers in distribution of 2d-class mail, 1924. 1924. 8 p. ‡

Mail-trains. Schedule of mail trains, no. 91, Apr. 1, 1924, 12th division, Railway Mail Service, comprising Louisiana and Mississippi. 1924. 77+[1] p. narrow 8° ‡

—— Schedule of mail trains, no. 449, Mar. 15, 1924, 7th division, Railway Mail Service, comprising Kansas and Missouri. 1924. 173+[1] p. narrow 8° ‡

Mississippi. Alphabetical scheme of Mississippi, for use of publishers in distribution of 2d-class mail, 1924. 1924. 19 p. ‡

Nevada. Alphabetical scheme of Nevada, for use of publishers in distribution of 2d-class mail, 1924. 1924. 5 p. ‡

Utah. Alphabetical scheme of Utah, for use of publishers in distribution of 2d-class mail, 1924. 1924. 9 p. ‡

Wisconsin. Alphabetical scheme of Wisconsin, for use of publishers in distribution of 2d-class mail, Apr. 1924. 1924. 18 p. ‡

TOPOGRAPHY DIVISION

Note.—Since February, 1908, the Topography Division·has been preparing rural-delivery maps of counties in which rural delivery is completely established. They are published in two forms, one giving simply the rural free delivery routes, starting from a single given post office, and sold at 10 cents each; the other, the rural free delivery routes in an entire county, sold at 35 cents each. A uniform scale of 1 inch to 1 mile is used. Editions are not issued, but sun-print copies are produced in response to special calls addressed to the Disbursing Clerk, Post Office Department, Washington, D. C. These maps should not be confused with the post route maps, for which see Monthly catalogue for February, 1924, page 486.

PRESIDENT OF UNITED STATES

Addresses. Address of President Coolidge at annual luncheon of Associated Press, at New York City, Apr. 22, 1924. 1924. [1]+10 p. †　　24—26420

—— Same, with title, New call for disarming, address by President of United States at annual luncheon of Associated Press Conference, New York City, Apr. 22, 1924. 1924. [1]+10 p. (S. doc. 94, 68th Cong. 1st sess.) 24—26421

—— Address [of President Coolidge, delivered before Daughters of American Revolution, Apr. 14, 1924, at Washington, D. C.]. [1924.] 6 p. ‡ 24—26422

Alaska. Executive order, Alaska [temporarily withdrawing certain described public lands in Alaska, pending determination as to advisability of including same in national monument]. Apr. 1, 1924. 1 p. f° (No. 3983.) ‡

Alien property. Executive order authorizing Alien Property Custodian to sell certain property at private sale [being real estate in Brooklyn, N. Y., belonging to John Kropp of Germany]. [Apr. 3, 1924.] 2 p. f° ([No. 3986.]) ‡

Birds. Amendments of migratory bird treaty act regulations, proclamation [further amending regulations proclaimed July 31, 1918]. Apr. 11, 1924. 1 p. f° (No. 1691.) †

Cereal Enforcement Division. Executive order [directing that all records and certain filing equipment of Cereal Enforcement Division of Food Administration be transferred from custody of comptroller general to Grain Corporation]. Apr. 17, 1924. 1 p. f° (No. 3990.) ‡

Colorado. Executive order, Colorado [revoking Executive order of Dec. 15, 1913, withdrawing certain described land in Colorado for use by Forest Service as Pagosa administrative site, ranger station in connection with administration of San Juan National Forest]. Apr. 17, 1924. 1 p. f° (No. 3991.) ‡

—— Executive order, Colorado [temporarily withdrawing, until Mar 5, 1925, certain described lands in Colorado, in aid of pending legislation embodied in H. R. 7998, granting public lands to Golden, Colo., to secure supply of water for municipal and domestic purposes]. Mar. 29, 1924. 1 p. f° (No. 3981.) ‡

Consuls. Executive order [amending Regulations governing consular service of United States, annotated to Dec. 31, 1922, concerning additional compensation for vice consuls]. Mar. 19, 1924. 1 p. f° (No. 3973.) ‡

Cutter, John D. Executive order [authorizing appointment of John D. Cutter to classified position in veterans' Bureau]. Apr. 14, 1924. 1 p. f° (No. 3989.) ‡

Dowling, Mrs. Florence R. Executive order [authorizing appointment of Mrs. Florence R. Dowling to clerical or stenographic position under Navy Department]. Mar. 26, 1924. 1 p. f° (No. 3979.) ‡

Foreign countries. Executive order [prescribing certain regulations for guidance of representatives of United States Government in foreign countries with view to giving unified direction to their activities in behalf of promotion and protection of commercial and other interests of United States, insuring effective cooperation, and encouraging economy in administration]. Apr. 4, 1924. 1 p. f° (No. 3987.) ‡

Honduras. Exportation of arms or munitions of war to Honduras unlawful, proclamation. Mar. 22, 1924. 1 p. f° (No. 1689.) †

Income tax. Executive order, inspection of income tax returns [authorizing that certain income tax returns shall be open to inspection in accordance and upon compliance with rules and regulations prescribed by Secretary of Treasury and approved by the President]. Mar. 15, 1924. 1 p. f° (No. 3971 A.) ‡

Indians. Executive order [providing that trust period on allotments made to Indians on Klamath River and Hoopa Valley reservations, Calif., which expires during calendar-year 1924, be extended for period of 15 years, except those named in order]. [Mar. 26, 1924.] 2 p. f° ([No. 3980.]) ‡

—— Executive order [providing that trust period on allotments made to Indians on Round valley Reservation, Calif., which expires during calendar year 1924, be extended for period of 10 years]. Apr. 19, 1924. (No. 3995.) ‡

—— Executive order [providing that trust period on allotments made to Sisseton and Wahpeton Band of Sioux Indians of Lake Traverse Reservation, N. Dak. and S. Dak., title to which has not passed from United States, be extended for period of 15 years]. Apr. 19, 1924. 1 p. f° (No. 3994.) ‡

Internal Revenue Bureau, Select Committee on Investigation of, Senate. Investigation of Internal Revenue Bureau, message transmitting letter from Secretary of Treasury relative to investigation of Bureau of Internal Revenue by select committee appointed under authority of Senate resolution 168, agreed to Mar. 12, 1924. Apr. 10, calendar day Apr. 11, 1924. 4 p. (S. doc. 87, 68th Cong. 1st sess.) *Paper, 5c.

Isle Royal. Executive order, Michigan [withdrawing public lands in Isle Royale. Mich., pending determination as to advisability of including such lands in national monument]. Mar. 22, 1924. 1 p. f° (No. 3976.) ‡

Keiser, Charles G. Executive order [authorizing reinstatement of Charles G. Keiser as clerk in post office at Indianapolis, Ind.]. Mar. 25, 1924. 1 p. f° (No. 3977.) ‡

Montana. Executive order, Montana [modifying Executive order of July 9. 1910, withdrawing certain lands in Miles City, Mont., land district for classification as to coal values, so as to permit Secretary of Interior to reinstate stock-watering reservoir declaratory statement filed by Ivory Brackett on Mar. 1, 1911]. Apr. 1, 1924. 1 p. f° (No. 3982.) ‡

National forests. Executive order, Elk City administrative site, near Nezperce National Forest, Idaho [temporarily withdrawing certain described land from settlement, etc., and reserving same for use by Forest Service as ranger station in connection with administration of Nezperce National Forest]. Mar. 21, 1924. 1 p. f° (No. 3975.) ‡

—— Executive order, Washington [amending proclamation of Jan. 16, 1924, excluding certain designated areas from Chelan National Forest so as to allow State of Washington to make selections of lands as indemnity in satisfaction of its common school grant, and adding certain described land to areas listed in said proclamation]. Apr. 17, 1924. 1 p. f° (No. 3992.) ‡

Naval Training Station, Great Lakes. Executive order [transferring certain land added to Naval Training Station, Great Lakes, Ill., by proclamation of Nov. 4, 1918, with certain exceptions herein listed, and all buildings and other improvements, from Navy Department to veterans' Bureau]. [Apr. 17, 1924.] 2 p. f° ([No. 3993.]) ‡

New Mexico. Executive order, New Mexico [temporarily withdrawing certain described public lands in New Mexico, for classification and pending determination as to advisability of reserving same for national park or monument purposes]. Apr. 2, 1924. 1 p. f° (No. 3984.) ‡

Pay, Army. Executive order [announcing that rates for rental and subsistence allowances of officers of various services entitled thereto as prescribed in act to readjust pay and allowances of commissioned and enlisted personnel of Army, Navy, Marine Corps, Coast Guard, Coast and Geodetic Survey, and Public Health Service, approved June 10, 1922, become effective for fiscal year 1925]. Apr. 21, 1924. 1 p. f° (No. 3996.) ‡

Registers (land offices). Executive order [consolidating offices of register and receiver of land office at Spokane, Wash., abolishing office of receiver, and transferring all powers, duties, obligations, and penalties imposed by law upon both register and receiver to register]. Mar. 21, 1924. 1 p. f° (No. 3974.) ‡

Richards, Mrs. Minnie. Executive order [authorizing appointment of Mrs. Minnie Richards to clerical position in Navy Department]. Mar. 26, 1924. 1 p. f° (No. 3978.) ‡

Seal and seal fisheries. Executive order [directing that Fisheries Bureau patrol boats named in order patrol waters frequented by seal herds and sea otters, and authorizing masters of these vessels to search any United States vessel suspected of violation of convention between United States, Great Britain, Japan, and Russia, for preservation and protection of fur seals and sea otters which frequent waters of north Pacific Ocean, and to bring such vessel into most accessible port of Alaska, California, Oregon, or Washington for trial]. Apr. 11, 1924. 1 p. f° (No. 3988.) ‡

Smith, Lucius M. Executive order [designating Lucius Meriwether Smith to be special judge for Canal Zone during absence of John D. Wallingford, district judge]. Apr. 3, 1924. 1 p. f° (No. 3985.) ‡

Virgin Islands. Further extending [period from May 1 to Nov. 1, 1924, for] establishment of adequate shipping service in, and deferring extension of coastwise laws of United States to Virgin Islands, proclamation. [Apr. 7, 1924.] 2 p. f° ([No. 1690.]) †

RAILROAD ADMINISTRATION

Casks. Before Interstate Commerce Commission, no. 13192, Lucas E. Moore Stave Company *v.* director general et al.; petition for reargument and reconsideration on behalf of defendants. 1924. cover-title, 8 p. ‡

Coal. Before Interstate Commerce Commission, no. 14227, W. D. Corley *v.* James C. Davis, director general of railroads, as agent; brief on part of director general. 1924. cover-title, 6 p. ‡

—— Before Interstate Commerce Commission, no. 15042, Romann & Bush Pig Iron & Coke Company *v.* director general; exceptions on behalf of director general to report of examiner. 1924. cover-title, 3 p. ‡.

Corona Coal Company. No. 819, in Supreme Court, Oct. term, 1923, Jas. C. Davis, director general of railroads, as agent of United States, *v.* Corona Coal Company, certiorari to court of appeal for parish of Orleans, La.; motion on behalf of plaintiff in error to advance for argument. 1924. cover-title, 3 p. ‡

Demurrage. No. —, in Supreme Court, Oct. term, 1923, James C. Davis, director general of railroads, *against* Wm. Radford Coyle, trustee in bankruptcy of Tidewater Coal Exchange; amended petition for writ of certiorari to circuit court of appeals for 2d circuit. 1924. cover-title, 12 p. ‡

Freight rates. Before Interstate Commerce Commission, no. 15092, National Supply Company *v.* director general; exceptions on behalf of director general to report of examiner. 1924. cover-title, 1 p. ‡

Industrial railroads. Before Interstate Commerce Commission, no. 12596, Pressed-Steel Car Company *v.* director general; director general's reply to complainant's exceptions to examiner's proposed report. 1924. cover-title, 14 p. ‡

Liquors. Before Interstate Commerce Commission, no. 15547, Woolner Distilling Company *v.* director general: brief for director general. 1924. cover-title, 8 p. ‡

Paper. Before Interstate Commerce Commission, no. 14462, Badger Bag & Paper Co. *v.* director general et al.; exceptions of director general to examiner's report. 1924. cover-title, 4 p. ‡

Petroleum. Before Interstate Commerce Commission, no. 14429, Continental Oil Company *v.* director general, as agent; brief on part of director general. 1924. cover-title, 8 p. ‡

—— Before Interstate Commerce Commission, no. 15069, subs. 1–9, Continental Oil Company [*v.* director general]; brief on part of director general. 1924. cover-title, 11 p. ‡

—— Before Interstate Commerce Commission, no. 15086, Continental Oil Company *v.* director general; brief on part of director general. 1924. cover-title, 7 p. ‡

Railroad ties. Before Interstate Commerce Commission, no. 15346, Walsh Tie and Lumber Company et al. *v.* director general, as agent; director general's exceptions to examiner's proposed report. 1924. cover-title, 5 p. ‡

Shipping. Docket nos. 905–911, memorandum in support of claims of director general of railroads before Mixed Claims Commission, United States and Germany [for vessels and cargoes lost through collision, grounding, mine explosion, or direct bombardment of German submarines]. 1924. cover-title, 14 p. ‡

Switching charges. Before Interstate Commerce Commission, no. 12821, Utah Fuel Company *v.* director general; brief on part of director general on rehearing. 1924. cover-title, 1+85 p. ‡ .

Waterloo, Cedar Falls and Northern Railway. Final settlement between director general of railroads and Waterloo, Cedar Falls and Northern Railway Company, Apr. —, 1924. 1924. 3 p. 4° †

Wool. Before Interstate Commerce Commission, no. 13318, Boston Wool Trade Association *v.* director general; answer of director general to exception brief and request for subpœna of plaintiff. 1924. cover-title, 3 p. ‡

—— Same; exceptions on part of director general to report proposed by examiner. 1924. cover-title, 3 p. ‡

RAILROAD LABOR BOARD

Railroad employees. Average daily wage rates of railroad employees on class 1 carriers; Feb. 1924. 1924. ii+12 p. 1 tab. (Wage series, report 4.) †
                                                                          A 24—691

SHIPPING BOARD

Duke. William B. No. 230, in Supreme Court, Oct. term, 1923, William Bernard Duke [et al.] *v.* United States, appeal from Court of Claims; brief for United States. 1924. cover-title, i+24 p. ‡

SHIPPING BOARD EMERGENCY FLEET CORPORATION

Ships. Schedule of sailings of Shipping Board vessels in general cargo, passenger & mail services, 1st of April to middle of May, 1924; issued by Traffic Department. [1924.] cover-title, iv+16 p. il. [Monthly. Text on p. 2–4 of cover.] †
                                                                          23—26331

SMITHSONIAN INSTITUTION

NOTE.—In a recent price-list the Smithsonian Institution publishes this notice: "Applicants for the publication in this list are requested to state the grounds for their requests, as the Institution is able to supply papers only as an aid to the researches or studies in which they are *especially* interested. These papers are distributed *gratis*, except as otherwise indicated, and should be ordered by the *publication numbers* arranged in sequence. The serial publications of the Smithsonian Institution are as follows: 1, Smithsonian contributions to knowledge; 2, Smithsonian miscellaneous collections; 3, Smithsonian annual reports. No *sets* of these are for sale or distribution, as most of the volumes are out of print. The papers issued in the series of Contributions to knowledge and Miscellaneous collections are distributed without charge to public libraries, educational establishments, learned societies, and specialists in this country and abroad; and are supplied to other institutions and individuals at the prices indicated. Remittances should be made payable to the 'Smithsonian Institution.' The Smithsonian report volumes and the papers reprinted in separate form therefrom are distributed *gratuitously* by the Institution to libraries and individuals throughout the world. Very few of the Report volumes are now available at the Institution, but many of those of which the Smithsonian edition is exhausted can be purchased from the Superintendent of Documents, Government Printing Office, Washington, D. C. The Institution maintains mailing-lists of public libraries and other educational establishments, but no *general mailing-list of individuals*. A library making application to be listed for Smithsonian publications should state the number of volumes which it contains and the date of its establishment, and have the endorsement of a Member of Congress."

The annual reports are the only Smithsonian publications that are regularly issued as public documents. All the others are paid for from the private funds of the Institution, but as they are usually regarded as public documents and have free transmission by mail they are listed in the Monthly catalogue.

Explorations and field-work of Smithsonian Institution in 1923. Washington, Smithsonian Institution, 1924. [3]+128 p. il. 1 pl. (Publication 2752: Smithsonian miscellaneous collections, v. 76, no. 10.) †   13—35550

NATIONAL MUSEUM

NOTE.—The publications of the National Museum comprise an annual report and three scientific series, viz., Proceedings, Bulletins, and Contributions from national herbarium. The editions are distributed to established lists of libraries, scientific institutions, and specialists, any surplus copies being supplied on application. The volumes of Proceedings are made up of technical papers based on the Museum collections in biology, geology, and anthropology, and of each of these papers a small edition, in pamphlet form, is issued in advance of the volume, for prompt distribution to specialists. No sets of any of these series can now be furnished.

Mermithidae. Remarkable new genus and species of Mermithid worms from Jamaica [with list of literature cited]; by G. Steiner. [1924.] 4 p. 2 p. of pl. [From Proceedings, v. 65; no. 2527.] †

NATIONAL SOCIETY OF DAUGHTERS OF AMERICAN REVOLUTION

Report. 26th report of National Society of Daughters of American Revolution, Mar. 1; 1922–Mar. 1, 1923. 1924. x+139 p. 1 pl. 6 p. of pl. (S. doc. 47, 68th Cong. 1st sess.) * Paper, 20c.   8—36850

STATE DEPARTMENT

Arbitration. Agreement between United States and Netherlands, arbitration, further extending duration of convention of May 2, 1908; signed Washington, Feb. 13, 1924, proclaimed Apr. 7, 1924. 1924. [1]+4 p. (Treaty series 682.) [English and Dutch.] †   24—26423

—— Agreement between United States and Norway, arbitration, further extending duration of convention of Apr. 4, 1908; signed Washington, Nov. 26, 1923, proclaimed Mar. 12, 1924. 1924. [1]+4 p. (Treaty series 680.) [English and Norwegian.] †   24—26277

China. Claim of Government of China, report in relation to claims presented by Government of China against Government of United States arising out of negligent or unlawful acts in China of persons connected with military and naval forces of United States. Apr. 21, calendar day Apr. 23, 1924. 4 p. (S. doc. 96, 68th Cong. 1st sess.) * Paper, 5c.

[Circulars] 922 and 923; Mar. 17 and 21, 1924. [1924.] Each 2 p. [General instruction circulars to consular officers.] ‡

Diplomatic list, Apr. 1924. [1924.] cover-title, i+34 p. 24° [Monthly.] ‡   10—16292

Extradition. Treaty between United States and Siam, extradition; signed Bangkok, Dec. 30, 1922, proclaimed Mar. 26, 1924. 1924. [1]+6 p. (Treaty series 681.) †   24—26367

Fees. Tariff of United States consular fees. [1924.] 3 p. [Chapter 13 from Register of Department of State, Jan. 1, 1924.] ‡

Government officials. Practice by ex-officials before Department of State, in response to resolution, report relative to appearance of ex-Members of Senate or ex-Cabinet officers as attorneys or agents before Department of State in advocacy of claims against Government of United States. Apr. 2, 1924. 2 p. (S. doc. 80, 68th Cong. 1st sess.) * Paper, 5c.   24—26424

Naturalization. To clerks of courts who take passport applications [circular letter concerning issue of duplicate certificates of naturalization]. Mar. 28, 1924. 1 p. 4° ‡

Rio de Janeiro, International Centennial Exposition, 1922. International Exposition in Rio de Janeiro, 1921 [1922], report forwarding, in conformity with joint resolution providing for participation by Government of United States in International Exposition held at Rio de Janeiro, departmental reports called for in resolution. Apr. 24, calendar day Apr. 25, 1924. 3 p. (S. doc. 98, 68th Cong. 1st sess.) [Departmental reports not included in this document.] * Paper, 5c.

SUPREME COURT

Cases. Docket [of cases pending in Supreme Court], Oct. term, 1923. [1924.] p. 285–300, 4° [Issued in loose-leaf form.] ‡

Graham, Samuel J. Transcript of record, Oct. term, 1923, no. 311, Joshua W. Miles, formerly collector of internal revenue for district of Maryland, *vs.* Samuel J. Graham, in error to district court for district of Maryland. [1924.] cover-title, i+17 p. ‡

[*Journal*] Apr. 7–30, 1924; [slips] 81–98. [1924.] leaves 204–253. ‡

Lorillard, P., Company, Incorporated. Transcript of record, Oct. term, 1923, no. 873, United States *vs.* P. Lorillard Company, appeal from Court of Claims. [1924.] cover-title, i+19 p. ‡

Official reports of Supreme Court, v. 263 U. S., no. 3; Ernest Knaebel, reporter. Preliminary print. 1924. cover-title, p. 365–536, 12° [Cases adjudged in Supreme Court at Oct. term, 1923 (opinions of Dec. 10, 1923 and Jan. 7, 1924, in part). Text on p. 2 and 4 of cover. From United States reports, v. 263.] * Paper, 25c. single copy, $1.00 per vol. (4 nos. to a vol.; subscription price, $3.00 for 12 nos.) ; foreign subscription, 5c. added for each pamphlet.

TARIFF COMMISSION

Wheat and wheat products, report [on] differences in costs of production of wheat, wheat flour, and wheat mill feed in United States and in Canada, as ascertained pursuant to provisions of sec. 315 of title 3 of tariff act of 1922; with appendix, proclamation by the President. 1924. iii+71 p. il. * Paper, 10c.
24—26366

TREASURY DEPARTMENT

Appeals pending before United States courts in customs cases, no. 74; Apr. 1924. 1924. [1]+14 p. [Quarterly.] * Paper, 5c. single copy, 15c. a yr.; foreign subscription, 20c.
10—4497

Bonds of officers. Companies holding certificates of authority from Secretary of Treasury, under acts of Aug. 13, 1894, and Mar. 23, 1910, as acceptable sureties on Federal bonds, also acceptable reinsuring companies under Department circular of July 5, 1922; revised as to process agents to Mar. 31, 1924. Mar. 31, 1924. 1 p. oblong large 8° [Semiannual.] †

Circular instructions of Treasury Department relative to tariff, internal revenue, liberty loan, and other laws, calendar year 1923 [title-page and index]. 1924. [1]+iii p. 4° †

Coins. values of foreign coins, Apr. 1, 1924. [1924.] 1 p. 4° (Department circular 1; Director of Mint.) [Quarterly.] †

Corporations. Distributed and undistributed earnings of corporations, letter, in response to resolution, furnishing information relative to profit, surplus, and dividends of corporations reporting net taxable income of $2,000 and over in 1922. 1924. iii+132 p. (S. doc. 85, 68th Cong. 1st sess.) * Paper, 15c.
24—26425

Finance. Daily statement of Treasury compiled from latest proved reports from Treasury offices and depositaries, Apr. 1–30, 1924. [1924.] Each 4 p. or 3 p. f° [Daily except Sundays and holidays.] † 15—3303

Ogdensburg, N. Y. Designating port of Ogdensburg, N. Y., as quarantine station for vessels destined via St. Lawrence River to ports on Great Lakes. Mar. 18. 1924. 1 p. 4° (Department circular 339; Public Health Service.) †

Portland, Me. Boundaries of quarantine anchorage in harbor at Portland, Me. Mar. 20. 1924. 1 p. 4° (Department circular 335 amended; Public Health Service.) †

Public debt. Statement of public debt of United States, Jan. 31. 1924. [1924.] [2] p. narrow f° [Monthly.] † 10—21268

Report. Annual report of Secretary of Treasury on state of finances, fiscal year 1923, with appendices. 1924· xxii+987 p. il. 1 pl. (Treas. Dept. doc. 2926.) * Cloth, $1.00. 8—32556

—— Same. (Treas. Dept. doc. 2926; H. doc. 63. 68th Cong. 1st sess.)

Telephone directory of Treasury Department, Jan. 1, 1924. 1924. ii+41 p. ‡

Treasury decisions under customs. internal revenue, and other laws, including decisions of Board of General Appraisers and Court of Customs Appeals, v. 45, no. 14–17; Apr. 3–24, 1924. 1924. various paging. [Weekly. Department decisions numbered 40087–130, general appraisers' decisions 8767–78, abstracts 47006–169, internal revenue decisions 3568–84 (except 3583, which has been printed as supplement to Treasury decisions, for which see, below, under Internal Revenue Bureau), and Tariff Commission Notices 35 and 36.] * Paper, 5c. single copy, $1.00 a yr.; foreign subscription. $2.00. 10—30490

APPRAISERS

Reappraisements of merchandise by general appraisers [on Mar. 24–Apr. 19, 1924]; Apr. 4–25, 1924. [1924.] various paging. (Reappraisement circulars 3503–6.) [Weekly.] * Paper, 5c. single copy, 50c. a yr.; foreign subscription, $1.05. 13—2916

BUDGET BUREAU

Foot-and-mouth disease. Eradication of foot-and-mouth and other contagious diseases of animals. supplemental estimate of appropriation for Department of Agriculture, fiscal year 1924, to remain available until June 30. 1925, for eradication of foot-and-mouth and other contagious diseases of animals, $1.500.000. Apr. 11, 1924. 3 p. (H. doc. 236, 68th Cong. 1st sess.) * Paper, 5c.

COAST GUARD

Circular letter 10; Feb. 28. 1924. [1924.] 9 p. ‡

Instructions, customs, navigation. and motor-boat laws and duties of boarding officers, 1923. 1924. iii p.+95 leaves. [Interleaved.] ‡ 24—26371

Register of commissioned and warrant officers and cadets. and ships and stations of Coast Guard, Jan. 1, 1924. [1924.] [1]+114· p. * Paper, 10c. 15—26584

COMPTROLLER OF CURRENCY

National banks. Monthly statement of capital. stock of national banks, national bank notes. and Federal reserve bank notes outstanding, bonds on deposit, etc. [Apr. 1, 1924]. Apr. 1, 1924. 1 p. narrow f° † 10—21266

GENERAL SUPPLY COMMITTEE

Government supplies. Specifications and proposals for supplies [fiscal year 1925]: class 14, Ice. [1924.] 2 p. 4° †

GOVERNMENT ACTUARY

Bonds of United States. Market prices and investment values of outstanding bonds and notes [of United States, Mar. 1924]. Apr. 1, 1924. 7 p. 4° (Form A.) [Monthly.] †

INTERNAL REVENUE BUREAU

Decisions. Citator of internal revenue Treasury decisions and regulations, showing where decisions nos. 1–3559 are cited, amended, reversed, etc., Dec. 29, 1899–Feb. 25, 1924. 1924. [1]+118 p. * Paper, 15c.

Income tax, community property, article 31, Regulations 62 (1922 edition), amended; [and] Community property, California, opinion of Attorney General [of United States]. [1924.] 12 p. ([Treasury decision] 3568–69.) [From Treasury decisions, v. 45, no. 14.] †

Internal revenue bulletin. Internal revenue bulletin, v. 3, no. 14–17; Apr. 7–28, 1924. 1924. various paging. [Weekly.] * Paper, 5c. single copy (for subscription price see note below). 22—26051

NOTE.—The Internal revenue bulletin service for 1924 will consist of weekly bulletins, quarterly digests, and semiannual cumulative bulletins. The weekly bulletins will contain the rulings to be made public and all internal revenue Treasury decisions. The quarterly digests, with the exception of the one to be published at the end of 1924, will contain digests of the rulings previously published in the weekly bulletins for 1924. The last digest for 1924 will also contain digests of the rulings published during 1922 and 1923. The semiannual cumulative bulletins will contain all new rulings published during the previous 6 months. The complete bulletin service may be obtained, on a subscription basis, from the Superintendent of Documents, Government Printing Office, Washington, D. C., for $2.00 a yr.; foreign subscription, $2.75.

—— Internal revenue bulletin, cumulative bulletin II–2, July–Dec. 1923. 1924. vii+404 p. [Semiannual.] * Paper, 40c. (for subscription price see note above). 22—27420

Liquors. Regulations 60 relative to intoxicating liquor. Revised Mar. 1924. 1924. vi+255 p. il. (Prohibition Unit.) * Paper, 30c. 24—26372

—— Same. Revised Mar. 1924. 1924. vi+255 p. il. (Prohibition Unit; [Treasury decision] 3583.) [Supplement to Treasury decisions, v. 45, no. 16.] * Paper, 30c.

Oleomargarin. Regulations 9 relating to taxes on oleomargarine, adulterated butter, and process or renovated butter under act of Aug. 2, 1886, as amended by act of May 9, 1902. Revised June, 1923. [Reprint] 1924. vi+101 p. * Paper, 10c. 24—26426

LOANS AND CURRENCY DIVISION

Bonds of United States. Caveat list of United States registered bonds and notes, Apr. 1, 1924. [1924.] 56 p. f° [Monthly.] †

MINT BUREAU

Coins. Information relating to United States coins and medals. 1924. [1]+l p. †

PUBLIC HEALTH SERVICE

Bedbug, its relation to public health, its habits and life history, and methods of control. Revised edition 1924. 1924. 8 p. (Reprint 626.) [Original article from Public health reports, Dec. 10, 1920.] * Paper, 5c. 24—26373

Conference of State Sanitary Engineers. Transactions of 4th annual Conference of State Sanitary Engineers, Washington, D. C., May 16 and 17, 1923. Apr. 1924. xii+82 il. map. (Public health bulletin 142.) * Paper, 15c. 19—27671

Diphtheria. Is prophylactic use of diphtheria antitoxin justified? [with list of references]; by James A. Doull and Roy P. Sandidge. 1924. [1]+12 p. (Reprint 901.) [Prepared in cooperation with Johns Hopkins University. From Public health reports, Feb. 15, 1924.] * Paper, 5c. 24—26377

Hygiene, Public. Municipal ordinances, rules, and regulations pertaining to public health, 1920–22; compiled by Jason Waterman and William Fowler. 1924. xiii+346 p. il. (Supplement 44 to Public health reports.) * Paper, 25c. 21—26956

Mercurial·poisoning. report on poisoning from small quantities of mercurial vapor; by J. A. Turner. 1924. [1]+13 p. (Reprint 903.) [From Public health reports, Feb. 22, 1924.] *Paper, 5c.   24—26427

Mosquitos. Some observations on dispersal of adult Anopheles; by M. A. Barber and T. B. Hayne. 1924. [1]+9 p. (Reprint 899.) [From Public health reports, Feb. 1, 1924.] * Paper, 5c.   24—26375

—— Some observations on winter activities of Anopheles in southern United States; by M. A. Barber, W. H. W. Komp, and T. B. Hayne. 1924. 16 p. (Reprint 900.) [From Public health reports, Feb. 8, 1924.] *Paper, 5c.   24—26376

Picrate. Preparation of crystalline picrate having antineuritic properties of vitamine B; by Atherton Seidell. 1924. [1]+6 p. (Reprint 902.) [From public health reports, Feb. 15, 1924.] *Paper, 5c. ·   24—26378

Public health reports. Public health reports, v. 38, pt. 2, nos. 27–52, July–Dec. 1923 [title-page and index]. 1924. [1]+3155–90 p. *Paper, 5c. single copy, included in price of Public health reports for subscribers.   6—25167

—— Same, v. 39, no. 14–17; Apr. 4–25, 1924. 1924. [xvi]+655–921 p. il. [Weekly.] *Paper, 5c. single copy, $1.50 a yr.; foreign subscription, $2.75.

· Special articles.—No. 14. Outbreaks of botulism at Albany. Oreg., and Sterling. Colo., Feb. 1924: Report on outbreak at Albany, Oreg., by Frederick D. Stricker and J. C. Geiger; [Report on outbreak at Sterling, Colo., by J. C. Geiger].—Goiter survey in Wexford County, Mich.—Mortality and birth rates for first 9 months of 1923, announcement of provisional figures made by Department of Commerce.—No. 15. Some tendencies indicated by new life tables; by Rollo H. Britten.—Method for estimation of total sulphur in neoarsphenamine and sulpharsphenamine; by Elias. Elvove.—Increase in automobile fatalities in Ohio.—No. 16. Sickness among 21,000 automobile workers, morbidity experience of Flint and Pontiac (Mich.) sick benefit associations in 1921 and 1922; by Dean. K. Brundage.—Studies on oxidation-reduction: 6, Preliminary study of ·indophenols, (A) dibromo substitution products· of phenol indophenol, (B) substituted indophenols of ortho type, (C) miscellaneous [with list of references]; by Barnett Cohen. H. D. Gibbs, and W. Mansfield Clark.—No. 17. Spontaneous hatching of Clonorchis ova, preliminary note on investigation to determine whether clonorchiasis may be disseminated on Pacific slope [with list of references]; by N. E. Wayson.—Factors in mental health of boys of foreign parentage, study of 240 boys of foreign parentage known to child welfare agency [Boston Children's Aid Society], 1916–23; by Mary ·C. Jarrett.—Reports of Health Section of·League of Nations.—Death rates in group of insured persons, comparison of principal causes of death, Jan. and Feb. 1924. and Feb. and year 1923.—Public Health Service publications, list of publications issued Oct. 1923–Apr. 1924.

Note.—This publication is distributed gratuitously to State and municipal health officers, etc., by the Surgeon General of the Public Health Service, Treasury Department. Others desiring these reports. may obtain them ·from the Superintendent of Documents, Washington, D. C., at the prices stated above.

Schick tests and immunization against diphtheria in 8th sanitary district of vermont; by C. W. Kidder. [Reprint] 1924. [1]+4 p. (Reprint 825.) [From Public health reports, Mar. 30, 1923.] * Paper, 5c.   24—26374

Venereal disease handbook for community leaders, program of venereal disease control [with bibliographies]; prepared by Public Health Service for use in its cooperative work with·State departments of health. 1924.··v+65·p. il. * Cloth, 50c.   ·   ◆

VENEREAL DISEASES DIVISION

Hygiene. Keeping fit [information for young men]. [Reprint 1924.] ii+11+ [1] p. il.·₁([V. D. B. 55.]) *

Red light districts. Case. against red light district. [Reprint with slight changes] 1924. 8 p. narrow 12° ([V. D. no. 54.]) [Prepared by American Social Hygiene Association.] †

Sex education in the home [with bibliography]. [Reprint with changes] 1924. 13 p. ([V. D. pamphlet 61.]) * Paper, 5c. .

SUPPLY BUREAU

Public buildings. · Proposal blank and specifications for miscellaneous supplies for all Federal buildings under control of Treasury Department and for ice for such buildings in New York, Brooklyn, Paterson,· and Newark, fiscal year 1925. 1924. [1]+37 p. 4° †

Public buildings—Continued. Soap scouring compound, specifications for sup-
plying public buildings under control of Treasury Department with soap
scouring compound, fiscal year 1925. [1924.] 6 p. f° †

VETERANS' BUREAU

Opinions. Digests of legal opinions relating to veterans' Bureau, including
opinions of general counsel of Veterans' Bureau, comptroller general, and
Attorney General, Oct. 1923; no. 2. 1924. vi+40 p. [Monthly.] * Paper,
5c.
24—26146
—— Same, Nov. 1923; no. 3. 1924. xi+29 p. [Monthly.] * Paper, 5c.

WAR DEPARTMENT

Army regulations. †

NOTE.—The Army regulations are issued in pamphlet form for insertion in loose-
leaf binders. The names of such of the more important administrative subjects as
may seem appropriate, arranged in proper sequence, are numbered in a single series,
and each name so numbered constitutes the title and number of a pamphlet containing certain administrative regulations pertaining thereto. Where more than one
pamphlet is required for the administrative regulations pertaining to any such title,
additional pamphlets will be issued in a separate sub-series.

15–5.   Adjutant General's Department: General provisions; Jan. 30, 1924. [1924.]
          4 p.
25–5.   Judge Advocate General's Department: General provisions; Mar. 12, 1924.
          [1924.] 2 p. [Supersedes AR 25–5, Mar. 16, 1922.]
30–2145. Quartermaster Corps: Unserviceable property, including waste material,
          Changes 3; Mar. 18, 1924. [1924.] 2 p. [Supersedes AR 30–2145,
          Changes 1 and 2, June 25 and Dec. 8, 1923. Date of Changes 2 incorrectly
          given on p. 1 as Dec. 30, 1923.]
35–860.   Finance Department: Inter-branch procurements; Jan. 8, 1924. [1924.] 2 p.
          [Supersedes AR 35–860, May 25, 1923.]
35–2360. Same: Pay of enlisted men, longevity pay; Jan. 26, 1924. [1924.] 2 p.
          [Supersedes AR 35–2360, Oct. 2, 1923.]
35–4520. Same: Monetary allowances in lieu of rations and quarters for enlisted men,
          Changes 2; Jan. 18, 1924. 1924. 1 p. [Supersedes AR 35–4520, Changes
          1, Sept. 1, 1923.]
35–6520. Same: Property accountability and responsibility; Dec. 13, 1923. [1924.]
          14 p.
35–6540. Same: Requisitioning property; Dec. 13, 1923. [1924.] 3 p.
35–6560. Same: Receipt, shipment, and issue of property, Dec. 13, 1923. [1924.] 8 p.
35–6580. Same: Accounting for subsistence supplies on Army transports; Dec. 13, 1923.
          [1924.] 2 p.
35–6600. Same: Accounting for property issued to rifle clubs; Dec. 13, 1923. [1924.]
          3 p.
35–6620. Same: Expendable property; Dec. 13, 1923. [1924.] 2 p.
35–6640. Same: Lost, destroyed, damaged, or unserviceable property, Changes 1; Feb.
          5, 1924. 1924. 1 p.
35–6660. Same: Sales of property; Dec. 13, 1923. [1924.] 4 p.
35–6680. Same: Transfers of property accountability; Dec. 13, 1923. [1924.] 3 p.
35–6700. Same: Property records; Dec. 13, 1923. 1924. 1 p.
35–6720. Same: Blank forms pertaining to property accounting; Dec. 13, 1923. [1924.]
          6 p.
35–6740. Same: Property auditing; Dec. 13, 1923. [1924.] 5 p.
40–80.   Medical Department: Medical Department Board; Jan. 22, 1924. 1924. 1 p.
40–215.   Same: Prevention of communicable diseases of man, immunization, Changes
          3; Mar. 7, 1924. [1924.] 3 p. [Supersedes AR 40–215, Changes 1 and
          2, Nov. 28 and Dec. 18, 1923.]
40–1195. Same: Identification record; Nov. 30, 1923. [1924.] 6 p. il.
100–50.   Corps of Engineers: Military railways, Changes 1; Jan. 29, 1924. 1924. 1 p.
105–25.   Signal Corps: Telegraph, cable, and radio service; Dec. 28, 1923. [1924.]
          6 p.
345–50.   Military records: Strength returns, general, Changes 1; Mar. 7, 1924. 1924.
          1 p.
350–110. Military education: General and special service schools, general provisions,
          Changes 2; Feb. 19, 1924. 1924. 1 p. [Supersedes AR 350–110, Changes
          1, Sept. 1, 1922.]
600–355. Personnel: Arrest and confinement, general; Feb. 19, 1924. [1924.] 4 p.
          [Supersedes AR 600–355, July 3, 1922.]
605–5.   Commissioned officers: Appointment in Regular Army, except in Medical
          Department and except chaplains, Changes 1; Feb. 28, 1924. 1924. 1p.
605–10.   Same: Appointment in Medical Corps, Regular Army; Mar. 8, 1924. [1924.]
          8 p. [Supersedes AR 605–10, Feb. 24, 1921.]
605–115. Same: Leaves of absence and delays, Changes 4; Mar. 7, 1924. [1924.] 3 p.
          [Supersedes AR 605–115, Changes 1–3, May 22–Oct. 5, 1923.]
605–245. Same: Retirement; Dec. 21, 1923. [1924.] 5 p. [Supersedes AR 605–245,
          Sept. 15, 1921.]

Army regulations.—Continued.

605–250.　Same: Army retiring boards; Jan. 19, 1924. [1924.]　10 p.　[Supersedes AR 605–250, Sept. 7, 1921.]

615–5.　Enlisted men: Appointment and reduction of noncommissioned officers and privates, 1st class, except in Medical Department; Dec. 13, 1923.　[1924.] 7 p.

615–15.　Same: Appointment and reduction of noncommissioned officers and privates, 1st class, Medical Department; Nov. 30, 1923.　[1924.]　8 p.

615–40.　Same: Clothing, allowances, accounts, and disposition, Changes 6; Feb. 12, 1924.　[1924.]　4 p.　[Supersedes AR 615–40, Changes 1–5, July 17, 1922–Nov. 24, 1923.]

850–20.　Standard specifications for marking shipments; Nov. 8, 1923.　[1923.]　4 p. il.

Japan. For relief of sufferers from earthquake in Japan, draft of proposed legislation for relief of sufferers from earthquake in Japan.　Apr. 22, 1924. 2 p.　(H. doc. 242, 68th Cong. 1st sess.)　* Paper, 5c.

Military Academy, West Point. Information relative to appointment and admission of cadets to Military Academy. 1924 edition.　[1924.]　40 p. il. 1 pl. 4 p. of pl.　†　　　　　　　　　　　　　　　　　　　　　　War 13—98

Training regulations.

NOTE.—The Training regulations are issued in pamphlet form for insertion in looseleaf binders.

50–25.　Soldier: Instruction and qualification with bayonet, prepared under direction of chief of infantry; Dec. 20, 1923.　[1924.]　48 p. il.　* Paper, 10c.

145–5.　Musketry, sec. 1–8 prepared under direction of chief of infantry, sec. 9 prepared under direction of chief of cavalry; Dec. 12, 1923.　[1924.]　55 p. il. 1 pl.　* Paper, 10c.

160–5.　Signal communication for all arms, prepared under direction of chief signal officer; Nov. 7, 1923.　[1924.]　73 p. il. 4 pl.　* Paper, 15c.

240–10.　Machine gun: Technique of machine-gun fire, direct laying, prepared under direction of chief of infantry; Dec. 19, 1923.　[1924.]　50 p. il.　* Paper, 10c.

ADJUTANT GENERAL'S DEPARTMENT

Bookkeeping, instructors guide for all arms; prepared at Finance School, Fort Hunt, Va., 1923. 1924.　iii+71 p. il.　(United States Army training manual 74.)　* Cloth, 25c.

Clerk, students manual for all arms; prepared under direction of quartermaster general, Army, 1923. 1924.　vi+185 p.　(United States Army training manual 75.)　‡

Flag circular.　[Mar. 28, 1924.]　6 p. 12°　†

Occupations. Minimum specifications and index for occupational specialists. Revised Feb. 15, 1924. 1924.　xxii+120 p.　(War Dept. doc. 1121.)　‡ War 24—15

U. S. Army, recruiting news, bulletin of recruiting information issued by direction of Adjutant General of Army, Apr. 1 and 15, 1924.　[Recruiting Publicity Bureau, Governors Island, N. Y., Apr. 1 and 15, 1924.]　Each 16 p. il. 4°　† Recruiting Publicity Bureau, Governors Island, N. Y.　War 22—1

AIR SERVICE

Aeronautical bulletin, no. 170, 185–200, State series; Feb. 15–Apr. 1, 1924. [1924.]　various paging, il. 12°　(Airways Section.)　[No. 200 is Index to Aeronautical bulletins 1–200.]　* Paper, 5c. each.　　　　　23—26231

Cameras. Instructions for installation of type L cameras on airplanes.　Reprint Mar. 1, 1924.　cover-title, 15 p. il. 3 pl. 12°　‡

ENGINEERING DIVISION

Rope. Addendum to [Air Service] information circular [aerostation] v. 1, no. 41, Development of manila balloon rope, Material Section report. 1924. ii+2 p. 4°　(Air Service. Air Service information circular, aerostation, v. 1, no. 41, addendum, Mar. 1, 1924.)　‡

ENGINEER DEPARTMENT

Cambridge Harbor, Md., reports on preliminary examination and survey of Cambridge Harbor, Md. Feb. 29, 1924.　14 p. map.　(H. doc. 210, 68th Cong. 1st sess.)　* Paper, 10c.

Chesapeake and Delaware Canal. Maintenance and improvement of existing river and harbor works, Chesapeake and Delaware Canal, advertisement [for constructing 3 highway bridges over inland waterway from Delaware River to Chesapeake Bay, Del. and Md. (Chesapeake and Delaware Canal)]. [1924.] 92 p. 4° †

Cowlitz River, Wash., report on preliminary examination of Cowlitz River, Wash., with view to preparing plans and estimates of cost for prevention and control of floods. Mar. 15, 1924. 15 p. (H. doc. 225, 68th Cong. 1st sess.) * Paper, 5c.

Deep River, Wash., reports on preliminary examination and survey of Deep River, Wahkiakum County, Wash., and entrance thereto. Mar. 13, 1924. 8 p. (H. doc. 218, 68th Cong. 1st sess.) * Paper, 5c.

Delaware River, Pa. and N. J., Philadelphia to Trenton, reports on preliminary examination and survey of Delaware River, Pa. and N. J., with view to securing increased depth and width in channels between Philadelphia and upper railroad bridge at Trenton. Mar. 24, 1924. 104 p. 1 tab. (H. doc. 228, 68th Cong. 1st sess.) * Paper, 15c.

Norfolk Harbor, Va., channels in southern and eastern branches of Elizabeth River, reports on preliminary examination and survey of Norfolk Harbor, Va., with view to securing increased depth and width in channel in south branch of Elizabeth River above inner end of 40-foot channel, also with view to securing increased depth and width in channel in eastern branch of Elizabeth River from Norfolk & Western Railway bridge to Virginian Railway bridge. Mar. 24, 1924. 27 p. 3 maps. (H. doc. 226, 68th Cong. 1st sess.) * Paper, 15c.

Onancock River, Va., reports on preliminary examination and survey of Onancock River, Va. Mar. 13, 1924. 16 p. (H. doc. 219, 68th Cong. 1st sess.) * Paper, 5c.

Puyallup River, Wash., report on preliminary examination of Puyallup River, Wash., with view to preparing plans and estimates of cost for prevention and control of floods on said river and its tributaries, and to determining extent to which United States and local interests should cooperate in carrying out any plans recommended. Mar. 13, 1924. 12 p. map. (H. doc. 220, 68th Cong. 1st sess.) * Paper, 10c.

St. Petersburg, Fla. Maintenance and improvement of existing river and harbor works, St. Petersburg Harbor and Boca Ceiga Bay, Fla., advertisement [for dredging and rock removal in Boca Ceiga Bay, Fla., and for construction of jetty at St. Petersburg (Bayboro Harbor), Fla.]. [1924.] 14 p. 4° †

CALIFORNIA DÉBRIS COMMISSION

Calaveras River, Calif., report on preliminary survey of Calaveras River, Calif., with view to control of its floods. Mar. 11, 1924. 36 p. (H. doc. 217, 68th Cong. 1st sess.) * Paper, 5c.

MISSISSIPPI RIVER COMMISSION

Stages of Mississippi River and of its principal tributaries, [calendar year] 1923. St. Louis, Mo., Mississippi River Commission Print [Apr. 10, 1924]. lxiv+79 p. ‡

8—5662

NORTHERN AND NORTHWESTERN LAKES SURVEY

NOTE.—Charts of the Great Lakes and connecting waters and St. Lawrence River to the international boundary at St. Regis, of Lake Champlain, and of the New York State canals are prepared and sold by the U. S. Lake Survey Office, Old Custom-house, Detroit, Mich. Charts may also be purchased at the following U. S. engineer offices: 710 Army Building, New York, N. Y.; 467 Broadway, Albany, N. Y.; 540 Federal Building, Buffalo, N. Y.; and Canal Office, Sault Ste. Marie, Mich. A catalogue (with index map), showing localities, scales, prices, and conditions of sale, may be had upon application at any of these offices.

A descriptive bulletin, which supplements the charts and gives detailed information as to harbors, shore lines and shoals, magnetic determinations, and particulars of changing conditions affecting navigation, is issued free to chart purchasers, upon request. The bulletin is revised annually and issued at the opening of navigation (in April), and supplements thereto are published monthly during the navigation season.

Complete sets of the charts and publications may be seen at the U. S. engineer offices in Duluth, Minn., Milwaukee, Wis., Chicago, Ill., Grand Rapids, Mich., Cleveland, Ohio, and Oswego, N. Y., but they are obtainable only at the sales offices above mentioned.

Great Lakes. Bulletin 33 [to supplement information given upon charts of Great Lakes]; edited by O. C. Hattery. Apr. 1924. 468 p. il. 2 tab. 4° †
8—35459

Note.—Includes a special article, Compass and magnetism of the earth in Lake region; by Thomas Russell.

Charts

Keweenaw Bay, including L'Anse [Mich.] and Portage Entry, Lake Superior. Scale 1:30,000. 3d edition. [U. S. Lake Survey Office, Detroit, Mich.] Feb. 6, 1924. 35.2×22.7 in. † 15c.

Michigan, Lake. North end of Lake Michigan, including Green Bay. Scale 1:240,000. 5th edition. [U. S. Lake Survey Office, Detroit, Mich.] Feb. 29, 1924. 32×45.5 in. † 30c.

Milwaukee, Wis. Milwaukee Harbor, Wis. Scale 1:15,000. 2d edition. [U. S. Lake Survey Office, Detroit, Mich.] Mar. 19, 1924. 31.3×33.6 in. † 15c.

St. Marys River, head of Hay Lake to Whitefish Bay; with inset, vicinity of Sault Ste. Marie, Mich. and Ontario, showing American and Canadian canals; chart 3. Scale 1:40,000. 10th edition. [U. S. Lake Survey Office, Detroit, Mich.] Feb. 28, 1924. 25.7×37.9 in. † 25c.

RIVERS AND HARBORS BOARD

New Orleans, La. Port of New Orleans, La. 1924. ix+230 p. il. 5 pl. 4 p. of pl. 5 maps, 1 mosaic map, 6 tab. (Port series 5.) [Prepared in co-operation with Research Bureau, Shipping Board.] * Paper, 75c.   24—26428

FINANCE DEPARTMENT

Finance circular. Finance circular 11 and 12 [1923]; Nov. 17 and Dec. 10, 1923. [1924.] Each 6 p. 12° ‡

—— Same 2 [1924]; Feb. 5, 1924. [1924.] 5 p. 12° ‡

GENERAL STAFF CORPS

Army. Changes 139 [for] Army regulations [1913]; Feb. 11, 1924. [1924.] 3 leaves. [Regulations issued by War Department.] †

Handbook for War Department General Staff, Oct. 1923. 1924. vii+52 p. 1 pl. (War Dept. doc. 1119.) * Paper, 10c.   War 24—14

INSULAR AFFAIRS BUREAU

HAITIAN CUSTOMS RECEIVERSHIP

Report of 7th fiscal period Haitian Customs Receivership, fiscal year Oct. 1, 1922–Sept. 30, 1923, with Summary of commerce for fiscal year. 1924. [1]+ 50 p. †

WORLD WAR FOREIGN DEBT COMMISSION

Hungary. Agreement made 25th day of April, 1924, at Washington, D. C., between Hungary and United States [concerning funding of indebtedness to United States through issue of bonds to United States]. [1924.] 11 p. 4° ‡
24—26429

—— Same, with report, and with title, Kingdom of Hungary, report, with agreement referred to therein, providing for settlement of indebtedness of Kingdom of Hungary to United States. Apr. 25, 1924. 10 p. (H. doc. 243, 68th Cong. 1st sess.) * Paper, 5c.   24—26430

Monthly Catalogue
United States
Public Documents

No. 353
May, 1924

ISSUED BY THE
SUPERINTENDENT OF DOCUMENTS

·· IRRAR OF

JUL

WASHINGTON
1924

Abbreviations

Appendix	app.	Page, pages	p.
Congress	Cong.	Part, parts	pt., pts.
Department	Dept.	Plate, plates	pl.
Document	doc.	Portrait, portraits	pl.
Facsimile, facsimiles	facsim.	Quarto	por.
Folio	fo	Report	4°
House	H.	Saint	rp.
House bill	H. R.	Section, sections	St.
House concurrent resolution	H. Con. Res.	Senate, Senate bill	sec.
House document	H. doc.	Senate concurrent resolution	S.
House executive document	H. ex. doc.	Senate document	S. Con. Res.
House joint resolution	H. J. Res.	Senate executive document	S. doc.
House report	H. rp.	Senate joint resolution	S. ex. doc.
House resolution (simple)	H. Res.	Senate report	S. J. Res.
Illustration, illustrations	il.	Senate resolution (simple)	S. rp.
Inch, inches	in.	Session	S. Res.
Latitude	lat.	Sixteenmo	sess.
Longitude	long.	Table, tables	16°
Mile, miles	m.	Thirtytwo-mo	tab.
Miscellaneous	mis., misc.	Treasury	32°
Nautical	naut.	Twelvemo	Treas.
No date	n. d.	Twentyfour-mo	12°
No place	n. p.	Versus	24°
Number, numbers	no., nos.	Volume, volumes	vs., v.
Octavo	8°	Year	v., vol.
			yr.

Common abbreviations for names of States and months are also used.
*Document for sale by Superintendent of Documents.
†Distribution by office issuing document, free if unaccompanied by a price.
‡Printed for official use.

NOTE.—Nearly all of the Departments of the Government make a limited free distribution of their publications. When an entry shows a * price, it is possible that upon application to the issuing office a copy may be obtained without charge.

Explanation

Words and figures inclosed in brackets [ ] are given for information, but do not appear on the title-pages of the publications catalogued. When size is not given octavo is to be understood. Size of maps is measured from outer edge of border, excluding margin. The dates, including day, month, and year, given with Senate and House documents and reports are the dates on which they were ordered to be printed. Usually the printing promptly follows the ordering, but various causes sometimes make delays.

SALES OF GOVERNMENT PUBLICATIONS

The Superintendent of Documents, Washington, D. C., is authorized to sell at cost, plus 10 per cent, without limit as to the number of copies to any one applicant who agrees not to resell or distribute the same for profit, any United States Government publication not confidential in character.

Publications can not be supplied free to individuals nor forwarded in advance of payment.

Publications entered in this catalogue that are for sale by the Superintendent of Documents are indicated by a star (*) preceding the price. A dagger (†) indicates that application should be made to the Department, Bureau, or Division issuing the document. A double dagger (‡) indicates that the document is printed for official use. Whenever additional information concerning the method of procuring a document seems necessary, it will be found under the name of the Bureau by which it was published.

In ordering a publication from the Superintendent of Documents, give (if known) the name of the publishing Department, Bureau, or Division, and the title of the publication. If the publication is numbered, give the number also. Every such particular assists in quick identification. Do not order by the Library of Congress card number.

The accumulation of publications in this Office amounts to several millions, of which over two million are assorted, forming the sales stock. Many rare books are included, but under the law all must be sold regardless of their age or scarcity. Many of the books have been in stock some time, and are apt to be shop-worn. In filling orders the best copy available is sent. A general price-list of public documents is not available, but lists on special subjects will be furnished on application.

MONTHLY CATALOGUE DISTRIBUTION

The Monthly catalogue is sent to each Senator, Representative, Delegate, Resident Commissioner, and officer in Congress; to designated depositories and State and Territorial libraries if it is selected by them; to substantially all Government authors; and to as many school, college, and public libraries as the limited edition will supply.

Subscription price to individuals, 50c. a year, including index; foreign subscription, 75c. a year. Back numbers can not be supplied. Notify the Superintendent of Documents of any change of address.

LIBRARY OF CONGRESS CARDS

Numbers to be used in ordering the printed catalogue cards of the Library of Congress are given at the end of entries for the more important documents. Orders for these cards, remittances in payment for them, and requests for information about them should be addressed to the Librarian of Congress, not to the Superintendent of Documents.

INDEX

An Index to the Monthly catalogue is issued at the end of the fiscal year. This contains index entries for all the numbers issued from July to June, and can be

bound with the numbers as an index to the volume. Persons desiring to bind the catalogue at the end of the year should be careful to retain the numbers received monthly, as duplicate copies can not be supplied.

HOW TO REMIT

Remittances for the documents marked with a star (*) should be made to the Superintendent of Documents, Washington, D. C., by coupons, postal money order, express order, or New York draft. Currency may be sent at sender's risk.

Postage stamps, foreign money, defaced or smooth coins, positively will not be accepted.

For the convenience of the general public, coupons that are good until used in exchange for Government publications sold by the Superintendent of Documents may be purchased from his Office in sets of 20 for $1.00. Address order to Superintendent of Documents, Government Printing Office, Washington, D. C.

No charge is made for postage on documents forwarded to points in United States, Alaska, Guam, Hawaii, Philippine Islands, Porto Rico, Samoa, or to Canada, Cuba, or Mexico. To other countries the regular rate of postage is charged, and remittances must cover such postage. In computing foreign postage, add one-third of the price of the publication.

CORRECTION FOR APRIL, 1924, MONTHLY CATALOGUE

For "xii+82 il. map." in last line of 2d entry under Public Health Service on p. 668, read "xii+82 p. il. map."

MONTHLY CATALOGUE

No. 353   MAY   1924

AGRICULTURE DEPARTMENT

NOTE.—Those publications of the Department of Agriculture which are for sale will be supplied by the Superintendent of Documents, Washington, D. C. The Department issues a monthly list of publications, which is mailed to all applicants, enabling them to select such reports and bulletins as interest them.

Cattle. [Bureau of Animal Industry] order 211 revised [amendment 2], 273 [amendment 3], 285 [amendment 1], 287 [amendment 8–15]; Mar. 31–May 26, 1924. 1924. Each 1 p. or 2 p. [Consist of orders concerning quarantine of cattle, etc.] †

Claims. Eight claims adjusted by Secretary of Agriculture, communication from Secretary of Agriculture, submitting estimate of appropriation to pay 8 claims for damages to or losses of privately owned property, which he has adjusted and which require appropriation for their payment. May 26, 1924. 4 p. (H. doc. 317, 68th Cong. 1st sess.) * Paper, 5c.

Crops and markets. Crops and markets, weekly, May 3–31, 1924; v. 1, no. 18–22. [1924.] p. 273–352, il. 4° * Paper, $1.00 a yr. (including monthly supplement); foreign subscription, $2.00.   Agr 24—113

—— Same, monthly supplement, May, 1924; v. 1, supplement 5. [1924.] p. 145–168, il. 4° [Included in price of weekly Crops and markets.]

Grain hulls. Effect of sodium hydroxid on composition, digestibility, and feeding value of grain hulls and other fibrous material [with list of literature cited]; by J. G. Archibald. 1924. cover-title, p. 245–265. [From Journal of agricultural research, v. 27, no. 5, Feb. 2, 1924.] ‡

Journal of agricultural research, v. 27, no. 5–8; Feb. 2–23, 1924. 1924. cover-titles, 231–616+[14] p.+[6] leaves, il. 9 pl. 18 p. of pl. [Weekly. Text on p. 2 of covers.] * Paper, 10c. single copy, $4.00 a yr.; foreign subscription, $5 25.   Agr 13—1837

CONTENTS.—No. 5. Blooming of wheat flowers [with list of literature cited]; by C. E. Leighty and W. J. Sando.—Effect of sodium hydroxid on composition, digestibility, and feeding value of grain hulls and other fibrous material [with list of literature cited]; by J. G. Archibald.—Tissue fluids of Egyptian and upland cottons and their F. hybrid [with list of literature cited]; by J. Arthur Harris, Zonja Wallen Lawrence, W. F. Hoffman, John V. Lawrence, [and] A. T. Valentine.—No. 6. Selective fertilization in cotton [with list of literature cited]; by Thomas H. Kearney and George J. Harrison.—Effect of fertilizers on development of stem rust of wheat [with list of literature cited]; by E. C. Stakman and O. S. Aamodt.—Morphological and physiological studies on resistance of wheat to Puccinia graminis tritici Eriкss. and Henn. [with list of literature cited]; by C. R. Hursh.—Function of grit in gizzard of fowl; by B. F. Kaupp.—Association of manganese with vitamins [with list of literature cited]; by J. S. McHargue.—No. 7. Experiments with flag smut of wheat and causal fungus, Urocystis tritici Keke. [with list of literature cited; by] Marion A. Griffiths.—Studies on parasitism of Urocystis tritici Kearn., organism causing flag smut of wheat [with list of literature cited]; by Robert J. Noble.—Inheritance of petal spot in Pima cotton; by Thomas H. Kearney.—Migration of Aphididae and appearance of sexual forms as affected by relative length of daily light exposure [with list of literature cited]; by S. Marcovitch.—No. 8. Breeding, feeding, and other life habits of meadow mice (Microtus) [with list of literature cited]; by Vernon Bailey.—Inheritance of crinkly, ramose, and brachytic characters of maize in hybrids with teosinte [with list of literature cited]; by J. H. Kempton.—Utilization of lactose by chicken [with list of literature cited]; by T. S. Hamilton and L. E. Card.—Occurrence of lactase in alimentary tract of chicken [with list of literature cited]; by T. S. Hamilton and H. H. Mitchell.—Life history of grape root rot fungus Roesleria hypogaea Thüm. et Pass. [with list of literature cited]; by Angie M. Beckwith.

NOTE.—This publication is published by authority of the Secretary of Agriculture, with the cooperation of the Association of Land-Grant Colleges. It is distributed free only to libraries of agricultural colleges and experiment stations, to large universities, technical schools, and to such institutions as make suitable exchanges with the Agriculture Department. Others desiring the Journal may obtain it from the Superintendent of Documents, Washington, D. C., at the prices stated above.

Manganese. Association of manganese with vitamins [with list of literature cited]; by J. S. McHargue. [1924.] p. 417–424+[1] leaf, 1 pl. [From Journal of agricultural research, v. 27, no. 6, Feb. 9, 1924.] ‡

Official record, Department of Agriculture, v. 3, no. 19–22; May 7–28, 1924. [1924.] Each 8 p. 4° [Weekly.] * Paper, 50c. a yr.; foreign subscription, $1.10.
Agr 22—146

Potatoes. Further observations on osmotic pressure of juices of potato plant; by B. F. Lutman. ·[1923.] p. 243–256. [From Journal of agricultural research, v. 26, no. 6, Nov. 10, 1923.] ‡

Quarantine. Modification of pink bollworm quarantine, Amendment 3 to 2d revision of regulations supplemental to Notice of quarantine 52, effective Apr. 5, 1924. [1924.] 4 p. (Federal Horticultural Board.) †

—— Quarantine on account of European corn borer, Notice of quarantine 43 (3d revision) [with rules and regulations], effective May 1, 1924. [1924.] 7 p. (Federal Horticultural Board.) †

Reports. Annual reports of Department of Agriculture, year ended June 30, 1923: Report of Secretary of Agriculture [with] reports of chiefs. 1924. ix+716 p. * Cloth, $1.00.
Agr 9—987

—— Same. (H. doc. 120, 68th Cong. 1st sess.)

Soybean mosaic, seed transmission and effect on yield [with list of literature cited]; by James B. Kendrick and Max W. Gardner. [1924.] p. 91–98. [From Journal of agricultural research, v. 27, no. 2, Jan. 12, 1924.] ‡

AGRICULTURAL ECONOMICS BUREAU

Accounting. Farm household accounts; [by] W. C. Funk. [June, 1918, reprint] 1924. ii+10 p. il. (Agriculture Dept. Farmers' bulletin 964.) * Paper, 5c.
Agr 18—571

Citrus fruit. Organization and development of cooperative citrus-fruit marketing agency [with list of literature cited]; by A. W. McKay and W. Mackenzie Stevens. May, 1924. cover-title, 68 p. il. (Agriculture Dept. Department bulletin 1237.) * Paper, 10c.
Agr 24—456

Cotton. Losses from selling cotton in seed; [by] Charles F. Creswell. [Nov. 10, 1916, reprint with changes] 1924. 12 p. il. (Agriculture Dept. Farmers' bulletin 775.) [Aug. 1921, on p. 2, is date of previous reprint.] * Paper, 5c.

Cotton-seed. Delinting and recleaning cottonseed for planting purposes; by J. E. Barr. Apr. 1924. 20 p. il. 8 p. of pl. (Agriculture Dept. Department bulletin 1219.) * Paper, 10c.
Agr 24—341

Europe. Agricultural survey of Europe: Danube Basin, pt. 1; by Louis G. Michael. Apr. 1924. cover-title, 111 p. il. (Agriculture Dept. Department bulletin 1234.) [Text on p. 2 of cover.] * Paper, 15c.
Agr 24—455

Farm labor in Massachusetts, 1921; by Josiah C. Folsom. Apr. 1924. 26 p. il. (Agriculture Dept. Department bulletin 1220.) * Paper, 5c.
Agr 24—342

Home supplies furnished by farm; [by W. C. Funk]. [Feb. 1920, reprint 1924.] 20 p. il. (Agriculture Dept. Farmers' bulletin 1082.) * Paper, 5c.
Agr 20—783

Sheep, lamb, mutton, and wool statistics, year ended Mar. 31, 1923, with comparable data for earlier years. May 9, 1924. cover-title, 100 p. (Agriculture Dept. Statistical bulletin 3.) [Text on p. 2 of cover.] * Paper, 15c.
Agr 24—466

Strawberries. Preparation of strawberries for market; [by] C. T. More [and] H. E. Truax. May, 1918 [reprint 1924]. 28 p. il. (Agriculture Dept. Farmers' bulletin 979.) [Imprint date incorrectly given on title-page as 1918.] * Paper, 5c.
Agr 18—437

Swine. Corn-belt farming system which saves harvest labor by hogging down crops; [by] J. A. Drake. [Revised Mar. 1917, reprint] 1924. 2+17 p. il. (Agriculture Dept. Farmers' bulletin 614.) * Paper, 5c.

Warehouses. Banker and United States warehouse act; [by H. S. Yohe]. 1924. [1]+12 p. il. narrow 8° [From Acceptance bulletin of American Acceptance Council, Feb. 1924.] †

Wheat. Experimental milling and baking, including chemical determinations; by J. H. Shollenberger, Walter K. Marshall, and D. A. Coleman. Apr. 1924. cover-title, 54 p. il. (Agriculture Dept. Department bulletin 1187.) [Includes list of Agriculture Department publications pertaining to grain standardization.] * Paper, 15c.   Agr 24—451

ANIMAL INDUSTRY BUREAU

Cotton-seed. Feeding cottonseed products to livestock; [by E. W. Sheets and E. H. Thompson]. [Nov. 1920, revised Apr. 1924.] [1924.] ii+14 p. il. (Agriculture Dept. Farmers' bulletin 1179.) * Paper, 5c.

Cows. Feeding of dairy cows; [by Helmer Rabild, H. P. Davis, and W. K. Brainerd]. [July, 1916, revised Apr. 1924.] [1924.] ii+21 p. il. (Agriculture Dept. Farmers' bulletin 743.) * Paper, 5c.

Dourine of horses; [by John R. Mohler and H. W. Schoening]. [Aug. 1920, revised June, 1923, reprint 1924.] ii+10 p. il. (Agriculture Dept. Farmers' bulletin 1146.) * Paper, 5c.

Goats. Milk goats; [by Edward L. Shaw]. [Feb. 1918, revised Mar. 1924.] 1924. 36 p. il. (Agriculture Dept. Farmers' bulletin 920.) * Paper, 5c.

Mycotic stomatitis of cattle; [by] John R. Mohler. May, 1924. 7 p. il. (Agriculture Dept. Department circular 322.) [Revision of Animal Industry Bureau Circular 51.] * Paper, 5c.   Agr 24—460

Posters. Report suspected cases of foot-and-mouth disease to nearest veterinarian or livestock official; [poster]. [1924.] 18×13 in. †

Service announcements. Service and regulatory announcements, Apr. 1924; [no.] 204. May 22, 1924. p. 41–51. [Monthly.] * Paper, 5c. single copy, 25c. a yr.; foreign subscription, 40c.   Agr 7—1658

Sheep. Breeds of sheep for farm; [by F. R. Marshall]. [May 2, 1914, revised Mar. 1923, reprint 1924.] ii+14 p. il. (Agriculture Dept. Farmers' bulletin 576.) * Paper, 5c.

Silos. Pit silos, [by T. Pryse Metcalfe and George A. Scott; revised by W. H. Black]. [June, 1917, slightly revised Jan. 1923, reprint 1924.] [2]+12 p. il. (Agriculture Dept. Farmers' bulletin 825.) * Paper, 5c.   Agr 23—409

Steers. Fattening steers in corn belt; [by Wm. H. Black]. [Apr. 1924.] ii+18 p. il. (Agriculture Dept. Farmers' bulletin 1382.) [Supersedes Farmers' bulletins 588 and 1218.] * Paper, 5c.   Agr 24—461

Tuberculosis in animals. Tuberculosis in livestock, detection, control & eradication; [by John A. Kiernan and Alexander E. Wight]. [Nov. 1919, revised Apr. 1924.] [1924.] 32 p. il. (Agriculture Dept. Farmers' bulletin 1069.) * Paper, 5c.

—— Tuberculosis of hogs; [by John R. Mohler and Henry J. Washburn]. [Feb. 1917, revised Apr. 1924.] [1924.] ii+14 p. il. (Agriculture Dept. Farmers' bulletin 781.) [Date of original issue incorrectly given on this publication as May, 1917, which is date of a reprint.] * Paper, 5c.

Turkey raising; [by Morley A. Jull and Alfred R. Lee]. [Apr. 1924.] ii+22 p. il. (Agriculture Dept. Farmers' bulletin 1409.) [Revision of Farmers' bulletin 791.] * Paper, 5c.   Agr 24—343

Woolly-pod milkweed (Asclepias eriocarpa) as poisonous plant; by C. Dwight Marsh and A. B. Clawson. Apr. 29, 1924. 14 p. il. (Agriculture Dept. Department bulletin 1212.) . * Paper, 5c.   Agr 24—340

BIOLOGICAL SURVEY BUREAU

Birds. Bird migration; by Wells W. Cooke. Apr. 17, 1915, [reprint] 1924. cover-title, 48 p. il. 4 p. of pl. (Agriculture Dept. [Department] bulletin 185.) * Paper, 10c.   Agr 15—507

—— How to attract birds in northeastern United States; [by W. L. McAtee]. [Dec. 14, 1914, revised Apr. 1924.] [1924.] 16 p. il. (Agriculture Dept. Farmers' bulletin 621.) * Paper, 5c.

—— Instructions for banding birds [with list of literature]; by Frederick C. Lincoln. May, 1924. cover-title, 28 p. il. (Agriculture Dept. Miscellaneous circular 18.) [Revision of Department circular 170. Includes lists of Agriculture Department publications on distribution and migration of birds.] * Paper, 10c.   Agr 24—464

Canaries, their care and management [with bibliography; by Alexander Wetmore]. [May, 1923, revised Apr. 1924.] [1924.] ii+22 p. il. (Agriculture Dept. Farmers' bulletin 1327.) * Paper, 5c.
Agr 23—743

English sparrow as pest; [by] Ned Dearborn. [Apr. 1912, revised Apr. 1917, reprint] 1924. 24 p. il. (Agriculture Dept. Farmers' bulletin 493.) [Includes lists of Agriculture Department publications relating to birds.] * Paper, 5c.

Rabbits. Cottontail rabbits in relation to trees and farm crops; [by D. E. Lantz]. [Jan. 17, 1916, revised Apr. 1924.] [1924.] 15 p. il. (Agriculture Dept. Farmers' bulletin 702.) [Includes lists of Agriculture Department publications relating to injurious wild animals and their control.] * Paper, 5c.

Rats. How to get rid of rats; [by James Silver]. [Apr. 1923, reprint 1924.] ii+14 p. il. (Agriculture Dept. Farmers' bulletin 1302.) * Paper, 5c.
Agr 23—594

Service announcements. Service and regulatory announcements, [no.] 59: Regulations for protection of game in certain localities in Alaska. May 6, 1924. 3 p. * Paper, 5c.
Agr 16—608

—— Same, [no.] 60: Regulations for protection of land fur-bearing animals in Alaska. May 29, 1924. 4 p. il. * Paper, 5c.

CHEMISTRY BUREAU

Food. Index to Notices of judgment [under food and drugs act] 11001–12000. [1924.] p. 559–571. [Notices of judgment 11001–12000 were issued in Service and regulatory announcement supplements 151–170 of the Chemistry Bureau.] * Paper, 5c.

Maple syrup. Production of maple sirup and sugar; [by A. Hugh Bryan, William F. Hubbard, and Sidney F. Sherwood]. [Reprint Feb. 1924.] 35 p. il. (Agriculture Dept. Farmers' bulletin 1366.) [Prepared in cooperation with Forest Service and Plant Industry Bureau.] * Paper, 5c.
Agr 24—209

Service announcements. Service and regulatory announcements, supplement 170. May 12, 1924. p. 533–558. [Contains Notices of judgment under food and drugs act 11951–12000.] * Paper, 5c.
Agr 14—194

ENTOMOLOGY BUREAU

Camphor thrips [with list of literature cited]; by W. W. Yothers and Arthur C. Mason. Apr. 30, 1924. 30 p. il. 6 p. of pl. (Agriculture Dept. Department bulletin 1225.) * Paper, 10c.
Agr 24—454

Carbon disulphid as insecticide; [by] W. E. Hinds. [June, 1917, revised Apr. 1924.] 1924. 22 p. (Agriculture Dept. Farmers' bulletin 799.) * Paper, 5c.

Grapes. Insect and fungous enemies of grape; [by A. L. Quaintance and C. L. Shear]. [Reprint with changes 1924.] 76 p. il. (Agriculture Dept. Farmers' bulletin 1220.) [Prepared in cooperation with Plant Industry Bureau. May, 1922, on p. 2, is date of previous reprint.] * Paper, 10c.

Insects. How to detect outbreaks of insects and save grain crops; [by W. R. Walton]. [June, 1917, revised Jan. 1924.] 1924. 24 p. il. (Agriculture Dept. Farmers' bulletin 835.) * Paper, 5c.

Mites and lice on poultry; [by] F. C. Bishopp and H. P. Wood. [May, 1917, revised Apr. 1924.] 1924. ii+30 p. il. (Agriculture Dept. Farmers' bulletin 801.) [Includes lists of Agriculture Department publications relating to poultry.] * Paper, 5c.

Oyster-shell scale and scurfy scale; by A. L. Quaintance and E. R. Sasscer. Apr. 26, 1916 [reprint 1924]. 16 p. il. (Agriculture Dept. Farmers' bulletin 723.) [Includes lists of Agriculture Department publications relating to insects injurious to deciduous fruits.] * Paper, 5c.
Agr 16—518

Parasites. Introduction of parasites of alfalfa weevil into United States; by Thomas R. Chamberlain. Apr. 1924. 9 p. il. (Agriculture Dept. Department circular 301.) * Paper, 5c.
Agr 24—458

EXPERIMENT STATIONS OFFICE

Experiment station record. Experiment station record, v. 50, no. 3; abstract number. Apr. 11, 1924. cover-title, x+201–300 p. [Text and illustration on p. 2 and 4 of cover.] * Paper, 10c. single copy, 75c. per vol. (2 vols. a yr.) ; foreign subscription, $1.25 per vol. (subscription price incorrectly given in publication).   Agr 9—832

    Note.—Mainly made up of abstracts of reports and publications on agricultural science which have recently appeared in all countries, especially the United States. Extra numbers, called abstract numbers, are issued, 3 to each volume. These are made up almost exclusively of abstracts, that is, they contain no editorial notes and only a limited number of current notes.

—— Same, v. 50, no. 4; Mar. 1924. 1924. cover-title, ix+301–400 p. [Text and illustration on p. 2 and 4 of cover.]

—— Same, v. 50, no. 5; Apr. 1924. 1924. cover-title, viii+401–500 p. [Text and illustration on p. 2 and 4 of cover.]

—— Same, v. 50, no. 6; abstract number. 1924. cover-title, ix+501–600 p. [Text and illustration on p. 2 and 4 of cover.]

FOREST SERVICE

National forests. Ideal vacation land, national forests in Oregon. 1923 [1924]. iv+56+[1] p. il. map. [Imprint date incorrectly given on title-page as 1923.] * Paper, 15c.   Agr 24—497

—— Information regarding employment on national forests. 9th revision. Dec. 15, 1921 [reprint 1924]. 4 p. †

Timber. Measuring and marketing farm timber ; [by Wilbur R. Mattoon and William B. Barrows]. [Sept. 1921, reprint 1924.] 62+[2] p. il. (Agriculture Dept. Farmers' bulletin 1210.) * Paper, 5c.   Agr 21—1164

Maps

Bighorn National Forest, Wyo., land of wealth and wonder. [1924.] 1 sheet (with map on verso), il. f°, folded into narrow 8° size and so printed as to number [1]+13+[1] p. †

Coconino National Forest, Ariz. [resources and recreation features]. [1924.] 1 sheet (with map on verso), il. oblong 8°, folded into narrow 8° size and so printed as to number [4] pages. †

Pisgah National Forest and game preserve, western North Carolina, information for visitors and tourists. [1924.] 1 sheet (with map on verso), il. oblong f°, folded into narrow 8° size and so printed as to number 8 pages. [The map is of the central portions of Pisgah National Forest.] †

Santa Fe National Forest, N. Mex. [resources and recreation features]. [1924.] 1 sheet (with map on verso), il. large 4°, folded into narrow 8° size and so printed as to number [1]+6+[1], p. †

GRAIN FUTURES ADMINISTRATION

Options and futures. Trading in grain futures, in response to resolution, report of Grain Futures Commission under grain futures act, in respect to trading in grain futures on Chicago Board of Trade. 1924. iii+12 p. (S. doc. 110, 68th Cong. 1st sess.) * Paper, 5c.   Agr 24—450

HOME ECONOMICS BUREAU

Canning and preserving. Time-tables for home canning of fruits and vegetables. May, 1924. 4 p. (Agriculture Dept. Miscellaneous circular 24.) * Paper, 5c.   Agr 24—465

Farm kitchen as workshop ; [by Anna Barrows]. [Jan. 1921, revised Sept. 1921, reprint with slight changes 1924.] ii+18 p. il. (Agriculture Dept. Farmers' bulletin 607.) * Paper, 5c.

Food. Directions for examining all canned food before use. May, 1924. 1 p. (Agriculture Dept. Miscellaneous circular 25.) [Prepared in cooperation with Chemistry Bureau and Plant Industry Bureau.] * Paper, 5c.

Honey and its uses in the home; [by Caroline L. Hunt and Helen W. Atwater]. [Apr. 7, 1915, slightly revised Aug. 1922, reprint with changes 1924.] ii+22 p. (Agriculture Dept. Farmers' bulletin 653.) *Paper, 5c.

Meat. Economical use of meat in the home; [by C. F. Langworthy and Caroline L. Hunt]. [1910, revised Nov. 1922, reprint 1924.] 30 p. (Agriculture Dept. Farmers' bulletin 391.) [Previously issued by States Relations Service.] *Paper, 5c.

PLANT INDUSTRY BUREAU

Beans; [by L. C. Corbett]. [Apr. 1907, revised Feb. 1923, reprint with changes 1924.] ii+18 p. il. (Agriculture Dept. Farmers' bulletin 289.) *Paper, 5c.

Bordeaux mixture. Commercial Bordeaux mixtures, how to calculate their values; [by] Errett Wallace and L. H. Evans. June, 1918, corrected Nov. 1922, [reprint] 1924. 12 p. il. (Agriculture Dept. Farmers' bulletin 994.) [Prepared in cooperation with Insecticide and Fungicide Board.] *Paper, 5c.

Box-elder. Red stain in wood of box elder; by Ernest E. Hubert. 1924. cover-title, 447-458+[2] p. il. 3 pl. [Prepared in cooperation with Forest Products Laboratory, Madison, Wis. From Journal of agricultural research, v. 26, no. 10, Dec. 8, 1923.] ‡

Bur clover; by Charles V. Piper and Roland McKee. Oct. 1915, corrected Mar. 1923 [reprint 1924]. 16 p. il. (Agriculture Dept. Farmers' bulletin 693.) [Includes lists of Agriculture Department publications relating to forage crops.] *Paper, 5c.

Cabbage. Cabbage; [by L. C. Corbett]. [Apr. 1911, revised Apr. 1924.] [1924.] ii+18 p. il. (Agriculture Dept. Farmers' bulletin 433.) *Paper, 5c.

—— Cabbage-seed treatment; [by] J. C. Walker. Apr. 1924. 4 p. il. (Agriculture Dept. Department circular 311.) *Paper, 5c.   Agr 24—459

Corn. Anchorage and extent of corn root systems; by James R. Holbert and Benjamin Koehler. 1924. cover-title, 71-78+[4] p.+[1] leaf, il. 5 p. of pl. [Prepared in cooperation with Illinois Agricultural Experiment Station and Funk Brothers Seed Company, Bloomington, Ill. From Journal of agricultural research, v. 27, no. 2, Jan. 12, 1924.] ‡

—— How to grow an acre of corn; [by] C. P. Hartley. [May, 1913, revised Sept. 1922, reprint with changes] 1924. 20 p. il. (Agriculture Dept. Farmers' bulletin 537.) *Paper, 5c.

Cotton. Selective fertilization in cotton [with list of literature cited]; by Thomas H. Kearney and George J. Harrison. [1924.] p. 329-340. [From Journal of agricultural research, v. 27, no. 6, Feb. 9, 1924.] ‡

Cow-pea. Cowpeas, culture and varieties; [by] W. J. Morse]. [Sept. 1920, revised Apr. 1924.] [1924.] ii+18 p. il. (Agriculture Dept. Farmers' bulletin 1148.) *Paper, 5c.

—— Cowpeas, utilization; [by] W. J. Morse]. [Sept. 1920, reprint 1924.] 24 p. il. (Agriculture Dept. Farmers' bulletin 1153.) *Paper, 5c.

Cranberry harvesting and handling; [by] Henry J. Franklin, George M. Darrow, and O. G. Malde]. [Apr. 1924.] ii+30 p. il. (Agriculture Dept. Farmers' bulletin 1402.) *Paper, 5c.   Agr 24—463

Drug plants under cultivation; [by] W. W. Stockberger]. [June, 1915, revised Aug. 1920, reprint 1924.] 52 p. il. (Agriculture Dept. Farmers' bulletin 663.) *Paper, 10c.

Emmer. Experiments with emmer, spelt, and einkorn [with list of literature cited]; by John H. Martin and Clyde E. Leighty. Feb. 1924. cover-title, 60 p. il. 3 p. of pl. (Agriculture Dept. Department bulletin 1197.) *Paper, 10c.   Agr 24—452

Foxtail millet, its culture and utilization in United States; [by] H. N. Vinall]. [Mar. 1917, revised Mar. 1924.] [1924.] 28 p. il. (Agriculture Dept. Farmers' bulletin 793.) *Paper, 5c.

Grape juice. Unfermented grape juice, how to make it in the home; [by Charles Dearing]. [Oct. 1919, reprint with slight changes 1924.] 32 p. il. (Agriculture Dept. Farmers' bulletin 1075.) *Paper, 5c.   Agr 19—994

Grapes. Home uses for muscadine grapes; [by] Charles Dearing. Aug., 1917, [reprint] 1924. 24 p. il. (Agriculture Dept. Farmers' bulletin 859.) *Paper, 5c.   Agr 17—829

Late-blight tuber rot of potato; [by] George K. K. Link and F. C. Meier. May, 1922, revised Feb. 1924. [1924.] 5 p. 2 p. of pl. (Agriculture Dept. Department circular 220.)   * Paper, 5c.   Agr 24—457

Peanut growing for profit; [by W. R. Beattie].   [July, 1920, revised Feb., 1924.] [1924.] 32 p. il. (Agriculture Dept.' Farmers' bulletin 1127.) * Paper, 5c.

Persimmons. Native persimmon; by W. F. Fletcher. Oct. 1915, revised Sept. 1923. [1924.] 24 p. il. (Agriculture Dept. Farmers' bulletin 685.)   * Paper, 5c.

Sorghum. Growing grain sorghums in San Antonio district of Texas; [by] C. R. Letteer. June, 1918, revised Apr. 1924. 1924. ii+9 p. il. (Agriculture Dept. Farmers' bulletin 965.)   * Paper, 5c.

Stinking smut. Studies in physiology and control of bunt, or stinking smut, of wheat [with .list of literature cited]; by Horace M. Woolman and Harry B. Humphrey. May, 1924. cover-title, 30 p. il. 5 p. of pl. (Agriculture Dept. Department bulletin 1239.) [Prepared in cooperation with Washington Agricultural Experiment Station.]   * Paper, 10c.   Agr 24—467

—— Summary of literature on bunt, or stinking smut, of wheat [with bibliography]; by Horace M. Woolman and Harry B. Humphrey. May 1, 1924. cover-title, 44 p. (Agriculture Dept. Department bulletin 1210.)   * Paper, 10c.   Agr 24—339

Strawberry culture, western United States; [by George M. Darrow]. [Apr. 1919, reprint 1924.] 31 p. il. (Agriculture Dept. Farmers' bulletin 1027.) [Mar. 1922, on p. 2, is date of previous reprint. Includes lists of Agriculture Department publications of interest in connection with this bulletin.] * Paper, 5c.

Sweet clover: Harvesting and thrashing seed crop; [by H. S. Coe]. [July, 1917, reprint 1924.] 24 p. il. (Agriculture Dept. Farmers' bulletin 836.) * Paper, 5c.   Agr 17—717

Vegetable seeds for home and market garden; [by W. W. Tracy, sr.,' and D. N. Shoemaker]. [Apr. 1924.] ii+14 p. il. (Agriculture Dept. Farmers' bulletin 1390.) [Supersedes Farmers' bulletin 884.]   * Paper, 5c.   Agr 24—462

Wheat. Blooming of wheat flowers [with list of literature cited]; by C. E. Leighty and W. J. Sando. [1924.] p. 231–244, il. [From Journal of agricultural research, v. 27, no. 5, Feb. 2, 1924.]   ‡

—— Culture of winter wheat in eastern United States; [by] Clyde E. Leighty. June 20, 1914, revised Aug. 1917, [reprint] 1924. 15 p. il. (Agriculture Dept. Farmers' bulletin 596.)   * Paper, 5c.

—— Effect of fertilizers on development of stem rust of wheat [with list of literature cited]; by E. C. Stakman and O..S. Aamodt. 1924. cover-title, 341–380+[2] p. il. 3 p. of pl. [Prepared in cooperation with Minnesota Agricultural Experiment Station. From Journal of agricultural research, v. 27, no. 6, Feb. 9, 1924.]   ‡

PUBLIC ROADS BUREAU

California. Report of traffic on State highways and county roads in California, 1922. California State Printing Office, Sacramento, 1924. 147 p. il. 3 pl. map. [Prepared in cooperation with California Highway Commission and 24 California counties.]   †   24—27088

Concrete. Plain concrete for farm use; [by T. A. H. Miller]. [Oct. 1922, reprint 1924.] [2]+28 p. il. (Agriculture Dept. Farmers' bulletin 1279.) * Paper, 5c.

Farm implements and machinery. Care and repair of farm implements: no. 4, Mowers, reapers, and binders; [by] E. B. McCormick [and] L. L. Beebe. Mar. 1918, [reprint with changes] 1924. 16 p. il. (Agriculture Dept. Farmers' bulletin 947.) [May, 1922, on title-page, is date of previous reprint.]   * Paper, 5c.

—— Care and repair of plows and harrows; [by] E. B. McCormick [and] L. L. Beebe. [Mar. 1918, reprinted with slight changes] 1924. 10 p. il. (Agriculture Dept. Farmers' bulletin 946.) [Apr. 1922, on p. 2, is date of previous reprint.]   * Paper, 5c.

Public roads. Public roads, journal of highway research, v. 5, no. 2; Apr. 1924. 1924. cover-title, 32 p. il. 4° [Monthly. Text on p. 2 and 4 of cover.]
* Paper, 10c. single copy, $1.00 a yr.; foreign subscription, $1.50.   Agr 18—322

—— Same, v. 5, no. 3; May, 1924. 1924. cover-title, 28 p. il. 4° [Monthly. Text on p. 2–4 of cover.]

Roads. Tentative standard methods of sampling and testing highway materials, adopted by American Association of State Highway Officials and approved by Secretary of Agriculture for use in connection with Federal-aid road construction. May, 1924. cover-title, 96 p. il. 1 pl. (Agriculture Dept. Department bulletin 1216.)   * Paper, 15c.
Agr 24—453

SOILS BUREAU

Adams County, Wis. Soil survey of Adams County, Wis.; by W. J. Geib, J. A. Weslow, F. J. O'Connell, Julius Kubier, T. J. Dunnewald, H. W. Stewart, and Oscar Magistad. 1924. iii+1121–52 p. il. map. [Prepared in cooperation with Wisconsin Geological and Natural History Survey and University of Wisconsin College of Agriculture. From Field operations, 1920.]   * Paper, 25c.

WEATHER BUREAU

Air. Determining atmospheric conditions of comfort [with bibliography]; by Frank M. Phillips. 1924. [1]+104–105 p. il. 4° [From Monthly weather review, Feb. 1924.] †

Climatological data for United States by sections, v. 11, no. 2; Feb. 1924. [1924.] cover-title, [202] p. il. 2 maps, 2 p. of maps, 4° [Text on p. 2 of cover.]   * Paper, 35c. complete monthly number, $4.00 a yr.   Agr 14—566

NOTE.—Made up of separate Climatological data issued from 42 section centers of the United States. Printed at the several section centers and assembled and bound at the Washington Office. Issued principally for service use and exchange. The separate Climatological data are sold by the Superintendent of Documents, Washington, D. C., at the rate of 5c. single copy, 50c. a yr. for each section.

Cloud forms according to international system of classification; prepared by Weather Bureau Cloud Committee [Mar. 1924]. [1924.] 22 p. il. large 4°
* Paper, 25c.

Colorado River. Problems of lower Colorado River; by James H. Gordon. 1924. [1]+95–98 p. il. 1 pl. 4° [From Monthly weather review, Feb. 1924.] †

Cyclones. Physical and geological traces of cyclone belt across North America; by Marsden Manson. 1924. [1]+102–104 p. il. 4° [From Monthly weather review, Feb. 1924.] †

Evaporation. [Charles H.] Lee on evaporation loss from water surfaces, moist soils with special reference to conditions in western America; [abstract] by A. J. Henry. 1924. [1]+99–101 p. il. 4° [From Monthly weather review, Feb. 1924.] †

Ice patrol. Cruise with international ice patrol; by R. De C. Ward. 1924. [1]+71–78 p. il. 4° [From Monthly weather review, Feb. 1924.] †

Meteorology. Monthly meteorological summary, Washington, D. C., Apr. 1924. [1924.] [2] p. f° †

Monthly weather review. Monthly weather review, v. 51, 1923 [title-page, corrections, index, etc.]. 1924. xiv p. 4° * Paper, 5c.   Agr 9—990

—— Same, v. 52, no. 2; Feb. 1924. [May 9] 1924. cover-title, p. 71–132, il. 2 pl. 13 p. of maps, 4° [Text on p. 2–4 of cover.] * Paper, 15c. single copy, $1.50 a yr.; foreign subscription, $2.25.

NOTE.—The Monthly weather review contains (1) meteorological contributions, and bibliography including seismology, (2) an interpretative summary and charts of the weather of the month in the United States, and on adjacent oceans, and (3) climatological and seismological tables dealing with the weather and earthquakes of the month. The contributions are principally as follows: (a) results of observational or research work in meteorology carried on in the United States or other parts of the world, (b) abstracts or reviews of important meteorological papers and books, and (c) notes.
SPECIAL ARTICLES.—Cruise with international ice patrol; by Robert De C. Ward.—Local forecast studies, winter precipitation [at Dubuque, Iowa]; by Thomas Arthur Blair.—New principle in analysis of periodicities; by Charles F. Marvin.—Fitting straight lines to data greatly simplified with applications to sun-spot epochs; by Charles F. Marvin.—On Krichewsky's method of fitting frequency curves; by Edgar W. Woolard.—Comments on Law of pressure ratios [and its application to charting of isobars in lower levels of troposphere by C. LeRoy Meisinger], by F. J. W. Whipple;

Monthly weather review—Continued.

[with discussion by C. LeRoy Meisinger].—Problems of lower Colorado River; by James H. Gordon.—Tidal bore at mouth of Colorado River, Dec. 8–10. 1923; by James H. Gordon.—[Charles H.] Lee on evaporation loss from water surfaces, moist soils with special reference to conditions in western America; [abstract] by A. J. Henry.—Course traveled by wind and weather in a day, aid in weather forecasting, by C. Kassner; [translated by C. LeRoy Meisinger].—Physical and geological traces of cyclone belt across North America; by Marsden Manson.—Determining atmospheric conditions of comfort [with bibliography]; by Frank M. Phillips.—High-altitude rocket; by R. H. Goddard.—Waterspout and tornado within typhoon area; by George B. Barbour.—Method of computing evaporation from temperature gradients in lakes and reservoirs, by Geo. E. McEwen; author's abstract.—Wind drift in relation to gipsy moth control work; [by W. R. G.].

Periodicity (meteorology). New principle in analysis of periodicities; Fitting straight lines to data greatly simplified with applications to sun-spot epochs: by C. F. Marvin. 1924. [1]+85–91 p. il. 4° [From Monthly weather review, Feb. 1924.] †

Rain. Local forecast studies, winter precipitation [at Dubuque, Iowa]; by T. A. Blair. 1924. [1]+79–85 p. il. 4° [From Monthly weather review, Feb. 1924.] †

Rockets. High-altitude rocket; by R. H. Goddard. [1924.] 1 p. 4° [From Monthly weather review, Feb. 1924, in which this material appears on 2 pages, 105–106.] †

Weather. Weekly weather and crop bulletin, May 6–27, 1924; no. 19–22, 1924. May 7–28, 1924. Each 4 p. il. 4° * Paper, 25c. a yr.   Agr 9—1305

Weather map. Daily weather map [of United States, containing forecasts for all States east of Mississippi River except Illinois, Wisconsin, Indiana, upper Michigan, and lower Michigan], May 1–31, 1924. 1st edition. [1924.] Each 16.4×22.7 in. [Not issued Sundays or holidays.] * Editions issued at Washington, D. C., 25c. a month, $2.50 a yr.; editions issued at about 65 stations throughout the United States, 20c. a month, $2.00 a yr.

—— Same [containing forecasts for United States], May 1–31, 1924. 2d edition. [1924.] Each 16.4×22.7 in. [The Sunday edition does not contain as much information as the edition for week days.] * 30c. a month, $3.00 a yr.

AMERICAN BATTLE MONUMENTS COMMISSION

Automobiles. War Department automobiles for American Battle Monuments Commission abroad, draft of proposed legislation to make appropriation for fiscal year 1924, for expenses of American Battle Monuments Commission, available for maintenance of War Department automobiles used by commission abroad. May 16, 1924. 3 p. (H. doc. 287, 68th Cong. 1st sess.) * Paper, 5c.

CIVIL SERVICE COMMISSION

NOTE.—The Commission furnishes its publications gratuitously to those who apply for them.

Mechanics. Instructions to applicants for examination for mechanical trades and similar positions in Departmental and Indian services. Apr. 1924. 4 p. (Form 1250.) †

COMMERCE DEPARTMENT

NOTE.—The Department of Commerce prints most of its publications in very limited editions, the distribution of which is confined to Government officers, libraries, etc. When a selling price is noted in this list, application for such publication should be submitted to the Superintendent of Documents, Washington, D. C., with remittance. For copies of charts, coast pilots, and tide tables, however, apply directly to the issuing office, the Coast and Geodetic Survey, Washington, D. C.

Claims. Claims adjusted by acting Secretary of Commerce, 2 communications from acting Secretary of Commerce submitting estimates of appropriations to pay claims for damages to or losses of privately owned property, which he has adjusted and which require appropriation for their payment. May 29, 1924. 4 p. (H. doc. 341, 68th Cong. 1st sess.) * Paper, 5c.

Claims—Continued. Four claims adjusted by commissioner of lighthouses, communication submitting claims for damages to privately owned property of 4 claimants, which claims have been adjusted by commissioner of lighthouses, and which require appropriation for their payment. May 2, 1924. 3 p. (H. doc. 262, 68th Cong. 1st sess.) *Paper, 5c.

—— Oregon Short Line Railroad, communication from acting Secretary of Commerce submitting claims of Oregon Short Line Railroad for damages to privately owned property, which claim has been adjusted by director of Coast and Geodetic Survey and which requires appropriation for its payment. May 2, 1924. 2 p. (H. doc. 256, 68th Cong. 1st sess.) *Paper, 5c.

CENSUS BUREAU

Note.—Persons desiring 14th census publications should address the Director of the Census, Department of Commerce, Washington, D. C. They are also sold by the Superintendent of Documents, Washington, D. C., at the price indicated.

Cotton. Cotton consumed, cotton on hand, active cotton spindles, and imports and exports of cotton, Apr. 1923 and 1924, with statistics of cotton consumed, imported, and exported for 9 months ending Apr. 30. May 14, 1924. oblong 32° [Preliminary report. This publication is issued in postal card form.] †

Cottonseed received, crushed, and on hand, and cottonseed products manufactured, shipped out, on hand, and exported covering 9-month period ending Apr. 30, 1924 and 1923. May 19, 1924. oblong 32° [Preliminary report. This publication is issued in postal card form.] †

Delaware. 14th census of United States: State compendium, Delaware, statistics of population, occupations, agriculture, and manufactures for State, counties, and cities. 1924. cover-title, 67 p. il. 4° [Text on p. 2–4 of cover.] *Paper, 15c.
24—26471

Florida. 14th census of United States: State compendium, Florida, statistics of population, occupations, agriculture, drainage, manufactures, and mines and quarries for State, counties, and cities. 1924. cover-title, 123 p. il. 4° [Text on p. 2–4 of cover.] *Paper, 20c.
24—26493

Lumber. Forest products, 1922: Lumber, lath, and shingles; compiled in cooperation with Department of Agriculture, Forest Service. 1924. 33 p. il. *Paper, 5c.
24—26494

Mortality statistics, [calendar year] 1921, 22d annual report. 1924. 774 p. il. 4° [Prepared under direction of William H. Davis, chief statistician for vital statistics, assisted by John B. Mitchell, expert chief of Division.] *Cloth, $1.75.
6—35268

Taxation. Digest of State laws relating to taxation and revenue, 1922, compiled with relation to statistics of taxation and revenue published by Bureau of Census in connection with decennial report on wealth, debt, and taxation. 1924. viii+544 p. [Prepared by Walter S. Gilchrist, under direction of Starke M. Grogan, chief statistician in charge of wealth, debt, and taxation.] *Cloth, $1.00.
24—26470

Tobacco. Leaf tobacco held by manufacturers and dealers, Apr. 1, 1924 and 1923, Jan. 1, 1924, and Oct. 1, 1923. Apr. 30, 1924. oblong 32° [This publication is issued in postal card form.] †

Vital statistics. Manual of international list of causes of death based on 3d decennial revision by International Commission [for Revision of International Classification of Nomenclature of Diseases and Causes of Death], Paris, Oct. 11–15, 1920. 1924. 302 p. [Prepared under direction of William H. Davis, chief statistician for vital statistics.] *Cloth, 70c.
24—26472

Note.—This is the 3d edition of the Manual of international list of causes of death and is based on the 3d decennial revision by the International Commission. The 1st edition was published in 1902, and the 2d edition, based on the 2d decennial revision by the International Commission (of which 3 reprints were issued) was originally published in 1911.

COAST AND GEODETIC SURVEY

Note.—The monthly Notice to mariners, formerly issued by the Coast and Geodetic Survey, has been consolidated with and made a part of the Notice to mariners issued by the Lighthouses Bureau, thus making it a joint publication. The charts, coast pilots, and tide tables of the Coast and Geodetic Survey are sold at the office of the Survey in Washington, and also by one or more sales agents in each of the important American seaports.

Coast and Geodetic Survey bulletin, Apr. 30, 1924; no. 107. [1924.] 8 p. [Monthly.] ‡
15—26512

Coast pilots. Supplement to Inside route pilot, New York to Key West, 5th edition. May 3, 1924. 16 leaves. (Serial 266.) †

—— Supplement to United States coast pilot, Philippine Islands: pt. 1. Luzon, Mindoro, and Visayas, 1st edition. Jan. 1, 1924. 13 leaves. (Serial 267.) †

—— Supplement to United States coast pilot, West Indies: Porto Rico and Virgin Islands. May 9, 1924. [1]+10 leaves. (Serial 265.) †

Charts

Balabac Strait and approaches, P. I., surveys to 1921 and other sources; chart 4720. [Scale 1:400,000.] Washington, Coast and Geodetic Survey, Feb. 1924. 41.2×30.6 in. † 75c.

Brazos River entrance, Tex., surveys in 1897, surveys by U. S. Engineers to Mar. 1924; chart 525. Scale 1:10,000. Washington, Coast and Geodetic Survey, Apr. 1924. 28.5×38.9 in. † 75c.

Coos Bay, Oreg., surveys 1861–90, surveys by Port of Coos Bay in 1915, surveys by U. S. Engineers to Nov. 1923; chart 5984. Scale 1:20,000. Washington, Coast and Geodetic Survey, May, 1924. 29.4×38.2 in. † 75c.

Florida, Chatham River to Clam Pass, surveys to 1890 and other sources; chart 1254. Scale 1:80,000. Washington, Coast and Geodetic Survey, Apr. 1924. 32.2×42.3 in. † 75c.

Inside route. Inside route, Norfolk to Gull Shoal, Va.–N. C., from latest surveys and other information; chart 3252. Scale 1:80,000. Washington, Coast and Geodetic Survey, Apr. 1924. 34×21.9 in. [Map is in 5 sections.] † 25c.

—— Same, Gull Shoal to Topsail Sound, N. C., from latest surveys and other information; chart 3253. Scale 1:80,000. Washington, Coast and Geodetic Survey, Apr. 1924. 34.1×22 in. [Map is in 4 sections.] † 25c.

—— Same, Topsail Sound to Midway Inlet, N. C.–S. C., from latest surveys and other information; chart 3254. Scale 1:80,000. Washington, Coast and Geodetic Survey, Apr. 1924. 34.2×22 in. [Map is in 3 sections.] † 25c.

—— Same, Midway Inlet to Charleston Harbor, S. C., from latest surveys and other information; chart 3255. Scale 1:80,000. Washington, Coast and Geodetic Survey, Apr 1924. 34.2×22 in. [Map is in 5 sections.] † 25c.

—— Same, Charleston Harbor to Sapelo Sound, S. C.–Ga., from latest surveys and other information; chart 3256. Scale 1:80,000. Washington, Coast and Geodetic Survey, May, 1924. 34×22 in. [Map is in 4 sections.] † 25c.

—— Same, Sapelo Sound to St. Augustine, Ga.-Fla., from latest surveys and other information; chart 3257. Scale 1:80,000. Washington, Coast and Geodetic Survey, Apr. 1924. 34.2×22 in. [Map is in 3 sections.] † 25c.

—— Same, St. Augustine to Titusville, Fla., from latest surveys and other information; chart 3258. Scale 1:80,000. Washington, Coast and Geodetic Survey, Apr. 1924. 34.1×19.3 in. [Map is in 3 sections.] † 25c.

—— Same, Titusville to Jupiter Inlet, Fla., from latest surveys and other information; chart 3259. Scale 1:80,000. Washington, Coast and Geodetic Survey, Apr. 1924. 34×22 in. [Map is in 3 sections.] † 25c.

—— Same, Jupiter Inlet to Barnes Sound, Fla., from latest surveys and other information; chart 3260. Scale 1:80,000. Washington, Coast and Geodetic Survey, Apr. 1924. 34×22 in. [Map is in 3 sections.] † 25c.

—— Same, Barnes Sound to Key West, Fla., from latest surveys and other information; chart 3261. Scale 1:80,000. Washington, Coast and Geodetic Survey, Apr. 1924. 34.2×22 in. [Map is in 4 sections.] † 25c.

Maine-New Hampshire, Cape Elizabeth to Portsmouth, surveys 1850–1923, surveys by U. S. Engineers to 1923 and other sources; chart 1205. Scale 1:80,000. Washington, Coast and Geodetic Survey, May, 1924. 30.4×37.1 in. † 75c.

Mississippi River, from passes to Grand Prairie, La., surveys 1859–1922, surveys by U. S. Engineers to 1923; chart 194. Scale 1:80,000. Washington, Coast and Geodetic Survey, Apr. 1924. 41.2×33.3 in. † 75c.

New York Harbor, surveys to 1920, surveys by U. S. Engineers to 1924 and other sources; chart 369. Scale 1:40,000. Washington, Coast and Geodetic Survey, Apr. 1924. 43.5×33.6 in. † 75c.

Portage Bay. Portage and Wide bays, Alaska Peninsula, surveys to 1923 and
other sources; chart 8666. Scale 1 : 50,000. Washington, Coast and Geodetic Survey, May, 1924. 30.4×34.2 in. † 75c.

Providence River and head of Narragansett Bay, surveys 1865–1913, surveys
by U. S. Engineers to 1924 and other sources [with insets] ; chart 278. Scale
1 : 20,000. Washington, Coast and Geodetic Survey, Apr. 1924. 38.3×31.3
in. † 75c.

> Greenwich Cove, Head of.
> Seekonk River, continuation to Pawtucket.

San Francisco entrance, Calif., surveys 1851–1921, surveys by U. S. Engineers
to 1923 and other sources; chart 5532. Scale 1 : 40,000. Washington, Coast
and Geodetic Survey, Apr. 1924. 33.4×41.3 in. † 75c.

South Carolina-Georgia, St. Helena Sound to Savannah River, surveys to 1921,
surveys by U. S. Engineers to 1924; chart 1240. Scale 1 : 80,000. Washington, Coast and Geodetic Survey, May, 1924. 31.7×40.7 in. † 75c.

FISHERIES BUREAU

Cold storage holdings of fish, Apr. 15, 1924. [1924.] 1 p. oblong 8° (Statistical bulletin 612.) [Statistics furnished by Agricultural Economics Bureau.] †

Fisheries service bulletin, May 1, 1924; no. 108. [1924.] 6 p. [Monthly.] ‡
                                                            F 15—76

Fishery products. Statement of quantities and values of certain fishery products landed at Boston and Gloucester, Mass., and Portland, Me., by American
fishing vessels, Mar. 1924. [1924.] 1 p. oblong f° (Statistical bulletin
610.) †

—— Same, Apr. 1924. [1924.] 1 p. oblong f° (Statistical bulletin 613.) †

—— Statement of quantities and values of certain fishery products landed at
Seattle, Wash., by American fishing vessels, Mar. 1924. [1924.] 1 p. oblong
12° (Statistical bulletin 611.) †

—— Same, Apr. 1924. [1924.] 1 p. oblong 12° (Statistical bulletin 614.) †

Oyster-cultural problems of Connecticut; by J. S. Gutsell. 1924. [1]+10 p. il.
(Bureau of Fisheries doc. 960.) [App. 10, report of commissioner of fisheries,
1923.] * Paper, 5c.
                                                            F 24—9

FOREIGN AND DOMESTIC COMMERCE BUREAU

Commerce. Monthly summary of foreign commerce of United States, Mar.
1924. 1924. 2 pts. p. 1–76 and ii+77–98 p. 4° * Paper, 10c. single copy
(including pts. 1 and 2), $1.00 a yr.; foreign subscription, $1.60. ·14—21465

—— Same. 1924. [2 pts. in 1], 98 p. 4° (H. doc. 15, 68th Cong. 1st sess.)

—— Same, Apr. 1924. 1924. 2 pts. p. 1–76 and ii+77–98 p. 4°

—— Same. 1924. [2 pts. in 1], 98 p. 4° (H. doc. 16, 68 Cong. 1st sess.)

Commerce reports. Commerce reports, weekly survey of foreign trade, reports from American consular officers and representatives of Department of
Commerce in foreign countries, no. 18–21; May 5–26, 1924. 1924. cover-
titles, p. 265–552, il. 4° [Text and illustrations on p. 2–4 of covers.] * Paper,
10c. single copy, $3.00 a yr.; foreign subscription, $5.00.

—— Same, nos. 1–13 [series 1924], v. 1, 27th year; Jan.–Mar. 1924 [title-page
and index]. 1924. [2]+xxxiv p. 4° [Quarterly.] * Paper, 5c. single copy,
20c. a yr.; foreign subscription, 30c.

—— Supplement to Commerce reports. [Included in price of Commerce reports for subscribers.]

Trade and economic review for 1923, no. 1 : United Kingdom ; by Robert P. Skinner,
assisted by Lowell C. Pinkerton, Eliot B. Coulter, Howard Donovan, Charles L.
DeVault, and Alfred Nutting. [1924.] 60 p.
Same, no. 2 : Netherlands ; [by] Eugene W. Nabel. [1924.] 33 p.
Same, no. 3 : France ; by A. M. Thackara, assisted by Charles D. Wescott, John F
Simons, J. R. Wood, Leonard G. Bradford, and George F. Wadley. [1924.] 30 p.
Same, no. 4 : France : Marseille ; by Wesley Frost, Alfred D. Cameron, and Hooker A.
Doolittle. [1924.] 19 p.

—— Supplement to Commerce reports: British dyestuffs industry; by Frederick E. Breithut. May 19, 1924. ii+30 p. (Trade information bulletin
231; Chemical Division.) †
                                                            24—26475

Commerce reports—Continued. Same: Colombia, commerce and industries, 1922 and 1923; prepared from reports submitted by Carlton Jackson, Maurice L. Stafford, Lester L. Schnare, Thomas McEnelly, and other authentic sources of information. Apr. 28, 1924. ii+21 p. (Trade information bulletin 223; Latin American Division.) †
24—26432

—— Same: European tariff policies since the war; by Henry Chalmers. May 12, 1924. ii+18 p. (Trade information bulletin 228; Division of Foreign Tariffs.) †
24—26435

—— Same: Foreign trade of United States, calendar year 1923; [by H. C. Campbell, assisted in preparation of tables by Grace Witherow]. May 5, 1924. [1]+109 p. il. (Trade information bulletin 225; [Research Division].) †
A 22—1744

—— Same: Franco-American trade, 1921, 1922, and 1923; by David S. Green. May 5, 1924. ii+13 p. (Trade information bulletin 227; Western European Division.) †
24—26434

—— Same: Ice-making and cold-storage plants in Mexico, Central America, and West Indies, reports of consular officers of Department of State. May 19, 1924. ii+66 p. (Trade information bulletin 229; Industrial Machinery Division.) †
24—26473

—— Same: Italian dyestuffs industry, production, export, and import statistics; by Frederick E. Breithut [and] J. Allen Palmer. May 26, 1924. ii+11 p. (Trade information bulletin 234; Chemical Division.) †
24—26495

—— Same: Latin American market for sporting and athletic goods; by C. J. North, prepared from reports by consular officers of State Department and by representatives of Department of Commerce. May 26, 1924. ii+34 p. (Trade information bulletin 232; [Specialties Division].) †   24—26496

—— Same: Market for athletic goods in Canada and Newfoundland; by C. J. North, prepared from reports by consular officers of State Department and by representatives of Department of Commerce. May 19, 1924. ii+13 p. (Trade information bulletin 230; [Specialties Division].) †   24—26474

—— Same: Nitrogen survey, pt. 2, General review of nitrogen situation in United States; by Harry A. Curtis. May 5, 1924. ii+63 p. il. (Trade information bulletin 226; [Nitrogen Division].) [Prepared as part of the investigation of essential raw materials authorized by the 67th Congress. For another print of this publication see, below, Nitrogen.] †   23—27477

—— Same: United States trade with Latin America in 1923; by J. R. McKey. Apr. 28, 1924. ii+48 p. (Trade information bulletin 224; Latin American Division.) †
24—26433

Nitrogen situation, general review of nitrogen situation in United States, by Harry A. Curtis; presented by Mr. Norris. 1924. [1]+63 p. il. (S. doc. 88, 68th Cong. 1st sess.) [Also issued as Trade information bulletin 226, for which see, above, Commerce reports, Supplement to Commerce reports: Nitrogen survey.] * Paper, 10c.
24—26441

LIGHTHOUSES BUREAU

Chesapeake Bay, Va., 35-foot channel to be changed; [all lettered poster]. May 16, 1924. 16×10.5 in. ([Poster] notice to mariners 92.) ‡

4th District. Atlantic Coast of United States, buoy list, Delaware Bay and River, including Philadelphia Harbor, 4th lighthouse district; 1924, corrected to Apr. 15. 1924. ii+30 p. * Paper, 20c.
11—20045

5th District. Atlantic Coast of United States, buoy list, Cape Henlopen to Cape Lookout, including Chesapeake Bay and North Carolina sounds, 5th lighthouse district; 1924, corrected to Apr. 1. 1924. [1]+142 p. * Paper, 20c.
11—32283

10th–12th Districts. Great Lakes of United States, buoy list, Great Lakes, 10th–12th lighthouse districts and Canadian lights; 1924, corrected to Mar. 15. 1924. [1]+149 p. * Paper, 30c.
12—29082

Lighthouse service bulletin, v. 3, no. 5; May 1, 1924. [1924.] p. 21–25. [Monthly.] †
12—35121

Massachusetts, Nantucket Sound, east entrance, Pollock Rip light vessel, light to be changed; [all lettered poster]. May 16, 1924. 16×10.5 in. ([Poster] notice to mariners 93.) †

Notice to mariners, weekly, no. 18–22, 1924; May 2–30 [1924]. 1924. various paging. [Issued jointly with Coast and Geodetic Survey.] † · 7–20609

Radio fog signals and their use in navigation in connection with radiocompass [with bibliography]; by George R. Putnam. 2d edition, 1924. 1924. [1]+28 p. il. 2 pl. 2 p. of pl. map. †
24—26478

NAVIGATION BUREAU

Ships. American documented seagoing merchant vessels of 500 gross tons and over, May 1, 1924. 1924. ii+67 p. 4° (Serial 78.) [Monthly.] *Paper, 10c. single copy, 75c. a yr.; foreign subscription, $1.25.
19—26597

RADIO SERVICE

Radio Service bulletin, May 1, 1924; no. 85. [1924.] 17 p. [Monthly.] *Paper, 5c. single copy, 25c. a yr.; foreign subscription, 40c.
15—26255

PUBLICATIONS DIVISION

Commerce Department. Supplement to annual List of publications [of Department of Commerce available for distribution], Apr. 30, 1924. [1924.] 4 p. [Monthly.] †

STANDARDS BUREAU

NOTE.—The Scientific papers will be supplied on subscription as issued at $1.25 per volume, paper bound. These volumes will afterwards be issued bound in cloth at $2.00 per volume; foreign subscription, paper $2.50 (sent in single numbers), cloth $2.35 (bound volumes). Single numbers vary in price. Address the Superintendent of Documents, Washington, D. C.

The Technologic papers will be issued first as separates and later in volume form in the same manner as the Scientific papers. Subscriptions will be accepted by the Superintendent of Documents at $1.25 per volume; foreign subscription, $2.50. Single numbers vary in price.

Asphalt. United States Government master specification for asphalt for mineral-surfaced roofing, Federal Specifications Board, Specifications 84, officially adopted by Federal Specifications Board, Dec. 29, 1923, for use of Departments and independent establishments of Government in purchase of asphalt for mineral-surfaced roofing. Apr. 8, 1924. 10 p. il. (Circular 159.) *Paper, 5c.
24—26436

—— United States Government master specification for asphalt for waterproofing and damp proofing, Federal Specifications Board, Specification 85. officially adopted by Federal Specifications Board, Dec. 29, 1923, for use of Departments and independent establishments of Government in purchase of asphalt for waterproofing and damp proofing. Apr. 8, 1924. 9 p. il. large 8° (Circular 160.) *Paper, 5c.
24—26477

—— United States Government master specification for asphalt primer for roofing and waterproofing, Federal Specifications Board, Specification 87, officially adopted by Federal Specifications Board, Dec. 29, 1923, for use of Departments and independent establishments of Government in purchase of asphalt primer for roofing and waterproofing. Apr. 8, 1924. 7 p. il. (Circular 162.) *Paper, 5c.
24—26437

Boilers. Range boilers and expansion tanks. Oct. 30, 1923, [published] 1924. 8 p. il. (Simplified practice recommendation no. 8.) [Title on cover is: Elimination of waste, simplified practice, range boilers and expansion tanks.] *Paper, 5c.

Coal-tar pitch. United States Government master specification for coal-tar pitch for roofing, Federal Specifications Board, Specification 80, officially adopted by Federal Specifications Board, Dec. 29, 1923, for use of Departments and independent establishments of Government in purchase of coal-tar pitch for roofing. Apr. 8, 1924. 10 p. il. large 8° (Circular 157.) *Paper, 5c.
24—26476

Files and rasps. Nov. 1, 1923, [published] 1924. 8 p. (Simplified practice recommendation no. 6.) [Title on cover is: Elimination of waste, simplified practice, files and rasps.] *Paper, 5c.

Paper. Elimination of waste: Paper, [circular] to manufacturers, distributors, jobbers, printers, and users of paper [asking indorsement of recommendations and pledge of their support for fiscal year 1925]. [1924.] 7 p. 4° †

Plumbing. Recommended minimum requirements for plumbing in dwellings and similar buildings, final report of Subcommittee on Plumbing of Building Code Committee, July 3, 1923; [issued by] Division of Building and Housing. 1924. xv+260 p. il. 2 p. of pl. (Commerce Dept. Elimination of waste series.) * Paper, 35c.

Radio apparatus and appliances. Some methods of testing radio receiving sets; by J. L. Preston [and] L. C. F. Horle. Mar. 26, 1924. [1]+203–228 p. il. 1 pl. (Technologic papers 256.) [From Technologic papers, v. 18.] * Paper, 10c. 24—26438

Steel barrels. Elimination of waste: Steel barrels and drums, [circular] to manufacturers and users of steel barrels and drums [asking indorsement of recommendations and pledge of their support for. calendar year 1925]. [1924.] 5 p. 4° †

Weights and measures. Program of 17th annual Conference on Weights and Measures of United States, at National Bureau of Standards, Washington, D. C., May 26–29, 1924. [1924.] cover-title, 8 p. 12° [Part of the pages are blank.] †

—— Weights and measures, [report of] 16th annual conference held at Bureau of Standards, Washington, D. C., May 21–24, 1923. 1924. 153 p. il. 1 pl. (Miscellaneous publications 55.) * Paper, 30c. 24—26439

STEAMBOAT INSPECTION SERVICE

Pilot rules. Pilot rules for certain inland waters of Atlantic and Pacific coasts and of coast of Gulf of Mexico. Edition, Mar. 1, 1924. 1924. 33 p. il. † 10—35955

—— Pilot rules for Great Lakes and their connecting and tributary waters [as far east as Montreal]. Edition, Mar. 1, 1924. 1924. 20 p. il. † 12—40699

—— Pilot rules for rivers whose waters flow into Gulf of Mexico and their tributaries and Red River of the North. Edition, Mar. 1, 1924. 1924. 22 p. il. † 11—35466

Steamboat Inspection Service bulletin, May 1, 1924; no. 103. [1924.] 2 p. [Monthly.] ‡ 15—26679

Steamboats. Ocean and coastwise, general rules and regulations prescribed by board of supervising inspectors, as amended Jan. 1924. Edition, Apr. 4, 1924. 1924. vi+202 p. il. † 24—26497

CONGRESS

Congressional record. Congressional record, proceedings and debates of 1st session, 68th Congress, and index, v. 65, pt. 2; Jan. 16–Feb. 7, 1924. [Permanent edition.] 1924. [1]+1019–2050 p. 4° [The index does not appear with this part but will be issued in the last volume.] * Price will be quoted when set is completed. 12—36438

NOTE.—In this permanent bound edition, the paging differs from that of the daily numbers, the text being revised, rearranged, and printed without break. The bound volumes of the Record are sold by the Superintendent of Documents. Prices will be furnished on application for the proceedings and debates of the 67th Congress, 1st–4th sessions, and prior Congresses. Send remittances for the bound volumes to the Superintendent of Documents, Washington, D. C. Stamps and foreign money will not be accepted.

—— Congressional record, 68th Congress, 1st session, v. 65, no. 117–146; May 1–31, 1924. [1924.] 7827–10373+[49] p. il. 4° 12—36438

NOTE.—The Congressional record, containing the proceedings and debates of Congress, is issued daily when Congress is in session, and indexes thereto are published fortnightly.
The Record is sold by the Superintendent of Documents on the following terms: Single copy, 3 cents, if not more than 24 pages, and 1 cent more for each additional 8 pages; per month, $1.50, foreign subscription, $2.50. Subscriptions are payable in advance. Prices for the bound volumes of the Record, 67th Congress, 1st–4th sessions, and prior Congresses, will be furnished on application. Send remittances to the Superintendent of Documents, Washington, D. C. Stamps and foreign money will not be accepted.

Congressional record—Continued.   Same, index, with title, Congressional record index, 68th Congress, 1st session, v. 65, nos. 114–127; Apr. 28–May 11, 1924. [1924.] no. 10; 34+14 p. 4° [Includes History of bills and resolutions.]

—— Same, v. 65, nos. 128–140; May 12–25, 1924. [1924.] no. 11; 41+30 p. 4° [Includes History of bills and resolutions.]

Directory. 68th Congress, 1st session, beginning Dec. 3, 1923, official Congressional directory; compiled by Elmer C. Hess. 3d edition, May, 1924. [1924.] xvi+583 p. il. 1 pl. * Cloth, 60c.

6—35330'

PRIVATE LAWS

NOTE.—The Publications Division, State Department, receives a small supply of the private acts which it distributes free upon application.

Private [act] 16–25, 68th Congress.

Con Rein, schooner. H. R. 2498, act for relief of East LaHave Transportation Company, Limited, owner, A. Picard and Company, owner of cargo, and George H. Corkum, Leopold S. Conrad, Wilson Zinck, Freeman Beck, Sidney Knickle, and Norman E. LeGay, crew of schooner Con Rein, sunk by United States submarine K-4. Approved May 23, 1924. 1 p. (Private 23.)

Fellows, Rush O. H. R. 3183, act for relief of Rush O. Fellows. Approved May 23, 1924. 1 p. (Private 24.)

Keegan, Peter C. S. 210, act for relief of Peter C. Keegan and others. Approved May 23, 1924. 1 p. (Private 20.)

Long Island Railroad. H. R. 1823, act for relief of Long Island Railroad Company. Approved May 19, 1924. 1 p. (Private 17.)

Mullen, William D., Company. S. 129, act for relief of William D. Mullen Company. Approved May 23, 1924. 1 p. (Private 18.)

New Jersey Shipbuilding and Dredging Company. S. 1572, act for relief of New Jersey Shipbuilding and Dredging Company, Bayonne, N. J. Approved May 23, 1924. 1 p. (Private 21.)

Nickles, George A. H. R. 3761, act for relief of George A. Nickles. Approved Apr. 28, 1924. 1 p. (Private 16.)

Tobin, George T., & Son. S. 130, act for relief of George T. Tobin and Son. Approved May 23, 1924. 1 p. (Private 19.)

Tozier, Dorr F. S. 1698, act granting permission to Commander Dorr F. Tozier, Coast Guard, retired, to accept gift from King of Great Britain. Approved May 23, 1924. 1 p. (Private 22.)

Williams, Edward T. H. R. 5808, act for relief of Edward T. Williams. Approved May 23, 1924. 1 p. (Private 25.)

Private [joint] resolution 1, 68th Congress.

Cumming, Hugh S. H. J. Res. 222, joint resolution granting permission to Hugh S. Cumming, surgeon general of Public Health Service, to accept certain decorations bestowed upon him by Republics of France and Poland. Approved Apr. 28, 1924. 1 p. (Private resolution 1.)

PUBLIC LAWS

NOTE—Public acts in slip form in the first prints may be obtained from the Superintendent of Documents, Washington, D. C., at a subscription price of $1.00 for the 68th Congress, 1st session, foreign subscription $1.25; single copies are usually 5c. each.

Public [act] 105–127, 68th Congress.

Andes, Lake. H. R. 4161, act authorizing commissioner of Indian affairs to acquire necessary rights of way across private lands, by purchase or condemnation proceedings, needed in constructing spillway and drainage ditch to lower and maintain level of Lake Andes, S. Dak. Approved May 20, 1924. 1 p. (Public 123.)

Chippewa Indians. H. R. 3684, act for enrollment and allotment of members of Lac du Flambeau band of Lake Superior Chippewas in Wisconsin. [Approved May 19, 1924.] 2 p. (Public 121.)

Cincinnati, Ohio. H. R. 4200, act to provide for cleaning of exterior of post-office building at Cincinnati, Ohio. Approved May 22, 1924. 1 p. (Public 126.)

Colville Reservation. H. R. 2878, act to authorize sale of lands allotted to Indians under Moses agreement of July 7, 1883. Approved May 20, 1924. 1 p. (Public 122.)

Cotton. S. 2112, act authorizing Department of Agriculture to issue semimonthly cotton crop reports and providing for their publication simultaneously with ginning reports of Department of Commerce. Approved May 3, 1924. 1 p. (Public 114.)

Crignier, Madame. S. 2392, act authorizing appropriation to indemnify damages [to property of Madame Crignier] caused by search for body of John Paul Jones. Approved May 13, 1924. 1 p. (Public 117.)

Crockett, Fort. S. 2736, act authorizing use of Government buildings at Fort Crockett, Tex., for occupancy during State convention of Texas Shriners. Approved Apr. 29, 1924. 1 p. (Public 109.)

Cumberland River. S. 431, act to extend time for construction of bridge across Cumberland River in Montgomery County, Tenn. [by said county, within 7 miles of Clarksville]. Approved Apr. 29, 1924. 1 p. (Public 107.)

District Courts. S. 1609, act to fix time for terms of district courts in western district of Virginia. Approved Apr. 30, 1924. 1 p. (Public 110.)

District of Columbia. H. R. 7962, act to extend for period of 1 year provisions of title 2 of food control and District of Columbia rents act, as amended. Approved May 17, 1924. 1 p. (Public 119.)

—— S. 1932, act to change name of 37th street between Chevy Chase circle and Reno road [to Chevy Chase drive]. Approved May 3, 1924. 1 p. (Public 113.)

Public [act] 105–127, 68th Congress—Continued.

Fort Hall Reservation. S. 2902, act authorizing acquiring of Indian lands on Fort Hall Indian Reservation, Idaho, for reservoir purposes in connection with Minidoka irrigation project. [Approved May 9, 1924.] 2 p. (Public 116.)

Kansa Reservation. S. 2798, act to authorize leasing for mining purposes of unallotted lands in Kaw [or Kansa] Reservation, Okla. Approved Apr. 28, 1924. 1 p. (Public 106.)

National McKinley Birthplace Memorial Association. S. 2821, act to amend sec. 3 of act to incorporate National McKinley Birthplace Memorial Association. Approved May 1, 1924. 1 p. (Public 111.)

National Society of Daughters of American Revolution. H. R. 837, act to exempt from taxation certain property of Daughters of American Revolution in Washington, D. C. Approved May 21, 1924. 1 p. (Public 125.)

Nisqualli Reservation. S. 1704, act for relief of dispossessed allotted Indians of Nisqually Reservation, Wash. Approved Apr. 28, 1924. 1 p. (Public 105.)

Reclamation of land. S. 1631, act to authorize deferring of payments of reclamation charges. [Approved May 9, 1924.] 2 p. (Public 115.)

Rio Grande. S. 2998, act providing for study regarding equitable use of waters of Rio Grande below Fort Quitman, Tex., in cooperation with Mexico. Approved May 13, 1924. 1 p. (Public 118.)

Seminole Indians. H. R. 5799, act conferring jurisdiction upon Court of Claims to hear, examine, adjudicate, and enter judgment in any claims which Seminole Indians may have against United States. [Approved May 20, 1924.] 2 p. (Public 124.)

Soldiers. H. R. 7959, act to provide adjusted compensation for veterans of World War. [Became law May 19, 1924, by two-thirds vote of each House, after veto by the President.] 12 p. (Public 120.)

Tennessee River. S. 2108, act to grant consent of Congress to Southern Railway Company to maintain bridge across Tennessee River, at Knoxville, in county of Knox, Tenn. Approved Apr. 29, 1924. 1 p. (Public 108.)

Washington, Mo. H. R. 6059, act authorizing conveyance to Washington, Mo., of 10 feet of Federal building site in said city for extension of existing public alley through entire block from Oak to Lafayette streets. Approved May 22, 1924. 1 p. (Public 127.)

William and Mary College. H. R. 1831, act to loan to College of William and Mary in Virginia 2 of cannon surrendered by British at Yorktown on Oct. 19, 1781. Approved May 2, 1924. 1 p. (Public 112.)

Public [joint] resolution 13–21, 68th Congress.

China. H. J. Res. 248, joint resolution for remission of further payments of annual installments of Chinese indemnity. Approved May 21, 1924. 1 p. (Public resolution 21.)

Foot-and-mouth disease. H. J. Res. 247, joint resolution making additional appropriation for Department of Agriculture, fiscal years 1924 and 1925 [for expenditures in connection with eradication of foot-and-mouth disease and other diseases of animals]. Approved Apr. 26, 1924. 1 p. (Public resolution 14.)

Inter-American Electrical Communications Committee. S. J. Res. 79, joint resolution for representation of United States at meeting of Inter-American Committee on Electrical Communications to be held in Mexico City in 1924. Approved Apr. 28, 1924. 1 p. (Public resolution 17.)

International Sanitary Conference of American Republics. S. J. Res. 77, joint resolution authorizing appropriation to provide for representation of United States at 7th Pan American Sanitary Conference to be held at Habana, Cuba. Approved Apr. 28, 1924. 1 p. (Public resolution 16.)

International Statistical Bureau. S. J. Res. 76, joint resolution authorizing appropriations for maintenance by United States of membership in International Statistical Bureau at The Hague. Approved Apr. 28, 1924. 1 p. (Public resolution 15.)

Interparliamentary Union. S. J. Res. 104, joint resolution requesting the President to invite Interparliamentary Union to meet in Washington City in 1925, and authorizing appropriation to defray expenses of meeting. Approved May 13, 1924. 1 p. (Public resolution 19.)

Loans. S. J. Res. 52, joint resolution for relief of drought-stricken farm areas of New Mexico. Approved Apr. 26, 1924. 1 p. (Public resolution 13.)

Narcotics. H. J. Res. 195, joint resolution authorizing appropriation for participation of United States in 2 international conferences for control of traffic in habitforming narcotic drugs. [Approved May 15, 1924.] 2 p. (Public resolution 20.)

United Confederate Veterans. H. J. Res. 163, joint resolution authorizing Secretary of War to loan tents, cots, and chairs, to executive committee of United Confederate Veterans for use at 34th annual reunion to be held at Memphis, Tenn., June, 1924. Approved Apr. 30, 1924. 1 p. (Public resolution 18.)

ADJUSTMENT OF SALARIES OF OFFICERS AND EMPLOYEES OF CONGRESS, JOINT SELECT COMMITTEE ON

Salaries. Adjustment of salaries of officers and employees of Congress, report to accompany H. R. 8262 [to fix compensation of officers and employees of legislative branch of Government]; submitted by Mr. Warren. Apr. 24, calendar day May 1, 1924. 16 p. (S. rp. 481, 68th Cong. 1st sess.) * Paper, 5c.

CONFERENCE COMMITTEES

Agriculture Department. Appropriations for Department of Agriculture [fiscal year 1925], conference report on bill (H. R. 7220); submitted by Mr. McNary. May 26, calendar day May 28, 1924. 4 p. (S. doc. 123, 68th Cong. 1st sess.) * Paper, 5c.

Agriculture Department—Continued. Department of Agriculture appropriation bill, [fiscal year] 1925, conference report to accompany H. R. 7220; submitted by Mr. Madden. May 28, 1924. 7 p. (H. rp. 895, 68th Cong. 1st sess.) * Paper, 5c.

Appropriations. Executive office and independent establishments appropriation bill, [fiscal year] 1925, conference report to accompany H. R. 8233; submitted by Mr. Wood. May 10, 1924. 4 p. (H. rp. 698, 68th Cong. 1st sess.) * Paper, 5c.

—— Independent offices appropriation bill [fiscal year 1925], conference report on bill (H. R. 8233) making appropriations for Executive Office and sundry independent executive bureaus, boards, commissions, and offices, fiscal year 1925; submitted by Mr. Warren. May 5, calendar day May 10, 1924. 2 p. (S. doc. 108, 68th Cong. 1st sess.) * Paper, 5c.

Army. To amend national defense act of June 3, 1916, conference report to accompany S. 2169; submitted by Mr. McKenzie. May 20, 1924. 2 p. (H. rp. 789, 68th Cong. 1st sess.) * Paper, 5c.

Cherokee Indians. Final disposition of affairs of eastern band of Cherokee Indians of North Carolina, conference report to accompany H. R. 3852; submitted by Mr. Snyder. May 23, 1924. 2 p. (H. rp. 832, 68th Cong. 1st sess.) * Paper, 5c.

—— Providing for final disposition of affairs of eastern band of Cherokee Indians of North Carolina, conference report on bill (H. R. 3852); submitted by Mr. Harreld. May 20, calendar day May 22, 1924. 1 p. (S. doc. 115,. 68th Cong. 1st sess.) * Paper, 5c.

Choctaw Indians. To adjudicate claims of Choctaw and Chickasaw Indians, conference report on bill (H. R. 5325), conferring jurisdiction upon Court of Claims to hear, examine, adjudicate, and enter judgment in any claims which Choctaw and Chickasaw Indians may have against United States; submitted by Mr. Harreld. May 20, calendar day May 22, 1924. 1 p. (S. doc. 114, 68th Cong. 1st sess.) * Paper, 5c.

—— To adjudicate claims of Choctaw and Chickasaw Indians, conference report on bill (H. R. 5325), conferring jurisdiction upon Court of Claims to hear, examine, adjudicate, and enter judgment in any claims which Choctaw and Chickasaw Indians may have against United States; submitted by Mr. Harreld. May 26, calendar day May. 29, 1924. 1 p. (S. doc. 124, 68th Cong. 1st sess.) * Paper, 5c.

—— To adjudicate claims which Choctaw and Chickasaw Indians may have against United States, conference report to accompany H. R. 5325 [conferring jurisdiction upon Court of Claims to hear, examine, adjudicate, and enter judgment in any claims which Choctaw and Chickasaw Indians may have against United States]; submitted by Mr. Snyder. May 23, 1924. 2 p. (H. rp. 833, 68th Cong. 1st sess.) * Paper, 5c.

District of Columbia. Extension of 14th street, conference report to accompany S. 114 [to vacate streets and alleys within area known as Walter Reed General Hospital, District of Columbia, and to authorize extension and widening of 14th street from Montague street to its southern terminus south of Dahlia street, Nicholson street from 13th street to 16th street, Colorado avenue from Montague street to 13th street, Concord avenue from 16th street to its western terminus west of 8th street west, 13th street from Nicholson street to Piney Branch road, and Piney Branch road from 13th street to Butternut street]; submitted by Mr. Zihlman. May 29, 1924. 2 p. (H. rp. 896, 68th Cong. 1st· sess.) * Paper, 5c.

Employers' liability and workmen's compensation. To amend employees' compensation act, conference report to accompany H. R. 7041 [to amend act to provide compensation for employees of United States suffering injuries while in performance of their duties]; submitted by Mr. Graham of Pennsylvania. May 28, 1924. 2 p. (H. rp. 894, 68th Cong. 1st sess.) * Paper, 5c.

Homestead. Stock-raising homesteads, conference report to accompany S. 381 [to amend sec. 2 of act to provide for stock-raising homesteads]; submitted by Mr. Sinnott. May 10, 1924. 2 p. (H. rp. 697, 68th Cong. 1st sess.) * Paper, 5c.

Immigration. Immigration of aliens into United States, conference report to accompany H. R. 7995 [to limit immigration of aliens into United States]; submitted by Mr. Johnson of Washington. May 12, 1924. 20 p. (H. rp. 716, 68th Cong. 1st sess.) * Paper, 5c.   24—26498

Immigration—Continued. Immigration of aliens, report to accompany H. R. 7995 [to limit immigration of aliens into United States]; submitted by Mr. Johnson of Washington. May 8, 1924. 22 p. (H. rp. 688, 68th Cong. 1st sess.) * Paper, 5c.   24—26500

Interior Department. Interior Department appropriation bill, [fiscal year] 1925, conference report to accompany H. R. 5078; submitted by Mr. Cramton. May 13, 1924. 1 p. (H. rp. 737, 68th Cong. 1st sess.) * Paper, 5c.

—— Interior Department appropriation bill, [fiscal year] 1925, conference report to accompany H. R. 5078; submitted by Mr. Cramton. May 29, 1924. 1 p. (H. rp. 902, 68th Cong. 1st sess.) * Paper, 5c.

Internal revenue. Revenue bill of 1924, conference report to accompany H. R. 6715; submitted by Mr. Green of Iowa. May 24, 1924. 34 p. (H. rp. 844, 68th Cong. 1st sess.) * Paper, 5c.   24—26499

Navy Department. Appropriations for Navy Department and naval service [fiscal year 1925], conference report on bill (H. R. 6820); submitted by Mr. Hale. May 14, calendar day May 17, 1924. 4 p. (S. doc. 112, 68th Cong. 1st sess.) * Paper, 5c.

—— Navy Department appropriation bill, [fiscal year] 1925, conference report to accompany H. R. 6820; submitted by Mr. French. May 17, 1924. 8 p. (H. rp. 776, 68th Cong. 1st sess.) * Paper, 5c.

Northern Pacific Railway. Northern Pacific land grants, conference report to accompany H. J. Res. 237 [directing Secretary of Interior to withhold his approval of adjustment of Northern Pacific land grants, and creating joint committee to investigate said land grants]; submitted by Mr. Sinnott, May 29, 1924. 2 p. (H. rp. 906, 68th Cong. 1st sess.) * Paper, 5c.

Ships. To amend merchant marine act of 1920, conference report to accompany H. R. 6202 [to amend sec. 11 and 12 of merchant marine act, 1920, so as to permit use of certain funds of Shipping Board for conversion of ships into motor ships]; submitted by Mr. Greene of Massachusetts. May 29, 1924. 2 p. (H. rp. 905, 68th Cong. 1st sess.) * Paper, 5c.

Soldiers. Veterans' adjusted compensation, conference report to accompany H. R. 7959; submitted by Mr. Green of Iowa. May 1, 1924. 8 p. (H. rp. 624, 68th Cong. 1st sess.) * Paper, 5c.

State Department. Appropriations for Departments of State and Justice and judiciary, and for Departments of Commerce and Labor [fiscal year 1925], conference report to accompany H. R. 8350; submitted by Mr. Shreve. May 15, 1924. 4 p. (H. rp. 761, 68th Cong. 1st sess.) * Paper, 5c.

—— Departments of State, Justice, Commerce, and Labor appropriation bill, [fiscal year] 1925, conference report to accompany H. R. 8350; submitted by Mr. Shreve. May 19, 1924. 2 p. (H. rp. 781, 68th Cong. 1st sess.) * Paper, 5c.

War Department. Military and nonmilitary activities of War Department, conference report to accompany H. R. 7877 [making appropriations for military and nonmilitary activities of War Department, fiscal year 1925]; submitted by Mr. Anthony. May 27, 1924. 8 p. (H. rp. 862, 68th Cong. 1st sess.) * Paper, 5c.

HOUSE OF REPRESENTATIVES

Appropriations. Contingent expenses, House of Representatives, deficiency estimate of appropriation for legislative establishment, fiscal year 1923. May 14, 1924. 2 p. (H. doc. 278, 68th Cong. 1st sess.) * Paper, 5c.

—— Miscellaneous items and expenses of special and select committees, House of Representatives, supplemental estimate of appropriation for legislative establishment, fiscal year 1924, miscellaneous items, contingent expenses, House of Representatives. May 26, 1924. . 2 p. (H. doc. 316, 68th Cong. 1st sess.) * Paper, 5c.

Calendars of House of Representatives, 68th Congress, 1st session, May 1–31, 1924; no. 110–136. 1924. various paging, large 8° [Daily when House of Representatives is in session.] ‡

Employees. Salaries, officers and employees, House of Representatives, 1925, supplemental estimates of appropriations for legislative establishments, fiscal year 1925, salaries, officers and employees, House of Representatives. May 26, 1924. 3 p. (H. doc. 320, 68th Cong. 1st sess.) * Paper, 5c.

Harding, Warren G. Providing for expenses incurred in Harding memorial exercises, report to accompany H. Res. 263; submitted by Mr. MacGregor. May 27, 1924. 1 p. (H. rp. 863, 68th Cong. 1st sess.) * Paper, 5c.

House of Representatives. Authorizing doorkeeper of House to detail page to House press gallery, report to accompany H. Res. 326; submitted by Mr. MacGregor. May 27, 1924. 1 p. (H. rp. 864, 68th Cong. 1st sess.) * Paper, 5c.

—— To pay 1 year's salary and funeral expenses to widows of deceased employees of House of Representatives, report to accompany H. Res. 293; submitted by Mr. MacGregor. May 27, 1924. 1 p. (H. rp. 866, 68th Cong. 1st sess.) * Paper, 5c.

—— To pay 6 months' salary and funeral expenses to relatives or representatives of deceased employees of House of Representatives, report to accompany H. Res. 292; submitted by Mr. MacGregor. May 27, 1924. 1 p. (H. rp. 865, 68th Cong. 1st sess.) * Paper, 5c.

Agricultural experiment stations. To authorize more complete endowment of agricultural experiment stations, report to accompany H. R. 157; submitted by Mr. Purnell. May 15, 1924. 1 p. (H. rp. 758, 68th Cong. 1st sess.) * Paper, 5c.

Agricultural products. McNary-Haugen bill, hearings on H. R. 5563, declaring emergency in respect to certain agricultural commodities and to promote equality between agricultural commodities and other commodities. 1924. [pt. 15], iii+729–746 p. (Serial E, pt. 15.) * Paper, 5c.

—— McNary-Haugen bill, minority report to accompany H. R. 9033 [declaring emergency in respect of certain agricultural commodities, to promote equality between agricultural commodities and other commodities, and for other purposes]; submitted by Mr. voigt. May 9, 1924. 20 p. (H. rp. 631, pt. 2, 68th Cong. 1st sess.) * Paper, 5c.

—— McNary-Haugen bill, report to accompany H. R. 9033 [declaring emergency in respect to certain agricultural commodities, to promote equality between agricultural commodities and other commodities, and for other purposes]; submitted by Mr. Haugen. May 2, 1924. 109 p. (H. rp. 631 [pt. 1], 68th Cong. 1st sess.) * Paper, 10c.

Birds. Migratory bird refuges, report to accompany H. R. 745 [for establishment of migratory-bird refuges to furnish in perpetuity homes for migratory birds, establishment of public shooting grounds to preserve American system of free shooting, provision of funds for establishing such areas, and furnishing of adequate protection for migratory birds]; submitted by Mr. Haugen. May 14, 1924. 4 p. (H. rp. 746, 68th Cong. 1st sess.) * Paper, 5c.

Bread bill, hearings on H. R. 4533, to establish standard weights for loaves of bread, Mar. 3 and May 5, 1924. 1924. [pt. 2], iii+67–115 p. (Serial M, pt. 2.) [Part 1 appeared in Monthly catalogue for Mar. 1924, p. 518.] * Paper, 5c.

Disbursing officers. To authorize designation of deputy fiscal or disbursing agents in Department of Agriculture stationed outside of Washington, report to accompany H. R. 8372; submitted by Mr. Haugen. May 29, 1924. 5 p. (H. rp. 904, 68th Cong. 1st sess.) [The committee recommends amendment of the bill by substituting bill containing general legislation relating to disbursing officers.] * Paper, 5c.

Loans, Oklahoma relief, hearings on H. J. Res. 202, for rlief of boll weevil, drought, and flood stricken farm areas of Oklahoma, Mar. 28 and Apr. 1, 1924. 1924. iii+18 p. (Serial T.) * Paper, 5c.

Packing industry. Packer act amendments, hearings on H. R. 6424 [to amend packers and stockyards act, 1921], Apr. 25, 1924. 1924. [pt. 2], iii+183–220 p. (Serial N, pt. 2.) [Part 1, which contains hearings on several bills amending the packers and stockyards act, appeared in Monthly catalogue for Apr. 1924, p. 604.] * Paper, 5c.

Upper Mississippi River Wild Life and Fish Refuge, report to accompany H. R. 4088 [to establish Upper Mississippi River Wild Life and Fish Refuge]; submitted by Mr. Haugen. May 14, 1924. 5 p. (H. rp. 747, 68th Cong. 1st sess.) * Paper, 5c.

APPROPRIATIONS COMMITTEE

Appropriations. Legislative appropriation bill, fiscal year 1925, report to accompany H. R. 9429; submitted by Mr. Dickinson of Iowa. May 24, 1924. 16 p. (H. rp. 841, 68th Cong. 1st sess.) * Paper, 5c.

—— Urgent deficiency appropriation bill, [fiscal year] 1924, hearing before subcommittee in charge of deficiency appropriations. 1924. ii+78 p. * Paper, 10c.

—— Urgent deficiency appropriation bill, fiscal year 1924, report to accompany H. R. 9192; submitted by Mr. Madden. May 13, 1924. 3 p. (H. rp. 718, 68th Cong. 1st sess.) * Paper, 5c.

Naval petroleum reserves. Appropriation for employing attorneys and agents in proceedings to cancel leases on oil lands [in former naval reserves], report to accompany H. J. Res. 160; submitted by Mr. Madden. Jan. 28, 1924. 1 p. (H. rp. 115, 68th Cong. 1st sess.) * Paper, 5c.

Senate. Contingent expenses of Senate, fiscal year 1924, report to accompany S. J. Res. 119 [making appropriation for contingent expenses of Senate, fiscal year 1924, for expenses of inquiries and investigations]; submitted by Mr. Madden. May 6, 1924. 1 p. (H. rp. 664, 68th Cong. 1st sess.) * Paper, 5c.

BANKING AND CURRENCY COMMITTEE

Federal Reserve Bank of Kansas City. Federal reserve bank building, Denver, Colo., report to accompany S. J. Res. 3 [authorizing Federal Reserve Bank of Kansas City to invest its funds in construction of building for its branch office at Denver, Colo.]; submitted by Mr. McFadden. May 8, 1924. 5 p. (H. rp. 686, 68th Cong. 1st sess.) [Includes views of minority signed by Mr. Steagall, Mr. Brand, Mr. Stevenson, Mr. Black, and Mr. Goldsborough.] * Paper, 5c.

—— · Federal reserve bank building, Omaha, Nebr., report to accompany S. J. Res. 51 [authorizing Federal Reserve Bank of Kansas City to invest its funds in construction of building for its branch office at Omaha, Nebr.]; submitted by Mr. McFadden. May 8, 1924. 5 p. (H. rp. 687, 68th Cong. 1st sess.) [Includes views of minority signed by Mr. Steagall, Mr. Brand, Mr. Stevenson, Mr. Black, and Mr. Goldsborough.] * Paper, 5c.

CLAIMS COMMITTEE

Abbott, James F. James F. Abbott, report to accompany H. R. 5759 [for relief of James F. Abbott]; submitted by Mr. Celler. May 13, 1924. 4 p. (H. rp. 733, 68th Cong. 1st sess.) * Paper, 5c.

Baumen, John. John Baumen, report to accompany H. R. 6506 [for relief of John Baumen]; submitted by Mr. Underhill. May 3, 1924. 3 p. (H. rp. 648, 68th Cong. 1st sess.) * Paper, 5c.

Blattmann & Co., report to accompany S. 555 [for relief of Blattmann and Company]; submitted by Mr. Fredericks. May 3, 1924. 19 p. (H. rp. 639, 68th Cong. 1st sess.) [Includes House report 1406, 67th Congress, 4th session.] * Paper, 5c.

Boyce, William H., sr. William Henry Boyce, report to accompany S. 2510 [for relief of William Henry Boyce, sr.]; submitted by Mr. Bulwinkle. May 19, 1924. 2 p. (H. rp. 782, 68th Cong. 1st sess.). * Paper, 5c.

Canadian Pacific Railway Co., report to accompany H. R. 8297 [for relief of Canadian Pacific Railway Company]; submitted by Mr. Edmonds. May 3, 1924. 9 p. (H. rp. 649, 68th Cong. 1st sess.) * Paper, 5c.

Church, Ernest F. Ernest F. Church, report to accompany H. R. 917 [for relief of Ernest F. Church]; submitted by Mr. Beck. May 21, 1924. 2 p. (H. rp. 807, 68th Cong. 1st sess.) * Paper, 5c.

Commercial Pacific Cable Co., report to accompany S. 709 [for relief of Commercial Pacific Cable Company]; submitted by Mr. Edmonds. May 10, 1924. 6 p. (H. rp. 703, 68th Cong. 1st sess.) * Paper, 5c.

Commercial Union Assurance Company, Limited. Commercial Union Assurance Co. (Ltd.) and others, report to accompany S. 1975 [for relief of Commercial Union Assurance Company (Limited), Federal Insurance Company, American and Foreign Marine Insurance Company, Queen Insurance Company of America, Fireman's Fund Insurance Company, United States Lloyds, and St. Paul Fire and Marine Insurance Company]; submitted by Mr. Edmonds. May 26, 1924. 18 p. (H. rp. 854, 68th Cong. 1st sess.) * Paper, 5c.

—— Commercial Union Assurance Co. (Ltd.) and others, report to accompany S. 1976 [for relief of Commercial Union Assurance Company (Limited), Federal Insurance Company, American and Foreign Marine Insurance Company, Queen Insurance Company of America, Fireman's Fund Insurance Company, St. Paul Fire and Marine Insurance Company, and United States Lloyds], submitted by Mr. Edmonds. May 26, 1924. 15 p. (H. rp. 855, 68th Cong. 1st sess.) * Paper, 5c.

Conniff, Mrs. Christina. Christina Conniff, report to accompany H. R. 9080 [for relief of Christina Conniff]; submitted by Mr. Edmonds. May 17, 1924. 3 p. (H. rp. 780, 68th Cong. 1st sess.) * Paper, 5c.

Cook, John W. J. W. Cook, report to accompany H. R. 3046 [for relief of J. W. Cook]; submitted by Mr. Fredericks. May 10, 1924. 11 p. (H. rp. 707, 68th Cong. 1st sess.) * Paper, 5c.

Disbursing officers. George M. Apple, report to accompany S. 1763 [to validate certain payments made to George M. Apple and to authorize General Accounting Office to allow credit to certain disbursing officers for payments of salaries made on properly certified and approved vouchers]; submitted by Mr. McReynolds. May 26, 1924. 7 p. (H. rp. 852, 68th Cong. 1st sess.) * Paper, 5c.

Eagle Pass Lumber Co., Eagle Pass, Tex., report to accompany H. R. 7122 [for relief of Eagle Pass Lumber Company, Eagle Pass, Tex.]; submitted by Mr. McReynolds. May 9, 1924. 12 p. (H. rp. 695, 68th Cong. 1st sess.) * Paper, 5c.

Eaton, John T. John T. Eaton, report to accompany S. 335 [for relief of John T. Eaton]; submitted by Mr. Fredericks. May 21, 1924. 4 p. (H. rp. 804, 68th Cong. 1st sess.) * Paper, 5c.

Erie Railroad Co., report to accompany S. 935 [for relief of Erie Railroad Company]; submitted by Mr. Black of New York. May 3, 1924. 7 p. (H. rp. 641, 68th Cong. 1st sess.) * Paper, 5c.

Farrell, J. M. J. M. Farrell, report to accompany H. R. 2745 [for relief of J. M. Farrell]; submitted by Mr. Black of New York. May 12, 1924. 20 p. (H. rp. 712, 68th Cong. 1st sess.) * Paper, 5c.

Gamboa, Mrs. Juana F. Juana F. Gamboa, report to accompany H. R. 8893 [for relief of Juana F. Gamboa]; submitted by Mr. Beck. May 3, 1924. 10 p. (H. rp. 650, 68th Cong. 1st sess.) * Paper, 5c.

Gardner, Bertram. Bertram Gardner, report to accompany H. R. 7194 [for relief of Bertram Gardner]; submitted by Mr. Celler. May 3, 1924. 2 p. (H. rp. 652, 68th Cong. 1st sess.) * Paper, 5c.

Glanville, J. B. J. B. Glanville and others, report to accompany S. 1253 [to reimburse J. B. Glanville and others for losses and damages sustained by them through negligent dipping of tick-infested cattle by Bureau of Animal Industry, Department of Agriculture]; submitted by Mr. Little. May 17, 1924. 21 p. (H. rp. 778, 68th Cong. 1st sess.) [Includes minority report signed by Mr. Underhill, Mr. McReynolds, Mr. Box, and Mr. Bulwinkle.] * Paper, 5c.

Glisson, Mrs. Janie B. Janie Beasley Glisson, report to accompany S. 648 [for relief of Janie Beasley Glisson]; submitted by Mr. Bulwinkle. May 21, 1924. 6 p. (H. rp. 805, 68th Cong. 1st sess.) * Paper, 5c.

Great Lakes Engineering Works, report to accompany S. 698 [for relief of Great Lakes Engineering Works]; submitted by Mr. Edmonds. May 26, 1924. 2 p. (H. rp. 849, 68th Cong. 1st sess.) * Paper, 5c.

Guess, Mrs. E. L. Mrs. E. L. Guess, report to accompany H. R. 2989 [for relief of Mrs. E. L. Guess]; submitted by Mr. Fredericks. May 3, 1924. 21 p. (H. rp. 645, 68th Cong. 1st sess.) * Paper, 5c.

Hall, John D. Mrs. John D. Hall, report to accompany S. 2187 [for relief of Mrs. John D. Hall, widow of John D. Hall]; submitted by Mr. Box. May 21, 1924. 7 p. (H. rp, 810, 68th Cong. 1st sess.) * Paper, 5c.

Healy, Daniel F. Daniel F. Healy, report to accompany H. R. 3595 [for relief of Daniel F. Healy]; submitted by Mr. Bulwinkle. May 12, 1924. 7 p. (H. rp. 713, 68th Cong. 1st sess.) * Paper, 5c.

Hennessee, Jim. Jim Hennessee, report to accompany H. R. 8343 [for relief of Jim Hennessee]; submitted by Mr. Edmonds. May 12, 1924. 3 p. (H. rp. 714, 68th Cong. 1st sess.) * Paper, 5c.

Jenkins, James F. James F. Jenkins, report to accompany H. R. 4750 [for relief of James F. Jenkins]; submitted by Mr. Thomas of Oklahoma. May 14, 1924. 20 p. (H. rp. 742, 68th Cong. 1st sess.) [Includes minority views signed by Mr. Underhill and Mr. Box.] * Paper, 5c.

Kessel, Henry A., Company, Incorporated. Henry A. Kessel Co. (Inc.), report to accompany H. R. 1082 [for relief of Henry A. Kessel Company (Incorporated)]; submitted by Mr. Box. May 5, 1924. 26 p. (H. rp. 659, 68th Cong. 1st sess.) * Paper, 5c.

Kettlewell, Mrs. Beatrice J. Beatrice J. Kettlewell, report to accompany H. R. 5774 [for relief of Beatrice J. Kettlewell]; submitted by Mr. Edmonds. May 3, 1924. 9 p. (H. rp. 651, 68th Cong. 1st sess.) * Paper, 5c.

Kin-Dave, steamship. Owners of steamship Kin-Dave, report to accompany S. 1894 [for relief of owners of steamship Kin-Dave]; submitted by Mr. Box. May 26, 1924. 3 p. (H. rp. 853, 68th Cong. 1st sess.) * Paper, 5c.

King, J. R. J. R. King, report to accompany S. 2669 [for relief of J. R. King]; submitted by Mr. Edmonds. May 26, 1924. 7 p. (H. rp. 856, 68th Cong. 1st sess.) * Paper, 5c.

Laird, Robert, sr. Robert Laird, sr., report to accompany H. R. 2309 [for relief of Robert Laird, sr.]; submitted by Mr. Fredericks. May 19, 1924. 4 p. (H. rp. 783, 68th Cong. 1st sess.) * Paper, 5c.

McCanna, P. F. Nelly McCanna, report to accompany H. R. 1889 [for relief of Nelly McCanna, residuary legatee and devisee under last will and testament of P. F. McCanna]; submitted by Mr. Thomas of Oklahoma. May 21, 1924. 2 p. (H. rp. 809, 68th Cong. 1st sess.) * Paper, 5c.

McCarty, Edward N. Edward N. McCarty, report to accompany S. 225 [for relief of Edward N. McCarty]; submitted by Mr. Celler. May 21, 1924. 10 p. (H. rp. 803, 68th Cong. 1st sess.) * Paper, 5c.

Malta Maru, Japanese steamer. Owners of steamship Malta Maru, report to accompany H. R. 6695 [authorizing Kokusai Kisen Kabushiki Kaisha, owners of steamship Malta Maru to bring suit against United States]; submitted by Mr. Edmonds. May 26, 1924. 5 p. (H. rp. 858, 68th Cong. 1st sess.) * Paper, 5c.

Maron, Frank A. F. A. Maron, report to accompany S. 799 [for relief of F. A. Maron]; submitted by Mr. Edmonds. May 3, 1924. 5 p. (H. rp. 640, 68th Cong. 1st sess.) * Paper, 5c.

Matlock, Albert S. Albert S. Matlock, report to accompany H. R. 8329 [for relief of Albert S. Matlock]; submitted by Mr. Edmonds. May 27, 1924. 10 p. (H. rp. 879, 68th Cong. 1st sess.) * Paper, 5c.

Mendoza, Mrs. Casimira. Casimira Mendoza, report to accompany H. R. 4294 [for relief of Casimira Mendoza]; submitted by Mr. Thomas of Oklahoma. May 21, 1924. 4 p. (H. rp. 808, 68th Cong. 1st sess.) * Paper, 5c.

Near East Relief (Inc.), report to accompany S. 87 [for relief of Near East Relief (Incorporated)]; submitted by Mr. Fredericks. May 3, 1924. 18 p. (H. rp. 638, 68th Cong. 1st sess.) [Includes Senate report 208 with Senate committee hearing of Jan. 24, 1924.] * Paper, 5c.   24—26501

New York Produce Exchange Bank. Mechanics & Metals National Bank, report to accompany H. R. 7118 [for relief of Mechanics and Metals National Bank, successor to New York Produce Exchange Bank]; submitted by Mr. Edmonds. May 26, 1924. 12 p. (H. rp. 859, 68th Cong. 1st sess.) * Paper, 5c.

Norman, Charles T. Charles T. Norman, report to accompany H. R. 1830 [for relief of Charles T. Norman]; submitted by Mr. McReynolds. May 3, 1924. 6 p. (H. rp. 643, 68th Cong. 1st sess.) * Paper, 5c.

Northampton, Mass. Chamber of Commerce, Northampton, Mass., report to accompany H. R. 4280 [for relief of Chamber of Commerce, Northampton, Mass.]; submitted by Mr. Edmonds. May 10, 1924. 8 p. (H. rp. 706, 68th Cong. 1st sess.) * Paper, 5c.

Oliver, William J. William J. Oliver, report to accompany H. R. 3132 [for relief of William J. Oliver]; submitted by Mr. Thomas of Oklahoma. Apr. 30, 1924. 9 p. (H. rp. 614, 68th Cong. 1st sess.) [Includes views of Mr. Box.] * Paper, 5c.

Oosterbaan, B. G. B. G. Oosterbaan, report to accompany H. R. 1699 [for relief of B. G. Oosterbaan]; submitted by Mr. Underhill. May 26, 1924. 2 p. (H. rp. 860, 68th Cong. 1st sess.) * Paper, 5c.

Payne, W. F. W. F. Payne, report to accompany H. R. 4290 [for relief of W. F. Payne]; submitted by Mr. Thomas of Oklahoma. May 3, 1924. 3 p. (H. rp. 646, 68th Cong. 1st sess.) * Paper, 5c.

Petrie, George A. George A. Petrie, report to accompany H. R. 5752 [for relief of George A. Petrie]; submitted by Mr. Bulwinkle. May 26, 1924. 3 p. (H. rp. 857, 68th Cong. 1st sess.) * Paper, 5c.

Picton Steamship Co. (Ltd.), report to accompany H. R. 6660 [for relief of Picton Steamship Company (Limited), owner of British steamship Picton]; submitted by Mr. Celler. May 19, 1924. 2 p. (H. rp. 784, 68th Cong. 1st sess.) * Paper, 5c.

Pond, Ezra S. Ezra S. Pond, report to accompany S. 1941 [for relief of Ezra S. Pond]; submitted by Mr. Underhill. May 10, 1924. 4 p. (H. rp. 704, 68th Cong. 1st sess.) * Paper, 5c.

Ryan, Joseph P. Joseph P. Ryan, report to accompany H. R. 1333 [for relief of Joseph P. Ryan]; submitted by Mr. McReynolds. May 10, 1924. 3 p. (H. rp. 705, 68th Cong. 1st sess.) * Paper, 5c.

Shymer, Mrs. Anne C. Estate of Anne C. Shymer, report to accompany H. R. 1824 [for relief of estate of Anne C. Shymer]; submitted by Mr. Edmonds. May 26, 1924. 6 p. (H. rp. 861, 68th Cong. 1st sess.) * Paper, 5c.

Spaight, Daniel A. Daniel A. Spaight and others, report to accompany H. R. 3071 [for relief of Daniel A. Spaight and others]; submitted by Mr. Underhill. Apr. 30, 1924. 24 p. (H. rp. 613, 68th Cong. 1st sess.) * Paper, 5c.

Standard Oil Co., report to accompany H. R. 2373 [for relief of Standard Oil Company, Savannah, Ga.]; submitted by Mr. Box. May 3, 1924. 7 p. (H. rp. 644, 68th Cong. 1st sess.) * Paper, 5c.

Stout, Harry B. H. B. Stout, report to accompany S. 831 [for relief of H. B. Stout]; submitted by Mr. Edmonds. May 26, 1924. 7 p. (H. rp. 851, 68th Cong. 1st sess.) * Paper, 5c.

Van Voorhis, David C. David C. Van Voorhis, adverse report to accompany H. R. 5638 [for relief of David C. Van Voorhis]; submitted by Mr. Edmonds. May 10, 1924. 4 p. (H. rp. 708, 68th Cong. 1st sess.) * Paper, 5c.

Vumbaca, Frank. Frank Vumbaca, report to accompany S. 243 [for relief of Frank Vumbaca]; submitted by Mr. Underhill. May 10, 1924. 2 p. (H. rp. 702, 68th Cong. 1st sess.) * Paper, 5c.

Weaver, Samuel S. Samuel S. Weaver, report to accompany S. 1573 [for relief of Samuel S. Weaver]; submitted by Mr. Vincent of Michigan. May 21, 1924. 12 p. (H. rp. 806, 68th Cong. 1st sess.) * Paper, 5c.

White, Adaline. Adaline White, report to accompany H. R. 1671 [for relief of Adaline White]; submitted by Mr. McReynolds. May 14, 1924. 12 p. (H. rp. 741, 68th Cong. 1st sess.) * Paper, 5c.

White, Mrs. Jessie M. Jessie M. White, report to accompany S. 827 [for relief of Jessie M. White]; submitted by Mr. Edmonds. May 26, 1924. 6 p. (H. rp. 850, 68th Cong. 1st sess.) * Paper, 5c.

COINAGE, WEIGHTS, AND MEASURES COMMITTEE

Weights and measures. Standardization of weights and measures used in trade and commerce, hearing on H. R. 4465, to regulate and control manufacture, sale, and use of weights and measures and weighing and measuring devices for use or used in trade or commerce, Apr. 18, 1924. 1924. pt. 2, ii+47–69 p. [Part 1 appeared in Monthly catalogue for Apr. 1924, p. 607.] * Paper, 5c.

DISTRICT OF COLUMBIA COMMITTEE

Accounts. · Adjustment of accounts between United States and District of Columbia, report to accompany S. 703; submitted by Mr. Beers. May 20, 1924. 1 p. (H. rp. 790, 68th Cong. 1st sess.) * Paper, 5c.

Alleys. Rearrangement of public alley facilities in square 616 in District of Columbia, and for other purposes, report to accompany S. 2265; submitted by Mr. Stalker. May 26, 1924. 2 p. (H. rp. 847, 68th Cong. 1st sess.) * Paper, 5c.

—— Rearrangement of public alley facilities in square 616 in District of Columbia, report to accompany H. R. 6297; submitted by Mr. Stalker. May 7, 1924. 2 p. (H. rp. 674, 68th Cong. 1st sess.) * Paper, 5c.

Architects. Regulating practice of architecture, report to accompany S. 933 [to provide for examination and registration of architects and to regulate practice of architecture in District of Columbia]; submitted by Mr. Zihlman. May 28, 1924. 2 p. (H. rp. 886, 68th Cong. 1st sess.) * Paper, 5c.

Burklin, George M. To remove remains of George Burklin and Anton Burklin, report to accompany H. R. 8686 [authorizing health officer of District of Columbia to issue permit for removal of remains of late George Mauger Burklin and remains of late Anton Lerch Burklin from Glenwood Cemetery, District of Columbia, to Fort Lincoln Cemetery, Prince Georges County, Md.]; submitted by Mr. Gilbert. May 23, 1924. 1 p. (H. rp. 836, 68th Cong. 1st sess.) * Paper, 5c.

Flag. To create commission to procure design for flag for District of Columbia, report to accompany S. 2480; submitted by Mr. Hammer. May 26, 1924. 1 p. (H. rp. 848, 68th Cong. 1st sess.) * Paper, 5c.

Land. To quiet title to lot 4, square 116, Washington [D. C.], report to accompany H. R. 8662; submitted by Mr. Hammer. May 27, 1924. 6 p. (H. rp. 872, 68th Cong. 1st sess.) * Paper, 5c.

Lincoln, Abraham. To declare Lincoln's birthday legal holiday in District of Columbia, report to accompany S. 1641; submitted by Mr. Keller. May 21, 1924. 3 p. (H. rp. 799, 68th Cong. 1st sess.) * Paper, 5c.

Parks. Comprehensive development of park and playground system of National Capital, report to accompany S. 112; submitted by Mr. Gibson. May 14, 1924. 10 p. (H. rp. 755, 68th Cong. 1st sess.) * Paper, 5c.

Policemen and firemen's relief fund of District of Columbia, report to accompany H. R. 5327 [for payment to retired members of Police and Fire departments of District of Columbia balance of retirement pay past due to them but unpaid from Jan. 1, 1911, to July 30, 1915]; submitted by Mr. Gibson. May 14, 1924. 3 p. (H. rp. 748, 68th Cong. 1st sess.) * Paper, 5c.

Workmen's compensation. Workmen's accident compensation, hearing on H. R. 487, creating District of Columbia insurance fund for benefit of employees injured and dependents of employees killed in employments, providing for administration of such fund by United States Employees' Compensation Commission, and authorizing appropriation therefor, Feb. 19–Mar. 6, 1924. 1924. pt. 3, ii+127–312 p. il. [Parts 1 and 2 have title District of Columbia insurance fund.] * Paper, 30c.

ELECTION OF PRESIDENT, VICE PRESIDENT, AND REPRESENTATIVES COMMITTEE

Corrupt practices. To prevent corrupt practices in Congressional elections, report to accompany H. R. 8956; submitted by Mr. Cable. May 13, 1924. 5 p. (H. rp. 721, 68th Cong. 1st sess.) * Paper, 5c.

ELECTIONS COMMITTEE, NO. 1

Contested elections. Contested-election case of Ansorge *v.* Weller, report [on contested-election case of Martin C. Ansorge *v.* Royal H. Weller from 21st Congressional district of New York]; submitted by Mr. Cole of Ohio. May 14, 1924. 3 p. (H. rp. 756, 68th Cong. 1st sess.) * Paper, 5c.

—— Contested-election case of Ansorge *v.* Weller, report to accompany H. Res. 242 [authorizing calling of persons and for papers in contested-election case of Ansorge *versus* Weller]; submitted by Mr. Cole of Ohio. Mar. 31, 1924. 1 p. (H. rp. 409, 68th Cong. 1st sess.) * Paper, 5c.

ELECTIONS COMMITTEE, NO. 3

Contested elections. Arguments and hearings, contested-election case of John J. Gorman *v.* James R. Buckley from 6th Congressional district of Illinois. 1924. ii+58 p. * Paper, 5c.

Contested elections—Continued. Contested-election case of Gorman *v.* Buckley, report on contested case of John J. Gorman *v.* James R. Buckley from 6th Congressional district of Illinois; submitted by Mr. Elliott. May 13, 1924. 3 p. (H. rp. 722, 68th Cong. 1st sess.) * Paper, 5c.

FOREIGN AFFAIRS COMMITTEE

Hassel, Norwegian steamship. Norwegian steamship Hassel, report to accompany H. R. 7558 [to authorize payment of indemnity to Government of Norway on account of losses sustained by owners of Norwegian steamship Hassel as result of collision between that steamship and American steamship Ausable]; submitted by Mr. Fairchild. May 13, 1924. 3 p. (H. rp. 731, 68th Cong. 1st sess.) * Paper, 5c.

Murphy, Dominic I. Authorizing Dominic I. Murphy, consul general of United States, to accept silver fruit bowl presented to him by British Government, report to accompany S. 1699; submitted by Mr. Cole of Iowa. May 27, 1924. 1 p. (H. rp. 880, 68th Cong. 1st sess.) * Paper, 5c.

Officers, Marine Corps. To authorize certain officers of Marine Corps to accept from Republic of Haiti medal for distinguished service, report to accompany H. J. Res. 249; submitted by Mr. Cole of Iowa. May 13, 1924. 1 p. (H. rp. 726, 68th Cong. 1st sess.) * Paper, 5c.

Rio Grande. Equitable use of waters of Rio Grande below Fort Quitman, Tex., hearings on H. R. 8371, for study regarding equitable use of waters of Rio Grande below Fort Quitman, Tex., in cooperation with Mexico, Apr. 17, 1924; statement of C. H. Pease. 1924. ii+45 p. * Paper, 5c.

—— Equitable use of waters of Rio Grande below Fort Quitman, Tex., report to accompany H. R. 8371 [for study regarding equitable use of waters of Rio Grande below Fort Quitman, Tex., in cooperation with Mexico]; submitted by Mr. Aldrich. May 6, 1924. 2 p. (H. rp. 667, 68th Cong. 1st sess.) * Paper, 5c.

—— Equitable use of waters of Rio Grande below Fort Quitman, Tex., report to accompany S. 2998 [for study regarding equitable use of waters of Rio Grande below Fort Quitman, Tex., in cooperation with Mexico]; submitted by Mr. Aldrich. May 6, 1924. 10 p. (H. rp. 666, 68th Cong. 1st sess.) * Paper, 5c.

IMMIGRATION AND NATURALIZATION COMMITTEE

Calendar. Legislative calendar, 68th Congress, May 2, 1924; no. 3. 1924. 15 p. large 8° ‡

INDIAN AFFAIRS COMMITTEE

Chippewa Indians. Adjudication of claims of Chippewa Indians of Minnesota, report to accompany H. R. 9343; submitted by Mr. Hudson. May 29, 1924. 1 p. (H. rp. 898, 68th Cong. 1st sess.) * Paper, 5c.

—— Chippewa Indians of Minnesota, hearing before subcommittee on H. R. 26, H. R. 27, H. R. 28, and H. R. 6493, Mar. 1–18, 1924. 1924. [1]+110 p. * Paper, 10c.

—— To amend act making appropriations for current and contingent expenses of Bureau of Indian Affairs, report to accompany H. R. 8086 [to amend act making appropriations for current and contingent expenses of Bureau of Indian Affairs, for fulfilling treaty stipulations with various Indian tribes, and for other purposes, fiscal year 1915, relative to reimbursable appropriation for education of Chippewa Indians provided by sec. 8 thereof]; submitted by Mr. Knutson. May 8, 1924. 2 p. (H. rp. 679, 68th Cong. 1st sess.) * Paper, 5c.

Croatan Indians. Designate Croatan Indians of Robeson and adjoining counties in North Carolina as Cherokee Indians, report to accompany H. R. 8083; submitted by Mr. Weaver. May 22, 1924. 1 p. (H. rp. 826, 68th Cong. 1st sess.) * Paper, 5c.

Fort Peck Reservation. Authorizing expenditure from fund to credit of Fort Peck Indians, report to accompany S. J. Res. 103 [authorizing expenditure of Fort Peck 4 per centum fund now standing to credit of Fort Peck Indians of Montana in Treasury]; submitted by Mr. Leavitt. May 19, 1924. 2 p. (H. rp. 785, 68th Cong. 1st sess.) *·Paper, 5c.

Indian Affairs Office. Quarters, fuel, and light for employees of Indian field service. report to accompany S. 2799; submitted by Mr. Snyder. May 27, 1924. 2 p. (H. rp. 869, 68th Cong. 1st sess.) * Paper, 5c.

Indians. Investigate Indian affairs in Oklahoma, report to accompany H. J. Res. 258 [authorizing Committee on Indian Affairs to investigate Indian affairs in Oklahoma]; submitted by Mr. Snyder. May 8, 1924. 3 p. (H. rp. 678, 68th Cong. 1st sess.) * Paper, 5c.

Klamath Indians of Oregon, hearings before subcommittee on H. R. 7351 [making appropriation for loan, reimbursable from tribal assets, to provide capital and credit for purpose of encouraging industry and self-support among Indians having tribal rights on Klamath Indian Reservation in Oregon], Apr. 11, 1924. 1924. ii+24 p. * Paper, 5c.

McAllister, James J. James J. McAllister, report to accompany H. R. 2258 [for relief of James J. McAllister]; submitted by Mr. Hayden. May 22, 1924. 9 p. (H. rp. 819, 68th Cong. 1st sess.) * Paper, 5c.

Menominee Reservation. Timber operations on Menominee Reservation, Wis., report to accompany H. R. 8356 [to amend law relating to timber operations on Menominee Reservation, Wis.]; submitted by Mr. Sproul of Kansas. May 8, 1924. 2 p. (H. rp. 681, 68th Cong. 1st sess.) * Paper, 5c.

Navajo Reservation. Appropriation for maintenance of Gallup-Durango highway across Navajo Indian Reservation, report to accompany S. 2159; submitted by Mr. Morrow. May 19, 1924. 2 p. (H. rp. 786, 68th Cong. 1st sess.) * Paper, 5c.

Omaha Indians of Nebraska, report to accompany H. R. 8965 [for relief of Omaha Indians of Nebraska]; submitted by Mr. Howard of Nebraska. May 22, 1924. 2 p. (H. rp. 828, 68th Cong. 1st sess.) * Paper, 5c.

Omaha Reservation. Disposal of unallotted lands on Omaha Indian Reservation. Nebr., report to accompany H. R. 6541 [to amend act for disposal of unallotted lands on Omaha Indian Reservation, Nebr.]; submitted by Mr. Howard of Nebraska. May 19, 1924. 2 p. (H. rp. 788, 68th Cong. 1st sess.) * Paper, 5c.

Pueblo Indians. To quiet title to lands within Pueblo Indian land grants, report to accompany S. 2932; submitted by Mr. Snyder. May 19, 1924. 10 p. (H. rp. 787, 68th Cong. 1st sess.) * Paper, 5c.

Rowell, James F. J. F. Rowell, report to accompany S. 2526 [providing for allotment of land from Kiowa, Comanche, and Apache Indian Reservation, Okla., to James F. Rowell, intermarried and enrolled member of Kiowa tribe]; submitted by Mr. Hastings. May 22, 1924. 2 p. (H. rp. 821, 68th Cong. 1st sess.) * Paper, 5c.

San Carlos irrigation project. Pima Indians and San Carlos irrigation project, information in connection with S. 966, for continuance of construction work on San Carlos Federal irrigation project in Arizona; special report on transportation and marketing conditions [by Arizona Industrial Congress]. 1924. iii+6 p. * Paper, 5c.

—— San Carlos irrigation project, report to accompany S. 966 [for continuance of construction work on San Carlos Federal irrigation project, Ariz.]; submitted by Mr. Snyder. May 1, 1924. 3 p. (H. rp. 618, 68th Cong. 1st sess.) * Paper, 5c.

Sanish, N. Dak. Authorizing repayment of excess amounts paid on certain lots in town site of Sanish, N. Dak., report to accompany H. R. 3387; submitted by Mr. Johnson of South Dakota. May 22, 1924. 6 p. (H. rp. 824, 68th Cong. 1st sess.) * Paper, 5c.

Shawnee Indians. Claims of loyal Shawnee and loyal absentee Shawnee Indians, hearing before subcommittee on H. R. 7324, Apr. 25, 1924. 1924. [1]+42 p. * Paper, 5c.

Stockbridge Indians. Claims of Stockbridge Indians before Court of Claims, report to accompany H. R. 8493 [conferring jurisdiction upon Court of Claims to hear, examine, adjudicate, and enter judgment in any claims which Stockbridge Indians may have against United States]; submitted by Mr. Hudson. May 8, 1924. 2 p. (H. rp. 682, 68th Cong. 1st sess.) * Paper, 5c.

Stockbridge Indians—Continued. To adjudicate claims of Stockbridge Indians, report to accompany S. 3111 [conferring jurisdiction upon Court of Claims to hear, examine, adjudicate, and enter judgment in any claims which Stockbridge Indians may have against United States]; submitted by Mr. Snyder. May 27. 1924. 1 p. (H. rp. 870, 68th Cong. 1st sess.) * Paper, 5c.

INDUSTRIAL ARTS AND EXPOSITIONS COMMITTEE

Washington, George. Bicentennial of birthday of George Washington, hearings on H. J. Res. 199, observance of bicentennial of birthday of George Washington, Apr. 21, 1924. 1924. ii+39 p. * Paper, 5c.

—— Participation of United States in observance of bicentennial of birthday of George Washington, report to accompany H. J. Res. 199 [authorizing appropriation for participation of United States in preparation and completion of plans for comprehensive observance of that greatest of all historic events, bicentennial of birthday of George Washington]; submitted by Mr. Reed of New York. May 13, 1924. 2 p. (H. rp. 732, 68th Cong. 1st sess.) * Paper, 5c.

INSULAR AFFAIRS COMMITTEE

Philippine Islands. Philippine local autonomy, hearings on H. R. 8856, to enable the people of Philippine Islands to adopt constitution and form government for Philippine Islands and to provide for future political status of same, Apr. 30–May 6, 1924. 1924. ii+157 p. * Paper, 15c.

—— To enable the people of Philippine Islands to adopt constitution and form government for Philippine Islands and to provide for future political status of same, minority report to accompany H. R. 8856; submitted by Mr. Kent. May 30, 1924. 3 p. (H. rp. 709, pt. 3, 68th Cong. 1st sess.) * Paper, 5c.

—— To enable the people of Philippine Islands to adopt constitution and form government for Philippine Islands and to provide for future political status of same, minority report to accompany H. R. 8856; submitted by Mr. Ragon. May 17, 1924. 17 p. (H. rp. 709, pt. 2, 68th Cong. 1st sess.) * Paper, 5c.

—— To enable the people of Philippine Islands to adopt constitution and form government for Philippine Islands and to provide for future political status of same, report to accompany H. R. 8856; submitted by Mr. Fairfield. May 10, 1924. 5 p. (H. rp. 709 [pt. 1], 68th Cong. 1st sess.) * Paper, 5c.

24—26502

INTERSTATE AND FOREIGN COMMERCE COMMITTEE

Chicago River. Abandonment of portion of present channel of South Branch of Chicago River, report to accompany H. R. 7757; submitted by Mr. Denison. May 20, 1924. 1 p. (H. rp. 791, 68th Cong. 1st sess.) * Paper, 5c.

Columbia River. Bridge across Columbia River at vantage Ferry, Wash., report to accompany H. R. 9177 [granting consent of Congress to counties of Kittitas and Grant, Wash., to construct bridge across Columbia River at or near vantage Ferry, Wash.]; submitted by Mr. Rayburn. May 16, 1924. 2 p. (H. rp. 769, 68th Cong. 1st sess.) * Paper, 5c.

Freight rates. Revision of railroad rate structure, report to accompany H. J. Res. 141 [directing Interstate Commerce Commission to take action relative to adjustments in rate structure of common carriers subject to interstate commerce act, and fixing of rates and charges]; submitted by Mr. Hoch. May 13, 1924. 3 p. (H. rp. 735, 68th Cong. 1st sess.) * Paper, 5c.

—— Revision of railroad rate structure, report to accompany S. J. Res. 107 [directing Interstate Commerce Commission to take action relative to adjustments in rate structure of common carriers subject to interstate commerce act, and fixing of rates and charges]; submitted by Mr. Hoch. May 27, 1924. 4 p. (H. rp. 867, 68th Cong. 1st sess.) * Paper, 5c.

—— To amend paragraph (3), sec. 16, of interstate commerce act [so as to extend time of filing claims for overcharge], report to accompany S. 2704; submitted by Mr. Newton of Minnesota. May 20, 1924. 3 p. (H. rp. 796, 68th Cong. 1st sess.) * Paper, 5c.

Mobile, Ala. Quarantine station at Fort Morgan, Ala., report to accompany H. R. 8090 [authorizing Secretary of Treasury to remove quarantine station now situated at Fort Morgan, Ala., to Sand Island, near entrance of port of Mobile, Ala., and to construct thereon new quarantine station]; submitted by Mr. Rayburn. May 16, 1924. 5 p. (H. rp. 768, 68th Cong. 1st sess.) * Paper, 5c.

Monongahela River. Bridge across Monongahela River near Masontown, Pa., report to accompany H. R. 9245 [granting consent of Congress to commissioners of Fayette and Greene counties, Pa., to construct bridge across Monongahela River near Masontown, Fayette County, Pa.]; submitted by Mr. Wyant. May 21, 1924. 2 p. (H. rp. 802, 68th Cong. 1st sess.) * Paper, 5c.

—— Bridge across Monongahela River, report to accompany H. R. 8438 [granting consent of Congress to county of Allegheny, Pa., to construct bridge across Monongahela River from Cliff street, McKeesport, to point opposite in Duquesne]; submitted by Mr. Wyant. May 8, 1924. 2 p. (H. rp. 683, 68th Cong. 1st sess.) [Corrected print.] * Paper, 5c.

Niagara River. Bridge across Niagara River, report to accompany H. R. 5434 [granting consent of Congress to construction of bridge across Niagara River and Black Rock Canal, near Buffalo, N. Y., by Buffalo and Fort Erie Public Bridge Company]; submitted by Mr. Parker. May 5, 1924. 3 p. (H. rp. 657, 68th Cong. 1st sess.) * Paper, 5c.

Ohio River. Bridge across Ohio River, report to accompany H. R. 9345 [granting consent of Congress for construction of bridge across Ohio River between Vanderburgh County, Ind., and Henderson County, Ky., by Kentucky and Indiana, through their respective highway commissions]; submitted by Mr. Barkley. May 29, 1924. 2 p. (H. rp. 900, 68th Cong. 1st sess.) * Paper, 5c.

Pearl River. Bridge across Pearl River, Miss., report to accompany H. R. 9077 [granting consent of Congress to board of supervisors of Hinds County, Miss., to construct bridge across Pearl River, Miss., at Jackson]; submitted by Mr. Huddleston. May 23, 1924. 2 p. (H. rp. 834, 68th Cong. 1st sess.) * Paper, 5c.

Peedee River. Bridge across Peedee River near Allisons Ferry, S. C., report to accompany H. R. 9176 [granting consent of Congress to counties of Marion and Florence, S. C., to construct bridge across Peedee River at or near Allisons Ferry, S. C.]; submitted by Mr. Wyant. May 13, 1924. 1 p. (H. rp. 736, 68th Cong. 1st sess.) * Paper, 5c.

Poteau River. Dam across Poteau River, report to accompany H. R. 9459 [granting consent of Congress to Fort Smith, Sebastian County, Ark., and Fort Smith waterworks district to construct dam across Poteau River]; submitted by Mr. Parks of Arkansas. May 28, 1924. 3 p. (H. rp. 887, 68th Cong. 1st sess.) * Paper, 5c.

Tallahatchie River. Dam in Tallahatchie River, report to accompany H. R. 9224 [granting consent of Congress to Panola-Quitman drainage district to construct dam in Tallahatchie River at or near Porters Ferry, Panola County, Miss]; submitted by Mr. Huddleston. May 23, 1924. 1 p. (H. rp. 835, 68th Cong. 1st sess.) * Paper, 5c.

White River. Bridge across White River near De valls Bluff, Ark., report to accompany S. 3116 [to authorize Choctaw, Oklahoma and Gulf Railway Company and Chicago, Rock Island and Pacific Railway Company to construct bridge across White River near De valls Bluff, Ark.]; submitted by Mr. Parks of Arkansas. May 5, 1924. 2 p. (H. rp. 658, 68th Cong. 1st sess.) * Paper, 5c.

INVALID PENSIONS COMMITTEE

Pensions. Granting pensions and increase of pensions to certain soldiers and sailors of Civil War, etc., report to accompany H. R. 9246 [substituted for H. R. 974 and other bills]; submitted by Mr. Fuller. May 15, 1924. 205 p. (H. rp. 760, 68th Cong. 1st sess.) * Paper, 20c.

103523—No. 353—24——3

Casper-Alcova irrigation project. Authorizing investigation of proposed Casper-Alcova irrigation project, Natrona County, Wyo., report to accompany S. J. Res. 114 [authorizing investigation of proposed Casper-Alcova irrigation project, Natrona County, Wyo., Deschutes project, Oreg., and Southern Lassen irrigation project, Lassen County, Calif.]; submitted by Mr. Sinnott. May 10, 1924. 2 p. (H. rp. 699, 68th Cong. 1st sess.) * Paper, 5c.

Bribery. Disposition of moneys paid as bribes, etc., report to accompany H. R. 5425 [for disposition of moneys paid to or received by any official as bribe, which may be used as evidence in any case growing out of any such transaction]; submitted by Mr. Graham of Pennsylvania. May 1, 1924. 1 p. (H. rp. 620, 68th Cong. 1st sess.) * Paper, 5c.

Calendar. Legislative calendar, 68th Congress, May 5 and 19, 1924; no. 12 and 13. 1924. 73 p. and 77 p. 4° ‡

Clerks of District Courts. To provide fees to be charged by clerks of District Courts, report to accompany H. R. 5420; submitted by Mr. Graham of Pennsylvania. Apr. 30, 1924. 2 p. (H. rp. 607, 68th Cong. 1st sess.) * Paper, 5c.

—— To provide for accounting by clerks of District Courts of fees received by them in naturalization proceedings, report to accompany H. R. 5428; submitted by Mr. Graham of Pennsylvania. May 1, 1924. 1 p. (H. rp. 621, 68th Cong. 1st sess.) * Paper, 5c.

Clerks of United States courts. Requiring clerks of courts to keep indices of judgment debtors, report to accompany H. R. 5423 [to amend sec. 2 of act of Aug. 1, 1888, to regulate liens of judgments and decrees of courts of United States, relative to indices of judgment debtors]; submitted by Mr. Graham of Pennsylvania. Apr. 30, 1924. 1 p. (H. rp. 610, 68th Cong. 1st sess.) * Paper, 5c.

—— To provide for reporting and accounting of fines, fees, forfeitures, and penalties, and all other moneys paid to or received by clerks of United States courts, report to accompany H. R. 5422; submitted by Mr. Graham of Pennsylvania. Apr. 30, 1924. 1 p. (H. rp. 608, 68th Cong. 1st sess.) * Paper, 5c.

Court of Claims. Additional judges, Court of Claims, hearings on H. R. 7650 [and] H. R. 7966, Apr. 17, 1924. 1924. ii+13 p. (Serial 32.) * Paper, 5c.

—— Additional judges, Court of Claims, report to accompany H. R. 7650 [to amend sec. 136 and 138 of judicial code so as to provide additional judges for Court of Claims and require 5 judges to constitute quorum]; submitted by Mr. Dyer. May 14, 1924. 3 p. (H. rp. 740, 68th Cong. 1st sess.) * Paper, 5c.

Courts of United States. To amend practice and procedure in Federal courts, report to accompany S. 624 [to amend practice and procedure in Federal courts, so that in jury trials presiding judge shall not express his opinion as to credibility of witnesses or weight of testimony involved in issue]; submitted by Mr. Major of Missouri. May 22, 1924. 1 p. (H. rp. 816, 68th Cong. 1st sess.) * Paper, 5c.

—— To provide for rendition of accounts by United States attorneys, United States marshals, clerks of United States courts, and United States commissioners, report to accompany H. R. 5424; submitted by Mr. Graham of Pennsylvania. May 1, 1924. 1 p. (H. rp. 619, 68th Cong. 1st sess.) * Paper, 5c.

District Courts. Changing time for holding court at Kansas City, Kans., report to accompany S. 2236 [to designate time and place of holding terms of district court in 1st division of district at Kansas City]; submitted by Mr. Graham of Pennsylvania. Apr. 30, 1924. 1 p. (H. rp. 611, 68th Cong. 1st sess.) * Paper, 5c.

—— Providing for holding of distrct court at Okmulgee, Okla., report to accompany H. R. 8683; submitted by Mr. Yates. May 29, 1924. 3 p. (H. rp. 898, 68th Cong. 1st sess.) * Paper, 5c.

District Courts—Continued. Term of court at Fayetteville, N. C., report to accompany H. R. 9314 [to amend sec. 98 of judicial code so as to provide that hereafter terms of district court for eastern district of North Carolina shall be held at Fayetteville instead of Laurinburg]; submitted by Mr. Graham of Pennsylvania. May 23, 1924. 2 p. (H. rp. 839, 68th Cong. 1st sess.) * Paper, 5c.

—— Term of court at Okmulgee, Okla., hearing on H. R. 8683, Apr. 29, 1924. 1924. ii+7 p. (Serial 34.) * Paper, 5c.

Judges. To relieve district judges from signing order admitting, denying, or dismissing each petition for naturalization, report to accompany H. R. 5421; submitted by Mr. Graham of Pennsylvania. Apr. 30, 1924. 1 p. (H. rp. 609, 68th Cong. 1st sess.) * Paper, 5c.

—— Western district of New York, hearing on H. R. 6491 [for appointment of additional judge of district court for western district of New York] and H. R. 8854 [to create additional judicial district in territory embraced within present western district of New York], Apr. 26 and May 9, 1924. 1924. ii+ 30 p. (Serial 37.) * Paper, 5c.

Marshals. Granting pension to deputy marshals of district court for western district of Arkansas, report to accompany H. R. 9364 [granting pension to deputy marshals of district court of western district of Arkansas who rendered special service prior to admission of Oklahoma into the Union]; submitted by Mr. Tillman. May 26, 1924. 4 p. (H. rp. 846, 68th Cong. 1st sess.) * Paper, 5c.

National Police Bureau. To create National Police Bureau [and] To create Bureau of Criminal Identification, hearing on H. R. 8580 [and] H. R. 8409, Apr. 17 and 24, 1924. 1924. ii+81 p. (Serial 31.) * Paper, 10c.

Negroes. To create a negro industrial commission [and] To create a commission on racial question, hearing on H. R. 3228 and H. R. 5564, Apr. 10– May 7, 1924. 1924. ii+74 p. (Serial 35.) * Paper, 10c.

Penitentiary, McNeil Island. To increase salary of warden of United States penitentiary at McNeil Island, Wash., report to accompany H. R. 1468; submitted by Mr. Graham of Pennsylvania. May 26, 1924. 1 p. (H. rp. 845, 68th Cong. 1st sess.) * Paper, 5c.

Prohibition Bureau. Establishment of Prohibition Bureau in Treasury Department, report to accompany H. R. 6645; submitted by Mr. Graham of Pennsylvania. May 5, 1924. 3 p. (H. rp. 663, 68th Cong. 1st sess.) * Paper, 5c.

Salaries. Salaries of officers and employees, Court of Appeals and Supreme Court, District of Columbia, United States Court of Claims, and United States Court of Customs Appeals, hearing on H. R. 8210, Apr. 23, 1924. 1924. ii+27 p. (Serial 33.) * Paper, 5c.

—— Salaries of officers and employees, Court of Appeals and Supreme Court of District of Columbia, United States Court of Claims, and United States Court of Customs Appeals, report to accompany H. R. 8210; submitted by Mr. Graham of Pennsylvania. May 8, 1924. 4 p. (H. rp. 680, 68th Cong. 1st sess.) * Paper, 5c.

Treasury Department. To amend act for retirement of employees in classified civil service [relative to payment of persons temporarily employed by Treasury Department who, before such employment, had reached age of retirement or who had been retired], report to accompany H. R. 8906; submitted by Mr. Hickey. May 22, 1924. 7 p. (H. rp. 827, 68th Cong. 1st sess.) * Paper, 5c.

Witnesses. Providing for calling of adverse parties for cross-examination, hearing on H. R. 6786, Mar. 24, 1924; statement of O. B. Burtness. 1924. [1]+8 p. (Serial 26.) * Paper, 5c.

LABOR COMMITTEE

Strikes and lockouts. Regulation of interstate transportation of labor, hearings on H. R. 7698, to regulate transportation and importation of labor from one State to any point in another State or District of Columbia, or any territorial possession of United States, or from District of Columbia or any territorial possession of United States into any State where labor lockout or strike is then in progress, Mar. 28 and Apr. 4, 1924. 1924. ii+64 p. * Paper, 10c.

710

Base-ball. Monument to symbolize national game of baseball, report to accompany S. J. Res. 7 [granting permission for erection in District of Columbia of monument to symbolize national game of baseball]; submitted by Mr. Luce. Apr. 30, 1924. 2 p. (H. rp. 604, 68th Cong. 1st sess.) * Paper, 5c.
24—26503

District of Columbia World War Memorial Commission, report to accompany S. J. Res. 73 [for appointment of commission for purpose of erecting in Potomac Park, in District of Columbia, memorial to those members of armed forces of United States from District of Columbia who served in Great War]; submitted by Mr. Luce. May 29, 1924. 1 p. (H. rp. 897, 68th Cong. 1st sess.) * Paper, 5c.

Lexington, Battle of, 1775. Observance of 150th anniversary of Battle of Lexington and Concord, report to accompany H. Joint Res. 259 [establishing commission for participation of United States in observance of 150th anniversary of Battle of Lexington and Concord, authorizing appropriation to be utilized in connection with such observance, and for other purposes]; submitted by Mr. Luce. May 9, 1914. 2 p. (H. rp. 696, 68th Cong. 1st sess.) * Paper, 5c.

—— One hundred and fiftieth anniversary of Battle of Lexington and Concord, hearings on H. J. Res. 259, establishing commission for participation of United States in observance of 150th anniversary of Battle of Lexington and Concord, May 8, 1924. 1924. ii+6 p. * Paper, 5c.

Lincoln, Abraham. Oldroyd collection of Lincoln relics, hearings on H. R. 9157, for purchase of Oldroyd collection of Lincoln relics, May 8, 1924. 1924. ii+3 p. * Paper, 5c.

—— Oldroyd collection of Lincoln relics, report to accompany H. R. 9157 [for purchase of Oldroyd collection of Lincoln relics]; submitted by Mr. Luce. May 14, 1924. 1 p. (H. rp. 753, 68th Cong. 1st sess.) * Paper, 5c. 24—26504

National Botanic Garden. Design for use of grounds in vicinity of Mall by Botanic Garden, report to accompany H. J. Res. 257 [for procurement of design for use of grounds in vicinity of Mall by Botanic Garden]; submitted by Mr. Luce. May 9, 1924. 1 p. (H. rp. 691, 68th Cong. 1st sess.) * Paper, 5c.

San Martin, José de. Statue of General San Martin, report to accompany S. J. Res. 106 [authorizing erection on public grounds in Washington, D. C., of equestrian statue of General San Martin which the people of Argentina have presented to United States]; submitted by Mr. Luce. Apr. 30, 1924. 2 p. (H. rp. 605, 68th Cong. 1st sess.) * Paper, 5c.

MEMBERS OF CONGRESS, SELECT COMMITTEE TO INVESTIGATE ALLEGED CHARGES AGAINST

House of Representatives. Charges against 2 Representatives in Congress, report relating to alleged charges against Representative Langley and Representative Zihlman; submitted by Mr. Burton. May 15, 1924. 2 p. (H. rp. 759, 68th Cong. 1st sess.) * Paper, 5c.

MERCHANT MARINE AND FISHERIES COMMITTEE

Freight rates. Providing for investigation in respect of suspension of operation of provisions of sec. 28 of merchant marine act of 1920 [relating to restriction on lower rail charges in connection with transportation by water to or from foreign countries, etc.], report to accompany H. J. Res. 253; submitted by Mr. Greene of Massachusetts. May 8, 1924. 1 p. (H. rp. 689, 68th Cong. 1st sess.) * Paper, 5c.

—— To amend sec. 28 of merchant marine act of 1920 [relating to restriction on lower rail charges in connection with transportation by water to or from foreign countries, etc., so as to postpone operation of provisions of section], hearings on H. R. 8091, Apr. 3–12, 1924. 1924. ii+620 p. * Paper, 60c.

Freight rates—Continued. To amend sec. 28 of merchant marine act of 1920 [relating to restriction on lower rail charges in connection with transportation by water to or from foreign countries, etc., so as to postpone operation of provisions of section], report to accompany H. R. 8638; submitted by Mr. Greene of Massachusetts. Apr. 30, 1924. 3 p. (H. rp. 617, 68th Cong. 1st sess.) * Paper, 5c.

Radio communication. Reaffirming use of the ether for radio communication or otherwise to be inalienable possession of the people of United States and their Government, report to accompany S. 2930; submitted by Mr. White of Maine. May 13, 1924. 7 p. (H. rp. 719, 68th Cong. 1st sess.) * Paper, 5c.   24—26505

MILITARY AFFAIRS COMMITTEE

Aber, Caleb. Caleb Aber, report to accompany H. R. 1539 [for relief of Caleb Aber]; submitted by Mr. Wurzbach. May 12, 1924. 8 p. (H. rp. 711, 68th Cong. 1st sess.) * Paper, 5c.

Armstrong, William H. William H. Armstrong, report to accompany H. R. 6442 [for relief of William H. Armstrong]; submitted by Mr. Hill of Alabama. May 2, 1924. 2 p. (H. rp. 635, 68th Cong. 1st sess.) * Paper, 5c.

Atherton, Francis M. Francis M. Atherton, report to accompany H. R. 6268 [for relief of Francis M. Atherton]; submitted by Mr. Frothingham. May 14, 1924. 2 p. (H. rp. 744, 68th Cong. 1st sess.) * Paper, 5c.

Baker, Walter. Walter Baker, report to accompany H. R. 5639 [for relief of Walter Baker]; submitted by Mr. Boylan. May 9, 1924. 2 p. (H. rp. 693, 68th Cong. 1st sess.) * Paper, 5c.

Brown, James M. James Madison Brown, report to accompany H. R. 3544 [for relief of James Madison Brown]; submitted by Mr. Wurzbach. May 28, 1924. 2 p. (H. rp. 888, 68th Cong. 1st sess.) * Paper, 5c.

Brown, Jesse P. Jesse P. Brown, report to accompany H. R. 4904 [for relief of Jesse P. Brown]; submitted by Mr. Wurzbach. May 14, 1924. 2 p. (H. rp. 751, 68th Cong. 1st sess.) * Paper, 5c.

Burgess, Thomas H. Thomas H. Burgess, report to accompany H. R. 2756 [for relief of Thomas H. Burgess]; submitted by Mr. Wurzbach. May 15, 1924. 3 p. (H. rp. 766, 68th Cong. 1st sess.) * Paper, 5c.

Caldwell, Robert W. Robert W. Caldwell, report to accompany H. R. 8672 [for relief of Robert W. Caldwell]; submitted by Mr. Speaks. May 27, 1924. 12 p. (H. rp. 878, 68th Cong. 1st·sess.) * Paper, 5c.

Carlisle Barracks. Sale of portion of Carlisle Barracks reservation, report to accompany H. R. 7731; submitted by Mr. Ransley. May 9, 1924. 4 p. (H. rp. 692, 68th Cong. 1st sess.) * Paper, 5c.

Choate, Joseph A. Joseph A. Choate, report to accompany H. R. 6824 [for relief of Joseph A. Choate]; submitted by Mr. Wurzbach. May 29, 1924. 2 p. (H. rp. 903, 68th Cong. 1st sess.) * Paper, 5c.

Corinth, Miss. Construction of water and sewer mains in Corinth, Miss., report to accompany S. 3026 [to permit Corinth, Miss., to construct water and sewer mains under and along Government approach roadway to Corinth National Cemetery]; submitted by Mr. Quin. May 27, 1924. 2 p. (H. rp. 871, 68th Cong. 1st sess.) * Paper, 5c.

Cowley, John H. John H. Cowley, report to accompany H. R. 4896 [for relief of John H. Cowley]; submitted by Mr. Wurzbach. May 14, 1924. 2 p. (H. rp. 750, 68th Cong. 1st sess.) * Paper, 5c.

Crum, Paul. Paul Crum, report to accompany H. R. 3388 [to place name of Paul Crum on muster rolls of Company E, 1st Regiment Nebraska Infantry, volunteers]; submitted by Mr. Hill of Maryland. May 13, 1924. 2 p. (H. rp. 723, 68th Cong. 1st sess.) * Paper, 5c.

Curran, Michael. Michael Curran, report to accompany H. R. 2419 [for relief of Michael Curran]; submitted by Mr. Reece. May 21, 1924. 2 p. (H. rp. 800, 68th Cong. 1st sess.) * Paper, 5c.

Dose, Josiah F. Josiah Frederick Dose, report to accompany H. R. 1415 [for relief of Josiah Frederick Dose]; submitted by Mr. Wurzbach. May 21, 1924. 2 p. (H. rp. 801, 68th Cong. 1st sess.) * Paper, 5c.

Douglas, John A.   John A. Douglas, report to accompany H. R. 1023 [for relief of John A. Douglas]; submitted by Mr. Wurzbach. May 16, 1924. 4 p. (H. rp. 770, 68th Cong. 1st sess.)   * Paper, 5c.

Engraving and Printing Bureau.   Engineer officer as director of Bureau of Engraving and Printing, report to accompany S. J. Res. 105 [authorizing the President to detail officer of Corps of Engineers as director of Bureau of Engraving and Printing]; submitted by Mr. Quin. Apr. 30, 1924. 2 p. (H. rp. 606, 68th Cong. 1st sess.)   * Paper, 5c.

Forbes, Francis.   Francis Forbes, report to accompany H. R. 6775 [for relief of Francis Forbes]; submitted by Mr. Wurzbach. May 20, 1924. 1 p. (H. rp. 798, 68th Cong. 1st sess.)   * Paper, 5c.

Fredericksburg, Battle of, 1862.   Inspection of battle fields in and around Fredericksburg and Spotsylvania Courthouse, Va., report to accompany H. R. 5567; submitted by Mr. McSwain. May 2, 1924. 3 p. (H. rp. 634, 68th Cong. 1st sess.)   * Paper, 5c.

Gardner, Thomas J.   Thomas J. Gardner, report to accompany H. R. 1962 [for relief of Thomas J. Gardner]; submitted by Mr. Wurzbach. May 22, 1924. 2 p. (H. rp. 818, 68th Cong. 1st sess.)   * Paper, 5c.

Gasparilla Island.   Sale of Gasparilla Island military reservation, report to accompany S. 3211 [authorizing sale of Gasparilla Island military reservation]; submitted by Mr. McSwain. May 20, 1924. 2 p. (H. rp. 795, 68th Cong. 1st sess.)   * Paper, 5c.

Getchell, Charles F.   Charles F. Getchell, report to accompany H. R. 1691 [for relief of Charles F. Getchell]; submitted by Mr. Wurzbach. May 22, 1924. 3 p. (H. rp. 811, 68th Cong. 1st sess.)   * Paper, 5c.

Glasson, William A.   William A. Glasson, report to accompany H. R. 1307 [for relief of William A. Glasson]; submitted by Mr. Wurzbach. May 27, 1924. 7 p. (H. rp. 876, 68th Cong. 1st sess.)   * Paper, 5c.

Harris, Pleasant R. W.   Pleasant R. W. Harris, report to accompany H. R. 7131 [for relief of Pleasant R. W. Harris]; submitted by Mr. Wurzbach. May 22, 1924. 2 p. (H. rp. 830, 68th Cong. 1st sess.)   * Paper, 5c.

Harrison, Ramon B.   Ramon B. Harrison, report to accompany H. R. 7508 [for relief of Ramon B. Harrison]; submitted by Mr. Hill of Maryland. May 13, 1924. 4 p. (H. rp. 725, 68th Cong. 1st sess.)   * Paper, 5c.

——   Relief of Ramon B. Harrison, hearings before subcommittee on H. R. 7508, Mar. 3, 1924; statements of John J. Eagan [and] Ramon B. Harrison. 1924. ii+54 p. * Paper, 5c.

Helium gas, report to accompany H. R. 5722 [authorizing conservation, production, and exploitation of helium gas, mineral resource pertaining to national defense and to development of commercial aeronautics]; submitted by Mr. Frothingham. May 2, 1924. 3 p. (H. rp. 627, 68th Cong. 1st sess.) * Paper, 5c.   24—26506

Hoboken Manufacturers' Railroad.   Sale of Hoboken Manufacturers' Railroad, report to accompany H. R. 7014 [to permit Secretary of War to dispose of and Port of New York Authority to acquire Hoboken Manufacturers' Railroad]; submitted by Mr. Wainwright. May 9, 1924. 7 p. (H. rp. 694, 68th Cong. 1st sess.)   * Paper, 5c.

——   Sale of Hoboken Manufacturers' Railroad, report to accompany S. 2287 [to permit Secretary of War to dispose of and Port of New York Authority to acquire Hoboken Manufacturers' Railroad]; submitted by Mr. Wainwright. May 16, 1924. 5 p. (H. rp. 767, 68th Cong. 1st sess.)   * Paper, 5c.

——   Sale of Hoboken Shore Line to Port of New York Authority, hearings on S. 2287 and H. R. 7014, to permit Secretary of War to dispose of and Port of New York Authority to acquire Hoboken Shore Line, May 1 and 2, 1924. 1924. ii+66 p. * Paper, 10c.

Hubbard, Samuel T., jr.   Samuel T. Hubbard, report to accompany H. R. 5813 [for relief of Samuel T. Hubbard, jr.]; submitted by Mr. Wainwright. May 14, 1924. 4 p. (H. rp. 743, 68th Cong. 1st sess.)   * Paper, 5c.

Japan.   For relief of sufferers from earthquake in Japan, report to accompany S. 3171; submitted by Mr. Hull of Iowa. May 28, 1924. 2 p. (H. rp. 893, 68th Cong. 1st sess.)   * Paper, 5c.

Kenly, William L.   Retirement of W. L. Kenly, hearings before subcommittee on H. R. 496, Mar. 26, 1924. 1924. ii+12 p.   * Paper, 5c.

Logan, Fort. Railroad across southwesterly portion of Fort Logan military reservation, Colo., report to accompany H. R. 7909 [granting consent of Congress to construction by Denver and Rio Grande Western Railroad Company of line of railroad across southwesterly portion of Fort Logan military reservation, Colo.]; submitted by Mr. Fisher. May 17, 1924. 1 p. (H. rp. 777, 68th Cong. 1st sess.) * Paper, 5c.

McCloud, Tennessee. Tennessee McCloud, report to accompany H. R. 8749 [to correct military record of Tennessee McCloud]; submitted by Mr. Reece. May 23, 1924. 1 p. (H. rp. 837, 68th Cong. 1st sess.) * Paper, 5c.

McHenry, Fort. Restoration of Fort McHenry in Baltimore, Md., report to accompany H. R. 5261 [to repeal and reenact chapter 100, 1914, public 108, to provide for restoration of Fort McHenry, Md., and its permanent preservation as national park and perpetual national memorial shrine as birthplace of immortal Star-spangled banner, written by Francis Scott Key, for appropriation of necessary funds, and for other purposes]; submitted by Mr. Hill of Maryland. May 13, 1924. 2 p. (H. rp. 720, 68th Cong. 1st sess.) * Paper, 5c.

—— To provide for restoration of Fort McHenry, hearings on H. R. 5261, to repeal and reenact chapter 100, 1914, public 108, to provide for restoration of Fort McHenry, Md., and its permanent preservation as national park and perpetual national memorial shrine as birthplace of immortal Star-spangled banner, written by Francis Scott Key, for appropriation of necessary funds, and for other purposes, Apr. 16, 1924. 1924. ii+27 p. * Paper, 5c.

Militia. To amend national defense act, report to accompany H. R. 8886 [providing for sundry matters affecting military establishment]; submitted by Mr. McKenzie. Apr. 30, 1924. 6 p. (H. rp. 612, 68th Cong. 1st sess.) [The sections of the bill relate exclusively to the National Guard.] * Paper, 5c.

Moore, Edward N. Edward N. Moore, report to accompany H. R. 5278 [for relief of Edward N. Moore]; submitted by Mr. Wurzbach. May 22, 1924. 2 p. (H. rp. 829, 68th Cong. 1st sess.) * Paper, 5c.

Mothers. To authorize mothers of deceased World War veterans buried in Europe to visit the graves, hearings, May 3, 1924, supplement, containing War Department study of proposed legislation. 1924. ii+27–37 p. * Paper, 5c.

New Orleans, Battle of, 1815. National military park to commemorate Battle of New Orleans, hearings on H. R. 4820 [4869], Mar. 27, 1924; statement of James O'Connor. 1924. ii+34 p. * Paper, 5c.

Officers, Army. Validating certain payments made by Army officers [for commutation of quarters, heat, and light under act of Apr. 16, 1918, and of rental and subsistence allowances under act of June 10, 1922], report to accompany H. R. 6065; submitted by Mr. Hull of Iowa. May 7, 1924. 2 p. (H. rp. 673, 68th Cong. 1st sess.) [Corrected print.] * Paper, 5c.

Pay, Navy. Pay of warrant and commissioned warrant officers, Navy, hearings, Apr. 22 [and] 29, 1924. 1924. pt. 2, ii+51–116 p. [Part 1 appeared in Monthly catalogue for Apr. 1924, p. 614.] * Paper, 10c.

Pike, Camp. Authorizing Arkansas to construct buildings, rifle ranges, and utilities at Camp Pike, Ark., report to accompany H. J. Res. 254; submitted by Mr. McSwain. May 7, 1924. 3 p. (H. rp. 669, 68th Cong. 1st sess.) * Paper, 5c.

Public Buildings and Grounds Office. Army officer of appropriate grade in charge of public buildings and grounds in District of Columbia, report to accompany H. R. 9012; submitted by Mr. McSwain. May 12, 1924. 3 p. (H. rp. 814, 68th Cong. 1st sess.) * Paper, 5c.

Quarles, William P. William P. Quarles, known as Qualls, report to accompany H. R. 9354 [for relief of William P. Quarles, known as Qualls]; submitted by Mr. Reece. May 22, 1924. 3 p. (H. rp. 813, 68th Cong. 1st sess.) * Paper, 5c.

Quinn, Leo P. Leo P. Quinn, report to accompany S. 2764 [authorizing the President to order Leo P. Quinn before retiring board for rehearing of his case and upon findings of such board either confirm his discharge or place him on retired list with rank and pay held by him at time of discharge]; submitted by Mr. Hill of Maryland. May 22, 1924. 3 p. (H. rp. 823, 68th Cong. 1st sess.) * Paper, 5c.

Rayburn, Harry D. Harry D. Rayburn, alias Daniel Harris, report to accompany H. R. 6554 [providing that records of War Department shall be amended to show services of Daniel Harris under his true name, Harry D. Rayburn]; submitted by Mr. Hill of Maryland. May 13, 1924. 6 p. (H. rp. 724. 68th Cong. 1st sess.) * Paper, 5c.

Rector, Frank. Frank Rector, report to accompany H. R. 8192 [for relief of Frank Rector]; submitted by Mr. Wurzbach. May 20, 1924. 8 p. (H. rp. 793, 68th Cong. 1st sess.) * Paper, 5c.

Reese, Isaac J. Isaac J. Reese, report to accompany H. R. 2958 [for relief of Isaac J. Reese]; submitted by Mr. Hill of Maryland. May 14, 1924. 8 p. (H. rp. 757, 68th Cong. 1st sess.) * Paper, 5c.

Russian Railway Service Corps. Give military status and discharges to members of Russian Railway Service Corps, report to accompany S. 1557; submitted by Mr. McSwain. May 13, 1924. 2 p. (H. rp. 727, 68th Cong. 1st sess.) * Paper, 5c.

—— Russian Railway Service Corps, providing honorable discharge for members of, from military service of United States, hearing on S. 1557, May 6, 1924. 1924. ii+43 p. * Paper, 5c.

Santa Rosa Island. To convey tract of land in military reservation of Santa Rosa Island, Fla., report to accompany S. 2676 [to lease or to convey by quit-claim deed tract of land in military reservation of Santa Rosa Island, Fla., to Thomas H. Hazelrigg and John A. Chumbley for ship canal]; submitted by Mr. Wright. May 22, 1924. 2 p. (H. rp. 822, 68th Cong. 1st sess.) * Paper, 5c.

Seattle, Wash. Old canal right of way between lakes Union and Washington, King County, Wash., report to accompany H. R. 3847 [granting right of way, with authority to improve same, across old canal right of way between lakes Union and Washington, King County, Wash., to Seattle, Wash.]; submitted by Mr. Sutherland. Apr. 30, 1924. 2 p. (H. rp. 615, 68th Cong. 1st sess.) * Paper, 5c.

Shekell, Alonzo C. Alonzo C. Shekell, report to accompany H. R. 5257 [for relief of Alonzo C. Shekell].; submitted by Mr. Wurzbach. May 20, 1924. 4 p. (H. rp. 797, 68th Cong. 1st sess.) * Paper, 5c.

Shook, James. James Shook, report to accompany H. R. 7133 [relief of James Shook]; submitted by Mr. Wurzbach. May 22, 1924. 2 p. (H. rp. 831, 68th Cong. 1st sess.) * Paper, 5c.

Solen, John. John Solen, report to accompany H. R. 7389 [for relief of John Solen]; submitted by Mr. Sutherland. Apr. 30, 1924. 3 p. (H. rp. 616, 68th Cong. 1st sess.) * Paper, 5c.

Sparks, Frederick. Frederick Sparks, report to accompany H. R. 1958 [for relief of Frederick Sparks]; submitted by Mr. Wurzbach. May 22, 1924. 1 p. (H. rp. 817, 68th Cong. 1st sess.) * Paper, 5c.

Strickland, Orrin F. Orrin F. Strickland, report to accompany H. R. 2107 [for relief of Orrin F. Strickland]; submitted by Mr. Wurzbach. May 27, 1924. 4 p. (H. rp. 877, 68th Cong. 1st sess.) * Paper, 5c.

Sussex County, Del. Conveying of lands to Delaware, report to accompany S. 2431 [conveying to Delaware land in county of Sussex, in that State]; submitted by Mr. Geran. May 7' 1924. 2 p. (H. rp. 672, 68th Cong. 1st sess.) * Paper, 5c.

Thomas, Matthew. Matthew Thomas, report to accompany H. R. 2421 [for relief of Matthew Thomas]; submitted by Mr. Wurzbach. May 22, 1924. 2 p. (H. rp. 812, 68th Cong. 1st sess.) * Paper, 5c.

Walker, John E. John E. Walker, report to accompany H. R. 6001 [for relief of John E. Walker]; submitted by Mr. Wurzbach. May 14, 1924. 2 p. (H. rp. 752, 68th Cong. 1st sess.) * Paper, 5c.

War. To promote peace and to equalize burdens and to minify profits of war, report to accompany H. J. Res. 128; submitted by Mr. McSwain. May 15, 1924. 3 p. (H. rp. 764, 68th Cong. 1st sess.) * Paper, 5c.

—— Universal mobilization for war purposes, hearings on H. J. Res. 128, H. R. 194, H. R. 4841, and H. R. 8111, Mar. 11, 13, and 20, 1924. 1924. iii+250 p. 1 tab. [The hearings held on Mar. 28, Apr. 9 and 10, and May 3 are included.] * Paper, 25c.

War Department. Sale of real property no longer required for military purposes, report to accompany H. R. 9124; submitted by Mr. McKenzie. May 12, 1924. 5 p. (H. rp. 710, 68th Cong. 1st sess.) * Paper, 5c.

—— Transfer of certain materials, machinery, and equipment from War Department to Department of Agriculture, report to accompany H. R. 7269; submitted by Mr. Reece. May 10, 1924. 4 p. (H. rp. 700, 68th Cong. 1st sess.) * Paper, 5c.

War trophies. Equitable distribution of captured war devices and trophies, report to accompany ·S. 1376 [for equitable distribution of captured war devices and trophies to States and Territories and to District of Columbia]; submitted by Mr. McKenzie. May 12, 1924. 1 p. (H. rp. 815, 68th Cong. 1st sess.) * Paper, 5c.

Westport, Battle of, 1864. To establish national military park at Kansas City, Mo., report to accompany H. R. 5417 [authorizing and directing Secretary of War to investigate feasibility and to ascertain and report cost of establishing national military park in and about Kansas City, Mo., commemorative of Battle of Westport, Oct. 23, 1864]; submitted by Mr. Reece. May 16, 1924. 8 p. (H. rp. 774, 68th Cong. 1st sess.) * Paper, 5c.

Woltman, Herman R. Herman R. Woltman, report to accompany H. R. 3556 [for relief of Herman R. Woltman]; submitted by Mr. Wurzbach. May 20, 1924. 2 p. (H. rp. 792, 68th Cong. 1st sess.) * Paper, 5c.

Yarbrough, Mrs. Rosa L. Rosa L. Yarbrough, report to accompany S. 1427 [for relief of Rosa L. Yarbrough]; submitted by Mr. Hill of Alabama. May 23, 1924. 2 p. (H. rp. 838, 68th Cong. 1st sess.) * Paper, 5c.

MINES AND MINING COMMITTEE

Alaska. To modify and amend mining laws in their application to Alaska, hearing on H. R. 4148, to modify and amend mining laws in their application to Alaska [so as to remove dimensional restriction where isolated parcels of unappropriated placer ground are surrounded on all sides by patented claims], Apr. 19, 1924. 1924. ii+13 p. * Paper, 5c.

Claims. Authorizing payment of claims under provisions of so-called war minerals relief act, hearing on S. 2797, Apr. 19, 1924. 1924. ii+17 p. * Paper. 5c.

NAVAL AFFAIRS COMMITTEE

Ames, Ray E. To change retired status of chief pay clerk R. E. Ames, Navy, report to accompany H. R. 1445; submitted by Mr. Woodruff. May 1, 1924. 3 p. (H. rp. 622, 68th Cong. 1st sess.) * Paper, 5c.

Bagshaw, Frank G. Frank George Bagshaw, report to accompany H. R. 909 [to remove charge of desertion against name of Frank George Bagshaw]; submitted by Mr. Burdick. May 3, 1924. 2 p. (H. rp. 653, 68th Cong. 1st sess.) * Paper, 5c.

Berry, George A. George A. Berry, report to accompany H. R. 7167 [for relief of George A. Berry]; submitted by Mr. Woodruff. May 6, 1924. 23 p. (H. rp. 668, 68th Cong. 1st sess.) * Paper, 5c.

Bostrom, Mrs. Elizabeth W. Elizabeth Walter Bostrom, report to accompany H. R. 1706 [granting 6 months' pay to Elizabeth Walter Bostrom, widow of Carl Augustus Bostrom]; submitted by Mr. Taylor of West Virginia. May 7, 1924. 2 p. (H. rp. 677, 68th Cong. 1st sess.) * Paper, 5c.

Calendar. Legislative calendar, 68th Congress, 1923–24; no. 4, May 14, 1924. 1924. 36 p. 4° ‡

Fenner, Milton M. Milton M. Fenner, report to accompany H. R. 2105 [for relief of Milton M. Fenner]; submitted by Mr. Andrew. May 3, 1924. 3 p. (H. rp. 656, 68th Cong. 1st sess.) * Paper, 5c.

Johnson, Russell W. Russell Wilmer Johnson, report to accompany H. R. 5061 [for relief of Russell Wilmer Johnson]; submitted by Mr. vinson of Georgia. May 2, 1924. 3 p. (H. rp. 629, 68th Cong. 1st sess.) * Paper, 5c.

Knox, Mrs. Lucy B. Lucy B. Knox, report to accompany H. R. 5456 [granting 6 months' pay to Lucy B. Knox, widow of Forney M. Knox]; submitted by Mr. Vinson of Georgia. May 2, 1924. 2 p. (H. rp. 630, 68th Cong. 1st sess.) * Paper, 5c.

Lindsay, Russell H. Russell H. Lindsay, report to accompany H. R. 2418 [for relief of Russell H. Lindsay]; submitted by Mr. Stephens. May 5, 1924. 8 p. (H. rp. 661, 68th Cong. 1st sess.) * Paper, 5c.

Little, Mrs. Joy B. Joy Bright Little, report to accompany H. R. 7018 [for relief of Joy Bright Little]; submitted by Mr. Patterson. May 17, 1924. 4 p. (H. rp. 779, 68th Cong. 1st sess.) * Paper, 5c.

MacDonald, Gordon G. Gordon G. MacDonald, report to accompany H. R. 2342 [for relief of Gordon G. MacDonald]; submitted by Mr. Swing. May 5, 1924. 9 p. (H. rp. 660, 68th Cong. 1st sess.) * Paper, 5c.

Martin, Joseph J. Authorizing payment of amount equal to 6 months' pay to Joseph J. Martin [father of George Russell Martin], report to accompany H. R. 1717; submitted by Mr. Stephens. May 3, 1924. 2 p. (H. rp. 642, 68th Cong. 1st sess.) * Paper, 5c.

Meehan, James J. James J. Meehan, report to accompany H. R. 3736 [for relief of James J. Meehan]; submitted by Mr. Magee of Pennsylvania. May 2, 1924. 2 p. (H. rp. 632, 68th Cong. 1st sess.) * Paper, 5c.

Naval Torpedo Station, Newport. To provide for reimbursement of certain civilian employees at Naval Torpedo Station, Newport, R. I., for value of personal effects lost, damaged, or destroyed by fire, report to accompany H. R. 6723; submitted by Mr. Burdick. May 7, 1924. 3 p. (H. rp. 675, 68th Cong. 1st sess.) * Paper, 5c.

Officers, Navy. To authorize accounting officers of Treasury to pay to certain supply officers of Regular Navy and Naval Reserve Force pay and allowances of their ranks for services performed prior to approval of their bonds, report to accompany H. R. 8263; submitted by Mr. Miller of Washington. May 13, 1924. 2 p. (H. rp. 717, 68th Cong. 1st sess.) * Paper, 5c.

Phillipson, William M. William M. Phillipson, report to accompany H. R. 2016 [for relief of William M. Phillipson]; submitted by Mr. Burdick. May 2, 1924. 6 p. (H. rp. 628, 68th Cong. 1st sess.) * Paper, 5c.

Steger, Isidor. Isidor Steger, report to accompany H. R. 6436 [for relief of Isidor Steger]; submitted by Mr. Burdick. May 8, 1924. 4 p. (H. rp. 684, 68th Cong. 1st sess.) * Paper, 5c.

Stevens, Herbert E. Herbert Elliott Stevens, report to accompany H. R. 2921 [for relief of Herbert Elliott Stevens]; submitted by Mr. Andrew. May 5, 1924. 3 p. (H. rp. 662, 68th Cong. 1st sess.) * Paper, 5c.

Stinchcomb, Frank. Frank Stinchcomb, report to accompany H. R. 8961 [for relief of Frank Stinchcomb]; submitted by Mr. Drewry. May 8, 1924. 7 p. (H. rp. 685, 68th Cong. 1st sess.) * Paper, 5c.

Sylvester, Garnet A. To correct naval record of Garnet A. Sylvester, report to accompany H. R. 4732; submitted by Mr. Stephens. May 1, 1924. 3 p. (H. rp. 623, 68th Cong. 1st sess.) * Paper, 5c.

Tribou, David H. Capt. D. H. Tribou, chaplain, Navy, report to accompany H. R. 5819 [for relief of estate of D. H. Tribou]; submitted by Mr. Stephens. May 3, 1924. 2 p. (H. rp. 647, 68th Cong. 1st sess.) * Paper, 5c.

PATENTS COMMITTEE

Garabed, means of utilizing free energy, hearings on H. J. Res. 190, to amend sec. 3 of joint resolution for purpose of promoting efficiency, for utilization of resources and industries of United States, and so forth, Apr. 11 and 15, 1924. 1924. [1]+53 p. * Paper, 5c.

PENSIONS COMMITTEE

Pensions and increase of pensions for certain soldiers and sailors of Regular Army and Navy, etc., report to accompany H. R. 9178 [substituted for H. R. 788 and other bills]; submitted by Mr. Knutson. May 12, 1924. 144 p. (H. rp. 715, 68th Cong. 1st sess.) * Paper, 15c.

POST OFFICE AND POST ROADS COMMITTEE

Air Mail Service. Contract Air Mail Service, report to accompany H. R. 7064 [to encourage commercial aviation and to authorize Postmaster General to contract for Air Mail Service]; submitted by Mr. LaGuardia. May 13, 1924. 1 p. (H. rp. 730, 68th Cong. 1st sess.) * Paper, 5c.

Air Mail Service—Continued.   Government owned and operated Air Mail Service, report to accompany H. R. 6942 [establishing transmission and carrying mail by airplane and flying machines]; submitted by Mr. La-Guardia. May 13, 1924. 2 p. (H. rp. 729, 68th Cong. 1st sess.)   * Paper, 5c.

Blind.   Transmission through mails of Bibles for the blind, report to accompany H. R. 8586 [for free transmission through mails of certain publications for the blind]; submitted by Mr. Kelly. May 2, 1924. 4 p. (H. rp. 633, 68th Cong. 1st sess.)   * Paper, 5c.

Firearms.   Carrying pistols, revolvers, and other firearms in mails, report to accompany H. R. 9093 [declaring pistols, revolvers, and other firearms capable of being concealed on the person nonmailable and providing penalty]; submitted by Mr. Ramseyer. May 15, 1924. 3 p. (H. rp. 762, 68th Cong. 1st sess.)   * Paper, 5c.

Postal service.   Reclassifying postal salaries, minority report to accompany H. R. 9035 [reclassifying salaries of postmasters and employees of postal service and readjusting their salaries and compensation on equitable basis]; submitted by Mr. Ramseyer. May 10, 1924. 9 p. (H. rp. 655, pt. 2, 68th Cong. 1st sess.)   [Corrected print.]   * Paper, 5c.

—— Reclassifying postal salaries, report to accompany H. R. 9035 [reclassifying salaries of postmasters and employees of postal service and readjusting their salaries and compensation on equitable basis]; submitted by Mr. Paige. May 3, 1924. 10 p. (H. rp. 655 [pt. 1], 68th Cong. 1st sess.)   [Corrected print. 1st print has 9 pages.]   * Paper, 5c.

PRINTING COMMITTEE

Immigration.   To print 600 additional copies of hearings on bills relating to restriction of immigration, report to accompany H. Res. 185; submitted by Mr. Kiess. Feb. 26, 1924. 1 p. (H. rp. 235, 68th Cong. 1st sess.)   * Paper, 5c.

PUBLIC BUILDINGS AND GROUNDS COMMITTEE

Astoria, Oreg.   Public buildings and grounds, hearings on H. R. 7821, conveyance of land to Astoria, Oreg., H. R. 8110, conveyance of land to Duluth, Minn., S. 1971, Glover parkway, S. 1918, officers in charge of public buildings and grounds, District of Columbia, H. J. Res. 31, survey of Potomac River banks and adjacent lands from Washington, D. C., to Great Falls, H. R. 2821, hospital, Santa Monica, Calif., Apr. 8, 1924. 1924. ii+14 p. (No. 7.)   * Paper, 5c.

New York City.   Public buildings and grounds, hearings on H. R. 5629, public building, borough of Richmond, New York, N. Y., Mar. 7 [11], 1924. 1924. ii+7 p. (No. 6.)   * Paper, 5c.

PUBLIC LANDS COMMITTEE

Arizona University.   Authorizing issuance of patent in fee simple to board of regents of University of Arizona, report to accompany S. 511; submitted by Mr. Richards. May 14, 1924. 1 p. (H. rp. 745, 68th Cong. 1st sess.)   * Paper, 5c.

Assinniboine, Fort.   Extension of time for payment of purchase money under homestead entries within former Fort Assiniboine military reservation, Mont., report to accompany H. J. Res. 210; submitted by Mr. Leavitt. May 13, 1924. 2 p. (H. rp. 734, 68th Cong. 1st sess.)   * Paper, 5c.

Battle Creek, Mich.   To relinquish to Battle Creek, Mich., all right, title, and interest of United States in 2 unsurveyed islands in Kalamazoo River, report to accompany H. R. 7144; submitted by Mr. Williams of Michigan. May 13, 1924. 3 p. (H. rp. 738, 68th Cong. 1st sess.)   * Paper, 5c.

Bowdoin, Mont.   Granting reappraisement of lots in town site of Bowdoin, Mont., report to accompany H. R. 7522; submitted by Mr. Leavitt. May 22, 1924. 2 p. (H. rp. 825, 68th Cong. 1st sess.)   * Paper, 5c.

Crooked Lake.   Disposal of certain lands on Crooked and Pickerel lakes, Mich., report to accompany H. R. 4482; submitted by Mr. Williams of Michigan. May 24, 1924. 2 p. (H. rp. 842, 68th Cong. 1st sess.)   * Paper, 5c.

Elstad, Lars O. For relief of Lars O. Elstad, report to accompany H. R. 7679 [for relief of Lars O. Elstad and exchange of certain lands owned by Northern Pacific Railway Company]; submitted by Mr. Sinnott. May 28, 1924. 2 p. (H. rp. 890, 68th Cong. 1st sess.) * Paper, 5c.

Game. Withdrawal of lands for protection of game animals and birds [in South Dakota], report to accompany S. 2761; submitted by Mr. Winter. May 27, 1924. 3 p. (H. rp. 868, 68th Cong. 1st sess.) * Paper, 5c.

Gladwin, Mich. First State Savings Bank of Gladwin, Mich., report to accompany H. R. 8226 [granting relief to First State Savings Bank of Gladwin, Mich.]; submitted by Mr. Williams of Michigan. May 13, 1924. 2 p. (H. rp. 739, 68th Cong. 1st sess.) * Paper, 5c.

Johnson, William G. Authorizing sale of land to William G. Johnson, report to accompany H. R. 9027 [authorizing Secretary of Interior to sell and patent to William G. Johnson lands in Louisiana]; submitted by Mr. Thomas of Oklahoma. May 28, 1924. 2 p. (H. rp. 892, 68th Cong. 1st sess.) * Paper, 5c.

La May, Fred J. Fred J. La May, report to accompany H. R. 7780 [for relief of Fred J. La May]; submitted by Mr. Williams of Michigan. May 24, 1924. 2 p. (H. rp. 843, 68th Cong. 1st sess.) * Paper, 5c.

Phoenix, Ariz. Granting lands to Phoenix, Ariz., report to accompany H. R. 8587; submitted by Mr. Richards. May 14, 1924. 1 p. (H. rp. 749, 68th Cong. 1st sess.) * Paper, 5c.

Redlands, Calif. Sale of public land to Redlands, Calif., report to accompany H. R. 166; submitted by Mr. Fredericks. May 28, 1924. 2 p. (H. rp. 883, 68th Cong. 1st sess.) * Paper, 5c.

Roosevelt-Sequoia National Park, hearings on H. R. 4095, to add certain lands to Sequoia National Park, Calif., and to change name of said park to Roosevelt-Sequoia National Park, Feb. 27 and 28, 1924. 1924. iii+122 p. * Paper, 10c.

Sweetgrass, Mont. For relief of First International Bank of Sweetgrass, Mont., report to accompany H. R. 6335; submitted by Mr. Leavitt. May 28, 1924. 2 p. (H. rp. 889, 68th Cong. 1st sess.) * Paper, 5c.

Taos County, N. Mex. Providing for acquirement by United States of privately owned lands within Rio Arriba and Taos counties, N. Mex., known as Las Trampas grant, by exchanging therefor timber within exterior boundaries of any national forest situated within New Mexico, report to accompany S. 3024; submitted by Mr. Morrow. May 27, 1924. 2 p. (H. rp. 882, 68th Cong. 1st sess.) *Paper, 5c.

—— Providing for acquirement by United States of privately owned lands within Taos County, N. Mex., known as Santa Barbara grant, by exchanging therefor timber, or lands and timber, within exterior boundaries of any national forest situated within New Mexico, report to accompany S. 1762; submitted by Mr. Morrow. May 27, 1924. 2 p. (H. rp. 881, 68th Cong. 1st sess.) * Paper, 5c.

Umatilla National Forest. Adding lands to Umatilla, Wallowa, and Whitman national forests, Oreg., report to accompany H. R. 6651; submitted by Mr. Sinnott. May 13, 1924. 2 p. (H. rp. 728, 68th Cong. 1st sess.) * Paper, 5c.

Wisconsin. Granting certain claimants preference right to purchase public lands [in Wisconsin], report to accompany H. R. 8522; submitted by Mr. Sinnott. May 28. 1924. 2 p. (H. rp. 885, 68th Cong. 1st sess.) * Paper, 5c.

RIVERS AND HARBORS COMMITTEE

Hilo, Honolulu, Kahului, and Nawiliwili harbors, Hawaii, hearings on subject of improvement of Hilo, Honolulu, Kahului, and Nawiliwili harbors, Hawaii. Jan. 8 and 9, 1924. 1924. [1]+35 p. * Paper, 5c.

Inland waterways. Louisiana and Texas intracoastal waterway, hearings on subject of improvement of Louisiana and Texas intracoastal waterway from Mississippi River, at or near New Orleans, La., to Corpus Christi, Tex., Apr. 5 and 11, 1924. 1924. [1]+61 p. * Paper, 5c.

Lake Drummond Canal, Va. and N. C., hearings on subject of acquisition of Lake Drummond (Dismal Swamp) Canal, Va. and N. C., Apr. 14, 1924. 1924. [1]+53 p. * Paper, 5c.

Mississippi, Missouri, and Ohio rivers, hearings on H. R. 3921, for improvement and completion of prescribed sections of Mississippi, Missouri, and Ohio rivers, Mar. 20–Apr. 4, 1924. 1924. iv+189 p. * Paper, 20c.

River and harbor bill, hearings on H. R. 8914, Apr. 3–22, 1924. 1924. [1]+139 p. * Paper, 15c.

Tennessee River. Survey of Tennessee River and its tributaries, hearings on subject of completion of survey of Tennessee River and its tributaries, N. C., Tenn., Ala., and Ky., Mar. 31 and Apr. 1, 1924. 1924. [1]+82 p. * Paper, 10c.

Water pollution. Oil pollution of coastal navigable waters, report to accompany S. 1942 [to protect navigation from obstruction and injury by preventing discharge of oil into coastal navigable waters of United States]; submitted by Mr. Lineberger. May 20, 1924. 4 p. (H. rp. 794, 68th Cong. 1st sess.) * Paper, 5c.

ROADS COMMITTEE

Roads. Federal aid in construction of roads, report to accompany H. R. 4971 [to amend act to provide that United States shall aid States in construction of rural post roads, approved July 11, 1916, as amended and supplemented]; submitted by Mr. Dowell. May 23, 1924. 3 p. (H. rp. 840, 68th Cong. 1st sess.) * Paper, 5c.

—— Roads, hearings on H. R. 63, H. R. 3232, H. R. 4971, H. R. 6133, Mar. 10–31, 1924. 1924. [2]+221 p. * Paper, 25c.

RULES COMMITTEE

Agricultural products. Consideration of H. R. 9033, report to accompany H. Res. 317 [for consideration of H. R. 9033, declaring emergency to exist in agricultural commodities, and so forth]; submitted by Mr. Snell. May 17, 1924. 1 p. (H. rp. 775, 68th Cong. 1st sess.) * Paper, 5c.

Arbitration. Consideration of H. R. 646, report to accompany H. Res. 299 [for consideration of H. R. 646, to make valid and enforceable written provisions or agreements for arbitration of disputes arising out of contracts, maritime transactions, or commerce among States or Territories or with foreign nations]; submitted by Mr. Snell. May 7, 1924. 1 p. (H. rp. 671, 68th Cong. 1st sess.) * Paper, 5c.

Cape Cod Canal. Consideration of H. R. 3933, report to accompany H. Res. 278 [for consideration of H. R. 3933, Cape Cod Canal bill]; submitted by Mr. Snell. May 3, 1924. 1 p. (H. rp. 636, 68th Cong. 1st sess.) * Paper, 5c.

Government Printing Office. Consideration of bill to regulate and fix rates of wages for employees of Government Printing Office, report to accompany H. Res. 315; submitted by Mr. Snell. May 16, 1924. 1 p. (H. rp. 773, 68th Cong. 1st sess.) * Paper, 5c.

Inland Waterways Corporation. Consideration of H. R. 8209, report to accompany H. Res. 279 [for consideration of H. R. 8209, Inland Waterways Corporation bill]; submitted by Mr. Snell. May 3, 1924. 1 p. (H. rp. 637, 68th Cong. 1st sess.) * Paper, 5c.

Judges. Consideration of H. R. 3318, report to accompany H. Res. 298 [for consideration of H. R. 3318, for appointment of 2 additional judges of district court for southern district of New York]; submitted by Mr. Snell. May 7, 1924. 1 p. (H. rp. 670, 68th Cong. 1st sess.) * Paper, 5c.

Rehabilitation of the disabled. Consideration of H. R. 5478, report to accompany H. Res. 274 [for consideration of H. R. 5478, to amend act providing vocational rehabilitation of persons injured in civil employment]; submitted by Mr. Snell. Apr. 30, 1924. 1 p. (H. rp. 602, 68th Cong. 1st sess.) * Paper, 5c.

Veterans' Bureau. Consideration of H. R. 5209, report to accompany H. Res. 275 [for consideration of H. R. 5209, to authorize additional hospital facilities for veterans' Bureau]; submitted by Mr. Snell. Apr. 30, 1924. 1 p. (H. rp. 603, 68th Cong. 1st sess.) * Paper, 5c.

SHIPPING BOARD AND EMERGENCY FLEET CORPORATION SELECT COMMITTEE

Shipping Board. United States Shipping Board and Emergency Fleet Corporation, hearings pursuant to House Resolution 186. 1924. pt. 1, ii+1–824 p. * Paper, 85c.

Alaska Railroad. Relief of special disbursing agents of Alaskan Engineering Commission, hearings on H. J. Res. 226, for relief of special disbursing agents of Alaskan Engineering Commission, authorizing payment of certain claims, and for other purposes, affecting management of Alaska Railroad, Mar. 24–26, 1924. 1924. ii+74 p. * Paper, 10c.

Hawaii. Electric light and power within district of Hamakua, hearings on H. R. 6070, for manufacture, maintenance, distribution, and supply of electric current for light and power within district of Hamakua, on island of Hawaii, Hawaii [by M. S. Botelho], Mar. 31, 1924. 1924. ii+6 .p. * Paper, 5c.

—— Land patents, Hawaii, hearings on H. R. 6303, to issue patents to certain persons who purchased government lots in district of Waiakea, island of Hawaii, in accordance with act 33, session laws of 1915, Legislature of Hawaii, Mar. 31, 1924. 1924. ii+6 p. * Paper, 5c.

Juneau, Alaska. Bond issue, Juneau, Alaska, hearings on H. R. 5558, to authorize Juneau, Alaska, to issue bonds in any sum not exceeding $200,000 for purpose of improving street and sewerage system of town, Mar. 29, 1924. 1924. ii+6 p. * Paper, 5c.

—— Bond issue, Juneau, Alaska, report to accompany H. R. 5558 [to authorize Juneau, Alaska, to issue bonds in any sum not exceeding $200,000 for purpose of improving street and sewerage system of town]; submitted by Mr. Abernethy. May 14, 1924. 2 p. (H. rp. 754, 68th Cong. 1st sess.) * Paper, 5c.

Seward Peninsula. Improvement of system of overland communications on Seward Peninsula, Alaska, hearings on H. J. Res. 60, Mar. 29, 1924. 1924. ii+14 p. [H. J. Res. 60 provides for the adoption of the Nome-Shelton-Kugruk River-Keewalik project.] * Paper, 5c.

Technical education. Establishment of industrial schools for Alaskan native children, and for other purposes, hearings on H. R. 4825, Mar. 29, 1924. 1924. ii+19 p. * Paper, 5c.

Adams, Byron S. Byron S. Adams, report to accompany H. R. 8298 [for relief of Byron S. Adams]; submitted by Mr. Williams of Michigan. May 28, 1924. 2 p. (H. rp. 891, 68th Cong. 1st sess.) * Paper, 5c.

Army. Payment of claims for damages to and loss of private property incident to training, practice, etc., of Army, report to accompany S. 2527; submitted by Mr. Williams of Michigan. May 27, 1924. 5 p. (H. rp. 875, 68th Cong. 1st sess.) * Paper, 5c.

Clayton, Charles T. Claims growing out of Houston riot, report to accompany H. R. 7631 [for relief of Charles T. Clayton and others]; submitted by Mr. Roach. May 22, 1924. 24 p. (H. rp. 820, 68th Cong. 1st sess.) * Paper, 5c.

Cobb, Murray A. Murray A. Cobb, report to accompany S. 1815 [for relief of Murray A. Cobb]; submitted by Mr. Williams of Michigan. May 27, 1924. 9 p. (H. rp. 874, 68th Cong. 1st sess.) * Paper, 5c.

De Kimpke Construction Co., report to accompany S. 970 [for relief of De Kimpke Construction Company, West Hoboken, N. J.]; submitted by Mr. Williams of Michigan. May 27, 1924. 3 p. (H. rp. 873, 68th Cong. 1st sess.) * Paper, 5c.

Fletcher, Ed. F. J. Belcher, jr., report to accompany H. R. 2336 [for relief of F. J. Belcher, jr., trustee for Ed Fletcher]; submitted by Mr. Williams of Michigan. May 2, 1924. 9 p. (H. rp. 626, 68th Cong. 1st sess.) * Paper, 5c.

—— F. J. Belcher, jr., report to accompany S. 1014 [for relief of F. J. Belcher, jr., trustee for Ed Fletcher]; submitted by Mr. Williams of Michigan. May 15, 1924. 1 p. (H. rp. 765, 68th Cong. 1st sess.) * Paper, 5c.

Gieriet, Andrew A. Andrew A. Gieriet, report to accompany H. R. 1569 [for relief of Andrew A. Gieriet]; submitted by Mr. Roach. May 16, 1924. 4 p. (H. rp. 771, 68th Cong. 1st sess.) * Paper, 5c.

Guenther, Mrs. G. A. Mrs. G. A. Guenther, report to accompany H. R. 8997 [for relief of Mrs. G. A. Guenther, mother of Gordon Guenther]; submitted by Mr. Roach. May 29, 1924. 3 p. (H. rp. 901, 68th Cong. 1st sess.) * Paper, 5c.

McCloud, Filer. Filer McCloud, report to accompany H. R. 4610 [for relief of estate of Filer McCloud]; submitted by Mr. Williams of Michigan. May 16, 1924. 2 p. (H. rp. 772, 68th Cong. 1st sess.) * Paper, 5c.

Pacific Commissary Co., report to accompany S. 2357 [for relief of Pacific Commissary Company]; submitted by Mr. Williams of Michigan. May 2, 1924. 7 p. (H. rp. 625, 68th Cong. 1st sess.) * Paper, 5c.

WAYS AND MEANS COMMITTEE

Cattle. Extending time during which certain domestic animals which have crossed boundary line into foreign countries may be returned duty free, report to accompany H. J. Res. 82; submitted by Mr. Hawley. Dec. 20, 1923. 1 p. (H. rp. 5, 68th Cong. 1st sess.) * Paper, 5c.

Hungary. Settlement of debt of Hungary to United States, report to accompany H. R. 8905 [to authorize settlement of indebtedness of Kingdom of Hungary to United States]; submitted by Mr. Crisp. May 3, 1924. 11 p. (H. rp. 654, 68th Cong. 1st sess.) * Paper, 5c.

Liquors. Abolition of 7-year regauge of distilled spirits, hearings on H. R. 9034, for regauging of distilled spirits, and for other purposes, May 7, 1924. 1924. ii+21 p. * Paper, 5c.

—— To abolish 7-year regauge of distilled spirits, report to accompany H. R. 9138 [to authorize discontinuance of 7-year regauge of distilled spirits in bonded warehouses]; submitted by Mr. Green of Iowa. May 10, 1924. 4 p. (H. rp. 701, 68th Cong. 1st sess.) * Paper, 5c.

Philadelphia, Pa. Relief of certain customs employees at port of Philadelphia, report to accompany H. R. 2858 [for relief of certain customs employees at port of Philadelphia who served as acting customs guards during war emergency]; submitted by Mr. Watson. May 28, 1924. 4 p. (H. rp. 884, 68th Cong. 1st sess.) * Paper, 5c.

War Department. Remission of customs duties on certain War Department property, hearings, Apr. 8, 1924. 1924. ii+6 p. * Paper, 5c.

—— To remit customs duties on certain War Department property, report to accompany H. R. 9111 [directing remission of customs duties on certain property of United States imported by War Department]; submitted by Mr. Green of Iowa. May 8, 1924. 3 p. (H. rp. 690, 68th Cong. 1st sess.) * Paper, 5c.

WORLD WAR VETERANS' LEGISLATION COMMITTEE

Pay, Army. World War veterans' legislation, hearing before subcommittee on H. R. 7845 and H. R. 8869. bills to amend sec. 210 of war risk insurance act, May 17, 1924. 1924. iii+12 p. * Paper, 5c.

Veterans' Bureau. To amend act to establish veterans' Bureau, etc., report to accompany S. 2257 [to amend act to establish veterans' Bureau and to improve facilities and service of such bureau, and further to amend and modify war risk insurance act, approved Aug. 9, 1921, and to amend and modify war risk insurance act, and to amend vocational rehabilitation act]; submitted by Mr. Johnson of South Dakota. May 15, 1924. 15 p. (H. rp. 763, 68th Cong. 1st sess.) [Corrected print.] * Paper, 5c.   24—26507

World War emergency officers retired list. Retirement of disabled emergency officers, report to accompany H. R. 6484 [making eligible for retirement under certain conditions officers and former officers of World War, other than officers of Regular Army, who incurred physical disability in line of duty while in service of United States during World War]; submitted by Mr. Fitzgerald. May 6, 1924. 2 p. (H. rp. 665, 68th Cong. 1st sess.) * Paper, 5c.

REORGANIZATION JOINT COMMITTEE

Executive Departments. Reorganization of Executive Departments, hearing on S. J. Res. 282, 67th Congress, to amend joint resolution to create Joint Committee on Reorganization of Administrative Branch of Government, Apr. 8, 1924, supplement. 1924. iii+787–834 p. * Paper, 5c.

722 MAY, 1924

SENATE

Appropriations. Contingent expenses, Senate, miscellaneous items, exclusive of labor, supplemental estimate of appropriation pertaining to legislative establishment, fiscal year 1924, for contingent expenses, miscellaneous items, exclusive of labor. May 12, 1924. 2 p. (H. doc. 273, 68th Cong. 1st sess.) * Paper, 5c.

—— Expenses of inquiries and investigations ordered by Senate, supplemental estimate of appropriation for legislative establishment of United States, fiscal year 1924, for expenses of inquiries and investigations ordered by Senate. May 2, 1924. 2 p. (H. doc. 254, 68th Cong. 1st sess.) * Paper, 5c.

Calendar of business, Senate, 68th Congress, 1st session, May 1–31, 1924; no. 97–122. [1924.] various paging, large 8° [Daily when Senate is in session. The legislative day of Apr. 24 extended through the calendar day May 1.] ‡

Employees. Salaries, officers and employees, Senate, supplemental estimates of appropriations for legislative establishment, fiscal year 1925, salaries, officers and employees, Senate. May 26, 1924. 2 p. (H. doc. 314, 68th Cong. 1st sess.) * Paper, 5c.

Homestead. Sixty-two years of homestead law, review of 62 years of homestead law, by George R. Wickham; presented by Mr. Cameron. 1924. [1]+6 p. (S. doc. 113, 68th Cong. 1st sess.) * Paper, 5c. 24—26468

International relations. Distinction between legal and political questions, paper read at Apr. 1924 meeting of American Society of International Law, by Edwin M. Borchard; presented by Mr. Borah. 1924. ii+6 p. (S. doc. 118, 68th Cong. 1st sess.) * Paper, 5c. 24—26508

Near East Relief, report of Near East Relief, year ending Dec. 31, 1923. 1924. iii+26 p. (S. doc. 111, 68th Cong. 1st sess.) * Paper, 5c. 21—26393

Peace. Organization of the world for peace, plan by which United States may cooperate with other nations to achieve and preserve peace of the world, by Chandler P. Anderson, to accompany Senate joint resolution 122; presented by Mr. Lodge. 1924. [1]+11 p. (S. doc. 107, 68th Cong. 1st sess.) * Paper, 5c. 24—26467

Permanent Court of International Justice, resolution advising adherence of United States to existing Permanent Court of International Justice with certain amendments, together with statute of the Court as amended in conformity with Senate resolution 234; presented by Mr. Pepper. 1924. [1]+16 p. (S. doc. 116, 68th Cong. 1st sess.) * Paper, 5c. 24—26469

Restaurant. Contingent expenses, Senate, kitchen and restaurant, supplemental estimate of appropriation for legislative establishment, fiscal year 1925, contingent expenses, Senate, kitchen and restaurant. May 26, 1924. 2 p. (H. doc. 321, 68th Cong. 1st sess.) * Paper, 5c.

AGRICULTURE AND FORESTRY COMMITTEE

Alaska. Protection of wild game animals and wild birds in Alaska, report to accompany S. J. Res. 127 [to provide that powers and duties conferred upon governor of Alaska under existing law for protection of wild game animals and wild birds in Alaska be transferred to and be exercised by Secretary of Agriculture]; submitted by Mr. Norbeck. May 20, calendar day May 21, 1924. 3 p. (S. rp. 573, 68th Cong. 1st sess.) * Paper, 5c.

Alien Property Trade Investment Corporation. Alien Property Investment Corporation, report to accompany S. J. Res. 121 [to create body corporate by name of Alien Property Trade Investment Corporation]; submitted by Mr. Harrison. May 5, calendar day May 9, 1924. 3 p. (S. rp. 511, 68th Cong. 1st sess.) * Paper, 5c.

—— Exportation of agricultural products and raw materials, hearings on S. 2710, to finance exportation of American agricultural products and raw materials, Apr. 2 and 3, 1924. 1924. iii+63 p. * Paper, 5c.

Birds. Establishing shooting grounds, game refuges, and breeding grounds for protecting migratory birds, report to accompany S. 2913 [for establishment of migratory-bird refuges to furnish in perpetuity homes for migratory birds, establishment of public shooting grounds to preserve American system of free shooting, provision of funds for establishing such areas, and furnishing of adequate protection for migratory birds]; submitted by Mr. Johnson of Minnesota. May 20, calendar day May 24, 1924. 4 p. (S. rp. 610, 68th Cong. 1st sess.) * Paper, 5c.

Calendar. Legislative calendar, 68th Congress, May 10 and 21, 1924; no. 9 and 10. 1924. Each 22 p. 4° ‡

Forests and forestry. Reforestation, hearing on S. 1182, for protection of forest lands, for reforestation of denuded areas, for extension of national forests, and for other purposes, in order to promote continuous production of timber on lands chiefly suitable therefor, Mar. 28 [and 29], 1924. 1924. ii+67 p. * Paper, 10c.

Marketing of farm produce. Yoakum plan for agricultural relief, hearing on S. 2844, to place agricultural industry on sound commercial basis, to encourage cooperative associations, and for other purposes, Apr. 1, 1924. 1924. ii+34 p. * Paper, 5c.

Muscle Shoals, hearings on S. 139, S. 2372, S. 2747, S. 3214, and H. R. 518, bills relative to completion of Muscle Shoals, Apr. 16 [-28], 1924. 1924. pts. 1, 2, [vii]+1-386 p. [The hearing for Apr. 28, 1924, noted on the title-page of pt. 2, is not contained in this publication.] * Paper, pt. 1, 20c.; * pt. 2, 15c.

Packing industry. Amendment to packers and stockyards act, hearings on S. 2089, to amend packers and stockyards act, 1921, Feb. 14-Mar. 19, 1924. 1924. iii+233 p. * Paper, 20c.

Potash. Investigation of potash deposits, hearing on S. 1925, authorizing investigation by Geological Survey to determine location and extent of potash deposits in United States, Apr. 4 and 5, 1924. 1924. ii+47 p. * Paper, 5c.

—— Potash investigations, report to accompany S. 3047 [authorizing joint investigations by Geological Survey and Bureau of Soils to determine location and extent of potash deposits or occurrence in United States and improved methods of recovering potash therefrom]; submitted by Mr. Ladd. May 20, calendar day May 21, 1924. 3 p. (S. rp. 572, 68th Cong. 1st sess.) * Paper, 5c.

Wheat. Adjustment of certain wheat prices, hearing on S. 2480, to determine and refund difference between price received for wheat of 1917, 1918, and 1919, fixed by United States and its agents, and price which wheat of 1917, 1918, and 1919 would have brought unfixed thereby, Feb. 19, 1924; [statement of Sterling P. Bond]. 1924. ii+14 p. * Paper, 5c.

APPROPRIATIONS COMMITTEE

Agriculture Department. Agricultural appropriation bill, [fiscal year] 1925, report to accompany H. R. 7220; submitted by Mr. McNary. May 13, 1924. 3 p. (S. rp. 531, 68th Cong. 1st sess.) * Paper, 5c.

Appropriations. Urgent deficiency bill, [fiscal year] 1924, report to accompany H. R. 9192; submitted by Mr. Warren. May 14, calendar day May 16, 1924. 3 p. (S. rp. 550, 68th Cong. 1st sess.) * Paper, 5c.

District of Columbia appropriation bill, [fiscal year] 1925, report to accompany H. R. 8889; submitted by Mr. Phipps. May 20, calendar day May 24, 1924. 8 p. (S. rp. 618, 68th Cong. 1st sess.) * Paper, 5c.

BANKING AND CURRENCY COMMITTEE

Silver. Pittman act, report to accompany S. 2917 [directing Secretary of Treasury to complete purchases of silver under act of Apr. 23, 1918, commonly known as Pittman act]; submitted by Mr. Phipps. May 26, calendar day May 29, 1924. 3 p. (S. rp. 658, 68th Cong. 1st sess.) * Paper, 5c.

—— Silver purchases under Pittman act, hearings on S. 2917, directing Secretary of Treasury to complete purchases of silver under act of Apr. 25 [23], 1918, commonly known as Pittman act, May 12 and 13, 1924. 1924. ii+41 p. * Paper, 5c.

CLAIMS COMMITTEE

Beaufort County Lumber Co. of North Carolina, report to accompany S. 2254 [for relief of Beaufort County Lumber Company of North Carolina]; submitted by Mr. Bayard for Mr. Bruce. May 26, calendar day May 28, 1924. 12 p. (S. rp. 647, 68th Cong. 1st sess.) * Paper, 5c.

Berwind-White Coal Mining Co., report to accompany S. 2992 [for relief of Berwind-White Coal Mining Company]; submitted by Mr. Bayard for Mr. Bruce. May 26, calendar day May 28, 1924. 3 p. (S. rp. 650, 68th Cong. 1st sess.) * Paper, 5c.

Bess, Gerard E. Gerard E. Bess, report to accompany H. R. 905 [for relief of Gerard E. Bess]; submitted by Mr. Trammell. May 20, calendar day May 23, 1924. 5 p. (S. rp. 598, 68th Cong. 1st sess.) * Paper, 5c.

Braznell, Benjamin. For relief of estate of Benjamin Braznell, report to accompany S. 1202; submitted by Mr. Stanfield. May 20, calendar day May 23, 1924. 2 p. (S. rp. 602, 68th Cong. 1st sess.) * Paper, 5c.

Bryson, Robert M. Estate of Robert M. Bryson, report to accompany S. 2223 [for relief of estate of Robert M. Bryson]; submitted by Mr. Trammell. May 20, calendar day May 23, 1924. 4 p. (S. rp. 595, 68th Cong. 1st sess.) * Paper, 5c.

Buxton, Grace. Grace Buxton, report to accompany H. R. 5967 [for relief of Grace Buxton]; submitted by Mr. Capper. May 20, calendar day May 23, 1924. 3 p. (S. rp. 606, 68th Cong. 1st sess.) * Paper, 5c.

Canada Steamship Lines (Ltd.), report to accompany S. 2860 [for relief of Canada Steamship Lines (Limited)]; submitted by Mr. Bayard for Mr. Bruce. May 26, calendar day May 28, 1924. 2 p. (S. rp. 656, 68th Cong. 1st sess.) * Paper, 5c.

Conniff, Mrs. Christina. Christina Conniff, report to accompany S. 3235 [for relief of Christina Conniff]; submitted by Mr. Trammell. May 20, calendar day May 23, 1924. 3 p. (S. rp. 597, 68th Cong. 1st sess.) * Paper, 5c.

Eagle Pass Lumber Co., Eagle Pass, Tex., report to accompany S. 2369 [for relief of Eagle Pass Lumber Company, Eagle Pass, Tex.]; submitted by Mr. Trammell. May 20, calendar day May 24, 1924. 12 p. (S. rp. 617, 68th Cong. 1st sess.) * Paper, 5c.

Export Oil Corporation, report to accompany S. 1599 [for relief of Export Oil Corporation]; submitted by Mr. Stephens. May 26, calendar day May 27, 1924. 8 p. (S. rp. 640, 68th Cong. 1st sess.) * Paper, 5c.

Ferlita, G. G. Ferlita, report to accompany S. 2774 [for relief of G. Ferlita]; submitted by Mr. Bayard for Mr. Bruce. May 26, calendar day May 28, 1924. 3 p. (S. rp. 649, 68th Cong. 1st sess.) * Paper, 5c.

Flaten, Emil L. Emil L. Flaten, report to accompany H. R. 2806 [for relief of Emil L. Flaten]; submitted by Mr. Johnson of Minnesota. May 26, 1924. 14 p. (S. rp. 621, 68th Cong. 1st sess.) * Paper, 5c.

Frazer, John. Estate of John Frazer, and others, report to accompany S. 2520 [to give Court of Claims jurisdiction to hear and adjudge claims of estate of John Frazer and others]; submitted by Mr. Stephens. May 26, 1924. 13 p. (S. rp. 622, 68th Cong. 1st sess.) * Paper, 5c.

Greenport Basin & Construction Co., report to accompany H. R. 3348 [to pay claim as result of damage sustained to marine railway of Greenport Basin and Construction Company]; submitted by Mr. Stanfield. May 20, calendar day May 23, 1924. 4 p. (S. rp. 604, 68th Cong. 1st sess.) * Paper, 5c.

Higgins, Mrs. Fannie M. Fannie M. Higgins, report to accompany H. R. 1860 [for relief of Fannie M. Higgins]; submitted by Mr. Trammell. May 20, calendar day May 23, 1924. 18 p. (S. rp. 599, 68th Cong. 1st sess.) * Paper, 5c.

Jenkins, James E. James E. Jenkins, report to accompany S. 2879 [for relief of James E. Jenkins]; submitted by Mr. Bayard. May 26, 1924. 2 p. (S. rp. 624, 68th Cong. 1st sess.) * Paper, 5c.

Jonas, Julius. Julius Jonas, report to accompany H. R. 5762 [for relief of Julius Jonas]; submitted by Mr. Bayard. May 26, 1924. 12 p. (S. rp. 625, 68th Cong. 1st sess.) * Paper, 5c.

Joshua Lovett, steam tug. Owners of steam tug Joshua Lovett, report to accompany S. 2568 [for relief of Taylor Dredging Company, owners of steam tug Joshua Lovett]; submitted by Mr. Bayard for Mr. Bruce. May 26, calendar day May 28, 1924. 2 p. (S. rp. 648, 68th Cong. 1st sess.) * Paper, 5c.

June, Robert. Robert June, report to accompany S. 2586 [for relief of Robert June]; submitted by Mr. Spencer. May 5, 1924. 5 p. (S. rp. 501, 68th Cong. 1st sess.) * Paper, 5c.

Kirk, Robert J. Robert J. Kirk, report to accompany H. R. 3009 [for relief of Robert J. Kirk] ; submitted by Mr. Trammell. May 20, calendar day May 23, 1924. 3 p. (S. rp. 600, 68th Cong. 1st sess.) * Paper, 5c.

Knapp, Mrs. Margaret B. Margaret B. Knapp, report to accompany S. 2794 [for relief of Margaret B. Knapp] ; submitted by Mr. Stanfield. May 26, 1924. 5 p. (S. rp. 626, 68th Cong. 1st sess.) * Paper, 5c.

Laxson, James W. James W. Laxson, report to accompany S. 367 [for relief of James W. Laxson] ; submitted by Mr. Bayard. Apr. 24, calendar day May 2, 1924. 2 p. (S. rp. 487, 68th Cong. 1st sess.) * Paper, 5c.

Louzau, José. José Louzau, report to accompany S. 1648 [for relief of José Louzau] ; submitted by Mr. Johnson of Minnesota. May 26, 1924. 6 p. (S. rp. 620, 68th Cong. 1st sess.) * Paper, 5c.

Lucas, Preston B. C. Almeda Lucas, report to accompany S. 149 [for relief of Almeda Lucas, widow of Preston B. C. Lucas] ; submitted by Mr. Bayard. Apr. 24, calendar day May 2, 1924. 5 p. (S. rp. 486, 68th Cong. 1st sess.) * Paper, 5c.

MacAdam, D. H. D. H. MacAdam, report to accompany H. R. 1438 [for relief of D. H. MacAdam] ; submitted by Mr. Spencer. May 5, 1924. 4 p. (S. rp. 502, 68th Cong. 1st sess.) * Paper, 5c.

Magoffin, Albert E. Albert E. Magoffin, report to accompany S. 3066 [for relief of Albert E. Magoffin] ; submitted by Mr. Stanfield. May 20, calendar day May 23, 1924. 3 p. (S. rp. 603, 68th Cong. 1st sess.) * Paper, 5c.

Maryland Casualty Company. Maryland Casualty Co. et al, report to accompany H. R. 6384 [for relief of Maryland Casualty Company, Fidelity and Deposit Company of Maryland, and United States Fidelity and Guaranty Company, Baltimore, Md.] ; submitted by Mr. Bayard for Mr. Bruce. May 26, calendar day May 28, 1924. 18 p. (S. rp. 652, 68th Cong. 1st sess.) * Paper, 5c.

—— Maryland Casualty Co., United States Fidelity & Guaranty Co., Baltimore, Md., and National Surety Co., report to accompany H. R. 6383 [for relief of Maryland Casualty Company, United States Fidelity and Guaranty Company, Baltimore, Md., and National Surety Company] ; submitted by Mr. Bayard for Mr. Bruce. May 26, calendar day May 28, 1924. 7 p. (S. rp. 651, 68th Cong. 1st sess.) * Paper, 5c.

Montana. Reimbursing Montana for expenses incurred in suppressing forest fires, report to accompany S. 308 ; submitted by Mr. Capper. May 20, calendar day May 24, 1924. 2 p. (S. rp. 614, 68th Cong. 1st sess.) * Paper, 5c.

Mosley, Rubie M. Rubie M. Mosley, report to accompany S. 1725 [for relief of Rubie M. Mosley] ; submitted by Mr. Stephens. May 14, calendar day May 17, 1924. 7 p. (S. rp. 562, 68th Cong. 1st sess.) * Paper, 5c.

Nash Motors Co., report to accompany S. 1893 [to refund duties paid by Nash Motors Company] ; submitted by Mr. Harreld. May 20, calendar day May 24, 1924. 2 p. (S. rp. 612, 68th Cong. 1st sess.) * Paper, 5c.

New York, ferryboat. Owner of ferryboat New York, report to accompany S. 2130 [for relief of Housing Corporation, owner of ferryboat New York; submitted by Mr. Bayard for Mr. Bruce. May 26, calendar day May 28, 1924. 3 p. (S. rp. 655, 68th Cong. 1st sess.) * Paper, 5c.

Nicholson, Francis. Francis Nicholson, report to accompany S 1022 [for relief of Francis Nicholson] ; submitted by Mr. Bayard for Mr. Bruce. May 26, calendar day May 28, 1924. 3 p. (S. rp. 653, 68th Cong. 1st sess.) * Paper, 5c.

Northampton, Mass. Chamber of Commerce. Northampton. Mass., report to accompany S. 2731 [for relief of Chamber of Commerce, Northampton, Mass.] ; submitted by Mr. Spencer. May 20, calendar day May 24, 1924. 7 p. (S. rp. 616, 68th Cong. 1st sess.) * Paper, 5c.

O'Brien Brothers, American steam tug. Owner of American steam tug O'Brien Brothers, report to accompany S. 2079 [for relief of O'Brien Brothers (Incorporated), owner of American steam tug O'Brien Brothers] ; submitted by Mr. Bayard for Mr. Bruce. May 26, calendar day May 28, 1924. 2 p. (S. rp. 654, 68th Cong. 1st sess.) * Paper, 5c.

Ogden, Utah. Ogden Chamber of Commerce, report to accompany S. 660 [for relief of Ogden Chamber of Commerce] ; submitted by Mr. Spencer. May 5, 1924. 4 p. (S. rp. 503, 68th Cong. 1st sess.) * Paper, 5c.

Oliver, William J. William J. Oliver. report to accompany S. 443 [for relief of William J. Oliver Manufacturing Company and William J. Oliver. Knoxville, Tenn.]; submitted by Mr. Harreld. May 20. calendar day May 24, 1924. 2 p. (S. rp. 613, 68th Cong. 1st sess.) * Paper, 5c.

Paul, Orville. Orville Paul, report to accompany H. R. 4432 [for relief of Orville Paul]; submitted by Mr. Spencer. May 20. calendar day May 23, 1924. 10 p. (S. rp. 503, 68th Cong. 1st sess.) * Paper, 5c.

Philadelphia, Pa. Claim of Philadelphia, Pa., hearing before subcommittee on S. 2171, for relief of Philadelphia, Pa., Apr. 9. 1924. 1924. [1]+11 p. * Paper, 5c.

Reaney, William B. Kate Reaney Zeiss. report to accompany S. 2478 [to carry out findings of Court of Claims in case of Kate Reaney Zeiss. administratrix of William B. Reaney. survivor of Thomas Reaney and Samuel Archbold, against United States] ; submitted by Mr. Bayard. May 26, 1924. 3 p. (S. rp. 623, 68th Cong. 1st sess.) * Paper, 5c.

Reiter, Mrs. Augusta. Augusta Reiter, report to accompany S. 1016 [for relief of Augusta Reiter]; submitted by Mr. Stanfield. May 26. 1924. 2 p. (S. rp. 627, 68th Cong. 1st sess.) * Paper, 5c.

Rheinlander, John H. John H. Rheinlander, report to accompany S. 893 [for relief of John H. Rheinlander]; submitted by Mr. Capper. Apr. 24, calendar day May 2, 1924. 3 p. (S. rp. 485, 68th Cong. 1st sess.) * Paper. 5c.

Rhode Island. State of Rhode Island, report to accompany S. 3252 [referring claim of Rhode Island for expenses during War with Spain to Court of Claims for adjudication] ; submitted by Mr. Spencer. May 20. calendar day May 23, 1924. 2 p. (S. rp. 605, 68th Cong. 1st sess.) * Paper, 5c.

Rinald Bros., Philadelphia, Pa., report to accompany S. 2833 [for relief of Rinald Brothers, Philadelphia. Pa.] ; submitted by Mr. Trammell. May 20, calendar day May 23, 1924. 4 p. (S. rp. 596, 68th Cong. 1st sess.) * Paper, 5c.

Scott, L. A. L. A. Scott, report to accompany H. R. 3537 [for relief of L. A. Scott] ; submitted by Mr. Trammell. May 20, calendar day May 23. 1924. 4 p. (S. rp. 601, 68th Cong. 1st sess.) * Paper, 5c.

Smith, Mrs. Ida. Ida Smith, report to accompany S. 3034 [for relief of Ida Smith] ; submitted by Mr. Spencer. May 26, calendar day May 28. 1924. 12 p. (S. rp. 643, 68th Cong. 1st sess.) * Paper, 5c.

Staples Transportation Co., report to accompany S. 1937 [for relief of Staples Transportation Company, Fall River, Mass.] ; submitted by Mr. Bayard for Mr. Bruce. May 26, calendar day May 28, 1924. 2 p. (S. rp. 646, 68th Cong. 1st sess.) * Paper, 5c.

Swartz, R. E. R. E. Swartz, W. J. Collier, and others, report to accompany S. 2778 [for relief of R. E. Swartz, W. J. Collier, and others]; submitted by Mr. Stephens. May 20, calendar day May 24, 1924. 7 p. (S. rp. 611, 68th Cong. 1st sess.) * Paper, 5c.

Turner Construction Co., report to accompany S. 3050 [for relief of Turner Construction Company, New York City]; submitted by Mr. Capper. May 20, calendar day May 24, 1924. 3 p. (S. rp. 615, 68th Cong. 1st sess.) * Paper, 5c.

Yearsley, A. V. A. V. Yearsley, report to accompany S. 1056 [for relief of A. V. Yearsley]; submitted by Mr. Capper. May 26. calendar day May 28, 1924. 2 p. (S. rp. 641, 68th Cong. 1st sess.) * Paper, 5c.

COMMERCE COMMITTEE

Chicago River. Abandonment of channel of South Branch of Chicago River, report to accompany S. 3188 [for abandonment of portion of present channel of South Branch of Chicago River]; submitted by Mr. Jones of Washington. May 26, calendar day May 29, 1924. 1 p. (S. rp. 660, 68th Cong. 1st sess.) * Paper, 5c.

Coast Guard cutters. Vessel for Coast Guard duty in Alaska, report to accompany H. R. 6817; submitted by Mr. Jones of Washington. Apr. 24, calendar day May 3, 1924. 1 p. (S. rp. 496, 68th Cong. 1st sess.) * Paper, 5c.

Fish cultural station at Orangeburg, S. C., report to accompany S. 3084 [to enlarge fish cultural station at Orangeburg, S. C.]; submitted by Mr. Dial. May 14, calendar day May 15, 1924. 2 p. (S. rp. 542, 68th Cong. 1st sess.) * Paper, 5c.

Floods. Preliminary examinations of sundry streams, report to accompany H. R. 8070 [authorizing preliminary examinations and surveys of sundry streams with view to control of their floods]; submitted by Mr. Jones of Washington. Apr. 24, calendar day May 3, 1924. 6 p. (S. rp. 497, 68th Cong. 1st sess.) * Paper, 5c.   24—26509

Inland Waterways Corporation, report to accompany S. 3161 [to create Inland Waterways Corporation for purpose of carrying out mandate and purpose of Congress as expressed in sec. 201 and 500 of transportation act]; submitted by Mr. Ransdell. May 14, calendar day May 15, 1924. 6 p. (S. rp. 538, 68th Cong. 1st sess.) * Paper, 5c.

Mississippi River. Bridge across Mississippi River at or near Hannibal, Mo., report to accompany S. 3292 [granting consent of Congress to Hannibal, Mo., to construct bridge across Mississippi River at or near Hannibal, Marion County. Mo.]; submitted by Mr. Ladd. May 20, calendar day May 22, 1924. 2 p. (S. rp. 591, 68th Cong. 1st sess.) * Paper, 5c.

Missouri River. Dam across Missouri River, report to accompany S. 2085 [to authorize Broadwater Irrigation District, Montana organization, to construct dam across Missouri River]; submitted by Mr. Jones of Washington. May 26, calendar day May 29, 1924. 3 p. (S. rp. 661, 68th Cong. 1st sess.) * Paper, 5c.

Monongahela River. Bridge across Monongahela River near Masontown, Pa., report to accompany S. 3395 [granting consent of Congress to commissioners of Fayette and Greene counties, Pa., to construct bridge across Monongahela River near Masontown, Fayette County, Pa.]; submitted by Mr. Ladd. May 26, calendar day May 28, 1924. 2 p. (S. rp. 645, 68th Cong. 1st sess.) * Paper, 5c.

Niagara River. Bridge across Niagara River and Black Rock Canal, report to accompany S. 3249 [granting consent of Congress to construction of bridge across Niagara River and Black Rock Canal near Buffalo, N. Y., by Buffalo and Fort Erie Public Bridge Company]; submitted by Mr. Ladd. May 14, calendar day May 15, 1924. 2 p. (S. rp. 543, 68th Cong. 1st sess.) * Paper, 5c.

Ohio River. Bridge across Ohio River, report to accompany S. 3350 [granting consent of Congress for construction of bridge across Ohio River between Vanderburgh County, Ind., and Henderson County, Ky., by Kentucky and Indiana, through their respective highway commissions]; submitted by Mr. Ladd. May 26, calendar day May 27, 1924. 2 p. (S. rp. 639, 68th Cong. 1st sess.) * Paper, 5c.

Pearl River. Bridge across Pearl River, Miss., report to accompany S. 3244 [granting consent of Congress to board of supervisors of Hinds County, Miss., to construct bridge across Pearl River, Miss., at Jackson]; submitted by Mr. Stephens. May 14, calendar day May 15, 1924. 2 p. (S. rp. 541, 68th Cong. 1st sess.) * Paper, 5c.

Peedee River. Bridge across Great Peedee River, report to accompany S. 3097 [to authorize building of bridge across Great Peedee River, S. C., at or near Yawhanna Ferry, by Highway Department of South Carolina in cooperation with Lower Peedee Bridge Commission]; submitted by Mr. Dial. Apr. 24, calendar day May 3, 1924. 2 p. (S. rp. 498, 68th Cong. 1st sess.) * Paper, 5c.

—— Bridge across Pedee River, S. C., report to accompany S. 3355 [granting consent of Congress to counties of Marion and Florence, S. C., to construct bridge across Peedee River at or near Savage Landing, S. C.]; submitted by Mr. Sheppard. May 26, calendar day May 28, 1924. 2 p. (S. rp. 644, 68th Cong. 1st sess.) * Paper, 5c.

Poteau River. Dam across Poteau River, report to accompany S. 601 [granting consent of Congress to Fort Smith, Sebastian County, Ark., to construct dam across Poteau River]; submitted by Mr. Sheppard. May 26, calendar day May 29, 1924. 2 p. (S. rp. 662, 68th Cong. 1st sess.) * Paper, 5c.

Ratigan, Luke. Luke Ratigan, report to accompany H. R. 1475 [for relief of Luke Ratigan]; submitted by Mr. Jones of Washington. Apr. 24, calendar day May 3, 1924. 2 p. (S. rp. 495, 68th Cong. 1st sess.) * Paper, 5c.

Ships. Marine Hospital Service, report to accompany S. 2232 [to amend sec. 2 of act granting additional quarantine powers and imposing additional duties upon Marine Hospital Service, so as to exempt from its provisions vessels operating exclusively between foreign ports on or near northern frontier of United States and ports in United States]; submitted by Mr. Jones of Washington. Apr. 24, calendar day May 3, 1924. 1 p. (S. rp. 494, 68th Cong. 1st sess.) * Paper, 5c.

Tallahatchie River. Dam in Tallahatchie River, report to accompany S. 3272 [granting consent of Congress to Panola-Quitman drainage district to construct dam in Tallahatchie River at or near Porters Ferry, Panola County, Miss.]; submitted by Mr. Stephens. May 14, calendar day May 16, 1924. 2 p. (S. rp. 553, 68th Cong. 1st sess.) * Paper, 5c.

DISTRICT OF COLUMBIA COMMITTEE

Buildings. To amend act regulating height of buildings in District of Columbia, report to accompany S. 3269; submitted by Mr. Edwards. May 26, 1924. 1 p. (S. rp. 619, 68th Cong. 1st sess.) * Paper, 5c.

Burklin, George M. Removal of remains of late George Mauger Burklin and Anton Lerch Burklin, report to accompany S. 3220 [authorizing health officer of District of Columbia to issue permit for removal of remains of late George Mauger Burklin and remains of late Anton Lerch Burklin from Glenwood Cemetery, District of Columbia, to Fort Lincoln, Prince Georges County, Md.]; submitted by Mr. Ball. May 5, calendar day May 9, 1924. 2 p. (S. rp. 510, 68th Cong. 1st sess.) * Paper, 5c.

Compulsory education. Compulsory school attendance and school census in District of Columbia, report to accompany S. 2842 [for compulsory school attendance, for taking of school census in District of Columbia, and for other purposes]; submitted by Mr. Capper. May 20, calendar day May 22, 1924. 3 p. (S. rp. 583, 68th Cong. 1st sess.) * Paper, 5c.

Deeds. To amend sec. 546 and 547 of code of law of District of Columbia, report to accompany S. 1935 [to amend, revise and reenact subchapter 3, sec. 546 and 547 of code of law of District of Columbia relating to recording of deeds of chattels]; submitted by Mr. Ball. May 20, calendar day May 22, 1924. 1 p. (S. rp. 586, 68th Cong. 1st sess.) * Paper, 5c.

Government officials and employees. Cooperative hotel for Government women employees in District of Columbia, hearing relative to construction of cooperative hotel for women employees of Federal Government in District of Columbia, Apr. 25, 1924. 1924. ii+14 p. * Paper, 5c.

Housing. Survey of housing and rental conditions in District of Columbia, report pursuant to S. Res. 158; submitted by Mr. Ball. May 12, 1924. 75 p. (S. rp. 530, 68th Cong. 1st sess.) * Paper, 10c.

Howard University. Athletic field and gymnasium for Howard University, report to accompany S. 2694 [to enable trustees of Howard University to develop athletic field and gymnasium project]; submitted by Mr. Ball. May 20, calendar day May 22, 1924. 2 p. (S. rp. 588, 68th Cong. 1st sess.) * Paper, 5c.

Land. To quiet title to original lot 4 in District of Columbia, report to accompany S. 3053 [to quiet title to original lot 4, square 116, Washington, D. C.]; submitted by Mr. Ball. May 20, calendar day May 22, 1924. 6 p. (S. rp. 590, 68th Cong. 1st sess.) * Paper, 5c.

Milk. Sale of milk, cream, and certain milk products in District of Columbia, report to accompany S. 2803 [to regulate within District of Columbia sale of milk, cream, and certain milk products]; submitted by Mr. Glass. May 5, calendar day May 8, 1924. 1 p. (S. rp. 508, 68th Cong. 1st sess.) * Paper, 5c.

—— To regulate sale of milk and cream containers in District of Columbia. report to accompany S. 3280; submitted by Mr. Copeland. May 20, calendar day May 22, 1924. 2 p. (S. rp. 589, 68th Cong. 1st sess.) * Paper, 5c.

Parks. Improvement of Rock Creek Parkway entrance, report to accompany S. 3016 [to enable Rock Creek and Potomac Parkway Commission to improve parkway entrance]; submitted by Mr. Ball. Apr. 24, calendar day May 2, 1924. 2 p. (S. rp. 482, 68th Cong. 1st sess.) * Paper, 5c.

—— Parkway connecting Civil War forts, report to accompany S. 1340 [to make necessary survey and to prepare plan of proposed parkway to connect old Civil War forts in District of Columbia]; submitted by Mr. Ball. May 20, calendar day May 22, 1924. 2 p. (S. rp. 585, 68th Cong. 1st sess.) * Paper, 5c.

Public Utilities Commission. To amend public utilities act of District of Columbia, report to accompany S. 3077 [to amend act creating Public Utilities Commission of District of Columbia so as to add 2 members to commission]; submitted by Mr. Ball. Apr. 24, calendar day May 2, 1924. 2 p. (S. rp. 483, 68th Cong. 1st sess.) * Paper, 5c.

Recorder of deeds. To amend sec. 549 of code of District of Columbia, report to accompany S. 1934 [to amend, revise, and reenact sec. 549 of subchapter 4 of code of law of District of Columbia relating to appointment of deputy recorder of deeds, and fixing compensation therefor]; submitted by Mr. Ball. May 20, calendar day May 22, 1924. 2 p. (S. rp. 587, 68th Cong. 1st sess.) * Paper, 5c.

Rent Commission. Extension of Rent Commission law, hearing on H. R. 7962, to extend for period of 2 years provisions of title 2 of food control and District of Columbia rents act, as amended, May 6, 1924. 1924. ii+12 p. * Paper, 5c.

—— Extension of time to District of Columbia Rent Commission, report to accompany H. R. 7962 [to extend for period of 2 years provisions of title 2 of food control and District of Columbia rents act, as amended]; submitted by Mr. Ball. May 5, calendar day May 9, 1924. 2 p. (S. rp. 509, 68th Cong. 1st sess.) * Paper, 5c.

Streets. Changing Jewett street west of Wisconsin avenue to Cathedral avenue, report to accompany H. R. 6628, submitted by Mr. Ball. Apr. 24, calendar day May 2, 1924. 1 p. (S. rp. 484, 68th Cong. 1st sess.) * Paper, 5c.

—— Closing certain streets, roads, or highways in District of Columbia, report to accompany S. 1179 [to authorize commissioners of District of Columbia to close certain streets, roads, or highways in District of Columbia rendered useless or unnecessary by reason of opening, extension, widening, or straightening, in accordance with highway plan of other streets, roads, or highways in District of Columbia]; submitted by Mr. Ball. May 20, calendar day May 22, 1924. 2 p. (S. rp. 584, 68th Cong. 1st sess.) * Paper, 5c.

Teachers. Teachers' salary and school reorganization bill for District of Columbia, report to accompany H. R. 6721 [to amend act to fix and regulate salaries of teachers, school officers, and other employees of Board of Education of District of Columbia, as amended, and for other purposes]; submitted by Mr. Capper. May 12, 1924. 32 p. (S. rp. 521, 68th Cong. 1st sess.) * Paper, 5c.

FINANCE COMMITTEE

Calendar. Legislative calendar, 68th Congress, May 5–26, 1924; no. 19–22. 1924. various paging, 4° ‡

Customs Service. Organization of Customs Service and enforcement of all customs revenue laws, report to accompany S. 3357 [to amend sec. 2 and 5 of act to provide necessary organization of Customs Service for adequate administration and enforcement of tariff act of 1922 and all other customs revenue laws]; submitted by Mr. Smoot. May 26, calendar day May 27, 1924. 2 p. (S. rp. 635, 68th Cong. 1st sess.) * Paper, 5c.

Freer, Charles L. Estate of Charles L. Freer, report to accompany H. R. 8100 [for relief of estate of Charles L. Freer]; submitted by Mr. Smoot. May 26, calendar day May 27, 1924. 2 p. (S. rp. 637, 68th Cong. 1st sess.) * Paper, 5c.

Heroin. Prohibiting importation of crude opium for manufacture of heroin, report to accompany H. R. 7079; submitted by Mr. Smoot. May 26, calendar day May 27, 1924. 3 p. (S. rp. 636, 68th Cong. 1st sess.) * Paper, 5c.

Soldiers. Adjusted compensation act, hearings on H. R. 7959, to provide adjusted compensation for veterans of World War, Mar. 25–29, 1924. 1924. ii+69 p. * Paper, 10c.

Baron Berwick, British steamship. British steamship Baron Berwick, report to accompany S. 2719 [to authorize payment of indemnity to British Government on account of losses sustained by owners of British steamship Baron Berwick as result of collision between that vessel and United States steamship Iroquois, now Freedom, and further collision with United States destroyer Truxtun]; submitted by Mr. Lodge. May 14, calendar day May 17, 1924. 3 p. (S. rp. 559, 68th Cong. 1st sess.) * Paper, 5c.

Calendar, 68th Congress, 1st session, May 5 and 26, 1924; no. 7 and 8. 1924. 16 p. and 19 p. 4° ‡

China. Remission of Chinese indemnity, report to accompany H. J. Res. 248 [for remission of further payments of annual installments of Chinese indemnity]; submitted by Mr. Lodge. May 12, 1924. 8 p. (S. rp. 518, 68th Cong. 1st sess.) * Paper, 5c.
                                                                24—26510

Diplomatic and consular service. Reorganization and improvement of foreign service, report to accompany H. R. 6357; submitted by Mr. Lodge. May 12, 1924. 18 p. (S. rp. 532, 68th Cong. 1st sess.) * Paper, 5c.   24—26511

Hassel, Norwegian steamship. Claim of Government of Norway, report to accompany S. 2718 [to authorize payment of indemnity to Government of Norway on account of losses sustained by owners of Norwegian steamship Hassel as result of collision between that steamship and American steamship Ausable]; submitted by Mr. Lodge. May 14, calendar day May 17, 1924. 3 p. (S. rp. 560, 68th Cong. 1st sess.) * Paper, 5c.

Lilly, Swedish fishing boat. Swedish fishing boat Lilly, report to accompany S. 2458 [to authorize payment of indemnity to Swedish Government for losses sustained by its nationals in sinking of Swedish fishing boat Lilly]; submitted by Mr. Lodge. May 14, calendar day May 17, 1924. 3 p. (S. rp. 561, 68th Cong. 1st sess.) * Paper, 5c.

Narcotics. Appropriation for participation of United States in 2 international conferences for control of narcotic drugs, report to accompany H. J. Res. 195; submitted by Mr. Lodge. May 5, 1924. 2 p. (S. rp. 499, 68th Cong. 1st sess.) * Paper, 5c.

Passports. To amend sec. 1 of act of June 4, 1920, as to passport fees, report to accompany S. 2172; submitted by Mr. Pepper. May 19, 1924. 2 p. (S. rp. 564, 68th Cong. 1st sess.) * Paper, 5c.

Permanent Court of International Justice. Permanent Court of International Justice, hearings before subcommittee relative to adhesion of United States to protocol under which Permanent Court of International Justice has been established at The Hague, Apr. 30 and May 1, 1924. 1924. iii+188 p. * Paper, 20c.

—— Permanent Court of International Justice, minority views to accompany S. Res. 234 [advising adherence of United States to existing Permanent Court of International Justice with certain amendments]; submitted by Mr. Swanson. May 31, 1924. 8 p. (S. rp. 634, pt. 2, 68th Cong. 1st sess.) * Paper, 5c.

—— Permanent Court of International Justice, report to accompany S. Res. 234 [advising adherence of United States to existing Permanent Court of International Justice with certain amendments]; submitted by Mr. Pepper. May 26, calendar day May 27, 1924. 10 p. (S. rp. 634 [pt. 1], 68th Cong. 1st sess.) * Paper, 5c.
                                                                24—26511

Chester Calf, Indian. Chester Calf and Crooked Nose Woman, report to accompany H. R. 6857 [for addition of names of Chester Calf and Crooked Nose Woman to final roll of Cheyenne and Arapahoe Indians, Seger jurisdiction, Okla.]; submitted by Mr. Harreld. May 14, calendar day May 15, 1924. 2 p. (S. rp. 547, 68th Cong. 1st sess.) * Paper, 5c.

Cowlitz Indians. Conferring jurisdiction upon Court of Claims in any claims which Cowlitz tribe of Indians may have against United States, report to accompany S. 2557; submitted by Mr. Harreld. May 26, calendar day May 28, 1924. 2 p. (S. rp. 642, 68th Cong. 1st sess.) * Paper, 5c.

Indian Affairs Office. To provide for quarters, fuel, and light for employees of Indian field service, report to accompany S. 2799; submitted by Mr. Harreld. May 19, 1924. 2 p. (S. rp. 565, 68th Cong. 1st sess.) * Paper, 5c.

Indian reservations. Leasing for oil and gas of unallotted lands, report to accompany H. R. 6298 [to authorize leasing for oil and gas mining purposes of unallotted lands on Indian reservations affected by proviso to sec. 8 of act of Feb. 28, 1891]; submitted by Mr. Harreld. May 14, calendar day May 15, 1924. 3 p. (S. rp. 546, 68th Cong. 1st sess.) * Paper, 5c.

Indians. To pay tuition of Indian children in public schools, report to accompany H. R. 4835; submitted by Mr. Harreld. May 19, 1924. 3 p. (S. rp. 568, 68th Cong. 1st sess.) * Paper, 5c.

Jocko Reservation. Addition of names to final roll of Indians of Flathead [or Jocko] Indian Reservation, Mont., report to accompany H. R. 2875; submitted by Mr. Harreld. May 14, calendar day May 15, 1924. 2 p. (S. rp. 544, 68th Cong. 1st sess.) * Paper, 5c.

Osage Indians. Osage fund restrictions, hearings on S. 2065 and S. 2933, bills to modify Osage fund restrictions, Mar. 28–Apr. 1, 1924. 1924. iii+248 p. * Paper, 25c.

Quinaielt Reservation. To authorize setting aside of certain tribal lands within Quinaielt Indian Reservation, Wash., for lighthouse purposes, report to accompany H. R. 5416; submitted by Mr. Harreld. May 19, 1924. 2 p. (S. rp. 566, 68th Cong. 1st sess.) * Paper, 5c.

Red Lake Reservation. Payment to Red Lake Indians for garden plats surrendered for school farm use, report to accompany H. R. 4460 [authorizing payment to Red Lake Indians, out of tribal trust funds, for garden plats surrendered for school-farm use]; submitted by Mr. Harreld. May 14, calendar day May 15, 1924. 2 p. (S. rp. 545, 68th Cong. 1st sess.) * Paper, 5c.

Stockbridge Indians. Conferring jurisdiction upon Court of Claims in any claims which Stockbridge Indians may have against United States, report to accompany S. 3111; submitted by Mr. Harreld. May 19, 1924. 2 p. (S. rp. 567, 68th Cong. 1st sess.) * Paper, 5c.

Wichita Indians. Wichita and affiliated bands of Indians of Oklahoma, report to accompany H. R. 731 [authorizing Wichita and affiliated bands of Indians in Oklahoma to submit claims to Court of Claims]; submitted by Mr. Harreld. May 14, calendar day May 15, 1924. 3 p. (S. rp. 548, 68th Cong. 1st sess.) * Paper, 5c.

INTERSTATE COMMERCE COMMITTEE

Industrial arbitration. Arbitration between carriers and employees, boards of adjustment, hearings before subcommittee on S. 2646, for expeditious and prompt settlement, mediation, conciliation, and arbitration of disputes between carriers and their employees and subordinate officials, supplement. 1924. ii+365–381 p. * Paper, 5c.

Railroad-cars. For protection of persons employed on railway express cars, railway baggage cars, and railway express baggage cars, report to accompany S. 863; submitted by Mr. Gooding. May 5, calendar day May 6, 1924. 2 p. (S. rp. 505, 68th Cong. 1st sess.) * Paper, 5c.

IRRIGATION AND RECLAMATION COMMITTEE

La Plata River compact, report to accompany S. 1656 [granting consent and approval of Congress to La Plata River compact]; submitted by Mr. Bursum. May 14, calendar day May 16, 1924. 1 p. (S. rp. 554, 68th Cong. 1st sess.) * Paper, 5c.

Reclamation of land. Extending period of payment under reclamation projects, hearing on S. 3186, amending sec. 1, 2, and 14 of act extending period of payment under reclamation projects, May 1, 1924. 1924. ii+32 p. * Paper, 5c.

JUDICIARY COMMITTEE

American War Mothers. To incorporate American War Mothers, joint hearing before Committees on Judiciary on H. R. 8980 and H. R. 9095, May 6, 1924. 1924. ii+12 p. (Serial 36.) [This hearing was held at a joint meeting of the Senate Committee on Judiciary and the House Committee on Judiciary and is published as Serial 36 of the House Judiciary Committee hearings.] * Paper, 5c.

Arbitration. To make valid and enforceable certain agreements for arbitration, report to accompany S. 1005 [to make valid and enforceable written provisions or agreements for arbitration of disputes arising out of contracts, maritime transactions, or commerce among States or Territories or with foreign nations]; submitted by Mr. Sterling. May 14, 1924. 4 p. (S. rp. 536, 68th Cong. 1st sess.) [Corrected print.] * Paper, 5c.

Bribery. Disposition of moneys paid as bribes, etc., report to accompany S. 2177 [to provide for disposition of moneys paid to or received by any official as bribe, which may be used as evidence in any case growing out of any such transaction]; submitted by Mr. Spencer. May 26, 1924. 1 p. (S. rp. 632, 68th Cong. 1st sess.) * Paper, 5c.

Calendar. Legislative calendar, 68th Congress, Apr. 12–May 17, 1924; no. 12–14. 1924. various paging, 4° ‡

Clerks of District Courts. To provide fees to be charged by clerks of District Courts, report to accompany S. 2173; submitted by Mr. Spencer. May 26, 1924. 2 p. (S. rp. 628, 68th Cong. 1st sess.) * Paper, 5c.

—— To provide for accounting by clerks of District Courts of fees received by them in naturalization proceedings, report to accompany S. 2174; submitted by Mr. Spencer. May 26, 1924. 1 p. (S. rp. 629, 68th Cong. 1st sess.) * Paper, 5c.

Clerks of United States courts. Requiring clerks of courts to keep indices of judgment debtors, report to accompany S. 2176 [to amend sec. 2 of act of Aug. 1, 1888, to regulate liens of judgments and decrees of courts of United States, relative to indices of judgment debtors]; submitted by Mr. Spencer. May 26, 1924. 1 p. (S. rp. 631, 68th Cong. 1st sess.) * Paper, 5c.

—— To provide for reporting and accounting of fines, fees, forfeitures, and penalties, and all other moneys paid to or received by clerks of United States courts, report to accompany S. 2175; submitted by Mr. Spencer. May 26, 1924. 1 p. (S. rp. 630, 68th Cong. 1st sess.) * Paper, 5c.

Courts of United States. To provide for rendition of accounts by United States attorneys, United States marshals, clerks of United States courts, and United States commissioners, report to accompany S. 2179; submitted by Mr. Spencer. May 26, 1924. 1 p. (S. rp. 633, 68th Cong. 1st sess.) * Paper, 5c.

District Courts. Judicial districts in Indiana, hearings before subcommittee on H. R. 62, to create 2 judicial districts within Indiana, establishment of judicial divisions therein, and for other purposes, Mar. 20 and 21, 1924. 1924. iii+156 p. * Paper, 15c.

—— Term of court at Casper, Wyo., report to accompanying H. R. 4445; submitted by Mr. Walsh of Montana. May 13, 1924. 2 p. (S. rp. 533, 68th Cong. 1st sess.) * Paper, 5c.

Enemy property. To amend sec. 9 of trading with the enemy act, report to accompany S. 1548 [to amend sec. 9 of act to define, regulate, and punish trading with the enemy, as amended, relative to claims against insurance companies for unpaid amounts for losses caused by San Francisco fire, 1906]; submitted by Mr. Shortridge. May 6, calendar day May 7, 1924. 2 p. (S. rp. 507, 68th Cong. 1st sess.) * Paper, 5c.

JUSTICE DEPARTMENT, SELECT COMMITTEE ON INVESTIGATION OF

Daugherty, Harry M. Investigation of Harry M. Daugherty, formerly Attorney General, hearings pursuant to S. Res. 157, directing committee to investigate failure of Attorney General to prosecute or defend certain criminal and civil actions wherein the Government is interested. Apr. 7 [–May 2], 1924. 1924. pts. 5–7, [xi]+1035–2023 p. * Paper, pts. 5 and 7, each 25c.; * pt. 6, 50c.

LIBRARY COMMITTEE

Lincoln, Abraham. Oldroyd collection of Lincoln relics, report to accompany S. 2434 [for purchase of Oldroyd collection of Lincoln relics]; submitted by Mr. Fess. Apr. 24, calendar day May 3, 1924. 1 p. (S. rp. 490, 68th Cong. 1st sess.) * Paper, 5c.

Washington, George. Celebration of bicentennial of birthday of George Washington, report to accompany S. J. Res. 85 [authorizing appropriation for participation of United States in preparation and completion of plans for comprehensive observance of that greatest of all historic events, bicentennial of birthday of George Washington]; submitted by Mr. Fess. Apr. 24, calendar day May 3, 1924. 2 p. (S. rp. 491, 68th Cong. 1st sess.) * Paper, 5c.

24—26513

MILITARY AFFAIRS COMMITTEE

Chaplains. To increase number of chaplains in Army, joint hearing before subcommittees of Committees on Military Affairs, Senate and House, on S. 2532 and H. R. 7038, to amend in certain particulars national defense act, as amended, [relative to Army chaplains], Apr. 16, 1924. 1924. ii+40 p. * Paper, 5c.

Commissions, Army. Posthumous commissions for certain enlisted men and posthumous promotions for certain commissioned officers, report to accompany S. J. Res. 124; submitted by Mr. Wadsworth. May 14, calendar day May 16, 1924. 1 p. (S. rp. 558, 68th Cong. 1st sess.) * Paper, 5c.

Dilks, John W. John W. Dilks, report to accompany H. R. 7296 [for relief of John W. Dilks]; submitted by Mr. Bruce. May 14, calendar day May 16, 1924. 1 p. (S. rp. 552, 68th Cong. 1st sess.) * Paper, 5c.

Fredericksburg, Battle of, 1862. Inspection of battle fields in and around Fredericksburg and Spotsylvania Courthouse, Va., report to accompany S. 3263; submitted by Mr. Wadsworth. May 14, calendar day May 16, 1924. 3 p. (S. rp. 555, 68th Cong. 1st sess.) * Paper, 5c.

Gasparilla Island military reservation, report to accompany S. 3211 [authorizing sale of Gasparilla Island military reservation]; submitted by Mr. Fletcher. May 14, calendar day May 15, 1924. 2 p. (S. rp. 549, 68th Cong. 1st sess.) * Paper, 5c.

Japan. Relief of sufferers from earthquake in Japan, report to accompany S. 3171; submitted by Mr. Wadsworth. May 5, calendar day May 10, 1924. 1 p. (S. rp. 513, 68th Cong. 1st sess.) * Paper, 5c.

Militia. National Guard amendments to national defense act, as amended, report to accompany S. 3248 [providing for sundry matters affecting military establishment]; submitted by Mr. Wadsworth. May 5, calendar day May 10, 1924. 5 p. (S. rp. 514, 68th Cong. 1st sess.) [The sections of the bill relate exclusively to the National Guard.] * Paper, 5c.

Nurse Corps, Army. Retirement for members of Nurse Corps of Army and Navy, report to accompany S. 3285; submitted by Mr. Wadsworth. May 14, calendar day May 16, 1924. 4 p. (S. rp. 556, 68th Cong. 1st sess.) * Paper, 5c.

Pay, Army. Readjust pay and allowances of commissioned and enlisted personnel of Army, Navy, Marine Corps, etc., report to accompany H. R. 4820 [to amend act to readjust pay and allowances of commissioned and enlisted personnel of Army, Navy, Marine Corps, Coast Guard, Coast and Geodetic Survey, and Public Health Service]; submitted by Mr. Wadsworth. May 20, calendar day May 23, 1924. 4 p. (S. rp. 594, 68th Cong. 1st sess.) * Paper, 5c.

Pike, Camp. National Guard buildings at Camp Pike, Ark., report to accompany S. J. Res. 89 [authorizing and permitting Arkansas to construct, maintain, and use permanent buildings, rifle ranges, and utilities at Camp Pike, Ark., as are necessary for use and benefit of National Guard of Arkansas]; submitted by Mr. Wadsworth. May 5, calendar day May 10, 1924. 2 p. (S. rp. 515, 68th Cong. 1st sess.) * Paper, 5c.

Santa Rosa Island, Fla., report to accompany S. 2676 [to lease or to convey by quitclaim deed tract of land in military reservation of Santa Rosa Island, Fla., to Thomas H. Hazelrigg and John A. Chumbley for ship canal]; submitted by Mr. Fletcher. May 5, calendar day May 10, 1924. 2 p. (S. rp. 517, 68th Cong. 1st sess.) * Paper, 5c.

Soldiers discharged during War for misrepresentation of age, report to accompany S. 3241 [for relief of soldiers who were discharged from Army during World War because of misrepresentation of age] ; submitted by Mr. Sheppard. May 5, calendar day May 10, 1924. 1 p. (S. rp. 512, 68th Cong. 1st sess.) * Paper, 5c.

Telegraphers. Persons who served in military telegraph corps during Civil War, report to accompany S. 1535 [granting relief to persons who served in military telegraph corps of Army during Civil War] ; submitted by Mr. Reed of Pennsylvania. May 14, calendar day May 16, 1924. 3 p. (S. rp. 551, 68th Cong. 1st sess.) * Paper, 5c.

Troup, Palestine. Palestine Troup, report to accompany S. 3090 [for relief of Palestine Troup] ; submitted by Mr. George. May 12, 1924. 2 p. (S. rp. 523, 68th Cong. 1st sess.) * Paper, 5c.

War Department. Authorizing sale of real property no longer required for military purposes, report to accompany S. 3276 ; submitted by Mr. Wadsworth. May 14, calendar day May 16, 1924. 5 p. (S. rp. 557, 68th Cong. 1st sess.) * Paper, 5c.

—— Sale of real property no longer required for military purposes, report to accompany H. R. 9124 ; submitted by Mr. Wadsworth. May 20, calendar day May 23, 1924. 10 p. (S. rp. 607, 68th Cong. 1st sess.) * Paper, 5c.

Winchell, Stephen A. Stephen A. Winchell, report to accompany S. 1232 [for relief of Stephen A. Winchell] ; submitted by Mr. Capper. May 5, calendar day May 10, 1924. 2 p. (S. rp. 516, 68th Cong. 1st sess.) * Paper, 5c.

York, Alvin C. Sergt. Alvin C. York, report to accompany S. 412 [to authorize President of United States to appoint Alvin C. York as captain in Army and then place him on retired list] ; submitted by Mr. Sheppard. May 5, calendar day May 7, 1924. 10 p. (S. rp. 506, 68th Cong. 1st sess.) * Paper, 5c.

24—26514

NAVAL AFFAIRS COMMITTEE

Berry, George A. For relief of George A. Berry, report to accompany S. 3073 ; submitted by Mr. Shortridge. May 26, calendar day May 29, 1924. 2 p. (S. rp. 657, 68th Cong. 1st sess.) * Paper, 5c.

Calendar. Legislative calendar, 68th Congress, 1st session, May 27, 1924 ; no. 5. 1924. 10 p. large 8° ‡

Maas, Charles O. To supplement military record of Charles O. Maas, report to accompany S. 1828 ; submitted by Mr. Copeland. May 26, calendar day May 29, 1924. 3 p. (S. rp. 659, 68th Cong. 1st sess.) * Paper, 5c.

Officers, Navy. To correct status of certain commissioned officers of Navy, report to accompany S. 483 [to correct status of certain commissioned officers of Navy appointed thereto pursuant to provisions of act approved June 4, 1920] ; submitted by Mr. Hale. May 12, 1924. 2 p. (S. rp. 519, 68th Cong. 1st sess.) * Paper, 5c.

PENSIONS COMMITTEE

Pensions. Pensions and increase of pensions for certain soldiers and sailors of Civil War, etc., report to accompany H. R. 6941 [substituted for H. R. 768 and other bills] ; submitted by Mr. Bursum. May 20, calendar day May 21, 1924. cover-title, 706 p. (S. rp. 571, 68th Cong. 1st sess.) * Paper, 55c.

—— Pensions and increase of pensions for certain soldiers and sailors of wars other than Civil War, etc., report to accompany H. R. 6426 [substituted for H. R. 792 and other bills] ; submitted by Mr. Bursum. May 20, calendar day May 21, 1924. 517 p. (S. rp. 570, 68th Cong. 1st sess.) * Paper, 50c.

Telegraphers. Persons who served in military telegraph corps during Civil War, report to accompany S. 1535 [granting relief to persons who served in military telegraph corps of Army during Civil War] ; submitted by Mr. Dale. May 20, calendar day May 23. 1924. 3 p. (S. rp. 592, 68th Cong. 1st sess.) * Paper, 5c.

POST OFFICES AND POST ROADS COMMITTEE

Air Mail Service. Payment of amounts expended in construction of hangars and maintenance of flying fields for use of Air Mail Service, report to accompany S. 1051 ; submitted by Mr. Oddie. Apr. 24, calendar day May 2, 1924. 3 p. (S. rp. 488, 68th Cong. 1st sess.) * Paper, 5c.

Blind. Free transmission through mails of certain publications for the blind, report to accompany S. J. Res. 115; submitted by Mr. Sterling. May 12, 1924. 3 p. (S. rp. 520, 68th Cong. 1st sess.)   [S. J. Res. 115, provides free transmission through mails for volumes of Holy Scriptures, or any part thereof, in raised characters for use of the blind.]   * Paper, 5c.

Postal service. Authorizing Postmaster General to contract for mail messenger service, report to accompany H. R. 6482; submitted by Mr. Sterling. May 14, 1924. 2 p. (S. rp. 535, 68th Cong. 1st sess.)   * Paper, 5c.

—— Postal salaries, extract from joint hearings before subcommittee of Committees on Post Offices and Post Roads on S. 1898, H. R. 4123, and H. R. 7016, bills relative to salaries and compensation of employees in postal service, Mar. 3–10, 1924; statement of Clarence Cannon. 1924. 4 p. * Paper, 5c.

—— Postal salaries, joint hearings before subcommittees of Committees on Post Offices and Post Roads on S. 1898, H. R. 4123, and H. R. 7016, bills relative to salaries and compensation of employees in postal service, Mar. 27–Apr. 28, 1924. 1924. pt. 2, ii+767–1102 p. 1 tab. [These hearings were held at joint meetings of the subcommittees of the Senate Committee on Post Offices and Post Roads and the House Committee on Post Offices and Post Roads.]   * Paper, 35c.

—— Reclassifying salaries of postmasters and employees of postal service and readjusting their salaries and compensation on equitable basis, report to accompany S. 1898; submitted by Mr. Edge. May 5, 1924. 15 p. (S. rp. 500, 68th Cong. 1st sess.)   * Paper, 5c.

PRINTING COMMITTEE

Calendar of bills, resolutions, petitions, manuscripts, communications, etc., referred to Committee on Printing for its consideration and action thereon, May 24, 1924; no. 1, 68th Congress, 1st session. 1924. 11 p. 4° [The number 1 on this issue for May 24 duplicates the number appearing on the previous calendar for Feb. 11.]   ‡

PRIVILEGES AND ELECTIONS COMMITTEE

Contested elections. Election contests in Senate, report to accompany S. 300 [to provide for election contests in Senate]; submitted by Mr. Ernst. May 26, calendar day May 27, 1924. 2 p. (S. rp. 638, 68th Cong. 1st sess.) * Paper, 5c.

PUBLIC BUILDINGS AND GROUNDS COMMITTEE

District of Columbia. Construction of Arlington Memorial Bridge across Potomac River and improvements in connection therewith, report to accompany S. 3173 [for construction of memorial bridge across Potomac River from point near Lincoln Memorial in Washington to appropriate point in Virginia]; submitted by Mr. Fernald. May 12, 1924. 2 p. (S. rp. 522, 68th Cong. 1st sess.)   * Paper, 5c.

—— Construction of certain public buildings in District of Columbia, report to accompany S. 2284; submitted by Mr. Keyes. Apr. 24, calendar day May 3, 1924. 11 p. (S. rp. 493, 68th Cong. 1st sess.)   * Paper, 5c.

Veterans' Bureau. Additional hospital facilities for patients of Veterans' Bureau, report to accompany S. 3181; submitted by Mr. McKinley. Apr. 24, calendar day, May 2, 1924. 3 p. (S. rp. 489, 68th Cong. 1st sess.) * Paper, 5c.

PUBLIC LANDS AND SURVEYS COMMITTEE

Benning National Forest. To establish Benning National Forest in Georgia [on military reservation at Camp Benning], report to accompany S. 1033; submitted by Mr. Norbeck. May 12, 1924. 2 p. (S. rp. 529, 68th Cong. 1st sess.)   * Paper, 5c.

Brockschmidt, William F. William F. Brockschmidt, report to accompany S. 1650 [for relief of William F. Brockschmidt]; submitted by Mr. Walsh of Montana. May 14, calendar day May 15, 1924. 2 p. (S. rp. 540, 68th Cong. 1st sess.)   * Paper, 5c.

Columbia Reservation. Authorizing acquisition of unreserved public lands in Columbia or Moses Reservation, Wash., report to accompany H. R. 7109 [to authorize acquisition of unreserved public lands in Columbia or Moses Reservation, Wash., under acts of Mar. 28, 1912 (isolated .tract) and Mar. 3, 1877 (desert land)]; submitted by Mr. Ladd. May 20, calendar day May 21, 1924. 1 p. (S. rp. 580, 68th Cong. 1st sess.) * Paper, 5c.

Crook National Forest. Recreational area within Crook National Forest, Ariz., report to accompany H. R. 498; submitted by Mr. Cameron. May 20, calendar day May 21, 1924. 2 p. (S. rp. 576, 68th Cong. 1st sess.) * Paper, 5c.

Crooked Lake. Disposal of lands on Crooked and Pickerel lakes, Mich., report to accompany S. 697; submitted by Mr. Ladd. May 19, 1924. 3 p. (S. rp. 563, 68th Cong. 1st sess.) * Paper, 5c.

Homestead. To extend provisions of homestead laws to Army, Navy, and Marine Corps, report to accompany S. 2979 [to extend provisions of homestead laws so as to allow certain credit, in lieu of permanent improvements, for period of enlistment to soldiers, nurses, and officers of Army and seamen, marines, nurses, and officers of Navy and Marine Corps, who have made or shall make entry under stock-raising homestead act]; submitted by Mr. Bursum. May 20, calendar day May 21, 1924. 2 p. (S. rp. 582, 68th Cong. 1st sess.) * Paper, 5c.

Hot Springs National Park. Land adjoining Hot Springs National Park, Ark., report to accompany S. 1528 [authorizing Secretary of Interior to accept fee-simple title to tract of land adjoining Hot Springs National Park, Ark., donated to United States for use in connection with Hot Springs National Park]; submitted by Mr. Cameron. May 12, 1924. 1 p. (S. rp. 524, 68th Cong. 1st sess.) * Paper, 5c.

Kildee, Nellie. Relief of Nellie Kildee, report to accompany S. 1607; submitted by Mr. Stanfield. May 12, 1924. 2 p. (S. rp. 528, 68th Cong. 1st sess.) * Paper, 5c.

Lundquist, Lyn. Relief of Lyn Lundquist, report to accompany S. 976; submitted by Mr. Kendrick. May 14, 1924. 2 p. (S. rp. 534, 68th Cong. 1st sess.) * Paper, 5c.

Lutsch, Johann J. Johann Jacob Lutsch, report to accompany H. R. 5169 [to grant patent to certain lands to Johann Jacob Lutsch]; submitted by Mr. Ladd. May 12, 1924. 1 p. (S. rp. 526, 68th Cong. 1st sess.) * Paper, 5c.

Medford, Oreg. Accepting tracts of land in Medford, Oreg. [to be used as sites for administration buildings for Crater Lake National Park], report to accompany S. 1987; submitted by Mr. Ladd. May 12, 1924. 2 p. (S. rp. 525, 68th Cong. 1st sess.) * Paper, 5c.

Montana. Claimants in township 16 north, ranges 32 and 33 east. Montana meridian, Montana, report to accompany H. R. 3511 [to extend relief to claimants in township 16 north, ranges 32 and 33 east, Montana meridian, Montana]; submitted by Mr. Walsh of Montana. May 20, calendar day May 24, 1924. 2 p. (S. rp. 609, 68th Cong. 1st sess.) * Paper, 5c.

Northern Pacific Railway. Northern Pacific land grants, report to accompany H. J. Res. 237 [directing Secretary of Interior to withhold his approval of adjustment of Northern Pacific land grants, and creating joint committee to investigate said land grants]; submitted by Mr. Ladd. May 5, calendar day May 6, 1924. 5 p. (S. rp. 504, 68th Cong. 1st sess.) * Paper, 5c.

Paiute Indians. Reservation of lands in Utah for Paiute Indians, report to accompany H. R. 2884; submitted by Mr. Smoot. May 20, calendar day May 21, 1924. 2 p. (S. rp. 575, 68th Cong. 1st sess.) * Paper, 5c.

Peterson, Laura C. Relief of Laura C., Ida E., Lulu P., and Esther Peterson, report to accompany S. 2087; submitted by Mr. Walsh of Montana. May 14, calendar day May 15, 1924. 2 p. (S. rp. 539, 68th Cong. 1st sess.) * Paper, 5c.

Phoenix, Ariz. Granting public lands to Phoenix, Ariz., report to accompany S. 3093; submitted by Mr. Cameron. May 20, calendar day May 21, 1924. 2 p. (S. rp. 569, 68th Cong. 1st sess.) * Paper, 5c.

Plumas National Forest. Plumas and Lassen national forests, Calif., report to accompany H. R. 656 [to add lands to Plumas and Lassen national forests, Calif.]; submitted by Mr. Ladd. May 20, calendar day May 21, 1924. 2 p. (S. rp. 577, 68th Cong. 1st sess.) * Paper, 5c.

Point of Woods Range Lights. Authorizing exchange of lands with Robert P. Hudson, report to accompany H. R. 4481 [authorizing Secretary of Commerce to exchange land formerly used as site for Point of Woods Range Lights, Mich., for other lands in vicinity]; submitted by Mr. Ladd. May 20, calendar day May 21, 1924. 2 p. (S. rp. 579, 68th Cong. 1st sess.) * Paper, 5c.

Pueblo Indians. To quiet title to lands within Pueblo Indian land grants, report to accompany S. 2932; submitted by Mr. Adams. Apr. 24, calendar day May 3, 1924. 11 p. (S. rp. 492, 68th Cong. 1st sess.) * Paper, 5c.

Shreveport, La. Granting lands to Shreveport, La., for reservoir purposes, report to accompany H. R. 5573; submitted by Mr. Ladd. May 12, 1924. 2 p. (S. rp. 527, 68th Cong. 1st sess.) * Paper, 5c.

Swanson, Charles. Issuance of patent to Charles Swanson, report to accompany H. R. 1442; submitted by Mr. Ladd. May 20, calendar day May 21, 1924. 3 p. (S. rp. 578, 68th Cong. 1st sess.) * Paper, 5c.

Sweetgrass, Mont. For relief of First International Bank of Sweetgrass, Mont., report to accompany S. 2689; submitted by Mr. Walsh of Montana. May 20, calendar day May 24, 1924. 2 p. (S. rp. 608, 68th Cong. 1st sess.) * Paper, 5c.

Taos County, N. Mex. Acquirement by United States of privately owned lands in New Mexico, report to accompany S. 3024 [for acquirement by United States of privately owned lands within Rio Arriba and Taos counties, N. Mex., known as Las Trampas grant, by exchanging therefor timber within exterior boundaries of any national forest situated within New Mexico]; submitted by Mr. Bursum. May 20, calendar day May 21, 1924. 2 p. (S. rp. 581, 68th Cong. 1st sess.) * Paper, 5c.

Ute Indians. Reservation of land in Utah as school for Ute Indians, report to accompany H. R. 2882; submitted by Mr. Smoot. May 20, calendar day May 21, 1924. 2 p. (S. rp. 574, 68th Cong. 1st sess.) * Paper, 5c.

TERRITORIES AND INSULAR POSSESSIONS COMMITTEE

Virgin Islands. Providing civil government for Virgin Islands, hearings on S. 2786, Mar. 15, 1924. 1924. pt. 1, ii+23 p. * Paper, 5c.

WHEELER, BURTON K., SELECT COMMITTEE ON INVESTIGATION OF CHARGES AGAINST

Wheeler, Burton K. Charges against Senator Burton K. Wheeler, of Montana, hearings pursuant to S. Res. 206, to investigate facts in relation to charges made in indictment returned against Senator Burton K. Wheeler in district court for Montana. 1924. iii+183 p. [These hearings, with the exception of p. 133–164, hearing of May 9, 1924, were also published in separate numbered parts.] * Paper, 20c.

—— Senator Burton K. Wheeler, minority views pursuant to S. Res. 206 [to investigate facts in relation to charges made in indictment returned against Senator Burton K. Wheeler in district court for Montana]; submitted by Mr. Sterling. May 19, 1924. 10 p. (S. rp. 537, pt. 2, 68th Cong. 1st sess.) * Paper, 5c.

—— Senator Burton K. Wheeler, report pursuant to S. Res. 206 [to investigate facts in relation to charges made in indictment returned against Senator Burton K. Wheeler in district court for Montana]; submitted by Mr. Borah. May 14, 1924. 3 p. (S. rp. 537 [pt. 1], 68th Cong. 1st sess.) * Paper, 5c.

24—26515

USELESS EXECUTIVE PAPERS, JOINT SELECT COMMITTEE ON DISPOSITION OF

Labor Department. Disposition of useless papers in Department of Labor, report; submitted by Mr. Moores of Indiana. May 7, 1924. 7 p. (H. rp. 676, 68th Cong. 1st sess.) * Paper, 5c.

COURT OF CLAIMS

American Tobacco Company. American Tobacco Company *v.* United States; evidence for defendant. [1924.] no. 34477, p. 135–180. ‡

—— Same; evidence for plaintiff in rebuttal. [1924.] no. 34477, p. 181–251. ‡

Chicago, Wilmington and Franklin Coal Company v. United States; findings of fact [conclusion of law, and opinion of court], decided May 19, 1924. [1924.] no. B–11, 8 p. ‡

Federal Sugar Refining Company. Federal Sugar Refining Company *v.* United States; evidence for defendant. [1924.] no. B–147, p. 97–107. ‡

—— Same; evidence for plaintiff in rebuttal. [1924.] no. B–147, p. 109–127. ‡

Howard, R. S., Company. R. S. Howard Company *v.* United States; findings of fact [and conclusion of law], decided May 19, 1924. [1924.] Congressional no. 17329, 6 p. ‡

Hygienic Fibre Company v. United States; findings of fact [conclusion of law, and opinion of court], decided Apr. 28, 1924. [1924.] no. 287–A, 10 p. ‡

Marion & Rye Valley Railway Company v. United States; [findings of fact, conclusion of law, and opinion of court] decided May 26, 1924. [1924.] no. C–699, 18 p. ‡

Moore. Girard Trust Company, George Stevenson, William R. Verner, and Robert Glendinning, trustees of estate of Alfred F. Moore, *v.* United States; findings of fact [conclusion of law, and memorandum], decided May 19, 1924. [1924.] no. C–972, 5 p. ‡

Peabody, Henry W., & Co. Henry W. Peabody & Co. *v.* United States; findings of fact [conclusion of law, and opinion of court], decided May 12, 1924. [1924.] no. B–425, 4 p. ‡

Ray Consolidated Copper Company v. United States; findings of fact [conclusion of law, and opinion of court], decided May 19, 1924. [1924.] no. B–160, 17 p. ‡

Semple. John B. Semple *v.* United States; findings of fact [conclusion of law, and opinion of court], decided May 12, 1924. [1924.] no. 34442, 7 p. [The 1st print of this publication bearing the signature mark 99400—24 was incorrect and was replaced by a 2d print with signature mark 100679—24.] ‡

State Savings Bank of Ortley, S. Dak., v. United States; findings of fact [conclusion of law, and opinion of court], decided Apr. 28, 1924. [1924.] no. B–35, 6 p. ‡

COURT OF CUSTOMS APPEALS

Crucifixes. No. 2398, United States *v.* A. B. Closson, jr., Co., transcript of record on appeal from Board of General Appraisers. [1924.] cover-title, i+7 p. ‡

Herring. No. 2377, United States *v.* F. W. Myers & Co., transcript of record on appeal from Board of General Appraisers. [1924.] cover-title, i+16 p. ‡

Jewelry. No. 2372, United States *v.* Doragon Company et al., transcript of record on appeal from Board of General Appraisers. [1924.] cover-title, i+32 p. ‡

Raisins. No. 2389, United States *v.* J. A. Barkey & Co., transcript of record on appeal from Board of General Appraisers. 1924. cover-title, i+9 p. ‡

Shortage of merchandise. No. 2391, United States *v.* Fensterer & Ruhe et al., transcript of record on appeal from Board of General Appraisers. [1924.] cover-title, i+7 p. ‡

Wool. No. 2384, United States *v.* Stone & Downer Co., transcript of record on appeal from Board of General Appraisers. [1924.] cover-title, i+50 p. ‡

DISTRICT OF COLUMBIA

Court of Appeals. Transcript of record, Apr. term, 1924 ,no. 4150, no. —, special calendar, indexed, Arthur B. White *vs.* District of Columbia, in error to Police Court of District of Columbia. [1924.] cover-title, i+8 p. ‡

FEDERAL BOARD FOR VOCATIONAL EDUCATION

National Conference on Vocational Rehabilitation of Civilian Disabled. Proceedings of National Conference on Vocational Rehabilitation of Civilian Disabled, held at Hotel Hamilton, Washington, D. C., Feb. 4–8, 1924. 1924. x+162 p. (Bulletin 93; Civilian vocational rehabilitation series 8.) *Paper, 20c.
E 24—450

Technical education. Trade and industrial education, organization and administration, all-day schools, part-time schools, evening schools, teacher training; [by Lewis H. Carris]. Revised edition, Mar. 1924. 1924. vii+112 p. (Bulletin 17; Trade and industrial education series 1.) [The revision of the bulletin and the preparation of new material, pt. 5, Teacher training, is the work of the entire staff of the Industrial Education Service.] *Paper, 10c.
E 24—449

FEDERAL RESERVE BOARD

Federal reserve bulletin, May, 1924; [v. 10, no. 5]. 1924. iv+325–454+ii p. il. 4° [Monthly. Includes Report of Committees of Experts to Reparation Commission which was also published separately. For separate issue see below, Germany.] †Paper, 20c. single copy, $2.00 a yr.   15—26318

NOTE.—The bulletin contains, in addition to the regular official announcements, the national review of business conditions, detailed analyses of business conditions, research studies, reviews of foreign banking, and complete statistics showing the condition of Federal reserve banks and member banks. It will be sent to all member banks without charge. Others desiring copies may obtain them from the Federal Reserve Board, Washington, D. C., at the prices stated above.

Federal reserve member banks. Federal reserve inter-district collection system, changes in list of banks upon which items will be received by Federal reserve banks for collection and credit, May 1, 1924. 1924. 15 p. 4° †   16—26870

Germany. Report of Committees of Experts to Reparation Commission, complete official English text with annexes. 1924. iii+67 p. 4° [From Federal reserve bulletin, May, 1924.] † Paper, 10c.   24—26395

NOTE.—Includes the report of the 1st Committee of Experts of which Charles G. Dawes was chairman, and the report of the 2d Committee of Experts with Reginald McKenna as chairman.

FEDERAL TRADE COMMISSION

NOTE.—The bound volumes of the Federal Trade Commission decisions are sold by the Superintendent of Documents, Washington, D. C. Separate opinions are sold on subscription, price $1.00 per volume; foreign subscription, $1.50; single copies, 5c each.

Bene, John, & Sons, Incorporated. United States circuit court of appeals for 2d circuit, John Bene & Sons, Inc., *v.* Federal Trade Commission; [petition for rehearing]. 1924. cover-title, 11 p. large 8° ‡

Caravel Company, Incorporated. Federal Trade Commission *v.* Caravel Company, Inc., [amended] complaint, [report] findings, and order; docket 792, June 21, 1923. 1924. [1]+198–202 p. ([Decision] 371.) [From Federal Trade Commission decisions, v. 6.] *Paper, 5c.

Fox Film Corporation. Federal Trade Commission *v.* Fox Film Corporation, complaint [report, findings, and order]; docket 901, June 6, 1923. [1924.] p. 191–197. ([Decision] 370.) [From Federal Trade Commission decisions, v. 6.] *Paper, 5c.

Gessler, Dudley D. Federal Trade Commission *v.* Dudley D. Gessler, complaint [report] findings, and order; docket 878, May 19, 1923. 1924. [1]+180–183 p. ([Decision] 368.) [From Federal Trade Commission decisions, v. 6.] *Paper, 5c.

Holsman Company. Federal Trade Commission *v.* Holsman Company, complaint [report, findings, and order]; docket 981, June 21, 1923. [1924.] p. 203–206. ([Decision] 372.) [From Federal Trade Commission decisions, v. 6.] *Paper, 5c.

Kraus & Co., Incorporated. Federal Trade Commission *v.* Kraus & Company, Inc., and Herman T. Weeks, complaint [report, findings, and order] ; docket 996. June 21, 1923. [1924.] 207–212+[1] p. ([Decision] 373.) [From Federal Trade Commission decisions, v. 6. Includes list of Cases in which orders for discontinuance or dismissal have been entered, June 22–25, 1923.] * Paper, 5c.

Penn Lubric Oil Company. Federal Trade Commission *v.* Penn Lubric Oil Company, complaint [report, modified] findings, and [modified] order ; docket 910, May 19, 1923. 1924. [1]+184–190+[1] p. ([Decision] 369.) [From Federal Trade Commission decisions, v. 6. Includes list of Cases in which orders for discontinuance or dismissal have been entered, May 23–June 4, 1923.] * Paper, 5c.

United States Steel Corporation. Docket no.. 760, Federal Trade Commission *v.* United States Steel Corporation et al. ; brief and argument by attorneys for Federal Trade Commission. 1924. cover-title, x+391 p. 10 pl. 5 maps, large 8° ‡

Western Meat Company. No. 4064, in circuit court of appeals for 9th circuit, Western Meat Company *v.* Federal Trade Commission ; brief and argument for respondent. 1924. cover-title, ii+100 p. ‡

GENERAL ACCOUNTING OFFICE

Decisions of comptroller general, v. 3, Mar. 1924, and index, Jan.–Mar. 1924 ; J. R. McCarl, comptroller general, Lurtin R. Ginn, assistant comptroller general. 1924. [1]+563–706+xx p. [Monthly.] †   21—26777

GOVERNMENT PRINTING OFFICE

DOCUMENTS OFFICE

Government publications. Information governing distribution of Government publications and Price lists by Office of Superintendent of Documents, Washington, D. C. [1924.] 4 p. †

Laws. Federal and State, opinions of Attorney General, decisions of courts, lists of publications for sale by superintendent of documents. Apr. 1924. [2]+20+[1] p. (Price list 10, 14th edition.) †   24—26479

Monthly catalogue, United States public documents, no. 352 ; Apr. 1924. 1924. p. 585–673. * Paper, 5c. single copy, 50c. a yr. ; foreign subscription, 75c.
4—18088

Public domain, Government publications concerning public lands, conservation, railroad land grants, etc. for sale by superintendent of documents. Mar. 1924. [2]+6 p. (Price list 20, 14th edition.) †   24—26442

Weights and measures. Standards of weight and measure, tests of metals, thermometers, concrete, iron, electricity, light, clay, radiotelegraphy, metric system, list of publications for sale by superintendent of documents. Mar. 1924. [2]+36+[1] p. (Price list 64, 9th edition.) †   24—26480

INTERIOR DEPARTMENT

NOTE.—The decisions of the Department of the Interior in pension cases are issued in slips and in signatures, and the decisions in land cases are issued in signatures, both being published later in bound volumes. Subscribers may deposit $1.00 with the Superintendent of Documents and receive the contents of a volume of the decisions of either kind in separate parts as they are issued ; foreign subscriptions, $1.25. Prices for bound volumes furnished upon application to the Superintendent of Documents, Washington, D. C.

Government officials. Practice by ex-officials before Interior Department, letter, in response to resolution, furnishing information relative to ex-Members of Congress and ex-Cabinet officers who, since Jan. 1, 1918, have appeared as attorneys or agents before Interior Department advocating claims against Government. Apr. 10, 1924. 58 p. (S. doc. 84, 68th Cong. 1st sess.) * Paper, 5c.
24—26516

Public lands. Decisions [of Department of Interior in cases] relating to public lands, v. 50, [signatures] 14–16. [1924.] p. 209–256. [For price, see note above under center head.]   7—23651

Reclamation of land. Federal reclamation by irrigation, message from President of United States transmitting report submitted to Secretary of Interior by committee of special advisers on reclamation. 1924. xvi+230 p. (S. doc. 92, 68th Cong. 1st sess.) * Paper, 25c.   24—26464

ARCHITECT OF CAPITOL

Capital power plant, supplemental estimate of appropriation for legislative establishment, fiscal year 1924 and to remain available during fiscal year 1925, for improving Capitol power plant. May 19, 1924. 2 p. (H. doc. 296, 68th Cong. 1st sess.) * Paper, 5c.

Employees. Salaries of employees under Architect of Capitol, supplemental estimates of appropriations for legislative establishment, fiscal year 1925, salaries of employees under Architect of Capitol. May 26, 1924. 2 p. (H. doc. 315, 68th Cong. 1st sess.) * Paper, 5c.

COLUMBIA INSTITUTION FOR THE DEAF

CONVENTION OF AMERICAN INSTRUCTORS OF THE DEAF

Proceedings. American Instructors of the Deaf, report of proceedings of 23d meeting of Convention of American Instructors of the Deaf, held June 25–30, 1923, at Belleville, Ontario, Canada. 1924. iv+278 p. (S. doc. 48, 68th Cong. 1st sess.) * Paper, 30c.   8—11184

EDUCATION BUREAU

Fiction. Thirty books of great `fiction; [prepared in] Home Education [Division]. [1924.] 4 p. 12° (Reading course 6 revised.) †

Industrial schools for delinquents, 1921–22; prepared by Division of Statistics. 1924. [1]+22 p. (Bulletin 2, 1924.) [Advance sheets from Biennial survey of education, 1920–22.] * Paper, 5c.   E 20—404

Parent-teacher associations and foreign-born women; by Caroline Hedger. Mar. 1924. 4 p. 12° (Home education circular 5.) †   E 24—452

School life, v. 9, no. 9; May, 1924. [1924.] cover-title, p. 193–224. il. 4° [Monthly except July and August. This is Bureau of Education number. Text and illustrations on p. 2–4 of cover.] * Paper, 5c. single copy, 30c. a yr. (10 months) ; foreign subscription, 55c.   E 18—902

Teaching costs in 39 junior high schools; [compiled by David H. Pierce]. Mar. 1924. 7 p. (City school leaflet 16.) * Paper, 5c.   E 24—451

GENERAL LAND OFFICE

NOTE.—The General Land Office publishes a large `general map of the United States, which is sold at $2.00; and also separate maps of the States and Territories in which public lands are to be found, which are sold at 25c. per sheet. The map of California is in 2 sheets. Address the Superintendent of Documents, Washington, D. C.

Public land system of United States, historical outline, by S. V. Proudfit; Rectangular system of surveying, by Frank M. Johnson. 1924. [1]+ 18 p. [The article by S. V. Proudfit was issued separately in Apr. 1923. The article by Frank M. Johnson originally appeared in Land service bulletin, Apr. 1918.] * Paper, 5c.   24—26517

GEOLOGICAL SURVEY

NOTE.—The publications of the United States Geological Survey consist of Annual reports, Monographs, Professional papers, Bulletins, Water-supply papers, chapters and volumes of Mineral resources of the United States, folios of the Topographic atlas of the United States and topographic maps that bear descriptive text, and folios of the Geologic atlas of the United States and the World atlas of commercial geology. The Monographs, folios, and maps are sold. Other publications are generally free as long as the Survey's supply lasts. Copies are also sold by the Superintendent of Documents, Washington, D. C., at the prices indicated. For maps and folios address the Director of the Geological Survey, Washington, D. C. A discount of 40 per cent is allowed on any order for maps or folios that amounts to $5.00 or more at the retail price. This discount applies to an order for either maps or folios alone or for maps and folios together but is not allowed on a few folios that are sold at 5c. each on account of damage by fire. Orders for other publications that are for sale should be sent to the Superintendent of Documents, Washington, D. C. For topographic maps see next page.

Enid, Okla. Additional ground-water supplies for Enid, Okla.; by B. Coleman Renick. May 27, 1924. ii+15–26 p. il. (Water-supply paper 520 B.) †

Mineral resources of United States, 1921: pt. 1. Metals [title-page, contents, Gold, silver, copper, and lead in Alaska, mines report, by Alfred H. Brooks, and index]. 1924. iv+599–617 p. †
4—18124

Publications. New publications, list 194; May 1, 1924. [1924.] 4 p. [Monthly.] †

Riddle, Oreg. Riddle folio, Oreg.; by J. S. Diller and G. F. Kay. [Library edition.] Washington, Geological Survey, 1924. cover-title. 8 p. il. 3 maps, large 4° (Geologic atlas of United States 218.) [Text and illustrations on p. 2–4 of cover.] † Paper, 25c.
- GS 24—105

Ruby, Alaska. Ruby-Kuskokwim region, Alaska; by J. B. Mertie, jr., and G. L. Harrington. 1924. vii+129 p. il. 1 pl. 4 p. of pl. 4 maps in pocket. (Bulletin 754.) * Paper, 50c.
GS 24—40

—— Same. (H. doc. 52, 68th Cong. 1st sess.)

Texas. Geology of coastal plain of Texas west of Brazos River; by Alexander Deussen. 1924. xii+139 p. il. 4 pl. 2 are in pocket, 30 p. of pl. 2 maps, 1 is in pocket, 4° (Professional paper 126.) * Paper, 40c.   GS 24—101

—— Same. (H. doc. 45, 67th Cong. 1st sess.)

Topographic maps

NOTE.—The Geological Survey is making a topographic map of the United States. The individual maps of which it is composed are projected without reference to political divisions, and each map is designated by the name of some prominent town or natural feature in the area mapped. Three scales are ordinarily used, 1:62,500, 1:125,000, and 1:250,000. These correspond, approximately, to 1 mile, 2 miles, and 4 miles to 1 linear inch, covering, respectively, average areas of 230, 920, and 3,700 square miles. For some areas of particular importance special large-scale maps are published. The usual size, exclusive of the margin, is 17.5 inches in height by 11.5 to 16 inches in width, the width varying with the latitude. The sheets measure 20 by 16½ inches. A description of the topographic map is printed on the reverse of each sheet.
More than two-fifths of the area of the country, excluding Alaska, has been mapped, every State being represented. Connecticut, Delaware, the District of Columbia, Maryland, Massachusetts, New Jersey, Ohio, Rhode Island, and West Virginia are completely mapped. Maps of the regular size are sold by the Survey at 10c. each, but a discount of 40 per cent is allowed on any order which amounts to $5.00 or more at the retail price. The discount is allowed on an order for either maps or folios alone or for maps and folios together, but does not apply to a few folios that are sold at 5c. each on account of damage by fire.

California, Gravelly Ford quadrangle, lat. 36° 45′–36° 52′ 30′′, long. 120° 07′ 30′′–120° 15′. Scale 1:31,680, contour interval 5 ft. [Washington, Geological Survey] edition of 1924. 17.3×13.9 in. † 10c.

Mississippi, Morton quadrangle, lat. 32° 15′–32° 30′, long. 89° 30′–89° 45′. Scale 1:62,500, contour interval 20 ft. [Washington, Geological Survey] edition of 1924. 17.5×14.8 in. † 10c.

Missouri, Polo quadrangle, lat. 39° 30′–39°45′, long. 94°–94° 15′. Scale 1:62,500, contour interval 20 ft. [Washington, Geological Survey] edition of 1924. 17.5×13.6 in. † 10c.

INDIAN AFFAIRS OFFICE

Employees. Roster of officers of Indian service; corrected to May 1, 1924. [Indian Print Shop, Chilocco Indian Agricultural School, Chilocco, Okla., May 5, 1924.] 8 p. †

MINES BUREAU

Marine boilers. Tests of marine boilers; [articles] by Henry Kreisinger, John Blizard, A. R. Mumford, B. J. Cross, W. R. Argyle, and R. A. Sherman. [1st edition.] [Jan.] 1924. xiv+309 p. il. 5 pl. 6 p. of pl. (Bulletin 214.) [Includes lists of Mines Bureau publications on design of boilers.] * Paper, 55c.
24—26443

CONTENTS.—Pt. 1. Tests of marine water-tube boilers; by Henry Kreisinger, A. R. Mumford, B. J. Cross, and W. R. Argyle.—Pt. 2. Steaming tests of Scotch marine boiler; by John Blizard, A. R. Mumford, and R. A. Sherman.

NATIONAL PARK SERVICE

Hot Springs National Park. Rules and regulations. Hot Springs National Park, Ark., 1924. [1924.] 32 p. il. †
21—26489

Mesa Verde National Park. Rules and regulations, Mesa Verde National Park, Colo., 1924, season May 15–Nov. 1 [with list of literature]. [1924.] iv+61 p. il. 2 p. of pl. †   21—26514

Wind Cave National Park. Rules and regulations, Wind Cave National Park, S. Dak., 1924, open all year, tourist season June 1–Sept. 30 [with list of literature]. 1924. 20 p. il. †   21—26490

Yellowstone National Park. Manual for railroad visitors, [with] time-tables Yellowstone Park tours, Yellowstone National Park, June 20–Sept. 15, 1924. [1924.] 24 p. il. 4°, folded into narrow 8° size. †

——— Rules and regulations. Yellowstone National Park, Wyo., 1924, season June 20–Sept. 20 [with list of literature]. 1924. 87 p. il. 2 p. of pl. map. †   21—26491

Maps

National parks. Map of national park-to-park highway, master scenic highway of America, showing every city, town, village, and hamlet throughout its entire length as developed by National Park-to-Park Highway Association. Scale 100 m.ʲ=1.6 in. [Washington] Geological Survey [1924]. 26.5×18.1 in. [Donated to National Park Service by National Highways Association for use of motorists visiting national parks.] †

PATENT OFFICE

NOTE.—The Patent Office publishes Specifications and drawings of patents in single copies. These are not enumerated in this catalogue, but may be obtained for 10c. each at the Patent Office.

A variety of indexes, giving a complete view of the work of the Patent Office from 1790 to date, are published at prices ranging from 25c. to $10.00 per volume and may be obtained from the Superintendent of Documents, Washington, D. C. The Rules of practice and pamphlet Patent laws are furnished free of charge upon application to the Patent Office. The Patent Office issues coupon orders in packages of 20 at $2.00 per package, or in books containing 100 coupons at $10.00 per book. These coupons are good until used, but are only to be used for orders sent to the Patent Office. For schedule of office fees, address Chief Clerk, Patent Office, Washington, D. C.

Classification bulletin [51], July 1–Dec. 31, 1923, containing classification of subjects of invention revised by Classification Division. 1924. 23 leaves, large 8° * Paper, 10c.   8—16238

Decisions. [Decisions in patent and trade-mark cases, etc.] May 6, 1924. p. 1–6, large 8° [From Official gazette, v. 322, no. 1.] † Paper, 5c. single copy, $2.00 a yr.   23—7315

——— Same. May 13, 1924. p. 263–268, large 8° [From Official gazette, v. 322, no. 2.]

——— Same. May 20, 1924. p. 499–504, large 8° [From Official gazette, v. 322, no. 3.]

——— Same. May 27, 1924. p. 733–738, large 8° [From Official gazette, v. 322. no. 4.]

——— Decisions of commissioner of patents and of United States courts in patent and trade-mark and copyright cases; compiled from Official gazette of Patent Office, [calendar] year 1923. 1924. xxv+757 p. il. * Cloth, $1.75.

——— Same. (H. doc. 77, 68th Cong. 1st sess.)

Official gazette. Official gazette. May 6–27, 1924; v. 322, no. 1–4. 1924. cover-titles, 973+[clxiv] p. il. large 8° [Weekly.] * Paper, 10c. single copy, $5.00 a yr.; foreign subscription, $11.00.   4—18256

NOTE.—Contains the patents, trade-marks, designs, and labels issued each week; also decisions of the commissioner of patents and of the United States courts in patent cases.

——— Same, weekly index, with title, Alphabetical list of registrants of trade-marks [etc., May 6, 1924]. [1924.] xlvi p. large 8° [From Official gazette, v. 322, no. 1.] † Paper, $1.00 a yr.

——— Same [May 13, 1924]. [1924.] xxxvi p. large 8° [From Official gazette, v. 322, no. 2.]

——— Same [May 20, 1924]. [1924.] xlii p. large 8° [From Official gazette, v. 322, no. 3.]

——— Same [May 27, 1924]. [1924.] xl p. large 8° [From Official gazette. v. 322, no. 4.]

Patents. Classification of patents issued May 6–27, 1924. [1924.] Each 2 p. large 8° [Weekly. From Official gazette, v. 322, no. 1–4.] †

Trade-marks. Trade-marks [etc., from] Official gazette. May 6, 1924. [1924.] 7–76+i–xx p. il. large 8° [From Official gazette. v. 322, no. 1.] † Paper, 5c. single copy, $2.50 a yr. •

—— Same. May 13, 1924. [1924.] 269–315+i–xii p. il. large 8° [From Official gazette, v. 322, no. 2.]

—— Same, May 20, 1924. [1924.] 505–558+i–xviii p. il. large 8° [From Official gazette, v. 322, no. 3.]

—— Same, May 27, 1924. [1924.] 739–788+i–xiv p. il. large 8° [From Official gazette, v. 322, no. 4.]

RECLAMATION BUREAU

New reclamation era, v. 15, no. 5; May, 1924. [1924.] cover-title, p. 65–84, il. 4° [Monthly. Text on p. 2–4 of cover.]

NOTE.—The New reclamation era is a magazine for the farmers and the personnel of the bureau. Its aim is to assist the settlers in the proper use of water, to help them in overcoming their agricultural difficulties. to instruct them in diversifying and marketing their crops, to inspire the employees of the bureau and chronicle engineering problems and achievements, and to promote a wholehearted spirit of cooperation, so that reclamation shall attain the greatest heights of success. The New reclamation era is sent regularly. to all water users on the reclamation projects under the jurisdiction of the bureau who wish to receive the magazine. To others than water users the subscription price is 75c. a year. payable in advance. Subscriptions should be sent to the Chief Clerk, Bureau of Reclamation. Washington. D. C., and remittance in the form of postal money order or New York draft should be made payable to the Chief Disbursing Clerk, Department of the Interior. Postage stamps are not acceptable in payment of subscription.

INTERSTATE COMMERCE COMMISSION

NOTE.—The bound volumes of the decisions. usually known as Interstate Commerce Commission reports, are sold by the Superintendent of Documents, Washington, D. C., at various prices, depending upon the size of the volume. Separate opinions are sold on subscription, price $1.00 per volume; foreign subscription, $1.50; single copies, usually 5c. each.

Akron Union Passenger Depot Company. Before Interstate Commerce Commission. valuation docket no. 316. in matter of tentative valuation of property of Akron Union Passenger Depot Company; brief in support of tentative valuation. 1924. cover-title, i+39 p. ‡

Alabama, Florida and Gulf Railroad. Finance docket no. 1420, public-convenience certificate to Alabama. Florida & Gulf R. R.; decided Mar. 20, 1924; supplemental report of commission. [1924.] p. 557–558. ([Finance decision] 1255.) [From Interstate Commerce Commission reports, v. 86.] * Paper, 5c.

Animal charcoal. No. 14036. Marine Products Company v. Southern Pacific Company et al.; decided Mar. 7. 1924; report [and order] of commission. [1924.] 227–228+[1] p. ([Opinion] 9323.) [Report from Interstate Commerce Commission reports. v. 88.] * Paper, 5c.

Apples. No. 14602. Board of Railroad Commissioners of Montana et al. v. Chicago. Milwaukee & St. Paul Railway Company et al.; decided Mar. 7, 1924; report [and order] of commission. [1924.] 183–184+[1] p. ([Opinion] 9308.) [Report from Interstate Commerce Commission reports, v. 88.] * Paper, 5c.

Arizona and New Mexico Railway. Finance docket no. 274. guaranty settlement with Arizona & New Mexico Ry.; [decided Apr. 15, 1924; report of commission]. 1924. [1]+698–700 p. ([Finance decision] 1299.) [From Interstate Commerce Commission reports, v. 86.] * Paper, 5c.

—— Finance docket no. 1293, deficit settlement with Arizona & New Mexico Ry.; decided Apr. 8, 1924; report of commission. [1924.] p. 679–680. ([Finance decision] 1293.) [From Interstate Commerce Commission reports, v. 86.] * Paper, 5c.

Asbestos. No. 14233, Cutler-Hammer Manufacturing Company v. director general, as agent, Grand Trunk Railway Company of Canada, et al.; [decided Apr. 2, 1924; report and order of commission]. 1924. [1]+600–604+ [1] p. ([Opinion] 9418.) [Report from Interstate Commerce Commission reports, v. 88.] * Paper, 5c.

Asphalt. No. 14897, Keystone Roofing Mfg. Company *v.* director general, as agent; decided Apr. 16, 1924; report of commission. [1924.] p. 707–708. ([Opinion] 9443.) [From Interstate Commerce Commission reports, v. 88.] * Paper, 5c.

Atlantic, Waycross and Northern Railroad. Finance docket no. 292, guaranty settlement with Atlantic, Waycross & Northern R. R.; decided Apr. 7, 1924; report of commission. [1924.] p. 643–645. ([Finance decision] 1281.) [From Interstate Commerce Commission reports, v. 86.] * Paper, 5c.

Baltimore and Ohio Railroad. Finance docket no. 3516, bonds of Baltimore & Ohio R. R.; decided Apr. 3, 1924; report of commission. [1924.] p. 671–673. ([Finance decision] 1290.) [From Interstate Commerce Commission reports, v. 86.] * Paper, 5c.

Barley. No. 15135, Milwaukee Grain Elevator Company *v.* director general, as agent; decided Mar. 20, 1924; report [and order] of commission. [1924.] 287–288+[1] p. ([Opinion] 9340.) [Report from Interstate Commerce Commission reports, v. 88.] * Paper, 5c.

Beet final molasses. No. 14426, Wyoming Sugar Company *v.* director general; decided Mar. 7, 1924; report [and order] of commission. [1924.] 213–216+[1] p. ([Opinion] 9318.) [Report from Interstate Commerce Commission reports, v. 88.] * Paper, 5c.

—— No. 14574, Utah-Idaho Sugar Company *v.* director general, as agent, Salt Lake & Utah Railroad Company, et al.; decided Mar. 7, 1924; report of commission. [1924.] p. 283–284. ([Opinion] 9338.) [From Interstate Commerce Commission reports, v. 88.] * Paper, 5c.

Beverages. No. 13703, L. M. Cohen et al. *v.* Atchison, Topeka & Santa Fe Railway Company et al.; decided Mar. 7, 1924; report [and order] of commission. [1924.] 143–146+ii p. ([Opinion] 9300.) [Report from Interstate Commerce Commission reports, v. 88.] * Paper, 5c.

Black Mountain Telephone Corporation. Finance docket no. 3520, purchase of telephone properties of Black Mountain Telephone Corporation by Southern Bell Telephone & Telegraph Co.; [decided Apr. 17, 1924; report of commission]. 1924. [1]+732–734 p. ([Finance decision] 1311.) [From Interstate Commerce Commission reports, v. 86.] * Paper, 5c.

Brass. No. 14366, Van Dyke Smelting & Refining Works, Incorporated, *v.* Pennsylvania Railroad Company; [no. 14366 (sub-no. 1), same *v.* Pennsylvania Railroad Company et al.]; decided Apr. 18, 1924; report [and order] of commission. [1924.] 743–744+[1] p. ([Opinion] 9447.) [Report from Interstate Commerce Commission reports, v. 88.] * Paper, 5c.

Bricks. Investigation and suspension docket no. 1885, brick and clay products from, to, and between points in southern territory; decided Apr. 5, 1924; [report and order of commission]. [1924.] 543–568+iii p. ([Opinion] 9411.) [Report from Interstate Commerce Commission reports, v. 88.] * Paper, 5c.

—— No. 14740, Sunderland Brothers Company *v.* director general, as agent, and Chicago, Rock Island & Pacific Railway Company; decided Apr. 2, 1924; report [and order] of commission. [1924.] 585–587+[1] p. ([Opinion] 9414.) [Report from Interstate Commerce Commission reports, v. 88.] * Paper, 5c.

Buffalo Creek Railroad. Finance docket no. 3406, bonds of Buffalo Creek R. R.; decided Mar. 25, 1924; supplemental report of commission. [1924.] p. 585–586. ([Finance decision] 1265.) [From Interstate Commerce Commission reports, v. 86.] * Paper, 5c.

Campbell's Creek Railroad. Finance docket no. 334, guaranty settlement with Campbell's Creek R. R.; decided Apr. 14, 1924; report of commission. [1924.] p. 695–697. ([Finance decision] 1298.) [From Interstate Commerce Commission reports, v. 86.] * Paper, 5c.

Cans. No. 14364, Iten Biscuit Company *v.* Atchison, Topeka & Santa Fe Railway Company et al.; decided Apr. 2, 1924; report [and order] of commission. [1924.] 653–658+ii p. ([Opinion] 9429.) [Report from Interstate Commerce Commission reports, v. 88.] * Paper, 5c.

Caretakers of cattle. No. 13259, Miller & Lux, Incorporated, *v.* director general, as agent, Southern Pacific Company, et al.; decided Apr. 2, 1924; report of commission. [1924.] p. 403–404. ([Opinion] 9371.) [From Interstate Commerce Commission reports, v. 88.] * Paper, 5c.

Cattle. No. 13965, Chicago Live Stock Exchange *v.* director general, as agent, et al.; [decided Mar. 7, 1924; report of commission]. 1924. [1]+202–204 p. ([Opinion] 9314.) [From Interstate Commerce Commission reports, v. 88.] * Paper, 5c.

Cement. Investigation and suspension docket no. 1727, rules for storing and sacking of cement in transit at Davenport, Iowa, on Chicago, Rock Island & Pacific Railway; [decided Apr. 14, 1924; report of commission on further hearing]. 1924. [1]+662–669 p. ([Opinion] 9431.) [From Interstate Commerce Commission reports, v. 88.] * Paper, 5c.

—— Investigation and suspension docket no. 2013, cement from eastern trunk line points to New England; decided Apr. 14, 1924; report [and order] of commission. [1924.] 605–609+[1] p. ([Opinion] 9419.) [Report from Interstate Commerce Commission reports, v. 88.] * Paper, 5c.

Central of Georgia Railway. Finance docket no. 3496, bonds of Central of Georgia Ry.; [decided Mar. 29, 1924; amended report of commission]. 1924. [1]+578–580 p. ([Finance decision] 1262.) [From Interstate Commerce Commission reports, v. 86.] * Paper, 5c.

Chesapeake and Ohio Railway. Finance docket no. 3439, bonds of Chesapeake & Ohio Railway; [decided Mar. 19, 1924; report of commission]. 1924. [1]+570–572 p. ([Finance decision] 1259.) [From Interstate Commerce Commission reports, v. 86.] * Paper, 5c.

Chicago, Harvard and Geneva Lake Railway. Finance docket no. 2934, deficit status of Chicago, Harvard & Geneva Lake Ry.; decided Mar. 31, 1924; report of commission. [1924.] p. 583–584. ([Finance decision] 1264.) [From Interstate Commerce Commission reports, v. 86.] * Paper, 5c.

Chicago Union Station Company. Finance docket no. 3461, bonds of Chicago Union Station Company; decided Mar. 10, 1924; report of commission. [1924.] p. 529–534. ([Finance decision] 1247.) [From Interstate Commerce Commission reports, v. 86.] * Paper, 5c.

Cleveland, Cincinnati, Chicago and St. Louis Railway. Finance docket no. 3336, C., C., C. & St. L. Ry.; decided Apr. 24, 1924; supplemental report of commission. [1924.] p. 787–788. ([Finance decision] 1327.) [From Interstate Commerce Commission reports, v. 86.] * Paper, 5c.

Coal. Investigation and suspension docket no. 1998, coal from Buffalo, Black Rock, and Suspension Bridge, N. Y., to Minnesota; decided Apr. 14, 1924; report [and order] of commission. [1924.] 631–639+[1] p. ([Opinion] 9425.) [Report from Interstate Commerce Commission reports, v. 88.] * Paper, 5c.

—— Investigation and suspension docket no. 2007, coal from Illinois, Indiana, Wisconsin, and St. Louis, Mo., to Iowa, Minnesota, North Dakota, and South Dakota; [4th section application no. 3400 on further hearing]; decided May 1, 1924; report [and orders] of commission. [1924.] 105–109+ii p. ([Opinion] 9472.) [Report from Interstate Commerce Commission reports, v. 89.] * Paper, 5c.

—— No. 11224, Chicago Coal Merchants Association *v.* director general, as agent, Atchison, Topeka & Santa Fe Railway Company, et al,; decided May 6, 1924; report [and order] of commission on reargument. [1924.] 137–140+ii p. ([Opinion] 9478.) [Report from Interstate Commerce Commission reports, v. 89.] * Paper, 5c.

—— No. 12328, Jeremy Fuel & Grain Company et al *v.* director general, as agent; [no. 12325, Wasatch Coal Company et al. *v.* same]; decided Apr. 2, 1924; report [and order] of commission. [1924.] 397–402+[1] p. ([Opinion] 9370.) [Report from Interstate Commerce Commission reports, v. 88.] * Paper, 5c.

—— No. 13445, Lackawanna Steel Company et al. *v.* Pennsylvania Railroad Company et al.; decided Apr. 21, 1924; report [and order] of commission. [1924.] 759–764+[1] p. ([Opinion] 9454.) [Report from Interstate Commerce Commission reports, v. 88.] * Paper, 5c.

Coal—Continued. No. 13949, Lincoln Gas Coal Company et al. v. Baltimore & Ohio Railroad Company et al.; portions of 4th section application no. 1571; decided Apr. 2, 1924; report [and orders] of commission. [1924.] 379–384+ iii p. ([Opinion] 9366.) [Report from Interstate Commerce Commission reports, v. 88.] * Paper, 5c.

—— No. 14180, Doniphan Brick Works, owned and operated by Klose Brick & Tile Company, Lincoln, Nebr., v. director general, as agent, Union Pacific Railroad Company, et al.; [decided Apr. 2, 1924; report of commission]. 1924. [1]+438–440 p. ([Opinion] 9383.) [From Interstate Commerce Commission reports, v. 88.] * Paper, 5c.

—— No. 14193, Great Western Paper Company v. Minneapolis, St. Paul & Sault Ste. Marie Railway Company; [decided Apr. 2, 1924; report and order of commission]. 1924. [1]+582–584+[1] p. ([Opinion] 9413.) [Report from Interstate Commerce Commission reports, v. 88.] * Paper, 5c.

—— No. 14271, Southern Cotton Oil Company v. director general, as agent; [no. 14331, same v. same; no. 14139, same v. same; decided Feb. 18, 1924; report of commission. 1924. [1]+280–282 p. ([Opinion] 9337.) [From Interstate Commerce Commission reports, v. 88.] * Paper, 5c.

—— No. 14315, Evansville Chamber of Commerce et al. v. Illinois Central Railroad Company et al.; decided Apr. 2, 1924; report [and order] of commission. [1924.] 389–394+[1] p. ([Opinion] 9368.) [Report from Interstate Commerce Commission reports, v. 88.] * Paper, 5c.

—— No. 14641, Midland Coal Company et al. v. Missouri Pacific Railroad Company, director general, as agent, et al.; decided May 1, 1924; report [and order] of commission. [1924.] 101–102+ii p. ([Opinion] 9470.) [Report from Interstate Commerce Commission reports, v. 89.] * Paper, 5c.

—— No. 14661, Southwestern Interstate Coal Operators' Association et al. v. Arkansas Western Railway Company et al.; decided Apr. 22, 1924; [report and order of commission]. [1924.] 73–86+ii p. ([Opinion] 9467.) [Report from Interstate Commerce Commission reports, v. 89.] * Paper, 5c.

—— No. 14809, Valley Camp Coal Company v. Baltimore & Ohio Railroad Company; [decided Apr. 16, 1924; report and order of commission]. 1924. [1]+682–686+[1] p. ([Opinion] 9436.) [Report from Interstate Commerce Commission reports, v. 88.] * Paper, 5c.

Coal-tar. No. 14216, Barrett Company v. director general, as agent, et al.; [nos. 14294–295, same v. same; decided Apr. 2, 1924; report [and order] of commission. [1924.] 459–462+[1] p. ([Opinion] 9391.) [Report from Interstate Commerce Commission reports, v. 88.] * Paper, 5c.

Coffee. No. 14825, Continental Coffee Company et al. v. Atchison, Topeka & Santa Fe Railway Company et al.; decided May 1, 1924; report [and order] of commission. [1924.] 159–161+[1] p. ([Opinion] 9485.) [Report from Interstate Commerce Commission reports, v. 89.] * Paper, 5c.

Condensed buttermilk. No. 15048, Consolidated Products Company v. Chicago, Burlington & Quincy Railroad Company; decided May 1, 1924; report [and order] of commission. [1924.] 103–104+[1] p. ([Opinion] 9471.) [Report from Interstate Commerce Commission reports, v. 89.] * Paper, 5c.

Cooperage. No. 13573, J. D. Hollingshead Company v. Deering Southwestern Railway et al.; decided Apr. 16, 1924; report [and order] of commission. [1924.] 659–661+ii p. ([Opinion] 9430.) [Report from Interstate Commerce Commission reports, v. 88.] * Paper, 5c.

Copper. No. 14010, United Verde Extension Mining Company v. Atchison, Topeka & Santa Fe Railway Company et al.; decided May 2, 1924; report [and order] of commission. [1924.] 95–100+[1] p. ([Opinion] 9469.) [Report from Interstate Commerce Commission reports, v. 89.] * Paper, 5c.

Copper Range Railroad. Finance docket no. 409, guaranty settlement with Copper Range Railroad; [decided Apr. 8, 1924; report of commission]. 1924. [1]+646–648 p. ([Finance decision] 1282.) [From Interstate Commerce Commission reports, v. 86.] * Paper, 5c.

Corn syrup. No. 14812, American Maize-Products Company v. director general, as agent; [no. 14812 (sub-no. 1), same v. same; decided Mar. 26, 1924; report and order of commission]. 1924. [1]+354–356+[1] p. ([Opinion] 9359.) [Report from Interstate Commerce Commission reports, v. 88.] * Paper, 5c.

Cotton. No. 13798, Japan Cotton Trading Company of Texas *v.* director general, as agent; decided Apr. 2, 1924; report of commission. [1924.] p. 407–409. ([Opinion] 9373.) [From Interstate Commerce Commission reports, v. 88.] * Paper, 5c.

—— No. 14413, Mississippi Railroad Commission et al. *v.* Alabama & Vicksburg Railway Company et al.; decided Apr. 24, 1924; [report and 4th section order no. 8904 of commission]. [1924.] 47–72+ii p. ([Opinion] 9466.) [Report from Interstate Commerce Commission reports, v. 88.] * Paper, 5c.

—— No. 14474, S. B. Locke & Company *v.* director general, as agent, and Kansas City Southern Railway Company; decided Apr. 2, 1924; report [and order] of commission. [1924.] 487–488+[1] p. ([Opinion] 9398.) [Report from Interstate Commerce Commission reports, v. 88.] * Paper, 5c.

Cotton-seed. Investigation and suspension docket no. 1995, oil cake and oil-cake meal, Wilmington, Calif., to stations in Idaho, Oregon, and Washington; decided Apr. 4, 1924; report [and order] of commission. [1924.] 421–423+[1] p. ([Opinion] 9377.) [Report from Interstate Commerce Commission reports, v. 88.] * Paper, 5c.

Cotton-seed meal. No. 14375, Arizona Egyptian Cotton Company *v.* director general, as agent; decided Mar. 7, 1924; report [and order] of commission. [1924.] 263–265+[1] p. ([Opinion] 9332.) [Report from Interstate Commerce Commission reports, v. 88.] * Paper, 5c.

—— No. 14833, Tallulah Cotton Oil Company, J. V. Wright, lessee, *v.* Vicksburg, Shreveport & Pacific Railway Company; decided May 1, 1924; report of commission. [1924.] p. 151–153. ([Opinion] 9482.) [From Interstate Commerce Commission reports, v. 89.] * Paper, 5c.

Crating charges. No. 15237, Gallaudet Aircraft Corporation *v.* New York, New Haven & Hartford Railroad Company et al.; [decided Apr. 16, 1924; report and order of commission]. 1924. [1]+750–752+[1] p. ([Opinion] 9450.) [Report from Interstate Commerce Commission reports, v. 88.] * Paper, 5c.

Cream. No. 14063, Kirschbraun & Sons, Incorporated, *v.* American Railway Express Company; [decided Apr. 19, 1924; report of commission]. 1924. [1]+670–672 p. ([Opinion] 9432.) [From Interstate Commerce Commission reports, v. 88.] * Paper, 5c.

Cumberland Northern Railroad. Finance docket no. 416, guaranty status of Cumberland Northern R. R.; decided Apr. 2, 1924; report of commission. 1924. p. 627. ([Finance decision] 1276.) [From Interstate Commerce Commission reports, v. 86.] * Paper, 5c.

Delaware, Susquehanna and Schuylkill Railroad. Finance docket no. 3382, control of Delaware, Susquehanna & Schuylkill R. R. by Lehigh Valley R. R.; decided Mar. 25, 1924; report of commission. [1924.] p. 567–569. ([Finance decision] 1258.) [From Interstate Commerce Commission reports, v. 86.] * Paper, 5c.

Demurrage. No. 14696, Empire Lumber Company *v.* director general, as agent, Southern Pacific Company, et al.; [decided Apr. 2, 1924; report and order of commission]. 1924. [1]+424–426+[1] p. ([Opinion] 9378.) [Report from Interstate Commerce Commission reports, v. 88.] * Paper, 5c.

East Jersey Railroad and Terminal Company. Finance docket no. 3549, East Jersey R. R. & Term. Co. equipment-trust notes; decided Apr. 17, 1924; report of commission. [1924.] p. 737–739. ([Finance decision] 1313.) [From Interstate Commerce Commission reports, v. 86.] * Paper, 5c.

Egg cases. Investigation and suspension docket no. 2002, classification exceptions on empty egg cases in western trunk-line territory; [decided Mar. 31, 1924; report and order of commission]. 1924. [1]+376–378+[1] p. ([Opinion] 9365.) [Report from Interstate Commerce Commission reports, v. 88.] * Paper, 5c.

Eggs. No. 13803, National Poultry, Butter & Egg Association et al. *v.* Ann Arbor Railroad Company et al.; decided Apr. 16, 1924; report [and order] of commission. [1924.] 673–676+[1] p. ([Opinion] 9433.) [Report from Interstate Commerce Commission reports, v. 88.] * Paper, 5c.

Electric locomotives. No. 14643, Colorado Fuel & Iron Company *v.* director general, as agent, and Colorado & Wyoming Railway Company; decided Apr. 2, 1924; report [and order] of commission. [1924.] 453–454+[1] p. ([Opinion] 9388.) [Report from Interstate Commerce Commission reports, v. 88.] * Paper, 5c.

Electric railroads. Finance docket no. 3392, application of sec. 15a of interstate commerce act to electric railway; report of commission. Apr. 30, 1924. [1924.] p. 751–754. ([Finance decision] 1315.) [From Interstate Commerce Commission reports, v. 86.] * Paper, 5c.

Farm implements and machinery. No. 14863, T. McCleland Hardware Company v. Illinois Central Railroad Company; decided May 1, 1924; report [and order] of commission. [1924.] 129–130+[1] p. ([Opinion] 9475.) [Report from Interstate Commerce Commission reports, v. 89.] * Paper, 5c.

Florida East Coast Railway. valuation docket no. 151, Florida East Coast Railway Company and Atlantic and East Coast Terminal Company; [decided Jan. 15, 1924; report of commission]. 1924. [2]+25–112 p. il. (B–9.) [From Interstate Commerce Commission reports, v. 84.] * Paper, 10c.

Florida Telephone Company. Finance docket no. 3494, purchase of properties of Florida Telephone Co. and East Florida Telephone Co. by Southern Bell Telephone & Telegraph Co.; decided Mar. 31, 1924; report of commission. [1924.] p. 603–605. ([Finance decision] 1270.) [From Interstate Commerce Commission reports, v. 86.] * Paper, 5c.

Frankfort and Cincinnati Railway. Finance docket no. 2954, abandonment of Frankfort & Cincinnati Ry.; [decided Apr. 19, 1924; report of commission]. 1924. [1]+740–750 p. ([Finance decision] 1314.) [From Interstate Commerce Commission reports, v. 86.] * Paper, 5c.

Freight-cars. No. 14678, Peerless Lumber Company v. director general, as agent; decided Apr. 2, 1924; report of commission. [1924.] p. 457–458. ([Opinion] 9390.) [From Interstate Commerce Commission reports, v. 88.] * Paper, 5c.

Freight rates. Fourth section applications nos. 2125, 12125, et seq., commodity rates to Gray's Harbor and Willapa Bay points; [decided Apr. 7, 1924; report and 4th section order no. 8890 of commission]. 1924. [1]+512–520+ii p. ([Opinion] 9406.) [Report from Interstate Commerce Commission reports, v. 88.] * Paper, 5c.

—— No. 11116, Beaver Sand Company et al. v. director general, as agent, Beaver valley Railroad Company, et al.; decided Mar. 10, 1924; report [and order] of commission on further hearing. [1924.] 115–119+[1] p. ([Opinion] 9294.) [Report from Interstate Commerce Commission reports, v. 88.] *Paper, 5c.

—— No. 11388, Public Service Commission of Indiana et al. v. Atchison, Topeka & Santa Fe Railway Company et al.; decided Apr. 8, 1924; [report of commission on further hearing]. [1924.] p. 709–724. ([Opinion] 9444.) [From Interstate Commerce Commission reports, v. 88.] * Paper, 5c.

—— No. 13384, Greene Cananea Copper Company v. Chicago, Rock Island & Pacific Railway Company et al.; decided Mar. 7, 1924; report [and order] of commission. [1924.] 225–226+[1] p. ([Opinion] 9322.) [Report from Interstate Commerce Commission reports, v. 88.] * Paper, 5c.

—— No. 13671, Public Service Commission of Indiana and Indiana Chamber of Commerce v. Atchison, Topeka & Santa Fe Railway Company et al.; [decided Apr. 8, 1924; report of commission]. 1924. [1]+728–742 p. ([Opinion] 9446.) [From Interstate Commerce Commission reports, v. 88.] * Paper, 5c.

—— No. 13721, International Harvester Company v. New York Central Railroad Company, director general, as agent, et al.; [decided Mar. 26, 1924; report of commission]. 1924. [1]+368–373 p. ([Opinion] 9363.) [From Interstate Commerce Commission reports, v. 88.] * Paper, 5c.

—— No. 13875, Oklahoma-Southwestern Railway Company v. St. Louis-San Francisco Railway Company et al.; decided Mar. 7, 1924; report [and order] of commission. [1924.] 235–246+[1] p. ([Opinion] 9326.) [Report from Interstate Commerce Commission reports, v. 88.] * Paper, 5c.

—— No. 14044, Metropolitan Utilities District of Omaha v. director general, as agent, Bauxite & Northern Railway Company et al.; decided Mar. 20, 1924; report of commission. [1924.] p. 331–337. ([Opinion] 9354.) [From Interstate Commerce Commission reports, v. 88.] * Paper, 5c.

—— No. 14167, Chicago, Milwaukee & St. Paul Railway Company v. Union Pacific Railroad Company et al.; [decided Mar. 20, 1924; report and order of commission]. 1924. [1]+312–318+[1] p. ([Opinion] 9349.) [Report from Interstate Commerce Commission reports, v. 88.] * Paper, 5c.

Freight rates—Continued. No. 14210, Lindeteves-Stokvis *v.* director general. as agent, et al.; decided Apr. 24, 1924; report of commission. [1924.] p. 3–6. ([Opinion] 9456.) [From Interstate Commerce Commission reports, v. 89.] * Paper, 5c.

Fruit. No. 13500, John F. Barker Produce Company et al. *v.* Southern Pacific Company et al.; decided Apr. 2, 1924; report [and order] of commission. ·[1924.] 385–388+[1] p. ([Opinion] 9367.) [Report from Interstate Commerce Commission reports, v. 88.] * Paper, 5c.

—— No. 14648, Babbitt Brothers Trading Company *v.* Atchison, Topeka & Santa Fe Railway Company et al.; [decided Apr. 2, 1924; report and order of commission]. 1924. [1]+614–616+[1] p. ([Opinion] 9421.) [Report from Interstate Commerce Commission reports, v. 88.] * Paper, 5c.

Fuel-oil. No. 14457, Alexander Milling Company et al. *v.* director general, as agent; decided Apr. 16, 1924; report [and order] of commission. [1924.] 677–678+[1] p. ([Opinion] 9434.) .[Report from Interstate Commerce Commission reports, v. 88.] * Paper, 5c,

Fullers' earth. No. 13587, Standard Oil Company (California) *v.* Atchison, Topeka & Santa Fe Railway Company et al.; decided Apr. 16, 1924; report of commission. [1924.] p. 27–32. ([Opinion] 9461.) [From Interstate Commerce Commission reports, v. 89.] * Paper, 5c.

Gasoline. No. 13629, Standard Oil Company (New Jersey) *v.* director general, as agent, Baltimore & Ohio Railroad Company, et al.; [no. 13629 (sub-nos. 1–5), same *v.* same; no. 13711, same *v.* same]; decided Apr. 21, 1924; report of commission. [1924.] p. 7–10. ([Opinion] 9457.) [From Interstate Commerce Commission reports, v. 89.] * Paper, 5c.

—— No. 15372, Standard Oil Company of Louisiana *v.* Yazoo & Mississippi Valley Railroad Company et al.; decided May 1, 1924; report of commission. [1924.] p. 157–158. ([Opinion] 9484.) [From Interstate Commerce Commission reports, v. 89.] * Paper, 5c.

Georgia and Florida Railway. Finance docket no. 3506, receiver's certificates of Georgia & Florida Ry. [John Skelton Williams, receiver]; decided Apr. 9, 1924; report of commission. [1924.] p. ·681–684. ([Finance decision] 1294.) [From Interstate Commerce Commission reports, v. 86.] * Paper, 5c.

Georgia Southern and Florida Railway.· Finance docket no. 3490, bonds of Georgia Southern & Florida Ry.; decided Apr. 9, 1924; report of commission. [1924.] p. 685–687. ([Finance decision] 1295.) [From Interstate Commerce Commission reports, v. 86.] * Paper, 5c.

Glass. No. 14636, Jackson Traffic Bureau, for Enochs Lumber & Manufacturing Company, Incorporated, *v.* St. Louis-San Francisco Railway Company et al.; [decided Mar. 7, 1924; report and order of commission]. 1924. [1]+188–190+[1] p. ([Opinion] 9310.) [Report from Interstate Commerce Commission reports, v. 88.] * Paper, 5c.

Grain. Investigation and suspension docket no. 1988, grain and grain products from defined territories to certain points in Texas; decided Apr. 16, 1924; report [and order] of commission. [1924.] 141–143+[1] p. ([Opinion] 9479.) [Report from Interstate Commerce Commission reports, v. 89.] * Paper, 5c.

—— Investigation and suspension docket no. 1994, routing on grain and grain products from stations in Oklahoma to Mobile, Ala.; decided Apr. 8, 1924; report [and order] of commission. [1924.] 505–506+[1] p. ([Opinion] 9404.) [Report from Interstate Commerce Commission reports, v. 88.] * Paper, 5c.

—— No. 13437, Traffic Bureau of Chamber of Commerce of Phoenix, Ariz., et al. *v.* Arizona Eastern Railroad Company et al.; [decided Mar. 7, 1924; report and order of commission]. 1924. [1]+250–254+[1] p. ([Opinion] 9328.) [Report from Interstate Commerce Commission reports, v. 88.] * Paper, 5c.

Grape juice. No. 12400, Armour and Company *v.* director general, as agent, Alabama Great Southern Railroad Company, et al.; decided Apr. 5, 1924; report [and orders] of commission. [1924.] 569–581+v p. ([Opinion] 9412.) [Report from Interstate Commerce Commission reports, v. 88.] * Paper, 5c.

Grate-bars. Investigation and suspension docket no. 2014, grate bars, East Birmingham, Ala., to Memphis, Tenn., for beyond; decided Apr. 23, 1924; report [and order] of commission. [1924.] 701–703+[1] p. ([Opinion] 9441.) [Report from Interstate Commerce Commission reports, v. 88.] * Paper, 5c.

Greene Railroad. Finance docket no. 3551, bonds of Greene R. R.; [decided Apr. 21, 1924; report of commission]. 1924. [1]+778–781 p. ([Finance decision] 1323.) [From Interstate Commerce Commission reports, v. 86.] * Paper, 5c.

Greenwich and Johnsonville Railway. Finance docket no. 505, guaranty settlement with Greenwich & Johnsonville Ry.; decided Apr. 26, 1924; report of commission. [1924.] p. 757–759. ([Finance decision] 1317.) [From Interstate Commerce Commission reports, v. 86.] * Paper, 5c.

Hay. No. 15174, National Hay & Milling Company *v.* Chicago, Burlington & Quincy Railroad Company; decided Apr. 21, 1924; report [and order] of commission. [1924.] 1–2+[1] p. ([Opinion] 9455.) [Report from Interstate Commerce Commission reports, v. 89.] * Paper, 5c.

Hides and skins. No. 14839, Charles Friend & Company *v.* Chicago, Burlington & Quincy Railroad Company et al,; [decided Mar. 7, 1924; report and order of commission]. 1924. [1]+288–292+.[1] p. ([Opinion] 9341.) [Report from Interstate Commerce Commission reports, v. 88.] * Paper, 5c.

Hill City Railway. Before Interstate Commerce Commission, valuation docket no. 223, in matter of tentative valuation of property of Hill City Railway Company; brief in support of tentative valuation. 1924. cover-title, i+29 p. ‡

Horses. No. 13001, Chamber of Commerce of Kansas City, Mo., *v.* Alexandria & Western Railway Company et al.; [decided Apr. 26, 1924; report and order of commission]. 1924. [1]+22–26+iii p. ([Opinion] 9460.) [Report from Interstate Commerce Commission reports, v. 89.] * Paper, 5c.

Houston and Brazos Valley Railway. Finance docket no. 3426, control of Houston & Brazos valley Ry. by New Orleans, Texas & Mexico Ry.; decided Mar. 28, 1924; report of commission. [1924.] p. 587–596. ([Finance decision] 1266.) [From Interstate Commerce Commission reports, v. 86.] * Paper, 5c.

Ice. No. 14388, Moline Ice Company *v.* director general, as agent, Chicago, Milwaukee & St. Paul Railway Company, et al.; [decided Apr. 2, 1924; report of commission]. 1924. [1]+444–446 p. ([Opinion] 9385.) [From Interstate Commerce Commission reports, v. 88.] * Paper, 5c.

Iron. Investigation and suspension docket no. 1984, scrap iron from East St. Louis, Ill., group to Terre Haute, Ind.; [decided Apr. 4, 1924; report and order of commission]. 1924. [1]+410–412+[1] p. ([Opinion] 9374.) [Report from Interstate Commerce Commission reports, v. 88.] * Paper, 5c.

—— Investigation and suspension docket no. 1997, iron and steel articles between points in Illinois, Indiana, and Missouri; decided Apr. 26, 1924; report [and order] of commission. [1924.] 17–21+[1] p. ([Opinion] 9459.) [Report from Interstate Commerce Commission reports, v. 89.] * Paper, 5c.

—— No. 15272, West End Scrap Iron & Metal Company *v.* director general, as agent, Duluth, South Shore & Atlantic Railway Company, et al.; decided May 1, 1924; report [and order] of commission. [1924.] 149–150+[1] p. ([Opinion] 9481.) [Report from Interstate Commerce Commission reports, v. 89.] * Paper, 5c.

Iron ores. No. 14386, Republic Iron & Steel Company *v.* director general, as agent, et al.; decided Apr. 16, 1924; report [and order] of commission. [1924.] 691–692+[1] p. ([Opinion] 9438.) [Report from Interstate Commerce Commission reports, v. 88.] * Paper, 5c.

Kansas and Missouri Railway and Terminal Company. Finance docket no. 3130, securities of Kansas & Missouri Railway & Terminal Co.; decided Feb. 16, 1924; report of commission. [1924.] p. 559–562. ([Finance decision] 1256.) [From Interstate Commerce Commission reports, v. 86.] * Paper, 5c.

Kansas and Missouri Railway and Terminal Company—Continued. Finance docket no. 3139, control of Kansas & Missouri Railway & Terminal Co. [by Kansas City, Kaw valley & Western Railway Company and Kansas City Southern Railway Company: and finance docket no. 3133]; decided Apr. 2, 1924; report of commission. [1924.] p. 631–636. ([Finance decision] 1278.) [From Interstate Commerce Commission reports, v. 86.] * Paper, 5c.

Keeseville, Ausable Chasm and Lake Champlain Railroad. Finance docket no. 1468, deficit settlement with Keeseville, Ausable Chasm & Lake Champlain R. R.; decided Apr. 16, 1924; report of commission. [1924.] p. 705–706. ([Finance decision] 1302.) [From Interstate Commerce Commission reports, v. 86.] * Paper, 5c.

Lake Superior and Ishpeming Railroad. Finance docket no. 3513, assumption of obligation and liability by Lake Superior & Ishpeming R. R.; [decided Apr. 2, 1924; report of commission. 1924. [1]+640–642 p. ([Finance decision] 1280.) [From Interstate Commerce Commission reports, v. 86.] * Paper, 5c.

Lake Tahoe Railway and Transportation Company. Finance docket no. 3540, notes of Lake Tahoe Railway & Transportation Co.; decided Apr. 19, 1924; report of commission. [1924.] p. 755–756. ([Finance decision] 1316.) [From Interstate Commerce Commission reports, v. 86.] * Paper, 5c.

Lamp-chimneys. No. 14415, Radiant Glass Company v. director general, as agent; [no. 14415 (sub-no. 1), same v. director general, as agent, Missouri, Oklahoma & Gulf Railway Company, et al.; decided Mar. 7, 1924; report [and order] of commission. [1924.] 295–297+[1] p. ([Opinion] 9343.) [Report from Interstate Commerce Commission reports, v. 88.] * Paper, 5c.

Lehigh Valley Railroad. Finance docket no. 3511, bonds of Lehigh valley R. R.; decided Apr. 18, 1924; report of commission. [1924.] p. 721–724. ([Finance decision] 1307.) [From Interstate Commerce Commission reports, v. 86.] * Paper, 5c.

Lemons. No. 14607, American Stores Company v. Pennsylvania Railroad Company; decided Apr. 16, 1924; report [and order] of commission. [1924.] 41–43+[1] p. ([Opinion] 9464.) [Report from Interstate Commerce Commission reports, v. 89.] * Paper, 5c.

Lighterage. No. 15067, American Woodpulp Corporation v. director general, as agent, and Baltimore & Ohio Railroad Company; decided Mar. 20, 1924; report [and order] of commission. [1924.] 277–279+[1] p. ([Opinion] 9336.) [Report from Interstate Commerce Commission reports, v. 88.] * Paper, 5c.

Limestone. Investigation and suspension docket no. 1948, limestone from . Illinois points to St. Louis, Mo.; decided Apr. 25, 1924; report [and order] of commission. [1924.] 11–16+[1] p. ([Opinion] 9458.) [Report from Interstate Commerce Commission reports, v. 89.] * Paper, 5c.

—— No. 14568, Amalgamated Sugar Company v. director general, as agent, Oregon Short Line Railroad Company, et al.; [decided Mar. 7, 1924; report of commission]. 1924. [1]+266–268 p. ([Opinion] 9333.) [From Interstate Commerce Commission reports, v. 88.] * Paper, 5c.

Linseed-oil. No. 13894, American Linseed Company v. New York Central Railroad Company et al.; [no. 14168, Midland Linseed Products Company v. Central Railroad Company of New Jersey et al.]; decided Apr. 2, 1924; report [and order] of commission. [1924.] 427–428+ii p. ([Opinion] 9379.) [Report from Interstate Commerce Commission reports, v. 88.] * Paper, 5c.

Logs. No. 14519. Thompson-Wells Lumber Company v. director general, as agent; decided Apr. 2, 1924; report [and order] of commission. [1924.] 395–396+[1] p. ([Opinion] 9369.) [Report from Interstate Commerce Commission reports, v. 88.] * Paper, 5c.

—— No. 14656. Murray & Nickell Manufacturing Company v. director general. as agent; decided Apr. 2, 1924; report [and order] of commission. [1924.] 455–456+[1] p. ([Opinion] 9389.) [Report from Interstate Commerce Commission reports, v. 88.] * Paper, 5c.

Lorain and Southern Railroad. Finance docket no. 167, deficit settlement with Lorain & Southern R. R.; decided Apr. 18, 1924; report of commission. [1924.] p. 711–712. ([Finance decision] 1304.) [From Interstate Commerce Commission reports, v. 86.] * Paper 5c.

Los Angeles and Salt Lake Railroad. In equity, no. H–44–T, in district court, southern district of California, southern division, Los Angeles & Salt Lake Railroad Company *v.* United States and Interstate Commerce Commission; brief for Interstate Commerce Commission. 1924. cover-title, ii+75 p. ‡

Lumber. No. 14459, Cyrus C. Shafer Lumber Company *v.* director general, as agent, Chicago, Rock Island & Pacific Railway Company, et al.; [decided Apr. 2, 1924; report and order of commission]. 1924. [1]+472–473+[1] p. ([Opinion] 9395.) [Report from Interstate Commerce Commission reports, v. 88.] * Paper, 5c.

—— No. 15056, Central Pennsylvania Lumber Company *v.* Tionesta Valley Railway Company et al.; decided Mar. 20, 1924; report [and order] of commission. [1924.] 303–304+[1] p. ([Opinion] 9346.) [Report from Interstate Commerce Commission reports, v. 88.] * Paper, 5c.

Maryland and Pennsylvania Railroad. Finance docket no. 3536, securities of Maryland & Pennsylvania R. R.; decided Apr. 17, 1924; report of commission. [1924.] p. 729–731. ([Finance decision] 1310.) [From Interstate Commerce Commission reports, v. 86.] ‡

—— Same; decided May 16, 1924; amended report of commission. Corrected reprint. [1924.] p. 729–732. ([Finance decision] 1310.) [From Interstate Commerce Commission reports, v. 86.] * Paper, 5c.

Maryland, Delaware and Virginia Railway. Finance docket no. 615, guaranty settlement with Maryland, Delaware & Virginia Ry.; [decided Apr. 21, 1924; report of commission]. 1924. [1]+760–762 p. ([Finance decision] 1318.) [From Interstate Commerce Commission reports, v. 86.] * Paper, 5c.

Meat. No. 14173, Swift & Company *v.* Texas & Pacific Railway Company et al.; [no. 14173 (sub-no. 1), Armour & Company *v.* same; decided Apr. 2, 1924; report of commission]. 1924. [1]+610–613 p. ([Opinion] 9420.) [From Interstate Commerce Commission reports, v. 88.] * Paper, 5c.

Milk. Investigation and suspension docket no. 1991, express rates on milk and cream via Chicago & North Western Railway; [decided Apr. 22, 1924; report and order of commission]. 1924. [1]+696–700+[1] p. ([Opinion] 9440.) [Report from Interstate Commerce Commission reports, v. 88.] * Paper, 5c.

—— Investigation and suspension docket no. 2003, express rates on milk and cream between stations in Virginia; decided Apr. 19, 1924; report [and order] of commission. [1924.] 687–690+[1] p. ([Opinion] 9437.) [Report from Interstate Commerce Commission reports, v. 88.] * Paper, 5c.

Minneapolis and St. Louis Railroad. Finance docket no. 632, guaranty settlement with Minneapolis & St. Louis R. R. [W. H. Bremner, receiver]; decided Apr. 14, 1924; report of commission. [1924.] p. 691–694. ([Finance decision] 1297.) [From Interstate Commerce Commission reports, v. 86.] * Paper, 5c.

Minneapolis, St. Paul and Sault Ste. Marie Railway. Finance docket no. 3457, notes of Minneapolis, St. Paul & Sault Ste. Marie Ry.; decided Mar. 19, 1924; report of commission. [1924.] p. 575–577. ([Finance decision] 1261.) [From Interstate Commerce Commission reports, v. 86.] * Paper, 5c.

Misrouting. No. 14043, M. T. Cummings, receiver of M. T. Cummings Grain Company, *v.* director general, as agent, and Chicago, Burlington & Quincy Railroad Company; decided Apr. 2, 1924; report of commission. [1924.] p. 429–431. ([Opinion] 9380.) [From Interstate Commerce Commission reports, v. 88.] * Paper, 5c.

—— No. 14228, B. Mifflin-Hood Brick Company *v.* director general, as agent; decided Mar. 7, 1924; report [and order] of commission. [1924.] 205–207+[1] p. ([Opinion] 9315.) [Report from Interstate Commerce Commission reports, v. 88.] * Paper, 5c.

—— No. 14796, Santa Rosa Mercantile Company *v.* director general, as agent; decided Apr. 21, 1924; report [and order] of commission. [1924.] p. 753, [1]. ([Opinion] 9451.) [Report from Interstate Commerce Commission reports, v. 88.] * Paper, 5c.

—— No. 15013, Consolidated Coal Company of St. Louis *v.* Missouri Pacific Railroad Company et al.; decided Apr. 2, 1924; report of commission. [1924.] p. 523–524. ([Opinion] 9408.) [From Interstate Commerce Commission reports, v. 88.] * Paper, 5c.

Missouri and North Arkansas Railroad. Finance docket no. 646, guaranty settlement with Missouri & North Arkansas R. R. [J. C. Murray, receiver; decided Apr. 4, 1924; report of commission]. 1924. [1]+654-656 p. ([Finance decision] 1285.) [From Interstate Commerce Commission reports, v. 86.] * Paper, 5c.

Missouri, Kansas and Texas Railway. Finance docket no. 647, guaranty settlement with Missouri, Kansas & Texas Ry.; [and finance dockets nos. 648 and 890]; decided Apr. 24, 1924; report of commission. [1924.] p. 763-768. ([Finance decision] 1319.) [From Interstate Commerce Commission reports, v. 86.] * Paper, 5c.

Missouri Pacific Railroad. Finance docket no. 3469, bonds of Missouri Pacific R. R.; decided Mar. 25, 1924; report of commission. [1924.] p. 573-574. ([Finance decision] 1260.) [From Interstate Commerce Commission reports, v. 86.] * Paper, 5c.

Missouri Southern Railroad. Finance docket no. 652, guaranty settlement with Missouri Southern Railroad; [decided Apr. 2, 1924; report of commission]. 1924. [1]+628-630 p. ([Finance decision] 1277.) [From Interstate Commerce Commission reports, v. 86.] * Paper, 5c.

Motor-trucks. No. 13026, Wichita Motors Company *v.* Alabama & Vicksburg Railway Company et al.; [decided Mar. 7, 1924; report and order of commission]. 1924. [1]+152-157+ii p. ([Opinion] 9302.) [Report from Interstate Commerce Commission reports, v. 88.] * Paper, 5c.

—— No. 14637, Arizona, ex rel. Arizona Corporation Commission, *v.* Arizona Eastern Railroad Company et al.; decided Apr. 16, 1924; report [and order] of commission. [1924.] 679-681+[1] p. ([Opinion] 9435.) [Report from Interstate Commerce Commission reports, v. 88.] * Paper, 5c.

New Jersey, Indiana and Illinois Railroad. Finance docket.no. 3324, stock of New Jersey, Indiana & Illinois R. R.; [decided Apr. 15, 1924; report of commission]. 1924. [1]+718-720 p. ([Finance decision] 1306.) [From Interstate Commerce Commission reports, v. 86.] * Paper, 5c.

Nitrostarch. No. 14432, Trojan Powder Company *v.* director general, as agent, and Southern Pacific Company; decided Apr. 2, 1924; report of commission. [1924.] p. 447-448. ([Opinion] 9386.) [From Interstate Commerce Commission reports, v. 88.] * Paper, 5c.

Norfolk and Portsmouth Belt Line Railroad. Finance docket no. 700, guaranty settlement with Norfolk & Portsmouth Belt Line R. R.; [decided Apr. 2. 1924; report of commission]. 1924. [1]+606-608 p. ([Finance decision] 1271.) [From Interstate Commerce Commission reports, v. 86.] * Paper, 5c.

North and South Railway. Finance docket no. 3287, construction of line by North & South Railway; decided Apr. 7, 1924; report of commission. [1924.] p. 663-670. ([Finance decision] 1289.) [From Interstate Commerce Commission reports, v. 86.] * Paper, 5c.

Northern Colorado and Eastern Railroad. Finance docket no. 3431, acquisition and stock issue by Northern Colorado & Eastern R. R.; decided Mar. 28, 1924; report of commission. [1924.] p. 617-622. ([Finance decision] 1274.) [From Interstate Commerce Commission reports, v. 86.] * Paper, 5c.

Northern Pacific Railway. Finance docket no. 3244, abandonment of Red Mountain branch by Northern Pacific Ry.; decided Apr. 1, 1924; report of commission. [1924.] p. 609-611. ([Finance decision] 1272.). [From Interstate Commerce Commission reports, v. 86.] * Paper, 5c.

—— Finance docket no. 3245, abandonment of Marysville branch by Northern Pacific Ry.; decided Apr. 1, 1924; report of commission. [1924.] p. 637-639. ([Finance decision] 1279.) [From Interstate Commerce Commission reports, v. 86.] * Paper, 5c.

Ohio and Kentucky Railway. Finance docket no. 716, guaranty settlement with Ohio & Kentucky Ry.; decided Apr. 3, 1924; report of commission. [1924.] p. 649-650. ([Finance decision] 1283.) [From Interstate Commerce Commission reports, v. 86.] * Paper, 5c.

—— Finance docket no. 1344, deficit status of Ohio & Kentucky Ry.; decided Apr. 1, 1924; report of commission. [1924.] p. 581-582. ([Finance decision] 1263.) [From Interstate Commerce Commission reports, v. 86.] * Paper, 5c.

Oil Fields Short Line Railroad. Finance docket no. 3495, abandonment of Oil Fields Short Line R. R.; decided Apr. 14, 1924; report of commission. [1924.] p. 701–702. ([Finance decision] 1300.) [From Interstate Commerce Commission reports, v. 86.] * Paper, 5c.

Oil-well machinery. No. 14464, Jackson Traffic Bureau et al. *v.* Chicago, Rock Island & Pacific Railway Company et al.; decided Mar. 31, 1924; report [and order] of commission. [1924.] 373–375+[1] p. ([Opinion] 9364.) [Report from Interstate Commerce Commission reports, v. 88.] * Paper, 5c.

Oklahoma City-Ada-Atoka Railway. Finance docket no. 3328, securities of Oklahoma City-Ada-Atoka Railway; [decided Mar. 10, 1924; report of commission]. 1924. [1]+512–515 p. ([Finance decision] 1242.) [From Interstate Commerce Commission reports, v. 86.] * Paper, 5c.

Paper. No. 13802, Texas Farm & Ranch Publishing Company *v.* Ahnapee & Western Railway Company et al.; portions of 4th section application no. 700; decided Apr. 5, 1924; report [and 4th section order no. 8894] of commission. [1924.] 417–420+[1] p. ([Opinion] 9376.) [Report from Interstate Commerce Commission reports, v. 88.] * Paper, 5c.

—— No. 14103, Universal Paper Bag Company *v.* Maine Central Railroad Company et al.; decided Apr. 2, 1924; report [and order] of commission. [1924.] 593–596+[1] p. ([Opinion] 9416.) [Report from Interstate Commerce Commission reports, v. 88.] * Paper, 5c.

—— No. 14635, Jackson Paper Company *v.* Beaumont, Sour Lake & Western Railway Company et al.; portions of 4th-section applications nos. 461 and 636; decided Mar. 7, 1924; report [and orders] of commission. [1924.] 219–220+ii p. ([Opinion] 9320.) [Report from Interstate Commerce Commission reports, v. 88.] * Paper, 5c.

Paper-stock. No. 12550, Barrett Company *v.* director general, as agent, Pennsylvania Railroad Company, et al.; decided Apr. 8, 1924; report [and order] of commission. [1924.] 535–542+[1] p. ([Opinion] 9410.) [Report from Interstate Commerce Commission reports, v. 88.] * Paper, 5c.

Passenger rates. No. 14786, Alabama passenger fares and charges, in matter of intrastate fares and charges of Alabama Great Southern Railroad Company and other carriers in Alabama; decided Apr. 14, 1924; report of commission. [1924.] p. 621–630. ([Opinion] 9424.) [From Interstate Commerce Commission reports, v. 88.] * Paper, 5c.‛

Peaches. No. 13718, M. Piowaty & Sons, Incorporated, *v.* director general, as agent, Idaho Central Railroad Company, et al.; decided Apr. 2, 1924; report [and order] of commission. [1924.] 597–599+[1] p. ([Opinion] 9417.) [Report from Interstate Commerce Commission reports, v. 88.] * Paper, 5c.

Peanuts. No. 13534, Tuscaloosa Cotton Seed Oil Company *v.* Alabama Great Southern Railway Company et al.; [decided Mar. 7, 1924; report and order of commission]. 1924. [1]+258–260+[1] p. ([Opinion] 9330.) [Report from Interstate Commerce Commission reports, v. 88.] * Paper, 5c.

—— No. 14177, Southern Cotton Oil Company *v.* director general, as agent; [decided May 1, 1924; report of commission]. 1924. [1]+154–156 p. ([Opinion] 9483.) [From Interstate Commerce Commission reports, v. 89.] * Paper, 5c.

Peoria Railway Terminal Company. Finance docket no. 736, guaranty settlement with Peoria Railway Terminal Co. [W. G. Bierd and H. J. Battles, receivers]; decided Apr. 4, 1924; report of commission. [1924.] p. 651–653. ([Finance decision] 1284.) [From Interstate Commerce Commission reports, v. 86.] * Paper, 5c.

Phosphates. No. 14854, Gulfport Fertilizer Company *v.* Louisville & Nashville Railroad Company; decided Mar. 7, 1924; report [and order] of commission. [1924.] 129–130+[1] p. ([Opinion] 9297.) [An incorrect print of this decision was also issued. Report from Interstate Commerce Commission reports, v. 88.] * Paper, 5c.

Phosphorus. No. 14194, Diamond Match Company *v.* director general, as agent, Lehigh Valley Railroad Company, et al.; decided Apr. 2, 1924; report [and order] of commission. [1924.] 435–437+[1] p. ([Opinion] 9382.) [Report from Interstate Commerce Commission reports, v. 88.] * Paper, 5c.

Pickles. No. 13758. Ridenour-Baker Mercantile Company et al. *v.* Atchison, Topeka & Santa Fe Railway Company et al.; decided Mar. 7. 1924; report [and order] of commission. [1924.] 273–276+ii p. ([Opinion] 9335.) [Report from Interstate Commerce Commission reports, v. 88.] *Paper, 5c.

Pipe. No. 11084, Prairie Pipe Line Company *v.* director general, as agent, St. Louis-San Francisco Railway Company, et al.; portions of 4th section applications nos. 630 and 799; decided Mar. 8, 1924; report [and orders] of commission. [1924.] 167–176+iii p. ([Opinion] 9305.) [Report from Interstate Commerce Commission reports, v. 88.] *Paper, 5c.

Pittsburg, Shawmut and Northern Railroad. Finance docket no. 3546, Pittsburg, Shawmut & Northern receiver's certificates and note [John D. Dickson, receiver; decided Apr. 18, 1924; report of commission]. 1924. [1]+734–736 p. ([Finance decision] 1312.) [From Interstate Commerce Commission reports, v. 86.] *Paper, 5c.

Pluto water. No. 14720, French Lick Springs Hotel Company *v.* Alabama Great Southern Railway Company et al.; decided Apr. 2, 1924; report of commission. [1924.] p. 503–504. ([Opinion] 9403.) [From Interstate Commerce Commission reports, v. 88.] *Paper, 5c.

Potatoes. No. 13578, Peycke Bros. Commission Company et al. *v.* director general, as agent; decided Apr. 16, 1924; report [and order] of commission. [1924.] 617–618+[1] p. ([Opinion] 9422.) [Report from Interstate Commerce Commission reports, v. 88.] *Paper, 5c.

Prescott and Northwestern Railroad. Finance docket no. 211, deficit settlement with Prescott & Northwestern R. R.; decided Apr. 11, 1924; report of commission. [1924.] p. 677–678. ([Finance decision] 1292.) [From Interstate Commerce Commission reports, v. 86.] *Paper, 5c.

Preserved fruit. No. 12253. Goodwin Preserving Company, Incorporated, *v.* Louisville Bridge & Terminal Railway Company et al.; decided Apr. 8, 1924; report [and order] of commission. [1924.] 725–727+ii p. ([Opinion] 9445.) [Report from Interstate Commerce Commission reports, v. 88.] *Paper, 5c.

Railroad accidents. Joint report of director of Bureau of Safety and chief inspector of Bureau of Locomotive Inspection in re investigation of accident which occurred on Pennsylvania Railroad near St. George, Pa., on Jan. 30, 1924. [1924.] 17 p. il. *Paper, 10c. A 24—717

Railroad employees. Wage statistics, class 1 steam roads in United States, including 15 switching and terminal companies, Jan. 1924; [prepared in] Bureau of Statistics. [1924.] [4] p. il. oblong large 8° [Imprint date incorrectly given on publication as 1923.] †

—— Same, Mar. 1924; [prepared in] Bureau of Statistics. [1924.] [4] p. il. oblong large 8° [Imprint date incorrectly given on publication as 1923.] †

Railroads. Freight and passenger service operating statistics of class 1 steam roads in United States, compiled from 160 reports of freight statistics representing 175 roads and from 158 reports of passenger statistics representing 173 roads (switching and terminal companies not included), Mar. 1924 and 1923 [and 3 months ended with Mar. 1924 and 1923; prepared in] Bureau of Statistics. Mar. 1924. [2] p. oblong large 8° [Subject to revision.] †

—— Operating revenues and operating expenses of class 1 steam roads in United States (for 193 steam roads, including 15 switching and terminal companies), Mar. 1924 and 1923 [and] 3 months ended with Mar. 1924 and 1923; [prepared in] Bureau of Statistics. Mar. 1924. 1 p. oblong large 8° [Subject to revision.] †

—— Operating revenues and operating expenses of large steam roads, selected items for roads with annual operating revenues above $25,000,000, Mar. 1924 and 1923 [and] 3 months ended with Mar. 1924 and 1923; [prepared in] Bureau of Statistics. Mar. 1924. [2] p. oblong large 8° [Subject to revision.] †

—— Operating statistics of large steam roads, selected items for Mar. 1924, compared with Mar. 1923, for roads with annual operating revenues above $25,000,000; [prepared in] Bureau of Statistics. Mar. 1924. [2] p. oblong large 8° [Subject to revision.] †

Railroads—Continued. Revenue traffic statistics of class 1 steam roads in United States, including mixed-train service (compiled from 162 reports representing 177 steam roads, switching and terminal companies not included), Feb. 1924 and 1923 [and] 2 months ended with Feb. 1924 and 1923; [prepared in] Bureau of Statistics. Feb. 1924. 1 p. oblong large 8° [Subject to revision.] †

Rails. No. 13378, Lakewood Engineering Company *v.* Baltimore & Ohio Railroad Company et al.; [decided Apr. 2, 1924; report of commission]. 1924. [1]+588–592 p. ([Opinion] 9415.) [From Interstate Commerce Commission reports, v. 88.] * Paper, 5c.

—— No. 14593, Mid-Continent Equipment & Machinery Company *v.* Manufacturers Railway Company et al.; decided Mar. 7, 1924; report [and order] of commission. [1924.] 217–218+[1] p. ([Opinion] 9319.) [Report from Interstate Commerce Commission reports, v. 88.] * Paper, 5c.

Reconsignment. No. 13705, Sam Litman and Ben Ossep *v.* director general, as agent; decided Mar. 7, 1924; report [and order] of commission. [1924.] 199–201+[1] p. ([Opinion] 9313.) [Report from Interstate Commerce Commission reports, v. 88.] * Paper, 5c.

—— No. 14705, C. W. Hull Company *v.* director general, as agent; [decided Apr. 21, 1924; report and order of commission]. 1924. [1]+44–46+[1] p. ([Opinion] 9465.) [Report from Interstate Commerce Commission reports, v. 89.] * Paper, 5c.

Refrigeration. No. 12158, Frye & Company *v.* Great Northern Railway Company et al.; [no. 12158 (sub-no. 1), Swift & Company et al. *v.* same]; decided Apr. 7, 1924: report [and order] of commission. [1924.] 477–486+ ii p. ([Opinion] 9397.) [Report from Interstate Commerce Commission reports, v. 88.] * Paper, 5c.

Roasted ore. No. 15080, Grasselli Chemical Company *v.* Baltimore & Ohio Railroad Company et al.: decided Mar. 20, 1924; report [and order] of commission. [1924.] 337–339+[1] p. ([Opinion] 9355.) [Report from Interstate Commerce Commission reports, v. 88.] * Paper, 5c.

Roll-scale. No. 14582, Hickman. Williams & Company *v.* director general, as agent; decided Apr. 2, 1924; report [and order] of commission. [1924.] 501–502+[1] p. ([Opinion] 9402.) [Report from Interstate Commerce Commission reports, v. 88.] * Paper, 5c.

Rollers (wooden). No. 14523, List & Gifford Construction Company *v.* Mobile & Ohio Railroad Company et al.; decided Apr. 2, 1924; report [and order] of commission. [1924.] 499–500+[1] p. ([Opinion] 9401.) [Report from Interstate Commerce Commission reports, v. 88.] * Paper, 5c.

Roofing. No. 12635, Co-Operative Oil & Paint Company et al. *v.* director general, as agent, Baltimore & Ohio Railroad Company, et al.; decided Apr. 16, 1924; report [and order] of commission. [1924.] 747–749+[1] p. ([Opinion] 9449.) [Report from Interstate Commerce Commission reports, v. 88.] * Paper, 5c.

Rosin. No. 14251. Sales Department Gillican-Chipley Company, Incorporated, *v.* director general. as agent; decided Apr. 2, 1924; report [and order] of commission. [1924.] 441–443+[1] p. ([Opinion] 9384.) [Report from Interstate Commerce Commission reports, v. 88.] * Paper, 5c.

Sand. No. 13959. Edward L. Scheidenhelm Company *v.* Chicago, Burlington & Quincy Railroad Company: decided Mar. 7, 1924; report [and order] of commission. [1924.] 319–320+[1] p. ([Opinion] 9350.) [Report from Interstate Commerce Commission reports, v. 88.] * Paper, 5c.

—— No. 14197. Edward L. Scheidenhelm Company *v.* Chicago, Milwaukee & St. Paul Railway Company et al.; [no. 14406, same *v.* Chicago & North Western Railway Company et al.]; decided Mar. 7, 1924; report of commission. [1924.] p. 321–324. ([Opinion] 9351.) [From Interstate Commerce Commission reports, v. 88.] * Paper, 5c.

—— No. 15088, Owens Bottle Company *v.* director general, as agent, Pennsylvania Railroad Company, et al.; decided Mar. 20, 1924; report [and order] of commission. [1924.] 285–286+[1] p. ([Opinion] 9339.) [Report from Interstate Commerce Commission reports, v. 88.] * Paper, 5c.

San Luis Central Railroad. Finance docket no. 3512, San Luis Central Railroad bonds; decided Apr. 17. 1924; report of commission. [1924.] p. 727–728. ([Finance decision] 1309.) [From Interstate Commerce Commission reports, v. 86.] * Paper, 5c.

San Luis Southern Railway. Finance docket no. 3533, San Luis Southern receiver's certificates [C. A. Robinson, receiver; decided Apr. 17, 1924; report of commission]. 1924. [1]+724–726 p. ([Finance decision] 1308.) [From Interstate Commerce Commission reports, v. 86.] * Paper, 5c.

Shooks. No. 14020, J. D. Hollingshead Company *v.* Aberdeen & Rockfish Railroad Company et al.; decided Mar. 7, 1924; report [and order] of commission. [1924.] 191–195+xv p. ([Opinion] 9311.) [Report from Interstate Commerce Commission reports, v. 88.] * Paper, 5c.

Silos. No. 15111, Michigan Silo Company *v.* Chicago & North Western Railway Company et al.; decided Apr. 2, 1924; report [and order] of commission. [1924.] 467–468+ii p. ([Opinion] 9393.) [Report from Interstate Commerce Commission reports, v. 88.] * Paper, 5c.

Sisal hemp. Investigation and suspension docket no. 2016, sisal from Gulf ports stored at Indianapolis, Ind., for reshipment (2); [decided Apr. 19, 1924; report and order of commission]. 1924. [1]+704–706+[1] p. ([Opinion] 9442.) [Report from Interstate Commerce Commission reports, v. 88.] * Paper, 5c.

South Georgia Railway. Finance docket no. 2615, South Georgia Railway capital stock; decided Apr. 8, 1924; report of commission on rehearing. [1924.] p. 713–717. ([Finance decision] 1305.) [From Interstate Commerce Commission reports, v. 86.] * Paper, 5c.

Southern Railway. Finance docket no. 3514, Southern Railway equipment trust, series Y; decided Mar. 31, 1924; report of commission. [1924.] p. 623–626. ([Finance decision] 1275.) [From Interstate Commerce Commission reports, v. 86.] * Paper, 5c.

Steam-turbines. No. 11911, General Electric Company *v.* director general, as agent, New York Central Railroad Company, et al.; decided Apr. 11, 1924; report [and order] of commission on further hearing. [1924.] 643–644+[1] p. ([Opinion] 9427.) [Report from Interstate Commerce Commission reports, v. 88.] * Paper, 5c.

Steamboats. Schedule of sailings (as furnished by steamship companies named herein) of steam vessels which are registered under laws of United States and which are intended to load general cargo at ports in United States for foreign destinations, May 15–June 30, 1924, no. 21; issued by Section of Tariffs, Bureau of Traffic. 1924. iii+43 p. 4° [Monthly. No. 21 cancels no. 20.] †

                                           22—26610

Stephenville North and South Texas Railway. Finance docket no. 3459, control of Stephenville North & South Texas Ry. by St. Louis Southwestern Ry. Co. of Texas; [decided Apr. 11, 1924; report of commission]. 1924. [1]+688–690 p. ([Finance decision] 1296.) [From Interstate Commerce Commission reports, v. 86.] * Paper, 5c.

Storage. Investigation and suspension docket no. 2061, storage in transit on apples at Alabama and Tennessee points; decided May 1, 1924; report [and order] of commission. [1924.] 135–136+[1] p. ([Opinion] 9477.) [Report from Interstate Commerce Commission reports, v. 89.] * Paper, 5c.

—— No. 14431, Hendee Manufacturing Company *v.* director general, as agent; [decided Apr. 16, 1924; report of commission]. 1924. [1]+38–40 p. ([Opinion] 9463.) [From Interstate Commerce Commission reports, v. 89.] * Paper, 5c.

Straw. No. 14939, Indiana Board & Filler Company *v.* Wabash Railway Company et al.; [decided Apr. 21, 1924; report of commission]. 1924. [1]+754–756 p. ([Opinion] 9452.) [From Interstate Commerce Commission reports, v. 88.] * Paper, 5c.

Strawberries. No. 14928, Headington & Hedenbergh *v.* director general, as agent; decided Apr. 16, 1924; report [and order] of commission. [1924.] 745–746+[1] p. ([Opinion] 9448.) [Report from Interstate Commerce Commission reports, v. 88.] * Paper, 5c.

Sugar. No. 13656, Early-Foster Company *v.* Atchison, Topeka & Santa Fe Railway Company et al.; portions of 4th section applications nos. 461 and 462; decided Apr. 7, 1924; report [and 4th section order no. 8896] of commission. [1924.] 507–511+[1] p. ([Opinion] 9405.) [Report from Interstate Commerce Commission reports, v. 88.] * Paper, 5c.

Sugar—Continued. No. 14650, Lynchburg Traffic Bureau *v.* Pennsylvania Railroad Company et al.; decided Apr. 2, 1924; report [and order] of commission. [1924.] 619–620+[1] p. ([Opinion] 9423.) [Report from Interstate Commerce Commission reports, v. 88.] * Paper 5c.

Sugar-beet. No. 14362, Interstate Sugar Company et al. *v.* Denver & Rio Grande Railroad Company et al.; [decided Apr. 2, 1924; report of commission]. 1924. [1]+432–434 p. ([Opinion] 9381.) [From Interstate Commerce Commission reports, v. 88.] * Paper, 5c.

—— No. 14562, Amalgamated Sugar Company *v.* director general, as agent, and Oregon Short Line Railroad Company; decided Mar. 7, 1924; report of commission. [1924.] p. 233–234. ([Opinion] 9325.) [From Interstate Commerce Commission reports, v. 88.] * Paper, 5c.

Sullivan County Railroad. Finance docket no. 3499, bonds of Sullivan County R. R.; decided Mar. 20, 1924; report of commission. [1924.] p. 601–602. ([Finance decision] 1269.) [From Interstate Commerce Commission reports, v. 86.] * Paper, 5c.

Sulphuric acid. No. 14013, Seaboard By-Product Coke Company *v.* director general, as agent; decided Mar. 7, 1924; report of commission. [1924.] p. 261–263. ([Opinion] 9331.) [From Interstate Commerce Commission reports, v. 88.] * Paper, 5c.

Switching. No. 13205, Chicago, Lake Shore & South Bend Railway Company *v.* Lake Erie & Western Railroad Company et al.; decided Apr. 2, 1924; [report and order of commission]. [1924.] 525–534+ii p. ([Opinion] 9409.) [Report from Interstate Commerce Commission reports, v. 88.] * Paper, 5c.

Switching charges. Investigation and suspension docket no. 2012; trackage charges at St. Louis, Mo.; decided Apr. 23, 1924; report [and order] of commission. [1924.] 693–695+[1] p. ([Opinion] 9439.) [Report from Interstate Commerce Commission reports, v. 88.] * Paper, 5c.

—— No. 11636, St. Louis-San Francisco Railway Company *v.* Northern Alabama Railway Company et al.; decided Mar. 13, 1924; report of commission. [1924.] p. 107–110. ([Opinion] 9292.) [From Interstate Commerce Commission reports, v. 88.] * Paper, 5c.

—— No. 11820, Missouri Portland Cement Company *v.* director general, as agent; [decided Apr. 7, 1924; report and order of commission on further hearing]. 1924. [1]+492–498+[1] p. ([Opinion] 9400.) [Report from Interstate Commerce Commission reports, v. 88.] * Paper, 5c.

—— No. 13367, Board of Commerce of Lockport, N. Y., *v.* New York Central Railroad Company et al.; [decided Apr. 30, 1924; report and order of commission]. 1924. [1]+144–148+[1] p. ([Opinion] 9480.) [Report from Interstate Commerce Commission reports, v. 89.] * Paper, 5c.

—— No. 14277, Barber Asphalt Company *v.* Louisville & Nashville Railroad Company et al.; [no. 14277 (sub-no. 1), Certain-teed Products Corporation *v.* same]; decided Mar. 15, 1924; report [and order] of commission. [1924.] 307–311+[1] p. ([Opinion] 9348.) [Report from Interstate Commerce Commission reports, v. 88.] * Paper, 5c.

—— No. 14674, Board of Trade of Detroit [Mich.] *v.* Wabash Railway Company et al.; decided Apr. 2, 1924; report [and order] of commission. [1924.] 413–416+[1] p. ([Opinion] 9375.) [Report from Interstate Commerce Commission reports, v. 88.] * Paper, 5c.

—— No. 14772, General Fire Extinguisher Company *v.* director general, as agent; decided Apr. 2, 1924; report [and order] of commission. [1924.] 521–522+[1] p. ([Opinion] 9407.) [Report from Interstate Commerce Commission reports, v. 88.] * Paper, 5c.

—— No. 15125, Crown Cork & Seal Company *v.* director general, as agent, and Baltimore & Ohio Railroad Company; decided Mar. 20, 1924; report of commission. [1924.] p. 305–306. ([Opinion] 9347.) [From Interstate Commerce Commission reports, v. 88.] * Paper, 5c.

Syrups. No. 14610, Steuart, Son & Company *v.* director general, as agent, and Baltimore & Ohio Railroad Company; decided Apr. 2, 1924; report [and order] of commission. [1924.] 469–471+[1] p. ([Opinion] 9394.) [Report from Interstate Commerce Commission reports, v. 88.] * Paper, 5c.

Tallow. No. 15054, Palmolive Company *v.* Chicago, Milwaukee & St. Paul Railway Company; [decided Apr. 21, 1924; report and order of commission]. 1924. [1]+756–758+[1] p. ([Opinion] 9453.) [Report from Interstate Commerce Commission reports, v. 88.] * Paper, 5c.

Tankage. No. 14205, Darling & Company *v.* director general, as agent; [decided Mar. 7, 1924; report and order of commission]. 1924. [1]+208–210+ [1] p. ([Opinion] 9316.) [Report from Interstate Commerce Commission reports, v. 88.] * Paper, 5c.

Tanks. No. 14525, Parkersburg Rig & Reel Company *v.* Texas & Pacific Railway Company et al.; decided Apr. 2, 1924; report [and order] of commission. [1924.] 463–466+ii p. ([Opinion] 9392.) [Report from Interstate Commerce Commission reports, v. 88.] * Paper, 5c.

Telegraph. No. 14797, Henry M. Davis, as mayor of St. Clairsville, Ohio, *v.* Western Union Telegraph Company; decided Apr. 2, 1924; report [and order] of commission. [1924.] 489–491+[1] p. ([Opinion] 9399.) [Report from Interstate Commerce Commission reports, v. 88.] * Paper, 5c.

Time. No. 10122, standard time zone investigation; decided Mar. 24, 1924; 11th supplemental report [and order] of commission. [1924.] 343–344+ [1] p. ([Opinion] 9357.) [Report from Interstate Commerce Commission reports, v. 88.] * Paper, 5c.

Tomatoes. No. 13859, Isabelle C. Gilbert and Addison E. Coddington, doing business as Harry C. Gilbert Company, *v.* Louisville & Nashville Railroad Company et al.; decided Apr. 2, 1924; report [and order] of commission. [1924.] 405–406+ii p. ([Opinion] 9372.) [Report from Interstate Commerce Commission reports, v. 88.] * Paper, 5c.

Trinity Valley and Northern Railway. Finance docket no. 1560, deficit settlement with Trinity valley & Northern Ry.; decided Apr. 8, 1924; report of commission. [1924.] p. 659–660. ([Finance decision] 1287.) [From Interstate Commerce Commission reports, v. 86.] * Paper, 5c.

Union Pacific Railroad. Finance docket no. 3519, Union Pacific equipment trust, series D; [decided Mar. 29, 1924; report of commission]. 1924. [1]+ 612–616 p. ([Finance decision] 1273.) [From Interstate Commerce Commission reports, v. 86.] * Paper, 5c.

United Railway. Finance docket no. 2570, deficit status of United Railway; decided Apr. 7, 1924; report of commission. [1924.] p. 661–662. ([Finance decision] 1288.) [From Interstate Commerce Commission reports, v. 86.] * Paper, 5c.

Upper Sandusky Telephone Company. Finance docket no. 3492, purchase of properties of Upper Sandusky Telephone Co. by Ohio Bell Telephone Co.; decided Mar. 29, 1924; report of commission. [1924.] p. 599–600. ([Finance decision] 1268.) [From Interstate Commerce Commission reports, v. 86.] * Paper, 5c.

Valley and Siletz Railroad. Finance docket no. 3389, construction of extension by Valley & Siletz R. R.; decided Mar. 19, 1924; report of commission. [1924.] p. 563–566. ([Finance decision] 1257.) [From Interstate Commerce Commission reports, v. 86.] * Paper, 5c.

Vegetables. No. 14469, Bender, Streibig & Company *v.* Illinois Central Railroad Company et al.; [decided Apr. 2, 1924; report and order of commission]. 1924. [1]+474–476+[1] p. ([Opinion] 9396.) [Report from Interstate Commerce Commission reports, v. 88.] * Paper, 5c.

Veneers. No. 14631, Boher & Hosfeld et al. *v.* Boston & Maine Railroad et al.; decided Apr. 2, 1924; report [and order] of commission. [1924.] 449–452+ [1] p. ([Opinion] 9387.) [Report from Interstate Commerce Commission reports, v. 88.] * Paper, 5c.

Visalia Electric Railroad. Finance docket no. 3428, acquisition and operation of line by Visalia Electric R. R.; [decided Apr. 9, 1924; report of commission]. 1924. [1]+674–676 p. ([Finance decision] 1291.) [From Interstate Commerce Commission reports, v. 86.] * Paper, 5c.

Warren and Ouachita Valley Railway. Finance docket no. 2461, deficit settlement with Warren & Ouachita Valley Ry.; decided Mar. 29, 1924; report of commission. [1924.] p. 597–598. ([Finance decision] 1267.) [From Interstate Commerce Commission reports, v. 86.] * Paper, 5c.

Wheat. No. 14542, Interstate Milling Company *v.* Baltimore & Ohio Railroad Company et al.; decided Mar. 7, 1924; report [and order] of commission. [1924.] 229–232+[1] p. ([Opinion] 9324.) [Report from Interstate Commerce Commission reports, v. 88.] * Paper, 5c.

White River Railroad. Finance docket no. 1365, deficit settlement with White River R. R.; decided Apr. 16, 1924; report of commission. [1924.] p. 703–704. ([Finance decision] 1301.) [From Interstate Commerce Commission reports, v. 86.] * Paper, 5c.

Wood-pulp. No. 13730, Pulp Wood Company et al. *v.* director general, as agent, Chicago & North Western Railway Company, et al.; [decided Mar. 7, 1924: report and order of commission]. 1924. [1]+196–198+[1] p. ([Opinion] 9312.) [Report from Interstate Commerce Commission reports, v. 88.] * Paper, 5c.

—— No. 13904, Iroquois Pulp & Paper Company *v.* Greenwich & Johnsonville Railway Company et al.; decided Mar. 7, 1924; report of commission. [1924.] p. 255–257. ([Opinion] 9329.) [From Interstate Commerce Commission reports, v. 88.] * Paper, 5c.

—— No. 14082, International Paper Company *v.* director general, as agent, et al.; decided Mar. 7, 1924; report [and order] of commission. [1924.] 211–212+[1] p. ([Opinion] 9317.) [Report from Interstate Commerce Commission reports, v. 88.] * Paper, 5c.

Wyoming Railway. Finance docket no. 1491, deficit settlement with Wyoming Ry.; decided Apr. 3, 1924; report of commission. [1924.] p. 657–658. ([Finance decision] 1286.) [From Interstate Commerce Commission reports, v. 86.] * Paper, 5c.

—— Finance docket no. 2839, construction of extension by Wyoming Ry.; decided Apr. 15, 1924; report of commission. [1924.] p. 707–710. ([Finance decision] 1303.) [From Interstate Commerce Commission reports, v. 86.] * Paper, 5c.

JUSTICE DEPARTMENT

American Hawaiian Steamship Co. v. United States and Prince Line (Ltd.) *v.* United States, judgments rendered against Government by District Courts as submitted by Attorney General. May 22, 1924. 4 p. (H. doc. 305, 68th Cong. 1st sess.) * Paper, 5c.

American Smelting and Refining Company. No. 2348, Court of Customs Appeals, American Smelting & Refining Co. *v.* United States; brief for United States. 1924. cover-title, 12 p. ‡

Anderson, Hubert C. In Court of Claims, Hubert C. Anderson *v.* United States, no. 167 Departmental; defendant's request for findings of fact, and brief. [1924.] p. 1–8, large 8° ‡

Andrus, John E. In Court of Claims, John E. Andrus *v.* United States, no. 242–A; defendant's objections to plaintiff's request for findings of fact, defendant's request for findings of fact, defendant's brief. [1924.] p. 295–322, large 8° ‡

Anglo American Industrial Diamond Company, Incorporated. No. 2371, Court of Customs Appeals, Anglo American Industrial Diamond Co., Inc., *v.* United States; brief for United States. 1924. cover-title, 11 p. ‡

Atlantic, Gulf and Pacific Steamship Corporation. No. 2222, circuit court of appeals for 4th circuit, United States *v.* L. vernon Miller, trustee in bankruptcy of Atlantic, Gulf & Pacific Steamship Corporation, bankrupt, and Merchants National Bank of Baltimore. Md., appeal from district court for district of Maryland, at Baltimore, in bankruptcy; brief of appellant. 1924. cover-title, i+15 p. ‡

Atwater, Wm. C., & Co. In Court of Claims, Wm. C. Atwater & Co. *v.* United States, no. D–125; special and general demurrer [and] brief. [1924.] p. 21–32, large 8° ‡

Bashara, M. J. No. 942, in Supreme Court, Oct. term, 1923, M. J. Bashara *v.* George C. Hopkins, collector of internal revenue [for 2d district of Texas], on petition for writ of certiorari to circuit court of appeals for 5th circuit; brief for respondent in opposition. 1924. cover-title, 4 p. ‡

Bernard, Judac & Co. No. 2363, Court of Customs Appeals, Bernard, Judae & Co. *v.* United States; brief for United States. 1924. cover-title, 16 p. ‡

Brilliant Coal Company. In Court of Claims, Brilliant Coal Company *v.* United States, no. C–671; defendant's motion for new trial. [1924.] p. 63–76, large 8° ‡

Brovig, Th. Th. Brovig *v.* United States (steamship Babcock), record of judgment rendered against Government by district court for eastern district of Virginia, sitting in admiralty. in case of Th. Brovig *v.* United States (steamship Babcock). May 22, 1924. 3 p. (H. doc. 302, 68th Cong. 1st sess.) * Paper, 5c.

Brown & Roese. No. 2373, Court of Customs Appeals, United States *v.* Brown & Roese; brief for United States. 1924. cover-title, 13 p. ‡

Butterworth-Judson Corporation. No. 912, in Supreme Court, Oct. term, 1923, United States et al. *v.* Butterworth-Judson Corporation et al., appeal from circuit court of appeals for 2d circuit; motion to advance. 1924. cover-title, 3 p. ‡

Childs, Edwards H. No. 992, in Supreme Court. Oct. term, 1923, Edwards H. Childs, trustee in bankruptcy, *v.* United States, on petition for writ of certiorari to circuit court of appeals for 2d circuit; brief for United States in opposition. 1924. cover-title, 1 p. ‡

Claims. Four judgments rendered against United States, list of judgments rendered against Government by District Courts, as submitted by Attorney General, which require appropriation for their payment. May 22, 1924. 4 p. (H. doc. 303, 68th Cong. 1st sess.) * Paper, 5c.

Commercial Diamond Company. No. 2326, Court of Customs Appeals, Commercial Diamond Company *v.* United States; brief for United States. 1924. cover-title, 12 p. ‡

Dorris Motor Car Company. In Court of Claims, Dorris Motor Car Company *v.* United States, no. 389–B; defendant's objections to claimant's request for findings of fact, defendant's request for findings of fact, defendant's brief. [1924.] p. 69–87, large 8° ‡

Farrell, James, & Co. No. 2350, Court of Customs Appeals, James Farrell & Co. *v.* United States; brief for United States. 1924. cover-title, 8 p. ‡

Ferries Company. No. 298, in Supreme Court, Oct. term, 1923, Ferries Company *v.* United States, appeal from Court of Claims; brief for United States. 1924. cover-title, 15 p. ‡

Fidelity and Deposit Company of Maryland. No. 938, in Supreme Court, Oct. term, 1923, United States *v.* Fidelity & Deposit Company of Maryland, appeal from Court of Claims; brief in opposition to appellee's motion to dismiss or affirm. 1924. cover-title, 4 p. ‡

Fish, O. B. No. 2266, Court of Customs Appeals. O. B. Fish *v.* United States; supplemental brief for United States. 1924. cover-title, 7 p. .‡

Former Corporation. In Court of Claims, Former Corporation (formerly Philipsborn's Corporation) *v.* United States, no. D–244; demurrer [and] brief. [1924.] p. 5–9, large 8° ‡

Frey & Son, Incorporated. No. 2194, circuit court of appeals, 4th circuit, Frey & Son, Inc., *v.* United States [and] Shipping Board Emergency Fleet Corporation; brief of appellees. 1924. cover-title, i+13 p. ‡

Fuller, George A., Company, Incorporated. No. 2485, in district court for district of Kansas, 1st division, United States *v.* George A. Fuller Company (Inc.); brief of plaintiff in support of amended petition and on damages. 1924. cover-title, iii+114 p. ‡

Grant, C. S., & Co., Incorporated. No. 2343, Court of Customs Appeals, C. S. Grant & Co., Inc., *v.* United States; brief for United States. 1924. cover-title, 8 p. ‡

Huron Navigation Corporation. In Court of Claims, Huron Navigation Corporation *v.* United States, no. 34755; defendant's objections to plaintiff's proposed findings of fact, defendant's request for findings of fact, and brief. [1924.] p. 439–488, large 8° ‡

Interocean Oil Company. In Court of Claims, Interocean Oil Company *v.* United States, no. D–267; demurrer [and] brief. [1924.] p. 13–19, large 8° ‡

Iselin, William, & Co. No. B–13, in Court of Claims, William E. Iselin [et al.], copartners, doing business under firm name of William Iselin & Company, *v.* United States; defendant's objections to plaintiffs' request for findings of fact, defendant's request for findings of fact, and brief. 1924· cover-title, p. 329–375. ‡

Jeffrey Manufacturing Company. In equity, no. —, in district court in and for southern district of Ohio, eastern division, United States *v.* Jeffrey Manufacturing Company et al.; petition. 1924. cover-title, 35 p. ‡

Kuttroff, Pickhardt & Co., Incorporated. No. 2347, Court of Customs Appeals, Kuttroff, Pickhardt & Company, Inc., *v.* United States; brief for United States. 1924. cover-title, 39 p. ‡

—— No. 2356, Court of Customs Appeals, Kuttroff, Pickhardt & Company, Inc., *v.* United States; brief for United States. 1924. cover-title, 7 p. ‡

—— No. 2365, Court of Customs Appeals, Kuttroff, Pickhardt & Company, Inc., *v.* United States; brief for United States. 1924. cover-title, 9 p. ‡

—— No. 2366, Court of Customs Appeals, Kuttroff, Pickhardt & Company, Inc., *v.* United States; brief for United States. 1924. cover-title, 18 p. ‡

Lafayette Warehouse Company. In Court of Claims, Harris P. Rallston, William F[D]. Maginnis, liquidators of Lafayette Warehouse Co., *v.* United States, no. 178–A; defendant's objections to claimants' request for findings of fact, defendant's request for findings of fact, and brief. [1924.] p. 37–54, large 8° ‡

Lake Calvenia, steamship. No. 2230, in circuit court of appeals, 4th circuit, United States, owner of steamship Lake Calvenia, *v.* Standard Oil Company of New Jersey, owner and claimant of steamship H. H. Rogers; brief for United States. 1924. cover-title, i+33 p. ‡

Lorillard, P., Company. No. [4], in Supreme Court, Oct. term, 1924, United States *v.* P. Lorillard Company, appeal from Court of Claims; brief for United States. 1924. cover-title, i+31 p. ‡

McClintic-Marshall Company. In Court of Claims, McClintic-Marshall Company *v.* United States, no. A–250; defendant's objections to claimant's request for findings of fact, defendant's request for findings of fact, defendant's brief. [1924.] p. 247–266, large 8° ‡

McKesson & Robbins, Incorporated. No. 2341, Court of Customs Appeals, McKesson & Robbins, Inc., *v.* United States; brief for United States. 1924. cover-title, 17 p. ‡

Maple Flooring Manufacturers Association. No. 920, in Supreme Court, Oct. term, 1923, Maple Flooring Manufacturers Association et al. *v.* United States, appeal from district court for western district of Michigan, southern division; motion by United States to advance. 1924. cover-title, 3 p. ‡

Middleton & Co. No. 2179, circuit court of appeals, 4th district, United States *v.* Middleton & Co., for themselves and as agents for and on behalf of Teikoku Menkwa Kabushiki Kaisha, Japanese corporation, and Teikoku Menkwa Kabushiki Kaisha, Carolina Company, and Standard Marine Insurance Company, Limited; brief for United States. 1924. cover-title, i+97 p. ‡

National Fruit Products Company. In Court of Claims, National Fruit Products Company *v.* United States, [no.] B–78; defendant's request for findings of fact, and brief. [1924.] p. 59–62, large 8° ‡

New York and Cuba Mail Steamship Company. No. —; in Supreme Court, Oct. term, 1923, United States *v.* New York and Cuba Mail Steamship Company; petition for writ of certiorari to circuit court of appeals for 2d circuit and brief in support thereof. 1924. cover-title, 5 p. ‡

—— United States circuit court of appeals for 2d circuit, decided Feb. 18, 1924, New York & Cuba Mail Steamship Company *v.* United States, no. 231, Oct. term, 1923, in error to district court for southern district of New York; [opinion of court]. [1924.] p. 25–29. ‡

Oklahoma. No. 15, original, in Supreme Court, Oct. term, 1923, Oklahoma *v.* Texas, United States, intervener; suggestions of United States in response to order of May 5, 1924. [1924.] cover-title, 20 p. ‡

Pearman, T. E. No. 2358, Court of Customs Appeals, T. E. Pearman and A. Murphy & Co. *v.* United States; brief for United States. 1924. cover-title, 9 p. ‡

Penick & Ford, Limited, Incorporated. No. 2345, Court of Customs Appeals, Penick & Ford, Ltd., Inc., *v.* United States; brief for United States. 1924. cover-title, 18 p. ‡

Reading Company. No. 34747, in Court of Claims, Reading Company [successor to Philadelphia & Reading Ry. Company], *v.* United States; defendant's objections to plaintiff's motion for amendment of findings of fact filed Nov. 5, 1923, and for new trial [defendant's request for additional findings of fact, and conclusion of law]. 1924. cover-title, p. 331–375, large 8° ‡

Real Estate Title Insurance and Trust Company of Philadelphia. No. —, in Supreme Court, Oct. term, 1923, Ephraim Lederer, collector of internal revenue [for 1st district of Pennsylvania], *v.* Real Estate Title Insurance & Trust Company of Philadelphia; petition for writ of certiorari to circuit court of appeals for 3d circuit and brief in support thereof. 1924. cover-title, 19 p. ‡

—— United States circuit court of appeals for 3d circuit, Oct. term, 1923, no. 3071 (list 70), Ephraim Lederer, collector [of internal revenue for 1st district of Pennsylvania], *vs.* Real Estate Title [Insurance and Trust Company of Philadelphia], in error to district court for eastern district of Pennsylvania; [transcript of record, opinion of court, etc.]. [1924.] p. 97–100 ‡

Richard, C. B., & Co. No. 2311, Court of Customs Appeals, United States *v.* C. B. Richard & Co. et al.; brief for United States in opposition to appellees' motion to dismiss. 1924. cover-title, 9 p. ‡

Rives, Logan. No. 783, in Supreme Court, Oct. term, 1923, Hubert Work, Secretary of Interior, *v.* United States ex rel. Logan Rives, in error to Court of Appeals of District of Columbia; brief of plaintiff in error in opposition to motion to affirm. 1924. cover-title, i+23 p. ‡

Roebling, Charles G. No. 954, in Supreme Court, Oct. term, 1923, Emily R. Cadwalader and Helen R. Tyson, as executors of Charles G. Roebling, *v.* Edward L. Sturgess, individually and as collector of internal revenue for 1st district of New Jersey, on petition for writ of certiorari to circuit court of appeals for 3d circuit; brief for respondent in opposition. 1924. cover-title, 4 p. ‡

Ross, Waldo A. Interference no. 47229, in Patent Office, before examiner of interferences, Waldo A. Ross *v.* George W. Burke, jr.; brief for George W. Burke, jr. 1924. cover-title, ii+57 p. ‡

Salsman, James. In Court of Claims, Eugene Hazelip, administrator of James Salsman, *v.* United States, no. 53–B; defendant's brief. [1924.] p. 29–31, large 8° ‡

Southern Pacific Company. In Court of Claims, Southern Pacific Company *v.* United States, [no.] B–69; defendant's brief. 1924. p. 117, large 8° ‡

—— In Court of Claims, Southern Pacific Company *v.* United States, no. B–371; defendant's request for findings of fact, defendant's brief. [1924.] p. 27–33, large 8° ‡

—— Same; stipulation of parties as to payment for transportation being made from certain appropriation. 1924. p. 25, large 8° ‡

Southern Paper Company, Limited. No. 2312, Court of Customs Appeals, United States *v.* Southern Paper Co., Ltd.; supplemental brief for United States. 1924. cover-title, 6 p. ‡

Southern Railway. In Court of Claims, Southern Railway Company *v.* United States, no. B–118; defendant's objections to plaintiff's request for additional findings of fact set out in its reply brief, defendant's request for additional findings of fact, and brief. [1924.] p. 107–123, large 8° ‡

Standard Transportation Company. No. 34216, in Court of Claims, Standard Transportion [Transportation] Company *v.* United States; objections to plaintiff's requests for findings of facts, Government request for findings of facts, and brief in support thereof. 1924. cover-title, i+996–1103 p. large 8° ‡

Swift & Co. No. 4–A, in Court of Claims, Swift & Company *v.* United States; defendant's motion to amend findings of fact filed herein by court, to make additional findings of fact, to set aside judgment for $1,077,386.30 rendered on Mar. 17, 1924, and to grant defendant new trial, with brief in support of same. 1924. cover-title, iii+3183–3258 p. large 8° ‡

Towar Cotton Mills, Incorporated. In Court of Claims, Towar Cotton Mills, Inc., *v.* United States, no. C–209; objections to plaintiff's request for findings of fact, defendant's request for findings of fact, statement, and brief. [1924.] p. 62–75, large 8° ‡

Tupman-Thurlow Company, Incorporated. No. 2349, Court of Customs Appeals, Tupman Thurlow Company, Inc.. *v.* United States; brief for United States. 1924. cover-title, 9 p. ‡

Wanamaker, John. No. 2353, Court of Customs Appeals. John Wanamaker, L. Bamberger & Co. *v.* United States; brief for United States on motion to dismiss. 1924. cover-title, 3 p. ‡

Washington Market Company. In Court of Appeals of District of Columbia, in re United States Commission to Appraise Washington Market Company Property, no. 685, original; [opinion of court]. [1924.] 12 p. ‡

—— No. —, in Supreme Court, Oct. term, 1923, United States *v.* Washington Market Company; petition for writ of certiorari to Court of Appeals of District of Columbia and brief in support thereof. 1924. cover-title 8 p. ‡

—— No. 993. in Supreme Court, Oct. term, 1923, United States *v.* Washington Market Company; additional suggestions in behalf of United States in support of petition for writ of certiorari. 1924. cover-title. 3 p. ‡

Weissman, Joseph. No. 1032, in Supreme Court, Oct. term, 1923, United States *v.* Joseph Weissman et al., in error to district court for district of Connecticut; motion to advance. 1924. cover-title, 1 p. ‡

Wheeler-Osgood Company. In equity no. —, in district court for district of Oregon, United States *v.* Wheeler-Osgood Company et al.; petition. 1924. cover-title, 14 p. ‡

Wyckoff Pipe and Creosoting Company, Incorporated. In Court of Claims. Wyckoff Pipe & Creosoting Company, Inc., *v.* United States, no. C–19; objections to plaintiff's request for findings of fact, defendant's request for findings of fact, statement, and brief. [1924.] p. 151–178, large 8° ‡

LABOR DEPARTMENT

Government Hotels. Additional laundry machinery and equipment for Government Hotels. Washington, D. C., draft of proposed legislation which will authorize Housing Corporation, Washington, D. C., to expend not exceeding $10,000 of appropriation for maintenance, operation, and management of Government Hotels for Government workers, Washington, D. C., for purchase of additional laundry machines and equipment. May 28, 1924. 3 p. (H. doc. 338, 68th Cong. 1st sess.) * Paper, 5c.

—— Government Hotels, Washington, D. C., supplemental estimate of appropriation for Housing Corporation, fiscal year 1925, for rent of grounds owned by Baltimore & Ohio Railroad Co., which is occupied by Government Hotel for Government workers. May 26, 1924. 3 p. (H. doc. 322, 68th Cong. 1st sess.) * Paper, 5c.

CHILDREN'S BUREAU

Cotton. Welfare of children in cotton-growing areas of Texas. 1924. v+83 p. 2 pl. 4 p. of pl. (Bureau publication 134.) * Paper, 15c. L 24—88

Habit clinics for child of preschool age, their organization and practical value; by D. A. Thom. 1924. v+71 p. il. (Bureau publication 135.) * Paper, 10c. L 24—89

EMPLOYMENT SERVICE

Industrial employment information bulletin, v. 4, no. 4; Apr. 1924. [1924.] 20 p. 4° [Monthly.] †

IMMIGRATION BUREAU

Immigration laws. Information relative to immigration laws and their enforcement in connection with admission of aliens. [Reprint with omissions] 1924. [1]+6 p. † L 24—90

LABOR STATISTICS BUREAU

Conference of Paper Box-Board Manufacturers on Shorter Working Hours. Proceedings of Conference of Paper Box-Board Manufacturers on Shorter Working Hours, Washington, D. C., May 2, 1924. 1924. v+33 p. * Paper, 5c.

L 24—91

Employment in selected industries, Apr. 1924. 1924. [1]+12 p. il. [Monthly.] †

L 23—234

Headlights. Specifications of laboratory tests for approval of electric headlighting devices for motor vehicles, Illuminating Engineering Society, New York, N. Y., sponsor; tentative American standard, approved Nov. 11, 1922, by American Engineering Standards Committee. [Reprint with changes] Jan. 1924. vii+7 p. il. (Bulletin 350; Safety code series.) [Title of previous print is: Rules governing approval of headlighting devices for motor vehicles.] * Paper, 5c.

L 24—92

Monthly labor review. Monthly labor review, index, [title-page] and contents, v. 15; July–Dec. 1922. 1924. [1]+1429–66+xvii p. * Paper, 10c.

15—26485

—— Same, v. 18, no. 5; May. 1924. 1924. v+933–1186 p. il. * Paper, 15c. single copy, $1.50 a yr.; foreign subscription, $2.25.

SPECIAL ARTICLES.—What 86 years have taught us about selecting labor; by Horace B. Cheney.—Administrative justice; by Reginald Heber Smith.—Conciliation work of Department of Labor, Mar. 1924; by Hugh L. Kerwin.—Statistics of immigration, Feb. 1924; by W. W. Husband.

NOTE.—The Review is the medium through which the Bureau publishes the results of original investigations too brief for bulletin purposes, notices of labor legislation by the States or by Congress, and Federal court decisions affecting labor, which from their importance should be given attention before they could ordinarily appear in the bulletins devoted to these subjects. One free subscription will be given to all labor departments and bureaus, workmen's compensation commissions, and other offices connected with the administration of labor laws and organizations exchanging publications with the Labor Statistics Bureau. Others desiring copies may obtain them from the Superintendent of Documents, Washington, D. C., at the prices stated above.

Prices. Wholesale prices of commodities for Apr. 1924. 1924. [1]+9 p. [Monthly.] †

L 22—229

WOMEN'S BUREAU

Women in industry. Radio talks on women in industry; [by Mary N. Winslow and Mary V. Robinson]. 1924. v+34 p. il. (Bulletin 36.) [Originally prepared for series of talks over the radio, which were broadcast during the winter 1922–23.] * Paper, 10c.

L 24—93

LIBRARY OF CONGRESS

COPYRIGHT OFFICE

Copyright. [Catalogue of copyright entries, new series, pt. 1, group 1, Books, v. 21] no. 16–26; May, 1924. May 1–31, 1924. p. 121–264. [Issued several times a week.]

6—35347

NOTE.—Each number is issued in 4 parts: pt. 1, group 1, relates to books; pt. 1, group 2, to pamphlets, leaflets, contributions to newspapers or periodicals, etc., lectures, sermons, addresses for oral delivery. dramatic compositions, maps, motion pictures; pt. 2, to periodicals; pt. 3, to musical compositions; pt. 4, to works of art, reproductions of a work of art, drawings or plastic works of scientific or technical character, photographs, prints, and pictorial illustrations.

Subscriptions for the Catalogue of copyright entries should be made to the Superintendent of Documents, Washington, D. C., instead of to the Register of Copyrights. Prices are as follows: Paper, $3.00 a yr. (4 pts.), foreign subscription, $5.00; pt. 1 (groups 1 and 2), 5c. single copy (group 1, price of group 2 varies), $1.00 a yr., foreign subscription, $2.25; pt. 3, $1.00 a yr., foreign subscription, $1.50; pts. 2 and 4, each 10c. single copy, 50c. a yr., foreign subscription, 70c.

—— Same, pt. 3, Musical compositions, v. 18, nos. 9 and 10. 1924. v+859–1066 p. [Monthly.]

—— Same, pt. 3, Musical compositions, v. 18, nos. 11 and 12. 1924. v+1067–1307 p. [Monthly.]

DOCUMENTS DIVISION

Government publications. Monthly check-list of State publications received dur'ng Mar. 1924; v. 15, no. 3. 1924. p. 97–141. * Paper, 10c. single copy, $1.00 a yr.; foreign subscription, $1.25.

10—8924

NATIONAL HOME FOR DISABLED VOLUNTEER SOLDIERS

Proceedings of board of managers of National Home for Disabled volunteer Soldiers. Mar. 26, 1924. Mar. 1924. [v. 4] p. 300-307. [Quarterly.] ‡

NAVY DEPARTMENT

Claims. Claims of Jeremiah E [J]. Kelley and 49 others, communication submitting estimate of appropriation to pay claims of Jeremiah J. Kelley and 49 others, which have been adjusted and which require appropriation for their payment. May 2, 1924. 11 p. (H. doc. 260, 68th Cong. 1st sess.) * Paper, 5c.

—— Claims of Texas Oil Co. and 22 other claimants, communication submitting estimate of appropriation to pay claims of Texas Oil Co., Port Arthur, Tex., and 22 other claimants, which have been adjusted and which require appropriation for their payment. May 2, 1924. 8 p. (H. doc. 261, 68th Cong. 1st sess.) * Paper, 5c.

—— Eight claims adjusted by Secretary of Navy, communication from Secretary of Navy, submitting estimate of appropriation to pay 8 claims which he has adjusted and which require appropriation for their payment. May 2, 1924. 5 p. (H. doc. 258, 68th Cong. 1st sess.) * Paper, 5c.

—— Nineteen claims adjusted by Secretary of Navy, communication submitting estimate of appropriation to pay 19 claims for damages for which Navy vessels were found to be responsible, which have been adjusted and which require appropriation for their payment. May 13, 1924. 6 p. (H. doc. 274, 68th Cong. 1st sess.) * Paper, 5c.

—— Thirteen adjusted claims, 2 communications from Secretary of Navy submitting estimate of appropriation to pay 13 claims which he has adjusted and which require appropriation for their payment. May 13, 1924. 6 p. (H. doc. 275, 68th Cong. 1st sess.) * Paper, 5c.

Court-martial order 3, 1924; Mar. 31, 1924. [1924.] 9 p. 12° [Monthly.] ‡

Reports. Annual reports of Navy Department, fiscal year 1923, including operations to Nov. 15, 1923. 1924. iii+995 p. il. 1 pl. * Cloth, $1.00.
14—11083

CONTENTS.—Annual report of Secretary of Navy.—Report of chief of naval operations.—Report of judge advocate general of Navy.—Report of chief of Bureau of Yards and Docks.—Report of chief of Bureau of Navigation.—Report of Hydrographic Office.—Report of superintendent of Naval Observatory.—Report of chief of Bureau of Ordnance.—Report of chief of Bureau of Construction and Repair.—Report of chief of Bureau of Engineering.—Report of surgeon general.—Report of Bureau of Aeronautics.—Report of paymaster general of Navy, chief of Bureau of Supplies and Accounts.—Report of major general commandant of Marine Corps.—Index.

—— Same. (H. doc. 150, 68th Cong. 1st sess.)

ENGINEERING BUREAU

Measuring instruments. Instructions for operation, care, and repair of measuring instruments; reprint of chapter 23 of Manual of engineering instructions. 1924. [1]+54 p. il. [The edition of the Manual of engineering instructions of which this chapter forms a part has not yet been issued.] * Paper, 10c.
24—26444

JUDGE ADVOCATE GENERAL

Court-martial orders. Index of Court-martial orders, year ending Dec. 31, 1923. 1924. [1]+9 p. 12° [Court-martial orders issued by Navy Department.] ‡

MARINE CORPS

Transportation. [Marine Corps manual: Chapter 16, Transportation.] [1924.] i+94 p. 4° [This chapter supersedes and is a modification of Instructions governing transportation of troops and supplies for Marine Corps, 1916, reprinted 1918, as amended by Changes 1-8. Issued in loose-leaf form for insertion in binder.] ‡

MEDICINE AND SURGERY BUREAU

Diet. Notes on dietetics taken at Miss Farmer's School of Cookery, Boston, Mass. [Apr. 1–June 30, 1923, with list of references]; compiled by Loretta Lambert. 1924. [1]+12 p. [From United States naval medical bulletin, v. 20, no. 5.] †

Instructions issued by Bureau of Medicine and Surgery. 1924. [1]+36 p. [From United States naval medical bulletin, v. 20, no. 5.] †

Naval medical bulletin. United States naval medical bulletin, published for information of Medical Department of service, May, 1924, v. 20, no. 5; edited by W. M. Kerr. 1924. vi+531–683 p. il. 1 pl. [Monthly.] * Paper, 15c. single copy, $1.50 a yr.; foreign subscription, $2.50.   8—35095

SPECIAL ARTICLES.—Account of Medical Department of Marine Corps east coast expeditionary force during fall maneuvers of 1923; by W. Chambers.—Pyelography [with list of references]; by Winfield S. Pugh.—Hydronephrosis; by R. B. Engle.—Treatment of bichloride of mercury poisoning with calcium sulphide as chemical antidote, preliminary report; by J. M. McCants.—Construction of vulcanite partial dentures; by L. M. Desmond.—Chronic duodenal ulcer; by O. A. Smith.—Malignant endocarditis following fracture of ribs, case report; by B. M. Summers.—Incontinence of urine; by E. M. Harris, jr.—Report of death occuring during treatment for leprosy with chaulmoogra oil derivatives; by F. L. McDaniel.—Notes on dietetics taken at Miss Farmer's School of Cookery, Boston, Mass. [Apr. 1–June 30, 1923, with list of references; compiled by Loretta Lambert].—Instructions issued by Bureau of Medicine and Surgery.—Notes on preventive medicine for medical officers, Navy.

Nurse Corps, Navy. Circular for information of nurses desiring to enter Navy Nurse Corps. Apr. 1924. [1]+6 p. 4° †

NAVIGATION BUREAU

Blowers. Instructions for operation, care, and repair of blowers, for use of enlisted men in preparation for advancement to ratings of machinist's mates and enginemen; compiled by Bureau of Navigation from publications of Bureau of Engineering. 1924. cover-title, 8 p. il. (Navy education-study courses.) ‡

Electric propulsion installations. Instructions for operation, care, and repair of electric-propulsion main drive installations, for use of enlisted men in preparation for advancement to ratings of machinist's mates and enginemen; compiled by Bureau of Navigation from publications of Bureau of Engineering. 1924. cover-title, 14 p. (Navy education-study courses.) ‡

Naval Academy, Annapolis. Regulations governing admission of candidates into Naval Academy as midshipmen, for class entering 1925 et seq. 1924. ii+30 p. †
                                                                     7—32069

Navy directory, officers of Navy and Marine Corps. including officers of Naval Reserve Force (active), Marine Corps Reserve (active), and foreign officers serving with Navy, May 1. 1924. 1924. iii+244 p. [Bimonthly.] * Paper, 25c. single copy, $1.25 a yr.; foreign subscription. $1.75.

Navy register. Register of commissioned and warrant officers of Navy and Marine Corps, Jan. 1. 1924. 1924. 543 p. * Paper, $1.00.   7—32070

—— Same. (H. doc. 156, 68th Cong. 1st sess.)

Office procedure. Office procedure. Navy, pt. 1, assignments 1–4. 1924. cover-title, i+1–21 p. il. (Navy education-study courses.) ‡

—— Same, pt. 2, assignments 5–8. 1924. cover-title, i+23–41 p. il. (Navy education-study courses.) ‡

Reciprocating steam engines. Instructions for operation, care, and repair of main propelling reciprocating steam engines, for use of enlisted men in preparation for advancement to rating of machinist's mates and enginemen; compiled by Bureau of Navigation from publications of Bureau of Engineering. 1924. cover-title, 32 p. (Navy education-study courses.) ‡

HYDROGRAPHIC OFFICE

NOTE.—The charts, sailing directions, etc., of the Hydrographic Office are sold by the office in Washington and also by agents at the principal American and foreign seaports and American lake ports. Copies of the General catalogue of mariners' charts and books and of the Hydrographic bulletins, reprints, and Notice to mariners are supplied free on application at the Hydrographic Office in Washington and at the branch offices in Boston, New York, Philadelphia, Baltimore, Norfolk, Savannah, New Orleans, Galveston, San Francisco, Portland (Oreg.), Seattle, Chicago, Cleveland, Buffalo, Sault Ste. Marie, and Duluth.

Africa. Supplement to publication 105, Africa pilot, v. 1, including summary of Notices to mariners and other information from date of publication (May 1, 1923) to Dec. 31. 1923. 1924. ii+6 leaves. †

Asia. Supplement to publication 123, Asiatic pilot, v. 2, including summary of Notices to mariners and other information from date of publication (Jan..15, 1920) to Dec. 31, 1923. 1924. ii+32 leaves, il. 3 maps. †

—— Supplement to publication 124, Asiatic pilot, v. 3, including summary of Notices to mariners and other information from date of publication (Nov. 1, 1919) to Dec. 31, 1923. 1924. ii+26 leaves, il. map. †

Great Britain. Supplement to publication 145, British Islands pilot, v. 2, including summary of Notices to mariners and other information from date of publication (Mar. 5, 1917) to Dec. 31, 1923. 1924. ii+35 leaves, il. †

Great Lakes. Supplement to publication 108A, Great Lakes pilot, v. 1, including summary of Notices to mariners and other information from date of publication (Feb. 26, 1921) to Dec. 31, 1923. 1924. ii+18 leaves, map. †

Hydrographic bulletin, weekly, no. 1809–12; May 7–28, 1924. [1924.] Each 1 p. f° and large 4° [For Ice supplements to accompany nos. 1809–12, see below under center head *Charts* the subhead *Pilot charts.*] †

Mexico. Supplement to publication 84, Mexican and Central American pilot (Pacific Coast), including summary of Notices to mariners and other information from date of publication (June 12, 1920) to Dec. 31, 1923. 1924. ii+22 leaves, map. †

New Zealand. Supplement to publication 171. New Zealand pilot, including summary of Notices to mariners and other information from date of publication (May 21, 1920) to Dec. 31, 1923. 1924. ii+19 leaves, 2 maps. †

Newfoundland. Supplement to publication 73, Newfoundland pilot, including summary of Notices to mariners and other information from date of publication (Nov. 1, 1918) to Dec. 31, 1923. 1924. ii+10 leaves, map. †

Notice to aviators 5, 1924; May 1 [1924]. [1924.] 3 p. [Monthly.] †
20—26958

Notice to mariners 18–22. 1924; May 3–31 [1924]. [1924.] [xlvi]+477–627 leaves. [Weekly.] †

Nova Scotia. Supplement to publication 99, Nova Scotia pilot, including summary of Notices to mariners and other information from date of publication (Feb. 12, 1920) to Dec. 31, 1923. 1924. ii+28 leaves, il. map. †

St. Lawrence River. Supplement to publication 100. St. Lawrence pilot, including summary of Notices to mariners and other information from date of publication (Feb. 19, 1917) to Dec. 31, 1923. 1924. ii+45 leaves, 2 maps. †

South America. Supplement to publication 172. South American pilot. v. 1, including summary of Notices to mariners and other information from date of publication (Sept. 1. 1919) to Dec. 31, 1923. 1924. ii+36 leaves, il. map. †

—— Supplement to publication 174. South America pilot, v. 3, including summary of Notices to mariners and other information from date of publication (Jan. 29. 1920) to Dec. 31. 1923. 1924. ii+39 leaves, il. 2 maps. [Includes index for chapter 6 of publication 174.] †

Tide calendars. Tide calendar [for Baltimore (Fort McHenry and Cape Henry], June. 1924. [1924.] 1 p. 4° [Monthly.] †

—— Tide calendar [for Norfolk (Navy Yard) and Newport News, Va.], June, 1924. [1924.] 1 p. 4° [Monthly.] †

Charts

Australia. south coast. Cape Otway to Rivoli Bay. from British survey in 1872, with additions to 1909 [with insets]; chart 3439. Scale 1° long.=11.7 in. Washington, Hydrographic Office, Apr. 1924. 26×45.6 in. † 50c.

Fairy, Port.
Portland Bay.
Warrnambool Harbor, Lady Bay.

Borneo. Bays and anchorages on east coast of Borneo. Eastern Archipelago, from Netherlands Government surveys between 1892 and 1904; chart 3053. Washington, Hydrographic Office, published Nov. 1913, 3d edition, Apr. 1924. 18.5×26.4 in. † 20c.

Borneo—Continued.
Balik Papan Bay.
Balik Papan Bay, Anchorage near east point of.
Buja and Manimbora anchorages.
Kaniungan Islands.
Kelumpang Bay.
Miang Besar, Anchorage north of.
Sangkulirang Bay.

Chile. Ports and channels south of Magellan Strait, Chile, South America, mainly from British surveys in 1829 and 1830; chart 452. Washington, Hydrographic Office, published Aug. 1922, 2d edition, Apr. 1924. 29.5×24.1 in. † 30c.

Adventure Cove.
Barbara Channel, Magellan Strait, mainly from British survey in 1829, with additions from Chilean survey in 1901.
Bedford Bay, Approaches to.
Dislocation Harbor.
Doris Cove.
Euston Bay and Laura Harbor.
Fury Harbor.
Hewett Bay.
Latitude Bay.
March Harbor, Waterman I.
Noir Road.
North Cove.
Smyth Harbor.
Stewart Harbor.
Townshend Harbor, from British survey in 1830.
Week Islands, Desolation I., Magellan Strait, from British survey, 1830.

Corisco Bay, Bight of Biafra, Africa, west coast, from French Government chart published in 1922 [with insets]; chart 2482. Scale naut. m.=0.7 in. Washington, Hydrographic Office, published Mar. 1918, 2d edition, Apr. 1924. 27.6×22.1 in. † 20c.

Little Elobey Anchorage.
Ukoko Road, from German Govt. chart publ. in 1919.

England, east coast, Outer Gabbard to Outer Dowsing, including coast from Orfordness to Blakeney, from latest British surveys; chart 4473. Scale naut. m.=0.4 in. Washington, Hydrographic Office, published Feb. 1917, 8th edition, Apr. 1924. 38.7×25.7 in. † 40c.

NOTE.—Contains on reverse: British Isles and North Sea [chart showing areas in which sunken mines exist].

Magellan Strait. Anchorages in Magellan Strait, Chile, South America, original British surveys in 1883; chart 1634. Washington, Hydrographic Office, published Sept. 1897, 9th edition, Apr. [1924]. 25×34 in. † 40c.

Baker Cove, Cordova Inlet.
Cripples Channel, Sea Reach.
Field Anchorage, Long Reach.
Havergal bays, Snowy Channel.
Marsh Basin, Arathoon Bay, Long Reach.
Rocky Inlet, Long Reach.
Sylvia Channel, Sea Reach.
Sylvia Cove, Providence Island, Sea Reach.

—— Channels between Magellan Strait and Gulf of Trinidad, lower part, chart 446. Scale 1° long.=9.2 in. Washington, Hydrographic Office, published May, 1885, 23d edition, Apr. [1924]. 25.3×25.5 in. †30c.

Marshall Islands. Plans of Marshall Islands, southern part, north Pacific Ocean, from latest information to 1923; chart 5429. Washington, Hydrographic Office, May, 1924. 26×39.3 in. † 50c.

Arno (Arhno) Atoll.
Darrit Anchorage.
Ebon or Boston Atoll.
Ine Anchorage.
Jabor Anchorage, Jaluit Atoll.
Jaluit or Bonham Atoll.
Majuro or Arrowsmith Atoll.
Mille or Mulgrave Atoll.
Namorik or Baring Atoll.
Reiher Pass (Jobenor Chan.), Mille or Mulgrave Atoll.
Rhin, Port, Mille or Mulgrave Atoll.

North Island, east & west coasts, New Zealand, Manukau Harbor to Maunganui Bluffs, and Tutukaka Harbor to Mayor Island, including Hauraki Gulf, from latest British surveys, with additions from other sources; chart 3338. Scale 1° long.=12 in. Washington, Hydrographic Office, Apr. 1924. 25.7×38.7 in. † 40c.

Patagonia. Plans on west coast of Patagonia, South America, mainly from British surveys between 1829 and 1879; chart 266. Washington, Hydrographic Office, published July, 1884, 14th edition, Apr. 1924. 25.5×19 in. † 20c.

Guia Narrows, Sarmiento Channel.
Isthmus Bay, Smyth Channel.
Puerto Bueno, Sarmiento Channel.
Puerto Caracciolo, West Channel, from Chilean plan published in 1914.
Victory Pass, Union Sound.
Welcome Bay and Port Mardon, Smyth Channel.

Pilot charts. Ice supplement to north Atlantic pilot chart; issue 109. Scale 1° long.=0.3 in. Washington, Hydrographic Office [1924]. 8.9×11.8 in. [To accompany Hydrographic bulletin 1809, May 7, 1924.] †

—— Same; issue 110. Scale 1° long.=0.3 in. Washington Hydrographic Office [1924]. 8.9×11.8 in. [To accompany Hydrographic bulletin 1810, May 14, 1924.] †

—— Same; issue 111. Scale 1° long.=0.3 in. Washington, Hydrographic Office [1924]. 8.9×11.8 in. [To accompany Hydrographic bulletin 1811, May 21, 1924.] †

—— Same; issue 112. Scale 1° long.=0.3 in. Washington, Hydrographic Office [1924]. 8.9×11.8 in. [To accompany Hydrographic bulletin 1812, May 28, 1924.] †

—— Pilot chart of Central American waters, June, 1924; chart 3500. Scale 1° long.=0.7 in. Washington, Hydrographic Office, May 15, 1924. 23.4×35.1 in. [Monthly. Certain portions of the data are furnished by the Weather Bureau.] † 10c.

NOTE.—Contains on reverse: Currents and navigational details in waters of Gulf of Mexico, Caribbean Sea, and west coast of Central America; by John C. Soley.

—— Pilot chart of Indian Ocean, July, 1924; chart 2603. Scale 1° long.=0.2 in. Washington, Hydrographic Office, May 15, 1924. 22.6×31 in. [Monthly. Certain portions of the data are furnished by the Weather Bureau.] † 10c.

NOTE.—Contains on reverse: Cyclonic storms.

—— Pilot chart of north Atlantic Ocean, June, 1924; chart 1400. Scale 1° long.=0.27 in. Washington, Hydrographic Office, May 15, 1924. 23.2×31.8 in. [Monthly. Certain portions of the data are furnished by the Weather Bureau.] † 10c.

14—16339

NOTE.—Contains on reverse: Cyclonic storms.

—— Pilot chart of north Pacific Ocean, July, 1924; chart 1401. Scale 1° long.=0.2 in. Washington, Hydrographic Office, May 15, 1924. 23.7×35.3 in. [Monthly. Certain portions of the data are furnished by the Weather Bureau.] † 10c.

NOTE.—Contains on reverse: Cyclonic storms.

Quintero Bay. Quintero and Horcon bays, Chile, from Chilean surveys between 1876 and 1903; chart 2246. Scale naut. m.=2.6 in. Washington, Hydrographic Office, published Oct. 1905, 5th edition, Apr. 1924. 20.5×17.1 in. † 20c.

Sakhalin Island. Anchorages on west coast of Sakhalin Island, Siberia, Asia, from Japanese surveys in 1920 and 1921; chart 5432. Washington, Hydrographic Office, Apr. 1924. 26.4×38 in. † 40c.

Agnevo Road.
Alexandrovski and Due roadsteads.
Mosiya Bay.
Pilevo Bay.
Rogati Road.

San Antonio, Chile. Ports San Antonio and San Antonio de las Bodegas, Chile, from Chilean surveys to 1922; chart 1485. Scale naut. m.=2.1 in. natural scale 1:36,481. Washington, Hydrographic Office, published Feb. 1895, 9th edition, May [1924]. 15.8×12.7 in. † 10c.

Savannah la Mar Anchorage, Jamaica, from British survey in 1876-78; chart 1296. Scale naut. m.=3.1 in., natural scale 1:24,321. Washington, Hydrographic Office, published Nov. 1891, 15th edition, May [1924]. 14.8×18.4 in. † 10c.

Siberia. Southeast coast of Siberia, Cape Biki to Cape Byelkin, and southern part of Sakhalin Island with La Perouse Strait, Gulf of Tartary and Okhotsk Sea, compiled from latest information; chart 1777. Natural scale 1:652,913, at lat. 48°. Washington, Hydrographic Office, published Aug. 1900, 9th edition, May [1924]. 31×41.8 in. † 60c.

Suwo Nada, Naikai or Inland Sea, Japan, Maruyama Zaki to Ominase, from Japanese surveys between 1884 and 1905; chart 2738. Natural scale 1:60,-171. Washington, Hydrographic Office, published Oct. 1911, 5th edition, May, 1924. 26.1×39 in. † 50c.

Toronto Harbor and approaches, Lake Ontario, Canada, from Canadian Government survey in 1913, topography and soundings inside harbor from plan by Toronto Harbor Commission; chart 1462. Scale 2000 yds.=6 in., natural scale 1:12,015. Washington, Hydrographic Office, published June, 1921, 2d edition, Apr. 1924. 27.2×32.6 in. † 40c.

Uruppu To and approaches, Chishima Retto (Kuril Islands), Japan, from Japanese surveys to 1916 [with insets]; chart 5326. Natural scale 1:242,-465, at lat. 46°. Washington, Hydrographic Office, May, 1924. 26.6×38.8 in. † 50c.

Futagojima Hakuchi, Uruppu To.
Tokotan Wan, Uruppu To.

Yap Island, Caroline Islands, north Pacific Ocean, from Japanese surveys between 1917 and 1921 [with insets]; chart 5421. Scale naut. m.=1 in., natural scale 1:72,585. Washington, Hydrographic Office, Apr. 1924. 25.2×38.3 in. † 40c.

Tarang I. approaches, Tomil Harbor, Yap Island.
Tomil Harbor, Yap Island.

RECRUITING BUREAU

[*Poster*] 259. [Press of Navy Recruiting Bureau, New York, Apr. 14. 1924.] 14×17 in. [Title is: Navy peace time activities; illustrator, C. McKnight-Smith.] †

SUPPLIES AND ACCOUNTS BUREAU

Manual. Standard organization of supply department ashore [changes for Manual of Supply Corps, Navy, 1922; Apr. 10, 1924]. 1924. cover-title, i p. 4° [Accompanied by reprints of certain pages to be inserted in their proper places in the original manual. A list of these reprinted pages is given in the publication here catalogued.] ‡

Supply Corps, Navy. Memorandum for information of officers of Supply Corps, commanding officers [of ships], and commandants 260; Apr. 1, 1924. [1924.] p. 8172–8259, 12° [Monthly.] ‡

YARDS AND DOCKS BUREAU

Power plants. General instructions for operation and maintenance of central power plants. United States navy yards and stations, revised; chapter 21 of Manual of Bureau of Yards and Docks. 1924. xv+86 p. 3 pl. ‡

Quarters. Maintenance and furnishing of quarters; chapter 25 of Manual of Bureau of Yards and Docks. 1924. iii+17 p. ‡

PAN AMERICAN UNION

NOTE.—The Pan American Union sells its own monthly bulletins, handbooks, etc., at prices usually ranging from 5c. to $2.50. The price of the English edition of the bulletin is 25c. a single copy or $2.50 a year, the Spanish edition $2.00 a year, the Portuguese edition $1.50 a year; there is an additional charge of 50c. a year on each edition for countries outside the Pan American Union. Address the Director General of the Pan American Union, Washington, D. C.

Antiquities. On certain antiquities in western Guatemala; [by T. T. Waterman]. 1924. [1]+22 p. il. [From Bulletin, Apr. 1924.] †

Argentina. Commerce of Argentina, latest reports from Argentine official sources. 1924. [1]+14 p. †
13—7277

——— Shaping destiny of Argentine farmer; [by John W. White]. 1924. [1]+6 p. [From Bulletin, May. 1924.] †

Bulletin (English edition). Bulletin of Pan American Union, May, 1924;
[v. 58, no. 5]. [1924.] iv+431–538 p. il. [Monthly.]   8—30967
—— Same. (H. doc. 6, pt. 11, 68th Cong. 1st sess.)
—— *(Portuguese edition)*. Boletim da União Pan-Americana, Maio, 1924,
edição portuguesa; [v. 26, no. 5]. [1924.] [iv]+305–380 p. il. [Monthly.
This number is entitled O problema de estradas publicas nas Americas.]
                                                                   11—27014

—— *(Spanish edition)*. Boletín de la Unión Panamericana, Mayo, 1924, sección española; [v. 58, no. 5]. [1924.] iv+437–541 p. il. [Monthly.]
                                                                   12—12555

Ecuador. Commerce of Ecuador, latest reports from Ecuadorean official
sources. 1924. [1]+4+[1] p. †   23—6433
Habana, metropolis of the Caribbean; [by W. A. R.]. 1924. [2]+38 p.
il. †   24—26518
Nicaragua, general descriptive data. 1924. [2]+30 p. il. †   11—35057
Oils, fats, and waxes in Latin America; [by Otto Wilson]. 1924. [2]+22 p.
il. †   24—26519
Quebracho forests of South America [personal notes and observations in
Argentina and Paraguay; by George A. Kerr]. 1924. [1]+27+[1] p. il. †
                                                                   24—26520
Salvador, general descriptive data. 1924. [2]+30 p. il. †   11—35843

PANAMA CANAL

NOTE.—Although The Panama Canal makes its reports to, and is under the supervision of, the Secretary of War, it is not a part of the War Department.

Panama Canal record, v. 17, no. 39–42; May 7–28, 1924. Balboa Heights,
C. Z. [1924]. . p. 553–622. [Weekly.]   7—35328

NOTE.—The yearly subscription rate of the Panama Canal record is 50c. domestic,
and $1.00 foreign, (single issues 2c.), except in the case of Government departments
and bureaus, Members of Congress, representatives of foreign Governments, steamship
lines, chambers of commerce, boards of trade, and university and public libraries, to
whom the Record is distributed free. The word "domestic" refers to the United
States, Canada, Canal Zone, Cuba, Guam, Hawaii, Manua, Mexico, the Philippines,
Porto Rico, Republic of Panama, Tutuila, and the Virgin Islands. Subscriptions will
commence with the first issue of the Record in the month in which the subscriptions
are received, unless otherwise requested. Remittances should be made payable to Disbursing Clerk, The Panama Canal, but should be forwarded to the Chief of Office. The
Panama Canal, Washington, D. C. The name and address to which the Record is to
be sent should be plainly written. Postage stamps, foreign money, and defaced or
smooth coins will not be accepted.

EXECUTIVE DEPARTMENT

EXECUTIVE OFFICE

Executive orders. Supplement 3 and 4 [to] ·Executive orders relating to
Panama Canal [Mar. 8, 1904–Dec. 31, 1921, annotated 1921]. Balboa Heights.
C. Z. [Apr. 5 and 21, 1924]. p. 339–362. [Executive orders relating to
Panama Canal published by The Panama Canal. Supplement 3 includes
Executive orders dated Oct. 16 and Dec. 20, 1923; Supplement 4 includes
Executive orders dated Feb. 26 and Mar. 5, 1924.] †

PURCHASING DEPARTMENT

'*Supplies*. Circular [proposals for supplies] 1607, 1611, and 1613; May 1–29,
1924. [1924.] various paging, f° †
—— Proposals [for supplies 1611, to accompany Circular proposals for supplies 1611]. [1924.] 1 p. 24° ‡

PERSONNEL CLASSIFICATION BOARD

Government officials and employees. Schedules in classification act, recommendations of Personnel Classification Board relative to amending compensation schedules in classification act of 1923, by F. J. Bailey, chairman;
presented by Mr. Sterling. 1924. [1]+1 p. (S. doc. 121, 68th Cong. 1st
sess.) * Paper, 5c.

POST OFFICE DEPARTMENT

Chicago, Ill. Scheme of station separation of post office at Chicago, Ill.; corrected to Feb. 11, 1924. 1924. 203 p. 12° ‡

Claims. One hundred and eighteen claims adjusted by Postmaster General, requiring appropriation for their payment. May 2, 1924. 13 p. (H. doc. 255, 68th Cong. 1st sess.) * Paper, 5c.

—— Twenty-four claims allowed by Postmaster General, 2 communications from Postmaster General submitting estimate of appropriation to pay claims for damages to or losses of privately owned property which he has adjusted and which require appropriation for their payment. May 17, 1924. 7 p. (H. doc. 293, 68th Cong. 1st sess.) * Paper, 5c.

Des Moines, Iowa. Scheme of Des Moines, Iowa, city carrier and station separation, for use of post office and railway post office clerks; corrected to Jan. 15, 1924. 1924. 55 p. ‡

Envelopes. Precautions to be taken in storing stamped envelopes; [issued by] 3d assistant Postmaster General. May 15, 1924. 1 p. 12° †

Mail matter. Ascertainment of cost of handling and transporting the several classes of mail matter and conducting special services: Instruction letter A-2, supplemental [May 15, 1924], Report showing, by subclasses, number of separately addressed pieces and bundles of publisher's 2d-class matter for domestic destinations by issues. [1924.] 2 p. ‡

—— Same: Instruction letter P-A [May 1, 1924], Parcel post, weighing of parcel post by subclasses and destinations. [1924.] 4 p. ‡

—— Same: Instruction letter P-C-w [May 1, 1924], Parcel post, record of revenues for 14-day statistical period, also weight and count of pieces of 4th-class (parcel post) mails by subclasses. [1924.] 4 p. ‡

—— Same: Instruction letter P-D-a [May 1, 1924], Parcel post, record of time consumed during 14-day statistical period in handling the several subclasses of parcel-post matter as described in instruction letter P-C-W. [1924.] 4 p. ‡

—— Same: Instruction letter P-D-T [May 1, 1924], Parcel post, test of outgoing and incoming mixed parcel post. [1924.] 3 p. ‡

—— Same: Instruction letter P-F-s-T [May 1, 1924], Parcel post, carrier tests. average time per stop for delivery and collection of single subclasses of parcel post. [1924.] 2 p. ‡

—— Same: Instruction letter P-F-T [May 1, 1924], Parcel post, tests in carrier service. [1924.] 4 p. ‡

—— Same: Instruction letter P-G-s-T [May 1, 1924], Parcel post, time studies of parcel post in 3d and 4th class post offices by departmental representatives. [1924.] 2 p. ‡

—— Same: Instruction letter P-K-T [May 1, 1924], Parcel post, rural delivery service. [1924.] 3 p. ‡

—— Same: Instruction letter P-R-T [May 1, 1924], Parcel post. [1924.] 3 p. ‡

—— Same: Instruction letter P-V-T [May 1, 1924], Parcel post, volume tests. [1924.] 3 p. ‡

—— Same: Instruction letter S-F-T [May 1, 1924], 2d class, tests in carrier service. [1924.] 4 p. ‡

—— Same: Instruction letter S-K-T [May 1, 1924], 2d class, rural delivery service. [1924.] 3 p. ‡

—— Ordinary and registered sealed articles from foreign countries containing dutiable merchandise not marked to indicate they may be opened for customs purposes. May 7, 1924. 1 p. 12° †

Postal bulletin, v. 45, no. 13459–484; May 1–31, 1924. [1924.] various paging, f° [Daily except Sundays and holidays.] * Paper, 5c. single copy, $2.00 a yr.
6—5810

Postal guide. United States official postal guide, 4th series, v. 3. no. 11; May, 1924, monthly supplement. 1924. cover-title, p. 1–56+leaves 57–60+p. 61–62 +[1] p. il. [Includes Modifications 35 and 36 of International money order list, pamphlet 14, and Insert 854 to Postal laws and regulations of United States. Text on p. 2–4 of cover.] * Official postal guide, with supplements, $1.00, foreign subscription, $1.50; July issue, 75c.; supplements published monthly (11 pamphlets), 25c.; foreign subscription, 50c. 4—18254

TOPOGRAPHY DIVISION

NOTE.—Since February, 1908, the Topography Division has been preparing rural-delivery maps of counties in which rural delivery is completely established. They are published in two forms, one giving simply the rural free delivery routes, starting from a single given post office, and sold at 10 cents each; the other, the rural free delivery routes in an entire county, sold at 35 cents each. A uniform scale of 1 inch to 1 mile is used. Editions are not issued, but sun-print copies are produced in response to special calls addressed to the Disbursing Clerk, Post Office Department, Washington, D. C. These maps should not be confused with the post route maps, for which see Monthly catalogue for February, 1924, page 486.

PRESIDENT OF UNITED STATES

Address [of President Coolidge dedicating building for National Academy of Sciences and National Research Council at Washington, D. C., Apr. 28, 1924].
[1924.] 3 p. †   24—26521

Alien property. Executive order, authorizing Alien Property Custodian to sell certain property at private sale [being real estate in Milwaukee, Wis., belonging to Helmuth Heyl and Reinhard Heyl of Germany]. Apr. 30, 1924.
1 p. f° (No. 4001.) ‡

—— Executive order, authorizing Alien Property Custodian to sell certain property at private sale [being certain other real estate in Milwaukee, Wis., belonging to Helmuth Heyl and Reinhard Heyl of Germany]. May 15, 1924.
1 p. f° (No. 4012.) ‡

—— Executive order, authorizing Alien Property Custodian to sell certain property at private sale [being real estate in Pasadena, Calif., belonging to Klara Kombst, Gertrude Luckhardt, and Ilka Wichmann of Germany]. May 13, 1924. 1 p. f° (No. 4010.) ‡

—— .Executive order authorizing Alien Property Custodian to sell certain property upon New York Stock Exchange [being 97,295 shares of capital stock of Standard Oil Company of New Jersey, corporation organized under laws of New Jersey, said stock belonging to Carl Schutte, Louise Braesecke, Gustav Schutte, Wilhelm A. Riedemann, and Meta Schutte]. May 8, 1924.
1 p. f° (No. 4007.) ‡

Arizona. Executive order, Arizona [temporarily withdrawing certain described land in Arizona for classification and pending enactment of legislation for its proper disposition]. Apr. 25, 1924. 1 p. f° (No. 3999.) ‡

—— Executive order, Arizona [temporarily withdrawing, until Mar. 5, 1925, certain described lands in Arizona, in aid of pending legislation authorizing Phoenix, Ariz., to purchase said land for public park purposes]. Apr. 23, 1924. 1 p. f° (No. 3998.) ‡

Arlington Memorial Bridge, message transmitting report of Arlington Memorial Bridge Commission on project to construct memorial bridge across the Potomac from vicinity of Lincoln Memorial to Arlington estate. Apr. 21, calendar day Apr. 23, 1924. 1 p. (S. doc. 95, 68th Cong. 1st sess.) [Letter of transmittal only.] *Paper, 5c.

Blackburn, James W. Executive order [rescinding Executive order dated Apr. 3, 1924, designating Lucius Meriwether Smith to be special judge for Canal Zone during absence of John D. Wallingford, district judge, and directing that James W. Blackburn be special judge of Canal Zone during absence of Judge Wallingford]. May 7, 1924. 1 p. f° (No. 4006.) ‡

Chaplains. Executive order [amending civil service rules relating to classified positions excepted from examination so as to permit chaplains in entire classified service to be excepted from examination, whereas only chaplains in United States penitentiaries or prisons under Justice Department were heretofore excepted]. May 7, 1924. 1 p. f° (No. 4005.) ‡

Civil service. Executive order [amending civil service rules relating to transfer so as to permit retransfer under certain conditions of persons who left classified service to enter service of State, county, municipality, or foreign government]. May 2, 1924. 1 p. f° (No. 4004.) ‡

Coast Guard. Executive order [authorizing Secretary of Treasury to cause to be prescribed such examinations as he may deem necessary governing original temporary appointments in commissioned grades in Coast Guard, and suitable regulations governing original temporary appointments of warrant officers or enlisted men of permanent Coast Guard and governing appointment of chief warrant officers]. Apr. 23, 1924. 1 p. f° (No. 3997.) ‡

Colorado. Executive order. Colorado [withdrawing certain described public lands in Colorado from settlement. etc.. pending resurvey, such withdrawal to remain in effect until resurvey is accepted and approved plat is officially filed in local land office]. Apr. 30, 1924. 1 p. f° (No. 4000.) ‡

Craters of the Moon National Monument. Idaho. proclamation. May 2, 1924. 1 p. map, f° (No. 1694.) †

Cuba. Exportation of arms or munitions of war to Cuba unlawful, proclamation. May 2, 1924. 1 p. f° (No. 1693.) †

Florida. Executive order [temporarily withdrawing certain described lands in Florida. from settlement, etc., in aid of pending legislation embodied in H. R. 8522, granting to certain claimants preference right to purchase unappropriated public lands]. May 22, 1924. 1 p. f° (No. 4014.) ‡

Government officials and employees. Executive order [further amending Executive order of Feb. 14, 1912, permitting employees in Executive civil service permanently residing in certain incorporated municipalities adjacent to District of Columbia to become candidates for or to hold municipal office therein, so as to include Berwyn Heights. Md., among those named in order]. May 19, 1924. 1 p. f° (No. 4013.) ‡

Honduras. Exportation of arms or munitions of war to Honduras unlawful except with consent of Secretary of State, proclamation. May 15, 1924. 1 p. f° (No. 1697.) †·

Hopkins. John J. Executive order [giving John J. Hopkins. parole officer at McNeil Island Penitentiary, Wash., classified status]. May 2, 1924. 1 p. f° (No. 4003.) ‡

Labor Department. Executive order [authorizing Theodore G. Risley, solicitor for Department of Labor. to perform duties of Secretary of Labor during absence of Secretary of Labor, assistant Secretary of Labor. and 2d assistant Secretary of Labor]. Apr. 28, 1924. 1 p. f° (No. 3999A.) ‡

Laufer, August F. Executive order [authorizing reinstatement of August F. Laufer, formerly printer and proof-reader in Government Printing Office. to appropriate position in any other Government Department or independent establishment]. May 10, 1924. 1 p. f° (No. 4009.) ‡

Mahoney, Mrs. Agnes E. Executive order [authorizing reinstatement of Mrs. Agnes E. Mahoney in suitable vacancy in Agriculture Department]. Apr. 30, 1924. 1 p. f° (No. 4002.) ‡

Pensions and increase of pensions to soldiers and sailors of Civil War, etc., message returning, without approval, bill (S. 5), granting pensions and increase of pensions to soldiers and sailors of Civil and Mexican wars and to widows, former widows, minor children. and helpless children of said soldiers and sailors, and to widows of War of 1812, and to Indian war veterans and widows, and to Spanish War soldiers, and certain maimed soldiers. Apr. 24, calendar day May 3, 1924. 5 p. (S. doc. 103, 68th Cong. 1st sess.) * Paper, 5c.
24—26522

Scotts Bluff National Monument. Executive order, Scotts Bluff National Monument. Nebr. [modifying proclamation of Dec. 12, 1919, reserving certain number of acres in Scotts Bluff County. Nebr.. as Scotts Bluff National Monument, so as to eliminate certain described land from said national monument]. May 9, 1924. 1 p. f° (No. 4008.) ‡

Sodium nitrite. Increasing rate of duty on sodium nitrite. proclamation [authorizing certain increase in duty on sodium nitrite, in order to equalize differences in costs of production in United States and Norway]. [May 6, 1924.] 2 p. f° ([No. 1696.]) †

Soldiers' adjusted compensation, message from President of United States returning, without approval, bill H. R. 7959. to provide adjusted compensation for veterans of World War. 1924. [1]+12 p. (H. doc. 281, 68th Cong. 1st sess.) * Paper, 5c.
24—26463

Teller, Harrison V. Executive order [waiving that part of Executive order of May 10, 1921, which pertains to residence requirement of candidates for Presidential postmaster examinations, so as to permit examination papers of Harrison V. Teller, candidate for position of postmaster at Windsor, Colo., to be rated by Civil Service Commission]. May 14, 1924. 1 p. f° (No. 4011.) ‡

RAILROAD ADMINISTRATION

Alfalfa. No. 114, in Supreme Court, Oct. term, 1923, James C. Davis, agent of the President and director general of railroads, *v.* Portland Seed Company, upon certiorari to circuit court of appeals for 9th circuit; [no. 123, same] *v.* A. J. Parrington, upon writ of error to circuit court of appeals for 9th circuit; petition by James C. Davis, agent of the President and director general of railroads, for further consideration. 1924. cover-title, 6 p. ‡

Chicago and Alton Railroad. In Court of Claims, no. D–301, United States and James C. Davis, director general of railroads, for benefit and in behalf of United States, *v.* Chicago & Alton Railroad Company and W. G. Bierd, receiver of Chicago & Alton Railroad; petition. [1924.] 56 p. ‡

Coal. Before Interstate Commerce Commission, no. 14710, Consolidated Coal Company of St. Louis *v.* director general et al.; exceptions on behalf of director general to proposed report of examiner. 1924. cover-title, 7 p. ‡

Cotton-seed. Nos. 2245, 2246, in circuit court of appeals, 4th circuit, James C. Davis, Federal agent for claims due in operation of Atlantic Coast Line Railway Company, *v.* E. H. Pringle, as trustee in bankruptcy of estate of Charles F. Boyd Company, Inc., bankrupt; James C. Davis, Federal agent for claims due in operation of Seaboard Air Line Railway Company *v.* [same], appeal from district court for eastern district of South Carolina, at Charleston, in bankruptcy; brief for appellant. 1924. cover-title, i+13 p. ‡

Demurrage. Before Interstate Commerce Commission, no. 12725, United States Steel Products Company *v.* director general of railroads, as agent; petition of director general for further consideration. 1924. cover-title, 6 p. ‡

Flour. Before Interstate Commerce Commission, no. 14503, Larabee Flour Mills Corporation *v.* director general; exceptions on part of director general to report proposed by examiner. 1924. cover-title, 13 p. ‡

Kangaroo skin. Before Interstate Commerce Commission, no. 13012, American Trading Company *v.* director general, as agent; exceptions on part of director general to report proposed by examiner. 1924. cover-title, 12 p. ‡

Leather, Imitation. Before Interstate Commerce Commission, no. 14889, Chevrolet Motor Company of California *v.* director general, as agent, Atchison, Topeka & Santa Fe Railway Company et al.; exceptions on part of director general to report proposed by examiner. 1924. cover-title, 9 p. ‡

Limitations (law). No. 819, in Supreme Court, Oct. term, 1923, Jas. C. Davis, director general of railroads, as agent of United States, *v.* Corona Coal Company, certiorari to court of appeal for parish of Orleans, La.; original brief on behalf of plaintiff in error. 1924. cover-title, i+13 p. ‡

Wheat. Before Interstate Commerce Commission, no. 14588, Royal Milling Company *v.* director general; answer on part of director general to complainant's exceptions to report proposed by examiner. 1924. cover-title, 4 p. ‡

Wood-pulp. Before Interstate Commerce Commission, no. 15289, Crown Willamette Paper Company *v.* director general et al.; brief for director general. [1924.] cover-title, 12 p. ‡

RAILROAD LABOR BOARD

Decisions. Decision 2374; Apr. 14, 1924. Chicago, Ill., Curtis-Johnson Printing Co. [Apr. 23, 1924]. 12 p. [Usually the decisions of the Railroad Labor Board are mimeographed and are not entered in this catalogue.] †

—— Interpretation 1 to Decision 757 and Interpretation 1 to Decision 2025 (dockets 2110 [et al.]); Apr. 15, 1924. Chicago, Ill., Curtis-Johnson Printing Co. [Apr. 23, 1924]. 4 p. †

SHIPPING BOARD

Government officials. Appearance of ex-government officials before Shipping Board or Emergency Fleet Corporation, letter transmitting, in response to resolution, information relative to appearance of ex-Cabinet officials and ex-Members of House of Representatives as agents or attorneys for claimants against Board or Emergency Fleet Corporation. Apr. 24, calendar day Apr. 29, 1924. 41 p. (S. doc. 101, 68th Cong. 1st sess.) * Paper, 5c.

SHIPPING BOARD EMERGENCY FLEET CORPORATION

Collisions at sea. Instructions to managers, charterers, and masters on reporting collision or salvage; revised to June 1, 1922. [Reprint 1924.] [1]+14 p. 12° ‡

Ships. Schedule of sailings of Shipping Board vessels in general cargo, passenger & mail services, 1st of May to middle of June, 1924; issued by Traffic Department. [1924.] cover-title, ii+15 p. il. [Monthly. Text on p. 2–4 of cover.] †

23—26331

SMITHSONIAN INSTITUTION

NATIONAL MUSEUM

NOTE.—The publications of the National Museum comprise an annual report and three scientific series, viz., Proceedings, Bulletins, and Contributions from national herbarium. The editions are distributed to established lists of libraries, scientific institutions, and specialists, any surplus copies being supplied on application. The volumes of Proceedings are made up of technical papers based on the Museum collections in biology, geology, and anthropology, and of each of these papers a small edition, in pamphlet form, is issued in advance of the volume, for prompt distribution to specialists. No sets of any of these series can now be furnished.

Asters. New American Asteraceae; by S. F. Blake. 1924. xi+587–661 p. il. 10 p. of pl. (Contributions from national herbarium, v. 22, pt. 8.) * Paper, 20c.

Agr 24—448

Barnacles. Miocene and Pleistocene Cirripedia from Haiti; by Henry A. Pilsbry. 1924. cover-title, 3 p. 1 pl. [From Proceedings, v. 65; no. 2515.] †

Cephalopods. New nautiloid cephalopod, Eutrephoceras sloani, from Eocene of South Carolina; by John B. Reeside, jr. 1924. cover-title, 4 p. il. 3 p. of pl. [From Proceedings, v. 65; no. 2518.] †

Clusiidae. Revision of 2-winged flies of family Clusiidae [with bibliography]; by A. L. Melander and Naomi George Argo. 1924. cover-title, 54 p. 4 p. of pl. [From Proceedings, v. 64; no. 2501.] †

Crinoids. Tertiary crinoid from West Indies; by Frank Springer. 1924. cover-title, 8 p. 1 pl. [From Proceedings, v. 65; no. 2516.] †

Entomostraca. Notes on Entomostraca from Colorado, Shantz collections from Pikes Peak region; by G. S. Dodds. 1924. cover-title, 7 p. il. [From Proceedings, v. 65; no. 2531.] †

Foraminifera of Atlantic Ocean: pt. 5, Chilostomellidae and Globigerinidae; by Joseph Augustine Cushman. 1924. v+55 p. 8 p. of pl. (Bulletin 104 [pt. 5].) * Paper, 15c.

18—26668

Ichneumon-flies. On genera of ichneumon-flies of tribe Paniscini Ashmead, with descriptions and discussion of related genera and species; by R. A. Cushman. 1924. cover-title, 48 p. il. [From Proceedings, v. 64; no. 2510.] †

Mammals. List of North American recent mammals, 1923, by Gerrit S. Miller, jr.; [with Guide to type localities, by Arthur J. Poole]. 1924. xvi+673 p. (Bulletin 128.) * Paper, 85c.

24—26445

Needle-grass. North American species of Aristida; by A. S. Hitchcock. 1924. viii+517–586 p. (Contributions from national herbarium, v. 22, pt. 7.) * Paper, 10c.

Agr 24—447

Plants. Economic fruit-bearing plants of Ecuador; by Wilson Popenoe. 1924. ix+101–134 p. 16 p. of pl. (Contributions from national herbarium, v. 24, pt. 5.) * Paper, 15c.

Agr 24—449

Termites. Descriptions of new species and hitherto unknown castes of termites from America and Hawaii; by Thomas E. Snyder. 1924. cover-title, 40 p. 5 p. of pl. [From Proceedings, v. 64; no. 2496.] †

STATE DEPARTMENT

Arbitration. Agreement between United States and Japan, arbitration, further extending duration of convention of May 5, 1908; signed Washington, Aug. 23, 1923, proclaimed Apr. 26, 1924. 1924. [1]+3 p. (Treaty series 683.) †
24—26481

[*Circular*] 924; May 7, 1924. 1924. 1 p. [General instruction circular to consular officers.] ‡

Claim for death of Juan Sariano [Soriano], report respecting claim for death of Juan Sariano [Soriano], subject of Dominican Republic, and recommending authorization of appropriation for its payment. Apr. 24, calendar day May 1, 1924. 3 p. (S. doc. 102, 68th Cong. 1st sess.)   * Paper, 5c.

Consuls. [Regulations governing consular service of United States, annotated to Dec. 31, 1922; reprint, with corrections, of pages containing Paragraphs 502–506½.] Apr. 1924. p. 3 and 4 [of Article 25]. ‡

Diplomatic and consular service of United States; corrected to Apr. 1, 1924. 1924. 67 p. ‡
10—16369

Diplomatic list, May, 1924. [1924.] cover-title, i+36 p. 24° [Monthly.] ‡
10—16292

Liquors. Convention between United States and Great Britain, prevention of smuggling of intoxicating liquors; signed Washington, Jan. 23, 1924, proclaimed May 22, 1924. 1924. [1]+3 p. (Treaty series 685.) †
24—26523

Naturalization. Treaty between United States and Bulgaria, naturalization; signed Sofia, Nov. 23, 1923, proclaimed May 6, 1924. 1924. [1]+3 p. (Treaty series 684.) †
24—26482

Oil concessions in foreign countries, in response to resolution, report of Secretary of State relative to diplomatic correspondence in connection with securing oil concessions for American citizens between this Government and Governments of certain foreign countries regarding oil concessions in those countries. Apr. 22, calendar day Apr. 23, 1924. 122 p. (S. doc. 97, 68th Cong. 1st sess.)   * Paper, 10c.
24—26524

Register of Department of State, Jan. 1, 1924. 1924. v+326 p. * Paper, 60c.
9—22072

Seville, International Exposition, 1927. International Exposition at Seville. Spain, report relative to participation by United States in international exposition of arts, sciences, history, industries, commerce, and resources of Spain, Portugal. and republics of America, beginning at Seville, Spain, Apr. 17, 1927. May 5, calendar day May 7, 1924. 6 p. (S. doc. 106, 68th Cong. 1st sess.)   * Paper, 5c.

Swains Island. Status of Swains Island, report from Secretary of State regarding status of Swains Island, recommending that it be placed under jurisdiction of Government established in American Samoa. May 20, calendar day May 23, 1924. 4 p. (S. doc. 117, 68th Cong. 1st sess.)   * Paper, 5c.

SUPREME COURT

Cases. Docket [of cases pending in Supreme Court], Oct. term, 1923. [1924.] p. 301–310, 4° [Issued in loose-leaf form.] ‡

Fidelity and Deposit Company of Maryland. Transcript of record, Oct. term, 1923, no. 938, United States *vs.* Fidelity & Deposit Company of Maryland, appeal from Court of Claims. [1924.] cover-title, i+7 p. ‡

[*Journal*] May 1–26, 1924; [slips] 99–104. [1924.] leaves 254–282. ‡

Official reports of Supreme Court, v. 263 U. S., no. 4; Ernest Knaebel, reporter. Preliminary print. 1924. cover-title, [1]+537–730 p. 12° [Cases adjudged in Supreme Court at Oct. term, 1923 (opinions of Jan. 7, in part, –Jan. 28, 1924). Text on p. 2 and 4 of cover. From United States reports, v. 263.] * Paper, 25c. single copy, $1.00 per vol. (4 nos. to a vol.; subscription price, $3.00 for 12 nos.) ; foreign subscription, 5c. added for each pamphlet.

Printing and binding, Supreme Court, supplemental estimate of appropriation for Supreme Court, fiscal year 1924, for printing and binding. May 8, 1924. 2 p. (H. doc. 269, 68th Cong. 1st sess.)   * Paper, 5c.

TREASURY DEPARTMENT

Claims. Judgments rendered by Court of Claims, list of judgments rendered by Court of Claims which have been submitted by Secretary of Treasury and require appropriation for their payment. May 22, 1924. 4 p. (H. doc. 301, 68th Cong. 1st sess.) *Paper, 5c.

9—6546

—— Laws and regulations governing recognition of attorneys, agents, and other persons representing claimants and others before Treasury Department and offices thereof. [1924.] 16 p. 4° (Department circular 230, with supplements 1–3; Chief Clerk.) [This circular supersedes Department circular 230, dated Feb. 15, 1921, and its several supplements.] †

—— Same. Apr. 15, 1924. 1 p. 4° (3d supplement to Department circular 230 dated Aug. 15, 1923; Chief Clerk.) †

—— Richard P. Moore, communication submitting claim of Richard P. Moore which has been adjusted and which requires appropriation for its payment. May 2, 1924. 2 p. (H. doc. 263, 68th Cong. 1st sess.) *Paper, 5c.

Finance. Daily statement of Treasury compiled from latest proved reports from Treasury offices and depositaries. May 1–31, 1924. [1924.] Each 4 p. or 3 p. f° [Daily except Sundays and holidays.] †

15—3303

Government securities. Letter from Secretary of Treasury to President of United States with respect to report submitted to Attorney General, Jan. 15, 1924, by Charles B. Brewer, special assistant to Attorney General, regarding alleged duplications of public debt. Apr. 26, 1924. [1]+186 p. 4° †

24—26525

Matthews, S. T. Rev. S. T. Matthews, communication submitting claim of S. T. Matthews which has been adjusted and which requires appropriation for its payment. May 17, 1924. 2 p. (H. doc. 291, 68th Cong. 1st sess.) *Paper, 5c.

Public debt. Statement of public debt of United States, Feb. 29, 1924. [1924.] [2] p. narrow f° [Monthly.] †

10—21268

Treasury decisions under customs, internal revenue, and other laws, including decisions of Board of General Appraisers and Court of Customs Appeals, v. 45, no. 18–22; May 1–29, 1924. 1924. various paging. [Weekly. Department decisions numbered 40131–210, general appraisers' decisions 8779–8807, abstracts 47170–306, internal revenue decisions 3585–94, and later Tariff Commission Notice 4.] *Paper, 5c. single copy, $1.00 a yr.; foreign subscription, $2.00.

10—30490

APPRAISERS

Reappraisements of merchandise by general appraisers [on Apr. 21–May 23, 1924]; May 2–29, 1924. [1924.] various paging. (Reappraisement circulars 3507–11.) [Weekly.] *Paper, 5c. single copy, 50c. a yr.; foreign subscription, $1.05.

13—2916

BUDGET BUREAU

Agricultural Economics Bureau. Bureau of Agricultural Economics, supplemental estimate of appropriation for Department of Agriculture, fiscal year 1925, for general expenses. Bureau of Agricultural Economics (crop and livestock estimates). May 19, 1924. 2 p. (H. doc. 295, 68th Cong. 1st sess.) *Paper 5c.

Census Bureau. Collecting statistics, Bureau of Census, supplemental estimate of appropriation for Department of Commerce, fiscal year 1925, for collecting statistics, Bureau of Census. May 19, 1924. 2 p. (H. doc. 297, 68th Cong. 1st sess.) *Paper, 5c.

Chemistry Bureau. General expenses, Bureau of Chemistry, supplemental estimate of appropriation for Department of Agriculture, fiscal year 1925, for purpose of enabling Secretary of Agriculture to carry into effect provisions of act of Mar. 3, 1923 [relating to naval stores]. May 26, 1924. 2 p. (H. doc. 323, 68th Cong. 1st sess.) *Paper, 5c.

Coconut palm scale. Coconut scale control in Guam, supplemental estimate of appropriation for Department of Agriculture, fiscal year 1924, for control and eradication of coconut scale on island of Guam, to remain available until June 30, 1925. May 5, 1924. 2 p. (H. doc. 268, 68th Cong. 1st sess.) *Paper, 5c.

District of Columbia. For bathing beach and bathhouse for colored population, Washington,.D. C,. supplemental estimate of appropriation for improvement and care of public buildings, District of Columbia, fiscal year 1924, for construction of bathing beach and bathhouse for colored population of Washington and care and maintenance of same, to remain available until June 30, 1925. May 26, 1924. 3 p. (H. doc. 325, 68th Cong. 1st sess.) * Paper, 5c.

—— Miscellaneous expenses, Supreme Court, District of Columbia [etc.], deficiency estimate of appropriation, fiscal year 1923, and supplemental estimates of appropriations, fiscal year 1924, for District of Columbia. May 14, 1924. 3 p. (H. doc. 279, 68th Cong. 1st sess.) * Paper, 5c.

—— Probation system, Supreme Court, District of Columbia, salaries and expenses, Court of Appeals, District of Columbia, supplemental estimates of appropriations, fiscal year 1925, required to provide for employees of field service of probation system, Supreme Court, District of Columbia, and for salaries and expenses, Court of Appeals, District of Columbia, comparable to those provided by classification act of 1923 for employees within District of Columbia. May 28, 1924. 2 p. (H. doc. 337, 68th Cong. 1st sess.) * Paper, 5c.

—— Recorder of deeds, supplemental estimate of appropriation for District of Columbia, fiscal year 1925, for rent of offices for recorder of deeds. Apr. 30. 1924. 2 p. (H. doc. 252. 68th Cong. 1st sess.) * Paper, 5c.

—— Rent Commission,. District of Columbia, 1924–25, supplemental estimate of appropriation for District of Columbia, fiscal year 1924, to pay salaries and expenses for continuance of Rent Commission, May 23, 1924–May 22. 1925 May 22, 1924. 3 p. (H. doc. 300, 68th Cong. 1st sess.) * Paper, 5c.

—— Supplemental and deficiency estimates of appropriations for District of Columbia [fiscal year 1924, and prior fiscal years], together with certain proposed legislation. May 2, 1924. 12 p. (H. doc. 265, 68th Cong. 1st sess.) * Paper, 5c.

Foot-and-mouth disease. Eradication of foot-and-mouth and other contagious diseases of animals, supplemental estimate of appropriation for Department of Agriculture, fiscal year 1924, to remain available until June 30, 1925, for eradication of foot-and-mouth and other contagious diseases of animals, $3,500,000. May 28, 1924. 2 p. (H. doc. 339, 68th Cong. 1st sess.) * Paper, 5c.

Government officials and employees. Estimates of appropriations for Government Departments, fiscal year 1925, supplemental estimates of appropriations, fiscal year 1925' required to provide for employees of field services of the several Departments and establishments at compensation rates comparable to those provided by classification act of 1923 for employees within District of Columbia. May 24, 1924. 12 p. (H. doc. 309, 68th Cong. 1st sess.) * Paper, 5c.

Hawaii. Cooperative vocational education in agriculture, trades. and industries in Hawaii, supplemental estimate of appropriation for Federal Board for Vocational Education, fiscal year 1925, to carry out provisions of act for cooperative vocational education in agriculture, trades, and industries in Hawaii. May 16, 1924. 2 p. (H. doc. 284, 68th Cong. 1st sess.) * Paper, 5c.

—— Promotion of welfare and hygiene of maternity and infancy in Hawaii, supplemental estimate of appropriation for Department of Labor, fiscal year 1925, to carry into effect provisions of act relative to promotion of welfare and hygiene of maternity and infancy in Hawaii. May 16, 1924. 2 p. (H. doc. 283, 68th Cong. 1st sess.) * Paper, 5c.

Immigration Bureau. Increasing appropriation to patrol Canadian and Mexican borders, draft of proposed legislation amending act making appropriations for Departments of State and Justice and for judiciary, and for Departments of Commerce and Labor, for personal services in District of Columbia, from not to exceed $50,000 to not to exceed $100,000. May 28, 1924. 2 p. (H. doc. 336, 68th Cong. 1st sess.) * Paper, 5c.

Inter-American Electrical Communications Committee. Meeting of Inter-American Committee on Electrical Communications, supplemental estimate of appropriation for Department of State, fiscal year 1924, to defray cost of representation of United States at meeting of Inter-American Committee on Electrical Communications to be held in Mexico City, Mexico, beginning May 27. 1924. May 2, 1924. 2 p. (H. doc. 264, 68th Cong. 1st sess.) * Paper, 5c.

Interior Department. Estimates of appropriations for Department of Interior. 1924 and 1925, deficiency estimates of appropriations for Department of Interior, 1923 and prior fiscal years. and supplemental estimates of appropriations, fiscal years 1924 and 1925. May 24, 1924. 7 p. (H. doc. 308. 68th Cong. 1st sess.) * Paper, 5c.

Interstate Commerce Commission. valuation of property of carriers, supplemental estimate of appropriation for Interstate Commerce Commission, fiscal year 1925, for valuation of property of carriers. May 21, 1924. 3 p. (H. doc. 299, 68th Cong. 1st sess.) * Paper, 5c.

Justice Department. Deficiency and supplemental estimates of appropriations for Department of Justice to June 30, 1924, deficiency estimates of appropriations, fiscal year 1923 and prior years, and supplemental estimates of appropriations, fiscal year 1924. May 16, 1924. 6 p. (H. doc. 285, 68th Cong. 1st sess.) * Paper, 5c.

—— Investigations in connection with war transactions. supplemental estimate of appropriation for Department of Justice, fiscal year 1924. for additional funds in connection with court appropriations and to provide supplemental amount sufficient to continue investigations in connection with war transactions. May 1, 1924. 3 p. (H. doc. 253, 68th Cong. 1st sess.) * Paper. 5c.

—— Lease of court room in New York City and appropriations for Department of Justice, deficiency estimates of appropriations, fiscal year 1923, and supplemental estimates of appropriations, fiscal year 1924. for Department of Justice, also draft of proposed legislation affecting appropriation for 1925. to authorize lease of court rooms in New York City for period of 5 years. May 2, 1924. 4 p. (H. doc. 257, 68th Cong. 1st sess.) * Paper, 5c.

Mexican Claims Commissions. General and Special Claims Commissions. United States and Mexico, supplemental estimate of appropriation for Department of State, fiscal year 1925, for General and Special Claims Commissions, United States and Mexico. May 9, 1924. 3 p. (H. doc. 270. 68th Cong. 1st sess.) * Paper, 5c.

Naval Observatory, supplemental estimate of appropriation for Navy Department, fiscal year 1924, to complete purchase of land lying within Naval Observatory Circle. May 5, 1924. 2 p. (H. doc. 266. 68th Cong. 1st sess.) * Paper, 5c.

Navy Department. Pay, miscellaneous, 1921, Navy Department. refund to Panama Railroad Co., 1924. also drafts of proposed legislation. deficiency estimate of appropriation, fiscal year 1921, and supplemental estimate of appropriation. fiscal year 1924, for Navy Department, also drafts of proposed legislation affecting certain existing appropriations. May 14, 1924. 4 p. (H. doc. 277, 68th Cong. 1st sess.) * Paper, 5c.

Nisqualli Reservation. Reimbursement to Nisqually Indians, Washington, supplemental estimate of appropriation for Department of Interior, fiscal year 1924, to compensate certain Nisqually Indians, of Washington, for lands and improvements given up for use by War Department. May 27, 1924. 2 p. (H. doc. 335, 68th Cong. 1st sess.) * Paper, 5c.

Post Office Department. Deficiency and supplemental estimates of appropriation for Post Office Department, deficiency estimates of appropriations for Post Office Department, fiscal year 1923 and prior fiscal years. and supplemental estimates of appropriations, fiscal year 1924. May 10, 1924. 7 p. (H. doc. 271, 68th Cong. 1st sess.) * Paper, 5c.

Public moneys. Contingent expenses, public moneys, supplemental estimate of appropriation for Treasury Department, fiscal year 1924. for expenses in connection with handling of public moneys. May 24, 1924. 2 p. (H. doc. 307, 68th Cong. 1st sess.) * Paper, 5c.

Reclamation Service, supplemental estimates of appropriations for Department of Interior, pertaining to Reclamation Service, fiscal year 1925. May 21. 1924. 5 p. (H. doc. 298, 68th Cong. 1st sess.) * Paper, 5c.

State Department. Appropriations for Department of State, 1924 and 1925. supplemental estimates of appropriations for Department of State, fiscal year 1924 and fiscal year 1925. also draft of proposed legislation making appropriation for embassy building in London, England, available until June 30, 1925. May 29, 1924. 5 p. (H. doc. 340, 68th Cong. 1st sess.) * Paper, 5c.

State, War, and Navy Department Building Office. Elevator repair, State, War, and Navy Department Building, supplemental estimate of appropriation for Office of Superintendent State, War, and Navy Building, fiscal year 1924, and to remain available until June 30, 1925, for rebuilding elevators. May 12, 1924. 2 p. (H. doc. 272, 68th Cong. 1st sess.) * Paper, 5c.

Story, Fort. For construction of road at Fort Story (Va.) military reservation, supplemental estimate of appropriation for War Department, fiscal year 1924, for construction of road at Fort Story, Va., to remain available until June 30, 1925, and draft of proposed legislation to make appropriation for fire control, Panama Canal, available until June 30, 1925. May 5, 1924. 3 p. (H. doc. 267, 68th Cong. 1st sess.) * Paper, 5c.

Treasury Department. Appropriations for Treasury Department, 1924 and 1925, supplemental estimates of appropriations for Treasury Department, fiscal year 1924 and fiscal year 1925, also proposed authorization to use an existing appropriation. May 17, 1924. 6 p. (H. doc. 292, 68th Cong. 1st sess.) * Paper, 5c.

Veterans' Bureau. Vocational rehabilitation, deficiency estimate of appropriation for veterans' Bureau, vocational rehabilitation, fiscal year 1923. May 14, 1924. 2 p. (H. doc. 280, 68th Cong. 1st sess.) * Paper, 5c.

War Department. Two drafts of proposed legislation affecting appropriations in War Department. May 26, 1924. 3 p. (H. doc. 324, 68th Cong. 1st sess.) * Paper, 5c.

War-ships. Scrapping of naval vessels, supplemental estimate of appropriation for Navy Department, fiscal year 1924, to remain available until 1925, for scrapping of naval vessels. May 16, 1924. 3 p. (H. doc. 290, 68th Cong. 1st sess.) * Paper, 5c.

World War adjusted compensation act. Administrative expenses, World War adjusted compensation act, Navy Department, supplemental estimate of appropriation for Navy Department, fiscal year 1925, for purpose of enabling Secretary of Navy to perform duties required of him by World War adjusted compensation act. May 24, 1924. 3 p. (H. doc. 310, 68th Cong. 1st sess.) * Paper, 5c.

—— Administrative expenses, World War adjusted compensation act, Veterans' Bureau, 1924, supplemental estimates of appropriations for Veterans' Bureau, fiscal years 1924 and 1925, to defray cost of adjusted compensation for veterans of World War. May 26, 1924. 3 p. (H. doc. 318, 68th Cong. 1st sess.) * Paper, 5c.

—— Administrative expenses, World War adjusted compensation act, War Department, supplemental estimate of appropriation for War Department, fiscal year 1924, to remain available until June 30, 1925, for purpose of enabling Secretary of War to perform duties required of him by World War adjusted compensation act. May 24, 1924. 3 p. (H. doc. 311, 68th Cong. 1st sess.) * Paper, 5c.

—— Salaries, General Accounting Office, 1925, supplemental estimate of appropriation for General Accounting Office, fiscal year 1925, for purpose of enabling comptroller general to meet additional work which will devolve upon him by reason of World War adjusted compensation act. May 27, 1924. 2 p. (H. doc. 334, 68th Cong. 1st sess.) * Paper, 5c.

COAST GUARD

Circular letter 11–14; Apr. 22–24, 1924. [1924.] various paging. ‡

Ice. International ice observation and ice patrol service in north Atlantic Ocean, season of 1923. 1924. iii+166 p. il. 2 pl. 6 p. of pl. 13 maps. (Bulletin 11.) * Paper, 40c.

Officers. Information relative to temporary appointment as commissioned officer in Coast Guard. [1924.] 5 p. †

COMPTROLLER OF CURRENCY

National banks. Abstract of reports of condition of national banks, Mar. 31, 1924; no. 143. [1924.] 13 p. f° †

—— Monthly statement of capital stock of national banks, national bank notes, and Federal reserve bank notes outstanding, bonds on deposit, etc. [May 1, 1924]. May 1, 1924. 1 p. f° †   10—21266

GENERAL SUPPLY COMMITTEE

Government supplies. Contract for supplies listed in General schedule of supplies [fiscal year 1925]. [1924.] [2] leaves, 4° [Blank form.] †

GOVERNMENT ACTUARY

Bonds of United States. Market prices and investment values of outstanding bonds and notes [of United States, Apr. 1924]. May 1. 1924. 7 p. 4° (Form A.) [Monthly.] †

INTERNAL REVENUE BUREAU

Internal revenue bulletin, v. 3, no. 18–21; May 5–26, 1924. 1924. various paging. [Weekly.] * Paper, 5c. single copy (for subscription price see note below).

24—26051

NOTE.—The Internal revenue bulletin service for 1924 will consist of weekly bulletins, quarterly digests, and semiannual cumulative bulletins. The weekly bulletins will contain the rulings to be made public and all internal revenue Treasury decisions. The quarterly digests, with the exception of the one to be published at the end of 1924, will contain digests of the rulings previously published in the weekly bulletins for 1924. The last digest for 1924 will also contain digests of the rulings published during 1922 and 1923. The semiannual cumulative bulletins will contain all new rulings published during the previous 6 months. The complete bulletin service may be obtained, on a subscription basis, from the Superintendent of Documents, Government Printing Office, Washington, D. C., for $2.00 a yr.; foreign subscription, $2.75.

Liquors. Statistics concerning intoxicating liquors, May, 1924. 1924. v+33 p. (Prohibition Unit.) * Paper, 5c.

24—26447

LOANS AND CURRENCY DIVISION

Bonds of United States. Caveat list of United States registered bonds and notes, May 1, 1924. [1924.] 56 p. f° [Monthly.] †

Money. Circulation statement of United States money, Apr. 1, 1924. [1924.] 1 p. oblong 8° [Monthly.] †

10—21267

—— Same, May 1, 1924. [1924.] 1 p. oblong 8° [Monthly.] †

PUBLIC HEALTH SERVICE

Botulism. Outbreaks of botulism at Albany, Oreg., and Sterling, Colo., Feb. 1924; [articles] by Frederick D. Stricker and J. C. Geiger. 1924. 11 p. (Reprint 911.) [From Public health reports, Apr. 4, 1924.] * Paper, 5c.

24—26526

Diphtheria immunization [with list of references]. Revised edition, 1924. 1924. [1]+5 p. (Reprint 698.) [Original article from Public health reports, Oct. 7, 1921.] * Paper, 5c.

24—26527

Malta fever, cattle suggested as possible source of infection, following serological study of human serums [with list of references]; by Alice C. Evans. 1924. [1]+18 p. (Reprint 906.) [From Public health reports, Mar. 14, 1924.] * Paper, 5c.

24—26483

Mosquitos. Effect of Chara robbinsii on mosquito larvæ [with list of references]; by M. A. Barber. 1924. [1]+5 p. (Reprint 910.) [From Public health reports, Mar. 28, 1924.] * Paper, 5c.

24—26528

Neoarsphenamine. Method for estimation of total sulphur in neoarsphenamine and sulpharsphenamine; by Elias Elvove. 1924. [1]+5 p. (Reprint 913.) [From Public health reports, Apr. 11, 1924.] * Paper, 5c.

24—26529

Nutrition. New Baldwin-Wood weight-height-age tables as index of nutrition, application of Baldwin-Wood standard of nutrition to 506 native white children without physical defects and good or excellent nutrition as judged from clinical evidence; by Taliaferro Clark, Edgar Sydenstricker, and Selwyn D. Collins. 1924. [1]+8 p. (Reprint 907.) [From Public health reports, Mar. 14, 1924.] * Paper, 5c.

24—26530

Public health reports, v. 39, no. 18–22; May 2–30, 1924. 1924. [xx]+923–1357 p. il. 2 p. of pl. [Weekly.] * Paper, 5c. single copy, $1.50 a yr.; foreign subscription, $2.75.

6—25167

Public health reports—**Continued.**

SPECIAL ARTICLES.—No. 18. Relative efficiency of methods of sterilization of milk bottles at pasteurization plants in Minnesota; by H. A. Whittaker, R. W. Archibald. and L. Shere.—Immigrants' hostel at Eastleigh, England.—Notifiable diseases, prevalence during 1922 in cities of 10,000 to 100,000 population.—No. 19, Tularæmia: 11, Tularæmia infection in ticks of species Dermacentor andersoni Stiles in Bitterroot Valley, Mont.; by R. R. Parker, R. R. Spencer, and Edward Francis.—Report of case of Dibothriocephalus latus (Diphyllobothrium latum); by T. B. H. Anderson.—School medical inspection in Hagerstown and Washington County, Md.; by C. V. Akin.—No. 20. Epidemiological principles affecting distribution of malaria in southern United States [with list of references]; by Kenneth F. Maxcy.—Extent of rural health service in United States, 1920–24; by L. L. Lumsden.—Whole time county health officers, 1924 [directory].—How Connecticut Department of Health tests clinical thermometers.—No. 21. Prevalence and trend of drug addiction in United States and factors influencing it [with list of references]; by Lawrence Kolb and A. G. DuMez.—Sins of the father [by John Norman Cruickshank]; abstract by Taliaferro Clark.—Reports of Health Section of League of Nations.—Summary of provisional birth and mortality figures, 1923.—No. 22. Some experiments on antigenic principles of ragweed pollen extract (Ambrosia elatior and Ambrosia trifida) [with list of references]; by W. T. Harrison and Charles Armstrong.—Health by radio.—Some publications suitable for general distribution [issued by Public Health Service].

NOTE.—This publication is distributed gratuitously to State and municipal health officers, etc., by the Surgeon General of the Public Health Service, Treasury Department. Others desiring these reports may obtain them from the Superintendent of Documents, Washington, D. C., at the prices stated above.

Summer schools. The 1924 public health summer schools to be held at Columbia University, University of California, University of Iowa, University of Michigan, in cooperation with Public Health Service. 1924. cover-title, xiii+128 p. [Final general announcement.]   * Paper, 15c.   24—26446

Workmen's compensation acts in United States, medical aspect, review [of Research report 61, of National Industrial Conference Board]; by E. C. Ernst. 1924. [1]+5 p. (Reprint 909.) [From Public health reports, Mar. 21, 1924.] * Paper, 5c.   24—26484

VENEREAL DISEASES DIVISION

Venereal disease information, issued by Public Health Service for use in its cooperative work with State health departments, v. 5, no. 4; Apr. 20, 1924. 1924. ii+163–222 p. [Monthly.] * Paper, 5c. single copy, 50c. a yr.; foreign subscription, 75c. . .   23—26719

SPECIAL ARTICLES.—Diagnostic signs of congenital syphilis [with bibliography]; by B. Bickel.—Study of attitude of group of male negroes toward venereal diseases.

Venereal diseases. Dividends from venereal disease control. [1924.] 16 p. 16° ([V. D. 70.]) †   24—26531

—— venereal disease menace, exhibit for adults; prepared by Public Health Service for use in its cooperative work with State departments of health: [posters] 1+1–50. [1924.] Each 12×9 in. [This set of posters consists of a title poster and 50 numbered posters.] * $1.00 per set.

Title poster and 4 introductory posters; [posters] 1 and 1–4.
[pt.] 1. Nature of venereal diseases; [posters] 5–12.
[pt.] 2. Effects of venereal diseases; [posters] 13–21.
[pt.] 3. Prevalence of venereal diseases; [posters] 22–25.
[pt.] 4. Control of venereal diseases; [posters] 26–46.
[pt. 5.] The aims; [posters] 47–50.

TREASURER OF UNITED STATES

Paper money. Monthly statement, paper currency of each denomination outstanding Mar. 31, 1924. Apr. 1 [1924]. 1 p. oblong 24° †

VETERANS' BUREAU

Claims. Seven claims adjusted by director of veterans' Bureau, communication from director of veterans' Bureau submitting estimate of appropriation to pay 7 claims for damages to or loss of privately owned property, which he has adjusted and which require appropriation for their payment. May 26, 1924. 4 p. (H. doc. 319, 68th Cong. 1st sess.) * Paper, 5c.

Opinions. Digests of legal opinions relating to veterans' Bureau, including opinions of general counsel of veterans' Bureau, comptroller general, and Attorney General, Dec. 1923; no. 4. 1924. viii+32 p. [Monthly.] * Paper, 5c.   24—26146

—— Same, Jan. 1924; no. 5. 1924. viii+33 p. [Monthly.] *Paper, 5c.

Regulations, Veterans' Bureau [1923]. supplement 3: Mar. 31. 1924. 1924. iv+9 p. ‡

WAR DEPARTMENT

Army regulations. †

NOTE.—The Army regulations are issued in pamphlet form for insertion in loose-leaf binders. The names of such of the more important administrative subjects as may seem appropriate, arranged in proper sequence, are numbered in a single series, and each name so numbered constitutes the title and number of a pamphlet containing certain administrative regulations pertaining thereto. Where more than one pamphlet is required for the administrative regulations pertaining to any such title, additional pamphlets will be issued in a separate sub-series.

20–20.   Inspector General's Department: Special and miscellaneous inspections, Changes 1; May 1, 1924. 1924. 1 p.
20–35.   Same: Inspection of property for condemnation, Changes 1; Apr. 10, 1924. 1924. 1 p.
30–455.   Quartermaster Corps: Branding and registration of public animals; Apr. 2, 1924. [1924.] 2 p.
35–2385. Finance Department: Additional compensation for enlisted men of Philippine Scouts for special qualification in use of arms; Mar. 15, 1924. 1924. 1 p.
40–1070. Medical Department: Clinical records and indexes, Changes 1; Apr. 9, 1924. 1924. 1 p.
40–1080. Same: Current statistical reports, tables, and charts; Jan. 29, 1924. [1924.] 20 p.
90–30.   Coast Artillery Corps: Coast artillery districts; Dec. 15, 1922. [1923.] 2 p. [Supersedes AR 90–30, Mar. 2, 1922.]
90–40.   Same: Coast defense command, Changes 2; Mar. 7, 1924. 1924. 1 p. [Supersedes AR 90–40, Changes 1, Nov. 15, 1922.]
95–10.   Air Service: Air Service troops; Apr. 16, 1924. [1924.] 2 p. [Supersedes AR 95–10, Apr. 20, 1923.]
170–10.   Corps areas, departments, and District of Washington; May 1, 1924. [1924.] 9 p.
260–10.   Flags, colors, standards, and guidons: Description and use, Changes 1; Apr. 1, 1924. 1924. 1 p.
345–800. Military records: Reports of changes, reports of casualties, and memoranda of transmittal, Changes 3; Mar. 21, 1924. [1924.] 3 p. [Supersedes AR 345–800, Changes 1 and 2, Mar. 7 and Apr. 17, 1923.]
350–105. Military education: General and special service schools, designations, locations, and organizations; May 1, 1924. [1924.] 2 p. [Supersedes AR 350–105, Nov. 8, 1922.]
615–5.   Enlisted men: Appointment and reduction of noncommissioned officers and privates, 1st class, except in Medical Department, Changes 1; Apr. 25, 1924. 1924. 1 p.
615–20.   Same: Rating and disrating of specialists, Medical Department, Medical, Dental, and Veterinary services; Nov. 30, 1923. [1924.] 19 p.
850–5.   Marking of clothing, equipment, animals, vehicles, and property, Changes 1; Apr. 2, 1924. 1924. 1 p.

Claims. Seven claims adjusted by Secretary of War, 2 communications submitting claims for damages to or loss of privately owned property of 7 claimants which have been adjusted and which require appropriation for their payment. May 2, 1924. 4 p. (H. doc. 259, 68th Cong. 1st sess.) * Paper, 5c.

Government officials. Practice of ex-officials before War Department, in response to resolution, information relative to appearance of ex-Senators and ex-Members of Cabinet who since Jan. 1, 1918, have appeared as attorneys or agents before War Department advocating claims against Government. Apr. 24, calendar day Apr. 28, 1924. 8 p. (S. doc. 99, 68th Cong. 1st sess.) * Paper, 5c.
                                                                    24—26532

Mexico. Shipment of arms to Mexico, letter submitting, in response to resolution concerning sale of arms and munitions to Government of Mexico, supplemental report containing remaining data not covered in letter of Mar. 31, 1924. 1924. ii+21 p. (S. doc. 104, 68th Cong. 1st sess.) * Paper, 5c.
                                                                    24—26465

Muscle Shoals. Lease of Muscle Shoals plant, proposal of Union Carbide Co., of New York, for lease of Government power and nitrate plants at Muscle Shoals and Sheffield, Ala. May 5, calendar day May 7, 1924. 12 p. (S. doc. 105, 68th Cong. 1st sess.) * Paper, 5c.
                                                                    24—26466

Training regulations.

NOTE.—The Training regulations are issued in pamphlet form for insertion in loose-leaf binders.

150–25.   Marksmanship: Pistol, mounted, prepared under direction of chief of cavalry; Jan. 28, 1924. [1924.] 19 p. il. * Paper, 5c.
420–70.   Infantry: Drill, service company, infantry regiment, prepared under direction of chief of infantry; Jan. 28, 1924. [1924.] 11 p. il. * Paper, 5c.
420–100. Same: Development of offensive combat, prepared under direction of chief of infantry; Mar. 21, 1924. [1924.] 19 p. il. * Paper, 5c.
420–180. Same: Combat principles, service company, infantry regiment, prepared under direction of chief of infantry; Feb. 1, 1924. [1924.] 16 p. il. * Paper, 5c.
425–75.   Cavalry: Cavalry machine-gun troop, prepared under direction of chief of cavalry; Mar. 3, 1924. [1924.] 21 p. il. * Paper, 5c.

Training regulations—Continued.

425–80. Same: Cavalry machine-gun squadron, prepared under direction of chief. of cavalry; Mar. 3, 1924. [1924.] 14 p. il. * Paper, 5c.

—— Changes in Training regulations for 1923. Feb. 8, 1924. xx leaves, il. [Some of these leaves are printed as pages. Training regulations amended are 50–15, 50–20, 50–45, 50–65, 50–70, 135–5, 165–5, 190–5, 420–45, 420–50, 420–85, 430–85, and 435–310.] * Paper, 5c.

NOTE.—The changes have been printed on one side only and of a size to permit of cutting and pasting each changed paragraph or subparagraph over the paragraph of the original.

ADJUTANT GENERAL'S DEPARTMENT

Army list and directory, May 1, 1924. 1924. v+278 p. large 8° [Bimonthly.] * Paper, 25c. single copy, $1.25 a yr.; foreign subscription, $1.85. 9—35106

Bookkeeping, students manual for all arms; prepared under direction of quartermaster general, Army, 1923. 1924. vi+162 p. (United States Army training manual 73.) * Cloth, 30c.

Citizenship. Studies in citizenship for citizens military training camps. 1924. 44 p. (United States Army training manual 4.) * Fabrikoid, 20c.

U. S. Army recruiting news, bulletin of recruiting information issued by direction of Adjutant General of Army, May 1 and 15, 1924. [Recruiting Publicity Bureau, Governors Island, N. Y., May 1 and 15, 1924.] Each 16 p. il. 4° † Recruiting Publicity Bureau, Governors Island, N. Y. War 22—1

AIR SERVICE

Aeronautical bulletins. Aeronautical bulletin, no. 125–139, Route information series; Apr. 15, 1924. [1924.] various paging, 12° (Airways Section.) [No. 125 is errata to no. 67, 70, 85.] * Paper, 5c. each. 23—26231

—— Aeronautical bulletin, no. 158, 201–228, 230, 232, State series; Feb. 15– May 1, 1924. [1924.] various paging, il. 12° (Airway Section.) [No. 220 is errata to no. 2, 16, 34, 59, 63, 72, 77, 109, 131–135.] * Paper, 5c. each.

ENGINEERING DIVISION

Airships. Lift of gases in practical balloon and airship operation, Lighter-than-Air Section report; by Ollie L. Lewis. 1924. ii+38 p. il. 4° (Air Service. Air Service information circular, aerostation, v. 1, no. 42, Mar. 1, 1924.) ‡

—— Speed and ceiling of U. S. Army airships, Lighter-than-Air Section report; by Ollie L. Lewis. 1924. ii+18 p. il. 4° (Air Service. Air Service information circular, aerostation, v. 1, no. 43, Mar. 1, 1924.) ‡

Wind tunnel tests. Aileron effectiveness, wind tunnel tests of U. S. A.–35 (half-span) airfoil with skewed ailerons, Airplane Section report; by A. L. Morse. 1924. ii+8 p. il. 4° (Air Service. Air Service information circular, aviation, v. 5, no. 454, Mar. 15, 1924.) ‡

—— Wind tunnel test of CO–2A model airplane, Airplane Section report; by C. E. Archer. 1924. ii+17 p. il. 4° (Air Service. Air Service information circular, aviation, v. 5, no. 453, Mar. 15, 1924.) ‡

—— Wind tunnel test of original TA–4 with following airfoils, USA–27C large, USA–27C small, Gottingen 387, Gottingen 255, Airplane Section report; by A. L. Morse. 1924. ii+27 p. il. 4° (Air Service. Air Service information circular, aviation, v. 5, no. 455, Mar. 15, 1924.) ‡

ENGINEER DEPARTMENT

Alligator Creek and Four Mile Creek, S. C., reports on preliminary examination and survey of Alligator Creek and Four Mile Creek, S. C. Apr. 12, 1924. 14 p. map. (H. doc. 237, 68th Cong. 1st sess.) * Paper, 10c.

Baltimore, Md. Maintenance and improvement of existing river and harbor works, harbor at Baltimore, Md., advertisement [for dredging]. [1924.] 14 p. 4° †

Fernandina Harbor, Fla., reports on preliminary examination and survey of
Fernandina Harbor, Fla. Mar. 24, 1924. 18 p. 3 maps. (H. doc. 227, 68th
Cong. 1st sess.) * Paper, 10c.

New York Harbor. Maintenance and improvement of existing river and harbor
works, New York and New Jersey channels, advertisement, no. 24–191 [for
dredging and rock removal]. [1924.] 14 p. 4° †

Officers. Statement showing rank, duties, and addresses of officers of Corps
of Engineers, Army, Apr. 1, 1924. 1924. [1]+25 p. 4° [Quarterly; none
issued for Jan. 1924.] ‡
                                                                War 14—114

St. Clair River. Maintenance and improvement of existing river and harbor
works, St. Clair River, Mich., advertisement [for dredging Russell Island
Shoal]. . [1924.] 13 p. 4° †

St. Marys Falls Canal, Mich., statistical report of lake commerce passing
through canals at Sault Ste. Marie, Mich. and Ontario, season of 1923, with
supplementary report of commerce passing through Detroit River [and
through St. Clair Flats Canal, Mich.; season of 1923]. . 1924. [1]+24 p. il.
11 p. of pl. map. . †
                                                                ES 20—21

NORTHERN AND NORTHWESTERN LAKES SURVEY

NOTE.—Charts of the Great Lakes and connecting waters and St. Lawrence River to
the international boundary at St. Regis, of Lake Champlain, and of the New York State
canals are prepared and sold by the U. S. Lake Survey Office, Old Custom-house, Detroit,
Mich. Charts may also be purchased at the following U. S. engineer offices: 710 Army
Building, New York, N. Y.; 467 Broadway, Albany, N. Y.; 540 Federal Building, Buffalo,
N. Y.; and Canal Office, Sault Ste. Marie, Mich. A catalogue (with index map), showing localities, scales, prices, and conditions of sale, may be had upon application at any
of these offices.
. A descriptive bulletin, which supplements the charts and gives detailed information as
to harbors, shore lines and shoals, magnetic determinations, and particulars of changing
conditions affecting navigation, is issued free to chart purchasers, upon request. The
bulletin is revised annually and issued at the opening of navigation (in April), and supplements thereto are published monthly during the navigation season.
Complete sets of the charts and publications may be seen at the U. S. engineer offices
in Duluth, Minn., Milwaukee, Wis., Chicago, Ill., Grand Rapids, Mich., Cleveland, Ohio,
and Oswego, N. Y., but they are obtainable only at the sales offices above mentioned.

Great Lakes. Supplement 1, May 22, 1924, corrections and additions to Bulletin
33; to supplement information given upon charts of Great Lakes. U. S.
Lake Survey Office, Detroit, Mich. [May 16, 1924]. 12 leaves+[2] p. 4° †

FINANCE DEPARTMENT

Finance circulars. Changes 3 [to] Finance circular 5, 1923; Mar. 29, 1924.
[1924.] 6 leaves, 12° ‡

—— Changes 4 [to] Finance circulars; Apr. 18, 1924. [1924.] 3 leaves, 12°. ‡

GENERAL STAFF CORPS

Field service regulations, Army, 1923. 1924. vii+195 p. il. (War Dept. doc.
1120.) * Cloth, 40c.
                                                                War 24–16

Quartermaster Corps. Changes 24 [for] Manual for Quartermaster Corps,
1916; Mar. 20, 1924. 1924. 1 p. [Manual issued by Quartermaster General
of Army.] †

ORDNANCE DEPARTMENT

Ordnance provision system: Group A, Browning tank machine gun, cal..30,
M1919, parts and accessories; Apr. 23, 1924. [1924.] 33 p. il. (Standard
nomenclature list A–6.) [Supersedes Standard nomenclature list A–6, Aug.
10, 1922.] ‡

Recoil mechanism. Handbook of St. Chamond recoil mechanism for 75-mm.
gun carriage, model of 1916M1, with instructions for its care, Jan. 15, 1924.
. 1924. . 44 p. il. (Ordnance Dept. doc. 2049.) ‡

Steel. Design of steel castings [with bibliography]. 1924. iii+36 p. il. 1 pl.
(Design manual, note no. 4, artillery; Ordnance Dept. doc. 2048.) ‡

Monthly Catalogue
United States
Public Documents

No. 354

June, 1924

THE LIBRARY OF THE

AUG 12 1924

UNIVERSITY OF ILLINOIS

ISSUED BY THE
SUPERINTENDENT OF DOCUMENTS

WASHINGTON
1924

Abbreviations

Appendix	app.	Page, pages	p
Congress	Cong.	Part, parts	pt., pts.
Department	Dept.	Plate, plates	pl.
Document	doc.	Portrait, portraits	por.
Facsimile, facsimiles	facsim.	Quarto	4°
Folio	f°	Report	rp.
House	H.	Saint	St.
• House bill	H. R.	Section, sections	sec.
House concurrent resolution	H. Con. Res.	Senate, Senate bill	S.
House document	H. doc.	Senate concurrent resolution	S. Con. Res.
House executive document	H. ex. doc.	Senate document	S. doc.
House joint resolution	H. J. Res.	Senate executive document	S. ex. doc.
House report	H. rp.	Senate joint resolution	S. J Res.
House resolution (simple)	H. Res.	Senate report	S rp .
Illustration, illustrations	il.	Senate resolution (simple)	S. Res.
Inch, inches	in.	Session	sess.
Latitude	lat.	Sixteenmo	16°
Longitude	long.	Table, tables	tab.
Mile, miles	m.	Thirtytwo-mo	32°
Miscellaneous	mis., misc.	Treasury	Treas.
Nautical	naut.	Twelvemo	12°
No date	n. d.	Twentyfour-mo	24°
No place	n. p.	Versus	vs., v.
Number, numbers	no., nos.	Volume, volumes	v., vol.
Octavo	8°	Year	yr.

Common abbreviations for names of States and months are also used.
*Document for sale by Superintendent of Documents.
†Distribution by office issuing document, free if unaccompanied by a price.
‡Printed for official use.
NOTE.—Nearly all of the Departments of the Government make a limited free distribution of their publications. When an entry shows a * price, it is possible that upon application to the issuing office a copy may be obtained without charge.

Explanation

Words and figures inclosed in brackets [ ] are given for information, but do not appear on the title-pages of the publications catalogued. When size is not given octavo is to be understood. Size of maps is measured from outer edge of border, excluding margin. The dates, including day, month, and year, given with Senate and House documents and reports are the dates on which they were ordered to be printed. Usually the printing promptly follows the ordering, but various causes sometimes make delays.

SALES OF GOVERNMENT PUBLICATIONS

The Superintendent of Documents, Washington, D. C., is authorized to sell at cost, plus 10 per cent, without limit as to the number of copies to any one applicant who agrees not to resell or distribute the same for profit, any United States Government publication not confidential in character.

Publications can not be supplied free to individuals nor forwarded in advance of payment.

Publications entered in this catalogue that are for sale by the Superintendent of Documents are indicated by a star (*) preceding the price. A dagger (†) indicates that application should be made to the Department, Bureau, or Division issuing the document. A double dagger (‡) indicates that the document is printed for official use. Whenever additional information concerning the method of procuring a document seems necessary, it will be found under the name of the Bureau by which it was published.

In ordering a publication from the Superintendent of Documents, give (if known) the name of the publishing Department, Bureau, or Division, and the title of the publication. If the publication is numbered, give the number also. Every such particular assists in quick identification. Do not order by the Library of Congress card number.

The accumulation of publications in this Office amounts to several millions, of which over two million are assorted, forming the sales stock. Many rare books are included, but under the law all must be sold regardless of their age or scarcity. Many of the books have been in stock some time, and are apt to be shop-worn. In filling orders the best copy available is sent. A general price-list of public documents is not available, but lists on special subjects will be furnished on application.

MONTHLY CATALOGUE DISTRIBUTION

The Monthly catalogue is sent to each Senator, Representative, Delegate, Resident Commissioner, and officer in Congress; to designated depositories and State and Territorial libraries if it is selected by them; to substantially all Government authors; and to as many school, college, and public libraries as the limited edition will supply.

Subscription price to individuals, 50c. a year, including index; foreign subscription, 75c. a year. Back numbers can not be supplied. Notify the Superintendent of Documents of any change of address.

LIBRARY OF CONGRESS CARDS

Numbers to be used in ordering the printed catalogue cards of the Library of Congress are given at the end of entries for the more important documents. Orders for these cards, remittances in payment for them, and requests for information about them should be addressed to the Librarian of Congress, not to the Superintendent of Documents.

INDEX

An Index to the Monthly catalogue is issued at the end of the fiscal year. This contains index entries for all the numbers issued from July to June, and can be

bound with the numbers as an index to the volume.   Persons desiring to bind the catalogue at the end of the year should be careful to retain the numbers received monthly, as duplicate copies can not be supplied.

HOW TO REMIT

Remittances for the documents marked with a star (*) should be made to the Superintendent of Documents, Washington, D. C., by coupons, postal money order, express order, or New York draft.   Currency may be sent at sender's risk.

Postage stamps, foreign money, defaced or smooth coins, positively will not be accepted.

For the convenience of the general public, coupons that are good until used in exchange for Government publications sold by the Superintendent of Documents may be purchased from his Office in sets of 20 for $1.00.   Address order to Superintendent of Documents, Government Printing Office, Washington, D. C.

No charge is made for postage on documents forwarded to points in United States, Alaska, Guam, Hawaii, Philippine Islands, Porto Rico, Samoa, or to Canada, Cuba, or Mexico.   To other countries the regular rate of postage is charged, and remittances must cover such postage.   In computing foreign postage, add one-third of the price of the publication.

Binding the Catalogue

The Documents Office will soon issue an index to all entries in the twelve numbers of the Monthly catalogue, July, 1923, to June, 1924.   A title-page for the twelve numbers of the catalogue will accompany the index. Duplicate numbers of the Monthly catalogue can not be supplied.

MONTHLY CATALOGUE

AGRICULTURE DEPARTMENT

NOTE.—Those publications of the Department of Agriculture which are for sale will be supplied by the Superintendent of Documents, Washington, D. C. The Department issues a monthly list of publications, which is mailed to all applicants, enabling them to select such reports and bulletins as interest them.

Cattle. [Bureau of Animal Industry] order 287 [amendment 16], relative to foot-and-mouth disease in cattle, sheep, other ruminants, and swine, effective June 5, 1924; June 5, 1924. [1924.] 1 p. †

Cotton. Modification of cotton regulations, amendment 1 of Rules and regulations governing importation of cotton and cotton wrappings into United States [revised Feb. 24, 1923], effective May 1, 1924. [1924.] 2 p. (Federal Horticultural Board.) †

Crops and markets. Crops and markets, weekly, June 7–28, 1924; v. 1, no. 23–26. [1924.] p. 353–416, il. 4° *Paper, $1.00 a yr. (including monthly supplement); foreign subscription, $2.00.   Agr 24—113

—— Same, monthly supplement, June, 1924; v. 1, supplement 6. [1924.] p. 169–208, il. 4° [Included in price of weekly Crops and markets.]

Forest fires. Fighting and preventing forest fires, supplemental estimate of appropriation for Department of Agriculture, fiscal year 1924, for fighting and preventing forest fires. June 3, 1924. 4 p. (H. doc. 347, 68th Cong. 1st sess.) *Paper, 5c.

Official record, Department of Agriculture, v. 3, no. 23–26; June 4–25, 1924. [1924.] Each 8 p. il. 4° [Weekly.] *Paper, 50c. a yr.; foreign subscription, $1.10.   Agr 22—146

Quarantine. Notice of quarantine 16: Sugar cane quarantine (domestic). June 6, 1914, [reprint] 1924. 1 p. (Federal Horticultural Board.) †

—— Quarantine on account of Japanese beetle [Notice of quarantine 48, with regulations (3d revision), effective Apr. 9, 1924]. [1924.] 11 p. map. (Federal Horticultural Board.) †

AGRICULTURAL ECONOMICS BUREAU

Farm labor. Sources of supply and conditions of employment of harvest labor in wheat belt; by Don D. Lescohier. May 23, 1924. 27 p. il. (Agriculture Dept. Department bulletin 1211.) *Paper, 5c.   Agr 24—502

Farms. Relation of land income to land value [with appendix]; by Clyde R. Chambers. June 11, 1924. cover-title, 132 p. il. (Agriculture Dept. Department bulletin 1224.) *Paper, 15c.   Agr 24—514

—— Same, appendix omitted. May, 1924. cover-title, p. 1–69, il. [From Department bulletin 1224.] †

—— Same, appendix only. May, 1924. cover-title, [1] + 70–132 p. [From Department bulletin 1224.] †

Hay. United States grades for timothy hay, clover hay, clover mixed hay, and grass mixed hay, effective Feb. 1, 1924, including outline of haymaking, baling, and loading methods essential to marketing of high grade hay; [by] Edward C. Parker. June, 1924. 24 p. il. (Agriculture Dept. Department circular 326.) *Paper, 5c.   Agr 24—521

Potatoes. Handling and loading southern new potatoes; [by] A. M. Grimes. [May 1, 1919, reprint] 1924. 19 p. il. (Agriculture Dept. Farmers' bulletin 1050.) [Mar. 1922, on p. 2, is date of previous reprint which was issued by the Markets and Crop Estimates Bureau.] *Paper, 5c.

Seed statistics, year ending May 31, 1923, with comparable data for earlier years. Apr. 1924. cover-title, 100 p. (Agriculture Dept. Statistical bulletin 2.) [Text and illustration on p. 2 and 3 of cover.] * Paper, 15c.

Agr 24—527

Service announcements. Service and regulatory announcements, no. 83: Regulations of Secretary of Agriculture under warehouse act of Aug. 11, 1916, as amended, regulations for potato warehouses, approved May 10, 1924. June, 1924. cover-title, i+27 p. * Paper, 5c.

Agr 15—199

—— Same, no. 84: Regulations of Secretary of Agriculture under warehouse act of Aug. 11, 1916, as amended, regulations for broomcorn warehouses, approved May 16, 1924. 1924. iii+27 p. * Paper, 5c.

ANIMAL INDUSTRY BUREAU

Cows. Relation of production to income from dairy cows; by J. C. McDowell. May 19, 1922, revised Mar. 29, 1924. [1924.] 20 p. il. (Agriculture Dept. Bulletin 1069.) * Paper, 5c.

Agr 24—529

Hog cholera [prevention and treatment; by M. Dorset and U. G. Houck]. [Aug. 1917, revised Apr. 1924.] [1924.] 32 p. il. (Agriculture Dept. Farmers' bulletin 834.) [Imprint date incorrectly given on last page as 1923.] * Paper, 5c.

Meadow death camas (Zygadenus venenosus) as poisonous plant [with list of literature cited]; by C. Dwight Marsh and A. B. Clawson. June 27, 1924. 14 p. il. 2 p. of pl. (Agriculture Dept. Department bulletin 1240.) * Paper, 5c.

Agr 24—517

Milk. City milk plants, construction and arrangement; by Ernest Kelly and Clarence E. Clement. July 16, 1920 [reprint 1924]. 36 p. il. (Agriculture Dept. Department bulletin 849.) * Paper, 10c.

Milk fever, its simple and successful treatment; [by] John R. Mohler. [Aug. 1904, revised Mar. 1918. reprint] 1924. 12 p. il. (Agriculture Dept. Farmers' bulletin 206.) [Apr. 1922, on p. 2, is date of previous reprint.] * Paper, 5c.

Poultry. Standard varieties of chickens: 4, Ornamental breeds and varieties; [by Rob R. Slocum]. [Oct. 1921, revised May, 1924.] [1924.] ii+25 p. il. (Agriculture Dept. Farmers' bulletin 1221.) * Paper, 5c. Agr 23—1234

Service announcements. Service and regulatory announcements, May, 1924; [no.] 205. June, 1924. p. 53–63. [Monthly.] * Paper, 5c. single copy, 25c. a yr.; foreign subscription, 40c.

Agr 7—1658

Sorghum. Feeding grain sorghums to livestock. [by George A. Scott; revised by Arthur T. Semple]. [June, 1916, revised May, 1924.] [1924.] ii+10 p. il. (Agriculture Dept. Farmers' bulletin 724.) * Paper, 5c.

Vesicular stomatitis of horses and cattle; by John R. Mohler. May, 1918, revised June, 1924. [1924.] 8 p. 1 pl. (Agriculture Dept. Department bulletin 662.) * Paper, 5c.

Agr 24—512

BIOLOGICAL SURVEY BUREAU

Birds. Food of some well-known birds of forest, farm, and garden; [by F. E. L. Beal and W. L. McAtee]. [Sept. 1912, revised Aug. 1922, reprint 1924.] 34 p. il. (Agriculture Dept. Farmers' bulletin 506.) * Paper, 5c.

Posters. Open seasons for game, 1924–25, compiled by George A. Lawyer and Frank L. Earnshaw; [all lettered poster]. June 30, 1924. 32×14.5 in. (Poster 43.) †

—— Ranchmen and stockmen of Wyoming, you claim that Wyoming hay is most nutritious in United States, rodent pests now eat grass which makes this hay; [poster]. [1924.] 21.5×15.7 in. † ·

CHEMISTRY BUREAU

Leather. Wearing qualities of shoe leathers; by F. P. Veitch, R. W. Frey, and I. D. Clarke. Sept. 5, 1923, revised Mar. 1924. [1924.] 24 p. il. 2 p. of pl. (Agriculture Dept. Department bulletin 1168.) * Paper, 10c. Agr 24—513

Service announcements. Service and regulatory announcements, supplement 171. June 12, 1924. p. 1–24. [Contains Notices of judgment under food and drugs act 12001–50.] * Paper, 5c.

Agr 14—194

COOPERATIVE EXTENSION WORK OFFICE

County agricultural agents. Methods and results of cooperative extension work, reported through county agricultural agents, 1922: [by] H. W. Hochbaum. May, 1924. 40 p. il. (Agriculture Dept. Department circular 316.) * Paper, 10c. Agr 24—520

ENTOMOLOGY BUREAU

Aspen borer and how to control it; [by George Hofer]. [Oct. 1920, reprint 1924.] 12 p. il. (Agriculture Dept. Farmers' bulletin 1154.) * Paper, 5c.

Bees. Transferring bees to modern hives; [by] E. L. Sechrist. [July, 1918, reprint] 1924. 16 p. il. (Agriculture Dept. Farmers' bulletin 961.) [Includes lists of Agriculture Department publications relating to bees. Apr. 1922, on p. 2, is date of previous reprint.] * Paper, 5c.

Flies. House fly and how to suppress it; [by] L. O. Howard and F. C. Bishopp]. [Apr. 1924.] ii+17 p. il. (Agriculture Dept. Farmers' bulletin 1408.) [Supersedes Farmers' bulletin 851.] * Paper, 5c. Agr 24—526

Mexican bean beetle in the East; [by Neale F. Howard]. [May, 1924.] ii+14 p. il. (Agriculture Dept. Farmers' bulletin 1407.) * Paper, 5c. Agr 24—525

Termites. Damage by termites in Canal Zone and Panama and how to prevent it [with list of literature cited]; by Thomas E. Snyder and James Zetek. June 27, 1924. 26 p. il. 8 p. of pl. 2 maps. (Agriculture Dept. Department bulletin 1232.) * Paper, 10c. Agr 24—516

Wood preservation. Tests of methods of protecting woods against termites or white ants, progress report; by Thomas E. Snyder. June 26, 1924. 16 p. il. 2 p. of pl. (Agriculture Dept. Department bulletin 1231.) * Paper, 5c. Agr 24—515

Maps

Boll weevils. Map showing spread of Mexican cotton boll weevil from 1892–1922. [Washington] Geological Survey, Mar. 1923. 11.4×23.1 in. †

EXPERIMENT STATIONS OFFICE

Agricultural experiment stations. List of bulletins of agricultural experiment stations in United States from their establishment to end of 1920: [prepared by E. Lucy Ogden, Martha L. Gericke, and others]. May 26, 1924. cover-title, 186 p. (Agriculture Dept. Department bulletin 1199.) [Text on p. 2 of cover.] * Paper, 20c. Agr 24—501

FEDERAL HORTICULTURAL BOARD

Service announcements. Service and regulatory announcements, Jan.-Mar. 1924; [no.] 78. June, 1924. p. 1–32, il. * Paper, 5c. Agr 14—383

FOREST SERVICE

Cattle. Constitution and by-laws of — Stock Association, adopted at —, —, 19–. [Reprint 1924.] [1]+10 p. 12° [Suggested constitution and by-laws for livestock association working in cooperation with the Forest Service in the administration and use of national forest grazing lands.] †

Forest Service directory, Apr. 1924; no. 8. [1924.] 43 p. 16° [Semiannual.] ‡ Agr 21—224

Forestry and farm income; [by Wilbur R. Mattoon]. [Aug. 1920, corrected Jan. 1923, reprint 1924.] 36 p. il. (Agriculture Dept. Farmers' bulletin 1117.) * Paper, 5c.

Lumber. Cooperative marketing of woodland products; [by A F. Hawes]. [Mar. 1920, revised May, 1924.] [1924.] 16 p. il. (Agriculture Dept. Farmers' bulletin 1100.) * Paper, 5c.

Slash disposal in western white pine forests in Idaho; [by] J. A. Larsen and W. C. Lowdermilk. Apr. 1924. 20 p. il. (Agriculture Dept. Department circular 292.) * Paper, 5c. Agr 24—518

Maps

Cochetopa National Forest, Colo., national forests are for your use and enjoyment. [1924.] 1 sheet (with map on verso), il. large 4°, folded into narrow 8° size and so printed as to number 15 pages. †

Colorado National Forest, Colo., wonderland of glaciers, peaks, canyons, lakes, and timber. [1924.] 1 sheet (with map on verso), il. large 4°, folded into narrow 8° size and so printed as to number 14+[1] p. †

Datil National Forest, N. Mex. [resources and recreation features, roads, trails, etc.]. [1924.] 1 sheet (with map on verso), il. oblong 8°, folded into narrow 8° size and so printed as to number [3] pages. † ·

Harney National Forest, S. Dak., national forests are for your use and benefit. [1924.] 1 sheet (with map on verso), il. large 4°, folded into narrow 8° size and so printed as to number 15 pages. †

Minnesota National Forest, information map. [1924.] 1 sheet (with map on verso), il. large 4°, folded into narrow 8° size and so printed as to number [1]+13+[1] p. †

Mount Baker National Forest, Wash., place it occupies in national and community life. [1924.] 1 sheet (with map on verso), il. oblong f°, folded into narrow 8° size and so printed as to number [1]+17 p. †

Mount Hood National Forest, Oreg., information for campers, tourists, and hikers. [1924.] 1 sheet (with map on verso), il. large 4°, folded into narrow 8° size and so printed as to number [1]+13+[1] p. †

Nebraska National Forest, Nebr. [resources and recreation features. roads, trails, etc.]. [1924.] 1 sheet (with map on verso), il. narrow f°, folded into narrow 8° size and so printed as to number [1]+14+[1] p. †

Routt National Forest, Colo. [resources and recreation features, roads, trails, etc.]. [1924.] 1 sheet (with map on verso), il. large 4°, folded into narrow 8° size and so printed as to number 15 pages. †

Shoshone National Forest, Wyo., oldest forest welcomes you. [1924.] 1 sheet (with map on verso), il. large 4°, folded into narrow 8° size and so printed as to number [1]+14 p. †

Washington State. Road and recreation map, Washington. [1924.] 1 sheet (with map on verso), il. f°, folded into narrow 8° size and so printed as to number 11 columns. †

PLANT INDUSTRY BUREAU

Alfalfa. How to grow alfalfa; [by R. A. Oakley and H. L. Westover]. [Dec 1922, reprint with slight changes 1924.] .ii+30 p. il. (Agriculture Dept. Farmers' bulletin 1283.) * Paper, 5c.

Apple scald and its control; [by Charles Brooks, J. S. Cooley, and D. F. Fisher]. [Oct. 1923, revised Apr. 1924.] [1924.] [2]+17 p. il. (Agriculture Dept. Farmers' bulletin 1380.) * Paper, 5c.

Apples. Apple-orchard renovation; [by H. P. Gould]. [Oct. 1922, revised May, 1924.] [1924.] ii+28 p. il. (Agriculture Dept. Farmers' bulletin 1284.) * Paper, 5c.

Brown-spot of corn, with suggestions for its control; [by W. H. Tisdale]. [Oct. 1920, reprint 1924.] ii+6 p. il. (Agriculture Dept. Farmers' bulletin 1124.) * Paper, 5c.

Cotton. Tissue fluids of Egyptian and upland cottons and their F_1 hybrid [with list of literature cited]; by J. Arthur Harris, Zonja Wallen Lawrence, W. F. Hoffman, John v. Lawrence, and A. T. valentine. 1924. cover-title, p. 267–328, il. 1 pl. [Prepared in cooperation with Minnesota Agricultural Experiment Station. From Journal of agricultural research, v. 27, no. 5, Feb. 2, 1924.] ‡

Cranberries. Establishing cranberry fields; [by George M. Darrow, Henry J. Franklin, and O. G. Malde]. [Mar. 1924.] ii+38 p. il. (Agriculture Dept. Farmers' bulletin 1400.) * Paper, 5c.   Agr 14—524

Flag smut. Experiments with flag smut of wheat and causal fungus, Urocystis tritici Kcke. [with list of literature cited]; by Marion A. Griffiths. 1924. cover-title, 425–450+[2] p. il. 3 p. of pl. [From Journal of agricultural research, v. 27, no. 7, Feb. 16, 1924.] ‡

Propagation. Solar propagating frame for rooting citrus and other subtropical plants; [by] Walter T. Swingle, T. Ralph Robinson, and E. May, jr. May, 1924. 14 p. il. (Agriculture Dept. Department circular 310.) * Paper, 5c.
Agr 24—519

Sudan grass; [by H. N. vinall]. [May, 1920, revised May, 1924.] [1924.] ii+22 p. il. (Agriculture Dept. Farmers' bulletin 1126.) * Paper, 5c.

Tree planting. Cooperative shelter-belt demonstrations on northern Great Plains. Revised [edition]. June 2, 1924. 4 p. [Title of 1st edition is: Cooperative shelter-belt planting on northern Great Plains.] † Agr 24—528

Urocystis tritici. Studies on parasitism of Urocystis tritici Koern., organism causing flag smut of wheat [with list of literature cited]; by Robert J. Noble. 1924. cover-title, p. 451–490+[2] leaves, il. 3 p. of pl. [From Journal of agricultural research, v. 27, no. 7, Feb. 16, 1924.] ‡

Vegetables. Diseases and insects of garden vegetables; [by W. W. Gilbert and C. H. Popenoe]. [Jan. 1924, revised May, 1924.] [1924.] ii+46 p. il. (Agriculture Dept. Farmers' bulletin 1371.) [Prepared in cooperation with Entomology Bureau.] * Paper, 10c.

Wheat. Morphological and physiological studies on resistance of wheat to Puccinia graminis tritici Erikss. and Henn. [with list of literature cited]; by C. R. Hursh. 1924. cover-title, 381–412+[1] p. il. 2 p. of pl. [Prepared in cooperation with Minnesota Agricultural Experiment Station. From Journal of agricultural research, v. 27, no. 6, Feb. 9, 1924.] ‡

PUBLIC ROADS BUREAU

Barns. Principles of dairy-barn ventilation; [by M. A. R. Kelley]. [Apr. 1924.] ii+22 p. il. (Agriculture Dept. Farmers' bulletin 1393.) * Paper, 5c.
Agr 24—523

Highways. Federal aid highway system, shown on map of United States, in 18 sections; approved by Henry C. Wallace, Secretary of Agriculture, Mar. 1, 1924. [Washington, Geological Survey, 1924.] [2] leaves, il. 18 maps, large 4° [Base maps adapted from copper plate base of General Land Office.] ‡

Pipe. Flow of water in concrete pipe; by Fred C. Scobey; with discussion by Kenneth Allen, Arthur S. Bent, F. C. Finkle, Allen Hazen, J. B. Lippincott, and H. D. Newell. Oct. 28, 1920, [reprint] 1924. cover-title, 100 p. il. 4 pl. 8 p. of pl. (Agriculture Dept. Bulletin 852.) * Paper, 25c.

Public roads, journal of highway research, v. 5, no. 4; June, 1924.   1924. cover-title, 20 p. il. 4° [Monthly. Text on p. 2–4 of cover.] * Paper, 10c. single copy, $1.00 a yr.; foreign subscription, $1.50.
Agr 18—322

Sewage and sewerage of farm homes; [by George M. Warren]. [Jan. 1922, reprint 1924.] 56 p. il. (Agriculture Dept. Farmers' bulletin 1227.) * Paper, 5c.

Terracing farm lands; [by C. E. Ramser]. [Feb. 1924.] ii+22 p. il. (Agriculture Dept. Farmers' bulletin 1386.) [Revision of Farmers' bulletin 997.] * Paper, 5c.
Agr 24—522

Wells. Pumping from wells for irrigation; [by Paul A. Ewing]. [May, 1924.] ii+28 p. il. (Agriculture Dept. Farmers' bulletin 1404.) * Paper, 5c.
Agr 24—503

SOILS BUREAU

Dallas County, Tex. Soil survey of Dallas County, Tex.; by William T. Carter, jr., A. H. Bauer, J. F. Stroud, W. B. Francis, and T. M. Bushnell. 1924. iii+1213–54 p. il. 2 pl. map. [Prepared in cooperation with Texas Agricultural Experiment Station. From Field operations, 1920.] * Paper, 15c.

Greenville County, S. C. Soil survey of Greenville County, S. C.; by W. I. Watkins, J. M. Snyder, and Howard C. Smith. 1924. iii+189–212 p. il. map. [From Field operations, 1921.] * Paper, 15c.

Winslow, Ariz. Soil survey of Winslow area, Ariz.; by A. T. Strahorn, Mark Baldwin, and E. J. Carpenter. 1924. iii+155–188 p. il. 4 p. of pl. map. [Prepared in cooperation with Arizona Land Department. From Field operations, 1921.] * Paper, 15c.

187—24—No. 354——2

WEATHER BUREAU

Climatological data. Climatological data for United States by sections, v. 10, no. 13; [calendar] year 1923. [1924.] cover-title, [248] p. il. 3 maps, 2 p. of maps, 4° [Text on p. 2 of cover.] *Paper, 35c. complete monthly number, $4.00 a yr.

Agr 14—566

NOTE.—Made up of separate Climatological data issued from 42 section centers of the United States. Printed at the several section centers and assembled and bound at the Washington Office. Issued principally for service use and exchange. The separate Climatological data are sold by the Superintendent of Documents, Washington, D. C., at the rate of 5c. single copy, 50c. a yr. for each section.

—— Same, v. 11, no. 3; Mar. 1924. [1924.] cover-title, [209] p. il. 2 maps, 2 p. of maps, 4° [Text on p. 2 of cover.]

Dust. Investigation of dust content of atmosphere, by H. H. Kimball and I. F. Hand; Note on organic bodies found in air of Washington and London, by Sir Napier Shaw; Dust fall of Mar. 29, 1924, preliminary note, by E. R. Miller. 1924. [1]+133-141 p. il. 1 pl. 2 p. of pl. 4° [From Monthly weather review, Mar. 1924.] †

Lava tide, seasonal tilt, and volcanic cycle, by T. A. Jaggar, assisted by R. H. Finch and O. H. Emerson; Borings at Kilauea Volcano, by T. A. Jaggar. 1924. [1]+142-147 p. il. 4° [From Monthly weather review, Mar. 1924.] †

Meteorology. Monthly meteorological summary, Washington, D. C., May, 1924. [1924.] [2] p. large 8° †

Monthly weather review, v. 52, no. 3; Mar. 1924. [June 2]1924. cover-title, p. 133-194, il. 1 pl. 2 p. of pl. 15 p. of maps, 4° [Text on p. 2-4 of cover.] *Paper, 15c. single copy, $1.50 a yr.; foreign subscription, $2.25. Agr 9—990

NOTE.—The Monthly weather review contains (1) meteorological contributions, and a bibliography including seismology, (2) an interpretative summary and charts of the weather of the month in the United States, and on adjacent oceans, and (3) climatological and seismological tables dealing with the weather and earthquakes of the month. The contributions are principally as follows: (a) results of observational or research work in meteorology carried on in the United States or other parts of the world, (b) abstracts or reviews of important meteorological papers and books, and (c) notes. SPECIAL ARTICLES.—Investigation of dust content of atmosphere; by Herbert H. Kimball and Irving F. Hand.—Note on organic bodies found in air of Washington and London; by Sir Napier Shaw.—Dust fall of Mar. 29, 1924, preliminary note; by Eric R. Miller.—Lava tide, seasonal tilt, and volcanic cycle; by T. A. Jaggar, assisted by R. H. Finch and O. H. Emerson.—Borings at Kilauea Volcano; by T. A. Jaggar.—On prediction of tidal waves; by R. H. Finch.—C. E. P. Brooks on variations in level of central African lakes, Victoria and Albert, by Alfred J. Henry; [with discussion by C. E. P. Brooks].—Frequency of winds of different speeds at flying levels between New York and Chicago, further analysis of records of Air Mail Service; by Willis Ray Gregg and J. Parker Van Zandt.—Results of measurements of solar radiation and atmospheric turbidity over Atlantic Ocean and in Argentina, preliminary report, by Franz Linke; translated from German by W. W. Reed.—Physical-meteorological observatory at Davos, Switzerland; by C. Dorno.—Movement of cyclone of Mar. 8, 1924, across Texas; [by] Alfred J. Henry.—Sleet, glaze, snow, and windstorm in Wisconsin, Feb. 3-6, 1924; by W. P. Stewart.—Note on partial correlation; by Edgar W. Woolard.—Gales off African coast and in Australian waters; by Albert J. McCurdy, jr.

Ocean. Weather of the oceans, Feb. 1924, with special reference to north Atlantic and north Pacific oceans (including charts), notes, abstracts, and reviews; issued by Marine Division. 1924. 8 p. il. 6 p. of maps, 4° [From Monthly weather review, Feb. 1924.] †

Weather. Weekly weather and crop bulletin, June 3-24, 1924; no. 23-26, 1924. June 4-25, 1924. Each 4 p. il. 4° *Paper, 25c. a yr. Agr 24—260

Weather map. Daily weather map [of United States, containing forecasts for all States east of Mississippi River except Illinois, Wisconsin, Indiana, upper Michigan, and lower Michigan], June 2-30, 1924. 1st edition. [1924.] Each 16.4×22.7 in. [Not issued Sundays or holidays.] *Editions issued at Washington, D. C., 25c. a month, $2.50 a yr.; editions issued at about 65 stations throughout the United States, 20c. a month, $2.00 a yr.

—— Same [containing forecasts for United States], June 1-30, 1924. 2d edition. [1924.] Each 16.4×22.7 in. [The Sunday edition does not contain as much information as the edition for week days.] *30c. a month, $3.00 a yr.

Winds. Frequency of winds at different speeds at flying levels between New York and Chicago, further analysis of Air Mail Service; by W. R. Gregg and J. P. Van Zandt. 1924. [1]+153-157 p. il. 4° [From Monthly weather review, Mar. 1924.] †

CIVIL SERVICE COMMISSION

NOTE.—The Commission furnishes its publications gratuitously to those who apply for them.

Civil service. Instructions to applicants, 13th civil service district, headquarters, Denver, Colo. May, 1924. [2]+26+[1] p. (Form 1372.) †

Eligibility and certification. Apr. 1924. 4 p. (Form 2424.) †

COMMERCE DEPARTMENT

NOTE.—The Department of Commerce prints most of its publications in very limited editions, the distribution of which is confined to Government officers, libraries, etc. When a selling price is noted in this list, application for such publication should be submitted to the Superintendent of Documents, Washington, D. C., with remittance. For copies of charts, coast pilots, and tide tables, however, apply directly to the issuing office, the Coast and Geodetic Survey, Washington, D. C.

Seasonal Operation in Construction Industries Committee. Seasonal operation in construction industries, summary of report and recommendations of a committee of the President's Conference on Unemployment; with foreword by Herbert Hoover. 1924. viii + 24 p. il. (Elimination of waste series.) [The complete report of the committee is published by the McGraw-Hill Book Company, New York, and is a non-Government publication.]
* Paper, 5c.   24—26568

CENSUS BUREAU

NOTE.—Persons desiring 14th census publications should address the Director of the Census, Department of Commerce, Washington, D. C. They are also sold by the Superintendent of Documents, Washington, D. C., at the price indicated.

Cotton. Cotton consumed, cotton on hand, active cotton spindles, and imports and exports of cotton, May, 1923 and 1924, with statistics of cotton consumed, imported, and exported for 10 months ending May 31. June 14, 1924. oblong 32° [Preliminary report. This publication is issued in postal card form.] †

—— Cotton production and distribution, season of 1922–23. 1924. 103 p. il. (Bulletin 153.) [Compiled by Division of Cotton and Tobacco Statistics under supervision of William L. Austin, chief statistician, assisted by Harvey J. Zimmerman, special agent.] *Paper, 15c.   24—26545

Cottonseed received, crushed, and on hand, and cottonseed products manufactured, shipped out, on hand, and exported covering 10-month period ending May 31, 1924 and 1923. June 19, 1924. oblong 32° [Preliminary report. This publication is issued in postal card form.] †

Industry. Integration of industrial operation, statistical and descriptive analysis of development and growth of industrial establishments and of size, scope, and structure of combinations of industrial establishments operated from central offices; by Willard L. Thorp. 1924. 272 p. il. large 8° (Census monographs 3.) *Cloth, $1.00.   24—26548

COAST AND GEODETIC SURVEY

NOTE.—The monthly Notice to mariners, formerly issued by the Coast and Geodetic Survey, has been consolidated with and made a part of the Notice to mariners issued by the Lighthouses Bureau, thus making it a joint publication. The charts, coast pilots, and tide tables of the Coast and Geodetic Survey are sold at the office of the Survey in Washington, and also by one or more sales agents in each of the important American seaports.

Coast and Geodetic Survey bulletin, May 31, 1924; no. 108. [1924.] 12 p. [Monthly.] ‡   15—26512

Figure of the earth. Effect of variations in assumed figure of the earth on mapping of large area [with list of references]; by Walter D. Lambert. 1924. iii + 35 p. il. (Special publication 100; serial 258.) *Paper, 5c.
                                                                                24—26549

Charts

Gastineau Channel and part of Stephens Passage, southeast Alaska, surveys to 1921 and other sources; chart 8235. Scale 1 : 40,000. Washington, Coast and Geodetic Survey, May, 1924. 27.9×31 in. † 50c.

Hilo Bay, Hawaii, surveys 1900–14, surveys by .U. S. Engineers to 1923 and other sources; chart 4103. Scale 1 : 10,000. Washington, Coast and Geodetic Survey, May, 1924. ˙39×28.1 in. † 75c.

Hudson River, N. Y., Coxsackie to Troy, surveys to 1863, surveys by U. S. Engineers to 1923 and from other sources; with inset, Albany to Troy; chart 284. Scale 1 : 40,000. Washington, Coast and Geodetic Survey, June, 1924. 40.7×20 in. † 50c.

Lingayen Gulf, west coast of Luzon, original surveys 1901–07, interior topography from various sources; chart 4209. [Scale 1 : 100,000.] Washington, Coast and Geodetic Survey, Mar. 1924. 30.8×41.6 in. † 75c.

Orca Bay, North end of Cordova Bay and Hetta Inlet, southeast Alaska, surveys to 1914 and other sources; with inset, Continuation of Hetta Inlet; chart 8147. Scale 1 : 50,000. Washington, Coast and Geodetic Survey, May, 1924. 41×32.8 in. † 75c.

Philadelphia water front, Delaware River, Pa., surveys 1878–1915, surveys by Dept. of Public Works to 1923, surveys by U. S. Engineers to Aug. 1923; chart 380. Scale 1 : 9,600. Washington, Coast and Geodetic Survey, May, 1924. 49.7×26 1 in. † 75c.

Polillo Islands, east coast of Luzon, surveys to 1921; chart 4275. Scale 1 : 80,-000. Washington, Coast and Geodetic Survey, Mar. 1924. 32.1×41.6 in. † 75c.

Providence Harbor, R. I., surveys 1865–78, surveys by U. S. Engineers to 1924, survey by City Engineers to 1915; chart 352. Scale 1 : 10,000. Washington, Coast and Geodetic Survey, May, 1924. 19.6×15.7 in. † 25c.

Puget Sound, Seattle to Olympia, Wash., surveys to 1920, surveys by U. S. Engineers to 1923 and other sources; chart 6460. Scale 1 : 80,000. Washington, Coast and Geodetic Survey, June, 1924. 32.3×38.9 in. † 75c.

Rapu Rapu Strait, east coast of Luzon, surveys to 1921; chart 4259. Scale 1 : 20,000. Washington, Coast and Geodetic Survey, Jan. 1924. 33.6×36.3 in. † 75c.

Raritan River from Raritan Bay to New Brunswick, N. J., original surveys to 1915, surveys by U. S. Engineers to 1923 and other sources; chart 375. Scale 1 : 20,000. Washington, Coast and Geodetic Survey, May, 1924. 19.6× 34.4 in. † 50c.

Tybee Roads, Savannah River, and Wassaw Sound, Ga., surveys 1852–1920, surveys by U. S. Engineers to 1924; with inset, Continuation of Savannah River; chart 440. Scale 1 : 40,000. Washington, Coast and Geodetic Survey, May, 1924. 31.1×40.2 in. † 75c.

Virginia, Cape Henry to Currituck Beach Light, surveys to 1922, surveys by U. S. Engineers to 1923 and other sources; chart 1227. Scale 1 : 80,000. Washington, Coast and Geodetic Survey, May, 1924. 32.1×41 3 in. †75c.

FISHERIES BUREAU

Cold storage holdings of fish, May 15, 1924. [1924.] 1 p. oblong 8° (Statistical bulletin 615.) [Statistics furnished by Agricultural Economics Bureau.] †

Fisheries of Key West and clam industry of southern Florida [with bibliography]; by William C. Schroeder. 1924. [1]+75 p. il. (Bureau of Fisheries doc. 962.) [App. 12, report of commissioner of fisheries. 1923.] * Paper, 20c.
                                                                    F 24—11

Fisheries service bulletin, June 2, 1924; no. 109. [1924.] 4 p. [Monthly.] ‡
                                                                    F 15—76

Fishery products. Statement of quantities and values of certain fishery products landed at Boston and Gloucester, Mass., and Portland, Me., by American fishing vessels, May, 1924. [1924.] 1 p. oblong f° (Statistical bulletin 616.) †

Oysters. Experiments in artificial propagation of oysters; by Herbert F. Prytherch. 1924. [1]+14 p. il. 4 p. of pl. (Bureau of Fisheries doc. 961.) [App. 11, report of commissioner of fisheries, 1923.] * Paper, 5c.   F 24—10

FOREIGN AND DOMESTIC COMMERCE BUREAU

Commerce reports. Commerce reports, weekly survey of foreign trade, reports from American consular officers and representatives of Department of Commerce in foreign countries, no. 22–26; June 2–30, 1924. 1924. cover-titles, p. 553–880, il. 4° [Text and illustrations on p. 2–4 of covers.] *Paper, 10c. single copy, $3.00 a yr.; foreign subscription, $5.00.

—— Supplement to Commerce reports. [Included in price of Commerce reports for subscribers.]

Trade and economic review for 1923, no. 5: Czechoslovakia; by C. S. Winans. [1924.] 12 p.
Same, no. 6: Canada: [by] John G. Foster. [1924.] 15 p.
Same, no. 7: Switzerland; by James R. Wilkinson. [1924.] 12 p.

—— Supplement to Commerce reports: Changes in representative wages in British industry; by H. B. Allin-Smith. June 30, 1924. ii+25 p. (Trade information bulletin 247.) †   24—26569

—— Same: Finance and industry in soviet Russia; by L. J. Lewery. June 30, 1924. ii+21 p. (Trade information bulletin 244; Eastern European and Levantine Division.) †   24—26570

—— Same: French possessions in tropical Africa; by Ellwood A. Welden. June 9, 1924. ii+22 p. (Trade information bulletin 239; Western European Division.) †   24—26571

—— Same: Italian hydroelectric industry; by Leon Dominian. June 2, 1924. ii+17 p. (Trade information bulletin 238; Electrical Division.) †   24—26552

—— Same: Italy's foreign trade in iron, steel, and nonferrous metals in 1923; by A. A. Osborne. June 2, 1924. ii+6 p. (Trade information bulletin 237; Iron and Steel Division.) †   24—26551

—— Same: Nitrogen survey, pt. 3, Air-nitrogen processes; by J. M. Braham. June 16, 1924. ii+41 p. 1 pl. (Trade information bulletin 240; [Nitrogen Division].) [Prepared as part of the nitrogen survey authorized by the 67th Congress.] †   23—27477

—— Same: Petroleum in Japan; by Albert T. Coumbe, jr. June 30, 1924. ii+27 p. (Trade information bulletin 245; Petroleum Division.) †   24—26572

—— Same: Selling American hosiery abroad, survey of principal markets for American hosiery based upon reports of consular officers of Department of State and representatives of Department of Commerce. June 2, 1924. ii+19 p. (Trade information bulletin 236; Textile Division.) †   24—26550

—— Same: Spain, resources, industries, and economic conditions; [articles] by Charles H. Cunningham and Philip M. Copp. June 23, 1924. ii+28 p. (Trade information bulletin 243; Western European Division.) †   24—26554

—— Same: Survey of world trade in agricultural products, no. 5, Foreign import duties on wheat, wheat flour, meat and meat products; by Frank W. Fetter and Henry Chalmers. June 2, 1924. ii+37 p. (Trade information bulletin 233; Foodstuffs and Foreign Tariff Divisions.) [Prepared as part of the study of world trade in agricultural products authorized by the 67th Congress.] †   24—26573

—— Same: Survey of world trade in agricultural products, no. 6, European economic conditions which affect markets for agricultural products; by H. B. Smith. June 2, 1924. ii+62 p. (Trade information bulletin 235; Foodstuffs Division.) [Prepared as part of the study of world trade in agricultural products authorized by the 67th Congress.] †   24—26574

—— Same: Survey of world trade in agricultural products, no. 7, Financing agricultural exports from United States; by George W. Edwards. June 23, 1924. ii+46 p. (Trade information bulletin 241; Foodstuffs Division.) [Prepared as part of the study of world trade in agricultural products authorized by the 67th Congress.] †   24—26555

Commerce reports—Continued. Same: Trading under laws of Argentina [with bibliography; articles] by Bernard S. Van Rensselaer, A. J. Wolfe [and Guerra Everett]. June 23, 1924. ii+37 p. (Trade information bulletin 242; Division of Commercial Laws.) †   24—26553
  CONTENTS.—Argentine company laws; by Bernard S. Van Rensselaer.—Notes on Argentine law and judiciary; by Guerra Everett.—Recent Argentine legislation and court decisions; by A. J. Wolfe.—Pointers on Argentine commercial law; by A. J. Wolfe.

—— Same: World survey of zinc industry, compiled from official statistics, reports of consular officers of State Department, and from other sources; with report on United States production and trade, by C. E. Siebenthal. June 30, 1924. ii+60 p. (Trade information bulletin 246; Mineral Section, Iron and Steel Division.) †   24—26330

—— Survey of current business, May, 1924, no. 33 [quarterly issue]; compiled by Bureau of Census, Bureau of Foreign and Domestic Commerce, [and] Bureau of Standards. 1924. cover-title, 239 p. il. 4° (Monthly supplement to Commerce reports.) [Contains statistics for Mar. 1924, the date given above. May, 1924, being the date of issue. Text on p. 2–4 of cover.]
* Paper, 10c. single copy, $1.00 a yr.; foreign subscription, $1.50. 21—26819
  NOTE.—Realizing that current statistics are highly perishable and that to be of use they must reach the business man at the earliest possible moment, the Department has arranged to distribute advance leaflets almost every week, whenever sufficient material is available, to those subscribers who request them. The leaflets are usually mailed on Tuesdays, and give such information as has been received during the preceding week. The information contained in these leaflets is also published in Commerce reports issued weekly by the Foreign and Domestic Bureau. The advance sheets will be mailed free of charge to all subscribers to the Survey who request them. Such requests should be addressed to the Bureau of the Census, Department of Commerce, Washington, D. C. Subscriptions, however, should be sent to the Superintendent of Documents, Washington, D. C., at the prices stated above.

—— Same, June, 1924, no. 34; compiled by Bureau of Census, Bureau of Foreign and Domestic Commerce, [and] Bureau of Standards. 1924. cover-title, 63 p. il. 4° (Monthly supplement to Commerce reports.) [Contains statistics for Apr. 1924, the date given above, June, 1924, being the date of issue. Text on p. 2–4 of cover.]

Dyes and dyeing. German dyestuffs industry [with bibliography]; by Thomas W. Delahanty. 1924. iv+63 p. il. 1 pl. (Miscellaneous series, 126.)
* Paper, 10c.   24—26575

LIGHTHOUSES BUREAU

California, seacoast, Farallon light station, light to be changed; [all lettered poster]. June 20, 1924. 16×10.5 in. ([Poster] notice to mariners 35.) †

2d District. Atlantic Coast of United States, buoy list, coast of Massachusetts, 2d lighthouse district; 1924, corrected to May 10. 1924. [1]+69 p.
* Paper, 20c.   11—29016

3d District. Atlantic Coast of United States, buoy list, Narragansett Bay to Cape May, including New York Harbor, 3d lighthouse district; 1924, corrected to Apr. 25. 1924. [1]+136 p. * Paper, 20c.   11—20037

Lighthouse service bulletin, v. 3, no. 6; June 2, 1924. [1924.] p. 27–31. [Monthly.] †   12—35121

Notice to mariners, weekly, no. 23–26, 1924; June 6–27 [1924]. 1924. various paging. [Issued jointly with Coast and Geodetic Survey.] †   7—20609

NAVIGATION BUREAU

Ships. American documented seagoing merchant vessels of 500 gross tons and over, June 2, 1924. 1924. ii+67 p. 4° (Serial 79.) [Monthly.] * Paper, 10c. single copy, 75c. a yr.; foreign subscription, $1.25.   19—26597

RADIO SERVICE

Radio Service bulletin, June 2, 1924; no. 86. [1924.] 18 p. [Monthly.]
* Paper, 5c. single copy, 25c. a yr.; foreign subscription, 40c.   15—26255

PUBLICATIONS DIVISION

Commerce Department. List of publications of Department of Commerce available for distribution. [Edition of] May 1, 1924. 1924. xi+100 p. †
                                                  14—30281

Commerce Department—Continued. Supplement to annual List of publications [of Department of Commerce available for distribution], May 31, 1924. [1924.] 4 p. [Monthly] †

STANDARDS BUREAU

NOTE.—The Scientific papers will be supplied on subscription as issued at $1.25 per volume, paper bound. These volumes will afterwards be issued bound in cloth at $2.00 per volume; foreign subscription, paper, $2.50 (sent in single numbers), cloth, $2.35 (bound volumes). Single numbers vary in price. Address the Superintendent of Documents, Washington, D. C.
  The Technologic papers will be issued first as separates and later in volume form in the same manner as the Scientific papers. Subscriptions will be accepted by the Superintendent of Documents at $1.25 per volume; foreign subscription, $2.50. Single numbers vary in price.

American Marine Standards Committee. Simplified practice in marine field : Organization of American Marine Standards Committee and its constitution and rules. 1924. ii+18 p. il. *.Paper, 5c. ·   24—26576

Ammonia. Large Mollier chart (foot-pound-Fahrenheit units) properties of ammonia, 1924. A. Hoen & Co. [Baltimore, Md.] May 15, 1924. 1 p. il. oblong f° (Miscellaneous publication 57.) [For explanation of use of chart, see Standards Bureau Circular 142, which was entered in Monthly catalogue for May, 1923, p. 707.] * Paper, 10c. ·   24—26577

Lumber. Elimination of waste : Lumber; [supplementary circular] to all organized consumers, technical experts, distributors, and manufacturers interested in lumber [asking indorsement of recommendations and pledge of their support for fiscal year 1925]. [1924.] 13 p. 4° * Paper, 5c.   24—26578

Molybdenite. Some new thermoelectrical and actinoelectrical properties of molybdenite; by W. W. Coblentz. Apr. 7, 1924. [1]+375–418 p. il; large 8° (Scientific papers 486.) [From Scientific papers, v. 19.] * Paper, 10c.
                                                                24—26579

Pulp and paper fiber composition standards, reference standards, showing color reactions of common paper-making fibers and standard fiber mixtures with various stains for use in identification and estimation of fiber composition of paper; by Muriel F. Merritt. Apr. 25, 1924. [1]+101–105 p. il. 9 pl. large 8° (Technologic papers 250.) [From Technologic papers, v. 18.] * Paper, 15c.   24—26580

Regeneration (radio communication). Quantitative study of regeneration by inductive feed back; by C. B. Jolliffe [and] J. A. Rodman. Apr. 22, 1924. [1]+419–428 p .il. large 8° (Scientific papers 487.) [From Scientific papers. v. 19.] .* Paper, 5c. (incorrectly given in publication as 10c.).   24—26581

Traps (plumbing). Elimination of waste : Brass lavatory and sink traps, [circular] to all manufacturers, distributors, jobbers, and consumers interested in brass traps [asking indorsement of recommendations and pledge of their support for calendar year 1925]. [1924.] 7 p. 4° *.Paper, 5c.
                                                                24—26582

STEAMBOAT INSPECTION SERVICE

Steamboat Inspection Service bulletin, June 2, 1924; no. 104· [1924.] 2 p. [Monthly.] ‡   15—26679

Steamboats. Great Lakes, general rules and regulations prescribed by board of supervising inspectors, as amended Jan. 1924. Edition, Apr. 4, 1924. 1924. vi+154 p. il. †   24—26557

CONGRESS

Congressional record. Congressional record, 68th Congress, 1st session, v. 65, no. 147–159; June 2–24, 1924. [1924.] 10375–11830+[15] p. il. 4° 12—36438
  NOTE.—The Congressional record, containing the proceedings and debates of Congress, is issued daily when Congress is in session, and indexes thereto are published fortnightly. The 1st session of the 68th Congress adjourned June 7, 1924; but 7 numbers of the Record, containing speeches, were issued June 9–24.
  The Record is sold by the Superintendent of Documents on the following terms: Single copy, 3 cents, if not more than 24 pages, and 1 cent more for each additional 8 pages; per month, $1.50, foreign subscription, $2.50. Subscriptions are payable in advance. Prices for the bound volumes of the Record, 67th Congress, 1st–4th sessions, and prior Congresses, will be furnished on application. Send remittances to the Superintendent of Documents, Washington, D. C. Stamps and foreign money will not be accepted.

Congressional record—Continued. Same, index, with title, Congressional record index, 68th Congress, 1st session, v. 65, nos. 141–159; May 26–June 7, 1924. [1924.] no. 12; 64+44 p. 4° [Includes History of bills and resolutions.]

Eulogies. John I. Nolan, memorial addresses. 1924. iii+[1]+110 p. 1 por. ‡
24—26565

—— Senators from Pennsylvania, memorial addresses delivered in memory of Philander C. Knox, Boies Penrose, William E. Crow. 1924. iii+[1]+172 p. 3 por. ‡
24—26566

PRIVATE LAWS

NOTE.—The Publications Division, State Department, receives a small supply of the private acts which it distributes free upon application.

Private [act] 26–65, 68th Congress.

Bess, Gerard E. H. R. 905, act for relief of Gerard E. Bess. Approved June 6, 1924. 1 p. (Private 48.)

Bruusgaard Klosteruds Dampskibs Aktieselskab. H. R. 8237, act for relief of Bruusgaard Klosteruds Dampskibs Aktieselskab, Norwegian corporation of Drammen, Norway. Approved June 7, 1924. 1 p. (Private 56.)

Burklin, George M. S. 3220, act authorizing health officer of District of Columbia to issue permit for removal of remains of late George Mauger Burklin and remains of late Anton Lerch Burklin from Glenwood Cemetery, District of Columbia, to Fort Lincoln, Prince Georges County, Md. Approved June 7, 1924. 1 p. (Private 61.)

Carson, C. C. H. R. 2126, act for relief of C. C. Carson. Approved June 7, 1924. 1 p. (Private 53.)

Comanche Indians. H. R. 2881, act to compensate [Nehio or Len Parker, Arrushe, and Neho], Comanche Indians of Kiowa Reservation. Approved May 24, 1924. 1 p. (Private 27.)

Commercial Pacific Cable Company. S. 709, act for relief of Commercial Pacific Cable Company. Approved June 6, 1924. 1 p. (Private 47.)

Eagle Pass Lumber Company. H. R. 7122, act for relief of Eagle Pass Lumber Company, Eagle Pass, Tex. Approved June 6, 1924. 1 p. (Private 50.)

Erie Railroad. S. 935, act for relief of Erie Railroad Company. Approved June 3, 1924. 1 p. (Private 37.)

Fallon, Henry N. S. 946, act for relief of Amy L. Fallon, mother of Henry N. Fallon. Approved May 31, 1924. 1 p. (Private 34.)

Flagg, William H. H. R. 4012, act to reimburse William' H. Flagg and others for property destroyed by mail aeroplane numbered 73, operated by Post Office Department. Approved June 7, 1924. 1 p. (Private 63.)

Frost, Arthur. S. 105, act for relief of Arthur Frost. Approved May 24, 1924. 1 p. (Private 29.)

Hutcheson, Bernice. H. R. 3143, act for relief of Bernice Hutcheson. Approved June 6, 1924. 1 p. (Private 44.)

Jack, Isaac. H. R. 1629, act authorizing removal of restrictions from 40 acres of allotment of ·Isaac Jack, Seneca Indian. Approved May 24, 1924. 1 p. (Private 26.)

Kernan, Harold. S. 1213, act for relief of· Harold Kernan. Approved June 4, 1924. 1 p. (Private 40.)

Kirk, Robert J. H. R. 3009, act for relief of Robert J. Kirk. Approved June 5, 1924. 1 p. (Private 42.)

Lexington, steamship. S. 81, act for relief of [Colonial Navigation Company], owners of steamship Lexington. Approved June 3, 1924. 1 p. (Private 35.)

Lutsch, Johann J. H. R. 5169, act to grant patent to certain lands to Johann Jacob Lutsch. Approved May 31, 1924. 1 p. (Private 32.)

MacAdam, D. H. H. R. 1438, act for relief of D. H. MacAdam. Approved June 7, 1924. 1 p. (Private 59.)

MacDonald, Gordon G. S. 1013, act for relief of Gordon G. MacDonald. Approved June 6, 1924. 1 p. (Private 45.)

McGuire, Henry. H. R. 1306, act for relief of Henry McGuire. Approved June 7, 1924. 1 p. (Private 58.)

Maron, Frank A. S. 799, act for relief of F. A. Maron. Approved June 5, 1924. 1 p. (Private 43.)

Meeks, Jesse L. H. R. 2607, act for relief of Jesse L. Meeks. Approved June 6, 1924. 1 p. (Private 49.)

Moran, James. S. 589, act for relief of James Moran. Approved May 28, 1924. 1 p. (Private 30.)

Nelson, William H. H. R. 6972, act for relief of William H. Nelson. Approved June 7, 1924. 1 p. (Private 65.)

Norman, Charles T. H. R. 1830, act for relief of Charles T. Norman. · Approved June 7, 1924. 1 p. (Private 60.)

Owens, Mrs. Lena G. H. R. 2647, act for relief of Lena Garagnon Owens. Approved June 7, 1924. 1 p. (Private 54.)

Pond, Ezra S. S. 1941, act for relief of Ezra S. Pond. Approved June 4, 1924. 1 p. (Private 41.)

Porter, James B. H. R. 3477, act for relief of James B. Porter. Approved June 7, 1924. 1 p. (Private 62.)

Ratigan, Luke. H. R. 1475, act for relief of Luke Ratigan. Approved May 31, 1924. 1 p. (Private 33.)

Reynolds, Hubert. H. R. 5541, act for relief of Hubert Reynolds. Approved June 7, 1924. 1 p. (Private 64.)

Schermerhorn, V. E. H. R. 6049, act for relief of V. E. Schermerhorn, E. C. Caley, G. W. Campbell, and Philip Hudspeth. Approved June 7, 1924. 1 p. (Private 55.)

Sharon, Mrs. Eva B. H. R. 5136, act for relief of Eva B. Sharon. Approved June 3, 1924. 1 p. (Private 38.)

Private [act] 26–65, 68th Congress—Continued.

Sonnenstrahl, Ely N. S. 1330, act for relief of estate of Ely N. Sonnenstrahl. Approved June 6, 1924. 1 p. (Private 46.)

Spaight, Daniel A. S. 588, act for relief of Daniel A. Spaight and others. Approved June 7, 1924. 1 p. (Private 57.)

Stinchcomb, Frank. H. R. 8961, act for relief of Frank Stinchcomb. Approved June 6, 1924. 1 p. (Private 51.)

Swanson, Charles. H. R. 1442, act authorizing issuance of patent to Charles Swanson. Approved May 31, 1924. 1 p. (Private 31.)

Thompson-Vache Boat Company, Bonnots Mill, Mo. H. R. 2123, act for relief of Thompson-Vache Boat Company, Bonnots Mill, Mo. Approved June 7, 1924. 1 p. (Private 52.)

Underwood Typewriter Company and Frank P. Trott. H. R. 4647, act for relief of Underwood Typewriter Company and Frank P. Trott. Approved May 24, 1924. 1 p. (Private 28.)

United Dredging Company. S. 593, act for relief of United Dredging Company. Approved June 3, 1924. 1 p. (Private 36.)

Vumbaca, Frank. S. 243, act for relief of Frank Vumbaca. Approved June 4, 1924. 1 p. (Private 39.)

PUBLIC LAWS

NOTE.—Public acts in slip form in the first prints may be obtained from the Superintendent of Documents, Washington, D. C., at a subscription price of $1.00 for the 68th Congress, 1st session, foreign subscription $1.25; single copies are usually 5c. each; no. 176, Internal revenue, p. 807, is 10c.

Public [act] 128–290, 68th Congress.

Adger, Idaho. H. R. 7500, act to authorize sale of lands at or near Adger, Ada County, Idaho, for railroad purposes, [to Oregon Short Line Railroad Company]. [Approved May 31, 1924.] 2 p. (Public 169.)

Agriculture Department. H. R. 7220, act making appropriations for Department of Agriculture, fiscal year 1925. [Approved June 5, 1924.] 32 p. (Public 201.)

Alaska. H. R. 8143, act for protection of fisheries of Alaska. [Approved June 6, 1924.] 3 p. (Public 204.)

Albany Institute and Historical and Art Society. H. R. 1018, act authorizing Secretary of Navy to deliver to custody of Albany Institute and Historical and Art Society of Albany, N. Y., silver service which was presented to cruiser Albany by citizens of Albany, N. Y. Approved June 4, 1924. 1 p. (Public 189.)

Alexandria Light and Power Company. H. R. 526, act authorizing Secretary of War to enter into arrangement, on behalf of United States, with Alexandria Light and Power Company, whereby civilians may obtain electric current from Government-owned transmission line extending from Alexandria to Fort Humphreys, Va. Approved June 7, 1924. 1 p. (Public 216.)

American Academy in Rome. S. 2834, act relating to American Academy in Rome. Approved June 7, 1924. 1 p. (Public 251.)

Appropriations. H. R. 8233, act making appropriations for Executive Office and sundry independent executive bureaus, boards, commissions, and offices, fiscal year 1925. [Approved June 7, 1924.] 15 p. (Public 214.)

—— H. R. 9192, act making appropriations to supply urgent deficiencies in appropriations, fiscal year 1924. [Approved May 26, 1924.] 2 p. (Public 140.)

—— H. R. 9429, act making appropriations for legislative branch of Government, fiscal year 1925. [Approved June 7, 1924.] 16 p. (Public 225.)

Army. S. 2169, act to amend in certain particulars national defense act, as amended. [Approved June 6, 1924.] 3 p. (Public 207.)

Bell, Richard. H. R. 3900, act to cancel 2 allotments made to Richard Bell, deceased, embracing land within Round Valley Indian Reservation, Calif. Approved May 24, 1924. 1 p. (Public 131.)

Blackfeet Reservation. H. R. 2879, act for disposal of homestead allotments of deceased allottees within Blackfeet Indian Reservation, Mont. Approved June 2, 1924. 1 p. (Public 173.)

Calumet River. H. R. 2665, act granting consent of Congress to Chicago to construct bridge across Calumet River in vicinity of 134th street in Chicago, county of Cook, Ill. Approved May 26, 1924. 1 p. (Public 142.)

—— H. R. 8304, act granting consent of Congress to Chicago to construct bridge across Calumet River at or near 100th street in Chicago, county of Cook, Ill. Approved May 26, 1924. 1 p. (Public 147.)

Carlisle Barracks. H. R. 7731, act authorizing Secretary of War to sell portion of Carlisle Barracks reservation. Approved June 7, 1924. 1 p. (Public 275.)

Chattahoochee River. H. R. 9457, act granting consent of Congress to Alabama and Georgia, through their respective highway departments, to construct bridge across Chattahoochee River at or near Alaga, Ala., connecting Houston County, Ala., and Early County, Ga. Approved June 7, 1924. 1 p. (Public 286.)

Cherokee Indians. H. R. 3852, act providing for final disposition of affairs of eastern band of Cherokee Indians of North Carolina. [Approved June 4, 1924.] 7 p. (Public 191.)

Chester Calf, Indian. H. R. 6857, act for addition of names of Chester Calf and Crooked Nose Woman to final roll of Cheyenne and Arapaho Indians, Seger jurisdiction, Okla. Approved June 2, 1924. 1 p. (Public 174.)

Chicago River. S. 3188, act for abandonment of portion of present channel of South Branch of Chicago River. Approved June 7, 1924. 1 p. (Public 259.)

Choctaw Indians. H. R. 4462, act to amend act authorizing payment of Choctaw and Chickasaw town-site fund, and for other purposes [so as to provide for payment of shares of deceased Indians to their heirs]. Approved May 24, 1924. 1 p. (Public 132.)

—— H. R. 5325, act conferring jurisdiction upon Court of Claims to hear, examine, adjudicate, and enter judgment in any claims which Choctaw and Chickasaw Indians may have against United States. [Approved June 7, 1924.] 2 p. (Public 222.)

Claims. S. 2797, act to authorize payment of claims under provisions of so-called war minerals relief act. Approved June 7, 1924. 1 p. (Public 249.)

187—24—No. 354——3

Public [act] 128–290, 68th Congress—Continued.

Columbia Reservation. H. R. 7109, act to authorize acquisition of unreserved public lands in Columbia or Moses Reservation, Wash., under acts of Mar. 28, 1912 [isolated tract] and Mar. 3, 1877 [desert land]. Approved June 3, 1924. 1 p. (Public 182.)

Columbia River. H. R. 9177, act granting consent of Congress to counties of Kittitas and Grant, Wash., to construct bridge across Columbia River at or near Vantage Ferry, Wash. Approved June 7, 1924. 1 p. (Public 280.)

Cordova, Alaska. H. R. 6950, act to authorize Cordova, Alaska, to issue bonds in any sum not exceeding $100,000 for purpose of constructing and equipping public school building in Cordova, Alaska. Approved June 7, 1924. 1 p. (Public 273.)

Crane, Mary. H. R. 3800, act to cancel allotment of land made to Mary Crane or Ho-tah-kah-win-kaw, deceased Indian, embracing land within Winnebago Indian Reservation, Nebr. Approved May 24, 1924. 1 p. (Public 130.)

Creek Indians. H. R. 7013, act conferring jurisdiction upon Court of Claims to hear, examine, adjudicate, and enter judgment in any claims which Creek Indians may have against United States. [Approved May 24, 1924.] 2 p. (Public 134.)

Crook National Forest. H. R. 498, act for recreational area within Crook National Forest, Ariz. Approved May 29, 1924. 1 p. (Public 154.)

Crooked Lake. S. 697, act for disposal of lands on Crooked and Pickerel lakes, Mich. Approved June 7, 1924. 1 p. (Public 228.)

Cumberland River. S. 3380, act to grant consent of Congress to Cincinnati, New Orleans and Texas Pacific Railway Company to construct bridge across Cumberland River, in county of Pulaski, Ky., near Burnside. Approved June 7, 1924. 1 p. (Public 265.)

Custer State Park Game Sanctuary. S. 2699, act to amend act creating Custer State Park Game Sanctuary in South Dakota [so as to authorize enlargement].. Approved June 7, 1924. 1 p. (Public 246.)

Dairying Bureau. H. R. 7113, act to establish Dairy Bureau in Department of Agriculture. Approved May 29, 1924. 1 p. (Public 156.)

Dakota Indians. S. 1174, act authorizing Secretary of Interior to investigate and report to Congress facts in regard to claims of certain members of Sioux Nation of Indians for damages occasioned by destruction of their horses. Approved June 7, 1924. 1 p. (Public 211.)

Detroit, Mich. H. R. 8588, act authorizing Secretary of Treasury to sell marine hospital reservation and improvements thereon at Detroit, Mich., and to acquire suitable site in same locality and to erect thereon modern hospital for treatment of beneficiaries of Public Health Service. Approved June 7, 1924. 1 p. (Public 278.)

Diplomatic and consular service. H. R. 6357, act for reorganization and improvement of foreign service of United States. [Approved May 24, 1924.] 8 p. (Public 135.)

District Courts. H. R. 169, act to amend act to amend sec. 73 of act to codify, revise, and amend laws relating to judiciary [so as to provide for terms of court to be held at Sterling, Colo.] Approved May 29, 1924. 1 p. (Public 157.)

—— H. R. 714, act to amend sec. 101 of judicial code [so as to provide for additional place for holding United States court in eastern district of Oklahoma at Ada, Okla.]. Approved June 5, 1924. 1 p. (Public 194.)

—— H. R. 4445, act to amend sec. 115 of act to codify, revise, and amend laws relating to judiciary [so as to provide term of court at Casper, Wyo.]. Approved June 5, 1924. 1 p. (Public 195.)

—— H. R. 8050, act to detach Reagan County, Tex., from El Paso division of western judicial district of Texas and attach said county to San Angelo division of northern judicial district of said State. Approved May 29, 1924. 1 p. (Public 159.)

—— H. R. 9314, act to amend sec. 98 of judicial code [so as to provide that hereafter terms of district court for eastern district of North Carolina shall be held at Fayetteville instead of Laurinburg]. [Approved June 7, 1924.] 2 p. (Public 281.)

—— S. 2236, act to designate time and place of holding terms of district court in 1st division of district at Kansas City [Kans.]. Approved June 7, 1924. 1 p. (Public 241.)

—— S. 3023, act designating New Mexico as judicial district, fixing time and place for holding terms of court therein, and for other purposes. Approved June 7, 1924. 1 p. (Public 254.)

District of Columbia. H. R. 3236, act to regulate practice of optometry in District of Columbia. [Approved May 28, 1924.] 6 p. (Public 151.).

—— H. R. 4122, act to amend act to revive, with amendments, act to incorporate Medical Society of District of Columbia, as amended. Approved May 24, 1924. 1 p. (Public 138.).

—— H. R. 5855, act to fix salaries of officers and members of Metropolitan Police Force, United States Park Police Force, and Fire Department of District of Columbia. [Approved May 27, 1924.] 3 p. (Public 148.).

—— H. R. 6628, act to change name of Jewett street west of Wisconsin avenue to Cathedral avenue. Approved May 27, 1924. 1 p. (Public 150.)

—— H. R. 6721, act to amend act to fix and regulate salaries of teachers, school officers, and other employees of Board of Education of District, of Columbia, as amended, and for other purposes. [Approved June 4, 1924.] 10 p. (Public 188.)

—— H. R. 8839, act making appropriations for government of District of Columbia and other activities chargeable in whole or in part against revenues of such District, fiscal year 1925. [Approved June 7, 1924.] 44 p. (Public 224.)

—— S. 112, act for comprehensive development of park and playground system of National Capital. [Approved June 6, 1924.] 2 p. (Public 202.)

—— S. 113, act changing name of Keokuk street, county of Washington, District of Columbia, to Military road. Approved June 7, 1924. 1 p. (Public 226.)

—— S. 1785, act to amend act for regulation of practice of dentistry in District of Columbia, and for protection of the people from empiricism in relation thereto, and acts amendatory thereof. [Approved June 7, 1924.] 6 p. (Public 237.)

—— S. 1971, act to authorize commissioners of District of Columbia to accept land in District of Columbia dedicated by Charles C. Glover for park purposes. Approved June 6, 1924. 1 p. (Public 203.)

—— S. 3269, act to amend act regulating height of buildings in District of Columbia. Approved June 7, 1924. 1 p. (Public 262.)

Public [act] 12S–290, 68th Congress—Continued.

Employers' liability and workmen's compensation. H. R. 7041, act to amend act to provide compensation for employees of United States suffering injuries while in performance of their duties. Approved June 5, 1924. 1 p. (Public 196.)

Flomaton, Ala. H. R. 4437, act to quiet titles to land in Flomaton, Ala. Approved May 31, 1924. 1 p. (Public 165.)

Floods. H. R. 8070, act authorizing preliminary examinations and surveys of sundry streams with view to control of their floods. Approved May 31, 1924. 1 p. (Public 170.)

Forests and forestry. H. R. 4830, act for protection of forest lands, for reforestation of denuded areas, for extension of national forests, and for other purposes, in order to promote continuous production of timber on lands chiefly suitable therefor. [Approved June 7, 1924.] 4 p. (Public 270.)

Fort Berthold Reservation. H. R. 4494, act authorizing extensions of time for payment of purchase money due under homestead entries and Government land purchases within Fort Berthold Indian Reservation, N. Dak. Approved May 24, 1924. 1 p. (Public 133.)

Fredericksburg, Battle of, 1862. S. 3263, act for inspection of battle fields in and around Fredericksburg and Spotsylvania Court House, Va. Approved June 7, 1924. 1 p. (Public 261.)

Freight rates. S. 2704, act to amend paragraph (3), sec. 16, of interstate commerce act [so as to extend time of filing claims for overcharge]. Approved June 7, 1924. 1 p. (Public 247.)

Game. S. 2761, act to authorize withdrawal of lands for protection of antelope and other game animals and birds [in South Dakota]. Approved June 7, 1924. 1 p. (Public 248.)

Golden, Colo. H. R. 7998, act granting public lands to Golden, Colo., to secure supply of water for municipal, domestic purposes. Approved June 7, 1924. 1 p. (Public 223.)

Government Printing Office. H. R. 7996, act to regulate and fix rates of pay for employees and officers of Government Printing Office. Approved June 7, 1924. 1 p. (Public 276.)

Grand Army of the Republic. H. R. 1869, act for incorporation of Grand Army of the Republic. [Approved June 3, 1924.] 2 p. (Public 184.)

Halibut. S. 3434, act for protection of northern Pacific halibut fishery. [Approved June 7, 1924.] 2 p. (Public 267.)

Hawaii National Park. H. R. 4985, act to repeal 1st proviso of sec. 4 of act to establish national park in Hawaii [relating to limitation on appropriations which may be made for improvement of said park]. Approved June 5, 1924. 1 p. (Public 198.)

Heroin. H. R. 7079, act prohibiting importation of crude opium for purpose of manufacturing heroin. Approved June 7, 1924. 1 p. (Public 274.)

Homestead. S. 381, ac to amend sec. 2 of act for stock-raising homesteads. Approved June 6, 1924. 1 p. t (Public 206.)

Howard University. S. 2694, act to enable trustees of Howard University to develop athletic field and gymnasium project. Approved June 7, 1924. 1 p. (Public 245.)

Hungary. H. R. 8905, act to authorize settlement of indebtedness of Kingdom of Hungary to United States. [Approved May 23, 1924.] 2 p. (Public 128.)

Immigration. H. R. 7995, act to limit immigration of aliens into United States. [Approved May 26, 1924.] 18 p. (Public 139.)

Indian Affairs Office. S. 2799, act to provide for quarters, fuel, and light for employees of Indian field service. Approved June 7, 1924. 1 p. (Public 250.)

Indian reservations. H. R. 6298, act to authorize leasing for oil and gas mining purposes of unallotted lands on Indian reservations affected by proviso to sec. 3 of act of Feb. 28, 1891. Approved May 29, 1924. 1 p. (Public 158.)

Indians. H. R. 4835, act to pay tuition of Indian children in public schools. Approved June 7, 1924. 1 p. (Public 220.)

—— H. R. 6355, act to authorize Secretary of Interior to issue certificates of citizenship to Indians. Approved June 2, 1924. 1 p. (Public 175.)

Inland Waterways Corporation. H. R. 8209, act to create Inland Waterways Corporation for purpose of carrying out mandate and purpose of Congress as expressed in secs. 201 and 500 of transportation act. [Approved June 3, 1924.] 3 p. (Public 185.)

Interior Department. H. R. 5078, act making appropriations for Department of Interior, fiscal year 1925. [Approved June 5, 1924.] 45 p. (Public 199.)

Internal revenue. H. R. 6715, act to reduce and equalize taxation, to provide revenue, and for other purposes. [Approved June 2, 1924.] 115 p. (Public 176.)

Jocko Reservation. H. R. 2875, act for addition of names of certain persons to final roll of Indians of Flathead [or Jocko] Indian Reservation, Mont. Approved May 31, 1924. 1 p. (Public 162.)

Kanawha River. S. 1614, act to repeal act authorizing construction of bridges across Great Kanawha River. Approved June 7, 1924. 1 p. (Public 236.)

Kansa Indians. H. R. 2887, act to authorize extension of period of restriction against alienation on homestead allotments made to members of Kansas or Kaw tribe of Indians in Oklahoma. Approved May 27, 1924. 1 p. (Public 149.)

Ketchikan, Alaska. H. R. 6255, act to amend act to authorize Ketchikan, Alaska, to issue bonds in any sum not to exceed $100,000 for purpose of constructing schoolhouse in said town and equipping same [so as to permit increase in amount of bond issue]. Approved June 7, 1924. 1 p. (Public 271.)

Lapwai Indian Sanatorium. H. R. 192, act to provide for girls' dormitory at Fort Lapwai Sanatorium, Lapwai, Idaho. Approved June 7, 1924. 1 p. (Public 215.)

Leavenworth, Fort. H. R. 6207, act authorizing and directing Secretary of War to transfer to jurisdiction of Department of Justice all that portion of Fort Leavenworth military reservation which lies in Missouri. Approved May 31, 1924. 1 p. (Public 168.)

Lights. S. 2887, act authorizing transfer of certain abandoned or unused lighthouse reservation lands by United States to State of New York for park purposes. Approved June 7, 1924. 1 p. (Public 252.)

Locomotives. H. R. 8578, act to amend act to promote safety of employees and travelers upon railroads by compelling common carriers engaged in interstate commerce to equip their locomotives with safe and suitable boilers and appurtenances thereto, as amended. [Approved June 7, 1924.] 2 p. (Public 277.)

Public [act] 128–290, 68th Congress—Continued.

Logan, Fort. S. 3420, act granting consent of Congress to construction by Denver and Rio Grande Western Railroad Company of line of railroad across southwesterly portion of Fort Logan military reservation, Colo. Approved June 7, 1924. 1 p. (Public 266.)

Long, Frederic K. S. 2922, act to authorize the President to reconsider case of Frederic K. Long and to reappoint him captain in Regular Army. Approved May 24, 1924. 1 p. (Public 137.)

MacArthur, Fort. H. R. 6652, act to authorize Los Angeles, Calif., to construct and operate line of railroad across Fort MacArthur military reservation, Calif. Approved June 7, 1924. 1 p. (Public 272.)

Mail matter. H. R. 4442, act to extend insurance and collect-on-delivery service to 3d-class mail. Approved June 7, 1924. 1 p. (Public 269.)

Medford, Oreg. S. 1987, act accepting tracts of land in Medford, Jackson County, Oreg. [to be used as sites for administration buildings for Crater Lake National Park]. Approved June 7, 1924. 1 p. (Public 239.)

Medicine Bow National Forest. S. 699, act authorizing addition of certain lands to Medicine Bow National Forest, Wyo. Approved June 7, 1924. 1 p. (Public 229.)

Militia. H. R. 8886, act providing for sundry matters affecting military establishment. [Approved June 3, 1924.] 4 p. (Public 186.) [The sections of the act relate exclusively to the National Guard.]

Mississippi River. H. R. 7063, act granting consent of Congress to Illinois and Iowa, or either of them, to construct bridge across Mississippi River, connecting county of Carroll, Ill., and county of Jackson, Iowa. Approved May 26, 1924. 1 p. (Public 144.)

——— H. R. 8229, act granting consent of Congress to St. Paul, Minn., to construct bridge across Mississippi River [in said city]. Approved May 26, 1924. 1 p. (Public 146.)

Monongahela River. S. 3395, act granting consent of Congress to commissioners of Fayette and Greene counties, Pa., to construct bridge across Monongahela River near Masontown, Fayette County, Pa. Approved June 4, 1924. 1 p. (Public 190.)

National Home for Disabled Volunteer Soldiers. H. R. 2821, act authorizing erection of sanitary fireproof hospital at National Home for Disabled Volunteer Soldiers, Santa Monica, Calif. Approved June 7, 1924. 1 p. (Public 217.)

Navajo Reservation. S. 2159, act authorizing annual appropriations for maintenance of that portion of Gallup-Durango highway across Navajo Indian Reservation and providing reimbursement therefor. Approved June 7, 1924. 1 p. (Public 240.)

Navy Department. H. R. 6820, act making appropriations for Navy Department and naval service, fiscal year 1925. [Approved May 28, 1924.] 25 p. (Public 152.)

Niagara River. S. 3249, act granting consent of Congress to construction of bridge across Niagara River and Black Rock Canal [near Buffalo, N. Y., by Buffalo and Fort Erie Public Bridge Company]. Approved June 3, 1924. 1 p. (Public 177.)

Oconee River. H. R. 9612, act granting consent of Congress to Georgia, through its Highway Department, to construct bridge across Oconee River. Approved June 7, 1924. 1 p. (Public 290.)

Ohio River. H. R. 9345, act granting consent of Congress for construction of bridge across Ohio River between Vanderburgh County, Ind., and Henderson County, Ky. [by Kentucky and Indiana, through their respective highway commissions]. Approved June 7, 1924. 1 p. (Public 282.)

——— H. R. 9402, act granting consent of Congress to Fullerton and Portsmouth Bridge Company to construct bridge across Ohio River to connect Portsmouth, Ohio, and Fullerton, Ky. Approved June 7, 1924. 1 p. (Public 284.)

Paiute Indians. H. R. 2884, act providing for reservation of lands in Utah for certain bands of Paiute Indians. Approved May 31, 1924. 1 p. (Public 164.)

——— S. 1203, act to amend act authorizing appropriation to meet proportionate expenses of providing drainage system for Piute Indian lands in Nevada within Newlands reclamation project of Reclamation Service. Approved June 7, 1924. 1 p. (Public 231.)

Pay, Army. H. R. 4820, act to amend act to readjust pay and allowances of commissioned and enlisted personnel of Army, Navy, Marine Corps, Coast Guard, Coast and Geodetic Survey, and Public Health Service. [Approved May 31, 1924.] 3 p. (Public 171.)

Pearl River. S. 3244, act granting consent of Congress to board of supervisors of Hinds County, Miss., to construct bridge across Pearl River, Miss. [at Jackson]. Approved June 7, 1924. 1 p. (Public 260.)

Peedee River. S. 3355, act granting consent of Congress to counties of Marion and Florence, S. C., to construct bridge across Peedee River at or near Savage Landing, S. C. Approved June 7, 1924. 1 p. (Public 264.)

Philadelphia, Pa. H. R. 4981, act to grant permission to Philadelphia, Pa., to widen Haines street in front of national cemetery, Philadelphia, Pa. Approved May 29, 1924. 1 p. (Public 155.)

Phoenix, Ariz. S. 3093, act granting public lands to Phoenix, Ariz., for municipal park, and other purposes. Approved June 7, 1924. 1 p. (Public 256.)

Plumas National Forest. H. R. 656, act to add lands to Plumas and to Lassen national forests, Calif. Approved June 3, 1924. 1 p. (Public 180.)

Point of Woods Range Lights. H. R. 4481, act authorizing Secretary of Commerce to exchange land formerly used as site for Point of Woods Range Lights, Mich., for other lands in vicinity. [Approved June 3, 1924.] 2 p. (Public 183.)

Porto Rico. S. 2572, act to purchase grounds, erect, and repair buildings for customhouses, offices, and warehouses in Porto Rico. Approved June 7, 1924. 1 p. (Public 243.)

——— S. 2573, act to amend and reenact sec. 20, 22, and 50 of act to provide civil government for Porto Rico [relating to salaries]. [Approved June 7, 1924.] 2 p. (Public 244.)

Postal service. H. R. 6482, act authorizing Postmaster General to contract for mail messenger service. Approved June 3, 1924. 1 p. (Public 179.)

Pueblo Indians. S. 2932, act to quiet title to lands within Pueblo Indian land grants. [Approved June 7, 1924.] 8 p. (Public 253.)

Public [act] 128–290, 68th Congress—Continued.

Pyramid Lake Reservation. S. 1309, act for relief of settlers and town-site occupants of lands in Pyramid Lake Indian Reservation, Nev. [Approved June 7, 1924.] 2 p. (Public 233.)

Quinaielt Reservation. H. R. 5416, act to authorize setting aside of tribal lands within Quinaielt Indian Reservation, Wash., for lighthouse purposes. Approved May 31, 1924. 1 p. (Public 167.)

Red Lake Reservation. H. R. 4460, act authorizing payment to Red Lake Indians, out of tribal trust funds, for garden plats surrendered for school-farm use. Approved June 3, 1924. 1 p. (Public 181.)

Red River. H. R. 9517, act granting consent of Congress to North Texas Company, St. Jo, Tex., to construct toll bridge across Red River in vicinity of Illinois Bend, Tex. Approved June 7, 1924. 1 p. (Public 288.)

Reformatories. S. 790, act for establishment of Federal industrial institution for women. [Approved June 7, 1924.] 2 p. (Public 209.)

Rehabilitation of the disabled. H. R. 5478, act to amend sec. 1, 3, and 6 of act for promotion of vocational rehabilitation of persons disabled in industry or otherwise and their return to civil employment. [Approved June 5, 1924.] 3 p. (Public 200.)

Rehoboth Beach, Del. H. R. 9515, act granting consent of Congress to Delaware State Highway Department to construct bridge across canal near Rehoboth, Del. Approved June 7, 1924. 1 p. (Public 287.)

Retired list, Army. S. 2450, act to amend sec. 2 of legislative, executive, and judicial appropriation act, approved July 31, 1894 [relative to holding of Government office by retired enlisted men and certain retired officers of Army, Navy, Marine Corps, or Coast Guard]. Approved May 31, 1924. 1 p. (Public 161.)

Rio Grande. H. R. 9361, act granting consent of Congress to construction of bridge across Rio Grande [by C. M. Newman]. Approved June 7, 1924. 1 p. (Public 283.)

Rocky Mountain National Park. H. R. 2713, act to transfer certain lands of United States from Rocky Mountain National Park to Colorado National Forest, Colo. Approved June 2, 1924. 1 p. (Public 172.)

Saginaw Indians. H. R. 694, act to amend act for relief of Saginaw, Swan Creek, and Black River band of Chippewa Indians in Michigan [so as to increase limit of attorneys' fees]. Approved May 24, 1924. 1 p. (Public 129.)

St. Marys River. H. R. 9434, act granting consent of Congress to Georgia and Florida, through their respective highway departments, to construct bridge across St. Marys River [at or near St. Marys, Ga.]. Approved June 7, 1924. 1 p. (Public 285.)

—— S. 2929, act granting consent of Congress to Georgia and Florida, through their respective highway departments, to construct bridge across St. Marys River at or near Wilds Landing, Fla. Approved June 6, 1924. 1 p. (Public 208.)

Salaries. H. R. 8262, act to fix compensation of officers and employees of legislative branch of Government. [Approved May 24, 1924.] 7 p. (Public 136.)

San Carlos irrigation project. S. 966, act for continuance of construction work on San Carlos Federal irrigation project, Ariz. [Approved June 7, 1924.] 2 p. (Public 210.)

Seal and seal fisheries. S. 1192, act to confer jurisdiction upon district court, northern district of California, to adjudicate claims of American citizens [who suffered damages or loss resulting from seizure, detention, sale, or interference by United States of vessels charged with unlawful sealing in Bering Sea during years 1886–96]. Approved June 7, 1924. 1 p. (Public 230.)

Ships. H. R. 6202, act to amend sec. 11 and 12 of merchant marine act, 1920 [so as to permit use of certain funds of Shipping Board for conversion of ships into motor ships]. [Approved June 6, 1924.] 3 p. (Public 205.)

Shreveport, La. H. R. 5573, act granting public lands to Shreveport, La., for reservoir purposes. Approved June 4, 1924. 1 p. (Public 192.)

Southern Pacific Company. H. R. 6012, act to confer jurisdiction upon Court of Claims to ascertain cost to Southern Pacific Company and amounts expended by it, Dec. 1, 1906–Nov. 30, 1907, in closing and controlling break in Colorado River, and to render judgment therefor. Approved May 26, 1924. 1 p. (Public 141.)

State Department. H. R. 8350, act making appropriations for Departments of State and Justice and for judiciary, and for Departments of Commerce and Labor, fiscal year 1925. [Approved May 28, 1924.] 41 p. (Public 153.)

Stevens County, Wash. H. R. 1414, act to authorize payment of certain taxes to Stevens and Ferry counties, Wash. Approved June 7, 1924. 1 p. (Public 235.)

Stockbridge Indians. S. 3111, act conferring jurisdiction upon Court of Claims to hear, examine, adjudicate, and enter judgment in any claims which Stockbridge Indians may have against United States. [Approved June 7, 1924.] 2 p. (Public 257.)

Susquehanna River. H. R. 6810, act granting consent of Congress to Millersburg and Liverpool Bridge Corporation to construct bridge across Susquehanna River at Millersburg, Pa. Approved May 26, 1924. 1 p. (Public 143.)

—— H. R. 7846, act to extend time for construction of bridge across North Branch of Susquehanna River from Wilkes-Barre to borough of Dorranceton, Pa. [by county of Luzerne, Pa.]. Approved May 26, 1924. 1 p. (Public 145.)

Sussex County, Del. S. 2431, act conveying to Delaware land in county of Sussex, in that State. Approved May 31, 1924. 1 p. (Public 160.)

Tallahatchie River. S. 3272, act granting consent of Congress to Panola-Quitman drainage district to construct dam in Tallahatchie River [at or near Porters Ferry, Panola County, Miss.]. Approved June 3, 1924. 1 p. (Public 178.)

Taos County, N. Mex. S. 3024, act for acquirement by United States of certain privately owned lands within Rio Arriba and Taos counties, N. Mex., known as Las Trampas grant, by exchanging therefor timber within exterior boundaries of any national forest situated within New Mexico. Approved June 7, 1924. 1 p. (Public 255.)

Temoak Indians. S. 1308, act authorizing appropriation to enable Secretary of Interior to purchase tract of land, with sufficient water right attached, for use and occupancy of Temoak band of homeless Indians, located at Ruby Valley, Nev. Approved June 7, 1924. 1 p. (Public 232.)

Public [act] 128–290, 68th Congress—Continued.

Tombigbee River. H. R. 9610, act granting consent of Congress to board of supervisors of Lowndes County, Miss., to construct bridge across Tombigbee River [at or near Columbus]. Approved June 7, 1924. 1 p. (Public 289.)

Trade-marks. S. 3324, act to amend sec. 5 of trade mark act of 1905, as amended, relative to unauthorized use of portraits. Approved June 7, 1924. 1 p. (Public 263.)

Tug Fork. H. R. 5218, act granting consent of Congress to Pittsburgh Coal, Land and Railroad Company to construct bridge across Tug Fork of Big Sandy River at or near Nolan, in Mingo County, W. Va., to Kentucky side, in Pike County, Ky. Approved May 31, 1924. 1 p. (Public 166.)

United States Blind Veterans of World War. H. R. 4526, act to incorporate United States Blind Veterans of World War. [Approved June 7, 1924.] 2 p. (Public 218.)

Upper Mississippi River Wild Life and Fish Refuge. H. R. 4088, act to establish Upper Mississippi River Wild Life and Fish Refuge. [Approved June 7, 1924.] 3 p. (Public 268.)

Utah National Park. S. 668, act to establish Utah National Park in Utah. Approved June 7, 1924. 1 p. (Public 227.)

Ute Indians. H. R. 2882, act for reservation of land in Utah as school site for Ute Indians. Approved May 31, 1924. 1 p. (Public 163.)

Veterans' Bureau. S. 2257, act to consolidate, codify, revise, and reenact laws affecting establishment of Veterans' Bureau and administration of war risk insurance act, as amended, and vocational rehabilitation act, as amended. [Approved June 7, 1924.] 26 p. (Public 242.)

—— S. 3181, act to authorize appropriation to enable director of Veterans' Bureau to provide additional hospital facilities. Approved June 5, 1924. 1 p. (Public 197.)

Vicksburg, Miss. H. R. 4816, act to permit Vicksburg, Miss., to construct water mains on and under National Cemetery road, Vicksburg, Miss. Approved June 7, 1924. 1 p. (Public 219.)

War Department. H. R. 7877, act making appropriations for military and nonmilitary activities of War Department, fiscal year 1925. [Approved June 7. 1924.] 48 p. (Public 213.)

—— H. R. 9111, act directing remission of customs duties on certain property of United States imported by War Department. Approved June 7, 1924. 1 p. (Public 279.)

—— H. R. 9124, act authorizing sale of real property no longer required for military purposes. [Approved June 4. 1924.] 6 p. (Public 193.)

War trophics. S. 1376, act for equitable distribution of captured war devices and trophies to States and Territories and to District of Columbia. [Approved June 7, 1924.] 2 p. (Public 234.)

Washington State. H. R. 5318, act to authorize exchange of lands with State of Washington. Approved June 7, 1924. 1 p. (Public 221.)

Water pollution. S. 1942, act to protect navigation from obstruction and injury by preventing discharge of oil into coastal navigable waters of United States. [Approved June 7, 1924.] 2 p. (Public 238.)

Western State College of Colorado. H. R. 3104, act granting 160 acres of land to Western State College of Colorado, Gunnison, Colo., for use of Rocky Mountain Biological Station of said college. Approved June 7, 1924. 1 p. (Public 212.)

White River. S. 3116, act to authorize Choctaw, Oklahoma and Gulf Railway Company and Chicago, Rock Island and Pacific Railway Company to construct bridge across White River near De Valls Bluff, Ark. Approved June 7. 1924. 1 p. (Public 258.)

Wichita Indians. H. R. 731, act authorizing Wichita and affiliated bands of Indians in Oklahoma to submit claims to Court of Claims. [Approved June 4. 1924.] 2 p. (Public 187.)

Public [joint] resolution 22–37, 68th Congress.

Alaska. S. J. Res. 127, joint resolution to provide that powers and duties conferred upon governor of Alaska under existing law for protection of wild game animals and wild birds in Alaska be transferred to and be exercised by Secretary of Agriculture. Approved June 7, 1924. 1 p. (Public resolution 34.)

Assinniboine, Fort. S. J. Res. 90, joint resolution providing extension of time for payment by entrymen of lands on Fort Assinniboine abandoned military reservation, Mont. Approved June 7, 1924. 1 p. (Public resolution 29.)

Blind. S. J. Res. 115, joint resolution for free transmission through mails of certain publications for the blind. Approved June 7, 1924. 1 p. (Public resolution 33.) [S. J. Res. 115 provides free transmission through mails for volumes of Holy Scriptures, or any part thereof, in raised characters for use of the blind.]

Casper-Alcova irrigation project. S. J. Res. 114, joint resolution authorizing investigation of proposed Casper-Alcova irrigation project, Natrona County, Wyo., Deschutes project, Oreg., and Southern Lassen irrigation project, Lassen County, Calif. Approved June 7, 1924. 1 p. (Public resolution 32.)

District of Columbia Memorial Commission. S. J. Res. 73, joint resolution for appointment of commission for purpose of erecting in Potomac Park, in District of Columbia, memorial to those members of armed forces of United States from District of Columbia who served in Great War. Approved June 7, 1924. 1 p. (Public resolution 28.)

Engraving and Printing Bureau. S. J. Res. 105, joint resolution authorizing the President to detail officer of Corps of Engineers as director of Bureau of Engraving and Printing. Approved May 31, 1924. 1 p. (Public resolution 23.)

Florida. S. J. Res. 142, joint resolution providing for United States Government to have representation at celebration of centennial of 1st meeting of Legislative Council of Territory of Florida [to be held at Tallahassee, Fla., Nov. 1924]. Approved June 6, 1924. 1 p. (Public resolution 26.)

Fort Peck Reservation. S. J. Res. 103, joint resolution authorizing expenditure of Fort Peck 4 per centum fund now standing to credit of Fort Peck Indians of Montana in Treasury. Approved June 7, 1924. 1 p. (Public resolution 30.)

Public [joint] resolution 22–37, 68th Congress—Continued.

Government officials and employees. S. J. Res. 146, joint resolution to amend sec. 13 of act for classification of civilian positions within District of Columbia and field service. Approved June 7, 1924. 1 p. (Public resolution 36.)

Grand Army of the Republic. H. J. Res. 194, joint resolution to print as House document proceedings of national encampments of Grand Army of the Republic, United Spanish War e erans, and American Legion, for use of House and Senate. Approved June 6, 1924. 1 p. (Public resolution 25.)

Immigration. H. J. Res. 283, joint resolution to permit to remain within United States certain aliens in excess of quotas fixed under authority of immigration act of May 19, 1921. Approved June 7, 1924. 1 p. (Public resolution 37.)

Northern Pacific Railway. H. J. Res. 237, joint resolution directing Secretary of Interior to withhold his approval of adjustment of Northern Pacific land grants. [and creating joint committee to investigate said land grants]. [Approved June 5, 1924.] 2 p. (Public resolution 24.)

Pike, Camp. S. J. Res. 89, joint resolution authorizing and permitting Arkansas to construct, maintain, and use permanent buildings, rifle ranges, and utilities at Camp Pike, Ark., as are necessary for use and benefit of National Guard of Arkansas. Approved May 29, 1924. 1 p. (Public resolution 22.)

San Martin, José de. S. J. Res. 106, joint resolution authorizing erection on public grounds in Washington, D. C., of equestrian statue of General San Martin which the people of Argentina have presented to United States. Approved June 7, 1924. 1 p. (Public resolution 31.)

Tax Appeals Board. S. J. Res. 137, joint resolution in respect of salaries of original appointees to Board of Tax Appeals. Approved June 7, 1924. 1 p. (Public resolution 35.)

Women. S. J. Res. 43, joint resolution in relation to [erection of American Red Cross memorial building as] monument to commemorate services and sacrifices of women of United States, its insular possessions, and District of Columbia in World War. Approved June 7, 1924. 1 p. (Public resolution 27.)

CONFERENCE COMMITTEES

Alaska. For protection of fisheries of Alaska, conference report to accompany H. R. 8143; submitted by Mr. Greene of Massachusetts. June 4, 1924. 2 p. (H. rp. 950, 68th Cong. 1st sess.) * Paper, 5c.

Appropriations. Deficiency appropriation bill, [fiscal year] 1924 [and prior fiscal years], conference report to accompany H. R. 9559; submitted by Mr. Madden. June 7, 1924. 6 p. (H. rp. 1019, 68th Cong. 1st sess.) * Paper, 5c.

—— Deficiency appropriation bill, [fiscal year] 1924 [and prior fiscal years], conference report to accompany H. R. 9559; submitted by Mr. Madden. June 7, 1924. 2 p. (H. rp. 1024, 68th Cong. 1st sess.) * Paper, 5c.

—— Executive and independent offices appropriation bill, [fiscal year] 1925. conference report to accompany H. R. 8233; submitted by Mr. Wood. June 5, 1924. 4 p. (H. rp. 976, 68th Cong. 1st sess.) * Paper, 5c.

—— Legislative appropriation bill [fiscal year 1925], conference report to accompany H. R. 9429; submitted by Mr. Dickinson of Iowa. June 7, 1924. 3 p. (H. rp. 1017, 68th Cong. 1st sess.) * Paper, 5c.

Choctaw Indians. To adjudicate claims which Choctaw and Chickasaw Indians may have against United States, conference report to accompany H. R. 5325 [conferring jurisdiction upon Court of Claims to hear, examine, adjudicate, and enter judgment in any claims which Choctaw and Chickasaw Indians may have against United States]; submitted by Mr. Snyder. May 30, 1924. 2 p. (H. rp. 908, 68th Cong. 1st sess.) * Paper, 5c.

District of Columbia. District of Columbia appropriation bill, [fiscal year] 1925, conference report to accompany H. R. 8839; submitted by Mr. Davis of Minnesota. June 2, 1924. 1 p. (H. rp. 925, 68th Cong. 1st sess.) * Paper, 5c.

—— District of Columbia appropriation bill, [fiscal year] 1925, conference report to accompany H. R. 8839; submitted by Mr. Davis of Minnesota. June 5, 1924. 1 p. (H. rp. 974, 68th Cong. 1st sess.) * Paper, 5c.

—— District of Columbia appropriation bill [fiscal year 1925], conference report to accompany H. R. 8839; submitted by Mr. Davis of Minnesota. June 6, 1924. 11 p. (H. rp. 1014, 68th Cong. 1st sess.) * Paper, 5c.

Freight rates. Agriculture basic industry of the country, conference report to accompany S. J. Res. 107 [directing Interstate Commerce Commission to take action relative to adjustments in rate structure of common carriers subject to interstate commerce act, and fixing rates and charges]; submitted by Mr. Hoch. June 7, 1924. 2 p. (H. rp. 1023, 68th Cong. 1st sess.) * Paper, 5c.

Indians. Tuition of Indian children, conference report to accompany H. R. 4835; submitted by Mr. Snyder. June 6, 1924. 1 p. (H. rp. 1007, 68th Cong. 1st sess.) *Paper, 5c.

Postal service. Reclassification of postal salaries, conference report to accompany bill (S. 1898), reclassifying salaries of postmasters and employees of postal service and readjusting their salaries and compensation on equitable basis; submitted by Mr. Edge. June 3, calendar day June 4, 1924. 19 p. (S. doc. 131, 68th Cong. 1st sess.) * Paper, 5c. 24—26583

Rehabilitation of the disabled. Industrial vocational rehabilitation, conference report to accompany H. R. 5478 [to amend sec. 1, 3, and 6 of act for promotion of vocational rehabilitation of persons disabled in industry or otherwise and their return to civil employment]; submitted by Mr. Dailinger. June 4, 1924. 2 p. (H. rp. 963, 68th Cong. 1st sess.) * Paper, 5c.

Veterans' Bureau. World War veterans' act, conference report to accompany S. 2257 [to consolidate, codify, revise, and reenact laws affecting establishment of Veterans' Bureau and administration of war risk insurance act, as amended, and vocational rehabilitation act, as amended]; submitted by Mr. Johnson of South Dakota. June 5 1924. 28 p. (H. rp. 1001, 68th Cong. 1st sess.) * Paper, 5c. 24—26584

HOUSE OF REPRESENTATIVES

Agricultural credit. Federal farm loan act, amendments, rules, and regulations: public law no. 158, 64th Congress, approved July 17, 1916; public law no. 271 (extract), 64th Congress, approved Sept. 8, 1916; public law no. 95, 65th Congress, approved Jan. 18, 1918; public law no. 182, 66th Congress, approved Apr. 20, 1920; public res. no. 45, 66th Congress, approved May 26, 1920; public law no. 334, 66th Congress, approved Feb. 27, 1921; public law no. 379, 66th Congress, approved Mar. 4, 1921; public law no. 32, 67th Congress, approved July 1, 1921; public law no. 50, 67th Congress, approved Aug. 13, 1921; public law no. 219 (extract), 67th Congress, approved May 15, 1922; public res. no. 104, 67th Congress, approved Mar. 4, 1923; public law no. 503, 67th Congress, approved Mar. 4, 1923. 1924. [1]+79 p. * Paper, 10c. 24—26609

Calendars. Calendars of House of Representatives, 68th Congress, 1st session, June 2–6, 1924; no. 137–141. 1924. various paging, large 8° [Daily when House of Representatives is in session.] ‡

—— Same, final edition, with title, Calendars and history of legislation of House of Representatives, 68th Congress, 1st session. 1924. 120 p. large 8° ‡

Grand Army of the Republic. Journal of 57th national encampment of Grand Army of the Republic, Milwaukee, Wis., Sept. 2–8, 1923. 1924. iv+328 p. 3 por. 12 p. of por. (H. doc. 604, 67th Cong. 4th sess.) * Paper, 30c. 16—15656

ACCOUNTS COMMITTEE

Alcoholic Liquor Traffic Committee, House. Providing for additional clerk to Committee on Alcoholic Liquor Traffic, report to accompany H. Res. 345; submitted by Mr. MacGregor. June 7, 1924. 1 p. (H. rp. 1026, 68th Cong. 1st sess.) * Paper, 5c.

Judiciary Committee, House. Authorizing select committee appointed under House resolution 325 to employ stenographic and other assistance, report to accompany H. Res. 336 [authorizing Judiciary Committee to employ stenographic and other assistance]; submitted by Mr. MacGregor. June 7, 1924. 1 p. (H. rp. 1025, 68th Cong. 1st sess.) * Paper, 5c.

McGinniss, William S. Daughter of William S. McGinniss, report to accompany H. Res. 265 [to pay daughter of William S. McGinniss]; submitted by Mr. MacGregor. June 7, 1924. 1 p. (H. rp. 1027, 68th Cong. 1st sess.) * Paper, 5c.

AGRICULTURE COMMITTEE

Agriculture Department. Administering oaths by certain employees of Department of Agriculture, report to accompany S. 2148 [to empower certain officers, agents, or employees of Department of Agriculture to administer and take oaths, affirmations, and affidavits in certain cases]; submitted by Mr. Haugen. June 5, 1924. 3 p. (H. rp. 994, 68th Cong. 1st sess.) * Paper, 5c.

Agriculture Department—Continued.   Transporting remains of employees of Department of Agriculture, report to accompany H. R. 9092 [to authorize transportation, at public expense, of remains of officers and employees of Department of Agriculture who die while away from their official stations] ; submitted by Mr. Haugen.   June 6, 1924.   3 p. ' (H. rp. 1010, 68th Cong. 1st sess.)   * Paper, 5c.

Alaska. Game administration in Alaska, report to accompany S. J. Res. 127 [to provide that powers and duties conferred upon governor of Alaska under existing law for protection of wild game animals and wild birds in Alaska be transferred to and be exercised by Secretary of Agriculture] ; submitted by Mr. Haugen. June 5, 1924. 3 p. (H. rp. 989, 68th Cong. 1st sess.) * Paper, 5c.

Alaska Game Commission, report to accompany S. 2559 [to establish Alaska Game Commission to protect game animals, land fur-bearing animals, and birds, in Alaska, and for other purposes] ; submitted by Mr. Haugen. June 5, 1924. 5 p. (H. rp. 993, 68th Cong. 1st sess.) * Paper, 5c. '

Bread. Federal bread bill, report to accompany H. R. 8981 [to establish standard weights for loaves of bread, to prevent deception in respect thereto, to prevent contamination thereof, and for other purposes] ; submitted by Mr. Haugen. June 5, 1924. 4 p. (H. rp. 990, 68th Cong. 1st sess.) * Paper, 5c.

Coates, Leonard R. Leonard R. Coates, report to accompany H. R. 5135 [for relief of Leonard R. Coates] ; submitted by Mr. Haugen. June 5, 1924. 3 p. (H. rp. 997, 68th Cong. 1st sess.) * Paper, 5c.

Dairying and livestock experiment stations. Dairying and livestock experiment station at Columbia, S. C., report to accompany H. R. 9398 [for establishment of dairying and livestock experiment station at Columbia, S. C.] ; submitted by Mr. Haugen. June 7, 1924. 1 p. (H. rp. 1030, 68th Cong. 1st sess.) * Paper, 5c.

—— Dairying and livestock experiment station at Dalhart, Tex., report to accompany H. R. 9362 [for establishment of dairying and livestock experiment station at Dalhart, Tex.] ; submitted by Mr. Haugen. June 7, 1924. 2 p. (H. rp. 1029, 68th Cong. 1st sess.) · * Paper, 5c.

—— Dairying and livestock experiment station at Mandan, N. Dak., report to accompany H. R. 4495 [for establishment of dairying and livestock experiment station at Mandan, N. Dak.] ; submitted by Mr. Haugen. June 6, 1924. 3 p. (H. rp. 1018, 68th Cong. 1st sess.) * Paper, 5c.

Pitt River Power Co. relief, report to accompany H. R. 7053 ; submitted by Mr. Haugen. June 5, 1924. 2 p. (H. rp. 999, 68th Cong. 1st sess.) * Paper, 5c.

Sugar. Watson sugar claim, hearings on S. J. Res. 49, authorizing the President to require Sugar Equalization Board (Incorporated) to adjust transaction relating to 3,500 tons of sugar imported from Argentine Republic, May 29, 1924. 1924. iii+15 p. (Serial X.) * Paper, 5c.

World's Poultry Congress, report to accompany S. J. Res. 98 [authorizing the President to extend invitation for holding of 3d World's Poultry Congress in United States in 1927, and to extend invitations to foreign governments to participate in this congress] ; submitted by Mr. Haugen. June 5, 1924. 3 p. (H. rp. 992, 68th Cong. 1st sess.) * Paper, 5c.

APPROPRIATIONS COMMITTEE

Appropriations. Legislative establishment appropriation bill, [fiscal year] 1925, hearings before subcommittee in charge of legislative establishment appropriation bill for 1925. 1924. ii+170 p. 1 tab. * Paper, 15c.

—— Second deficiency appropriation bill, [fiscal year] 1924 [and prior fiscal years], hearing before subcommittee in charge of deficiency appropriations. 1924. ii+682 p. * Paper, 65c.

—— Second deficiency appropriation bill, fiscal year 1924 [and prior fiscal years], report to accompany H. R. 9559 ; submitted by Mr. Madden. May 30, 1924. 19 p. (H. rp. 907, 68th Cong. 1st sess.) * Paper, 5c.

Government officials and employees. Adjustment of compensation of civilian employees in certain field services, fiscal year 1925, report to accompany H. R. 9561 ; submitted by Mr. Madden. June 3, 1924. 5 p. (H. rp. 938, 68th Cong. 1st sess.) * Paper, 5c.

—— Adjustment of compensation to employees in field service, [fiscal year] 1925, hearing before subcommittee in charge of deficiency appropriations. 1924. ii+23 p. * Paper, 5c.

187—24—No. 354—4

Admiralty. Authorizing suits against United States in admiralty, report to accompany H. R. 9535 [authorizing suits against United States in admiralty for damage caused by and salvage services rendered to public vessels belonging to United States]; submitted by Mr. Edmonds. May 31, 1924. 23 p. (H. rp. 913, 68th Cong. 1st sess.) * Paper, 5c.
24—26535

Canadian Car & Foundry Co. (Ltd.), report to accompany H. R. 8879 [for relief of Canadian Car and Foundry Company, Limited]; submitted by Mr. Edmonds. June 7, 1924. 30 p. (H. rp. 1020, 68th Cong. 1st sess.) * Paper, 5c.

Itasca, schooner. Owner of schooner Itasca, report to accompany S. 51 [for relief of owner of schooner Itasca]; submitted by Mr. Edmonds. June 6, 1924. 4 p. (H. rp. 1013, 68th Cong. 1st sess.) * Paper, 5c.

Kiener, Christian. Emma Kiener, report to accompany S. 1605 [for relief of Emma Kiener, widow of Christian Kiener]; submitted by Mr. Fredericks. May 30, 1924. 7 p. (H. rp. 922, 68th Cong. 1st sess.) * Paper, 5c.

State Bank & Trust Co., Fayetteville, Tenn.; report to accompany H. R. 1076 [for relief of State Bank and Trust Company, Fayetteville, Tenn.]; submitted by Mr. Edmonds. May 31, 1924. 4 p. (H. rp. 920, 68th Cong. 1st sess.) * Paper, 5c.

Accounts. Adjustment of accounts between United States and District of Columbia, hearings before subcommittee on S. 703, May 12 and 13, 1924. 1924. ii+23 p. * Paper, 5c.

—— Adjustment of accounts between United States and District of Columbia, minority views to accompany S. 703; submitted by Mr. Blanton. June 5, 1924. 29 p. (H. rp. 790, pt. 2, 68th Cong. 1st sess.) .* Paper, 5c.

Biological products. Regulation of sale of viruses, serums, toxins, and analogous products, etc., hearings before subcommittee on H. R. 5845, H. R. 7366, and H. R. 8618, bills to amend sec. 2 of act to regulate sale of viruses, serums, toxins, and analogous products in District of Columbia, to regulate interstate traffic in said articles, and for other purposes, Feb. 21–May 6, 1924. 1924. ii+230 p. * Paper, 20c.

Buildings. To amend act regulating height of buildings in District of Columbia, report to accompany S. 3269; submitted by Mr. Zihlman. May 31, 1924. 2 p. (H. rp. 919, 68th Cong. 1st sess.) * Paper, 5c.

Howard University athletic field and gymnasium project, report to accompany S. 2694 [to enable trustees of Howard University to develop athletic field and gymnasium project]; submitted by Mr. Zihlman. June 5, 1924. 3 p. (H. rp. 984, 68th Cong. 1st sess.) * Paper, 5c.

Park and playground system, hearings before subcommittee on H. R. 8055, for comprehensive development of park and playground system of National Capital, Apr. 21, 1924. 1924. ii+26 p. * Paper, 5c.

Streets. Changing name of 3d place ne. to Abbey place, report to accompany H. R. 8410; submitted by Mr. Zihlman. June 2, 1924. 1 p. (H. rp. 935, 68th Cong. 1st sess.) * Paper, 5c.

—— Widening of Nichols avenue between Good Hope road and S street se., report to accompany S. 1782; submitted by Mr. Hammer. June 4, 1924. 2 p. (H. rp. 951, 68th Cong. 1st sess.) * Paper, 5c.

Contested elections. Proceedings in cases of contested elections of Members of House of Representatives, report to accompany H. R. 9493; submitted by Mr. Dallinger. June 2, 1924. 4 p. (H. rp. 927, 68th Cong. 1st sess.) * Paper, 5c.

Packers and stockyards act, hearings, Apr. 3–30, 1924. 1924. pt. 1, ii+100 p. * Paper, 10c.

Immigration. Permitting certain aliens to remain within United States, report to accompany. H. J. Res. 283 [to permit to remain within United States certain aliens in excess of quotas fixed under authority of immigration act of May 19, 1921]; submitted by Mr. Johnson of Washington. June 5, 1924. 4 p. (H. rp. 995, 68th Cong. 1st sess.) * Paper, 5c.

Immigration Bureau. Changing title of commissioner general of immigration, report to accompany H. R. 9639 [to change title of commissioner general of immigration to 3d assistant Secretary of Labor]; submitted by Mr. Johnson of Washington. June 5, 1924. 2 p. (H. rp. 991, 68th Cong. 1st sess.) * Paper, 5c.

Lipman, Leia. Leia, Gersch, and Civia Lipman, report to accompany S. J. Res. 110 [to admit Leia, Gersch, and Civia Lipman, 3 Russian orphan children, to United States]; submitted by Mr. Johnson of Washington. June 5, 1924. 2 p. (H. rp. 996, 68th Cong. 1st sess.) * Paper, 5c.

Florida. Centennial celebration of 1st meeting of Legislative Council of Territory of Florida, Tallahassee, Fla., report to accompany H. J. Res. 281 [authorizing the President to appoint representative of United States Government to attend celebration of centennial of 1st meeting of Legislative Council of Territory of Florida, to be held at Tallahassee, Fla., Nov. 1924]; submitted by Mr. Reed of New York. June 3, 1924. 1 p. (H. rp. 945, 68th Cong. 1st sess.) * Paper, 5c.

Seville, International Exposition, 1927. Accepting invitation to participate in international exposition at Seville, Spain, in 1927, hearings on H. J. Res. 268, May 21, 1924. 1924. ii+14 p. * Paper, 5c.

—— International exposition, Seville, Spain, report to accompany H. J. Res. 268 [for participation of United States in international exposition to be held at Seville, Spain, in 1927]; submitted by Mr. Reed of New York. May 31, 1924. 6 p. (H. rp. 918, 68th Cong. 1st sess.) * Paper, 5c.

Chattahoochee River. Bridge across Chattahoochee River, report to accompany H. R. 9457 [granting consent of Congress to Alabama and Georgia, through their respective highway departments, to construct bridge across Chattahoochee River at or near Alaga, Ala., connecting Houston County, Ala., and Early County, Ga.]; submitted by Mr. Huddleston. June 4, 1924. 2 p. (H. rp. 957, 68th Cong. 1st sess.) * Paper, 5c.

Coosa River. Bridge across Coosa River, Ala., report to accompany H. R. 9518 [granting consent of Congress to Alabama, through its Highway Department, to construct bridge across Coosa River at or near Leesburg, Ala.]; submitted by Mr. Huddleston. June 4, 1924. 2 p. (H. rp. 961, 68th Cong. 1st sess.) * Paper, 5c.

Cumberland River. Bridge across Cumberland River, report to accompany H. R. 9456 [to grant consent of Congress to Cincinnati, New Orleans and Texas Pacific Railway Company to construct bridge across Cumberland River, in county of Pulaski, Ky., near Burnside]; submitted by Mr. Barkley. June 4, 1924. 2 p. (H. rp. 956, 68th Cong. 1st sess.) * Paper, 5c.

Fort Gratiot Light, Mich. Transfer to Port Huron, Mich., of portion of Fort Gratiot lighthouse reservation, Mich., report to accompany H. R. 9537; submitted by Mr. Mapes. June 6, 1924. 1 p. (H. rp. 1005, 68th Cong. 1st sess.) * Paper, 5c.

Lights. Authorizing exchange of lands between United States and State of New York, report to accompany S. 2887 [authorizing transfer of certain abandoned or unused lighthouse reservation lands by United States to State of New York for park purposes]; submitted by Mr. Parker. June 5, 1924. 2 p. (H. rp. 985, 68th Cong. 1st sess.) * Paper, 5c.

Mississippi River. Bridge across Mississippi River in Aitkin County, Minn., report to accompany H. R. 9380 [granting consent of Congress to board of county commissioners of Aitkin County, Minn., to construct bridge across Mississippi River]; submitted by Mr. Newton of Minnesota. June 3, 1924. 2 p. (H. rp. 943, 68th Cong. 1st sess.) * Paper, 5c.

Missouri River. Bridge across Missouri River, report to accompany H. R. 9516 [granting consent of Congress to South Sioux City, Nebr., to construct bridge across Missouri River between Nebraska and Iowa]; submitted by Mr. Shallenberger. June 4, 1924. 2 p. (H. rp. 959, 68th Cong. 1st sess.) * Paper, 5c.

New York Canal and Great Lakes Corporation. Modification of contracts with New York Canal and Great Lakes Corporation, report to accompany S. J. Res. 102 [authorizing Secretary of War to modify certain contracts entered into for sale of boats, barges, tugs, and other transportation facilities intended for operation upon New York State Barge Canal]; submitted by Mr. Corning. June 4, 1924. 10 p. (H. rp. 949, 68th Cong. 1st sess.) * Paper, 5c.

—— New York State Barge Canal, hearings before subcommittee on S. J. Res. 102 [authorizing Secretary of War to modify certain contracts entered into for sale of boats, barges, tugs, and other transportation facilities intended for operation up New York State Barge Canal]. May 23, 1924. 1924. iii+28 p. * Paper, 5c.

Oconee River. Bridge across Oconee River, report to accompany H. R. 9612 [granting consent of Congress to Georgia, through its Highway Department, to construct bridge across Oconee River]; submitted by Mr. Huddleston. June 5, 1924. 2 p. (H. rp. 982, 68th Cong. 1st sess.) * Paper, 5c.

Ohio River. Bridge across Ohio River, report to accompany H. R. 9402 [granting consent of Congress to Fullerton and Portsmouth Bridge Company to construct bridge across Ohio River to connect Portsmouth, Ohio, and Fullerton, Ky.]; submitted by Mr. Barkley. June 4, 1924. 2 p. (H. rp. 954, 68th Cong. 1st sess.) * Paper, 5c.

Peedee River. Bridge across Peedee River, S. C., report to accompany S. 3355 [granting consent of Congress to counties of Marion and Florence, S. C., to construct bridge across Peedee River at or near Savage Landing, S. C.]; submitted by Mr. Huddleston. June 4, 1924. 2 p. (H. rp. 962, 68th Cong. 1st sess.) * Paper, 5c.

Red River. Bridge across Red River, report to accompany H. R. 9517 [granting consent of Congress to North Texas Company, St. Jo, Tex., to construct toll bridge across Red River in vicinity of Illinois Bend, Tex.]; submitted by Mr. Rayburn. June 4, 1924. 2 p. (H. rp. 960, 68th Cong. 1st sess.) * Paper, 5c.

Rehoboth Beach, Del. Bridge across canal near Rehoboth, Del., report to accompany H. R. 9515 [granting consent of Congress to Delaware State Highway Department to construct bridge across canal near Rehoboth, Del.]; submitted by Mr. Wyant. June 4, 1924. 2 p. (H. rp. 958, 68th Cong. 1st sess.) * Paper, 5c.

Rio Grande. Bridge across Rio Grande, report to accompany H. R. 9361 [granting consent of Congress to construction of bridge across Rio Grande by C. M. Newman]; submitted by Mr. Rayburn. June 4, 1924. 2 p. (H. rp. 953, 68th Cong. 1st sess.) * Paper, 5c.

St. Marys River. Bridge across St. Marys River, report to accompany H. R. 9434 [granting consent of Congress to Georgia and Florida, through their respective highway departments, to construct bridge across St. Marys River at or near St. Marys, Ga.]; submitted by Mr. Huddleston. June 4, 1924. 2 p. (H. rp. 955, 68th Cong. 1st sess.) * Paper, 5c.

Tombigbee River. Bridge across Tombigbee River, report to accompany H. R. 9610 [granting consent of Congress to board of supervisors of Lowndes County, Miss., to construct bridge across Tombigbee River at or near Columbus]; submitted by Mr. Rayburn. June 5, 1924. 2 p. (H. rp. 981, 68th Cong. 1st sess.) * Paper, 5c.

United States. Completion of topographical survey of United States, report to accompany H. R. 4522; submitted by Mr. Wyant. June 6, 1924. 6 p. (H. rp. 1011, 68th Cong. 1st sess.) * Paper, 5c.

24—26539

Wool. Truth in fabrics and merchandise misbranding bills, hearings on H. R. 16, H. R. 732, H. R. 739, H. R. 3225, and H. R. 4141. 1924. iii+473 p. * Paper, 45c.

IRRIGATION AND RECLAMATION COMMITTEE

Colorado River. Protection and development of lower Colorado River basin, hearings on H. R. 2903, Mar. 14–21, 1924. 1924. pt. 4, iii+541–813 p. * Paper, 25c.

Hiersche, Anton. Providing for exchange of lands between Anton Hiersche and United States in connection with North Platte Federal irrigation project, report to accompany H. R. 5170; submitted by Mr. Simmons. June 3, 1924. 3 p. (H. rp. 947, 68th Cong. 1st sess.) * Paper, 5c.

Macdonald, Mrs. Katherine. Katherine Macdonald, report to accompany H. R. 5812 [for relief of Katherine Macdonald]; submitted by Mr. Leavitt. June 5, 1924. 2 p. (H. rp. 969, 68th Cong. 1st sess.) * Paper, 5c.

Reclamation of land. Extension of time of payment for settlers on Government reclamation projects, report to accompany H. R. 9611 [to provide safeguards for future Federal irrigation development, and equitable adjustment of existing accounts on Federal irrigation projects]; submitted by Mr. Smith. June 3, 1924. 16 p. (H. rp. 942, 68th Cong. 1st sess.) * Paper, 5c.

24—26536

JUDICIARY COMMITTEE

Admiralty. Appeals from interlocutory decrees in admiralty cases, report to accompany H. R. 9162 [to amend sec. 128 of judicial code, relating to appeals in admiralty cases]; submitted by Mr. Graham of Pennsylvania. June 2, 1924. 1 p. (H. rp. 932, 68th Cong. 1st sess.) * Paper, 5c.

—— Appeals in admiralty cases, hearing on H. R. 9162, May 21, 1924. 1924. ii+3 p. (Serial 40.) * Paper, 5c.

American War Mothers. To incorporate American War Mothers, report to accompany H. R. 9095; submitted by Mr. Graham of Pennsylvania. June 2, 1924. 1 p. (H. rp. 931, 68th Cong. 1st sess.) * Paper, 5c.

Constitution of United States. Proposal and ratification of amendments to Constitution of United States, report to accompany H. J. Res. 68; submitted by Mr. Graham of Pennsylvania. June 3, 1924. 1 p. (H. rp. 944, 68th Cong. 1st sess.) * Paper, 5c.

Gambling. To punish unlawful transmission in interstate commerce or through mails of gambling machines, fraudulent devices, pistols, and revolvers, etc., report to accompany H. R. 9179; submitted by Mr. Dyer. May 30, 1924. 2 p. (H. rp. 910, 68th Cong. 1st sess.) * Paper, 5c.

National banks. Preservation of oaths of bank directors, report to accompany S. 2209 [to amend sec. 5147, Revised statutes, relative to preservation of oaths of bank directors]; submitted by Mr. Graham of Pennsylvania. June 2, 1924. 2 p. (H. rp. 933, 68th Cong. 1st sess.) * Paper, 5c.

Negroes. To create a negro industrial commission, report to accompany H. R. 3228; submitted by Mr. Foster. June 2, 1924. 4 p. (H. rp. 936, 68th Cong. 1st sess.) [Corrected print.] * Paper, 5c.

Prohibition. Proposed modification of prohibition law to permit manufacture, sale, and use of 2.75 per cent beverages, hearing, Apr. 21 [–June 4], 1924. 1924. [pts. 1, 2, viii]+1–653 p. 1 pl. (Serial 39, pts. 1, 2.) * Paper, pt. 1, 50c.; * pt. 2, 10c.

Writs of error. With reference to writs of error, report to accompany S. 2693; submitted by Mr. Graham of Pennsylvania. June 2, 1924. 1 p. (H. rp. 934, 68th Cong. 1st sess.) * Paper, 5c.

LIBRARY COMMITTEE

American Academy in Rome, report to accompany S. 2834 [relating to American Academy in Rome]; submitted by Mr. Luce. May 30, 1924. 2 p. (H. rp. 911, 68th Cong. 1st sess.) * Paper, 5c.

Arlington, Va. Restoration of Lee mansion in Arlington National Cemetery, report to accompany H. J. Res. 264; submitted by Mr. Luce. June 3, 1924. 1 p. (H. rp. 941, 68th Cong. 1st sess.) * Paper, 5c.

MERCHANT MARINE AND FISHERIES COMMITTEE

Halibut. Protection of northern Pacific halibut fisheries, report to accompany H. R. 9632; submitted by Mr. Greene of Massachusetts. June 5, 1924. 3 p. (H. rp. 988, 68th Cong. 1st sess.) * Paper, 5c.

MILITARY AFFAIRS COMMITTEE

Bills for relief and restoration, hearings before subcommittee no. 7, Feb. 15, 1924, H. R. 204, to reappoint and immediately discharge or retire certain warrant officers of Army Mine Planter Service, H. R. 5465, for advancement on retired list of Regular Army of Ambrose I. Moriarty; Feb. 18, 1924, H. R. 6972, for relief of William H. Nelson, H. R. 4679, for relief of George Barrett; [etc.] 1924. li+130 p. * Paper, 10c.

Camp, Thomas J. Thomas James Camp, report to accompany H. R. 9553 [to authorize appointment of Thomas James Camp as major of infantry, Regular Army]; submitted by Mr. McKenzie. May 31, 1924. 1 p. (H. rp. 915, 68th Cong. 1st sess.) * Paper, 5c.

Cemeteries, National. Approach roads to national cemeteries and national military parks, report to accompany S. 2745 [to authorize Secretary of War to convey to States in which located Government owned or controlled approach roads to national cemeteries and national military parks]; submitted by Mr. Hill of Alabama. May 31, 1924. 1 p. (H. rp. 916, 68th Cong. 1st sess.) * Paper, 5c.

MacArthur, Fort. Railroad across Fort MacArthur military reservation, Calif., report to accompany H. R. 6652 [to authorize Los Angeles, Calif., to construct and operate line of railroad across Fort MacArthur military reservation, Calif.]; submitted by Mr. Hull of Iowa. May 31, 1924. 2 p. (H. rp. 924, 68th Cong. 1st sess.) * Paper, 5c.

Mothers. Authorizing mothers of deceased World War veterans to visit graves in Europe, report to accompany H. R. 9538 [to authorize mothers of deceased World War veterans buried in Europe to visit graves of their sons at expense of United States]; submitted by Mr. McKenzie. May 30, 1924. 12 p. (H. rp. 909, 68th Cong. 1st sess.) * Paper, 5c.

24—26534

Woodruff, William S. William Schuyler Woodruff, report to accompany S. 1199 [authorizing appointment of William Schuyler Woodruff as infantry officer, Army]; submitted by Mr. Reece. May 31, 1924. 5 p. (H. rp. 923, 68th Cong. 1st sess.) * Paper, 5c.

NAVAL AFFAIRS COMMITTEE

Betts, Claude S. Claude S. Betts, report to accompany H. R. 8566 [for relief of Claude S. Betts]; submitted by Mr. Drewry. June 5, 1924. 3 p. (H. rp. 971, 68th Cong. 1st sess.) * Paper, 5c.

Bonds of United States. Reimbursement of certain persons for loss of liberty bonds, report to accompany H. R. 5705 [for reimbursement of certain persons for loss of liberty bonds and victory notes while naval general court-martial prisoners]; submitted by Mr. Burdick. June 5, 1924. 2 p. (H. rp. 1003, 68th Cong. 1st sess.) * Paper, 5c.

Byrd, Richard E., jr. Lieut. Richard Evelyn Byrd, jr., Navy, report to accompany H. R. 9461 [for relief of Richard Evelyn Byrd, jr.]; submitted by Mr. Britten. June 5, 1924. 4 p. (H. rp. 973, 68th Cong. 1st sess.) * Paper, 5c.

Calendar. Legislative calendar, 68th Congress, 1923–24; no. 5, June 30, 1924. 1924. 40 p. 4° ‡

Conroy, John I. First Lieut. John I. Conroy, report to accompany H. R. 5143 [for relief of John I. Conroy]; submitted by Mr. Stephens. June 4, 1924. 3 p. (H. rp. 965, 68th Cong. 1st sess.) * Paper, 5c.

Dobbertin, John J. John J. Dobbertin, report to accompany H. R. 8169 [for relief of John J. Dobbertin]; submitted by Mr. Britten. June 5, 1924. 2 p. (H. rp. 979, 68th Cong. 1st sess.) * Paper, 5c.

Fechteler, Mrs. Maude M. Maud [Maude] Morrow Fechteler, report to accompany H. R. 6755 [granting 6 months' pay to Maude Morrow Fechteler, mother of Frank C. Fechteler]; submitted by Mr. Britten. June 5, 1924. 1 p. (H. rp. 977, 68th Cong. 1st sess.) * Paper, 5c.

Froemke, Fayette L. Fayette L., Froemke, report to accompany H. R. 8234 [for relief of Fayette L. Froemke]; submitted by Mr. Woodruff. June 5, 1924.' 4 p. (H. rp. 1000, 68th Cong. 1st sess.) .* Paper, 5c.

Gray, William C. William C. Gray, report to accompany H. R. 7825 [for relief of William C. Gray]; submitted by Mr. Darrow. June 5, 1924. 5 p. (H. rp. 978, 68th Cong. 1st sess.) * Paper, 5c.

Grimes, Edward A. Edward A. Grimes, report to accompany H. R. 1343 [for relief of Edward A. Grimes]; submitted by Mr. Vinson of Georgia. June 5, 1924. 15 p. (H. rp. 1002, 68th Cong. 1st sess.) * Paper, 5c.

Herrick, Mrs. Flora M. Flora M. Herrick, report to accompany H. R. 8741 [for relief of Flora M. Herrick]; submitted by Mr. Butler. June 6, 1924. 2 p. (H. rp. 1012, 68th Cong. 1st sess.) * Paper, 5c.

Holland, John P. John P. Holland, report to accompany H. R. 5779 [to place John P. Holland on retired list of Navy]; submitted by Mr. Vinson of Georgia. June 5, 1924. 17 p. (H. rp. 998, 68th Cong. 1st sess.) * Paper, 5c.

Lathrop, Mrs. Constance D. Granting 6 months' pay to Constance D. Lathrop [widow of Patrick T. M. Lathrop], report to accompany H. R. 9204; submitted by Mr. Drewry. June 5, 1924. 3 p. (H. rp. 972, 68th Cong. 1st sess.) * Paper, 5c.

Marshall, Frederick. Frederick Marshall, report to accompany H. R. 811 [for relief of Frederick Marshall]; submitted by Mr. Burdick. June 5, 1924. 5 p. (H. rp. 967, 68th Cong. 1st sess.) * Paper, 5c.

Mulloy, Henry F. Henry F. Mulloy, report to accompany H. R. 9308 [to authorize appointment of machinist Henry F. Mulloy, Navy, as ensign in Regular Navy]; submitted by Mr. Stephens. June 5, 1924. 2 p. (H. rp. 1004, 68th Cong. 1st sess.) * Paper, 5c.

Naval Reserve. To provide for creation, organization, administration, and maintenance of Naval Reserve and Marine Corps Reserve, report to accompany H. R. 9634; submitted by Mr. Britten. June 4, 1924. 8 p. (H. rp. 964, 68th Cong. 1st sess.) * Paper, 5c.

Shea, John C. John Clarence Shea, report to accompany H. R. 3771 [for relief of John Clarence Shea]; submitted by Mr. Magee of Pennsylvania. June 5, 1924. 3 p. (H. rp. 968, 68th Cong. 1st sess.) * Paper, 5c.

Zembsch, Mrs. Emma. Emma Zembsch, report to accompany H. R. 8072 [for relief of Emma Zembsch]; submitted by Mr. Swing. June 5, 1924. 3 p. (H. rp. 970, 68th Cong. 1st sess.) * Paper, 5c.

PATENTS COMMITTEE

Trade-marks. To amend sec. 5 of trade-mark act of 1905, as amended, relative to unauthorized use of portraits, report to accompany S. 3324; submitted by Mr. Perkins. June 3, 1924. 1 p. (H. rp. 946, 68th Cong. 1st sess.) * Paper, 5c.

POST OFFICE AND POST ROADS' COMMITTEE

Air Mail Service. Air mail, Government owned and operated and contract service, hearings before subcommittee on H. R. 6942 and H. R. 7064, Apr. 29, 1924. 1924. ii+32 p. * Paper, 5c.

—— Extension and operation of transcontinental Airplane Mail Service to Boston, Mass., report to accompany S. 3319; submitted by Mr. LaGuardia. June 6, 1924. 1 p. (H. rp. 1008, 68th Cong. 1st sess.) * Paper, 5c.

—— To authorize and provide for payment of amounts expended in construction of hangars and maintenance of flying fields for use of Air Mail Service of Post Office Department, report to accompany S. 1051; submitted by Mr. LaGuardia. June 2, 1924. 1 p. (H. rp. 929, 68th Cong. 1st sess.) * Paper, 5c.

Blind. Free transmission through mails of certain publications for the blind, report to accompany S. J. Res. 115; submitted by Mr. Kelly. June 2, 1924. 1 p. (H. rp. 930, 68th Cong. 1st sess.) [S. J. Res. 115 provides free transmission through mails for volumes of Holy Scriptures, or any part thereof, in raised characters for use of the blind.] * Paper, 5c.

Books. Postage rates on books to and from certain public libraries, hearings before subcommittee on H. R. 7218, Apr. 24, 1924. 1924. ii+30 p. * Paper, 5c.

Mail equipment shops. Sick leave of employees of mail equipment shops, report to accompany H. R. 6353 [to grant sick leave to employees of mail equipment shops]; submitted by Mr. Kelly. June 2, 1924. 1 p. (H. rp. 928, 68th Cong. 1st sess.) * Paper, 5c.

PUBLIC BUILDINGS AND GROUNDS COMMITTEE

Cradock, Va. Public buildings and grounds, hearings on H. J. Res. 124, relief of citizens of Cradock, Va., H. R. 4177, public building, Spartanburg, S. C., May 21, 1924. 1924. ii+40 p. (No. 8.) * Paper, 5c.

Detroit, Mich. Sale of marine hospital reservation and erection of Public Health Service hospital, Detroit, Mich., report to accompany H. R. 8588; submitted by Mr. Elliott. June 7, 1924. 3 p. (H. rp. 1022, 68th Cong. 1st sess.) * Paper, 5c.

District of Columbia. Public buildings and grounds, hearings on H. R. 8916, Arlington Memorial Bridge, May 22, 1924. 1924. ii+16 p. (No. 9.) * Paper, 5c.

Knoxville, Iowa. Right of way over Veterans' Bureau hospital reservation at Knoxville, Iowa, report to accompany S. J. Res. 61 [to grant right of way over Veterans' Bureau hospital reservation at Knoxville, Iowa, to State and municipal authorities]; submitted by Mr. Elliott. May 31, 1924. 2 p. (H. rp. 914, 68th Cong. 1st sess.) * Paper, 5c.

Sapulpa, Okla. Public buildings and grounds, hearing on H. R. 9401, purchase of site and building, Sapulpa, Okla., [and] Uniformity and character of public buildings, statement of Jas. A. Wetmore, June 3, 1924. 1924. ii+22 p. (No. 11.) * Paper, 5c.

Washington Gaslight Company. Agreement between Secretary of War and Washington Gas Light Co., report to accompany S. 2848 [to validate agreement between Secretary of War, acting on behalf of United States, and Washington Gas Light Company]; submitted by Mr. Elliott. May 31, 1924. 3 p. (H. rp. 917, 68th Cong. 1st sess.) * Paper, 5c.

—— Public buildings and grounds, hearing on S. 2848, to validate agreement between Secretary of War and Washington Gas Light Co., May 31, 1924. 1924. ii+8 p. (No. 10.) * Paper, 5c.

PUBLIC LANDS COMMITTEE

Homestead. To restore homestead rights in certain cases, report to accompany H. R. 8333; submitted by Mr. Leavitt. June 5, 1924. 2 p. (H. rp. 986, 68th Cong. 1st sess.) * Paper, 5c.

Medford, Oreg. Accepting tracts of land in Medford, Oreg. [to be used as sites for administration buildings for Crater Lake National Park], report to accompany S. 1987; submitted by Mr. Sinnott. June 5, 1924. 2 p. (H. rp. 983, 68th Cong. 1st sess.) * Paper, 5c.

Nevada National Forest. Adding lands to Nevada National Forest, report to accompany H. R. 9063; submitted by Mr. Richards. June 5, 1924. 3 p. (H. rp. 987, 68th Cong. 1st sess.) * Paper, 5c.

Red River, Okla., oil-land royalties, hearings on H. R. 178, authorizing payment of all money received as royalty from Red River oil lands to Kiowa, Comanche, and Apache tribes of Indians, Apr. 30, 1924. 1924. iii+51 p. * Paper, 5c.

RIVERS AND HARBORS COMMITTEE

River and harbor bill, report to accompany H. R. 9672; submitted by Mr. Dempsey. June 4, 1924. 63 p. (H. rp. 952, 68th Cong. 1st sess.) * Paper, 5c. 24—26537

Water pollution. Oil pollution of navigable rivers of United States, report to accompany H. R. 9199 [to prevent pollution by oil of navigable rivers of United States]; submitted by Mr. O'Connor of Louisiana. June 2, 1924. 4 p. (H. rp. 926, 68th Cong. 1st sess.) [Corrected print. First print has title: Oil pollution of coastal navigable rivers.] * Paper, 5c. 24—26610

ROADS COMMITTEE

Mount Vernon, Va. Roads, hearings on H. R. 524 [to authorize and direct construction and maintenance of memorial highway connecting Mount Vernon, Va., with Washington, D. C.], Apr. 25, 1924. 1924. ii+30 p. * Paper, 5c.

Roads, hearings on H. R. 8885 and H. R. 8907 [bills to amend Federal highway act by including nontaxable Indian lands in class with unappropriated public lands], Apr. 25, 1924. 1924. ii+7 p. * Paper, 5c.

RULES COMMITTEE

Bankruptcy law, report to accompany H. Res. 350 [to appoint subcommittee of Committee on Judiciary to examine into bankruptcy law of United States]; submitted by Mr. Snell. June 5, 1924. 1 p. (H. rp. 975, 68th Cong. 1st sess.) * Paper, 5c.

National banks. For consideration of H. R. 8887, report to accompany H. Res. 343 [for consideration of H. R. 8887, to amend act for consolidation of national banking associations, to amend sec. 5136 as amended, 5137, 5138 as amended, 5142, 5150, 5155, 5190, 5200 as amended, 5202 as amended, 5208 as amended, 5211 as amended, Revised statutes, and to amend sec. 9, 13, 22, and 24 of Federal reserve act]; submitted by Mr. Snell. June 3, 1924. 1 p. (H. rp. 940, 68th Cong. 1st sess.) * Paper, 5c.

Soldiers. Survey and investigation of soldiers' homes, hospitals, and hospital facilities, report to accompany H. Res. 351 [to empower World War veterans' Legislation Committee, or any subcommittee thereof, to make survey of soldiers' homes, hospitals, and hospital facilities, including contract hospitals]; submitted by Mr. Johnson of South Dakota. June 6, 1924. 1 p. (H. rp. 1016, 68th Cong. 1st sess.) * Paper, 5c.

TERRITORIES COMMITTEE

Alaska. Reapportionment of Alaska Legislature, hearings on H. R. 8114, to amend sec. 4 of act to create Legislative Assembly in Alaska, to confer legislative power thereon, and for other purposes, Mar. 27-29, 1924. 1924. ii+99 p. * Paper, 10c.

WAR CLAIMS COMMITTEE

Hoar, Roger S. Roger Sherman Hoar, report to accompany H. R. 8727 [for relief of Roger Sherman Hoar]; submitted by Mr. Winter. June 5, 1924. 2 p. (H. rp. 980, 68th Cong. 1st sess.) * Paper, 5c.

Janowitz, Mrs. Martha. Martha Janowitz, report to accompany H. R. 9131 [for relief of Martha Janowitz]; submitted by Mr. Winter. May 31, 1924. 2 p. (H. rp. 921, 68th Cong. 1st sess.) * Paper, 5c.

Officers, Army. Relief of certain officers in Army, report to accompany S. 1568 [for relief of Horace P. Hobbs, Charles B. Stone, Henry M. Bankhead, and Louis F. Garrard, jr., officers in Army]; submitted by Mr. Winter. June 3, 1924. 2 p. (H. rp. 948, 68th Cong. 1st sess.) * Paper, 5c.

WAYS AND MEANS COMMITTEE

Appraisers of merchandise, Baltimore, Md., report to accompany H. R. 7918 [to diminish number of appraisers at port of Baltimore]; submitted by Mr. Mills. June 6, 1924. 1 p. (H. rp. 1009, 68th Cong. 1st sess.) ' * Paper, 5c.

Customs Service. Organization of Customs Service for administration and enforcement of customs laws, report to accompany H .R. 9076 [to amend sec. 2 of act to provide necessary organization of Customs Service for adequate administration and enforcement of tariff act of 1922 and all other customs revenue laws]; submitted by Mr. Green of Iowa. May 31, 1924. 2 p. (H. rp. 912, 68th Cong. 1st sess.) * Paper, 5c.

Tax Appeals Board. Board of Tax Appeals, salaries of original appointees, report to accompany H. J. Res. 278; submitted by Mr. Green of Iowa. June 3, 1924. 2 p. (H. rp. 939, 68th Cong. 1st sess.) * Paper, 5c.

Pay, Army. Recovery of allotments, report to accompany H. R. 7845 [to amend sec. 210 of war risk insurance act so as to regulate recovery of allotments and allowances heretofore paid to designated beneficiaries]; submitted by Mr. Johnson of South Dakota. June 7, 1924. 2 p. (H. rp. 1028, 68th Cong. 1st sess.) * Paper, 5c.

REORGANIZATION JOINT COMMITTEE

Executive Departments. Reorganization of Executive Departments, report to accompany H. R. 9629 [to provide for reorganization and more effective coordination of executive branch of Government, to create Department of Education and Relief, and for other purposes]; submitted by Mr. Mapes. June 3, 1924. 32 p. (H. rp. 937, 68th Cong. 1st sess.) [Includes supplemental report signed by Mr. Harrison and Mr. Moore.] * Paper, 5c.

24—26538

—— Same, with additions, and with title, Reorganization of Executive Departments, report of Joint Committee on Reorganization created under joint resolution adopted Dec. 17, 1920, as amended by resolution approved May 5, 1923; presented by Mr. Mapes. June 3, 1924. [1]+52 p. 2 tab. (H. doc. 356, 68th Cong. 1st sess.) [Includes supplemental report signed by Mr. Harrison and Mr. Moore and appendices A–C.] * Paper, 10c.

—— Same; presented by Mr. Smoot. June 3, 1924. [1]+50 p. 2 tab. (S. doc. 128, 68th Cong. 1st sess.) [Includes supplemental report signed by Mr. Harrison and Mr. Moore and appendices A–C.] * Paper, 10c. 24—26567

SENATE

Calendar. Calendar of business, Senate, 68th Congress, 1st session, June 2–7, 1924; no. 123–128. [1924.] various paging, large 8° [Daily when Senate is in session. The legislative day of May 31 extended through the calendar day June 2.] ‡

—— Same, 68th Congress, 2d session, Dec. 1, 1924; no. 129. [1924.] 40 p. large 8° [Printed in advance.] ‡

General Staff Corps. Creation of American General Staff, personal narrative of General Staff system of American Army, by William Harding Carter; presented by Mr. Wadsworth. 1924. iii+65 p. (S. doc. 119, 68th Cong. 1st sess.) * Paper, 5c.

24—26546

Russia. Conditions in Russia, speech of William H. King, Senator from Utah, delivered in Senate Jan. 22 and Apr. 24, 1924; presented by Mr. Lodge. 1924. [1]+127 p. (S. doc. 126, 68th Cong. 1st sess.) * Paper, 10c.

24—26547

Agricultural products. To encourage and promote sale and export of agricultural products, report to accompany S. 3459; submitted by Mr. Norbeck. June 6, 1924. 1 p. (S. rp. 795, 68th Cong. 1st sess.) * Paper, 5c.

Calendar. Legislative calendar, 68th Congress, June 3, 1924; no. 11. 1924. 22 p. 4° ‡

McGuire, Henry. Henry McGuire, report to accompany H. R. 1306 [for relief of Henry McGuire]; submitted by Mr. Morris [Norris]. June 6, 1924. 2 p. (S. rp. 777, 68th Cong. 1st sess.) * Paper, 5c.

Marketing of farm produce. Interstate Farm Marketing Association, report to accompany S. 2844 [to place agricultural industry on sound commercial basis, to encourage agricultural cooperative associations, and for other purposes]; submitted by Mr. Kendrick. June 6, 1924. 5 p. (S. rp. 787, 68th Cong. 1st sess.) * Paper, 5c.

24—26542

—— To provide for cooperative marketing of agricultural commodities, report to accompany S. 3327; submitted by Mr. Smith. June 6, 1924. 2 p. (S. rp. 776, 68th Cong. 1st sess.) * Paper, 5c.

Muscle Shoals. Muscle Shoals, hearings on S. 139, S. 2372, S. 2747, S. 3214, and H. R. 518, bills relative to completion of Muscle Shoals, Apr. 28 [–May 20], 1924. 1924. pts. 3–5, [xi]+387–1122 p. map. * Paper, pt. 3, 30c.; * pt. 4, 10c.; * pt. 5, 25c.

Muscle Shoals—Continued. Muscle Shoals, report to accompany H. R. 518 [to provide for manufacture of explosives for use of Army and Navy, to provide for manufacture of fertilizer and other agricultural products, to incorporate Federal Power Corporation, and for other purposes]; submitted by Mr. Norris. May 31, calendar day June 2, 1924. 31 p. (S. rp. 678 [pt. 1], 68th Cong. 1st sess.) * Paper, 5c.   24—26540

—— Muscle Shoals, views to accompany H .R. 518 [to provide for manufacture of explosives for use of Army and Navy, to provide for manufacture of fertilizer and other agricultural products, to incorporate Federal Power Corporation, and for other purposes]; submitted by Mr. E. F. Ladd. June 3, 1924. 20 p. (S. rp. 678, pt. 2, 68th Cong. 1st sess.) * Paper, 5c.

APPROPRIATIONS COMMITTEE

Agriculture Department. Agriculture appropriation bill, [fiscal year] 1925, hearings before subcommittee on H. R. 7220. 1924. ii+177 p. * Paper, 15c.

Appropriations. Legislative appropriation bill, [fiscal year] 1925, report to accompany H. R. 9429; submitted by Mr. Warren. May 31, 1924. 2 p. (S. rp. 663, 68th Cong. 1st sess.) * Paper, 5c.

District of Columbia appropriation bill, [fiscal year] 1925, hearings before subcommittee on H. R. 8839. 1924. ii+195 p. * Paper, 15c.

Freer, Charles L. Estate of Charles L. Freer, report to accompany S. 3368 [to cancel additional taxes together with all penalties and other charges assessed against estate of Charles L. Freer, and to remit any further taxes, penalties, or charges, which may hereafter be found due from said estate]; submitted by Mr. Warren. June 3, calendar day June 5, 1924. 8 p. (S. rp. 772, 68th Cong. 1st sess.) * Paper, 5c.

Navy Department appropriation bill, [fiscal year] 1925, hearings before subcommittee on H. R. 6820. 1924. ii+287 p. * Paper, 25c.

State Department. Departments of State, Justice, Commerce, and Labor appropriation bill, [fiscal year] 1925, hearings before subcommittee on H. R. 8350. 1924. ii+49 p. * Paper, 5c.

BANKING AND CURRENCY COMMITTEE

Federal Farm Loan Board, hearings on nominations of members of board. 1924. iii+475 p. · * Paper, 45c.

National banks. Consolidation of national banking associations, report to accompany S. 3316 [to amend act for consolidation of national banking associations, to amend sec. 5136 as amended, 5137, 5138 as amended, 5142, 5150, 5155, 5190, 5200 as amended, 5202 as amended, 5208 as amended, 5211 as amended, Revised statutes, and to amend sec. 9, 13, 22, and 24 of Federal reserve act]; submitted by Mr. Pepper. May 31, 1924. 8 p. (S. rp. 666, 68th Cong. 1st sess.) * Paper, 5c.

CLAIMS COMMITTEE

American Surety Co. of New York, report to accompany H. R. 4374 [for relief of American Surety Company of New York]; submitted by Mr. Capper. May 31, calendar day June 2, 1924. 5 p. (S. rp. 696, 68th Cong. 1st sess.) * Paper, 5c.

Ashley, Grover. Grover Ashley, report to accompany S. 615 [for relief of Grover Ashley]; submitted by Mr. Trammell. June 3, calendar day June 5, 1924. 11 p. (S. rp. 767, 68th Cong. 1st sess.) · * Paper, 5c.

Baumen, John. John Baumen, report to accompany H. R. 6506 [for relief of John Baumen]; submitted by Mr Mayfield. June 3, calendar day June 5, 1924. 3 p. (S. rp. 757, 68th Cong. 1st sess.) * Paper, 5c.

Black, Clara T. Clara T. Black, report to accompany H. R. 1326 [for relief of Clara T. Black]; submitted by Mr. Capper. June 3, calendar day June 5, 1924. 9 p. (S. rp. 756, 68th Cong. 1st sess.) * Paper, 5c.

Brennan, Leslie W. Leslie Warnick Brennan, report to accompany S. 2552 [for relief of Leslie Warnick Brennan]; submitted by Mr. Bruce. June 3, 1924. 11 p. (S. rp. 706, 68th Cong. 1st sess.) * Paper, 5c.

Cole, C. M. ,Estate of C. M. Cole, report to accompany H. R. 4760 [for relief of estate of C. M. Cole] ; submitted by Mr. Bayard. June 3, calendar day June 5, 1924. 14 p. (S. rp. 759, 68th Cong. 1st sess.) . * Paper, 5c.

Cook, John W. J. W. Cook, report to accompany H. R. 3046 [for relief of J.. W. Cook] ; submitted by Mr. Capper. June 3, 1924. 11·p. (S. rp., 713, 68th Cong. 1st sess.) * Paper, 5c.

Dixon, Mrs Wynona .A. Wynona A. Dixon, report to accompany S. 594 [for relief of Wynona A. Dixon] ; submitted by Mr. Mayfield. June 3, calendar day June 4, 1924. 4 p. (S. rp. 739, 68th Cong. 1st sess.) * Paper, 5c.

Durkee, Mrs. Alice M. Alice M. Durkee, report to accompany S. 52 [for relief of Alice M. Durkee] ; submitted by Mr. Harreld. June 3, calendar day June 4, 1924. 8 p. (S. rp. 737, 68th Cong. 1st sess.) * Paper, 5c.

Farrell, J. M. J. M. Farrell, report to accompany H. R. 2754 [for relief of J. M. Farrell] ; submitted by Mr. Spencer. . June 3, 1924. 20 p. (S. rp. 718, 68th Cong. 1st sess.) * Paper, 5c.

Fuller, Stansfield A. Stanfield [Stansfield] A. and Elizabeth G. Fuller, report· to accompany H. R. 914 [granting 6 months' gratuity pay to Stansfield A. and Elizabeth G. Fuller, parents of Stansfield A. Fuller] ; submitted by Mr. Capper. June 3, calendar day June 5, 1924. 2 p. (S. rp. 755, 68th Cong. 1st sess.) . * Paper, 5c.

Gamboa, Mrs. Juana F. Juana F. Gamboa, report to accompany H. R. 8893 [for. relief of Juana F. Gamboa] ; submitted by Mr. Mayfield. June 3, 1924. 10 p.. (S. rp. 709, 68th Cong. 1st sess.) * Paper, 5c.

Gardner, Bertram. Bertram Gardner, report to accompany H. R. 7194 • [for relief of Bertram Gardner] ; submitted by· Mr. Bayard. June 3, calendar day June 4, 1924. 2 p. ÙS. rp. 728, 68th Cong. 1st sess.) * Paper, 5c.

Geere, Frank. Capt. Frank Geere, report to accompany H. R. 8258 ·[for relief of Frank Geere] ; submitted by Mr. Bayard. June 3, calendar day June 5, 1924. 4 p. (S. rp. 762, 68th Cong. 1st sess.) * Paper, 5c.

Gosnell, Fred A. Fred A. Gosnell and estate of Richard C. Lappin, report to accompany S. 2976 [to authorize comptroller general to relieve Fred A. Gosnell and estate of Richard C. Lappin in settlement of certain accounts] ; submitted by Mr. Capper. June 3, calendar day June 5, 1924. 3 p. (S. rp. 754, 68th Cong. 1st sess.) * Paper, 5c.

Guess, Mrs. E. L. Mrs. E. L. Guess, report to accompany H. R. 2989 [for relief of Mrs. E. L. Guess] ; submitted by Mr. Spencer. June 3, 1924. 21 p. (S. rp. 719, 68th Cong. 1st sess.) * Paper, 5c.

Healy, Daniel F. Daniel·F. Healy, report to accompany H. R. 3595 [for relief of Daniel F. Healy] ; submitted by Mr. Capper. May 31, calendar day June 2, 1924. 7 p. (S. rp. 695, 68th Cong. 1st sess.) * Paper, 5c.

Hennessee, Jim. Jim Hennessee, report to accompany H. R. 8343 [for relief of Jim Hennessee] ; submitted by Mr. Spencer. June 3, 1924. 3 p. · (S. rp. 721, 68th Cong. 1st sess.) * Paper, 5c.

Hilton, Robert G. Robert G. Hilton, report to accompany H. R. 2656 [to permit correction of general account of Robert G. Hilton, former assistant treasurer of United States at Baltimore, Md.] ; submitted by Mr. Bruce. June 3, calendar day June 4, 1924. 4 p. (S. rp. 736, 68th Cong. 1st sess.) *.Paper, 5c.

Hopkins, Mrs. Evalyn. Mrs. John P. Hopkins, report to accompany H. R. 3411 [for relief of Mrs. John P. Hopkins] ; submitted by Mr. Mayfield. June 3, 1924. 13 p. (S. rp. 707, 68th Cong. 1st sess.) * Paper, 5c.

Hunt, Geston P. Geston P. Hunt, report to accompany H. R. 7052 [for relief of Geston P. Hunt] ; submitted by Mr. Mayfield. June 3, calendar day June 5, 1924. 8 p. (S. rp. 758, 68th Cong. 1st sess.) * Paper, 5c.

Jessop, J. J. Jessop and sons, report to accompany H. R. 2335 [for relief of J. Jessop and sons] ; submitted by Mr. Capper. June 3, calendar day June 4, 1924. 3 p. (S. rp. 730, 68th Cong. 1st sess.) . * Paper, 5c.

Jones, Fred E., Dredging Company. Fred E. Jones Dredging Co., report to accompany H. R. 1078 [for relief of Fred E. Jones Dredging Company] ; submitted by Mr. Capper. June 3, calendar day June 4, 1924. 5 p. (S. rp. 729, 68th Cong. 1st sess.) * Paper, 5c.

Kessel, Henry A., Company, Incorporated. Henry A. Kessel Co. (Inc.), report to accompany H. R. 1082 [for relief of Henry A. Kessel Company (Incorporated)]; submitted by Mr. Spencer. June 3, 1924. 26 p. (S. rp. 715, 68th Cong. 1st sess.) * Paper, 5c.

Kettlewell, Mrs. Beatrice J. Beatrice J. Kettlewell, report to accompany H. R. 5774 [for relief of Beatrice J. Kettlewell]; submitted by Mr. Capper. June 3, calendar day June 4, 1924. 9 p. (S. rp. 733, 68th Cong. 1st sess.) * Paper, 5c.

King, William H. W. H. King, report to accompany S. 2503 [for relief of W. H. King]; submitted by Mr. Capper. May 31, calendar day June 2, 1924. 3 p. (S. rp. 697, 68th Cong. 1st sess.) * Paper, 5c.

Lamberton, U. S. S. Relief of various owners of vessels and cargoes damaged by U. S. S. Lamberton, report to accompany S. 708; submitted by Mr. Harreld. June 3, calendar day June 5, 1924. 5 p. (S. rp. 766, 68th Cong. 1st sess.) * Paper, 5c.

Laxton, Albert E. Albert E. Laxton, report to accompany H. R. 7420 [for relief of Albert E. Laxton]; submitted by Mr. Bayard. June 3, calendar day June 5, 1924. 6 p. (S. rp. 761, 68th Cong. 1st sess.) * Paper, 5c.

Lebanon National Bank, Lebanon, Tenn., report to accompany H. R. 3748 [for relief of Lebanon National Bank]; submitted by Mr. Spencer. June 3, calendar day June 4, 1924. 7 p. (S. rp. 724, 68th Cong. 1st sess.) * Paper, 5c.

Lehigh Valley Railroad Co. and McAllister Lighterage Line (Inc.), report to accompany S. 2293 [for relief of Lehigh Valley Railroad Company and McAllister Lighterage Line (Incorporated)]; submitted by Mr. Bruce. June 6, 1924. 4 p. (S. rp. 780, 68th Cong. 1st sess.) * Paper, 5c.

McAllister, Edwin J. Lieut. E. J. McAllister, report to accompany H. R. 6241 [for relief of E. J. McAllister]; submitted by Mr. Trammell. June 3, calendar day June 5, 1924. 2 p. (S. rp. 769, 68th Cong. 1st sess.) * Paper, 5c.

McGee, William J. William J. McGee, report to accompany H. R. 2005 [for relief of William J. McGee]; submitted by Mr. Spencer. June 3, 1924. 12 p. (S. rp. 717, 68th Cong. 1st sess.) * Paper, 5c.

Malley, John F. John F. Malley, report to accompany S. 2714 [for relief of John F. Malley]; submitted by Mr. Walsh of Massachusetts for Mr. Caraway. June 3, calendar day June 5, 1924. 14 p. (S. rp. 773, 68th Cong. 1st sess.) * Paper, 5c.

Neil, J. W. J. W. Neil, report to accompany S. 1221 [for relief of J. W. Neil]; submitted by Mr. Harreld. June 3, calendar day June 5, 1924. 5 p. (S. rp. 748, 68th Cong. 1st sess.), * Paper, 5c.

Norman, Charles T. Charles T. Norman, report to accompany H. R. 1830 [for relief of Charles T. Norman]; submitted by Mr. Bayard. June 6, 1924. 6 p. (S. rp. 778, 68th Cong. 1st sess.) * Paper, 5c.

Northampton, Mass. Chamber of Commerce, Northampton, Mass., report to accompany H. R. 4280 [for relief of Chamber of Commerce, Northampton, Mass.]; submitted by Mr. Spencer. June 3, calendar day June 4, 1924. 8 p. (S. rp. 725, 68th Cong. 1st sess.) * Paper, 5c.

Payne, W. F. W. F. Payne, report to accompany H. R. 4290 [for relief of W. F. Payne]; submitted by Mr. Mayfield. June 3, 1924. 3 p. (S. rp. 708, 68th Cong. 1st sess.) * Paper, 5c.

Peirce, Charles F. Charles F. Peirce, Frank T. Mann, and Mollie V. Gaither, report to accompany H. R. 6328 [for relief of Charles F. Peirce, Frank T. Mann, and Mollie V. Gaither]; submitted by Mr. Bayard. June 3, calendar day June 4, 1924. 2 p. (S. rp. 727, 68th Cong. 1st sess.) * Paper, 5c.

Porter, James B. James B. Porter, report to accompany H. R. 3477 [for relief of James B. Porter]; submitted by Mr. Spencer. June 3, 1924. 6 p. (S. rp. 720, 68th Cong. 1st sess.) * Paper, 5c.

Post, Philip T. Philip T. Post, report to accompany S. 2033 [for relief of Philip T. Post]; submitted by Mr. Bruce. June 3, calendar day June 4, 1924. 4 p. (S. rp. 735, 68th Cong. 1st sess.) * Paper, 5c.

Rich, Walter A. Estate of Walter A. Rich, report to accompany S. 2139 [for relief of estate of Walter A. Rich]; submitted by Mr. Harreld. June 3, 1924. 6 p. (S. rp. 712, 68th Cong. 1st sess.) * Paper, 5c.

Richards, Margaret. Margaret Richards, report to accompany S. 854 [for relief of Margaret Richards]; submitted by Mr. Harreld. June 6, 1924. 5 p. (S. rp. 775, 68th Cong. 1st sess.) * Paper, 5c.

Ryan, Joseph P. Joseph P. Ryan, report to accompany H. R. 1333 [for relief of Joseph P. Ryan]; submitted by Mr. Spencer. June 3, 1924. 3 p. (S. rp. 716, 68th Cong. 1st sess.) * Paper, 5c.

Saucier, J. E. J. E. Saucier, report to accompany S. 2534 [for relief of J. E. Saucier]; submitted by Mr. Stephens. June 3, 1924. 2 p. (S. rp. 701, 68th Cong. 1st sess.) * Paper, 5c.

Scheibe, Edward S. Edward S. Scheibe, report to accompany H. R. 4318 [for relief of Edward S. Scheibe]; submitted by Mr. Johnson of Minnesota. June 3, 1924. 12 p. (S. rp. 704, 68th Cong. 1st sess.) * Paper, 5c.

Seibel, Clifford W. Clifford W. Seibel and Frank A. Vestal, report to accompany H. R. 5448 [for relief of Clifford W. Seibel and Frank A. Vestal]; submitted by Mr. Capper. June 3, calendar day June 4, 1924. 6 p. (S. rp. 732, 68th Cong. 1st sess.) * Paper, 5c.

Sharp, Mrs. May A. May Adelaide Sharp, report to accompany H. R. 6498 [for relief of May Adelaide Sharp]; submitted by Mr. Capper. June 3, calendar day June 4, 1924. 3 p. (S. rp. 734, 68th Cong. 1st sess.) * Paper, 5c.

Smith, Mrs. Ella H. Ella H. Smith, report to accompany S. 1885 [for relief of Ella H. Smith]; submitted by Mr. Johnson of Minnesota. June 3, 1924. 13 p. (S. rp. 703, 68th Cong. 1st sess.) * Paper, 5c.

Standard Oil Co., report to accompany H. R. 2373 [for relief of Standard Oil Company, Savannah, Ga.]; submitted by Mr. Capper. June 3, calendar day June 4, 1924. 7 p. (S. rp. 731, 68th Cong. 1st sess.) * Paper, 5c.

Stickney, Fred W. Fred W. Stickney and H. A. Reynolds, report to accompany H. R. 3505 [for relief of Fred W. Stickney and H. A. Reynolds]; submitted by Mr. Capper. June 3, 1924. 2 p. (S. rp. 714, 68th Cong. 1st sess.) * Paper, 5c.

Stone Towing Line, report to accompany H. R. 1682 [for relief of Stone Towing Line]; submitted by Mr. Trammell. June 3, calendar day June 5, 1924. 7 p. (S. rp. 768, 68th Cong. 1st sess.) * Paper, 5c.

Therrien, Mrs. Yvonne. Yvonne Therrien, report to accompany S. 54 [for relief of Yvonne Therrien]; submitted by Mr. Harreld. June 3, calendar day June 4, 1924. 6 p. (S. rp. 738, 68th Cong. 1st sess.) * Paper, 5c.

Tower, Mrs. Cornelia M. A. Cornelia M. A. Tower, report to accompany H. R. 3504 [for relief of Cornelia M. A. Tower]; submitted by Mr. Capper. May 31, calendar day June 2, 1924. 4 p. (S. rp. 694, 68th Cong. 1st sess.) * Paper, 5c.

Tribou, David H. Capt. D. H. Tribou, chaplain, Navy, report to accompany H. R. 5819 [for relief of estate of D. H. Tribou]; submitted by Mr. Bayard. June 3, calendar day June 5, 1924. 2 p. (S. rp. 760, 68th Cong. 1st sess.) * Paper, 5c.

Wright, Ralph O. Ralph Ole Wright and Varina Belle Wright, report to accompany S. 3281 [for relief of Ralph Ole Wright and Varina Belle Wright]; submitted by Mr. Stephens. June 3, calendar day June 5, 1924. 3 p. (S. rp. 747, 68th Cong. 1st sess.) * Paper, 5c.

COMMERCE COMMITTEE

Appraisers. Appointment of appraiser of merchandise at Portland, Oreg., report to accompany S. 3352; submitted by Mr. McNary. June 3, calendar day June 5, 1924. 1 p. (S. rp. 764, 68th Cong. 1st sess.) * Paper, 5c.

Chicago River. Examination of Chicago River, report to accompany S. 3192 [to provide for examination of Chicago River and its branches]; submitted by Mr. Jones of Washington. June 3, 1924. 1 p. (S. rp. 723, 68th Cong. 1st sess.) * Paper, 5c.

Cumberland River. Bridge across Cumberland River, report to accompany S. 3380 [to grant consent of Congress to Cincinnati, New Orleans and Texas Pacific Railway Company to construct bridge across Cumberland River, in county of Pulaski, Ky., near Burnside]; submitted by Mr. Ladd. June 3, 1924. 2 p. (S. rp. 710, 68th Cong. 1st sess.) * Paper, 5c.

Lafayette River. Dam across Lafayette River, Va., report to accompany S. 3398 [to authorize Norfolk, Va., to construct combined dam and bridge in Lafayette River at or near Granby street, Norfolk, Va.]; submitted by Mr. Sheppard. June 6, 1924. 2 p. (S. rp. 781, 68th Cong. 1st sess.) * Paper, 5c.

Lights. Lighthouse lands for park purposes, New York, report to accompany S. 2887 [authorizing transfer of certain abandoned or unused lighthouse reservation lands by United States to State of New York for park purposes]; submitted by Mr. Willis. June 3, 1924. 3 p. (S. rp. 702, 68th Cong. 1st sess.) * Paper, 5c.

Ohio River. Bridge across Ohio River, report to accompany H. R. 9345 [granting consent of Congress for construction of bridge across Ohio River between Vanderburgh County, Ind., and Henderson County, Ky., by Kentucky and Indiana, through their respective highway commissions]; submitted by Mr. Ladd. June 6, 1924. 2 p. (S. rp. 784, 68th Cong. 1st sess.) * Paper, 5c.

Rehoboth Beach, Del. Bridge across canal near Rehoboth, Del., report to accompany S. 3409 [granting consent of Congress to Delaware State Highway Department to construct bridge across canal near Rehoboth, Del.]; submitted by Mr. Ladd. June 3, calendar day June 4, 1924. 2 p. (S. rp. 741, 68th Cong. 1st sess.) * Paper, 5c.

St. Marys River. Bridge across St. Marys River, report to accompany S. 3464 [granting consent of Congress to Georgia and Florida, through their respective highway departments, to construct bridge across St. Marys River at or near St. Marys, Ga.]; submitted by Mr. Sheppard. June 3, calendar day June 5, 1924. 2 p. (S. rp. 771, 68th Cong. 1st sess.) * Paper, 5c.

EDUCATION AND LABOR COMMITTEE

Diploma mills, hearings before subcommittee pursuant to S. Res. 61, authorizing Committee on Education and Labor to inquire into certain abuses in medical education, Jan. 19–Mar. 28, 1924. 1924. ii+98 p. * Paper, 5c.

FINANCE COMMITTEE

Army General Hospital, Fort Bayard. Director of Veterans' Bureau to take assignments of certain claims at Fort Bayard, N. Mex., report to accompany S. J. Res. 131 [authorizing director of Veterans' Bureau to take assignments of certain claims of patients of General Hospital numbered 55, Fort Bayard, N. Mex.]; submitted by Mr. Reed of Pennsylvania. June 3, 1924. 2 p. (S. rp. 700, 68th Cong. 1st sess.) * Paper, 5c.

Calendar. Legislative calendar, 68th Congress, June 3–13, 1924; no. 23–25. 1924. Each 54 p. 4° ‡

Internal revenue. Revenue act of 1924, hearings on H. R. 6715, to reduce and equalize taxation, to provide revenue, and for other purposes, Mar. 7–Apr. 8, 1924. 1924. ii+456 p. * Paper, 45c.

—— Statement of changes made in revenue act of 1921 by H. R. 6715 and reasons therefor. 1924. ii+38 p. (Senate committee print, 68th Cong. 1st sess.) ‡   24—26585

Liquors. To refund taxes paid on distilled spirits in certain cases, report to accompany S. 3072; submitted by Mr. Ernst. May 31, calendar day June 2, 1924. 1 p. (S. rp. 690, 68th Cong. 1st sess.) * Paper, 5c.

FOREIGN RELATIONS COMMITTEE

Calendar, 68th Congress, 1st session, June 7, 1924; no. 9. 1924. 20 p. 4° [Complete.] ‡

Russia. Recognition of Russia, hearings before subcommittee pursuant to S. Res. 50, declaring that Senate favors recognition of present Soviet Government in Russia; letter from Secretary of State transmitting information relative to propaganda carried on in United States, directed from Russia. 1924. pt. 2, iii+159–530 p. 1 tab. * Paper, 50c.

IMMIGRATION COMMITTEE

Calendar. Legislative calendar, 68th Congress, June 7, 1924; no. 3. 1924. 6 p. 4° ‡

Chippewa Indians. To amend act making appropriations for current and contingent expenses of Bureau of Indian Affairs, report to accompany H. R. 8086 [to amend act making appropriations for current and contingent expenses of Bureau of Indian Affairs, for fulfilling treaty stipulations with various Indian tribes, and for other purposes, fiscal year 1915, relative to reimbursable appropriation for education of Chippewa Indians provided by sec. 8 thereof]; submitted by Mr. Harreld. June 7, 1924. 2 p. (S. rp. 796, 68th Cong. 1st sess.) *Paper, 5c.

—— To provide for payment of claims against Chippewa Indians of Minnesota, report to accompany H. R. 4461; submitted by Mr. Harreld. May 31, calendar day June 2, 1924. 2 p. (S. rp. 687, 68th Cong. 1st sess.) *Paper, 5c.

Cowlitz Indians. Authorizing Cowlitz tribe of Indians in State of Washington to submit claims to Court of Claims, report to accompany H. R. 71; submitted by Mr. Harreld. June 6, 1924. 2 p. (S. rp. 789, 68th Cong. 1st sess.) *Paper, 5c.

Crew, Jacob. Providing for payment of any unappropriated moneys belonging to Apache, Kiowa, and Comanche Indians to Jacob Crew, report to accompany S. 3247; submitted by Mr. Harreld. June 3, calendar day June 5, 1924. 3 p. (S. rp. 751, 68th Cong. 1st sess.) *Paper, 5c.

Five Civilized Tribes. To amend act fulfilling treaty stipulations with various Indian tribes, report to accompany H. R. 7077 [to amend act to amend act making appropriations for current and contingent expenses of Bureau of Indian Affairs, for fulfilling treaty stipulations with various Indian tribes, and for other purposes, fiscal year 1914, relating to certain payments from funds of Five Civilized Tribes of Oklahoma for cost of street paving and construction of sidewalks and sewers]; submitted by Mr. Harreld. June 6, 1924. 2 p. (S. rp. 792, 68th Cong. 1st sess.) *Paper, 5c.

Gauthier, Mrs. Benjamin. Mrs. Benjamin Gauthier, report to accompany S. 1897 [for relief of Mrs. Benjamin Gauthier]; submitted by Mr. Harreld. May 31, calendar day June 2, 1924. 1 p. (S. rp. 683, 68th Cong. 1st sess.) *Paper, 5c.

Indian reservations. To provide for disposition of bonuses, rentals, and royalties from unallotted lands in Executive order Indian reservations, report to accompany S. 876 [to provide for disposition of bonuses, rentals, and royalties received under provisions of act to promote mining of coal, phosphate, oil, oil shale, gas, and sodium on public domain, from unallotted lands in Executive order Indian reservations]; submitted by Mr. Harreld. May 31, 1924. 2 p. (S. rp. 669, 68th Cong. 1st sess.) *Paper, 5c.

Indian trust funds. To provide for expenditure of tribal funds of Indians for construction repair, and rental of agency buildings and related purposes, report to accompany S. 2838; submitted by Mr. Harreld. May 31, calendar day June 2, 1924. 1 p. (S. rp. 684, 68th Cong. 1st sess.) *Paper, 5c.

Indians occupying railroad lands in Arizona, New Mexico, or California, report to accompany S. 369 [to amend act for relief of Indians occupying railroad lands in Arizona, New Mexico, or California, so as to extend provisions of act to Mar. 4, 1925]; submitted by Mr. Harreld. May 31, 1924. 2 p. (S. rp. 667, 68th Cong. 1st sess.) *Paper, 5c.

Ko-mo-dal-kiah. Heirs of Ko-mo-dal-kiah, Moses agreement allottee no. 33, report to accompany S. 1705 [for relief of heirs of Ko-mo-dal-kiah, Moses agreement allottee numbered 33]; submitted by Mr. Harreld. May 31, calendar day June 2, 1924. 2 p. (S. rp. 679, 68th Cong. 1st sess.) *Paper, 5c.

Kramer, Forrest J. For relief of Forrest J. Kramer, report to accompany H. R. 7249; submitted by Mr. Harreld. May 31, calendar day June 2, 1924. 2 p. (S. rp. 688, 68th Cong. 1st sess.) *Paper, 5c.

Kuca, H. E. H. E. Kuca and V. J. Koupal, report to accompany H. R. 2977 [for relief of H. E. Kuca and v. J. Koupal]; submitted by Mr. Harreld. May 31, calendar day June 2, 1924. 2 p. (S. rp. 686, 68th Cong. 1st sess.) *Paper, 5c.

Menominee Reservation. To amend law relating to timber operations on Menominee Reservation, Wis., report to accompany S. 3036; submitted by Mr. Harreld. May 31, calendar day June 2, 1924. 2 p. (S. rp. 685, 68th Cong. 1st sess.) * Paper, 5c.

Navajo Reservation. Authorizing expenditure for certain purposes of receipts from oil and gas on Navajo Indian Reservation, Ariz., and N. Mex., report to accompany S. 1653; submitted by Mr. Harreld. May 31, calendar day June 2, 1924. 2 p. (S. rp. 681, 68th Cong. 1st sess.) * Paper, 5c.

Paiute Indians. Providing for reservation of lands in Utah for certain bands of Paiute Indians, report to accompany S. 879; submitted by Mr. Harreld. May 31, 1924. 2 p. (S. rp. 671, 68th Cong.1st sess.) * Paper, 5c.

Ponca Indians. Authorizing Ponca tribe of Indians residing in Oklahoma and Nebraska to submit claims to Court of Claims, report to accompany H. R. 4275; submitted by Mr. Harreld. June 6, 1924. 2 p. (S. rp. 790, 68th Cong. 1st sess.) * Paper, 5c.

—— Authorizing Ponca tribe of Indians residing in Oklahoma and Nebraska to submit claims to Court of Claims, report to accompany S. 1392; submitted by Mr. Harreld. June 3, calendar day June 5, 1924. 2 p. (S. rp. 750, 68th Cong. 1st sess.) * Paper, 5c.

Potawatomi Indians. Authorizing Secretary of Interior to pay certain funds to various Wisconsin Pottawatomi Indians, report to accompany H. R. 7239; submitted by Mr. Harreld. May 31, calendar day June 2, 1924. 2 p. (S. rp. 691, 68th Cong. 1st sess.) * Paper, 5c.

Quapaw Agency. Removal of restrictions on alienation of lands of allottees of Quapaw Agency, Okla., report to accompany H. R. 7453 [to amend act for removal of restrictions on alienation of lands of allottees of Quapaw Agency, Okla., and sale of all tribal lands, school, agency, or other buildings on any of reservations within jurisdiction of such agency, so as to permit sale of homestead allotments]; submitted by Mr. Harreld. June 6, 1924. 2 p. (S. rp. 793, 68th Cong. 1st sess.) * Paper, 5c.

—— To perfect title of purchasers of Indian lands, report to accompany H. R. 4818 [to perfect title of purchasers of Indian lands sold under provisions of act of Congress of Mar. 3, 1909, and regulations pursuant thereto as applied to Indians of Quapaw Agency]; submitted by Mr. Harreld. June, 6, 1924. 2 p. (S. rp. 791, 68th Cong. 1st sess.) * Paper, 5c.

Red Lake Reservation. Payment of $50 each to members of Red Lake band of Chippewa Indians, report to accompany H. R. 25 [authorizing per capita payment of $50 each to members of Red Lake band of Chippewa Indians from proceeds of sale of timber and lumber on Red Lake Reservation]; submitted by Mr. Harreld. June 6, 1924. 2 p. (S. rp. 788, 68th Cong. 1st sess.) * Paper, 5c.

San Juan River. To provide for payment of ½ cost of construction of bridge across San Juan River, N. Mex. [near Bloomfield], report to accompany S. 1665; submitted by Mr. Harreld. May 31, calendar day June 2, 1924. 2 p. (S. rp. 682, 68th Cong. 1st sess.) * Paper, 5c.

Santee Indians. Adjudicating alleged claims of Sisseton and Wahpeton bands of Sioux Indians against United States, report to accompany S. 3346 [to provide that jurisdiction shall be conferred upon Court of Claims, notwithstanding lapse of time or statutes of limitation, to hear, examine, and adjudicate and render judgment in any and all legal and equitable claims arising under or growing out of any treaty or agreement between United States and certain bands of Indians]; submitted by Mr. Harreld. May 31, calendar day June 2, 1924. 2 p. (S. rp. 692, 68th Cong. 1st sess.) * Paper, 5c.

Stevens County, Wash. To authorize payment of certain taxes to Stevens and Ferry counties, Wash., report to accompany H. R. 1414; submitted by Mr. Dill. June 3, calendar day June 5, 1924. 5 p. (S. rp. 765, 68th Cong. 1st sess.) * Paper, 5c.

Uinta Indians. For relief of Uintah and White River tribes of Ute Indians of Utah, report to accompany S. 3080; submitted by Mr. Harreld. June 3, calendar day June 5, 1924. 2 p. (S. rp. 752, 68th Cong. 1st sess.) * Paper, 5c.

Umatilla Reservation. Allotment of lands to Indians residing upon Umatilla Reservation, Oreg., and granting patents therefor, report to accompany S. 994 [to amend act for allotment of lands in severalty to Indians residing upon Umatilla Reservation, Oreg., and granting patents therefor, so as to withhold from sale or disposition certain lands for use as tribal grazing grounds]; submitted by Mr. Harreld. May 31, calendar day June 2, 1924. 2 p. (S. rp. 680, 68th Cong. 1st sess.) * Paper, 5c.

Ute Indians. Reservation of land in Utah as school site for Ute Indians, report to accompany S. 875; submitted by Mr. Harreld. May 31, 1924. 2 p. (S. rp. 668, 68th Cong. 1st sess.) * Paper, 5c.

Walapai Reservation. To provide for exchanges of Government and privately owned lands in Walapai Indian Reservation, Ariz., report to accompany S. 877; submitted by Mr. Harreld. May 31, 1924. 2 p. (S. rp. 670, 68th Cong. 1st sess.) * Paper, 5c.

INTERSTATE COMMERCE COMMITTEE

Freight rates. Transportation rates of common carriers, hearings on S. 91, S. 1227, S. 1919, and S. 2951, bills for repeal or amendment of sec. 15a of interstate commerce act as amended. 1924. iii+818 p. * Paper, 80c.

Industrial arbitration. Arbitration between carriers and employees, boards of adjustment, report to accompany S. 2646 [for expeditious and prompt settlement, mediation, conciliation, and arbitration of disputes between carriers and their employees and subordinate officials]; submitted by Mr. Smith. June 6, 1924. 4 p. (S. rp. 779, 68th Cong. 1st sess.) * Paper, 5c.

Locomotives. To promote safety of employees and travelers on railroads, report to accompany H. R. 8578 [to amend act to promote safety of employees and travelers upon railroads by compelling common carriers engaged in interstate commerce to equip their locomotives with safe and suitable boilers and appurtenances thereto, as amended]; submitted by Mr. Smith, June 3, calendar day June 4, 1924. 8 p. (S. rp. 740, 68th Cong. 1st sess.) * Paper, 5c.

Railroads. Consolidation of railway properties, hearings on S. 2224, May 21, 1924. 1924. iii+63 p. * Paper, 5c.

IRRIGATION AND RECLAMATION COMMITTEE

Reclamation of land. Development of Federal irrigation projects, report to accompany S. 3372 [to provide safeguards for future Federal irrigation development and equitable adjustment of existing accounts on Federal irrigation projects]; submitted by Mr. Gooding. June 4 [3], calendar day June 3 [4], 1924. 4 p. (S. rp. 726, 68th Cong. 1st sess.) * Paper, 5c.

JUDICIARY COMMITTEE

Bankruptcy. Amendment of national bankruptcy act, report to accompany S. 1649 [to amend act to establish uniform system of bankruptcy throughout United States, and acts amendatory thereof and supplementary thereto]; submitted by Mr. Walsh of Montana. June 3, calendar day June 5, 1924. 8 p. (S. rp. 774, 68th Cong. 1st sess.) * Paper, 5c.   24—26611

Birth control. Cummins-vaile bill, joint hearings before subcommittees of Committees on Judiciary on H. R. 6542 and S. 2290, Apr. 8 and May 9, 1924. 1924. iii+79 p. (Serial 38.) [These hearings were held at joint meetings of the subcommittees of the Senate Committee on Judiciary and the House Committee on Judiciary and is published as Serial 38 of the House Judiciary Committee hearings.] * Paper, 10c.

Judges. Two additional circuit judges for 8th circuit, report to accompany S. 99 [authorizing the President to appoint 2 additional circuit judges for 8th circuit]; submitted by Mr. Spencer. June 3, 1924. 12 p. (S. rp. 705, 68th Cong. 1st sess.) * Paper, 5c.

Negroes. Commission on racial question, hearing before subcommittee on S. 291; creating a commission on racial question, May 24, 1924. 1924. ii+22 p. * Paper, 5c.

Pay, Army. To confer jurisdiction on Court of Claims, report to accompany S. 4 [to confer jurisdiction on Court of Claims to certify findings of fact heretofore made for claimants in claims of officers of Army for longevity pay]; submitted by Mr. Caraway. June 3, 1924. 1 p. (S. rp. 699, 68th Cong. 1st sess.) * Paper, 5c.

Daugherty, Harry M. Investigation of Harry M. Daugherty, formerly Attorney General, hearings pursuant to S. Res. 157, directing committee to investigate failure of Attorney General to prosecute or defend certain criminal and civil actions wherein the Government is interested, May 5–14, 1924. 1924. pt. 8, iii+2025–2293 p. 2 p. of pl.　* Paper, 25c.

LAWS, SELECT COMMITTEE ON REVISION OF

Codification of laws, report to accompany S. J. Res. 141 [for appointment of commission to consolidate, codify, revise, and reenact general and permanent laws of United States in force Dec. 2, 1923] ; submitted by Mr. Ernst. June 3, 1924. 71 p. (S. rp. 722, 68th Cong. 1st sess.) [S. J. Res. 141 is reported in lieu of H. R. 12, to consolidate, codify, revise, and reenact general and permanent laws of United States in force Dec. 22, 1923.] * Paper, 5c.
24—26541

MILITARY AFFAIRS COMMITTEE

Aber, Caleb. Caleb Aber, report to accompany H. R. 1539 [for relief of Caleb Aber] ; submitted by Mr. Wadsworth. June 3, calendar day June 4, 1924. 1 p. (S. rp. 742, 68th Cong. 1st sess.)　* Paper, 5c.

Camp, Thomas J. Thomas J. Camp, report to accompany S. 3416 [to authorize appointment of Thomas James Camp as major of infantry, Regular Army] ; submitted by Mr. Wadsworth. May 31, 1924. 1 p. (S. rp. 672, 68th Cong. 1st sess.)　* Paper, 5c.

Carlisle Barracks. Sale of portion of Carlisle Barracks reservation, report to accompany H. R. 7731 ; submitted by Mr. Wadsworth. June 6, 1924. 4 p. (S. rp. 782, 68th Cong. 1st sess.)　* Paper, 5c.

Claims. Settlement of admiralty claims resulting from World War and sale of ordnance stores to Cuba, report to accompany S. 3408 [to amend act to give indemnity for damages caused by American forces abroad, and for other purposes] ; submitted by Mr. Wadsworth. May 31, 1924. 1 p. (S. rp. 677, 68th Cong. 1st sess.)　[Sec. 2 of S. 3408 amends existing law relating to sale of ordnance to Cuba.]　* Paper, 5c.

Harpham, George E. George E. Harpham, report to accompany S. 1543 [for relief of George E. Harpham] ; submitted by Mr. Bursum. May 31, 1924. 2 p. (S. rp. 673, 68th Cong. 1st sess.)　* Paper, 5c.

Logan, Fort. Railroad across southwesterly portion of Fort Logan military reservation, Colo., report to accompany S. 3420 [granting consent of Congress to construction by Denver and Rio Grande Western Railroad Company of line of railroad across southwesterly portion of Fort Logan military reservation, Colo.] ; submitted by Mr. Warren. May 31, calendar day June 2, 1924. 1 p. (S. rp. 698, 68th Cong. 1st sess.)　* Paper, 5c.

MacArthur, Fort. Railroad across Fort MacArthur military reservation, Calif., report to accompany H. R. 6652 [to authorize Los Angeles, Calif., to construct and operate line of railroad across Fort MacArthur military reservation, Calif.] ; submitted by Mr. Wadsworth. June 6, 1924. 2 p. (S. rp. 785, 68th Cong. 1st sess.)　* Paper, 5c.

McNickle, John. John McNickle, report to accompany S. 2950 [to define and determine character of service represented by honorable discharge issued to John McNickle, of company I, 7th regiment New York volunteer heavy artillery, under date of Sept. 27, 1865] ; submitted by Mr. Wadsworth. May 31, 1924. 2 p. (S. rp. 676, 68th Cong. 1st sess.)　* Paper, 5c.

National Home for Disabled Volunteer Soldiers. Hospital at National Home for Disabled volunteer Soldiers. Santa Monica, Calif., report to accompany H. R. 2821 ; submitted by Mr. Wadsworth. June 3, calendar day June 4, 1924. 2 p. (S. rp. 743, 68th Cong. 1st sess.)　* Paper, 5c.

Nelson, William H. William H. Nelson, report to accompany H. R. 6972 [for relief of William H. Nelson] ; submitted by Mr. George. June 6, 1924. 1 p. (S. rp. 783, 68th Cong. 1st sess.)　* Paper, 5c.

Rethers, Harry F. Permission to Col. Harry F. Rethers to accept statuette Le courage militaire, report to accompany H. R. 5661 [granting permission to Colonel Harry F. Rethers, Quartermaster Corps, Army, to accept gift of Sevres statuette entitled Le courage militaire tendered by President of French Republic] ; submitted by Mr. Reed of Pennsylvania. June 3, calendar day June 4, 1924. 2 p. (S. rp. 745, 68th Cong. 1st sess.) *Paper; 5c.

Vicksburg, Miss. Construct water mains on National Cemetery road at Vicksburg, Miss., report to accompany H. R. 4816 [to permit Vicksburg, Miss., to construct water mains on and under National Cemetery road, Vicksburg, Miss.] ; submitted by Mr. Wadsworth. June 3, calendar day June 4, 1924. 2 p. (S. rp. 744, 68th Cong. 1st sess.) *Paper, 5c.

War Department. Transfer of trucks and tractors for road building purposes, report to accompany H. R. 7269 [to authorize and direct Secretary of War to transfer certain materials, machinery, and equipment to Department of Agriculture] ; submitted by Mr. Wadsworth. May 31, 1924. 1 p. (S. rp. 675, 68th Cong. 1st sess.) *Paper, 5c.

NAVAL AFFAIRS COMMITTEE

Becker, Joseph F. For relief of Joseph F. Becker, report to accompany S. 747; submitted by Mr. Swanson. May 31, 1924. 2 p. (S. rp. 674, 68th Cong. 1st sess.) *Paper, 5c.

Byrd, Richard E., jr. Lieut. Richard Evelyn Byrd, jr., Navy, report to accompany S. 3433 [for relief of Richard Evelyn Byrd, jr.] ; submitted by Mr. Swanson. June 3, calendar day June 5, 1924. 2 p. (S. rp. 763, 68th Cong. 1st sess.) *Paper, 5c.

Calendar. Legislative calendar, 68th Congress, 1st session, June 7, 1924; no. 6. 1924. 7 p. large 8° ‡

Naval Reserve. To provide for Naval Reserve and Marine Corps Reserve; report to accompany S. 1807; submitted by Mr. Oddie. June 3, calendar day June 5, 1924. 9 p. (S. rp. 749, 68th Cong. 1st sess.) *Paper, 5c.

Rush, William R. To commission Capt. William Rees Rush, report to accompany S. 1187 [to commission Captain William Rees Rush as rear admiral on retired list of Navy] ; submitted by Mr. Lodge. May 31, 1924. 1 p. (S. rp. 665, 68th Cong. 1st sess.) *Paper, 5c.

Stinchcomb, Frank. Frank Stinchcomb, report to accompany H. R. 8961 [for relief of Frank Stinchcomb] ; submitted by Mr. Swanson. May 31, calendar day June 2, 1924. 7 p. (S. rp. 693, 68th Cong. 1st sess.) *Paper, 5c.

War-ships. Alterations to certain naval vessels and construction of additional vessels, hearing on H. R. 8687, May 31, 1924. 1924. ii+24 p. *Paper, 5c.

—— To authorize alterations to certain naval vessels and to provide for construction of additional vessels, report to accompany H. R. 8687; submitted by Mr. Hale. May 31, 1924. 10 p. (S. rp. 664, 68th Cong. 1st sess.) *Paper, 5c.

Webb, Leland D. To compensate L. D, Webb, report to accompany S. 1569 [to compensate L. D. Webb for damages to household effects while being transported by Government conveyance] ; submitted by Mr. Pepper. June 3, calendar day June 5, 1924. 1 p. (S. rp. 753, 68th Cong. 1st sess.) *Paper, 5c.

PATENTS COMMITTEE

Patents. To amend patent and trade-mark laws, and for other purposes, report to accompany H. R. 21; submitted by Mr. Ernst. June 3, calendar day June 4, 1924. 1 p. (S. rp. 746, 68th Cong. 1st sess.) *Paper, 5c.

Radio communication. To amend copyright act, hearings before subcommittee on S. 2600, to amend sec. 1 of act to amend and consolidate acts respecting copyright, Apr. 9–18, 1924. 1924. iii+277 p. *Paper, 25c.

POST OFFICES AND POST ROADS COMMITTEE

Air Mail Service. Authorizing extension and operation of transcontinental Airplane Mail Service to Boston, Mass., report to accompany S. 3319; submitted by Mr. Sterling. June 3, calendar day June 5, 1924. 1 p. (S. rp. 770, 68th Cong. 1st sess.) *Paper, 5c.

PRINTING COMMITTEE

Calendar of bills, resolutions, petitions, manuscripts, communications, etc., referred to Committee on Printing for its consideration and action thereon, June 3, 1924; no. 2, 68th Congress, 1st session. 1924. 11 p. 4° ‡

PRIVILEGES AND ELECTIONS COMMITTEE

Mayfield, Earle B. Senator from Texas, hearings before subcommittee pursuant to S. Res. 97, authorizing investigation of alleged unlawful practices in election of Senator from Texas, May 8–16, 1924. 1924. pt. 1, iii+1–185 p. * Paper, 15c.

PUBLIC LANDS AND SURVEYS COMMITTEE

Calendar. Legislative calendar, 68th Congress, Dec. 1, 1924; no. 8. [1924.] 39 p. 4° [Printed in advance.] ‡

Metcalfe, Mary T. Mary T. Metcalfe, report to accompany S. 3370 [for relief of Mary T. Metcalfe]; submitted by Mr. Bursum. June 3, 1924. 3 p. (S. rp. 711, 68th Cong. 1st sess.) * Paper, 5c.

Naval petroleum reserves. Leases upon naval oil reserves, minority views pursuant to S. Res. 147; submitted by Mr. Spencer. June 6, 1924. 2 p. (S. rp. 794, pt. 2, 68th Cong. 1st sess.) * Paper, 5c.

—— Leases upon naval oil reserves, report pursuant to S. Res. 147; submitted by Mr. Walsh of Montana. June 6, 1924. 36 p. 1 pl. (S. rp. 794 [pt. 1], 68th Cong. 1st sess.) * Paper, 5c.   24—26543

Washington State. Authorizing exchange of lands with State of Washington, report to accompany H. R. 5318; submitted by Mr. Dill. June 6, 1924. 3 p. (S. rp. 786, 68th Cong. 1st sess.) * Paper, 5c.

TERRITORIES AND INSULAR POSSESSIONS COMMITTEE

Hawaii National Park. To repeal 1st proviso of sec. 4 of act to establish national park in Hawaii [relating to limitation on appropriations which may be made for improvement of said park], report to accompany H. R. 4985; submitted by Mr. Bayard. May 31, calendar day June 2, 1924. 2 p. (S. rp. 689, 68th Cong. 1st sess.) * Paper, 5c.

Porto Rico. Civil government of Porto Rico, hearings on S. 2448, to amend organic act of Porto Rico, S. 2571, to extend provisions of certain [Federal aid] laws to Porto Rico, S. 2572, to purchase grounds, erect, and repair buildings for customhouses, offices, and warehouses in Porto Rico, S. 2573, to amend and reenact sec. 20, 22, and 50 of act to provide civil government for Porto Rico [relating to salaries], Feb. 16–Mar. 7, 1924. 1924. pt. 2, ii+87–105 p. [The title-page of pt. 2, through an error, bears the dates of the hearings contained in pt. 1, which appeared in Monthly catalogue for Apr. 1924, p. 635.' Part 2 contains only the hearing of Mar. 9, 1924.] * Paper, 5c.

USELESS EXECUTIVE PAPERS, JOINT SELECT COMMITTEE ON DISPOSITION OF

Government Printing Office. Disposition of useless executive papers in Government Printing Office, report; submitted by Mr. Moores of Indiana. June 7, 1924. 3 p. (H. rp. 1021, 68th Cong. 1st sess.) * Paper, 5c.

Navy Department. Disposition of useless executive papers in Department of Navy, report; submitted by Mr. Moores of Indiana. June 6, 1924. 4 p. (H. rp. 1015, 68th Cong. 1st sess.) * Paper, 5c.

State Department. Disposition of useless executive papers in Department of State, report; submitted by Mr. Moores of Indiana. June 6, 1924. 2 p. (H. rp. 1006, 68th Cong. 1st sess.) * Paper, 5c.

Treasury Department. Disposition of useless executive papers in Treasury Department, report; submitted by Mr. Moores of Indiana. June 5, 1924. 48 p. (H. rp. 966, 68th Cong. 1st sess.) * Paper, 5c.

COURT OF CLAIMS

Collier Manufacturing Company, Inc., v. United States; evidence for plaintiff. [1924.] no. C–1030, p. 43–71. ‡

Howard, R. S., Company. R. S. Howard Co., findings of court in case of R. S. Howard Co. against United States. June 3, calendar day June 4, 1924. 4 p. (S. doc. 133, 68th Cong. 1st sess.) * Paper, 5c.

National Fruit Products Company v. United States; findings of fact [conclusion of law, and memorandum] decided June 2, 1924. [1924.] no. B–78, 16 p. ‡

Reynolds, R. J., Tobacco Company. R. J. Reynolds Tobacco Co. v. United States; evidence for plaintiff. [1924.] no. B–282, p. 45–86. ‡

Wyckoff Pipe & Creosoting Co. (Inc.) v. United States; findings of fact [and conclusion of law] decided June 2, 1924. [1924.] no. C–19, 7 p. ‡

COURT OF CUSTOMS APPEALS

Dolls. No. 2339, United States v. Geo. Borgfeldt & Co., transcript of record on appeal from Board of General Appraisers. [1924.] cover-title, i+15 p. ‡

Fish as food. No. 2404, United States v. Aki Company, transcript of record on appeal from Board of General Appraisers. [1924.] cover-title, i+6 p. ‡

DISTRICT OF COLUMBIA

Court of Appeals. Transcript of record, Apr. term, 1924, no. 4155, no. —, special calendar, United States vs. William A. Starrett et al., appeal from Supreme Court of District of Columbia. [1924.] cover-title, i+90 p. il. ‡

FEDERAL BOARD FOR VOCATIONAL EDUCATION

Rehabilitation. Civilian vocational rehabilitation, act to provide for promotion of vocational rehabilitation of persons disabled in industry or otherwise and their return to civil employment (public no. 236, 66th Congress, as amended by public no. 200, 68th Congress). [1924.] 4 p. †

Yearbook, 1923, general description of outstanding developments and summary of progress by States. Jan. 1924. xiii+443 p. il. 2 pl. 3 tab. * Paper, 60c.

　　　　　　　　　　　　　　　　　　　　　　　　　　　　　　· E 24—471

CONTENTS.—Sec. 1, Administrative activities of Federal Board for Vocational Education in 1923.—Sec. 2, General survey and progress of vocational education: pt. 1, Agricultural education; pt. 2, Industrial education; pt. 3, Home economics education; pt. 4, Commercial education.—Sec. 3, Civilian vocational rehabilitation.

FEDERAL RESERVE BOARD

Federal reserve bulletin, June, 1924; [v. 10, no. 6]. 1924. iv+455–528+ii p. il. 4° [Monthly.] † Paper, 20c. single copy, $2.00 a yr. 15—26318

NOTE.—The bulletin contains, in addition to the regular official announcements, the national review of business conditions, detailed analyses of business conditions, research studies, reviews of foreign banking, and complete statistics showing the condition of Federal reserve banks and member banks. It will be sent to all member banks without charge. Others desiring copies may obtain them from the Federal Reserve Board, Washington, D. C., at the prices stated above.

Federal reserve member banks. Abstract of condition reports of State bank and trust company members, and of all member banks of Federal reserve system, Mar. 31, 1924. May 17, 1924. 12 p. f° (Report 24.) †

—— Federal reserve inter-district collection system, changes in list of banks upon which items will be received by Federal reserve banks for collection and credit, June 1, 1924. 1924. 16 p. 4° † 16—26870

FEDERAL TRADE COMMISSION

NOTE.—The bound volumes of the Federal Trade Commission decisions are sold by the Superintendent of Documents, Washington, D. C. Separate opinions are sold on subscription, price $1.00 per volume; foreign subscription, $1.50; single copies, 5c. each.

Aluminum Company of America. No. 2721, in circuit court of appeals for 3d circuit, Oct. term, 1921, Aluminum Company of America *v.* Federal Trade Commission, re application by Federal Trade Commission for modification of order; supplemental and reply brief of Federal Trade Commission. 1924. cover-title, i+74 p. large 8° ‡

American Tobacco Company. In Supreme Court, Oct. term, 1923, no. 206, Federal Trade Commission *v.* American Tobacco Company; no. 207, [same] *v.* P. Lorillard Company, Inc.; brief and argument in support of petition for rehearing. 1924. cover-title, i+33 p. ‡

—— Nos. 206 and 207, in Supreme Court, Oct. term, 1923, no. 206, Federal Trade Commission *v.* American Tobacco Company; no. 207, [same] *v.* P. Lorillard Company, Inc.; petition for rehearing. 1924. cover-title, 6 p. ‡

Decisions. Federal Trade Commission decisions, findings and orders of Federal Trade Commission, May 22, 1922–Feb. 13, 1923; [edited by Richard S. Ely]. 1924. v. 5, xvii+628 p. * Cloth, $1.50. 20—26411

Prichard & Constance, Incorporated. Federal Trade Commission *v.* Prichard & Constance, Inc. [amended] complaint, [report] findings, and order; docket 740, July 9, 1923. 1924. [1]+244—252 p. ([Decision] 375.) [From Federal Trade Commission decisions, v. 6.] * Paper, 5c.

Pure Silk Hosiery Mills, Incorporated. No. —, in circuit court of appeals for 7th circuit, Federal Trade Commission *v.* Pure Silk Hosiery Mills, Inc.; application for enforcement of order of Federal Trade Commission. 1924. cover-title, i+20 p. large 8° ‡

Rochester Clothing Company. Federal Trade Commission *v.* Philip Moskowitz, trading under name and style of Rochester Clothing Company, complaint [report, findings, and order]; docket 826, July 11, 1923. [1924.] p. 259–266. ([Decision] 377.) [From Federal Trade Commission decisions, v. 6.] * Paper, 5c.

Swift & Co. No. 3215, in circuit court of appeals for 7th circuit, Oct. term, 1922, Swift & Company *v.* Federal Trade Commission; supplemental brief. 1924. cover-title, ii+30 p. large 8° ‡

Thatcher Manufacturing Company. Federal Trade Commission *v.* Thatcher Manufacturing Company, complaint [report, findings, and order]; docket 738, June 26, 1923. [1924.] 213–243+[1] p. ([Decision] 374.) [From Federal Trade Commission decisions, v. 6. Includes list of Cases in which orders for discontinuance or dismissal have been entered, July 7, 1923.] * Paper, 5c.

GENERAL ACCOUNTING OFFICE

Claims. Claims allowed by General Accounting Office, schedules of claims allowed by the various divisions of General Accounting Office, as covered by certificates of settlement. May 22, 1924. 123 p. (H. doc. 304, 68th Cong. 1st sess.) * Paper, 10c.

—— Schedule of claims allowed for service of the several Departments and independent offices, schedules of claims allowed by the various divisions of General Accounting Office under appropriations balances of which have exhausted or carried to surplus fund. June 3, calendar day June 4, 1924. 27 p. (S. doc. 136, 68th Cong. 1st sess.) * Paper, 5c.

Decisions of comptroller general, v. 3, Apr. 1924; J. R. McCarl, comptroller general, Lurtin R. Ginn, assistant comptroller general. 1924. [1]+706–819 p. [Monthly.] † 21—26777

Government salary tables, showing basic salaries in accordance with provisions of classification act approved Mar. 4, 1923, 2½ per cent deduction in accordance with civil service retirement act approved May 22, 1920, as well as basic salaries less 2½ per cent. June, 1924. iii+108 p. * Cloth, 60c. 24—26586

GOVERNMENT PRINTING OFFICE

DOCUMENTS OFFICE

Foods and cooking, canning, cold storage, home economics, list of publications for sale by superintendent of documents. Apr. 1924. [2]+14 p. (Price list 11, 13th edition.) †
24—26558

Geological Survey. Publications of Geological Survey, geology, mineral resources, and water supply, list of publications for sale by superintendent of documents. Apr. 1924. [2]+46 p. (Price list 15, 14th edition.) †
24—26587

Government specifications. Authorized Government standards and specifications [list of publications for sale by superintendent of documents]. May, 1924. 1 p. 4° †
24—26612

Mines, explosives, fuel, gas, gasoline, petroleum, list of publications for sale by superintendent of documents. Apr. 1924. [2]+24+[1] p. (Price list 58, 11th edition.) †
24—26588

Monthly catalogue, United States public documents, no. 353; May, 1924. 1924. p. 675–788. * Paper, 5c. single copy, 50c. a yr.; foreign subscription, 75c.
4—18088

INTERIOR DEPARTMENT

NOTE.—The decisions of the Department of the Interior in pension cases are issued in slips and in signatures, and the decisions in land cases are issued in signatures, both being published later in bound volumes. Subscribers may deposit $1.00 with the Superintendent of Documents and receive the contents of a volume of the decisions of either kind in separate parts as they are issued; foreign subscription, $1.25. Prices for bound volumes furnished upon application to the Superintendent of Documents, Washington, D. C.

General information regarding Department of Interior, Feb. 1924. 1924. vi+23 p. †
24—26589

Pensions. [Decisions of Department of Interior in appealed pension and bounty land claims, v. 21, slips] 103–106 pension. [1924.] various paging. [For price, see note above under center head.]
12—29422

ARCHITECT OF CAPITOL

Capitol. Completion of frieze in rotunda of Capitol, supplemental estimate of appropriation for legislative establishment, for amount required in connection with completion of frieze in rotunda of Capitol, fiscal years 1924 and 1925. June 3, 1924. 2 p. (H. doc. 348, 68th Cong. 1st sess.) * Paper, 5c.

EDUCATION BUREAU

Athletics for women; [by] J. F. Rogers. Apr. 1924. 4 p. (Physical education series 4.) * Paper, 5c.
E 24—474

High schools. Statistics of private high schools and academies, 1921–22; prepared by Statistical Division. 1924. [1]+53 p. (Bulletin 60, 1923.) [Advance sheets from Biennial survey of education in United States, 1920–22.] * Paper, 10c.
E 20—424

Kindergarten progress from 1919–20 to 1921–22 [with list of references]; by Nina C. vandewalker. May, 1924. 4 p. (Kindergarten circular 16.) [From School life, v. 9, no. 8, Apr. 1924.] * Paper, 5c.
E 24—472

National Conference on Foreign Service Training. Practices and objectives in training for foreign service, report of National Conference on Foreign Service Training, Washington, Dec. 26, 1923; by Glen Levin Swiggett. 1924. iii+27 p. (Bulletin 21, 1924.) * Paper, 5c.
E 24—473

National Conference on Secretarial Training. Secretarial training, report of national conference held at College of Secretarial Science of Boston University, Oct. 27, 1923; by Glen Levin Swiggett. 1924. [1]+33 p. (Bulletin 12, 1924.) * Paper, 5c.
E 24—457

National Education Association of United States. Program of activities of Bureau of Education for 62d annual meeting, National Education Association, Washington, D. C., June 29–July 4, 1924. 1924. 7 p. narrow 8° †

Publications available May, 1924. [1924.] 24 p. †   E 15—1070

Salaries of country teachers in 1923; by Alex Summers. Apr. 1924. 29 p. il.
(Rural school leaflet 24.)   * Paper, 5c.   E 24—463

School life, v. 9, no. 10; June, 1924. [1924.] cover-title, p. 225–256, il. 4°
[Monthly except July and August. This is Department of Interior number.
Text and illustration on p. 2–4 of cover.] * Paper, 5c. single copy, 30c. a
yr. (10 months) ; foreign subscription, 55c.   E 18—902

Teachers, Training of. Evaluation of kindergarten-primary courses of study
in teacher-training institutions [with list of references on teacher training] ;
by Nina C. Vandewalker. 1924. iii+44 p. (Bulletin 3, 1924.) * Paper, 5c.
                                                                      E 24—465

GENERAL LAND OFFICE

NOTE.—The General Land Office publishes a large general map of the United States,
which is sold at $2.00 ; and also separate maps of the States and Territories in which
public lands are to be found, which are sold at 25c. per sheet. The map of California
is in 2 sheets. Address the Superintendent of Documents, Washington, D. C.

Roster of field officers, June 1, 1924. [1924.] 4 p. †   20—6103

GEOLOGICAL SURVEY

NOTE.—The publications of the United States Geological Survey consist of Annual
reports, Monographs, Professional papers, Bulletins, Water-supply papers, chapters and
volumes of Mineral resources of the United States, folios of the Topographic atlas of the
United States and topographic maps that bear descriptive text, and folios of the Geologic atlas of the United States and the World atlas of commercial geology. The
Monographs, folios, and maps are sold. Other publications are generally free as long as
the Survey's supply lasts. Copies are also sold by the Superintendent of Documents,
Washington, D. C., at the prices indicated. For maps and folios address the Director
of the Geological Survey, Washington, D. C. A discount of 40 per cent is allowed on
any order for maps or folios that amounts to $5.00 or more at the retail price. This
discount applies to an order for either maps or folios alone or for maps and folios
together but is not allowed on a few folios that are sold at 5c. each on account of
damage by fire. Orders for other publications that are for sale should be sent to the
Superintendent of Documents, Washington, D. C. For topographic maps see next page.

Alaska. Geology and mineral resources of region traversed by Alaska Railroad ;
by Stephen R. Capps. 1924. iv+73–150 p. il. 7 maps. (Bulletin 755 C.) †

Coal resources of Ratou coal field, Colfax County, N. Mex.; by Willis T. Lee.
1924. vi+254 p. il. 18 pl. 2 p. of pl. 2 maps, 1 is in pocket. (Bulletin 752 ;
H. doc. 50, 68th Cong. 1st sess.) * Paper, 50c.   GS 24—39

Gold and silver in 1922, general report; by J. P. Dunlop. June 4, 1924. iv+
595–635 p. il. 1 pl. [From Mineral resources, 1922, pt. 1.] †

Mineral resources. Mineral resources of United States, 1921: pt. 1, Metals
[title-page, contents, index, etc.]. 1924. iv+1a–130a+599–617 p. †
                                                                      4—18124

CONTENTS.—Introduction ; by G. F. Loughlin.—Summary ; by Martha B. Clark.—
Prefatory note to reports on gold, silver, copper, lead, and zinc ; by G. F. Loughlin.—
Gold, silver, copper, and lead in Alaska, mines report; by Alfred H. Brooks.—Index.

—— Same: pt. 2, Nonmetals [title-page, contents, and index]. 1924. v+663–
682 p. †

Ohio River. Surface water supply of United States, 1919–20; pt. 3, Ohio River
basin ; Nathan C. Grover, chief hydraulic engineer, Oliver W. Hartwell, Guy
C. Stevens, Warren E. Hall, Warren R. King, and Carl G. Paulsen, district
engineers. 1924. vi+257 p. 2 p. of pl. (Water-supply paper 503.) [Pre-
pared in cooperation with Pennsylvania, West Virginia, Kentucky, Illinois,
and Tennessee.] * Paper, 25c.   GS 10—293

—— Same. (H. doc. 441, 67th Cong. 3d sess.)

Publications. New publications, list 195; June 1, 1924. [1924.] 2 p.
[Monthly.] †

Maps

Alaska Railroad, Seward to Matanuska coal field; reconnaissance map. Scale
1 : 250,000, contour interval 200 ft. [Washington] Geological Survey, 1924.
39.5×36 in. † 50c.

Kentucky. Relief map, Kentucky. Scale 1 : 500,000. [Washington] Geological
Survey, 1924. 24.6×54.6 in. [Relief shading by Jno. H. Renshawe.] † 25c.

Topographic maps

NOTE.—The Geological Survey is making a topographic map of the United States. The individual maps of which it is composed are projected without reference to political divisions, and each map is designated by the name of some prominent town or natural feature in the area mapped. Three scales are ordinarily used, 1 : 62,500, 1 : 125,000, and 1 : 250,000. These correspond, approximately, to 1 mile, 2 miles, and 4 miles to 1 linear inch, covering, respectively, average areas of 230, 920, and 3,700 square miles. For some areas of particular importance special large-scale maps are published. The usual size, exclusive of the margin, is 17.5 inches in height by 11.5 to 16 inches in width, the width varying with the latitude. The sheets measure 20 by 16½ inches. A description of the topographic map is printed on the reverse of each sheet.

More than two-fifths of the area of the country, excluding Alaska, has been mapped, every State being represented. Connecticut, Delaware, the District of Columbia, Maryland, Massachusetts, New Jersey, Ohio, Rhode Island, and West Virginia are completely mapped. Maps of the regular size are sold by the Survey at 10c. each, but a discount of 40 per cent is allowed on any order which amounts to $5.00 or more at the retail price. The discount is allowed on an order for either maps or folios alone or for maps and folios together, but does not apply to a few folios that are sold at 5c. each on account of damage by fire.

California. California, Conejo quadrangle, lat. 36° 30'–36° 37' 30'', long. 119° 37' 30''–119° 45'. Scale 1 : 31,680, contour interval 5 ft. [Washington, Geological Survey] edition of 1924. 17.3×13.9 in. † 10c.

—— California, Selma quadrangle, lat. 36° 30'–36° 37' 30'', long. 119° 30'–119° 37' 30''. Scale 1 : 31,680, contour interval 5 ft. [Washington, Geological Survey] edition of 1924. 17.3×13.9 in. † 10c.

Maine, Farmington quadrangle, lat. 44° 30'–44° 45', long. 70°–70° 15'. Scale 1 : 62,500, contour interval 20 ft. [Washington, Geological Survey] edition of 1924. 17.5×12.7 in. † 10c.

MINES BUREAU

Safety-lamps. Flame safety lamps [with bibliography] ; by J. W. Paul, L. C. Ilsley, and E. J. Gleim. [1st edition.] [Jan.] 1924. xii+212 p. il. 12 pl. 22 p. of pl. (Bulletin 227.) * Paper, 50c.
                                                                        24—26590

NATIONAL PARK SERVICE

Sequoia National Park. Rules and regulations, Sequoia and General Grant National Parks, 1924, season May 24–Oct. 10 and earlier and later for motorists carrying own camp equipment [with list of literature]. [1924.] iv+33 p. il. 2 p. of pl. map. †
                                                                        21—26445
Yosemite National Park. Rules and regulations, Yosemite National Park, Calif., 1924 [with list of literature]. 1924. iv+76 p. il. 2 p. of pl. map. †
                                                                        21—26446

PATENT OFFICE

NOTE.—The Patent Office publishes Specifications and drawings of patents in single copies. These are not enumerated is this catalogue, but may be obtained for 10c. each at the Patent Office.

A variety of indexes, giving a complete view of the work of the Patent Office from 1790 to date, are published at prices ranging from 25c. to $10.00 per volume and may be obtained from the Superintendent of Documents, Washington, D. C. The Rules of practice and pamphlet Patent laws are furnished free of charge upon application to the Patent Office. The Patent Office issues coupon orders in packages of 20 at $2.00 per package, or in books containing 100 coupons at $10.00 per book. These coupons are good until used, but are only to be used for orders sent to the Patent Office. For schedule of office fees, address Chief Clerk, Patent Office, Washington, D. C.

Decisions. [Decisions in patent and trade-mark cases, etc.] June 3, 1924. p. 1–6, large 8° [From Official gazette, v. 323, no. 1.] † Paper, 5c. single copy, $2.00 a yr.
                                                                        23—7315
—— Same. June 10, 1924. p. 227–234, large 8° [From Official gazette, v. 323, no. 2.]

—— Same. June 17, 1924. p. 477–482, large 8° [From Official gazette, v. 323, no. 3.]

—— Same. June 24, 1924. p. 727–730, large 8° [From Official gazette, v. 323, no. 4.]

Official gazette. Official gazette, June 3–24, 1924 ; v. 323, no. 1–4. 1924. cover-titles, 954+[clxiv] p. il. large 8° [Weekly.] * Paper, 10c. single copy, $5.00 a yr.; foreign subscription, $11.00.
                                                                        4—18256
NOTE.—Contains the patents, trade-marks, designs, and labels issued each week; also decisions of the commissioner of patents and of the United States courts in patent cases.

Official gazette—Continued. Same [title-page, contents, errata, etc., to] v. 321; Apr. 1924. 1924. [2] leaves, large 8° *Paper, 5c. single copy, included in price of Official gazette for subscribers.

—— Same, weekly index, with title, Alphabetical list of registrants of trade-marks [etc., June 3, 1924]. [1924.] xlii p. large 8° [From Official gazette, v. 323, no. 1.] † Paper, $1.00 a yr.

—— Same [June 10, 1924]. [1924.] xlii p. large 8° [From Official gazette, v. 323, no. 2.]

—— Same [June 17, 1924]. [1924.] xl p. large 8° [From Official gazette, v. 323, no. 3.]

—— Same [June 24, 1924]. [1924.] xl p. large 8° [From Official gazette, v. 323, no. 4.]

Patents. Classification of patents issued June 3-24, 1924. [1924.] Each 2 p. large 8° [Weekly. From Official gazette, v. 323, no. 1-4.] †

Trade-marks. Trade-marks [etc., from] Official gazette, June 3, 1924. [1924.] 7-62+i-xvii p. il. large 8° [From Official gazette, v. 323, no. 1.] † Paper, 5c. single copy, $2.50 a yr.

—— Same, June 10, 1924. [1924.] 235-286+i-xvi p. il. large 8° [From Official gazette, v. 323, no. 2.]

—— Same, June 17, 1924. [1924.] 483-540+i-xiv p. il. large 8° [From Official gazette, v. 323, no. 3.]

—— Same, June 24' 1924. [1924.] 731-775+i-xv p. il. large 8° [From Official gazette, v. 323, no. 4.]

RECLAMATION BUREAU

New reclamation era, v. 15, no. 6; June, 1924. [1924.] cover-title, p. 85-100, il. 4° [Monthly. Text on p. 2-4 of cover.]

NOTE.—The New reclamation era is a magazine for the farmers and the personnel of the bureau. Its aim is to assist the settlers in the proper use of water, to help them in overcoming their agricultural difficulties, to instruct them in diversifying and marketing their crops, to inspire the employees of the bureau and chronicle engineer-ing problems and achievements, and to promote a wholehearted spirit of cooperation, so that reclamation shall attain the greatest heights of success. The New reclamation era is sent regularly to all water users on the reclamation projects under the juris-diction of the bureau who wish to receive the magazine. To others than water users the subscription price is 75c. a year, payable in advance. Subscriptions should be sent to the Chief Clerk, Bureau of Reclamation, Washington, D. C., and remittance in the form of postal money order or New York draft should be made payable to the Chief Disbursing Clerk, Department of the Interior. Postage stamps are not acceptable in payment of subscription.

INTERSTATE COMMERCE COMMISSION

NOTE.—The bound volumes of the decisions, usually known as Interstate Commerce Commission reports, are sold by the Superintendent of Documents, Washington, D. C., at various prices, depending upon the size of the volume. Separate opinions are sold on subscription, price $1.00 per volume; foreign subscription, $1.50; single copies, usually 5c. each.

Accounting. Order [promulgated] at session of Interstate Commerce Commis-sion, division 4, on 2d of June, 1924, [in] matter of uniform system of ac-counts to be kept by steam roads. [1924.] 3 p. *Paper, 5c.

Alabama and Vicksburg Railway. Finance docket no. 3558, Alabama & Vicks-burg bonds; decided May 12, 1924; report of commission. [1924.] p. 49-50. ([Finance decision] 1357.) [From Interstate Commerce Commission reports, v. 90.] *Paper, 5c.

Asherton and Gulf Railway. Finance docket no. 3554, securities of Asherton & Gulf Railway; decided May 2, 1924; report of commission. [1924.] p. 9-10. ([Finance decision] 1344.) [From Interstate Commerce Commission reports, v. 90.] *Paper, 5c.

Baltimore, Chesapeake and Atlantic Railway. Finance docket no. 297, guar-anty settlement with Baltimore, Chesapeake & Atlantic Ry.; decided May 23, 1924; report of commission. [1924.] p. 81-83. ([Finance decision] 1369.) [From Interstate Commerce Commission reports, v. 90.] *Paper, 5c.

Brevard County Telephone Company. Finance docket no. 3535, purchase of properties of Brevard County Telephone Co. by Southern Bell Telephone & Telegraph Co.; decided May 2, 1924; report of commission. [1924.] p. 27–28. ([Finance decision] 1350.) [From Interstate Commerce Commission reports, v. 90.] * Paper, 5c.

Cabbage. No. 13806, Meyer-vasquez Produce Company *v.* director general, as agent; decided May 24, 1924; report of commission. [1924.] p. 437–439. ([Opinion] 9536.) [From Interstate Commerce Commission reports, v. 89.] * Paper, 5c.

Carbon black. No. 14818, Goodyear Tire & Rubber Company *v.* Akron, Canton & Youngstown Railway Company et al.; decided May 17, 1924; report of commission. [1924.] p. 401–404. ([Opinion] 9531.) [From Interstate Commerce Commission reports, v. 89.] * Paper, 5c.

Cast-iron. Investigation and suspension docket no. 2028, pig iron between Florence and Sheffield, Ala., when for beyond; [decided May 15, 1924; report and order of commission]. 1924. [1]+324–326+[1] p. ([Opinion] 9508.) [Report from Interstate Commerce Commission reports, v. 89.] * Paper, 5c.

—— No. 4800, Sloss-Sheffield Steel & Iron Company et al. *v.* Louisville & Nashville Railroad Company et al.; [decided Apr. 14, 1924; 8th supplemental report and order of commission]. 1924. [1]+640–642+vii p. ([Opinion] 9426.) [Report from Interstate Commerce Commission reports, v. 88.] * Paper, 5c.

Central New York Southern Railroad. Finance docket no. 2722, abandonment of Central New York Southern R. R.; [decided Apr. 29, 1924; report of commission]. 1924. [1]+830–834 p. ([Finance decision] 1335.) [From Interstate Commerce Commission reports, v. 86.] * Paper, 5c.

Central of Georgia Railway. Finance docket no. 3489, public-convenience application of Central of Georgia Ry.; decided May 2, 1924; report of commission. [1924.] p. 19–23. ([Finance decision] 1348.) [From Interstate Commerce Commission reports, v. 90.] * Paper, 5c.

—— Finance docket no. 3577, Central of Georgia Railway deposited cash; decided May 8, 1924; report of commission. [1924.] p. 1–2. ([Finance decision] 1341.) [From Interstate Commerce Commission reports, v. 90.] * Paper, 5c.

Central Railroad of New Jersey. Finance docket no. 3568, Central of New Jersey equipment bonds; [decided May 1, 1924; report of commission]. 1924. [1]+42–44 p. ([Finance decision] 1355.) [From Interstate Commerce Commission reports, v. 90.] * Paper, 5c.

Chesapeake and Ohio Railway. Finance docket no. 3586, bonds of Chesapeake & Ohio Ry.; decided May 8, 1924; report of commission. [1924.] p. 39–41. ([Finance decision] 1354.) [From Interstate Commerce Commission reports, v. 90.] * Paper, 5c.

Chicago, Indianapolis and Louisville Railway. Finance docket no. 4039, bonds of Chicago, Indianapolis & Louisville Railway; decided May 24, 1924; report of commission. [1924.] p. 95–96. ([Finance decision] 1372.) [From Interstate Commerce Commission reports, v. 90.] * Paper, 5c.

Chicago, Rock Island and Pacific Railway. Finance docket no. 2926, abandonment of branch line by Chicago, Rock Island & Pacific Ry.; decided May 2, 1924; report of commission. [1924.] p. 15–18. ([Finance decision] 1347.) [From Interstate Commerce Commission reports, v. 90.] * Paper, 5c.

Cincinnati, Georgetown and Portsmouth Railroad. Finance docket no. 3581. Cincinnati, Georgetown & Portsmouth. equipment trust, series B; [decided May 8, 1924; report of commission]. 1924. [1]+24–27 p. ([Finance decision] 1349.) [From Interstate Commerce Commission reports, v. 90.] * Paper, 5c.

Coal. Lake dock coal cases, no. 14476, Northwestern Coal Dock Operators' Association *v.* Chicago & Alton Railroad Company et al.; [decided May 6, 1924; report and orders of commission]. 1924. [1]+170–211+vi p. ([Opinion] 9487.) [Report from Interstate Commerce Commission reports, v. 89.] * Paper, 5c.

—— No. 13220, Cincinnati Association of Purchasing Agents *v.* Louisville & Nashville Railroad Company; decided May 17, 1924; report [and order] of commission. [1924.] 285–295+[1] p. ([Opinion] 9505.) [Report from Interstate Commerce Commission reports, v. 89.] * Paper, 5c.

Copper. No. 14747, Afterthought Copper Company *v.* director general, as agent, California, Shasta & Eastern Railway Company, et al.; [decided May 17, 1924; report and order of commission]. 1924. [1]+346–348+[1] p. ([Opinion] 9514.) [Report from Interstate Commerce Commission reports, v. 89.] * Paper, 5c.

Cotton-seed. No. 14668, Pinson Brokerage Company *v.* Columbus & Greenville Railroad Company et al.; decided May 1, 1924; report [and order] of commission. [1924.] 125–128+[1] p. ([Opinion] 9474.) [Report from Interstate Commerce Commission reports, v. 89.] * Paper, 5c.

—— No. 15190, Roberts Cotton Oil Company *v.* Butler County Railroad Company et al.; decided May 7, 1924; report [and order] of commission. [1924.] 255–256+[1] p. ([Opinion] 9497.) [Report from Interstate Commerce Commission reports, v. 89.] * Paper, 5c.

Decisions of Interstate Commerce Commission, June–Aug. 1923. 1923. xxx+ 960 p. (Interstate Commerce Commission reports, v. 81.) [Contains also decisions of Sept. 7 and 10, 1923.] * Cloth, $2.00.   8–30656

Demurrage. Investigation and suspension docket no. 2035, demurrage rules on coal and coke; [decided May 8, 1924; report and order of commission]. 1924. [1]+230–232+[1] p. ([Opinion] 9491.) [Report from Interstate Commerce Commission reports, v. 89.] * Paper, 5c.

—— No. 13404, Walter Wallingford Coal Company *v.* director general, as agent; decided May 17, 1924; report of commission. [1924.] p. 353–355. ([Opinion] 9517.) [From Interstate Commerce Commission reports, v. 89.] * Paper, 5c.

—— No. 14262, Toberman, Mackey & Company *v.* director general, as agent; decided May 17, 1924; report [and order] of commission. [1924.] 365–366 +[1] p. ([Opinion] 9522.) [Report from Interstate Commerce Commission reports, v. 89.] * Paper, 5c.

Evaporated milk. No. 14203, Nestle's Food Company, Incorporated, *v.* director general, as agent, Chicago & North Western Railway Company, et al.; [no. 14202, same *v.* same; decided May 17, 1924; report and order of commission]. 1924. [1]+340–342+[1] p. ([Opinion] 9512.) [Report from Interstate Commerce Commission reports, v. 89.] * Paper, 5c.

Express. No. 13930, express rates, 1922; decided May 17, 1924; supplemental report [and order] of commission. [1924.] 297–323+v p. ([Opinion] 9507.) [Report from Interstate Commerce Commission reports, v. 89.] * Paper, 5c.

Flour. No. 13556, C. E. Grosjean Rice Milling Company *v.* director general, as agent; decided May 17, 1924; report [and order] of commission. [1924.] 395–398+[1] p. ([Opinion] 9529.) [Report from Interstate Commerce Commission reports, v. 89.] * Paper, 5c.

Freight. Summary of freight commodity statistics of class 1 roads [having annual operating revenues above $1,000,000], quarter ended Mar. 31, 1924; [prepared in] Bureau of Statistics. [1924.] [4] p. oblong large 8°

Freight rates. Ex parte no. 86, in re sec. 28 of merchant marine act, 1920; decided Apr. 19, 1924; [report and 5th supplemental order of commission]. [1924.] 645–652+[1] p. ([Opinion] 9428.) [Report from Interstate Commerce Commission reports, v. 88.] * Paper, 5c.

—— Investigation and suspension docket no. 2005, burlap bags and certain iron and steel articles from Central Freight Association territory to Mississippi Valley; decided May 1, 1924; report [and order] of commission. [1924.] 131–134+[1] p. ([Opinion] 9476.) [Report from Interstate Commerce Commission reports, v. 89.] * Paper, 5c.

—— No. 14822, Traffic Bureau, Chamber of Commerce, La Crosse, Wis., et al. *v.* Great Lakes Transit Corporation et al.; [decided May 17, 1924; report and order of commission]. 1924. [1]+386–391+[1] p. ([Opinion] 9527.) [Report from Interstate Commerce Commission reports, v. 89.] * Paper, 5c.

Fruit. No. 14719, Buxton-Smith Company *v.* Atchison, Topeka & Santa Fe Railway Company et al.; decided May 17, 1924; report of commission. [1924.] p. 373–378. ([Opinion] 9524.) [From Interstate Commerce Commission reports, v. 89.] * Paper, 5c.

Gas oil. No. 14086, Atlantic Refining Company *v.* Atlanta, Birmingham & Atlantic Railway Company et al.; decided May 14, 1924; report [and order] of commission. [1924.] 279–281+[1] p. ([Opinion] 9503.) [Report from Interstate Commerce Commission reports, v. 89.] * Paper, 5c.

Gasoline. No. 14127. J. M. McLeod et al. *v.* Texas & Pacific Railway Company et al.; [decided May 17, 1924; report of commission]. 1924. [1]+356–358 p. ([Opinion] 9518.) [From Interstate Commerce Commission reports, v. 89.] * Paper, 5c.

—— No. 14419, Atlantic Refining Company *v.* director general, as agent, Baltimore & Ohio Railroad Company, et al.; decided May 17, 1924; report of commission. [1924.] p. 391–394. ([Opinion] 9528.) [From Interstate Commerce Commission reports, v. 89.] * Paper, 5c.

Georgia, Florida and Alabama Railway. Finance docket no. 3588, notes of Georgia, Florida & Alabama Ry.; decided May 8, 1924; report of commission. [1924.] p. 11–12. ([Finance decision] 1345.) [From Interstate Commerce Commission reports, v. 90.] * Paper, 5c.

Grain. Investigation and suspension docket no. 2036, transit rules on grain at stations in Missouri; decided May 21, 1924; report [and order] of commission. [1924.] 349–350+[1] p. ([Opinion] 9515.) [Report from Interstate Commerce Commission reports, v. 89.] * Paper, 5c.

Great Northern Railway. Finance docket no. 2853, bonds of Great Northern Ry.; [decided May 16, 1924; supplemental report of commission]. 1924. [1]+66–67 p. ([Finance decision] 1364.), [From Interstate Commerce Commission reports, v. 90.] * Paper, 5c.

Hides. No. 15136, Eagle-Ottawa Leather Company *v.* director general, as agent; decided May 7, 1924; report [and order] of commission. [1924.] 233–235+ [1] p. ([Opinion] 9492.) [Report from Interstate Commerce Commission reports, v. 89.] * Paper, 5c.

High Point, Thomasville and Denton Railroad. Finance docket no. 3338, acquisition of line by High Point, Thomasville & Denton Railroad; [decided May 20, 1924; report of commission]. 1924. [1]+72–74 p. ([Finance decision] 1366.) [From Interstate Commerce Commission reports, v. 90.] * Paper, 5c.

Illinois Bell Telephone Company. Finance docket no. 3531, acquisition of properties by Illinois Bell Telephone Co. and Commercial Telephone & Telegraph Co.; decided May 9, 1924; report of commission. [1924.] p. 57–59. ([Finance decision] 1360.) [From Interstate Commerce Commission reports, v. 90.] ;* Paper, 5c.

Indiana Harbor Belt Railroad. Finance docket no. 3593, Indiana Harbor Belt equipment trust of 1924; decided May 16, 1924; report of commission. [1924.] p. 77–80. ([Finance decision] 1368.) [From Interstate Commerce Commission reports, v. 90.] * Paper, 5c.

Industrial railroads. Wasteful service by tap lines, investigation and suspension docket no. 11, Prescott & Northwestern Railroad Company and Ouachita & Northwestern Railroad Company; [no. 9024, Oakdale & Gulf Railway Company]; decided May 5, 1924; report [and order] of commission on further hearing. [1924.] 327–331+ii p. ([Opinion] 9509.) [Report from Interstate Commerce Commission reports, v. 89.] * Paper, 5c.

Jefferson Southwestern Railroad. Finance docket no. 2556, construction of line by Jefferson Southwestern; [decided Apr. 15, 1924; report of commission on rehearing]. 1924. [1]+796–804 p. il. ([Finance decision] 1330.) [From Interstate Commerce Commission reports, v. 86.] * Paper, 5c.

Kansas City Southern Railway. Valuation docket no. 4, Kansas City Southern Railway Company et al.; decided Mar. 4, 1924; supplemental report of commission. [1924.] p. 113–149. (B–10.) [From Interstate Commerce Commission reports, v. 84.] * Paper, 5c.

Lake Champlain and Moriah Railroad. Finance docket no. 2176, deficit settlement with Lake Champlain & Moriah R. R.; decided May 9, 1924; report of commission. [1924.] p. 7–8. ([Finance decision] 1343.) [From Interstate Commerce Commission reports, v. 90.] * Paper, 5c.

Limestone. No. 14363, C. H. Young et al. *v.* Chicago, Indianapolis & Louisville Railway Company et al.; [decided May 20, 1924; report and order of commission]. 1924. [1]+428–436+[1] p. ([Opinion] 9535.) [Report from Interstate Commerce Commission reports, v. 89.] * Paper, 5c.

Linseed-meal. No. 12290, Midland Linseed Products Company *v.* director general, as agent, Erie Railroad Company, et al.; [decided May 6, 1924; report of commission on further hearing]. 1924. [1]+260–266 p. ([Opinion] 9499.) [From Interstate Commerce Commission reports, v. 89.] * Paper, 5c.

Maine Central Railroad. Finance docket no. 3591, Maine Central equipment trust of 1924; [decided May 14, 1924; report of commission]. 1924. [1]+ 60–63 p. ([Finance decision] 1361.) [From Interstate Commerce Commission reports, v. 90.] * Paper, 5c.

Marion and Eastern Railroad. Finance docket no. 610, guaranty status of Marion & Eastern R. R.; [decided May 16, 1924; report of commission]. 1924. [1]+64–65 p. ([Finance decision] 1363.) [From Interstate Commerce Commission reports, v. 90.] * Paper, 5c.

Matches. Investigation and suspension docket no. 2065, matches from Bellefonte, Pa., to Chattanooga group and Knoxville, Tenn.; decided May 15, 1924; report [and order] of commission. [1924.] 337–339+[1] p. ([Opinion] 9511.) [Report from Interstate Commerce Commission reports, v. 89.] * Paper, 5c.

Meat. No. 12423, Armour and Company et al. *v.* Atlantic Coast Line Railroad Company, director general, as agent, et al.; [investigation and suspension docket no. 1494; decided May 6, 1924; report and order of commission]. 1924. [1]+162–169+ii p. ([Opinion]9486.) [Report from Interstate Commerce Commission reports, v. 89.] * Paper, 5c.

Muscatine, Burlington and Southern Railroad. Finance docket no. 3180, abandonment of Muscatine, Burlington & Southern R. R. [Arthur Hoffman, receiver]; decided May 10, 1924; report of commission. [1924.] .p. 31–35. ([Finance decision]1352.) [From Interstate Commerce Commission reports, v. 90.] * Paper, 5c.

Nevada County Narrow Gauge Railroad. Finance docket no. 1757, deficit settlement with Nevada County Narrow Gauge R. R.; decided May 20, 1924; report of commission. [1924.] p. 75–76. ([Finance decision]1367.) [From Interstate Commerce Commission reports, v. 90.] * Paper, 5c.

New York, New Haven and Hartford Railroad. Finance docket no. 3386, abandonment of branch line by New York, New Haven & Hartford R. R.; decided May 8, 1924; report of commission. [1924.] p. 3–6. ([Finance decision] 1342.) [From Interstate Commerce Commission reports, v. 90.] * Paper, 5c.

—— Finance docket no. 3590, New Haven equipment trust FF; [decided May 12, 1924; report of commission]. 1924. [1]+36–38 p. ([Finance decision] 1353.) [From Interstate Commerce Commission reports, v. 90.] * Paper, 5c.

Norfolk and Western Railway. Finance docket no. 701, guaranty settlement with Norfolk & Western Ry.; decided Apr. 30, 1924; report of commission. [1924.] p. 847–849. ([Finance decision]1340.) [From Interstate Commerce Commission reports, v. 86.] * Paper, 5c.

Oats. No. 13394, Atlas Cereal Company *v.* Atchison, Topeka & Santa Fe Railway Company et al.; [decided Apr. 30, 1924; report and order of commission]. 1924. [1]+212–218+[1] p. ([Opinion]9488.) [Report from Interstate Commerce Commission reports, v. 89.] * Paper, 5c.

Paper. Investigation and suspension docket no. 2051, paper stock from St. Louis, Mo., to Illinois; decided May 10, 1924; report [and order] of commission. [1924.] 267–270+[1] p. ([Opinion]9500.) [Report from Interstate Commerce Commission reports, v. 89.] * Paper, 5c.

Pelham and Havana Railroad. Finance docket no. 3373, abandonment of Pelham & Havana R. R. [Alvin Wight, receiver]; decided May 12, 1924; report of commission. [1924.] p. 51–53. ([Finance decision]1358.) [From Interstate Commerce Commission reports, v. 90.] * Paper, 5c.

Pennsylvania Railroad. Finance docket no. 3565, Pennsylvania general equipment trust, series B; decided Apr. 28, 1924; report of commission. [1924.] p. 841–844. ([Finance decision] 1338.) [From Interstate Commerce Commission reports, v. 86.] * Paper, 5c.

Petroleum. Investigation and suspension docket no. 2024, petroleum oil and its products from Kansas, Missouri, and Oklahoma to Belleville, Ill.; decided May 15, 1924; report [and order] of commission. [1924.] 295–296+[1] p. ([Opinion]9506.) [Report from Interstate Commerce Commission reports, v. 89.] * Paper, 5c.

Pipe. No. 14729, Standard Oil Company (California) *v.* Atchison, Topeka & Santa Fe Railway Company et al.; decided May 20, 1924; report [and order] of commission. [1924.] 425–427+[1] p. ([Opinion]9534.) [Report from Interstate Commerce Commission reports, v. 89.] * Paper, 5c.

Potatoes. No. 14847, Pikes Peak Co-operative Lettuce & Produce Growers As-sociation *v.* Midland Terminal Railway Company et al.; [no. 14847, sub-no. 1, same *v.* same]; decided May 17, 1924; report [and order] of commission. [1924.] 379–382+ii p. ([Opinion] 9525.) [Report from Interstate Com-merce Commission reports, v. 89.] * Paper, 5c.

Railroad accidents. Accident bulletin 91, collisions, derailments, and other ac-cidents resulting in injury to persons, equipment, or roadbed, arising from operation of steam roads used in interstate commerce, Oct.–Dec. 1923; [prepared in] Bureau of Statistics. 1924. iii+16 p. 4° .[Quarterly.] * Paper, 5c. single copy quarterly issue, 25c. a yr ,: foreign subscription, 40c.

5—41547

—— Report of director of Bureau of Safety in re investigation of accident which occurred, on Richmond, Fredericksburg & Potomac Railroad near Woodford, Va., on Apr. 2, 1924 [accompanied by report of engineer-physicist]. [1924.] 7 p. il. .* Paper, 5c.

A 24—737

Railroads. Freight and passenger service operating statistics of class 1 steam roads in United States, compiled from 160 reports of freight statistics repre-senting 175 roads and from 158 reports of passenger statistics representing 173 roads (switching and terminal companies not included), Apr. 1924 and 1923 [and 4 months ended with Apr. 1924 and 1923; prepared in] Bureau of Statistics. Apr. 1924. [2] p. oblong large 8°. [Subject to revision.] †

—— Operating revenues and operating expenses of class 1 steam roads in United States (for 193 steam roads, including 15 switching and terminal companies), Apr. 1924 and 1923 [and] 4 months ended with Apr. 1924 and 1923; [prepared in] Bureau of Statistics, Apr. 1924. 1 p. oblong large 8° [Subject to revision.] †

—— Operating revenues and operating expenses of large steam roads, selected items for roads with annual operating revenues, above $25,000,000, Apr. 1924 and 1923 [and] 4 months ended with Apr. 1924 and 1923; [prepared in] Bureau of Statistics. Apr. 1924. [2] p. oblong large 8° [Subject to re-vision.] †

—— Operating statistics of large steam roads, selected items for Apr. 1924, compared with Apr. 1923, for roads with annual operating revenues above $25,000,000; [prepared in] Bureau of Statistics. Apr. 1924. [2] p. oblong large 8° [Subject to revision.] †

—— Revenue traffic statistics of class 1 steam roads in United States, in-cluding mixed-train service (compiled from 162 reports representing 177 steam roads, switching and terminal companies not included), Mar. 1924 and 1923 [and] 3 months ended with Mar. 1924 and 1923; [prepared in] Bureau of Statistics. Mar. 1924. 1 p. oblong large 8° [Subject to revision.] †

Rails. No. 14230, Duluth Iron & Metal Company *v.* director general, as agent; decided May 17, 1924; report [and order] of commission. [1924.] 343–345+ [1] p. ([Opinion] 9513.) [Report from Interstate Commerce Commission reports, v. 89.] * Paper, 5c.

Reconsignment. No. 12921, Chesnutt Lumber Company *v.* director general, as agent; [decided Apr. 14, 1924; report and order of commission]. 1924. [1]+236–240+[1] p. ([Opinion] 9493.) [Report from Interstate Commerce Commission reports, v. 89.] * Paper, 5c.

—— No. 13563, Western Petroleum Refiners Association *v.* Chicago, Rock Island & Pacific Railway Company et al.; decided Apr. 14, 1924; report [and order] of commission. [1924.] 241–244+iv p. ([Opinion] 9494.) [Report from Interstate Commerce Commission reports, v. 89.] * Paper, 5c.

—— No. 14176, Flanley Grain Company *v.* director general, as agent; [no. 13263, Washburn-Crosby Company *v.* same; no. 14175, Turner Grain Com-pany *v.* same]; decided Apr. 16, 1924; report of commission. [1924.] p. 33–37. ([Opinion] 9462.) [From Interstate Commerce Commission reports, v. 89.] * Paper, 5c.

Refrigeration. Investigation and suspension docket no. 1842, rules, regula-tions, and charges for protective service on perishable freight; decided Apr. 30, 1924; report [and order] of commission. [1924.] 87–94+[1] p. ([Opinion] 9468.) [Report from Interstate Commerce Commission reports, v. 89.] * Paper, 5c.

Refrigeration—Continued. No. 13715, Fairmont Creamery Company *v.* director general, as agent; decided May 17, 1924; report of commission. [1924.] p. 359–361. ([Opinion] 9519.) [From Interstate Commerce Commission reports, v. 89.] * Paper, 5c.

Rome and Northern Railway. Finance docket no. 3523, abandonment of Rome & Northern Ry.; [decided May 10, 1924; report of commission]. 1924. [1]+54–56 p. ([Finance decision] 1359.) [From Interstate Commerce Commission reports, v. 90.] * Paper, 5c.

Routing. Investigation and suspension docket no. 2039, routing of lumber from Pacific Coast to stations on Copper Range Railroad in Michigan; decided May 21, 1924; report [and order] of commission. [1924.] 351–352+ [1] p. ([Opinion] 9516.) [Report from Interstate Commerce Commission reports, v. 89.] * Paper, 5c.

Rutland Railroad. Finance docket no. 3597, Rutland Railroad equipment trust, 1924; [decided May 16, 1924; report of commission]. 1924. [1]+68–71 p. ([Finance decision] 1365.) [From Interstate Commerce Commission reports, v. 90.] * Paper, 5c.

St. Louis-San Francisco Railway. Finance docket no. 3530, securities of St. Louis-San Francisco Ry. and certain subsidiaries; [and finance docket 3530 (sub-nos. 1–5); decided Apr. 29, 1924; report of commission]. 1924. [1]+ 818–826 p. ([Finance decision] 1333.) [From Interstate Commerce Commission reports, v. 86.] * Paper, 5c.

Saltpeter, Chile. No. 14553, New Orleans Joint Traffic Bureau *v.* Alabama & Vicksburg Railway Company et al.; decided May 10, 1924; report [and orders] of commission. Corrected report and order. [1924.] 223–229+ iii p. ([Opinion] 9490.) [Report from Interstate Commerce Commission reports, v. 89.] * Paper, 5c.

Sand. No. 14178, Liberty Glass Company *v.* Missouri Pacific Railroad Company et al.; [decided May 17, 1924; report and order of commission]. 1924. [1]+362–364+[1] p. ([Opinion] 9521.) [Report from Interstate Commerce Commission reports, v. 89.] * Paper, 5c.

Shearwood Railway. Finance docket no. 791 guaranty settlement, with Shearwood Ry.; decided Apr. 30, 1924; report of commission. [1924.] p. 827–829. ([Finance decision] 1334.) [From Interstate Commerce Commission reports, v. 86.] * Paper, 5c.

Shingles. No. 11982, A. & C. Mill Company et al. *v.* director general, as agent, Aberdeen & Rockfish Railroad Company, et al.; decided Apr. 15, 1924; report of commission on further hearing. [1924.] p. 245–250. ([Opinion] 9495.) [From Interstate Commerce Commission reports, v. 89.] * Paper, 5c.

Shooks. Investigation and suspension docket no. 2022, combination rule on box shooks from Pacific Coast to Colorado; decided May 10, 1924; report [and order] of commission. [1924.] 219–222+[1] p. ([Opinion] 9489.) [Report from Interstate Commerce Commission reports, v. 89.] * Paper, 5c.

Southern Pacific Company. Finance docket no. 3589, Southern Pacific equipment trust, series G; decided May 14, 1924; report of commission. [1924.] p. 45–48. ([Finance decision] 1356.) [From Interstate Commerce Commission reports, v. 90.] * Paper, 5c.

Staves. No. 14757, Jackson Traffic Bureau *v.* Alabama & Vicksburg Railway Company et al.; decided May 17, 1924; report [and order] of commission. [1924.] 399–400+[1] p. ([Opinion] 9530.) [Report from Interstate Commerce Commission reports, v. 89.] * Paper, 5c.

Steamboats. Schedule of sailings (as furnished by steamship companies named herein) of steam vessels which are registered under laws of United States and which are intended to load general cargo at ports in United States for foreign destinations, June 15–July 31, 1924, no. 22; issued by Section of Tariffs, Bureau of Traffic. 1924. iii+46 p. 4°. [Monthly. No. 22 cancels no. 21.] †   22—26610

Stone. No. 14472, Dolese Brothers Company et al. *v.* Atchison, Topeka & Santa Fe Railway Company et al.; [no. 14450, Edward L. Scheidenhelm Company *v.* Chicago, Rock Island & Pacific Railway Company et al.; decided May 1, 1924; report of commission]. 1924. [1]+110–124 p. ([Opinion] 9473.) [From Interstate Commerce Commission reports, v. 89.] * Paper, 5c.

Stoneware. No. 14929, Northwestern Terra, Cotta Company *v.* Pittsburgh, Cincinnati, Chicago & St. Louis Railroad Company et al.; decided May 7, 1924; report of commission. [1924.] p. 257–259. ([Opinion] 9498.) [From Interstate Commerce Commission reports, v. 89.] * Paper, 5c.

Straw. No. 14627, American Box Board Company *v.* director' general, as agent, Pere Marquette Railway Company, et al.; decided May 14, 1924; report [and order] of commission. [1924.] 271–273+[1] p. ([Opinion] 9501.) [Report from Interstate Commerce Commission reports, v. 89.] * Paper, 5c.

Sulphur. No. 14544, Grasselli Chemical Company *v.* Baltimore & Ohio Railroad Company et al.; decided May 16, 1924; report of commission. [1924.] p. 383–385. ([Opinion] 9526.) [From Interstate Commerce Commission reports, v. 89.] * Paper, 5c.

—— No. 14618, Jackson Traffic Bureau (for Jackson Fertilizer Company) *v.* Brimstone Railroad & Canal Company et al.; [decided May 14, 1924; report and order of commission]. 1924. [1]+282–284+[1] p. ([Opinion] 9504.) [Report from Interstate Commerce Commission reports, v. 89.] * Paper, 5c.

Superheaters. No. 13961, Power Specialty Company *v.* Dansville & Mount Morris Railroad Company et al.; decided Apr. 16, 1924; report [and order] of commission. [1924.] 251–254+[1] p. ([Opinion] 9496.) [Report from Interstate Commerce Commission reports, v. 89.] * Paper, 5c.

Tennessee, Alabama and Georgia Railway. Finance docket no. 3567, notes of Tennessee, Alabama & Georgia Ry.; decided Apr. 28, 1924; report of commission. [1924.] p. 839–840. ([Finance decision] 1337.) [From Interstate Commerce Commission reports, v. 86.] * Paper, 5c.

Terminal charges. Investigation and suspension docket no. 1962, terminal charges, privileges, and allowances applicable on transcontinental traffic; [decided Mar. 22, 1924; report and order of commission]. 1924. [1]+332–336+[1] p. ([Opinion] 9510.) [Report from Interstate Commerce Commission reports, v. 89.] * Paper, 5c.

Texas and Pacific Railway. Finance docket no. 3399, Texas & Pacific readjustment; [decided Apr. 25, 1924; report of commission]. 1924. [1]+808–817 p. ([Finance decision] 1332.) [From Interstate Commerce Commission reports, v. 86.] * Paper, 5c.

Valdosta, Moultrie and Western Railway. Finance docket no. 862, guaranty settlement with Valdosta, Moultrie & Western Ry.; decided May 5, 1924; report of commission. [1924.] p. 13–15. ([Finance decision] 1346.) [From Interstate Commerce Commission reports, v. 90.] * Paper, 5c.

Vegetables. No. 14820, W. B. Ahern Brokerage Company et al. *v.* Atlantic Coast Line Railroad Company et al.; [decided May 13, 1924; report and order of commission]. 1924. [1]+274–278+[1] p. ([Opinion] 9502.) [Report from Interstate Commerce Commission reports, v. 89.] * Paper, 5c.

Vitrolite. No. 14623, Vitrolite Company *v.* Atchison, Topeka & Santa Fe Railway Company et al.; decided May 20, 1924; report [and order] of commission. [1924.] 367–372+iv p. ([Opinion]9523.) [Report from Interstate Commerce Commission reports, v. 89.] * Paper, 5c.

Western Pacific Railroad. Finance docket no. 3505, Western Pacific equipment trust, series C; decided Apr. 25, 1924; report of commission. [1924.] p. 835–838. ([Finance decision]1336.) [From Interstate Commerce Commission reports, v. 86.] * Paper, 5c.

Wisconsin Central Railway. Finance docket no. 4009, Wisconsin Central securities; decided May 24, 1924; report of commission. [1924.] p. 89–94. ([Finance decision]1371.) [From Interstate Commerce Commission reports, v. 90.] * Paper, 5c.

Yreka Railroad. Finance docket no. 915, guaranty settlement with Yreka R. R.; decided May 12, 1924; report of commission. [1924.] p. 29–30. ([Finance decision]1351.) [From Interstate Commerce Commission reports, v. 90.] * Paper, 5c.

JUSTICE DEPARTMENT

Baltimore and Ohio Railroad. In Court of Claims, Baltimore & Ohio Railroad Company *v.* United States, no. B–73; defendant's objections to plaintiff's request for findings of fact, defendant's request for findings of fact, and brief. [1924.] p. 83–135, large 8° ‡

—— In Court of Claims, Baltimore & Ohio Railroad Company *v.* United States, no. B–87; defendant's objection to plaintiff's request for findings of fact, defendant's request for findings of fact, and brief. [1924.] p. 70–93, large 8° ‡

Bradford Company. No. 2386, Court of Customs Appeals, Bradford Company and Adolph Frankau & Co., Inc. (importers), United States impleaded, *v.* American Lithographic Company (American manufacturer); brief for United States. 1924. cover-title, 16 p. ‡

Byrnes, Bertha M. In Court of Claims, Bertha M. Byrnes *v.* United States, no. 1076–C; defendant's brief. 1924. p. 13, large 8° ‡

California Cooperative Canneries. No. 4071, in Court of Appeals of District of Columbia, Jan. term, 1924, California Cooperative Canneries *v.* United States, Swift & Company, et al., appeal from Supreme Court of District of Columbia; brief on behalf of United States in answer to brief on behalf of Swift and Armour groups of appellees. 1924. cover-title, 9 p. ‡

Chestatee Pyrites and Chemical Corporation. No. —, in Supreme Court, Oct. term, 1923, Hubert Work, Secretary of Interior, *v.* United States ex rel. Chestatee Pyrites and Chemical Corporation, in error to Court of Appeals of District of Columbia; motion to advance. 1924. cover-title, 3 p. ‡

Cheyenne Milling Company. In Court of Claims, Cheyenne Milling Co. *v.* United States, no. 34739; defendant's objections to claimant's request for findings of fact [defendant's request for findings of fact, and defendant's brief]. [1924.] p. 123–173, large 8° ‡

Childs, Edward H. In Supreme Court, Oct. term, 1923, Edward H. Childs, trustee in bankruptcy, *v.* United States, no. 992; on petition for writ of certiorari to circuit court of appeals for 2d circuit. 1924. 1 p. ‡

Claims. Judgments by District Courts *v.* Government, list of judgments rendered against Government by District Courts as submitted by Attorney General, which require appropriation for payment. June 3, calendar day June 4, 1924. 3 p. (S. doc. 135, 68th Cong. 1st sess.) * Paper, 5c.

Coamo, steamship. No. 301, in Supreme Court, Oct. term, 1923, United States *v.* steamship Coamo, her engines, etc., New York & Porto Rico Steamship Company, on certificate from circuit court of appeals for 2d circuit; brief for United States. 1924. cover-title, 17 p. ‡

Dayton Airplane Company. No. 107, district court, southern district of Ohio, western division, United States *v.* Dayton Airplane Company; answer to cross petition. 1924. cover-title, 4 p. ‡

—— Same; reply to 2d amended answer. 1924. cover-title, 15 p. ‡

Durbrow & Hearne. No. 2338, Court of Customs Appeals, Durbrow & Hearne *v.* United States; brief for United States in opposition to application for rehearing. 1924. cover-title, 4 p. ‡

Early & Daniel Company. In Court of Claims, Early & Daniel Company *v.* United States, no. 238–A; defendant's objections to claimant's request for findings of fact, defendant's request for findings of fact, defendant's brief. [1924.] p. 117–136, large 8° ‡

Forbes, Charles R. No. 12511, in district court for northern district of Illinois, eastern division, United States *v.* Charles R. Forbes and John W. Thompson; indictment, viol. sec. 37, criminal code, conspiracy to defraud United States in construction of veterans' hospitals. 1924. cover-title, 14 p. ‡

—— No. 12512, in district court for northern district of Illinois, eastern division, United States *v.* Charles R. Forbes; indictment, viol. sec. 117, criminal code, director of Veterans' Bureau accepting bribe. 1924. cover-title, 5 p. ‡

—— No. 12513, in district court for northern district of Illinois, eastern division, United States *v.* Charles R. Forbes and John W. Thompson; indictment, viol. sec. 37, criminal code, conspiracy to commit bribery offenses in connection with construction of veterans' hospitals. 1924. cover-title, 9 p. ‡

Gunn, Margaret G. In Court of Claims, Margaret G. Gunn *v.* United States, no. 1079–C; defendant's brief. 1924. p. 15, large 8° ‡

Illinois Central Railroad. No. 248, in Supreme Court, Oct. term, 1923, Illinois Central Railroad Company *v.* United States, appeal from Court of Claims; brief for United States. 1924. cover-title, ii+18 p. ‡

International Sales Company. No. 2299, Court of Customs. Appeals, International Sales Co. et al. *v.* United States; brief for appellee in answer to appellant's reply to reply brief for United States. 1924. cover-title, 6 p. ‡

—— Same; brief for United States [in reply to supplemental memorandum of appellant]. 1924. cover-title, 14 p. ‡

Kent, Charles A. No. —, in Supreme Court, Oct. term, 1923, John A. Grogan, collector of internal revenue [for 1st district of Michigan], *v.* Bryant Walker, executor of Charles A. Kent; petition for writ of certiorari to circuit court of appeals for 6th circuit, and brief in support thereof. 1924. cover-title, 11 p. ‡

—— Same, proceedings in circuit court of appeals for 6th circuit; appearance of counsel [etc.]. 1924. p. 43. [This is printed without title. The signature mark reads: 103284—24.] ‡

Kuttroff, Pickhardt & Co., Incorporated. No. 2347, 2356, 2365, 2366, Court of Customs Appeals, Kuttroff, Pickhardt & Co., Inc., *v.* United States; reply brief for United States. 1924. cover-title, 11 p. ‡

Ladenburg, Thalmann & Co. No. —, in Supreme Court, Oct. term, 1923, Thomas W. Miller, as Alien Property Custodian, and Frank White, as Treasurer of United States, *v.* Benjamin Guinness [et al.], copartners doing business under firm name and style of Ladenburg, Thalmann & Company; petition for writ of certiorari to circuit court of appeals for 2d circuit, and brief in support thereof. 1924. cover-title, 20 p. ‡

Lake Calvenia, steamship. No. 2240, in circuit court of appeals, 4th circuit, United States, owner of steamship Lake Calvenia, *v.* Standard Oil Company of New Jersey, owner and claimant of steamship H. H. Rogers; reply brief for United States. 1924. cover-title, 20 p. ‡

Leiter, Levi Z. In Court of Claims, Joseph Leiter [et al.], trustees of estate of Levi Z. Leiter, *v.* United States, no. D–262; demurrer [and] brief. [1924.] p. 59–68, large 8° ‡

Liu Kah. In Supreme Court, Oct. term, 1923, United States ex rel. Joseph M. Singleton, next friend of Liu Kah, *v.* Robert E. Tod, commissioner of immigration at port of New York, no. 482; on petition for writ of certiorari to circuit court of appeals for 2d circuit. 1924. 1 p. ‡

Louisville Bedding Company. No. 1022, in Supreme Court, Oct. term, 1923, Louisville Bedding Co. *v.* United States, appeal from Court of Claims; answer of appellee to appellant's motion to remand. 1924. cover-title, 4 p. ‡

Meissner, Alexander. United States district court, district of Delaware, United States and Alexander Meissner *v.* Deforest Radio Telephone and Telegraph Company [et al.], in equity no. —, action under sec. 4915 U. S. Revised statutes; bill of complaint. [1924.] 7 p. ‡

Mitchell, Irvine. In Court of Claims, Irvine Mitchell *v.* United States, no. D–255; demurrer [and] brief in support of demurrer. [1924.] p. 5–9, large 8° ‡

Myers, F. W., & Co. No. 2377, Court of Customs Appeals, United States *v.* F. W. Myers & Co.; brief for United States. 1924. cover-title, 7 p. ‡.

Opinions. [Official opinions of Attorneys General] v. 34, [signatures] 5–8. [1924.] p. 65–128.

12—40693

NOTE.—The opinions of the Attorney General are first issued in signatures being published later in bound volumes. Subscribers may deposit 75c. with the Superintendent of Documents and receive the contents of a volume of the opinions in separate parts as they are issued. Prices for bound volumes furnished upon application to the Superintendent of Documents, Washington, D. C.

Provost Brothers & Co. No. B–112, in Court of Claims, George D. Provost and Cornelius W. Provost, copartners, composing firm of Provost Bros. & Co., *v.* United States; defendant's request for findings of fact and brief. 1924. cover title, ii+153–267 p. large 8° ‡

Rickard, George L. In district court for district of New Jersey, United States *v.* George L. Rickard et al.; indictment, viol. sec. 37, cr. code, and act July 31, 1912, interstate transportation of prize-fight films. 1924. cover-title, 14 p. ‡

Rodman, Hugh. Interference no. 46630, in Patent Office, before board of examiners-in-chief, Hugh Rodman *v.* John C. Woodruff; brief for Woodruff. 1924. cover-title, 62 p. ‡

Scalione, Charles C. In Patent Office, before board of examiners in chief, interference no. 48046, Charles C. Scalione *v.* Heinrich Herman [Heimann]; brief for Scalione. 1924. cover-title, 57 p. ‡

—— In Patent Office, before board of examiners in chief, Scalione *v.* Heimann, interference no. 48046; Scalione's reply brief. [1924.] 11 p. ‡

—— In Patent Office, before board of examiners in chief, Scalione *v.* Heimann *v.* Bosch, interference no. 48044; reply brief for Scalione. [1924.] 17 p. ‡

Schumann, Adam. In Court of Claims, Adam Schumann *v.* United States, no. D–363; demurrer [and] brief. [1924.] p. 1–6. ‡

Soo Hoo Hong. In Supreme Court, Oct. term, 1923, United States ex rel. Soo Hoo Hong *v.* Robert E. Tod, commissioner of immigration [at port of New York], no. 454; on petition for writ of certiorari to circuit court of appeals for 2d circuit. 1924. 1 p. ‡

Standard Oil Company. United States circuit court of appeals, 4th circuit, no. 2189, Standard Oil Company, California corporation, *v.* United States, Shipping Board, and Shipping Board Emergency Fleet Corporation, as owners of steamships Liberator [etc.], and L. Vernon Miller, as trustee of estate of Atlantic Gulf and Pacific Steamship Corporation, bankrupt respondent, impleaded, appeals from district court for district of Maryland, at Baltimore; brief of appellees, United States, Shipping Board, and Shipping Board Emergency Fleet Corporation. 1924. cover-title, i+39 p. ‡

Standard Steel Car Company. In Court of Claims, no. 307–A, Standard Steel Car Company *v.* United States; defendant's brief in answer to plaintiff's brief on demurrer. 1924. cover-title, iii+1361–1422 p. large 8° ‡

Stegemann, E., jr. No. 2367, Court of Customs Appeals, United States *v.* E. Stegemann, jr.; application for rehearing on behalf of United States. 1924. cover-title, 9 p. ‡

Stone & Downer Company. No. 2384, Court of Customs Appeals, United States *v.* Stone & Downer Co.; brief for United States. 1924. cover-title, 10 p. ‡

Sun Shipbuilding Company. In Court of Claims, Sun Shipbuilding Company *v.* United States, no. 317–B; defendant's objections to plaintiff's request for findings of fact, defendant's request for findings of fact, and brief. [1924.] p. 1–22, large 8° ‡

Texas and Pacific Railway. In Court of Claims, J. L. Lancaster and Charles L. Wallace, receivers of Texas and Pacific Railway, *v.* United States, no. C–112; defendant's objections to plaintiff's request for findings of fact, defendant's request for findings of fact, defendant's brief. [1924.] p. 47–54, large 8° ‡

Thompson, John W. No. 12514, in district court for northern district of Illinois, eastern division, United States *v.* John W. Thompson; indictment, viol. sec. 39, criminal code, giving bribe to director, Veterans' Bureau. 1924. cover-title, 6 p. ‡

Thorsch, Hugo. No. 4130, in Court of Appeals of District of Columbia, Hugo Thorsch *v.* Thomas W. Miller, as Alien Property Custodian, Frank White, as Treasurer of United States, Richard Werner and Otto Werner; brief on behalf of Thomas W. Miller, as Alien Property Custodian, and Frank White, as Treasurer of United States. 1924. cover-title, 1+26 p. ‡

Union Twist Drill Company. In Court of Claims, Union Twist Drill Company *v.* United States, no. 316–A; defendant's requests for amended findings of fact and supplemental brief. [1924.] p. 38–45, large 8° ‡

United Gas and Electric Engineering Corporation. No. 1060, in Supreme Court, Oct. term, 1923, United Gas & Electric Engineering Corporation *v.* United States, appeal from Court of Claims; answer of appellee to appellant's motion to remand. 1924. cover-title, 4 p. ‡

Von Bremen, Asche & Co. No. 2370, Court of Customs Appeals; Von Bremen, Asche & Co. v. United States; brief for United States. 1924. cover-title, 16 p. ‡

Wells, Julia L. In Court of Claims, Julia L. Wells v. United States, no. 1067–C; defendant's brief. 1924. p. 13, large 8° ‡

LABOR DEPARTMENT

EMPLOYMENT SERvICE

Directory of public employment offices, May, 1924. 1924. 20 p. narrow 12° †

Employment agencies. Monthly report of activities of State and municipal employment services cooperating with U. S. Employment Service, Apr. 1924. 1924. iv+12 p. †
L 24—62

Industrial employment information bulletin, v. 4, no. 5; May, 1924. [1924.] 20 p. 4° [Monthly.] †
L 21—17

Wheat. Harvesting in "big wheat belt"; [prepared in U. S. Farm Labor Bureau, Kansas City, Mo.]. 1924. [1]+10 p. (Bulletin H–24; Farm labor series.) †
L 24—94

IMMIGRATION BUREAU

Immigration laws. Information relative to immigration laws and their enforcement in connection with admission of aliens. [1924.] 4 p. [This publication takes the place of the 1+6 page publication entered in the Monthly catalogue for May, 1924, p. 765.] †

LABOR STATISTICS BUREAU

Employment in selected industries, May, 1924. 1924. [1]+10 p. [From Monthly labor review, July, 1924.] †

Monthly labor review, v. 18, no. 6; June, 1924. 1924. v+1187–1398+vi p. il. * Paper, 15c. single copy, $1.50 a yr.; foreign subscription, $2.25. ·15—26485

SPECIAL ARTICLES.—Conference of paper box-board manufacturers on shorter working hours, Washington, D. C., May 2, 1924.—Coal-mine explosions and their prevention; by H. Foster Bain.—Prevention of coal-dust explosions and other accidents in coal mines.—New arbitration machinery in Germany; by Boris Stern.—Labor law of Jalisco, Mexico; by Ethel Yohe Larson.—Conciliation work of Department of Labor, Apr. 1924; by Hugh L. Kerwin.—Statistics of immigration, Mar. 1924; by W. W. Husband.

NOTE.—The review is the medium through which the Bureau publishes the results of original investigations too brief for bulletin purposes, notices of labor legislation by the States or by Congress, and Federal court decisions affecting labor, which from their importance should be given attention before they could ordinarily appear in the bulletins devoted to these subjects. One free subscription will be given to all labor departments and bureaus, workmen's compensation commissions, and other offices connected with the administration of labor laws and organizations exchanging publications with the Labor Statistics Bureau. Others desiring copies may obtain them from the Superintendent of Documents, Washington, D. C., at the prices stated above.

Prices. Prices and cost of living. [1924.] p. 961–1022, il. [From Monthly labor review, May, 1924.] †

—— Prices and cost of living. [1924.] p. 1223–51, il. [From Monthly labor review, June, 1924.] †

Tires. Wages and hours of labor in automobile tire industry, 1923. Apr. 1924. iii+58 p. (Bulletin 358; Wages and hours of labor series.) * Paper, 10c.
L 24—95

—— Same. (H. doc. 244, 68th Cong. 1st sess.)

Wages. Union scale of wages and hours of labor, May 15, 1923. Apr. 1924. iii+196 p. (Bulletin 354; Wages and hours of labor series.) * Paper, 20c.
L 13—159

—— Same. (H. doc. 93, 68th Cong. 1st sess.)

NATURALIZATION BUREAU

English language. Federal textbook on citizenship training: pt. 1, Our language, conversational and language lessons for use in public schools by candidate for citizenship learning to speak English; by Lillian P. Clark. 1924. iii+198 p. il. map. †

Naturalization laws and regulations, June 15, 1924. 1924. 58 p. * Paper, 10c.
                                                                      11—35337

WOMEN'S BUREAU··

Alabama. Women in Alabama industries, study of hours, wages, and working,
conditions; [by Kathleen B. Jennison]. .1924. vii+86 p. il. (Bulletin 34.)
* Paper, 15c.   L24—96
Home work laws in United States [Jan. 1, 1924]. 1924. [1]+10 p. [Advance
  section from Bulletin 40.] * Paper,· 5c.·

LIBRARY· OF CONGRESS ·

COPYRIGHT OFFICE

Copyright. [Catalogue of copyright entries, new series, pt. 1, group 1, Books,
v. 20] no. 125; May, 1924. May 12, 1924. p. 1425–35. [Issued several times
a week.]   6—35347
    NOTE.—Each number is issued in 4 parts: pt. 1, group 1, relates to books; pt. 1,
group 2, to pamphlets, leaflets, contributions to newspapers or periodicals, etc., lectures, sermons, addresses for oral delivery, dramatic compositions, maps, motion pictures; pt. 2, to periodicals; pt. 3, to musical compositions; pt. 4, to works of art, reproductions of a work of art, drawings or plastic works of scientific or technical character, photographs, prints, and pictorial illustrations.
    Subscriptions for the Catalogue of copyright entries should be made to the Superin-
tendent of Documents, Washington, D. C., instead of to the Register of Copyrights.
Prices are as follows: Paper, $3.00 a yr. (4 pts.), foreign subscription, $5.00; pt. 1
(groups 1 and 2), 5c. single copy (group 1, price of group 2 varies), $1.00 a yr.,
foreign subscription, $2.25; pt. 3, $1.00 a yr., foreign subscription, $1.50; pts. 2 and
4, each 10c. single copy, 50c. a yr., foreign subscription, 70c. ·
—— Same [pt. 1, group 1, Books, v. 21] no. 27–35; June, 1924. June 4–27,
1924. p. 265–408. [Issued several times a week.]
—— Same, pt. 2, Periodicals, v. 18, no. 4 [with index and title-page to new
series, pt. 2, v. 18, nos. 1–4, Jan.–Dec. 1923]. 1924. iii+267–428+[1] p.
[Quarterly.]
—— Same, pt 4, Works of art, reproductions of a work of art, drawings or
plastic works of scientific or technical character, photographs, prints and
pictorial illustrations,·v. 18, no. 4 .[with index and·title-page to new series,
pt. 4, v. 18, nos. 1–4, calendar year 1923]. 1924. iii+275–443+[1] p.
[Quarterly.]·

NATIONAL ADVISORY COMMITTEE FOR AERONAUTICS

Wings. Elements of wing section theory and of wing theory ·[with, list of
references]; by Max M. Munk. 1924. cover-title, 25 p. il. 4° (Report 191.)
[Text and illustration on p. 2 and 3 of cover.] * Paper, 10c.   24—26591

NAVY DEPARTMENT

Court-martial order 4, 1924; Apr. 30, 1924. [1924.] 12 p. 12° [Monthly.] ‡
Orders. General order 127 [6th series]; May 23, 1924. [1924.] 20 p. 4° ‡

CONSTRUCTION AND REPAIR BUREAU

War-ships. Unit weights of materials adopted by Navy Department for purposes of estimate and design. Edition, Mar. 1924. 1924. 5 p. [Issued
jointly with Bureaus of Engineering, Ordnance, Aeronautics, and Yards and
Docks. Supersedes Appendix 18 to General specifications for building ships
of Navy.] †   24—26592

ENGINEERING BUREAU

Bulletin of engineering information 11; Jan. 1, 1924. 1924. [1]+29 p. il. 2
  pl. ‡   22—26665

Electric apparatus and appliances. Instructions for operation, care, and repair of generating sets, motors, and motor control panels; reprint of chapter 24 of Manual of engineering instructions. 1924. [1]+22 p. [The edition of the Manual of engineering instructions of which this chapter forms a part has not yet been issued.]   * Paper, 5c.

24—26593

Marine engineering. Changes in Manual of engineering instructions, no. 21; Dec. 15, 1923. [1924.] i+54 p. il. [Changes 21 is chapter 23 of the new edition of the Manual of engineering instructions. This chapter has also been issued in pamphlet form with the title Instructions for operation, care, and repair of measuring instruments, for which see Monthly catalogue for May, 1924, p. 767.]   * Paper, 10c.

MARINE CORPS

Orders. Marine Corps orders 3 and 4, 1924; May 1 and 16, 1924. [1924.] 2 p. and 1 p. 4° ‡

Training regulations. [Circular letter, May 27, 1924, to all officers concerning Training regulations prepared by Army and to be distributed to Marine Corps.] [1924.] 5 p. ‡

MEDICINE AND SURGERY BUREAU

Field supply table of Medical Department, Navy, with special instructions for medical officers on expeditionary service, 1923. 1924. [1]+69 p. ‡

24—26594

Manual. Changes in Manual for Medical Department [Navy, 1922], no. 2; Jan. 1924. [1924.] ii p. [Accompanied by reprints of certain pages to be inserted in their proper places in the original manual. A list of these reprinted pages is found on p. ii of Changes 2 here catalogued.] ‡

Naval medical bulletin. United States naval medical bulletin, published for information of Medical Department of service, June, 1924, v. 20, no. 6; edited by W. M. Kerr. 1924. vi+685–818+viii p. [Monthly.] * Paper, 15c. single copy, $1.50 a yr.; foreign subscription, $2.50.

8—35095

SPECIAL ARTICLES.—Diagnosis of early pulmonary tuberculosis [with list of references]; by W. L. Rathbun.—Early diagnosis and tretement [treatment] of pulmonary tuberculosis; by J. B. Pollard.—Extensive superficial burns [with list of references]; by G. W. Shepard.—Sulpharsphenamine, report on its use at Mayo Clinic, Rochester, Minn.; by R. Hayden.—Leprosy in Hawaiian Islands [with bibliography]; by J. M. McCants.—Kondoleon operation and filariasis; by H. M. Stenhouse.—Maxillary sinusitis of dental origin; by E. B. Howell.—Report of case of large solitary tuberculous abscess of liver; by L. F. Robinson.—Case of far-advanced tuberculosis unsuccessfully treated by artificial pneumothorax, complicated by pyo-pneumothorax and treatment by thoracoplasty; by E. W. Gutzmer.—My first duty aboard ship, U. S. S. Relief; by Thomasina Libby.—Notes on preventive medicine for medical officers, Navy [including Studies of submarine ventilation in tropical waters, by R. F. Jones and G. H. Mankin; Epidemiological report of outbreak of bacillary dysentery at marine barracks rifle range, Santo Domingo City, Dominican Republic, by H. B. La Favre].—Index to United States naval medical bulletin, v. 20.

NAVIGATION BUREAU

Deck seamen. Deck seamanship branch: Instructions for boatswain's mate 1c in preparation for rating of chief boatswain's mate, assignment 1. 1924. cover-title, i+7 p. il. (Navy education-study courses.) ‡

—— Same, assignment 2. 1924. cover-title, 6 p. (Navy education-study courses.) ‡

—— Same, assignment 3. 1924. cover-title, 7 p. (Navy education-study courses.) ‡

—— Deck seamanship branch: Instructions for boatswain's mate 2c in preparation for rating of boatswain's mate 1c, assignment 1. 1924. cover-title, i+9 p. il. (Navy education-study courses.) ‡

—— Same, assignment 2. 1924. cover-title, 9 p. (Navy education-study courses.) ‡

—— Deck seamanship branch: Instructions for coxswain in preparation for rating of boatswain's mate 2c, assignment 1. 1924. cover-title, i+9 p. (Navy education-study courses.) ‡

—— Same, assignment 2. 1924. cover-title, 10 p. il. (Navy education-study courses.) ‡

Deck seamen—Continued. Same, assignment 3. 1924. cover-title, 8 p. (Navy education-study courses.) ‡

—— Same, assignment 4. 1924. cover-title, 8 p. (Navy education-study courses.) ‡

—— Same, assignment 5. 1924. cover-title, 8 p. il.ʹ (Navy education-study courses.) ‡

—— Deck seamanship branch: Instructions for quartermaster 1c in preparation for rating of chief quartermaster, assignment 1. 1924. cover-title, i+11 p. (Navy education-study courses.) ‡

—— Same, assignment 2. 1924. cover-title, 10 p. il. (Navy education-study courses.) ‡

—— Same, assignment 4. 1924. cover-title, 23 p. (Navy education-study courses.) ‡

—— Same, assignment 5. 1924. cover-title, 5 p. (Navy education-study courses.) ‡

—— Deck seamanship branch: Instructions for quartermaster 2c in preparation for rating of quartermaster 1c, assignment 1. 1924. cover-title, i+7 p. (Navy education-study courses.) ‡

—— Same, assignment 2. 1924. cover-title, 8 p. (Navy education-study courses.) ‡

—— Same, assignment 3. 1924. cover-title, 9 p. (Navy education-study courses.) ‡

—— Deck seamanship branch: Instructions for quartermaster 3c in preparation for rating of quartermaster 2c, assignment 2. 1924. cover-title, 31 p. (Navy education-study courses.) ‡

—— Same, assignment 3. 1924· cover-title, 11 p. (Navy education-study courses.) ‡

—— Same, assignment 4. 1924. cover-title, 7 p. (Navy education-study courses.) ‡

—— Same, assignment 5. 1924. cover-title, 1+6 p. 3 pl. (Navy education-study courses.) ‡

—— Same, assignment 6. 1924. cover-title, i+16 p. (Navy education-study courses.) ‡

—— Deck seamanship branch: Instructions for seaman in preparation for rating of quartermaster 3c, assignment 1. 1924· cover-title, i+8 p. (Navy education-study courses.) ‡

—— Same, assignment 2. 1924. cover-title, 12 pp. il. (Navy education-study courses.) ‡

—— Same, assignment 3. 1924. cover-title, 9 p. (Navy education-study courses.) ‡

—— Same, assignment 4. 1924. cover-title, i+10 p. il. (Navy education-study courses.) ‡

—— Same, assignment 5. 1924. cover-title, 11 p. 2 pl. (Navy education-study courses.) ‡

—— Deck seamanship branch: Instructions for seaman 1c in preparation for rating of coxswain, assignment 1. 1924. cover-title, i+8 p. (Navy education-study courses.) ‡

—— Same, assignment 2. 1924. cover-title, 14 p. (Navy education-study courses.) ‡

—— Same, assignment 3. 1924. cover-title, S p. (Navy education-study courses.) ‡

—— Same, assignment 4. 1924. cover-title, 14 p. il. (Navy education-study courses.) ‡

—— Same, assignment 5. 1924. cover-title, 8 p. il. (Navy education-study courses.) ‡

Radio communication. Communications, radio and sound, instructions and exercises to be used in preparation for advancement to rating of radioman, 3d class, pt. 2, assignment 1, procedure and material; prepared by Office of Naval Operations, Communications Division. 1923 [1924]. [1]+4 p. (Navy education-study courses.) [Date incorrectly given on title-page but correct on cover.] ‡

—— Same, pt. 2, assignment 2, procedure and material; prepared by Office of Naval Operations, Communications Division. 1924. [1]+10 p. il. (Navy education-study courses.) ‡

—— Same, pt. 2, assignment 3, procedure and material; prepared by Office of Naval Operations, Communications Division. 1924. cover-title, 6 p. (Navy education-study courses.) ‡

—— Same, pt. 2, assignment 4, procedure and material; prepared by Office of Naval Operations, Communications Division. 1924. cover-title, 25 p. il. (Navy education-study courses.) ‡

—— Same, pt. 2, assignment 5, procedure and material; prepared by Office of Naval Operations, Communications Division. 1924. cover-title, 15 p. il. (Navy education-study courses.) ‡

—— Same, pt. 2, assignment 6, procedure and material; prepared by Office of Naval Operations, Communications Division. 1924. [1]+13 p. il. (Navy education-study courses.) ‡

—— Same, pt. 2, assignment 7, procedure and material; prepared by Office of Naval Operations, Communications Division. 1924. cover-title, 11 p. il. (Navy education-study courses.) ‡

—— Same, pt. 2, assignment 8, procedure and material; prepared by Office of Naval Operations, Communications Division. 1924. cover-title, 14 p. il. (Navy education-study courses.) ‡

—— Same, pt. 2, assignment 9, procedure and material; prepared by Office of Naval Operations, Communications Division. 1924. cover-title, 16 p. il. 1 pl. (Navy education-study courses.) ‡

—— Same, pt. 2, assignment 10, procedure and material; prepared by Office of Naval Operations, Communications Division. 1924. cover-title, 15 p. il. (Navy education-study courses.) ‡

—— Same, pt. 2, assignment 11, procedure and material; prepared by Office of Naval Operations, Communications Division. 1924. cover-title, 12 p. il. (Navy education-study courses.) ‡

—— Same, pt. 2, assignment 12, procedure and material; prepared by Office of Naval Operations, Communications Division. 1924. cover-title, 20 p. il. (Navy education-study courses.) ‡

HYDROGRAPHIC OFFICE

NOTE.—The charts, sailing directions, etc., of the Hydrographic Office are sold by the office in Washington and also by agents at the principal American and foreign seaports and American lake ports. Copies of the General catalogue of mariners' charts and books and of the Hydrographic bulletins, reprints, and Notice to mariners are supplied free on application at the Hydrographic Office in Washington and at the branch offices in Boston, New York, Philadelphia, Baltimore, Norfolk, Savannah, New Orleans, Galveston, San Francisco, Portland (Oreg.), Seattle, Chicago, Cleveland, Buffalo, Sault Ste. Marie, and Duluth.

Hydrographic bulletin, weekly, no. 1813–16; June 4–25, 1924. [1924.] Each 1 p. large 4°. [For Ice supplements to accompany nos. 1813–16, see below under center head *Charts* the subhead *Pilot charts.*] †

Lights. List of lights, with fog signals and visible time signals, including uniform time system, radio time signals, radio weather bulletins, and radio compass stations of the world: v. 3, West coast of Europe and Africa, Mediterranean Sea, Black Sea, and Sea of Azov; corrected to Apr. 26, 1924. 1924. 582 p. map. ([Publication] 32.) † Paper, 60c.   7—24403

—— Same: v. 6, Baltic Sea, with Kattegat, Belts and Sound, and Gulf of Bothnia; corrected to Mar. 22, 1924. 1924. ii+482 p. map. ([Publication] 35.) † Paper, 60c.

Notice to aviators 6, 1924; June 1 [1924]. [1924.] 9 p. [Monthly.] †
                                                    20—26958

Notice to mariners 23–26, 1924; June 7–28 [1924]. [1924.] [xxxviii]+628–756 leaves. 6 maps. [Weekly.] †

Signals. International code of signals. American edition. 1923. 558 p. il. 8 pl. large 8° ([Publication] 87.) † Fabrikoid, $1.50.   24—26559

Tide calendars. Tide calendar [for Baltimore (Fort McHenry) and Cape Henry], July, 1924. [1924.] 1 p. 4° [Monthly.] †

—— Tide calendar [for Norfolk (Navy Yard) and Newport News, Va.], July, 1924. [1924.] 1 p. 4° [Monthly.] †

Charts

Almirante Bay and Chiriqui Lagoon, north coast of Panama, compiled from latest information; chart 1384. Natural scale 1:71,424 at lat. 9° 10'. Washington, Hydrographic Office, published May, 1915, 7th edition, May, 1924. 32.8×46.5 in. † 70c.

Anticosti Island and adjacent coast of Quebec, Gulf of St. Lawrence, Canada, compiled from latest information; chart 1109. Natural scale 1:291,946 at lat. 49° 20'. Washington, Hydrographic Office, published June, 1889, 30th edition, May [1924]. 43.2×29.2 in. † 40c.

Arafura Sea, eastern part of Banda Sea, and northwestern portion of New Guinea, Eastern Archipelago, eastern portion, sheet 2, from Netherlands Government and British surveys; chart 3003. Natural scale 1:1,566,257 at lat. 6°. Washington, Hydrographic Office, May, 1924. 38.7×26.5 in. † 40c.

Atlantic Coast of United States, Boston to Cape Hatteras, compiled from latest United States coast surveys; chart 942. Natural scale 1:759,495 at lat. 39°. Washington, Hydrographic Office, published Oct. 1885, 14th edition, May, 1924. 45.1×31.8 in. † 70c.

Baltic Sea, Giedser Odde (Point) to Bornholm, from latest Swedish, Danish, & German surveys; chart 4853. Natural scale 1:297,864 at lat. 55°. Washington, Hydrographic Office, published Apr. 1915, 13th edition, May, 1924. 25.6×38.5 in. † 40c.

Brazil. East coast of Brazil, Comoxatiba Point to Rio Doce, compiled from latest information; chart 1672. Natural scale 1:290,780 at lat. 18° 20'. Washington, Hydrographic Office, published Aug. 1898, 9th edition, May, [1924]. 40.7×27.9 in. † 50c.

Collingwood, Ontario. Approaches to Collingwood, Georgian Bay, Lake Huron, Ontario, Canada, from Canadian Government survey in 1888; with inset, Collingwood Harbor; chart 1461. Scale naut. m.=2.3 in., natural scale 1:31,123. Washington, Hydrographic Office, published Dec. 1894, 7th edition, May [1924]. 26.7×18.8 in. † 20c.

Cook Strait, North and South islands, New Zealand, from British surveys between 1849 and 1854, with additions from local and topographic surveys to 1885; chart 3376. Natural scale 1:148,627 at lat. 41°. Washington, Hydrographic Office, May, 1924. 38.7×33.3 in. † 50c.

English Channel, middle sheet, compiled from latest information; chart 4433. Natural scale 1:397,965 at lat. 50°. Washington, Hydrographic Office, published Jan. 1915, 15th edition, May, 1924. 38.8×26.3 in. † 50c.

NOTE.—Contains on reverse: British Isles and North Sea [chart showing areas where sunken mines exist].

La Ceiba, Honduras. Port Ceiba, Honduras, from reconnaissance by U. S. S. Rochester in 1924; chart 5393. Natural scale 1:7,200. Washington, Hydrographic Office, June, 1924. 25×21.6 in. † 20c.

North Island, New Zealand, Cape Egmont to Manukau Harbor, from British surveys between 1849 and 1851, with additions from other sources [with insets]; chart 3342. Natural scale 1:303,784 at lat. 38°. Washington, Hydrographic Office, May, 1924. 36.3×23.9 in. † 40c.

Aotea Harbor, from British survey in 1854.
Mokau River, from British survey in 1854.
New Plymouth or Taranaki Road from British survey in 1849, with later additions from other sources.
Waikato River, from British survey in 1853, with additions in 1863.

Pilot charts. Ice supplement to north Atlantic pilot chart; issue 113. Scale 1° long.=0.3 in. Washington, Hydrographic Office [1924]. 8.9×11.8 in. [To accompany Hydrographic bulletin 1813, June 4, 1924.] †

—— Same; issue 114. Scale 1° long.=0.3 in. Washington, Hydrographic Office [1924]. 8.9×11.8 in. [To accompany Hydrographic bulletin 1814, June 11, 1924.] †

Pilot charts—Continued. Same; issue 115. Scale 1° long.=0.3 in. Washington, Hydrographic Office [1924]. 8.9×11.8 in. [To accompany Hydrographic bulletin 1815, June 18, 1924.] †

—— Same; issue 116. Scale 1° long.=0.3 in. Washington, Hydrographic Office [1924]. 8.9×11.8 in. [To accompany Hydrographic bulletin 1816, June 25, 1924.] †

—— Pilot chart of Central American waters, July, 1924; chart 3500. Scale 1° long.=0.7 in. Washington, Hydrographic Office, June 16, 1924. 23.4×35.1 in. [Monthly. Certain portions of the data are furnished by the Weather Bureau.] † 10c.

NOTE.—Contains on reverse: Cyclonic storms.

—— Pilot chart of Indian Ocean, Aug. 1924; chart 2603. Scale 1° long.=0.2 in. Washington, Hydrographic Office, June 16, 1924. 22.6×31 in. [Monthly. Certain portions of the data are furnished by the Weather Bureau.] † 10c.

NOTE.—Contains on reverse: Cyclonic storms.

—— Pilot chart of north Atlantic Ocean, July, 1924; chart 1400. Scale 1° long.=0.27 in. Washington, Hydrographic Office, June 16, 1924. 23.2×31.8 in. [Monthly. Certain portions of the data are furnished by the Weather Bureau.] † 10c.

                                                          14—16339

NOTE.—Contains on reverse: Cyclonic storms.

—— Pilot chart of north Pacific Ocean; Aug. 1924; chart 1401. Scale 1° long. =0.2 in. Washington, Hydrographic Office, June 16, 1924. 23.7×35.3 in. [Monthly. Certain portions of the data are furnished by the Weather Bureau.] † 10c.

NOTE.—Contains on reverse: Cyclonic storms.

Romana River and entrance, Dominican Republic, Haiti, from surveys by U. S. S. Castine and Department of Public Works, Dominican Government, in 1915, scale 2000 yds.=8 in., natural scale 1:9,072; Enlarged plan of Romana River, scale 400 yds.=7.2 in., natural scale 1:2,016; chart 2772. Washington, Hydrographic Office, published Apr. 1916, 5th edition, May, 1924. 21.8×27.7 in. † 20c.

St. Lawrence River, Canada, Pointe des Monts to Saguenay River, from Canadian surveys between 1905 and 1916; chart 1111. Natural scale 1:193,-338 at lat. 48° 40'. Washington, Hydrographic Office, published July, 1889, 34th edition, May, 1924. 26×33.3 in. † 40c.

Suwo Nada. Suo [Suwo] Nada, Naikai or Inland Sea, Japan, Shimonoseki Kaikyo to Maruyama Zaki, from Japanese surveys between 1884 and 1918; chart 2737. Natural scale 1:50,574 at lat. 33° 55'. Washington, Hydrographic Office, published Feb. 1912, 7th edition, May, 1924. 26.1×38.9 in. † 50c.

Tonkin Gulf, Tonkin, French Indo-China, Lakh entrance to Kaotao Islands, including delta of Ka River, from latest French surveys; chart 3160. Natural scale 1:234, 805 at lat. 20° 30'. Washington, Hydrographic Office, published Dec. 1916, 2d edition, May, 1924. 25.9×38.6 in. † 40c.

NAVAL ACADEMY

Report. Board of visitors to Naval Academy, 1924, letter from Rear Admiral W. L. Rodgers, Navy, transmitting report of board of visitors to Naval Academy, 1924. June 7, 1924. 8 p. (S. doc. 152, 68th Cong. 1st sess.) * Paper, 5c.
                                                          8—7222

RECRUITING BUREAU

[*Poster*] 260. [Press of Navy Recruiting Bureau, New York, May 29, 1924.] 14×17 in. [Title is: Future admirals.]

ORDNANCE BUREAU

Craven, Francis S. Interference no. 46578, in Patent Office, Francis S. Craven *v.* Hamilton Foley; brief for Craven. 1924. cover-title, 26 p. ‡

SUPPLIES AND ACCOUNTS BUREAU

Pay, Navy. Changes in Instructions for carrying into effect joint service pay bill (act of June 10, 1922) [sec. A–H, revised to Sept. 21, 1923] ; June 1, 1924. [1924.] 1 p. 4° [Accompanied by reprints of certain pages and additional pages to be inserted in their proper places in the original publication. A list of these pages is given on the first page.] ‡

Supply Corps, Navy. Memorandum for information of officers of Supply Corps, commanding officers [of ships], and commandants 261; May 1, 1924. [1924.] p. 8260–8353, 12° [Monthly.] ‡

YARDS AND DOCKS BUREAU

Drawings. Requirements of Bureau of Yards and Docks in preparation of drawings, surveys, and other technical records; chapter 14 of Manual of Bureau of Yards and Docks. 1924. iii+38 p. 13 pl. 16 p. of pl. ‡

PAN AMERICAN UNION

NOTE.—The Pan American Union sells its own monthly bulletins, handbooks. etc., at prices usually ranging from 5c. to $2.50. The price of the English edition of the bulletin is 25c. a single copy or $2.50 a year, the Spanish edition $2.00 a year, the Portuguese edition $1.50 a year; there is an additional charge of 50c. a year on each edition for countries outside the Pan American Union. Address the Director General of the Pan American Union, Washington, D. C.

Brazil. Commerce of Brazil, latest reports from Brazilian official sources. 1924. [1]+17 p. † 23–·6435

Bulletin (English edition). Bulletin of Pan American Union, June, 1924; [v. 58, no. 6]. [1924.] iv+539–646 p. il. [Monthly.] 8—30967

—— Same. (H. doc. 6, pt. 12, 68th Cong. 1st sess.)

—— *(Portuguese edition).* Boletim da União Pan-Americana, Junho, 1924, edição portuguesa; [v. 26, no. 6]. [1924.] iv+381–456 p. il. [Monthly.] 11—27014

—— *(Spanish edition).* Boletin de la Unión Panamericana, Junio, 1924, sección española; [v. 58, no. 6]. [1924.] iv+543–650 p. il. [Monthly.] 12—12555

Latin America. A glance at Latin American civilization; by Francisco J. Yánes. 1924. 16 p. † 24—26595

—— Latin America, suggestions for teachers [with bibliographies]. 1924. [2]+14 p. il. (Educational series, Monograph 2.) † 24—26596

Mexico as an industrial nation; [by Hector Lazo]. 1924. [2]+14 p. il. [From Bulletin, May, 1924.] †

Pan American Child Congress. Cuarto Congreso Panamericano del Niño [Santiago, Chile, Oct. 12–19, 1924]. 1924. [1]+8+[1] p. il. [From Boletin, May, 1924.] †

PANAMA CANAL

NOTE.—Although The Panama Canal makes its reports to, and is under the supervision of, the Secretary of War, it is not a part of the War Department.

Panama Canal record, v. 17, no. 43–46; June 4–25, 1924. Balboa Heights, C. Z. [1924.] p. 623–674. [Weekly.] 7—35328

NOTE.—The yearly subscription rate of the Panama Canal record is 50c. domestic, and $1.00 foreign, (single issues 2c.), except in the case of Government departments and bureaus, Members of Congress, representatives of foreign Governments, steamship lines, chambers of commerce, boards of trade, and university and public libraries, to whom the Record is distributed free. The word, "domestic" refers to the United States, Canada, Canal Zone, Cuba, Guam, Hawaii, Manua, Mexico, the Philippines, Porto Rico, Republic of Panama, Tutuila, and the Virgin Islands. Subscriptions will commence with the first issue of the Record in the month in which the subscriptions are received unless otherwise requested. Remittances should be made payable to Disbursing Clerk, The Panama Canal, but should be forwarded to the Chief of Office, The Panama Canal, Washington, D. C. The name and address to which the Record is to be sent should be plainly written. Postage stamps, foreign money, and defaced or smooth coins will not be accepted.

EXECUTIVE DEPARTMENT

EXECUTIVE OFFICE

Executive orders. Supplement 5 [to] Executive orders relating to Panama Canal [Mar. 8, 1904–Dec. 31, 1921, annotated 1921]. Balboa Heights, C. Z., June 7, 1924. p. 363. [Executive orders relating to Panama Canal published by The Panama Canal. This supplement includes Executive orders dated Apr. 3 and May 7, 1924.] †

PURCHASING DEPARTMENT

Supplies. Circular [proposals for supplies]' 1616; June 18. 1924. [1924.] 18+[1] p. f° †

—— Proposals [for supplies 1616 and 1617, to accompany Circular proposals for supplies 1616 and 1617]. [1924.] Each 1 p. 24° ‡

PERSONNEL CLASSIFICATION BOARD

Government officials and employees. Classification of field service, communication submitting separate views relative to classification of field service of Government by Guy Moffett, member representing Civil Service Commission; presented by Mr. Sterling. 1924. iii+7 p. (S. doc. 122, 68th Cong. 1st sess.) * Paper, 5c.

POST OFFICE DEPARTMENT

Envelopes. Proposal and specifications for stamped envelopes and newspaper wrappers for postal service, for 4 years, beginning Jan. 1, 1925, 1924. ii+18 p. 4° †

Labels of sacks of 2d-class matter made up by publishers should show name of post office of publication; [issued by] 3d assistant Postmaster General. June 30, 1924. 1 p. oblong 32° †

Letter-boxes. Apartment house mail receptacles. May 28, 1924. 1 p. narrow 8° †

Mail matter. Foreign countries now selling international reply coupons of new style unsurcharged; Special care must be exercised in addressing mail for post offices having same or similar names; [issued by] 3d assistant Postmaster General. [1924.] 1 p. narrow 8° †

—— Name and address of sender must be placed on 4th-class mail; [issued by] 3d assistant Postmaster General. June 5, 1924. 1 p. oblong 32° †

Motion pictures. Importance of proper address labels on shipments of motion-picture films; [issued by] 3d assistant Postmaster General. June 5, 1924. 1 p. †

Postal bulletin, v. 45, no. 13485–509; June 2–30, 1924. [1924.] Each 2 leaves or 1 p. f° [Daily except Sundays and holidays.] * Paper, 5c. single copy, $2.00 a yr.
6—5810

Postal guide. United States official postal guide, 4th series, v. 3, no. 12; June, 1924, monthly supplement. 1924. cover-title, 62 p. [Includes inserts 1–11 to Postal laws and regulations of United States. Text on p. 2–4 of cover.] * Official postal guide, with supplements, $1.00; foreign subscription, $1.50; July issue, 75c.; supplements published monthly (11 pamphlets), 25c.; foreign subscription, 50c.
4—18254

Postal laws and regulations of United States. Edition of 1924, in effect July 1, 1924. 1924. xiv+706 p. * Cloth, $1.00.
24—26560

Reports of unrated, short-paid matter on Form 3580 should include name of station where mailed, if known; [issued by] 3d assistant Postmaster General. June 19, 1924. 1 p. oblong 48° †

FOREIGN MAILS DIVISION

Postal Union transit statistics, Oct. 15–Nov. 11, 1924, instructions to postmasters. [1924.] 24 p. ‡

POST OFFICE INSPECTORS DIVISION

Post offices. [Circular to be used in inspection of 1st and 2d class post offices and filed in inspected office.] Revised July 1, 1924. [1924.] 4 p. 4° ‡

—— [Circular to be used in inspection of 3d and 4th class post offices and filed in inspected office.] Revised July 1, 1924. [1924.] 4 p. 4° ‡

Telegraph code as embodied in Circular letter no. 439 addressed to post office inspectors under date of June 12, 1924. 1924. iv+26 p. 24° ‡

PURCHASING AGENT

Envelopes. Award of contracts for envelopes for use of departments of Government during fiscal year 1925. 1924. cover-title, ii+13 p. 4° ‡

RAILWAY MAIL SERVICE

Mail-trains. Schedule of mail trains, no. 92, June 1, 1924, 12th division, Railway Mail Service, comprising Louisiana and Mississippi. 1924. 77+[1] p. narrow 8° ‡

—— Schedule of mail trains, no. 370, May 19, 1924, 2d division, Railway Mail Service, comprising New York, New Jersey, Pennsylvania, Delaware, eastern shore of Maryland, Accomac and Northampton counties, Va., Porto Rico, and virgin Islands. 1924. 302+[1] p. narrow 8° ‡

—— Schedule of mail trains, no. 445, May 20, 1924, 3d division, Railway Mail Service, comprising District of Columbia, Maryland, North Carolina, Virginia, and West Virginia (except peninsula of Maryland and Virginia). 1924. 150+[1] p. narrow 8° ‡

—— Schedule of mail trains, no. 450, May 14, 1924, 7th division, Railway Mail Service, comprising Kansas and Missouri. 1924. 174+[1] p. narrow 8° ‡

TOPOGRAPHY DIVISION

NOTE.—Since February, 1908, the Topography Division has been preparing rural-delivery maps of counties in which rural delivery is completely established. They are published in two forms, one giving simply the rural free delivery routes, starting from a single given post office, and sold at 10 cents each; the other, the rural free delivery routes in an entire county, sold at 35 cents each. A uniform scale of 1 inch to 1 mile is used. Editions are not issued but sun-print copies are produced in response to special calls addressed to the Disbursing Clerk, Post Office Department, Washington, D. C. These maps should not be confused with the post route maps, for which see *Monthly catalogue* for February, 1924, page 486.

PRESIDENT OF UNITED STATES

Addresses. Address of President Coolidge at Confederate Memorial, Arlington National Cemetery, Va., May 25, 1924. 1924. [1]+2 p. †   24—26597

—— Address of President Coolidge at National Conference on Outdoor Recreation at Washington, D. C., May 22, 1924. 1924. [1]+4 p. †. 24—26598

—— Address [of President Coolidge, delivered at Arlington National Cemetery, May 30, 1924]. [1924.] 6 p. †   24—26599

—— Address [of President Coolidge, delivered at dedication of Arizona State stone in Washington Monument, Apr. 15, 1924]. [1924.] 3 p. † 24—26600

Alaska. Executive order, Alaska, Sitka National Cemetery [revoking Executive order of June 21, 1890, in so far as it withdrew 10 acre tract at Sitka, Alaska, and withdrawing certain described tract of land at Sitka, Alaska, from settlement, etc., reserving same for cemetery purposes, said reservation to be known as Sitka National Cemetery]. June 12, 1924. 1 p. f° (No. 4025.) ‡

Alaska Peninsula Fisheries Reservation. Executive order [revoking Executive order of Feb. 17, 1922, creating Alaska Peninsula Fisheries Reservation for protection of fisheries in Alaskan waters]. June 7, 1924. 1 p. f° (No. 4020.) ‡

Aliens. Executive order, documents required of aliens entering United States. [June 14, 1924.] [2] p. f° ([No. 4027.]) ‡

Barium dioxid. Increasing rate of duty on barium dioxide, proclamation [authorizing certain increase in duty on barium dioxide, in order to equalize differences in costs of production in United States and Germany]. [May 19, 1924.] 2 p. f° ([No. 1698.]) †

Civil service. Executive order [amending civil service rules relating to reinstatement and revoking certain clauses of said rules so as to remove time limitation of 5 years on reinstatement of those eligible by reason of military service]. June 19, 1924. 1 p. f° (No. 4031.) ‡

Crow Reservation. Extension of time for payments for Crow Indian lands, Mont., proclamation. [June 9, 1924.] [2] p. f° ([No. 1701.]) †

Deboe, William J. Executive order [waiving Executive order of May 10, 1921, requiring candidates to take civil service examinations for Presidential postmasterships, so as to permit appointment of William J. Deboe to position of postmaster at Marion, Ky., without examination]. June 3, 1924. 1 p. f° (No. 4017.) ‡

Diplomatic and consular service. Executive order [prescribing certain rules and regulations for administering foreign service on interchangeable basis, and creating and defining duties, etc., of Foreign Service Personnel Board and its executive committee, Board of Examiners, and Foreign Service School]. [June 7 ,1924.] 4 p. f° ([No. 4022.]) ‡

Government officials and employees. Executive order [revoking civil service rules requiring employees to serve 3 years in Executive Department or independent establishment at Washington, D. C., before transfer to another Department, and directing that employees be permitted to remain in positions to which they have been allocated by classification act of 1923, but shall not thereby be given any different status for promotion or transfer than they had acquired under civil service rules prior to such allocation]. June 19, 1924. 1 p. f° (No. 4030.) ‡

—— Executive order [stating that from 2d Saturday of June to 2d Saturday of September, both inclusive, of each year until further notice, 4 hours shall constitute day's work on Saturdays for all clerks and other employees of Federal Government, wherever employed, except where same conflicts with existing law, and revoking all Executive or other orders in conflict herewith, except Executive order of Apr. 4, 1908, relating to certain naval stations]. June 13, 1924. 1 p. f° (No. 4026.) ‡

Indians. Executive order [providing that trust period on allotments made to Indians on Umatilla Reservation, Oreg., which expires during calendar year 1924, be extended for period of 10 years, except those named in order]. June 10, 1924. 1 p. f° (No. 4024.) ‡

—— Executive order [providing that trust period on allotments made to Mexican-Kickapoo Indians in Oklahoma, which expires during calendar year 1924, be extended for period of 10 years]. June 19, 1924. 1 p. f° (No. 4029.) ‡

Lay, Julius G. Executive order [authorizing reinstatement of Julius G. Lay in grade of consular service from which he resigned when vacancy shall occur]. June 3, 1924. 1 p. f° (No. 4016.) ‡

Montana. Executive order, Montana [modifying Executive order of July 9, 1910, withdrawing certain lands in Miles City, Mont., land district for classification as to coal values, so as to permit Secretary of Interior to reinstate stock-watering reservoir declaratory statement filed by Ivory Brackett on May 1, 1911, and revoking Executive order of Apr. 1, 1924]. May 31, 1924. 1 p. f° (No. 4015.) ‡

National forests in Idaho, proclamation [modifying proclamations affecting Kaniksu National Forest, so as to exclude certain designated areas and so as to allow Idaho to make selection of lands as indemnity in partial satisfaction of its common school grant]. [June 4, 1924.] 2 p. f° ([No. 1700.]) †

Panama. Abrogation of so-called Taft agreement between United States and Panama, proclamation. May 28, 1924. 1 p. f° (No. 1699.) †

Panama Canal. Executive order establishing and declaring certain property in Republic of Panama to be part of Canal Zone for construction, maintenance, operation, sanitation, and protection of Panama Canal [and setting forth correct description of Alhajuela Lake basin area]. [June 5, 1924.] 2 p. f° ([No. 4019.]) ‡

Postal service. Reclassification of postal salaries, message returning, without approval, bill (S. 1898) reclassifying salaries of postmasters and employees of postal service and readjusting their salaries and compensation on equitable basis. June 7, 1924. 17 p. (S. doc. 149, 68th Cong. 1st sess.) * Paper, 5c.

Southwestern Alaska Fisheries Reservation. Executive order [revoking Executive order of Nov. 3, 1922, creating Southwestern Alaska Fisheries Reservation for protection of fisheries in Alaskan waters]. June 7, 1924. 1 p. f° (No. 4021.) ‡

Treasury Department. Executive order [amending civil service rules relating to classified positions which may be filled upon noncompetitive examination so as to include classified positions in custodian service of Treasury Department when filled by promotion of unclassified laborers, subject to approval of Civil Service Commission]. June 4, 1924. 1 p. f° (No. 4018.) ‡

Veterans' Bureau. Executive order [directing that such of commissioned personnel of Public Health Service, heretofore detailed to veterans' Bureau and now performing service in said bureau, as may be designated by director of veterans' Bureau, may be appointed and employed in veterans' Bureau at such compensation and for such time as director thereof may direct without regard to provisions of civil service law and regulations]. June 7, 1924. 1 p. f° (No. 4023.) ‡

Wyoming. Executive order, Wyoming [temporarily withdrawing, until Mar. 5, 1925, certain described lands in Wyoming, in aid of pending legislation embodied in S. 3452, to adjust portion of eastern boundary of Shoshone National Forest, Wyo.]. June 17, 1924. 1p. f° (No. 4028.) ‡

RAILROAD ADMINISTRATION

Bills of lading. Before Interstate Commerce Commission, no. 15201, Liggett & Myers Tobacco Company v. director general; defendant's exceptions to proposed report of examiner. 1924. cover-title, 8 p. ‡

Coal. Before Interstate Commerce Commission, no. 15640, Beacon Coal Company v. director general; brief on part of director general. 1924. cover-title, 6 p. ‡

Creosote. Before Interstate Commerce Commission, no. 14514, Shreveport Creosoting Company v. director general, as agent; interest on reparation awards against director general, as agent of the President. 1924. cover-title, ii+38 p. ‡

Freight rates. Before Interstate Commerce Commission, no. 14210, Lindeteves-Stokvis v. director general, as agent, Baltimore & Ohio Railroad Company, et al.; petition for further consideration or further hearing. 1924. cover-title, 8 p. ‡

Liquors. Before Interstate Commerce Commission, no. 15547, Woolner Distilling Company v. director general; exceptions on behalf of director general to examiner's proposed report. 1924. cover-title, 6 p. ‡

Matches. Before Interstate Commerce Commission, no. 15421, Diamond Match Company v. director general et al.; brief for defendants. 1924. cover-title, 12 p. ‡

Sweet potatoes. Before Interstate Commerce Commission, no. 14943, Fort Smith Commission Company v. director general et al.; exceptions on behalf of director general to report proposed by examiner. 1924. cover-title, 6 p. ‡

Wood flour. Before Interstate Commerce Commission, no. 14467, Hercules Powder Company v. director general; exceptions on part of director general to report proposed by examiner. 1924. cover-title, 5 p. ‡

Wood-pulp. Before Interstate Commerce Commission, no. 15441, Kieckhefer Container Company, successor to Kaukauna Pulp Company, v. Chicago & North Western Railway Company, director general, as agent; exceptions on part of director general to report proposed by examiner. 1924. cover-title, 5 p. ‡

SHIPPING BOARD

Brooks-Scanlon Corporation. In Supreme Court, Oct. term, 1923, Brooks-Scanlon Corporation v. United States, no. 367; United States v. Brooks-Scanlon Corporation, no. 385, appeals from Court of Claims; motion of United States to extend time for purpose of filing petition for rehearing or in alternative for modification of opinion and mandate. 1924. cover-title, 3 p. ‡

SHIPPING BOARD EMERGENCY FLEET CORPORATION

Ships. Schedule of sailings of Shipping Board vessels in general cargo, passenger & mail services, 1st of June to middle of July, 1924; issued by Traffic Department. [1924.] cover-title, ii+18 p. il. [Monthly. Text on p. 2 and 3 of cover.] †

23—26331

SMITHSONIAN INSTITUTION

NOTE.—In a recent price list the Smithsonian Institution publishes this notice: "Applicants for the publications in this list are requested to state the grounds for their requests, as the Institution is able to supply papers only as an aid to the researches or studies in which they are *especially* interested. These papers are distributed *gratis*, except as otherwise indicated, and should be ordered by the *publication numbers* arranged in sequence. The serial publications of the Smithsonian Institution are as follows: 1, Smithsonian contributions to knowledge; 2, Smithsonian miscellaneous collections; 3, Smithsonian annual reports. No *sets* of these are for sale or distribution, as most of the volumes are out of print. The papers issued in the series of Contributions to knowledge and Miscellaneous collections are distributed without charge to public libraries, educational establishments, learned societies, and specialists in this country and abroad; and are supplied to other institutions and individuals at the prices indicated. Remittances should be made payable to the 'Smithsonian Institution.' The Smithsonian report volumes and the papers reprinted in separate form therefrom are distributed *gratuitously* by the Institution to libraries and individuals throughout the world. Very few of the Report volumes are now available at the Institution, but many of those of which the Smithsonian edition is exhausted can be purchased from the Superintendent of Documents, Government Printing Office, Washington, D. C. The Institution maintains mailing-lists of public libraries and other educational establishments, but no *general mailing-list of individuals.* A library making application to be listed for Smithsonian publications should state the number of volumes which it contains and the date of its establishment, and have the endorsement of a Member of Congress."

The annual reports are the only Smithsonian publications that are regularly issued as public documents. All the others are paid for from the private funds of the Institution, but as they are usually regarded as public documents and have free transmission by mail they are listed in the Monthly catalogue.

Cambrian geology. Cambrian geology and paleontology [v.] 4: no. 9, Cambrian and Ozarkian Brachiopoda, Ozarkian Cephalopoda and Notostraca; by Charles D. Walcott. Washington, Smithsonian Institution, June 3, 1924. [2]+477—554 p. 21 p. of pl. (Publication 2753; Smithsonian miscellaneous collections, v. 67, no. 9.) † Paper, 70c.

8—35374

—— Same [v.] 5: no. 1, Geological formations of Beaverfoot-Brisco-Stanford Range, British Columbia, Canada; by Charles D. Walcott. Washington, Smithsonian Institution, June 28, 1924. [2]+1—51 p. il. 1 pl. 6 p. of pl. map. (Publication 2756; Smithsonian miscellaneous collections, v. 75, no. 1.) † Paper, 45c.

24—26621

NATIONAL MUSEUM

NOTE.—The publications of the National Museum comprise an annual report and three scientific series, viz., Proceedings, Bulletins, and Contributions from national herbarium. The editions are distributed to established lists of libraries, scientific institutions, and specialists, any surplus copies being supplied on application. The volumes of Proceedings are made up of technical papers based on the Museum collections in biology, geology, and anthropology and of each of these papers a small edition, in pamphlet form, is issued in advance of the volume, for prompt distribution to specialists. No sets of any of these series can now be furnished.

Benjaminite, new sulphosalt mineral of klaprotholite group; by Earl V. Shannon. 1924. cover-title, 9 p. il. [From Proceedings, v. 65; no. 2537.] †

Chloropidae. New genus and species of 2-winged flies of family Chloropidae injuring Manihot in Brazil; by J. M. Aldrich. 1924. cover-title, 2 p. [From Proceedings, v. 65; no. 2534.] †

Mammals. East African mammals in National Museum: pt. 3, Primates, Artiodactyla, Perissodactyla, Proboscidea, and Hyracoidea; by N. Hollister.. 1924. viii+164 p. il. 56 pl. map. (Bulletin 99 [pt. 3].) * Paper, 40c.
                                                                            18—26736

Moths. New species of moths in National Museum; by William Schaus. 1924. cover-title, 74 p. [From Proceedings, v. 65; no. 2529.] †

Wasps. Revision of mutillid wasps of genera Myrmilloides and Pseudomethoca occurring in America north of Mexico [with bibliography]; by Clarence E. Mickel. 1924. cover-title, 51 p. 4 p. of pl. [From Proceedings, v. 64; no. 2505.] †

—— Revision of North American wasps of subfamily Platygasterinae; by Robert M. Fouts. 1924. cover-title, 145 p. il. 1 pl. [From Proceedings, v. 63 ; no. 2484.] †

STATE DEPARTMENT

Claims for damages to foreign vessels, report in relation to claims presented by Governments of Denmark, Sweden, and Norway against Government of United States on account of damages sustained by vessels owned by their nationals in collision with vessels in public service of United States. May 31, 1924. 6 p. (S. doc. 127, 68th Cong. 1st sess.) * Paper, 5c.

Diplomatic and consular service. Living and office facilities at Tokyo, report by Secretary of State concerning living and office facilities at Tokyo, Japan, for diplomatic and consular officers of United States. June 3, 1924. 4 p.. (S. doc. 129, 68th Cong. 1st sess.) * Paper, 5c.

Diplomatic list, June, 1924. [1924.] cover-title, i+33 p. 24° [Monthly.] ‡
                                                                            10—16292

SUPREME COURT

Cases. Docket [of cases pending in Supreme Court], Oct. term, 1923. [1924.] p. 311–330, 4° [Issued in loose-leaf form.] ‡

[*Journal*] June 2–9, 1924; [slips] 105–108. [1924.] leaves 283–306. ‡

Official reports of Supreme Court, v. 264 U. S., no. 1; Ernest Knaebel, reporter. Preliminary print. 1924. cover-title, p. 1–171, 12° [Cases adjudged in Supreme Court at Oct. term, 1923 (opinions of Feb. 18, 1924, in part). Text on p. 2 and 4 of cover. From United States reports, v. 264.] * Paper, 25c. single copy, $1.00 per vol. (4 nos to a vol.; subscription price, $3.00 for 12 nos.) ; foreign subscription, 5c. added for each pamphlet.

TARIFF COMMISSION

Cotton. 100 imported cotton cloths, showing cloth particulars, invoice prices in 1913 and 1920, and rates of duty applicable under acts of 1909, 1913, and 1922. 1923. iii+54 p. il. 4 tab. (Tariff information survey I–3a.) * Paper, 10c.

Tariff. Industries requesting tariff investigations, letter in response to resolution requesting Tariff Commission to inform Senate of number of industries which have made requests for tariff investigations and cost of obtaining data for trade information for tariff adjustment. June 6, 1924. 16 p. (S. doc. 142, 68th Cong. 1st sess.) * Paper, 5c.   24—26601

—— Tariff information surveys. Revised edition. 1923. [First edition was issued by Ways and Means Committee. Other parts of Tariff information surveys appeared in previous Monthly catalogues.]

I–3a. [Published under title: 100 imported cotton cloths, and entered in this catalogue under Tariff Commission, Cotton.]

I–4. On articles in paragraph 254 of tariff act of 1913 and related articles in other paragraphs, Cotton cloths provided for eo nomine. vii+51 p. il. * Paper, 10c.   20—27464

—— Tariff information surveys. 1923.

J–8. On articles in paragraphs 1009–11 of tariff act of 1922 and related articles in other paragraphs, Woven fabrics of flax, hemp, and ramie. vi+37 p. il. * Paper, 5c.

TREASURY DEPARTMENT

Certificates of indebtedness. United States of America, 2¾ per cent Treasury certificates of indebtedness, series TD2-1924, dated and bearing interest from June 16, 1924, due Dec. 15, 1924. June 9, 1924. 1 p. 4° - (Department circular 341; Public Debt [Commissioner]. †

Claims. Judgments rendered by Court of Claims, list of judgments rendered by Court of Claims, which have been submitted by Secretary of Treasury and require appropriation. June 3, calendar day June 4, 1924. 4 p. (S. doc. 132, 68th Cong. 1st sess.) * Paper, 5c.
9—C546

Finance. Daily statement of Treasury compiled from latest proved reports from Treasury offices and depositaries, June 2–30, 1924. [1924.] Each 4 p. or 3 p. f° [Daily except Sundays and holidays.] †
15—3303

New Orleans, La. Boundaries of quarantine anchorage in harbor at New Orleans, La. May 19, 1924. 1 p. 4° (Department circular 340; Public Health Service.) †

Plant quarantine act [of Aug. 20, 1912, as amended], compiled regulations. [1924.] 8 p. ([Treasury decision] 40134.) [From Treasury decisions, v. 45, no. 18.] †

Public debt. Statement of public debt of United States, Mar. 31, 1924. [1924.] [2] p. narrow f° [Monthly.] †
10—21268

Telephone. Amendment to Telephone instructions [Coast Guard, 1919] no. 2 [new series]; May 14, 1924. 1924. 1 p. [Telephone instructions issued by Coast Guard.] ‡

Treasury decisions under customs, internal revenue, and other laws, including decisions of Board of General Appraisers and Court of Customs Appeals, v. 45, no. 23–26; June 5–26, 1924. 1924. various paging. [Weekly. Department decisions numbered 40144 corrected, 40211–274, general appraisers' decisions 8781 corrected, 8808–22, abstracts 47307–491 and 47329 corrected, internal revenue decisions 3595–3607, Tariff Commission Notice 37 and Notice dated June 6, 1924.] * Paper, 5c. single copy, $1.00 a yr.; foreign subscription, $2.00.
10—30490

APPRAISERS

Reappraisements of merchandise by general appraisers [on May 27–June 21, 1924]; June 6–27, 1924. [1924.] various paging. (Reappraisement circulars 3512–15.) [Weekly.] * Paper, 5c. single copy, 50c. a yr.; foreign subscription, $1.05.
13—2916

BUDGET. BUREAU

Alaska. Protecting Alaskan seal and salmon fisheries, supplemental estimate of appropriation for Department of Commerce, fiscal year 1925, protecting seal and salmon fisheries in Alaska. June 6, 1924. 2 p. (S. doc. 147, 68th Cong. 1st sess.) * Paper, 5c.

Boyer, James W., jr. James W. Boyer, jr., draft of proposed legislation for relief of James W. Boyer, jr. May 31, 1924. 2 p. (H. doc. 345, 68th Cong. 1st sess.) * Paper, 5c.

Carson Indian School. Rebuilding of dairy barns at Indian school, Carson City, Nev., supplemental estimate of appropriation for Interior Department Indian service, fiscal year 1924, for rebuilding dairy and horse barns, Carson Indian School, Carson City, Nev. June 3, calendar day June 5, 1924. 2 p. (S. doc. 139, 68th Cong. 1st sess.) * Paper, 5c.

District of Columbia. Estimates of appropriations for Metropolitan police, 1925 [etc.], supplemental estimates of appropriations for District of Columbia, 1 for fiscal year 1924, and 5 for fiscal year 1925. May 31, 1924. 4 p. (H. doc. 342, 68th Cong. 1st sess.) * Paper, 5c.

—— Public schools, District of Columbia, 1925' supplemental estimates of appropriations for District of Columbia, fiscal year 1925, for public schools. June 4, 1924. 3 p. (H. doc. 351, 68th Cong. 1st sess.) * Paper, 5c.

Executive Mansion. Salaries and equipment, White House police, fiscal year 1925, supplemental estimates of appropriations, fiscal year 1925, for additional personnel and equipment for White House police force required in accordance with provisions of act approved May 27, 1924. May 31, 1924. 2 p. (H. doc. 343, 68th Cong. 1st sess.)   * Paper, 5c.

Floods. Supplemental estimate for War Department, flood control, supplemental estimate of appropriation for War Department, preliminary examination and surveys for flood control, fiscal year 1924. June 3, calendar day June 4, 1924. 2 p. (S. doc. 134, 68th Cong. 1st sess.)   * Paper, 5c.

Fort Hall Reservation. Relocating main canal, Fort Hall Reservation, Idaho; 1924 and 1925, supplemental estimate of appropriation for Department of Interior of amount required to be withdrawn from Indian tribal funds, fiscal years 1924 and 1925. May 31, 1924. 2 p. (H. doc. 344, 68th Cong. 1st sess.)   * Paper, 5c.

Income tax. Refunding income taxes under title 12 of revenue act of 1924, 1924 and 1925, supplemental estimate of appropriation for Treasury Department pertaining to Internal Revenue Service, fiscal year 1924. June 4, 1924. 2 p. (H. doc. 352, 68th Cong. 1st sess.)   * Paper, 5c.

Inland Waterways Corporation. Purchase of capital stock of Inland Waterways Corporation, supplemental estimate of War Department, fiscal year 1924, for purchase of capital stock of Inland Waterways Corporation act, June 3, 1924. June 3, calendar day June 5, 1924. 2 p. (S. doc. 140, 68th Cong. 1st sess.)   * Paper, 5c.

Missouri River. Repair of Government-owned bridge across Missouri River at Fort Leavenworth, Kans., supplemental estimate of appropriation for Department of Justice, fiscal year 1924, to remain available until June 30, 1925, for repairs to Government-owned bridge across Missouri River at Fort Leavenworth, Kans. June 3, 1924. 2 p. (H. doc. 346, 68th Cong. 1st sess.)   * Paper, 5c.

Northern Pacific Railway. Land grants Northern Pacific Railway Co., supplemental estimate of appropriation for Department of Interior, fiscal year 1925, to provide for expenses of joint committee of Congress created by House joint resolution 237. June 6, 1924. 2 p. (S. doc. 143, 68th Cong. 1st sess.)   * Paper, 5c.

Oil-shales. Development of oil shale, supplemental estimate of appropriation for Department of Interior, Bureau of Mines, fiscal year 1924, to remain available until June 30, 1925, for development of oil shale. June 3, calendar day June 5, 1924. 2 p. (S. doc. 141, 68th Cong. 1st sess.)   * Paper, 5c.

Pearl Harbor. Acquiring fishery rights in Pearl Harbor, Hawaii, supplemental estimate of appropriation for Navy Department, fiscal year 1924, to pay expenses of condemnation in connection with acquisition of private rights of fishery in and about Pearl Harbor, Hawaii. June 3, calendar day June 4, 1924. 2 p. (S. doc. 137, 68th Cong. 1st sess.)   * Paper, 5c.

Rehabilitation of the disabled. Rehabilitation of persons disabled in industry, supplemental estimate of appropriation for Federal Board for Vocational Education for cooperative vocational rehabilitation of persons disabled in industry, fiscal year 1925. June 6, 1924. 2 p. (S. doc. 145, 68th Cong. 1st sess.)   * Paper, 5c.

Secret Service, suppressing counterfeiting and other crimes, 1923, deficiency estimate of appropriation for Treasury Department, pertaining to Secret Service, fiscal year 1923. June 4, 1924. 2 p. (H. doc. 353, 68th Cong. 1st sess.)   * Paper, 5c.

Transportation, Army. Army transportation, supplemental estimate of appropriation for Army transportation for War Department, fiscal year 1924. June 6, 1924. 2 p. (S. doc. 146, 68th Cong. 1st sess.)   * Paper, 5c.

Veterans' Bureau. United States veterans' Bureau, supplemental estimate of appropriation for Veterans' Bureau, fiscal year 1924, for hospital facilities and services for patients. June 6, 1924. 2 p. (S. doc. 144, 68th Cong. 1st sess.)   * Paper, 5c.

COAST GUARD

Warrant officers. Information relative to appointment as temporary warrant officer in Coast Guard. [1924.] 6 p. †

COMPTROLLER OF CURRENCY

National banks. Monthly statement of capital stock of national banks, national bank notes, and Federal reserve bank notes outstanding, bonds on deposit, etc. [June 2, 1924]. June 2, 1924. 1 p. f° †
10—21266

ENGRAVING AND PRINTING BUREAU

Historical sketch of Bureau of Engraving and Printing and its work. [Bureau of Engraving and Printing] City of Washington, 1921 [published 1924]. 30 +[1] p. [Title on cover is: Brief history of Bureau of Engraving and Printing and its work. Illustrations on p. 1 and 2 of cover.] †
24—26602

FEDERAL FARM LOAN BUREAU

Agricultural credit. Financing the farmer. n. p. [1924]. [2] p. narrow f°, folded into narrow 8° size. (Circular 16.) †
24—26603
Mortgages. Semiannual installment 5½ per cent amortization tables for use of Federal land banks, joint stock land banks, and national farm loan associations. Mar. 1924. ii+86 p. (Circular 17.) †

GENERAL SUPPLY COMMITTEE

Government supplies. Specifications and proposals for supplies [fiscal year 1925]: class 8, Gasoline and kerosene. [1924.] 4 p. 4° †
—— Same: class 10, Meat, fish, lard, and oleomargarine. [1924.] 4 p. 4° †

GOVERNMENT ACTUARY

Bonds of United States. Market prices and investment values of outstanding bonds and notes [of United States, May, 1924]. June 2, 1924. 7 p. 4° (Form A.) [Monthly.] †

INTERNAL REVENUE BUREAU

Internal revenue bulletin. Internal revenue bulletin, v. 3, no. 22–26; June 2–30, 1924. 1924. various paging. [Weekly.] * Paper, 5c. single copy (for subscription price see note below).
22—26051

NOTE.—The Internal revenue bulletin service for 1924 will consist of weekly bulletins, quarterly digests, and semiannual cumulative bulletins. The weekly bulletins will contain the rulings to be made public and all internal revenue Treasury decisions. The quarterly digests, with the exception of the one to be published at the end of 1924, will contain digests of the rulings previously published in the weekly bulletins for 1924. The last digest for 1924 will also contain digests of the rulings published during 1922 and 1923. The semiannual cumulative bulletins will contain all new rulings published during the previous 6 months. The complete bulletin service may be obtained, on a subscription basis, from the Superintendent of Documents, Government Printing Office, Washington, D. C., for $2.00 a yr.; foreign subscription, $2.75.

—— Internal revenue bulletin, digest no. 9; Jan. 1922–Dec. 1923. 1924. xiii+402 p. [Quarterly.] * Paper, 25c. (for subscription price see note above).
22—26463
—— Same, digest no. 10; Jan.–Mar. 1924. 1924. vi+70 p. [Quarterly.] * Paper, 10c.

LOANS AND CURRENCY DIVISION

Bonds of United States. Caveat list of United States registered bonds and notes, June 1, 1924. [1924.] 56 p. f° [Monthly.] †
Money. Circulation statement of United States money, June 1, 1924. June 6 [1924]. 1 p. oblong 8°. [Monthly.] †
10—21267

PUBLIC HEALTH SERVICE

Fluke-worms. Spontaneous hatching of Clonorchis ova, preliminary note on investigation to determine whether clonorchiasis may be disseminated on Pacific slope [with list of references]; by N. E. Wayson. 1924. [1]+2 p. (Reprint 916.) [From Public health reports, Apr. 25, 1924.] * Paper, 5c.
24—26564

Oxidation. Studies on oxidation-reduction: 5, Electrode potentials of simple indophenols, each in equilibrium with its reduction product [with list of references]; by Barnett Cohen, H. D. Gibbs, and W. Mansfield Clark. 1924. [1]+34 p. il. (Reprint 904.) [From Public health reports, Feb. 29, 1924.]
24—26604
* Paper, 5c.

—— Same: 6, Preliminary study of indophenols, (A) dibromo substitution products of phenol indophenol, (B) substituted indophenols of ortho type, (C) miscellaneous [with list of references]; by Barnett Cohen, H. D. Gibbs, and W. Mansfield Clark. 1924. [1]+20 p. il. (Reprint 915.) [From Public health reports, Apr. 18, 1924.] * Paper, 5c.
24—26605

Public health reports, v. 39, no. 23–26; June 6–27, 1924. 1924. [xvi]+1359–1609 p. il. [Weekly.] * Paper, 5c. single copy, $1.50 a yr.; foreign subscription, $2.75.
6—25167

SPECIAL ARTICLES.—No. 23. Absenteeism because of sickness in certain schools in Cleveland [Ohio], 1922–23; by G. E. Harmon and G. E. Whitman.—Sanitary problem. address delivered at University of Chile, July 28, 1923, by Alejandro Del Rio.—Hayfever plants of Kansas City [Mo.] district.—No. 24. Disabling sickness in cotton mill communities of South Carolina in 1917, study of sickness prevalence and absenteeism, as recorded in repeated canvasses, in relation to seasonal variation, duration, sex, age, and family income; by Dorothy Wiehl and Edgar Sydenstricker.—City health officers, 1924, directory of those in cities of 10,000 or more population.—No. 25. Prevention and treatment of hay fever; by William Scheppegrell.—Adsorption by aluminium hydrate considered as solid solution phenomenon [with bibliography]; by Lewis B. Miller.—Virginia law requiring sanitary privies or closets.—No. 26. Past incidence of certain communicable diseases common among children, occurrence of measles, whooping cough, mumps, chicken pox, scarlet fever, and diphtheria among school children in various localities in United States; by Selwyn D. Collins.—Iodine deficiency and prevalence of simple goiter in Michigan.—Current world prevalence of disease, review of monthly epidemiological report for May, 1924, issued by Health Section of League of Nations; by Edgar Sydenstricker.
NOTE.—This publication is distributed gratuitously to State and municipal health officers, etc., by the Surgeon General of the Public Health Service, Treasury Department. Others desiring these reports may obtain them from the Superintendent of Documents, Washington, D. C., at the prices stated above.

Railroads. Standard railway sanitary code, approved by Conference of State and Provincial Officers of Health, and recommended to the several States for adoption May 25, 1920, and amended June 2, 1921. 1924. [1]+13 p. (Supplement 46 to Public health reports.) * Paper, 5c.
24—26606

Sickness among 21,000 automobile workers, morbidity experience of Flint and Pontiac (Mich.) sick benefit associations in 1921 and 1922; by Dean K. Brundage. 1924. [1]+13 p. il. (Reprint 914.) [From Public health reports, Apr. 18, 1924.] * Paper, 5c.
24—26607

VENEREAL DISEASES DIVISION

Sex instruction. Wonderful story of life, a father's talks with his little son regarding life and its reproduction. [1924.] iv+18 p. ([V. D. 59 B.]) * Paper, 5c.
24—26608

Venereal disease information, issued by Public Health Service for use in its cooperative work with State health departments, v. 5, no. 5; May 20, 1924. 1924. ii+225–292+iii p. [Monthly.] * Paper, 5c. single copy, 50c. a yr.; foreign subscription, 75c.
23—26719

SPECIAL ARTICLES.—Tabes dorsalis; by Paul E. Bowers.—Syphilis and chancroid, brief history, differential diagnosis, prophylaxis, and treatment, [by] P. H. Bailhache; from Annual report of Marine Hospital Service, fiscal year 1875.

TREASURER OF UNITED STATES

Paper money. Monthly statement, paper currency of each denomination outstanding Apr. 30, 1924. May 1 [1924]. 1 p. oblong 24° †

—— Same, May 31, 1924. June 2 [1924]. 1 p. oblong 24* †

VETERANS' BUREAU

Opinions. Digests of legal opinions relating to veterans' Bureau, including opinions of general counsel of Veterans' Bureau, comptroller general, and Attorney General, Feb. 1924; no. 6. 1924. vi+21 p. [Monthly.] * Paper, 5c.
24—26146

—— Same, Mar. 1924; no. 7. 1924. vi+18 p. [Monthly.] * Paper, 5c.

Property regulations, Veterans' Bureau, 1924. 1924. v+49 p. ‡

WAR DEPARTMENT

Army regulations. †

NOTE.—The Army regulations are issued in pamphlet form for insertion in loose-leaf binders. The names of such of the more important administrative subjects as may seem appropriate, arranged in proper sequence, are numbered in a single series, and each name so numbered constitutes the title and number of a pamphlet containing certain administrative regulations pertaining thereto. Where more than one pamphlet is required for the administrative regulations pertaining to any such title, additional pamphlets will be issued in a separate sub-series.

30–960. Quartermaster Corps: Transportation of baggage, Changes 1; Apr. 14, 1924. 1924. 1 p.

30–2145. Same: Unserviceable property, including waste material, Changes 4; Apr. 10, 1924. [1924.] 2 p. [Supersedes AR 30–2145, Changes 1–3, June 25, 1923–Mar. 18, 1924.]

35–2380. Finance Department: Additional compensation for enlisted men, except Philippine Scouts, for special qualification in use of arms; Mar. 4, 1924. [1924.] 8 p. [Supersedes AR 35–2380, Apr. 28, 1923.]

35–4520. Same: Monetary allowances in lieu of rations and quarters for enlisted men, Changes 3; Apr. 28, 1924. [1924.] 2 p. [Supersedes AR 35–4520, Changes 1 and 2, Sept. 1, 1923 and Jan. 18, 1924.]

40–30. Medical Department: Contract surgeons; Jan. 4, 1924. [1924.] 2 p.

40–2080. Same: Veterinary sanitation, Changes 1; Apr. 14, 1924. 1924. 1 p.

60–5. Chaplains: General provisions; Feb. 15, 1924. [1924.] 5 p.

605–175. Commissioned officers: Foreign service; Apr. 29, 1924. [1924.] 2 p. [Supersedes AR 605–175, Apr. 20, 1923.]

615–175. Enlisted men: Detached enlisted men's list; Apr. 30, 1924. 1924. 1 p.

615–275. Same: Furloughs, passes, and delays, Changes 2; Apr. 25, 1924. [1924.] 2 p. [Supersedes AR 615–275, Changes 1, Dec. 16, 1921. Date of Changes 1 incorrectly given on p. 1 as Dec. 16, 1924.]

775–15. Ammunition allowances: Coast artillery target practice; Mar. 22, 1924. [1924.] 7 p.

Flag day, June 14, 1924, ceremonies on the Ellipse. [1924.] [4] p. il. narrow large 8° †

Training regulations.

NOTE.—The Training regulations are issued in pamphlet form for insertion in loose-leaf binders.

320–15. Ordnance Department: Automatic pistol, caliber .45, model of 1911, prepared under direction of chief of ordnance; Mar. 3, 1924. [1924.] 21 p. il. * Paper, 5c.

420–170. Infantry: Combat principles, infantry regiment, prepared under direction of chief of infantry; Apr. 2, 1924. [1924.] 17 p. il. * Paper, 5c.

420–185. Same: Combat principles, infantry brigade, prepared under direction of chief of infantry; Apr. 2, 1924. [1924.] 8 p. * Paper, 5c.

435–20. Coast Artillery Corps: Emplacement and tactical employment of coast artillery in harbor defense, prepared under direction of chief of coast artillery; Apr. 4, 1924. [1924.] 10 p. * Paper, 5c.

435–210. Same: Gunnery for antiaircraft machine guns, prepared under direction of chief of coast artillery; Mar. 21, 1924. [1924.] 20 p. il. * Paper, 5c.

435–290. Same: Fire command, prepared under direction of chief of coast artillery; May 7, 1924. [1924.] 9 p. * Paper, 5c.

435–295. Same: Fort command, prepared under direction of chief of coast artillery; May 7, 1924. [1924.] 11 p. * Paper, 5c.

ADJUTANT GENERAL'S DEPARTMENT

Posters. 'Round the world flight [with] map showing flight route; [poster]. n. p. [May 5, 1924]. 27×20 in. †

—— Stop! look! read! enlist with U. S. Army, good pay, enjoyable, inspiring work, recreation and man building, earn! learn! travel! [all-lettered poster]. n. p. [May 16, 1924]. 38×25 in. †

Recruiting and enlistment. Army training develops system, health, loyalty, courage, initiative, education, character, leadership, self control, responsibility, essentials of success in life. [Recruiting Publicity Bureau, Governors Island, N. Y., Apr. 30, 1924.] [6] p. il. narrow 16° †

—— I am merely a little folder passing from hand to hand and as I pass along I ask each and every one this question, are you satisfied? [circular of information concerning opportunities, pay, etc., of enlisted men in Army]. [Recruiting Publicity Bureau, Governors Island, N. Y., May 10, 1924.] [4] p. il. 16° †

—— United States Army builds men. [Recruiting Publicity Bureau, Governors Island, N. Y., Apr. 1, 1924.] [8] p. il. narrow 12° †

U. S. Army recruiting news, bulletin of recruiting information issued by direction of Adjutant General of Army, June 1 and 15, 1924. [Recruiting Publicity Bureau, Governors Island, N. Y., June 1 and 15, 1924.] Each 16 p. il. 4° † Recruiting Publicity Bureau, Governors Island, N. Y. War 22–1

AIR SERVICE

Aeronautical bulletins. Aeronautical bulletin, no. 140–163, Route information series; May 1–15, 1924. [1924.] various paging, 12° (Airways Section.) * Paper, 5c. each.   23—26231

—— Aeronautical bulletin. no. 229, 231, 233–237, State series; May 1–15, 1924. [1924.] Each 2 p. il. 12° (Airways Section.) * Paper, 5c. each.

ENGINEER DEPARTMENT

Hilo Harbor, Hawaii, reports on preliminary examination and survey of Hilo Harbor, Hawaii. Apr. 10, 1924. 21 p. map. (H. doc. 235, 68th Cong. 1st sess.) * Paper, 10c.   24—26533

Hudson River Channel at Weehawken and Edgewater, N. J., reports on preliminary examination and survey of Hudson River Channel, along water front of Weehawken and Edgewater, N. J., with view to providing depth of 40 feet at mean low water or such lesser depth as may be necessary to serve interests of navigation and extending in straight line in front of dock of Edgewater about three-quarters of mile farther north. May 26, 1924. 18 p. (H. doc. 313, 68th Cong. 1st sess.) * Paper, 5c.

Sabine-Neches Waterway (salt water guard lock), Tex., supplementary report on survey of Sabine-Neches Waterway (salt water guard lock), Tex. Apr. 10, 1924. 24 p. map. (H. doc 234, 68th Cong. 1st sess.) [Supplementary to report contained in House document 975, 66th Congress, 3d session.] * Paper, 10c.

NORTHERN AND NORTHWESTERN LAKES SURVEY

NOTE.—Charts of the Great Lakes and connecting waters and St. Lawrence River to the international boundary at St. Regis, of Lake Champlain, and of the New York State canals are prepared and sold by the U. S. Lake Survey Office, Old Custom-house, Detroit, Mich. Charts may also be purchased at the following U. S. engineer offices: 710 Army Building, New York, N. Y.; 467 Broadway, Albany, N. Y.; 540 Federal Building, Buffalo, N. Y., and Canal Office, Sault Ste. Marie, Mich. A catalogue (with index map), showing localities, scales, prices, and conditions of sale, may be had upon application at any of these offices.
A descriptive bulletin, which supplements the charts and gives detailed information as to harbors, shore lines and shoals, magnetic determinations, and particulars of changing conditions affecting navigation, is issued free to chart purchasers, upon request. The bulletin is revised annually and issued at the opening of navigation (in April), and supplements thereto are published monthly during the navigation season.
Complete sets of the charts and publications may be seen at the U. S. engineer offices in Duluth, Minn.. Milwaukee, Wis., Chicago, Ill., Grand Rapids, Mich., Cleveland, Ohio, and Oswego, N. Y., but they are obtainable only at the sales offices above mentioned.

Charts

Ashtabula, Ohio. Ashtabula Harbor, Ohio. Scale 1 : 5,000. 7th edition. [U. S. Lake Survey Office, Detroit, Mich.] May 31, 1924. 32.7×20.7 in. † 15c.

Champlain, Lake. Lake Champlain, from Rouses Point to Cumberland Head; chart. 1. Scale 1 : 40,000. 4th edition. [U. S. Lake Survey Office, Detroit, Mich.] May 10, 1924. 37.1×27.5 in. † 20c.

Menominee, Mich. Chart of Menominee Harbor, Green Bay, including Marinette, Wis., and Menominee, Mich. Scale 1 : 15,000. 3d edition. [U. S. Lake Survey Office, Detroit, Mich.] Apr. 25, 1924. 26×23.2 in. † 15c.

Michigan, Lake. Lake Michigan, Port Washington, Wis., to Waukegan, Ill. [with insets]; coast chart 4. Scale 1 : 120,000. 2d edition. [U. S. Lake Survey Office, Detroit, Mich.] May 28, 1924. 41×28.2 in. † 30c.
Port Washington Harbor, Wis.
Waukegan Harbor, Ill.

Superior, Lake. East end of Lake Superior, from Cape Gargantua, Ont., to mouth of Big Two Hearted River, Mich., including Whitefish Bay and head of St. Marys River; with inset. Gargantua Harbor, Ont.; coast chart 1. Scale 1 : 120,000. 4th edition. [U S. Lake Survey Office, Detroit, Mich.] May 8, 1924. 44.9×29.4 in. † 30c.

—— General chart of Lake Superior. Scale 1 : 500,000. 10th edition. [U. S. Lake Survey Office, Detroit, Mich.] Apr. 22, 1924. 28×49 in. † 30c.

FINANCE DEPARTMENT

Finance circular 3 and 4 [1924] ; Mar. 3 and Apr. 18, 1924. [1924.] 6 p. and 5 p. 12° [Finance circular 4 is an advance copy.] ‡

GENERAL STAFF CORPS

Army. Changes 140 [for] Army regulations [1913] ; Mar. 21, 1924. [1924.] 7 leaves. [Regulations issued by War Department.] †

MEDICAL DEPARTMENT

Empyema [with lists of references], excerpt from Medical Department' of United States Army in World War ; by Edward K. Dunham.' 1924. xvi+ 33–392 p. il. 8 pl. 2 tab. large 8° [Though Lieut. Col. Dunham did not live to complete the compilation of the data embodied in the manuscript on empyema, it was so well forward at the time of his death, that what remained could be done by his collaborators in accordance with his plans. Certain chapters were prepared by Franklin A. Stevens, Evarts A. Graham, and William L. Keller.] ‡

Index-catalogue. Synopsis of style, Index-catalogue of library ' of. Surgeon General's Office. 1924. cover-title, 16 p. [Interleaved.] ‡. 24—26563

ORDNANCE DEPARTMENT ,.

Ballistics. Exterior ballistic tables based on numerical integration :' v. 1, Summital arguments. 1924. [1]+xxii+689 p. il. large 4° (War Dept.' doc. 1107.) * Cloth, $1.50. War 24—17

Orders. General orders 2 [1924; June 12, 1924]. [1924.] 12 leaves, 12° [Mimeographed. Title is: Appropriations for.'fiscal year, 1925.] ‡.,

QUARTERMASTER GENERAL OF ARMY

Specifications.' Index to Army. Quartermaster 'Corps' specifications ;' revised' to Dec. 1, 1923. 1923. 61 p. 12° ‡

Index to

Monthly Catalogue
United States
Public Documents

Nos. 343-354
July, 1923–June, 1924

ISSUED BY THE
SUPERINTENDENT OF DOCUMENTS

WASHINGTON
1924

INDEX

To Monthly Catalogue, July, 1923—June, 1924

NOTE.—*Entries appear in this index (1) under names of Government or corporate authors; (2) under personal authors; (3) under series titles or titles of publications, if distinctive; (4) under subjects. Specific subjects are not duplicated under the Government authors.*

The list of page numbers immediately following the name of any Executive Department, bureau, office, etc., refers to all entries under the corresponding center head on those pages of the Monthly Catalogue proper. Inclusive paging is not given.

Page

14763—25†——3

Lightning Source UK Ltd.
Milton Keynes UK
UKHW010617201218
334296UK00010B/1251/P

9 780428 614584